Handbook of Research on Teacher Education, Third Edition

D0074234

This volume provides a balance and perspective that enhances inquiry into teacher education. What the editors and authors have accomplished is to put research in context, apply research findings to relevant current issues, and draw on influential documents and current scholarship.

W. Robert Houston, University of Houston, United States;
Editor, *Handbook of Research on Teacher Education*, First Edition—
From the Foreword

The *Handbook of Research on Teacher Education* was initiated to ferment change in education based on solid evidence. The publication of the First Edition was a signal event in 1990. While the preparation of educators was then—and continues to be—the topic of substantial discussion, there did not exist a codification of the best that was known at the time about teacher education. The Second Edition (1996) built on the first to extend this comprehensive knowledge base. Reflecting the needs of educators today, this Third Edition takes a new approach to achieving the same purpose. Beyond simply conceptualizing the broad landscape of teacher education and providing comprehensive reviews of the latest research for major domains of practice, this edition aims to:

- stimulate a broad conversation about foundational issues;
- bring multiple perspectives to bear, including historical perspectives;
- provide new specificity to topics that have been undifferentiated in the past; and
- include diverse voices in the conversation.

Taking all of these aspirations into account, the Editors, with the help of an Advisory Board, identified nine foundational issues and, to bring these issues to life, translated them into a set of focal questions:

- What's the point? The purposes of teacher education
- What should teachers know? Teacher capacities: knowledge, beliefs, skills, and commitments
- Where should teachers be taught? Settings and roles in teacher education
- Who teaches? Who should teach? Teacher recruitment, selection, and retention
- Does difference make a difference? Diversity and teacher education
- How do people learn to teach? Teacher learning over time
- Who's in charge? Authority in teacher education and licensure policy
- How do we know what we know? Research and teacher education
- What good is teacher education? The place of teacher education in teachers' education

The *Handbook* is organized around these questions, with a common four-part structure in each section. The Introduction, by the section editor, explains why the core issue has persisted, how it has been conceptualized over time, and why the particular framing chapters, artifacts, and commentators were chosen for the section. The framing chapters focus on different dimensions or facets of the issue as well as different ways of thinking about it. The artifacts—historical and contemporary documents, many of them classics in teacher education—demonstrate the enduring nature of the issue and how it has been conceptualized or debated over time. Each section concludes with commentaries written by researchers, teachers, teacher educators, policy makers, or foundation directors that reflect a wide spectrum of political and ideological stances.

Handbook of Research on Teacher Education

Enduring Questions in Changing Contexts
Third Edition

Edited by

Marilyn Cochran-Smith
Boston College

Sharon Feiman-Nemser
Brandeis University

D. John McIntyre
Southern Illinois University

and

Kelly E. Demers

Associate Editor
Boston College

Co-published by
Routledge, Taylor & Francis Group
and the Association of Teacher Educators

 Routledge
Taylor & Francis Group

NEW YORK AND LONDON

First edition published 1990 by Macmillan Reference Library
Second edition published 1996 by Macmillan Reference Library

This edition published 2008
by Routledge
270 Madison Ave, New York, NY 10016

Simultaneously published in the UK
by Routledge
2 Park Square, Milton Park, Abingdon, Oxon OX14 4RN

Routledge is an imprint of the Taylor & Francis Group, an informa business

First edition © 1990 Houston
Second edition © 1996 Sikula

Third edition © 2008 by Association of Teacher Educators

Typeset in Sabon by
RefineCatch Limited, Bungay, Suffolk
Printed and bound in the United States of America on acid-free paper by
Edwards Brothers, Inc.

Library of Congress Cataloging-in-Publication Data
Handbook of research on teacher education : enduring questions in changing
contexts.— 3rd ed. / edited by Marilyn Cochran-Smith, Sharon Feiman-Nemser,
D. John McIntyre ; Kelly E. Demers, associate editor.
     p. cm.
   "Published for the Association of Teacher Educators by Lawrence Erlbaum
Associates/Taylor & Francis Group."
   Includes bibliographical references and index.
   ISBN 978-0-8058-4776-5 (hb : alk paper)—ISBN 978-0-8058-4777-2
(pb : alk. paper)   1. Teachers—Training of—United States.   I. Cochran-Smith,
Marilyn, 1951–   II. Feiman-Nemser, Sharon.   III. McIntyre, D. John.
IV. Association of Teachers Educators.
   LB1715.H274 2008
   370.71′1—dc22
                                                          2007026180

ISBN10: 0–8058–4776–6 (hbk)
ISBN10: 0–8058–4777–4 (pbk)
ISBN10: 0–2039–3869–0 (ebk)

ISBN13: 978–0–8058–4776–5 (hbk)
ISBN13: 978–0–8058–4777–2 (pbk)
ISBN13: 978–0–2039–3869–0 (ebk)

Contents

Artifacts   937

List of figures

List of tables

Notes on contributors

Vonzell Agosto is a former special education teacher with the Chicago Public Schools. As a doctoral student in the department of Curriculum and Instruction at the University of Wisconsin-Madison, her research interests include teacher education with a focus on multicultural education and special education.

Soyeon Ahn is a Doctoral Candidate in Measurement and Quantitative Methods in the College of Education at Michigan State University and is interested in developing statistical models for complicated data structures. Her current research focuses on the application of latent variable models to synthesizing evidence in education.

Glenda R. Aleman is an Assistant Professor in the Teacher Education Department at California State University, Dominguez-Hills.

Michael W. Apple is John Bascom Professor of Curriculum and Instruction and Educational Policy Studies at the University of Wisconsin-Madison and Professor of Educational Policy Studies at the Institute of Education, University of London. Among his recent books are *Education the "Right" Way: Markets, Standards, God, and Inequality*, 2nd edition (2006), *The Subaltern Speak* (2006), and *Democratic Schools: Lessons in Powerful Education*, 2nd edition (2007).

Katherine C. Boles is a Lecturer on Education at the Harvard Graduate School of Education, teaches about school reform and new forms of teacher leadership. A classroom teacher for over 25 years, she co-founded (with Vivian Troen) one of the first professional development schools in the country, and co-authored (with Troen) *Who's Teaching Your Children? Why the Teacher Crisis is Worse Than You Think and What Can Be Done About It*.

Hilda Borko is a Professor in the School of Education, University of Colorado at Boulder. A member of the National Academy of Education, she was President of the American Educational Research Association 2003–2004, Editor of the *American Educational Research Journal*, Section on Teaching, Learning and Human Development 1988–1992, and is currently editor (with Dan Liston and Jennie Whitcomb) of the *Journal of Teacher Education*.

Marilynne Boyle-Baise is a Professor in the Department of Curriculum and Instruction at Indiana University's School of Education. She was a member of the Board of Directors for the National Council for the Social Studies (NCSS) from 2004–2007. She was selected as a Faculty Fellow for Service Learning for 2006–2007. She currently serves as an Academic Advisor for the Center on Congress.

Anthony L. Brown is an Assistant Professor in the Department of Curriculum and

Instruction at the University of Texas at Austin. He completed his Ph.D. in curriculum and instruction from the University of Wisconsin-Madison. Anthony is a former classroom teacher and school administrator. His scholarly interests focus on the educational experiences of African American males and curriculum studies.

Kathryn Byrnes is a Doctoral Candidate in Instruction and Curriculum at the University of Colorado at Boulder. Her research interests include contemplative education, spirituality and education, and teacher education. She is the former managing editor of the *Journal of Teacher Education* and is a visiting instructor at Colorado College, teaching Educational Psychology and Introduction to Psychology courses.

Jinyoung Choi is a recent graduate of Michigan State University, where she received a Ph.D. in Curriculum, Teaching, and Educational Policy. She is currently a Full-Time Instructor in the Department of Elementary Education at Ewha Women's University in South Korea.

Victoria Chou is Dean and Professor of the University of Illinois at Chicago College of Education. She chairs UIC's Council on Teacher Education and recently served as Chair of the Governing Board of the National Teachers Academy in Chicago.

Mary Clevenger-Bright is a Doctoral Student in Teacher Education, a Research Assistant in the Teacher Education Program, and a University Supervisor at the University of Washington in Seattle. A former kindergarten and primary grade teacher and literacy leader in the public schools, she is interested in researching, writing, and teaching about connections within and between settings in teacher preparation, and about sociocultural influences in early childhood development and education.

Reneé T. Clift is a Professor in the Department of Curriculum and Instruction at the University of Illinois at Urbana-Champaign and is the Director of the Illinois New Teacher Collaborative. Her research interests include teacher learning and development and the use of technology for preservice and continuing teacher education.

Marilyn Cochran-Smith is the John E. Cawthorne Millennium Chair in Education and directs the Doctoral Program in Curriculum and Instruction at Boston College's Lynch School of Education. She was President of the American Educational Research Association in 2004–2005, co-chair of the AERA Panel on Research and Teacher Education and Editor of the *Journal of Teacher Education* from 2000–2006.

Hilary G. Conklin is an Assistant Professor in the Department of Elementary and Social Studies Education at the University of Georgia. She teaches undergraduate and graduate courses in social studies education and has research interests in the preparation of middle school teachers, social studies teacher education, and teacher learning.

Elizabeth Craig is Assistant Professor in the Master of Arts in Teaching program at Bard College. Scholarly interests focus on the demographics and quality of the public school teaching force; student resistance and school failure; and the development of pedagogical content knowledge in social studies teachers. Recent publications include chapters in *Studying Teacher Education: The Report of the AERA Panel on Research and Teacher Education* (co-authored with Karen Zumwalt).

Edward Crowe is a consultant on teacher quality reform, K-16 policy, and higher education information systems and strategic planning. He was the first director of the federal Title II Grants Program, and now works with the Carnegie Corporation, the

NYC Partnership for Teacher Excellence, the Hunter Foundation of Scotland, the Committee on Teacher Preparation of the National Research Council, and the National Commission on Teaching and America's Future.

Linda Darling-Hammond is the Charles E. Ducommun Chair in Education at Stanford University and is co-director of the Stanford Educational Leadership Institute and School Redesign Network. She is a past president of AERA, a member of the National Academy of Education, and author or editor of more than 250 publications on education policy and practice, including, most recently, *Powerful Teacher Education: Lessons from Exemplary Programs.*

Danné E. Davis is an Assistant Professor of Elementary Education at Montclair State University. Her primary research centers on the process of "consultative interaction" between student teachers and schoolchildren. Dr. Davis is currently examining the contribution of Elizabeth Jennings, an African American public school teacher involved in issues of social justice during the nineteenth century.

Kelly E. Demers is a Doctoral Candidate in Curriculum and Instruction at Boston College. Her research interests include multicultural education and anti-racist education. She is currently completing her doctoral dissertation, which focuses on the way that White teachers' ideology informs their construction of race.

Mary E. Dilworth is Vice President for Higher Education and Research at the National Board for Professional Teaching Standards. Prior to joining the Board, she was a senior officer with AACTE. She is nationally known for her work in the areas of teaching and teachers' professional development with an emphasis on racial, ethnic and linguistic diversity.

Daniel Fallon is Program Director for Higher Education at Carnegie Corporation of New York. He designed and has administered *Teachers for a New Era*, a national program of philanthropic support to selected institutions leading efforts to rethink teacher education. He is Professor Emeritus of Psychology and Professor Emeritus of Public Policy at the University of Maryland, College Park.

Sharon Feiman-Nemser is the Mandel Professor of Jewish Education at Brandeis University and founding director of the Mandel Center for Studies in Jewish Education. Before coming to Brandeis, she was a Professor of Teacher Education at Michigan State University where she served as Senior Researcher with several national research centers. A leading scholar of teacher education, she has written extensively about mentoring, new teacher induction, teacher learning and the curriculum and pedagogy of teacher education.

Robert E. Floden is University Distinguished Professor of Teacher Education, Measurement and Quantitative Methods, and Educational Psychology at the Michigan State University College of Education. He is a member of the National Academy of Education and has been Editor of *Review of Research in Education*, Features Editor of *Educational Researcher*, and President of the Philosophy of Education Society.

Susan Florio-Ruane is Professor of Teacher Education at Michigan State University and recipient of the university's Distinguished Faculty Award. Her book, *Teacher Education and the Cultural Imagination*, won awards from the National Reading Conference and the American Educational Research Association. She served as President of the Council on Anthropology and Education and the National Council for Research on Language and Literacy.

Kim Fries is an Assistant Professor at the University of New Hampshire. Her areas of interest include research on teaching and teacher education. She is presently the President of the New England Educational Research Organization (the regional affiliate to the American Educational Research Association). She served as the Project Manager for the AERA Panel on Research and Teacher Education.

Mary H. Futrell is the Dean of the George Washington University Graduate School of Education and Human Development and is a Former President of the National Education Association. Dr. Futrell is chair of the Holmes Partnership Board and is a member of the Boards of the National Society for the Study of Education, The National Commission on Teaching and America's Future, The Kettering Foundation, Lynchburg College and the Teachers Support Network.

Maureen D. Gillette is Dean of the College of Education at Northeastern Illinois University in Chicago. Her research focuses on urban education and preparing culturally responsive teachers. As former director of the Paterson Teachers for Tomorrow project, she designed and implemented a teacher education pipeline project to recruit and prepare teachers of color. Maureen is co-author of the book, *Learning to Teach Everyone's Children: Equity, Empowerment, and Education that is Multicultural.*

Donna M. Gollnick is Senior Vice President of the National Council for Accreditation of Teacher Education (NCATE) where she oversees accreditation activities. She is the co-author of the textbook, *Multicultural Education in a Pluralistic Society* and other teacher education textbooks. She is past-president of the National Association for Multicultural Education (NAME).

John I. Goodlad is a Senior Fellow in the College of Education of the University of Washington and President of the Institute for Educational Inquiry in Seattle. He is author, co-author, or editor of approximately 40 books and yearbooks. He is past-president of AERA and AACTE and has received various awards, primarily for his work in public schooling, as well as honorary degrees from 20 universities in the United States and Canada.

A. Lin Goodwin is Professor of Education in the Department of Curriculum and Teaching at Teachers College, Columbia University, and has been engaged in the preparation of teachers for over 20 years. She also serves as Associate Dean for Teacher Education and School-Based Support Services, a position she has held since September 2005.

Carl A. Grant is a Hoefs-Bascom Professor in the Department of Curriculum and Instruction and Professor in the Afro-American Studies Department at the University Wisconsin-Madison. He is a past President of the National Association For Multicultural Education and Chair of the AERA Publication Committee 2004–2007.

Jaime Grinberg is a Professor of Educational Foundations at Montclair State University. He has published journal articles, books, and book chapters in Spanish and English on teacher education and professional development vis-à-vis the education of Latina/o students. He has been the director, co-director, and presently the faculty advisor to the Montclair State University Network for Educational Renewal.

Pam Grossman is Professor of Education at Stanford University. Her research interests include teacher education, the teaching of English in secondary schools, and the teaching of practice in professional education. A Past-President of Division K (Teaching and Teacher Education) of AERA, she served as a member of both the AERA Panel on

Research and Teacher Education and the National Academy of Education's Committee on Teacher Education.

Karen Hammerness is a Research Associate with Stanford University. In Spring, 2007, she was a Visiting Professor at Leiden University in The Netherlands. Her research focuses upon teacher preparation practices and policies, as well as upon teacher's ideals and visions. Her book, *Seeing Through Teachers' Eyes: Professional Ideals and Classroom Practices.* was published last year by Teachers College Press.

David T. Hansen is Professor and Director of the program in Philosophy and Education at Teachers College, Columbia University. He is the author of *The Call to Teach, Exploring The Moral Heart of Teaching*, and other works on the practice of teaching. He was President of the John Dewey Society in 2003–2005 and is President-Elect of the Philosophy of Education Society for 2008–2009.

Frederick M. Hess is a Resident Scholar and Director of Education Policy studies at the American Enterprise Institute. He is executive editor of *Education Next* and a member of the review board for the Broad Prize in Urban Education. His many books include *Spinning Wheels, Common Sense School Reform*, and *No Child Left Behind: A Primer.*

W. Robert Houston is the John and Rebecca Moores Professor and Executive Director, Institute for Urban Education at the University of Houston. Author of over 40 books and hundreds of journal articles and research papers, he was Editor of the first *Handbook of Research in Teacher Education* in 1990. In 1997 ATE named him the first Distinguished Educator of the year. In 2002, he received the prestigious Pomeroy award from AACTE for his contributions to education.

Tyrone C. Howard is an Associate Professor of Education in the Graduate School of Education and Information Studies at the University of California, Los Angeles. His research interests include teacher education, multicultural education, and the social and political context of urban schools. He is the past chair of the College University Faculty Assembly and Associate Editor of *Theory and Research in Social Education.*

David G. Imig is a Professor of Practice at the University of Maryland, College Park and serves as Coordinator for the Carnegie Project on the Education Doctorate for the Carnegie Foundation and the Council of Academic Deans in Research Education Institutions. Dr. Imig served as President and CEO of AACTE from 1980–2005. He currently is serving as chair of the National Society for the Study of Education.

Scott R. Imig is an Assistant Professor at the University of North Carolina Wilmington's Watson School of Education. He directs the University's curriculum, instruction, and supervision program. From 2003–2006 he ran the University of Virginia's Teaching Assessment Initiative, the research component of UVA's Teachers for a New Era grant.

Richard M. Ingersoll is a Professor of Education and Sociology at the University of Pennsylvania. His book, *Who Controls Teachers' Work? Power and Accountability in America's Schools*, published by Harvard University Press, was awarded the 2004 Outstanding Writing Award from the American Association of Colleges for Teacher Education.

Jacqueline Jordan Irvine is the Charles Howard Candler Professor of Urban Education at Emory University. Her books include *Black Students and School Failure, Growing Up African American in Catholic Schools, Critical Knowledge for Diverse Students,*

Culturally Responsive Lesson Planning, In Search of Wholeness: African American Teachers and Their Culturally Specific Pedagogy, and *Seeing with the Cultural Eye.*

Tina Jacobowitz is Professor of Education at Montclair State University. She founded Montclair's Office of the Agenda for Education in a Democracy, sponsoring professional development and research on teaching in a democracy and for social justice. She is co-author of *Introduction to Education: Teaching in and for a Democracy,* forthcoming from McGraw Hill.

Susan Moore Johnson is the Pforzheimer Professor of Teaching and Learning at the Harvard Graduate School of Education, where she served as Academic Dean from 1993 to 1999. She is director of the Project on the Next Generation of Teachers, which examines how best to recruit, support, and retain a strong teaching force.

Susan M. Kardos is the director of a large community fund and school improvement project in greater-Boston and a researcher at the Project on the Next Generation of Teachers at Harvard University. Her research includes work on professional culture, new teacher induction and mentoring, school leadership, and education policy. She is co-author of *Finders and Keepers: Helping New Teachers Survive and Thrive in Our Schools.*

Mary M. Kennedy is Professor of Teacher Education at Michigan State University. She has published numerous articles and books about teacher knowledge and teacher thinking and about the role of policy and research in influencing teaching.

Joyce E. King is the Benjamin E. Mays Chair for Urban Teaching, Learning, and Leadership and Professor in the Department of Educational Policy Studies at Georgia State University. Her scholarship addresses the role of culture and community knowledge in effective teaching and teacher preparation, Black studies epistemology and curriculum change, and she is co-editor of *The Review of Educational Research.*

Kevin K. Kumashiro is an Associate Professor of Policy Studies at the University of Illinois-Chicago College of Education, and the founding director of the Center for Anti-Oppressive Education. He is author of the award-winning book, *Troubling Education,* and more recently, *Against Common Sense: Teaching and Learning toward Social Justice.*

David F. Labaree is a Professor and Associate Dean for student affairs in the Stanford University School of Education. He was President of the History of Education Society (2004–2005), Vice President for Division F (History of Education) of the American Educational Research Association (2003–2006), and member of the AERA executive board (2004–2006).

Meghna Antani Lipcon is a fifth grade math and science teacher at Broad Acres Elementary School in Silver Spring, Maryland. She received her master's degree in elementary education from Teachers College in 2001. Since achieving National Board Certification in 2005, Meghna has coordinated the candidate support program in Howard County, Maryland. In addition, Meghna supports National Board candidates in Montgomery County, Maryland by planning and implementing effective Saturday Candidate Support Sessions and coaching individual candidates.

John Loughran is the Foundation Chair in Curriculum and Professional Practice in the Faculty of Education, Monash University and Associate Dean. His research has spanned both science education and the related fields of professional knowledge, reflective practice and teacher research. He was co-editor of the International Handbook of Teaching and Teacher Education and is co-editor of the journal *Studying Teacher Education*.

Tamara Lucas is Associate Dean of the College of Education and Human Services at Montclair State University. Her work has focused on the education of culturally and linguistically diverse students and the preparation of their teachers. Her publications include two books—most recently, *Educating Culturally Responsive Teachers: A Coherent Approach*, with Ana María Villegas (2002).

G. Williamson McDiarmid is the Boeing Professor of Teacher Education in the University of Washington's College of Education. He previously served as Co-Director of the National Center for Research on Teacher Learning at Michigan State University and Director of the Institute of Social and Economic Research at the University of Alaska.

Morva McDonald is an Assistant Professor of Education in the areas of teacher education and curriculum and instruction at the University of Washington's College of Education. Her research interests include a focus on teacher education and the preparation of teachers for diversity as well as students' opportunities to learn in and out of school.

D. John McIntyre is a Professor in the Department of Curriculum and Instruction with a specialization in teacher leadership at Southern Illinois University Carbondale. He was President of the Association of Teacher Educators (ATE) in 1992–1993, a recipient of ATE's Distinguished Research Award in Teacher Education and co-editor of ATE's Research in Teacher Education Yearbook series from 1995–2000.

Nicholas M. Michelli is Presidential Professor in the Ph.D. program in urban education at City University of New York's Graduate Center, serves as a member of the New York State Professional Standards and Practices Board for Teaching, the Executive Committee of the National Network for Educational Renewal, and is editor of the McGraw Hill Teacher Education Series. He received AACTE's Pomeroy Award for Contributions to Teacher Education.

David H. Monk is Professor of Educational Administration and Dean of the College of Education at Pennsylvania State University. He is the author of numerous publications dealing with economic aspects of education policy and is the co-editor of *Education Finance and Policy* (MIT Press). He is a past president of the American Education Finance Association.

Frank B. Murray is H. Rodney Sharp Professor in the School of Education and the Department of Psychology at the University of Delaware and served as Dean of the College of Education between 1979 and 1995. Currently, he is President of the Teacher Education Accreditation Council in Washington, DC. For his contributions to the fields of child development and teacher education, he was awarded an honorary doctorate from Heriot-Watt University in Edinburgh, Scotland.

Karla Oakley serves as Vice President of Training and Certification for the New Teacher Project (TNTP), a national non-profit organization that has recruited, trained or certified approximately 23,000 teachers since 1997. Karla began her career in education as a teacher in 1991, and has since worked as a teacher developer, assessor, curriculum developer, and program manager.

Celia Oyler is an Associate Professor in the Department of Curriculum and Teaching at

Teachers College, Columbia University. She directs the Inclusive Education Program and is the author of *Learning to Teach Inclusively: Student Teachers' Classroom Inquiries* and *Making Room for Students: Sharing Authority in Room 104*. Before obtaining her Ph.D., she was a classroom teacher for 15 years.

Diane Ravitch is Research Professor of Education at New York University's Steinhardt School of Education. She is a historian of education and the author of many books, including *Left Back: A Century of Battles Over School Reform, The Great School Wars: New York City, 1805–1973,* and *The Language Police: How Pressure Groups Restrict What Students Learn*. She served as a member of the National Assessment Governing Board from 1997–2004.

Michell Rhee founded The New Teacher Project in 1997 and served as its CEO and President for 10 years. Today, the organization is recognized as an authority on the recruitment, selection, training and hiring of new teachers for urban and high-poverty schools. Ms. Rhee left the organization in 2007 to become Chancellor of the Washington, DC public school system.

Emily Robertson is dual Associate Professor of Education and Philosophy at Syracuse University. She is former interim dean and associate dean of the School of Education and a past president of the Philosophy of Education Society. Her research focuses on philosophy of education, especially on the civic, moral, and epistemic ends of education.

Sharon P. Robinson is currently AACTE President and Chief Executive Officer. She is the former president of the ETS's Educational Policy Leadership Institute, served as Assistant Secretary of Education with the U.S. Department of Education's Office of Educational Research and Improvement and held a variety of leadership positions in the National Education Association. She was also interim deputy director of the National PTA's Programs and Legislation office.

Carol R. Rodgers is an Associate Professor of Education at the University at Albany, State University of New York. Her interests include reflective practice, John Dewey, presence in teaching, the inner life of the teacher, and the history of progressive teacher education. Her most recent publications include "Presence in teaching," *Teachers and Teaching: Theory and Practice* (2006, co-authored with Miriam Raider-Roth), and "Attending to student voice," *Curriculum Inquiry* (2006).

Matthew Ronfeldt is a doctoral candidate in Teacher Education at the Stanford University School of Education. His research focuses on the adaptation process of novice teachers and clinical psychologists during their first year of professional preparation. Previously he taught middle school math and science in Oakland, CA and coordinated a teacher research group.

Cheryl L. Rosaen is Associate Professor of Teacher Education at Michigan State University and a faculty Team Leader in a five-year Teacher Preparation Program. She teaches courses in literacy methods and teacher education, and conducts research on learning to teach literacy, and the role technology can play in supporting teacher learning.

Karen Sakash is a Clinical Associate Professor in Education at the University of Illinois at Chicago. She coordinates the graduate elementary education program and is a bilingual teacher educator in the Department of Curriculum and Instruction. She has a Ph.D. from the University of Illinois at Chicago in Public Policy Analysis with a specialization in educational program evaluation and administration.

Brian D. Schultz is an Assistant Professor at Northeastern Illinois University in Chicago. His research focuses on developing democratic curricula surrounding students' concerns. His forthcoming book, *Spectacular Things Happen Along the Way: Lessons from an Urban Classroom* (Teachers College Press), details a yearlong justice-oriented project where his fifth-grade students from Chicago's Cabrini Green fought for an equitable school building.

Katherine H. Scott is a developmental psychologist whose work focuses on adult development. She is an independent scholar and educational consultant in Cambridge, Massachusetts.

Michael W. Sedlak is a Professor of History of Education and Associate Dean for Academic Affairs in the College of Education at Michigan State University. He also coordinates the doctoral program in Educational Policy. He has published widely in the history of professional education and American high school policy and reform.

Christine E. Sleeter is Professor Emerita in the College of Professional Studies at California State University, Monterey Bay. Her research focuses on anti-racist multicultural education and teacher education. She is the author of about 100 articles and book chapters, and several books, including *Facing Accountability in Education* and *Un-Standardizing Curriculum* (Teachers College Press), and *Doing Multicultural Education for Achievement and Equity* (with Carl Grant, Routledge).

Hugh Sockett is Professor of Education at George Mason University (GMU) in the Department of Public and International Affairs of the College of Humanities and Social Studies. He was Dean of Education at the University of East Anglia (UK) (1982–1986) and Director of the GMU Institute for Educational Transformation (1991–1998). He has been a member of the AACTE Task Force on Teacher Education as a Moral Community since 1997.

Eran Tamir is a Post-Doctoral Research Fellow at the Mandel Center, Brandeis University. A sociologist and educational policy analyst, his research focuses on the social and political context of educational policy and teacher professionalism. He is currently leading the "Choosing to Teach" project, a collaborative study of new teachers in Jewish, Catholic and public schools.

Vivian Troen is a Lecturer at Brandeis University and a consultant on professional development school initiatives. An elementary school teacher for over two decades, she now lectures and leads workshops nationally and internationally on teaming, mentoring and teacher development. With Katherine Boles, she is co-founder of one of the first professional development schools in the country and co-author of *Who's Teaching Your Children? Why The Teacher Crisis is Worse Than You Think and What Can Be Done About It.*

Ana María Villegas is Professor of Curriculum and Teaching at Montclair State University. Her research focuses on culturally responsive teaching, preparing teachers for a diverse student population, and preparing and retaining a diverse teaching force. She was the 2004 recipient of the Margaret B. Lindsay Award for Distinguished Research in Teacher Education from the American Association of Colleges for Teacher Education.

Vanessa Siddle Walker is a Professor of Educational Studies at Emory University. Her research articles and books on the segregated schooling of African American children in the south have received numerous regional and national awards, including the Grawmeyer Prize for Education and the AERA Raymond Cattell Early Career Award for Programmatic Research. Her research has also appeared on the PBS Series, *School: The Story of American Education*.

Steven Weiland is Professor of Teacher Education and Higher Education at Michigan State University. Prior to his appointment at MSU he taught English and American Studies at the Universities of Michigan, Iowa, and Minnesota.

Joel Westheimer is University Research Chair in Democracy and Education at the University of Ottawa where he founded and co-directs *Democratic Dialogue*, (www.democraticdialogue.com). He is editor and contributing author, most recently, of the book *Pledging Allegiance: The Politics of Patriotism in America's Schools* (www.pledgingallegiance.org) and author of *Among Schoolteachers: Community, Autonomy, and Ideology in Teachers' Work* (Teachers College Press).

Jennifer A. Whitcomb is the Assistant Dean for Teacher Education at the University of Colorado at Boulder. She is co-editor of the *Journal of Teacher Education* (2006–2009). Her research interests focus on the intersection between and among the practice and structure of teacher education and teacher learning.

Suzanne M. Wilson is Chair and Professor in the Department of Teacher Education at Michigan State University. She also directs the Center for the Scholarship of Teaching. She has written widely on teacher education and curriculum policy, teacher learning and professional development, and mathematics and history teaching.

Kenneth Zeichner is Hoefs-Bascom Professor of Teacher Education and Associate Dean of the School of Education at the University of Wisconsin-Madison.

Karen Zumwalt is the Edward Evenden Professor of Education in the Department of Curriculum and Teaching, Teachers College, Columbia University where she works with doctoral and master's students. She served as Dean of the College and Vice President for Academic Affairs from 1995–2000. Along with Elizabeth Craig, she wrote two chapters for AERA's (2005) *Studying Teacher Education: The Report of the AERA Panel on Research and Teacher Education*.

Foreword

W. Robert Houston

Few matters are more important to our nation's future than the education of its future citizens—or so neglected. At a time when competition throughout the world increases the need for more effective education, our nation vacillates in its support. With the advent of comprehensive post-industrial changes, the necessity of a strong, effective education has become even more vital. The technological era has ushered in a world-wide revolution whose implications are at least as far-reaching as the industrial revolution of over a century earlier.

Teacher education today is far different than it was 50 or 100 years ago. Teacher preparation and professional development are provided by a wider range of institutions; their programs are more complex and their quality more divergent. Prospective teachers have a broader array of potential professions from which to choose and researchers are exploring more varied problems. Yet, despite all the changes in teacher education, the major issues under-girding the profession are as paramount as ever. Understanding these changes and their effects on educational practice, and considering them in light of several enduring issues, requires careful and continual examination.

Educational research, the industrial revolution, and technology

The industrial revolution reshaped education in its image. Schools were expected to instruct children and youth based on the needs of industry (i.e. reading, writing, and arithmetic). Schools were organized along factory lines with groups of students following directions and individual students advancing from one grade to the next each year).

The technological revolution has radically changed society, the workplace, and the knowledge needed in the twenty-first century. One only has to compare agrarian life in America in 1907, 100 years ago, with the horseless carriage and airplane flight in their infancy, or even 1957, fifty years ago, to recognize the vast differences from today. The computer, internet, email, i-pods, cell phones, digital technology, color television, and instant communication have reshaped not only business but also education and the activities and values of children and youth. The population of the country has not only increased from 87 million in 1907 to 172 million in 1957 to over 300 million in 2007, but shifted from primarily rural to urban, with concomitant changes in culture, experiences, and aspirations.

Educational institutions, however, have been slow to engage the new reality—to draw on world-wide communication, massive data storage, retrieval, and analysis, and transportation that shrinks the globe. Evidence indicates this is changing. Schools have wireless connectivity and an increasing number of computers and advanced technology. Three years ago, the Houston Independent School District purchased 15,000 laptop computers so all teachers in the district would have one to bolster their lessons.

Technological challenges have been intensified by increased ethnic and socio-economic diversity in American schools and world-wide competition for well-educated graduates and economic dominance. In the next decade, at-risk students may be defined more by lack of access to technology in their homes than by their ethnicity, gender, or economic status.

Technology is beginning to reshape schooling. Elementary school students are communicating via the internet with children in other countries, not only learning to write but also learning about another culture. The evening news brings world events into the home. High school students are conducting science experiments about phenomena that were unknown fifty years ago. American enterprises compete with industries throughout the world while political events ricochet around the earth. Education is more vital than ever because students today will be competing for the best jobs with people throughout the world. We have indeed moved into the global village where events anywhere affect people everywhere. Such tsunami events are fostering massive changes in the education of teachers.

Enduring issues

Change is an inherent part of our culture, our environment, our heritage, and our future. Despite programmatic changes and extensive research, a number of issues in teacher education have persisted. How extensive should knowledge of content and pedagogy be in preparing teachers? What is the balance between them and what is the best institution (workplace or academic institution) in which to prepare teachers? To what extent should teachers be prepared to meet the special needs of individual students from varied ethnicities, economic conditions and disadvantages, learning disabilities, and special gifts and talents? In what ways does brain research contribute to improved learning? What is the role of research in teacher preparation?

The symbiotic relationship between research and practice continues to be a Gordian Knot that has yet to be untied, although several generations of researchers have contributed to our understanding. Change in human knowledge and behavior is so complex but research relies on proxies for learning and generalizations that mask underlying differences.

Effective programs built on knowledge

Isaac Newton once said, "If I have seen farther, it is because I stood on the shoulders of giants." Until research is systemic, developmental, and focused on the real needs of educational enterprises, little progress will be made. Without a firm foundation, programs and innovations are based on slogans and panaceas. Many educators and concerned citizens admit that no simple solution can correct the problems of education, yet simple remedies abound.

Knowledge is not static but dynamic, changing, growing, evolving. What is known today may be antiquated tomorrow, and perhaps even wrong. Those persons who are not able to inquire into their discipline soon find themselves unable to contribute to it nor even to understand it. The half-life of most innovations in education is about three years, the time required to complete an externally funded project. Nominal mutations occur as the nomenclature changes—goals and objectives, competencies and proficiencies, outcomes, and now standards, all basically deal with similar concepts.

If education is to approach the stature of the sciences, educational researchers will need to build on previous explorations, sharpen their studies, and provide a basis for further, more refined research agendas. Such continuity requires teams of researchers, not individuals exploring complex issues. With innovations in communication and transportation, collaborators no longer need to be physically near each other. Science research teams (and their publications) often include the names of 50 or more scientists working on similar problems and sharing their results, even though they may reside continents apart.

In 1989, as I prepared the Preface for the first *Handbook of Research on Teacher Education*, I expressed concern about the extensiveness and quality of research in the field. Teachers had little research to guide their actions, making most decisions on the basis of how they were taught, what they found in textbooks, and what their colleagues were doing. At every educational level, too many decisions were being made on the basis of personal experiences, too little on comprehensive research conducted about relevant and important issues, and too few educators were committed to building a solid research foundation. Some progress has been made in the intervening years, but the preponderance of decisions are still not informed by dependable evidence.

Educators and researchers face daunting challenges when they try to base their research and practice on previous findings and conclusions and methodology. The easy availability of literature on the internet and in the thousands of local journals, monographs, and private publications without controls imposed by careful editors, has intensified the problem. As a result, too many published studies have been poorly conceived, inconsequential, unimaginative, insignificant, and simply mirror their author's biases rather than contributing to sound research. The uneven quality of educational literature requires each researcher to assess the validity and relevance of sources before basing processes and hypotheses on them. Winnowing out valid studies so that education can become a progressing field becomes vital to relevant education in an increasingly changing twenty-first century.

The *Handbook of Research on Teacher Education*

The *Handbook of Research on Teacher Education* was initiated to ferment change in education based on solid evidence. The first Handbook was conceptualized twenty years ago in February 1987 and published three years later, thanks to the prodigious work of committed educators. I was privileged to serve as Editor and to work with two talented Associate Editors, Martin Haberman and John Sikula. Six years later the Second Handbook was published with John Sikula as Editor and Thomas Buttery and Edith Guyton as Associate Editors.

Editors and their Editorial Boards of these two handbooks examined current educational literature and invited educators who were conducting sound research and providing leadership to serve as chapter authors. The purpose was to synthesize current research findings, interpret and critique them, delete questionable findings, and provide a sound basis for further explorations. In addition to the editors of the first two handbooks and their editorial boards and advisory committees, 160 coauthors contributed their expertise to the ninety-six chapters that analyzed and summarized educational research.

The two volumes organized teacher education into recognizable sections and chapters that mirrored teacher preparation and professional development. The second handbook built on the first. Several fields seemed to require more extensive exploration or had undergone rapid change in the previous six years. The two handbooks, while formatted in similar ways, complemented each other by focusing on different areas.

Just as the world environment and education have changed since the last Handbook was published ten years ago, so too have the needs for research handbooks. Since the second Handbook was published, more than a dozen reviews of research in different fields of education have been published, including the work of AERA's Panel on Research and Teacher Education, *Studying Teacher Education*, edited by Marilyn Cochran-Smith and Kenneth M. Zeichner (2005).

The third Handbook is organized in a different way from the first two volumes to reflect the needs of educators today. In its developmental stages, the third Handbook was often referred to as the "unhandbook" to denote its unique approach to achieving the same purpose. The Editors and the Editorial Board believed that only a new approach would meet the needs of researchers and practitioners today.

The third Handbook is organized around nine sections. Each section includes an introduction and three types of documents: framing chapters by distinguished researchers, commentaries that provide different perspectives on the central issue, and artifacts—documents, treatises and articles that have formed the basic fabric of teacher education over the past century. The combination of thoughtful essays and equally thoughtful commentaries complemented by careful attention to historically significant documents provides a balance and perspective that enhances the inquiry into teacher education. As I read the chapters, commentaries, and artifacts in the third Handbook, I was impressed by the perspectives gained from the volume. What the editors and authors have accomplished is to put research in context, apply research findings to relevant current issues, and draw on influential documents and current scholarship.

The profession and the Association of Teacher Educators are indebted to the four editors of the *Handbook of Teacher Education*, Third Edition, Marilyn Cochran-Smith, Kelly Demers, Sharon Feiman-Nemser, and John McIntyre, who have devoted extensive time over the past four years to bring together a volume that provides the base for improved education and educational research. They have introduced major changes in the format of the Handbook. And the new organization brings the best of education's historical roots through artifacts combined with fresh insights into teacher education's most vexing challenges, and commentaries on chapters that broaden the research perspectives. The leadership of the four co-editors as well as the contributions of the exceptional authors and commentators emulate the finest in professional service and scholarship. More than 70 distinguished educators and researchers have contributed to the Handbook of Research on Teacher Education, Third Edition which also contains over 30 historically significant artifacts. To each of them we as a profession owe a deep sense of gratitude for their vision, diligence, and contributions to education.

W. Robert Houston
John and Rebecca Moores Professor of Education
University of Houston
Editor, *Handbook of Research on Teacher Education*, First Edition

Preface

The growing consensus that teachers matter is not matched by a growing consensus that teacher education matters. In fact, the value of teacher education remains as contested today as it was in the era of the normal school. And yet, given the importance of education in our global society, one could surely make the case that the education of teachers is indispensable in shaping the quality of life for individual learners, for communities, for our nation, and for the world.

This *Handbook of Research on Teacher Education* appears at a volatile time in the history of the field. Alternative pathways into teaching have proliferated. Accreditation is no longer the monopoly of a single organization. The accountability movement drives reform initiatives at every level of the educational system. There is a renewed confidence in the power of scientific research to solve social and educational problems. Yet the achievement gap between majority and minority students persists. As the subtitle of this Handbook suggests, the fundamental issues facing teacher education are not new. They have persisted over time despite economic, political, and social changes.

One reason why these issues endure is that teacher education is a value-driven enterprise. A central purpose of this Handbook is to help readers sort out which of the enduring issues is primarily values-based and cannot be settled by science alone and which of the issues depends on empirical study. For example, empirical research can tell us who is going into teaching and what teachers actually learn in teacher preparation, but research alone cannot determine who is qualified to teach. Decisions about teacher quality and qualifications depend on beliefs about what good teaching entails and these beliefs ultimately derive from what we value most in teachers. Since people have different views about what makes a good teacher, they will hold different expectations about what teachers should know, care about, be able to do. Hopefully this Handbook will help readers appreciate the power and limits of "science" in addressing some of the normative issues that confront teacher education.

A second purpose of the Handbook is to help the diverse community of teacher educators connect their own work to contemporary conceptual and empirical scholarship and to historicize our collective understanding of teacher education. In order to generate new knowledge and build a dependable foundation for policy and practice, teacher educators need to understand how others have framed and investigated the issues and problems they face and how their own experiences and insights relate to existing knowledge. Not every teacher educator needs to do original research, but anyone who aspires to be a professional teacher educator needs to stay abreast of new developments in the field and read research with a critical eye.

A third and related purpose is to challenge conventional thinking and practice and disturb the status quo not by polarizing issues or ignoring problems, but by presenting evidence, arguments and diverse perspectives in critical, clear-minded ways. Hopefully this Handbook will help advocates, critics and skeptics consider what we do well and where we fail, what we agree on and where we legitimately disagree, what dependable evidence exists and where opinion and ideology cloud our thinking.

This Handbook is addressed to the growing community of practitioners, researchers and policy makers involved or interested in the education of quality teachers. This includes teacher educators and other faculty who teach teachers in universities, colleges and community colleges as well as those involved in alternate route recruitment programs like Teach for America, alternative preparation programs recognized by state agencies, distance-based teacher preparation curriculum, for-profit providers of teacher training, school-based administrators and teachers who participate in a variety of teacher education and induction programs and policy makers who formulate and enact policy at multiple levels. We target this mixed audience because we believe that, in teacher education, research, policy and practice are intertwined. We also hope that the volume or at least sections will be useful to observers, skeptics and critics of teacher education.

When the leadership of the Association of Teacher Educators invited us to co-edit the third *Handbook of Research on Teaching*, we were skeptical about the need for another conventional handbook. Since 2000, there had been a steady stream of commission reports, blue ribbon panels, research syntheses, report cards, manifestos and white papers on teacher quality and teacher preparation. In addition, two major research reviews were in the works. The American Educational Research Association (Cochran-Smith and Zeichner, 2005) had commissioned an analysis of empirical evidence regarding key policies and practices in preservice teacher education with the goal of generating a new research agenda. The National Academy of Education through its Committee on Teacher Education (Darling-Hammond and Bransford, 2005) was preparing a major synthesis of research on teaching, learning, teacher education and teacher learning in order to develop recommendations for the curriculum of teacher education.

Instead of going forward with a conventional handbook, we conceived of what we informally call the "unhandbook." Rather than conceptualize the broad landscape of teacher education and commission comprehensive reviews of the latest research for major domains of practice and inquiry as is usually the case with something called a "handbook," we took a different tack. We wanted to stimulate a broad conversation about foundational issues, bring multiple perspectives to bear, including historical perspectives, provide new specificity to topics that have been undifferentiated in the past, and include diverse voices in the conversation. Taking all these aspirations into account, we conceptualized a unique "unhandbook" with a thematic focus and distinctive structure.

With the help of an Advisory Board who met in Boston in 2003, we identified nine foundational issues in teacher education. To bring these issues to life, we translated them into set of focal questions, for example, What's the point? Who's in charge? Who should teach? How do people learn to teach? Does difference make a difference? How do we know what we know? We organized the volume around the nine issues with a common structure for each of the sections.

Each section includes an introduction, a set of framing chapters, a collection of artifacts and some commentaries. The introduction, written by the section editor, explains why the core issue has persisted, how it has been conceptualized over time, and why the particular framing chapters, artifacts and commentators were chosen for the section. The framing chapters focus on different dimensions or facets of the issue as well as different ways of thinking about it. These chapters offer a more nuanced discussion than is usually possible with a single, comprehensive research review. For instance, in the section on diversity, one chapter considers the preparation of white teachers to teach diverse students, while a second chapter deals with the preparation needs of minority teachers. The framing chapters are followed by a set of artifacts, historical and contemporary documents that demonstrate the enduring nature of the issue and illustrate how it has been conceptualized or debated over time. Many are classics in teacher education and they contribute to the unique character of the Handbook. Each section concludes with two or three commentaries written by researchers, teachers, teacher educators, policy makers and/or foundation directors representing diverse perspectives.

Each section was developed by a member of the Advisory Board who took responsibility for conceptualizing the issue, inviting authors of framing chapters and commentators, selecting artifacts and writing the introduction. Some sections, like the one on accreditation or the demographics of the teaching force, are more self contained; others deal with cross-cutting themes. For example, the issue of diversity receives a fresh treatment in its own section but also permeates the entire book. The section on the purposes of teacher education is a first. No previous handbook of research on teacher education has dealt with this enduring and foundational topic.

Over eighty authors, ranging from established scholars and teacher education leaders to emerging researchers and new entrants to the field, have contributed to this volume. The Handbook contains a wealth of artifacts spanning two centuries and offering rich and varied evidence that the central concerns in teacher education have persisted although they have been understood in different ways at different times. The commentators reflect a wide spectrum of political and ideological stances. We deliberately sought out thoughtful people with divergent views on teaching and teacher education to provoke critical thinking and stimulate engagement with fundamental questions about teacher education.

No Handbook is meant to be read cover to cover, and we fully expect that readers of this Handbook will be drawn to different sections. We hope that they will be stimulated and stretched by the opportunity to think about fundamental issues from multiple perspectives, to gain historic perspective and conceptual clarity, to consider where dependable evidence exists and where belief and ideology cloud thinking. Ultimately we hope this Handbook will contribute to more informed and equitable practice and policy in teacher education and move the field toward more rigorous and relevant research.

Acknowledgments

As with any project of the size of this Handbook, this project could never have been completed without the assistance of many people. We are grateful to all of them. The editors especially want to acknowledge the members of the Handbook Advisory Board who helped to conceptualize this handbook and offered excellent advice about enduring issues in teacher education. Many of the board members eventually became section editors, chapter authors, and commentators for this volume. As the editors of this volume, we want to acknowledge their efforts: Renée Clift (University of Illinois), Carl Grant (University of Wisconsin), David Hansen (Teachers College), Andy Hargreaves (Boston College), Bob Houston (University of Houston), David Imig (AACTE), Mary Kennedy (Michigan State University), Susan Moore-Johnson (Harvard University), Sonia Nieto (University of Massachusetts), Ed Pultorak (Southern Illinois University), and Ken Zeichner (University of Wisconsin). We also want to thank Renée Clift, in particular, who served on ATE's Research Committee, and was instrumental in encouraging us and ATE to take on the editorship of this volume. We also want to thank Bob Houston, Editor of the first *Handbook of Research on Teacher Education*, who provided a valuable historical perspective on this project and graciously agreed to write the volume's Foreword. Finally, we would like to thank Allen Warner (University of Houston) who was ATE president when the third edition was proposed and was influential in the original contacts with our publisher.

There is no way this project would ever have been completed without the thoughtful, always positive, and tireless efforts of Kelly Demers, who began to work on this project as a graduate student assisting in the organization of the board meeting. Over time, Kelly became the manager of the project and eventually Associate Editor of this volume. She also served as co-editor of one of the volume's major sections. Kelly worked with the editors to conceptualize the volume and its many chapters. She kept all of the contributors to the volume organized and on track. There were 83 authors in total, so this was no small task. She handled all of the administration, logistics and permissions related to the project over four years. Her efforts were absolutely indispensable, and her pleasant diplomacy and consistent grace under the most trying circumstances were inspiring. Her contributions to the project and to this volume are immense.

We are also grateful to the many graduate students who assisted faculty members in their preparation of chapters and commentaries. In particular, we want to thank Ann Marie Gleeson, a doctoral student at Boston College, who worked on the formatting of the chapters in this volume; her attention to detail was invaluable.

Finally, we would like to acknowledge the editorial assistance and overall encouragement and support of Naomi Silverman, who worked with us on this project from the beginning. Her unfailing positive attitude and her enthusiasm for the project sustained us.

Marilyn Cochran-Smith
Sharon Feiman-Nemser
John McIntyre

Part 1

What's the point?

The purposes of teacher education

Editor: David T. Hansen

Part 1
Framing chapters

1 Introduction

Why educate teachers?

David T. Hansen
Teachers College, Columbia University

Every philosophy of teacher education presupposes underlying assumptions about teaching and education. These assumptions are not easy to keep in view. As every seasoned teacher educator can attest, the work is all-encompassing, sometimes exhaustively so. The press of time, of building programs, of dealing with bureaucracies, of endless meetings with collaborators, of countless hours with candidates, of getting from one school to another, of applying for grants, and more, can make philosophical reflection seem like a remote luxury, perhaps for sabbatical or a weekend retreat. Moreover, the politicized environment surrounding teacher education generates anxiety, anger, distraction, and confusion. The environment places relentless pressure on teacher educators to showcase and defend their work, however experimental and in transition it may properly be (because dedicated teacher educators, like good teachers everywhere, are constantly seeking to improve their work, it often has an experimental character). This pressure can lead teacher educators to dig in their heels and dogmatically cling to particular values and aims, rather than to subject them to ongoing criticism and judgment. All of these factors militate against calm, tenacious, and honest reflection on purpose.

Even in settled moments it is not easy to return to one's philosophical starting points. And yet, this kind of inquiry can be a source of immense intellectual satisfaction and personal growth. On the one hand, it can trigger fresh, revitalized thinking for programs, policies, and practices. On the other hand, it can spin out new and stronger threads for the fabric of one's work as a teacher educator. The effort to philosophize makes it possible to articulate why teacher education is worthwhile. It positions teacher educators to gauge whether their views and values have matured over time. Such inquiry makes it possible to consider alternative outlooks, an experience that in itself can have significant consequences for educational thought and action.

The goal of this section of the handbook is to undertake an intellectual excavation. The authors of the chapters that follow identify bedrock values that underlie the stated purposes of teacher education most prominently in circulation today. The authors also describe additional values, outlooks, and programmatic approaches that might be of service to teacher educators as they ponder their reasons for being. All three authors are philosophers of education who have played sometimes intensive roles in the practical work of teacher education. As they elucidate concepts and ideas, they aspire to be critical, clear, and analytic. Their concerns and values will be apparent, even as they seek to keep open to question their own assumptions and those that characterize the current ethos in teacher education.

In Chapter 2, I discuss the educational values of (1) preparation for productive life, (2) academic learning, (3) human development, and (4) social justice, with the latter sometimes associated with multiculturalism, at others with civic and democratic education. I identify core meanings that advocates perceive in these values, and I raise questions about them. To provide philosophical assistance in criticizing them, I sketch two alternative standpoints for assessing the purposes of teacher education. They are what can be called "public interest" and "the cultivation of personhood" (or individuality). The chapter concludes with suggestions on how to sustain a critical dialogue about purpose in a climate where, to many, the issue has long been settled in favor of one value or another. Because no previous handbook of research on teacher education has addressed the question of purpose in a direct or systematic way, I write in the form of an essay, hoping to sketch perspectives that can propel future reflection and research.

Emily Robertson, in Chapter 3, examines the relation between teacher education and democracy. She takes as her context several interlocking circumstances: the evident decline in democratic participation in the United States, pressures to standardize curriculum and teaching through broad testing schemes, questions about the worthiness of schools of education to house teacher education, growing interest in civic education on the part of higher education institutions, and what she and many critics characterize as a polarized political and educational discourse in the nation. She asks: What dispositions and abilities can strengthen a genuinely democratic way of life? What roles can education, including teacher education, play in developing them? In response, Robertson focuses on how schools can assist the young to develop the arts of deliberation, negotiation, and activism in the name of justice and freedom. She addresses how teacher education can help new teachers grasp and teach these arts. (These tools can also be useful to teacher educators themselves as they debate purpose and substance in their programs.) Robertson concludes that schools of education can prepare good teachers capable of fulfilling this democratic purpose only if they sustain meaningful autonomy from centers of societal power, which might otherwise coopt teacher preparation in pursuit of their own particular ends.

In Chapter 4, Hugh Sockett describes four models of the epistemic and moral purposes of teacher education. Sockett takes as a point of departure conceptions of a profession, and raises questions about the appropriateness and likelihood of school-teaching becoming a full-blown profession. He examines the often conflicting claims about the knowledge base in teacher education. With this discussion in hand, Sockett elucidates four models of teacher preparation which he calls (1) the scholar-professional, (2) the nurturer-professional, (3) the clinician-professional, and (4) the moral agent-professional. Each harbors a distinctive moral and epistemological standpoint, such that each, as he shows, is both a model of practice and a model for practice. Sockett deploys his analysis of the models to underscore the fact that diversity of outlook continues to prevail both within and outside the teacher education community. As such, debate about the purposes and substance of teacher education, rather than consensus, will likely continue far into the future.

The inclusion and structure of the three chapters mirrors the aims of this section of the handbook. I hope my lead-off chapter helps readers come to grips with their most fundamental beliefs and convictions, as well as their deepest doubts and questions, about the purposes of teacher education. Emily Robertson seeks to shed light on the thorny and urgent issue of the place of teacher education in a society that purports to be democratic. Hugh Sockett foregrounds the epistemological and moral aspects of teacher preparation not only because it is timely to do so given contemporary discourse on teacher education, but also to illuminate what it means to speak of teacher *education* rather than, say, merely job training as if teaching were a mode of rote skill work.

These core chapters are followed by four readings selected to provide an intellectual, aesthetic, and ethical backdrop to this section of the handbook. They are written by, respectively, Ralph Waldo Emerson, Jane Addams, W. E. B. Du Bois, and John Dewey.

From an intellectual point of view, the readings demonstrate that questions about the purposes of education have been around for a long time because they are unavoidable, challenging, and inviting. In aesthetic terms, the readings illuminate how shriveled and dry conceptions of education can become if they are divorced from what renders life beautiful and meaningful. The readings provide an ethical backdrop because virtually every sentence in them addresses the reader, asking her or him to confront questions about value and purpose in education. Put another way, the readings cannot be heard if approached solely through an historical or sociological lens. Those lenses categorize the texts before they have even been opened, putting them in their (or a) place rather than considering the fresh voice they provide if one seeks to listen.

In "The American Scholar," an address at Harvard College given in 1837, Ralph Waldo Emerson fashions a provocative image of what it means to be an educator in a new society that has not yet "found" its identity (a condition that some might say continues to describe the United States). Such an educator takes seriously his or her mind and its powers to think, imagine, and question. For Emerson, this posture is requisite for taking seriously the minds of others. An educator does not pre-judge self or others, but rather arrives at or reaches a judgment after inquiry, reflection, and communication. The teacher and scholar also is a person immersed in the richest curriculum available, which constantly pushes him or her to expand horizons and perspectives. Emerson illustrates his argument by spotlighting reading. He contends that reading should constitute not merely the acquisition of information but should also be a formative experience in its own right. Reading should show the teacher and scholar the tremendous range and depth of human accomplishment across time, even as it demonstrates the many challenges in living. As a consequence, reading should compel the teacher and scholar onward, and outward, to realize as fully as possible his or her unique talents and bent. This experience positions the individual to assist others in what Emerson regards as the great and boundless human adventure of education. For Emerson, education should support every person's entry to a life of purpose and meaning rather than to one of subservience, whether the latter be to a class, a geographic region, an idea, or an idol.

W. E. B. Du Bois's tale, "Of the Coming of John," published in 1903 in his *The Souls of Black Folk*, is at once a story of the costs of racism and of the dangers of education. A young black man, John, leaves his southern town to obtain an education in the north. After nearly failing because of youthful frivolity, he reverses course and succeeds brilliantly as a student. The consequences are both beautiful and devastating. On the one hand, John perceives how miraculous and magnificent are the accomplishments of humanity in realms such as art, science, and literature. He has an Emersonian insight into his own unfathomable potential to create and be a purposive being. On the other hand, he also sees how unjust his society has become under the pressure of racism and its associated social, political, economic, and educational inequities. At one and the same time, John experiences inexpressible joy and indescribable despair. His newly won vision is dangerous both to a racist social order and to his own community's self-containment, and he becomes a foreigner to both. In between the lines of this story, Du Bois seconds Emerson's call for an education in meaning for all persons, and also indicates that political, economic, and social change must accompany such a call for it to become a reality. At the same time, Du Bois leaves on the table the idea that genuine education will generate confusion, doubt, and suffering as much as their opposites. He asks, in effect, whether teachers (and their teachers) can accept this condition or whether they will seek safety and consolation by adopting a one-sided view of what is entailed in becoming educated.

Jane Addams advances a complementary view in her essay, "Socialized Education," published in 1910 in her book about the settlement house movement, *Twenty Years at*

Hull-House. Addams' view of education fuses the values of individual development and community enrichment. She and her colleagues treat every immigrant who crosses the threshold of the settlement house as a unique, unprecedented being, but also as a person who can go on to share his or her educational experiences with others. It becomes an informally understood obligation for residents and immigrants alike that to receive positions one to give. Through a myriad of examples in this essay and throughout her book, Addams describes an education in and for the arts of communication and meaningful interaction with other people. "Socialized education" points to a merger of academic, trade, and civic education, as the immigrant children and adults participate in the comprehensive programs she and her colleagues tirelessly create and reconstruct. But the term suggests more than this, as a brief analogy with an idea from John Dewey will illustrate. Dewey highlights the need to "psychologize" subject matter if the young are to grasp its logic. They cannot immediately perceive knowledge in the same way an experienced scholar or teacher does. Knowledge must first be connected with their experience (see Chapter 2 in this section). On her part, Addams emphasizes the need to "socialize" the subject matter of both school and life in order to render it into something other than merely a personal possession. She grants a necessary space for solitude and private self-cultivation. But their fruitfulness is immensely enriched through a generous social and public life (and vice versa), however modest in scale it may be.

In the final selection, on "The Need for a Philosophy of Education" published in 1934, Dewey argues that in a rapidly changing world educators must be ever vigilant and ever articulate about their aims and methods. They must wed flexibility with principle, adaptability with conviction, and experimentation with commitment. A democratic way of life calls for these and associated dispositions precisely because such a life refuses to pre-determine peoples' destinies. For Dewey, education in modern times carries a special burden: to make available to all children and youth, on a regular basis, genuine educational opportunities. This unending task requires both excellent preparation of educators and consistent social, economic, and political support from society. At the same time, in accepting this burden educators experience a special democratic grace. More than most other groups and individuals in society, they have the privileged opportunity to engage in a systematic educational relationship with children, youth, adults, and their peers. They can bear witness to democratic transformation every day, if by "transformation" is meant the expansion and enrichment of communication between people however small in scale when compared to the social whole.

These cursory summaries illustrate why the readings remain fresh even as their influence has percolated through culture up to the present moment. They challenge the dominance of theory in approaches to reading, whether of books, persons, or events. The four figures would understand the claim that each of them could be read historically, as subject to particular influences, pressures, values, precedents, and so forth that in an a priori fashion are taken to determine the boundaries of thought and expressivity. They would understand the notion that each could be read as the embodiment of a particular gendered, raced, classed, and otherwise sociologically bounded standpoint or location. In a marvelous way, however, the four figures question the privileging of any perspective that presumes to hold "the key" to "the right way" to read the world. Through a variety of tropes and viewpoints, they dramatize the question of what degrees of freedom human beings enjoy to be creative in the very midst of psychological and social pushes and pulls. These and other factors account for why their work remains young, and for why it provides an appropriate backdrop for a fundamental inquiry into the purposes of teacher education. (For a detailed and closely related examination of the readings as a set, see Hansen *et al.*, in press.)

The concluding portion of Part 1 of the handbook features commentaries by Michael Apple, John Goodlad, and Vanessa Siddle Walker. As editor, I invited them to serve as commentators because of their lengthy and varied experience as scholars, and because of their long-standing concern for education. Apple has examined ways in which the structures and ideologies of a capitalist political economy interface with the workings of the educational system. Goodlad has undertaken extensive studies of the functioning of teaching, schooling, and teacher education. Walker has researched in depth the education of blacks during the historical period of de jure segregation in the United States. In asking these scholars to comment, I also believed they would offer contrasting perspectives on the question of purpose in teacher education. They have fulfilled that expectation.

The core chapters, reading selections, and commentaries underscore the idea that education is a value-laden endeavor. Every curriculum and every mode of instruction embodies a judgment that *this* is important to learn and *this* is the way to teach it. This expression of judgment holds for the most advanced doctoral study and it holds for the most bare-bones job preparation program. The unavoidable presence of values in all educational work thus raises the question of which values ought to be given priority in a given system. In turn, this question illuminates why all genuinely educational purposes are bound to spark tension and controversy, precisely because they rest upon values that may not be shared or prioritized by others.

These points hold for the purposes of teacher education. As this section of the handbook demonstrates, there is significant disagreement among teacher educators, teachers, administrators, policy-makers, researchers, and others regarding the purposes of teacher preparation. Some critics would do away with formal preparation entirely, while others advocate for rigorous training programs modeled after those in law and medical schools. In between these endpoints are a host of perspectives that regard teacher education as a mode of socializing new candidates into an occupation, or as a means of inducting them into a profession, or as a vehicle for initiating them into a social and moral vocation. Taken as a whole, this section provides one way to sketch the contemporary debate about purpose and prospect in teacher education. Hopefully, it will be useful to all who aspire to greater clarity about purpose and to a greater sense of agency in participating in the ongoing debate.

REFERENCES

Addams, J. (1990) Socialized education. In Addams, *Twenty years at Hull-House*, 244–258. Urbana: University of Illinois Press.

Dewey, John (1989) The need for a philosophy of education. In J. A. Boydston (ed.), *John Dewey, the later works 1925–1953: Vol. 9. Essays, reviews, miscellany, and a common faith*, 194–204. Carbondale: Southern Illinois University Press.

Du Bois, W. E. B. (1990) Of the coming of John. In Du Bois, *The souls of black folk*, 165–179. New York: The Library of America.

Emerson, R. W. (1983) The American scholar. In *Ralph Waldo Emerson: Essays & lectures*, 51–71. New York: The Library of America.

Hansen, D. T., Anderson, R. F., Frank, J., & Nieuwejaar, K. (in press) Re-envisioning the progressive tradition in curriculum. In M. Connelly, J. Phillion, & M. F. He (eds.), *Handbook of research on curriculum*. New York: Sage.

2 Values and purpose in teacher education

David T. Hansen
Teachers College, Columbia University

To ask what the purposes of teacher education are is to presume such an education is necessary. However, from the time that schools for children and youth emerged on a wide scale in the nineteenth and twentieth centuries, many critics have asserted teachers do not require formal, professional preparation. They need to know the basics of the subjects they teach, how to keep order in the classroom, how to get along with people, and how to abide by administrative regulations. An adequate secondary and college education, so the argument goes, will give them the requisite subject matter knowledge. Experience will teach them how to organize the classroom and cooperate with institutional authority. This familiar point of view goes hand-in-hand with the idea that schools exist to socialize the young to fit into society. Since teachers have themselves been socialized in this system, they do not need any distinctive background or preparation for the work. In this outlook, the idea of formal teacher preparation makes no more sense then instituting a "socialization preparation program" for teacher candidates.

To talk about the purposes of teacher education is also to presume such an education is worthwhile, that it makes a difference in how teachers conduct themselves and in the influence they have on children and youth. However, since the beginning of widespread schooling around the globe many critics have asserted that teachers are basically technicians serving the interests of those with economic and political power. Despite their good intentions and best efforts, so the argument goes, teachers labor in highly constrained circumstances that undermine the possibility of meaningful education. Their factory-like schools embody hierarchical economic, social, and class structures characteristic of the larger society. Their work is subject to constant bureaucratic and administrative control, itself shaped by the same societal forces and conditions. Writing from the perspective of the 1960s, Harry Braverman captured the spiritual consequences of what he and other critics regarded as a lockstep system:

> . . . [T]here is no longer any place for the young in this society other than school. Serving to fill a vacuum, schools have themselves become that vacuum, increasingly emptied of content and reduced to little more than their own form. Just as in the labor process, where the more there is to know the less the worker need know, in the schools the mass of future workers attend the more there is to learn, the less reason there is for teachers to teach and students to learn. In this more than in any other single factor—the purposelessness, futility, and empty forms of the educational system—we have the source of the growing antagonism between the young and their schools which threatens to tear the schools apart.
>
> (1974, p. 440)

Given this picture of the world, formal teacher education can be seen as a waste of time, if not a cruel hoax perpetrated on unsuspecting young candidates about to run into a wall.

These long-standing viewpoints differ in their fundamental assumptions about education and society. The one sees schools as benign agents of social continuity, the other as an embodiment of social ills. They share the presupposition that formal education, including the education of future teachers, must be understood through a functionalist lens.

In this chapter, I will argue that there remain good reasons for talking about the purposes rather than solely the functions of teacher education. Purpose and function are not synonyms. As Dorothy Emmet (1958) has shown, function supports maintenance while purpose mirrors creativity. Maintenance and creativity are both indispensable to society, though they may co-exist uneasily. To conceive education in functional terms presumes that the terms of the work are not set by its practitioners but rather by larger societal forces. There is truth in this outlook. Broad social, economic, political, cultural, and other forces will always influence educational practice, as well they should. A permanent aim of schooling in any society is renewal and continuity, without which the society would simply collapse. Even in the most democratically constituted community, teachers will always undertake important functions that differ from the functions of other societal actors (for example, lawyers and judges who preserve law, airline pilots who make the air fleets run, garbage collectors who keep towns and cities clean).

However, my premise in this chapter is that there can be significant consequences when educators ask What do we want to do, and how are we going to do it? The consequences may affect a single student, a classroom, a school, a district, or a larger entity, even a nation. If a "purpose" is understood as something envisaged that is to be brought about through human creativity, then it remains legitimate, coherent, and necessary to speak of the purposes rather than merely the functions of teacher education.

Put another way, there are excellent reasons for talking about *education* rather than presuming human conduct reduces to preset modes of formation. For one thing, even an insightful (and anguished) critic like Braverman acknowledges in the very act of his writing that it is important to strive for societal improvement. For another thing, the very existence of multiple and incommensurable theories of social determinism—consider the ways in which Karl Marx, Sigmund Freud, and Michel Foucault have been appropriated—calls one to look again at human possibilities and prospects. Moreover, the unpredictable and the uncanny continue to emerge in human affairs, sundering time and again theoretical attempts to categorize or pin them down. A few thousand votes out of tens of millions in 2000 would have altered the outcome of the presidential election in the United States. Would a President Gore have advanced the same educational agenda as President Bush, embodied, for example, in the No Child Left Behind legislation passed in 2001?

Education as compared with functionalist reproduction continues to happen whenever teachers and students ask meaningful questions, share their interpretations and arguments surrounding subject matter, conceive and complete projects, and cultivate their individual talents and bents. Such happenings take place countless times even in large, bureaucratic schools. They happen all the more frequently in schools with thoughtful administrators, dedicated teachers, imaginative curricula, engaged parents, and structures conceived experimentally that range from block scheduling, to regular faculty meetings, to "schools within schools" that can support meaningful teaching and learning.[1] These points do not obviate genuine concerns about today's schools. But they do call into question overarching claims about "the way education is."

Furthermore, as both teacher testimonials and systematic research have demonstrated (see, for example, Connelly *et al.*, in press, and Richardson, 2001), to *enact* what it means to be a successful teacher requires ongoing teacher education understood in both its formal and informal senses. Any serious reader of this literature, it seems to me, cannot help but perceive how complicated the work is. In no particular order, teachers need to consider (1) the psychological, social, and cultural aspects of students' learning and conduct, (2) the logical and substantive aspects of subject matter, (3) the social, moral, intellectual, even aesthetic dimensions of interaction in classrooms and schools, and (4) the politics of parent–teacher, teacher–administrator, and teacher–teacher relations in the school setting. And there is more. Teachers need to cultivate an articulate perspective on today's rapidly changing world with its economic, social, technological, and environmental problems and prospects. They need this outlook because the young will invariably look to them for structures of meaning and significance in response to the often stark transformations they hear about (and perhaps experience). Unless teachers cultivate a sense of purpose allied with a feeling for the larger human affairs of our time, they may themselves feel solely like functionaries. This call does not imply they must become philosophers, theorists, or public intellectuals. Rather, it means appreciating why they teach, why their subjects are important, and why it matters to pay attention to students, parents, colleagues, and others involved in the educational process.

Given this portrait of the complexity of teaching and human life today, I believe teacher education remains both necessary and worthwhile. It is also highly complex in its own right. Most teacher educators concur that a college degree is insufficient to render a person a successful teacher, just as a degree does not automatically make a person a successful doctor, businesswoman, policeman, or botanist. The complexities in teaching, which themselves evolve alongside the changing complexity of society, demand ongoing teacher education in both its formal and informal senses. However, teacher educators, teachers, school administrators, policy-makers, researchers, and others disagree about what constitutes the *best* education for teachers. These differences mirror contrasting values regarding the purpose of education, and thus of the education that teachers need— and, one might add, deserve—to perform their work well.

In the first section of this chapter, I will touch on what I take to be some of the most widely lauded values people perceive in education. I will address the consequences of these values for teacher education. The subsequent two sections provide alternative standpoints for assessing the purposes of teacher education. The first is what can be called "public interest," and the second can be called "the cultivation of personhood" (or individuality). These alternatives are not incompatible with one another nor with the values outlined in the first section. However, they generate a larger backdrop or horizon for discussion than what any single conception of teacher education on the table today can provide. In the concluding section of the chapter, I address the vexing but unavoidable question of how the educational community, in interaction with other sectors of society, can sustain a dialogue about purpose in the very midst of strident claims that this issue has been settled.

A SKETCH OF THE CURRENT VALUES LANDSCAPE IN TEACHER EDUCATION

Among the most prominent values influencing the scope and structure of teacher education programs today are preparation for work and life, academic learning, human development, and social justice, with the latter cast in some cases as respect for cultural diversity or multicultural education, and in others as civic or democratic education. For heuristic purposes, I will address each of these values separately. However, in actual practice they often overlap and even fuse.

From the very inception of schooling many educators and members of the public have understood its primary purpose to be the preparation of the young for economic and social life. This widely held value exerts continuous pressure on teacher education programs. It does so because many parents conceive this value first and last when they think of their children's education, even while they may differ radically from one another with regards to political, cultural, or religious values. Moreover, the idea of preparation for the future endures because few educators would claim that schools should play no role whatsoever in readying the young for adult life. Quite on the contrary, this value may be the most widely shared among teacher educators. The differences between them boil down to how they conceive enacting it. Many believe this value should be seen as immanent, as a natural or constitutive outcome of a good education rather than as an explicit force driving program structures and content.

For example, teacher educators who esteem the values in academic subjects believe that excellent teaching equips the young with the knowledge and intellectual skills to confront the challenges of adulthood. Often associated with a particular subject such as art, English, mathematics, history, or science, these teacher educators believe their programs should cultivate candidates' disciplinary knowledge in conjunction with instructional knowledge about how to bring subject matter to life. They take seriously, if not in so many words, John Dewey's (1976) distinction between the logical and psychological aspects of a discipline. Logic points to methods of inquiring and thinking that form the structure of a field of knowledge. These methods are the bread and butter of scholars and experienced teachers in the field. However, Dewey argues that in a teaching and learning environment this material must be psychologized if students are to move beyond mindless memorization into genuine understanding. When they first encounter a new domain of knowledge, students cannot immediately grasp the logic which scholars have at their command. Consequently, the teacher's charge, at whatever level of the system, is to generate activities that engage students' powers to understand, explain, and come to grips with the significance of new academic knowledge. Teacher educators who heed this outlook draw upon, or produce themselves, research that illuminates ways to deepen candidates' academic strengths and related pedagogical ability. Some take their point of departure from a sense that academic disciplines constitute beautiful, ever-evolving human achievements, and that it constitutes an injustice not to initiate the young into their mind-expanding and enriching values.

Other teacher educators esteem first and foremost particular conceptions of learning and the values associated with them. For example, some teacher education programs seek to enact a constructivist perspective, in which academic learning is highly prized and yet premised centrally on notions of the learner's agency, initiative, and imagination. Other teacher educators highlight multiple intelligence theory, with its pantheon of ways of knowing the world (artistic, mathematical, etc.). Still others turn to Maria Montessori, Jean Piaget, Lev Vygotsky, and others who have articulated highly detailed accounts of human development. In a deep and perhaps inexpressible sense (save by poets), these teacher educators are often inspired by the sheer fact that human beings can indeed learn and grow in remarkable, unfathomable ways. They are moved by the facts of human generativity and meaning-making.

Other teacher educators conceive social justice as the core value in the preparation of teachers. For many, this value emerges from a commitment to rectify, through teacher education and (hence) schooling, historic injustices in society based on racism, sexism, classism, homophobia, and other forms of systematic prejudice. These teacher educators envision teacher preparation as a dynamic vehicle for equipping new generations of teachers to play a part in societal transformation. This value also springs, for others, from a desire to ensure that today's immigrant children experience genuine education. These teacher educators look at the rapidly evolving cultural tapestry of the nation and call for teacher education and school programs that respond to the changing scene.

In some cases, the call for social justice materializes in a focus on cultural diversity as the guiding theme in everything from crafting lessons, to organizing the classroom, to assessment. The call also takes form in various models of multicultural education, which again becomes the orienting perspective for selecting curricula, pedagogical method, and so forth. Proponents of cultural diversity and multicultural education argue that such an education is necessary for the young to ready themselves for a changing and, according to this view, a better world. They do not necessarily marginalize the marvels of academic learning, the beauties of individual human development, or the need to be prepared to lead a productive life, even though they may not privilege these values. This posture mirrors the fact that those who esteem first and foremost academic learning, life preparation, or human development are not necessarily sidelining issues of social justice. However, there are tensions (to which I will return) between these standpoints with their varying emphases on what is central in teacher preparation.

Other teacher educators translate social justice into a call for civic and democratic education. Proponents draw on a variety of political and social theorists to argue that a central purpose of schooling in a democracy is to equip the young with the skills, knowledge, and dispositions that can enable them to act as citizens, rather than, say, solely as producers and consumers in the economic system. Advocates share common ground with multiculturalists in the sense that schooling cannot be, in their view, merely a preparation for life in society as it is currently constituted. Their eyes are directly on what they envision as a better world for all. However, they argue that multiculturalism may become incoherent and fragmented without a democratic education that cultivates an abiding disposition among all citizens to engage others with different values, outlooks, backgrounds, and concerns. For those dedicated to this outlook, teacher education becomes a site for preparing teachers of all subjects to bring to their work the commitment and the know-how to infuse civic and democratic interaction into school life (see Chapter 3 by Emily Robertson in this section of the handbook). Moreover, proponents also conceive the purpose of teacher education as helping practitioners learn to extend their teaching outside the boundaries of the school, either through forms of what is called experiential learning or through establishing connections with local communities and agencies. These activities would flow from a desire to help students develop democratic attitudes and skills alongside their learning of academic subject matter.

For heuristic reasons, I have characterized these various purposes of teacher education as inhabiting distinct, clearly demarcated realms of theory and practice. However, according to both research and extensive testimonials, teacher educators often adopt and fuse particular aspects of them in constructing their programs. Put another way, it is hard to name a single teacher education program that endorses one of the purposes while systematically excluding the others. No doubt some programs have transformed these purposes into approaches for which the field lacks an adequate description or name. They may have done so because there are pressing questions to be asked about all the values undergirding teacher education that I have sketched here.

For example, those who value above all the idea of schooling as preparation for a productive life must confront the question of what kind of "productive life" they have in view. To pose the matter in provocative terms, is it a life of fitting into the current socioeconomic system, marked as it is by inequity along the lines of quality of work (ranging from little to considerable autonomy and initiative), quality of compensation (including pecuniary and health benefits), and quality of housing and community well-being? Or is it a life that in its modest, local way offers a contrast to accepting inequity precisely because the person has had a school education that equips him or her with the outlook, skills, and dispositions to act creatively and imaginatively in the face of social problems?

Proponents of life preparation may have multiple responses to these questions. For example, they might argue that societal transformation—presuming there is agreement about this aim and its meaning—is the work of adults rather than of children, who need solid training in skills and know-how to develop their capacity to decide and act on life matters. More provocatively, advocates might argue that because teacher educators often strain to cultivate the right political and ethical outlook, they end up privileging the health of their consciences and the imprint of those consciences on their programs more than they attend to concrete realities facing today's young. For proponents of life preparation, the goals of teacher preparation are specific and focused, at all points tied to equipping teachers with the ability to teach skills and information effectively.

Nonetheless, the question of what kind of life one has in view as the outcome of education always remains on the table, at least in a society that styles itself as democratic. Even libertarians need to argue, rather than merely assert, that it is democratic to leave the question entirely up to individuals.

Those who value first and last academic learning face not only comparable questions but also queries about the constitution and meaning of academic knowledge. Whose knowledge? is the first question they are likely to have hurled at them. What knowledge is of most worth, and who decides? Teacher educators in this camp can point to the evolution of disciplines and emphasize that much of what is in them arose in the face of political and cultural opposition. For example, the very existence of history as a field of study and teaching can be seen as a human project of critical understanding (as contrasted, say, with one of mute acquiescence to the status quo). A field of work and teaching such as art can be viewed as a human response to universal experiences of wonder, joy, suffering, and beauty. Teacher educators can juxtapose these insights with an argument that the issue of academic knowledge raises dynamic educational and philosophical questions that are not reducible to ideological standpoint. The very concept "ideology," they might underscore, emerged from systematic inquiry and knowledge rather than vice versa.

However defensible these responses may or may not be, there remain contentious questions such as When and how should academic knowledge be introduced to students? How can teachers learn to work effectively with the distinction between the logical and the psychological aspects of knowledge? Why do academic disciplines so often seem to morph into "school knowledge"? Put in stronger terms, how can academic disciplines help but be watered down, fractured, and distorted given the realities of school structure, of complicated lives students lead, and so forth? Is the account of the values in academic learning too idealistic, on the one hand, and too isolated from social realities, on the other hand? Or can it withstand this criticism? Teacher educators who esteem various conceptions of human development face similar probing into the nature and consequences of their values.

The values of academic learning and human development reach back several millennia and are among the most enduring in the world's educational community. However, teacher educators who support them will have to respond to the equally long-standing view of humans as fundamentally economic beings. Can they demonstrate that pursuing academic learning and human development accomplishes the aims of preparation for productive life, only better so? Put another way, can a humanistic education that cultivates the mind, the hand, the heart, indeed the whole person, prepare people for the concrete challenges of life? Or should schools focus tightly on training in skills and practical know-how, and be staffed by teachers who function more like technicians than educators acting on a sense of purpose?

Those who value social justice as the aim of teacher education can ponder what they mean by justice. One way to do so is to ask why this value trumps or is preferable to others such as freedom, peace, compassion, truth, and love, all of which have been advanced for centuries as core values in education. It would also be productive to engage contrasting views of justice that have emerged from human history and that continue to influence contemporary debate. Finally, it would be valuable to question what it means to put educational processes in the service of overtly political objectives, however estimable the latter may be. The mirror twin here is the first value touched on above, preparing to lead a productive life. In that outlook, education takes its identity not from being an end in its own right but rather from being merely a means to an end.

All teacher educators, regardless of their values, can benefit from being critical of their views. However, for those who put forward democratic or multicultural education there is an additional self-imposed responsibility (even if not recognized as such) to be clear, articulate, and self-questioning precisely because they claim explicitly to be acting in the very name of justice and democracy. To assert a claim to the moral high ground in debate is no light matter. Can this claim be harmonized with an image of clearing new moral ground? How would proponents respond to the critic Susan Sontag (2001) when she states (thinking of writers): "Should we serve justice or truth? It has to be truth, in order to serve a justice which is not yet." Sontag does not mean that justice and truth cannot be reconciled. She means that the idea of truth presupposes a commitment to inquiry into values rather than solely advocacy on their behalf (see the second section below on public interest).

Advocates of social justice, whether in the form of advancing cultural diversity, democratic education, or some combination thereof, can reply by underscoring the sheer longevity of inequity and inequality in society—literally, from before the founding of the republic itself. They could argue that in a society that purports to be democratic, public resources in the areas of health, housing, employment, community development, and so forth must be redirected to equip all to realize the risky promise, or promising risk, of reaching out for genuine education (see the third section below on cultivating personhood). Put another way, access by everyone to the adventure of education is not something that can be brought about by fiat or by philosophical argument. Proponents of social justice would argue that this accomplishment will take long-term social dedication, political will, and thoughtful policy, in conjunction with reconstructed teacher education programs.

These and other responses do not mute the questions posed above nor others that have become familiar in teacher education circles. For example, how might multicultural education avoid essentializing cultural differences and therefore distorting our understanding of both human community and the development of individuality? How can civic and democratic education avoid predetermining the scope and substance of teaching and curriculum? Such an undemocratic outcome would be ironic, to say the least, if one takes the view that democracy's deepest and most radical prospect is that it refuses to preset the terms of the future, even while working tirelessly in the present to expand communication and possibilities for all.

John Wilson (1975) urges his fellow educators to be clear "whether we are, at any one time, seeking for what is educationally desirable or what is desirable on other grounds—and the fact that we might want both, if we can get them, only makes it more important to keep the distinction clear in the first place. Effective compromises can only be made if we know what we are compromising between" (p. 45). Academic learning and preparation for work, human development and democracy, truth and justice—these are among the distinct values at play in the contemporary landscape of teacher education. Can they be harmonized and realized at one and the same time? Or are tradeoffs, compromises, and differences in what to emphasize endemic to teacher education, much as they appear to be in every other social practice that comes to mind? In the ensuing two sections, I portray a horizon broader than any single value addressed in this cursory review. This horizon does not in itself constitute a larger, encompassing value or purpose. Instead, it provides an additional philosophical lens, or handhold, that can be of use as the debates about purpose go on, as hopefully they will.

PUBLIC INTEREST AS A CRITERION FOR ASSESSING PURPOSE

In this section I build upon Dewey's theory of public interest. I will emphasize the difference between interest, in the singular, and interests, in the plural, because the distinction between them resides at the heart of Dewey's outlook and its consequences for criticizing the purposes of teacher education. Dewey puts forward what is at first glance a breathtaking ideal, and yet one that can in fact be embraced by every person in society although never in a complete or final way. It is an ideal according to which life in its everyday manifestations can constitute an ongoing education, in the fullest intellectual, aesthetic, and moral sense of that term. To elucidate this outlook, I will discuss what I take Dewey to mean by the trio of concepts public, interest, and public interest. Then, I turn to how his notion of public interest provides a useful backdrop against which to reconsider the purposes of teacher education outlined in the previous section.

Human beings are members of various groups and social entities. They are associated with families, neighborhoods, churches, synagogues, mosques, schools, political parties, clubs and other local organizations, etc. Contemporary society is saturated with such groups, and people have a host of varied memberships in them. However, none of these groupings, either in their singularity or collectivity, constitute what Dewey calls a public. Rather, the public is an always emergent, always evolving entity. Dewey argues that a public comes into being when (1) the consequences of human activity in any particular group or association spill out beyond those local social boundaries and affect people elsewhere, and when (2) the affected people take note of these consequences and seek to respond to them.

> The perception of consequences which are projected in important ways beyond the persons and associations directly concerned in them is the source of a public . . . The public consists of all those who are affected by the indirect consequences of transactions to such an extent that it is deemed necessary to have those consequences systematically cared for . . . Indirect, extensive, enduring and serious consequences of conjoint and interacting behavior call a public into existence having a common interest in controlling these consequences.
>
> (Dewey, 1988, pp. 244–245, 314)

I understand Dewey to be suggesting that there is no such thing as a fixed or permanent public—unlike, say, various long-established associations and institutions—and nor is there any public at all if people remain enclosed within their various groupings. A public only emerges when people are drawn outside their local spheres and seek to address the consequences of action that are affecting them all in one way or another. Put another way, a public comes into being when people act with one foot outside the boundaries of their particular interests, whether the latter be economic, moral, cultural, religious, artistic, political, or educational.

Here is where the distinction between interests, in the plural, and interest, in the singular, that can be found in Dewey's work becomes useful. Interests in the plural are like possessions. I have my interests and you have yours. This social group has its interests, that one has others. People seek out those with similar interests. In politics, business, and elsewhere, various groups with comparable interests come together to advance them in the face of competing interests. This language is familiar and useful in understanding social and political life.

In contrast, Dewey deploys the term interest, in the singular, to denote an attitude, orientation, or disposition that is bound up in the completion of an activity. While interests denote discrete *objects* or *possessions* which people can name, interest constitutes a *movement* or *process*. In various writings Dewey reminds us that a core meaning of interest is that which stands between two otherwise distant entities, or between the beginning and completion of an undertaking. Thus, interest is not a starting point or precondition of activity, and nor is it an outcome per se. Interest is a transactive concept, capturing a process that resides neither in the head nor wholly outside the head. The concept points to a process that is always forward-looking, prospective, uncertain, and yet also potentially generative in meaning and consequence as persons seek to bring activity to fruition. As such, interest forms a key concept in Dewey's overall view of human growth.

What happens if we fuse Dewey's framing of the terms public and interest? For one thing, public interest differs substantively from anything that can be captured by the term interests. Public interest is not another name for just another, perhaps larger "interest group," to use the well-known term. Moreover, public interest is something other than a summation of localized interests; it is not merely a sum of the parts. To put it another way, there is no such thing as "the" public interest in the sense in which individuals and various groupings and associations can point to their interests. Public interest, framed now as a single concept, denotes an attitude, disposition, orientation that both emerges from and is enacted by human beings seeking to bring activity to meaningful completion. In what kind of activity is public interest expressed? Precisely in that which is called out by the emergence of consequences whose reach and effects have spilled out beyond localized boundaries, and which are of moment to people from various groupings and associations.

Teaching and teacher education are practices whose consequences percolate throughout society, thereby giving rise to a public concerned with their substance, quality, and effects. This public exists alongside others called out by the consequences of action in other domains such as health and sport. (Thus, a person can participate in many publics, while also pursuing various localized interests.) The public concerned about teaching and teacher education is never fully determinable because it is dynamic. It is diffuse, diverse, ebbing and flowing in its activity. Its constituents are rarely in agreement because the consequences of teaching and teacher education affect people and their particular groupings differently, in perception if not in concrete result.

Can this public develop *public interest* understood as a responsive disposition, orientation, attitude toward others and their concerns? Posed differently, can this public enact interest that reaches outside or beyond its many localized *interests*? According to Dewey, the existence and cultivation of such interest depends upon communication and education. At the conclusion of his *Democracy and Education* (1985), he describes what he regards as an ongoing, never fully achieved communicative and educational need: "Interest in learning from all the contacts of life is the essential moral interest" (p. 370). The idea of "learning from all the contacts of life" infuses a democratic aspect to interest. It does so because, according to Dewey, a democracy "is more than a form of government; it is primarily a mode of associated living, of conjoint communicated experience" (1985, p. 93). Democracy as a way of life, as an organic commitment to meaningful communication, necessitates interest in learning from all one's contacts in life. Democracy can neither function nor expand if persons remain cocooned within their respective domains. Such a posture, in Dewey's view, constitutes a refusal of the priceless opportunity to learn from others and is thus, inadvertently, a form of self-diminishment. He calls especially upon those with the greatest economic, cultural, and political power to recognize the many short- and long-term costs of their isolation.

Dewey argues that all people can be educated in an interest in learning from experience. If students are provided with sustained educational encouragement that incorporates quality academic materials in conjunction with interacting with diverse people and situations, they can learn to enact as a matter of course such an interest. They can learn to respond habitually not only to pleasurable and pleasing events, but equally so to challenging and thorny circumstances. They can learn to address new consequences, including those in which conflicting interests are at work. In other words, interest in the singular sense of a process of involvement can lead people to deal with the consequences of different interests when they meet head to head. Dewey calls this interest in learning from all the contacts of life "the essential moral interest" not because he subscribes to an a priori human essence, but because if this interest saturates peoples' dispositions and attitudes it propels them into the public world, however localized it may be, in the very face of misunderstanding, miscommunication, disagreement, and conflict. The term "moral" captures the sense of commitment and concern implied in an interest in learning from all one's contacts and encounters.

Dewey concludes *Democracy and Education* on this note because, for him, democracy implies much more than a set of institutional structures, important as they remain. Democracy presumes expansive forms of communication, interaction, and mutual regard constitutive of everyday life. In a democracy understood as "a mode of associated living, of conjoint communicated experience," life metamorphoses into a permanent, ongoing education. To learn from *all* the contacts one has means not just being a spectator and looking on, although careful observation of surrounding human affairs and attentive listening are vital. Rather, such learning necessitates participating, sharing views and perceptions, and more. Dewey's (1985, pp. 7–9) notion of communication is germane here, predicated as it is on the fundamental idea that every genuine communication (as contrasted with an exchange of information) implies a transformation in participants' outlooks and dispositions, however subtle or imperceptible it may be. Furthermore, people not only find themselves transformed through the course of genuine communication. They also find that this give-and-take can transform their interests, a consequence of great importance for the growth of both individuals and of democracy.

Dewey's provocative closing sentence to *Democracy and Education*—"Interest in learning from all the contacts of life is the essential moral interest"—captures the core of his philosophy of education. I believe it points to an image of a dynamic public forum for debating purpose in teacher education and for acting, experimentally, on various conceptions of purpose. To sketch this image, I want to substitute the terms "consequences" and "public" for "contacts" and "moral" in Dewey's phrase. The result is what could have served, in my view, as the concluding sentence of *The Public and Its Problems* (1988), one of Dewey's major statements about society: interest in learning from all the consequences of life is the essential public interest.

This interest implies learning not just from *some* contacts or consequences, those, for example, which help people serve their own interests. Rather, the approach obliges persons to try to learn from all contacts and consequences, including those that may call their interests into question. Thus it fosters a critical attitude toward one's own desires, aims, and conduct, as well as those of the various groupings and associations of which one is a member. In this light, according to Dewey, public interest is not a thing, entity, object, or possession. It is not a claim, argument, opinion, or belief. It is not a standpoint, position, posture, or platform. Public interest constitutes a living, dynamic process that pivots around a concern for the very next moment of associated human life in a particular domain of ideals and action. Public interest constitutes an orientation or point of view premised on the idea that persons can learn to learn from their experience. It points to a disposition of inquiry that ideally would saturate public affairs.

What might such an interest look like in practice, particularly with regards to the relation between education, teacher education, and society? For one thing, this interest would imply reconstructing how teacher educators perceive their various interests and commitments. Consider the values illustrated in the previous section of the chapter: preparation for life, academic learning, human development, and social justice. From one point of view, this diversity of values in itself is both intellectually and politically consequential. It reflects the fact that nobody has "the last word" on the nature and purposes of teacher preparation. It also makes possible a practical focus on specific dimensions of educational reality and need.

However, understood from the point of view of public interest as outlined here, these values can advance a parochial, territorial mentality. They can function as perceived end points, destinies, or king-of-the-hill interests, and oblige educators to bend their activity toward them rather than toward the situations and circumstances in front of their very noses. Teacher educators might instead consider values such as academic learning, diversity, and civic education as productive points of departure, or as beginnings, for further inquiry, test, and trial on how to create the richest educational experience possible. Like democracy itself—"a mode of associated living, of conjoint communicated experience"—teacher education perceived through the lens of public interest reaches beyond any single theoretical outlook or domain of value however estimable it may otherwise be.

Dewey's image of public interest provides teacher educators a backdrop against which to weigh their values in comparison with values put forth by their peers and by other sectors of society. They can speak articulately on behalf of their values even while recognizing their contested and dynamic nature. They can inquire into the values other societal actors advance in order to appreciate their origins, appeal, and possible consequences if acted upon in teacher education and in teaching. Just as teacher educators urge teacher candidates to take all students seriously, despite any number of differences between them, so they can learn to learn from all the contacts they have in their own professional work. The values in such learning include becoming clearer, more discerning, and more critical about their own and others' values and educational purposes. They include becoming more dedicated to modes of communication that are constituted by a passionate, disinterested interest—an interest not in the triumph of one's values or interests but in their continued improvement, and perhaps transformation, through the crucible of educational thought, dialogue, and practice.

THE CULTIVATION OF PERSONHOOD AS A CRITERION FOR ASSESSING PURPOSE

Dewey's conception of public interest generates a broad social criterion for assessing purpose in teacher education. A second, equally broad criterion springs from the question of what it means to be an educated person. In one sense, this question was answered in the first section of the chapter. Depending on their outlook, teacher educators would argue that an educated person is prepared to lead a productive life, has studied academics systematically, has been taught and supported through developmentally appropriate methods, has a democratic outlook, respects and understands diversity, and so forth. In other words, an educated person is a human being who embodies one or another of the cardinal values advanced by teachers and teacher educators.

However, there is another view of an educated person that emerges from the very same democratic notion Dewey puts forward in conceiving public interest. If democracy constitutes "more than a form of government" but rather "is primarily a mode of associated living, of conjoint communicated experience," what does it take for an individual human being to participate in such experience? At a minimum, it seems, the person must understand how to "associate" with others through "communication" that is shared, interactive, and "conjoint." That capacity implies social knowledge, social skill, and social commitment. But it also necessitates having something to contribute that nobody else can put forward, however modest it may be in comparison with the whole. Social change and, in particular, social improvement are inconceivable without *individual* response, imagination, and action.

The improvement may materialize in how a parent and child interact thanks to an idea one or the other conceives. It may surface in enhanced interaction between teacher and student, judge and jury, friend and friend, cabdriver and passenger, doctor and client, etc. The improvement may be in policy or in governance. In every case one or another person has to step forward, metaphorically speaking, into new terrain. Someone must advance an idea, notion, image, or possibility. Without these individual initiatives, there can be no association, no conjoint communicated experience, no education, no politics, in short nothing people mark out as remarkable and noteworthy in life.

Individuality is not necessarily coterminous with self (nor is it identical with "individualism" as a social or political theory). Every culture has a conception of the self or person that differs in substantive ways from other cultures. The self may be regarded as an autonomous entity or as a social, spiritual, natural, or composite entity. Regardless of these differences, however, what remains universal about culture is the recognition of individuality—for example, that he is a particularly talented shoe-maker, that she gardens more effectively than others, that he has greater patience as a painter, that she sings with greater range and nuance. Consider other lines of work undertaken today. Dentists the world over differ widely in ability, tact, insight, knowledge, personality, and stamina. So do bus drivers, storekeepers, school principals, hair stylists, and professional sports players. In one way or another, every culture both features and thrives on individuality, just as it does on understandings of community.

Dewey and other critics have argued that individual distinctiveness is crucial and precious in a society that aspires to be democratic in its life and practices. It is so, in part, because improvement in any domain of the human cannot emerge without individual initiative (which is not to imply such initiative is sufficient, as the previous section suggests). Individuality is also prized by democracy because this mode of life depends fundamentally on courage, hope, and faith in human possibility. Those qualities find embodiment in individual human beings, and they help form the moral structure of "associated living, of conjoint communicated experience." This conception of the person-in-democracy is at once both challenging and realizable.

It is challenging because to participate in democratic life implies having the courage to engage new ideas and perspectives. To recall Dewey's terms addressed previously, it takes courage to cultivate interest "in learning from all the contacts of life." That prospect can be frightening because the process of education always implies giving things up, however minute or modest they are in scope. When I learn to see history in a broader light I have to give up my previous, more narrow way of looking at the past. When I learn to interpret poetry I have to let go of previous assumptions about what language can do. When I grasp the insights of biology I take leave of former, perhaps highly bounded images of physical processes in nature. "The way of life is wonderful," wrote Ralph Waldo Emerson; "it is by abandonment" (1983, p. 414). Emerson meant quite literally that wonder dwells only in the moment of encountering the new; it emerges only in the moment of risking the old. Put differently, education only happens when a person engages and lets in the new, which means abandoning one's prior state of understanding. This posture necessitates courage, and thus steady encouragement from one's teachers as well as supportive conditions in the environment.

It does not require heroism, save in particular circumstances. The changes denoted here are typically small if not microscopic in comparison with the totality of a person's and community's life. Nonetheless these modest changes have summative force. In addition, they stand as a permanent example to others of what transformation means and what it looks like in everyday human affairs. Thus, the perspective framed here is inhabitable or realizable precisely because it takes seriously the promise in each succeeding moment of human interaction. Each moment can be marked by a perhaps tiny but nonetheless additional and cumulative increment of awareness, mindfulness, appreciation, and concern. This conception of the person opens the door to endless individuality and multiple modes and expressions of identity (it also illustrates why the idea of personhood is larger than what is typically captured by the psychological concept human development). The conception conjures the idea of life as an ongoing education. To learn from all the contacts one has constitutes a life of expanding, deepening meaning and communication, however confusing and unsettling the process will sometimes be. It bears emphasizing that this image of an educated person is not dependent upon the individual's particular station, formal degrees, or any other institutional criteria. A day care worker or waiter can display greater curiosity, wonder, and capacity to learn than the richest executive or most powerful scientist.

Teacher educators, who are themselves noninterchangeable, distinctive human beings, cannot help but hold a conception of personhood that informs their sense of purpose. It may not be articulate or thought through to a logical and practical conclusion, but it is operative. Consequently, teacher educators can only benefit from rendering visible their notions of personhood and how these jibe with their assumptions about education and society. It is a truism that education occurs one human being at a time. Moreover, no two persons learn in identical fashion, just as no two classrooms and no two schools feature the same ethos. The most glorious, inspiring ideals of social and political purpose will founder unless they are fused with a fine-grained image of the cultivation of individuality—and vice versa. The idea of public interest sketched previously and the notion of cultivating personhood outlined here constitute, together, a conceptual diptych useful for criticizing the underlying values in teacher education.

CONCLUSION: SUSTAINING DIALOGUE ON VALUE AND PURPOSE

What is the purpose of talking about the purposes of teacher education? Is it to hammer out a final version of "the" purpose which everyone can accept? Is it to elucidate a clearer understanding of the influence that conceptions of purpose have on teacher education practice? Is it a political mechanism for the educational community to demonstrate to the larger society that it knows what it is doing? Or is such talk a waste of time, as the long-standing presumptions about schooling with which this chapter opened suggest?

I hope the analysis here makes plain that it is important to distinguish between function and purpose. Function denotes maintenance, purpose the possibility of transformation. People may never be able to tell just how many social or psychological degrees of freedom they have to be creative—in other words, to conceive and realize purposes. But they do know the domain is larger than zero, perhaps larger than any teacher, philosopher, politician, or artist has yet shown. I believe this outlook renders it worthwhile and necessary to consider the purposes of teacher education.

Should such inquiry strive to produce a final agreement about values? Should teacher educators conclude that either preparation for productive life, academic learning, human development, or social justice captures "the" core value? Or should they encourage a thousand flowers to bloom, and assume that the purpose of teacher education includes all of these values and goals as well as others that might emerge over time? Should there be unity or diversity in values and purpose (see the chapter by Hugh Sockett in this section)?

Such questions are intimidating, at least at first glance, but they do not imply that teacher educators must choose between an absolutist or relativist standpoint. Neither posture appears to be tolerable or sustainable in a democratic society that is dependent, in turn, on education. Absolutism is not tolerable because a democracy, understood through a Deweyan lens, generates a multiplicity of points of view. It presumes that new values, aims, and hopes are constantly surfacing. Relativism is not tolerable because democracy rejects the premise that anything goes; it assumes that with rights come obligations and responsibilities. It presumes that it is both individually and communally demanding to dwell in a democracy. It presupposes a place for public interest rather than solely for particular interests.

Thus, to examine purpose in teacher education implies something other than a process that would terminate dialogue through a final agreement. Rather, inquiry into purpose is crucial to maintain dialogue. It functions to keep the conversation vibrant, dynamic, and consequential. Such talk is indispensable to the very existence of a sense of purpose. Without dialogue on purpose people can quickly become passive if not resigned to "the way things are." Looked at from another angle, communication about purpose is not solely instrumental. It is not a mere means to an end, whether the latter be a new program, new protocol, or new institutional structure. Such interaction can certainly lead to these changes and, some would argue, is a sine qua non if the changes are to be intelligent and wise. However, dialogue about purpose embodies its own values, among them sustaining a sense of value (again, as contrasted with becoming passive), a sense of community (which often translates into critical energy), a sense of individuality (as each person articulates her or his outlook), and a sense of hope (that values matter in the world precisely because human life is not predetermined or predestined).

These points suggest that a core purpose of teacher education is to cultivate an open mind toward multiple views of educational purpose, and yet without lapsing into an uncritical or bland relativism (as if the mind were empty rather than open). Proponents of life preparation, academic learning, human development, and social justice can do more than presume "others have their values, we have ours" and proceed to operate in isolation one from the other. Such a strategy is self-defeating. It generates increasing strain, anxiety, and wasted energy—not to mention rigid thinking—since it is much harder to sustain isolation than it is to accept the possibility of communication, however challenging the latter is to initiate and support. In some respects, it is more vital to retain an interest in learning from all the contacts of life than it is to bind oneself to a particular position, platform, or standpoint. To adopt this course, teacher educators will need both courage and the ability to become articulate in a new key. This posture does not imply abandoning their values. It is not a diminishment of commitment, but rather constitutes an escalation of commitment into a more complicated but ultimately more enriching democratic space. That space will always be both unsettling and inspiring; unsettling because nobody in it (including oneself or one's community of purpose) has the last word, and inspiring precisely because nobody has that last word. The word—the purposes of teacher education and of education itself—is something for all to participate in generating anew.

This view of purpose, and of why it matters to communicate about purpose, can support the two additional aims of engagement mentioned at the start of this section. First, the dialogue creates a supportive ethos for research in teacher education. At one and the same time, this ethos encourages research and the criticism of its results. It fuels systematic inquiry into the consequences of differing values and purposes on teacher education. Second, the dialogue fortifies, edifies, and educates the participants in the teacher education community, such that when they interact with various societal constituents—policy makers, parents, community and business leaders, politicians, and so forth—they bring to the table a richer language, a broader vision, and a deeper sense of value and justification. They can juxtapose communication about what teachers need in their preparation programs with dialogue about what teachers deserve if they are to carry out the distinctive, complex, and indispensable tasks that society sets before them.

NOTE

1 I use the term "experimentally" in the Deweyan sense of practices formed through an intelligent trial of ideas and methods. This use should not be conflated with the formal meaning of a scientific experiment that deploys control and treatment groups, etc.

REFERENCES

Note: In addition to works referenced directly in the chapter, the readings below provide useful perspectives and background for engaging the question of purpose in teacher education.

Beyer, L. E., Feinberg, W., Pagano, J. A., & Whitson, J. A. (1989) *Preparing teachers as professionals: the role of educational studies and other liberal disciplines*. New York: Teachers College Press.

Borrowman, M. L. (ed.) (1965) *Teacher education in America: a documentary history*. New York: Teachers College Press.

Braverman, H. (1974) *Labor and monopoly capital: the degradation of work in the twentieth century*. New York: Monthly Review Press.

Broudy, H. S. (1977) Types of knowledge and purposes of education. In *Schooling and the acquisition of knowledge*, ed. R. C. Anderson, R. J. Spiro, & W. E. Montague, 1–17. Hillsdale, NJ: Erlbaum.

Buchmann, M. & Floden, R. E. (1993) *Detachment and concern: conversations in the philosophy of teaching and teacher education*. New York: Teachers College Press.

Cochran-Smith, M. & Fries, M. K. (2001) Sticks, stones, and ideology: the discourse of reform in teacher education. *Educational Researcher*, 30 (8), 3–15.

Combs, A. W., Blume, R. A., Newman, A. J., & Wass, H. L. (1974) *The professional education of teachers: a humanistic approach to teacher preparation*, 2nd edition. Boston: Allyn & Bacon.

Connelly, M., Phillion, J., & He, M. F. (eds.) (in press) *Handbook of research on curriculum*. New York: Sage.

Dewey, J. (1972) Interest in relation to the training of the will. In *The early works of John Dewey 1882–1898: Vol. 5. Early essays*, ed. J. A. Boydston, 111–150. Carbondale, IL: Southern Illinois University Press.

Dewey, J. (1976) The child and the curriculum. In *The middle works of John Dewey 1899–1924: Vol. 2. Essays on logical theory 1902–1903*, ed. J. A. Boydston, 271–291. Carbondale, IL: Southern Illinois University Press.

Dewey, J. (1977) The relation of theory to practice in education. In *The middle works of John Dewey 1899–1924: Vol. 3. Essays on the new empiricism*, ed. J. A. Boydston, 249–272. Carbondale, IL: Southern Illinois University Press.

Dewey, J. (1985) Democracy and education. In *John Dewey, the middle works 1899–1924: Vol. 9. Democracy and education 1916*, ed. J. A. Boydston, 3–370. Carbondale, IL: Southern Illinois University Press.

Dewey, J. (1988) The public and its problems. In *John Dewey, the later works 1925–1953: Vol. 2. Essays, reviews, miscellany, and The public and its problems*, ed. J. A. Boydston, 235–372. Carbondale, IL: Southern Illinois University Press.

Dewey, J. (1989) How we think. In *The later works of John Dewey 1925–1953: Vol. 8. Essays and how we think, Revised edition*, ed. J. A. Boydston, 105–352. Carbondale, IL: Southern Illinois University Press.

Elliott, J. (ed.) (1993) *Reconstructing teacher education: teacher development*. London: Falmer Press.

Emerson, R. W. (1983 [1841]) Circles. In *Ralph Waldo Emerson: essays & lectures*, 401–414. New York: The Library of America.

Emmet, D. (1958) *Function, purpose, and powers*, 2nd edition. Philadelphia: Temple University Press.

Feiman-Nemser, S. (1990) Teacher preparation: structural and conceptual alternatives. In *Handbook of research on teacher education*, ed. W. R. Houston, 212–233. New York: Macmillan.

Feiman-Nemser, S. (2001) From preparation to practice: designing a continuum to strengthen and sustain teaching. *Teachers College Record*, 103 (6), 1013–1055.

Fenstermacher, G. D. & Amarel, M. (1983) The interests of the student, the state, and humanity in education. In *Handbook of teaching and policy*, ed. L. Shulman & G. Sykes, 392–407. New York: Longman.

Floden, R. E. & Buchmann, M. (1990) Philosophical inquiry in teacher education. In *Handbook of research on teacher education*, ed. W. R. Houston, 42–58. New York: Macmillan.

Green, T. F. (1983) Excellence, equity, and equality. In *Handbook of teaching and policy*, ed. L. Shulman & G. Sykes, 318–341. New York: Longman.

Greene, M. (1981) Contexts, connections, and consequences: the matter of philosophical and psychological foundations. *Journal of Teacher Education*, 32 (4), 31–37.

Griffin, G. A. (ed.) (1999) *The education of teachers: ninety-eighth yearbook of the National Society for the Study of Education*, Part I. Chicago: University of Chicago Press.

Grow-Maienza, J. (1996) Philosophical and structural perspectives in teacher education. In *The teacher educator's handbook: building a knowledge base for the preparation of teachers*, ed. F. B. Murray, 506–525. San Francisco: Jossey-Bass.

Grubb, W. N. & Lazerson, M. (2004) *The education gospel: the economic power of schooling*. Cambridge, MA: Harvard University Press.

Hansen, D. T. (2001) Teaching as a moral activity. In *Handbook of research on teaching*, Fourth Edition, ed. V. Richardson, 826–857. Washington, DC: American Educational Research Association.

Hansen, D. T. (ed.) (2006) *John Dewey and our educational prospect: a critical examination of Dewey's Democracy and Education*. Albany: State University of New York Press.

Hirsch, Jr., E. D. (1999) *The schools we need and why we don't have them*. New York: Anchor Books.

Joyce, B. (1975) Conceptions of man and their implications for teacher education. In *Teacher education: the 74th yearbook of the National Society for the Study of Education*, ed. K. Ryan, 111–145. Chicago: University of Chicago Press.

Kennedy, M. M. (1987) Inexact sciences: professional development and the education of expertise. In *Review of Research in Education*, 14, ed. E. Z. Rothkopf. Washington, DC: American Educational Research Association.

Kessels, J. P. A. M. & Korthagen, F. A. (1996) The relationship between theory and practice: back to the classics. *Educational Researcher*, 25 (3), 17–22.

Korthagen, F. A. J. (2001) *Linking practice and theory: the pedagogy of realistic teacher education*. Mahwah, NJ: Lawrence Erlbaum Associates.

Labaree, D. F. (1997) Public goods, private goods: the American struggle over educational goals. *American Educational Research Journal*, 34 (1), 39–81.

Ladson-Billings, G. (1994) *The dreamkeepers: successful teachers of African American children*. San Francisco: Jossey-Bass.

Peters, R. S. (1977) *Education and the education of teachers*. London: Routledge & Kegan Paul.

Proefriedt, W. A. (1994) *How teachers learn: toward a more liberal teacher education*. New York: Teachers College Press.

Richardson, V. (ed.) (2001) *Handbook of research on teaching*, Fourth Edition. Washington, DC: American Educational Research Association.

Russell, T. & Korthagen, F. (eds.) (1995) *Teachers who teach teachers: reflections on teacher education*. London: Falmer Press.

Scheffler, I. (1968) University scholarship and the education of teachers. *Teachers College Record*, 70 (1), 1–12.

Schrag, F. (1995) *Back to basics: fundamental educational questions reexamined*. San Francisco: Jossey-Bass.

Schwartz, H. (1996) The changing nature of teacher education. In *Handbook of research on teacher education*, Second Edition, ed. J. Sikula, T. J. Buttery, & E. Guyton, 3–13. New York: Macmillan.

Shulman, L. S. (1998) Theory, practice, and the education of professionals. *The Elementary School Journal*, 98 (5), 511–526.

Sontag, S. (2001) A dialogue with W. G. Sebald on the writer's task. A public forum at the Ninety-Second Street YMCA, New York City.

Wilson, J. (1975) *Educational theory and the preparation of teachers*. Windsor, Berks.: NFER Publishing Company.

3 Teacher education in a democratic society

Learning and teaching the practices of democratic participation

Emily Robertson
Syracuse University

> The essential feature of a democratic polity is its concern for the participation of the member in the process by which the community is governed.
>
> (Tussman, 1960, p. 105)

TEACHER EDUCATION AND THE CONTEMPORARY POLITICAL CONTEXT FOR CIVIC PARTICIPATION

It is frequently claimed that many United States citizens are politically ill informed and fail to participate in the political process. More people can name the Three Stooges than can name the three branches of government (Westheimer & Kahne, 2004). Only 8 percent of college graduates from 1982 to 1992 who were surveyed in the National Election Studies had ever written a letter to a public official and only 7 percent had worked for a party or candidate (Nie & Hillygus, 2001). Not all the news is bad. American youth are increasingly engaged in community service: Eighty-two percent of 2004 first year college students surveyed reported engaging in volunteer work as high school seniors (Williams, 2005). Yet volunteer work, unlike the war protests and civil rights movements of earlier generations, involves students in serving the public good but not necessarily in distinctively democratic political action.

In the wake of the last presidential election, the *quality* of public political discourse has been under attack. In a *New York Times* Op-Ed piece, "Is Persuasion Dead?" Matt Miller (2005) asked: "Is it possible in America today to convince anyone of anything he doesn't already believe? If so, are there enough places where this mingling of minds occurs to sustain a democracy?" (p. A15). Miller's question was echoed by Paul Krugman's (2005) complaint that neither politicians nor the electorate are willing to change their views when confronted with decisive contrary evidence. Ideological polarization, the "red" states versus the "blue" states, is evident not only in the electorate but also in the House, whose members are often elected from districts created by partisan gerrymandering. Both a gerrymandered House and the niche market media create situations in which people have no need to speak to any but the like-minded (Rosen, 2005; Posner, 2005). Richard Posner (2005) holds that people read newspapers, not to become well informed, but to find "information that will support rather than undermine their existing beliefs" (p. 9).

Education has been identified as both part of the cause of the current state of democratic political participation and as part of the potential solution, although where the solution lies is contested. Diane Ravitch and Joseph P. Viteritti (2001a) say that, while Americans have traditionally relied on public schooling to transmit "deeply cherished democratic values," there is currently concern that schools are no longer playing this role. In their view, today's students fail to acquire core civic knowledge, such as an understanding of how our government works, but rather encounter in public schools a multiculturalist curriculum that does not aim at "the overarching civic ideals of the American community" (p. 5). Ravitch and Viteritti's critique shares common ground with Steiner and Rozen's claim that teachers are trained in education schools that are lacking in "balance" and are dominated by "progressivist" and "constructivist" visions where they encounter a "countercultural" curriculum, "instilling mistrust of the system that teachers work in" (as cited in Hartocollis, 2005, p. 25). In general, those who take this perspective favor greater teacher and school accountability through the standards and assessment movements and legislation such as No Child Left Behind (NCLB). Their view of civic education focuses on the acquisition of knowledge about American history and government and on sharing common civic ideals.

On the other hand, there are those who believe that education for democracy in the United States must involve a commitment to social justice, which requires attention to diversity in an increasingly multicultural society. Walter C. Parker (2003), for example, holds that democratic citizens require a conception of justice that includes a "capacity for recognizing patterns of domination and unfairness that may be lodged comfortably in everyday life and for working toward alternative ways of living together" (p. 73). The implications of this view for principles of teacher education as drawn by Marilyn Cochran-Smith (2004) include making "inequity, power, and activism explicit parts of the curriculum" (p. 77).

Advocates of the social justice perspective are by no means convinced that theirs is the dominant view in teacher education, unlike the critics cited above. Jacqueline Jordan Irvine's (2004) assessment is that the "field of teacher education has not taken seriously its role to prepare teachers as activists and advocates of social justice" (p. xii). She holds that the leadership of schools of education must create an environment that exemplifies and values diversity and that faculty committed to social justice must make their political stances clear. Although in agreement with NCLB's goal of eliminating the gaps in group achievement levels, the supporters of democratic education for social justice generally believe that NCLB's implementation has resulted in methods of teaching and a narrow curriculum that do not serve the goal of democratic education. High stakes testing and the standards movement have similar effects, it is said (Michelli & Keiser, 2005).

Thus the debates about educating democratic citizens, and the knowledge and commitments their teachers should have, seem as polarized as the rest of the political landscape. The differences in perspective can be exaggerated: likely everyone thinks it would be good if students knew more about the workings of government and likely everyone believes that achieving greater social justice is an important democratic goal, even if there is disagreement about what these objectives mean. Nevertheless, democratic education of students and its implications for teacher education are contested terrains—what democracy is; what constitutes appropriate participation; how to educate for democracy; the contributions of higher education generally and teacher education in particular are all disputed. For example, Derek Heater (2004) provides the following list of contemporary controversies concerning American civic education: "multicultural *vs.* national cohesion objectives, national *vs.* world citizenship, structure of the disciplines *vs.* problems of democracy approaches, learning about institutions *vs.* learning civic behavior, academic study *vs.* community service" (p. 124).

The contentiousness of civic education is not simply a contemporary phenomenon. While historically Americans have expected schools to prepare future citizens, what that participation entailed—and who counted as a "citizen"—depended on the dominant political values and prejudices of the period. Areas of focus have included moral virtue, American history, the principles of the Constitution and of American government, patriotism and nationalism, world citizenship and tolerance, social issues, and civic participation (Reuben, 2005; Heater, 2004). Injustices related to race, ethnicity, gender, and religion have represented repeated challenges to the democratic rhetoric of political equality. Current attempts at civic education at the elementary level include celebrating national holidays, learning about community helpers, and a focus on the rule of law, American history, the Bill of Rights, and the Constitution. At the secondary level, students typically have at least a year of American history and one semester of government (Heater, 2004).

Given this background of polarization and controversy, any discussion of democratic education must occupy a non-neutral terrain. Accordingly, my treatment of teacher education and its relation to democracy takes place within a particular context that gives salience to some issues rather than others. (And that's a good thing, given that searches for key terms in my university's library consistently turned up more than 10,000 entries for each term, the system's maximum reporting capacity.) The social and political context for this essay includes the perceived state of democratic participation in the United States, the polarized political climate, the educational assessment and accountability movements, challenges to schools of education as the best location for teacher education, and the growing interest in civic education on the part of higher education institutions. Also, I have chosen to focus on civic education in the United States, although I am well aware that democracy is a global phenomenon and that many who live in the United States and participate in democratic life are not citizens. The specific focus of this chapter is on modes of democratic participation and their implications for pre-service teacher education.

The virtues we imagine citizens should possess depend in part on our conception of political life. What is the political domain, the sphere of civic action? And what actions are called for in that domain? My conception of the domain of political action in this chapter is an expansive one. My main focus is, in Dewey's (1966/1916) terms, on democracy as "a mode of associated living, of conjoint communicated experience" (p. 87). No doubt United States citizens should study American history and government. But the fundamental commitments of citizens of a liberal democratic society to the political equality of all citizens and to all citizens' rights to basic liberties and opportunities that are protected even against the majority are formed through participation with others in democratic modes of communication and action. What are the "habits of the heart" that sustain a democratic mode of life and what roles can education, including teacher education, play in cultivating them (Bellah *et al.*, 1985)?

I will argue that the role of citizen in a liberal democracy requires the ability to engage in multiple practices through which citizens co-determine the goods they will pursue together as citizens and negotiate the differences that divide them. The fact that citizens hold different and conflicting views about how individual and public life should be led, as well about what justice demands, makes these negotiations necessary. The freedom a liberal democratic society provides for voicing differences of opinion and acting on them, within the limits of the law, makes continuous conversation about public matters a requirement of democratic life. The political polarization described earlier represents a failure of engagement in this fundamental democratic task: if there is no "mingling of minds," no willingness to change one's views in the give and take of conversation, no openness to engaging with any but the likeminded, can democracy worthy of the name be sustained?

Further, I will argue that the knowledge, skills, and virtues required to participate in democratic practices of engagement set goals for the education of democratic citizens, as well as supplying goals for the education of the teachers who will help develop these capacities in each new generation. Finally, I suggest that the ability of schools of education, and higher education institutions generally, to contribute to civic education depends on creating and maintaining their autonomy from centers of power in the society that might corrupt this mission.

THE CIVIC SPHERE AND THE PRACTICES OF DEMOCRATIC CITIZENS

The contexts that come readily to mind when democratic political action is invoked are places such as legislatures, town councils, and school boards where participants are making decisions that are binding for a particular polity. Recently, however, theorists have explored the potential of civil society for democratic action. "Civil society" refers to the social sphere of voluntary associations formed by citizens to express their interests and commitments, associations that are largely outside the spheres of the economy and the state. As Iris Marion Young (2000) says: "In the associations of civil society people co-ordinate their actions by discussing and working things out, rather than by checking prices or looking up the rules" (p. 159). Civil society, in this sense, includes churches, neighborhood associations, workers' organizations, political action groups, clubs, cultural organizations, non-profit service providers, civic associations, and many others. Such groups may provide services for their members, can expose injustice in the political and economic spheres, and sometimes succeed in placing limits on state and economic power. Young suggests categorizing these associations as private, civic, and political. Although not all associations in civil society are positive (e.g. the Ku Klux Klan), in their civic and political forms, these associations have the potential for strengthening democratic life. The inclusion of civil society in the political domain extends the possibilities for political action beyond the sphere of the state and opens up wider possibilities for democratic participation. The expansion of the political sphere to include civil society mirrors Dewey's expansive and inclusive conception of democratic life previously invoked.

Further, Jane Mansbridge (1999) argues for including what she calls "everyday talk" as a potential site for political action. Mansbridge defines as political " 'that which the public ought to discuss' when that discussion forms part of some, perhaps highly informal, version of a collective 'decision' " (p. 214). While legislatures aim at decisions that will be binding on the participants, everyday talk creates the climate of opinion within which binding decisions can be made (or through which such decisions are realized). From this perspective, Mansbridge suggests, "The snort of derision one might give at a sexist television character while watching with friends" is a political act (p. 214).

What types of actions do we engage in as citizens, not only in contexts where authoritative decisions are being made, but also in associational life and through everyday talk? And what knowledge, skills, and virtues do these forms of action require? Michael Walzer (2004) has emphasized the variety of forms of political participation, including (among others) political education, voting, campaigning, fund raising, demonstrating, and "scut work," such as stuffing envelopes. Yet these particular activities are embedded in more general types of practices that orient our engagement with other citizens around the issues that divide us.

With these political contexts in mind, I will consider three categories of interpersonal relationships among democratic citizens: (1) deliberation; (2) negotiation and bargaining; and (3) activism. These practices represent different visions of the work of citizens and their proper orientation to each other. Moreover, these forms of interaction are often in tension with each other, as we shall see. Yet my thesis is that democratic political life requires them all. While some citizens may specialize in one category or another as life stances, most of us are called upon to engage in all three categories of action, at least within the sphere of civil society and everyday talk. The role of formal education in developing them is what I want to explore, along with what these practices imply for the purposes of teacher education in a democratic society.

Deliberation

Many of the recent discussions of civic virtue assume that the prime thing citizens ought to do together is deliberate. I have in mind here theories of what is called "deliberative democracy" (Gutmann & Thompson, 2004; Gutmann & Thompson, 1996; Macedo, 1999). From this perspective, when confronted with a public problem, citizens should try to figure out the best solution to the problem through joint consideration of the reasons for and against proposed courses of action. Alan Wertheimer (1999) says that: "In general, we deliberate with each other when we think that (1) there is a right answer to an issue and (2) discussion will move us closer to that answer" (p. 171). Walzer (2004) character-izes deliberation as "a rational process of discussion among equals, who listen respect-fully to each other's views, weigh the available data, consider alternative possibilities, argue about relevance and worthiness, and then choose the best policy for the country or the best person for the office" (p. 91). When citizens deliberate, then, they seek the best policy or the best course of action through analysis of the available evidence in a process of rational discussion with fellow participants. Deliberation is not just a sharing of per-spectives but rather "discussion with an eye toward decision making" even when the participants are not themselves the primary decision makers (Parker, 2003, p. 81).

Juries are examples of citizen deliberation. We assume that there is a truth of the matter—the person charged is either guilty or innocent. The jury's task is to assess the evidence and decide on a verdict. We do not think that jurors should compromise or "split the difference" when there is disagreement. If the charge is murder in the first degree and some jurors believe that the defendant is guilty while others think he is totally innocent, it would be wrong of them to compromise by convicting him of a lesser charge, say manslaughter. Their task is to agree on the direction the available evidence points or to acknowledge that they cannot reach a verdict. Negotiations may take place behind the scenes among lawyers, defendants, and prosecutors; but juries should not negotiate. On the other hand, friends debating which movie to see normally do not think there is an objectively right answer. They seek to accommodate each other, to find a movie each wants to see. They do not, in the sense described above, "deliberate" (Walzer, 2004; Wertheimer, 1999).

All theories of deliberative democracy attempt to specify the conditions under which public deliberations can be regarded as legitimate (e.g. that all citizens should have an equal and effective right to participate) and they attempt to specify the citizen virtues that are required for successful public deliberation (e.g. willingness to listen to and seriously entertain other citizens' points of view). The point of the deliberation is to convert dis-agreement into agreement about what to do by determining which proposals are sup-ported by the best reasons. Deliberative democrats recognize that disagreement may be persistent. Nevertheless, they believe that the mutual respect involved in the process of deliberation will enhance the legitimacy of whatever decision is ultimately made even in the eyes of those who lose out.

While deliberation is a familiar activity, it is perhaps not often realized quite how strenuous the ideal is. Deliberation is not merely talking nor is it a debate. As Deborah Tannen ([1998] 1999) puts the point in *The Argument Culture*: "Public discourse requires *making* an argument for a point of view, not *having* an argument—as in having a fight" (p. 4). In a debate, the opponents are trying to win, not to discover the truth. They may present the evidence that favors their case and suppress the contrary evidence, for example. Debaters are not trying to find the best solution by keeping an open mind about the opponent's point of view. Unlike deliberators, debaters are typically not open to the possibility of being shown wrong (Walzer, 2004). Neither is deliberation simply a matter of the airing of opinions in which each participant is regarded as having a right to his or her own point of view. Deliberation involves joint inquiry in which evidence is collected and brought to bear on a problem and multiple theories and interpretations are examined. Thus that participants change their views as the deliberations unfold is one indication that real deliberation is taking place (Simon, 2005).

Preparing future citizens to deliberate, then, requires a focus on a particular set of skills and dispositions. Effective deliberators should be able to construct sound arguments for their positions but should also be open to changing their views when confronted with better arguments. Like Dewey, deliberative democrats see communal political discourse as joint inquiry that is self-correcting given the right conditions (Michelli, 2005). Deliberation is, as previously noted, not a debate but rather a collaborative inquiry into questions affecting the public good: seeing what is at stake, bringing evidence and alternative perspectives to bear on the question, developing an opinion, assessing the fairness of the decision-making process (Simon, 2005).

Since diversity of perspective is a deliberative asset, willingness to listen to others who disagree with you is a deliberative virtue. So also is support for the principles that constitute the grounds for free and fair exchange of ideas: respect for the rights of others; nondiscrimination; the freedom and equality of all citizens; civility; mutual respect; tolerance of dissent; openness to different points of view. As deliberative democrat Amy Gutmann (2005) puts the point, the goal of civic education is to prepare citizens with "the ability to argue and appreciate, understand and criticize, persuade and collectively decide in a way that is mutually respectable even if not universally acceptable" (p. 358). Since, as Gutmann suggests, consensus may not be reached on contentious issues, citizens must be willing to respect decisions reached through fair procedures even if they disagree and intend to continue trying to persuade their fellow citizens to change their judgments.

There is a considerable consensus in the literature that one of the best ways to develop deliberative capacities in students is to engage them in discussion of controversial issues (Gutmann, 2005; Johnson *et al.*, 2000; Parker, 2003; Simon, 2005). If the issues were not controversial, deliberation would not be required. Sometimes the preferred issues are those close to home, such as classroom and school policies, where students may be able to influence the outcome. But often students are engaged in deliberating public policy questions such as free trade or environmental treaties. Parker (2003) offers a curriculum for a high school course in deliberation that teaches students a framework for policy analysis. The National Issues Forum (NIF) network promotes a deliberative focus on policy issues, using material provided through the Public Agenda Foundation. In Project 540, students define their own topics for deliberation. This program has involved 250 high schools and over 140,000 students since 2002 (Johanek & Puckett, 2005).

In her study of 50 secondary schools in five countries (England, Denmark, Germany, the Netherlands, and the United States), Hahn (1998) found that students who had opportunities to discuss controversial issues in classrooms where they felt free to express their views developed more positive political attitudes than students lacking such experiences. Such discussions were most effective when the classroom was open to multiple points of view and students felt able to express views that differed from those of their peers or their teacher. Students having such experiences expressed "higher levels of political efficacy, interest, trust, and confidence" (p. 245).

The implication of a focus on developing students' deliberative capacities for teacher education is that teachers should learn how to conduct deliberative discussions and create supportive classroom environments. If we are to encourage deliberation in students "we would have to incorporate facilitation skills in significant ways into teacher education programs and ongoing professional development efforts," notes Simon (2005, p. 112). Simon contrasts classroom deliberation with the simple acquisition and recall of information that she believes dominates classrooms. Of course, deliberative discussions need to be informed, but Simon argues that such discussions take longer than straightforward knowledge acquisition and hence there will be some tradeoff between deliberative discussion and content coverage. Standardized tests and high stakes testing are often barriers to classroom deliberation, she says, because deliberative capacities are not tested for and teachers are reluctant to spend time on things that are not tested. They may also be afraid of getting into trouble through discussion of controversial issues. Parker (2003) offers an account, based on his own experience, of how pre-service teachers can learn to lead deliberative discussions (Chapter 7). Drawing on the work of Morton Deutsch on conflict resolution, Johnson, Johnson, and Tjosveld (2000) have trained teachers and administrators in techniques of "constructive controversy," which engage students in deliberative discussion of controversial issues.

Is deliberation a frequent component of public political life? Admittedly, it does not seem to capture the real world very well. If we think about the quality of conversation in the last Presidential election, reasonableness, open-mindedness, willingness to be shown wrong, are not the first adjectives that come to mind. Even advocates of the deliberative view acknowledge that the actual political process does not often exemplify deliberation, so students may have rarely seen examples (Simon, 2005). But the model offers an ideal to be aspired to, not a description of reality. To what extent *should* political discussion depend on mutual persuasion about the rightness of particular policies and courses of action? Can democratic interpersonal political communication rightly take other forms? Are these alternatives morally second best to deliberation even if they may be more efficient or expedient? Advocates of deliberation do not generally argue that deliberation is the only acceptable political activity, but they do tend to think that it has moral advantages over other activities and should be preferred when possible. Is this true?

Dewey (1966/1916) modeled public political discourse as joint inquiry. But others have held that in a *democratic* society, deliberation plays a more limited role. Some believe that the deliberative stance pays too little attention to "the degree to which moral disagreements in politics are shaped by differences of interest and power" (Shapiro, 1999, p. 29). Daniel Bell (1999) argues that if a country is deeply divided between rich and poor and lacks a sense of community and mutual trust, "the solution might be expropriation rather than deliberation" (p. 73). The political philosopher Will Kymlicka (2003) has recently suggested that cooperation among diverse groups may be "more a matter of bargaining and negotiation than of genuinely shared deliberation or mutual understanding" (p. 165). Are advocates of deliberation attempting to transcend politics—are they trying to create "a world where political conflict, class struggle, and cultural difference are all replaced by pure deliberation?" asks Walzer (2004, p. 105).

Deliberation can enhance disagreement rather than bringing about convergence. Religious differences may prove irreconcilable, for example, or citizens may become more aware of their class interests through discussion and hence more aware of how their interests diverge from those of other citizens. In a liberal democratic society such as the United States where there are diverse groups with different perspectives as well as conflicting interests, reaching agreement on what is true or best as a way of deciding what to do may be less likely to produce a solution acceptable to all than accommodation of conflicting interests. A political order based on agreement about what is true (a theocracy, for example) is different from a liberal democratic political order that attempts to encompass citizens with different conceptions of the good.

Negotiation and bargaining

Bargains represent the balance of power not the force of the arguments. The parties trying to reach agreement are seeking to secure their own interests, not necessarily to transcend them through appeal to a common conception of justice or concern for the common good, as the deliberative democrat might want. However, since agreements are more likely to be stable if they give each party a decent measure of satisfaction of their interests, accommodating each other will generally be in the interest of each of the negotiating parties. Wertheimer (1999) says that "We may seek to accommodate each other when we believe that there is no right answer to an issue or that continued deliberation will not likely resolve the dispute (even if there is a right answer)" (p. 171). An accommodation attempts to reach an agreement all can accept. Nevertheless, a mutually agreed to bargain or accommodation may not represent anyone's idea of the *best* solution. It may not coincide with either party's conception of the just outcome or the one best supported by the available reasons.

Advocates of deliberative democracy are wary of negotiation even as they sometimes acknowledge the need for it. Parker (2003), for example, distinguishes negotiation from deliberation by noting that bargaining assumes competing interests and involves "at least two groups present in the same forum engaged in an adversarial contest" (p. 81). Gutmann (2005) says that bargaining is "self-interested or group-interested"—a "politics of manipulation and coercion" rather than "a politics of reasoning and persuasion" (p. 354). And she notes: "Without the capacity to deliberate, there would be no escaping from power politics—which give power priority over both justice and deliberation—which all moral conceptions of democracy are intent on avoiding" (p. 353). Gutmann does acknowledge, however, that bargaining and negotiation might be called for in situations where no moral issue is at stake or at least one party to the dispute is unwilling to take a moral point of view and so those who did so would be disadvantaged.

Gutmann and Thompson (1999) contrast "the positive case of finding grounds of moral accommodation with similarly motivated political adversaries and the negative case of reaching compromises that undermine one's fundamental principles" (p. 266). New York Senator Hilary Clinton's suggestion that both pro-life and pro-choice advocates can support a program for preventing unwanted pregnancies is an example of positive moral accommodation. A hypothetical case in which a pro-life person proposes giving up the effort to make abortion illegal in exchange for a pro-choice advocate's support of the Hyde amendment (which denies federal funds for abortions for poor women) would be an example of the latter, of compromising one's principles.

Skepticism about the morality of bargaining in politics may be part of what gives politics a bad name. Hahn (1998) found low levels of political trust among all adolescents in her multi-country study of secondary school students. Only about 20 percent of adolescents said that they respect those who hold public office. She notes that few students reported ever meeting a politician. They gained their views from media reports of scandals, especially in the tabloid press, and from their parents. Hahn asks what these attitudes mean for the survival of the ideal of representative democracy.

But is negotiation or bargaining necessarily morally suspect? Strategies for forging agreements among opposing parties obviously vary. A winner take all power politics leaves a few crumbs at best for the loser. Competitive struggles are determined by the balance of power or by force. Yet bargains are required when each side needs the other. If one side can force its will on others, there is no need to negotiate. Generally, parties in a bargaining or negotiating situation have interdependent interests; they need each other's cooperation to some extent in order to serve their own interests. Each has some power either to promote or to frustrate the other's satisfaction of their needs.

Morton Deutsch's theory of negotiation emphasizes this interdependence rather than competitive struggle (2000a). From this perspective, constructive conflict resolution requires shifting perspective from conflicts in world-views or moral principles (which usually are non-negotiable) toward the primary interests of the conflicting parties. What is required is to enlist the parties in a collaborative investigation of how to satisfy the primary interests of each in the specific context. In a sense, this strategy transforms negotiations into deliberation about how to reach an agreement all can accept. Yet the agreement sought is not the objectively right outcome but an arrangement that accommodates each of the parties.

Some of the most difficult conflicts are those where moral principles cannot be set aside because the conflict concerns different interpretations of principles of justice. Deutsch (2000b) offers an example of a mediated conflict resolution where the conflict involved how teacher representatives to a site-based management team should be selected. The issue was whether seats should be designated for teachers from minority groups that were heavily represented among the students but not among the teachers. The school's Black Teacher Caucus held that the management team needed their input, given the diversity of the student body and the importance of the school's dealing with increases in bias related incidents and developing a curriculum more relevant to the current student population. The majority of council members held that all members should be elected through democratic procedures and that setting aside a seat for an African American teacher would open the door to still other seats dedicated to other minority groups. With the help of a mediator, they were ultimately able to agree on a solution that involved the principal's appointing a seven person multicultural task force each year from which two members of the council would be selected, one at large by vote of the task force and one from the ethnic group most prevalent in the student population (pp. 3–4). The challenge in such cases is to find a creative solution that allows the claims of each side to be represented and the principles that each invokes to be included (Deutsch, 2000a).

Despite the disdain sometimes expressed by deliberative democrats of negotiation as a moral enterprise, democratic citizens arguably need the virtues and skills of conflict resolution that are useful in finding peaceful accommodation of others' interests or creative solutions to conflicts of moral principles. Aside from skills in conflict resolution, citizens prepared to engage in constructive negotiation require problem-solving skills, self-control, ability to take the perspectives of others, ability to communicate well, cooperativeness, and awareness of bias (Sandy & Cochran, 2000).

There are numerous programs for teaching conflict resolution skills to children and adolescents in schools, as well as to their teachers through in-service workshops. Since the 1980s, Educators for Social Responsibility (2005) has advocated teaching students ways of peaceably and creatively resolving conflicts as a way of producing safe and supportive learning environments. In 2003, their Resolving Conflict Creatively Program for grades K-8, originally developed with the New York City Schools, was in 400 schools in the

United States. Sandy and Cochran (2000) provide examples of programs serving youth from early childhood to adolescence, including the Peaceful Kids Early Childhood Social-Emotional Learning Program developed in 1998 at the International Center for Cooperation and Conflict Resolution at Teachers College (Columbia University, New York City).

The most frequently mentioned aims of these programs include: reducing school violence; generating positive inter-group relations; reducing prejudice; creating good learning environments; helping students develop pro-social skills that will aid their personal growth and their success in school and in the workplace; and fostering responsible citizenship. That conflict resolution skills might make a contribution to the practices of democratic citizenship can certainly be inferred from these aims, but the connections are not fully developed in the materials surveyed for this chapter. However, given the persistence of disagreement among citizens about which policies and practices are best, the attitudes and strategies fostered by training in creative conflict resolution offers a positive alternative to the polarization we currently confront. If teachers were to help students develop such capacities, they would need training, not only in conflict resolution strategies, but also in how to teach such strategies to others. The experiences of numerous practitioners who have conducted workshops in conflict resolutions in various settings could be a resource for such training (Raider *et al.*, 2000).

There are, however, limitations to the scope of constructive conflict resolution. When conflict is generated by injustice, especially injustice that is difficult to recognize by those who perpetrate it because it is embedded within major social institutions, a reorientation of thinking is required, not simply creative solutions. Some citizens must learn to enlarge the scope of their moral communities and recognize their complicity in the persistence of unjust treatment of other citizens. Those who have been unjustly treated are often more likely to recognize their situation and organize to become forces for social change. This work exemplifies the final practice of democratic citizenship surveyed here, activism oriented toward social justice.

Activism

Activism can be engaged in from any point in the political spectrum and for different purposes. Here I will focus on activism that is oriented toward achieving greater social justice, a form of activism especially relevant to democratic citizenship.

While deliberating and bargaining tend to take place within given social structures, activists work to change structures they view as unjust. They attend to differences of power, to the way the context of discussion has been framed by actions outside its scope. The activist believes that deliberation typically occurs in contexts that have been structured in ways that serve the interests of those in power. Thus deliberation is not likely to be effective in securing greater social justice or advancing the interests of the oppressed. Activists employ other strategies of mobilization, protest, and disruption that call attention to their causes. Unlike bargainers, activists are not usually motivated solely by their own or their group's interests. Rather, they see themselves as acting in the interest of principles of justice (Young, 2002). Some citizens make activism their life's work, their profession in effect. They identify with a social movement and devote themselves to realizing its goals. The civil rights movement, feminist movements, disability rights, gay pride, PETA, ACT UP are but part of a long list of causes.

Citizens may have moments of activism within everyday talk even if it is not a major part of their identities. The following example is taken from Jane Mansbridge's (1999) research. An African American woman went with her husband to his family's home in the South. At dinner, the men gathered at the table while the women went into the kitchen and came back with plates filled with food for the men. The visiting woman had remained seated at the table. Her husband asked her to fill his plate. She said, "I don't fill your plate at home. Why would I do it here?" And the other women sat down as well and stopped waiting on the men. The woman said, "Well, what I did was I ended up like liberating the other women in the family." Mansbridge comments: "With this small act— a combination of speech, and, in this case, nonperformance of an expected action—[she] . . . intervened in her own and others' lives to promote a relatively new ideal of gender justice, exemplified by her verb 'liberating' " (pp. 217–218).

The contradiction between democratic commitment to political equality and fair opportunity and disparities in schooling help fuel a commitment to teaching for social justice and a conception of teachers as change agents (Cochran-Smith, 2004; Hytten, 2006; Villegas & Lucas, 2002). Villagas and Lucas (2002) assert: "The consistent gap between racial/ethnic minority and poor students and their white, middle-class peers in scores on standardized tests is indicative of the inability of the educational system to effectively teach students of color as schools have traditionally been structured" (p. 9). Advocates of teaching for social justice argue that the gap cannot be closed simply by training prospective teachers in research-based pedagogical practices, but rather requires challenging the "structural inequalities embedded in the United States' system of school-ing [that] perpetuate hierarchies of domination closely linked to race and class . . . Activ-ism, and analysis of power and social inequalities [must be made] part of the curriculum" (Rubin & Justice, 2005, p. 80).

Educating teachers for activism, then, requires fostering a strong commitment to social justice, but that commitment alone is not enough. Teacher educators committed to teach-ing for social justice help pre-service teachers to see injustice related to race and class in tracking or in lowered expectations and in differences in school facilities, for example, and to understand the dynamics of power and privilege as they are manifest in the "systematic production of inequality" (Parker, 2003, p. 154). They help pre-service teachers develop teaching stances and styles that engage, and are sensitive to, their stu-dents' experiences and perspectives. They challenge pre-service teachers to examine their own perspectives for the ways they have been shaped by their social and cultural loca-tions and hence may harbor biases and stereotypes (Applebaum, 2004). They encourage pre-service teachers in developing ways to engage effectively with others from different backgrounds (Rubin & Justice, 2005; Lucas, 2005). They help pre-service teachers to see the diverse backgrounds and perspectives of their students as assets rather than deficits, and they encourage teaching techniques and assessment practices that promote learning for all students (Villegas & Lucas, 2002). But beyond acquiring and transmitting to their own students the perspectives, knowledge, and skills described above, activist teachers require the courage to challenge injustice in the educational system.

As noted above, activism is not the sole province of any one political perspective. Students can be taught to critically examine existing practices and to advocate for the social and political changes they believe are justified whatever their particular view-points. Teaching for social justice, however, does involve substantive political commit-ments, as we have seen. Some critics are concerned that such teaching is partisan. Ruth Grant (1996) argues that classrooms should engage students in "conversation aimed at genuine inquiry" rather than conversation "aimed at producing a consensus on a predetermined position or point of view" (pp. 476–477). While commitment to social justice is a constitutive feature of liberal democracy, citizens have different conceptions of what justice is and what it requires. The danger of activism from the perspective of deliberative democracy is that the activists will be so persuaded of the rightness of their own positions that they will be unwilling to engage in genuine deliberation with those who hold opposing views. And once the issues have been framed as matters of justice, the prospects for negotiation and compromise will be limited.

DEMOCRATIC PRACTICES: MUST WE CHOOSE?

A democratic citizen should have the knowledge, skills, and commitments necessary for the various practices required by a democratic life that likely will always be full of contention. Deliberation, negotiation, and activism are core practices in which citizens engage with each other over the issues that divide them. The democratic culture sets the ground rules for engagement: a commitment to the freedom and equality of all citizens (Rawls, 1993). A robust civic education, fueled in part through democratic-minded teacher education, fosters the democratic culture through preparing future citizens for participation in the basic practices of democratic life.

There are both commonalities and tensions among these practices. For example, both deliberation and activism, as I have portrayed them, aim at the common good. In deliberative fora, citizens speak from their own perspectives, of course, but they are expected to be open to rational persuasion about which solution to their common problem is best. Activism that aims at social justice seeks to educate, and appeal to, a conception of the appropriate treatment of persons and the equality of citizens. While redistribution of social goods may advantage some more than others, for example, the reason for the redistribution activists seek is remedying injustice, not responding to special interests.

By contrast, negotiation aims at mutual accommodation of interests and thus has appeared to some to be inferior to the moral stances of deliberation and the demand for social justice. Bargaining is not oriented toward the common good and it is extremely doubtful that a "hidden hand" will see to it that the common good is served by the pursuit of individual and group interests. Yet deliberative democrats acknowledge that agreement is not always forthcoming. Disagreement is a ubiquitous fact of democratic political life. John Rawls (1993) has argued that such disagreement can persist without anyone's being ill-informed or mistaken about the facts, because, for example, different groups may assign different weightings to competing values. Joseph M. Schwartz (1995) argues for the "permanence of the political." By that phrase, he means that even in "a relatively egalitarian political community" there will still be "spirited political disagreement and contestation" (p. 19). He suggests that radical democratic theorists have underestimated the persistence of conflict and have supposed that politics as the mediation of conflicting interests could be eliminated in a truly just and egalitarian society. Deliberation and activism share a hope that conflict can be eliminated by seeking truth, whether it is the truth about which policy is best or how justice can be achieved. Negotiation (or "politics" in Schwartz's formulation) acknowledges the radical pluralism of interests and cultural commitments that makes overcoming conflict unlikely except through repression.

While the deliberative forum strives to be a power free zone, negotiation and activism recognize, in their own ways, the reality of differential distribution of power. Each is willing to use power in pursuit of its goals, unlike the deliberator's focus on rational persuasion. While activism aimed at social justice seeks a redistribution of power, negotiation acknowledges the existing power relationships. Yet constructive negotiation relies on the interdependence of even those with unequal power and the capacity of each party to thwart the interests of the others.

How, then, shall we live together as democratic citizens in the face of continuing disagreement? Should we choose among these practices? Deliberation has much to recommend it even if agreement is not always reached. In public political contexts, voting or the courts may decide the matter for the time being, while deliberation continues. But in civil society or everyday life, beyond the reach of voting and courts, trying to achieve mutual accommodation with others through agreements that satisfy the primary interests of each group seems equally a staple of democratic life. And legislative proposals themselves typically embody bargains based on accommodation of different interests. Lack of willingness to accommodate others, insisting on one's own claim to truth, thwarts legislative action and polarizes the electorate. But when conflict is generated by injustice, especially injustice that is difficult to recognize by those who perpetrate it because it is embedded within major social institutions, a reorientation of thinking is required, not simply creative accommodations of interests. Thus activism oriented to social justice has its distinct claim on democratic life.

Thus it is no surprise that, while I have described each of these political practices independently, in reality, they often appear in combination. For example, a *New York Times'* reporter was struck by the oddity of two Act-Up (the Aids Coalition to Unleash Power) protesters engaged in a "die-in" while wearing sports jackets and ties. When she followed up, she learned that, after the protest, they were attending a meeting at the office of the United States trade representative (as cited in Levinson, 2002). Activism aimed at changing citizens' awareness of issues is not incompatible with employing deliberative strategies when they are available.

In *Democracy and Disagreement*, deliberative democrats Gutmann and Thompson (1996) consider the example of the strategies used by Senator Carol Moseley Braun to defeat efforts to renew the Daughters of the Confederacy's patent on the Confederate flag insignia. After the amendment passed a test vote, Moseley Braun took to the Senate floor. She argued that putting the Senate's "imprimatur" on a racist symbol was an "outrage" and "insult" that was "absolutely unacceptable" to her and millions of Americans both black and white. Her speech was described as an "oratory of impassioned tears and shouts" and she threatened a filibuster. At the end of a three-hour debate, the amendment failed. Commenting on this example, Gutmann and Thompson write: "even extreme non-deliberative methods may be justified as necessary steps to deliberation" (p. 135). Yet they also point out that her appeal might not have succeeded if it had been "purely strategic, asserting only a claim of interest and making no appeal to moral principle" (p. 258). That is, if she had made the issue a matter of bargaining or accommodation to ensure the interests of African Americans as a group, rather than making a moral appeal, based on justice, she would have been less effective. Yet Moseley Braun cannot have been unaware that the interests in re-election of the Senators who initially opposed her were part of what made them yield. In this case, deliberation, negotiation, and activism combined to generate a resolution. Choosing among these practices, then, is not only not required, but also not a good idea. Each has its place in the repertoire of a democratic citizen.

The goal of democratic education for both teachers and teacher educators might be to educate citizens who would realize the following ideals, as represented by Walzer's (2004) thought experiments:

> We can imagine the party platform drawn up by a group of people who are not only good negotiators but reflective men and women aiming at proposals that are morally justified and economically realistic as well as politically appealing. We can imagine a negotiating process in which people try to understand and accommodate the interests of the other side (while still defending their own) rather than just driving the hardest possible bargain. We can imagine parliamentary debates where the rival

speakers listen to one another and are prepared to modify their positions. And finally, we can imagine citizens who actually think about the common good when they evaluate candidates, or party programs, or the deals their representatives strike, or the arguments they made.

(pp. 107–108)

SCHOOLING AND THE FOSTERING OF DEMOCRATIC PRACTICES

Even if my argument is persuasive that democratic citizens need the dispositions, knowledge, and skills required to participate in the practices of deliberation, negotiation, and activism, that fact does not settle the question of what the roles of public schooling and higher education are in developing these capacities. Closest to the heart of the current curriculum of education at all levels are aspects of the practice of deliberation. Fostering capacities for rational persuasion is simply part of what a good liberal education involves. Even without aiming at civic education, universities will enhance the civic virtue of their students, including prospective teachers, simply by developing the knowledge, attitudes, and skills required for serious inquiry. By teaching students how to engage in the search for truth, they will enhance the quality of public reason. As Dewey often argued, inquiry is not the sole provenance of a special class of persons called "researchers," but is both the right and the duty of democratic citizens.

Thus liberal education has significance for democratic life. And the inequality of our current system that denies a strong liberal education to some citizens is not only unjust but also undermines democratic participation. Yet acquiring knowledge of the liberal arts does not in itself foster willingness to listen to others' points of view, openness to being shown wrong, or willingness to modify one's understanding in light of new evidence— the virtues required for genuine deliberation. Thus democratic education requires more explicit attention to virtues often thought to be embedded in the curriculum of liberal education, but surely not always realized.

The place of the knowledge, attitudes, and skills associated with negotiation in the curriculum of schooling at all levels is less secure than those associated with deliberation. While there are programs for teaching students and their teachers conflict resolution techniques, as noted earlier in this chapter, these practices are not as deeply embedded in the educational curriculum of either public schooling or higher education as the practices of deliberation. I have suggested that it may be that suspicions about the morality of bargaining as opposed to deliberation may be part of the explanation. But it may also simply be that these techniques are thought of as "add-ons" that are less central to the educational missions of schools at all levels. But the enduring reality of disagreement in democratic political life makes the willingness to accommodate others' legitimate interests and the ability to devise creative solutions to conflicts important democratic virtues. If the educational system does not foster these capacities, what other institutions will?

Fostering a commitment to social justice and social activism within schooling has been controversial, as noted earlier in this chapter. Some question whether schools of education, or universities more generally, should make commitment to social justice and activism a part of the curriculum. Stanley Fish (2004) has argued that urging students to engage in political acts, even fostering "the practices of responsible citizenship," is not the business of the university. "Universities," he writes, "could engage in moral and civic education only by deciding in advance which of the competing views of morality and citizenship is the right one, and then devoting academic resources and energy to the task of realizing it.

But that task would deform (by replacing) the true task of academic work: the search for truth and the dissemination of it through teaching" (n.p.). Further, some worry about the prospects of indoctrination. While classifying himself as within the radical democratic tradition, Schwartz (1995) nevertheless claims:

> A pluralist democrat would argue that schools should impart a minimalist democratic ideology to students involving a capacity for critical reasoning (even about democracy itself) and a commitment to the equal rights of democratic citizens. To inculcate a thicker, more comprehensive political ideology would cross the line between democratic schooling and ideological indoctrination.
>
> (pp. 10–11)

So there is contestation about the role of schools in promoting activism.

Yet social criticism has long been an established part of the university's function in American society. And while there are legitimate disagreements about what justice requires, that teachers in a democratic society should be committed to a just distribution of educational resources does not seem an inappropriate expectation. More challenging, but also clearly necessary for democratic life, is creating awareness of systematic injustice and the role citizens play in perpetuating it, even without being aware of their complicity. Of course, the line between education and political indoctrination can be crossed. But teachers who have acquired the deliberative capacities described above will be better able to draw that line.

Deliberation, negotiation, and activism are all possible stances for democratic citizens to take. A case can be made that that these practices are rightly fostered through the educational system. The commitment to developing citizens who can participate in these practices sets a complex agenda for teacher education. As I have suggested in this essay, teachers in a democratic society should be able to: lead deliberative discussions where students learn to formulate their own arguments, engage others' points of view, and be open to changing their minds when given good reasons to do so; teach the skills and attitudes of negotiation that include the willingness to accommodate others' interests in ways that do not deny fundamental democratic principles, as well as the ability to generate creative solutions to conflicts; and encourage students to be alive to injustice in social practices as well as in themselves and others and to be willing to challenge injustice when they see it.

It should be plain from the discussion thus far that the democratic practices considered in this chapter are more than mere sets of skills. They have ethical dimensions that involve qualities of character and attitudes toward other participants that are required to make them constitutive of democratic practices (Grant, 1996). Mere training in skills of conflict resolution, for example, will not necessarily foster willingness to accommodate others' interests. Thus democratic practices cannot be communicated in a few training workshops. Rather, the whole educational process in teacher education programs as well as in K-12 education must provide forums for the reflective appropriation of these practices.

The limited success of effects to "export democracy" shows that learning and teaching the practices of democratic participation are not simple matters. Children need to experience these practices as part of a democratic political culture if they are to fully develop the complex "habits of the heart" that sustain democracy. As Dewey (1966/1916) noted, "the main texture of disposition is formed, independently of schooling" through the "unconscious influence of the environment" (p. 17). On the other hand, schooling is not inert: it provides "a special social environment which shall especially look after nurturing the capacities of the immature" (Dewey, 1966/1916, p. 22). Schooling that consciously fosters democratic practices makes its contribution to revitalizing and improving democratic life.

A CONCLUDING POSTSCRIPT: HIGHER EDUCATION, TEACHER EDUCATION, AND CIVIC EDUCATION

Teacher education is located within colleges and universities that have increasingly embraced a role in civic education. A few years ago 500 university presidents called upon colleges and universities to help students "realize the values and skills of our democratic society" (as cited in Fish, 2004). Many colleges and universities include a commitment to civic education within their mission statements. Indeed Fullinwider and Lichtenberg (2004) claim that higher education's understanding of the benefits of liberal education has shifted from acquiring liberal culture to preparation for social and civic engagement (Chapter 3).

Yet the university's capacity to play a role in civic education depends on its protecting its institutional autonomy. To maintain its social roles as truth seeker and social critic, the university needs the capacity to speak truth to power whatever the dominant sources of power are at a given historical moment. While contemporary university scholars attack the injustices embedded in our social and political life, universities as institutions are increasingly connected to the agendas of state governments and corporations.

The Martin Luther King Day dinner at my university is held in the campus' main athletic facility. It is a large event and some people have distant views of the stage and the speaker, so the instant replay screen normally used for athletic events is pressed into service. At a recent dinner, during the opening moments, old television footage of the civil rights movement was projected onto the screen, which is surrounded by advertisements for several corporations. I found it a disquieting moment to view images of nonviolent protesters being beaten by the police in juxtaposition with the advertisements. Later the image of our speaker, President Ruth Simmons of Brown University, was on the same screen. As she challenged our students to be less concerned with Hummers and bling-bling and more concerned with social justice, the advertisements surrounded her face.

That image stayed with me as a metaphor of the moral and political challenges facing contemporary universities. Examining the curriculum and the education provided to students is only one part of the civic mission of higher education. Universities—and that includes colleges and schools of education—need to examine their own actions as corporate agents for consistency with maintaining the ability to speak truth to power and their role as civic educators.

I am not saying that it is necessarily wrong for universities to have corporate sponsors for their enterprises. Nor am I saying that business is necessarily a morally contaminated activity from which universities should keep their distance in order to maintain purity. But universities do need to think hard about structuring government and corporate partnerships in ways that do not compromise their essential roles as truth seeker and social critic. Without returning to the idea of the university as an ivory tower, unengaged in the affairs of the community, it is important to maintain institutional autonomy if universities are to fulfill their civic role. That role includes the preparation of the nation's teachers who can help our children and youth develop the arts of deliberation, negotiation, and activism.

REFERENCES

Applebaum, B. (2004) Social justice education, moral agency, and the subject of resistance. *Educational Theory*, 54, 59–72.

Bell, D. A. (1999) Democratic deliberation: the problem of implementation. In Macedo (pp. 70–87).

Bellah, R. N., Madsen, R., Sullivan, W. M., Swidler, A., & Tepton, S. M. (1985) *Habits of the heart: individualism and commitment in American life*. Berkeley: University of California Press.

Cochran-Smith, M. (2004) *Walking the road: race, diversity, and social justice in teacher education*. New York: Teachers College Press.

Deutsch, M. (2000a) Cooperation and competition. In Deutsch & Coleman (pp. 21–40).

Deutsch, M. (2000b) Introduction. In Deutsch & Coleman (pp. 1–17).

Deutsch, M. & Coleman, P. T. (eds.) (2000) *The handbook of conflict resolution: theory and practice*. San Francisco: Jossey-Bass.

Dewey, J. (1966/1916) *Democracy and education*. New York: The Free Press.

Educators for Social Responsibility Homepage (2005) Information retrieved from http://www.esrnational.org/homehtm, September 15, 2005.

Fish, S. (2004) Why we built the ivory tower. NYTimes.com. Retrieved May 25, 2004, from http://www.nytimes.com/2004/05/21/opinion/21FISH.html?ex=1086167589&ei=1&en=7959c8d2cfff8d1b. Originally published, *New York Times* (May 21, 2004).

Fuhrman, S. & Lazerson, M. (eds.) (2005) *The public schools*. Oxford: Oxford University Press.

Fullinwider, K. and Lichtenberg, J. (2004) *Leveling the playing field: justice, politics, and college admissions*. Lanham, MD: Rowman & Littlefield.

Grant, R. W. (1996) The ethics of talk: classroom conversation and democratic politics. *Teachers College Record*, 97, 470–482.

Gutmann, A. (2005) Afterword: democratic disagreement and civic education. In Fuhrman & Lazerson (pp. 347–359).

Gutmann, A. & Thompson, D. (1996) *Democracy and disagreement*. Cambridge, MA: Belknap Press of Harvard University Press.

Gutmann, A. & Thompson, D. (1999) Democratic disagreement. In Macedo (pp. 243–279).

Gutmann, A. & Thompson, D. (2004) *Why deliberative democracy?* Princeton, NJ: Princeton University Press.

Hahn, C. L. (1998) *Becoming political: comparative perspectives on citizenship education*. Albany, NY: State University of New York Press.

Hartocollis, A. (2005, July 31) Who needs education schools? *New York Times Education Life*, Section 4A, p. 25.

Heater, D. (2004) *A history of education for citizenship*. New York: Routledge.

Hytten, K. (2006) Education for social justice: provocations and challenges. *Educational Theory*, 56, 221–236.

Irvine, J. J. (2004) Forward. In Cochran-Smith (pp. xi–xiv).

Johanek, M. C. & Puckett, J. (2005) The state of civic education: preparing citizens in an era of accountability. In Fuhrman & Lazerson (pp. 130–159).

Johnson, D. W., Johnson, R. T., & Tjosvold, D. (2000) Constructive controversy: the value of intellectual opposition. In Deutsch & Coleman (pp. 65–85).

Krugman, P. (2005, July 15) Karl Rove's America. *The New York Times*, p. A19.

Kymlicka, W. (2003) Multicultural states and intercultural citizens. *Theory and Research in Education*, 1, 147–169.

Levinson, N. (2002) Deliberative democracy and justice. In Rice (pp. 56–59).

Lucas, T. (2005) Fostering a commitment to social justice through service learning in a teacher education course. In Michelli & Keiser (pp. 167–188).

Macedo, S. (ed.) (1999) *Deliberative politics: essays on democracy and disagreement*. New York: Oxford University Press.

Mansbridge, J. (1999) Everyday talk in the deliberative system. In Macedo (pp. 211–239).

Michelli, N. M. (2005) Education for democracy: What can it be? In Michelli & Keiser (pp. 3–30).

Michelli, N. M. & Keiser, D. L. (eds.) (2005) *Teacher education for democracy and social justice.* New York: Routledge.

Miller, M. (2005, June 4) Is persuasion dead? *The New York Times,* p. A15.

Nie, N. & Hillygus, D. S. (2001) Education and democratic citizenship. In Ravitch & Viteritti (2001b, pp. 30–57).

Parker, W. C. (2003) *Teaching democracy: unity and diversity in public life.* New York: Teachers College Press.

Posner, R. A. (2005, July 31) Bad news. *The New York Times,* Book Review, pp. 1, 8–11.

Raider, E., Coleman S., & Gerson, J. (2000) Teaching conflict resolution skills in a workshop. In Deutsch & Coleman (pp. 499–521).

Ravitch, D. & Viteritti, J. P. (200la) Introduction. In Ravitch & Viteritti (2001b, pp. 1–14).

Ravitch, D. & Viteritti, J. P. (eds.) (2001b) *Making good citizens: education and civil society.* New Haven, CT: Yale University Press.

Rawls, J. (1993) *Political liberalism.* New York: Columbia University Press.

Reuben, J. A. (2005) In Fuhrman & Lazerson (pp. 1–24).

Rice, S. (ed.) (2002) *Philosophy of education 2001.* Urbana, IL: Philosophy of Education Society.

Rosen, J. (2005, June 12) Center court. *The New York Times,* Magazine, Section 6, pp. 17–18.

Rubin, B. S. & Justice, B. (2005) Preparing social studies teachers to be just and democratic: problems and possibilities. In Michelli & Keiser (pp. 79–103).

Sandy, S. V. & Cochran, K. M. (2000) Constructive controversy: the development of conflict resolution skills in children: preschool to adolescence. In Deutsch & Coleman (pp. 316–342).

Shapiro, I. (1999) Enough of deliberation: politics is about interests and power. In Macedo (pp. 28–38).

Schwartz, J. M. (1995) *The permanence of the political: a democratic critique of the radical impulse to transcend politics.* Princeton: Princeton University Press.

Simon, K. G. (2005) Classroom deliberations. In Fuhrman & Lazerson (pp. 107–129).

Tannen, D. ([1998] 1999) *The argument culture.* New York: Ballantine Books.

Tussman, J. (1960) *Obligation and the body politic.* New York: Oxford University Press.

Villegas, A. M. & Lucas, T. (2002) *Educating culturally responsive teachers: a coherent approach.* Albany, NY: State University of New York Press.

Walzer, M. (2004) *Politics and passion: toward a more egalitarian liberalism.* New Haven, CT: Yale University Press.

Wertheimer, A. (1999) Internal disagreements: deliberation and abortion. In Macedo (pp. 170–183).

Westheimer, J. & Kahne, J. (2004) *What to teach to teach democracy?* Virginia Education Association. Retrieved June 17, 2005, from http://69.13.212.9/articles_archives_detail.asp?ContentID=1023.

Williams, A. (2005, September 11) Realistic idealists. *The New York Times,* Sunday Styles, Section 9, pp. 1, 17.

Young, I. M. (2000) *Inclusion and democracy.* Oxford: Oxford University Press.

Young, I. M. (2002) Activist challenges to deliberative democracy. In Rice (pp. 41–55).

4   The moral and epistemic purposes of teacher education

Hugh Sockett
George Mason University

To identify an occupation as a profession minimally describes a community in which autonomous members see themselves in practical service to individual clients and to society, a practice which requires the use of judgment on the basis of a body of scholarly knowledge and professional experience (Jackson, 1970; Hoyle, 1980; Sockett, 1990, 1993; Shulman, 1998). The two concepts of service and knowledge imply that a profession has both moral and epistemic purposes. The ideal of a profession furthermore implies that the community is self-governing, primarily through determining admission criteria, with a code of ethics backed by sanctions including expulsion from the community. For an occupation to achieve this status demands a process of professionalization in two major ways: first, it must continually enhance its professionalism, i.e. the quality of its service and of its knowledge, and second, it must seek public recognition of its merits through appropriate financial rewards, autonomy and respect, i.e. its occupational status.

The moral and epistemic purposes of teacher education are therefore critical not only in enhancing the quality of practitioners in teaching, but also in contributing to the development of the public status of the occupation of teaching, for, as Sullivan (2004) reminds us, ". . . professionals are inescapably moral agents whose work depends upon public trust for its success." Most entrants to the profession are now graduates in the liberal arts or sciences and can be assumed to have developed some habits of critical inquiry germane to their field of study, although, like many serving teachers, they may have been given only a weak and intellectually uncritical base in educational theory (Clifford & Guthrie, 1990; Goodlad, 1990; Griffin, 1999). Yet though teacher education is by definition parasitic on the practices of teaching, there is little shared professional identity or equivalence of status between the practitioner and the academic. Indeed not all academics in education units of higher education institutions have responsibility for programs of teacher education, and many of those that do see themselves driven only by the research purposes of the academy (Clifford & Guthrie, 1990; Goodlad, 1990), where they enjoy the professional status of the academic. Yet these institutions have begun to feel the thrust of federal and state policy in the last decade to increasing teacher quality, and the accrediting organizations have become more tough-minded with the aim of improving the professional quality of graduates (NCATE, 2002; TEAC, 2005).

The professional aspiration for teaching is thus intertwined with the practices of teacher education, but in terms of autonomy, an ideal of service or self-government the aspiration may be chimerical. First, the autonomy of the profession may be an anachronism because public and political control increasingly dominates the work of the public school teacher, and such talk seems meaningless or merely rhetorical, especially in the context of high-stakes testing. Second, the ideal of service, set out in the Anglo-American ideal (Jackson, 1970) has been corrupted. Fareed Zakaria (2003) argues that "professions are the shadow of their former selves. They have been crushed by a pincer movement with the market increasing competition on one side and the state on the taking over many of the functions of professions and private business" (p. 222). Third, the ideal of self-government with sanctions based in a code of ethics is equally out-of-date. Some professions seem unable or unwilling to police their members effectively, notoriously in the pedophilia scandals among Catholic clergy made public in 2003, with egregious behavior stretching back three or four decades. For teaching, without any apparatus for professional policing, instances of teacher malfeasance are ignored. Teacher unions have other priorities and show little enthusiasm for sanctioning incompetent or wayward teachers, thereby casting doubt on whether the occupation of school-teaching is prepared to develop the institutional muscle needed to be regarded as a profession. The call for professionalism and professionalization in teaching may not therefore be practical, even if it were coherent.

If these three constituents of what we understand as criteria of a profession, namely autonomy, service and self-government are so fragile in the contemporary social context, how is the fourth essential element, a knowledge base for practice, to be regarded? A quite different line of criticism about teaching as a profession comes from those who regard the notion of there being education-specific specialist knowledge as mistaken. Educational research and teacher education as currently practiced is viewed as a doomed enterprise (Hirsch, 1996; Finn, 1991; Ravitch, 2000) because it has embraced unsound epistemologies, neglected what is regarded as the palpable need for education in a traditional framework of knowledge with its Platonic and medieval origins, and complicated the teaching task with illusions of technique based on science (Regnier, 1994) rather than accepting it as a task of initiating children into the life of the mind and developing wisdom and virtue through knowledge of content.

Yet while this is the most politically developed and well-known line of criticism of the profession having a distinctive knowledge base, it should not be viewed just as ideological chatter. It is one relatively small part of a profound and widespread controversy among those academics and politicians interested in matters of both moral and epistemic purpose in teaching and teacher education in particular. At the root of such controversy is the fundamental but complex three-legged conflict of purpose: Is education (a) a vocational and socializing endeavor, or (b) for the transmission of knowledge and culture, or (c) focused on the development of the individual (Egan, 1997; see also Bruner, 1996, Chapter 3)? Viewed as epistemological, this three-way conflict indicates that talk of the knowledge base of teaching as a body of scholarly knowledge for a profession is a minefield of epistemological controversy, with positivists, post-positivists, objectivists, post-modernists, feminists, constructivists, and pragmatists, each vying for dominance in research and school curricula. Viewed as moral, the conflict finds Platonists, Aristotelians, Kantians, Deweyans, Buberians and various kinds of existentialists pitted against each other in terms of their moral perspectives on society, the individual, his or her moral development and place in society, with the differing emphases in moral language (e.g. duty v. virtue) which that implies. Clearly a coherent knowledge base for the profession of teaching could not be an amalgam of such severely conflicting moral and epistemological viewpoints. In this respect, teaching is unlike medicine where there is a scientific epistemology that dominates that profession, marginalizing those with claims to alternative healing powers or therapies, such as homeopathy, which lack the widely accepted authority of the testable empirical base. Professional medicine, it should be noted, goes to some lengths to keep out those it regards as outside this epistemological tradition: chiropractors or acupuncturists need not apply.

While it is not possible here to give comprehensive attention to the heterogeneity of perspective on moral and epistemic purpose in education, it must be constantly recognized that this diversity forms a necessary and perplexing background for the idea of teaching being a profession, a matter not solved, in my view, by declarations that this or that somehow constitutes the knowledge base, as if consensus were all that were needed. To illustrate the characteristics of this diversity in this essay, I articulate four models of teaching from amongst a plethora of choice, each of which implies how teacher education should be conducted. Each also has a different emphasis in terms of the three-way paradigm of educational purposes and each, in my view, has a strong claim in principle for providing an account of moral purposes and the knowledge base for teaching.

FOUR MODELS OF MORAL AND EPISTEMOLOGICAL PURPOSES IN TEACHER EDUCATION

The justification for this approach through models is two fold. First it is grounded in the belief that teacher education in general needs a much more rigorous examination of the moral and epistemological underpinnings of practice, if the professional aspiration is to be coherent. Teacher education programs must be grounded philosophically and driven by intellectual rigor in their construction (Sockett, 1993). Second, in so far as the drive for professionalism is not merely an interest of the research community but a target many practitioners might embrace, that would seem to necessitate some form of consensus and agreement. That putative consensus would describe how the profession manifests the varied elements of being a profession, such that the agreed elements provide criteria of "correctness" upon which strong guidelines for "proper" professional teacher education praxis can be constructed. But can consensus exist without ignoring or obscuring profound moral and epistemological issues, and marginalizing significant perspectives on the professional aspiration, treating constructivists as chiropractors or Aristotelians as acupuncturists? Opening up different kinds of models, though it cannot be complete, may serve to promote that profound moral and epistemological debate and the question of whether consensus is viable. Certainly one possible outcome is that there could be several coherent models of teacher professionalism, with differing moral and epistemological underpinnings, and the level of consensus between them limited. Diversity in describing teacher professionalism, it might emerge, should be welcomed and consensus eschewed.

The four models I will articulate through the main body of this chapter are described in terms of the professional teacher's moral and epistemological stances. They are:

a the scholar-professional
b the nurturer-professional
c the clinician-professional, and
d the moral agent-professional

A model here is seen as an ideal type, with the label acting as a rough and ready descriptor of emphasis, and not carrying exclusivity, i.e. (d) does not mean that (a), (b), or (c), individually or severally, lack a moral perspective. How in general might such models be articulated? One could pick out, say, the central tenets of Dewey's moral and epistemological stances to education, including other scholars in this tradition, and describe therefrom a Deweyan model of teacher education (see, for example, Dottine, 2006). Different institutions using a Deweyan model would not be in lockstep, any more than those using a Christian model would be. Rather there would distinctive interpretations and practices, rooted in a common adherence to the central tenets of the Deweyan model.

Other institutions might display elements of the Deweyan model, say in terms of Dewey's emphasis on democratic society, but not carry the whole model through their practices.

A different approach to this description of a model which begins with a theorist, would be to look at practice and seek to build a model from different elements of practice, e.g. how children learn, the teacher's responsibility, managing a classroom and so on, notwithstanding that such observations embody theoretical frameworks. So, as will be seen in the clinician-professional model (see pp. 54–59), practices may vary in their moral and epistemological frameworks but their coherence as a model rests on some form of consensus about specific moral and epistemological positions set within an overarching ambition, in this case, of professionalism. Once again, there will be differences between the scholars, just as there are between institutions, in the theoretical articulation of the model, and in the extent to which they adhere to the central tenets of that model. Both these approaches to the characterization of models are used here.

However, a model of teacher education presupposes a picture of a good teacher. What counts as "good" is culturally and morally heterogeneous. Socrates, Aristotle, Jesus of Nazareth, Mohammed, Saint Thomas Aquinas, Confucius, Jean-Jacques Rousseau and Julia Child each provide us with glimpses into different aspects of teaching quality, not forgetting such literary heroes as Mr. Chips, or those men and women celebrated across the nation with different forms of good teaching awards and by success, for example, in the standards elaborated by the National Board. Models reveal differences in the conception of the "good teacher." The four models described here are, to repeat, not exclusive. They are articulations of distinctive moral and epistemological positions on teacher education: they are therefore both models *of* practice and also models *for* practice. (While each model cites specific authors, it should not be assumed that all features of a model are exclusively that scholar's or that the named scholar is only to be associated with that model.)

The scholar-professional

This first model regards knowledge as the purpose of education, so that the teacher is dedicated to imparting wisdom and fostering the life of the mind (Oakeshott, 1967, 1975; Hirst, 1972; Barzun, 1991). Moral purpose here is a matter of traditional, even conventional virtue. Epistemic purposes for teacher educators and teachers will not simply be focused on what is regarded as the unique character of disciplines (e.g. History) or inter-disciplines (e.g. Classics) being studied, but will also focus on epistemological battles within disciplines and on the nature of knowledge, perhaps with some attention to what has come to be called pedagogical content knowledge (for a recent account of this, see Grossman & Schonfield, 2005).

The nurturer-professional

The second model is primarily focused on the development of the individual. It describes a teacher whose primary focus is on relationships with children: as Noddings (1984) puts it, the child is infinitely more important than the subject. It interprets the parent of *in loco parentis* as the mother. It can encompass such perspectives as Van Manen's (1991) with his emphasis on intuition and the "personal embodiment of a pedagogical thoughtfulness" (p. 9). In other iterations (see Belenky *et al.*, 1986), as teachers educators work with novice or serving teachers, both moral and epistemic purposes are connected to individual development. Throughout, the emphasis is on individual nurture: care or tact demands self-understanding of the teacher and the cognitive is subsumed within the affective.

The clinician professional

The third model starts from an account of the work of the professional public school teacher in a democratic society, emphasizes the teacher's adaptive expertise, with moral emphases geared to social purposes, such as social justice with socialization as the educational aim (see, for instance, Darling-Hammond & Bransford, 2005). Its epistemic character is a strong if guarded belief in the integrity of educational research as a social science with explicit assumptions about knowledge, truth and belief, and the significance of the scientific method (see, for instance, Phillips & Burbules, 2004).

The moral agent-professional

The fourth model accepts the legitimacy of the three conflicting educational purposes and regards none as having priority since its focus is on teaching as primarily, predominantly, and pervasively a moral activity (for example, see Tom, 1984; Hansen, 1995, 2001; Campbell, 2003). Although Aristotle and his followers provide the ethics of virtue examined in this essay, the model would have different interpretations dependent on the ethic depicted; e.g. that of Kant or Dewey. Social and moral in education are *a fortiori* epistemic purposes, in the Aristotelian tradition, uniting moral and intellectual virtues (Norton, 1991; Williams, 2002). The model describes the individual teacher with a primarily moral purpose focused on the child's comprehensive development and growth, and its epistemic purposes, for teachers as well as children, are to integrate academic content with intellectual and moral virtues, such as accuracy, consistency, courage, and open-mindedness.

Each model can now be examined in turn.

THE SCHOLAR-PROFESSIONAL

The education of the scholar-professional consists primarily in an intellectual endeavor which will enlighten his or her teaching of a discipline within an academic curriculum in schools. Ravitch writes of this as

> the systematic study of language and literature, science and mathematics, history, the arts and foreign languages: these studies, commonly described today as a "liberal education" convey important knowledge and skills, cultivate aesthetic imagination, and teach students to think critically and reflectively about the world in which they live.
>
> (p. 15; see also Finn, 1991, p. 252)

The nineteenth-century English Cardinal John Henry Newman argued in *The Idea of the University* that "Liberal Education, viewed in itself, is simply the cultivation of the intellect, as such, and its aim is nothing more or less than intellectual excellence" (see Pring, 2004: 43). Philosopher Allan Bloom (1987) has a different emphasis: a liberal education, he argues, means that students seek to investigate the question "What is man?" "in relation to his highest aspirations as opposed to his low and common needs" (p. 21). The life men lead and the cultivated intellect which helps them in their respective quests implies that "the proper and effective exercise of reason must take place against the background of inherited forms of thought and experience" (O'Hear, 1994: 20), which Oakeshott (1967) has described both as modes of experience and as the different conversations of mankind. Education, Peters (1966) argued, is initiation into "worthwhile activities," i.e. those forms of thought developed across the centuries. This general culture provides the basis for scholar teachers to illuminate the particularities of their professional work.

The moral purposes of the education of a scholar-professional are therefore classical, historical, and conventional; acquiring knowledge to become more virtuous, thereby yielding good members of a democratic society. Ravitch makes the important claim that as the academic curriculum lost its importance in the twentieth century, schools lost "their intense moral commitment to the *intellectual* development of each child" (p. 16, my italics). Such a child would be guided by a scholar-professional toward intellectual autonomy, which will inform moral choice through the human issues embedded in the content and the intellectual and moral virtues needed to address those issues seriously. Understanding such a complex character as Claudius the King in Shakespeare's *Hamlet* or Raskolnikov in Dostoevsky's *Crime and Punishment*, for instance, is to learn of human guilt and responsibility. Differently, grappling with calculus is not merely finding answers to problems, but coming to value accuracy and the unremitting struggle of handling success and failure. The moral purpose of the "engagement," as Oakeshott (1975) describes education, is to enhance individuality of expression and thought rooted in traditional modes of experience, and to find ways to examine a student's success which facilitates the teacher's discovery of that individuality. The life of the mind is a (moral) good for its own sake, and the educational task is primarily to develop in children an intrinsic motivation for it, eschewing such external motivations as a good career. Such moral claims, heavily disputed then as now, were exemplified in a continuing debate based on the contest between C. P. Snow (Snow, 1998, 1959) and F. R. Leavis (1962) who argued the relative moral merits of the sciences and the humanities. The education of the scholar-professional however places firm moral emphasis on the "scholar" who will likely use the models of intellect he or she has experienced, and fashion a professional persona therefrom.

That the scholar-professional is today something of a rare breed is indicative of the wide range of criticisms that have been leveled at knowledge and the life of the mind as a moral purpose for education. It has been seen as elitist, historically developed to create leaders, irrelevant to modern life, lacking in instrumental purpose, and based in an out-dated epistemology, each of which criticism was reflected in the debates about the Western Canon (Bloom, H., 1994). Even those who are its advocates (e.g. Hirsch, 1996, 1987) now provide instrumental arguments for the life of the mind, such as being able to read the Science columns in the *Washington Post* (Hazen & Trefil, 1991) rather than the intrinsic justifications apparent in Newman.

Its epistemic purpose, however, is to develop teachers who see themselves *as* scientists, historians, philosophers, geographers etc., who teach their discipline, not merely deliverers of perspectives on these disciplines. In that sense, the identity of the school teacher with the academic community is strongly sustained. (A paradigm example of that identity is William Everdell of St. Ann's School Brooklyn, who in 1997 published *The First Moderns*, a widely acclaimed 800 page book of cultural analysis of the turn of the twentieth century.) Intellectual discipline is the pre-occupation of the scholar-professional: it takes a form both specific to a discipline (e.g. methodology in science), and fosters the emergence of attitudes and propensities, capacities and virtues germane to the life of the mind, including a "fanaticism for veracity, which is a greater possession than much learning ... as the moral nature of man is greater than the intellectual; for veracity is the heart of morality" (Huxley, 1874).

Disciplines, on this model, are the primary influence on teaching with different types of influence dependent on the methodology of the discipline. Science teaching will be experimental—in a laboratory or field, philosophy will be taught in seminars, history will demand work on primary sources, often with implications for the acquisition of another language, all of which will be reflected in teacher education. Scholar-professionals will thus see themselves as working within a tradition of inquiry, into which they have been initiated as children and as scholars, which may account for what is perceived as the inherent conservatism of this model.

Becoming a scholar-professional therefore demands both a rigorous understanding of one or more disciplines from within, and being active in the raging epistemological controversies that many disciplines offer. For the life of the mind means immersion in controversy and uncertainty, rather than consensus and certainty, with implications both for teaching and teacher education. It is not clear, for example, whether there is a consensus about the teaching of mathematics, since arguments about math teaching seem to be settled more by political fiat than philosophical consensus on the nature of mathematics (see LePage & Sockett, 2002, pp. 21–36). English teachers in the United States too "cannot seem to agree on a definition of the subject-matter" (Darling-Hammond & Bransford, p. 211), and, "there are many competing definitions of social studies, some of which feature the importance of history, whereas others stress the centrality of civics" (p. 209). Familiar too are the disagreements among historians, geographers and political scientists or indeed commentators who deplore the dissolution of literature in language arts and history into social studies.

There are at least three kinds of epistemic conflict for the scholar-professional to enjoy. First, there is frequent dispute about the central characteristics of the discipline. In the case of history, while methodologies may not differ much, political perspective does: compare the work of Howard Zinn or Eric Hobsbawm with David McCullough or Shelby Steele, as well as pervasive debate about an emphasis on social history and social movements or individual heroes. Second, there is disagreement about the merits of different potential topics to be taught, e.g. *Chaucer v. J. D. Salinger*, partly exemplified, once again, in debates about the Western Canon. Third, however, the most pervasive contemporary struggle is one deeply rooted in the claims of postmodernism which simply rejects the view of knowledge represented in this tradition of distinctive disciplines as the source of all scholarly knowledge.

The scholar-professional may sympathize with Shulman's (1987) comment that "Effective teachers know much more than their students, and more than good pedagogy. They know how students tend to understand (and *mis*-understand) their subjects; they know how to anticipate and diagnose such misunderstanding; and they know how to deal with them when they arise," and they may seek to emulate it. Course content will focus on how to achieve what Bruner (1963) called "courteous translation" in the belief that the basic principles of a discipline are available to all, a principle espoused by those who teach Philosophy to young children (see Lipman, 1988). Yet the scholar-professional may not read much non-subject-based educational research, as teaching is seen as a common engagement for teacher and learner with the subject: indeed, in some cases notions from educational research, e.g. developmentally appropriate practice, are trenchantly criticized and dismissed (see Matthews, 1994).

Since the publication of the Harvard (1942) Report *General Education in a Free Society* notions of common intellectual or "communicative" skills, or the "general powers of the mind" have become an alternative currency to that of the discipline. Benjamin Bloom and his colleagues (1972) boosted this psychological conceptual approach to knowledge, driven by the measurement of outcomes. The scholar-professional resists such conceptualizations of the curriculum, for such skills, they argue, have to be located in a disciplinary base: "Analyzing" in history, for instance, is so far different an intellectual exercise from "analyzing" in chemistry (see Hirst, 1972) that talk of the ability "to analyze" as a general power of the mind is just muddled. Thus the approach to a curriculum of teacher education for this model would be firmly located in a discipline and the belief that developing intellectual power in a disciplined framework itself provides intellectual virtue, and that moral virtue will inevitably follow.

THE NURTURER-PROFESSIONAL

The nurturer-professional is focused on the individual and on personhood but primarily on the relations between the child and the teacher. It would be mistaken to assume that this is just one of the many classic models of that view of the purposes of education which is "child-centered." The European tradition includes Rousseau, with the emphasis on the uninhibited development of the child, Froebel with the emphasis on play in the child's garden (the kindergarten), Makarenko with his attempts after the 1917 Russian Revolution to build communal school government with orphans, and A. S. Neill with his puritanical zeal for the removal of authority in the child's life. The American tradition comprises mavericks such as Homer Lane, a follower of Neill, the innovator Jane Addams, and influential pioneers such as W. H. Kilpatrick and his Project Method. Dewey too wanted public education to provide an education determined, in a complex sense, by a child's interests and capacities, but his educational perspective is set firmly within his project for democratic society. The corpus of Dewey's work, in Alan Ryan's memorable phrase, is a "gospel for democrats" (Ryan, 1996, p. 31).

Many different types of educator used to define the moral role of the teacher professional as *in loco parentis*, although it is now viewed as an untenable idea of the professional role primarily because it has largely been replaced by due process in teacher-parent relationships. The model of the nurturer-professional, however, is singularly distinctive in the child-centered tradition in that it puts the figure of the mother at the center of a revitalized concept of *in loco parentis*. Not the neutral "good parent," not the father or the mother, but the *mother*.

Notwithstanding its ancestry in child-centered education, this model is rooted firmly in the feminism of the second half of the twentieth century, developed by Betty Freidan and others. However, it is to Carol Gilligan that belongs the original development of a feminist understanding of education through her important thesis that women did not think about moral issues in terms of rules and principles, but in terms of relationships. This was a strong gender-based counterpoint to an ethic of rules derived from Kohlberg's interpretation of the central moral principles of classical liberalism (Gilligan, 1979, 1982; Gilligan & Attanucci, 1988). Numerous and significant additional steps have since been taken by feminist scholars (e.g. Belenky *et al.*, 1986), some of whom have articulated the sense of moral purpose in education focused on the child, not on the individual teacher or parent caring for the child. The moral focus in this nurturer-professional model is therefore on motherliness, the *relationship* between what Noddings calls "the one-caring" and the "one cared-for," with acknowledged philosophical roots in the "I–Thou" work of Martin Buber (1970). So justice, especially social justice, is not thought of in this model as detached or paternal with desired social ends, but as maternal, with the receptivity, relatedness and responsiveness characteristic of caring, an extension of Gilligan's line of thought (Noddings, 1999).

Centering the moral in relationships focuses on how "we meet the other morally" (Noddings, 1984, p. 5) and on the uniqueness of human encounters. It is empirically obvious, but worth indicating philosophically, that the experiences everyone has, including the challenges of caring-for and being cared-for are complex and highly intricate, often idiosyncratic, e.g. relationships within a family, with our children, our parents, or our siblings. From the inside, on Noddings' view, for the one caring there is a displacement of interest from my own reality to the reality of others. I feel your pain, as it were. This goes well beyond a feeling of empathy, even beyond a sense of compassion: rather we see the other person's reality in the perspective of caring as a real possibility for *me*. "I must make a commitment to act. The commitment to act on behalf of the cared-for, a continued interest in his or her reality through an appropriate time-span, and the continuing renewal of that caring are the essential elements of caring" are the demands of caring (Noddings, 1984, p. 16). For the one cared-for, on the other hand, the reception of the authentic attitude of the one caring transforms the relationship.

Three major concepts are at the core of this moral idea of caring on Noddings' account. Receptivity defines a relationship in which both are open to the other, building a context of trust and understanding. Relatedness suggests the ability of both to fashion the relationship, to contribute to it, to have it grow, and responsiveness implies the readiness to commit to a relationship, whatever it brings. A similar orientation is found in Van Manen's account of pedagogical understanding: "What could be more important than to have a sense of what things are like for a particular child and what is necessary to help young people to stand more fully, more strongly on their own two feet in a moral, aesthetic, social and vocational sense?" (1991, p. 83).

The epistemic purpose is also one of building relationships which presupposes knowledge of the disciplines. For the nurturer-professional embraces intellectual life, but seeks to move beyond the bureaucratic and technical framework of modern schooling, and places the desirability of relationships in the epistemic context (Noddings, 1984). Learning the disciplines (however they are to be construed) is therefore integral to learning how to teach, but each discipline has relationships with other disciplines. If we attend to what might be called the latitude and longitude of any discipline, we must not treat it as detached or impersonal, but to switch the metaphor, as part of the family of human understanding. Mathematics education should not therefore be perceived as detached from other types of study. For a comprehensive integrated understanding of that subject, explorations into history and philosophy will be needed. Any disciplined perspective can yield further understanding through the exploration of such relationships.

This epistemic purpose of the model is embedded in its moral purpose and suggests a still more extensive view of relationships and caring. We cannot appropriately understand a discipline and its constituents without caring for them and understanding their relationship with us. That human beings care and are cared for extends into the real world of the planet, its nature and the world of human artifacts: the dimensions of caring in the nurturer-professional model extend to all aspects of our world, plants, animals, works of art and, of course, disciplines or school subjects however construed. The model thus prescribes teacher education curricula which integrate discipline and pedagogy, implying that education specialists work consistently and jointly with, say, mathematicians, exemplifying the reach of relationships. Such ambitions are, in many ways, extremely exacting moral and epistemic purposes.

Yet, of course, it is this bureaucratic and technical framework of modern schooling that makes it difficult to imagine such a concept of the nurturer-professional gaining any credibility in public schooling. Due process has brought a legalistic view of what the teacher's relationships should be with tougher accountability and systems of control. Due process undermines the centrality of relationships implicit in the model, and makes the character of the moral relationships demanded practically impossible to implement.

Using this model demands much more autonomy and freedom for the teacher than contemporary systems allow. Therefore, like radical child-centered education practitioners before it (Neill, Homer Lane, Makarenko) it may seem more easily fully deployed with children in alternative schooling, children who are delinquent or for different reasons outside the public school mainstream.

THE CLINICIAN-PROFESSIONAL

The clinician-professional model celebrates the development of teaching as a profession, with medicine being seen as the benchmark for its development. This model is articulated most clearly and recently in *Preparing Teachers for a Changing World* (Darling-Hammond & Bansford, 2005) which seeks to "codify the (scholarly) knowledge base for professional practice and standards for the work of practitioners" (p. vii). The conclusions and ideas "represent the considered judgments of a large number of experienced practitioners and scholars in the field of education" (p. 21). It may be regarded as the most widely accepted of the four models under discussion, in teacher education if not in teaching, and *Preparing Teachers for a Changing World* thus forms an appropriate source for this model.

The epistemic content of this model contains an extensive range of scholarly knowledge relevant to the professional aspiration. It includes basic research on how people (specifically children) learn, and the influences of different conditions, including teaching strategies on that learning (see Darling-Hammond & Bransford, pp. 40–88). It includes a focus on how teachers learn, especially those practices that influence student learning (see pp. 358–390) and it equips them to use developmentally appropriate practices (see pp. 88–126). In particular, research provides knowledge of learning in different social contexts and contributes strongly to understanding the development and the significance of language for students (see pp. 126–169). Curriculum in teacher education further implies knowledge of subject matter, pedagogical content knowledge, the skills and social purposes of schooling, on which basis the individual student-teacher develops what is called a curricular vision (see pp. 169–232). Teaching diverse learners, subject matter, managing and assessing learning complete the range of research topics and scholarly knowledge needed by a teacher educator and a novice student (see Chapters 7, 8 and 9, pp. 232–358). The teacher educator will thus need to follow the research on student-teachers' learning particularly as the latter become "adaptive experts," with the demands such expertise makes on the processes of observation, enactment and complexity (see Chapters 10 and 11, pp. 358–442).

Under the influence of the medical profession's development, this extensive knowledge base is regarded as research-driven. So successful has this approach been from its initial formulation by Shulman (1987) that the primary emphasis in the practice of teacher education in the 1990s has been the development of this knowledge base (see for instance Reynolds, 1989; Murray, 1995). Thus a model built from this perspective on the profession and its knowledge-base is appropriately described as the (medically-derived) notion of the clinician, i.e. a person who reflectively uses research-based knowledge to inform practice, either by simply applying scientifically grounded conclusions somewhat like a technician, or more positively in making reflective judgments about research conclusions and their applicability to his or her own practice. However, given that the aspiration is a knowledge base for the whole profession, the broad comprehensive character of professional scholarly implies a search for consensus between epistemological positions. Both the moral and epistemological perspectives of the model can now be elaborated and the status of this model requires more critical examination than description.

Moral purposes

The moral content of the model is one in which a teacher forges his or her own identity against the moral purposes of a democratic society. That identity has both common and divergent purposes.

In common,

> Teachers need to think about the subject matters they teach in a broader context that includes an understanding of the social purposes of education, including the many functions of schools—academic, vocational, social and civic, and personal—that must be *balanced* in classrooms every day. In a democratic society, students must also evaluate their teaching decisions against the goals of preparing students to be *equitable* participants in a society that relies on *interdependence*. An important component of preparing students to participate in democracy is to allow them to experience democratic classrooms and schools. This includes a commitment to eliminate disparities in *educational opportunities* among students, especially those students who have been poorly served by our current system. It also includes ambitious learning opportunities and, in today's society, equitable access to the technological tools that citizens need to succeed.
>
> (Darling-Hammond & Bransford, p. 35; my italics)

This common emphasis is therefore on social morality, i.e. interdependence and equality of educational opportunities as a goal for classrooms and for the development of learning communities in schools. Equality of educational opportunity is viewed as a necessary constituent in matters of teaching diverse learners, and in the construction of equitable classrooms. So, "The core purpose of formal education is to enable the development of *all* children to take their place in adult society with the competencies to be positively contributing members to the society (p. 125) for ... curriculum goals are, or should be, shaped by the requirements of preparation for citizenship in a democratic society" (p. 170). The primary moral principles, as opposed to goals for schooling, are those of distributive justice and equality of treatment, framed within a democratic society, which serves to emphasize the "social perspective, that of the local community as well as the broader society, not just an unconsidered personal perspective" (p. 175). Teacher education programs will thus emphasize issues of diversity and the complexity of multi-cultural contexts for teaching, framed in a rhetoric of social justice.

From this common base, there is diversity: each clinician-professional will develop his or her own identity and curricular vision. It is suggested, for example, that individual teachers might see themselves as professionals, as scholars, as change agents, as nurturers and child advocates or as moral agents. Forging this identity of their own "is an important part of securing teachers' commitment to their work and adherence to professional norms of practice" (Darling-Hammond & Bransford, 2005, p. 383).

Three critical matters arise from this characterization of the model's moral purposes. First, the model carves the teacher's professional role out of the goals of a democratic society: but it states these goals as if they were not controversial but certain, agreed upon, and fundamental to the beliefs of the teacher in a democratic society. Yet, it is clearly not a matter of general agreement in this society that social justice is more important than individual liberty, or that the schools have to be vehicles for the former (see Brighouse,

2000 for an extended discussion of social justice). Indeed, whether parents should view schools as providing their children with public (i.e. valuing social justice) or positional (i.e. getting on a career ladder) goods or whether teachers should likewise view schools one way or the other depends on alternative conceptions of democratic society, its conflicting principles and the purposes of schooling outlined on page 4. Nor is equality of educational opportunity bereft of ambiguity and debate—in both concept and in application. Incumbent on teacher educators, it can be argued against the model's certitude, is that their students get strong understanding of these disagreements and complexities in a democratic society upon which the specifics of a professional role can be based. Without that kind of understanding, teacher education on this model would short-change student teachers on the diversity of public and intellectual opinion and beliefs.

Second, the model describes teachers as building an identity for themselves on to the norms of the professional role and indeed sometimes the place of that moral identity seems like an afterthought: e.g. "Teachers will need a moral compass that enables them to follow through on their commitments for all children. This requires some explication of ethical issues that arise in teaching" (p. 173). If this interpretation of the model is correct, individual identity is secondary to the demands of the role. But moral identity is not like a good bedside manner, something to be acquired in dealing with patients as you get to know the ropes. How one performs in a role is dependent on profound moral beliefs and attitudes, not the other way round. In practice, too, students teachers should not be treated as a moral or religious blank slate on to which professional norms have to be etched. Students need, morally speaking, to be seen as individuals:

> In terms of my religion, I am invisible. My professors, they look at me, see the color of my skin and think they know my story. I am African-American, I am Jewish. How can they see me if they do not know me? How can they teach me if they do not see me?
>
> (Kazanjian, 1999, para 1, quoted in Sockett, 2006)

The demands of the role are secondary to the individual beliefs and attitudes which need to be educated and the quality of the teacher–student relationships implied for teacher education.

Third, a similar problem occurs in the relationship between promoting the goals of a democratic society and becoming a democratic citizen. That is, the strong emphasis on teaching in a democratic society risks neglecting the conceptually, if not logically, prior notion of what it is to be a democratic citizen, engaging with the kinds of inevitable controversies such a society welcomes. Commitment to independence, balance, social justice and equality of opportunity, seen as objectives for teacher education, should necessarily be premised on the student's acquiring a sense of him or herself as possessing not just knowledge of the controversies for the sake of his or her job, but of those personal virtues and propensities characteristic of the democratic citizen. On Thomas Ehrlich's (2003) interpretation, this means such intellectual virtues as truth, respect, openness, impartiality alongside the social-moral virtues of tolerance, reason, compassion, and alongside a core knowledge of ethical principles, necessary to being an effective citizen (Ehrlich, 2003: but see also Soder et al., 2000; Guttman, 2001). On this model, it seems, the teacher's moral compass is at the periphery of teacher education. (It should also be noted, in terms of moral purposes, that such "individual" matters as the moral problems inherent in a teacher's authority (see Peters, 1966) or the "manner" of the teacher (Fenstermacher & Richardson, 2001) are not seen as necessary to adequate functioning in the role.)

Epistemological purpose

The clinician-professional model describes professional practices rooted in research-based scholarly knowledge. Two significant matters rise from this account: (1) How does the clinician-professional justify or warrant what he or she does? (2) How does the clinician professional grapple with the epistemic complexity inherent in the model?

Research-based scholarly knowledge is defined primarily as empirical, often quantitative, with some recognition of a place for what is usually referred to as qualitative research. The empirical tradition in general assumes, (boldly perhaps in the knowledge that these epistemological matters are contested), that by knowledge is meant the beliefs (held by a person), the evidence (accessible to a person in justification of the beliefs held) and the truths (statements which the individual believes but which are independent of an individual). (For access to these discussions, see, for instance, Hamlyn, 1970; Zagzebski, 1996; Lehrer, 2004; Phillips & Burbules, 2000.)

The epistemic purpose of teacher education will therefore be to acquaint novice teachers with the findings of such research, which becomes theory for use in their practice (hence the notion of the clinician applying, with more or less skill and judgment, what the research and scholarship reveals). However, to be serious about the clinician-professional having knowledge, mere acquaintanceship will not be enough. For emphasizing *knowledge* of scholarship and research in the tradition, rather than, say, knowledge as an epistemological construction (see Phillips, 2000), is to require that the clinician-professional *accept as true* findings from the range of research work of specific relevance to the practical arts of teaching and to have the evidence for the truths such that the hypotheses which are the subject of the knowledge claim can in principle be falsified. Such capacity is needed in order that practices dependent on that knowledge can be warranted. However, the model does not seem to be clear as to whether scholarly theories function primarily as a set of prescriptions *for* action, or as hypotheses to be tested *in* action. This is a distinction made familiar by Bruner in his distinction between knowers, who follow prescriptions, and seekers who challenge hypotheses.

The model thus contains ambiguity, at least in the Darling-Hammond and Bransford iteration, as to the relationship between the clinical-professional and the scholarly knowledge acquired. There seem to be three possibilities: (a) that the teacher simply applies whatever "the research says" should be done, like a skilled technician; (b) that the teacher can appraise the effectiveness of the ideas, learn from them, and adapt them to practice, like a skilled knower, or (c) that the teacher is able to use scholarly knowledge, and understand it in such a way that he or she can test the conclusions of the research, and maybe falsify it, since the knowledge will be seen as testable hypotheses, not conclusions to be followed, like a skilled seeker. The professional ideal would suggest (c), primarily because of the professional autonomy it implies for teachers to be able to warrant autonomously their actions effectively rather than simply pointing to the authority of research.

For the clinician-professional model does imply teacher autonomy as the ideal. Its general respect for reflectiveness in teaching leads toward (c), i.e. in the same direction for the resolution of the ambiguity. Reflectiveness goes beyond mere puzzlement or giving the matter a bit of thought, into careful reflective examination, not just of practices themselves, but of research on teaching itself (see Schon, 1986 for an alternative way of understanding professional action). This will extend to understanding the relationship between individual values and teaching, and looking for the ways in which teachers may interpret situations in classrooms and schools with open-mindedness and objectivity. To be a reflective teacher suggests preparedness to embrace spirited inquiry into the foundations of one's action and what empirical research and values-inquiry suggests and which can falsified. The central characteristic of teacher reflectiveness will be a research-driven characteristic, that is, to be critics of scholarly knowledge and to hold their beliefs in such a way that the practices they deploy are seen as hypotheses constantly being tested (see Phillips & Burbules, 2004), an impetus familiar from the Teacher-Researcher Movement.

In addition to the problem of warrant, the model's comprehensive range of research suggests epistemic complexity. While it is clear that drawing on a vast body of scholarly knowledge and in different idioms is a major challenge, one politically charged example of the complexity is the specific problem of the relation of fact and value and what that implies for teacher education. In the normative business of education the clinician-professional will be able to examine and critique the research knowledge being offered for use, and be able to make judgments about the application or develop skills related thereto. Teacher education must thus provide for detailed examination of values and norms, not just empirical research, and mastering this complexity will contribute towards justifiable warrant. The model's stance towards the goals of a democratic society (see pp. 21–22) does not indicate that serious normative inquiry is essential.

Yet, the clinician-professional is commonly presented by politicians, administrators, principals, parents and teacher educators with policies or programs purportedly based on "what the research says" which does not articulate the value-laden nature of the enquiry (and is often about as reliable as "History tells us"). Research conclusions (especially on controversial topics like whole language or phonics, the teaching of mathematics, even class size) frequently vary depending on the political and social perspective which underpins the researcher's (and thence the politician's or administrator's) arguments, indicating that conclusions in educational research, as in social science generally need to be approached with some caution. Not being able to face up to such complexity may leave the teacher ill-equipped to provide satisfactory warrant, i.e. where research conclusions are not empirically pure, with embedded norms and values left unexamined. This suggests that in teacher education, research and its conclusions will need to be examined not just as fact-based empirical research, but also in an idiom appropriate to values.

This example points up the problem:

> ... In contrast to earlier views of development as a set of biologically related stages clearly determining what students can do, current research shows that development, knowledge and learning are related to one another. The older belief that development proceeds at a fixed pace that determines children's "readiness" for learning is no longer accepted by current developmental theorists. Instead research demonstrates how learning can affect development, as well as the reverse. New studies show that, in addition to their age or apparent "stage," people's prior knowledge and experience with specific content affects the sophistication of their thinking."
>
> (p. 93)

The widespread use in teaching young children of the notion of developmentally appropriate practice will require both examination of the empirical side of the research and of the value-systems which determine what counts as development in a teacher education curriculum. Development is not an incontrovertible notion in human growth, like homeostasis, i.e. something to be understood solely through scientific endeavor. Development must be a normative concept because it describes *desirable* ends to which human beings *should* develop or be led, socially, intellectually, aesthetically and morally

(Peters, 1972). Thus, notwithstanding ongoing argument about Piagetian *epistemologie genétique* and the critiques of modern developmental theorists, "developmentally appropriate practice" looks like a claim for *empirical* validity, but only if its normative and ideological foundation is accepted. This is not to say that those promoting "developmentally appropriate practice" are mistaken, but that in teacher education the normative concept of the development prescribed must be examined. Without that sophisticated values-inquiry, the epistemic purpose of this model in teacher education would start to look more like ideological training rather than engagement with scholarly knowledge (for a reinterpretation of the empirical tradition's epistemology, see Phillips & Burbules, 2004).

THE MORAL AGENT-PROFESSIONAL

This model is dubbed the moral agent-professional model because its proponents hold that the moral is primary, predominant and pervasive in teaching the young and educating their teachers (see for instance, Peters, 1966; Noddings, 1984; Goodlad *et al.*, 1990; Tom, 1984, 1997; Sockett, 1993; Hansen, 1995, 2001; Fenstermacher & Richardson 2001; Campbell, 2003). It is *primary*, because the educational engagement is a specific endeavor in the development of persons for which teachers are given moral authority. It is *predominant*, because the ends of the engagement are moral, and the means (technique for instance) are subservient to and only justifiable through moral ends with the implication that teachers cannot withdraw from the moral obligations or commitments of the role, as they can eschew certain techniques or bodies of knowledge. It is *pervasive*, because there is no aspect of the engagement to which the moral is irrelevant, not merely in the social day-to-day of the classroom, but in curriculum choice, in subject matter, in the manner of the teacher, the efficacy of teaching methods and the teacher's practical wisdom, the conduct of schools, and in the individual student perspectives which teachers hope to educate. To have a moral purpose *is* thus to have an epistemic purpose.

The weaknesses of such a model are diverse. First, it is unlikely that the success of school students will ever be judged in terms of their intellectual and moral virtues, as opposed to SAT scores. Second, public discussions of moral life are frequently entangled with religious beliefs, whether about day-to-day morality or matters of ultimate justification. Third, thereby, assumptions that one can choose any god one likes extend into the moral sphere and its "democracy of values," i.e. where one person's choices are as good as another's, and where teachers are worried about imposing their values. It thereby becomes difficult for the model to establish its credentials in public discussion and in public education. Fourth, such moral discussion of education as exists is often limited to those concerned with moral and character education which, while important, does not yield a comprehensive model for teacher education, and ignores the complex relationship with curriculum content. Fifth, the legacy of the fact-value distinction and, on some views, the impossibility of moral *knowledge* has left scholars in this endeavor unable to penetrate the epistemological issues the moral perspective on education raises. Finally, the historical record of "education for character" (see Hartshorne & May, 1928; Kohlberg, 1981) has left a legacy of contemporary academic ignorance of the model and its possibilities, and some scholars therefore follow Kohlberg's original thesis, arguing that talk of virtues is just talk of personality, and since it resists empirical verification, can be of little use in educational research (Oser, 1994).

Perspectives on ethics and morality vary. The model would yield very different accounts dependent on the specifics of the ethical position adopted. For example, the model could be characterized through Dewey's view of ethics, or perhaps through a religious Thomist account, visible in some parochial schools. The moral agent-professional could also be cast within an ethics of rules, rooted in the classical liberalism of Hobbes, Kant, and Mill, or an ethics of character (or virtue) derived from Aristotle's account of εὐδαιμονια (Norton, 1991), both of which could also in principle provide an account of the moral agent-professional. All such putative models, (with the probable exception of Mill whose Theory of Logic demand a tough-minded separation of fact and value built on Comte's account of positivism), will portray a close affinity between the moral position espoused and the epistemic purpose of the educational enterprise.

For the purposes of this chapter, the moral agent-professional model will be derived from Aristotle and his contemporary followers, where the distinction between moral and epistemic purpose evaporates, since they are necessarily integrated in an ethics of virtue (or character), and where the moral end for humankind is εὐδαιμονια. (Norton's (1991) focus on development, linked strongly to John Dewey's views of both democracy and growth, requires separate treatment, as does the highly significant emergence of Virtue Epistemology (Fairweather & Zagzebski, 2001; DePaul & Zagzebski, 2003) in the past decade.)

Although εὐδαιμονια is often translated as happiness, Norton holds that it is better understood as a self-actualizing life and self-fulfilling conduct from which a non-hedonic condition and feeling of "happiness" is derived. The moral target, in Norton's arresting phrase, is "meaningful work to meaningful living." The ethic is dedicated to the ". . . 'enhancement of the quality of life for human beings . . .' " This means the acquisition of moral virtues "where moral virtues are understood as dispositions of character that are (1) personal utilities; (2) intrinsic goods, and (3) social utilities" (Norton, pp. 80–81). This triad reflects, though does not quite instantiate the three general educational purposes of (1) the individual's development; (2) knowledge as valuable in itself, and (3) those virtues important for social life and citizenship in a democratic society, none which can be salient for the model, since each has moral legitimacy and moral importance. This acquisition takes place as the individual, at his or her own initiative, takes into him or herself values which form an identity comprised of virtues, e.g. the person who comes to value honesty and the absence of deceit thus becoming a truthful person. Education supplies many of the conditions under which such self-direction can be facilitated—and the task of politics in a democratic society, on Norton's view, is to remove obstacles (like poverty or injustice) which prevent that fulfillment.

Teacher Education would therefore be centered on the process of self-discovery as a teacher through the development of those virtues germane to the task of teaching, congruent with personal virtues. This is developing an identity primarily out of personal values and commitments, not out of adherence to professional norms. The teacher educator's role in facilitating this self-discovery by students through practices involving learning disciplines, classroom experience, community service, or the arts and crafts of democratic citizenship, will necessitate an encounter with values inherent, often through tradition (Hansen, 2001) in these practices including those intellectual and moral virtues necessary for learning a discipline. Moral identity is therefore built out of commitment to the values which the individual encounters and which become dispositions of character and thereby virtues. However, such virtues are not merely the property of the individual but of the institutions. To describe an institution is to describe its values: both schools and schools of education would, on this model, perceive these values as characteristics of their ethos, and regard them as primary, predominant and pervasive (see MacIntyre, 1984; Zagzebski, 1996).

Typical "individual" virtues include sincerity, care, integrity, honesty, empathy, imaginativeness, and courage (moral and intellectual) and such virtues of the will as persistence, perseverance and courage (Sockett, 1988). Typical "social" virtues include commitments to justice, temperance, tact, discretion, civility, tolerance and liberality. Typical "knowledge" virtues (what Phillips and Burbules (2000) call "cognitive values") are accuracy, clarity, open-mindedness, humility, and fair-mindedness. Manifestly there is overlap and integration between these categories and the dispositions typical of each. For the moral agent-professional model, however, the school curriculum and the teacher education curriculum would be conceptualized as much through the development of these virtues as through the acquisition of knowledge items, for these qualities range over intellectual, social, personal life, and life in the workplace. They are part of who one is.

Bernard Williams (2002) in *Truth and Truthfulness* provides an argument which can be used to understand how the moral agent-professional model might integrate moral and epistemic purpose in teacher education, as he specifically explores two virtues both of which are significant for truth (and thereby for knowledge)—accuracy and sincerity. Both provide examples of (a) how the moral and the epistemic purposes are integrated, and (b) of how the model could construe the connections implied in this moral-epistemic reciprocity, for example, how the epistemic notion of belief is connected to open-mindedness and tolerance, or differently to intellectual courage.

Following Williams, we can connect the moral and epistemic in this way. Truth is a property of statements whereas truthfulness is a property of persons. In educating teachers, the model would claim, it is desirable that they come to believe what is true, and make true statements, assertions and claims about what they believe. So we connect these epistemic characteristics to the claim that, morally, teachers should be or become truthful people especially, we might say, in being truthful to themselves and not becoming victims of self-deceit, a condition Shulman detects in the contemporary undergraduate (Shulman, 1999). Truthfulness is seen as a desirable disposition, i.e. a stable characteristic of the ways a person acts (see the NCATE emphasis on teacher dispositions, and Sockett, 2006 (ed.)). Stability implies consistency, so teachers cannot be people who tell the truth only when it suits them, so they must come to be truthful people and truthful teachers. Yet truthfulness, on Williams' (2002) account, is a virtue or disposition of character with two constituent "basic virtues of truth"—accuracy and sincerity. Accuracy connects to acquiring a correct belief, and sincerity to the motivation to say what one actually believes, both of which are critical to the establishment of a relationship of trust, morally crucial in classrooms and schools. These intimate connections between truth, accuracy, sincerity and trust are thus at once moral and epistemic and they serve as illustrations of how, in the moral agent-professional model, the character of research and scholarly knowledge will be somewhat different from other models.

For the purposes of illustrating the link between the moral and the epistemic in this model, the focus here will be only on accuracy. Dispositions of character are seen as virtues because they counter human failings and foibles which, in this case of accuracy, are the "motivations to conceal or dissimulate" (Williams, 2002, p. 124). Accuracy "... lies in the skills and attitudes that resist the pleasure principle, in all its forms, from a gross need to believe the agreeable, to mere laziness in checking one's investigations" (Williams, p. 125). The core attitude needed is a concern for truth, indeed "a passion for getting it right" (p. 127) such that it can be a matter of honor, or conscience, or self-respect to do just that. The specific skills needed will vary from context to context in the public world, and in the school from discipline to discipline. Accuracy thus implies "care, reliability and so on in discovering and coming to believe the truth" (p. 127), recognizing the differences within disciplines but the coherence of it as an intellectual and moral virtue. On the moral epistemic connection, it is as important to teach children to be accurate as it is to teach them mathematics: yet of course, the one cannot be done without the other.

This brief account of accuracy illustrates the moral-epistemic relationship as conceived by the model. For teachers, it is not simply prudent to have children get the sums right, or to have the facts clear, but to have them come to value accuracy as important (when sloppiness, laziness, tiredness, and the attractions of the TV seem overwhelming) and to identify with that specific value a disposition of their character. In psychological terms, the target is not just intrinsic motivation, but motivation directed to who one is. So the model would expect from teachers a double duty: to be accurate themselves, both for their own character and as an example, and to teach children this specific, but not exclusive, virtue of truth. For accuracy, on this account, could not be regarded as some kind of virtuous skill to be taught outside a context: it would be seen as being developed in terms of the intellectual content which poses intellectual challenges, e.g. the academic disciplines (Sockett, 2000). Unsurprisingly, the moral agent-professional model characterizes the teacher as continuously facing complex moral problems, specifically but not exclusively in the *moral* content of what is being taught (e.g. Is what I am teaching true? Am I being truthful? Does my playing devil's advocate here undermine my sincerity? Should I have let these inaccuracies slip by? Am I trustworthy?) but in the moral responsibilities the teacher has to the school as an institution and its ethos.

Manifestly this model is not on the horizons of most contemporary thought about teacher education, except in so far as NCATE is urging institutions to define those dispositions it wishes to foster in novice teachers (see Sockett (ed.), 2006). Proponents of the model, derived from Aristotle, would urge a radical re-thinking of teacher education, rooted in an institutional ethos, intellectual rigor and the articulation and discussion of the profound character of moral issues confronting the teacher, specifically in terms of how they begin to articulate their moral identity, which can only be achieved on their own initiative. Yet a model derived from Dewey, with a very different set of moral and epistemic assumptions, would urge a similar radical re-thinking.

CONCLUSION

These four models provide one incomplete panorama of the conceptualization of moral and epistemic purposes in teacher education. If the implicit aim of the movement for teaching as a profession is consensus, it is extremely difficult to see how the differing moral and epistemic perspectives can easily be reconciled. The difficulty of some form of reconciliation and common base is fourfold: first, educational research is divided by paradigms of method and approach and it is in no one's self-interest in the academy to search for reconciliation. Second, the bureaucracy of public education is conducted in a discourse to which the clinician-professional model is the closest, but even that does not come near the language of the free market. Third, the thrust towards professionalization is connected with the academic's identification of professionalism than the teacher's, with the absence of partnership that suggests. Finally, teacher education thus requires more significant philosophical inquiry at institutional, curriculum and pedagogical levels if the complexities of moral and epistemic purposes are to be fully articulated. That would probably mean abandoning the attempt at consensus around the medical model of professionalism and the development of alternative models, each of which might gain public acceptance.

REFERENCES

Barzun, Jacques (1991) *Begin here: the forgotten conditions of teaching and learning*. Chicago: Chicago University Press.

Belenky, M. F., Clinchy, B. M., Goldberger, N. R., & Tarule, J.M. (1986) *Women's ways of knowing*. New York: Basic Books.

Buber, Martin (1970) *I and thou*. New York: Scribner.

Bloom, A. (1987) *The closing of the American mind*. New York: Simon and Schuster.

Bloom, B. S. & Krathwohl, D. R. (1956) *Taxonomy of educational objectives. Handbook 1: cognitive domain*. New York: Longman.

Bloom, B., Krathwohl, D., & Masia, B. (1963) *A Taxonomy of educational objectives*. London: Longman.

Bloom, H. (1994) *The Western canon: the books and school of the ages*. New York: Harcourt Brace.

Brighouse, H. (2000) *School choice and social justice*. Oxford: Oxford University Press.

Bruner, J. S. (1963) *The process of education*. New York: Vintage.

Bruner, J. S. (1996) *The culture of education*. Harvard: Harvard University Press.

Buber, M. (1996: translated by Walter Kaufmann) *I and thou*. Touchstone: New York

Campbell, E. (2003) *The ethical teacher*. Philadelphia, PA: Open University Press.

Clifford, G. & Guthrie, J. W. (1990) *Ed school*. Berkeley: University of California Press.

Darling-Hammond, L. & Bransford, J. (2005) *Preparing teachers for a changing world*. San Francisco: Jossey-Bass.

DePaul, M. & Zagzebski, L. (2003) *Intellectual virtue*. Oxford: Oxford University Press.

Dottine, E. (2006) A Deweyan approach to the development of moral dispositions in professional teacher education communities: using a conceptual framework. In Sockett, H. (ed.) *Teacher dispositions: building a teacher education framework of moral standards*. Washington, DC: American Association of Colleges for Teacher Education.

Egan. K (1997) *The educated mind*. Chicago: University of Chicago Press.

Ehrlich, T. (2003) *Civic responsibility and higher education*. Westport, CT: Oryx Press.

Everdell, William (1997) *The first moderns*. Chicago: Chicago University Press.

Fairweather, A., & Zagzebski, L. (2001) *Virtue epistemology: essays on epistemic virtue and responsibility*. Oxford: Oxford University Press.

Fenstermacher, Gary D. & Richardson, Virginia (2001) Manner in teaching: the study in four parts. *Journal of Curriculum Studies* 33(6): 631–639.

Finn, Chester. (1991) *We must take charge: our schools and our future*. New York: Free Press.

Gilligan, C. (1979) Woman's place in man's life cycle. *Harvard Educational Review* 49(1): 431–446.

Gilligan, C. (1982) *In a different voice*. Cambridge MA: Harvard University Press.

Gilligan, C. & Attanucci J. (1988) Two moral orientations: gender differences and similarities. *Merrill-Palmer Quarterly* 34(3): 223–237.

Goodlad, John I. (1990) *Teachers for our nation's schools*. San Francisco: Jossey-Bass.

Goodlad, J. I., Soder, R., & Sirotnik, K. (eds.) (1990) *The moral dimensions of teaching*. San Francisco: Jossey-Bass.

Griffin, Gary A. (ed.) (1999) *The education of teachers*. Ninety-Eighth Yearbook of the National Society for the Study of Education, Part I. Chicago: Chicago University Press.

Grossman, P. & Schonfield A. (2005) Teaching subject matter. In Darling-Hammond, L. & Bransford, J. (2005) *Preparing teachers for a changing world*. San Francisco: Jossey-Bass (Chapter 6, pp. 201–232).

Guttman, Amy (1999) *Democratic education*. Princeton: Princeton University Press.

Hamlyn, D. W. (1970) *The theory of knowledge*. London: Macmillan.

Hansen. David T. (1995) *The call to teach*. New York: Teachers College Press.

Hansen, David T. (2001) *Exploring the moral heart of teaching*. New York: Teachers College Press.

Hartshorne, H. & May, M. (1930) *Studies in the nature of character* (3 volumes). New York: Macmillan.

Harvard University (1942) *General education in a free society.* Harvard: Harvard University Press.

Hazen, Robert M., & Trefil, James S. (1991) *Science matters: achieving scientific literacy.* New York: Anchor Books.

Hirsch, E. D. Jr. (1987) *Cultural literacy.* New York: Doubleday.

Hirsch, E. D. Jr. (1996) *The schools we need.* New York: Doubleday.

Hirst, P. H. (1972) *Knowledge and the curriculum.* London: Routledge and Kegan Paul.

Hoyle, E. (1980) Professionalization and deprofessionalization in education. In E. Hoyle & J. E. Megarry (eds.) *The Professional development of teachers* (pp. 42–57), London: Kogan Press.

Huxley, Thomas (1874) *Universities: actual and ideal.* Rectorial Address to Aberdeen University. http://worldebooklibrary.com/eBooks/Adelaide/aut/huxley_th.html

Jackson, J. A. (1970) *Professions and professionalization.* Cambridge: Cambridge University Press.

Kazanjian, Victor (1999) Religion, identity and intellectual development: forging powerful learning communities. *Diversity Digest*, American Association of Colleges and Universities. Spring 1999 (see http://www.diversityweb.org/Digest/Sp99/religious.html).

Kohlberg, L. (1981) *Essays on moral development. Volume I: the philosophy of moral development.* San Francisco: Harper and Row.

Leavis, F. R. (1962) *Two cultures? The significance of C. P. Snow.* London: Chatto and Windus.

Lehrer, K. (2004) *Theory of knowledge.* Boulder, CO: Westview Press.

LePage, P. & Sockett, H. (2002) *Educational controversies: towards a discourse of reconciliation.* London: Falmer.

Lipman, M. (1988) *Philosophy goes to school.* Philadelphia, PA: Temple University Press.

MacIntyre, A. (1984) *After virtue* (2nd edition). Notre Dame, IN: University of Notre Dame Press.

Matthews, G. (1994) *The philosophy of childhood.* Cambridge, MA: Harvard University Press.

Murray, F. (1995) *The teacher educator's handbook: building a knowledge base for the preparation of teachers.* San Francisco: Jossey-Bass.

National Council for the Accreditation of Teacher Education (2005) *Professional standards for the accreditation of schools, departments and colleges of education.* Washington, DC: NCATE.

Noddings, N. (1984) *Caring: a feminine approach to ethics and moral education.* Berkeley: University of California Press.

Noddings, N. (1988) An ethic of caring and its implications for instructional arrangements. *American Journal of Education* 96(2): 215–231.

Noddings, N. (1999) Care, justice and equity. In Katz, M., Noddings, N., & Strike, K. A. (eds.) *Justice and caring: the search for common ground in education.* New York: Teachers College Press (pp. 7–21).

Norton, D. L. (1991) *Democracy and moral development: a politics of virtue.* Berkeley: University of California Press.

Oakeshott, M. (1967) *Rationalism in politics and other essays.* London: Methuen.

Oakeshott, M. (1975) *On human conduct.* Oxford: Oxford University Press.

O'Hear, A. (1994) "Education, values and the state." Victor Cook Memorial Lecture, Center for Philosophy and Public Affairs, University of St. Andrews, Scotland.

Oser, Fritz (1994). Moral perspectives on teaching. In Darling-Hammond, L. (ed.) *Review of research in education.* Washington, DC: AERA (pp. 57–129).

Peters, R. S. (1966) *Ethics and education.* London: Allen and Unwin.

Peters, R. S. (1972) Education and human development. In Dearden, R. F., Hirst, P. H., & Peters R. S. (eds.) *Education and the development of reason*, pp. 501–521. London: Routledge and Kegan Paul.

Phillips, D. C. (ed.) (2000) *Constructivism in education.* Ninety-Ninth Yearbook of the National Society for the Study of Education, Part I. Chicago: Chicago University Press.

Phillips, D. C. & Burbules, Nicholas C. (2000) *Post-positivism and educational research.* Lanham, MD: Rowman and Littlefield.

Pring, Richard A. (2000) *Philosophy of educational research.* London: Continuum.

Pring, Richard A. (2004) *Philosophy of education: aims, theory, common sense and research.* London: Continuum.

Ravitch, D. (2000) *Left back: a century of failed school reforms*. New York: Simon and Schuster.

Regnier, P. (1994) The illusion of technique and the intellectual life of schools, *Phi Delta Kappan*, September, 1994.

Reynolds, M. (1989) *Knowledge base for the beginning teacher*. New York: Pergamon.

Ryan, A. (1996) *John Dewey and the high tide of American liberalism*. New York: Norton.

Schon, D. (1986) *The reflective practitioner*. London: Temple Smith.

Shulman, L. (1987) Knowledge and teaching: foundations of the new reform. *Harvard Educational Review*, 57(1): 1–22.

Shulman, L. (1998) Theory, practice and the education of professionals. *Elementary School Journal*, 98(5): 511–526.

Shulman. L. (1999) Taking learning seriously. *Change* (July August 1999): 11–17.

Snow, C. P. (1998: 1959) *The two cultures (Canto)*. Cambridge: Cambridge University Press.

Sockett, H. (1988) Education and will: aspects of personal capability. *American Journal of Education*, 98(2): 195–215.

Sockett, H. (1990) Accountability, trust and ethical codes of practice. In Goodlad, J. I., Soder, R. & Sirotnik, K. (eds.) (1990) *The Moral Dimensions of Teaching*. San Francisco: Jossey-Bass (pp. 224–251).

Sockett, H. (1993) *The moral base for teacher professionalism*. New York: Teachers College Press.

Sockett, H. (2000) Creating a culture for the scholarship of teaching. *Inventio*. 2:1.

Sockett, H. (ed.) (2006) *Teacher dispositions: building a teacher education Framework of Moral Standards*. Washington, DC: American Association of Colleges of Teacher Education.

Soder, R., Goodlad, J. I., and McMannon, T. (eds.) (2000) *Developing democratic character in the young*. San Francisco: Jossey-Bass.

Sullivan, W. (2004) Preparing professionals as moral agents. *Carnegie Perspectives*: http// www.carnegiefoundation.org/perspectives/perspectives2004

Teacher Education Accreditation Council (2005): see http://www.teac.org

Tom, Alan (1984) *Teaching as a moral craft*. New York: Longman.

Tom, Alan (1997) *Redesigning teacher education*. Albany, NY: State University of New York Press.

Van Manen, Max (1991) *The tact of teaching*. New York: State University of New York Press.

Williams, B. (2002). *Truth and truthfulness*. Princeton: Princeton University Press.

Zakaria, F. (2003) *The future of freedom: illiberal democracy at home and abroad*. New York: Norton Press.

Zagzebski, L. (1996) *Virtues of the mind*. Cambridge: Cambridge University Press.

Part 1
Artifacts

1.1 The American scholar

Ralph Waldo Emerson

Source: Ralph Waldo Emerson, *Essays and Lectures*. New York: Library of America, 1983, pp. 51–71.

Mr. President and Gentlemen,

I greet you on the re-commencement of our literary year. Our anniversary is one of hope, and, perhaps, not enough of labor. We do not meet for games of strength or skill, for the recitation of histories, tragedies, and odes, like the ancient Greeks; for parliaments of love and poesy, like the Troubadours; nor for the advancement of science, like our contemporaries in the British and European capitals. Thus far, our holiday has been simply a friendly sign of the survival of the love of letters amongst a people too busy to give to letters any more. As such, it is precious as the sign of an indestructible instinct. Perhaps the time is already come, when it ought to be, and will be, something else; when the sluggard intellect of this continent will look from under its iron lids, and fill the postponed expectation of the world with something better than the exertions of mechanical skill. Our day of dependence, our long apprenticeship to the learning of other lands, draws to a close. The millions, that around us are rushing into life, cannot always be fed on the sere remains of foreign harvests. Events, actions arise, that must be sung, that will sing themselves. Who can doubt, that poetry will revive and lead in a new age, as the star in the constellation Harp, which now flames in our zenith, astronomers announce, shall one day be the pole-star for a thousand years?

In this hope, I accept the topic which not only usage, but the nature of our association, seem to prescribe to this day,—the AMERICAN SCHOLAR. Year by year, we come up hither to read one more chapter of his biography. Let us inquire what light new days and events have thrown on his character, and his hopes.

It is one of those fables, which, out of an unknown antiquity, convey an unlooked-for wisdom, that the gods, in the beginning, divided Man into men, that he might be more helpful to himself; just as the hand was divided into fingers, the better to answer its end.

The old fable covers a doctrine ever new and sublime; that there is One Man,—present to all particular men only partially, or through one faculty; and that you must take the whole society to find the whole man. Man is not a farmer, or a professor, or an engineer, but he is all. Man is priest, and scholar, and statesman, and producer, and soldier. In the *divided* or social state, these functions are parceled out to individuals, each of whom aims to do his stint of the joint work, whilst each other performs his. The fable implies, that the individual, to possess himself, must sometimes return from his own labor to embrace all the other laborers. But unfortunately, this original unit, this fountain of power, has been so distributed to multitudes, has been so minutely subdivided and peddled out, that it is spilled into drops, and cannot be gathered. The state of society is one in which the members have suffered amputation from the trunk, and strut about so many walking monsters,—a good finger, a neck, a stomach, an elbow, but never a man.

Man is thus metamorphosed into a thing, into many things. The planter, who is Man sent out into the field to gather food, is seldom cheered by any idea of the true dignity of his ministry. He sees his bushel and his cart, and nothing beyond, and sinks into the farmer, instead of Man on the farm. The tradesman scarcely ever gives an ideal worth to his work, but is ridden by the routine of his craft, and the soul is subject to dollars. The priest becomes a form; the attorney, a statute-book; the mechanic, a machine; the sailor, a rope of a ship.

In this distribution of functions, the scholar is the delegated intellect. In the right state, he is, *Man Thinking*. In the degenerate state, when the victim of society, he tends to become a mere thinker, or, still worse, the parrot of other men's thinking.

In this view of him, as Man Thinking, the theory of his office is contained. Him nature solicits with all her placid, all her monitory pictures; him the past instructs; him the future invites. Is not, indeed, every man a student, and do not all things exist for the student's behoof? And, finally, is not the true scholar the only true master? But the old oracle said, "All things have two handles: beware of the wrong one." In life, too often, the scholar errs with mankind and forfeits his privilege. Let us see him in his school, and consider him in reference to the main influences he receives.

I The first in time and the first in importance of the influences upon the mind is that of nature. Every day, the sun; and, after sunset, night and her stars. Ever the winds blow; ever the grass grows. Every day, men and women, conversing, beholding and beholden. The scholar is he of all men whom this spectacle most engages. He must settle its value in his mind. What is nature to him? There is never a beginning, there is never an end, to the inexplicable continuity of this web of God, but always circular power returning into itself. Therein it resembles his own spirit, whose beginning, whose ending, he never can find,—so entire, so boundless. Far, too, as her splendors shine, system on system shooting like rays, upward, downward, without centre, without circumference,—in the mass and in the particle, nature hastens to render account of herself to the mind. Classification begins. To the young mind, every thing is individual, stands by itself. By and by, it finds how to join two things, and see in them one nature; then three, then three thousand; and so, tyrannized over by its own unifying instinct, it goes on tying things together, diminishing anomalies, discovering roots running under ground, whereby contrary and remote things cohere, and flower out from one stem. It presently learns, that, since the dawn of history, there has been a constant accumulation and classifying of facts. But what is classification but the perceiving that these objects are not chaotic, and are not foreign, but have a law which is also a law of the human mind? The astronomer discovers that geometry, a pure abstraction of the human mind, is the measure of planetary motion. The chemist finds proportions and intelligible method throughout matter; and science is nothing but the finding of analogy, identity, in the most remote parts. The ambitious soul sits down before each refractory fact; one after another, reduces all strange constitutions, all new powers, to their class and their law, and goes on for ever to animate the last fibre of organization, the outskirts of nature, by insight.

Thus to him, to this school-boy under the bending dome of day, is suggested, that he and it proceed from one root; one is leaf and one is flower; relation, sympathy, stirring in every vein. And what is that Root? Is not that the soul of his soul?—A thought too bold,—a dream too wild. Yet when this spiritual light shall have revealed the law of more earthly natures,—when he has learned to worship the soul, and to see that the natural philosophy that now is, is only the first gropings of its gigantic hand, he shall look forward to an ever expanding knowledge as to a becoming creator. He shall see, that nature is the opposite of the soul, answering to it part for part. One is seal, and one is print. Its beauty is the beauty of his own mind. Its laws are the laws of his own mind. Nature then becomes to him the measure of his attainments. So much of nature as he is ignorant of, so much of his own mind does he not yet possess. And, in fine, the ancient precept, "Know thyself," and the modern precept, "Study nature," become at last one maxim.

II The next great influence into the spirit of the scholar, is, the mind of the Past,—in whatever form, whether of literature, of art, of institutions, that mind is inscribed. Books are the best type of the influence of the past, and perhaps we shall get at the truth,—learn the amount of this influence more conveniently,—by considering their value alone.

The theory of books is noble. The scholar of the first age received into him the world around; brooded thereon; gave it the new arrangement of his own mind, and uttered it again. It came into him, life; it went out from him, truth. It came to him, short-lived actions; it went out from him, immortal thoughts. It came to him, business; it went from him, poetry. It was dead fact; now, it is quick thought. It can stand, and it can go. It now endures, it now flies, it now inspires. Precisely in proportion to the depth of mind from which it issued, so high does it soar, so long does it sing.

Or, I might say, it depends on how far the process had gone, of transmuting life into truth. In proportion to the completeness of the distillation, so will the purity and imperishableness of the product be. But none is quite perfect. As no air-pump can by any means make a perfect vacuum, so neither can any artist entirely exclude the conventional, the local, the perishable from his book, or write a book of pure thought, that shall be as efficient, in all respects, to a remote posterity, as to contemporaries, or rather to the second age. Each age, it is found, must write its own books; or rather, each generation for the next succeeding. The books of an older period will not fit this.

Yet hence arises a grave mischief. The sacredness which attaches to the act of creation,—the act of thought,—is transferred to the record. The poet chanting, was felt to be a divine man: henceforth the chant is divine also. The writer was a just and wise spirit: henceforward it is settled, the book is perfect; as love of the hero corrupts into worship of his statue. Instantly, the book becomes noxious: the guide is a tyrant. The sluggish and perverted mind of the multitude, slow to open to the incursions of Reason, having once so opened, having once received this book, stands upon it, and makes an outcry, if it is disparaged. Colleges are built on it. Books are written on it by thinkers, not by Man Thinking; by men of talent, that is, who start wrong, who set out from accepted dogmas, not from their own sight of principles. Meek young men grow up in libraries, believing it their duty to accept the views, which Cicero, which Locke, which Bacon, have given, forgetful that Cicero, Locke, and Bacon were only young men in libraries, when they wrote these books.

Hence, instead of Man Thinking, we have the bookworm. Hence, the book-learned class, who value books, as such; not as related to nature and the human constitution, but as making a sort of Third Estate with the world and the soul. Hence, the restorers of readings, the emendators, the bibliomaniacs of all degrees.

Books are the best of things, well used; abused, among the worst. What is the right use? What is the one end, which all means go to effect? They are for nothing but to inspire. I had better never see a book, than to be warped by its attraction clean out of my own orbit, and made a satellite instead of a system. The one thing in the world, of value, is the active soul. This every man is entitled to; this every man contains within him, although, in almost all men, obstructed, and as yet unborn. The soul active sees absolute truth; and utters truth, or creates. In this action, it is genius; not the privilege of here and there a favorite, but the sound estate of every man. In its essence, it is progressive. The book, the college, the school of art, the institution of any kind, stop with some past utterance of genius. This is good, say they,—let us hold by this. They pin me down. They look backward and not forward. But genius looks forward: the eyes of man are set in his forehead, not in his hindhead: man hopes: genius creates. Whatever talents may be, if the man create not, the pure efflux of the Deity is not his;—cinders and smoke there may be, but not yet flame. There are creative manners, there are creative actions, and creative words; manners, actions, words, that is, indicative of no custom or authority, but springing spontaneous from the mind's own sense of good and fair.

On the other part, instead of being its own seer, let it receive from another mind its truth, though it were in torrents of light, without periods of solitude, inquest, and self-recovery, and a fatal dis-service is done. Genius is always sufficiently the enemy of genius by over influence. The literature of every nation bear me witness. The English dramatic poets have Shakspearized now for two hundred years.

Undoubtedly there is a right way of reading, so it be sternly subordinated. Man Thinking must not be subdued by his instruments. Books are for the scholar's idle times. When he can read God directly, the hour is too precious to be wasted in other men's transcripts of their readings. But when the intervals of darkness come, as come they must,—when the sun is hid, and the stars withdraw their shining,—we repair to the lamps which were kindled by their ray, to guide our steps to the East again, where the dawn is. We hear, that we may speak. The Arabian proverb says, "A fig tree, looking on a fig tree, becometh fruitful."

It is remarkable, the character of the pleasure we derive from the best books. They impress us with the conviction, that one nature wrote and the same reads. We read the verses of one of the great English poets, of Chaucer, of Marvell, of Dryden, with the most modern joy,—with a pleasure, I mean, which is in great part caused by the abstraction of all *time* from their verses. There is some awe mixed with the joy of our surprise, when this poet, who lived in some past world, two or three hundred years ago, says that which lies close to my own soul, that which I also had wellnigh thought and said. But for the evidence thence afforded to the philosophical doctrine of the identity of all minds, we should suppose some preestablished harmony, some foresight of souls that were to be, and some preparation of stores for their future wants, like the fact observed in insects, who lay up food before death for the young grub they shall never see.

I would not be hurried by any love of system, by any exaggeration of instincts, to underrate the Book. We all know, that, as the human body can be nourished on any food, though it were boiled grass and the broth of shoes, so the human mind can be fed by any knowledge. And great and heroic men have existed, who had almost no other information than by the printed page. I only would say, that it needs a strong head to bear that diet. One must be an inventor to read well. As the proverb says, "He that would bring home the wealth of the Indies, must carry out the wealth of the Indies." There is then creative reading as well as creative writing. When the mind is braced by labor and invention, the page of whatever book we read becomes luminous with manifold allusion. Every sentence is doubly significant, and the sense of our author is as broad as the world. We then see, what is always true, that, as the seer's hour of vision is short and rare among heavy days and months, so is its record, perchance, the least part of his volume. The discerning will read, in his Plato or Shakespeare, only that least part,—only the authentic utterances of the oracle;—all the rest he rejects, were it never so many times Plato's and Shakespeare's.

Of course, there is a portion of reading quite indispensable to a wise man. History and exact science he must learn by laborious reading. Colleges, in like manner, have their indispensable office,—to teach elements. But they can only highly serve us, when they aim not to drill, but to create; when they gather from far every ray of various genius to their hospitable halls, and, by the concentrated fires, set the hearts of their youth on flame. Thought and knowledge are natures in which apparatus and pretension avail nothing. Gowns, and pecuniary foundations, though of towns of gold, can never countervail the least sentence or syllable of wit. Forget this, and our American colleges will recede in their public importance, whilst they grow richer every year.

III There goes in the world a notion, that the scholar should be a recluse, a valetudinarian,—as unfit for any handiwork or public labor, as a penknife for an axe. The so-called "practical men" sneer at speculative men, as if, because they speculate or *see*, they could do nothing. I have heard it said that the clergy,—who are always, more universally than any other class, the scholars of their day,—are addressed as women; that the rough, spontaneous conversation of men they do not hear, but only a mincing and diluted speech. They are often virtually disfranchised; and, indeed, there are advocates for their celibacy. As far as this is true of the studious classes, it is not just and wise. Action is with the scholar subordinate, but it is essential. Without it, he is not yet man. Without it, thought can never ripen into truth. Whilst the world hangs before the eye as a cloud of beauty, we cannot even see its beauty. Inaction is cowardice, but there can be no scholar without the heroic mind. The preamble of thought, the transition through which it passes from the unconscious to the conscious, is action. Only so much do I know, as I have lived. Instantly we know whose words are loaded with life, and whose not.

The world,—this shadow of the soul, *or other me*, lies wide around. Its attractions are the keys which unlock my thoughts and make me acquainted with myself. I run eagerly into this resounding tumult. I grasp the hands of those next me, and take my place in the ring to suffer and to work, taught by an instinct, that so shall the dumb abyss be vocal with speech. I pierce its order; I dissipate its fear; I dispose of it within the circuit of my expanding life. So much only of life as I know by experience, so much of the wilderness have I vanquished and planted, or so far have I extended my being, my dominion. I do not see how any man can afford, for the sake of his nerves and his nap, to spare any action in which he can partake. It is pearls and rubies to his discourse. Drudgery, calamity, exasperation, want, are instructors in eloquence and wisdom. The true scholar grudges every opportunity of action past by, as a loss of power.

It is the raw material out of which the intellect moulds her splendid products. A strange process too, this, by which experience is converted into thought, as a mulberry leaf is converted into satin. The manufacture goes forward at all hours.

The actions and events of our childhood and youth, are now matters of calmest observation. They lie like fair pictures in the air. Not so with our recent actions,—with the business which we now have in hand. On this we are quite unable to speculate. Our affections as yet circulate through it. We no more feel or know it, than we feel the feet, or the hand, or the brain of our body. The new deed is yet a part of life,—remains for a time immersed in our unconscious life. In some contemplative hour, it detaches itself from the life like a ripe fruit, to become a thought of the mind. Instantly, it is raised, transfigured; the corruptible has put on incorruption. Henceforth it is an object of beauty, however base its origin and neighborhood. Observe, too, the impossibility of antedating this act. In its grub state, it cannot fly, it cannot shine, it is a dull grub. But suddenly, without observation, the selfsame thing unfurls beautiful wings, and is an angel of wisdom. So is there no fact, no event, in our private history, which shall not, sooner or later, lose its adhesive, inert form, and astonish us by soaring from our body into the empyrean. Cradle and infancy, school and playground, the fear of boys, and dogs, and ferules, the love of little maids and berries, and many another fact that once filled the whole sky, are gone already; friend and relative, profession and party, town and country, nation and world, must also soar and sing.

Of course, he who has put forth his total strength in fit actions, has the richest return of wisdom. I will not shut myself out of this globe of action, and transplant an oak into a flower-pot, there to hunger and pine; nor trust the revenue of some single faculty, and exhaust one vein of thought, much like those Savoyards, who, getting their livelihood by carving shepherds, shepherdesses, and smoking Dutchmen, for all Europe, went out one day to the mountain to find stock, and discovered that they had whittled up the last of their pine-trees. Authors we have, in numbers, who have written out their vein, and who, moved by a commendable prudence, sail for Greece or Palestine, follow the trapper into the prairie, or ramble round Algiers, to replenish their merchantable stock.

If it were only for a vocabulary, the scholar would be covetous of action. Life is our dictionary. Years are well spent in country labors; in town,—in the insight into trades and manufactures; in frank intercourse with many men and women; in science; in art; to the one end of mastering in all their facts a language by which to illustrate and embody our perceptions. I learn immediately from any speaker how much he has already lived, through the poverty or the splendor of his speech. Life lies behind us as the quarry from whence we get tiles and copestones for the masonry of to-day. This is the way to learn grammar. Colleges and books only copy the language which the field and the work-yard made.

But the final value of action, like that of books, and better than books, is, that it is a resource. That great principle of Undulation in nature, that shows itself in the inspiring and expiring of the breath; in desire and satiety; in the ebb and flow of the sea; in day and night; in heat and cold; and as yet more deeply ingrained in every atom and every fluid, is known to us under the name of Polarity,—these "fits of easy transmission and reflection," as Newton called them, are the law of nature because they are the law of spirit.

The mind now thinks; now acts; and each fit reproduces the other. When the artist has exhausted his materials, when the fancy no longer paints, when thoughts are no longer apprehended, and books are a weariness,—he has always the resource *to live*. Character is higher than intellect. Thinking is the function. Living is the functionary. The stream retreats to its source. A great soul will be strong to live, as well as strong to think. Does he lack organ or medium to impart his truths? He can still fall back on this elemental force of living them. This is a total act. Thinking is a partial act. Let the grandeur of justice shine in his affairs. Let the beauty of affection cheer his lowly roof. Those "far from fame," who dwell and act with him, will feel the force of his constitution in the doings and passages of the day better than it can be measured by any public and designed display. Time shall teach him, that the scholar loses no hour which the man lives. Herein he unfolds the sacred germ of his instinct, screened from influence. What is lost in seemliness is gained in strength. Not out of those, on whom systems of education have exhausted their culture, comes the helpful giant to destroy the old or to build the new, but out of unhandselled savage nature, out of terrible Druids and Berserkirs, come at last Alfred and Shakespeare.

I hear therefore with joy whatever is beginning to be said of the dignity and necessity of labor to every citizen. There is virtue yet in the hoe and the spade, for learned as well as for unlearned hands. And labor is everywhere welcome; always we are invited to work; only be this limitation observed, that a man shall not for the sake of wider activity sacrifice any opinion to the popular judgments and modes of action.

I have now spoken of the education of the scholar by nature, by books, and by action. It remains to say somewhat of his duties.

They are such as become Man Thinking. They may all be comprised in self-trust. The office of the scholar is to cheer, to raise, and to guide men by showing them facts amidst appearances. He plies the slow, unhonored, and unpaid task of observation. Flamsteed and Herschel, in their glazed observatories, may catalogue the stars with the praise of all men, and, the results being splendid and useful, honor is sure. But he, in his private observatory, cataloguing obscure and nebulous stars of the human mind, which as yet no man has thought of as such,—watching days and months, sometimes, for a few facts; correcting still his old records;—must relinquish display and immediate fame. In the long period of his preparation, he must betray often an ignorance and shiftlessness in popular arts, incurring the disdain of the able who shoulder him aside. Long he must stammer in his speech; often forego the living for the dead. Worse yet, he must accept,—how often! poverty and solitude. For the ease and pleasure of treading the old road, accepting the fashions, the education, the religion of society, he takes the cross of making his own, and, of course, the self-accusation, the faint heart, the frequent uncertainty and loss of time, which are the nettles and tangling vines in the way of the self-relying and self-directed; and the state of virtual hostility in which he seems to stand to society, and especially to educated society. For all this loss and scorn, what offset? He is to find consolation in exercising the highest functions of human nature. He is one, who raises himself from private considerations, and breathes and lives on public and illustrious thoughts. He is the world's eye. He is the world's heart. He is to resist the vulgar prosperity that retrogrades ever to barbarism, by preserving and communicating heroic sentiments, noble biographies, melodious verse, and the conclusions of history. Whatsoever oracles the human heart, in all emergencies, in all solemn hours, has uttered as its commentary on the world of actions,—these he shall receive and impart. And whatsoever new verdict Reason from her inviolable seat pronounces on the passing men and events of to-day,—this he shall hear and promulgate.

These being his functions, it becomes him to feel all confidence in himself, and to defer never to the popular cry. He and he only knows the world. The world of any moment is the merest appearance. Some great decorum, some fetish of a government, some ephemeral trade, or war, or man, is cried up by half mankind and cried down by the other half, as if all depended on this particular up or down. The odds are that the whole question is not worth the poorest thought which the scholar has lost in listening to the controversy. Let him not quit his belief that a popgun is a popgun, though the ancient and honorable of the earth affirm it to be the crack of doom. In silence, in steadiness, in severe abstraction, let him hold by himself; add observation to observation, patient of neglect, patient of reproach; and bide his own time,—happy enough, if he can satisfy himself alone, that this day he has seen something truly. Success treads on every right step. For the instinct is sure, that prompts him to tell his brother what he thinks. He then learns, that in going down into the secrets of his own mind, he has descended into the secrets of all minds. He learns that he who has mastered any law in his private thoughts, is master to that extent of all men whose language he speaks, and of all into whose language his own can be translated. The poet, in utter solitude remembering his spontaneous thoughts and recording them, is found to have recorded that, which men in crowded cities find true for them also. The orator distrusts at first the fitness of his frank confessions,—his want of knowledge of the persons he addresses,—until he finds that he is the complement of his hearers;—that they drink his words because he fulfill for them their own nature; the deeper he dives into his privatest, secretest presentiment, to his wonder he finds, this is the most acceptable, most public, and universally true. The people delight in it; the better part of every man feels, This is my music; this is myself.

In self-trust, all the virtues are comprehended. Free should the scholar be,—free and brave. Free even to the definition of freedom, "without any hindrance that does not arise out of his own constitution." Brave; for fear is a thing, which a scholar by his very function puts behind him. Fear always springs from ignorance. It is a shame to him if his tranquility, amid dangerous times, arise from the presumption, that, like children and women, his is a protected class; or if he seek a temporary peace by the diversion of his thoughts from politics or vexed questions, hiding his head like an ostrich in the flowering bushes, peeping into microscopes, and turning rhymes, as a boy whistles to keep his courage up. So is the danger a danger still; so is the fear worse. Manlike let him turn and face it. Let him look into its eye and search its nature, inspect its origin,—see the whelping of this lion,—which lies no great way back; he will then find in himself a perfect comprehension of its nature and extent; he will have made his hands meet on the other side, and can henceforth defy it, and pass on superior. The world is his, who can see through its pretension. What deafness, what stone-blind custom, what overgrown error you behold, is there only by sufferance,—by your sufferance. See it to be a lie, and you have already dealt it its mortal blow.

Yes, we are the cowed,—we the trustless. It is a mischievous notion that we are come late into nature; that the world was finished a long time ago. As the world was plastic and fluid in the hands of God, so it is ever to so much of his attributes as we bring to it. To ignorance and sin, it is flint. They adapt themselves to it as they may; but in proportion as a man has any thing in him divine, the firmament flows before him and takes his signet and form. Not he is great who can alter matter, but he who can alter my state of mind. They are the kings of the world who give the color of their present thought to all nature and all art, and persuade men by the cheerful serenity of their carrying the matter, that this thing which they do, is the apple which the ages have desired to pluck, now at last ripe, and inviting nations to the harvest. The great man makes the great thing. Wherever Macdonald sits, there is the head of the table. Linnaeus makes botany the most alluring of studies, and wins it from the farmer and the herb-woman; Davy, chemistry; and Cuvier, fossils. The day is always his, who works in it with serenity and great aims. The unstable estimates of men crowd to him whose mind is filled with a truth, as the heaped waves of the Atlantic follow the moon.

For this self-trust, the reason is deeper than can be fathomed,—darker than can be enlightened. I might not carry with me the feeling of my audience in stating my own belief. But I have already shown the ground of my hope, in adverting to the doctrine that man is one. I believe man has been wronged; he has wronged himself. He has almost lost the light, that can lead him back to his prerogatives. Men are become of no account. Men in history, men in the world of to-day are bugs, are spawn, and are called "the mass" and "the herd." In a century, in a millennium, one or two men; that is to say,—one or two approximations to the right state of every man. All the rest behold in the hero or the poet their own green and crude being,—ripened; yes, and are content to be less, so *that* may attain to its full stature. What a testimony,—full of grandeur, full of pity, is borne to the demands of his own nature, by the poor clansman, the poor partisan, who rejoices in the glory of his chief. The poor and the low find some amends to their immense moral capacity, for their acquiescence in a political and social inferiority. They are content to be brushed like flies from the path of a great person, so that justice shall be done by him to that common nature which it is the dearest desire of all to see enlarged and glorified. They sun themselves in the great man's light, and feel it to be their own element. They cast the dignity of man from their downtrod selves upon the shoulders of a hero, and will perish to add one drop of blood to make that great heart beat, those giant sinews combat and conquer. He lives for us, and we live in him.

Men such as they are, very naturally seek money or power; and power because it is as good as money,—the "spoils," so called, "of office." And why not? for they aspire to the highest, and this, in their sleep-walking, they dream is highest. Wake them, and they shall quit the false good, and leap to the true, and leave governments to clerks and desks. This revolution is to be wrought by the gradual domestication of the idea of Culture. The main enterprise of the world for splendor, for extent, is the upbuilding of a man. Here are the materials strown along the ground. The private life of one man shall be a more illustrious monarchy,—more formidable to its enemy, more sweet and serene in its influence to its friend, than any kingdom in history. For a man, rightly viewed, comprehendeth the particular natures of all men. Each philosopher, each bard, each actor, has only done for me, as by a delegate, what one day I can do for myself. The books which once we valued more than the apple of the eye, we have quite exhausted. What is that but saying, that we have come up with the point of view which the universal mind took through the eyes of one scribe; we have been that man, and have passed on. First, one; then, another; we drain all cisterns, and, waxing greater by all these supplies, we crave a better and more abundant food. The man has never lived that can feed us ever. The human mind cannot be enshrined in a person, who shall set a barrier on any one side to this unbounded, unboundable empire. It is one central fire, which, flaming now out of the lips of Etna, lightens the capes of Sicily; and, now out of the throat of Vesuvius, illuminates the towers and vineyards of Naples. It is one light which beams out of a thousand stars. It is one soul which animates all men.

But I have dwelt perhaps tediously upon this abstraction of the Scholar. I ought not to delay longer to add what I have to say, of nearer reference to the time and to this country.

Historically, there is thought to be a difference in the ideas which predominate over successive epochs, and there are data for marking the genius of the Classic, of the Romantic, and now of the Reflective or Philosophical age. With the views I have intimated of the oneness or the identity of the mind through all individuals, I do not much dwell on these differences. In fact, I believe each individual passes through all three. The boy is a Greek; the youth, romantic; the adult, reflective. I deny not, however, that a revolution in the leading idea may be distinctly enough traced.

Our age is bewailed as the age of Introversion. Must that needs be evil? We, it seems, are critical; we are embarrassed with second thoughts; we cannot enjoy any thing for hankering to know whereof the pleasure consists; we are lined with eyes; we see with our feet; the time is infected with Hamlet's unhappiness,—"Sicklied o'er with the pale cast of thought." Is it so bad then? Sight is the last thing to be pitied. Would we be blind? Do we fear lest we should outsee nature and God, and drink truth dry? I look upon the discontent of the literary class, as a mere announcement of the fact, that they find themselves not in the state of mind of their fathers, and regret the coming state as untried; as a boy dreads the water before he has learned that he can swim. If there is any period one would desire to be born in,—is it not the age of Revolution; when the old and the new stand side by side, and admit of being compared; when the energies of all men are searched by fear and by hope; when the historic glories of the old, can be compensated by the rich possibilities of the new era? This time, like all times, is a very good one, if we but know what to do with it.

I read with joy some of the auspicious signs of the coming days, as they glimmer already through poetry and art, through philosophy and science, through church and state.

One of these signs is the fact, that the same movement which effected the elevation of what was called the lowest class in the state, assumed in literature a very marked and as benign an aspect. Instead of the sublime and beautiful; the near, the low, the common, was explored and poetized. That, which had been negligently trodden under foot by those who were harnessing and provisioning themselves for long journeys into far countries, is suddenly found to be richer than all foreign parts. The literature of the poor, the feelings of the child, the philosophy of the street, the meaning of household life, are the topics of the time. It is a great stride. It is a sign,—is it not? of new vigor, when the extremities are made active, when currents of warm life run into the hands and the feet. I ask not for the great, the remote, the romantic; what is doing in Italy or Arabia; what is Greek art, or Provencal minstrelsy; I embrace the common, I explore and sit at the feet of the familiar, the low. Give me insight into to-day, and you may have the antique and future worlds. What would we really know the meaning of? The meal in the firkin; the milk in the pan; the ballad in the street; the news of the boat; the glance of the eye; the form and the gait of the body;—show me the ultimate reason of these matters; show me the sublime presence of the highest spiritual cause lurking, as always it does lurk, in these suburbs and extremities of nature; let me see every trifle bristling with the polarity that ranges it instantly on an eternal law; and the shop, the plough, and the ledger, referred to the like cause by which light undulates and poets sing;—and the world lies no longer a dull miscellany and lumber-room, but has form and order; there is no trifle; there is no puzzle; but one design unites and animates the farthest pinnacle and the lowest trench.

This idea has inspired the genius of Goldsmith, Burns, Cowper, and, in a newer time, of Goethe, Wordsworth, and Carlyle. This idea they have differently followed and with various success. In contrast with their writing, the style of Pope, of Johnson, of Gibbon, looks cold and pedantic. This writing is blood-warm. Man is surprised to find that things near are not less beautiful and wondrous than things remote. The near explains the far. The drop is a small ocean. A man is related to all nature. This perception of the worth of the vulgar is fruitful in discoveries. Goethe, in this very thing the most modern of the moderns, has shown us, as none ever did, the genius of the ancients.

There is one man of genius, who has done much for this philosophy of life, whose literary value has never yet been rightly estimated;—I mean Emanuel Swedenborg. The most imaginative of men, yet writing with the precision of a mathematician, he endeavored to engraft a purely philosophical Ethics on the popular Christianity of his time. Such an attempt, of course, must have difficulty, which no genius could surmount. But he saw and showed the connection between nature and the affections of the soul. He pierced the emblematic or spiritual character of the visible, audible, tangible world. Especially did his shade-loving muse hover over and interpret the lower parts of nature; he showed the mysterious bond that allies moral evil to the foul material forms, and has given in epical parables a theory of insanity, of beasts, of unclean and fearful things.

Another sign of our times, also marked by an analogous political movement, is, the new importance given to the single person. Every thing that tends to insulate the individual,—to surround him with barriers of natural respect, so that each man shall feel the world is his, and man shall treat with man as a sovereign state with a sovereign state;—tends to true union as well as greatness. "I learned," said the melancholy Pestalozzi, "that no man in God's wide earth is either willing or able to help any other man." Help must come from the bosom alone. The scholar is that man who must take up into himself all the ability of the time, all the contributions of the past, all the hopes of the future. He must be an university of knowledges. If there be one lesson more than another, which should pierce his ear, it is. The world is nothing, the man is all; in yourself is the law of all nature, and you know not yet how a globule of sap ascends; in yourself slumbers the whole of Reason; it is for you to know all, it is for you to dare all.

Mr. President and Gentlemen, this confidence in the unsearched might of man belongs, by all motives, by all prophecy, by all preparation, to the American Scholar. We have listened too long to the courtly muses of Europe. The spirit of the American freeman is already suspected to be timid, imitative, tame. Public and private avarice make the air we breathe thick and fat. The scholar is decent, indolent, complaisant. See already the tragic consequence. The mind of this country, taught to aim at low objects, eats upon itself. There is no work for any but the decorous and the complaisant. Young men of the fairest promise, who begin life upon our shores, inflated by the mountain winds, shined upon by all the stars of God, find the earth below not in unison with these,—but are hindered from action by the disgust which the principles on which business is managed inspire, and turn drudges, or die of disgust,—some of them suicides. What is the remedy? They did not yet see, and thousands of young men as hopeful now crowding to the barriers for the career do not yet see, that, if the single man plant himself indomitably on his instincts, and there abide, the huge world will come round to him. Patience,—patience;—with the shades of all the good and great for company; and for solace, the perspective of your own infinite life; and for work, the study and the communication of principles, the making those instincts prevalent, the conversion of the world. Is it not the chief disgrace in the world, not to be an unit;—not to be reckoned one character;—not to yield that peculiar fruit which each man was created to bear, but to be reckoned in the gross, in the hundred, or the thousand, of the party, the section, to which we belong; and our opinion predicted geographically, as the north, or the south? Not so, brothers and friends,—please God, ours shall not be so. We will walk on our own feet; we will work with our own hands; we will speak our own minds. The study of letters shall be no longer a name for pity, for doubt, and for sensual indulgence. The dread of man and the love of man shall be a wall of defence and a wreath of joy around all. A nation of men will for the first time exist, because each believes himself inspired by the Divine Soul which also inspires all men.

1.2 Of the coming of John

by W. E. B. Du Bois

Source: W. E. B. Du Bois, *The Souls of Black Folk*. New York: Library of America, 1990, pp. 165–179

> What bring they 'neath the midnight,
>   Beside the River-sea?
> They bring the human heart wherein
>   No nightly calm can be;
> That droppeth never with the wind,
>   Nor drieth with the dew;
> O calm it, God; thy calm is broad
>   To cover spirits too.
>   The river floweth on.
>   Mrs. Browning.

Carlisle Street runs westward from the centre of Johnstown, across a great black bridge, down a hill and up again, by little shops and meat-markets, past single-storied homes, until suddenly it stops against a wide green lawn. It is a broad, restful place, with two large buildings outlined against the west. When at evening the winds come swelling from the east, and the great pall of the city's smoke hangs wearily above the valley, then the red west glows like a dreamland down Carlisle Street, and, at the tolling of the supper-bell, throws the passing forms of students in dark silhouette against the sky. Tall and black, they move slowly by, and seem in the sinister light to flit before the city like dim warning ghosts. Perhaps they are; for this is Wells Institute, and these black students have few dealings with the white city below.

And if you will notice, night after night, there is one dark form that ever hurries last and late toward the twinkling lights of Swain Hall,—for Jones is never on time. A long, straggling fellow he is, brown and hard-haired, who seems to be growing straight out of his clothes, and walks with a half-apologetic roll. He used perpetually to set the quiet dining-room into waves of merriment, as he stole to his place after the bell had tapped for prayers; he seemed so perfectly awkward. And yet one glance at his face made one forgive him much,—that broad, good-natured smile in which lay no bit of art or artifice, but seemed just bubbling good-nature and genuine satisfaction with the world.

He came to us from Altamaha, away down there beneath the gnarled oaks of Southeastern Georgia, where the sea croons to the sands and the sands listen till they sink half drowned beneath the waters, rising only here and there in long, low islands. The white folk of Altamaha voted John a good boy,—fine plough-hand, good in the rice-fields, handy everywhere, and always good-natured and respectful. But they shook their heads when his mother wanted to send him off to school. "It'll spoil him,—ruin him," they said; and they talked as though they knew. But full half the black folk followed him proudly to the station, and carried his queer little trunk and many bundles. And there they shook and shook hands, and the girls kissed him shyly and the boys clapped him on the back. So the train came, and he pinched his little sister lovingly, and put his great arms about his mother's neck, and then was away with a puff and a roar into the great yellow world that flamed and flared about the doubtful pilgrim. Up the coast they hurried, past the squares and palmettos of Savannah, through the cotton-fields and through the weary night, to Millville, and came with the morning to the noise and bustle of Johnstown.

And they that stood behind, that morning in Altamaha, and watched the train as it noisily bore playmate and brother and son away to the world, had thereafter one ever-recurring word,— "When John comes." Then what parties were to be, and what speakings in the churches; what new furniture in the front room,—perhaps even a new front room; and there would be a new schoolhouse, with John as teacher; and then perhaps a big wedding; all this and more—when John comes. But the white people shook their heads.

At first he was coming at Christmas-time,—but the vacation proved too short; and then, the next summer,—but times were hard and schooling costly, and so, instead, he worked in Johnstown. And so it drifted to the next summer, and the next,—till playmates scattered, and mother grew gray, and sister went up to the Judge's kitchen to work. And still the legend lingered,—"When John comes."

Up at the Judge's they rather liked this refrain; for they too had a John—a fair-haired, smooth-faced boy, who had played many a long summer's day to its close with his darker namesake. "Yes, sir! John is at Princeton, sir," said the broad-shouldered gray-haired Judge every morning as he marched down to the post-office. "Showing the Yankees what a Southern gentleman can do," he added; and strode home again with his letters and papers. Up at the great pillared house they lingered long over the Princeton letter,—the Judge and his frail wife, his sister and growing daughters. "It'll make a man of him," said the Judge, "college is the place." And then he asked the shy little waitress, "Well, Jennie, how's your John?" and added reflectively, "Too bad, too bad your mother sent him off,—it will spoil him." And the waitress wondered.

Thus in the far-away Southern village the world lay waiting, half consciously, the coming of two young men, and dreamed in an inarticulate way of new things that would be done and new thoughts that all would think. And yet it was singular that few thought of two Johns,—for the black folk thought of one John, and he was black; and the white folk thought of another John, and he was white. And neither world thought the other world's thought, save with a vague unrest.

Up in Johnstown, at the Institute, we were long puzzled at the case of John Jones. For a long time the clay seemed unfit for any sort of moulding. He was loud and boisterous, always laughing and singing, and never able to work consecutively at anything. He did not know how to study; he had no idea of thoroughness; and with his tardiness, carelessness, and appalling good-humor, we were sore perplexed. One night we sat in faculty-meeting, worried and serious; for Jones was in trouble again. This last escapade was too much, and so we solemnly voted "that Jones, on account of repeated disorder and inattention to work, be suspended for the rest of the term."

It seemed to us that the first time life ever struck Jones as a really serious thing was when the Dean told him he must leave school. He stared at the gray-haired man blankly, with great eyes. "Why,—why," he faltered, "but—I haven't graduated!" Then the Dean slowly and clearly explained, reminding him of the tardiness and the carelessness, of the poor lessons and neglected work, of the noise and disorder, until the fellow hung his head in confusion. Then he said quickly, "But you won't tell mammy and sister,—you won't write mammy, now will you? For if you won't I'll go out into the city and work, and come back next term and show you something." So the Dean promised faithfully, and John shouldered his little trunk, giving neither word nor look to the giggling boys, and walked down Carlisle Street to the great city, with sober eyes and a set and serious face.

Perhaps we imagined it, but someway it seemed to us that the serious look that crept over his boyish face that afternoon never left it again. When he came back to us he went to work with all his rugged strength. It was a hard struggle, for things did not come easily to him,—few crowding memories of early life and teaching came to help him on his new way; but all the world toward which he strove was of his own building, and he builded slow and hard. As the light dawned lingeringly on his new creations, he sat rapt and silent before the vision, or wandered alone over the green campus peering through and beyond the world of men into a world of thought. And the thoughts at times puzzled him sorely; he could not see just why the circle was not square, and carried it out fifty-six decimal places one midnight,—would have gone further, indeed, had not the matron rapped for lights out. He caught terrible colds lying on his back in the meadows of nights, trying to think out the solar system; he had grave doubts as to the ethics of the Fall of Rome, and strongly suspected the Germans of being thieves and rascals, despite his text-books; he pondered long over every new Greek word, and wondered why this meant that and why it couldn't mean something else, and how it must have felt to think all things in Greek. So he thought and puzzled along for himself,—pausing perplexed where others skipped merrily, and walking steadily through the difficulties where the rest stopped and surrendered.

Thus he grew in body and soul, and with him his clothes seemed to grow and arrange themselves; coat sleeves got longer, cuffs appeared, and collars got less soiled. Now and then his boots shone, and a new dignity crept into his walk. And we who saw daily a new thoughtfulness growing in his eyes began to expect something of this plodding boy. Thus he passed out of the preparatory school into college, and we who watched him felt four more years of change, which almost transformed the tall, grave man who bowed to us commencement morning. He had left his queer thought-world and come back to a world of motion and of men. He looked now for the first time sharply about him, and wondered he had seen so little before. He grew slowly to feel almost for the first time the Veil that lay between him and the white world; he first noticed now the oppression that had not seemed oppression before, differences that erstwhile seemed natural, restraints and slights that in his boyhood days had gone unnoticed or been greeted with a laugh. He felt angry now when men did not call him "Mister," he clenched his hands at the "Jim Crow" cars, and chafed at the color-line that hemmed in him and his. A tinge of sarcasm crept into his speech, and a vague bitterness into his life; and he sat long hours wondering and planning a way around these crooked things. Daily he found himself shrinking from the choked and narrow life of his native town. And yet he always planned to go back to Altamaha,—always planned to work there. Still, more and more as the day approached he hesitated with a nameless dread; and even the day after graduation he seized with eagerness the offer of the Dean to send him North with the quartette during the summer vacation, to sing for the Institute. A breath of air before the plunge, he said to himself in half apology.

It was a bright September afternoon, and the streets of New York were brilliant with moving men. They reminded John of the sea, as he sat in the square and watched them, so changelessly changing, so bright and dark, so grave and gay. He scanned their rich and faultless clothes, the way they carried their hands, the shape of their hats; he peered into the hurrying carriages. Then, leaning back with a sigh, he said, "This is the World." The notion suddenly seized him to see where the world was going; since many of the richer and brighter seemed hurrying all one way. So when a tall, light-haired young man and a little talkative lady came by, he rose half hesitatingly and followed them. Up the street they went, past stores and gay shops, across a broad square, until with a hundred others they entered the high portal of a great building.

He was pushed toward the ticket-office with the others, and felt in his pocket for the new five-dollar bill he had hoarded. There seemed really no time for hesitation, so he drew it bravely out, passed it to the busy clerk, and received simply a ticket but no change. When at last he realized that he had paid five dollars to enter he knew not what, he stood stock-still amazed. "Be careful," said a low voice behind him; "you must not lynch the colored gentleman simply because he's in your way," and a girl looked up roguishly into the eyes of her fair-haired escort. A shade of annoyance passed over the escort's face. "You *will* not understand us at the South," he said half impatiently, as if continuing an argument. "With all your professions, one never sees in the North so cordial and intimate relations between white and black as are everyday occurrences with us. Why, I remember my closest playfellow in boyhood was a little Negro named after me, and surely no two,—*well!*' The man stopped short and flushed to the roots of his hair, for there directly beside his reserved orchestra chairs sat the Negro he had stumbled over in the hallway. He hesitated and grew pale with anger, called the usher and gave him his card, with a few peremptory words, and slowly sat down. The lady deftly changed the subject.

All this John did not see, for he sat in a half-maze minding the scene about him; the delicate beauty of the hall, the faint perfume, the moving myriad of men, the rich clothing and low hum of talking seemed all a part of a world so different from his, so strangely more beautiful than anything he had known, that he sat in dreamland, and started when, after a hush, rose high and clear the music of Lohengrin's swan. The infinite beauty of the wail lingered and swept through every muscle of his frame, and put it all a-tune. He closed his eyes and grasped the elbows of the chair, touching unwittingly the lady's arm. And the lady drew away. A deep longing swelled in all his heart to rise with that clear music out of the dirt and dust of that low life that held him prisoned and befouled. If he could only live up in the free air where birds sang and setting suns had no touch of blood! Who had called him to be the slave and butt of all? And if he had called, what right had he to call when a world like this lay open before men?

Then the movement changed, and fuller, mightier harmony swelled away. He looked thoughtfully across the hall, and wondered why the beautiful gray-haired woman looked so listless, and what the little man could be whispering about. He would not like to be listless and idle, he thought, for he felt with the music the movement of power within him. If he but had some master-work, some life-service, hard,—aye, bitter hard, but without the cringing and sickening servility, without the cruel hurt that hardened his heart and soul. When at last a soft sorrow crept across the violins, there came to him the vision of a far-off home,—the great eyes of his sister, and the dark drawn face of his mother. And his heart sank below the waters, even as the sea-sand sinks by the shores of Altamaha, only to be lifted aloft again with that last ethereal wail of the swan that quivered and faded away into the sky.

It left John sitting so silent and rapt that he did not for some time notice the usher tapping him lightly on the shoulder and saying politely, "Will you step this way, please, sir?" A little surprised, he arose quickly at the last tap, and, turning to leave his seat, looked full into the face of the fair-haired young man. For the first time the young man recognized his dark boyhood playmate, and John knew that it was the Judge's son. The white John started, lifted his hand, and then froze into his chair; the black John smiled lightly, then grimly, and followed the usher down the aisle. The manager was sorry, very, very sorry,—but he explained that some mistake had been made in selling the gentleman a seat already disposed of; he would refund the money, of course,—and indeed felt the matter keenly, and so forth, and—before he had finished John was gone, walking hurriedly across the square and down the broad streets, and as he passed the park he buttoned his coat and said, "John Jones, you're a natural-born fool." Then he went to his lodgings and wrote a letter, and tore it up; he wrote another, and threw it in the fire. Then he seized a scrap of paper and wrote: "Dear Mother and Sister—I am coming—John."

"Perhaps," said John, as he settled himself on the train, "perhaps I am to blame myself in struggling against my manifest destiny simply because it looks hard and unpleasant. Here is my duty to Altamaha plain before me; perhaps they'll let me help settle the Negro problems there,— perhaps they won't. 'I will go in to the King, which is not according to the law; and if I perish, I perish.' " And then he mused and dreamed, and planned a life-work; and the train flew south.

Down in Altamaha, after seven long years, all the world knew John was coming. The homes were scrubbed and scoured,—above all, one; the gardens and yards had an unwonted trimness, and Jennie bought a new gingham. With some finesse and negotiation, all the dark Methodists and Presbyterians were induced to join in a monster welcome at the Baptist Church; and as the day drew near, warm discussions arose on every corner as to the exact extent and nature of John's accomplishments. It was noontide on a gray and cloudy day when he came. The black town flocked to the depot, with a little of the white at the edges,—a happy throng, with "Good-mawnings" and "Howdys" and laughing and joking and jostling. Mother sat yonder in the window watching; but sister Jennie stood on the platform, nervously fingering her dress,—tall and lithe, with soft brown skin and loving eyes peering from out a tangled wilderness of hair. John rose gloomily as the train stopped, for he was thinking of the "Jim Crow" car; he stepped to the platform, and paused: a little dingy station, a black crowd gaudy and dirty, a half-mile of dilapidated shanties along a straggling ditch of mud. An overwhelming sense of the sordidness and narrowness of it all seized him; he looked in vain for his mother, kissed coldly the tall, strange girl who called him brother, spoke a short, dry word here and there; then, lingering neither for hand-shaking nor gossip, started silently up the street, raising his hat merely to the last eager old aunty, to her open-mouthed astonishment. The people were distinctly bewildered. This silent, cold man,—was this John? Where was his smile and hearty hand-grasp? " 'Peared kind o' down in the mouf," said the Methodist preacher thoughtfully. "Seemed monstus stuck up," complained a Baptist sister. But the white postmaster from the edge of the crowd expressed the opinion of his folks plainly. "That damn Nigger," said he, as he shouldered the mail and arranged his tobacco, "has gone North and got plum full o' fool notions; but they won't work in Altamaha." And the crowd melted away.

The meeting of welcome at the Baptist Church was a failure. Rain spoiled the barbecue, and thunder turned the milk in the ice-cream. When the speaking came at night, the house was crowded to overflowing. The three preachers had especially prepared themselves, but somehow John's manner seemed to throw a blanket over everything,—he seemed so cold and preoccupied, and had so strange an air of restraint that the Methodist brother could not warm up to his theme and elicited not a single "Amen"; the Presbyterian prayer was but feebly responded to, and even the Baptist preacher, though he wakened faint enthusiasm, got so mixed up in his favorite sentence that he had to close it by stopping fully fifteen minutes sooner than he meant. The people moved uneasily in their seats as John rose to reply. He spoke slowly and methodically. The age, he said, demanded new ideas; we were far different from those men of the seventeenth and eighteenth centuries,—with broader ideas of human brotherhood and destiny. Then he spoke of the rise of charity and popular education, and particularly of the spread of wealth and work. The question was, then, he added reflectively, looking at the low discolored ceiling, what part the Negroes of this land would take in the striving of the new century. He sketched in vague outline the new Industrial School that might rise among these pines, he spoke in detail of the charitable and philanthropic work that might be organized, of money that might be saved for banks and business. Finally he urged unity, and deprecated especially religious and denominational bickering. "To-day," he said, with a smile, "the world cares little whether a man be Baptist or Methodist, or indeed a churchman at all, so long as he is good and true. What difference does it make whether a man be baptized in river or wash-bowl, or not at all? Let's leave all that littleness, and look higher." Then, thinking of nothing else, he slowly sat down. A painful hush seized that crowded mass. Little had they understood of what he said, for he spoke an unknown tongue, save the last word about baptism; that they knew, and they sat very still while the clock ticked. Then at last a low suppressed snarl came from the Amen corner, and an old bent man arose, walked over the seats, and climbed straight up into the pulpit. He was wrinkled and black, with scant gray and tufted hair; his voice and hands shook as with palsy; but on his face lay the intense rapt look of the religious fanatic. He seized the Bible with his rough, huge hands; twice he raised it inarticulate, and then fairly burst into the words, with rude and awful eloquence. He quivered, swayed, and bent; then rose aloft in perfect majesty, till the people moaned and wept, wailed and shouted, and a wild shrieking arose from the corners where all the pent-up feeling of the hour gathered itself and rushed into the air. John never knew clearly what the old man said; he only felt himself held up to scorn and scathing denunciation for trampling on the true Religion, and he realized with amazement that all unknowingly he had put rough, rude hands on something this little world held sacred. He arose silently, and passed out into the night. Down toward the sea he went, in the fitful starlight, half conscious of the girl who followed timidly after him. When at last he stood upon the bluff, he turned to his little sister and looked upon her sorrowfully, remembering with sudden pain how little thought he had given her. He put his arm about her and let her passion of tears spend itself on his shoulder.

Long they stood together, peering over the gray unresting water.

"John," she said, "does it make every one—unhappy when they study and learn lots of things?"

He paused and smiled. "I am afraid it does," he said.

"And, John, are you glad you studied?"

"Yes," came the answer, slowly but positively.

She watched the flickering lights upon the sea, and said thoughtfully, "I wish I was unhappy,—and—and," putting both arms about his neck, "I think I am, a little, John."

It was several days later that John walked up to the Judge's house to ask for the privilege of teaching the Negro school. The Judge himself met him at the front door, stared a little hard at him, and said brusquely, "Go 'round to the kitchen door, John, and wait." Sitting on the kitchen steps, John stared at the corn, thoroughly perplexed. What on earth had come over him? Every step he made offended some one. He had come to save his people, and before he left the depot he had hurt them. He sought to teach them at the church, and had outraged their deepest feelings. He had schooled himself to be respectful to the Judge, and then blundered into his front door. And all the time he had meant right,—and yet, and yet, somehow he found it so hard and strange to fit his old surroundings again, to find his place in the world about him. He could not remember that he used to have any difficulty in the past, when life was glad and gay. The world seemed smooth and easy then. Perhaps,—but his sister came to the kitchen door just then and said the Judge awaited him.

The Judge sat in the dining-room amid his morning's mail, and he did not ask John to sit down. He plunged squarely into the business. "You've come for the school, I suppose. Well, John, I want to speak to you plainly. You know I'm a friend to your people. I've helped you and your family, and would have done more if you hadn't got the notion of going off. Now I like the colored people, and sympathize with all their reasonable aspirations; but you and I both know, John, that in this country the Negro must remain subordinate, and can never expect to be the equal of white men. In their place, your people can be honest and respectful; and God knows, I'll do what I can to help them. But when they want to reverse nature, and rule white men, and marry white women, and sit in my parlor, then, by God! we'll hold them under if we have to lynch every Nigger in the land. Now, John, the question is, are you, with your education and Northern notions, going to accept the situation and teach the darkies to be faithful servants and laborers as your fathers were,—I knew your father, John, he belonged to my brother, and he was a good Nigger. Well—well, are you going to be like him, or are you going to try to put fool ideas of rising and equality into these folks' heads, and make them discontented and unhappy?"

"I am going to accept the situation, Judge Henderson," answered John, with a brevity that did not escape the keen old man. He hesitated a moment, and then said shortly, "Very well,—we'll try you awhile. Good-morning."

It was a full month after the opening of the Negro school that the other John came home, tall, gay, and headstrong. The mother wept, the sisters sang. The whole white town was glad. A proud man was the Judge, and it was a goodly sight to see the two swinging down Main Street together. And yet all did not go smoothly between them, for the younger man could not and did not veil his contempt for the little town, and plainly had his heart set on New York. Now the one cherished ambition of the Judge was to see his son mayor of Altamaha, representative to the legislature, and—who could say?—governor of Georgia. So the argument often waxed hot between them. "Good heavens, father," the younger man would say after dinner, as he lighted a cigar and stood by the fireplace, "you surely don't expect a young fellow like me to settle down permanently in this—this God-forgotten town with nothing but mud and Negroes?" "I did," the Judge would answer laconically; and on this particular day it seemed from the gathering scowl that he was about to add something more emphatic, but neighbors had already begun to drop in to admire his son, and the conversation drifted.

"Heah that John is livenin' things up at the darky school," volunteered the postmaster, after a pause.

"What now?" asked the Judge, sharply.

"Oh, nothin' in particulah,—just his almighty air and uppish ways. B'lieve I did heah somethin' about his givin' talks on the French Revolution, equality, and such like. He's what I call a dangerous Nigger."

"Have you heard him say anything out of the way?"

"Why, no,—but Sally, our girl, told my wife a lot of rot. Then, too, I don't need to heah: a Nigger what won't say 'sir' to a white man, or—"

"Who is this John?" interrupted the son.

"Why, it's little black John, Peggy's son,—your old playfellow."

The young man's face flushed angrily, and then he laughed.

"Oh," said he, "it's the darky that tried to force himself into a seat beside the lady I was escorting—"

But Judge Henderson waited to hear no more. He had been nettled all day, and now at this he rose with a half-smothered oath, took his hat and cane, and walked straight to the schoolhouse.

For John, it had been a long, hard pull to get things started in the rickety old shanty that sheltered his school. The Negroes were rent into factions for and against him, the parents were careless, the children irregular and dirty, and books, pencils, and slates largely missing. Nevertheless, he struggled hopefully on, and seemed to see at last some glimmering of dawn. The attendance was larger and the children were a shade cleaner this week. Even the booby class in reading showed a little comforting progress. So John settled himself with renewed patience this afternoon.

"Now, Mandy," he said cheerfully, "that's better; but you mustn't chop your words up so: 'If—the—man—goes.' Why, your little brother even wouldn't tell a story that way, now would he?"

"Naw, suh, he cain't talk."

"All right; now let's try again: 'If the man—' "

"John!"

The whole school started in surprise, and the teacher half arose, as the red, angry face of the Judge appeared in the open doorway.

"John, this school is closed. You children can go home and get to work. The white people of Altamaha are not spending their money on black folks to have their heads crammed with impudence and lies. Clear out! I'll lock the door myself."

Up at the great pillared house the tall young son wandered aimlessly about after his father's abrupt departure. In the house there was little to interest him; the books were old and stale, the local newspaper flat, and the women had retired with headaches and sewing. He tried a nap, but it was too warm. So he sauntered out into the fields, complaining disconsolately, "Good Lord! how long will this imprisonment last!" He was not a bad fellow,—just a little spoiled and self-indulgent, and as headstrong as his proud father. He seemed a young man pleasant to look upon, as he sat on the great black stump at the edge of the pines idly swinging his legs and smoking. "Why, there isn't even a girl worth getting up a respectable flirtation with," he growled. Just then his eye caught a tall, willowy figure hurrying toward him on the narrow path. He looked with interest at first, and then burst into a laugh as he said, "Well, I declare, if it isn't Jennie, the little brown kitchen-maid! Why, I never noticed before what a trim little body she is. Hello, Jennie! Why, you haven't kissed me since I came home," he said gaily. The young girl stared at him in surprise and confusion,—faltered something inarticulate, and attempted to pass. But a wilful mood had seized the young idler, and he caught at her arm. Frightened, she slipped by; and half mischievously he turned and ran after her through the tall pines.

Yonder, toward the sea, at the end of the path, came John slowly, with his head down. He had turned wearily homeward from the schoolhouse; then, thinking to shield his mother from the blow, started to meet his sister as she came from work and break the news of his dismissal to her. "I'll go away," he said slowly; "I'll go away and find work, and send for them. I cannot live here longer." And then the fierce, buried anger surged up into his throat. He waved his arms and hurried wildly up the path.

The great brown sea lay silent. The air scarce breathed. The dying day bathed the twisted oaks and mighty pines in black and gold. There came from the wind no warning, not a whisper from the cloudless sky. There was only a black man hurrying on with an ache in his heart, seeing neither sun nor sea, but starting as from a dream at the frightened cry that woke the pines, to see his dark sister struggling in the arms of a tall and fair-haired man.

He said not a word, but, seizing a fallen limb, struck him with all the pent-up hatred of his great black arm; and the body lay white and still beneath the pines, all bathed in sunshine and in blood. John looked at it dreamily, then walked back to the house briskly, and said in a soft voice, "Mammy, I'm going away,—I'm going to be free."

She gazed at him dimly and faltered, "No'th, honey, is yo' gwine No'th agin?"

He looked out where the North Star glistened pale above the waters, and said, "Yes, mammy, I'm going—North."

Then, without another word, he went out into the narrow lane, up by the straight pines, to the same winding path, and seated himself on the great black stump, looking at the blood where the body had lain. Yonder in the gray past he had played with that dead boy, romping together under the solemn trees. The night deepened; he thought of the boys at Johnstown. He wondered how Brown had turned out, and Carey? And Jones,—Jones? Why, *he* was Jones, and he wondered what they would all say when they knew, when they knew, in that great long dining-room with its hundreds of merry eyes. Then as the sheen of the starlight stole over him, he thought of the gilded ceiling of that vast concert hall, and heard stealing toward him the faint sweet music of the swan. Hark! was it music, or the hurry and shouting of men? Yes, surely! Clear and high the faint sweet melody rose and fluttered like a living thing, so that the very earth trembled as with the tramp of horses and murmur of angry men.

He leaned back and smiled toward the sea, whence rose the strange melody, away from the dark shadows where lay the noise of horses galloping, galloping on. With an effort he roused himself, bent forward, and looked steadily down the pathway, softly humming the "Song of the Bride,"—

Freudig geführt, ziehet dahin.

Amid the trees in the dim morning twilight he watched their shadows dancing and heard their horses thundering toward him, until at last they came sweeping like a storm, and he saw in front that haggard white-haired man, whose eyes flashed red with fury. Oh, how he pitied him,—pitied him,—and wondered if he had the coiling twisted rope. Then, as the storm burst round him, he rose slowly to his feet and turned his closed eyes toward the Sea.

And the world whistled in his ears.

1.3 Socialized education

Jane Addams

Source: Jane Addams, *Twenty Years at Hull-House*. Urbana:
University of Illinois Press, 1990, pp. 244–258

In a paper written years ago I deplored at some length the fact that educational matters are more democratic in their political than in their social aspect, and I quote the following extract from it as throwing some light upon the earlier educational undertakings at Hull-House:—

> Teaching in a Settlement requires distinct methods, for it is true of people who have been allowed to remain undeveloped and whose facilities are inert and sterile, that they cannot take their learning heavily. It has to be diffused in a social atmosphere, information must be held in solution, in a medium of fellowship and good will.
>
> Intellectual life requires for its expansion and manifestation the influences and assimilation of the interests and affections of others. Mazzini, that greatest of all democrats, who broke his heart over the condition of the South European peasantry, said: "Education is not merely a necessity of true life by which the individual renews his vital force in the vital force of humanity; it is a Holy Communion with generations dead and living, by which he fecundates all his faculties. When he is withheld from this Communion for generations, as the Italian peasant has been, we say, 'He is like a beast of the field; he must be controlled by force.'" Even to this it is sometimes added that it is absurd to educate him, immoral to disturb his content. We stupidly use the effect as an argument for a continuance of the cause. It is needless to say that a Settlement is a protest against a restricted view of education.

In line with this declaration, Hull-House in the very beginning opened what we called College Extension Classes with a faculty finally numbering thirty-five college men and women, many of whom held their pupils for consecutive years. As these classes antedated in Chicago the University Extension and Normal Extension classes and supplied a demand for stimulating instruction, the attendance strained to their utmost capacity the spacious rooms in the old house. The relation of students and faculty to each other and to the residents was that of guest and hostess, and at the close of each term the residents gave a reception to students and faculty which was one of the chief social events of the season. Upon this comfortable social basis some very good work was done.

In connection with these classes a Hull-House summer school was instituted at Rockford College, which was most generously placed at our disposal by the trustees. For ten years one hundred women gathered there for six weeks, in addition there were always men on the faculty, and a small group of young men among the students who were lodged in the gymnasium building. The outdoor classes in bird study and botany, the serious reading of literary masterpieces, the boat excursions on the Rock River, the cooperative spirit of doing the housework together, the satirical commencements in parti-colored caps and gowns, lent themselves toward a reproduction of the comradeship which college life fosters.

As each member of the faculty, as well as the students, paid three dollars a week, and as we had little outlay beyond the actual cost of food, we easily defrayed our expenses. The undertaking was so simple and gratifying in results that it might well be reproduced in many college buildings which are set in the midst of beautiful surroundings, unused during the two months of the year when hundreds of people, able to pay only a moderate price for lodgings in the country, can find nothing comfortable and no mental food more satisfying than piazza gossip.

Every Thursday evening during the first years, a public lecture came to be an expected event in the neighborhood, and Hull-House became one of the early University Extension centers, first in connection with an independent society and later with the University of Chicago. One of the Hull-House trustees was so impressed with the value of this orderly and continuous presentation of economic subjects that he endowed three courses in a downtown center, in which the lectures were free to anyone who chose to come. He was much pleased that these lectures were largely attended by workingmen who ordinarily prefer that an economic subject shall be presented by a partisan, and who are supremely indifferent to examinations and credits. They also dislike the balancing of pro and con which scholarly instruction implies, and prefer to be "inebriated on raw truth" rather than to sip a carefully prepared draught of knowledge.

Nevertheless Bowen Hall, which seats seven hundred and fifty people, is often none too large to hold the audiences of men who come to Hull-House every Sunday evening during the winter to attend the illustrated lectures provided by the faculty of the University of Chicago and others who kindly give their services. These courses differ enormously in their popularity: one on European capitals and their social significance was followed with the most vivid attention and sense of participation indicated by groans and hisses when the audience was reminded of an unforgettable feud between Austria and her Slavic subjects, or when they wildly applauded a Polish hero endeared through his tragic failure.

In spite of the success of these Sunday evening courses, it has never been an easy undertaking to find acceptable lectures. A course of lectures on astronomy illustrated by stereopticon slides will attract a large audience the first week, who hope to hear of the wonders of the heavens and the relation of our earth thereto, but instead are treated to spectrum analyses of star dust, or the latest theory concerning the milky way. The habit of research and the desire to say the latest word upon any subject often overcomes the sympathetic understanding of his audience which the lecturer might otherwise develop, and he insensibly drops into the dull terminology of the classroom. There are, of course, notable exceptions; we had twelve gloriously popular talks on organic evolution, but the lecturer was not yet a professor—merely a university instructor—and his mind was still eager over the marvel of it all. Fortunately there is an increasing number of lecturers whose matter is so real, so definite, and so valuable, that in an attempt to give it an exact equivalence in words, they utilize the most direct forms of expression.

It sometimes seems as if the men of substantial scholarship were content to leave to the charlatan the teaching of those things which deeply concern the welfare of mankind, and that the mass of men get their intellectual food from the outcasts of scholarship, who provide millions of books, pictures, and shows, not to instruct and guide, but for the sake of their own financial profit. A Settlement soon discovers that simple people are interested in large and vital subjects, and the Hull-House residents themselves at one time, with only partial success, undertook to give a series of lectures on the history of the world, beginning with the nebular hypothesis and reaching Chicago itself in the twenty-fifth lecture! Absurd as the hasty review appears, there is no doubt that the beginner in knowledge is always eager for the general statement, as those wise old teachers of the people well knew, when they put the history of creation on the stage and the monks themselves became the actors. I recall that in planning my first European journey I had soberly hoped in two years to trace the entire pattern of human excellence as we passed from one country to another, in the shrines popular affection had consecrated to the saints, in the frequented statues erected to heroes, and in the "worn blasonry of funeral brasses"—an illustration that when we are young we all long for those mountaintops upon which we may soberly stand and dream of our own ephemeral and uncertain attempts at righteousness. I have had many other illustrations of this; a statement was recently made to me by a member of the Hull-House Boys' club, who had been unjustly arrested as an accomplice to a young thief and held in the police station for three days, that during his detention he "had remembered the way Jean Valjean behaved when he was everlastingly pursued by that policeman who was only trying to do right"; "I kept seeing the pictures in that illustrated lecture you gave about him, and I thought it would be queer if I couldn't behave well for three days when he had kept it up for years."

The power of dramatic action may unfortunately be illustrated in other ways. During the weeks when all the daily papers were full of the details of a notorious murder trial in New York and all the hideous events which preceded the crime, one evening I saw in the street a knot of working girls leaning over a newspaper, admiring the clothes, the beauty, and "sorrowful expression" of the unhappy heroine. In the midst of the trial a woman whom I had known for years came to talk to me about her daughter, shamefacedly confessing that the girl was trying to dress and look like the notorious girl in New York, and that she had even said to her mother in a moment of defiance, "Some day I shall be taken into court and then I shall dress just as Evelyn did and face my accusers as she did in innocence and beauty."

If one makes calls on a Sunday afternoon in the homes of the immigrant colonies near Hull-House, one finds the family absorbed in the Sunday edition of a sensational daily newspaper, even those who cannot read, quite easily following the comic adventures portrayed in the colored pictures of the supplement or tracing the clew of a murderer carefully depicted by a black line drawn through a plan of the houses and streets.

Sometimes lessons in the great loyalties and group affections come through life itself and yet in such a manner that one cannot but deplore it. During the teamsters' strike in Chicago several years ago when class bitterness rose to a dramatic climax, I remember going to visit a neighborhood boy who had been severely injured when he had taken the place of a union driver upon a coal wagon. As I approached the house in which he lived, a large group of boys and girls, some of them very little children, surrounded me to convey the exciting information that "Jack T. was a 'scab'," and that I couldn't go in there. I explained to the excited children that his mother, who was a friend of mine, was in trouble, quite irrespective of the way her boy had been hurt. The crowd around me outside of the house of the "scab" constantly grew larger and I, finally abandoning my attempt at explanation, walked in only to have the mother say: "Please don't come here. You will only get hurt, too." Of course I did not get hurt, but the episode left upon my mind one of the most painful impressions I have ever received in connection with the children of the neighborhood. In addition to all else are the lessons of loyalty and comradeship to come to them as the mere reversals of class antagonism? And yet it was but a trifling incident out of the general spirit of bitterness and strife which filled the city.

Therefore the residents of Hull-House place increasing emphasis upon the great inspirations and solaces of literature and are unwilling that it should ever languish as a subject for class instruction or for reading parties. The Shakespeare club has lived a continuous existence at Hull-House for sixteen years during which time its members have heard the leading interpreters of Shakespeare, both among scholars and players. I recall that one of its earliest members said that her mind was peopled with Shakespeare characters during her long hours of sewing in a shop, that she couldn't remember what she thought about before she joined the club, and concluded that she hadn't thought about anything at all. To feed the mind of the worker, to lift it above the monotony of his task, and to connect it with the larger world, outside of his immediate surroundings, has always been the object of art, perhaps never more nobly fulfilled than by the great English bard. Miss Starr has held classes in Dante and Browning for many years, and the great lines are conned with never failing enthusiasm. I recall Miss Lathrop's Plato club and an audience who listened to a series of lectures by Dr. John Dewey on "Social Psychology" as genuine intellectual groups consisting largely of people from the immediate neighborhood, who were willing to make "that effort from which we all shrink, the effort of thought." But while we prize these classes as we do the help we are able to give to the exceptional young man or woman who reaches the college and university and leaves the neighborhood of his childhood behind him, the residents of Hull-House feel increasingly that the educational efforts of a Settlement should not be directed primarily to reproduce the college type of culture, but to work out a method and an ideal adapted to the immediate situation. They feel that they should promote a culture which will not set its possessor aside in a class with others like himself, but which will, on the contrary, connect him with all sorts of people by his ability to understand them as well as by his power to supplement their present surroundings with the historic background. Among the hundreds of immigrants who have for years attended classes at Hull-House designed primarily to teach the English language, dozens of them have struggled to express in the newly acquired tongue some of these hopes and longings which had so much to do with their emigration.

A series of plays was thus written by a young Bohemian; essays by a Russian youth, outpouring sorrows rivaling Werther himself and yet containing the precious stuff of youth's perennial revolt against accepted wrong; stories of Russian oppression and petty injustices throughout which the desire for free America became a crystallized hope; an attempt to portray the Jewish day of Atonement, in such wise that even individualistic Americans may catch a glimpse of that deeper national life which has survived all transplanting and expresses itself in forms so ancient that they appear grotesque to the ignorant spectator. I remember a pathetic effort on the part of a young Russian Jewess to describe the vivid inner life of an old Talmud scholar, probably her uncle or father, as of one persistently occupied with the grave and important things of the spirit, although when brought into sharp contact with busy and overworked people, he inevitably appeared self-absorbed and slothful. Certainly no one who had read her paper could again see such an old man in his praying shawl bent over his crabbed book, without a sense of understanding.

On the other hand, one of the most pitiful periods in the drama of the much-praised young American who attempts to rise in life, is the time when his educational requirements seem to have locked him up and made him rigid. He fancies himself shut off from his uneducated family and misunderstood by his friends. He is bowed down by his mental accumulations and often gets no farther than to carry them through life as a great burden, and not once does he obtain a glimpse of the delights of knowledge.

The teacher in a Settlement is constantly put upon his mettle to discover methods of instruction which shall make knowledge quickly available to his pupils, and I should like here to pay my tribute of admiration to the dean of our educational department, Miss Landsberg, and to the many men and women who every winter come regularly to Hull-House, putting untiring energy into the endless task of teaching the newly arrived immigrant the first use of a language of which he has such desperate need. Even a meager knowledge of English may mean an opportunity to work in a factory versus nonemployment, or it may mean a question of life or death when a sharp command must be understood in order to avoid the danger of a descending crane.

In response to a demand for an education which should be immediately available, classes have been established and grown apace in cooking, dressmaking, and millinery. A girl who attends them will often say that she "expects to marry a workingman next spring," and because she has worked in a factory so long she knows "little about a house." Sometimes classes are composed of young matrons of like factory experiences. I recall one of them whose husband had become so desperate after two years of her unskilled cooking that he had threatened to desert her and go where he could get "decent food," as she confided to me in a tearful interview, when she followed my advice to take the Hull-House courses in cooking, and at the end of six months reported a united and happy home.

Two distinct trends are found in response to these classes; the first is for domestic training, and the other is for trade teaching which shall enable the poor little milliner and dressmaker apprentices to shorten the years of errand running which is supposed to teach them their trade.

The beginning of trade instruction has been already evolved in connection with the Hull-House Boys' club. The ample Boys' club building presented to Hull-House three years ago by one of our trustees has afforded well-equipped shops for work in wood, iron, and brass; for smithing in copper and tin; for commercial photography, for printing, for telegraphy, and electrical construction. These shops have been filled with boys who are eager for that which seems to give them a clew to the industrial life all about them. These classes meet twice a week and are taught by intelligent workingmen who apparently give the boys what they want better than do the strictly professional teachers. While these classes in no sense provide a trade training, they often enable a boy to discover his aptitude and help him in the selection of what he "wants to be" by reducing the trades to embryonic forms. The factories are so complicated that the boy brought in contact with them, unless he has some preliminary preparation, is apt to become confused. In pedagogical terms, he loses his "power of orderly reaction" and is often so discouraged or so overstimulated in his very first years of factory life that his future usefulness is seriously impaired.

One of Chicago's most significant experiments in the direction of correlating the schools with actual industry was for several years carried on in a public school building situated near Hull-House, in which the bricklayers' apprentices were taught eight hours a day in special classes during the non-bricklaying season. This early public school venture anticipated the very successful arrangement later carried on in Cincinnati, in Pittsburgh and in Chicago itself, whereby a group of boys at work in a factory alternate month by month with another group who are in school and are thus intelligently conducted into the complicated processes of modern industry. But for a certain type of boy who has been demoralized by the constant change and excitement of street life, even these apprenticeship classes are too strenuous, and he has to be lured into the path of knowledge by all sorts of appeals.

It sometimes happens that boys are held in the Hull-House classes for weeks by their desire for the excitement of placing burglar alarms under the door mats. But to enable the possessor of even a little knowledge to thus play with it, is to decoy his feet at least through the first steps of the long, hard road of learning, although even in this, the teacher must proceed warily. A typical street boy who was utterly absorbed in a wood-carving class, abruptly left never to return when he was told to use some simple calculations in the laying out of the points. He evidently scented the approach of his old enemy, arithmetic, and fled the field. On the other hand, we have come across many cases in which boys have vainly tried to secure such opportunities for themselves. During the trial of a boy of ten recently arrested for truancy, it developed that he had spent many hours watching the electrical construction in a downtown building, and many others in the public library "reading about electricity." Another boy who was taken from school early, when his father lost both of his legs in a factory accident, tried in vain to find a place for himself "with machinery." He was declared too small for any such position, and for four years worked as an errand boy, during which time he steadily turned in his unopened pay envelope for the use of the household. At the end of the fourth year the boy disappeared, to the great distress of his invalid father and his poor mother whose day washings became the sole support of the family. He had beaten his way to Kansas City, hoping "they wouldn't be so particular there about a fellow's size." He came back at the end of six weeks because he felt sorry for his mother who, aroused at last to a realization of his unbending purpose, applied for help to the Juvenile Protective Association. They found a position for the boy in a machine shop and an opportunity for evening classes.

Out of the fifteen hundred members of the Hull-House Boy's club, hundreds seem to respond only to the opportunities for recreation, and many of the older ones apparently care only for the bowling and the billiards. And yet tournaments and match games under supervision and regulated hours are a great advance over the sensual and exhausting pleasures to be found so easily outside the club. These organized sports readily connect themselves with the Hull-House gymnasium and with all those enthusiasms which are so mysteriously aroused by athletics.

Our gymnasium has been filled with large and enthusiastic classes for eighteen years in spite of the popularity of dancing and other possible substitutes, while the Saturday evening athletic contests have become a feature of the neighborhood. The Settlement strives for that type of gymnastics which is at least partly a matter of character, for that training which presupposes abstinence and the curbing of impulse, as well as for those athletic contests in which the mind of the contestant must be vigilant to keep the body closely to the rules of the game. As one sees in rhythmic motion the slim bodies of a class of lads, "that scrupulous and uncontaminate purity of form which recommended itself even to the Greeks as befitting messengers from the gods, if such messengers should come," one offers up in awkward prosaic form the very essence of that old prayer, "Grant them with feet so light to pass through life." But while the glory stored up for Olympian winners was at the most a handful of parsley, an ode, fame for family and city, on the other hand, when the men and boys from the Hull-House gymnasium bring back their cups and medals, one's mind is filled with something like foreboding in the reflection that too much success may lead the winners into the professionalism which is so associated with betting and so close to pugilism. Candor, however, compels me to state that a long acquaintance with the acrobatic folk who have to do with the circus, a large number of whom practice in our gymnasium every winter, has raised our estimate of that profession.

Young people who work long hours at sedentary occupations, factories and offices, need perhaps more than anything else the freedom and ease to be acquired from a symmetrical muscular development and are quick to respond to that fellowship which athletics apparently affords more easily than anything else. The Greek immigrants form large classes and are eager to reproduce the remnants of old methods of wrestling, and other bits of classic lore which they still possess, and when one of the Greeks won a medal in a wrestling match which represented the championship of the entire city, it was quite impossible that he should present it to the Hull-House trophy chest without a classic phrase which he recited most gravely and charmingly.

It was in connection with a large association of Greek lads that Hull-House finally lifted its long restriction against military drill. If athletic contests are the residuum of warfare first waged against the conqueror without and then against the tyrants within the State, the modern Greek youth is still in the first stage so far as his inherited attitude against the Turk is concerned. Each lad believes that at any moment he may be called home to fight this long-time enemy of Greece. With such a genuine motive at hand, it seemed mere affectation to deny the use of our boys' club building and gymnasium for organized drill, although happily it forms but a small part of the activities of the Greek Educational Association.

Having thus confessed to military drill countenanced if not encouraged at Hull-House, it is perhaps only fair to relate an early experience of mine with the "Columbian Guards," an organization of the World's Fair summer. Although the Hull-House squad was organized as the others were with the motto of a clean city, it was very anxious for military drill. This request not only shocked my nonresistant principles, but seemed to afford an opportunity to find a substitute for the military tactics which were used in the boys' brigades everywhere, even in those connected with churches. As the cleaning of the filthy streets and alleys was the ostensible purpose of the Columbian guards, I suggested to the boys that we work out a drill with sewer spades, which with their long narrow blades and shortened handles were not so unlike bayoneted guns in size, weight, and general appearance, but that much of the usual military drill could be readapted. While I myself was present at the gymnasium to explain that it was nobler to drill in imitation of removing disease-breeding filth than to drill in simulation of warfare; while I distractedly readapted tales of chivalry to this modern rescuing of the endangered and distressed, the new drill went forward in some sort of fashion, but so surely as I withdrew, the drillmaster would complain that our troops would first grow self-conscious, then demoralized, and finally flatly refuse to go on. Throughout the years since the failure of this Quixotic experiment, I occasionally find one of these sewer spades in a Hull-House storeroom, too truncated to be used for its original purpose and too prosaic to serve the purpose for which it was bought. I can only look at it in the forlorn hope that it may foreshadow that piping time when the weapons of warfare shall be turned into the implements of civic salvation.

Before closing this chapter on Socialized Education, it is only fair to speak of the education accruing to the Hull-House residents themselves during their years of living in what at least purports to be a center for social and educational activity.

While a certain number of the residents are primarily interested in charitable administration and the amelioration which can be suggested only by those who know actual conditions, there are other residents identified with the House from its earlier years to whom the groups of immigrants make the historic appeal, and who use, not only their linguistic ability, but all the resource they can command of travel and reading to qualify themselves for intelligent living in the immigrant quarter of the city. I remember one resident lately returned from a visit in Sicily, who was able to interpret to a bewildered judge the ancient privilege of a jilted lover to scratch the cheek of his faithless sweetheart with the edge of a coin. Although the custom in America had degenerated into a knife slashing after the manner of foreign customs here, and although the Sicilian deserved punishment, the incident was yet lifted out of the slough of mere brutal assault, and the interpretation won the gratitude of many Sicilians.

There is no doubt that residents in a Settlement too often move toward their ends "with hurried and ignoble gait," putting forth thorns in their eagerness to bear grapes. It is always easy for those in pursuit of ends which they consider of overwhelming importance to become themselves thin and impoverished in spirit and temper, to gradually develop a dark mistaken eagerness alternating with fatigue, which supersedes "the great and gracious ways" so much more congruous with worthy aims.

Partly because of this universal tendency, partly because a Settlement shares the perplexities of its times and is never too dogmatic concerning the final truth, the residents would be glad to make the daily life at the Settlement "conform to every shape and mode of excellence."

It may not be true

> That the good are always the merry
> Save by an evil chance,

but a Settlement would make clear that one need not be heartless and flippant in order to be merry, nor solemn in order to be wise. Therefore quite as Hull-House tries to redeem billiard tables from the association of gambling, and dancing from the temptations of the public dance halls, so it would associate with a life of upright purpose those more engaging qualities which in the experience of the neighborhood are too often connected with dubious aims.

Throughout the history of Hull-House many inquiries have been made concerning the religion of the residents, and the reply that they are as diversified in belief and in the ardor of the inner life as any like number of people in a college or similar group, apparently does not carry conviction. I recall that after a house for men residents had been opened on Polk Street and the residential force at Hull-House numbered twenty, we made an effort to come together on Sunday evenings in a household service, hoping thus to express our moral unity in spite of the fact that we represented many creeds. But although all of us reverently knelt when the High Church resident read the evening service and bowed our heads when the evangelical resident led in prayer after his chapter, and although we sat respectfully through the twilight when a resident read her favorite passages from Plato and another from Abt Vogler, we concluded at the end of the winter that this was not religious fellowship and that we did not care for another reading club. So it was reluctantly given up, and we found that it was quite as necessary to come together on the basis of the deed and our common aim inside the household as it was in the neighborhood itself. I once had a conversation on the subject with the warden of Oxford House, who kindly invited me to the evening service held for the residents in a little chapel on the top floor of the Settlement. All the residents were High Churchmen to whom the service was an important and reverent part of the day. Upon my reply to a query of the warden that the residents of Hull-House could not come together for religious worship because there were among us Jews, Roman Catholics, English Churchmen, Dissenters, and a few agnostics, and that we had found unsatisfactory the diluted form of worship which we could carry on together, he replied that it must be most difficult to work with a group so diversified, for he depended upon the evening service to clear away any difficulties which the day had involved and to bring the residents to a religious consciousness of their common aim. I replied that this diversity of creed was part of the situation in American Settlements, as it was our task to live in a neighborhood of many nationalities and faiths, and that it might be possible that among such diversified people it was better that the Settlement corps should also represent varying religious beliefs.

A wise man has told us that "men are once for all so made that they prefer a rational world to believe in and to live in," but that it is no easy matter to find a world rational as to its intellectual, aesthetic, moral, and practical aspects. Certainly it is no easy matter if the place selected is of the very sort where the four aspects are apparently furthest from perfection, but an undertaking resembling this is what the Settlement gradually becomes committed to, as its function is revealed through the reaction on its consciousness of its own experiences. Because of this fourfold under-taking, the Settlement has gathered into residence people of widely diversified tastes and interests, and in Hull-House, at least, the group has been surprisingly permanent. The majority of the present corps of forty residents support themselves by their business and professional occupations in the city, giving only their leisure time to Settlement undertakings. This in itself tends to continuity of residence and has certain advantages. Among the present staff, of whom the larger number have been in residence for more than twelve years, there are the secretary of the City club, two practicing physicians, several attorneys, newspapermen, businessmen, teachers, scientists, artists, musicians, lecturers in the School of Civics and Philanthropy, officers in The Juvenile Protective Association and in The League for the Protection of Immigrants, a visiting nurse, a sanitary inspector, and others.

We have also worked out during our years of residence a plan of living which may be called cooperative, for the families and individuals who rent the Hull-House apartments have the use of the central kitchen and dining room so far as they care for them; many of them work for hours every week in the studios and shops; the theater and drawing-rooms are available for such social organization as they care to form; the entire group of thirteen buildings is heated and lighted from a central plant. During the years, the common human experiences have gathered about the House; funeral services have been held there, marriages and christenings, and many memories hold us to each other as well as to our neighbors. Each resident, of course, carefully defrays his own expenses, and his relations to his fellow residents are not unlike those of a college professor to his colleagues. The depth and strength of his relation to the neighborhood must depend very largely upon himself and upon the genuine friendships he has been able to make. His relation to the city as a whole comes largely through his identification with those groups who are carrying forward the reforms which a Settlement neighborhood so sadly needs and with which residence has made him familiar.

Life in the Settlement discovers above all what has been called "the extraordinary pliability of human nature," and it seems impossible to set any bounds to the moral capabilities which might unfold under ideal civic and educational conditions. But in order to obtain these conditions, the Settlement recognizes the need of cooperation, both with the radical and the conservative, and from the very nature of the case the Settlement cannot limit its friends to any one political party or economic school.

The Settlement casts aside none of those things which cultivated men have come to consider reasonable and goodly, but it insists that those belong as well to that great body of people who, because of toilsome and underpaid labor, are unable to procure them for themselves. Added to this is a profound conviction that the common stock of intellectual enjoyment should not be difficult of access because of the economic position of him who would approach it, that those "best results of civilization" upon which depend the finer and freer aspects of living must be incorporated into our common life and have free mobility through all elements of society if we would have our democracy endure.

The educational activities of a Settlement, as well its philanthropic, civic, and social under-takings, are but differing manifestations of the attempt to socialize democracy, as is the very existence of the Settlement itself.

1.4 The need for a philosophy of education

John Dewey

Source: John Dewey, *The Later Works, 1925–1953, Volume 9: 1933–1934*, ed. Jo Ann Boydston. Carbondale: Southern Illinois University Press, 1989, pp. 194–204

"Progressive education" is a phrase at least of contrast with an education predominantly static in subject-matter, authoritarian in methods, and mainly passive and receptive from the side of the young. But the philosophy of education must go beyond any method of education that is formed by way of contrast, reaction, and protest, as an attempt to discover what education *is* and how it takes place. Only as identified with schooling does a definition of actual education seem simple, though such definition gives the only criterion for judging and directing the work of schools.

Some suppose that the philosophy of education should tell what education *should* be and set up ideals and norms for it. In a sense this proposition is true, but not in the sense usually implied. For the only way of deciding what education should be, and which does not take us too far away from actual conditions and from tangible processes, is discovery of what actually takes place when education really occurs. Any ideal that is a genuine help in carrying on activity must rest upon a prior knowledge of concrete actual occurrences. A metallurgist's ideal of the best possible steel must rest upon knowledge of actual ores and of natural processes. Otherwise his ideal is not a directive idea but a fantasy.

So too with the ideal of education as affecting the philosophy of education we have to know how human nature is constituted in the concrete just as the steel-worker has to know about his raw material, to know about the working of actual social forces and about the operations through which basic raw materials are modified into things of greater value. The need for a philosophy of education *is* thus fundamentally the need for finding out what education really is. We have to take those cases in which we find there is a real development of desirable powers, find out how this development took place, and then project what has taken place as a guide for directing our other efforts. The need for this discovery and this projection is the need for a philosophy of education.

What then is education when we find actual satisfactory specimens of it in existence? Firstly, it is a process of development—of growth, and the *process*, not merely the end result, is important. A truly healthy person is not something fixed and completed. He is one who through his processes and activities will continue to be healthy. He cannot say "I am healthy" and stop at that as if health were bound to continue automatically, otherwise he would soon find himself ill. Similarly, an educated person has the power to go on and get more education, to grow and to expand his development. Hence sometimes learned, erudite persons, as having parted with the capacity to grow, are not educated.

What is growth? What is development? Early philosophers, like Rousseau and his followers, made much use of the analogy of the development of a seed into the full-grown plant, deducing the conclusion that in human beings there are latent capacities which, left to themselves, will ultimately flower and bear fruit. So they framed the notion of a *natural* development, as far as possible left alone, as opposed to a directed growth, direction here being an interference resulting in distortion and corruption of natural powers.

This idea has two fallacies. In the first place seed-growth is limited as compared with human growth; its future is much more prescribed by its antecedent nature; its line of growth is comparatively fixed; it has not the capacities for growth in different directions toward different outcomes characteristic of the human young, which is also, if you please, a seed embodying germinal powers but may develop any of many forms.

This fact suggests the second fallacy. Even the seed of a plant does not grow simply of itself without atmospheric aids. Its development is controlled by external conditions and forces. Native inherent forces must interact with external if there is to be life and development. In brief, development, even with a plant, depends on the *kind of interaction* between itself and its environment. A stunted oak, or a stalk of maize with few ears of scattered grains, exhibits natural development as truly as the noblest tree or the prize-winning ear of maize. The difference in result is due not only to native stock but also to environment; the finest native stock would come to an untimely end, or give a miserable product, if its own energies could not interact with favourable atmospheric conditions.

There being two factors involved in any interaction (and hence in every kind of growth) the idea and ideal of education must take account of both. Native capacities of growth and inherent traits provide the raw material. What is lacking cannot interact with even the very best of conditions; there is then no leverage, nothing with which to cooperate. Traditional school methods and subject-matter fail in three ways to take this factor into account. In the first place, they ignore the *diversity* of capacities and needs of different human beings which constitute *individuality*. They virtually assume that, for purposes of education, all human beings are as much alike as peas in a pod, hence their provision of a uniform curriculum, the same lessons assigned for all, and the same conduct of the recitation.

In the second place, they fail to recognize that the *initiative* in growth comes from the needs and powers of the pupil. The *first* step in the interaction for growth comes from the reaching out of the tentacles of the individual, from an effort, at first blind, to procure the materials that his potentialities demand if they are to come into action and find satisfaction. With the body, hunger and power of taking and assimilating food are the first necessities. Without the inner demand and impetus the most nutritious food is offered in vain; repulsion and indigestion result. No proper system of education could tolerate the common assumption, that the mind of the individual is naturally averse to learning, and has to be either browbeaten or coaxed into action. Every mind, even of the youngest, is naturally seeking for those modes of active operation within the limits of its capacities. The problem is to discover what tendencies are especially seeking expression at a particular time and just what materials and methods will serve to evoke and direct a truly educative development.

The practical counterpart of this failure to see the source of initiative lies in the method of imposition by the teacher and of reception by the pupil. The idea of drill is only too suggestive of drilling a hole into a hard and resistant rock by means of repeated monotonous blows. Unwillingness to learn naturally follows failure to take into account tendencies urgent in the existing make-up of an individual. All sorts of external devices then are needed to achieve absorption and retention of imposed subject-matter and skills. This method of teaching may be compared to inscribing records upon a passive phonograph disc to secure their return when the proper button is pressed. Or again the pupil's mind is treated as an empty cistern passively waiting to be filled, while teacher and text-book form the reservoir from which pipelines lead.

The third failure is the result of the two already mentioned. Every teacher must observe that there *are* real differences among pupils. But, because these are not carried back to concrete differences of individuality in needs, in desires, in direction of native interest, they are too often generalized under two main heads. Some pupils are bright, others dull and stupid! Some are docile and obedient, others unruly and troublesome! Inability to fit into a cast-iron scheme of subject-matter or to meet the requirements of the set discipline is taken as a sign of either radical intrinsic incapacity or deliberate wilfulness. Conformity then becomes the criterion of judgment in spite of the value of initiative, originality and independence in life.

While the raw material and the starting-point of growth are found in native capacities, the environing conditions to be furnished by the educator are the indispensable means of their development. They are not, and do not of themselves decide, the end. A gardener, a worker of metals, must observe and pay attention to the properties of his material. If he permits these properties in their original form to dictate his treatment, he will not get *anywhere*. If they decide his end, he will fixate raw materials in their primitive state. Development will be arrested, not promoted. He must bring to his consideration of his material an idea, an ideal, of possibilities not realized, which must be in line with the constitution of his plant or ore; it must not do violence to them; it must be *their* possibilities. Yet it cannot be extracted from any study of their present form but from seeing them imaginatively, reflectively, and hence from another source.

Similarly with the educator, save that the demand on him for imaginative insight into possibilities is greater. The gardener and worker in metals may take as their measures results already achieved with plants and ores, although originality and invention will introduce some variation. But the true educator while using results already accomplished cannot make them his final and complete standard. Like the artist he has the problem of creating something that is not the exact duplicate of some previous creation.

In any case, development and growth involve change and modification in definite directions. A teacher, under the supposed sanction of the idea of cultivating individuality, may fixate a pupil more or less at his existing level, confusing respect for individual traits with a catering for their present estate. Respect for individuality is primarily the *intellectual* study of the individual to discover material. With this sympathetic understanding the *practical* work then begins of modification, of changing, of reconstruction continued without end. The change must at least be toward more effective techniques, greater self-reliance, a more thoughtful and inquiring disposition more capable of persistent effort in meeting obstacles.

Some would-be progressive schools and teachers in their reaction from the method of external imposition stop short with the recognition of the importance of giving free scope to native capacities and interests. They do not examine closely or long enough what these may actually be; they judge too much from superficial and transitory reactions to accidental circumstances. In the second place, they are inclined to take the evident individual traits as finalities instead of as possibilities for suitable direction into something of greater significance. Under the alleged sanction of not violating freedom and individuality the responsibility for providing development conditions is overlooked. The idea persists that evolution and development are simply matters of automatic unfolding from within.

This is a natural reaction from the manifest evils of external imposition. But there is a radically different alternative between thinking of the young as clay to be molded into traditional patterns and thinking of existing capacities and present interests and desires as laying down the whole law of development. Existing likes and powers are to be treated as possibilities necessary for any healthy development. But development involves a point of direction as well as a starting-point with constant movement in that direction, and the direction-point, as the temporary goal, is reached only as the starting-point of further reconstruction. The great problem of the educator is to see intellectually, and to feel deeply, the forces moving in the young as possibilities, as signs and promises, and to interpret them in the light of what they may become. Nor does the exacting task end there: it is bound up with the judging and devising of the conditions, the materials, the tools—physical, moral, and social—which will, once more by *interaction* with existing powers and preferences, bring about the desired transformation.

The old education emphasised the necessity for provision of definite subject-matter and activities, which *are* necessities for right education. The weakness was that its imagination did not go beyond provision of a rigid environment of subject-matter drawn from sources remote from any concrete experiences of the taught. Its conception of techniques was derived from the conventions of the past. The New Education needs more attention, not less, to subject-matter and to progress in technique for getting satisfactory results. More does not, however, mean more in quantity of the same old kind but an imaginative vision, which sees that no prescribed and ready-made scheme can determine the exact subject-matter for the educative growth of each individual, since each sets a new problem and calls for at least a somewhat different emphasis in either subject-matter or angle of presentation. Only blindly obtuse convention supposes that the actual contents of text-books will further the educational development of all children, or of any one child, if they be regarded as the prescription of a doctor to be taken just as they are. As Louis Stevenson remarked, "the world is full of a number of things," and no teacher can know too much or have too ingenious an imagination in selecting and adapting this and that aspect of some of the many things in the world to meet the requirements that make for growth in this and that individual.

In short, departure from the rigidity of the old curriculum is only the negative side. If we do not go on and go far in the positive direction of providing, through persistent intelligent study and experiment, a body of subject-matter much richer, more varied and flexible, and also more definite in terms of the experience of those being educated, we shall tend to leave an educational vacuum in which anything may happen. The old saying that "nature abhors a vacuum" embodies a definite truth. Complete isolation is impossible in nature. The young live in some environment constantly interacting with what the young bring to it, and the result is the shaping of their interests, minds and characters—either educatively or mis-educatively. If the professed educator abdicates his responsibility for judging and selecting the kind of environment conducive, in his best understanding, to growth, then the young are left at the mercy of all the unorganized and casual forces that inevitably play upon them throughout life. In the educative environment the knowledge, judgment, or experience of the teacher becomes a greater, not a smaller factor. He now operates not as a magistrate set on high and possessed of arbitrary authority but as a friendly co-partner and guide in a common enterprise.

There is a further truism about education as development, difficult to carry out in practice and easily violated. Development is a *continuous* process and continually signifies consecutiveness of action—the strong point of the traditional education at its best. The subject-matter of the classics and mathematics involved a consecutive and orderly development along definite lines. In the newer education it is comparatively easy to improvise, to try a little of this to-day and something else to-morrow, on the basis of some immediate stimulus but without sufficient regard to its objective or whether or not something more difficult is led up to naturally, raising new questions and calling for acquisition of more adequate technique and for new modes of skill. There is genuine need for taking account of spontaneous interest and activity but, without care and thought, it readily results in a detached multiplicity of isolated brief-lived activities or projects, not in continuity of growth. Indeed, the new educational processes require much more planning ahead by the teachers, for whom the old planning was all effected in advance by the fixed curriculum, etc.

But a sound philosophy of education also requires that the general term environment be specified as dominantly human with its values social. Through its influence each person becomes saturated with the customs, the beliefs, the purposes, skills, hopes and fears, of his own cultural group. The features of even his physical surroundings come to him through the eyes and ears of his community. His geographical, climatical, and atmospherical experiences are clothed with the memories and traditions, the characteristic associations, of his particular society. In the early stages, then, it is particularly important that subject-matter be presented in its human context and setting. Here the school often fails when, in proceeding from the concrete to the abstract, it forgets that to the child only that which has human value and function is concrete. In his nature study and geography, physical things are presented to him from the standpoint of the adult specialist as if independent and complete in themselves. But to the child these things have a meaning only as they enter into human life. Even those distinctively human products, reading and writing, whose purpose is the furthering of human communication and association, are treated as if they were subjects of and in themselves, not used as is friendly everyday speech, and so for the child they become abstract, a mystery belonging to the school but not to daily life.

The same separation of school studies from social or human setting and function deadens the traditional recitation which, instead of being a scene of friendly intercourse as are the conversations of home and of ordinary life, clarified and organized by definite purpose, becomes an artificial exercise in repeating uniformly the identical material of some one text-book and a mere test of the faithfulness of the preparation. It thus becomes a first cause of the isolation of school from out-of-school life and experience.

As the material of genuine development is that of human contacts and associations, so the end, the value that is the criterion and directing guide of educational work, is social. The acquisition however perfectly of skills is not an end in itself. They are things to be put to use as a contribution to a common and shared life. They are intended, indeed, to make an individual more capable of self-support and of self-respecting independence. But unless this end is placed in the context of services rendered to others, services which they need to the fulfillment also of their lives, skills gained will be put to an egoistic and selfish use as means of a trained shrewdness for personal advantage at the cost of others' claims and opportunities for the good life. Too often, indeed, the schools, through reliance upon the spur of competition and the bestowal of special honours and prizes as for those who excel in a competitive race or even battle, only build up and strengthen the disposition that in after-school life employs special talents and superior skill to outwit others and "get on" personally without respect for their welfare.

And as with skills acquired in school so also with knowledge gained in school. The educational end and the ultimate test of the value of what is learned is its use and application in carrying on and improving the common life of all. The background of the traditional educational system is a class society, and opportunity for instruction in certain subjects, especially literary ones, and in mathematics beyond the rudiments of simple arithmetical subjects was reserved for the well-born and the well-to-do, and thus knowledge of these subjects became a badge of cultural superiority and social status, which marked off those who had it from the vulgar herd and for many persons was a means of self-display. Useful knowledge, on the other hand, was necessary only for those compelled by their class status to work for a living. A class stigma attached to it, and the uselessness of knowledge, save for purely personal culture, was proof of its higher quality.

Even after education in many countries was made universal for all, these standards of value persisted. There is no greater egotism than that of learning when treated simply as a mark of personal distinction to be cherished for its own sake. Yet to eliminate this quality of exclusiveness all conditions of the school environment must tend in actual practice to develop in individuals the realization that knowledge is a trust for the furthering of the well-being of all.

Perhaps the greatest need of and for a philosophy of education to-day is the urgent need that exists for making clear in idea and effective in practice the social character of its end and that the criterion of value of school practices is social.

The aim of education is development of individuals to the utmost of their potentialities. But this statement as such leaves unanswered the question of the measure of the development to be desired and worked for. A society of free individuals in which all, in doing each his own work, contribute to the liberation and enrichment of the lives of others is the only environment for the normal growth to full stature. An environment in which some are limited will always in reaction create conditions that prevent the full development even of those who fancy they enjoy complete freedom for unhindered growth.

There are two outstanding reasons why in existing world conditions a philosophy of education must make the social aim of education the central article in its creed. The world is being rapidly industrialized. Individual groups, tribes and races, once living completely untouched by the economic regime of modern capitalistic industry, now find almost every phase of their lives affected by its expansion. The principle of a report of the Geneva Commission based on a study of conditions of life of mine-Natives in South Africa holds good of peoples all over the world, "The investment of Western capital in African industries has made the Native dependent upon the demand of the world markets for the products of his labour and the resources of his continent." In a world that has so largely engaged in a mad, often brutal, race for material gain by means of ruthless competition the school must make ceaseless and intelligently organized effort to develop above all else the will for cooperation and the spirit which sees in every other individual an equal right to share in the cultural and material fruits of collective human invention, industry, skill and knowledge. The supremacy of this aim in mind and character is necessary, not merely as an offset to the spirit of inhumanity bred by economic competition and exploitation but to prepare the coming generation for an inevitable new and more just and humane society which, unless hearts and minds are prepared by education, is likely to come attended with all the evils of social changes by violence.

The other especially urgent need is connected with the present unprecedented wave of nationalistic sentiment, of racial and national prejudice, of readiness to resort to force of arms. For this spirit to have arisen on such a scale the schools must have somehow failed grievously. Their best excuse is maybe that schools and educators were caught unawares. But that excuse is no longer available. We now know the enemy; it is out in the open. Unless the schools of the world can unite in effort to rebuild the spirit of common understanding, of mutual sympathy and goodwill among all peoples and races, to exorcise the demon of prejudice, isolation and hatred, they themselves are likely to be submerged by the general return to barbarism, the sure outcome of present tendencies if unchecked by the forces which education alone can evoke and fortify.

It is to this great work that any ideal worthy of the name of education summons the educational forces of all countries.

Part 1
Commentaries

5 Is deliberative democracy enough in teacher education?

Michael W. Apple
University of Wisconsin, Madison

SITUATING EDUCATION

The chapters in this section are wide ranging, thoughtful, and well-written. Each is well worth its own lengthy discussion and the issues that they collectively and individually raise deserve careful consideration. In a relatively brief commentary such as this, I have chosen to focus on one particular set of assumptions and one particular claim that underpin many of the arguments the authors make. I applaud each of the authors for their evident commitment to deliberative processes; but as you will see I have some reservations about its limits and efficacy. But before I make my own arguments about this, I need to situate these arguments in their larger context.

By its very nature the entire schooling process—how it is paid for, what goals it seeks to attain and how these goals will be measured, who has power over it, what textbooks are approved, who has the right to ask and answer these questions, and so on—is political. The educational system will constantly be in the middle of crucial struggles over the meaning of democracy, over definitions of legitimate authority and culture, and over who should benefit the most from government policies and practices. That this is not of simply academic interest is made more than a little visible in the current attempts in many nations to radically transform education policy and practice.

These proposals involve conscious attempts to institute neo-liberal "reforms" in education (such as plans for marketization through voucher and privatization plans), neo-conservative reforms (such as national or state-wide curriculum and national or state-wide testing, a "return" to a "common culture," and the English only movement in the United States), and policies based on "new managerialism" with its focus on strict accountability and constant assessment. When the efforts of authoritarian populist religious conservatives to install *their* particular vision of religiosity into state institutions are also added to this mix, this places education at the very core of an entire range of political and cultural conflicts (Apple, 2006).

In teacher education such pressures are increasingly visible in the proposals, among others, to privatize and/or deregulate the education of teachers, in the increasingly common reductive entry and exit tests for prospective teachers, in differential funding to those teacher education institutions whose students score higher, and in the steady growth of home schooling where parents have decided to school their children outside formal educational institutions and to reject the very notion of professionally educated teachers (Apple, 2006; Apple & Buras, 2006).

In many ways there has been a loss of collective memory of the rich history of reflections on the complex role of education in general, and of teacher education in particular, in society. One of the benefits of chapters such as those included in this section—and of the material by Addams, Dewey, Du Bois, and Emerson that accompanies them—is to help restore the memory of these debates. Indeed, Hansen, Roberson, and Sockett each contribute in very interesting ways to the restorative project by making public the long history of debates and thoughtful positions on what teacher education—and education in general—should do, how this should be decided, and what principles might guide our deliberations.

THE POLITICS OF DELIBERATION

Much of what Hansen, Roberson, and Sockett argue for—and they do so in clear and articulate ways—is grounded in what we would now recognize as a rather Habermasian or Rawlsian position of communicative competence and deliberation in what might be called "ideal speech situations" (see e.g. Habermas, 1984; Crosley & Roberts, 2004; Rawls, 1971), one that has gone beyond Aristotle, Dewey, and others in sophistication. These kinds of positions have much to commend them. And they are important first steps, especially in a time when the arrogance of rightist policies in combination with such things as No Child Left Behind and similar "reforms" have not only denigrated, but have left little time for, deliberation. Many educators and teacher educators face a situation of what might best be called "management by stress."

However, even with their importance, models based on deliberative democracy—of extending the "public sphere" of debate—are not only too general at times, but unless they are employed with a serious critical economic, political, and cultural understanding, they may ignore the fact that there is a danger of romanticizing the public sphere. As Nancy Fraser (1997) has reminded us, both the public sphere and its accompanying vision of free and open discussions and debate have been grounded in unacknowledged gender relations. And as Charles Mills (1997) has also documented, the theories of liberal democracy that stand behind such visions are based on an unacknowledged racial contract, something Du Bois also understood. Thus, by speaking so generally about public deliberations as their grounding, we may lose the power of speaking equally elegantly and honestly about the specificities of actually existing and very real relations of dominance and subordination—and of the struggles against them—that serve to organize the very structures of the societies in which we live.

This overly general perspective, one that risks romanticizing the public sphere, points to another problem I wish to note. Even with their evident strengths, strengths witnessed in each of the chapters, when we talk about relations of dominance such perspectives have a history of talking about social justice all too vaguely. Hence, they may paradoxically cause us to prepare our teachers less than adequately to deal with the utter complexities associated with concerns surrounding the structures of inequalities in schools and the larger society so well documented for example in the work of Kozol (2005) and Davis (2006). Thus, in our attempts to create critical dispositions in general, we may also risk deskilling current and future teachers. Teachers may understand critical inquiry *as a process*, but they may not have the knowledge and critical social understanding that might enable them to reposition themselves to see the world through the eyes of those with least in this society. In my mind, it is this act of *repositioning* that is crucial for a more thorough understanding of social justice and of the role of education and teacher education in the struggles over it (Apple, 1995). A disposition of critical dialogue in general does not necessarily lead to such repositioning.

Yet there is a vital tradition of thinking seriously about what we mean when we want our teachers to be committed both to "thick democracy" and to social justice. This task is appropriately theoretical and political at one and the same time. Once again Fraser is helpful.

Fraser (1997) reminds us that we can (analytically) distinguish two kinds of political movements, a politics of redistribution and a politics of recognition. Neither is a substitute for the other. Both are crucial at this historic moment. Our task is to work on both simultaneously so that gains along one set of dynamics (class and the economy, for example) do not contradict and are not contradicted by the other set of dynamics (struggling for curricula and teaching that respond to oppressed groups' cultures, identities, and histories, for example, and expanding our concerns about justice, say, to include disability and the politics of the body). Of course, in the real world it is almost impossible to differentiate totally between redistributive movements and those involving recognition. For instance, African Americans and Latino/as suffer economic discrimination and levels of exploitation at a tragic rate and this has predictable effects on educational finance, the realities of schools, and the ways in which education is experienced (see Dance, 2002). But this can more easily occur because of the history of racism and of being constructed as a category of "despised others." Thus, racism and a retrogressive politics of whiteness cohere with exploitative economic relations.

The implications of Fraser's points are important for my discussion here. We need to attach our commitment to deliberation to the *specific* relations of dominance that are so powerful in this society and that are ever present in schools. We need to do so in a way that documents the range of these relations so that our current and future teachers do not engage in actions that have contradictory effects (i.e. that efforts on recognition do not interrupt efforts on redistribution). And we need to do this in such a way that current and future teachers can reposition themselves so that they see what reality looks like if one is subject to the massive inequalities that are so ever-present to millions of people. This can be done by examining the ways in which all too many economic and educational reforms now operate (Apple, 2006; Smith *et al.*, 2004; Valenzuela, 2005; Lipman, 2004). But it also may require that people examine their own lives—their buying habits; where, by whom, and under what conditions their consumer products are made; their hidden feelings about race; the ways they think about who is and is not "deserving"; etc. (Apple, 1996) This process may be uncomfortable, but I believe that it is necessary.

The language of "deliberation" is crucial in establishing a dream of full participation over important issues; but it does not specify in enough detail what these issues actually should be. Nor as I mentioned does it necessarily enable the act of repositioning that I noted earlier was so important. Finally, it does not necessarily lead to action that might interrupt the structural and ideological conditions under which so many of us operate. This does not mean that it can't. Rather, I fear that under current conditions the tools of deliberation can serve as a limited discursive resource. It will largely be rhetorical, if it is not expressly connected to a larger agenda of social and cultural transformation.

Let me say more about what I mean by this last point. It has become something of a truism in the literature in analytic philosophy that language does and can do many things, all of them valuable. It can be used to describe, explain, control, critique, legitimate, affiliate, and mobilize (Austin, 1962; see also Wittgenstein, 1963). Rhetorical language is associated with legitimation, affiliation, and mobilization; but it is often a poor tool for the other tasks that language must perform. And the tasks of critical educational work are multiple.

THE TASKS OF CRITICAL WORK

In general, there are five tasks in which critical work in education must engage.

1 It must "bear witness to negativity." That is, one of its primary functions is to illuminate the ways in which educational policy and practice are connected to the relations of exploitation and domination in the larger society.

2 In engaging in such critical analyses and understanding, it also must point to contradictions and to spaces of possible action. Thus, its aim is to critically examine current realities with a conceptual/political framework that emphasizes the spaces in which "counter-hegemonic" actions can be or are now going on.

3 At times, this also requires a redefinition of what counts as "research." Here I mean acting as "secretaries" to those groups of people and social movements who are now engaged in challenging existing relations of unequal power or in what elsewhere I have called "non-reformist reforms" in education and elsewhere (Apple, 1995).

4 In the process, critical work has the task of keeping traditions of progressive work alive. In the face of organized attacks on the "collective memories" of difference and struggle, attacks that make it increasingly difficult to retain academic and social legitimacy for multiple critical approaches that have proven so valuable in countering dominant narratives and relations, it is absolutely crucial that these traditions be kept alive, renewed, and when necessary criticized for their conceptual, empirical, historical, and political silences or limitations. This includes not only keeping theoretical, empirical, historical, and political traditions alive—and very importantly, extending and (supportively) criticizing them. But it also involves keeping alive the dreams, utopian visions, and "non-reformist reforms" that are so much a part of them (see, e.g. Jacoby, 2005; Teitelbaum, 1993).

5 Such work must also assist in the building of critical communities, supporting social movements and mobilizations, engaging with them and learning from them so that we all can go forward. Thus, all of the work of critical education is *dependent on* having real connections—not simply rhetorical ones—to these social movements and mobilizations (Anyon, 2005; Apple & Buras, 2006). And it is dependent on our willingness to take risks and to not be defensive when those with whom we are working are critical of our efforts.

I note these five tasks because I believe that theories of education, including teacher education, that derive their grounding from theories of deliberation are sufficient for some of these roles. But they are not adequate for all of these tasks. They provide rhetorical resources for pointing to where we might like to go in terms of a general process of debate. In doing so, they enable us to connect to a valued past and act to legitimate that past as well. But they are less than powerful in illuminating the ways in which differential power now operates. They are a bit too utopian in their hopes that all can be or are willing to be equally involved in a "talking cure" for the dilemmas we face as educators. And they are at too general a level to specify the content of what these deliberations must be about if we are to deal with specific economic, political, cultural, and educational relations that condemn identifiable people to lives of misery.

Do not misinterpret me. I support the utopian goal of a society in which all people can and will engage in democratic (and critical) deliberation. But the steps that are required to get there do not automatically arise in a time of anti-democratic sentiment and, especially, in a time when neoliberals are changing our very idea of democracy from more political and collective understandings to a purely economic understanding of democracy as consumer choice (Apple, 2006). Much harder conceptual and political/educational work needs to be done around this, work that recognizes the hidden gendered and raced construction of the public sphere and also develops a sense of how commitments toward expanding it also can enable the act of repositioning that seems essential to actual challenges to actual inequalities.

Are we starting out anew here in dealing with such issues? Of course not. There are examples of what can be done in teacher education from the continuing efforts of Kenneth Zeichner and Marilyn Cochran Smith (see Liston & Zeichner, 1991; Zeichner & Liston, 1996; Cochran-Smith, 2004) to the ongoing attempts at building and defending critically and ethically responsive models of teacher education in institutions throughout the United States (see, e.g. McDonald, in press), to so many others. And these examples can be linked concretely to much more critically democratic educational practices in real schools in real communities throughout the world, from the United States (Apple & Beane, 2007) to places such as Brazil (Apple *et al.*, 2003).

In my mind, the experiences of Porto Alegre are essential here. Critical educators at schools and universities, government officials, and community activists, have taken up a model of critical deliberation and dialogue based on some of the work of Paulo Freire. They have recast it to make it more inclusive of multiple dynamics of power (both redistribution and recognition) and have made it more sensitive to the realities of the conditions of the poor and disenfranchised. The results are striking, both in terms of the kinds of deliberation that go on and in terms of the content of these deliberations—and especially in terms of the concrete interruptive actions that are the results of this ongoing process. I urge all of us to pay close attention to what is happening there. This example may provide us with a model of critical deliberation that has more bite than those with which we are used to dealing. Furthermore, the international focus would be salutary, since it would enable our teachers and others to understand that we may have much to learn from places outside our borders. In both of these ways, then, our deliberations may run less of a risk of being "free-floating" and may actually be much more adequately connected to a series of well thought out and active interruptions of dominance in educational and social policies and practices.

There are of course dangers in what I have proposed here and in the arguments I have made. The debate over indoctrination that played a key role in the history of education in the United States comes to mind. And I am certain that not everyone will agree with the points I have made here. However, it is to the credit of the chapters by Hansen, Roberson, and Sockett included in this section that they have opened the space for these considerations and debates. Let the debates continue.

REFERENCES

Anyon, J. (2005) *Radical possibilities*. New York: Routledge.

Apple, M. W. (1995) *Education and power*, 2nd edition. New York: Routledge.

Apple, M. W., Aasen, P., Cho, M. K., Gandin, L. A., Oliver, A., Sung, Y. K., Tavares, H., & Wong, T. H. (2003) *The State and the politics of knowledge*. New York: Routledge.

Apple, M. W. (2006) *Educating the "right" way: markets, standards, God, and inequality*, 2nd edition. New York: Routledge.

Apple, M. W. & Buras, K. L. (eds.) (2006) *The subaltern speak: curriculum, power, and educational struggles*. New York: Routledge.

Apple, M. W. & Beane, J. A. (eds.) (2007) *Democratic schools*, 2nd edition. Portsmouth, NH: Heinemann.

Austin, J. L. (1962) *How to do things with words*. Cambridge, MA: Harvard University Press.

Cochran-Smith, M. (2004) *Walking the road: race, diversity, and social justice in teacher education*. New York: Teachers College Press.

Crosley, N. & Roberts, J. M. (2004) *After Habermas: new perspectives on the public sphere*. Oxford: Blackwell Publishing.

Dance, L. J. (2002) *Tough fronts: the impact of street culture on schooling*. New York: Routledge.

Davis, M. (2006) *Planet of slums*. New York: Verso.

Fraser, N. (1997) *Justice interruptus*. New York: Routledge.

Habermas, J. (1984) *The theory of communicative action*. Boston: Beacon Press.

Jacoby, R. (2005) *Picture imperfect: utopian thought for an anti-utopian age*. New York: Columbia University Press.

Kozol, J. (2005) *The shame of the nation: the restoration of apartheid schooling in America*. New York: Crown.

Lipman, P. (2004) *High stakes education*. New York: Routledge.

Liston, D. & Zeichner, K. (1991) *Teacher education and the social conditions of schooling*. New York: Routledge.

McDonald, M. (in press) *The integration of social justice: reshaping teacher education*. New York: Routledge.

Mills, C. (1997) *The racial contract*. Ithaca, NY: Cornell University Press.

Rawls, J. (1971) *A theory of justice*. Cambridge, MA: Belknap Press of Harvard University Press.

Smith, M. L., Miller-Kahn, L., Heinecke, W., & Jarvis, P. (2004). *Political spectacle and the fate of American schooling*. New York: Routledge.

Teitelbaum, K. (1993) *Schooling for good rebels*. New York: Teachers College Press.

Valenzuela, A. (ed.) (2005) *Leaving children behind*. Albany, NY: State University of New York Press.

Wittgenstein, L. (1963) *Philosophical investigations*. Oxford: Blackwell.

Zeichner, K. & Liston, D. (1996) *Reflective teaching*. Mahwah, NJ: L. Erlbaum Associates.

6 Advancing the public purpose of schooling and teacher education

John I. Goodlad
University of Washington

The people of this nation have extraordinary expectations for those who teach the young in schools and very diverse views on the preparation necessary for their work. As David Hansen points out in his opening chapter of this handbook, there are those who believe that teachers need no formal, professional preparation. But what he and his colleagues perceive to be the purposes of teacher education calls for immersing future practitioners in educational agendas that one would be hard-pressed to find in our colleges and universities.

Studying the history of professions reveals that all have intensely debated the purposes of educating practitioners. Those put forward for medical education in Abraham Flexner's groundbreaking report of 1910 fueled heated debate for several decades over issues that remain central today in making curricular and other decisions. The issue of gaining the right balance of general education, scientific studies, and clinical apprenticeship remains at the forefront of debate, as Flexner predicted.

One of the most interesting agreements about the purposes of teacher education put forward by Hansen, Emily Robertson, and Hugh Sockett is the interface between their comprehensive high-level take on the topic and thoughtful consideration of *what* preparation teachers would need if serious attention were given to meeting the public's expectations for our schools. From our respective studies of schooling conducted in the early 1980s, Ernest Boyer and I concluded, quite independently with respect to each other's ongoing work, that "we want it all": the personal, social, vocational, and intellectual development of the child (1983, 1984). Surely we can assume that what we want our schools to do is what we want teachers to be able to do.

THE PURPOSES OF SCHOOLING

As with most social science research, particularly surveys, one must take great care in interpreting findings and conclusions. Many surveys of public expectations for schooling either leave respondents free to state their preferences or to choose among the alternatives provided for them. The dominant response over a long period of years has given preference to the academic—that is, the teaching of departmentalized subject matter and basic skills of reading, writing, figuring, etc. But this finding should not be interpreted to mean that respondents reject other categories of learning. Indeed, most would oppose the neglect of students' personal, social, and vocational development. In our study of 8,624 parents, 1,350 teachers, and many thousands of students, colleagues and I called for their rating of all of these. The only category not rated "very important" by every group was the vocational, which elementary school teachers considered to be only "somewhat important" (Goodlad, 1984).

Parents and teachers of our sample rated "personal development" as a goal for schools only a little behind "intellectual development." Large percentages of all three groups of respondents would opt for more attention to the personal, especially in those schools viewed by their clientele as providing well for students' intellectual development. These findings do not surprise me.

Most parents perceive schools to be responsible for educating what was once commonly referred to as "the whole child." The concept fell into disfavor in the 1950s when the attack on anything considered to be "Progressive Education" was in high gear. The term is once more gaining legitimacy today as we appear to be moving out of a longstanding cycle of "hard-and-tough" expectations for schooling into the more "soft-and-tender."

Jane Roland Martin (1992) and Nel Noddings (2003), among others, have had the splendid audacity to propose for schools the cultivation of happiness in the young. Since schools have played a major role in the creation of childhood as a distinctive phase in the life cycle, it is past time for us to ensure that parents support and teachers provide educational environments that truly implement the common rhetoric of school reform: "It's all for the children."

Having written the above, I already begin to feel uneasy. I have been around this fingerpost[1] of the domain of schooling before—several times. One finger points to "Children's Interests," another to "Academic Rigor," another to "Responsible Adulthood," and still another to "Economic Productivity." Because the fingers are at right angles to one another, the more one moves in the direction to which each points, the further one gets from the paths that reach out from the other fingers. And the less attention is given to the existence of these other paths.

Several decades ago, I was approached by an enthusiastic group of teachers who sought my support for "the open classroom." They were correct in assuming that some of my educational views were compatible with some of those guiding their interpretation of this innovation. But we were not long into our conversation before I realized that they advocated a curriculum that would emerge entirely out of children's interests. This and several of their other views would put them on a collision course with all those people who follow other paths, particularly the one to which the finger labeled "Academic" points. The more these teachers followed exclusively the finger pointing to the "Children's Interests," the more they would fuel the nonproductive debate and struggle over the soul of the American public school. I declined their invitation. My mother's voice has come back to me again and again to guide me in matters carried to indefensible extremes: "Practice moderation in all things." I do not want to be perceived as dedicated to only one path of educational preference.

Currently, the No Child Left Behind (NCLB) Act is directing schools to follow a narrow academic path that ignores the fingerpost of the comprehensive mission for schooling consistently endorsed by a very large majority of the American people. The major danger is not that hundreds of thousands of children and youths are being denied the breadth and depth of education they need for making the most of themselves in this complex world, serious though this danger is. The even greater danger is that, should NCLB or similar successor mandates prevail through the next decade, our educational system will fail in its major purpose—that is, to provide for all the comprehensive education that ensures a democratic public (Barber, 1997).

THE PURPOSES OF TEACHER EDUCATION

Productively helping the young to gain some fundamental understanding of concepts such as time, space, light, gravity, and the tides; appreciation of the arts; the structure of our federal government; and why there are night and day and summer and winter is pedagogically challenging. It requires of each teacher of the physical sciences, the arts, the humanities, and the social sciences a deeper understanding of the subject matter than is expected of the students. But it also requires a repertoire of teaching skills and sensitivities grounded in knowledge of cognition and honed in practice: pedagogy, the art and science of teaching.

That teachers of both elementary and secondary school classes should be quite well versed in the subject matter they teach and the methods of teaching they will use is a longstanding assumption of the public, those who teach persons aspiring to teach, and those who establish the entry requirements. All groups also agree that teachers should have some understanding of the role schooling has played in our society, the social and economic values that have influenced educational policies and school curricula, and the developmental characteristics of the young. As a consequence of this interface, the educational requirements each state sets for certification to teach are rather closely matched by the preparation programs of colleges and universities.

Were it not for the fact that teachers of elementary school classrooms usually teach all the subjects of the curriculum (with those of the larger schools commonly relieved of the arts and physical education, if such are provided at all), much of the intense debate over the professional education of teachers would never have arisen. Given this daunting requirement, it is understandable that college faculty members responsible for preparing elementary school teachers would insist on teachers at this level gaining some educational background and pedagogical competence in all the relevant fields.

Understandable though this position is, it has spawned a host of problems: near impossibility of future elementary school teachers' completing both college graduation and teacher certification requirements in the normal time of 120 semester or 180 quarter hours, course overloads, reduction of education in the arts and sciences, and severe criticism of schools of education. Pundit George Will has been erroneously reporting for decades that most future teachers are majoring in a field of education devoid of intellectual content. A large segment of the public now believes this to be true.

We found in our study of a representative sample of colleges and universities that the undergraduate curriculum of teacher education in professional studies was very much like that of other fields such as business, journalism, and engineering in sharing their time with the arts and sciences. A dean of the arts and sciences in a major university we visited was highly critical of its school of education's usurping too much of the undergraduate curriculum. He held up the journalism program as having the ideal distribution. I found that it required more courses in the vocational field than did the secondary teacher education program and came close to meeting that of elementary preparation.

There is a myth about the course demands of college and university teacher education that just does not go away. Unfortunately, it is kept alive in part by the existence of some programs that come close to replicating the critical stereotype. We found no programs where general and special subject courses took up less than half of the four-year curriculum. But we did find a couple where getting two years of general education and completing the teacher preparation requirements required crowded programs of well over 120 semester or 180 quarter hours of credit—situations much in need of substantial improvement. Interestingly, the deans of education of universities in the same states were very much aware of these programs, regarded then as institutional cash cows, and thought it was high time for them to be revised or discontinued.

I realize that most readers of this handbook are well aware of the realities described and perhaps are wondering why I am giving them so much attention in a short commentary. My reasons pertain to the gulf between the purposes of teacher education put forward by Hansen, Robertson, and Sockett and those embedded in the long-term struggle over the preparation teachers need for fulfilling much more modest expectations. The gulf between what some of our most thoughtful educators have proposed for both schooling and teacher education over the past half-century and what James B. Conant recommended nearly fifty years ago (Conant, 1959 and 1963) and a host of federal and state commissions have recommended is substantial. Consequently, there must be an ethos of policy and public support, or what is so gratifying to read in the section of this handbook on the purposes of teacher education will become just one more script for educational theater.

ON IMPLEMENTATION AND RENEWAL

Twenty-nine editorials written by Marilyn Cochran-Smith during the six years she was editor of the *Journal of Teacher Education* are available in a single volume (2006). She refers frequently to the necessity of educators' being much more involved in the determination of educational policy and practice. I have referred from time to time to a cautionary stance of some educators that comes close to giving up rights of citizenship. School teachers and administrators and teacher educators should be educational leaders in their communities. They not only should be communicating with the public regarding what they are doing and why but also about needed improvements based on trial and solid inquiry.

Good ideas come and go, sometimes are resurrected and then fade, perhaps after they have had brief flowering in a few boutique gardens. David Tyack and Larry Cuban describe some of this in their historical analysis of schooling in the twentieth century, aptly titled *Tinkering Toward Utopia* (1995). They offer no blueprints for change but do conclude that improvement would be more likely to occur if more power were shifted to the local level and if there were closer linkages of schools and their communities. I agree.

Most readers of this handbook will resonate with the rich array of purposes for teacher education that Hansen, Robertson, and Sockett have set before us. Their menu encompasses and enriches the personal, social, vocational, and intellectual domains described by that large sample of people polled over the last several decades. But the devil is in the details.

Hansen writes: "If a 'purpose' is understood as something anticipated or envisaged that is to be brought about through human agency and creativity, then it remains legitimate, coherent, and necessary to speak of the purposes rather than merely the functions of teacher education." Sockett writes that "the moral and epistemic purposes of teacher education are . . . critical not only in enhancing the quality of practitioners in teaching, but also in contributing to the development of the public status of the occupation of teaching," and then goes on to quote Sullivan (2004): "Professionals are inescapably moral agents whose work depends upon public trust for its success." I agree.

On assuming the above paragraph presents logical truth, educators had better not also assume this to be truth widely shared. "Moral" is a word of many interpretations. One might expect the high public expectation for personal development of the young in schools to include moral denotations and connotations, but some of the advocates of this school purpose view it as excluding any teaching of moral values.

Hugh Sockett was a member of a group of educators who wrote a book entitled *The Moral Dimensions of Teaching* (Goodlad *et al.* eds., 1990). If his subsequent experiences were anything like mine, he would have quickly encountered both puzzled and negative reactions even to the title. Following a speech I made on the topic, a man in a rather selective, university-based audience expressed pleasure over educators becoming concerned at long last about sins such as drinking, taking drugs, and sexual activity not condoned by marriage. Readers in Moscow, just as the U.S.S.R. was breaking up, and in Buenos Aires, however, viewed the book as contributing to the very essence of democracy—how we should behave with one another as members of humankind.

In another chapter of that book, Sirotnik (1990) describes the American democracy as "a moral community that transcends the special interests of individuals, families, groups, that stand for what this country is all about: liberty and *justice* for all . . . It is a 'moral ecology' held together by a political democracy and the fundamental values embedded in the system" (p. 307). He then poses the question "What could be more central to education generally and public schooling particularly than moral commitments to inquiry, knowledge, competence, caring, and social justice?" (p. 308). Sirotnik put forward a public democratic purpose for schooling. But a significant segment of the public harbors a private purpose: both democracy and the public school are to take care of their needs, wants, and individual (rather than collective) goals. World historian Alan Wood notes that we cherish freedom as the essence of the American democracy but have given too little attention to our responsibilities for its care (2001).

What Emily Robertson sees as central to the care of our democracy is widespread practice of democratic participation. The knowledge, competence, and inquiry required presumably are what Sirotnik viewed as central to education generally and public schooling particularly. But Robertson makes it clear that these attributes are learned through disciplined participation, whether as students in schools or adults in the daily life of communities. They are not "delivered" by teachers and teacher educators. Indeed, educators must learn them through the participatory route of all other members of a democratic public. And educators are likely to have just as much difficulty as others will have in debating issues grounded in moral values.

Hansen, Robertson, and Sockett do a magnificent job of presenting the case for purposes of teacher education that take us far beyond the traditional scope of the enterprise, a scope dominated by issues of what academic content to teach and how to teach it. Implemented in practice, these purposes would shift the public status of teaching from a minor to a major profession.

But even the implementation of the traditional purpose was fraught with controversy. Robertson cautions us: "The debates about educating democratic citizens, and the knowledge and commitments their teachers should have, seem as polarized as the rest of the political landscape . . . Democratic education of students and its implications for teacher education are contested terrains." And embedded in these contested terrains also are the comprehensive scope of the intellectual purpose put forward by Hansen and, most certainly, the moral and epistemic purposes elaborated by Sockett. It is essential to remember how very *public* schooling is, without backing off from advancing the education of the public the care our democracy requires (Goodlad *et al.* 2004).

It becomes obvious that teacher educators must play an active role in addressing the challenge of significantly broadening the purposes of this critically important educational endeavor. A major component of this challenge is that of engaging the public—not just a few of its leaders—in sustained discourse followed by action regarding the purposes and conduct of public education and schooling. Clearly, the Founding Fathers did not intend for the nation's capital to be the epicenter of educational debates and policy making. History has shown us but not as yet taught us how wise they were.

NOTE

1 *Webster's International Dictionary*—"Fingerpost": a guidepost bearing one or more index fingers.

REFERENCES

Barber, Benjamin R. (1997) "Public schooling: education for democracy," in John I. Goodlad & Timothy J. McMannon (eds.), *The public purpose of education and schooling*. San Francisco: Jossey-Bass.

Boyer, Ernest L. (1983) *High school: a report on secondary education in America*. New York: Harper & Row.

Cochran-Smith, Marilyn (2006) *Policy, practice, and politics in teacher education*. Thousand Oaks, CA: Corwin Press.

Conant, James B. (1959) *The American high school today*. New York: McGraw-Hill.

Conant, James B. (1963) *The education of American teachers*. New York: McGraw-Hill.

Flexner, Abraham (1910) *Medical education in the United States and Canada*. New York: Carnegie Foundation for the Advancement of Teaching.

Goodlad, John I. (1984) *A place called school*. New York: McGraw-Hill.

Goodlad, John I. (1990) *Teachers for our nation's schools*. San Francisco: Jossey-Bass.

Goodlad, John I. (1994) *Educational renewal: better teachers, better schools*. San Francisco: Jossey-Bass.

Goodlad, John I., Soder, Roger, & Sirotnik, Kenneth A. (eds.) (1990) *The moral dimensions of teaching*. San Francisco: Jossey-Bass.

Goodlad, John I., Mantle-Bromley, Corinne, & Goodlad, Stephen John (2004) *Education for everyone: agenda for education in a democracy*. San Francisco: Jossey-Bass.

Martin, Jane Roland (1992) *The schoolhome: rethinking schools for changing families*. Cambridge, MA: Harvard University Press.

Noddings, Nel (2003) *Happiness and education*. New York: Cambridge University Press.

Sirotnik, Kenneth A. (1990) "Society, schooling, teaching, and preparing to teach," in Goodlad, Soder, & Sirotnik (eds.), *The moral dimensions of teaching* (pp. 296–327). San Francisco: Jossey-Bass.

Sullivan, William (2004, December) "Preparing professionals as moral agents," *Carnegie Perspectives*. Stanford, CA: The Carnegie Foundation for the Advancement of Teaching.

Tyack, David & Cuban, Larry (1995) *Tinkering toward utopia: a century of public school reform*. Cambridge, MA: Harvard University Press.

Wood, Alan T. (2001) *What does it mean to be human?* New York: Peter Lang.

7   A thought from another world

The professional education of Black teachers in Georgia, 1930–1965

Vanessa Siddle Walker
Emory University

Three assumptions undergird the excellent essays on teacher education presented in this section of the handbook. The first suggests that constructing and transmitting knowledge for teachers is primarily a conversation for teacher educators in academic institutions. This assumption emerges despite Hansen's admonition that teacher education should be ongoing, both formal and informal. The second assumption implies that historical ideas and theorists, rather than historical actors and practices, provide the most salient context for contemporary conversations. Amplified by the artifacts presented, this assumption is threaded throughout and reinforced through recurring portraits of teacher educators such as John Dewey. Finally, the essays decontextualize the diversity of teacher educators, teachers, and local contexts and assume the general purposes of teacher education are broadly applicable across these contexts. Although Dewey's artifact reminds readers that, for purposes of education, we too often assume that "all human beings are as much alike as peas in a pod," the essays fail to problematize differences in ethnicity, historical period, and region. This occurs despite the important attention given to a social justice agenda.

This commentary proposes to extend the conversation on teacher education by providing an alternative world view on the assumptions identified, specifically utilizing the lens of Black teachers in Georgia during a historical period of de jure segregation (Walker, in press). The utilization of a Black teacher sample to contribute to a professional conversation about teaching remains an embryonic idea. The more frequent depiction of Black teachers and teaching is embedded in the W. E. B. Du Bois artifact, which recounts the story of low pay, poor teaching circumstances, and oppression by White superintendents that permeated the world of John and other Black teachers of his era. However, as poignant and accurate as is John's story, the professional activity of Black teachers in the decades following John's escape reveals the narrowness of the historical lens that has reduced the story of Black teachers primarily to one of inequality. To fail to include the professional activity of Black teachers in constructing an understanding of the aims of teacher education is to ignore, as Ralph Waldo Emerson notes, "the mind of the past." Or, as Du Bois eloquently describes the disconnect between Black and White Georgians: "And neither world thought the other world's thought."

To elevate the Black teaching profession during segregation into a contemporary conversation on teacher education requires some contextualization. For example, many Black teachers during this period, despite the devaluing of teachers generally, and Black teachers especially, referred to themselves as "professionals" and embraced practices that incorporate much of Sockett's description of a professional group. That is, they maintained a code of professional practices, sought the elevation of the profession through attempts to raise teacher standards and increase financial rewards, and existed in local settings where Black principals could, and sometimes did, apply sanctions to teachers who did not abide by the commonly-accepted teaching code. This degree of self-governance was possible as a result of the isolation imposed by White superintendents who often ignored the activity of Black teachers unless behaviors were exhibited that challenged the status quo (and these activist behaviors were generally carefully concealed). However, the result was a world in which Black educators were often able to function with a semblance of the autonomy Robertson values.

Three characterizations of the professional education and activities of Black teachers are useful to extend the current dialogue. These are: (1) that the education of teachers and the discussion of the purposes of education were broader than teacher education institutions, (2) that practices in teacher education were not disconnected from the larger academic world of teacher educator personalities and ideas, and (3) that social justice and curricular focus existed as a merged agenda, rather than a separately codified explanation of options. These characterizations are drawn largely from the archival records of the Black teachers association in Georgia and are discussed in more detail in Walker (2005) and my forthcoming work, *Hello Professor: The Professional Development World of the Black Principal Leader*.

PROPOSITION ONE: THE EDUCATION OF TEACHERS WAS BROADER THAN TEACHER EDUCATION INSTITUTIONS

Black teachers during the 1930s and 1940s were faced with the Herculean task of improving the educational knowledge base and certification level of their peers, many of whom held earlier state certifications that did not require a college degree. Black teacher education institutions in the South played the dominant role in this initial certification process. Although the teacher education activities of these institutions beg additional research, ads from the quarterly publication of Black teachers, the *Herald*, provide data demonstrating the ongoing commitment of these institutions to providing continuing coursework to expand the disciplinary training of teachers. Additionally, articles reveal the ways Black colleges sought to prepare teachers who would be sensitive to the particular needs within the state, the ways they worked cooperatively to develop a state vision for Black teacher education, and the type of professional conversations they had, such as appropriate evaluative criteria for prospective teachers (e.g. "Georgia's New Education Program," p. 8; Bolden, 1963, p. 6). The role played by these institutions in developing teachers was considered to be so substantial that educators during the era argued that "The Negro College in the south can potentially in no other way at this time contribute so much to the race and to society as by devoting its best efforts to the development of a superior profession of teachers . . ." ("What Every Teacher Should Know," 1941, pp. 12–13).

Ironically, however, despite the visibility of the teacher education institution in disseminating and structuring the aims of education, oral historical accounts by Black educators in Georgia seldom attribute their professional beliefs to the teacher education curriculum in these undergraduate institutions. Rather, the professional association of Black teachers, the Georgia Teachers and Education Association (GTEA), appears to have played the more substantial educative role over time. In the professional meetings designed in corporation with this structure, Black educators report that they were revitalized professionally, able to experiment with their own ideas, and inspired to learn from the practices of colleagues who were working under similar restricted conditions. Opportunities for professional education that existed through GTEA included teacher study groups, organized across the state with the direct purpose being to "raise the standards of work of the teachers" ("Georgia Jeanes Supervisors," 1937, pp. 9–10). They likewise included district and state meetings, where yearly and quarterly programs consistently included ongoing dialogue and sharing of professional practices among participants. The tenor of many of these meetings is captured in the minutes of a 1941 district meeting: "The groups entered into a thorough discussion of their problems—how the school is meeting the mental, physical, and moral needs of the child … The meeting was outstanding for the spontaneity of group participation and enthusiasm ("What the Districts are Doing," 1941, p. 17).

Purist historians will cringe at the imposition of a presentivist framework on an historical practice; however, the professional programming of Black teachers across the state correlate in significant ways with "deliberative democracy" that Robertson argues is essential if teachers are to model discussion capacity with their students. Importantly, the activity also demonstrates the ways in which institutional structures joined in teacher education. Importantly, this focus included teacher education departments, but the talk was not confined to academics in departments of teacher education.

PROPOSITION TWO: THAT PRACTICES IN TEACHER EDUCATION IN THE FIELD WERE CONNECTED TO TEACHER EDUCATOR PERSONALITIES AND IDEAS

Sockett bemoans the disconnectedness between practitioners and academics that characterizes the current teacher education climate. However, similar to the University of Chicago professors who are reported to have frequented the Hull-House on Sunday evenings, Black teachers of Georgia lived in a world closely connected to the leading educational thought of their day. For example, in a speech at the GTEA convention in 1937, and later reprinted in their professional journal and distributed throughout the state, Du Bois embraces Hansen's first purpose of teacher education, to esteem the value of academic subjects ("Curriculum Revision, 1937, p. 15). Du Bois argues that the foundation of 'an intelligent citizenship' was based on teaching students to read, to write, and to use numbers" (pp. 13–17). Indeed, he rails that "the school has but one way to cure the ills of society and that is by making men intelligent." Du Bois's connection to Black Georgia teachers, though unchartered in his biographies, is unsurprising in light of his service as a member of the advisory board of their association in 1937.

Yet, having a scholar of the reputation of Du Bois participate in their professional educative circle was not a unique occurrence. In the 1940s, Horace Mann Bond edited the teachers' journal while he served as president of Fort Valley State. Although Bond's biographers note that he did little scholarly writing during this period, his articles in the journal demonstrate the ways in which he exploited his position as "editor" to provide detailed information to Black teachers on the educational terrain inside and outside of Georgia. Teacher Educator William Kilpatrick, a Georgia native, also appears in their journal and at their professional meetings, as do other prominent educators such as Allison Davis and Charles Thompson.

A point about the intersection of Dewey with Black educators is also important, given the prominence of Dewey in the current conversation. In ways uncaptured in most descriptions of his work, Dewey figures prominently in the professional talk of Black educators in Georgia. Black teachers of the era adopted Dewey's beliefs about schools, and myriad references occur to life teaching, community study, and knowing the needs of the child exist in their district, state, and local talk. (e.g. "Reports from Department

Meetings," 1938, p. 11; "Conference of Principals of Negro High Schools," 1940, pp. 8–9; "Programs of District Teachers Meetings Held," 1941, p. 19). Even the language that has been captured in oral history accounts detailing the professional vision of Black educators on the education of Black children is reflective of their familiarity with Dewey's philosophy: the child is to progress from the known to the unknown; the teacher can't teach a child he/she doesn't know; every child must be given the opportunity to reach his highest potential. Reinforced by a new Georgia state curriculum, Black teachers built a professional view of teaching that heavily incorporated Dewey's ideas and extended throughout the decades of Black segregated education.

In sum, the Black historical actors of this period did not exist estranged in a segregated world; rather, many lived in a close professional world with leading theorists. They were not all intimately acquainted with each person; however, the mechanisms of professional training in which they participated cultivated a knowledge base of ideas that became part of their general ideology of teaching. In this history, the disconnect between practitioners and academics does not appear to be so broad a divide.

PROPOSITION THREE: THAT SOCIAL JUSTICE AND CURRICULAR FOCUS EXISTED AS A MERGED AGENDA

Throughout its history, GTEA used its leadership structure to focus on improving teaching conditions, even as it structured and supported the ongoing professional talk described above. Du Bois's speech, noted earlier, captures the duality Black teachers confronted. Although Du Bois admonished teachers to hold high curricular standards, he also stressed that teachers should also be concerned about lengthening the school term, making attendance mandatory, and selecting teachers (p. 17). For Black teachers, the teaching act could not be separated from the teaching environment. In this compilation of academic standards and social justice that characterized the talk of their era, Black teachers provide an example of Hansen's wondering of what it would mean to put "educational processes in the service of overtly political objectives" (p. 12).

One way in which this practice is most repeatedly observed is in the Black teachers' application of Dewey and their co-opting of his use of democratic aims of education. In the artifact in this section, Dewey critiques racial and national prejudice, noting that schools must "rebuild the spirit of common understanding, or mutual sympathy and goodwill among all people and races to exercise the demon of prejudice." Black educators took Dewey at his word.

Despite the segregated circumstances in which they lived, Black teachers widely embraced teaching Black children to participate in a democratic society. The focus on democratic living embraced by Black teachers was part of a social studies curriculum, as Patrice Grimes has documented in a doctoral dissertation on their teaching activities during this era (Grimes, 2005). However, their focus on democratic living was broader than a particular disciplinary initiative. Theirs was the embodiment of Dewey's challenge to prepare a new generation for a "new and more just and humane society." This belief is woven throughout their professional talk. Moreover, the ways in which students verbally embraced these ideas is exemplified in a speech given on Citizenship Day in 1939. The recent graduate notes that

> . . . things will not always be the same. Perhaps not in our day will any great changes come about. But the time will surely come when no one, regardless of race, creed or color, will be denied his full constitutional rights and privilege. Then we, as citizens,

can feel that we played a definite part—although we were but a small cog in the wheel—in the fight to bring about freedom for all.

(Irby, 1940, p. 6)

In sum, Black teachers used their teaching to prepare children for a world that did not yet exist. This social justice agenda was mediated by the cultural and social needs of their children and not subordinated to a curricular discussion. Rather, curricular focus and social justice existed co-dependently.

This overview of the practices of Black teachers is not posited to suggest that the practices of Black teachers were unique. White teachers of the era also engaged in professional training through their teaching association. However, White teachers of the era do not embrace social justice in the same manner, a point that is significant in considering the ways in which region and culture influence the aims of education. Of certainty, the ideas are also not posed to suggest direct correlations with contemporary ideas. Sockett makes an important point exemplifying this difference when he notes that ideas such as in loco parentis (which Black teachers uniformly embraced) have been replaced in contemporary climates with due process.

However, the inclusion of the historical Black teaching world in a conversation on teacher education unmasks how culture and local circumstances might transform political ideas. It may move us beyond the assumption that teacher education institutions must singularly dispense professional ideas and generate an impetus to forge collaborative educative relationships with other stakeholders. We might also be reminded that social justice and academic excellence do not have to live disconnected—and, for that matter, neither do teacher educator professors and classroom teachers. Perhaps another world could provide context that will prompt a new thought.

REFERENCES

Bolden, W. S. (1963) Improving selection process in preservice teacher education. *Herald*, 24 (4), 6–7, 15.

Conference of principals of Negro high schools (1940) *Herald*, 6 (3), 8–9.

Du Bois, W. E. B. (1937) Curriculum Revision. *Herald*, 3 (3), 13–18.

Georgia Jeanes supervisors (1937) *Herald*, 4 (1), 9.

Georgia's new education program (1938) *Herald*, 4 (3), 8.

Grimes, P. (2005) *Teaching democracy: civic education in Georgia's African American schools, 1930–1954*. Unpublished doctoral dissertation, Emory University, Atlanta, Georgia.

Irby, D. (1940) The viewpoint of a new citizen. *Herald*, 6 (3), 6.

Programs of district teachers meetings held (1941) *Herald*, 7 (2), 18–20.

Reports from department meetings (1938) *Herald*, 4 (3), 11.

Walker, V. S. (2005) Organized resistance and Black educators' quest for school equality, 1878–1938. *Teachers College Record*, 107 (3), 355–388.

Walker, V. S. (in press) *Hello professor*. Chapel Hill: University of North Carolina Press.

What Every Teacher Should Know (1941) *Herald*, 8 (1), 11–13.

What the Districts are Doing (1941) *Herald*, 8 (3), 17.

Part 2

What should teachers know?

Teacher capacities: knowledge, beliefs, skills, and commitments

Editor: Carl A. Grant

Part 2
Framing chapters

8 Teacher capacity

Introduction to the section

Carl A. Grant
University of Wisconsin-Madison

Initially many of us associate the word "capacity" with the natural sciences—with units of measure such as pints, quarts, teaspoons and liters. Having earned an undergraduate degree in science, I initially learned about capacity with the experiments I conducted in my physics classes. Over the past few decades, however, capacity has increasingly become a concept in social science scholarship, including research in education. Conduct a Google search for "teacher capacity," and the results reveal thousands of documents using this term in many different ways. In this chapter, we define teacher capacity as a teacher's knowledge, skills and dispositions.

HISTORICAL INFLUENCES ON THE DEFINITION OF TEACHER CAPACITY IN THE UNITED STATES

Debates about what makes a good teacher and what capacities teachers need to be good teachers have flourished both inside educational institutions and in the greater society for decades. McDiarmid and Clevenger-Bright (this volume, Chapter 9), for instance, tell us that as early as 1830, at Barre Normal School in Massachusetts, Governor Everett identified four core areas of study for teachers. Then, as now, the focus was on teacher knowledge, skills and dispositions.

However, as time and context change, as events with wide-ranging consequences occur, and as developments in science lead to technological advancements, society and government have made demands for standards and accountability that require teachers not only to keep pace with the change, but to lead the change. This, in turn, has required the definitions of teacher capacity to be altered and amended. For example, in order for students to meet curriculum/performance standards and for schools to meet accountability requirements, teachers' knowledge has had to become deeper and more flexible. This now includes having an understanding of the relationship between content knowledge and pedagogical content knowledge. Teacher capacity must also include such essential skills such as having a wide array of grouping strategies and assessments techniques. In addition, teachers must have dispositions that foster positive attitudes toward change as well as a commitment to student learning. They must also be committed to the paramount perspective that all students can learn.

Three examples from recent history

Three examples illustrate how our concept of what constitutes acceptable teacher capacity has changed during the course of the twentieth century. The first example comes from the early 1900s when scientific management and educational efficiency based upon business and industrial values and practices arose in response to the nation's rapid industrialization and urbanization. These influenced definitions of teacher capability. The second example is from the middle of the century, after the Soviet Union launched the Sputnik satellite into orbit in 1957. The third example is from the latter part of the century, after the 1983 publication of the National Commission on Excellence in Education's report, *A Nation at Risk.*

Agriculture increasingly gave way to manufacturing in the late 1800s and early 1900s in the United States. Industrialization led to urbanization, as many Americans—black and white—moved into cities. Additionally, the early 1900s saw numerous miraculous technological achievements such as the Wright brothers first controlled, powered, heavier-than-air human flight in 1903; the construction of skyscrapers such as the Cass Gilbert-designed Woolworth Building, which opened in New York City in 1913; the opening of the Panama Canal in 1914; and Henry Ford's development of the assembly line which led to mass production of automobiles. All of these greatly increased America's international trade activity (Nash *et al.*, 1990; Yapp, 2000).

Industrialization, urbanization, and international trade influenced the questions being asked and debated with regard to teacher knowledge, skills and dispositions. This was especially true after a new concept about industrial management, known as "scientific management" or the "Taylor System," emerged from hearings before the Interstate Commerce Commission in Washington, D.C. in 1910, which dazzled American society (Callahan, 1962, p. 19).

In 1913, Franklin Bobbitt addressed the application of scientific management to education in the Twelfth *Yearbook of the National Society for the Study of Education* titled, *Supervision of City Schools.* Although scientific management was forwarded as an idea to be employed by school superintendents and principals, it also had implications for teacher capacity. Bobbitt argued that an educator's knowledge "must be kept up to standard qualifications for his kind of work for his entire service" (cited in Callahan, 1962, p. 89). He also insisted that school systems had the right to tell teacher training institutions what their specifications for teachers were, saying, "They have the same right to say to colleges what products shall be sent to them as a transportation system has to say to a steel plant what kind of rails shall be sent to it" (cited in Callahan, 1962, p. 89).

In 1957, when the Soviet Union launched the space satellite, "Sputnik," politicians and pundits severely criticized the curriculum of the education system in the United States. Critics claimed that the science and technology instruction offered in public schools was vastly inferior to that offered to students in the Soviet Union. Conant (1963), for example, claimed that educational requirements were too low; Koerner (1963) argued that there was "inferior intellectual quality of the education faculty" (p. 73); and Rickover (1959) contended that the neglect of science and mathematics in the schools had weakened the American capacity to survive in a dangerous world. Along related lines, Bestor (1955) claimed that teachers needed increased understanding of the separate disciplines. He described social studies as "social stew" and argued that teachers should have a knowledge base in history, geography, and political science. The social policies adopted in the late 1950s were in part a response to the perceived Soviet lead in science and technology; these required that teachers' knowledge and skills reflect a high level of understanding of science and mathematics. This was done with the intention of helping the United States regain global eminence in science and technology through teachers' excellence in teaching.

In 1983, the publication of the National Commission on Excellence in Education (1983) report, *A Nation at Risk*, again raised the debate about teacher capacity. The report called attention to the dismal failure of public schools in the U.S. in comparison with the educational systems in other countries. A much-quoted line from the report captures the harshness of the criticism toward American public education: "If an unfriendly foreign power had attempted to impose on America the mediocre educational performance that exists today, we might well have viewed it as an act of war" (p. 5).

A Nation at Risk called for major reforms in teacher preparation, with particular attention to the knowledge, skills, and dispositions that enabled teachers to to teach higher-level thinking in the areas of mathematic and science. Two other influential reports followed *A Nation at Risk*: *Teachers for Tomorrow's Schools* from the Holmes Group (1986) and *A Nation Prepared: Teachers for the 21st Century* from the Carnegie Corporation (Carnegie Forum on Education and the Economy, 1986). Both reports argued that teachers' capacity should be grounded in the humanities and sciences, and both recommended the elimination of undergraduate teacher education programs, instead suggesting that teacher education be a post-baccalaureate program and that teacher candidates hold a bachelor's degree in an academic discipline in addition to a degree in education.

What we see from these three examples is that debates about what teachers need to know, including their skills and dispositions, change and evolve in response to changing social, economic, and political agendas. However, these examples also make clear that while attention to mathematics, science, and technology is often at the forefront in discussions about what teachers need to know, attention to issues of diversity have for the most part been marginalized or omitted from the discourse.

The approach to teacher capacity we took in this section

This section of the handbook could have been conceptualized in many ways. However, as section editor and chapter authors, what we saw missing or lacking in much of the literature on teacher capacity was scholarship about teacher capacity as it relates to knowledge, skills, and dispositions for teaching non-white students and other traditionally marginalized groups. Also, what we saw that needed attention and direction were discussions that explore the multiple relationships and discourses between teachers' knowledge, skills, and dispositions and social justice, as well as what teacher candidates need to know, care about, and be able to do to work in classrooms that are becoming increasingly diverse. Additionally, we noticed that a good deal of the literature on teacher capacity lacks new insights, is too selective, or is limited in its discussion of historical ideas and events that would help teacher candidates to better understand teacher capacity today.

As editor of this section, I am not suggesting that there is no scholarship that seeks to show a relationship between social justice and teachers' knowledge or that seeks to inform teacher candidates about the knowledge, skills, and dispositions they need to teach socially and racially diverse groups of students. There is scholarship along these lines, and the chapters in this section have richly benefited from it. However, much of this scholarship points out that the work examining the relationship between social justice and teacher capacity is limited, and that questions about what teachers need to know, care about, and be able to do need more in-depth study.

In response to these gaps in the education literature, we decided to develop and organize this section of the handbook so that it addresses diversity within the teacher capacity discourse. Having decided upon the approach, we next discussed the purpose and goal for each of the three chapters, including artifacts that would enrich and inform the discussion, and who would write commentaries that would "trouble" the teacher capacity discourse, and even our arguments in the chapters. The chapter authors first wanted to provide readers with a history of teacher capacity so readers could understand how, why and to what end teachers' knowledge, skills and dispositions have been conceptualized in the earlier years of the country. Second, the authors wanted to call attention to the many recent changes in U.S. social and political policies that have influenced the way teacher capacity is formulated, the most important of which is the significant population growth and demographic changes in urban and rural areas. Although the United States has grown and prospered over the decades in part because of its demographic diversity, the increasing diversity of the student population challenges and continues to challenge the teaching force, which for the most part remains white and monolingual. Third, the authors of this section believed it was important to address the relationship between social justice and teacher capacity. We believed that teacher educators would appreciate an in-depth and comprehensive discussion of this relationship to assist them as they consider what they are doing programmatically and in their own research and scholarship in the name of social justice. In sum, the three chapters in this section provide the reader with a historical as well as a present day view of teacher capacity and how enduring questions such as, "What do teachers need to know, care about, and be able to do?" are considered.

ORGANIZATION OF THE SECTION

This section begins with three stand-alone, but complementary and inter-connected framing chapters, which collectively illuminate the historical and ongoing evolution of the conceptualization and understanding of teacher capacity. G. Williamson McDiarmid and Mary Clevenger-Bright's chapter *Rethinking Teacher Capacity* helps us to examine and learn from past efforts as we look forward to enhancing and improving programs of teacher preparation and the scholarship of teacher educators. They inform us about how teacher capacity was conceptualized and formulated from the "days of the normal school" to the present day. Here the discussion is not only about what teachers should come to know, believe and care about, but also what they bring with them to the teaching experience. Reflecting on their review of the education literature and the state of the scene in teacher education McDiarmid and Mary Clevenger-Bright argue that it now time to rethink "teacher capacity."

Tyrone C. Howard and Glenda R. Aleman's chapter, *Teacher capacity for diverse learners: what do teachers need to know?*, is a response to McDiarmid and Clevenger's call to rethink teacher capacity. They interject a good deal of present day reality from the schools and teacher education programs into the discourse on teacher capacity and recommend a critical approach to preparing teacher candidates that connects critical multicultural theory and practice (e.g. problem-posing /Praxis: critical literacy). Howard and Aleman argue that this approach is needed in order to develop teacher capacity to change the environments in schools. They claim that, "What teachers need to know, care about, and be able to do can/should no longer be thought about in a context where inequities that relate to race, class and gender and other markers of identity are ignored or tolerated." They point out that although the past thirty years have witnessed a good deal of research concerned with preparing teachers with knowledge, skills, and dispositions to effectively teach in a culturally diverse and low-income classrooms, this effort has fallen far short.

Carl A. Grant and Vonzell Agosto's *Teacher Capacity and Social Justice in Teacher Education* is also a response to McDiarmid and Clevenger's call to rethink teacher capacity, as well as to add to critical discourse on teacher capacity that we see in Howard and Aleman's chapter. Implicitly these authors argue that in the U.S., people of color have historically always had thoughts of "justice" in their knowledge, skills, and dispositions when considering both schooling for their children and the preparation of teachers—both black and white—who would teach their children and other children. Also, the authors contend that over the past two decades there has been a reawakening of attention to social justice, which a number of educators are trying to make catch hold in all of education, especially teacher education. However, Grant and Augusto argue that before the concept and practice of social justice can become embedded in teacher education generally, and teacher capacity specifically, much basic work needs to take place and be in place including, for example, definitions, guiding theories, understanding and acknowledgement of the role of context, and conceptual tools for adjudication of these issues.

The artifacts included in this section pay attention to the idea of freedom and educational opportunities for traditionally marginalized groups. They challenge members of mainstream and non-mainstream groups alike to strive for human rights and civil rights in education and all other areas of life. All the writings in this section were selected because of their elegance, advocacy, and candor.

James Baldwin's *A Talk to Teachers*, which is a piece that has been used over the years in many teacher education programs, introduces numerous ideas that educators should contemplate when considering teacher capacity. In addition, Baldwin asserted a revealing truth in 1974, which continues to have currency today. He stated "What is upsetting the country is a sense of its own identity. If, for example, one managed to change the curriculum in all the schools so that Negroes learned more about themselves and their real contributions to this culture, you would be liberating not only Negroes, you'd be liberating white people who know nothing about their history" (p. 4).

The artifact by Maxine Greene, excerpted from *The Dialectic of Freedom* (1988), demands that we step away from the technical and rational discourse often found in discussions of teacher capacity and attend instead to the challenges and possibilities of "freedom" available in thinking about teacher capacity. "Freedom," according to Green is "about overcoming barriers and obstacles that challenge and impede individuals from finding their true selves and realizing their potential" (Reed & Johnson, 2000, p. 125). Green argues that education should help individuals reach beyond themselves "by means of education they may be empowered to think about what they are doing, to become mindful, to share meanings, to conceptualize, to make varied sense of their worlds" (cited in Reed & Johnson, 2000, p. 126). Teacher capacity, according to Green would embrace teachers' actions and practice which are actions of freedom.

All of Paulo Freire's writings have major implications for thought and action about teacher capacity. *Teachers as Cultural Workers: Letters to Those who Dare Teach* (2006) is no exception. In fact, it speaks directly to the attitude/disposition dimension of teacher capacity. Freire identifies eight qualities that are indispensable to the progressive teacher; qualities he believes are acquired gradually through practice and are developed concurrently). Each of the qualities, while readily associated with teacher dispositions; also have meaning for how knowledge and skills are exercised by teachers.

Katrina B. Flores' *They're Calling Us Names* is the fourth and final artifact in this section—and it differs in format from the other three. It is a poem that speaks provocatively about the knowledge, skills, and attitude/dispositions teachers must have, while implicitly supporting what McDiarmid and Clevenger and others in this section argue, namely that, "the old formula of knowledge, skills and disposition are now too static and individualistic a framework for thinking about teacher capacity, limiting our understanding of what teachers need to know, be able to do and care about." As a student who very recently lived the P/K-12 classroom experience, Flores demands that educators rethink their notion of teacher capacity and respond to the needs and contributions of students today in order to promote their achievements and pride.

The significance of the four commentaries to the section is multiple. Each brings powerful insights that add to and extend the discussion of teacher capacity in the section. Each brings sophistication and independence of thought since they are written by scholars who are major stakeholders occupying a particular critical space within the field of education.

Chicago educators Maureen Gillette's and Brian Schultz's commentary, *Do You See What I See? Teacher Capacity as a Vision for Education in a Democracy*, is written from their perspectives as teacher educators at a large urban state institution noted as being the most ethnically diverse university in the Midwest. They argue that teacher candidates need to acquire content knowledge base that is multicultural and develop critical thinking skills in order to help their students succeed. Another important contribution their commentary makes to the section is the argument about the importance of collaboration between the faculty in teacher education and the faculty in the liberal sciences.

Donna M. Gollnick's *Teacher Capacity for Diversity* locates the discussion of teacher capacity within larger issues of accreditation, particularly the work of the National Council for Accreditation of Teacher Education (NCATE). Gollnick help us to understand how teacher capacity is defined within an accreditation agency. She explains the tensions between different stakeholders regarding where emphasis on capacity should be placed in teacher education and tells us about how NCATE has been a strong advocate for diversity and social justice. In addition, Gollnick helps us to see how the meaning of social justice is in the eye of the beholder, and that a negative interpretation of this concept can lead to an attack by those who believe that "social justice" embedded within teacher capacity articulates a disposition based in leftist ideology and is politicizing teacher education.

Pam Grossman, Morva McDonald, Karen Hammerness and Matthew Ronfeldt's *Dismantling Dichotomies in Teacher Education* argues that we should step outside of the box as we think about teacher capacity and consider it less about distinct forms of knowledge and beliefs and more about classroom practices, emphasizing the importance of integrating theoretical principles with the enactment of practice in the preparation of teachers. Grossman *et al.* claim that the current debate on teacher capacities has a dichotomy at its core. They contend that research in multicultural education rarely references the teaching of subject matter and that those who teach subject matter overlook issues of race, class, and language. Grossman and her colleagues offer a model of teacher capacity that views preparing teachers to teach subject matter and teaching for social justice as interdependent. To this end, they argue that three fundamental shifts are required on the part of teacher educators: (1) undo the dichotomies between subject matter and social justice; (2) focus upon helping novices develop and refine practices; and (3) explicitly prepare teacher candidates for the schools attended by the lowest achieving students.

The final commentary is Kevin's K. Kumashiro's *Partial Movements Toward Teacher Quality . . . and their potential for advancing social justice*. Kumashiro, from the Center for Anti-Oppressive Education and the University of Illinois-Chicago, reminds us that at a time when the official discourse in the country is narrowly defining teacher quality, it is important to remember that teacher educators have long argued that teacher capacity cannot be defined without considering its context. Using an anti-oppressive lens, Kumashiro introduces three enduring questions about the necessary and troubling relation between teacher quality and (anti)oppressive movements in school and society. Kumashiro's queries push us to consider partiality, paradox, and resistance as we teach for change and social justice.

The overarching importance of teacher capacity

Finally, this section on teacher capacity has an exceedingly strong connection to, and in many ways helps to shape the arguments in the other sections. These include arguments about the purpose of teacher education, where teachers should acquire their professional knowledge and skills, who should be allowed to enter the profession, how teachers learn, who should govern teacher education, how do we determine teacher quality are critical and fundamental questions to improving education in the United States. In addition, these questions provide much of the contextual influences for asking "What teachers need to know, care about, and be able to do?"

REFERENCES

Bestor, A. E. (1955) *The restoration of learning*. New York: Alfred A. Knopf.

Callahan, R. E. (1962) *Education and the cult of efficiency*. Chicago: University of Chicago Press.

Carnegie Forum on Education and the Economy (1986) *A Nation prepared: teachers of the 21st century*. Washington, DC: Author.

Conant, J. B. (1963) *The education of American teachers*. New York: McGraw-Hill.

Holmes Group (1986) *Tomorrow's teachers: a report of the Holmes Group*. East Lansing, MI: Author.

Koerner, J. (1963) *The miseducation of American teachers*. Boston: Houghton Mifflin.

Nash, G. B., Howe, J. R., Davis, A. F., Jeffrey, J. R., Frederick, P. J., & Winkler, A. M. (1990) *The American people*. New York: Harper & Row.

Reed, R. F. & Johnson, T. W. (2000) *Philosophical documents in education*, 2nd edition. New York: Longman.

Rickover, H. G. (1959) *Education and freedom*. New York: E. P. Dutton.

Yapp, N. (2000) *The American millennium*. London: Konemann/Hulton.

9 Rethinking teacher capacity

G. Williamson McDiarmid and
Mary Clevenger-Bright
University of Washington

INTRODUCTION

In their 1861 petition, the Committee on State Normal Schools urged the California Superintendent of Public Instruction to create such schools because "a very learned man may profoundly understand a subject himself, and yet fail egregiously in elucidating it to others" (State Office, 1889). The authors then identified the areas in which teachers needed to demonstrate competence:

> ... the powers, capacities, and laws of growth of the mind; the order, as to time, in which the different faculties are to be addressed and developed; the best modes of their development; the special adaptation of each school study to the particular necessities and faculties of the juvenile mind; the laws of bodily health as to ventilation, posture, school calisthenics and gymnastics; ... the moral natures of children ... best methods of school organization, classification, programmes of daily exercises, and modes of teaching, as exemplified in the best systems and best schools in the world; and the knowledge so acquired is practically applied in the model or experimental school (a necessary part of a Normal School) in the presence of competent and experienced teachers.

Nearly a century and a half later, we continue to revisit what we believe teachers need to know, be able to do, and care about. This long-standing conversation about teacher capacity exhibits both continuities and discontinuities. Although policymakers, regulators, researchers, critics, and teacher educators have disagreed about how each is defined, weighted in importance, learned, and assessed, three broad categories appear to capture the spectrum of teacher capacities across time: (1) *knowledge*, including subject matter, pedagogical content knowledge, curriculum, pedagogy, educational foundations (multicultural as well as historical, philosophical, sociological, and psychological), policy context, diverse learners (including those with special needs) and their cultures, technology, child and adolescent development, group processes and dynamics, theories of learning, motivation, assessment; (2) *craft skills*, including planning, organizing, and orchestrating instruction, using instructional materials and technology, disciplining pupils, managing groups, monitoring and evaluating learning, collaborating with colleagues, parents, and community and social service agencies; and (3) *dispositions*, including beliefs, attitudes, values, and commitments.

As we will see, debates and assertions about the teacher preparation curriculum tend to focus on what teachers need to know and are able to do. Although no less controversial, specifying dispositions—what teachers should believe and care about—and how these are to be developed has proven more elusive. To some degree, programs have used admissions processes and standards to address dispositions. Normal school candidates were required to demonstrate "high moral character," presumably through the testimonies of referees. Today, selective programs, in search of candidates with dispositions the faculty deem essential, may ask for evidence of particular experiences, such as living or working in a cross-cultural setting, as a proxy for desired dispositions. Meanwhile, finger printing and background checks have formalized the process of ensuring minimally acceptable "moral character."

Of course, teacher candidates also begin their teacher preparation programs with varying knowledge and skills, many absorbed unconsciously from observing their own teachers (Lortie, 1975). Teacher educators rely on others, such as colleagues in arts and science departments, to ensure that future teachers possess certain essential knowledge such as subject matter (McDiarmid, 1994). Building teacher capacity, thus, depends, to some considerable extent, on what teacher candidates bring with them and on the knowledge, skills, and dispositions they develop in other settings.

In what follows, we examine some of these continuities and discontinuities across time and describe developments in the social, political, and intellectual context that shape our current understandings. We also want to identify some of the key debates over teacher capacity, particular debates about dispositions. Our goal is to offer a framework for thinking both about what constitutes teacher capacity as well as how it can be best developed. In particular, we want to argue, based on what we have discovered about teacher learning and knowledge and changes in the broader context, for rethinking the timeframe, opportunities, and contexts for developing critical knowledge, skills, and dispositions. We also want to argue that the developing culture of evidence in education, fostered in large part by accountability policies, holds the promise of more rigorous approaches to assessing teacher capacity.

DEFINING TEACHER CAPACITY

"[T]he ability to receive, hold, or absorb" is the first definition of "capacity" offered by the *American Heritage Dictionary*. A subsequent definition, perhaps most pertinent for this chapter, is: "The power to learn or retain knowledge; mental ability." Yet another definition suggests a dynamic dimension of capacity: "Innate potential for growth, development, or accomplishment." All three of these definitions have implications for how we conceptualize what it is that teachers bring to teaching.

"Capacity" rarely stands alone but rather in relationship to some purpose or goal—a capacity to accomplish or perform X. When we speak of the "capacity of an organization," for example, we are usually referring to its ability to carry out certain functions, meet particular goals and expectations. Currently, the term is used in policy circles typically referring to the efforts of schools, districts, and states to enhance the human resources needed to bring about curricular and instructional reform (Barnes, 2002; Cohen & Ball, 1999; Corcoran & Lawrence, 2003; Massell, 1998, 2000). Thus, in the current educational context, the meaning of "capacity" seems closer to the idea of "potential for growth" than to "ability to receive."

Such an interpretation of "capacity" is also consistent with the growing understanding of learning to teach as a nearly life-long phenomenon. The journey begins with Lortie's (1975) "apprenticeship of observation" in P-12 classrooms and continues through preservice—including both arts and sciences as well as professional preparation programs—into the induction years and beyond (Feiman-Nemser, 2001). The term "teacher capacity" suggests the potential for teachers to continue to develop their knowledge, skills, and dispositions along the continuum.

The idea of enhancing teachers' capacity along the learning continuum has a particular appeal because of the ever-rising expectations for teachers. As we will see, expectations, always high, have, in recent years, risen almost exponentially. Driving these expectations are a range of forces—changing demographics, policy initiatives, technology, and phenomenal growth of knowledge as well as in our growing understanding of what successful teaching requires. As we will argue, understanding teacher learning and knowledge across time also requires attention to the social contexts in which teachers find themselves.

CONCEPTIONS OF TEACHER CAPACITY OVER TIME

As the authors of a recent review of research on teachers' knowledge point out, the category of "teacher knowledge"—connoting propositional and procedural knowledge as well as dispositions—as an object of study is relatively new, appearing only in the last two and a half decades (Munby et al., 2001). The term "teacher capacity" seems to have entered the conversation fairly recently, although the underlying concept has, of course, been around for years. Over time, the job of ensuring that teachers have the requisite capacities to meet public expectations for schools has fallen to those who have provided—or overseen those who provide—professional preparation. The curricular requirements established by those who have educated and certified teachers reveal what teachers have been thought to need to know, be able to do, and care about. Using the lens of curriculum and standards to explore the history of "teacher capacity" reveals a concept that, at least superficially, appears, at least until recently, stable over time.

In the United States, the normal school movement of the nineteenth century was an occasion for defining requisite teacher knowledge, skills, and dispositions. On the occasion of opening the normal school at Barre in 1839, Massachusetts Governor Everett, foreshadowing the standard normal school curriculum well into the twentieth century, described the four "core" areas of study for teachers (Everett, 1839, quoted in Ogren, 2005). These were: (1) subject matter: "careful review of the branches of knowledge required to be taught in out common schools" (p. 42); (2) pedagogical methods: "the art of teaching ... those principles of our nature on which education depends; the laws which control the faculties of the youthful mind in pursuit and attainment of the truth; and the moral sentiments on the part of teacher and pupil which must be brought into harmonious action" (p. 48); (3) "the government of the school" which included the moral influence of teachers; and (4) practice teaching (Ogren, 2005). To ensure that candidates exhibited the proper ethical dispositions, "good moral character" was an admissions requirement, vouchsafed, apparently, by recommendation letters to this effect (Ogren, 2005).

Sixty years after the California Committee on Normal Schools described at the outset of this chapter, the official view of what teaching required had changed relatively little (Ogren, 2005). According to the Course of Study and Syllabus for the College Graduate Certificates (1922), the University of the State of New York instructed the state schools of education to ensure that graduates seeking provisional teaching certificates were knowledgeable in four areas: (1) psychology, both "general and educational"; (2) history of education; (3) principles of education; (4) subject matter and methods of teaching (University of the State of New York, 1922, p. 5).

These historical documents, particularly the 1922 syllabus, suggest a broad view of teacher capacity. Teachers were expected to know the content of the core school disciplines, differentiated between elementary and secondary, as well as how to teach these subjects. In addition, they were also expected to have mastered a broad range of foundational knowledge, especially psychology and history but also sociology, school governance, philosophy and "educational theory." Methods included "no more than 2 [out of the six prescribed for methods] semester hours . . . [of] observation and practice" (University of the State of New York, 1922, p. 5). In-school practica, often in affiliated demonstration or laboratory schools, were standard fare in the normal school and teacher college curriculum.

The idea that teachers' capacities would need to continue developing across their careers does not appear in these documents. This may have been due to the expectation that most teachers would enter the profession on a temporary basis before moving on to other careers (Ogren, 2005). This is also consistent with an era in which general knowledge growth was comparatively slow. Changes in disciplinary and pedagogical knowledge and in demographics were not so rapid as to require teachers to frequently update their knowledge. In addition, expectations for what pupils needed to know were fairly low; few continued on into higher education, most entering the work force right out of school. With the notable exception of urban school systems, classrooms tended to be considerably more ethnically, racially, and socially homogenous than they have become and special needs pupils were either educated separately or not at all.

The Great Depression was an occasion for a re-examination of expectations for schools and teachers—at least among progressive educators. John Dewey and George Counts, in particular, argued that teachers must commit to and pursue social reconstruction, captured in the title of Counts' controversial work, *Dare the Schools Build a New Social Order?* (1932). Although teaching as a social and moral calling pervaded earlier commentaries and preparation programs, Counts went further. He argued that teachers were "under a heavy social obligation to protect and further" the interests of the people against those of the failed capitalist class (Counts, 1932, quoted in Cremin, 1988, p. 188). Dewey, for his part, believed that schools and teachers should "form the understanding and the dispositions necessary for movement in the direction of social change" (Cremin, 1988, p. 195)—a theme that continues to echo down to the present.

A contemporary of Dewey and Counts, Robert Hutchins, President of the University of Chicago, spoke for a more traditional stance toward the purpose of schools—and of teaching—in 1936: "Education implies teaching. Teaching implies knowledge. Knowledge implies truth. Truth is everywhere the same" (Hutchins, 1936). For Hutchins and others who rejected the social reconstruction agenda, teachers principally needed knowledge of the "eternal truths" available through the great books of the Western world and the classical curriculum—rhetoric, logic, grammar, and mathematics. It was up to a Hutchins's protégé, Mortimer Adler, to subsequently popularize such a curriculum through his *Paideia Proposal* (1982), adding the pedagogical gloss of Socratic seminars. Teacher capacity appears, from this viewpoint, to consist in being liberally educated and capable of orchestrating such seminars.

This debate about the purpose and goals of teaching—central to specifying "teacher capacity"—continues today. Critics of traditional university-based teacher preparation charge, in line with Hutchins, that these programs typically pursue a social reconstruction agenda and, as a consequence, fail to adequately prepare teachers (Steiner, 2003). Social reconstruction proponents continue to argue that teachers need to be committed to and pursue a social justice agenda (Cochran-Smith, 1999, 2004; McLaren, 1995; see also Howard and Aleman in this volume, Chapter 10). We will revisit this debate below.

A key related and consequential curriculum development, chronicled by Urban, was the foundations movement of the late 1920s. A group of scholars at Teachers College, strongly influenced by Dewey and their colleague William Kilpatrick, developed a curriculum for non-methods courses that focused less on the concerns of the constituent foundational disciplines and more on educational issues through disciplinary lenses. In addition, in the tradition of both Dewey and Counts, the curriculum was intended to encourage prospective teachers to question how well schools and classrooms served democratic goals and values (Urban, 1990). Arguably, encouraging prospective teachers to take a critical stance toward schools and the status quo has frequently brought university teacher educators and preservice teachers into conflict with practicing educators.

Throughout the 1940s and 1950s, while the debate on expectations seems to have focused less on teacher dispositions and more on the school curriculum, antagonism between the social reconstructionists and the classicists continued to fuel the debate (Cremin, 1988). Those, in the Hutchins tradition, who felt that the school curriculum had been hijacked by the "life-adjustors" (Bestor, 1953)—thereby fatally diluting the intellectual and academic purposes of public schools—were in particularly high dudgeon after the launch of "Sputnik" (Rickover, 1993). For them and some part of the public, the U.S. had fallen behind the Soviets in science and technology because of the tepid "life-adjustment" fare served up by schools and teachers. Koerner (1963), speaking for others in the academy and beyond, placed the blame squarely on the doorstep of schools and colleges of education.

Other than the transformation of foundations, most elements of the curriculum remained stable while the institutional setting changed markedly (Caliver, 1933: Orgen, 2005; Pangburn, 1932). State normal schools transformed into state colleges—in response, partially, to the influx of WWII veterans—and state colleges, over time, into universities. After WWII, attention was increasingly riveted on producing a sufficient number of teachers to staff schools running double shifts to accommodate the post-war baby boom. As the number of universities housing departments of education increased, educational faculty, seeking to establish status parity with colleagues in the arts and sciences, increased their research reach and activity. Programs of research focused on teachers and teaching began to emerge. Thus, a new community—researchers—joined the conversation about teachers' knowledge, skills, and dispositions.

An early foray into research on teacher capacity was studies to identify the personal characteristics of effective teachers (Ryans, 1960; Gage, 1963). This research sought to identify observable patterns of "classroom behaviors, attitudes, viewpoints, and intellectual and emotional qualities which may characterize teachers" (Ryans, 1960, p. 9). Absent—at least in the study that Ryans (1960) reports—is any attempt to associate characteristics with pupil learning. The findings seem to have added little to understanding teacher capacity. For instance, teachers whose principals rated them highly were found to be more favorable toward their pupils and teachers judged "warm and understanding" had more favorable attitudes toward pupils and administrators.

The alarm that Admiral Rickover and others raised over losing the scientific and technological lead to the Soviets prompted the National Science Foundation, in the 1960s, to make sizeable grants to universities and educational development organizations to overhaul school curricula and retrain teachers, particularly in mathematics and sciences but also in social sciences (Dow, 1991). Not only were teachers expected to know more about the disciplines—especially mathematics, sciences, and social sciences—but the new curricula were also grounded in the idea that pupils need to conduct their own inquiries, to act as scientists, mathematicians, and social scientists (Dow, 1991).

Against the backdrop of the Great Society and the War on Poverty, the 1960s were a time of great faith in social science as a means to solve societal problems, including low-performing African American pupils. James Coleman, a sociologist, brought sophisticated statistical models to bear on large-scale data sets to identify the factors influencing pupil achievement (Coleman, 1966). Ironically, this research was to raise questions about the influence of teachers and other in-school factors—other than the race and class of one's classmates—on pupil achievement (Jencks, 1972).

In the 1970s, educational researchers endeavored to establish a new science of teaching by first correlating observations of teachers' behaviors with pupil test scores and, subsequently, experimentally testing the causal nature of particular behaviors (Gage, 1963, 1971; Rosenshine & Furst, 1972). This "process-product" research focused on identifying specific behaviors or skills—question asking, explaining, wait time, time on task, classroom management techniques, and so on—that produced pupil learning (for reviews, see Brophy & Good, 1986; Gage, 1978; Waxman & Walberg, 1991; Zumwalt, 1988). The hallmark of teacher capacity, thus, was knowledge and application of these research-validated behaviors.

This research coincided with an increasing push for accountability of public institutions in the political arena and the idea of scientifically validated, observable teaching skills resonated with policy makers (Linn, 2001). The result was state policies to ensure teacher competence, based at least in part on the findings from process-product research. Practically, these policies often manifest as extensive checklists of skills against which the classroom performances of beginning teachers were judged (Hall, 1981). This, in turn, shaped the curricula of teacher preparation programs, many of which introduced "research on teaching" courses and student-teaching evaluation forms that mimicked the state competency checklists (Cooper & Weber, 1973; Dodl & Schalock, 1973). This skills-dominated view of teaching and teachers mirrored the "back-to-basics" curriculum movement in the K-12 system.

Just as process-product researchers had reacted to the limitations they saw in research on teacher characteristics during the 1950s, researchers in the 1980s responded to the limitations they saw in process-product research. This coincided with a growing interest in developing approaches to studying and understanding learning in what has been termed the "cognitive revolution" (Gardner, 1985). Some teacher researchers explored the "interior" lives of teachers—their decision- and sense-making, thinking, and learning processes as well as their knowledge and dispositions (Clark & Peterson, 1986; Feiman-Nemser & Floden, 1986; Lampert, 1985). Teacher education programs incorporated formal opportunities for preservice teachers to "reflect," to make manifest—for themselves and others—their interpretations of what they were experiencing in classrooms, and to take a critical stand toward their assumptions and actions (Calderhead & Gates, 1993; Schon, 1984, 1990; Zeichner & Liston, 1996). A view of teaching as continually responding to changing circumstances and interacting with the curriculum and diverse learners challenged earlier views of teaching as applying scientifically validated methods in covering the curriculum.

In the policy arena, evidence that policymakers found compelling began to mount that teachers—and their relative capacities—do, indeed, make a difference. Using econometric statistical tools, researchers found that teacher "quality"—defined by degrees, credentials, and experience—was the single most significant in-school influence on student achievement (Ferguson, 1991; Ferguson & Ladd, 1996; Greenwald et al., 1996). These findings spurred policymakers in a number of states, particularly those that had launched ambitious standards-based reforms, to increase their investment in teacher development. In Kentucky, for example, state funding for professional development increased from less than a dollar per student in the late 1980s to $24 per student by the mid-1990s (Foster, 1999).

Standards-based reforms, beginning in the 1990s, raised expectations for teacher capacity dramatically. No longer was meeting minimum academic levels of competence sufficient; all pupils were expected to meet publicly established standards. Public account-ability systems raised stakes even higher. What teachers were expected to know, be able to do, and care about had not only increased markedly but had become substantially more complex. The forces that have fueled this increase in expectations and complexity show no signs of abating.

EVOLVING AND EXPANDING CONCEPTIONS OF CAPACITY

As suggested above, the past two decades have seen more attention focused on teacher capacity than at any previous time in history. This is, as we have seen, due to a confluence of factors: research underlining teachers' significance in pupil learning; various reports—from the Holmes Group (1988, 1990), the Carnegie Task Force on Teaching as a Profession, (1986), and the National Commission on Teaching and America's Future (1996, 2003)—focused on improving teacher quality; and state and federal policies of high-stakes assessments and accountability. The conception of teacher capacity embed-ded in the curricula of normal schools and, later, state colleges and, finally, universities has burgeoned dramatically. The areas of expansion, described below, reflect currents not only in academia and policy but also in society at large.

Rethinking teacher knowledge of subject matter

A major criticism leveled at the exclusively skilled-focused view of teacher capacity was the lack of attention to teachers' knowledge and understanding of their subject matter as a major factor in pupil learning (Shulman, 1986). Shulman and his students explored the role that teachers' knowledge of subject matter for teaching—what Shulman termed "pedagogical content knowledge"—played in their capacity (Grossman, 1990; Wilson *et al.*, 1987; Wilson & Wineburg, 1988). These case studies interjected into the con-versation much richer and more textured accounts of teachers' subject matter knowledge than ever before. Teachers need to know not only the substance of the discipline—long recognized as vital to teacher capacity—but also how to best represent the content to diverse learners. To do this well requires knowledge of curriculum materials, common pupil difficulties with the content, the context of learning, and the goals of the enterprise (Shulman, 1987).

Whether they acknowledge it or not, teachers draw on their typically tacit understand-ings of the various dimensions—substance, structure, and syntax (Schwab, 1962)—of subject matter knowledge when they plan, carry out, and assess instruction as well as when they interact with colleagues, parents, and others. To claim that this is a much richer and more textured conception of teachers' subject matter knowledge than that on which educators and others have previously operated understates the difference. Although arguing for rich subject matter understanding, researchers in this area did not claim this is sufficient for successful teaching. Recent research, using large data sets rather than the earlier case study approach, seems to confirm what many believed self-evident: differences in teachers' knowledge of teaching particular subject matter, which also involves substantive knowledge of the subject, produces differences in pupil learning (Hill *et al.*, 2005).

Moreover, such rich understandings may also be necessary to ensure that pupils with diverse interests and backgrounds have equitable access to knowledge. The better teachers know the landscape of the subject matter they teach, the better able they are to find productive points of access for different pupils (McDiarmid, 1991, 1993). This view of the role of teachers' subject matter knowledge overlaps with the idea of teachers' responsibilities for providing equitable access to knowledge.

Revisiting teachers' social responsibilities

The modern civil rights movement prompted scholars and advocates to agitate for greater attention to teaching poor children and those of color and to addressing the effects of race, social class, and gender differences on learning opportunities (Banks, 1988; Grant & Sleeter, 1996; see Grant & Agosto, this volume, Chapter 11). In the wake of the *Brown* decision, African Americans, Mexican Americans, American Indians and other groups demanded school curricula that reflect the range of experiences, histories, and cultures that make up the U.S.—as well as teachers with the knowledge, skills, and dispositions to work successfully with children of color (Banks, 1988). By 1977, the National Council for the Accreditation of Teacher Education *Standards* required teacher preparation programs to include multicultural courses and components (NCATE, 1977). In addition to knowing the history and cultures of ethnic, racial, and social groups, teachers were expected to know about the learning preferences and linguistic challenges of pupils from different backgrounds (Banks, 1988; Grant & Sleeter, 1996).

As the accountability movement picked up steam during the 1990s, states implemented pupil assessment and school accountability systems to identify "failing" or "at-risk" schools. This drew renewed attention to the disparities in test scores between and among schools serving different groups of pupils—Euro-American, Latinos, African Americans, American Indians; rural, urban, and suburban; rich and poor; native speakers and English language learners; regular and special needs (Johnston & Viadero, 2000; Farkas, 2003; Jencks & Phillips, 1998). Assessment results from schools and districts around the country provided yet more evidence that teachers, especially those in high-needs schools, needed better preparation to work with pupils who came from historically under-served populations (Ladson-Billings, 1999, 1994; Gay, 2002; Sleeter & Grant, 1987).

Beginning in 2001, federal No Child Left Behind (NCLB) legislation raised the heat on educators even higher by requiring that assessment data be disaggregated by subgroups and that schools meet improvement goals for all the subgroups or face sanctions. The persistent "gaps" in test scores between students of Euro-American origins and those of color have prompted states and districts to develop and publish standards for "cultural competency" to which teacher preparation programs must respond (for example, see Alaska Department of Education and Early Childhood, 1999; Oregon Department of Education, 2004; Seattle Public Schools, 2005). In addition to greater knowledge of various groups as well as their own cultural viewpoints, teachers are expected to teach in "culturally responsive" ways (Gay, 2002; Ladson-Billings, 1999).

Rethinking teachers and democratic education

In a related vein, John Goodlad and his colleagues, building on a theme central to Dewey and earlier progressives, have argued, over the past two decades, for greater attention to the unique and critical role that schooling and teachers play in a democratic society (Goodlad, 1997; Goodlad & McMannon, 1997; Soder, 1995; Soder *et al.*, 2001). In this view, teachers are responsible for nurturing the democratic dispositions, habits, and practices of their pupils even as they ensure pupils learn academic knowledge and skills. At the heart of their argument is the fundamental democratic value of ensuring equitable access to knowledge for every pupil—a theme central in multicultural arguments as well

(Goodlad & Keating, 1994). Although this presupposes some minimal level of classroom skills and knowledge, teaching in support of the "democratic agenda" is primarily dispositional. That is, possessing and acting on commitments to access to knowledge for all learners, cultivation of democratic values, and stewardship of public schools.

For some—heirs to George Counts' "social reconstruction" mission—educating pupils to be knowledgeable, participating, and productive citizens of their communities and the country is not enough. They argue that teachers must help their pupils understand the inequities—of power as well as wealth—inherent in capitalist social and economic institutions and society at large (McLaren, 1995). For these critics, multicultural education is insufficient to the task; conditions call for a "multicultural revolution." From this viewpoint, teacher capacity includes not only the knowledge of how the economic and social system operate to maintain a repressive status quo but also commitment and actions to change the world, to change the distribution of power and resources. As we argued above, the implications for teacher capacity are primarily in the arena of dispositions.

Rethinking standards and accountability for teachers

In *A Nation Prepared* (1986), the Carnegie Task Force on Teaching as a Profession provided a view of teachers' work that is notably ambitious and comprehensive. Partly a response to *A Nation At Risk*—the 1983 report decrying the economic crisis purportedly created by substandard public education in the U.S.—the report describes what pupils and their teachers need to know to keep up with a rapidly changing world of work:

> Teachers should have a good grasp of the ways in which different kinds of physical and social systems work; a feeling for data and what uses to which they can be put; an ability to help students see patterns where others see only confusion; an ability to foster genuine creativity . . .; and the ability to work with other people in work groups that decide for themselves how to get a job done. They must be able to learn all the time . . . Teachers will not come to school knowing all they have to know, but knowing how to figure out what they need to know . . .
>
> (p. 25)

To help recognize teachers with these capacities, the report called for the creation of a National Board for Professional Teaching Standards "to establish standards for high professional teaching competence" (p. 66). This reflected a broader movement toward establishing standards for teachers as well as pupils. Professional associations such as the National Association of Teachers of Mathematics (1989) and the American Association for the Advancement of Science (Rutherford & Ahlgren, 1990) led the way, publishing standards for both pupils and teachers. Individual states, prompted in part by the federal Goals 2000 legislation, also developed standards for pupils and teachers.

Perhaps no single development has raised the profile of teacher capacity more than the implementation of pupil assessment and accountability systems in virtually all the states (Linn, 2000). State departments of education and districts as well as schools invested heavily in increasing teacher capacity through professional development. Many states also instituted tests for teachers—at first, in basic skills and, subsequently, in subject matter and pedagogical knowledge (Darling-Hammond, 1999).

Close on the heels of state-developed standards, assessments, and accountability systems, the federal government entered the fray directly. Until the end of the last century, determining the adequacy of teachers' knowledge, skills, and dispositions was left to the states. The reauthorized Higher Education Act, in 1998, forced states to report to the

U.S. Department of Education a range of data intended to capture the quality of teacher preparation in the state. NCLB legislation requires that states and districts ensure that all pupils are taught by a federally defined "highly qualified" teacher. In defining what this means, the architects of the legislation reveal their conception of teacher capacity: "To be deemed highly qualified, teachers must have: (1) a bachelor's degree, (2) full state certification or licensure, and (3) prove that they know each subject they teach" (U.S. Department of Education, n.d.). Although this appears to reduce teacher capacity largely to knowing the subjects taught, the requirement for state certification suggests that teachers also need professional knowledge, as defined by the state.

Equally important, the federal government has, concurrently, attempted to wrest control of certification away from the states as well. The U.S. Department of Education has supported—to the tune of $40 million to date—the creation of the American Board for Certification of Teaching Excellence (ABCTE), an alternative to state certification. Applicants must pass online tests in both subject matter knowledge and professional knowledge, acknowledging, as does NCLB, that teaching requires more than knowledge of content alone (American Board for Certification of Teaching Excellence, n.d.).

ABCTE proponents are vocal in their determination to end the "educational establishment's" purported "monopoly" on teacher standards and licensing (Blair, 2003). Yet, standards for ABCTE and those for the National Board for Professional Teaching Standards (NBPTS) overlap considerably, although the former has, to date, published standards only for beginning teachers (the NBPTS Standards are designed for experienced teachers). Both sets of standards include; (1) knowledge of content areas; (2) classroom skills, including organizing, planning, and designing lessons; managing diverse groups of pupils; using a range of instructional approaches; differentiating instruction according to individual needs; and monitoring and evaluating pupil learning; and (3) working with parents.

Areas where the standards differ represent, on the other hand, markedly divergent conceptions of teacher capacity. Perhaps because their audience is beginning teachers, the ABCTE Standards tend to be more prescriptive ("communicating by listing the lesson objectives" "present material in a logical sequence with small steps") and appear to draw heavily on practices identified as effective in process-product research—questioning techniques, time on task, graphic organizers, and so on. In short, ABCTE has taken a "social efficiency" (Zeichner & Liston, 1990) view of teacher capacity.

The NBPTS, on the other hand, includes practices that seem as much dispositions as skills, such as "thinking systematically about . . . practice and learning from experience" and "working collaboratively with other professionals on instructional policy curriculum development and staff development." The NBPTS standards appear informed by a broader conception of teacher capacity, a conception that is infused with the rethinking of teacher knowledge, skills, dispositions, and learning that has occurred over the past couple of decades.

Another area of teacher capacity that has emerged in the last decade, has been strongly supported by federal and state agencies, and, yet, figures marginally if at all in standards is the classroom use of information and instructional technology. The federal government has made substantial investments in improving the classroom technological knowledge and skills of educators—practicing teachers, preservice teachers, and teacher educators alike. NCLB includes support for enhancing teachers' ability to use informational technology in the classroom (Department of Education, n.d.). At least ten states have explicit educational technology standards (Council of Chief State School Officers, n.d.). Yet, knowledge of informational and instructional technology does not appear in the ABCTE standards (American Board for Certification of Teaching Excellence, n.d.) and receives only brief mention in other standards. One need not accept exaggerated claims for the power of informational technology to revolutionize education to acknowledge the potential of this technology to significantly enhance both teaching and learning.

Rethinking teacher learning and expertise

As noted above, over the past three decades, evolving understandings of how we learn and how we develop expertise have influenced profoundly how we think about what teachers need to know, be able to do, and care about. Specifically, two areas seem to bear, in particular, on our current understanding of teacher capacity: the first is the role that social context plays in our learning and understanding of ourselves, our actions, and our surround; the second is how we develop and deploy our understanding and knowledge over time.

Teaching knowledge and practice as socially mediate

The growing understanding of teaching as a practice that is mediated by the social contexts in which it occurs has profoundly influenced thinking about how to support teachers in maximizing their capacities. Research has deepened our understanding that our experiences are filtered through our socio-cultural surround and the language we use to represent these experiences (Brown *et al.*, 1991; Luria, 1976; Vygotsky, 1962, 1978; Wertsch, 1985). The knowledge, skills, and dispositions that individual teachers bring to teaching are, to a large extent, the products of the social contexts in which these were developed. The "apprenticeship of observation" is not confined to schools. The conceptions of "knowledge," "teaching," "learning," and so on that pervade actions, organizational structures, social relations, and curriculum materials in schools reflect those that pervade experiences outside school and the broader culture (Cohen, 1988). This suggests that the context in which "capacity" is developed is defining, however imperfectly.

We come to understand core concepts—"knowledge," "content," "knowing," "teaching," "learning," and so on—through our interactions with others and our environment. Viewed in a political context, social cognition theory intersects with critical theory: our concepts and the language we use to express them are not value-neutral, socio-cultural constructs; they are shaped by the socio-historical circumstances of unevenly distributed political and economic power (Lakoff, 2000). That is, our concept of "knowledge" itself is defined through a political process. In this process, particular social groups, because of their resources, are able to shape, however imperfectly, fundamental concepts and how they are represented. Not only are our understandings socially mediated but specific historical and political forces also shape the social contexts in which the mediation occurs, as well as the process of mediation itself. Clearly, this is not a rigidly deterministic process—if it were, critical theorists would not exist.[1] It does suggest, however, the profoundly social, cultural, and political character of our understandings, including our understanding of "teacher capacity."

The act of teaching is socially and politically negotiated. What teachers can and cannot do within their classrooms depends, in large part, on others in their surround—colleagues, pupils, administrators, parents, journalists, civic leaders, taxpayers, policymakers, textbook publishers, and so on. The content they teach as well as how they teach it are the products of negotiations between the teacher and a range of policies, materials, and key others. Content standards, curricula, standardized assessments, textbooks, software, and other instructional materials typically represent the ideas of others about what should be taught and how. Thus, to establish their practice, to act in concert with their knowledge, beliefs, purposes, and commitments, teachers must negotiate with key others. Yet the skills, knowledge, and dispositions required for productive social and political negotiations are rarely included in various conceptions of teacher capacity.

Also informing our understanding of teacher capacity is the concept of "situated learning" (Lave & Wenger, 1991). Closely related to socio-cultural theories of learning, the concept captures the idea that learning is, to a substantial degree, a function of the context in which it takes place. A particular idea or practice encountered in a K-12 classroom will be understood differently than if encountered at the university. This helps explain the "two worlds" phenomenon so familiar in teacher education; generations of student teachers have found themselves caught between the expectations of university educators and the realities of school classrooms (Feiman-Nemser & Buchmann, 1983). Such an understanding of learning has implications for both preservice preparation and professional development.

The socially mediated and contextually situated nature of learning also suggests that resources and attention have been disproportionately focused on the development of teachers as individual practitioners, as opposed to members of local "communities of practice" (Little, 1993; Wenger, 1998). School cultures and climate are collective products of educators, pupils, parents, and others in the setting. Even in those instances where teachers isolate themselves, confine themselves to their classrooms and avoid engaging colleagues, they are contributing to a particular school culture and climate. Much of what teachers do, they do in groups, especially creating learning opportunities through choosing, using, and evaluating curricular materials, instructional and assessment methods, and classroom management approaches. In the process, they undergo change and contribute, unwittingly at times, to shared understandings of practice, however tacit these may be.

> Workplace learning is best understood, then, in terms of the communities being formed or joined and personal identities being changed. The central issue in learning is *becoming* a practitioner not learning *about* practice. This approach draws attention away from abstract knowledge and cranial processes and situates it in the practices and communities in which knowledge takes on significance.
>
> (Brown & Duguid, 1991, p. 48)

The argument for purposefully transforming schools into "learning communities" rests on the idea that teaching practices and their under-girding, often tacitly-held understandings need to be made explicit and examined collaboratively. The process of "*becoming* a practitioner" needs to be an explicit and collective subject of focus for collegial learning communities (Kardos *et al.*, 2001).

Thus, teacher capacity, in this view, includes productive participation in these processes of building, collectively, school cultures and "communities of practice."[2] As the work of McLaughlin and Talbert (2001) suggests, however, professional collaboration is not sufficient to improve teaching practice. A critical stance toward practice, one that relies on evidence of practice and pupil learning, may be a necessary corollary.

Although this may have always been a dimension of teacher capacity, our growing understanding of practice as socially mediated has dramatically raised its profile. This suggests that changing the social contexts in which teachers learn and develop may be necessary for real changes in their understanding of their role, the purposes of schooling, and core educational concepts and skills.

Adaptive expertise

A second area of investigation in the learning sciences that speaks to teacher capacity is expertise—specifically, the idea of "adaptive expertise." Expertise itself has been a focus of research for several decades with increasing attention to the concept in teaching (Bereiter & Scaradamalia, 1993; Chi *et al.*, 1988; Leinhart, 1988; Steinberg & Grigorenko, 2003). Summarizing the results of recent studies of expertise, Hatano and Oura (2003) distinguish between "routine" experts "who have had years of problem-solving experiences in a given domain, can solve familiar types of problems quickly and accurately," but often fail to go beyond "procedural efficiency" and "adaptive" experts who "can go beyond the routine competencies, and can be characterized by their flexible, innovative, and creative competencies within the domain, rather than in terms of speed, accuracy, and automaticity of solving familiar problems" (p. 28).

Growing interest in adaptive expertise coincides with increasing attention within the field of teacher education to the idea of a continuum of teacher learning across preparation, induction, and career mentioned above. Viewing teacher development in this way draws attention to the lack of coordination and collaboration at the transition points along the continuum but also to the need to reconsider what teachers need to learn at different points. Educating teachers who develop into adaptive experts within a few years requires a rethinking of not only appropriate learning opportunities but their timing as well.

Viewed as the development of expertise, teacher capacity encompasses teaching as a continuously and rapidly evolving activity. Not only are the demographics of schools and classrooms changing but so too is our knowledge of the social, technological, and natural world (Hage & Powers, 1992; NCTAF, 2003). In addition, federal, state, and local mandates, reforms, and programs come and go, creating a turbulent policy environment (Tyack & Cuban, 1995). At a more micro-level, classrooms and schools are dynamic environments, changing according to the pupils present as well as the curriculum, the time of day, week, and year, and in response to outside events—in the school, families, communities, and beyond. Pupils themselves, as individuals and in groups, are constantly changing—intellectually, physically, socially, and emotionally.

As a consequence, the concept of teacher capacity must include how teachers adapt to these changes and manage the dynamics of the classroom and the school. On the one hand, such constantly changing circumstances and the normal busy-ness of classrooms demand the establishment of routines just to make the teaching enterprise manageable. On the other, the unpredictability of how these changes in so many different spheres will interact over time suggests adaptability as a critical dimension of teacher capacity. Indeed, as Grossman (1995) has pointed out, teachers are constantly creating new knowledge on the fly. That is, they are digesting and interpreting information from their immediate situation through the filters of past experiences, their social context, and their accumulated knowledge, skills, and dispositions. The resulting knowledge is the basis for their decisions and actions that, in turn, initiates a new round of gathering and digesting information. Thus, teachers' capacities are in constant development and change.

Ball and Cohen (1999) have argued that teachers learn "in and from" practice. As they have written, "Teaching occurs in particulars—particular students interacting with particular teachers over particular ideas in particular circumstances ... no amount of knowledge can fully prescribe appropriate or wise practice" (p. 10). Teacher capacity, from this point of view, consists both in establishing routines and being prepared to adapt to specific circumstances that change rapidly and often unpredictably. In the first instance, developing routine expertise consists in learning to solve a particular set of problems—say, the repeated failure of pupils in particular circumstances to turn in homework. As long as the teacher-expert continues to work with pupils in the same circumstances, the routines work. If the pupils change, the routine expert may be stuck with approaches that do not work well (and may end up blaming the pupils). Teaching, therefore, like other occupations pursued under conditions of uncertainty and rapid change, require the purposeful development of adaptive expertise (Bransford *et al.*, 2005).

As we argued above, teaching has increasingly been understood as a socially mediated practice. This suggests that the development of expertise must similarly be understood not merely as an individual phenomenon but a collective outcome. Whether or not teachers develop either routine or adaptive expertise depends, to a great extent, to the contexts in which they work. Indeed, developing adaptive teaching expertise may depend on contexts in which flexible, innovative, even adventuresome practice is supported and encouraged—or, at the very least, not punished. This speaks to the importance of the school context and communities of practice as well as policy contexts in which teachers are, at the very least, comfortable trying out, evaluating, and refining innovative practices.

The old formula of "knowledge, skills, and dispositions" now seems too static and individualistic a framework for thinking about teacher capacity, limiting both our understanding of what teachers need to know, be able to do, and care about and how to ensure they develop their capacities over time. The collaborative framing of the particular circumstances, events, and problems teachers encounter—so critical to their choosing a course of action—is a more specific, dynamic, fluid, uncertain, and socially mediated activity than is captured in these categories. In addition, perhaps central to the entire enterprise is the disposition and ability to step outside of one's practice and examine it in good company and in light of a range of data. The data need to include not only evidence on pupil learning, growth, and development as individuals, workers, community members, and citizens but also colleagues' insights and perspectives as well as community expectations, needs, and goals.

THE DEVELOPING CULTURE OF EVIDENCE

As noted above, much current policy is directed toward increasing accountability for teachers and for teacher preparation programs. In response, many schools are currently engaged in trying to change their cultures so that decisions about instruction and curriculum are based on the analysis of pupil data in which teachers are collectively involved. This represents attempts to change the way schools make decisions by fostering a "culture of evidence" within the school, a culture in which decisions are based on a careful consideration of quality data.

States, districts, and schools have been collecting masses of evidence for many years. This evidence has, apparently, seldom been analyzed and interpreted in ways that drive curricular and instructional decisions toward continuous improvement (Fitz-Gibbon, 2002; Hedges, 2003). Drawing on Toulmin's conception of "warrants" as the vital link between data and conclusions in an argument, Hedges writes,

> . . . a culture of evidence must pay attention not only to evidence, but also to the warrants that link evidence of various kinds to conclusions. Warrants clearly encompass ideas about methods for drawing conclusions given evidence. One of the major contributions of a culture of evidence is not only to make use of evidence, but to make the process of drawing conclusions transparent. That is, a culture of

evidence makes explicit what particular evidence may be linked to a conclusion, but also makes the methodological assumptions, the link between the evidence and the conclusions, explicit.

(p. 3)

Hedges' argument underlines the need to engage teachers, in communities of practice, in making sense of data and implications for practice. Such an approach differs significantly from one in which an administrator interprets the data and attempts to direct classroom practice.

Participating in a culture of evidence suggests that conceptions of teacher capacity include the skills, knowledge, and dispositions to collaboratively collect, analyze, and interpret evidence and translate interpretations of evidence into improved learning opportunities. Classroom assessment has long been a commonplace in some, but by no means all, teacher preparation programs. The inclusion of such courses may not, however, be enough. As schools, under various pressures, move toward greater collective attention to disaggregated evidence of pupil learning, novice as well as experienced teachers may need collaborative opportunities to learn these skills applied to a variety of evidence—both evidence generated as a part of instruction as well as external assessments (Hedges, 2003; Taylor & Nolen, 2004).

As recent reviews of the research on teacher preparation suggest, teacher educators have not systematically and convincingly examined the effects that preparation programs and professional development have had on both classroom teaching practices and pupil learning (Wilson *et al.*, 2001; Cochran-Smith & Zeichner, 2005). Developing cultures of evidence within such programs may be a necessary prerequisite to preparing teachers to participate in similar cultures in schools. Not only could analyzing and interpreting evidence—of program impact both on current students and on graduates and their pupils—improve programs, such an orientation provides a model for prospective teachers.

CONCLUSION

Continuities and discontinuities characterize thinking and writing about teacher capacity across time. Schwab's (1973) "commonplaces" of teaching and curriculum building—the learner, the teacher, the milieu, and the subject matter—continue to be useful categories. We continue to debate what teachers need to know, be able to do, and care about. At the same time, our understanding of all these concepts has changed radically over time in response to a range of forces—intellectual, social, technological, and political.

Heightened expectations for teachers, driven in part by changes in the policy environment, have also changed our concept of teacher capacity. Published test scores have forced schools and teachers into a harsh public spotlight—or, perhaps more aptly, into the headlights. At the same time, we have also learned a great deal about what teachers need to do to be successful with every learner. Increasingly, we are recognizing that teachers cannot possibly learn all that they need to know in preservice programs. States and districts are responding by devoting more attention to induction supports for novices. Recognition that teachers must adapt to rapidly changing circumstances in classrooms, curriculum, and policy has prompted rethinking of the supports and learning opportunities teachers are provided across their careers. Increased understanding of the socially mediated nature of practice is also forcing a reconsideration of the pervasively individualistic approach to teacher development.

To develop their capacities, teachers may require improved opportunities to collaborate with colleagues in rethinking their practice based on various evidence of pupil learning. This, in turn, posits schools in which administrators, pupils, parents, community members, and key others understand that to improve pupil learning teachers need time and opportunities to collaborate. For genuine learning communities to develop, school schedules, teacher workloads, and district policies must reflect this understanding.

Merely affording teachers time to get together will not, however, automatically produce better practice. Such opportunities must be focused on evidence of learning and the implications of the evidence for practice. Developing cultures of evidence in schools—as well as in higher education—will require time but appears essential to improve learning. Teachers need opportunities to develop the knowledge, skills, and dispositions necessary to collaboratively analyze evidence of pupil learning and determine implications for practice. During the induction years, novice teachers, as they develop their practice, need opportunities to collaborate with veteran colleagues in examining evidence of practice (Johnson *et al.*, 2004a; Johnson, *et al.*, 2004b; Kardos, 2004; Kardos *et al.*, 2001). Because not all schools are true learning communities, teachers may also need to develop the political skills necessary for building such communities.

Developing teacher capacity to succeed with every pupil, especially those historically under-served and those with special learning needs, similarly requires rethinking. Pre-service programs have, for many years, included courses on multicultural education and at least some exposure to special education issues. Yet, the gaps in pupil achievement, high school graduation, and college attendance persist and inclusion continues to be a problem in some schools. This raises a question about the efficacy of the approaches teacher educators have been taking. The expectation that increasing teachers' propositional knowledge about the cultural background and social circumstances of under-served pupils, culturally responsive teaching, and special education generally would, by itself, produce classroom practices that lead to learning for all pupils may have been misplaced.

To better prepare teachers to succeed in helping under-served pupils requires greater attention to the efficacy of current approaches. Developing a culture of evidence is as essential to improving teacher preparation as it is to improving schools. Teacher educators and their Arts and Sciences colleagues need to collect evidence of the impact of their practices on preservice teachers and the subsequent impact of these teachers on their P-12 pupils. Far from a simple task, such evidence-based examination of practice and programs is critical for enhancing teacher capacity. The challenge for teacher educators, as it is for P-12 teachers, is not merely to collect valid data but to make analysis, interpretation, and practice and program adjustment a regular part of their collective work.

Another apparent continuity is recognition of public education's and, therefore, teachers' central role in maintaining and extending democracy. Yet, the assessment and accountability policies emanating from state and federal government over the past two decades seem to have narrowed the purposes of schooling.[3] Despite the protestations of accountability advocates, large majorities of teachers report that state assessments drive what and how they teach (Pedulla *et al.*, 2003). While acknowledging that academic knowledge and skills are essential, proponents of democratic education worry that the dispositions, knowledge, and skills necessary for informed and productive engagement in the public arena are being ignored.

Fostering the disposition to engage and contribute in the public arena is necessary for maintaining a democratic society. Enhancing pupils' sense of agency—a sense that, in conjunction with others, they can influence their social, political, and natural surround—underpins such a disposition. Direct experience of efficacious agency promotes this sense. From this point of view, teacher capacity thus includes creating opportunities for pupils to experience agency. Supporting pupils in changing their environment, however immediate and small-scale that may be, provides that experience.

Similarly, creating classroom and school-wide norms that ensure that adults and pupils feel comfortable speaking—from their direct experience as well as from other sources—on public issues, listen closely and respectfully to others, and engage in reasoned debate are not measured on any assessment yet arguably teach the very dispositions and skills essential for a democratic society. A definition of teacher capacity that ignores educators' responsibility to establish, teach, and enforce these norms contributes to the erosion of a primary rationale for "common schools."

In short, we cannot go back to a time when prospective teachers were taught a menu of knowledge, skills, and dispositions, given a few weeks of practice teaching, certified, sent out into classrooms, and "inserviced" a few times each year. The enterprise is too demanding, the consequences of failure too dire for pupils, their families, and our democracy. In the past two decades, we have learned much more than ever before about both what teachers need to know, be able to do, and care about and how these things are learned. At the core of these understandings is new appreciation for the degree to which teacher capacity and learning are social phenomena that occur across time and settings. At the same time, changes in the policy context threaten to narrow our concept of teacher capacity in ways that short-change the values and knowledge vital to a democratic society. Programs and opportunities to learn—at the preservice, induction, and inservice levels—intended to support teachers need to catch up with our expanded understanding of teacher capacity.

NOTES

1 Although this may be obvious, we need to keep in mind that our ideas are not strictly determined by the social, political, ideological, and economic forces that dominate at any given historical moment. "Functionalist fantasies" (Cohen & Rosenberg, 1977), however tempting, deny human agency and reduce complexities to corrupting oversimplifications.
2 The widespread adoption of cohort models in preservice teacher education is, in part, an effort to promoted the dispositions, habits, and skills needed to build and maintain professional communities. Some graduates of cohort-based programs report, however, that the schools in which they are hired do little or nothing to encourage the collaboration fostered in their preservice programs.
3 The irony is that the NCLB legislation was designed to address the unequal results of schooling, requiring schools to disaggregate standardized pupil assessment data by under-served race and/ or ethnic groups, English language proficiency, and special needs and penalizing schools that fail to improve results for every subgroup. By placing such an emphasis on a single annual assessment in a few subject areas—typical, mathematics, reading, and writing—the legislation pushes the teaching of other vital knowledge, skills, and dispositions to the margins—or, off the table completely.

REFERENCES

Adler, M. J. (1982) *The Paideia proposal: an educational manifesto.* New York: Macmillan.
Alaska Department of Education and Early Childhood (1999) *Guidelines for preparing culturally-responsive teachers for Alaska's schools.* Juneau, AK: Author.
American Board for Certification of Teaching Excellence (n.d.) http://www.abcte.org/. Retrieved September 12, 2005.
Ball, D. L. & Cohen, D. K. (1999) Developing practice, developing practitioners: toward a

practice-based theory of professional education. In L. Darling-Hammond and G. Sykes (eds.), *Teaching as the learning profession: handbook of policy and practice* (pp. 3–32). San Francisco: Jossey-Bass.

Banks, J. (1988) *Multicultural education: theory and practice (second edition)*. Boston, MA: Allyn and Bacon.

Barnes, C. (2002) *Standards reform in high-poverty schools: managing conflict and building capacity*. New York: Teachers College Press.

Bereiter, C. & Scardamalia, M. (1993) *Surpassing ourselves: an inquiry into the nature and implications of expertise*. Chicago: Open Court.

Bestor, A. (1953) *Educational wastelands: the retreat from learning in our public schools*. Urbana, IL: University of Illinois Press.

Blair, J. (2003, June 18) Congress to probe teacher education group and its president. *Education Week*, 22, 41, pp. 1, 24.

Bransford, J., Darling-Hammond, L., & Lepage, P. (2005) Introduction. In L. Darling-Hammond and J. Bransford (eds.), *Preparing Teachers for a changing world* (1–39). San Fransisco: Jossey-Bass.

Brophy, J. & Good, T. L. (1986) Teacher behavior and student achievement. In M. C. Wittrock (ed.), *Handbook of research on teaching* (3rd ed.) (pp. 328–375). New York: Simon & Schuster.

Brown, J. S. & Duguid, P. (1991) Organizational learning and communities-of-practice: Toward a unified view of working, learning and innovation. *Organization Science*, 2 (1), 40–57.

Brown, J., Collins, A., & Duguid, P. (1989) Situated cognition and the culture of learning. *Educational Researcher*: 18 (1), 32–42.

Bruner, J. (1960) *The process of education*. New York: Vintage Books.

Calderhead, J. & Gates, P. (1993) *Conceptualizing reflection in teacher development*. London: Routledge Falmer.

Caliver, A. (1933) Secondary education for negroes. *The School Review*, 41(3), 231–232.

Carnegie Corporation. (2001) *Teachers for a new era: a national initiative to improve the quality of teaching*. New York: Author.

Carnegie Task Force on Teaching as a Profession (1986) *A nation prepared: teachers for the 21st century: the report of the task force on teaching as a profession*. New York: Author.

Center for Educational Renewal (n.d.) *Agenda for education in a democracy*. Retrieved September 12, 2005. http://depts.washington.edu/cedren/AED.htm

Chi, M. T. H., Glaser, R., & Farr, M. J. (1988) *The nature of expertise*. Hillsdale, NJ: Erlbaum.

Clark, C. & Peterson, P. (1986) Teachers' thought processes. In M. Wittrock (ed.). *Handbook of research on teaching* (3rd edition) (pp. 255–296). New York: Macmillan.

Cochran-Smith, M. (1999) Learning to teach for social justice. In G. Griffin (ed.), *The education of teachers: ninety-eighth yearbook of the National Society for the Study of Education* (pp. 114–144). Chicago: University of Chicago.

Cochran-Smith, M. (2004) *Walking the road: race, diversity, and social justice in teacher education*. New York: Teachers College.

Cochran-Smith, M. & Zeichner, K. (2005) *Studying teacher education: the report of the AERA Panel on Research and Teacher Education*. Hillsdale, NJ: Erlbaum.

Cohen, D. K. (1988) *Plus ça change . . .* Issue Paper 88–3. East Lansing, MI: Michigan State University, National Center for Research on Teacher Learning.

Cohen, D. K. & Ball, D. L. (1999) *Instruction, capacity, and improvement. CPRE Research Report Series (RR-043)*. Philadelphia: Consortium for Policy Research in Education.

Cohen, D. K. & Rosenberg, B. H. (1977) Functions and fantasies: understanding schools in capitalist America. *History of Education Quarterly*, 17(2), 113–137.

Coleman, J. S., Campbell, E. Q., Hobson, C. J., McPartland, J., Mood, A. M., Weinfeld, F. D., & York, R. L. (1966) *Equality of educational opportunity*. Washington, DC: U.S. Government Printing Office.

Cooper, J. M. & Weber, W. A. (1973) A competency based systems approach to teacher education. In J. M. Cooper, W. A. Weber, & C. E. Johnson (eds.), *A systems approach to program design: Vol. 2. Competency based teacher education* (pp. 7–18). Berkeley, CA: McCutchan.

Corcoran, T. & Lawrence, N. (2003) *Changing district culture and capacity: the impact of the Merck Institute for Science Education Partnership.* (Policy Brief 54). Philadelphia, PA: Consortium for Policy Research in Education, University of Pennsylvania.

Council of Chief State School Officers (n.d.) *State Content Standards.* Retrieved January 13, 2006. http://www.ccsso.org/Projects/state_education_indicators/key_state_education_policies/3160.cfm

Counts, G. (1932) *Dare the school build a new social order?* New York: The John Day Company.

Cremin, L. (1988) *American education, the metropolitan experience, 1876–1980.* New York: Harper and Row.

Darling-Hammond, L. (1999) *Teacher quality and student achievement: a review of state policy evidence.* Seattle, WA: Center for the Study of Teaching and Policy.

Delpit, L. (1995) *Other people's children: cultural conflict in the classroom.* New York: The New Press.

Dodl, N. R. & Schalock, H. D. (1973) A competency based teacher preparation. In D. W. Anderson, J. M. Cooper, M. V. DeVault, G. E. Dickson, C. E. Johnson, & W. A. Weber (eds.), *Competency based teacher education* (pp. 45–52). Berkeley, CA: McCutchan.

Dow, P. (1991) *Schoolhouse politics: lessons from the Sputnik era.* Cambridge, MA: Harvard.

Farkas, G. (2003) Racial disparities and discrimination in education: what do we know, how do we know it, and what do we need to know? *Teachers College Record*, 105 (6), 1119–1146.

Feiman-Nemser, S. (2001) From preparation to practice: designing a continuum to strengthen and sustain teaching. *Teachers College Record*, 103 (6), 1013–1055.

Feiman-Nemser, S. & Buchmann, M. (1983) *Pitfalls of experience in teacher education* (Occasional Paper 65). East Lansing: Michigan State University, Institute for Research on Teaching.

Feiman-Nemser, S. & Buchman, M. (1987) When is student teaching teacher education? *Teaching and Teacher Education*, 3, 255–273.

Feiman-Nemser S. & Floden R.E. (1986) The cultures of teaching. In M. C. Wittrock (ed.), *Handbook of research on teaching*, 3rd edition (pp. 505–526). New York: Macmillan.

Ferguson, R. F (1991) Paying for public education: new evidence on how and why money matters. *Harvard Journal on Legislation*, 28, 465–498.

Ferguson, R. & Ladd, H. (1996) How and why money matters: an analysis of Alabama schools. In H. Ladd (ed.) *Holding schools accountable: performance-based reform in education.* Washington, DC: Brookings Institution.

Fitz-Gibbon, C. T. (ed.) (2002) *Evidence-based policies and indicator systems.* Durham, UK: University of Durham.

Foster, J. (1999) *Redesigning public education.* Lexington, KY: Diversified Services.

Gage, N. (1963) Paradigms for research on teaching. In N. L. Gage (ed.), *Handbook of research on teaching* (pp. 91–141). Chicago: Rand McNally.

Gage, N. (1971) *Tools of the trade: an approach to enhancing the teacher's ability to make a difference.* Washington, DC: U.S. Department of Education, Bureau of Educational Personnel Development.

Gage, N. (1978) *The scientific basis of the art of teaching.* New York: Teachers College Press.

Gardner, H. (1985) *The mind's new science: a history of the cognitive revolution.* New York: Basic Books.

Gay, G. (2002) Preparing for culturally responsive teaching. *Journal of Teacher Education*, 53(2), 106–117.

Goodlad, J. (1997) *In praise of education.* New York: Teachers College.

Goodlad, J. & Keating, P. (1994) *Access to knowledge: the continuing agenda for our nation's schools.* Princeton, NJ: The College Board.

Goodlad, J. & McMannon, T. (1997) *The public purpose of education and schooling.* San Francisco, CA: Jossey-Bass.

Grant, C. A. & Sleeter, C. E. (1996) *After the school bell rings.* Bristol, PA: Falmer Press.

Griffin, A. & Hett, A. (2004, June) *Performance-based pedagogy of teacher candidates.* Olympia, WA: Office of the Superintendent of Public Instruction.

Greenwald, R., Hedges, L. V. & Laine, R. D. (1996) Have times changed? The effect on school resources on student achievement. *Review of Educational Research*, 66(3), 361–396.

Grossman, P. L. (1990) *The making of a teacher: teacher knowledge and teacher education*. New York: Teachers College Press.

Grossman, P. (1995) Teachers' knowledge. In L. W. Anderson (ed.), *International encyclopedia of teaching and teacher education* (2nd ed., pp. 20–24). Kidlington, Oxford: Elsevier Science Ltd.

Hage, J. & Powers, C. (1992) *The post-industrial lives: roles and relationships in the 21st century*. Thousand Oaks, CA: Sage.

Hall, G. E. (1981) Competency-based teacher education: where is it now? *New York University Education Quarterly*, 12(4), 20–27.

Hatano, G. & Oura, Y. (2003) Commentary: reconceptualizing school learning using insight from expertise research. *Educational Researcher*, 32(8), 26–29.

Hedges, L. (2003) *The culture of evidence*. A paper presented at the meeting of the National Science Foundation Math Science Partnerships. January 30, 2003.

Hill, H., Rowan, B. & Ball, D. (2005) Effects of teachers' mathematical knowledge for teaching on student achievement. *American Educational Research Journal*, 42(2), 371–406.

Holmes Group (1988) *Tomorrow's teachers*. East Lansing, MI: Author.

Holmes Group (1990) *Tomorrow's schools*. East Lansing, MI: Author.

Hunt, T. (2002) *The impossible dream: education and the search for panaceas*. New York: Peter Lang.

Hutchins, R. M. (1936) *The higher learning in America*. New Haven, CT: Yale University Press.

Jencks, C. (1972) *Inequality: a reassessment of the effect of family and schooling in America*. New York: Basic Books.

Jencks, C. & Phillips, M. (1998) *The black-white test score gap*. Washington, DC: The Brookings Institute.

Johnston, R. C. & Viadero, D. (2000, March 15) Unmet promise: raising minority achievement. *Education Week*, 19, 27, pp. 1, 18–19.

Johnson, S. M. & The Project on the Next Generation of Teachers (2004a) *Finders and keepers: helping new teachers survive and thrive in our schools*. San Francisco: Jossey-Bass.

Johnson, S., Kardos, S., Kaufman, D., Liu, E., & Donaldson, M. (2004b) The support gap: new teachers' early experiences in high-income and low-income schools. *Education Policy Analysis Archives*, 61(12). http://epaa.asu.edu/epaa/v12n61/

Kardos, S. M. (2004) *Supporting and sustaining new teachers in schools: the importance of professional culture and mentoring*. Cambridge, MA: Harvard University.

Kardos, S. M., Johnson, S. M., Peske, H. G., Kauffman, D., & Liu, E. (2001) Counting on colleagues: new teachers encounter the professional cultures of their schools. *Educational Administration Quarterly*, 37(2), 250–290.

Koerner, J. (1963) *The miseducation of American teachers*. Boston: Houghton Mifflin, 1963.

Ladson-Billings, G. (1994) *The dreamkeepers: successful teachers of African American children*. San Francisco: Jossey-Bass.

Ladson-Billings, G. (1999) Preparing teachers for diverse student populations: a critical race theory perspective. In A. Iran-Nejad & D. Pearson (eds.), *Review of Research in Education* (24) (pp. 211–248). Washington, DC: AERA.

Lakoff, R. (2000) *The language war*. Berkeley, CA: University of California Press.

Lampert, M. (1985) How do teachers manage to teach? Perspectives on problems in practice, *Harvard Educational Review*, 55(2), 178–194.

Lave, J. & Wenger, E. (1991) *Situated learning: legitimate peripheral participation*. Cambridge, UK: Cambridge University Press.

Leinhardt, G. (1988) Situated learning and expertise in teaching. In J. Calderhead (ed.). *Teachers' professional learning* (pp. 146–168). London: Falmer.

Linn, R. L. (2000) Assessments and accountability. *Educational Researcher*, 29(2), 4–16.

Linn, R. L. (2001) *The design and evaluation of educational assessment and accountability systems*

(CSE. Tech. Rep. No. 539). Los Angeles: University of California, Center for Research on Evaluation, Standards and Student Testing.

Little, J. W. (1993) Teachers' professional development in a climate of educational reform. *Educational Evaluation and Policy Analysis*, 15(2), 129–151.

Lortie, D. (1975) *Schoolteacher: a sociological study*. Chicago: University of Chicago Press.

Luria, A. R. (1974) *Cognitive development: its cultural and social foundations*. Cambridge, MA: Harvard University.

Luria, A. R. (1976) *Cognitive development: its cultural and social foundations*. Cambridge, MA: Harvard University.

McDiarmid, G. W. (1991) What do prospective teachers need to know about culturally different children? In M. M. Kennedy (ed.), *Teaching academic subjects to diverse learners* (pp. 257–269). New York: Teachers College Press.

McDiarmid, G. W. (1993) Teacher education: a vital part of the equity issue. *State Education Leader*, 12(1), 11.

McDiarmid, G. W. (1994) The arts and science as preparation for teaching. In K. Howey and N. Zympher (eds.), *Informing faculty development for teacher educators* (pp. 99–138). Norwood, NJ: Ablex.

McLaren, P. (1995) *Critical pedagogy and predatory culture*. New York: Routledge.

McLaughlin, M. & Talbert, J. (2001) *Professional communities and the work of high-school teaching*. Chicago: University of Chicago Press.

Massell, D. (1998) *State strategies for building capacity in education: progress and continuing challenges*. Philadelphia, PA: Consortium for Policy Research in Education, University of Pennsylvania.

Massell, D. (2000) *The district role in building capacity: four strategies (CPRE Policy Brief No. RB-32)*. Philadelphia: Consortium for Policy Research in Education, University of Pennsylvania.

Mayer, R. (2003) What causes individual differences in cognitive performance? In R. Steinberg & E. Grigorenko (eds.), *The psychology of abilities, competencies, and expertise* (pp. 263–274). New York: Cambridge University Press.

Michelli, N. M. & Keiser, D. L. (2005) *Teacher education for democracy and social justice*. New York: Routledge.

Munby, H. Russell, T., & Martin, A. K. (2001) Teachers' knowledge and how it develops. In V. Richardson (ed.), *Handbook of research on teaching* (4th ed.) (pp. 877–904). Washington, DC: American Educational Research Association.

National Board for Professional Teaching Standards (n.d.) Retrieved August 26, 2005. http://www.nbpts.org/standards/stds.cfm

National Council for the Accreditation of Teacher Education (NCATE) (1977) *Standards for the accreditation of teacher education*. Washington, DC: Author.

National Council for Accreditation of Teacher Education (NCATE) (2001) *Professional standards for the accreditation of schools, colleges, and departments of education*. Washington, DC: Author.

National Commission of Teaching and America's Future (1996) *What matters most: teaching for America's future*. New York: Author.

National Commission of Teaching and America's Future (2003) *No dream denied: a pledge to America's children*. Washington, DC: Author.

National Council of Teachers of Mathematics (1989) *Curriculum and evaluation sandards for school mathematics*. Reston, VA: Author.

Ogren, C. (2005) *The American state normal school : "An instrument of great good."* New York: Palgrave Macmillan.

Oregon Department of Education. (May, 2004) *Cultural competency summit proceedings*. Salem, OR: Author.

Pangburn, J. M. (1932) *The evolution of the American teachers college*. New York: Teachers College, Columbia University.

Pedulla, J., Abrams, L., Madaus, G., Russell, M., Ramos, M. & Miao, J. (2003) *Perceived effects of state-mandated testing programs on teaching and learning: findings from a national survey of teachers.* Boston, MA: National Board on Educational Testing and Public Policy, Boston College.

Rickover, H. (1963) *American education-a national failure: the problem of our schools and what we can learn from England.* New York: Dutton.

Rosenshine, B. & Furst, N. (1973) Research on teacher performance criteria. In B. O. Smith (ed.), *Research in teacher education—A symposium* (pp. 37–72). Englewood Cliffs, NJ: Prentice-Hall.

Rutherford, J. & Ahlgren, A. (1990) *Science for all Americans: Project 2061.* New York: Oxford.

Ryans, D. (1960) *Characteristics of teachers: their description, comparison, and appraisal.* Washington, DC: American Council on Education.

Schon, D. (1984) *The reflective practitioner: how professionals think in action.* New York: Basic Books.

Schon, D. (1990) *Educating the reflective practitioner: toward a new design for teaching and learning in the professions.* San Francisco, CA: Jossey-Bass.

Schwab, J. J. (1962) The concept of a structure of a discipline. *Educational Record,* 43, 197–205.

Schwab, J. J. (1973) The practical 3: translation into curriculum. *School Review,* 81, 501–522.

Seattle Public Schools (2005) *What is cultural competence?* Retrieved September 9, 2005. http://www.seattleschools.org/area/equityandrace/culturalcompetency.xml

Shulman, L. S. (1986) Those who understand: knowledge growth in teaching. *Educational Researcher,* 15(2), 4–14.

Shulman, L. S. (1987) Knowledge and teaching: foundations of the new reform. *Harvard Educational Review,* 57(1), 1–22.

Sleeter, C. & Grant, C. (1987) An analysis of multicultural education in the United States. *Harvard Educational Review,* 57 (4), 421–444.

Soder, R. (1995) *Democracy, education, and the schools.* San Francisco, CA: Jossey-Bass.

Soder, R., Goodlad, J. & McMannon, T. (2001) *Developing democratic character in the young.* San Francisco, CA: Jossey-Bass.

State Office (1889) *Historical sketch of the State Normal School at San José, California, with a catalogue of its graduates and a record of their work for twenty-seven years [1862–1889].* (J. D. Young, Supt. State Printing). Sacramento, CA. http://www.cagenweb.com/archives/schools/sns/sns89001.htm. Retrieved August 28, 2005.

Steiner, D. (2003) *Preparing teachers: are American schools of education up to the task?* Paper presented at the conference of the American Enterprise Institute for Public Policy Research: A Qualified Teacher in Every Classroom. October 23, 2003, Washington, DC.

Steinberg, R & Grigorenko, E. (2003) *The psychology of abilities, competencies, and expertise.* New York: Cambridge University Press.

Taylor, C. & Nolen, S. (2004) *Classroom assessment.* Upper Saddle River, NJ: Prentice.

Toulmin, S. E. (1958) *The uses of argument.* Cambridge: Cambridge University Press.

Tyack, D. & Cuban, L. (1995) *Tinkering towards utopia: a century of public school reform.* Cambridge, MA: Harvard University Press.

United States Department of Education (n.d.a) *Fact sheet: new No Child Left Behind flexibility: highly qualified teachers.* Retrieved September 4, 2005. http://www.ed.gov/nclb/methods/teachers/hqtflexibility.html

United States Department of Education (n.d.b) *Elementary & Secondary Education: Part D— Enhancing Education Through Technology.* Retrieved January 13, 2006. http://www.ed.gov/policy/elsec/leg/esea02/pg34.html12c2401

University of the State of New York (1922) *Course of study and syllabus for the college graduate certificates.* Albany, NY: Author.

Urban, W. J. (1990) Historical studies of teacher education. In W. H. Houston (ed.) *Handbook of research on teacher education* (pp. 59–71). New York: Macmillan.

Vygotsky, L. S. (1962) *Thought and language.* Cambridge, MA: MIT Press.

Vygotsky, L. S. (1978) *Mind in society.* Cambridge, MA: Harvard University Press.

Waxman, H. & Wahlberg, H. (eds.) (1991) *Effective teaching: current research.* Berkeley, CA: McCutchan.

Wenger, E. (1998) *Communities of practice: learning, meaning, and identity*. Cambridge, UK: Cambridge University Press.

Wertsch, J. V. (1985) *Cultural, communication, and cognition: Vygotskian perspectives*. Cambridge University Press.

Wilson, S. M., Shulman, L. S., & Richert, A. (1987) 150 different ways of knowing: representations of knowledge in teaching. In J. Calderhead (ed.), *Exploring teachers' thinking* (pp. 104–124). Sussex, England: Holt, Rinehart & Winston.

Wilson, S. M., & Wineburg, S. (1988) Peering at history through different lenses: the role of disciplinary perspectives in teaching history. *Teachers College Record*, 89, 525–539.

Wilson, S. M., Floden, R. E., & Ferrini-Mundy, J. (2001) *Teacher preparation research: current knowledge, gaps, and recommendations*. Seattle, WA: Center for the Study of Teaching and Policy.

Zeichner, K. & Liston, D. (1990) *Traditions of reform in U.S. teacher education (Issue paper 90–1)*. East Lansing, MI: Michigan State University, National Center for Research on Teacher Learning.

Zeichner, K. & Liston, D. (1996) *Reflective teaching: an introduction*. Mahwah, NJ: Lawrence Erlbaum Associates.

Zumwalt, K. (1988) Are we improving or undermining teaching? *Yearbook (National Society for the Study of Education)* v. 87, pt. 1, 148–174. Chicago: University of Chicago.

10 Teacher capacity for diverse learners

What do teachers need to know?

Tyrone C. Howard
University of California, Los Angeles

Glenda R. Aleman
California State University Dominguez Hills

ABSTRACT

Teacher capacity has concerned itself with the knowledge and dispositions that are required to teach in P-12 classrooms. However, some suggest that many of these efforts have fallen short in helping to create equitable learning environments for all students. In this work, we examine the historical depictions of teacher capacity, examine the salient research on teacher knowledge for diverse learners, and finally we offer recommendations for reconceptualizing teacher capacity for diverse learners.

Only within the past 30 years has the issue of student diversity been part of the teacher capacity discourse. The AACTE endorsed multicultural education in 1973. In the document *No One Model American*, they call for the profession to respond to the increase in cultural pluralism (Nieto, 2000). AACTE's push for addressing diversity in teacher education was followed up by NCATE's call for all member institutions to place more attention on preparing its candidates for teaching in diverse school settings. However, a review by Gollnick in 1995 revealed that most teacher education programs still had few substantive programs or courses that addressed issues of diversity. Other reviews on the topic of preparing teachers for diverse school settings have reached similar conclusions, arguing that while there is a pressing need to prepare teachers for teaching diverse learners, issues pertaining to diversity have typically been separated from the rest of the teacher education curriculum (Cochran-Smith *et al.*, 2003; Ladson-Billings, 1995; Hollins & Guzman, 2006; Zeichner & Hoeft, 1996).

The history of teacher preparation reveals an ongoing search to identify the most useful means of preparing teachers and to characterize the capacity that each teacher must possess to help educate the nation's student body population. Yet, mostly absent from the discourse, research, and recommendations have been discussions of teachers' capacity to teach non-mainstream students—those who are poor and/or who come from culturally diverse backgrounds. Despite years of committees, consortiums, and task forces dedicated to the creation of core standards, essential knowledge, and effective practices in the field of teacher education, more attention is needed to the changing demographics in the nation's schools.

In this chapter we examine teacher capacity for teaching diverse populations. Building on the work of McDiarmid & Clevenger-Bright and Grant & Agosto (this volume) we define teacher capacity as the core knowledge, skills, and dispositions that teachers should possess to teach in today's classrooms. More specifically, we define these knowledge and skills as the command of subject matter and pedagogical content knowledge. We also include in our description of capacity an awareness of the social and political contexts of education and the development of critical consciousness about issues such as race, class, gender, culture, language, and educational equity. We emphasize teachers' capacity to teach diverse learners because of the need to prepare teachers for the growing ethnic, racial, linguistic, and social class diversity in the nation's schools. According to the U.S. Department of Education, students of color currently comprise close to 40 percent of the U.S. school population (National Center for Education Statistics, 2003). The U.S. Census Bureau (2000) estimates that by the year 2050 African American, Asian American, and Latino students will constitute close to half of the entire U.S. student population. In a number of cities such as New York, Los Angeles, Chicago, Philadelphia, and Washington D.C., students of color already make up the overwhelming majority of the student population (Hodgkinson, 2002). Furthermore, the number of students whose primary language is not English has increased dramatically over the last 20 years, going from 1.5 million in 1985 to 5.5 million in 2005 (Villegas & Lucas, 2002; U.S. Department of Education, 2002).

In this chapter, we pose fundamental questions that are at the core of teachers' capacity to teach in a diverse society, including: what are the essential skills, knowledge, and dispositions that are needed to educate students in a diverse society? Are teacher education programs aptly suited to teach this capacity to pre-service teachers? One of our primary objectives is to frame the discourse about teacher capacity in a manner that is inclusive of the dynamics and complexities involved in preparing teachers to teach in classrooms that look drastically different from schools in years past. We believe it is imperative to frame an analysis of teacher capacity squarely within the context of the diversity that has become the fabric of the country and of the nation's schools. Unfortunately, historical understandings of teacher capacity have generally failed to incorporate important variables involved in teaching diverse populations.

Despite dramatic changes in the school population, discussions about teachers' core knowledge generally focus primarily on subject matter and pedagogy. These are certainly very important. We recommend, however, that the inclusion of empirical and conceptual research that has examined effective teaching practice with diverse learners be given much more serious consideration in descriptions of teacher capacity. Thus we organize the following discussion around three aspects of teachers' capacity to teach diverse learners: (1) subject matter and pedagogical content knowledge, (2) knowledge of effective practice about teaching in diverse settings, and (3) the development of a critical consciousness.

SUBJECT MATTER AND PEDAGOGICAL CONTENT KNOWLEDGE

Amidst ongoing debates regarding the professionalization of teaching, the role of varying governing bodies over certification, and the essential skills needed to teach, subject matter knowledge has arguably emerged as the most important area of teacher capacity. The importance of subject matter knowledge has been part of the discourse regarding teacher preparation for at least the last two centuries (Darling-Hammond, 2005). The challenge has always been clear: teachers should have a deep knowledge of the subject matters that they teach (Shulman, 1987; Munby et al., 2001; Wilson et al., 1987). More important, a long line of research has revealed that teachers who have strong background knowledge in their content areas produce higher outcomes in student learning in certain subject areas (Darling-Hammond, 2000; Goldhaber & Brewer, 2000). At the extreme, the U.S. Department of Education (U.S. DOE, 2002) and the American Board for the Certification of Teacher Excellence (2003) both assert that mastery of subject matter knowledge and verbal ability are the only empirically supported characteristics of high quality teachers.

Although some research has maintained that mastery of subject matter is the most essential aspect of teacher capacity, others state that the mere knowledge of subject matter alone is insufficient for teachers. Equally crucial for teachers is accurate command of the subject in ways that can be communicated to diverse learners. This includes breadth and depth in the critical concepts, themes, and skills most germane to the subject, which would allow the content to be presented in a multitude of ways (Grossman *et al.*, 2005). Each of the major areas of study, English/Language Arts, mathematics, social studies and science have established essential content standards that embody central concepts of the discipline, and each area stresses content and process as part of the mastery of the subject. Some research has shown while teachers who have majored in the area they are teaching is an important predictor of student achievement (Monk, 1994; Monk & King, 1994) teachers who have a rich, deep, or organizationally clear concept of their subject area in a manner suitable for teaching may be more effective in teaching that material to students (Ball & Bass, 2000; Ma, 1999); hence the important of pedagogical content knowledge.

An increasing amount of research has been dedicated to examining the influence of subject matter knowledge on teacher effectiveness and student learning, and the findings of these studies have been less than conclusive. Floden and Meniketti (2005) provide an exhaustive review of the correlation between subject matter study and teacher effectiveness. What we infer from their findings is that the mere exposure to subject matter alone does not ensure teacher effectiveness. In short, Floden and Meniketti argue that additional empirical research about the relationship between subject area study and teacher effectiveness is needed. The area where there appears to be the most empirical research is in the field of secondary mathematics, where a positive association between the study of math and the learning of math by students was found in several studies (see Wenglinsky, 2002; Wilson *et al.*, 2001; Wilson & Floden, 2003). Monk (1994) using data from the Longitudinal Study of American Youth found that the amount of college coursework math and science teachers have taken in their content areas was positively related to student achievement gains. Similar research by Begle (1979) and Goldhaber and Brewer (2000) also found that content area expertise makes a difference in student learning. However, in the areas of English and social studies there is very little research about the benefits of course study and teacher practice and effectiveness on student learning. However, Floden and Meniketti's (2005) review that in the area of science, the more science courses that teachers had taken the more positive the students' dispositions were toward science. Therefore, while we would suggest that subject matter knowledge continues to be an essential component of teacher capacity, it is clear that additional research is needed to assess the relationship between teachers' content knowledge, practice, and student learning. Additional investigations are needed to assess not simply the quantity of subject matter content pre-service teachers receive, but also the quality and type of exposure. Historically, discussions about teacher capacity have taken the stance that the more exposure pre-service teachers have to subject matter content, the better command they have of it. However, findings from several of the studies mentioned above suggest that additional research is needed to examine what, if any, correlations exist between subject matter command, teaching practice, and student learning—with particular attention being given to these influences across diverse learners.

Increasing concerns about teachers' knowledge of their subject matter has resulted in the implementation in many states of subject matter assessment exams before teachers can gain full certification. As of 2005–2006, 42 states and the District of Columbia required that new high school teachers pass a subject matter assessment, and 33 required subject area majors for high school teachers. Assessment measures such as the Praxis I and Praxis II exams, which assess teaching skill and subject area content knowledge, have gained increasing prominence in states across the country. A number of educational organizations have challenged the prevalence of such exams, contending that historically they have served as an obstacle for potential teachers from ethnically and racially diverse backgrounds (Irvine, 2003). Despite debates, however, it is clear is that ensuring teachers' knowledge of subject matter is non-negotiable, although the amount of content preparation and the manner in which that knowledge ought to be evaluated remain points of contention.

An increasing numbers of states also now require that teachers show command of subject matter within the contexts of other variables that are critical to teaching such as human development, professional growth, and teacher leadership to name a few. In the state of California, for example, teachers are required to show competence according to the California Teaching Performance Expectations (TPE). Designed to improve teacher quality in California classrooms TPE are centered in the belief that effective teacher competence takes numerous years to develop and is an ongoing process. The TPE were designed as a set of outcomes specifically for pre-service teachers and intended to address multiple and overlapping knowledge and skills in domains such as pedagogical knowledge, personal growth, and the needs of English Language Learners. In short, these principles are intended to represent the core knowledge base that beginning teachers must have as they take on the demanding and complex challenges of California classrooms.

The assessment of subject matter knowledge is not limited to individual state frameworks but is also present at the national level. Since its inception more than 12 years ago, the National Board for Professional Teaching Standards (NBPTS) has sought to advance the quality of teaching and learning in U.S. schools through a rigorous certification process. The NBPTS requires teachers to show mastery and integration of content *and* pedagogical knowledge. It also requires teachers to possess a repertoire of instructional strategies to help all students meet high standards (NBPTS, 2001). Intended as the teaching profession's highest credential, National Board Certification is based on five core propositions in relation to which teachers must show evidence of mastery by submitting a portfolio. The propositions are as follows:

1   Teachers are committed to students and their learning.
2   Teachers know the subjects they teach and how to teach those subjects to students.
3   Teachers are responsible for managing and monitoring student learning.
4   Teachers think systemically about their practice and learn from experience.
5   Teachers are members of learning communities.

The NBPTS has provided an important mechanism to establish what would be considered exemplary teaching standards across all areas and has gained increased prominence over the past decade as a set of standards that define excellence in the field. Moreover, the emphasis on having teachers demonstrate command of subject matter in a manner that contributes to student learning is an essential part of teacher capacity. However, some researchers have called into question the equity and cultural assumptions implicit in National Board Certification, arguing that the disproportionate numbers of teachers of color who fail to certify may reflect a major flaw with the process

(Goldhaber *et al.*, 2003). Ladson-Billings and Darling-Hammond (2000), for example, contend that culturally responsive teaching practices may not be consistent with the measures used by the National Board. In their research, they examined the practices of successful teachers in urban schools and argued that the characteristics of these teachers were not well represented, specifically in the National Board Early Adolescent/English Arts assessment. They also argued that the National Board for Professional Teaching Standards assessments have an adverse impact with respect to race, meaning that teachers of color and teachers in urban schools certify at significantly lower rates than White teachers and teachers in more affluent schools. Therefore, while the NBPTS offers important promise for recognizing the highest standard of teaching, consideration must be given to further evaluation of its ability to capture commendable teaching in all of its manifestations.

PEDAGOGICAL CONTENT KNOWLEDGE

Any discussion of fundamental capacity or essential knowledge for teachers should pay careful consideration to the importance of how content is delivered or made accessible to learners. During the early part of the twentieth century, the issue of pedagogy became increasingly common in discussions of teacher training and was considered an important attribute of teacher capacity. Shulman (1986) helped to advance the thinking on pedagogical content knowledge by stating that:

> The most regularly taught topics in one's subject area, the most useful forms of representations of those ideas, the most powerful analogies, illustrations, examples, explanations, and demonstrations, in a word, ways of representing and formulating the subject that make it comprehensible to others. Pedagogical content knowledge also includes an understanding of what makes the learning of specific topics easy or difficult; the conceptions and preconceptions that students of different ages and backgrounds bring with them to the learning of those most frequently taught topics and lessons.
>
> (pp. 9–10)

Shulman's notion of pedagogical content knowledge was predicated on his contention that subject matter and pedagogy were too often treated as two different domains. He suggested instead that the intersection of the two concepts provided a clear blending of how subject matter content and concepts within it could be organized in a manner that make them accessible to learners. Although, Shulman dramatically influenced thinking in the field regarding pedagogical content knowledge, he was not the first to discuss the importance of the role of pedagogy in teaching. John Dewey (1897) suggested that the educational process should be looked at as a complex endeavor which required knowledge and understanding of multiple domains of teaching and learning. He asserted that the educational process "has two sides-one psychological and one sociological; and that neither can be subordinated to the other or neglected without evil results following" (p.78). Drawing on Dewey's and/or Shulman's ideas, teacher educators across the nation have restructured training programs to emphasize the role of pedagogy and pedagogical content knowledge in teacher capacity. Some have suggested, however, that the shift to pedagogical content knowledge has come at the expense of the necessary emphasis on content knowledge (Ball & McDiarmid, 1990).

Teaching is a highly complex activity, which requires intellectual sophistication in a dynamic space (Leinhardt & Greeno, 1986; Spiro *et al.*, 1991). The concept of pedagogical content knowledge has been widely cited in the professional literature on essential knowledge for teachers in training (Grossman, 1990; Ma, 1999; Shulman, 1987; Wilson *et al.*, 1987). The manner in which pedagogical content knowledge intersects with subject matter areas varies across disciplines. Wineburg & Wilson (1988), for example, found that social studies teachers' disciplinary backgrounds significantly influenced the manner in which they represented historical knowledge for high school students. Grossman (1990) reached similar conclusions with regard to the preparation of English teachers, particularly that with regard to teachers' pedagogical approaches to literature influenced the manner in which textbooks were utilized. Our point in this chapter is that conceptions of teacher capacity for diverse learners must include continued attention to pedagogical content knowledge. In particular, we suggest that a notion of pedagogy must recognize complexity in students' learning, especially with regard to background knowledge and individual culture.

PEDAGOGY, LEARNING, AND CULTURE: THEORIES OF SITUATED COGNITION

While we have learned much from the research on pedagogical content knowledge, we maintain that teacher capacity for diverse learners can be enhanced by the intersection of pedagogical content knowledge along with a complex notion of culture and learning. This intersection is necessary because it helps to provide insight about the type of knowledge that can be useful in teaching diverse learners. Some scholars have suggested that the importance of pedagogy is largely tied to an understanding of the cultural context in which students learn and grow, thus the importance of human development and cultural context is essential (Cole, 1996, 2000; Erickson, 2002; Gutiérrez, 2002). Further development of a model to establish a meaningful knowledge base about teacher capacity should be cognizant of the connection between pedagogy, culture, and cognition.

A plethora of research has examined the manner in which human development influences student cognition (Gutiérrez & Rogoff, 2003; Gutiérrez *et al.*, 2000). In light of increasing student diversity in schools, sociocultural theory has gained increased prominence in teacher training, and we would argue that this should be a fundamental part of conceptualizations of teacher capacity for teaching diverse learners. Drawing heavily on the works of Vygotsksy (1986), sociocultural theories purport that children's development cannot be understood simply by studying the individual, but that development must be understood within the participation of activities that require cognitive and communicative functions. This type of situated learning draws attention to learning and how it occurs in authentic situations (Brown *et al.*, 1996). Another domain of the sociocultural paradigm, cultural historical theory, asserts that the process of learning requires the use of signs, symbols, and other cultural tools (e.g. language, skills, knowledge, and beliefs) used by individuals to embody their collective experiences in external forms such as material objects (words, pictures, books, etc.,) which is the essence of learning. Teachers who have an understanding of these aspects of student learning and cognition are better equipped to teach students who come from a variety of diverse cultural and linguistic backgrounds.

Sociocultural theorists have posited that a nuanced and complex notion of culture is necessary to understand the culture-pedagogy-cognition connection. They suggest examining culture as a construct that influences cognition, motivation, modes of interaction, means of interaction, and ways of viewing the world. Renaldo (1989) argues that culture is pervasive; that it represents a social system of accumulated beliefs, attitudes, habits, values which serve as a response to particular set of circumstances; and that all human conduct is culturally mediated. Understanding student learning from the perspective of sociocultural theory alters notions of teacher capacity in ways that are critical for teaching an increasingly diverse student population. Currently, most descriptions of teacher capacity rely on mainstream learning theories such as behaviorism, information processing, and cognitive constructivism, which fail to take into consideration the influence of culture and environment on thinking and learning (Artilles *et al.*, 2004).

A number of theorists have discussed how culture shapes student thinking, learning, situated cognition, and the social context of cognition (Rogoff, 1990; Tharp & Gallimore, 1988). These ideas are important for teachers to understand because they move beyond traditional methods of conceptualizing learning and beyond superficial and essentialized notions of student and group culture. Rogoff and Andelillo (2002), for example, talk about the mainstream essentialized view of culture as the "box problem" wherein individuals from various ethnic groups are viewed as highly homogeneous. More comprehensive and complex accounts of culture suggest instead that educators need to understand that students bring diverse cultural and social capital to the classroom that is often drastically different from mainstream norms and worldviews and that differs greatly among members of the same ethnic group.

A growing number of scholars have posited that effective teaching practices must recognize and respect the intricacies of cultural differences in order to be culturally recognizable and socially meaningful. Geneva Gay (2000) suggests that culturally responsive pedagogy recognizes the uniqueness of students' culture by using "the cultural knowledge, prior experiences, frames of reference, and performance styles of ethnically diverse students to make learning more relevant to and effective for them. It teaches *to and through* strengths of these students. It is culturally *validating and affirming*" (p. 29). Ladson-Billings describes the concept as one that "empowers students intellectually, socially, emotionally, and politically by using cultural referents to impart knowledge, skills, and attitudes," (p. 18).

Research on pedagogy will continue to inform the discourse on teacher capacity. From the perspectives of advocates of pedagogical content knowledge, the discourse about teacher capacity must be informed by reliable research and empirical evidence which helps to shed light on how teacher educators can effectively teach the skills and knowledge around pedagogical knowledge to pre-service teachers.

TEACHER CAPACITY AND KNOWLEDGE OF EFFECTIVE PRACTICE FOR TEACHING IN DIVERSE SETTINGS

Multicultural education emerged in the 1980s in an attempt to provide teachers with the necessary knowledge and skills to teach diverse learners. Among its aims were to interrupt the cycle of hegemony, inequality, and oppression that results in lack of achievement among students of diverse backgrounds (Banks, 2002). Multicultural education was conceptualized as a reform movement that should be infused throughout school curriculum and policy, pedagogical strategies, and school culture that embraces the homes and communities of all children to create an equitable educational system so that all children may become knowledgeable, caring, reflective, and active citizens in a global and multicultural society (Banks, 2002, 2004; Bennett, 2003; Sleeter & Grant, 2003).

Multicultural educators would argue that any attempt to construct a knowledge base for classroom teachers should recognize the important roles that race, culture, language, gender, and class currently play in the United States. Moreover, multicultural teacher educators would argue that teachers must teach with what Jackie Irvine (2003) refers to as "the cultural eye," wherein teachers view their world and the work that they do through a cultural lens that allows them to be change agents in the academic performance of culturally diverse students.

Banks' (2002) five dimensions of multicultural education attempt to move the field from one centered primarily on content infusion to a more comprehensive and complex area of study. Each of Banks' (1995) dimensions—content integration, knowledge construction, equity pedagogy, prejudice reduction, and empowering school culture—are viewed as a starting point to look at the breadth and depth of multicultural education theory and practice particularly in teacher education, and can be a core feature of teacher capacity for diverse learners. While some may critique Banks' model as not being radical or reconstructive enough (Kanpol & McClaren, 1995; Obidah, 2000), there are other multicultural scholars who also take a holistic approach to reforming the educational process to reflect diversity, address curriculum concerns, and question institutional discrimination with the intent of improving academic achievement for all students such as Sonia Nieto (2004) in her list of "multicultural is" and Bennett's (2003) "core values and goals" of multicultural education.

Based on an extensive review of the multicultural literature, Cochran-Smith (2003) offered a "conceptual structure [for] interrogating the multiple meanings of multicultural teacher education" (p. 8). Her framework includes eight penetrating questions such as investigating the complexity of student diversity, examining the purpose of schooling, assessing which knowledge is most useful, evaluating the importance of teacher outcomes, and continuing to document best practices. Cochran-Smith recommends that a more comprehensive and complex understanding of multicultural teacher education can inform teacher practice, and also recognizes the salience of research for policy regarding ways to recruit, retain, prepare, support, and assess high quality teachers for multicultural schools.

A plethora of empirical research has contributed to the knowledge base on effective teaching practices to improve the school performance for diverse learners. Au and Jordan (1981), for example, conducted a case study of the Kamehameha Early Education Program (KEEP), a language arts development project, to examine how a team of teachers, psychologists, anthropologists, and linguists devised methods to teach native Hawaiian children to read. Au and Jordan found KEEP's method of reading instruction to be successful because greater emphasis was placed on comprehension as opposed to sound-symbol relationships. In addition, reading instruction was organized into a system of learning centers, which made instruction more individualized. However, Au and Jordan attributed the majority of KEEP's success to the similarities between how the reading lessons were conducted and the linguistic patterns frequently found in native Hawaiian culture, namely "talk-story."

Lee (1995) examined the efficacy of signifying, a form of social discourse in the African American community, as a scaffold for teaching skills in literary interpretation. She hypothesized that teachers who demonstrated the ability to signify and had prior knowledge about social discourse, values, and themes on which instructional texts were based would positively influence the ability of African American students to interpret fiction. Lee (1995) explained student improvement in terms of schema theory, which asserts that when analogies are used to connect unfamiliar information with existing schemata, unfamiliar information is placed within a recognizable context. This familiarity often leads to better comprehension and high mastery of skills (Collins *et al.*, 1991; Resnick, 1987). Lee concluded that there is a need to further analyze classroom environments wherein teachers create learning strategies out of metacognitive experiences involving the analysis of culturally specific texts and culturally familiar experiences.

In an effort to examine the schooling experiences of Puerto Rican girls, Rolon-Dow (2005) used "critical care praxis" as a conceptual framework to examine how teachers connected with students. They found that teachers who had a historical understanding of students' lives were able to translate race conscious orientations into pedagogical benefits and use counter narratives to create more intimate caring connections between themselves and the communities in which their students lived. These findings were similar to what Valenzuela (1999) found in her work with Mexican immigrant and U.S. born students. She discovered that when there was "authentic caring"—wherein students' cultural capital was affirmed and validated by teachers—the students were more engaged and willing to assert effort to be academically successful. This was in stark contrast to teachers who used "subtractive" methods of teaching which frequently ignored students' cultural and social capital.

Nasir (2002) found that the relationship between identity and schooling was integral to mathematics proficiency for African American adolescents. Building on the students' knowledge of dominoes, Nasir found that in practices such as games of dominoes, mathematical goals arose in the context of activity wherein math concepts became a normalized and mandatory part of particular activity. Nasir (2000) found similar types of connections between culture and learning when she explored how basketball afforded different levels of engagement of statistical thinking and reasoning for African American males. Nasir suggests that when students' cultural experiences and contributions were not recognized as valuable parts of the learning process, students often assumed that their poor performance was a result of race-based failure. Thus, she makes an important call for linking classroom-learning goals with essential learning goals.

A number of other scholars have offered frameworks for the preparation of teachers for work in diverse school settings. Nieto (2000) has articulated three key factors that teacher education programs must consider if they are to seriously prepare teacher education students for diverse classrooms, (1) take a stand of social justice and diversity, (2) make social justice ubiquitous in teacher education and (3) promote teaching as a life-long journey of transformation. Each of these areas serve as a challenge to teacher education programs to probe the manner in which they seek to have candidates think about beliefs, attitudes, and knowledge that they have about diverse learners. The works done by the aforementioned scholars offers important conceptual and empirical works that can inform the reconceptualization of teacher capacity for diverse learners. However, we maintain that the use of the models from the multicultural paradigm must be equipped with a set of dispositions, beliefs, and commitments to equity in schools which we address as part of critical consciousness.

CRITICAL CONSCIOUSNESS AND REFLECTION

While much of the research on teacher capacity has centered on professional aspects of teaching such as subject matter knowledge, pedagogy, and cognition, more recent attention has been given to the political values and beliefs and to the importance of teachers' critical consciousness about the social and political contexts of society and education. Moll & Arnot-Hopffer (2004), for example, talk about the need for teachers to have "ideological clarity," about the work they do, and to recognize that teaching is always a political endeavor. They stress that ideological clarity requires teachers to have an awareness of the cultural capital that students bring to the classroom and know how to take advantage of the rich array of cultural, social, and community resources at their disposal within the classrooms and communities they teach. The idea here is that when teachers foster positive teacher-student and teacher-family relationships, there is a much better opportunity to understand how to structure learning situations without requiring students to relinquish their cultural integrity in pursuit of academic success. Villegas and Lucas (2003) call for teachers to acquire "sociocultural consciousness," which means recognizing that people's ways of thinking are significantly influenced by race, class, gender, and language, and the hierarchical social systems in which they are located.

Much of the discourse on critical consciousness emerges from the concept of critical pedagogy, and critical educational theorists in particular. Critical educational theorists clearly advocate that teachers must first understand that schools are—"agencies of social legitimization" (Anyon, 1988). Moreover, they assert that schools are spaces where social hierarchies and social practices are reified through curriculum, policy, pedagogy, daily interactions, and discipline. Because all school practices are embedded in these larger institutional social structures, many critical theorists see educational institutions as prime contributors to ideological hegemony (Anyon, 1988; Giroux, 1988; Macedo, 2000; McLaren, 2003a; McCarthy & Crichlow, 1997). It is the ideological structure of institutional hegemony that allows social prejudice and deficit thinking to flourish uncontested in schools, thus institutionalizing the failure of working-class students and students of color (Hatcher & Troyna, 1993).

We posit that these critical works should be definitions of teacher capacity for diverse learners. Critical educational theorists differ from many multicultural education scholars in that they do not see individual prejudice or ignorance as the problem in education, but rather that it is the systemic institutionalization of such prejudice which allows it to remain hidden and thriving. Looking at schools through the lens of political structure necessitates that teachers understand their role in such a structure (Bell *et al.*, 2003; hooks, 1994). Given the widespread complexity of how education is delivered in the twenty-first century, it can be argued that pre-service teachers need to examine their perspectives on schooling and ideology because these frameworks may play useful roles in the overall knowledge base that pre-service teachers develop.

Reflection as part of critical consciousness

A central part of teacher capacity is examining one's own ideas and how these influence the work of teachers. A number of scholars have provided frameworks for thinking about how to engage pre-service teachers in this important reflection (Milner, 2003; Howard, 2003). A critical consciousness would take teacher's hegemonic thinking to task, and require them to reflect on the effects of their practice on the students they teach. This means that the preparation of critical educators begins with "consciousness" about their role in the institution and their ability to see themselves as agents of change. "To insist that teachers recognize the political nature of their own work can be understood as part of a broader critical effort to make them self-reflective of the interests and assumptions that shape their classroom practices" (Giroux, 1994, p 36). Parker (1987) states that one of our goals as educators is to help students develop "critical habits of mind" in which they judge whether conclusions are supported by sufficient evidence, including investigation of the accuracy of historical events as they have traditionally been told.

It is the inclusion of social and political consciousness in teacher preparation that unnerves many critics of teacher education, who argue that teacher preparation should be devoid of politics, and soft pedagogy, and should be steeped in rigorous subject matter (Ravitch, 2000; Schlesinger, 1991). From a critical pedagogy approach, teachers play the role of facilitators of discussion and critical dialogue. They do not seek to provide students with "right" answers, but push them to collect information to support their beliefs. However, Freire (1989) advises teachers to be knowledgeable in their field and to apply a challenging curriculum. Engaging in "problem posing" education, does not imply that there is a lack of rigor or that content knowledge is not being obtained by the students. Instead, students are receiving a quality education that also includes "humanizing pedagogy" where teachers and student dialogically engage in discovering and transforming their world. Does knowledge about the politics of education infer that teachers should be trained in certain types of pedagogy? Critical pedagogy seeks to counter what Bartolomé (2003) calls the "methods fetish." According to Bartolomé it matters not what type of methods teachers engage in as long as the goal is the same—to empower marginalized students. Thus, "the actual strengths of methods depend, first and foremost, on the degree to which they embrace a humanizing pedagogy" (p. 425).

Teachers who have a critical or problem posing approach to teaching engage students in the spirit of critical inquiry on an ongoing basis. Coincidentally, in standards related to teaching in each of the primary content areas, teachers are encouraged to promote and teach inquiry based skills tied to specific content areas. Freire's problem posing begins with the curiosity of the learner; critical inquiry entails not only asking questions, but investigating potential solutions, creating new knowledge, seeking an understanding of various phenomenon, discussing discoveries and experiences, and then engaging in reflection and application of new found knowledge. Today's teachers should have the capacity to challenge students to question the world around them, including issues in their communities, topics in the nation, problems in the world, and problematizing ways to identify interventions for these occurrences.

TEACHER CAPACITY: IMPLICATIONS FOR RESEARCH AND PRACTICE

How teacher preparation will continue to evolve is unclear on multiple levels. Regardless, teachers will continue to enter classrooms with unprecedented ethnic, racial, linguistic, and social class diversity. We suggested at the outset of this chapter that historically teacher capacity has been narrowly defined in terms of core knowledge and skills, without careful consideration to diverse populations. McDiarmid and Clevenger-Bright (in this volume, Chapter 9) argue that enhancing teacher capacity is contingent upon a number of factors such as technology, policy, and changing demographics. To that end, we posit the need for research that examines whether and how teachers who are equipped with the capacities we have outlined are influencing learning for diverse students. Teacher education practitioners and researchers must be equally committed to, on one hand, creating and examining programs designed to ensure that teachers entering classrooms with the capacity to teach in today's diverse learning communities, and, on the other, to documenting how student learning is improved when teachers have these capacities.

It is imperative for teacher education researchers to concern themselves with establishing a "culture of evidence" which documents, when, where, and how teacher education programs are making an impact on teacher quality and student learning. Cochran-Smith and Zeichner (2005) argue that we need "studies from differing paradigmatic and epistemological perspectives that examine the links between . . . teacher preparation context for learning, what teacher candidates actually learn, how their learning is played out in practice in K-12 schools and classrooms, and how this influences pupils' learning" (p. 2).

It is absolutely essential that researchers produce evidence that speaks to the best and most effective means to prepare teachers for diverse school settings. Furthermore, teacher educators must remain mindful of the politics of debate about how to prepare high quality teachers to teach in diverse schools—particularly in light of persistent low performance in low-income, culturally diverse school settings. Therefore, it is essential that not only the technical knowledge base be established to prepare teachers, but also that a political infrastructure be developed that recognizes the difficulty of articulating the manner in which most teachers are prepared in this country, and a structure that can withstand the large scale attacks on the profession.

We offer three considerations that we believe can inform the future direction, research and thinking regarding teacher capacity for diverse learners in a manner that speaks directly from the research base on teacher preparation.

1   Given the type of scrutiny that has been given to multicultural interventions for teacher capacity, we call for more empirical research on the correlation between multicultural concepts, content, and paradigms and student learning. Questions to be considered might entail: how does mathematics content situated in a multicultural framework influence students' math proficiency? Or, what are the academic outcomes of students who are placed in classrooms where teachers utilize culturally responsive teaching practices? What do curriculum design and pedagogical practices look like for teachers who employ a critical consciousness in their teaching? How do low performing readers respond to a critical pedagogy orientation? The answers to these questions are vital to the continued push to expand the paradigm of teacher capacity for diverse learners. Extensive systematic research on what is working and what is inadequate in the training of teachers for diverse school settings is crucial to ensure that the attributes of teacher capacity remain informed by current research, the latest policy initiatives, and reliable data on student demographics and learning outcomes.

2   Much of the argument about revising teaching capacity for diverse learners has implications for teacher education programs. Therefore, future research should also investigate the effectiveness of teachers who come from more social justice oriented programs. A growing number of programs have made explicit mention of their programs being dedicated to the implementation of social justice theory and practice. Teacher capacity for diverse learners can be fortified by taking note of the practices, coursework, theory, and ongoing supervision given to teachers who attend such programs. And ask pointed questions such as: are these teachers better prepared to teach diverse learners? Do they remain in hard-to-staff schools longer? Ongoing research with these programs can investigate the manner of how students achieve with teachers from these programs. Indices do not have to be restricted to test scores, but could include indices such as graduation rates, attendance, college enrollment, grade point average, behavioral issues, and overall student engagement in course material.

3   The documentation of best practices will continue to be instrumental in teacher capacity for diverse learners. While a necessary component of teacher capacity is centered on what teachers need to know, more attention should be placed on what they *do* in classrooms. In particular, when teaching practices seem to be contributing to the academic success of diverse learners, they should be assessed for potential replication. While many novice teachers are equipped with sound theoretical knowledge of subject matter, pedagogy, and critical consciousness, the transfer of that knowledge into meaningful teaching practices is frequently an insurmountable

obstacle. Further examination and documentation of best practices can serve as useful models to help provide novice and experienced teachers with the type of capacity that can contribute to their effectiveness of teachers in diverse classrooms.

CONCLUSION

One of the biggest challenges we face in helping to redefine teacher capacity in a manner that is reflective of the needs of diverse learners is to assess the moral, political, and professional will of those involved in teacher development to do what is right for today's student population. The importance of rethinking teacher capacity for diverse learners is underscored by the persistent and disproportionate academic underachievement of scores of culturally diverse and low-income students. The need to rethink teacher capacity is essential because recent data from student academic outcomes informs us that many of the attributes of current teacher capacity are falling terribly short in helping all students learn. Moreover, in an era of increased accountability, high stakes testing, and decreased funding for schools it is absolutely essential for teachers to be the best that they can be in all facets of their work—their students deserve nothing short. While we make a call for additional research and analysis of what teachers should know and do to reach all learners, we already have at our disposal a multitude of evidence which provides educators with information of what does work, what does not, and how to transform various aspects of teaching and learning. We cannot afford to ignore these worthwhile and informative contributions.

We conclude with the point with which we began. How we think about teacher capacity—their knowledge, skills and dispositions—must be informed by the complexities of the changing demographics of the students they are teaching. This has major implications for how we think and care about young people in a diverse society and how we view equity, justice, and students' opportunities. It is our hope that the preceding discussion will inform ongoing empirical research, analysis, and dissemination of information about how we can establish a comprehensive and critical conception of teacher capacity for teaching diverse learners. The gravity of this challenge is underscored by the millions of school children who depend on educators to help them reach their full potential in every aspect of their development as citizens. Not only does this have ramifications for the work that we do as educators, but it has consequential effects on the very fabric of our democracy and the greater global community as well.

REFERENCES

Anderson, J.D. (1988) *The education of blacks in the south 1860–1935*. Chapel Hill, NC: University of North Carolina Press.

American Board for the Certification of Teacher Excellence (2003) *American Board for the Certification of Teacher Excellence: promoting teacher quality—impacting student learning*. Available from http://www.abcte.org.

Angus, D.L. (2001) *Professionalism and the public good: a brief history of teacher certification*. Fordham Foundation: Washington, DC.

Anyon, J. (1988) Schools as agencies of social legitimation. In W. Pinar (ed.) *Contemporary curriculum discourses* (pp. 175–200). Arizona: Gorsuch Scarisbrick Publishers.

Artilles, A.J., Trent, S.C., & Palmer, J.D. (2004) Culturally diverse students in special education. In J.A. & C.A.M. Banks (eds.), *Handbook of research on multicultural education* (pp. 716–735). San Francisco: Jossey-Bass.

Au, K.H. & Jordan, C. (1981) Teaching reading to Hawaiian children: finding a culturally appropriate solution. In H. Trueba, G.P. Guthrie, & K.H. Au (eds.), *Culture in the bilingual classroom: studies in classroom ethnography* (pp. 139–152). Rowley, MA: Newbury House.

Bagley, W. (1939) Basic problems in teacher education. *Teacher Education Journal*, 1, 100–105.

Ball, D.L. & McDiarmid, G.W. (1990) The subject matter preparation of teachers. In W.R. Houston (ed.), *Handbook of research on teacher education* (pp. 437–449). New York: Macmillan.

Ball, D.L. & Bass, H. (2000) Interweaving content and pedagogy in teaching and learning to teach: knowing and using mathematics. In J. Boaler (ed.), *Multiple perspectives on the teaching and learning of mathematics* (pp. 83–104). Westport, CT: Ablex.

Ballou, D. & Podgursky, M. (2000) Reforming teacher preparation and licensing: what is the evidence? *Teachers College Record*, 102(1), 5–27.

Banks, J.A. (1995) Multicultural education: historical development, dimensions, and practice. In J.A. Banks and C.A.M. Banks (eds.), *The handbook of research on multicultural education*. (pp. 3–24). New York: Macmillan.

Banks, J.A. (2002) *Introduction to multicultural education* (Third ed.). Boston: Allyn Bacon.

Banks, J.A. (2004) Multicultural education: historical development, dimensions, and practice. In J.A. Banks & C.A.M. Banks (eds.), *Handbook of research on multicultural education* (Second ed., pp. 3–29). San Francisco: Jossey-Bass.

Bartolomé, L.I. (2003) Beyond the methods fetish. In A. Darder, M. Baltodano, & R. Torres (eds.) *The critical pedagogy reader* (pp. 408–429). New York: RoutledgeFalmer.

Begle, E.G. (1979) *Critical variables in mathematics education: findings from a survey of the empirical literature*. Washington, DC: Mathematical Association of America.

Bell, L.A., Washington, S., Weinstein, G., & Love, B. (2003) Knowing ourselves as instructors. In A. Darder, M. Baltodano, & R. Torres. (eds.) *The critical pedagogy reader* (pp. 408–429). New York: RoutledgeFalmer.

Bennett, C. (2003) *Comprehensive multicultural education: theory and practice* (Fifth ed.). Boston: Allyn & Bacon.

Bigelow, K. (1958) New direction in teacher education appraised. *Teachers College Record*, 59, 350–356.

Brown, J.S., Collins, A., & Duguid, P. (1989, January–February) Situated cognition and the culture of learning. *Educational Researcher*, 18(1) pp. 32–42.

Cochran-Smith, M. (2003) The multiple meanings of multicultural teacher education: a conceptual framework. *Teacher Education Quarterly*, Spring 2003, 7–26.

Cochran-Smith, M. (2004) The problem of teacher education (Editorial) *Journal of Teacher Education*, 55, 295–299.

Cochran-Smith, M. & Fries, K. (2005) Researching teacher education in changing times: politics and paradigms. In M. Cochran-Smith & K.M. Zeichner (eds.), *Studying teacher education* (pp. 69–110). Washington, DC: American Educational Research Association.

Cochran-Smith, M. & Zeichner, K.M. (2005). *Studying teacher education*. Washington, DC: Erlbaum.

Cochran-Smith, M., Davis, D., & Fries, M.K. (2004) Multicultural teacher education: research practice and policy. In J.A. Banks & C.A.M. Banks (eds.), *Handbook of research on multicultural education* (pp. 936–978). San Francisco: Jossey-Bass.

Cole, M. (1996) *Cultural psychology: a once and future discipline*. Cambridge, MA: The Belknap Press.

Cole, M. (2000) Struggling with complexity: the handbook of child psychology at the millennium. Essay review. *Human Development*, 6, 369–375.

Collins, A., Brown, J.S., & Holum, A. (1991) Cognitive apprenticeship: making thinking visible. *American Educator*, 6–11, 38–46.

Darling-Hammond, L. (1988) Teacher quality and educational equality. *College Board Review*, 148, Summer, 16–23, 39–41.

Darling-Hammond, L. (2000) Teacher quality and student achievement: a review of state policy evidence. *Education Policy Analysis Archives*, 8(1), Retrieved October 3, 2004 from http:// epaa.asu.edu/epaa/v8n1.

Darling-Hammond, L. (2004) From "Separate but equal" to "No child left behind": the collision of new standards and old inequalities. In D. Meier, A. Kohn, L. Darling-Hammond, T.R. Sizer, & G. Wood (eds.), *Many children left behind* (pp. 3–32). Boston: Beacon Press.

Darling-Hammond, L. (2005) Teaching as a profession: lessons in teacher preparation and professional development. *Phi Delta Kappan*, 87(3), 237–240.

Darling-Hammond, L., Chung, R., & Frelow, F. (2002) Variation in teacher preparation: how well do different pathways prepare teachers to teach? *Journal of Teacher Education*, 53(4), 286–302.

Dewey, J. (1897) My pedagogic creed. *The School Journal, LIV*, Number 3, 77–80.

Erickson, F. (2002) Culture and human development. *Human Development*, 45(4), 299–306.

Floden, R.E. & Meniketti, M. (2005) Research on the effects of coursework in the arts and sciences and in the foundations of education. In M.C. Smith & K.M. Zeichner (eds.), *Studying Teacher Education* (pp. 261–308). New Jersey: Erlbaum Publishers.

Fraser, J.W. (2001) *The school in the United States: a documentary history*. New York: McGraw Hill.

Freire, P. (1989) *Pedagogy of the oppressed*. New York: The Continuum Publishing Company.

Gay, G. (2000) *Culturally responsive teaching*. New York: Teachers College Press.

Gay, G. & Howard, T.C. (2001) Multicultural education for the 21st century. *The Teacher Educator*, 36(1), 1–16.

Giroux, H.A. (1988) Border Pedagogy in the age of postmodernism. *Journal of Education*, 170(3), 162–181.

Giroux, H.A. (1993) *Border Crossings: cultural workers and the politics of education*. New York: Routledge.

Giroux, H.A. (1994) Teachers, public life, and curriculum reform. In *Peabody Journal of Education* (69), 3, pp. 35–47.

Goldhaber, D., Perry, D., & Anthony, E. (2003) *NBPTS certification: who applies and what factors are associated with success?* (National Partnership for Excellence and Accountability in Teaching Report). Washington, DC: Office of Educational Research and Improvement (ERIC Document No. ED 448 152).

Goldhaber, D.D. & Brewer, D.J. (1998) When should we reward degrees for teachers? *Phi Delta Kappan*, 80(2), 134, 136–138.

Goldhaber, D.D. & Brewer, D.J. (2000) Does teacher certification matter? High school teacher certification status and student achievement. *Educational Evaluation and Policy Analysis*, 22(2), 129–145.

Gollnick, D.M. (1995) National and state initiatives for multicultural education. In J.A. Banks & C.A.M. Banks (eds.), *Handbook of research on multicultural education* (pp. 44–64). New York: Macmillan.

Grant, C.A. & Secada, W. (1990) Preparing teachers for diversity. In W.R. Houston, M. Haberman, & J. Sikula (eds.), *Handbook of research on teacher education* (pp. 403–422). New York: Macmillan.

Green, A. (1997) *Education, globalization and the nation state*. London: Macmillan.

Grossman, P.L. (1990) *The making of a teacher: teacher knowledge and teacher education*. New York: Teachers College Press.

Grossman, P.L. & Richert, A. (1988) Unacknowledged knowledge growth: a re-examination of the effects of teacher education. *Teaching and Teacher Education*, 4(1), 53–62.

Grossman, P.L., Schoenfeld, A., & Lee, C.D. (2005) Teaching subject matter. In L. Darling-Hammond & J. Bransford (eds.), *Preparing teachers for a changing world* (pp. 201–231). San Francisco: Jossey-Bass.

Gutiérrez, K. (2002) Studying cultural practices in urban learning communities. *Human Development*, 45(4), 312–321.

Gutiérrez, K. & Rogoff, B. (2003) Cultural ways of learning: individual traits or repertoires of practice. *Educational Researcher*, 32(5), 19–25.

Gutiérrez, K.D., Baquedano-López, P., & Tejada, C. (2000) Rethinking diversity: hybridity and hybrid language practices in the third space. *Mind, Culture, and Activity*, 6, 286–303.

Hatcher, R. & Troyna, B. (1993) Racialization and children. In C. McCarthy & W. Crichlow (eds.), *Race, identity, and representation in education*. New York: Routledge.

Hill, H.C., Rowan, B., & Ball, D.L. (2005) Effects of teachers' mathematical knowledge for teaching on student achievement. *American Educational Research Journal*, 42(2), 371–406.

hooks, b. (1994) *Teaching to transgress: education as the practice of freedom*. New York: Routledge.

Hodgkinson, H. (2002) Demographics and teacher education—an overview. *Journal of Teacher Education*, 53(2), 102–105.

Hollins, E.R. & Guzman, M.T. (2006) Research on preparing teachers for diverse populations. In M. Cochran-Smith & K.M. Zeichner (eds.), *Studying teacher education* (pp. 477–548).

Howard, T.C. (2003) Culturally relevant pedagogy: ingredients for critical teacher reflection. *Theory Into Practice*, 42(3), 195–202.

Irvine, J.J. (2003) *Educating teachers for diversity: seeing with a cultural eye*. New York: Teachers College Press.

Jencks, C. & Phillips, M. (eds.) (1998) *The black-white test score gap*. Washington, DC: Brookings Institution Press.

Kanpol, B. & McClaren, P. (eds.) (1995) *Critical multiculturalism*. Buckingham, England: Open University Press.

Ladson-Billings, G. (1995) Toward a theory of culturally relevant pedagogy. *American Educational Research Journal*, 32(3), 465–491.

Ladson-Billings, G. & Darling-Hammond, L. (2000) The validity of National Board for Professional Teaching Standards (NBPTS)/Interstate New Teacher Assessment and Support Consortium (INTASC) Assessments for Effective Urban Teachers: findings and implications for assessments. (National Partnership for Excellence and Accountability in Teaching Report). Washington, DC: Office of Educational Research and Improvement. (ERIC Document No. 448 152).

Lagemann, E. (2000) *An elusive science: the troubling history of educational research*. Chicago: The University of Chicago Press.

Lanier, J. & Little, J. (2986) Research on teacher education. In M. Wittrock (ed.), *Handbook of research on teaching* (3rd. ed.) (pp. 527–569). Washington, DC: American Educational Research Association.

Lave, J. (1996) Teaching, as learning, in practice. *Mind, Culture, and Activity*, 3, 149–164.

Lee, C.D. (1995) Signifying as a scaffold for literary interpretation. *Journal of Black Psychology*, 21(4), 357–381.

Leinhardt, G. & Greeno, J.G. (1986) The cognitive skill of teaching. *Journal of Educational Psychology*, 78(2), 75–95.

McCarthy, C. & Crichlow, W. (1993) Introduction: theories of identity, theories of representation, theories of race. In C. McCarthy & W. Crichlow (eds.) *Race, identity, and representation in education*. New York: Routledge.

McLaren, P. (1991) Critical pedagogy: constructing an arch of social dreaming and a doorway to hope. *Journal of Education*, 173(1), 9–34.

McLaren, P. (2003a) *Life in schools: an introduction to critical pedagogy in the foundations of education* (4th edition). New York: Addison Wesley Longman Inc.

Ma, L. (1999) *Knowing and teaching elementary mathematics: teachers' understanding of fundamental mathematics in China and the United States*. Mahway, NJ: Erlbaum.

Macedo, D. (2000) *Chomsky on miseducation*. New York: Rowan & Littlefield Publishers, Inc.

Milner, H.R. (2003) Teacher reflection and race in cultural contexts: history, meanings, and methods in teaching. *Theory into Practice*, 42(3), 173–180.

Moll, L.C. & Ruiz, R. (2002) The schooling of Latino students. In M. Suarez-Orozco & M. Paez (eds.), *Latinos: Remaking America* (pp. 362–374). Berkeley: University of California Press.

Moll, L.C. & Arnot-Hopffer, E. (2004) Sociocultural competence in teacher education. *Journal of Teacher Education*, 56(3), 242–247.

Monk, D.H. (1994) Subject area preparation of secondary mathematics and science teachers and student achievement. *Economics of Education Review*, 13(2), 125–145.

Monk, D.H., & King, J. (1994) Multilevel teacher resource effects on pupil performance in secondary mathematics and science: the role of teacher subject matter preparation. In R.G.

Ehrenberg (ed.), *Contemporary policy issues: choices and consequences in education* (pp. 29–58). City: ILR Press.

Munby, H., Russell, T., & Martin, A.K. (2001) Teachers' knowledge and how it develops. In V. Richardson (ed.), *Handbook of research on teaching* (4th ed.) (pp. 877–905). Washington, DC: American Educational Research Association.

Nasir, N. (2000) Points ain't everything: emergent goals and average and percent understandings in the play of basketball among African-American students. *Anthropology and Education Quarterly*, 31(3), 283–305.

Nasir, N. (2002) Identity, goals, and learning: mathematics in cultural practice. In N. Nasir & P. Cobb (eds.) *Mathematical Thinking and Learning*, 4 vols. (2&3), 213–248.

National Board for Professional Teaching Standards (2001) *Report on issues referred to the working groups by the Equal Opportunity Coordinating Committee (EOCC)*, Arlington, VA.

National Commission on Teaching and America's Future (1996) *What matters most: teaching for American's future*. New York: Teachers College, Columbia University.

NCES (2003) *School and Staffing Survey, 1999–2000*. Washington, DC: National Center for Education Statistics, U.S. Department of Education. Retrieved October 3, 2003, from http://www.nces.ed.gov/surveys/sass

Nieto, S. (2000) Placing equity front and center: some thoughts on transforming teacher education for a new century. *Journal of Teacher Education*, 51(3), 180–187.

Nieto, S. (2004) *Affirming diversity. The sociopolitical context of multicultural education*. Boston: Pearson.

Obidah, J.E. (2000) Mediating boundaries of race, class, and professional authority as a critical multiculturalist. *Teachers College Record*, 102(6), 1035–1060.

Palmer, P.J. (1997) *The courage to teach*. San Francisco: Jossey-Bass Publishers.

Parker, W.R. (1987) Navigating the Unity/Diversity Tension in Education. *Social Studies* 88(1): 12–18.

Ravitch, D. (2000) *Left back, a century of failed school reforms*. New York: Simon & Schuster.

Renaldo, R. (1989) *Culture and truth: the remaking of social analysis*. Boston: Beacon Press.

Resnick, L. (1987) *Education and learning to think*. Washington, DC: National Academy Press.

Richardson, V. (2001) *Handbook of research on teaching*. American Educational Research Association: Washington, DC.

Rogoff, B. (1990) *Apprenticeship in thinking: cognitive development in social context*. New York: Oxford University Press.

Rogoff, B. (2003) *The cultural nature of human development*. New York: Oxford University Press.

Rogoff, B. & Angelillo, C. (2002) Investigating the coordinated functioning of multifaceted cultural practices in human development. *Human Development*, 45(4), 211–225.

Rolon Dow, R. (2005) Critical care: a color(full) analysis of care narratives in the schooling experiences of Puerto Rican girls. *American Educational Research Journal*, 42(1), 77–111.

Schlesinger, A. (1991) The disuniting of America: what we all stand to lose if multicultural education takes the wrong approach. *American Educator*, 15(3) 21–33.

Shulman, L.S. (1986) Those who understand: knowledge growth in teaching. *Educational Researcher*, 15(2), 4–14.

Shulman, L.S. (1987) Knowledge and teaching: foundations of the new reform. *Harvard Educational Review*, 57, 1–22.

Siddle Walker, V. (1996) *Their highest potential: an African American school community in the segregated south*. Chapel Hill, NC: University of North Carolina Press.

Sikula, J., Buttery, T., & Guyton, E. (eds.) (1996) *Handbook of research on teacher education* (2nd ed.) New York: Macmillan.

Sleeter, C. & Grant, C. (2003) *Making choices for multicultural education: five approaches to race, class, and gender* (4th ed.). New York: John Wiley & Sons, Inc.

Spiro, R.J., Feltovich, P.J., Jacobson, M.J., & Coulson, R.L. (1991) Cognitive flexibility, constructivism, and hypertext: random access instruction for advanced knowledge acquisition in ill-structured domains. *Educational Technology*, 31(1), 24–33.

Spring, J. (2006) *Deculturalization and the struggle for equality*. Columbus, OH: McGraw-Hill Publishers.

Stigler, J.W. & J. Hiebert (2003) Improving mathematics teaching, *Educational Leadership*, 61(5), 12–17.

Tharp, R. & Gallimore, R. (1988) *Rousing minds to life: teaching, learning and schooling in social context*. Cambridge: Cambridge University Press.

Tyack, D. (2003) *Seeking common ground*. Cambridge: Harvard University Press.

U.S. Census Bureau (2000) *Statistical abstract of the United States* (120th edition). Washington, DC: U.S. Government Printing Office.

U.S. Department of Education, National Center for Education Statistics (2002) *Early estimates of public elementary and secondary education statistics: school year 2001–2002*. Retrieved December 27, 2002, from http://nces.ed.gov/edstats/

U.S. Department of Education, National Center for Education Statistics (2003) *Digest for education statistics*, 2002, NCS 2003–060, Washington, DC.

U.S. Department of Education (2002) *Meeting the highly qualified teachers challenge: the secretary's annual report on teacher quality*. Washington, DC: Author, Office of Postsecondary Education.

Valenzuela, A. (1999) *Subtractive schooling: U.S. Mexican youth and the politics of caring*. New York: State University New York Press.

Villegas, A.M. & Lucas, T. (2003) Preparing culturally responsive teachers: rethinking the curriculum. *Journal of Teacher Education*, 53(1), 20–32.

Vygotsky, L. (1986) *Thought and language*. Cambridge, MA: The MIT Press.

Wallerstein, N. & Bernstein, E. (1988) Empowerment education: Freire's ideas adapted to health education. *Health Education Quarterly* (15), 4, 379–394.

Wenglinsky, H. (2002) How schools matter: the link between teacher classroom practices and student academic performance. *Education Policy Analysis Archives*, 10(12). Retrieved January 2, 2004, from http://epaa.Asu.edu/epaa/v10n12?

Wilson, S.M. & Floden, R.E. (2003) Creating effective teachers—Concise answers for hard questions: an addendum to the report *Teacher preparation research: current knowledge, gaps and recommendation*. Washington, DC: ERIC Clearinghouse on Teaching and Teacher Education.

Wilson, S.M., Shulman, L.S., & Richert, A.E. (1987) 150 different ways of knowing: representations of knowledge in teaching. In J. Calderhead (ed.), *Exploring teachers' thinking* (pp. 104–124). London: Cassell.

Wilson, S.M., Floden, R.E., & Ferrini-Mundy, J. (2001) *Teacher preparation research: current knowledge, gaps, and recommendations*. Seattle: Center for the Study of Teaching and Policy.

Wineburg, S.S. & Wilson, S.M. (1988) Models of wisdom in teaching of history. *Phi Delta Kappan*, 70(1) 50–58.

Wink, J. (1997) *Critical pedagogy: notes from the real world*. Boston: Pearson.

Wink, J. & Wink, D. (2004) *What's love got to do with it?* Boston: Pearson.

Wise, A.E. & Darling-Hammond, L. (1987) *Licensing teachers: design for a profession*. Santa Monica, CA: RAND

Wise, A.E. & Leibbrand, A. (1993) Accreditation and the creation of a profession of teaching. *Phi Delta Kappan*, 75(2), 133–173.

Wittrock, M. (ed.) (1986) *Handbook of research on teaching* (3rd ed.). New York: Macmillan.

Zeichner, K. (1993) Traditions of practice in U.S. preservice teacher education programs. *Teaching and Teacher Education*, 9, 1–13.

Zeichner, K. (1999) The new scholarship of teacher education. *Educational Researcher*, 28(9), 4–15.

Zeichner, K.M. & Hoeft, K. (1996) Teacher socialization for cultural diversity. In J. Sikula, T.J. Buttery, & E. Guyton (eds.), *Handbook of research on teacher education* (2nd ed., pp. 525–547). New York: Macmillan.

Zumwalt, K. (1989) The need for curricular vision. In M.C. Reynolds (ed.), *Knowledge base for beginning teachers* (pp. 173–184). New York: Pergamon Press.

11 Teacher capacity and social justice in teacher education

Carl A. Grant and Vonzell Agosto
University of Wisconsin-Madison

INTRODUCTION

Education is "the great equalizer of the conditions of man," declared Horace Mann, in his annual report to the Massachusetts State Board of Education in 1848 (Cremin, 1957). Mann, who became known as the father of the American common school, believed public education could be transformed into a powerful instrument for social unity by providing all children with a common set of values and skills.

More than 150 years later, Mann's vision of education as an equalizer has not been realized in the United States, despite the multitude of federal, state, and local policies devoted to achieving this goal. Today in a nation where power and privilege in our society remain stratified by race, gender, and socio-economic status, we are engaged in an ongoing debate about what constitutes educational policies based on equality, equity or social justice.

In this chapter we discuss social justice and teacher capacity, an amalgam of teachers' knowledge, skills and dispositions, by posing and answering three questions. How should education professionals define the concept of social justice? What is the relationship between teacher capacity and social justice? What are teacher educators doing in scholarship and practice to bring about social justice? Our purpose is to provide teacher educators with an overview of the concepts of social justice and teacher capacity, so they may understand the relationship between the two and consider how well they are contributing to Horace Mann's vision of education as the "great equalizer."

We draw on literature from the field of teacher education, but also borrow from the literature of moral and political philosophy as well as social policy. In addition, we examine a particular body of teacher education literature—articles from four journals that focus on social justice over the past three decades—in order to identify the characteristic practices associated with social justice efforts in education

The chapter is organized around three major ideas each of which are presented in the following three sections: (1) an overview of the history and evolution of the concept of social justice; (2) an examination of the relationship between teacher capacity and the implementation of social justice; and (3) a review of the literature from four journals to examine how educators are currently attempting to implement social justice.

AN OVERVIEW OF THE HISTORY AND EVOLUTION OF THE CONCEPT OF SOCIAL JUSTICE

The term social justice was first used by Luigi Taparelli d'Azeglio, an Italian Catholic scholar, in his *Theoretical Treatise on Natural Right Based on Fact*, published during the period from 1840–1843. However, it was John Stuart Mill who, according to Michael Novak (2000), gave this "anthropomorphic approach to social questions almost canonical status for modern thinkers" when, in 1863, he wrote in *Utilitarianism* that:

> Society should treat all equally well who have deserved equally well of it, that is, who have deserved equally well absolutely. This is the highest abstract standard of social and distributive justice; towards which all institutions, and the efforts of all virtuous citizens, should be made in the utmost degree to converge.

Although Mill's ideas about social justice held sway for decades, in the aftermath of World War II, scholars began to re-examine the concept of social justice. This came after it was apparent that Mills' ideas about "the greatest good for the greatest number" could be twisted or abused to lead to a "tyranny of the majority" such as Nazi Germany's mistreatment of the Jews and the United States' mistreatment of African Americans. One of the most important and influential modern examinations of the concept of social justice is John Rawls' *A Theory of Justice* (1971), which is credited with re-awakening an interest in political philosophy in the United States.

Rawls (1971) writes that, "Justice is the first virtue of social institutions, as truth is of systems of thought." He asserts that, "Each person possesses an inviolability founded on justice that even the welfare of society as a whole cannot override" (p. 3). Writing about the enduring significance of Rawls' work, Martha Nussbaum (2001) asserts that:

> The intuitive idea from which Rawls's theory starts is simple and profound: "Each person possesses an inviolability founded on justice that even the welfare of society as a whole cannot override." In other words, the pursuit of a greater social good should not make us mar the lives of individuals by abridging their basic rights and entitlements. In particular, Rawls is concerned with the many ways in which attributes that have no moral worth—like class, race, and sex—frequently deform people's prospects in life. Even if racism and sexism could be shown to maximize social utility, he says, they would still violate our basic sense of fairness.
>
> (p. 3)

During the 1950s and 1960s, when Rawls was starting his academic career, major social justice events and movements for civil rights were taking place in the United States. These had significant implications for education, as well as for the kinds of teacher capacity necessary for dealing with these issues.

Although President Harry S. Truman's 1945 creation of the President's Committee on Civil Rights and the subsequent desegregation of the United States armed forces were among the first postwar steps toward making social justice a reality, the most important public policy changes arose in 1954 with the Supreme Court's unanimous decision in *Brown v. Board of Education*, 347 U.S. 483 (1954). The decision struck down the separate but equal doctrine of *Plessey v. Ferguson*. Chief Justice Earl Warren, delivering the opinion of the court wrote:

> Does segregation of children in public school solely on the basis of race, even though the physical facilities and other "tangible" factors may be equal, deprive the children of equal education opportunity? We believe it does.

In the aftermath of the *Brown* decision, the Civil Rights Movement became a major force in reshaping the philosophy, implementation, and practice of social justice in the United States. Events such as the following propelled the Civil Rights Movement:

- The brutal death of Emmett Till in Mississippi in August 1955, and the acquittal by an all-White jury of the two men who were arrested for the murder and who subsequently boasted about committing the murder in a *Look* magazine interview.
- Rosa Parks' decision on December 1, 1955 not to surrender her seat to a White man on the Montgomery bus. This led to a boycott which did not end until the buses were desegregated more than a year later.
- President Eisenhower's decision to send in federal troops to intervene on behalf of the students who were trying to integrate Little Rock High School.
- The 1965 Selma-to-Montgomery march for voting rights.

The Civil Rights Movement of the 1960s was followed by the second wave of the feminist movement, Chicano and American Indian movements, the Individuals with Disabilities Educational Act and movement, and the gay rights movement, all of which sought increased social justice. For example, the feminist movement of the 1970s, like the Civil Rights Movement of the 1960s included actions for social justice at the federal, state and local levels in such areas as employment and education.

Since the publication of *A Theory of Justice*, there has been an ongoing debate and discussion about the meaning of social justice. In his article "Defining Social Justice" Michael Novak takes note of the work of British born economist and political philosopher Friedrich Hayek's assertion that social justice is a mirage:

> Hayek points out that whole books and treatises have been written about social justice without ever offering a definition of it. It is allowed to float in the air as if everyone will recognize an instance of it when it appears.
>
> (Novak, 2000, p. 11)

Novak continues his observations about the difficulty of defining social justice by further reference to Hayek's assertions that social justice is a mirage:

> Hayek points out another defect of twentieth-century theories of social justice. Most authors assert that they use it to designate a virtue (a moral virtue, by their account). But most of the descriptions they attach to it appertain to impersonal states of affairs: high unemployment, or inequality of incomes or lack of a living wage are cited as instances of social injustice. Hayek goes to the heart of the matter: social justice is either a virtue or it is not. If it is, it can properly be ascribed only to the reflective and deliberate acts of individual persons. Most who use the term, however, ascribe it not to individuals but to social systems. They use "social justice" to denote a regulative principle of order; again, their focus is not virtue but power.

Goodlad (2002) is among a number of scholars (e.g. North, in press; Sturman, 1997) who contend that social justice is a contested and normative concept and that theoreticians and policymakers use the term to mean different things (e.g. equal opportunity, equity). Bell (1997), for example, defines social justice as both a process and a goal. The goal of social justice is full participation of all groups in a society that is mutually shaped to meet their needs. Social justice includes "a vision of society . . . [where] members are physically and psychologically safe and secure" (p. 3).

Barry (2005) argues that "social justice is, and is normally understood to be, a question of equal opportunities" (p. 7). In addition, he contends, "Social justice is about the treatment of inequalities of all kinds" (p. 10). Smith's (1994) argument about social justice, while somewhat similar to Barry's, employs the concept of fairness and equity. In addition, Smith is concerned with both fairness in the distribution of outcomes and how distributive injustices come about:

> The term social justice is taken to embrace both fairness and equity in the distribution of a wide range of attributes, which need not be confined to material things. Although the primary focus is on attributes, which have an immediate bearing on people's well-being or the quality of their lives, our conception of social justice goes beyond patterns of distribution, general and spatial, to incorporate attributes relevant to how these come about. While fairness is sometimes applied to procedures and justice to outcomes (Barry, 1989), we are concerned with both. Preference for the term social justice rather than justice in general is explained not by preoccupation with the distribution of attributes which might be labeled as social, but by a concern with something which happens socially among people in a society . . . Thus the meaning of socially justice adopted here is simultaneously distributional and relational.
>
> (p. 26)

According to Young (1990), "social justice aims for the elimination of institutionalized domination and oppression" (p. 15). She believes that social justice should facilitate: (1) "developing and exercising one's capacity and expressing one's experiences" and (2) "participating in and determining one's action" (p. 37).

Fraser (1997) introduces the "recognition" of "culturally defined groups" into the social justice discourse and contends that social justice must be defined within a framework that includes both economic redistribution and cultural recognition.

> Many actors appear to be moving away from a socialist political imaginary, in which the central problem of justice is redistribution to a "postsocialist" political imaginary, in which the central problem of justice is recognition. With this shift, the most salient social movements are no longer economically defined "classes" who are struggling to defend their "interest," end "exploitation," and win "redistribution." Instead, they are culturally defined "groups" or "communities of value" who are struggling to defend their "identities," end "cultural domination," and win "recognition."
>
> (pp. 8, 9)

TRACING THE RELATIONSHIP BETWEEN SHIFTING DEFINITIONS OF SOCIAL JUSTICE AND THEIR ROLE IN TEACHER EDUCATION AND THE DEVELOPMENT OF TEACHER CAPACITY

Social justice and teacher education

Implicitly and explicitly, the various civil right movements of the 1960s and 1970s raised fundamental questions about teacher capacity and spoke to the necessity of embedding social justice issues within the knowledge, skills, and dispositions of teacher education programs, as well as the scholarship and actions of teacher educators.

Two ideas a reader of the social justice literature may come away with are: (1) changes in society, such as the social inclusion of groups (people of color and other marginalized groups), the Civil Movements, progress toward gender equity, technological advances over the past sixty years continue to affect the ways social justice is defined, policies are written and implemented, and the ways people accept and act on a particular meanings of social justice; and (2) Rawls' notion of social justice as fairness holds an influential position in social justices discourses and, therefore, may be a useful tool for teacher educators to use as they examine both their scholarship and practice and teacher education program policies and practices.

It is important to locate social justice within the theories that are being used. Theoretical perspectives allow us to ask different questions about social injustices and contribute to a deeper understanding of justice or injustice concerning, for example, the distribution of attributes and resources or the recognition of culturally defined groups. More specifically, for instance, feminist theories, with their attention to how gender plays a role in shaping human consciousness and patriarchy functions within educational systems, ask somewhat different questions from those of post-colonial theories that focus on explaining the role of colonialism in persistent relations of domination and subordination in a multicultural, democratic society.

Since the publication of Rawls' book in 1971, social justice has been reinterpreted in light of the contemporary theories of equality, participation, and recognition (Miller, p. 2). Arguably, these theories became major criteria for addressing public policy in the 1960s. The passage of the Elementary and Secondary Education Act (ESEA) in 1965, for example, illustrates how these theories informed a political action aimed at correcting a failing education system for poor children. This legislation was based upon the theories of: (1) equality (i.e. equal opportunity); (2) participation (e.g. Latino children enjoying the privileges of public education, where their home language (Spanish) was the language of instruction and bilingual policies were in place to maintain the language); and (3) recognition (e.g. awareness of Asian American, Native American, and African children "as somebody").

Similarly, theories of equality, participation, and recognition influenced the funding of Head Start programs. Poor students and/or students of color were recognized and given access to an enriched social environment, where they received health and social services and education (Illinois Head Start Association, 2006). Likewise, the 1965 funding of Teacher Corps to prepare teachers for urban and rural schools and to improve home-school relationships was also a social justice act based on theories of equality, participation, and recognition. Teacher Corps recognized parents as a significant stakeholder in the education of their children, and they (parents and care-givers) were encouraged to participate in developing school policy and procedures that affected students in the school community.

Additionally, the reauthorization of ESEA in 2001, also known as *No Child Left Behind (NCLB)* legitimates this legislation in terms of equality, participation, and recognition. As the authors of *NCLB* state, "In America, no child should be left behind. Every child should be educated to his or her potential" (p. 3) *NCLB* is largely aimed at inner city students and is, in theory, supposed to empower parents and bring about an increase in teacher/school accountability for students' academic performance.

Over the past two decades, teacher educators have increasingly focused attention on how teachers' knowledge, skills and dispositions relate to social justice. For example, Giroux (1992), Kumashiro (2002), and Cochran-Smith (2003) each describe a different approach, idea or method for integrating social justice into teacher capacity and many of their claims address power and the distribution of resources. Giroux (1992) focuses on teacher pedagogy, Kumashiro (2002) takes a more global view of education, and Cochran-Smith (2003) speaks about teacher preparation.

In the early 1990s, Giroux (1992) argued for a pedagogy that would help teachers gain the capacity to teach for social justice:

> Learning to teach that is premised on a stance for social justice recognizes the importance of social justice pedagogy. This social justice pedagogy refers to a deliberate attempt to construct authentic conditions through which educators and students can think critically about what stands as knowledge, how knowledge is produced, and how knowledge is transformed by a particular relationship between the self, others, and the larger world.
>
> (p. 99)

Giroux (1992) went on to assert that:

> A social justice stance is, in part, a disposition through which teachers reflect upon their own actions and those presented by others. Rather than passively accepting information or embracing a false consciousness, teachers take a much more active role in leading, learning, and reflecting upon their relationship with their practice and the social context in which the practice is situated.
>
> (p. 99)

Kumashiro (2002) advocates "anti-oppressive education," that is based on four approaches to education. The first approach includes developing education for the Other, by making schools helpful, safe spaces for all students. The second approach is education about the Other. This approach seeks "to enrich all students' understanding of different ways of being" (p. 42). The third approach, education that is critical of privileging and "othering," advocates "a critical awareness of oppressive structures and ideologies, and strategies to change them" (p. 45). The fourth approach promotes an education that changes students and society. This approach argues for "curricular and pedagogical reforms that help to address the complexities of anti-oppressive education by developing such notions as partiality, resistance, crisis, and unknowability as they apply to teaching and learning" (p. 68).

Cochran-Smith (2003) argues for a major overhauling of university-based teacher education programs that prepare teachers. She makes a strong case for a *new* teacher education, one that works both to challenge historical ideological underpinnings of traditional programs and to situate knowledge about culture and racism at the forefront of the teacher education curriculum. Included in this re-imagining of teacher education is teaching for social justice as an imperative and outcome of learning to teach as well as understanding the importance of valuing the cultural knowledge of local communities.

Although attention to social justice has increased over the past two decades, it has been more in name than substance. Zeichner (2006) states, "It has come to the point that the term social justice in teacher education is so commonly used now by colleges and university teacher educators that it is difficult to find a teacher education program in the United States that does not claim to have a program that prepares teachers for social justice" (p. 328). Additionally, he reports that except for greater attention being given to the role of communities in the preparation of teachers most of the work toward social justice in the United States seems to focus on classroom-based activities of individual teacher. Zeichner's comment suggests that a number of problems and challenges are facing teacher education programs, such as the seriousness with which programs address the conceptual underpinnings and context of social justice. We need to examine if and how social justice is defined in teacher education programs as well as the conceptual tools being used to assess how well programs are meeting social justice goals.

Defining teacher capacity in addition to knowledge, skills and dispositions

Conceptions of teacher capacity that include attention to the dimensions of knowledge, skills, and dispositions are evolving and expanding, as McDiarmid & Clevenger-Bright (this volume) point out. Part of the growing conception of teacher capacity includes the dimension "views of self," described as "their beliefs about their role in classroom activity, and the persona they adopt in the classroom" (O' Day *et al.*, 1995; CPRE Policy Brief, 1995). All of these dimensions are "interdependent and interactive" (O'Day *et al.*, 1995).

According to the National Council for Accreditation of Teacher Education (NCATE, 2003), teacher capacity involves candidates' "knowledge, skills, and dispositions." However, NCATE goes on to link the quality of disposition, to for example, professionalism in working with students, families, and communities. Target performance for the teacher disposition standard involves candidates working "with students, families, and communities in ways that reflect the dispositions expected of professional educators as delineated by the institutions as well as professional and state standards." Target performance is therefore realized when candidates' views of self include acknowledging that their own "dispositions may need to be adjusted" and they are able to "develop plans to do so." Significantly, this performance standard suggests that institutions should define and standardize teacher disposition.

However, NCATE places the onus of delineating the teacher dispositions that "help all students learn" on the unit (college, department, programs), which may be influenced by professional and state standards but not necessarily by theories of social justice. Calling attention to this procedure, Cochran-Smith (2004) declares, "It is not clear . . . whether this emerging professional image also includes images of the teacher as activist, as agent for social change, or as ally in antiracist initiatives" (p. 117). She further argues, "As we construct the outcomes question in teacher education, we need to clarify and interrogate what it means to teach 'all students' well and/or what is means to adjust teaching practices according to the needs and interests of 'all children' " (p. 117). Cochran-Smith's questions go to the core of discussing the relationship between social justice and teacher capacity, and education as "the great equalizer of the conditions of man."

Although discussions of teacher capacity generally refer to knowledge, skills, and dispositions, Freire (1998) lists other "essential qualities of progressive teachers" (p. 45). He warns that his list, which includes humility, lovingness, courage, tolerance, decisiveness, security, the tension between patience and impatience, verbal parsimony, competence, and the joy of living, is not exhaustive and that these qualities must develop over time. These qualities are less present in the literature where the focus is on teacher capacity without attention to social justice.

Historical tracing: teacher capacity and social justice

For years, the explicit and implicit thinking regarding the issue of teacher capacity often centered on the capacity of White teachers to teach White students without much attention to the racism embedded within this thinking. When the question of teacher capacity began to include the teaching of Black students, questions of race (and racism) became more visible.

An earlier formulation of the teacher capacity question was thus, "Can/should White teachers teach Black children; and if so, what are the knowledge, skills, and implicit disposition they have (or need to have) other than the color of their skin?" Mabee (1979) in *Black Education in New York State* argued that there was considerable debate among African Americans in New York throughout most of the nineteenth century over whether Whites should teach in Black schools. A reading of Mabee's text shows that the enduring question about teacher capacity, in relation to the White Quaker woman who taught the children of Frederick Douglas in Rochester, New York, was one of skin color. In other words, at that time many Whites did not believe that a White person should teach Black children.

Mabee (1979) additionally argues that there was debate over who should teach Black students within the Black community. Here again teacher capacity was related to the color of a teacher's skin and Whites' dispositions toward Blacks. Mabee claims that Blacks were by no means united on calls for Black teachers in Black schools. For example, the *Christian Recorder*, a publication of the African Methodist Church, argued that for Blacks' demands for Black teachers for their children strengthened "the color line," which was in fact the "death line" for Blacks. Moreover, school officials often believed that Black parents preferred White teachers. In Brooklyn in 1863, when attendance at a Black school dropped, a White school board member declared that it would improve attendance at the school if it had a White teacher because Black parents preferred White teachers. Lending support to this belief, a Black school principal explained that some Black parents thought White teachers would prepare the community for the abolishment of Black schools (p. 95).

Nevertheless, some Blacks were not in favor of White teachers because they believed that White teachers did not have the capacity (i.e. dispositions) to do well by Black students. Mabee (1979) writes:

> Early in the nineteenth century, William Hamilton a Black carpenter argued that White teachers did not expect enough of Black pupils. Hamilton states, "It has been the policy of White men," he said in an address to Black youths in 1827, "to give you a high opinion of your advancement when you have made but smattering attainments. They know that a little education is necessary for better accomplishing the menial services you are in the habit of performing for them. They do not wish you to be equal with them—much less superior . . . They will take care that you do not rise above mediocrity."
>
> (Hamilton, quoted in Mabee, 1997, p. 95)

Note that teacher capacity as modeled from Mabee's book is about White and Black teachers teaching Black students and not about Black teachers teaching White students, which suggests that the answer to the enduring question about what teachers need to know, care about, and be able to do (i.e. knowledge, skills and dispositions) needs to be critiqued for its racist origins.

The skin color of teachers, along with their racialized experience and positionality, was further acknowledged in an observation made by Phillips (1940) when he drew on a 1936 study to argue that the qualification most needed by secondary teachers was social intelligence. However, he also pointed out additional qualifications that African American teachers needed, besides social intelligence. Accordingly, Phillips (1940) suggested that Negro [sic] secondary teachers should possess three additional qualifications: (1) "knowledge of the history of one's race, and understanding of the problems of one's racial group"; (2) "keen insight into the current social, economic, and political issues in relation to the problems peculiar to minority groups, vocational opportunities for one's group, and a willingness to assume educational leadership"; and (3) full appreciation of "the fact that his [sic] responsibility reaches far beyond the confines of his classroom" (p. 485). The term *social intelligence* and the additional qualities Phillips lists integrated social consciousness into discussions of teacher capacity.

Since Phillips wrote this piece in 1940, the framing of teacher capacity is no longer explicitly situated within a legally racially segregated society where teachers are predominately concerned about teaching students of their own racial group and/or teaching minority group students to model the dominant social group. As noted above, the Civil Rights Movements of the 1960s and 1970s spoke to the necessity of embedding social justice issues within the knowledge, skills, and dispositions of teacher education programs, as well as the scholarship and actions of teacher educators. The Civil Rights Movements (1) stimulated the rise of recognition and redistribution theories (Fraser, 1997); (2) played a major role in generating several theories and activities that placed race, class, gender, and other social and political inequities within the teacher capacity discourse; (3) acknowledged that White teachers had a responsibility to teach racially diverse groups of students in a manner that respected and promoted each group's culture and each student's self-identity; and (4) advocated that teachers of color accept responsibility for creating "an educational experience powerful and enduring enough to breach the walls of oppression and open pathways to freedom" (Ayers, 1997).

The Civil Rights Movement also generated the reform of curriculum materials so they were more racially inclusive and gender fair and addressed historical inaccuracies and omissions, particularly in terms of teachers' knowledge of the history and culture of students of color and other marginalized students (Sleeter & Grant, 1991) Additionally, instructional materials were developed that addressed the teaching skills, dispositions, and strategies that teachers needed to successfully teach students of color and other marginalized students (Grant & Sleeter, 2003). In addition to developing a more culturally inclusive and relevant curriculum, consultants and speakers provided teachers with a realistic assessment of the challenges they faced, the knowledge, skills and disposition they needed to have, and the changes that were needed in the education system and within them as individuals.

When writer James Baldwin spoke to a group of 200 New York teachers in 1963, he took a view of teacher capacity that drew on social justice and was set within social justice theories of equality, participation, and recognition. Baldwin began his "Talk to Teachers" by claiming "[We] are living through a very dangerous time." He then defined how equality, participation and recognition in U.S. society were denied to Blacks:

> [A]ny Negro who is born in this country and undergoes the American educational system runs the risk of becoming schizophrenic. On the one hand he is born in the shadow of the stars and stripes and he is assured it represents a nation which has never lost a war. He pledges allegiance to that flag which guarantees "liberty and justice for all." He is a part of a country in which anyone can become president, and so forth. But on the other hand he is also assured by his country and his countrymen that he has never contributed anything to civilization—that his past is nothing more than a record of humiliations gladly endured.
>
> (p. 326)

In concluding his remarks, Baldwin declared, "I began by saying that one of the paradoxes of education was that precisely at the point when you begin to develop a conscience, you must find yourself at war with your society. It is your responsibility to change society if you think of yourself as an educated person" (p. 331). He cautioned the teachers, "[Y]ou will meet the most fantastic, the most brutal, and the most determined resistance" since "what societies really, ideally want is a citizenry which will simply obey the rules of society" (p. 331). Baldwin's comments about education and society find expression in questions about the kinds of knowledge, skills, dispositions, and views of self that are required to participate in an improved and more desirable form of social life. Notions of teacher capacity need to attend to the same questions.

Baldwin's metaphor of "a dangerous time" was revisited by Ladson-Billings (1999) when she reminded educators that destabilizing dominant discourses of prospective teachers is "dangerous work" (p. 240). Ladson-Billings' comment—made 36 years after Baldwin's scathing commentary—continues to raise questions about both the knowledge, skills and dispositions that participation in an improved and more desirable form of social life requires for groups of people who have historically been marginalized, and the teacher capacity needed to develop those knowledge, skills, and dispositions. The metaphors "dangerous time" and "dangerous work" also call attention to issues of power and privilege, which are the center of the social justice relationship to teacher capacity. Walker (2003) reminds us that a social justice discourse in education needs to allow teacher educators to ascertain how power (e.g. pedagogical and institutional) and resources (e.g. material, opportunity and outcomes) are distributed to individuals and social groups.

Conceptual tools for the adjudication of actions

Meaning(s), theories, and understandings of the context of social justice are important, but separately or collectively they are not enough. Scholars such as O'Neil (1996) demand conceptual tools for adjudication of action that include principles/criteria for the construction of institutions and practices *and* evaluations of those constructions. Regarding the latter, O'Neil (1996) states, "Just institutions and practices provide the specifications for judging the justice of particular acts or decisions" (p. 182).

Similarly, Walker (2003) wants educators to do more than provide a definition of social justice. She argues that educators need conceptual tools that will tell us how well we are doing. Are our actions moving us closer to social justice or further away? As Walker states, "We need a theory of principles of justice which enables us to adjudicate between our actions so that we can say with some confidence this action is more just than that" (p. 169). Using the making of a quilt as a metaphor for actions for social justice, Walker states,

> Patchwork actions, the individual pieces of cloth, however bright and lively, are just bits of cloth. Only when we stitch the piece (our actions) together to make a quilt do the patterns emerge and transform the pieces into something new; we need to know what we are trying to make and to be able to judge whether we have made it well.
>
> (p. 169)

To illustrate her idea of such a conceptual tool, Walker (2003) suggests using Nussbaum's (2000) "Capabilities Approach." In *Women and Human Development: The Capabilities Approach*, Nussbaum identities ten capabilities: (1) life; (2) bodily health; (3) bodily integrity; (4) senses, imagination, thought; (5) emotion; (6) practical reason; (7) affiliation; (8) other species; (9) play; and (10) control over one's environment (pp. 78–80). She claims these capabilities are essential to the flourishing life of an individual but are not limited to the capacity for economic participation. She also focuses on personal and interpersonal development, as well as wider environmental, political, and social contexts and interactions. Walker (2003) argues that although Nussbaum's approach offers only one way to assess how well we are doing, it frames education within social justice and serves as a good starting place. Walker (2003) is worth quoting at length at this point:

> The attraction for education in the capabilities approach is fivefold. First, its emphasis on the flourishing of each and every person and hence a challenge, for example, to university "drop out" statistics which say nothing useful about individual experiences of higher education, even while glossing over success for many. Secondly, the approach points to what "people are actually able to do and to be" (Nussbaum, 2000, p. 5). As a social practice education is fundamentally about what we learn to be as much as about what knowledge we acquire. It is, above all, a domain of activity requiring thinking and judgment not only about what has been done but as a guide to future action. Thirdly, many if not all, of the ten capabilities advocated by Nussbaum point at least in some way to educational conditions and practices. To which stories of educational practice might we point to show capability development (interruption, disruption, transformation) and capability deformation (reproduction)? Finally, this approach suggests a view of (higher) education as more than education for economic development, and incorporates an implicit view of education both as and for democratic citizenship, and understanding and solidarity under conditions of cultural difference and diversity.
>
> (p. 170)

The development of conceptual tools for adjudication of action criteria which can help to determine whether or not program policies acknowledge and tackle lack of recognition, exclusion and the powerlessness associated with race, class, gender, sexuality, disability, language, religion and other cultural and social differences. In other words, teacher educators will need to ask: "Does program policy seek to enhance the life opportunities for teacher education students who are disadvantaged by cultural and economic differences, including any stigma associated with being included in the program because they are from a group of people who are historically, economically and/or socially disadvantaged?"

Pitt (1998) contends that program policies should address the ways education and the disadvantage of not attending and/or earning a university degree are implicated as causes or consequences in social justice. In addition, university policy and procedures should not compound the challenge of receiving a college education and should, instead, facilitate a teacher education program that enhances the life chances for people who are disadvantaged (and come to the university disadvantaged) because of major obstacles in society.

In summary, Pitt (1995) argues that criteria for assessing social justice in teacher education programs should include policies that address structural disadvantages, such as the distribution of education goods like knowledge, skills and dispositions; recognize the ideology underlying the prevailing economic discourse(s) (e.g. market place economy); and acknowledge (i.e. respect and affirm) cultural differences. Further, program policies must indicate who is responsible for seeing that students receive policy entitlements and who and what office are responsible for distributing the resources needed for implementation and executing that implementation.

Not nailing down the evaluation tools for how well a teacher education program is establishing and developing a relationship between social justice and teacher capacity undercuts an analysis and interpretation of the two concepts. In addition, the lack of an evaluation framework may leave teacher candidates and teacher educators conflicted about their actions for social justice. For example, many teacher candidates regularly undertake activities in their programs in the name of social justice. However, accountability measures (e.g. high-stake tests) may confuse their understanding of social justice. Here we are reminded of Walker's (2003) statement, "We need a theory or principles of justice which enables us to adjudicate between our actions so that we can say with some confidence this action is more just than that" (p. 169). When teacher candidates hear citizens who take action for certain social and political causes (e.g. immigration, homelessness, poverty) refer to their genre of work as "social justice," will they understand social justice and its relationship to teacher capacity differently or more fully? Will teacher candidates' understanding of social justice be related to equality, participation, recognition and/or access? When some less well-off and/or non-White students are allowed to enter the teacher education program, but a White, middle-class friend is not admitted, will the teacher candidate and her friends view the admittance of the student from a systemically/historically disadvantaged group as an act of social justice? Will the teacher candidates appeal to a meritocratic argument and become conflicted about the meaning of social justice? In other words, will they see a contradiction between Rawls' (1971) principles that the most deprived and needy should receive the greater attention and/but that those with talent and potential should be educated to their highest capacity? Will they understand social justice as "the obligation to help those less advantaged" for the benefit of the whole (Rawls, 1971, pp. 100–101)?

Institutions that claim they are using social justice to inform teacher candidates' knowledge, skills and dispositions must spell out their meaning of social justice, and conceptual tools which will adjudicate the actions of the teacher candidates and teacher educators involved should be in place and functioning.

SOCIAL JUSTICE IN TEACHER EDUCATION: WHAT DO JOURNAL ARTICLES SAY?

Reviewing teacher education journals

One way scholars keep up with the development of their field is by reading the journals in their area. Articles published in refereed journals are not only fundamental to promotion and tenure of professors, they also inform scholars about the history of the field, ongoing changes and emerging concepts, and current problems and issues. Journal publications present the latest research and scholarship in a timely manner. In addition, journal articles serve as curriculum material for both graduate and undergraduate programs. To examine when, how, and to what extent social justice has become associated with teacher education and the preparation of teacher candidates in the United States, we reviewed articles in four teacher education journals: *Action in Teacher Education, Equity and Excellence, Journal of Teacher Education*, and *Teacher Education Quarterly* published between 1985 and 2006.

Our review identifies characteristics and/or characteristic practices discussed in the articles that are associated with social justice (teacher) education. In addition, the review explores the meaning assigned to social justice, the theoretical lenses in use, the conceptual tools used to evaluate social justice in teacher education programs, and the context in which social justice is discussed. Our search of the four journals yielded 39 articles published between 1991 and 2005 that used the term "social justice" in their title or abstract. Before the 1990s, education journals published few, if any, articles using the term social justice in their discussion of teacher education. Social justice began to become popular in the 1990s because, according to North (in press), the highly publicized war over the meaning of terms like multiculturalism, encouraged "educational researchers like Griffith (1998) to intentionally use social justice to describe the subject and methodology of their work." North goes on to say that Griffiths believed that since "social justice was not appearing frequently in academic or media and popular culture outlets, it had not yet, suffered the kind of attack that more well known terms have" (Griffiths, 1998, p. 85).

In these 39 articles, we note that authors writing about social justice generally do not offer a definition. An exception appears in an article by Carlisle, Jackson, and George (2006) who define social justice education "as the conscious and reflexive blend of content and process intended to enhance equity across multiple social identity groups (e.g. race, class, gender, sexual orientation, ability), foster critical perspectives, and promote social action" (p. 57). The authors outline five principles of social justice education in schools based on their work at an elementary school: Inclusion and Equity; High Expectations; Reciprocal Community Relationships; System Wide Approach; and Direct Social Justice Education and Intervention. They also discuss equity-oriented models that have demonstrated academic outcomes, current research related to student achievement and a systems approach to bringing social justice education to school communities.

In a study of faculty members' and administrators' understandings of social justice at Boston College (Zollers *et al.*, 2000), participants met to investigate their shared understandings of social justice. All embraced the goal to teach for social justice. However, they had a range of definitions. The authors noticed that there were divergent categories related to equity and fairness, institutional versus individual understandings of injustice, and individuals' responsibility to advocate for social justice.

The 39 articles use a range of perspectives to address social justice within teacher education. In addition, while authors are more frequently offering start-up approaches, plans or methods for implementing social justice in teacher education programs, these approaches are not accompanied by benchmarks, staffing needs, and/or conceptual tools for the adjudication of actions. On the other hand, scholars who invoke social justice as central to their scholarship often share a similar vision or perspective and address it similarly. These scholars generally describe social justice as an ethic, concern, sense or orientation. Within these descriptions, a meaning of social justice is sometimes given, and sometimes implied, but is not usually fully articulated. McLaren and Fishchman (1998), for example, refer to an ethic of social justice. According to Murrell (2006), social justice indicates a disposition toward recognizing and eradicating all forms of oppression and differential treatment extant in the practices and policies of institutions, as well as an appeal to participatory democracy as a means of realizing social justice. Garmon (2004) argues that a "sense of social justice is a commitment to equity and equality for all people in society" (p. 206). According to Nieto (2000), a concern for social justice is an ideology and pedagogy which takes into account individuals and institutions. Nieto (2000) argues that teacher education programs need to "(a) take a stand on social justice and diversity, (b) make social justice ubiquitous in teacher education, and (c) promote teaching as a life-long journey of transformation" (p. 182). Nieto also claims that social justice is an individual, collective, and institutional journey that involves self-identity awareness, learning with students, developing meaningful relationships, developing multilingual/multicultural knowledge, challenging racism and other biases, having a critical stance, and working with a community of critical friends (p. 5).

As we reviewed these articles, we come away with the idea that teachers' "capacities" suggests a kind of "package" of understandings, skills, and commitments (or knowledge, skills and dispositions)—a much broader notion than just "what do teachers need to know?" or just what "skill" they should have. When social justice is embedded within or connected to teacher capacity, it should include the characteristics that Nieto (2000) articulates and those which emerge in our content analysis of the journal articles. These characteristic practices include: (1) critical pedagogy, (2) community and collaboration, (3) reflection, (4) social (critical) consciousness, (5) social change and change agents, (6) culture and identity and (7) analyses of power.

The role of critical pedagogy

Several articles argued that by using critical pedagogy, teachers and teacher educators are encouraged to understand social justice and/or work toward it. According to Beyer (2001), one reason for advocating critical pedagogy is to "focus on the social dimensions and consequences of educational practice, the ideological meaning of texts and experiences, the power relations in schools and other institutions, and the need to integrate theory and practice in new ways" (p. 155). Nieto (2000) argues that the reason a program should adopt critical pedagogy is to help prospective teachers develop a critical stance to challenge racism and other biases. McLaren and Fischman (1998) state that teacher education programs should be "committed to the development of critical epistemologies, ethics of caring, compassion, and solidarity" (p. 131), strive to heighten students' understandings of social relations of production, and consider alternatives to existing structural arrangements that are conducive to economic inequality and exploitation.

Although there is an emphasis on critical pedagogy in teacher education programs and professional development within this literature, there is little attention to how teachers translate critical pedagogy into P-12 classroom practice. Ball (2000) recognizes this problem and suggests that researchers attempt to "extrapolate the tenets of critical pedagogy from the interactive classroom practices of those teachers who attempt to operationalize such a philosophy in their day-to-day teaching" (p. 1007). Similarly, Hoffman-Kipp suggests that more attention be paid to the "actual activities in which teachers engage both from a process and content point of view" (p. 28).

Whereas these authors persuasively advocate for the use of "critical pedagogy," the argument is constructed as a general call and not a call for pedagogy based upon a particular critical theory or combination of critical theories. Critical theories and the pedagogies they foster differ somewhat in purpose and focus. For example, both Black feminist theory and pedagogy and social/radical feminist theory and pedagogy challenge male domination and female oppression. However, Black feminist theory and pedagogy challenge perspectives and practices among White feminists that marginalize or exclude Black women. Black feminist theory has a different purpose and focus than social/radical feminist theory and pedagogy that mainly challenges male supremacy or patriarchy (Welch, 2001). Although most if not all critical theories and pedagogies may be employed in a teacher education program that advocates social justice, what teacher candidates learn or take away from the program may differ in accordance with the theories employed and the pedagogy taught and demonstrated. The intention here is not to advocate for a particular theory and/or pedagogy but to call attention to the differences within the same genre of theories and the pedagogies they foster and to ask, when teacher educators or teacher education programs say our program uses "critical theory," have they said enough about their purposes and foci and nature of the pedagogy they use?

Community and collaboration

Many of the articles reviewed contend that community and collaboration are as significant to social justice as ideology and practice. Although working with others suggests a general practice, the articles argue that the terms and phrases such as "community of learners," "communities of practice," "collective action" and "collaboration" imply solidarity or working together (Cochran-Smith, 2001; Garmon, 2004; Glass & Wong, 2003; Greenman & Dieckmann, 2004; Hoffman-Kipp, 2003; Jennings, 1995; Johnson, 2002; Kurth-Schai, 1991; Lane et al., 2003; McLaren & Farahmandpur, 2001; McLaren & Fischman, 1998; Merryfield, 2001; Morrell, 2003; Moscovici, 2003; Murrell, 2006; Nieto, 2000; Quartz & TEP Research Group, 2003; Rios et al., 1997). According to several articles, a community of practice is a site of learning and action where participants engage in a joint enterprise to develop a whole repertoire of activities, common stories, and ways of speaking and acting for social justice. This endeavor diminishes the borders between community and school, as well as between virtual spaces and physical spaces in education enabling other social arenas to incite new ways of relating and inciting solidarity that is characterized by conviviality and criticality.

Wenger (1998) argues that communities of practice constitute reality in a particular manner and encourages specialized ways of acting and thinking. The community approach to teaching and learning for social justice suggests replacing the image of teachers working alone to images of teachers collaborating with(in) and across communities of practice or communities of learners (broadly defined), thereby challenging the narratives of individual heroism. Addressing the significance of a community of learners or the importance of a team effort in developing pedagogy for social justice, Quartz and the TEP Research group (2003) state:

> The real heroes of urban schools are those who figure out ways to stay connected to their profession, their pursuit of social justice, their colleagues, their students, and their communities. These heroes are not born; they emerge from an extensive network of supports and a solid understanding of pedagogy.
>
> (p. 105)

In addition, some of the articles offered suggestions for working together, including joining organizations, working with community members and forming critical friendship circles and/or inquiry groups.

The idea of collaborative support (Weinstein et al., 2004; Luna et al., 2004) figures strongly in these articles. Collaborative support tends to occur in reciprocal relationships that are beneficial and supportive to teachers (Garmon, 2004) and the community or group in which they participate. In Luna et al.'s (2004) article, a participant in an inquiry group describes the concept of "support" as it was experienced in his/her group: "Support in our group had more to do with being listened to, challenged, and validated as we took risks in our classrooms and in our lives" (p. 79). Other collaborative efforts mentioned include capitalizing on parents' strengths (Cooper, 2003) and participating as members in social movements (McLaren & Fischman, 1998; Hoffman & Kipp, 2003) by linking/connecting individual efforts for change to collective and institutional changes (Nieto, 2000). Merryfield (2001), among others, argues that models and ways of creating communities and collaborating must be continually interrogated, critiqued, and reformed.

Overall, the articles contend that community and collaboration, both of which are fundamental elements of social change, require collective action in solidarity. Missing from the articles is attention to the effects of unequal power relations in communities and other social networks and how assymetrical power relations can undermine the struggle for social justice.

The role of reflection

Some articles suggest reflection as a practice for social justice (Lane *et al.*, 2003; Morrell, 2003; Glass & Wong, 2003). Glass and Wong (2003) argue that engaged pedagogy involves continuous critical reflection and professional development, linked to classroom and school-level reform. They contend that the presence of teaching candidates as observers in classrooms forces guiding teachers to critically reflect on their own practice. Similarly, Morrell (2003) reports that conversations between teachers in a professional development research seminar and six other professionals "forced teachers to reflect more fully on their own practice as they witnessed others in action" (p. 95).

However, across most of these articles, reflection is presented as an unproblematic practice that teacher education and professional development programs expect their students to develop. The common assumptions are: reflection will occur through a critical lens that takes social justice concerns into consideration; reflection and subsequent changes in thinking are guided by particular motivations and interests which spawn questions; and reflection influences and is influenced by the processes involved in dialogical teaching, identity and cultural formation, and collaboration.

The role of critical social consciousness

Multiple types of consciousness are discussed across the articles with numerous references to Paulo Freire's (1970/1974/2000) concept "*conscientização.*" This represents the *development* of the awakening of critical awareness, which "must grow out of a critical educational effort based on favorable historical conditions" (Freire, 1974, p. 15). An assumption underlying the call for critical consciousness is that educators who "develop high levels of critical social consciousness are likely to begin their teaching careers attentive to their role in redressing social injustice" (Jennings, 1995, p. 243). Jennings (1995) adds that although this assumption awaits systematic investigation, it has "enough face validity to suggest that the development of critical social consciousness deserves the attention of teacher educators who take seriously the links between affirming diversity and educating for social justice" (p. 243).

Jennings (1995) also examines critical social consciousness through the lens of developmental psychology and argues that "because critical social consciousness involves a developmental process related to identity and cognitive growth, those students who find the examination of oppression threatening must themselves be respected as being in process without being patronized" (p. 248). Jennings therefore suggests that teacher educators have a goal of keeping "resistant students" engaged in the classroom dialogues as part of the process of sensitizing them to issues of social justice and diversity. His reference to dispositions (e.g. sensitizing, resistant) within the context of raising student critical social consciousness integrates teacher capacity and social justice

Within this literature base, minimum consideration is given to the consciousness of P-12 students. Exceptions include Beyer (2001) who suggests that teachers should use their knowledge of social inequality to raise student consciousness, Glass & Wong (2003) who argue that students should understand that race, class, and linguistic discrimination persists even for the most educated members of their communities, and Ríos *et al.* (1997)

who argue for a social justice approach at the middle school level that raises students' consciousness. Ríos *et al.*'s (1997) argument for a social justice curriculum which takes students' lives into account and facilities classroom critique is consistent with the ideas articulated in the Rethinking Schools article by Bob Peterson (1994): "Teaching for Social Justice: One Teacher's Journey." Peterson lists the following goals a of social justice classroom: a curriculum grounded in the lives of the students, dialogue, a questioning/ problem posing approach, an emphasis on critiquing bias and attitudes, and the teaching of activism for social justice.

What remains to be examined in this genre of research is the impact that teachers who exhibit a high level of critical social consciousness have on student performance. Furthermore, the articles that include suggestions for classroom teachers and the development of critical social consciousness often fail to include the following characteristics, suggested in the other articles, that are essential to the preparation of teachers for social justice education: analysis of power, (self) reflective practice, and collaboration/ community. In addition, this literature does not include discussions of teacher capacity, especially teachers' knowledge and skills.

Social change and change agents

A thread throughout the articles is the need to reform education so that it becomes a system that embodies and promotes social justice in all of its components. This reform effort would be proactive, responsive to change, and demonstrate a commitment to the struggle for social justice (e.g. Wallace, 2000). A common perspective in this social justice discourse is that no one is completely outside the social system and that practices and people are not neutral. Additionally, a prominent claim is that teachers should become agents for social change or activists. Cochran-Smith (2001), for example, offered the following statement in an editorial, "Learning to Teach Against the (New) Grain":

> A major goal of the project of teacher education for social change has been helping prospective teachers think deeply about and deliberately claim the role of educator as well as activist based on political consciousness and ideological commitment to combating the inequities of American life.
>
> (p. 3)

An example of a teacher candidate performing as a change agent is illustrated in an article by Lane *et al.* (2003). They investigated how the teacher education program at U.C.L.A.-Center X develops their students as change agents during their student teaching. Student teachers in the study were given the charge to "reform the schools while learning how to teach children in urban schools" (p. 65). Lane *et al.* conclude that student teachers became change agents by having an impact on the practice of their guiding teachers. This approach challenges traditional student teacher placements, most of which do not emphasize the role of the student teacher as an agent for social change.

Another central message in this literature is that social justice includes supporting students in understanding and transforming their own positions in society and as citizens in a democracy. Nevertheless, there is little attention given to student agency and, more specifically, possibilities for students to negotiate the forces that work to regulate their positionalities and the subsequent material effects of this regulation. Linking positionality and agency makes different questions available. For instance, what possibilities can be created to maintain or access that would improve the quality of life given the way we are situated within matrices of positionalities by those with the influence to shape public sentiment and therefore societal perceptions of our gender(s) race(s), sexuality, etc.

McLaren and Farahmandapur (2001) describe agency as "a form of intellectual labor and concrete social practice-in short, a critical praxis" (p. 149). Their discussion includes attention to students in general, not just preservice or inservice teachers as learners, and how the legacies of historical conditions, and not just one's subjectivity, determine subject positions. They state, "We need to identify the historical determinations of domination and oppression as part of the struggles to develop concrete practices of counter representation" (p. 146). However most of the discussions of teachers as change agents in this body of literature do not relate the idea of *change agent* to particular knowledge, skills, or dispositions. Moreover, attention to student agency and, more specifically, student resistance is minimal (exceptions are Cooper, 2003; McCall & Andringa, 1997; Pohan & Mathison, 1999).

Culture and identity

Social justice and multicultural education discourses largely overlap in this literature. Perhaps this is so because proponents of multicultural education, especially those who espouse social reconstructionist multicultural education (Martin, 2005; Martin & Van Gunten, 2002; McCall & Andringa, 1997), connect social justice to teacher education and education more generally. Beyer (2001) uses both terms when discussing teachers: "Teachers who embody these orientations [social justice and multicultural education] will intervene in the lives of their students so as to help them construct futures that are personally rewarding, socially responsible, and morally compelling" (p. 156). In a number of articles, social justice is described as a goal of multicultural education (Cochran-Smith, 2003; Ríos *et al.*, 1997; Martin & Van Gunten, 2002). Zeichner (2003) argues that multicultural education can function as an approach with similar and overlapping goals of social justice education and, at times, it and diversity are used synonymously in education with the term social justice.

Martin and Van Gunten (2002) suggest that teachers use multicultural education that is social reconstructionist, an approach that shares many of the same concerns as critical theory, to examine their own positionalities. Cooper (2003) supports the idea of "teacher education programs training social justice educators to be knowledgeable about the positionality of the students and families they serve" (p. 102). She adds, "I stress the need for teachers to recognize schools as sites of political resistance, which they must work to improve" (p. 102).

In this strand of literature, there are some salient conversations about diversity and equity that include culture and identity. The argument is that these concepts are intertwined and that our ways of being in the world (including the classroom) are not isolated from how we activate or alter our roles. McLaren and Fischman (1998) argue there is an absence of the "construction of identity" and "critical citizenship" in teacher education discussions and suggest that these absences diminish "the capacity of teacher education programs to participate in the formation of teachers as critical agents of social justice" (p. 125). Three years later, McLaren and Faramandapur (2001) state that "critical pedagogy has, of late, drifted dangerously toward the cultural terrain of identity politics in which class is reduced to an effect rather than understood as a cause" (p. 136). These two articles were indicators of an increase in attention to identity and culture in teacher education reform and the need for teachers, teacher education programs, and professional development to consider how class, identity, and culture influences teacher education. The arguments in these articles have resulted in research studies that examine how teachers' identity affects their ability to work toward social justice goals (e.g. Garmon, 2004; Martin & Van Gunten, 2002; Johnson, 2002). However, these articles also introduce a concern that the way identity has been introduced is problematic in that it frequently ignores the need for economic redistribution—not just group recognition— when discussing equality. Fraser (1997) argues that identity politics should not eclipse the need for economic redistribution.

Analyses of power

A few of the articles we reviewed discussed teachers in relation to the effects of power. For three consecutive years, Moscovici (2003) examined how teachers working on emergency permits used inquiry to understand their positions of power, the effect of these power positions on classroom practice, and how they might change their practice as a result of knowledge gained through inquiry. In addition, the teachers in the study were encouraged to examine their own power positions in the classroom using critical theory and concepts of power by Yukl (1989) and Foucault (1979). Moscovici (2003) reports, "As a result of their own personal analyses, many of the teachers in the study changed their practices to encourage their students to participate in scientific inquiries and become skeptics" (p. 47).

The argument made in this literature is that by understanding the effects of power, educators can move from a focus on individual psychological factors to larger societal factors that affect social relations, including the extent to which they can transcend the constraints that impinge on their ability to prepare students for socially-conscious (critical) citizenship. Cooper (2003) points to the significance of teachers' understanding of the effects of power when she writes, "Educators who do not recognize the power they possess are likely to abuse it or fail to maximize it for their students' benefit" (p. 104).

DISCUSSION

Several significant observations came out of reviewing the journal articles. We found overlaps and gaps between the key themes and the characteristic practices that we identified in the review. Similarly, we found overlaps and gaps between the characteristic practices and the "principles of practice" of classroom based pedagogy for social justice that Cochran-Smith (1999) outlines (e.g. communities of learning, dialogic and multi-culturally sensitive classrooms, knowledge).

In reviewing research between 1992 and 2002, Wiedeman (2002) identified key themes that define teacher education for social justice as: (1) diversity and difference, (2) multi-cultural education, (3) critical theory, (4) critical multiculturalism, (5) care theory, (6) antiracist education and (7) critical race theory. Identifying the general themes, principles, and/or characteristic practices of social justice in teacher education, classroom contexts, and education contributes to developing a deeper understanding of relationship between teacher capacity and social justice.

Across the articles, there is an emphasis on dialogue as central to the development of communities and an indication of learning, reflection, and social-consciousness. Yet none of the studies we reviewed explain how dialogue is interpreted, or if discourse analysis or some other form of analysis was used to analyze the relationship between dialogue and practice. Often, the studies do not reveal the source of the participants' statements, such as whether they are excerpted from dialogues generated during interviews or reflections on dialogues recorded in journals. Thus, educators and students have little information to guide their understanding about how dialogue shaped community building in the context of the studies.

Research focusing on social justice in teacher education may help to redefine teacher capacity by communicating a changing expectation in teacher education, one that can be recognized through the identification, promotion, and integration of these characteristic practices. Together, these characteristic practices support a conceptual orientation that moves teacher educators toward developing their capacity to approach education in ways that integrate social justice theories and practices.

There is a limited amount of empirical research that examines the classroom practices of teachers who claim to work toward social justice and/or the practices of those who were prepared in teacher education programs or professional development programs where social justice is the conceptual orientation (Hollins & Torres-Guzman, 2005). Exceptions to this pattern were Hoffman-Kipp's (2003) and Moscovici's (2003) studies. Although, Moscovici reports that teachers' practice changed after they analyzed their power positions, the author does not provide evidence of this change.

Moreover, because this body of research lacks attention to definition, context, and assessment, it tends to contribute to the gap in the literature on the impact that teacher education for social justice and/or specific characteristic practices have on student performance. Three exceptions are the articles by Murrell (2006) who focuses on the assessment of teacher practice as social justice education; Brown (2004) who reviews measures used to assess preservice leaders' beliefs, attitudes, and values regarding issues of diversity, social justice and equity; and Carlisle *et al.* (2006) who focus on the assessment of teacher education programs.

Furthermore, when the qualities associated with teacher capacity are included in social justice discourses, they are usually not central or explicit, but implied or assumed. We wish to note that although we discuss the often cited characteristics associated with social justice literature separately, they overlap and interrelate in the articles. Usually multiple characteristic practices are present, as one might expect given the complexities of learning and teaching. Neither we nor the authors of these articles suggest that these characteristic practices should be developed in isolation from one another, positioned hierarchically in practice or policy, or developed by one person or program without a network of support. The characteristics and practices of one's teaching and one's ways of being a teacher inform, support, and challenge one another. Together, they can serve as a guide in the continuous processes of re(de)fining the teacher characteristics associated with social justice and posing further questions about one's actions in particular contexts.

Our reading of the literature confirms our idea that teacher "capacities" is best understood as a package of understandings, skills and commitments. It is a broader notion than simply "what teachers need to know," what "skills" they should have or be seeking to learn, or what "dispositions" they should have or be seeking to acquire. We want to stress here that this "package" of teacher capacity also needs to include conceptual tools for the adjudication of actions for social justice.

CONCLUSIONS

Social justice is a well-intended idea in the teacher education literature and a popular slogan among teacher educators. However, a definition of social justice is rarely included in teacher education policy statements, practices, or the expectations for teacher candidates. To reiterate Hayek's observation, "It is allowed to float in the air as if everyone will recognize an instance of it when it appears" (quoted in Novak, p. 1). By not defining social justice and addressing what it means, or by narrowly defining social justice in relation to teacher candidates' knowledge, skills, and disposition, teacher educators' and teacher candidates' actions in the name of social justice are often superficial, ineffective and uniformed.

The theoretical framing of social justice lacks craftsmanship and is often reduced to employing one of many concepts—including equality, equal opportunity and sometimes equity—without elaborating their meanings, putting them in context, noting the differences between and among these concepts and/or acknowledging that they have different implications for education policies and procedures (North (in press); Secada, 1989; Sturman, 1997). A well established tradition in social science scholarship is to acknowledge the theoretical shoulders upon which one's own work stands. This kind of historical acknowledgment is not found in most of the articles on social justice we reviewed, which contributes to the confusion over the meaning and theoretical framing of social justice.

The literature is also silent about the assessment of social justice in teacher education programs. Very little discussion is offered about the extent to which social justice principles and practices are being used. Observations such as Walker's (2003) about the necessity of evaluative conceptual tools for social justice should force the question: "Are our actions moving us closer to social justice or further away?" However, judging claims about social justice and teacher capacity in teacher education rarely occurs. Zeichner (2006) makes clear that such conceptual tools are needed when he reminds us that everyone in teacher education these days claims to be working for social justice.

There is some acknowledgement of the context in which education is taking place (e.g. rapid fire technological innovation, globalization, economic imperatives, and accountability measurers) during discussions of social justice and teacher capacity. For the most part, a language of economic and U.S competitiveness is inherent in the discussion along with some acknowledgment that preparing students of color and poor students to take their place within a global society is important.

There is very little discussion that connects social justice and teacher capacity to the good of society, unless the discussions connect to the political economy and social cohesion. An exception is Britzman's (2000) discussion of capacity, knowledge, and social concerns. She asks, "What inhibits our capacity to respond ethically to others, to learn something from people we will never meet and to be affected by histories that we many never live?" (p. 202). Instead, the focus is on the changing relation between local and global, and thinking globally becomes the major goal. It is this context which fosters the creation of hyper-individuals "who place value on individual rights, competition and individual achievement" (Pitts, 1998, p. 2).

Finally, we have entered the moment in which teacher education and social justice are sharing a discursive space in mainstream teacher education. The increasing number of statements about the importance of social justice in the focus and scope of major teacher education journals and books, publication of articles that explicitly refer to social justice and number of teacher education programs and professional development programs that endeavor to prepare teachers for social justice are indicative of the increasing focus on social justice in teacher education.

The development of social justice discourse(s) in teacher education appears to be due to the increasing public awareness of and rallying against long standing inequities in areas like academic achievement, school funding, faculty and staff hiring procedures, and the allocation and types of resources. Also contributing to the development of social justice discourses in teacher education is the rising recognition and acknowledgment of the complexity of education, as communicated by a growing community of scholars across the field of education. Still, as Nieto (2000) laments, we are faced with the "the sluggish pace with which teacher education programs are addressing social justice and equity" (p. 181). Thus, if we return to Horace Mann's statement that "Education, then, beyond all other devices of human origin, is the great equalizer of the conditions of man,—the balance-wheel of the social machinery," and we consider the efforts thus far to embed social justice in the development of teacher capacity, we have to admit that much, much work remains to be done.

Acknowledgment

We wish to thank Nadine Goff and Connie E. North for their comments and suggestions on this manuscript.

REFERENCES

Ayers, W. (1998) Foreword: popular education: teaching for social justice. In W. Ayers, J.A. Hunt, & T. Quinn (eds.), *Teaching for social justice*. New York: Teachers College Press.

Baldwin, J. (1963) A talk to teachers. *Saturday Review*, December 21, 42–44.

Ball, A. (2000) Empowering pedagogies that enhance the learning of multicultural students. *Teacher College Record*, 102(6), 1006–1034.

Barry, B. (2005) *Why social justice matters*. Cambridge: Policy Press.

Bell, L.A. (1997) Theoretical foundations for social justice education. In M. Adams, L.A. Bell, & P. Griffin (eds.), *Teaching for diversity and social justice* (pp. 3–15). New York: Routledge.

Beyer, L.E. (1991) Schooling, moral commitment, and the preparation of teachers. *Journal of Teacher Education*, 42(3), 205–215.

Beyer, L.E. (2001) The value of critical perspectives in teacher education. *Journal of Teacher Education*, 52(2), 151–163.

Britzman, D. (2000) Teacher education in the confusion of our times. *Journal of Teacher Education*, 51(3), 200–205.

Brown v. Board of Education, 347 U.S. 483 (1954) (p. 2).

Brown, K.M. (2004) Assessing preservice leaders' beliefs, attitudes, and values regarding issues of diversity, social justice, and equity: a review of existing measures. *Equity & Excellence in Education*, 37, 332–342.

Carlisle, L.R., Jackson, B.W., & George, A. (2006) Principles of social justice education: the social justice education in schools project. *Equity & Excellence in Education*, 39, 55–64.

Cochran-Smith, M. (1999) Learning to teach for social justice. In G. Griffin (ed.) *The education of teachers: ninety-eighth year book of the National Society for the Study of Education* (pp. 114–144). Chicago: University of Chicago Press.

Cochran-Smith, M. (2001) Learning to teach against the (new) grain. *Journal of Teacher Education*, 52(1), 3–4.

Cochran-Smith, M. (2002) Reporting on teacher quality: the politics of politics. *Journal of Teacher Education*, 53(5), 379–382.

Cochran-Smith, M. (2003, Spring) The multiple meanings of multicultural teacher education: a conceptual framework. *Teacher Education Quarterly*, 7–26.

Cochran-Smith, M. (2004) *Walking the road: race, diversity, and social justice in teacher education*. New York: Teachers College Press.

Consortium for Policy Research in Education (CPRE) (1995) Dimension of capacity. www.ed.gov/pubs/CPRE/rb18/rb18b.html

Cooper, C.W. (2003, Spring) The detrimental impact of teacher bias: lessons learned from the standpoint of African American mother. *Teacher Education Quarterly*, 101–116.

Cremin, L.A. (1957) *The republic and the school: Horace Mann on the education of free men.* New York: Teachers College.

Foucault, M. (1979) *Discipline and punish: the birth of the prison*, Translated by Alan Sheridan. New York: Vintage Books.

Fraser, N. (1997) *Justice interruptus: critical reflections on the post-socialist condition.* New York: Routledge.

Fraser, N. (1997) *Justice interruptus. Critical reflections on the "post socialist" condition.* New York: Routledge.

Freire, P. (1970) *Pedagogy of the oppressed*, New York: Continuum.

Freire, P. (1974) *Education for critical consciousness.* New York: Continuum.

Freire, P. (1998) *Teachers as cultural workers: letters to those who dare teach.* Translated by D. Macedo, D. Koike, & A. Oliveira. Boulder, CO: Westview Press.

Freire, P. (2000) *Pedagogy of the oppressed*, 30th anniversary edition. New York: Continuum.

Friedman, T.L. (2005) *The world is flat: a brief history of the twenty-first century.* New York: Farrar, Straus, & Giroux.

Garmon, M.A. (2004) Changing preservice teachers' attitudes/beliefs about diversity: what are the critical factors? *Journal of Teacher Education*, 55(3), 201–213.

Giroux, H.A. (1992) *Border crossings: cultural workers and the politics of education.* London: Routledge.

Giroux, H.A. (2005) *Border crossings: cultural workers and the politics of education.* 2nd ed. New York: Routledge.

Glass, R.D. (2000) Education and the ethics of democratic citizenship. *Studies in Philosophy and Education.* 19(3), May, 275–296.

Glass, R.D. & Wong, P.L. (2003, Spring) Engaged pedagogy: meeting the demands for justice in urban professional development schools. *Teacher Education Quarterly*, 30(2), 69–87.

Goodlad, J. (2002) *A place called school.* New York: McGraw-Hill.

Grant, C.A. & Sleeter, C.E. (2003) *Turning on learning: five approaches for multicultural teaching plans for race, class, gender, and disability.* 3rd ed. New York: John Wiley & Sons, Inc.

Greenman, N.P. & Dieckmann, J.A. (2004) Considering criticality and culture as pivotal in transformative teacher education. *Journal of Teacher Education*, 55(3), 240–255.

Griffiths, M. (1998) *Educational research and social justice: getting off the force*, Buckingham: Open University Press.

Grutter v. Bollinger (02–241) 539 U.S. 306 (2003).

Hayek, F. A. (1997) *The mirage of social justice.* Chicago: University of Chicago Press.

Hoffman-Kipp, P. (2003, Spring) Model activity systems: dialogic teacher learning for social justice teaching. *Teacher Education Quarterly*, 27–40.

Hollins, E.R. & Torres-Guzman, M. (2005) Research on preparing teachers for diverse populations. In M. Cochran-Smith & K.M. Zeichner (eds.), *Studying teacher education: the report on the AERA panel on research and teacher education* (pp. 477–548). Mahwah, NJ: Lawrence Erlbaum.

Irvine, J.J. (2003) *Educating teachers for diversity: seeing with a cultural eye.* New York: Teachers College Press.

Jenlink, P.M. & Jenlink, K.E. (2005) *Portraits of teacher preparation: learning to teach in a changing America.* Lanham, MD: Rowman & Littlefield Education.

Jennings, T.E. (1995) Developmental-psychology and the preparation of teachers who affirm diversity: strategies promoting critical social consciousness in teacher preparation programs. *Journal of Teacher Education* 46(4), 243–250.

Johnson, L. (2002) "My eyes have been opened": white teachers and racial awareness. *Journal of Teacher Education*, 53(2), 153–167.

Kumashiro, K. (2002) *Troubling Education: queer activism and anti-oppressive.* New York Routledge.

Kurth-Schai, R. (1991) The peril and promise of childhood: ethical implications for tomorrow's teachers. *Journal of Teacher Education*, 42(3), 196–204.

Ladson-Billings, G. (1999) Preparing teachers for diverse student populations: a critical race theory perspective. *Review of Research in Education*, 24, 211–247.

Lane, S., Lacefield-Parachini, N., & Isken, J. (2003, Spring) Developing novice teachers as change agents: student teacher placements "Against the grain." *Teacher Education Quarterly*, 55–68.

Long, S. (2004) Separating rhetoric from reality: supporting teachers in negotiating beyond the status quo. *Journal of Teacher Education*, 55(2), 141–153.

Luna, C., Botelho, M.J., Fontaine, D., French, K., Iverson, K., & Matos, N. (2004, Winter) Making the road by walking the talking: critical literacy and/as professional development in a teacher inquiry group. *Teacher Education Quarterly*, pp. 67–80.

McDonald, M.A. (2005) The integration of social justice in teacher education: Dimensions of prospective teachers' opportunities to learn. *Journal of Teacher Education*, 56(5), 418–435.

McLaren, P.L., & Fischman, G. (1998, Fall) Reclaiming hope: teacher education and social justice in the age of globalization. *Teacher Education Quarterly*, (25)4, 125–133.

McLaren, P. & Farahmandpur, R. (2001) Teaching against globalization and the new imperialism: toward a revolutionary pedagogy. *Journal of Teacher Education*, 52(2), 136–150.

McCall. A.L. & Andringa, A. (1997) Learning to teach for social justice and equality in a multi-cultural social reconstructionist teacher education course. *Action in Teacher Education* 18, 57–67.

Martin, R.J. (2005, Spring) An American dilemma: using action research to frame social class as an issue of social justice in teacher education courses. *Teacher Education Quarterly*, 32(2), 5–22.

Martin, R.J. & Van Gunten, D.M. (2002) Reflected identities: Applying positionality and multi-cultural social reconstructionism in teacher education. *Journal of Teacher Education*, 53(1), 55–54.

Mabee, C. (1979) *Black education in New York State: from colonial to modern times*. New York: Syracuse University.

Meacham, J. (ed.) (2001) *Voices in our blood: America's best on the civil rights movement*. New York: Random House.

Merryfield, M.M. (2001) The paradoxes of teaching a multicultural education course online. *Journal of Teacher Education*, 52(4), 283–299.

Morrell, E. (2003, Spring) Legitimate peripheral participation as professional development: lessons from a summer institute. *Teacher Education Quarterly*, 89–99.

Moscovici, H. (2003, Spring) Secondary science emergency permit teachers' perspectives on power relations in their environments and the effects of these powers on classroom practices. *Teacher Education Quarterly*, 41–54.

Murrell, P.C. (2006) Toward social justice in urban education: a model of collaborative cultural inquiry in urban schools. *Equity & Excellence in Education*, 39(1), 81–90.

National Council for Accreditation of Teacher Education (2002) *Professional standards for the accreditation of schools, colleges, and departments of Education.*

National Council for Accreditation of Teacher Educators (NCATE) (2003) *Professional Standards for the Accreditation of Schools, Colleges, and Departments of Education.* Washington, DC. Author

Neubauer, D. (2005) Globalization, interdependence and education. Paper presented to the International Seminar on "Education in China: the dialectics of the global and the local", November 15.

Nieto, S. (2000) Placing equity front and center: some thoughts on transforming teacher education for a new century. *Journal of Teacher Education*, (51)3, 180–187.

North, C. (in press) What is all this talk about "social justice"? Mapping the terrain of education's latest catch phrase. *Teachers College Record*.

Novak, M. (2000) Defining social justice. *First Things*, 108, 11–13.

Nussbaum, M.C. (2000) *Women and human development: the capabilities approach*. Cambridge: Cambridge University Press.

Nussbaum, M.C. (2001, 7/20) The enduring significance of John Rawls. *The Chronicle Review, The Chronicle of Higher Education*. Retrieved November 15, 2006 from http://chronicle.com/free/v47/i45/45b00701.htm, pp. 1–7.

O'Day, J.A., Goertz, M.E., & Floden, R.A. 1995 *Building Capacity for Education Reform*. New Brunswick, NJ: Consortium for Policy Research in Education.

O'Neil, O. (1996) *Towards justice and virtue*. Cambridge: Cambridge University Press.

Peterson, B. (1994) Teaching for social justice: one teacher's journey. *Rethinking our Classrooms* V. 2. Rethinking Schools, Ltd.

Phillips, M.R. (1940) The negro secondary school teacher. *The Journal of Negro Education*, 9(3), 482–497.

Pitt, J. (1995) Social justice in contemporary schooling: some methodological considerations. Paper presented at the Australian Association for Research in Education, November 26–30.

Pitt, J. (1998) Social justice in education in "new times." Paper presented at the Australian Association for Research in Education Annual Conference, December 2.

Pohan, C. & Mathison, C. (1999) Dismantling defensiveness and resistance to diversity and social justice issues in teacher preparation. *Action in Teacher Education*, 20(1), 15–22.

Popkewitz, T.S. (1988) Culture, pedagogy, and power: issues in the production of values and colonization. *Journal of Education*, 170(2), 77–90.

Quartz, K.H. & TEP Research Group (2003) "Too angry to leave": supporting new teachers' commitment to transform urban schools. *Journal of Teacher Education*, 54(2), 99–111.

Rawls, J. (1971) *A theory of justice*. Cambridge, MA: The Belknap Press of Harvard University Press.

Rethinking Schools, Ltd. (1994) *Rethinking our classrooms: teaching for equity and justice*. Milwaukee, WI: Rethinking Schools, Ltd.

Ríos, F. & Montecinos, C. (1999) Advocating social justice and cultural affirmation: ethnically diverse preservice teachers' perspectives on multicultural education. *Equity & Excellence*, 32(3), 66–76.

Ríos, F.A., Stowell, L.P., Christopher, P.A., & McDaniel, J.E. (1997, Fall) Looking over the edge: preparing teachers for cultural and linguistic diversity in middle schools. *Teacher Education Quarterly*, 67–83.

Schultz, B.D. & Oyler, C. (2006) We make this road as we walk together: sharing teacher authority in a social action curriculum project. *Curriculum Inquiry*, 36(4) 423–451.

Secada, W. (ed.) (1989) *Equity in education*. New York: Falmer Press.

Sleeter, C.E., & Grant, C.A. (1991) Race, class, gender, and disability in current textbooks. In M.W. Apple & L.K. Christian-Smith (eds.), *The politics of the textbook*, pp. 78–110. New York: Routledge.

Smith, D.M. (1994) *Geography and social justice*. Cambridge, MA: Blackwell.

Solórzano, D. (1997, Summer) Images and words that wound: critical race theory, racial stereotyping and teacher education. *Teacher Education Quarterly*, 5–19.

Spring, J. (1972) *Education and the rise of the corporate state*. Boston: Beacon Press.

Sturman, A. (1997) *Social justice in education*. Melbourne, Victoria: ACER Press.

Uniqueness of Head Start. Retrieved December 17, 2006 from http://www.ilheadstart.org/uniqueness.html.

U.S. Department of Education, (2002, June) *Meeting of the highly-qualified teachers challenge: the secretary's annual report on teacher quality*. Washington, DC: U.S. Department of Education, Office of Postsecondary Education.

Walker, M. (2003, June) Framing social justice in education: what does the "capabilities" approach offer? *British Journal of Educational Studies*, 51(2), pp. 168–187.

Wallace, B.C. (2000) A call for change in multicultural training at graduate schools of education: Educating to end oppression and for social justice. *Teachers College Record*, 102(6), 1086–1111.

Weinstein, C.S., Tomlinson-Clark, S., & Curran, M. (2004) Toward a conception of culturally-responsive classroom management. *Journal of Teacher Education*, 55(1), 25–38.

Welch, P. (2001) Strands of feminist theory. Retrieved August 27, 2007 from http://pers-www.wlv.ac.uk/nle1810/femin.htm.

Wenger, E. (1998) *Communities of practice: learning, meaning, and identity*. New York: Cambridge University Press.

The White House President George W. Bush. No Child Left Behind. Retrieved December 18, 2006 from http://www.Whitehouse.gov/news/reports/no-child-left-behind.html.

Wiedeman, C.R. (2002) Teacher preparation, social justice, equity: a review of the literature. *Equity & Excellence in Education*, 35(3), 200–211.

Young, I.M. (1990) *Justice and the politics of differences*. Princeton, NJ: Princeton University Press.

Yukl, G.A. (1989) *Leadership in organizations*. Englewood Clifts, NJ: Prentice Hall.

Zeichner, K.M. (2003) The adequacies and inadequacies of three current strategies to recruit, prepare, and retain the best teachers for all students. *Teachers College Record*, 105(3), 490–519.

Zeichner, K.M. (2006) Reflection of a university-based teacher educator on the future of college- and university-based teacher education, *Journal of Teacher Education*, 57(3), 326–340.

Zollers, N.J., Albert, L.R., & Cochran-Smith, M. (2000) In pursuit of social justice: Collaborative research and practice in teacher education. *Action in Teacher Education*, 22(2), 1–14.

Part 2
Artifacts

2.1 A talk to teachers

James Baldwin

Source: James Baldwin, "A talk to teachers," *Saturday Review*, December 21, 1963, pp. 42–44

About 200 New York City teachers are taking a special in-service course this year on "The Negro: His Role in the Culture and Life of the United States." The course meets at Public School 180 in Harlem. At the October 16 session the speaker was James Baldwin, who was born and brought up in Harlem and attended Harlem schools. His topic was "The Negro Child—His Self Image." Mr. Baldwin spoke extemporaneously, and without notes, but his remarks were recorded on tape. By special arrangement with Mr. Baldwin and the New York Board of Education, his talk to the teachers is presented herewith.

Let's begin by saying that we are living through a very dangerous time. Everyone in this room is in one way or another aware of that. We are in a revolutionary situation, no matter how unpopular that word has become in this country. The society in which we live is desperately menaced, not by Khrushchev, but from within. So any citizen of this country who figures himself as responsible—and particularly those of you who deal with the minds and hearts of young people—must be prepared to "go for broke." Or to put it another way, you must understand that in the attempt to correct so many generations of bad faith and cruelty, when it is operating not only in the classroom but in society, you will meet the most fantastic, the most brutal, and the most determined resistance. There is no point in pretending that this won't happen.

Now, since I am talking to school-teachers and I am not a teacher myself, and in some ways am fairly easily intimidated, I beg you to let me leave that and go back to what I think to be the entire purpose of education in the first place. It would seem to me that when a child is born, if I'm the child's parent, it is my obligation and my high duty to civilize that child. Man is a social animal. He cannot exist without a society. A society, in turn, depends on certain things which everyone within that society takes for granted. Now, the crucial paradox which confronts us here is that the whole process of education occurs within a social framework and is designed to perpetuate the aims of society. Thus, for example, the boys and girls who were born during the era of the Third Reich, when educated to the purposes of the Third Reich, became barbarians. The paradox of education is precisely this—that as one begins to become conscious one begins to examine the society in which he is being educated. The purpose of education, finally, is to create in a person the ability to look at the world for himself, to make his own decisions, to say to himself this is black or this is white, to decide for himself whether there is a God in heaven or not. To ask questions of the universe, and then learn to live with those questions, is the way he achieves his own identity. But no society is really anxious to have that kind of person around. What societies really, ideally want is a citizenry which will simply obey the rules of society. If a society succeeds in this, that society is about to perish. The obligation of anyone who thinks of himself as responsible is to examine society and try to change it and to fight it—at no matter what risk. This is the only hope society has. This is the only way societies change.

Now, if what I have tried to sketch has any validity, it becomes thoroughly clear, at least to me, that any Negro who is born in this country and undergoes the American educational system runs the risk of becoming schizophrenic. On the one hand he is born in the shadow of the stars and stripes and he is assured it represent a nation which has never lost a war. He pledges allegiance to that flag which guarantees "liberty and justice for all." He is part of a country in which anyone can become President, and so forth, But on the other hand he is also assured by his country and his countrymen that he has never contributed anything to civilization—that his past is nothing more than a record of humiliations gladly endured. He is assured by the republic that he, his father, his mother, and his ancestors were happy, shiftless, watermelon-eating darkies who loved Mr. Charlie and Miss Ann, that the value he has as a black man is proven by one thing only—his devotion to white people. If you think I am exaggerating, examine the myths which proliferate in this country about Negroes.

Now all this enters the child's consciousness much sooner than we as adults would like to think it does. As adults, we are easily fooled because we are so anxious to be fooled. But children are very different. Children, not yet aware that it is dangerous to look too deeply at anything, look at everything, look at each other, and draw their own conclusions. They don't have the vocabulary to express what they see, and we, their elders, know how to intimidate them very easily and very soon. But a black child, looking at the world around him, though he cannot know quite what to make of it, is aware that there is a reason why his mother works so hard, why his father is always on edge. He is aware that there is some reason why, if he sits down in the front of the bus, his father or mother slaps him and drags him to the back of the bus. He is aware that there is some terrible weight on his parents' shoulders which menaces him. And if isn't long—in fact it begins when he is in school—before he discovers the shape of his oppression.

Let us say that the child is seven years old and I am his father, and I decide to take him to the zoo, or to Madison Square Garden, or to the U.N. Building, or to any of the tremendous monuments we find all over New York. We get into a bus and we go from where I live on 131st Street and Seventh Avenue downtown through the park and we get into New York City, which is not Harlem. Now, where the boy lives—even if it is a housing project—is in an undesirable neighborhood. If he lives in one of those housing projects of which everyone in New York is so proud, he has at the front door, if not closer, the pimps, the whores, the junkies—in a word, the danger of life in the ghetto. And the child knows this, though he doesn't know why.

I still remember my first sight of New York. It was really another city when I was born—where I was born. We looked down over the Park Avenue street-car tracks. It was Park Avenue, but I didn't know what Park Avenue meant *downtown*. The Park Avenue that I grew up on, which is still standing, is dark and dirty. No one would dream of opening a Tiffany's on that Park Avenue, and when you go downtown you discover that you are literally in the white world. It is rich—or at least it looks rich. It is clean—because they collect garbage downtown. There are doormen. People walk about as though they owned where they were—and indeed they do. And it's a great shock. It's very hard to relate yourself to this. You don't know what it means. You know—you know instinctively that none of this is for you. You know this before you are told. And who is it for and who is paying for it? And why isn't it for you?

Later on when you become a grocery boy or messenger and you try to enter one of those buildings a man says, "Go to the back door." Still later, if you happen by some odd chance to have a friend in one of those buildings, the man says, "Where's your package?" Now this by no means is the core of the matter. What I'm trying to get at is that by this time the Negro child has had, effectively, almost all the doors of opportunity slammed in his face, and there are very few things he can do about it. He can more or less accept it with an absolutely inarticulate and dangerous rage inside—all the more dangerous because it is never expressed. It is precisely those silent people whom white people see every day of their lives—I mean your porter and your maid, who never say anything more than "Yes Sir" and "No Ma'am." They will tell you it's raining if that is what you want to hear, and they will tell you the sun is shining if *that* is what you want to hear. They really hate you—really hate you because in their eyes (and they're right) you stand between them and life. I want to come back to that in a moment. It is the most sinister of the facts, I think, which we now face.

There is something else the Negro child can do, too. Every street boy—and I was a street boy, so I know—looking at the society which has produced him, looking at the standards of that society which are not honored by anybody, looking at your churches and the government and the politicians, understands that this structure is operated for someone else's benefit—not for his. And there's no room in it for him. If he is really cunning, really ruthless, really strong—and many of us are—he becomes a kind of criminal. He becomes a kind of criminal because that's the only way he can live. Harlem and every ghetto in this city—every ghetto in this country—is full of people who live outside the law. They wouldn't dream of calling a policeman. They wouldn't, for a moment, listen to any of those professions of which we are so proud on the Fourth of July. They have turned away from this country forever and totally. They live by their wits and really long to see the day when the entire structure comes down.

The point of all this is that black men were brought here as a source of cheap labor. They were indispensable to the economy. In order to justify the fact that men were treated as though they were animals, the white republic had to brainwash itself into believing that they were, indeed, animals and *deserved* to be treated like animals. Therefore it is almost impossible for any Negro child to discover anything about his actual history. The reason is that this "animal," once he suspects his own worth, once he starts believing that he is a man, has begun to attack the entire power structure. This is why America has spent such a long time keeping the Negro in his place. What I am trying to suggest to you is that it was not an accident, it was not an act of God, it was not done by well-meaning people muddling into something which they didn't understand. It was a deliberate policy hammered into place in order to make money from black flesh. And now, in 1963, because we have never faced this fact, we are in intolerable trouble.

The Reconstruction, as I read the evidence, was a bargain between the North and South to this effect: "We've liberated them from the land—and delivered them to the bosses." When we left Mississippi to come North we did not come to freedom. We came to the bottom of the labor market, and we are still there. Even the Depression of the 1930s failed to make a dent in Negroes' relationship to white workers in the labor unions. Even today, so brainwashed is this republic that people seriously ask in what they suppose to be good faith, "What does the Negro want?" I've heard a great many asinine questions in my life, but that is perhaps the most asinine and perhaps the most insulting. But the point here is that people who ask that question, thinking that they ask it in good faith, are really the victims of this conspiracy to make Negroes believe they are less than human.

In order for me to live, I decided very early that some mistake had been made somewhere. I was not a "nigger" even though you called me one. But if I was a "nigger" in your eyes, there was something about *you*—there was something *you* needed. I had to realize when I was very young that I was none of those things I was told I was. I was not, for example, happy. I never touched a watermelon for all kinds of reasons. I had been invented by white people, and I knew enough about life by this time to understand that whatever you invent, whatever you project, is you! So where we are now is that a whole country of people believe I'm a "nigger," and I *don't*, and the battle's on! Because if I am not what I've been told I am, then it means that *you're* not what you thought *you* were *either*! And that is the crisis.

It is not really a "Negro revolution" that is upsetting this country. What is upsetting the country is a sense of its own identity. If, for example, one managed to change the curriculum in all the schools so that Negroes learned more about themselves and their real contributions to this culture, you would be liberating not only Negroes, you'd be liberating white people who know nothing about their own history. And the reason is that if you are compelled to lie about one aspect of anybody's history, you must lie about it all. If you have to lie about my real role here, if you have to pretend that I hoed all that cotton just because I loved you, then you have done something to yourself. You are mad.

Now let's go back a minute. I talked earlier about those silent people—the porter and the maid—who, as I said, don't look up at the sky if you ask them if it is raining, but look into your face. My ancestors and I were very well trained. We understood very early that this was not a Christian nation. It didn't matter what you said or how often you went to church. My father and my mother and my grandfather and my grandmother knew that Christians didn't act this way. It was as simple as that. And if that was so there was no point in dealing with white people in terms of their own moral professions, for they were not going to honor them. What one did was to turn away, smiling all the time, and tell white people what they wanted to hear. But people always accuse you of reckless talk when you say this.

All this means that there are in this country tremendous reservoirs of bitterness which have never been able to find an outlet, but may find an outlet soon. It means that well-meaning white liberals place themselves in great danger when they try to deal with Negroes as though they were missionaries. It means, in brief, that a great price is demanded to liberate all those silent people so that they can breathe for the first time and *tell* you what they think of you. And a price is demanded to liberate all those white children—some of them near forty—who have never grown up, and who never will grow up, because they have no sense of their identity.

What passes for identity in America is a series of myths about one's heroic ancestors. It's astounding to me, for example, that so many people really appear to believe that the country was founded by a band of heroes who wanted to be free. That happens not to be true. What happened was that some people left Europe because they couldn't stay there any longer and had to go someplace else to make it. That's all. They were hungry, they were poor, they were convicts. Those who were making it in England, for example, did not get on the *Mayflower*. That's how the country was settled. Not by Gary Cooper. Yet we have a whole race of people, a whole republic, who believe the myths to the point where even today they select political representatives, as far as I can tell, by how closely they resemble Gary Cooper. Now this is dangerously infantile, and it shows in every level of national life. When I was living in Europe, for example, one of the worst revelations to me was the way Americans walked around Europe buying this and buying that and insulting everybody—not even out of malice, just because they didn't know any better. Well, that is the way they have always treated me. They weren't cruel, they just didn't know you were alive. They didn't know you had any feelings.

What I am trying to suggest here is that in the doing of all this for 100 years or more, it is the American white man who has long since lost his grip on reality. In some peculiar way, having created this myth about Negroes, and the myth about his own history, he created myths about the world so that, for example, he was astounded that some people could prefer Castro, astounded that there are people in the world who don't go into hiding when they hear the word "Communism," astounded that Communism is one of the realities of the twentieth century which we will not overcome by pretended that it does not exist. The political level in this country now, on the part of people who should know better, is abysmal.

The Bible says somewhere that where there is no vision the people pariah. I don't think anyone can doubt that in this country today we are menaced—intolerably menaced—by a lack of vision.

It is inconceivable that a sovereign people should continue, as we do so abjectly, to say, "I can't do anything about it. It's the government." The government is the creation of the people. It is responsible to the people. And the people are responsible for it. No American has the right to allow the present government to say, when Negro children are being bombed and hosed and shot and beaten all over the deep South, that there is nothing we can do about it. There must have been a day in this country's life when the bombing of four children in Sunday School would have created a public uproar and endangered the life of a Governor Wallace. It happened here and there was no public uproar.

I began by saying that one of the paradoxes of education was that precisely at the point when you begin to develop a conscience, you must find yourself at war with your society. It is your responsibility to change society if you think of yourself as an educated person. And on the basis of the evidence—one is compelled to say that this is a backward society. Now if I were a teacher in this school, or any Negro school, and I was dealing with Negro children, who were in my care only a few hours of every day and would then return to their homes and to the streets, children who have an apprehension of their future which with every hour grows grimmer and darker, I would try to teach them—I would try to make them know—that those streets, those houses, those dangers, those agonies by which they are surrounded are criminal. I would try to make each child know that these things are the results of a criminal conspiracy to destroy him. I would teach him that if he intends to get to be a man, he must at once decide that he is stronger than this conspiracy and that he must never make his peace with it. And that one of his weapons for refusing to make his peace with it and for destroying it depends on what he decides he is worth. I would teach him that there are currently very few standards in this country which are worth a man's respect. That it is up to him to begin to change these standards for the sake of the life and the health of the country. I would suggest to him that the popular culture—as represented, for example, on television and in comic books and in movies—is based on fantasies created by very ill people, and he must be aware that these are fantasies that have nothing to do with reality. I would teach him that the press he reads is not as free as it says it is—and that he can do something about that, too. I would try to make him know that just an American history is longer, larger, more various, more beautiful, and more terrible than anything anyone has ever said about it, so is the world larger, more daring, more beautiful and more terrible, but principally larger—and that it belongs to him. I would teach him that he doesn't have to be bound by the expediencies of any given Administration, any given policy, any given time—that he has the right and the necessity to examine everything. I would try to show him that one has not learned anything about Castro when one says, "He is a Communist." This is a way of *not* learning something about Castro, something about Cuba, something, in fact, about the world. I would suggest to him that he is living, at the moment, in an enormous province. America is not the world and if America is going to become a nation, she must find a way—and this child must help her to find a way—to use the tremendous potential and tremendous energy which this child represents. If this country does not find a way to use that energy it will be destroyed by that energy.

2.2 Teachers as cultural workers
Letters to those who dare teach

Paulo Freire
Translated by
Donaldo Macedo, Dale Koike, and Alexandre Oliveira

Source: Paulo Freire, *Teachers as Cultural Workers: Letters to Those Who Dare Teach*, Westview Press, 1998, pp. 39–46.

FOURTH LETTER

On the indispensable qualities of progressive teachers for their better performance

I would like to make it clear that the attributes I am going to speak about, which seem to me to be indispensable to the progressive teacher, are qualities acquired gradually through practice. Furthermore, they are developed through practice in concurrence with a political decision that the educator's role is crucial. Thus the attributes I am going to speak about are not attributes that we can be born with or that can be bestowed upon us by decree or as a gift. In addition, the order in which I list them here is not intended to rank their value. They are all necessary for a progressive educational practice.

I shall start with *humility*, which here by no means carries the connotation of a lack of self-respect, or resignation, or of cowardice. On the contrary, humility requires courage, self-confidence, self-respect, and respect for others.

Humility helps us to understand this obvious truth: No one knows it all; no one is ignorant of everything. We all know something; we are all ignorant of something. Without humility, one can hardly listen with respect to those one judges to be too far below one's own level of competence. But the humility that enables one to listen even to those considered less competent should not be an act of condescension or resemble the behavior of those fulfilling a vow: "I promise the Virgin Mary that, if the problem with my eyes turns out not to be serious, I will listen to the rude and ignorant parents of my students with attention." No. None of that. Listening to all that come to us, regardless of their intellectual level, is a human duty and reveals an identification with democracy and not with elitism.

In fact, I cannot see how one could reconcile adherence to an ideal of democracy and of overcoming prejudice with a proud or arrogant posture in which one feels full of oneself. How can I listen to the other, how can I hold a dialogue, if I can only listen to myself, if I can only see myself, if nothing or no one other than myself can touch me or move me? If while humble, one does undermine oneself or accepts humiliation, one is also always ready to teach and to learn. Humility helps me avoid being entrenched in the circuit of my own truth. One of the fundamental auxiliaries of humility is *common sense*, which serves to remind us that certain attitudes may lead us too close to becoming lost.

The arrogance of "You don't know who you are dealing with . . .," the *conceit* of the know-it-all with an unrestrained desire to make his or her knowledge known and recognized—none of this has anything to do with the *tameness* (which is not apathy) of the humble. Humility does not flourish in people's insecurities but in the insecure security of the more aware, and thus this insecure security is one of the expressions of humility, as is uncertain certainty, unlike certainty, which is excessively sure of itself. The authoritarians' stance, in contrast, is sectarian. Theirs is the only truth, and it must be imposed on others. It is in their truth that others' salvation resides. Their knowledge "illuminates" the obscurity or the ignorance of others, who then must be subjected to the knowledge and arrogance of the authoritarian.

I will return to my analysis of authoritarianism, whether that of parents or teachers. As one might expect, authoritarianism will at times cause children and students to adopt rebellious positions, defiant of any limit, discipline, or authority. But it will also lead to apathy, excessive obedience, uncritical conformity, lack of resistance against authoritarian discourse, self-abnegation, and fear of freedom.

In saying that authoritarianism may generate various types of reactions, I understand that on a human level things do not happen so *mechanically* and happily. Thus it is possible that certain children will go through the rigors of arbitrariness unscathed, which does not give us the license to gamble on that possibility and fail to make an effort to become less authoritarian. And if we can't make that effort for our dream for democracy, we should make it out of respect for beings in development, our children and our students.

But to the humility with which teachers perform and relate to their students, another quality needs to be added: *lovingness*, without which their work would lose its meaning. And here I mean lovingness not only toward the students but also toward the very process of teaching. I must confess, not meaning to cavil, that I do not believe educators can survive the negativities of their trade without some sort of "armed love," as the poet Tiago de Melo would say. Without it they could not survive all the injustice or the government's contempt, which is expressed in the shameful wages and the arbitrary treatment of teachers, not coddling mothers, who take a stand, who participate in protest activities through their union, who are punished, and who yet remain devoted to their work with students.

It is indeed necessary, however, that this love be an "armed love," the fighting love of those convinced of the right and the duty to fight, to denounce, and to announce. It is this form of love that is indispensable to the progressive educator and that we must all learn.

It so happens, however, that this lovingness I speak about, the dream for which I fight and for whose realization I constantly prepare myself, demands that I invent in myself, in my social experience, another quality: *courage*, to fight and to love.

Courage, as a virtue, is not something I can find outside myself. Because it comprises the conquering of my fears, it implies fear.

First of all, in speaking about fear we must make sure that we are speaking of something very concrete. In other words, fear is not an abstraction. Second, we must make sure that we understand that we are speaking of something very normal. And, when we speak about fear, we are faced with the need to be very clear of our choices, and that requires certain concrete procedures and practices, which are the very experiences that cause fear.

To the extent that I become clearer about my choices and my dreams, which are substantively political and attributively pedagogical, and to the extent that I recognize that though an educator I am also a political agent, I can better understand why I fear and realize how far we still have to go to improve our democracy. I also understand that as we put into practice an education that critically provokes the learner's consciousness, we are necessarily working against myths that deform us. As we confront such myths, we also face the dominant power because those myths are nothing but the expression of this power, of its ideology.

When we are faced with concrete fears, such as that of losing our jobs or of not being promoted, we feel the need to set certain limits to our fear. Before anything else, we begin to recognize that fear is a manifestation of our being alive. I do not need to hide my fears. But I must not allow my fears to immobilize me. If I am secure in my political dream, having tactics that may lessen my risk, I must go on with the fight. Hence the need to be in control of my fear, to *educate* my fear, from which is finally born to my courage.[1] Thus I must neither, on the one hand, deny my fears nor, on the other, surrender myself to them. Instead, I must control them, for it is in the very exercise of this control that my necessary courage is shared.

That is why though there may be fear without courage, the fear that devastates and paralyzes us, there may never be courage without fear, that which "speaks" of our humanness as we manage to limit, subject, and control it.

Tolerance is another virtue. Without it no serious pedagogical work is possible; without it no authentic democratic experience is viable; without it all progressive educational practice denies itself. Tolerance is not, however, the irresponsible position of those who play the game of make-believe.

Being tolerant does not mean acquiescing to the intolerable; it does not mean covering up disrespect; it does not mean coddling the aggressor or disguising aggression. Tolerance is the virtue that teaches us to live with the different. It teaches us to learn from and respect the different.

On an initial level, tolerance may almost seem to be a favor, as if being tolerant were a courteous, thoughtful way of accepting, of *tolerating*, the not-quite-desired presence of one's opposite, a civilized way of permitting a coexistence that might seem repugnant. That, however, is hypocrisy, not tolerance. Hypocrisy is a defect; it is degradation. Tolerance is a virtue. Thus if I live tolerance, I should embrace it. I must experience it as something that makes me coherent first with my historical being, inconclusive as that may sound, and second with my democratic political choice. I cannot see how one might be democratic without experiencing tolerance, coexistence with the different, as a fundamental principle.

No one can learn tolerance in a climate of irresponsibility, which does not produce democracy. The act of tolerating requires a climate in which limits may be established, in which there are principles to be respected. That is why tolerance is not coexistence with the intolerable. Under an authoritarian regime, in which authority is abused, or a permissive one, in which freedom is not limited, one can hardly learn tolerance. Tolerance requires respect, discipline, and ethics. The authoritarian, filled with sexual, racial, and class prejudices, can never become tolerant without first overcoming his or her prejudices. That is why a bigot's *progressive* discourse, which contrasts with his or her practice, is a false discourse. That is also why those who embrace scientism are equally intolerant, because they take science for the *ultimate truth*, outside of which nothing counts, believing that only science can provide certainty. Those immersed in scientism cannot be tolerant, though that fact should not discredit science.

I would also like to add *decisiveness, security*, the tension between *patience and impatience*, and *joy of living* to the group of qualities to be nourished in ourselves if we are to be progressive educators.

An educator's ability to make decisions is absolutely necessary to his or her educational work. It is by demonstrating an ability to make decisions that an educator teaches the difficult virtue of decisiveness. Making decisions is difficult to the extent that it signifies breaking free to choose. No one ever decides anything without making a trade-off, weighing one thing against another, one point against another, one person against another. Thus every choice that follows a particular decision calls for careful evaluation in comparing and opting for one of the possible sides, persons, or positions. It is evaluation, with all of its implications, that helps us to finally make choices.

Decision making is rupture and is not always an easy experience. But it is not possible to exist without rupturing, no matter how hard it may be.

One of the deficiencies that an educator may possess is an inability to make decisions. Such *indecision* is perceived by learners as either moral weakness or professional incompetence. Democratic educators must not nullify themselves in the name of being democratic. On the contrary, although they cannot take sole responsibility for the lives of their students, they must not, in the name of democracy, evade the responsibility of making decisions. At the same time, they must not be arbitrary in their decisions. Setting an example, as an authority figure, of not taking responsibility for one's duties, of allowing oneself to fall into permissiveness, is even more somber a fate for a teacher than abusing authority.

There are plenty of occasions when a good democracy-oriented pedagogical example is to make the decision in question with the students, after analyzing the problem. Other times, when the decision to be made is within the scope of the educator's expertise, there is no reason not to take action, to be negligent.

Indecision reveals a lack of confidence; but confidence is indispensable for anyone with responsibilities in government, whether of a class, a family, an institution, a company, or the state.

Security, confidence, on the other hand, requires scientific competence, political clarity, and ethical integrity.

One cannot be secure in one's actions without knowing how to support those actions scientifically, without at least some idea of what one does, why, and to what end. The same is true of allegiance: One must know whom or what one is for or against. Nor can one be secure in one's actions without being moved by them, or if one hurts the dignity of others, exposing them to embarrassing situations. Such ethical irresponsibility and cynicism show an inability to live up to the educator's task, which demands critically disciplined performance with which to challenge learners. On the one hand, such discipline reflects the educator's competence, as it is gradually revealed to the learners, discreetly and humbly, without arrogant outbursts; on the other it affects the balance with which the educator exercises authority—secure, lucid, and determined.

None of this, however, can be realized if an educator lacks a taste for permanently seeking justice. No one can prevent a teacher from liking one student more than another, for any number of reasons. That is a teacher's right. What a teacher must not do is disregard the rights of the other students in favoring one student.

There is another fundamental quality that the progressive educator must not lack: He or she must exercise wisdom in experiencing the tension between *patience* and *impatience*. Neither *patience* nor *impatience* alone is what is called for. Patience alone may bring the educator to a position of resignation, of permissiveness, that denies the educator's democratic dream. Unaccompanied patience may lead to immobility, to inactivity. Conversely, impatience alone may lead the educator to blind activism, to action for its own sake, to a practice that does not respect the necessary relationship between tactics and strategy. Isolated patience tends to hinder the attainment of objectives central to the educator's practice, making it soft and ineffectual. Untempered impatience threatens the success of one's practice, which becomes lost in the arrogance of judging oneself the owner of history. Patience alone consumes itself in mere prattle; impatience alone consumes itself in irresponsible activism.

Virtue, then, does not lie in experience either without the other but, rather, in living the permanent tension between the two. The educator must live and work impatiently patiently, never surrendering entirely to either.

Alongside this harmonious, balanced way of being and working there must figure another quality, which I have been calling *verbal parsimony*. Verbal parsimony is implied in the assumption of patience-impatience. Those who live impatient patience will rarely lose control over their words; they will rarely exceed the limits of considered yet energetic discourse. Those who predominantly live patience along stifle their legitimate anger, which then is expressed through weak and resigned discourse. Those, on the other hand, who are all uncontrolled impatience tend toward lack of restraint in discourse. The patient person's discourse is always *well-behaved*, whereas that of the impatient person generally goes beyond what reality itself could withstand.

Both of these kinds of discourse, the overly controlled as well as the undisciplined, contribute to the preservation of the status quo. The first falls short of the demands of the status quo; the second surpasses its limits.

The benevolent classroom discourse and practice of those who are only patient suggest to learners that anything, or almost anything, goes. There is in the air a sense of a nearly infinite patience. Nervous, arrogant, uncontrolled, unrealistic, unrestrained discourse will find itself immersed in inconsequence and irresponsibility.

In no way do these discourses contribute to the learners' education.

There are also those who are excessively restrained in their discourse but who once in a while lose control. From absolute patience, they leap unexpectedly into uncontainable impatience, creating a climate of insecurity for everyone around them, always with terrible effects.

Countless mothers and fathers behave so. Today their words and their actions are permissive, but they transform tomorrow into the opposite, a universe of authoritarian discourse and orders, which not only leaves their sons and daughters appalled but, above all, makes them insecure. Such immoderate parental behavior limits children's emotional balance, which they need to grow up. Loving is not enough; one must know how to love.

Though I recognize that these reflections on qualities are incomplete, I would also like to briefly discuss *joy of living* as a fundamental virtue for democratic educational practice.

By completely giving myself to life rather than to death—without meaning either to deny death or the mythicize life—I can free myself to surrender to the joy of living, without having to hide the reasons for sadness in life, which prepares me to stimulate and champion joy in the school.

Whether or not we are willing to overcome slips or inconsistencies, by living humility, loving-ness, courage, tolerance, competence, decisiveness, patience-impatience, and verbal parsi-mony, we contribute to creating a happy, joyful school. We forge a school-adventure, a school that marches on, that is not afraid of the risks, and that rejects immobility. It is a school that thinks, that participates, that creates, that speaks, that loves, that guesses, that passionately embraces and says *yes* to life. It is not a school that quiets down and quits.

Indeed the easy way out in dealing with the obstacles posed by governmental contempt and the arbitrariness of antidemocratic authorities is the fatalist resignation in which many of us find ourselves.

"What can I do? Whether they call me *teacher* or coddling mother, I am still underpaid, dis-regarded, and uncared for. Well, so be it." In reality, this is the most convenient position, but it is also the position of someone who quits the struggle, who quits history. It is the position of those who renounce conflict, the lack of which undermines the dignity of life. There may not be life or human existence without struggle and conflict. Conflict[2] shares in our conscience. Denying con-flict, we ignore even the most mundane aspects of our vital and social experience. Trying to escape conflict, we preserve the status quo.

Thus I can see no alternative for educators to unity within the diversity of their interests in defending their rights. Such rights include the right to freedom in teaching, the right to speak, the right to better conditions for pedagogical work, the right to paid sabbaticals for continuing educa-tion, the right to be coherent, the right to criticize the authorities without fear of retaliation (which entails the duty to criticize truthfully), the right to the duty to be serious and coherent and to not have to lie to survive.

We must fight so that these rights are not just recognized but respected and implemented. At times we may need to fight side by side with the unions; at other times we may need to fight against them, if their leadership is sectarian, whether right or left. At other times we also need to fight as a progressive administration against the devilish anger of the obsolete; of the tradition-alists, some of whom judge themselves progressive; and of the neoliberals, who see themselves as the culmination of history.

NOTES

1 See Paulo Friere and Ira Shor, *Medo e Ousadia, o Cotidiano do Professor* (Rio de Janeiro: Paz e Terra, 1987).
2 See Moacir Gadotti, Paulo Freire, and Sergio Guimarães, *Pedagogy: Dialogue and Conflict* (Rio de Janeiro: Cortex, 1989).

2.3 The dialectic of freedom

M. Greene

Source: M. Greene, *The Dialectic of Freedom*, Teachers College Press, 1988, pp. 117–135.

Our exploration began in an awareness of a taken-for-grantedness and a void where present-day thinking is concerned, of a lassitude and a lack of care. The void exists with regard to the question of freedom, the givenness of which is taken for granted. We have, in the course of this inquiry, distinguished freedom from liberty for the purpose of highlighting the tension and the drama of personal choosing in an intersubjective field—choosing among others in a conditioned world. Liberty may be conceived of in social or political terms: Embodied in laws or contracts or formulations of human rights, it carves out a domain where free choices can be made. For Isaiah Berlin, the sense of freedom entails "the absence of obstacles to possible choices and activities— absence of obstructions on roads along which a man can decide to walk" (1970, p. xxxix). We recognize, as he did, that among the obstructions to be removed (and preferably through social action) are those raised by poverty, sickness, even ignorance. We recognize as well that the removal of obstacles to "possible choices and activities" may, in many cases, lead to domination by the few and the closing off of opportunities for the many. We know too that, even given conditions of liberty, many people do not act on their freedom; they do not risk becoming different; they acceded; often, they submit.

The problems for education, therefore, are manifold. Certain ones cluster around the presumed connection between freedom and autonomy; certain ones have to do with the relation between freedom and community, most significantly moral community. Autonomy, many believe, is a prime characteristic of the educated person. To be autonomous is to be self-directed and responsible; it is to be capable of acting in accord with internalized norms and principles; it is to be insightful enough to know and understand one's impulses, one's motives, and the influences of one's past. There are those who ascribe to the autonomous person a free and rational will, capable of making rational sense of an extended objective world. Values like independence, self-sufficiency, and authenticity are associated with autonomy, because the truly autonomous person is not supposed to be susceptible to outside manipulations and compulsions. Indeed, he/she can, by maintaining a calm and rational stance, transcend compulsions and complexes that might otherwise interfere with judgment and clarity.

As is well known, the attainment of autonomy characterizes the highest state in the developmental patterns devised by Jean Piaget (1977) and, later, by Lawrence Kohlberg (1971). Piaget saw autonomy as emergent from experience of mutual reciprocity and regard. A life plan, he wrote, is "an affirmation of autonomy"; and "a life plan is above all a scale of values which puts some ideals above others and subordinates the middle-range values to goals thought of as permanent" (p. 443). For Kohlberg, whose primary interest was in moral development, people who reach a high-enough cognitive stage of development become autonomous enough to guide their choices by universalizable principles of justice and benevolence. "That welfare and justice," he said, "are guiding principles of legislation as well as of individual moral action points to the fact that a principle is always a maxim or a rule for making rules or laws as well as a maxim of individual situational conduct" (p. 60). If the presumption is that autonomy is associated with "higher order" thinking and with the ability to conceptualize abstractions like human rights and justice, and if indeed such principles become maxims of individual conduct, many conclude that autonomous persons can be considered free persons. To abide by internalized principles, after all, is to acknowledge the rule of "ought" or "should." R. M. Hare has written that it is because we *can* act in this way or that, that we ask whether we ought to do this or that (1965, p. 51ff.). Granting the various usages of words like "ought" and "should," we can still understand why persons who are capable of principled action and who are responsive to ideals they have incarnated for themselves are considered self-determining and therefore free.

The implications for education have had to do with cognition—with logical thinking, the resolution of moral dilemmas, the mastery of interpersonal rules. For R. S. Peters, this kind of education involves the nurture of a "rational passion" associated with commitment to the worthwhile. Peters wrote: "Respect for truth is intimately connected with fairness, and respect for persons, which together with freedom, are fundamental principles which underlie our moral life and which are personalized in the form of the rational passions" (1970, p. 55). The problem with this highly cognitive focus in the classroom has in part to do with what it excludes. Also, it has to do with whether or not reasoning is enough when it comes to acting in a resistant world, or opening fields of possibilities among which people may choose to choose. There have been many reports on classroom discussions of issues ostensibly of moment to the students: cheating, betraying confidences, nonviolent resistance, sexual relations, discrimination. Not only has there been little evidence that the participants take such issues personally; there has been little sigh of any transfer to situations in the "real world," even when there were opportunities (say, in a peace demonstration) to act on what were affirmed as guiding principles. We will touch, before long, on the importance of imagination and the exploration of alternative possibilities. It seems clear, as Oliver and Bane have said, that young people "need the opportunity to project themselves in rich hypothetical worlds created by their own imagination or those of dramatic artists. More important, they need the opportunity to test out new forms of social order—and only then to reason about their moral implications" (1971, p. 270).

Most of the writers to whom we have referred in these paragraphs are, or course, interested primarily in moral commitments, not freedom *per se*. It does appear, as has been said, that there is a presupposition linking autonomy to personal freedom, autonomy in the sense of rational and principled self-government. For many, a movement out of heteronomous existence, with all its conditioning and shaping factors, cannot but be a movement in the direction of a kind of rule-governed self-sufficiency and independence. And this (at least where qualified students are concerned) is viewed by numbers of educators as the most desirable end of pedagogy, to be achieved by liberal education and commitment to the worthwhile.

Such inquiries into women's moral development as Carol Gilligan's *In a Different Voice* (1981) and into women's distinctive modes of reflection as *Women's Ways of Knowing* by Mary Field Belenky and her colleagues (1986) have, at the very least, made problematic the focal emphasis on separateness and responsiveness to purely formal principle. Gilligan has pointed time and time again to the neglect of the patterns of women's development, whose "elusive mystery . . . lies in its recognition of the continuing importance of attachment in the human life cycle. Woman's place in man's life cycle is to protect this recognition while the developmental litany intones the celebration of separation, autonomy, individuation, and natural rights" (p. 23). Belenky's work emphasizes the relational thinking and the integration of voices that characterize women's life stories. Where freedom is concerned (and it is rarely mentioned in contemporary women's literature), it is taken to signify either liberation from domination of the provision of spaces where choices can be made. There is a general acknowledgement that the opening of such spaces depends on support and connectedness. "Connected teaching," for example, involves what Nel Noddings describes as "care" (1984, pp. 15–16). Rather than posing dilemmas to students or presenting models of expertise, the caring teacher tries to look through students' eyes, to struggle *with* them as subjects in search of their own projects, their own ways of making sense of the world. Reflectiveness, even logical thinking remain important; but the *point* of cognitive development is not to gain an increasingly complete grasp of abstract principles. It is to interpret from as many vantage points as possible lived experience, the ways there are of being in the world.

This recent attentiveness to mutuality and to responsiveness to others' wants and concerns cannot but recall the contextual thinking of Dewey, Merleau-Ponty, Hannah Arendt, Michel Foucault, and others. Dewey wrote of the habit of viewing sociality as a trait of an individual "isolated by nature, quite as much as, say, a tendency to combine with others in order to get protection against something threatening one's own private self" (1938/1963, p. 22). He believed it essential to consider the problem of freedom within the context of culture, surely within a context of multiple transactions and relationships. Part of the difficulty for him and those who followed him had to do with the positing of a "free will" associated with a mysterious interiority, even as it had to do with a decontextualization that denied the influences of associated life. Hannah Arendt found some of the century's worst contradictions in the distinction made between "inner" freedom and the kind of outward "unfreedom" or causality described by Immanuel Kant and his successors. The search for a freedom within, she said, denied notions of *praxis* and the public space. For her, as we have seen, freedom was identified with a space that provided room for human action and interaction. She believed that freedom was the major reason persons came together in political orders; it is, she wrote, "the *raison d'être* of politics" and the opposite of "inner freedom," which she called "the inward space into which we may escape from external coercion and *feel* free" (1961, pp. 141–146).

The relationships and responsibilities stressed by women inquirers are not to be identified entirely with the cultural matrix of such importance to Dewey; nor is either emphasis precisely the same as Arendt's concern with the public space. Nonetheless, all these strains of thought are significant responses to present calls, in philosophy and the human sciences, for some reconstitution of core values, some rebuilding of community today. Attention is being repeatedly called to the crucial good of "friendship" in the Aristotelian qualitative-moral sense (see *Nichomachean Ethics*, Bk. VIII)—the relation between those who desire the good of friends for their friends' sake, no matter how different that "good" may be from what a companion chooses and pursues. In some degree, this is a way of acknowledging and respecting another's freedom to choose among possibilities, as it involves a desire to foster that choosing, because the other is a friend. There is talk of "solidarity" as well, as in the case of Richard Rorty talking about human beings giving sense to their lives by placing them in a larger context. There are two ways of doing this, he says: "by telling the story of their contribution to a community" or "by describing themselves as standing in immediate relation to a nonhuman reality." He calls the first story an example of the desire for solidarity, the second an example of the desire for objectivity. "Insofar as a person is seeking solidarity, he or she does not ask about the relation between the practices of the chosen community and something outside that community" (1985, p. 3). Rorty associates the notion of solidarity with pragmatism, especially when the suggestion is made that the only foundation for the sense of community is "shared hope and the trust created by such sharing." This removes not only objectivism but absoluteness; it returns us to the ideas of relatedness, communication, and disclosure, which provide the context in which (according to the viewpoint of this book) freedom must be pursued.

It is because of people's embeddedness in memory and history, because of their incipient sense of community, that freedom in education cannot be conceived either as an autonomous achievement or as merely one of the principles underlying our moral life, personalized (as R. S. Peters said) "in the form of rational passions." It is because of the apparent normality, the givenness of young people's everyday lives, that intentional actions ought to be undertaken to bring things within the scope of students' attention, to make situations more palpable and visible. Only when they are visible and "at hand" are they likely to cry out for interpretation. And only when individuals are empowered to interpret the situations they live together do they become able to mediate between the object-world and their own consciousness, to locate themselves so that freedom can appear.

Aware of how living persons are enmeshed, engaged with what surrounds them, Merleau-Ponty wrote:

> It is because we are through and through compounded of relationships with the world that for us the only way to become aware of the fact is to suspend the resultant activity . . . to put it out of play. Not because we reject the certainties of common sense and a natural attitude to things—they are, on the contrary, the consistent theme of philosophy—but because, being the presupposed basis of any thought, they are taken for granted and go unnoticed, and because in order to arouse them and bring them into view we have to suspend for a moment our recognition of them.
>
> (1962/1967, p. xiii)

He was not talking about withdrawing into some interior domain. Nor was he calling for a deflection of attention from ordinary life. Rather, he was exploring the possibilities of seeing what was ordinarily obscured by the familiar, so much part of the accustomed and the everyday that it escaped notice entirely. We might think about the clocks that play such important parts in schoolrooms, or school bells, or loudspeakers blaring at the beginning and end of the day; about calling individual children "third graders" or "lower track"; about threats to summon the remote principal; even about the Pledge of Allegiance, and about the flags drooping in the public rooms. Why *should* these phenomena be presupposed as a "basis" for thought and self-identification? We might think of the way the chalkboard is placed, of the peculiar distancing of the teacher at the front desk, of books firmly shut before the reading is done. The point is to find a means of making all this an object of thought, of critical attention. And we may be reminded again of Foucault's remark that "thought is freedom in relation to what one does." Part of the effort might be to defamiliarize things, to make them strange. How would a Martian view what was there, a "boat person" newly arrived? What would happen if the hands were removed from the clock? (No one, for instance, who has read William Faulkner's *The Sound and the Fury* is likely to forget the strangeness of what happens when Quentin pulls the hands off his watch on the day of his suicide. "Hearing it, that is," thinks Quentin, "I don't suppose anybody ever deliberately listens to a watch or a clock. You don't have to. You can be oblivious to the sound for a long while, then in a second of ticking it can create in the mind unbroken the long diminishing parade of time you didn't hear" [1946, p. 96]. Later, he remembers that "Father said clocks slay time. He said time is dead as long as it is being clicked off by little wheels; only when the clock stops does time come to life" [p. 104]. Reading that, one cannot but find the clock-field, the clock-world, expanding. And the possibilities of thinking multiply.) What of paper? Why is there so much paper? So many files? (George Konrad's novel about a Hungarian social worker, called *The Caseworker*, prove, comfort, threaten, grant, deny, demand, approve . . . the order I defend is brutal though fragile, it is unpleasant and austere; its ideas are impoverished and its style is lacking in grace . . . I repudiate the high priests of individual salvation and the sob sisters of altruism, who exchange commonplace partial responsibility for the aesthetic transports of cosmohistorical guilt or the gratuitous slogans of universal love. I refuse to emulate these Sunday-school clowns and prefer—I know my limitations—to be the sceptical bureaucrat that I am. My highest aspiration is that a medium-rank, utterly insignificant civil servant should, as far as possible, live with his eyes open" [1974, p. 168]. Again, familiar bureaucratic orders in one's own world thrust themselves into visibility. Seeing more, feeling more, one reaches out for more to do.)

Walker Percy's narrator in *The Moviegoer* says it in another way. He is trying to relieve his own boredom, a boredom verging on despair; and the idea of a search suddenly occurs to him.

What is the nature of the search? you ask.

Really, it is very simple, at least for a fellow like me; so simple that it is easily overlooked.

The search is what anyone would undertake if he were not sunk in the everydayness of his own life. This morning, for example, I felt as if I had come to myself on a strange island. And what does such a castaway do? Why, he pokes around the neighborhood and he doesn't miss a trick.

To become aware of the possibility of the search is to be onto something. Not to be onto something is to be in despair.

(1979, p. 13)

To undertake a search is, of course, to take an initiative, to refuse stasis and the flatness of ordinary life. Since the narrator says he was "sunk in everydayness," his search is clearly for another perspective, one that will disclose what he has never seen. Even to realize that he can be "onto something" is to begin perceiving lacks in his own life. The question as to what the "neighborhood" holds and implies remains open. He may be moved to "poke around" because others have taken heed of him, because he has appeared in the open for almost the first time. If this is so, he may acquire the space that will free him from his environment of everydayness. The experience may be one denoting a willingness "to learn again to see the world"—and to restore "a power to signify, a birth of meaning, or a wild meaning, an expression of experience by experience" (Merleau-Ponty, 1962/1967, p. 60). I am suggesting that there may be an integral relationship between reaching out to learn to learn and the "search" that involves a pursuit of freedom. Without being "onto something," young people feel little pressure, little challenge. There are no mountains they particularly want to climb, so there are few obstacles with which they feel they need to engage. They may take no heed of neighborhood shapes and events once they have become used to them—even the figures of homelessness, the wanderers who are mentally ill, the garbage-strewn lots, the burned-out buildings. It may be that no one communicates the importance of thinking about them or suggests the need to play with hypothetical alternatives. There may be no sense of identification with people sitting on the benches, with children hanging around the street corners after dark. There may be no ability to take it seriously, to take it personally. Visible or invisible, the world may not be problematized; no one aches to break through a horizon, aches in the presence of the question itself. So there are no tensions, no desires to reach beyond.

There is an analogy here for the passivity and the disinterest that prevent discoveries in classrooms, that discourage inquiries, that make even reading seem irrelevant. It is not simply a matter of motivation or interest. In this context, we can call it a question having to do with freedom or, perhaps, the absence of freedom in our schools. By that I do not necessarily mean the ordinary limits and constraints, or even the rules established to ensure order. I mean, in part, the apparent absence of concern for the ways in which young people feel conditioned, determined, even *fated* by prevailing circumstances. Members of minority groups, we are repeatedly informed, do not see the uses of commitment to schooling and studying. No matter how they yearn for success in society, they are convinced of inimical forces all around them, barricades that cannot be overcome. Poor children and others often experience the weight of what is called "cultural reproduction," although they cannot name it or resist it. By that is meant not only the reproduction of ways of knowing, believing, and valuing, but the maintenance of social patternings and stratifications as well. The young people may not chafe under the inequities being kept alive through schools, as inequities often are; they are likely to treat them as wholly "normal," as predictable as natural laws. The same might be said about advantaged children who grow up with a sense of entitlement and privilege, but still feel they have no choice.

The challenge is to engage as many young people as possible in the thought that is freedom—the mode of thought that moved Sarah Grimké, Elizabeth Cady Stanton, Septima Clark, Leonard Covello, the Reverend King, and so many others into action. Submergence and the inability to name what lies around interfere with questioning and learning. Dewey had something much like this in mind when he emphasized the dangers of "recurrence, complete uniformity," "the routine and mechanical" (1934, p. 272). What he sometimes called the "anaesthetic" in experience is what numbs people and prevents them from reaching out, from launching inquiries. For Dewey, experience becomes fully conscious only when meanings derived from earlier experience enter in through the exercise of the imaginative capacity, since imagination "is the only gateway through which these meanings can find their way into a present interaction; or rather . . . the conscious adjustment of the new and the old *is* imagination" (p. 272). The word, the concept "conscious" must be emphasized. Experience, for Dewey, becomes "human and conscious" only when what is "given here and now is extended by meanings and values drawn from what is absent in fact and present only imaginatively." Conscious thinking always involves a risk, a "venture into the unknown"; and it occurs against a background of funded or sedimented meanings that must themselves be tapped and articulated, so that the mind can continue dealing consciously and solicitously with lived situations, those situations (as Dewey put it) "in which we find ourselves" (p. 263).

Education for freedom must clearly focus on the range of human intelligences, the multiple languages and symbol systems available for ordering experience and making sense of the lived world. Dewey was bitterly opposed to the anti-intellectual tendencies in the culture and frequently gave voice to what he called "a plea for casting off that intellectual timidity which hampers the wings of imagination, a plea for speculative audacity, for more faith in ideas, sloughing off a cowardly reliance upon those partial ideas to which we are wont to give the name facts" (1931, p. 12). He spoke often as well about the kinds of inquiry that deliberately challenge desires for certainty, for fixity. He would undoubtedly have agreed with John Passmore's more recent call for "critico-creative thinking," the kind that is consciously norm-governed but at once willing to challenge rules that become irrelevant or stultifying. No principle, Passmore wrote, no person or text or work of art should be kept beyond the reach of rational criticism. There should nonetheless be a continuing initiation into the great traditions in which we are all, whether we are aware of it or not, embedded. Passmore went on:

> Critical thinking as it is exhibited in the great traditions conjoins imagination and criticism in a single form of thinking; in literature, science, history, philosophy or technology, the free flow of the imagination is controlled by criticism and criticisms are transformed into a new way of looking at things. Not that either the free exercise of the imagination or the raising of objections is in itself to be despised; the first can be suggestive of new ideas, the second can show the need for them. But certainly education tries to develop the two in combination. The educator is interested in encouraging critical discussion as distinct from the mere raising of objections; and discussion is an exercise of the imagination.
>
> (1975, p. 33)

A concern for the critical and the imaginative, for the opening of new ways of "looking at things," is wholly at odds with the technicist and behaviorist emphases we still find in American schools. It represents a challenge, not yet met, to the hollow formulations, the mystifications so characteristic of our time. We have taken note of the forms of evangelism and fundamentalism, the confused uneasiness with modernism that so often finds expression in anti-intellectualism or an arid focus on "Great Books." Given the dangers of small-mindedness and privatism, however, I do not think it sufficient to develop even the most variegated, most critical, most imaginative, most "liberal" approach to the education of the young. If we are seriously interested in education for freedom as well as for the opening of cognitive perspectives, it is also important to find a way of developing a *praxis* of educational consequence that opens the spaces necessary for the remaking of a democratic community. For this to happen, there must of course be a new commitment to intelligence, a new fidelity in communication, a new regard for imagination. It would mean fresh and sometimes startling winds blowing through the classrooms of the nation. It would mean the granting of audibility to numerous voices seldom heard before and, at once, an involvement with all sorts of young people being provoked to make their own the multilinguality needed for structuring of contemporary experience and thematizing lived worlds. The languages required include many of the traditional modes of sensemaking: the academic disciplines, the fields of study. But none of them must ever be thought of as complete or all-encompassing, developed as they have been to respond to particular kinds of questions posed at particular moments in time. Turned, as lenses or perspectives, on the shared world of actualities, they cannot but continue resonating and reforming in the light of new undercurrents, new questions, new uncertainties.

Let us say young high school students are studying history. Clearly, they require some under-standing of the rules of evidence where the historical record is concerned. They need to dis-tinguish among sources, to single out among multiple determinants those forces that can be identified as causal, to find the places where chance cuts across necessity, to recognize when calculations are appropriate and when they are not. All this takes reflective comprehension of the morns governing the discipline of history. But this does not end or exhaust such study. There is a consciousness now, as there was not in time past, of the significance of doing history "from the ground up," of penetrating the so-called "cultures of silence" in order to discover what ordinary farmers and storekeepers and elementary schoolteachers and street children and Asian new-comers think and have thought about an event like the Holocaust or the Vietnam War or the bombing of Hiroshima or the repression in South Africa that continues to affect them directly or indirectly even as it recedes into the visualizable past. And they may be brought to find out that a range of informed viewpoints may be just as important when it comes to understanding the Civil War, or the industrial revolution, or the slave trade, or the Children's Crusade. Clearly, if the voices of participants or near-participants (front-line soldiers, factory workers, slaves, crusaders) could be heard, whole dimensions of new understanding (and perplexity and uncertainty) would be disclosed. The same is true with respect to demographic studies, studies based on census rolls or tax collections, studies that include diaries and newspaper stories and old photographs. Turning the tools and techniques of history to resources of this kind often means opening up new spaces for study, metaphorical spaces sometimes, places for "speculative audacity." Such efforts may provide experiences of freedom in the study of history, because they unleash imagination in unexpected ways. They draw the mind to what lies beyond the accustomed boundaries and often to what is not yet. They do so as persons become more and more aware of the unanswered questions, the unexplored corners, the nameless faces behind the forgotten windows. These are the obstacles to be transcended if understanding is to be gained. And it is in the transcending, as we have seen, that freedom is often achieved.

The same can be said for the other disciplines and fields of study in the social and natural sciences; and, even among the exact sciences, a heightened curiosity may accompany the growth of feelings of connection between human hands and minds and the objects of study, whether they are rocks or stars of memory cores. Again, it is a matter of questioning and sense-making from a grounded vantage point, an interpretive vantage point, in a way that eventually sheds some light on the commonsense world, in a way that is always perspectival and therefore forever incomplete. The most potent metaphor for this can be found at the end of Melville's chapter called "Cetology" in the novel *Moby Dick*. The chapter deals with the essentially futile effort to provide a "systematized exhibition of the whale in his broad genera," or to classify the constituents of a chaos. And finally:

It was stated at the outset, that this system would not be here, and at once, perfected. You cannot but plainly see that I have kept my word. But now I leave my cetological System standing thus unfinished, even as the great Cathedral of Cologne was left, with the crane still standing upon the top of the uncompleted tower. For small erections may be finished by their first architects; grand ones, true ones, ever leave the copestone to posterity. God keep me from ever completing anything. This whole book is but a draught—nay, but the draught of a draught. Oh, Time, Strength, Cash, and patience!

(1851/1981, p. 148)

To recognize the role of perspective and vantage point, to recognize at the same time that there are always multiple perspectives and multiple vantage points, is to recognize that no accounting, disciplinary or otherwise, can ever be finished or complete. There is always more. There is always possibility. And this is where the space opens for the pursuit of freedom. Much the same can be said about experiences with art objects—not only literary texts, but music, painting, dance. They have the capacity, when authentically attended to, to enable persons to hear and to see what they would not ordinarily hear and see, to offer visions of consonance and dissonance that are unfamiliar and indeed abnormal, to disclose the incomplete profiles of the world. As importantly, in this context, they have the capacity to defamiliarize experience: to begin with the overly familiar and transfigure it into something different enough to make those who are awakened hear and see.

Generalizations with regard to what forms possess such potential for different people are tempting, but they must be set aside. Jazz and the blues have long had a transformative, often liberating effect on many populations, for example. We have only to read the musical history of our country, recall the stories of our great black musicians, heed such novels as *Invisible Man* (constructed, its author said, according to the patterns of the blues), take note of the importance of jazz in European art forms throughout the century, see how the Jazz Section of the Czech dissident movement has become the live center of dissent. The ways in which the blues have given rise to rock music and what are called "raps" testify as well to a power, not merely to embody and express the suffering of oppressed and constricted lives, but to name them some-how, to identify the gaps between what is and what is longed for, what (if the sphere of freedom is ever developed) will some day come to be.

Recent discoveries of women's novels, like discoveries of black literature, have certainly affected the vision of those reared in the traditions of so-called "great" literature, as they have the constricted visions of those still confined by outmoded ideas of gender. The growing ability to look at even classical works through new critical lenses has enabled numerous readers, of both genders, to apprehend previously unknown renderings of their lived worlds. Not only have many begun coming to literature with the intent of *achieving* it as meaningful through realization by means of perspectival readings. Many have begun engaging in what Mikhail Bakhtin called "dialogism," viewing literary texts as spaces where multiple voices and multiple discourse inter-sect and interact (1981, pp. 259–422). Even to confront what Bakhtin calls "heteroglossia" in a novel is to enlarge one's experience with multiplicity of perspectives and, at once, with the spheres that can open in the midst of pluralities.

With *Invisible Man* in mind, we might recall the point that invisibility represents a condition in the mind of the one who encounters the black person and draw implications for the ways we have looked at other strangers, and even for the ways we have looked at those posited as "other" or as enemies. We can find ourselves reading so-called canonical works like *Jane Eyre* and become astonished by a newly grasped interpretation of the "madwoman" imprisoned upstairs in Mr. Rochester's house. Shocked into a new kind of awareness, we find ourselves pushing back the boundaries again, hearing new voices, exploring new discourses, unearthing new possi-bilities. We can ponder such works as Tillie Olsen's "I Stand There Ironing" or "Tell Me a Riddle" and uncover dimensions of oppression, dream, and possibility never suspected before. We can look again at Gabriel Garcia Márquez's *One Hundred Years of Solitude* and find ourselves opening windows in our experience to startling renderings of time, death, and history that subvert more of our certainties. It is not only, however, in the domains of the hitherto "silent" cultures that transformations of our experience can take place. There is a sense in which the history of any art form carries with it a history of occasions for new visions, new modes of defamiliarization, at least in cases where artists thrust away the auras, and broke in some way with the past.

It has been clear in music, pushing back the horizons of silence for at least a century, opening new frequencies for ears willing to risk new sounds. It has been true of dance, as pioneers of movement and visual metaphor uncover new possibilities in the human body and therefore for embodied consciousnesses in the world. In painting, it has been dramatically the case. An example can be found in the work of the painter John Constable, who abandoned old paradigms of studio painting and studio light and began sketching his subjects in the open air. Breaking through "horizons of expectation," as the critic Ernst Gombrich writes (1965, p. 34), Constable enabled spectators to perceive green in the landscape, rather than rendering it in the traditional manner in gradations of brown. He defamiliarized the visible world, in effect, making accessible shadings and nuances never suspected before. We can say similar things about numerous visual artists, we are enabled, say, to see them against their forerunners; moving through the "museums without walls," listening to those Merleau-Ponty called the "voices of silence," we can discover ourselves variously on an always-changing place on earth. Giotto, della Francesca, Botticelli, Michelangelo, Raphael, Poussin: The names sound, the doors open to vista after vista. Exemplary for moderns may be Claude Monet making visible the modeling effects of light on objects once seen as solidly and objectively *there*. Some can recall the multiple studies of haystacks in his garden at different seasons of the year or of Rouen Cathedral at different times of the day. Recalling, we are reminded again how visions of fixity can be transformed, how time itself can take on new meanings for the perceiver, for the one choosing to journey through works of visual art. And we can (we ought to) recall Pablo Picasso's abrupt expansion of Western observers' conceptions of humanity and space with his "Demoiselles d'Avignon" and its African and Iberian visages, or his imagining of unendurable pain in "Guernica."

Of course, such visions are unknown in most of our classrooms; and relatively few people are informed enough or even courageous enough actually to "see." And it must be acknowledged that, for all their emancipatory potential, the arts cannot be counted on to liberate, to ensure an education for freedom. Nonetheless, for those authentically concerned about the "birth of meaning," about breaking through the surfaces, about teaching others to "read" their own worlds, art forms must be conceived of as ever-present possibility. They ought not to be treated as decorative, as frivolous. They ought to be, if transformative teaching is our concern, a central part of curriculum, wherever it is devised. How can it be irrelevant, for example, to include such images as those of William Blake, with contraries and paradoxes that make it forever impossible to place the "lamb" and the "tiger" in distinctive universes, to separate the "marriage" from the "hearse"? How can it be of only extracurricular interest to turn to Emily Dickinson, for instance, and find normal views of experience disrupted and transformed? She wrote:

I stepped from plank to plank
  So slow and cautiously;
The stars about my head I felt,
  About my feet the sea.
I know not but the next
  Would be my final inch,—
This gave me that precarious gait
  Some call experience.
        (1890/1959, p. 166)

The spaces widen in the poem—from plank to plank under an open sky. She identifies experience itself with a "precarious gait"; and the risk involved is emphasized. Reading such a work, we cannot but find our own world somehow defamiliarized. Defamiliarized, it discloses aspects of experience ordinarily never seen. Critical awareness may be somehow enhanced, as new possibilities open for reflection. Poetry does not offer us empirical or documentary truth, but it enables us to "know" in unique ways. So many poems come to mind, among them W. H. Auden's "Surgical Ward," which may emerge from memory because of the AIDS epidemic, or because of a concern about distancing and lack of care. He wrote of the remoteness of those who "are and suffer; that is all they do" and of the isolation of the sufferers compared with those who believe "in the common world of the uninjured and cannot imagine isolation—" (1970, pp. 44–45). Any one of a hundred others might have come to mind: the choice is arbitrary. A writer, like the writer of this book, can only hope to activate the memories of *her* readers, to awaken, to strike sparks.

The same is true, even more true, when it comes to novels and plays: The occasions for revelation and disclosure are beyond counting. In my train of thought (and readers will locate themselves in their own), I find Antigone, committed to her sense of what is moral and dying for her cause; King Lear, with all artifice and "superfluity" abandoned on the heath in the raging storm. I somehow see Lucifer falling in *Paradise Lost* and continually falling, reappearing at the end of James Joyce's *A Portrait of the Artist as a Young Man* when Stephen Dedalus says, "I will not serve." And then, remembering Joyce, I hear that resounding "Yes" at the end of Molly Bloom's soliloquy in *Ulysses*. In the background, softly, stubbornly, there is Bartleby's "I prefer not to" in the Melville story; there is the dying Ivan Ilyitch in the Tolstoy story; speaking of himself as "little Vanya" to the peasant holding his legs; there is the shadow of the little girl who hung herself in Dostoevsky's *The Possessed*. There are the soldiers described in Malraux's *Man's Fate*, young soldiers about to be executed on the Lithuanian front and forced to take off their trousers in the snow. They begin to sneeze, "and those sneezes were so intensely human in that dawn of execution, that the machine-gunners, instead of firing, waited—waited for life to become less indiscreet" (1936, p. 76). Indiscreet—and I see the house beaten by the storms and the dilapidations of time in the "Time Passes" section of Virginia Woolf's *To the Lighthouse*; Willa Cather's Paul (in "Paul's Case") and the winter roses and a boy's death on the railroad tracks. There are the spare, lace-curtained bedrooms and the slave women in red in Margaret Atwood's *The Handmaid's Tale*; and, in another future, there is the stark transcendence of the rocket in *Gravity's Rainbow* by Thomas Pynchon. There is Mark Helprin's white horse in the snow-bound city in *Winter's Tale*, the "air-borne toxic event" in Don DeLillo's *White Noise*.

Any reader might go on to recall how, as Herbert Marcuse has put it, "art is committed to that perception of the world which alienates individuals from their functional existence and performance in society" (1978, p. 9). An education for freedom must move beyond function, beyond the subordination of persons to external ends. It must move beyond mere performance to action, which entails the taking of initiatives. This is not meant to imply that aesthetic engagements, because they take place in domains of freedom, separate or alienate learners so fully from the tasks of the world that they become incapacitated for belonging or for membership or for the work itself. Marcuse also spoke of an aesthetic transformation as a "vehicle of recognition," drawing the perceiver away from "the mystifying power of the given" (1978, p. 72). He was pointing to an emancipatory possibility of relevance for an education in and for freedom. Encounters with the arts alone will not realize it; but the arts will help open the situations that require interpretation, will help disrupt the walls that obscure the spaces, the spheres of freedom to which educators might some day attend.

With situations opening, students may become empowered to engage in some sort of *praxis*, engaged enough to name the obstacles in the way of their shared becoming. They may at first be identified with the school itself, with the neighborhood, with the family, with fellow-beings in the endangered world. They may be identified with prejudices, rigidities, suppressed violence: All these can petrify or impinge on the sphere of freedom. As Foucault would have it, persons may be made into subjects, docile bodies to be "subjected, used, transformed, and improved" (1977, p. 136). It is not merely the structures of class, race, and gender relations that embody such power and make it felt in classrooms. Much the same can happen through the differential distribution of knowledge, through a breaking of what is distributed into discrete particles, through an unwarranted classification of a "chaos."

Having attended to women's lives and the lives of many strangers, we are aware of the relation between the subjugation of voices and the silencing of memories. All these have often been due to the insidious workings of power or the maintenance of what has been called "hegemony" (Entwhistle, 1979, pp. 12–14). Hegemony, as explained by the Italian philosopher Antonio Gramsci, means direction by moral and intellectual persuasion, not by physical coercion. That is what makes it a matter of such concern for those interested in education for freedom. The persuasion is often so quiet, so seductive, so disguised that it renders young people acquiescent to power without their realizing it. The persuasion becomes most effective when the method used obscures what is happening in the learners' minds. Strangely, the acquiescence, the acceptance, may find expression through dropping out or other modes of alienation, as much as through a bland compliance to what is taken to be the given. This may be because the message or the direction emphasizes an opportunity system or a stratification system offering a limited range of possibilities, apparently attentive to but a few modes of being. This becomes most drastically clear in the case of youngsters whose IQs, according to current testing practices, are low. Ours is not a society that ponders fulfilling options for people with low IQs. Lacking an awareness of alternatives, lacking a vision of realizable possibilities, the young (left unaware of the messages they are given) have no hope of achieving freedom.

In the classroom opened to possibility and at once concerned with inquiry, critiques must be developed that uncover what masquerade as neutral frameworks, or what Rorty calls "a set of rules which will tell us how rational agreement can be reached on what would settle the issue on every point where statements seem to conflict" (1979, p. 315). Teachers, like their students, have to learn to love the questions, as they come to realize that there can be no final agreements or answers, no final commensurability. And we have been talking about stories that open perspectives on communities grounded in trust, flowering by means of dialogue, kept alive in open spaces where freedom can find a place.

Looking back, we can discern individuals in their we-relations with others, inserting themselves in the world by means of projects, embarking on new beginnings in spaces they open themselves. We can recall them—Thomas Jefferson, the Grimké sisters, Susan B. Anthony, Jane Addams, Frederick Douglass, W. E. B. Du Bois, Martin Luther King, John Dewey, Carol Gilligan, Nel Noddings, Mary Daly—opening public spaces where freedom is the mainspring, where people create themselves by acting in concert. For Hannah Arendt, "power corresponds to the human ability . . . to act in concert. Power is never the property of an individual; it belongs to a group and remains in existence only so long as the group keeps together" (1972, p. 143). Power may be thought of, then, as "empowerment," a condition of possibility for human and political life and, yes, for education as well. But spaces have to be opened in the schools and around the schools; the windows have to let in the fresh air. The poet Mark Strand writes:

> It is all in the mind, you say, and has
> nothing to do with happiness. The coming of cold,
> The coming of heat, the mind has all the time in the world.
> You take my arm and say something will happen,
> something unusual for which we were always prepared,
> like the sun arriving after a day in Asia,
> like the moon departing after a night with us.
>   (1984, p. 126)

And Adrienne Rich, calling a poem "Integrity" and beginning, "A wild patience has taken me this far" (1981, p. 8). There is a need for a wild patience. And, when freedom is the question, it is always a time to begin.

REFERENCES

Arendt, H. (1961). *Between Past and Present.* New York: The Viking Press.
——. (1972). *Crises of the Republic.* New York: Harcourt Brace Jovanovich.
Atwood, M. (1986). *The Handmaid's Tale.* New York: Houghton Mifflin Co.
Auden, W. H. (1970). *Selected Poetry of W. H. Auden.* New York: Vintage Books.
Bakhtin, M. M. (1981). *The Dialogic Imagination.* Austin: University of Texas Press.
Belenky, M. F., et al. (1986). *Women's Ways of Knowing.* New York: Basics Books.
Berlin, I. (1973). *Four Essays on Liberty.* New York: Oxford University Press.
DeLillo, D. (1985). *White Noise.* Viking Penguin Press.
Dewey, J. (1931). *Philosophy and Civilization.* New York: Minton, Balch & Co.
——. (1934). *Art as Experience.* New York: Minton, Balch & Co.
——. (1938). *Experience and Education.* New York: Collier Books, 1963.
Dickinson, E. (1890). *Selected Poems & Letters of Emily Dickinson.* Ed. R. N. Linscott. Garden City, NY: Doubleday Anchor Books, 1959.
Entwhistle, H. (1979). *Antonio Gramsci.* London: Routledge & Kegan Paul.
Faulkner, W. (1946). *The Sound and the Fury.* New York: Modern Library.
Foucault, M. (1977). *Language, Counter-Memory, Practice.* Ed. D. F. Bouchard. Ithaca: Cornell University Press.
Garcia Marquez, G. J. (1967). *One Hundred Years of Solitude.* Trans. G. Rabasso. New York Harper & Row, 1970.
Gilligan, C. (1982). *In a Different Voice.* Cambridge: Harvard University Press.
Gombrich, E. (1965). *Art and Illusion.* New York: Pantheon Press.
Hare, R. M. (1965). *Freedom and Reason.* New York: Oxford University Press.
Helprin, M. (1983). *Winter's Tale.* New York: Pocket Books.
Joyce, J. (1916). *A Portrait of the Artist as a Young Man.* New York: Viking Press, 1955.
Kant, I. (1797). *The Doctrine of Virtue.* Part II of *The Metaphysics of Morals.* Trans. Mary J. Gregor. New York: Harper Torchbooks, 1964.
Kohlberg, L. (1971). "Stages of Moral Development as a Basis for Moral Education." In *Moral Education: Interdisciplinary Approaches,* ed. C. M. Beck, B. S. Crittenden, & E. V. Sullivan. New York: Newman Press.
Konrad, G. (1974). *Caseworker.* New York: Harcourt Brace Jovanovich.
Malraux, A. (1936). *Man's Fate.* New York: Modern Library.
Marcuse, H. (1978). *The Aesthetic Dimension.* Boston: Beacon Press.
Melville, H. (1851). *Moby Dick.* Berkeley: University of California Press, 1981.
Merleau-Ponty, M. (1962). *Phenomenology of Perception.* New York: Humanities Press, 1967.
Noddings, N. (1984). *Caring: A Feminine Approach to Ethics and Moral Education.* Berkeley: University of California Press.
Oliver, D. W. & Bane, M. J. (1971). "Moral Education: Is Reasoning Enough?" In *Moral Education: Interdisciplinary Approaches,* ed. C. M. Beck, B. S. Critenden, & E. V. Sullivan. New York: Newman Press.
Olsen, T. (1978). *Silences.* New York: Delacorte Press.
Passmore, J. (1975). "On Teaching to Be Critical." In *Education and Reason,* ed. R. F. Dearden, P. H. Hirst, & R. S. Peters, pp. 415–433. London: Routledge & Kegan Paul.
Percy. W. (1979). *The Moviegoer.* New York: Alfred A. Knopf.
Peters, R. S. (1970). "Concrete Principles and the Rational Passions." In *Education and Reason,* ed. N. F. Sizer & T. R. Sizer. Cambridge: Harvard University.
Piaget, J. (1977). *The Essential Piaget.* Ed. H. E. Gruber & J. J. Voneche. New York: Basic Books.
Pynchon, T. (1973). *Gravity's Rainbow.* New York: Viking Press.
Rorty, R. (1979). *Philosophy and the Mirror of Nature.* Princeton: Princeton University Press.
——. (1985). "Solidarity or Objectivity?" In *Post-Analytic Philosophy,* ed. J. Rajchman & West. New York: Columbia University Press.
Strand, M. (1939). "So You Say." In *Selected Poems.* New York: Viking Press.
Woolf, V. (1938). *To the Lighthouse.* London: J. M. Dent & Sons, 1962.

2.4 They're calling us names

Katrina B. Flores

Katrina B. Flores, "They're calling us names"

You see they're calling us names-playing games, keeping us confused.
Identities change every few decades.
More options to check so I can move myself smaller into a box.
Lines drawn all sides around to keep us in because according to their world created mixing is a sin.

Like flashback, walking four deep-fourteen years old in our neighborhood streets.
Migrating dangerously close to the other side.
To their drawn lines of districting.
Not knowing our place is the crime.

Being chased like a fox.
Flashlight bright light in our dark as night eyes.
Pupils dilate with fear of getting stopped and interrogated for being brown in this town.

See you in school . . . not too often chola cuz I'm not going to be looking the fool.
Again getting thrown in the blue room-after school detention-for throwing down for being called a garden tool by some guera chick for wearing the same brown eye liner she bought outlining my voluptuous lips.

No I'm not on the college bound plan . . . Doesn't seem like you're ever going to understand why I'm tracked like an animal in sciences of household chores and family because I'm just a baby machine . . . the next pregnant teen drop out.

Because that's all you've seen in me.
You my teacher, you who's helped me learn that little brown girls with big mouths, big hips and big hair are only good for just one thing—if you know what I mean.
Unless you give me a broom so I can clean your house all SPIC and span.
And my boys-hairnet wearing-butt ends of your jokes stuffed into the kitchens the backrooms.

Let me tell you how it is when everything you say and do counts against you, when it's a struggle even to come to class.
But you'll never know what it's like to be sitting in this room, in this row of desks getting called on as an expert only when we read the two paragraphs about Dr. Martin Luther King Jr. and non-violent protests in our text.

When I tried to learn about my peoples history in building this country you had nothing to feed my mentality and changed the subject hurriedly.
All were trying to do is wipe clean the slate of built up check marks against our names—you can't even pronounce and you're telling me to enunciate.

And you wonder why it took until 1997 for my family to go to college?

Just one of us-sent off with all the hopes and dreams of her people in her backpack. Shouldering the weight of the world and not equally prepared because my grandmother never made it past the 5th grade picking grapes, picking cucumbers and cotton.
A migrant worker-modern day slave.

And my father had to choose helping provide for his sisters and brothers instead of education to alleviate the immediate risks of starvation.
Compounded by the fact he didn't believe he could make it to another graduation.

He called the first time luck—I call it pushing children through or out of the system where teachers guard the golden gates.

Because you see, all too often La Raza has in the minds of those that teach illiteracy, welfare misusing, illegal, poverty stricken sealed fates.

Part 2
Commentaries

12 Do you see what I see?

Teacher capacity as vision for education in a democracy

Maureen D. Gillette and
Brian D. Schultz
Northeastern Illinois University

We were asked to write a commentary on teacher capacity based on the framing papers and artifacts in this section. Our commentary is written from our positions as teacher educators at a large, urban state institution that has been characterized as the most ethnically diverse university in the Midwest. In our roles within the College of Education, we prepare teacher candidates for Chicago and the surrounding suburbs. The diversity of this geographic area represents what some would argue are intractable gaps in educational access and outcomes. For example, recent research has documented that only about 30 percent of students graduating from Chicago Public Schools enroll in a four-year college and of that number, only 35 percent graduate (Chicago Consortium for School Research, 2006). Students from families with the highest incomes in Illinois are more likely to attend out-of-state, four-year institutions and are least likely to attend a two-year institution (IERC, 2005). Like our colleagues at other large, urban institutions, this context reminds us on a daily basis of the immediate need to prepare all teacher candidates be educators who understand and are committed to teaching for social justice.

The teacher candidates with whom we work mirror the diversity found in today's P-12 schools. Many attended under-resourced urban schools and struggled academically upon entrance into college. As a designated Hispanic-serving institution, many of our candidates began their own schooling in the United States unable to speak English. A significant number of them work full-time by necessity, have immediate and extended families to support, and are older than traditional undergraduates. We are keenly aware of immigration issues as some of our students are undocumented. Our teacher candidates are typically the first in their family to attend college. Because most work and attend school part-time, it is not unusual to find that some of our students take eight or more years to graduate, a timeline that is not only acceptable to them but may be one that is essential to their success. This portion of our teacher candidate population is often unaware of the type resources available in nearby wealthy districts and thus does not have first-hand knowledge of the magnitude of the inequities that existing between school districts across our geographic area.

At the same time, we have a large number of suburban students who grew up in nearby middle or upper-class homes. They may never have developed a strong relationship with peers who do not share their ethnic and socioeconomic characteristics. Many are fearful of completing clinical experiences in an urban school and often argue that it is unneces-sary for them to do so because they have no intention of teaching in city schools. For instance, when reading Kozol's (2005) *The Shame of the Nation: The Restoration of Apartheid in Schooling in America* as a required text for a course, many of the students from this demographic do not believe that the conditions Kozol describes actually exist in schools, even though some of the data and anecdotes in the book were collected in the Chicago Public Schools.

We see first-hand every day that developing teacher capacities for social justice is not just an enterprise for candidates intending to teach in urban or rural poverty areas, but an imperative for all teacher candidates. We have an obligation to foster teachers who are committed to social justice and have the knowledge, skills, and dispositions to work toward equitable access and outcomes for all, regardless of where or who they teach. In this chapter, we elaborate on two salient characteristics of teacher education programs raised by the framing papers: the commitment to inquiry-based critical pedagogy and the development of communities of practice. We use these points to argue for a specific type of "teacher vision," one that is rooted in social justice. As an aspect of teacher capacity we believe this is essential to the development of teachers who can and will prepare all young people for meaningful participation in our society.

THE ROLE OF VISION IN DEVELOPING TEACHER CAPACITY FOR EMANCIPATORY EDUCATION

The framing papers in this section can be synthesized and seen through a conceptual lens of teacher vision. The comprehensive book, *Teachers for a Changing World: What Teachers Should Learn and Be Able To Do* (Darling-Hammond & Bransford, 2005), contains a chapter entitled, "How Teachers Learn and Develop" (Hammerness *et al.*, 2005) that underscores the importance of new teachers learning to teach in a community that enables them to develop a vision for practice (pp. 385–386). Vision, or imaging what is possible, is seen by these researchers as an essential component of overcoming the "apprenticeship of observation" that has long been recognized as a roadblock to emancipatory teaching. The model developed by Hammerness *et al.* (2005) places teacher vision at the center of a large, outer circle that represents the "learning community." This exemplifies the optimal situation for teacher development. Surrounding the "vision" centerpiece are four key, yet general concepts that align with those described in the framing papers: Understanding, Practices, Dispositions, and Tools. *Understanding* is defined as "deep knowledge of content, pedagogy, students, and social contexts." The "Developing, practicing, and enacting a beginning repertoire" comprises *Practice*. *Dispositions* includes "habits of thinking and action regarding children and teaching," and *Tools* encompasses the conceptual and practical resources that teachers must have to be effective (p. 386).

The Hammerness *et al.* model, as presented, does not speak specifically to the types of knowledge, the forms of practice, the specific dispositions, or the appropriate tools that might help teacher candidates develop their own social justice teacher vision. We believe this vision for justice-oriented teaching is central, as well as critical, to addressing the question of teacher capacity today. The specific knowledge, understandings, practices, dispositions, and tools for social justice teaching discussed in the framing papers can be used to describe teacher vision for emancipatory teaching. We believe it is necessary for teacher candidates to develop such a imagination for what is possible. They not only need the capacity to see that which they may initially struggle to operationalize, they need a commitment to equity and a trust in themselves and their students in order to take the risks necessary to eventually succeed.

Teacher candidates need to see and analyze models of teaching that embody social justice teaching that reflect such vision. In doing so, they can be guided to develop, implement, and reflect on enactments of their own vision to move beyond traditional classroom practices that, as James Baldwin (1963) noted in *A Talk to Teachers*, maintain the status quo in society rather then develop in students the capacity for critical thought and action. Further, they can learn effective ways to interrupt those practices, policies, and procedures that have exacerbated current gaps in educational access and outcome.

TEACHER CAPACITY FOR SOCIAL JUSTICE AS A DEVELOPMENTAL, COLLABORATIVE, COMMUNITY-ORIENTED PROCESS

Helping candidates develop a vision for teaching with social justice at the core or foundation cannot be accomplished within programs and courses where components and people are in isolation. Appropriately, the model presented by Hammerness *et al.* (2005) places the Understandings, Practices, Dispositions, and Tools within a larger circle that represents the "learning community." The concept of learning community is broad and deep in regards to preparing teachers for social justice. As McDiarmid and Clevenger-Bright pointed out in their framing paper, teacher education is developmental, beginning when candidates enter college and continuing through the life-cycle of teaching. When teacher development for social justice is viewed on such a continuum, the need for collaboration between multiple constituencies within the context of a learning community becomes clear. Teacher educators have long known that teacher capacity cannot be built within teacher preparation programs alone. It is incumbent upon teacher educators to build such communities throughout the university career of prospective teachers as well as to create those connections in P-12 schools. What, then, is necessary in order to model for candidates the type of collaborative, democratic practice we espouse? How can we create and then deconstruct campus and classroom experiences that are illustrative of our vision of democratic practice so that our candidates learn how to do the same in their own P-12 classrooms?

The framing papers briefly addressed the need for collaboration between faculty in teacher education and those in the liberal arts and sciences. Teacher candidates must develop a content-knowledge base that is multicultural, come to see themselves as cultural beings with a plurality of identities, develop the type of critical thinking and analytic skills necessary for problem-posing, critical inquiry, and reflective thinking, and acquire the skills necessary to help P-12 students succeed (e.g. technological competence, community-based learning). The foundation for these competencies must be set within the liberal arts and it must be done in collaboration with education faculty. Additionally, many teacher educators will need to consider forging partnerships with community college colleagues where many of our candidates get their general education and beginning teacher education course work.

To make this collaboration both a tool for modeling and a reality, teacher educators must engage their liberal arts and science colleagues in discussions about teacher capacity. They must share their mission and vision for teacher preparation. Teacher educators must be able to clearly articulate the conceptual underpinnings of their programs. Questions about the perspectives and emphases in the general education curriculum and the major or minor areas of study must be raised and discussions invited. They must be willing to explore areas of congruence and dissonance between and within the university-wide components of teacher-education programs. It means that, for example, models of effective practice in team-teaching, collaborative student research, and integrated, student-centered curriculum and pedagogy must be exemplified between and among faculty from diverse disciplines. Perhaps one type of learning community that would lead students to develop a vision for critical pedagogy might be represented by a partnership between liberal arts and sciences, teacher candidates, and teacher education faculty.

The faculty who prepare candidates are themselves often compartmentalized into departments or areas that fail to create a learning community within schools or colleges of education. Programs are typically comprised of isolated course work in educational foundations, educational psychology, curriculum and methods, and field experiences. Faculty members hold beliefs about teacher capacity and the purpose of teacher education that are not shared, discussed, debated, and deliberated with colleagues. How do schools, departments, and colleges of education foster teacher vision for democratic community by themselves operating as a disconnected learning community? How is vision developed by teacher educators themselves? How often are candidates engaged in intellectual, social, or professional endeavors with faculty and administrators from across the college or university? In order for candidates to develop a vision of classroom community where teachers and students are partners in the learning journey, they must see it modeled and should participate in such experiences at the campus level as well as in the classroom.

Another aspect noted by the framing papers was the importance of collaboration with P-12 partners. It is typically assumed that in clinical teacher preparation, the primary learning community is comprised of teacher candidates, P-12 students, cooperating teachers, and university supervisors. It is rare to hear teacher educators discussing the candidate's learning community in a broader context that might include other teacher education faculty, liberal arts and sciences faculty, school administrators, parents, and other community members. While research underscores the importance of the principal as instructional leader in high-achieving schools, schools where community-building is a priority, and schools where teachers feel valued and affirmed, there is very little evidence outside of the professional development school literature that indicates that building and district administrators are included in preservice learning communities. Further, this is especially the case of parents and other community members. Research on the perceptions of first-year teachers about their preparation indicates that one area where they believe they were least prepared is in working with administrators and parents (IADPCE, 2005). Candidates must develop a vision of education that is community-based, one where parents and administrators are allies.

Collaboration in teacher education can and should exist in some form or another in colleges and universities. The challenge is to begin considering strategies for altering traditional boundaries and practices in our own settings. Mandates such as teacher standardized test score reporting and federal and state requests for grant proposals requiring various partnerships have raised the prominence of teacher education on many campuses, but it is fair to say that it is currently not the developmental, collaborative process that we suggest in this section. We cannot expect candidates to envision democratic practice nor come to understand implementation strategies if they do not see it, experience it, and participate in guided deconstruction of such experiences.

TEACHER VISION FOR AN INQUIRY-BASED, STUDENT-CENTERED, CRITICAL PEDAGOGY

The final section of our commentary raises questions about three areas of the teacher education that we believe are essential components of the development of teacher vision for social justice: curriculum, foundations, and the moral impulse. All three areas were addressed by the framing papers but we raise the following questions within the context of our argument that the type of capacities we are advocating must be built within communities of learners if candidates are to transfer their vision into pedagogical action.

The capacity to envision curriculum and curriculum development as tools of emancipation for learners requires teacher candidates to understand and be willing to confront, critique, and subsequently deconstruct the traditional power structure of the classroom. Candidates must have faith in democratic practice and trust in a student-centered model in order to find out through practice that powerful, student-centered curriculum will engage learners and that learners can be partners in curriculum development. This trust is difficult to develop when school administrators and outside societal pressures, especially in urban areas, place increasing emphasis on control rather than emancipation of learners. In learning communities where teacher education faculty, candidates, teachers and administrators have support for risk-taking and experimentation, it is possible to ask the types of questions that help structure democratic vision and facilitate trust in the process. Such organizational questions might be: How can Schwab's (1969) commonplaces of curriculum (subject matter, teacher, students, milieu) contribute to what will motivate and "work" successfully in a given classroom? How can meaningful, engaged curricula that is both justice-oriented and standards-aligned be developed and encouraged? How does a teacher's vision account for and encompass what may be called inverted curriculum (Schultz, 2008), null curriculum (Eisner, 1994) or out-of-school curriculum (Schubert, 1986) and make such concepts and strategies a part of an explicit classroom curriculum? What is it that allows for the creation of rich curriculum in under-resourced schools? How can teachers come to see students as curricularists (Schubert, 1992)? How can social action be seen as curriculum and curriculum be one of social action (Schultz & Oyler, 2006)?

The foundational aspects of education are often seen as useless by teacher candidates. Many candidates leave foundational course work unable to connect the historical, philosophical, sociocultural, and political dimensions of education to their role in the classroom. How do we assist candidates in developing a vision that is underpinned by a foundational context in order to justify their ideas and ideals about what is possible? How do candidates come to understand that the attainment of their vision is an evolutionary process, one that can be informed by scholarly examination of the social justice vision of others who have come before them? How do teacher educators and teacher candidates share the foundational dimensions of their vision? When do teacher candidates get opportunities to hear from exemplar teachers who are committed to equity about the theories and philosophies that drive their daily practice?

We consider these questions an entrée to understanding moral aspects of teacher vision. The moral aspects encompass democratic, emancipatory, and community-oriented impulses. These impulses enable effective teachers to take action challenging the status quo and interrupting conventional practices when those practices do not lead to more equitable educational outcomes. A vision for social justice is a necessary foundation, but vision without the courage and support to act will perpetuate the state of affairs that currently exists. How do self-awareness, identity, and culture play a role in the translating vision to action? How are reflection and action, for students and the teacher, encompassed within teacher vision? How are justice themes rooted in the idea of vision-based classroom action (Kesson & Oyler, 1999)? How do candidates come to see teaching as a moral action and ethical enterprise (Ayers, 2004)?

CONCLUSION

The gospel song *Faith* by God's Property (1997) contains the refrain, "I can do the impossible, I can see the invisible." These lyrics describe the foundation of teacher vision for social justice. It is the capacity to envision learners and learning experiences in ways that they may never have experienced during the "apprenticeship of observation." Teacher educators must also develop the same capacity in order to develop new models for practice and structures for implementation.

Our task in this commentary was to add to the discussion on teacher capacity by reflecting on the framing papers and artifacts included in this section in light of our own beliefs about teacher capacity. Our focus has been on the need to help our candidates develop the capacity for a specific vision, one of democratic education rooted in social justice. We cannot help but note that those teachers we know who teach with such vision exhibit those characteristics that Paulo Freire enumerated in his Fourth Letter: humility, courage, tolerance, decisiveness, security, patience/impatience, and joy of living. These teachers love their job and continue to work in high-need schools year after year because they can see their students as successful adults. They understand that all parents want their children to be successful, even though they may not be know how or be able to help them attain that success. These teachers come back day after day in difficult situations because they believe that they can make a difference in the lives of the children and in society by teaching the young people who sit before them each day to be critical thinkers and actors. They hold a student-centered vision for collaborative, emancipatory learning environments. They understand that attaining their vision is an ongoing process that is created and recreated with students, colleagues, parents, and the community. They espouse and enact their vision and that vision sustains them as lifelong educators.

Teacher educators must develop a vision of emancipatory teacher education practice and act on that vision through the creation of communities of practice that include our partners in the liberal arts, in the schools, and in our communities. We must be willing to practice what we preach if we expect to foster the capacities described in the framing papers in our teacher candidates.

In James Baldwin's (1963), *A Talk To Teachers*, he states, "I don't think anyone can doubt that in this country today we are menaced—intolerably menaced—by a lack of vision." He notes that it is inconceivable that people continued, during the horror of incidents such as the Birmingham Sunday School bombing, to say, "I can't do anything about it. It's the government." It seems to us that in many ways, the country is gripped by the same type of feeling about education today and that we, as teacher educators, may be complicit. We look at the problems in high-need schools and tell ourselves that the issues are complex. We say that we are addressing teacher capacity for democratic education in our courses but it's the "adjuncts" or the "liberal arts faculty" or the "schools" or "bureaucracy" that thwart our efforts. If we are serious about fostering an environment that encourages our teacher candidates to take action and teach for change in the roles as teachers, we must not only facilitate environments that encourage such practice, but also model what we envision in our own daily practice as teacher educators.

REFERENCES

Ayers, W. C. (2004) *Teaching toward freedom: moral commitment and ethical action in the class-room*. Boston: Beacon Press.
Baldwin, J. (1963, December 21) A talk to teachers. *Saturday Review*, 45(51).

Darling-Hammond, L. & Bransford, J. (2005) *Preparing teachers for a changing world: what teachers should know and be able to do*. San Francisco, CA: Jossey-Bass.

De Angelis, K. J., Presley, J. B., & White, B. R. (2005) *The distribution of teacher quality in Illinois* (IERC 2005–1), Illinois Education Research Council.

Eisner, E. W. (1994) *The educational imagination: on the design and evaluation of school programs* (3rd ed.). Upper Saddle River, NJ: Merrill Prentice Hall.

God's Property from Kirk Franklin's Nu Nation (1997). Inglewood, CA: B-Rite Music.

Gong, Y. & Presley, J. B. (2006) *The demographics and academics of college going in Illinois— Summary brief*. Edwardsville, IL: Illinois Education Research Council.

Hammermess, K., Darling-Hammond, L., Bransford, J., Berliner, D., Cochran-Smith, M. McDonald, M., & Zeicher, K. (2005) How teachers learn and develop. In L. Darling-Hammond & J. Bransford (eds.), *Preparing teachers for a changing world: what teachers should know and be able to do*. San Francisco, CA: Jossey-Bass.

Illinois Association of Deans of Public Colleges of Education (2005) Teacher graduate survey. Eastern Illinois University.

Kesson, K. & Oyler, C. (1999) Integrated curriculum and service learning: linking school-based knowledge and social action. *English Education* 31, 135–49.

Kozol, J. (2005) *The shame of the nation: the restoration of apartheid in America*. New York: Crown.

Schubert, W. H. (1986) *Curriculum: perspective, paradigm, and possibility*. New York: Macmillan.

Schubert, W. H. (1992) Personal theorizing about teachers' personal theorizing. In E. W. Ross, *et al.* (eds.) (1992) *Teacher personal theorizing: connecting curriculum, practice, theory, and research*. Albany, NY: State University of New York Press.

Schultz, B.D. & Oyler, C. (2006) We make this road as we walk together: sharing teacher authority in a social action curriculum project. *Curriculum Inquiry*. 36(4), 423–451.

Schultz, B.D. (2008) *Spectacular things happen along the way: lessons from an urban classroom*. New York: Teachers College Press.

Schwab, J. J. (1969) The practical: a language for curriculum. *School Review*, 78, 1–23.

13 Partial movements toward teacher quality . . . and their potential for advancing social justice

Kevin K. Kumashiro
University of Illinois-Chicago

At a time when official discourses in the United States are narrowly defining teacher quality, it is helpful to be reminded that the field of teacher education has long grappled with the notion that teacher quality cannot be defined independently of the context—and the oppressive as well as anti-oppressive movements within that context—in which the teaching occurs. The framing papers and artifacts in this section not only serve as this reminder, but as well, suggest to me at least three enduring and provocative questions about the necessary and troubling relation between teacher quality and (anti)oppressive movement in schools and society.

HOW IS TEACHING NECESSARILY PARTIAL, AND HOW CAN PARTIALITY BE USED TO ADVANCE SOCIAL JUSTICE?

The papers and artifacts in this section illustrate how teaching is not a neutral act. What gets taught is framed by only certain people using certain criteria to include certain things according to only certain perspectives in the curriculum. Similarly, how that then gets taught makes use of selected instructional methods that favor some learning styles over others and that strive towards only some pedagogical goals. Saying what and how to teach simultaneously requires saying what and how not to teach. Even with the best of intentions, teaching cannot help but to be partial.

Yet, current movements to reform education often overlook this necessary partiality of teaching. Currently in the United States, for example, the official discourse on improving teacher quality, as reflected in federal legislation (i.e. No Child Left Behind) and agencies (such as the U.S. Department of Education's Institute of Education Sciences), suggests that learning to teach means learning to use only those instructional methods that somehow have been proven to be effective in raising student achievement (as exemplified by the What Works Clearinghouse, established by IES to provide "scientific evidence" of what works in education), despite competing visions of what it is that schools should be working towards, and despite questions raised about the methods used to evaluate what works.

This official discourse of how to teach (via methods that "work") is not unlike the official discourse of what to teach, i.e. the "official knowledge" of schools that often becomes institutionalized as standards for learning, as what all students should know and be able to do. Both discourses are partial—reflecting only certain perspectives, advancing only certain goals, enabling only certain kinds of learning and growth. This narrowing of what and how to teach can be viewed as assimilationist when it demands conformity (think like this, teach like this, perform like this) while hindering opportunities to think outside the box and challenge the status quo via alternative perspectives, alternative methods, even alternative goals.

Calls to be more inclusive cannot solve this problem since full inclusion is not possible—there will always be things that get left out or prevented from coming in, intentionally or not. Even initiatives from within the profession to improve teacher quality and teacher education—embodied by such organizations or programs as the National Council for Accreditation of Teacher Education and the National Board for Professional Teaching Standards, and leaders who identify as social justice advocates— leave some teacher educators feeling that the professional requirements they put forth regarding what and how to teach teachers (or what/how to demonstrate what/how teachers learned) can and do hinder anti-oppressive education. Why? Because the requirements are partial, and problematically so, particularly when they presume to say what it means to engage in anti-oppressive approaches to education, and more importantly, when they simultaneously raise barriers to engaging in competing approaches.

This is not to say that there should not be standards. Standards, after all, make explicit the knowledge, skills, and dispositions that are valued in schools and society, as well as the unspoken rules or assumptions or practices for succeeding and getting ahead. But there are different ways to talk about the standards. Teaching to standards should not mean teaching that *this* is how things are and should be. Teaching to standards must involve teaching about the partiality of those very standards. It must involve teaching how any set of standards, or any curriculum, or any teaching and learning moment, is partial, is framed by only certain questions, is able to include some things but must exclude others, is helpful for achieving certain goals but a hindrance to achieving others. Any lesson, for example, will both include and exclude certain perspectives, will favor some interests over others, will challenge some inequities but reinforce others, will raise some questions or insights but mask others. Across the spectrum of grade level, subject matter, and cultural context, students need to see these partialities. And teachers need to treat these partialities not as things that make a lesson a failure, or ineffective for teaching and learning, but rather, as the very things that can make anti-oppressive education possible. Teaching students to think independently means teaching students to see that every lesson—even with the best of intent—is partial, and that this partiality will always have (educational, material, political) consequence.

Quality teachers need certain knowledge, but also need to know the limits of their knowledge. They need certain skills, but also need the skill of troubling whatever they do. They need certain dispositions, but also need to be disposed to uncomfortable changes in these very dispositions. Anti-oppressive teaching and teacher education are as partial as other forms of teaching and teacher education, but they make use of that partiality in ways that are uncommon, unsettling, even paradoxical.

HOW IS TEACHING PARADOXICAL, AND HOW CAN PARADOX SUGGEST DIFFERENT METAPHORS FOR TEACHING?

The partiality of teaching makes the process of teaching (and of learning) paradoxical, and necessarily so: It requires that teaching and learning aim to trouble the very things being taught and learned, and the very ways that the teaching/learning are happening. This does not mean that learners reject everything that they are learning; rather, it means that they examine how everything that they learn is partial, and how this partiality always has consequence. This metaphor of *troubling* contrasts with metaphors that currently frame dominant discourses of teacher quality. Examples of dominant metaphors include metaphors of repetition, transmission, and accumulation that are akin to Paulo Freire's characterization of "banking education," as is apparent when expecting that quality teachers will delineate what all students (or student teachers) should know and be able to do (via standards); will use instructional methods that transmit this effectively (via "what works"); and will assess that students (or student teachers) indeed acquired what they were to learn (via high achievement on standardized assessments). This is not to say that anti-oppressive teaching involves avoiding standards, or methods that "work," or standardized assessments, as if such avoidance were even possible. Rather, anti-oppressive teaching involves simultaneously engaging in and challenging how we commonly think of "teaching"; it involves engaging in and challenging what I noted earlier to be its own assimilationist moves. And therein lies the paradox.

Teaching is paradoxical because it is both excessive and subtractive. Teaching is excessive in the sense that it always includes or accomplishes more than what was intended. And, given that learners will always view and respond to what is being taught in multiple and unpredictable ways (because they view themselves and the world through various "lenses" that have been colored by their unique histories and identities and experiences and prior learnings), teaching can never be foretold or contained, and it can even contradict what it aimed to accomplish. Teaching is also subtractive, not merely "subtractive" in the sense that it disadvantages the students academically (although such a form of subtractive schooling indeed characterizes what too often is happening in schools), but also "subtractive" in the sense that it takes away from what the teacher is teaching, or what the learner already thought was learned, or even how the learner has come to make sense of and feel about him/herself. Teaching/learning involves not only gaining something, but also losing something. And this subtractive relation can be anti-oppressive when it troubles the identities and knowledge that help to maintain the status quo.

It is in this loss, in this process of raising challenging questions, that teaching and learning should expect to coincide with discomfort, particularly if the knowledge being troubled is knowledge about oneself or one's relation to others or the world in which one lives. After all, learning that *the very ways we make sense of the world is partial, and this partiality can have harmful consequence*, can be an upsetting process. Yet, in school, space is not always opened up for such discomfort. Too often, teachers seem to hope that discomfort does not arise in their teaching (as when talking about racism and hoping that crisis does not erupt), and then overlook discomfort when it inevitably arises. This is a problem because discomfort is not something that often leads a learner to want to learn more, to want to ask even more troubling questions. Discomfort can lead to resistance to further learning. Thus, it is important for teachers to learn how to structure learning such that students anticipate discomfort and are able to find ways to work through it so that they continue learning. Teachers need to come to view discomfort as a part of learning that is not only unavoidable, but also potentially productive.

Teacher education does not often prepare teachers for addressing discomfort in this way. And perhaps this is because teacher educators, themselves, are not often prepared for it.

HOW IS TEACHING HINDERED BY RESISTANCE WITHIN TEACHER EDUCATION, AND HOW CAN WE BRING ABOUT CHANGE?

More and more teacher education programs are teaching about anti-oppressive approaches to education (including approaches that are multicultural, critical, feminist, and queer), but barriers persist in getting such approaches into K-12 schools. Some barriers come from the structure of the teaching contexts (such as requirements to teach only certain things in only certain ways), and some from the teachers themselves (as when believing that the teachings of the university are out of touch with the realities of schools). But some barriers come in the form of mixed messages from within teacher education, as when teacher educators do not trouble their own partialities, and in the process, indirectly and, perhaps, unintentionally model a resistance to and impossibility of putting anti-oppressive theory into practice.

An example would be the message of hypocrisy. Such was the criticism about the field of teacher education when some teacher educators spoke out against the Passport to Teaching, a program of the American Board for Certification of Teaching Excellence (ABCTE), with substantial funding by the federal government, that would award initial teacher certification based almost entirely on content knowledge (as demonstrated in a standardized test). In 2004, ABCTE was picking up steam, on its way to getting five states to adopt the Passport in some form, and scheduled to make a bid for a sixth state, California. A coalition of teacher educators, K-12 educators, and community activists spoke through letters, testimonies, media releases, e-mails, and other outlets to make clear to leaders and the public how the Passport would not increase the number of quality teachers because it did not provide a mechanism for teacher candidates to learn about and develop skills in teaching the subject matter, particularly to a diverse student population with a range of needs, learning styles, and cultural influences. Quality or effective teachers must not only know the content, but also be skilled in how to teach the content, and the Passport did not ensure such skills. The Passport was not adopted by CA, but the struggle left a lingering question in the minds of some observers, who asked why teacher educators were arguing that educators in K-12 schools must formally learn how to teach before being hired when teacher educators themselves (and other educators in colleges and universities) do not face a similar requirement. Teacher educators may be experts in their context (as represented in their earning a Ph.D.) but their criticism of ABCTE was precisely that content knowledge alone does not make for teacher quality. By not institutionalizing their own learning of how to teach, teacher educators seemed resistant to troubling their own teaching.

Of course, a growing number of teacher educators are arguing that teacher educators, too, should be formally learning how to teach. But there are challenges: opportunities for professional development on teaching are rare, rewards are few (as in the tenure process), and resistance is strong (among those who value their independence). A philosophical challenge also exists to institutionalizing that type of professional development, namely, the lack of consensus, even among education scholars, on what exactly it means to learn to teach, be it "effectively" or "anti-oppressively" or otherwise. Presumably, learning to teach would mean learning to teach in ways that contrast what is traditionally or commonly done, or what common sense would have us believe should be done—i.e. the whole point of learning to teach is to learn not to rely on tradition or common sense. This turn to alternatives is important if traditional or common ways of teaching are deemed to be ineffective, either in raising student achievement (as reflected in standardized tests), in managing the classroom (as is often a primary challenge of and concern for beginning teachers), or even in advancing social justice through critical consciousness and engagement. But who defines the alternative? And how does that definition, which cannot help but to be partial, necessarily lead to problematic consequences? There are competing ways of defining what is ineffective and what is desired. Are those groups that are currently driving education reform by institutionalizing their perspectives into policy, including and especially those who identify as advocates for social justice, acknowledging their own partiality, and institutionalizing ways to trouble it?

Policies and practices in teacher education are no less partial than those in K-12 schools, no less likely to have both oppressive and anti-oppressive consequence, and thus, are in no less need of bring troubled. As the field of teacher education continues to grapple with the question of teacher quality in K-12 schools, we in teacher education should continue to bring the questions and insights of this grappling to bear on ourselves and our ongoing work. This new handbook is an important resource for doing this, and I look forward to seeing the changes that we make happen.

14 Dismantling dichotomies in teacher education

Pam Grossman
Stanford University

Morva McDonald
University of Washington

Karen Hammerness
Stanford University

Matthew Ronfeldt
Stanford University

INTRODUCTION

For more than forty years, the achievement gap between middle-class, white students and students of color has persisted. At the turn of the twenty-first century, the average African American or Latino high school student performs at about the level of an eighth grade white student in reading and mathematics (Resnick, 2004). The lower achievement of minority and poor students results from numerous factors: for example, they are more likely to attend poorly resourced schools, to be taught by uncertified teachers, to encounter lower teacher expectations and rote curriculum, and experience a revolving door of teachers. In addition, they face higher drop out rates, higher rates of suspension, and higher rates of placement in special education than their white middle class peers (e.g. Anyon, 1997; Darling-Hammond, 1995; Jacobsen *et al.*, 2001; Lankford *et al.*, 2002).

Increasingly, educational scholars of all stripes agree that teacher quality is critical to improving access to intellectually rigorous content and ultimately, to efforts to narrow the achievement gap. Less clear, however, is how we might select, prepare, and support teachers to meet this challenge, and how we might define the capacity teachers require to narrow the gap. In this chapter, we conceptualize teacher capacity as less about distinct forms of knowledge and belief than about classroom practices, emphasizing the importance of integrating theoretical principles with the enactment of practice in the preparation of teachers.

DANGEROUS DICHOTOMIES

The current debate on teacher capacities has a curious dichotomy at its core. While teacher educators proclaim the need to prepare teachers to teach for social justice (e.g. Cochran-Smith, 2004; Grant & Agosto, this volume; Howard & Aleman, this volume), critics of teacher education decry the lack of attention to teachers' preparation to teach subject matter knowledge (e.g. Will, 2006). With a few notable exceptions (e.g. Au, 1980; Boaler, 1997; Lee, 1995; Gutstein *et al.*, 1997; Moses & Cobb, 2001; Warren *et al.*, 2001), researchers in multicultural education rarely reference the teaching of subject matter. On the other hand, those who study the teaching of subject matter often overlook issues of race, language, and class.

This dichotomy has deep roots, as McDiarmid and Clevenger-Bright (this volume) illustrate. And as Dewey long ago observed, such educational dichotomies (content versus process; child versus curriculum) are rarely useful and often dangerous. We argue that re-conceptualizing teacher capacity, particularly with regard to reducing educational inequality, requires dismantling this particular dichotomy. Carol Lee (1995) demonstrated the value of scaffolding from African American students' cultural knowledge in order to help them read complex literary texts; in her work culturally-relevant pedagogy targets deep disciplinary understandings of literature. In mathematics, Gutstein and his colleagues (1997) observed effective mathematics teachers in the Mexican American community provide students with tools for active participation in society through the teaching of mathematics content. Consistent with this line of work, we propose a model of teacher capacity that views preparing teachers to teach subject matter well and teaching for social justice as interdependent.

Talking about teaching for social justice without addressing the importance of content is like giving people the right to vote without handing them a ballot—the substance is missing. As Freire recognized long ago, the pedagogy of the oppressed is centrally about empowering students as readers, writers, and thinkers; literacy is at the core of Freire's early work (1970). In arguing for algebra as the new civil right, Bob Moses makes a similar claim about the centrality of content in addressing educational inequality. Reducing educational inequality means taking on the challenge to prepare students from historically oppressed groups to tackle intellectually ambitious subject matter in mathematics, science, history, and literature, among other areas. It is not enough to prepare teachers with the dispositions to teach all students, or with knowledge of their students' cultural and linguistic resources. Teachers need to know how to use such knowledge in order to help students develop intellectual skills and to succeed academically.

Teaching reading well requires professional knowledge, skill, craft, professional judgment, and the ability to use curricular resources (Snow *et al.*, 2005). We know more than ever before about approaches to teaching early reading to prevent reading problems (Snow *et al.*, 1998), yet we can't be sure that all prospective teachers have the opportunity to develop their ability to teach reading well, especially in settings where many children struggle with reading. This may require teacher educators to rethink how they prepare novices to teach in high-poverty schools. Not preparing teachers to teach decoding or phonemic awareness right along with approaches that focus on the meaning of text, simply perpetuates inequality (Delpit, 1996). Not preparing novice teachers to use and adapt the kinds of curriculum materials that are increasingly being mandated in high-poverty schools is irresponsible. Teacher educators may rail against the limitations of Open Court, for example, but they have a professional responsibility to ensure that novices learn to use such curricula to promote student learning, even as they work to change policy. Otherwise, we risk preparing teachers for schools that do not exist rather than preparing them to negotiate the expectations that they will meet in today's schools. By choosing to ignore these expectations, we fail both the students, and the teachers who teach them.

At the same time, policies that prevent students in high-poverty schools from engaging in more sophisticated forms of literacy (including interpretation, extended writing and analysis) because of their exclusive focus on easily tested basic skills, also perpetuate inequality. For example, scholars suggest that although the academic achievement gap in reading has narrowed for students in the early grades, the gap persists as students enter middle and high schools where literacy achievement demands greater knowledge and understanding of content (Hirsch, 2006). Preparing teachers to teach for social justice requires that novices develop intellectually ambitious goals for their students and learn ways to enact these teaching goals in their classrooms. As Megan Franke of Center X teaches her novice teachers, even in the most rigid of pacing plans, there is room to attend to and develop students' conceptual understanding of mathematics. But novices must learn not only that this kind of intellectually ambitious teaching is possible—they must learn to enact these practices in their classrooms, a challenge we take up below.

Teaching reading well is also a matter of experience. No matter how well we prepare teachers initially, much of their learning will be on the job. Placing the least experienced teachers with the most needy students—what we routinely do now—ensures social injustice. To talk seriously about teacher capacity is to acknowledge the continuum of teacher learning (Feiman-Nemser, 2001) and the differential kinds of support that teachers need throughout their careers. Getting serious about supporting the learning of new teachers means changing entrenched policies that place the least experienced teachers in the most challenging settings.

A FOCUS ON PRACTICES ACROSS THE CURRICULUM

Teaching for social justice must happen through the teaching of subject matter. But learning how to help struggling students succeed in algebra or read *Beloved* is no simple task for teachers. To teach effectively, teachers must develop both conceptual and practical tools. Conceptual tools are the principles, frameworks, or guidelines that teachers use to guide their decisions about teaching and learning (Grossman *et al.*, 1999). These tools may include general, applicable theories such as constructivist theories of learning, motivation, and instructional scaffolding or more philosophical views related to the purposes of schooling such as social justice and the goal of improving educational opportunities for students. Conceptual tools facilitate teachers' framing and interpretations of practice, but they do not offer specific solutions for negotiating the dilemmas that arise in interactions with students. Practical tools encompass the kinds of practices, strategies, and relationships that teachers can enact in classrooms as they strive to accommodate the needs of students and challenge them with intellectually, rigorous content. To paraphrase a debate between Nate Gage and Lee Shulman, two venerable researchers of teaching, without practical tools, teachers may be lost in thought; without conceptual tools to make sense of practice, teachers may be missing in action.

From this perspective, increasing teachers' capacity requires the development of both conceptual and practical tools. For example, proponents of preparing teachers for social justice argue that teachers' ability to accommodate the cultural and community resources students bring with them to school is an important principle for teachers to learn (cf. Gandara, 2002; Ladson-Billings, 1997; Moll *et al.*, 1992). In order for new teachers to enact that principle in the context of their work with students, however, they must also cultivate classroom practices for identifying students' cultural and community resources as well as adapting subject matter curriculum and instruction to build on and draw from those resources (e.g. Richert, 2006). Similarly, given the increasing number of English language learners in many of today's urban public schools, teachers must not only understand the particular language needs of English learners, but have access to practices that enable them to address those needs in the context of subject matter instruction. Abstract knowledge of either students' needs or ways to address them will not suffice; teachers also need opportunities to try out and refine practices that embody such knowledge.

Without opportunities to develop and refine practices for the teaching of specific subject matter areas to minority and poor students, teachers' capacities to provide high quality learning opportunities for their students are severely limited.

UNDOING DICHOTOMIES IN TEACHER EDUCATION

The conception of teacher capacity put forward in this commentary requires three fundamental shifts in emphasis to be made on the part of teacher educators: first, that teacher educators work to develop programs that undo the dichotomies between subject matter and social justice; second, that they focus upon helping novices develop and refine practices; and finally, that they prepare teachers explicitly for the schools attended by our lowest achieving students. While these alterations may not represent wholecloth reform, they are also difficult changes to make. They necessitate shifts in focus both at the course and program level as well as in the field.

Such an effort, for example, may require blurring curricular lines between what are typically called "foundations" courses and those that focus on "methods" or teaching (Howard, this volume). Foundational courses in multicultural education, for instance, may need to go beyond their focus upon conceptual understandings of racism, injustice, or urban schools. They must not only help novices understand the presence of inequities in our schools and understand what it means to support a "socially just" educational system; they also need to help prospective teachers develop a set of specific classroom practices that will help them succeed with students from historically oppressed groups. And in turn, methods courses that have typically focused upon teaching subject matter must also address issues of inequity directly, through introducing students to the practices associated with teaching intellectually ambitious subject matter to historically underserved children.

In this new framing of teacher preparation, methods courses are not only inherently about subject matter and the methods of teaching—about classroom *practices*—but also deeply about teaching for social justice. And in this new framing of teacher preparation, foundations courses are not only inherently about conceptual tools, but also come to represent a deep form of learning about practices. In her study of how two teacher education programs prepare new teachers for diversity, McDonald (2005) describes one particular course that provides an interesting example of how a carefully structured course can help new teachers develop practices for teaching English language learners. This course, focused on the teaching of English language learners, skillfully provided prospective teachers with broad principles for making decisions about how best to teach ELLs as well as specific strategies for doing so. For example, the instructor stressed the importance of accommodating ELLs' literacy needs but also walked prospective teachers through specific adaptations to the strategy of reciprocal teaching as a specific tool aimed at supporting ELLS in the classroom. Prospective teachers in this class repeatedly commented that they learned not only how to *think about* English Language Learners, but also how to *teach* them. This example points to the possibility and the potential power of providing prospective teachers with opportunities to develop both concepts and practices for teaching specific types of students within the context of teacher education.

Finally this new conception of teacher preparation may require that teacher educators prepare teachers for classrooms and schools *as they are*, while still giving prospective teachers opportunities to consider what they could become. While it is imperative that new teachers are supported in developing powerful images of good teaching, it is also unfair to prepare new teachers to expect to enact their ideals immediately. To do so, may in fact, set new teachers up for disappointment and increase the risk that they leave the profession (e.g. Achinstein *et al.*, 2006). As Hargreaves and Jacka (1999) argue: "Initial teacher education may increasingly be a process of soft seduction into images and practices of teaching that prepare new teachers neither to adjust to the unchanged realities of the schools in which they will begin their paid teaching careers, nor to develop the intellectual understanding and political skills which would enable them to critique and challenge those realities" (p. 58). This may mean achieving a delicate balance in teacher education between *preparing new teachers for schools as they might be* and *acknowledging and thoroughly preparing teachers for schools as they are*; to achieve this balance might also require developing what Freire terms a patient impatience (p. 64). For example, teacher educators must not only offer novice teachers skills and opportunities to develop curriculum on their own "from scratch" so that they understand how to plan, develop appropriate assessments, identify big ideas in the discipline, and develop their ability to engage in pedagogical thinking; teacher educators must also give new teachers sufficient opportunities to use, adapt, enact, and critique the existing curricula they may be required to use in their classrooms.

Grant and Agosto (this volume) observe that the qualities typically associated with a conception of teacher capacity are "entangled, slippery and vague." Yet if we define teacher capacity as enacted in particular practices, practices that embody theoretical principles of instruction, learning, development, and culture, practices that can be developed and refined over time, we begin to move away from an amorphous conception of capacity toward a more concrete understanding of what teachers really need to know and be able to do.

REFERENCES

Anyon, J. (1997) *Ghetto schooling: a political economy of urban educational reform.* New York: Teachers College Press.

Achinstein, B. & Ogawa, R.T. (2006) (In)Fidelity: what the resistance of new teachers reveals about professional principles and prescriptive educational policies. *Harvard Educational Review,* 76, 30–63.

Au, K.H. (1980) Participation structures in a reading lesson with Hawaiian children: analysis of a culturally appropriate instructional event. *Anthropology and Education Quarterly,* 1(2), 91–115.

Boaler, J. (1997) *Experiencing school mathematics: teaching styles, sex and setting.* Philadelphia, PA: Open University Press.

Cochran-Smith, M. (2004) *Walking the road: race, diversity, and social justice in teacher education.* New York: Teachers College Press.

Cochran-Smith, M. & Fries, M.K. (2002) The discourse of reform in teacher education: extending the dialogue. *Educational Researcher,* 31(6), 26–28.

Darling-Hammond, L. (1995) Inequality and access to knowledge. In J. Banks & C. Banks (eds.) *Handbook of research on multicultural education* (pp. 465–483). New York: Macmillan.

Delpit, L. (1996) *Other people's children: cultural conflict in the classroom.* San Francisco: The New Press.

Education Commission of the States (2003) The progress of education reform 2003: closing the achievement gap. *The Progress of Education Reform 2003,* 4(1).

Feiman-Nemser, S. (2001) From preparation to practice: designing a continuum to strengthen and sustain teaching. *Teachers College Record,* 103(6), 1013–1055.

Freire, P. (1970) *Pedagogy of the oppressed* (30th anniversary edition). New York: Continuum Publications Press.

Freire, P. (2006) *Teachers as cultural workers: letters to those who dare teach* (D. Macedo, D. Koike, & A. Oliviera, Trans.). Boulder, CO: Westview Press.

Gandara, P. (2002) A study of High School Puente: what we have learned about preparing Latino youths for postsecondary education. *Educational Policy Special Issue: The Puente Project— Issues and perspectives on preparing Latino youth for higher education*, 16(4), 474–495.

Grossman, P.L., Smagorinsky, P., & Valencia, S.W. (1999) Appropriating tools for teaching English: a theoretical framework for research on learning to teach. *American Journal of Education*, 108(1), 1–29.

Gutstein, E., Lipman, P., Hernandez, P., & de los Reyes, R. (1997) Culturally relevant mathematics teaching in a culturally relevant context. *Journal for Research in Mathematics Education*, 28(6), 709–737.

Hargreaves, A. & Jacka, N. (1995) Induction or seduction? Postmodern patterns of preparing to teach. *Peabody Journal of Education*, 70(3), 41–63.

Heath, S.B. (1982) *Ways with words: language, life, and work in communities and classrooms.* Cambridge, UK: Cambridge University Press.

Hirsch, E.D. (2006) The case for bringing content into the language arts block and for a knowledge-rich curriculum core for all children. *American Educator* (Spring).

Jocabsen, J., Olsen, K.R., Sweetland, S., & Ralph, J. (2001) *Educational achievement and black and white inequality* (No. 2001061). Washington, DC: National Center for Educational Statistics.

Ladson-Billings, G. (1997) *The dreamkeepers: successful teachers of African-American children.* San Francisco: Jossey-Bass.

Lankford, H., Loeb, S., & Wycoff, J. (2002) Teacher sorting and the plight of urban schools. *Educational Evaluation and Policy Analysis*, 24(1), 37–62.

Lee, C.D. (1995) A culturally based cognitive apprenticeship: teaching African-American high school students skills in literary interpretation. *Reading Research Quarterly*, 30(4), 608–630.

McDonald, M.A. (2005) The integration of social justice in teacher education. *Journal of Teacher Education*, 56(5), 418–435.

Moll, L.C., Amanti, C., Neff, D., & Gonzalez, N. (1992) Funds of knowledge for teaching: using a qualitative approach to connect homes and classrooms. *Theory into Practice*, 31(1), 132–141.

Moses, R.P. & Cobb, C.E. (2001) *Radical equations: math literacy and civil rights.* Boston: Beacon Press.

Resnick, L. (ed.) (2004) Closing the achievement gap: high achievement for students of color. *Research Points: Essential Information for Education Policy*, 2(3), 2–4.

Richert, A.E. (2006, April) When you ask: learning from the families of the children we teach. Paper presented at the annual meeting of the American Educational Research Association, San Francisco, CA.

Snow, C.E., Burns, S.M., & Griffin, P. (eds.) (1998) *Preventing reading difficulties in young children.* Washington, DC: National Academy Press.

Snow, C.E., Burns, S.M., & Griffin, P. (eds.) (2005) *Knowledge to support the teaching of reading: preparing teachers for a changing world.* San Francisco: Jossey-Bass.

Tharp, R. (1982) The effective instruction of comprehension: results and description of the Kamehameha early education program. *Reading Research Quarterly*, 17(4), 503–527.

Warren, B., Ballenger, C., Ogonowski, M., Rosebery, A. S., & Hudicourt-Barnes, J. (2001). Rethinking diversity in learning science: the logic of everyday sense-making. *Journal of Research in Science Teaching*, 38(5), 529–552.

15 Teacher capacity for diversity

Donna M. Gollnick
National Council for Accreditation of Teacher
Education (NCATE)

For the purposes of accreditation, the National Council for Accreditation of Teacher Education (NCATE) would define teacher *capacity* as what teachers and other school professionals should know, be able to do, and be disposed to. In fact, NCATE's Standard 1 is entitled "Candidate Knowledge, Skills, and Dispositions."[1] However, teachers, teacher educators, policymakers, parents, and critics do not always agree on the capacities that teachers should develop. They agree that teachers should know the subjects they teach, and should be able to help students learn those subjects. Consensus has not been reached on whether "good teaching transcends settings and populations" (Howard and Aleman in this volume, Chapter 10). Many teacher educators, particularly multiculturalists and critical theorists, believe that teachers must understand the power dimensions of society as well as the cultures and prior experiences of students, their families, and communities to help *all* students learn and become active participants in a democracy. Others are not so sure.

Critics of teacher education charge that teacher education prepares teachers with "warm and fuzzy" notions about teaching such as developing self-esteem and helping students feel good about themselves at the expense of in-depth study of content or subject matter. In fact most secondary teacher candidates do major in their subjects. Requirements for mathematics and literacy in elementary and special education are increasing. The NCATE program standards for elementary education require candidates to develop content proficiencies in reading and English language arts, mathematics, science, and social studies. The number of credit hours required for a baccalaureate degree is often limited to around 120 hours, limiting the amount of time for both in-depth study of content and the study of teaching and learning in professional education courses. A number of institutions have decided that a four-year program does not provide enough time to adequately prepare candidates to work in schools, and have moved teacher preparation to the graduate level in master's, post baccalaureate, and fifth year programs. Others are offering graduate pathways into teacher education for candidates who have already completed a bachelor's program in a content field.

A part of the debate around teacher capacity focuses on what teachers should know. Is there a set of proficiencies that teachers should develop and who should determine them? Beginning in the late 1980s, teacher educators, researchers, and policymakers developed national and state standards for what students and teachers should know and be able to do. The teacher standards focus on the subjects being taught and the age/grade of students. These are generally accepted for state program approval and national accreditation by the National Council for Accreditation of Teacher Education (NCATE). The Council of Chief State School Officers (CCSSO) has incorporated very similar standards in the model licensure standards of the Interstate New Teacher Assistance and Support Consortium (INTASC), which many states have adopted or adapted. Similar standards have also been developed for the national board certification of teachers by the National Board for Professional Teaching Standards (NBPTS).

However, not everyone agrees that the profession should set its own standards. A number of national committees with business representatives, policy makers, and other non-educators have produced reports with recommendations about teacher education. They call for a greater emphasis on academics, the elimination of teacher education, and testing of teachers. The U.S. Department of Education promotes a curriculum based solely on scientifically based research in reading, mathematics, etc. A recent study by the National Council on Teacher Quality (NCTQ) ranked 72 institutions based on an examination of the syllabi and textbooks of reading courses in their elementary education programs for references to the five components of effective reading instruction (phonemic awareness, phonics, fluency, vocabulary, and comprehension) identified by the National Reading Panel in its report to the National Institute of Child Health and Human Development in 2000. President George W. Bush has now appointed a similar panel on mathematics to determine the critical components of mathematics that should be taught in the nation's schools. When this report is complete, states and schools may receive federal funding to implement the recommendations in a way similar to the Reading First projects. When it comes to what should be included in the teacher education curriculum related to diversity, the disagreement can become very polarized as will be discussed later.

Another part of the debate on teacher capacity focuses on when teachers learn the expected proficiencies. Some critics of teacher education believe that professional knowledge and skills are more effectively developed on the job after receiving a college degree rather than as part of the college degree. The question is not so much whether teachers should have the capacity to teach all students, but whether they learn their profession in college or in schools when they accept their first teaching job.

As part of the accreditation process, NCATE is concerned with the impact of a program on a candidate's capacity. It has worked with numerous professional associations to determine the capacity a teacher needs to ensure that all P-12 students learn the subject and other important proficiencies. With this goal, NCATE's Standard 1 asks institutions to provide evidence that teacher candidates and candidates preparing for other professional school roles have the knowledge, skills, and dispositions outlined in professional, state, and institutional standards. McDiarmid and Clevenger-Bright earlier in this volume (Chapter 9) suggest that the focus on knowledge, skills, and dispositions may be an "old formula" that is "too static and individualistic a framework for thinking about teacher capacity." They suggest that teaching is too complex and contextually based to be captured in this way. At the same time, they suggest that a disposition(s) might capture the milieu in which teachers work. It is "ability to step outside of one's practice and examine it in good company and in light of a range of data" that might include community expectations and the insights and perspectives of colleagues. The concern that knowledge, skills, and dispositions is an old formula might be correct if candidates' proficiencies were static and prescriptive. NCATE and its member organizations have tried to keep their standards current with research in the field by reviewing them every seven years. Most standards are framed in terms of broad statements of knowledge, skills, and dispositions and are not specific and narrow.

McDiarmid and Clevenger-Bright also highlight the importance of a *culture of evidence* in schools and teacher education. NCATE agrees, requiring institutions to show that candidates are meeting standards through assessments. In addition, Standard 2 on the unit assessment system requires that faculty, candidates, and other members of the professional community regularly review the assessment data to improve programs and candidate performance.

DIVERSITY IN TEACHER EDUCATION PROGRAMS

Since 1979, NCATE has expected accredited institutions to prepare candidates to work with diverse student populations. The 1979 standards included a standard on multicultural education. Today, Standard 4 on diversity has requirements for curricula, field experiences, faculty, candidates, and the P-12 students with which teacher candidates work. It requires candidates to acquire and demonstrate the capacity to help all students learn as shown below:

> The unit designs, implements, and evaluates curriculum and provides experiences for candidates to acquire and demonstrate the knowledge, skills, and professional dispositions necessary to help all students learn. Assessments indicate that candidates can demonstrate and apply proficiencies related to diversity. Experiences provided for candidates include working with diverse populations, including higher education and P-12 school faculty, candidates, and students in P-12 schools.
>
> (NCATE, 2006b)

In addition, all accredited institutions are expected to have a conceptual framework that includes diversity. Diversity could be one of the lens through which all teacher education is delivered as some multiculturalists and critical theorists suggest. The closest that NCATE comes to identifying teacher capacity related to diversity is in the first rubric for the diversity standard. At the acceptable level, the following proficiencies for candidates' capacity related to diversity are indicated:

- understand diversity, including English language learners and students with exceptionalities;
- be aware of different learning styles and adapt instruction or services appropriately for all students;
- connect lessons, instruction, or services to students' experiences and cultures;
- communicate with students and families in ways that demonstrate sensitivity to cultural and gender differences;
- incorporate multiple perspectives in the subject matter being taught or services being provided;
- develop a classroom and school climate that values diversity;
- demonstrate classroom behaviors that are consistent with the ideas of fairness and the belief that all students can learn.

(NCATE, 2006b)

These expectations also reflect the knowledge, performance, and dispositions in the INTASC principles. They address some of the proficiencies that multiculturalists and critical multiculturalists raise in the literature, but they do not address many of the issues that these theorists think are important. Accreditation agencies balance among best practices, what is known from research, and what should or could be. The NCATE requirements push institutions to design curriculum and experiences for education candidates to help them learn how to work with diverse students and to value the diversity of the United States. They do not require the inclusion of the issues identified by multicultural theorists although faculty may decide to include study beyond that required by the NCATE standard. Other than ensuring that candidates can help students learn or support student learning in non-teaching roles, NCATE does not specifically require social action or the reconstruction of schools to eliminate inequality. The intent of the diversity standard is to close the achievement gap among students from diverse groups.

McDiarmid and Clevenger-Bright report that many institutions have courses on multicultural education and special needs students, but "the gaps in pupil achievement, high school graduation, and college attendance persist and inclusion continues to be a problem in some schools." Howard and Aleman contend in this volume that teacher education programs are not preparing teachers to be critical multicultural educators because (1) multicultural and diversity issues are addressed in separate classes and not integrated through all classes and (2) fieldwork does not help them acquire the necessary skills. They suggest that the second is, in part, the fault of critical theorists who have not posited a set of proficiencies that critical teachers should have. However, attention to the needs of diverse learners or social justice may not be developed at all if courses specifically on multicultural education and special education did not exist. On entrance into teacher education, most teacher candidates have limited knowledge of and experience with people different from themselves. Although diversity should be integrated in all courses, a multicultural education course can provide the basic knowledge base on diversity and related equity issues.

Howard and Aleman report that some critics of multicultural education indicate that it "relies too heavily on theory with few, if any, implications for practice." They recommend increased attention to field experiences and criteria for school and university supervisors. I agree that ideals like social justice, if a part of the teacher education unit's[2] conceptual framework, need to be incorporated into methods courses and field experiences. At the same time, leading scholars and practitioners in the field should provide examples and themselves model the practices that they are promoting.

The closest the NCATE standards come to addressing faculty capacity is in the rubric, which accompanies each standard, on faculty diversity in which professional education faculty, including the school and university supervisors of student teaching, "have knowledge and experiences related to preparing candidates to work with diverse student populations, including English language learners and students with exceptionalities." Standard 5 on faculty qualifications expects them to "integrate diversity and technology throughout their teaching." Teacher educators are expected to regularly and systematically examine candidate assessment data. If completers of teacher education programs are not helping students learn once they are in the classroom, it is time for faculty to chart a different course.

SOCIAL JUSTICE

The meaning of social justice appears to be in the eyes of the beholder. The papers and artifacts in this volume have presented numerous definitions from the literature. In 1988 Maxine Greene believed that it was the removal of "obstacles" such as poverty, sickness, and ignorance. James Baldwin did not use the words, *social justice*, when he spoke to teachers in 1963, but he did speak to one's responsibility "to examine society and try to change it and to fight it—at no matter what risk." The same sentiment is reflected in Paulo Freire's "Letters to Those Who Dare Teach."

The literature refers to equality within schools, teaching as a political act, social responsibility, caring, ethics, concern, sense, an orientation, concern with quality of life, and social consciousness about injustice, discrimination, racism, power, etc. Many authors link the concepts of democracy, justice, and struggle (Grant & Agosto in this volume). A number of teacher education units list social justice as part of their conceptual framework or identify other related concepts such as urban teaching, teaching all students, etc. However, conceptual frameworks are not always explicit about the capacities that a candidate should have to reflect social justice or multicultural education in their teaching.

What does NCATE say about social justice? Social justice is included as an example of a disposition in the NCATE standards used for visits between 2001 and 2008. NCATE does not define social justice, but it has defined dispositions as

> The values, commitments, and professional ethics that influence behaviors toward students, families, colleagues, and communities and affect student learning, motivation, and development as well as the educator's own professional growth. Dispositions are guided by beliefs and attitudes related to values such as caring, fairness, honesty; responsibility, and social justice. For example, they might include a belief that all students can learn, a vision of high and challenging standards, or a commitment to a safe and supportive learning environment.
>
> (NCATE, 2006a)

As part of the revision of the NCATE standards that will become effective in 2008, the term, dispositions, has been changed to *professional dispositions* to more clearly indicate that NCATE is primarily concerned with teacher behavior in classrooms and schools. The new definition, which indicates that teacher educators should base their assessments on behaviors rather than beliefs and values, reads as follows:

> *Professional dispositions*: The behaviors demonstrated as educators interact with students, families, colleagues and communities, which are expected of professionals and support student learning and development. NCATE expects candidates to demonstrate classroom behaviors that are consistent with the ideas of fairness and the belief that all students can learn. Based on their mission, professional education units may determine additional professional dispositions they want candidates to develop. NCATE expects institutions to assess professional dispositions based on observable behavior in educational settings.
>
> (NCATE, 2006b)

NCATE's new definition of professional dispositions does not identify social justice as an example or requirement. It also does not prevent an institution from including social justice as a part of its conceptual framework or as the centerpiece of its mission and work.

SOCIAL JUSTICE UNDER ATTACK

Social justice in teacher education became part of the mainstream news in 2005. The first report of a few students resisting "social justice" and threatening law suits appeared in *The New York Sun* on May 31, 2005. Several teacher candidates had charged an instructor with discrimination based on their political beliefs, which they perceived as not aligned with the School of Education's conceptual framework, which included "social justice." A professor of history and another of business and economics sided with the students, charging that the assessment of dispositions was leading to indoctrination into leftist ideology. They blamed NCATE's requirement for dispositions for politicizing teacher education

Soon afterwards the National Association of Scholars (NAS) weighed in on the issue with a letter to the U.S. Assistant Secretary of Education requesting that NCATE be stripped of its authority to accredit. The NAS did not limit its attack to NCATE, it also asked that the right to accredit be withdrawn from the National Association of Social Workers (NASW) because of its social justice requirement. The Thomas B. Fordham Foundation published an article by a professor at Stanford that equated dispositions with personality and attacked NCATE's requirement for the assessment of dispositions as giving education schools "unbounded power over what candidates may think and do" through "ideological arm-twisting and Orwellian mind-control" (Damon, 2005, p. 1). The Foundation for Individual Rights in Education (FIRE) has been working with candidates in these schools to make sure their First Amendment rights are not violated by social justice assessments.

The news then escalated to the national level with an article in *U.S. News & World Report* by John Leo. Leo repeated the accusations from candidates at Brooklyn College and added the woes of a student at Washington State University who complained that faculty had failed him on his professional disposition evaluations because he expressed conservative opinions in his classes. Again, the claim was that NCATE required accredited institutions to incorporate social justice in their curriculum. Articles in the *Chronicle of Higher Education* expanded the stories to include the University of Alabama and University of Alaska. In January 2006 George Will joined the bandwagon in a commentary in *Newsweek* that suggested that students with conservative views were being weeded out of teacher education programs. He claimed that NCATE focused on a candidate's beliefs and attitudes and cared not whether teachers understand the subjects they will teach.

Following NCATE's hearing for re-recognition by the U.S. Department of Education, an article in the online *Chronicle of Higher Education* announced that NCATE had dropped its *standard* on social justice. Of course, as noted, NCATE never had a standard on social justice. The only reference to social justice was an example in the glossary definition of dispositions. NCATE continues to have a standard on diversity that has become stronger with each iteration of the standards since 1978. The debate about dispositions and social justice has continued in *Inside Higher Education*'s blog, "A Spirited Disposition Debate," at http://www.insidehighered.com/news/2006/06/06/disposition.

Why the attack? Maybe some teacher education programs have begun to include a critical multicultural perspective, which some conservatives connect to the liberal faculty members they perceive as dominating universities. On the one hand, critics view social justice as attacking our social and political system that causes the inequities. NCATE has been attacked for years by right-wing groups for its standard on diversity. Robert Holland from the Lexington Institute in Virginia was quoted as saying "The tight link between the accreditors and multiculturalists indicates that social justice is being defined by those who despise the very ideal of an American common culture—considering it irredeemably racist, sexist, homophobic, etc" (Gershman, 2005, p. 6). One group periodically contacts policymakers and chief state school officers suggesting that NCATE and the National Association for Multicultural Education (NAME) are corrupting the minds of children with their attention to diversity.

The American Bar Association (ABA) is the latest accrediting group to be attacked for including diversity in standards. The U.S. Commission on Civil Rights attacked the group in June 2006 for proposed standards that the Commission perceives as requiring racial preferences for hiring and admission. The Center for Equal Opportunity joined NAS in protesting the standards, threatening to sue the ABA if the standards are adopted.

CONCLUSIONS

When social justice refers to working with the least advantaged students to ensure that they are provided all of the opportunities necessary to learn at the same levels as advantaged students, most people see it as a laudable goal. Even No Child Left Behind requires the disaggregation of test data by race, sex, native languages, and ability to determine the group of students not being well served in school. When the discussion of equity in a teacher education course begins to question the current distribution of goods and benefits in society, many conservatives see it as an attack on the American way of life. They may believe that racism, sexism, classism, and homophobia do not exist or are inflated beyond their actual occurrence. Perspectives on social justice vary across a cohort of teacher education candidates. Some are very supportive because of their religious background or their intense concern and empathy for less advantaged families. Others argue that white privilege and oppression do not exist.

Faculties who are reforming their programs to reflect multiculturalism or social justice should consider how they will help candidates understand diversity or social justice and develop educational strategies for ensuring that P-12 students achieve at equitable levels. Howard and Aleman identify several strategies being used by faculty to increase candidates' awareness of the issues and develop their commitment to overcoming existing inequities among students.

As Howard and Aleman point out, examples of integrating multiculturalism or social justice into classrooms can help candidates understand how they could be reflected in classrooms. The teachers who write in the periodical, *Rethinking Teachers*, describe their work at engaging students with real world issues such as child labor, homelessness, and immigration throughout the school year. Teachers tell their stories about working with students from low-income families, students with disabilities, English language learners, and students of color in segregated schools in a number of books. During their preparation programs, teacher candidates should have the opportunity to observe and collaborate with teachers who have eliminated the achievement gap between groups of students. Programs that are serious about social justice help candidates understand the courage it takes to deliver social justice in classrooms. The realities of student, and sometimes community, resistance to multicultural education or social justice should be discussed along with ways to gain support and not become discouraged.

A number of accrediting agencies include diversity or social justice in their standards, in part, because the clients that will be served by the professionals who complete programs are increasingly diverse in race, ethnicity, language, and religion. They are more likely to be in poverty, have low-incomes, or have a disability than in the past. The professionals who write standards believe that the graduates of accredited programs should be able to serve these populations effectively, equitably, and without bias. As part of learning how to work with diverse clients, most professional groups think that society, its institutions, and the profession itself need to be studied and understood for the way clients from different groups have been treated over time. This study almost always reveals inequality and discrimination. It seems quite appropriate that accrediting agencies require programs in their fields to incorporate attention to diversity or social justice in the curriculum.

NCATE not only requires accredited schools, colleges, and departments of education to incorporate diversity into the curriculum and experiences of programs, it also requires an institution's conceptual framework to identify the proficiencies related to diversity that candidates should develop. Diversity proficiencies include knowledge, skills, and dispositions. NCATE's standard on diversity does identify some proficiencies for which there is general professional consensus. However, NCATE gives education faculty a great deal of latitude in identifying proficiencies not included in other sets of standards to which they are being held such as the content standards for mathematics or early childhood teachers. A number of religious institutions include social justice in both their conceptual framework and institutional mission. The faculty in a growing number of public institutions, especially those serving urban areas, have also adopted social justice.

Whatever proficiencies the faculty includes in their conceptual framework, candidates must be assessed to determine if they are developing those proficiencies. The assessments used to determine whether candidates are developing explicit proficiencies are developed by faculty. For the assessment of dispositions, which could include social justice, NCATE recommends against the use of attitude or belief scales. Instead, NCATE recommends that dispositions be assessed as candidates work with students, parents, and colleagues at the university, in schools, and in communities. The NCATE standards do not require the development of critical multiculturalists as described in the Howard and Aleman chapter. However, they do push teacher education programs to incorporate some multicultural concepts and develop some of the dispositions that are inherent in social justice such as fairness and the belief that all students can learn.

As professions think about the proficiencies that their members need to provide effective services to their clients, an understanding of their clients and communities is important. Teachers need first to have an in-depth understanding of the subjects they teach. In addition, they need to know how to help the P-12 student learn what is being taught. To do that, they need to know the culture and prior experiences of their students and be able to draw on representations from the real worlds of their students. To provide a quality education to students who have limited economic and educational advantages requires educators who are advocates for their students. Accreditation standards, at a minimum, should expect graduates of its schools to have the knowledge, skills, and dispositions to help all students learn.

NOTES

1 NCATE has the following six standards: 1-Candidate Knowledge, Skills, and Dispositions; 2-Assessment System and Unit Evaluations; 3-Field Experiences and Clinical Practice; 4-Diversity; 5-Faculty Qualifications, Performance and Development; and 6-Unit Governance and Resources.
2 A teacher education unit is usually the Department, School, or College of Education at a college or university.

REFERENCES

Damon, W. (2005, September 8) Personality test: the dispositional dispute in teacher preparation today, and what to do about it. Washington, DC: Thomas B. Fordham Foundation. Retrieved July 10, 2006 from http//www.edexcellence.net/foundation/publication/publication.cfm?id=343%20.
Gershman, J. (2005, May 31) "Disposition" emerges as issue at Brooklyn College. *The New York Sun*. Retrieved June 7, 2005 from http://www.nysun.com/article/14604.
Jacobson, J. (2006, June 30) Conservative groups threaten to sue bar association. *The Chronicle of Higher Education, LII* (43): A13–A15.
National Council for Accreditation of Teacher Education (NCATE) (2006a) *Professional standards*

for the accreditation of schools, colleges, and departments of education. Washington, DC: Author.

National Council for Accreditation of Teacher Education (NCATE) (2006b) *Proposed revision: professional standards for the accreditation of schools, colleges, and departments of education.* Washington, DC: Author.

Part 3

Where should teachers be taught?

Settings and roles in teacher education

Editor: Kenneth Zeichner

Part 3
Framing chapters

16 Introduction

Settings for teacher education

Kenneth Zeichner
University of Wisconsin-Madison

One of the most vigorously debated issues throughout the history of formal teacher education has been concerned with the role of various settings on the formation of teachers. Since the mid-nineteenth century, institutions have existed in the U.S. that have had as part of their mission the preparation of teachers for America's public schools. Throughout the history of formal teacher education in the U.S. which began in the early nineteenth century with academies, normal schools, and teacher institutes, a variety of models for preparing teachers have emerged that have emphasized the role of different settings in the education of teachers.

For example, the Master of Arts in Teaching model which was initiated at Harvard in 1936 (Zeichner, 1988) has emphasized the liberal arts and content preparation of teachers in colleges and universities along with learning from firsthand teaching experience in schools while providing a very limited preparation in professional education coursework. This lack of emphasis on formal class work preparation in the professional education aspects of learning to teach such as classroom management, curriculum, instructional practices and conducting assessment (Darling-Hammond & Bransford, 2005) in favor of learning about the professional aspect of being a teacher on the job has also characterized some of the school-based alternative routes into teaching that have emerged in recent years.

Also, arguments have been set forth for many years for extending the pre-service education of teachers from the standard four-year college and university preparation to five or more years so that teachers can begin teaching with a good grasp of the content that they will teach and its pedagogical implications as well as having studied the professional knowledge base that some claim is necessary to acquire to teach successfully (Denemark & Nutter, 1984).

Other models of teacher preparation such as the National Teacher Corps which existed from 1965 through 1981 (Smith, 1980) have stressed the role of local communities in educating teachers for its schools and have expanded the definition of field experiences in teacher education to include experiences for prospective teachers in the communities served by the schools in which they work as student teachers. The idea of community field experiences in a pre-service teacher education program to contribute to developing the cultural competence of teachers to teach in community responsive schools that are anchors in their communities has been around a long time (see e.g. Flowers *et al.*, 1948).

The emphasis of different settings in the education of teachers has reflected different visions of the role of the teacher and of the school in relation to the community which can be in tension with one another. For example, there is a danger that too much of an emphasis on professionalizing teaching through mastery of the knowledge base for teaching can, unless steps are taken to balance this aspect of the teacher's role with other aspects, serve to undermine teachers responsiveness to parents and local communities (Zeichner, 1991).

This section examines a variety of perspectives on the contributions of different settings to the education of teachers. The issue of settings for teacher education has become particularly significant in recent years in the U.S. as the pathways into teaching have increased. There are many different ways to become a teacher now in the U.S. that emphasize the role of different settings in educating teachers. The role of universities, schools and communities in teacher education are explored in this section through the framing papers, artifacts, and commentaries. So too is the position that the personal characteristics of prospective teachers rather than the settings in which they are prepared is the key element in the preparation of teachers.

FRAMING PAPERS

Universities as settings for teacher education

David Labaree examines the evolution of teacher education in universities in the U.S. and illuminates several of the enduring issues that have faced teacher educators within these institutions. He identifies two different patterns in teacher education's existence within universities and argues that the effects of universities on teacher education depend on the type of university in question. The two patterns Labaree identifies are the evolution of teacher education from normal schools and state teachers colleges into regional state universities and the evolution of teacher education within elite research universities from single education professorships to departments to schools and colleges of education. He discusses what is potentially gained and lost both by teacher education and by the university in both regional state universities and research universities and how this has affected the relationship between teacher education and their institutional homes.

Labaree discusses the enduring tension between the professional and academic missions of Education schools and colleges and shows how this tension has been resolved differently within regional state universities and research intensive universities. He argues that a major challenge for leaders of Education schools has been to be able to maintain a delicate balance between their academic and professional missions. He claims that this task has been particularly difficult to achieve in elite research universities where he feels that the professional mission associated with teacher education has been most at risk.

A second enduring tension that Labaree identifies in American teacher education is between quantity and quality in the education of teachers. He discusses the dilemma of wanting to maintain high quality in the preparation of teachers who have a grasp of the knowledge base for teaching (Darling-Hammond & Bransford, 2005) and the market pressures that demand filling empty classrooms with large numbers of teachers who have been less well trained that is desired. He argues that these market forces as well as characteristics of the work of teaching have historically undermined efforts to prepare professional teachers.

Schools and communities as settings for teacher education

Marilynne Boyle-Baise and John McIntyre address the ways in which professional development schools and communities serve as settings for preparing teachers to teach culturally diverse students in our public schools. Their chapter considers the range of knowledge, skills, and dispositions that the authors think teachers need to have to do this job well including mastery of content knowledge, multicultural understanding, and an asset-based view of students and their families.

Boyle-Baise and McIntyre explore the tensions between emphasizing the preparation of teachers who have gained mastery over a body of professional knowledge (the professional teacher) and teachers who are responsive to and build upon the cultural resources brought to school from their families local communities (the community teacher). They attempt to resolve the tensions between these two different views of the role of the teacher and of the place of the school in communities by broadening the way in which professionalism is viewed to include the development of community knowledge and the ability to engage in culturally responsive teaching practices.

Boyle-Baise and McIntyre discuss a variety of experiences in pre-service teacher education programs such as the completion of field experiences in professional development schools that aim to more closely connect course work and clinical experiences, service learning, cultural immersion, and various experiences in studying the assets and resources in communities that they argue will serve under certain conditions to prepare teachers to successfully serve culturally diverse students and their families in today's public schools.

Teacher education programs as settings for teacher education

Zeichner and Conklin explore various issues related to teacher education programs as settings for educating teachers. Rejecting the simplistic distinctions that have dominated the literature and policy discussions (e.g. traditional vs. alternative certification and 4-year vs. 5-year vs. postgraduate programs) they propose a conceptual framework that identifies the various structural and substantive dimensions along with teacher education programs differ from one another.

This conceptual framework considers both the structural aspects of teacher education programs such as how long they are, whether they are located at the undergraduate or post graduate level and the type of institution that sponsors them. It also considers a number of substantive aspects of programs including the nature and coherence of a program's mission, its admission processes, curriculum, the nature of field experiences, various internal organizational features such as staffing patterns, instructional practices, and the ways in which data are used to make programmatic decisions. Zeichner and Conklin draw on several national case studies of teacher education programs to identify what research suggests makes an exemplary teacher education in relation to the various program elements in their conceptual framework. They argue that there is likely to be a variety of effective pathways into teaching rather than one effective program model and that the challenge that lies ahead is to ensure that elements of program excellence are present in all of the various pathways into teaching.

Although this section examines the implications for teacher preparation of different settings on teachers learning to teach, there are other settings and contexts that are relevant to understanding teacher education that are not fully explored in this set of documents. These include the growing influence of state and national policy contexts on the education of teachers and as commentator Sharon Robinson points out, the growing use of online learning environments for teachers.

ARTIFACTS

Three artifacts are included in this section that highlight various aspects of the role of settings in educating teachers. The first artifact, a 1999 chapter by Linda Darling-Hammond, responds to critiques of university-based teacher education and while acknowledging several longstanding shortcomings of university programs such as fragmentation of the curriculum, she argues the case regarding the importance of universities to educating teachers for the complex and demanding work that teaching entails. She outlines what she feels teachers need to learn and be able to do, and explains why she thinks it is necessary for universities to play an important role in helping them learn these things. Her solution to the weaknesses of university teacher education is to develop more powerful teacher education programs in universities (e.g. Darling-Hammond, 2006) not to eliminate the university's role as some have suggested in recent years.

In contrast to Darling-Hammond's defense of the university's role in teacher education Martin Haberman and Linda Post in a paper published in 1998 argue based on their experience in their recently closed Metropolitan Multicultural Teacher Education Program that the personal characteristics of prospective teachers together with what they learn on the job from credible mentors are the most important factors in preparing teachers to be successful in multicultural urban schools serving children in poverty. Haberman and Post outline a set of personal characteristics of successful teachers in urban schools ("star teachers") that they feel are the key elements in teaching success in high poverty urban schools including such traits as self-knowledge and self-acceptance, empathy, being able to function in chaos, and awareness of and working on one's own racism, classism and other prejudices.

Haberman and Post believe that for urban teaching, teacher education is only useful for those who have the personal characteristics of "star teachers" and feel that colleges and universities "should be involved in but not in control of the preparation of teachers for children in poverty" (p. 104). Their position is that research and theory should complement the appropriate personal characteristics and careful mentoring on the job by successful urban teachers.

The final artifact, a 2002 paper by Barbara Seidl and Gloria Friend emphasizes the role of communities in the preparation of teachers who develop more mature anti-racist identities, bicultural competence, and the ability to teach in more culturally responsive ways. Their paper describes a community-based internship at a large African American church in Columbus OH that is part of a five quarter post baccalaureate teacher education program at Ohio State University. This experience involves prospective teachers in working for two to three hours per week with adults from the church community in programs for children developed by the community.

Seidl and Friend identify several aspects of this cross-cultural community internship that they think are responsible for the growth they were able to stimulate in three cohorts of mostly white teacher education students. These include the importance of student teachers working with equal-status (in economic and professional terms) adults over time so that they could develop cross-cultural caring relationships and the careful mediation of prospective teachers' community experiences through coursework (e.g. on the sociopolitical context of racism) and planned and structured group conversations between the teacher education students and members of the church community.

COMMENTARIES

Three discussants respond to these papers and artifacts that represent different points of view. First, Michelle Rhee, the director of the "New Teacher Project," an alternative route program that recruits, selects trains, and facilitates the hiring of new teachers for placement in high need urban school districts across the U.S. This program includes a rigorous selection process, a very brief pre-service training period of six to eight weeks focusing on teaching in high-need urban schools, and a carefully structured seminar series provided by experienced teachers after the new teachers assume full responsibility for an urban classroom. The program emphasizes the selection of teacher candidates who are deeply committed to working in high need urban communities over time. Rhee contrasts her approach in this alternative route with university-based programs which she feels do not adequately prepare teachers to work in urban schools.

The second discussant, Sharon Robinson, the president and CEO of the American Association of Colleges for Teacher Education, comments on the papers and artifacts from her position of close contact with national and state policy makers. She rejects the position that there is a single best model for educating teachers and raises the issue of how all of the various settings discussed in this section (schools, communities, arts and science faculties and ed schools) can best be brought together in the service of designing the best possible teacher preparation programs. The measure of a successful education for teachers according to Robinson must be determined in relation to its ability to promote both teacher and student learning.

Finally, Bob Houston, a long time professor of teacher education at the University of Houston, discusses the ways in which settings for teacher education have shifted over time in relation to various cultural changes in the society and within particular institutions like universities. Houston notes the emergence of several new hybrid settings for teacher education such as the school or center of pedagogy (Goodlad, 1994; Smith, 1980). He discusses the broad spectrum of factors that effect how particular settings for teacher education influence the character and quality of teacher education.

REFERENCES

Darling-Hammond, L. (1999) The case for university-based teacher education. In R. Roth (ed.) *The role of the university in the preparation of teachers* (pp. 8–24). London: Falmer Press.

Darling-Hammond, L. (2006) *Powerful teacher education: lessons from exemplary programs.* San Francisco: Jossey-Bass.

Darling-Hammond, L. & Bransford, J. (2005) (eds.) *Preparing teachers for a changing world.* San Francisco: Jossey-Bass.

Denemark, G. & Nutter, N. (1984) The case for extended programs of initial teacher education. In L. Katz & J. Raths (eds.) *Advances in teacher education* (pp. 203–246). Norwood NJ: Ablex.

Flowers, J., Patterson, A., Stratemeyer, F., & Lindsay, M. (1948) *School and community laboratory experiences in teacher education.* Oneata, NY: American Association of Teachers Colleges.

Goodlad, J. (1994) *Educational renewal.* San Francisco: Jossey-Bass.

Haberman, M. & Post, L. (1998) Teachers for multicultural schools: the power of selection. *Theory into Practice,* 37(2), 96–104.

Seidl, B. & Friend, G. (2002) Leaving authority at the door: equal-status community-based experiences and the preparation of teachers for diverse classrooms. *Teaching and Teacher Education,* 18(4), 421–433.

Smith, B.O. (1980) *A design for a school of pedagogy.* Washington, DC: U.S. Department of Education.

Smith, W. (1980) The American teacher corps programme. In E. Hoyle & J. Megarry (eds.) *World yearbook of education: the professional education of teachers* (pp. 204–218). New York: Nichols.

Zeichner, K. (1988) Learning from experience in graduate teacher education. In A. Woolfolk (ed.) *The graduate preparation of teachers* (pp. 12–29). New York: Random House.

Zeichner, K. (1991) Contradictions and tensions in the professionalization of teaching and democratization of schools. *Teachers College Record*, 92(3), 363–379.

17 Teacher education programs as sites for teacher preparation

Kenneth Zeichner
University of Wisconsin-Madison

Hilary G. Conklin
University of Georgia at Athens

We are divided about whether the primary faculty should be academics or practitioners. We disagree about whether the curriculum should be largely coursework or field experience. And, of course, we differ regarding the amount of education students require before entering the classroom. The enormous diversity of practices within university and non university teacher education muddles the path further.

(Levine, 2006, p. 17)

This chapter explores issues related to the idea of teacher education programs as sites for the preparation of teachers and the varying dimensions of these programs that may contribute to effective teacher preparation. When debates about the efficacy of different forms of teacher education have occurred, they mostly have been framed around arguments about the advantages and disadvantages of different program models. While the literature discusses many different ways in which teacher education programs can be distinguished from one another, empirical research on the consequences of entering teaching through different kinds of programs has typically taken into account a very narrow range of these program features. In this chapter, following a discussion of how the empirical research has defined teacher education programs and has begun to identify program characteristics that are related to desired outcomes for teachers and their pupils, we will broaden the discussion by outlining a conceptual framework for thinking about programs that takes additional elements into account. We will conclude with a discussion of how we think the broader framework that we present for thinking about teacher education programs can be useful to both researchers and teacher educators as they design research and plan and renew teacher education programs.

TEACHER EDUCATION PROGRAMS AS DESCRIBED IN EMPIRICAL RESEARCH

Between 1999 and 2004, we conducted a review of peer-reviewed research on teacher education programs in the U.S. conducted between 1985 and 2004 as part of the work of the American Educational Research Association Panel on Research and Teacher Education (Zeichner & Conklin, 2005). In this review, we analyzed 37 studies that used a variety of teacher and pupil outcome measures to assess the effectiveness of different kinds of teacher education programs. The programs were assessed in relation to a variety of teacher and pupil outcomes including teacher efficacy, evaluations of teachers' practices, teacher retention and student learning. The most common distinction that was made among programs in these studies was in terms of program structure such as length (e.g. 1, 4, 5 years), when they are offered (undergraduate, graduate), and by the institutions that sponsor them (e.g. college or university, school district).

Much of the discussion about teacher education program reform in the U.S. has focused on the impact of teacher education programs' structural characteristics. For example, there have been numerous proposals to lengthen undergraduate preservice teacher education to 5-years or to move it to the graduate level entirely (e.g. Denemark & Nutter, 1984; Holmes Group, 1986). There have also been arguments to preserve the four-year undergraduate model as the dominant pathway into teaching (e.g. Hawley, 1987). Arends and Winitzky (1996) provide a summary of the different structural models that have existed and of the debates about their merits and shortcomings.

In our AERA panel work, we grouped the studies that we analyzed into several categories according to the comparisons made by researchers. These were: four-year programs vs. five-year programs, state sponsored alternative programs vs. traditional programs, university-sponsored alternative programs vs. traditional programs, school district sponsored alternative programs vs. traditional programs, studies involving "Teach for America," and comparisons of multiple alternative and traditional programs. In grouping programs as alternative or traditional, we defined an alternative program as any program other than a four or five year undergraduate program at a college or university.[1] One problem with the classification of programs into alternative and traditional which was made necessary because of the nature of the research we were examining is the tremendous variation that exists within each of these categories. Shulman (2005a) has argued that "the claim that traditional programs can be contrasted with alternative programs is a myth. We have only alternative routes into teaching." This same problem exists for four-year and five-year programs and with the categories of graduate and undergraduate programs. Our analysis showed that Shulman is right because there was a lack of clear and consistent findings about the effects of any particular type of teacher education program only defined by a four-year or five-year or traditional or alternative designation.

In addition to the differences within these categories, programs also exist in different kinds of institutional contexts (e.g. research universities, liberal arts colleges) and in different state policy contexts. Goodlad's (1990) national study of teacher education suggests that institutional variation is a major source of difference among teacher education programs. State policy contexts also vary in significant ways that help define the character and quality of teacher education programs. For example, a four-year program in Texas where the state has capped the number of education courses in preservice programs will be very different in significant ways from a four-year program in a state like Wisconsin where the state has maintained a strong emphasis on the professional component of preservice programs. Also, although the INTASC standards (Council of Chief State School Officers, 1992) have had much influence on state standards across the U.S., there is much variation in what states require to obtain an initial teaching license. For example, some states require elementary education teachers to complete academic majors for a teaching license while others do not require this and allow students to major in education at the undergraduate level with varying levels of preparation in academic content knowledge.

Neither teacher educators nor policymakers are well served by the current emphasis in research on comparing the efficacy of teacher education programs that are only described by general labels such as those discussed above. Kliebard (1973) noted during the era of teacher effectiveness research in the U.S. that research on teaching was structured mostly in the form of a horse race: "Sometimes one horse wins, sometimes the other; often it is a tie" (p. 21). Kliebard argued that this kind of research will never result in useful findings with explanatory value. This same argument can be applied to the current wave of studies comparing so called traditional vs. so called alternative certification programs and four-year vs. five-year programs. More attention to the substantive aspects of teacher education programs and to the contexts in which they exist needs to be part of research on teacher education programs, teacher education planning and renewal efforts, and policy discussions (Zeichner, 2006).

CASE STUDIES OF THE CHARACTERISTICS OF EXEMPLARY TEACHER EDUCATION PROGRAMS

In addition to the bulk of studies which have compared the effects of different pathways into teaching defined only by their surface level structural characteristics (e.g. their length, sponsor, etc.), a few multi-site case studies have been conducted that have begun to illuminate more specific aspects of programs that appear to be related to program effectiveness.[2] These include Howey and Zimpher's (1989) study of six Midwestern elementary teacher education programs, the National Center for Research on Teacher Education's "Teacher Education and Learning to Teach" (TELT) study (NCRTE, 1991; Kennedy, 1998; Tatto, 1996), the Education of Educator's study of a nationally representative sample of 29 teacher education programs led by John Goodlad (Goodlad, 1990), case studies of seven exemplary preservice programs sponsored by the National Commission of Teaching for America's Future (Darling Hammond, 2000, 2006), a national study of alternative certification programs conducted by researchers at SRI (Humphrey & Wechsler, 2005; Humphrey *et al.*, 2005), case studies of teacher preparation in 28 schools, colleges and departments of education across the nation (Levine, 2006) completed by the Education Schools Project, and case studies of teacher education programs that prepare teachers to specialize in the field of bilingual education, ESL, and/or multicultural teacher education sponsored by the Center for Research on Education, Diversity and Excellence (Walton *et al.*, 2002).

Although these studies do not provide definitive evidence linking particular program components to specific teacher and pupil outcomes (see Zeichner & Conklin, 2005), they suggest some elements of teacher education programs that should be further investigated by researchers. They also suggest a way to think and talk about teacher education programs that is more meaningful than what is present in the dominant discourse on this issue in the literature. In general, these case studies point to the need to look beyond the surface structural features of teacher education programs in order to understand the key elements of program effectiveness. In addition to understanding the elements of successful teacher education programs, we also need to understand how to transform programs so that they embody these characteristics (Hammerness, 2006).

Following are some examples of some of what these case studies have to say about the critical components of effective pre-service teacher education programs. We look first at the institutional context of teacher education programs, considering the social and political context attributes that are important to the functioning of programs. We then examine important attributes at the program level such as how a program is organized and program goals. Next we consider the people involved in a teacher education program, both teacher educators, and teacher candidates. Finally we explore the substance of teacher education programs and discuss the nuances of coursework, field experiences, the ways in which candidates are taught, and the data that informs how they are taught. Following this discussion of the empirical case literature on teacher education programs, we will present a conceptual framework for thinking about teacher education programs that draws on the extant research but that also goes beyond the limited empirical categories that have been investigated by researchers.

The social and institutional context of teacher education programs

Goodlad (1990) bases his assumptions about the elements of good teacher education programs on a moral commitment to the role of education in democratic societies rather than on empirical data.[3] He draws our attention to the importance of the policy and institutional contexts in which programs are located. First, he argues that in order for programs to have the potential to thrive and produce exemplary teachers, they must have strong institutional support in terms of physical and budgetary resources and ideological support needed to prepare future teachers well. This means that teacher education faculty would have comparable standing, workloads and other rewards to other faculty within an institution. Goodlad's research team found that this support was present to varying degrees in different kinds of institutions (e.g. liberal arts colleges, research universities), but generally they concluded that teacher educators lacked the infrastructure support and advocacy in their institutions needed to enable exemplary teacher education programs to exist.

Program level characteristics

At the program level, all of the case studies help us to think about the way a teacher education program is organized and the overarching beliefs and intellectual quality that drive a program. Organizationally, the cases suggest we need to think about how program components and people are related to one another, and how they come together to form a whole program. Howey and Zimpher (1989) for example, argue that exemplary teacher education programs organize prospective teachers into cohort groups so that they develop a sense of shared identity and accomplishments as they move through particular benchmarks in their programs. All of the case studies emphasize the value of connectedness, coursework and fieldwork being closely tied together and people who work in different parts of a program having strong relationships with one another. Some programs that were deemed by researchers to be exemplary however, were able to establish this connectedness and coherence without the use of student cohort groups (e.g. Darling-Hammond, 2000, 2006).

Similarly, the cases suggest that we should consider how program components are conceptually connected. The TELT study (NCRTE, 1991; Kennedy, 1998) found that the substantive orientation of a teacher education program (rather than its structure) had the greatest impact on what candidates learned.[4] The case studies suggest that it is the guiding ideas of a program that are likely to have the most influence on what prospective teachers learn and suggest that the more coherent a program is with regard to the ideas about teaching and learning and schooling that underlie it, the more powerful the influence is likely to be. The cases as a group suggest that program impact is strengthened by a clear and common vision of teaching and learning that permeates all coursework and field experiences.

For example, in Tatto's (1996) study of the impact of different teacher education programs on teachers' beliefs about teaching diverse learners using TELT data, she concluded:

Our findings across the field of teacher education seem to indicate that in those few cases where faculty espoused more coherent views around professional norms, student teachers tended to show more definite movement toward developing views that were in turn congruent with those espoused by the faculty. Thus coherence around program norms and professional norms seem to play an important role in the influence of teacher education on student teachers' beliefs about teaching diverse students.

(p. 175)

The particular philosophy or mission of a program is a point worth considering further. Both Goodlad (1990) and Darling-Hammond (2000) correctly note that the particular vision of good teaching a program espouses is necessarily a value-laden judgment that has ethical and moral implications. Goodlad (1990) argues that the mission of teacher education programs needs to be viewed in the context of a democratic society and that doing this provides a certain direction to a program (also see Michelli & Keiser, 2005). Darling- Hammond (2000, 2006) elaborates on the direction that she sees as appropriate in a democratic context and equates the achievement of the goals preparing teachers who can engage in "learner-centered" and "learning-centered" teaching with program excellence.[5]

There are of course also other visions of what teachers need to know and be able to do that are very different from these "democratic-oriented" views of teaching expertise which prioritize the development of teachers' abilities to exercise their judgment in the classroom to adapt instruction to the backgrounds and needs of their diverse learners (Zeichner, 2003). For example, there are those who have argued that preparing teachers to faithfully follow teaching scripts based on methods that allegedly have been shown by research to promote student learning is a more appropriate path for teacher education than developing teachers' abilities to make decisions about which methods to use with particular students at specific times (e.g. Walsh et al., 2006).

Because of these different visions of the appropriate ends of teacher education, strengthening program impact is not necessarily a desirable thing to those who do not share the particular goals of a teacher education program. For example, for those educators concerned about preparing teachers to exercise their judgment in the classroom, making a program more effective in preparing teachers to be compliant implementers of teaching scripts is not a good thing. Similarly, strengthening the ability of a teacher education program to prepare teachers who are proactive decision makers and who are critical of school policies that they do not judge to be in the best interests of their students would not be a desirable outcome for advocates of the idea of teachers as compliant implementers of scripts. In the end, the determination of "excellence" is always dependent on moral and ethical questions and cannot be determined by empirical research alone.

The case studies also suggest that it is important to consider the intellectual quality of teacher education programs. For example, Howey and Zimpher (1989) argue that one of the key attributes of effective teacher education programs is that they are characterized by high levels of rigor and academic challenge. Goodlad (1990) similarly breaks down particular intellectual attributes that he argues are critical to preparing teachers who will be stewards of schools. He contends that teacher education programs must enable teachers to address the tensions inherent in teaching practice, providing them with the intellectual tools needed to negotiate the inevitable issues associated with the disconnect between theory and practice, and tensions between the role of the school in society and individual interests. Goodlad envisions teacher education as an enterprise that prepares teachers to think beyond the status quo and equips them with the ability to bring about change. Although Goodlad's (1990) research team did not find a lot of this academic rigor in the 29 teacher education institutions they examined, this is certainly an issue that teacher educators need to consider when looking for markers of program excellence.

Finally, the case studies direct us to consider a teacher education program's sources of information in evaluating itself and in conducting its daily work. Goodlad (1990) and Howey and Zimpher (1989) contend that high quality teacher education programs have systems in place for evaluating programs based on data including soliciting feedback from its graduates. A sign of program excellence according to this view is the use of data in making decisions about the program.

The people in teacher education programs

The case studies identify several elements related to the people who inhabit teacher education programs (teacher educators and their students). For example, in their case studies of alternative certification programs Humphrey *et al.* (2005) found that the most effective mentors for prospective teachers were those who knew how to work with adults and were trained in and knowledgeable about specific mentoring strategies. In recent years, there has been increased attention to the fact that teacher educators often receive little preparation in their doctoral programs for the work of teacher education (Cochran-Smith, 2003; Zeichner, 2005). The cases suggest that good programs provide preparation and ongoing support to the teacher educators who work with teacher candidates.[6]

The case studies also address aspects of the candidates who enroll in teacher education programs. For example, the TELT study (Kennedy, 1998; NCRTE, 1991) discovered that recruitment into programs was a crucial element in determining the learning that took place for prospective teachers. This study found that in some cases, programs recruited candidates who already shared the substantive orientation of the program, thereby contributing to outcomes they called "enrollment influences" as opposed to "learning influences" that occurred as a direct result of the impact of the program. Goodlad (1990) suggested that recruitment and admission are fundamentally connected to realizing the goals of a program and argued that teacher education programs should specifically select candidates who possess an initial commitment to moral and ethical aspects of teaching in a democratic society.

The substance of a teacher education program

The case studies also address the character and quality of the coursework and curriculum in teacher education programs including the attributes of the field experiences and the school contexts in which prospective teachers learn to teach, and the ways in which they are taught by their teacher educators.

For example, Darling-Hammond (2000, 2006) argues that exemplary teacher education programs offer extensive course work in child and adolescent development, learning theory, and theories about cognition and motivation and subject matter pedagogy that is taught in the context of practice.[7] Howey and Zimpher (1989) assert that exemplary programs offer a balance between pedagogical knowledge and general knowledge so that teacher candidates do not come away from their preparation with ideas about teaching that are too narrow or technical.

Goodlad (1990) also suggests that good teacher education programs should provide opportunities for candidates to become more "other-oriented" and identify with a broader culture of teaching. Similarly, he argues that programs should help teachers shift from only being consumers of educational knowledge to also becoming inquirers into knowledge and the nature of schooling.

The case studies also address the attributes of the school contexts in which prospective teachers complete their practicum, student teaching and internship experiences. Goodlad (1990) argues that programs should only admit as many candidates as there are exemplary field placements. Darling-Hammond's (2000, 2006) case studies suggest that good programs have extended field experiences (at least 30 weeks) that reflect a program's vision of good teaching and are interwoven with coursework and where the teaching of prospective teachers is carefully mentored.

Finally, Humphrey *et al.*'s (2005) studies of alternative certification programs highlight salient features of high quality school sites for teacher learning. They found that candidates in effective alternative programs had field placements characterized by collegial relationships, strong leadership and adequate materials and supplies. For example, the candidates in the programs they studied learned more from field placements in which teachers got along and discussed their teaching practice with one another, in schools where principals were supportive and where candidates had access to the materials and resources that they needed to teach. This study also identified several additional opportunities that contributed to program effectiveness: candidates having opportunities to observe other teachers teach, to discuss instruction with colleagues, to get materials and resources from colleagues, and to have others observe their instruction and provide them with feedback. While Humphrey *et al.*'s (2005) analysis acknowledges that individual candidates will not always benefit from the exactly the same kind of field experience supports, they argue that all good alternative programs provide both emotional and instructional support focused on issues of teaching and learning.

Not surprisingly, the case studies have also addressed the ways in which candidates are taught in their teacher education programs. The cases converge on the conclusion good teacher education programs operate under the same conditions that they advocate for educating K-12 students. As Kennedy (1998) argues, teacher candidates should experience the learning of teaching practices firsthand, as learners themselves; they should have opportunities to consider why new practices are better than conventional ones; and they should have on-site assistance as they learn to implement these new practices themselves.

Finally, the case studies suggest that good programs integrate the instruction of candidates into the context of practice through the use of instructional strategies such as case studies, teacher research, performance assessments and portfolios that connect learning about teaching to the actual problems of teaching practice (Darling-Hammond, 2000, 2006).

While all of these examples of program characteristics that are associated with program effectiveness in accomplishing their goals have received only partial and tentative empirical support in the case studies, they clearly suggest that it is within the substance of teacher education programs and not only in their structural characteristics that clues about program effectiveness are to be found. We will now draw on these case studies which have begun to uncover key elements of program excellence and the broader literature in teacher education to suggest a framework for thinking about the dimensions of a teacher education program. This framework can be used by researchers who study the efficacy of different pathways into teaching, by policy makers, and by teacher educators who want to examine their programs as part of a continual process of self-study and improvement.

A FRAMEWORK FOR THINKING ABOUT TEACHER
EDUCATION PROGRAMS

Although most empirical studies of teacher education programs have focused on the structural differences between programs such as their length and who sponsors them, the literature suggests a number of additional features of teacher education programs that should be taken into account by both researchers who study programs and teacher educators who want to improve them (see Figure 17.1). This conceptual framework draws on the case studies just discussed and also on the broader teacher education literature.

We propose this framework as a way to highlight the substantive features of teacher education programs and thereby provide a guide for teacher education research and reform efforts. The program features we discuss below are dimensions along which

- Social and Institutional Context
  - Institutional type and mission.
  - Structure of program (length, undergraduate or graduate).
  - Institutional support for teacher education.
  - State policy context.

- View of Teaching, Learning, Schooling, the Teacher's Role and Learning to Teach in the Program's Mission
  - How clearly are they defined?
  - How widely are they shared?
  - Degree of commitment to them.

- Admissions Process
  - Content of admissions criteria.
  - Link to program mission.
  - How selective is the process?

- Curriculum in Course work
  - Emphasis on different aspects of preparation.
  - Placement within the program of different curricular components.
  - Connection to program mission.
  - Representation of different perspectives in the curriculum.
  - Academic rigor.
  - Integration of major topics (preparation to teach diverse learners) into the whole curriculum or in particular courses.
  - Preparation to teach different subject areas.
  - Preparation for teaching students at different age levels.

- Field Experiences
  - Number, length, and placement of field experiences in the curriculum.
  - How closely they are connected to the rest of the program?
  - Teaching responsibility provided.
  - Extent to which they build on prior field experiences.

- Instructional Strategies
  - What are the strategies?
  - How are the strategies used? For what purposes? How are they introduced and supported?
  - Are the strategies advocated for candidate use modeled by teacher educators?

- Internal Organizational Features
  - Use of student cohorts or not.
  - Staffing:
    Horizontal/vertical.
    Who are the teacher educators?
    How were they prepared for their roles and how are they supported in their roles?
  - Level of coherence between field and campus components.

- Use of Data
  - How are data collected about the program used to inform decisions about the program?

Figure 17.1 A framework for thinking about teacher education programs.

programs vary. In order to understand the particular practices and features of teacher education programs that may matter in terms of desired outcomes for teacher education, we need to understand how different program features are implemented, the extent to which they exist, and the particular quality and focus of their existence. We suggest that attention to these different dimensions and their implementation can help us understand the particular program attributes that lead to effective teacher preparation. As we discuss each of these dimensions below, we offer some specific examples to illustrate the ways in which these different dimensions may look in particular institutions and highlight program attributes that may be productive places for researchers, teacher educators, and policymakers to focus their attention.

Social and institutional context

As we discussed earlier in the chapter, we need to consider the type of institution in which as teacher education is housed, the nature of institutional support for teacher education, and the state policy context in order to understand a program. For example, state policies will influence the nature of teacher education programs, just as the size and kind of institution in which a teacher education program is housed will shape a program's character.

Key ideas in a program's mission

Another element of this model is the view of teaching, learning, schooling and the role of teachers that underlies a program. A number of different general frameworks have been proposed over the years for distinguishing the conceptual orientations of teacher education programs from one another (e.g. Cochran-Smith & Fries, 2005; Feiman-Nemser, 1990; Zeichner, 1993, 2003). In addition to variation in the content of teacher education program orientations or conceptual frameworks there are a number of other aspects to the variation in these orientations such as how clearly defined or elaborated the orientations are, how widely they are shared among teacher educators in the program including school-based teacher educators (Barnes, 1987), and the degree of commitment to them by those who affiliate with them. For example just because programs claim to be organized around slogans such as teachers as decision makers or teaching for social justice does not mean that they have similar orientations (McDonald & Zeichner, in press). It depends on what these terms actually mean in particular contexts when they are elaborated and enacted.

Teacher education programs that undergo the process of accreditation by the National Council for Accreditation of Teacher Education (NCATE) are required to articulate a conceptual framework for their teacher education programs. Although no one has published an analysis of the frameworks that NCATE approved institutions have used to organize their programs, periodically frameworks that organize teacher education programs are reported in the literature as part of descriptions of programs or studies of aspects of particular programs. In recent years, we have seen programs that have been organized around a commitment to such things as teaching as principled practice (Mills College, Kroll *et al.*, 2005), and teaching for social justice (UCLA, Oakes & Lipton, 1999). Although it is fairly easy to gather together the teaching standards used by teacher education programs to evaluate their students, we don't have a good picture currently of the conceptual orientations that are connected to these standards in programs across the nation.

The admissions process

The next aspect of this model for thinking about teacher education programs is the admissions process, the specific requirements and procedures that are used by faculty to decide who is allowed to enter a program. There are at least two aspects of admissions that need to be considered: (a) the relationship between admissions criteria and processes and the stated mission or conceptual framework for a program; and (b) how selective the program is on these criteria (e.g. highly selective, not selective). For example, if preparation for teaching for social justice is the expressed mission of a program, how is the potential of individuals to enact this vision of teaching considered in admissions to the program?

The curriculum

Another dimension of teacher education programs is their curriculum. Here one can distinguish programs according to a number of factors such as the amount of emphasis placed on different components of the curriculum such as subject matter preparation and preparation in pedagogical knowledge as well as the amount of time spent in supervised clinical experiences. Programs also differ in the way these various components are placed within the teacher education program (Tom, 1997). For example, the coursework and fieldwork candidates experience prior to assuming full responsibility for a classroom is one aspect of the curriculum that often distinguishes programs from one another with the growing prevalence of "fast track" alternative programs. One can also ask about the strength of the connection between the curriculum of a program and its stated mission as well as the academic rigor of the curriculum. For example, to what degree has the vision for teaching and learning guiding the program been transformed into clear performance standards and assessment criteria? What are the cognitive demands made upon candidates in readings, assignments, and assessments?

Recently Steiner and Rozen (2004) have criticized teacher education programs in university colleges and schools of education for not including a variety of viewpoints, but especially conservative ones, on different issues in required coursework. Apart from the accuracy of these charges and the desirability of the kind of curriculum they propose, the issue of the inclusion of different perspectives on issues is certainly an aspect of curriculum along which programs vary.

Another aspect of the teacher education curriculum that should be taken into account is the way in which certain substantive issues are addressed. For example, with regard to an important issue like preparing teachers to teach diverse learners, what elements of diversity are included in this preparation and how is the content addressed? Taking this one example, it has become clear that programs' claim to address student diversity vary according to how much attention is given to linguistic diversity and preparation to teach English Language Learners (Zeichner, 2003). In some programs, multicultural education includes an applied linguistics and ESL and/or bilingual teaching component while in many others it does not. We can also examine a program's attention to specific content like preparation to teach diverse learners as to whether the content is infused into various courses and experiences, is addressed as a stand alone course or experience (e.g. a course on teaching diverse learners), or both (Zeichner & Hoeft, 1996).

Another issue is preparation in methods to teach particular subject areas. Some programs emphasize subject specific methods preparation such as courses in the teaching of mathematics and social studies, others focus on generic methods preparation for groups of candidates preparing to teach different subjects (e.g. methods in teaching secondary school), while other programs use a combination of both approaches. Programs also vary in terms of who provides methods instruction to teaching candidates. For example, preparation to teach specific subjects like history or biology might utilize faculty in Colleges of Letters and Science who are specialists in these disciplines, School of Education faculty who are specialists in a discipline, but also usually have a K-12 education background, practitioners in elementary and secondary schools who teach these subjects, or some combination of these approaches.

A final issue with regard to curriculum is the extent to which there is a focus on teaching specific students at different age levels (e.g. a specialized middle level program) vs. a focus on general principles that apply to a broad range of age levels (e.g. an elementary education or secondary education program that includes the teaching of middle level students but is not focused on it) (Conklin, 2006).

Field experiences

With regard to the field experience component of programs, there are a number of dimensions that can distinguish programs from one another. For example, some programs include a student teaching semester while others include a year-long internship. Some programs include field experiences throughout the program while others have them only at the end. In some programs the student teaching or internship experience is completed as a teacher of record while in others it is not. Some field experiences may only be in schools, while others may include experiences with children and/or adults in the community or other settings.

There is also the issue of how closely connected the field and course components of the program are. At one extreme, supervision of candidates' teaching is carried out by staff that is unconnected and often ignorant about the course components of the program while at the other extreme the field and campus components for programs are closely linked within the context of a professional development school or other form of school and university partnership.

Closely connected can also be defined in terms of the degree to which the classrooms in which field experiences are completed reflect the vision of teaching and learning emphasized in program courses. Hammerness (2006) describes a recent effort in Stanford's teacher education program to take the degree of correspondence in teaching and learning between what is advocated in courses and in potential placement sites into account in choosing places for teacher candidates to complete their field experiences.

A final issue with regard to field experiences is the nature and degree of teaching responsibility provided to prospective teachers in these experiences. Programs vary according to how explicitly the requirements for field experiences are laid out before hand or near the beginning of the experience, who is involved in making the decisions about these requirements (e.g. the university only or school and university personnel together), in how much teaching responsibility is provided in an experience, and in the degree to which each field experience builds on the ones which preceded it in terms of adding more responsibility and complexity (Brouwer & Korthagen, 2005).

Instructional strategies

The next aspect of teacher education programs that should be taken into account is the teaching strategies that are used to instruct candidates. Research has been conducted on a number of instructional strategies used in teacher education programs such as microteaching, computer simulations, the use of video technology and hypermedia, case methods, autobiography, portfolios, and practitioner research (Carter & Anders, 1996; Darling-Hammond *et al.*, 2005; Grossman, 2005). Shulman (2005b) has criticized the great variety of instructional approaches that exist in different teacher education programs and calls for a consensus on a small set of "signature pedagogies" that would characterize all teacher education programs as he claims exist in other professions such as law and medicine.[8]

In addition to the variation in instructional approaches within and across programs, the same instructional approaches such as portfolios or case methods are implemented for different purposes and in different ways by different teacher educators. For example, the use of portfolios in some programs focuses on the documentation that standards have been met as opposed to an emphasis on using the portfolio as a tool for reflection about teaching in other situations. Portfolios are introduced and supported in different ways by different teacher educators. The same can be said about any instructional strategy in teacher education. When instructional approaches used in teacher education programs are studied and/or discussed the purposes toward which they are used in different settings and the conditions of their use must be considered.

One question of importance with regard to instructional strategies is the degree to which teaching strategies advocated for prospective teachers to use with PK-12 students are modeled in the teacher education classroom. Teacher education sites vary in the degree to which this modeling occurs.

Internal organizational features

The next aspect of teacher education programs is a variety of staffing and internal organizational aspects within programs including the nature of social relations within a program. Here such issues are addressed as whether or not candidates enter and proceed through a program in intact cohorts or whether they can proceed through the program in more individualized ways (Arends & Winitzky, 1996). There is also the issue of how the staff is organized to work with students. Tom (1997) has identified two patterns of staffing in teacher education programs (horizontal and vertical) that will influence how candidates experience their programs. In a horizontal staffing pattern which is organized by subject specialty,

> Prospective teachers proceed from course to course, as if on an elevator moving from floor to floor. Professors of education stand at the elevator doors and dispense ideas and attitudes to the students, who methodically stop at each floor on the way to student teaching on the top floor. Teachers-in-training accept the bits of professional knowledge in the hope that they will have some value when the elevator finally arrives at student teaching.
>
> (p. 145)

In this horizontal staffing pattern which minimizes the intellectual and practical demands on teacher educators by enabling them to focus only on one piece of the teacher education curriculum, candidates meet a different group of teacher educators at each floor who often do not communicate with each other about the contents of the different floors. The result is often a fragmented curriculum where both redundancy and absence of content are significant problems. Tom (1997) calls for a form of vertical staffing which helps bridge areas of specialized knowledge and practice. Here faculty assume responsibility for more than one course or experience in the program or for helping candidates analyze and make sense of different pieces of their program. An example of vertical staffing is where a faculty member is responsible for a cohort of candidates as they move through the different layers of a program helping them to make connections across the different components of the program.

In models like this, even if individual teacher educators only teach in a particular part of the program, they have knowledge of the whole program rather than only one part, and they can deliberately build coherence into the program. The knowledge that teacher educators have of the whole program and of all of its individual components is a critical dimension along which programs vary. Although the common situation especially in large programs is for teacher educators to have little knowledge of the whole program and of parts in which they are not directly involved (Lanier & Little, 1986), there are some programs like those at Alverno College in Milwaukee where teacher educators are very knowledgeable about every aspect of their programs even though they may not be directly involved in all of them (Zeichner, 2000).

Another aspect of staffing that affects program coherence is related to who staffs a program. For example, if a program relies mostly on adjunct staff or faculty or graduate students who come and go frequently, it is less likely to be able to create a coherent program with a shared vision and purpose than in a program where more permanent faculty and staff are engaged in educating teachers. In some situations though, programs that utilize adjunct staff to teach course and supervise field experiences have closely integrated these staff into the program through regular seminars and support. The University of California at Santa Cruz is an example of a teacher education institution that has closely integrated its adjunct staff into its teacher education programs.[9]

The common pattern in many teacher education programs in research intensive universities that prepare teacher educators in doctoral programs and where pressure on faculty to do research is particularly intense is for graduate students and/or adjuncts to assume much responsibility for the teaching and clinical supervision of teacher candidates. In situations like these, the quality of faculty oversight and mentoring of the staff that do the work of teacher education is a key to developing program coherence.

There is also the issue of coherence between the field and campus components of the program that have been mentioned earlier. A number of programs in an effort to develop stronger connections between the coursework and fieldwork have created new boundary spanning staff and faculty roles where university staff work directly in schools helping candidates to make connections between the different elements of their programs. These include placing university supervisors of student teachers and interns within specific schools (Zeichner & Miller, 1997), and doing some teaching of courses and seminars in schools where deliberate links are made between practices in the schools and concepts and practices addressed in the courses. Other programs have brought expert P-12 teachers to the university campus for a year or two as teachers- in-residence to work along side university faculty in teaching campus methods and foundations courses and in some cases subject matter content courses in the arts and sciences (e.g. Benyon *et al.*, 2004; Post *et al.*, 2006).

Using data to make program decisions

There is also the issue of the degree to which teacher educators use data to inform their decision making about their programs. It has been argued that there is very little use of data in making decisions about programs (Houston, 1990) and there have been recent calls for more "evidence-based practice" in the pre-service education of teachers (Fallon, 2006). Although in many programs, teacher educators conduct the often mandatory graduate follow up studies that are required by state and national accrediting agencies, there is not always evidence that they use this data to make improvements in their programs. As was pointed out earlier, it is the use of the data rather than its generation that has been suggested as an element of effective programs.

One of us has been evaluating two sites of the Teachers for a New Era Program during the past two years and has discovered through observing teacher educators in these programs,[10] a variety of ways in which teacher educators can use data to inform decision making about program renewal. For example, these teacher educators in these two TNE sites have conducted surveys and interviews of program graduates and current faculty, staff and students, conducted case studies of the teaching of program graduates, surveyed the research literature, and examined practices at other institutions. Essentially this use of data to inform decision making with regard to teacher education involves a much more deliberate and systematic approach to teacher education program renewal than has been common.

Structural features

In addition to these dimensions of teacher education programs typically not accounted for in research comparing the efficacy of different program models, the structural features of programs should also be considered. These include such things as whether the program is undergraduate or graduate, the length of the program, and who sponsors it. If these structural features of programs are considered in addition to the substantive program dimensions discussed above in discussions about improving teacher education programs and in research studies, these activities will begin to get at the things inside teacher education programs that truly distinguish them from one another.

We will now consider three general issues that have negatively influenced the character and quality of research about teacher education programs and teacher education program renewal efforts: the problem of ambiguous comparisons between programs, the reliance on self-descriptions of programs for an understanding of programs and the problem of unwarranted generalizations about programs that exist in multiple sites.

The problem of ambiguous comparisons

Some researchers have sought to compare what candidates learn about teaching and the quality of their teaching in programs that designate the schools where the clinical experiences take place as "professional development schools" with programs that do not do so. It is not common however, for researchers to describe these partnerships with enough specificity and in common enough ways for comparisons to be made across research studies. For example, a recent study compared the effects on the quality of teaching practice of doing practicum experiences and student teaching/internship experiences in professional development schools or non professional development schools at George Mason University (Castle *et al.*, 2006). The researchers describe the differences in the two pathways at this university (PDS and non PDS) as one of length (a fifteen-week student teaching experience in the non PDS track vs. a year-long internship in the PDS track), the timing of methods courses (during the internship for the PDS track vs. prior to student teaching for the non PDS track), and whether the program is completed as a part time student (non PDS track) or fulltime student (PDS track). Students were admitted into the program according to the same criteria but then self-selected into either the PDS or non PDS track.

Another recently published comparison between the effects of professional development schools and traditional field placements (Ridley *et al.*, 2005) distinguished professional development school placements from traditional placements according to the amount of time candidates spent in field experiences and how often they were supervised by university staff. In this particular study, the PDS graduates had about three times the amount of field experience in their program as the other graduates and were supervised by university staff each semester rather than only at the end of the program like the other graduates. Although both of these studies presented data supporting that the teaching effectiveness of the PDS graduates was superior to that of the non PDS graduates on specific dimensions, it is difficult to know what the findings mean. The definitions of professional development schools used in these studies are different from each other and from other depictions of this innovation elsewhere. What are the particular aspects of these placements that influenced the higher teaching ratings? If it was just a longer field experience or more frequent supervision, these conditions can be created without having placements in a professional development school.

This comparison of one model of teacher education against another model based on only surface level information about the two alternatives being compared is very common in the literature. Castle *et al*. (2006) conclude their analysis with the statement that "the case may be made that PDS graduates may affect student learning sooner than traditionally trained beginning teachers" (p. 65). We need to move beyond these comparisons of alternatives that are defined differently by various researchers and use specific and similar sets of elements that define alternative approaches under investigation by researchers.[11] The National Council of Accreditation for Teacher Education has developed a set of standards for professional development schools that could be a source from which to develop a common definition of professional development schools that can be used in both discussions and research (NCATE, 2001).

Going beyond reliance on teacher educators' program descriptions

Another aspect of teacher education programs that should be taken into account is the difference between programs as described by teacher educators and in written materials and how the programs are enacted for different individuals. Much of the research on teacher education programs that we reviewed for the AERA panel relied on documents about programs and on statements from teacher educators rather than on first hand examination of programs in action. Relying on these secondhand sources to understand the characteristics of programs could cause problems because of the gaps that often exist between how programs are described and what they actually represent when implemented.

For example, in the Teacher Education and Learning to Teach (TELT) study conducted by researchers at Michigan State's National Center for Research on Teacher Education between 1986 and 1990 researchers found that in one of the five-year programs in their sample, relatively few students were actually enrolled in the program for five years. Many students spent their first two years in a community college and transferred to the university in their third year and; some either could not get admitted to the graduate school for the fifth year or left to complete student teaching as teachers of record because of a severe teaching shortage in the state (Kennedy, 1998).

Another example of the gap between program rhetoric and reality is in an alternative certification program in the Houston school district where although the program was described as providing a mentor to every intern in the alternative certification program, a study of the program revealed that many of the interns had not met their mentors and in some cases did not even know who their mentors were (Stevens & Dial, 1993). Humphrey *et al*. (2005) also found a gap in their case studies of seven alternative certification programs between mentoring described in program documents and what candidates actually experienced. Thirteen percent of the candidates in Teach for America and eleven percent of the candidates in the New Jersey state alternative certification program reported that they received no mentor support. Researchers and others need to look beyond the claim that a practice exists in a teacher education program and investigate how that practice has been elaborated and enacted. It is in the enactment of these program elements that the features of program effectiveness will be found not in cursory statements about the presence of particular practices.

Generalizing about programs that exist in multiple sites

A final issue has to do with the assumption in discussions and the literature that programs that exist at more than one site are the same and provide a common preparation for teaching that can be compared to other types of preparation. The clearest example right now of this problem at the preservice level is the assumption that "Teach for America" provides a common training experience that can be compared to other preparation experiences. Here, although there is a common five-week summer institute for teachers and some support structures that exist in all TFA regions, the preparation received by TFA teachers varies considerably because they are enrolled in a variety of college and university-based and other preservice certification programs to meet the highly qualified provisions of NCLB. Because of the wide variation in the preparation for teaching received by Teach for America teachers, it makes little sense to compare TFA teachers to other beginning teachers without describing the specific nature of the preparation of the teachers being compared.

CONCLUSION

The conceptual framework that we have offered in this chapter provides suggestions for researchers and others to move beyond the simplistic traditional vs. alternative and other surface level comparisons that have dominated the literature and policy discussions. In conversations among teacher educators and between teacher educators and policy makers and in research studies, we need to begin to be more specific about the features of teacher education programs that we are discussing and/or studying. The various dimensions that we have just elaborated suggest particular features of teacher education programs that could lead us to better understandings of how to prepare effective teachers.

We are beginning to see a shift in two recent large scale studies of the effects of different pathways into teaching in how teacher education programs are described. In the first study being conducted by researchers at Mathematica Policy Research (Decker, 2005), teacher education programs are distinguished by their admissions processes (highly selective vs. less selective) and by the required professional education course load (minimal vs. substantial). Although this depiction of programs does not even begin to deal with the complexities of preparation that we will eventually need to understand, it is a step beyond merely labeling a program alternative or traditional.

In a second study conducted by researchers in the Teacher Policy Research Consortium at Stanford University and SUNY Albany (Boyd et al., 2006), researchers are probing more deeply into the differences among programs than has been common. In addition to taking into account various program characteristics such as program length, whether it is graduate or undergraduate, whether it uses student cohorts, faculty and student characteristics, the nature of graduate follow-up, researchers are conducting in-depth exam-inations of the nature of preparation to teach reading and mathematics, to teach diverse learners, and the features of field experiences. Rather than relying on the surface descriptions that have dominated discussions and research, they are examining the character and quality of student assignments and assessments, noting the topics and readings that are part of the preparation in these areas.

It is obviously expensive to perform this kind of in-depth analysis of the elements of different pathways into teaching. Both the TELT and NCTAF case studies discussed earlier and these two current studies were all supported by large grants. Although it is not possible for every research study to include this kind of detailed analysis of program features, it is possible for individual studies to link themselves to particular programs of research about the nature and effects of different program characteristics and consciously build upon one another's work, defining practices and program elements in consistent ways and even using the same instruments and methods to gather data about these practices in different contexts. As Shulman (2004) suggests, it is in these programs of research rather than in individual studies that we will be able to deal with the complexity of teacher education programs. There has been very little evidence to date of teacher education researchers consciously building upon one another's work (Zeichner, 2005).

The complexity of teacher education programs and program elements as has been portrayed in this chapter also has implications for how discussions should be framed between and among teacher educators and policymakers. Figure 17.1 summarizes some of the factors that need to be taken into account when studying the links between teacher education, teacher learning, and student learning.

We have argued in this chapter that the meaning of a teacher education program is to be found in its substance as well as in its structural characteristics. We have further argued that with regard to the substantive aspects of teacher education programs, their meanings are to be found in the elaboration and enactment of particular program features rather than in their mere presence or absence. Just as the question of whether alternative programs are more effective than traditional programs will never be able to be answered in a meaningful way, we will never settle the question of what effects the mere presence of certain practices in a teacher education program have (e.g. portfolios, action research, professional development schools) independent of an understanding of the ways in which these practices have been defined and implemented and knowledge of the contexts in which they have been enacted. Also, the search for the universally best practices in teacher education for all types of candidates in all types of settings is likely to be a futile one.

Given the diversity of who comes in to our teacher education programs and the settings for which they are prepared to teach, there is likely to be a variety of effective pathways into teaching and a variety of elements of effective teacher education programs. The most important task that lies ahead is to ensure that elements of excellence in teacher education are present in all of these various pathways into teaching.

NOTES

1 Not all of the researchers used the same definitions of alternative and traditional programs and this definition which was originally proposed by Adelman (1986) and has been more recently used by others enabled us to make the most use of the data in the 37 studies.
2 Effectiveness in accomplishing its particular goals. As will be discussed below, there are a number of different views of what teachers need to know, be like, and be able to do.

3 The purpose of these case studies of teacher education programs in 29 institutions was to verify the extent to which these conditions existed in U.S. teacher education programs.

4 Tatto (1996) in her study of the impact of programs on preparing teachers to teach diverse learners distinguished the substance of programs in TELT by contrasting a "constructivist" from a "conventional" or "transmission" approach. Kennedy (1998), in her TELT study of learning to teach writing, distinguished "reform-oriented" from "traditional" programs.

5 According to Darling-Hammond (2000) "learning-centered" instruction refers to a focus on in-depth learning and understanding and "learner-centered" instruction refers to instruction that is responsive to students' cultural backgrounds, experiences, needs and talents.

6 Because most college and university-based teacher educators are prepared for their work in the doctoral programs in research intensive universities, interventions to improve the quality of teacher education in these institutions can potentially have a widespread effect throughout higher education. Ironically, these institutions with the most troubled history with regard to teacher education (e.g. Labaree, 2004) have the major responsibility for preparing the nation's teacher educators.

7 See Darling-Hammond and Bransford (2005) for an elaboration of what Darling-Hammond believes is minimally necessary for teacher education programs to teach.

8 In an effort to move toward the identification of signature pedagogies in teacher education, the Carnegie Foundation for the Advancement of Teaching has initiated a new web-based collection of K-12 and teacher education teaching practices (http://gallery.carnegiefoundation.org/insideteaching.

9 One of us conducted an external review of the education department at the University of California at Santa Cruz a few years ago and this was one of the findings in this review.

10 The two sites that are being referred to here are the University of Wisconsin-Milwaukee and the University of Washington in Seattle.

11 In both of these professional development school/non professional development school comparisons, students self-selected into the PDS track of their program. Because of the design of these studies, there is no basis for attributing the results found by researchers to the programs as opposed to differences in the characteristics of the individuals who entered the different program tracks.

REFERENCES

Adelman, N. (1986) *An exploratory study of teacher alternative certification and retraining programs.* Washington, DC: U.S. Department of Education.

Arends, R. & Winitzky, N. (1996) Program structures and learning to teach. In F. Murray (ed.) *The teacher educator handbook* (pp. 526–536). San Francisco: Jossey-Bass.

Barnes, H. (1987) The conceptual basis for thematic teacher education programs. *Journal of Teacher Education*, 38(4), 13–18.

Benyon, J., Grout, J., & Wideen, M. (2004). *From teacher to teacher educator: collaboration within a community of practice.* Vancouver, Canada: Pacific Educational Press.

Boyd, D., Grossman, P., Langford, H., Loeb, S., Michelli, N., & Wyckoff, J. (April, 2005) Complex by design: investigating pathways into teaching in New York City schools. *Journal of Teacher Education*, 57(2), 155–166.

Brouwer, N. & Korthagen, F. (2005) Can teacher education make a difference? *American Educational Research Journal*, 42(1), 153–224.

Carter, K. & Anders, D. (1996) Program pedagogy. In F. Murray (ed.) *The teacher educator's handbook* (pp. 537–592). San Francisco: Jossey-Bass.

Castle, S., Fox, R., & O'Hanlan Souder, K. (2006) Do professional development schools (PDSs) make a difference? A comparative study of PDS and non PDS teacher candidates. *Journal of Teacher Education*, 57(1), 65–80.

Cochran-Smith, M. (2003) Learning and unlearning: the education of teacher educators. *Teaching & Teacher Education*, 19(1), 5–28.

Cochran-Smith, M. & Fries, M.K. (2005) Researching teacher education in changing times:

politics and paradigms. In M. Cochran-Smith & K. Zeichner (eds.) *Studying teacher education*. Mahwah, NJ: Lawrence Erlbaum.

Conklin, H. (2006) *Learning to teach social studies at the middle level: a case study of preservice teachers in the elementary and secondary pathways*. Unpublished doctoral dissertation, University of Wisconsin-Madison School of Education.

Council of Chief State School Officers (1992) *Model standards for beginning teacher licensing, assessment and development: a resource for state dialogue*. Washington, DC: Interstate New Teacher Assessment and Support Consortium of the Council of Chief State School Officers.

Darling-Hammond, L. (2000) (ed.) *Studies of excellence in teacher education*. Washington, DC: American Association of Colleges for Teacher Education.

Darling-Hammond, L. (2006) *Powerful teacher education: lessons from exemplary programs*. San Francisco: Jossey-Bass.

Darling-Hammond, L. & Bransford, J. (2005) (eds.) *Preparing teachers for a changing world*. San Francisco: Jossey-Bass.

Darling-Hammond, L., Hammerness, K., Grossman, P., Rust, F., & Shulman, L. (2005) The design of teacher education programs. In L. Darling-Hammond & J. Bransford (eds.) *Preparing teachers for a changing world* (pp. 390–441). San Francisco: Jossey-Bass.

Decker, P. (September, 2005) *The evaluation of teacher preparation models*. Paper presented at the Forum on Highly Rigorous Research on Alternative Certification, Washington, DC. Washington, DC: Institute for Educational Sciences.

Denemark, G. & Nutter, N. (1984) The case for extended programs of initial teacher education. In L. Katz & J. Raths (eds.) *Advances in teacher education* (pp. 203–246). Norwood NJ: Ablex.

Fallon, D. (2006). The buffalo upon the chimneypiece: the value of evidence. *Journal of Teacher Education*, 57(2), 139–154.

Feiman-Nemser, S. (1990) Teacher education: structural and conceptual alternatives. In W.R. Houston (ed.) *Handbook of research on teacher education* (pp. 212–223). New York: Macmillan.

Goodlad, J. (1990) *Teachers for our nation's schools*. San Francisco: Jossey-Bass.

Grossman, P. (2005) Pedagogical approaches in teacher education. In M. Cochran-Smith & K. Zeichner (eds.) *Studying teacher education* (pp. 425–476). Mahwah, NJ: Lawrence Erlbaum.

Hammerness, K. (2006) From coherence in theory to coherence in practice. *Teachers College Record*, 108(7), 1241–1265.

Hawley, W.D. (1987) The high costs and doubtful efficacy of extended teacher preparation programs. *American Journal of Education*, 95, 275–313.

Holmes Group (1986) *Tomorrow's teachers*. East Lansing MI: Author.

Houston, W.R. (1990) Preface. *Handbook of research on teacher education* (pp. ix–xi). New York: Macmillan.

Howey, K. & Zimpher, N. (1989) *Profiles of preservice teacher education: inquiry into the nature of programs*. Albany, NY: SUNY Press.

Humphrey, D. & Wechsler, M. (2005) Insights into alternative certification: initial findings from a national study. *Teachers College Record*. Retrieved from the web www.tcrecord.org 9/2/05.

Humphrey, D., Wechsler, M., & Hough, H. (July, 2005) *Characteristics of effective alternative teacher certification programs*. Menlo Park, CA: SRI.

Kennedy, M. (1998) *Learning to teach writing: does teacher education make a difference?* New York: Teachers College Press.

Kliebard, H. (1973) The question in teacher education. In D. McCarty (ed.), *New perspectives on teacher education* (pp. 8–24). San Francisco: Jossey-Bass.

Kroll, L., Cossey, R., Donahue, D., Galguera, T., Laboskey, V., Richert, A., & Tucher, P. (2005) *Teaching as principled practice: managing complexity for social justice*. Thousand Oaks, CA: Sage.

Labaree, D. (2004) *The trouble with ed schools*. New Haven, CT: Yale University Press.

Lanier, J. & Little, J.W. (1986) Research on teacher education. In M. Wittrock (ed.) *Handbook of research on teaching* (3rd edition, pp. 527–569). New York: Macmillan.

Levine, A. (September, 2006) *Educating school teachers*. Washington, DC: Education Schools Project. Downloaded from http://www.edschools.org on October 2, 2006.

Liston, D. & Zeichner, K. (1991) *Teacher education and the social conditions of schooling*. New York: Routledge.

McDonald, M. & Zeichner, K. (in press) Social justice teacher education. In W. Ayers, T. Quinn, & D. Stovall (eds.) *Handbook of social justice in education*. Mahwah, NJ: Lawrence Erlbaum.

Michelli, N. & Keiser, D.L. (2005) (eds.) *Teacher education for democracy and social justice*. New York: Routledge.

National Center for Research on Teacher Education (1991) *Findings from the teacher education and learning to teach study*. East Lansing, MI: National Center for Research on Teacher Education/Learning.

National Council for Accreditation of Teacher Education (2001) *Standards for professional development schools*. Retrieved from ncate.org on January 5, 2006.

Oakes, J. & Lipton, M. (1999) *Teaching to change the world*. Boston: McGraw-Hill.

Post, L., Pugach, M., Harris, S., & Hedges, M. (2006) The teachers-in-residence program: Veteran urban teachers as teacher leaders in boundary-spanner roles. In K. Howey & N. Zimpher (eds.) *Boundary spanners*. Washington, DC: American Association of State Colleges and Universities.

Ridley, D.S., Hurwitz, S., Hackett, M.R.D., & Miller, K.K. (2005) Comparing PDS and campus-based preservice teacher preparation: is PDS preparation really better? *Journal of Teacher Education*, 56(1), 46–56.

Shulman, L. (2004) Truth and consequences: inquiry and policy in research on teacher education. *Journal of Teacher Education*, 53(3), 248–253.

Shulman, L. (2005a) Teacher education does not exist. *Stanford University School of Education Alumni Newsletter*, Fall, 2005. Retrieved from http://stanford.edu on January 6, 2006.

Shulman, L. (February, 2005b) *The signature pedagogies of the professions of law, medicine, engineering, and the clergy: potential lessons for the education of teachers*. Talk presented at the Math Science Partnerships (MSP) workshop: Teacher education for effective teaching and learning, Irvine, CA.

Steiner, D. & Rozen, S. (2004) Preparing tomorrow's teachers: an analysis of syllabi from a sample of schools of education. In F. Hess, A. Rotherham, & K. Walsh (eds.) *A qualified teacher in every classroom?* (pp. 119–148). Cambridge, MA: Harvard Education Press.

Stevens, C.L. & Dial, M. (1993) A qualitative study of alternatively certified teachers. *Education & Urban Society*, 26(1), 63–77.

Tatto, M.T. (1996). Examining values and beliefs about teaching diverse students: understanding the challenges for teacher education. *Education Evaluation and Policy Analysis*, 18(2), 155–180.

Tom, A. (1997) *Redesigning teacher education*. Albany, NY: SUNY Press.

Valli, L. (1992) (ed.) *Reflective teacher education: cases and critiques*. Albany, NY: SUNY Press.

Walsh, K., Glaser, D., & Wilcox, D. (May, 2006) *What education schools aren't teaching about reading and what elementary teachers aren't learning*. Washington, DC: National Council on Teacher Quality.

Walton, P., Baca, L. & Escamilla, K. (2002) *A national study of teacher education preparation for diverse student populations*. Santa Cruz, CA: National Center for Education, Diversity, and Excellence. Executive summary was retrieved on July 1, 2006. The full case studies were obtained from Priscilla Walton and Leonard Baca.

Zeichner, K. (1993) Traditions of practice in U.S. preservice teacher education programs. *Teaching & Teacher Education*, 9(1), 1–13.

Zeichner, K. (2000) Ability-based teacher education: elementary teacher education at Alverno College. In L. Darling-Hammond (ed.) *Studies of excellence in teacher education, the undergraduate years* (pp. 1–66). Washington, DC: American Association of Colleges for Teacher Education.

Zeichner, K. (2003) The adequacies and inadequacies of three current strategies to recruit, prepare, and retain the best teachers for all students. *Teachers College Record*, 105(3), 490–515.

Zeichner, K. (2005) A research agenda for teacher education. In M. Cochran-Smith & K. Zeichner (eds.) *Studying teacher education* (pp. 737–760). Mahwah, NJ: Erlbaum.

Zeichner, K. (2006) Studying teacher education programs: enriching and enlarging the inquiry. In C. Conrad & R. Serlin (eds.) *The sage handbook for research in education* (pp. 79–94). Thousand Oaks, CA: Sage.

Zeichner, K. & Conklin, H. (2005) Teacher education programs. In M. Cochran-Smith & K. Zeichner (eds.) *Studying teacher education* (pp. 645–736) Mahwah, NJ: Erlbaum.

Zeichner, K. & Hoeft, K. (1996) Teacher socialization for cultural diversity. In J. Sikula (ed.) *Handbook of research on teacher education (2nd edition)* (pp. 525–547). New York: Macmillan.

Zeichner, K. & Miller, M. (1997) Learning to teach in professional development schools. In M. Levine & R. Trachtman (eds.) *Making professional development schools work: politics, practice, and policy* (pp. 15–32). New York: Teachers College Press.

18 An uneasy relationship
The history of teacher education in the university

David F. Labaree
Stanford University

For better and for worse, teacher education in the United States has come to be offered primarily within the institutional setting of the university. In many ways, this came about by historical accident. In the nineteenth century, teacher education, if it took place at all, occurred in a variety of organizational settings, until the state normal school emerged in the last quarter of the century as the emergent (if not yet predominant) model. In the early twentieth century, however, this model went through a rapid evolution, from normal school to state teachers college to general-purpose state college to regional state university. Since the 1970s, teacher education has been a wholly owned subsidiary of the university.

Ironically, although teacher education was a latecomer to the university in the U.S., it was at the core of the original form of the university that emerged in medieval Europe. Early in this institution's history, an advanced liberal arts education was primarily intended to prepare teachers. The university was then constituted as a craft guild for teachers, whose highest degrees (the master's and doctorate) were badges of admission to the status of master teacher and whose oral examinations were tests of the candidate's teaching ability (Shulman, 1986; Durkheim, 1938/1969). But over the years teacher education was gradually pushed from the center to the periphery of higher education, which is where it was found in the early nineteenth century when American teacher education started its long march back.

In this chapter I examine the history of teacher education in the U.S. for insight into the situation facing teacher education today. As it turns out, the relationship between the university and teacher education has been an uneasy one for both parties. There has been persistent ambivalence on both sides. Each needs the other in significant ways, but each risks something important by being tied to the other. The university offers status and academic credibility, and teacher education offers students and social utility. But in maintaining this marriage of convenience, the university risks undermining its academic standing, and teacher education risks undermining its professional mission. I explore some of the central issues that surround this awkward relationship: the centrality of teacher education's status problem in shaping its relationship with the university; the roots of this problem, both in the market pressures that shaped teacher education's history and in the problems of practice that shaped its professional role; the status politics that shaped the situation of teacher education within the university; and the differences in the relationship between TE and university that come with the latter's location in the university status order.

THE HISTORY

Teaching existed long before teacher education.[1] In the years preceding the emergence of the normal school in the mid-nineteenth century and continuing afterward, prospective teachers in the U.S. followed many routes into the classroom. In general, the assumption was that anyone who had completed a given level of education could turn around and teach it. Teachers needed no special preparation in the art of teaching; they just needed modest familiarity with the subject matter they would teach. This lack of formal training in pedagogy was not unique to teaching. Before the twentieth century, most professionals did not learn their craft by enrolling in a program of professional education but rather by pursuing an apprenticeship with an experienced practitioner. What was distinctive about the preparation of teachers, however, was that it involved neither formal instruction nor informal apprenticeship. Instead, the rule was simply: take the class, teach the class.

EARLY FORMS OF TEACHING AND TEACHER EDUCATION

In early nineteenth century America, education took place in a wide variety of settings: home, where children acquired basic literacy and numeracy skills; church, where children learned via sermons, study groups, and Sunday schools; a variety of lyceums and public lectures; apprenticeships, which required the master artisan to provide some general education as well as trade craft; dame schools, in which students learned elementary skills in the home of a neighbor; private tutors; private schools relying on tuition; free schools for paupers operated by the local municipality; public schools in New England towns; academies, providing secondary education; and colleges, operating preparatory departments. The setting determined the identity of the teacher, who could be any of a number of persons: a parent, a preacher, a master craftsman, an association leader, an adult in the neighborhood, an itinerant tutor, a private contractor, a town official, a corporate employee, or a college professor.

The arrival of the common school in the 1830s initiated a process of simplifying this complex structure of education and making it look more like the system we have today. The emerging model was the community elementary school, operated by local public officials and supplemented over time by a grammar school and a high school. In this new structure, teachers were public employees, appointed by a school board acting as the agent for the community. The criteria for hiring teachers varied. Perhaps the most important characteristic was the ability to maintain order among the students (Sedlak, 1989). It also helped if the candidate was local and needed the work. As for educational qualifications: at the very least, you needed to have completed the level at which you would be teaching. As standards increased over time, the educational requirement became completion of the level above that. Grammar school graduates thus were viewed as prospective elementary teachers, and high school graduates as grammar school teachers. College students often taught in the summer, and college graduates frequently taught for a while until something better came along.

With the development of the common school system, however, came the first effort to establish a system of formal preparation of teachers for these schools. Leaders of the common school movement, like James Carter, Horace Mann, and Henry Barnard, were also strong advocates for teacher education. One innovation that became prominent during the middle of the century was the summer teacher institute, which was a set of lectures and classes aimed at developing the skills of teachers in both pedagogy and subject matter. These institutes constituted a form of on-the-job training for teachers, the first formal effort to provide teachers with professional development opportunities. They typically took place during the summer, over a period ranging from one to eight weeks, usually organized by the county school superintendent or a group of school districts (Mattingly, 1975).

THE NORMAL SCHOOL

The major teacher education initiative that came out of the common school movement, however, was the state normal school. One reason for this was the sharp increase in the demand for teachers that arose with the adoption of the common school model. In place of the vast array of mechanisms for providing instruction that marked education at the start of the nineteenth century, the common school system established a single standard model, the publicly operated community school. The process of creating these schools all over the country produced an enormous and continuing shortage of teachers who could be employed to occupy the new classrooms. The normal school was to be the primary means of providing these teachers. However, the common school movement generated not only a demand for teachers but also a demand for higher teacher qualifications. When education shifted from an *ad hoc* and voluntaristic mode of delivery to a systematic and publicly sponsored form, teaching became a kind of public trust, which required systematic training and professional certification for teachers in order to insure that they were capable of meeting their new public responsibility for educating the nation's children. As their name suggested, normal schools were expected to set the standard—the norm—for good teaching.

Normal schools took a variety of forms. Major cities set up their own normal schools, or normal departments within the high school, in order to train teachers for the local system. Often counties established normal schools to feed into their own school districts. But the most prominent and ultimately most influential form was the state normal school, the first of which opened in Lexington, Massachusetts in 1839. The state normal school, which started out at the level of a high school, was a single-purpose professional school for future teachers. In order to accomplish this end, the curriculum had to be a mix of liberal arts courses, to give prospective teachers the grounding in subject matter they had not received in their earlier education, and professional courses, to give them a grounding in the arts of teaching. Initially the course of study lasted for one or two years.

In the eyes of reformers like Mann, the primary aim of the state normal school was to prepare a group of well educated and professionally skilled teachers who could serve as the model for public school teachers throughout the country. Here is the way Cyrus Pierce, the founder of the Lexington normal school, put it in a letter to Henry Barnard:

> I answer briefly, that it was my aim, and it would be my aim again, to make better teachers, and especially, better teachers for our common schools; so that those primary seminaries, on which so many depend for their education, might answer, in a higher degree, the end of their institution. Yes, to make better teachers; teachers who would understand, and do their business better; teachers who should know more of the nature of children, of youthful developments, more of the subject to be taught, and more of the true methods of teaching; who would teach more philosophically, more in harmony with the natural development of the young mind, with a truer regard to the order and connection in which the different branches of knowledge should be presented to it, and, of course, more successfully.
>
> (Borrowman, 1965, p. 65)

This was a noble professional mission for the normal school; one can hear echoes of it in the debates about today's university-based schools of education. But it directly conflicted with the other main purpose of the normal school, which was to fill empty classrooms with much-needed teachers. It is hard to see how the normal school could have satisfied both of these aims at the same time. From the very beginning, it was caught in a classic bind between quality and quantity. It could provide a few model teachers with a high degree of professional training; or it could provide the large number of teachers needed for the expanding common school system by skimping on professional preparation. It could be professionally strong but functionally marginal, leaving the vast majority of teachers to reach the classroom with less rigorous training; or it could be professionally weak and functionally central, turning out large numbers of graduates with minimal preparation.

It should surprise no one that normal school leaders ended up choosing relevance over rigor. Doing otherwise would have been difficult. To preserve academic rigor would have meant opting for professional purism over social need; it would have meant leaving mass teacher preparation to less qualified providers; and it would have meant depriving their institutions of the funding, power, and opportunities for expansion that would come with making themselves useful. As I examine in more detail later, this same debate about the role of teacher education continues today. Schools of education at elite universities generally have opted for rigor over relevance, with boutique teacher education programs that provide academically credible preparation for a small and highly selective group of students. But schools of education at regional state universities—the heirs of the normal schools, which reside at the bottom of the university status order—have opted for programs that mass produce teachers to fill the continuing demand in schools. This tension between rigor and relevance, it seems, is endemic to teacher education, and criticisms customarily descend on the heads of education schools for erring in both directions. A recent report by Arthur Levine (2006), *Educating School Teachers*, is only the latest in a long line of polemics that lambaste the university school of education for being both academically weak and professionally irrelevant.[2]

Under these conditions, the number of state normal schools grew rapidly. After their start in 1839, they grew to 39 in 1870, 103 in 1890, and 180 in 1910 (Ogren, 2005, pp. 1–2). Enrollments at public normal schools (which included a few city and county normals) grew from about 26,000 in 1879–80 to 68,000 in 1899–1900 and 111,000 in 1909–10 (Ogren, 2005, Table 2.1, p. 58). This rapid increase had the effect of dramatically lowering both the status of these institutions and the quality of their programs, a point I develop later. Even though they were running hard to catch up with the demand for teachers, by the end of the century normal schools still had not been able to do so. As David Tyack has pointed out, "By 1898 the number of public normal schools had reached 127, with about the same number of private ones. But all the normal schools together graduated no more than one-quarter of the new teachers" (Tyack, 1967, p. 415).

THE EVOLUTION OF THE NORMAL SCHOOL INTO THE REGIONAL STATE UNIVERSITY

At the same time that normal schools were under pressure to meet the demand from school districts for more teachers, they were also experiencing another kind of demand, this coming from their own students. If the first kind of pressure sought to turn normal schools into teacher factories, the second sought to turn them into people's colleges.

From the perspective of their students, normal schools were more than just a way to become a teacher. They were also a way to acquire a local, affordable, and accessible form of higher education. Private colleges were expensive. State universities were almost as expensive, they were usually far away, and gaining admission was not easy. But normal schools were less expensive; they were located at geographically accessible points around the state, allowing students to commute and thus keep down living costs; and admission was easy. The only problem was that normal schools focused entirely on preparing students for a single occupation, teaching. But on this point, it turns out, the normal school was prepared to be flexible. It really had no choice.

Like American higher education in general, both then and now, state normal schools were dependent on student tuition. They received appropriations from state government, but these funds were only adequate to support a portion of the costs of educating students. The rest had to come from tuition. With money comes power. In order to survive and prosper, normal schools needed to keep attracting student tuition dollars, which meant competing with other higher education providers in their market area to offer students the kinds of educational services they wanted. What these consumers wanted was not a single, narrowly-defined program for preparing teachers, but instead an array of programs that offered broad access to a variety of possible jobs. They did not want a normal school; they wanted an open-access liberal arts college. Adapting to this consumer demand was mandatory for the normal schools; if they failed to do so, students would go to competitor institutions that had already made the adjustment. And adapting to this demand was also relatively easy. In order to provide prospective teachers with the subject matter knowledge they needed, normal schools already had a group of professors who were teaching history, English, math, science, and the rest of the core liberal arts curriculum, in addition to courses in pedagogy. It was thus a simple matter for normal schools to supplement their core teacher education program with a series of programs of study that drew on these liberal arts courses. And that is what they did.

In his book *And Sadly Teach*, Jurgen Herbst (1989) describes in detail the process by which normal schools gradually abandoned their commitment to professional education and allowed themselves to be lured into mimicking the liberal arts college. For proponents of high quality professional education for teachers, this is not a pretty story. But for those who see education as an important way to allow individuals to get ahead in society, it is a heartening tale of expanding educational opportunity and social mobility.[3] As was the case when normal schools expanded to meet the demand from school districts for more teachers, they were just doing what people wanted them to do. The market spoke—first employers, then consumers—and normal schools responded. Depending on one's point of view, this response may or may not be admirable, but it is certainly understandable.

The evolution of the normal school into a people's college helps explain the rapid expansion and proliferation of these institutions in the late nineteenth century. It also helps explain why this expansion was insufficient to meet the demand for teachers, since an increasing share of the normal school student body was there to pursue other professional goals. But the process by which the normal school adapted to consumer pressure from students did not stop with the development of a multipurpose institution. If students wanted the normal school to be a local, inexpensive, and accessible form of a liberal arts college, then it made no sense to stop with the addition of a few new programs. After all, the normal school was still more high school than college, so it could not provide the kind of social mobility opportunities that a real college could. Students wanted college status for the normal school, and so did its faculty members and administrators, all of whom would benefit from being able to ride this institution to a higher level in the educational system. The same was true of members of the community surrounding the normal school, local legislators, and also communities that were hoping to open new such institutions in their own areas.

Given the array of constituencies supporting this elevation, it was inevitable that by the start of the twentieth century state legislatures would begin transforming normal schools into teachers colleges, and between 1911 and 1930 there were 88 such conversions (Tyack, 1967, p. 417). With this change, the former normal schools could grant bachelor's degrees, giving heft and credibility to all their programs. But the process did not end there. These teachers colleges had already diversified their programs, turning themselves into de facto liberal arts colleges, with teacher education playing a smaller role in the curriculum every year. So it made sense to recognize this fact, remove the word "teachers" from their letterhead, and change to a more generally recognized and marketable label, "state college." This started happening in the 1920s, and by the 1950s the last of the normal schools were formally disappearing from the scene. Finally, this process of institutional evolution reached its culmination in the 1950s, 1960s, and 1970s, when one after another of these former normal schools took the last step by seeking and winning the title "university." In the century-long race to adopt the most attractive institutional identity, being a college was no longer good enough; only becoming a university would do. The large majority of the old normal schools followed this route—from normal school to teachers college to state college to state university—with only minor variations in labeling and timing. For example:

State Normal School, Albany, NY, 1844; State Normal College, 1890; State College for Teachers, 1914; State University College of Education, 1959; State University College, 1961; State University of New York at Albany, 1962.

State Normal School, Millersville, PA, 1859; State Teachers College, 1927; State College, 1959; Millersville University of Pennsylvania, 1983.

State Normal School, Mankato, MN, 1868; State Teachers College, 1921; State College, 1957; State University, 1975; now Minnesota State University, Mankato.

Northern State Normal School, De Kalb, IL, 1899; Northern State Teachers College, 1921; Northern State College, 1955; Northern State University, 1957.

State Normal School, Montclair, NJ, 1908; State Teachers College, 1929; State College, 1958; Montclair State University, 1994 (Ogren, 2005, appendix).

An alternate route: education in elite universities

There was another route that brought teacher education into the university, this one much more direct though much less common. In the late nineteenth century, universities started adding chairs in pedagogy or education. These were flagship state universities and private universities, which were destined to occupy the top tier in the emerging hierarchy of higher education in the twentieth century (with the former normal schools, now regional state universities, occupying the lower tier). Historians generally give University of Iowa credit for establishing the first permanent professorship in pedagogy in 1873 (Tyack, 1967, p. 415; Clifford & Guthrie, 1988, p. 62), but University of Michigan claims this honor for itself with a chair established in 1879 (University of Michigan, 2005). Others quickly followed: Columbia (Teachers College) in 1887; Chicago, Stanford, and Harvard in 1891; Berkeley in 1892; and Ohio State in 1895 (Clifford & Guthrie, 1988, pp. 62–63). Education began at these institutions as individual professorships and then quickly evolved into departments and finally schools or colleges of education. The latter stage arrived at Ohio State and Iowa in 1907, Berkeley in 1913, Stanford in 1917, Harvard in 1920, and Michigan in 1921 (Clifford & Guthrie, 1988, p. 64).

These education schools saw themselves playing a markedly different role from the one assumed by normal schools (Powell, 1976). Whereas the latter focused on meeting the central needs of an expanding education system, by preparing a large number of teachers for the elementary schools, university education professors focused on the preparation of a much smaller number of high school teachers and school administrators and on the production of educational research. Not by accident, the large majority of these university education students were men, whereas most normal school students were women. This sharp divergence in mission laid the groundwork for the continuing dichotomy in education roles that characterizes the contemporary university, with education schools at former normal schools going one way and those at elite universities going another. I will have more to say about that issue later in the chapter.

Converging on a canonical model

By the 1960s, through the diverse processes I have outlined here, teacher education in United States had stumbled upon a model of organization that quickly became canonical. Teacher education, it turned out, was going to be carried out within a university, under the leadership of professors in a school or college of education located there. By this time, the former normal schools had evolved into universities, and once they achieved this status they naturally imitated the structure of existing universities by setting up education schools and then assigning them the work that had once constituted the normal school's entire mission, preparing teachers.

In allowing itself to become incorporated within the university, teacher education was just following in the path of the other more prestigious professions. As I noted earlier, until the late nineteenth century the primary route into all of the professions was apprenticeship (Brubacher & Rudy, 1997). A prospect would work out an arrangement with an experienced practitioner: to learn by doing, in the manner of an apprentice carpenter or shoemaker; and to study the books in the practitioner's library. The traditional high professions—clergy, law, and medicine—have had a place in university faculties from medieval times to the present, but only the pinnacle of the practitioners in these professions studied there; the large majority had always followed the route of apprenticeship. By the eighteenth and nineteenth centuries, colleges and universities were providing the liberal component of the education of the high professions, but apprenticeship was still the means of acquiring the skills of professional practice. Gradually, individual practitioners started specializing in professional preparation, gathering groups of apprentices together into what amounted to proprietary professional schools. Then, in the last quarter of the nineteenth century, universities started establishing formal professional schools that incorporated both academic study and guided practice, and this spelled the beginning of the end of independent professional preparation.

The university was emerging as a powerful new form of American higher education during this period (Veysey, 1965). As Clark Kerr (2001) has noted, it combined the British college, which focused on undergraduate education, with the German graduate school, which focused on advanced studies and research, and then added the American land grant college, which focused on practical-vocational education. In this setting, professional schools were a natural addition, drawing on the German and American elements to produce a graduate school for practice. And the growing prestige of the new university made it attractive for prospective practitioners to start seeking professional education there instead of through apprenticeship. By 1900, more than 10 percent of doctors, lawyers, clergymen, and college professors had received training at a university professional school (Brubacher & Rudy, 1997, p. 383). Abraham Flexner's 1910 report on medical education set off a cascade of demands for reform of professional education more generally, seeking to improve the quality of this preparation by reinforcing the connection with the research university. Soon it became difficult and eventually unthinkable for professional schools in any major field to exist on their own. Only schools for training practitioners of the lesser trades—like cosmetology and truck driving—could survive independently. For teacher education, as with other programs of professional preparation, there was really nowhere else to go but the university.

Teacher education and the university: the nature of the relationship

This is how teacher education ended up in the university. Now we need to explore the kind of home it found there: the nature of the relationship between the education school and the larger institution, and the consequences of this arrangement for both parties. In particular, I focus on the kind of exchange that has been involved in maintaining this relationship. As I suggested at the beginning, the university provides status and academic credibility for its part of the bargain, and in return teacher education provides students and social utility. Below I explore the terms of this exchange: the roots of teacher education's status problem, the programmatic and professional consequences of using university status to remedy this problem, and the significant differences in the nature of the bargain with education at elite universities vs. regional state universities (the former normal schools).

Education's status problem

Teacher education has long suffered from low status.[4] Everyone picks on it: professors, reformers, policymakers, and teachers; right wing think tanks and left wing think tanks; even the professors, students, and graduates of teacher education programs themselves. In part this status problem is a legacy of the market pressures that shaped the history of the normal school; in part it is a side effect of the bad company that teacher education is seen as keeping; and in part it is a result of the kind of work that teachers and teacher educators do. Let us consider each of these in turn.

Legacy of market pressures

At the core of teacher education's status problem are the market pressures that shaped the history of the normal school. One kind of market pressure came from employer demand. There was a seemingly endless call for warm bodies to fill the ever expanding number of classrooms in a school system that was increasing in size both horizontally (incorporating the entire age cohort) and vertically (extending the school career from elementary school to grammar school to high school). Normal schools expanded to meet this demand, and in doing so they necessarily relaxed professional standards for teacher preparation. This meant making teacher education easy to enter, short in duration, modest in academic rigor, and inexpensive to maintain. The normals were being asked to turn out large numbers of teachers at low cost and with minimal qualifications, and they did so. But, of course, being accommodating in this manner sharply lowered their institutional status. And this stigma has stuck with teacher education as it migrated into the university, where it has retained the reputation for being an academically weak program produced on the cheap for students of modest intellect.

Another kind of market pressure on teacher education came from consumer demand. Students entering the normal school wanted a credential that would open a much wider array of occupational doors than a simple teaching degree, and the normal school obliged by expanding programs and evolving into a college and then university. In the process of doing so, however, the normal school had to abandon its focus on the professional preparation of teachers. Teacher preparation became increasingly marginal within the expanding college and university context. No longer the centerpiece of the institution as it was in the normal school, education was now just one school among many; and the responsibility for teacher education itself became diffused across the entire university. Prospective teachers acquired general education and knowledge of the school subjects they would teach in departments elsewhere on campus, leaving the education school with responsibility only for courses in pedagogy. Thus the evolution into a university meant that the normal school lost both its professional mission and its control over the education of teachers. This left the university education school with a function that seemed vestigial. It looked like the "real" education of teachers in academic subject matter took place elsewhere, whereas the education school seemed responsible only for the vocational side of things—teaching lesson planning and classroom management, and supervising student teachers. In the status hierarchy of the university, which values the academic over the vocational and the theoretical over the practical, this put education on the lowest tier.

Bad company

Another source of teacher education's low esteem is the apparently bad company it keeps. Teacher education serves stigmatized populations, as defined by gender, class, and age. This is a problem, since professions derive much of their esteem from the quality of their associations. For one thing, the emergence of the common school movement quickly turned teaching from men's work into women's work. In part this change was ideological, grounded in a vision that nurturing the young was best handled by women. In part it was practical, grounded in the need for vast numbers of teachers, and the understanding that women were willing to work at half the pay demanded by men. Becoming defined as women's work has never helped the status of an occupation.

In addition, teaching was not an exclusive profession but more like a mass occupation. As such it drew a large number of practitioners from the working class and lower middle class, whereas the more esteemed professions drew aspirants from the higher classes. At the same time—unlike the prestigious professions, whose clients were among the more elevated members of society—public school teaching expended its efforts on behalf of a clientele of students who were concentrated at the lower parts of the social spectrum. As the most accessible of the professions serving the least advantaged members of society, teachers—and the programs for preparing them—carry a stigma of class.

Finally, there is the issue of age. If professionals earn part of their status from the status of their clients, then teaching's focus on children works against it since adult clients carry more cachet. Doctors, lawyers, accountants, and architects deal primarily with adults; even if a doctor has a child as a patient, the clients are the parents. The rungs in the status ladder of teaching correspond to the age of the student, with professors in graduate programs at the top and early childhood educators at the bottom. Elementary teachers are just a rung above the latter and high school teachers a rung above that.

The nature of the work

A third factor in the low status of teacher education is the nature of the work that teachers do. Teaching is an extraordinarily difficult job that looks easy, which is a devastating combination for its professional standing and for the standing of its professional educators. Why is teaching so difficult? One reason is that teaching cannot succeed without the compliance of the student. Most professions can carry out their work independent of the client; surgeons operate on the anesthetized and lawyers defend the mute. But teachers can only accomplish their goals if students are willing to learn. They exert their efforts to motivate student compliance in the task of learning, but they cannot on their own make learning happen.

Compounding this problem is the fact that students are generally in the classroom under duress. Pressure from parents, truancy laws, and the job market bring them and keep them there. But unlike the clients of most professionals, they are not contracting with the teacher to deliver services that they themselves want. Add to this another complication, which is that teachers usually carry out their practice under conditions of isolation, in a self-contained classroom where they are the only professional and only adult in the room. Finally, teachers have to function in a situation in which they lack a proven technology that works, a clear definition of success, or even a definite fix on the identity of the client (who can be construed simultaneously as the student, the parent, and the community).

Teaching is therefore a very difficult form of professional practice, which makes teacher preparation equally difficult. Complicating this challenge, however, is the general perception that teaching is actually easy. As Dan Lortie (1975) has explained and generations of teacher educators continually rediscover, one reason for this perception is that teaching is extraordinarily visible. We all undergo a 12-year apprenticeship of observation in the elementary and secondary classroom, watching teachers on the job. Compared to our knowledge about other professions, whose work we encounter only occasionally and whose workings we see only obliquely, we think we really know what teaching is all about: maintaining order, asking questions, grading tests, assigning work. As a result, prospective teachers think they know how to teach before entering teacher education programs, which allows little authority or esteem for these programs. In addition, teaching appears to be a natural skill rather than one that one needs to learn through a rigorous program of professional education. We think of it as something that individuals either have or they do not have: a way with kids, a confident and forceful personality. Whatever it is, no one can really learn it in a teacher education program. Finally, teaching is a rare profession in which practitioners succeed by making themselves dispensable. Most professions rent their expertise, which requires clients to return every time they need help. But teachers give away their expertise, by showing children how to learn on their own. This makes the skills of the teacher seem transparent and ordinary, whereas the skills of other professionals seem obscure and remote. If teaching is this difficult and if it appears this easy and commonplace, there is really little need for, and no special esteem associated with, the work of preparing teachers.

In light of all these factors, teacher education's status problem is understandable. It bears the legacy of a historical evolution that undermined its commitment to professionalism and marginalized it within a university setting where it is given little respect; it lacks the high status associations that enhance the prestige of the major professions; and it is stuck with problems of professional practice that are overwhelmingly difficult but that earn it little public credit. Under these circumstances, the advantages for teacher education in migrating from the normal school to the university seem compelling, as compelling as the advantages that lured European peasants to Ellis Island. In status terms, there seemed to be everything to gain and nothing to lose.

The exchange: its costs and benefits

Benefits to education

Teacher education desperately needed a status boost, and the university had status to spare. So to incorporate the former into the latter seemed to provide the answer to teacher education's big problem. By making this move, normal school teachers became university professors, teacher candidates became university students, and education schools assumed a proud place alongside law schools and medical schools. Teachers would now enter the profession with the blessing of the most potent credentialing institution of the modern era.

Not only would this connection with the university grant teacher education the status it craved; it would also imbue this program of professional preparation with the academic credibility it had so sorely lacked in the days of the normal school and teachers college. By the twentieth century, the university had a monopoly on the highest levels of learning. It was the place that brought together the top experts in their fields, who generated the most important forms of new knowledge, and who taught this knowledge to the leaders of the next generation. Being there meant that education school faculty members were now anointed the experts in their domain, who could be trusted to develop the knowledge base for the whole field of education and then imbue this knowledge into the newly emerging members of the teaching profession.

Benefits to the university

Bringing teacher education into the university offered great benefits to the education, but what was in it for the university? One benefit was that teacher education brought with it a large number of students. Like the rest of American higher education, the university has long been heavily dependent on tuition to pay the bills. This is most obviously the case with private institutions, but it holds for public institutions as well. State appropriations pay only part of the cost of running a public university, so student tuition is crucial for its ability to maintain itself and to expand. And state appropriations themselves are usually prorated according to the number of students. So no university can afford to ignore a large pool of potential students who could contribute to the institution's greater welfare. Teacher education offers such a pool. Teaching is by far the largest of the professions, so the demand for teachers, and thus for teacher education programs, is substantial and enduring. Even today, after a long period during which the number of students enrolling in higher education has expanded much faster than the number of openings for new teachers, teaching still employs about 15 percent of all college graduates every year. That is a market that is too big to pass up.

What makes teacher education so attractive to universities, however, is not only the numbers of students it brings but their low cost. Universities have long treated teacher education as what has come to be known as a "cash cow." In these programs, if one is not too punctilious about maintaining high professional standards, an education school can generate a nice profit for the rest of the university. This is possible if the school keeps class sizes large and faculty salaries low, and if it dispenses with the need for the kinds of expensive laboratories and extensive libraries and intimate seminars that drive up the costs in more prestigious programs.

Of course greater numbers of students, by themselves, are not necessarily beneficial for a university, even if the costs are low. Elite universities are careful to limit access in order to maintain exclusivity and thus drive up the exchange value of their credentials.

Opening the doors to a flood of education students, especially if this means lowering academic standards, would be counterproductive to this strategy. But even in this elite sector of higher education, teacher education has its advantages. For one thing, it provides support for a number of large academic departments, whose graduate programs offer prestige to the university but whose undergraduate programs are often unattractive to potential majors. Programs in English and history and music and art, for example, benefit greatly by being able to offer potential majors the possibility that they could actually make a living in this field by teaching the subject at the secondary level. For these departments, it is critical to have a viable and sizeable teacher education program on campus.

For the university more generally, teacher education helps out with another related problem: relevance. Prestige accrues to a university for having the most advanced graduate programs and generating the most esoteric research. But public support for the university depends on being able to make a claim for its public usefulness. Legislators and voters want to know what benefits the state gains through its support of the university. One of these benefits is providing access to higher education for the state's young people, which means that the university cannot take the pursuit of exclusivity too far. It pays to have some open access programs for ordinary folk, programs like teacher education that have traditionally provided easy entry into higher education. Another public benefit the university can claim is that that through education it makes a contribution to solve pressing social problems in the state. The work of education school faculty members can support this claim, both as researchers exploring educational problems and as teacher educators preparing teachers for the state's schools.

This analysis points back to Clark Kerr's insight about the kind of balance that is so critical to the American university. This institution needs to combine the British focus on the undergraduate college (providing a basic college education for a large number of tuition paying students), the German focus on research and advanced graduate study (providing the advanced knowledge and highly selective graduate programs that are so critical to university status), and the American focus on vocational-professional education and practical problem solving. Teacher education thus helps the university with the first and third components of this triad, by providing a large number of undergraduates and a strong practical-vocational rationale, both which serve to support (both financially and politically) the other component, those prestigious and costly graduate programs. What makes the university work is striking the right balance between the *elite* on the one hand and the *populist and the practical* on the other, and teacher education is key to achieving this balance.

Costs to education

The primary price that teacher education pays for its affiliation with the university is the potential loss of its professional mission. This is the Faustian bargain identified by critics of the university school of education like Herbst (1989) and Clifford and Guthrie (1988), in which the education school accepts university status in exchange for its professional soul. As we have seen, this bargain took form early in the history of the normal school— when normal schools agreed to expand beyond their ability to preserve high quality professional programs, and when they adapted to consumer pressure by increasing academic programs and marginalizing teacher education. By the time normal schools became universities in the mid-twentieth century, the terms of the deal were already in place. The last stage in this evolutionary path simply formalized the situation, making education just one school among many and assigning it a supporting role in the larger university enterprise (to provide low cost students and a practical rationale).

Costs to the university

The most significant potential cost of this bargain for the university is that incorporating teacher education can undercut its own academic credibility and thus institutional status. The university in general has unassailable standing in the American educational scene. But individual universities operate in an extraordinarily competitive environment, in which they much constantly attend to the possible loss of their position in the academic hierarchy. This is a main theme of Jerome Karabel's book on the history of admissions at Harvard, Yale, and Princeton in the twentieth century (Karabel, 2005). All three institutions were running scared during this entire period. They were afraid of being pushed aside by one of their longstanding competitors (like the other ivies) or by an upstart (like Stanford or NYU). Universities look like they have status to burn, but the market in higher education means that they have to worry constantly about losing position to their peers. This means that they cannot afford to preserve academically weak programs, even if these programs offer great ancillary benefits. Therefore teacher education is on the radar of every university administrator. As a weak program with benefits, it is useful to have around as long as it is not embarrassing; but its position in the university is never completely secure. As we will see next, however, this is particularly the case with universities at the top of the pecking order.

Different bargains at the top and bottom of the university status order

As we have seen, university schools of education came about through two different mechanisms—*evolution into a university*, from normal school to teachers college to state college to state university (the route followed by Millersville, Mankato, and Montclair), and *evolution within a university*, from chair to department to school of education (the route followed by Harvard, Michigan, and Berkeley). These differences in origin have carried over to the present as differences in orientation.[5]

Education schools at regional state universities, many of which evolved from normal schools, focus primarily on the preparation of future teachers and the professional development of current teachers, and they maintain close connections with the profession and the schools; they devote little time to doctoral study or research. Their identity is clear: they are professional schools. As a result, in general they tend to be professionally strong but academically weak. On the other hand, education schools at top-ranked universities focus primarily on doctoral programs and research; they spend relatively little time preparing teachers or maintaining ties to the profession and the schools. Their identity is more academic than professional, since they construct themselves more as graduate schools of educational studies than schools of teacher education. As a result, in general they tend to be academically strong but professionally weak. Overall, education schools tend toward one pole or the other in these terms, with relatively few occupying the middle ground.

These two types of education schools present strengths and weaknesses that are mirror images of each other. In theory, therefore, both would seem to be at risk of appearing misplaced at the university, each in its own way. Education schools at the regional state universities make a clear case for their inclusion in the university on professional grounds (they are unquestionably professional schools of education), but their weakness in research and advanced degree programs calls into question their suitability on academic grounds. Conversely, those at elite universities make a clear case for their inclusion in the university on academic grounds (they devote nearly all their energies to enhancing their scholarly credibility); but their weakness in teacher education and in connections with schools calls into question their suitability on professional grounds.

In practice, however, only one of these types of education schools is truly at risk of being drummed out of the university, and that, ironically, is the education school at the pinnacle. Consider recent history. Education schools were eliminated at Yale and Johns Hopkins in the 1950s, Duke in the 1980s, and Chicago in the 1990s. This almost happened at Berkeley in the 1980s, at the same time that there were scares at Michigan and Stanford. Meanwhile education schools at regional state universities have remained unthreatened.

The reason for this striking difference in viability is in the differences in the bargain struck between the education school and the university at the opposite ends of the status ladder. At the low end, education schools bring the expected benefits to the university: a large number of low-cost students (regional state universities produce the large majority of the country's teachers) and a strong reputation for relevance to community concerns. The modest academic reputation of these schools is not a problem, since universities at this level have only a modest academic reputation themselves. These universities there-fore have less status to lose by including education; like education, they justify their programs more on practical than academic grounds. At the same time, these education schools have less status to gain from the exchange. This means that, unlike their counter-parts at the other end of the scale, they are not under compulsion to emphasize the academic at the expense of the professional. They do not feel the same need to sell out their professional mission in order to maintain academic credibility.

At the high end of the spectrum, education schools occupy shakier ground. Such a conclusion seems odd, at first glance, since these are the education schools with the strongest publication records, the biggest research grants, the most successful doctoral programs (measured by size, selectivity of admissions, and placement of graduates), and the top rankings in *U.S. News and World Report*. Life is good at such institutions—until the ax falls. The problem is that, compared with their counterparts at the former normal schools, they are in a situation where the university has more status to lose from its association with education and the education school has more status to gain from this arrangement. This means that these education schools have a very powerful incentive to abandon their professional mission in order to establish the highest possible level of academic credibility.

Consider the situation of today's elite education schools in the years after World War II, when established research universities were desperately seeking to distinguish them-selves from the lower tier of colleges and universities, which were rapidly expanding in response to the G.I. Bill. They did so by visibly increasing academic standards. In part this meant identifying weak programs and telling them to become more academic or risk elimination, which made both education and business schools obvious targets on these campuses. Both types of schools ended up adopting the same basic strategy for responding to this pressure: they abandoned undergraduate programs of professional preparation, refocused their instructional efforts at the graduate level, drew heavily on academic disciplines, and started churning out a lot of research. This strategy was mark-edly successful for both: the universities found these reconstructed schools worthy of inclusion academically, and most of these education and business schools are now at the top of their respective fields.

But this strategy had its down side. Education schools on these elite campuses had established strong academic credibility, as requested, but they had done so at the expense of their identities as professional schools. Business schools managed to avoid this prob-lem through the invention of the Masters in Business Administration, which they turned into a high status program for the professional preparation of business leaders and made the keystone of the new business school, thereby reinforcing its connection with the profession. There has been no parallel program in elite education schools, which have focused instructionally on a variety of doctoral programs while maintaining boutique programs in teacher education. As a result, these schools have come to face another threat from the university. They may be academically strong, but they can also appear professionally irrelevant. They do serious research on education, applying the disciplines of sociology, psychology, anthropology, political science, history, philosophy, statistics, linguistics, and so on. But research universities already have separate departments in each of these areas, where scholars have the high academic standing that comes with full disciplinary credibility. So administrators can easily ask: why do we have an education school to carry out disciplinary work in education, when we have the real thing elsewhere on campus? If the school of education is not a professional school, then why do we need one? If it is neither disciplinary nor professional, it has no rationale for existence as a separate school in a research university.

Therefore, a number of these elite education schools disappeared in the last 50 years, and others escaped after a close call. Many of the survivors have learned a lesson from this experience, which is that life at the top of the rankings requires a delicate balance between the academic and professional. These education schools need to be academically strong, while at the same time maintaining a modest but credible professional profile. Watching what happened to institutions that failed to heed this lesson, deans at many top education schools have worked carefully in the last 20 years to move their institutions one or two steps in the direction of the professional without threatening their academic credibility. This has meant shoring up connections with local schools, modestly increasing the education of teachers and administrators, and augmenting master's programs for practitioners.

Conclusions

Starting in independent professional schools 150 years ago, teacher education in the United States ended up in universities. This was not the result of a plan to enhance the quality of professional education for teachers. Instead, it was a side effect of the growing dominance of the university over all matters educational, which meant that teacher education, like other professional domains, had no other place to go. Education gained access to the inner sanctum of higher learning on terms that were not of its own making and that have been often problematic for its professional mission. In the terms of this bargain between the two parties, teacher education has ceded control over its professional programs, cooperated in undermining the professional quality of these programs, and allowed these programs to become marginalized within a university setting that grants them little respect. In return it has been allowed to bask in the glow of the university's high status.

The effects on professional education, however, have varied according to the university's location in the academic hierarchy. At the low end, the modest status benefits of affiliation with regional state universities have permitted education schools to maintain a relatively strong professional identity, although often at the expense of both academic and professional quality. The resulting accommodation has shown remarkable stability over time. But the same cannot be said about the situation of teacher education at the high end. Leading research universities have exerted strong pressures on education schools to pursue academic credibility at the expense of professional mission, while at the same time requiring them to maintain sufficient professional identity to differentiate themselves from the disciplines. This accommodation has been more unstable. Education schools at these institutions find it difficult to strike the right balance of the academic and professional, since the terms of that balance vary according to time and place, and the consequences of erring too far in either direction can be fatal.

NOTES

1 This section draws from Labaree, 2004, Chapter 2.
2 Chapter headings in the report tell the story of an institution failing in both dimensions: The Pursuit of Irrelevance; Inadequate Preparation; A Curriculum in Disarray; A Disconnected Faculty; Low Admission Standards; Insufficient Quality Control; Disparities in Institutional Quality (Levine, 2004). Earlier attacks in this genre include: *The Miseducation of American Teachers* (Koerner, 1963); *Ed School Follies* (Kramer, 1991); and *Tomorrow's Schools of Education* (Holmes Group, 1995).
3 For other accounts of this process, see Altenbaugh and Underwood, 1990; Eisenmann, 1990; and Labaree 2004.
4 This section draws from Labaree, 2004, Chapters 2 and 3.
5 This section draws from Labaree, 2004, Chapter 6.

REFERENCES

Altenbaugh, Richard J. & Underwood, Kathleen (1990) The evolution of normal schools. In John I. Goodlad, Roger Soder, & Kenneth A. Sirotnik (eds.), *Places where teachers are taught* (pp. 136–186). San Francisco: Jossey-Bass.

Borrowman, Merle L. (ed.) (1965) *Teacher education in America: a documentary history*. New York: Teachers College Press.

Brubacher, John S. & Rudy, Willis (1997) Professional education. In Lester F. Goodchild & Harold S. Wechsler (eds.), *ASHE reader on the history of higher education*, 2nd ed. (pp. 379–393). Boston: Pearson Custom Publishing.

Clifford, Geraldine Joncich & Guthrie, James W. (1988) *Ed school: a brief for professional education*. Chicago: University of Chicago Press.

Durkheim, Emile (1938/1969) *The evolution of educational thought: lectures on the formation and development of secondary education in France*. Boston: Routledge and Kegan Paul.

Eisenmann, Linda (1990) The influence of bureaucracy and markets: teacher education in Pennsylvania. In J.I. Goodlad, R. Soder, & K.A. Sirotnik (eds.) *Places where teachers are taught* (pp. 287–329). San Francisco: Jossey-Bass.

Flexner, Abraham (1910) *Medical education in the United States and Canada: a report to the Carnegie Foundation for the Advancement of Teaching*. New York: Carnegie Foundation for the Advancement of Teaching.

Herbst, Jurgen (1989) *And sadly teach: teacher education and professionalization in American culture*. Madison, WI: University of Wisconsin Press.

Holmes Group (1995) *Tomorrow's schools of education*. East Lansing, MI: Author.

Karabel, Jerome (2005) *The chosen: the hidden history of admission and exclusion at Harvard, Yale, and Princeton*. Boston: Houghton Mifflin.

Kerr, Clark (2001) *The uses of the university*, 5th ed. Cambridge, MA: Harvard University Press.

Koerner, James (1963) *The miseducation of American teachers*. Boston: Houghton Mifflin.

Kramer, Rita (1991) *Ed school follies: the miseducation of America's teachers*. New York: Free Press.

Labaree, David (2004) *The trouble with ed schools*. New Haven: Yale University Press.

Levine, Arthur (2006) *Educating school teachers*. Washington, DC: The Education Schools Project.

Lortie, Dan C. (1975) *Schoolteacher: a sociological study*. Chicago: University of Chicago.

Mattingly, Paul (1975) *The classless profession: American schoolmen in the nineteenth century*. New York: New York University Press.

Ogren, Christine (2005) *The American state normal school: "An instrument of great good."* New York: Palgrave Macmillan.

Powell, Arthur G. (1976) University schools of education in the twentieth century. *Peabody Journal of Education*, 54(1), 3–20.

Sedlak, Michael W. (1989) Let us go and buy a schoolmaster. In Donald Warren (ed.) *American teachers: histories of a profession at work* (pp. 257–290). New York: Macmillan.

Shulman, Lee S. (1986) Those who understand: knowledge growth in teaching. *Educational Researcher*, 15(1): 4–14

Tyack, David B. (ed.) (1967) *Turning points in American educational history*. Waltham, MA: Blaisdell Publishing Company.

University of Michigan (2005) Teaching the disciplines and the discipline of teaching: celebrating 125 years of the art and science of teaching at the University of Michigan. Conference program. Ann Arbor: University of Michigan.

Veysey, Laurence R. (1965) *The emergence of the American university*. Chicago: University of Chicago Press.

19 What kind of experience?

Preparing teachers in PDS or community settings

Marilynne Boyle-Baise
Indiana University

D. John McIntyre
Southern Illinois University

WHAT KIND OF EXPERIENCE? PREPARING TEACHERS IN PDS OR COMMUNITY SETTINGS

Where are different groups of teachers being educated, by whom, and toward what ends? What do we know about the impact of different settings and educators on teachers' knowledge and practice, on students' learning and on school change? Educational researchers and policy makers are posing these questions in an effort to find optimal conditions and settings in which to prepare future teachers.

Our purpose is to compare and consider two contexts for teacher education: professional development schools (PDSs) and community oriented settings. Both contexts can be described as efforts for reform, improving student learning and teacher preparation, but they differ considerably in the kinds of experiences teacher candidates receive. Our goal is to ponder the potential of each setting to ready teachers to serve culturally diverse students and families, especially from high poverty communities, and to explore possible linkages between the contexts that promote this end.

One of us is a scholar and advocate of the Professional Development School (PDS) Movement, the other is a student and supporter of community oriented teacher education. Both of us find traditional models of teacher preparation inadequate, especially when schools and universities are separated as sites of theory and practice, or when schools and communities are disconnected as sites for student learning. However, like the contexts we consider, we perceive good teaching and learning somewhat differently.

In order to organize our comparison, we borrow from a pamphlet published by the Institute for Educational Leadership (IEL): *Education and Community Building: Connecting Two Worlds* (Jehl *et al.*, 2001). In this work, IEL seeks to bridge gulfs between schools and community builders, by demonstrating how school reform and community development can work in unison to benefit youth and families. IEL describes positions for each group, points out tensions between them, and, then, suggests strategies for improved working relationships. Just so, we delineate dimensions of teacher training in PDSs or community settings, indicate sticking points, and ponder intersections. We begin with a snapshot of teacher education in each setting. Next, we describe principles, perspectives, and practices for each. Last, we propose a blending of experiences for an alternative view of teacher preparation.

Snapshot: a community's school

Envision the following school. The school is situated in an urban context marked by cultural diversity. It serves students and families from multiple, ethnic groups, many of whom speak languages other than English. Many families are new immigrants to the United States, struggling with poverty. This school could exist in many cities today.

This school is place where diverse families feel at home. It is a place that is student-centered, treating each student as a highly valued individual. It is a place that works with its neighbors; students do research about local concerns and help immigrants with naturalization processes. Residents think of the school as the heart of the community. They refer to it as the "community's school."

The school is guided by a dynamic, multi-lingual, locally attuned principal. He believes that a school should lead constructive change in its community. He hires multi-lingual home visitors, familiar with the neighborhood, to explain school programs to parents in their mother tongue. He organizes committees of parents, students, teachers, and community leaders to take on important decision-making tasks. He involves young people, in and out of school, with issues that concern the community.

On-site, in-service training is provided for teachers, focused on issues of race and culture. Teachers form literary groups, reading and discussing books about ethnicity. They gather information via questionnaires about students, and they begin to incorporate their knowledge into curriculum. Teachers hold themselves directly accountable to the community they serve. They speak with parents during a weekly open house at school. They are evaluated by students and use the feedback to improve their teaching.

This school is not visionary. It thrived in the 1930s, 1940s, and 1950s. The school was the Benjamin Franklin High School (BFHS) for boys in East Harlem, New York City, and the principal was Leonard Covello (e.g. Covello, 1936; McGee Banks, 2005; Peebles, 1969). Today, similar efforts go by many names: Beacons, Bridges to Success, Caring Communities, and University-assisted Community Schools (Dryfoos, 2002). Often called full-service schools, they locate educational, social, and health services under one roof (Blank *et al.*, 2003). Like BFHS, they tend to serve economically stressed, urban locales where the population is ethnically and racially diverse (Dryfoos, 2002).

Snapshot: a professional development school

Envision the following school. This school is a place where student's academic achievement is uppermost. The school has forged new relationships with the university to reform teacher education and to improve student learning. University faculty can be seen in the school's halls everyday; they teach their classes on school grounds. Teacher education faculty focus on state standards, as hallmarks of academic excellence, and teach pre-service teachers "best" practices for meeting them.

Teacher candidates learn on-site, remaining at one school for several semesters and becoming well acquainted with school aims, policies, and procedures and with teachers, students, and classrooms. They collaborate with university faculty and teachers to undertake action research projects aimed at the improvement of student learning. A problem-solving atmosphere prevails.

Parents have high expectations for their children in this school. They are satisfied with its strong focus on academics, especially when "dumbing down" of curriculum often seems the rule in high poverty schools. They look forward to regular communication with teachers, including frequent parent-teacher conferences, about the academic progress of their children. They expect higher test scores on standardized, state exams than was the rule in more traditional settings.

Teacher candidates see themselves as professionals, honing their skills in a model atmosphere, underpinned by research and aimed toward their development of expertise. They are mentored by teachers, as in conventional teacher education programs, but teacher educators mentor them as well. The school, like the medical model it emulates, is a clinical site for excellence in regard to student achievement, educational research, and teacher training.

KEY IDEAS, AND PRINCIPLES: A COMMUNITY ORIENTED VIEW

Community oriented teacher education is not easily defined because the term serves as an umbrella for diverse initiatives. For our focus, it means field placement in schools or field experiences, like service learning, in communities with culturally diverse and/or lower income populations. We examine ways in which service learning, cultural immersion, and participation in community schools impacts teacher education.

Service learning

Service learning probably is the most common effort to address community issues in teacher education. Service learning eases a community orientation into teacher education because it can be included as an "add-on" to conventional courses, without disrupting or displacing other subject matter. Service learning allows pre-service teachers to work with and learn from local youth and adults in the process of doing something worthwhile. It can foster greater comfort with people unlike oneself. And, it can cultivate the idea that teaching is public service and that teachers serve as educational leaders for an increasingly diverse public.

Many practices are identified as service learning; not all support a community orientation to teaching (e.g. Boyle-Baise, 1999; Densmore, 2000; Butin, 2003). Charitable endeavors meet immediate needs, but leave deficit views of others in tact (e.g. Henry, 2003). Tutoring helps pre-service teachers hone their teaching skills, but provides few contacts with adults and limited opportunities to understand the social context in which learners live (e.g. Boyle-Baise & Kilbane, 2000).

Critical service learning (e.g. Rhoads, 1997; Rosenberger, 2000), justice oriented service learning (e.g. Wade, 2001) or multicultural service learning (Boyle-Baise, 2002) aims to affirm diversity, build community, and question inequity. Culturally diverse and/or high poverty communities are viewed from an asset-based position: as places with resources and strengths, not only as sites with problems (e.g. Kretzmann, 1992). Learners work with constituents, developing relationships of trust. Issues of race, culture, and power are discussed as part of reflection upon field work (e.g. Jones et al., 2005; Pompa, 2005). Critical service learning strongly supports a community orientation to teaching.

Cultural immersion

In a study of 100 members of the National Association for Multicultural Education, cultural immersion was one of the key factors that influenced respondents' commitment to multicultural education (Paccione, 2000). Cultural immersion experiences helped educators venture outside their cultural comfort zone and transformed their understanding of others.

For more than thirty years, cultural immersion projects at Indiana University-Bloomington (IU) have supplemented conventional student teaching, providing prospective teachers with cultural insights and developing community teacher knowledge (e.g. Stachowski & Mahan, 1998). The American Indian Reservation Project (AIRP) prepares and places student teachers for 17-week teaching assignments in schools across the Navajo Nation.

During the academic year prior to student teaching, pre-service teachers undergo extensive cultural education for their placement sites, including sessions with consultants from host groups. During student teaching, they live in Bureau of Indian Affairs dormitories, providing tutoring, companionship, and activities for Navajo youth. Participants teach and immerse themselves in the lives and cultures of the people with whom they work (Stachowski & Mahan, 1998). They perform at least one service learning project and submit reports in which they reflect on cultural values and issues.

Through immersion, pre-service teachers gain deep, cultural knowledge of their sites, recognize the worth of local wisdom, commit to service learning, and create culturally relevant curricula (Stachowski & Brantmeier, 2002; Stachowski & Frey, in press; Zeicher & Melnick, 1996). The idea of immersion suggests the need for long-term, local, interaction to gain cultural insights about one's future students.

Community schools

Community schools are a definitive location for teachers prepared to serve community. Community schools are not a new idea. Fueled by the Charles Stewart Mott Foundation, a community education movement gained national visibility in the 1930s. In 1933, Frank Manley initiated "lighted schools" in Flint Michigan. Eventually, 50 school buildings offered after school and summer programs, health services, and community education programs (Dryfoos, 2002).

Beginning in the mid-1980s, community schools took root anew. Community schools built on the experience of lighted schools to in order to help contemporary young people succeed. In 1997, a group of educators and social service leaders formed the Coalition for Community Schools to support an array of school-based, community education endeavors (Dryfoos *et al.*, 2005). The Coalition for Community Schools defines a community school as a "set of partnerships and a place where services, supports, and opportunities lead to improved student learning, stronger families, and healthier communities" (2000, p. 1). Over 1,000 schools are now in operation (Dryfoos, 2002).

While community schools are well underway, efforts to prepare teachers to work in them are almost non-existent. Thirty-five years ago, Leonard Covello suggested teachers for community schools should: "should get the major part of their training on the job" (Peebles, 1969, p. 19). Recently, Martin Blank, Staff Director for the Coalition for Community Schools, suggested the same thing (Martin Blank, personal communication, June 27, 2005). Teachers, he said, bring "personal conviction" to community schools and, then, "learn the rest on the job."

We can find seeds of principles for community teacher preparation in words and deeds from earlier days. Leonard Covello wanted prospective teachers to "get off the college campus and rub elbows with the people they will later be dealing with" (Peebles, 1969, p. 17). He wanted them to understand youth and their families through personal involvement. "The child will have a different meaning to the teacher if the teacher has been directly involved in the child's life in the child's own community" (Peebles, p. 19).

As noted in our snapshot, Covello initiated comprehensive in-service programs for his faculty (McGee Banks, 2005). At BFHS, in-service training focused on learning about student's cultural backgrounds, addressing family concerns, and participating in neighborhood affairs. Education was perceived broadly, as something that took place in and out of school. We daresay these aims retain legitimacy for community oriented teacher preparation today.

Recently, Peter Murrell (2001, pp. 5–7) delineated principles that restate Covello's proposals and reiterate roles for service learning and cultural immersion in community oriented teacher preparation.

1 Schools of education should help urban teachers develop a system of accomplished practice, or professional and instructional activities that promote academic and personal development for diverse learners.
2 Accomplished practice should be articulated as a set of standards for urban schools with diverse student bodies.
3 Community teachers should participate in a rich array of field experiences, including immersion in collaborative, inquiry oriented contexts and in urban, community settings.
4 Any candidate can become a community teacher, given sufficient opportunity to learn accomplished practice and to gain cultural insights.
5 The development of community teachers requires assistance from a network of colleagues, including successful urban teachers, parents, and community members, rather than from a single mentor teacher.
6 The right context for teacher development is community-dedicated, practice-oriented, urban-focused field work.
7 Teacher education should be considered ecological, with intersecting, mutually reinforcing, levels of experience and expertise.

Murrell introduces the idea of accomplished practice to our discussion, as learning successful, teaching strategies for particular populations with whom teachers work.

PRINCIPLES: A PDS VIEW

The Holmes Group originated the term professional development school in their 1986 publication of *Tomorrow's Teachers*. A PDS is expected to create a new kind of partnership between universities and P-12 schools. University faculty and P-12 teachers work together for joint aims as expectations and roles of each become more complex and intertwined than in traditional field placements (Book, 1996). The Holmes Group (1986) envisioned partnerships between universities and P-12 schools that provide opportunities for teachers and administrators to influence the development of their profession while, at the same time, university faculty have the opportunity to increase the relevance of their work. Collaboration occurs through mutual problem solving on issues related to student learning, shared teaching at the university and schools, and cooperative, innovative supervision of teacher candidates.

The concept of PDSs was influenced by the medical profession's teaching hospitals (Book, 1996; Koehnecke, 2001). In these settings, future physicians are placed in hospitals with licensed doctors, and their training is supported by interaction with medical researchers. The physician-trainee practices with real patients under the tutelage of a practicing doctor, gaining experience in actual, rather than simulated, medical situations and emergencies. In many ways, this approach mirrors Covello's assertion that a major part of a prospective teacher's training should be on the job.

This is not to say that collaboration and partnerships are new to teacher education. The need for novice teachers to gain experiences during their early preparation historically led to arrangements between colleges/universities and school districts. Staff development for licensed teachers also provided opportunities for higher education and school districts to work together. However, collaboration is fraught with potential problems and risks. Byrd and McIntyre (1999) suggest that one unanticipated outcome of the PDS movement may be better understanding of these obstacles and more incentive to collaborate in schools and universities.

Several groups developed principles to guide the development and implementation of PDSs. For example, in 1993 Frank Murray articulated features of effective PDSs. These include:

1   Understanding the content by all teachers is the goal of the school.
2   It is the intention to teach important knowledge and for students to master that even if it means that they have exposure to less information.
3   The goals of the school apply to all pupils, including those who are hard to teach.
4   Teachers use dialectical instruction, which is more responsive to the needs and understanding of the individual students.
5   Students are required to be active in their interaction with the knowledge because it is perceived their understanding is dependent on the context for knowledge.
6   Valid assessment is used to determine the students' abilities to use the information gained in real-world contexts.
7   The learning community in a PDS models the values students are to acquire, including the demonstration of a negotiated, dialectical learning process.
8   The professional teacher is a continual learner who seeks to collaborate with others to respond to the learning needs of students.
9   The school organization is structured to allow teachers to have time for reflection, planning, and consultation necessary for a dialectical learning environment.
10 The goal is to bring integrated support services to the needs of the students.
11 The PDS is a center of inquiry that contributes to the scholarly literature and that works to solve practical problems related to teaching and learning.

According to these principles, teachers should master content, become students of teaching, collaborate with peers on inquiry, gain expertise in constructed learning, and use valid forms of assessment to determine what students learned.

From the Holmes Group, the Holmes Partnership evolved. This network of universities, schools, community agencies and national professional organizations work together to improve teaching and learning for all children by creating high quality professional development and by fostering significant school renewal. The Holmes Partnership (1996) put forth six goals to assist the development and assessment of quality PDS partnerships. These include:

- Goal 1: High Quality Professional Preparation—provide exemplary professional preparation and development programs for public school educators.
- Goal 2: Simultaneous Renewal—engage in simultaneous renewal of public K-12 schools and teacher education programs.
- Goal 3: Equity, Diversity, Cultural Competence—actively work on equity, diversity and cultural competence in K-12 schools, higher education, and the education profession.
- Goal 4: Scholarly Inquiry and Programs of Research—conduct and disseminate educational research and engage in scholarly activities that advance knowledge, improve teaching and learning for all youth, inform the preparation and development of educators, and influence educational policy and practice.
- Goal 5: School and University-Based Faculty Development—provide high quality doctoral programs for the future education professoriate and for advanced professional development of school-based educators.
- Goal 6: Policy Initiation—engage in policy development and analysis related to public schools and the preparation of educators.

These goals reiterate the importance of professionalizing teachers, through exemplary teacher preparation and professional development programs (based on the latest research). School renewal is centered on student learning, again based on research. A new aim is to affirm diversity and to develop cultural competence through teacher education and professional development.

In 2001, the National Council for the Accreditation of Teacher Education (NCATE) introduced standards to define and guide PDSs. NCATE defines a PDS as an environment that supports candidate and faculty development within the context of meeting all children's needs. PDS partners must be guided by a common vision of teaching and learning grounded in research, share responsibility for teacher preparation, blend their expertise to meet common goals, hold themselves publicly accountable for meeting common goals, and commit themselves to prepare teacher candidates and faculty to meet the needs of diverse student populations.

So, what does teacher education mean in a PDS? PDSs should be places of professional excellence and inquiry where teacher candidates practice innovative techniques, under the tutelage of fine teachers and scholars, like the medical profession.

STICKING POINTS

PDSs seek to professionalize the teacher, developing a culture of academic expertise. Community oriented efforts downplay specialization, fearing that it distances teachers from communities. Instead, teachers are urged to blend school and community cultures. PDSs focus primarily on students' academic achievement, while community schools take a broad view of student development as academic progress, personal well-being, cultural affirmation, and social engagement. PDSs emphasize linkages between schools and universities. Community oriented efforts stress connections between schools and communities. PDSs aim to be centers of educational excellence. Community oriented schools aim to be anchors of communities.

While PDSs call for attention to diversity, particularly in terms of student achievement, there is little indication that it is central to the movement. Alternatively, the affirmation of diversity is the "lingua franca" of community-dedicated initiatives. PDSs call for integrated services to support youth, but, again, there is little indication of its centrality.

Education of the whole child, meeting education, health, and social needs, is paramount for community initiatives.

PERSPECTIVES: A COMMUNITY ORIENTED VIEW

Leonard Covello (1958/1970) entitled his autobiography, *The Heart is the Teacher*. His heart literally beat with the pulse of his East Harlem neighborhood. His students' issues were his issues, affecting him personally and professionally. Covello believed that the school should be a major force in community development. He utilized school resources to assist student growth, provide adult education, challenge ethnic denigration, and combat disruptive forces of urban poverty. Covello thought of himself as a teacher with heart. What modes of thought and action might ground community oriented teachers— teachers with heart?

Multicultural understanding

One of the problems Leonard Covello faced was a dearth of multicultural understanding among his faculty. The teachers were subject matter specialists who did not know how to address issues of culture and race in the classroom (McGee Banks, 2005). In his auto-biography, Covello (1958/1970) recalled a time when an English teacher asked him to expel a boy who was troublesome in her class. The boy wanted to finish high school and asked for a second chance. The teacher was: "young, new to East Harlem, and could not wait to be reassigned to a school in a better neighborhood ... She had been raised in Pelham, a peaceful suburb of New York, and this was her first regular job" (p. 200). Covello advised the teacher:

> It's easier for me ... because I was raised in the same way and have lived all my life in the same neighborhood ... But, if you convince yourself deep down that these boys ... are basically not much different from others you have known, and that they would like to be liked by you, then most of your troubles will be over."
> (Covello, 1958/1970, p. 200)

Not much has changed. Today, teachers rarely understand a community to which they do not belong as well as they think they do (Sleeter, 2000). They assume they know students well because they see them in school everyday. They think of multicultural education narrowly, as the addition of cultural information to lessons. Teacher education courses can begin to help teachers understand issues of culture, race, and power, but community knowledge can not be learned in college classrooms alone. Community teachers need to learn about their school communities by participating in them.

Ethic of service

An ethic of service is a "habit of the heart" (Bellah *et al.*, 1985, p. 37), or a conviction that can ground community teaching. Several concepts can assist teacher's development of a service ethic. They can imagine themselves as servant leaders (Greenleaf, 1977), or leaders who see themselves as servants first. Servant leaders are learners who respond to problems by listening and, then, by offering their resources to assist the aims of those they serve. As they genuinely serve others, their effort is recognized as local leadership.

Jane Addams, leader of Hull-House, a settlement house in Chicago in the early 1900s, demonstrated servant leadership (Daynes & Longo, 2004). She started her career thinking that Hull-House would provide cultural uplift to immigrant families. But, as Addams spent time with her neighbors, she realized that families brought cultural traditions with them to their new country. She began to work collaboratively with her neighbors to develop educational, cultural, and political programs that served their needs.

Nel Noddings (1984) proposed another idea that can underpin a service ethos: an ethic of care. To care is to feel and act in empathy *with* the concerns and hopes of others. Of course, the crux of the matter is making connections with others, who may be different from oneself. Care *with* not *for* as a collaborative mood of mutual human-ness must be at the root of a community orientation toward teaching.

Community teachers need to think of teaching as public service and of themselves as public servants. Accountability should be redefined to mean a sense of responsibility for child, family, and community development. A sense of dedication to the greater good should underpin teachers' work.

Asset-based view

From a needs-based perspective, distressed, city neighborhoods are overwhelmed with problems. They are places where helpless individuals and hapless organizations predominate. This view prevails among those who make policy and distribute resources. It is often taken up by the media, and, eventually, it sifts down to pre-service teachers (Boyle-Baise & Sleeter, 2000).

From an asset-based perspective, needs in neighborhoods, while very real, describe only part of a community's reality. The other part is local strengths, wisdom, and resources. It is what people know and can do. It is its formal and informal organizations, its businesses, its buildings, and, especially, its schools (Kretzmann, 1992). Teachers are key assets; they are a pool of highly educated adults who contribute to efforts of local groups.

Community teachers need to perceive even the most devastated neighborhoods as places with internal strengths. They need to see themselves as people with skills and knowledge who can assist neighborhood improvement. They need to view school-community partnerships as promising avenues for community development and empowerment.

Broad, relational view of education

Jane Addams claimed that "the settlement is a protest against a restricted view of education" (Addams, cited in Daynes & Longo, 2004). She perceived education broadly, relationally, and publicly. Education was not distanced from a community, but instead drew from it. Education was not specialized, but something of public, universal interest.

Hull-House was a model of learning that took place outside the school and involved children and adults from diverse backgrounds. It offered a kindergarten, music school, drama training, citizenship classes, and general adult education. It served as a mediator between neighborhood residents and other institutions, including schools. The Hull-House experience exemplifies an inclusive, interactive, locally attentive view of what it means to be educated.

Leonard Covello (Peebles, 1969) found it natural that teachers would think of education as something that occurred in classrooms—they spent the better part of their lives there. He submitted that even practicing teachers saw only the four walls of the school not the community in which the school was located. He thought it was extremely important to get teacher candidates out of university classrooms and into community experiences as soon as possible.

Community teacher knowledge

Murrell envisions the "community teacher," as someone who "possesses contextualized knowledge of the culture, community, and identity of the children and families he or she serves and draws on this knowledge to create the core teaching practices necessary for effectiveness in a diverse setting" (2001, p. 52). Community teacher knowledge is knowledge of the lives, cultural traditions, and experiences of students.

Community teacher knowledge is called by many names, including culturally relevant teaching (Ladson-Billings, 1994) and culturally responsive pedagogy (Gay, 2000). Characteristics include: validation of the cultural knowledge, prior experiences, and frames of reference of ethnically diverse students; attention to cultural responsiveness in curriculum content, classroom climate, and instructional techniques and assessments; commitment to student success, and promotion of student engagement as productive members of their ethnic groups and of the national society (Gay, 2000, pp. 29–34).

Murrell (2001) submits that most teacher candidates drawn to community oriented teaching will come from urban neighborhoods, like those served, but that any person can become a community teacher if he/she makes an effort to gain local knowledge. A community teacher needs to gain community teacher knowledge and to practice culturally responsive teaching.

PERSPECTIVES: A PDS VIEW

From a PDS perspective, teachers should be content experts, helping all students learn constructively, in interaction with knowledge. Teachers should be learners, continually striving, through inquiry, to comprehend and improve student learning. Teachers should be collaborators, working with university partners and school peers to reform schools (Murray, 1993; NCATE, 2001). Teachers should be accountable for what students learn. The following notions ground the preparation of teachers for PDSs.

Mastery of content knowledge

A call for enhanced teacher content knowledge helped propel the PDS movement (Teitel, 2003). Federal, Title II legislation, in the late 1990s, resulted in Teacher Report Cards, requiring teacher education programs to report the pass rates of teacher candidates on content exams. Title II Legislation also required arts and science faculty to become more involved in teacher education programs as in collaborations with schools. NCATE then required an 80 percent pass rate on content-area exams for completers of teacher education programs.

Obviously teachers must be competent in their content knowledge to effectively and efficiently present this subject matter to students. This point grounds the No Child Left Behind Act's (2002) definition of a "highly qualified teacher" as a person who passes a test of content knowledge. This definition assumes that subject matter, which can be assessed on a standardized test, is what teachers need to know to teach well (Cochran-Smith, 2004). Teacher education programs have responded to this political pressure with renewed emphasis on the acquisition of subject matter knowledge. However, Wise (2005) argues that this restricted definition of a "highly qualified teacher" does not emanate from the teaching profession's values and beliefs.

Those in the PDS movement argue that, although knowledge of subject matter is essential, it must be linked to practice in classrooms that meets the needs of all students.

This aim is accomplished by having courses taught in the schools, by collaborating with practicing teachers as well as with arts and science faculty, and by increasing the time teacher candidates spend in classrooms observing, tutoring, and teaching students. PDSs aim to increase teacher candidates' subject matter knowledge as well as their understanding of the school and student culture. However, a question remains. Does a strong emphasis on subject matter knowledge interfere with the teacher candidates' understanding of student and community needs?

Learning through inquiry

The Holmes Partnership (1996) established scholarly inquiry as one of its primary goals for effective PDSs. This Partnership urges PDSs to conduct and disseminate educational research in order to advance knowledge, improve teaching and learning for all youth, inform teacher preparation and professional development, and influence educational policy.

The emphasis on research is no surprise given PDSs' comparison to teaching hospitals where future doctors learn on-site and where researchers conduct studies to advance knowledge and skills within their profession. Similarly, inquiry has been implemented in PDSs through several avenues. First, teacher education scholars have begun to conduct research on teacher development, supervisory and collaborative practices, and student achievement. Second, inquiry within PDSs focuses on action research conducted by teacher candidates, practicing teachers, and university faculty on site. Dana *et al.*, (2001) argue that inquiry must be a central feature of a PDS. Teitel (2003) claims that the conduct of inquiry in PDSs helps ensure that new practices, strategies and/or policies actually lead to improved learning of students and adults. Although much can be learned from conducting action research projects in PDSs, there is still much to learn about the actual process of inquiry and how it contributes to teacher development (Crocco *et al.*, 2003; Price & Valli, 2005).

Collaboration/partnership

Teitel (2003) asserts that the words "collaboration" and "partnership" are two of the most overused and misused words in the late twentieth and early twenty-first centuries. Yet, authentic collaboration and partnership between institutions of higher education and P-12 schools are at the core of the PDS concept. As Teitel (2003) reminds us, however, some schools call themselves PDSs simply because a university places student teachers in their building with no other substantive changes in program, philosophy, or policy. So, whereas the school may be "cooperating" with the university, there is little, if any, "collaboration" that can result in transformative change at the school or university level. Teitel (2003) describes collaboration as "complex interpersonal and inter-organizational undertakings" (p. 10).

PDS advocates believe that schooling and teacher education are intertwined and that transformative change of either endeavor cannot occur without collaboration between the two partners. Valli (1999) states that the existence of collaborative partnerships represents a sea of change in the way higher education and school systems have typically related in the past. She reminds us that school-university partnerships must transform the cultures of both contexts to become more than individualized initiatives by committed educators.

Accountability for student learning

Dedication to P-12 student needs is a cornerstone of the PDS movement. In an era of accountability, however, this focus has narrowed to concern with student academic achievement. Few educators question the right of the public to hold teachers accountable for student learning and to expect higher education institutions to take some responsibility for this aim. Unfortunately, as Cochran-Smith (2003) argues, this charge for accountability has often been interpreted solely as higher scores on standardized achievement tests.

The emphasis on improving student achievement is linked commonly to the PDS goal of promoting equity in the classroom, especially of decreasing the achievement gap between students of different race and class backgrounds. Teitel (2003) cites an example of the Boston public school system providing over a quarter of a million dollars annually to fund local PDS interns. He pressed for evidence that PDS preparation made the interns more effective in reducing the achievement gap among Boston students. However, as noted later in this chapter, PDSs have been criticized for focusing so much on academic achievement that they have not lived up to their promise to promote equity in schools. It is interesting to note O'Sullivan's (2005) description of her interviews with potential teacher candidates:

> For many years, I have been interviewing candidates who hope to come into our teacher education program. One of the questions we always ask is, "Why do you want to be a teacher?" The answers to this question are remarkably similar across time, major, race, and gender, nearly all candidates answer this question with the same version of "I think I can make a difference here." When pressed to clarify what "make a difference" means, I have yet to have a candidate dream of raising the end-of-the-year achievement scores for children. What candidates do mention when trying to articulate making a difference is a vision of helping children become better people, of helping them become more competent and more caring.
>
> (O'Sullivan, 2005, p. 3)

O'Sullivan's statement reminds those of us involved in PDS work that while focusing on improved student achievement and decreased achievement gaps between different races and class backgrounds is a worthy goal, it should not be our sole focus for equity.

STICKING POINTS

Teacher candidates who participate in PDS or in community oriented initiatives are encouraged to develop very different mindsets. Imagine their confusion when they undertake service learning in one part of their program and end up student teaching in a PDS! In community oriented activities, pre-service teachers are urged to gain cultural knowledge and cross-cultural experiences. In PDSs, pre-service teachers are urged to become subject matter specialists, possibly at the cost of learning about diversity.

Where community oriented teachers are invited to consider themselves as public servants, PDS teachers are encouraged to think of themselves as professionals. One perspective can bring teachers closer to those they serve; the other can distance them from constituents. For a community emphasis, teachers are asked to think of education broadly, but for a PDS focus, teachers are expected to concentrate on what happens inside schools.

Both contexts support an inquiry stance for teachers, but, the focus of research differs. In PDSs, inquiry should aim to decrease achievement test gaps. In community engagements, inquiry should aim to learn more about students as whole human beings. Inquiry, as a potential intersection between contexts, is discussed later in the chapter.

PRACTICES: A COMMUNITY ORIENTED VIEW

How can teacher candidates deepen their multicultural understandings, practice an ethic of service, grasp education broadly, identify local assets, and gain community wisdom? A body of evidence is growing in regard to these questions, and we share it here. We organize these findings by topics of our discussion, but they are overlapping and interdependent.

Gaining community teacher knowledge

Prospective teachers can learn through service to local communities, especially when service is collaborative in nature and augmented by course work. Seidl (Seidl *et al.*, in press) arranged an internship for pre-service teachers at an African American Baptist church. Pre-service teachers worked with adults in programs created for children from the community, such as tutoring or latchkey programs. Their field experience was supported by course work focused on racism, privilege, and African American culture, and by reflection guided by university instructors and by church members. Prospective teachers considered themes that arose from their work with church youth. Through this process, prospective teachers identified specific information that could help them teach in culturally responsive ways.

Kidd *et al.* (2003) contribute findings that support Seidl's work. As part of a class in early childhood education, pre-service teachers developed a relationship with a family whose cultural was different from their own. Their listened to family stories and used the information to plan learning experiences responsive to the family's needs. Most pre-service teachers met with their selected families three or four times, often in their homes. Pre-service teachers reported that they: understood a culture different from their own, felt able to work with their focus family, and felt able to transfer their learning to work with other families.

Another way to link pre-service teachers to local wisdom is to involve people intimately acquainted with localities in a community of practice as co-teacher educators (Murrell, 2001). A community of practice is marked by mutual engagement, joint enterprise, and shared repertoire (Wenger, 1998). The most common, teacher preparation collaboration is the clinical triad which counsels student teachers. Murrell (2001) suggests opening the triad to a range of advisors for teachers' practice. Parents, university faculty, teachers, and community leaders could serve as a community of practice for student teachers.

One of us witnessed the power of community people as educators for prospective teachers. Lynne worked with a community partnership to co-teach a service learning component for a multicultural education course (Boyle-Baise *et al.*, 2001). Her partners represented a variety of positions and roles: from church leaders to Head Start staff, to community center directors. They helped plan, implement, and evaluate service learning. Their input greatly diversified the knowledge pre-service teachers gained.

Identifying local assets

Teachers can gain community teacher knowledge and identify local assets through the study of community-as-text (Blank et al., 2003). This approach uses the history, culture, and conditions of the community as content for learning. Pre-service teachers' role is that of a facilitator, co-learner, and link to community resources for students. Place-based education is another derivation of this focus. Students "go local" (Smith, 2002, p. 30) to learn more about the historical issues, cultural traditions, environmental issues, and civic processes in their home space.

Several projects illustrate ways in which studies of community-as-text reveal local assets. Under the auspices of the West Philadelphia Improvement Corps college history majors, high school students, and former neighborhood residents teamed up to study the history of a community displaced by urban renewal. College and high school students gained a wealth of knowledge from local residents, resulting in "Black Bottom Sketches," plays about the community in earlier days (Coalition for Community Schools, 2000, p. 9).

For the Banneker History Project (Boyle-Baise, 2005), pre-service teachers helped high school students reconstruct the history of a once segregated school in their town. Under pre-service teacher's guidance, high school students interviewed surviving alumni of the school. They tapped into funds of wisdom (Moll et al., 1992) in the form of personal stories about school segregation. Prospective teachers identified elders of color as significant sources of knowledge about past and present racism. They started to wonder about ways that local residents might serve as resources for historic studies of their home towns.

Practicing an ethic of service

Educators have utilized service learning to help prospective teachers (and other service providers): question assumptions, confront racism, consider cultural difference, and begin to think about positively about serving in pluralistic contexts (e.g. Rosner-Salazar, 2003; Wade, 2000). However, much depends on the rationale for and type of service learning. As Morton (1995) notes, a mismatch of course goals and service work can stymie course aims. For example, a charitable experience does not prod critical, social insights (e.g. Cipolle, 2004). Further, unless a service ethic is incorporated through out teacher education programs; pre-service teachers can see service learning as something peripheral to teacher preparation (e.g. Boyle-Baise, 2005).

When service is considered integral to teacher education, as in the AIRP, pre-service teachers can gain cultural insights and cultivate an ethic of service. In Navajo communities, pre-service teachers believed that their service efforts boosted their acceptance, as local residents recognized their willingness to work and learn. Pre-service teachers began to see themselves as community members and to look for ways to continue to serve. They started to rethink their roles as educators to include both teaching and community service (Stachowski & Frey, in press).

Participating in cultural immersion

Cultural immersion is an experience with multiple benefits for a community orientation to teaching. It can foster deep learning about another culture, assist the identification of local resources, and prompt commitment to service learning. In studies of the AIRP, Mahan and Stachowski (1993–1994) found that student teachers identified community people, such as American Indian dorm staff and parents of students as important sources for their learning. Their service learning projects fostered greater community teacher knowledge and more commitment to making service part of the curriculum. Further, Stachowski (1997) found that 26 percent of student teachers used their local awareness to create culturally relevant teaching units.

Even short-term immersion projects seem to help develop dispositions, knowledge, and skills needed to become a community teacher. Amazingly, Wiest (1998) found that when students spent at least one hour, alone, participating fully in a cultural context quite foreign to them they: dispelled stereotypes, grasped different cultural frames of reference, and increased their ability to take perspectives of others.

Ference and Bell (2004) found that pre-service teachers deepened their understanding of Latino, Spanish-speaking youth in just two weeks of field experience. Their work compares with AIRP, suggesting components for effective cultural immersion: intensive cultural education prior to field work, lived experiences with host families, involvement in community activities, and regular reflection on issues of culture, race, and power.

PRACTICES: A PDS VIEW

Does the PDS model hold promise for transforming the learning community in schools? Can teachers learn to be masters of content knowledge, investigators of learning, collaborative educational partners, and experts in student achievement? We explore bodies of research in response to these questions. Findings should be considered overlapping and interdependent.

Mastering content

We did not find much evidence that focused expressly on teacher's content knowledge, although a firm grasp of subject matter is key to the PDS movement. Instead, teacher knowledge is defined as pedagogical content knowledge.

Paese (2003) examined two groups of teacher candidates who had different types of PDS experiences. The first had two PDS experiences prior to student teaching and a PDS student teacher experience. The other group had two PDS experiences prior to student teaching, but had a traditional, non-PDS student teaching experiences. At the conclusion of student teaching there were significant differences in favor of the Total PDS group in areas of role preparedness, personal teacher efficacy and general teacher efficacy. Ridley *et al.* (2005) conducted a two-year study that compared the lesson planning, teaching effectiveness, post-lesson reflectivity and content retention of professional teaching knowledge for candidates at a PDS or a campus-based program. Scores of PDS-prepared student teachers were consistently higher than their campus-prepared peers, but no statistically significant differences were discovered. However, during the first year of teaching, PDS-prepared teachers scored significantly higher than campus-prepared teachers on: managing student behavior, maintaining students' interest during instruction, and providing immediate feedback. This finding is supported by previous studies conducted by Houston *et al.* (1999); Sharpe *et al.* (1999); Stallings (1991) and Wait (2000).

Acting as inquirers

Although inquiry is a cornerstone of the PDS movement, there is very little research that looks at its effectiveness. Galassi *et al.* (1999) reported on a PDS project that focused on collaborative inquiry as a vehicle for developing teachers and for enhancing student achievement at a middle school. Inquiry groups focused on looping, working with book groups, and resiliency of students. Anecdotal evidence suggests that the inquiry group activities had an empowering effect on teachers and that teaching practices were refined.

Rock and Levin (2002) conducted a study that examined the effect of collaborative action research on teacher candidates. Data were obtained from five teacher candidates, each of whom worked with an on-site teacher educator mentor. Engagement in action research provided teacher candidates with an opportunity to explore images of themselves as teachers, to wrestle with novice concerns of teaching, to interact with and study students in systematic ways, to gain valuable insights into the curriculum and their roles and responsibilities, and to realize the importance of focused inquiry for their professional development.

Participating in collaboration

McBee and Moss (2002) reported on the efforts of a PDS to address teacher and student needs at a time when inclusion began to increase in a large, urban, P-8 school. Workshops on collaborative learning and teaching as well as developing caring communities were offered to teacher candidates and experienced teachers. Test performance of special education students in the inclusion classrooms improved despite reading skills that were well below grade level.

Fisher *et al.* (2004) reported that students in classrooms with student teachers in a PDS had significantly higher achievement gains than those students who were in classrooms taught by classroom teachers alone. The presence of the student teacher allowed for more small group instruction and for more co-teaching, improving achievement.

Fischetti *et al.* (2000) examined the benefits of a yearlong experience for teacher candidates in a high school PDS. Interviews revealed that the candidates felt more comfortable with their classroom and more knowledgeable about their teacher's planning and responsibilities, and that they developed more meaningful relationships with their cooperating teachers. They felt at ease in talking with teachers about instructional issues.

Fostering student achievement

Student achievement is the sin qua non of PDSs, without proof of student learning there is little reason to promote the PDS model. We culled through the research, looking for varied foci on student learning and for strength of findings. We report a sample of the research here.

Houston *et al.* (1999) described a consortium of four universities and three school districts designed to prepare teachers for urban settings. They reported that, over a three-year period, student achievement in reading, mathematics and writing on the Texas Assessment of Academic Skills (TAAS) increased in PDS schools as opposed to non-PDS schools. Also, a greater proportion of PDS students passed the ExCET tests than their peers in the traditional programs. PDS students were significantly more on-task than their non-PDS peers. In addition, PDS students were more likely to be placed in small group instruction and less frequently placed in whole group activities than were students in the non-PDS classes.

Klingner *et al.* (2004) examined the possibility of enhancing the achievement of special education students in an urban PDS. Students' standardized test scores increased over an eight-year period and were higher than the scores of students in non-PDS schools. Interviews with teachers and administrators revealed that they perceived students benefited in academic, social/affective and general domains.

Several studies found pre-service teachers focused on classroom management as their key concern. We group them here to indicate the centrality of this concern.

Neubert and Binko (1998) studied the effectiveness of a PDS in Maryland. Their study consisted of two groups of teacher candidates. One group consisted of 11 teacher candidates who enrolled in a discipline-specific methods class and a three-credit internship at a PDS. The second group of ten candidates also was enrolled in the same discipline methods class but elected not to do the internship in the PDS. Data showed that PDS teacher candidates performed "at a competent level" while non-PDS candidates performed at a "minimally satisfactory" level. Researchers concluded that the PDS experience was more effective in preparing the teacher candidates to maintain classroom discipline, use technology effectively for instruction, and reflect upon their own teaching.

Conaway and Mitchell (2004) studied the impact of a year-long internship on 22 interns in a PDS setting. Interview questions focused instructional responsibilities and decision-making, behavior management, interactions with mentor teachers, university supervisor support, and content of seminars. PDS interns consistently reported an emphasis on "positive management techniques." PDS interns reported more responsibility for making and implementing instructional decisions than one-semester student teachers.

McIntyre *et al.* (2006) examined the impact of a yearlong, induction, field-based master's degree program for recently certified teachers: Teaching Fellows. Teaching Fellows believed that they were better prepared for the classroom than their non-PDS peers in the areas of classroom management and the ability to meet the needs of their students.

A similar study was conducted by Giles *et al.* (2001). Teaching Fellows answered questions about their greatest satisfaction in teaching and about their greatest concerns. Professional survival and classroom management were the top categories cited by the Teaching Fellows. Most of the Fellows were focused on their desire to manage the classroom better so that more learning could take place.

Summary

In each of these cases, the programs delivered through the PDSs resulted in improved preparation of teacher candidates when compared to the non-PDS programs. While we found few studies on teachers' content knowledge, or on their abilities to investigate student learning, many studies indicate that PDSs improve teachers' capacities to foster student achievement, and some show teachers are more able to collaborate with peers.

STICKING POINTS

Our comparisons continue to suggest an inside/outside emphasis. From a community view, future teachers need to make connections outside schools, in communities. From a PDS view, future teachers need to concentrate on what happens inside schools, on student learning.

We get the sense that PDS practices are not transformative, instead prospective teachers instruct students effectively in conventional settings. PDS teachers are concerned with time on task, maintenance of interest, prompt feedback, and, above all, successful classroom management. Extended time in student teaching, more than anything, seems to increase effectiveness on these factors. More local, cultural, social knowledge of students and their families and communities should heighten teacher effectiveness. Students seem to be faceless in PDS research.

Several scholars have criticized PDS practice, and we include those criticisms here. Peter Murrell (1998, 2001) claims that the PDS structure is culturally and politically neutral. He believes that PDS must challenge the status quo in urban communities. He thinks that PDSs exclude key partners, like parents and community activists, who could help transform the school and the local community.

Abdal-Haqq (1998) argues that PDSs attend to the establishment of relationships between schools and universities and to the transformation of roles for teachers and university faculty at the expense of attention to issues of equity. He wants PDSs to increase diversity in the teaching force and prepare teachers to work in communities with diverse student bodies. Teitel's (1998), review of PDS literature revealed little evidence of progress toward meeting goals of equity. Valli *et al.* (1997) share similar findings in their review of the literature.

A COMMUNITY-ORIENTED PDS: BRIDGING TWO WORLDS

Our comparison points out ideological and pedagogical barriers to easy connections between these two worlds. Yet, the struggle has merit. We return to our sticking points, considering possible connections. Then, we propose principles, perspectives, and practices for teacher education in a community-oriented PDS.

Intersections

Reasonably, teacher education should develop professional behavior, but what counts as professionalism might be redefined. A professional might be perceived not only as a subject matter specialist, but as one who takes special care to learn about the home places from which students come. A focus on teacher practice *within* the school community can be broadened to include teacher understanding of the *school's community*.

PDS and community-oriented teacher education stress collaboration, but with different groups. While complicated, it is possible to develop partnerships among universities, schools, and communities. Service learning illustrates a moment of such partnership. Pre-service teachers might engage in service learning and, then, try it out with youth. The student teaching triad offers another space to substantially involve community people in new teacher development. Service by teachers, parents, and local leaders on policy-making school committees suggests yet another avenue for partnership. Teacher candidates might observe and/or participate in committee work.

PDS and community-oriented teacher education are vitally interested in school renewal, particularly in improved student learning. Both urge prospective teachers to reach out to youth, helping them learn constructively. Both aim to address diverse constituencies, though the PDS response is tepid at best. Culturally responsive teaching, grounded in community teacher knowledge, arguably is integral to constructive learning. Prospective teachers might participate in cultural immersion and service projects, as well as rehearse interactive teaching strategies.

PDS and community-oriented education emphasize inquiry. Years ago, teachers in Covello's community school conducted surveys to learn more about their students' interests, backgrounds, and concerns. Action research is a centerpiece of PDSs, but the topics seem to conceive of instruction narrowly, as something that happens inside school walls. Research also can be seen as a service project, helping local entities address concerns or improve programs. Further, research can focus on local history, telling forgotten stories that deserve attention. Prospective teachers might use action research to investigate a local problem, or uncover lost history, and, in so doing, learn about local assets and affairs.

New visions

In light of the insights gleaned from our comparisons and analyses, we propose the following framework for community-oriented PDSs.

Professional: what counts as professional dispositions, skills, and actions?

- *Teachers with heart*: teachers need to connect with students as members of families and communities. Teachers need to regard school communities as their communities. Local issues should become their issues. Teaching should be personal; teachers should care that students succeed.
- *Teachers with connections*: teachers should do more than go to school, then go home. They might coach volleyball or guide a school club. They might participate on school and neighborhood committees with peers and community people to address issues related to the school. Teachers should also connect with universities, engaging in life long learning.
- *Teachers with knowledge*: teachers should seek community teacher knowledge as well as subject matter expertise. Local issues should shape curriculum, involving students deeply in constructive learning.

Development: what might it mean in its broadest sense?

- *Student Development*: student development should remain at the core of the educational enterprise. Student development should include academic achievement, cultural awareness and ethnic identification, and health and general well-being.
- *Community development*: citizens pay for schools, gaining rights and responsibilities related to them. Citizens should be able to use "their" buildings for adult education and community meetings. Citizens also should shoulder some responsibility to assist schools, taking part in the education of "their" children. Schools should serve as an anchor for community, and, possibly, act as an advocate in regard to local concerns.
- *Teacher development*: future teachers should learn from a synergy of university-related and community-oriented activities. They should learn to teach innovatively, but also particularly, experimenting with teaching specific populations of students well. They need to gain wisdom of practice from accomplished teachers, especially for high poverty, rural and urban youth.

School: whose school is it anyway?

- *School renewal*: some old ideas deserve new life. The history of lighted schools and community schools like Benjamin Franklin High School should light the way for community-oriented PDSs. A community focus needs to be perceived as supportive of student learning.
- *School partnership*: links should be made between schools and universities. Connections need to be made with community organizations too. Service learning projects

offer a wonderful means to give and receive from neighborhoods, but parents, elders, and local leaders should serve on integral, significant school positions as well. Community participation in the student teaching "triad" seems like an excellent place to begin.

Where are different groups of teachers being educated, by whom, and toward what ends? What do we know about the impact of different settings and educators on teachers' knowledge and practice, on students' learning and on school change? We have explored two very different contexts for teacher education, probing their differences, and suggesting their intersections. We conclude that PDSs offer crucial teacher preparation, focused on student learning and grounded in teacher inquiry. However, attention to equity, diversity, family, and community needs to become an integral aspect of PDS principles, perspectives, and practices. It is vital to think of students as members of certain contexts, with particular educational needs. We propose a community-oriented vision for PDSs. We invite your further consideration of these issues.

REFERENCES

Abdal-Haqq, I. (1998) *Professional development schools: weighing the evidence.* Thousand Oaks, CA: Corwin Press.

Bellah, R., Madsen, R., Sullivan, W., Swidler, A., & Tipton, S. (1985) *Habits of the heart: individualism and commitment in American life.* New York: Harper & Row.

Blank, J., Johnson, S., & Shah, B. (2003) Community as text: using the community as a resource for learning in community schools. *New Directions for Youth Development,* 97 (Spring), 107–120.

Book, C. (1996) Professional development schools. In. J. Sikula (ed.), *Handbook of research on teacher education* (pp. 194–210). New York: Macmillan.

Boyle-Baise, M. (1999) As good as it gets? The impact of philosophical orientations on community-based service learning for multicultural education. *Educational Forum,* 63 (Summer), 310–32.

Boyle-Baise, M. (2002) *Multicultural service learning: educating teachers in diverse communities.* New York: Teachers College.

Boyle-Baise, M. (2005) Preparing community teachers: reflections from a service learning project. *Journal of Teacher Education* (Nov-Dec).

Boyle-Baise, M. & Kilbane, J. (2000) What really happens? A look inside a community service learning field experience for multicultural teacher education. *Michigan Journal of Community Service Learning,* 7 (Fall), 54–64.

Boyle-Baise, M., Epler, B., Clark, J., McCoy, W., Paulk, G., Slough, N., & Truelock, C. (2001) Shared control: Community voices in community service learning. *Educational Forum,* 65 (Summer), 344–353.

Boyle-Baise, M. & Sleeter, C. (2000) Community-based service learning for multicultural teacher education. *Educational Foundations,* 14 (2), 33–50.

Butin, D. (2003) Of what use is it? Multiple conceptions of service learning in education. *Teachers College Record,* 105 (9), 1674–1692.

Byrd, D. & McIntyre, D. (1999) Introduction: professional development schools—promise and practice. In D. Byrd & D. McIntyre (eds.), *Research on professional development schools. Teacher education yearbook VII* (vii–xii). Thousand Oaks, CA: Corwin Press.

Cipolle, S. (2004) Service-learning as a counter-hegemonic practice: evidence pro and con. *Multicultural Education,* 11 (3), 12–23.

Coalition for Community Schools (2000) *Community schools: partnerships for excellence.* Washington, DC: Author.

Cochran-Smith, Marilyn (2003) Inquiry and out comes: learning to teach in an age of accountability. *Teacher Education and Practice,* 15(4) 12–34.

Cochran-Smith, M. (2004) Taking stock in 2004: teacher education in daugerons times, *The Journal of Teacher Education*, Vol. 55(1).

Conaway, B.J. & Mitchell, M.W. (2004) A comparison of the experiences of yearlong interns in a professional development school and one-semester student teachers in a non-PDS location. *Action in Teacher Education*, 26 (3), 21–28.

Covello, L. (1936) A high school and its immigrant community: a challenge and an opportunity. *Journal of Educational Sociology*, 9 (6), 331–346.

Covello, L. (1958/1970) *The heart is the teacher: the teacher in the urban community*. Totowa, NJ: Littlefield, Adams, & Co.

Crocco, M.S., Faithfull, B., & Schwartz, S. (2003) Inquiring minds want to know: action research at a New York City professional development school. *Journal of Teacher Education*, 4 (1), 19–30.

Dana, N. F., Gimbert, B.G., & Silva, D.Y (2001) Teacher inquiry as protessional development for the 21st century in the United States. *Change: Transformations in Education*, 4 (2), 51–59.

Daynes, G. & Longo, N. (2004) Jane Addams and the origins of service-learning practice in the United States. *Michigan Journal of Community Service Learning*, 11 (1), 5–13.

Dryfoos, J. (2002) Full-service community schools: creating new institutions. *Phi Delta Kappan* (January), 393–398.

Dryfoos, J., Quinn, J., & Barkin, C. (2005) *Community schools in action: lessons from a decade of practice*. New York: Oxford University Press.

Ference, R. & Bell, S. (2004) A cross-cultural immersion in the US: changing pre-service teacher attitudes toward Latino ESOL students. *Equity and Excellence in Education*, 37, 343–350.

Fischetti, J., Garrett, L., Gilbert, J.I., Johnson, S., Johnston, P., Larson, A., Kenealy, A., Schneider, E., & Streible, J. (2000) This just makes sense: yearlong experience in a high school professional development school. *Peabody Journal of Education*, 73 (3/4), 310–318.

Fisher, D., Frey, N., & Farnan, N. (2004) Student teachers matter: the impact of student teachers on elementary-aged children in a professional development school. *Teacher Education Quarterly*, 31(2), 43–56.

Gay, G. (2000) *Culturally responsive teaching*. New York: Teachers College.

Galassi, J.P., Brader-Araje, L., Brooks, L., Dennison, P., Jones, M.G., Mebane, D.J., Parrish, J., Richer, M., White, K., & Vesilind, E.M. (1999). Emerging results from a middle school professional development school: the McDougle-University of North Carolina collaborative inquiry partnership groups. *Peabody Journal of Education*, 74 (3/4), 236–254.

Giles, C., Cramer, M.M. & Hwang, S.K. (2001) Beginning teacher perceptions of concerns: a longitudinal look at teacher development. *Action in Teacher Education*, 23 (3), 89–98.

Greenleaf, R. (1977) *Servant leadership: a journey into the nature of legitimate power and greatness*. New York: Paulist Press.

Henry, S.E. (2005) "I can never turn my back on that": liminality and the impact of class on service-learning experience. In D. Butin (ed.), *Service-learning in higher education: critical issues and directions* (pp. 45–66). New York: Palgrave Macmillan.

Holmes Group (1986) *Tomorrow's teachers*. East Lansing, MI: Author

Holmes Partnership Goals (1996) Holmes Partnership. Retrieved July 2005 from http://www.holmespartnership.org/goals.html.

Houston, W.R., Hollis, L.Y., Clay, D., Ligons, C.M., & Roff, L. (1999) Effects of collaboration on urban teacher education programs and professional development schools. In D.M. Byrd and D.J. McIntyre (eds.), *Research on professional development schools. Teacher education yearbook VII* (6–28). Thousand Oaks, CA: Corwin Press.

Jehl, J., Blank, M., & McCloud, B. (2001) *Education and community building: connecting two worlds*. Washington, DC: Institute for Educational Leadership.

Jones, S., Gilbride-Brown, J., & Gasiorski, A. (2005) Getting inside the "underside" of service-learning: student resistance and possibilities. In D. Butin (ed.), *Service-learning in higher education: critical issues and directions* (pp. 3–24). New York: Palgrave Macmillan.

Klingner, J.K., Leftwich, S., & van Garderen, D. (2004). Closing the gap: enhancing student outcomes in an urban professional development school. *Teacher Education and Special Education*, 27(3), 292–306.

Kidd, J., Sanchez, S., & Thorp, E. (2003, April) Gathering family stories: facilitating pre-service teacher's cultural awareness and responsiveness. Paper presented at the annual meeting for the American Educational Research Association, Chicago, IL.

Koehnecke, D.S. (2001) Professional development schools provide effective theory and practice. *Education*, 121 (3), 589–91.

Kretzman, J. (1992) Community-based development and local schools: a promising partnership. Chicago: Institute for Policy Research, Northwestern University.

Ladson-Billings, G. (1994) *The dreamkeepers: successful teachers of African American children*. San Francisco: Jossey-Bass.

Mahan, J. & Stachowski, L. (1993–4) Diverse, previously uncited sources of professional learning reported by student teachers serving in culturally different communities. *National Forum of Teacher Education Journal*, 3 (1), 21–28.

McBee, R.H. & Moss, J. (2002) PDS partnerships come of age. *Educational Leadership*, 59 (6), 61–64.

McGee Banks, C. (2005) *Improving multicultural education: Lessons from the Intergroup Education Movement*. New York: Teachers College.

McIntyre, D.J., Smith, L.C., Gilbert, S.L., & Hillkirk, R.K. (2006) The perceived effectiveness of a graduate teaching fellows program. In Julie Rainer Dangel (ed.), *Research in Teacher Induction: ATE Teacher Education Yearbook XIV* (pp. 243–258). Lanham, MD: Rowan & Littlefield Education.

Moll, L., Amanti, C., Neff, D., & Gonzalez, N. (1992) Funds of knowledge for teaching: using a qualitative approach to connect homes and classrooms. *Theory Into Practice*, 31 (2), 132–140.

Moore, S., Brennan, S., Garrity, A., & Godecker, S. (2000) Winburn Community Academy: a university-assisted community school and a professional development school. *Peabody Journal of Education*, 75 (3), 33–50.

Morton, K. (1995) The irony of service: charity, project, and social change in service learning. *Michigan Journal of Community Service Learning*, 2, 19–32.

Murray, F.B. (1993) "All or none" criteria for professional development schools. In P. Altebach, H. Petrie, M. Shujaa, & L. Weiss (eds.), *Educational policy: 7, 1. Professional development schools* (pp. 66–73). Newbury Park, CA: Corwin Press.

Murrell, P. (1998) *Like stone soup: the role of the professional development school in the renewal of urban schools*. Washington, DC: American Association of Colleges for Teacher Education.

Murrell, P. (2001) *Community teacher*. New York: Teachers College Press.

National Council for the Accreditation of Teacher Education (2001) *Standards for professional development schools*. Washington, DC: Author.

Noddings, N. (1984) *Caring: a feminine approach to ethics and moral education*. Berkeley: University of California Press.

O'Sullivan, S. (2005) The soul of teaching. Education teachers of character. *Action in Teacher Education*, 26(4) 3–9.

Nuebert, G.A. & Binko, J.B. (1998) Professional development schools: the proof is in the performance. *Educational Leadership*, 55 (5), 44–46.

Paccione, A. (2000) Developing a commitment to multicultural education. *Teachers College Record*, 102 (6), 980–1005.

Paese, P.C. (2003) Impact of professional development schools through induction. *Action in Teacher Education*, 25 (1), 83–88.

Peebles, R. (1969) Interview with Leonard Covello. *Urban Review*, 3 (3), 1969.

Pompa, L. (2005) Service-learning as crucible: reflections on immersion, context, power, and transformation. In D. Butin (ed.), *Service-learning in higher education: critical issues and directions* (pp. 173–192). New York: Palgrave Macmillan.

Rhoads, R. (1997) *Community service and higher learning: explorations of the caring self*. New York: SUNY.

Ridley, D.S., Hurwitz, S., Hackett, M.R.D., & Miller, K.K. (2005) Comparing PDS and campus—

based preservice teacher preparation. Is PDS-based preparation really better? *Journal of Teacher Education*, 56 (1), 46–56.

Rock, T.C. & Levin, B. (2002) Collaborative action research projects: enhancing pre-service teacher development in professional development schools. *Teacher Education Quarterly*, 29 (1), 7–21.

Rosenberger, C. (2000) Beyond empathy: developing critical consciousness through service learning. In C. O'Grady (ed.) *Integrating service learning and multicultural education in colleges and universities* (pp. 23–43). Mahwah, NJ: Erlbaum.

Rosner-Salazar, T. (2003) Multicultural service learning and community based research as a model to promote social justice. *Social Justice*, 30 (4), 64–76.

Seidl, B. (2007) Push, double images, and raced talk: working with communities to explore and personalize culturally relevant pedagogies. *Journal of Teacher Education*.

Sharpe, T., Lounsbery, M.F., Golden, C., & Deibler, C. (1999) Analysis of an on-going, district-wide approach to teacher education. *Journal of Teaching in Physical Education*, 19(3), 79–96.

Sleeter, C. (2000) Strengthening multicultural education with community-based service learning. In C. O'Grady (ed.), *Integrating service learning and multicultural education in colleges and universities* (pp. 263–276). Mahwah, NJ: Erlbaum.

Smith, G. (2002) Going local. *Educational Leadership*, 60 (1), 30–33.

Stachowski, L.L. & Visconti, V. (1997) Adaptations for success: U.S. student teachers living and teaching abroad. *International Education*, 26 (2), 5–20.

Stachowski, L. & Mahan, J. (1998) Cross-cultural field placements: student teachers learning from schools and communities. *Theory Into Practice*, 37 (2) 155–162.

Stachowski, L. & Brantmeier, E. (2002) Understanding self through other: changes in student teacher perception of home culture from immersion in Navajoland and overseas. *International Education*, 32 (1), 5–18.

Stachowski, L, & Frey, C. (2005) Student teachers' reflections on service and learning in Navajo Reservation communities: contextualizing the classroom experience. *The Community School Journal*, 15 (2), 101–120.

Stallings, J.A. (1991, April) Connecting preservice teacher education and inservice professional development: a professional development school. Paper presented at the annual meeting of the American Educational Research Association, Chicago.

Teitel, L. (1998) Professional development schools: a literature review. in M. Levine (ed.), *Designing Standards that Work for Professional Development Schools* (pp. 33–80). Washington, DC: National Council for the Accreditation of Teacher Education.

Teitel, L. (2003) *The Professional development schools handbook*. Thousand Oaks, CA: Corwin Press.

Valli, L., Cooper, D., & Frankes, L. (1997) Professional development schools and equity: a critical analysis of rhetoric and research. In M. Apple (ed.), *Review of Research in Education* (Vol. 22), Washington, DC: American Educational Research Association.

Wade, R. (2000) Service learning for multicultural teaching competency: insights from the literature for teacher education. *Equity & Excellence in Education*, 33 (3), 21–30.

Wade, R. (2001) ". . . And justice for all." Community service-learning for social justice. Denver, CO: Education Commission of the States.

Wait, D.B. (2000) *Are professional development school trained teachers really better?* Paper presented at the annual meeting of the National PDS Conference, Columbia, SC.

Wenger, E. (2002) *Communities of practice: learning, meaning, and identity*. Cambridge, MA: Cambridge University Press.

Wiest, L. (1998) Using immersion experiences to shake up pre-service teachers' views about cultural difference. *Journal of Teacher Education*, 49 (5) 358–365.

Wise, A. (2005) Establishing teaching as a profession: The essential role of professional accreditation. *Journal of Teacher Education*, 56(4), 318–331.

Zeichner, K. & Melnick, S. (1996) Community field experiences and teacher preparation for diversity. In D. Byrd & D. J. McIntyre (eds), *Preparing tomorrow's teachers: the field experience*. Thousand Oaks, CA: Corwin Press.

Part 3
Artifacts

3.1 The case for university-based teacher education

Linda Darling-Hammond

Source: R. Roth (ed.), *The Role of the University in the Preparation of Teachers*. NewYork: Routledge/Falmer, 1999, pp. 13–30

For a number of years, public dissatisfaction with schools has been coupled with dissatisfaction with schools of education as well. Education schools have been variously criticized as ineffective in preparing teachers for their work, unresponsive to new demands, remote from practice, and barriers to the recruitment of bright college students into teaching. In more than 40 states policy makers have enacted alternate routes to teacher certification to create pathways into teaching other than those provided by traditional 4-year undergraduate teacher education programs. Upon his election in 1988, President Bush's only education proposal was the encouragement of alternative teacher certification to allow more flexible teacher recruitment. In 1995, Newt Gingrich proposed the elimination of teacher certification rules, which require preparation for teaching, as his major education initiative.

Voices of dissatisfaction have been raised from within the profession as well. During the past decade, significant critiques of traditional teacher education practices have been raised by the Holmes Group of education deans (Holmes Group, 1986) and the Carnegie Task Force on Teaching as a Profession (1986), along with scholars like John Goodlad (1990), Ken Howey and Nancy Zimpher (1989), and Ken Zeichner (1993), among others. These voices, however, have urged the redesign of teacher education to strengthen its knowledge base, its connections to both practice and theory, and its capacity to support the development of powerful teaching.

Proposals at the far ends of this continuum stand in stark contrast to one another: on the one hand, university-based preparation would be replaced by "onthe-job" training that focuses on the pragmatics of teaching, while on the other, more extensive professional training would aim to prepare teachers for much more adaptive, knowledge-based practice while tackling the redesign of schools and teacher education in tandem. Which of these routes holds the most promise? What would the implications be for teachers' knowledge, skills, and commitments and, most important, for the education-of children?

While the debates on these questions have been largely ideological, there is a growing body of empirical evidence about the outcomes of different approaches to teacher education and recruitment, ranging from quick alternative routes into the classroom to traditional university-based approaches to newer models that are 5-year extended programs or 5th year postbaccalaureate programs. As I describe in this chapter, the evidence strongly suggests that "on-the-job" preservice training leaves teachers seriously underprepared. Most alternative routes sponsored by school districts, states, and other vendors have been found to be significantly less effective at preparing and retaining recruits than university-based teacher education programs. Furthermore, these truncated programs tend to feature regressive approaches to teaching practice that are seriously out of synch with new standards for student learning.

Although traditional teacher education programs differ significantly from one another and some have major shortcomings, as a group they produce teachers who are more highly rated and effective with children than are teachers who enter teaching without training or through quick alternate routes. Furthermore, more extensive redesigned programs that have resulted from recent reforms are even more successful than traditional four-year models. In short, teacher education matters, and more teacher education is better than less. In what follows, I discuss why.

WHAT TEACHERS NEED TO KNOW AND BE ABLE TO DO

Central to any discussion of teacher preparation is a judgment about what it is teachers must be prepared to do. If teachers are viewed primarily as purveyors of information for students, one could argue that they need little more than basic content knowledge and the ability to string together comprehensible lectures in order to do an adequate job. For this kind of teaching, it is easy to believe that a liberal arts education could be sufficient preparation. But if teachers need to be able to ensure successful learning for students who learn in different ways and encounter a variety of difficulties, then teachers need to be diagnosticians and planners who know a great deal about the learning process and have a repertoire of tools at their disposal. This kind of teaching is not intuitively obvious. And it is this kind of teaching that current social demands increasingly require.

In today's complex society and economy, much greater numbers of students need to be prepared for much more challenging forms of learning than ever before in our history. In order to meet the ambitious standards for student learning currently being developed by states and professional associations, teachers must learn to teach for understanding and to teach for diversity—that is, to teach in ways that enable a wide range of learners to succeed at very demanding intellectual tasks (National Commission on Teaching and America's Future, 1996).

What do teachers need to know to teach all students in the way new standards suggest? First of all, teachers need to understand subject matter in ways that allow them to organize it so that students can create useful cognitive maps of the terrain. They need more than formulaic or procedural understanding of the core ideas in a discipline and how these help to structure knowledge, how they relate to one another, and how they can be tested, evaluated, and extended. Teachers also need to be able to use their knowledge of subject matter flexibly to address ideas as they come up in the course of learning. They need to understand how inquiry in a field is conducted and what reasoning entails—such as what counts as "proving" something in mathematics as compared with proving something in history (Ball & Cohen, in press). And they need to see ways that ideas connect across fields, and to everyday life, so that they can select and use examples, problems, and applications well.

Understanding subject matter in this way provides a foundation for pedagogical content knowledge (Shulman, 1987), which enables teachers to represent ideas so that they are accessible to others. Knowledge of the domain of study is critical: the teacher needs to understand what ideas can provide important foundations for other ideas and how they can be usefully linked and assembled. The audience is also key: people will understand ideas differently depending on their prior experiences and context. A skillful pedagogue figures out what a particular audience is likely to know and believe about the topic under study, and how learners are likely to "hook into" new ideas, so as to create productive learning experiences. Knowledge of cognition, information processing, and communication are also important so that teachers can shape lectures, materials, learning centers, projects, and discussions in useful ways.

Interpreting learners' statements and actions and framing productive experiences for them requires knowledge of development—how children and adolescents think and behave, what they are trying to accomplish, what they find interesting, what they already know and what they are likely to have trouble with in particular domains at particular ages in particular contexts. This knowledge includes an understanding of how to support further growth in a number of domains—social, physical, and emotional, as well as cognitive.

Teaching in ways that connect with students also requires an understanding of differences that may arise from culture, language, family, community, gender, prior schooling, or other factors that shape people's experiences, as well as differences that may arise from developed intelligence, preferred approaches. to learning, or specific learning difficulties. Teachers need to be able to inquire sensitively and productively into children's experiences and their understandings of subject matter so that they can interpret curriculum through their students' eyes and shape lessons to connect with what students know and how they learn well. To get non-stereotypic information that can help them come to understand their learners, teachers need to know how to listen carefully to students and look at their work as well as to structure situations in which students write and talk about their experiences and what they understand. This builds a foundation of pedagogical learner knowledge (Grimmett & MacKinnon, 1992) which grows as teachers examine how particular learners think and reason, where they have problems, how they learn best, and what motivates them.

An understanding of motivation is critical in teaching for understanding, because achieving understanding is difficult. Teachers must know how to structure tasks and feedback so as to encourage extensive effort without either relinquishing the press for understanding when the going gets tough or discouraging students so that they give up altogether. Motivating students not only requires understanding general principles about how to engage young people and sustain their interest at different ages, but also understanding what individual students believe about themselves and their abilities, what they care about, and what tasks are likely to give them enough success to encourage them to continue to work hard to learn.

Teachers need several kinds of knowledge about learning. Since there are many kinds of learning—for example, learning for recognition or appreciation vs. learning for various kinds of applications or performances—teachers need to think about what it means to learn different kinds of material for different purposes, how to support different kinds of learning with distinctive teaching strategies, and how to make judgments about which kinds of learning are most necessary in different contexts. Not everything can be learned deeply—that is, with opportunities for extensive application—but some things must be deeply understood as foundations for work that is to follow and as a means for developing specific skills and performances. Other ideas may be understood more superficially to create a map of the domain, but learned so that they connect to concepts that are meaningful.

Teachers need to understand what helps children (or anyone) learn in these different ways. They need to be able to construct and use a variety of means for assessing students' knowledge, as well as for evaluating student's approaches to learning. To be effective, they must be able to identify the strengths of different learners while addressing their weaknesses—those who rely more on visual or oral cues; those who tend to reason from the specific to the general or vice-versa; those who use spatial or graphic organizers vs. those who are more text-oriented; those who bring a highly developed logical/mathematical intelligence and those who bring a strong aesthetic sense.

Using this information well requires a command of teaching strategies that address a variety of ways to learn and a variety of purposefully selected goals for learning. Strategies that regularly use multiple pathways to content are one major part of a teacher's repertoire. In addition, more than ever before in the past, all teachers need tools to work with the students in their classrooms who have specific learning disabilities or needs—the estimated 15 to 20 percent of students who are dyslexic or dysgraphic, who have particular visual or perceptual difficulties or difficulties with information processing. There are useful teaching strategies for these relatively commonplace problems, but they have been rarely taught to "regular" education teachers. And, because language is the gateway to learning, teachers need an understanding of how students acquire language, both native English speakers and students who start from other languages, so that they can build language skills and create learning experiences that are accessible. This may mean strategies ranging from explicit teaching of key vocabulary or use of an array of visual and oral cues and materials to the creation of collaborative learning settings in which students use language extensively.

Teachers need to know about curriculum resources and technologies. They need to be able to connect their students with sources of information and knowledge that extend beyond textbooks that allow for the exploration of ideas, the acquisition and synthesis of information, and the development of models, writings, designs, and other work products. The teacher's role will be to help students learn to find and use a wide array of resources for framing and solving problems, rather than to remember only the information contained in one source.

And they need to know about collaboration. They need to understand how interactions among students can be structured to allow more powerful shared learning to occur. They need to be able to shape classrooms that sponsor productive discourse that presses for disciplined reasoning on the part of students. They need to understand how to collaborate with other teachers to plan, assess, and improve learning within and across the school, as well as how to work with parents to learn more about their students and to shape supportive experiences at school and home.

Finally, teachers need to be able to analyze and reflect on their practice, to assess the effects of their teaching and to refine and improve their Instruction. When teaching for understanding, teachers must maintain two intertwining strands of thought at all times. How am I doing at moving the students toward high levels of understanding and proficient performance and how am I taking into account what students know and care about in the process of moving them toward these curriculum goals and developing their talents and social abilities? Teachers must continuously evaluate what students are thinking and understanding and reshape their plans to take account of what they've discovered as they build curriculum to meet their goals.

These demands that derive from the desire to teach a much wider range of students for much higher standards of performance are new ones for most teachers. With few having experienced this kind of learning themselves, how can it be possible to create a different kind of teaching on a wide scale? The only plausible answer is to develop much more powerful forms of teacher education—both before entry and throughout the teaching career—that systematically provide experience with the kinds of knowledge and forms of practice described above, and then to make that kind of education available to all teachers, not just a few. As Gary Fenstermacher (1992) observes:

> In a time when so many advocate for restructured schools, for greater decision autonomy for teachers, and for connecting the schools more intimately with homes and communities, it is more important than ever that teachers have the capacity to appraise their actions, evaluate their work, anticipate and control consequences, incorporate new theory and research into practice, and possess the skills and understanding needed to explain their work to other teachers, and to students and their parents . . .
>
>   These reflective capacities are not innate to human beings, nor are they acquired quickly. They are not acquired during a planning period sandwiched somewhere in between classes, or during evening "mini-courses" after a full day's work. They are, rather, the outcome of sustained and rigorous study, and of dialogue and exchange with master teacher educators.
>
> (35, in manuscript)

Developing the kinds of knowledge I have described requires that most teachers move far beyond what they themselves experienced as students, and thus that they learn in ways that are more powerful than simply reading and talking about new pedagogical ideas (Ball & Cohen, in press). Learning to practice in substantially different ways than one has oneself experienced can occur neither through theoretical imaginings alone, nor on unguided experience alone. It requires a much tighter coupling of the two.

Teachers learn just as students do: by studying, doing, and reflecting; by collaborating with other teachers; by looking closely at students and their work; and by sharing what they see. This kind of learning cannot occur either in college classrooms divorced from engagement in practice or in school classrooms divorced from knowledge about how to interpret practice. Good settings for teacher learning—in both colleges of education and schools—provide lots of opportunities for research and inquiry, for trying and testing, for talking about and evaluating the results of learning and teaching. The "rub between theory and practice" (Miller & Silvernail, 1994) occurs most productively when questions arise in the context of real students and real work-in-progress where research and disciplined inquiry are also at hand.

DO EDUCATION SCHOOLS HELP TEACHERS LEARN?

Even if one agrees that there are desirable knowledge and skills for teaching, many people sincerely believe that anyone can teach, or, at least, that knowing a subject is enough to allow one to teach it well. Others believe that teaching is best learned, to the extent it can be learned at all, by trial-and-error on the job. The evidence strongly suggests otherwise. Reviews of research over the past 30 years summarizing hundreds of studies have concluded that, even with the shortcomings of current teacher education and licensing, fully prepared and certified teachers are better rated and more successful with students than teachers without this preparation (Evertson *et al.*, 1985; Ashton & Crocker, 1986; Ashton & Crocker, 1987; Greenberg, 1983; Haberman, 1984; Olsen, 1985). As Evertson and colleagues conclude in their research review:

> The available research suggests that among students who become teachers, those enrolled in formal preservice preparation programs are more likely to be effective than those who do not have such training. Moreover, almost all well planned and executed efforts within teacher preparation programs to teach students specific knowledge or skills seem to succeed, at least in the short run.
>
> (Evertson *et al.*, 1985, 8)

The importance of full preparation holds across specific subject-matter fields. A review of research on science education, incorporating the results of more than 65 studies, found consistently positive relationships between students' achievement in science and their teacher's background in both education courses and science courses (Druva & Anderson, 1983; see also Davis, 1964; Taylor, 1957). The effects of teacher training are particularly noticeable when achievement is measured on higher order tasks such as students' abilities to apply and interpret scientific concepts (Perkes, 1967–8). Students' performance in mathematics is also strongly related to their teachers' preparation in teaching methods as well as in mathematics content (Begle, 1979; Begle & Geeslin, 1972; Hawk *et al.*, 1985). The importance of teachers' education preparation has also been established for teachers of vocational education (Erekson and Barr, 1985), teachers of reading and elementary education (Hice, 1970; LuPone, 1961; McNeil, 1974), teachers in early childhood education (Roupp *et al.*, 1979), and teachers of gifted students (Hansen, 1988).

Other studies point out the differences in the perceptions and practices of teachers with differing amounts and kinds of preparation. A number of studies suggest that the typical problems of beginning teachers are lessened for those who have had adequate preparation prior to entry (Adams *et al.*, 1980; Glassberg, 1980; Taylor & Dale, 1971). Teachers who are well prepared are better able to use teaching strategies that respond to students' needs and learning styles and that encourage higher order learning (Perkes, 1967–8; Hansen, 1988; Skipper & Quantz, 1987). Since the novel tasks required for problem-solving are more difficult to manage than the routine tasks associated with rote learning, lack of knowledge about how to manage an active, inquiry-oriented classroom can lead teachers to turn to passive tactics that "dumb down" the curriculum (Carter & Doyle, 1987; Doyle, 1986), busying students with workbooks rather than complex tasks that require more skill to orchestrate (Cooper & Sherk, 1989).

Studies of teachers admitted with less than full preparation—with no teacher preparation or through quick alternate routes—reveal serious shortcomings: Recruits tend to be dissatisfied with their training; they have greater difficulties planning curriculum, teaching, managing the classroom, and diagnosing students' learning needs. They are less able to adapt their instruction to promote student learning and less likely to see it as their job to do so, blaming students if their teaching is not effective. Principals and colleagues rate them less highly on their instructional skills, and they leave teaching at higher-than-average rates. Most important, their students learn less, especially in areas like reading, writing, and mathematics, which are critical to later school success. These feelings undoubtedly contributed to the high attrition rate of TF A recruits. TF A statistics show that of those who started in 1990, 58 percent had left by the third year, a two-year attrition rate more than twice the national average for new teachers, including those in cities. The Maryland State Department of Education reported that 62 percent of corps members who started in Baltimore in 1992 had left within two years.

This track record is not unusual for alternative certification programs. Stoddart's (1992) analysis reveals that 53 percent of Los Angeles' alternative certification recruits (prepared in an eight-week summer program run by the district) had left within the first six years of program operation. California's state evaluation found that 20 percent of recruits dropped out before completing the training. Of those who completed the training, 20 percent left during the first two years of teaching, and another 20 percent of the remainder were not deemed ready for employment by the end of year two (Wright et al., 1987).

Of 110 Dallas recruits, only 54 percent had successfully "graduated" to become full-fledged teachers after their first year as interns (Lutz & Hutton, 1989). Of this group, 24 had the possibility of "graduating" at some point in time if deficiencies in meeting program requirements were cleared up, along with 14 who were requested to continue as interns for another year in hopes that they could improve their performance sufficiently. Only 40 percent of these alternate route interns said they planned to stay in teaching, as compared to 72 percent of traditionally trained recruits.

Across a range of nontraditional programs reviewed by the Rand Corporation, 75 percent of recruits who had not previously been teachers remained in teaching after two years, while only half planned to make it their career. Among these, candidates admitted through short alternative routes were least likely to say they planned to stay in teaching; mid-career recruits trained in master's degree programs were most likely to plan to stay in teaching (Darling-Hammond et al., 1989).

THE CAPACITY OF SCHOOL DISTRICTS TO PREPARE TEACHERS

The idea that school districts have the will and the capacity to train and mentor teachers unilaterally and well has been tested repeatedly without success. The literature of the late 1960s and early 1970s was full of such proposals, and the schools were full of pilots very much like today's short-term alternative routes. The reasons are simple: the districts where most new teachers are hired are poor urban and rural districts with high turnover and few resources. They do not have the level of fiscal or pedagogical resources to take on this job. Neither do they have a strong self-interest in investing thousands of dollars in the preparation of beginners, most of whom will leave for other occupations or suburban schools as soon as they are able. Over and over again, reviews of such district-based efforts find that they leave their candidates underprepared, undersupported, and less effective than candidates who received systematic university-based preparation for teaching.

There are at least three kinds of problems studies have noted with these programs: the amount of time for training, the nature of teaching knowledge conveyed, and the extent and nature of supervision.

School districts are necessarily impatient about the time teachers spend learning rather than covering classes that need to be taught. Virtually all district-run and vendor-provided programs for training teachers are extremely short, generally ranging from three to eight weeks in duration.

Because they are short-term, alternative certification programs provide little pedagogical coursework and no subject matter coursework or extended practicum experience; recruits' "practicum" consists of their first year(s) of full-time teaching. Pedagogical training tends to focus on generic teaching skills rather than subject-specific pedagogy, on singular techniques rather than a range of methods, and on specific, immediate advice rather than research or theory (see Stoddart, 1992; Bliss, 1992; Zumwalt, 1990). These choices are a necessary consequence of the short period of time available. As one program coordinator in New Jersey's Provisional Teacher program explained: "The condensed time frame of 200 hours of formal instruction places serious limitations on the amount of curriculum content that can be covered (Brown, 1990).

These constraints, and the current status of teaching knowledge in many of the districts that mount their own programs or hire teachers with little preparation, lead to a predilection for teacher-proof approaches to training and curriculum that undermine most of the current reforms in teaching and learning. Packaged programs like Distar, ITIP, and Assertive Discipline are frequently used. Although these approaches do not allow teachers to teach diagnostically or in ways that support the acquisition of higher order thinking skills, they can be "taught" in a day-long workshop and require almost no sophisticated knowledge or skill on the part of teachers. When these programs fail to meet many of the teacher's goals and the students' needs, teachers. have no powerful theories or alternative techniques to marshal.

The lack of traditional coursework (and, often, student teaching) in these programs is generally supposed to be compensated for by intensive mentoring and supervision in the initial months of full-time teaching. However, promised mentors do not always materialize. As the RAND report on nontraditional programs noted:

> . . . Ironically, given that these (alternative certification) programs presumably emphasize on-the-job training in lieu of standard coursework, the alternative program recruits in our sample received substantially less assistance and supervision than recruits in any of the other types of programs.
>
> (Darling-Hammond et al., 1989, 106)

In this study, fewer than a third of alternative certification recruits spent an hour or more each week working with a support person as compared to threequarters of the recruits in graduate school programs. Other studies have also commented on the unevenness of supervision in AC programs, particularly those that rely on local district resources (Adelman, 1986; Cornett, 1992).

Several studies found that New Jersey's alternate route teachers rarely received the combination of supervision, training, and mentoring services required by the program (Gray & Lynn, 1988; Smith, 1990a, 1990b). For example, 99 percent of AC candidates had no meeting with their support team and 67 percent did not meet with their mentors within the first four weeks of teaching, when their teaching was supposed to be "intensively supervised." Over two-thirds did not receive the daily supervision they were to receive, and nearly one-quarter were not observed by anyone at all during this time. By comparison, 96 percent of student teachers were supervised daily (Smith, 1990a, 1990b). School districts were generally unable to provide these services, given the fiscal resources and staff time available to them (Smith, undated).

Even where state resources are available, the promise of serious supervision is not always easy to meet. Despite state funding for mentors, 15 percent of California's alternative certification trainees reported that they had not met with any support person at all during their first year of teaching; fewer than 20 percent had the advantage of meeting at least once a week with a support person (Wright *et al.*, 1987, 82–3).

Reviews of the availability and quality of preparation and supervision offered by university-based programs, on the other hand, have generally been positive (see e.g. Coley & Thorpe, 1985; Darling-Hammond *et al.*, 1989; Sundstrom & Berry, 1989; Smith, 1990b). Many studies have found that, over time, alternative certification programs have added coursework requirements as gaps in teachers' preparation have been identified, and states and districts have increasingly turned to universities to provide coursework and supervision (Hudson *et al.*, 1988; Carey *et al.*, 1988; Cornett, 1992).

Programs launched by states, districts, and other non-university sponsors have also been unstable. One recent study of nontraditional programs for preparing mathematics and science teachers found that during the year in which a survey was being conducted, eight out of 64 programs had already disappeared, while several others were unsure as to whether they would continue in the following year (Carey *et al.*, 1988). Discontinuation was related to funding, reputation, availability of recruits, and stability of the agency operating the program. Programs that survived had broadened their target recruitment pools, refined their programs, and had become attached to university-based teacher education programs, if they were not already part of such programs.

Similarly, Lutz and Hurron (1989, 251) point out the dramatic shrinkage over several years in the alternative certification programs operated by the Houston and Dallas Independent School Districts, speculating that the decline may be attributed "to a shrinking pool of qualified applicants or the high financial cost of such programs, which are carried by the local school district." For these and other reasons—including a preference for traditionally trained and certified candidates—most districts in states that allow alternative certification programs do not participate in them (Gray & Lynn, 1988; Wright *et al.*, 1987; Mitchell, 1987).

RECENT RESPONSES TO CRITIQUES OF TRADITIONAL TEACHER EDUCATION

Lest schools of education become sanguine, however, there are grounds for concern about traditional preparation programs as well. One major aspect of the critique of teacher education is that, particularly in the years after normal schools were abandoned for university departments, and in the places where lab schools or other kinds of partner schools never emerged, many teacher education programs seemed to separate theory and application to a large extent. In some places, teachers were taught to teach in lecture halls from texts and teachers who frequently had not themselves ever practiced what they were teaching. Students' courses on subject matter topics were disconnected from their courses on teaching methods, which were in turn disconnected from their courses on foundations and psychology. Students completed this coursework before they began student teaching, which was a brief taste of practice typically appended to the end of their program with few connections to what had come before. Many encountered entirely different ideas from those they had studied in the classrooms where they. did their student teaching, because university and school-based faculty did little planning or teaching together. Sometimes, their cooperating teachers were selected with no regard for the quality or kind of practice they themselves engaged in. When new teachers entered their own classrooms; they could remember and apply little of what they had learned by reading in isolation from practice. Thus, they reverted largely to what they knew best: the way they themselves had been taught.

The often-repeated critiques of traditional teacher education programs include:

- Traditional views of schooling: because of pressures to prepare candidates for schools as they are, most prospective teachers learn to work in isolation, rather than in teams, and to master chalkboards and textbooks instead of computers and CD-ROMS (National Commission on Teaching and America's Future, 1996, p. 32).
- Inadequate time: the confines of a four-year undergraduate degree make it hard to learn subject matter, child development, learning theory, and effective teaching strategies. Elementary preparation is considered weak in subject matter; secondary preparation, in knowledge of learning and learners.
- Fragmentation: elements of teacher learning are disconnected from each other. Coursework is separate from practice teaching; professional skills are segmented into separate courses; faculties in the arts and sciences are insulated from education professors. Would-be teachers are left to their own devices to put it all together.
- Uninspired teaching methods: for prospective teachers to learn active, hands-on and minds-on teaching, they must have experienced it for themselves. But traditional lecture and recitation still dominates in much of higher education, where faculty do not practice what they preach.
- Superficial curriculum: once-over-lightly describes the curriculum. Traditional programs focus on subject-matter methods and a smattering of educational psychology. Candidates do not learn deeply about how to understand and handle real problems of practice.

Over the past decade, many schools of education and school districts have begun to change these conditions. Stimulated by the efforts of the Holmes Group and the National Network for Educational Renewal, more than 300 schools of education have created programs that extend beyond the confines of the traditional 4-year bachelors degree program, thus allowing more extensive study of the disciplines to be taught along with education coursework that is integrated with more extensive clinical training in schools. Some are one- or two-year graduate programs that serve recent graduates or mid-career recruits. Others are five-year models that allow an extended program of preparation for prospective teachers who enter teacher education during their undergraduate years. In either case, because the fifth year allows students to devote their energies exclusively to the task of preparing to teach, such programs allow for year-long school-based internships that are woven together with coursework on learning and teaching.

These approaches resemble reforms in teacher education abroad. Countries like Germany, Belgium, and Luxembourg have long required from two to three years of graduate level study for prospective teachers on top of an undergraduate degree—sometimes with two disciplinary majors—in the subjects to be taught. Education courses include the study of child development and learning, pedagogy, and teaching methods, plus an intensively supervised internship in a school affiliated with the university. Many other nations have recently launched similar reforms.

In 1989, both France and Japan undertook major teacher education reforms to extend both university- and school-based training. In France, all candidates must now complete a graduate program of teacher education in newly created University Institutes for the Preparation of Teachers that are closely connected to schools in their regions. In Japan, although most candidates still prepare in undergraduate programs, they have lessened responsibilities in their first year of teaching and continue to engage in significant study through a highly structured induction program. Recent reforms in Taiwan include graduate-level preparation for teachers plus a yearlong induction program.

A number of recent studies have found that graduates of extended (typically five year) programs are not only more satisfied with their preparation, they are viewed by their colleagues, principals, and cooperating teachers as better prepared, are as effective with students as much more experienced teachers, and are much more likely to enter and stay in teaching than their peers prepared in traditional four-year programs (Andrew, 1990; Andrew & Schwab, 1995; Arch, 1989; Denton & Peters, 1988; Dyal, 1993; Shin, 1994).

Many of these programs have joined with local school districts to create professional development schools where novices' clinical preparation can be more purposefully structured. Like teaching hospitals in medicine, these schools aim to provide sites for state-of-the-art practice which are also organized to support the training of new professionals, extend the professional development of veteran teachers, and sponsor collaborative research and inquiry. Programs are jointly planned and taught by university-based and school-based faculty. Cohorts of beginning teachers get a richer, more coherent learning experience when they are organized in teams to study and practice with these faculty and with one another. Senior teachers report that they deepen their knowledge by serving as mentors, adjunct faculty, co-researchers, and teacher leaders. Thus, these schools can help create the rub between theory and practice that teachers need in order to learn, while creating more professional roles for teachers and building knowledge in ways that are more useful for both practice and ongoing theory-building (Darling-Hammond, 1994).

These new programs typically engage prospective teachers in studying research and conducting their own inquiries through cases, action research, and the development of structured portfolios about practice. They envision the professional teacher as one who learns from teaching rather than one who has finished learning how to teach, and the job of teacher education as developing the capacity to inquire sensitively and systematically into the nature of learning and the effects of teaching. This is an approach to knowledge production that John Dewey (1929) sought one that aims to empower teachers with greater understanding of complex situations rather than to control them with simplistic formulas or cookie-cutter routines for teaching.

> Command of scientific methods and systematized subject matter liberates individuals; it enables them to see new problems, devise new procedures, and in general, makes for diversification rather than for set uniformity (12). This knowledge and understanding render (the teacher's) practice more intelligent, more flexible, and better adapted to deal effectively with concrete phenomena of practice . . . Seeing more relations he sees more possibilities, more opportunities. His ability to judge being enriched, he has. a wider range of alternatives to select from in dealing with individual situations.
>
> (Dewey, 1929, pp. 20–1)

If teachers investigate the effects of their teaching on students' learning, and if they read about what others have learned, they come to understand teaching "to be an inherently problematic endeavor, rather than a highly routinized activity" (Houston, 1993, p. 126). They become sensitive to variation and more aware of what works for what purposes in what situations. Access to nuanced knowledge allows them to become more thoughtful decision makers.

Training in inquiry also helps teachers learn how to look at the world from multiple perspectives; including those of students whose experiences are quite different from their own, and to use this knowledge in developing pedagogies that can reach diverse learners. Learning to reach out to students—those who are difficult to know as well as those who are easy to know—requires boundary crossing, the ability to elicit knowledge of others and to understand it when it is offered. As Lisa Delpit (1995) notes, "we all interpret behaviors, information, and situations through our own cultural lenses; these lenses operate involuntarily, below the level of conscious awareness, making it seem that our own view is simply 'the way it is' " (p. 151). Teachers concerned with democratic education must develop an awareness of their perspectives and how these can be enlarged to avoid a "communicentric bias" (Gordon, 1990) which limits understanding of areas of study as well as of those who are taught.

Developing the ability to see beyond one's own perspective—to put "oneself in the shoes of the learner and to understand the meaning of that experience in terms of learning—is, perhaps, the most important role of universities in the preparation of teachers. One of the great flaws of the "bright person myth" of teaching is that it presumes that anyone can teach what he or she knows to anyone else. However, people who have never studied teaching or learning often have a very difficult time understanding how to convey material that they themselves learned effortlessly and almost subconsciously. When others do not learn merely by being told, the intuitive teacher often becomes frustrated and powerless to proceed. This frequently leads to anger directed at the learner for not validating the untrained teacher's efforts. Furthermore, individuals who have had no powerful teacher education intervention often maintain a single cognitive and cultural perspective that makes it difficult for them to understand the experiences, perceptions, and knowledge bases that deeply influence the approaches to learning of students who are different from themselves. The capacity to understand another is not innate. It is developed through study, reflection, guided experience, and inquiry.

A commitment to open inquiry, the enlargement of perspectives, and the crossing of boundaries are critical features of the ideal of university education. In fact, the basis of the very earliest universities was that they tried to bring together scholars from all over the known world. They sought to create ways to share diverse perspectives from various geographic areas, cultures, and disciplines as the basis for developing knowledge and finding truth. If universities are to continue to make the important contribution to the education of teachers that they can make, they need to pursue these ideals of knowledge-building and truth-finding by creating a genuine praxis between ideas and experiences—by honoring practice in conjunction with reflection and research and by helping teachers reach beyond their personal boundaries to appreciate the perspectives of those whom they would teach.

REFERENCES

Adams, R.D., Hutchinson, S., & Martray, C. (1980) "A developmental study of teacher concerns across time," Paper presented at the American Educational Research Association Annual Meeting, Boston, MA.

Adelman, N.E. (1986) *An Exploratory Study of Teacher Alternative Certification and Retraining Programs*, Washington, DC: Policy Study Associates.

Andrew, M. (1990) "The differences between graduates of four-year and five-year teacher preparation programs", *Journal of Teacher Education*, 41, pp. 45–51.

Andrew, M. & Schwab, R.L. (1995) "Has reform in teacher education influenced teacher performance? An outcome assessment of graduates of eleven teacher education programs," *Action in Teacher Education*, 17, pp. 43–53.

Arch, E.C. (1989) "Comparison of student attainment of teaching competence in traditional preservice and fifth-year master of arts in teaching programs," Paper presented at the annual meeting of the American Educational Research Association, San Francisco, CA.

Ashton, P. & Crocker, L. (1986) "Does teacher certification make a difference?" *Florida Journal of Teacher Education*, 3, pp. 73–83.

Ashton, P. & Crocker, L. (1987) "Systematic study of planned variations: the essential focus of teacher education reform," *Journal of Teacher Education*, May–June, pp. 2–8.

Ball, D. & Cohen, D. (in press) "Developing practice, developing practitioners: toward a practice-based theory of professional education," in Darling-Hammond, L. & Sykes, G. (eds.) *The Heart of the Matter: Teaching as the Learning Profession*, San Francisco: Jossey-Bass.

Begle, E.G. (1979) *Critical Variables in Mathematics Education*, Washington, DC: Mathematical Association of American and National Council of Teachers of Mathematics.

Begle, E.G. & Geeslin, W. (1972) "Teacher effectiveness in mathematics instruction," National Longitudinal Study of Mathematical Abilities Reports No. 28, Washington, DC: Mathematical Association of America and National Council of Teachers of Mathematics.

Bents, M. & Bents, R. (1990) "Perceptions of good teaching among novice, advanced beginner and expert teachers," Paper presented at the Annual Meeting of the American Educational Research Association, Boston, MA.

Bliss, T. (1992) "Alternate certification in Connecticut: reshaping the profession," *Peabody Journal of Education*, 67, 3.

Brown, E.J. (1990) "New Jersey provisional teacher program: model of support for beginning teachers," Paper presented at the Annual Meeting of the American Association of Colleges for Teacher Education, Chicago, IL.

Carey, N.B., Mittman, B.S., & Darling-Hammond, L. (1988) *Recruiting Mathematics and Science Teachers through Nontraditional Programs*, Santa Monica: RAND Corporation.

Carnegie Task Force On Teaching As A Profession (1986) *A Nation Prepared: Teachers for the 21st century*, Washington, DC, Author.

Carter, K. & Doyle, W. (1987) "Teachers' knowledge structures and comprehension processes," in Calderhead, J. (ed.) *Exploring Teacher Thinking*, London: Cassell, pp. 147–60.

Coley, R.I. & Thorpe, M.E. (1985) *Responding to the Crisis in Math and Science Teaching: Four Initiatives*, Princeton, NJ: Educational Testing Service.

Cooper, E. & Sherk, I. (1989) "Addressing urban school reform: issues and alliances," *Journal of Negro Education*, 58, 3, pp. 315–31.

Cornett, L.M. (1992) "Alternative certification: state policies in the SREB states," *Peabody Journal of Education*, 67, 3.

Darling-Hammond, L. (1992) "Teaching and knowledge: Policy issues posed by alternative certification for teachers," *Peabody Journal of Education*, 67, 3, pp. 123–54.

Darling-Hammond, L. (1994) *Professional Development Schools: Schools for Developing a Profession*, NY: Teachers College Press.

Darling-Hammond, L., Hudson, L., & Kirby, S. (1989) *Redesigning Teacher Education: Opening the Door for New Recruits to Science and Mathematics Teaching*, Santa Monica: The Rand Corporation.

Davis, C.R. (1964) "Selected teaching-learning factors contributing to achievement in chemistry and physics," Unpublished doctoral dissertation, University of North Carolina, Chapel Hill.

Delpit, L. (1995) *Other People's Children: Cultural Conflict in the Classroom*, New York: New Press.

Denton, U. & Peters, W.H. (1988) "Program assessment report: curriculum evaluation of a non-traditional program for certifying teachers," Texas A and M University, College Station, TX.

Dewey, J. (1929) *The Sources of a Science of Education*, New York: Horace Liveright.

Doyle, W. (1986) "Content representation in teachers' definitions of academic work," *Journal of Curriculum Studies*, 18, pp. 365–79.

Druva, C.A. & Anderson, R.D. (1983) "Science teacher characteristics by teacher behavior and by student outcome: a meta-analysis of research," *Journal of Research in Science Teaching*, 20, 5, pp. 467–79.

Dyal, A.B. (1993) "An exploratory study to determine principals' perceptions concerning the effectiveness of a fifth-year preparation program," Paper presented at the annual meeting of the Mid-South Educational Research Association, New Orleans, LA.

Erekson, T.L. & Barr, L. (1985) "Alternative credentialing: lessons from vocational education," *Journal of Teacher Education*, 36, 3, pp. 16–19.

Evertson, C., Hawley, W., & Zlotnick, M. (1985) "Making a difference in educational quality through teacher education," *Journal of Teacher Education*, 36, 3, pp. 2–12.

Feiman-Nemser, S. & Parker, M.B. (1990) *Making Subject Matter Part of the Conversation or Helping Beginning Teachers Learn to Teach*, East Lansing, MI: National Center for Research on Teacher Education.

Fenstermacher, G.D. (1992) "The place of alternative certification in the education of teachers," *Peabody Journal of Education*, 67, 3.

Glassberg, S. (1980) "A view of the beginning teacher from a developmental perspective," Paper presented at the American Educational Research Association Annual Meeting, Boston, MA.

Gomez, D.L. & Grobe, R.P. (1990) "Three years of alternative certification in Dallas: Where are we?," Paper presented at the Annual Meeting of the American Educational Research Association, Boston, MA.

Goodlad, J. (1990) *Teachers for Our Nation's Schools*, San Francisco, CA: Jossey-Bass.

Gordon, E.W. (1990) "Coping with communicennic bias in knowledge production in the social sciences," *Educational Researcher*, 19, p. 19.

Grady, M.P., Collins, P., & Grady, E.L. (1991) "Teacher for American 1991 summer institute evaluation report," Unpublished manuscript.

Gray, D. & Lynn, D.H. (1988) *New Teachers, Better Teachers: A Report on Two Initiatives in New Jersey*, Washington, DC: Council for Basic Education.

Greenberg, J.D. (1983) "The case for teacher education: open and shut," *Journal of Teacher Education*, 34, 4, pp. 2–5.

Grimmett, P. & Mackinnon, A. (1992) "Craft knowledge and the education of teachers," in Grant, G. (ed.) *Review of Research in Education*, vol. 18, pp. 385–456, Washington, DC: American Educational Research Association.

Grossman, P.L. (1989) "Learning to teach without teacher education," *Teachers College Record*, 91, 2, pp. 191–208.

Guyton, E. & Farokhi, E. (1987) "Relationships among academic performance, basic skills, subject matter knowledge and teaching skills of teacher education graduates," *Journal of Teacher Education* (Sept–Oct), pp. 37–42.

Haberman, M. (1984) "An evaluation of the rationale for required teacher education: beginning teachers with or without teacher preparation," Prepared for the National Commission on Excellence in Teacher Education, University of Wisconsin-Milwaukee, September.

Hansen, J.B. (1988) "The relationship of skills and classroom climate of trained and untrained teachers of gifted students," Unpublished doctoral dissertation, Purdue University.

Hawk, P., Coble, C.R., & Swanson, M. (1985) "Certification: it does matter," *Journal of Teacher Education*, 36, 3, pp. 13–15.

Hice, J.L. (1970) "The relationship between teacher characteristics and first-grade achievement," *Dissertation Abstracts International*, 25, 1, p. 190.

Holmes Group (1986) *Tomorrow's Teachers: A Report of the Holmes Group*, East Lansing, MI, Author.

Howey, K.R. & Zimpher, N.L. (1989) *Profiles of Preservice Teacher Education*, Albany, NY: State University of New York.

Hudson, L., Kirby, S.N., Carey, N.B., Mittman, B.S. & Berry, B. (1988) *Recruiting Mathematics and Science Teachers through Nontraditional Programs: Case Studies*, Santa Monica: Rand Corporation.

Kopp, W. (1992) "Reforming schools of education will not be enough," *Yale Law and Policy Review*, 10, 58, pp. 58–68.

Lenk, H.A. (1989) "A case study: the induction of two alternate route social studies teachers," Unpublished doctoral dissertation, Teachers College, Columbia University.

Lupone, L.J. (1961) "A comparison of provisionally certified and permanently certified elementary school teachers in selected school districts in New York State," *Journal of Educational Research*, 55, pp. 53–63.

Lutz, F.W. & Hurron, J.B. (1989) "Alternative teacher certification: its policy implications for classroom and personnel practice," *Educational Evaluation and Policy Analysis*, 11, 3, pp. 237–54.

McNeil, J.D. (1974) "Who gets better results with young children—experienced teachers or novices?," *Elementary School Journal*, 74, pp. 447–51.

Miller, L. & Silvernail, D. (1994) "Wells junior high school: evaluation of a professional development school," in Darling-Hammond, L. *Professional Development Schools: Schools for Developing a Profession*, NY: Teachers College Press.

Mitchell, N. (1987) *Interim Evaluation Report of the Alternative Certification Program* (REA87-027-2), Dallas, TX: DISD Department of Planning, Evaluation, and Testing.

National Commission On Teaching And America's Future (1996) "What matters most: teaching for America's future," NY, Author.

Natriello, G., Zumwalt, K., Hansen, A., & Frisch, A. (1990) "Characteristics of entering teachers in New Jersey," Revised version of a paper presented at the 1988 Annual Meeting of the American Educational Research Association.

Olsen, D.G. (1985) "The quality of prospective teachers: Education vs. non-education graduates," *Journal of Teacher Education*, 36, 5, pp. 56–9.

Perkes, V.A. (1967–8) "Junior high school science teacher preparation, teaching behavior, and student achievement," *Journal of Research in Science Teaching*, 6, 4, pp. 121–6.

Popkewitz, T.S. (1995) "Policy, knowledge, and power: some issues for the study of educational reform," in

Cookson, P. & Schneider, B. (eds.) *Transforming Schools: Trends, Dilemmas and Prospects* New York: Garland Press.

Roth, R.A. (1986) "Alternate and alternative certification: purposes, assumptions, implications," *Action in Teacher Education*, 8, 2, pp. 1–6.

Roth, R.A. (1993) "Teach for America 1993 summer institute: program review," Unpublished report.

Rottenberg, C.J. & Berliner, D.C. (1990) "Expert and novice teachers' conceptions of common classroom activities," Paper presented at the Annual Meeting of the American Educational Research Association, Boston, MA.

Roupp, R., Travers, J., Glantz, F., & Coelen, C. (1979) *Children at the Center: Summary Findings and Their Implications*, Cambridge, MA: Abt Associates.

Schorr, J. (1993, December) "Class action: what Clinton's national service program could learn from 'Teach for America,' " *Phi Delta Kappan*, pp. 315–18.

Sciacca, J.R. (1987) "A comparison of levels of job satisfaction between university-certified first-year teachers and alternatively-certified first-year teachers," Unpublished doctoral dissertation, East Texas State University.

Shapiro, M. (1993) *Who Will Teach for America?*, Washington, DC: Farragut Publishing Co.

Shin, H. (1994) "Estimating future teacher supply: an application of survival analysis," Paper presented at the annual meeting of the American Educational Research Association, New Orleans, LA.

Shulman, L. (1987) "Knowledge and teaching: foundations of the new reform," *Harvard Educational Review*, 57, 1, pp. 1–22.

Skipper, C.E. & Quantz, R. (1987) "Changes in educational attitudes of education and arts and science students during four years of college," *Journal of Teacher Education*, May–June, pp. 39–44.

Smith, J.M. (1990a) "School districts as teacher training institutions in the New Jersey alternate route program," Paper presented at the Annual Meeting of the Eastern Educational Research Association, Clearwater, FL, February.

Smith, J.M. (1990b) "A comparative study of the state regulations for and the operation of the New Jersey provisional teacher certification program," Paper presented at the Annual Meeting of the American Educational Research Association Meeting, April.

Smith, J.M. (undated) "Supervision, Mentoring and the 'Alternate Route'," Mimeograph.

Stoddart, T. (1992) "An alternate route to teacher certification: preliminary findings from the Los Angeles unified school district intern program," *Peabody Journal of Education*, 67, 3.

Sundstrom, K. & Berry, B. (1989) *Assessing the Initial Impact of the South Carolina Critical Needs Certification Program*, Report to the State Board of Education.

Taylor, T.W. (1957) "A study to determine the relationships between growth in interest and achievement of high school students and science teacher attitudes, preparation, and experience," Unpublished doctoral dissertation, North Texas State College, Denton.

Taylor, J.K. & Dale, R. (1971) *A Survey of Teachers in the First Year of Service*, Bristol: University of Bristol, Institute of Education.

Texas Education Agency (1993) *Teach for America Visiting Team Report*, Austin: Texas State Board of Education Meeting Minutes, Appendix B.

Wright, D.P., McKibboN, M., & Walton, P. (1987) *The Effectiveness of the Teacher Trainee Program: An Alternate Route into Teaching in California*, California Commission on Teacher Credentialing.

Zeichner, K. (1993, February) "Traditions practice in US preservice teacher education programs," *Teaching and Teacher Education*, 9, pp. 1–13.

Zumwalt, K. (1990) *Alternate Routes to Teaching: Three Alternative Approaches*, NY: Teachers College, Columbia University.

3.2 Leaving authority at the door

Equal-status community-based experiences and the preparation of teachers for diverse classrooms

Barbara Seidl and Gloria Friend

Source: Barbara Seidl and Gloria Friend, "Leaving authority at the door," *Teaching and Teacher Education*, 18(4), 2002, pp. 421–433

In a time when the society in the United States is becoming increasingly culturally and socioeconomically diverse we are all called upon to become bicultural or multicultural people, capable of moving competently between sociocultural worlds in ways that honor and respect and do not dominate, appropriate, and oppress others. We are called upon to explore more profoundly our human capacity to love, care for, and support others, and, in particular, those whose lives and social realities differ from our own, and to, as Delpit (1995, p. 151) demands, engage "in the hard work of seeing the world as others see it". We are also called upon to define our positions as antiracist individuals within a commitment to social justice. This challenge is felt urgently in the preparation of teachers for public schools where it is estimated that by the year 2050, students of color will exceed 50 percent of the total population while the teaching force will remain predominantly white (American Association of Colleges of Teacher Education, 1994).

The question of how to prepare teachers for culturally rich and economically diverse classrooms is central to teacher education efforts in many countries. Teacher educators in the US, like their counterparts in Canada (Darling & Ward, 1995; Ward, 1998), have tried numerous approaches, but the question remains, for the most part, unanswered. Coursework on multicultural education, workshops, and placements in urban schools have been a popular response to the challenge, but these attempts have produced mixed (Melnick & Zeichner, 1998) and often negative results (Haberman & Post, 1992; Zeichner, 1992). Prospective teachers often continue to view diversity within a deficit framework and use individual explanations for success and failure with little awareness of the larger social context in which opportunity is distributed (Paine, 1990; Sleeter, 1997). Courses aimed at helping white students deconstruct white privilege have produced positive, but limited, results in supporting the development of mature anti-racist identities. The short duration of these courses, the difficulty of such work in a racist society, and lack of support for continued development make it easy for students to slip from more advanced forms of an anti-racist identity into a stage of reintegration resulting in a perceived lack of efficacy around social justice issues and/or blaming people of color for their oppression (Lawrence & Bunche, 1996; Sleeter, 1997). More recently, community service has been used as a vehicle through which to provide prospective teachers with cross-cultural experiences. Again, such experiences have produced mixed results, often acting to confirm stereotypes and reinforce privilege and cultural authority (Kahne & Westheimer, 1996; McCann, 1996; Morton, 1995). Finally, a factor that further complicates multicultural teacher education is the lack of faculty of color within teacher education programs. It is all too common to find predominantly white teacher education faculty who have had little experience in diverse settings (Ducharme & Agne, 1989) teaching white students about how best to teach children of color. In short, teacher education continues to struggle to find experiences sufficiently powerful to support students in deconstructing the messy tangle of racism, classism, poverty, sexism, and opportunity and is much less successful in helping students reconstruct maintainable positions within a commitment to social justice.

COMMUNITY PARTNERSHIPS: RELATIONSHIPS AND TRANSFORMATION

> The personhood of each of us is shaped by a moving inward intersection of numerous selves-family and friends and colleagues and strangers. If we are to grow as persons and expand our knowledge of the world, we must consciously participate in the emerging community of our lives, in the claims made upon us by others as well as our claims upon them. Only in community does the person appear in the first place, and only in community can the person continue to become.
>
> (Palmer, 1983, p. 57)

We believe, as Palmer describes, that we emerge as beings through our interactions and relationships with others. And, if our identities are shaped through our relationships with certain people, then they are equally influenced by our lack of contact with others. That is, in a divided and racist society where it is quite common for people, and especially whites, to live largely monocultural lives, and where there are few opportunities to develop significant and caring relationships across ethnic and class lines, many people lack access to the very relationships that might help to create and nurture multicultural identities. Our prospective students are like many of their counterparts in other areas of the country and of the world, in that they have grown up in largely homogeneous cultural communities and have had few cross-cultural experiences (Howey & Zimpher, 1990; Ward, 1998) even with the non-dominant cultural groups that are visible within the community.

In describing what it means to be committed to anti-racist, culturally and racially nuanced social practices, Thompson (1998) challenges these segregated social patterns and calls on white theorists and others to step outside the comfortable, narrow community of relationships that define their personal worlds to,

> [. . .] change how we live: our habits, our neighborhoods, our circumstances, our political activities, our relationships. If the relationships and situations that we live with on a day-to-day basis allow us to rest comfortably in the knowledge that works best for us, we will not see any reason to change or to inquire into the lives of others.
>
> (p. 544)

We believe that if teacher education is committed to preparing teachers for diverse classrooms, then we must take seriously the challenge of "changing our habits". If our communities of relationships limit the very relations that are essential for helping to develop anti-racist identities and bicultural competency, then we must move to forge broader communities through which to learn and grow.

MT. OLIVET AND THE LEADS PROGRAM

Forging bridges between traditionally divided communities to create broader communities of relationships has been the goal of a 3-yr partnership between a Masters in Education program at The Ohio State University and the Mt. Olivet Baptist community located in the same city. The Literacy Education and Diverse Settings, Masters of Education (LEADS M.Ed.) program is a five-quarter, fifth year, teacher certification program. As in most teacher education programs, the students in the LEADS program (~30 per year) are predominantly white, as is the university faculty, and most students lack experience with diverse socioeconomic and cultural communities. The program, however, is committed to preparing teachers for diverse classrooms and, specifically, for preparing teachers for local public schools where over 60 percent of the students are African American. The Mt. Olivet community is a large, socioeconomically diverse, African American community with a congregation of ~1400 members. The church operates and houses Mt. Olivet Christian Academy (MOCA), a private Christian school serving children from kindergarten through sixth grade, as well as many other programs for children and adults from the Mt. Olivet community and from the surrounding neighborhood.

Throughout the life of our partnership, we have attempted to develop a relationship that is mutually beneficial and reciprocal; that is, both partners benefit in ways particular to their needs and share expertise particular to their strengths (Seidl & Friend, 2002). Thus, while the Mt. Olivet community provides support for our teacher education students, university faculty works to connect the Mt. Olivet community with resources and expertise available through the university. We have also attempted to avoid, the traditional authoritative stance universities occupy in such partnerships and the damaging and exploitive effects universities and, particularly, research institutions, have on culturally diverse communities. In such relationships, the push to do research positions communities as data collection sites and produces a racist research discourse, while the relationship often ends when the grant runs out or when the research is concluded. Within our partnership we have worked to develop a mutually beneficial relationship; one in which a research agenda is collaboratively constructed.

Our partnership holds multiple goals for our prospective teachers. Our overall goal is to support them towards mature anti-racist identities so that their future work with children is situated within a more sophisticated understanding of racism and inequity. We use the terms anti-racist identities and anti-racist commitments instead of other terms, such as multicultural or culturally competent, because we believe that the term anti-racist represents a commitment to an overt and activist personal and political stance (Lee, 1997). This commitment encompasses the knowledge of diverse ways of living and the need for bicultural or multicultural competency and, for teachers, the need for developing culturally relevant pedagogies. In addition, anti-racist education challenges the structural inequities that are rendered legitimate through policies, laws, and social norms (Thompson, 1997) and that are invisible to many whites. Anti-racist terminology can be found in multicultural scholarship in both the United States and Canada (Lee, 1997; Nieto, 2000; Thompson, 1998). We draw from the work of scholarship in anti-racist identity development (Derman-Sparks & Phillips, 1997; Helms, 1990; Tatum, 1992) to situate our efforts within a developmental pedagogy. The work of these scholars demonstrates the positive outcomes associated with concerted and deliberate efforts to help white students and students of color grow in their ability to identify and work against the personal, institutional, and cultural patterns of racism. Our aims are not to replicate their work, nor use it to evaluate our effectiveness. We are more interested in understanding the attitudes, beliefs, and behaviors that are common for students within that process of growth and development as well as the kinds of experiences that support growth toward more mature identities.

There is little research regarding anti-racist teacher education curricula and increased student achievement. However, we draw from research that documents the work of exemplary teachers for children of color (Foster, 1997; Irvine, 1992; Ladson-Billings, 1994). This research indicates that these teachers have had the life experiences that have helped them learn to recognize and work against racism. Their intercultural competencies allow them to act as cultural interpreters who support their students' identity development as well as support them in acquiring competency in the mainstream discourse. In short, these teachers have mature anti-racist identities and have developed culturally relevant pedagogies in response to this commitment. It is toward the exemplary vision of these teachers that we work. We do not claim, given the limited time we have with students, that it is possible for them to develop mature anti-racist identities, nor can they develop culturally relevant pedagogies, within a year. While some students move a great deal towards these goals, growth depends upon prior experiences. Given that most of our students enter our program with very little cross-cultural experience, our primary goal is to nurture a disposition and commitment to sustaining the personal and professional work they begin during their experience within the partnership.

AN EQUAL-STATUS, CROSS-CULTURAL INTERNSHIP

Towards these ends, we have constructed an equal-status, community-based internship for our prospective teachers, described in greater detail elsewhere (Seidl & Friend, 2002). LEADS M.Ed. students spend two to three hours a week at Mt. Olivet working with adults from Mt. Olivet in programs for children developed by the community. There are a number of different options through which to fulfill the requirements of the community-based internship. Some students work with an extended care program that is part of the Mt. Olivet Christian Academy. They work with teacher assistants from the Academy to help children finish homework and to plan and implement learning and recreational activities. Other students work with a male-mentoring program in the church, I'm Making a Godly Expression (IMAGE). The IMAGE program is organized by a men's group in the church. and serves fourth and fifth grade boys from a nearby public school. These students work with the men to provide tutoring in reading and math and to plan and participate in recreational activities for the boys. They also have the privilege of being part of the unity circle—an experience intended to provide spiritual and cultural education for the boys. LEADS students have also had the opportunity to work as interns with teachers in the Mt. Olivet Christian Academy and with Sunday School classes.

Mediation of our students' experiences is very important to our work, with the two authors of this chapter bearing primary responsibility for this mediation. Dr. Friend is a member of the Mt. Olivet community, the principal of the Mt. Olivet Christian Academy, and minister in the church. Dr. Seidl is a faculty member at the university, responsible for coordination between the university and Mt. Olivet. Coursework at the university in literacy, foundations classes, and other methods classes requires that students read, think, and write about the sociopolitical context of racism, the role of education in an inequitable society, and their responsibilities as teachers with children from diverse backgrounds. The internship is also mediated in planned and structured conversations facilitated by faculty from the university and members of Mt. Olivet. In addition, students have opportunities to talk with parents, teachers, and different members of the Mt. Olivet Community.

EQUAL-STATUS CONTACT

We have been committed to developing the internship as an equal-status experience; a goal aligned with our commitment to rethinking and reconstructing the social relations that characterize relationships in a racist and classist society. The concept of equal-status contact can be traced back to Allport's (1954) work in prejudice reduction and is also located in mainstream multicultural theory (Banks & Banks, 1997; Grant, 1990). Allport, summarizing work in intercultural contact, maintained that when whites experience contact with African Americans who are of equal or greater economic or professional status, there is greater likelihood for a reduction in bias and/or prejudice. On the other hand, contact between whites and blacks where blacks occupy a lower occupational or economic status is "an active factor in creating and maintaining prejudice" (p. 274). Until recently, defining and pursuing such contact as a part of teacher education has remained largely unexplored. A recent exception to this is work at the University of New Mexico (Smolkin & Suina, 1999), where the teacher education faculty is committed to an "equal other" experience for their Native American students.

We believe that equal-status, cross-cultural experiences are critical to anti-racist identity development. Too often a white student's initial contact with a community of color is one of unequal status in which they occupy privileged cultural and economic positions and maintain a sense of cultural authority. In such cases they often perceive their role as charitable or helping "those less fortunate." Such positioning promotes the likelihood that they will evaluate different cultural contexts as deficient, appropriate diverse cultural patterns within a dominant framework, or resist recognition of inequity by drawing from available racist ideologies (Sleeter, 1992; Thompson, 1998). We believe that, for white students who have had few significant cross-cultural experiences, unequal status contact such as service projects or placements in urban schools remain situated within the dominant Eurocentric cultural paradigm and allow students to maintain a privileged cultural authority. On the other hand, an equal-status partnership is better positioned to de-center this privileged cultural stance and help them begin to question their own hegemonic cultural beliefs and the racist social ideologies that sustain them.

While equal-status relationships may assume many forms, we feel that there are a number of characteristics that are essential to such an experience. First, equal-status, cross-cultural experiences place students not as helpers within a context, but as learners and participants in a community that is not essentially dependent upon their service. As partners, the Mt. Olivet community and the LEADS M.Ed. program come together in a mutual dependency, each with different needs and contributions, to pursue particular and common goals. No one partner holds the monopoly on knowledge and no one partner is placed in the role of receiving charity from the other--each brings an expertise that enriches the other. For example, our teacher education students understand that they are learners in a position of receiving invaluable support and information on their journeys to become teachers. None of the programs they work with are dependent upon their services. On the other hand, their contributions to the programs and their emerging expertise in teaching are publicly valued by the community.

Second, an equal-status experience places our prospective teachers in working relationships with adults. It is quite common for white prospective and practicing teachers to feel comfortable in developing what are often problematic relationships with children of color. Many teachers adopt a "Messiah" complex (Thompson, 1998) where their relationships are based on feelings of pity and a desire to save children from what they perceive to be uncaring families and communities. Peer relationships with people of color are far less commonly negotiated by whites, especially when outside of a helping role. Engaging in equal-status, peer relationships with adults requires developing a bicultural competency that we feel is critical to teachers who will need to build strong and positive relationships with parents, teachers of color, and other community members. Third, as Mt. Olivet is a socioeconomically diverse community, our students meet and work with adults who are their peers, economically and professionally. Such equal-status contacts with adults of color challenge the stereotypes of people of color most commonly forwarded through the media-stereo types based in youth culture and/or conditions of poverty. In addition, witnessing the many images of parenting available within such a context challenges our students' perceptions and generalizations that African American children need to be "saved."

Finally, an equal-status experience places our students within an intact, African American cultural milieu. Mt. Olivet, like many black churches in both the United States and Canada, has remained somewhat economically and politically independent of the dominant society (Poole, 1990; Walker, 1979), preserving African American traditions, norms, values, and cultural patterns to provide a protective environment within which its members can grow and thrive (hooks, 1992; West, 1993). That white students participate in a strong and intact African American cultural context is important. First, the context itself initiates an awareness of our students' cultural and raced identities. Students find themselves in situations where they are uncertain of the norms and mores that govern patterns of social interaction, whether it be in the church school context or in attending a church service. They are also exposed to the role the church has played in supporting the physical survival and dignity of African Americans in a racist society. Race, and consequently, racism, as issues to be dealt with cannot be avoided within this co ext. Third, in this society, a history of racism and discrimination has created a disproportionate number of people of color in situations of long-term, generational poverty. Public images that portray welfare mothers as predominantly black, violence as endemic to the black community, and black children as behavioral problems in schools, make it easy for whites to equate the outcomes of racism and poverty with African American culture (Sleeter, 1997). Mt. Olivet represents a diverse economic context ranging from families who struggle economically to economic, professional, and political leaders from the black community. In addition, a number of the programs in the church serve children from surrounding neighborhoods—communities impacted by long-term and generational poverty. The diverse economic context and the strong cultural context of the Mt. Olivet community make it possible to begin to deconstruct this culture/poverty conflation. In sorting out the differences between culture and the effects of poverty, we attempt to move our students toward an understanding of the relationship between racism and classism.

Overall, we believe that the equal-status internship requires that our students leave their cultural authority at the door. In becoming tentative learners in an unfamiliar cultural and political space, we hope they experience, to some degree, what it means to cross borders and to be humble in the face of the unknown. We also hope that they gain a new form of confidence that rests, not upon privileged cultural authority, but in the shedding of conscious and unconscious racist beliefs and practices and the emerging knowledge and bicultural competencies that will allow them to be active participants in the creation of a more just society.

LEARNING TOGETHER

We have worked and grown together for over three years now. No two years have been exactly alike, as we have found it necessary each year to respond to specific university and community needs. However, equal-status experiences and mediation have been central to our work each year. Over these three years we have maintained field notes of community/university meetings, classroom dialogue, and mediation meetings. Student works we have collected include reflective journals, assignments from a number of different courses, and final Masters papers. The data we have collected across this three year period has shaped our understanding of how students grow and develop within the partnership as well as guided our efforts in framing the internship and organizing experiences between our communities. The two authors of this paper, a white university professor and a black minister and principal from Mt. Olivet, have been engaged in a reiterative analysis of this data. Methodologically we employ a grounded process (Strauss & Corbin, 1994) situated within a recursive, collaborative dialogue between the two authors. Within this process of recursive analysis we have been committed to a reflective comparison of our two cultural interpretations.

Overall, we are interested in supporting our students toward more mature anti-racist identities, toward bicultural competency, and toward a commitment to culturally relevant teaching. Thus, we have considered our students' work and our discussion group data with an eye toward the attitudes, beliefs, and/or behaviors that we feel represent movement toward or away from that goal. What we share here are the patterns we have found repeated among the three cohorts of students who have been involved in the partnership. We have chosen quotes from reflective journals, Masters' papers, and class discussions that we feel are representative of those patterns. We are optimistic. Many of our students do develop more mature and sophisticated understandings of issues of culture, racism, and education and, depending upon their prior experiences, many are well on their way to developing more mature anti-racist identities. On the other hand, we are also reminded of the resiliency of long-held social and cultural beliefs as some students demonstrate little growth, remaining within a fixed dominant paradigm and displaying many of the ideological defenses white students utilize to resist personal and social transformation.

DEFINING POSITIVE GROWTH

One of our primary goals is to challenge our students' sense of cultural authority; we consider it a positive step when students express a sense of uneasiness upon their first visits to Mt. Olivet. This communicates to us that they are *de-centering cultural authority*—that they are aware of being in an unfamiliar cultural context where they are outsiders with little awareness of the cultural norms being practiced. In addition, we believe this uneasiness also means that our students are aware of the state of race relations within the world and that there is increased probability that they will move out of a naïve racial innocence in which feeling comfortable and getting along are the primary desired outcomes (Thompson, 1998). Shelly, a young white woman from an affluent suburb who had had little experience with cultural diversity, demonstrates, we believe, an appropriate and positive initial awareness of a racialized identity and the need to be thoughtful of her position within a raced world.

> In my life, I have dealt with a lot of different sorts of people. African Americans, though, is one group I have not dealt with to a very large degree . . . I can't think of a highly influential relationship I have had with a Black person (who was not a kid). This fact, combined with the fact that (I feel) interactions between White and Black people in the US are so hyped up, that I find myself very nervous about dealing with black people in peer-type relationships. I know that my nervousness is a symptom of my intense desire for things to "just go well", but in any case, it is unproductive. I think I need to work to get rid of my paranoia that everything I do or say is being examined for racist content. I wonder sometimes why I have this paranoia. I feel defensive at times, like "hey, just because I am White doesn't mean . . ." But why am I so defensive? This is definitely something I might re-examine.
>
> Even here, in a personal piece of writing I feel self-conscious, lest I make some politically incorrect remark, or indicate that I am not enlightened in some way.
>
> (Shelly, Reflective Journal, 2000)

The development of sophisticated, culturally relevant pedagogies is a process that requires commitment over time and lived experience. It is impossible for our students to unlearn years of racist socialization and develop anti-racist and sophisticated bicultural identities in one year. Thus, what we hope for is that our students begin to understand the difficulties that arise when schools are not responsive to children's sociocultural experiences. Jill's journal illustrates the degree to which her experiences with a program at Mt. Olivet helped her more fully appreciate the *sociocultural incongruity* that many children of color experience in public schools.

Sometimes when you read something or hear something it makes sense intellectually but it just doesn't feel right. In many of the readings over the last year that had to do with culture, they made sense intellectually but I had a hard time feeling they were correct or real. That little things that are different between the dominant white culture and nondominant cultures could cause minority children not to perform as well as children from the dominant culture didn't feel like an adequate explanation. I thought that it may have some part but surely couldn't explain it fully. I still did not feel that cultural differences could fully explain failure till I started in the summer camp/summer school program at Mt. Olivet. . . . After a couple of days I could see many similarities between my experience and that of a young black child entering a school and classroom that is based on white culture and has as its directors people from that culture. It was a rare event in my life and I felt lost as if everyone knew what was going on but me.

(Jill, Final Masters' Paper, 1998)

The degree to which she felt "lost" supported Jill in understanding how what appeared to her to be the "invisible" values, assumptions, and patterns of communications in schools advantage certain children while simultaneously disadvantaging others. While she must maintain a commitment to efforts to identify these conditions, her experience is one that we believe will help her first question the viability and supportiveness of the context of education before she questions the abilities of children.

It is important that prospective teachers begin to understand the *political context* of education for African American children and to think about how they might deliberately construct curriculum aimed at helping children identify and deal with racism. Thus, we want our students to begin to recognize the alternative social reality constructed at Mt. Olivet, a social reality in which culturally affirming images and patterns of interaction become cultural resources for resisting the negative images of the larger social world. Peggy's journal entry captures her understanding of the political context of education within the Mt. Olivet Community.

It is amazing to me that so many adults work so hard to create an environment in the school that is effective. The purpose of such commitment is to raise confident, able African-American children. This is their life. With racism active in society, with the rebellious acts of African American children, with schools that continually and unconsciously pass down hegemony of discrimination, it seems only natural that the members of Mt. Olivet band together to create a place to conflict these social realities. Unfortunately, Mt. Olivet is the only place I've seen such unified dedication.

[. . .] It's almost as if someone sat down and thought of necessary concepts for survival as an African-American and then constructed a school to implement those concepts.

(Peggy, Reflective Journal, 1998)

RECOGNIZING OUR CHALLENGES

As optimistic as we feel about the growth and development of many of our students, we recognize that some of them do not experience a displacement of their cultural authority and maintain encapsulated world views or dysconcious racist beliefs (King, 1991) in which they acknowledge their privilege but feel little responsibility for transforming social inequity. For instance, while many LEADS students come to understand caring as culturally and politically defined, many do not. Some do not suspend their own understandings of what constitutes appropriate and "good" authority, discipline, and structure in order to understand the way in which roles and relationships are culturally and politically situated at Mt. Olivet. Some students, like Kathy, learn to talk about differences but judge these differences from their own personal framework, maintaining a patronizing and judgmental attitude typical of a *patronizing cultural authority*.

For me, I kind of already knew what to expect in this program, as I was introduced and already had prior experiences working with the Mt. Olivet students and staff. I believed that the after school program was run much like the school day-very structured, and strict. My first night doing service at Mt. Olivet, I realized that my expectations were right-especially for the older students. They are not allowed to talk to one another, or even look around without having permission. I understand however, that this is what is believed is best for them-to get their homework done before going home, and keeping the same expectations on them as they have during the day. The younger students however, get free time, where they are able to make a choice to color or read. They also play games. When I experienced this, I was kind of upset because I think the older kids need to experience some fun as well, instead of constantly being hounded to do homework, and getting yelled at for getting distracted. [. . .]

I have a personal conflict with this because I do not agree with how the older students are treated. However, it is the structure that they are used to, and obviously works well for them. I have come to accept it, and constantly remind myself that it is best for them, and the philosophy of the school.

(Kathy, Reflective Journal, 1999)

Other students, no matter what the support for thinking otherwise, assimilate an understanding of diversity as individual difference. These students maintain, as Thompson (1998) describes, a "racially innocent" narrative where being natural or good means being color-blind. These students *white-out difference*, in that they assimilate "the experience of people of color to that of whites" (p. 524). Consider Georgia's final reflection on her experience at Mt. Olivet.

One thing that frustrated me earlier in the year was that I did not feel that I was learning what I needed to be learning. There was so much talk in seminar and in my classes about how we need to learn to work within different communities. Therefore, I thought that we were doing the community based education experience to learn how to work with students across diverse settings. However, I noticed that my interactions and relationships with the students at Mt. Olivet did not differ from the relationships I had with my students at Starling. I finally realized that there was not something I needed to learn how to do in order to be able to relate to these students. The students at Mt. Olivet are just like students anywhere. They are all different and have unique personalities. I think in order to be able to work with students across diverse settings, teachers need to take the time to get to know the individual students because this will help you relate to them and therefore, teach them more effectively and teachers need to have a genuine concern for their students. I think all students need this regardless of race or background.

(Georgia, Reflective Journal, 1998)

Finally, some of our students, instead of seeing themselves as learners within a new cultural context, maintain a dominant cultural authority in that they insist on situating the experience as "service" and seeing themselves as "*helpers*" within the context. These students are often those who do not (cannot) develop relationships with the adults in the context, seeking instead the relative safety of *inequitable power relationships* with children. Consider Lynn's last journal entry. She focuses on how "welcome" she felt in the context, but did not feel needed. The role she was most comfortable with was helper, not learner, and the relationships she focuses on as valuable are those relationships with children with no mention of the adults at Mt. Olivet.

My experience with Mt. Olivet has been overall a valuable one. [. . .] I feel a little confused about the role I played in my Mt. Olivet partnerships, however. I was always treated with an enormous amount of respect from children, parents, and staff at Mount Olivet, and though I was constantly thanked for the time that I spent there, I never left feeling that my contribution was necessary or even a help to anyone involved.

Looking back now on my Mount Olivet experience, I wish that I had done things a little differently. I wish that I would have taken more initiative in the extended care program and taken a bigger leadership role in that situation. Though I did get to make a small difference answering questions one-on-one, I never really had a chance to TEACH those kids, and I would have liked to have had that experience. {. . .} I also wish that I had pushed myself a little more in getting to know the boys in the Men of the Manna program.

(Lynn, Reflective Journal, 1998)

Georgia, who earlier had insisted that differences of ethnicity and race did not matter, reflects upon her relationship with children at Mt. Olivet-positioning these relationships in a completely unproblematized, patronizing and "safe" paradigm where "learning to relate to children of all ages, background, and race" is completely absent in terms of any attention to the political nature of her relationship with them and lacks any mention of the need to understand the sociocultural and political context of their lives.

It was such a treat for me to spend time with the kindergartners and first graders. I enjoyed talking with them and getting to know them better. They are so sweet and they would always make me laugh. It is a good experience to learn to relate to children of all ages, background, and race.

(Georgia, Reflective Journal, 1998)

WHAT WE KNOW ABOUT SUPPORTING GROWTH

As we have reflected upon how our students develop, and, in particular, the experiences students describe as most powerful, several themes have emerged. For example, we have always believed that the most powerful vehicles through which to learn about diversity are caring human relationships. The students who experienced the most growth and who were most accepted at Mt. Olivet as allies in an anti-racist effort were those who developed close, *caring relationships* with an adult in the community. Keith was such a young man. Consider his description of his work at Mt. Olivet.

Probably the most valuable part of the Mt. Olivet experience was working with Ms. Jordan. I really learned a lot from Ms. Jordan. I mean, I grew up in a diverse community so I went to school with kids from lots of different ethnic backgrounds, but I've never really had conversations about differences. Ms. Jordan and I got to know each other. We became friends. I would come in the mornings early and we would watch the kids and talk. I learned about things like "ashy skin" and what that means and I learned about greens. We talked a lot about racism and what that meant. We talked about our lives. We talked about what's important for education for African American kids. I don't think I would be able to be as effective in my job where I am now if I hadn't had those conversations.

(Keith, Classroom Discussion, 1999)

An intellectual approach to learning about racism that remains at an abstract level is difficult for many students to understand or recognize. In relationships, our students are able to begin to see and understand the results and impact of racism on the lives of those they care for and, in caring, are called upon to change and to act.

Furthermore, within this relational context, students learn a great deal from the *stories* that are shared. For white students, stories offer a concrete representation of what has largely been abstract and invisible. Stories of racism and antiracism are contextualized lessons that embed theories of racism and cultural diversity in lived experience. Students gather stories and retell them. These stories act as monikers in naming racism, as vicarious memories that they refer to in their efforts to deconstruct the tangled racist ideologies in which they have been socialized. It is quite common to hear students say, "I remember the story Dr. Friend told," in an effort to understand and connect class readings to concrete examples.

Finally, students learned when engaged in extended *dialogue* within a diverse group.

> The other aspect of our partnership I felt to be most meaningful was our group "community" meetings and discussions with Mt. Olivet staff, parents, etc. I thought it was a very effective way to talk about our differences and similarities and to put these things on the table. I know from experience that bringing two homogeneous groups together can be uncomfortable if there is no discussion about what makes the groups different and how each side can address those differences. I felt these community meetings provided an outlet to talk about some issues that could be analyzed from a multitude of viewpoints. In other words, it was a good way to eliminate any ignorance or generalizations that existed between the two groups.
>
> (Randy, Reflective Journal, 1998)

Randy's comment captures the manner in which he experienced reciprocity and respect for both sides to be important to the integrity of such dialogue. Such a dialogue does not situate either side as "right" or "wrong", but instead honors the commitment that each party brings to the pursuit of understanding and growing.

RETHINKING OUR WORK: NEXT STEPS

Developing an anti-racist identity is not a natural, or a frequent, occurrence for most whites in our society. In a world as divided and fractured as ours, such identities must be deliberately nurtured, and opportunities for such development cannot be left to chance. Thus, in evaluating the effectiveness of our internship, we have focused more on the quality of the opportunities we are able to provide our students and less on assessing their progress through pre-established identity development stages. While, as stated earlier, we draw heavily from the work of scholars in antiracist identity development, we are more interested in fleshing out the attitudes, behaviors, and experiences characteristic of students engaged in this work so that we can be more supportive more deliberate-in our efforts with them. We have come to see the development of relationships, the opportunities to share stories, and engagement in extended dialogue as key to supporting the growth and development of our students. However, finding ways to more fully support these experiences is our challenge. In a teacher education program where students complete both degree and certification in a year, there is often less time than needed to organize for these critical exchanges across the partnership.

Yet, we are hopeful. As we finished our third year together we organized an opportunity for the students who were working with the partnership to complete their Masters' project through involvement in a co-operative inquiry with members of the Mt. Olivet community and university faculty. Within co-operative inquiry (Heron, 1981), "all those involved in the research are both co-researchers, whose thinking and decision making contribute to generating ideas, designing and managing the project, and drawing conclusions from the experience, and also co-subjects, participating in the activity being researched" (Reason, 1994, p. 326). The focus of this inquiry was the question of each of our roles in a commitment to an anti-racist and socially just society. We met each week to engage in extended dialogue around many facets of this question. The contents of our conversations emerged from shared readings, shared experiences (such as attending a Mt. Olivet service or talking with the pastor or a parent group), and shared stories. Participation in this inquiry provided more of an opportunity for our students to develop relationships with members of the Mt. Olivet community, to share stories, and to engage in reciprocal dialogue. The outcome of our inquiry was a collectively constructed product and the result of a collaborative analysis of the themes, stories, patterns, experiences, etc. that emerged as important to our question.

In conclusion, we believe that cross-cultural encounters that are mutually beneficial and equal status are necessary in the construction of a multicultural and socially just society. If teacher education is to take seriously the preparation of teachers for diverse student populations, then more teacher education students must be engaged in cross-cultural experiences for extended periods of time. Further, the necessary supports must be in place to help mediate these experiences if we are to help prospective teachers begin to develop multicultural competency and anti-racist commitments. We look forward to extended conversations with others around such work.

REFERENCES

Allport, G. W. (1954) *The nature of prejudice*. Cambridge, MA: Addison-Wesley.

American Association of Colleges of Teacher Education (1994) *Briefing books*. Washington, DC: Author.

Banks, J. A. & Banks, C. A. (1997) *Multicultural education: issues and perspectives*. Boston: Allyn & Bacon.

Darling, L. & Ward, A. (1995) Understanding the school community: a field-based experience in teacher education. *Teaching Education*, 7(1), 85–93.

Delpit, L. (1995) *Other people's children*. NY: New York Press.

Derman-Sparks, L. & Phillips, C. B. (1997) *Teaching/learning anti-racism: a developmental approach*. New York: Teachers College Press.

Ducharme, E. & Agne, R. (1989) Professors of education: uneasy residents of academe. In R. Wisniewski & E. Ducharme (eds.), *The professors of teaching: An inquiry* (pp. 67–86). Albany: State University of New York Press.

Foster, M. (1997) *Black teachers on teaching*. New York: Free Press.

Grant, C. (1990) Desegregation, racial attitudes, and intergroup contact: a discussion of change. *Phi Delta Kappan*, 70, 25–32.

Haberman, M. & Post, L. (1992) Does direct experience change education students' perceptions of low-income minority children? *Midwestern Educational Researcher*, 5(2), 29–31.

Helms, J. E. (ed.) (1990) *Black and white rqcial identity: theory, research and practices*. Westport, CT: Greenwood Press.

Heron, J. (1981) Experiential research methodology. In P. Reason & J. Rowan (eds.), *Human inquiry: a sourcebook of new paradigm research*. Chichester, UK: John Wiley.

hooks, b. (1992) *Black looks*. Boston: South End Press.

Howey, K. & Zimpher, N. (1990) Professors and deans of education. In W. R. Houston (ed.), *Handbook of research on teacher education* (pp. 349–370). New York: Macmillan.

Irvine, J. J. (1992) Making teacher education culturally responsive. In M. Dilworth (ed.), *Diversity in teacher education* (pp. 79–92). San Francisco: Jossey-Bass.

Kahne, J. & Westheimer, J. (1996) In the service of what? The politics of service learning. *Phi Delta Kappan*, 7(9), 592–599.

King, J. (1991) Dysconscious racism: ideology, identity and the miseducation of teachers. *Journal of Negro Education*, 60, 133–146.

Ladson-Billings, G. (1994) *Dreamkeepers: Successful teachers of African American children*. San Francisco: Jossey-Bass.

Lawrence, S. M. & Bunche, T. (1996) Feeling and dealing: teaching white students about racial privilege. *Teaching and Teacher Education*, 12(5), 531–543.

Lee, E. (1997) Antiracist education: pulling together to close the gaps. In E. Lee, D. Menkart, & M. Okazawa-

Rey (eds.), *Beyond heroes and holidays: a practical guide to K-12 antiracist, multicultural education and staff development* (pp. 26–34). Washington, DC: Network of Educators on the Americas.

McCann, B. (1996) *Implementing a reciprocal dimension to service learning: participatory research as a pedagogical enterprise.* Eric Document No. ED 404692.

Melnick, S. L. & Zeichner, K. M. (1998) Teacher education's responsibility to address diversity issues: enhancing institutional capacity. *Theory Into Practice*, 37(2), 88–95.

Morton, K. (1995) The irony of service: charity, project, and social change in service-learning. *Michigan Journal of Community Service Learning*, 2, 19–32.

Nieto, S. (2000) *Affirming diversity: the sociopolitical context of multicultural education.* New York: Addison Wesley Longman, Inc.

Paine, L. (1990) *Orientation towards diversity: what do prospective teachers bring?* Research Report 89–9. The National Center for Research on Teacher Education, Michigan State University, East Lansing, MI.

Palmer, P. (1983) *To know as we are known.* San Francisco: Harper.

Poole, T. G. (1990) Black families and the black church: a sociohistorical perspective. In H. Cheatham & J. Stewart (eds.), *Black families: Interdisciplinary perspectives* (pp. 334–338). New Brunswick, NJ: Transaction Publishers.

Reason, P. (1994) Three approaches to participatory inquiry. In N. Denzin & Y. Lincoln (eds.), *Handbook of qualitative research* (pp. 324–339). Thousand Oaks, CA: Sage.

Seidl, B. L. & Friend, G. (2002) Unification of church and state: universities and churches working together to nurture anti-racist, biculturally competent teachers. *Journal of Teacher Education*, 53(2), 142–152.

Sleeter, C. E. (1992) *Keepers of the American dream.* London: Falmer Press.

Sleeter, C. E. (1997) Teaching whites about racism. In E. Lee, D. Menkart, & M. Okazawa-Ray (eds.), *Beyond heroes and holidays: a practical guide to K-12 anti-racist, multicultural education and staff development.* Washington, DC: Network of Educators on the Americas.

Smolkin, L. B. & Suina, J. H. (1999) Cross-cultural partnerships: acknowledging the "equal other" in The Rural/Urban American Indian Teacher Education Program. *Teaching and Teacher Education*, 15, 571–590.

Strauss, A. & Corbin, J. (1994) Grounded theory methodology: an overview. In N. Denzin & Y. Lincoln (eds.), *Handbook of qualitative research* (pp. 273–285). Thousand Oaks, CA: Sage Publications.

Tatum, B. D. (1992) Talking about race, learning about racism: the application of racial identity development theory in the classroom. *Harvard Educational Review*, 62(1), 1–24.

Thompson, A. (1997) For: anti-racist education. *Curriculum Inquiry*, 27(1), 7–44.

Thompson, A. (1998) Not the color purple: Black feminist lessons for educational caring. *Harvard Educational Review*, 68(4), 522–554.

Walker, J. W. (1979) *Identity: the black experience.* Toronto: Ontario Educational Communications Authority.

Ward, A. (1998) The role of mentorship in a Saskatchewan cross-cultural teacher education project. *McGill Journal of Education*, 33(3), 285–297.

West, C. (1993) *Keeping the faith.* NY: Routledge.

Zeichner, K. M. (1992) *Educating teachers for cultural diversity.* NCRTL Special Report. National Center for Research on Teacher Learning, East Lansing, MI.

3.3 Teachers for multicultural schools

The power of selection[1]

Martin Haberman and Linda Post

Source: Martin Haberman and Linda Post, "Teachers for multicultural schools," *Theory into Practice*, 37(2), 1998, pp. 97–104

Multicultural education has much to offer our schools, particularly our urban schools, but simply adding a course or two will not bring about the changes that are needed. Likewise, adding multicultural education to the teacher education curriculum will not be sufficient. In this article, we argue that only teachers with a particular set of attributes and ideology can offer a multicultural curriculum. The stated goals of these curricula emphasize students' personal development. The achievement of such critically important but elusive objectives requires outstanding teachers.

We propose here 12 teacher attributes for offering a multicultural program, focusing on specific teacher qualities and ideology. We describe ways in which teachers explain how they learn, and present a profile of such teachers. Our argument proposes "what" (the content to be learned), "how" (the way it is learned), and "who" seems likely to learn it. The basic contention is that in order to perform the sophisticated expectations of multicultural teaching, selecting those predisposed to do it is a necessary precondition. Training, while vital, is only of value to teacher candidates whose ideology and predispositions reflect those of outstanding, practicing teachers. The article is prefaced by a brief analysis of the challenge presented by street values to multicultural initiatives.

THE URBAN SETTING

Urban schools are the battleground of a culture war. Traditional societal values are pitted against street values and are being beaten-badly. Not only are schools unable to contravene street values, they actually adopt and promulgate many of them. Elsewhere we have described 14 values that constitute unemployment training and by which urban schools systematically predispose graduates as well as dropouts to a life of unemployment and nonparticipation (Haberman, 1997).

Street values do not represent the diverse, minority culture groups that comprise urban communities any more than they represent the traditional American values promulgated in public schools. Being a member of a particular culture group is a source of strength and provides a platform for living a life of high self-esteem and self realization. Living by street values portends a life of poverty, poor health, and antisocial behavior.

Before urban schools can become more multicultural, they must first become effective in resisting street values which, like other viruses, are carried into school each day by infected children. At present, students control the urban school's agenda by making educators spend most of their time and energy reacting to street values rather than proactively implementing the stated curriculum. Responding to street values is the school's primary business because maintaining a safe environment is a prerequisite for learning. But street values ultimately coalesce into an integrated behavior pattern that "works" for youngsters in urban schools.

For example, one street value is that personal relationships are determined by "who has the power to hurt you." This supports the tacit but ever-present threat of violence. One way students demonstrate this power value in school is by manifesting a "make me" attitude. This street value, which defines all interactions and relationships on the basis of power, forms the basis for the school game in which it becomes the job of the teachers to force students to learn and the role of the students to resist by functioning as observers rather than participants. Once the game is in progress, school authorities respond with more and more rules and attempts at greater coercion; students respond with noncompliance. This leads to even more complex rules which in turn engender more sophisticated forms of student resistance and detachment. The net effect is that urban students who have assimilated this street value do as little as possible, indeed nothing more than show up, and finesse the schools into legitimizing this "activity" with passing grades. The technical term for this exchange in which students are passed for merely showing up and not being disruptive is "the deal" and has been carefully documented (Payne, 1984).

Enter all those interested in restructuring or reform, including advocates for multicultural curriculum. Unfortunately, making school curriculum more multicultural will not necessarily decrease the power of street values. The communal and face-to-face values that characterize the minority cultures in our cities have been just as ineffective at overcoming the power of street values as the traditional associational values taught in public schools. (The Black Muslim community is a notable exception to this pattern and actually does contravene some street values.) Scenes of distraught family members and ministers sitting in courts, hospitals, and funeral parlors and wondering how they lost their children are just as well documented as those of educators expressing failure at turning their students on to learning or keeping them in school.

STREET VALUES AND MULTICULTURALISM

The goal of overcoming street values must be separated from the goal of making schools more multicultural. The former deals with issues such as whether or not schools should use metal detectors; the latter deals with teaching and learning about self-identity, enhancing community cultures, and functioning effectively in American society. Making the school curriculum more multicultural will not necessarily decrease violence, dropout rates, or gang activity. These are not valid criteria for initiating or judging the effects of multicultural curriculum. Greater multiculturalism in school programs has the potential for providing students with (a) powerful ideas for how to live successfully in the general American society, (b) useful skills for succeeding in the world of work, (c) understanding various culture groups, (d) gaining identity and strength from participating in one's own culture group, and (e) learning ways to contribute to greater equity and opportunity for all individuals and groups.

Some teachers offer such a curriculum by engaging, motivating, and interesting their students in ways that actively involve them and make them responsible for their learning. This leads to higher achievement in traditional school subjects. More importantly, it also leads students to demonstrate high level skills for solving real life problems—even how to resist street values in some cases. We designate such teachers "stars" using the following criteria: they work in districts serving a majority of students in poverty; their classes surpass the average achievement level of their building; they are identified by other teachers, their principals, students' parents, outside observers, and themselves as superior or excellent. We estimate that even the most chaotic systems have as many as 8 percent of the teachers who meet these criteria (Haberman, 1995b).

Whether or not having a multicultural curriculum can overcome street values or merely provides a better education for youngsters who would resist street values anyway is a question in need of substantial future study. What we can be sure of is that multicultural curricula focus students on their current lives by studying real world problems rather than preparing them only for living later on in the best of all nonexistent worlds. In a society with the stated goals of equal opportunity and the enhancement of all culture groups, multicultural curriculum becomes a fundamental mission of public education.

Officially approved school-board positions adopting multiculturalism as a top priority are not typically found in small town or suburban school districts. "Can we all learn to live together?" is not a mission given schools in advantaged communities or in communities in which people expect societal institutions (i.e. government, the criminal justice system, health care, education) to function in their interest and actually meet their needs. Typically, multicultural mission statements are adopted in the 120 major urban districts that serve 7 million students in poverty and in which a majority of students are from diverse minority backgrounds. Consider the following statement of definition:

> Multicultural education is a process built on respect and appreciation of cultural diversity. Central to this process is gaining understanding of the cultures of the world and incorporating these insights into all areas of the curriculum and school life with a particular emphasis on those cultures represented in our school community. Growing from these insights is a respect for all cultures and commitment to creating equitable relationships between men and women, among people of different ethnic backgrounds, and for all categories of people. Viewed in this manner multicultural education builds respect, self-esteem, and appreciation of others and provides students with the tools for building a just and equitable society.
>
> (Milwaukee Public Schools, 1995)

The statement goes on to spell out an exhaustive list of goals for students that include an extensive understanding of American society derived from anthropological, historical, and economic concepts: sophisticated communication concepts and skills: the willingness and ability to self-reflect and change oneself; the causes and cures of a low self-concept; and in-depth knowledge of the causes of all forms of societal inequity as well as the proclivity and skills for making the world a better place.

THE KNOWLEDGE BASE

Over the last 40 years we (Haberman and colleagues) have had the opportunity to develop, evaluate, and offer more teacher education programs preparing more teachers than anyone in the history of American teacher education. These programs have been notable failures if we use criteria such as the following: Did these models become institutionalized in universities after external funding was discontinued? Did the graduates remain as teachers in poverty schools longer than 3 years? Within each of these models, however, we have been able to identify program elements that do predict which candidates will be effective with children in poverty, who will remain as classroom teachers, what is the ideology of such teachers, and how are they selected and trained. In our current Metropolitan Multicultural Teacher Education Program (which is now replicated in several cities), we have a 7-year record of 97.5 percent retention of a teacher population that is 75 percent minority in the Milwaukee Public Schools.

In considering what we know about our teachers that predisposes them to offer multicultural programs as an integral part of their teaching, we have identified the nature of their knowledge base. Following are some of the essential elements of this knowledge base.

Self-knowledge—a thorough understanding of one's own cultural roots and group affiliations. An individual who says, "I'm not a member of any culture group, I'm just an American," is not sufficiently grounded to teach a multicultural curriculum. Teachers encourage students to search for more knowledge about their own and classmates' roots by sharing their own.

Self-acceptance—a high level of self-esteem derived from knowing one's roots. Nobodies do not make somebodies. It takes somebodies to make somebodies. Teachers foster self-confidence and pride of group identity by demonstrating a confident acceptance of their own.

Relationship skills—the ability to work with diverse children and adults who are different from oneself in ways that these others perceive as respectful and caring. The teacher shows "we can all live together" by treating all groups as equally fine.

Community knowledge—a knowledge of the cultural heritages of the children and their families. Teachers who make home visits and have continuing experiences in the community's churches, stores, businesses, and parks are able to offer a multicultural curriculum that derives from the specific life experiences of the children in their classes.

Empathy—a deep and abiding sensitivity and appreciation to the ways in which children and their families perceive, understand, and explain their world. The teacher truly understands what parents in particular culture groups may want for their children without lowering standards and expectations.

Cultural human development—a understanding of how the local community influences development. The teacher knows more than what is supposedly universal for all 7-year-olds or all 13year-olds. What does it mean for a toddler, child, preadolescent, or adolescent who is of a particular language, racial, cultural, or economic group to "grow up" in this community?

Cultural conflicts—an understanding of the discrepancies between the values of the local community groups and the traditional American values espoused in schools. The teacher expects, prepares for, and deals with issues that arise from differences in religion, gender roles, and values.

Relevant curriculum—a knowledge of connections that can be made between general societal values and those of the culture groups in the community, and the skills needed to implement this knowledge. The teacher connects specific content goals to specific uses in the students' lives.

Generating sustained effort—a knowledge and set of implementation skills that will engage youngsters from this community to persist with schoolwork. The teacher's daily instruction is organized around and rewards effort rather than perceived ability.

Coping with violence—skills for preventing and de-escalating violence and the potential for violence. How do I work in and help students succeed in an environment where violence is a constant fact of life? The teacher demonstrates forms of conflict resolution based on criteria other than power.

Self-analysis—a capacity for reflection and change. How can I use my experiences to continue to learn, grow, and change? Teachers engage in systematic self-reflection. They develop and implement plans for professional development that impact on their classrooms.

Functioning in chaos—an ability to understand and the skills to cope with a disorganized environment. Urban school systems reflect the unstable, dysfunctional nature of their communities. Teachers who remain effective in such environments know and can implement behaviors that enable them to function effectively in spite of the irrationality of their school bureaucracies.

HOW DO TEACHERS LEARN THESE THINGS?

Teachers who can work with children in poverty in multicultural ways are neither born nor made; they develop as they integrate significant life experiences. A consideration of the elements of the knowledge base described above reveals that they are not forms of knowledge found in genes or gained in university courses. How then are these forms of knowledge developed and learned?

Star teachers of children in poverty offer some interesting perceptions and beliefs regarding how they got where they are in their development as teachers. Telling their stories, they state some things directly about their own development. In other cases they offer explanations after we ask them to explain things we have observed them doing in their teaching. The discussion that follows describes most, not all, of how they learned to teach. While the content of these learnings has changed, the procedures for learning them has remained fairly constant over the last 4 decades in which we have witnessed instruction and listened to teachers in urban schools across the nation.

Almost everything star teachers do that they regard as important is something they believe they learned on the job after they started teaching. When asked, "Where did you learn that?" about a practice or idea, they almost never attribute their learning to a university course, experience, or faculty. Teachers' preferred way of learning is to observe colleagues whom they regard as credible because they are successful with similar students in the same school system. Their focus is on craft knowledge. They are the ultimate pragmatists. Their test for knowledge is that they have seen it "work."

Having a credible teacher mentor actively coach them in their own classroom is the way star teachers prefer to practice and learn more effective procedures and make them their own. "Credible" mentors are teachers observed actually performing what they advise. Being part of an effective teacher team is also a powerful influence on teaching practice. Teaming is so influential that even when the team is functioning negatively it may continue to dominate their thinking and learning. Since teacher teams typically deal with the same students, teachers are especially sensitive to other teachers' practices that may be generating different student behaviors.

The perceived need to learn more subject matter is an unusual and minor influence on development of teachers. Practicing teachers rarely if ever attribute their students' lack of interest or achievement to their "inadequate" content knowledge. They strongly reject the contention that children in poverty are not learning more because their teachers do not know enough.

Developing more knowledge of teaching methods is regarded as an unimportant or easily met need. Teachers do not believe they need more workshops on teaching methods. They do seek more specific ways of making any method meet the particular needs of their students. They seek solutions to their perceived problems, not more subject matter content or teaching methodologies. Teachers regard workshops as useful if they come away with (a) specific strategies they can use to resolve their problems or (b) specific new materials or resources they can use in their classrooms. Again, such workshops must be offered by practicing teachers they regard as credible.

Networking with other teachers trying to resolve similar problems in the same school system seems to further teacher development and combat burnout. Some of the more influential activities frequently relate to methods of coping with system-imposed policies regarding new programs, testing, grade level requirements, recordkeeping, discipline, and school rules. The body of knowledge teachers learn in order to cope with such school mandates and other required conditions of employment constitutes a major portion of the knowledge they develop in the course of their careers. This essential knowledge for functioning in chaotic systems is shared by classroom teachers but is ignored in the professional literature. If it is noted it is deprecated as situation-specific information, or craft know-how, and not considered "professional knowledge."

Teacher practice is not seriously affected by theory or research. Rival explanations of human intelligence or summaries of phonics versus whole language research is not a determinant of how they plan or make instructional decisions. Activities that impact on teacher development in unimportant ways, if at all, include reading reports of research findings; listening to experts who are not regarded as credible because they are not teaching children in poverty; and reading analyses of "hot" topics at particular times, such as bilingual versus English-only instruction, or the pros and cons of tracking.

Substantial teacher development comes from using the lives of children as a rich source of study. Star teachers are constantly involved in learning more about their children, their families and communities, and what it means to grow up in particular settings. By using children's life experiences as a fundamental part *of* the classroom program, teachers continually learn more about children and community cultures. Teachers attribute almost all they know about child development to what they have learned about the lives of their students.

Much teacher development comes from the process of sharing their own interests, experiences, and talents with their students. The children, in effect, reward and shape their teachers *by* accepting and affirming what they share. The teachers, in turn, see the need for children to share their own backgrounds.

A great source of teacher development occurs by serendipity. Urban schools "try" almost everything. While projects are not systematically offered or evaluated, they abound. Inevitably this plethora *of* projects ("projectitis") has unintended consequences and unforeseen impact. Urban teachers and students who live with these erratic initiatives, reforms, programs, and models have daily encounters with unplanned events. In addition to developing general coping principles (e.g. "Just wait a year and it will go away"), teachers learn much from the specifics of each initiative. Working in chaotic systems—and urban school systems are examples *of* chaos theory in action-is a powerful learning opportunity. Teachers in large urban settings become experts in discerning what to ignore, what to cope with, and what to learn from.

The most important source of teacher development is their ideology; that is, what they believe about the nature of teaching and learning, the nature of development, and the nature of the setting. They bring this ideology with them, but it is imbedded in a casing of prejudices, biases, preferences, beliefs, values, and perceptions. As they begin and move through their teaching experiences, some resist any new input. Such teachers have one year of experience 30 times. Others seek to reconcile their ideology with their experiences and have 30 years of growth-much of it on a painfully steep learning curve.

But the teachers' experiences do not automatically lead to positive growth. We know that many teachers use their teaching experiences to solidify and rationalize their prejudices (Sleeter, 1992). Other teachers use their direct experiences to become increasingly supportive of children. Teaching is a process in which selective perception enhances what the teacher believes at the start. The ideology with which teachers begin their teaching has been shown to determine whether or not they will use their subsequent teaching experience to become more positive or more negative (Haberman & Post, 1992).

There are, of course, other ways in which teachers learn. Since Haberman started preparing teachers for children in poverty in the late 1950s, what teachers need to know has changed appreciably, but how teachers learn has not. Effective, growing teachers continue to use the same fundamental learning modes as practitioners of other human service crafts.

WHO SHOULD PREPARE FOR MULTICULTURAL TEACHING

In the programs we offer, we begin with college graduates (from all fields) who have had in-depth experiences with children and youth. They have initial summer experiences teaching children so that we can verify our selection interviews. In effect, how they actually interrelate with children in poverty is their final selection. They are hired as teachers by the Milwaukee Public Schools each September. The process by which they are prepared includes careful mentoring (one full-time mentor for each four teachers) and weekly classes. The mentors are star urban teachers as are the resource people who lead their weekly meetings. The role of university faculty, health and human service professionals, business consultants, parents, computer experts, and community resource people is to supplement the knowledge base of the practitioners who serve as mentors and resource people.

Not surprisingly, the "best and the brightest" teachers of children in poverty who complete this program at not young White females from small towns or suburbs with grades of A in student teaching and high grade point averages (GPAs) who "always wanted to teach." The profile of the "best and the brightest" for culturally diverse children in urban poverty includes demographic as well as personal attributes such as the following:

- Did not decide to teach until after graduation from college.
- Tried (and succeeded) at several jobs or careers. Is between 30 and 50 years of age.
- Attended an urban high school.
- Has raised several children, is a parent, or has had close, in-depth, meaningful relations with children and youth.
- Currently lives in the city and plans to continue to do so.
- Is preparing for a teaching position in an urban school system.
- Doesn't believe "kids are kids" but comprehends and appreciates how cultural forces impact human development.
- Has had personal and continuing experiences with violence and of living "normally" in a violent community and city.
- Has majored in just about anything at the university.
- May or may not have an above-average grade point average.
- Expects to visit the homes of the children.
- Has some awareness of or personal experience with a range of health and human services available in the urban area.
- Expects that the school bureaucracy will be irrational and intrusive.
- Is likely not to be of Euro-American background but a person of color.
- Is likely to be sensitive to, aware of, and working on one's own racism, sexism, classism, or other prejudices.

These are some of the attributes that, taken together, provide a thumbnail sketch. Taken singly, each has no predictive validity. They characterize but do not explain teaching success. They are cited here merely to provide the real-world alternative to "the best and the brightest" stereotype that emphasizes high GPA college youth and continues to emanate from blue-ribbon committees, national panels, private foundations, the Office of Education, and other fantasy factories. High GPA has nothing to do with teaching children in poverty effectively or predicting who will remain in teaching. Indeed, we have much evidence that using high GPA to recruit and select will identify quitters and failures (Corwin, 1973).

In our current Milwaukee program (which has been replicated seven times in 7 years), we prepare individuals who share most if not all of the attributes cited- above. They also share the experience of living in poverty for substantial periods themselves. Indeed, many of them are currently living in poverty and need not recollect former periods of their lives. In many ways these new teachers are "at risk" themselves because they live in communities characterized by violence. Since they are all carefully selected as having a commitment to the behaviors and ideology that matches those of star urban teachers, we know they will be successful. What we did not anticipate were the effects of their own low economic level on their lives and the stress this creates during their first year.

For example, we have had resident teachers die. They have also experienced the following: the death of a child; critical, life-threatening injuries to members of their immediate family; violence at home (either abuse from a spouse or child abuse); bankruptcy; forced moving, that is, the need to find a new residence for the family; inability to secure an affordable home or car insurance; serious illnesses requiring unforeseen surgery or rehabilitation; chemical or drug dependency; serious and continuing transportation problems; marital problems of all types and severity; child custody problems; lawsuits related to a variety of out-of-school issues for which the teacher could not afford counsel; poor nutrition, exercise, and sleep habits; no preventive medicine for themselves or their families: mental and emotional problems, treated and untreated; and fear of deportation as illegal aliens.

We have been impressed, "floored" would be more accurate, by the ability of our resident teachers to both learn from and overcome their life experiences at the same time they were learning to teach in extremely demanding, urban poverty schools. The lesson we have learned is that carefully selected "best and brightest" (i.e. our definition) are individuals who are themselves frequently in poverty, close to poverty, or grew up in poverty. They are sensitive to what it means for a child to have to sneak to school early to avoid being beaten up by a gang, and why it is important for schools to have unlocked doors and serve breakfast. They not only show great understanding for the children but for the parents or caregivers.

At the same time such teachers follow through and insist upon parents and caregivers performing their responsibilities. While they appreciate and empathize with their students' stressful life conditions, they expect students to work at being successful in school. This profile has not precluded us from finding some teacher candidates from advantaged backgrounds. Our experience has been that one out of ten full-time, undergraduate students under 25 years of age, in full-time preservice teacher education programs, can pass our selection procedures.

One focus of our program is on preparing the interprofessional practitioner. This is no small feat. Anyone who has ever offered a teacher education program for children in poverty knows that it is typical for student teachers, beginning interns, and first-year resident teachers to be fearful: they fixate on the question, "Will I be able to control the children and manage what happens in my class." To shift the focus off themselves and onto the total wellness of children frequently living in debilitating life conditions, once again, requires careful. appropriate selection of teacher candidates. The assumption that training alone can be sufficiently powerful to transform the immature and fearful into interprofessional practitioners is contrary to our experience. Teachers cannot themselves perform the range of health and human services their children need, but they can learn to identify conditions (such as abuse) and even more, expect and anticipate the needs of their children for services. Teachers can also be taught to help their children's families to make the connections they will need to get services they do not know they need, do not know are available, or do not know who to contact to access them. In poverty schools the client is not only the child but the child's family.

CAREFUL SELECTION AS A NECESSARY CONDITION

No school can be better than its teachers. And the surest and best way to improve the schooling for children and youth in poverty is to provide them with better teachers. The strategy for doing this is not mysterious. The premise is simple: Selection is more important than training. We have elsewhere described the attributes that predict success in urban poverty schools and the ones that may be identified in interviews (Haberman, 1995a).

Training is useful only for those with appropriate predispositions. The reason for this is that the functions performed by effective urban teachers are undergirded by a clear ideology derived from life experiences. Such teachers not only perform functions that quitters and burnouts do not, they also know why they do what they do. They have a coherent vision. It is a humane, respectful, caring, and nonviolent form of "gentle teaching" that we have described elsewhere (Haberman, 1994). Our point here is that star teachers' behaviors and the ideology that undergirds their behaviors cannot be unwrapped. They are of a piece.

Nor can this ideology be taught in traditional programs of teacher preparation. Writing a term paper on Piaget's concept of conservation or learning the seven steps in direct instruction will not provide neophytes with the ideology or skills of star teachers. This ideology and craft is open to development only in those predisposed to selectively perceive from their experiences in positive ways. What can be taught are effective teaching behaviors that are built on an already functioning belief system. Like the ideology, the teaching behaviors are not typically learned in coursework or in student teaching but on the job, with mentoring by a star teacher/coach, a support network, and some specific workshops and classes.

Reviews of college student learning and teaching provide overwhelming evidence that what students expect and value will determine what they will derive from their teacher education (Pintrich, 1990). Reviews of the relationship between development and learning indicate that what is learned is determined by the students' developmental stage. They must have attained an adult stage of development to benefit from teacher training (Sprinthall *et al.*, 1996). But knowing that college students' learning is controlled by their values and whether or not they have reached adulthood still has not changed the way they are selected into traditional programs of teacher education. GPA and written test scores still control the admission of late adolescents into traditional preparation programs (Haberman, 1996).

IMPLICATIONS FOR THE LOCUS OF PROGRAMS

We have earlier discussed the ways in which teachers learn most effectively. Each of these ways is incorporated into an effective training program. Teachers-to-be should be actually engaged in responsible teaching; be able to observe star teachers in action; have a mentor who is a star teacher coaching them; be part of a team; participate in a network coping with a highly bureaucratized system; be students of their communities; and continually be faced with problems that cause them to reshape their ideology. In addition, the training is most effective when it is offered in the worst schools under the worst conditions of work.

Traditional teacher education and state certification agencies make the reverse assumption. They create professional development centers engaged in best practices and then certify graduates universally. The naive assumption is that graduates will be able to function in the worst school situations because they have observed good practices.

We make a more realistic assumption: Carefully selected and well prepared teachers who are educated to function in the worst situations will be able to function in poverty schools and other schools as well. They will not quit if they are "forced" to teach smaller classes, have fewer inclusion students, or receive adequate supplies and materials. Neither will they be shocked if every student has a seat and enough textbooks.

Since states assume license holders can teach all students in all situations, our philosophy of training in and for the worst situations is also the ethical position. In these "worst" training sites we have always found star teachers who can demonstrate that their ideology works (Haberman, 1995b). The fact that star teachers can actually function effectively in such "intolerable" situations has great impact on neophytes. Beginners are much more impressed by greatness operating in the real world than by observing best practices in a situation they will never again find. Our approach is to also work toward zero transfer, that is, learning to teach is most powerful when it is under the actual conditions in which one will serve. This means that ideal preparation would occur in the very school and community where one will remain as a teacher.

CONCLUSION

We believe that getting better teachers is the best engine for driving school reform in poverty schools. The success of our program over the last 7 years tells us that implementing multicultural programs requires melding an extensive knowledge base with teacher ideology. The knowledge base can be identified in the work of star urban teachers, and neophytes with the ideology can be selected and then trained.

Emphasizing the work of star teachers means that the role of university education faculty with specific expertise must be reconceptualized from that of primary educator to resource person. We argue that the knowledge base is learned best in particular, specific school sites in the worst urban poverty schools and only those predisposed to learn what star teachers already know will accept and internalize the training. We make the issue *of* transfer of learning moot by preparing teachers to work in the very schools and communities where they will continue to teach after certification. After careful selection, training does have important value, provided such training emphasizes being mentored while on the job as a fully accountable teacher.

Our work has also identified neophytes who are "best and brightest" in ways not recognized by traditional teacher education programs. Successful candidates are over 30 years of age, frequently minorities, and have life experiences in urban areas. We have also shown that some European Americans may also demonstrate the predispositions of star teachers and are able to function effectively in poverty schools.

We hold several undergirding beliefs as guiding principals that need to be developed elsewhere to complement our argument. University faculty should be involved in but not in control *of* the preparation of teachers for children in poverty. Research and theory in the preparation of urban teachers must complement teacher ideology and the practices of star urban teachers. The university dedicated to accepting any candidate's belief system in a context of academic freedom is not the ideal place for selecting future teachers with an appropriate ideology. The process of mentoring on the job is extremely more powerful training than taking classes or going through traditional forms of laboratory experiences. Finally, and of greatest importance, is our contention that all teacher education programs for children in poverty must require candidates to demonstrate that the children they teach are actually learning important things (e.g. multicultural concepts) before granting certification.

NOTE

1 Reprinted from *Theory into Practice*, Volume 37, Number 2, Spring 1998.

REFERENCES

Corwin, R. (1973) *Reform and organizational survival: the Teacher Corps as an instrument of educational change.* New York: Wiley.

Haberman, M. (1994) Gentle teaching in a violent society. *Educational Horizons*, 72(3), 131–136.

Haberman, M. (1995a) Selecting star teachers *for* children and youth in urban poverty. *Phi Delta Kappan*, 76, 777–781.

Haberman, M. (1995b) *Star teachers of children in poverty.* West Lafayette, IN: Kappa Delta Pi.

Haberman, M. (1996) Selecting and preparing culturally competent teachers *for* urban schools. In J. Sikula (ed.), *Handbook for research on teacher education* (2nd ed.; pp. 747–760). New York: Macmillan.

Haberman, M. (1997) Unemployment training: the ideology of nonwork learned in urban schools. *Phi Delta Kappan*, 78(7), 499–503.

Haberman, M. & Post, L. (1992) Does direct experience change students' perceptions of low income minority children? *Midwestern Educational Research*, 5(2), 29–31. (Special multicultural issue, University of Akron.)

Milwaukee Public Schools (1995, January). MPS *Proposed Definition of Multicultural Education.* Adopted by the Multicultural Curriculum Council of the Milwaukee Public Schools, Milwaukee, WI.

Payne, C.M. (1984) *Getting what we ask for: the ambiguity of success and failure in urban education.* Westport, CT: Greenwood Publishing.

Pintrich, P. (1990) Implications of psychological research on student learning and college teaching for teacher education. In W.R. Houston (ed.), *Handbook for research on teacher education* (pp. 826–857). New York: Macmillan.

Sleeter, C.E. (1992) *Keepers of the American dream: a study of staff development and multicultural education.* London: The Falmer Press.

Sprinthall, N.A., Reiman, A.J., & Thies-Sprinthall, L. (1996) Teacher professional development. In J. Sikula (ed.), *Handbook for research on teacher education* (2nd ed., pp. 666–703). New York: Macmillan.

Part 3
Commentaries

20 Rigor and relevance in teacher preparation

Michelle Rhee
Former CEO, The New Teacher Project

Karla Oakley
Vice President of Training and Certification,
The New Teacher Project

Over the past decade, The New Teacher Project has been engaged in the processes of recruiting, selecting, training, and hiring new teachers for placement in high-need urban school districts across the country. We have started over 55 initiatives and programs in 26 states and have succeeded in recruiting, training, placing, and/or certifying over 28,000 teachers to work in under-performing schools across the nation. In our work, we have learned several things. First, there is an abundance of people who truly want to work in urban districts and who are driven by the idea of having an impact on public education by being classroom teachers. Both traditionally trained or certified teachers and young and mid-career professionals can be compelled to work in challenging environments if the right messages are sent, rigorous standards are held to in the selection of candidates, and high quality training and induction are in place to orient the new teachers to their classroom environments.

THE WORK WE DO

In our alternate route programs, we aggressively recruit career changers to make the switch into education. We start with very stark, but compelling recruitment campaigns that make clear the social injustices in our public education system. We utilize a call to action surrounding the need for outstanding community members to make the commitment to changing life outcomes for poor and minority youth. Our recruitment campaigns across the country have been incredibly successful in attracting a large pool of potential teaching applicants, with the average applicant to vacancy ratio in our programs being 12:1.

Once we attract this pool of applicants we implement a rigorous screening process to cull the best candidates from the pool. We eliminate between 30 to 40 percent of the pool based on a paper screen of their cover letter, résumé, writing sample, and transcripts. The remaining 60–70 percent of applicants are invited to a day-long interview. During the interview day we assess the candidates through a variety of lenses. First, the candidates conduct a mock lesson in which they are required to state the objective of the lesson and grade level of the instruction and then deliver a five-minute lesson to meet that objective. As career changers, we do not expect them to be able to teach a full lesson, but we are looking for their capacity to organize their activity around a clear objective. Second, the candidates self-facilitate a group discussion around a reading chosen for its focus on student achievement or the achievement gap in urban districts. We also require candidates to respond to a writing prompt to gauge their ability to think critically and write compellingly in a short amount of time. Lastly, we conduct a one-on-one interview with candidates where we ask them specific questions about the interview day, their application and work histories, and additional questions that probe for the attributes that we believe are necessary in any successful urban school teacher. Our selection process is intense, highly competitive, and results in very few of the candidates ultimately being chosen for participation in the program.

Once a candidate is accepted into the program, we enroll him or her in a six- to eight-week intensive pre-service training. The training largely takes place in summer school classrooms in the hiring district in order to give the teachers first-hand experience with students. We inculcate the teachers with the belief that they, personally, are responsible for ensuring the achievement of every child in their classroom, no matter the external influences at play. We train teachers that understanding the whole child, including community/environment/home life, is a crucial aspect in order to see the child reach his or her fullest academic potential, but we send and reinforce the explicit message that the teacher still has personal responsibility for the outcomes that are achieved in his or her classroom.

As the candidates continue through the pre-service training, we facilitate their hiring and placement in the district and ensure that they are enrolled in a state-approved certification or credentialing program in order to comply with NCLB "highly qualified" provisions. Our candidates are selected for their extremely strong content knowledge in their subject area and rarely have problems passing the required content exams. They are enrolled in certification programs in order to learn the theory, methodology, and pedagogy involved in being a successful teacher.

WORKING WITH UNIVERSITY-BASED ALTERNATE
CERTIFICATION PROGRAMS

Our experiences with more than two dozen institutions of higher education providing programs to our participants have been mixed. With few exceptions, we have found the programs to be cumbersome, expensive, not academically rigorous, and mostly irrelevant to the day-to-day professional lives of our "Teaching Fellows." Feedback from our Fellows indicate that university-based programs overall do not take into account who they are as learners, specifically (1) that many are working professionals with a significant amount of content knowledge and work experience; (2) they are in high-need urban classroom settings; and (3) that they are teaching full-time concurrent with learning how to teach. In other words, the typical Fellow's experiences are very different from 18-year-old undergraduates who are entering schools of education with limited content knowledge and work experience and who typically do not commence the field placement portion of their program until the latter part of their four- (or five-) year degree program.

Yet, most university-based alternate certification programs geared toward career changers simply offer the same program of study delivered to undergraduates, with the course times changed from the middle of the day to the evenings. Our Fellows report that their courses are often developed and taught by professors who appear far removed from the current realities and demands of teaching in urban classrooms. The content (syllabi, including text/reading selections) of the courses do not take into account that Fellows are likely to be responsible for teaching students who are two to four grade levels below where they should be in terms of reading, writing, and mathematical proficiency. Given the challenges they and their students face, Fellows understandably expect coursework that accommodates their need for concrete, effective instructional strategies and interventions that they can apply immediately in the classroom to accelerate their students' academic growth and success. Finally, Fellows report that the overall rigor and expectations for coursework, academic engagement, and discussion are extremely low.

Despite the fact that our programs across the country are a pipeline for a significant number of shortage subject area teachers, we have found little interest from colleges and universities in working to adapt or modify their certification programs to better serve our Fellows. Fellows continue to be required to take generalized courses (with a physics teacher sitting next to a kindergarten teacher) in which neither of them is getting real value out of the coursework content or experience. Education schools and divisions, often tied by state regulations around what programs must look like, feel compelled to or choose to adhere to a traditional structure and delivery of the mandated program of study.

We have also found through our experiences bringing career changers into the teaching profession the limits of how education schools and divisions often theorize and view the work of teaching and teacher education. In the Boyle-Baise and McIntyre essay, for example, we are offered two competing theories of teacher preparation: Community School Models versus Professional Development Schools. Our organizational experiences suggest this to be a false dichotomy. While researchers have not fully settled the question of what teacher qualities predict student achievement, there is strong consensus that both content knowledge and verbal ability are linked to a teacher's ability to increase student achievement;[1] therefore, a core part of our selection model screens for people with strong verbal abilities and deep content knowledge in a subject area. In addition, because we are seeking people willing to take a tremendous risk in changing careers into what is well known as an extremely difficult profession, we typically recruit locally, seeking people who have a deep commitment to the community in which they will be teaching. In our experience it is not an either/or but our starting premise that Fellows must have both significant content knowledge and a strong community orientation with requisite cultural sensitivity in order to maximize the achievement of every child.

PRACTITIONER TEACHER PROGRAMS: MEETING THE NEEDS OF BEGINNING TEACHERS

It was not TNTP's intention to go into the teacher certification business. Our original program design entailed finding high-quality university partners who would certify and prepare our alternate route candidates. Our initial core competencies were teacher recruitment, selection and pre-service training. We felt compelled, however, to move into the certification arena by the overwhelming feedback from our Teaching Fellows, who told us that their university-based alternate certification programs were not meeting their needs. In 2002 we launched our first certification program, called the Practitioner Teacher Program, in Louisiana. At the heart of this alternate certification program lies the *Teaching for Results* content seminar series, a design and delivery approach that focuses on meeting the needs of alternate route beginning teachers.

Standards-focused, content-specific pedagogy

In 2002, we developed and began implementing the *Teaching for Results* (TfR) content seminar series to support new teacher development in content-specific pedagogy with a deliberate focus on teaching for student achievement. TNTP commissioned practitioners and scholars within specific fields to develop a series of seminars ranging from Elementary Literacy to Secondary Science, in which new teachers could hone their skills in the design and delivery of high-quality, standards-based instruction to their students.[2]

The conceptual framework for the TfR series blends a backwards design instructional approach, content-specific pedagogy, and action research to provide continuous, ongoing support and professional development for participants. The beginning of the series coincides with the first months of school so teachers spend those first sessions drilling down into state- or district-specified grade and content standards, identifying critical priority standards, and then choosing, modifying, or creating assessments that demonstrate student proficiency in those priority standards. Once new teachers are grounded in the "what" of the standards, they move into the "how"—in each seminar session they tackle a new chunk of student standards and they choose, model, discuss and critique which instructional approaches are most appropriate for those priority standards; these choices are always rooted in their understanding of what a valid assessment of that standard would look like. Finally, as new teacher proficiency in selecting assessments and instructional choices grows, they bring their own practice into the session by presenting lessons they design or adapt and share student work to critically examine with the group whether the lessons resulted in achievement of or student progress towards the standard.

The series is specifically focused on working in high-need urban schools, closing the achievement gap and working with learners who are often two to three grade levels behind their peers. Seminar participants also receive support in classroom management that is specific to the subject and the grade level they teach. This dual approach—the art of teaching, coupled with subject-specific classroom management strategies—is what makes *Teaching for Results* different from other new teacher support programs.

Content seminar leaders: academic practitioners

Content Seminar Leaders (CSLs) are experienced teachers hired by The New Teacher Project to formally train, support, and facilitate the content seminar series for our beginning teachers. In keeping with our belief that connection to the community is a critical element of effective professional development for teachers, CSLs are deliberately recruited from within the districts and communities in which our teachers work. CSLs are responsible for implementing the TfR curriculum and planning two seminar sessions per month. During these sessions, they model high-impact instructional strategies and engage seminar participants in reflective practice, including individual and collective analysis of participants' lesson plans, assessments, and student work. CSLs are also available to teachers outside the seminar sessions through phone and email. CSLs formally evaluate participants' progress during the year and help enforce programmatic requirements by keeping seminar meeting attendance records and monitoring assignments.

All CSLs participate in an intensive five-day training based on "strategic design," a framework to help new teachers align standards-based assessment and instruction with unit and lesson planning. During the training, CSLs discuss and practice strategies to help seminar participants do the following: prioritize content standards; identify and choose from among a variety of assessment strategies; make appropriate instructional choices based on content and assessment; and benchmark student progress toward standards by analyzing student work and using that work to inform their teaching practice.

Content Seminar Leaders provide a critical link between new teachers' pedagogical development and their classroom-based experiences. Therefore, TNTP carefully evaluates the effectiveness of these leaders through regularly-solicited informal feedback from seminar participants, ongoing CSL observations by TNTP staff, and mid- and end-of-year written assessments of their performance and usefulness of the seminars by seminar participants.

School site-based input on certification decisions

At the end of their first year of teaching, in addition to successfully passing their content seminar series, completing a portfolio assessment that complies with state standards, and passing state-mandated pedagogical and subject-specific standardized exams, participants must also receive the recommendation of their principal or site-based administrator in order to gain certification. Our program differs from many university-based alternate certification programs in that it involves the employment manager in the certification decision. Typically, beginning teachers are certified based on coursework completion (what we call "seat time") and classroom observations. Unfortunately, observations provide only a snapshot of teaching performance, often only highlighting engagement or lack of engagement in students; they do not provide a comprehensive view of the teacher's capacity to move all of his or her students toward academic mastery of content standards. Our experiences suggest that input from a school leader or principal, who can assess teacher performance as compared to grade level peers and who is accountable for the overall impact of his/her teaching staff, is instrumental in making an informed program decision when it comes to teacher certification.

Response from participants

Of participants who completed our PTP certification programs, TNTP found:

- Eighty-four percent agree that the TfR content seminar series was relevant to their experiences in the classroom (in comparison, in TNTP's surveys of new teachers in university-based alternate certification programs, 62 percent agree that their university coursework was relevant to their teaching needs).
- Sixty-eight percent report that the PTP improved their classroom management skills.
- Seventy-nine percent report that the PTP improved their instructional planning skills.
- Seventy-four percent report that that the PTP improved their student assessment skills.
- Ninety-six percent agree that their Content Seminar Leader helped them become a more effective teacher.
- Eighty-four percent agree that they are satisfied with the TfR content seminars overall (as compared to new teachers in university-based alternate certification programs, of whom 67 percent were satisfied with their university, overall).

Conclusion

Our experiences to date in developing and running our PTP alternate certification programs underscore our belief that the most effective way to prepare teachers for urban classroom settings entails recruiting and selecting candidates with substantive content knowledge and a keen commitment to working in high-need communities, and then ensuring they are prepared and certified through programs that are highly responsive to their unique pathway into high-need, urban school settings. The learning curve during the first years of classroom teaching is precipitous, and the stakes for urban school districts are enormous. We will continue to challenge our university-based certification program partners to meet these demands or provide alternatives that can; it is our hope that certification providers will align their programs to the very real needs of new teachers and provide rigorous, relevant programs like the PTP.

NOTES

1 Ferguson, R. F. (1991) "Paying for Public Education: New Evidence on How and Why Money Matters". *Harvard Journal on Legislation* 28(2): 465–98; Ferguson, R. F. & Ladd, H. F. 1996. "How and Why Money Matters: An Analysis of Alabama Schools." In Ladd, ed. *Holding Schools Accountable*. Washington, DC: Brookings.
2 The series was designed with financial support from Washington Mutual Bank.

21 Settings for teacher education
Challenges in creating a stronger research base

Sharon P. Robinson
American Association of Colleges for
Teacher Education

Why does the question of settings for teacher education matter? One could argue that—if teacher education settings are regarded as an "input" or "process" dimension—then attending to this issue runs counter to the focus on teacher performance. But for the same reason, this issue may be more relevant than ever. As formats and delivery modes through which teacher preparation takes place continue to multiply, learning how various preparation settings influence growth and professional development of teachers may become critical to sorting out what is valuable and what is ineffective in the expanding array of teacher education models. If we envision an investigative framework that includes the major variants in teacher education settings tied to systematic data collection and analysis of correlation with student learning results, the resulting research could contribute an absolutely essential piece in linking professional preparation methods with measures of student success.

So, as we look at previous studies and commentaries on teacher education settings, we need to look at these with an eye to:

- understanding whether and how the mode of preparation influences how teachers practice;
- learning how to identify professional development needs for teachers and other professionals currently in practice; and
- making decisions about how to design and implement teacher preparation settings in order to achieve the best results for students and their teachers.

There is an important link between the settings in which professional educators are prepared and the overall coherence of their preparation programs. Clift and Brady (2005) note that most research on teacher education courses and field settings is done without considering overall program coherence, making it difficult to determine in isolation the effectiveness of a particular course or field experience. Moreover, Darling-Hammond and Hammerness (2005), argue that programs lacking in coherence and lacking in "a common conception of teaching and learning have been found to be relatively feeble change agents for affecting practice among new teachers." While it is important to turn our attention specifically to the issue of professional preparation settings, it is equally important to link these studies back to comprehensive structure of the program.

SETTINGS FOR TEACHER EDUCATION:
OBSERVATIONS ON THE DIALOGUE

Papers and artifacts present divergent views, not only on perspectives about teacher education settings but in how they even conceive the topic. Labaree (2004), for instance, observes that "teacher education" can mean preparing new teachers for the profession, or it can mean conducting research on the enterprise, or it can mean training superintendents and school leaders. Some of the variation in definitions reflects a breadth of roles and contexts for professional practice, some differences stem from the individual researcher, and some reflect the history of a not-yet-fully-formed professional teacher preparation enterprise that has grown from both primary/secondary and normal school roots. The conceptions of teacher education underlying these studies are not always stated by their authors, but they do surface in the nature of the discussions—for instance, the basic framework from which the teacher preparation enterprise is viewed. Some researchers write from a clear commitment to supporting equity for particular groups of students, and while this may be a common stance for most educators, it is not as explicitly addressed in other studies that direct more of their attention to structural or curricular aspects of teacher education. The commitment to equity may itself be grounded in larger conceptions of the role of teaching as a moral enterprise. Hansen (2001) describes how the conception of teaching as a job, an occupation, or a profession impacts the perceived ends of teaching and the terms by which the teaching activity is framed—a critical foundation for designing and selecting the settings in which expectations are conveyed to candidates and to new teachers.

Divergent views lead to different descriptors about teacher education and teaching. Authors who frame observations about settings for teacher education from a definitional or normative starting point offer criteria for determining successful teacher education. Zeichner and Conklin (this volume) suggest four critical components for exemplary preservice teacher education programs: (1) institutional context which considers the social and political context attributes important to the functioning of the programs; (2) the program level which looks at the how a program is organized and its goals; (3) the teacher educators and candidates in the program; and (4) the substance of the program which looks at coursework, field experiences, ways candidates are taught and the data that informs how candidates are taught. Haberman and Post (1998) suggest that indicators of effective settings to prepare the best teachers for culturally diverse children in urban poverty would take into account the connection between classroom placement for clinical experiences and candidates' personal background and attributes.

Darling-Hammond (1999) addresses settings from the perspective that programs preparing successful teachers provide appropriate contexts for engaging several kinds of knowledge about learning such as what it means to learn different kinds of material for different purposes, how to support different kinds of learning with distinctive teaching strategies, and how to make judgments about which kinds of learning are most necessary in different contexts. In this frame of reference, successful teacher preparation settings would be those that best help candidates acquire knowledge and skills. This brings into the picture other aspects of the setting decision, i.e. adequate time for a complete preparation program, linking particular learning contexts relating to the nature of teaching knowledge being conveyed, extent and nature of candidate supervision, provision of pedagogical and subject matter coaching, and the candidate's access to an extended practicum experience (Darling-Hammond, 1999).

The research field as a whole has yet to fully expand analysis of teacher education settings to develop a convincing case or effective methodology that grounds study of successful teacher preparation in the performance of P-12 students. In particular, we need to connect varying perspectives on successful teacher preparation to academic standards that constitute the predominant structure for current education policy and practice at the P-12 level. Rarely do our studies probe connections between specific settings for teacher education, students' work toward standards-based learning expectations, and capacity of teachers to support effective instruction with constructive feedback to students on their academic work products.

Cognitive development researchers argue that it is essential for teacher preparation to be "linked to actual experience in classrooms in assessing and interpreting the development of student competence" (National Research Council, 2001, p. 309). Designing the settings for this all-important link between teacher understanding and student learning is a critical contribution to teacher quality. It also requires that teacher educators develop a plan for expansion of their own professional knowledge in areas such as cognitive science and assessment at both student and candidate levels as a prerequisite to the program design work that shapes field and clinical experiences for teacher education.

Researchers' perspectives also differ on rationales for decisions about teacher education settings. Authors of these papers reflect different starting points for basing significant decisions on the structure and design of settings in which candidates learn to teach. Seidl and Friend (2002) contend that White people need specific training in anti-racist behavior and attitudes to be successful teachers in urban settings. Others focus on the placement level for which teachers are being prepared as an important determinant. For example, Labaree (this volume) suggests that teacher education is very different—in substance, reputation, mission—for elementary teachers than for high school teachers. He points out that elite universities historically have seen themselves playing a different role than the education schools at regional state universities with the latter focused on preparing a large number of elementary school teachers—primarily women—and the former focused on preparing school administrators and a small number of high school teachers and on the production of educational research, primarily men.

Research approaches that focus on *candidates' needs* appear to ground decisions about settings in the needs of (all or particular) teacher candidates (Seidl & Friend, 2002). This rationale implies that teacher education should attend to the individual needs of its own learners—in effect, should model learner-centered approaches of P-12 teaching practice. Another research perspective, the focus on school level (Labaree, this volume), makes the school configuration or the content level—or both—the key factors. And another assumption, the focus on context (Seidl & Friend, 2002), seems to raise the question of knowing in advance where teachers will be placed in order to provide appropriate settings, or alternatively, preparing teachers for all possible settings.

This variety of approaches presents us with strategic questions: Do we actually need to select from these viewpoints? Should we consider these factors together as they help us understand the complexity of designing university-based, field, clinical, and induction settings? How do we bring the intricate collage of all these factors to bear in configuring the best settings for new teacher learning?

Zeichner and Conklin suggest that the way to understand the substance and effect of particular teacher education approaches is by looking inside the program or academic structures to identify important factors related to the view of teaching, learning, schooling. This leads us back to the pivotal focus raised earlier: Do any of these structural factors really matter in and of themselves, if the primary purpose is to tie preparation settings to teacher support for student learning? Do the underlying views on teaching, learning, and schooling impact how well a particular approach supports P-12 student learning—and if so, how?

These studies help us think about alternative routes to teaching. Across these studies, teacher preparation approaches are discussed as if decisions about design of field, clinical, and induction settings are the products of intentional and collaborative planning on the part of researchers and teacher educators. In fact, moving such an expectation for teacher preparation design to become the standard of practice has been a goal of accrediting agencies (see Unit Standard 3, National Council for Accreditation of Teacher Education; Quality Principles 1.3, 2.2 and Capacity 4.3, Teacher Education Accreditation Council (NCATE, 2002; TEAC, 2004)). Over 600 institutions and programs have demonstrated their ability to meet such a standard.

This expectation for rational design of teacher preparation settings may be honored in some district-based alternative preparation programs, but it probably does not characterize the reality for many alternative programs geared up quickly in response to policy mandates whose aim is primarily the urgent reduction of teacher shortages. A major challenge for alternate route programs is to provide adequate and appropriate settings that support new teacher learning and assessment, particularly when individuals with no previous professional preparation are placed into classrooms as the teacher of record. Research studies that show uneven evidence on the impact of alternative preparation programs have cited the lack of uniformity in settings across and within such program structures (Humphrey & Wechsler, 2005). Concerns about attrition levels among alternative preparation candidates add to the significance of this point; the impact of quality in classroom setting and support may be critical not only as a contributor to teacher success, but may also contribute to the predisposition of new teachers to leave the profession when faced with challenges in the early years of practice (Shen, 1997).

These studies on teacher education settings also raise other issues that need attention in research and in the practice of structuring teacher education. There is, for instance, the role of student poverty as an important (some would say primary) factor in the context of school—and therefore in teacher preparation settings; Haberman and Post (1998) give this issue significant consideration. Beyond the need to help candidates understand critical research on the role of poverty and effective approaches to enhance student learning, the factor of poverty needs to be seriously considered by faculty in designing systematic placement and preparation of candidates for field and clinical work (Payne & Biddle, 1999; WEAC, 2006).

Teacher ideology as a factor in effective teaching practice is another significant issue raised by Haberman and Post (1998). In fact, the authors raise a challenge that teacher behaviors critical to success in urban classrooms are intrinsically linked to appropriate teacher ideology, and they assert that this ideology cannot be taught within the structure of traditional teacher education programs. This discussion brings us directly into the professional and public dialogue on defining professional dispositions, relating psychological constructs to professional standards for teacher practice and behavior, and practical or legal constraints on preparation programs. Research studies could contribute significantly to our understanding of how effective settings support development and assessment of professionally-accepted teaching practice. Extending research in this area is especially critical because of the complexities involved in assessing professional dispositions of alternate route teachers whose initial preparation setting is a classroom for which he/she has full responsibility.

OTHER ASSUMPTIONS ABOUT THE ENTERPRISE OF PREPARING TEACHERS: WHAT WE HAVE NOT YET FULLY ADDRESSED

Impact of the growth of online program and/or programs delivered through blended modes

The very concept of "settings" for teacher preparation raises one of the most intriguing of challenges that face professional preparation of teachers in the near term: the inclusion of clinical and field settings in the context of online teacher preparation. Indeed, a major attraction of online programs is the ease of physical access, especially reduction of location and time challenges for the second-career candidates. But the challenges of school settings and supervisory arrangements for professional preparation still matter greatly—in fact, perhaps to an even greater degree when the physical and collegial structures of traditional programs are substituted by distance-delivery tools and dialogue formats (Marra, 2004; Rovai, 2003). As research studies addressing online teacher preparation increase, attention to the field and clinical component of distance-delivery programs can build understandings as to what are the true qualitative distinctions.

Differences in the work to prepare mature learners for teaching

Relatively little attention in these studies links decisions on professional preparation settings to specific research on who teacher candidates are. Increasingly smaller proportions of these candidates come from the 18–24 traditional college student cohort, with increasing numbers representing 27-and-older age groups (NCES, 1997). This trend is accentuated by the growth of alternative route and career-switcher programs in traditional teacher education institutions and in distance-delivery programs. For teacher education to ground design of settings and learning approaches in knowledge of learners' prior knowledge and in understanding of teaching strategies for adult learners, the research agenda will need to incorporate studies that point toward effective models in teacher preparation.

Content preparation for alternate route candidates

Candidates in alternate route programs are often assumed to have adequate and appropriate content knowledge based on an undergraduate content major, with only the preparation in pedagogy left to be addressed. The reality of differences across undergraduate curricula and assessment measures, however, makes this a questionable assumption. Alternate route programs need to incorporate the same kind of pedagogical content assessment that is conducted in high-quality preservice programs, with special attention to the kinds of knowledge that help students reach learning goals identified in state and national P-12 standards. Settings that provide content knowledge assessment and developmental support for alternate route teachers present a challenge, especially coupled with the need to build teachers' ability to assess content development in their own students. The initial classroom placement for alternate route teachers becomes a critical factor since it also serves as the basic preparation setting.

A longstanding issue: relationship between theory and practice in learning to teach

Studies of teacher education have often addressed the challenge of bringing educational theory and practice into meaningful and practical balance for beginning teachers. Knowles and Cole note that:

> [t]he understanding is that theory and practice are distinct entities; the theory learned at the university and the practice residing and experienced in schools have little connection. The problem is systemic. From the university perspective, there is a concern that the activities taking place during field experiences are often too focused on the immediacy of classroom action, narrowly defined, and too technically oriented. Frequently, preservice teachers enter preparation programs with preconceptions that experiences in the field are all that really matter in the learning-to-teach endeavor, that the university component is to be endured but not taken seriously. These preconceived ideas all too often become reinforced in the field by those with whom they interact.
>
> (Knowles & Cole, 1998, p. 669)

This theory/practice conundrum has enormous implications for design of settings in which teachers are prepared. One aspect is noted by Haberman and Post in their observations on the importance of immersion in the P-12 classroom to effectively prepare teachers for urban classrooms, but the issue grows in complexity when we expect a results-oriented marker for successful teacher preparation. What can research tell us about linking specific theory-practice designs and settings for professional preparation to new teachers' effectiveness in supporting student learning gains?

CONCLUSIONS

We return to the question originally posed: What should we expect from research on settings in teacher education? This dialogue among researchers on settings for teacher preparation gives us the opportunity to . . .

Bring additional perspectives to bear

Hammerness *et al.* (2005) suggest certain aspects of how teachers learn and develop as being critical components for decisions about teacher education settings. Among these aspects are enabling teachers to develop their own metacognitive knowledge and regulation—in order to reflect systematically and effectively about their own practice, and to develop metacognitive abilities in students. These authors cite a "strong research literature demonstrating that efforts to help students become more active monitors of their own learning facilitate their performances." Similarly, National Research Council reports describe teaching approaches that facilitate transfer and development of meta-cognition, including technology-based tools that support learning about the process of inquiry (1999). The papers included in this dialogue tend to separate discussion of settings and context for teacher education from cognitive and academic development, but context and supportive settings are key to helping candidates take on the challenging intellectual aspects of teaching. A goal for future research might be to identify indicators of teachers' intellectual and cognitive growth that can help link this aspect of teaching effectiveness with specific professional preparation settings.

Influence not only the particular choices about settings for teacher education, but the larger political context of how those decisions are made

Along with the engagement in this academic and rational dialogue, we need also to take cognizance of (and some responsibility for) action within the real contexts in which decisions about settings for teacher preparation are determined; many if not most decisions on teacher preparation are made or heavily impacted by market and political forces. The question for teacher educators and researchers is how to have impact on that dynamic in a way that makes all of this research actually matter.

Move beyond thinking of teacher preparation settings in ways that are unnecessarily oppositional

One way in which professional educators' political voice might gain more impact is to treat seriously the issue of coming to consensus on the research and practice base, and to find more productive ways of casting our research frames. Zeichner and Conklin reference fruitless "horse race" approaches to research, and their proposed structure is suggested in part as an avenue to bypass more limited frameworks for program comparison. Researchers and practitioners in teacher education need to avoid framing studies as unproductive comparisons or forced choices between either/or options. We do this when we position a choice between either institution-based or school-based models; or when we claim that it is either the settings or the selection of individuals that matters most; or when we position teaching as either an intellectual endeavor or a craft. Other established professions do not see questions of preparation as mutually exclusive choices, but as balances and interwoven components. When we look at the example of medical education, for instance, there is clearly not a triumph of either academic preparation or clinical preparation over the other—both are given due place, time, and role in the structure of professional programs and the elements work in tandem to produce what we consider an appropriately qualified professional practitioner.

What would teacher education look like if we could take advantage of the opportunities embedded in each of these papers? Who in the public or professional community would not be in favor of:

- programs that provide the support and analytical strengths of academic teacher preparation (Darling-Hammond, 1999) with the intensive classroom experience more characteristic of alternate route programs?
- programs that attend carefully to the aspect of selection and admission to teacher preparation (Zeichner & Conklin, this volume), making use of more traditional measures alongside the dynamic ideology and practice-based factors (Haberman & Post, 1998)?
- Programs that retain the academic strength of the PDS model and enhance student learning by greater attention to the diversity of student context and community that characterizes other models (Boyle-Baise & McIntyre, this volume)?

The history of teacher preparation provides ample evidence of tensions between the liberal arts and professional conceptions, between theoretical and clinical preparation, between university-based and school-based approaches. Can we use a more goal-oriented framework for research and experimentation with promising practice to elicit productive gain from complementary strengths found in different approaches? When student learning and student development become the touchstone evidence, it changes the conversation, and research can help us understand how a variety of approaches contribute to the challenge of preparing today's students and prospective teachers.

REFERENCES

Clift, R. T. & Brady, P. (2005) Research on methods courses and field experiences. In M. Cochran-Smith & K. M. Zeichner (eds.), *Studying teacher education: the report on the AERA panel on research and teacher education*. Washington, DC: American Educational Research Association.

Darling-Hammond, L. (1999) The case for university-based teacher education. In R. A. Roth (ed.), *The role of the university in the preparation of teachers*. London: Falmer Press.

Darling-Hammond, L., Hammerness, K., Grossman, P., Rust, F., & Shulman, L. (2005) The design of teacher education programs. In L. Darling-Hammond & J. Bransford (eds.), *Preparing teachers for a changing world: what teachers should learn and be able to do* (pp. 390–441). San Francisco: Jossey-Bass.

Haberman, M. & Post, L. (1998, Spring) Teachers for multicultural schools: the power of selection. *Theory into Practice*, 37 (2), 96–104.

Hanson, D. T. (2001) *Exploring the moral heart of teaching: toward a teacher's creed*. New York: Teachers College Press.

Hammerness, K., Darling-Hammond, L., Bransford, J., Berliner, D., Cochran-Smith, M., McDonald, M., & Zeichner, K. (2005) How teachers learn and develop. In L. Darling-Hammond & J. Bransford (eds.), *Preparing teachers for a changing world: what teachers should learn and be able to do* (pp. 358–389). San Francisco: Jossey-Bass.

Humphrey, D. C. & Wechsler, M. E. (2005, September 2) Insights into alternative certification: initial findings from a national study. *Teachers College Record*, Id Number: 12145. Retrieved June 21, 2006, from http://www.sri.com/policy/cep/pubs/teachers/AltCert_TCR_article.pdf

Knowles, J. G. & Cole, A. L. (1996) Developing practice through field experiences. In F. B. Murray (ed.), *The teacher educator's handbook: building a knowledge base for the preparation of teachers* (pp. 648–688). San Francisco: Jossey-Bass.

Marra, R. M. (2004) An online course to help teachers "use technology to enhance learning": successes and limitations. *Journal of Technology and Teacher Education*, 12 (3), 411–429.

National Center for Education Statistics (NCES) (1997) *America's teachers: profile of a profession, 1993–94*. Retrieved June 21, 2006 from http://nces.ed.gov/pubs97/97460.pdf

National Council for Accreditation of Teacher Education (NCATE) (2002) *Professional standards for the accreditation of schools, colleges, and departments of education*. Washington, DC.

National Research Council (1999) *How people learn: brain, mind, experience, and school*. Washington, DC: National Academy Press.

National Research Council (2001) *Knowing what students know: the science and design of educational assessment*. Washington, DC: National Academy Press.

Payne, K. J. & Biddle, B. J. (1999) Poor school funding, child poverty, and mathematics achievement. *Educational Researcher*, 28 (6), 4–13.

Rovai, A. P. (2003) A political framework for evaluating online distance education programs. *Internet and Higher Education*, 6 (2), 109–124.

Seidl, B. & Friend, G. (2002) Leaving authority at the door: equal-status community-based experiences and the preparation of teachers for diverse classrooms. *Teaching and Teacher Education*, 18, 421–433.

Shen, J. (1997, Autumn). Has the alternative certification policy materialized its promise? A comparison between traditionally and alternatively certified teachers in public schools. *Educational Evaluation and Policy Analysis*, 19 (3), 276–283. Retrieved June 21, 2006, from http://links.jstor.org/sici?sici=01623737(199723)19%3A3%3C276%3AHTACPM%3E2.0. CO%3B2-Z

Teacher Education Accreditation Council (TEAC) (2004) *Accreditation goals and principles.* Retrieved June 21, 2006, from http://www.teac.org/accreditation/goals/index.asp

Wisconsin Education Association Council (WEAC) (2006) *Great schools issue paper: socio-economic conditions and student behavior.* Retrieved June 21, 2006, from http://www.weac.org/GreatSchools/Issuepapers/socioconditions.htm

22 Settings are more than sites

W. Robert Houston
University of Houston

While only one of many factors that characterize teacher education programs, the *settings* in which programs are located determine in large part their potential effectiveness. The dichotomy often is posed between a strong conceptual/knowledge frame and practical knowledge of schooling, with the university representing one and school-based education the other position. The issues involved are much broader and deeper than the relative roles of universities and schools as sites. Power and prestige, funding and profit margins, definitions of high quality teachers, emphases on academic content or community all are embedded in competing and hotly debated philosophies of teacher education.

SETTINGS FOR TEACHER EDUCATION ARE MORE THAN SITES

The *setting* for teacher education is not the same as the *site*, one of its components. The setting is more than the location(s) in which teacher education is practiced. Settings reflect a broad spectrum of factors, including resources available (personnel and equipment/materials), conceptual framework of the teacher education program, prospective teachers (including criteria for admission to the program), sites where prospective teachers learn about effective teaching, cultural and economic contexts, and sponsoring organizations (e.g. universities, for-profit institutions, local educational agencies). Settings also reflect the interrelation of these various factors, the extent to which each is effectively implemented the configuration of their various components, the decision-makers and the decision-making process, and the identified organization in a partnership that is empowered by the state to make recommendations for certification of teachers. Settings refer to the totality of the places, people, and programs that are part of teacher education. Identifying settings that are relevant and drawing on their strengths is one of the issues in educating teachers.

When one uses *setting* as the focus for examining teacher education, other aspects of the program are put in perspective; because of their interrelationships, the *settings* for preparing teachers not only influence other factors but are influenced by them. Sites of teacher education (e.g. school, university, store front, web-based technology) structure which programs or resources are appropriate and potentially effective, influence on the curriculum and instructional strategies, and often determine the school in which graduates ultimately will teach.

POLITICS AND POWER

The setting for teacher education and the institution responsible for anointing teachers is a major political and economic factor in America. Prestige and power are generated because of the potential impact of such programs on schools and society. Various agencies have assumed this responsibility over the past century—individual schools, county judges, state boards of education, professional organizations, universities, school districts, and private companies. And, in time, each has begun to take its responsibility and authority for granted, been criticized for the quality of its programs, and been replaced by another agency. Legislatures at the state and national levels, reflecting public sentiment and political power, have enacted laws and regulations governing teacher education, provided funding for special projects or research as well as teacher education programs, and have increasingly required accountability for outcomes.

The process (and the settings for teacher education) is dynamic and continually changing. Settings are not neutral—neutral in terms of their potential power, neutral in terms of their potential training outcomes, nor neutral in terms of their potential for employment. Settings for teacher preparation have changed over the past century as a result of cultural trends and political realities.

SETTINGS FOR TEACHER EDUCATION IMPACTED
BY CHANGING CULTURAL CONTEXT

The settings for teacher education are intertwined with their historic, cultural, and economic roots. Settings have changed over the years to meet varying contexts and needs of our nation. Teacher education in the nineteenth century involved primarily practical, on-the-job training, and the basic site was the school. Its settings varied from that of 16-year-old Laura Ingalls Wilder who taught in a one-room school in Minnesota using techniques she had learned as a student, to the state normal schools that provided teacher training for schools in more industrialized areas.

Following World War II, as a result of the GI Bill of Rights, universities provided programs and college degrees to upgrade the knowledge and skills of returning service men and women. Education became an important function in the country, keeping millions temporarily out of the workforce, and in the process, drastically increasing the number of students in universities, the prestige of and need for a university education, and the size and power of universities.

For fifty years, the university has served as the major setting for teacher education. As regional universities matured and expanded their missions, they became less focused on teacher education. Initially, schools of education formed the core of their programs, supported by academic fields to increase prospective teachers' knowledge of the content they would be teaching. As academic units grew in size and power, faculty in education became less central in the institutions they once dominated. Within colleges of education, teacher education was marginalized as the colleges assumed broader professional missions. Even the names were modified to reflect the broader mission (from College of Education to, for example, College of Professional Studies, College of Education, Health, and Human Performance; School of Business, Education, and Social Work).

The university reward structure in education began to recognize research and publication more than teaching and working in schools, reflecting the criteria of academic departments. As universities shifted their priorities and values, they increased their emphasis on conceptual and theoretical aspects of teacher education and decreased their focus on practical approaches to teaching. The basic tenets of professional schools (focus on the profession, the market place, and practitioners) were violated, and teacher education more connected to university values.

Schools became less central in preparing teachers. The primary setting became the university campus, with some observation and student teaching occurring at school sites. Schools became "field sites," teachers referred to as "cooperating teachers," and control of the process and program, college grades, and authority for certification became the purview of the university, distinctions that signaled the peripheral status of schools in teacher education. One colleague told me thirty years ago during the height of this period that he did not need to go to schools to learn about them; I could go and observe, tell him what I saw, and he would apply his model of teaching to my description to inform me of the validity of what I observed and the potential effectiveness of the teacher. It was an arrogant attitude and philosophy, but pervaded teacher education at the time. The work place (schools) became *incidental* to learning to teach.

MAINTAINING SETTINGS AS AN EVOLUTIONARY PROCESS

Criticism by teachers, combined with the increasing shortage of teachers able to complete extensive teacher preparation led to compressed internship models of teacher education. School districts, particularly in urban areas, opened fast-track alternative certification programs as a way to decrease the teacher shortage in their communities. Supported by state and federal legislatures, alternative certification programs were initiated by inter-mediate school districts, medical schools, and for-profit institutions. Universities, not to be out-done, also initiated fast-track alternative certification programs.

Alternative certification programs were touted by educators and the U.S. Department of Education as effective training modes that prepared highly qualified teachers—particularly males and minorities. Like normal school models, they involved in their pro-grams "relevance over rigor" (Labaree, 2003, p. 14) as contrasted with university pro-grams that emphasized rigor and knowledge over relevance and practical preparation.

Darling Hammond in one of her continuing analyses of teacher education quality, charged "that 'on-the-job' preservice training leaves teachers seriously underprepared" (Darling-Hammond, 1999, p. 39). The first signs of dissatisfaction with alternative prep-aration programs began appearing in 2005; school district administrators and human resources specialists began expressing concerns about the effects on student achievement of alternatively certified teachers, preferring teachers with preparation that includes an internship prior to becoming the teacher-of-record.

As these analyses become more widespread, yet another cycle of changes will emerge. Current preparation settings and programs may evolve into new institutions such as Goodlad's "Centers of Pedagogy" that is designed to bring schools and universities together in a closer, renewing partnership (Goodlad, 1994), increased leadership by pri-vate corporations, and institutions aligned with professional organizations, or some yet unforeseen setting.

Technology will no doubt be an important factor in any of the potential futures of teacher education; however, it cannot focus primarily on using technology as an informa-tion-downloading resource, thus contributing to "the 'isolated teacher' phenomenon. In contrast, focusing on technology's use for collaboration and communication opens" extended opportunities (Fulton *et al.*, 2005, pp. 300–301).

SETTINGS INVOLVE BASIC ASSUMPTIONS ABOUT
TEACHER EDUCATION

Settings are influenced by basic assumptions and theoretical constructs of education's role in society. Two chapters in this section of the *Handbook* illustrate these differences. Boyle-Baise and McIntyre contrast two teacher education programs with different basic assumptions about education. Professional Development Schools (Castle *et al.*, 2006) assume that the purpose of teacher education is increased student cognition, focusing its attention on standards and effective practices that increase student achievement. Community oriented teacher education (Seidl & Friend, 2002) assumes the purpose of schools is improving the community, relying on strategies such as "service learning, cultural immersion, and participation in community schools" (Boyle-Baise & McIntyre, this volume). Both rely on strong partnerships between universities and schools but their *settings* are radically different. Each involves very different content and processes in their teacher education programs, different strategies in schools, and different outcomes by graduates. The same sites could provide different settings as a result.

The quality of the site influences the setting. Boyle-Baise and McIntyre insist that teacher education is improved through an integrated school site jointly managed by the university and school, whether in the Professional Development School model or the Community oriented model. By working in the most effective environment, prospective teachers tend to gain the skills they need to be effective. Haberman and Post, on the other hand, state that "training is most effective when it is offered in the worst schools under the worst conditions of work" (Haberman & Post, 2001, p. 103). One believes prospective teachers should be exposed to the best teaching while the other points out that because prospective teachers are likely to be placed in the most troubled inner-city schools, they should have experience in those environments. Basic assumptions of teacher education as well as the quality of schools are infused into the selection of sites, activities that occur in those sites (e.g. community studies and interviews; lesson plans and instruction), persons involved in the program, and relations with schools and communities.

SETTINGS INVOLVE CULTURAL CONTEXTS AND
CURRENT EVENTS

Settings for teacher preparation and the nature of that preparation are interrelated with the evolving culture of our nation. The purpose of schools in the nineteenth century was to prepare children in reading, 'riting, and 'rithmetic, the three r's needed to work in the factory. The environment of Laura Ingalls Wilder at the turn of the twentieth century was quite different in her agrarian community from that of the workers in Lexington, Massachusetts with its tightly packed population and factory-dominated community. Schools were different. Laura's dozen students were of multiple ages and stages in their education, some as old as eighth-grade-educated Laura. The education of teachers in Minnesota and Massachusetts was different. Both were educated on the job—Laura by remembering what and how she had been taught, while in Massachusetts a "principal teacher" supervised teachers as schools reflected the factory model of the evolving industrial age.

The purpose of schools today has become more complex and related to a world-wide culture with increased communication and transportation, world-wide economic conditions, and systemic impact of events half a world away. Reports of our nation's poor achievement on mathematics tests and shortage of professionals in Science, Technology,

Engineering, and Mathematics (STEM) or a report of the influx of immigrants creates renewed interest in these areas to the diminution of others. The United States has become a multicultural society, not only in regard to ethnicity, but also to religion, gender, and conservative/liberal traditions.

Immigration has changed our nation and in the process changed teacher education. At the turn of the twentieth century, the majority of immigrants were from northern Europe, either well-educated or with advanced technological or professional expertise. Protectionism during the 1930s and 1940s lowered the number of immigrants, and then increased with immigrants from southern Europe. Near the end of the century, waves of immigrants from Central and South America and from Asia sought to move from poverty or war to the United States with its reputation for wealth. Complex interaction of employment options, health and retirement benefits, global economy, US status in the world, age and ethnicity of population, educational level of new immigrants—boat people from Cuba and southeast Asia—all are interrelated with the setting of teacher education. Education in schools and teacher education has responded to the new needs promulgated by immigrants; bilingual programs and English as a Second Language, for example, have become vital with the influx of Hispanics and Southeast Asians in the past decade.

DIGITAL DIVIDE AS SETTINGS

A rapidly expanding setting for teacher education involves increasingly sophisticated technology and prospective teachers (and their students) who are more comfortable and uninhibited with technology than their parents. They readily engage in multitasking while using their cell phones, i-pods, digital cameras, blogs, chat rooms, maintaining virtual relationships, using Google or some other search engine to conduct a literature review instead of going to the library, sending and reading e-mail, turning in assignments via the internet, observing a classroom using a miniature camera while located in the university or at home, engaging in distance learning, and making power point in presentations. Using this increasingly sophisticated technology becomes a challenge in preparing teachers—not only in most effectively using it in teacher education, but also supporting prospective teachers' appropriate use of technology in their classrooms.

What is critical about technology in teacher education is not so much developing an understanding of how to use various modes and to maintain currency in their use, but to derive the greatest strengths from them. For example, search engines such as Google have become popular in conducting research or finding information about a particular topic; it is faster and more efficient than going to the library. The quality of outputs, however, varies widely as some sites reflect extensive thought and research while others are shallow and often involve propaganda or radical perspectives. Being able to analyze sources, inquire into relevant areas, and use judgment in making decisions are vital qualities in teacher education. Settings involve not only the use of technology but how technology is used, the thought processes involved in solving problems by drawing on technological innovations.

HUMAN SUPPORT SYSTEMS AS SETTINGS

The setting for preparing prospective and novice teachers includes the quality and attentiveness of the persons with whom they work in the program. This includes course instructors with their knowledge of their fields as well as staff in their preservice and beginning teaching assignments. Often referred to as mentors or coaches, some organizations have paid and trained them while others have relied on the good will of their teachers to work with beginning teachers, interns, student teachers, or pre-student teachers. Some are part of the preparation program; others volunteers who take on an additional assignment. The prospective teacher may interact with them only for short periods, have only superficial contacts, or work with them for extended periods. The quality of this support varies widely; they may have a coach who is concerned about them, advises and counsels them, and makes the program more useful. This human support system defines a vital aspect of setting.

Relationships among teacher educators in the university (or other sponsoring agencies) and schools is another aspect of setting. The contributions of each partner, the personal relations among them, and the integration of program content are part of the psychological settings of teacher education.

SETTINGS AS INTEGRAL TO TEACHER EDUCATION

The various components of teacher education are connected to one another in such a way that each contributes to the others and draws from them. As we examine the settings of teacher education, we recognize that they influence the curriculum, the instructional strategies, even the persons who select that setting for their education, and the school in which they will teach.

An analysis of the settings for teacher education identifies the maze of interrelationships that are involved and the relative impact each has on all the others; teacher education, indeed, is a system that can be defined by its setting. Settings change in response to political trends, hypotheses of quality teacher education, cultural and technological contexts, and economic conditions. It is in the continued exploration of these factors that teacher education can become more effective with greater impact on the education of future generations.

REFERENCES

Castle, S., Fox, R.K., & Souder, K.O. (2006, January/February) Do professional development schools (PDSs) make a difference? A comparative study of PDS and non-PDS teacher candidates. *Journal of Teacher Education*, 57 (1), 65–80.

Darling-Hammond, L. (1999) *Teacher quality and student achievement: a review of state policy evidence*. Seattle, WA: Center for the Study of Teaching and Policy, University of Washington.

Fulton, K., Burns, M., & Goldenberg, L. (2005, December) Teachers learning in networked communities: the TLINC strategy. *Phi Delta Kappan* 87 (4), 298–303; 305.

Goodlad, J. I. (1994). *Educational renewal*. San Francisco: Jossey-Bass Publishers.

Haberman, M. & Post, L. (1998) Teachers for multicultural schools: the power of selection. *Theory into Practice*, 37 (2), 96–104.

Labaree, D.F. (2003) The peculiar problems of preparing and becoming educational researchers. *Educational Researcher*, 32 (4).

Seidl, B. & Friend, G. (2002) Leaving authority at the door: E-status community-based experiences and the preparation of teachers for diverse class rooms. *Teaching and Teacher Education*, 18 (4), 421–433.

Part 4
Framing chapters

23 Defining teacher quality

Is consensus possible?

A. Lin Goodwin
Teachers College, Columbia University

INTRODUCTION

In the Ninety-eighth Yearbook (Part 1), of the National Society for the Study of Education (NSSE)—a volume devoted to the critical analysis of teacher education—editor Gary Griffin states:

> Whoever teaches in our schools, we must reaffirm and strengthen our intentions to recruit into teacher education the capable rather than settle on the available. At issue, of course, is the initial determination and subsequent monitoring of capability.
>
> (1999, p. 7)

Twenty-five years prior, NSSE's Seventy-fourth Yearbook focused also on the education of teachers, and editor Kevin Ryan articulated a similar question "Where do we get the teachers who can do these things?" by which he meant those who can "be effective teachers of our children" (1975, p. ix). The issue of capable or qualified teachers is clearly one that has endured in the teaching profession and in U.S. society. Who teaches? Who should teach?

There is no argument that everyone is interested in capable, qualified and quality teachers for all our nation's classrooms, from the families who send their children to school, to policy-makers who shape the structure, governance, and funding of the education enterprise, to multi-national corporate conglomerates eyeing the next generation of skilled workers. Indeed, the question—who does or should teach—is an enduring one in large part because *everyone* is interested in and concerned about the capabilities and qualifications of teachers. However, the heart of the concern is not simply *that* teachers should be capable or qualified, but *what constitutes* capableness or qualification. Thus, each constituency comes at the question with different definitions of teacher quality and different ideas about what teachers should know and be able to do, ideas and definitions that are framed by different values, socio-cultural norms, and aims.

A closer examination of the contexts surrounding and informing these different values, norms and aims offers additional insight into the longevity of this question of who should or can teach. First, as crucibles of culture and historical memory, schools—and the curriculum—play a key role in the socialization of citizens and the conveyance of national priorities. Because teachers occupy a central position in the educational enterprise and interact directly with developing citizens (i.e. children and youth) as they implement, deliver, direct, and often even create, the curriculum, they become, in essence, guardians of the country's collective socio-cultural legacy. What knowledge is of most worth and whose values are emphasized or understated represent fundamental battles that continuously play out over time and surely will never be resolved. It is no surprise then that the part teachers play in this fundamental battle fuels keen and universal interest in who is permitted to teach.

Second, the state and quality of schooling and academic achievement are consistently linked to the economic health of the country. Our ability to compete internationally is increasingly measured in terms of students' performance on large-scale standardized assessments, and how their scores compare to the performance of their counterparts in other countries. Students' performance levels are seen as a reflection of teacher quality, competence, and preparation—better teachers are presumed to lead to better test scores. Maintaining our economic edge keeps our attention on teacher quality.

Third, the struggle for equal educational access is a theme that undergirds the U.S. story. The opportunity to learn is/should be a fundamental right for all citizens in a democracy. In the history of this country, that right has been systematically denied many groups, and the fight for educational equity and parity continues today, even while gains have been made. Who can or should teach is a question that is inextricably tied to definitions and enactments of diversity, democracy, and equality because it brings into the foreground issues such as the representativeness of the teaching force, teacher preparation for diverse school populations, and the (un)even distribution of quality teachers across dissimilar communities. In a diverse democracy, where the common good constantly competes against individual interests, debates about how teachers should be prepared, what their knowledge base and skill sets—not to mention mindsets—should include, and who should be deemed fit for practice, will be ongoing.

Clearly, consensus around definitions of capability, qualification, and quality continues to be elusive, despite sustained discussion throughout educational history on these very matters, discussion that remains robust and very contemporary, as a glance at any educational journal or newspaper will reveal. Thus, the teaching profession continues to struggle with a fundamental dilemma. On the one hand, we must decide who should be in the teaching force and therefore enticed to teaching. On the other hand, we must weigh who should be allowed to teach, or is considered ready for teaching. In the current context of teacher shortages in some areas and surpluses in others, a teaching force that is far from representative of the population of schools, and sharp disagreements about how teachers should be prepared, we are required to simultaneously recruit and reject, draw people to the profession and sift through them to weed some out. Undoubtedly, the questions surrounding the composition and competence of the teaching force have perennially perplexed the profession and constitute the core of this section.

Through a series of four framing chapters, the section examines the challenges of recruiting, preparing, and retaining teachers of diversity and quality given shifting demographics and evolving global economies. What lessons does history offer in terms of attracting teachers and meeting teacher shortages? How has the demographic makeup of teachers changed over time and in what ways have our efforts to build a representative teaching force had any impact on who enters the classroom? On what basis has the profession made decisions about who is fit to teach and can be recommended for certification? How do these issues of diversity, quality, representation, readiness, and recruitment intersect and what kinds of dilemmas do they raise for teacher educators?

In the initial chapter, Karen Zumwalt and Elizabeth Craig provide a backdrop for the section by profiling today's teaching force according to demographic and quality characteristics. Their discussion is framed by four questions: "Who is teaching? Where are they prepared? Where do they teach? How long do they stay?" They then sift through these background characteristics, using extant research studies, in an effort to ascertain possible relationships between demographic variables or quality indicators and student learning outcomes. From analysis at a macro level, Zumwalt and Craig shift to a more

focused examination of one specific demographic characteristic—teachers' race/eth-
nicity—and one specific quality indicator—teachers' academic ability/achievement—as a
way of detailing and illuminating the complexity surrounding any effort to draw a relationship between teacher variables and learning outcomes for students. Their chapter
offers considerable insight into the issues surrounding recruitment, pedagogical competence, and definitions of quality teaching. More importantly, their work gives us pause
in terms of the importance of certain characteristics or variables, *regardless* of whether
they are supported by empirical evidence or have been proven to positively impact student achievement. Some of these characteristics carry a moral or social value that cannot
be measured but instead speaks volumes about what we care about as a society and who
we are.

Zumwalt and Craig's work segues nicely into the chapter authored by Susan Moore
Johnson and Susan Kardos, which focuses on the recruitment and retention of teachers.
Thus, the section moves from a broad, overarching portrait of who is teaching or present
in the teaching force, to the work of Johnson and Kardos that addresses specifically why
teachers are drawn to the profession (or repelled/deflected from it), and what structures,
incentives, and strategies seem to keep them in the profession. Johnson and Kardos deftly
link the past with the future by comparing what seemed to work in terms of recruitment
or retention for the previous generation of teachers, with what will need to be in place
or factored into the equation when we think about attracting the next generation of
classroom practitioners. Their analysis concretely reveals that today's potential teacher
candidate or new teacher holds fundamentally different ideas about career trajectories,
workplace environments, and what Lortie (1975) calls "psychic rewards." Their expectations and the experiences they bring to the profession, differ dramatically from those of
veteran teachers currently in the profession and winding down to retirement. Changes in
labor market conditions and in opportunities for skilled workers, particularly women
and people of color, mean that the teaching profession cannot, as it did in the past, rely
on a readily *available* pool of candidates, as Griffin describes in the opening of this
introduction, and must think imaginatively about how to recruit and retain those who
are *capable*.

Mary Dilworth and Anthony Brown address the critical shortage of teachers of color
by tackling the question—what do teachers of color bring to the classroom and does it
matter? Coming on the heels of an in-depth discussion of recruitment and retention,
it is fitting that Dilworth and Brown should examine closely the value teachers of color
add to the profession, so as to underscore the ways in which a representative teaching
force is so much more than simply a superficial demographic concern. In their chapter,
Dilworth and Brown take a historical perspective and chronicle the presence, preparation, and practice of African American, Hispanic American, Chinese American, and
Native American teachers. Their analysis underscores the important role these teachers
of color played as socio-cultural stewards and translators, as culturally responsive pedagogues, and as key community members imbued with the spirit of racial uplift. Their
discussion also sheds light on how families of color struggled to ensure that their children
received quality education and were instructed by quality teachers from within their
community. While much of the chapter is located in the past, Dilworth and Brown use
history to inform contemporary dilemmas and current practice. They suggest that today's
challenges surrounding the appropriate education of children of color, whether in rural
schools or central cities, would undoubtedly benefit from the wisdom inherent in the
practice of teachers of color, wisdom that too often goes untapped or unacknowledged.

The final chapter authored by A. Lin Goodwin and Celia Oyler departs from the
other chapters which focus on who is in the profession or should be, and attends to the

question of teacher readiness and who should be *allowed* into the profession. The issue of teacher quality is currently very salient. Yet, prevailing discussions about teacher quality have emphasized teacher characteristics prior to entry into the profession—such as GPA or subject matter knowledge, and teacher performance—on teacher tests for instance, post entry into the field. Goodwin and Oyler suggest that what is missing from these discussions is an examination of the learning-to-teach process and teacher educators' roles as gatekeepers for the profession. In their chapter, Goodwin and Oyler analyze the role, structure, and function of teacher education programs within the context of teacher certification. They then describe practices, procedures, policies, and assessments that teacher preparation programs employ as they make decisions about teacher candidates' readiness to teach, using data gleaned from the literature as well as from a representative sample of teacher preparation programs across the country. Finally, the chapter presents the dilemmas and issues teacher educators face as they struggle to uphold standards of quality teaching in the face of competing demands as well as teacher candidates who bring many needs and diversities to the table.

Each of these four chapters offers a different view point of and response to the central questions of the section: Who teaches? Who should teach? While each offers a particular conversation, all four speak through shared lenses—social milieu (economic, political, sociological), diversity, and shifting social norms. Together, they make us aware of the numerous factors, structures, policies, and players involved (entangled?) in the development of an excellent teaching force, even while they remind us that definitions of quality and excellence depend on a wide range of contextual variables, ideologies and political forces, and are often in conflict as a consequence.

As a collection, the chapters are framed by a variety of artifacts, some historical, some contemporary, some text-based, others visual, some in narrative form, still others organized as a series of bullets. These artifacts also offer varied perspectives on issues of teacher quality, characteristics, recruitment, retention, and diversity. They help to expand the discussion and add texture and richness; they become a series of different lenses through which to contemplate the perennial concern with teacher quality.

Three commentaries written by scholar educators conclude the section. Each commentary is designed to be an integrative statement on the central focus of the section by drawing upon, or spring boarding from, the framing chapters in concert with the artifacts. The commentaries simultaneously insert the voices of diverse educators who are situated very differently and therefore speak from the unique space in which they are located.

The commentary written by Mary Futrell offers the perspective of a teacher educator who is also a seasoned education Dean. It is no surprise then that Futrell's commentary takes a broad look at teacher preparation with an eye toward teachers for the next century. Futrell challenges the teacher education profession to dramatically change what it has been doing in the name of teacher preparation, if it is to keep pace with changing technology, demographics, and a global economy, and produce teachers for the future, not the past. In order to accomplish this, Futrell acknowledges that the teacher education professoriate needs to "consider the implications of the emerging societal challenges, the changing roles of faculty and what their priorities should be as they prepare tomorrow's teachers, counselors, and school administrators." In other words, teacher preparation will not change if teacher educators don't also change.

As a sociologist, Richard Ingersoll argues that "fully understanding issues of teacher quality requires examining the character of the teaching occupation and the social and organizational contexts in which teachers work." In his commentary, Ingersoll deconstructs commonplace explanations for low teacher quality, and suggests that three primary explanations are largely inaccurate. These explanations include: restrictive occupational entry barriers; teacher shortages; and under-qualified teachers. Ingersoll discusses each in turn and counters conventional perspectives by offering alternative explanations and identifying weakness in each argument. He concludes that conventional explanations for low teacher quality are incomplete if they do not take in consideration the nature of teacher's work and the organizational structure of schools.

The third commentary is authored by a practicing teacher. Meghna Antani Lipcon exemplifies the talented liberal arts graduate who has many vocational choices and is therefore less likely to go into teaching. Yet, Antani Lipcon not only chose to go into teaching via a university-based teacher preparation program, but also chose to teach in a "challenging" school (i.e. one that served culturally and linguistically diverse, poor children who were not achieving academically). Her commentary clearly shows that attracting bright, academically prepared people to teaching—and keeping them—requires giving them the opportunity to use their minds, to participate in decision-making at the school as respected instructional leaders, and to develop professionally. Antani Lipcon also speaks passionately about the importance of a diverse teaching force, and uses her own experience as a teacher of color as an example. Ultimately, she says, "those who choose to teach come for the kids, but stay because of the intellectual stimulation and ability to truly make a difference."

REFERENCES

Griffin, G. (1999) Changes in teacher education: looking to the future. In G. Griffin (ed.), *The Education of teachers, Ninety-eighth Yearbook of the National Society for the Study of Education, Part I* (pp. 1–28). University of Chicago Press: NSSE.

Lortie, D. (1975) *School teacher: a sociological study*. Chicago: University of Chicago Press.

Ryan, K. (1975) Editor's preface. In K. Ryan (ed.), *Teacher education, Seventy-fourth Yearbook of the National Society for the Study of Education, Part II* (pp. xi–xiii). University of Chicago Press: NSSE.

24 Who is teaching? Does it matter?

Karen Zumwalt
Teachers College, Columbia University

Elizabeth Craig
Bard College

Three million teachers work in our nation's public schools teaching almost 50 million children and adolescents. In this chapter, we describe these teachers in terms of background characteristics and then look at whether these characteristics make a difference in the education of their students. The characteristics we look at include demographic characteristics (i.e. gender, race/ethnicity, socioeconomic background, age) and other background characteristics that have been used as indicators of teacher quality (i.e. college entrance tests, college GPA, college major, status of college attended, teacher tests and teacher certification).

In essence, these background characteristics are what teachers bring to teacher preparation programs and then to K-12 classrooms. Taken together, these characteristics are often used to describe the demographic and quality profile of the teaching force. The demographic profile, while sensitive to policy, is largely influenced by individual career decisions, shaped by larger social forces evolving over time. In contrast, teacher educators, state education officials and school administrators have more impact on the quality profile of the teaching force, within the parameters of those who choose to teach. Hence, we are looking at background characteristics that have different susceptibility to being directly shaped by policy makers and teacher educators. In turn, these background characteristics may have differential impact on the education of students.

Before turning to issues raised by these background characteristics of the teaching force, we describe how the demographic and quality profiles look in response to four questions: Who is teaching? Where are they prepared? Where do they teach? How long do they stay? Then, we look at what the research indicates about the relationship of these characteristics to student achievement. The chapter ends with a consideration of whether these background demographic and quality characteristics of teachers matter.

WHO IS TEACHING?

Most teachers are female, White and monolingual. Approximately, 75 percent are female (U.S. Department of Education, 2005) and 84 percent are White (Snyder *et al.*, 2004). While the percentage of teachers of color, especially prospective teachers, has increased slightly in recent years, it does not match the increase in student diversity. While more minorities are graduating from college, a smaller percentage of Black college graduates now chooses teaching than in the past when teaching was one of the few professions open to them (Murnane *et al.*, 1991).

Historically, teaching has attracted people from all socioeconomic backgrounds, but, as a middle class occupation, it has been an upwardly mobile choice for those from the working and lower-middle classes. The majority of teachers' parents still do not have high school or college degrees, but they are more likely to have college-educated parents than in the past, reflecting the increased educational level of Americans (National Education Association [NEA], 2003). While more teachers are coming from higher SES backgrounds, a counter trend is that higher SES females and minorities now have a range of other job possibilities that were not previously available to them and are not choosing teaching in as high proportion.

The average age of teachers is in the low 40s, reflecting in part the graying of the work force, as well as the older age of college graduates and the growth of graduate and alternative programs. The average age of prospective teachers has been rising. The majority of teachers now enter teaching between the ages of 25 and 29, rather than under the age of 25, as in the past (Provosnik & Dorfman, 2005).

Recent studies of teachers' academic ability and achievement have produced a somewhat more positive picture than the dismal one portrayed in the late 1970s and early 1980s which echoed earlier perceptions of the teaching as a "failure belt" (Waller, 1932). This improved picture probably reflects both the results of teacher education reform efforts and better research methods.

Studies that have followed cohorts of students through the teacher education pipeline have been particularly informative. Five findings have emerged from recent data. (1) Researchers have clearly demonstrated that earlier studies relying on high school students' career intentions are misleading since these students are not the same population that actually prepares to teach or becomes teachers. (2) When differences among college students are reported, prospective teachers tend to have lower college entry test scores but higher academic achievement, as measured by high school GPA and rank, and college GPA. However, these differences may largely reflect gender imbalances, since women generally earn higher grades and under-perform on entrance tests. (3) More lower ability students exit the teacher pipeline at each successive stage (high school graduation, college entry, entry into teacher education programs, graduation from college.) By graduation, those prepared to teach have higher than average SAT/ACT scores compared to students entering college. (4) While their average scores are slightly lower than all college graduates, those preparing for secondary teaching have comparable scores. (5) Those in the top SAT/ACT quartile are less likely to take jobs as teachers and, once in the classroom are less likely to stay (Zumwalt & Craig, 2005b).

WHERE ARE THEY PREPARED?

Although there are a growing number of extended teacher education programs and 46 states now offer alternative programs, most prospective teachers are still prepared in baccalaureate programs at public institutions (Feistritzer, 1999; U.S. Department of Education, 2005). Graduates of selective institutions are less likely to become teachers than those at colleges and universities ranked as average or below average in selectivity (Ballou, 1996; Henke *et al.*, 1996; Henke *et al.*, 2005). However, because of changing state and institutional requirements, more teachers now graduate with regular content majors rather than just education majors.

The numbers of prospective teachers of color vary widely by region and by institution. They are more likely than Whites to start their higher education at two-year colleges and transfer to four-year public institutions for teacher preparation.

Teachers with higher SES backgrounds are more likely to have attended private institutions. Although there are few studies, there is some indication that those with higher SES backgrounds are more highly represented in alternative programs that recruit from elite, private institutions, more likely to be "late entrants" to teaching, and more likely to have graduate degrees at entry (Heyns, 1988; Wenglinsky, 2000).

Despite fears that extended teacher education programs would create another barrier for students of color, graduate and alternative programs attract similar or higher proportions of students of color (Andrew, 1990; Cornett, 1992; Darling-Hammond *et al.*, 1989; Feistritzer, 2003; Kirby *et al.*, 1989; Kirby *et al.*, 1999; Kopp, 1994; Lutz & Hutton, 1989; Natriello & Zumwalt, 1993; Shen, 1998; Stafford & Barrow, 1994). While still predominantly female, graduate level and alternative programs also attract proportionately more males than undergraduate teacher education programs (Jelmberg, 1996; Kopp, 1994; Wright *et al.*, 1987).

Research on the quality profile of graduate and alternatively prepared teachers compared to those prepared at the undergraduate level is scant and inconclusive, although those who pursue post-baccalaureate education are generally presumed to have higher academic achievement than those who do not. By design, alternatively prepared teachers did not major in education, but that does not necessarily mean that they majored in the subjects they are teaching. In fact, teachers prepared in undergraduate and graduate programs may be more likely to have majored in subjects they are teaching because of stricter state regulations governing these programs. As a growing number of colleges— many NCATE-accredited—offer alternative programs, the assumed differential between the quality of alternative and regular programs may diminish, as well as any differences in the background quality indicators of their students.

Teacher test scores, taken as either entry requirements to teacher education or just after teacher education programs as students seek state certification, indicate some demographic differences. The highest SAT and teacher test scores were found among students attending private universities, which generally enroll students with higher SES backgrounds (Wenglinsky, 2000). Teachers graduating from teacher education programs had higher test scores than those who were not prepared in such programs. An ETS study found that graduates of NCATE accredited institutions were more likely to pass the PRAXIS II content tests than graduates of non-NCATE institutions, when controlling for students' college entry scores (Gitomer *et al.*, 1999). White applicants had higher passing rates on teacher tests; higher proportions of minorities, particularly Blacks and Hispanics, did not pass the tests. Hence, the effect of these tests raises the quality profile but may restrict the diversity of the teaching force.

Given the very inclusive definitions of certification often used, most teachers have been counted as "certified" and, therefore, deemed qualified. The actual proportion certified depends on the types of certification counted (e.g. regular, alternative, provisional, transitional, emergency) which vary greatly by state and even locale. Hence, without specific analysis of how "certified" is being defined, using certification status as a quality indicator is problematic.

WHERE DO THEY TEACH?

Teachers' reasons for teaching and their expectations show some variation by gender, race/ethnicity, SES and age. Fewer than half those prepared to teach actually teach the next year (Henke *et al.*, 2000). Some delay entry but others never teach (Heyns, 1988; Murnane & Olsen, 1988). Prospective elementary teachers are more likely to enter teaching than secondary teachers (Murnane & Schwinden, 1989). Prospective teachers in the top SAT/ACT quartile are less likely to take jobs after becoming prepared as teachers (Kerr, 1983; Pigge, 1985; Wirt & Livingston, 2002).

New first time teachers represent an increasing proportion of the teaching force; they are older, more diverse and include more males than in previous years (Broughman & Rollefson, 2000; U.S. Department of Education, 2005). These new teachers are more likely to find their first jobs in harder-to-staff, lower performing rural and central city schools with high proportions of minority and low-income students (Henke *et al.*, 2000; Lankford *et al.*, 2002; Wirt *et al.*, 2001.) Alternatively prepared teachers, especially non-Whites, initially are more likely to take positions in urban schools (Natriello & Zumwalt, 1993; Shen, 1998).

Teachers of color disproportionately teach at the elementary level and are found more often in central cities and schools serving high proportions of minority and low-income students (Henke *et al.*, 1997). Females and elementary school teachers are slightly younger than male teachers and secondary teachers. Rural teachers are younger than their counterparts in urban and suburban schools, reflecting the greater proportion of new teachers hired in rural schools.

Teachers with master's degrees are more likely to be found in the suburbs, in high schools and in the Northeast (Feistritzer, 1996). Some studies have found that fewer teachers hold masters degrees at schools with large numbers of low-income students (Lewis *et al.*, 1999).

The high proportion of reportedly certified teachers drops considerably when looking at whether teachers are certified in the areas in which they teach most of their classes ("main field") or in the other areas they teach. Most uncertified or partially certified teachers are recent entrants to teaching (U.S. Department of Education, 2005). Besides its relation to experience, certification status also varies by teaching field. Teachers in departmentalized contexts (e.g. many middle and high schools) are less likely to be certified than elementary teachers. Bilingual and special education teachers are the least likely to be certified. Schools serving low-income and minority students have more inexperienced teachers and teachers without full certification (Darling-Hammond, 2004; Henke *et al.*, 1997; Kirby *et al.*, 1999). Some studies also indicate that these schools are more likely to have teachers from lower SAT quartiles, teachers from lower status colleges and teachers more likely to have failed at least one teacher test. Data on "out-of-field" teaching is less conclusive because of differing definitions, but often indicates more "out-of-field" teachers in poor and central city schools (Lewis *et al.*, 1999).

As states have raised criteria for certification as well as entry into and graduation from teacher education programs, it is not surprising that the quality profile of teachers looks better than it did prior to reforms instituted over the past 20 years. There is concern, however, that shortages of fully certified teachers in "hard to staff schools" serving lower SES students combined with demands from No Child Left Behind (NCLB) have put increased pressure to adjust definitions of "certified" to include those who would not previously have been labeled "certified" to meet compliance regulations.

HOW LONG DO THEY STAY?

Teacher turnover is the largest determinant of demand for new teachers. Average turnover is about 30 percent, with about 17 percent switching teaching assignments, 7 percent moving to another school and about 6 percent leaving, either temporarily or permanently (Boe *et al.*, 1998). Of those leaving, more than half return to teaching after a break. In recent years, a growing proportion of teachers are staying in their classroom positions for longer periods of time. Attrition is expected to rise as more teachers reach retirement age and younger teachers, who traditionally have higher attrition rates, replace them.

Age is the prime demographic contributor to attrition, with the highest rates among the youngest and oldest teachers, creating the "U" shaped curve consistently found in retention studies (Ingersoll, 1999; Whitener & Gruber, 1997). Attrition rates are confounded by the fact that more women take breaks from teaching, primarily for child-bearing and rearing (NEA, 1997). Although female teachers take more breaks, findings on overall rates of attrition by gender are mixed (Boe *et al.*, 1998; Hanushek & Pace, 1995; Whitener & Gruber, 1997). For instance, while attrition rates are higher for secondary teachers, who are less likely to be female, they are also higher for special education teachers, who are more likely to be female (Boe *et al.*, 1996). Attrition rates are slightly higher for teachers of color than for White teachers, primarily because of recent high attrition rates amongst Hispanics (Whitener & Gruber, 1997). Teachers from higher SES backgrounds and those from higher SAT/ACT quartiles are less likely to stay in teaching. The relationship between attrition and teacher test scores is inconclusive.

Findings comparing attrition rates between alternatively and traditionally prepared teachers and between those with undergraduate and graduate degrees are also mixed, indicating the need to look at school level, subject, type of school, time frame, race/ethnicity of teacher. Despite expectations, yearly attrition rates for math and science teachers are near average (Ingersoll, 1999; Texas Education Agency [TEA], 1995; Whitener & Gruber, 1997), and the highest attrition rates are in small private schools, not large urban public schools (Ingersoll, 1999).

RESEARCH ON THE RELATIONSHIP AMONGST DEMOGRAPHIC VARIABLES, QUALITY INDICATORS AND STUDENT ACHIEVEMENT

Most of the "impact" research in teacher education is actually correlational research, where student outcomes are operationalized as students' scores on standardized achievement tests (Cochran-Smith & Zeichner, 2005). This being said, there are not many studies that assess the impact of the demographic characteristics of teachers on student achievement. While the large number of female teachers may have an impact on the public and prospective teachers' perceptions about teaching, the evidence indicates that generally it is not related to student learning, as measured by achievement tests (Brophy, 1985; Evans, 1992; Gold & Reis, 1982; Humrich, 1988). The impact of the aging teaching force has been studied primarily with a view toward its consequences for potential teacher shortages rather than its relationship to student achievement. The impact of the dominant monolingual teaching force, despite the growing number of limited English proficient students, and the SES background of teachers have not been studied.

The demographic variable of most concern is the racial/ethnic composition of the teaching force, particularly since there is an increasing gap between its diversity and the diversity of the student population. Research on the relationship between the match between a teacher and student race/ethnicity and student learning is mixed. Several studies (Ehrenberg & Brewer, 1994; Ehrenberg *et al.*, 1995; Farkas *et al.*, 1990) found little association between race, gender, and ethnicity of the teacher and of the students, and how much students learned. Contrary evidence has been found by Ehrenberg and Brewer (1995) in a re-analysis of the Coleman *et al.* (1966) data and in several recent studies in relation to Black teachers and students (Clewell & Puma, 2003; Dee, 2001; Evans, 1992; Hanuschek, 1992). The findings may be mixed in part because many of the studies ignore SES of students and teachers (Zumwalt & Craig, 2005a).

While the relationship of the ability/achievement profile of teachers and student achievement might seem obvious, the research support for such claims is not as strong as might be expected. Studies exploring the impact of differences in teacher ability, largely measured by test scores, have focused on the relationship to student test scores, rather than teachers' actual classroom practices. Analyses generally provide mixed results, such as different relationships between teacher test scores and student reading, vocabulary or math test scores or differences depending on the match between the race of the teacher and the students. While several recent studies provide stronger evidence of a relationship between teachers' verbal ability and student achievement, there is no evidence about the relative importance of verbal ability compared to other aspects of teacher quality (Zumwalt & Craig, 2005b).

Research on the impact of subject matter knowledge, another quality indicator often expressed as majoring in a content area rather than education, is scant and inconclusive, except in the area of mathematics. Studies of secondary mathematics teachers generally show a positive relationship between teachers' study of mathematics and the mathematics learning of high school students (Floden & Meniketti, 2005).

The mostly inconclusive research on the impact of master's degrees is confounded by the lack of information about the content of the degree and whether or not it is a preservice or inservice education degree. However, Rivkin *et al.* (2005) conclude that a masters degree is not significantly related to student achievement. In contrast, Rowan *et al.* (2002) report that having a teacher with advanced degrees in mathematics had a negative relationship to student achievement in math. They speculate that advanced degrees in math may have substituted for pedagogical preparation in mathematics or that these teachers' advanced understandings made it more difficult for them to explain the knowledge in simple terms to elementary school students.

Although accreditation, teacher testing, and certification are seen as important elements in maintaining and improving the quality profile of teachers, there is little conclusive research which links these regulatory mechanisms to improved student achievement (Wilson & Youngs, 2005).

DOES IT MATTER?

Parents and students know on a personal level that teachers make a difference—it does matter who teaches them. And politicians and the public generally agree that teachers are a significant factor in students' learning. Yet there is not strong research evidence that teachers' demographic characteristics and most of the quality indicators described here make a difference in student learning. Are we left to conclude that perhaps the only demographic or quality characteristic that matters is teachers' verbal ability, as measured by standardized tests? Is there no need to attract and retain a diverse group of teachers to our public schools? Should teacher verbal test scores be the critical background criterion used in setting admissions standards to teacher education programs and establishing standards for teacher certification?

Although strong empirical research evidence has become the sine qua non in current policy debates, we believe there are compelling reasons not to answer the "what matters" question only by marshalling existing "scientific" evidence. First of all, just because there is no or little research demonstrating relationships does not mean the relationships do not exist. Current research is mostly correlational, not causal, because it is hard to set up the conditions of experimental research, such as randomized sampling and control of independent variables in the midst of providing equal educational opportunity to public school students. Teaching is a tremendously complex act, involving numerous variables and on-the spot decision making by teachers that defy easy operationalization and control. What works for different groups of students and for individual students within those groups provides incredible variation that interacts differentially with teachers' background demographic and quality characteristics.

For obvious reasons, most of the correlational research looks at the relationship between demographic and quality characteristics and student learning, without making the connection between intervening variables such as teacher knowledge, beliefs and practice, and student attitudes and behavior. The background quality indicators used here are proxies for the quality that really matters—quality teaching. They obviously cannot be equated with quality teaching, but since they are relatively easily obtained and measurable, it is clear why they are used in research. And for equally understandable reasons, student learning is most frequently limited to the kind of learning that is measured on standardized tests—an important but narrow view of the intended outcomes of public education. Are other cognitive outcomes, attitudes, healthy self-concept, cultural identity, graduation, college entry, avoidance of risky behavior and good citizenship—to name a few of the other goals of public education—affected by teacher characteristics?

What is needed are large, longitudinal studies, using quantitative and qualitative methods, that take into consideration multiple and related student, family, teacher and school variables, capture intervening variables such as teacher and student knowledge, beliefs and behavior, as well as more robust definitions of student outcomes. The research challenge is substantially beyond anything we have been able to do. Add into this mix the fact that teachers, individual students and groups of students all have personalities and experiences that may connect or not connect in meaningful ways and the research challenge appears overwhelming. We also need to remember that even if more empirical research were available about background demographic and quality characteristics of teachers, while informative, it would never be able to provide definitive criteria for policy makers in relation to recruitment, preparation, placement, and retention of teachers because teaching is such a complex, value-laden social and political activity.

One could argue, whatever the extant research about impact on student outcomes, that there are good reasons to be concerned about the demographic diversity of the teaching force and its "quality" as described by common quality indicators. Public perception of the profession—both in terms of demography and quality characteristics of teachers—influences support for teachers, schools, and education. The profile also sends messages about teaching and teachers that influence who is attracted to teaching, where they choose to teach, and who decides to stay in teaching. The differential distribution of teachers, particularly in terms of perceived "quality" indicators, sends a powerful message. A society committed to equal educational opportunity for all children cannot afford to ignore the messages the public, teachers and prospective teachers receive about the demographic and quality characteristics of the teaching force.

While aiming for demographic diversity, a quality teaching force may seem like an indisputable goal on the face of it. Despite the lack of definitive research evidence that these particular characteristics make a difference, they do raise a series of issues and challenges for teacher educators and policy makers. In the remainder of this chapter, we illustrate this complexity by focusing on one demographic characteristic, race/ethnicity of teachers, and one quality characteristic, academic ability/achievement of teachers. We choose these two characteristics because we believe they do matter. In one case, the research about the impact of race/ethnicity of teachers on student learning is mixed. In the other case, while the research on the academic ability/achievement of teacher is not conclusive, there is a stronger, more consistent relationship between teacher verbal ability and student learning outcomes. However, the implications of such a relationship pose other kinds of challenges for teacher educators and policy makers that could impact the racial and ethnic profile of the teaching force. After considering these two characteristics of teachers, we return briefly to issues raised by the other demographic and quality characteristics of teachers which add further complexity for those hoping to directly and indirectly shape the profile of the teaching force.

Race/ethnicity of teachers

The question here is whether it matters that public school teachers are predominantly White, non-Hispanic (84.3 percent) while the student population is increasingly diverse (42 percent minority). Although minority teachers are more likely to teach in schools serving high proportions of minority and low-income students, even students of color are more likely to have White teachers.

Nationally, the teaching force has ranged from 84 to 92 percent White in the past 30 years, with the highest percentages in the mid-1980s. There is some recent indication that prospective teachers in undergraduate programs are more diverse and that graduate and alternative programs are attracting a higher proportion of minorities. Although the proportion of teachers of color, especially prospective teachers, has increased slightly in recent years, it does not match the increase in student diversity.

There are several factors that appear to have been working against increasing the numbers of non-Whites in teaching. While more minorities are graduating from college, a smaller percentage of African American college graduates now choose teaching than in an earlier era when teaching was one of the few professions open to them (Zumwalt & Craig, 2005a). Besides access to other opportunities, minority college graduates are now actively recruited by higher status and higher paid professions and businesses seeking to diversify their own labor force at all levels. At the same time, in light of the unequal educational opportunities provided many minorities, moves by some institutions and states to raise cut-off scores for admission to teacher education programs and on teacher certification tests have the potential to decrease the pool of minorities who actually enter teaching (Gitomer et al., 1999; Smith et al., 1988; TEA, 1994).

Since there seem to be countervailing societal, economic and political forces over time that have shaped the proportion of teachers of color, one might argue that little can or should be done to try to increase the race/ethnicity profile of the teaching force. However, we believe that there are compelling arguments to take a pro-active stance here even if policy makers and teacher educators have limited ability to alter the demographic pro-file of the teaching force. If one accepts these arguments, there are considerable challenges for research and practice confronting teacher educators and institutional and governmental policy makers.

Arguments for increasing racial/ethnic diversity

Much of the argument for increasing the racial/ethnic diversity of the teaching force to better reflect the diversity of the student population is predicated on the belief that a diverse teaching force is good for all children, regardless of their racial and ethnic back-ground. The health of our democracy requires attention to the messages children receive about others who are not like them and to providing them with experiences in diverse classroom and school communities. The authority of knowledge should not be seen as the special privilege of Whites, implying the legitimacy of power of one group over all others. Teachers of different races/ethnicities can better prepare children for life in a multi-cultural society committed to equal opportunity.

This prima-facie argument for a diverse teaching force is accompanied by the argument that there are particular benefits for children of color in having a teacher of their own race/ethnicity. Some have suggested that the predominately White teaching force contributes to the continuing "achievement gap" between White students and students who are Black, Hispanic or Native American (Downey & Pribesh, 2004; Farkas, 2003; Ferguson, 1998). The federally mandated No Child Left Behind Act (NCLB) with its specific consequences for not remedying the gap between standardized test scores of different racial and ethnic student groups has raised the stakes for schools and school districts. NCLB, despite its controversial aspects, has heightened attention to increasing the diversity of teachers in our schools and improving the effectiveness of all teachers working with students from diverse races and cultures. As the student population in America's schools continues to grow increasingly diverse, the necessity for addressing these needs grows even more critical.

Research suggests that same race/ethnicity teachers may act as role models who can instill positive attitudes toward school and provide culturally relevant pedagogy that will also increase students' chances of academic success (Clewell & Puma, 2003; Dee, 2001; Ladson-Billings, 1992, 1994; King, 1993; NCTAF, 1996). Early studies in this area focused on cultural synchronicity or cultural compatibility of same-race teachers and the extent of which shared language, perspectives, and community values create a classroom climate and relationships that lead to greater academic success among minority students (Au & Jordan, 1981; Erickson & Mohatt, 1982; Irvine, 1990). Other work, most notably the 1994 study by Ladson-Billings, has identified specific pedagogical practices that are linked to effective teaching of African American students. Among these are practices grounded in: a mastery of subject knowledge; an authoritative classroom style in combination with a warm personal relationship; respect for the importance of African American identity and local community values; and high expectations for all students (Foster, 1997; Ladson-Billings, 1994, 1995; Siddle Walker, 1996). (See chapters by Howard and Villegas & Davis in this volume.) While knowledge is accumulating to help teachers and teacher educators understand the diverse needs of their students, many challenges face researchers, teacher educators, and policy makers as they attempt to address these complex issues.

Challenges for research and practice

There is much that we do not know. We do not know enough about how the non-representative racial/ethnic profile of the public school teaching force and the uneven distribution of these teachers across regions and schools affects what children and adolescents learn in school and, in particular, what they learn about race and ethnicity in our society. Nor do we know whether and how the racial/ethnic mis-match between individual teachers and students might contribute to inequities in educational achievement for students. These are questions that do matter.

Doing such research is quite challenging, but figuring out what to do with findings that might be uncomfortable might be just as challenging. If we find that certain groups of teachers might be more effective with students in general or students of a particular race/ethnicity (or gender, SES background, or age), what do we do with such a finding? That, however, is not a reason to avoid research of this type nor to conclude that such evidence should be used to support discriminatory policies in admission to teacher education programs or in hiring teachers. It would suggest that efforts to recruit and retain teachers of color be given a high priority.

It also suggests that a focus on how race/ethnicity (and other demographic variables) relates to teacher knowledge, beliefs and teaching practice might provide new insights into some intractable issues related to student achievement and help teacher educators prepare prospective teachers who can meet the increasingly diverse needs of all students. For instance, research suggests that White teachers who demonstrate teaching qualities similar to African American teachers can be as successful with African American students (Cooper, 2003; Ladsen-Billings, 1994). (See also chapter by Sleeter in this volume.) As mentioned earlier, there is a growing body of literature about culturally relevant pedagogy that can provide teachers with a repertoire of practices that might be more effective with certain learners.

While more research is needed in this area, teacher educators have access to enough knowledge to make all prospective teachers, regardless of their backgrounds, aware that some of their underlying assumptions about teaching and learning emanating from their own experience may be affecting their effectiveness with students who come from different racial, ethnic, and social class backgrounds than they do. The challenge, of course, is that awareness and knowledge do not automatically translate into attitudes and behaviors that make a difference in the classroom. Sometimes the schools where student teachers are placed are not as diverse as might be desired. Sometimes the cooperating teachers reject or dismiss as impractical the ideas about culturally relevant pedagogy or differentiation of curriculum that prospective teachers learn in their teacher education programs. Sometimes teacher educators themselves have not had enough personal or professional experience with students of different racial and ethnic groups to help prospective teachers enact what they are learning about diversity in their teacher education programs. Sometimes the challenges of learning to teach—to manage a class, try out basic instructional strategies, implement the required curriculum—are about all student teachers can handle during their student teaching placements. Sometimes some knowledge about racial and ethnic differences leads to miscues, as the impact of social class background is ignored or research on one sub-group is generalized to all members of the group (e.g. research on Vietnamese immigrant students is seen as applicable to all Asian Americans). Even experienced teachers are challenged by what to do with the growing knowledge about how racial and ethnic differences could and should be accommodated in the classroom to provide all students with an opportunity to learn.

Besides informing teacher educators and prospective teachers about addressing the needs of diverse learners, research about the impact of teachers of diverse racial/ethnic backgrounds could add further impetus to current institutional and governmental policy and program efforts to recruit, prepare, and retain teachers of color. Designing and carrying out effective policies and programs have their own set of challenges. One of the challenges is how these efforts mesh with efforts that focus on raising test scores of prospective teachers as the means to increase the quality of the teaching force.

Academic ability/achievement of teachers

The question here is whether it matters that public school teachers have a certain level of academic ability/achievement. As part of teacher education reform efforts, many institutions and states have raised minimum SAT/ACT test scores and/or GPAs for admission into and graduation from teacher education programs, and established or raised cut-off scores for teacher tests required for certification.

Recent interest in quality characteristics of teachers has focused on intellectual competence in comparison to earlier interests in personal qualities and behavioral performance (Lanier & Little, 1986). The most frequently used measures have been academic ability as measured by the SAT or ACT college entry tests and academic achievement as measured by college GPA. Also used are the basic skills sections of various teacher tests now utilized primarily for certification purposes, but sometimes for entry or graduation from teacher education programs. Whether these measure ability or achievement is worthy of debate; for our purposes, we are calling them measures of academic ability/achievement.

The belief in the relative inferiority of American teachers is not a new phenomenon (Conant, 1963; Flexner, 1930; Waller, 1932). In "A Nation at Risk," Americans were warned that "not enough of the academically able students are attracted to teaching ... Too many teachers are being drawn from the bottom quarter of graduating high school and college students" (National Commission on Excellence in Education, 1983, p. 22). Research indicates that the most academically able are less likely to enter teaching and more likely to leave sooner than their peers (Chapman & Hutcheson, 1982; Kerr, 1983; Sykes, 1983; Vance & Schlechty, 1982; Weaver, 1983).

As we described earlier in this chapter, the dismal portrayal of teachers in the early 1980s has been replaced in the research literature, if not public perception, by a more positive picture over the last twenty years. This improvement probably reflects both the results of teacher education reform efforts and better research methods. Although the general picture is improved, particularly in regard to the finding that lower ability students exit the teacher pipeline at higher rates at each successive stage, there are still some concerns. White teacher applicants have higher passing rates on teacher tests; higher proportions of minorities, particularly Blacks and Hispanics do not pass the tests. Those in the top SAT/ACT quartile are less likely to take jobs as teachers and, once in the classroom, are less likely to stay. Schools serving low-income and minority students are more likely to have teachers from lower SAT quartiles and teachers who are more likely to have failed at least one teacher test (Zumwalt & Craig, 2005b).

Whether these differences in academic ability/achievement have an impact in terms of student learning is not as definitively clear from research evidence as it might seem from the policy imperatives to raise minimum required SAT/ACT scores, GPAs, and teacher test scores. It just seems to make sense that more academically able teachers would be desirable. As Vegas *et al.* (2001, p. 4) express it, "Teaching well is seen as a complex, cognitive challenge requiring the ability to think and reason clearly." Smarter teachers are assumed to be better teachers; hence, more able to produce higher student achievement.

Issues related to higher standards for teachers' academic ability/achievement

Concerns relate to the limitations of standardized tests and GPAs as measures of academic ability/achievement, how to interpret quality profiles and whether a focus on narrowly defined intellectual attributes captures the qualities important for good teaching. A major issue involves the consequences of the push to raise minimum criteria for entry into teaching on the diversity of the teaching force, especially in light of the lack of supporting research evidence demonstrating an impact on student learning.

Measures of academic ability/achievement

Recently, almost universally, researchers offer caveats about the use of SAT/ACT scores as indicators of intellectual competence and the use of GPAs as comparable, credible measures. Heavily correlated with SES, it is debatable whether the SAT/ACT tests actually measure ability or achievement. However, college entry test scores do provide comparable, standardized national data for student cohorts. And unlike teacher test scores, they provide data for a more inclusive group, not just those preparing to teach. However, the fact that these tests taken in high school are used as an indicator of quality is ironic since their use implies that there is relatively no value added by the college experience or at least that students graduate from college with the same relative abilities with which they entered. The relative ease of collecting SAT/ACT scores, GPA information and other basic skills test scores, however, means that they will remain the most frequently used measure of intellectual competence of teachers, despite their acknowledged limitations.

Interpretation of quality profiles

Concern has been expressed that teacher candidates from the top quartiles of SAT/ACT scores are less likely to take teaching jobs since they are more likely to continue with graduate education or pursue more attractive career options. Once teaching, those in the top quartile are more likely to leave.

This raises questions about realistic expectations for the ability profile of teachers. As Lanier and Little (1986) point out, the annual demand for teachers means that even if all the top quintile of college graduates went into teaching, there still would not be enough teachers for our nation's schools. Obviously, it is unrealistic to expect all top college graduates to become teachers, particularly since there are so many higher status, higher paid careers that are open to them, many of which also need highly able people.

So what would an appropriate profile look like? Should any students in the bottom quartile be permitted to become teachers? Should the ability distribution of teachers match the ability profile of all college graduates? Or should it match the distribution of college graduates going into medicine, law, architecture, business, social work, journalism, nursing? Lack of comparable data with other professions limits our ability to interpret appropriate expectations for the ability profile of teachers.

Comparisons with other professions might provide some realistic expectations for the teaching profession, but the question remains about how much it matters in terms of teacher practice and student learning. There is no empirical evidence indicating what GPA (which is extremely sensitive to institutional variability), SAT/ACT scores and teacher test scores are minimally acceptable in terms of teacher performance and student achievement. Cut-off scores are largely based on what politically and intuitively seem like a minimal level to convey a message of quality and provide an adequate number of qualified teachers of diverse backgrounds for an institution or state. There is always the danger that cut-offs may keep effective teachers out of classrooms and give a false sense of confidence about those who are teaching. Predictive validity studies of GPAs, SAT/ACT scores and teacher cut-off scores in terms of teacher performance and student achievement are needed to see at what level they really do matter.

Definition of quality

The intellectual ability of teachers, although it has not been definitely tied to teacher practice and student outcomes, has long dominated discussions of the quality profile. The transition of teacher preparation from normal schools to colleges and universities, not completed until 1940, was not easy because the public perception of normal schools and teachers had been shaped "by the intellectual limitations then commonly believed to be inherent in the female sex" (Lagemann, 2000, p. 6). Although teachers' intellectual competence was questioned, they were seen as possessing compensating personal qualities such as "altruism or idealism . . . in abundance" (p. 16). The perceived intellectual inferiority of teachers and education as a field of study helped make standardized test scores the most used indicator of quality.

When Dewey spoke of the "intellectual equipment" of teachers being key to the success of teaching, he was not referring to college entrance tests. "[I]t is a question of not only what is known, but of how it is known" he said (1902, p. 398). As he noted,

> ... just in the degree in which the teacher's understanding of the material of the lesson is vital, adequate and comprehensive, will that material come to the child in the same form; in the degree in which the teacher's understanding is mechanical, superficial and restricted, the child's appreciation will be correspondingly limited and perverted.
>
> (pp. 397–398)

Understanding and appreciation of subject matter and pedagogy are other aspects of intellectual competence critical to teaching. However, such knowledge is not captured in current quality profiles of teachers based on college entry tests.

Even more broadly defined, intellectual competence would not be sufficient for quality teaching. Some prospective teachers from the highest quartile decide not to teach after struggling in student teaching with learners for whom school is not as easy as it was for them. Some, encouraged by others because they are "good with kids" find the organizational and intellectual challenges of teaching overwhelming. The reality is that teaching requires a mix of intellectual and personal qualities. As Howey and Strom (1987) suggest:

> Given the complex, interactive and moral nature of teaching and the rapid changes and diversity in schools (and in society), we maintain that the professional preparation of teachers should have as its basic goal of development of teachers as persons who have conceptual systems characterized by the qualities of being adaptable, questioning, critical, inventive, creative, self-renewing and oriented to moral principles.
>
> (p. 8)

Needless to say, profiles based on assessment of all these qualities do not exist. Figuring out how to collect valid measures of such data about large numbers of college students would be a major challenge. Given these challenges and the public's less complex vision of teaching, it is likely that quality as measured by text scores will continue to dominate research and policy.

Impact on diversity

Raising minimum academic standards for teachers appears commonsensical if the aim is to increase quality of teaching in our schools and to raise the public perception of teaching. Yet, because of inequities of educational opportunities for students in this country, there is tension between the goal of increasing the diversity of the teaching force and the goal of increasing the quality profile of teachers by establishing higher GPA, SAT/ACT scores, and teacher test scores for admission, graduation and certification. The effect of raising minimum cut-off scores raises the quality profile but may restrict the diversity of the teaching force. Since a diverse teaching pool is seen by many as a critical element of a quality teaching pool, the raising of minimum cut-off scores can be seen as having contradictory influences on quality.

The need to provide an adequate number of teachers for our nation's public schools also places parameters on the setting of minimum standards. Within these parameters, the tension between the two goals of quality and diversity is undoubtedly the major issue facing teacher educators and policy makers in relation to setting minimum academic standards.

In conclusion, whether these measures of academic ability/achievement make as much difference as the public thinks, they will still make a difference in terms of the public image of teaching which affects support for education and helps influence peoples' decisions about entering and staying in teaching. The potential impact on the diversity of the teaching force is a sensitive topic not receiving the attention it deserves. It must also be remembered that larger social and economic factors, the ethos of the occupation and the structure of schools also shape the quality profile of the teaching force by affecting interest in teaching, the selectivity of teacher education and alternative programs, whether and where teacher candidates decide to teach, and how long they stay.

Demographic and quality characteristics

In this chapter, we have focused on one demographic and one quality background characteristic of the teaching force to illustrate the complexity of the issues in relating them to student learning. Regardless of the status of research surrounding them, the racial/ethnic diversity of the teaching force, the academic ability of teachers and the interaction between them are issues that do and should matter to policy makers, teacher educators, and the public. The other background demographic and quality characteristics are also important in themselves and also in how they interact with ethnicity/race and academic ability/achievement. While space prevents full consideration of these other characteristics here (see Zumwalt & Craig, 2005a, 2005b) we want to end by briefly noting some of them.

Even if the research indicates that gender imbalance has little or no impact on student achievement as measured by test scores, some believe that gender diversity is not only intrinsically valuable, but important for the symbolic messages it sends about teachers and education. The perception that teaching is a "female" career is seen by some as having a negative impact on efforts to improve working conditions and the status of the profession, as well as possibly discouraging half the population from considering teaching when making career decisions. We do not know enough about the impact of gender on other student outcomes nor its interaction with other variables such as race/ethnicity and SES background of teachers. For instance, minority male teachers, serving as role models, may have a differential impact on low-income minority males' persistence in school.

We know the least about teachers' SES background and how it may affect their teaching practice and student learning. Teachers from different SES backgrounds may bring different knowledge, attitudes, and practices to the classrooms that affect students differentially. For policy makers, SES background may matter in terms of recruitment strategies, while for teacher educators it may matter in terms of their program. The SES background of teacher education students is likely to be highly correlated with the quality and types of teaching they experienced in their own K-12 education (Popkewitz et al., 1982). Such knowledge could affect the content and strategies teacher educators use in their programs if they want students to enact teaching that goes beyond that which they have experienced as students.

Teacher educators—in undergraduate, graduate, and alternative programs—are all working with students older than the previously typical 18–22 year old college students. Undergraduates are taking more than four years to complete their programs and older adults, many with parenting experience, are returning to college to start or complete their bachelor's degrees. Graduate and alternative programs are designed for older adults who did not prepare for teaching in college; these prospective teachers range from new college graduates to retirees. Age is not a perfect proxy for maturity and experience, but if the candidates are getting older, teacher educators might want to reconsider elements of preparation programs that were appropriate for unmarried, college-age students but less so for older students with children of their own. Also, as the age of prospective teachers increases, the initial attractions of teaching, as well as future career paths, change. The ubiquitous linear connection between teacher age and attrition labeled the "U-shape" phenomenon by researchers may be modified. Teacher educators need to become familiar with the expectations and career decisions facing older adults preparing to teach.

Whether age matters may depend on how it interacts with experience. While research linking teacher experience with student achievement has been inconsistent, generally a relationship is most evident in the early years of teaching at the elementary level and a longer effect at the secondary level (Rice, 2003). Regardless of research findings, the aging of the teaching pool has been cause for both concern and celebration. On the one hand, the greater maturity, experience, and stability of the teaching pool and the ability of graduate and alternative programs to attract older candidates are viewed as positive. On the other hand, the "graying" of the teaching pool is seen as alarming—too many burned out teachers holding on to old (e.g. progressive or traditional) ways of teaching, resisting new demands for accountability. The differential distribution of young and inexperienced teachers, with their typically higher attrition rates, in urban schools serving low-income, minority students is one particular concern seen as a contributory factor to the persistent achievement gap.

While the ability/achievement of teachers has dominated public discussion and research, other indicators of background quality characteristics of teachers also need attention. Whether or not there is ever research evidence that supports a content major instead of an education major (Floden & Meniketti, 2005), it has face validity for policy makers and the public. It serves the purpose of seeming to upgrade teacher quality, whether or not it improves the academic ability profile of teachers, affects the quality of their preparation or makes them better teachers.

The unequal distribution of other background quality indicators, besides academic ability and achievement, raise questions that matter. Teachers who attend less competitive colleges are more likely to teach non-White, low-achieving students and more likely to have failed one teacher test (Lankford *et al.*, 2002). Public schools with higher proportions of minority or low-income students are more likely to have uncertified teachers and teachers teaching "out-of-field" (Darling-Hammond & Cobb, 1996; Henke *et al.*, 1997; Ingersoll, 1996; Zeichner & Schulte, 2001).

Whether certification matters is increasingly debated as the struggle between professionalizaton and deregulation takes center-stage and in light of federal legislation requiring all classrooms to be staffed by "qualified" teachers. A major challenge in using it as a quality indicator is that each state has different certification requirements and multiple certificates. What one can say is that being "certified" is an indicator of what a particular state deems as its minimal "safe to practice" criterion. Complexity is added when different criteria are used to judge "out-of-field" teaching—most may be certified to teach, but not necessarily to teach all the courses they are assigned to teach. To meet new standards for "qualified" teachers, sometimes definitions of who is "certified" have been adjusted to include those who previously would not have been labeled certified.

CONCLUSION

While the research evidence about the impact of the background demographic and quality characteristics discussed in this chapter on student learning is not overwhelming, hopefully, our consideration of the issues leaves the reader with the sense that the demographic and quality profile of the teaching force does matter.

In highlighting one demographic characteristic—the race/ethnicity of teachers—and one quality indicator—the academic ability/achievement of teachers—it becomes clear that these two highly salient characteristics actually both contribute to the quality of the teaching force. A diverse teaching force, desirable for a variety of intrinsic and extrinsic reasons, itself becomes a quality indicator.

Seen in this light, the seemingly obvious goal of raising minimum standards of academic ability/achievement of teachers that may restrict the diversity of the teaching force creates a tension not just between quality and diversity, but really a tension between different aspects of a quality teaching force. With all the issues associated with measures of quality discussed here and the lack of definitive evidence indicating the impact of certain test scores and GPAs, the rationale for further increasing cut-off scores on these measures of academic ability/achievement is questionable. Additionally, as Rivkin *et al.* (2005) conclude, there is such substantial difference in quality among those with similar traditional quality attributes (e.g. masters degree, experience), that focusing policy in the hiring, mentoring, firing and promotion at the school level probably makes more sense than adjusting state cut-off scores.

Whether policy makers and teacher educators can do much to substantially change the demographic and quality profile in light of larger social forces is debatable. However, that does not absolve them from taking a pro-active stance on one of the major issues— the consequences of a predominantly White teaching force and a growing minority public school population. While efforts to recruit and retain more teachers of color are certainly desirable and should be accelerated, so should the efforts to understand how race and ethnicity relate to teachers' beliefs, knowledge, and classroom practices in order to prepare teachers who can better meet the diverse needs of all their students.

REFERENCES

Andrew, M. (1990) Differences between graduates of 4-year and 5-year teacher preparation programs. *Journal of Teacher Education*, 41(2), 45–51.

Au, K. & Jordan, C. (1981) Teaching reading to Hawaiian children: finding a culturally appropriate solution. In H. Trueba, G. Guthrie, & K. Au (eds.) *Culture and the bilingual classroom: studies in classroom ethnography* (pp. 139–152). Rowley, MA: Newbury.

Ballou, D. (1996) Do public schools hire the best applicants? *Quarterly Journal of Economics*, 111(1), 97–133.

Boe, E. E., Cook, L. H., Kaufman, M. J., & Danielson, L. C. (1996) Special and general education teachers in public schools: sources of supply in national perspective. *Teacher Education and Special Education*, 19(1), 1–16.

Boe, E. E., Bobbitt, S. A., Cook, L. H., Barkanic, G., & Maislin, G. (1998) *Teacher turnover in eight cognate areas: national trends and predictors*. Philadelphia, PA: Center for Research and Evaluation in Social Policy.

Brophy, J. (1985) Interactions of male and female teachers with male and female students. In C. Wilkinson (ed.) *Gender influences in classroom interaction* (pp. 115–142). Madison, WI: University of Wisconsin Press.

Broughman, S. P. & Rollefson, M. R. (2000) *Teacher supply in the United States: sources of newly hired teachers in the public and private schools, 1987–88 to 1993–94.* Washington, DC: National Center for Education Statistics, U.S. Department of Education.

Chapman, D. W. & Hutcheson, S. M. (1982) Attrition from teaching careers: a discriminate analysis. *American Educational Research Journal*, 19, 93–105.

Clewell, B. C. & Puma, M. (2003, April) *Does it matter if my teacher looks like me? The impact of teacher race and ethnicity on student academic achievement.* Paper presented at the Annual Meeting of the American Association of Colleges of Teacher Education, New Orleans, LA.

Cochran-Smith, M. & Zeichner, K. M. (eds.) (2005) *Studying teacher education: the report of the AERA Panel on Research and Teacher Education.* Mahwah, NJ: Lawrence Erlbaum Associates.

Coleman, J. S., Campbell, E. Q., Hobson, C. J., McPartland, J., Mood, A. M., Weinfeld, F. D., & York, R. L. (1966) *Equality of educational opportunity.* Washington, DC: U.S. Government Printing Office.

Conant, J. B. (1963) *The education of American teachers.* New York: McGraw-Hill.

Cooper, P. M. (2003) Effective white teachers of black children: teaching within a community. *Journal of Teacher Education*, 54(5), 413–427.

Cornett, L. M. (1992) Alternative certification: state policies in the SREB states. *Peabody Journal of Education*, 67(3), 55–83.

Darling-Hammond, L. (2004) Inequality and the right to learn: access to qualified teachers in California's public schools. *Teachers College Record*, 106(10), 1936–1966.

Darling-Hammond, L. & Cobb, V. L. (1996) The changing context of teacher education. In F. Murray (ed.), *Teacher educator's handbook* (pp. 14–62). Washington, DC: AACTE.

Darling-Hammond, L., Hudson, L., & S. N. Kirby (1989) *Re-designing teacher education: opening the door for new recruits to science and mathematics teaching.* Washington, DC: Rand Corporation.

Dee, T. S. (2001) *Teachers, race, and student achievement in a randomized experiment.* Cambridge, MA: National Bureau of Economic Research.

Dewey, J. (1902) The educational situation: as concerns the elementary school. Reprinted in *Journal of Curriculum Studies* (Electronic Version), 34(3), 387–403.

Downey, D. B. & Pribesh, S. (2004) When race matters: teachers' evaluations of students' classroom behavior. *Sociology of Education*, 72(4) 267–82.

Ehrenberg, R. G. & Brewer, D. J. (1994) Do school and teacher characteristics matter? Evidence from *High School and Beyond. Economics of Education Review*, 13(1), 1–17.

Ehrenberg, R. G. & Brewer, D. J. (1995) Did teachers' verbal ability and race matter in the 1960s? Coleman revisited. *Economics of Education Review*, 14(1), 1–21.

Ehrenberg, R. G., Goldhaber, D. D., & Brewer, D. J. (1995) Do teachers' race, gender and ethnicity matter? Evidence from the National Educational Longitudinal Study of 1988. *Industrial and Labor Relations Review*, 48, 547–561.

Erickson, F. & Mohatt, G. (1982) Cultural organization and participation structures in two classrooms of Indian students. In G. Spindler (ed.) *Doing the ethnography of schooling* (pp. 131–174). New York: Holt, Rinehart, & Winston.

Evans, M. O. (1992) An estimate of race and gender role-model effects in teaching high school. *Journal of Economic Education*, 29(3), 209–17.

Farkas, G. (2003) Racial disparities and discrimination in education: what we know, how do we know it, and what do we need to know. *Teachers College Record*, 105(6), 1119–1146.

Farkas, G., Grobe, R., Sheehan, D., & Shuan, Y. (1990) Cultural resources and school success: gender, ethnicity and poverty groups within an urban school district. *American Sociological Review*, 55, 127–142.

Feistritzer, C. E. (1996) *Profile of teachers in the US.* Washington, DC: National Center for Education Information.

Feistritzer, C. E. (1999) *The making of a teacher: a report on teacher preparation in the United States.* Washington, DC: National Center for Education Information.

Feistritzer, C. E. (2003) *Alternative teacher certification: a state-by-state analysis 2003.* Washington, DC: National Center for Education Information.

Ferguson, R. (1998) Teachers' perceptions and expectations and the Black-White test score gap. In

J. Christopher & M. Phillips (eds.) *The Black-White test score gap* (pp. 273–317). Washington, DC: The Brookings Institution.

Flexner, A. (1930) *Universities: American, English, German*. London: Oxford University Press.

Floden, R. E. & Meniketti, M. (2005) Research on the effects of coursework in the arts and sciences and in the foundations of education. In M. Cochran-Smith & K. Zeichner (eds.) *Studying teacher education: the report of the AERA Panel on Research and Teacher Education* (pp. 261–308), Mahwah, NJ: Lawrence Erlbaum Associates.

Foster, M. (1997) *Black teachers on teaching*. New York: New Press.

Gitomer, D. H., Latham, A. S., & Ziomek, R. (1999) *The academic quality of prospective teachers: the impact of admissions and licensure testing*. Princeton, NJ: Educational Testing Service.

Gold, D. & Reis, M. (1982) Male teacher effects on young children: a theoretical and empirical consideration. *Sex Roles: A Journal of Research* 8(5), 493–513.

Hanushek, E. A. (1992) The trade-off between child quantity and quality. *Journal of Political Economy*, 100, 84–118.

Hanushek, E. A. & Pace, R. R. (1995) Who chooses to teach (and why)? *Economics of Education Review*, 14(2), 101–117.

Henke, R. R., Chen, X., & Geis, S. (2000) *Progress through the teacher pipeline: 1992–93 college graduates and elementary/secondary school teaching as of 1997*. Washington, DC: National Center for Education Statistics, U.S. Department of Education.

Henke, R. R., Choy, S. P., Geis, S., & Broughman, S. P. (1997) *Schools and staffing in the U.S.: a statistical profile, 1993–94*. Washington, DC: National Center for Education Statistics, U.S. Department of Education.

Henke, R. R., Geis, S., Giambattista, J., & Knepper, P. (1996) *Out of the lecture hall and into the classroom: 1992–93 college graduates and elementary/secondary school teaching*. Washington, DC: National Center for Education Statistics, U.S. Department of Education.

Henke, R. R., Peter, K., Li, X., & Geis, S. (2005) *Elementary/secondary school teaching among recent college graduates: 1994 and 2001 (NCES 2005–161)*. Washington, DC: U.S. Department of Education, National Center for Education Statistics.

Heyns, B. (1988) Educational defectors: a first look at teacher attrition in the NLS-72. *Educational Researcher*, 17, 24–32.

Howey, K. & Strom, S. (1987) Teacher selection reconsidered. In G. Katz & J. Rath (eds.) *Advances in Teacher Education* (vol. 3, pp. 1–34). Norwood, NJ: Ablex.

Humrich, E. (1988, April) *Sex differences in the second IEA science study—U.S. results in an international context*. Paper presented at the Annual Meeting of the National Association for Research in Science Teaching, Lake of the Ozarks, MO.

Ingersoll, R. M. (1996) *Out-of-field teaching and educational equality*. Washington, DC: National Center of Education Statistics, U.S. Department of Education.

Ingersoll, R. M. (1999) The problem of underqualified teachers in American secondary schools. *Educational Researcher*, 28(2), 26–37.

Irvine, J. (1990) *Black students and school failure: policies practices and prescriptions*. New York: Greenwood.

Jelmberg, J. (1996) College-based teacher education versus state-sponsored alternative programs. *Journal of Teacher Education*, 47(1), 60–66.

Kerr, D. H. (1983) Teaching competence and teacher education in the United States. *Teachers College Record*, 84(3), 525–52.

King, S. H. (1993) The limited presence of African-American teachers. *Review of Educational Research*, 63(2), 115–149.

Kirby, S. N., Berends, M., & Naftel, S. (1999) Supply and demand of minority teachers in Texas: problems and prospects. *Educational Evaluation and Policy Analysis*, 21(1), 47–66.

Kirby, S. N., Darling-Hammond, L., & Hudson, L. (1989) Nontraditional recruits to mathematics and science teaching. *Educational Evaluation and Policy Analysis*, 11(3), 301–323.

Kirby, S. N., Naftel, S., & Berends, M. (1999) *Staffing at-risk school districts in Texas: problems and prospects*. Santa Monica, CA: Rand Corporation.

Kopp, W. (1994) Teach for America: moving beyond the debate. *The Educational Forum*, 58, 187–192.

Ladson-Billings, G. (1992) Liberatory consequences of literacy: a case of culturally relevant instruction for African-American students. *Journal of Negro Education*, 61(3), 378–391.

Ladson-Billings, G. (1994) *The dreamkeepers: successful teachers of Black children*. San Francisco: Jossey-Bass.

Ladson-Billings, G. (1995) Toward a theory of culturally relevant pedagogy. *American Educational Research Journal*, 32(3), 465–491.

Lagemann, E. C. (2000) *An elusive science: the troubling history of educational research*. Chicago: University of Chicago Press.

Lanier, J. E. & Little, J. W. (1986) Research on teacher education. In M. C. Wittrock (ed.) *Handbook of Research on Teaching* (pp. 527–569). New York: Macmillan.

Lankford, H., Loeb, S., & Wykoff, J. (2002) Teacher sorting and the plight of urban schools. *Educational Evaluation and Policy Archives* 24(1), 37–62.

Lewis, L., Parsad, B., Carey, N., Bartfai, N., & Farris, E. (1999) *Teacher quality: a report on the preparation and qualifications of public school teachers*. Washington, DC: National Center of Education Statistics, U.S. Department of Education.

Lutz, F. W. & Hutton, J. B. (1989) Alternative teacher certification: its policy implications for classroom and personnel practice. *Educational Evaluation and Policy Analysis*, 11(3), 237–254.

Murnane, R. J. & Olsen, R. J. (1988, April) *Factors affecting the length of stay in teaching*. Paper presented at the Annual Meeting of the American Educational Research Association, New Orleans, LA.

Murnane, R. J. & Schwinden, M. (1989) Race, gender, and opportunity: supply and demand for new teachers in North Carolina, 1975–1985. *Educational Evaluation and Policy Analysis*, 11(2), 93–108.

Murnane, R. J., Singer, J. D., Willett, J. B., Kemple, J. J., & Olsen, R. J. (1991) *Who will teach? Policies that matter*. Cambridge, MA: Harvard University Press.

National Commission on Excellence in Education (1983) *A nation at risk: a report to the nation and the Secretary of Education*. Washington, DC: United States Department of Education.

National Commission on Teaching and America's Future (1996) *What matters most: teaching for America's future*. New York: Author.

National Education Association (1997) *Status of the American public school teacher, 1995–96*. Washington, DC: Author.

National Education Association (2003) *Status of the American public school teacher, 2000–2001*. Washington, DC: Author.

Natriello, G. & Zumwalt, K. K. (1993) New teachers for urban schools? The contribution of the provisional teacher program in New Jersey. *Education and Urban Society*, 26(1), 49–62.

Pigge, F. L. (1985) Teacher education graduates: comparisons of those who teach and do not teach. *Journal of Teacher Education*, 36(4), 27–28.

Popkewitz, T. S., Tabachnik, B. R., & Wehlage, G. (1982) *The myth of educational reform: a study of school responses to a program of change*. Madison, WI: University of Wisconsin Press.

Provasnik, S. & Dorfman, S. (2005) *Mobility in the teacher workforce. Findings from* The condition of education, 2005. Washington, DC: National Center for Education Statistics, U.S. Department of Education.

Rice, J. K. (2003) *Teacher quality: understanding the effectiveness of teacher attributes*. Washington, DC: Economic Policy Institute.

Rivkin, S. G., Hanushek, E. A., & Kain, J. F. (2005) Teachers, schools and academic achievement. *Econometrica*, 73(2), 417–458.

Rowan, B., Correnti, R., & Miller, R. J. (2002) What large-scale, survey research tells us about teacher effects on student achievement: insights from the *Prospects* study of elementary schools. *Teachers College Record*, 104(8), 1525–1567.

Shen, J. (1998) The impact of alternative certification on the elementary and secondary public teaching force. *Journal of Research and Development in Education*, 32(1), 9–16.

Siddle Walker, E. V. (1996) *Their highest potential: a Black school community in the segregated South*. Chapel Hill: University of North Carolina Press.

Smith, G. P., Miller, M. C., & Joy, J. (1988) A case study of the impact of performance-based testing on the supply of minority teachers. *Journal of Teacher Education*, 39(4), 45–53.

Snyder, T., Tan, A. G., & Hoffman, C. M. (2004) *The digest of education statistics, 2003*. Washington, DC: U.S Department of Education, National Center for Education Statistics.

Stafford, D. & Barrow, G. (1994) Houston's alternative certification program. *The Educational Forum*, 58, 193–200.

Sykes, G. (1983) Caring about teachers. Response to Donna Kerr. *Teachers College Record*, 84(3), 579–92.

Texas Education Agency (1994) *Texas teacher diversity and recruitment: teacher supply, demand, and quality policy research project, report no. 4*. Austin, TX: Author.

Texas Education Agency (1995) *Texas teacher retention, mobility, and attrition: teacher supply, demand, and quality policy research project, report no. 6*. Austin, TX: Author.

U.S. Department of Education (2005) *The condition of education, 2005*. Washington, DC: National Center for Education Statistics, U.S. Department of Education.

Vance, V. S. & Schlechty, P. C. (1982) The distribution of academic ability in the teaching force: policy implications. *Phi Delta Kappan*, 64(1), 22–27.

Vegas, E., Murnane, R. J., & Willett, J. B. (2001) From high school to teaching: many steps, who makes it? *Teachers College Record*, 103(3), 427–449.

Waller, W. (1932) *The sociology of teaching*. New York: Wiley & Sons.

Weaver, W. T. (1983) *America's teacher quality problem: alternatives for reform*. New York: Praeger.

Wenglinsky, H. (2000) *Teaching the teachers: different settings, different results*. Princeton, NJ: Educational Testing Service.

Whitener, S.D. & Gruber, K. (1997) *Characteristics of stayers, movers, and leavers: results from the teacher follow-up survey: 1994–5*. Washington, DC: National Center for Education Statistics, U.S. Department of Education.

Wilson, S. & Youngs, P. (2005) Research on accountability processes in teacher education. In M. Cochran-Smith & K. Zeichner (eds.) *Studying teacher education: the report of the AERA Panel on Research and Teacher Education* (pp. 591–643). Mahwah, NJ: Lawrence Erlbaum Associates.

Wirt, J. & Livingston, A. (2002) *The condition of education 2002 in brief*. Washington, DC: National Center for Education Statistics, U.S. Department of Education.

Wirt, J., Choy, S., Gerald, D., Provasnik, P. R., Watanabe, S., Tobin, R., & Glander, M. (2001) *The condition of education, 2001*. Washington, DC: National Center for Education Statistics, U.S. Department of Education.

Wright, D. P., McKibbin, M. D., & Walton, P. A. (1987) *The effectiveness of the teacher trainee program: an alternative route into teaching in California*. Sacramento, CA: California Commission on Teacher Credentialing.

Zeichner, K. M. & Schulte, A. K. (2001) What we know and don't know from peer-reviewed research about alternative teacher certification programs. *Journal of Teacher Education*, 5(4), 266–282.

Zumwalt, K. K. & Craig, E. (2005a) Teachers' characteristics: research on the demographic profile. in M. Cochran-Smith & K. Zeichner (eds.) *Studying teacher education: the report of the AERA Panel on Research and Teacher Education* (pp. 111–156). Mahwah, NJ: Lawrence Erlbaum Associates.

Zumwalt, K. K. & Craig, E. (2005b) Teachers' characteristics: research on the indicators of quality. In M. Cochran-Smith & K. Zeichner (eds.) *Studying teacher education: the report of the AERA Panel on Research and Teacher Education* (pp. 157–260). Mahwah, NJ: Lawrence Erlbaum Associates.

25 Teachers of color

Quality and effective teachers one way or another

Mary E. Dilworth
National Board for Professional
Teaching Standards

Anthony L. Brown
University of Texas at Austin

AN ENDURING QUESTION

What is the inherent value of teachers of color—to the teaching force, to society and most importantly to students? These questions are asked today in somewhat the same manner as they were posed more than a century ago. Do these teachers provide a necessary service to the students and communities? Is their training, knowledge or ability consistent with that of other teachers? Is there a value-added dimension in their craft wisdom? Yes. We argue that teachers of color have made and continue to make a substantial contribution to the quality of instruction and student achievement in this nation. We understand that teachers of color frequently teach with a greater level of social consciousness than others. This difference, along with imposed and self-imposed responsibilities, is prompted by a commitment to the maintenance or assimilation of cultures, racial uplift, and socioeconomic necessity and survival.

In this chapter, we describe how the presence, preparation, and practice of African American, Hispanic, Asian American and Native American teachers has been addressed in the literature and perceived in society. Our discussion is premised on the notion that the role and treatment of all teachers has changed over time, but these changes do not influence teachers of differing racial/ethnic and linguistic backgrounds in the same way. We begin with a historical overview of the educational experiences of African Americans, Mexican Americans, Chinese Americans and Native Americans. We then offer observations on similarities in the perceptions of these groups toward schools, the curriculum and the role of teachers of color. We include discussion of contemporary enduring issues that build on this history.

THE AFRICAN AMERICAN HISTORICAL CONTEXT

The expectations and practices of African American teachers during the late nineteenth century and early twentieth century have been duly noted by educational historians (Anderson, 1988; Fultz, 1995a; 1995b). This literature consistently illustrates that the African American teacher was a central figure of discussions regarding the educational and social progress of African Americans. Indeed, the historical period and region of the country made for varied aims and contexts for African American education, yet the educational discourse regarding the role and expectations for the African American teacher has remained quite stable. In fact, there has been a rather persistent discussion since the early nineteenth century and continuing to the present, relating to issues surrounding the role and expectations of African American teachers working with African American students (Campbell, 1970; Dubois, 1935; Lynn, 2002; Mabee, 1979).

For example, during the late 1800s in the state of New York, African American educators, community leaders and parents advocated for school officials to hire African American teachers to teach African American students (Mabee, 1979; Rury, 1983). Advocates for such a change contended that African American teachers could serve as role models to incite African American students to succeed. After Reconstruction, similar arguments supported the idea that the African American teacher could serve as a pillar of "moral righteousness," social uplift and educational excellence (Fultz, 1995a). Embedded in such an argument was a belief that African American students would better comprehend the value and importance of education by hearing, seeing, and learning the implicit and explicit messages of "education for social uplift," from a person of their racial background.

Historical arguments for African American teachers, 1805–1900

In 1789, the New York Manumission Society founded the *New York African Free School* to serve the growing population of free African Americans to the area (Rury, 1983). The board of trustees from the Manumission Society insisted that by teaching the free African American child and adolescent about different aspects of "sobriety" and "industry," "they could make them more orderly and tractable as they emerged from slavery" (Rury, 1983, p. 187). Through the late 1800s, mostly White teachers taught at these schools. However, during this period there was an emerging debate about whether Black teachers would better serve the mission of educating the African American child. For example, in 1805, members at the *American Convention of Abolitionist Societies* declared that African American children would benefit from the instruction of African American teachers. At the convention, members maintained that the instruction of African American teachers would "kindle a spirit of emulation" in Black children (Mabee, 1979, p. 93). In addition, historian John Rury (1983) found that Black parents consistently declared to the Manumission Society the importance of Black teachers educating their children. Through the late 1800s and 1900s there were also countless arguments made at local districts in the North, and after Reconstruction, in the South, for the importance of Black teachers educating Black children (Blackshear, 1969 [1922]; Mabee, 1979). This quote from noted African American educator E. L. Blackshear (1969 [1902]) highlights a common sentiment about why African American teachers could best serve the specific needs of Black children:

> The colored teacher has been a herald of civilization to the youth of his people. His superior culture and character have acted as a powerful stimulus to the easily roused imagination of the colored youth, and the black boy feels the presence of the black "professah," to him the embodiment of learning, that he too can be "something." At first he does not know what that something is, but he determines to be "somebody" and to make a place and a standing for himself in the world.
>
> (p. 337)

While this quote reflects a common argument made about the practice and value of Black teachers, African American educators and leaders simultaneously expressed the importance of African American teachers receiving "proper" educational training (Bond, 1934;

Caliver, 1933; Johnson, C., 1930). Historian Michael Fultz (1995b) notes that African American community leaders, scholars, and teacher associations insisted that more rigorous teacher training programs would assist African American teachers' instructional practices.

Early arguments for African American teacher training

During the decades immediately following the Civil War, the nation moved cautiously towards educational access for children of the poor and working poor as a means to advance society. Once the merits of an elementary level education were established, local communities, particularly in the North, worked to determine minimum academic standards that suited their vicinities (Grant & Murray, 1999). In contrast, the segregated South was obstinate in using public education as a vehicle to move their community forward and consequently offered limited academic opportunity for its citizens. African American children of former slaves were especially perceived as expendable for reasons other than labor; consequently, the poor conditions of their schools were of little interest to the majority population and were unsupported by their jurisdictions. Thus, southern rural schools for African American children were established, financed and supported by and large by Northern philanthropic organizations and churches of various denominations. For instance, the Jeanes teachers, a corps of African American and White teachers financially supported by the General Education Board, are frequently noted in the literature for their efforts in the rural south. Their work was intended to improve the knowledge and skills of African American teachers operating in isolation (Tillman, 2004). Indeed, reports of over-crowded, grade-less classrooms, minimal supplies, books and other resources, were surpassed only by reports of teachers who themselves had received very limited and inadequate educations.

African American educators insisted that teacher training for Black teachers would provide more "competent professionalism" and "improved instruction" (Fultz, 1995b). For example, Fultz (1995b) found that several Black state teacher associations, including the National Association of Teachers in Colored Schools, "carried the banner of improved training and instruction" (p. 205). In addition to the growing interest of African American colleges to provide rigorous instruction and professionalism, some sociologists and educational scholars (Bond, 1934; Caliver, 1933; Johnson, C. 1930) adamantly expressed that the future of Black education was incumbent upon the advanced pedagogical training of Black teachers. For example, sociologist Charles Johnson, in his assessment of the educational conditions of African American children in rural schools, contended that, "these poorly trained teachers . . . will inflict the accumulated deficiencies of the system in which they have been trained upon their pupils, and so perpetuate it" (Fultz, 1995b, p. 197). Educational scholar, Ambrose Caliver, who conducted one of the first comprehensive studies about the education and training of African American teachers, also suggested that African American education could not progress unless changes occurred in the selection and training of African American teachers. The following are two of his recommendations:

- Teacher-preparing institutions for Negroes should raise their entrance requirements, making them more selective, and should improve their admission procedures in order to assure to the teaching profession recruits with better background and preparation.
- More attention should be given by school officials to the qualifications and certification of Negro applicants, and appointments should be made solely on merit.

(Caliver, 1933, pp. 117–118)

Therefore, while there was strong advocacy for Black teachers' social practices (i.e. community leadership and role modeling), African American educators consistently argued that improved educational outcomes *must* equally occur through sound educational training and professionalism.

At the advent of the landmark *Brown v. Board of Education* Supreme Court decision, historically Black colleges and universities (HBCUs) were solely responsible for the preparation of African American teachers for segregated "Negro" schools (Groff, 1961, p. 8). Groff, in a survey reported approximately 5 years following the *Brown* decision, found a general sense of optimism among responding HBCUs in the south. The majority of respondents indicated that they did not anticipate a decrease in enrollments or a reduction of financial support. They did anticipate greater competition among students and better pre-college preparation of students. According to Groff (1961), one respondent reported, "this would raise academic standards, better social manners and speech habits and help reduce the need of removing undesirable feelings toward White people" (p. 10). Groff (1961) further reports that HBCU administrators felt that their teacher education students had a stronger urge to achieve and make greater contributions to uplifting the race through education. Their students also had greater anticipation of the challenges of future employment opportunities, of professional welfare and advancement, and "less obsequiousness" (p. 10). Lastly, HBCUs exhibited greater pride in preparing teachers and providing "quality preparation."

Closing thoughts on history: African American teachers

Much of the early debates and discussions about the roles and responsibilities of African American teachers emerged out of larger political concerns of racial and social justice. While racial and cultural identification was a central argument made for the placement of Black teachers in African American classrooms, several African American educators and scholars expressed a deep concern that African American teachers must also receive sound instructional training in order to effectively address the educational needs of African American children. Fultz (1995b) summarizes, "[T]he fate of the race depended on the types of schools it had, the types of schools Blacks possessed depended on the quality of the teacher available to them, and the quality of the teachers depended upon sterling character and professional training" (p. 197). In summary, while the historical contexts of the debate for Black teachers have changed since the early 1900s, recent educational literature reveals the sustained political nature of discussions about whether Black teachers can best serve the educational needs of African American students.

AMERICANIZATION AND LATINO EDUCATION

The ideological practice of "Americanization" during the mid-1800s had an immediate impact on the educational experiences of Latino communities (San Miguel & Valencia, 1998). "Americanization" was a political movement that aimed at teaching, acculturating and educating U.S. economic, political, religious, and cultural forms. San Miguel and Valencia (1998) point out that "Americanization" was not undertaken just to inculcate "American" ways, but also to discourage the maintenance of a "minority group's" own culture (p. 358). In the case of Mexican Americans, public school officials instituted "Americanization" practices by banning the use of Spanish in schools and the removal of all content and pedagogical practices associated with Mexican culture. Certainly, such policies did not affect every state in the nineteenth century. However, by the early twentieth century, English-only policies became common practice throughout most Western and Southwestern states. San Miguel and Valencia (1998) argue that the effort to remove Spanish and Mexican culture from the schools was part of a national campaign against diversity. These authors state, "The primary goals of this campaign were to promote the purity of Anglo-American culture, [and] unify the country on the basis of a common culture and language" (p. 361).

Despite such practices, however, various Mexican American and Latino communities developed educational and social interventions to meet the needs of Latino communities. For example, several educational historians (DeLeon, 1982; San Miguel, 1987; San Miguel & Valencia, 1998) note that from the late 1800s through the early 1900s, there were several examples of Mexican and Latino teachers and educators who worked to meet the specific educational needs of Spanish-speaking children.

Exclusionary practices and Latino teachers

Richard Valencia (2005) argues that *Mendez v. Westminster*, a 1946 class action suit on behalf of 5,000 California Mexican American students was an important precursor to the *Brown* decision. He notes that "Racial/ethnic isolation of school children was a normative practice in the Southwest, despite the fact that these states had no legal statutes by which they could legally segregate Mexican American from White students" (p. 394). However, despite such exclusionary policies including English-only instruction and curriculum, Mexican American community leaders as early the late 1800s, opened their own schools and hired Spanish-speaking teachers of Mexican and Latino descent, to meet the cultural and linguistic needs of Latino students (DeLeon, 1982). One case occurred during the late 1800s, when several Tejano[1] communities in El Paso opened schools with Spanish-speaking teachers who taught Mexican children to become literate in both English and Spanish (DeLeon, 1982). Another example was during the 1880s, when Mexican American parents developed a school to teach English to Mexican students with limited English proficiency because the local El Paso school officials refused to teach English to Spanish-speaking students. The community turned to an elderly man named Olivas Villanueva Aoy, who agreed to open a private school with the sole purpose of teaching Mexican children English to prepare them for public schools. Historian Mario Garcia (1981) notes that by the 1890s, Aoy, with the help of two Mexican assistants, was able to teach close to one hundred first and second graders. Such examples, according to DeLeon (1982), illustrate how Spanish and Mexican teachers and parents persistently fought against exclusionary educational practices. This type of determination was also apparent in the political and social practices of Hispano[2] communities in New Mexico. In fact, by the early 1900s, some Latino community leaders and educational advocates were able to gain support for teacher training programs for Latino teachers working in rural Spanish-speaking regions.

Teacher training and Latino teachers

During the early 1900s in New Mexico, after the Hispano community established political influence in the region, they were able to develop a bilingual teacher training school named the "Spanish-American Normal School at El Rito." In 1909, Latino leaders Veneslao Jaramillo and Solomon Luna, joined forces with the former territorial governor L. Bradford Prince, to lobby for a normal school to be opened for Spanish-speaking teachers (Getz, 1997). The purpose of the school was to educate, "Spanish-speaking natives of New Mexico for the vocation of teachers in the public schools of the counties and districts where the Spanish language is prevalent" (MacDonald, 2004, p. 120). By 1918, over one hundred future teachers enrolled in the teacher-training program, with it eventually becoming part of the New Mexico higher education system.

Getz (1997) argues that some teacher training efforts for Hispano communities only served to enhance the already accepted roles of teachers as "community leaders, role models, and members of community networks" (Getz, 1997, p. 90). However, despite such community advocacy, university scholars insisted that if Latino teachers received more training in "new ideas and advanced teacher methods," they could better serve the educational needs of rural Hispano children (Getz, 1997, p. 92). For example, during the 1930s, with the political and social aims of the New Deal and philanthropic organizations such as the General Education Board, University of New Mexico teacher educator and social activist Lloyd Tireman was able to pursue educational reform efforts such as the San José school, to provide rural Spanish-speaking teachers exposure to new teaching methods (Getz, 1997). Tireman tirelessly reiterated the benefits of Latino children receiving instruction in their "mother tongue"; however he also argued that such teachers would also require training in advanced pedagogical practices (Getz, 1997, p. 74).

As a way to provide such training, Latina teachers were awarded scholarships to attend the College of Education at the University of New Mexico. There, they too learned methods thought necessary for learners to thrive in a rural school context. In addition, the teachers regularly attended "demonstration schools" to observe models of instruction that they could transfer to their own school sites. As a whole, "progressive"[3] educational philosophies guided the efforts to train community teachers, drawing from the assumption that the combination of sound instructional training and the culturally congruent instruction offered by Latina teachers would have a profound impact on the rural education of Hispano students.

Closing thoughts on history: Latino teachers

As several historians illustrate, the efforts of Latino teachers were at the center of social change for Latino communities during the late nineteenth century and early twentieth century (DeLeon, 1982; Garcia, 1981; MacDonald, 2004). Although the ideological practice of "Americanization" became a common educational approach in California, Texas, and Southwestern U.S. schools, the efforts of Mexican and Latino teachers consistently served to meet the specific cultural and linguistic needs of Spanish-speaking children. Additionally, these histories illustrate that the issues over cultural synchronization and relevance were critical in discussions about education for Mexican and Latino communities as early as 1850. Indeed, as subsequent history would tell, issues of language maintenance and cultural competence have remained a central debate within educational discourse for Latino and Hispanic communities.

THE HISTORICAL CONTEXT OF CHINESE AMERICANS

The educational experience of Asian Americans provides one of the earliest accounts of how race, culture, and language shaped the practice of teaching.[4] The case of Asian Americans historically illustrates how various exclusionary practices in the U.S. led to the call for alternative educational interventions in meeting the social and cultural needs of Asian American students. For example, the early history of Chinese Americans reveals how immigration laws and anti-Asian sentiment catalyzed community efforts at developing language schools with teachers of Chinese descent. Although there is a dearth of historical literature about the specific practices of Chinese-American teachers in language schools in the U.S., some of the available literature illustrates how various exclusionary practices and racial discrimination led to the development of language schools. More importantly, some of this literature discusses the cultural and pedagogical relevance of Chinese-American students having teachers from their specific cultural and linguistic backgrounds.

Chinese-Americans in the U.S.: migration and exclusion

The history of Chinese Americans reads much like an epic novel, filled with long journeys, dreams, ambitions, struggles and perseverance. The story begins during the mid-1800s with the rapid increase of Chinese immigration to the United States. Daniels (1988) notes that between 1849 and 1882, a little over 300,000 Chinese immigrants arrived in the U.S. By the late 1870s, it was quite clear that the new Chinese immigrants had become an integral and vital part of the labor force. However, what started out as a journey for Chinese immigrants filled with possibility, was quickly decimated by increased levels of nativism from labor leaders, politicians, journalists, and school board officials.

Anti-Chinese sentiment: schools and society

Although there were nationwide economic hardships during the 1870s, the working people of California tended to place the blame for these hardships on the presence of Chinese workers. Such an atmosphere helped to influence anti-Chinese legislative practices in California at the state and municipal level. Thus, at the state and municipal level, a number of absurd ordinances were passed to drive the Chinese immigrants to other states. For example, the California state legislature passed an act that prohibited Chinese "to land without a bond unless they could convince the State Commissioner of Immigration of their 'good character' " (Daniels, 1988, p. 38). Similarly, at the municipal level, California cities such San Francisco also passed capricious ordinances to drive the Chinese immigrants to other states. For instance, because Chinese families generally had to live in crammed housing in "Chinatown," the city of San Francisco passed the Cubic Air Ordinance calling for tenants to have at least 500 cubic feet of air for each inhabitant. To no surprise, under this ordinance, Chinese residents received several citations, but not the White property owners (Daniels, 1988). This atmosphere of anti-Chinese sentiment led to the eventual passing of the Chinese Exclusion Act of 1882, which barred the immigration of Chinese laborers for ten years (Kitano & Daniels, 2001). In California schools, similar exclusionary practices existed, having a significant impact on the early educational experience of Chinese American children.

In 1857, the San Francisco school board rejected the request of Chinese leaders to admit Chinese children into the public schools. The following year, the school board allowed Chinese students to enroll, but only at the segregated African American school. The Chinese parents refused, arguing that they would only attend schools integrated or segregated for Chinese (Weinberg, 1997). For close to ten years, the school board continued to open and close temporary quarters specifically for Chinese students. Although Chinese leaders persistently complained to the school board about such inequitable treatment, the school and governmental authorities continued to ignore Chinese leaders' consistent appeals to enroll Chinese students in San Francisco public schools. The U.S. governmental authorities even ignored the provisions of the Burlingame Treaty of 1868 that "required the public educational rights of citizens of both countries [United States and China] be respected while those citizens resided in the other country" (Weinberg, 1997, p. 18). In addition, the United States government ratified the treaty stating that their only responsibility was to "protect all Chinese subjects from abuse and mistreatment" (Weinberg, 1997, p. 18). By 1871, the state authorities had developed exclusionary laws that claimed that Chinese American children had no legal claim to education, and subsequently Chinese American students were barred from public schools from 1871 to 1884 (Weinberg, 1997). However, this did not mean that Chinese American children went without schooling. In fact, for families that wished to have their children in an educational setting less hostile to Chinese culture, they generally placed their children in Chinese-language schools.

Chinese-language schools and teachers

Chinese language schools were small, privately operated, and maintained by Chinese immigrants. These schools were called *kuan* in Chinese, meaning, "[A] private institute under the supervision of a tutor" (Morimoto, 1997, p. 11). Chinese-language schools generally enrolled twenty to thirty pupils ranging in age from seven to eighteen. In many of the schools, classes were taught on weeknights, and they provided instruction in subjects such as Confucian classics, Chinese language, philosophy, calligraphy, and poetry. Chinese educators focused the curriculum on the traditional values, language and culture of China as way to buffer the racism Chinese American students faced in schools and society. Here, Chinese scholar Kim-Fong Tom (1941) elaborates on the necessity of Chinese-language schools:

> Chinatown has been described by some American writers as a place of opium dens and gambling houses. The pulp magazines and some motion pictures have served to keep this illusion alive. Even today, many Americans still have the notion that [Chinese] people are inferior and backward. Living in a country where the Chinese have been looked down upon and ill-treated, it is easy for them to develop inferiority complexes. To prevent the children from falling into conviction, it is necessary for them to have a correct knowledge of China and the Chinese civilization.
>
> (p. 559)

Tom (1941) further pointed out that the Chinese-language school helped to instill in students a rich and positive appreciation of Chinese ancient culture and respect for their race. Besides instilling racial and cultural pride, Tom (1941) also argued that Chinese-language schools helped students negotiate their new cultural context of being both Chinese and American. Along this same vein, Louis (1932) suggests that because Chinese American students had to learn how to negotiate Chinese and American culture, leaders from the Chinese community should help students with strategies for accommodating the cultural worlds of United States and China. Chinese teachers served such a purpose.

The Chinese-language teachers were generally well-educated community leaders who had the capacity to help Chinese American students negotiate their social and educational worlds of being both Chinese and American. During the 1930s, sociologist Francis Chang (1934) argued that although there were conscientious non-Chinese teachers in public schools, he felt that they did not "understand the children's language, home conditions, and future cultural and vocational possibilities" (p. 542). He further pointed out that Chinese teachers in Chinese-language schools had an advantage over public school teachers, because the Chinese teachers spoke the children's language and had the capacity to approach parents more readily. As a whole, the discussion about

Chinese teachers focused on aspects of culture and race. Given the onslaught of racial antagonism towards and exclusion of Chinese Americans during this period, Chinese-language schoolteachers appeared to serve three central purposes: (a) maintaining the culture and language of Chinese tradition; (b) countering negative stereotypes and racial images of the Chinese community; (c) helping second-generation Chinese-American students negotiate Chinese and American culture. Given the context of anti-Chinese sentiment, it seems fair to argue that Chinese teachers at this time fulfilled not only a linguistic or cultural gap, but may have also served as advocates of social change for Chinese American students. The history of Chinese American education therefore, illustrates one of the earliest accounts of Asian American teachers for Asian American students.

Closing thoughts on history: Chinese American education

The educational experience of Chinese Americans illustrates that the discussion around cultural synchronization and teaching is hardly new. Many of the questions asked in the contemporary literature about Asian American teachers parallel the concerns of Chinese families and community leaders during the late nineteenth and early twentieth century. During this period, the concerns of culture, language, and tradition were all key arguments for having teachers of Chinese backgrounds. Another central concern during this early history was the effect that anti-Asian sentiment would have on the self-worth of Chinese second-generation children. The role of the Chinese teacher was to provide a positive image of the culture and infuse children with a sense of racial and cultural pride to buffer against the ideological practice of U.S. schools and society. In recent years, educational scholars concerned with education of Asian-American students have continued to explore these issues. The question that remains is: What impact does having a teacher of an Asian American background have on the social and educational development of Asian American students?

THE HISTORICAL CONTEXT OF NATIVE AMERICAN EDUCATION

Historians have consistently argued that the education of Native American students during the late nineteenth and early twentieth century was unquestionably a movement toward cultural annihilation (Adams, 1995; Coleman, 1993; Szasz, 1999 [1974]). Much of this literature asserts that the discussion of Native American education in the 1880s emerged out of a theme of educating Native Americans to "save" the Native American (Adams, 1988, 1995; Lomawaima, 1993). This theme of "saving" was based on an ideological belief that Native American culture was "inferior" and "savage," while White protestant culture was "superior" and "civilized." Therefore, education for American Indians served to remove all aspects of Native American language, culture, and traditions, with the ultimate aim of total assimilation into "American-Protestant" culture (Adams, 1995; Reyhner & Eder, 2004; Witmer, 1993).

Education for cultural annihilation

During the late nineteenth century, it was quite clear that the aims of education for American Indian children served one purpose—Americanization (Adams, 1988; Lomawaima, 1993). White educators proposed three specific aims to meet this goal:

(1) academic development, (2) individuation, and (3) Christianization (Adams, 1995, pp. 21–23). According to Adams (1995), one of the first priorities of educating the Native American child was to ensure that she/he could read, speak and write the English language. Mastery of such skills, according to White school officials, was a measure of acquired "civilized knowledge." However, White educators insisted that in order for Native American children to internalize school knowledge, they had to develop an individual identity disconnected from their tribal identities (Adams, 1995; Lomawaima, 1993; Reyhner & Edner, 2004). One strategy used to foster individual identity was to separate students from their families and siblings—and in some cases separate them from all American Indians (Reyhner & Edner, 2004). Another pedagogical strategy employed to assimilate the Native American child was to Christianize their spiritual beliefs (Lomawaima, 1993). School officials insisted that the Native American child would reach the highest level of social evolution through a firm foundation of Christian morals. Again, this aim emerged because of ensuing beliefs among White school officials that American Indian religious practices were hedonistic and "savage," while Christianity was a "civilized" spiritual practice. In short, through the process of academic development, individuation and Christianization, White educators sought two purposes: (1) to *deculturate* the tribal identity of the Native American child, and (2) to acculturate them to White Protestant ways of thinking and living (Coleman, 1993, p. 53). Certainly, such a schooling context did not come without its share of student resistance.

Native American students' resistance started first with their deep resentment toward the schools for pulling them away from their families. Students resisted in a variety of ways such as running away, day-to-day protests of school policies and in some cases, burning down buildings (Coleman, 1993). Other forms of resistance included, "willful acts of defiance, disruptive pranks, 'work slow downs,' refusing to participate in competitive exercises, and perhaps most common, adopting a general posture of nonreponsiveness" (Adams, 1995, p. 231). In addition to students' persistent direct and indirect challenges to both policy and curriculum, the growing presence of Native American teachers at American Indian boarding schools during the early twentieth century, implicitly and explicitly helped Native American students to cope within a school context that devalued American Indian culture.

Historical perspectives on Native American teachers

Although much of American Indian education was clearly Eurocentric during the late nineteenth century, some White educators introduced the importance of including the cultural and linguistic backgrounds of Native American students, including the benefits of having a teacher of American Indian descent. For example, in 1886, Elizabeth Peabody, the famous Boston educator, spoke of Native American teacher Sarah Winnemucca's qualifications:

> The only vital education that can be given to Indians must be given by Indians themselves who have spoken both languages from childhood, and are able to ground their methods, as she [Winnemucca] does, upon their own inherited natural religion and family moralities.
>
> (Gere, 2005, p. 6)

Peabody arrived at such insights directly from Sarah Winnemucca's work at the Peabody Institute for Native American students. Educational historian Ann Ruggles Gere (2005) notes that during the four-year history of the school, Winnemucca was able to create a learning environment that affirmed American Indian culture while providing a western-style academic curriculum. For her efforts as a teacher, she gained praise and admiration from the local community, including American Indian parents and students. However, not all White school officials agreed on Winnemucca's approach, which led to the school's ultimate closing. Although the school did not remain open, Gere (2005) notes that Winnemucca's methods of teaching would remain a modeled approach employed by other Native American teachers. A critical aspect of Winnemucca's method was her raced-based connection to American Indian students and community. These insights were apparent in a letter she wrote to the parents of the Peabody Institute:

> You all know me; many of you are my aunts and cousins. We are one race—your blood is my blood—so I speak for your good. I can speak five tongues—three Indian tongues, English and Spanish. I can read and write, and [I] am a school teacher. Now I say this not to boast, but to simply show you what can be done.
>
> (Gere, 2005, p. 8)

This theme of racial identification was a key ideal taken up by several other Native American teachers after Winnemucca. For example, in 1906 after school officials insisted that Indian culture and arts be infused into the curriculum for off-reservation boarding schools, the first Native American art course was taught by an American Indian woman, Angel De Cora. De Cora taught her course by infusing Native American cultures with western ideals of "economic practicality" (Witmer, 1993). Another Native American teacher (the husband of Angel De Cora) hired at Carlisle during this period was Lone Star Dietz, who also was noted for his innovative culturally relevant teaching strategies.

In addition to racial identification, Native American teachers and some supportive White educators (such as Elizabeth Peabody) argued that an integral aspect to Native American pedagogy was the teacher's ability to use bi-lingual practices. Native American teachers' ability to speak both the students' language and the English language made it easier for students to comprehend various academic disciplines. Gere (2005) notes that in some contexts where English-only policies pervaded, Native American teachers found different ways to provide home language instruction despite such policies.

While there was little support specifically for culturally relevant practices for Native Americans students, as indicated by the closing of the Peabody Institute, a growing number of American Indian teachers worked at off-reservation boarding schools during the early 1900s. In fact, with a growing demand for teachers at American Indian schools, the U.S. federal government created teacher-training programs at the largest off-reservation schools, including Carlisle, Haskell, Genoa, Salem and Chilocco (Gere, 2005). These programs offered courses in pedagogy and classroom practice, and also included lab schools for pre-service teachers. Ben Nelson, a Haskell normal school graduate, commented on the impact that trained American Indian teachers could have on American Indian students:

> The Indian students now have as their ideal teachers of their own race. The student-teachers that leave this institution and go back among their people, will not only be of infinite value to their community but will stimulate a desire for higher learning in the hearts and minds of the younger generation.
>
> (cited in Gere, 2005, p. 17)

A Shoshone teacher Essie Horne, commented that it was her childhood experiences with Native American teachers that had left the strongest impression on her life, including her decision to become a teacher. Here she comments on the pedagogical practice of American Indian teachers, Ella Deloria and Ruth Muskrat Bronson:

> Ruth and Ella listened to us. They were interested in what we thought about the subject material and interested in our lives. They taught us that we could accomplish anything that we set our minds to.
>
> (Horne & McBeth, 1998, p. 42)

This theme of racial identification and cultural competence resonated in the stories of many Native American students and teachers during the early twentieth century. These narratives also illustrated Native American students' and teachers' persistent efforts to challenge the hegemonic efforts of cultural annihilation within Native American boarding schools.

Closing thoughts on history: early history of Native American teachers

Historians have documented the pedagogies and social practices of Native American teachers such as Alice Callahan, Angel DeCora, Ella Deloria, Lone Star Dietz, and countless other teachers, highlighting the importance race and culture played in their work with Native American students (Coleman, 1993; Gere, 2005; Witmer, 1993). In 1928, with the publication of *The Problem of Indian Administration*—also known as the Merriam Report—a team of experts funded by the Brookings Institute, alluded to the importance of race and culture to Native American education, suggesting that school officials infuse cultural practices into the pedagogical practice and curriculum of Native American boarding schools. They also included recommendations to provide post-secondary opportunities for the training of more Native American teachers. As stated in the Merriam Report (Institute of Government Research in Administration, 1928):

> Plans for higher educational opportunities for Indian young men and women should include scholarship and loan aids for students who show promise of being especially helpful among their own people. Indian teachers and nurses, for example, are likely to have a special field of service for some time to come.
>
> (p. 62)

While the report recommendations clearly revealed the necessity of providing more culturally-informed curriculum and pedagogy, it should be noted that prior to 1928, there were several documented accounts of Native American teachers already implementing strategies suggested by the Merriam Report. The narratives of Native American teachers during the early 1900s provide an essential historical context to the enduring importance of teaching as a cultural and political practice. In recent years, the literature on education and Native American students has continued to emphasize the importance of language and cultural competence.

SITUATING HISTORICAL DISCUSSIONS WITHIN THE PRESENT

The right to a quality education for any child regardless of race/ethnicity or language has been debated and re-defined numerous times in this nation's history. The conversation invariably comes too late and is typically prompted by pressures of civil unrest, or recognition of economic and demographic realities. In the past as well as in the present, questions of who is best prepared to educate youngsters who are poor, non-White and often underserved are incessantly debated once there is a general consensus as to whether and to what extent they should be educated at all.

Once the established educational rights and privileges of the majority are extended to students of all racial, ethnic and linguistic backgrounds, valuable history is frequently lost. There is little acknowledgement of what communities of color had accomplished in providing quality instruction to their children, and the methods that they used to meet their respective goals. For instance, the Emancipation Proclamation abolished slavery and also gave license for pre-existing underground African American educational institutions in the South to legally exist and to be recognized. Although Historically Black Colleges and Universities (HBCUs) continued to yield a far greater proportion of degreed and qualified African American professionals, there is little to suggest that newly integrated majority institutions sought their counsel in working with African American students. Similarly, *Brown v. Topeka Board of Education* in 1956 and *Lau v. Nichols* in 1974 brought to the forefront discrepancies in educational access, resources, and quality in public schools. Yet for decades, these discrepancies were addressed through private and community supported schools. In the post-*Brown* era, approximately 31,584 African American teachers lost their jobs in 17 southern and border states (Ethridge, 1979), and were not welcome in newly integrated schools. More than a quarter of a century after *Lau*, those who have the pedagogical training and fluency in languages other than English are precluded in many states from teaching students in ways that they understand will enhance student achievement. Thus, the wealth of skills, knowledge and abilities that educators of color possess are frequently diluted or ignored in policies that are crafted to "enhance" equal educational opportunity.

For one and for all: perceptions and reality

For the nineteenth and most of the twentieth century, the societal role for people of color was distinct from that perceived for the dominant majority. There was the perception that African Americans, Latinos, Asian and Native Americans would serve a supportive role to the majority population's goals and that their education should be framed within this context. They were to reside in segregated communities and adhere to the cultural norms of the majority. This would be their American Dream. It was difficult for many individuals of color to see beyond these expectations as they struggled day to day to provide for their own and survive. Still, there were some from these communities who saw beyond the socio-economic and political limitations of the time and led the masses through more ambitious and liberating agendas (Moore, 1999).

Still, Tippiconnic (2000) contends that very little has changed for Native American Indian education since the seminal Merriam report was issued in 1928. Similarly, scores of researchers and scholars reported similar sentiments during the 2004 fiftieth anniversary of the *Brown v. Board of Education* decision. Yet, as Huntley (2004) notes, ". . . there is a sense of bridled optimism about the future in part because of what *Brown*, against the odds, was able to set in motion" (p. 3). Fairclough (2004) reminds us that all changes in teaching and the composition of the teaching force—good or bad—need not be attributed to the *Brown* decision and had little connection to integration. He argues that all was not good in segregated society, that "the post integration literature on segregated schools, often celebratory and sometimes hagiographic, must be treated with caution" (p. 45). He notes also that features attributed to African American teachers' effectiveness in segregated schools, e.g. corporal punishment, were abandoned in all schools for a reason, and that many African American teachers who lost their positions to integration were ill-educated and poorly trained.

The tumultuous 1960s and 1970s brought racial/ethnic identity to bear on education and teaching. In similar, but louder, voices than in the past, African, Latino, Asian, and Native Americans redefined their missions and goals to focus explicitly on the needs and desires of their communities and youth. Public and private schools and educational programs that were situated in communities of color were established and controlled by the parents and students who attended them. These community or alternative schools were condoned by public agencies as experiments. Still, the efficacy of these schools' teaching practices and curriculum were often called into question and dismissed by some as pacifiers to civil unrest.

In some ways, the sentiments and approaches to these community schools were consistent with those of previous decades. In the classic book, *An American Dilemma*, Gunnar Myrdal (1944) illustrates this point:

> Concerning the content of teaching in other respects, Negroes are also divided. On the one hand, they are inclined to feel that the Northern system, where standardized teaching is given students independent of whether they are Whites or Negroes, is the only right thing. On the other hand they feel that the students get to know too little about Negro problems. They thus want an adjustment of teaching toward the status of Negroes, usually not in order to make the Negroes weak and otherwise fit into the White man's wishful picture about "good niggers" but, on the contrary to make Negroes better prepared to fight for their rights. They feel that education should not be accepted passively but should be used as a tool of concerned action to gain the equal status they are seeking. For this reason, all if not most, Negro leaders desire that Negro students should get special training in the Negro problems.
>
> (p. 901)

The efforts of community-controlled education were in part an effort to avoid what Anderson (1988) notes:

> When you look at the curricula that was developed—domestic science for women, industrial education for African Americans, boarding schools for Native Americans—much of what developed under the guise of a demographic and differentiated curriculum was in fact a way to reinforce the kind of class, gender, and race prejudice that existed in society.
>
> (p. 112)

Given the new focus on cultural identity, it is not surprising that the 1960s also prompted the establishment of a number of race/ethnic specific organizations for teachers. Lomawaima (1995) offers that the Native American takeover of Alcatras Penitentiary had much to do with the type and quality of education provided by their community. During this period, the Native American Education Association, Aspira—the organization devoted solely to the education and leadership of Puerto Rican and other Latino youth, and the National Alliance for Black School Educators, were established. Unlike the segregated local, state and national organizations of earlier decades, these organizations were able to openly engage teachers from these groups, formally establish relationships with each other, and engage majority organizations and colleagues on issues of policy and practice relating to education and society.

It is interesting to note that following this period of engagement in the 1960s and

1970s, there began a precipitous decline in the number of teachers of color. Given access to careers that were previously prohibited, women generally and women of color specifically began to pursue careers in other fields, leaving a significant void in the teaching ranks (Darling-Hammond, Dilworth, & Bullmaster, 1996; Dilworth, 1984; Garibaldi, 1986). Thus as the nation's student population became increasingly diverse, those most prepared and knowledgeable about culturally responsive practice were absent. What we eventually found in the 1980s and 1990s were seasoned teachers of color retiring. They left the profession, taking with them the heritage and knowledge of previous decades and the spirit of *racial uplift*; they were lost to the nation's educational system at the time of greatest need.

Snyder notes that after World War II, 79 percent of African American female graduates were employed as teachers, but by the mid-1980s, this number had fallen to 23 percent (1998, cited in Zumwalt & Craig, 2005). Throughout the late 1980s and early 1990s, significant support—primarily by private philanthropic organizations and agencies—encouraged participation of teachers of color by establishing targeted recruitment programs in schools, colleges, and departments of education (SCDEs), as well as community colleges and high schools (Darling-Hammond *et al.*, 1996). Recent data indicate that

> The numbers of prospective and practicing teachers of color vary widely by region and by institution. They are more likely than Whites to start their higher education at 2-year colleges and transfer to 4-year public institutions for teacher preparation . . . Minority teachers disproportionately teach at the elementary level and are found more often in central cities and schools serving high proportions of minority and low-income students.
>
> (Zumwalt & Craig, 2005, p. 140)

While we speculate that all licensed teachers have the ability to educate students to their full academic potential, teachers of color offer a value-added dimension of racial/ethnic or linguistic relationship. At the same time, it is important to acknowledge that similar teacher-student race, ethnicity and language do not ensure enhanced teaching and learning (Banks *et al.*, 2005). However, while there are similarities among all effective teachers, there are also differences. The cultural backgrounds of educators help illuminate these differences:

> Given their culturally diverse backgrounds, and academic training defined by the White majority, Black, Hispanic and other minority teachers possess a consummate understanding of the relationship between education and this society. This knowledge enhances the quality of education when these teachers offer their students broader and more complex interpretations of the educational curriculum, and when they translate and interpret for their majority peers, in educational terms, the cultural backgrounds of their students.
>
> (Dilworth, 1990, p. xi)

Same goals, varying perspectives

Rong and Preissle (1997) in their discussion of Asian American teachers posit that while the literature on teachers of color typically combines and treats all such groups generically, there are apparent differences that evolve from ancestry, language, immigration, and access and participation in higher education. Indeed, there are factors that distinguish teachers of differing cultures but there are also commonalities of roles and practice. For instance, when describing African American teachers with whom she worked, Irvine (1999) provides:

> The pedagogy and mastery of the content standards were less important than these teachers' beliefs about the nature of teaching itself. Teachers, in my research, not only viewed teaching as telling, guiding, and facilitating mastery of the much-heralded content standards, but they also believed teaching is defined as caring, "other mothering" believing, demanding the best, responding to one's calling and disciplining.
>
> (p. 249)

Similarly, Nieto (1994; 1998) reflects on characteristics of effective Latino teachers who, like Irvine's "other mother" teachers, tend to practice with the notion of extended family relationships. She cites Montero-Sieburth and Perez's (1987) identifiers used by a bilingual teacher as "teacher, friend, mother, social worker, translator, counselor, advocate, prosecutor, group therapist, hygienist, and monitor" (p. 158). Nieto notes that the caring characteristic is often attributed to Puerto Rican and other Latino teachers, however these features can be found in teachers of any culture if the intent and understanding exists.

The present day demands made of those who know how to engage, challenge and teach youngsters, are enormous. Significant philanthropic efforts of the late 1980s and sometimes desperate efforts, e.g. alternative teaching licensure routes, to recruit and license more teachers of color, have just begun to bear fruit. At the same time, we acknowledge that for the foreseeable future, the teaching force will remain largely White. Research and knowledge of diverse cultures and ways of knowing are now at a premium in teacher education and professional development. Virtually all state and disciplinary teaching standards and assessments address matters of student diversity, yet this information must be shared in formats that are consistent with the academy or else they will be/ are lost. The burden of everyday practice—teaching well—often precludes culturally responsive teachers from contributing to meaningful initial and continuing professional development (Johnson, S. M., 1990; Rios et al., 1998). A number of contemporary scholars provide us with significant examples of the strength of practice that teachers of color provide (Foster, 1994; Henry, 1998; Ladson-Billings, 1994; Pang & Sablan, 1997; Siddle Walker, 2005). Exhibiting the cultural teaching styles of their predecessors, teachers of color are often observed and discussed in the literature. Authors such as Cochran-Smith, Fraser and Perry, Zimpher and Ashburn, and Sleeter aptly relay their understanding of these practices to those teachers who will educate an increasing number of youngsters from non-White cultures, as well as to teacher educators who prepare prospective teachers who, for the foreseeable future, will remain predominantly White.

Reviewing the preparation and practices of teachers over time allows us to understand and substantiate society's values towards education as well as towards difference. The criteria for acceptance into the profession, time and attention to preparation, the caliber of those who teach teachers, and the contexts and situations that inform the curriculum all contribute to a weak or strong teaching force. Yet as Hollins and Guzman (2005) offer, research on teachers of color focuses primarily on three areas: retention in teacher education programs, alternative experiences, and program experiences. Indeed, until the 1990s, issues regarding the preparation of teachers of color were rarely studied or analyzed as anything other than a problem, i.e. supply and demand. As Sedlak and Schlossman (1987) note, "without intensive, in-depth analyses of the broad trends … historians' and policymakers' understanding of why and how major changes in the teaching force have come about will inevitably remain superficial" (p. 94).

In recent times, preparation and pedagogy have been examined more closely in search of guidance in educating the increasing number of youngsters from racial, ethnic, and linguistically diverse cultures. In fact, there is a perception among members of all communities of color that they are frequently reviewed and scrutinized by others. For instance, it is interesting to note that McWilliams (1943), as well as Deyhle and Swisher (1997), contend that African American and American Indians respectively are the most studied ethnic groups in the literature. Nieto (1998) and Rong and Preissle (1997) also note a proliferation of education studies in recent decades focusing on Puerto Ricans and Asian Americans respectively. Given the disparities in the academic achievement of some of these groups, these perceptions suggest that the findings may not resonate or find an audience with those responsible for teaching students from these groups. It is apparent that culturally responsive themes are an important component in the education research literature. To ignore or avoid their importance is counter-productive to efforts to close the achievement gap.

Conclusions

In the case of teachers of color, we find the determination of their respective communities and commitment of philanthropic and religious organizations forging quality preparation and effective practice despite lack of support from the general population. Disenfranchised racial, ethnic, and linguistically diverse groups for the past centuries have endured for three primary reasons: the uplift of the race, maintenance of culture and the pursuit of social–economic justice. In reviewing the literature, we note how educational events and policies impact or situate teachers of color in schools and practice. We note occasions where "minority" teachers and communities craft schools and other educational experiences that supplement standard—and sub-standard—educational offerings. From the nineteenth century until today, these groups have established for themselves, in segregated settings, syllabi, and program designs that best suit their goals. There is a similar message in all of these efforts, that while there is something of value, usefulness, and necessity in the educational offerings of standard basic education, rich educational experiences can be created by engaging teachers and communities of color in a greater way than they are, typically, or at this time. This century's teachers are more formally prepared, degreed and licensed than at any point in the history of this nation. While the teaching force is by and large White, there is a cadre of African, Latino, Asian and Native American teachers, who by virtue of their heritage and culture, offer a value-added dimension to effective teaching and learning. Given the challenges of today where the educational environment for the poor and students of color is fraught with inequities (Kozol, 1991), and far too many students of color find schools and teachers unwelcoming (Macedo & Bartolomé, 1999), it is apparent that we have not fully recognized and empowered of teachers of color in a manner that will help reconcile the issues that we face.

NOTES

1 A "Tejano" is a person of Mexican heritage born and living in Texas (San Miguel, 1987).
2 The term "Hispano" refers to people of Hispanic descent living in New Mexico (Getz, 1997).
3 During this period, "progressive" educator John Dewey's ideas of community education were widely recognized within educational discourses.
4 The early history of Japanese-Americans also provides an important historical perspective about how culture, language and race informed the early educational experiences of Asian American

students. This history also elaborates on how and why Japanese Americans communities hired teachers of Japanese background to teach their children in Japanese-language schools. See the following references: Bell, R. (1978). *Public school education of second generation Japanese in California*. California: Stanford University Press; Daniels, R. (1988). *Asian America: Chinese and Japanese in the United States since 1850*. Seattle: University of Washington Press; Svensrud, M. (1932). Attitudes of Japanese towards their language schools. *Sociology and Social Research*, 11, 259–264; Tsuboi, S. (1926). Japanese language school teacher. *Sociology and Social Research*, 11, 160–165.

REFERENCES

Adams, D. (1988) Fundamental considerations: the deep meaning of Native American schooling, 1880–1900. *Harvard Educational Review*, 58(1), 1–28.

Adams, D. (1995) *Education for extinction: American Indians and the boarding school experience, 1875–1928*. Lawrence, KS: University Press of Kansas.

Anderson, J. A. (1988) *The education of Blacks in the South, 1860–1935*. Chapel Hill, NC: University of North Carolina Press.

Banks, J., M. Cochran–Smith, M., Moll, L., Richert, A., Zeichner, K., *et al.* (2005) Teaching diverse learners. In Darling-Hammond & Bransford (ed.), *Preparing teachers for a changing world* (pp. 232–274). San Francisco: Jossey-Bass.

Bell, R. (1978) *Public school education of second generation Japanese in California*. New York: Arno.

Blackshear, E. L. (1969 [1902]) What is the Negro teacher doing in the matter of uplifting the race? In D. W. Culp (ed.), *Twentieth century Negro literature* (pp. 334–338). New York: Arno.

Bond, H. M. (1934) *The education of the Negro in the American social order*. New York: Octagon Books.

Caliver, A. (1933) *Education of Negro teachers*. Westport, CT: Negro Universities Press.

Campbell, L. (1970). The Black teacher and Black power. In N. Wright (ed.), *What Black educators are saying* (pp. 23–25). New York: Hawthorn Books.

Chang, F. (1934) An accommodation program for second-generation Chinese. *Sociology and Social Research*, 18, 541–553.

Coleman, M. (1993) *American Indian children at school, 1850–1930*. Jackson, MS: University Press of Mississippi.

Daniels, R. (1988) *Asian America: Chinese and Japanese in the United States since 1850*. Seattle: University of Washington Press.

Darling-Hammond, L., Dilworth, M. E., & Bullmaster, M. (1996) *Educators of color* (commissioned paper). Washington, DC: Office of Educational Research and Improvement (OERI)/U.S. Department of Education.

DeLeon, A. (1982) *The Tejano community, 1836–1900*. Albuquerque, NM: University of New Mexico.

Deyhle, D. & Swisher, K. (1997) Research in American Indian and Alaskan Native Education: from assimilation to self-determination. *Review of Education Research*, 113–194.

Dilworth, M. E. (1984). *Teachers' totter: a report on teacher certification issues*. (Occasional paper of the Institute for the Study of Educational Policy No. 6). Howard University, Washington, DC: Institute for the Study of Educational Policy. (ERIC Document Reproduction Service No. ED266086).

Dilworth, M. E. (1990) *Reading between the lines: teachers and their racial/ethnic cultures*. (Teacher Education Monograph no. 11). Washington, DC: ERIC Clearinghouse on Teacher Education. (ERIC Document Reproduction Service No. ED322148).

Du Bois, W. E. B. (1935) Does the Negro need separate schools? *Journal of Negro Education*, 4(3), 328–335.

Ethridge, S. (1979) Impact of the 1954 Brown v. Topeka Board of Education decision on Black educators. *Negro Educational Review*, 30(3–4), 217–232.

Fairclough, A. (2004) The costs of *Brown*: Black teachers and school integration. *Journal of American History*, 91(1), 43–55.

Foster, M. (1994) Effective Black teachers: a literature review. In E. R. Hollins, J. E. King, & W. C. Hayman (eds.), *Teaching diverse populations: formulating a knowledge base* (pp. 225–241). Albany: SUNY Press.

Fultz, M. (1995a) African American teachers in the South, 1890–1940: powerlessness and the ironies and expectations and protest. *History of Education Quarterly*, 35(4), 401–422.

Fultz, M. (1995b) Teacher training and African American education in the South, 1900–1940. *Journal of Negro Education*, 64(2), 196–210.

Garcia, M. (1981) *Desert immigrants: the Mexicans of El Paso, 1880–1920*. New Haven, CT: Yale University.

Garibaldi, A. M. (1986) *The decline of teacher production in Louisiana (1976–83) and attitudes toward the profession*. Atlanta: Southern Education Foundation (ERIC Micro film Document No. ED 268 108).

Gere, A. R. (2005) Indian heart/white man's head: native American teachers in Indian schools, 1880–1930. *History of Education Quarterly*, 45(1), 38–65. Retrieved July 18, 2005, from http://www.historycooperative.org.

Getz, L. (1997) *Schools of their own: the education of Hispanos in New Mexico: 1850–1940*. Albuquerque, NM.

Grant, G. & Murray, C. E. (1999) *Teaching in America: the slow revolution*. Cambridge, MA: Harvard University Press.

Groff, P. J. (1961) School desegregation and the education of Negro teachers in the south. *Journal of Teacher Education*, 12, 8–11.

Henry, A. (1998) *Taking back control: African Canadian women teachers' lives and practice*. Albany: SUNY Press.

Hollins, E. R. & Guzman, M. T. (2005) Research on preparing teachers for diverse populations. In M. Cochran-Smith & K. M. Zeichner (eds.), *Studying teacher education: the report of the AERA Panel on research and teacher education* (pp. 477–548). Mahwah, NJ: Lawrence Erlbaum Associates.

Horne, E. B. & McBeth, S. (1998) *Essies's story: the life and legacy of a Shoshone teacher*. Lincoln, NE: University of Nebraska Press.

Huntley, L. (2005) Brown v. Board of Education: message for the future. *Lessons from Brown*. Atlanta: Southern Education Foundation, 1–18.

Institute of Government Research in Administration (1928) *The Problem of Indian Administration* (Merriam Report). Retrieved October 9, 2005, from http://www.alaskool.org/native_ed/research_reports/IndianAdmin/Indian_Admin_Problms.html

Irvine, J. J. (1999) The education of children whose nightmares come both day and night. *Journal of Negro Education*, 68(3), 244–253.

Johnson, C. (1930) *The Negro in American civilization*. New York: Henry Holt.

Johnson, S. M. (1990) *Teachers at work: achieving success in our schools*. New York: Basic Books.

Kitano, D. & Daniels, R. (2001) *Asian Americans: emerging minorities*. Upper Saddle River, NJ: Prentice Hall.

Kozol, J. (1991) *Savage inequities: children in America's schools*. New York: HarperCollins.

Ladson-Billings, G. (1994) *Dreamkeepers: successful teachers for African American children*. San Francisco: Jossey-Bass.

Lomawaima, K. T. (1993) Domesticity in the federal Indian schools: the power of authority over mind and body. *American Ethnologist*, 20(2), 227–240.

Lomawaima, T. (1995) Educating Native Americans. In J. A. Banks & C. A. M Banks (eds.), *Handbook of research on multicultural education* (pp. 331–347). New York: Macmillan.

Louis, K. K. (1932) Program for second generation Chinese. *Sociology and Social Research*, 16, 455–462.

Lynn, M. (2002) Critical race theory and the perspectives of Black men teachers in the Los Angeles public schools. *Equity & Excellence in Education*, 35(2), 119–130.

Mabee, C. (1979) *Black Education in New York State: from colonial to modern times*. Syracuse, NY: Syracuse University Press.

MacDonald, V. M. (ed.) (2004) *Latino education in the United States: a narrated history from 1513–2000*. New York: Palgrave.

Macedo, D. & Bartolomé, L. (1999) *Dancing with bigotry: beyond the politics of tolerance*. New York: Palgrave.

McWilliams, C. (1943) *Brothers under the skin*. Boston: Little, Brown and Co.

Montera Sieburth, M. and Perez, M. (1987) Echar pa'lante, moving onward: the dilemmas and strategies of a bilingual teacher. *Anthropology and Education Quarterly*, 18, 180–189.

Moore, J. (1999) Leading the race: the transformation of the black elite in the nation's capital 1880–1920. Charlottesville, VA: University Press of Virginia.

Morimoto, T. (1997) *Japanese Americans and cultural continuity: maintaining language and heritage*. New York: Garland.

Myrdal, G. (1944) *An American dilemma: the Negro problem and modern democracy*. New York: Harper & Row.

Nieto, S. (1994) Lessons from students on creating a chance to dream. *Harvard Educational Review* 64, (4) 392–426.

Nieto, S. (1998) Fact and fiction: stories of Puerto Ricans in U.S. schools. *Harvard Educational Review*, 68(2), 133–163.

Pang, V. O. & Sablan, V. A. (1997) Teacher efficacy: how do teachers feel about their ability to teach African American students. In M. E. Dilworth (ed.), *Being responsive to cultural differences: how teachers learn* (pp. 39–58). Thousand Oaks: Corwin Press.

Reyhner, J. & Eder, J. (2004) *American Indian education: a history*. Norman, OK: University of Oklahoma Press.

Rios, F., McDaniel, J., & Stowell, L. P. (1998) Pursuing the possibilities of passion: the affective domain of multicultural education. In M. E. Dilworth (ed.), *Being responsive to cultural differences: how teachers learn* (pp. 160–179). Thousand Oaks, CA: Corwin Press.

Rong, X. L. & Preissle, J. (1997) The continuing decline in Asian American teachers. *American Educational Research Journal*, 34(2), 267–293.

Rury, J. L. (1983) The New York African free school, 1827–1836: conflict over community control of Black education. *Phylon*, 44(3), 187–197.

San Miguel, G., Jr. (1987) *"Let them all take heed:" Mexican Americans and the campaign for educational equity in Texas, 1910–1981*. Austin, TX: University of Texas Press.

San Miguel, G., Jr. & Valencia, R. R. (1998) From the Treaty of Guadalupe Hidalgo to Hopwood: the educational plight and struggle of Mexican Americans in the Southwest. *Harvard Educational Review*, 68(3), 353–412.

Sedlak, M. & Schlossman, S. (1987) Who will teach? Historical perspectives on the changing appeal of teaching as a profession. *Review of Research in Education*, 14, 93–131.

Siddle Walker, V. (2005) Organized resistance and the Black educators' quest for school equality, 1878–1938. *Teachers College Record*, 107(3), 355–388.

Svensrud, M. (1932) Attitudes of the Japanese towards their language schools. *Sociology and Social Research*, 11, 259–264.

Szasz, M. C. (1999 [1974]) *Education and the American Indian: the road to self-determination since 1928*. New Mexico: University of New Mexico Press.

Tillman, L. (2004) (Un)Intended Consequences? The impact of the Brown v. Board of education decision on the employment status of Black educators. *Education and Urban Society*, 36, 280–303.

Tippiconnic, J. (2000) Reflecting on the past: some important aspects of Indian education to consider as we look toward the future. *Journal of American Indian Education*, 39(2), 39–48.

Tom, K. F. (1941) Function of Chinese-language schools. *Sociology and Social Research*, 25(7), 557–571.

Tsuboi, S. (1926) Japanese language school teacher. *Sociology and Social Research*, 11, 160–165.

Valencia, R. (2005) The Mexican American struggle for equal educational opportunity in Mendez v.

Westminster: helping to pave the way for Brown v. Board of Education. *Teachers College Record*, 107(3), 398–423.

Weinberg, M. (1997) *Asian-American education: historical background and current realities.* Mawah, NJ: Lawrence Earlbaum.

Witmer, L. (1993) *The Indian Industrial school: Carlisle, PA.* Carlisle, PA: Cumberland County Historical Society.

Zumwalt, K. & Craig, E. (2005) Teachers' characteristics: research on the demographic profile. In M. Cochran-Smith & K.M. Zeichner (eds.), *Studying teacher education: the report of the AERA Panel on Research and Teacher Education* (pp. 111–156). Washington, DC; Mahwah, NJ: Lawrence Erlbaum.

26 The next generation of teachers

Who enters, who stays, and why

Susan Moore Johnson
Harvard Graduate School of Education

Susan M. Kardos
Independent Researcher

Before the 1960s, teaching was largely a short-term career chosen by men on their way to another line of work and women who taught until they married or had children (Lortie, 1975). Leaving teaching was not always a matter of choice for women, since many school districts required them to resign once they married or became pregnant. However, as the demand for teachers grew and sanctions on women teachers relaxed in the 1950s, the teaching force stabilized. In the late 1960s and early 1970s, public schools hired the first cohort of teachers who would make teaching a lifelong career (Grant & Murray, 1999; Rury, 1989; Spencer, 2001; Teacher Quality Clearinghouse).

By 2000, however, analysts began to predict that the teaching force would again be transformed. Hussar (1999) projected the need to hire 2.2 million new teachers by 2010. In 2001, more than one-third of all teachers had more than 20 years of experience (National Education Association, 2003) and could be expected to retire soon. Forecasts of continued change were further substantiated in 2005 by results from a survey of U.S. public school teachers, 40 percent of whom said that they would not be teaching in 2010 (Feistritzer, 2005). At the high school level, that percentage was even higher (50 percent). Given that 27 percent of the respondents had been teaching 25 years or more, approaching retirement explained much of the projected turnover. However, there was more to the story than the predictable retirement of an aging teaching force.

Since they were hired in the late 1960s and early 1970s, the generation of teachers approaching retirement has continuously constituted the largest cohort of the teaching force (Wirt, 2000). Because of their high retention rates and the decline of student enrollments during the 1980s, far fewer teachers were hired in the 1980s and 1990s. Since 2001, however, when substantial numbers of veteran teachers began to retire, school districts have aggressively recruited and hired the next generation of teachers. The profile of experience in the teaching force has become increasingly U-shaped with two distinct cohorts, one entering and one leaving with relatively few teachers in between (Johnson & The Project on the Next Generation of Teachers, 2004; National Education Association, 2003). Differences in the priorities and expectations of these two groups have led researchers to call the valley between these two peaks a "generation gap" (Johnson & The Project on the Next Generation of Teachers, 2004).

In the 40 years since the last major wave of hiring, the work of teaching has changed dramatically. Schools today serve much larger and more diverse student populations than ever before due to increased immigration, higher birth rates, and policies adopted to improve education for a wider range of students, especially those from low-income communities, those with disabilities, and English language learners. Overall, state and federal policy has increasingly required teachers not only to serve all students, but to succeed with them as well. Under the *No Child Left Behind Act*, low-performing schools face unprecedented sanctions if they fail to make steady gains.

With these new demands on public education has come increased concern about the quality of teachers, since research clearly demonstrates that teachers are the most important factor in students' learning (Haycock, 1998; McCaffrey *et al.*, 2003; Sanders & Rivers, 1996). However, with the impending retirement of such a large segment of the teaching force, it is not clear if public education can attract and retain a new cohort of teachers sufficiently skilled and committed to meet the growing demands on schools. Many potential teachers never consider a career in the classroom (Public Agenda, 2000) and attrition rates among those who enter teaching are surprisingly high (Ingersoll, 2001a). In this chapter, we consider what is known about the next generation of teachers, how current patterns of attrition undermine the stability of the teaching force, what factors affect new teachers' career decisions, and what reforms are underway to support and retain them.

A DIFFERENT LABOR CONTEXT

When teachers of the retiring generation were hired 35 to 40 years ago, the labor market for teaching was much different than it is today. Other professions were closed, either tacitly or explicitly, to the women and people of color who comprised education's traditional labor pool. This group of well-educated recruits to the classroom provided their talents and knowledge at a discount since they would have earned more had they been hired to work in other fields; thus they have become known as the "hidden subsidy" of public education. At the same time, politicians lauded public service as respectable work, and teachers retained a certain status, even though their comparatively low pay signaled otherwise. Moreover, long-term careers were the norm in society four decades ago. Whether individuals entered banking, accounting, or nursing, they typically chose a career for life, often working for a single organization. Thus, the cohort of teachers now retiring often chose teaching by default, never seriously weighing the benefits and limitations of other lines of work. Large numbers of them made a lifetime commitment to the classroom.

Those considering teaching today do so within a very different labor context. All career options, from engineering and medicine to business and finance, are open to them. In fact, today many professions actively recruit the very candidates they excluded before 1970. Teaching thus has become one of the many possible career choices for women and people of color, who once could be counted on to enter teaching in large numbers.

The newer career opportunities competing directly with classroom teaching today have certain advantages. For example, law offices, architecture firms, and advertising agencies typically provide more comfortable and attractive work environments than schools and usually offer greater support for their employees' work. Recruits can expect to earn much more on entry than they would in teaching, and they can anticipate far higher wages over time than the standard salary scale teaching promises (Allegretto *et al.*, 2004). In addition, the prospect of high pay in other lines of work also brings a level of status that classroom teaching lacks. Other fields also offer a job candidate the possibility of expanded responsibility and recognition within a relatively short time.

Further complicating the challenge of staffing schools for the long term is a shift in people's expectations about the nature of career. Long-term careers, once the norm across the society, are far less common today. According to a recent study, the average American 32 year old already has worked for nine firms (Editors, 2000). Thus, there can be no certainty that an entrant to teaching will remain in the classroom for 35 years until retirement. Given the attractions of competing work environments—more comfortable and supportive workplaces, higher pay and status, greater opportunities for advancement—and decreased commitment to any long-term career, it is unlikely that the public schools can replace the teachers of the retiring generation with a similarly skilled and steadfast cohort.

THE NEW GENERATION OF TEACHERS

Given this context, what is known about the current entrants to teaching? First, the group of teachers being hired today is far more diverse in age and experience than ever before. Whereas most of the retiring generation entered teaching soon after college, far more of today's entrants are choosing teaching at mid-career. Random sample surveys of first-year and second-year teachers conducted between 1999 and 2003 in seven states (California, Florida. Massachusetts, Michigan, North Carolina, New Jersey, and Washington) revealed that a large proportion of new teachers are entering at mid-career, at ages 35 to 38 (Kardos, 2004; Kauffman, 2005; Liu, 2004). In these surveys, mid-career entrants to teaching comprised between 28 percent of new teachers in Michigan and 47 percent in California. These mid-career entrants bring to teaching a different set of skills, experiences, and expectations (Johnson *et al.*, 2005; Johnson & The Project on the Next Generation of Teachers, 2004). Unlike the first-career entrants who moved directly from *being* students to *teaching* students, mid-career entrants have been away from school for a substantial period of time, working in other types of settings that offer greater support and earning potential than schools. Often these mid-career entrants had supervisory responsibilities and worked on teams with other employees. They have chosen to teach at mid-career largely because they were dissatisfied with the values or demands of their prior workplaces; for them, teaching offers the promise of more meaningful work (Feistritzer, 2005; Johnson *et al.*, 2005). Many bring to teaching knowledge, skill, and experiences they gained in real-world enterprises as chemists, engineers, or journalists. Often they are parents who enter the classroom more confident than their first-career counterparts about their role as an authority figure. Many, though certainly not all, express a commitment to remain in teaching long-term (Johnson *et al.*, 2005).

The first-career entrants, by contrast, are both younger and less experienced in other types of work and organizations. Although many have always planned to be teachers and anticipate a long career in the classroom, more of them approach teaching tentatively (Peske *et al.*, 2001). They talk of exploring teaching. If they find success there, they may stay; if not, they will move on (Johnson & Birkeland, 2003). Others plan to make a short-term contribution to teaching by committing a few years to public education before entering another line of work (Peske *et al.*, 2001). First-career entrants are well aware that teaching is publicly held in low regard, that they could earn more in another field, and that the day-to-day work of teaching is very demanding. They are not certain that they will be satisfied with the conditions of work or succeed with today's students.

The cohort of new teachers today also enters schools with differing levels of preparation. Some have majored in the subject they will teach and have completed undergraduate or graduate programs in education, including a substantial period of student teaching under the supervision of experienced, expert teachers. Others enter teaching through alternative routes. Nearly all states today authorize and often fund alternative certification programs through which prospective teachers can attain a provisional license after five to eight weeks of coursework and part-time student teaching in a summer school

(Feistritzer & Chester, 2003). These fast-track programs often are designed to prepare mid-career entrants for a quick transition into the classroom. In addition to these entrants who are traditionally or alternatively prepared, there are many new teachers with no formal preparation. Although the regulations of No Child Left Behind make it increasingly difficult for school districts to employ teachers on an emergency license, many still do since fully licensed teachers are not always available. Thus, there is a tremendous range of preparation among new teachers entering schools today.

As a group these new teachers vary widely in their expectations, experience, and training. However, their schools are remarkably similar—flat organizations, with the majority of teachers working independently and reporting directly to one or two administrators. Compared with the more complex and varied workplaces that many mid-career entrants have known, schools are far less flexible in structure, seldom reorganizing in response to new demands or evidence that they are ineffective. Most new teachers continue to work in "egg-crate" schools, where they are assigned to separate classrooms and given sole responsibility for a group of students throughout the school year. They can anticipate doing the same work in the same way on the first and last day of their career. Pay is predictable since all teachers within a district are paid according to a single salary scale, compensating them modestly for earning advanced degrees and continuing to teach from year to year. Unless they take on an extra assignment as an athletic coach or student club sponsor, teachers in most districts can never expect to earn more than another colleague with similar degrees and years of experience.

Increasingly, evidence shows that such "egg-crate" schools are no longer effective, if they ever were. Schools found to support the improvement of instruction for all students tend to be far more flexible, responsive, and team-based (Rosenholtz, 1989). They distribute leadership, making good use of teachers who offer greater expertise or specialized knowledge and skills (Elmore, 2004a). They have a coherent curriculum and demonstrate consistent instructional practices school-wide (Abelmann & Elmore, 1999; Elmore, 2004b). They promote positive norms for students' behavior and teachers' professional practice, while building trust among all parties (Bryk & Schneider, 2002). They have deliberate strategies for socializing and supporting new teachers; novices are not left to sink or swim (Berry et al., 2002). These are the kinds of schools needed today, given the extensive turnover in the teaching force and the wide range of needs and experience among new entrants. Although the retiring generation of teachers largely found that the schools they entered fit their expectations, early research on the current cohort of new teachers entering the classroom suggests that many are dissatisfied with their schools and know that they have other workplace options (Boston Plan for Excellence, 2005).

TEACHER TURNOVER

For almost four decades, teacher turnover was a minor concern for school administrators and policymakers. However, since 2000, it has become increasingly apparent that schools are no longer retaining teachers as they once did, and thus teacher retention has replaced teacher recruitment as the first priority of many states and districts (National Commission for Teaching and America's Future, 2003), since high rates of teacher turnover introduce unprecedented costs—financial, instructional, and organizational.

Researchers use the term "attrition" to denote the loss of teachers from the profession and "migration" to denote teachers' movement from one district or school to another. "Turnover" is an umbrella term used for both (Ingersoll, 2001b). The policy implications for attrition and migration differ. For example, a state official with a goal of maintaining the size of the teaching force statewide, will be far more concerned about rising attrition rates than high rates of migration. A local school official is more likely to focus on the causes of teacher migration from district to district, while a school principal will attend to movement from school to school. For those working in schools, the consequences of migration and attrition are much the same. Whether a teacher leaves the profession entirely or moves to the school across town, the loss disrupts continuity and introduces new demands. Ongoing turnover is costly and disabling to schools, districts, and states.

Currently, turnover rates among teachers are relatively high and thought by many to be growing. In 2000–2001, the most recent year for which there are national data on teacher turnover, 7.4 percent of public school teachers left the teaching profession and 7.7 percent moved to a different school for a total turnover rate of 15.1 percent, which exceeds by 2 to 3 percent that of the prior decade. Attrition rates among white, non-Hispanic teachers (7.5 percent), Hispanic teachers (7.5 percent) and black, non-Hispanic teachers (7.4 percent) were much the same. However, migration rates varied somewhat more among these three groups; 7.6 percent of white, non-Hispanic teachers changed schools, while 8.3 percent of black, non-Hispanic teachers and 7.1 percent of Hispanic teachers did so. Teachers who self-identified as Native American or Alaskan Native had generally the same attrition rates as these other groups (7.5 percent), but substantially lower migration rates (4.7 percent). Asian and Pacific Islander teachers left the classroom at far lower rates (2.1 percent) and moved at far higher rates (16.2 percent) than the other groups (Luekens *et al.*, 2004).

Ingersoll (2001b) found that retiring teachers comprised only 12.3 percent of those who left teaching in 1991, but by 2001 they represented 27 percent of the leavers. As Feistritzer's data suggest, the proportion of turnover that can be attributed to retirement is likely to increase through at least 2010 (Feistritzer, 2005). However, there is evidence that new teachers today are leaving the classroom after a short time in their career. Recent analysis (Luekens *et al.*, 2004) reveals that teachers under 30 were the least likely of four age cohorts to remain in their schools from 1999 to 2000. The Boston Public Schools reports losing half of their new teachers in three years (Boston Plan for Excellence, 2005). If other districts experience comparable attrition, the cohort of new teachers may leave schools at rates that rival those of their retiring colleagues.

Notably, turnover is not equally distributed across subjects or schools. Researchers have found higher turnover rates for teachers of mathematics, science and special education than for teachers of other subjects, although studies using different data sets do not report consistent findings (Ingersoll, 2001b; Kirby *et al.*, 1999; Murnane *et al.*, 1991). There is little current research documenting turnover rates in separate subjects, although anecdotal reports from districts suggest that staffing these fields continues to be very difficult.

Schools that experience high rates of turnover typically serve low-income communities. Ingersoll (2001b) reports that among public schools in 1990–1991, those serving high-poverty communities experienced higher turnover rates (15.2 percent) on average than did low-poverty schools (10.5 percent). Similarly, schools enrolling higher proportions of minority students experienced higher rates of turnover. Luekens *et al.* (2004) report that 16.8 percent of teachers left schools enrolling more than 35 percent minority students; 14.7 percent of teachers left schools enrolling between 10 and 35 percent minority students; and 13.5 percent of teachers left schools with a minority enrollment of less than 10 percent. Hanushek *et al.* (2004), who report a similar pattern in Texas schools, also found that schools where students scored within the bottom quartile on state tests had annual attrition rates of 20 percent, while those achieving average scores experienced rates of 15 percent. Combined, these studies suggest that "students at lower-performing, lower-income, higher-minority schools are more likely to have inconsistent staffing from year to year and to be taught by a greater number of inexperienced teachers than their counterparts are at higher-achieving, more affluent, and predominantly white schools" (Johnson *et al.*, 2005, p. 6). It is not clear from this line of research, however, whether teachers choose to leave because of their low-income, low-performing, minority students or because the schools attended by such students fail to support effective teaching and learning.

WHY RETENTION MATTERS

Many who express concern about the quality of teachers today criticize efforts to retain them at high rates. Clearly, schools will not improve if ineffective teachers are encouraged to stay, and many analysts make the point that 100 percent retention is an unwise objective (Ballou & Podgursky, 1997; Guarino *et al.*, 2004; Hanushek *et al.*, 2004). However, there is evidence based on teachers' test scores that schools experiencing turnover tend to lose their more able rather than their less able teachers (Lankford *et al.*, 2002; Murnane & Olsen, 1989; Podgursky *et al.*, 2004; Stinebrickner, 2001). If the quality of the teaching force is to improve, especially in low-income, low-performing schools, policy and practice must provide support and reinforcement for promising teachers, while ensuring that those who fail are dismissed in a timely way.

Financial costs

Researchers have begun to document the substantial financial costs of turnover, although their approaches and results vary. Most calculations include the personnel costs of recruitment, hiring, induction, professional development, substitutes' pay, and separation expenses, such as unemployment pay. Some also include the lost investment in teacher preparation. Again, it makes a difference whether one assesses the costs from the perspective of the state, district, or school. Districts that invest most in their new teachers have the most to lose when they leave and, thus, their per-teacher turnover costs tend to be highest. The Texas Center for Educational Research (2000) found that per-teacher turnover costs ranged from $354.92 in a district with relatively low turnover and recruiting problems, to $5165.76 in a district with high turnover. A 2003 study of 64 elementary schools by the Chicago Association of Community Organizations for Reform Now (ACORN) (2003) used three models for calculating the costs of turnover. The first, based on schools' reported costs, averaged 20 percent of the leaving teacher's salary ($10,329). The second, using an industry model, estimated the costs at 150 percent of the leaving teacher's salary ($77,470.50). The third estimated the costs at 2.5 times the average per-teacher expense of teacher preparation statewide ($63, 689.00). Birkeland and Curtis (2006) examined the costs to the Boston Public Schools of recruiting, hiring, providing professional development, and processing the job terminations of new teachers who leave. They found that replacement costs were $10,547 for a first-year teacher, $18,617 for a second-year teacher, and $26,687 for a third-year teacher, annual increases that are largely due to the district's investment in professional development. A recent analysis by the Alliance for Excellent Education reports a "conservative" estimate of turnover costs nationally at $2.2 billion per year; when the costs of migration are added, the total reaches $4.9 billion (2005).

Instructional and organizational costs

Beyond these financial expenses, turnover carries instructional and organizational costs. New teachers have been shown to improve over the first few years of teaching (Ballou & Podgursky, 1998; Hanushek *et al.*, 2004; Murnane & Phillips, 1981; Rockoff, 2003). Therefore, when schools lose them, they also lose the investment made in their new teachers' induction. Because schools tend to fill the resulting vacancies with more novices, they are unlikely to improve the quality of instruction over time. When teachers "repeatedly leave a school before they become competent in their practice, students will be taught by a string of teachers who are, on average, less effective than more experienced teachers" (Johnson *et al.*, 2005, p. 7). Moreover, as noted above, because teachers with the highest qualifications leave teaching in greater proportions than those with lower qualifications, the instructional costs are compounded.

Research on turnover conducted in Philadelphia from 1999–2000 to 2002–2003 (Neild *et al.*, 2003) revealed that the schools serving the highest poverty communities had the most difficulty retaining teachers and filling vacancies. These authors identified the far-reaching organizational costs of such turnover, noting that it "impede[d] development of a coherent educational program, institutional memory, and staff cohesion" (p. 14). Therefore, students lose when a teacher who knows the curriculum or the community leaves and is replaced by a novice who must start afresh. At the same time, teachers and administrators lose a colleague with whom they may have had productive professional relationships or looked to for schoolwide leadership. They must then invest scarce time and resources to find a replacement and rebuild shared practices.

WHY DO TEACHERS LEAVE? WHY DO TEACHERS STAY?

Over time, teachers offer the same explanations for why they leave teaching. One is low pay. Another is unsatisfactory working conditions. However, these are not independent factors in teachers' career decisions, for often teachers report that poor working conditions exacerbate their dissatisfaction with pay. Combined, low pay and substandard working conditions underscore the lack of status that teaching has in society today. When teachers leave, they seldom attribute their departure to a single factor, instead citing some combination of inadequate pay, unacceptable working conditions, and low status. The following discussion reviews what is known about the role of pay and various aspects of working conditions in teachers' career decisions.

Pay

Prospective and current teachers often cite pay as one factor dissuading them from entering or remaining in teaching. Although there is dispute among policy analysts about whether pay in teaching is low relative to that of comparable fields, there is evidence that pay is a factor in non-entry, dissatisfaction, migration, and attrition. Also, there is some evidence that teachers are attracted by districts offering higher pay.

Are teachers underpaid?

Most researchers have found that teachers are paid less than employees with comparable education, and that the gap between the two groups is growing. For example, an analysis conducted for *Education Week/Quality Counts* (Olson, 2000) shows that in 1994, teachers with a bachelor's degree made $11,035 less (in 1998 dollars) than non-teachers with a bachelor's degree. By 1998, the gap was $18,000. The pay discrepancy between teachers and non-teachers holding a master's degree is even more dramatic, having doubled between 1994 ($12,918) and 1998 ($24,684). Similarly, Henke *et al.* (2000) examined the pay of bachelor's recipients after five years of full-time work and found that teachers' salaries were lower than those of any other professionals. Loeb and Reininger's (2004) review of research studies based on national data led them to conclude that "teachers' salaries are close to those of social workers, ministers, and clerical staff. Lawyers, doctors, scientists, and engineers earn substantially more, as do managers and sales and financial workers" (p. 40). Allegretto *et al.* (2004) reached similar conclusions when they compared the weekly salaries of employees whose work required similar levels of skill and had similar market value. By their calculations, teachers earn an average of 12 percent less per week than the composite salary of the other groups.

Those who report significantly different findings often are counting only the hours for which teachers are contractually required to be on duty in schools. Using such an approach, Vedder (2003) concluded that teachers' pay is much higher than that of other workers with comparable education, such as architects, mechanical and civil engineers, and nurses. Unlike Vedder, most researchers take into account teachers' additional preparation time and conclude that teachers are underpaid.

How does pay affect decisions about teaching?

There is some evidence that many prospective teachers never enter the profession because of low pay (Public Agenda, 2000) and a widespread belief that the problems of teacher quality and teacher shortages could be best addressed by substantially increasing pay for all teachers (Moulthrop *et al.*, 2005). However, far more is known about how pay affects current teachers' decisions.

Economists have studied the effects of different pay levels on teachers' decisions to accept a district's initial job offer or to transfer from one district to another. An analysis of national data about the graduating high school class of 1972 led Ballou and Podgursky to conclude that a raise for all teachers within a district would enable the district to attract teachers with higher test scores (1995). Similarly, Figlio (2002) concluded that districts with higher pay could attract teachers holding degrees from more selective colleges. Lankford *et al.* (2002) analyzed New York teachers' employment records and found that their income increased by 4 to 15 percent when they transferred to a new district, suggesting that they were drawn by the prospect of higher pay.

Just as higher pay has been found to attract teachers, it has been shown to retain them, especially early in their career. Dolton and von der Klaauw (1995) studied first-career entrants to teaching in the UK and concluded that a 10 percent salary increase was associated with a 9 percent reduction in the probability that they would have left teaching after five years. Similarly, Murnane *et al.* (1991) concluded that North Carolina and Michigan teachers who worked in districts with comparatively higher salaries stayed in teaching longer than those employed by districts with lower salaries. Stinebrickner (2001) examined the career decisions of a national sample of teachers during their first nine years and also found that higher salaries are associated with longer retention.

Much of this research is conducted using the average pay figure for teachers within a district. However, some districts deliberately "front-load" their pay scale to attract new teachers, while others reward long-serving teachers at the top of the scale. Little is known about how different approaches to distributing pay on the salary scale affect teachers' decisions to enter or remain in teaching.

Often researchers analyze the effects of pay without attending to the role that working conditions play as teachers decide whether to transfer or to leave teaching. Teachers interviewed in two studies (Johnson, 1990; Johnson & The Project on the Next Generation of Teachers, 2004) reported that they expected to earn enough in teaching to live a comfortable, middle-class lifestyle. Younger teachers told of stress when they could not pay their bills or finance vacations, while those with more experience complained about not being able to afford a house or to send their children to college. However, along with expressing dissatisfaction with their paycheck, many complained about the difficulties they encountered day to day on the job. Often pay took on greater importance in the face of unsatisfactory working conditions.

Working conditions

The teacher's workplace is composed of many elements that can make teaching productive and satisfying or unsuccessful and dispiriting work, particularly for new teachers. Important factors include teachers' assignments; their working relationships with colleagues; access to curriculum and resources; the organization and leadership of the school; the abilities, attitudes, and behavior of students; and the quality of facilities in which they teach. These factors take on different levels of importance for different individuals working in different settings.

Appropriate and fair teaching assignments

Having a teaching assignment that is manageable and within a new teacher's field is critical to satisfaction. Qualitative research shows that new teachers decide to leave teaching or transfer to another school in response to excessively large classes or teaching loads; assignments that are split across grades, subjects or schools; or assignments outside one's field (Johnson & The Project on the Next Generation of Teachers, 2004). Often new teachers are assigned the courses or classes that are left, once more experienced teachers are given their preference. The importance of having an appropriate and fair teaching assignment is apparent when one considers the great difficulty that most new teachers face as they first enter the classroom. Analyzing national survey data on teacher attrition and mobility, Luekens *et al.* (2004) found that 40 percent of teachers who move to another school seek an opportunity of a better teaching assignment. Of those in the sample who left teaching, 13.1 percent said that dissatisfaction with their job responsibilities was a "very important" or "extremely important" factor in their decisions.

Out-of-field assignments are common in public education. According to research by the National Education Association (2003), 19 percent of teachers spent time teaching outside their field of license. Ingersoll found that large proportions of secondary school teachers lack a major or minor in the subject they teach or in a related discipline: one-third of mathematics teachers, one-fourth of all English teachers, one-fifth of science teachers, and one-fifth of social science teachers (2002). Similarly, he found that 12 percent of those teaching self-contained elementary school classes do not have a degree in pre-elementary, early childhood, or elementary education. Often critics of out-of-field assignments focus on the effects on students of being taught by an under-prepared teacher. However, out-of-field assignments surely affect the confidence and satisfaction of the teachers as well, further compounding the consequences for students.

Luekens *et al.* (2004) report that 24.2 percent of teachers who left the profession in 2000–2001 and 20.3 percent of those who changed schools agreed with the statement, "I often felt that my teaching workload was too heavy" (p. 21). Large class size was reported to be "continually raised as a source of dissatisfaction" by teachers who were surveyed by the Public Education Network (2004, p. 19). Given evidence that new teachers' career decisions will depend on whether they experience a "sense of success" with their students (Johnson & Birkeland, 2003), ensuring that their teaching assignments are reasonable may greatly increase the chance of retaining them.

Working relationships with colleagues

Although many teachers in the retiring generation preferred to work independently (Lortie, 1975), new teachers today report an increased interest in collegial work (Kardos, 2004; Kardos & Johnson, 2007). The National Education Association (2003) randomly samples teachers' views every five years. When the survey was first administered in 1956, respondents chose having "cooperative/competent teachers colleagues/mentors" as one of the top six factors that "helped [them] teach well." Since 1996, teachers have ranked this factor as more important than all others.

Studies about school reform conducted by Rosenholtz (1989), Louis *et al.* (1996), Bryk *et al.* (1999), McLaughlin and Talbert (2001), Little (1982), and Bryk and Schenider (2003) all document the importance of collegial work to strengthening instruction and advancing school improvement. However, large proportions of newly hired teachers report that they continue to be isolated in their classrooms. Qualitative research on new teachers has found that they are more likely to stay in teaching and at their schools if they perceive those schools to be places that promote frequent and reciprocal interaction among faculty members across experience levels, recognize new teachers' needs as beginners, and develop shared responsibility among teachers for the school and its students (Johnson & The Project on the Next Generation of Teachers, 2004; Kardos *et al.*, 2001). Indeed, national survey research has found that the largest reductions in teacher turnover are "associated with activities that tied new teachers into a collaborative network of their more experienced peers" (Smith & Ingersoll, 2005, p. 704). Despite new teachers' need for collegial exchange, random sample survey analysis (Kardos, 2004; Kardos & Johnson, 2007) has shown that new teachers report that their work is solitary and that they mostly plan and teach alone. Furthermore, they are expected to be expert and independent from the start. For example, about half (49 percent) of new teachers in the 4 states included in the study report that they usually plan and teach alone, and only 44 percent report that extra assistance is available to them (Kardos, 2004; Kardos & Johnson, 2007).

Curriculum resources and accountability

Curriculum is central to teachers' day-to-day work with their students (Cohen & Ball, 1996). The need for a comprehensive curriculum and the resources to support its use is particularly great for novice teachers who are just learning their craft. With heightened standards for student performance and public demands for accountability, teachers increasingly expect a curriculum that is aligned with state frameworks and assessments. However, recent surveys reveal that often teachers lack both.

Although studies document teachers' support for higher standards (Doherty, 2001; Public Agenda, 2003), fewer than half of teachers surveyed in one study said they "have 'plenty' of access to curriculum guides or textbooks and other materials that match state standards" (2001, p. 45). In an interview study of 50 new Massachusetts teachers, the majority reported that they "either had no curriculum at all—leaving them without guidance about both what to teach and how to teach it—or a curriculum that included only lists of topics and skills—suggesting only very generally what to teach but not how to teach it" (Kauffman *et al.*, 2002, p. 280). The materials they had often were not aligned with the frameworks or assessments. In 2003, Kauffman (2004) surveyed elementary school teachers in Massachusetts, North Carolina, and Washington. Three-fourths (75.4 percent) reported that they had not received sufficient curricular direction in a least one core subject, with the problem being more severe in science (56.2 percent) and social studies (69.2 percent), than in mathematics (20.5 percent) and language arts (31.7 percent). Grossman and Thompson (2004) report similar findings in their four-year study of novice language arts teachers. Research also suggests that, although most beginning teachers want to have rich and detailed curriculum materials, they expect to use them flexibly and resent efforts to regulate how they teach (Kauffman, 2004).

Whether or not schools provide an ample and aligned curriculum, many require teachers to spend substantial time on test preparation and they intensify pressure for higher test scores (Banicky & Noble, 2001; Doherty, 2001; Olson, 2001; Wong *et al.*, 1999). Tye and O'Brien (2002) report that among graduates of one teacher education program, those who left teaching "ranked the pressures of increased accountability (high-stakes testing, test preparation, and standards) as their number-one reason for leaving" (p. 27).

Not only do new teachers seek guidance about what to teach, they also need instructional resources to conduct class day to day. Qualitative studies and popular accounts of teachers' work repeatedly report that teachers lack basic supplies, such as textbooks, paper, pencils, paperback books, and supplies for science experiments (Corcoran *et al.*, 1988; Johnson, 1990; Moulthrop *et al.*, 2005). One study concluded that in 2001 teachers spent an average of $443 each on instructional resources (The National Education Association, 2003, p. 51), while another reported that first-year elementary teachers spent far more—$701 (Quality Education Data, 2002).

School organization and leadership

There is strong evidence that schools differ in the extent to which they support good teaching and learning, and that new teachers' decisions about whether to remain in their school or in teaching often hinge on how well that school is organized and led (Johnson *et al.*, 2004). Researchers frequently conclude that the success or dysfunction of schools results from the quality of the principal's leadership (Rosenholtz, 1989; Louis *et al.*, 1996; Bryk *et al.*, 1999). Analysis of surveys of teachers new to Boston in 2003 showed that those who returned in September 2004 "felt that they received better support from their principals-headmasters than those who left after their first year" (Boston Plan for Excellence, 2005, p. 5). Analyzing data from the national Teacher Follow-up Survey, 2000–2001, Luekens *et al.* found that over one-third (38.2 percent) of teachers who transferred to new schools reported that their dissatisfaction with "support from administrators" was either a "very" or "extremely important" reason for leaving their school. Research in Philadelphia also shows that new teachers leave schools that have neglectful or arbitrary principals (Useem, 2003).

The principal is important not only as the teacher's direct supervisor, but also as the broker of working conditions throughout the school, linking it with the district office and local community and, in the process, garnering resources and ongoing support or generating opposition or unwarranted scrutiny. The principal often sets the tone for the school, be that one of collaboration and confidence or blame and defeat (Blase & Blase, 2004; Bryk & Schneider, 2003; Drago-Severson, 2004; Murphy, 1994).

Students

Since Lortie's classic study of teachers in 1975, it has been clear that students introduce the greatest source of uncertainty in teachers' work. Teachers repeatedly report that they enter teaching because they want to "help young people learn and develop" (Feistritzer, 2005) or to "work with young people" (National Education Association, 2003). In one study conducted by Public Agenda (2000), the primary source of satisfaction for new teachers who said they planned to continue teaching was their confidence that they were making a difference in the lives of their students. New teachers leave the profession when they find that they cannot achieve a "sense of success" with their students (Johnson & Birkeland, 2003).

Little effective teaching or learning can occur when schools are disorderly or dangerous. Over half of the teachers responding to a 2004 survey by the Public Agenda reported that there was a "somewhat serious" or "very serious" discipline problem in their school. One-third of the respondents said they had "seriously considered quitting the teaching profession because student discipline and behavior was such a problem" and the same proportion reported knowing someone who had left teaching for the same reasons (Public Agenda, 2004, pp. 43–44). Useem (2003) found that 52 percent of the third-year Philadelphia teachers in her sample who planned to leave teaching cited dissatisfaction with student behavior as the primary factor in their decision.

Some schools support effective work with students by endorsing strong, positive norms for behavior, providing extensive supports for students, and maintaining well-conceived, effective approaches to discipline (Johnson & The Project on the Next Generation of Teachers, 2004). Further, research suggests that when a school works closely with parents, there are instructional benefits for students and teachers (Bryk & Schneider, 2002; Dauber & Epstein, 1993; Rosenholtz, 1989).

Facilities

The literal workplace of teachers—the buildings and classrooms within which they teach—affects what they teach and their sense of security and comfort on the job. Although it would seem obvious that schools in disrepair are unfit for instruction, a surprising number of school facilities remain hazardous and ill-equipped, particularly in low-income communities (Carroll et al., 2004; General Accounting Office, 1995; Public Education Network, 2004).

Recent quantitative studies by Schneider (2003) and Buckley et al. (2004) focus exclusively on the role that facilities play in teachers' work in Chicago and Washington, D.C. In addition to reporting wide dissatisfaction with the buildings, "more than one-quarter of the Chicago teachers and about one-third of the Washington teachers reported suffering health problems rooted in poor environmental conditions in their schools" (Schneider, 2003, p. 2). The researchers surveyed teachers about their career plans and found that "the probability of retention increases" as the "perceived quality of the school facilities improves, *ceteris paribus*" (p. 7). Although there is little evidence that teachers leave their school solely because it is in poor repair, Carroll et al. (2004) have found that such dissatisfaction contributes to turnover.

Thus, a seemingly straightforward factor—the state of repair of a school building—interacts with much more complex factors, such as the effectiveness of a principal's leadership or the character of work with colleagues, to determine the overall quality of working conditions. Given the importance that teachers place on achieving success with students, poor working conditions that interfere with good teaching are particularly noteworthy. Dissatisfaction with working conditions often fuels the discontent teachers already feel about low pay and prestige, and the combined result is increased turnover. When teachers of the retiring generation were disturbed by the pay and circumstances of their work, they had little option but to endure. However, today's new teachers have many alternative options for employment, and early evidence suggests that, as a cohort, they are unwilling simply to cope while waiting for better times.

PROMISING APPROACHES TO RETAINING GOOD TEACHERS

Some approaches to attracting and retaining good teachers are obvious. If strong candidates are to enter and remain in teaching, they must be paid a decent salary that is competitive with what they might earn in a comparable field. Their teaching assignment must be fair and reasonable, making good use of their knowledge and skills. In deciding what and how to teach, new teachers need a curriculum that is well-aligned with standardized assessments, and they must have the resources required to teach that curriculum. They should be able to count on strong, knowledgeable and collaborative principals, who can ensure that the school is orderly and has the supporting services required to meet students' needs. The buildings they work in must be safe, clean, and well-equipped. These are the basics.

However the priorities of the new generation of teachers suggest that more must be done if the best among them are to commit a substantial part of their career to public education. Given their inclination to make quick decisions about their career, more must be done to ensure that the school where they begin teaching offers a good match for their professional priorities. Given their need for collegial support and their preference for team-based work, profound reforms are called for in the egg-crate structure of their schools. Given their expectations for ongoing professional growth and expanded responsibility, new opportunities for career development are in order. Given their interest in linking performance and pay, efforts should be made to rework the standard salary scale. Currently some promising policies and practices are underway that begin to address each of these needs.

Timely and information-rich hiring

For many years, school districts—particularly large ones—screened and hired their teachers centrally and then assigned them to schools (Murnane *et al.*, 1991). Implicit in this practice was the assumption that schools and teaching positions are essentially the same within a district, one placement being much like another. However, educators today recognize that schools differ in important ways, and that a teacher who is just right for one school might be out of place in another.

There is evidence that new teachers often decide whether to remain in the profession on the basis of their early experience; many of those who are dissatisfied with their first school simply leave teaching (McCarthy & Guiney, 2004). Although more districts today are moving to school-based hiring, which might lead to better matches between teachers and schools, recent research nevertheless suggests that the hiring process is often delayed and deficient (Liu, 2004).

Studies show that, on average, new teachers are hired late. A survey of new teachers in four states (Liu & Johnson, 2006) found that only one-third had their jobs more than a month before school started; one-third accepted jobs during the month before school opened; and one-third were hired after school began. Thus, most teachers had little time to prepare for their new courses, curriculum, and students. Late hiring is especially common in large, urban districts (Levin & Quinn, 2003; Useem & Farley, 2004). In 2003, almost half of the new teachers in Boston were hired after September 1, and only 11 percent were hired before August 1 (Boston Plan for Excellence, 2005).

In addition to being late, hiring tends to be "information-poor," with little exchange of information about what a school would expect from and offer a new teacher or what the new teacher might contribute to the school (Liu & Johnson, 2006). Inevitably, when hiring is late, rushed, and conducted haphazardly, poor matches result. Liu (2005) found that teachers who experience "information-rich" hiring and report having a good preview of their job, are more satisfied than teachers who did not.

Many changes in hiring practice are underway, particularly in large urban districts. These reforms are designed to increase the capacity of human resource offices to track candidates and make timely job offers, to streamline seniority-based transfer procedures that delay hiring, and to prepare schools for more effective site-based hiring (Johnson & Donaldson, 2006; Useem & Farley, 2004).

Mentoring and support

Formal mentoring programs for new teachers are often used to moderate teacher isolation and to support new teachers in their early years. Analysts conclude that, in fact, mentoring is good for new teachers (Berry *et al.*, 2002; Evertson & Smithey, 2000; Feiman-Nemser, 1996; Humphrey *et al.*, 2000; Ingersoll & Kralik, 2004; Wilson *et al.*, 2001). Thus, policymakers, central office administrators, and school leaders have sponsored mentoring programs to induct new teachers, improve their effectiveness, and reduce their attrition. Recent analysis of NCES's School and Staffing Survey data shows that induction and mentoring practices for new teachers have greatly expanded over the past decade (Smith & Ingersoll, 2004).

Studies show that new teachers who are mentored early in their careers are more effective (Evertson & Smithey, 2000; Feiman-Nemser, 1983; Humphrey *et al.*, 2000) and are likely to remain in their schools or in teaching longer than those who are not (Humphrey *et al.*, 2000; Smith & Ingersoll, 2004). In the ideal scenario, new teachers have mentors who help them meet the challenges of being a beginning teacher (Feiman-Nemser, 1983, 2001; Gold, 1996; Veenman, 1984). Mentors assist novice teachers as they decide what to teach and how to teach it, and help them manage classrooms and develop strategies for succeeding with particular students. At their best, mentors observe new teachers in their classroom, model good teaching, and share materials and ideas. In short, the ideal mentor's work with the new teacher focuses on the central components of teaching: classroom instruction, curriculum and lesson planning, and classroom management (Darling-Hammond, 1999; Evertson & Smithey, 2000; Feiman-Nemser, 1983; Holloway, 2001; Humphrey *et al.*, 2000; Smylie, 1994; Wilson *et al.*, 2001). Mentors also help new teachers acclimate to the modes of professional practice in the school and acculturate them to the particular norms of their school and the families it serves (Kardos *et al.*, 2001; Villani, 2002).

However, mentoring programs vary in origin and design. They can be statewide, district-wide, school-based, or informal (Feiman-Nemser, 2001). Some programs are short-sighted and ill-conceived and therefore difficult to implement, monitor, and evaluate. While most U.S. new teachers are currently assigned mentors, large proportions of them are inappropriately matched, are rarely or never observed in their classroom, and hardly ever discuss issues of instruction and lesson planning with their mentors (Kardos, 2004; Kardos & Johnson, 2007).

Researchers who study mentoring caution against assuming the simplistic view that the new teachers' school-site induction needs will be fully met if only each is assigned an experienced teacher as mentor (Johnson & The Project on the Next Generation of Teachers, 2004; Kardos, 2004; Little, 1990; Stansbury & Zimmerman, 2000). However, thoughtful, carefully implemented, school-based mentoring programs can serve new teachers extremely well (Berry *et al.*, 2002; Feiman-Nemser & Floden, 1986; Gold, 1996; Johnson & The Project on the Next Generation of Teachers, 2004; Villani, 2002; Wilson *et al.*, 2001). The New Teacher Center, for example, which sponsors various initiatives to support new teachers, reports measurable success in their mentoring program (www.newteachercenter.org).

It appears that mentoring programs having certain features and being embedded in certain contexts are more likely to provide new teachers with the type of support they need. For example, mentoring programs are more likely to succeed if new teachers are matched with their mentors according to their subjects (Smith & Ingersoll, 2004). They are more likely to be successful if they are embedded in a professional culture that anticipates new teachers' need for help, and not only encourages them to seek it out but also provides easy access to it (Feiman-Nemser, 1996; Johnson & The Project on the Next Generation of Teachers, 2004; Kardos *et al.*, 2001; Little, 1990; Rosenholtz, 1989). New teachers are more likely to get the support they need when they experience mentoring as one feature among many in the context of an ongoing, comprehensive, school-based induction program (Johnson & The Project on the Next Generation of Teachers, 2004).

Differentiated roles and career growth

The prospect of a static and stagnant career in the classroom dissuades many from teaching, while the reality of a fixed and undifferentiated role for all teachers drives others from the classroom. Early research shows that few in the new generation expect to remain full-time classroom teachers over decades, even those who anticipate having a long-term career in education (Peske *et al.*, 2001). Yet, the teaching roles that these new entrants seek—academic coaches, team leaders, mentors, or curriculum specialists—are only beginning to emerge as schools respond to new demands for student success (Mangin, 2005; Neufeld & Roper, 2003).

Career ladders for teachers, including differentiated roles for master or lead teachers, were first introduced in the 1980s. Despite great enthusiasm for their potential to improve schools and enrich the career of teaching (Carnegie Forum on Education and the Economy, 1986), they proved difficult to establish and sustain. Successful implementation of differentiated roles or a career ladder requires a district to create a credible, reliable selection process; establish roles and training for lead teachers or coaches; schedule teachers' time to accommodate new approaches to professional development; and to ensure sustained funding and public support. Some studies show that career ladders have positive effects on teachers' morale, commitment, satisfaction, and sense of efficacy (Ebmeier & Hart, 1992), while others report negative effects of increased stress, misdirected energy, and opportunism (Henson & Hall, 1993).

Although there is evidence that poorly implemented career ladders can introduce new problems (Rosenholtz, 1987), it is clear that many new teachers today seek the kind of differentiated role that career ladders might provide. Hart and Murphy (1990) found that new teachers with high promise and ability assess career ladders more favorably than those with lower promise and ability, suggesting that effectively implemented career ladders might be a mechanism for attracting and retaining strong teachers.

Career ladder programs sometimes falter because they have no means of selecting expert teachers for differentiated roles. However, the National Board for Professional Teaching Standards, which had certified 32,000 "accomplished" teachers by November 2005 (www.nbpts.org), offers a new method of selection that would be untainted by local patronage and politics and, in many states and districts, provide salary bonuses that might be integrated with a career ladder. Notably, over half of the teachers whom the Board had certified by 2004 were early in their careers, suggesting that there is a core of teachers in the new generation of teachers who seek recognition and compensation for their instructional expertise as well as the potential to influence education beyond their classroom (Berg, 2005).

Performance-based pay

New teachers regularly report their dissatisfaction with the standardized pay scale. Why, they ask, should effective and ineffective teachers be paid the same? (Johnson & The Project on the Next Generation of Teachers, 2004). However, like career ladders, merit pay plans have been hard to implement. Those introduced in the 1980s widely failed because they did not have defensible approaches to assessment, were poorly funded, or turned out to be no more than extra pay for extra work (Murnane & Cohen, 1986). New teachers express great interest in pay plans that would reward them on the basis of performance, but they remain skeptical that even-handed judgments will be made (Public Agenda, 2003).

Public support for merit pay is high today, although policymakers often recommend or mandate performance-based pay policies without resolving the difficulties and short-comings experienced by failed plans of the 1980s. Nationwide, a few schools, districts, and states have implemented performance-based pay plans, although most are relatively small programs (see the web site of the University of Wisconsin's Consortium for Policy Research on Education: www.wcer.wisc.edu/cpre). Large unionized districts have encountered more difficulty designing and gaining approval for such reforms. For example, in 2000, Cincinnati approved a comprehensive performance-based pay plan in collective bargaining. However it was abandoned two years later, before it was fully implemented when the teachers challenged the quality of the evaluation process on which the plan was based (Keller, 2002). Currently, the Denver Public Schools, in partnership with the local teachers union, is implementing a pay system that rewards teachers with bonuses for a variety of skills and behaviors, including completing relevant courses or degrees, earning National Board Certification, receiving a satisfactory evaluation, teaching in hard-to-staff schools or subjects, and teaching in classes and schools where students demonstrate progress on standardize tests (Jupp, 2005). Each accomplishment adds additional pay to the teacher's base salary and there is no limit on the number of bonuses that can be earned or on the number of teachers who can qualify. Denver piloted and refined this program over four years and subsequently teachers voted to approve it. In November 2005, Denver voters approved a property tax increase needed to fund the program. Although initial experience with the plan is encouraging (Slotnik, 2005), it is not yet clear whether this plan can be sustained over time financially, organizationally, or politically.

Ideally, merit pay plans for teachers would rest on evidence of students' learning, although currently there are no measures of student learning that all parties agree are legitimate. Critics contend that standardized tests are flawed because they provide only narrow or misguided measures of teaching and learning (Kohn, 2000). Nonetheless, the introduction of "valued-added" measures of teachers' performance, which analyze the standardized test scores of their students over a number of years (McCaffrey *et al.*, 2003; Sanders & Rivers, 1996) offer the prospect that teachers eventually might be paid on the basis of their students' performance (Carey, 2004).

CONCLUSION

If public education is to ensure that all students have able and committed teachers, policymakers and practitioners must comprehend the enormous challenge of attracting and retaining a new generation of teachers. Because of transformations in the job market and society, there is no longer a steady supply of men of color and women to replace the large number of teachers due to retire by 2010. Public schools must now compete with all other workplaces for talented employees, and the evidence suggests that they are ill-equipped to do so. Prospective teachers today, who have many employment options in various lines of work, critically assess their opportunities. What will they earn and what kind of work environment will they have? In order to successfully recruit these individuals, schools must respond to their desire for a workplace that supports successful teaching and learning. Those who enter the classroom expecting more than they find may well leave after a short time. Moreover, because workers nationwide are far less likely today than 30 years ago to commit to a lifelong career in any field, schools must change in order to accommodate the frequent entry and exit of teachers.

Schools are remarkably resilient organizations that generally do not change rapidly or deeply, and are more likely to adopt reforms reluctantly and gradually, if at all (Tyack & Cuban, 1995). Therefore, it seems unlikely that they will respond quickly or adequately to the current labor market for teachers or to the priorities of those entering teaching today. Some reforms being adopted by various states, districts, and schools offer promise, but there is no certainty that schools can fulfill the public's goal of truly educating all students.

REFERENCES

Abelmann, C. & Elmore, R. (1999) *When accountability knocks, will anyone answer?* Philadelphia: Consortium for Policy Research in Education: University of Pennsylvania Graduate School of Education.

Allegretto, S. A., Corcoran, S. P., & Mishel, L. (2004) *How does teacher pay compare? Methodological challenges and answers.* Washington, DC: Economic Policy Institute.

Alliance for Excellent Education (2005) *Teacher attrition: a costly loss to the nation and the states.* Washington, DC: Alliance for Excellent Education.

Ballou, D. & Podgursky, M. (1995) Recruiting smarter teachers. *The Journal of Human Resources,* 30 (2), 326–338.

Ballou, D. & Podgursky, M. (1997) *Teacher pay and teacher quality.* Kalamazoo, MI: W. E. Upjohn Institute for Employment Research.

Ballou, D. & Podgursky, M. (1998) Teacher recruitment and retention in public and private schools. *Journal of Policy Analysis and Management,* 17(3), 393–417.

Banicky, L. A. & Noble, A. J. (2001) *Detours on the road to reform: when standards take a backseat to testing.* Wilmington, DE: Delaware Education Research and Development Center.

Berg, J. H. (2005, April) *Board certification during teaching's second stage: professionalizing teaching through differentiated roles.* Paper presented at the Annual Meeting of the American Educational Research Association, Montreal, CA.

Berry, B., Hopkins-Thompson, T., & Hoke, M. (2002) *Assessing and supporting new teachers:*

lessons from the Southeast. North Carolina: The Southeast Center for Teaching Quality at the University of North Carolina.

Birkeland, S. E. & Curtis, R. (2006) *Ensuring the support and development of new teachers in the Boston public schools: a proposal to improve teacher quality and retention.* Boston, MA: The Boston Public Schools.

Blase, J. & Blase, J. (2004) *Handbook of instructional leadership: how successful principals promote teaching and learning.* Thousand Oaks, CA: Corwin Press.

Boston Plan for Excellence (2005) *Building a professional teaching corps in Boston: survey of teachers new to the Boston Public Schools in SY2003–2004.* Boston, MA: Boston Plan for Excellence.

Bryk, A. & Schneider, B. (2002) *Trust in schools: a core resource for improvement.* New York: Russell Sage Foundation.

Bryk, A. S. & Schneider, B. (2003) Trust in schools: a core resource for reform. *Educational Leadership,* 60(6), 40–44.

Bryk, A., Camburn, E., & Louis, K. S. (1999) Professional community in Chicago elementary schools: facilitating factors and organizational consequences. *Educational Administration Quarterly,* 35, 751–781.

Buckley, J., Schneider, M., & Shang, Y. (2004) *The effects of school facility quality on teacher retention in urban school districts.* Chestnut Hill, MA: National Clearinghouse for Educational Facilities.

Carey, K. (2004) The real value of teachers: using new information about teacher effectiveness to close the achievement gap. *Thinking K-16,* 8(1), 3–40.

Carnegie Forum on Education and the Economy (1986) *A nation prepared: teachers for the 21st century.* New York: Carnegie Forum on Education and the Economy.

Carroll, T. G., Fulton, K., Abercrombie, K., & Yoon, I. (2004) *Fifty years after Brown v. Board of Education: a two-tiered education system.* Washington, DC: National Commission on Teaching and America's Future.

Chicago Association of Community Organizations for Reform Now (ACORN) (2003) *Where have all the teachers gone? The costs of teacher turnover in ACORN neighborhood schools in Chicago.* Retrieved September 9, 2004, from http://www.acorn.org/index.php?id=315

Cohen, D. K. & Ball, D. L. (1996) Reform by the book: what is—or might be—the role of curriculum materials in teacher learning and instructional reform? *Educational Researcher,* 25(9), 6–8.

Corcoran, R., Walker, L. J., & White, J. L. (1988) *Working in urban schools.* Washington, DC: The Institute for Educational Leadership.

Darling-Hammond, L. (1999) *Solving the dilemmas of teacher supply, demand, and standards: how we can ensure a competent, caring, and qualified teacher for every child.* Washington, DC: National Commission on Teaching and America's Future.

Dauber, S. L., & Epstein, J. L. (1993) Parents' attitudes and practices of involvement in inner-city elementary and middle schools. In N. F. Chavkin (ed.), *Families and schools in a pluralistic society.* Albany, NY: State University of New York Press.

Doherty, K. M. (2001, January 11) Poll: Teachers support standards—with hesitation. *Education Week/Quality Counts 2001,* p. 20.

Dolton, P. & von der Klaauw, W. (1995) Leaving teaching in the UK: a duration analysis. *The Economic Journal,* 105(429), 431–444.

Drago-Severson, E. (2004) *Helping teachers learn: principal leadership for adult growth and development.* Thousand Oaks, CA: Corwin Press.

Ebmeier, H. & Hart, A. W. (1992) The effects of a career-ladder program on school organizational process. *Educational Evaluation & Policy Analysis,* 14, 261–281.

Editors (2000, January 29) The future of work: career evolution. *The Economist,* 89–90.

Elmore, R. (2004a) Building a new structure for school leadership. In R. Elmore (ed.), *School reform from the inside out* (pp. 41–88). Cambridge, MA: Harvard Education Publishing.

Elmore, R. (2004b) Doing the right thing, knowing the right thing to do. In R. Elmore (ed.), *School reform from the inside out* (pp. 227–258). Cambridge, MA: Harvard Education Publishing.

Evertson, C. & Smithey, M. (2000) Mentoring effects on proteges' classroom practice: an experimental field study. *Journal of Educational Research*, 93(5), 294–304.

Feiman-Nemser, S. (1983) Learning to teach. In L. S. Shulman & G. Sykes (eds.), *Handbook of teaching and policy* (pp. 150–170). New York: Longman.

Feiman-Nemser, S. (1996) *Mentoring: a critical review*. Washington, DC: ERIC Clearinghouse on Teaching and Teacher Education.

Feiman-Nemser, S. (2001) From preparation to practice: designing a continuum to strengthen and sustain teaching. *Teachers College Record*, 103(6), 1013–1055.

Feiman-Nemser, S. & Floden, R. E. (1986) The cultures of teaching. In M. C. Witrock (ed.), *Handbook of research on teaching* (3rd ed., pp. 505–526). New York: Macmillan.

Feistritzer, C. E. (2005) *Profile of teachers in the U.S. 2005*. Washington, DC: National Center for Education Information.

Feistritzer, C. E. & Chester, D. (2003). *Executive summary: alternative teacher certification: a state-by-state analysis 2003*. Washington, DC: National Center for Education Information.

Fideler, E. F. & Haselkorn, D. (1999) *Learning the ropes: urban teacher induction programs and practices in the United States*. Belmont, MA: Recruiting New Teachers, Inc.

Figlio, D. N. (2002) Can public schools buy better-qualified teachers? *Industrial and Labor Relations Review*, 55(4), 686–699.

General Accounting Office (1995) *School facilities: America's schools not designed or equipped for 21st century* (No. HEHS-95-95). Washington, DC.

Gold, Y. (1996) Beginning teacher support: attrition, mentoring, and induction. In J. Sikula, T. J. Buttery, & E. Guyton (eds.), *Handbook of research on teacher education* (2nd ed., pp. 548–594). New York: Simon & Schuster Macmillan.

Grant, G. & Murray, C. (1999) *Teaching in America: the slow revolution*. Cambridge, MA: Harvard University Press.

Grossman, P. & Thompson, C. (2004) *Curriculum materials: scaffolds for new teacher learning?* Seattle, WA: Center for the Study of Teaching and Policy.

Guarino, C., Santibañez, L., Daley, G., & Brewer, D. (2004) *A review of the research literature on teacher recruitment and retention* (No. TR-164-EDU). Santa Monica, CA: Rand Corporation.

Hanushek, E. A., Kain, J. F., & Rivkin, S. G. (2004) Why public schools lose teachers. *Journal of Human Resources*, 39(2), 326–354.

Hart, A. W. & Murphy, M. J. (1990) New teachers react to redesigned teacher work. *American Journal of Education*, 98, 224–250.

Haycock, K. (1998) Good teaching matters: how well-qualified teachers can close the gap. *Thinking K-16*, 3(2), 3–14.

Henke, R. R., Chen, X., & Geis, S. (2000) *Progress through the teacher pipeline: 1992–93 college graduates and elementary/secondary school teaching as of 1997*. Washington, DC: National Center for Educational Statistics, U.S. Department of Education.

Henson, B. E. & Hall, P. M. (1993) Linking performance evaluation and career ladder programs: reactions of teachers and principals in one district. *The Elementary School Journal*, 93(4), 323–353.

Hoff, D. J. (2001, January 11) Missing pieces. *Education Week/Quality Counts 2001*, pp. 43–45, 48.

Holloway, J. H. (2001) The benefits of mentoring. *Educational Leadership*, 58(8), 85–86.

Humphrey, D. C., Adelman, N., Esch, C. E., Riehl, L. M., Shields, P. M., & Tiffany, J. (2000) *Preparing and supporting new teachers: a literature review*. Menlo Park, CA: SRI International.

Hussar, W. J. (1999) *Predicting the need for newly hired teachers in the United States to 2008–09*. Washington, DC: National Center for Education Statistics, U.S. Department of Education.

Ingersoll, R. M. (2001a) *A different approach to solving the teacher shortage problem*: Seattle, WA: Center for the Study of Teaching and Policy.

Ingersoll, R. M. (2001b). Teacher turnover and teacher shortages: an organizational analysis. *American Educational Research Journal*, 38(3), 499–534.

Ingersoll, R. M. (2001c) *Teacher turnover, teacher shortages, and the organization of schools*. Seattle, WA: Center for the Study of Teaching and Policy.

Ingersoll, R. M. (2002) *Out-of-field teaching, educational inequality, and the organization of schools: an exploratory analysis.* Seattle, WA: Center for the Study of Teaching and Policy.

Ingersoll, R. M. & Kralik, J. M. (2004) *The impact of mentoring on teacher retention: what the research says.* Denver, CO: Education Commission of the States.

Johnson, S. M. (1990) *Teachers at work: achieving success in our schools.* New York: BasicBooks.

Johnson, S. M. & The Project on the Next Generation of Teachers (2004) *Finders and keepers: helping new teachers survive and thrive in our schools.* San Francisco, CA: Jossey-Bass.

Johnson, S. M. & Donaldson, M. (2006) The effects of collective bargaining on teacher quality. In Hannaway, J. & Rotherham, A., *Collective bargaining in education: negotiating change in today's schools.* Cambridge, MA: Harvard Education Press, 111–140.

Johnson, S. M., Berg, J. H., & Donaldson, M. (2005) *Who stays in teaching and why: a review of the literature on teacher retention.* Washington, DC: NRTA.

Johnson, S. M. & Birkeland, S. E. (2003) Pursuing a "sense of success": new teachers explain their career decisions. *American Educational Research Journal,* 40(3), 581–617.

Johnson, S. M., Birkeland, S. E., & Peske, H. G. (2005) *A difficult balance: incentives and quality control in alternative certification programs.* Cambridge, MA: Project on the Next Generation of Teachers at Harvard University.

Jupp, B. (2005) The uniform salary schedule. *Education Next* (2005, Winter), 5 (2), 10–12.

Kardos, S. M. (2004) *Supporting and sustaining new teachers in schools: the importance of professional culture and mentoring* (unpublished dissertation). Cambridge, MA: Harvard University.

Kardos, S. M. & Johnson, S. M. (2007) On their own and presumed expert: new teachers' experiences with their colleagues. *Teachers College Record,* 109(12).

Kardos, S. M., Johnson, S. M., Peske, H. G., Kauffman, D., & Liu, E. (2001) Counting on colleagues: new teachers encounter the professional cultures of their schools. *Educational Administration Quarterly,* 37(2), 250–290.

Kauffman, D. (2004) *Second-year teachers' experiences with curriculum materials: results from a three-state survey.* Paper presented at the Annual Meeting of the American Educational Research Association, San Diego.

Kauffman, D. (2005) *Second-year teachers' experiences with curriculum materials: results from a three-state survey* (unpublished dissertation). Cambridge, MA: Harvard University.

Kauffman, D., Johnson, S. M., Kardos, S. M., Liu, E., & Peske, H. G. (2002) "Lost at sea": new teachers' experiences with curriculum and assessment. *Teachers College Record,* 104(2), 273–300.

Keller, B. (2002, May 29) Cincinnati teachers rebuff performance pay. *Education Week,* p. 5.

Kirby, S. N., Naftel, S., & Berends, M. (1999) *Staffing at-risk school districts in Texas: problems and prospects.* Santa Monica, CA: Rand.

Kohn, A. (2000) *The case against standardized testing.* Portsmouth, NH: Heinemann.

Lankford, H., Loeb, S., & Wyckoff, J. (2002) Teacher sorting and the plight of urban schools: a descriptive analysis. *Educational Evaluation and Policy Analysis,* 24(1), 37–62.

Levin, J. & Quinn, M. (2003) *Missed opportunities: how we keep high quality teachers out of urban classrooms.* Washington, DC: New Teacher Project.

Little, J. W. (1982) Norms of collegiality and experimentation: workplace conditions of school success. *American Educational Research Journal,* 19(3), 325–340.

Little, J. W. (1990) The mentor phenomenon and the social organization of teaching. In C. Cazden (ed.), *Review of Research in Education* (Vol. 16, pp. 297–351). Washington, DC: American Educational Research Association.

Liu, E. (2004) *Information-rich, information-poor: new teachers' experiences of hiring in four states.* Unpublished doctoral dissertation. Cambridge, MA: Harvard University.

Liu, E. (2005) *Hiring, job satisfaction, and fit between new teachers and their schools.* Paper presented at the Annual Meeting of the American Educational Research Association, Montreal, Canada.

Liu, E. & Johnson, S. M. (2006). New teachers' experiences of hiring: late rushed and information-poor *Educational Administration Quarterly,* 42(3), pp. 324–360.

Loeb, S. & Reininger, M. (2004) *Public policy and teacher labor markets: what we know and why it matters* (policy report). East Lansing: The Education Policy Center at Michigan State University.

Lortie, D. C. (1975) *Schoolteacher: a sociological study*. Chicago: University of Chicago Press.

Louis, K. S., Marks, H. M., & Kruse, S. (1996) Teachers' professional community in restructuring schools. *American Educational Research Journal*, 33(4), 757–798.

Luekens, M. T., Lyter, D. M., Fox, E. E., & Chandler, K. (2004) *Teacher attrition and mobility: results from the teacher follow-up survey, 2000–01*. Washington, DC: National Center for Education Statistics.

McCaffrey, D. F., Lockwood, J. R., Koretz, D. M., & Hamilton, L. S. (2003) *Evaluating value-added models for teacher accountability*. Santa Monica, CA: Rand Corporation.

McCarthy, M. & Guiney, E. (2004) *Building a professional teaching corps in Boston: baseline study of new teachers in Boston's public schools*. Boston, MA: Boston Plan for Excellence.

McLaughlin, M. W. & Talbert, J. E. (2001) *Professional communities and the work of high school teaching*. Chicago: The University of Chicago Press.

Mangin, M. M. (2005) *Designing instructional teacher leadership positions: lessons learned from five school districts*. Paper presented at the annual meeting of the American Educational Research Association, Montreal, Canada.

Moulthrop, D., Calegari, N. C., & Eggers, D. (2005) *Teachers have it easy: the big sacrifices and small salaries of America's teachers*. New York, NY: The New Press.

Murnane, R. J. & Cohen, D. K. (1986) Merit pay and the evaluation problem: why some merit pay plans fail and a few survive. *Harvard Educational Review*, 56(1).

Murnane, R. J. & Olsen, R. J. (1989) Will there be enough teachers? *The American Economic Review*, 79(2), 242–246.

Murnane, R. J. & Phillips, B. R. (1981) What do effective teachers of inner city children have in common? *Social Science Research*, 10, 83–100.

Murnane, R. J., Singer, J. D., Willett, J. B., Kemple, J., & Olsen, R. (1991) *Who will teach? Policies that matter*. Cambridge: Harvard University Press.

Murphy, J. (1994) Transformational change and the evolving role of the principal: early empirical evidence. In Murphy, J. & Louis, K. S. (eds.), *Reshaping the principalship: insights from transformational reform efforts*. Thousand Oaks, CA: Corwin Press.

National Commission for Teaching and America's Future (2003) *No dream denied: a pledge to America's children*. Stanford, CA: Author.

National Education Association (2003) *Status of the American public school teacher 2000–2001*. Washington, DC: National Education Association.

Neild, R. C., Useem, E., Travers, E. F., & Lesnick, J. (2003) *Once and for all: placing a highly qualified teacher in every Philadelphia classroom*. Philadelphia, PA: Research for Action.

Neufeld, B. & Roper, D. (2003) Growing instructional capacity in two San Diego middle schools. Cambridge, MA: Education Matters.

Olson, L. (2000, January 13) Finding and keeping competent teachers. *Education Week/Quality Counts 2000*, pp. 12–18.

Olson, L. (2001, January 11) Finding the right mix. *Education Week*, pp. 12–20.

Peske, H. G., Liu, E., Johnson, S. M., Kauffman, D., & Kardos, S. M. (2001) The next generation of teachers: changing conceptions of a career in teaching. *The Phi Delta Kappan*, 83(4), 304–311.

Podgursky, M., Monroe, R., & Watson, D. (2004) The academic quality of public school teachers: an analysis of entry and exit behavior. *Economics of Education Review*, 23(5), 507–518.

Public Agenda (2000) *A sense of calling: who teaches and why*. Washington, DC: Public Agenda.

Public Agenda (2003) *Stand by me: what teachers really think about unions, merit pay and other professional matters*. Washington, DC: Public Agenda.

Public Agenda (2004) *Teaching interrupted: do discipline policies in today's public schools foster the common good?* Washington, DC: Public Agenda.

Public Education Network (2004) *The voice of the new teacher*. Washington, DC: Public Education Network.

Quality Education Data (2002) *QED's school market trends: teacher buying behavior and attitudes 2001–2002 (Press Version)*. Denver, CO: Quality Education Data, Inc.

Rockoff, J. (2003) *The impact of individual teachers on student achievement: evidence from panel data*. Cambridge, MA: National Bureau of Economic Research.

Rosenholtz, S. J. (1987) Education reform strategies: will they increase teacher commitment? *American Journal of Education*, 95(4), 534–562.

Rosenholtz, S. J. (1989) *Teachers' workplace: the social organization of schools*. New York: Longman.

Rury, J. L. (1989) Who became teachers? The social characteristics of teachers in American history. In D. Warren (ed.), *American teachers: histories of a profession at work* (pp. 7–48). New York: Macmillan.

Sanders, W. L. & Rivers, J. C. (1996) *Cumulative and residual effects of teachers on future student academic achievement* (research progress report). Knoxville, TN: University of Tennessee Value-Added Research and Assessment Center.

Schneider, M. (2003) *Linking school facility conditions to teacher satisfaction and success*. Washington, DC: National Clearinghouse for Educational Facilities.

Slotnik, W. J. (2005, September 28) Mission possible: tying earning to learning. *Education Week*, pp. 32–33, 40.

Smith, T. M. & Ingersoll, R. M. (2004) What are the effects of induction and mentoring on beginning teacher turnover? *American Educational Research Journal* 41(3), 681–714.

Smylie, M. A. (1994) Redesigning teachers' work: connections to the classroom. In L. Darling-Hammond (ed.), *Review of Research in Education*, Vol. 20 (pp. 129–177). Washington, DC: American Educational Research Association.

Spencer, D. A. (2001) Teachers' work in historical and social context. In V. Richardson (ed.), *Handbook of research on teaching* (4th ed., pp. 803–825). Washington, DC: American Educational Research Association.

Stansbury, K. & Zimmerman, J. (2000) *Lifelines to the classroom: designing support for beginning teachers*. San Francisco: WestEd.

Stinebrickner, T. R. (2001) Compensation policies and teacher decisions. *International Economic Review*, 42(3), 751–779.

Teacher Quality Clearinghouse. Retrieved from http://www.tqclearinghouse.org/bulletin/v2n5.html

Texas Center for Educational Research (2000) *The cost of teacher turnover*. Austin: Texas State Board for Educator Certification.

Tyack, D. & Cuban, L. (1995) *Tinkering toward utopia: a century of public school reform*. Cambridge, MA: Harvard University Press.

Tye, B. B. & O'Brien, L. (2002) Why are experienced teachers leaving the profession? *Phi Delta Kappan*, 84(1), 24–32.

Useem, E. (2003, March 1) *The retention and qualifications of new teachers in Philadelphia's high-poverty middle schools: a three-year cohort study*. Paper presented at the Annual Conference of the Eastern Sociological Society, Philadelphia, PA.

Useem, E. & Farley, E. (2004) *Philadelphia's teacher hiring and school assignment practices: comparisons with other districts* (research brief). Philadelphia: Research for Action.

Vedder, R. (2003) Comparable worth. *Education Next: A Journal of Opinion and Research* (Summer), 3(3), 14–19.

Veenman, S. (1984) Perceived problems of beginning teachers. *Review of Educational Research*, 54(2), 143–178.

Villani, S. (2002) *Mentoring programs for new teachers: models of induction and support*. Thousand Oaks, CA: Corwin Press.

Wilson, S., Darling-Hammond, L., & Berry, B. (2001) *A case of successful teaching policy: connecticut's long-term efforts to improve teaching and learning*. Seattle, WA: Center for the Study of Teaching and Policy.

Wirt, J. (2000) *The condition of education, 1999; indicator of the month: salaries of teachers* (No. NCES 2000–011). Washington, DC: National Center for Educational Statistics, U.S. Department of Education.

Wong, K. K., Anagnostopoulos, D., Rutledge, S., Lynn, L., & Dreeben, R. (1999) *Implementation of an educational accountability agenda: integrated governance in the Chicago public schools enters its fourth year*. Chicago, IL: Irving B. Harris Graduate School of Public Policy Studies, The University of Chicago.

27 Teacher educators as gatekeepers

Deciding who is ready to teach

A. Lin Goodwin
Teachers College, Columbia University

Celia Oyler
Teachers College, Columbia University

INTRODUCTION: FRAMING THE ISSUE

The current teacher education context

Without a doubt, the issue of teacher quality is currently one of the most pressing concerns expressed by policy makers, the media, the public at large, and by educators themselves. Within the national educational discourse, there are a multitude of opinions about how teacher quality should be defined, and these opinions are not only varied but often contradictory. We are immersed in debates regarding what teachers should know and be able to do, the qualities and preparation teachers should have, where teacher preparation should take place (if at all), and what this preparation should include—or exclude (Berry *et al.*, 2004; Cochran-Smith, 2001b; Cochran-Smith & Fries, 2005; Lasley *et al.*, 2002). The widespread perception that teaching ability is more innate than learned continues to fuel arguments that pedagogy is unnecessary and that good teaching relies primarily on content knowledge and "verbal ability" (Goldhaber & Brewer, 1995; Hess, 2004; Kanstroroom & Finn, 1999; U.S. Department of Education, 2002; Walsh, 2001). In contrast, others—particularly educators—are of the opinion that learning to teach is complex and difficult and requires the acquisition of specialized knowledge and professional methods through formal study and apprenticeship (Cochran-Smith, 2004; Holt-Reynolds, 1999; Monk, 1994; National Commission on Teaching and America's Future (NCTAF), 1996, 1997; Shulman, 1987).

It would be difficult to succinctly characterize or categorize the wide range of opinions, debates and public policy discussions surrounding what constitutes teacher quality. However, these discussions all appear to uniformly define learning to teach and teacher assessment as a process of inputs and outputs. Inputs include academic credentials and professional knowledge such as GPA, content majors, subject matter knowledge, pedagogical knowledge, field experience, instructional methods; outputs include so-called indicators of teacher knowledge and quality such as performance on teacher tests, students' standardized test scores, artifacts and work samples and teacher certification. Such variables are assumed to be indicators of quality and consequently, much of the research seeking to identify predictors of teacher quality has focused on describing what candidates know or the characteristics and skills they do or need to possess *before* certification (inputs), and what candidates do or how they perform *after* certification (outputs) (Zumwalt & Craig, 2005).

Undoubtedly, the relationship between teachers' knowledge and skills prior to or upon certification, and teachers' performance post-certification is critical to understanding what separates a quality teacher from those unqualified. This kind of "impact research" has been called for, yet such research is far from plentiful or definitive (Cochran-Smith & Zeichner, 2005; Zumwalt & Craig, 2005). Indeed there continues to be differences of opinion about whether teacher certification does have an impact on student outcomes. Thus, research and scholarship supporting the positive impact of teacher certification and preparation on student achievement sits alongside reports that argue the exact opposite (Darling-Hammond, 2000, 2001; Darling-Hammond *et al.*, 2002; Darling-Hammond & Youngs, 2002; Fetler, 2001; Goldhaber & Brewer, 2000; Walsh, 2001; Wilson & Youngs, 2005; Zumwalt & Craig, 2005). Still, these differences of opinion aside, teacher certification continues, apparently, to be perceived as a gatekeeping mechanism that controls who can enter into the profession, and as a key indicator of teacher quality. Thus, even those who have called for the dismantling of formal or university-based teacher preparation, have also implicitly supported teacher certification, For example, former secretary of education Rod Paige defines teacher certification as "broken" but still recommends that "states will need to streamline their certification system" (U.S. Department of Education, 2002, p. 40), and the language of the *No Child Left Behind Act of 2001* (NCLB) (Pub. Law 107–110) underscores the need for quality teachers, defined in large part as state certified teachers (Cochran-Smith, 2004).

As teacher educators who prepare candidates to be certified, we agree that teacher certification is a crucial aspect of any definition of teacher quality, and through our work we enact our belief that a teacher with certification is ultimately more qualified than someone who practices without certification. Of course we acknowledge that possession of teacher certification does not imply a certain (or minimum) level or length of preparation—or any preparation at all—given the existence of alternate routes to certification which vary greatly in terms of requirements and standards. Still, in this discussion, it is important for us to position ourselves from the outset as teacher educators who have been classroom practitioners and who work in a university-based teacher preparation program. Thus, we stand behind the necessity for formal, professional study prior to entry into the classroom (and certification), and see teaching as work that demands specialized knowledge and skills. So our purpose in this piece is not to debate the value of formal teacher education—we believe it is essential to the development of good teachers, a stance that consciously underlies our chapter. However, we worry that measures of teacher quality that rely solely on inputs and outputs leave unexamined a major dilemma in teacher preparation—how do teacher educators know when a preservice student teacher is ready for independent practice or certification? Given our on-the-ground work in the preparation of teachers, our perspective regarding teacher quality naturally encompasses the space between inputs and outputs, and causes us to ask different questions about teacher quality. What indicators do teacher educators look for? What kinds of gatekeeping mechanisms are in place—at entry, during coursework, during fieldwork and at completion? Do certain characteristics or dispositions figure into whether a teacher candidate is ready to—or can—teach?

In this chapter, we wrestle with the question of teacher quality from the perspective of teacher educators who must decide *during* the learning-to-teach-process which teacher candidate can continue in the program through to a recommendation for certification, who might continue given additional support and intervention, and who must be barred from teaching practice. These questions illuminate the issues and dilemmas teacher educators must resolve on the journey *towards* certification which represent a missing component of the national discussion about teacher quality. Yes, it is important to know about what happens when teachers finish their program, but we argue that it is equally important to analyze the decision-making points and assessments that teacher educators use to answer the question, who is ready teach? However, little scholarship currently exists to help policy-makers and researchers understand the local practices that programs routinely use to separate competent from incompetent teachers. Our chapter then, targets two major areas: (1) front end requirements for entrance into programs; and (2) assessment and support mechanisms related to readiness to teach. Each area connects to a specific question—who is fit to teach? who is ready to teach?—and takes us across university sites to examine the role teacher educators play as gatekeepers for the teaching profession.

Our chapter begins with an overall description of the structure, role, and function of teacher education programs vis-à-vis the certification process, both historically and contemporarily. We then present practices, procedures, policies, and assessments that teacher preparation programs employ as they make decisions about teacher candidates' readiness to teach and the dilemmas and issues teacher educators face as they make these decisions. For this documentation and analysis, we rely upon three sources: (1) peer-reviewed scholarship from the last ten years; (2) data from structured interviews with 12 teacher educators representing a range of institutional types and geographic regions; and (3) examples from our own teacher education program. Using these bodies of information, we present ways in which the field can conceptualize what we are calling the gatekeeping function of teacher educators. Our chapter ends with recommendations for research.

The structure, role and function of teacher education in the teacher certification process

There is no shortage of condemnation of teacher education—what it should or should not do and whether it should even exist (Ballou & Podgursky, 2000; Berliner, 2000; Hess, 2004; U.S. Department of Education, 2002; Walsh, 2001; Weitman & Colbert, 2003; Zeichner, 2006). However, almost from the start of formal teacher preparation, criteria and requirements for teacher licensing and certification have been mandated from outside the academy by boards of education and state departments (Conant, 1964; Hodenfield & Stinnett, 1961; Koerner, 1968; Wilson & Youngs, 2005), a practice that has continued through to the present (Darling-Hammond & Cobb, 1995; Goodlad, 1990; Tom; 1996; Wayne & Youngs, 2003). In fact, a look at current state certification mandates reveals a move towards additional regulation, so that "new regulations represent unprecedented moves to establish external control of nearly every aspect of teacher preparation" (Cochran-Smith, 2001b, p. 264). Thus, it could be said that teacher educators find themselves the brunt of criticism for a situation not entirely of their own making and not entirely within their control as they respond to standards and curriculum guidelines laid down by bodies that govern teacher certification rather than by those who engage firsthand in the preparation of teachers.

This external governance of teacher education is the likely reason why teacher education programs across states are remarkably similar in terms of structures and requirements, and remarkably dissimilar in terms of certifications offered, individual practices and interpretations of standards. Typically, teacher preparation programs encompass four components: general or content knowledge, the foundations of education, professional knowledge and methods, and field experience. But the implementation and practical enactment of these four components can—and does—differ widely across and within states, because neither course titles nor program descriptions can truly indicate what individual faculty do in their own classes or within their own programs. This perhaps explains why there is widespread disapproval of teacher educators' work at the same time that "for most of the 20th century, candidates were eligible for certification as long as they completed a state-approved teacher preparation program" (Wayne & Youngs, 2003, p. 90).

This should not be construed as criticism of teacher educators or of state authorities. The reality is that no matter how tightly regulated teacher education is, short of prescribing every aspect of the teacher preparation curriculum, state agencies are not in the position financially or personnel-wise to oversee every minute aspect of every program (even if they were inclined to do so). Thus, state departments and teacher education programs enter into an explicit agreement—states agree to certify those individuals that teacher education programs endorse if teacher education programs comply with preparation requirements dictated by the state. In essence then, teacher educators become gatekeepers for the state as well as for the profession, assuring the state that candidates recommended for certification will have met the state's criteria for "quality." This means that programs must articulate to varying state mandates as they engage in the day-to-day work of judging the fit and readiness of individual candidates, which, in turn, requires teacher educators to erect several gatekeeping hurdles in the form of varying experiences, requirements, assessments, and supports for students as they progress through the program.

Examining gatekeeping: integrating the literature with data from the field

As we began this work on the practices of gatekeeping, we were struck by the dearth of literature, documentation or research on these varying experiences, requirements, assessments, and supports for students employed by teacher educators in their individual programs to determine fitness to teach—who gets into teacher preparation—and readiness to teach—who is allowed out into the profession. Spanning the last ten years, literature that does address this issue, while minimal, offers some important insights about teacher exams, field-based assessments, and approaches to understanding and theorizing student teacher competence and incompetence. Seeking to expand upon this literature and to portray some typical programmatic practices around fit and readiness to teach, and then analyze common issues surrounding these decisions, we held twelve telephone conversations with teacher educators around the United States focused on questions of program structure, decision-making, and practices that fall under the rubric of "gatekeeping." Although not designed as a representative sampling, or even a systematic research project, we did use three criteria in generating our list of twelve program contacts: (1) a focus on elementary education programs as a way to delimit our inquiry (given our own program experience); (2) regional diversity, knowing that state mandates differ widely and are often the source of at least some requirements related to fit and readiness; and (3) variety of institutional types, using AACTE's (American Association of Colleges for Teacher Education) categories.

Table 27.1 portrays the regions and institutional types we contacted by telephone. Promising confidentiality to our colleagues, we are not including the name of the institution, although we did have conversations with people from New York, New Jersey, Massachusetts, Pennsylvania, Florida, Kentucky, Ohio, Illinois, California, Utah, and Alaska. The programs ranged in size from very small, certifying 25 or 30 new teachers a year, to those which were quite large and prepared several hundred teacher candidates per year. Conversations lasted anywhere from 20 minutes to over one hour and were based on a list of questions (Appendix 1) that we had sent each respondent ahead of time. Many of these colleagues were people we know, but some of the people with whom we spoke were solicited because of the institutional type (using Peterson's on-line index) or region (using AACTE's categories).

Table 27.1 Types and regions of colleges and universities contacted by telephone regarding their elementary education program

	Northeast	Southeast	Central	West	Totals
Large (9000+) public Ph.D.		✓			1
Large (9000+) private Ph.D.	✓		✓		2
Large (9000+) public comprehensive	✓			✓	3
				✓	
Large private comprehensive					0
Small public comprehensive	✓				1
Small private comprehensive			✓	✓	2
Private baccalaureate		✓	✓		2
Private specialized	✓				1
Totals	4	2	3	3	12

What emerged, and what we present below (interwoven with a review of the literature) was a fascinating portrait of a wide range of program practices, some influenced by state requirements, many emerging from the students enrolled in their programs, some in place because of long-standing collaborative relationships with school districts, some due to organizational structures of the wider universities, and a few based on long-range planning by faculty involved in the teacher education program. Although we found it quite interesting to compare practices and problems across programs, we do not present a list and description of these practices, but rather, we seek to analyze issues that cross the various contexts.

FIT TO TEACH? CONTENT KNOWLEDGE AND ACHIEVEMENT

The importance of content knowledge and academic achievement has been much debated and discussed in reference to teacher preparation in the United States. Although no one will disagree that knowledge of content is central to good teaching, it is much harder to determine which content knowledge is of most value and then agree on valid and reliable measures of achievement. While this critical debate is beyond the scope of our chapter, it is important to note that many teacher education programs emphasize content knowledge and achievement by requiring specific university course work, using student GPAs for admission or continuation in their programs, and stipulating higher scores than the state's cut-off on teacher exams. The programs we spoke with are no exception: most require minimum GPAs of 2.75 (the range was 2.5 to 3.0); more than half have course prerequisites (typically involving a practicum or field placement) or require applicants to achieve a minimum grade in specified courses prior to admissions (usually, these are basic skills courses such as English and mathematics); eight of the twelve require applicants to take or pass some form of standardized test such as Praxis I to demonstrate basic skills or content knowledge (primarily), or in lieu of SATs or ACTs.

State requirements and teacher exams

While teacher education programs within particular states can show great variation in their interpretations and implementations of state guidelines for approved teacher education programs, the requirement of passing standardized teacher examinations is one that is most common, least open to interpretation, and in most cases is not subject to negoti-ation. Although 42 states have licensing exams required for certification (Cochran-Smith & Zeichner, 2005), many also require teacher education programs to measure fitness to teach through the Praxis Series, developed by the Educational Testing Service. As of 2005, 30 states and the District of Columbia required the Praxis I—or Pre-professional Skills Test (PPST)—for either entrance into teacher education programs or licensure (Educational Testing Service, 2005).

Common practice notwithstanding, researchers of teacher education have raised crit-ical questions about the usefulness and validity of Praxis I as a tool to sort qualified from unqualified teachers and teacher candidates (Cobb *et al.*, 1999; Garcia, 1987; Mitchell & Barth, 1999). Although the PPST was developed and is used to identify students likely to succeed in teacher education programs, the subtests themselves—which states often spe-cify with specific "cut-scores" (Educational Testing Service, 2005)—have not proven valid for separating students who succeed in teacher education programs from those who fail (Memory *et al.*, 2003; Mikitovics, 2002; Wilson & Youngs, 2005). Furthermore, three studies undertaken to explore the relationship between students' PPST scores and student teaching evaluations could find none (Mikitovics, 2002).

Most disturbingly, however, the PPST does function as an identifier by ethnicity, and the "supply of minority teacher candidates appears to be negatively affected by the use of PPST as a screening device" (Mikitovics, 2002, p. 221; see also Wilson & Youngs, 2005; and Zumwalt & Craig, 2005). Although few programs or states use *only* a standardized assessment measure to determine entry or licensure, cut-scores and passing scores are often set by state regulations, leaving individual teacher preparation programs little lee-way in balancing performance assessments with standardized ones. Strong warnings have been sounded by researchers such as Strosnider and Blanchett (2003) that such practices not only violate the recommendations of the American Association of Colleges for Teacher Education (AACTE 1992, 1999), but can also be seen as resulting in dis-criminatory practices. With this, and other state-mandated requirements, we can see how teacher education programs function within certain constraints that do not necessarily place the teacher educators as the creators of the gatekeeping mechanisms. We are, however, mandated by our agreements with state licensing authorities to enact the decisions of regulatory agencies.

Still, admission is not the only gatekeeping point in teacher education programs: in our sample, the programs in Florida, New Jersey, Kentucky, Alaska, Massachusetts, Illinois, and California also use teacher tests such as the Illinois Assessment of Profes-sional Teaching, as well as basic skills tests such as the MTEL (Massachusetts Test for Educator Licensure) literacy test for entrance into student teaching or for certification recommendations to the state. Thus, one very strong gate that we *do* see in teacher education programs is attaining a particular score on a state-mandated standardized exam. Said one teacher educator in our sample, "(the basic skills test) keeps them from getting in (to the teacher preparation program), and the general knowledge test keeps them from getting out (i.e. graduating and getting certified)."

Accordingly, many programs offer a variety of "test-prep" supports. Some programs in our sample offer tutoring to individual students, and others offer non-credit classes for students to develop their test-taking skills. However, such measures are not always suf-ficient to ensure that all candidates are able to move forward. One program coordinator explained that although students are sometimes able to pass the first standardized test which admits them into the College of Education, they are not able to pass the next exam which allows them to student teach, or the final exam that is required for the capstone course that follows student teaching. As she explained, all students are required to pass each test before moving forward. No exceptions are granted. She termed this state mandate the "100 percent solution," and added that if a student fails the test three times, it is very unlikely that she or he will ever pass it.

Academic difficulties beyond testing and GPA

Assessing teacher candidates' content knowledge and achievement through tests and GPA is no guarantee that they will be able to be successful in teacher education courses that often require extensive writing and critical analysis, or K-12 classrooms that require a wide range of skills and knowledge. Such skill deficits are fairly easy to spot (based on weak papers and course assignments, or frequent errors with students) but are quite troubling and perplexing for teacher educators to handle. Thus, related gates tend to be more idiosyncratic and local; for instance, many universities have writing programs or tutorials designed to help students with the demands of academic writing. One program director with whom we spoke described students who were required to take time away from the program and remediate basic skill deficits through community-college programs. However, most of the pin-pointing of academic skill deficits is conducted on an *ad hoc* basis, and remedial interventions are similarly *ad hoc*.

The issue of academic performance is sometimes intertwined with a diagnosis of learning disabilities. Complying with the Americans with Disabilities Act (P.L. 101–336), campuses have varying levels of supports for students with diagnosed disabilities. Yet, there is little research or documentation of how programs think about fitness and readiness to teach of teacher candidates with disabilities. Of course, under Section 504 of the Rehabilitation Act of 1973 (P.L. 93–112), employers are required to make reasonable accommodations. Yet if an elementary teacher cannot read out loud, will the school district be willing to have the teacher use recordings or guest readers? What is the role of teacher education programs in advising students with disabilities who seek to become teachers?

One group of researchers studying preservice teachers with learning disabilities points out that field placements may require special consideration. They advise that preservice students be exposed to the realistic demands of teaching, but be placed in classrooms where their strengths can be maximized (Wertheim *et al.*, 1998). This entails a careful needs assessment of both the student teacher and the receiving classroom. Additionally, these same authors have a set of important recommendations for the student, including ways to foster honest and on-going communication with the cooperating teacher,[1] supervisor and teacher education faculty about specific and individual needs.

This careful attention to clinical experiences is often required with other disabilities such as deafness and blindness. For instance, a Deaf student teacher who recently graduated from Teachers College did her general education placement (required by New York State for special education certification programs) in an elementary classroom with only hearing children. Two interpreters worked full-time with this preservice teacher, one voicing what she signed to the students, and the other signing what the children said. Is this a "reasonable accommodation" as required by Section 504? Although there are some court cases that set precedent and can offer guidance for program faculty, in most cases, we make these decisions at a very local level.

Sometimes such decisions are made in the midst of crisis; in our own program we have found an increase in the number of students who are receiving medication and/or psychotherapy for mental health issues. Even students without disabilities are often seriously challenged by the rigors and stress of student teaching. As Shively and Poetter note, "Student teaching can be overwhelming, extremely difficult, even harrowing. Difficulties in one or two areas can seem to drag down the entire experience" (2002, p. 294). When student teachers are unable to meet program demands due to mental health issues, what is a reasonable accommodation? There is little guidance forthcoming on this issue from the law, the states have not yet weighed in with regulations in this regard (nor would we want them to!), and yet, many teacher education programs face decisions each year about how best to respond to and accommodate preservice teachers whose mental health is compromised during (and perhaps due to) student teaching.

When asked what particular student problems, challenges, and dilemmas they face, many of the twelve faculty with whom we spoke mentioned psychiatric disorders, mental health issues, or emotional needs. Frequently, we heard stories of students' crises from the field. Often, program decisions are made with the assistance of legal counsel, who let the program know if removing the student from the program is an option, or if they need (legally) to be given another field placement because the case is not strong enough to support removal. In almost all cases, faculty spoke of interventions and counseling services that are recommended or required. In many cases, once the student receives the appropriate treatment, s/he is able to re-enter the program and successfully complete the certification program. In a recent case from our own program, after an emergency hospitalization, increased family support, and a change in medication, the student was able to complete her field work requirement successfully.

Language proficiency and fitness to teach

As the number of immigrants in this country continues to rise, the number of English Language Learners enrolled in teacher education programs increases. Many programs across the United States—particularly in larger East and West Coast cities—have students who speak a first language besides English. Various programs have a language requirement or courses related to English or speech; one program from our conversations—located in a high-immigration area—requires the TOEFL (Test of English as a Foreign Language) as a requirement for entrance for all students whose first language is not English.

At one university, the elementary program includes an interview as a requirement for entrance into the program, a requirement mirrored by several other programs in our sample. At this particular university, the interview was developed in the 1990s to find out about spoken language ability, not as a gate for program acceptance, but rather as a way to recommend remediation. Currently, however, due to an increase of students in their program, the interviews are group interviews and the possible English language services are weak or non-existent. Since the university does not have "good mechanisms for language remediation," and faculty are not comfortable turning students down because of English language proficiency, this is a very "sensitive issue." Thus, students are admitted into the program and most do quite well in the university-based coursework; however, when they become student teachers, their English language production sometimes becomes a barrier to successful ratings from cooperating teachers and supervisors. When this occurs, students are given a different placement or are required to spend additional semesters student teaching.

ADVOCACY vs. GATEKEEPING

Given our discussion thus far, it is easy to see how decisions about fitness and readiness to teach resist simple formulas, scores on exams, or grade point averages. These questions are entangled with cultural/political values and with program organization, design, and resources (for example, would all programs be able to provide two full-time American Sign Language interpreters for a Deaf student teacher?). Clearly teacher education programs have responsibilities to not only determine fitness and readiness to teach, but to also scaffold students' fitness and readiness. As the above examples demonstrate, there are many students who need extra support, resources, and accommodations because of individual circumstances. Thus, teacher educators assume the dual role of helping students construct their teaching identities and knowledge and skills of teaching, while at the same time serving as gatekeepers for the state and the profession.

This dual role is explored in some detail by Paris and Gespass (2001) who document the tensions that arise when teacher educators must measure student teachers' discrete behaviors against set standards while attempting simultaneously to be learner-centered. They conclude that ultimately teacher educators' gatekeeping role dominates, resulting in a "technical rationality that emphasizes the uncritical performance of generalizable teaching strategies" (p. 398).

Similarly, seeing the potential conflict between scaffolding the developmental process of learning to teach and simultaneously having to recommend—or not recommend—for licensure, researchers from Minnesota (Page *et al.*, 2004) used case studies of student teachers to explore the relationship between gatekeeping and advocacy in teacher preparation. They explain the gatekeeping role of the teacher educator is to, "clarify and enforce programmatic expectations; implement learning plans and probationary procedures; [and] counsel candidates into other areas of study" (p. 37). Concerned that their gatekeeping did not prematurely dismiss students from the program, and that their advocacy did not license inadequate teachers, the authors analyzed specific student teachers' cases along two dimensions: ability (GPA, course exams, performance tasks) and teachability (openness to feedback and self-reflection). With students who present as having low ability and also low teachability, teacher educators must assume the role of gatekeeper. It is the combination of low ability and low teachability that can result in students not meeting minimum program expectations.

The judgment of minimum standards or program expectations requires summative evaluation by program faculty. Yet, Raths and Lyman (2003) claim that teacher education programs do not necessarily always do a good job of ferreting out incompetent teachers. Many evaluations throughout teacher education programs are formative in nature (e.g. portfolios and observations) and often the roles of formative assessor and summative assessor are conflated, which is one reason why incompetent students are sometimes recommended for certification (Raths & Lyman, 2003). Other explanations include: those making summative judgments about student teachers often occupy "minor roles within the larger teacher education setting"; pressure from students, parents, and lawyers to back down on decisions made that have career altering consequences; and a "rhetoric of excellence" that often pervades student teaching evaluations with benchmarks such as *superior* and *excellent* (p. 208; emphasis in original).

One reason why teacher educators conflate formative and summative assessment may be a key assumption undergirding teacher educators' work—that learning to teach does not rest on techno-rational skills (Hinchman & Oyler, 2001; Paris & Gespass, 2001) or proceed in a linear, predictable fashion. Rather, we know that learning to teach is complex, contextually specific, autobiographically grounded, and informed by socio-political understandings (Goodwin 2002a, 2002b). Accordingly, we do not expect to see students progressing at predictable rates or steps during field placements. We spoke with many faculty (and see evidence in the literature) of strong gates to exit student teaching successfully. However, the other program assessments are not typically used to keep students from graduating, from certification, or from continuing in the program. Rather, they are used to scaffold students' success, thus acting as advocacy mechanisms, rather than gatekeeping devises. We are referring here to typical program assessments such as portfolios, disposition checklists, action research projects, reflective journals, and culminating projects. Students, of course, experience these assessments as stressful, often challenging, and sometimes anxiety-producing. However, we have found no evidence in the literature, nor in our informal conversations with colleagues, that such assessments are ever gates that keep students from moving on. Therefore, much of our own efforts in scaffolding field-based experiences in learning to teach must center on designing specific interventions when difficulties do arise.

READINESS TO TEACH: FIELDWORK AS A GATE

Evaluations of students' progress in teacher education programs must be understood in relationship to the multiple stake-holders with whom teacher educators work. Our programs are: subject to agreements with our respective state departments of education, usually dependent on approval by national accrediting agencies (such as NCATE), and always functioning within larger college or university guidelines and standards. Preservice students must be evaluated by us for both licensure and degree requirements, and both of these are dependent on successful completion of fieldwork.

This responsibility—that embeds decisions about graduation and licensure in evaluations of clinical experiences—increases the significance of teacher education assessments and requires that they not be only formative in nature, but demands they also be summative. However, there is little research available that documents or analyzes our assessments in light of high-stakes decisions, such as graduation and licensure. Instead, teacher educators have been strangely silent on this matter.

Student teaching: measuring competence, deciding incompetence

State Departments of Education do not typically outline how to measure satisfactory performance in the required field work experiences. Although states usually specify the minimum number and length of field experiences, they have not explicitly defined what it means to be a competent *student* teacher. Yes, many states have developed standards to which they hold individual teacher education programs and individual teacher candidates responsible, and some states even require that teacher candidates submit evidence to their programs of satisfactory performance in each standard. However, it is obviously much harder (if not impossible) for states to judge the performance qualifications of individual teacher candidates. It is that judgment that has been placed in the hands of teacher educators via state-approved programs.

Certainly, the student teaching experience is understood by teacher educators and teacher candidates as a centerpiece of the preparation experience. Although some literature exists delineating what makes a "good" student teaching experience (Beck & Kosnick, 2002; Cochran-Smith, 1991; Koerner *et al.*, 2002; LaBoskey & Richert, 2002), there is little research documenting how programs evaluate teacher candidates' performance and subsequent readiness to teach during and immediately after the student teaching experience, elaborate practices (supervisors, observations, check-lists, evaluation forms, etc.) notwithstanding.

A few case studies or narrative accounts of student teaching difficulties have been published or presented that illustrate some of the challenges and decision-points that teacher educators face in assisting students along the developmental continuum to become a teacher (Dubetz *et al.*, 1997; Gray, 1998; Oyler *et al.*, 2001). Still, cases of individual students being removed from field placements are scarce in the research on learning to teach, or are mentioned but not elaborated upon.

When students are evaluated as not successful in student teaching, various studies report that they may be asked to withdraw from student teaching, or may be allowed to re-enroll in student teaching in a different semester (Farkas & Johnson, 1997; Johnson & Yates, 1982; Knudson & Turley, 2000; Raths & Lyman, 2003; Sudzina & Knowles, 1993). However, as Suzdzina and Knowles noted (1993), "teacher educators rarely talk about 'failure' in their programs," . . . perhaps because it is "unwelcome, unanticipated, and often embarrassing" (p. 254). Thus, incompetence, and the reasons behind it, is not well theorized, operationalized, or explored in the scholarship from inside teacher education.

Accordingly, Raths and Lyman (2003) offer a "classification scheme of teaching behaviors—ranging from the most egregious to those representing good practices" (p. 210). Their continuum includes: criminality, malpractice, lack of basic skills, incompetence in teaching, plain teaching, and teaching with best practices (p. 214). Clearly, it is the categories in the middle (lack of basic skills, incompetence, and plain teaching) that offer the greatest challenge to teacher educators. To that end, these authors also include a 2-page chart with "Indicators of Incompetence in Student Teaching" (2003, pp. 212–213) designed to help teacher educators counsel out preservice teachers who are not exhibiting evidence of competency in the field.

How students are identified to be "at risk" was the focus of a study conducted in California (Knudsen & Turley, 2000). In this study of two teacher education programs at one university, the supervisor was the person who raised a concern in 50 percent of all cases. The reasons that students were red-flagged differed depending on the point in both the program (first or second placement) and in the semester, but included: problems with instructional strategies, difficulties with either the supervisor, the cooperating teacher, or the university requirements, not managing time well, difficulties establishing management skills or rapport with students, lack of knowledge of subject matter, or incompatible ideas of what it meant to be a teacher.

Interventions

Making the decision to not recommend a candidate for certification is a difficult one. Although not all the programs with whom we spoke had experience with this, the ones that did all remarked about the time and energy involved in this process. In our own program, we spend enormous numbers of hours developing special intervention programs for and with student teachers experiencing difficulty in field work. What is clear to us from both our interviews with colleagues and our own experience, is that the needs of certain preservice teachers often consume much additional time, require greater program flexibility, and challenge the capacity of typical university services. As one colleague told us, "For one student with a problem, it could take 50–100 hours to resolve."

The judgment of when it is "appropriate" to intervene, and what interventions are developed is, of course, a local program decision. Although state mandates are clear regarding teacher certification exams, and sometimes even detail standards to meet, the day-to-day decisions about readiness to teach remain squarely in the hands of teacher education programs.

How programs intervene to assist "at-risk" student teachers, is an area that has received little focused attention in studies of preservice teacher education. According to Sudzina and Knowles (1993), "A major weakness in the literature on "failure" is the lack of attention to collective programmatic actions and the consequences of particular preservice teacher education practices within institutions" (p. 256). Depending on the severity of the issue, students may be required to demonstrate they have taken specific courses, or received specific treatment as a condition of continuing in the program; for instance, one student teacher who went to two different placements obviously inebriated and was removed twice from student teaching, was required to show evidence of substance abuse treatment before being considered for re-admission.

When the problem that surfaces is most egregious—what Raths and Lyman (2003) would term criminality or malpractice, the decisions are more straightforward. They often involve consultation with university lawyers, but offer little confusion to faculty regarding an appropriate line of action. The student is removed from the placement, often exited from the program, and sometimes dismissed from the university. Of course, we also realize that given the large number of "back-door" routes to teacher certification, it is possible that students we have failed and even dismissed find other ways into teaching.

Drastic cases involving such egregious behavior are thankfully rare (according to our anecdotal evidence; again this has not been a subject for systematic inquiry), and call for fairly unambiguous decision-making. Much more commonly, when we need to intervene, it is with a student who falls into one of the next categories of Raths and Lyman's typology (2003): unethical behavior; lack of basic skills; incompetence as a teacher; and even "plain teaching," defined as strong in one or two areas, but overall "mediocre, uninspiring, and tedious" (p. 214).

Similar to the majority of programs with whom we spoke, when a student is rated below satisfactory for student teaching, in our program we will require a third, or sometimes, even a fourth placement. Completing this additional placement, however, is no guarantee of success. Although continued poor ratings from new supervisors and new cooperating teachers does help make the teacher educator's case stronger, it provides little comfort for the prospective teacher. Particularly challenging in these cases is the large amounts of time and money that have been invested up to the point of final decision. Because of this, over half of the programs with whom we spoke have developed, or are developing, degree programs that offer graduation without certification. This is typically an "Educational Studies" degree and the program recommendation for certification is withheld.

However, this action is not without consequence. Students in possession of a university degree that includes education course work can—as we mentioned earlier, and our colleagues echoed—still find ways to achieve "certification" via emergency, temporary, or alternative routes, and/or enter the classroom, especially in hard-to-staff schools or shortage areas such as special education or science. A number of our colleagues, especially at the undergraduate level, also related stories of angry parents, anxious university administrators, and subsequent communication from lawyers seeking to overturn the negative decisions. Accordingly, the most common practice when dealing with students experiencing difficulty at any point in our teacher education programs (but particularly at the fieldwork stage) is the strategy of "counseling out."

"Counseling out" is a skill that many teacher educators hone over the years and refers to the common practice of advising preservice students of other academic and career options available besides the certification programs in which they are enrolled. Again, we could find no systematic data or study of this practice, although in our conversations with all the teacher educators, this was a practice in which we had all engaged, and was recommended by researchers of teacher education (Sudzina & Knowles, 1993) as "direct exit counseling" (p. 261).

Other steps short of not recommending for certification and counseling out, are developed by the individual teacher education programs and may include changing supervisors or cooperating (mentor) teachers, or bringing in faculty for the creation of individual action plans. One university has developed a "Communication of Concern" form that can be filled out by university professors, PDS faculty-school liaisons, or the cooperating teacher. These forms are placed in the students' files and serve as data if "Intensive Action Plans" need to be created for individual students.

Whatever the student teaching problem, and regardless of the planned intervention, this is time- and emotion-intensive work. As Raths and Lyman write (2003), "The challenge of making judgments about student teaching is akin to those facing a jury. There are rarely ever tight and precise definitions of what composes guilt or innocence in a jury trial . . . . however the process still calls for informed judgments" (p. 215).

Negotiating field placements and school partners

These informed judgments are not made by university-based teacher educators alone, but must be made in collaboration with our school partners. Teacher education programs are inextricably dependent upon field placements for student teachers. Yet the issues of control over the placements and communication with the placement often present challenges that can have a direct impact on teacher educators' gatekeeping practices. It is a rare program that hand-picks cooperating teachers and makes individual matches between mentor teacher and student teacher. Although we could locate no large-scale studies that document student teaching placement practices, we do know that programs have a range of agreements with the field and a variety of administrative supports at the university level.

The majority of the programs in our sample reported little control, or even input, over the decisions about which cooperating teachers to use. Some of the programs have centralized, field placement services. Often, these offices have agreements with schools or school districts and it is personnel at the school end that either make the matches or develop the lists of classroom teachers. As one of our colleagues related, "We have lots of students in placements that are not ideal . . . we tried to maintain a list of teachers we didn't want to use again, but they would re-appear on the lists." (This experience was repeated by a number of faculty with whom we spoke.)

This lack of control of placements has implications for how much field-based information can be used by teacher educators to make gatekeeping decisions, and how much of a role the school-partners can and do play as gatekeepers. One faculty coordinator of a large program explained that, "school partners are not at the place where they truly see themselves as gatekeepers." Another faculty member told of a case of a student from his social studies methods course who submitted a unit plan she had taught in an area high school. This professor assessed the unit plan as unacceptable, as the lessons did not maintain sufficient boundaries between church and state. However, the student teacher's field evaluations were exemplary and the cooperating teacher rated the unit and the woman's teaching most highly. Frustrated by the lack of influence on school-based curriculum planning, this faculty member characterized the lack of decision-making about placements and the weak link between field and campus as a "major program issue." Other researchers (Knudsen & Turley, 2000) have explained some cooperating teachers' reluctance to critique inadequate student teachers as a result of the close personal relationship that often develops. Cooperating teachers know more about the personal lives of the student teacher and might even make excuses for a student teacher's lapses or lower their expectations.

Smaller programs or universities that use a Professional Development School (PDS) model, are often able to build strong communication systems, including faculty-school liaisons who develop long-term relationships with a small number of teachers or schools. In these situations, faculty report that cooperating teachers move from a less critical stance toward a more rigorous stance after working with the program for a few years. Clearly, the ongoing presence of faculty in the schools, and conferences about specific problem students, helps create a sense of shared gatekeeping responsibility among the school-based partners.

MONKEY IN THE MIDDLE OR PARTICIPATION IN THE ABSENCE OF CONTROL

Any random glance at the educational history of this country, especially over the past half century or so, reveals schools and teachers as lightening rods for all manner of social critique. Crime, economic instability, teenage pregnancy, loss of a global competitive edge, and so on, have been laid at the feet of schools and teachers who have been blamed wholesale for a host of societal failings and ills. Likewise, teacher educators and their university-based programs have become the sole scapegoat for all that is wrong with teachers and schools, with no acknowledgement of the vast enterprise that surrounds the preparation of teachers. There are many groups and constituencies engaged and invested in teacher preparation for reasons beyond ensuring quality teachers, including financial profit, political advancement, access to public and private funding, or personal notoriety. Thus, as teacher preparation has become highly politicized and political, it becomes more apparent that teacher quality is less a matter of competence versus incompetence, and more a fundamental battle for *control* in/of the gatekeeping process. Our examination in this chapter of the role of university-based teacher preparation in deciding who can or should teach illuminates the major dilemma facing teacher educators—they are held accountable for ensuring quality and blamed for teacher incompetence, but have little input in defining what quality means and minimal control over who enters and who is kept out of the profession. This lack of control is the consequence of a variety of factors and historical circumstances including teacher preparation as a collective enterprise, the place of teacher education in the academy, and the impact of the external socio-cultural context.

Teacher preparation as a collective enterprise

University-based teacher preparation is an enterprise that relies on the joint efforts of several different groups, some of whom are in the academy but sit outside the field, others of whom are in the field but are outside the academy. Thus teacher educators depend on arts and science colleagues, and school partners such as district administrators and teachers, to maintain their programs and enact their curricula. This alliance across these three groups is, and has historically been, uneasy, typically characterized by a lack of respect in the academy for education as an intellectual, or even a bona fide discipline, and mistrust of university-based educators on the part of school-based practitioners. Thus, teacher educators are placed in the unhappy position of working with reluctant or critical collaborators who may not always uphold the same goals or assume responsibility for quality teacher preparation, *even while teacher preparation cannot occur without their participation.*

Thus, several of the teacher educators we spoke with shared their frustration of having almost no hand in the selection of student teaching placements and cooperating teachers, resulting in "lots of students in placements that are not ideal," despite the reality that the field placement is a critical component of teacher preparation. Others described needing to rely on school partners such as principals or cooperating teachers for candid assessments of student teachers—particularly candidly critical assessments—in order to make a poor or failing grade "stick," despite having little leverage to hold these partners accountable for student teacher quality. As one teacher educator stated, incompetence on the part of a student teacher will not necessarily affect certification in the absence of "a very vigilant supervisor, a teacher concerned about quality, [and] a principal who will back you up."

Much of the discussion about teacher quality has emphasized subject matter preparation and teacher education has been criticized for devoting the majority of its programs to professional preparation over content knowledge. In reality, the opposite is true: historically, general education requirements or "academic" courses consume the majority of credits (as much as 75 percent) required for elementary or secondary teacher certification, and reform in university-based teacher preparation curricula over the past 50 years has consistently resulted in more academic courses and fewer education courses (Conant, 1964; Goodlad, 1990; Howey, 1983), and these academic courses are offered by arts and sciences faculty, not those in teacher education. Still, teacher educators continue to be faulted for new teachers' lack of content knowledge, or their inability to pass subject matter tests, even while they are not directly responsible for candidates' academic preparation, and have little authority over those who do.

The place of teacher education in the academy

The movement of teacher education from normal schools into the universities as a state-initiated reform resulted in an implicit agreement between teacher educators and states that has positioned teacher education as subordinate to the state for the past 100 years (Goodlad, 1990; Haberman, 1983; Melnick, 1996).

> The state's role in helping to establish teacher education departments in universities, became a legitimate license to exercise power and control over the curriculum in schools of education. . . . Once schools of education relied on the support of state education agencies for recognition and approval of their teacher education programs, they were compelled to accept the role and authority of the state in order to justify their own existence.
>
> (Schneider, 1987, p. 215)

University-based teacher preparation programs cannot exist without state sponsorship and therefore are not always in a position to resist or question state mandates. Indeed, "no higher education specialty approaches teacher education in the degree of influence exerted by outside agencies, particularly state agencies controlling entry into public school teaching" (Goodlad, 1990, p. 93), an observation echoed, as we noted earlier, during different eras by numerous scholars. Ironically, it is the promise of certification that makes university-based programs marketable. By approving teacher education programs as conduits for teacher certification, states in essence protect or enhance program viability and attractiveness to students, yet teacher certification is an outcome that can only be granted by the state; teacher preparation programs do not control the certification process nor can they offer certification or deny it. They can, and do, offer or withhold their endorsement for certification, but the absence of their endorsement does not necessarily keep low performing student teachers out of the classroom since graduates can still—often easily—achieve certification regardless via alternate routes, certification through testing, emergency licenses, etc. Even school districts are now in the business of certifying teachers, bypassing university-based teacher preparation altogether. Teacher educators find themselves caught in a paradox—over-regulation on the part of state agencies alongside vociferous calls for the de-regulation of teacher preparation (Cochran-Smith, 2001a).

It is not surprising then that our conversations found teacher educators to be the keepers of gates without locks. Thus, many of the faculty with whom we spoke characterized most of the gates through which students pass as "not rigorous," not in terms of the robustness of individual assessments, but in terms of a gate's ultimate capacity to keep students out of the profession or out of the teacher preparation program. Those gates that have the most teeth are those linked to state certification requirements—teaching test scores and indications of content knowledge, i.e. GPA, which measure concrete and discrete knowledge and skills. In all of the programs we canvassed, it was students not meeting minimum grade requirements or test scores who were most likely to be barred from entering—or exiting—the teacher preparation program.

Those gates that seemed to have very little teeth were invariably those conceptualized or developed by teacher educators themselves—disposition charts, teaching/INTASC standards, reflections on ethics and philosophy, observations and assessments of classroom performance. In fact, the majority of the programs with which we spoke include the assessment of candidates' dispositions as a significant aspect of their teacher preparation and evaluation; in conversations with teacher education colleagues, all except one named dispositions such as flexibility, reflectivity, openness to learning, commitment to multiculturalism, as key qualities for student teachers to possess. Such skills, knowledge, and dispositions are often not easily quantifiable or discrete and do not lend themselves to standardized or mass assessment, yet they encompass professional knowledge and behaviors that teacher educators believe are essential to good teaching. Therefore, the gates built around this set of knowledge and skills must similarly be fluid and open-ended, offering students more than one opportunity to "get it" and offering teacher educators many different avenues for assessment. Thus, the designation of these gates as "lockless" is not meant to be pejorative but instead is an indication of a philosophical mindset that pervades teacher education and views teachers as advocates, and learning to teach as a developmental and complicated process. These gates do not, however, represent what the state and the public underscore as essential teacher knowledge, and therefore, do not necessarily lock individuals out of the teaching profession even while the teacher educators with whom we spoke do use them to keep applicants out of their programs and to stop students from continuing through to university endorsement for certification.

The impact of the external socio-cultural context

Teacher education is not, of course, immune to a changing socio-cultural context; no profession is. However, some of the changes have further affected, complicated or even eroded the level of control teacher educators exert as gatekeepers for teaching. First, as attested by our conversations with colleagues across the country, continued legislation to widen access to education has meant greater diversity among teacher candidates, more of whom exhibit complex and serious needs that must be accommodated if they are to grow into teachers. We certainly applaud ongoing efforts, both grass-roots and bureaucratic, that render schooling and professional study more inclusive. However, the question of who can teach or who is ready to teach becomes even more difficult to address and requires teacher educators to balance ever more precariously their role as advocates with their responsibility as gatekeepers.

Teacher education programs have also been experiencing a period of growth in enrollments, beginning in the late 1980s. However, despite dramatic increases in enrollments, most teacher education programs have not yet recovered from the severe budget cuts that accompanied the teacher surplus of the 1970s. Teacher education programs continue to be under-resourced and rely heavily on adjuncts, doctoral students, and non-tenure-line faculty to operate even while they are pressured by university administrators to admit additional students given their continued ability to attract applicants. Several faculty with whom we spoke invoked the image of teacher education as "cash cow," either in direct statements, or by implication when they talked about "pressure to keep enrollments high" or "not turning [applicants] away." Pressure to admit students means that admissions criteria may or may not be applied to keep out candidates of questionable quality, yet once in the program, teacher educators are held accountable for ensuring that these very same candidates achieve minimum standards. This pressure may also, in part, represent a reaction to for-profit or alternative teacher certification routes that threaten to pull potential students away from university-based teacher preparation.

Finally, in a social environment characterized by consumerism, teacher educators' ability to gatekeep with conviction may be thwarted by students (and their representatives) advocating for themselves, rejecting professional assessments, or threatening litigation. As discussed earlier, almost all of our colleagues spoke of parents becoming "heavily involved" in difficult decisions surrounding students' apparent lack of fitness for teaching, of students resisting intervention options, or of needing the advice of legal counsel before making a decision to discontinue a student or take a particular action.

WHAT NEXT?

According to Cochran-Smith and Fries, researchers on teacher education have "worked from quite different constructions of the problem" and "that simply asking a different question about the quality and depth of the research base on teacher education can produce a different answer" (2005, p. 99). This chapter offers a perspective on and analysis of learning to teach that suggest there *are* some different questions we as teacher educators can ask that may expand our research agenda to allow the possibility of alternate explanations for and definitions of teacher quality. The questions we posed at the beginning of our discussion bear repeating. What indicators of teacher quality do teacher educators look for as they engage in the daily work of teacher preparation? What kinds of gatekeeping mechanisms are in place in teacher education programs—at entry, during coursework, during fieldwork and at completion—to ensure teachers of quality are selected and then certified? Do certain characteristics beyond GPA, test scores and race (including, for instance, academic difficulties, disabilities, mental health, standard English language proficiency) or dispositions (such as commitment to diversity, openness to learning and change, an ethical stance, etc.) figure into whether a teacher candidate is ready to—or can—teach?

Research on teacher education over the past 50 years has focused on teacher education as a training problem, a learning problem, and a policy problem (Cochran-Smith & Fries, 2005). The intersection of these three research strands, gatekeeping in teacher education, and the questions we pose above allow us to make specific recommendations about future empirical work. Teacher education as a training problem emphasizes "transportable training procedures that [have] an impact on teacher behaviors" (Cochran-Smith & Fries, 2005, p. 16). Thus, gatekeeping in teacher education as a training problem points to the need to document and examine the practices, interventions, and programmatic structures embedded in teacher preparation programs that serve as major assessment points and mechanisms throughout the learning-to-teach process. We need to know what kinds of strategies teacher educators use—and when—and how these strategies, interventions and gates impact, support or impede teacher learning and teacher success. We also need to know what works and what does not and under what circumstances—what kinds of gates should be in place in teacher education programs so as to ensure teacher quality.

Teacher education as a learning problem looks at how teachers acquire the "knowledge, skills and dispositions needed to teach, and how they [interpret] their experiences in teacher preparation courses" (Cochran-Smith & Fries, 2005, p. 29). When gatekeeping is inserted as a variable, teacher education as a learning problem must ask how teacher educators measure, recognize, and remediate student teacher learning *and* quality, and what factors teacher educators weigh as they ultimately decide who is fit or ready to teach. Some of these factors may involve student teacher characteristics and dispositions that have received very little attention from the research community. Yet teacher educators would argue that dispositions play an important role in fitness to teach, while certain characteristics that student teachers present require supports and accommodations that are difficult to provide and also raise ethical dilemmas because the rights of students must be balanced against the rights of teachers who are also students.

Finally, teacher education as a policy problem aims to "provide evidence about how teacher education as an overall enterprise can be successful and cost effective" (Cochran-Smith & Fries, 2005, p. 47). Studying gatekeeping practices in teacher education could provide much data about the supports, decisions, policies, and interventions that need to be (or are) in place during the learning-to-teach process that likely enhance success in teacher education. It follows that effective gatekeeping practices increase cost effectiveness because resources and time are targeted to specific student teacher needs, and decisions regarding appropriateness and fit are embedded into programs and are made deliberately and consistently—another lens through which to examine teacher education. Gatekeeping in teacher education as a policy problem also suggests that we need to study assessment and accountability policies across institutions in order to understand how gatekeeping policies support the work of teacher educators, make explicit definitions of teacher quality, and keep weak teacher candidates out of the profession. Given the current push for evidence-based judgments, such studies should also focus on gathering data that illuminates whether gatekeeping policies currently in place in teacher education programs actually ensure teaching readiness on the part of graduates in their initial years of practice.

Our recommendations are not intended to be comprehensive or exhaustive. Rather, we offer them as a way to highlight how little we know about what goes on in teacher education programs or what teacher educators do in their daily work with student teachers, how notions of teacher quality, fitness, and readiness are fluid, contingent and program-specific even while there appears to be more in common across programs and practices than is acknowledged or recognized, and how the current policy debate about quality teachers focuses on the big picture of state standards, teacher tests, and subject matter knowledge, but attends minimally to the space between entry into teacher preparation and exit into the profession, where teacher candidates are actually engaged in the process of becoming teachers.

NOTE

1 "Cooperating teacher" (CT) is the term we use throughout this paper; we realize the terms "mentor teacher" and "associate teacher" are often used, and that these terms convey subtle differences of program philosophy.

REFERENCES

American Association of Colleges for Teacher Education (1992) *Teacher education pipeline III: schools, colleges and departments of education enrollment by race, ethnicity and gender.* Washington, DC: Author.

American Association of Colleges for Teacher Education (1999) *Teacher education pipeline IV: schools, colleges and departments of education enrollment by race, ethnicity and gender.* Washington, DC. Author.

Ballou, D. & Podgursky, M. (2000) Reforming teacher preparation and licensing: what is the evidence? *Teachers College Record*, 102(1), 5–27.

Beck, C. & Kosnick, C. (2002) Components of a good practicum placement: student teacher perceptions. *Teacher Education Quarterly*, 29(2), 81–98.

Berliner, D. (2000) A personal response to those who bash teacher education. *Journal of Teacher Education*, 51(5), 358–371.

Berry, B., Hoke, M., & Hirsch, E. (2004) The search for highly qualified teachers. *Phi Delta Kappan*, 85(9), 684–689.

Cobb, B. R., Shaw, R., Millard, M., & Bomotti, S. (1999) An examination of Colorado's teacher licensure testing. *The Journal of Educational Research*, 92, 161–175.

Cochran-Smith, M. (1991) Reinventing student teaching. *Journal of Teacher Education*, 42, 104–118.

Cochran-Smith, M. (2001a) Reforming teacher education: competing agendas. *Journal of Teacher Education*, 52(4), 263–265.

Cochran-Smith, M. (2001b) The outcomes question in teacher education. *Teaching and Teacher Education*, 17(5), 527–546.

Cochran-Smith, M. (2004) Taking stock in 2004: teacher education in dangerous times. *Journal of Teacher Education*, (55)1, 3–7.

Cochran-Smith, M. & Fries, K. (2005) Researching teacher education in changing times: politics and paradigms. In M. Cochran-Smith & K. Zeichner (eds.), *Studying teacher education: the report of the AERA panel on research and teacher education* (pp. 69–110). Mahwah, NJ: Erlbaum.

Cochran-Smith, M. & Zeichner, K. (2005) *Studying teacher education: the report of the AERA panel on research and teacher education.* Mahwah, NJ: Erlbaum.

Conant, J. B. (1964) *The education of American teachers.* NY: McGraw-Hill.

Darling-Hammond, L. (2000) Teacher quality and student achievement: a review of state policy evidence. *Education Policy Analysis Archives*, 8(1). Retrieved May 1, 2006, from http://epaa.asu.edu/epaa/v8n1

Darling-Hammond, L. (2001) *The research and rhetoric on teacher certification: a response to "teacher certification reconsidered."* Retrieved June 15, 2006 from http://www.nctaf.org/documents/nctaf/abell_response.pdf

Darling-Hammond, L. & Cobb, V. (1995) The changing context of teacher education. In F. Murray (ed.), *The teacher educator's handbook: building a knowledge base for the preparation of teachers* (pp. 14–53). San Francisco: Jossey-Bass.

Darling-Hammond, L. & Youngs, P. (2002). Defining "highly qualified teachers": what does "scientifically-based research" actually tell us? *Educational Researcher*, 31(9), 13–25.

Darling-Hammond, L., Chung, R., & Frelow, F. (2002) Variation in teacher preparation: how well do different pathways prepare teachers to teach? *Journal of Teacher Education*, 53(4), 286–302.

Dubetz, N., Turley, S., & Erickson, M. (1997) Dilemmas of assessment and evaluation in preservice teacher education. In A. L. Goodwin (ed.), *Assessment for equity and inclusion: embracing all our children* (pp. 197–210). New York: Routledge.

Educational Testing Service (2005) The Praxis series: state requirements. Retrieved July 6, 2005, from http://www.ets.org/portal/site/ets/menuitem

Farkas, S. & Johnson, J. (1997) *Different drummers: how teachers of teachers view public education*. New York: Public Agenda.

Fetler, M. (2001) Student mathematics achievement test scores, dropout rates, and teacher characteristics. *Teacher Education Quarterly*, 28(1), 151–168.

Garcia, P. A. (1987) A study on teacher competency testing and test validation with implications for minorities and the results and implication of the use of the Pre-Professional Skills Test (PPST) as a screening device for entrance into teacher education programs in Texas (ERIC Document Reproduction Service No. ED270389).

Goldhaber, D. & Brewer, D. J. (1995) Why don't schools and teachers seem to matter? Assessing the impact of unobservables on educational productivity. *Journal of Human Resources*, 32(3), 505–523.

Goldhaber, D. D. & Brewer, D. J. (2000) Does teacher certification matter? High school certification status and student achievement. *Educational Evaluation and Policy Analysis*, 22, 129–145.

Goodlad, J. I. (1990) *Teachers for our nation's schools*. San Francisco: Jossey-Bass.

Goodwin, A. L. (2002a) The case of one child: making the shift from personal knowledge to professionally informed practice. *Teaching Education*, 13(2), 137–154.

Goodwin, A. L. (2002b) The social/political construction of low teacher expectations for children of color: re-examining the achievement gap. *Journal of Thought*, 37(4), 83–103.

Gray, J. (1998, April) *Paradox and pathos: who fails the preservice teacher?* Paper presented at the annual meeting of the American Educational Research Association, San Diego, CA.

Haberman, M. (1983) Research on preservice laboratory and clinical experiences: implications for teacher education. In K. R. Howey & W. E. Gardner (eds.), *The education of teachers: a look ahead* (pp. 98–117). New York: Longman.

Hess, F. (2004) *Common sense school reform*. New York: Palgrave Macmillan.

Hinchman, K. & Oyler, C. (2000) Us and them: finding irony in our teaching methods. *Journal of Curriculum Studies*, 32(4), 495–508.

Hodenfield, G. K. & Stinnett, T. M. (1961) *The education of teachers*. Englewood Cliffs, NJ: Prentice-Hall.

Holt-Reynolds, D. (1999) Good readers, good teachers? Subject matter expertise as a challenge in learning to teach. *Harvard Educational Review*, 69(1), 29–50.

Howey, K. R. (1983) Teacher education: an overview. In K. R. Howey & W. E. Gardner (eds.), *The education of teachers: a look ahead* (pp. 6–39). New York: Longman.

Johnson, J. & Yates, J. (1982) *A national survey of student teaching programs*. DeKalb, IL: Northern Illinois University (ERIC Document Reproduction Service NO. ED232963).

Kanstoroom, M. & Finn, C. E. (1999) *Better teachers, better schools*. Washington, DC: Thomas B. Fordham Foundation.

Knudson, R. E. & Turley, S. (2000) University supervisors and at-risk student teachers. *Journal of Research and Development in Education*, 33(3), 175–186.

Koerner, J. D. (1968) *Who controls American education?* Boston: Beacon Press.

Koerner, M., Rust, F. O., & Baumgartner, F. (2002) Exploring roles in student teaching placements. *Teacher Education Quarterly*, 29(2), 35–58

LaBoskey, V. K., & Richert, A. E. (2002) Identifying good student teaching placements: a programmatic perspective. *Teacher Education Quarterly*, 29(2), 1–34.

Lasley, T., Bainbridge, W.L., & Berry, B. (2002) Improving teacher quality: ideological perspectives and policy prescriptions. *Educational Forum*, 67(1), 14–25.

Levin, R. A. (1990) Recurring themes and variations. In J. I. Goodlad, R. Soder, & K. A. Sirotnik (eds.), *Places where teachers are taught* (pp. 40–83). San Francisco: Jossey-Bass.

Melnick, S. (1996) Reforming teacher education through legislation: a case study from Florida.

In K. Zeichner, S. Melnick, & M. L. Gomez (eds.), *Currents of reform in preservice teacher education* (pp. 30–61). NY: Teachers College Press.

Memory, D. M., Coleman, C. L., & Watkins, S. D. (2003) Possible tradeoffs in raising basic skills cutoff scores for teacher licensure: a study with implications for participation of African Americans in teaching. *Journal of Teacher Education*, 54(3), 217–227.

Mikitovics, A. (2002) Pre-professional Skills Test scores as college of education admission criteria. *Journal of Educational Research*, 95(4), 215–223.

Mitchell, R. & Barth, P. (1999). How teacher licensing tests fall short. *Thinking K-16*, 3(1), 3–23.

Monk, D. H. (1994) Subject area preparation of secondary mathematics and science teachers. *Economics of Education Review*, 13(2), 125–145.

National Commission on Teaching and America's Future (1996) *What matters most: teaching for America's future*. New York: Author.

National Commission on Teaching and America's Future (1997) *Doing what matters most: investing in teacher quality*. New York: Author.

Oyler, C., Jennings, G., & Lozada, P. (2001) Silenced gender: the construction of a male primary educator. *Teaching and Teacher Education*, 17, 367–379.

Page, M. L., Rudney, G. L., & Marxen, C. E. (2004) Leading preservice teachers to water . . . and helping them drink: how candidate teachability affects the gatekeeping and advocacy roles of teacher educators. *Teacher Education Quarterly*, 31(2) 25–41.

Paris, C. & Gespass, S. (2001) Examining the mismatch between learner-centered teaching and teacher-centered supervision. *Journal of Teacher Education*, 52(5), 398–412.

Raths, J. & Lyman, F. (2003) Summative evaluation of student teachers: an enduring problem. *Journal of Teacher Education*, 54(3), 206–216.

Schneider, B. L. (1987) Tracing the provenance of teacher education. In T. Popkewitz (ed.), *Critical studies in teacher education* (pp. 211–241). London: Falmer Press.

Shiveley, J. M. & Poetter, T. S. (2002) Exploring clinical, on-site supervision in a school-university partnership. *The Teacher Educator*, 37(4), 282–301.

Shulman, L. (1987) Knowledge and teaching: foundations of the new reform. *Harvard Educational Review*, 51, 1–22.

Strosnider, R. & Blanchett, W. J. (2003) A closer look at assessment and entrance requirements: implications for recruitment and retention of African American special educators. *Teacher Education and Special Education*, 26(4), 304–314.

Sudzina, M. R. & Knowles, J. G. (1993) Personal, professional and contextual circumstances of student teachers who "fail": setting a course for understanding failure in teacher education. *Journal of Teacher Education*, 44(4), 254–262.

Tom, A. R. (1996) External influences on teacher education programs: national accreditation and state certification. In K. Zeichner, S. Melnick and M. L. Gomez (eds.), *Currents of reform in preservice teacher education* (pp. 11–29). NY: Teachers College Press.

U.S. Department of Education, Office of Postsecondary Education, Office of Policy Planning and Innovation (2002) *Meeting the highly qualified teachers challenge: the secretary's annual report on teacher quality*, Washington, DC: Author.

Walsh, K. (2001) *Teacher certification reconsidered: stumbling for quality*. Baltimore, MD: Abell Foundation.

Wayne, A. R. & Youngs, P. (2003) Teacher characteristics and student achievement gains: a review. *Review of Educational Research*, 73(1), 89–122.

Weitman, C. J. & Colbert, R. P. (2003) *Are elementary teacher education programs the real problem of unqualified teachers?* Paper presented at the Annual Meeting of American Association of Colleges for Teacher Education, New Orleans, LA (ERIC Document Reproduction Service No. ED346082).

Wenglinksy, H. (2002) How schools matter: the link between teacher classroom practices and student academic performance. *Education Policy Analysis Achives*, (10)12. Retrieved April 25, 2006 from http://epaa.asu.edu/epaa/v10n12/.

Wertheim, C., Vogel, S. A., & Brulle, A. R. (1998). Students with learning disabilities in teacher education programs. *Annals of Dyslexia*, 48(1), 293–309.

Wilson, S. M. & Youngs, P. (2005) Research on accountability processes in teacher education. In M. Cochran-Smith & K. Zeichner (eds.) *Studying teacher education: the report of the AERA Panel on Research and Teacher Education* (pp. 591–643). Mahwah, NJ: Lawrence Erlbaum Associates.

Zeichner, K. (1996) Designing educative practicum experiences for prospective teachers. In K. Zeichner, S. Melnick, & M. L. Gomez (eds.), *Currents of reform in preservice teacher education* (pp. 215–234). NY: Teachers College Press.

Zeichner, K. (2006) Reflections of a university-based teacher educator on the future of college- and university-based teacher education. *Journal of Teacher Education*, 57(3), 326–340.

Zumwalt, K. K. & Craig, E. (2005) Teachers' characteristics: research on the indicators of quality. In M. Cochran-Smith & K. Zeichner (eds.) *Studying teacher education: the report of the AERA Panel on Research and Teacher Education* (pp. 157–260). Mahwah, NJ: Lawrence Erlbaum Associates.

APPENDIX 1

Gatekeeping in teacher education
Conversations protocol

Approximate number of students your institution admits each year to teacher preparation programs:

Approximate number of teachers your institution certifies each year:

Who makes admissions decisions (for teacher preparation programs)?

Who makes student teaching placement decisions—selection and assignment?

1 *Requirements and process for entrance in the elementary teacher preparation program*

- What are the minimum requirements for acceptance into your program (e.g. GPA, GRE/SATs, other test scores, experience with children, experience in urban settings, strong writing, dispositions, certain/prerequisite coursework, faculty recommendation, other)?
- If there are any special steps involved in the acceptance process (interview, entrance portfolio, group exercise, etc.), what are they?
- If you had to say the two most important qualities/characteristics/dispositions, and/or experiences, you look for in prospective teachers, what would these be?

2 *Gatekeeping as students progress through the elementary teacher preparation program*

- What are the gates (assessments that determine continuation in the program)?
- Have there been students who did not continue in the program and/or were not recommended for certification? At what points/stages in the program were they asked/did they choose not to continue?
- Have there been students who did complete the program and were recommended for certification, but required special support/intervention/extra time in order to be successful? What did these interventions entail? (List.)

3 *Problems, dilemmas, and challenges*

- What types of problems/dilemmas/challenges have you dealt with in the past few years related to candidates readiness to teach? (List.)

Part 4
Artifacts

4.1 Meeting the highly qualified teachers challenge

The secretary's annual report on teacher quality

U.S. Department of Education
Rod Paige
Secretary
2002 Executive Summary

Source: U.S. Department of Education, Office of Postsecondary Education, Office of Policy Planning and Innovation, *Meeting the Highly Qualified Teachers Challenge: The Secretary's Annual Report on Teacher Quality*, Washington, DC, 2002, pp. vii–9

THE TITLE II REPORTING SYSTEM

Under the 1998 reauthorization of Title II of the *Higher Education Act*, the secretary of education is required to issue annual reports to Congress on the state of teacher quality nationwide. *Meeting the Highly Qualified Teachers Challenge* is the inaugural report on this important issue. The 1998 reauthorization also established a reporting system for states and institutions of higher education to collect information on the quality of their teacher training programs. Data collected under the Title II reporting system are available at www.title2.org and include information on state teacher certification requirements, the performance of prospective teachers on state licensure tests and the number of teachers hired on temporary or emergency certificates.

THE VITAL ROLE OF TEACHERS IN LEAVING NO CHILD BEHIND

As President Bush said recently, "We give our teachers a great responsibility: to shape the minds and hopes of our children. We owe them our thanks and our praise and our support." Because of the vital role that teachers play in the lives of our children, the No Child Left Behind Act requires that all teachers in core academic subjects be highly qualified by the end of the 2005–2006 school year.

As part of the new law, Congress defines highly qualified teachers as those who not only possess full state certification but also have solid content knowledge of the subjects they teach. For example, beginning Fall 2002, all new elementary school teachers will have to pass tests in subject knowledge and teaching skills in math, reading, and writing, while new middle and high school teachers must pass rigorous subject-matter tests or have the equivalent of an undergraduate major, graduate degree or advanced certification in their respective fields. As this report details, research suggests teachers with strong academic backgrounds in their subjects are more likely to boost student performance.

The Title II reporting system reveals that states have a long way to go in meeting these requirements, largely because of states' outdated certification systems. Many academically accomplished college graduates and mid-career professionals with strong subject matter backgrounds are often dissuaded from entering teaching because the entry requirements are so rigid. At the same time, too many individuals earn certification even though their own content knowledge is weak. States' systems seem to maintain low standards and high barriers at the same time.

A BROKEN SYSTEM

The data collected for this report suggest that schools of education and formal teacher training programs are failing to produce the types of highly qualified teachers that the No Child Left Behind Act demands. Some highlights from the Title II reporting system:

- Only 23 states to date have implemented teacher standards tied to their respective academic content standards for grades K-12.
- Academic standards for teachers are low. On one popular teacher licensure test used by 29 states, only one state set its passing score near the national average in reading, while 15 set their respective passing scores below the 25th percentile. On math and writing tests, only one state set its passing score above the national average. Not surprisingly, more than 90 percent of teachers pass these tests.
- Forty-five states have developed alternative routes into the profession to bypass some of the burdensome requirements of the traditional system. While performance on licensure tests is higher among alternative route teachers than traditionally prepared teachers in most states, alternative routes are still larded with a variety of requirements.
- States are increasingly relying on teachers who are hired on waivers and lack full certification (a practice that is to be phased out under the new law). Nationwide, 6 percent of teachers lack full certification, but the share of uncertified teachers is higher in high- poverty schools and certain fields like special education, math and science.

ENSURING A HIGH QUALITY TEACHER IN EVERY CLASSROOM

Data collected for this report, and outside sources, confirm that states have a long way to go in aligning their certification regimes with the requirements of the No Child Left Behind Act. In order to comply with the new law, states and universities may well have to transform their preparation and certification systems, by basing their programs on rigorous academic content, eliminating cumbersome requirements not based on scientific evidence and doing more to attract highly qualified candidates from a variety of fields.

Across the country, there are several promising experiments that recruit highly qualified candidates who are interested in teaching but did not attend schools of education and place them quickly into high-need schools, providing training, support and mentoring. If states are to meet the requirements of the *No Child Left Behind Act* these programs should become models for the future, as states make it less burdensome for exceptional candidates to find teaching positions in our nation's schools.

In order to leave no child behind, we need a highly qualified teacher in every classroom. Clearly, states and universities have much work to do in the years ahead. This report points the way.

INTRODUCTION

Background on the secretary's report

Few adults are as important in the lives of children as teachers are. Ensuring that all students have access to highly qualified teachers is of paramount importance, especially for disadvantaged children. Fulfilling the promise of leaving no child behind rests on our ability to staff our schools with the best teachers our nation can produce.

Recognizing the vital role that teachers play: Congress recently required the secretary of education to issue an annual report on the state of teacher quality and teacher preparation in the 50 states. This is the first full report submitted to Congress on these topics.

This report contains a variety of data collected under the requirements of Title II of the Higher Education Act. Last amended in 1998, Title II requires three annual reports on teacher preparation. First, institutions of higher education are to report various data to states. These data include the pass rates on state certification and licensure examinations of students completing their teacher-training programs.

Second, using reports from institutions of higher education as well as other sources, states are to report the following information to the U.S. Department of Education:

- state certification and licensure requirements for completers of traditional and alternative teacher preparation programs;
- statewide pass rates on the most recent state assessments of graduates of teacher preparation programs, pass rates disaggregated by institution, and quartile rankings of their institutions based on their pass rates;
- the number of teachers on waivers or emergency and temporary permits;
- Information on teacher standards and their alignment with student standards; and
- criteria for identifying low-performing schools of education.

Finally, the secretary of education is to report to Congress on national patterns and their implications (the topics of this document and related material found at www.title2.org).

Outline of the secretary's report

This report attempts to do more than present the key findings from the Title II reporting system. It also seeks to place these findings within the context of state and federal policy and rigorous scientific research. Here is a brief overview:

Chapter 1: "The Quest for Highly Qualified Teachers." This chapter will provide a summary of the sweeping reforms enacted by the No Child Left Behind Act, especially the new requirement that all teachers be "highly qualified" by 2005–2006. It also draws upon solid research to answer the question: What do we know about highly qualified teachers?

Chapter 2: "Preparing and Certifying Highly Qualified Teachers: Today's Broken System and Its Alternative." Chapter 2 investigates how teacher recruitment, preparation and certification systems in place today impede the development of highly qualified teachers and presents a more promising model for the future.

Chapter 3: "Are States Doing Enough to Produce Highly Qualified Teachers? Lessons from the Title II Reporting System." Chapter 3 presents findings from the Title II reporting system, as well as rigorous evidence from other sources, about the "state of the states" vis-à-vis the preparation and certification of highly qualified teachers.

Chapter 4: "Looking Forward: A Highly Qualified Teacher in Every Classroom." The concluding chapter presents some final insights into the state of teacher quality today and offers suggestions for states as they seek to meet the requirements of the No Child Left Behind Act to provide a highly qualified teacher in every classroom.

CHAPTER 1: THE QUEST FOR HIGHLY QUALIFIED TEACHERS

The No Child Left Behind Act is the most fundamental transformation of federal education policy in at least 35 years. Upon its signing, President George W. Bush said: "Today begins a new era, a new time in public education in our country. As of this hour, America's schools will be on a new path of reform and a new path of results." Congress signaled its support by passing the law by an overwhelming bipartisan majority.

The No Child Left Behind Act brings new thinking and new resources to the challenge of educating all of the nation's children. Many of the new ideas and new funds are directed at the issue of improving teacher quality. Here is a snapshot of some of the most important initiatives in this area:

Teacher quality state grants: under the new law, states and school districts will be eligible for almost $3 billion in flexible grants to improve the quality of teachers and principals using research-based strategies. In return, districts must demonstrate annual progress in ensuring that all teachers teaching in core academic subjects are highly qualified.

Reading first: this major new initiative is aimed at helping every student become a successful reader by the end of third grade. The president has requested $1 billion for this program in 2003. Most of these funds will support professional development in research-based reading instruction.

Troops to teachers and transition to teaching: both programs seek to streamline the entry of talented mid-career professionals into the classroom through alternate routes to certification.

Other formula-based programs will also provide substantial resources for professional development, including Title I ($11.4 billion proposed for 2003), Educational Technology State Grants ($700 million) and the English Language Acquisition State Grants ($665 million). Access to information about all U.S. Department of Education teacher quality grants is available through a searchable database at http://www.ed.gov/offices/OESE/TPR/index.html.

In addition, the president's budget for 2003 calls for a major expansion of loan forgiveness for teachers serving in high-poverty schools, from the current maximum of $5,000 to a maximum of $17,500.

Demanding highly qualified teachers

These bold initiatives represent the federal government's serious commitment to improving teacher quality. But perhaps the most dramatic policy shift in No Child Left Behind is the new requirement that all teachers of core academic subjects be "highly qualified." What are the consequences of this new requirement? For school districts receiving Title I funds, the consequences are dramatic and immediate. Starting in the coming school year—that is, Fall 2002—Title I funds may not be used to hire new teachers in targeted assistance Title I programs who do not meet the definition of "highly qualified." Though final regulations are forthcoming, the Department has indicated that Title I schools using a schoolwide approach may not hire *any* new teachers to teach in the core academic areas who are not highly qualified. Schools using a pullout approach may not use their Title I funds to support teachers who do not meet the definition of "highly qualified." School districts that are out of compliance could lose their Title I dollars.

Non-Title I schools will be affected as well. States must ensure that by the end of the 2005–2006 school year, all teachers teaching in core academic subjects must be highly qualified. In addition, states must ensure that districts make annual progress toward that end.

With such large consequences at stake, understanding the definition of "highly qualified" teachers becomes imperative. It is worth quoting part of the No Child Left Behind Act, Public Law 107–110, Section 9 101(23). First, it establishes the definition of "highly qualified" for all teachers of core academic subjects:

The term "highly qualified"—

(A) when used with respect to any public elementary school or secondary school teacher teaching in a State, means that—

(i) the teacher has obtained full State certification as a teacher (including certification obtained through alternative routes to certification) or passed the State teacher licensing examination, and holds a license to teach in such State, except that when used with respect to any teacher teaching in a public charter school, the term means that the teacher meets the requirements set forth in the State's public charter school law; and

(ii) the teacher has not had certification or licensure requirements waived on an emergency, temporary, or provisional basis;

Therefore, except for charter school teachers, all teachers of core academic subjects must have full state certification or licensure to be considered "highly qualified." But new teachers of core academic subjects face even stricter requirements:

[The term "highly qualified"—]

(B) when used with respect to—

(i) an elementary school teacher who is new to the profession, means that the teacher—

(I) holds at least a bachelor's degree; and

(II) has demonstrated, by passing a rigorous State test, subject knowledge and teaching skills in reading, writing, mathematics, and other areas of the basic elementary school curriculum (which may consist of passing a State-required certification or licensing test or tests in reading, writing, mathematics, and other areas of the basic elementary school curriculum); or

(ii) a middle or secondary school teacher who is new to the profession, means that the teacher holds at least a bachelor's degree and has demonstrated a high level of competency in each of the academic subjects in which the teacher teaches by—

(I) passing a rigorous State academic subject test in each of the academic subjects in which the teacher teaches (which may consist of a passing level of performance on a State-required certification or licensing test or tests in each of the academic subjects in which the teacher teaches); or

(II) successful completion, in each of the academic subjects in which the teacher teaches, of an academic major, a graduate degree, coursework equivalent to an undergraduate academic major, or advanced certification or credentialing;

Notice that these additional requirements focus entirely on rigorous subject matter preparation, demonstrated either through adequate performance on a test or through successful completion of a major, graduate degree, or advanced credentialing. Next, the law provides further detail on the definition of "highly qualified" as it applies to existing teachers of core academic subjects:

[The term "highly qualified"—]

(C) when used with respect to an elementary, middle, or secondary school teacher who is not new to the profession, means that the teacher holds at least a bachelor's degree and—

(i) has met the applicable standard in clause (i) or (ii) of subparagraph (B), which includes an option for a test; or

(ii) demonstrates competence in all the academic subjects in which the teacher teaches based on a high objective uniform State standard of evaluation that—

(I) is set by the State for both grade appropriate academic subject matter knowledge and teaching skills;

(II) is aligned with challenging State academic content and student academic achievement standards and developed in consultation with core content specialists, teachers, principals, and school administrators;

(III) provides objective, coherent information about the teacher's attainment of core content knowledge in the academic subjects in which a teacher teaches;

(IV) is applied uniformly to all teachers in the same academic subject and the same grade level throughout the State;

(V) takes into consideration, but not be based primarily on, the time the teacher has been teaching in the academic subject;

(VI) is made available to the public upon request; and

(VII) may involve multiple, objective measures of teacher competency.

Again, the focus of the law is on "content knowledge." Congress has made it clear that it considers content knowledge to be of paramount importance. The law also implies, through these detailed definitions, that Congress suspects that current state certification systems are not doing enough to ensure preparation in solid content knowledge—otherwise the definition could have ended after subparagraph (A). As we will learn, from both research and the Title II data, these concerns are well founded.

What we know about highly qualified teachers

By adding strict new mandates about "highly qualified" teachers, Congress indicated the importance of teacher quality in improving the nation's schools. By focusing its definition of "highly qualified" teachers on preparation in content knowledge, as opposed to components such as pedagogy or teaching practicums, it expressed its opinion of what matters most. Is teacher quality an important indicator of school success? Does content knowledge relate to academic achievement? Aren't other things, like methods courses or practice teaching, essential as well? Let us turn to the scientific evidence for guidance.

Evidence that good teachers matter

For many years, research has found teacher quality to be a key determinant of student success. Large-scale studies suggest that teacher quality is more closely related to student achievement than other factors, such as class size, spending and instructional materials. As part of his landmark 1966 study, *Equality of Educational Opportunity*, sociologist James Coleman noted that among African American students, there was a correlation between student achievement and teachers' scores on vocabulary tests. Among students generally, however, Coleman found no discernable pattern.

But Coleman's evaluation was aggregated at the school level, meaning important variations among individual teachers and classrooms within the same school were not measured. In recent years, a new approach to measuring teacher quality has been developed, focusing on the value that teachers provide to individual students in their classrooms. By testing students annually and comparing the growth of individual students and individual classrooms, researchers can pinpoint the effect teachers are having on their students. Because the analysis is focused on learning gains, and not absolute test scores, the influence of background characteristics like socioeconomic status can be parsed out. Not surprisingly, researchers have found that some teachers are much more effective than others.

Value-added measures also permit researchers to examine the cumulative effects a string of high-quality versus low-quality teachers can have on student performance over several years. Some of the best research on this subject has been done by statistician William Sanders in

Tennessee. The state of Tennessee evaluates all of its teachers based on the learning gains individual students make while in their respective classrooms. Using this information, Sanders categorized the state's teachers into quintiles based on the performance of their students. As part of his research, he tracked two comparable sets of third- graders: one group which had three successive teachers from the top quintile, and the other that had three successive teachers from the bottom quintile. By the end of fifth grade, the set with the least effective teachers posted academic achievement gains of 29 percent, compared to gains of 83 percent by the set assigned to the most effective teachers—a gap of more than 50 percent. Moreover, Sanders found that the effect was both additive and cumulative, denying students the full opportunities they might have had to acquire an excellent education.

Similar studies in Boston and Dallas have confirmed these findings. According to some estimates, the difference in annual achievement growth between having a good teacher and having a bad teacher can be more than one grade level of achievement in academic performance. The implication is that not only does teacher quality matter—it matters a lot. Students unfortunate enough to face several bad teachers in a row face devastating odds against success.

Evidence of the importance of verbal ability and content knowledge

Ever since the publication of the Coleman report, studies have consistently documented the important connection between a teacher's verbal and cognitive abilities and student achievement. Teachers' verbal ability appears to be especially important at the elementary level, perhaps because this is when children typically learn to read. Stanford University economist Eric Hanushek, who has conducted extensive academic literature reviews on teacher quality, said, "[P]erhaps the closest thing to a consistent conclusion across studies is the finding that teachers who perform well on verbal ability tests do better in the classroom [in boosting student achievement]."

More recent studies suggest that subject-matter background can also have a positive effect on student performance. Research has generally shown that high school math and science teachers who have a major in the subjects they teach elicit greater gains from their students than out-of-field teachers, controlling for student's prior academic achievement and socioeconomic status. These same studies also suggest that possessing an undergraduate major in math and science has a greater positive effect on student performance than certification in those subjects. Research has not always produced consistent results on the effects of teachers having a masters degree, but in the better designed studies the effects are weak, at best.

Yet even as research demonstrates the importance of content knowledge, new data from the National Center for Education Statistics (NCES) suggests that too many students, especially in the middle-school grades, have teachers who are not fully qualified in their subject areas. For example, in 1999–2000, 15 to 22 percent of middle-grade students in English, math and science had teachers who lacked a postsecondary major, minor or certification in the subject taught. In biology and life science, physical science and English as a Second Language (ESL) or bilingual education classes, the data are even more troubling. Between 30 and 40 percent of middle-grade students had teachers who lacked a major, minor or certification in these subjects.

The evidence on pedagogy and education degrees

This report shows that verbal ability and content knowledge of teachers have been linked to higher student achievement, but what about other attributes, like knowledge of pedagogy, degrees in education, or amount of time spent practice teaching? After all, these are the requirements that make up the bulk of current teacher certification regimes.

There is a great deal of contention surrounding the evidence on these components, with some studies linking these requirements to improved student achievement. However, the quality of many of these studies has been called into question. A report by the Abell Foundation evaluated approximately 175 studies spanning the past 50 years, all of which purported to demonstrate a connection between certification and improved student outcomes. The analysis found that virtually all of these evaluations were not scientifically rigorous, did not use generally accepted statistical techniques to gather data and relied too much on anecdotal evidence.

Scientific evidence also raises questions about the value of attendance in schools of education. In a recent study, economists Dan Goldhaber and Dominic Brewer found that while certified math and science teachers outperformed those who lack certification (as measured by their students' achievement), there was no statistical difference in performance between teachers who attended conventional training programs and received traditional teaching licenses versus those who did not complete such programs and were teaching on emergency or temporary certificates.

Conclusion: the challenge of highly qualified teachers

As this chapter made clear, the federal government is serious about raising the quality of the nation's teaching force. And because the best available research shows that solid verbal ability and content knowledge are what matters most, it is clear that Congress wrote its definition of "highly qualified teachers" wisely.

What are the implications of this new law for state policy? How can states design preparation and certification systems that produce enough highly qualified teachers for every classroom? These and other questions will be answered in Chapter 2.

4.2 Assessment of diversity in America's teaching force

A call to action

Presented by the National Collaborative on Diversity in the Teaching Force

Source: National Collaborative on Diversity in the Teaching Force, *Assessment of Diversity in America's Teaching Force: A Call to Action*. Washington, DC: National Education Association, October 2004, pp. 3–10

INTRODUCTION

In late 2001, Congress passed the reauthorization of the Elementary and Secondary Education Act (ESEA), also known as the No Child Left Behind Act (NCLB). The goal of this legislation is to improve the academic performance of all students, while simultaneously closing achievement gaps that persist between students from different ethnic groups and economic backgrounds. The law includes a number of elements considered essential for reaching this goal, including ensuring that all teachers are "highly qualified." Yet, despite this focus on teacher quality, little attention has been paid to the issues of cultural competence and diversity in the teacher workforce—critical factors in improving the performance of students of color.

To examine the relationships among educational opportunity, educational achievement, educator diversity, and teacher quality, more than 20 of the nation's leading education and advocacy organizations came together in November 2001 for a three-day conference entitled "Losing Ground: A National Summit on Diversity in the Teaching Force."

Focusing specifically on the roles ethnicity and cultural competence play in student achievement, participants reviewed research on the impact of culturally responsive pedagogy on children. They also studied demographic data on the growing diversity of America's schoolchildren and the static composition of the teaching force. After this review, participants voiced widespread concern about these demographic disparities and their negative impact on the quality of education for all children. In addition, participants noted that although teacher quality has been accepted and internalized as a mantra for school reform, the imperative for diversity is often marginalized rather than accepted as central to the quality equation in teaching.

As a result, the participating organizations agreed on the need to create the National Collaborative on Diversity in the Teaching Force (the Collaborative). The Collaborative's primary mission is to infuse the issues of teacher diversity and cultural competence into the education policy debate, at both state and national levels, with the same vigor and frequency as the issue of teacher quality.

Since the 2001 Summit, partner organizations have worked to achieve that mission. While the organizations vary in size, years of existence, number of staff, geographical location, and budget, they are committed to the following goals:

- coalescing and increasing the research base on culturally responsive teaching;
- identifying and eliminating obstacles to expanding the pool of prospective teachers of color and to increasing the cultural competence of all teachers;

- insisting that resources needed for successful teaching be equitable, no matter what school the teachers work in; and
- demanding that significantly greater resources be targeted to the recruitment, preparation, and support of a teaching cadre that is fully qualified, ethnically diverse, and culturally competent.

However, as controversies continue to swirl around NCLB and achievement gaps continue to widen in too many communities, the Collaborative is more concerned than ever that the issues of diversity and cultural competence in the teaching force have not received the attention they deserve from policymakers.

Recognizing the dearth of meaningful research on the number and impact of teachers of color, as well as on state efforts to recruit and retain teachers of color, the Collaborative commissioned three significant reports (These reports are available online at the primary partners web sites):

- *The Presence and Performance of Teachers of Color in the Profession* (Gay *et al.*, 2003)
- *Recruiting Teachers of Color: A 50-State Survey of State Policies* (Education Commission of the States, 2003)
- *Recruiting Teachers of Color: A Program Overview* (Education Commission of the States, 2003)

These reports, along with the expertise and vision of the members of the Collaborative, form the foundation of this assessment, which is organized into the following sections:

I   The Current State of Diversity and Cultural Competence in the Classroom briefly addressed the representation of teachers of color in the teaching force and their impact on student achievement.
II   The Future of Diversity in Public School Classrooms looks at efforts taken by states to recruit a diverse teaching force, trends in test scores for teacher candidates of color, and the implications of NCLB.
III Conclusion and Implications for Research and Policymakers summarizes the beliefs of the Collaborative and provides a list of recommendations for increasing the percentages of teachers of color in the workforce.
IV   The appendices include a list of 2001 Summit participants and a list of the Collaborative's primary partners.

Taken together, these findings present an important first step toward creating a truly qualified, diverse teacher workforce that meets the needs and potential of all public school students. Additional research is needed, but time is passing quickly, and action is vital. We cannot continue to wait as more children of color fail to reach their potential and as fewer teachers of color join and remain in the education community.

I THE CURRENT STATE OF DIVERSITY AND CULTURAL COMPETENCE IN THE CLASSROOM

The challenges of ensuring teacher excellence and diversity are not new. However, only recently have these issues begun to garner the public attention needed to bring about actual change in the composition of the teacher workforce.

Representation of teachers of color in the workforce

According to the National Center for Education Statistics (NCES, 2003), the number of minority teachers (teachers of color) nationwide is not representative of the number of minority students (students of color). For example,

- In 2001–2002, data shows that 60 percent of public school students were White, 17 percent Black, 17 percent Hispanic, 4 percent Asian/Pacific Islander, and 1 percent American Indian/Alaska Native.
- In contrast, 2001 data shows that 90 percent of public school teachers were White, 6 percent Black, and fewer than 5 percent of other races.
- Some 40 percent of schools had no teachers of color on staff.

Digging beneath the surface of the data (NCES, 2003), further trends emerge.

- The percentage of teachers of color does not even approximate the percentage of students of color in any state with a sizable population of diverse residents except Hawaii. The District of Columbia also is an exception.
- Across the states, the larger the percentage of students of color is, the greater the disparity with the percentage of teachers of color. Ironically, these are the areas with the greatest need for teachers of color.
- Teachers of color come closest to having proportional representation in large, urban school districts.
- Most teachers of color are employed in schools that have 30 percent or more students of color. For American Indians/Alaska Natives, these schools are located in rural areas and small towns, rather than urban centers.
- Teachers of color tend to teach in schools that have large numbers of students from their own ethnic groups.
- Teachers of color are found in states and regions of the United States with large percentages of their own ethnic groups. Thus, the highest percentages of African American teachers are found in the Southeast, Latinos in the West and in the Northeast, American Indians/Alaska Natives in the central and western regions, and Asian Americans in the West. Attendance at colleges and schools of education follow similar patterns.
- Teachers of color largely are geographically isolated from each other and from their White colleagues, in terms of both where they enroll in teacher education programs and where they are employed.
- Within ethnic groups, teachers of color are about equally represented in elementary and secondary schools.

Furthermore, statistical projections show that while the percentage of students of color in public schools is expected to increase, the percentage of teachers of color is not expected to rise— unless action is taken on the state and national levels.

The impact of teachers of color on student achievement

Policymakers, teacher educators, members of ethnic communities, and school leaders agree that the education profession needs more teachers of color. More teachers of color would

- increase the number of role models for students of color;
- provide opportunities for all students to learn about ethnic, racial, and cultural diversity;
- be able to enrich diverse students' learning because of shared racial, ethnic, and cultural identities; and
- serve as cultural brokers, able not only to help students navigate their school environment and culture, but also to increase the involvement of other teachers and their students' parents.

Although their contributions are sometimes identified as having more of an impact on the social and relational areas than on academic performance, increasing the percentage of teachers of color in the workforce is connected directly to closing the achievement gap of students.

Most of the data currently available on connections between teachers of color and student performance are generated from small-scale qualitative research involving single or multiple case studies. These data focus on a number of significant, though under-recognized, school achievement markers, including attendance records, disciplinary referrals, dropout rates, overall satisfaction with school, self-concepts, cultural competence, and students' sense of the relevance of school.

While additional data about the positive impact of teachers of color on student achievement need to be gathered, the limited number of studies indicate that

- Students of color tend to have higher academic, personal, and social performance when taught by teachers from their own ethnic groups. (However, this finding does not suggest that culturally competent teachers could not achieve similar gains with students of color from different ethnic groups.)
- Teachers from different ethnic groups have demonstrated that when students of color are taught with culturally responsive techniques and with content-specific approaches usually reserved for the gifted and talented, their academic performance improves significantly.
- Teachers of color have higher performance expectations for students of color from their own ethnic group.

II THE FUTURE OF DIVERSITY IN PUBLIC SCHOOL CLASSROOMS

Efforts by states to recruit and retain teachers of color

States across the country are recognizing the urgent need to recruit and retain teachers of color and are implementing a variety of programs and policies that complement traditional teacher recruitment methods. Some of these approaches include the following:

- Alternative programs, in which teacher candidates are appointed as the teacher-of-record in a classroom after initial training of six months or less. These alternatively trained teachers tend to complete their preparation program while employed as teachers.
- Early outreach/precollegiate programs, which are designed to expose middle and high school students to teaching as a profession.
- Community college outreach programs, which steer teacher candidates toward completion of an associate's and then a bachelor's degree. Community colleges have proven to be a

highly effective resource for preparing new teachers—approximately 20 percent of the current teacher workforce began their education in community colleges.

- Paraeducator (often referred to as paraprofessionals or teachers' aides) outreach programs, which target and recruit paraeducators to become fully licensed teachers. In some states, these programs are called "career ladder" approaches.
- Scholarships, grants, and fellowships, which provide financial incentives and are among the most popular strategies to recruit teachers.
- Loans and loan forgiveness programs, which are offered by several states to help prospective teachers defray the cost of their education.

Testing among teacher candidates of color

Most states and schools of education require some form of standardized testing for entry into teacher education programs. As an exit criterion, a large number of states also require standardized testing of teacher candidates to assess their knowledge in subject matter areas that must be passed in order to become a licensed teacher. The majority of states use the Praxis series created by the Educational Testing Service—Praxis I is a basic skills test used for entry into teacher education programs and Praxis II is designed to assess the knowledge of beginning teachers in a specific subject or content area. It is important to understand that passing scores alone do not guarantee teachers will be highly effective, nor does failing the tests automatically mean teachers will be ineffective. However, the tests do assess what a beginning teacher should know.

Limited data are available on the testing results of teachers of color, partly because the national pool of teachers—both in the classroom and in the pipeline—contains far fewer teachers of color than teachers who are not of color. However, the data does reveal specific trends:

- In most instances, fewer than 50 percent of African Americans pass teacher tests. This pattern prevails across time, location, and types of tests.
- Overall, more teacher candidates of color pass Praxis II subject matter content tests than Praxis I basic skills tests. The pass rates on Praxis II are greater for secondary than for elementary teachers.
- All teacher candidates of color (African Americans, Asian Americans, Latino Americans, and American Indians/Alaska Natives) who passed both Praxis I and II scored much higher on the SAT than their ethnic group peers who did not pass. They also scored higher on the SAT than those in the general population who took Praxis I and II.
- There are positive correlations between SAT and ACT scores, grade point averages, and performance on teacher tests for all ethnic groups.
- Teacher candidates of color who took the SAT tend to perform better on the Praxis I certification tests than those who took the ACT college entrance examination. The reverse is true for Praxis II for all ethnic groups, except African Americans.

Clearly, much more research is needed on the impact of practices that may facilitate or obstruct the entry of teachers of color into the profession. Additional research is needed to find out why these disparities exist and what the best solutions are to closing this gap. The Collaborative is firmly committed to identifying and decreasing the obstacles that currently impede efforts to expand the pool of prospective teachers of color.

The implications of No Child Left Behind legislation

Since the No Child Left Behind legislation was passed in 2001, several substantive changes have been made, and additional revisions no doubt will take place in the coming years. Members of this Collaborative support the legislation's goals of improving student performance and closing achievement gaps. They particularly are interested in the timely, adequate provision of resources necessary for improving student achievement.

However, one of the resources necessary for improving the performance of students of color is a teacher workforce that is culturally competent and diverse. Even though the legislation calls for "highly qualified" teachers and leaves the actual implementation and assessment to each state, the logistics of this complex legislation continue to create significant barriers to recruiting teachers of color. The Collaborative is concerned about the long-term implications of this legislation if future revisions do not remove these barriers and clearly spell out cultural competence and diversity as critical elements of a highly-qualified teacher workforce.

III CONCLUSION AND IMPLICATIONS FOR RESEARCH AND POLICYMAKERS

The Collaborative believes that:

- Diversity and cultural competence are key factors in improving the quality of America's teaching force.
- The issues of teacher diversity and cultural competence must be infused into state and national education policy agendas.
- Teachers of color and culturally competent teachers must be actively recruited and supported.
- Barriers for candidates of color across the teacher development continuum must be identified and reduced.
- Institutional resources to meet the growing need for teachers of color must be increased.
- Toxic institutional and program practices—including institutional and individual racism—in schools and colleges must be eliminated.
- Highly qualified teachers must be equitably distributed to ensure that students in high-poverty and high-minority schools receive their fair share of the best and experienced teachers.

To do this, significantly greater resources need to be targeted to the recruitment, preparation, and support of a teaching cadre that is fully qualified, ethnically diverse, and culturally competent. Although the members of the Collaborative recognize that there is no "one-size-fits-all" solution, the following recommendations are a major step toward addressing this problem.

Federal, state, and local governments should:

- enact more legislation to increase and support the number of teachers of color both in the pipeline and in the classroom.
- provide additional, meaningful resources and financial support to programs that result in the successful recruitment and training of teachers of color.
- create policies to strengthen professional development programs for public school teachers in high-poverty, high-minority areas, with particular emphasis on cultural competency and mentoring.
- examine trends in teacher performance within different content areas.
- ensure that future teachers are trained with a solid, substantive curriculum, particularly in the social foundations of education. (Without understanding the historical, social, and political underpinnings of how disenfranchised groups have been systematically excluded from receiving a fair and equitable education, there will continue to be a shallow approach to understanding diversity issues.)

- encourage higher education institutions to use responsible recruitment strategies to increase the number of faculty of color in colleges and universities, particularly in colleges of education.
- provide a supportive environment at institutions of higher learning for culturally and linguistically diverse students and faculty.
- conduct research on how different ethnic groups are performing on different teacher tests as well as on who is not taking the tests and why they are not. In other words, are some prospective teachers of color leaving the field before testing because they are afraid of failing? Are some not even considering the profession because of the negative press around rates of failure by candidates of color?
- conduct research on successful efforts to increase the rate of test passage by teacher candidates of color and work with higher education institutions to develop, implement, and evaluate appropriate resources to help more teacher candidates of color pass tests.
- promote strategies for increased retention of both diverse students and diverse teachers.
- increase the amount and quality of research on all issues related to the presence, preparation, and performance of teachers of color and to culturally responsive teaching.
- include and maintain more detailed variables on race an ethnicity for all groups in research, policies, and practices about teacher education and student achievement.

The Collaborative urges all those involved in education and education policy to consider carefully the current research, to recognize the value and validity of diversity, and to join us in calling for a qualified and diverse teaching force for America's public schools.

4.3 African American Teacher, Samuel R. Ward

". . ., Samuel R. Ward, who had himself taught in blacks schools in both New Jersey and New York. He emphasized that blacks should insist on black teachers because blacks ought to support black talent."

(Mabee, 1979, p. 95)

Photo from: Mabee, C. (1979) *Black Education in New York State: From Colonial to Modern Times.* Syracuse, NY: Syracuse University Press.

4.4   First Mexican School

The first Mexican school in El Paso during the 1880s. Mexican American parents developed a school to teach English to Mexican students with limited English proficiency because the local El Paso school officials refused to teach English to Spanish-speaking students. The community turned to an elderly man named Olivas Villanueva Aoy, who agreed to open a private school with the sole purpose of teaching Mexican children English to prepare them for public schools. Historian Mario Garcia (1981) notes that by the 1890s Aoy, with the help of two Mexican assistants, was able to teach close to one hundred first and second graders.

(Text by Anthony L. Brown)

Photo from: Garcia, M. (1981) *Desert Immigrants: The Mexicans of El Paso, 1880–1920*. New Haven, CT: Yale University.

4.5   The Carlisle School

A Native American teacher at the Carlisle School during the early 1900s teaching American Indian weaving. The school during this period began to hire more Native American teachers and they often infused into the school curriculum the cultural and ethnic backgrounds of the students.

(Text by Anthony L. Brown)

Photo from: Witmer, L. (1993) *The Indian Industrial School: Carlisle, PA*. Carlisle, PA: Cumberland County Historical Society.
Permission to reprint from Cumberland County Historical Society, Carlisle, PA.

4.6 Asian American Scholar, Francis Chang

The teachers in the Chinese-language schools have a good many advantages over public school teachers in a matter of practical education for the Chinese children. They speak the children's language. They approach the parents easily and understand the pupils' home conditions, if they would like to do so. By their experience in China and in America, they should also be able to understand the needs of the children with regard to their future cultural and vocational possibilities. As Chinese parents generally respect the teachers, according to Chinese tradition, the teachers in the Chinese school should be in the position to determine what will be most practical and useful for the children to learn in school.

(Chang, 1934, pp. 542–543)

Chang, F. (1934) An accommodation program for second-generation Chinese. *Sociology and Social Research*. 18, 541–553.

4.7 INTASC model standards

INTASC, "Model standards for beginning teacher licensing, assessment and development: a resource for state dialogue"

Source: *INTASC*, Washington, DC: Council of Chief State School Officers, 1992

Principle 1:   Content knowledge
The teacher understands the central concepts, tools of inquiry, and structures of the discipline(s) he or she teaches and can create learning experiences that make these aspects of subject matter meaningful for students.

Principle 2:   Child development and learning
The teacher understands how children learn and develop, and can provide learning opportunities that support their intellectual, social, and personal development.

Principle 3:   Diverse learning styles
The teacher understands how students differ in their approaches to learning and creates instructional opportunities that are adapted to diverse learners.

Principle 4:   Instructional strategies
The teacher understands and uses a variety of instructional strategies to encourage students' development of critical thinking, problem solving, and performance skills.

Principle 5:   Learning environment
The teacher uses an understanding of individual and group motivation and behavior to create a learning environment that encourages positive social interaction, active engagement in learning, and self-motivation.

Principle 6:   Communication
The teacher uses knowledge of effective verbal, nonverbal, and media communication techniques to foster active inquiry, collaboration, and supportive interaction in the classroom.

Principle 7:   Instructional planning
The teacher plans instruction based upon knowledge of subject matter, students, the community, and curriculum goals.

Principle 8:   Assessment
The teacher understands and uses formal and informal assessment strategies to evaluate and ensure the continuous intellectual, social, and physical development of the learner.

Principle 9:   Professional development and reflection
The teacher is a reflective practitioner who continually evaluates the effects of his/her choices and actions on others (students, parents, and other professionals in the learning community) and who actively seeks out opportunities to grow professionally.

Principle 10:   Collaboration and relationships
The teacher fosters relationships with school colleagues, parents, and agencies in the larger community to support students 'learning and well-being.

4.8 Schoolteacher

Dan C. Lortie

Source: Dan C. Lortie, *Schoolteacher*. Chicago: University of Chicago Press, 1975, pp. 26–40 (notes pp. 261–262)

RECRUITMENT AND REAFFIRMATION

The attractions of teaching

We can find what occupational characteristics attract people to a given line of work by using a model of career decisions as choices among competing alternatives. In such a model a particular occupation is presumed to "win out" over competitors because it offers greater advantage to those making choices. To identify which characteristics elicit commitments, I questioned those within the occupation, asking them to describe the attractions they saw in it and to identify those which made it more attractive than the alternatives they seriously considered. I developed this approach during earlier work on legal careers (Lortie 1958).

This section has two major parts. In the first we will review data in which teachers described the attractions they saw in teaching; the data consist of intensive interviews in five towns in the Boston metropolitan area, hereafter referred to as "Five Towns" . . ., and national surveys conducted by the National Education Association (NEA).[1] Although the interviews were conducted and analyzed before I encountered the NEA surveys, there is sufficient convergence for joint use. The second part of the section concentrates specifically on the material benefits of teaching and their differential meaning for men and for women.

Five attractors to teaching

The interpersonal theme

One of the most obvious characteristics of teaching is that it calls for protracted contact with young people. To cite this as an attraction seems almost tautological, but this is not so when we compare teaching with other kinds of work; very few occupations involve such steady interaction with the young. It led the list of attractions among Five Towns teachers, although it is interesting that some respondents did not specify that the interactions were primarily with children—they simply said they liked "to work with people."[2]

"Desire to work with young people" led the selections of NEA respondents: 34 percent of the 2,316 teachers answering the questionnaire chose it. It appealed equally to men and women in the total sample, but 10 percent more elementary than secondary teachers checked it as their predominant reason for choosing teaching careers (NEA 1967, p. 47).

Contact with young people helps teaching in its competition for members; on reflection, we observe that it occupies a favored competitive position in this regard. Unlike other major middle-class occupations involving children, such as pediatric nursing and some kinds of social work, teaching provides the opportunity to work with children who are neither ill nor especially disadvantaged. Those who want such contact can visualize it taking place under "normal" conditions which do not include sickness, poverty, or emotional disturbance. The psychological needs which underlie an interest in working with children are undoubtedly varied and complex, and there is no research which justifies the concept of a single personality type among teachers (Getzels and Jackson 1963). The care of youngsters is generally said to be especially consistent with the social definition of women's work in our society. It is interesting therefore that the data do not show that women have a marked preference for this attraction. Perhaps it is a matter of intensity rather than extensity; but we will need subtler measures before we can settle this point.

Some Five Towns teachers preferred to talk about teaching as "work with people," not emphasizing the age differences involved. This rhetoric suggests that they perceive interpersonal work as valuable. Rosenberg (1957) found that a large proportion of college students sought work which offered much contact with people. It is provocative, moreover, that the highest-ranked occupations in our society (high government office, the learned professions, and positions of business leadership) reveal a gregarious cast. "Working with people" carries a certain aura, and to so define the work of teachers adds dignity and enhances the self-esteem of members of the occupation.

Teachers are involved with knowledge and its diffusion; their work has also been described as an "art" requiring special sensitivity and personal creativity. Involvement with knowledge and the call for creativity could quite logically serve as foci for attraction to teaching. It is therefore interesting that neither of these aspects of the role receives as much attention as the interpersonal. More than twice as many NEA respondents chose the interpersonal theme as chose "interest in a subject-matter field," the alternative closest to expressing intellectual interests. The NEA survey did not include interest in creativity as an option, an omission which is itself suggestive. And at most a handful of Five Towns teachers gave responses which could be construed as concern with creativity. Perhaps this points to conventionality in the sense that classroom teachers are closer to popular culture and less differentiated than, for example, artists and certain categories of intellectuals.

The service theme

Although their status has been shadowed, teachers have been perceived as performing a special mission in our society, and we see the continuation of that conception among those engaged in the work today. The idea that teaching is a valuable service of special moral worth is a theme in the talk of Five Town teachers.[3] Respondents in the NEA national survey chose the option "opportunity for rendering important service" in 28 percent of the instances, making it the second most frequent response. Women were a little more inclined to stress it than were men, selecting it 29 percent of the time compared with 25 percent among men; and elementary teachers were even more inclined to favor it with a percentage of 32 compared with 23 percent of the secondary teachers.

One can argue that teaching as service is grounded in both sacred and secular aspects of American culture. To Christians, Jesus is "the Great Teacher"; teaching has been an honored vocation within the Roman Catholic church for centuries; the Jewish tradition is steeped in the love of learning. Thus those who define work as an expression of their religious faith can connect teaching with their beliefs; this gives teaching a resource of considerable potency. As we saw in Chapter 1, Americans respect the secular version of the service ideal, ranking occupation partially in such terms. The definition of teaching as service to others is a recruitment resource of some significance.

The service appeal of teaching, however, cannot be described as universal, for to see teaching as service, one must attach a certain degree of efficacy to it. It makes little sense to define teaching as service if one is skeptical about its conduct or value. One might, of course, enter teaching to change it; but as we shall see later, it is difficult to find members of the occupation who so describe their entry. One can infer that teaching as service is more likely to appeal to people who approve of prevailing practice than to those who are critical of it.

The continuation theme

Sociologists normally depict schools as socialization agencies charged with preparing students for adult roles in other parts of the society. It is clear, however, that some who attend school become so attached to it that they are loath to leave. Five Towns teachers talked of such attachments and referred to them as attractions to the occupation.[4] Some said they "liked school" and wanted to work in that setting; others mentioned school-linked pursuits and the difficulty of engaging in them outside educational institutions. A teacher might, for example, have affection for a hard-to-market subject like ancient history or be interested in athletics but not have the ability needed for a professional career in sports. Each can find in teaching a medium for expressing his interests. Some high school teachers told how teaching "came close" to a primary, but blocked, aspiration; an English teacher, for example, may substitute directing school plays for an earlier hope to act. Teaching can serve as the means of satisfying interests which might have originally been fostered and reinforced in school; this attraction has a built-in quality.

The NEA survey did not ask about continuing such interests, but perhaps some of those selecting "interest in a subject-matter field" fall into this category. That response drew many more high school than elementary teachers (23 percent versus 5 percent), but that could be a result of the wording, which designated specialized interest in one subject rather than general attachment to school.

A mass system of public schooling means that millions of young people move through the schools, it is hardly surprising that some develop lasting affiliations. Widespread contact with each generation is a powerful recruitment resource possessed by few occupations. Yet we must recall that the attraction of continuation is not universal among the young. The concept will probably be unattractive to those who look forward to new experience and novel challenges; to "stay in school" will strike some as surrendering their passport to engage in specifically adult activities. Is it not likely, therefore, that fewer of those who opt to continue with school will have a strong interest in the new and untried? It also seems probable that those who feel positive enough about school to stay with it will be more likely to approve of existing arrangements and will be less motivated to press for change. The continuation theme, in short, appears to have a conservative bias.

Material benefits

There are reasons why teachers underplay the role of material rewards in their decision to enter the occupation. Historically the status has been defined as under rewarded; teachers addressing others may hesitate to cite material benefits when in the public eye such rewards are said to be inadequate. But I suspect that the emphasis on service, on teachers as "dedicated," is a more potent source of inhibition, since many people both inside and outside teaching believe that teachers are not supposed to consider money, prestige, and security as major inducements. Such normative pressures make it probable that material benefits influence teachers' decisions more than their answers indicate. There is indirect evidence, at least, that such normative inhibition is at work; we will discuss it after summarizing the direct data.

More Five Towns teachers were willing to list material benefits as attractions to teaching than as key factors in their decision to teach[5] (these benefits include money, prestige, and employment security). The NEA study included two benefits as possible "predominant reasons"; 6 percent chose "security" and only 2 percent "financial rewards." Men were slightly readier to cite security (8 percent versus 5 percent) and women, money benefits (2.1 percent versus 0.6 percent). The NEA options did not include prestige.

There are two aspects of teaching which make the few references to material benefits puzzling. Viewed in the context of occupations with a large proportion of *women*, teaching salaries are not notably deficient, particularly when the relatively fewer working days per year are taken into account. The usual alternatives considered by women teachers normally offer no greater income and may, in fact, offer less. The other fact that leads one to expect greater emphasis on material rewards is that a significant proportion of men who teach come from homes marked by economic insecurity and low social status.

The thought that normative inhibitions reduce teachers' readiness to include material benefits among the major attractions gains support from indirect data gathered in Five Towns. Respondents were asked why *other* teachers were in the occupation—they were asked to project motivations onto unnamed others rather than to talk about themselves (question 39, Appendix B-1). Using categories for money, security, and prestige and an additional one for time compatibility, we find provocative differences in the distributions of self-ascribed and other-ascribed motivations. The theme of service increases on the "projective" item, suggesting that if normative inhibitions are indeed less there may be more references to idealistic considerations: 42 percent of the answers about others refer to service compared with 17 percent in the self-descriptive, major factors question. The most striking difference, however, refers to material benefits. In the projective item, the general category had to be subdivided to accommodate the more frequent mentions. Although all material benefits together were mentioned only 6 percent of the time on the self-descriptive item, each single benefit elicited frequent mentions in the projective question (money, 37 percent; security, 34 percent; and prestige, 12 percent). Respondents who were reluctant to depict material benefits as influential in their own cases show no such hesitation when interpreting the behavior of teachers in general. Interpretation of such a difference is hazardous—it might, for example, imply depreciation of colleagues rather than a projection of personal feelings. But it does at least suggest that these respondents are aware of the drawing power of material benefits.

The differences by sex in the question about other teachers' interests are also provocative. A category had to be included for those who said, one way or another, that "teaching is a good job for women." (The 19 percent involved both men and women.) But men and women differed in their emphasis on money as an attraction; 54 percent of the women and 39 percent of the men alluded to it. The fact that more than half the women teachers saw money as a positive feature in attracting and holding others indicates that we should be skeptical about the 2 percent statistic in the NEA study. One is forced to wonder, in fact, at the reliability of subjective testimony on this matter. I suspect that the research we need to estimate the effects of material benefits on recruitment should focus on the decisions people make rather than on their later interpretation.

The theme of time compatibility

The working schedules of teachers have always been special; although the length of the school year has increased steadily over the last century, most Americans are required to work considerably more days per year than the average teacher.[6] Teachers are sensitive to criticism about this, and one senses that reaction in the statistics their national association gathers to show that teachers actually work longer hours than formal school schedules require (NEA 1972, p. 34). The fact remains, however, that the teacher's schedule features convenient gaps which play a part in attracting people to the occupation. Work days which are finished in midafternoon, numerous holidays, and long summer vacations do not go unnoticed by young people comparing teaching with alternative possibilities.

As with material benefits, more Five Towns teachers listed the work schedule as an attraction than were ready to accord it a major role.[7] It figured prominently, however, in the question where respondents were asked to interpret the behavior of other teachers; in that context, 44 percent mentioned it, and women did so oftener than males—54 percent versus 26 percent.[8]

Five Towns respondents who said that schedules attracted them related working hours to other obligations and pursuits. The dominant obligations referred to were those associated with wifehood and motherhood; the schedule permits time for shopping, household duties, and so on, and matches the schedules of school-age children. Although a few men mentioned compatibility with family life as an attraction, more pointed out that teaching schedules allowed them to undertake further study or do other kinds of work.

The compatibility of teaching schedules is probably a potent recruitment resource; few occupations can offer men and women with other interests such flexibility. Yet it has some disadvantages. Teachers are sometimes criticized for having "easy jobs" (Vidich and Bensman 1958). Occupational leaders do not seem inclined to use this attraction to obtain recruits; they probably feel that it is inconsistent with the occupation's status as a service field and that treating teaching as a means to other ends tends to reduce its intrinsic value. One suspects, moreover, that those who are drawn into teaching primarily by this attractor are less likely to identify strongly with the occupation and its interests. One would not expect people who selected teaching because it made limited claims on their time to give long hours of extra service. If this is so, compatibility is also indirectly conservative in its effects; change in an occupation normally requires extra effort from its members.

The testimony of classroom teachers makes it clear that the occupation possesses potent attractors. Teaching is special in at least two respects: few occupations can offer similar opportunities for protracted contact with normal children, and few can provide such compatible work schedules. The definition of teaching as service (the aura of its mission) sets it apart from many other ways to earn a living. Schools instill interests and attitudes which help recruit the next generation of faculty members. Although muted, material benefits play their part in drawing persons into the occupation.

Analysis of the appeal of the several attractors, however, reveals important limits on their scope; taken together, they affect the distribution of values we would expect to find among new entrants. There is a reiterated emphasis on conserving the past rather than changing educational institutions, implicit in the themes of service and continuation. The tendency of teachers to stress the interpersonal suggests conventionality rather than a special, deviant point of view; the operation of time compatibility is probably indirectly conservative. We are speaking, of course, of propensities and probabilities rather than of absolutes, of a bias toward continuity rather than of a uniform predisposition common to all teachers. What makes these propensities of special interest, however, is that they reappear when we examine the circumstances which facilitate entry to teaching. Those circumstances and the accompanying facilitators will be discussed immediately after the next section.

Material benefits and sex differences

The reluctance of teachers to link their entry to material benefits need not deter us from trying to understand how such attractions affect recruitment and, in particular, influence the sex composition of the occupation. In Chapter 1, I pointed out that the types of material benefits proffered by teaching are likely to operate somewhat differently for men and women. Although each attracts members of both sexes, each appears to vary in the meaning (and possible intensity) it has for them. I will review three kinds of material benefits from this point of view, using data from Five Towns and from national surveys.

Money income and alternatives foregone

Occupational choice is an either-or decision where one selection rules out others, most likely permanently. Economists have a useful concept which they use as part of the calculus of rational choice—the idea of "alternatives foregone." We can extend the concept and think of any given selection as being more of less subjectively costly to individuals (and categories of individuals) when we take into account the aspirations set aside when, for whatever reasons, they enter a given line of work. When we make this transposition into a social psychological definition, we need not assume that rational choices were made or, in fact, that the sacrificed aspirations were indeed assured. Approached this way, it turns out that entering teaching is subjectively more costly for men than for women.

Approximately three-quarters of the Five Towns teachers considered another occupation before entering teaching (question 9, Appendix B-1). *All* the alternatives they mentioned were middle-class and upper-middle class occupations, and 59 percent were interpersonal work with some element of public service. They were not aiming low in their work aspirations. But men and women did not choose teaching from the same list of possibilities. Whereas the men considered business administration and the professions, women thought about semiprofessions (nursing, library work, and social work), office positions, and the performing arts. Except for a small number of women who entertained hope of working in the high-prestige professions, there was no overlap in the alternatives men and women considered. Teaching is the one occupation on which bother sexes converged.

It is evident that men and women will feel that they sacrificed different levels of income (and prestige) in order to teach. With the exception of the performing arts, the women's alternatives are marked by similar or lower earnings. One can become rich and famous in the performing arts but such success is rare. Young women who opt for teaching (or parents who influence them to do so) are not usually following a course which involves material sacrifice. Men who enter teaching, however, find it less difficult to avoid feeling that their teaching careers have brought them less than the alternatives would have yielded; the lifetime earnings of business executives and professionals (and their social positions) clearly exceed those of classroom teachers.

Economists will argue that what has been said will make teaching less attractive to men than to women and that this will perpetuate female dominance of teaching ranks. Granted. What I wish to point out, however, is that some men do become teachers and that their sense of loss has a depressing effect on the recruitment of younger men. We can reason that male teachers will have greater material motives for regretting their fates and are thus less likely to project high enthusiasm for their work. We will see later that identification with teachers plays an important part in recruitment and that young men and women tend to identify with members of the same sex. To the extent that a subjective sense of deprivation makes male teachers less acceptable as models, there is a systematic tendency for the occupation to attract more women than men. The differential distribution by sex of material rewards of money and prestige therefore probably has effects beyond its role in the original calculus of choice.

Social mobility

The special mission of teachers gives their occupation a standing somewhat higher than we would expect solely on the basis of income. We have just alluded to the limits on the prestige of the occupation when it is compared with the highest ranked fields; it is useful, however, to examine the other side of the stratification equation. Teaching is clearly white-collar, middle-class work, and as such offers upward mobility for people who grew up in blue-collar or lower-class families.

Although it is a truism that teaching has benefited from its position as a mobility ladder, it remains difficult to obtain precise information on how many teachers have ascended by entering the occupation. There are thorny technical problems in making estimates on the matter, especially in classifying the original social rank of teachers whose parents were engaged in farming.[9] We can, however, confirm the presence of considerable upward mobility by making conservative use of available data.

A national sample study conducted by the NEA reveals that "the social backgrounds of teachers come close to representing a cross-section of the American public," except for a slight upward bias (NEA 1963, p. 15). Thirty percent of the teachers sampled came from homes where the father was a blue-collar worker. A crude index of mobility within teaching, therefore, is provided by the difference between offspring and their parents; since teaching outranks blue-collar occupations, the sons and daughters of blue-collar parents have climbed significantly by entering teaching (National Opinion Research Center 1953). The procedure is conservative, however, in that it disregards mobility among those who came from lower-status rural families. Using the 30 percent figure, we can estimate that in an occupation now numbering over two million members, somewhere around six hundred thousand persons have crossed the boundary between blue-collar and white-collar work. Teaching appears to be one of the more important routes into the middle class.

Men and women do not benefit equally from these mobility gains. The NEA data disclose that women teachers typically originate in higher-status homes than men in the occupation; for example, more men teachers' fathers were blue-collar workers.[10] Perhaps the disparity stems in part from the differential opportunities perceived by women and men. We noted that within the usual framework of possibilities considered by women, teaching ranks high; it can appeal, therefore, to relatively advantaged women. With their wider range of possibilities, men are less likely to choose teaching if they have socioeconomic advantages. But whatever underlies the disparity, teaching is a more important medium of upward mobility for men than for women.

The subtle differences in the meaning of mobility and prestige for men and women in teaching makes it risky to assign it much greater salience for one or the other. From available data we can infer that mobility as such draws in more men. Yet the acceptability of the occupation for women of higher social background also facilitates their entry. It seems, then, that the social rank of the occupation recruits differentially among men and women, influencing members of both sexes but producing recruits of somewhat different social class backgrounds.

Employment security

American work ideologies tend to denigrate impulses toward employment security, and occupations are sometimes derided by calling their incumbents "security-seekers." This ideology seems a poor description, however, of the economic behavior of many who voice it: the readiness to take protracted risk does not appear abundant. Our task here, however, is not to analyze the gap between ideology and reality in American society, but to uncover some of the meanings security has for men and women in teaching. Employment security is basic to other work rewards; the unemployed earn none.

Anyone studying teaching during the sixties was bound to encounter men whose fathers were on the fringes of the economy during the Great Depression of the thirties. Teachers who grew up in those years (particularly in working-class homes) can have sharp recollections of the pain of economic insecurity.[11] The NEA survey I have referred to makes it clear that a noteworthy proportion of male teachers came from homes where the breadwinner had little protection against unemployment or underemployment during the depression. It seems highly probable, therefore, that some of these men, upon being discharged from the armed services at the end of World War II, chose to use their educational subsidies to prepare for work which was more secure than their fathers'. The flow of veterans into teaching during the postwar years is therefore related to the depression; college education was an unexpected boon for some, and although they may have dreamed of higher-income occupations, it seems likely that they valued the security proffered by classroom teaching.

Women have somewhat different reasons to appreciate the security of teaching. Fewer women grew up in economically vulnerable homes and even fewer would have expected to play the role of principal breadwinner. Employment security can, however, be meaningful to both single and married women. The single woman is assured of a predictable income without having to compete aggressively with men. For those who marry, the economic aspects of security are probably less important, but there are psychological and family-connected benefits. The absence of employment anxiety after tenure has been attained helps to make teaching compatible with marriage and motherhood. If these married women were forced to compete actively to hold their jobs, it would be considerably more difficult for them to balance rival claims of work and family. Employment security makes it easier for married women "to keep work in its place." If they must miss time at work, as when a child is ill, they need not fear discharge. Given the complexities which confront women who combine marriage and motherhood with full-time employment, security gives leverage in an intrinsically delicate situation.

Security is an important recruitment resource for teaching, and I suspect that it exerts more influence than teachers are ready to accord it. The NEA survey indicated that more men than women were ready to assign it a key role in their entry, but the difference was only 3 percent. Since it serves valued purposes for members of both sexes, it is not critical in perpetuating the predominance of women. But we should not be surprised when teachers react strongly to perceived threats to their economic security—a case in point is the New York strike of 1968 (Mayer 1969).

Among the material benefits of teaching, it appears that money most clearly differentiates the appeal of teaching for men and women. Men place teaching salaries in a different comparative context, and they are thus considerably more attractive to women than to men. What makes great change unlikely is that the marginal utility of additional salary is greater for women than for men; attempts to draw in more men by raising general salaries are likely to produce a greater number of highly qualified women applicants. Employers are faced with a dilemma. Are there controlling reasons to hire men even where their qualifications are less impressive than those of available women? Even if some employers were so convinced, could they implement such policies in view of the adverse public sentiment symbolized by the Women's Liberation Movement, laws proscribing discrimination against women, and the collective power of women in teacher organizations? It seems most doubtful. Traditional modes of compensating teachers are likely to enhance the continued preponderance of women in classroom teaching.

TWO GENERAL FACILITATORS

We observed in Chapter 1 that entry to teaching has been facilitated by such mechanisms as highly accessible training and nonelitist admission standards. Two other ways entry to teaching is eased have something in common—each broadens the pool of potential candidates for the occupation.

The wide decision range

Some occupations have a narrow "decision range" because they are not visible to the very young or because they require that the first of a mandatory series of decisions be made at an early point. Few youngsters, for example, are sufficiently aware of actuarial science to choose it at an early age; at the other end of the scale, it is difficult to become a concert musician or a physician if one has not taken the preparatory steps early in life. Occupations which discourage early decisions or constrict later ones will at any time have smaller pools of potential candidates than those with wide "decision ranges."

People can decide to become teachers at any of a number of points. Since the occupation is ubiquitous and highly visible in the lives of children, it can easily figure in their fantasies about adult occupational activity; even young children can make persisting decisions to enter teaching. At the other end of the continuum, it is possible to decide on teaching late and still implement the decision: in Five Towns, for example, several people decided in their thirties to enter teaching. There are supports for decisions made both early and late; since teaching is perceived as among the more accessible occupations, adults feel less pressure to protect youngsters who wish to teach against their possible disappointment; and training institutions have been ready to admit, and school systems to hire, "older" people.

There are indications in Five Towns and in other samples that variations in the age of decision are patterned by sex and school level. Thus 63 percent of the women teachers in Five Towns decided before they graduated from high school, but only 24 percent of the men did so; 41 percent of the men, in fact, waited until their last year in college or later to commit themselves to teaching (question 6, Appendix B-1). Kronus found a similar sex difference in her sample, and Benjamin Wright found that women considered teaching earlier than men did (Kronus 1969, p. 23; Wright, personal communication). With sex held constant, elementary teachers in Five Towns and in Wright's sample decided earlier than secondary teachers. Women, especially those who select elementary teaching, are the most eager recruits; men are more hesitant.

A wide decision range has other consequences in addition to enlarging the candidate pool: one is heterogeneity in patterns of entry. One might expect early decisions to show more affective properties than those made by older people, who have more information; late decisions, on the other hand, may point to considerable "compromise" as hopes and plans are realistically assessed (Ginzberg *et al.*, 1951). Some teachers, therefore, will talk about teaching in glowing terms, as a "calling" they chose early and have given unwavering commitment; others will talk about their choice as a compromise with reality's demands. This is a potential source of cleavage among teachers since those at each extreme may be uncomfortable about the others' valuations of teaching.

The heterogeneity of entry patterns indicates that teaching is not, in this regard, standardized by professional consensus, nor is its membership carefully screened through shared criteria for admission. Consequently there is considerable *self-selection*; the motivation, orientations, and interests candidates bring are not systematically assessed to eliminate those whose characteristics fail to fit a particular model. As we shall note in later chapters, diversity so permitted has important consequences for the inner life of the occupation.

The subjective warrant

Licenses to practice regulated occupations are issued by governments after candidates have passed the stipulated examinations. But this is the culmination of a longer process during which individuals have played a critical part by qualifying or disqualifying themselves; those who sustain an ambition have tested and retested themselves in terms of a personal conception of what their goal will demand, and have in their own eyes passed those tests. We find examples in adolescent boys' testing their dexterity to see whether they have "surgeon's hands" or arguing with peers to see whether they might succeed in law. It is instructive to know what people think is required for success in a given work role, for this indicates the subjective filters associated with the occupation—its "subjective warrant." Occupations with stringent warrants will lose more would-be members through self-discouragement than will those with permissive warrants.

Given the tendency to ease entry into teaching, we might expect to find that subjective tests are also less than stringent. We can examine this possibility with data gathered in Five Towns, where teachers told what personal qualities they thought suited them for teaching (question 11, App. B-1). Analysis produced three types of answers: (1) statements of personal preference; (2) references to interpersonal capacities and dispositions; and (3) allusions to intellectual interests and abilities. A quarter of the responses fell into the first category, with such answers as

"I liked children and wanted to work with them." The model response, however, dealt with personal characteristics like patience, a sense of humor, leadership ability, and a calm and self-possessed nature (slightly over half selected those). The third category, intellectual strengths and interests, was mentioned least, getting fewer than a fifth of the responses. These responses included knowledge of a subject, intelligence, being well-organized, and enjoying learning. Interpersonal qualities and preferences were mentioned more than three times as often as intellectual attributes in Five Towns; such differences, even in a limited sample, command attention. This emphasis on the interpersonal is consistent with the themes of attraction we examined earlier.

The subjective warrant implied by the Five Towns data is not stringent. The preferential responses are logically circular: wanting to teach becomes justification for doing so. Interpersonal qualities, even though not possessed by everyone, suggest a plastic rather than a resistant warrant—one which an individual can shape to suit his purposes. It is difficult, after all, to be sure one does *not* possess the cited qualities. Intellectual criteria, on the other hand, are rendered "scarce" by academic grading systems which depend upon ranking. The question is not whether respondents selected "the best criteria" but rather the effects of using a particular set of criteria. The attributes teaches chose—preferences and interpersonal characteristics—were less likely to force self-elimination than would more stringent standards of self-assessment. The data suggests that there is a social psychological correlate to structurally eased entry; in both instances the hurdles are set at the lower notches.

A final comment. It is interesting that the permissive warrant fits so neatly with the existence of early and late deciders. It prevents those making early decisions from seeing the aspiration to teach as ridiculously high. It also helps those making late decisions to avoid worry about their lack of protracted and specialized preparation for the role: since personality and preference rule, other considerations are secondary. One also observes that the content of the warrant has a "feminine ring"; it emphasizes expressive qualities which, as Parsons and Bales (1955) point out, are presumed to differentiate women in the American division of labor between the sexes.

NOTES

1   This chapter was planned and written before the publication of the 1972 report from the National Education Association (*Status of the American Public-School Teacher, 1970–1971* [Washington, D.C.: Research Division, National Education Association, research report 1972-R3]). It is based primarily on two earlier reports (NEA 1963-M2 and 1967-R4); I have, however, added observations from the later report in the notes where it seems appropriate.

2   The wording of the questions can be found in Appendix B [removed]; for Five Towns, see Appendix B-1. In this instance, the two questions are numbers 8 and 10 in the Five Towns interview. Henceforth, I shall indicate the relevant question in parentheses in the text.

3   On question 8 (attractions to teaching), 14.4 percent of the respondents made reference to teaching as valuable service. On question 10 (most important factors in your decision), 17.3 percent responded in this fashion.

4   6.7 percent said that they "like school" and wished to continue in work related to it; 12.2 percent said they were interested in a particular subject. The last NEA survey (1972-R3) asked specifically about "interest in a subject-matter field," and 34.5 percent of the respondents selected it as one of *three* reasons they decided to become teachers. Men chose it more often than women (46.6 percent verses 28.2 percent) and high school teachers more often than elementary teachers (57.0 percent compared with 14.3 percent). The survey does not break data down by sex within level of schooling, but it appears that interest in a particular subject is highly associated with level of schooling.

5   References to material benefits total 16.7 percent including money, prestige, and security in the attractions question and 6.2 percent in the key factors question.

6   The mean number of days teachers reported as scheduled for their regular school year in 1970–71 was

181 (National Education Association 1972, p. 134). Americans who work five days a week with three weeks vacation and eight holidays annually put in 237 days a year.

7 Although 13 percent included work schedule among the attractions, only 4 percent listed it among the major factors influencing their decision to enter teaching.

8 The most recent NEA survey included a reference to "long summer vacation"; 14.4 percent of all respondents included it as one of three reasons for entering teaching (NEA 1972, p. 160).

9 A refined estimate of social mobility would have to include measurement of *net* upward mobility—some teachers occupy statuses lower than their parents'. Given the data in hand, it is not wise to undertake anything more precise than the discussion in the text. Farmer fathers, for example, can be owners or renters, prosperous leaders in their communities or impecunious sharecroppers. The same problems hold for self-employed fathers, who can own major or minor enterprises.

10 In 1971, 43.9 percent of men in teaching had fathers who were unskilled, semiskilled, or skilled workers compared with 29.0 percent of the women (NEA 1972, p. 61).

11 In one of the pilot interviews I conducted, one teacher told of a fisherman father who, after four days at sea, was forced to sell his share of the catch for twenty-five cents.

REFERENCES

Getzels, J. W. & Jackson, P. W. (1963) The teacher's personality and characteristics. In *Handbook of research on teaching*, ed. N. L. Gage, pp. 506–582. Chicago: Rand McNally.

Ginzberg, E., Ginzberg, S. W., Axelrad, S., & Herma, J. L. (1951) *Occupational choice*. New York: Columbia University Press.

Kronus, C. (1969) Occupational career decisions: temporal patterns and sociological correlates. Ph.D. dissertation, University of Chicago.

Lortie, D. C. (1958) The striving young lawyer: a study of early career differentiation in the Chicago bar. Ph.D. dissertation, University of Chicago.

Mayer, M. (1969) *The teachers' strike, New York, nineteen sixty-eight*. New York: Harper and Row.

National Education Association (1963) *The American public-school teacher, 1960–61*. Washington, DC: Research Division, research monograph 1963-M2.

National Education Association (1967) *The American public-school teacher, 1965–66*. Washington, DC: Research Division, research report 1967-R4.

National Education Association (1972) *Status of the American public-school teacher, 1970–71*. Washington, DC: Research Division, research report 1972-R3.

National Opinion Research Center (1953) Jobs and occupations: a popular evaluation. In *Class, status, and power*, ed. R. V. Bendix & S. M. Lipser, pp. 411–425. Glencoe, IL: Free Press.

Parsons, T. V. & Bales, R. F (1955) *Family socialization and interaction process*. Glencoe, IL.: Free Press.

Rosenberg, M. (1957) *Occupations and values*. Glencoe, IL: Free Press.

Vidich, A. J. & Bensman, J. (1958) *Small town in mass society*. Princeton: Princeton University Press.

Part 4
Commentaries

28 The teacher quality problem[1]

Richard M. Ingersoll
University of Pennsylvania

Few educational issues have received more attention in recent times than the problem of ensuring that our nation's elementary and secondary classrooms are all staffed with quality teachers. There is a general consensus that the quality of teachers and teaching matter—both are undoubtedly among the most important factors shaping the learning and growth of students. Moreover, there is a general consensus that serious problems exist with the quality of teachers and teaching in the U.S. Beyond that, however, there appears to be little consensus and much disagreement over what teacher quality entails, who should and should not be allowed to teach, and especially what are the sources of, and solutions to, the teacher quality problem. In this commentary section, I will briefly discuss three related diagnoses and their attendant prescriptions: restrictive occupational entry barriers; shortages of teachers; inadequate teacher preparation. These three are not the only explanations given for the purported problem of low quality of teachers and teaching. Nor are these views universally believed—indeed each is the subject of much contention—and proponents of one are at times opponents of another. But all are prominent views, all are part of the conventional wisdom as to what ails teaching and all have had an impact on research, reform and policy.

The thesis of this commentary is, however, that each of these three views is largely incorrect. My theoretical perspective is drawn from the sociology of organizations, occupations and work. My operating premise, drawn from this perspective, is that fully understanding issues of teacher quality requires examining the character of the teaching occupation and the social and organizational contexts in which teachers work. In the following sections I briefly review each of the above views and explain why I believe each provides an inaccurate explanation of, and inadequate solutions to, the quality problems plaguing the teaching occupation.

OVERLY RESTRICTIVE OCCUPATIONAL ENTRY

There is much debate over the qualifications deemed necessary for entry into, and success in, the teaching occupation. How much and what kinds of preparation, training and certification should we require in order to yield quality classroom teachers? On one side of the debate, are those who argue that a primary source of low-quality teaching has been a lack of depth, rigor, and breadth in pre-service training and certification (Interstate New Teacher Assessment and Support Consortium, 1992; National Commission on Teaching and America's Future, 1996, 1997). This viewpoint, to which I will return to in the last section of this commentary, holds that we simply have had too few requirements and too low standards. Accordingly, proponents of this view seek to upgrade and expand the education, training, and certification standards required of new teachers.

On the other side, are those who hold that entry into the teaching occupation is already plagued by unusually restrictive and unnecessary rigid bureaucratic entry barriers (Finn *et al.*, 1999; Hanushek & Rivkin, 2004; U.S. Department of Education, 2002; Walsh, 2001). From this latter viewpoint, traditional teacher training and state certification requirements are akin to monopolistic practices. These critics argue that there is no solid empirical research documenting the value of such entry requirements. These regulations, such critics charge, are less motivated by an interest in protecting the public and are really about protecting the self interest of key constituencies involved with the education system. As a result, this view holds, large numbers of high quality candidates are discouraged from getting into the occupation. By doing away with these impediments, this argument concludes, schools could finally recruit the kinds and numbers of candidates they deem best and this would solve the quality problems that plague the teaching force.

There are a number of different variants of this anti-restrictive-entry perspective. One of the more popular favors a training model analogous to that dominant in higher education. The pre-service preparation of professors often includes little formal training in instructional methods. Similarly, from this viewpoint, having an academic degree in a subject is sufficient to be a qualified secondary school teacher in that subject. From this viewpoint, content or subject knowledge—knowing what to teach—is considered of primary importance for a qualified teacher. Formal training in teaching and pedagogical methods—knowing how to teach—is considered less necessary (Finn *et al.*, 1999).

Another variant of the anti-restrictive-entry perspective is motivated by concern for the demographic diversity of the teaching force. From this viewpoint, teaching's entry requirements result in reduced numbers of minority candidates entering the occupation, either because the requirements are themselves racially or ethnically biased, or because they screen out otherwise worthwhile candidates who are unable to pass over particular hurdles because of an underprivileged background (National Collaborative on Diversity in the Teaching Force, 2004; Villegas & Lucas, 2004).

Proponents of these various anti-restrictive-entry perspectives have pushed a range of initiatives, all of which involve a loosening of the traditional entry gates, including alternative certification programs, and Peace Corps-like programs, such as Teach for America.

To be sure, there are at least two problems with existing teaching entry requirements. First, such requirements sometimes keep out capable candidates. In short, not everyone needs such qualifications to be a quality teacher. Second, and conversely, entry requirements sometimes do *not* keep out some who ought not be in this particular line of work. That is, having obtained credentials and completed exams does not, of course, guarantee an individual will be a quality teacher, nor even a qualified teacher.

But, these two problems are true in all occupations and professions. For example, there are no doubt otherwise highly capable individuals who cannot practice law because they did not complete a law school program and pass a state bar exam. Alternatively, there are no doubt individuals who completed law school, passed a bar exam, but who ought not to be lawyers.

It is useful to place teaching's entry and training requirements in context. The restrictiveness of occupational entry requirements is relative and when evaluating the norms and rules governing a particular occupation the question must always be posed—compared to what?

One useful comparison is cross-national. Compared to the U.S., how restrictive and rigorous is entry into the teaching occupation in other developed nations? Interestingly, one recent comparative study has concluded that the filters and requirements embedded in the process of becoming a teacher in the U.S. are less rigorous, less arduous and less lengthy than those in a number of other nations, including Australia, England, Japan, Korea, Netherlands, Hong Kong, and Singapore (Wang *et al.*, 2003). This warrants further investigation—a project I am now undertaking.

Another useful comparison is cross-occupational. Sociologists of work, organizations and occupations have traditionally characterized teaching as a relatively complex form of work, characterized by uncertainty, intangibility, and ambiguity, and requiring as high a degree of initiative, judgment, and skill to perform at a high level as do some of the traditional professions (Bidwell, 1965; Kohn & Schooler, 1983; Lortie, 1975). However, in contrast to the deregulation perspective, sociologists of work, organizations and occupations have also traditionally characterized teaching as a relatively easy-in/easy-out occupation, with a relatively low entry bar, and a relatively wide entry gate, especially in comparison to the traditional professions (Etzioni, 1969). In his classic study of the teaching occupation, Dan Lortie (1975) drew attention to a number of aspects and mechanisms that facilitate ease of entry. Most of those who desire to enter the teaching occupation are free to do so—a characteristic Lortie labeled the "subjective warrant." In contrast, the opposite prevails in many occupations and most traditional professions. Especially in the latter, occupational gatekeepers have a large say in choosing new members and not all who desire to enter are allowed to do so.

Ironically, although teaching's entry training and licensing requirements are lower than those for many other occupations in the U.S., and lower than in some other nations, they appear to be subject to far more scrutiny than those in other occupations. There is an extensive body of empirical research, going back a couple of decades, devoted to evaluating the effects of teacher credentials on student performance and, not surprisingly, the results from this literature are often contradictory (Allen, 2003). But, a number of studies have indeed found teacher education or licensure, of one sort or another, to be significantly related to increases in student achievement (Greenberg *et al.*, 2004; Greenwald *et al.*, 1996; Raudenbush *et al.*, 1999).

Scrutiny of the added value of entry requirements is, of course, useful from the perspective of the public interest. But, it can also be useful to place this research itself in a cross-occupational comparison. Typically for most occupations and professions, there is little or no empirical research done assessing the value added of practitioners having a particular credential, license or certification (American Educational Research Association, American Psychological Association, & National Council on Measurement in Education, 1999; Kane, 1994). Such research can be difficult to undertake; for instance, if licensure is mandatory in an occupation, it may be impossible to compare the performance of those licensed with those unlicensed. Nevertheless, occupational entry requirements, whether by precedent, or by law, are common. For example, almost all universities require a doctorate for full-time academic positions. However, there are very few examples of a "professor effects" literature that examines whether professors' qualifications have a positive effect on student achievement or on research quality (Pascarella & Terenzini, 1991). In other words, in academia as in most occupations and professions, it appears that it is taken as a given that particular credentials are necessary to practice particular kinds of work. Hence, from a cross-occupational perspective, the interesting research question is not solely, 'Do qualifications matter for teachers?', but also, 'Why do so many find this an important question?' Is teaching held to up to more scrutiny and skepticism than other occupations and, if so, why?

Regardless of their impact on recruitment, the data also suggest that increasing or decreasing entry qualifications, alone, will not solve the problem of ensuring a quality teacher in every classroom if it does not also address the issue of teacher retention—the subject of the next section.

TEACHER SHORTAGES

A second and related explanation for the problem of low quality teaching in American schools is teacher shortages. In this view, the main source of the problem is that the supply of new teachers is insufficient to keep up with the demand. Restrictive entry requirements may exacerbate this condition, but the root of this gap, it is widely believed, is a dramatic increase in the demand for new teachers primarily resulting from two converging demographic trends—increasing student enrollments and increasing teacher retirements due to a "graying" teaching force. Shortfalls of teachers, this argument continues, have meant that many school systems have not been able to find qualified candidates to fill their openings, inevitably resulting in the hiring of underqualified teachers, ultimately lowering school performance.

The prevailing policy prescription and response to these school staffing problems has been to attempt to increase the quantity of teachers supplied through a wide range of recruitment initiatives. Some of these involve a loosening of entry requirements, some do not. Overseas recruitment, financial incentives, such as signing bonuses, student loan forgiveness, housing assistance, and tuition reimbursement have all been used (Hirsch et al., 2001).

The data, however, raise serious doubts for the success of these kinds of initiatives. In my own research I have shown that the main source of school staffing problems is not shortages—in the sense of too few new candidates being produced—but rather too many existing teachers leaving their jobs (Ingersoll, 2001, 2003b). Most of the demand for new teachers is not driven by student enrollment or teacher retirement increases, but from pre-retirement teacher turnover. The data portray a "revolving door" occupation in which there are relatively large flows in and out of a significant portion of schools each year. It is also an occupation that loses many of its newly trained members very early in their careers. The data indicate that as many as half of those trained to be teachers never enter teaching, and another 40–50 percent of those who do enter, leave the teaching occupation either temporarily or permanently in the first five years on the job. Moreover, the data tell us that the overall amount of turnover accounted for by retirement is relatively minor when compared to that resulting from other causes, such as teacher job dissatisfaction and teachers seeking better jobs or other careers.

These findings have large implications for current policy—they suggest prescriptions must focus less on recruitment and more on retention. In short, recruiting more teachers will not solve the teacher crisis if large numbers of such teachers then leave. The image that comes to mind is a bucket rapidly losing water because of holes in the bottom. Pouring more water into the bucket will not be the answer if the holes are not first patched.

THE PROBLEM OF UNDERQUALIFIED TEACHERS

A third prominent explanation of low-quality teaching focuses on the adequacy of the qualifications of prospective teachers. In this view, as noted earlier, a major source of low quality teaching is low quality pre-service education, training and certification standards (National Commission on Teaching and America's Future, 1996, 1997). In contrast to the deregulation perspective, this group seeks to expand the training and certification standards traditionally required of new teachers. In response, reformers in many states have pushed tougher certification requirements and more rigorous coursework requirements for teaching candidates.

Upgrading teacher preparation programs and teacher certification standards certainly may be necessary and helpful. However, like many similarly worthwhile reforms, these efforts *alone* will also not solve the problem of underqualified teachers because they do not address some key causes. One of the least recognized of these causes is the problem of out-of-field teaching—teachers being assigned to teach subjects which do not match their training or education. From a policy perspective, this is a crucial issue because highly qualified teachers may become highly unqualified if they are assigned to teach subjects for which they have little training or education.

In my own research I have found that out-of-field teaching is a chronic and widespread problem. For example, about one third of all secondary (grades seventh to twelfth) math classes are taught by teachers who do not have either a major or a minor in math, or related disciplines such as physics, statistics, engineering or math education. Almost one quarter of all secondary school English classes are taught by teachers who are not certified in English. Some out-of-field teaching takes place in well over half of all secondary schools in the U.S. in any given year. Each year over one fifth of the public seventh to twelfth grade teaching force does some out-of-field teaching (Ingersoll, 1999, 2004a).

Typically, policy-makers and analysts have assumed that the problem of out-of-field teaching is a result of teacher shortages. The conventional wisdom holds that shortfalls in the number of available teachers have led many school systems to resort to assigning teachers to teach out of their fields (National Commission on Teaching and America's Future 1996, 1997). This is clearly a factor, but, out-of-field teaching cannot be entirely explained by teacher shortages. The data show, for example, high levels of out-of-field teaching exist in fields, such as English and social studies, long been known to have surpluses.

Rather than deficits in the qualifications and quantity of teachers, the data point in another direction—out-of-field teaching is really an issue of human resource management and mismanagement. The data tell us that decisions concerning the allocation of teaching assignments are usually the prerogative of school principals (Ingersoll, 2003a). School managers are charged with the often difficult task of providing a broad array of programs and courses with limited resources, limited time, a limited budget, and a limited teaching staff (Delany, 1991). In this context, principals appear to find that assigning teachers to teach out of their fields is often more convenient, less expensive and less time consuming than the alternatives. For example, rather than find and hire a new part-time science teacher to teach two sections of a newly state-mandated science curriculum, a principal may find it more convenient to assign a couple of English and social studies teachers to each "cover" a section in science. If a teacher suddenly leaves in the middle of a semester, a principal may find it faster and cheaper to hire a readily available, but not fully qualified, substitute teacher, rather than conduct a formal search for a new teacher. When faced with a tough choice between hiring an unqualified candidate for a science teacher position or doubling the class size of one of the fully qualified science teachers in the school, a principal might opt for the former choice—resulting in a smaller class, but taught by a lesser qualified teacher. If a full-time music teacher is under contract, but student enrollment is sufficient to fill only three music classes, the principal may find it both necessary and cost effective in a given semester to assign the music teacher to teach two classes in English, in addition to the three classes in music, in order to employ the teacher for a regular full-time complement of five classes per semester. All of these managerial choices to misassign teachers may save time and money for the school, and ultimately for the taxpayer, but they are not cost free. They are a large, and until recently, under-recognized source of the problem of underqualified teachers in classrooms.

These findings have implications for current policy. The efforts by many states to recruit new teachers, to enhance their training, to enact more stringent certification standards, and to increase the use of testing for teaching candidates, although perhaps highly worthwhile, will not eliminate out-of-field teaching assignments and, hence, alone will not solve the problem of underqualified teaching in our nation's classrooms. In short, bringing in thousands of new candidates and mandating more rigorous coursework and certification requirements will help little if large numbers of such teachers continue to be assigned to teach subjects other than those for which they were educated or certified.

Rather than deficits in the quantity or quality of teachers, the data point in another direction. As with the two other views (restrictive occupational entry barriers and teacher shortages), the data indicate much of the conventional thinking on the sources of the teacher quality problem suffers from serious limitations. Rather the data suggest that if we want to fully understand and also address these problems, we must also examine the character of teaching as an occupation and the character of schools as organizations.

NOTE

1 This commentary draws from an earlier paper (Ingersoll, 2004b) published as chapter 1 in Mark Smylie and Debra Miretzky (eds.) 2004, *Developing the Teacher Workforce*, the *103rd Yearbook of the National Society for the Study of Education*. Chicago: National Society for the Study of Education.

REFERENCES

Allen, M. (2003) *Eight questions on teacher preparation: what does the research say?* Denver, CO: Education of the States.

American Educational Research Association, American Psychological Association, & National Council on Measurement in Education (1999) *Standards for educational and psychological testing*. Washington, DC: Author.

Bidwell, C. (1965) The school as a formal organization. In J. March (ed.), *Handbook of Organizations* (pp. 973–1002). Chicago: Rand McNally.

Delany, B. (1991) Allocation, choice and stratification within high schools: how the sorting machine copes. *American Journal of Education*, 99(2), 181–207.

Etzioni, A. (1969) (ed.), *The semi-professions and their organizations: teachers, nurses and social workers*. New York: Free Press.

Finn, C., Kanstoroom, M., & Petrilli, M. (1999) *The quest for better teachers: grading the states*. Washington, DC: Thomas B. Fordham Foundation.

Greenberg, E., Rhodes, D. A., & Ye, X. L. (2004) *Teacher preparation and student achievement in mathematics*. Paper presented at the Annual Meeting of the American Educational Research Association, San Diego.

Greenwald, R., Hedges, L., & Laine, R. (1996) The effect of school resources on student achievement. *Review of Educational Research*, 66(3), 361–396.

Hanushek, E. & Rivkin, S. (2004) How to improve the supply of high-quality teachers. In D. Ravitch (ed.), *Brookings Papers on Education Policy: 2004* (pp. 7–44). Washington, DC: Brookings Institution.

Hirsch, E, Koppich, J., & Knapp, M. (2001) *Revisiting what states are doing to improve the quality of teaching: an update on patterns and trends*. Seattle, WA: University of Washington, Center for the Study of Teaching and Policy.

Ingersoll, R. (1999) The problem of underqualified teachers in American secondary schools. *Educational Researcher*, 28(2), 26–37.

Ingersoll, R. (2001) Teacher turnover and teacher shortages: an organizational analysis. *American Educational Research Journal*, 38(3), 499–534.

Ingersoll, R. (2003a) *Who controls teachers' work?: power and accountability in America's schools*. Cambridge, MA: Harvard University Press.

Ingersoll, R. (2003b) *Is there really a teacher shortage?* Seattle, WA: University of Washington, Center for the Study of Teaching and Policy.

Ingersoll, R. (2004a) Why some schools have more underqualified teachers than others. In D. Ravitch (ed.), *Brookings Papers on Education Policy: 2004* (pp. 45–88). Washington, DC: Brookings Institution.

Ingersoll, R. (2004b) Four myths about America's teacher quality problem. In M. Smylie & D. Miretzky (eds.), *Developing the teacher workforce: the 103rd yearbook of the National Society for the Study of Education* (pp. 1–33). Chicago: University of Chicago Press.

Interstate New Teacher Assessment and Support Consortium (1992) *Model standards for beginning teacher licensing, assessment and development*. Washington, DC. Council of Chief State School Officers.

Kane, M. (1994) Validating interpretive arguments for licensure and certification examinations. *Evaluation & the Health Professions*, 17(2), 133–159.

Kohn, M. & Schooler, C. (1983) *Work and personality*. Norwood, NJ: Ablex.

Lortie, D. C. (1975) *Schoolteacher: a sociological study*. Chicago: University of Chicago Press.

National Collaborative on Diversity in the Teaching Force (2004) *Assessment of diversity in America's teaching force*. Washington, DC: National Education Association.

National Commission on Teaching and America's Future (1996) *What matters most: teaching for America's future*. New York: NCTAF.

National Commission on Teaching and America's Future (1997) *Doing what matters most: investing in quality teaching*. New York: NCTAF.

Pascarella, E. & Terenzini, P. (1991) *How college affects students: findings and insights from twenty years of research*. San Francisco: Jossey-Bass.

Raudenbush, S., Fotiu, R., & Cheong, Y. (1999) Synthesizing results from the trial state assessment. *Journal of Educational and Behavioral Statistics*, 24(4), 413–438.

U.S. Department of Education (2002) *Meeting the highly qualified teachers challenge: the secretary's annual report on teacher quality*. Washington, DC: U.S. Department of Education, Office of Postsecondary Education.

Villegas, A. & Lucas, T. (2004) Diversifying the teacher workforce: a retrospective and prospective account. In M. Smylie & D. Miretzky (eds.), *Developing the teacher workforce: the 103rd yearbook of the National Society for the Study of Education* (pp. 70–104). Chicago: University of Chicago Press.

Walsh, Kate (2001) *Teacher certification reconsidered: stumbling for quality*. Baltimore, MD: Abell Foundation.

Wang, A., Coleman, A., Coley, R., & Phelps, R. (2003) *Preparing teachers around the world*. Princeton, NJ: Educational Testing Service.

29 Changing the paradigm

Preparing teacher educators and teachers for the twenty-first century

Mary H. Futrell
George Washington University

> Tell me, and I forget. Teach me, and I may remember.
> Involve me, and I learn.
>
> Benjamin Franklin

One of the longest reform movements in recent United States history has focused on the need to improve the quality of our education system. For more than 50 years, local, state and federal leaders have been engaged in a debate about why the education system should be transformed, how much and by whom. As early as the 1950s, when the *Brown vs. Board of Education* decision desegregated the public school system, followed by the minimum standards movement imposed by the states in the 1960s and 1970s, we have been engaged in heated discussions about educational access and quality in America. That debate continued in the 1980s with the release of the report, "A Nation at Risk: the Imperative for Educational Reform" (1983), and the National Education Goals (1989), both of which raised concern about the quality of P-12 education and, by association, the quality of teaching in America.

During this same period, The Carnegie Corporation issued its report, "A Nation Prepared: Teachers for the 21st Century," in which it identified the need to more clearly define what we mean by accomplished teaching and how to recognize teachers who demonstrate those attributes. The report linked the quality of teaching to the successful reform of America's schools. As a result, the Carnegie Corporation created the National Board for Professional Teaching Standards (NBPTS) in order to define highly accomplished teaching and to provide national certification to teachers who exemplify those qualities.

More recently, the issue of teacher quality has become a federal issue as government officials express growing concern about the future of the American workforce. The 2001 Congressional reauthorization of the Elementary and Secondary Education Act (No Child Left Behind, NCLB) catapulted the issue of teaching quality and teacher education to the top of the education reform agenda as a critical factor in improving student learning. The NCLB Act developed its own definition of what it means to be a highly qualified teacher in the core subject areas and mandated states to use its criteria in defining highly qualified teachers.

And just last year, Congress called for a study of teacher preparation programs, to be conducted by the National Research Council (NRC), the principal operating agency of the National Academies of Sciences and Engineering in Washington, DC (U.S. Department of Education, 2002). The NRC was asked to assess the state of the nation's teacher preparation programs and publicly report its findings in 2007. Specifically, the NRC must synthesize data and conduct research on the academic preparation and educational characteristics of candidates in pre-service, graduate, and alternative certification programs; the specific content and experiences that are provided to candidates for degrees and alternative certification in education; the consistency of the required course work and experiences in reading and mathematics across teacher preparation programs; and the degree to which the content and experiences are based on converging scientific evidence.

I can only presume that Congress commissioned this study because it believes, as do I, that the key to America's future health and well-being is education. In order for America to be able to grow and thrive in today's global society, it must rethink the way it educates and prepares its citizens—from pre-kindergarten through graduate school and beyond. From an economic standpoint, Americans today are competing for jobs with people from around the world and, therefore, in order to be successful, require an education that will better prepare them for a complex, more culturally-diverse environment. Further, the increased mobility of knowledge and capital, along with lower wages in many other countries, erodes the United States' ability to keep industry and jobs on its own soil. Lockheed Martin Chief Executive Norman Augustine recently observed, "In the five decades since I've been working in the aerospace industry, I have never seen American business and academic leaders as concerned about this nation's future prosperity as they are today" (*The Washington Post*, December 6, 2005). Augustine further argues that to address this issue, the United States must focus more on fundamentals such as recruiting more teachers, providing them with more financial support, and improving the skills of teachers through enhanced education and preparation.

The complexity of our education system and the nuances of what the future will bring mean that we need to be willing to change the education paradigm to more effectively prepare our graduates to be educationally and, thus, economically competitive. In other words, we need to address the inadequacies of our classrooms as well as the philosophy, practices and politics of teaching and learning. As a global pace-setter, the United States' commitment to better-educating its citizenry will not only benefit its own future but will influence the educational and economic transformation of other countries. A century ago, America adapted its education system to the needs of a newly industrialized nation. The system must now evolve again, to reflect explosive growth in technology and communications, increased access to information and rapidly changing demographics. By commissioning the NRC study, Congress has acknowledged the vital role of schools of education in ensuring that the United States remains one of the most socially, economically and politically advanced countries in the world.

How can schools of education better prepare twenty-first-century teachers, counselors and administrators (hereafter referred to as teachers) to more fully equip citizens for the global society in which we live? Much has been written on this topic by organizations like the NBPTS, The Interstate New Teacher Assessment and Support Consortium (INTASC), the National Commission on Teaching and America's Future (NCTAF), the National Council for the Accreditation of Teacher Education (NCATE) and other groups. Two main themes are stressed.

First, today's teacher must be prepared for the increasingly diverse U.S. classroom and be committed to educating all children, especially those who have traditionally struggled to meet high academic standards—the economically disadvantaged, minorities and those for whom English is not the first language—and must recognize that all students are integral to America's future.

Second, in order to ensure that each student is prepared to succeed, teachers should be able to teach in ways that promote deep understanding of the subject matter and have a repertoire of pedagogical strategies that addresses the needs of different learners. They must be able to design a curriculum that is aligned with what students are expected to learn, as defined by state and national standards, and, as part of our global learning community, they must know how to use data to assess and then adapt lessons so that all students have an opportunity to achieve at higher levels.

Thus, a key question is whether we are preparing educators, especially teachers, for the knowledge-based, global society in which we now live, or whether we are still preparing them for the industrial era that is long past? The model of schools as cubicles—in which teachers teach their classes in isolation using the didactic method, or where subjects are taught as though they, too, are isolated disciplines—is no longer the most practical nor effective way to teach and learn. Today, students need to understand the interdisciplinary relationship between, for example, technology, English and biology. Such courses could be taught by teams of teachers using strategies like block scheduling to allow more time for students to develop strong social and academic foundations, and to learn how to learn together. In these environments, students would discover how to ask real world questions and research, synthesize and effectively communicate the answers. Thus, they would have more opportunities to become self-motivated and inquisitive, and to become leaders in their learning environment. Throughout their educational experience and beyond, students will be able to draw upon these valuable skills.

But, some would say our classrooms are actually becoming *more* didactic and our curricula *more* narrow in response to an increasing emphasis on standards-based testing. Indeed, this method of learning appears to be on a collision course with mediated and distance learning methodologies, and we, therefore, need to re-examine how we teach standards-based curricula and how the school day is structured to maximize learning. In order to allow more time for students to work in the aforementioned learning communities, schools need to introduce flexible formats that can accommodate integrated learning models, distance learning or other strategies designed to expand and strengthen the depth of their learning experiences. This means that teachers need to know how to use a variety of technologies as part of their repertoire of teaching and learning tools, how to design course offerings that reinforce high standards of learning for the individual student, as well as for the class as a whole, and must be able to teach in teams—either face-to-face or by using, for example, video conferencing.

But, before teachers can do so, schools need to be structured and equipped to ensure that they have the fiscal and physical capacity to accommodate these new learning tools. For example, teachers are expected to prepare students for an information-communications, technological society, yet, in too many schools, the electrical facilities are so outdated that, even if they had the technologies, it would be too dangerous to plug them in. Many schools, colleges and departments of education (SCDEs) also need to be modernized to assure that they, too, have the resources to prepare teachers for the realities of teaching and learning in a knowledge based and diverse society.

We often hear policymakers express concern about America's teacher shortage (which, I might add, is a worldwide crisis) and the need for teachers to be better qualified. There are more than 3.1 million teachers in the U.S., of which about 50 percent are expected to retire or simply leave by 2015 (National Education Association, 2002). The shortage is expected to be even more dramatic for school administrators and higher education faculty. The shortage is even more acute among educators from minority groups and in communities whose student populations are primarily minority and/or poor. This means that, as America's student population grows more diverse, the diversity within the teaching profession is diminishing at a time when we need to grow the size and quality as well as enhance diversity within the teaching profession. As we struggle with the issue of the teacher shortage, we must also address the issue of the teaching paradigm and its effect on our ability to attract and retain highly qualified teachers in our schools.

I believe that we need to redefine the roles and responsibilities of teachers as key players in determining what we mean by quality education, accountability and effective teaching and learning. Communities should build upon the talents, knowledge and skills of their teachers as teachers, but also as mentors to teacher interns, curriculum developers, clinical practitioners, staff development providers, peer coaches for their teacher colleagues, researchers and leaders of reforms to improve teaching and learning in their schools (Futrell, 2004). Such distributive leadership can strengthen teaching, the school environment and the profession itself. Teacher educators, therefore, should prepare teachers for these differentiated, integral roles rather than continue year after year the paradigm of teaching as an isolated discipline. These are roles and responsibilities that I believe will enhance the learning community and teaching as a profession.

Before entering the classroom, future teachers must fully demonstrate mastery of their content area and pedagogical skills through well-mentored, diverse field experiences. Teacher candidates at The George Washington University, for example, are required to intern in two different settings, at least one of them urban, for a minimum of two semesters while being supervised and evaluated by faculty and veteran teachers. Through partnerships with eleven school districts—rural, suburban and urban—our students are exposed to a variety of experiences that enrich and strengthen their teaching and leadership expertise even before they graduate.

Once novice teachers are in the classroom, veteran teachers, administrators and teacher educators should work together to help keep them there. Attrition, particularly in urban school districts where the need for highly qualified teachers is the greatest, is a major contributor to America's teacher shortage. Schools should work with school districts to create induction programs that more effectively mentor and retain new teachers. For example, novice teachers should not enter the profession through the traditional "baptism by fire" method in which they are assigned to teach the toughest classes with little, if any, support or mentoring. Rather, novice teachers should be inducted into the profession and the classroom over a period of one to three years through programs that are carefully designed and staffed by accomplished teachers who help them gain the self confidence and the expertise they will need to become successful teachers.

This brings me back to the point of teacher educators and their capacity to help the United States maintain its leadership role in the world. Studies have repeatedly shown that teacher quality is one of the most important factors influencing educational success (Sanders & Rivers, 1996). Studies have also shown that the quality of preparation and support teachers receive will determine their effectiveness in the classroom, the confidence they have in themselves as teachers and whether or not they will remain in the profession (Alliance for Excellent Education, 2002; Lieberman & Miller, 1999; NCTAF, 2003; Southeast Center for Teaching Quality, 2003). The same logic applies to teacher preparation programs: we need to ensure that teacher educators have the institutional support to successfully recruit and prepare candidates who are highly qualified and committed to teaching as a profession. We also need to more clearly define and support the scholarship of teaching and learning, including field experiences and other forms of engagement.

Yet, in too many instances, despite the increasing national demand for more and better prepared teachers, SCDEs remain low on the higher education hierarchy. The institutional commitment to strengthening teacher preparation programs is weak, which is ironic because the quality of teacher preparation programs is a major determinant of the quality of the teaching force, which, in turn, affects the quality of the high school graduates who will become the students attending these very same higher education institutions. Colleges and universities seem more willing to pay billions of dollars for remediation programs for students rather than invest in programs that enhance faculty development, improve teacher preparation and provide sophisticated teaching tools and environments on par with those their graduates will be required to use when they enter their chosen profession. And, as we induct teacher educators into the professoriate, we should consider the implications of the emerging societal challenges, the changing roles of faculty and what their priorities should be as they prepare tomorrow's teachers, counselors, and school administrators.

The process of education reform is very complex, but it continues to evolve steadily. Schools, colleges and departments of education, especially teacher preparation programs, must maintain and improve ongoing efforts to redesign the teaching-learning paradigm to more effectively ensure that American citizens are well-educated and well-prepared for our global society. As part of the changing environmental context, we should celebrate our achievements, but also recognize that if we are to achieve the goal of a better educated America, we, too, must change, and we must have the institutional support to help us do so. As Wynn Calder, associate director of University Leaders for a Sustainable Future, said, the future calls on us to "... look forward ..., to envision what we hope to achieve, and to create a strategy for getting there" (UNESCO Education Today Newsletter, 2006, p. 3).

The ability of teacher educators to successfully fulfill our mission of preparing highly qualified teachers will be a key factor in determining how we, the United States, as a nation respond to challenges facing us now and in the future, whether they are educational, political or economic. Citizens will need to understand the interrelated nature of those challenges and have the knowledge, diverse skills and leadership abilities to work together in order to address them. Our success also will be contingent upon how committed, determined and successful we are in redefining the philosophical, political and practical paradigm of teaching as a profession, from pre-school through graduate school. Teacher educators have played and will continue to play a key role in ensuring that Americans are educationally prepared to help sustain and strengthen the foundations of our nation's democracy in a global society.

REFERENCES

Alliance for Excellent Education (December, 2002) *New teacher excellence: retaining our best.* Washington, DC: Author.

Augustine, Norman as quoted in *The Washington Post*, December 6, 2005.

Calder, Wynn (March 16, 2006) quoted in *Educating for tomorrow's world.* UNESCO Education Today Newsletter, p. 3. Paris, France: UNESCO.

Futrell, Mary H. (Winter 2003) Teaching tomorrow's citizens today: the need for more highly qualified teachers. *Teacher Education and Practice*, 16(4), 355–368.

Lieberman, A. & Miller, L. (1999) *Teachers—transforming their world and their work.* New York: Teachers College Press; Alexandria, VA: Association for Supervision and Curriculum Development.

National Commission on Teaching and America's Future (NCTAF) (September, 1996) *What matters most: teaching for America's future.* New York: Author.

National Education Association (2002) *Attracting and keeping quality teachers* (pp. 1–2) http://www2.nea.org/teachershortage/

Sanders, W. L. & Rivers. J. C. (1996) *Cumulative and residual effects of teachers on future academic achievement.* Knoxville, TN: University of Tennessee Value Added Research and Assessment Center.

Southern Center for Teaching Quality (2003) How do teachers learn to teach effectively? Quality indicators from quality schools. Teaching quality in the southeast: best practices and policies brief (Vol. 2, No. 7) Chapel Hill, NC: Author.

United States Department of Education (2002) P. L. 107–110, the No Child Left Behind Act of 2001. Washington, DC: U.S. Department of Education.

30 The perspective of a national board certified teacher on who should teach

Meghna Antani Lipcon
National Board Certified Teacher, Broad Acres
Elementary School, Silver Spring, Maryland

"Why do you want to be a teacher?" When I first decided to pursue a career in teaching, I heard that question many times. My answer was always the same: "I love learning and I want to share my passion with others." My family instilled that passion in me, and the teachers I was fortunate to have throughout my schooling shaped my vision of "good" teachers. Good teachers had great power—to inspire students to strive for success, to make ideas come alive in the classroom, and to respond to a wide range of student needs. My love of learning, combined with this favorable view of the teaching profession, influenced my decision to become a teacher. Despite my passion for the profession, I had not always considered teaching as a career. I graduated from a highly rigorous and prestigious university with a degree in psychology. It was not until my junior year that my love for teachers, children, and learning came back to me, and I decided to become a teacher.

Soon after I applied to graduate school for education, the questions began. I received mixed responses—some from my former teachers—ranging from surprise, to support, to flat-out discouragement. Many wondered why I would graduate from one of the nation's top universities and choose "just to be a teacher." The prevailing sentiment was that students who were successful in school, and could do "anything they wanted" should not settle for teaching as a career. To me, this seemed counterintuitive. Wouldn't any profession—especially one charged with educating the next generation, need and *want* to attract men and women with strong educational backgrounds?

Teaching is referred to as a "profession" or a "career." However, it is not held with the same regard as traditional professions, such as medicine, law or business. A reason for this is historically, teaching has been a "female" career. Women, who were barred from many other types of work, generally chose to be teachers. Since "teaching was largely a short-term career chosen by men on their way to another line of work and women who taught until they married or had children" (Johnson & Kardos, framing chapter in this section), wages were not comparable to other professions. Male teachers would move on to more lucrative careers, and after a woman got married, her husband would provide for her, eliminating the need to increase teacher salaries. Times have changed, and women now have a multitude of opportunities. They do not have to choose between a career and family. However, since women still make up the majority of the teaching force, many perceptions of teaching have not changed.

These perceptions have a major impact on who does or does not choose to teach. Teaching faces many hurdles in the twenty-first century. It does not pay a salary comparable to other professions which require specialized skills and knowledge. This, combined with the challenges of being a teacher today (high percentage of non-native English speaking students, youth violence and poverty, standardized testing, scripted curricula, increased pressure, and decreased autonomy), speaks to why teaching must strive to change the "status quo" if it is to recruit a workforce comprised of individuals from diverse backgrounds and experiences. All U.S. schoolchildren deserve and require teachers who represent the diversity and cultural richness of our nation. The composition of the mostly white, female teaching work force does not match the increasingly diverse student body in the United States. If our young people are to develop an appreciation and understanding of people from all walks of life, they must be exposed to a variety of experiences and people. Having a teaching workforce that more closely matches the students we serve increases the probability that we meet the social, emotional, and academic needs of all children and provide all children with a deep, rich education. While some critics contend that demographic diversity among teachers does not correlate with better test scores, the fact remains that students and the public at large need to see that knowledge belongs to all people, and that is best demonstrated through an economically and culturally diverse workforce. Thus, teaching needs to attract and retain teachers of color, male teachers, and candidates from the top of their graduating classes—individuals who normally do not consider teaching.

Teaching is an intellectual profession—and teachers *are* intellectuals. Accomplished teachers know how to effectively manage classrooms of upwards of 20 unique learners. Teachers are not only responsible for teaching factual knowledge, but must facilitate students' acquisition of essential higher-order, analytical skills. Teachers must merge in-depth knowledge of the state/district curriculum with numerous other resources to deliver the content and skills students need to know in a *developmentally appropriate* way. Students are children, and children have interests, concerns, and emotions. A teacher must take in a multitude of inputs that include but are not limited to academic information, and make decisions to tailor their lessons to each child they teach. For example, these are some questions I have asked myself during *one day of teaching*: "Did Anita have breakfast this morning? Did Carmen fight with a friend? How will David's parents' divorce affect his motivation? How do I engage Jake in science? Are my materials provisioned correctly? Who needs to work on long division in a small group? Does Amjad miss his friends back in Bangladesh? Is Joey still worried about the gunshots he heard last night?"

If teaching continues to attract only a narrow slice of graduates, the status of the profession will remain what it is today—below that of other professions that require a similar level of intellect, resolve, creativity, and preparation. It is essential that teachers possess a certain level of intellect so that they are able to process information quickly and make instructional decisions based on their understanding of how essential skills are applied in a variety of settings. For example, a teacher who simply shows students how to conduct a science experiment is not as accomplished as one who leads students to a deeper understanding of the nature of inquiry. However, this intellect is not comprised solely of verbal ability and the teacher's college GPA. While the teacher's academic preparation is, of course, an asset to the students he or she teaches, a teacher must also have the ability to understand children, determine the vital concepts and skills they need to acquire, *and* construct a lesson sequence which engages students in meaningful experiences, leading them to discovery of said skills and concepts. While student-teaching first grade, I definitely possessed a high level of verbal ability and had a strong academic background. However, it took weeks of teaching, observation, and collaboration with my cooperating teacher and university advisor to effectively engage my first graders in instruction crafted to their unique strengths and needs. In addition, a teacher is a model of a learned person, someone who is passionate about knowledge and provides students with opportunities to see the world beyond the classroom, and beyond their neighborhoods. A teacher is a scholar who, through personal rapport with students, can inspire them to set and achieve high goals. If the composition of the teaching profession were to more closely match the racial and ethnic demographics of students, as stated earlier, then there would be teachers providing students from all walks of life an authentic role model of an educated person.

The question remains as to how to attract and retain a wider range of individuals to the profession. In large part the answer is money. Our society equates money with status and prestige. If teaching wants to attract candidates on par with those considering medicine, law, business, and engineering careers, salaries *must* be competitive. The notions that teaching is "noble" and that "teachers don't go into it for the money" are limiting to the profession, and propagate other common sayings, such as "those who can't do, teach." As Lortie states, "historically [teachers'] status has been defined as underrewarded . . . the emphasis on service, on teachers as 'dedicated,' is a more potent source of inhibition, since many people both inside and outside teaching believe that teachers are not supposed to consider money, prestige and security as major inducements" (1975, p. 30).

In the twenty-first century, employees perceive work differently than they did thirty years ago. According to Johnson and Kardos (this section), "the average American thirty-two year old has worked for nine firms." I have worked with many accomplished teachers who have left their schools or even the profession because of low pay, high-stress and a stifling work environment. The creativity of teaching often takes a back seat to constant preparation for high-stakes tests, especially at low-income schools, increasing teacher "burn-out." Other factors in addition to salary come into play when attracting and retaining accomplished teachers. Schools must be structured in a way that teachers' expertise and intellect are utilized. Exceptional teachers must be rewarded and recognized for their accomplishments. If graduates perceive teaching as a profession in which they will be able to sustain a comfortable life-style and one in which they will enjoy autonomy and opportunity for professional advancement, they are more likely to choose teaching as a career.

In its 2002 annual report on teacher quality, the U.S. Department of Education states that, "the best available research shows that solid verbal ability and content knowledge are what matters most" (U.S. Department of Education, 2002, p. 18). However, teaching and learning are highly complex and therefore difficult to quantify; the absence of data to expand definitions of teacher quality beyond content knowledge (as measured by GPA or test scores) does not mean that teacher quality does not encompass numerous characteristics and skills. Teaching is an intricate act involving a range of skills—from seemingly routine tasks such as constructing seating charts and calculating grades, to making countless split second decisions based on student needs, planning instruction and assessment, and playing the role of psychologist, parent, mentor and disciplinarian (sometimes simultaneously!). These skills are not innate, or solely intuitive. They are skills that the teacher must learn prior to entering the classroom, and in the years of practice that follow.

While it is obvious to teachers, parents, and students that a good teacher possesses many qualities, there are many others who seek to distill "good teaching" into a simple formula. This simply cannot be done. Quantifying the science and art of teaching shortchanges it. There is more to being a good teacher than content knowledge and verbal ability. Teacher preparation programs do and must continue to emphasize teachers' ability to work with young people effectively. Thus, teacher candidates graduating from teacher preparation programs must be deemed knowledgeable in their subject area, as well as in their ability to relate to the students they teach, to engage them in meaningful instruction, and to use assessments to inform appropriate instruction. I do not believe that content knowledge should be disregarded—broad content knowledge and academic ability are essential aspects of accomplished teaching. However, they constitute *only one part*. When readiness to teach is indicated by a passing score on a simple standardized (often multiple choice) exam, we are afforded only a snapshot of a candidate's abilities (Goodwin & Oyler, this section). A single test score cannot reveal how "good" of a teacher she or he will be. Thus, evaluation of a student teacher's interaction with students should take a greater role. A teacher ill-prepared in managing a classroom of diverse learners with multiple needs will most likely leave the profession in frustration. In addition, highly able teachers will (and do) leave the profession if not given a chance to use their professional teaching knowledge to affect and inform educational change.

Two major aspects of my teaching career thus far have made my experience as a classroom practitioner a rewarding and fulfilling one. The first is the school in which I have worked for the last seven years. The second is achieving National Board Certification. I hope that by sharing my experiences, I can provide clear examples of how teaching can draw top candidates, retain talent and elevate the status of the profession in the eyes of the public.

Too often, promising young teachers leave teaching due to increased pressure from standardized tests, "teacher proof" curricula, and top-down mandates which hardly seem to relate to children at all. Research shows that it is often the best teachers who leave (Johnson & Kardos, this section). The pressures of state and government mandates (and resultant teacher turn-over) more acutely affect low-income schools, leaving the poorest children with the least experienced teachers. I teach fourth and fifth grade at a school outside of Washington, D.C. The student population is greatly impacted by poverty. About 90 percent of our students are eligible for Free and Reduced Meals (FARMS), which is an indicator of poverty, and 40 percent of the students receive "English for Speakers of Other Languages" (ESOL) services. Our mobility rate is high—over a third of our students change during the course of a year. Five years ago, only 13 percent of third graders scored at a proficient level on the Maryland state assessments, and only 5 percent were proficient in math. A large part of our student population is made up of brand-new immigrants from all over the globe. We face many challenges besides low test scores: adult illiteracy, neighborhood gang violence, students affected deeply by the war-torn homelands they left, students and parents' beliefs that intelligence and academic success are innate, and of course, poverty. Communicating expectations of a U.S. school to parents who are unfamiliar with the role they play in their children's education is also a challenge we face. Our students often lack the background knowledge that is taken for granted in middle-class schools. However, they do have rich cultural backgrounds and stories of their own. Unfortunately, standardized tests do not always take these experiences into account.

Due to our low test scores, the state threatened to reconstitute the school and hire an entirely new administration and staff. However, through a unique partnership between the teachers' union and the school district, a teacher-led restructuring program began in 2001. The principal stayed, and teachers were given a choice to leave or stay. Twelve first-year teachers were hired that year. All teachers made a three year commitment to our school. We were required to work (and were compensated for) the equivalent of 15 extra days collaborating with colleagues, planning instruction, and analyzing student work. The focus of every decision was *doing what's best for children*. With support from administration, the union, and the school district, teachers became "teacher-leaders." Teachers were given a voice in the operations and structure of the school and the education it provided for students. For example, two years after the initial restructuring, the teaching and instructional support staff voted to departmentalize. Collectively, we felt stretched thin, and chose departmentalization as an alternative structure that would benefit students, because teachers would be able to specialize in two content areas (math/science or literacy/social studies). We decided to structure our planning time to allow us to work in vertical (Pre K-5) teams as well as with our grade level content team (e.g. fourth grade math/science teachers). Staff also designed and implemented sessions on examining student work or studying professional books, and developed committees that focused on meeting the social/emotional needs of students, recognizing and instructing gifted-talented students, and initiating parent/community outreach. Everything we chose to do as a staff had a purpose—to positively impact our students' learning and their lives as a whole.

Over the next five years, test scores improved dramatically, increasing to 75 percent of third graders proficient in reading and 67 percent of third graders proficient in math. Test scores weren't the only improvement. Students and parents alike became accustomed to the school philosophy—that all children can learn, given enough time and support. Students began seeing the value of effort and its correlation with achievement. Our school's "4 Key Messages" include, "Effective effort and strategies will lead to success." The culture of the school is one of academic rigor and respect for students' cultural backgrounds and the knowledge they bring to the classroom. I believe that the reason our school continues to succeed in educating our students is because teachers, instructional assistants, administration—even the cafeteria and custodial staff—are all accountable to each other and to themselves. Though the restructuring was initially driven by low test scores, the ownership of the process by staff has enabled our school to create professional accountability—not the kind that teachers shudder at the thought of (sanctions, penalties, programs imposed by outside agencies), but the kind that demands that everyone in the building takes responsibility for educating children, the kind which attracts and retains strong, accomplished teachers by giving them a voice in the way their school works. In the process of reforming our school, ten teachers achieved National Board Certification. We currently have five National Board Certified Teachers, including the 2006 National Teacher of the Year. Five additional teachers are currently pursuing National Board Certification.

In addition to strong, teacher-led schools, the profession needs to support teachers' continual quest for knowledge and passion for learning. If we are to attract and retain lifelong learners to teaching, then we must allow teachers an opportunity to break out of the traditional salary lane, to advance professionally and intellectually. Sure, teachers love working with children, but this alone is not enough to keep them in the profession. The National Board for Professional Teaching Standards (NBPTS) set forth its Five Core Propositions in 1989 (NBPTS, 2002), articulating a vision of accomplished teaching. NBPTS states that proficient teaching calls for the teacher to have a broad knowledge of the liberal arts and sciences; to know the subjects and skills they teach students; to understand and utilize curriculum materials and assessments; to use a variety of teaching and assessment methods. Teachers must also possess "knowledge of students and human development; skills in effectively teaching students from racially, ethnically, and socio-economically diverse backgrounds; and the skills, capacities and dispositions to employ such knowledge wisely in the interest of students" (NBPTS, 2002, p. 2). The policy statement contends that:

> This enumeration suggests the broad base for expertise in teaching but conceals the complexities, uncertainties and dilemmas of the work. The formal knowledge teachers rely on accumulates steadily, yet provides insufficient guidance in many situations. Teaching ultimately requires judgment, improvisation, and conversation

about means and ends. Human qualities, expert knowledge and skill, and professional commitment together compose excellence in this craft."

(NBPTS, 2002, p. 2)

To achieve National Board Certification, there were many skills I had to demonstrate. As a teacher of upper-elementary students, I had to demonstrate in-depth content knowledge of national standards in literacy, mathematics, science, social studies, health and the arts. However, this was only *one part* of my certification requirements. In accordance with NBPTS standards, I had to demonstrate knowledge of students' strengths and needs, monitor student learning, think systematically about my practice, engage parents in two-way communication, and be an active member of a learning community. Research conducted by numerous universities and independent agencies show that students of teachers who meet NBPTS standards improved an average of 7 percent more on their year-end math and reading tests than pupils whose teachers attempted but failed to gain certification. There were even more significant gains (up to 15 percent) with younger and lower-income students. This gain was statistically significant even when controlling for years of experience, degree level and scores on licensing exams (Goldhaber & Anthony, 2005).

So what does this all mean? First, if we, as a nation, are to provide a well-balanced, culturally relevant, cutting-edge education to all children, we must strive to attract and retain diverse, well-prepared, accomplished, *vocal* teachers. Those who choose to teach come for the kids, but stay because of the intellectual stimulation and ability to truly make a difference (in education as well as children's lives). Second, all teachers must be empowered to speak out on what we know is good for learners. It is up to those of us working in the profession, and those preparing the next generation of teachers, to ensure that we work towards strengthening our profession by increasing teacher voice in policy-making decisions. It is only by bolstering teachers and teaching through better pay, increased opportunities for advancement, and a greater voice in curricular and policy decisions, that we will attract the highest quality candidates from varied backgrounds and experiences who will commit to teach our nation's greatest resource: its children.

REFERENCES

Goldhaber, D. & Anthony, E. (2005) *Can teacher quality be effectively assessed? National board certification as a signal of effective teaching.* Retrieved June 10, 2006, from http://www.crpe.org/workingpapers/pdf/NBPTSquality_report.pdf

Lortie, D. C. (1975) *Schoolteacher: a sociological study.* Chicago: University of Chicago Press.

National Board for Professional Teaching Standards. (2002) *What teachers should know and be able to do.* Retrieved June 10, 2006, from http://www.nbpts.org/pdf/coreprops.pdf

U.S. Department of Education, Office of Postsecondary Education, Office of Policy Planning and Innovation (2002) *Meeting the highly qualified teachers challenge: the secretary's annual report on teacher quality*, Washington, DC: Author.

Does difference make a difference?

Diversity and teacher education

Editor: Ana María Villegas

Part 5
Framing chapters

31 Diversity and teacher education

Ana María Villegas
Montclair State University

The population of the United States has always been characterized by racial, ethnic, and linguistic diversity. While formal histories of the country have given center-stage to Anglo-Saxon English speakers, a large percentage of the populace has always been of other racial, ethnic, and linguistic backgrounds. These groups have included the Native people who were on this continent before Northern Europeans arrived; African people brought here as slaves; Spanish-speaking people (some of European heritage and some *mestizos*) in what was Northern Mexico before it was appropriated to become the American Southwest; the Chinese men who came to build the railroads; a large influx of European immigrants, mostly from Southern and Eastern Europe, who began arriving in the latter part of the nineteenth century; and more recently, an even larger and more diverse wave of immigrants from all over the world.

The need to unify these varied groups equitably into one political entity has made diversity an enduring and tension-laden issue in the United States. The public schools of this country are said to have a major role in bringing about this unification by providing a "common education" to students from diverse groups. Theoretically, the "great equalizer" of public education offers everyone the knowledge and skills they need for successful integration into American society, regardless of differences in backgrounds. The underlying assumption is that if students work hard in school and prove themselves deserving, they will ultimately reap the benefits of education in their adult lives. Despite these lofty ideals, American society has failed at the task of equitably integrating people of diverse backgrounds—particularly people of color—into its economic, social, and political structures. Neither have schools fulfilled their promise of providing an equitable opportunity for every person to prove his or her merit.

Until slaves were emancipated in 1862, people of African descent living in this country were prohibited by law and/or custom from formal education (Woodson, 1919). After emancipation, public schooling became available to Black children, but they were required to attend segregated schools, particularly in the South, where the overwhelming majority of the Black population lived. The "separate but equal" doctrine notwithstanding, segregated schools were clearly not equal. While the Brown decision of 1954 dismantled the legal basis for a dual system of education in this country, the pre-Brown legacy endures to the present in that many if not most U.S. schools remain largely segregated by race, ethnicity, and social class (Orfield & Lee, 2006). Like African Americans, Native American and Hispanic students have also suffered from a pattern of segregation and inequitable schooling. Such exclusionary practices have resulted in a considerable academic gap between students of color and their White peers over time. This contradiction between the espoused principles of equal educational opportunities on one hand and well-document disparities in the treatment and educational outcomes of different groups of students on the other hand has framed discussions of issues related to diversity in American education, particularly during the past 50 years.

Conflicting views of how schools should prepare children and youth from diverse backgrounds for social, economic, and political participation in American society reflect different conceptions of diversity that have coexisted in this country over the years. Historically, cultural and linguistic assimilation has been the prevalent goal of American education. From this perspective, a prime objective of schools is to eradicate cultural and linguistic differences and instill in all children a common set of values—namely, those of the White, Protestant, middle-class, English-speaking dominant group in American society. In its extreme form, this view is reflected in Federal policies of the post-Civil War era that called for Indian children to be removed from their families and enrolled in boarding schools where they were immersed in the language, values, and practical knowledge of the dominant society while being stripped of their traditional language and culture. Assimilationist thinking has also informed public school practices aimed at Americanizing immigrants, whether they came to this country voluntarily or became part of it through colonization or annexation (MacDonald, 2004). Underlying such assimilationist school policies and practices is a deep-seated fear that cultural and linguistic diversity threatens the unity of society. Implicit in this thinking is also the general belief that the language and culture of the dominant group in the United States are inherently superior to the languages and cultures of other groups, especially those of people of color.

Countering the assimilationist position is a pluralistic perspective that has gained some support in the United States over the past four decades. The latter viewpoint contends that diversity is a valuable aspect of U.S. society and the presence of a variety of cultures and languages enriches the nation as a whole. As such, advocates of pluralism encourage the preservation of linguistic and cultural differences, but not the separation of different groups from one another. To the contrary, they believe that respectful interaction and communication across differences is essential for the well-being of all. In its purest form, pluralism embraces the belief that no one group is superior to others and all cultures are equally valuable. From this perspective, a salient goal of schools is to incorporate and respond positively to the diverse ways of knowing, learning, and behaving of different cultural groups. This thinking is manifested in the concept of multicultural education articulated by the American Association of Colleges for Teacher Education (AACTE) in its 1972 position paper entitled *No One Model American*. Because this position paper has helped define issues of diversity in teacher education since its publication, it is included as an artifact in this section of the Handbook. Interestingly, Glazer (1993) contended that assimilation as an ideal came into disrepute in the late 1960s due to the country's failure to integrate the Black population into its social and economic structures. Such failure, he argued, was based on racist attitudes and behaviors that have historically prevailed in the U.S. He further contended that the inability to integrate Black Americans equitably brought to surface the problems inherent in assimilationist thinking and lent political support to pluralist views, a shift in perspectives that he thinks resulted in calls for multicultural education. This provocative article is also included in the artifact portion of this section of the Handbook.

DIVERSITY AND TEACHER EDUCATION IN A CHANGING CONTEXT

This section of the Handbook focuses on how teacher education has responded to student diversity, attending specifically to developments of the past 50 years. Among several key factors that have shaped this response, three merit special attention: (1) changes in the demographic makeup of the K-12 student population; (2) changes resulting from the Brown decision; and (3) changes in conceptions of learning.

Changes in the demographics of the K-12 student population

Since the 1970s, the K-12 student population has become increasingly diverse racially and ethnically. In 1971, students of color accounted for 22 percent of enrollments in elementary and secondary public schools. Today they account for over 41 percent of the total K-12 student population (NCES, 2004). It is projected that schools will become even more heterogeneous in the future, with students of color attaining the numerical majority by 2035 (U.S. Department of Education, 2002). Growth is particularly evident among Hispanics, who are already the single largest minority group in the United States, and Asians, who are the fastest growing minority group here. Numerical and proportional gains among these groups signal an increase in the number of young people who speak a language other than English at home, which is already having a significant impact in schools. For example, one in five students attending public schools in the United States today is an English language learner (NCES, 2005). These demographic changes are exerting considerable pressure on programs of teacher education to address issues of racial, ethnic, and linguistic diversity.

Changes resulting from the Brown decision

The Brown decision of 1954 also helped to define teacher education over the past half century. While the overall intent of the Brown decision was to provide equal educational opportunities for African Americans, school desegregation significantly changed the role of White teachers in elementary and secondary public schools. In the segregated system, White teachers had taught only White children. After 1954, however, they were also responsible for teaching the children of color assigned to their classes, an undertaking for which most were unprepared. This lack of preparation is evident in numerous studies conducted in racially/ethnically integrated classrooms during the 1960s, 1970s, and 1980s, the results of which showed that White teachers generally held lower expectations for students of color and often treated them less favorably. This sobering realization led to some modification of the teacher education curriculum with the overall goal of preparing White candidates to teach students from diverse backgrounds equitably and effectively. The addition of a multicultural education standard by the National Council for the Accreditation of Teacher Education (NCATE) in 1979 as part of the accreditation process for schools and colleges of education and its revision in 2000 provided support for these changes.

The Brown decision had another unintended consequence. Ironically, school desegregation dramatically reduced the presence of Black teachers in public elementary and secondary schools. Ethridge (1979) conservatively estimated that by 1970 at least 38,000 Black educators who had staffed Black schools prior to *Brown* lost their jobs through dismissal or non-renewal of contracts. According to Irvine (1988), the massive loss of Black teachers severed the cultural links between home and school that had existed for African American students prior to desegregation. Since the late 1980s, programs of teacher education have been pressed to recruit and prepare more people of color for the profession. (The Ethridge article is included as a section artifact to give insight into the historical roots of the existing shortage of teachers of color.)

Changing conceptions of learning

Changing conceptions of learning over the past three decades—from transmission to constructivist views—also have profound implications for the teaching of diverse student populations. Historically, transmission views of learning have guided the work of teachers and schools. Within a transmission framework, the role of students is largely that of "receiving" the knowledge comprising the curriculum. From this perspective, learning is viewed as the consumption, storage, and recall of information by individual students. The prevalent image of the learner is that of a receptacle or container waiting passively to be filled with knowledge. Accordingly, teaching involves transmitting the content of the curriculum to students. Because it is assumed that all students (should) learn the same way and that their background experiences play no appreciable role in learning, teachers are thought to need only knowledge of their subject matter and a uniform method of instruction.

Since the 1960s, transmission views of learning have been challenged by critics who argue that what is learned is always filtered through the learner's frame of reference. From this interpretive perspective, learning is defined as the process by which students construct meaning in response to new ideas and experiences. In so doing, learners are said to use their prior knowledge and beliefs—which they have stored in memory as mental structures (described variously by cognitive scientists as knowledge frameworks, schemata, or personal theories)—to make sense of the new input (von Glaserfeld, 1995). Good teaching, therefore, involves helping students build bridges between their prior knowledge and experiences—both personal and cultural—and the material to be learned. This requires that in addition to knowing their subject matter, teachers need to know their students well in order to help them build these bridges. They also need to be able to use a variety of pedagogical strategies to involve students of diverse backgrounds in learning.

By acknowledging that children's pre-existing knowledge and experiences—both personal and cultural—serve as the foundation for learning, constructivists position student diversity in a positive light. As constructivist views gain acceptance, teacher educators are necessarily pressed to question the pervasive belief that the language and culture of children who are different from the dominant mainstream group are problems to be remedied. Similarly, teacher educators are finding that they must address the deficit attitudes toward diversity that many White pre-service teachers have derived from a lifetime of socialization in a racist and mostly segregated society.

The aforementioned changes in the demographics of schools, in educational policies and practices resulting from the *Brown* decision, and in conceptions of learning inform the content addressed throughout the Diversity section of the Handbook.

ORGANIZATION OF THE SECTION

The section opens with three distinct but complementary framing chapters, each of which addresses issues of diversity in teacher education from a different angle. The chapters were conceptualized not only to provide much-needed updates on relevant issues, but also to make conceptually and practically important distinctions that tend to be obscured in the literature on preparing teachers for diversity. Because White teacher candidates and candidates of color enter teacher education programs with substantially different understandings of matters of diversity based on their life experiences, their preparation needs can differ dramatically. Unfortunately, most of the existing literature ignores such differences. Since the vast majority of teacher candidates are White, most of the literature on the preparation of teachers to teach students of color focuses on the needs of White teachers—often without making that focus explicit. The section tackles this conceptual confusion by purposefully including separate chapters on the preparation of White teachers and on the preparation of teachers of color. This strategy enabled the authors of the two chapters to provide greater conceptual clarity regarding specific preparation issues of relevance to the particular population of teachers on which they focused their analysis. Similarly, the preparation of teachers to teach English language learners (ELLs) has tended to be subsumed under general discussions of teacher preparation for diversity or of preparing culturally responsive teachers. Teacher educators have had almost nowhere to turn to in the literature to learn about the language-related knowledge, skills, and dispositions classroom teachers need to teach ELLs successfully or to learn about ways to help preservice and inservice teachers develop in these areas. The third framing chapter in the section makes a major contribution to the field of teacher education by explicitly distinguishing linguistic diversity from other types of diversity and in examining the preparation of all teachers to teach linguistically diverse student populations.

In the following chapter, Christine Sleeter offers a detailed and thoughtful analysis of the preparation of White teachers for diverse students. Drawing on the available research, she makes a convincing case that preparing White educators for diverse student populations involves much more than equipping otherwise culturally neutral and unbiased candidates with pedagogical knowledge and skills. The chapter presents a comprehensive research-based framework that can assist teacher educators in rethinking the preparation of White teachers for diverse students from the preservice level through the initial year of teaching. The framework gives detailed attention to cross-cultural community-based learning and to coursework and preparation in classrooms, while promoting a coherent approach to teacher education. In addition to its unique and explicit focus on White teachers, Sleeter's chapter is distinct from previous reviews of the literature on preparing teachers for diversity in its developmental conceptualization of the process for learning to teach from preservice preparation through the inservice years. The chapter offers implications for research and sketches recommendations for teacher education practice that are warranted by the existing research base.

In the next chapter, Villegas and Davis shift the focus of analysis from the preparation of White candidates for teaching diverse students to the recruitment, preparation, and retention of candidates of color for the teaching profession. Situating policies and practices aimed at diversifying the teaching force within the context of the racial/ethnic achievement gap, the chapter offers the most up-to-date review of a relatively small but expanding body of empirical studies that examine the relationship between teacher race/ethnicity and student learning. Based on this review, Villegas and Davis conclude that increasing the diversity in the ranks of teachers has the potential for changing the dynamics of classrooms and schools, and ultimately for improving the academic outcomes of students of color. The chapter also chronicles the shortage of teachers of color from 1971 to the present, explores the reasons for their short supply, and details policy and programmatic initiatives implemented since the early 1990s to remedy the problem. The authors present evidence that minority recruitment policies and programs in the past decade have succeeded in increasing the percentages of Hispanic and Asian teachers, but not the percentage of African American teachers. They warn, however, that while issues of minority recruitment into teacher education and teaching continue to attract the attention of educators, policymakers and researchers, relatively little is being done to prepare these recruits to use their insiders' knowledge about the experiences of students from racial/ethnic minority groups in their own teaching and to retain them in the profession.

As mentioned above, the final framing chapter breaks new ground in its focus on the preparation of regular classroom teachers to teach ELLs, a topic addressed only superficially—if at all—in previously published reviews of the literature on preparing teachers for diversity. In this chapter, Lucas and Grinberg address three fundamental questions. Why should we devote attention to preparing all teachers to teach ELLs? What do classroom teachers need to know and be able to do to teach ELLs well? What do we know about how classroom teachers are currently being prepared to teach ELLs? The authors draw on empirical, theoretical, and descriptive literature to answer each of these questions. The chapter makes a case for the preparation of all teachers to teach ELLs; provides frameworks for thinking about the content, structures, and processes of such preparation; and gives much needed examples of initiatives that provide such preparation in pre-service and in-service contexts. They also make recommendations for sorely needed research.

The framing chapters are followed by four artifacts (previously published works) that were carefully selected to help the reader understand better how the conflict between assimilationist and pluralist ideologies has played out over time in American society in general and in its schools in particular. Two of the pieces are scholarly articles and two are position statements by the American Association of Colleges for Teacher Education. The first artifact is a 1993 article by Nathan Glazer, an influential sociologist who has written extensively on issues of immigration, multiculturalism, and social policy. As mentioned above, Glazer argues in this article that assimilation as an ideal for immigrants and minorities in the United States fell into disrepute in the late 1960s as a result of the country's inability to assimilate Black Americans because of deep-rooted prejudices and discrimination against this group. The article illustrates the profound tension between the forces of assimilation and pluralism, particularly as they confronted each other in the United States during the twentieth century. Glazer concludes that multicultural education is a compelling option for Black Americans, given the group's long history of cultural and structural exclusion.

The second article in this group was written in 1979 by Samuel Ethridge, a prominent official at the National Education Association (NEA) in the 1960s and 1970s who was recently recognized by the NEA for his work to desegregate teacher organizations in this country. By painstakingly documenting the loss of numerous Black educators through dismissals and non-renewal of contracts following the 1954 *Brown* decision, Ethridge provides insight into the profound racial prejudices that exist in this country. He also sheds light on the historical roots of the current shortage of teachers of color, especially Black teachers.

The last two artifacts—both policy statements endorsed by AACTE—focus directly on issues of diversity in teacher education. In its *No One Model American* statement of 1972, AACTE concisely articulated the pluralistic perspective discussed above and its implications for teacher education, explicitly rejecting both assimilation and separatism as educational goals. This was a groundbreaking statement at a time when assimilation was still widely embraced. Thirty years later, AACTE published *Educators' Preparation for Cultural and Linguistic Diversity: A Call to Action*. In this more recent position paper, AACTE once again rejected assimilation and articulated support for both linguistic and cultural pluralism. The 2002 statement is as bold as the earlier one in its explicit "call to action" for teacher education institutions to strive for educational equity for English language learners in U.S. schools by supporting such measures as native language development and "mutual accommodation" of native and mainstream U.S. cultures. The focus on culturally and linguistically diverse students in 2002 reflects the demographic changes over the previous 30 years—particularly the increased presence of students who speak languages other than English at home.

The section ends with three commentaries written by individuals positioned differently in terms of their cultural, linguistic, and professional backgrounds. In their thoughtful commentaries, the authors explore a broad range of implications for research, policy, and practice that flow from the literature reviewed in the framing chapters. In the first commentary, Jacqueline Jordan Irvine draws on her broad and rich experience as a scholar and researcher with a substantial body of work focusing on matters of diversity. Irvine offers insightful observations regarding the tensions surrounding issues of diversity in teacher education as related to people, pedagogy, and politics. The theme threaded throughout her commentary is that advocates of multicultural education must accept that efforts to integrate diversity into teacher education inevitably involve conflict.

In the second commentary, Tina Jacobowitz and Nicholas Michelli make use of their extensive work with the National Network for Educational Renewal and the Agenda for Education in a Democracy, both of which are based on the work of John Goodlad, to frame their observations. They contend that teacher educators—broadly defined to include faculty in education, in the arts and sciences, and in elementary and secondary schools—need to work together in order to prepare future teachers to address the achievement gap. They argue that such work involves the simultaneous renewal of K-12 schools and teacher education. Jacobowitz and Michelli also offer insightful comments about the purposes of public education in a democracy and the appropriateness of focusing on candidates' dispositions in programs of teacher education.

In the final commentary, Victoria Chou and Karen Sakash respond to key ideas presented in the framing chapters from the perspective of teacher educators at a land-grant institution with an explicit commitment to serve an urban environment. After illustrating their points clearly with examples from their own practice, they conclude that teacher educators must break with tradition to prepare teacher candidates to ground their teaching in the language and culture of their future students.

Taken together, the works in this section provide rich complementary perspectives on how to prepare teachers for a diverse student population. The changing demographics of elementary and secondary schools coupled with persistent racial/ethnic achievement gaps demand fundamental changes in the ways teachers are prepared. While the goal of providing all children, regardless of backgrounds, with an equal opportunity to learn and ultimately to become active participants in a democratic society has endured across time, approaches to this overarching goal must be adapted to suit the historical moment. The framing chapters offer distinctly new ways of looking at the issues as well as helpful suggestions regarding the types of changes needed today to prepare teachers who have the knowledge, skills, and commitment to educate students of diverse racial, ethnic, cultural and linguistic backgrounds. The artifacts and commentaries help us better understand why such changes are needed.

REFERENCES

American Association of Colleges for Teacher Education Commission on Multicultural Education (1972) *No one model American*. Washington, DC: Author.

American Association of Colleges for Teacher Education (2002) *Educators' preparation for cultural and linguistic diversity: a call to action*. Washington, DC: Author.

Ethridge, S. (1979) Impact of the 1954 *Brown v. Topeka Board of Education* decision on Black educators. *The Negro Educational Review*, 30(4), 217–232.

Glasersfeld, E. von (1995) *Radical constructivism: a way of knowing and learning*. London: Falmer.

Glazer, N. (1993, November) Is assimilation dead? *The Annals of the American Academy of Political and Social Sciences*, 530, 122–136.

Irvine, J. J. (1988) An analysis of the problem of the disappearing Black educator. *Elementary School Journal*, 88(5), 503–514.

MacDonald, V. M. (2004) Americanization and resistance. In V. M. MacDonald (ed.), *Latino education in the United States: a narrated history from 1513–2000* (pp. 55–73). New York: Palgrave Macmillan.

National Center for Education Statistics (2002) Digest for education statistics tables and figures. Washington, DC: U.S. Government Printing Office. Retrieved 5/6/06 from http://nces.ed.gov/programs/digest/d04/dt04.asp.

National Conter for Education Statictics (2004) *Digest for education statistics*, Table 42. Percentage distribution of enrollment in public elementary and secondary schools, by race/ethnicity and state or jurisdiction: Fall 1992 and fall 2002. Retrieved 4/30/06 from http://nces.ed.gov/programs/digest/d 04/tables/dt 04–042.asp.

National Center for Educational Statistics (2005) The condition of education 2005. Indicator 5: Language minority school-age children. Washington, DC: U.S. Department of Education. Retrieved 7/16/05 from http://nces.ed.gov/programs/coe/2005/section1/indicator05.asp.

National Center for Educational Statistics (2002) *The condition of education 2002*. Washington, DC: U.S. Government Printing Office.

Orfield, G. & C. Lee (2006) *Racial transformation and the changing nature of segregation.* Cambridge, MA: The Civil Rights Project at Harvard University.

Woodson, C. G. (1919, July) Negro life and history in our schools. *Journal of Negro History*, 4, 273–280.

32 Preparing White teachers for diverse students

Christine E. Sleeter
California State University Monterey Bay

Beginning in the 1960s, desegregation was intended to make schools more equitable and responsive to communities of color. I will not review the extent to which this intention was actually fulfilled, but will focus on one result: problems associated with the Whitening of the teaching force. In the wake of desegregation, because Whites perceived Black schools and teachers as inferior, numerous Black schools were closed and almost 40,000 Black teachers and administrators lost their positions (Milner & Howard, 2004). Currently less than 16 percent of the teaching force is of color, in contrast to about 42 percent of public K-12 students (National Center for Education Statistics, 2002). The demographic gap between students and teachers is growing as the student population continues to diversify but the teaching population does not.

This gap matters because it means that students of color—especially Black and Latino students—are much more likely than White students to be taught by teachers who question their academic ability, are uncomfortable around them, or do not know how to teach them well. For example, researchers consistently find teachers to see White and Asian students as more teachable than Black or Latino students, and White teachers to be more likely than teachers of color to hold lower expectations for Black and Latino students (Hauser-Cram *et al.*, 2003; Pang & Sablan, 1998; Warren, 2002). White teachers often have more difficulty forming constructive relationships with students of color, particularly African American students, than with White students. Commonly assuming that African American and Latino parents do not value education, White teachers are much less likely to build relationships with them than are teachers of color. Lacking familiarity with communities their students of color come from, many White teachers are unable to build bridges between students and curriculum, but then interpret students' lack of engagement as disinterest in learning, or their academic problems as inability to learn. Due to a combination of low expectations and cultural mismatch, White teachers appear to refer students of color to special education more than do teachers of color. As a result, students of color tend to be overrepresented in special education, while White students—particularly those from affluent backgrounds—overpopulate gifted programs (Harry & Klingner, 2006). White teachers who are ill-equipped to teach students of color, particularly those in low-income communities, often seek jobs elsewhere as soon as they can, leading to high levels of teacher turn-over in many urban and poor rural schools.

Empirical research documents that White preservice students commonly bring into teacher education attitudes and experiences that eventually lead to the patterns above. As members of the most segregated and isolated racial category in the U.S. (Orfield & Lee, 2005), most White candidates enter teacher education with very little cross-cultural background, knowledge and experience, although they often bring naive optimism that coexists with unexamined stereotypes taken for granted as truth (Barry & Lechner, 1995;

Law & Lane, 1987; Schultz, *et al.*, 1996; Smith, *et al.*, 1997; Terrill & Mark, 2000). Four interrelated problems affect teaching if not addressed directly.

First, bringing little awareness or understanding of discrimination, especially racism (Avery & Walker, 1993; McIntyre, 1997; Su, 1996), most White preservice teachers are "dysconscious" of how racism works in schools and society at large, and how it is reproduced daily (King, 1991). They tend to see racism as a problem of interpersonal interactions, which they believe that an open attitude toward others solves. They generally do not see racism as patterned institutionalized structures and processes that allocate social resources differentially based on race and that have long historical roots. For example, White preservice teachers commonly assume that schools are no longer segregated and that everyone has access to the same quality of education. To attempt to understand race, they usually rely on their own family ethnic history with assimilation and upward mobility, assuming that experiences of White ethnics are the same as those of non-Whites. As a result, many characterize calls for culturally relevant teaching, bilingual education, or multicultural education as "whining" or unnecessary demands for "special treatment."

Second, because they bring virtually no conceptual framework for understanding visible inequalities other than the dominant deficit framework, studies find White preservice teachers generally assume lower expectations for the achievement of students of color than for White students, without seeing this as a manifestation of racism (Marx, 2003; Schultz, *et al.*, 1996). For example, Richman and colleagues (1997) found twenty such students in a small college estimated the grade point average and IQ of African American children lower than that of White children based *only* on viewing photographs of children. Like White practicing teachers, White preservice teachers generally assume that underachievement of students of color, particularly African American students, is due to their families not valuing education (e.g. Avery & Walker, 1993; Irvine & York, 1993) rather than to factors under control of classroom teachers. Such a deficit view affects a teacher's willingness to work to figure out how to reach and challenge students of color. It is unlikely that White preservice teachers will act to close achievement gaps without directly confronting deficit views of students of color and their communities.

Third, White preservice teachers are generally ignorant of communities of color, fearing them and fearing discussing race and racism (Martin & Williams-Dixon, 1994). White teachers commonly sidestep fear through colorblindness, claiming, "I don't see color, I just see children" (McIntyre, 1997; Valli, 1995). Part of this fear has to do with teachers' perceptions of themselves as good people. For example, Marx (2003) pointed out that, as her White students began to recognize some of their own actions as racist, they were shocked and disappointed in themselves. Many are also afraid of emotions and tensions that accompany discussions of racism (O'Brien, 2004), and fear saying the wrong thing. Even those who grew up in diverse communities have been found to assume they understand other groups much better than they actually do (Powell *et al.*, 2001). Fear probably makes so many White preservice teachers resistant to examining long-held beliefs (Smith *et al.*, 1997) and hearing people of color talk about racial concerns that can be addressed. Yet, if fear and ignorance are not directly dealt with, White preservice teachers become classroom teachers who are not able to examine racism in their own workplaces, hear what students or parents of color say about teaching and working with them more appropriately, or facilitate conversations about differences with racially diverse students in their own classrooms.

Fourth, White preservice teachers commonly lack awareness of themselves as cultural beings (Schmidt, 1999), assuming that their own beliefs and ways of behaving are "the norm to which others should aspire" (Valli, 1995). In addition, they have usually spent very little time in cultural communities unfamiliar to them, so have not developed cross-cultural awareness or tools for viewing another community as a cultural site (Barry & Lechner, 1995; Gilbert, 1995; Hlebowitsh & Tellez, 1993; Larke, 1990; Taylor & Sobel, 2001). As long as they see themselves as normal but not cultural, they use their own unexamined frames of reference against which to judge students, students' families, and their communities. This practice unfortunately reinforces deficit thinking. For example, a teacher who believes that learning behavior involves sitting quietly will not recognize learning behavior in students who are active and noisy, nor accurately differentiate learning behavior from off-task or disruptive behavior.

There is an urgent need to improve substantially White teachers' preparation for diverse students.[1] While White teachers can learn to teach diverse student populations well, this does not happen automatically. Preparing White teachers is not simply a matter of equipping presumably unbiased individuals with additional skills and strategies to use with diverse populations. If it were that simple, patterns of racial bias and exclusion would not continue to permeate schooling.

This chapter develops a research-based framework for considering programmatically coherent preparation at the preservice level and subsequent support through the first years of teaching. I selected data-based research studies published after 1980 in which the great majority of the preservice or inservice teachers (usually 90 percent or above) were White. I looked particularly for empirical studies examining effects of an intervention or teacher education experience (such as student teaching) on the attitudes, knowledge, or teaching behaviors of White teachers relative to teaching students of color and/or language minority students. None of the studies linked teacher education with student learning in the K-12 classroom. Given the absence of this type of work, I sought studies that demonstrated a connection between teacher education and teacher learning in areas relevant to quality teaching for diverse students (Alton-Lee, 2003; Gay, 2000). Most of the studies were published in refereed journals, although a few were reported in book chapters.

Throughout I will argue that it is not enough to prepare White teachers to teach *as well as* the average White teacher does currently. Doing so would only perpetuate lower expectations, discomfort, and lack of appropriate pedagogical knowledge. Instead, if we are serious about preparing White teachers who are able to help close the racial achievement gap, we need to prepare them to teach *better* and *more equitably* than the average White teacher does currently. I will use research evidence to show that this cannot be done with one course, one field experience, or one student teaching experience. Instead, research suggests that teacher education programs that are coherently organized to develop teaching practices, with supporting attitudes and knowledge, have the potential to enable White teacher candidates to confront and move beyond twenty-odd years of prior socialization, in order to learn to teach diverse students well.

RETHINKING TEACHER PREPARATION

Teacher education faces the challenge of preparing teachers who will become better than established teachers at confronting and transcending patterns of racism in schools. Teacher education must be powerful enough to counter at least three forms of on-going socialization that White teachers, both preservice and inservice, experience. First, the on-going lived experiences of White people usually take place in relatively homogeneous neighborhoods, in which White individuals associate mainly with other White people, experiencing the everyday privileges that accrue to looking White without being aware of this (Sleeter, 1992). In this context, not only does cross-cultural and cross-racial aware-ness not come naturally, but White people often have so little awareness of the experi-ences of people unlike themselves that they generally deny what people of color say about their own experiences, aspirations, and communities. Second, the ongoing experience of school and classroom life, first as a K-12 student, then as a university student, and subsequently as a new teacher, solidifies taken-for-granted conceptions of how schooling should go and what teaching should look like, making it difficult to envision alternatives (Lortie, 1975). Third, the everyday conditions of teacher work generally structure teach-ing as transmission of prescribed content to crowds of students following a "banking" model of teaching and learning. When teaching is experienced this way and supported by testing, teachers learn to see differences among students primarily as differences in ability to learn what is prescribed (Prawat, 1992).

Most teacher education programs lack a coherent and sustained approach to counter-ing these on-going forms of socialization. Case studies have found programs in pre-dominantly White institutions to provide disjointed preparation for diversity and equity, dependent on the interests of individual professors rather than on a comprehensive conception of preparation for excellent teaching in racially diverse contexts. Some topics recur in several classes (such as textbook bias), while others are not addressed at all. Student teachers may develop a superficial understanding of multicultural teaching, but in the classroom follow the lead of their cooperating teachers (Cannella & Reiff, 1994; Davis, 1995; Grant & Koskela, 1986; Miller *et al.*, 1997). Many student teachers from such programs have been found to flounder if placed in classrooms in which most stu-dents are culturally or linguistically different from themselves (Birrell, 1994; Goodwin, 1994; Weiner, 1990).

There is evidence that well-planned, coherent programs can make an impact that persists beyond preservice preparation. By coherence, I mean two related things. First, the faculty and cooperating teachers who work with preservice students share norms and a vision regarding the purpose of education, the nature of teaching and learning, and the nature and value of equity and diversity. Second, this vision guides planning a teacher preparation curriculum and set of experiences that intentionally build preservice stu-dents' conceptual foundation and pedagogical skill. Ideally, everyone who works with preservice students—including arts and sciences faculty, university administrators who support teacher preparation programs, and teachers and administrators in partner schools—would share the same vision and orient their work toward it. In practice, it is difficult enough to get the teacher education faculty and a core of cooperating teachers to agree on a shared vision and to plan a program together. But doing even that much matters.

Two comparative studies examined program capacity to produce teachers with a con-structivist, socio-cultural approach to teaching and learning, demonstrating the power of program coherence. Tatto (1998), in a comparison of nine teacher education programs (five preservice, one induction, one alternate route, and two inservice), found that those with the most internal coherence most strongly guided the development of teachers' beliefs. Internal coherence meant that faculty shared a defined philosophy and norms, used those to guide curriculum development and implementation, and provided students with context-relevant opportunities to learn. Brouwer and Korthagen (2005), in a longi-tudinal study of graduates of four teacher education programs, found programs with an impact that was visible in teachers' second and third years of teaching were the most coherently planned. Cooperating teachers and field supervisors developed a shared vision of classroom teaching. Classroom field experiences introduced preservice teachers grad-ually to increasingly complex teaching, and programs alternated intentionally between field experiences and college classes. In both studies, the strength of well-planned, coherent programs blunted the impact of other forms of socialization.

The remainder of this chapter considers research-based components of teacher education programs that show promise for strengthening preparation and professional support so that White teachers can learn to teach students of racially, ethnically, and linguistically diverse backgrounds well, first at the preservice level, then after completing teacher certification.

PRESERVICE PREPARATION

At the preservice level, teacher education programs commonly attend to the theory-practice linkage through university-based coursework and school-based fieldwork. In addition to those two broad sites for learning, research suggests that teacher education develop out-of-school cross-cultural community-based learning experiences. These three sites offer different kinds of knowledge and experiential resources that, when intentionally connected, have the potential to interrupt racist attitudes and understandings, and help White teachers learn to teach diverse students well. Together, they constitute a three-legged platform for preparing White teachers at the preservice level. All three legs are needed; if one or two are weak or absent, the platform does not stand.[2]

Cross-cultural community-based learning

Cross-cultural community-based learning involves learning about a community that is culturally different from one's own by spending time there, equipped with learning strategies such as active listening and guidance in what to observe. Most White teachers have had little experience learning how to learn from someone else's community, yet this is exactly what they will need to do in order to build pedagogy that is culturally and contextually relevant to students from backgrounds different from their own. Effective teachers of students who are racially, ethnically, culturally different from themselves have learned how to recognize and build on assets students bring, interpret students' classroom behavior accurately, contextualize problems students bring within a sociopolitical rather than cultural deficiency analysis, and communicate constructively with adults in students' lives. As Villegas and Lucas (2002) explained,

> To help students from diverse backgrounds build bridges between home and school, teachers need to know about the lives of the specific children they teach. While prospective teachers cannot develop this knowledge in advance in programs of preservice teacher education, they should be helped to understand what they need to know about their future students and to develop strategies for familiarizing themselves with those students.
>
> (p. 80)

Community-based learning, when carefully planned to guide learning and reflection, can help White preservice as well as inservice teachers learn to construct intellectually inclusive classrooms. Noordhoff and Kleinfeld's (1993) case study of the impact on a cohort of student teachers of a semester-long immersion experience in a small indigenous Alaskan community demonstrated the potential of community-based learning. The student teachers lived in the community and became involved in activities such as sewing or beading groups, local church activities, or cross-country skiing. Noordhoff and

Kleinfeld videotaped them student teaching three times over the semester. Videotapes showed them learning to shift from teaching as telling, to teaching as engaging the children with culturally relevant knowledge to connect academic knowledge with what children know.

Autobiographical accounts of White educators having learned to teach in urban schools and work against racism emphasize the power of community-based learning (Johnson, 2002; Merryfield, 2000; Smith, 1998; Yeo, 1997). Of the three legs on the platform, this may well be the most powerful venue for helping White preservice teachers begin to critically examine racism, move beyond fear, and see teaching with "a cultural eye" (Irvine, 2003). Yet, this is the leg most often missing from the platform.

Cross-cultural community-based learning experiences can vary widely in intensity and duration. Immersion experiences involve living in another cultural context for a period of time, while short visitations do not. Extended immersion experiences have potential to promote the deepest learning, mainly because they compel a person to deal with discomfort and confusion, and to learn from other people in the host cultural context. In short cross-cultural visits (say, for a few hours or a day), one immediately returns to what is known and comfortable, and may never need to question fundamental assumptions and feelings. Nonetheless, shorter, less intensive experiences are easier to construct, and can also be valuable.

Indiana University provides an example of an extended immersion experience. Since the mid-1970s, it has offered semester-long cross-cultural immersion experiences in placement sites that include the Navajo Nation, the lower Rio Grande Valley, inner-city Indianapolis, and overseas. The academic year prior to their immersion experience, preservice teachers complete intensive preparatory coursework in which they study the culture, history, lifestyle, and education of the group with which they will be placed. During the immersion experience, they carry out their student teaching while engaging in ongoing substantive community involvement in a project they co-plan with a community member. According to follow-up surveys of graduates, as well as case studies by external researchers, this experience has a strong impact on attitudes and knowledge. It helps student teachers learn to make "efforts to connect their classrooms to community people, practices, and values" (Melnick & Zeichner, 1996, p. 185). Graduates report interaction with community residents as particularly significant to their learning (Estrada, 1999; Mahan, 1982; Mahan & Stachowski, 1993–4; Stachowski & Mahan, 1998).

Shorter immersion experiences also have value. For example, Aguilar and Pohan (1998) took nine students from Nebraska to the Southwest for four and a half weeks, where they lived in Mexican households and worked on a three-week arts program for children. Riojas Clark and Bustos Flores (1997) took teacher education students for a week to Monterrey, Mexico, where they studied and experienced the prior schooling of Mexican children who had immigrated to the United States. Case studies report that, in well-structured experiences, preservice teachers see functioning communities and everyday cultural patterns first-hand, form relationships with people, confront stereotypes, and hear stories of lives that reflect abstractions they may have read about in textbooks (Aguilar & Pohan, 1998; Canning, 1995; Cooper et al., 1990; James & Haig-Brown, 2002; Marxen & Rudney, 1999; Riojas Clark & Bustos Flores, 1997; Sconzert et al., 2000). This kind of learning provides a basis for developing an alternative to deficit thinking.

The least intensive type of community-based learning involves visiting rather than living in another community. Preservice or inservice teachers visit neighborhoods or communities that differ from their own by factors such as social class, ethnicity, race, or primary language. While there, they have a role to play (such as tutoring) or a specific guided learning activity (such as interviewing senior citizens or constructing a community portrait). Such experiences often take the form of service learning, in which the teacher's role serves a community-identified need, such as assisting in a food bank or a homework center (Boyle-Baise, 2002).

Numerous case studies of these shorter forms of community-based learning have found most White preservice teachers to grow conceptually and attitudinally, and to show greater willingness to consider teaching in a community like the one in which they were involved (Barton, 1999; Bondy & Davis, 2000; Bondy et al., 1993; Moule, 2004; Narode et al., 1994; Olmedo, 1997; Rodriguez, 1998; Seidl & Friend, 2002; Sleeter, 1996). For example, Burant and Kirby (2002) found that community-based learning connecting White preservice teachers with urban parents sensitized teacher candidates to struggles parents faced, showed them that parents valued education, and taught them to see the community as a resource for learning.

At the same time, short community-based learning experiences may not move some White preservice teachers beyond "eye opening" (Boyle-Baise & Sleeter, 2000; Burant & Kirby, 2002). Some researchers have noted White preservice teachers' reluctance to contextualize communities within broader relations of power, particularly racism. A few researchers found the experience to confirm stereotypes some preservice teachers brought with them (Murtadha-Watts, 1998; Ross & Smith, 1992). Seidl and Friend (2002) described the difficulty of trying to give White preservice teachers depth of knowledge in a short experience:

> The development of sophisticated, culturally relevant pedagogies is a process that requires commitment over time and lived experience. It is impossible for our students to unlearn years of racist socialization and develop anti-racist and sophisticated bicultural identities in one year. Thus, what we hope for is that our students begin to understand the difficulties that arise when schools are not responsive to children's sociocultural experiences.
>
> (p. 427)

Community-based learning experiences that are most productive are well-planned, linked directly to teacher education, and involve guided reflection. Before teachers enter someone else's community, they learn something of its history and current issues, as well as ethnographic research tools such as interviewing, active listening, and careful observation. Throughout the experience, the instructor helps them make sense of what they are learning and link it to teaching. For example, for several years, I had preservice teachers in my multicultural education course work 30 to 50 hours in predominantly African American or Latino community centers, where they tutored children, provided recreational support, or assisted in other ways. After teaching them active listening, I assigned them to interview adults they were working with, assisting them in selecting interview topics and questions. I also taught observation skills, such as how to discern cultural patterns in interpersonal interaction styles, and developed guides for exploring the community (see Sleeter, 2001). Throughout the semester, as students brought data into the classroom, I helped them interpret and develop pedagogically-relevant implications of what they learned.

Taken by itself, cross-cultural community-based learning does not necessarily lead to excellent multicultural teaching. However, it provides an experiential foundation, which most White teachers lack, for coursework and school-based learning.

Professional coursework on culture and equity pedagogy

Earlier I summarized research that finds White preservice teachers entering teacher education with (1) little awareness or understanding of discrimination, especially racism, (2) depressed expectations for the achievement of students of color buttressed by a taken-for-granted deficiency orientation, (3) ignorance and fear of communities of color, and of discussing race and racism, and (4) lack of awareness of themselves as cultural beings, and of communities and classrooms as cultural sites. Professional coursework, especially when linked with community-based learning, can help to address these problems.

The last 25 years have seen considerable development of such coursework. It most commonly takes the form of a separate course in multicultural education, urban education, or teaching English language learners, although a more comprehensive integration of such coursework through a program is desirable. There is a fair amount of agreement about the kinds of concepts such coursework should include. Zeichner (1996, p. 159), for example, recommended that it include the following: development of clearer ethnic and cultural self-identity; self-examination of ethnocentrism; dynamics of prejudice and racism, including implications for teachers; dynamics of privilege and economic oppression, and how schools contribute to these inequities; multicultural curriculum development; the promise and potential dangers of learning styles; relationships between language, culture, and learning; and culturally appropriate teaching and assessment. Organizationally, coursework generally begins with a sociological examination of institutional racism, historically as well as currently, an anthropological examination of culture, and a personal examination of teacher candidates' own identities, histories, and experiences. The reason for beginning with a "big picture" rather than with specific teaching techniques is that most White preservice teachers do not understand what needs to be changed and why, and therefore tend to accept or reject what they see as appropriate practices based on their own experiences, without necessarily recognizing alternatives or harmful implications of practices they take for granted.

Many small-scale studies have examined the extent to which such a course changes the attitudes or perceptions of predominantly White groups of preservice teachers, most commonly by surveying them at the beginning and conclusion of the course. The majority of these studies found that attitudes were a bit better at the end of the course than at the beginning (Bennett et al., 1990; Bondy et al., 1993; Grottkau & Nickolai-Mays, 1989; Hennington, 1981; Lawrence & Bunche, 1986; Martin & Koppelman, 1991; Middleton, 2002; Rios et al., 1998; Tran et al., 1994; Weisman & Garza, 2002). However, most studies found very small gains; when gains were noted, they generally involved acceptance of specific teaching strategies, but not a deeper understanding of racism (VanGunten & Martin, 2001), or negligible gains (Guillaume et al., 1995, 1998). The small reported gains in most studies may be due partly to limitations of survey instruments. Using a measure of conceptual growth as well as an attitude survey, Artiles and McClafferty (1998) found conceptual growth that was not captured on the attitude survey. This insight led them to recommend using multiple measures of growth and learning rather than a single survey.

A more significant question is how much impact a multicultural or diversity course has on subsequent teaching. The few studies that have followed preservice students into the classroom after completing coursework report mixed results, juxtaposing the power of coursework with prior life experience. Vavrus (1994) found that White student teachers in Iowa, who had earlier taken a multicultural education course, modeled themselves after their cooperating teachers, most adding a bit of ethnic content to curriculum but doing little else. Smith (2000) compared two White preservice teachers on their willingness to use principles of multicultural education when student teaching. One, who brought prior diversity experiences, used awareness of culture as a pedagogical tool for relating to students and constructing lessons, while the other, who was otherwise a comparable and caring teacher, lacked such prior experiences and pedagogical tools. Similarly, Causey *et al.* (2000) found one White teacher in a three-year follow-up study to have largely forgotten equity issues and reverted to stereotypic notions about students, while the other continued to develop an activist approach to equity. They speculated that predisposition to reflection might differentiate the two (see also Lawrence, 1997).

These follow-up studies speak to the power of prior socialization and on-going everyday life experiences of White people in a racist society. While some reconsider how to interpret students from historically marginalized communities and how to teach in order to break patterns of racism in schooling, many do not or do so only to a limited degree. Adding a course into an otherwise traditional teacher education program is probably insufficient to counter such ongoing socialization and limited life experiences. Further, when the rest of the program fails to build on the course, White preservice teachers who find its content threatening often dismiss it (much as they see the rest of the program doing), turning their anger toward the course instructor (often an untenured faculty member of color).

There is evidence that preservice teachers learn more from multicultural courses that model and use the kinds of active instructional processes that work best in culturally and linguistically diverse classrooms, than from those that take a more didactic approach (Villegas & Lucas, 2002). For example, Torok and Aguilar (2000) examined what their largely White preservice teachers learned from a multicultural education course in which they were expected to read, write daily reflective journals, complete an in-depth project about a self-selected issue, and engage in a short, self-selected cross-cultural experience. The preservice teachers attributed their growth mainly to the course's open environment in which they could discuss controversial issues and learn from each other. Similarly, Rodriguez (1998) found that when he used the same sociocultural constructivist teaching processes in his science methods course that good science teachers use to engage diverse students, including "dialogic conversation, authentic activity, metacognition, and reflexivity," his preservice teachers learned to make science relevant to diverse students (p. 616; see also Brown, 2004).

Many active learning and reflection strategies that connect conceptual frameworks with personal experience, examine diverse points of view, and model pedagogical strategies have been the focus of action research studies. For example, shared journaling is a process in which the instructor pairs students and then assigns them to write reflections that connect reading assignments or class discussions with their own experience. Student pairs exchange journals and then read and write reactions to their partner's journal entries; the instructor also may read and respond to journal entries. Those who have studied shared journaling in multicultural education coursework report that it prompts considerable constructive reflection (Milner, 2003; Garmon, 1998; Pewewardy, 2005).

Other active learning strategies that have been studied include the following: reading, writing, and discussing autobiographies, including one's own autobiography (Clark & Medina, 2000; Dillard, 1996; Florio-Ruane, 1994; Rubin, 1995; Xu, 2000); engaging preservice teachers in a cross-cultural exchange through the mail (Fuller & Ahler, 1987) or through email (Lacina & Sowa, 2005; Schoorman, 2002); reading and discussing contemporary ethnic children's literature (LaFramboise & Griffith, 1997; Nathenson-Mejía & Escamilla, 2003); using simulations (Frykholm, 1997) or debates (Marshall, 1998); involving White preservice teachers in direct discussions of racism and White privilege (Lawrence, 1997; Lawrence & Bunche, 1996; Marx & Pennington, 2003), and involving White preservice teachers in guided research projects (Brown, 2004; Sleeter, 1996).

Active learning strategies appear to help White preservice teachers work through their defenses by engaging them in reflection about connections between key concepts and their own experiences and beliefs. Sustained didactic presentations, on the other hand, do not do this. Based on interviews with participants in a teacher education program, McDiarmid (1992) found didactic presentations about different racial or ethnic groups inadvertently to teach stereotypes and generalizations.

As preservice teachers gain awareness of what needs to be changed and why, coursework can shift to pedagogical applications for the classroom, such as how to teach content and skills using student life experiences, how to promote positive student-student relationships in the classroom, or how to assess student learning in culturally appropriate ways. The more such pedagogical coursework is directly integrated into subject-specific methods coursework, the more likely preservice teachers will make sense of it, as Rodriguez (1998) has found in his case studies of science methods taught through a multicultural and equity lens.

Villegas and Lucas (2002) recommend organizing professional coursework around six strands that move from broad awareness and attitude development, through cultivation of pedagogical skills. These strands include: (1) gaining a sociocultural consciousness, (2) developing an affirming attitude toward students from culturally diverse backgrounds, (3) developing the commitment and skills to act as change agents, (4) understanding the constructivist foundations of culturally responsive teaching, (5) learning about students and their communities, and (6) cultivating culturally responsive teaching practices. Learning experiences for these strands can be packaged in different ways. Least effective is cramming them into one separate course, or infusing the strands throughout the program in such a way that they become lost. Instead, Villegas and Lucas suggest designating courses in which each strand is addressed either as the course's central theme, or as a significant theme among others. Offering the example of Montclair State University's curriculum, they show how each teacher education course addresses two to five of the strands, each strand being emphasized as a central theme in at least one course. They note that planning such coursework takes a good deal of time, effort, and faculty development, but the result is a coherent rather than piecemeal curriculum.

Although it is relatively easy for programs to add or reconstruct a single course as a way of addressing diversity, little research supports this by itself as effective in preparing White teachers for racially diverse or urban schools. At the same time, there is a fairly extensive knowledge base for building a coherent curriculum, and teaching it through active learning strategies that model those that enable teachers to relate curriculum to diverse students.

Preparation in the classroom

Classroom work constitutes the third leg of the platform outlined in this chapter. Feiman-Nemser and Buchmann (1985) noted, "Teachers claim that most of what they know about teaching came from first-hand experience" (p. 53). Classroom teaching experience is essential, although a challenge for teacher education is preparing teachers who do not simply *replicate* prevailing practices. Feiman-Nemser and Buchmann identified three pitfalls of classroom experience: familiarity that reinforces taking much for granted rather than questioning, divergent demands of universities and classrooms that prompt teachers to bifurcate rather than synthesize what they learn in each context, and the reality that because classrooms are not set up as learning labs for teachers, novices are incorporated into already-running systems. Feiman-Nemser and Buchmann explained that,

> These pitfalls arrest thought or mislead prospective teachers into believing that central aspects of teaching have been mastered and understood . . . future teachers get into them without knowing it and have a hard time getting out. What makes them even more treacherous is that they may not look like pitfalls to an insider, but rather like a normal place to be.
>
> (p. 63)

These challenges are particularly salient in the preparation of White teachers for schools in historically oppressed communities. Although excellent teachers exist, in most such schools a good deal of teaching is mediocre and not well-crafted to build on students' strengths, particularly in low-income schools that have high teacher turnover. Further, considerable teaching in such schools currently is heavily didactic and scripted, with curricula focusing strongly on test preparation. How can teacher education programs work with the schools that exist to prepare White teachers to work with diverse students *more effectively* than is the case at present?

Early field experiences and student teaching have usually been studied separately. Most studies of White preservice teachers in early field experiences examined attitude change through work in urban schools. Most of these early field experiences were connected with a course such as literacy or multicultural education.

About half of the studies reported that a field experience in an urban school made a positive impact on preservice teachers' perceptions of urban students, particularly African American students (Aaronsohn *et al.*, 1995; Chance *et al.*, 1996; Fry & McKinney, 1997; Larke *et al.*, 1990; Lazar, 1998; Reed, 1993), although one noted that the impact was quite small (Reed, 1993). The rest found such field experiences either to result in negligible change, or to confirm preservice teachers' racial and social class stereotypes (Deering & Stanutz, 1995; Haberman & Post, 1992; Marx, 2000; Tiezzi & Cross, 1997; Wiggins & Follo, 1999). As Tiezzi and Cross (1997) observed,

> The necessity of providing direct experiences as early as possible in urban schools is fully understood. However, a dilemma arises . . . When we immerse inexperienced, misinformed, and sometimes resistant prospective teachers in urban classrooms by themselves for their first field experience, the result is predictable. The prospective teachers are overwhelmed by the urban context and focus primarily on problems rather than possibilities in teaching and learning. Our prospective teachers rely on what they've learned about the urban context through families, communities, churches, and media to frame their observations. For the majority of the prospective teachers we serve, this is problematic.
>
> (p. 122)

In classrooms, preservice teachers see students reacting to institutions that, depending on the specific school or classroom, may not support the students' cultures, identities, and intellectual capabilities. Students' behavior in such settings often ends up reinforcing unexamined assumptions that White preservice teachers bring.

More useful than the question of whether field experiences in classrooms that serve students of color improve White preservice teachers' attitudes and perceptions, is the question of how to construct field experiences that do so. Early field experiences commonly involve observing, helping the teacher, or tutoring children. Simply doing these things, however, does not necessarily prompt preservice teachers to question their assumptions. Engaging preservice teachers in planned field-based learning can prompt such questioning.

Classroom field experiences that include guided inquiry with planned, extended reflection prompt more learning and questioning of assumptions than those that do not (Armaline, 1995; Brookhart, 1997). For example, Lazar (1998) had her preservice teachers interview children in urban classrooms about home literacy activities. Although some asked more and better questions than others, most of them discovered much more literacy activity and value for literacy in urban households than they had been aware of, causing many to rethink deficit assumptions about urban students' home environments (see also Pucci *et al.*, 2000).

Multiple field experiences in classrooms modeling different kinds of instruction seem to help preservice teachers to see the interaction between children and teaching. Commonly, White preservice teachers assume that the learning and behavior of children of color are products of the home environment rather than reactions to what happens in the classroom. Two studies examined what preservice teachers learned in classrooms that used a transmission mode of teaching compared to those using a constructivist mode (Richards *et al.*, 1996; Ross & Smith, 1992). The researchers came to somewhat different conclusions regarding which kind of classroom prompted more preservice teacher learning, but they agreed that preservice teachers benefit when they see urban children respond to different kinds of classroom contexts. As Ross and Smith (1992) put it, "contrasting experiences may help students analyze the effect of curriculum and instruction on student learning," especially if preservice teachers are guided in reflecting on connections between what happens in the classroom and how children respond (p. 102). Such guided reflection can help them view learning and behavior as not simply characteristics of the students themselves, but rather a result of the interaction between students and what teachers do. The benefit of comparative placements is important, particularly since teacher education programs struggle to locate optimal classrooms for field experiences. While it is imperative that novice teachers see excellent teaching of children from historically oppressed communities, excellent teachers are usually in short supply. In that case, excellent teachers can be videotaped, and videos used to help preservice teachers compare student learning and behavior in classrooms that are structured differently.

Teacher education programs often struggle with how to construct student teaching so it equips novices with practical strategies as well as helping them to question common structures and practices that do not serve historically underserved students well. Studies that focus directly on the preparation of White preservice teachers during student teaching can be examined through an analytical framework that differentiates among possible goals of student teaching. According to Cochran-Smith (1991a), the *consonance* approach links student teachers with school-based mentors in order to induct student teachers into using best practices. For example, Stallings and Quinn (1991) reported a study of a collaborative project between the University of Houston and the Houston Independent School District in which the main goal of student teaching was for preservice teachers to model themselves after good classroom teachers and adopt "best practices" recommended in the literature. Based in an inner city academy, the project involved close collaboration between teachers, the principal, and university faculty, offering preservice teachers a weekly seminar and daily interaction with cooperating teachers that reinforced university coursework. In a comparison of 65 graduates of this program with 20 controls, the researchers found the program's graduates to spend less time on classroom behavior and more time on instruction, and to use more higher order questions and more positive support for students, showing that they had learned to use teaching processes they were taught.

Cochran-Smith's second approach, *critical dissonance*, emphasizes preparing student teachers to contextualize schools within broader relations of power in order to question prevailing school practices, and construct alternatives. Artiles *et al.* (1998) reported a small case study of graduates of an urban program based on this model. The graduates reported navigating disconnected discourses during the program: their own prior beliefs, conflicting theoretical perspectives within the program (such as critical theory versus behaviorism), and beliefs of teachers in the schools. As a result, they discarded much of what they had learned in the program and learned to teach "on the job." Student teaching that emphasizes critique appears to leave novices unclear about what to do when they begin to teach.

Cochran-Smith's third approach, *collaborative resonance*, offers an alternative that connects critique with practice. This approach prepares student teachers to inquire into practice by collaborating with practicing teachers who are engaged in school-based reform. Cochran-Smith (1991b) and Cochran-Smith and Lytle (1992) studied school-based inquiry teams composed of experienced and preservice teachers who were involved in reforming culturally diverse urban schools. The experienced teachers were interested in improving their practice through reflective inquiry. Teams used school or classroom data to help generate solutions to problems, such as how to handle children who had been in kindergarten two years but were not yet ready for first grade. The preservice teachers observed good teaching, and engaged in rich conversations with practicing teachers about their methods, reasons for using them, and questions or problems they were grappling with. But rather than simply modeling themselves after practicing teachers, the preservice teachers were also learning to construct practice on classroom-based inquiry.

Research on how fieldwork in classrooms contributes to the growth of White preservice teachers is fairly limited. Not only are there relatively few studies, but they also do not follow teachers into the classroom through their first years of teaching in order to assess the impact of various configurations of field experiences. Further, early field experiences and student teaching are addressed separately in most research on preparing teachers for diverse students, although they should be connected programmatically. Professional development schools lend themselves to building seamless fieldwork (e.g. Cristol & Gimbert, 2002; Sconzert *et al.*, 2000), although as Murrell (1998) noted, many do not explicitly address urban education, including the issues discussed in this chapter.

Learning to teach is a developmental process in which the novice typically progresses from concerns about self, to concerns about students and their learning. Learning to teach in a different cultural context can be complicated by culture shock, which is rarely discussed in the teacher education literature. This has implications for the length of student teaching and the nature of support that may be needed. Rushton (2000, 2001) studied the experiences of White preservice teachers in a Master's degree program that focused on urban and multicultural teaching, and included a full year internship in a low-income urban school. He documented a growth process that began with culture shock, moved through various conflicts and difficulties, and then toward development of a sense of teaching efficacy by the end of the year. He noted that it took the full year, with classroom support, for the interns to shift from focusing on their personal struggles, to students' learning and development of a sense of teaching efficacy. Had student teaching lasted only a semester, it would have ended while the interns were still navigating culture shock (see also Luft *et al.*, 1999). While Rushton noted the value of a full year of student teaching, I suspect that student teaching need not last a year if the program is purposefully designed to move White preservice teachers in a coherent way through culture shock and toward culturally relevant pedagogy that centers on students' intellectual needs.

Some would argue that content acquisition and classroom experience are the *only* form of preparation teachers need, that community-based learning is unnecessary, and that professional coursework breeds mediocrity. Such is the assumption behind test-only certification programs (e.g. the American Board for Certification of Teaching Excellence) and abbreviated programs (e.g. Teach for America). While some researchers have found alternatives to teacher education to produce teachers whose students' test scores are comparable to those of teachers from conventional teacher education programs (Decker *et al.*, 2004), others have found students of teachers from such alternatives to score significantly lower (Laczko-Kerr & Berliner, 2002). Notably, one does not find abbreviated teacher certification programs helping White teachers become *better* at closing racial achievement gaps. Such programs do little or nothing to confront teaching inadequacies that stem from race- and class-related beliefs, fears, ignorance, and limited life experience.

Connecting the three legs

I have maintained that a coherently-planned teacher education program that explicitly addresses issues and concerns of White preservice teachers can prepare them to teach diverse populations more effectively than can traditional programs of teacher education or certification routes that by-pass teacher education. I build this case mainly on pieces of evidence rather than on a comprehensive study of such a program. Here, I examine the very small body of comparative research that sheds light on this topic.

There is evidence that community-based learning linked with professional coursework is more powerful than either by itself. Bondy *et al.* (1993) compared the effects of community-based learning alone and paired with a multicultural education course on White preservice teachers' perspectives about urban students. They concluded that "fieldwork alone, even when it involved direct contact with children who were different from the tutors, did not change tutors' beliefs about the causes and consequences of being different" (p. 61). In a study comparing the impact of a stand-alone cultural diversity course with a course linked with community-based learning, Brown (2004) reported a similar finding. Most community-based learning projects discussed earlier were linked with coursework, and these two comparative studies confirm the importance of such linking.

Some evidence suggests that community-based learning should occur early in a teacher preparation program. Based on a study of the relationship between community-based and school-based fieldwork, Burant and Kirby (2002) found the former to provide a foundation for the latter. For example, they reported that preservice teachers "who interacted with parents overwhelmingly reported much greater understandings about the structural obstacles parents face and were convinced that the majority of parents were doing their best to make wise choices for their children" (p. 571). Such preservice teachers were in a better position to respect the parents and children than were those who had not interacted with parents. Further, the researchers stressed the value preservice teachers found in learning how to learn about students through the community before teaching them.

Imagine, then, a program that includes: (1) community-based learning connected with professional coursework emphasizing reflection; followed by (2) early field experiences in culturally diverse classrooms connected with professional coursework that examines culture, language and learning; continuing with (3) foundations and methods coursework that is explicitly designed around teaching diverse students; and culminating in (4) student teaching in a school that serves a historically oppressed community, designed around a model of collaborative resonance. Further, the whole program is long enough to support preservice teachers through culture shock, to respectful engagement. To what extent does such a program make an impact? Unfortunately, data are far too thin to know. Three studies of programs designed around diversity examined their impact on predominantly White preservice teachers' beliefs. One reported a positive impact (Capella-Santana, 1989) and two reported limited impact (Artiles *et al.*, 1998; Burstein & Cabello, 1989). None described the programs in much detail, however, nor did they examine the impact of the program on the teacher candidates' classroom teaching abilities.

The research reviewed above, while too fragmented to be conclusive, suggests that coherent programs that are designed explicitly to address the limited experiences, knowledge gaps, fears, and biases common among White preservice teachers are likely to produce educators who are at least as effective, if not more so, than traditional programs tend to do. The research does not suggest, however, that even a strong, coherently planned program will overcome the prior socialization of all White preservice teachers. Many of the studies mentioned above identified White preservice teachers who continued to resist or dismiss what the program was trying to teach related to diversity. For example, Smith (2000) and Causey *et al.* (2000) found that some White graduates of programs that aimed to prepare them to teach cross-culturally "forgot" what they had learned once they began to teach.

The above research suggests that predisposition to working with students from non-mainstream cultures and languages and to equity matters, should be taken into consideration when selecting applicants into teacher education. Consider the teacher who knows algebra well and knows how to teach it to children much like herself, but believes that her low-income Black, Latino, and Indian students are not only too far behind to learn algebra, but also too uninterested and too lacking in home support. She does not lack teaching methods or content knowledge, but rather belief in the academic capabilities of her students and willingness to gear her teaching toward those students.

I believe that, rather than admitting White preservice teachers on the basis of grade point average and test scores alone, we need to become much more intentional about selecting or counseling out those prospective teachers who lack the willingness (or maturity) to learn to teach cross-culturally. Currently, although some teacher education programs are experimenting with ways to do this fairly, there are few tested systems for doing so. Haberman (1995; 1996), based on his observations of star urban teachers, developed an interview process that helps identify prospective teachers who have dispositions (such as a strong belief in children, capacity to learn from mistakes, and willingness to explore and try alternatives) that will enable them to learn to teach well in urban schools. Preservice teachers who have these dispositions are generally older (thirty to fifty years of age) and usually bring experience living in an urban environment. Adopting his interview is not a panacea, but it offers a way of conceptualizing program admission based on willingness and ability to learn to teach cross-culturally.

MENTORING AND RETAINING WHITE TEACHERS IN DIVERSE SCHOOLS

The first two to three years of teaching are critical. During that time, many patterns of teaching, believing, and relating to students become solidified. Novice White teachers face at least three challenges. First is ongoing socialization in the forms of everyday life experience in a relatively racist and segregated society, as well as socialization into the beliefs and practices of other, more experienced teachers. Very often, both reinforce a tacit belief in the superiority of the White ways of doing things and perceiving the world, and a colorblind perspective toward race (Sleeter, 1992). Second is the crucible of the classroom, in which novice teachers form relationships with students and figure out what seems to work with them. From the first day, through an interactive process, teachers and students size each other up and establish patterns that can range from supportive to punitive, intellectually demanding to deadening. Race, culture, and social class are highly potent filters through which teachers and students interpret each other; the intensity of classroom life wears quickly on shallow good intentions. Third is the task of connecting professional knowledge with practice, and continuing to deepen both in order to develop teaching efficacy. While there is a significant body of professional knowledge related to excellent teaching of students from historically oppressed communities, novice teachers who are unsure how to connect professional knowledge with everyday classroom practice are likely to dismiss it as "theory" that does not "work." Failure to address these three issues quite often results in White teachers giving up and either leaving the profession, taking jobs in the suburbs as quickly as possible, or adopting a custodial model of teaching students.

The professional literature on mentoring, retaining, and professionally developing White teachers in diverse or urban schools is quite thin. Nevertheless, it offers some guidance. One-shot workshops, still common in multicultural education, have little if any effect. As with preservice teacher education, didactic presentations about groups are more likely to teach stereotypes than improve teaching (McDiarmid, 1992). Staff development projects that are too broad, attempting to re-work teachers' worldviews, are often met with resistance and conflict (Leistyna, 2001; Sleeter, 1992).

Professional development programs with the most promise combine ongoing practice-based inquiry with classroom-based coaching. These processes can occur through a variety of staff development venues, including beginning teacher induction, professional development schools, teacher networks, school reform projects, or university coursework. The venue appears itself to be less important than the extent to which it (1) involves teachers in thinking deeply about their own practice and assumptions; (2) supportively stretches novice White teachers beyond their existing beliefs and understandings; (3) is facilitated by someone with a deep commitment to and knowledge about education in communities of color; and (4) maintains a clear and consistent focus on helping teachers meet the intellectual needs of their students, without becoming sidetracked. Below are examples.

Several studies have found sustained workshops combined with classroom coaching beneficial to teachers, particularly those in historically low-achieving schools. For example, Johnson and Kean (1992) developed and evaluated a project that involved intensive summer workshops on teaching science in multicultural settings. The workshops focused on matters such as using classroom-based processes for identifying strengths of students, problem solving in science, and cooperative learning. General meetings of participants were held quarterly for discussion and problem solving. Classroom-based coaching twice per month provided teachers with additional support. The researchers documented positive changes in teacher-student interactions, and classroom pedagogy (see also Lindley & Keithley, 1991). Many teacher induction programs are built on this model, although as Mendoza Reis (2001) found in her research on California's teacher induction program, classroom support providers who lack knowledge about culturally relevant teaching cannot help novices learn to do this very effectively.

Inquiry-based teacher networks and inquiry-based graduate coursework can help support novice White teachers when the focus is on teaching excellence in culturally diverse contexts (Exposito & Favela, 2003; Jennings & Smith, 2002; Moss, 2001; Sleeter, 2005).

For example, the University of Pennsylvania has been involved in a teacher network inquiry project that has been in existence for over two decades; Cochran-Smith's (1991b) work, noted earlier, was part of this network. As El-Haj (2003) explains, working in collaborative inquiry groups, the teachers (most of whom are White) focus deeply on one child, analyzing the child's work in order to construct a portrait of him or her as an intellectual. The inquiry process moves outward, from the particulars of one child, situating the child in a social and cultural context. Through this inquiry process, teachers develop genuine respect for children's intellectual abilities, and learn to navigate the sometimes conflicting demands of individual children and broad systems in which children need to learn to succeed.

In the context of graduate coursework, Moll and González (1994) helped teachers improve their teaching through structured home visits, a form of community-based learning. After instructing teachers how to conduct interviews, they had teachers identify children whose families they would like to learn more about in the context of non-intrusive home visits. While in the home, teachers learned about household "funds of knowledge," areas of expertise that family members have as a part of everyday life, such as carpentry, cooking, or mechanical repair. Teachers also learned about family social networks to become acquainted with various people in the community who interact with children and the family. After the home visits, Moll and González helped teachers to build curriculum to connect academic knowledge with the knowledge family members teach their children.

Professional development that is embedded within a larger school reform project can support novice White teachers, if it is not excessively top-down and attends to the needs of novice teachers. Darling-Hammond and colleagues (2003) studied a district-wide professional development program in San Diego that focused on improving literacy instruction, then expanded to other subject areas. The project involved principal professional development, teacher workshops, and the nurturing of a network of well-trained peer coaches who worked directly with teachers in their classrooms. The researchers were able to document a significant improvement in student achievement, particularly among students who had been previously least-well served. They noted, however, that teacher satisfaction with the program varied. Many teachers saw it as too centralized and standardized; the school district was in the process of experimenting with more flexibility and school-based decision-making. The researchers stressed the importance of reform projects striking a productive balance between bottom-up and top-down planning and decision-making.

CONCLUSION

It is urgent that teacher educators work much more purposefully toward developing coherent programs that can help White teachers learn to teach diverse populations well; it is also urgent that systematic research on such programs be conducted. Although we do not yet have research data that confirm the effectiveness of programs following the model I have sketched in this chapter, we do have research that confirms the limited experiences, misconceptions, fears, and biases that White preservice and inservice teachers bring to the profession, and the negative impact on those on classroom practice. There is also enough research suggesting interventions and supports that make a difference, to warrant taking action. Improving schools that serve students from historically underserved communities demands that we do so.

NOTES

1 There is also an urgent need to diversify the teaching force, and to prepare all teachers to teach diverse students well. Since other chapters in this handbook take up these issues, this chapter focuses on preparation of White teachers.
2 This platform is not intended to substitute for other important components of teacher education, including content preparation, but rather to complement them.

REFERENCES

Aaronsohn, E., Carter, C., & Howell, M. (1995) Preparing monocultural teachers for a multi-cultural world. *Equity & Excellence in Education* 29(1): 5–9.

Aguilar, T. E. & Pohan, C. A. (1998) A cultural immersion experience to enhance cross-cultural competence. *Sociotam* 8(1): 29–49.

Alton-Lee, A. (2003) *Quality teaching for diverse students in schooling: a best evidence synthesis.* Wellington, New Zealand: Ministry of Education.

Armaline, W. D. (1995) Reflecting on cultural diversity through early field experiences: pitfalls, hesitations, and promise. In R. J. Martin (ed.) *Practicing what we teach: confronting diversity in teacher education*, pp. 163–180. Albany, NY: SUNY Press.

Artiles, A. J. & McClafferty, K. (1998) Learning to teach culturally diverse learners. *The Elementary School Journal* 98(3): 189(32).

Artiles, A. J., Barreto, R. M., Peña, L., & McClafferty, K. (1998) Pathways to teacher learning in multicultural contexts. *Remedial and Special Education* 19(2): 70–90.

Avery, P. G. & Walker, C. (1993) Prospective teachers' perceptions of ethnic and gender differences in academic achievement. *Journal of Teacher Education* 44(1): 27–37.

Barry, N. H. & Lechner, J. V. (1995) Preservice teachers' attitudes about and awareness of multi-cultural teaching and learning. *Teaching and Teacher Education* 11(2): 149–161.

Barton, A. C. (1999) Crafting a multicultural science teacher education: a case study. *Journal of Teacher Education* 50(4): 303–314.

Bennett, C., Niggle, T., & Stage, F. (1990) Preservice multicultural teacher education: predictors of student readiness. *Teaching and Teacher Education* 6(3): 243–254.

Birrell, J. R. (1994) Coping with the culturally unpredictable: an ethnically encapsulated beginning teacher's struggle with African-American students' ethnic behavior. *Professional Educator* 16(2): 27–37.

Bondy, E. & Davis, S. (2000) The caring of strangers: insights from a field experience in a culturally unfamiliar community. *Action in Teacher Education* 22(2), 54–66.

Bondy, E., Schmitz, S., & Johnson, M. (1993) The impact of coursework and fieldwork on student teachers' reported beliefs about teaching poor and minority students. *Action in Teacher Education* 15(2): 55–62.

Boyle-Baise, M. (2002) *Multicultural service learning.* New York: Teachers College Press.

Boyle-Baise, L. & Sleeter, C. E. (2000) Community-based service learning for multicultural teacher education. *Educational Foundations* 14(2): 33–50.

Brookhart, S. M. (1997) A field-based introduction to urban education at the middle school. *Mid-Western Educational Researcher* 10(2): 2–8.

Brouwer, N. & Korthagen, F. (2005) Can teacher education make a difference? *American Educational Research Journal* 42(1): 153–224.

Brown, E. L. (2004) What precipitates change in cultural diverse awareness during a multicultural course? *Journal of Teacher Education* 55(4): 325–340.

Burant, T. J. & Kirby, D. (2002) Beyond classroom-based early field experiences: understanding an "educative practicum" in an urban school and community. *Teaching and Teacher Education* 18(5): 561–575.

Burstein, N. D. & Cabello, B. (1989) Preparing teachers to work with culturally diverse students: a teacher education model. *Journal of Teacher Education* 40(5): 9–16.

Cannella, G. S. & Reiff, J. C. (1994) Teacher preparation for diversity. *Equity and Excellence in Education* 27(3): 28–33.

Canning, C. (1995) Getting from the outside in: teaching Mexican Americans when you are an "Anglo." *The High School Journal* 78(4): 195–205.

Capella-Santana, N. (2003) Voices of teacher candidates: positive changes in multicultural attitudes and knowledge. *Journal of Educational Research* 96(3): 182–90.

Causey, V. E., Thomas, C. D., & Armento, B. J. (2000) Cultural diversity is basically a foreign term to me. *Teaching and Teacher Education* (16)1: 33–45.

Chance, L., Morris, V. G., & Rakes, S. (1996) Fostering sensitivity to diverse cultures through an early field experience collaborative. *Journal of Teacher Education* 47(5): 386–389.

Clark, C. & Medina, C. (2000) How reading and writing literacy narratives affect preservice teachers' understandings of literacy, pedagogy, and multiculturalism. *Journal of Teacher Education* 51(1): 63–76.

Cochran-Smith, M. (1991a) Reinventing student teaching. *Journal of Teacher Education* 42(2): 104–118.

Cochran-Smith, M. (1991b) Learning to teach against the grain. *Harvard Educational Review* 61(3): 279–310.

Cochran-Smith, M. & Lytle, S. L. (1992) Interrogating cultural diversity: inquiry and action. *Journal of Teacher Education* 43(2): 104–115.

Cooper, A., Beare, P., & Thorman, J. (1990) Preparing teachers for diversity: a comparison of student teaching experiences in Minnesota and South Texas. *Action in Teacher Education* 12 (3): 1–4.

Cristol, D. S. & Gimbert, B. G. (2002) A case study of an urban school-university partnership: designing and implementing curriculum for contextual teaching and learning. *Professional Educator* 25(1): 43–54

Darling-Hammond, L., Hightower, A. M., Husbands, J. I., LaFors, J. R., Young, V. M., & Christopher, C. (2003) *Building instructional quality*. Seattle, WA: Center for the Study of Teaching and Policy.

Davis, K. A. (1995) Multicultural classrooms and cultural communities of teachers. *Teaching and Teacher Education* 11(6): 553–563.

Decker, P. T., Mayer, D. P., & Glazerman, S. (2004) *The effects of Teach for America on students: findings from a national evaluation*. Princeton, NJ: Mathematica Policy Research, Inc.

Deering, T. E. & Stanutz, A. (1995) Preservice field experience as a multicultural component of a teacher education program. *Journal of Teacher Education* 46(5): 390–394.

Dillard, C. B. (1996) From lessons of self to lessons of others. *Multicultural Education* 4(2): 33–37.

El-Haj, T. R. (2003) Practicing for equity from the standpoint of the particular: exploring the work of one urban teacher network. *Teachers College Record* 105: 817–845.

Exposito, S. & Favela, A. (2003) Reflective voices: valuing immigrant students and teaching with ideological clarity. *Urban Review* 35(1): 73–91.

Estrada, V. L. (1999) Living and teaching along the U.S./Mexico border. *Bilingual Research Journal* 23(2–3): 247–276.

Feiman-Nemser, S. & Buchmann, M. (1985) Pitfalls of experience in teacher preparation. *Teachers College Record* 87(1): 53–65.

Florio-Ruane, S. (1994) The future teachers' autobiography club. *English Education* 26(11): 52–56.

Fry, P. G. & McKinney, L. J. (1997) A qualitative study of preservice teachers' early field experiences in an urban, culturally different school. *Urban Education* 32(2): 184–201.

Frykholm, J. A. (1997) A stacked deck: addressing issues of equity with preservice students. *Equity and Excellence in Education* 30(2): 50–58.

Fuller, M. L. & Ahler, J. (1987) Multicultural education and the monocultural student: a case study. *Action in Teacher Education* 9(3): 33–40.

Garmon, M. A. (1998) Using dialogue journals to promote student learning in a multicultural teacher education course. *Remedial & Special Education* 19(1): 32–45.

Gay, G. (2000) *Culturally responsive teaching: theory, research, and practice*. New York: Teachers College Press.

Gilbert, S. L. (1995) Perspectives of rural prospective teachers toward teaching in urban schools. *Urban Education* 30(3): 290–305, 2 charts.

Goodwin, A. L. (1994) Making the transition from self to other: what do preservice teachers really think about multicultural Education? *Journal of Teacher Education* 45(2): 119–131.

Grant, C. A. & Koskela, R. A. (1986) Education that is multicultural and the relationship between campus learning and field experiences. *Journal of Educational Research* 79(4): 197–204.

Grottkau, B. J. & Nickolai-Mays, S. (1989) An empirical analysis of a multicultural education paradigm for preservice teachers. *Educational Research Quarterly* 13(4): 27–33.

Guillaume, A., Zuniga C., & Lee I. (1995) Prospective teachers' use of diversity issues in a case study analysis. *Journal of Research and Development in Education* 28(2): 69–78.

Guillaume, A., Zuniga C., & Lee I. (1998) What difference does preparation make? In M. E. Dilworth (ed.), *Being responsive to cultural differences*, pp. 143–159. Washington, DC: Corwin Press.

Haberman, M. (1995) *Star teachers of children in poverty*. West Lafayette, IN: Kappa Delta Pi.

Haberman, M. (1996) Selecting and preparing culturally competent teachers for urban schools. In J. Sikula, T. J. Buttery, & E. Guyton (eds.) *Handbook of Research on Teacher Education*, 2nd ed. (pp. 747–760). New York: Macmillan.

Haberman, M. & Post, L. (1992) Does direct experience change education students' perceptions of low-income minority students? *Midwest Educational Researcher* 5(2): 29–31.

Harry, B. & Klingner, J. (2006) *Why are so many minority students in special education?* New York: Teachers College Press.

Hauser-Cram, P., Sirin, S. R., & Stipek, D. (2003) When teachers' and parents' values differ: teachers' ratings of academic competence in children from low-income families. *Journal of Educational Psychology*, 95(4).

Hennington, M. (1981) Effect of intensive multicultural non-sexist instruction on secondary student teachers. *Educational Research Quarterly* 6(1): 65–75.

Hlebowitsh, P. S. & Tellez, K. (1993) Pre-service teachers and their students: early views of race, gender, and class. *Journal of Education for Teaching*, 17(1), 41–52.

Irvine, J. J. (2003) *Educating for diversity: seeing with a cultural eye*. New York: Teachers College Press.

Irvine, J. J. & York, D. E. (1993) Teacher perspectives: why do African American, Hispanic, and Vietnamese students fail? In S. E. Rothstein (ed.). *Handbook of schooling in urban America* (pp. 161–173). Westport, CT: Greenwood Press.

James, C. E. & Haig-Brown (2002) "Returning the dues." Community and the personal in a university-school partnership. *Urban Education* 36(2): 226–255.

Jennings, L. B. & Smith, C. P. (2002) Examining the role of critical inquiry for transformative practices. *Teachers College Record* 104(3): 456–481.

Johnson, J. & Kean, E. (1992) Improving science teaching in multicultural settings: a qualitative study. *Journal of Science Education and Technology* 1 (4): 275–287.

Johnson, L. (2002). "My eyes have been opened": white teachers and racial awareness. *Journal of Teacher Education* 53(2): 153–167.

King, J. E. (1991) Dysconscious racism: ideology, identity, and the miseducation of teachers. *Journal of Negro Education* 60(2): 133–146.

Laczko-Kerr, I. & Berliner, D. C. (2002, September 6) The effectiveness of "Teach for America" and other under-certified teachers on student academic achievement: a case of harmful public policy. *Education Policy Analysis Archives*, 10(37). Retrieved January 12, 2005 from http://epaa.asu.edulepaalvl0837/.

Lacina, J. G. & Sowa, P. (2005) Preparing for multicultural schools. *Teacher Education Quarterly* 32(1): 61–76.

LaFramboise, K. L. & Griffith, P. L. (1997) Using literature cases to examine diversity issues with preservice teachers. *Teaching and Teacher Education*, 13(4), 369–382.

Larke, P. J. (1990) Cultural diversity awareness inventory: assessing the sensitivity of pre-service teachers. *Action in Teacher Education* 12(3): 23–30.

Larke, P. J., Wiseman, D. & Bradley, C. (1990) The Minority Mentorship Project: changing attitudes of preservice teachers for diverse classrooms. *Action in Teacher Education* 12(3); 5–11.

Law, S. & Lane, D. (1987) Multicultural acceptance by teacher education students: a survey of attitudes. *Journal of Instructional Psychology* 14(1): 3–9.

Lawrence, S. M. (1997) Beyond race awareness: white racial identity and multicultural teaching. *Journal of Teacher Education*, 48(2), p108, 10p.

Lawrence, S. M. & Bunche, T. (1996) Feeling and dealing: teaching white students about racial privilege. *Teaching and Teacher Education*, 12(5), 531–542.

Lazar, A. (1998) Helping preservice teachers inquire about caregivers: a critical experience for field-based courses. *Action in Teacher Education* 19(4): 14–28.

Leistyna, P. (2001) Extending the possibilities of multicultural professional development in public schools. *Journal of Curriculum and Supervision* 16(4): 282–304.

Lindley, H. A. & Keithley, M. E. (1991) Gender expectations and student achievement. *Roeper Review* 13(4).

Lortie, D. (1975) *Schoolteacher*. Chicago: University of Chicago Press.

Luft, J. A., Bragg, J., & Peters, C. (1999) Learning to teach in a diverse setting: a case study of a multicultural science enthusiast. *Science Education* 83(5): 527–43.

McDiarmid, G. W. (1992) What to do about differences? A study of multicultural education for teacher trainees in the Los Angeles Unified School District. *Journal of Teacher Education* 43(2): 83–93.

McIntyre, A. (1997) Constructing an image of a white teacher. *Teachers College Record* 98(4), 653–681.

Mahan, J. (1982) Native Americans as teacher trainers. *Journal of Educational Equity and Leadership* 2(2): 100–110.

Mahan, J. M. & Stachowski, L. (1993–4) Diverse, previously uncited sources of professional learning reported by student teachers serving in culturally different communities. *National Forum of Teacher Education Journal* 3(1): 21–28.

Marshall, P. L. (1998) Toward developmental multicultural education: case study of the issues exchange activity. *Journal of Teacher Education* 49(1): 57–65.

Martin, O. & Williams-Dixon, R. (1994) Overcoming social distance barriers. *Journal of Instructional Psychology*, 21(1): 76–82.

Martin, R. & Koppelman, K. (1991) The impact of a human relations/multicultural education course on the attitudes of prospective teachers. *Journal of Intergroup Relations* 18(1): 16–27.

Marx, S. (2000) An exploration of preservice teacher perceptions of second language learners in the mainstream classroom. *Texas Papers in Foreign Language Education* 5(1): 207–221.

Marx, S. (2003). Entanglements of altruism, whiteness, and deficit thinking. *Education for Urban Minorities* 2 (2): 41–46.

Marx, S. & Pennington, J. (2003) Pedagogies of critical race theory: Experimentations with European-American pre-service teachers. *Qualitative Studies in Education* 16(1): 91–110.

Marxen, C. E. & Rudney, G. L. (1999) An urban field experience for rural preservice teachers. *Teacher Education Quarterly*, winter, 61–74.

Melnick, S. & Zeichner, K. (1996) The role of community-based field experiences in preparing teachers for cultural diversity. In K. Zeichner, S. Melnick, & M. L. Gomez (eds.) *Currents of reform in preservice teacher education* (pp. 176–196). New York: Teachers College Press.

Mendoza Reis, N. (2001) *A case study on the impact of professional development grounded in multicultural education on improving the quality of teachers of Latino students*. Unpublished doctoral dissertation, LaVerne University, LaVerne, CA.

Merryfield, M. M. (2000) Why aren't teachers being prepared to teach for diversity, equity, and global interconnectedness? *Teaching and Teacher Education* 16: 429–443.

Middleton, V. A. (2002) Increasing preservice teachers' diversity beliefs and commitment. *The Urban Review* 34(4): 343–361.

Miller, S. M., Miller, K. L., & Schroth, G. (1997) Teacher perceptions of multicultural training in preservice programs. *Journal of Instructional Psychology*, 24(4): 222–232.

Milner, H. R. (2003) Teacher reflection and race in cultural contexts: history, meanings, and methods in teaching. *Theory into Practice* 42(3): 173–180.

Milner, R. & Howard, T. C. (2004) Black teachers, Black students, Black communities, and *Brown*. *Journal of Negro Education* 73(3): 285–297.

Moll, L. C. & González, N. (1994) Lessons from research with language-minority children. *Journal of Reading Behavior* 26(4): 439–456.

Moss, G. (2001) Critical pedagogy: translation for education that is multicultural. *Multicultural Education* 9(2): 2–11.

Moule, J. (2004) Safe and growing out of the box: immersion for social change. In J. Romo, P. Bradfield, & R. Serrano (eds.), *Working in the margins: becoming a transformative educator* (pp. 147–171). Upper Saddle River: Merrill Prentice Hall.

Murrell, P. C., Jr. (1998) *Like stone soup: the role of the professional development school in the renewal of urban schools*. Washington, DC: AACTE.

Murtadha-Watts, K. (1998) Teacher education in urban school-based, multiagency collaboratives. *Urban Education*, 32(5): 616–631.

Narode, R., Rennie-Hill, L. & Peterson, K. (1994) Urban community study by preservice teachers. *Urban Education*, 29(1): 5–21.

Nathenson-Mejía, S. & Escamilla, K. (2003) Connecting with Latino children: bridging cultural gaps with children's literature. *Bilingual Research Journal*, 27(1): 101–116.

National Center for Education Statistics (2002) *Selected characteristics of students, teachers, parent participation, and programs and services in traditional public and public charter elementary and secondary schools: 1999–2002*. Retrieved 9/16/04, http://nces.ed.gov/

Noordhoff, K. & Kleinfeld, J. (1993) Preparing teachers for multicultural classrooms. *Teaching and Teacher Education* 9(1): 27–39.

O'Brien, E. (2004) "I could hear you if you would just calm down." In V. Lea & J. Helfand (eds.) *Identifying race and transforming whiteness in the classroom* (pp. 68–86). New York: Peter Lang.

Olmedo, I. M. (1997) Challenging old assumptions: preparing teachers for inner city schools. *Teaching and Teacher Education* 13(3): 245–258.

Orfield, G. & Lee, C. (2005) *Why segregation matters*. Boston: The Harvard University Civil Rights Project.

Pang, V. O. & Sablan, V. A. (1998) Teacher efficacy. In M. E. Dilworth (ed.), *Being responsive to cultural differences*, pp. 39–58. Washington, DC: Corwin Press.

Pewewardy, C. (2005) Shared journaling: a methodology for engaging white preservice students into multicultural education discourse. *Teacher Education Quarterly* 32(1): 1–20.

Powell, R. R., Sobel, D., Hess, R. S., & Verdi, M. (2001) The relationships between situated cognition and rural preservice teachers' knowledge and understanding of diversity. *Journal of Research in Rural Education* 17(2): 71–83.

Prawat, R. (1992) Teachers' beliefs about teaching and learning: a constructivist perspective. *American Journal of Education*, 100(3), 354–395.

Pucci, S. L., Ulanoff, S. H., & Orellana, M. F. (2000) Se hace camino al andar: reflections on the process of pre-service teacher inquiry. *Educators for Urban Minorities* 1(2): 17–26.

Reed, D. F. (1993) Multicultural education for preservice students. *Action in Teacher Education* 15(3): 27–34.

Richards, J. C., Moore, R. C. & Gipe, J. P. (1996) Preservice teachers in two different multicultural field programs: the complex influences of school context. *Research in the Schools* 3(2): 23–34.

Richman, C. L., Bovelsky, S., Kroovand, N., Vacca, J., & West, T. (1997). Racism 102: the classroom. *Journal of Black Psychology*, 23(4): 378–387.

Riojas Clark, E. & Bustos Flores, B. (1997) Instructional Snapshots (IS) in Mexico: pre-service bilingual teachers take pictures of classroom practices. *Bilingual Research Journal*, 21(2 & 3): 273–282.

Rios, F. A., McDaniel J. E., & Stowell, L. P. (1998) Pursuing the possibilities of passion: the affective domain of multicultural education. In M. E. Dilworth (ed.), *Being responsive to cultural differences* (pp. 160–181). Washington, DC: Corwin Press.

Rodriguez, A. J. (1998) Strategies for counterresistance: toward sociotransformative constructivism and learning to teach science for diversity and understanding. *Journal of Research in Science Teaching* 35(6): 589–622.

Ross D. D. & Smith, W. (1992) Understanding preservice teachers' perspectives on diversity. *Journal of Teacher Education* 43(2): 94–103.

Rubin, L. (1995) The strange and the familiar: using multicultural autobiography to stimulate critical thinking. *CEA Forum* 25(1–2): 4–9.

Rushton, S. P. (2000) Student teacher efficacy in inner-city schools. *Urban Review* 32 (4): 365–383.

Rushton, S. P. (2001) Cultural assimilation: a narrative case study of student-teaching in an inner-city school. *Teaching and Teacher Education* 17(2): 147–60.

Schmidt, P. R. (1999) Know thyself and understand others. *Language Arts* 76(4): 332–340.

Schoorman, D. (2002) Increasing critical multicultural understanding via technology. *Journal of Teacher Education* 53(4): 356–69.

Schultz, E. L., Neyhart, K., & Reck, U. M. (1996) Swimming against the tide: a study of prospective teachers' attitudes regarding cultural diversity and urban teaching. *Western Journal of Black Studies* 20(1): 1–7.

Sconzert, K., Iazzetto, D., & Purkey, S. (2000) Small-town college to big-city school: Preparing urban teachers from liberal arts colleges. *Teaching and Teacher Education* 16(4): 465–90.

Seidl, B. & Friend, G. (2002) Leaving authority at the door. *Teaching and Teacher Education* 18(4): 421–433.

Sleeter, C. E. (1992) *Keepers of the American dream*. London: The Falmer Press.

Sleeter, C. E. (1996) *Multicultural education as social activism*. Albany, NY: SUNY Press.

Sleeter, C. E. (2001) *Culture, difference and power*. New York: Teachers College Press.

Sleeter, C. E. (2005) *Un-standardizing curriculum: multicultural teaching in the standards-based classroom*. New York: Teachers College Press.

Sleeter, C. E. (in press) Preparing teachers for multiracial and historically underserved schools. In G. Orfield & E. Frankenburg (eds.) *Can we make a rainbow? From segregation to integration*. University of Virginia Press.

Smith, G. P. (1998) Who shall have the moral courage to heal racism in America? *Multicultural Education* 5(3): 4–10.

Smith, R. W. (2000) The influence of teacher background on the inclusion of multicultural education: a case study of two contrasts. *The Urban Review* 32(2): 155–176.

Smith, R., Mollem, M., & Sherrill, D. (1997) How preservice teachers think about cultural diversity. *Educational Foundations* 11(2): 41–62.

Stachowski, L. L. & Mahan, J. M. (1998) Cross-cultural field placements: student teachers learning from schools and communities. *Theory into Practice*, 37(2): 155–162.

Stallings, J. A. & Quinn, L. F. (1991) Learning how to teach in the inner city. *Educational Leadership* 49(3): 25–27.

Su, Z. (1996) Why teach: profiles and entry perspectives of minority students as becoming teachers. *Journal of Research and Development in Education* 29(3): 117–133.

Tatto, T. M. (1998) The influence of teacher education on teachers' beliefs about purposes of education, roles, and practice. *Journal of Teacher Education* 49(1): 66 (12).

Taylor, S. V. & Sobel, D. M. (2001) Addressing the discontinuity of students' and teachers' diversity. *Teaching and Teacher Education* 17: 487–503.

Terrill, M. & Mark, D. L. H. (2000) Preservice teachers' expectations for schools with children of color and second-language learners. *Journal of Teacher Education*, 51(2): 149–155.

Tiezzi, L. J. & Cross, B. E. (1997) Utilizing research on prospective teachers' beliefs to inform urban field experiences. *The Urban Review* 29(2): 113–125.

Torok, C. E. & Aguilar, T. E. (2000) Changes in preservice teachers' knowledge and beliefs about language issues. *Equity & Excellence in Education* 33(2): 24–31.

Tran, M. T., Young, R. L., & DiLella, J. D. (1994) Multicultural education courses and the student teacher. *Journal of Teacher Education* 45(3): 183–189, 3 charts.

Valli, L. (1995) The dilemma of race: learning to be color blind and color conscious. *Journal of Teacher Education*, 46(2): 120–129.

VanGunten, D. M. & Martin, R. J. (2001) Complexities and contradictions: a study of teacher education courses that address multicultural issues. *Journal of Intergroup Relations* 28(1): 31–42.

Vavrus, M. (1994) A critical analysis of multicultural education infusion during student teaching. *Action in Teacher Education* 16(3): 45–57.

Villegas, A. M. & Lucas, T. (2002) *Educating culturally responsive teachers*. Albany, NY: SUNY Press.

Warren, S. R. (2002) Stories from the classroom: how expectations and efficacy of diverse teachers affect the academic performance of children in poor urban schools. *Educational Horizons* 80(3): 109–116.

Weiner, L. (1990) Preparing the brightest for urban schools. *Urban Education* 25(3): 258–273.

Weisman, E. M. & Garza, S. A. (2002) Preservice teacher attitudes toward diversity: can one class make a difference? *Equity & Excellence in Education* 35(1): 28–34.

Wiggins, R. A. & Follo, E. J. (1999) Development of knowledge, attitudes, and commitment to teach diverse student populations. *Journal of Teacher Education* 50(2): 94–105.

Xu, H. (2000) Preservice teachers integrate understandings of diversity into literacy instruction. *Journal of Teacher Education* 51(2): 135–142.

Yeo, F. L. (1997) *Inner-city schools, multiculturalism, and teacher education*. New York: Garland.

Zeichner, K. (1996) Educating teachers for cultural diversity. In K. Zeichner, S. Melnick, & M. L. Gomez (eds.), *Currents of reform in preservice teacher education* (pp. 133–175). New York, NY: Teachers College Press.

33 Preparing teachers of color to confront racial/ethnic disparities in educational outcomes

Ana María Villegas and
Danné E. Davis
Montclair State University

Many advocates of educational equity look back to the 1970s and early 1980s as a time of hope. During that period, the Black-White and Hispanic-White achievement gaps narrowed in both reading and mathematics (Lee, 2002). These welcome changes were attributed, at least in part, to the implementation of policies initiated in the 1960s for the purpose of equalizing educational and economic opportunities in the United States (Hedge & Nowell, 1998; Grissmer *et al.*, 1998). Such efforts included federally-funded preschool programs, special programs in elementary schools with high concentrations of poor children, attempts to broaden the participation of students of color in post-secondary education, and expanded welfare and employment initiatives for families living below the poverty line. In the latter part of the 1980s, however, progress toward eliminating the racial/ethnic achievement gap stalled. While African American and Hispanic students continued to make modest gains at the basic skills level, the gap in achievement at the advanced skills level began to widen substantially around 1988, a trend that has continued (Campbell *et al.*, 2000; Lee, 2002).[1] Interestingly, this setback occurred precisely at a time when African Americans began to experience stagnation in their economic position relative to White Americans, and Hispanics began to suffer a substantial economic decline (Smith, 2001).

The test score gap is not the only evidence of disparity in educational outcomes. Relative to White students, African American and Hispanic students are overrepresented in special education programs (Coutinho & Oswald, 2000) and lower academic tracks (Lucas, 2001); are more apt to repeat a grade (Campbell *et al.*, 2000) and/or drop out of high school (Swanson, 2003); and are less likely to enroll in and graduate from college (Havey & Anderson, 2005). Such differential outcomes have profound consequences for students of color, limiting their future employment, earnings, and overall life chances (Carnevale, 1999). Those consequences are magnified in the current global information-based economy, in which people lacking a strong basic education are apt to become part of the unemployed or underemployed classes. Given the stakes involved, it is not surprising that the racial/ethnic achievement gap has generated increasing unease among equity-minded citizens, educators, researchers, and policymakers. The urgency of this problem, which has both moral and economic implications, is exacerbated by the growing numbers of students of color in elementary and secondary schools.

To make serious progress toward eradicating the achievement gap, policymakers will have to address the considerable economic disparities that currently exist between people of color and White people in the United States. Clearly, with the current poverty rate as high as 34 percent among African American children and 30 percent among Hispanic children (U.S. Census Bureau, 2005), schools are seriously challenged in their efforts to improve the academic success rates of these student groups (Berliner, 2005). At the same time, educators and policymakers must take measures that have the potential to change the dynamics of classrooms and schools with the goal of improving the academic out-comes of students of color. Increasing the diversity of the teaching force is one such measure that merits public attention.

Three major arguments for diversifying the ranks of teachers are posited in the litera-ture. The most widely cited rationale is that teachers of color can serve as role models for students of color, inspiring them to believe that they too can become successful profes-sionals if they apply themselves academically (Stewart *et al.*, 1989). A second rationale, mentioned less frequently, is that teachers of color tend to have higher expectations for students of color than White teachers do, and are more apt to place greater academic demands on them, thereby enhancing these students' school performance (Irvine, 1990). A third argument has been voiced more recently. It is said that racial/ethnic minority teachers are uniquely positioned to use their first-hand knowledge about the cultural background and everyday life experiences of students of color to help them build bridges to learning. The notion is that what these teachers know about the communities students of color come from as well as barriers they face in life enable them to work more effect-ively with this population (Irvine & Armento, 2001; Villegas & Lucas, 2002). Under-lying each of these rationales for increasing the diversity of the teaching force is the assumption that students of color will benefit academically from exposure to teachers who are racially/ethnically similar to them. Acting on this assumption, 30 states have developed teacher diversity policies since 1990 (ECS, 2003).

In this chapter, we assess the merit of policies that aim to recruit more people of color into the teaching profession, review the impact of those policies to date, and identify gaps in teacher education programs that require immediate attention if ongoing teacher recruitment efforts are to fulfill their promise to improve the school performance of minority students. First, we review the expanding empirical literature regarding the effect of teacher race/ethnicity on student learning. We then describe the salient elements of minority recruitment policies developed in the 1990s, discuss the impact of those policies on the racial/ethnic composition of the teaching force, and identify potential problems that could derail ongoing efforts to diversify the ranks of teachers. In the third section, we argue that teacher education programs, even when designed to address issues of diversity, focus their attention almost exclusively on the preparation needs of White candidates while ignoring the needs of minority candidates. We also present several strategies intended to improve the preparation of candidates of color. In the final section we offer a brief summary and recommendations.

The chapter draws on different types of data. Our analysis of the effect of teacher race/ethnicity on student learning is built on quantitative empirical studies conducted primar-ily by economists and sociologists, and reported for the most part in peer-reviewed journals of those fields. Many of these studies draw on national databases, such as the National Educational Longitudinal Study (NELS) of 1988. We also build on a com-prehensive synthesis of research on teacher-student interactions that includes experi-mental studies, survey studies, and classroom observation studies. Our discussion of minority recruitment policies and the events that led to the adoption of such policies is informed by the following: teacher and student demographic data collected by the National Center for Education Statistics as part of its Schools and Staffing Survey; influential reports issued by well-respected education-related organizations and agencies; and descriptive and evaluative studies of programs and strategies for recruiting people of color into teaching. Our assessment of existing problems regarding the preparation of candidates of color in teacher education as well as the strategies we propose for address-ing them draw on two emerging lines of research—one focusing on the experiences of candidates of color in teacher education and the other on culturally-relevant practices of teachers of color. Much of this work uses a case study methodology. All empirical studies reviewed in this chapter are consistent with the principles of scientific research identified by the National Research Council (Shavelson & Towne, 2003), which, although debated in the education community, are used widely.

DOES TEACHER RACE/ETHNICITY MATTER? A LOOK AT THE EVIDENCE

As mentioned above, minority teacher recruitment policies are motivated largely by the poor school performance of students of color. An assumption underlying these policies is that minority teachers, considered as a group, are more adept at teaching minority students than are White teachers. To judge the merit of this assumption, we identified 15 empirical studies that addressed this issue. The result of our review is presented in three parts. We first consider six studies that examined the effects of teacher race/ethnicity on student achievement as measured by scores on standardized tests. We then review five studies that explored the relationships between teacher race/ethnicity and student outcomes as measured by indicators other than test scores (e.g. absenteeism, high school dropout rates, college going rates, and enrollment rates in advanced-level high school courses). Finally, we focus on research that examined whether teacher-student racial/ethnic pairings influence teachers' perceptions, expectations, and treatment of students.

Student test scores as outcome measures

We examined six empirical studies of the effect of a teacher's race/ethnicity on student learning as measured by students' performance on tests. To determine how having a same-race teacher influences student learning, Dee (2004) reanalyzed test score data from the Tennessee Project STAR class-size experiment conducted in the late 1980s, in which students and teachers in the participating schools were randomly assigned to one another. In the original experiment, scaled scores from the Stanford Achievement Test in math and reading were used as the outcome measures. Dee discovered that racial pairing of teachers and students significantly increased the reading and mathematics achievement scores of both African American and White students by approximately three to four percentage points. He also found that racial pairing had cumulative effects on student learning, with students gaining two to four percentile points in both mathematics and reading for each additional year of exposure to a same-race teacher. The race effects were particularly strong among poor African American children attending segregated schools. Because students and teachers were randomly assigned to each other as part of the original class-size experiment, the results reported by Dee effectively control for unobserved student level determinants of educational achievement. These results support the assumption that increasing the racial/ethnic diversity of the teaching force can improve the academic achievement of students of color. However, given that the sample included students only from Tennessee, the generalizability of the findings is limited.

Clewell *et al.* (2005) used data from Prospects—a congressionally mandated study of educational growth and opportunities for American students—to investigate whether exposure to a same-race teacher was related to the reading and mathematics achievement of African American and Hispanic students in elementary schools. Scaled scores from the Comprehensive Test of Basic Skills were used as learning outcomes in this study. Clewell and associates found that for Hispanic fourth- and sixth-grade students, having a Hispanic teacher resulted in higher test score gains in mathematics. The same effect was noted in reading, but only in the fourth grade. For Black students, the effect of having a same-race teacher was somewhat weaker. Nevertheless, Black students in the fourth grade demonstrated significantly higher score gains in mathematics when taught by a Black teacher.

As part of a broad investigation of the effects of family and schools on children's scholastic achievement, Hanushek (1992) examined the impact of selected teacher characteristics, including race, on student learning. The empirical analysis drew on data about the family generated between 1971 and 1975 by the Gary Income Maintenance Experiment. These data were merged with school information on the children from the families in the experimental group. All students in the sample were Black. The school data included scores from the Iowa Reading Comprehension and Vocabulary tests, along with background information about the teachers of those students. Hanushek's analysis showed that White teachers in the sample were significantly less successful than Black teachers in increasing student achievement in both vocabulary and reading comprehension. Because the study did not include controls for teacher background variables, Hanushek concluded that either the Black teachers in the sample were more effective teachers of Black students or the White teachers who were attracted to the Gary schools (settings with a high concentration of poor Black students) were less skilled overall than their Black colleagues.

Evans (1992) investigated the influence of having a same-race teacher on the economic literacy of African American high school students. Data for this study were drawn from the National Assessment of Economic Education Survey administered in 1987 by the Joint Council on Economic Education. The survey included information for 3,266 students relating to their education, family background, teachers, schools, and school districts. Evans focused his analysis on the subset of 2,440 surveyed students who had taken an economics course. Scores on the Test of Economic Literacy, which all students in the sample had completed at the end of their economics course, was the dependent measure used in this study. Evans found that after controlling for teacher and student ability, African American students taught by African American teachers scored 2.25 points higher on the test than African American students taught by teachers of another race/ethnicity. The effect was particularly strong among students whose mother/female guardian was not college-educated. Based on these findings, Evans argued that increasing the representation of African Americans in the teaching profession would appear to have important academic benefits for Black students.

Ehrenberg and Brewer (1995) reanalyzed data from the Coleman Report of 1966 to determine whether the characteristics of teachers in a school (including the racial composition of the teaching staff) influenced the "synthetic gain scores" of the students. Synthetic gain scores were defined as the difference between the average test scores of students in upper and lower grades. The researchers restricted their analysis to the 969 schools for which test scores on verbal aptitude, nonverbal aptitude, reading, and mathematics were available for both third- and sixth-grade students. At the high school level, they limited their attention to the subset of 256 high schools for which the aforementioned data were available for ninth- and twelfth-grade students. The study used an econometric model that allowed the researchers to account for the non-random nature of teacher assignment to schools. Holding teacher characteristics other than race constant, the researchers found that an increase in the percentage of Black teachers in a school was associated with higher gain scores for Black high school students. However, no effects were detected for Black students in elementary school.

Using the National Educational Longitudinal Study (NELS) of 1988, Ehrenberg et al. (1995) examined the effect of teacher race on the academic achievement of students of different races. Scores on tests of reading comprehension, science, history/social studies, and mathematics developed by the Educational Testing Service were used as measures of student outcomes. In contrast to the results reported above, Ehrenberg and his colleagues found no evidence that a racial/ethnic match between teachers and their students was related to how much the students learned between the eighth and tenth grades in each of the four subject areas.

It is impossible to reach any definitive conclusion about the merit of teacher diversity policies based solely on the results of the six studies discussed above. For one thing, the evidence is thin, and although a clear pattern emerges, the results are not uniformly supportive. Furthermore, because data involving studies of real students in real classrooms cannot be collected under "pristine" laboratory conditions, it is nearly impossible to isolate the effects of teacher race/ethnicity on student learning from other potentially intervening teacher, student, and school variables. As a result, all six studies suffer from some sort of limitation. Even when random assignment of students and teachers is used, as in the Dee study, the generalizability of inferences that can logically be made from the findings is limited, given that the sample included students, teachers, and schools from a single state. Despite these limitations, the evidence generated by the six studies reviewed above cannot be ignored. Collectively, these works suggest that a teacher's race/ethnicity plays an important role in how much his or her students will learn, as measured by tests. There is also some evidence that teacher race/ethnicity influences student learning both at the classroom level (with students of color who are paired with a same-race/ethnicity teacher experiencing favorable academic effects) and at the school level (with schools that have a large concentration of teachers of color producing larger effects on student learning). These works, however, provide no insight into the underlying mechanisms by which teacher race/ethnicity influences student learning.

Outcomes other than test scores

While test score gains are critically important indicators of learning, there are other important student outcomes that also warrant attention (Cochran-Smith & Fries, 2001). We now turn to a subset of studies that examined whether benefits other than test score gains accrue to students of color when they are taught by teachers of color. Farkas *et al.* (1990) used the Southwestern City School District Data Set to determine the relationship between teacher race/ethnicity and absenteeism among African American students in large urban high schools. Because absenteeism reduces students' instructional time, it limits their opportunities to learn. Farkas and colleagues found a strong inverse relationship between the two variables of interest in this investigation. That is to say, African American students who were taught by a same-race teacher displayed markedly lower rates of absenteeism.

Using data collected during the 1980s from 82 urban school districts in this country, England and Meier (1986) set out to determine the effect of various district variables—including the proportion of Black teachers—on a summary variable they called "second generation discrimination." As used in this study, second generation discrimination consisted of eight specific indicators—placement in special education, placement in classes for the educable mentally retarded, admission to gifted programs, admission to enriched classes, suspension from schools, dropping out of school, attending vocational schools, and attending college. The regression model used by these researchers showed that as the proportion of Black teachers in a district increased, incidents of second generation discrimination decreased significantly. Taking a similar tack, Klopfenstein (2005) examined the impact of the percentage of Black mathematics teachers in a school on the likelihood that Black students who completed a geometry course would enroll in an Algebra II class the following year. She found that Black students' enrollment in Algebra II increased significantly as the percentage of mathematics teachers who were Black increased. Given the critical role that advanced courses such as Algebra II play in high school students' access to college, Klopfenstein's finding is particularly relevant for those interested in increasing the college-going rate of African American high school students.

There is also evidence that an increase in the proportion of racial/ethnic minority teachers in a high school reduces the dropout rates of minority students and boosts their college-going rates. Fraga *et al.* (1986) showed both of these effects to be true for Hispanic students enrolled in large urban school systems that have a sizeable concentration of Hispanic teachers. Similarly, Hess and Leal (1997) found that after controlling for relevant factors, large urban school districts with a high percentage of teachers of color had significantly higher overall college matriculation rates.

The five studies reviewed above suggest that students of color are likely to derive academic benefits from exposure to teachers of color. These works further suggest that such benefits can result from direct contact with a teacher of color in a given classroom (as illustrated in the Farkas *et al.* study) as well as from exposure to school settings with a large concentration of teachers of color. Yet as we observed in our discussion of studies that focused on student test score gains, this second set of works sheds little light on the dynamics of interaction between teachers and students that influence student outcomes. To seek insight into this topic, we turned to an extensive body of research that examines whether pairings by race/ethnicity influence teachers' perceptions, expectations, and treatment of students. Arguably, teachers' perceptions and expectations of students have an impact on the learning opportunities they create in the classroom. This line of research dates back to the 1960s, a time when many educators, researchers, and policymakers were concerned about the impact of school desegregation on students. Their concern was related to the fact that the Brown v. Topeka Board of Education decision of 1954 had been based largely on the assumption that students of color would make substantial academic gains when taught in integrated classrooms. While a review of this vast literature is beyond the scope of this chapter, highlights drawn from a frequently-referenced synthesis of research are instructive. We supplement those highlights with several more recent studies of teacher perceptions, expectations, and treatment of students that have direct bearing on the theme of this chapter.

Teacher perceptions, expectations, and treatment of students

Irvine (1990) conducted a comprehensive synthesis of studies that focused on teacher expectations as related to teacher and student race. Specifically, she reviewed 35 studies, all conducted between 1964 and 1983, that examined the expectations of Black and White teachers for Black students. Five of the studies used an experimental design in which the teachers were told to expect certain achievement performance from the students. Eighteen other studies, all of which involved the administration of questionnaires, compared teachers' perceptions of and attitudes toward African American students to their perceptions of and attitudes toward White students. The remaining 12 studies examined teacher expectations of students in actual classroom settings.

Based on her review, Irvine concluded that White teachers' perceptions of Black students tend to be less favorable than their perceptions of White students, and they tend to expect less of Black students than Black teachers do. For instance, in the studies Irvine reviewed, White teachers used negative terms such as "lazy" and "rebellious" to describe African American children. Furthermore, they thought them to be less skilled in language and mathematics, believed they had less potential for achievement, found them more disruptive, and considered them less attractive physically than White children. These unfavorable views were conveyed to the students in unambiguous ways. For instance, White teachers tended to give Black learners less attention, less encouragement, less eye contact, more verbal and non-verbal criticism (especially to Black boys), and less positive feedback after correct responses to questions. Irvine contended that this differential treatment in turn affected Black students' self-concept, classroom conduct, achievement, motivation, and level of aspiration. She also asserted that such disparities in teacher expectations and treatment of students contribute in a very significant way to the lower academic achievement of Black children.

As Irvine's conclusions were based on research conducted more than 20 years ago, it might be tempting to dismiss them. Issues of cultural diversity have received considerable attention in elementary and secondary schools, as well as teacher education, over the past two decades. Even so, while it is likely that teachers have become more culturally aware, such exposure does not necessarily translate into improved patterns of classroom inter-action. In a more recent study, Casteel (1998) examined White teachers' interactions with Black and White students in racially integrated classrooms, focusing specifically on the amount of acceptance and feedback students received. The 417 students in this study were all considered low academic achievers and had been placed in their classes based on test scores. The 16 White teachers, all experienced educators, had recently received favorable evaluations from their principals. Each teacher was observed teaching two full class periods during the school year. Data were collected by using the Brophy-Good Dyadic Interaction Observation System. Casteel found that compared to White students, Black youngsters were asked fewer of the more demanding process questions, were offered guided clues following an incorrect response less frequently, were praised after giving a correct answer less frequently, and were encouraged to ask questions less frequently. The results of this study suggest that in spite of the passage of time and increased attention being given to matters of diversity in K-12 schools and programs of teacher education, Black students continue to experience more negative interactions with their teachers than their White counterparts, even when they are at a comparable skills level.

The attitudes of teachers toward students of color have been the focus of several other recently published studies. In a complex investigation that drew on NELS 1988 data, Oates (2003) set out to determine, among other things, the effect of racial pairing of teachers and students on teachers' perceptions of African American and White tenth graders. The dependent variable for this aspect of the study was a composite construct that included whether the teacher expected the student to go to college, as well as her/his appraisal of the frequency with which the student completed assigned homework, was tardy, was attentive, and was disruptive. Oates found that White teachers had signifi-cantly less favorable perceptions of Black students than of White students, even when controlling for relevant student variables (e.g. prior GPA, prior scores on standardized tests, and current grade track placement). By contrast, African American teachers' per-ceptions of students were based on observable indicators of their performance. According to Oates, the pairing of Black students with Black teachers "shielded" the students from the anti-Black perceptions of White teachers.

Dee (2005) also analyzed NELS 1988 data to determine the effect of racial pairing of teachers and students on teachers' subjective assessments of student behavior and performance. Because the NELS database includes student-specific evaluations from teachers in two different subject areas, he was able to use a fixed-effect econometric model that identified how two racially different teachers assessed the same student. This innovative aspect of the analysis allowed Dee to control for potential bias created by the non-random assignment of students within and across schools. Focusing on negative teacher assessments, he looked specifically at the frequency with which a teacher perceived a student to be disruptive, inattentive, and unlikely to complete homework assignments. Dee found that both African American and Hispanic students were more likely to be viewed unfavorably by a teacher who was not of the same race/ethnicity. These teacher effects were most striking for students from economically poor families.

The results reported by Oates (2003) and Dee (2005) are consistent with those published earlier by Alexander *et al.* (1987), Ehrenberg *et al.* (1995), Farkas *et al.* (1990), and Irvine (1990). These findings are particularly disturbing in light of evidence that to succeed academically, students of color depend more on their teachers than White students do (Ferguson, 2002; Jussim *et al.*, 1996). While it is still an open question whether observed disparities in teacher expectations are biased by racial stereotypes or conditioned on observable indicators of student performance, the empirical literature overwhelmingly shows that racially dissimilar teacher-student pairings result in poor subjective assessments of students of color. Considered together, the evidence suggests that same-race pairings offer students of color a supportive environment that protects them to some extent from disproportionately negative subjective teacher appraisals and the potentially harmful consequences of such judgments for their academic performance.

To summarize, the evidence reviewed in this section supports the assumption that a diverse teaching force can generate important academic gains for students of color. Five of the six studies dealing with the effect teachers have on their students' test scores showed that, under certain conditions, exposure to a minority teacher results in higher test scores for minority students. If one broadens student outcomes to include other academic indicators—such as absenteeism, placement in special education, suspension from school, enrollment in advanced mathematics classes, high school dropout rates, and college matriculation rates—the case for diversifying the teaching force is made even stronger. Moreover, if one also considers the results of studies that tested for the effect of racial/ethnic pairing of teachers and students on teachers' subjective assessments of students of color, the case for minority recruitment policies becomes compelling.

We suspect that the dynamics of racial interactions in classrooms aptly described by Irvine (1990) explain, to a large extent, the teacher effects reported in most of the studies we reviewed. Another plausible explanation is that these teacher effects are conditioned by the phenomenon Steele (1997) calls "stereotype threat." According to this theory, students of color experience anxiety in situations where they perceive that stereotypes are likely to be perpetuated (e.g. students of color might think their White teachers believe them to be inferior academically). Such anxiety could interfere with the learning process and lower the students' academic outcomes. Interactions with teachers of color might reduce or eliminate the stereotype threat for minority students, allowing them to focus more directly on learning. Still another credible explanation for the beneficial academic outcomes that minority students derived from exposure to minority teachers reported in nearly all the studies reviewed above is that educators of color are able to draw on their own cultural experiences to help students of color (who are culturally similar to them) engage in learning. Clearly, additional research is needed to understand more fully the intricacies of the relationship between teacher race and student academic gains. Nevertheless, on the basis of available evidence, we believe that existing minority recruitment policies warrant continued support.

The merit of policies that seek to diversify the teaching force should not be decided solely on the basis of empirical evidence. One could legitimately argue that diversity in teaching is in keeping with the values of our pluralistic, democratic society. Schools not only facilitate the development of knowledge and skills, they also send powerful messages about what is valued by local communities and the larger society. If youngsters of color are exposed to a disproportionately small number of teachers of color, they could learn implicitly that people who are like them racially/ethnically are unsuited to be conveyers of the knowledge and skills valued by our society. Similarly, if White students do not see racial and ethnic diversity among their teachers, they may not come to value such diversity in their fellow citizens.

By advocating for minority teacher recruitment policies, we are not suggesting that White teachers are incapable of teaching students of color effectively. In fact, there are many well-documented examples of White teachers who have been highly successful in teaching students of color (see Ladson-Billings, 1994; Lucas *et al.*, 1990; Paley, 1989). Neither are we suggesting that people of color, merely by virtue of their complexion or ethnicity, possess a natural aptitude for teaching students of color. We are also not proposing that teachers be assigned to students based on their race and ethnicity. Instead, we believe that the teaching profession as a whole stands to gain from the infusion of expertise about minority cultures, perspectives, and experiences that people of color would bring to it. For example, teachers of color can help to expand our understanding of culturally responsive teaching. They also can help their White colleagues interpret the cultural backgrounds of students of color. In short, people of color can diversify the teaching profession by bringing alternative perspectives to problem solving. Ultimately, their increased presence in the teaching force can provide a means for improving the preparation of all teachers who work with students of color. At the same time, all White teachers at both the pre-service and in-service levels need intensive preparation to help them become responsive educators for an increasingly diverse elementary and secondary student population (see chapter by Sleeter in this volume). Similarly, prospective and in-service teachers of color need support to incorporate their personal understanding of students of color into pedagogical practices, as we discuss in a subsequent section of this chapter.

The minority teacher shortage: sources of the problem and proposed solutions

The shortage of teachers of color first gained national attention toward the end of the 1980s when conflicting trends in the racial/ethnic compositions of the K-12 student population and the teaching force became evident. Figure 33.1 illustrates these trends for the 15-year period from 1971 through 1986. The figure shows that as student enrollments became more diverse over time, the teacher population became less so. Specifically, the racial/ethnic disparity between students and educators more than doubled during this

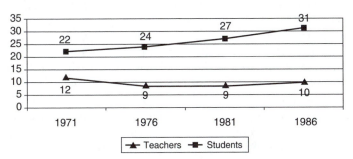

Figure 33.1 Percentage of minority teachers and minority students in public elementary and secondary schools, 1971–1986.

Sources: Student data derived from U.S. Department of Education 2001; teacher data derived from NEA 2003.

15-year period. Concerned by these conflicting demographic trends, leaders in communities of color argued that without active intervention, the cultural divide already obvious in many classrooms across the country would become even more striking in the future (Graham, 1987; Irvine, 1988; Tomás Rivera Center, 1993).

The reasons for the short supply of teachers of color are complex. A leaky pipeline is an apt representation for the dynamics of the shortage (Villegas & Lucas, 2004). In this metaphor, the pipeline represents the educational path that leads to a teaching career, beginning at entry into schools in kindergarten. There are critical junctures along this path—completion of high school, enrollment in post-secondary education, enrollment in a program of teacher education, completion of college, and completion of requirements for a teaching certificate. The shortage of minority teachers can be attributed to a sizeable loss of students of color at each critical juncture in the pipeline.

Historically, students of color have had significantly lower high school completion rates than White students. In 2000, for instance, the high school completion rate was 91.8 percent for White students, compared to 83.7 percent for Blacks and a dismal 64.1 percent for Hispanics (NCES, 2001). Such losses of minority students at this critical juncture in the education pipeline substantially reduce the pool of eligible candidates of color for higher education, especially among Hispanics.

Of those who complete high school and pursue a post-secondary education, most begin by enrolling in two-year colleges (Chronicle of Higher Education, 1999). To become teachers, they must transfer to four-year colleges, but a disappointingly small proportion of them do so (Palmer, 2005). A major part of the problem is that articulation agreements between two- and four-year colleges tend to lack clarity regarding the transfer of courses, especially as it pertains to teacher education. Consequently, transfer students often find themselves having to repeat courses they completed at the junior college. The necessity of additional coursework prevents many transfer students of color from going into teacher education (Villegas & Clewell, 1998).

Ironically, another barrier to increasing the number of teachers of color is the fact that in the early 1970s, professional options outside the field of education began to open up to minorities as a result of the Civil Rights movement. Because of other options, teacher education programs have experienced increasing difficulty attracting students of color from the traditional college-bound pool. This population has defected in large numbers to non-education fields that offer graduates the promise of higher salaries and greater prestige, such as business, engineering, and the health professions (Carter & Wilson, 1992). According to Gordon (1997), middle-class minority parents—especially within the African American and Asian communities—have contributed to this exodus by encouraging their children to pursue lucrative careers that command more status than teaching.

Even when efforts to recruit students of color into teacher education succeed, they are insufficient. If the representation of people of color in the teaching profession is to grow, institutions of higher education must retain the new recruits through graduation. Unfortunately colleges and universities, especially predominantly White ones, have a dismal record on the retention of minority students. This is particularly true for first-generation students from low-income backgrounds (Seidman, 2005). Factors contributing to the low retention rates for minorities in higher education include the lack of attention given to cultural diversity on most college/university campuses, insufficient academic and social support, and the resulting sense of alienation that many minority students experience in predominantly White colleges/universities (Feagin *et al.*, 1996). Thus, even when teacher education programs are successful in recruiting minority students, attrition within this group significantly constrains the pool of candidates of color for the teaching profession.

Increased use of teacher testing since the 1980s is another factor restricting the flow of people of color through the teacher education pipeline. In 1980, for example, only 15 states required prospective teachers to pass a standardized test to be certified. Now 43 states have testing requirements for initial certification. Because the passing rates of candidates of color on standardized tests tend to be lower than those of their White counterparts, the teacher testing movement has resulted in the exclusion of disproportionately large numbers of people of color from the profession (Memory *et al.*, 2003). Given the limited and contested evidence regarding the predictive validity of existing teacher tests (Haney *et al.*, 1999; Melnick & Pullin, 2000), the intensified use of teacher testing associated with the No Child Left Behind Act of 2001 raises serious legal questions. While we believe that the quality of public education needs to be improved, we fear that the narrow definition of teacher quality and accompanying methods for identifying "highly qualified teachers" inherent in NCLB will result in a further whitening of the teaching force.

The factors discussed above have seriously limited the representation of people of color in teaching just as the representation of students of color in elementary and secondary schools has grown significantly. In response to the widening demographic gap between teachers and their students, a number of school districts, colleges and universities, and state departments of education have adopted minority recruitment policies and programs over the past 15 years. Such policies and programs seek to expand the pool of potential teachers of color by focusing recruitment efforts on non-traditional candidates and offering new recruits support services specifically designed to increase their completion of high school, enrollment and retention in college, completion of teacher education programs and the requirements associated with a teaching certificate, and placement in teaching positions. These are some the most frequently used strategies: targeting middle and high school students to prepare them for college while motivating them to pursue a teaching career; creating career ladder programs for paraeducators; developing clear and strong articulation agreements between two- and four-year colleges to facilitate the transfer of students of color into teacher education at four-year institutions; and creating programs of alternative routes to certification to attract career switchers and retirees from other professions. A brief description of each of these strategies follows.

Early recruitment programs identify potential minority candidates before their senior year in high school, often as early as middle school, and involve them in interventions designed to foster their interest in teaching and enhance their preparation for college. These programs entail partnerships between the school districts in which the students are enrolled and teacher education programs of nearby colleges. Among the variety of strategies used to attain their dual goals are the following: Future Educators Clubs; introductory teacher education courses that offer college credit to high school juniors and seniors; mentor teachers and invited speakers who provide students with information about the teaching profession and inspire them to pursue a college education and become teachers; summer programs that give students intensive teaching experiences as well as academic support; and work study programs in which minority students in the upper high school grades tutor young children in community programs (Recruiting New Teachers, 1997).

Paraeducator-to-teacher programs also entail collaboration between teacher education programs and neighboring school districts. Given that many paraeducators are of racially and ethnically diverse backgrounds and have extensive teaching experience, they are a strong pool from which to draw candidates of color for teaching. In initiatives of this type, paraeducators continue to work in their salaried positions and enroll in courses each semester toward the completion of requirements for teaching certification and, in most cases, for a bachelor's degree as well. Since the ultimate goal of these programs is to place graduates in permanent teaching positions, active involvement of partner district staff in the selection of participants is essential. The teacher education curriculum is specifically designed to help participants explore the connection between the theories studied in college/university classes and their practice in classrooms as paraeducators. Tuition assistance is a key feature of these programs. In addition, participants receive a wide variety of support services, including preparation for certification exams and mentoring to assist them with their teaching (Clewell & Villegas, 2001; Villegas & Clewell, 1998).

Partnerships between two- and four-year colleges are another effective strategy for recruiting and preparing more teachers of color. As mentioned above, most students of color who pursue a college education first matriculate into two-year colleges. Critical to these partnerships is a dual admissions system that guarantees two-year college students entry into selected teacher education programs at a four-year institution if they complete the specified course of general studies successfully. Effective partnerships require that faculties of the two- and four-year colleges be involved in decisions regarding the general education courses that will transfer. Students also receive counseling to facilitate a smooth transfer (Hudson *et al.*, 2002).

Alternative certification programs target for recruitment individuals who already hold a bachelor's degree in a non-education field, including midlife career changers, retirees from professions outside education, and emergency certified or substitute teachers. Alternative route programs that have successfully prepared people of color for teaching provide recruits with rigorous training in pedagogy and intensive classroom support during their first year as teachers (Clewell & Villegas, 1999).

Have existing minority teacher recruitment programs succeeded in increasing the diversity within the ranks of public school teachers? The data summarized in Table 33.1 suggest progress has been made toward this end. The table provides information about the racial/ethnic distribution of public school teachers taken from the National Center for Educational Statistics' last three administrations of the Schools and Staffing Survey. As shown, the overall composition of the teaching force was more diverse in 1999–2000 than in 1987–1988. Specifically, teachers of color accounted for 15.7 percent of the teaching force in 1999–2000, up from 13.1 percent twelve years earlier. However, the gains were not evenly distributed across the different minority groups. While the fraction of American Indian/Alaska Native teachers remained at about the same level, there were gains in the percentages of Hispanic and Asian/Pacific Island teachers. In contrast, the share of African Americans declined from 8.2 percent in 1887–88 to 7.4 percent in 1993–94, where it has held steady since (NCES, 1995; 2002). We suspect that in addition to the factors discussed above, the waning presence of African American teachers is

Table 33.1 Racial/ethnic distribution of public school teachers for selected years

Racial/ethnic group	1987–1988	1993–1994	1999–2000
African American	8.2	7.4	7.5
Asian/Pacific Islander	0.9	1.1	1.6
American Indian/Alaskan Native	1.0	0.8	0.9
Hispanic	2.9	4.2	5.6
White	86.9	86.5	84.3

Source: NCES, 1995, 2002

influenced by a large wave of retirements within this group. Clearly, the diminishing representation of African Americans in teaching is an issue that demands immediate attention and further investigation.

A review of information pertaining to the racial/ethnic backgrounds of new teachers— that is, those who have been *teaching for three years or less*—also affirms the success of ongoing minority recruitment efforts. Table 33.2 summarizes the relevant information for the 12-year period between 1987 and 1999. As shown, 13.0 percent of all new teachers were of minority backgrounds in 1987. That figure rose to 17.4 percent in 1993. Six years later, it reached a high of nearly 23 percent. According to Shen (1998), this increase in diversity among new teachers can be attributed in large measure to the growth of programs that offer alternative routes to teaching, the path of choice for most people of color since 1990.

The favorable trend noted above suggests that the goal of diversifying the teaching force appreciably is attainable. Even so, it will require more than active recruitment. Focused attention must also be given to issues of retention. As Ingersoll (2004) argues persuasively, the inability of school systems to retain teachers of all backgrounds contributes significantly to the short supply of educators in the United States. Because the overwhelming majority of teachers of color are placed in hard-to-staff urban schools (Villegas, 2005), they are especially vulnerable to attrition.

Urban schools are plagued by chronic teacher shortages. To cope with this problem, school officials often resort to a strategy of moving staff around for coverage, even if this results in assigning teachers to teach subjects that do not match their academic preparation. A second strategy used frequently by school officials is to increase the size of classes in order to reduce the number of teachers a school requires. Because these administrative practices intensify the work load of teachers, they increase the odds of attrition among those affected. Unfortunately, teachers of color are more likely than their White colleagues to receive out-of-field assignments for at least a portion of their time, and also to have large classes (Villegas, 2005). The relevant information for the 15-year period between 1986 and 2001 is summarized in Table 33.3. As shown, out-of-field assignments increased for minority teachers from 1986 through 2001. Particularly problematic is the change noted from 1996 to 2001, when misassignments spiked from 23 to 30 percent among minorities. In contrast, misassignments held steady over the years at 16 to 17 percent among White teachers. The table also shows dramatic differences between the average size of classes taught by minority and White teachers in departmentalized settings. Among minorities, the average class size ranged from a low of 30 students in 1991 to a high of 46 students in 1996. Even though class size decreased for minorities in 2001, the 38-student average observed that year is far from optimal. The average class size for White teachers was never higher than 29 students during the same 15-year period.

The data presented above suggest that without strong mentoring programs for novice minority teachers and improved working conditions in urban schools—where the majority of these teachers are employed—gains made toward diversifying the teaching force through recruitment could be negated by the premature loss of teachers of color through

Table 33.2 Distribution of White and minority new teachers in public school for selected years

Racial/ethnic group	1987–1988	1993–1994	1999–2000
White	87.0	82.6	77.1
Minority	13.0	17.4	22.9

Source: Shen *et al.*, 2003

Table 33.3 Teaching assignment/class size by teacher race/ethnicity, 1981–2001

Teacher race/ethnicity	1986	1991	1996	2001
Percentage of teachers assigned outside their major field of college preparation for at least a portion of time				
Minority	16	19	23	30
White	17	16	16	17
Average number of students taught per class (departmentalized settings—elementary/secondary)				
Minority	36	30	46	38
White	25	25	29	26

Source: NEA, 2003

attrition. This concern is magnified by the recent growth of minority teachers in the novice category. Research shows that the highest attrition from teaching tends to occur among the most junior teachers, partly as a result of difficulties in adjusting to the profession.

ATTENDING TO THE PREPARATION OF CANDIDATES OF COLOR

To maximize the benefits that can be derived from a diverse teaching force, we must go beyond issues of recruitment and retention and attend to the preparation of candidates of color. Unless minority candidates are appropriately prepared to use the unique qualities and perspectives they bring to teaching, the yield of those resources will be limited at best. More to the point, it would be unfair to expect people of color to help narrow the racial/ethnic achievement gap without the benefit of professional growth experiences that enable them to use their cultural knowledge and expertise in teaching. Unfortunately, teacher education programs are evading their responsibility in this matter (Montecinos, 1994; 2004; Rios & Montecinos, 1999).

While there has been some progress over the past 15 years toward making the teacher education curriculum more multicultural, the intended beneficiaries of those efforts have largely been White pre-service teachers (Cochran-Smith, 1995; Knight, 2002; Montecinos, 2004; Rios & Montecinos, 1999; Sheets & Chew, 2002). Part of the problem is that empirical studies of multicultural teacher education conducted to date have tended to focus on approaches for helping White pre-service teachers—who represent the overwhelming majority of the pre-service teacher population—to teach students who are racially and ethnically different from themselves. This literature pays scant attention to strategies that teacher educators might use to help candidates of color build on the unique strengths they bring to teaching—that is, their knowledge about students of color and their insiders' experiences as members of minority groups—to shape their pedagogy and define their roles as teachers. Thus, candidates of color are left to figure out on their own how best to use their cultural knowledge and life experiences in classrooms and schools. Lacking this preparation, teachers of color—most of whom teach in school districts with high minority enrollments—become increasingly vulnerable to attrition (Parker & Hood, 1995).

In the remainder of this section, we present three strategies that could make programs of teacher education more responsive to minority teacher candidates: (a) preparing teachers of color to be agents of change; (b) preparing teachers of color to be culturally responsive; and (c) creating a safe environment conducive to critical dialogue.

Preparing teachers of color to be agents of change

In spite of progress over the years toward making schools more equitable and just, schools continue to place poor and minority students at a learning disadvantage. Eradicating the deeply ingrained inequities demands a cadre of teachers who understand the political nature of schools and teaching, and who are adept at identifying biases in their own teaching and skilled in reconstructing the culture of their classrooms to make them fully inclusive. Compared to their White peers, people of color are more likely to enter teacher education with the attitudes and dispositions needed to become agents of change. They know from experience what it is like to be a person of color in the United States. Most come from economically poor backgrounds. If they are not poor themselves, they often have close relatives or friends who are. They also know from first-hand experience that schools are not level playing fields on which all students can prove their merit. They understand that built into virtually every school system are practices that put minority students at a decided disadvantage (Kauchak & Burback, 2003; Rios & Montecinos, 1999; Su, 1997; Wilder, 1999). If properly tapped by teacher educators, these experiences and insights—and the sociocultural consciousness they engender—could serve as a powerful resource for cultivating commitment on the part of minority candidates to engage in the future reconstruction of schools. In fact, we believe that the addition of large numbers of teachers of color who are well prepared to act as agents of change represents our best chance to make schools more democratic and just.

To use minority teacher candidates' understanding of inequalities in schools and society for political change, teacher education programs must address thorny issues of racism and ethnocentrism openly. Unfortunately, many programs are silent on these topics or address them only in simplistic and superficial ways. Among programs that promote more thoughtful discussions of issues related to social inequalities, usually in the one required multicultural education course, the focus generally is on helping White teacher candidates recognize that schools and society are not neutral and that "white privilege" does exist. The intense focus on the needs of White candidates leaves little or no space in the curriculum for students of color (who are already well aware that racism and ethnocentrism are ingrained in our society) to develop the skills they need to respond constructively to the inequities they will encounter in schools as teachers. This gap in the curriculum seriously undermines the gains that could be derived from ongoing efforts to diversify the teacher workforce.

Preparing teachers of color to be culturally responsive

Minority recruitment policies assume that teachers of color will be effective teachers of students of color because they are knowledgeable about those students' cultures. While the cultural knowledge people of color bring to teaching gives them an advantage over their White colleagues in teaching students of color, it would be simplistic to assume that people of color can become culturally responsive educators on their own. To accomplish this, they need a framework that makes the connection between culture and pedagogy explicit. A constructivist conception of learning could serve as such a framework (Villegas & Lucas, 2002)

From a constructivist perspective, learning is seen as a process by which students generate meaning in response to new ideas and experiences they encounter in school. In this interpretive process, they use their prior knowledge and beliefs to make sense of new input (Glasersfeld, 1995). This suggests that learners' preexisting knowledge, derived from personal and cultural experiences, gives them access to learning. To ignore the experiences that children bring to school is to deny them access to the knowledge construction process. Thus, a salient role of the teacher is to help students connect learning in school to their everyday life experiences outside school.

Guided by this theory of learning, a culturally responsive teacher uses such practices as the following: activating students' prior knowledge and beliefs related to the topic being studied; building instruction on students' interests in order to engage them in learning; selecting instructional materials that are relevant to students' experiences; making use of pertinent examples and analogies drawn from students' lives to introduce or clarify new concepts; building on students' linguistic resources; creating different paths to learning by using varied instructional approaches; managing the classroom in ways that take into consideration cultural differences in interaction styles; and using a variety of assessment strategies to maximize students' opportunities to demonstrate what they know about the topic at hand in ways that are familiar to them (Villegas & Lucas, 2002).

This framework or a similar one would enable candidates of color to envision a variety of ways in which to use their knowledge of minority cultures for pedagogical purposes. To facilitate the development of culturally responsive teaching practices, teacher educators could ask minority candidates to read about and discuss the practices of effective teachers of color (see for example Irvine, 2002; Monzó & Rueda, 2001). Teacher educators also need to support minority teacher candidates in applying principles of culturally responsive teaching in culturally diverse classroom settings.

If a teacher does not have a firm grasp of the subject being taught, the teacher's ability to help students make connections between their cultural backgrounds and the content of the lesson will be limited. To be successful, all teachers, regardless of their backgrounds, need to have a deep understanding of the concepts in their respective academic disciplines and how those concepts relate to one another; the structures, principles, and nature of discourse in those disciplines; and the role that those disciplines play in society. Whatever the candidates' ethnicity, the preparation of culturally responsive teachers involves providing a strong foundation in the subject matter they will teach. Because minority teacher candidates tend to be the products of urban elementary and secondary schools that often provide a watered-down academic experience, many are likely to need additional support in their disciplinary majors. Colleges and universities that do not offer such support are not seriously committed to diversifying the teacher workforce, even if their mission statements and policies claim otherwise.

Creating a safe environment conducive to critical dialogue

A theme that emerges from studies on the experiences of minority candidates in teacher education programs, especially at predominantly White institutions, is the profound sense of alienation this population commonly experiences (Bennet *et al.*, 2000; Cochran-Smith, 2000; Sheets & Chew, 2002). Such alienation stems from what Sleeter (2001) aptly describes as an "overwhelming presence of whiteness." Candidates of color constitute a small fraction of the enrollment in teacher education classes. They encounter relatively few faculty members who are like them racially and ethnically, and are generally exposed to a curriculum that ignores their strengths and needs. In this context of overwhelming whiteness, it is not surprising that minority candidates frequently report feeling unsafe in class, especially when discussing issues of diversity with peers and faculty whom they perceive as insensitive to these topics and disinterested in hearing what they have to offer. The resulting sense of alienation increases the odds of minority candidates' attrition from teacher education programs. From another perspective, the withdrawal of students of color from in-class discussions deprives everyone, including White students, of opportunities to engage in the critical dialogue they need to become agents of change.

To retain students of color through program completion, teacher educators must find ways of building a learning community in which minority candidates feel both safe and respected. This goal can be attained by creating a space in the curriculum (e.g. a seminar) for students of color to talk openly among themselves about issues they consider important to their own professional development as teachers (Bennett *et al.*, 2000). In such a seminar, for example, students of color might reflect on characteristics they bring to teaching that are unique and inherently of value in our increasingly diverse elementary and secondary schools (Dillard, 1994).

Teacher educators also need to find ways of involving students of color in productive conversations across racial/ethnic lines in classrooms where they are a small minority, if not the only one. Unless steps are taken toward this end, the overwhelming number of White students in teacher education classes can drown out the voices of even the most outspoken students of color. Such conversations are necessary if teacher educators are to prepare candidates of all racial/ethnic backgrounds to develop the skills required to exchange ideas across differences in professional contexts and to build coalitions for change (Knight, 2002). To this end, teacher educators will need to articulate clear rules for discussing differences in a manner that is respectful of all. These conversations would benefit from having teacher educators pose critical questions to the group about who speaks or is silent in the program, in what settings, and on which topics. Clearly, to orchestrate these potentially difficult dialogues, teacher educators will require considerable professional development themselves. Such conversations are not likely to occur in the absence of faculty diversity.

CONCLUSION

As women of color, we (the authors) cannot claim to be uninterested in the subject examined in this chapter. We acknowledge that our own personal and professional experiences suggest that the presence of teachers of color makes a difference in the learning of students of color. However, as educational researchers, we also know that our own experiences do not constitute evidence for drawing conclusions about the experiences of others. Therefore, we began the review of the literature for this chapter with a commitment to follow the empirical evidence wherever it would lead us. Having examined the empirical literature, we are now convinced there is sufficient evidence to suggest that teacher race and ethnicity do matter in the education of students of color. Our review does not support a color-blind perspective on the relationship between teacher and student race/ethnicity.

While the available research is insufficient to provide a clear understanding of exactly how and why teacher race/ethnicity matters, it allows us to draw some tentative conclusions. Teacher perceptions and expectations of students play a critical role in the racial dynamics of classrooms. There is substantial evidence that these factors influence the opportunities teachers create for students to learn. Because teachers of color tend to have more favorable (or at least more neutral) views of students of color, it is likely that they structure their teaching in ways that are more supportive of student achievement. In effect, they protect students of color from the potentially pernicious effects of negative stereotyping and low expectations. Research also suggests that teachers of color who are considered effective by parents and principals use their cultural knowledge to help students of color build bridges to learning and tend to establish relationships of care and trust with their students. Clearly, teachers who know their students well and are adept at communicating with them in culturally appropriate ways are better able to engage students in the learning process. While the existing research suggests that these are two ways in which teacher race/ethnicity has a positive impact on the learning of students of color, there is a need for further research to test these conclusions and provide a more nuanced understanding of the roles played by and the impact of teacher race/ethnicity.

The evidence that teacher race/ethnicity can make a positive difference in the learning of students of color supports efforts to increase the number of teachers of color. In this chapter we reviewed minority teacher recruitment policies and programs adopted by school districts, institutions of higher education, and state education departments over the past 15 years and their impact on the racial/ethnic composition of the teacher workforce. Because the shortage of teachers of color derives from the loss of students of color at different junctures along the educational pipeline, recruitment initiatives have been developed to help more minority candidates qualify for postsecondary education in general and for teaching in particular. Recruitment programs target different pools of potential teachers, including pre-college students, community college students, paraprofessionals, mid-life career changers, and retirees from other professions. Evidence regarding the success of such efforts is promising with regard to increasing the number of Hispanic and Asian teachers, but it is less promising regarding Black teachers. The proportion of teachers who are Black is decreasing and is likely to continue to do so as large numbers of older Black teachers reach retirement age. Alternative routes for bringing mid-career-changing adults into teaching appear to offer the best hope for increasing the number of Black Americans in the profession.

Regardless of the success of some recruitment efforts, recruitment alone is woefully inadequate as a strategy for increasing the diversity of the teaching force. The almost exclusive focus on recruitment efforts is shortsighted. Unless we want to perpetuate a revolving door for teachers of color, we must turn our attention to retaining them once they have entered the profession. Research is needed to identify factors that influence teachers of color to leave or to remain in the classroom. A number of factors discussed in the literature seem to merit exploration. One, for example, is the fact that a large proportion of teachers of color are employed in urban schools, where conditions tend to interfere with teaching and learning. There is also evidence that teachers of color are more likely to have large classes and to be assigned to teach in fields or disciplines for which they are unprepared. The more responsible and committed a teacher is, the less willing she or he may be to continue working in a situation where success seems impossible. In addition to these issues, all aspects of the retention of teachers of color should be explored empirically.

Similarly, more attention should be given to providing relevant preparation for prospective teachers of color and to studying such preparation. Culturally responsive teacher education is as essential as culturally responsive teaching in K-12 schools. A great deal of attention has been given to designing teacher education so that the large majority of future teachers who are White will be prepared to teach culturally and linguistically diverse students—and rightfully so. However, teachers of color also need preparation that is designed specifically for them. A person of color cannot be expected to know how to use his or her cultural knowledge for pedagogical purposes without being taught how to do so. Teachers of color who are not adequately supported in learning how to use their insights and experiences may make less difference in the lives of their students than they could, and they may be among those who do not remain in teaching. This is another area for research.

We began this chapter by suggesting that a more diverse teaching force might contribute to the reduction of the achievement gap. Evidence we reviewed generally supports the argument that teachers of color can promote the learning of students of color. However, as we pointed out earlier, the strategy must involve much more than simply increasing the number of teachers who reflect the diversity of the student population. A comprehensive effort is needed to recruit, prepare, and retain people of color in teaching. In addition, a multifaceted research agenda must be undertaken to gain a better understanding of how and why teacher race/ethnicity makes a difference for students and of how a diverse teaching force can be successfully recruited, prepared, and nurtured.

NOTE

1 Murname and Levy (1996) suggest that to qualify for a middle-class job, 17-year-olds must attain a scaled score of 300 or higher in NAEP tests of reading and mathematics. That is, they must reach the basic skills proficiency level designated by the 300 scaled score. In 1999, 70 percent of White 17-year-olds performed at or above the basics skills level in reading and mathematics, compared to only 27 percent of Black students and 38 percent of Hispanic students (Lee, 2002).

REFERENCES

Alexander, K. L., Entwistle, D. R., & Thompson, M. S. (1987) School performance, status relations, and the structure of sentiment: bringing the teacher back in. *American Sociological Review*, 52 (October): 665–682.

Bennett, C., Cole, D., & Thompson, J. N. (2000) Preparing teachers of color at a predominantly White university: A case study of project TEAM. *Teaching and Teacher Education*, 16, 445–464.

Berliner, D. (August 2, 2005) Our impoverished view of educational research. *Teachers College Record*. Retrieved December 28, 2005: http://www.tcrecord.org/Home.asp

Campbell, J. R., Hombo, C. M., & Mazzeo, J. (2000) *NAEP 1999 trends in academic progress: three decades of student performance*. Washington, DC: OERI, U.S. Department of Education.

Carter, D. J. & Wilson, T. (1992) *Minorities in higher education: tenth annual report*. Washington, DC: American Council on Education.

Casteel, C. A. (1998) Teacher-student interactions and race in integrated classrooms. *Journal of Educational Research*, 92 (Nov/Dec), 115–120.

Carnevale, A. P. (1999) *Education = success: empowering Hispanic youth and adults*. Princeton, NJ: Educational Testing Service.

Chronicle of Higher Education (1999, August) 1999–2000 *Almanac Issue* 46, no. 1.

Clewell, B. C. & Villegas, A. M. (Summer 1999) Creating a nontraditional pipeline for urban teachers: the Pathways to Teaching Careers model. *The Journal of Negro Education*, 68(3), 306–317.

Clewell, B. C. & Villegas, A. M. (2001) *Ahead of the class: a handbook for preparing new teachers from new source*. Washington, DC: The Urban Institute.

Clewell, B. C., Puma, M. J., & McKay, S. A. (2005) *Does it matter if my teacher looks like me? The impact of teacher race and ethnicity on student academic achievement*. Paper presented at an Invited Presidential Session of the Annual Meeting of the American Educational Research Association, Montreal, Canada, April 2005.

Cochran-Smith, M. (1995) Uncertain allies: understanding the boundaries of race and teaching. *Harvard Educational Review*, 65(4), 541–570.

Cochran-Smith, M. (2000) Blind vision: unlearning racism in teacher education. *Harvard Educational Review*, 70, 541–570.

Cochran-Smith & Fries, K. (2001) Sticks, stones, and ideology: the discourse of teacher education. *Educational Researcher*, 30(8), 3–15.

Coutinho, M. J. & Oswald D. P. (2000) Disproportionate representation in special education: a synthesis and recommendations. *Journal of Child and Family Studies* 9(2), 135–152.

Dee, T. (2004) Teachers, race, and student achievement in a randomized experiment. The *Review of Economics and Statistics*, 86(1), 195–210.

Dee, T. (2005) *A teacher like me: does race, ethnicity or gender matter?* Paper presented at an Invited Presidential Session of the Annual Meeting of the American Educational Research Association, Montreal, Canada, April 2005.

Dillard, C. (1994) Beyond supply and demand: critical pedagogy, ethnicity, and empowerment in recruiting teachers of color. *Journal of Teacher Education*, 45(1), 9–17.

Education Commission of the States (2003) *Recruiting teachers of color: a 50-state survey of sate policies*. Denver, CO: Author.

Ehrenberg, R. G. & Brewer, D. J. (1995) Did teacher's verbal ability and race matter in the 1960s? Coleman revisited. *Economics of Education Review*, 14(1), 1–21.

Ehrenberg, R. G., Goldhaber, D. D., & Brewer, D. J. (1995) Do teachers' race, gender, and ethnicity matter? Evidence from the National Educational Longitudinal Study of 1988. *Industrial and Labor Relations Review*, 48(3), 547–561.

England, R. E. & Meier, K. J. (1986) From desegregation to integration: Second generation school discrimination as an institutional impediment. *American Politics Quarterly*, 13(2), 227–247.

Evans, M. O. (1992) An estimate of race and gender role-model effects in teaching high school. *Journal of Economic Education*, 10, 209–227.

Farkas, G., Grobe, R., Sheehan, D., & Shuan, Y. (1990) Cultural resources and school success: gender, ethnicity, and poverty groups within an urban school district. *American Sociological Review*, 55, 127–142.

Feagin, J. R., Vera, H., & Imain, N. (1996) *The agony of education: Black students at white colleges and universities*. New York: Routledge.

Fraga, L. R., Meier, K. J., & England, R. E. (1986) Hispanic Americans and educational policy: limits to equal access. *The Journal of Politics*, 48(4), 850–876.

Ferguson, R. (2002) What doesn't meet the eye: understanding and addressing racial disparities in high-achieving suburban schools. North Central Regional Educational Laboratory. Retrieved February 11, 2005: http://www.ncrel.org/gap/research.htm.

Glasersfeld, E. von (1995) *Radical constructivism: a way of knowing and learning*. London: Falmer.

Gordon, J. (1997) Teachers of color speak to issues of respect and image. *The Urban Review*, 29(1), 41–66.

Graham, P. A. (1987) Black teachers: a drastically scarce resource. *Phi Delta Kappan*, 68(3), 598–605.

Grissmer, D., Fanagan, A., & Williamson, S. (1998) Why did the Black-White score gap narrow in the 1970s and 1980s? In C. Jencks and M. Phillips (eds.), *The Black-White test score gap* (pp. 182–226). Washington, DC: Brookings Institution Press.

Haney, W., Fowler, C., & Wheelock, A. (1999) *Less truth than error? An independent study of the Massachusetts teacher test*. Chestnut Hill, MA: Boston College, Center for the Study of Testing, Evaluation, and Policy.

Hanushek, E. A. (1992) The trade-off between child quantity and quality. *Journal of Political Economy*, 100(1), 84–117.

Havey, W. B. & Anderson, E. L. (2005) *Minorities in higher education 2003–2004: Twenty-first annual status report (2005)*. Washington, DC: American Council on Education.

Hedge, L.V. & Nowell, A. (1998) Black-White test score convergence since 1965. In C. Jencks and

M. Phillips (eds.), *The Black-White test score gap* (pp. 149–181). Washington, DC: Brookings Institution Press.

Hess, F. M. & Leal, D. L. (1997) Minority teaches, minority students, and college matriculation: a new look at the role-modeling hypothesis. *Policy Studies Journal*, 25(2), 235–248.

Hudson, M., Foster, E., Irvine, J. J., Holmes, B., & Villegas, A. M. (2002) *Tapping potential: community college students and America's teacher recruitment challenge*. Belmont, MA: Recruiting New Teachers.

Ingersoll, R. (2004) Four myths about America's teacher quality problems. In M. A. Smylie and D. Miretzky (eds.), *Developing the teacher workforce: 103rd yearbook of the National Society for the Study of Education* (pp. 1–33). Chicago, IL: University of Chicago Press.

Irvine, J. J. (1988) An analysis of the problem of the disappearing Black educator. *Elementary School Journal*, 88(5), 503–514.

Irvine, J. J. (1990) *Black students and school failure*. New York: Greenwood Press.

Irvine, J. J. (2002) *In search of wholeness: African American teachers and their culturally specific classroom practices*. NY: Palgrave.

Irvine, J. J. & Armento, B. J. (2001) Culturally responsive teaching: Lesson planning for elementary and middle grades. NY: McGraw-Hill.

Jencks, C. & Phillips, M. (1998) The Black-White test score gap: an introduction. In C. Jencks & M. Phillips (eds.), *The Black-White test score gap* (pp. 1–51). Washington, DC: The Brookings Institute.

Jussim, L., Eccles, J., & Madon, S. (1996) Social perception, social stereotypes, and teacher expectations: accuracy and the quest for the powerful self-fulfilling prophecy. *Advances in Experimental Social Psychology*, 28, 281–388.

Kauchak, D. & Burback, M. D. (2003) Voices in the classroom: case studies of minority teacher candidates. *Action in Teacher Education*, 25(1), 63–75.

Klopfenstein, K. (2005) Beyond test scores: the impact of Black teacher role models on rigorous math-taking. *Contemporary Economic Policy*, 23(3), 416–428.

Knight, M. G. (2002) The intersections of race, class, and gender in the teacher preparation of an African American social justice educator. *Equity & Excellence in Education*, 35(3), 212–223.

Ladson-Billings, G. (1994) *The dreamkeepers: successful teachers of African American children*. San Francisco, CA: Jossey-Bass.

Lee, J. (2002) Racial and ethnic achievement gap trends: reversing the progress toward equity? *Educational Researcher*, 31(1), 3–12.

Lucas, S. R. (2001) Effectively maintained inequality: education transitions, track mobility, and social background effects. *American Journal of Sociology*, 106, 1642–1690.

Lucas, T. L., Henze, R., & Donato, R. (1990) Promoting the success of Latino language-minority students: an exploratory study of six high schools. *Harvard Educational Review*, 60(3), 315–340.

Melnick, S. L. & Pullin, D. (2000) Can you take a dictation? Prescribing teacher quality through testing. *Journal of Teacher Education*, 51(4), 262–280.

Memory, D. M., Coleman, C. L., & Watkins, S. D. (2003) Possible tradeoffs in raising basic skills cutoff scores for teacher licensure: a study with implications for participation of African Americans in teaching. *Journal of Teacher Education*, 54(3), 217–228.

Montecinos, C. (1994) Teachers of color and multiculturalism. *Equity & Excellence in Education*, 27(3), 34–42.

Montecinos, C. (2004) Paradoxes in multicultural teacher education research: students of color positioned as objects while ignored as subjects. *International Journal of Qualitative Studies in Education*, 17(2), 167–181.

Monzó L. D. & Rueda, R. S. (2001) Sociocultural factors in social relationships: examining Latino teachers' and paraeducators' interactions with Latino students. Santa Cruz, CA: Center for Research on Education, Diversity & Excellence. Retrieved January 10, 2005 from http://repositories.cdlib.org/crede/rsrchrpts/rr09.

Murname, R. J. & Levy, R. J. (1996) *Teaching the new basic skills*. NY: The Free Press.

National Center for Education Statistics (1995) *Digest of educational statistics, 1995*. Washington, DC: U.S. Government Printing Office.

National Center for Education Statistics (2002) *Dropout rates in the United States: 2000*. Washington, DC: U.S. Government Printing Office. Retrieved on 12/20/2005 from http://nces.ed.gov/pubs2002/droppub_2001/12.asp.

National Center for Education Statistics (2002) *Digest for education statistics tables and figures*. Washington, DC: U.S. Government Printing Office. Retrieved on 7/16/2005 from http://nces.ed.gov/programs/digest/d02/dt066.asp.

National Education Association (2003) *Status of the American Public School Teacher*. Washington, DC: Author.

Oates, G. L. (2003) Teacher-student racial congruence, teacher perceptions, and test performance. *Social Science Quarterly*, 8(3), 508–525.

Paley, V. (1989) *White teacher*. Cambridge, MA: Harvard University Press.

Palmer, J. C. (2005) What do we know abut student transfer? An overview. In R. Shoenberg (ed.), *General education and student transfer: fostering intentionality and coherence in state systems* (pp. 25–28). Washington, DC: Association of American Colleges and Universities.

Parker, L. & Hood, S. (1995) Minority students vs. majority faculty and administrators in teacher education: perspectives on the clash of cultures. *The Urban Review*, 27(2), 159–174.

Recruiting New Teachers (1997) Teaching's next generation: a national study of precollegiate teacher recruitment. Belmont, MA: Author.

Rios, F. & Montecinos, C. (1999) Advocating social justice and cultural affirmation: ethnically diverse preservice teachers' perspectives on multicultural education. *Equity & Excellence in Education*, 32(3), 66–76.

Seidman, A. (2005) Minority student retention: resources for practitioners. In G. H. Gather (ed.), *Minority retention: what works* (pp. 7–24), San Francisco, CA: Jossey-Bass.

Shavelson, R. J. & Towne, L. (2003) *Scientific research in education*. Washington, DC: National Academy Press.

Sheets, R. H. & Chew, L. (2002) Absent from the research, present in our classrooms: Preparing culturally responsive Chinese American teachers. *Journal of Teacher Education*, 53(2), 127–141.

Shen, J. (1998) Alternative certification, minority teachers, and urban education. *Education and Urban Society*, 31(1), 30–41.

Shen, J., Wegenke, G. L., & Cooley, V. E. (2003) Has the public teaching force become more diversified? National and longitudinal perspectives on gender, race, and ethnicity. *Educational HORIZONS*, Spring, 112–118.

Sleeter, C. (2001) Preparing teachers for culturally diverse school: research and the overwhelming presence of whiteness. *Journal of Teacher Education*, 52(2), 94–107.

Smith, J. P. (2001) Race and ethnicity in the labor market: trends over the short and long run. In N. Smelser, W. J. Wilson, & F. Mitchell (eds.), *America becoming: racial trends and their consequences, Volume I* (pp. 52–97). Washington, DC: National Academy Press.

Steele, C. M. (1997) A threat in the air: how stereotypes shape intellectual identity and performance. *American Psychologist*, 52(6), 613–629.

Stewart, J., Meier, K., & England, R. (1989) In quest of role models: change in black teacher representation in urban school districts, 1968–1986. *Journal of Negro Education*, 58, 140–152.

Su, Z. (1997) Teaching as a profession and as a career: minority candidates' perspectives. *Teaching and Teacher Education*, 13(3), 325–340.

Swanson, C. B. (2003) *Who graduates? Who doesn't? A statistical portrait of public high school graduation, Class of 2001*. Washington, DC: Urban Institute.

Tomás Rivera Center (1993) *Resolving a crisis in education: Latino teachers for tomorrow's classrooms*. Claremont, CA: Tomas Rivera Center.

U.S. Census Bureau (2005) *Historical poverty tables*. Washington, DC: Author. Retrieved on 12/16/2005 from http://www.census.gov/hhes/www/poverty/histpov/hstpov3.html.

Villegas, A. M. (2005) Racial/ethnic diversity in the public school teaching force: a look at trends. Paper commissioned by the National Education Association.

Villegas, A. M. & Clewell, B. C. (1998) Increasing the numbers of teachers of color for urban schools: lessons from the Pathways National Evaluation. *Education and Urban Society*, 31(1), 42–61.

Villegas, A. M. & Lucas, T. (2002) Educating culturally responsive teachers: a coherent approach. Albany, NY: SUNY.

Villegas, A. M. & Lucas, T. (2004) Diversifying the teacher workforce: a retrospective and prospective analysis. In M. A. Smylie and D. Miretzky (eds.), *Developing the teacher workforce: 103rd yearbook of the National Society for the Study of Education* (pp. 70–104). Chicago, IL: University of Chicago Press.

Wilder, M. (1999) Re-examining the African American teacher shortage: building a new professional image of teaching for the 21st century. *Equity & Excellence in Education*, 32(3), 77–82.

34 Responding to the linguistic reality of mainstream classrooms

Preparing all teachers to teach English language learners

Tamara Lucas and
Jaime Grinberg
Montclair State University

INTRODUCTION

Until recently, little thought was given to preparing regular classroom teachers to teach students who speak native languages other than English. English language learners (ELLs) have been expected to develop proficiency in English before they enter the main-stream classroom[1] by taking classes taught by specialists in English as a second language (ESL) or, in some contexts, participating in programs that allow them to learn in their native language while developing English proficiency. However, in reality, many ELLs have no access to instruction by specially-prepared teachers. ELLs who are not fully proficient in English are placed in classes with teachers who are not prepared to teach them, and they are expected to "pick up" English—along with academic content and skills—by swimming (rather than sinking) in the mainstream. As the number of ELLs across the country continues to grow (Kindler, 2002), the problematic nature of this practice becomes increasingly evident. Even after spending time in special classes, most ELLs enter the mainstream needing some extra support to have full access to academic content. The failure to prepare all teachers to provide the support needed by ELLs has had negative repercussions for generations of young people who have entered regular classrooms (Grinberg *et al.*, 2005; Marquez-Lopez, 2005).

In this chapter, we examine the literature on the preparation of non-specialist class-room teachers (hereafter referred to as *classroom teachers*) to teach ELLs. We see this chapter as closely related to the literature on preparing culturally responsive teachers (e.g. Cochran-Smith *et al.*, 2004; Gay, 2000; Grant & Secada, 1990; Grinberg *et al.*, 2005; Ladson-Billings, 1995; Villegas, 1991; Villegas & Lucas, 2002). However, this review departs in major ways from that literature and from previous reviews of the literature on the preparation of teachers for diverse populations (see, for example, Hollins & Guzman, 2005). While the existing literature tends to treat linguistic and cultural diversity as one largely undifferentiated set of factors and to treat language as one of many aspects of culture, we explicitly distinguish linguistic diversity from other types of diversity, focusing squarely on linguistic issues. We pull the threads related to language that get lost in the larger fabric of culturally responsive teacher preparation and bring them to the surface. We also show why more attention must be devoted to preparing all teachers to teach ELLs. It is time that we stop subsuming the preparation of classroom teachers to teach English language learners within more general considerations of the preparation of teachers for diverse populations. This review is an attempt to move the field of teacher education away from that practice.

The literature on the preparation of classroom teachers to teach ELLs—especially reports of rigorous empirical research—is sparse, as noted by August and Hakuta (1997), Merino (1999), and Zeichner (2005). In this chapter, we concentrate on literature related to the pre-service and in-service preparation of classroom teachers to teach ELLs published within the last 20 years. Our selection of empirical literature was guided by the principles of scientific inquiry articulated by Shavelson and Towne (2002). We identified 17 relevant empirical studies—eight that focused directly on the preparation of classroom teachers to teach ELLs[2] and nine that examined some aspect of the education of ELLs in mainstream classrooms.[3] While we made every effort to identify the relevant empirical literature, we did not privilege empirical evidence; we also included literature that provided well-developed arguments and assertions grounded in philosophical, historical, sociological, and wisdom-of-practice traditions. We included articles in peer-reviewed journals, book chapters, reports prepared for government agencies and professional organizations, and conference presentations.

We believe the diversity of genres and publication types we have used in preparing the chapter is warranted. First, very little empirical research on preparing teachers to teach ELLs has been conducted, particularly on preparing regular classroom teachers. Second, and in our view more importantly, empirical evidence alone cannot explain what education is or should be. Because of the importance of values and the wisdom of practice in educational decision making—especially with regard to subordinated groups such as ELLs and their families—we considered conceptual, theoretical, and policy literature as well as reports of empirical research in preparing this chapter.

Limited as it is in many respects, the literature we reviewed could have led us in a number of directions in our efforts to give the material structure and coherence. However, our iterative process of analysis and synthesis of the literature led us to address three questions. First, to establish the importance of preparing classroom teachers to teach ELLs—and to problematize the marginal treatment of such preparation in mainstream teacher education literature—we begin by explicitly addressing the following question. Why should we devote attention and resources to preparing all teachers to teach ELLs? Our answers come from demographic, empirical, and conceptual literature. Second, to construct a foundation for curriculum and instruction to prepare all teachers to teach ELLs, we ask what teachers need to know and be able to do to teach ELLs successfully. We draw on empirical and theoretical literature to identify language-related experiences, attitudes, beliefs, knowledge, and skills that are particularly relevant for classroom teachers of ELLs. Finally, we ask: What do we know about how classroom teachers are being prepared to teach ELLs? Drawing on empirical and descriptive literature, we describe structural and process strategies for the pre-service and in-service preparation of classroom teachers to teach ELLs. We conclude with a brief overview of key issues and recommendations for policy and research.

WHY MORE ATTENTION SHOULD BE GIVEN TO PREPARING CLASSROOM TEACHERS TO TEACH ELLs

While the literature on preparing teachers to teach culturally diverse student populations often mentions language as a factor to consider, language-related issues are seldom addressed in depth. Diversity is frequently treated as a general and undifferentiated concept (Goodwin, 2002). Commonly used phrases such as *culturally and linguistically diverse students* tend to obscure the particular linguistic issues relevant to teaching ELLs. A number of arguments have been made in support of increased attention to those issues in preparing all teachers to teach ELLs. Because of the invisibility of this issue, we believe an elaboration on these arguments is warranted.

The increasing likelihood that classroom teachers will have ELLs in their classes

The demographic argument is perhaps the most compelling. The increasing number of ELLs in schools across the country means that many classroom teachers who never expected to have ELLs in their classes are finding them there. Between 1979 and 2003, the proportion of 5- to 17-year-olds in the United States who spoke a language other than English grew by 161 percent (from 8.5 percent to 18.7 percent), and the proportion who reported speaking English less than "very well" grew by 124 percent (from 2.8 percent to 5.5 percent) (NCES, 2005). Between 1990–91 and 2000–01, the LEP[4] enrollment in U.S. schools increased by 105 percent, compared to a relatively small 12 percent overall enrollment increase (Kindler, 2002). An estimated 4 million LEP students (8.4 percent of all students) enrolled in U.S. schools in 2001–02—an increase of 72 percent over 1992 (Zehler *et al.*, 2003). It is projected that, by 2030, 40 percent of the K-12 age population in the U.S. will be children whose first language is not English (AACTE, 2002). While the growth in the Asian population (from 2.8 percent of the U.S. population in 1986 to 4.1 percent in 2000 [NCES, 2002d]) contributes to this trend, the increase in the Hispanic population is the most influential factor. Hispanic students accounted for 6 percent of public school enrollment in 1972, 11 percent in 1986, and 17 percent in 2000 (NCES, 2002a). Half of Hispanic immigrants are under age 27, and 20 percent of all children under the age of 5 years in the U.S. is now Hispanic (Files, 2005). In 1999, 71 percent of Hispanic children ages 5–17 spoke a language other than English at home, compared to 4 percent of White and Black children (NCES, 2003a).

Although ELLs continue to be concentrated in a few states and metropolitan areas, their presence is also being felt in other areas across the U.S. These changes are noteworthy because the presence of even a few ELLs can have a significant impact on schools and teachers with no relevant prior experience. According to Zehler and associates (2003), 43 percent of districts and 50 percent of schools in the U.S. enroll one or more LEP students. Hopstock and Stephenson (2003) reported that 43 percent of all K-12 teachers in 2001–2002 worked with at least one LEP student, up from 15 percent ten years earlier. This shift also means that LEP students are spread across more classes and that the diversity of English language abilities among students in mainstream classes has increased.

Besides the statistical fact that ELLs constitute a growing proportion of the U.S. student population, there are other reasons for their increasing numbers in mainstream classes. First, as a result of political opposition to the use of languages other than English that began in the 1980s, the number of bilingual programs and therefore bilingual teachers has diminished (Crawford, 1992; Rumberger & Gándara, 2004). This means that classroom teachers are increasingly responsible for providing the majority of instruction to ELLs (Menken & Antunez, 2001). Second, the passage of the No Child Left Behind (NCLB) Act in 2001 contributed to this trend by requiring that LEP students be tested in English after they have been in the U.S. for three years or longer. The urgency of trying to prepare these students for standardized tests in English within three years has pushed many districts to speed up the process of enrolling them in mainstream classes (Cornell, 1995) and put greater pressure on the teachers of those classes (Wong-Fillmore & Snow, 2005). Third, the fact that placing ELLs in mainstream classes is less costly than providing special classes provides additional impetus for this process (Cornell, 1995).

For all these reasons, classroom teachers may spend more time with ELLs overall than ESL and bilingual specialists do and they therefore have a major impact on their achievement. Given this reality, mainstream teachers must be prepared to teach ELL students.

Special challenges faced by classroom teachers with ELLs in their classes

The second argument for preparing classroom teachers to teach ELLs is that teachers of ELLs face a number of special challenges for which current pre-service and in-service teacher education programs generally do not prepare them. Perhaps the most obvious challenge is the need to teach both content and English language to students who are not native speakers of English. In an influential essay, Wong-Fillmore and Snow (2005) make the case that teachers need extensive language-related knowledge and skills to successfully play their roles as communicators, educators, evaluators, educated human beings, and agents of socialization. They argue that, given few U.S. elementary and secondary schools today require the formal study of the structure of English or the study of foreign languages, most classroom teachers are not equipped to teach ELLs successfully. Other special challenges of teaching ELLs identified by teachers in 22 California districts (Gándara *et al.*, 2005) included difficulty communicating with students and their families, insufficient time to teach English and subject matter to ELLs, missed class time for students attending pull-out ESL classes, widely varying levels of English proficiency and academic preparation of ELLs in one class, lack of appropriate instructional materials, and general lack of teacher preparation.

Clearly some of these challenges cannot be addressed through teacher preparation, but most of them can be. Classroom teachers' lack of knowledge about language, difficulties communicating with ELLs and their families, and inability to successfully address widely differing linguistic and academic skills in one class are exacerbated by common myths and misconceptions about ELLs and about learning a second language (Walker *et al.*, 2004)—all of which lead to the mis-education of ELLs. Appropriate preparation can directly address such misconceptions and ameliorate many of the challenges. Without preparation, classroom teachers are left to sink or swim, much as the ELLs in their classes are expected to do.

The inadequacy of the current preparation of classroom teachers to teach ELLs

The great majority of U.S. teachers—74 percent of them in 2000—have had no recent professional development for working with ELLs, and most teachers who have participated in relevant professional development activities have spent only a few hours in those activities (NCES 2002c). Particularly troubling is the fact that between 1998 and 2000, the percent of all teachers who had participated in relevant professional development decreased from 31 percent to 26 percent (NCES, 1999, 2002c). A more promising indicator is that participation in professional development varies by minority enrollment and number of ELLs in teachers' classes. Appropriately, the larger the minority student enrollment in districts (NCES, 1997, 1999) and the more ELLs in teachers' classes (at least in California) (Gándara *et al.*, 2005), the more likely teachers are to have had at least some professional development related to teaching ELLs. Still, we cannot be certain about the quality of such professional development or about the sustainability and support available for teachers after such experiences.

The extent of pre-service preparation of teachers is another aspect of their inadequate preparedness. Less than one-sixth (17 percent) of schools, colleges, and departments of education report that they require a course focused on issues related to ELLs (Menken & Antunez, 2001). With regard to teachers' level of education, the 1999–2000 Schools and Staffing Survey (NCES, 2002b) found that the higher the proportion of LEP students in a school, the fewer teachers there were with master's degrees.

Teaching experience and proficiency in a second language are other indicators of how well-prepared teachers are to teach ELLs. While available data make it difficult to draw firm conclusions about the experience of teachers of ELLs, the 1999–2000 Schools and Staffing Survey indicated that public and private schools "with the highest percentages of limited-English-proficient (LEP) students were more likely to employ beginning teachers than schools . . . with the lowest percentages of LEP students" (NCES 2003b, p. 59). We were not able to identify any agency or organization that regularly collects data on the native languages of teachers or the extent to which teachers have studied foreign languages.

Teachers' perceptions of their preparedness to teach ELLs offer a different sort of insight about the adequacy of their preparation. The evidence suggests that large proportions of classroom teachers do not feel prepared to successfully teach ELLs. A 1998 U.S. Department of Education survey found that 54 percent of teachers taught "limited English proficient or culturally diverse students,"[5] but only 20 percent of those teachers felt very well prepared and 17 percent felt not at all prepared to meet their needs (NCES, 1999). Teachers in schools with higher minority enrollments and teachers who had participated in relevant professional development reported feeling more prepared than others. A study of California teachers also revealed that teachers with more pre-service and in-service preparation were more confident in their ability to teach ELLs (Gándara *et al.*, 2005). A study of the attitudes, beliefs, and knowledge of teachers in a medium-sized (15,000 students) Midwestern school district, one-third of whose students were identified as LEP, complements the national and California-based studies (Karabenick & Noda, 2004). The authors obtained survey data from 729 teachers (98 percent of the total), 88 percent of whom had had ELLs in their classes. They concluded that teachers did not have a clear understanding of second language acquisition (including the role of the first language in learning a second language), the difference between oral communication proficiencies and cognitive-academic language proficiencies, bilingualism, and approaches to bilingual education.

Given the increasing numbers of ELLs in mainstream classrooms and the special challenges faced by their teachers, it is incumbent upon teacher educators to provide all teachers with the necessary preparation for teaching ELLs. If teachers are not appropriately prepared to provide the linguistic, academic, and personal support needed by ELLs, then these students are being denied their civil rights (AACTE, 2002)—that is, they are being denied instruction they can understand and from which they can learn. Some of the evidence presented above is promising with regard to the potential impact of professional development. However, overall, it is clear that teachers are not well prepared to successfully educate ELLs. In the next section, we turn to what well-prepared teachers need to know and be able to do.

EXPERIENCES, ATTITUDES, BELIEFS, KNOWLEDGE, AND SKILLS FOR TEACHING ELLs

While there is little literature focused on approaches and strategies for preparing classroom teachers to teach ELLs, some attention has been given to identifying the knowledge, skills, and dispositions teachers need to instruct this student population (e.g. August & Hakuta, 1997; García, 1993, 1996, 1999; González & Darling-Hammond, 1997; Milk *et al.*, 1992; Wong-Fillmore & Snow, 2005). This section of the chapter reviews that literature, which draws on the wisdom of practice and theoretical work as well as empirical research. We remind readers that our focus is on those *language-related* qualities particularly important for classroom teachers of ELLs that too often are obscured in discussions on preparing culturally responsive teachers. We are purposefully silent about the many essential qualities that apply to all good teachers (e.g. deep content knowledge, pedagogical content knowledge, reflection). As shown in Figure 34.1, we have organized the language-related qualities into four broad categories—experiences, attitudes and beliefs, knowledge, and skills.

Language-related experiences teachers need for teaching ELLs

Teachers, like everyone else, are shaped by their experiences. Although it is beyond the scope of this chapter to elaborate on the relationship between personal experience and learning to teach (see Feiman-Nemser & Buchmann, 1986; Grinberg, 2002), suffice it to say that teachers' professional perspectives and actions are influenced by what they have seen, heard, and done in their lives. Below we consider two types of language-related experiences—studying a foreign/second language and having contact with people who speak languages other than English—that could promote teachers' deep connections with their ELLs.

Studying a foreign/second language

The experience of studying a second language contributes to the preparation of teachers to teach ELLs by giving them insight into the language learning process and the experiences of their students—even if they are not fully fluent in the language and even if they have not studied the particular languages spoken by their students (Baca & Escamilla, 2005; Wong-Fillmore & Snow, 2005). This personal experience can "open teachers' eyes and hearts" to the language-learning experiences of ELLs (Nieto & Rolón, 1997, p. 113).

A *Language-related experiences for teaching ELLs*
    1 Study of a foreign/second language
    2 Contact with people who speak languages other than English

B *Language-related attitudes and beliefs for teaching ELLs*
    1 Affirming views of linguistic diversity and bilingualism
    2 Awareness of the sociopolitical dimension of language use and language education
    3 Inclination to collaborate with colleagues who are language specialists

C *Language-related knowledge for teaching ELLs*
    1 The language backgrounds, experiences, and proficiencies of their students
    2 Second language development
    3 The connection between language, culture, and identity
    4 Language forms, mechanics, and uses

D *Language-related skills for teaching ELLs*
    1 Skills for conducting basic linguistic analysis of oral and written texts
    2 Skills for participating in cross-cultural and cross-linguistic communication
    3 Skills for designing instruction that helps ELLs learn both language and content

---

Figure 34.1 Language-related qualities teachers need for teaching ELLs.

Evidence of the benefits of teachers' language learning experience comes from two empiri-cal studies. A survey of 143 secondary mainstream teachers in a Great Plains community with a population of approximately 80,000 found that teachers who had completed one or more years of foreign language classes in high school or college were "significantly more positive about teaching ESL students than were teachers who had not taken foreign language classes" (Youngs & Youngs, 2001, p. 110). Qualitative case studies of eight pre-service teachers studying a language unfamiliar to them indicated that they had developed a better understanding of language as a system, were more aware of the difficulties ELLs might face, and were able to identify more and less successful approaches to teaching language (Hyatt & Beigy, 1999).

Having contact with speakers of languages other than English

The second type of experience that has been shown to influence teacher attitudes toward ELLs is contact with people who speak languages other than English. Youngs and Youngs (2001) found that classroom teachers who had lived or taught outside the U.S. had significantly more positive attitudes toward ELLs than those lacking such experiences. Simply traveling abroad and hosting a foreign student were not significantly related to teachers' attitudes. This latter finding points to the importance of extended contact. Another study showed that experience with ELLs in U.S. schools can also have a positive impact on teachers' attitudes. Byrnes *et al.* (1997) administered the Language Attitudes of Teachers Scale (LATS) to 191 regular classroom teachers in Arizona, Utah, and Virginia (see also Byrnes & Kiger, 1994; Byrnes *et al.*, 1996). They found that teachers who had had more experience with ELLs had more positive attitudes toward them. While this study suggests that contact with ELLs can have a positive impact on teachers' attitudes, teacher educators have argued that contact alone does not guarantee this impact (Evans *et al.*, 2005; Zeichner & Melnick, 1996). A qualitative study of community service learning in a teacher education course found that, without skillful guided reflection on their experiences, some prospective teachers interpreted their experiences in ways that perpetuated stereotypes (Lucas, 2005b).

Language-related attitudes and beliefs teachers need for teaching ELLs

As presented in Figure 34.1, the second language-related quality teachers need for teach-ing ELLs encompasses relevant attitudes and beliefs. Distinctions between attitudes and beliefs are often imprecise, largely because there are overlaps in the conceptual territory covered by these concepts. Given this lack of clarity in the literature, we will treat these two concepts together here. Attitudes and beliefs have been examined at length and consist-ently found to be influential in teachers' interactions with their students (Richardson, 1996). Three specific attitudes/beliefs associated with teaching ELLs are discussed below—affirming views of linguistic diversity and bilingualism, awareness of the socio-political dimension of language use and language education, and inclination to collaborate with colleagues who are language specialists.

Affirming views of linguistic diversity and bilingualism

The literature on multicultural education and culturally responsive teaching is unani-mous in its emphasis on the critical role played by the extent to which teachers have affirming, positive attitudes toward their students and their students' home cultures

(Villegas & Lucas, 2002). Because of the strong connection between language and identity (Delpit, 1998; Nieto, 2002; Rickford & Rickford, 2000), teachers' attitudes toward their students' languages and language proficiencies send powerful messages about their attitudes toward the students and their families. Teachers who view linguistic diversity and bilingualism as resources rather than deficiencies are also more likely to recognize that limited proficiency in English is not equated with limited ability to learn (González & Darling-Hammond, 1997; Lucas *et al.*, 1990; Maxwell-Jolly & Gándara, 2002). Empirical evidence suggests that teachers' attitudes and beliefs about their students' language uses and language learning have an impact on their expectations of ELLs, the nature of their interactions with ELLs, and their instructional practices (Byrnes *et al.*, 1997; Byrnes, *et al.*, 1996; Platt & Troudi, 1997; Walker *et al.*, 2004; Youngs & Youngs, 2001).

Awareness of the sociopolitical dimension of language use and language education

Although people tend to see language as a politically neutral set of skills, language is intimately tied to its social and political context. Therefore, the second fundamental attitude for classroom teachers of ELLs is awareness of the sociopolitical dimension of language. Such awareness is a prerequisite for understanding linguistic diversity and avoiding erroneous assumptions about students' language abilities and uses. Villegas and Lucas (2002) have argued that culturally responsive teachers have developed socio-cultural consciousness—that is, awareness that each person's worldview is influenced by such factors as class, race, and gender; that people of different sociocultural backgrounds are likely to have different and equally valid worldviews; and that power is differentially distributed in society so that the worldviews of people from some groups are valued more highly than those of others. Equally important for teachers of ELLs is sociolinguistic consciousness—the understanding that language variation, both within and across languages, is a natural social phenomenon; that no language or language variety is inherently better than another; and that the dominant position of a language or language variety within a particular social context derives from the power of the speakers of that language rather than from any linguistic factors (De Jesus, 2005; Delpit, 1995; Fasold, 1990; Grinberg & Saavedra, 2000). Teachers with sociolinguistic consciousness understand their students' experiences as speakers of subordinated languages and recognize that the challenges they face go beyond the cognitive difficulties of learning a second language (see Olsen, 1997). Such teachers are vigilant in reflecting on their own assumptions about ELLs, and cognizant of the fact that their perceptions of language, language use, and language learning are shaped by their own and their students' sociocultural positioning.

Bartolomé (2000, 2002) has argued that *ideological clarity* is fundamental to teachers' ability to fully grasp the political nature of language and to foster academic success for language minority students. Ideological clarity is "the process by which individuals achieve a deepening awareness of the sociopolitical and economic realities that shape their lives and their capacity to transform them" (p. 167). Similarly, Villegas and Lucas (2002) argue that, to develop affirming rather than deficit views of children from diverse backgrounds, teachers must recognize that there are *structured inequalities* at all levels in society that ultimately result in lower academic achievement of students from subordinated groups—including language minorities (see also Grinberg & Saavedra, 2000 for a discussion of this phenomenon with regard to immigrants).

Inclination to collaborate with colleagues who are language specialists

Another important attitude for classroom teachers of ELLs—especially for those who have not developed expertise for teaching ELLs—is the willingness to collaborate with colleagues who are language specialists (Lucas, 1997; Maxwell-Jolly & Gándara, 2002; Milk *et al.*, 1992). By sharing their knowledge and expertise, teachers not only learn from each other but also create a sense of collective responsibility for educating ELLs. It is especially helpful for classroom teachers to communicate and collaborate with ESL and bilingual educators. The classroom teachers benefit from the expertise of the specialists, and the specialists benefit from learning more about the expectations and priorities of the regular classroom. Even if there are no ELL specialists in a school, teachers can collaborate to build individual and collective knowledge and skills. They can also reach out to aides and community members with relevant linguistic, cultural, and professional knowledge and experience. To make use of these resources, teachers must be open to working closely with others.

Language-related knowledge teachers need for teaching ELLs

Common misconceptions about language learning and teaching can lead to the miseducation of ELLs. Responsible preparation of classroom teachers to teach ELLs includes facilitating the development of knowledge to dispel those misconceptions. Knowledge in four broad areas is of particular help to teachers: (a) the language backgrounds, experiences, and proficiencies of their students; (b) second language development; (c) the connection between language, culture, and identity; and (d) language forms, mechanics, and uses. These are discussed below.

The language backgrounds, experiences, and proficiencies of their ELL students

The first type of language-related knowledge that is essential for classroom teachers of ELLs is knowledge of their students' linguistic backgrounds, experiences, and proficiencies. This knowledge is important for two reasons. One reason is that relationships are central to healthy human development and to students' academic engagement (Comer, 1993; Cummins, 2000; Palinscar, 1996). To develop relationships with students, teachers need to know what language students are most fluent and comfortable in, what language(s) they use at home, and how they feel about the uses of their native language and English. The second reason is that, to facilitate students' learning, teachers need to be able to help them build on their prior linguistic knowledge, experiences, abilities, and resources. Students' linguistic resources can be used to support their learning (Moll & González, 2004). Therefore, teachers need to know about a student's oral and written proficiency in the native language as well as in English, what language is spoken at home, how language is used and by whom in the student's community, and how strongly the student's family and community feels about maintaining the native language (Lucas, 1997; Villegas & Lucas, 2002).

Second language development

To make sense of ELLs' oral and written performance and to facilitate their instructional decision making, teachers also need knowledge of second language development. Teachers of ELLs need to be able to draw on established principles of second language acquisition (SLA) (Carlson & Walton, 1994; Gándara *et al.*, 2005; González & Darling-Hammond, 1997). While the field of SLA research has examined many facets of the second-language-learning process, we have distilled seven principles of SLA that are commonly highlighted in the literature as having especially important implications for teaching. It is beyond the scope of this chapter to elaborate on these principles; we can only provide brief explanations of each below.

First, mainstream teachers need to know that learners with strong native language and literacy skills learn second languages more easily and more fully than those with weak native language skills (Thomas & Collier, 2002; Cummins, 1981, 2000). Teachers, therefore, should learn about and draw on the native language abilities of ELLs in their classes and support further development of those abilities. The second principle of second language learning is that cognitive and linguistic benefits derive from additive bilingualism (that is, the addition of a second language to a first language) while deficits derive from subtractive bilingualism (that is, the replacement of the first language by the second language) (Cummins, 1976, 2000). As such, teachers should encourage ELLs to continue to develop their native languages and should recognize their native language as a resource for learning.

Third, teachers need to know that for students to learn a second language, they must have direct and frequent contact with people who are fluent in the language (Wong-Fillmore & Snow, 2005). This principle reflects Vygotsky's influential theory that individual learning originates in social interaction (1978). It suggests that teachers should design instruction so that ELLs can actively engage in meaningful interactions with their English-speaking peers. Designing such instruction requires special skills, which we discuss below.

Fourth, teachers need to understand that conversational language proficiency is fundamentally different from academic language proficiency. This is largely because the cognitively demanding and decontextualized discourse involved in learning academic concepts poses greater challenges than the cognitively undemanding and contextualized discourse involved in conversations (Cummins, 1979, 1981, 2000). As this principle suggests, teachers cannot assume that children who are conversationally fluent have developed sufficient academic language proficiency to be successful in school. They need to consider all the modes of language—listening, speaking, reading, and writing—in their approaches to teaching ELLs.

The fifth principle of second language learning is that, for SLA to occur, the language that a learner encounters must be comprehensible to him or her (Krashen, 1982, 2003). It does no good for a learner to listen to hours of lectures in the second language if she cannot understand what is being said. Therefore, teachers need to give conscious thought to how they can modify the spoken and written language for ELLs in their classes. A related principle is that the best linguistic input for language learners needs to be just slightly beyond the learners' current level of proficiency (Krashen, 1982, 2003). Language that is too easy does not result in new learning, and language that it too difficult is not comprehensible. Together, the fifth and sixth principles of SLA suggest that teachers must think carefully about how they use language and how they scaffold language for ELLs.

The final principle of second language learning we want to highlight is that anxiety in the language learning situation can be an obstacle to language learning. Not only can anxiety distract learners from the linguistic "input" they encounter (Krashen, 1982, 2003), it can also lead them to withdraw from social interaction, which is critical to language learning (Pappamihiel, 2002). The implication for teachers is that they need to avoid placing ELLs in embarrassing or stressful situations and to prevent ridicule of ELLs by their English-speaking peers.

The connection between language, culture, and identity

The third essential type of knowledge for classroom teachers of ELLs is an understanding of the powerful link between a person's language and his/her sense of affiliation, or belonging, to social and cultural groups (Rickford & Rickford, 2000; Romaine, 1994). If teachers understand the connection between language, culture, and identity, they will be more likely to develop respectful, affirming attitudes toward linguistic diversity, which we discussed above. Teachers' understanding of the relationship between language and culture can also prevent miscommunication resulting from cultural differences that are expressed through language (Wolfram *et al.*, 1999). An influential body of research in the 1970s and 1980s identified cross-cultural differences in communication and interaction patterns that can interfere with student learning (e.g. Au, 1980; Heath, 1983; Michaels, 1981; Philips, 1972, 1983). If teachers understand that the way students express themselves reflects different cultural values and expectations, they can learn not to make assumptions about students' intentions based solely on their own cultural framework (Price & Osborne, 2000; Valdés, 2001).

Language forms, mechanics, and uses

Finally, classroom teachers of ELLs need knowledge of language forms, mechanics, and uses. González and Darling-Hammond (1997) have argued that "language is the most visible aspect of student diversity that schools encounter and that the school staff are least prepared to address in a manner that demonstrates reciprocal respect" (p. 12). In the past, everyone in U.S. schools studied the structure of English. In recent decades, however, the teaching of grammar has come to be seen as a quaint practice of earlier generations, and no other study of language *as language* has replaced it in undergraduate education (Wong-Fillmore & Snow, 2005). Study of a foreign language could give teachers a sense of language structure, but many teacher education programs do not require candidates to study a foreign language. To facilitate students' language development, teachers must understand the forms, mechanics, and uses of language in general and of the particular language(s) in which they are teaching (Gándara *et al.*, 2005; Valdés *et al.*, 2005; Wong-Fillmore & Snow, 2005). A number of educational linguists have specified the linguistic knowledge needed by teachers (e.g. Freeman & Freeman, 2004; Justice, 2004; Valdés *et al.*, 2005; Wong-Fillmore and Snow, 2005).

Language-related skills teachers need for teaching ELLs

The fourth and final set of language-related qualities for teaching ELLs presented in Figure 34.1 entails skills for conducting basic linguistic analyses of oral and written texts, skills for engaging in cross-cultural and cross-linguistic communication, and skills for designing instruction that helps ELLs learn both language and content.

Skills for conducting basic linguistic analysis of oral and written text

The challenge of learning *through* academic language in English while still in the process of learning English *as* a language of communication is daunting and greatly underestimated by most monolingual people. To promote language development in the context of learning academic content and skills, teachers of ELLs need to be able to analyze the linguistic demands of oral and written discourse and design instruction accordingly (Cummins, 2000; Wong-Fillmore & Snow, 2005). For teachers of particular disciplines, this means being able to identify the vocabulary, syntax, and discourse patterns of their discipline that are likely to be especially challenging for ELLs (Valdés et al, 2005). For English/Language Arts teachers, it also means being able to provide explicit instruction in language structures and uses (Wong-Fillmore & Snow, 2005) and to explain grammatical errors in ways that can help ELLs edit their writing (Walker *et al.*, 2005).

Skills for participating in cross-cultural and cross-linguistic communication

As we discussed above, culture influences the ways people express themselves and interact with others. While an understanding of this connection between language and culture is essential for teachers of ELLs, an understanding alone is not sufficient; teachers must be able to use this understanding to communicate with students and their families who are from diverse cultural and linguistic backgrounds. They need strategies for learning about the students' culturally-based communication patterns and for responding in ways that facilitate communication across cultural and linguistic differences (Gándara *et al.*, 2005). Wolfram *et al.* (1999) recommend that teachers conduct research on the ways language is used in interactions in their classes. They also recommend that teachers thoughtfully examine whether they might be misunderstanding speech acts (e.g. explaining, reporting, requesting, denying) and participation structures by students of different cultural backgrounds in their classes. Teachers also must be able to communicate successfully with the families of their students (Goldfarb, 1998; Nieto, 2000). Engaging them in school-related activities requires reaching out to them in ways that are culturally congruent and linguistically accessible for them. One way to reach out to parents and to ELLs is to develop some ability to communicate in their native language—even if only minimally. This ability can facilitate communication as well as build trust and rapport (Stanton-Salazar, 2001). Pre-service teachers at Boston College found "even minimal proficiency in Spanish invaluable" in providing a meaningful connection to the Spanish speaking children with whom they were working (Friedman, 2002, p. 214).

Skills for designing instruction to help ELLs learn both language and content

The final language-related skill for teaching ELLs is that of designing instruction to facilitate the learning of both English and content. There is a growing body of work focused on the academic instruction of ELLs in content classes (e.g. Echevarria & Graves, 2003; Echevarria *et al.*, 2004; Gibbons, 2002). While most of this work involves bilingual and ESL teachers, the pedagogical strategies considered effective for these specialized instructors are applicable for use by regular classroom teachers. Drawing on this literature, we highlight nine instructional strategies that regular classroom teachers could use to facilitate ELLs' learning of both language and content. These highlights are presented in Figure 34.2. Preparing classroom teachers to use these strategies would considerably improve the experiences of ELLs in their classrooms.

Summary

We noted at the beginning of this section that we were going to highlight only the experiences, attitudes and beliefs, knowledge, and skills that are particularly relevant to language issues. Still, teachers with no previous cross-linguistic or cross-cultural experience and no experience teaching ELLs could easily be overwhelmed by the scope of the

1   *Identify and build on students' prior knowledge and linguistic resources* (González & Darling-Hammond, 1997; Leighton *et al.*, 1995; Milk *et al.*, 1992; Villegas & Lucas, 2002).

2   *Facilitate students' use of their native languages* for instruction, even if English is the language of the classroom (August & Hakuta, 1997; Lucas & Katz, 1994).

3   *Create language-rich classrooms* in which students have many varied opportunities to speak, listen, read, and write in English and their native languages (August & Hakuta, 1997; Maxwell-Jolly & Gándara, 2002; Milk *et al.*, 1992; Villegas & Lucas, 2002).

4   *Engage students in varied and frequent interactions with other students*, including native English speakers, about meaningful content (Gibbons, 2002; Wong-Fillmore & Snow, 2005).

5   *Scaffold students' learning of language and content*—that is, provide temporary assistance so that a student can later complete a similar process or task alone (Gibbons, 2002, p. 10).

6   *Establish and facilitate heterogeneous, cooperative groups* in which language can be practiced in authentic communication situations and authentic learning tasks (Gibbons, 2002; González & Darling-Hammond, 1997).

7   *Provide explicit instruction in academic skills and language structures and uses* (August & Hakuta, 1997; Wong-Fillmore & Snow, 2005).

8   *Use varied approaches* to make content in English comprehensible and accessible to ELLs (Echevarria *et al.*, 2004; Leighton *et al.* 1995).

9   *Reduce the anxiety* associated with learning a second language, and be especially vigilant about teasing by native English-speaking students (Krashen, 1982, 2003; Pappamihiel, 2002).

Figure 34.2 Instructional strategies classroom teachers can use to facilitate ELLs' learning.

expectations for teachers of ELLs we have presented. We acknowledge that advocates for preparing classroom teachers to teach ELLs need to be "honest with ourselves about the enormous complexity of what we are asking teachers to do" and to know and to believe (Palinscar, 1996, p. 223). The responsibility, however, lies not only with teachers but also with pre-service and in-service teacher educators. We need to find ways to begin to help future and current teachers develop these experiences, dispositions, knowledge, and skills. The following section of the chapter describes what the literature tells us about efforts already underway.

EFFORTS TO PREPARE CLASSROOM TEACHERS TO TEACH ENGLISH LANGUAGE LEARNERS

Teacher educators, especially in geographic areas with substantial language minority populations, are beginning to recognize the necessity of preparing classroom teachers to teach the ELLs they are likely to have in their classes. There is increasing evidence in the literature of efforts to provide the types of experiences and cultivate the dispositions, knowledge, and skills described above. To learn about those efforts, we turn to a body of literature which includes some small-scale qualitative and evaluation studies (Delaney-Barmann & Minner, 1995; Evans *et al.*, 2005; Hadaway, 1993; Levy *et al.*, 2002; Lucas, 2005a; Zetlin *et al.*, 1998), but which is largely descriptive. No doubt there are many innovative efforts to prepare classroom teachers to teach ELLs that are not represented in the literature. We hope that those involved in such efforts will write about them and will conduct research to examine their functions and impact. We also recognize that changes may have occurred in the programs included here. However, the lack of currency of some examples does not make them any less useful for envisioning possibilities.

From our examination of the literature, we identified seven strategies used to prepare classroom teachers to teach ELLs in pre-service and in-service contexts, which we present in this section. These are listed in Figure 34.3, which provides an outline of this section of the chapter. The four *structural strategies* require some redesign and reorganization of the curriculum in teacher education programs in institutions of higher education (IHEs). While structures need to be put in place to support the three *process strategies*, they can be implemented without restructuring the curriculum and they can take place in schools as well as IHEs. Therefore, they are better characterized as processes for teacher preparation than as strategies for modifying program structure. We describe these seven strategies below. For purposes of brevity, we present only one or two examples to illustrate each. The examples show multiple approaches to cultivating the experiences, knowledge, skills, and dispositions discussed above.

Structural strategies to prepare teachers to teach ELLs

Add a course

To address issues or populations that have not previously been included in mainstream pre-service teacher education programs (e.g. teaching students of diverse racial and ethnic backgrounds and students with disabilities), teacher educators have generally added a course on the topic or tried to infuse attention to the issue throughout the curriculum (Villegas & Lucas, 2002). The first structural strategy to prepare teachers to teach ELLs is to add a course to the curriculum. The obvious benefit of this strategy—assuming the course is required of all teacher candidates—is that it signals the importance of preparing all teachers to teach ELLs and ensures that future teachers give their full attention to becoming prepared to teach ELLs. On the other hand, adding a course poses a challenge for most teacher education programs because of the limited number of teacher education credits allowed in many states. Still, some institutions have taken this approach.

At the University of Minnesota, as a result of pre-service teachers' expressed need for better preparation to teach ELLs, a one-credit course was added to the pre-service curriculum (Walker *et al.*, 2005). Guided by the "fundamental premise" that "the best teaching [of ELLs] . . . requires an effective integration of language and content" (p. 318), faculty teach special sections of the course for elementary teacher candidates and for candidates in different content area programs. Though only for one-credit, this course appears to provide a comprehensive overview of relevant issues. Every section of the course

---

Structural strategies
- Add a course.
- Modify existing courses and field experiences to infuse attention to teaching ELLs across the curriculum.
- Add or modify pre-program requirements.
- Add a minor or supplemental certificate program.

Process strategies
- Offer mentoring for practicing teachers.
- Foster collaboration across institutional boundaries.
- Provide professional development for teacher education faculty.

Figure 34.3 Strategies to prepare classroom teachers to teach ELLs.

addresses some common issues and engages in some common activities, including in-school experiences working with ELLs, principles of second language learning, demographic information about ELLs in the U.S. and in the local area, cultural information about immigrant groups in the local area, and curricular and instructional practices for successfully teaching ELLs. In addition, the section of the course for candidates in the elementary program emphasizes different models of ESL services and "the importance of collaboration between the classroom teacher and the ESL teacher" (p. 320). Candidates in the disciplinary sections of the course analyze the vocabulary and syntax of textbooks to determine challenges ELLs might face in using them, and the English/Language Arts section introduces ways teachers can explain grammatical errors to their future students. Courses added at two other institutions concentrate on linguistic knowledge and skills: an introductory linguistics course for teachers taught by Valdés at University of California, Berkeley (Valdés *et al.*, 2005), and a Spanish for Teachers course at Northern Arizona University (NAU) (Delaney-Barmann & Minner, 1995).

Modify existing courses and field experiences to infuse attention to teaching ELLs across the curriculum

A second major approach to addressing new issues within an existing pre-service teacher education curriculum is to infuse the issues throughout the curriculum by modifying existing courses and field experiences. In this vein, Valdés *et al.* (2005) argue that "a language strand [should] become an integral part of the required program for all teachers" (p. 161). Infusing attention to language and to teaching ELLs across the curriculum is theoretically preferable to adding a course because it makes these concerns integral to all aspects of teaching and of becoming a teacher. However, in practice, infusion often does not live up to its potential. It requires that teacher education faculty have the knowledge, skills, and commitment to address the issues in a less-than-superficial way (Villegas & Lucas, 2002). (We discuss the need for professional development for faculty at the end of this section.)

A number of teacher education programs have taken the infusion approach to improving the preparation of classroom teachers to teach ELLs. For some, the goal was infusion of relevant cultural and linguistic issues across all courses (Bermúdez *et al.*, 1989; González & Darling-Hammond, 1997 [UC Santa Barbara]; Merino, 1999). One infusion strategy at NAU is to address issues relevant to ELLs in "special enrichment activities" such as seminars, guest lectures, and special field trips (Delaney-Barmann & Minner, 1995, p. 7).

Other institutions targeted one particular course for modification rather than the entire curriculum (e.g. methods courses at San Diego State University (SDSU) [González & Darling-Hammond, 1997]). Hadaway (1993) describes the details of one effort to infuse attention to ELL issues in a required multicultural education course at a state university in a culturally and linguistically homogeneous area. The course had not previously addressed linguistic diversity in depth and included no field experience. To give the largely monolingual pre-service teachers the opportunity to interact with ELLs, faculty instituted a pen-pal program through which each teacher candidate in the course was paired with an ELL in one of eight schools in four districts. The written interactions with the children provided the first exposure to children of different cultural and linguistic backgrounds for many of these teacher candidates. They had practice communicating across cultural and linguistic boundaries for the first time. In class, the teacher candidates engaged in discussions of their experiences and confronted some negative attitudes and stereotypes, guided by the course instructor. Through pre- and post-semester surveys,

Hadaway determined that the teacher candidates learned about the "culture, language, family traditions, and customs" of the ELLs (p. 28) and developed more positive attitudes about having ELLs in their future classes. One teacher candidate wrote that she had come to better understand "how it feels to be a non-native speaker in the United States" (p. 28).

Add or modify pre-program requirements

Another structural strategy described in the literature for preparing teachers to teach ELLs is to add or modify requirements for candidates prior to formal entry into a pre-service teacher education program. In practice, this strategy is equivalent to a modification of criteria for admission to teacher education. While we found only minimal evidence that institutions are using this strategy, we include it because of its potential to improve the preparation of teachers of ELLs. One advantage of this strategy is that, because prerequisite courses are not part of the professional education sequence, they can be added without reducing the number of education credits already required. This strategy can also ensure that future teachers have developed particular knowledge and skills before they begin their formal preparation program. The strategy is problematic, however, for students who transfer from community colleges to four-year institutions and in institutions where there are already many lower-division requirements.

Study of a second language is one logical prerequisite for admission to teacher education, given the association between having studied a foreign language and positive attitudes toward ELLs (Hyatt & Biegy, 1999; Youngs & Youngs, 2001) and the commonly recognized benefits of language study for all citizens. Because pre-service teachers at Boston College "found even minimal proficiency in Spanish invaluable as they developed and implemented instruction for mainstream classrooms," Friedman (2002) reported that Boston College was considering adding a second/foreign language requirement for admission to teacher education (p. 214). Knowledge of a second language is already a prerequisite for admission to the minor in Teaching English Language Learners (TELL) that is available to candidates in Early Childhood, Elementary, and Secondary Education certificate programs at Boston College. Courses in linguistics are also potential prerequisites for teacher candidates (Wong-Fillmore & Snow, 2005), such as the introductory linguistics course taught at UC Berkeley by Valdés (Valdés *et al.*, 2005).

Add a minor or supplemental certificate program

The fourth structural strategy to prepare teachers to teach ELLs is to offer a minor or supplemental certificate program related to teaching ELLs that pre-service teachers can pursue along with their major field of study. Because it generally involves a coherent sequence of several courses, this strategy provides the most comprehensive pre-service preparation for classroom teachers of ELLs of all the strategies we identified. For the same reason, it is the most difficult to require; institutions are reluctant to add to the time students must spend taking courses—especially given the already lengthy undergraduate careers of many students.

As mentioned above, Boston College has developed a minor in Teaching English Language Learners (TELL) for candidates in Early Childhood, Elementary, and Secondary Education (Friedman, 2002). Intended to provide "a systematic and extended study of theory and pedagogy . . . for students interested in teaching in urban and changing suburban environments" (p. 213), the minor requires four courses—Linguistic Structure of English, Classroom Assessment, Teaching Bilingual Students, and Second Language

Acquisition. Candidates also complete a field experience in a mainstream classroom with a teacher with ESL preparation. (See details on the Boston College Lynch School of Education website: www.bc.edu.) Other minors/supplemental certificates are offered at Temple University (Nevárez-La Torre *et al.*, 2005) and at NAU, where it is called a "special content emphasis" (Delaney-Barmann & Minner, 1995).

California's Cross-Cultural, Language, and Academic Development (CLAD) certificate, instituted in 1992 in California to provide teachers with basic knowledge and skills for teaching ELLs, was not technically a minor; it was the enactment of a state policy rather than a program of study at one university. However, it had a similar function and structure in that its certified teachers had developed particular knowledge, skills, and dispositions for teaching ELLs in addition to the knowledge, skills, and dispositions required for teaching particular grades and academic subjects (see August & Hakuta, 1997; Carlson & Walton, 1994; Kuhlman & Vidal, 1993; Merino, 1999). To be awarded the CLAD certificate, teachers had to have a valid California teaching credential, satisfy a second-language requirement, and show that they had developed knowledge of three domains—(a) language structure and first- and second-language development; (b) methodology of bilingual instruction, instruction for English language development, and specially designed academic instruction delivered in English; and (c) culture and cultural diversity (California Commission on Teacher Credentialing, 2004). Teachers could earn a CLAD certificate by taking 12 upper-division credits in the three domains above, or they could take an examination. The CLAD certificate has been supplanted by a requirement that all teacher education programs infuse methods for teaching ELLs across the curriculum—an approach that has diluted the preparation of classroom teachers for teaching ELLs (J. Maxwell-Jolly, personal communication, 8/22/05). We include this brief description of the CLAD certificate program because it represented a large-scale and intensive effort to ensure that all classroom teachers were fully prepared to teach ELLs. As such, it can serve as a model for other institutions (see González & Darling-Hammond, 1997; Kuhlman & Vidal, 1993; Merino, 1999).

Process strategies to prepare teachers to teach ELLs

The four previous strategies for preparing teachers to teach ELLs require structural changes in the teacher education curriculum. We now turn to three process strategies that can be implemented without restructuring the curriculum and that can take place in schools as well as institutions of higher education. While these approaches are not dependent upon curriculum change, they do require educators in universities and in schools to function in new and often unfamiliar ways. The first two of these strategies—mentoring and collaboration across institutions—can be successful only if the participants develop new kinds of working relationships. The third strategy—providing professional development for teacher educators—requires "experts" to acknowledge and act on their need to develop new knowledge and skills.

Offer mentoring for practicing teachers

The first process strategy we identified is mentoring for teachers already in the classroom. Formal and informal mentoring can be effective in facilitating the development of practicing teachers' knowledge and skills for teaching ELLs. The Language Minority Teacher Induction Project (LMTIP) at George Mason University, which received funding from 1998 to 2004, brought together teams of four to six beginning teachers, a mentor, and a university professor for the purpose of providing support to beginning teachers in schools with large numbers of ELLs (Levy *et al.*, 2002). The teams met regularly and designed and carried out action research projects with the support of their mentors, which served as "the driving force behind the growth and improvement of ELL education" at the schools involved (p. 273). Levy and colleagues drew conclusions about the impact of the initiative from examining the action research projects conducted by 66 teachers, all of which included some form of assessment of student growth. The researchers concluded that teachers engaged in ongoing reflection on their practice, enhanced their understanding of and skills for modifying instruction for ELLs and for communicating with students across different cultures, learned about their students' cultural backgrounds and prior knowledge, and developed more positive perceptions of their students. Mentoring is also a central feature of the Bilingual/ESL Teacher Leadership Academy (BETLA), an initiative at Bank Street College to develop leadership skills in exemplary bilingual and ESL teachers in the New York City Public Schools so they can become leaders in their schools and mentors for their colleagues regarding the education of ELLs (Hernandez, 2005; Lucas, 2005a). Retired bilingual and ESL teachers provide extensive mentoring for the teachers for a year.

Foster collaboration across institutional boundaries

The most frequently discussed process strategy for preparing both prospective and current teachers to teach ELLs is collaboration across institutional boundaries. The argument for collaboration between classroom teachers of ELLs and their colleagues (especially specialists in ELL education) is compelling, given the increasing number of ELLs in classes with teachers who are not prepared to teach them, as we previously discussed. Through collaboration, both pre-service and practicing teachers can gain experience and develop dispositions, knowledge, and skills for teaching ELLs. Bermúdez *et al.* (1989), Evans *et al.* (2005), Gebhard *et al.* (2002), Kaufman and Brooks (1996), and Levy *et al.* (2002) describe initiatives in which faculty in different pre-service programs and university departments have collaborated to teach courses taken by candidates in different programs. Here, we elaborate on one of these efforts.

At the University of Arizona, three faculty members (a bilingual social studies instructor, a math and science instructor, and an English language arts instructor) taught their respective courses to a group of pre-service teachers, ten of whom were in the bilingual education program and 18 of whom were in the mainstream teacher education program (Evans *et al.*, 2005). After the semester, Evans and her co-authors examined course syllabi, fieldnotes by the bilingual instructor, fieldnotes by another of the authors who was not an instructor, and two sets of written reflections by the students. The participants reported that the most "cherished" aspects of the experience were "the opportunities to 'live multiculturalism' and to form a sense of collegiality in a consciously multicultural-bilingual community" (p. 81). Instructors stressed collegiality and respect, and tried to allay fears of potential cross-cultural conflict. In the social studies class, students had multiple opportunities to reflect on and discuss "issues of race, prejudice, cultural difference, and equity," with the goal of strengthening intercultural sensitivity, promoting cross-cultural communication, and helping students to "learn from one another in a safe and respectful multicultural setting" (p. 81). Because instruction was conducted in both English and Spanish, students interacted at times "in their weaker language" (p. 83). The native English speakers recognized the inequity in the fact that the great majority of instruction in the courses was in English and they advocated for more use of Spanish. This experience helped sensitize them to "the treatment of bilingualism as a problem" (p. 84) and led them to see the need to advocate for greater recognition and value for bilingualism.

Evans and her colleagues concluded that the bilingual, bicultural learning community that developed was beneficial for the future mainstream teachers, who developed greater cross-cultural understanding and greater sensitivity to the challenges of ELLs and to the subordinate position of non-English languages in the U.S. However, they do not recommend the replication of their collaborative initiative without some modifications, largely because the bilingual education candidates were not as well prepared as they would have been as a result of reduced modeling of bilingual instruction and less opportunity to use Spanish in the classroom. The authors do argue that combining bilingual and mainstream teacher candidates in some courses and for some purposes can be beneficial in helping future teachers develop skills and confidence for building cross-cultural collegial relationships.

Professional development initiatives for practicing teachers also highlight the importance of collaboration (Alfred, 1994; González & Darling-Hammond, 1997 [International High School, in NYC]; Sakash & Rodriguez-Brown, 1995; Walqui, 2000; Zetlin *et al.*, 1998). Because of the fragmented and specialized nature of teaching and schooling, teachers in different departments or programs rarely have extended interactions about students, though each group (e.g. classroom teachers, ESL specialists, bilingual specialists) has expertise that could benefit the other (Kaufman & Brooks, 1996; Lucas, 1997). While many of these collaborative professional development efforts are instructive, we can highlight only one here—the description of professional development over four years at Harden Middle School (HMS) in Salinas, CA (Walqui, 2000).

Opened in 1992, HMS was a year-round school organized according to "houses," with 68 percent of the students designated as limited English proficient. The focus of professional development for faculty at the school evolved over the four years described by Walqui, but collaboration continued to be a central element of it. During the first year, faculty decided that professional development would focus on developing collaborative working relationships among the interdisciplinary teams within the houses. During the second year, they decided to concentrate on preparing all teachers at the school to earn the California Language Development Specialist (LDS) certificate. Groups of faculty members participated in sessions on cultural, linguistic, and educational theories fundamental to the education of ELLs; the native languages and cultures of the ELLs in the school; and research on promising instructional practices for ELLs. For the third year, faculty decided to focus on teaching challenging academic content in English to ELLs. To support their learning, faculty engaged in team planning and team teaching activities, wrote and shared reflective journals, and carried out peer observations. They were supported by two resource teachers hired with federal funds to spend half their time at the school and serve as mentors for the teachers. In-service sessions offered opportunities for teachers to examine and discuss issues of social justice as they relate to ELLs. In the fourth year, professional development focused on the development of interdisciplinary thematic units by teams of teachers. Walqui's description captures the complex, evolving, and collaborative nature of professional development at the school, as the faculty grappled with trying to develop the knowledge, skills, and dispositions they needed to teach ELLs successfully.

Provide professional development for teacher education faculty

The final process strategy for preparing classroom teachers to teach ELLs is to provide professional development for teacher education faculty. Even if all the structural changes previously described were instituted in a teacher education program, they would have little impact if the faculty teaching the courses did not have the knowledge and skills to prepare teachers to teach ELLs. Since teacher educators generally do not have such knowledge and skills, professional development for them must be an integral part of any effort to modify teacher education to prepare classroom teachers to teach ELLs (Steffens, 1992). A number of professional development efforts have been undertaken in recognition of this imperative (Costa *et al.*, 2005; González & Darling-Hammond, 1997 [San Diego State University]; Nevárez-La Torre *et al.*, 2005). We describe only one of these.

Faculty at Boston College developed a three-year federally-funded professional development initiative, one part of which addressed the preparation of faculty to prepare their students to work with linguistically and culturally diverse students (Costa *et al.*, 2005). During the spring semester, faculty volunteers participated in a seven-session seminar. They read and discussed literature on the education of ELLs, and were expected to explore ways to modify their syllabi to incorporate more attention to ELLs and then to implement the changes. Topics addressed in the seminar included "current and historical controversies in bilingual education" (p. 108), local language policy and programs, social and cognitive factors of bilingualism, attitudes toward bilingualism, strategies for differentiating instruction, culture and identity development, and the nature and process of second language development. Participants analyzed the language of textbooks and state assessments to determine difficulties they might pose for ELLs. They visited a school and observed classes with ELLs, reflecting on what they had seen and the implications for classroom teachers of ELLs. During the summer following the seminar, participants presented their plans for modifying their courses to their colleagues, and in the fall they began implementing the changes to incorporate more attention to language and linguistic diversity.

Summary

Some strategies teacher educators are using to prepare classroom teachers to teach ELLs require structural modifications in teacher education programs at institutions of higher education (adding a course, modifying existing courses to infuse ELL issues, modifying pre-program requirements, and adding a minor or certificate). Others are more accurately characterized as processes than as structures (offering mentoring for practicing teachers, fostering collaboration across institutional boundaries, and providing professional development for faculty). The first two of these processes apply largely to practicing teachers, but they involve participants from different institutional contexts. Several of the above descriptions emphasize the evolutionary nature of these initiatives, and many of them are, no doubt, still evolving (e.g. González & Darling-Hammond, 1997; Walqui, 2000; Zetlin *et al.*, 1998). This is a reminder that quick-fixes—whether for pre-service teacher education programs or in-service professional development—are not realistic. Learning to be a successful teacher of ELLs takes time, and so does developing strategies for supporting such learning.

Many complex contextual factors determine which of these strategies, or others, will be most workable for a particular teacher education program, school, or school district. For that reason, the variety of strategies teacher educators are using to improve the preparation of classroom teachers to teach ELLs is heartening. At IHEs, the most comprehensive approach that also ensures direct focus on issues related to ELLs is to add a minor or supplemental certificate. But adding a course or requiring foreign language credits before program entry can also contribute to the preparation of teachers to teach ELLs. Infusion across the curriculum is theoretically comprehensive and, in its ideal form, the most desirable strategy, but in practice too few faculty members are sufficiently knowledgeable of the issues to fully infuse them into the curriculum. For preparing practicing teachers who are not enrolled in formal teacher education programs, efforts that emphasize collaboration seem to offer the most comprehensive approach to develop knowledge and expertise in teaching ELLs.

Clearly, other efforts can and are being undertaken in pre-service and inservice teacher education to better prepare classroom teachers to teach ELLs. Teachers, prospective teachers, teacher educators, and, most importantly, ELL students will benefit from greater dissemination of current efforts. However, while data were reported for several of the initiatives described above, we need far more rigorous, systematic studies. Such research is desperately needed for teacher education in general and for the preparation of teachers of ELLs even more so. In the final section of the chapter, we make recommendations for such research as well as for policy.

CONCLUSION AND RECOMMENDATIONS

This chapter has examined the literature on the preparation of non-specialist classroom teachers to teach English language learners. We have argued that more attention should be given to such preparation because of the increasing likelihood that ELLs will be in mainstream classes, because of the special challenges faced by classroom teachers of ELLs, and because classroom teachers are not now adequately prepared to meet those challenges. We then identified language-related experiences, attitudes and beliefs, knowledge, and skills needed by classroom teachers of ELLs. While some of these characteristics are alluded to in the literature on preparing culturally responsive teachers, they tend to be treated superficially, if at all. We argue that teacher educators need to give more attention to cultivating these characteristics in all teachers. Finally, drawing on both descriptive and empirical literature, we identified four structural strategies and three process strategies for preparing teachers to teach ELLs in pre-service and in-service contexts. In the following pages, we will highlight a few themes that emerged from our examination of the literature and then make recommendations for policy and research.

One theme that runs through the chapter is the importance of teachers having a variety of language experiences (Byrnes *et al.*, 1996, 1997; Griego-Jones, 2002; Youngs & Youngs, 2001). These include exposure to languages other than English, contact with people who speak other languages, and spending an extended period of time in a context where English is not the dominant language. The importance of these experiences is distinct from knowledge about language structures and uses. Teachers of ELLs gain something more than knowledge when they observe people interacting in different languages for different purposes and in different contexts, speak a language that is not the dominant language, and go through the process of trying to learn a second language—with all the accompanying challenges, anxiety, and exhilaration. While the knowledge and skills gained from such exposure is important, it is the complete *experience* of these phenomena that gives teachers a deep understanding—physical, emotional, and social as well as cognitive—that they can bring to interactions with English language learners.

The second theme emerging from our review of the literature is the critical importance of linguistic knowledge for teachers. We have used two metaphors—pulling language threads from the larger cloth of the preparation of culturally and linguistically responsive teachers, and challenging the invisibility of language issues in teacher preparation. These are akin to Nieto's (2000) call to bring bilingual education out of the basement. All three are, we believe, apt metaphors, given the marginality of language issues, linguistic diversity, and the education of English language learners in the literature on teacher education. In fact, considering language *as language* has become a marginal activity in U.S. schools at all levels, including teacher education (Wong-Fillmore & Snow, 2005). The literature suggests that teachers in particular need to be comfortable and competent with the linguistic elements of English and the processes of first and second language learning to be competent teachers of ELLs and, in fact, of all students. We believe there is an urgent need to reconsider the trivialization of the study of language in U.S. schools—from elementary school through college.

The final theme we highlight is that of collaboration. Some efforts to prepare classroom teachers to teach ELLs treat collaboration as a defining feature, as we discussed in the previous section. But, at some level, the sharing of expertise and hard work cuts across all the strategies we discussed. One reason the preparation of teachers to teach ELLs remains in the shadows is that the education of ELLs is perceived as something special, not part of the routine responsibilities of mainstream teachers. Therefore, faculty in mainstream pre-service teacher education programs generally have not seen it as their responsibility to prepare teachers to teach ELLs, nor do most teacher educators have the expertise to do so. Similarly, faculty in TESL or bilingual education programs have not thought of themselves as responsible for preparing mainstream teachers. This same specialization characterizes K-12 schools; regular classroom teachers, ESL teachers, and bilingual teachers are seen as having very different roles and responsibilities. Educating ELLs in mainstream classes requires collaboration across these institutional and professional boundaries. Collaborations might involve higher education faculty in different departments (e.g. linguistics, English, and curriculum and teaching) jointly designing and teaching a course in Linguistics for Educators. Retired ESL and bilingual teachers might mentor current ESL and bilingual teachers, who in turn serve as peer mentors for classroom teachers in their schools. A group of classroom teachers might form a study group and conduct peer observations to develop their knowledge and skill for teaching ELLs, serving as "a community of critical friends" (Nieto, 2000, p. 204). Whatever the particulars, collaboration is essential for providing challenging and appropriate education for ELLs in regular classrooms.

From our review of the literature, we have drawn some recommendations for policy. First, a coordinated effort is needed to collect relevant language data about teachers, teacher candidates, teacher educators, and language education. We were unable to locate comprehensive data on teachers' native languages, their levels of proficiency in languages other than English, their experiences studying foreign/second languages (how long they studied, in what contexts, through what methods, at what ages), their experiences traveling and living for extended periods of time in other countries, and their exposure to language minority groups in the U.S. While periodic data collection efforts such as *The Schools and Staffing Survey* (e.g. NCES, 1997) and *The Descriptive Studies* of LEP students (Fleischman & Hopstock, 1993; Zehler *et al.*, 2003) provide some language-related information about teachers, we believe more such data should be collected routinely at the national level. Similarly, language-related data on teacher candidates and teacher educators should be routinely collected. Zeichner (2005) has called for the construction of a national data set about teacher education candidates and teacher educators; such a data set must include the kinds of information about language we have listed above.

Second, funding is needed to support innovative pre-service and in-service efforts to develop classroom teachers' knowledge, skills, and dispositions for teaching ELLs. Five of the reports of pre-service and in-service initiatives described in the previous section were developed with federal funding (Bermúdez *et al.*, 1989; Costa *et al.*, 2005; Levy *et al.*, 2002; Nevárez *et al.*, 2005; Sakash & Rodriguez-Brown, 1995), and one wonders if they would have taken place at all without the funding. If already over-burdened faculty must initiate and implement innovations without additional funding, it seems safe to assume that there will be fewer of them, they will be less comprehensive, and less data will be collected through formal evaluations than if these innovations receive external funding.

Finally, we recommend that teacher educators advocate for an additional endorsement or certificate at the state level, following the now-defunct model of the CLAD certificate in California. Such a certificate may be premature in states with very few ELLs or with highly concentrated linguistic minority populations, but in several states ELLs are already a notable presence in mainstream classes. Realistically, it will be many years before teacher education programs or school districts make the necessary adjustments on their own to ensure that all teachers have the knowledge, skills, and dispositions to teach ELLs successfully. If states require that teachers of ELLs complete a specified number of credits or hours focused on the education of ELLs, teacher educators will have the support, motivation, and funding (through tuition) to make the needed changes.

We now turn to our recommendations for research, many of which echo the recommendations of Zeichner (2005) for the development of a research agenda for teacher education as a whole. We identified 17 reports of empirical studies related to the preparation of teachers to teach ELLs that met our criteria for selection. Eight of them focused directly on such preparation, and three of those involved large-scale surveys. Nine studies were indirectly related to teacher preparation, six of which examined teachers' attitudes and beliefs—the only area in which there was evidence of a body of research. Thirteen were published in peer review journals, one was a book chapter, one was prepared for the U.S. Department of Education, one was prepared for three policy organizations in CA, and one was a paper presented at AERA. Consistent with other research on teacher education, several of the studies (seven) were done at the researchers' own institutions and focused on their own students. Even assuming that we failed to include every relevant study and acknowledging the rigor of many of these studies, this body of work is sadly inadequate. Research is needed in every area.

We believe, therefore, that the first priority should be to conduct research to get a better sense of where we are starting from. While the published studies and descriptions of initiatives we identified are heartening, they leave us wanting a comprehensive and systematic study of what is now being done to prepare classroom teachers to teach ELLs. Nationally, how many institutions of higher education are taking steps to prepare pre-service and in-service teachers for ELLs? What are the characteristics of such efforts? What structural and process strategies are being used? What are the "curriculum and instructional practices and organizational arrangements" of these initiatives (Zeichner, 2005, p. 21)? How do these characteristics and strategies vary by institutional context? What are the characteristics of those who are teaching in these programs? Gathering descriptive data on in-service initiatives not associated with IHEs poses great challenges given the more diffuse and unregulated nature of most professional development. But we need to find ways to identify in-service initiatives and to gather descriptive data about them as well. Once descriptive data have been collected about pre-service and in-service initiatives, a series of detailed case studies of a representative sample of those initiatives could be conducted to provide "rich descriptions of what . . . the programs actually do to address cultural and linguistic diversity" (Maxwell-Jolly & Gándara, 2002, p. 60).

Beyond such descriptive studies, research that examines the implications and impacts of the various efforts to prepare classroom teachers to teach ELLs is needed. What are the impacts on teachers' experiences, dispositions, knowledge, and skills? On their teaching practices? On the learning of the ELLs in their classes? In addition, variations in outcomes related to program characteristics and to institutional and community contexts need to be studied. How do outcomes vary according to the different strategies, characteristics, and models used? For example, "do teachers prepared in a program that gives greater emphasis to the role of culture function differently than those in programs giving more importance to language issues" (Merino, 1999, p. 245)? What is the relationship of the sociocultural context of institutions and communities to the extent to which and ways in which teachers are prepared to teach ELLs, and to their outcomes (Walker *et al.*, 2004; Zeichner, 2005)?

Research is also needed on teacher educators who are attempting to prepare teachers to teach ELLs through both pre-service and in-service initiatives at IHEs, in school districts, and in other contexts. We need to understand the relationship between the characteristics of teacher educators, what they teach, how they teach, and how successful they are. How do their personal backgrounds and experiences, their linguistic and cultural knowledge and expertise, and their professional knowledge and skills influence their practices and the learning of their students? As Zeichner (2005) posed the question: "... How do various demographic and quality indicators associated with teacher educators ... influence the character and quality of instruction in teacher education programs" (p. 20)?

Finally, with regard to research methods, we want to echo Zeichner's (2005) recommendations that the peer review process be strengthened so that published research meets more rigorous standards and that greater attention be given to preparing educational researchers and to mentoring beginning researchers. We reviewed many reports of empirical work that were lacking clearly articulated research questions, a coherent theoretical framework, an adequate explanation of the research design or data collection procedures, an explanation of how the sample was selected, and/or a description of the context for the research. We read reports in which the implications did not logically grow out of the study findings. To enhance the credibility of research on preparing teachers in general, and preparing them to teach ELLs in particular, we in the research community must hold ourselves accountable for producing high quality research and reports of that research.

When we began writing this chapter, we imagined that we would end with recommendations for practice. What steps do we suggest teacher educators take to prepare classroom teachers to teach English language learners? Now that we come to our final comments, however, we feel it is premature to make recommendations for the design of pre-service and in-service programs to prepare classroom teachers to teach ELLs. The examples included in the chapter can provide inspiration and direction. But without research to examine the functions and outcomes of these strategies, we have no basis on which to recommend one over the other or to suggest that one strategy is more successful in one context or with one population than another. Therefore, we conclude by expressing our hope that educators will recognize the urgency to bring the education of English language learners in mainstream classes out of the shadows. The extent to which teachers are prepared to teach all students reflects the value we place on the education of all students. It also plays a major role in determining the quality of life of individuals and groups within our society. The academic success and future life possibilities of ELLs depend to a large extent on the assistance and quality of instruction they receive in mainstream classes. To continue to deny them the best teachers possible is to turn our backs on our professional responsibilities as educators.

ACKNOWLEDGMENT

The authors would like to thank Julie Maxwell-Jolly, University of California, Davis, for her comments on a draft of this chapter, and Revital Israeli, Tamara's Graduate Assistant at Montclair State University, whose assistance was invaluable.

NOTES

1 In this chapter, we use the terms *mainstream classroom* and *regular classroom* to refer to classes that assume students are native English speakers. This is in contrast to *special classes* (ESL or bilingual classes) designed for ELLs.

2 Abramson *et al.*, 1993; Evans *et al.*, 2005; Gándara *et al.*, 2005; Hyatt & Beigy, 1999; Menken & Antunez, 2001; Rhine, 1995; Torok & Aguilar, 2000; Zetlin *et al.*, 1998.

3 Byrnes *et al.*, 1996, 1997; Gersten, 1999; Griego-Jones, 2002; Karabenick & Noda, 2004; Pappamihiel, 2002; Penfield, 1987; Platt & Troudi, 1997; Walker *et al.*, 2004; Youngs & Youngs, 2001.

4 The official term used in government documents for speakers of other languages who are not yet proficient in English is *limited English proficient* (LEP).

5 The survey did not make a distinction between linguistic minority students and culturally diverse students, so it is impossible to determine teachers' feelings of preparedness related only to teaching ELLs.

REFERENCES

Abramson, S., Pritchard, R., & Garcia, R. (1993) Teacher education and limited-English-proficient students: are we meeting the challenge? *Teacher Education Quarterly*, 20(3), 53–65 (ERIC Document Reproduction Service No. EJ471882).

Alfred, I. (1994, March) *ESL in the mainstream: challenges and possibilities*. Paper presented at the TESOL '94, 28th Annual Convention and Exposition, Baltimore, Maryland (ERIC Document Reproduction Service No. ED385120).

American Association of Colleges for Teacher Education, Committee on Multicultural Education (2002, March) *Educators' preparation for cultural and linguistic diversity: a call to action*. Accessed 6/28/05 at http//:www.aacte.org/Programs/Multicultural/ culturallinguistic.pdf.

Au, K. H. (1980) Participation structures in a reading lesson with Hawaiian children: an analysis of a culturally appropriate instructional event. *Anthropology and Education Quarterly* 11(2), 93–115.

August, D. & Hakuta, K. (eds.) (1997) *Improving schooling for language-minority children: a research agenda*. Washington, DC: National Academy Press.

Baca, L. & Escamilla, K. (2005) Educating teachers about language. In C. T. Adger, C. E. Snow, & D. Christian (eds.), *What teachers need to know about language*, 71–84. Washington, DC: Center for Applied Linguistics.

Bartolomé, L. I. (2000) Democratizing bilingualism: the role of critical teacher education. In Z. F. Beykont (ed.), *Lifting every voice: pedagogy and politics of bilingualism* (pp. 167–186). Cambridge, MA: Harvard Education Publishing Group.

Bartolomé, L. I. (2002) Creating an equal playing field: teachers as advocates, border crossers, and cultural brokers. In Z. F. Beykont (ed.), *The Power of culture: teaching across language difference* (pp. 167–191). Cambridge, MA: Harvard Education Publishing Group.

Bermúdez, A. B., Fradd, S. H., Haulman, A., & Weismantel, M. J. (1989) Developing a coordination model for programs preparing personnel to work with LEP students. *The Journal of Educational Issues of Language Minority Students*, 5, 79–95.

Byrnes, D. A. & Kiger, G. (1994) Language attitudes of teachers scales (LATS). *Educational and Psychological Measurement*, 54(1), 227–231.

Byrnes, D. A., Kiger, G., & Manning, L. (1996) Social psychological correlates of teachers' language attitudes. *Journal of Applied Social Psychology*, 26(5), 455–467.

Byrnes, D. A., Kiger, G., & Manning, L. (1997) Teachers' attitudes about language diversity. *Teaching and Teacher Education*, 13(6), 637–644.

California Commission on Teacher Credentialing (2004) Crosscultural, Language, and Academic Development (CLAD) Certificates. Leaflet Number CL-628C. Accessed 6/17/04 at http://www.ctc.ca.gov/credentialinfo/leaflets/c1628c.html.

Carlson, R. & Walton, P. (1994, February) *CLAD/BCLAD: California reforms in the preparation and credentialing of teachers for a linguistically and culturally diverse student population.* Paper presented at the 23rd Annual International Bilingual/Multicultural Education Conference, Los Angeles, CA (ERIC Document Reproduction Service No. ED 374670).

Cochran-Smith, M., Davis, D., & Fries, K. (2004) Multicultural teacher education: research, practice, and policy. In J. A. Banks & C. A. M. Banks (eds.), *Handbook of research on multicultural education* (2nd ed.), pp. 931–975. San Francisco: Jossey-Bass.

Comer, J. P. (1993) The potential effects of community organizations on the future of our youth. In R. Takanishi (ed.), *Adolescence in the 1990s: risk and opportunity*, pp. 203–206. New York: Teachers College Press.

Cornell, C. (1995, Winter) Reducing failure of LEP students in the mainstream classroom and why it is important. *The Journal of Educational Issues of Language Minority Students*, 15.

Costa, J., McPhail, G., Smith, J., & Brisk, M. E. (2005) The challenge of infusing the teacher education curriculum with scholarship on English language learners. *Journal of Teacher Education*, 56(5), 104–118.

Crawford, J. (1992) *Hold your tongue: the politics of "English Only."* Reading, MA: Addison Wesley.

Cummins, J. (1976) The influence of bilingualism on cognitive growth: a synthesis of research findings and explanatory hypotheses. *Working Papers on Bilingualism* 9, 1–43.

Cummins, J. (1979) Cognitive/academic language proficiency, linguistic interdependence, the optimum age question and some other matters. *Working Papers on Bilingualism* 19, 121–129.

Cummins, J. (1981) The role of primary language development in promoting educational success for language minority students. In California State Department of Education, *Schooling and language minority students: a theoretical framework*, pp. 3–49. Sacramento, CA: CA DOE.

Cummins, J. (2000) *Language, power, and pedagogy: bilingual children in the crossfire.* Clevedon, UK: Multilingual Matters.

De Jesus, A. (2005) Theoretical perspectives on the underachievement of Latino/a students in U.S. schools: toward a framework for culturally additive schooling. In P. Pedraza & M. Rivera (eds.), *Latino education: an agenda for community action research* (pp. 343–374). Mahwah, NJ: Lawrence Erlbaum Associates.

Delany-Bermann, G. & Minner, S. (1995, November) *Development and implementation of a program of study to prepare teachers for diversity at Northern Arizona University: a preliminary report.* Paper presented at the annual conference of the AERO, Sedona, AZ (ERIC Document Reproduction Service No. ED391792).

Delpit, L. (1995) *Other people's children: cultural conflict in the classroom.* New York: The New Press.

Delpit, L. (1998) What should teachers do? Ebonics and culturally responsive instruction. In T. Perry & L. Delpit (eds.), *The real Ebonics debate: power, language, and the education of African-American Children* (pp. 17–26). Boston: Beacon Press.

Echevarria, J. & Graves, A. (2003) *Sheltered content instruction: teaching English-language learners with diverse abilities.* Boston: Allyn & Bacon.

Echevarria, J., Vogt, M., & Short, D. J. (2004) *Making content comprehensible for English language learners: the SIOP Model* (Second ed.). Boston: Allyn & Bacon.

Evans, C., Arnot-Hopffer, E., & Jurich, D. (2005) Making ends meet: bringing bilingual education and mainstream students together in preservice teacher education. *Equity and Excellence in Education*, 38, 75–88.

Fasold, R. (1990) *The sociolinguistics of language.* Oxford, UK: Blackwell.

Feiman-Nemser, S. & Buchmann, M. (1986) The first year of teacher preparation: transition to pedagogical thinking. *Journal of Curriculum Studies*, 18(3): 239–56.

Files, J. (2005, June 10). Report describes immigrants as younger and more diverse. *New York Times*.

Fleischmann, H. L. & P. J. Hopstock (1993) *Descriptive study of services of limited English proficient students*. Volume 1, Summary of findings and conclusions. Arhugton, VA: Developments Associates, Inc.

Freeman, D. E. & Freeman, Y. S. (2004) *Essential linguistics: what you need to know to teach reading, ESL, spelling, phonics, grammar.* Portsmouth, NH: Heinemann.

Friedman, A. A. (2002) What we would have liked to know: preservice teachers' perspectives on effective teacher preparation. In Z. F. Beykont (ed.), *The power of culture: teaching across language difference* (pp. 193–217). Cambridge, MA: Harvard Education Publishing Group.

Gándara, P., Maxwell-Jolly, J., & Driscoll, A. (2005) *Listening to teachers of English language learners: a survey of California teachers' challenges, experiences, and professional development needs.* Santa Cruz, CA: The Center for the Future of Teaching and Learning.

García, E. E. (1993) Language, cuture, and education. In L. Darling-Hammond (ed.), *Review of Research in Education*, 19 (pp. 51–98). Washington, DC: American Educational Research Association.

García, E. E. (1996) Preparing instructional professionals for linguistically and culturally diverse students. In J. Sikula (ed.), *Handbook of research on teacher education, 2nd edition*, pp. 802–813. New York: Macmillan.

García, E. E. (1999) *Student cultural diversity: understanding and meeting the challenge. Second edition.* Boston: Houghton Mifflin.

Gay, G. (2000) *Culturally responsive teaching: theory, research, and practice.* NY: Teachers College Press.

Gebhard, M., Austin, T., Nieto, S., & Willett, J. (2002) "You can't step on someone else's words": preparing all teachers to teach language minority students. In Z. F. Beykont (ed.), *The Power of culture: teaching across language difference* (pp. 219–243). Cambridge, MA: Harvard Education Publishing Group.

Gersten, R. (1999) Lost opportunities: challenges confronting four teachers of English-language learners. *The Elementary School Journal*, 100(1), 37–56.

Gibbons, P. (2002) *Scaffolding language, scaffolding learning: teaching second language learners in the mainstream classroom.* Portsmouth, NH: Heinemann.

Goldfarb, K. (1998) Creating sanctuaries for Latino immigrant families: a case for the schools. *The Journal for a Just and Caring Education*, 4(4), 454–466.

González, J. M. & Darling-Hammond, L. (1997) *New concepts for new challenges: professional development for teachers of immigrant youth.* Washington, DC: Center for Applied Linguistics.

Goodwin, A. L. (2002) Teacher preparation and the education of immigrant children. *Education and Urban Society*, 34(2), 156–172.

Grant, C. A. & Secada, W. (1990) Preparing teachers for diversity. In R. Houston (ed.), *Handbook of research in teacher education* (pp. 403–422). New York: Macmillan.

Griego Jones, T. (2002) Relationship between pre-service teachers' beliefs about second language learning and prior experiences with non-English speakers. In L. Minaya-Rowe (ed.), *Teacher training and effective pedagogy in the context of student diversity*, pp. 39–64. Greenwich, CT: Information Age Publishing.

Grinberg, J. (2002) "I had never been exposed to teaching like that": progressive teacher education at Bank Street during the 1930's. *Teachers College Record*, 104(7), 1422–1460.

Grinberg, J. & Saavedra, E. (2000) The constitution of bilingual/ESL education as a disciplinary practice: genealogical explorations. *Review of Educational Research*, 70(4), 419–441.

Grinberg, J., Goldfarb, K., & Saavedra, E. (2005) *Con coraje y con pasión*: The schooling of Latinas/os and their teachers' education. In P. Pedraza & M. Rivera (eds.), *Latino education: an agenda for community action research* (pp. 227–254). Mahwah, NJ: Lawrence Erlbaum Associates.

Hadaway, N. (1993) Encountering linguistic diversity through letters: preparing preservice teachers for second language learners. *Equity & Excellence in Education*, 26(3), 25–30 (ERIC Document Reproduction Service No. EJ480461).

Heath, S. B. (1983) *Ways with word: language, life, and work in communities and classrooms.* London, UK: Cambridge University Press.

Hernandez, L. (2005) Building capacity in schools to educate English language learners: the Bilingual/ESL Teacher Leadership Academy (BETLA). Paper presented at the annual meeting of the American Educational Research Association, Montreal, Canada.

Hollins, E. R. & Guzman, M. T. (2005) Research on preparing teachers for diverse populations. In M. Cochran-Smith & K. Zeichner (eds.), *Studying teacher education: the report of the AERA Panel on Research and Teacher Education* (pp. 477–548). Mahwah, NJ: Lawrence Erlbaum.

Hopstock, P. J. & Stephenson, T. G. (2003) *Descriptive study of services to LEP students and ELP students with disabilities. Special Topic Report #1*. Washington, DC: U.S. Department of Education. Accessed 7/6/05 at http://www.ncela.gwu.edu/stats/2_nation.htm.

Hyatt, D. F. & Beigy, A. (1999) Making the most of unknown language experience: pathways for reflective teacher development. *Journal of Education for Teaching*, 25(1), 31–40.

Justice, P. W. (2004) *Relevant linguistics: an introduction to the structure and use of English for teachers, 2nd Edition*. Stanford, CA: CSLI Publications.

Karabenick, S. A. & Noda, P. A. C. (2004) Professional development implications of teachers' beliefs and attitudes toward English language learners. *Bilingual Research Journal*, 28(1), 55–75.

Kaufman, D. & Brooks, J. G. (1996) Interdisciplinary collaboration in teacher education: a constructivist approach. *TESOL Quarterly*, 30(2), 231–251.

Kindler, A. L. (2002) Survey of the states' limited English proficient students and available educational programs and services: 2000–2001 summary report. Washington, DC: National Clearinghouse for English Language Acquisition.

Krashen, S. D. (1982) *Principles and practices in second language acquisition*. NY: Pergamon Press.

Krashen, S. D. (2003) *Explorations in language acquisition and use*. Portsmouth, NH: Heinemann.

Kuhlman, N. A. & Vidal, J. (1993) Meeting the needs of LEP students through new teacher training: the case in California. *The Journal of Educational Issues of Language Minority Students*, 12, 97–113.

Ladson-Billings, G. (1995) Multicultural teacher education: research, practice, and policy. In J. A. Banks & C. A. M. Banks (eds.), *Handbook of research on multicultural education*, pp. 747–759. New York: Macmillan.

Leighton, M. S., Hightower, A. M., & Wrigley, P. (1995) *Model strategies in bilingual education: professional development*. Washington, DC: U.S. Department of Education. Available at www.ed.gov/pubs/ModStrat/title.html.

Levy, J., Shafer, L., & Dunlap, K. (2002) Advancing the professional development of beginning teachers through mentoring and action research. In L. Minaya-Rowe (ed.), *Teacher training and effective pedagogy in the context of student diversity*, pp. 269–296. Greenwich, CT: Information Age Publishing.

Lucas, T. (1997) *Into, through, and beyond secondary school: critical transitions for immigrant youths*. Washington, DC: Center for Applied Linguistics.

Lucas, T. (2005a) The Bilingual/ESL Teacher Leadership Academy (BETLA): Evaluation results. Paper presented at the annual meeting of the American Educational Research Association, Montreal, Canada.

Lucas, T. (2005b) Fostering a commitment to social justice through service learning: hopes, plans, and realities in a teacher education course. In N. M. Michelli & D. L. Keiser (eds.), *Education for democracy and social justice* (pp. 167–188). New York: Routledge.

Lucas, T. & Katz, A. (1994) Reframing the debate: the Roles of native languages in "English-Only" programs for language minority students. *TESOL Quarterly*, 28(3), 537–561.

Lucas, T., Henze, R., & Donato, R. (1990) Promoting the success of Latino language minority students: an exploratory study of six high schools. *Harvard Educational Review*, 60(3), 315–340.

Marquez-Lopez, T. (2005) California's standards movement: how English learners have been left out of the equation for success. In P. Pedraza & M. Rivera (eds.), *Latino education: an agenda for community action research* (pp. 205–230). Mahwah, NJ: Lawrence Erlbaum Associates.

Maxwell-Jolly, J. & Gándara, P. (2002) A quest for quality: providing qualified teachers for California's English learners. In Z. F. Beykont (ed.), *The power of culture: teaching across language difference* (pp. 43–70). Cambridge, MA: Harvard Education Publishing Group.

Menken, K. & Antunez, B. (2001) *An overview of the preparation and certification of teachers working with limited English proficient (LEP) students.* Washington, DC: National Clearinghouse for Bilingual Education.

Merino, B. (1999) Preparing secondary teachers to teach a second language: the case of the United States with a focus on California. In C. J. Faltis & P. Wolfe (eds.), *So much to say: adolescents, bilingualism, & ESL in the secondary school* (pp. 225–254). New York: Teachers College Press.

Michaels, S. (1981) Sharing time: children's narrative styles and differential access to literacy. *Language in Society* 10(3), 423–442.

Milk, R., Mercado, C., & Sapiens, A. (1992) *Re-thinking the education of teachers of language-minority children: developing reflective teachers for changing schools.* Available from the National Clearinghouse for Bilingual Education, Washington, DC (ERIC Document Reproduction Service No. ED350877).

Moll, L. & Gonzalez, L. (2004) Engaging life: a funds of knowledge approach to multicultural education. In J. A. Banks & C. A. M. Banks (eds.), *Handbook of research on multicultural education* (2nd ed., pp. 699–715). San Francisco: Jossey-Bass.

National Center for Educational Statistics (1997) *1993–94 Schools and staffing survey: a profile of policies and practices for limited English proficient students: screening methods, program support, and teacher training.* Washington, DC: U.S. Department of Education. Available at http://nces.ed.gov/pubs97/97472.pdf.

National Center for Educational Statistics (1999) *Teacher quality: a report on the preparation and qualifications of public school teachers.* Washington, DC: U.S. Department of Education. Available at http://nces.ed.gov/surveys/frss/publications/1999080/.

National Center for Educational Statistics (2002a) The condition of education 2002. Indicator 3: racial/ethnic distribution of public school students. Washington, DC: U. S. Department of Education. Available at http://nces.ed.gov/pubsearch/pubsinfo.asp?pubid=2002025.

National Center for Educational Statistics (2002b) The condition of education 2002. Indicator 32: educational background of teachers. Washington, DC: U.S. Department of Education. Available at http://nces.ed.gov/pubsearch/pubsinfo.asp?pubid=2002025.

National Center for Educational Statistics (2002c) The condition of education 2002. Contexts of elementary and secondary education. Indicator 33: participation in professional development. Retrieved July 6, 2005 from http://nces.ed.gov/Programs/coe/2002/section4/indicator33.asp.

National Center for Educational Statistics. (2002d). Table 42: percentage distribution of enrollment in public elementary and secondary schools, by race/ethnicity and state: Fall 1986 and Fall 2000. Retrieved July 7, 2005 from http://nces.ed.gov/Programs/digest/d02/dt042.asp.

National Center for Educational Statistics (2003a) The condition of education 2003. Indicator 4: language minority students. Washington, DC: U. S. Department of Education. Available at http://nces.ed.gov/pubsearch/pubsinfo.asp?pubid=2003067.

National Center for Educational Statistics (2003b) The condition of education 2003. Indicator 29: beginning teachers. Washington, DC: U. S. Department of Education. Available at http://nces.ed.gov/pubsearch/pubsinfo.asp?pubid=2003067.

National Center for Educational Statistics (2005) The condition of education 2005. Indicator 5: language minority school-age children. Washington, DC: U.S. Department of Education. Retrieved 7/16/05 at http://nces.ed.gov/programs/coe/2005/section1/indicator05.asp.

Nevárez-la Torre, A. A., Sanford-De Shields, J. S., Soundy, C., Leonard, J., & Woyshner, C. (2005) Faculty perspectives on integrating linguistic diversity issues into a teacher education program. Paper presented at the Annual Meeting of the American Educational Research Assocation, Montreal, Canada.

Nieto, S. (2000) Bringing bilingual education out of the basement, and other imperatives for teacher education. In Z. F. Beykont (ed.), *Lifting every voice: Pedagogy and politics of bilingualism* (pp. 187–207). Cambridge, MA: Harvard Education Publishing Group.

Nieto, S. (2002) *Language, culture, and teaching: critical perspectives for a new century.* Mahwah, NJ: Lawrence Erlbaum.

Nieto, S. & Rolón, C. (1997) Preparation and professional development of teachers: a perspective from two Latinas. In J. J. Irvine (ed.), *Critical knowledge for diverse teachers and learners* (pp. 89–123). Washington, DC: American Association of Colleges for Teacher Education.

Olsen, L. (1997) *Made in America: immigrant students in our public schools.* NY: The New Press.

Palincsar, A. S. (1996) Language-minority students: instructional issues in school cultures and classroom social systems. *The Elementary School Journal*, 96(3), 221–226.

Pappamihiel, N. E. (2002) English as a second language students and English language anxiety: issues in the mainstream classroom. *Research in the Teaching of English*, 36, 327–355.

Penfield, J. (1987) ESL: the regular classroom teacher's perspective. *TESOL Quarterly*, 21(1), 21–39.

Phillips, S. (1972) Participant structures and communicative competence: warm Springs children in community and classroom. In C. Cazden, V. John, and D. Hymes (eds.), *Functions of language in the classroom*, pp. 370–394. New York: Teachers College Press.

Phillips, S. (1983) *The invisible culture: communication in classroom and community on the Warm Springs Indian Reservation.* New York: Longman.

Platt, E. & Troudi, S. (1997) Mary and her teachers: a Grebo-speaking child's place in the mainstream classroom. *The Modern Language Journal*, 81, 28–49.

Price, J. N. & Osborne, M. D. (2000) Challenges of forging a humanizing pedagogy in teacher education. *Curriculum and Teaching*, 15 (1), 27–51.

Rhine, S. (1995) The challenges of effectively preparing teachers of limited-English-proficient students. *Journal of Teacher Education*, 46(5), 381–389 (ERIC Document Reproduction Service No. EJ523838).

Richardson, V. (1996) The role of attitudes and beliefs in learning to teach. In J. Sikula (ed.), *Handbook of research on teacher education, 2nd edition*, pp. 102–119. New York: Macmillan.

Rickford, J. R. & Rickford, R. J. (2000) *Spoken soul: the story of Black English.* New York: John Wiley.

Romaine, S. (1994) *Language in society: an introduction to sociolinguistics.* Oxford: Oxford University Press.

Rumberger, R. W. & Gándara, P. (2004) Seeking equity in the education of California's English learners. *Teachers College Record*, 106(10), 2032–2056.

Sakash, K. & Rodriguez-Brown, F. V. (1995) *Teamworks: mainstream and bilingual/ESL teacher collaboration.* Washington, DC: National Clearinghouse for Bilingual Education.

Shavelson, R. & Towne, L. (2002) *Scientific research in education: report of the National Research Council's Committee on Scientific Principles in Education Research.* Washington, DC: National Academy Press.

Stanton-Salazar, R. D. (2001) *Manufacturing hope and despair: the school and kin support networks of U.S.-Mexican youth.* New York: Teachers College Press.

Steffens, J. E. (1992) Will the LEP train reach its destination? Designing the IHE teacher training program for specific LEP student instructional needs. In: *Focus on evaluation and measurement* (pp. 393–416). Proceedings of the National Research Symposium on Limited English Proficient Student Issues, Washington, DC (ERIC Document Reproduction Service No. ED349832).

Thomas, W. P. & Collier, V. P. (2002) *A national study of school effectiveness for language minority students' long-term academic achievement.* University of California, Santa Cruz: Center for Research on Education, Diversity, and Excellence.

Torok, C. E. & Aguilar, T. E. (2000) Changes in preservice teacher's knowledge and beliefs about language issues. *Equity & Excellence in Education*, 33(2), 24–31 (ERIC Document Reproduction Service No. EJ614021).

Valdés, G. (2001) *Learning and not learning English: Latino students in American schools.* New York: SUNY Press.

Valdés, G., Bunch, G., Snow, C., & Lee, C. (2005) Enhancing the development of students' language(s). In L. Darling-Hammond & J. Bransford (eds.), *Preparing teachers for a changing world: what teachers should learn and be able to do* (pp. 126–168). San Francisco: Jossey-Bass.

Villegas, A. M. (1991) *Culturally responsive teaching for the 1990s and beyond.* Washington, DC: American Association of Colleges for Teacher Education.

Villegas, A. M. & Lucas, T. (2002) *Educating culturally responsive teachers: a coherent approach.* Albany, NY: SUNY Press.

Vygotsky, L. (1978) *Mind in society.* Cambridge: Cambridge University Press.

Walker, C. L., Ranney, S., & Fortune, T. W. (2005) Preparing preservice teachers for English language learners: a content-based approach. In D. J. Tedick (ed.), *Second language teacher education, international perspectives* (pp. 313–333). Mahwah, NJ: Lawrence Erlbaum.

Walker, A., Shafer, J., & Iiams, M. (2004) "Not in my classroom": teacher attitudes towards English language learners in the mainstream classroom. *NABE Journal of Research and Practice,* 2(1), 130–160.

Walqui, A. (2000) *Access and engagement: program design and instructional approaches for immigrant students in secondary school.* Washington, DC: Center for Applied Linguistics.

Wolfram, W., Adger, C. T., & Christian, D. (1999) *Dialects in schools and communities* (Second ed.). Mahwah, NJ: Lawrence Erlbaum.

Wong-Fillmore, L. & Snow, C. (2005) What teachers need to know about language. In C. T. Adger, C. E. Snow, & D. Christian (eds.), *What teachers need to know about language* (pp. 7–54). Washington, DC: Center for Applied Linguistics.

Youngs, C. S. & Youngs, G. A. (2001) Predictors of mainstream teachers' attitudes toward ESL students. *TESOL Quarterly* 35(1), 97–120.

Zehler, A. M., Fleischman, H. L., Hopstock, P. J., Stephenson, T. G., Pendzick, M. L., & Sapru, S. (2003) *Descriptive study of services to LEP students and LEP students with disabilities. Policy report: summary of findings related to LEP and SPED-LEP students.* Washington, DC: U.S. Department of Education.

Zeichner, K. (2005) A research agenda for teacher education. In M. Cochran-Smith & K. Zeichner (eds.), *Studying teacher education: the report of the AERA Panel on Research and Teacher Education* (pp. 737–759). Mahwah, NJ: Lawrence Erlbaum.

Zeichner, K. M. & Melnick, S. (1996) The role of community field experiences in preparing teachers for cultural diversity. In K. Zeichner, S. Melnick, & M. L. Gomez (eds.), *Currents of reform in preservice teacher education* (pp. 176–196). New York: Teachers College Press.

Zetlin, A. G., Macleod, E., & Michener, D. (1998, April). *Professional development of teachers of language minority students through university-school partnership.* Paper presented at the Annual Meeting of the American Educational Research Association, San Diego, CA (ERIC Document Reproduction Service No. ED421877).

Part 5
Artifacts

5.1 Is assimilation dead?

Nathan Glazer

Source: Nathan Glazer, "Is assimilation dead?" *The Annals of the American Academy of Political and Social Sciences*, 530, November 1993, pp. 122–136

Assimilation is not today a popular term. Recently I asked a group of Harvard students taking a class on race and ethnicity in the United States what their attitude to the term "assimilation" was. The large majority had a negative reaction to it. Had I asked what they thought of the term "Americanization," the reaction, I am sure, would have been even more hostile. Indeed, in recent years it has been taken for granted that assimilation, as an expectation of how different ethnic and racial groups would respond to their common presence in one society or as an ideal regarding how the society should evolve or as the expected result of a sober social scientific analysis of the ultimate consequence of the meeting of people and races, is to be rejected. Our ethnic and racial reality, we are told, does not exhibit the effects of assimilation; our social science should not expect it; and as an ideal, it is somewhat disreputable, opposed to the reality of both individual and group difference and to the claims that such differences should be recognized and celebrated.

One might think there is nothing left to say. The idea that it would happen, that it should happen, has simply been discredited, and we live with a new reality. It was once called cultural pluralism, it is now called multiculturalism, and whatever the complications created by the term for educational policy; or for public policy in various other realms, that is what we must live with, and all of us must be ranged along a spectrum of greater or lesser enthusiasm and acceptance of the new reality. Even critics of the new multiculturalism take their place within this spectrum. Those who truly stand against it, the true advocates and prophets of a full assimilationism, are so minuscule in American public and intellectual life that they can scarcely be discerned in public discussion. One can point to the journal *Chronicles* and scarcely anything else. Neither liberals nor neoliberals, conservatives nor neoconservatives, have much good to say about assimilation, and only a branch of paleoconservatism can now be mustered in its defense. It is only they who would agree that even if it has not yet happened, it is something that, despite the reverses of the past thirty years, should have happened and should still happen.

My purpose is not to present a eulogy over a dead hope or demeaning concept. It is rather to argue that properly understood, assimilation is still the most powerful force affecting the ethnic and racial elements of the United States and that our problem in recognizing this has to do with one great failure of assimilation in American life, the incorporation of the Negro, a failure that has led in its turn to a more general counterattack on the ideology of assimilation.

THE HISTORY OF AN IDEA

But to go back: what was assimilation? It was the expectation that a new man would be born, was being born, in the United States. We can go back to that much quoted comment on what was the American, in Crevecoeur's *Letters from an American Farmer* of 1782:

> What then is the American, this new man? He is either a European or the descendant of a

European, hence that strange mixture of blood, which you will find in no other country. I could point out to you a family whose grandfather was an Englishman, whose wife was Dutch, whose son married a French woman, and whose present four sons have four wives of four different nations. *He* is an American, who, leaving behind him all his ancient prejudices and manners, receives new ones from the new mode of life he has embraced, the new government he obeys, and the new rank he holds.[1]

This passage, which Philip Gleason tells us "has probably been quoted more than any other in the history of immigration," has, of course, been generally cited to celebrate American diversity and the general acceptance of this diversity as forming the basis of a new nation, a new national identity, but in 1993 we will look at it with more critical eyes and note what it does not include as well as what it does: there is no reference to Africans, who then made up a fifth of the American population, or to American Indians, who were then still a vivid and meaningful, on occasion menacing, presence in the American world. In this article, I will refer to many other passages that to our contemporary eyes will express a similar surprising unconsciousness, or hypocrisy, or unawareness. Today we would cry out, "There are others there you are not talking about! What about them, and what place will they have in the making of the new American?"

The concept of assimilation looked toward Europe. It referred to the expected experience and fate of the stream of immigrants who were a permanent part of American life and consciousness from the time of the first settlements on the Atlantic seaboard to the 1920s, when it was thought—incorrectly—that we were now done with mass immigration of varied backgrounds to the United States.

There has been a good deal of discussion of a major characteristic of the emerging American national consciousness, or, we would say today, the emerging American identity. That is, that in many authoritative formulations, from the Declaration of Independence on, the American, the new nationality being formed here, is not defined ethnically, as deriving from an ancient common stock or stocks, as almost all other major modern nations define themselves. I may point out as an aside that while the term "identity" is almost essential in any discussion of this emerging American national character, it is a relative latecomer to the discussion. Philip Gleason tells us,

The term "identity" has become indispensable in the discussion of ethnic affairs. Yet it was hardly used at all until the 1950's. The father of the concept, Erik H. Erikson, remarked on its novelty in . . . *Childhood and Society* (1950): "We begin to conceptualize matters of identity . . . in a country which attempts to make a super-identity of all the identities imported by its constituent immigrants." In an autobiographical account published 20 years later, Erikson . . . quoted this passage and added that the terms "identity" and "identity crisis" seemed to grow out of "the experience of emigration, immigration, and Americanization."[2]

Many could be quoted on this surprising characteristic of American identity, its avoidance of explicit ethnic reference. Despite the fact that the American revolution was fought almost exclusively by men who traced their origins to the British Isles, and primarily to England, and that the signers of the Declaration of Independence and the framers of the Constitution were almost exclusively of this stock, they did not define their Americanness as an ethnic characteristic. They emphasized its dependence on adherence to ideals, to universal principles. Perhaps, as Gleason points out, this was because it was necessary for the rebels and revolutionaries to distinguish themselves from the ethnically identical country against which they were rebelling. But in any case, the ideological formulation of the definition of the American was there at the beginning. Years ago I quoted Hans Kohn, Yehoshua Arieli, and S. M. Lipset on this characteristic of American identity.[3] One could add other voices. As Gleason writes,

The ideological quality of American national identity was of decisive importance, vis-à-vis the question of immigration and ethnicity. To become an American, a person did not have to be of any particular national, linguistic, religious, or ethnic background. All he had to do was to commit himself to the political ideology centered on the abstract ideals of liberty, equality, and republicanism. Thus the universalist ideological character of American nationality meant that it was open to anyone who willed to become an American.[4]

As anyone writing in 1980 must be, he is aware of the exclusions, not remarked on by the writers of those early ringing documents, perhaps exclusions of which they were not even aware, the blacks and Indians and, later, groups not in the beginning present in the new United States. Certainly, even if not specifically excluded, they were not intended to be included in these ringing affirmations of universality.

One could find here and there before the 1940s a few voices of significance who seem to make no exclusion. There was Emerson in 1845:

> In this continent-asylum of all nations—the energy of Irish, Germans, Swedes, Poles, and Cossacks, and all the European tribes,—of the Africans, and of the Polynesians,—will construct a new race, a new religion, a new state, a new literature, which will be as vigorous as the new Europe which came out of the smeltingpot of the Dark Ages.[5]

There was Whitman. But one can ask even of Emerson, Did he mean it? What did he know of Polynesians, after all? And one can ask of the term he introduced to characterize the assimilation of the different elements, the "smelting pot," later to achieve fame in this discussion in the form of the "melting pot," Was that not too brutal, too strong, a metaphor for what was to be lost, to disappear, in order to make this new race? The groups were to be more than melted, smelted, as in two or more metals becoming one (the Emerson passage begins with a reference to "Corinthian brass"). But for the moment ignoring the question of whether assimilation was too strong a demand, it is necessary to focus on who was to be assimilated.

FORGETTING THE BLACKS

In almost all the discussion of Americanization or assimilation until about World War II, the discussants had only Europeans in mind. This is true whether they favored or opposed assimilation and Americanization efforts. A reader today of the documents of the great Americanization drive of the second decade of this century will find no reference to blacks, then as now our largest minority. It is as if the turmoil of abolitionism, slavery, the Civil War, Reconstruction did not exist. All concern was with the "new" immigrants, that is, the mass immigration from Eastern and Southern Europe that brought enormous numbers of kinds of Europeans different from those the nation had become accustomed to. Admittedly, one could make the argument that "Americanization," the name of the assimilation movement of the time, could address only those who were not Americans, and were not blacks American-born and formally citizens? So, one could argue, this was the reason they were ignored in the great debate that finally degenerated into a resurgent Ku Klux Klan and the closing of the gates to the new immigrants.

Yet, when one looks at the aims of the Americanization movement, one asks, And why not blacks, too? The aims of the movement, in its earlier, benign form, were to make the newcomers citizens and encourage them to participate as individuals in politics (as against their domination by urban bosses), to teach them English (and here one main argument was to make them better and safer workers, in view of the huge toll of industrial accidents), to break up immigrant colonies ("distribution" it was called), and to teach American customs, which meant primarily sanitation and hygiene. All this would make the immigrants better Americans. One major motivation was concern that the new immigrants would not become good Americans, owing to lack of English, citizenship, and knowledge of American customs. With World War I, to this motivation was added fear of lack of patriotism or disloyalty. But the vigorous advocates of Americanization—social workers and businessmen, a strange mix that nevertheless characterized much of the progressivism of the time—were also trying to plead the case of the new immigrants against the arguments of their countrymen who increasingly favored immigration restriction. The social workers, we know, pled this case out of understanding and sympathy for the new immigrants; the businessmen, we may assume, out of self-interest, much as the *Wall Street Journal* of today argues for free immigration. But if these were the aims of the Americanization movement, why were not the blacks included?

Their exclusion is even more striking to the current reader in view of the language of the time, in which ethnic groups are referred to as "races"—but the first group that comes to mind when we speak of "race" today is not in the minds of these earnest and energetic advocates of assimilation and Americanization.

Consider one of the most authoritative statements of what was hoped for from Americanization, from Frances Kellor, a progressive woman social worker who was the heart and soul of the movement, indefatigably organizing committees, conventions, statements, programs:

> Americanization is the science of racial relations in America, dealing with the assimilation and amalgamation of diverse races in equity into an integral part of the national life. By "assimilation" is meant the indistinguishable incorporation of the races into the substance of American life. By "amalgamation" is meant so perfect a blend that the absence or imperfection of any of the vital racial elements available, will impair the compound. By "an integral part" is meant that, once fused, separation of units is thereafter impossible. By "inequity" is meant impartiality among the races accepted into the blend with no imputations of inferiority and no bestowed favors.[6]

This is a late statement, made when the movement was taking on a harsher tone, and rather stronger than we would find from most advocates of Americanization, in particular in the emphasis on "amalgamation," which can only mean intermarriage to the point of the indistinguishability of any distinct group. My concern here, however, is with the remarkable absence of the blacks, despite the continual emphasis on the word "race."

One of the early climaxes of the movement was a great meeting in Philadelphia, on 10 May 1915. Woodrow Wilson addressed a huge throng—5,000 newly naturalized citizens, 8,000 previously naturalized, a chorus of 5,000 voices, and the like. He does not use the term "race" in his paean to the all-inclusiveness of America, but all races are clearly implied in his term "the people of the world":

> This is the only country in the world which experiences this constant and repeated rebirth. Other countries depend upon the multiplication of their own native people. This country is constantly drinking strength out of new sources by the voluntary association with it of great bodies of strong men and forward-looking women out of other lands . . . It is as if humanity had determined to see to it that this great Nation, founded for the benefit of humankind, should not lack for the allegiance of the people of the world.[7]

But we might again ask, Where were the blacks? Clearly, Wilson did not have them in mind.

This great meeting was the prelude to Americanization Day on 4 July 1915, when many meetings to welcome new citizens were held all over the country. One of them was in Faneuil Hall in Boston, addressed by Justice Louis Brandeis. He asserted that what was distinctly American was "inclusive brotherhood." America, as against other nations, "has always declared herself for equality of nationalities as well as for equality of individuals. It recognizes racial equality as an essential of full human liberty and true brotherhood. . . . It has, therefore, given like welcome to all the peoples of Europe."[8] He did not seem to have blacks in mind.

Most ironically, we find that one of the most active of the postwar Americanization groups was the Inter-Racial Council. We know what the name of the council would mean had it been used 20 years later. But in 1919 it struck no one as odd, apparently, that it did not refer to blacks and that it did not include blacks. Among a host of names of leading businessmen and bankers and political dignitaries we find some prominent immigrant names—Dr. Antonio Stella, M. 1. Pupin, Gutzon Borglum, Jacob Schiff—but none belonging to blacks.[9]

As the Americanization movement began to shift from one befriending the immigrant, bringing him closer together to Americans, to one that seemed increasingly hostile, in which the generous offer of citizenship and full participation became the compulsory demand that the immigrant must learn the English language and American government, the Carnegie Corporation, trying to defend the earlier openness toward the immigrant, in the spirit of Jane Addams and Lillian Wald, sponsored a series of Americanization studies. Once again the language will surprise in its unconsciousness of the fact that "race" might include other than Europeans. In James A. Gavit's *Americans by Choice* on the issue of naturalization, we find again the argument with which we are familiar: that the American is not defined ethnically but by allegiance to an ideology. "The American Has No Racial Marks," one subtitle asserts. The text continues,

> This absence of exclusive racial marks is the distinguishing physical characteristic of the American. True of him as of no other now or ever in the past is the fact that he is, broadly speaking, the product of *all* races . . .
>
> We are in the midst of the making of the "American." He does not yet appear what he shall be but one thing is certain, he is not to be of any particular racial type now distinguishable. Saxon, Teuton, Kelt, Latin and Slav—to say nothing of any appreciable contribution by yellow and brown races as yet negligible . . .—each of the races that we now know on this soil will have its share of "ancestorial" responsibility for the "typical American" that is to be.

The next heading reads, "Not Racial, But Cultural."[10]

Dealing as he does with naturalization, Gavit cannot, as more celebratory advocates of Americanization can, totally ignore the racial aspect: naturalization was racially limited. He does write:

> It is not yet true—perhaps it will be very long before it can be true—that there is absolutely no bar to any person on account of race; for the law and its interpretations exclude from citizenship Chinese, Japanese, and certain people of India not regarded as "white"—although the blacks of Africa are expressly admitted. Nevertheless, it may be said broadly that regardless of race, the immigrant can come to America and win his way upon his own merits into the fellowship all the world calls "Americans."[11]

As we know, the Americanization movement lost its aspect of welcome and inclusion in the midst of the passions aroused by World War I and the postwar fear of Bolshevism and radicalism. It turned into something harsh and oppressive, in which the issue became less the opportunity to learn English than the insistence that nothing but English be learned; less the generous offer of citizenship than the widespread fear of subversion from aliens and naturalized citizens. Americanization developed a bad name among liberals. Insofar as there was still concern for the living and working conditions of immigrants, this became encompassed in a larger liberal movement for improving the conditions of working men, a movement that was easily capable of reconciling commitment to the cause of working people with opposition to further immigration. If the word "assimilation" now makes us suspicious, and "Americanization" even more so, among the older and more knowing it may be because of the excesses of the 1920s.

"Americanization" is no longer to be found in encyclopedias of the social sciences,[12] but it does appear in the first great *Encyclopedia of the Social Sciences* of 1930, and the comment we find there on the fate of Americanization will to some extent explain to us why we do not hear much about it today:

> This emphasis on the learning of English and naturalization, together with the unfortunate atmosphere of coercion and condescension in which so many war time Americanization efforts were conceived, had the effect of bringing the word into a disrepute from which it has never fully recovered. Contributing to the same result, in the period following the war, were the widely expressed fear and suspicion of the immigrant, his frequent indictment as a radical, attempts to suppress his newspapers and organizations, the ignoring of his own culture and aspirations, the charge that certain nationalities and races were inferior and unassimilable, and the use of intimidating slogans. Americanization work too frequently made the assumption that American culture was something already complete which the newcomer must adopt in its entirety. Such attitudes and activities were important factors in promoting restriction of immigration, but they did not advance the assimilation of the immigrants who were already in America.[13]

THE LIMITED VISION OF CULTURAL PLURALISM

But the point of this recital of the history of Americanization is not to add to the extensive literature that explores the neglect of and ignoring of the key question of the treatment of blacks in American society, nor to argue—although it is true—that immigrants were better treated and taken more seriously from the point of view of their inclusion in American society, nor to attack the Americanization movement for its excesses—all legitimate responses to it. It is to set the stage for something that has also received little attention: that the critics of Americanization and assimilation had little to say about blacks. However passionate in their defense of the contribution to American economy, culture, and politics of immigrants and immigrant groups, however strong in their resistance to the demand for assimilation, whatever arguments they raised in resistance to the expectation of assimilation, the critics—let us call them for convenience the "cultural pluralists," for it was they who raised the strongest objections—had little to say, indeed nothing to say, about adding blacks to the series of groups who they felt had every right to maintain their separate identity. Maybe they believed blacks should; maybe they never thought of them: they just never entered them into the argument.

There were, of course, critics of Americanization. There were fewer during its earlier, more benign form; more when it evolved under the pressures of war into an attack on "hyphenated Americanism," led by former President Theodore Roosevelt; more when it further evolved into the repression of the postwar years, through laws restricting aliens and imposing English, through administrative actions expelling aliens, through waves of public opinion against further mass immigration from Europe, and into the mass hysteria of the Ku Klux Klan and similar organizations. But those few voices of cultural pluralism that were then raised, and that we have in recent decades disinterred, had almost nothing to say about blacks in their celebration of a possible "Transnational America," as in Randolph Bourne's phrase, in their attack on the critics of "hyphenated Americanism," in their insistence that each group, each "race," in the language of the time, had an inherent genius or character that should not be suppressed but allowed to flower, as in the argument of Horace Kallen. We search this modest literature in vain for any reference to black Americans.

Thus, when John Dewey spoke to the National Education Association in 1916 to defend the value of cultural pluralism, he did not seem to have blacks in mind. Of course, he was speaking in the context of an attack on the loyalty of Europeans. Nevertheless, one would have thought that America's largest minority might have entered into the discussion. Many groups were mentioned in his talk:

> Such terms as Irish-American or Hebrew-American or German-American are false terms, because they seem to imply something which is already in existence called America, to which the other factors may be hitched on. The fact is, the genuine American, the typical American, is himself a hyphenated character. It does not mean he is part American and some foreign ingredient is added. It .means that . . . he is international and interracial in his make-up. He is not American plus Pole or German. But the American is himself Pole-German-English-French-Spanish-Italian-Greek-Irish-Scandinavian-Bohemian-Jew-and so on.[14]

One searches Horace Kallen's *Culture and Democracy in the United States*, the fullest statement of the cultural-pluralist view of the time, almost in vain for any reference to blacks. They cannot be fully escaped: after all, the introductory chapter is titled "Culture and the Ku Klux Klan," and Negroes are listed as among its targets. There are two other slightly fuller references. In speaking of the spirit of Know-Nothingism, he writes,

> What differs from ourselves we spontaneously set upon a different level of value. If it seems to be strong it is called wicked and is feared; if it is regarded as weak, it is called brutish and exploited. Sometimes, as in the attitude toward the negro [sic], the emotions interpenetrate and become a sentiment focalizing the worst qualities of each.

There is one more reference. Kallen is concerned in this passage with whether the current hysteria will wane, the integration of immigrants into American life under a liberal regime will continue (here "integration" clearly does "not mean "assimilation"). But it may not happen. The immigrant may be fixed in the inferior economic position he now holds: "One need only cast an eye over the negro-white relations in the South to realize the limit that such a condition would, unchecked, engender."[15] Perhaps it is reading too much into very little, but one detects in this passage no expectation that there will be much change in this condition.

The significance of this episode in the history of American thinking about race and ethnicity is that the argument over assimilation and Americanization evoked by the mass immigration of the period 1880–1924 and by the pressures of World War I simply did not take blacks, let alone Mexican Americans or Asians, into account.

Thus the evolution of the argument did not take account of the groups that came in time to stand for both American minorities and immigrants. After World War II, Europeans did not stand for either. Discrimination against European groups declined rapidly after World War II. Thus they began to lose their status as minorities. Immigration, when it recovered after World War II, encompassed a rather modest stream of Europeans. When it grew, after 1965, into a volume rivaling that of earlier periods of mass immigration, it included very few Europeans: it became an immigration predominantly of Asians of varying nations, of Latin Americans of many nations, of Caribbean blacks of many nations. The European component was reduced to a small fraction.

Now blacks and others had to be included in the discussion. As something like cultural pluralism began to raise its head again with the coming of Hitler and the fear of a future war, the growing concern was no longer with European immigrants alone, as it was in the buildup to World War I. Americans generally and security agencies specifically were concerned about German American adherents of Nazism, with Italian adherents of Italian Fascism—many fewer than Nazi adherents—and most with Japanese Americans, who were the only group to be affected by a

World War I-style hysteria. There was, then, a reprise to some extent of World War I concern with immigrant loyalty. Indeed, we even had a revival of something like the Americanization Day spectacles of the earlier period in the creation and brief history of "I Am an American Day." But the tone of the new movement was different in some key respects.

First, mass immigration had come to an end, and no one expected it to revive, whatever the needs of persecuted Jews and other groups harried by the Nazis. Perhaps this explains a greater degree of benignity.

But second, blacks and Hispanics and Asians were now definitely part of the story. Because we were fighting Hitler and his ideology of racial superiority, we had to take into account our own groups of racially defined second-class citizens, all suffering under a weight of legal as well as informal segregation, discrimination, and prejudice. Cultural pluralism, which had been in World War I and its aftermath only the evanescent hope of a few philosophers and journalists, became a sturdy growth, under a new name, intercultural education. The focus began to shift, from European immigrant groups to minorities of color. European immigrant groups were already well on the way to assimilation. In addition, Hitler had antagonized so many of them that disloyalty did not seem the great problem it had appeared in World War I; suspicion touched only the Japanese. And in fighting the ideology of race—physical race, biological race—how could we not be concerned with how we treated our racial minorities?

What was to be the fate of assimilation in this new dispensation? Whatever the new degree of tolerance for diversity, it was generally expected that assimilation would continue. Intercultural education was a far cry from a full-bodied cultural pluralism and presented no resistance to assimilation. It stood for tolerance, not for the maintenance of cultural difference and identity. Indeed, even if the term was not used, assimilation was what the advocates for our largest and most oppressed minority also wanted.[16]

WAS ASSIMILATION INEVITABLE?

The term "assimilation" was a key concept in the thinking of our most important sociologist of race and ethnicity, Robert E. Park, founder of the school of sociology at the University of Chicago, which went deeply into questions of race and ethnicity. Park and his colleagues had participated in the Carnegie Americanization studies I have referred to. Opponents of forceful Americanization, they nevertheless believed social trends were bringing an inevitable assimilation. They did not decry this; rather, they felt that this was the unavoidable result in time of the meeting of peoples. Park saw that the great problem in the way of assimilation was the blacks.

His 1930 article on assimilation in the *Encyclopedia of the Social Sciences* perceptively points to this as the stumbling block in the way of assimilation:

> In a vast, varied and cosmopolitan society such as exists in America, the chief obstacle to assimilation seems to be not cultural differences but physical traits . . . The Negro, during his three hundred years in this country, has not been assimilated. This is not because he has preserved in America a foreign culture and alien tradition . . . no man is so entirely native to the soil . . . To say the Negro is not assimilated means no more than to say that he is still regarded in some sense a stranger, a representative of an alien race. . . . This distinction which sets him apart from the rest of the population is real, but is not based upon cultural traits but upon physical and racial characteristics."

As for Europeans: "The ease and rapidity with which aliens have been able to take over American customs and manners have enabled the United States to digest every sort of normal human difference, with the exception of the purely external ones like that of the color of the skin."[17]

Park saw the key problem. Of course, he was not alone. Black intellectuals and leaders also saw where they stood. They were not even participants in the debate over assimilation and Americanization. Nevertheless, they strove for assimilation, or, rather, for the rights that they assumed would lead to assimilation. American liberals generally, supporters of black aims, saw no argument against assimilation in principle, for all groups. Park had set forth a scheme, which became quite influential in sociology, in which groups in contact moved through various phases, such as conflict and accommodation, ending in assimilation. Fifteen years ago, pondering the rise then of an earlier phase of multiculturalism, I noted this assimilationist stance of both sociologists who studied race and ethnicity and black scholars and leaders.

Park and his leading students, I pointed out, while they did not put forth their preferences sharply, assumed assimilation was not only inevitable but would be all for the best. Thus

> Louis Wirth, who was the chief successor to Park, made clear in *The Ghetto* that his preference was for assimilation: the Jew continued to exist only because of prejudice and discrimination; all the reactions of the Jew to this antagonism were humanly limiting; and assimilation, which to be sure required lowering the barriers to assimilation, was the desirable end result of the interaction of Jews and non-Jews in contemporary society.
>
> The major works of E. Franklin Frazier on the black family went in the same direction. Insofar as the black family was stable and puritanical it was good-that was unquestioned. There was no hint, or scarcely any, that any distinctive cultural feature should survive as specifically Negro or black, or that there should be any effort to seek for such features.
>
> This was not cultural arrogance or imperialism; instead, it was the point of view of the best-informed, most liberal, and most sympathetic analysts of the ethnic and racial scene. Assimilation was a desirable consequence of the reduction of prejudice and discrimination, while acculturation, that is, becoming more like the majority, would contribute to the reduction of discrimination and prejudice. This was the dominant liberal view until at least the 1950's.
>
> It was also the view, insofar as a view could be discerned, of the representatives of racial and ethnic groups. The NAACP and the Urban League were clearly "assimilationist." Although it was clear that blacks could never because of race be indistinguishable from whites, it was desirable that they become culturally, socially, economically, and politically assimilated, that they be simply Americans with dark skins. All public agencies, including the government and the schools, and all private agencies that affected individual circumstances, including banks, businesses, housing producers, and landlords, were to be "color blind." In the 1950's the only legitimate form of differentiation proposed for American life was religious . . .
>
> Admittedly, in each group there were the maintainers and upholders of the ethnic conscience and consciousness, including schools, churches, philanthropic and civic organizations, networks of insurance societies, and social groups, but except by those whose direct interest was in maintaining them and the jobs they offered, these were regarded as survivals, fated to fall away as acculturation and assimilation progressed.
>
> Acculturation and assimilation, if not the cruder "Americanization," were thus not simply the positions of the old Americans who were antagonistic to new immigrants and non-white races; they were also the positions of those who were most sympathetic to these groups and who understood them best, and even of the representatives of these groups.[18]

Of course, as we know, we are now very far from all this. The voices of opposition to integration burst out in the late 1960s and have gone through many permutations since. Bland intercultural education has succumbed to the rather more forceful multicultural education-though that too comes in all brands, from the mildest recognition of differences to a rather hysterical and irrational

Afrocentrism. We even had, in the late 1960s and 1970s, a brief explosion of revived ethnic assertiveness among white European ethnic groups, the heirs of the immigrants of the early decades of the century. It could not survive; assimilation had gone too far. We have a few modest programs in Italian American studies, and a sturdier growth of Jewish programs, which are able to draw not only on ethnic attachments that tend to be stronger than that for most white Europeans but also on religion, which creates a firmer body of institutions to parallel the purely ethnic and which has greater prestige and receives more tolerance in the American setting.

We come now to our question: is assimilation then dead? The word may be dead, the concept may be disreputable, but the reality continues to flourish. As so many observers in the past have noted, assimilation in the United States is not dependent on public ideology, on school curricula, on public approbation; factors in social and economic and cultural life foster it, and it proceeds apace. Read Lewis was right when, in his article on Americanization in the *Encyclopedia of the Social Sciences*, now more than sixty years old, he wrote:

> Important as these conscious efforts are toward Americanization, they represent only a part of the social forces which play continuously upon the immigrant and determine the degree and rapidity of his assimilation. A conspicuous force which makes for adjustment is the urge to material success, which makes the immigrant adapt himself to American ways of work and business. This usually involves learning the English language as quickly as possible. Standardizing forces such as national advertisements, ten-cent store products, movies, radio and the tabloid press play also upon the immigrant.[19]

Correct for inflation, add television, baseball, football, basketball, and so on, and it is clear that the forces pressing assimilation have not lost power.

Call it "acculturation" if you will. But assimilation in its least deniable and strongest form, what was once called "amalgamation," also proceeds apace. The rates of intermarriage among all European ethnic groups is very high.[20] Even Jews, with their bar against intermarriage posed by religion, and who maintained a rather low rate of intermarriage through the 1940s, now show the very high rates at which individuals commonly marry outside their ethnic group, however defined. With these high rates in the postwar period, it is hardly clear what one's ethnic group is and how it is to be defined. Mary Waters, in *Ethnic Options*, shows how thin any sense of ethnicity among Americans of European origin has become.[21] But there is the great exception.

SEPARATENESS

If intermarriage is taken as key evidence for powerful assimilatory forces, then blacks are not subject to these forces to the same degree as others. Hispanic groups and Asian groups, despite the recency of the immigration of so many of them, and thus the greater power of family and group attachment, show rates of intermarriage approaching the levels of Europeans. Blacks stand apart, with very low rates of intermarriage, rising slowly. They stand apart, too, in the degree of residential segregation.[22] Thirty years of effort, public and private, assisted by antidiscrimination law and a substantial rise in black earnings, have made little impact on this pattern.

This is not the place to explain all this, but the apartness is real. And it is this that feeds multiculturalism. For one group, assimilation, by some key measures, has certainly failed. For others, multicultural education may be a matter of sentiment. But most black children do attend black-majority schools. Most live in black neighborhoods. Why should not multiculturalism, in the form of the examination of group history, characteristics, problems, become compelling as one way of understanding one's situation, perhaps overcoming it? The large statements of an American national ideal of inclusion, of assimilation, understandably ring false.

For Hispanics and Asian Americans, marked in varying degree by race, it is in large measure a matter of choice, their choice, just how they will define their place in American society. We see elements in these groups who, in their support of bilingual education and other foreign-language rights, want to establish or preserve an institutional base for a separate identity that may maintain some resistance to the forces of assimilation. For blacks, too, there are choices—we see the existence of choices in the writings of black intellectuals who oppose the stronger tendencies of multiculturalism. But the difference that separates blacks from whites, and even from other groups "of color" that have a history of discrimination and prejudice in this country, is not to be denied. It is this that is the most powerful force arguing for multiculturalism and for resistance to the assimilatory trend of American culture and of American society.

NOTES

1 Michel Guillaume Jean de Crevecoeur, *Letters from an American Farmer*, as quoted in Philip Gleason, "American Identity and Americanization," in *Harvard Encyclopedia of American Ethnic Groups* (Cambridge, MA: Harvard University Press, 1980), p. 33.
2 Gleason, "American Identity," p. 31.
3 Nathan Glazer, *Affirmative Discrimination* (New York: Basic Books, 1975).
4 Gleason, "American Identity," p. 32.
5 Harold J. Abramson, "Assimilation and Pluralism," in *Harvard Encyclopedia of American Ethnic Groups*, p. 152.
6 Frances A. Kellor, "What is Americanization?" *Yale Review* (Jan. 1919), as reprinted in Philip Davis, *Immigration and Americanization: Selected Readings* (Boston: Ginn, 1920), pp. 625–626.
7 Davis, *Immigration and Americanization*, p. 612; for a description of the meeting, see Edward George Hartman, *The Movement to Americanize the Immigrant* (New York: AMS Press, 1967), p. 11 n.
8 Davis, *Immigration and Americanization*, pp. 642–643.
9 Hartman, *Movement to Americanize the Immigrant*, pp. 220–221.
10 James A. Gavit, *Americans by Choice* (New York: Harper, 1922), pp. 10, 11–12.
11 Ibid., pp. 7–8.
12 Nor can we find what was once a key sociological concept, "assimilation, n among the entries in the recent four-volume *Encyclopedia of Sociology* by C. F. Borgatta and M. L. Borgatta (New York: Macmillan, 1992).
13 Read Lewis, "Americanization," in *Encyclopedia of the Social Sciences* (New York: Macmillan, 1930), 2:33.
14 John Dewey, as quoted in Horace M. Kallen, *Culture and Democracy in the United States* (New York: Boni Liveright, 1924), pp. 131–132.
15 Kallen, pp. 127, 165.
16 For a characterization of the movement, see Nathan Glazer, *Ethnic Dilemmas, 1964–1982* (Cambridge, MA: Harvard University Press, 1983), pp. 104–108.
17 Robert E. Park, "Assimilation," in *Encyclopedia of the Social Sciences*, 2: 282.
18 Glazer, *Ethnic Dilemmas*, pp. 100–101.
19 Lewis, "Americanization," p. 34.
20 Stanley Lieberson and Mary Waters, *From Many Strands: Ethnic and Radical Groups in Contemporary America* (New York: Russell Sage Foundation, 1988).
21 *Ethnic Options* (Berkeley: University of California Press, 1990).
22 Douglas S. Massey and Nancy A. Denton, *American Apartheid* (Cambridge, MA: Harvard University Press, 1993).

5.2 Impact of the 1954 *Brown v. Topeka Board of Education* decision on Black educators

Samuel B. Ethridge

Source: Samuel B. Ethridge, "Impact of the 1954 *Brown v. Topeka Board of Education* decision on Black educators," *The Negro Educational Review*, 30(4), 1979, pp. 217–232

The impact of the 1954 Supreme Court Decision on education on the employment of Black professionals for the first eleven years was absolutely devastating. In spite of a series of improvements, both in the laws and in enforcement efforts, the fallout from those devastating years (1954–1965) is being compounded alarmingly each year in the seventeen states covered by Brown.

In my opinion, there is a five-fold reason for this. First, the Judges had before them the question of inferior schools. (Subconsciously, this meant inferior teachers). Second, at that time judges were reluctant to invade the domain of the school boards and respected even their right to make errors in administration. Third, since the previous decisions in the field were against colleges and universities that had carried out Court orders, even though with great reluctance, the Court had no experience with the kind of massive resistance which the Decision would engender at the elementary and secondary levels. The fourth reason for the Decision's devastating effects on teachers and students, as well, was the lack of information on the result of the orders. Fifth, the 1954 Decision was not really an education decision. It was the first in a long series of civil rights cases. I will treat each of these reasons separately.

PSYCHOLOGICAL ATTITUDES OF WHITES AND SOME BLACKS

The unconscious psychological attitudes of the lawyers, the judges and the expert witnesses did not take into account either the rights of students to an integrated staff or their right to non-racist texts and curriculum.

The language of the Decision, as well as the sociological evidence put before the Court, set the stage for twenty-five years of sacrifice on the part of Black educators in the South.

"Schools separated by race are inherently unequal,"[1] translated by the average every day school board member, means "Black schools, no matter how good, no matter how well trained their faculties, are unequal."

One of the questions asked by lawyers for the students was, "If two schools were in separate parts of town with teachers of equal experience and equal degrees, with equal facilities, could the Black students receive an equal education?"

The reply from the witness was, "No, the other neighborhood has better houses and a better surrounding. Therefore, they could not receive an equal education."[2]

At a national conference of Black teachers, one of the chief expert witnesses in the case told the audience, "If Black children have not learned, it is because Black teachers have not taught them and because Black principals have not seen that they were taught." His solution was that the Black[3] principals should be replaced by white principals who will see that they learn.

This kind of thinking set the stage for unceremonious dismantling of hundreds of Dunbars, Booker T. Washingtons, Lincolns, Phyllis Wheatleys, and Maggie Walkers around the South.

In 1965, a task force survey by the National Education Association concluded the following:

> It is clear, that in the past, Negro teachers were employed specifically and exclusively for the purpose of teaching Negro pupils in segregated schools. Segregated schools required segregated faculties. Since Negro teachers were employed to teach Negro pupils, there were relatively few positions for Negro teachers in a school system with few classes for Negroes. In a system with no classes for Negroes, there were simply no positions for Negro teachers. It has been, and still is, widely assumed by many school board members that Negroes, both students and teachers, are intellectually inferior. From this specious premise, it follows that "quality education" can be obtained only when schools, even after being integrated, remain in spirit and often in name "white schools." White schools are viewed as having no place for Negro teachers.

The emphasis of these early suits on specific students and specific schools rather than on state systems and school districts revealed that both lawyers and judges had a lot to learn before the real intent of the Brown Decision could be implemented.[4]

In the eleven southern states, from 1954 to 1965, little integration of faculties took place in the vast majority of school districts. The border states of Oklahoma, Missouri, Kentucky, West Virginia, Maryland and Delaware, having few district concentrations of Black students, found it relatively easy to close most of the Black schools and send the children to the schools nearest to their homes. This resulted in the dismissal of more than 6,000 teachers and more than 50 percent of the Black principals between 1954 and 1965.[5]

RELUCTANT JUDGES AND LAWYERS

In 1954, in Mobley, Missouri, fourteen fully certified Black educators, including one with a doctorate degree, were dismissed. All 125 white educators remained, including those white teachers who had only provisional certificates. The judge in the case ruled that the Mobley Board of Education had the "right to make that decision" even though he personally felt that it was the wrong thing to do.[6]

For ten long years, all cases involving Black educators charging discrimination were dismissed on the basis of the Mobley Decision.

In 1964, a similar incident occurred in Giles County, Virginia.[7] The Virginia Teachers Association, headed by J. Rupert Picott, with the support of the NEA, brought suit against the County on behalf of all seven Black educators who were dismissed when the one Black school in the County was closed and the students sent to the school nearest their homes. Fortunately for the case, Giles County had experienced a number of school closings due to the school consolidation movement.

The judge put aside all of the testimony about the certification and excellent ratings of the Black teachers, waived aside the fact that the system had hired seven more white teachers than it needed the previous year, and ruled that the letter of dismissal indicating that the teachers and the principal were no longer needed because their school was closed was, in itself, discriminatory. He stated that teachers are hired *by* and work *for* the school *system*, not for a *school*, and that they should have been reassigned as had been the custom of the system in other school consolidation cases.

The case was appealed and upheld, and thus became the first in a series of cases that began to protect Black teachers against discriminatory dismissals. From this point, the legal emphasis began to shift to systems rather than to school and individuals.

When the Civil Rights Act was passed, Black teachers rejoiced because we thought that at last we were protected. To our disappointment and chagrin, the original Guidelines for Desegregation of Schools (1966) contained no mention of teacher desegregation or the hiring, dismissal, or promotion of teachers. To add insult to injury, a young lawyer for HEW, in explaining the Guidelines, was quoted in the *Washington Post* as having said, "In a war there must be some casualties, and perhaps the Black teachers will be the casualties in the fight for equal education of Black students."[8]

As a participant in the 1967 conference to revise the HEW Guidelines, I had a single purpose: To convince David Seeley and his staff, and the HEW lawyers, that the 1954 Decision and the 1964 Civil Rights Act did not cancel the Bill of Rights or the 13th, 14th, and 15th Amendments for Black educators. It was no coincidence that the revised guidelines contained some language directly from the NEA Professional Rights and Responsibilities Commission position papers on the retention of teachers:

"Race shall not be a factor in the hiring, firing, promotion or demotion of staff."[9]

The Guidelines required that all teachers be considered for dismissal in case of surplus teachers and that dismissed teachers be recalled before new teachers be added.

The revised Guidelines, combined with less reluctance by the judges to intervene in staff decisions, began to slow the tide of mass dismissals.

In the Montgomery County, Alabama case, the judge agreed with attorneys that one should not be able to look at a faculty and decide for what race the school was meant. He ordered that the faculty in each school should represent within ten percent the ratio of Black to white teachers in the County. No school could have less than ten percent Black teachers and no school could have more than thirty percent of Black teachers in order to reflect the two-to-eight ratio.[10]

In my opinion, the Decision after Mobley which had had the most impact on the employment of Black professionals is *Singleton v. Jackson Municipal District.*"[11] It is basically a decision for good, but it has been interpreted in ways which have reduced or limited the number of Black educators in small districts where white students have withdrawn and in large cities, like New Orleans and Memphis, where the Black population is increasing. It states that staff members who work directly with children, and professional staff who work on the administrative level, will be hired, assigned, promoted, paid, demoted, dismissed, or otherwise treated without regard to race, color, or national origin, and that the district shall assign staff so that the ratio of Negro to white teachers in each school and the ratio of other staff are substantially the same as each such ratio is to the teachers and other staff in the entire school system. The decision is troublesome primarily because of misuse and misinterpretation.

WITH ALL DELIBERATE SPEED

I think that the judges made a tactical error in that they misjudged the mood of school people when they issued a statement in 1955 indicating that systems need not comply forthwith, but indicated that they could proceed with "All Deliberate Speed."[12] My own system, and many other systems, had their maps drawn assigning students to the nearest school. They were waiting for the Court to say "Go."

Most school central office staffs were tired of the dual school system which meant two principals' meetings, two PTA Council meetings, two teachers' meetings, two curriculum council meetings, two textbook committee meetings, etc., etc., etc. They secretly welcomed the 1954 Decision for physical reasons.

After the 1954 Decision, the maps disappeared and many of the dual meetings were restored. By this time, the politicians, governors, senators, and congressmen got into the act, and no superintendent who wanted to work was going to integrate schools in the face of this kind of pressure, Court or no Court, and the move to suburbia was on. (The neighborhood patterns in the South in 1954 made desegregation without busing a very simple matter.)

One problem with desegregation is that by and large many of the same people who were in charge in 1954 are still in charge—"The foxes are in charge of the chickens."[13] So devastation of Black teachers continues in the South in spite of the Guidelines and in spite of the Court Decisions. The foxes have learned how to hide their displacements. They know that they can't overtly discriminate; so they have new ways of displacement.

Black teachers who retired or moved away were either not replaced or replaced by whites. Standardized tests, such as NTE and GRE, were used to evaluate teachers or screen out teachers. Responding to the court requirement that objective criteria be used in dismissing Black teachers under a desegregation order, West Feliciana Parish, Louisiana[14] utilized a form of NTE to dismiss twenty-nine teachers. An injunction was secured by LEA and NEA to prevent their dismissal.[15] In Columbus, Mississippi, ten teachers were dismissed on the basis of NTE scores. The teachers were ordered reinstated with over $100,000 in back pay and legal fees.

Fewer and fewer Black recruits are able to find teaching positions in either rural or city systems in the South. Many tenured Black teachers have been placed in federal programs with contracts that indicate their rehiring is dependent on refunding. Some Black teachers are placed out of their fields so that their dismissal can be justified on the basis of poor performance.

NO MONITORING AND LACK OF INFORMATION

The lack of effective data collection throughout the first fourteen years of desegregation will prevent the true impact of the Brown Decision on Black educators from ever being really known.

Soon after I arrived at NEA in 1964, I heard rumors that large numbers of Black teachers had lost their jobs in Oklahoma and Missouri, and perhaps a few other places, on the basis of desegregation. We also received a number of requests from Black teachers associations in the South asking that the NEA establish programs to prevent such mass dismissals when the expected desegregation came to the eleven Deep South states as a result of implementation of the Civil Rights Act of 1964.

On the basis of this sketchy information, I approached the powers that be in the NEA and requested that programs be instituted. I received a series of questions which I shall never forget. "Where?" "How many?" "What is your source?" "Can't be documented?" "Why can't their place-ment offices in their Alma Maters find them new positions?"

I assumed that this would be a relatively easy task. I would check with the Department of Education in each state, and it would be a simple matter of computation. I was to receive another rude awakening.

The Departments of Education in the seventeen southern states allegedly stopped keeping school statistics by race after 1954. Thus, it became almost impossible to find out comparative official racial employment figures between 1954 and 1964. The only reliable source of racial data on either faculty or students in the seventeen southern states for the period in question was the Ford Foundation-supported Nashville-based Southern Education Reporting Service. From SERS files we were able to document that approximately 3,000 Black educators had lost their jobs in Oklahoma, Missouri, Kentucky, West Virginia, Maryland and Delaware from 1954 to 1964.[16] Even though the actual number of Black educators was believed to be much higher, these statistics gave the first credibility to our predictions that many more Black educators might lose their jobs unless HEW and the Courts made special efforts to prevent a rerun of the saga of the border states.

A reporter from one of the major daily newspapers got wind of my concerns and predictions, and in the resulting interview pushed me for a figure. "How many people will lose their jobs?" "I don't know!" "But what is your best guess?" "5,500 over a period of several years" was my reply, even though I believed strongly that it would be much higher. (But it is my style to err on the side of understatement rather than overstatement.) The 5,500 figure was big enough to capture the imagination of the press and the Civil Rights activists. Soon the 5,500 figure became gospel rather than an educated guess of one person who was willing to express an opinion on the matter.[17]

The first hard data on the subject was gathered by an NEA Task Force survey on Teacher Displacement, under a grant from HEW.[18]

Directed by Robert Cousins, coordinated for HEW by Allan Lesser, and coordinated by the author for NEA, the task force of twenty-five researchers and scholars documented through personal interview and inventory 668 cases of displacement of Black educators for the year 1965 alone. Thus, the Congress saw the need for such data. By 1970, the Office of Civil Rights of HEW started to develop nationwide reliable comprehensive racial data by school, district and state.

When these raw data were released in 1972, Don Shire, Boyd Bosma, and I did an analysis of the data and developed comparative losses based on the projected number of teaching positions that would have been available to Black teachers had the schools remained segregated.

At the NAACP Legal Defense Fund workshop, May 19, 1972, the nation was shocked when we announced that 31,584 teaching positions had been lost by Black teachers in the seventeen southern states by 1970, as a result of desegregation.[19]

Based on the average salary for each state, we computed the loss in income to the Black community in those seventeen states for 1970–71 alone as $240,564,911.00, nearly a quarter of a billion dollars. The cumulative amount is staggering to the imagination.

Two years later, this displacement factor had increased to 39,386 in those states (see Table A5.1). The Black student population in the South had increased from twenty-one percent to twenty-three percent, while the Black teacher population had decreased from nineteen to seventeen percent.[20]

In 1972, at the annual meeting of the Association for the Study of Afro-American Life and History, I was asked to give equal treatment to the North, the East, and the West on employment discrimination. In response, I reported that the nation needed 210,000 more minority teachers in order to achieve any kind of equity in hiring based on the presence of minorities in the public schools.

"To the 186,000 Black teachers now employed, we need to add another 116,000; to the 23,000 Spanish-speaking, we need to add 85,000 (almost 300 percent); to the 7,300 Asian and Pacific Islanders, we need to add 3,000; and to the 2,900 Native Americans, we need to add another 7,400."[21]

The school systems of Boston and New York City stood out as the most flagrant violators. On the basis of statistical projections and evidence of discriminatory hiring practices brought by local groups, judges in both cities have since ordered the school boards in both cities to significantly increase the numbers of minority teachers and administrators.

At the 1975 Southern Christian Leadership Conference in Anniston, Alabama, we projected that the nation would have to employ 5,368 more Black principals to reach equity and parity.[22] The estimated loss of Black principals due to discrimination in the seventeen southern and border states is 2,235. This formula takes into consideration the number of schools closed for consolidation and other reasons as well as new schools which have opened. Since Texas had more than 700 Black principals in 1964, we could have used that figure, but we have used a projected number of 581. In 1966, North Carolina had more than 625 Black principals; yet, we

Table A5.1 1972 impact on desegregation on Black teaching positions 1954–1972

State	State totals			Non-minority					Black					Projection + or −	
	Students	Teachers	Pupil teacher ratio	Students number	%	Teachers number	%	Pupil teacher ratio	Students number	%	Teachers number	%	Pupil teacher ratio	Projection	Actual # of Black teachers needed
Alabama	761,502	30,806	25	508,964	66.8	22,058	71.6	24	251,578	33.0	8,721	28.3	29	10,063	1,342
Alaska	83,233	3,862	22	64,970	78.1	3,657	97.7	17	2,410	2.9	88	2.3	27	110	22
Arizona	468,446	19,663	24	332,008	70.9	18.160	92.4	18	18,327	3.9	381	1.9	48	764	363
Arkansas	417,390	18,510	23	315,697	75.6	15,596	84.3	20	100,291	24.0	2,883	15.6	35	4,361	1,476
California	4,441,309	175,599	25	3,145,657	70.8	156,719	89.2	20	429,731	9.7	9,029	5.1	46	17,189	6,160
Colorado	556,679	24,362	23	452,920	81.4	22,961	94.2	20	22,204	4.0	503	2.1	44	956	453
Connecticut	673,769	33,813	20	588,131	87.3	32,388	95.8	18	60,856	9.0	1,173	3.5	52	3,043	1,870
Delaware	133,516	5,949	23	103,943	77.9	5,031	84.6	21	28,113	21.1	885	14.9	32	1,222	337
D.C.	140,000	5,902	24	4,928	3.5	875	14.8	6	133,638	95.5	4,995	84.6	27	5,568	573
Florida	1,494,729	63,614	23	1,065,050	71.3	50,881	80.0	21	344,865	23.1	11,533	18.1	30	14,994	3,461
Georgia	1,084,830	45,546	24	710,619	65.5	33,242	73.0	22	371,034	34.2	12,224	26.8	30	15,460	3,236
Idaho	172,869	7,625	23	164,421	95.1	7,569	99.3	22	448	0.3	10	0.1	45	19	9
Illinois	2,262,463	99,630	23	1,738,909	76.9	88,056	88.4	20	423,707	18.7	10,765	10.8	39	18,422	7,657
Indiana	1,206,942	50,113	24	1,074,610	89.0	47,114	94.0	23	113,762	9.4	2,782	5.6	41	4,740	1,958
Iowa	632,638	30,821	21	617,154	97.6	30,551	99.1	20	10,741	1.7	182	0.6	59	511	329
Kansas	502,975	24,311	21	456,287	90.7	23,440	96.4	19	32,691	6.5	677	2.8	48	1,557	880
Kentucky	722,125	30,466	24	658,706	91.2	28,925	94.9	23	62,587	8.7	1,519	5.0	41	2,608	1,089
Louisiana	851,018	36,797	23	499,375	58.3	24,378	66.8	20	345,967	40.7	12,165	33.1	28	15,042	2,877
Maize	207,402	9,487	22	206,055	99.4	9,470	99.8	27	405	0.2	6	0.1	68	18	12
Maryland	921,050	38,385	24	679,450	73.8	30,469	79.4	21	232,033	25.2	7,731	20.1	30	9,668	1,937
Massachusetts	1,173,237	59,473	20	1,098,248	93.2	58,353	98.1	19	57,584	4.9	873	1.5	66	2,879	2,006
Michigan	2,173,211	86,234	25	1,825,724	81.0	78,158	90.6	23	304,852	14.0	7,529	8.7	41	12,194	4,665
Minnesota	926,446	43,315	21	898,059	96.9	42,853	98.9	21	11,132	1.2	293	0.7	38	530	237
Mississippi	521,723	23,529	22	257,887	49.2	14,048	59.7	18	262,952	50.6	9,436	40.1	28	12,043	2,607
Missouri	1,004,310	44,201	23	849,197	82.5	39,912	90.3	21	149,028	14.8	4,019	9.2	37	6,479	2,430
Montana	136,458	6,204	22	128,458	94.1	6,237	99.3	21	338	0.2	6	0.1	56	15	9
Nebraska	262,168	12,613	21	243,043	92.7	12,344	97.9	20	13,495	3.1	226	1.8	60	643	417
Nevada	130,751	5,290	25	111,341	85.2	4,938	93.4	23	11,109	8.5	241	4.6	46	444	203

(continued overleaf)

Table A5.1 Continued

State	State totals			Non-minority					Black					Projection + or −	
	Students	Teachers	Pupil teacher ratio	Students number	%	Teachers number	%	Pupil teacher ratio	Students number	%	Teachers number	%	Pupil teacher ratio	Projection	Actual # of Black teachers
N. Hampshire	161,988	7,841	21	160,799	99.3	7,613	99.6	21	630	0.4	17	0.2	37	30	13
N. Jersey	1,468,899	33,402	30	1,155,924	78.7	67,232	91.6	17	231,324	15.7	5,467	7.4	42	11,566	6,099
N. Mexico	281,823	11,960	24	141,771	50.3	9,536	79.7	15	6,221	2.2	139	1.2	45	259	120
N. York	3,436,980	171,926	20	2,536,389	73.4	162,317	94.4	16	956,187	16.1	7,461	4.3	128	47,809	40,346
N. Carolina	1,180,050	48,065	25	813,393	69.1	36,788	76.3	22	347,783	29.5	10,248	22.4	32	14,491	3,743
N. Dakota	118,484	3,844	20	113,350	95.7	3,802	99.3	30	526	0.4	4	0.1	132	26	22
Ohio	2,404,743	99,323	24	2,085,602	86.7	92,873	93.5	22	293,877	12.2	6,176	6.2	48	12,245	6,069
Oklahoma	544,495	23,978	23	448,589	82.4	21,580	90.0	21	55,345	10.2	1,514	6.3	33	2,406	892
Oregon	458,698	22,129	21	446,422	95.2	23,672	97.9	21	8,518	1.8	152	0.7	56	406	254
Pennsylvania	2,305,158	101,624	23	2,014,127	87.4	96,006	94.5	21	269,579	11.7	5,462	5.4	49	11,721	6,239
Rhode Island	185,786	9,049	21	176,148	94.3	8,903	98.4	20	7,753	4.2	118	1.3	66	369	251
S. Carolina	629,893	26,880	23	366,935	58.3	18,521	68.9	20	261,346	41.5	8,321	31.0	31	11,363	3,042
S. Dakota	153,624	7,493	21	143,470	93.4	7,445	99.4	19	439	0.3	17	0.2	26	21	4
Tennessee	896,942	35,952	25	702,924	78.4	30,082	83.7	23	192,483	21.5	5,844	16.3	33	7,699	1,855
Texas	2,611,177	117,341	22	1,595,363	61.1	96,378	82.1	17	418,298	16.0	13,118	11.2	32	19,014	5,896
Utah	312,417	12,032	26	292,874	91.7	11,882	98.8	25	1,381	0.5	26	0.2	61	61	35
Vermont	72,054	3,995	18	71,737	99.6	3,982	99.7	18	149	0.2	7	0.2	21	9	2
Virginia	1,060,147	47,474	22	791,602	74.1	38,451	81.0	21	260,956	24.6	8,903	18.8	29	11,862	2,959
Washington	786,929	31,795	25	725,001	92.1	10,856	97.0	23	20,937	2.7	387	1.2	54	873	486
W. Virginia	410,184	17,300	23	391,013	95.3	16,891	96.5	23	18,197	4.4	591	3.4	31	791	200
Wisconsin	984,326	44,761	22	920,412	93.3	43,620	97.5	21	45,445	4.6	953	2.1	47	2,066	1,103
Wyoming	80,431	4,267	19	73,670	91.6	4,201	98.5	18	784	1.0	4	0.1	196	41	37

Table A5.2 In southern and border states, 1972

17 southern and border states	Total no. of principals	Projected no. of Black principals	Current no. of Black principals	Number needed	Present loss
West Virginia	835	33	12	21	65
Kentucky	1144	98	36	62	64
Arkansas	723	174	75	99	57
Texas	3632	581	258	323	55+
Delaware	174	37	19	18	45+
Florida	1832	421	246	175	42
Tennessee	1232	259	151	108	42
Alabama	1122	370	222	148	40
Mississippi	676	342	204	138	40
Oklahoma	791	79	47	32	40
Missouri	1434	234	143	91	39
Louisiana	1386	568	353	215	38
Georgia	1785	607	388	219	36
South Carolina	761	424	274	150	36
Maryland	1267	317	209	108	35
North Carolina	1848	536	348	188	35
Virginia	1636	402	262	140	35
		5308	3172	2234	

Projections prepared by Samuel B. Ethridge for presentation at SCLC National Conference, Anniston, Alabama; August 14, 1975. Projections are based on data from the HEW Office of Civil Rights 1972 Reports.

have used a projected figure of 536. In Kentucky, the actual number of Black principals was over 400, yet we have used a 1972 projection of only 98. If we were interested in rhetoric, we could use the 1954 number of Black schools and show high losses, many of which are due to population decline, shifting population, and school consolidation (see Table A5.2).

San Antonio, Texas is the only large school district in the nation where the Black principal ratio and the Black student ratio are equal (16 percent and 16 percent). But San Antonio has a significant disparity in the ratio of Spanish-speaking principals to Spanish-speaking students. Washington, D.C. is the only other major city which comes close. Boston is consistent in that it is public enemy number one for the Black principal as it was for the Black teacher and, more recently, the Black student.

NEED FOR MONITORS

As helpful as the Office of Civil Rights data have been in making the judges, news media and the people aware of the inequities in hiring in their districts, there is almost a two-year time lag between the collection and the release of the data in meaningful form.

The NEA Task Force on Louisiana and Mississippi recommended, among other things, that the judges appoint monitors to observe the desegregation process and report back to the judges on progress.

On September 9, 1970, we inadvertently discovered the importance of monitoring after the Attorney General of Mississippi placed an injunction on the NEA Associate Director of the Atlanta Region, Jimmy Williams, and on me, and threatened to jail us because we attempted to monitor the desegregation process in several Mississippi school districts. No doubt, they had something to hide.

Since 1968, it has become a common practice for judges to establish biracial committees and monitoring groups to help them evaluate the reports supplied by the system. In some instances, judge have dismissed the school board and appointed themselves or someone else to oversee the school operation on a temporary basis. Such practices are long overdue and should be expanded.

1975 DATA ENCOURAGING

Boyd Bosma, in a study for the National Institute for Education, has done an analysis of 1975 OCR data which yields some interesting things. His findings are summarized below:[23]

1   Affirmative action in education seems to be working in some places. Minority teachers (primarily Spanish-speaking) account for nearly 40 percent of the 150,230 new teaching jobs which were added between 1970–71 and 1975–76; but not nearly enough to reach the 210,000 called for on the basis of 1972 data.
2   Nationwide, Black teacher employment increased from 9.4 percent of the teaching population to 10.2 percent. This increase represents a 15 percent decrease in their actual numbers.
3   Hispanic teacher employment increased by almost 15,000, from 1 percent to 1.6 percent of the teaching population. This represents an increase of 79.3 percent since 1972, but is still a long way from 85,500 which I projected at the Tucson Conference.
4   Asian American teacher employment increased by 52.6 percent and First Americans increased by 103.5 percent. But this represents relatively low numerical gains in spite of the impressive percent gains.

Keep in mind that the above figures represent national gains and will be misleading for this paper without some analysis of the data for the South where the Brown Decision had its original focus. Bosma's summary of the 1975 data for the South is as follows:[24]

1   Approximately 65 percent of the national increase in the number of white teachers between 1970–71 and 1975–76 occurred in the South.
2   The 49,306 white teachers hired during this period were more than the total number (48,444) minorities hired throughout the nation.
3   Six white teachers were employed for every Black teacher employed in the South during this period.
4   In addition to the 39,386 displacement factor shown in the 1972 data in seventeen states, additional 8,430 position losses were projected in the eleven states alone (47,816).
5   In spite of the increase in the teacher population, the total number of Black teachers employed decreased in Alabama and South Carolina. In addition to the above, the ratio of Black to white teachers decreased in Arkansas, Florida, Mississippi, North Carolina and Virginia. Increases in the ratio of Black to white are reported in Georgia, Louisiana, Tennessee and Texas.

I believe that most judges, even those who are hard to convince, are honorable persons and that if the disproportionate burden of desegregation which was placed upon the backs of Black educators and students had been known to them, it would not have been allowed to the same degree.

NOT AN EDUCATION DECISION

As stated at the outset, the impact of *Brown v. the Board of Education* on Black educators in terms of employment opportunities lost during the first twenty-five years was devastating. If the

Brown Decision was a decision about education *per se*, I would be the first to criticize it. As I view the Decision, it was a decision about rights and in the scheme of things education just happened to come first and took a terrible beating for it.

In my view, it was a decision about the right to the best public education the nation could afford. It was not a desegregation plan. It was about the right to be served a hamburger at any counter in the store. It was about the right to sit or stand in any section of the bus. It was about the right to buy a house and live in it in any neighborhood one can afford.

It was about the right to secure training in any occupation to get a job in it at the end of that training.

It was about the right to vote and the right to run and hold office.

The statistics reveal that the Decision has not been all losses. There have been some gains which were hard to discern at first but now may have some relevance for a reversal of some of the losses in the South and acceleration of gains in the North.

In 1954, there were no Black superintendents, and less than a dozen at the assistant superintendent level. There were approximately 200 Black persons called "Jean's Supervisors" or "Jean's Teachers" who could be counted as part of the central office staffs. The 1975 OCR data indicate that more than 1,000 Black educators hold central office jobs, including several superintendents, including major cities such as Richmond, Atlanta and Miami; scores of assistant superintendents and hundreds of directors of various federal programs (see Table A5.3).

Black administrators make up 17.2 percent of the central office staff personnel in Louisiana; 15.5 percent in Mississippi; 14.2 percent in Maryland; 14.1 percent in Alabama; 12.9 percent in South Carolina; 11.7 percent in Georgia and 11.5 percent in North Carolina.

Some of these gains are a result of HEW requirements, some the result of Court orders. But most are the result of political power which has accrued from electing people friendly to "Black enlightened self-interest" and by electing Black officials. The number of Black elected officials had grown from about 1,200 in 1969 to 4,500 in 1978, an increase of 280 percent.

Table A5.3 Employment status of Black central office administrators, officials, managers—1975

State	Total employment	Number of Blacks	Percentage of Blacks	Number of minorities	Percentage of minorities
Alabama	384	54	14.1	54	14.1
Arkansas	536	34	6.4	34	6.4
Delaware	188	15	8.0	15	8.0
Florida	1,371	98	7.2	115	8.4
Georgia	736	86	11.7	87	11.8
Kentucky	831	38	4.5	38	4.5
Louisiana	552	95	17.2	100	18.1
Maryland	620	88	14.2	90	14.6
Mississippi	373	58	15.5	58	15.5
Missouri	991	64	6.4	68	6.8
North Carolina	704	81	11.5	84	12.0
Oklahoma	715	17	2.4	57	7.9
South Carolina	523	67	12.9	70	13.4
Tennessee	404	34	8.4	34	8.4
Texas	3,461	173	5.0	457	13.2
Virginia	767	67	8.7	69	9.0
West Virginia	365	12	3.3	12	3.3

Source: Equal Employment Opportunity Commission, 2401 E Street, North West, Washington, D.C. 20506.

CONCLUSION

Thousands of educational positions which would have gone to Black people in the South under a segregated system have been lost for them since desegregation, and the number increases with each report. In the North, East and West, where it has been traditionally hard for minority teachers to be employed, recent gains are being made.

More Blacks are being elected to school boards and, as the population trends change, more systems are gaining Black majorities. As this happens, more Black educators are being hired in decision-making positions in the administration. As more Blacks, other minorities, and other fair-minded persons are placed in these sensitive positions, the opportunities for equal job opportunity in education will increase and hopefully reverse the steady eroding of job opportunities for Blacks which has been going on in the South since 1954.

NOTES

1 *Brown v. Board of Education of Topeka, Kansas, et al.* U.S. 493 (1954).

2 James Nabritt, one of the legal counsels for plaintiffs *Brown v. Board of Education*, unpublished lecture, May 1948.

3 *American Teachers Association Bulletin XXXVI*, #1, October 1962.

4 National Education Association, *Task Force Survey of Displacement in Seventeen Southern States*, Washington, D.C., 1965.

5 Samuel B. Ethridge, *Jet*, May 18, 1979, p. 17.

6 *Brooks v. School District of Mobley, Missouri.* 267 F. 2nd 733.

7 *Franklin v. County School Board of Giles County, Virginia.*

8 *Washington Post*, September 21, 1965.

9 U.S. Office of Education, *Desegregation Guidelines of 1966*, as revised in 1967.

10 *Carr v. Montgomery County Board of Education.* 289 F. Supp. 647 (1968).

11 *Singleton v. Jackson Municipal Separate School District.* 419 F. 2nd 1213.

12 *Brown v. Board of Education of Topeka, Kansas, et al.*, 439 U.S. 294 (1955).

13 Samuel B. Ethridge, National Conference of Christians and Jews, Annual Conference of Christians and Jews, Nov. 18–21, 1972.

14 *Carter v. School Board of West Feliciana Parish*, 432 F. 2nd 875 (1970).

15 *Baker v. Columbus*, 71 5th Cir. 2531 (1972).

16 *Southern Education Reporting Service*, "Statistical Survey, Segregation-Desegregation in Southern and Boarder States." Nashville, Tennessee, Nov. 1964.

17 Samuel B. Ethridge, *Washington Daily News*, 1965.

18 The National Education Association—*Task Force Report on Displacement*.

19 Samuel B. Ethridge, Comments to luncheon meeting, NAACP Legal Defense Fund Seminar on Brown, May 19, 1972, *Washington Post*, May 20, 1972.

20 Samuel B. Ethridge, *Helping America Understand: Integration and Employment of Black School Principals and Teachers*, remarks to Association for the Study of Afro-American Life and History, New York City, *New York Times*, October 19, 1973.

21 Ibid.

22 Samuel B. Ethridge, remarks to *Southern Cristian Leadership Conference*, Anniston, Alabama, August 14, 1973—*Atlanta Journal*, August 15, 1973.

23 Dr. Boyd Bosma, *Teachers, Teachers Associations, and School Desegregation*, an unpublished study—National Institute for Education, 1979.

24 Ibid.

5.3 No one model American

American Association of Colleges for Teacher Education

Source: American Association of Colleges for Teacher Education
Commission on Multicultural Education, *No One Model American*.
Washington, DC: Author, 1972

A STATEMENT ON MULTICULTURAL EDUCATION

In an action reflecting its commitment to alleviating social problems through education, the American Association of Colleges for Teacher Education established the Commission on Multicultural Education. The Commission, formed in the aftermath of the Kent State and Jackson State tragedies, is the outgrowth of the Association's long history of involvement in building a more effective and humane society through the betterment of teacher education.

The Multicultural Statement is a significant product of the Commission's work. The Statement, which was adopted officially in November 1972 by the AACTE Board of Directors, was prepared for AACTE, its member institutions, and other centers of higher learning as a guide for addressing the issue of multicultural education.

Commission members caution that the term "multicultural" is not a euphemism for "disadvantaged." Rather, the Statement encompasses broad ethnic and cultural spheres.

The Statement, a product of Commission interaction with a number of higher education institutions and personnel, is presented here in the interest of improving the quality of society through an increased social awareness on the part of teachers and teacher educators.

Multicultural education is education which values cultural pluralism. Multicultural education rejects the view that schools should seek to melt away cultural differences or the view that schools should merely tolerate cultural pluralism. Instead, multicultural education affirms that schools should be oriented toward the cultural enrichment of all children and youth through programs rooted to the preservation and extension of cultural alternatives. Multicultural education recognizes cultural diversity as a fact of life in American society, and it affirms that this cultural diversity is a valuable resource that should be preserved and extended. It affirms that major education institutions should strive to preserve and enhance cultural pluralism.

To endorse cultural pluralism is to endorse the principle that there is no one model American. To endorse cultural pluralism is to understand and appreciate the differences that exist among the nation's citizens. It is to see these differences as a positive force in the continuing development of a society which professes a wholesome respect for the intrinsic worth of every individual. Cultural pluralism is more than a temporary accommodation to placate racial and ethnic minorities. It is a concept that aims toward a heightened sense of being and of wholeness of the entire society based on the unique strengths of each of its parts.

Cultural pluralism rejects both assimilation and separatism as ultimate goals. The positive elements of a culturally pluralistic society will be realized only if there is a healthy interaction among the diverse groups which comprise the nation's citizenry. Such interaction enables all to share in the richness of America's multicultural heritage. Such interaction provides a means for coping with intercultural tensions that are natural and cannot be avoided in a growing, dynamic society. To accept cultural pluralism is to recognize that no group lives in a vacuum—that each group exists as part of an interrelated whole.

If cultural pluralism is so basic a quality of our culture, it must become an integral part of the educational process at every level. Education for cultural pluralism includes four major thrusts: (1) the teaching of values which support cultural diversity and individual uniqueness; (2) the encouragement of the qualitative expansion of existing ethnic cultures and their incorporation into the mainstream of American socioeconomic and political life; (3) the support of explorations in alternative and emerging life styles; and (4) the encouragement of multiculturalism, multilingualism, and multidialectism. While schools must insure that all students are assisted in developing their skills to function effectively in society, such a commitment should not imply or permit the denigration of cultural differences.

Educational institutions play a major role in shaping the attitudes and beliefs of the nation's youth. These institutions bear the heavy task of preparing each generation to assume the rights and responsibilities of adult life. In helping the transition to a society that values cultural pluralism, educational institutions must provide leadership for the development of individual commitment to a social system where individual worth and dignity are fundamental tenets. This provision means that schools and colleges must assure that their total educational process and educational content reflect a commitment to cultural pluralism. In addition, special emphasis programs must be provided where all students are helped to understand that being different connotes neither superiority nor inferiority; programs where students of various social and ethnic backgrounds may learn freely from one another; programs that help different minority students understand who they are, where they are going, and how they can make their contribution to the society in which they live.

Colleges and universities engaged in the preparation of teachers have a central role in the positive development of our culturally pluralistic society. If cultural pluralism is to become an integral part of the educational process, teachers and personnel must be prepared in an environment where the commitment to multicultural education is evident. Evidence of this commitment includes such factors as a faculty and staff of multiethnic and multiracial character, a student body that is representative of the culturally diverse nature of the community being served, and a culturally pluralistic curriculum that accurately represents the diverse multicultural nature of American society.

Multicultural education programs for teachers are more than special courses or special learning experiences grafted onto the standard program. The commitment to cultural pluralism must permeate all areas of the educational experience provided for prospective teachers.

Multicultural education reaches beyond awareness and understanding of cultural differences. More important than the acceptance and support of these differences is the recognition of the right of these different cultures to exist. The goal of cultural pluralism can be achieved *only* if there is full recognition of cultural differences and an effective educational program that makes cultural equality real and meaningful. The attainment of this goal will bring a richness and quality of life that would be a long step toward realizing the democratic ideals so nobly proclaimed by the founding fathers of this nation.

Members of AACTE's Commission On
Multicultural Education
Chairman—James Kelly, Jr., dean. School of Education, University of Pittsburgh. Pittsburgh, Pennsylvania

Dwight Billedeaux, coordinator for Indian Culture and assistant professor, Eastern Montana College. Billings, Montana.

AACTE Officers 1973

President—William A. Hunter, One Dupont Circle Washington, DC

President-elect—Sam P. Wiggins, dean, College of Education, Cleveland State University, Cleveland, Ohio

Richard H. Davis, dean, School of Education, University of Wisconsin—Milwaukee. Milwaukee, Wisconsin

Carl J. Dolce, dean, School of Education, North Carolina State University. Raleigh, North Carolina.

Hilda Hidalgo, chairman, Department of Urban Studies and Community Development, Livingston College, Rutgers University. New Brunswick, New Jersey

Charles F. Leyba, associate professor, California State University, Los Angeles. Los Angeles, California

Elaine Witty, chairman, Department of Elementary Education, Norfolk State College. Norfolk, Virginia

Executive Director—Edward C. Pomeroy, AACTE, One Dupont Circle, Suite 610 Washington, DC

American Association of Colleges for Teacher Education
1307 New York Avenue NW, Suite 300
Washington, DC 20005-4701
www.aacte.org

5.4 Educators' preparation for cultural and linguistic diversity

A call to action

Committee on Multicultural Education

Source: Committee on Multicultural Education, *Educators' Preparation for Cultural and Linguistic Diversity: A Call to Action.* Washington, DC: American Association of Colleges for Teacher Education, 2002

INTRODUCTION

The guiding motivation of this policy paper is to provide information about issues surrounding the education of culturally and linguistically diverse [CLD] student populations. Preparation of non-English speakers to survive in English-dominant schools and society is more complex than current policy debates would suggest. Of paramount concern in this paper is the need for teachers who can deliver classroom practice that respects the language and culture of the child, and effective, accommodative, instruction that results in literacy and academic success for second-language learners.

Of equal concern is the context that distinctly favors the assimilation of CLD students. There is little thought given to their rich cultural heritage or the language knowledge they bring to the classroom. At the policy level, this sociopolitical context poses a distinct challenge for future support and development. At the level of praxis, this context threatens efforts to better prepare school educators for the differential learning and transition needs of CLD students.

This paper is arranged in seven sections addressing key terminology, demographics and the achievement gap of CLD students, preparation of public school teachers and administrators, the legal context of teacher preparation for diversity, challenges for the field of education, implications of these challenges, and a call to action.

TERMINOLOGY OF THE ARENA

The phrase *culturally and linguistically diverse [CLD] student*, is in our view, most holistically descriptive of a student whose culture and/or language are assets for learning, but nonetheless different, from that of the dominant culture and/or language in American society. Since diversity implies a multi-dimensional learning environment, CLD is also affirmatively descriptive of students who will need *accommodative programming and instruction* to facilitate their cultural and linguistic development within a content-focused learning context.

Acculturation defines the process of learning about and living in another/second culture. Individuals who acculturate by *assimilation* are expected to relinquish their own cultural (and sometimes language) identity. Individuals who acculturate by *adaptation* maintain their own cultural heritage (and frequently language) as they learn another.

Accommodation is best understood, according to the notion of mutual (two-way) accommodation (Nieto, 2000). According to Nieto, a belief in one-way accommodation is at the heart of educational strategies which view academically unsuccessful students as culturally deprived or genetically inferior to those who are successful. *Mutual accommodation*, on the other hand, enables teachers and schools to recognize and build upon the resources and assets that CLD students bring to the school. These resources, when used as a basis for instruction, enhance students' capacities and abilities to reach academic success.

THE CLD STUDENT

The rapid increase in the CLD student population is changing the fabric of the American classroom. At the same time, the academic achievement gap between these students and others in the schools is widening.

DEMOGRAPHICS

In the last decade, the enrollment of CLD students across the nation has grown at a phenomenal rate of 104.97 percent (National Center of Educational Statistics, NCES, 2002). This growth rate represents an annual increase equal to five times that of the total enrollment in public schools. Today, one in five students throughout the nation comes from a home in which a language other than English is spoken (Crawford, 2000). Additionally, the patterns of migration among CLD students and families within the United States are also changing. The largest and fastest growing CLD student populations continue to concentrate in such coastal states as Florida, California, and Texas. In addition, Midwestern states such as Kansas, Indiana, Iowa, and Nebraska have experienced a dramatic increase in CLD student enrollments over the past two decades. Such increases have exceeded 200 percent per annum in many Midwestern states (NCELA, 2002). This current pattern is a precursor of what is yet to come. Current projections indicate that school-aged children whose first language is not English will constitute an estimated 40 percent of the K-12 age population in the U.S. by the year 2030 (U.S. Census Bureau, 2000). Similarly, if current trends continue, Hispanics will account for 25 percent of the total U.S. population by 2050, and may constitute 33.3 percent of the population by 2100 (U.S. Census Bureau, 2000).

There are over 400 languages currently represented in U.S. schools. Spanish-speaking students comprise 77 percent of the total CLD, K-12 population. Indeed, by far the most common language, other than English, spoken across the nation is Spanish. Other languages representing the remaining 23 percent include Vietnamese, Hmong, Haitian Creole, and Korean, which round out the top five languages spoken by CLD, K12 students in the U.S. Each comprise 1 to 3 percent of this total population (USDE, 2002).

ACHIEVEMENT GAP

Perhaps the central concern regarding CLD students across the nation's schools is how well they are performing. Unfortunately, national data on the performance of CLD students is very limited. This is most certainly the case with immigrant students. These students constitute one of the fastest growing groups of CLD students, yet sound and valid data on their achievement, school and grade completion rates, and college attendance patterns remain exceptionally limited. Although many reasons account for limited data on CLD student achievement, the number of

CLD students across the nation who are consistently exempted from standardized tests is particularly problematic. Regrettably, as the pressure for test-measured accountability increases, so do the number of CLD students exempted from standardized testing.

What we do know is that CLD students are more likely to drop out of school, have disrupted schooling, lower attendance, and be under-represented in higher level courses in high school. Additionally, among students who score below the 35th percentile on national achievement tests, about 13 percent of the first and third graders and about 6 percent of the lowest achievers in seventh grade are CLD students (NCES, 1999). The drop out rate among these students continues to average over 40 percent, especially where native language- to- English transitions have proven difficult (NCES, 1999). Not surprisingly, the USCCR (1997) found that CLD students, nationally, are three times more likely to be low achievers than high achievers; two times more likely to be at least one grade level behind in school; and four times more likely to drop out than their native-English-speaking peers.

PUBLIC SCHOOL EDUCATORS

Increases in the number of CLD students in U.S. schools are placing greater demands on teacher preparation as well as professional development programs for inservice educators. School educators need support in developing the capacity to provide appropriate and effective instruction for CLD students. According to the National Center of Educational Statistics [NCES] (1997), only 2.5 percent of teachers who teach CLD students hold a degree in either Bilingual or English as a Second Language (ESL) education. States that have the least experience with CLD student populations face the greatest shortage of certified bilingual and (ESL) teachers (AAEE, 2001). Although most CLD students spend the majority of their school day in grade-level classrooms, most teachers in these classrooms have little or no training in the differential learning and development needs of these students. Of the total number of public school teachers across the nation, only 12 percent of teachers who have CLD students in their classrooms have had eight or more hours of professional development specific to the needs of this student population (NCES, 2002). Consequently, few teachers are prepared to provide instruction specifically designed to meet the linguistic, cognitive, academic, and emotional development needs of these students.

As the diversity of the grade-level classroom has increased, the instructional practices to address this diversity have, for many teachers, remained unchanged. They use curricula and materials that do not adequately serve the needs of their CLD learners. According to Short, "The lack of familiarity with their students' cultures, learning styles, and communication patterns translates into teachers holding negative expectations for students, while inappropriate curricula, assessments, and instructional materials are used with these students, compounding the problem" (Short, 1999, p.107).

LEGAL CONTEXT

The American Association of Colleges for Teacher Education is cognizant of the legal context of teacher preparation for diversity. Multiple court decisions have varied with respect to the support of using the native language of students as the basis for instruction. The landmark Supreme Court case, *Lau v. Nichols* (1974), ruled that schools had an obligation to adequately prepare CLD students. The justices did not propose solutions due to the fact that they believed that only educators could recommend specific remedies for the education of CLD students. Instead, in *Castañeda v. Pickard* (1981), the Court stated that programs should be based on sound educational theory (a theory supported by experts). As a result of the particular theory adopted, using only English for instruction of CLD students was considered acceptable.

Presently, state referenda are changing the mandates on education of CLD students. Short-term English-only instruction in special classes, followed by integration in mainstream classrooms are replacing bilingual education programs. As a result, increasing numbers of unprepared students are entering classes with unprepared teachers. We encourage school educators to acquaint themselves with the legal precedents and mandates for educating CLD students.

Regardless of mandates, educators should be mindful of the words of Justice Douglas in the *Lau v. Nichols* ruling:

> There is no equality of treatment merely by providing students with the same facilities, textbooks, teachers, and curriculum; for students who do not understand English are effectively foreclosed from any meaningful, education.
>
> Basic English skills are at the very core of what these public schools teach. Imposition of a requirement that, before a child can effectively participate in the education program, he must have already acquired those basic skills is to make a mockery of public education. We know that those who do not understand English are certain to find their classroom experiences wholly incomprehensible and in no way meaningful.
>
> (*Lau v. Nichols*, 1974)

CHALLENGES

AACTE recognizes that changing demographics and sociocultural dynamics in public schools require the following:

- teachers/administrators who are better prepared to critically reflect upon the complex dynamics of appropriate accommodations for cultural and linguistic diversity;
- teachers/administrators who advocate for CLD students;
- teachers/administrators who are better prepared to analyze, plan, deliver, and evaluate curriculum and instruction that has been modified and adapted for the differential learning and transition needs of CLD students;
- teachers/administrators who are better prepared to critically evaluate widespread and popular curriculum initiatives, especially pre-packaged curricula, for their applicability with and potential impact on CLD student achievement;
- a curriculum for the preparation of school leaders which prompts them to value and explore both the biographical assets which the CLD student brings to school and the valuable contribution of caregivers, extended family members, and community;
- an enhanced emphasis on advocacy for norm- and criterion-referenced testing in schools which accommodates CLD students at their level of readiness and development, and which is not culturally or linguistically focused to the extent that purposive monitoring and evaluation of process and product gains are precluded.

AACTE must exhibit leadership in these matters. In complex environments of practice, creativity, flexibility, professional development, and collaboration, the American Association of Colleges for Teacher Education seeks to set a new direction, which incorporates these essentials, in a unified effort of proactive leadership.

IMPLICATIONS

As educators, the foundation upon which we practice our craft is rapidly changing. Either we and our respective institutions adjust to meet this change, or the scenario will be one of institutional failure. First, education is the bedrock of the national economy, providing a capable work force that is prepared to participate in a competitive, global market place. Clearly, CLD students now constitute the fastest growing segment of the educational systems in the nation. Concomitantly, this segment demonstrates unacceptably low levels of achievement, coupled with the highest dropout rates. This scenario is fast becoming untenable. What is the purpose of our school systems if the fastest growing segment of their student populations are consistently unable to complete the program, or unable to graduate with a diploma? Qui bono?

Second, the inequitable education of CLD students, as a result of cultural and linguistic differences, is a denial of their civil rights. Currently, these students arrive in the system with needs and differences for which the current system is unprepared. It is the system that must adjust to accommodate these increasingly prevalent differences through differentiated curriculum and instruction. Culturally and linguistically diverse students cannot change their prior socialization in a particular culture or in a particular language. Instead, the system must adjust its practices, build capacity for diversity, and professionally accommodate these differences.

Inevitably, the policies and infrastructures of the institution we call schooling must change to accommodate the changing foundation upon which their existence rests. However, change must also begin with the educators who deliver the services of this institution in society. School educators, especially classroom teachers, must be better prepared for the changing fabric of the American classroom.

CALL TO ACTION

AACTE is committed to supporting and moving forward the agenda of ensuring an equitable education for students whose primary language is not English. The Association challenges institutions of higher education to commit to transforming the preparation of educators at all levels to address the changing demographics of American public schools. To this end, AACTE will support partnerships to unite and begin the transformation process in teacher/administrator preparation. Specifically, AACTE invites all member institutions to collaborate in addressing the inclusion of diversity in teacher preparation.

- *Sociocultural*: diversity in teacher preparation must emphasize the sociocultural struggles that CLD students endure. These include learning another culture, acquiring a second language, integrating their world views, performing well in the content areas, and adapting their personal knowledge within the American classroom. Teachers must be prepared to understand and support the acculturation process in a mutually adaptive way, building bridges between the student's prior cultural knowledge and that of a new cultural environment, including the culture of the school. Teachers must be professionally prepared to explicitly teach the norms, beliefs and expectations of school contexts and society-at-large while affirming the student's cultural heritage, previous knowledge, and native language proficiency.

  This preparation for diversity must begin with the teacher. Teachers must be taught to explore their own socialization in a particular culture as a basis for understanding perspectives on, attitudes toward, and professional responsibility with CLD students and families. They must learn to test the validity of the influence of their own cultural filters upon their own perspectives and actions in practice. Moreover, teachers must be prepared to value, affirm, and maximize the rich cultural heritage that CLD students bring to the school. Ultimately, teachers must be prepared to acquire the field experiences and learning necessary to understand the acculturation process of students from cultures and languages different than their own.

- *Language*: teacher preparation and professional development for diversity should explore and discuss theories and stages of the second language acquisition (SLA). Teachers need experiences in their preparation that allow them to understand the realities of negotiating academic instruction in another language. Teachers should understand why native language and associated cognitive development are critical to academic success and language acquisition in English. They should incorporate the use of the students' native language in their teaching, and support language and academic learning objectives as well as literacy development in English. Teachers must be prepared to distinguish social from academic language proficiency, so as to avoid erroneous assumptions about the learner's preparedness for academic learning. They must be prepared, through well-designed field experiences, to structure environments that promote accumulative, communicative, and constructive language acquisition and literacy development in a second language.

- *Cognitive*: teacher preparation and professional development for diversity must encompass a deep understanding of cognitive development challenges and processes for CLD students. In this regard, prospective teachers must be prepared to differentiate curriculum, instruction, and assessment to accommodate differences in preferred learning styles. Teachers' field experiences should emphasize the use of context and prior knowledge. Furthermore, teachers must also be prepared to teach students strategies that maximize their cognitive, metacognitive, and social-affective skills in problem solving and critical thinking.

- *Academic*: teacher preparation and professional development for diversity must include an understanding of culturally and linguistically mediated instruction in all content areas. This instruction must be scaffolded and/or sheltered, process and product driven, and grounded in sound theory and methodologies explicitly designed for CLD students. Reductionistic curricula, programs, and instruction may seem sufficient to target social language learning among CLD students, but will not develop the academic language and content learning necessary for successful performance in school.

Ultimately, institutions of higher education must demonstrate critical reflexivity regarding the readiness of their faculties to achieve these benchmarks of teacher preparation and professional development for diversity. Prior socialization is as much an issue for collegiate faculty as it is for grade-level classroom teachers. It requires the capacity to influence perspectives on preparation, attitudes toward the accommodation of diversity, and actions in practice. Accordingly, cross-culturally sensitive professional development and accommodation training are each equally as applicable to college faculty members as they are to public school educators.

Vavrus (2002) suggests that teacher education programs play a crucial role in determining teachers' attitudes toward diversity and the accommodation of that diversity within their teaching. He strongly recommends that faculty members engage themselves in self-study and internal evaluations to better understand their capacity to infuse diversity issues throughout the curriculum.

REFERENCES

American Association of Employment in Education (AAEE), (2001) Educator Supply and Demand in the U.S. Retrieved December 27, 2002 from http://www.ub-careers.buffalo.edu/aaee/

Castañeda v. Pickard, 648 F.2d 989 (5th cir. 1981).

Crawford, J. (2000) At War With Diversity: "U.S. Language Policy in an Age of Anxiety." Clevedon, England: Multilingual Matters.

Lau v Nichols, 414 U.S. 563 (1974).

National Center for Education Statistics (NCES) (2002) Early Estimates of Public Elementary and Secondary Education Statistics: school year 2001–2002. Retrieved December 27, 2002 from http://nces.ed.gov/edstats/

National Clearinghouse for English Language Acquisition (NCELA), (2002) State Elementary and Secondary LEP Enrollment Growth and Top Languages. Retrieved December 27, 2002, from http://www.ncela.gwu.edu/states/index.htm

Nieto, S. (2000) *Affirming diversity: The Sociopolitical Context of Multicultural Education* (third ed.). Reading, MA: Longman.

Short, D. J. (1999) Integrating Language and Content for Effective Sheltered Instruction Programs. In C. J. Faltis (ed.), *So Much To Say* (pp. 105–137). New York: Teachers College Press.

United States Census Bureau. (2000) *American Fact Finder*, (Tables and Charts). Available: http://factfinder.census.gov/servlet/BasicFactsServlet (2002, 3/13/02).

United States Commission on Civil Rights (USCCR). Equal Education Opportunities and Nondiscrimination for Students with Limited English Proficiency (1997). Retrieved December 27, 2002 from http://www.usccr.gov/

United States Department of Education. No Child Left Behind: Educating Linguistically and Culturally Diverse Students (2002). Retrieved December 27, 2002 from http://www.ed.gov/index.jsp

Vavrus, M. (2002). *Transforming the Multicultural Education of Teachers*. New York: Teachers College Press.

BIBLIOGRAPHY

August, D. & Hakuta, K. (1997) *Improving Schooling for Language Minority Children*. Washington, DC: National Academy Press.

Brisk, M. E. (1998) *Bilingual Education: From Compensatory to Quality Schooling*. Mahwah, NJ: Lawrence Erlbaum.

Cummins, J. (2000) *Language, Power and Pedagogy*. Clevedon, England: Multilingual Matters.

Fillmore, L. W. (1991) Second-Language Learning in Children: A Model of Language Learning in Social Context. In E. Bialystok (ed.), *Language Processing in Bilingual Children*. Cambridge: Cambridge University Press.

Fillmore, L. W. & Snow, C. (2002) What Teachers Need to Know About Language. In C. T. Adger, C. Snow, & D. Christian (eds.), *What Teachers Need to know about Language* (pp. 7–53). McHenry, IL: Delta Systems Inc. & The Center for Applied Linguistics (CAL).

Gándara, P. (2000) In the Aftermath of the Storm: English Learners in the Post-227 Era. *Bilingual Research Journal*, 24 (1 & 2), 1–13.

García, G. E. (2000) Bilingual Children's Reading. In M. Kamil, P. S. Mosenthal, P. D. Pearson, & R. Barr (eds.), *Handbook of Reading Research: Volume III* (pp. 813–834). Mahwah, NJ: Lawrence Erlbaum Associates.

Gebhard, M., Austin, T., Nieto, S., & Willett, J. (2002) You Can't Step On Someone Else's Words: Preparing All Teachers to Teach Language Minority Students. In Z. Beykont (ed.), *The Power of Culture: Teaching Across Language Difference* (pp. 219–243). Cambridge, MA: Harvard Education Publishing Group.

Herrera, S. (Kansas State U.) and Ronald Rochon (U. of Wisconsin) for the AACTE Committee on Multi-cultural Education.

Hudelson, S., Poynor, L., & Wolfe, P. (2002) Teaching Bilingual and ESL Children and Adolescents. In J. Flood, D. Lapp, J. R. Squire, & J. M. Jensen (eds.), *Handbook of Research on Teaching the English Language Arts* (pp. 421–434). Mahwah, NJ: Lawrence Erlbaum.

Jacobs, D. & Reyhner, J. (2002) *Preparing Teachers to Support American Indian and Alaska Native Student Success and Cultural Heritage*. Eric Digest, May.

Milk, R. (1992) Re-Thinking the Education of Teachers of Language Minority Children: Developing Reflective Teachers for Changing Schools. *Focus*, 6, 2–17.

National Center for Education Statistic (1999) *The condition of education*. Washington, DC: U.S. Department of Education.

Portes, A. & Rumbaut, Rubén (2001) *Legacies: The Story of the Immigrant Second Generation*. Berkeley, CA: The University of California Press.

Ruiz-de-Velasco, J., Fix, M., & Clewell, B. (2000) *Overlooked and Underserved: Immigrant Students in U.S. Secondary Schools*. Washington, DC: The Urban Institute Press.

Suárez-Orozco, C. & Suárez-Orozco, M. (2001) *Children of Immigration*. Cambridge, MA: Harvard University Press. (Chapter 4) Prepared by Maria Estela Brisk (Boston College), Ray Barnhardt (University of Alaska), Socorro.

Part 5
Commentaries

35 Diversity and teacher education
People, pedagogy, and politics

Jacqueline Jordan Irvine
Emory University

Although the inclusion of diversity in teacher education has made significant progress, success is not easily measured. Success is difficult to gauge because the field has developed as a series of overlapping "struggles" with peaks and valleys in a changing landscape of different proponents and opponents, political contexts, institutional climates, and demographic changes. Struggles in the teacher education diversity domain continue today as we advocate for our rightful place in the larger fields of educational research and teacher education. We often speak in one united multicultural voice, but many times there are conflicting and competing voices in different conversations. Hence measuring success, in a traditional sense, is difficult if one does not come to grips with the fact that the struggle for inclusion of diversity in teacher education is, and always will be, a contentious battleground that often pits the field against itself as well as against mainstream hegemonic forces. These tensions are reflected in issues related to people, pedagogy, and politics.

PEOPLE

The first proponents of diversity in teacher education operated simultaneously as both insiders and outsiders in the field of education. In order to understand the evolution of these insider-outside perspectives, it is necessary to understand the historical context in which diversity emerged in teacher education. According to Banks (1996) the early multicultural education movement started with a small group of African Americans who applied the campus activism they learned in ethnic studies programs, the Civil Rights Movement, and the War Against Vietnam to the field of teacher education.

By the early 1970s, these former outsiders were insiders. They were professors in schools and colleges of education who were using their activist strategies of the past to push for the adoption in 1972 of the *No One Model American*, a groundbreaking statement by the American Association for Colleges of Teacher Education (AACTE). This document called for support for cultural diversity, alternative and emerging lifestyles, multiculturalism, and multilingualism. This landmark document was a bold and significant statement for its time.

AACTE's approval of the *No One Model American* was followed by the adoption of a multicultural education standard by the National Council for the Accreditation of Teacher Education (NCATE). That standard, which became effective in 1979, aimed "to help institutions become more responsive to the human condition, individual cultural integrity, and cultural pluralism in society" (McCormick, 1984, p. 3).

This brief historical context provides the background for the identification of other stakeholders in multicultural teacher education, primarily pre- and in-service teachers in our preparation programs. Research shows that students in such programs are mostly

White females with limited exposure to or experiences with people of color, and often resist their professors' attempts to teach them about English language learners (ELLs) and issues related to structural inequalities, racism, and White privilege. Sleeter, in this Handbook, states that White preservice teachers are generally fearful both of students of color and of discussing race and racism. Additionally, they tend to rely on the ethnic history and assimilation of their own families, and in turn, assume that the experiences of people of color are or should be the same.

I believe we need to examine the predispositions of students we admit to our programs. One sobering finding in multicultural teacher education that resurfaces continuously is that our programs and courses may have some short-term effect on changing students' beliefs and attitudes about diversity, but their long-term influence is most likely minimal. It has been my experience that some students enter our programs with prior experiences and predispositions we can build on to help them become *more* effective multicultural teachers. This group includes: students who are older and have relevant work experiences; students who are parents themselves; students of color; students who have lived, worked, or attended schools in integrated communities; and students with international experiences (e.g. returning Peace Corps volunteers or participants of Study Abroad programs) who have some skills in learning about cultures other than their own.

We need to find ways to identify pre-service teachers who are persistent, open-minded, reflective and complex thinkers, and risk takers. I believe that Diane Goodman (2000) was correct when she concluded that those more likely to be committed to multiculturalism are people of color, people with strong moral and spiritual orientations for social justice, and people who have experienced injustices in our society. Goodman's conclusion does not bode well for teacher education for diversity. We have to find ways to motivate and educate people from privileged groups and mono-cultural backgrounds to teach in culturally diverse urban schools.

There are also too few preservice teacher candidates of color. Currently, 80 percent of teacher candidates are White (Zumwalt & Craig, 2005). Teachers of color are needed in the profession because their teaching beliefs and instructional practices are related in positive ways to the school achievement of students, especially African American and Latino students, who continue to lag behind their White and Asian counterparts academically. Villegas' and Davis' piece in this volume summarizes the research on this topic and concludes that teacher race/ethnicity does influence student learning as well as other important student outcomes like absenteeism, enrollment in advanced courses, and dropout rates.

PEDAGOGY

The people involved in and influencing our work in teacher education represent only one aspect of the larger picture. The pedagogy we use to prepare future teachers is a second aspect that needs to be considered. Beverly Armento and I (2001) argue that the demographic changes in today's schools demand new ways of organizing and implementing instruction. Teachers have to be prepared as culturally responsive educators who understand that students bring a range of cultural and everyday experiences that may differ from their own and certainly differ from the dominant norms of the school.

Teacher education candidates must be taught how to motivate learners and maximize instruction for diverse students. As part of meaningful instruction, teacher educators must consider the language and textbooks used in K-12 schools to represent concepts and ideas, and find better ways to help preservice and inservice teachers connect with the realities students know and live, in order to help them understand what they are taught. The goal of teacher education for diversity is to produce culturally responsive teachers who:

- are well prepared and competent in their subject matter;
- are advocates for their students;
- teach their students about issues of social justice;
- are change agents and leaders in their schools and in the communities served by those schools;
- understand how to involve their students' parents;
- know how to teach ELLs and communicate with their parents;
- are problem solvers who search for insight in how culture and ethnicity influence teaching and learning;
- include the history of diverse groups in whatever content area they teach;
- use culturally relevant and student-generated images, examples, and metaphors in their teaching;
- understand students' learning preferences;
- share ownership of the lessons with students; and
- use a variety of formative and summative assessments to inform their teaching.

POLITICS

Reflecting on the history of diversity in teacher education reveals that our work is as much about politics as it is the people we prepare as teachers and the pedagogy we teach. In fact, AACTE's *A Call for Action on Educators' Preparation for Cultural and Linguistic Diversity* (2002) asserted that the inequitable education of culturally and linguistically diverse students is a denial of their basic civil rights. As such, these implications suggest that we, as well as the students we teach, have to be more informed about and active in politics. We have to claim our personal, professional, and political worldviews, even when these might conflict with the views held by colleagues who do not embrace the diversity agenda. We must be social reconstructivists committed to the transformation of systems of racism, inequality, and oppression. Too frequently we hesitate to share our beliefs and political stance; however, we need to speak up.

We need to attend to politics at the federal, state, and local levels. Lucas and Grinberg, in their chapter on preparing teachers to teach English Language Learners, point out how political opposition that started in the 1980s decreased the number of bilingual teachers and bilingual programs. State and federal initiatives have circumvented schools and departments of education by offering alternative routes for certification with scant attention to issues of diversity. This growing trend is influenced and supported by the U.S. Department of Education's current emphasis on mastery of subject matter as the sole criterion for effective teaching.

The No Child Left Behind Act, for example, has made a mockery of the definition of a highly qualified teacher. States can now individually decide what a qualified teacher is. My state, Georgia, defines a highly qualified teacher (with a full not temporary license) as a person who holds a bachelor's degree in almost any subject and passes PRAXIS I and II. These newly proclaimed "highly qualified" teachers with little or no formal preparation in issues of diversity will not be teaching in the suburban schools of middle class students. Instead, they will teach in the schools with the most vacancies—segregated rural and urban schools with large numbers of low income, diverse students.

I do not want to end this commentary by giving the impression that teacher education for diversity has not made gains over time or that the goal is too difficult and challenging to pursue. Indeed there have been many accomplishments. Over the years, multiculturalism has gained support in universities, colleges and schools of education, and society at large. We need to recognize, however, that the future of diversity in teacher education will be similar to its past. It will inevitably involve struggles for acceptance and inclusion around themes of people, pedagogy, and politics. Perhaps Marilyn Cochran-Smith (2004) is correct when she reminds us that the mere battle for social justice is, in and of itself, an acceptable measure of success.

REFERENCES

American Association of Colleges for Teacher Education (2002) *Educators' preparation for cultural and linguistic diversity: a call to action*. Washington, DC: Author.

Banks, J. A. (1996) The African American roots of multicultural education. In J. A. Banks (ed.) *Multicultural education: transformative knowledge and action* (pp. 30–45). New York: Teachers College Press.

Cochran-Smith, M. (2004) *Walking the road: race, diversity, and social justice in teacher education*. New York: Teachers College Press.

Goodman, D. J. (2000) Motivating people from privileged groups to support social justice. *Teachers College Record*, 102(6), 1061–1085.

Irvine, J. J. & Armento, B. J. (2001) *Culturally responsive teaching*. Boston: McGraw-Hill Publishers.

McCormick, T. E. (1984) Multiculturalism: some principles and issues. *Theory into Practice*, 28(2), 93–97.

Zumwalt, K. & Craig, E. (2005) Teachers' characteristics: research on the demographic profile. In M. Cochran-Smith & K. M. Zeichner (eds.) *Studying teacher education* (pp. 111–156). Mahwah, NJ: Lawrence Erlbaum Associates.

36 Diversity and teacher education

What can the future be?

Tina Jacobowitz
Montclair State University

Nicholas M. Michelli
The City University of New York

The juxtaposition of the artifacts for this section calling for dramatic change in our commitment to enhancing diversity and increasing our success with diverse students, some going back 30 years, and the calls in the three framing chapters for attention to diversity and teaching diverse learners can only infuriate anyone who sees a connection between education, democracy, and social justice. What is it about this society that allows us to satisfy our deep concerns about children who need the best education and fail to get it by simply making recommendations and not acting on them? The recommendations continue. In 2006 the College Board, in its report *Teachers and the Uncertain American Future*, makes this statement:

> We recommend abandoning the expectation that teacher-diversity goals will take care of themselves. Higher education must mount intense and targeted recruitment for minority students, programs that emphasize financial aid, along with loan forgiveness tied to years of teaching service.
>
> (The College Board, 2006, p. 21)

The report doesn't end there. It calls for making teaching a "preferred profession" by enhancing salaries for teachers as well as other measures, and undertaking "a national effort designed to *create a teaching force that looks like America*—that is to say, a teaching workforce in which the proportion of minority teachers matches the proportion of minority students" (The College Board, 2006, p. 22). In this report there also are bold recommendations about funding, and how to find the funds. But given the history of such recommendations, why should we be optimistic? We know that we continue to fail minority children. In New York City, for example, the high school graduation rate reported in 2004 was 58 percent for whites (not so great), but it was 32 percent for African Americans and 30 percent for Latinos (Orfield, 2004, p. 57). While we have not made progress, we know much more than we did when past recommendations were made. The new recommendations have the power of research to support them. This may be our last chance to make a difference. Having nearly 70 percent of minority children failing to graduate from high school in a great urban center is abysmal. Knowing that this is happening in a society that within 30 years will serve a majority of minority K-12 students is as uncomfortable a future as we can imagine. Indeed the title of Orfields's study, "Losing our Future," may well come to pass if we don't act this time.

The chapter authors, all of whom are cautious in avoiding over-interpreting the research they report on, provide significant evidence that attending to diversity in teacher education is critically important for improving the quality of education for a growing portion of our student population. Attending to diversity in teacher education means taking clear and unequivocal steps to ensure that the teaching force itself becomes more diverse to mirror the diversity of the student population *and* that all teachers learn how to effectively teach the diverse populations they will face in the course of their careers. It is our contention that we have failed to address this critical issue. Why have we ignored the clarion calls made ten, twenty and thirty years ago to increase the diversity of the teaching force and to improve the success rate of students of color, as discussed in the artifacts included in this section? The data presented in the three framing chapters confirm such failures and underscore the continuing challenge to all of us. We must think about what we want the future to be and how best to get there.

We could blame ourselves, and there is no doubt we have responsibility, but who are *we*, the teacher educators? Historically, "we" meant the faculty and administrators in schools, colleges and departments of education (SCDEs), but if we are determined to address issues of diversity appropriately, that description is not adequate. Our colleagues in arts and sciences must see themselves as teacher educators as well. In fact, most of the undergraduate students in teacher education spend the bulk of their coursework with arts and sciences faculty, not with faculty in the colleges of education. Similarly, students entering teaching at the graduate level have by and large completed full undergraduate programs in the arts and sciences without taking any education courses. Our colleagues in the public schools must identify themselves as teacher educators as well. There is compelling evidence, some of it reported in these chapters, of the critical impact that field experiences make on students' success in becoming teachers.

If we are serious about teaching to diversity, educators in arts and sciences and in elementary and secondary schools must be substantively involved with education faculty in preparing future teachers. Students must become aware of the inequalities that exist in the U.S. among our diverse populations before they enter the professional program so they can apply these understandings in their practice. Therefore, arts and sciences faculty must develop courses that focus on issues of diversity and multiculturalism and those courses should be required as part of their general education experience. Additionally, arts and sciences faculty must encourage their students, in particular students of color, to consider teaching as a career. Too often, students enter teaching as a fall-back career, because they fail to see it valued by their arts and sciences professors. And, as all of the chapter authors propose, our colleagues in the public schools must structure field experiences for our students that are rich in opportunities to practice culturally responsive teaching. We realize that the responsibility for promoting these actions falls primarily with faculty and administrators in education who must advocate for both diversification of the teacher candidate population and assure that the professional curriculum adequately prepares them for the diversity they will encounter in their future classrooms. That part of the "we," the teacher educators in the SCDEs, needs to make arts and sciences and public school faculty aware of the research reported here and the importance to our democracy of attending to the needs of all students. We can think of few more important actions that educators can take in the national interest than assuring that the increasingly diverse students in our schools have access to knowledge and the ability to think critically—thus closing the achievement gaps and providing them with enhanced opportunities for success in their lives.

There are examples of college, university and public school partnerships that have taken on this commitment to ensure that all these groups—faculty and administrators in education, arts and sciences, and the public schools—recognize their responsibility for preparing future teachers. Forty such settings are members of the National Network for

Educational Renewal, founded by John Goodlad. We do not mean to suggest that all of these partnerships have succeeded with this commitment or extended it adequately to addressing the diversity issues discussed in these chapters. Each of these settings, however, has an obligation to engage in research to test the assertion that when all three groups take on this challenge, we might make some headway in reducing the racial/ethnic achievement gap.

Another area for examination is the commitment to diversity embedded in the process that SCDEs seeking national accreditation must undergo. The National Council for the Accreditation of Teacher Education (NCATE), one of the two nationally recognized accrediting agencies, requires that several conditions regarding diversity be met. Standard 4, for instance, states:

> The unit designs, implements, and evaluates curriculum and experiences for candidates to acquire and apply the knowledge, skills, and dispositions necessary to help all students learn. These experiences include working with diverse higher education and school faculty, diverse candidates, and diverse students in P-12 schools.
>
> (NCATE, 2002)

The rubric used to assess the design, implementation, and evaluation of curriculum and experiences for this standard reads as follows:

> The unit clearly articulates the proficiencies that candidates are expected to develop during their professional program. Curriculum and accompanying field experiences are designed to help candidates understand the importance of diversity in teaching and learning. Candidates learn to develop and teach lessons that incorporate diversity and develop a classroom and school climate that values diversity. Candidates become aware of different teaching and learning styles shaped by cultural influences and are able to adapt instruction and services appropriately for all students, including students with exceptionalities. They demonstrate dispositions that value fairness and learning by all students. Assessments of candidate proficiencies provide data on the ability to help all students learn. Candidates' assessment data are used to provide feedback to candidates for improving their knowledge, skills and dispositions.
>
> (NCATE, 2002, p. 29)

This is quite a complete statement of what we need—curriculum, clear statements of dispositions, knowledge, and skills, and data to provide evidence that graduates "help all students learn." While the standard does not tell us how to go about reaching the goal, these framing chapters begin to. It should be noted that in addition to calling for a diverse cohort of future teachers who work with diverse students, the standard rightly expects a diverse faculty of teacher educators. If the standard were seriously applied, then half the teacher education programs in the nation, those accredited by NCATE, would be doing much of what the chapters in this section call for. It would be productive to determine whether differences exist in the extent to which graduates of NCATE accredited institutions that meet and do not meet the diversity standard (which would not disqualify them necessarily for accreditation) succeed in teaching students of racial/ethnic backgrounds.

Another aspect of teacher education that is part of the current landscape, and addressed in this section of the Handbook, is the appropriateness of assessing and developing dispositions during the admissions process and throughout the program. Increasingly, commentators writing in major news magazines and newspapers are challenging the use of dispositions for assessing teacher candidates. Their argument is that developing dispositions in candidates is a form of "mind control" and "left-leaning politics" when dispositions hint of elements of social justice. We believe instinctively, and with some evidence, that dispositions—which we view as comprised of attitudes, values, beliefs and actions—are important, particularly in preparing teachers to work effectively with students of cultural backgrounds different than their own. The dispositions often mentioned include respect for others who come from diverse backgrounds, belief in the importance of multiculturalism to a democracy, and empathy for those not treated equitably in society because of their difference. These dispositions are very complex sets of attributes and behaviors, and programs should use them as one factor in assessing students. We believe, for example, that if a teacher education student does not have a firm conviction that all children should have equal learning opportunities, there is likely insufficient time in the professional sequence of courses to change such a disposition. Additional research is needed to probe the links between teacher dispositions towards diversity and student learning.

Concern for the values and beliefs of teachers and their students on important issues related to cultural differences is not a new concept in teacher education. More than 30 years ago the American Association of Colleges for Teacher Education's issued its "No One Model American" statement which called for *the teaching of values that support cultural diversity and individual uniqueness* (AACTE, 1973). That document called for teaching such values at every level, including within programs for teacher education. Opposition to such long-standing positions are not based on new evidence—in fact as we see in these chapters we have, if anything, more of a basis for concern about such values and belief. Clearly the opposition has a basis in political dogma and ideology, which will unfortunately make further change in support of this work even more difficult.

The concern about dispositions raises another issue important to this discussion. Many critics of the work described in these chapters believe that the purposes of public education are narrowly constrained to clearly measurable knowledge and skills. Certainly the basis for adequate yearly progress that is part of No Child Left Behind would suggest that achievement on standardized tests is the single most important variable in judging a school. A very telling statement that illustrates this narrow position, especially in the context of multicultural education, comes from Chester Finn, President of the Fordham Foundation, who wrote:

> Civic education may sound like a good idea in theory, but in practice public schools could even do harm in this realm. Some educators harbor worrisome values: moral relativism, atheism, doubts about the superiority of democracy, undue deference to the "pluribus" at the expense of the "unum," discomfort with patriotism, cynicism toward established cultural conventions and civic institutions. Transmitting those values to children will gradually erode the foundations of a free society. Perhaps society would be better off if its schools stuck to the three R's and did a solid job in domains where they enjoy both competence and wide public support.
>
> (Finn, 2004, p. 14)

The research and recommendations reported in this section indicated the need for increased deference to the "pluribus" rather than the "unum." We can only reach the goal of "one out of many" when we attend to the needs of the many and equip them for full participation in society. Furthermore, a focus on "the three R's" is too narrow a definition of what we should expect of education in a democracy. We argue that we need educators who understand the full scope of the following four enduring purposes for public education:

- preparing each new generation to live in a socially just democratic society;
- providing access to knowledge and critical thinking for all students;
- helping students imagine and achieve all the possibilities for their place in society, and to have full access to life's chances; and
- enabling students to lead rich and rewarding personal lives characterized by understanding all aspects of human knowledge, including aesthetics, creativity, and personal health.

(Michelli, 2005)

What about the claim that No Child Left Behind, by requiring the disaggregated reporting of student achievement scores, will shine the light on inadequacies and foster reform? Several states, including New York, have reported disaggregated data for some time, and that alone has not led to reform. In fact, despite a court order mandating redistribution of educational resources to those cities in New York with the largest populations of students of color, the governor and legislature have yet to act on the order. But the kind of data NCLB yields may help in some jurisdictions. One affluent Virginia district recently "discovered" that African American students in the district were doing less well than students in large cities in Virginia, including Richmond and Norfolk. The superintendent said, "We had a perception that our performance is higher than the data would indicate, in part because of the accolades our schools get. Until you peel back the onion a little bit, you may not see areas where you are not successful" (*The Washington Post*, April 14, 2006, p. A01). So this is important information for the district, and it is of course surprising that they didn't know already. How will the district react? Time will tell, but what has happened elsewhere is that instead of focusing on the ability of teachers to successfully teach students of color, there has been a narrowing of the curriculum and an increased focus on what gets measured (Center of Education Policy, 2006). Not all of the purposes of education are served by this focus on standardized test scores. We cannot assume that even by exposing disparities like the one in Virginia the solution will be in keeping with all the recommendations of the chapters in this section.

There is still another factor that explains this failure to adequately prepare future teachers to ensure the success of all students, one that has already been alluded to in this commentary, and perhaps the most difficult one to overcome: the lack of political will to address the issues. Where are the policymakers in this? Where in policy do we find evidence that they have acted to assure that teacher education programs are designed to prepare teachers who can meet the standards we aspire to? Where are the resources to support excellent education and professional development in high need districts? Where is policy that requires public schools and arts and sciences departments to participate in teacher preparation? They are largely absent and we need to find out why. What drives policy makers? What prevents them from taking the actions we think they should take? Is it our failure to adequately educate them or the populace that elected them? Or is the problem rooted in ideological differences that are impossible to reconcile? George Lakoff's (2002) concept of "world view" may be applicable here. Is it possible that politicians and educators hold different world views—that is, different attitudes, values, beliefs about, and goals for, public education—that preclude a meeting of the minds?

Several principles of practice related to preparing teachers to teach diverse populations emerge from our experiences. We suggest that each can be the basis for research. First, those preparing teachers and other public school educators must have a clear, unambiguous shared vision that addresses the four enduring purposes of public education listed above. The vision must be the basis for all important academic decisions. A shared vision, as Peter Senge (1993) has suggested, is very powerful. When there is a shared vision, all participants understand with clarity what the goals are and what must be done to achieve them. A part of that shared vision must focus squarely on issues of diversity and meeting the needs of all students in schools. We cannot, for example, hide behind a program standard, including an accreditation one, without being clear about what it means to really meet it. Decisions about admission, curriculum, assessment, research agendas, and resource distribution, to name a few, must flow from the vision. A professional program needs a shared vision to make it effective, coherent, and distinctive. Developing such a vision requires a great deal of collaboration and professional development of all involved in educating educators and P-12 students. It is only through common readings, in-depth discussions, and a focused research agenda that we reach a shared vision. This is especially true in an area as complex as dealing with diversity in these times.

Second, teacher preparation programs and programs in public elementary and secondary schools must be renewed simultaneously. We cannot achieve our goals for diversity from either the vantage point of higher education or from the P-12 schools alone. It makes no sense to prepare teachers with the knowledge, skills and dispositions they need to be successful with all students if the system they work in does not embrace these goals overtly and consciously work towards them. We need to develop our research and educational agendas together, not separately.

Third, faculty and administrators in education, the arts and sciences, and the public schools must work together as equal partners in the preparation of future educators and in the renewal of education. To successfully diversify our faculties and reach all children, all must share both authority and accountability. Formal structures to support this collaboration and appropriate reward systems need to be developed. A failure to include all who must be involved inevitably leads to finger pointing. We are all in this together! Admittedly, this is an incomplete list of who must be involved. By mentioning faculty and administrators we mention only those directly involved in this work on a daily basis. We cannot forget the importance of collaboration with policy makers, parents, business and community leaders.

Fourth, teacher educators must collectively advocate for teaching for democracy and social justice to ensure equity for all children. The authors of these chapters have set goals that are not only educational, but political and moral as well. Teacher educators must be grounded in all of these perspectives in order to successfully advocate for programs that meet the needs of all students, especially those from high need areas. Unless we are active in doing this, we have not fulfilled our professional responsibilities.

Lastly, excellent programs assess their outcomes regularly, and provide evidence relating to the full range of their vision for public schools and the education of educators. We must be willing to assemble the evidence about what works in achieving our goals. This is an important, but daunting task. Even when we focus on what one would expect to be the most easily measured outcome of schools—student knowledge—the task is complex. A research project underway in New York City is described in an article appropriately entitled *Complex by Design* (Boyd *et al.*, 2006). In that study, researchers seek to determine the effectiveness of the many pathways into teaching in New York City using a variety of measures, including value added assessment (where adequate data are present). This research needs to be extended to determine the success of teachers who complete different programs with a variety of school populations that differ in race, culture and language. This is a measure of only one of the outcomes we hope for in education, and each college and university must use qualitative and quantitative measures where appropriate to examine their impact on the full range of sought after outcomes.

Programs also need to assess themselves with respect to factors that affect their ability to prepare teachers of color by examining barriers to program completion. The work at the University of Illinois at Chicago is an excellent example of a program that found factors working against African American students' success and made programmatic changes that eliminated the barriers (see Chou *et al.*, 2006). Similarly, work at Boston College (see Cochran-Smith *et al.*, 2006) and at Montclair State University (see Villegas & Lucas, 2006) that aims to assess achievement of difficult to measure outcomes related to social justice and diversity represent promising lines of research and development.

What can we conclude? The authors of the framing chapters in the diversity section of the Handbook have added to our knowledge base and we clearly know more than ever before about the connections among diversity, student learning, and a commitment to social justice. There is more to be done to test our assertions and common convictions. We need evidence of what works across the broad spectrum of the purposes of education in a democracy and the political will to make a difference. We need to examine ourselves, perhaps even redefine who we are and how we hold ourselves accountable. The changing demographics of the next several decades require that we take action through research and practice to assure that all children reach their fullest potential in life.

REFERENCES

American Association of Colleges for Teacher Education (1973) *No one model American.* Washington, DC: Author.

Boyd, W., Grossman, P., Lankford, H., Loeb, S., Michelli, N., & Wyckoff, J. (2006) Complex by design: investigating pathways into teaching in New York City schools. *Journal of Teacher Education*, 57(2), 155–166.

Center of Education Policy (2006) *From the capital to the classroom: year four of No Child Left Behind.* Washington, DC: Author.

The College Board (2006). *Teachers and the uncertain American future.* New York: Author.

Chou, V., Fleming, J., Radinsky, J., & Miltner, D. (April 2006) *How are we doing? Reframing accountability as an opportunity for institutional reflection.* Paper presented at the Annual Meeting of the American Educational Research Association, San Francisco.

Cochran-Smith, M., Shakeman, K., & Barnatt, J. (April 2006) *Learning to teach for social justice: complex matters, complex measures.* Paper presented at the Annual Meeting of the American Educational Research Association, San Francisco.

Finn, C. E. (2004) Faulty Engineering. *Education Next* 4(2), 14.

Lakoff, G. (2002) *Moral politics.* Chicago: The University of Chicago Press.

Michelli, N. M. (2005) Education for democracy: what can it be? In N. M. Michelli and D. Keiser (eds.), *Teacher Education for Democracy and Social Justice*, pp. 3–30. New York: Routledge.

NCATE (2002) *Professional standards for the accreditation of schools, colleges, and departments of education.* Washington, DC: Author.

Orfield G. (2004) *Losing our future: how minority children are being left behind by the graduation rate crisis.* Cambridge, MA: The Civil Rights Project.

Senge, P. (1993). *The Fifth Discipline.* New York: Doubleday.

The Washington Post (April 14, 2006) *Fairfax success masks gap for Black students: test scores in county lag behind state's poorer areas* (p. A01). Washington, DC: Author.

Villegas, A. M. & Lucas, T. (April 2006) *Holding ourselves accountable: assessing preservice teachers' development as culturally and linguistically responsive educators.* Paper presented at the Annual Meeting of the American Educational Research Association, San Francisco.

37 Troubling diversity

Victoria Chou and Karen Sakash
University of Illinois at Chicago

The construct "diversity" is vague enough that it can mean almost anything to anyone. It is both inoffensive and plastic, so it can fit very different ideological and educational orientations. And when no rationale for privileging one kind of diversity over another is readily available, all are equally valid or easily trivialized. It is safe to say that virtually every teacher education program in the nation claims to teach for diversity, despite the evidence that our graduates are not serving the educational needs of all groups equitably.

This section of the Handbook offers a clear focus on how diversity operates in three distinctive sectors of teacher education: the preparation of White teachers to teach students of diverse backgrounds (Sleeter), the recruitment and preparation of teachers of color (Villegas and Davis), and the preparation of all teachers—regardless of their backgrounds—to teach English language learners (Lucas and Grinberg). Our essay builds on the discussions of these three aspects of teacher education, as developed in the framing chapters, and raises additional questions about how race and language are or ought to be addressed in the education of teachers today. By way of conclusion, we discuss how schools of education must "trouble diversity," to borrow Kevin Kumashiro's (2002) language of complicating existing paradigms, to create a truly pluralistic approach to teacher preparation.

ON PREPARING WHITE PRESERVICE TEACHERS TO TEACH STUDENTS OF DIVERSE BACKGROUNDS

Sleeter's platform for preparing White preservice teachers to teach students of diverse backgrounds rests on three supports: (1) cross-cultural community-based learning, (2) professional coursework on culture and equity pedagogy, and (3) field experiences in classrooms that serve students of color.

We emphatically agree with Sleeter that White teacher candidates need *community-based learning experiences* to build an experiential foundation for teaching students from cultures other than their own. We have learned that this cannot be accomplished on the fly during student teaching, however. Finding time, curricular space, and adequate funding for these experiences is challenging. There may be insufficient time in the typical teacher preparation program for the necessary cultural learning to go beyond eye-opening. Can a semester- or even a year-long experience effect deep attitudinal change? Or should we select into teacher education only those applicants who already possess dispositions that are supportive of diversity? Cross-cultural community-based learning is insufficient to prepare White preservice candidates to teach "other people's children" well, unless they are already favorably inclined toward diversity from the start of the program.

Like Sleeter, we believe that cross-cultural community-based learning experiences must be "well-planned, linked directly to teacher education, and involve guided reflection." We recognize, however, that the vast majority of teacher educators themselves have received little or no preparation to support preservice candidates in these experiences. Without understanding how our own dysconscious racism, to use Joyce King's (1990) phrase, operates in schools and communities, we (teacher educators) may unwittingly perpetuate stereotypes by positioning our teacher candidates as naive voyeurs who barge carelessly into community places and make uninformed critical judgments about what they are seeing.

We also endorse Sleeter's recommendation for *professional coursework on culture and equity pedagogy*. Such coursework can map a progression from big-picture analyses of culture and institutional racism—such as those posed in the Glazer (1993) artifact—to self-examination, to pedagogical applications for the classroom. In our particular institutional context, our biggest challenge lies in getting teacher education faculty to make the shared programmatic commitment that results in a coherent curriculum organized around culture and equity pedagogy. Albeit challenging, it is critical for teacher educators to make the shared programmatic commitment that results in a coherent curriculum organized around culture and equity pedagogy. Despite our own university's avowed commitment to serving its urban community, we know that the problems of institutional racism pervade all of the nation's schools in urban, suburban and rural locales, our own included. As such, the University of Illinois at Chicago (UIC) is a land-grant institution with an avowed commitment to serving the urban context. We recognize that most institutions do not have such an explicitly urban mission. We know, however, that the problems of institutional racism pervade the nation's schools in urban, suburban, and rural locales. As such, every teacher education program needs to place at the center of its work the preparation of teachers to counter the effects of that racism.

The segregated disciplinary spaces within schools and colleges of education make it difficult for us to act as a holistic and reflective learning community. While exceptions exist, faculty taking an explicitly "critical" theoretical orientation often reside in social foundations departments. Methods faculty, in the typical division of program labors, are often focused on more disciplinary concerns, while faculty who supervise student teachers are generally more interested in basic pedagogical development. Faculty responsibilities are frequently divided between teacher preparation and advanced graduate programs related to specialized disciplinary and research interests, with the infelicitous outcome that many faculty view their teacher education work as little more than "service" contributions which are not central to their research agendas. Add to this a general education curriculum that usually resides outside the school/college of education and must respond to the always-changing State curriculum mandates. Given these divergent interests and perspectives, the development of a coherent curriculum that can equip candidates to challenge the status quo presents a seemingly insurmountable challenge.

How to secure teacher educator buy-in to create a coherent curriculum that focuses on culture and equity pedagogy is a major challenge to us all. We are well aware of the problematic nature of approaching this task by "going with the goers" (Au, 2005). Such an approach tends to divide the faculty, build resistance among those who elect not to go, and lower trust all around. We need to think seriously about the kinds of conversations and professional development needed to foster common understandings about the desired curriculum. We also need to explore the kinds of institutional incentives that must be in place to make this happen.

We have dedicated considerable efforts and resources to developing *field experiences in classrooms that serve students of color*, the third leg of Sleeter's platform. As such, we are acutely familiar with the challenges of developing excellent field experiences in schools in economically oppressed communities. We realize that many teacher educators are disinclined to place teacher candidates in classrooms where practicing teachers are perceived to engage largely in didactic, scripted teaching and test preparation —strategies that sadly abound in urban schools. In these settings, the *collaborative resonance* approach proposed by Cochran-Smith (2004), which calls for teacher candidates to work with practicing teachers to connect critique with practice, would be most appropriate. We submit the following cautions, however. The data on the effects of didactic, scripted teaching on student learning are decidedly mixed, as are the data on more inquiry-based teaching approaches. Moreover, schools in historically oppressed communities, many of which fall under NCLB sanctions, are not offered the curricular and instructional freedoms afforded other schools. It is also important to remember that White, "progressive" teacher educators' perspectives on what is good teaching often differ from the perspectives of good teaching held by members of racial/ethnic minority groups. So long as members of the teaching profession are predominantly White, the language and programmatic emphasis of social justice are likely to prevail over programmatic emphases that enable African American and Latino teachers to teach the children and youth of their own communities of color.

So long as members of the teaching profession are predominantly white and middle-class, we need to stay alert to the fact that their programmatic preferences and emphases may be unjustifiably privileged over those of African American and Latino teachers who are teaching the children and youth of their own communities of color. When we attempt to place teacher candidates in exclusively Black schools, however, at least some teacher candidates and faculty employ "diversity" in a rationale of resistance, i.e. claiming that schools with a homogeneous Black student body are not sufficiently diverse. This is especially problematic in school districts like Chicago in which 46 percent of all schools have student enrollments that are at least 90 percent African American. As teacher educators, we must confront and address our own and teacher candidates' discomforts and fears about working with "others."

ON RECRUITING AND PREPARING TEACHERS OF COLOR FOR STUDENTS OF COLOR

We could not agree more with the arguments of Villegas and Davis for increasing the recruitment of people of color into the teaching profession. Their "leaky pipeline" metaphor describes the terrible loss of students of color at every point along the educational continuum. Consequences of such losses echo the devastating impact of the dismissal of more than 38,000 Black educators in the decade following the 1954 *Brown v. Board of Education of Topeka* decision, as Ethridge (1979) aptly points out. A disproportionate number of the overwhelmingly Black and Latino graduates of urban public school systems nationwide who enter college do so with academic gaps that must be addressed before they can be admitted to teacher preparation programs. Rather than merely serving as gatekeepers, it behooves us in schools and colleges of education to join our arts and sciences colleagues to help address the learning gaps among students of color at our institutions. Once students of color are in our programs, we must remain vigilant to ensure they are well supported through graduation and beyond in their teaching careers.

Otherwise, the cycle of negative consequences for students of color in this country will never be broken.

Villegas and Davis argue that teacher preparation programs concentrate almost exclusively on the needs of White teacher candidates, overlooking the needs of prospective teachers of color. We find historical resonance in Glazer's (1993) account of the way in which the concept of assimilation never embraced African Americans. Like Villegas and Davis, we think it is of paramount importance for teacher educators to devote significantly more attention to the needs of preservice candidates of color. In our view, the needs of this group cannot be adequately addressed without a critical mass of teacher educators of color. The American Association of Colleges of Teacher Education's "Multicultural Statement No One Model American" recognized this in 1972. Evidently, it is harder to apply the lesson than to make a statement. And just as teacher educators must create a safe environment for dialogue among teacher candidates, so too must teacher educators of color be assured of a safe environment for dialogue among their colleagues. Faculty members of color bring distinctive perspectives that enrich the content and conduct of teacher preparation programs. While their numbers are increasing, many more are needed.

While prospective teachers of color enter their preparation programs with cultural knowledge and experiences that place them at an advantage over their White counterparts in teaching students of color, Villegas and Davis affirm that they nevertheless also need support translating such knowledge and experience into sound pedagogical practices. If we take seriously Gloria Ladson-Billings' (1995) assertion about inserting education into the culture, rather than vice versa—and at UIC we do—then we have to consider the cultural backgrounds of our teacher candidates just as we ask them to consider the cultural backgrounds of their future students. Given that most teacher preparation programs draw at least some students from non-mainstream backgrounds, we ourselves need to engage in differentiated instruction to prepare future teachers, regardless of their race/ethnicity, to teach racially and ethnically diverse student populations. That is, we need to model what we teach.

ON PREPARING ALL TEACHERS TO TEACH ENGLISH LANGUAGE LEARNERS (ELLs)

Lucas and Grinberg explain why, in recent years, greater numbers of English language learners have been taught in mainstream classrooms by teachers who have received no special preparation for undertaking this task. As these authors point out, content related to teaching English language learners too often is absent from the curricula of teacher preparation programs in early childhood, elementary, and secondary education. If second language learning issues are addressed, they either are melded into an unwieldy multicultural course or loosely bundled with other multicultural content into the overall teacher preparation curriculum. In the former case, teacher candidates have no access to key language-related topics; in the latter case, those issues are submerged in a host of competing "diversity" topics. And in neither case are classroom teachers provided with direct experience working with English language learners. Fortunately, in recent years, federal funding focusing on programs that target "all" teachers has enabled more teacher candidates to take coursework leading to ESL endorsements and credentials. Such efforts have the potential for breaking down some of the attitudinal barriers pointed out by Lucas and Grinberg.

There are other ways that teacher education programs can prepare prospective mainstream classroom teachers to teach ELLs. For example, placing non-bilingual teacher candidates to learn side-by-side with bilingual teacher candidates could help both groups naturally develop new understandings related to language and culture. Non-specialists could also be placed in bilingual/ESL classrooms for at least a portion of their field experiences. And pairing bilingual and non-bilingual teacher candidates in field experiences can facilitate richer conversations about appropriate instruction for ELL students.

We see these pairings between bilingual and non-bilingual teacher candidates mirrored in the increasing collaborations between regular classroom and bilingual/ESL teachers (Mosca, 2006). We know that greater communication between these two groups at the preservice level can be key to promoting knowledge-sharing in their future work as teachers in schools. Both sets of teachers benefit from collaborative relationships, and when the students are mixed for instruction, everyone learns more about language and culture (Whitmore & Crowell, 2006).

Another trend that parallels teacher collaboration is the increase in dual language programs which are implemented using many different models, but often result in a whole-school focus on valuing two languages for instruction (Cloud *et al.*, 2000). Often, teachers proficient only in English become involved in the English instructional component in dual language instruction. We are also seeing increased attention to professional development to prepare regular teachers to support English language learners through content-based ESL instruction (Echevarria *et al.*, 2000). More regular classroom math, science, social studies, and other content-specific teachers have come to understand their role in making their lessons comprehensible for English language learners. We believe teacher candidates would benefit from experiencing the variety of learning environments available to English language learners.

Similar to the argument made above for teacher educators of color, if more bilingual/ESL faculty were hired into general teacher education positions, the knowledge base regarding English language learners would grow. Whether or not a teacher educator is bilingual may matter less than the individual's informed understanding of current assessment and instruction policies at the local, state, and national levels. All teacher educators need to know the current policies regarding the education of English language learners. The recruitment of more bilingual individuals into the teaching profession continues to be important, and more so now that federal and state policies are de-emphasizing native language instruction and fewer federal scholarship opportunities for preparing bilingual teachers are available. Perhaps teacher accreditation bodies such as the National Council for the Accreditation of Teacher Education (NCATE) can grapple with the "Call to Action" outlined by AACTE's Committee on Multicultural Education (2002) to shed light on the specific teacher preparation work needed to advance the field beyond a surface understanding of the concept of "diversity" and recognize the urgency of providing the best education possible for English language learners and those who educate them. But teacher education programs need not wait for NCATE to act on this matter.

IN CLOSING

Our essay suggests how schools of education might "trouble diversity." In our combined 56 years of higher education experience, developing an effective approach to culturally pluralistic teacher preparation is the hardest job we have ever tackled. Traditional teacher preparation for a predominantly White teacher force—most often grounded in mainstream values and principles—make it much easier to go with the cultural and linguistic assimilation flow. Breaking with this tradition involves helping teacher candidates ground their teaching in the culture and language of the students they teach. This requires that future teachers develop a deep understanding of the ways of knowing, learning, and behaving of others who are different from themselves. Equally important, they must learn to see themselves in relation to those others. Accomplishing this is no easy task.

It is time to take a critical, reflexive look at how poorly we are serving the learning needs of millions of African American and Latino students who continue to be left behind. We must move beyond so-called diversity standards to familiarize ourselves and our teacher candidates with the cultural particulars of the students we serve and the concomitant implications for teaching and teacher preparation.

REFERENCES

American Association of Colleges for Teacher Education Commission on Multicultural Education (1972) *No one model American.* Washington, DC: Author.

American Association of Colleges for Teacher Education (2002) *Educators' preparation for cultural and linguistic diversity: a call to action.* Washington, DC: Author.

Au, K. H. (2005) Negotiating the slippery slope: school change and literacy achievement. *Journal of Literacy Research,* 37, 267–288.

August, D. (n.d.) *Developing literacy in second language-learners. A report of the National Literacy Panel on language-minority children and youth. Executive summary.* Retrieved March 21, 2006 from the Center for Applied Linguistics, Web site: http://www.cal.org/natl-lit-panel/reports/Executive_Summary.pdf

Cochran-Smith, M. (2004) *Walking the road: race, diversity, and social justice in teacher education.* New York: Teachers College Press.

Cloud, N., Genesee, F., & Hamayan, E. (2000) *Dual language instruction: a handbook for enriched education.* Boston, MA: Heinle & Heinle Publishers.

Echevarria, J., Vogt, M., & Short, D. J. (2004) *Making content comprehensible for English language learners: the SIOP model* (Second ed.). Boston: Allyn & Bacon.

Ethridge, S. (1979) Impact of the 1954 *Brown v. Topeka Board of Education* decision on Black educators. *The Negro Educational Review,* 30(4), 217–232.

Glazer, N. (1993, November) Is assimilation dead? *The Annals of the American Academy of Political and Social Sciences,* 530, 122–136.

King, J. (1990) Dysconscious racism: ideology, identity, and the miseducation of teachers. *Journal of Negro Education,* 60, 133–146.

Kumashiro, K. K. (2002) *Troubling education: queer activism and antioppressive pedagogy.* New York: RoutledgeFalmer.

Ladson-Billings, G. (1995) But that's just good teaching! The case for culturally relevant teaching. *Theory into Practice,* 34, 159–165.

Mosca, C. (2006) How do you ensure that everyone in the school shares the responsibilities for educating English language learners, not just those who are specialists in the field? In E. Hamayan & R. Freeman (eds.), *English language learners at school: a guide for administrators* (pp. 109–110). Philadelphia, PA: Caslon Publishing.

Whitmore, K. F. & Crowell, C. G. (2005) Bilingual education students reflect on their language education: reinventing a classroom 10 years later. *Journal of Adolescent & Adult Literacy,* 49, 270–285.

Part 6

How do people learn to teach?

Teacher learning over time

Editor: Sharon Feiman-Nemser

Part 6
Framing chapters

38 Teacher learning

How do teachers learn to teach?

Sharon Feiman-Nemser
Brandeis University

INTRODUCTION

A recent publication sponsored by the National Academy of Education carries the title, "Preparing teachers for a changing world: What teachers should learn and be able to do" (Darling-Hammond and Bransford, 2005). The formulation of the sub-title with its explicit use of the verb "learn" reflects a subtle but important shift in how researchers are beginning to think about and study the professional education and development of teachers. The more common and related question, What do teachers need to know, care about, and be able to do, has preoccupied teacher educators and scholars of teacher education for over a century and continues to do so. At the same time, researchers have come to appreciate that learning to teach extends beyond the boundaries of formal teacher education. Moreover, questions about the content of teacher learning are not the same as questions about how teachers acquire, generate and learn to use knowledge in teaching. Influenced by developments in learning theory and new understandings of teaching, scholars are shaping a new area of research on teacher learning with important implications for teacher education policy and practice.

A messy problem space

When we talk about research on teacher learning, we generally mean research on how people learn to teach and develop their practice over time. But this seemingly straightforward statement embraces conceptual and empirical questions about the content, processes, opportunities and contexts of teacher learning. It also implies questions about the consequences of teacher learning. What do teachers need to learn in order to help all students achieve their potential? What kinds of intentional learning opportunities help teachers acquire and develop the vision, knowledge, practices, frameworks and dispositions they need to promote student learning? Since becoming an accomplished teacher happens over time across settings, research on teacher learning includes studies of what teachers learn from teacher preparation and professional development and how they use what they learn in teaching. It also includes studies of what teachers learn from the daily experiment of teaching and from informal interactions with colleagues. Ultimately research on teacher learning must consider how the outcomes of teacher learning contribute to student learning. How else will we know whether teachers' newly acquired knowledge and skills are helping them become more effective teachers?

Research on teacher learning involves value-based considerations as well. The knowledge, skills and commitments that teachers need to learn derive from a conception of accomplished teaching which in turn reflects a view of what students should learn and what schools are for. The connection between public expectations for schooling and requirements for teacher learning is expressed in prescriptions for the curriculum of teacher education, in professional teaching standards, and even in expectations for research on teacher learning. For example, the rationale for linking evidence of teacher learning with evidence of student learning comes in part from the educational imperative to enhance learning outcomes for a diverse student population.

Research on teacher learning is a complex area of inquiry that sits at the intersection of several fields of research and areas of study, including research and theories of learning, studies of teaching and teacher knowledge, research on teacher preparation, new teacher induction and professional development, studies of school change and teaching culture. This explains the inevitable overlap between the contents of this section and other sections in this Handbook, especially "Teacher Capacities: Knowledge, Beliefs, Skills and Commitments," and "Diversity and Teacher Education." It also underscores the challenge of designing the kind of research that considers the interaction of person, program and school setting; accounts for changes in what teachers know, do, think and feel over time; and addresses the question of how teacher learning promotes student learning.

The diverse intellectual roots of research on teacher learning, the need to connect different lines of work, the mix of descriptive and normative issues, and the variety of frameworks and paradigms that researchers have used to study teacher learning complicate the task of synthesizing what we know and what we need to learn. Still, we have made some progress in conceptualizing and studying what learning to teach entails since the 1980s when teacher learning emerged as a new focus of research (Cochran-Smith and Fries, this volume).

A thematic framework of learning to teach

Learning to teach can be conceptualized around four broad themes—learning to *think* like a teacher, learning to *know* like a teacher, learning to *feel* like a teacher and learning to *act* like a teacher. This formulation highlights major theories and findings in research on teacher learning. Compatible with contemporary frameworks for understanding teaching and learning, it underscores the interconnections of content, process and contexts in learning to teach.

The first theme—learning to think like a teacher—points to the intellectual work of teaching and the influence of cognitive science on studies of teacher learning. Learning to think like a teacher requires a critical examination of one's existing beliefs, a transition to pedagogical thinking, and the development of meta-cognitive awareness. A substantial body of research documents the beliefs that teachers hold and the ways in which these beliefs influence what teachers do and do not learn from professional education and teaching. (For reviews, see Richardson and Placier, 2001; Wideen *et al.*, 1998). Without an opportunity to examine critically their existing beliefs in light of new possibilities and understandings, teachers may ignore or distort new ideas and practices.

Learning to think like a teacher means moving beyond naïve beliefs, for example, that teaching is easy and learning involves the simple transfer of information from teacher to student, to embrace more defensible views of teaching, learning, subject matter and students. It means learning to place the activities of teaching and learning in a pedagogical framework that links ends and means (Lortie, 1975; Feiman-Nemser & Buchmann, 1986). It means developing the capacity to think on one's feet, reflect on and adjust one's practice.

The second theme—learning to know like a teacher—highlights the different kinds of knowledge that good teaching depends on, including the knowledge teachers generate in practice. (For a discussion of views of knowledge and their implications for teacher learning, see Cochran-Smith & Lytle, 1999.) Teachers need to know a great deal in order to enhance the academic learning of all students. They need deep knowledge of subject matter and how to teach it to diverse learners (Ball & McDiarmid, 1990; Kennedy, 1991). They need to understand how children grow and learn and how culture and language influence their learning. They need to know about curriculum, pedagogy, classroom organization and assessment. They need to understand the broad purposes of schooling and how those purposes affect their work. (For a recent synthesis of knowledge for teaching, see Darling-Hammond & Bransford, 2005.)

Depth and breadth are two important dimensions of teacher knowledge. Equally important is how teachers organize and "hold" their knowledge. Considerable research on learning indicates that competence in a given area depends on having a solid foundation of factual knowledge organized around a conceptual framework and held in ways that facilitate retrieval and use (National Research Council, 2000). This principle has important implications for the curriculum of teacher education and professional development, and for our understanding of teaching and teacher learning.

Besides knowledge *for* teaching which can be learned outside practice, teachers need knowledge *of* teaching which can only be gained in the context of their work. For example, teachers may anticipate what students will find difficult or confusing, but they cannot know ahead of time how particular students will make sense of what they are learning. This underscores the importance of learning to learn in and from teaching.

The third theme—learning to feel like a teacher—signals the fact that teaching and learning to teach are deeply personal work, engaging teachers' emotions and identity as well as their intellect. Forming a professional identity is a complex process that fuses past, present and future ideals and realities (Featherstone, 1993). What kind of self-knowledge do teachers need, especially when they teach students whose backgrounds differ from their own? How do teachers manage the gap between their vision of the kind of teacher they want to be and the realities and challenges they face (Hammerness, 2006; Ladson-Billings, 2001)? How do teachers reconcile different images of themselves as teachers and colleagues and develop an earned sense of intellectual and moral authority (Roosevelt, 2007)?

For some time, discussions of teacher capacity have been framed in terms of knowledge, skills and dispositions. Dispositions unite ability with desire, orienting teachers to act in particular ways (Schwab, 1976). For example, the disposition to see all children as capable of learning leads teachers to hold high standards, to seek out students' strengths and interests as a foundation for learning, and to persist in helping all students find success. Accomplishing these goals may require collaboration with colleagues' more than heroic efforts on the part of individual teachers. McDiarmid and Clevenger-Bright (this volume) criticize prevailing views of teacher capacity as "too static and individualistic" and argue that teachers need the dispositions to participate productively in communities of practice and to examine their teaching in light of a range of evidence.

Ultimately teachers must learn to integrate ways of thinking, knowing, feeling and acting into a principled and responsive teaching practice. Inside the classroom, teachers engage in a wide range of activities—explaining, listening, questioning, managing, demonstrating, assessing, inspiring. Outside the classroom, teachers must plan for teaching, collaborate with colleagues, work with parents and administrators. The complex, uncertain, multidimensional nature of teaching exacerbates what Mary Kennedy (1999) calls the "problem of enactment"—putting one's intentions into action.

To act like a teacher, teachers need a repertoire of skills, strategies and routines and the judgment to figure out what to do when. The normal busyness of classrooms requires the establishment of routines to make teaching manageable. At the same time, the unpredictability of teaching means that teachers are constantly absorbing new information and using it to decide what to do next. So learning to act like a teacher means developing what cognitive scientists call "adaptive expertise" (Hatano & Oura, 2003).

Cognitive science and teacher learning

New understandings from cognitive science about how people learn are beginning to influence our understanding of how teachers learn to teach and develop their practice over time. In a review of research on learning to teach, Borko and Putman (1996) offer a succinct definition of learning from a cognitive science perspective. Learning is "an active, constructive process that is heavily influenced by an individual's existing knowledge and beliefs and is situated in particular contexts" (pp. 674–675). This definition highlights two key ideas. Learning is not a passive process of absorbing new information. Like all learners, teachers interpret new knowledge and experience through their existing beliefs and modify and reinterpret new ideas on the basis of what they already know and believe. What teachers learn is also influenced by the social and cultural contexts where knowledge is acquired and used, including the particulars of subject matter and students.

Many early studies of teacher learning focused on individual teachers and the changes that did or did not occur in their knowledge and beliefs as they participated in teacher education and professional development. More recently, researchers have adopted broader perspectives that consider the interactions between what teachers bring and what they encounter, including the contexts of their learning. Socio-cultural theories are particularly useful in longitudinal studies of learning to teach because they focus on how the various settings in which teachers learn—university courses, student teaching, schools and classrooms, mentoring relationships—enable and constrain their adoption and use of new knowledge and practices and their ongoing learning.

In one study, for example, researchers (Grossman *et al.*, 1999) followed a group of beginning elementary and secondary teachers from their last year of teacher education through their first three years of teaching. They found that the teachers used the reflective stance they had developed during their teacher education program to make sense of their teaching situation. Although some struggled as first year teachers, by the second year, most were able to use specific pedagogical tools (e.g. Writers Workshop) they had learned about in teacher education. The research team also identified particular aspects of the school and district context, including access to particular curricular materials and professional development opportunities, which dramatically affected teachers' on-the-job learning and their ability to use ideas and strategies introduced in teacher education. Some of these ideas and perspectives are taken up in the framing chapters and artifacts which make up this section.

The framing chapters

Each of the three framing chapters deals with an enduring aspect of teacher learning. Cheryl Rosaen and Susan Florio-Ruane examine the necessary but problematic role of experience in learning to teach. Carol Rodgers and Katherine Scott focus on the process of identity formation in teachers. Joel Westheimer considers colleagues as a salient resource and context for teacher learning. These chapters examine familiar issues in new ways and introduce emerging areas of scholarship on teacher learning.

While no one denies the essential role of experience in learning to teach, we may not appreciate the role that language plays in mediating what teachers can and do learn from first hand experience. In "The Metaphors By Which We Teach: Experience, Metaphor and Culture in Teacher Education," Rosaen and Florio-Ruane look at the experience of teaching and learning to teach through a socio-cultural lens, asking what and how prospective teachers learn in terms of their work and identity. They argue that experience is not only an essential activity by means of which a beginner learns to teach and is inducted into a practice and community of practitioners, it is fundamentally shaped by pervasive metaphors in our culture. To illustrate their argument that metaphors influence what teachers learn from university and school-based experiences, the authors examine the meanings and potential impact of three common metaphors—field experience, struggling reader and at risk learners. One implication is that novices may have difficulty learning well from experience without professional education that equips them with frameworks to interpret and organize their insights about students and to sort out the implications for teaching.

In "The Development of the Personal Self and Professional Identity in Learning to Teach," Carol Rodgers and Katherine Sullivan open up an important aspect of teacher learning that has not been the subject of much empirical investigation. Teachers construct a sense of themselves as professionals by combining parts of their past and pieces of their present with images of the kind of teacher and colleague they want to become and the kind of classroom they want to have (Featherstone, 1993). The identities teachers form influence where they put their effort and guide them in carrying out their responsibilities (Hammerness, 2006). But teacher identity is not fixed and unchanging. Reviewing contemporary conceptions of identity, Rodgers and Sullivan point out that teacher identity is shifting, multi-faceted, formed in relationships, influenced by contexts, constructed in stories. Rodgers and Sullivan are especially interested in how teachers can learn to "author" their own professional identity. They introduce Robert Kegan's constructivist-developmental theory as one framework for thinking about the psychological circumstances under which this is more or less possible. They also provide examples of historical and contemporary teacher education programs that take identity formation seriously and suggest needed research, including attention to issues of race, class and gender in teacher identity formation.

Two decades of research on teacher community and teacher collaboration have produced compelling evidence that improvements in teaching are most likely to occur in schools where teachers work together. Whether the focus is on novices learning to teach in the company of mentors or teachers at different career stages coming together to develop curriculum, analyze student work, discuss problems of practice or implement a new instructional program, researchers are demonstrating the power (some would say necessity) of collective activity to strengthen teaching and enhance student learning. Joel Westheimer reviews much of this research in his chapter, "Learning Among Colleagues: Teacher Community and the Enterprise of Education." The chapter is organized around five goals that researchers and reformers have set for professional learning communities among teachers. Westheimer also discusses challenges to teacher learning in community such as teacher isolation, the constraints of time and space, and the tension between inclusivity and competing ideologies. Finally he shows how the community metaphor intersects with notions of democracy, social justice, and visions of the good society.

The artifacts

The three artifacts that accompany this section span the twentieth century, illustrating the persistence of concerns about teacher learning. Although empirical studies of teacher learning did not emerge until the 1980s, the idea of teachers as learners was articulated decades earlier by progressive educators like John Dewey and Lucy Sprague Mitchel whose views of learning are compatible with contemporary socio-cultural theories. The Dewey essay examines the proper focus of teacher preparation in laying a foundation for continued learning from teaching. The Mitchel chapter outlines a large-scale experiment in inservice education that transformed urban teachers' practice and identity. Berliner's essay on the development of expertise in teaching lends empirical support to the fact that learning to teach well happens over time and does not automatically result from teaching experience. Read as a set, the artifacts offer different answers to the question of how teacher preparation and professional development can assist teachers along the path toward adaptive expertise.

In his 1904 essay on "The Relation of Theory to Practice in Education," Dewey distinguishes two approaches to practice work in teacher education, the laboratory approach and the apprenticeship. Influenced by the rise of the research university, Dewey favored the laboratory approach. In his view, teacher preparation should develop the intellectual habits needed for personal mastery of practical skills rather than focusing on developing technical proficiency "lest immediate skill be got at the cost of the power to go on growing." For Dewey, the supreme mark of the teacher is the ability to interpret and activate students' motivational and intellectual processes. To do this, teachers need the capacity to see what is going on in the minds of their students and to figure out how to engage them in worthwhile learning. If student teachers are faced with the challenge of managing a class before they become students of subject matter and learning, they will develop their teaching habits on the basis of "what works" to maintain order rather than what pupils need to move their learning forward.

It is easy to misread Dewey as making the case for studying theory before encountering practice. Actually the sequence he outlines involves the study of subject matter and educational psychology *in conjunction with* critical reflection on personal learning experiences, focused classroom observations, tutoring, curriculum investigation and curriculum development as foundations for more practical experience. Although his language may be quaint, Dewey's recommendations for inquiry-oriented, content-rich, learning-centered teacher preparation foreshadow contemporary teacher education programs committed to laying a foundation for learning in and from teaching (see Darling-Hammond, 2000).

The second artifact from *Our Children, Our Schools* by Lucy Sprague Mitchel, founder of Bank Street College, describes a system-wide inservice experiment in the 1940s which introduced progressive educational ideas and practices to teachers in the New York City public schools. The chapter, "Growth of Teachers in Professional Maturity," documents the stages teachers went through as they unlearned traditional attitudes and pedagogies, constructed a new professional identity, and learned new ways of working with children and content.

In the beginning, teachers were impatient with talk by the Bank Street Workshop staff about what children are like or how to fit a curriculum to their needs. They wanted practical help in implementing approaches which they had never seen or experienced. The first stage of growth emerged as teachers acquired enough confidence to try something new and not be overly worried if it did not work perfectly. In the second stage, teachers realized that they did not know enough to teach in the new ways. The Workshop spent considerable time helping teachers acquire relevant background knowledge. In the third stage, teachers' growing interest in and understanding of children and their expanding subject matter knowledge merged into the concept of curriculum building. Topics that seemed excessively theoretical at the beginning of the experiment—what children are like, what subject matter and activities further their growth—came to seem relevant and timely as teachers worked with Bank Street staff to create a system-wide social studies curriculum. In the fourth stage teachers began to relate their job to broader social problems in the world.

The Bank Street Workshop exhibited many of the features currently associated with effective professional development (Borko and Putnam, 1996; Knapp, 2003; Wilson and Berne, 1999). By documenting the practices of the Workshop as well as its impact on teachers and on the learning opportunities they provided to students, *Our Children, Our Schools* also offers an early example of research on teacher learning through professional development. Finally, Mitchel's analysis of how the hierarchical school system worked against the formation of self confidence, intellectual curiosity and professional judgment foreshadows recent efforts to document the impact of school cultures and structures on teacher's stance toward teaching and their own learning.

The third artifact, "The Nature of Expertise in Teaching," illustrates the influence of cognitive science on the study of teacher learning and the value and limits of efforts to describe stages of teacher development. (For reviews and critiques of this work, see Feiman-Nemser, 1983; Grossman, 1992; Richardson and Placier, 2001.) Written by David Berliner and organized around seven propositions, the chapter reviews studies that compare the thinking of novice and expert teachers in order to generate "a deeper understanding of the sophisticated forms of pedagogical knowledge used by expert teachers to accomplish instructional goals in the complex social environment called the public school classroom." By detailing differences in the way expert teachers "read" classrooms, interpret problems, and frame responses to students, these comparative studies demonstrate that accomplished teaching takes time to develop. Although the research does not tell us how novice teachers become competent performers or how competent performers become experts, it demonstrates that even well-started novices cannot have the flexibility or practical knowledge of a master teacher.

One proposition states that experts develop routines to deal with repetitive aspects of their work. Berliner speculates that routinizing certain teaching functions like taking attendance, handing out paper, reviewing homework frees the teacher's mind to focus on other aspects of the situation, to be flexible, even opportunistic in responding to students' comments and questions. What emerges is an image of the expert teacher as an "improvisational performer" able to draw connections between students' questions and comments and the goals of the lesson. This fits with more recent discussions of teachers as "adaptive experts" able to balance efficiency and innovation (Darling-Hammond and Bransford, 2005).

While efficiency and innovation may be complementary, it is also true that well-learned routines can be difficult to unlearn and may prevent teachers from experimenting with new approaches or responding in flexible ways to unanticipated situations. What kind of teacher preparation lays a foundation for the development of adaptive expertise in teaching? What kinds of working conditions and professional learning opportunities increase the likelihood that advanced beginners will become competent performers and that competent performers will develop proficiency and even expertise? Ultimately these questions call for longitudinal research that traces teacher learning across the multiple settings where teachers learn to teach and develop their practice. Such research can shed light on how and why teachers adopt particular ways of thinking and acting in response to the realities they face in a given setting and how, in the process, they form a sense of themselves as teachers.

Commentaries

The three commentaries open up the discussion of teacher learning from multiple perspectives. Teacher/scholars Vivian Troen and Katherine Boles draw on years of co-teaching in public schools and continuing work in teacher education to reflect on teaching and teacher learning from the inside. The Learning/Teaching Collaborative which they founded and which they describe fits well within the progressive traditions represented by Dewey and Mitchel. Renée Clift, experienced teacher educator/researcher, takes a different tack, highlighting some of the pressures and challenges researchers face in forming research teams and designing longitudinal studies of teacher learning. She calls for a different kind of doctoral training for those who aspire to an academic career, including exposure to a broader set of research models and paradigms. Daniel Fallon, architect of Teachers for a New Era, observes that the research literature on teacher education and teacher learning is "richly endowed with normative and logical arguments," but lacks "empirical evidence to support a program of teacher learning." Nevertheless, Fallon is optimistic about the prospects of financing sophisticated empirical research on teacher learning that uses student learning as the measure of effectiveness.

Expanding demands on America's teachers and the centrality of teacher learning in serious efforts to improve the quality of teaching have led to increased interest in research on teacher learning. Researchers are investigating teacher learning in intentional settings like teacher preparation and professional development, and studying the influence of collegial interaction on teaching and teacher learning. We have some evidence that high quality preparation, induction and professional development can promote changes in teachers' knowledge, skills and dispositions. We also have evidence that it is easier to become a good teacher in schools with a collaborative culture. Still, we know little about what teachers actually learn in reform-minded and traditional programs, why particular activities promote teacher learning, what enables teachers to act on what they have learned, how teacher learning contributes to student learning.

We need more conceptual work on the content, mechanisms and contexts of teacher learning, more longitudinal studies of teacher learning over time, more attention to the learning of teachers with different cultural and educational backgrounds, and more thoughtful efforts to link teacher learning to meaningful student learning. As Wilson and Berne (1999) conclude in their review of research on teacher learning and the acquisition of professional knowledge, "The future of good research on teacher learning lies in our ability to weave together ideas of teacher learning, professional development, teacher knowledge and student learning—fields that have largely operated independent of one another" (p. 204). The quality of teaching and learning in our nation's schools depends on it.

REFERENCES

Ball, D. L. & McDiarmid, G. W. (1990) The subject matter preparation of teachers. In W. R. Houston (ed.), *Handbook of research on teacher education* (pp. 437–449). New York: Macmillan.

Borko, H. & Putnam, R. T. (1996) Learning to teach. In D. Berliner & R. Calfee (eds.), *Handbook of educational psychology* (pp. 673–708). New York: Simon & Shuster Macmillan.

Cochran-Smith, M. & Lytle, S. L. (1999) Relationships of knowledge and practice: teacher learning in communities. In *Review of research in education* (Vol. 24), pp. 249–306. Washington, DC: American Education Research Association.

Cochran-Smith, M. & Fries, K. (2005) Researching teacher education in *Changing times: politics and paradigms.* In M.Cochran-Smith & K. Zeichner, *Studying teacher education* (pp. 69–109) Washington, DC: American Education Research Association.

Darling-Hammond, L. (ed.) (2000) *Studies of exellence in teacher education* (3 volumes). Washington, DC: American Association of Colleges for Teacher Education.

Darling-Hammond, L. & Bransford, J. (eds.) (2005) *Preparing teachers for a changing world. Report of the Committee on Teacher Education of the National Academy of Education.* San Francisco: Jossey-Bass.

Featherstone, H. (1993) Learning from the first years of classroom teaching: the journey in, the journey out. *Teachers College Record,* 95 (1), 93–112.

Feiman-Nemser, S. (1983) Learning to teach. In L. S. Shulman and G. Skyes (eds.), *Handbook of teaching and policy* (pp. 150–171). New York: Longman.

Feiman-Nemser, S. (2000) From preparation to practice: designing a continuum to strengthen and sustain teaching. *Teachers College Record,* 103 (6), 1013–1055.

Feiman-Nemser, S. (2006) A teacher educator looks at *Democracy and Education.* In D. Hansen (ed.), *John Dewey and Our Educational Prospect.* New York: SUNY Press, 207–232.

Feiman-Nemser, S. & Buchmann, M. (1986) The first year of teacher preparation: transition to pedagogical thinking? *Journal of Curriculum Studies,* 18 (3), 239–256.

Grossman, P. L. (1992) Why models matter: an alternative view on professional growth in teaching. *Review of Educational Research,* 62 (2), 171–179.

Grossman, P. L., Smagorinsky, P. & Valencia, S. (1999) Appropriating tools for teaching English: a theoretical framework for research on learning to teach. *American Journal of Education,* 108 (1), 1–29.

Hammerness, K. (2006) *Seeing through teachers eyes: professional ideas and classroom practices.* New York: Teachers College Press.

Hatano, G. & Oura, Y. (2003) Commentary: reconceptualizing school learning using insights from expertise research. *Educational Researcher,* 32 (8), 26–29.

Kennedy, M. M. (ed.) (1991) *Teaching academic subjects to diverse learners.* New York: Teachers College Press.

Kennedy, M. M. (1999) The role of preservice teacher teacher education. In Darling-Hammond, L. & Sykes, G. (eds.), *Teaching as the learning profession: handbook of teaching and policy* (pp. 54–86). San Francisco: Jossey Bass.

Knapp, M. S. (2003) Professional development as a policy pathway. *Review of Research in Education,* 27, 109–158.

Ladsen-Billings, G. (2001) *Crossing over to Canaan: the journey of new teachers in diverse classrooms.* San Francisco: Jossey-Bass.

Lortie, D. (1975) *Schoolteacher: a sociological study.* Chicago: University of Chicago Press.

National Research Council (2000) How *people learn: brain, mind, experience, and school* (expanded ed.). Washington, DC: National Academies Press.

Richardson, V. and Placier, P. (2001) Teacher change. In V. Richardson (ed.), *Handbook of research on teaching* (4th ed., pp. 905–947). Washington, DC: American Educational Research Association.

Roosevelt, D. (2007) Keeping real children at the center of teacher education: child study and the local construction of knowledge in teaching. In D. Carroll, H. Featherstone, J. Featherstone, S. Feiman-Nemser & D. Roosevelt (eds.), *Transforming teacher education: notes from the field.* Cambridge, MA: Harvard Education Press.

Schwab, J. J. (1976) Education and the state: learning community. In *Great ideas today.* Chicago: Encyclopedia Britannica.

Wideen, M., Mayer-Smith, J. & Moon, B. (1998) A critical analysis of the research on learning to teach: making the case for an ecological perspective on inquiry. *Review of Educational Research,* 68 (2), 130–178.

Wilson, S. & Berne, J. (1999) Teacher learning and acquisition of professional knowledge: an examination of research on contemporary professional development. In A. Iran-Nejad & P. D. Pearson (eds.), *Review of Research in Education,* Vol. 24 (pp. 173–209). Washington, DC: American Educational Research Association.

39 The metaphors by which we teach

Experience, metaphor, and culture in teacher education [1]

Cheryl Rosaen and Susan Florio-Ruane
Michigan State University

Humans do not converse because they have thoughts to express, but they have thoughts to express because they converse.[2]

INTRODUCTION

In this chapter we examine a topic of perennial interest in teacher education: the role of experience in learning to teach. Rather than reviewing a particular literature dealing explicitly with the topic, our point of entry is "metaphor," a process comparing one thing to another that is used not only by poets, but by all of us—tacitly and explicitly—to weave individual with society, experience with concept, and word with activity. Building upon work of linguists who investigated the relationship between metaphor and thought (e.g. Ortony, 1979/1993), Lakoff and Johnson (1980) argued, "metaphor is pervasive in everyday life, not just in language but in thought and action. Our ordinary conceptual system, in terms of which we both think and act, is fundamentally metaphorical in nature" (p. 3). In these ways, metaphors are central to how we experience and understand the world because they provide an experiential framework for making sense of abstract concepts. We often experience one thing in terms of another.

Connecting the ideas of metaphor and experience with teaching, learning and teacher education is not new. Some scholars have used metaphors descriptively to help us understand classroom life by characterizing teachers as supply sergeants, traffic cops and time keepers (Jackson, 1968) and by identifying roles for teachers such as executive, therapist or liberationist (Fenstermacher & Soltis, 1986). Others have investigated what metaphors reveal about beginning and experienced teachers' conceptions of teaching and their emerging sense of self (Bullough, 1991; Bullough *et al.*, 1991; Bullough & Stokes, 1994; Grant, 1992; Munby, 1986; Munby & Russell, 1990), and the images that guide their actions (Clandinin, 1985, 1986). For example, knowing that some teachers see themselves as a "butterfly" or "chameleon," or conceive of their role as that of "parenting," provides insights into how they view the work of teaching, and allows us to explore whether their conceptions change and evolve over time (Bullough, 1991). Exploration of teachers' metaphors for teaching can help us understand the conceptual systems that guide their work (Berliner, 1990; Collins & Green, 1990; Cohen & Lotan, 1990; Shuell, 1990). Some teacher educators have taken the concept of metaphor a step further and used it as a heuristic to get preservice teachers to be more reflective (de Guerrero & Villamil, 2002; Hunt & Gow, 1984; Marshall, 1990; Tobin, 1990; Weade & Ernst, 1990) and to help collaborating teachers learn productive ways to talk with student teachers (Carter, 1990).

In this chapter we investigate metaphors and learning from experience from a slightly different angle. We take a close look at how metaphors that are pervasive in our culture and profession have the potential to influence how preservice teachers make sense of their experiences in teacher preparation programs and classrooms where they learn to teach. We argue that metaphors, if left unexamined, have the potential to limit or constrain what novices learn from experience.

The chapter is organized into four sections. The first section, *Experience and Learning as Social Processes*, discusses theories of experience and learning as social processes, pointing out the importance of language in mediating stimuli and developing concepts. We show how people use language to describe activities and to make of them what Dewey (1938) called, "educative experience." It is through the use of figurative language, which is culturally patterned and shared, that people learn actively and form concepts and networks of concepts. We draw on the work of Soviet psychologist Vygotsky (1981), who studied learning in the context of social interaction, and argue that people develop understandings in social interaction with others and, in this way, thought begins on the social plane before becoming internalized on the individual plane. Metaphors we use to represent our experience help us know what we are experiencing, which is why study of experience is important to the education of a teacher.

In the second section, *Understanding Experience through Language, Metaphor and Representation*, we draw on the work of Lakoff and Johnson (1980) and Donald Schon (1979/1993) to focus on metaphors as one form of representation that is often hidden and embedded in our everyday language. We explain how different types of metaphors influence the ways in which we experience the world. Three common metaphors found in educational discourse are examined: field experience; struggling readers; and at risk learners.

"Field experience" is examined as a root metaphor that is so embedded in the language and culture of teacher education that we often do not recognize it as a metaphor at all. It is a root metaphor from which other metaphors spring. We argue that this metaphor influences how teacher educators conceive of and organize university- and school-based experiences for novices. An alternative metaphor, ecological environment, is explored in terms of its potential for reinventing the social dimensions of learning to teach.

The second metaphor, "struggling reader," was selected as an example of an ontological metaphor. An ontological metaphor takes an abstraction (how one experiences learning to read) and expresses a certain version of that experience (a great deal of effort may be put forth by the reader without success) as a certain type of person (struggling reader). Because reading is so central to all learning, and because metaphors like this are found in common parlance and in professional discourse, it is important to consider how metaphors of this type position learners and where they focus novices' attention.

A third metaphor, "at risk learners," was selected because it is another example of an ontological metaphor (the abstraction of danger and threat are expressed as a certain type of learner). It also illustrates what Schon (1979/1993) calls a generative metaphor. Generative metaphors suggest a particular way of looking at a situation (i.e. there is a danger or threat to our educational system when the number of certain types of learners increases) and that way of seeing the world or framing a problem suggests (or generates) its own solution (i.e. fix what is wrong with the learner and the danger/threat will go away).

Thus, the second section illustrates how these three common metaphors are used in teacher education and in teaching to represent complex ideas by associating them with the familiar. We maintain that these metaphors can limit how beginning teachers make sense of experience and what they think is possible to attain. In addition, we argue that as conceptual networks of terms used in common parlance make their way into professional conversations, teacher educators and beginning teachers alike are in danger of falling prey to them instead of learning from them.

In the third section, *Teacher Educators as Designers of Experience*, we suggest both a means and an end for re-considering the metaphors embedded in our language and culture, and for recognizing how teaching and learning need not be limited to what we can know by means of extant, culturally patterned, and largely tacit representations. We imagine a new metaphor, teaching as weaving, that brings into consideration multiple layers and dimensions of teaching, learning, and learning to teach. This metaphor suggests new designs for teacher education. We draw on our own work in teacher education and the work of others to provide examples of pedagogical tools and practices for helping novices develop explicit metacognitive awareness of the ways educators, politicians, and the general public use their implicit theories to interpret experiences. We argue that awareness and understanding of the metaphors by which we teach—their stability as well as their contingent, situated nature—is fundamental to thoughtful practice and also to the beginning teacher's educative experiencing of that practice.

In the final section, *Where Does Understanding Experience, Metaphor and Culture Lead Us?*, we identify questions for future research. For example, we call for investigating the extent to which beginning teachers' explicit examination of metaphors that are pervasive in our profession and culture influences what they pay attention to as they experience various aspects of teacher preparation. We also call for empirical study of the alternative metaphors for designing and redesigning teacher education offered in the chapter—the field as an ecological environment, and teaching as weaving—to understand more fully what contribution they make, if any, to creating alternative structures for social interaction and transforming our own practices as teacher educators.

EXPERIENCE AND LEARNING AS SOCIAL PROCESSES

Experience pervades everyday life, and we all learn by means of our cultural transactions within it. Our encounters with the social and natural world are woven into meaning by language. Accordingly, cognition and culture grow for the beginner and also for the community of which he or she is a part. For example, when a grandfather walks with his young grandson and a hairy, four-legged creature approaches them wagging a tail, the child may shout, "Max!" In response, grandfather is apt to say something like, "Yes, this is a dog and you have a dog, too. Your dog is named Max." In this exchange so much has happened by way of the linguistic mediation of experience and the authentic engagement of a more and a less experienced member of the culture. Most important perhaps is that in the intimacy of adult-child interaction, language and concept development proceed almost incidentally, and context is immensely important to the process. Initiates' repertoires for speaking and thinking about complex ideas are limited. But with growing interaction within the physical world and among experienced members of a culture, beginners' thought and language become increasingly complex. Vygotsky studied learning in the context of social interaction, and he referred to this linking process as "inner speech." He asserted that, "any function in children's cultural development appears twice, or on two planes. First it appears on the social plane ... Social relations or relationships among people ... underlie all higher functions and their relationships (Vygotsky in Wertsch (1981, p. 163), cited in Cole 1996, pp. 110–111). Ultimately, thought, which began on the social plane, is internalized and personalized in cognitive networks of words, ideas, and experiences, which have been learned and have meaning in the company of others (Vygotsky, 1981)."[3]

Learning to teach as situated activity

What in large part makes the teaching profession and the process of learning to teach different from everyday life among youngsters is that prospective teachers engage in various planned activities in classrooms such as observing, planning and teaching lessons, assessing learners, and talking with mentor teachers. Some, like Dewey (1915, 1938), would not even call being swept along in the flow of classroom talk or activity a learning experience—not unless it was social, authentically oriented to a purpose, and guided with curricular ends in view. In fact, Dewey was the first philosopher to stress the importance of situation to learning and to presage the idea that situations or contexts are not the theater sets on which life is enacted. Situational contexts are, in fact, made up of an array of props, tools, artifacts, and message systems that we take for granted. For Dewey, the situation, as it was co-created in classroom activities and guided by the teacher toward curricular "ends-in-view," was the key linkage of language, experience, and the development of thought.

We know that experience is hard to recognize precisely because we make it, and tacitly, we take our message systems for granted. Sometimes it takes a breakdown in our assumed common understanding to find that while we have a consensus that is workable generally, not all members of the community think the same way. Oftentimes, for instance, teacher educators' ideas about fruitful experiences differ from our students' expectations of what it takes to learn to teach. Consider, for example, what Lana, a senior in a literacy methods course, had to say about an assignment that required her to plan, teach and reflect on a language arts lesson in an elementary classroom: "Real world experience is the best kind!" And about course reading assignments Lana commented, "I feel that experience is more helpful, but the readings were a good place to start." We see that while reading has some value to her as a launching point for her learning, getting "real world experience" in learning to teach is most important to her.

Considering Lana's comments in rhetorical terms suggests the question: What is implied by the terms "real world" and "experience"? Metaphorically, the "real world" is located in elementary classrooms, not in the university classroom or at Lana's apartment while she reads. "Experience" in elementary classrooms could mean many things to Lana that may or may not foster her learning: participation; imitation through apprenticeship; trial and error experimentation; discovery; implementation of methods for teaching literacy, and so on. While the sense of the *authority* of experience persists for Lana and many teacher candidates, the question of what and how novices actually have opportunities to *learn from* experience is important to consider (Feiman-Nemser & Buchmann, 1985; Munby & Russell, 1994).

Learning to teach in "activity settings"

Scholars have argued that carefully designed experiences in classrooms have the potential to help novices go beyond *having experiences* to helping them *learn from them* by developing their abilities to perceive and assess a classroom situation, make judgments, formulate goals, choose a course of action and reflect on consequences (Dewey, 1904/1964; Kennedy, 1987, 1999; Kessels & Korthagen, 1996; Schon, 1983, 1987). For the practicing teacher the tools that are used to prepare and enact learning experiences are both practical and conceptual (Grossman *et al.*, 1999). According to socio-cultural theory, learning to teach takes place in various "activity settings" that contain tools, artifacts and message systems. Conceptual tools include the guiding principles, frameworks, and theories that help teachers interpret their practice and make decisions

(Grossman *et al.*, 1999). These include broad concepts such as adopting a diverse social constructivist orientation (Au, 1998) as well as ideas that fit with a particular stance such as teaching for social justice (Ayers *et al.*, 1998; Cochran-Smith, 1998), culturally relevant teaching (Ladson-Billings, 1995), or critical and feminist pedagogies (Gore, 1993). Practical tools include the resources and teaching ideas used in daily teaching (Grossman *et al.*, 1999). These consist of knowledge of curriculum materials and pedagogical and assessment strategies that enable teachers to provide instruction that is responsive to a range of learners (Au, 1993; Villegas & Lucas, 2002).

From this viewpoint, concepts and theories are not learned as ends in themselves. Novices require support in learning to use them interpretively as instruments to explore their perceptions, generate questions, examine points of view or arguments, and make judgments about means and ends. As they gain language for communicating about their work, novice teachers begin to see that their craving for experience-as-action is necessary but not sufficient for learning to occur. Beginning teachers must temper the tendency to describe and understand their work with pupils as exclusively a matter of "doing." They also "do" in their planning in the empty classroom after their students have gone home at the end of the day. And, as we have already noted, learning in teacher education involves a variety of experiences and so must entail both kinds of doing—"hands on" teaching and analytic work that includes talking about and writing about ideas with others. Consequently, in order to learn from experiences, beginning teachers need both analysis and action in order to see the connections between the two (Dewey, 1904/1964; Kennedy, 1987).

This is why penetrating study of experience—not only study by means of *having experience*—is important to the education of a teacher. This kind of study is not merely a matter of learning the ordinary. It is learning to understand one another's understandings, since even the same word can function metaphorically, yet in different ways, depending on the perspective, prior knowledge, purposes and role of the speakers. This in fact exemplifies the situated nature of metaphors and how they help us understand complex ideas such as "real world," "experience" or "learning." If we are aware of these ideas and learn with and from one another about such differences, we are engaging in an aspect of learning to teach that is not easily observed but fundamental to good teacher education.

UNDERSTANDING EXPERIENCE THROUGH LANGUAGE, METAPHOR AND REPRESENTATION

Experience is expressed metaphorically in ways so common that they and their meanings can become tacit, and widely held as local or "folk" knowledge (Geertz, 1983; Bruner, 1996). Much of this knowledge derives from metaphors of place and movement, or what Lakoff and Johnson (1980) refer to as "orientation metaphors," which are systematic and organize "a whole system of concepts with respect to one another, and have a basis in our physical and cultural experience" (p. 14). An example familiar to most of us is the metaphor "sunrise." Because orientation is a common, shared phenomenon, we know "rising" as going upward, as when we awaken and rise from our beds. We can talk of the sun similarly "rising," because it changes in orientation from below the horizon (having previously "set"). Even though the sun does not literally rise and fall relative to us, the metaphor is resonant with our immediate experience of position. It also extends to a network of related associations—we lie down at night just as the sun sets to give us nightfall. We awaken and rise at sunrise, and we think of dawn as a time of revival after sleep.

This metaphor powerfully organizes how we think about daily cycles, cycles in nature, and life cycles. We die and are placed in prostrate positions down in the ground. But many believe that we rise—as in the Christian resurrection—and, like the sun, ascend into a high place we might call heaven. Few of us stop to think about all this when we get up in the morning or even when we note the beautiful "sunrise." Fewer still connect this discourse with formal study of astronomy or physics. There is no need for most of us to do so, because meaning need not be "true" to be sensible and shared.

Metaphors simplify and are selective; this is at once their power and problem. Simplifications can make it easier to view aspects of a complex phenomenon—but they do so by framing out of view other aspects which, had they been included, might change an image entirely. They also caricature, exaggerating some features to make them more salient and easier to view. But what we may get is a distortion, not an enhancement. Finally, metaphors offer enticing—and confusing—multiplicities. Some can turn on a tiny detail in the reading of a situation, while others depend on perspective or position.

When, for example, we also extend orientation metaphors to social relationships, we do more than wax poetic or reveal lack of knowledge of astronomy. Unaware, we can characterize learners, for example, in ways that are damaging to them. Consider that teachers sometimes refer to the "low" readers in their classrooms and restrict access to rich learning materials for that population, based on the assumption that low readers are incapable of learning from complex texts. Or a teacher might say that a student doesn't want to "aim high" and settle for minimal performance as good enough for that learner's goals. Teachers might want to encourage their students to "raise their grades" and foster inadvertently a misplaced focus on extrinsic versus intrinsic rewards. In other words, educators might assimilate such ways of speaking and thinking without awareness and critical reflection. Used by teachers, such metaphors transcend the vernacular and have the power of a profession behind them. Thus metaphors may not only limit understanding, but may also limit opportunities for students to learn. Below we consider three metaphors that, left unexamined, have the potential to shape how we organize experiences for beginning teachers and influence the systems of thought that guide our work as educators: "field experience," "struggling readers," and "at risk learners."

"Field experience": an unexamined root metaphor

As we pointed out earlier with Lana's comments, when asked to evaluate their program of study, new teachers are apt to report that they learned little from their university courses but a great deal from their "field experience." While teacher educators cringe at what seems to them to be a reductive model, a second look at the term and its use by students of teaching is revealing. "Field experience" in teacher candidates' lexicons is what linguists call a "root" metaphor. Root metaphors are embedded in our language and culture and thus are often overlooked as metaphors; they also spawn other metaphors. There is a clear and fundamental physical connection between "field-as-place" for growth and nurturance, but it is also a metaphor connected to place in the sense that the classroom is itself a place. Ironically, though their instructors may miss this aspect of beginners' ways of representing learning to teach, it is for teacher educators part of a hybrid of meanings linking "hands on" and "real world," but also a metaphor that abstracts from physical place to "discourse-as-place."

Different "activity systems" for course and field work

Thus teacher educators do, in fact, place a great deal of time and emphasis on students' observation of and work with children and teachers in schools. But we take pains to accompany the pragmatic "hands on" with thought about activity—and with thought about the concepts such activity might help students to develop. These activities are linked metaphorically to the field in the sense that a professional field is a sociolinguistic place—and identity—that includes speaking, thinking and understanding as well technique.

Nevertheless, it is commonplace to speak and act in ways that differentiate between field experience as one activity system and university coursework as yet another activity system. We lend "experiential" status to the former and run the risk of separating doing from thinking in the latter. We also run the risk of reifying this representation when we create very different activity systems for learning in each context. These activity systems differ in participants, speakers' rights, social roles, ways of speaking, tools, artifacts, purposes, and physical settings. For instance, in teacher education course work we tend to focus on the conceptual tools associated with teaching: reading about and discussing theories and concepts found in the professional literature; writing analytic papers that help teacher candidates make sense of theories and concepts; and talking about appropriate teaching methods that are consistent with the theoretical orientations featured in the course. Opportunities to "use" or "apply" these concepts and ideas—through the use of practical tools—occur in "the field" where teacher candidates select resources and methods to design and teach lessons to "real" children in "real" classrooms. Subsequently, reflection on these "real world" experiences takes place away from the field—by writing a course paper, or by engaging with peers in discussions back on campus. Only recently have some teacher educators begun to hold their teacher education courses in schools where the lines between learning versus doing and the theoretical versus the practical can be blurred more easily. Even then, however, the activity settings for course work (e.g. reading, writing, discussing the literature in a room where adults gather) versus the "real work" of teaching in the classroom (e.g. interacting with children using educational resources) remain strikingly different. As a consequence, our students quite appropriately divide their professional education into two unrelated parts as they are expected effectively to change discourses and cross culturally determined borders in order to learn.

Field experience and the "hidden curriculum"

There is a powerful "hidden curriculum" (Jackson, 1968) in the field experience metaphor. That is, there are things outside the stated objectives of a given teacher education program or course that prospective teachers learn as they prepare for practice by coming to campus and going back to the school. They experience learning largely on their own by being "placed" individually with one collaborating teacher. This learning is different from what they are able to get from studying theory by reading about it in articles and books. For instance, beginners learn to see teaching as isolated within a classroom with a closed door (Jackson, 1968; Lortie, 1975) and compartmentalized within grade levels or subject matter departments (McLaughlin & Talbert, 2001; Siskin, 1994, 1995). The meaning being the message, beginning teachers may personalize problems, hold themselves to unrealistic standards of knowledge and performance, blame themselves when difficulty arises, and make (or abandon) the crossing from the student to teacher essentially alone (Britzman, 1991). These are not planned as learning outcomes for beginning teachers, but nevertheless represent how some novices experience "the field."

Positioning the field as a more productive learning environment

Thus, field experience is a metaphor that links two ambiguous terms into a unified, comprehensible object. It is an accessible way of speaking about a complex educational accomplishment involving multiple sites, situations, ways of speaking, and social roles. At the same time, the metaphor effectively sets up the experience of many teacher candidates as learning little in one setting and a lot in another. It contrasts the outdoors, green and growing, with the enclosed, remoteness of staying inside. We are physically more constrained indoors. We are active outdoors. The air is stale indoors but fresh outside. We think within but act without. Hands on, experience-based, practical, and real all associate with the word "field," as does tilling soil, growing, and nurturing. Indoors we mind our manners, speak more softly and have little connection with nature. Our indoor environment is ornamented by material objects—irrelevant to our growth and survival. In nature, we are encompassed by a powerful life force we cannot tame but of which we are a part.

Thus we see the power of familiar associations is such that we organize institutions, activities, tools, language, and social identity in ways that reinforce them. The metaphor is sufficiently useful in its simplicity that it becomes part of our stock of common knowledge. Yet, as Scribner (1984) found when she studied metaphor in literacy education, its very shared, simplified characteristics limit possibility and leave us mostly trying to refine, assess or otherwise modify what we have come to know rather than thinking about how else experience might be understood. Scribner argued for literacy, as we argue here, that simplifying metaphors for variable, situated activities invites thinking of activity as object rather than a process and the individual as a recipient rather than a co-creator of experience and learning.

Examining an alternative metaphor to envision enhanced social interaction

Looking closer at the metaphor and interpreting rather than living by it, we can see how it shapes meaning—and also how it might be re-thought—in freeing, critical ways. If, for example, we re-think the field as a metaphor, we might compare education to the field as an ecological environment,[4] and find ourselves conceptualizing experience and learning in very new ways. With the ecological environment metaphor we note, for example, that growth involves interdependence as well as interaction among organisms. Thinking of the field as an ecological environment, teacher educator, teacher candidate, and practicing teacher work together to make meaning and depend on one another to do so. From this view, teacher educators would not dismiss the ways today's practicing teachers mediate the daily challenges they face in their classrooms—such as preparing students for standardized tests—as "maintaining the status quo" or "teaching to the test." Instead, they would encourage teacher candidates to ask questions so they can understand how these challenges become powerful forces that shape teachers' everyday practice. In this way, the practicing teacher provides access for both teacher educators and prospective teachers to the complex context in which novices learn to enact their practice. That same teacher also shares ways in which she manages the tensions and dilemmas in making curricular decisions that fulfill school and district mandates while also following her professional judgment regarding what constitutes good teaching (e.g. Johnson, 2001; Lampert, 2001). Subsequently, both teacher educators and practicing teachers share responsibility in helping teacher candidates see and understand the forces that shape the teaching context.

By rethinking the field as a metaphor we also contemplate the balance of diverse ingredients needed for growth. As we have seen, ingredients for teaching and learning include conceptual tools, such as theories and concepts used to guide and interpret practice, as well as the practical tools familiar to teachers' daily work, such as curriculum materials, textbooks, trade books, math manipulatives, or microscopes. Working with conceptual tools without consideration of the practical tools needed to plan, and teach lessons or assess learners' progress has the potential to make those tools seem distant, or even irrelevant to the real work of teaching. On the other hand, only working with practical tools without consideration of guiding principles and theories can reduce practice to implementing a series of "fun" or "neat" activities that may not lead to educative experiences for children and may not help the beginning teacher understand whether or why certain practices are effective. Teacher educators, beginning teachers and experienced teachers all play a part in working with, and talking or writing about the tools. That is, if we separate these ingredients from one another or an organism from the ecology, we risk the growth of the individual and also the growth and health of the community.

Reading "field experience" this way, we see the social dimensions of learning to teach include enacting practice and analysis of practice through conversation and writing. We also see the necessary interdependence of a variety of experiences, and the cultural nature of experience in root, radical terms—culture as in agriculture—as the nurturing of the young plant into maturity. Teacher educators, teacher candidate and practicing teachers all play a part in this interactive, meaning-making process.

"The struggling reader": metaphors as powerful organizers of experience

Shared metaphors develop shared concepts and systems of thought (Lakoff & Johnson, 1980). These systems quickly become sedimented as they shape subsequent activity and understanding and are passed on. In effect, they become phenomena. Largely taught and learned in ordinary situations, metaphors and the concepts they engender are often tacitly held. And, as Bruner (1996) observed, as local or folk knowledge, they do not require empirical testing to be taken as true. They are believed to be explanatory and predictive and this believing makes it so. We learn that grandfather's aching toe predicts a coming storm. We do not question how and why "it works."

Much has been written in teacher education about the intrinsic difficulty of making what has become a familiar context (with shared and taken-for-granted ways of speaking, acting, participating, and thinking), the classroom and school, into a newly unfamiliar one. To become a professional educator the student must see, hear, feel, speak, and learn from familiar stimuli in new ways (Florio-Ruane, 1990; Frank & Uy, 2004). This is a cognitive change very closely tied to communication. Teachers' language and meta-linguistic awareness are extremely important aspects of their professional education and practice. Critical awareness of language—its forms, functions, and power to shape activity, learning, and learners—is perhaps the most important and most difficult task of becoming a teacher, yet it is something teachers must learn in order to teach it to their students.

An ontological metaphor categorizes learners

Consider, for example, the metaphor "the struggling reader." As discussed in this chapter's introduction, this is an ontological metaphor that takes an abstraction (how one experiences learning to read) and expresses a certain version of that experience (a great deal of effort may be put forth by the reader without success) as a certain type of person (struggling reader). The popular media and the ordinary citizen may freely speak of struggling readers. Unless they are teachers, however, most have little influence on reading education and little more than passing interest in the topic. There is nothing to cause these speakers to pause and think about their words. They rarely ask, "Why do I associate struggle with reading?" or "With whom or what is the reader struggling?" and "What does it mean to characterize someone as struggling?" or "How did I decide whom to label that way—and why?" (Florio-Ruane & Raphael, 2004; Rogoff, 1990).

So we see that when beginning teachers spend time in local classrooms and gloss a child or group of children as "struggling readers," they are using a metaphor available in both common parlance and in teachers' talk. These teachers must learn that the term is being used, however, inappropriately to construct difference as a deficit within individual readers; this construction runs the risk of missing other issues that require attention, such as structural or institutional inequalities that may contribute to whether or not a given group of students is learning to read at a desired rate (Gutierrez & Orellana, 2006). In a chapter titled "Struggling and Difficulty in Reading: Managing Vulnerability," two experienced educators, Randy and Katherine Bomer, engage in an important analysis of how the "struggling reader" metaphor positions children:

> Who is the struggling reader? The term itself is suspect, since it implies that all struggling readers belong to a single category. Anyone can struggle, and no one struggles all the time. No two readers struggle in the same ways. A poor score on a test may mean simply that a reader struggles with tests, not with reading something she is interested in. Often the perception of struggling is not coming from the reader at all, but from grade-level expectations or similar setups of the system.
>
> (Bomer & Bomer, 2001, p. 89)

These authors go on to acknowledge that some students do not learn to read without struggling with some aspect of the process but they are careful to point out that different readers wrestle with different aspects of making meaning from text. They also point out that struggling is not the same thing as failing, since, "Struggling implies *trying*, intentionally putting forth effort. When we watch readers in trouble, we see them struggle. Struggling implies that the effort is unnecessarily great, that reading should be easier and more energy efficient" (Bomer & Bomer, 2001, p. 89).

This analysis points out the pitfalls of importing folk knowledge into professional discourse and using the shorthand of metaphors in technical ways to describe students as all fitting into one single category. The use of one single category provides a false sense of confidence that there is one way to help that category of students, when any experienced teacher would readily dispute that claim. Yet this is a subtle distinction since it is human nature to think we know something because we have a way of speaking about it. This shorthand feature of metaphor is troublesome for the same reason it is useful: in simplifying, it focuses on the individual and takes both the reader and reading as isolated and isolating. Consequently, reading and learning to read are not viewed in social perspective.

Moreover, the "struggling reader" metaphor relates closely to the orientation metaphor of reading development where "We think of a line on a graph that shows nothing but profit, continual improvement in a given direction. When we see readers struggling, we imagine that they are at a lower point on the line than those who don't struggle" (Bomer & Bomer, 2001, p. 96). This feeds into thinking that there is one process called reading and a single path to learning to read. Those who are not as far along the path are viewed as deficient.

Learning to analyze assumptions embedded in language

Beginning teachers can learn to think critically about the talk they hear among the general public and educators in schools by playing what Elbow (1986) calls the "believing game" and the "doubting game." He describes these processes as disciplined approaches to (a) working to "believe" particular interpretations, even when they don't easily fit with their presuppositions in order to understand them thoroughly; and (b) working to critically and systematically "doubt" or appraise underlying assumptions. Elbow explains,

> As intellectuals we need to learn to doubt things by weaning ourselves from ideas, particularly our own. We need to learn how to cease experiencing an idea while still holding it, that is, to drain the experience from an idea and see it in its pure propositionality . . . Methodological doubt represents the human struggle to free ourselves from parochial closed-mindedness, but it doesn't go far enough. Methodological belief comes to the rescue at this point by forcing us genuinely to enter into unfamiliar or threatening ideas instead of just arguing against them without experiencing them or feeling their full force.
>
> (Elbow, 1986, p. 263)

It is important to make explicit the metaphors we take for granted and look closely at the concepts and ideologies they support. Using Elbow's approach, rather than throw out entirely the word "struggle" from their vocabulary (and thus only "doubting" its merits), beginning teachers can learn to distinguish *categorizing* students (as struggling readers) from *describing readers' experience* (noting how a particular reader struggles with a particular aspect of the reading process). This subtle distinction shifts the novice's attention from thinking of those who struggle as being all the same to focusing on identifying individual learning needs. A professional educator is expected to ask these questions precisely because he or she has rhetorical force by virtue of professional identity and status. As a gatekeeper, what a teacher says about a child who is learning to read can make an enormous difference in that child's educational biography and life chances.

A key point here is that the language teachers and other professionals use to describe and interpret those in their care and the meanings they make of their own lived experiences can distort, alienate, silence, and preclude examination of what others find uncomfortable or threatening. But metaphors are taken up precisely because they "work" by simplification, association, and giving members of a community a handle on—or shorthand for—something complex. We assume these tools enable us both to understand complexity and hold that understanding in common. Because professionals have often found that it is difficult to break the frames accepted in their extant discourse communities, it is necessary to step outside a familiar discourse in order to look at it critically and see it as contingent. Our familiar discourse can sustain and enable practice or it can truncate it.

"At risk learners": metaphor, ideology and power

By stopping to think about the metaphoric nature of our descriptions and the power we as teachers have to describe, we can see our practice as far more than a pragmatic exercise in prediction and control. The agency teachers have in this transformative work is considerable. It is also ideological. This aspect of teaching does not come naturally or easily. It needs to be taught, learned, and practiced (Shannon, 1992). Moreover, an important part of the professional's work is, according to Cochran-Smith, "taking account of the ways metaphors, narratives and literary devices are used strategically to garner support for the approaches various groups favor and also for their ways of understanding the issues in the first place" (2005, pp. 4–5).

Viewed this way, neither our talk nor our actions as teachers and teacher educators are, again quoting Cochran-Smith, "politically neutral." Our work is intrinsically ideological and undertaken in the crucible of culture, where ideologies intensify and harden in the heat of discourse. By the same logic, "experience" is not neutral and, thus, learning, too, is ideological in nature, serving to enhance our understanding of nature and human society but with particular ends-in-view. Teaching and teacher education are of necessity pragmatic enterprises. But a learning environment which tends to operate in terms of the "what" and the "how" to the exclusion of the "why" and "wherefore" can become reductive, reproductive, and mute. Thus, understanding the cultural and historical origins of metaphors can provide insight into their political and ideological power.

Metaphors make their way into our common stock of knowledge

In Biblical scholarship there is a Greek word standing in tension with "chronos." We understand that chronos refers to the experience of time, one instant after another. We live primarily in chronological time and mostly tell stories (even if they contain flashbacks) chronologically: "And then what happened? What happened after that?" This way of experiencing time, language, and activity tends to limit our seeing to one dimension, to chains of cause and effect, to sequences that, though unique in content, are repetitive in form and function.

Kairos, in contrast, is quite another kind of time. It is not clock-time but interruption of it—another kind of time where we are called to act, think, or speak in a different way from the usual. This change in the nature of our language and relationships is referred to rhetorically as "kairos." This is the Greek word for "opportunity," "occasion," or "turning point" (Erickson, 2004). It can be invoked by powerful people and interests, but it is also the province of all members of a culture; it is one way that people can shape as well as be shaped by culture (Eisenhart, 1995). Especially at times of major significance, change or crisis in the wider society, professionals, such as teachers and teacher educators, are called into question in ways that affect their organization, knowledge base, activities, and professional education. Because teaching is a public, applied profession, examination and reform of practice takes place both inside the practice and outside it. When people believe that education is failing society or that society is failing and education is a likely solution, the profession emerges as a focal point of public debate and discussion. Increasingly central to the debate at such times of apparent crisis are the preparation of teachers and assessment of their mastery of specialized knowledge and their competence effectively to practice their craft.

Thus, the metaphors dominating the national discourse about education, teaching, and teacher education are not so much imposed deliberately by virtue of some kind of power (political, economic, spiritual, etc.), but instead are circulated or seeded in the common cultural ground through every day discussions among the citizenry, news reporting and dialogue among professionals. As metaphors are taken up, even for purposes of rejecting, critiquing, or debating them, they find their way into the stock of common cultural knowledge, preoccupying and shaping subsequent thought and speech.

"Generative" metaphors suggest their own solutions

For example, it is not uncommon for a teacher (experienced or beginner) to speak of a child as being "at risk." The visibility and conceptual ante was raised on this metaphor in

1983 when the Federal government issued a report titled "A Nation at Risk" (National Commission on Excellence in Education, 1983). Calling a crisis in U.S. public education relevant to competitiveness in a global economy, the report used "risk" to evoke a sense of danger and to describe the likelihood of failure or of the nation being overcome. Like the "struggling reader," the "at risk learner" is an ontological metaphor that locates the problem within the child, rather than portraying a competent child who is placed in a dangerous situation. This metaphor is also generative (Schon, 1979) in that it suggests a particular way to frame the situation: our educational system becomes more threatened as the number of "at risk learners" increases. Framed in this way, with all the relevant facts apparently embedded within the metaphor itself, the metaphor suggests, or generates, its own solution: fix the learners and the threat will diminish.

For the nation, the risk, too, was internal. Because of falling standards in education, for example, the report described students leaving U.S. schools as not ready to compete successfully in the global economy. Subsequently in the early 1990s, curriculum standards meant to address the identified "risks" soon became standardization, thus extending the network of metaphors that shape experience and the conceptual and practical tools novice teachers have available to them to learn in practice.

As this example illustrates, novice teachers need to develop awareness that the language of others—and others' interests—shapes thinking and sense-making. In times of crisis, people tend to opt for the simplicity and reliability of hierarchy. Borders harden, and horizontal structures—from collaboration across disciplines to flexible scheduling, or even to school architecture—are set aside. The language of others also shapes the tools that are available to teachers to learn and enact their practice. When curriculum materials, approaches to assessments, and professional development experiences are all "aligned" with curriculum standards for schools and professional standards for teachers, the conceptual and practical tools available to teachers become constrained. There is an implicit message that these tools provide the solutions to "the problem" of "at risk learners."

Now that the more recent policy No Child Left Behind (2002) has become part of public and professional discourse and teacher candidates, teacher educators, and practicing teachers alike speak of NCLB and nod knowingly, we must acknowledge that rhetorical work has been done somewhere, somehow, and by someone (or some group). And when rhetorical work is examined carefully within the social and historical contexts from which it emerged, we uncover ideological and political stances that have the potential to shape what and how beginning teachers learn from experience.

TEACHER EDUCATORS AS DESIGNERS OF EXPERIENCE

Given the powerful role metaphors play in shaping what teachers perceive and learn from experience, there are important design implications for teacher educators. One way to approach design is to consider an alternative metaphor for educating beginning teachers. We often describe or think of teaching as historically a "woman's profession" in which craft, relationship, and care are as important as objectivity, reason, and proof. It seems appropriate, therefore, to suggest weaving as a metaphor for teaching since it befits the concepts powerfully associated with our work. It offers alternatives to the rigid, encapsulating metaphors of structure in which we have little apparent means to change our circumstances.

What does this metaphor bring into view? Weaving involves work on multiple levels and in multiple color and tensions. The project is to move among these levels in a creative yet patterned way to make a unified and aesthetically pleasing work. It also can be a simpler activity in which yarn is strung and repeatedly moved in two directions to make fabric—more intended, perhaps to warm our bodies. In either case weaving has associations that bring together characteristics we often put in opposition: strength and flexibility; structure and agency; individual and collective work; unfolding and design; beauty and utility. Teachers are weavers of meaning in language, by means of experience, in the context of culture, and with their students.

The metaphor of weaving helps us to understand many layers and dimensions of education. Together these layers and dimensions are complex and rich accomplishments. They are learned and taught. Teacher candidates participate peripherally at first but view the expert weaver and the fruits of her labors (Wenger, 1998). They also view the raw material and tools the weaver needs, and gradually they learn to do individually what they could only watch or do with assistance as novices. The rules we frame and follow to make communication possible and allow for its artful improvisational character are very much like the skills, knowledge and creativity of the weaver. They require not only expertise at weaving, but deep understanding of learning to share as educative experience with beginners.

With this metaphor in mind, we can make a different analysis of teachers' experience and practice. It is not only local and pragmatic, but it is also conceptual and, as such, unfolding. Those who dominate the rhetoric of teaching and teacher education are able to thread their interests strongly into the weave of American education. Ironically, if teachers are not critically aware of the metaphors by which they teach, they cannot speak and see in new ways. If they abdicate the potential of their profession to other speakers, teachers cannot be part of the educational fabric or its weaving, no matter how hard they work or how well they are educated. In helping beginning teachers to make and share educative experience, the teacher educator's educational responsibility is to support and extend the development of new weavers—who will not only learn the enduring knowledge and practices of a culture, but will transform them as they play with variations upon them, and ultimately as they assume the responsibility of weavers. The examples discussed below provide images of social arrangements and use of conceptual and practical tools that have the potential to guide teacher educators, prospective teachers and classroom teachers in coming to a richer understanding of language, learning and experience in teacher education.

Learning a professional discourse

Examining rhetorical work requires developing meta-awareness, stepping out of our familiar discourse and seeing metaphors as constructs, as examples of many versions of how people have characterized and interpreted experience. A longstanding practice for teacher educators is to work with what teacher candidates bring to their professional preparation: their preconceptions about children, subject matter, schools and schooling, along with their own prior experiences as students. Typically, we design experiences that help teacher candidates make explicit their preconceptions and recount their experiences for closer examination and critique. However, research has shown that these entering beliefs are powerful and difficult to change (Feiman-Nemser, 2001; Wideen et al., 1998).

Pondering the metaphorical nature of language and its relationship to thought in literary analysis, Lentriccia and McLaughlin (1990) ask, "How does any word make sense? It makes sense by being a part of a system of meanings, a set of contrasts and comparisons. No word has meaning in isolation but only insofar as it relates to and differs from other words in the language system" (pp. 85–86). As discussed earlier, part of the joint work of teacher educators, novices and experienced teachers who mentor novices is to understand how the system of meanings—especially what is contrasted or compared or what is framed in certain ways—varies along with context and ideology. Usually, when we look closely at our use of language, we lay bare our biases and open ourselves up to other possible perspectives. In language we not only find metaphors amplifying meaning, but we find metaphors that push us to think about something familiar in new ways. Or, by juxtaposing unlikely images, we open up new ways of seeing, speaking, and thinking about them. In that sense, teacher educators, teacher candidates, and practicing teachers create openings to work together to uncover hidden meanings associated with their experiences so they can become more open to what else future experiences might hold, or what alternative explanations might be.

We are suggesting that when teacher educators and mentor teachers take on the responsibility to help novices become part of a community of practice, they are helping them learn a professional discourse. Linguist James Gee describes a "Discourse," or a particular kind of community in which specialized cultural practices and uses of language along with other identifiable accoutrements of status and role are conferred on people who have undertaken specialized learning. These people can be identified as practitioners whose professional identity deeply penetrates their lives and relationships. For them, language is now related to culture and learning in new and particular ways. Gee writes,

> Discourses are ways of being in the world, of forms of life which integrate words, acts, values, beliefs, attitudes, and social identities, as well as gestures, glances, body positions, and clothes. A Discourse is a sort of identity kit which comes complete with the appropriate costume and instructions on how to act, talk, and often write, so as to take on a particular social role that others will recognize.
>
> (1996, p. 127)

When they investigate their own language use, professionals use language tentatively and judiciously, and they exercise the disposition to inquire into the hidden meanings behind their language. That means that they work with novices to avoid confusing naming (e.g. the "struggling reader") with knowing how to enact practices that support all learners become successful readers. They take time to investigate meaning, pay attention to the rhetoric of teaching, what it is like, and what it reveals.

Creating new discourse communities

What are some examples of ways in which teacher educators can engage novices in this investigative work? Whatever the design, it must maintain complexity in teaching and learning and avoid simplification. As such, teacher educators work jointly with practicing teachers and teacher candidates to become weavers of experience. As weavers, there is the end in view of learning from experience, while still maintaining openness to experiencing and re-experiencing the ordinary in new ways. One design option is to partner with teacher study groups to co-create new discourse communities in which novices can participate. We offer three examples of educators' efforts to stand outside familiar professional ways of thinking, speaking, and interacting. These examples address the figurative language—narrative and metaphorical—of our practice critically and imaginatively.

Descriptive review

The Philadelphia Teachers Learning Cooperative (TLC) found ways to investigate alternative meanings as they work to make sense of classroom life. They engage in oral inquiries called "descriptive reviews" where teachers bring questions to the group that will help the teacher learn something new—about an approach to addressing a problem, a particular child, a discrepancy between a child's work and behavior, and so on (Carini, 2000; Kanevsky, 1993). Presenting information to the group regarding five categories—children's physical presence and gesture; disposition; relationships with children and adults; activities and interests; and modes of thinking and learning—teachers emphasize description and are open to alternative ideas. As Patricia Carini explained,

> What does it mean to speak descriptively and provisionally? It means to set aside heavy judgmental language and diagnostic or other categorizing labels such as "hyperactive" or "learning disabled" or "developmentally delayed." The chair [leading the discussion] explains that no child is *always* moving or invisible or pestering or whatever—not matter how much it seems that way to the harried or concerned parent or teacher. She suggests that phrases like "it seems to me" or "from my perspective" leave room for the child to be other than what any of us might think. The chair stresses that what is most important is to ground language used to describe the child in examples and illustrations so that the language is well rooted in observation.
>
> (Carini, 2000, p. 14, emphasis in original)

In these ways, many perspectives on an issue or question are considered to make the issue more, not less, complex. Avoiding shorthand labels such as "hyper" or "disabled" or "delayed" permits teachers to focus on what the child *can* do, adding ". . . depth and dimension to the picture of the child" (Carini, 2000, p. 15) rather than speaking metaphorically about what the child cannot do relative to others.

Teacher study groups

In a second example, Anne Haas Dyson and her teacher colleagues gathered twice monthly during a full school year to explore the central question, "[W]hat difference does 'difference' make in our experience of the daily work of teaching?" (Dyson, with The San Francisco East Bay Teacher Study Group, 1997, p. 3). As the group explored this broad question in the context of teaching writing, they developed a more specific set of questions:

- What do we mean by "difference"?
- Who decides what or who is "different"?
- How and when do we experience "differences" in the course of our daily teaching? Are there particular dimensions of classroom life in which differences become salient in positive or negative problematic ways? What makes them "positive" or "problematic"?
- How do we make literacy curricula open to children's diverse experiences and resources? How do we keep our activities flexible and our expectations forward looking?
- How do we help children themselves live in a world of differences?

(Dyson *et al.*, 1997, pp. 3–4)

The group's consideration of these questions from multiple angles yielded understandings of "horizontal differences among children (e.g. differences of language, cultural style, familial circumstance . . . and vertical differences (i.e. differences where children fall on the very narrow band of abilities and skills that mark even young children as 'smart' or 'not,' 'ready' or 'not,' 'at risk' or 'not')" (p. 11). By thinking about learners as situated in classrooms and schools as institutions, these inquiring teachers probed ways in which language has the potential to shape what we see and understand about learners (or not) and to influence our curricular and pedagogical decisions.

Professional networks

In a third example, the Book Club Plus Network created in Michigan by Taffy Raphael and Susan Florio-Ruane linked teachers across urban, rural, and suburban districts in Michigan for inquiry-based professional development. The common project of the network was designing and researching ways to re-engage youngsters who, after several years of identification as struggling or slow readers, had disengaged from school-based literacy and adopted self-images as non-readers. The network was a collaborative. Running for five years, it involved teachers from many communities (K though middle school) with teacher educators and merged designs for educational improvement with their own professional growth. By designing, teaching, and assessing pilot curriculum, members of the network sustained and deepened relationships and created a field-tested conceptual framework for classroom literacy focused on the re-engagement of youngsters for whom reading has been a difficult, frustrating experience. They sustained the network by writing and publishing together, taking part in face-to-face discussions, visiting one another's classrooms and homes, speaking on the telephone, communicating over the Internet, and coming together periodically for retreats (Florio-Ruane *et al.*, 2004; Raphael *et al.*, 2001).

Like the first two examples discussed above, these educators made language a focus of their inquiry and challenged the metaphors of "struggling" or "slow" readers as inadequate and inappropriate for effecting meaningful improvements in curriculum and instruction. They emphasized the nature of experiences children encounter in school and considered how those experiences make learning possible (or not), rather than labeling the children themselves with language that locates the problem within the individual child.

Investigating culture, language and meaning

Across these three examples, we see that variations in meaning of terms such as "struggle" or "difference" have profound implications for the choices beginning teachers make regarding teaching methods and materials and ways in which they organize their classrooms for learning. They have profound implications, as well, for which children are included or excluded in rich learning opportunities. For if the novice teacher concludes that the "struggling reader" must only read texts that simplify language and reduce struggle, then that reader may never have opportunities to work with rich, descriptive language that makes texts inherently artistic, poetic and interesting.

These educators are already engaged in important investigations into culture, language and meaning. As Cochran-Smith proposed years ago (1991), working alongside reform-minded teachers creates a rich learning context for novices and teacher educators alike because the joint work involves more than doing—it includes inquiry into current practices for the purpose of ongoing learning and educational reform.

Using technological tools

More recent technological innovations such as the use of multi-media video cases provide another avenue for investigating classroom life and meanings associated with it (e.g.

Kinser & Risko, 1998; Koehler *et al.*, 1999; Lambdin *et al.*, 1996; Lampert & Ball, 1998; Rosaen, 2002; Rosaen *et al.*, 2004; Rosaen *et al.*, 2002). Video cases can be created using a multi-media editor that lets users view, analyze, organize and comment on artifacts from classrooms (video, photographs, audio and a range of text files) to investigate the visible practice of teaching and raise questions about the associated thinking of teachers and students. These cases, designed with multiple paths to follow and a range of records of practice (Ball & Cohen, 1999) to investigate, are pedagogical tools that can help teacher candidates adopt an inquiring stance and flexible thinking about teaching and learning (Spiro & Jeng, 1990). Moreover, because video can be viewed repeatedly, there is the potential to slow down the rapid pace of classroom life and help novices learn to use concepts and theories to make sense of complex classroom interactions.

Close study of teaching and learning

For instance, teacher candidates can work in small groups and engage in multiple viewings of video clips and student work associated with a particular lesson. They can be encouraged to make explicit their assumptions about teaching and learning and compare and contrast their own interpretations with those of their peers. They can also be encouraged to ask questions (versus giving answers or explanations) about what they are seeing. Here is what one pair of students in Rosaen's literacy methods class asked after viewing a guided reading lesson with James, an emergent reader, in a second grade classroom:

1 [We would like to know] what does the next day's lesson look like to better help James [the focal student in the video] and other struggling readers to comprehend what [the book] they have looked at in this [video] clip?
2 How many other students are at James's level and how does she [the teacher] help them? If there are multiple students at his level, why didn't she take them into a small group and work on this text with them too?
3 Did it benefit James to work one-on-one with the teacher as opposed to working with a small group of students?
4 What was the rest of the class doing while [the teacher] was working solely with James?

(Student Work 11/9: Mary and Arlene)

Here we note that Mary and Arlene labeled James a "struggling reader," which clues their instructor in to their use of the metaphor to interpret a student's participation in the classroom. It also provides an opening to explore their interpretation further: Do they think James is "struggling" because he is reading at an emergent level while other second graders are reading chapter books? Or is this because they notice that James mentioned to the teacher that he read the same book in Kindergarten? What else did they notice during the lesson that indicates to them that he is "struggling"?

We also see that this pair of students is thinking about issues related to James' membership in the learning community (e.g. how he is similar to or different from other readers and what sorts of social interaction might be beneficial for him). Additionally, they are questioning how the classroom is organized so the teacher can work one on one with a particular student. These questions indicate an awareness that there are many aspects teachers need to pay attention to during reading instruction—materials, grouping, student ability, classroom organization, and so on—that affect the learning of "struggling" readers.

Learning to notice across contexts

Learning to notice particular practices and connect them to broader understandings of meaningful instruction is complicated, especially during the rush of classroom activities and routines (Mason, 2002; Schultz, 2003; Sherin & van Es, 2002). The use of video cases in teacher education classes can blur the distinction between "the course" and "the field" and help prepare teacher candidates to perceive aspects of instruction in "real life" classrooms as well as to add to their developing repertoire of teaching practices, strategies and resources for teaching. Mary spent time in a third grade classroom and Arlene in a fourth grade setting as part of the methods course requirements. They noticed both similarities and differences in their beliefs and ideas about effective literacy instruction. When thinking about why these exist, they named several types of experiences that may have influenced their views:

> Similarities exist due to the fact that we are both in the same section of [this course] and we are reading the same informational texts, discussing the same things, and even viewing the same [video] clips, as we frequently work together.
> We feel that differences exist due to our varying experiences in our different classrooms. One may see something that works, while the other one may not experience it. Personal views may also come into play as we place emphasis on different things and feel that some things are more important than others.
>
> (Student Work 11/16: Mary and Arlene)

Here it appears that Mary and Arlene see how a set of experiences—course readings and discussions, viewing video cases, and classroom participation—all contribute to their views. They attribute their areas of agreement to having shared experiences in the course, while areas of difference emerge from participating in different classroom settings for field experiences. They also assume their prior knowledge and beliefs interact with their current thinking. It is not clear whether they would agree with Lana's comments, shared earlier, that "real world" (classroom) experience is the best kind, with course readings only contributing as a starting point for learning in the classroom.

Investigating curriculum, policies, and standards

Earlier we discussed ways in which teacher's work and the metaphors embedded in it are both ideological and political. This suggests that "classroom life" is not all novices need to experience or think about. Other aspects of schooling such as curriculum materials, standards documents, and policies such as No Child Left Behind (2002) influence what teachers need to attend to in their work. They also affect teachers' sense of agency regarding the type and amount of autonomy they have in the classroom (Pardo, 2006). Sometimes when we think of teachers' needs across the career stages, we think of helping them first and foremost learn to manage and teach in the classroom and we tend to assume novices will leave other roles such as curriculum development work and taking on leadership roles to their more experienced colleagues. As Feiman-Nemser (2001) points out, teacher educators can design the progression of experiences novices are exposed to over time, centered on the central tasks of teaching. The curriculum can vary the level of responsibility, focus of attention and types of mentoring available and match beginning teachers' developmental readiness and needs. She suggests a continuum that expands out from a focus on the classroom during the preservice years to include the community in the induction years and leadership roles in the broader profession in subsequent years.

However, a close look at ways in which the standards movement and pressures from policies such as NCLB and other high-stakes testing initiatives are currently impacting all teachers' classroom practices (Anagnostopoulos, 2003; Copenhaver, 2001; Johnson, 2001; Johnson *et al.*, 2003) suggests the need to rethink whether it is possible or even desirable to delay focusing novices' attention on the communities in which learners in their field placement classrooms live and the larger issues that impinge on the work the teachers in field placement classrooms do. If novices are to perceive their experiences as events over which they have some control (versus being controlled by them), then they need to understand how they can and do take part in their own weaving of experience.

Learning to question

For instance, there are five skill areas included in No Child Left Behind (2002) legislation that are promoted as research based practices for literacy teaching and learning: phonemic awareness, phonics, vocabulary development, reading fluency, and reading comprehension. Yet the new Grade Level Content Expectations developed by the State of Michigan (released in the fall of 2004) include some additional categories that are deemed important to literacy teaching and learning: word study (as a part of vocabulary development), metacognition, critical standards and reading attitudes. There is ample research evidence that these areas are equally important to effective instruction as those targeted by NCLB (Palincsar & Brown, 1989; Pressley *et al.*, 1987).

Novices who are taught to ask the question: *Who would have me believe what about this?* about any materials and requirements they confront as teachers would notice quickly that the additional areas of focus in the Michigan document move literacy teaching and learning beyond what might be considered "the basics" to engaging as well in higher level, critical thinking. Based on their analysis, novices might ask a follow-up question, *What does it mean to "leave no child behind" if all children are only getting "the basics"?* Even if they teach eventually in a "Reading First" School where funds are allocated to help states and local school districts offer effective reading instruction in grades K through 3 in very specific and prescribed ways, novice teachers must realize that they still have some instructional choices. They also must realize that they can justify their choices based on what is also expected by their own state and argue that these additional expectations are complementary to those found at the national level. In short, they can learn to view themselves as having some power over critical decisions regarding the learning opportunities available to children in their classrooms (Cochran-Smith & Lytle, 1999; Darling-Hammond, 1998; Firestone & Pennell, 1997). They can also learn to provide solid documentation regarding their students' growth as readers, writers and thinkers (Bauer & Garcia, 2002).

WHERE DOES UNDERSTANDING EXPERIENCE, METAPHOR AND CULTURE LEAD US?

In a recent review of research on methods courses and field experiences, Clift and Brady (2005) concluded that there is a need in teacher education for rich, complex socio-cultural approaches to studying how beginners make sense of and interpret experiences. Our consideration of how metaphor brings together language, culture, activity and thought in ways that can both help and limit what beginners learn from experience suggests a similar need. As discussed in the introductory section of this chapter, prior research on metaphors that reflect teachers' conceptions of teaching and sense of self provides a foundation for further empirical work. We see a need to investigate ways in which beginning teachers' explicit examination of metaphors that are pervasive in our culture and profession influence what they pay attention to as they experience various aspects of teacher preparation. For example, if teacher candidates have opportunities to investigate metaphorical language as part of study groups comprised of experienced teachers and teacher educators, what do these activities help novices notice and pay attention to? How does participation influence their understanding of their own responsibilities toward subject matter and learning? How do various metaphors shape how they name and frame instructional issues and what conceptual and practical tools do they use to address them? In what ways does looking at social, historical, political and ideological influences on language help them interpret experience? These are interesting questions worth investigating to understand more fully the metaphors by which beginners teach and how to help them consider alternative metaphors.

In this chapter we have also offered some alternative metaphors that could guide the design of teacher education. We suggested that thinking of the field as an ecological environment has the potential to foster interdependence and interaction among teacher candidates, teacher educators, and classroom teachers, rather than positioning learning experiences as taking place either "out there" in the field or "in here" on campus. We also suggested that thinking of teaching as weaving brings many layers into view, allowing for multi-dimensional investigation of discourse, classroom practice, curriculum, policy and standards. If these metaphors were used to design and redesign teacher education experiences, to what extent would the designs represent real change in how teacher education is carried out and evaluated? How would beginning teachers make sense of their experiences? To what extent do the experiences support novices in learning to think critically about ways in which metaphorical language shapes and structures experience? To what extent would they learn to choose metaphors that work in productive ways to guide their practice as opposed to working within tacit structures of which they are unaware? In offering new metaphors it is important to stand back from them and appraise them for their contributions to our work.

In the end, we need to learn more about how engaging in analysis of experience as the relationship among language, culture, activity and thought have the potential to transform teacher education to provide more powerful learning experiences. Because the metaphors that structure and guide our work as educators are rooted deeply in our culture and our profession and thus hold a great deal of power, it is important not only to understand them, but to make our own choices regarding their influence on what we do as educators.

NOTES

1 Partial support for the preparation of the chapter was provided by the Michigan State University Literacy Achievement Research Center (LARC). We acknowledge the encouragement we received from the late Dr. Michael Pressley, who served as the Director of LARC while we were writing this chapter. We also thank the students in our doctoral seminar, *Using literacy to learn: curriculum and pedagogy*, for many lively discussions that encouraged us to explore many of the ideas we developed this chapter. All ideas presented in this chapter are the sole responsibility of the authors.
2 Billig, M. (1987) *Arguing and thinking: a rhetorical approach to social psychology*. Cambridge: Cambridge University Press. Cited in Engestrom (1994).

3 The ideas and illustrative example are adapted from the essay, "How shall a thing be called?" by Roger Brown and Albert Gilman (1970).
4 Barton (1994) chose this metaphor as an alternative way to think about "literacy" because it introduced the idea of situated growth, the idea that growth happens in complex contexts.

REFERENCES

Anagnostopoulos, D. (2003) Testing and student engagement with literature in urban classrooms: a multi-layered approach. *Research in the teaching of English*, 38(2), 177–212.

Au, K. (1993) *Literacy instruction in multicultural settings*. Fort Worth, TX: Harcourt, Brace, Jovanovich.

Au, K. (1998) Social constructivism and the school literacy learning of students of diverse backgrounds. *Journal of Literacy Research*, 30, 297–319.

Ayers, W., Hunt, J. A., & Quinn, T. (eds.) (1998) *Teaching for social justice*. New York: Teachers College Press.

Ball, D. L. & Cohen, D. K. (1999) Developing practice, developing practitioners: toward a practice-based theory of professional development. In L. Darling-Hammond & G. Sykes (eds.), *Teaching as the learning professional: handbook of policy and practice* (pp. 3–32). San Francisco: Jossey-Bass.

Barton, D. (1994) *Literacy: an introduction to the ecology of written language*. London: Blackwell.

Bauer, E. B. & Garcia, G. E. (2002) Lessons from a classroom teacher's use of alternative literacy assessment. *Research in the Teaching of English*, 36, 462–494.

Berliner, D. C. (1990) If the metaphor fits, why not wear it? The teacher as executive. *Theory Into Practice*, 29(2), 85–93.

Billig, M. (1987) *Arguing and thinking: a rhetorical approach to social psychology*. Cambridge: Cambridge University Press.

Bomer, R. & Bomer, K. (2001) *For a better world: reading and writing for social action*. Portsmouth, NH: Heinemann.

Britzman, D. (1991) *Practice makes practice: a critical study of learning to teach*. Albany, NY: State University of New York Press.

Brown, R. & Gilman, R. (1970) How shall a thing be called? In Brown, R. (ed.) *Psycholinguistics: selected papers by Roger Brown*, pp. 3–15. New York: The Free Press.

Bruner, J. (1996) *The culture of education*. Cambridge, MA: Harvard University Press.

Bullough, R. V. (1991) Exploring personal teaching metaphors in preservice teacher education. *Journal of Teacher Education*, 42(1), 43–51.

Bullough, R. V. & Stokes, D. K. (1994) Analyzing personal teaching metaphors in preservice teacher education as a means for encouraging professional development. *American Educational Research Journal*, 31(1), 197–224.

Bullough, R. V., Knowles, J. G., & Crew, N. A. (1991) *Emerging as a teacher*. New York: Routledge.

Carini, P. F. (2000) Prospect's descriptive process. In M. Himley with P. F. Carini (eds.), *From another angle: children's strengths and school standards* (pp. 8–22). New York: Teachers College Press.

Carter, K. (1990) Meaning and metaphor: case knowledge in teaching. *Theory Into Practice*, 29(2), 109–115.

Clandinin, D. J. (1985) Personal practical knowledge: a study of teachers' classroom images. *Curriculum Inquiry*, 15(4), 361–385.

Clandinin, D. J. (1986) *Classroom practice: teacher images in action*. London: The Falmer Press.

Clift, R. T. & Brady, P. (2005) Research on methods courses and field experiences. In M. Cochran-Smith & K. M. Zeichner (eds.), *Studying teacher education: the report of the AERA panel on research and teacher education* (pp. 309–424). Mahwah, NJ: Lawrence Erlbaum.

Cochran-Smith, M. (1991) Learning to teach against the grain. *Harvard Educational Review*, 51(3), 279–310.

Cochran-Smith, M. (1998) Teaching for social justice: toward a grounded theory of teacher education. In A. Hargreaves, A. Lieberman, M. Fullan, & D. Hopkins (eds.), *The international handbook of educational change* (pp. 916–951). The Netherlands: Kluwer Academic.

Cochran-Smith, M. (2005) The new teacher education: for better or for worse? *Educational Researcher* 34(6), 3–17.

Cochran-Smith, M. & Lytle, S. (1999) Relationships of knowledge and practice: teacher learning in community. In *Review of Research in Education*, 24 (pp. 249–305). Washington, DC: American Educational Research Association.

Cohen, E. G. & Lotan, R. A. (1990) Teacher as supervisor of complex teaching. *Theory Into Practice* (29)2, 78–84.

Collins, E. C. & Green, J. L. (1990) Metaphors: the construction of a perspective. *Theory Into Practice* (29)2, 71–77.

Cole, M. (1996) *Cultural psychology: a once and future discipline.* Cambridge, MA: Harvard University Press.

Copenhaver, J. F. (2001) Running out of time: rushed read-alouds in a primary classroom. *Language Arts*, 79(2), 148–158.

Darling-Hammond, L. (1998) Teacher learning that supports student learning. *Educational Leadership*, 55(5), 6–11.

de Guerrero, M. C. M & Villamil, O. S. (2002) Metaphorical conceptualizations of ESL teaching and learning. *Language Teaching Research*, 6(2), 195–120.

Dewey, J. (1904/1964) The relation of theory to practice in education. In R. D. Archambault (ed.), *John Dewey on education*, pp. 313–338. Chicago: University of Chicago Press.

Dewey, J. (1915) *The School and the society/The child and the curriculum.* Chicago: University of Chicago Press.

Dewey, J. (1938) *Experience and education.* New York: Macmillan.

Dyson, A. H. with the San Francisco East Bay Teacher Study Group (1997) *What difference does difference make?* Urbana, IL: National Council of Teachers of English.

Eisenhart, M. (1995) The fax, the jazz player, and the self-story teller: how do people organize culture? *Anthropology and Education Quarterly*, 26(2), 3–26.

Engestrom, Y. (1994) Teachers as collaborative thinkers: activity-theoretical study of an innovative teacher team. In Carlgren, I., Handal, G., & Vaage, S. (eds.) *Teachers' minds and actions: research on teachers' thinking and practice* (pp. 43–61). Bristol: Falmer.

Erickson, F. (2004) *Talk and social theory: ecologies of speaking and listening in everyday life.* Cambridge: Polity Press.

Elbow, P. (1986) *Embracing contraries: explorations in learning and teaching.* Oxford: Oxford University Press.

Feiman-Nemser, S. (2001) From preparation to practice: designing a continuum to strengthen and sustain teaching. *Teachers College Record*, 103(6), 1013–1055.

Feiman-Nemser, S. & Buchmann, M. (1985) Pitfalls of experience in teacher education. *Teachers College Record*, 87(1), 53–65.

Fenstermacher G. D. & Soltis J. F. (1986) *Approaches to teaching.* New York: Teachers College Press.

Firestone, W. A. & Pennell, J. R. (1997) Designing state-sponsored teacher networks: a comparison of two cases. *American Educational Research Journal*, 34, 237–266.

Florio-Ruane, S. (1990) Creating your own case studies: a guide for early field experience. *Teacher Education Quarterly*, 1, 29–41.

Florio-Ruane, S. & Raphael, T. E. (2004) Reconsidering our research: collaboration, complexity, design, and the problem of "Scaling up what works." In Worthy, J., Maloch, B., Hoffman, J. V., Schallert, D. L., & Fairbanks, C. M. (eds.), *53rd Yearbook of the National Reading Conference* (pp. 170–188). Oak Creek, WI: National Reading Conference.

Florio-Ruane, S., Raphael, T. E., Highfield, K., & Berne, J. (2004) Reengaging youngsters with reading difficulties by means of innovative professional development. In Strickland, D. & Kamil, M. L. (2004) *Improving reading through professional development* (pp. 129–148). Norwood: Christopher-Gordon.

Frank, C. R. & Uy, F. L. (2004) Ethnography for teacher education. *Journal of Teacher Education*, 55(3), 269–283.

Gee, J. P. (1996) *Social linguistics and literacies: ideology in discourse* (Second edition). London: Routledge-Falmer.

Geertz, C. (1983) "From the native's point of view": on the nature of anthropological understanding. In Geertz, C. (1983) *Local knowledge: further essays in interpretive anthropology* (pp. 55–72), Third edition. New York: Basic Books.

Gore, J. (1993) *The struggle for pedagogies: Critical land feminist discourses as regimes of truth*. New York and London: Routledge.

Grant, G. E. (1992) The sources of structural metaphors in teacher knowledge: Three cases. *Teaching and Teacher Education*, 8(5–6), 433–440.

Grossman, P., Smagorinsky, P., & Valencia, S. (1999). *Appropriate conceptual and pedagogical tools for teaching English: a conceptual framework for studying professional development*. Albany, NY: National Research Center on English Learning Achievement.

Gutierrez, K. D. & Orellana, M. F. (2006) The "problem" of English learner: constructing genres of difference. *Research in the Teaching of English*, 40, 502–507.

Hunt, D. E. & Gow, J. (1984) How to be your own best theorist II. *Theory Into Practice*, 23(1), 64–71.

Jackson, P. (1968) *Life in classrooms*. New York: Holt, Rinehart & Winston.

Johnson, J. E. (2001) Overcoming the challenge of mandated instructional time. *Primary Voices K-6* (9) 3, 8–13. Urbana, IL: National Council of Teachers of English.

Johnson, T. W., Smagorinsky, P., Thompson, L., & Fry, P. (2003) Learning to teach the five-paragraph theme. *Research in the Teaching of English*, 38(2), 136–176.

Kanevsky, R. D. (1993) Descriptive review of a child: a way of knowing about teaching and learning. In M. Cochran-Smith & S. Lytle (eds.), *Inside/outside: teacher research and knowledge* (pp. 150–162). New York: Teachers College Press.

Kennedy, M. (1987) Inexact sciences: professional education and the development of expertise. In E. Z. Rothkopf (ed.), *Review of research in education*, Volume 14, 133–167. Washington, DC: American Educational Research Association.

Kennedy, M. (1999) Ed schools and the problem of knowledge. In J. D. Raths & A. C. McAninch (eds.), *Advances in teacher education Volume 5: what counts as knowledge in teacher education?* (pp. 29–45). Stamford CT: Ablex Publishing Corp.

Kessels, J. & Korthagen, F. (1996) The relationship between theory and practice: back to the classics. *Educational Researcher*, 25(3), 17–22.

Kinzer, C. K. & Risko, V. J. (1998) Multimedia and enhanced learning: transforming preservice education. In D. Reinking, M. D. McKenna, L. D. Labbo, & R. D. Keiffer (eds.), *Handbook of literacy and technology* (pp. 185–202). Mahwah, NJ: Erlbaum.

Koehler, M. J., Petrosino, A. J. & Lehrer, R. (1999) Elements of case design for hypermedia environments in teacher education. *World conference on educational hypermedia, hypermedia and telecommunications*, 1999(1), 1414–1415.

Ladson-Billings, G. (1995) Toward a theory of culturally relevant pedagogy. *American Educational Research Journal*, 32(3), 465–491.

Lakoff, G. & Johnson, M. (1980) *Metaphors we live by*. Chicago: University of Chicago Press.

Lambdin, D., Duffy, T., & Moore, J. (1996) *A hypermedia system to aid in preservice teacher education: instructional design and evaluation*. ERIC Document 397 808.

Lampert, M. (2001) *Teaching problems and problems in teaching*. New Haven, CT: Yale University Press.

Lampert, M. & Ball, D. (1998) *Teaching multimedia: investigations of real practice*, New York: Teachers College Press.

Lentriccia, F. & McLaughlin, T. (1990) *Critical terms for literary study*. Chicago: University of Chicago Press.

Lortie, D. (1975). *Schoolteacher*. Chicago: University of Chicago Press.

Marshall, H. H. (1990) Metaphor as an instructional tool in encouraging student teacher reflection. *Theory Into Practice* 29(2), 128–132.

Mason, J. (2002) *Researching your own practice: the discipline of noticing.* New York: Routledge.

McLaughlin, M. W. & Talbert, J. E. (2001) *Professional communities and the work of high school teaching.* Chicago: University of Chicago Press.

Munby, H. (1986) Metaphor in the thinking of teachers: an exploratory study. *Journal of Curriculum Studies,* 18(2), 197–209.

Munby, H. & Russell, T. (1990) Metaphor in the study of teachers' professional knowledge. *Theory Into Practice,* 29(2), 116–121.

Munby, H. & Russell, T. (1994) The authority of experience in learning to teach: messages from a physics methods class. *Journal of Teacher Education,* 45(2), 86–95.

National Commission on Excellence in Education (1983) *A nation at Risk: the imperative for educational reform.* Retrieved February 22, 2006 from http://www.goalline.org/Goal%20Line/NatAtRisk.html

No Child Left Behind Act (2002) U.S. Department of Education. Retrieved February 22, 2006 from http://www.ed.gov/nclb/landing.jhtml?src=pb

Ortony, A. (ed.) (1979/1993) *Metaphor and thought,* Second edition. Cambridge: Cambridge University Press.

Palincsar, A. S. & Brown, A. L. (1989) Classroom dialogues to promote self-regulated comprehension. In J. Brophy (ed.), *Advances in research on teaching, Volume 1,* pp. 35–71. Greenwich, CT: JAI Press.

Pardo, L. (2006) The role of context in learning to teach writing: what teacher educators need to know to support beginning urban teachers. *Journal of Teacher Education,* 57(4), 378–394.

Pressley, M., Borkowski, J. G., & Schneider, W. (1987) Good strategy users coordinate metacognition, strategy use, and knowledge. In R. Vasta and G. Whitehurst (eds.), *Annals of child development,* Volume 4, pp. 89–130. Greenwich, CT: JAI Press.

Raphael, T. E., Florio-Ruane, S., Kehus, M. J., George, M., Hasty, N. L., & Highfield, K. (2001) Thinking for ourselves: literacy learning in a diverse teacher inquiry network. *The Reading Teacher, March* 54(6), 596–607.

Rogoff, B. (1990) *Apprenticeship in thinking: cognitive development in social context.* New York: Oxford University Press.

Rosaen, C. L. (2002) Designing and using hypermedia materials to investigate language use in a culturally diverse classroom. *Journal of Educational Multimedia and Hypermedia,* 11(2), 155–175. (Online). Available: http://www.aace.org/dl/index.cfm/fuseaction/View/paperID/9214

Rosaen, C. L., Degnan, C., VanStratt, T., & Zietlow, K. (2004) Designing a virtual K-12 classroom literacy tour: learning together as teachers explore "best practice." In J. Brophy (ed.), *Advances in research on teaching, volume 10: Using video in teacher education,* pp. 169–199. New York: Elsevier Science.

Rosaen, C. L., Schram, P., & Herbel-Eisenmann, B. (2002) Using technology to explore connections among mathematics, language and literacy. *Contemporary Issues in Technology and Teacher Education.* (Online serial), 2(3). Available: http://www.citejournal.org/vol2/iss3/mathematics/article1.cfm

Schon, D. (1979/1993) Generative metaphor: a perspective on problem-setting in social policy. In Ortony, A. (ed.), *Metaphor and thought,* Second edition (pp. 137–163). Cambridge: Cambridge University Press.

Schon, D. (1983) *The reflective practitioner.* New York: Basic Books.

Schon, D. (1987) *Educating the reflective practitioner.* San Francisco: Jossey-Bass.

Schultz, K. (2003) *Listening: a framework for teaching across differences.* New York: Teachers College Press.

Scribner, S. (1984) Literacy in three metaphors. *American Journal of Education* (November), 6–20.

Shannon, P. (1992) *Becoming political: readings and writings in the politics of literacy education.* Portsmouth, NH: Heinemann.

Shuell, T. J. (1990) Teaching and learning as problem solving. *Theory Into Practice* (29)2, 102–108.

Sherin, M. & van Es, E. (2002) Using video to support teachers' ability to interpret classroom interactions. *Society for Information Technology and Teacher Education International Conference 2002* (1), 2532–2536. (Online). Available: http://dl.aace.org/11510

Siskin, L. S. (1994) *Realms of knowledge*. New York: Routledge/Falmer.

Siskin, L. S. (1995) *The subjects in question: departmental organization and the high school*. New York: Teachers College Press.

Spiro, R. J. & Jehng, J. (1990) Cognitive flexibility theory and hypertext: theory and technology for the nonlinear and multidimensional traversal of complex subject matter. In D. Nix & R. Spiro (eds.), *Cognition, education, and multimedia: exploring ideas in high technology* (pp. 163–205). Hillsdale, NJ: Lawrence Erlbaum Associates.

Tobin, K. (1990) Changing metaphors and beliefs: a master switch for teaching? *Theory Into Practice*, 29(2), 122–127.

Weade, R. & Ernst, G. (1990) Pictures of life in classrooms, and the search for metaphors to frame them. *Theory Into Practice* 29(2), 133–140.

Villegas, A. M. & Lucas, T. (2002) *Educating culturally responsive teachers: a coherent approach*. Albany, NY: State University of New York Press.

Vygotsky, L. S. (1981) The genesis of higher mental functions. In J.V. Wertsch (ed.), *The concept of activity in Soviet psychology* (pp. 144–188). Armonk, NY: M. E. Sharpe.

Wenger, E. (1998) *Communities of practice: learning, meaning, and identity*. Cambridge: Cambridge University Press.

Wideen, M., Mayer-Smith, J., & Moon, B. (1998) A critical analysis of the research on learning to teach: making the case for an ecological perspective on inquiry. *Review of Educational Research*, 68(2), 130–178.

40 The development of the personal self and professional identity in learning to teach

Carol R. Rodgers
University at Albany

Katherine H. Scott
Independent scholar

INTRODUCTION

The previous *Handbook on Research in Teacher Education* (Sikula, 1996) includes two chapters dealing with the "inner life" of the teacher: Virginia Richardson's review of research on teacher attitudes and beliefs, and Kathy Carter and Walter Doyle's review of research on personal narrative and life history. Richardson dismisses attitudes as weak indicators of teacher learning, while endorsing beliefs as important determinants of action. She defines beliefs as "psychologically held understandings, premises, or propositions about the world that are felt to be true," (p. 103; Feiman-Nemser & Floden, 1986) and that stem from personal experience, experience with school, and experience with formal knowledge (Clandinin & Connelly, 1987; Elbaz, 1983). Given the tenacity of beliefs that spring from previous life history and student teaching, she concludes that teacher education is a relatively "weak intervention". Although beliefs are clearly part and parcel of who one is as a teacher, Richardson does not directly address issues of identity and self.

Carter and Doyle take on the question of self and identity indirectly, through the lenses of personal narrative and life history research. Their research rests on the premise that "the process of learning to teach, the act of teaching and teachers' experiences and choices are deeply personal matters inexorably linked to their identity and life story" (p. 120). Life history research highlights the social contexts that shape identity, while personal narrative emphasizes the fact that learning, including learning to teach, involves the construction of personal stories. Carter and Doyle conclude by stating that "from a biographical frame . . . becoming a teacher means (a) transforming an identity, (b) adapting personal understandings and ideals to institutional realities, and (c) deciding how to express one's self in classroom activity" (p. 139). Clearly teachers are people who bring themselves into the classroom and the formation of their identities involves an interplay between external and internal forces.

This chapter does not refute these findings and perspectives. Rather, it shows how research over the past ten years has deepened and complicated our understanding of the role of self and identity in learning to teach, particularly by critical theorists (e.g. Britzman, 2003; Cochran-Smith, 2004; Giroux, 2005; Zembylas, 2003). Specifically, identity and identity formation have taken center stage, subsuming the categories of belief, attitude, life history, and personal narrative. In addition, research on the role of emotion in learning to teach and the development of teacher identity has gained a foothold. At the same time, the distinction and relationship between one's self/ves and one's identity/ies remains murky. Finally, and importantly, there is a call from theorists for teachers to become aware of their identities and the political, historical, and social forces that shape them—in Britzman's (1993) words, to "acknowledge the politics of identity." In addition, theorists exhort teachers to assume agency, find their voice, and take the authority to shape their own professional paths and identities. Left largely unexplored by this literature, however, is the black box of *how*—how teachers should go about making the psychological shift from being authored by these forces to authoring their own stories, and how teacher educators might facilitate this process. This black box represents a psychological shift; it leads us to explore what developmental psychologists might contribute to the discussion. In particular, we take into account the view of constructive developmental psychologists who offer a potentially useful way to think about this shift. Many of the studies reviewed for this chapter were conceptual rather than empirical in nature. We hope that the introduction of a psychological frame will move the field of teacher education towards more empirical work in the development of self and identity in learning to teach.

This chapter is divided into four parts. We begin by exploring contemporary conceptions of identity and self, drawing on the teacher education and professional development literature. We follow this with a discussion of how constructive-developmentalists might illuminate our understanding of the development of self and identity. The third section looks at some promising programs from the past and present that support the development of teachers' selves and identities. The final section concludes with a discussion of these model programs in light of constructive-developmental theory, and suggests directions for further research.

Definitions of self and identity

It is necessary to carve out of the vast literature on self and identity a workable set of definitions.[1] For the purposes of this chapter, we have drawn our definitions from within the fields of teacher education and adult development.

The past ten years have seen a burgeoning of articles and books on teacher identity development. At the same time, studies of identity have cast doubt on the very concept of a "self," which may explain why much less has been written about self as teacher. Still, confusion between the terms remains. As Beijaard *et al.* (2004) note in their review of research on teachers' professional identity, "it remains unclear how exactly the concepts of 'identity' and 'self' are related" (p. 124). We first look at the larger field of identity formation, followed by the more elusive notion of self.

Contemporary conceptions of identity share four basic assumptions: (1) that identity is dependent upon and formed within multiple *contexts* which bring social, cultural, political, and historical forces to bear upon that formation; (2) that identity is formed in *relationship* with others and involves *emotions*; (3) that identity is *shifting, unstable, and multiple*; and, (4) that identity involves the construction and reconstruction of meaning through *stories* over time. Embedded in these assumptions is an implicit charge: that teachers should work towards an *awareness* of their identity and the contexts, relationships, and emotions that shape them, and (re)claim the authority of their own *voice*. This calls upon teachers to make a psychological shift in how they think about themselves as teachers. Contexts and relationships describe the *external* aspects of identity formation; and stories and emotions, the *internal*, meaning-making aspects. Awareness and voice represent the "contested" place where the normative demands of the external encounter the internal meaning making and desires of the teacher.

Identity as contextual

Identity is dependent upon the contexts in which we immerse ourselves: schools, teacher education programs, study groups, family, religious groups, political parties and so forth (Gee, 2001; Fitzgerald, 1993; Coldron & Smith, 1999; Beijaard *et al.*, 2000, 2004; Britzman, 2003; Carter & Doyle, 1996; MacLure, 1993; Smagorinsky *et al.*, 2004; Clandinin & Huber, 2005; Agee, 2004). Clandinin and Huber (2005) refer to context as "the landscapes past and present in which [a teacher] lives and works" (p. 4). Most definitions of identity take into consideration all four assumptions named above. A few, however, define identity solely as a matter of context. Fitzgerald (1993) writes that ". . . identity is defined as *the academic metaphor for self-in-context*" (italics in original, p. 3). Coldron & Smith (1999) speak of context as a matter of "space and location" and the identity of a teacher as "a matter of where, within the professional pertinent array of possibilities, a particular person is located" (p. 714). Contexts inevitably shape our notions of who we perceive ourselves to be and how others perceive us. We do not necessarily perceive contexts (which include ways of thinking and knowing) as much as we absorb them, often taking them for granted as what is "real." Britzman (1993) for example, argues that contextual forces are normative and determined by those in authority who have a vested interest in the compliance of those under their authority. Within each context there exists a set of norms, and it is expected that these norms will be upheld by the participants within the given community. Lack of awareness of these norms and pressures to assimilate, keep teachers subject to contextual forces, robbing them of agency, creativity and voice.

James Gee (2001) provides the most elaborate view of these contextual forces, identifying four interrelated perspectives on identity: the nature perspective (N-identity, or those parts of who we are that have their source in nature rather than society, e.g. a tall person); the institutional perspective (I-identity, or those parts of who we are that have their source in institutional authority, e.g. a school teacher); the discourse perspective (D-identity, or those parts of who we are that have their source in the discourse or dialogue of other people, e.g. someone who is deemed by others to be a "charismatic" person); and the affinity perspective (A-identity, or those parts of who I am that have their source in a "distinctive set of practices," e.g. a Red Sox fan). Each of these perspectives provides an "*interpretive system* underwriting the recognition of [one's] identity" by others:

> The *interpretive system* may be people's historically and culturally different views of nature; it may be the norms, traditions and rules of institutions; it may be the discourse and dialogue of others; or it may be the working of affinity groups. What is important about identity is that almost any identity trait can be understood in terms of any of these different interpretive systems.
>
> (italics in original, p. 108)

Gee uses the example of a label like "African American." This label, viewed through different interpretive systems can be understood differently. Through the institutional lens of school, for example, being an "African American" child might be equated with being "at risk." Alternatively, "African American" understood as an A-Identity, points to an affiliation with groups who share certain practices. "Here," writes Gee, "people do not see themselves as African American primarily because of 'blood' (an N-Identity), because of an institutional category (an I-Identity), or because others respond to them, for better or worse, in certain distinctive ways (a D-Identity)" (p. 108). He suggests that in this case, a "Black" person could claim that they have chosen not to be African American and a "White" person could claim to be African American. In this way identities are a matter of negotiation with others. "Thus," writes Gee, "people can accept, contest, and negotiate identities in terms of whether they will be seen primarily (or in some foregrounded way) as N-, I-, D-, or A-Identities. What is at issue, though, is always how and by whom a particular identity is to be *recognized*" (italics in original, p. 109). And this points to the second assumption of identity: that it is relational, and hence, also emotional.

Identity as relational and emotional

Within multiple contexts one forms multiple relationships, and brings forth multiple aspects of oneself. Gee (2001) points out that relationship cuts across all four of his perspectives on identity. Relationship is essential to identity primarily because to have an identity one must be recognized as a particular "kind of person" by others.

Smagorinsky *et al.* (2004), in their study of identity formation among new teachers, conclude that identity is co-constructed "through engagement with others in cultural practice" (p. 21). Samuel and Stephens (2000) observe multiple layers of relationship and negotiation in their work with black South African teachers, where teachers "walk a tightrope in both developing a personal teacher identity which sits comfortably with their own sense of self," and satisfying state requirements, while at the same time embodying reform by being "the impetus for change," including acting as critics to the very teachers who are assigned to be their mentors (p. 478). Complicated identities, indeed!

That the complex relationships between teacher, students, colleagues, mentor, school, community and state would provoke emotion is no surprise. Emotions have been taken up increasingly as a critical aspect of identity formation (Britzman, 1993; Hargreaves, 2001; Zembylas, 2002, 2003; Winograd, 2003). "Feelings," Britzman asserts, "are made in social relationships." In particular, she cites the friction created between institutional structures and expectations of how teachers *should* behave and feel and the actual "structure of feelings" that teachers already hold because of who they are, and "the lives they live" (p. 252).

In his discussion of "emotional geographies," Hargreaves (2001) also takes up the ways in which teachers' emotions are "embedded in the conditions and interactions of their work." Emotional geographies consist of "the spatial and experiential patterns of closeness and/or distance in human interactions and relationships that help create, configure and color the feelings and emotions [he does not distinguish between the two] we experience about ourselves, our world and each other" (p. 1061). In other words, teachers' emotions are shaped by the conditions of their work (for example, high-stakes tests) and are then manifest in their interactions with students, parents, administrators and others. In his interviews of 53 elementary and secondary Canadian schoolteachers, Hargreaves identifies five different emotional geographies: socio-cultural, moral, professional, political, and physical. Each involves either a closeness or a distance—distance driving wedges between people, and closeness forming bonds. For example, a socio-cultural distance might exist between a white middle-class teacher and her less-economically secure students. Moral distance exists when "teachers feel their purposes are being threatened or have been lost" by those around them (p. 1067), for example, when a school's priority is high test scores rather than student learning. Hargreaves advocates a deeper understanding of these geographies as key to making the relationships of school work, and, by implication, making teacher identity less fractured.

Zembylas (2002, 2004) echoes Hargreaves' notion of distance when he speaks of the "emotional labor" in which teachers must engage in an effort to conform to what is deemed appropriate within schools (the "emotional rules" of school): "teacher identity and emotion discourses are formed within specific school political arrangements, in relation to certain expectations and requirements, ones that presume a teacher should conform to particular emotional rules (e.g. teachers should leave their emotions 'outside' the classroom . . .)" (p. 226). Winograd (2003), an education professor who returned to elementary school teaching for a year, brought the theories of emotion outlined above to bear on his experience back in the classroom. During his year as a teacher, Winograd faced challenges, particularly in classroom management, that caused him to question his own identity as an effective educator. He found himself caught in a cycle of self-blame, often experienced by new teachers, where the school culture made it easy "to conclude that failure or struggle is [teachers'] fault alone and that structural conditions are less influential than the individual's own failings" (p. 1669). Feelings of anger, for example, were experienced as bad in the face of a culture that see teachers as restrained, gentle, and nurturing.

Identity as shifting and multiple

As implied above, when teachers' identities are shaped, at least in part, by the external forces of context and relationships, identity necessarily becomes a multiple and shifting affair, in process and changeable. As Gee writes, "The 'kind of person' one is recognized as 'being,' at a given time and place, can change from moment to moment in the interaction, can change from context to context, and of course, can be ambiguous or unstable" (p. 99). Identity is therefore not only shifting but also multiple. Beijaard *et al.* (2004) in their review of the research on teachers' professional identity, note that because identity is relational, it is also shifting, and constantly in the process of becoming.

> [Identity] is not a fixed attribute of a person, but a relational phenomenon. Identity development occurs in an intersubjective field and can be best characterized as an ongoing process, a process of interpreting oneself as a certain kind of person and being recognized as such in a given context. In this context then, identity can also be seen as an answer to the recurrent question: "Who am I at this moment?"
>
> (p. 108)

What is important here is that identity: (1) is always "in the making," rather than stable, (2) shifts according to context and relationships, and (3) is therefore varied and multiple.

Identity as storied

Thus far, identities appear to be like a deck of cards spread out on a tabletop; any one might be turned up at any time, depending upon the who, what, and where of circumstance. Continuity and coherence suggested by the terms identity *formation* or identity *development* feel elusive. There is a need for making sense—an internal arrangement and control of things so that the shifting, multiple, constructed, contradictory, confusing, cubistic thing called identity becomes useful. The most widely embraced way of making sense is through the practice of narrative, or the telling of our stories. "Nowadays," as Beijaard *et al.* (2000) note, "identity formation is conceived as an ongoing process that involves the interpretation and reinterpretation of experiences as one lives through them" (Kerby, 1991, as cited in Beijaard *et al.*, 2000). The foremost proponents of this point of view are Michael Connelly and D. Jean Clandinin (1986, 1995, 1999, 2000). Based on

Spence's (1984) notion of the narrative construction of the self (side-stepping for a moment any definition of self), Connelly and Clandinin understand a teacher's identity as "a unique embodiment of his/her stories to live by, stories shaped by the landscapes past and present in which s/he lives and works . . ." (as cited in Clandinin & Huber, p. 4). Sfard and Prusak (2005), equate identity with the construction of stories. They parse the process further by articulating a tripartite picture of identity: first-person identities (stories a person tells himself about himself), second person identities (stories told about oneself to oneself by a second person), and third person identities (stories told about oneself by a second person to a third person). Identity, then, is both interpreted and constructed through the stories that one tells oneself and that others tell. These stories change over time, across contexts, and depend upon relationship.

Awareness and voice

The four assumptions described above address the nature of identity. Awareness and voice, however, point to what theorists believe teachers *do* in light of those assumptions. Identities form and develop as a result of interactions, but not necessarily as a result of awareness. Theorists, however, call for teachers to develop an awareness of the normative contextual and relational forces that shape their identities. They exhort new and experienced teachers alike to "resist" these normative forces, forces which are "overburdened with the meanings of others," and author their own identities according to their own "deep convictions, investments, and desires" (Britzman, 1993, p. 33). Voice, Britzman contends, struggles to emerge from the confluence of forces that compete for a teacher's allegiance: the schools and universities in which she works and learns, her past experiences and identities as a learner, and her desires and images of herself as a teacher. Finding one's voice implies not having others (researchers, school boards, text books) speak for us, not being silenced by authorities or normative notions of who teachers should be, in effect, to be the *author* of one's identity.

Like Britzman, Zembylas (2002, 2004) advocates developing an awareness of and resistance to the normative forces of school, and encourages teachers to "try to think differently, to ask themselves not only how discourses on emotions and the various norms in their school have shielded them from their desires, but also how it [normative discourse] has installed those desires as what they presume themselves to be" (p. 229). Awareness of the emotions (as manifested in the body—e.g. facial gesture, the eyes, the gut) that are triggered within the context of school, and the forces that bring them about, he argues, prepares the road to voice, agency and self-transformation, especially when done in the company of others.

Winograd (2003), reflecting on his year as an elementary school teacher, advocates teachers forging relationships with other teachers in order to "study, share, and use their emotions for social change," by holding up for critique the kind of "emotional rules" that schools can impose (p. 1670).

What it takes to move from being "authored by" to "authoring" oneself is not, however, addressed in detail in the literature. It also begs the question of self in contrast to identity. If one's identities are to be "self-authored," then who is the "self" doing the authoring? It is at this juncture that discussion of an aware, active *self* is useful.

Self as maker of meaning and agent

The literature on the self reviewed here (Dewey, 1938; Kegan, 1983; Gee, 2001; Nias, 1989; Palmer, 1998) assumes that there is more to a self than simply an array of shifting identities. There is a notion of continuity and coherence that signals a self, even as there are discontinuities, shifts, and crises that signal an *evolving* self. In effect, the self can be seen as the meaning maker, or the teller of stories. If our identities are stories, then our selves might be the storytellers. As a bridge to this notion of self, we again turn to Gee who, in his discussion of identities, speaks briefly of a "core identity." One's "core identity," he writes, is different from one's "identities" which are multiple and connected "not to [one's] 'internal states' but to [one's] performances in society." One's core identity, in contrast, is something "that holds more uniformly, for ourselves and others, across contexts" (p. 99).

John Dewey references the importance of such coherence across contexts. He writes that when coherence is lacking, a person, in a sense, "cracks up":

> A divided world, a world whose parts and aspects do not hang together [for a person], is at once a sign and a cause of a divided personality. When the splitting-up reaches a certain point we call the person insane. A fully integrated personality . . . exists only when successive experiences are integrated with one another.
>
> (p. 44)

The integration, he argues, is a matter of the meaning that is made of experience through reflection. Similarly, Polkinghorne (as cited in Bruner, 1990) spoke of the self as "a configuring of personal events into an historical unity" (p. 116).

Jennifer Nias (1989), citing Foulkes (1975) and Mead (1934) distinguishes between a substantial self (I) and situational selves (me). The substantial self, formed primarily at, and even before, birth and in the early years, is embodied in values shaped by family and one's immediate culture. The substantial self remains relatively impervious to change. One's situational selves can be thought of here as one's identities. Our situational selves, she argues, "incorporate those beliefs, values, and attitudes which we feel to be most self-defining" (p. 163). The I-substantial self is subject and the me-situational self, object. The former is not knowable except as it becomes object. Reflection is the tool the self uses to know one's situational selves, which change over time. What Nias and others call the self or the private self, Britzman refers to as "being." It is both conscious and unconscious and therefore can really only "hint at itself":

> In my view, the self and identity are maybe two sides of the same coin. I have come to believe that there is an unknowable core, something that resists sociality, and can only hint at itself. I would not locate this core in identity, which I tend to think of as the social clothing plus desire for recognition. Within this clash or conflict, there is something called the private self, which I would call "being." Here is where I would locate interiority that may fuel the need for identity but in and of itself the self is not coextensive with identity, or another way of saying this is the self is not identical to itself as the philosophers might say.
>
> (Personal communication, August 2005)

Parker Palmer (1998), educator and author of the popular book, *The Courage to Teach*, distinguishes between identity and integrity in defining the self. Identity, he says, is the "evolving nexus where all the forces that constitute life converge in the mystery of self . . . In the midst of that complex field, identity is a moving intersection of the inner and outer forces that make me who I am, converging in the irreducible mystery of being human" (p. 13). Integrity differs from identity in that it suggests a conscious weaving together of some kind of meaning out of the experiences that comprise one's identity. It is "whatever wholeness I am able to find within that nexus [of identity] as its vectors form and re-form the pattern of my life. Integrity requires that I discern what is integral to my selfhood, what fits and what does not—and that I choose life-giving ways of relating to the forces that converge within me" (p. 13).

Psychologist Robert Kegan (1982), writing from a constructive-developmental perspective, holds that at every stage of development, the "self" coheres in an organized system of meaning and meaning making. It coheres differently at each stage (something which we explore more extensively below), but there is a balance in place that allows one to *be*. "There is presumed to be a basic unity to personality, a unity best understood as a process rather than an entity. This process, according to [Carl] Rogers' conception, gives rise to the 'self,' the meaning-making system with which the process gets identified" (p. 5).

Self, then, might be thought of as the meaning *maker* and identity as the meaning *made*, even as the self and identity evolve and transform over time. The self in its completeness, however, remains unknowable. It is, as Palmer says, an elusive reality "that can be caught only out of the corner of the eye." Still, despite the inevitable discontinuities and change and the intangible nature of self, there is a belief that there exists over time a "Self" that is recognizable and a coherence that allows one to move in the world with a certain confidence. For the purposes of this discussion, then, *self will subsume identity(ies) and will be understood as an evolving yet coherent being, that consciously and unconsciously constructs and is constructed, reconstructs and is reconstructed, in interaction with the cultural contexts, institutions, and people with which the self lives, learns, and functions.*

Looking at self and identity formation through a constructive-developmental lens

Because Kegan (1982, 1994) clearly articulates a process of growth and change as well as distinct developmental stages in adulthood, his theoretical framework is a useful lens with which to consider the hidden developmental demands that are at work in the literature on teacher identity. *How* a teacher makes sense of her teacher identity evolves out of the developmental capacities of the self. That is, lying underneath the four basic assumptions about teacher identity is the question: *how? How* does the teacher make sense of social, cultural, political, and historical forces? *How* does she make sense of her relationships with others? *How* does she construct and reconstruct meaning through stories? It is in the answer to this question, *how*, that we are able to identify qualitatively different ways that teachers make sense of their experiences; these differences reflect the differing developmental capacities of teachers' selves, and therefore, color and shape how they make sense of their identities.

The different ways in which teachers might answer these questions are reflected in Table 40.1 below.

Kegan's conception of self suggests that the way the teacher self makes sense of his/her experience is, in fact, different at different developmental stages, and that it evolves over time. These differences reflect teachers' varying capacities to take a perspective on their experiencing (i.e. their developmental *structure)* as distinct from differences in the *content* of their teaching (i.e. their discipline, teaching strategies, area of discipline), teacher education experiences (the philosophy of the program, the expectations of the program), or identity (i.e. sex, socio-economic status, religion, political position, etc.). Developmental structure or stage reveals the specific ways in which individuals make sense out of experiences that are seemingly similar.

Table 40.1   Differences in how teachers make sense of their teacher identities revealed through the lens of constructive developmental theory

	How does the teacher make sense of social, political, and historical forces?	*How does she make sense of her relationship with others?*	*How does she construct and reconstruct meaning through stories? What meaning does she make of story telling? What are the developmental limitations of the stories she tells?*
Stage 2: The instrumental knower	• She views them as concrete states outside of herself.	• Concrete conception of teacher role. • Interactions with others are rule bound. • No perspective on oneself in relationship to others. • "Golden Rule: I'll do to you what you do to me" (Popp & Portnow, 1998).	• External, concrete rendering of experiences • Views experiences in black and white; self-reflection eludes her.
Stage 3: The socializing knower	• The self is identified with these forces; readily conforms to them—is defined by them. • Not yet able to take a perspective on them—threatened by values associated with social/political/historical forces that are not one's own.	• Self is defined through relationships—the opinions and expectations of others. • Feels empathy for others; feels responsible for others' feelings and holds others responsible for her feelings. • Because she seeks to stay in the good graces of others, she struggles with conflicting agendas or needs. • Criticism experienced as an assault to the self. • "Golden Rule: I should do for you what I hope and need and expect you should do for me" (Popp & Portnow, 1998).	• Able to report on feelings and emotions that surround teaching. • Stories bound by relationships—impact that she has on students/teachers/institution and vice versa. • Because self made up of these relationships, not yet able to reflect on or story ways in which her own thinking or teaching is colored by her relationships to her students, her history, and vice versa. • Stories likely to be shaped by what she thinks people want to hear.

Stage 4: The self-authoring knower	• Has a perspective on these forces, and the ways in which they shape the self. • Holds a perspective on how she knows the world, and how she is known in the world. • Able to define for oneself where she stands in relationship to these forces, rather than being defined by them.	• Clear sense of self; takes responsibility for own feelings as separate and distinct from others. • Integrates others' perspectives, including criticism according to one's own internally generated standards and values. • Can hold contradictory feelings simultaneously. • "Golden Rule: Doing for each other supports each of us in meeting our defined values, ideals, goals, and helps us preserve the social order." (Popp & Portnow, 1998)	• Author of one's experiences; best able to engage in self-reflection. • Tells stories according to her own internal standards. • Because she holds a perspective on herself, she is better able to see the ways in which her relationships impact upon her teaching.

Kegan delineates five developmental stages; however, for the purposes of this discussion, we will only address stages two through four.[2] At Kegan's stage 2, or the Imperial Balance (Kegan, 1982, 1994) one has the capacity to take the role of another person, and to view oneself as distinct from the other. At this point in development, there is an emergence of self-concept, a consistent notion of me, an enduring set of dispositions (Kegan, 1982, p. 89). While the success of this developmental stage is that one is in a "project for oneself" (p. 89), one is not yet able to coordinate the perspective of another with one's own perspective and one understands the world in highly concrete terms. The teacher at this developmental stage is likely to conceive of the teacher role as a means to fulfilling her own purposes (or her own project in some way—as a fulfillment of herself [Scott, 1999]). Because she does not yet have a perspective on her own needs, desires or interests, she is not able to articulate them. Her self is made up of these needs, desires, and interests. As a result, any attempt to engage in self-reflection would be characterized by a very concrete, black and white analysis.

At Kegan's stage 3, or the Interpersonal Balance (also known as the "socialized self"), the self "embodies a plurality of voices" (1982, p. 96). The teacher self at this developmental stage is subject to the demands of her surround; as such, the notion of multiple identities, may be a developmental notion. The self is authored by the context of relationship. Teachers at this developmental stage are likely to *enact* the teacher role that is ascribed by the culture generally, or the most significant contexts of which the teachers are a part (i.e. teacher education program, school context). They take their cues from the cultural surround and seek approval and feedback from their surround as a measure of how well they are doing (Scott, 1999). Thus, their measurement of success or well-being is defined according to *external* standards rather than according to *internal* standards defined by them. Although they are able to engage in self-reflection, the nature of their reflection is focused on the way they view their teaching in relationship to the expectations or demands that are defined by the "authorities"—those who author or define their experiences for them (i.e. the institution of school, teacher education programs).

At Kegan's stage 4, or the Institutional Balance (also known as the "self-authoring self"), the self moves from being defined by external sources to being defined internally. The self is its own system with a clearly defined set of values, a clear philosophy. One is no longer pushed and pulled by the needs, wants, or expectations of others. Rather, the self is able to take a perspective on information, evaluate it, and then decide how to act upon it. Teacher identity at this stage is defined *internally*; it is no longer subject to the demands/expectations of the cultural surround. Teachers at this stage are able to take a perspective on their identities; it is at this developmental stage that they are able to evaluate the ways in which the different aspects of their selves (i.e. their identities: socio-economic class, race, culture, history, etc.) are borne out in their teaching and in their relationships with their students, and engage in a critique of their teaching according to their own standards rather than by the standards of others.

Kegan's view of an evolving self sheds new light on the literature on teacher identity. It helps to illuminate the varying capacities of teachers to respond to the calls that they: (1) become aware of their identities and the political, historical, and social forces that shape them; (2) assume agency, find their voice, and take the authority to shape their own professional paths and identities. Clearly, these calls assume that these teachers are self-authoring in their developmental orientation; in fact, this claim may put teachers at risk for being "in over their heads" (Kegan, 1994). Nevertheless, what is revealed is that there is a hidden developmental expectation that teachers do, in fact, possess these developmental capacities. Returning to the question that we posed at the beginning of this chapter: *how should teachers go about making the psychological shift from being authored by these forces to authoring their own stories and how should teacher educators facilitate this process?* we now give consideration to the necessary components of an environment or program that does facilitate the ongoing growth and development of its members so that they can successfully fulfill the expectations held of them. First, we will consider the importance of a good developmental match between program and student, and then we will explore model teacher education programs that do seek to support the growth and development of their students, or the emergence of a teacher's voice.

The way that teachers construct their relationship to their teacher role does not by itself indicate how teachers will fare in teacher education, nor how they will fare as beginning teachers. Rather, there is an interaction between how teachers make sense of their role, the norms/values of the culture in which they are situated (the culture of the graduate school curriculum, the culture of the school in which they are teaching), and the available supports. To be at a higher developmental stage could be an asset or a risk. Likewise, to be at a lower developmental stage could be an asset or a risk. To determine whether developmental capacity, or the way that a teacher makes sense of his/her experience is an asset or a risk, consideration must be given to the developmental demands of the context (teacher education program, the culture of school) and the available supports (Berger, 2002; Daloz, 1999; Drago-Severson, 2004; Kegan, 1982, 1994; Scott, 1999). In this regard, Kegan states,

> If I were to stand on one leg, like Hillel, and summarize my readings of centuries of wise reflection on what is required of an environment for it to facilitate the growth of its members, I would say this: people grow best where they continuously experience an ingenious blend of support and challenge; the rest is commentary. Environments that are weighed too heavily in the direction of challenge without adequate support are toxic; they promote defensiveness and constriction. Those weighed too heavily

toward support without adequate challenge are ultimately boring; they promote devitalization. Both kinds of imbalance lead to withdrawal or dissociation from the context. In contrast, the balance of support and challenge lead to vital engagement.

(1994, p. 42)

Daloz (1999) illustrates this relationship between support and challenge to engagement or disengagement in the following diagram:

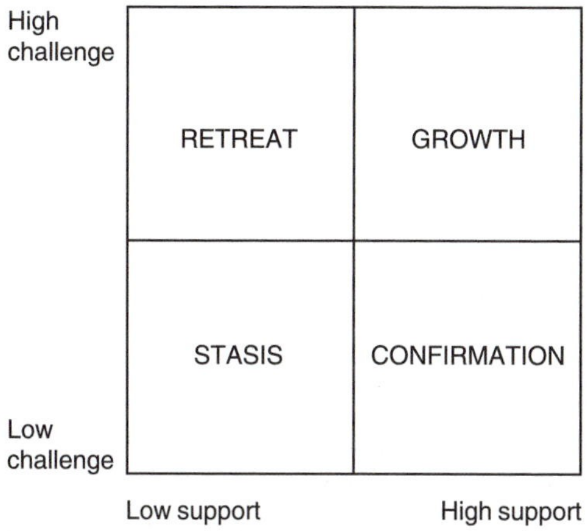

Figure 40.1 Daloz's matrix of support and change.

Daloz states that the function of support is "to affirm the validity of one's senses" and the function of challenge is to "open a gap between students and environment, a gap that creates tension in the student—calling out for closure" (p. 213). Like Kegan, he suggests that a balance of support and challenge is what will best promote the growth or evolution of the student's or the teacher's self. Both Kegan (1994) and Daloz (1999), however, caution that what one person (teacher) may experience as support may be experienced as challenge by another, and vice versa. Thus, from a developmental perspective, an effective teacher education program must take into account the goodness of fit between how its students are making sense (developmental structure) and the developmental demands of the curriculum. If the program assumes that all teachers make sense in one way—that they all have the same developmental perspective—some students will likely meet with success and others will not. However, their success or failure will have as much to do with the developmental demands of the program, as with the effort, motivation, or determination of the students. In other words, a student could be very motivated to participate in the program, but because there is a mismatch between her way of knowing (developmental stage), and the developmental demands of the environment, she could become disengaged. Without attention given to the goodness of fit between the developmental demands of teacher education programs, and the developmental capacities of prospective teachers, we will fail to understand why teacher education programs are successful in promoting/supporting the development of the teacher self for some students, while they are not for others (Berger, 2002).

TEACHER EDUCATION PROGRAMS THAT EDUCATE SELF AND IDENTITY

The programs outlined below, both historical and current, offer examples of ways in which teachers can be both challenged to become aware of the ways in which their identities are shaped by their contexts and relationships, and supported in reflection upon those forces in order to become more self-determining. We look at four historical teacher education programs that explicitly educated the personal/critical/social self, and current efforts to educate awareness of self and identity.

A short history of teacher education and the personal/critical/ social self

In Feiman-Nemser's (1990) outline of conceptual orientations in teacher education, the personal and critical/social orientations (which are most closely aligned with work on self and identity) are included along with the academic, practical, and technological orientations. Where the practical and technical orientations emphasize "additive" knowledge and skills, the personal and critical/social orientations demand awareness and a transformation of the "self," (of the meanings one makes and the internal and external forces that shape those meanings), and encourage teachers to take action based on their learning. The programs described below affirm the unique humanity of the teacher, but also ask new and prospective teachers to take a critical look at themselves and the privileges and inequities of their own and their students' lives. In this section we describe how four early, alternative teacher education programs, the teacher center movement and several contemporary efforts sought/seek to support teachers in the development of self-awareness and voice, or to make that psychological shift from being authored by external forces (e.g. historical, political, social) to authoring their own teacher identities.

Leading teacher education programs regarded the growth of teachers as inseparable from the growth of persons, in both humanistic and critical/social terms. Among the teacher education programs embodying this stance were Bank Street College, (started in 1930 under Lucy Sprague Mitchell), The Prospect School Teacher Education Program (1968–1990, initially under the direction of Patricia Carini), New College (1932–1939) of Columbia Teachers College, and the Putney Graduate School of Teacher Education (1950–1965, under the direction of Morris R. Mitchell). These private programs operated with small numbers of students. Variously influenced by the thinking of John Dewey, Maurice Merleau-Ponty, Alfred North Whitehead, and Theodore Brameld, they had well-articulated philosophies and values regarding teaching and learning, which included the importance of self-knowledge. One might say they had strong programmatic identities. They valued close observation of and inquiry into children's learning as well as the world around them and recognized the role that the teacher's perceptions and preconceptions played in learning to see children and their learning. As Morris Mitchell wrote, "A teacher teaches who he is." In other words, since a teacher teaches from herself, self-awareness is an ethical necessity. It is also the source of her power. These programs also emphasized the teachers' role as citizen and educator of citizens in a democracy. As Jaime Grinberg (2002) noted of Bank Street, it "assume[d] a need for teachers' own social perspectives to be explored and the need for teachers to engage actively as participants in social and civic responsibilities" (p. 1430).

Teacher education programs

These programs shared several characteristics which influenced the ways in which they challenged new teachers to become aware of and to interrogate their past experiences, their beliefs and assumptions about school, schooling, and the contexts within which they lived and worked, while offering them the necessary support to make a transition from old perspectives to new ones. First, each program had a clearly defined mission that saw education as a key to a democratic society. They linked teachers' personal and professional identities to the larger societal causes that reached beyond the circumscribed world of the classroom or their personal lives (e.g. social justice, racial equality). Second, as progressive programs, their approach to learning and teaching was experiential and necessarily included both experience and reflection. The experiences included one's own past, one's existing perspectives on learning, teaching, and school, and the decisions made in one's teaching present. As such, reflection on experience was meant to lead to self-awareness.

Mission

All these programs, but most clearly the Putney Graduate School and New College of Columbia, saw their purpose as the building of a better society. The development of the person was not their end goal. Rather such development was in service of the larger goals of children's own learning and development and eventual transformation of society. New College, which suffered an early demise (Teachers College News, 2001), was an experimental undergraduate, four-year teacher education program within Columbia Teachers College. It combined a liberal arts curriculum with a focus on social problems which future teachers were expected to address. Students spent their time between New York City and the New College Community, a student-run farm in Ashville, North Carolina. They also studied abroad for at least a summer in an effort to experience peoples and cultures different from their own.

Once a faculty member at New College, Morris Mitchell, who later directed the Putney Graduate School of Teacher Education, wrote that education should "become a dynamic for peace" in the world. This was accomplished, he believed, by immersing students in a variety of experiences that awakened them to problems of poverty, war, and racial injustice. This usually involved a long trip, or Study Tour, South, often to sites of what Mitchell termed, "quiet revolution," where people involved in the Civil Rights movement and sustainable land development were working.

Bank Street and Prospect also adhered to purposes beyond the bounds of school and test results, and saw education as linked to principles of democracy. Bank Street took teachers into the streets of New York City to explore the workings of the city and on Long Trips to explore the larger issues of the nation. As Grinberg (2002) notes, "Bank Street . . . emphasized that teachers ought to engage in systematic investigation of communities and social relations as an integral part of learning to teach . . . [and that] issues of social justice not only have to be studied but also must be experienced, lived" (p. 1431).

While Prospect's mission was less overtly attuned to broad political and social issues, it was grounded in questions that mattered. What makes us human? How can teaching bring forth and nurture the humanity of a child? What resources and activities manifest the complexity and humanness of the child? How are universal human themes reflected in the disciplines? These commitments lifted the sense of oneself above the particular. Yet deep knowledge of the particulars of experience (as revealed through reflection) grounded teachers' (and students') investigations (Rodgers, in press).

Experiential learning, reflection, and self-awareness

In each program, awareness of oneself was developed through recollection of past experience, interaction with the "stuff" of the world, and observation of children's interactions. At Prospect and Bank Street, especially, teacher-students were asked to recall their own experiences as children, to play with blocks, clay, and wax, for example, and to closely observe children on a daily basis. They were asked to both describe their own and others' experiences with awareness of the potential interference of pre-conceptions, and to reflect on the meaning of what they had observed (either from childhood or in the present). Carini (like Dewey) believed that a human being is knowable in his or her interactions with the world. It is therefore important to observe those interactions closely and carefully. In the observing of the other, one gains knowledge of one's own self. Carini (1979) writes:

> When the perception of the other person is based on direct access through the expressiveness of the body in its engagement with things-in-the-world, there is an assumption of co-extensive beings united through the shared world setting. From that assumption, it can be derived that self-knowledge and knowledge of others are achieved reciprocally and intersubjectively.
>
> (p. 29)

At Bank Street, student teachers "engaged in treating their own learning experiences as a subject matter of study" (Grinberg, 2002, p. 1429). Bank Street sought "to promote the development of personal powers . . . to treat the student-teachers as we should treat children—only on a higher level" (Lucy Sprague Mitchell, 1931, as quoted in Grinberg, 2002, p. 1430). As Grinberg (2002) explains,

> the purpose was to further the connections with children's learning. After the student teachers learned the content, understood relationships [through reflection], and had a powerful personal experience that helped them construct personal meanings, they had to plan the environment to provide their own students in their particular classrooms with concrete experiences that would further learning.
>
> (p. 1435)

New College and Putney also relied on experience and reflection as the vehicles of learning. In each case, students would come up against themselves and the assumptions and prejudices that resulted from their own particular histories. Putney students began the year by writing an autobiography that was read aloud to their fellow students. "Writing the autobiography was one way of sorting through what brought students to the Graduate School and getting at what was termed 'felt needs.' . . . Once uncovered, these needs or desires served as the impetus for study" (Rodgers, 1998, p. 102). To a large extent, though not exclusively, students at Putney determined their own course of study. Throughout their time in the program, they kept reflective journals of their experiences, met regularly with director, Morris Mitchell, and with his guidance, structured and restructured their course of study, as well as their stories of their experiences—in short, their identities.

Each of these progressive teacher education programs relied heavily upon advising systems that allowed students to explore in depth their personal experiences as both learners and teachers, one-on-one and in small groups with a faculty advisor. In large part, these sessions were forums for reflection, which, coupled with their experiences, provided a bridge that carried teachers from a place of being authored by their past, (e.g. traditional school systems, a racist society, or a world of privilege) to one where they might question these systems and assumptions and begin to construct a learning environment that resonated with their own emerging voice. For the most part, these private programs sent teachers into private schools where teachers' emerging voice resonated with the song of the institution they had chosen, and which had chosen them.

Contemporary approaches and programs

Echoing these older programs contemporary progressive programs (e.g. Cook-Sather, in press; Smulyan, 2004; Elbaz-Luwisch, 2002; Korthagen and Vasalos, 2005; Feather-stone, 1993; Abu El-Haj, 2003; Palmer, 1998; Intrator, 2002) advocate *creating time and space* for *reflection*, creating *communities of trust* and *making sense of experience through stories*. They, too, ask teachers to *confront and speak back to the external forces that shape and limit who and what a teacher is*, that is, using the language of today, to become aware of one's various identities and to cultivate a teaching self that is self-authored.

As we have already mentioned, most of the studies reviewed for this chapter were theoretical in nature, and either speculated about practices that might support teachers' identity formation, contained first person teacher reports on identity transformations, or exhorted teacher education and professional development programs to address teacher identity. Empirical studies are relatively scarce. Of the more than 40 articles and books reviewed, only about a third reported on courses or programs that worked explicitly with teachers' identity formation. Many of those were self-reports. Of these, three reported on isolated courses and seven described substantial programs. Nonetheless, promising contemporary programmatic efforts rely on familiar tools, techniques, and structures like journals and autobiographies, teacher study groups and book groups, action research and collaborative research. In addition, some initiatives embed these strategies in a larger mission and set of beliefs that may potentially provide the kind of developmental bridge of challenge and support of which Kegan and Daloz speak. However, it is important to note that none of them addresses the fact that developmentally, not all new teachers may be ready to cross that bridge. A description of a selection of these efforts follows.

One useful concept that resonates with Kegan's idea of a developmental bridge, is the idea of "liminal" time and space. Alison Cook-Sather (2005), drawing on the work of anthropologist Victor Turner, describes liminality as "outside of standard, hierarchical structures of institutional relationship, power, and action," and between one way of being and another, new way (p. 7). In Cook-Sather's program, pre-service teachers work with experienced teacher partners in a liminal time and space created by e-mail. The experienced teachers are not students' cooperating teachers but participate actively in the design and delivery of the teacher education program. The outside-of-time-and-space aspect of the e-mail environment provides an opportunity "both for initial processing and then dialogue" that allows new teachers to "re-imagine" and "transform" themselves from students to teachers in an unpressured environment, hearing their own voices against the backdrop of the normative voices they hear so loudly in the context of school.

Smulyan (2004), in her ten-year study of female graduates of an elite liberal arts college, speaks of the college experience in general as a time and space where her students were encouraged by the institution as a whole to redefine what it means to be a "success-ful" woman. Students came to this college with the externally crafted notion that success meant a lucrative career as a doctor, lawyer, or engineer. Through the course of their education, their concept of success changed to a more internally defined set of criteria. This happened through a process of reflection on "social and internalized frameworks," and included a reframing of teaching not merely as a helping, woman's profession, but as a means to "change a society that they see as inequitable and unjust" (p. 535). Smulyan attributed this shift in part to the knowledge, skills, and language the college provided to describe and explain students' gendered experiences as teachers.

Another example comes from Elbaz-Luwisch's (2002) work with "storying the teacher-self in writing workshops." Elbaz-Luwisch sees autobiography as a place, again, in the liminal space between identity as student and that as teacher, for the persuasive inner voice (the self?) to counter authoritative social discourse (Britzman, 2005, personal communication). Through describing, storying, and questioning in small groups of trusted colleagues, the self reframes experience and begins to assume the *authority* of his or her identity instead of ceding it to external forces. Writing, Elbaz-Luwisch says, acts as mid-wife to the teacher's own "becoming."

While several programs refer to reflection as a necessary tool for making meaning, questioning external authorities, and constructing identities, many left the actual process of reflection undefined. A few, however, were specific in describing the reflective processes to which they refer. Elbaz-Luwisch (2002), for example, outlines a clear process of description, storying, and questioning, a process she calls "restorying."

Korthagen and Vasalos (2005) describe a Dutch teacher education program that utilizes "core reflection." Core reflection aims at an awareness of the "core of one's personality," namely, *identity* (the kind of teacher one wants to be) and *mission* (why a person teaches, their calling) and the emotions that accompany such work. The teacher, in partnership with an empathetic and skilled supervisor, goes through an iterative process of action, looking back at action, developing awareness of the mission and identity played out in— or missing from—that action, and devising plans for alternative actions. In the process, the teacher becomes aware of the "less rational" sources of behavior: one's self-concept, fears, desires, and "deepest motives for becoming a teacher." The authors argue that such awareness can effect change in teacher behavior, and even in the school.

The reflective practices of groups like the Philadelphia Teachers Learning Cooperative (PTLC) (Featherstone, 1998; El-Haj, 2003), affiliated with the Prospect Center for Education and Research in North Bennington, Vermont and the Teacher Knowledge Project of the School for International Training in Brattleboro, Vermont are also clearly spelled out. The PTLC has met as a group of new and experienced teachers once a week for over 25 years. It (along with several other similar groups across the country) continues to follow the descriptive processes developed at the Prospect School. These include descriptive reviews of children, descriptions of student work and descriptions of practice. The objective of these processes is to carefully gather evidence that allows a teacher to see a child and his or her work without resorting to labels, or jumping to judgments based on unexamined assumptions about the child. The Teacher Knowledge Project, which, like the PTLC, works with teachers across subject areas and age groups, operates study groups across the country (Rodgers, 2002). It, too, follows a process that moves from description of experience to analysis to "intelligent action." Based on Dewey's conception of reflection, teachers are encouraged to "slow down" to see students and their learning. While the purpose of these two programs is not explicitly the development of the teacher's self and identity, by training teachers' attention on what *is*, rather than what they think *should* be or what they *wish* were so, these programs bring into focus the ways in which the fears and desires of the self can make assumptions which might not be borne out by evidence. They are then confronted with the gap between what *is* and what either they or the system thinks *should* be. The challenge then becomes one of choice—to act according to one's own perceptions of what is necessary or according to the demands of the system.

Finally, it seems important to include in this discussion the work of Parker Palmer. With the Fetzer Foundation, Palmer has established a series of workshops and retreats that ask, "Who is the self that teaches? How does the quality of my selfhood form—or deform—the way I relate to my students, my subject, my colleagues, my world? How can educational institutions sustain and deepen the selfhood from which good teaching comes" (Intrator, 2002, p. 288). Palmer (1998), a college professor, writes, "In every class I teach, my ability to connect with my students and to connect them with the subject depends less on the method I use than on the degree to which I know and trust my own selfhood—and am willing to make it available and vulnerable in the service of learning" (p. 11). His workshops draw upon teachers' "personal stories, reflections on classroom practice, and insights from poets, storytellers, and various wisdom traditions" (Intrator, 2002, p. 288). Palmer views teacher formation as a spiritual (though not explicitly religious) practice and intentionally structures his work with teachers along a retreat model. Time and space is built in for contemplation and solitude within a context of supportive community.

Analysis

These model teacher education and professional development programs share the following expectations: (1) teachers must know themselves and their own frames of reference, values and biases; (2) teachers should take a critical look at themselves and the privileges and inequities of their own and their students' lives; (3) teachers should explore their own social perspectives; (4) teachers should reflect upon their educational experiences as children, and recognize how these experiences impact upon how they think about teaching; (5) teachers should be exposed to perspectives different from their own. Some consider the capacity to engage in this kind of self-reflection to be an "ethical necessity." Each program offered processes that both challenged and supported teachers in confronting and changing their practices and conceptions: i.e. in developing their teacher selves and identities.

Constructive developmental theory helps us unpack the hidden developmental demands of these teacher education programs. It reveals that even model programs may not be good matches for all teachers who are enrolled (Berger, 2002, Drago-Severson, 2004, Kegan, 1982, 1994) and it highlights the importance of attending to the developmental diversity of students enrolled in such programs. As such, to assume that there is a static notion of identity or self puts even the best teacher education programs at risk for alienating certain groups of students.

These model teacher education programs may be best suited to the prospective teacher who is making sense somewhere between a stage three and a stage four way of knowing. For the stage three/stage four student, such programs provide the three necessary components of a "holding environment" that is designed to support the growth/development of its members' selves.

> A holding environment is a tricky transitional culture, an evolutionary bridge, a context for crossing over. It fosters developmental transformation or the process by which the whole ("how I am") becomes gradually a part ("who I was") of a new whole ("how I am now").
>
> (Kegan, 1994, p. 43)

These programs provide *support* ("to affirm the validity" of one's experiences), *challenge* (to "open a gap between students and environment, a gap that creates tension in the student—calling out for closure") and *vision* (Daloz, 1999) suited to this subgroup of students. In his discussion about the supportive function of mentors to adult learning Daloz defines *vision*:

> It [providing vision] is similar to Kegan's idea of the confirming function. Mentors hang around through transitions, a foot on either side of the gulf; they offer a hand to help us swing across. By their very essence, mentors provide proof that the journey can be made, the leap taken. In helping their charges look ahead, form a dream, sketch their own maps, mentors offer a fair chance of 'winning through' as the Old Man said to Telemakhos.
>
> (p. 207)

These teacher education programs (appreciating the stage three side of students) provide a context of affiliation by offering a defined set of values, a common purpose that generates a common language, or a norm of which students can be a part. As such, there are clear values, expectations, and purposes that are defined *by the program*. This creates a safe space in which students can begin to define themselves and their own purposes. The *challenge* function of these teacher education programs (appreciating the student's movement towards a more self-authoring self) is the encouragement for students to engage in self-reflection, to know/understand the limits of their own thinking, values, histories, and the ways in which these limitations could influence their teaching. As such, there is encouragement/support for students to become self-authoring. Finally, the *vision* function of these programs is the belief that students' teaching holds a bigger purpose; it is for the greater good of a democratic society.

If prospective teachers are making sense in a stage 3 way (the socialized self, according to Kegan), they are likely to feel "in over their heads" (Kegan, 1994). As a result, they may experience disappointment and frustration because the program did not provide the degree of clarity or the specific guidelines and direction that the students felt they needed. The teacher educators may also experience disappointment and frustration because, in their view, their students *should* take more risks, be independently minded, and refrain from leaning on them. Teacher educators may desire their students to be more "self-authoring" than they are capable of being. As such, there is a developmental mismatch between the students and the developmental demands of the program. Using Daloz's model, the programs offer high challenge and low support. Unless supports are put into place—a developmental bridge that attends to both who the teacher is now (her current way of making meaning; stage three), and to who she may become (stage 4, a more self-authored self)—students may disengage. (Daloz, 1999; Kegan, 1994).

It is also possible for prospective teachers operating in a stage four way (self-authoring) or beyond to feel alienated in these model teacher education programs. While these programs espouse values such as independence, self-motivation, and the capacity for self-reflection/self-critique, they assume that students will espouse *their* values and beliefs about teaching. Thus, a conflicting message is put forth. On the one hand, independence and self-authoring are desired; yet, there is an unspoken expectation that students will tow the party line (a stage three way of knowing). As a result, students who are independent-minded, and hold a different set of values about teaching may, in fact, challenge the very fabric of the program. These students may feel that asserting their voice puts them at risk within the context of the program (i.e. maintaining the good graces of their professors, achieving good grades, getting along with fellow students). Because they hold a perspective on their conflict, they can make a conscious *choice* about whether to "play the game" to get through the program successfully, to take the risk of asserting their voice, or to leave the program. Teacher educators who themselves are not stage 4 or beyond may experience these students as a threat to the program, resistant (to upholding the values of the program), or self-absorbed. Using Daloz's model there is low challenge and low support; unless both support and challenge are increased, there is the potential for disengagement.

Constructive developmental theory, then, helps us to better understand why some students' may fare better than others in these model teacher education programs (Berger, 2002; Drago-Severson, 2004; Kegan, 1982, 1994). This perspective suggests that if our mission is to design teacher education programs that will support the growth and development of teacher selves, we need to attend to the developmental diversity students bring, as well as the developmental demands inherent in the program. A developmental perspective helps us to "see more clearly" and to have greater compassion for prospective teachers (Kegan, 1982). Rather, than focusing on *behaviors* (e.g. needy, resistant, etc.), we can attend to the *meaning* that these behaviors have to the students who are displaying them. This attention leads to better understanding of students and compels us to develop teacher education programs that attend to the developmental diversity of its students. In doing so, we are more likely to achieve the goal of graduating teachers who have successfully developed their own voice, and who can take a critical perspective on their teaching.

Finally, a note of caution. Implicit in this discussion is the notion that the growth and development of teachers' selves is a worthy goal. It is the mission of these programs for students to become more self-authoring, self-motivated, and self-directed. However, prospective teachers leave these programs to enter school contexts that may, in fact, value a more stage three way of knowing. Schools, in fact, may prefer that their teachers enact a role that has been defined by the system, rather than that they self-author their role (see Achinstein and Ogawa, 2006 for an exploration of just this). Teachers who enter the system hoping to define their role may be at risk for a developmental mismatch between themselves and the context in which they find themselves teaching. Thus, teacher education programs must also give consideration to the developmental demands of the educational system and how to prepare students to negotiate that system in a way that is productive for them and their students.

CONCLUSION

In this chapter we have sorted through recent conceptions of teacher identity and teacher self to arrive at a new definition of teacher identity and teacher self. As we stated earlier, we define *self to subsume teacher identities and to be an evolving, yet, coherent being that consciously and unconsciously constructs and is constructed, reconstructs and is reconstructed in interaction with cultural contexts, institutions, and people with which the self lives, learns, and functions.* Drawing upon the psychological literature of constructive developmental theory, we highlight that the sense the self makes of her experiences is distinctly different at different levels of meaning making (i.e. the varying capacities to take a perspective on oneself), and that these differences color how the teacher self makes sense of her teacher identity, emotions that are evoked for her within the context of her teaching, and the level of connection or involvement that she may feel as a participant in her teacher education program.

In the face of such developmental diversity, there is nevertheless a hidden developmental expectation or assumption held by teacher educators and teacher education program that teachers should, in fact, make sense of their experiences at a particular level of development. They assume that prospective teachers should have the capacity to be self-authoring, and self-critical. In our discussion, we have emphasized that without attention given to the developmental diversity of students, both they and their professors are at risk for disappointment, and even disengagement.

Clearly, what is still missing from the literature and the field is empirical work that seeks to better understand the role of psychology in teacher education. While there is an evolving literature on teacher emotion, the literature that brings in the psychological development of the self to bear on the effectiveness of teacher education programs is in its infancy. It is our hope that over the next decade this research will evolve so that we can better answer the questions that we posed at the beginning of this chapter: (1) How might teachers go about making the psychological shift from being authored by these forces to authoring their own stories? (2) How might teacher educators facilitate this process? (3) What is the impact on the practice of teachers who participate in such programs? And finally, (4) What is the impact on their students' learning?

NOTES

1 It is well beyond the scope of this chapter to do this exhaustively. Conceptions of the self and identity reside in nearly every field of study from psychology to philosophy, from literature to cognitive science.
2 We exclude stage 1, the latency age child, and stage 5, a developmental achievement that is not usually achieved until middle age or later.

REFERENCES

Abu El-Haj, T.R. (2003) Practicing for equity from the stand point of the particular: exploring the work of the urban teacher network. *Teachers College Record*, 105(5), 817–845.

Achinstein, B. & R.T. Ogawa (2006) (In)fidelity: what the resistance of new teachers reveals about professional principles and prescriptive educational policies. *Harvard Educational Review* 76(1), 80–109.

Agee, J.M. (2004) Negotiating a teacher identity: an African-American teacher's struggle to teach in test-driven contexts. *Teachers College Record*, 106(4), 747–774.

Athanases, S.Z. & B. Achinstein (2003) Focusing new teachers on individual and low performing students: the centrality of formative assessment in the mentor's repertoire of practice. *Teachers College Record*, 105(8), 1486–1520.

Antonek, J.L., D.E. McCormack, & R. Donato (1997) The student teacher portfolio as auto-biography: developing a professional identity. *Modern Language Journal*, 81, 15–27.

Barty, L. (2004) Embracing ambiguity in the artefacts [sic] of the past: teacher identity and pedagogy. *Canadian Social Studies*, 38(3), www.quasar.ualberta.ca/css.

Beijaard, D., N. Verloop, & J.D. Vermunt (2000) Teachers' perceptions of professional identity: an exploratory study from a personal knowledge perspective. *Teaching and Teacher Education*, 16, 749–764.

Beijaard, D., P.C. Meijer, & N. Verloop (2004) Reconsidering research on teachers' professional identity. *Teaching and Teacher Education*, 20, 107–128.

Benger, J. (2002) *Exploring the connection between teacher education practice and adult development theory*. Unpublished dissertation. Cambridge, MA: Harvard University Graduate School of Education.

Britzman, D. (1992) Structures of feeling in curriculum and teaching. *Theory Into Practice*, 31(3), 252–258.

Britzman, D.P. (1993) The terrible problem of knowing thyself: toward a poststructuralist account of teacher identity. *Journal of Curriculum Theorizing*, 9, 23–46.

Britzman, D. (2003) *Practice makes practice: a critical study of learning to teach*. Revised edition. Albany, NY: State University of New York Press.

Brott, P.E. and L.T. Kajs (nd). *Developing the professional identity of first year teachers through a "working alliance."* Retrieved April 5, 2006 from http://www.alt-teachercert.org/Working%20Alliance.html.

Bruner, J. (1990) *Acts of meaning*. Cambridge, MA: Harvard University Press.

Carini, P.F. (1979) *The art of seeing and the visibility of the person*. North Dakota Study Group on Evaluation, Grand Forks: University of North Dakota.

Carini, P.F. (2002) *Starting strong: a different look at children, schools, and standards*. New York: Teachers College Press.

Carter, K. & Doyle, W. (1996) Personal narrative and life history in learning to teach. In J. Sikula, T.J. Buttery, & E. Guyton (eds.), *Handbook on Research in Teacher Education*. New York: Simon & Schuster Macmillan.

Clandinin, D.J. & F.M. Connelly (1986) *Classroom practice: teacher images in action*. London: Falmer Press.

Clandinin, D.J. & F.M. Connelly (1987) Teachers' personal knowledge: what counts as "personal" in studies of the personal. *Journal of Curriculum Studies*, 19(6), 487–500.

Clandinin, D.J. & F.M. Connelly (1989) Developing rhythm in teaching: the narrative study of a beginning teacher's personal practical knowledge of classrooms. *Curriculum Inquiry*, 19(2), 121–141.

Clandinin, D.J. & F.M. Connelly (1995) *Teachers' professional knowledge landscapes*. New York: Teachers College Press.

Clandinin, D.J. & M. Huber (2005) Shifting stories to live by: interweaving the personal and the professional in teachers' lives. In D. Beijaard, P. Meijer, G. Morine-Dershimer & H. Tillema (eds.) *Teacher professional development in changing conditions*. Dordrecht: Springer.

Cochran-Smith, M. (2004) *Walking the road: race, diversity, and social justice in teacher education*. New York: Teachers College Press.

Coldron, J. & R. Smith (1999) Active location in teachers' construction of their professional identities. *Journal of Curriculum Studies*, 31(6), 711–726.

Connelly, F.M. and Clandinin, D.J. (1999) *Shaping a professional identity: stories of educational practice*. New York: Teachers College Press.

Cook-Sather, A. (submitted) Newly betwixt and between: revising liminality in the context of a contemporary rite of passage.

Daloz, L. (1999) *Mentor: guiding the journey of adult learners*. San Francisco, CA: Jossey-Bass.

Devaney, K. (1977) *Surveying teachers' centers: from grassroots beginnings to federal support*. Washington, DC: Department of Health, Education, and Welfare (Education Division), National Institute of Education.

Devaney, K. (1982) *Networking on purpose: a reflective study of the Teachers' Centers Exchange*. San Francisco: Far West Laboratory for Educational Research and Development.

Dewey, J. (1938) *Experience and education*. New York: Collier Macmillan.

Drago-Severson, E. (2004) *Helping teachers learn: principal leadership for adult growth and development*. Thousand Oaks, CA: Corwin Press.

Elbaz-Luwisch, F. (2002) Writing as inquiry: storying the teaching self in writing workshops. *Curriculum Inquiry* 32(4), 403–428.

Featherstone, H. (1993) Learning from the first years of classroom teaching: the journey in, the journey out. *Teachers College Record*, 95(1), 93–112.

Feiman-Nemser, S. (1990) Teacher preparation: structural and conceptual alternatives. In W.R. Houston (ed.), *Handbook on teacher education* (pp. 212–223). New York: Macmillan.

Feiman-Nemser, S. (2001) From preparation to practice: designing a continuum to strengthen and sustain teaching. *Teachers College Record*, 103(6), 1013–1055.

Feiman-Nemser, S. & Floden, R.E. (1986) The cultures of teaching. *Handbook of research on teaching*, 3rd edition (ed. M.C. Wittrock) (pp. 505–526). New York: Macmillan.

Fenstermacher, G.D. (2001) Manner in teaching: the study in four parts. *Journal of Curriculum Studies*, 33(6), 631–637.

Fitzgerald, T.K. (1993) *Metaphors of identity*. Albany, NY: State University of New York Press.

Foulkes, S.H. (1975) A short outline of therapeutic processes in group analytic psychotherapy. *Group Analysis* 8, 59–63.

Gee, J. P. (2001) Identity as an analytic lens for research in education. In W.G. Secada (ed.) *Review of research in education, 25, 2000–2001*. Washington, DC: American Educational Research Association.

Gilligan, C. (2003) *The birth of pleasure*. New York: Vintage Books.

Giroux, H.A. (2005) *Schooling and the struggle for public life: critical pedagogy in the modern age*. Boulder, CO: Paradigm Publishers.

Greene, M. (1984) How do we think about our craft? *Teachers College Record*, 86(1), 55–67.

Greene, M. (1995) *Releasing the imagination: essays on education, the arts, and social change*. San Francisco: Jossey-Bass.

Grinberg, J.G.A. (2002) "I had never been exposed to teaching like that": progressive teacher education at Bank Street during the 1930s. *Teachers College Record*, 104(7), 1422–1460.

Hargreaves, A. (2001) The emotional geographies of teaching. *Teachers College Record*, 103(6), 1056–1080.

Hopper, T. & K. Sanford (2004) Representing multiple perspectives of self-as-teacher: integrated teacher education and self-study. *Teacher Education Quarterly* 31(2), 57–74.

Huberman, M. (1982) Making changes from exchanges: some frameworks for studying the teachers' centers exchange. In K. Devaney, *Networking on purpose*, San Francisco: Far West Laboratory.

Intrator, S. (2002) *Stories of the courage to teach: honoring the teacher's heart*. San Francisco: Jossey-Bass.

Jennings, L.B. & Smith, C.P. (2002) Examining the role of critical inquiry for transformative practices: two joint case studies of multicultural teacher education. *Teachers College Record*, 104(3), 456–481.

Johnson, K. (2003) "Every experience is a moving force:" Identity & growth through mentoring. *Teaching and Teacher Education*, 19, 787–800.

Kegan, R. (1982) *The evolving self*. Cambridge, MA: Harvard University Press.

Kegan, R. (1994) *In over our heads*. Cambridge, MA: Harvard University Press.

Korthagen, F. & A. Vasalos (2005) Levels in reflection: core reflection as a means to enhance professional growth. *Teachers and Teaching: Theory and Practice*, 11(1), 47–71.

Levine, K.P. (2004) The birth of the citizenship school: entwining the struggles for literacy and freedom. *History of Education Quarterly*, 44(3), 388–414.

MacLure, M. (1993) Arguing for yourself: identity as an organizing principle in teachers' jobs and lives. *British Educational Research Journal*, 19(4), 311–323.

McGowen, K.R. & L.E. Hart (1990) Still different after all these years: gender differences in professional identity formation. *Professional Psychology: Research and Practice*, 21(2), 118–123.

Marsh, M.M. (2002) Examining the discourses that shape our teacher identities. *Curriculum Inquiry*, 32(4), 453–469.

Mead, G.H. (1934) *Mind, self and society*. Chicago: University of Chicago Press.

Mitchell, A. (1997) Teacher identity: a key to increased collaboration. *Action in Teacher Education*, 19, 1–14.

Moore, A., G. Edwards, D. Halpin, & R. George (2002) Compliance, resistance and pragmatism: the reconstruction of schoolteacher identities in a period of intensive educational reform. *British Educational Research Journal*, 28(4), 551–565.

Nias, J. (1989) Teaching and the self. In M.L. Holly & C.S. Mcloughlin (eds.), *Perspectives on teacher professional development*, London: The Falmer Press, 155–173.

Noddings, N. (2003) *Caring: a feminine approach to ethics and moral education*, Second edition. Berkeley: University of California Press.

Palmer, P.J. (1998) *The courage to teach: exploring the inner landscape of a teacher's life*. San Francisco: Jossey-Bass.

Rex, L. & M.C. Nelson (2004) How teachers' professional identities position high-stakes test preparation in their classrooms. *Teachers College Record*, 106(6), 1288–1331.

Richardson, V. (1996) The role of attitudes and beliefs in learning to teach. In J. Sikula, T.J. Buttery, & E. Guyton (eds.), *Handbook of Research on Teacher Education*. New York: Simon & Schuster Macmillan.

Rodgers, C.R. (1998) Morris R. Mitchell and the Putney Graduate School of Teacher Education, 1950–1964. Unpublished dissertation, Harvard University Graduate School of Education.

Rodgers, C.R. (2002) Seeing student learning: teacher change and the role of reflection. *Harvard Educational Review*, 72(2), 230–253.

Rodgers, C.R. (in press) Learning to teach as an art: John Dewey and the Prospect Teacher Education Program (1967–1991). *Teacher Education Practice*.

Rodgers, C.R. (in press) "The Turning of One's Soul:" learning to teach for social justice: The Putney Graduate School of Teacher Education (1950–1964). *Teachers College Record*, 108(7).

Samuel, M. & D. Stevens (2000) Critical dialogues with self: developing teacher identities and roles—a case study of South African student teachers. *International Journal of Educational Research*, 33, 475–491.

Schoomaker, F. (1998) Promise and possibility: learning to teach. *Teachers College Record*, 99(3), 559–591.

Scott, K. (1999) *Parenting boys identified as having learning disabilities: a meaning-making perspective*. Unpublished Doctoral Dissertation, Harvard University Graduate School of Education.

Sfard, A. & A. Prusak (2005) Telling identities: in search of an analytic tool for investigating learning as a culturally shaped activity. *Educational Researcher*, 34(4), 14–22.

Sikula, J.P. (ed.) *Handbook of research on teacher education*, Second edition. New York: Macmillan.

Smagorinsky, P., L.S. Cook, C. Moore, A.Y. Jackson, & P.G. Fry (2004) Tensions in learning to teach: accommodations and the development of a teaching identity. *Journal of Teacher Education*, 55(1), 8–24.

Smulyan, L. (2004) Choosing to teach: reflections on gender and social change. *Teachers College Record*, 106(3), 513–543.

Spence, D. (1984) *Narrative truth and historical truth: meaning and interpretation in psychoanalysis*. New York: Norton.

Stengle, B. & A.R. Tom (1995) Taking the moral nature of teaching seriously. *The Educational Forum* 59(2), 154–169.

Sterling, M. (2005) *Influences on professional learning: five teachers' stories*. Unpublished doctoral dissertation, Lesley University (pp. 24–57).

Van Manen, M. (1994) Pedagogy, virtue, and narrative identity in teaching. *Curriculum Inquiry*, 4(2), 135–170.

Van Manen, M. (1999) The practice of practice. In M. Lange, J. Olson, H. Hansen, & W. Bünder (eds.), *Changing schools/changing practices: perspectives on educational reform and teacher professionalism*. Louvain, Belgium: Garant.

Van Manen, M. (2000) Moral language and pedagogical experience. *Journal of Curriculum Studies*, 32(2), 315–327.

Watts, H. (2005) The legacy of teachers' centers. Unpublished Monograph, Keene, NH: Antioch New England.

Williams, R. (1961) *The long revolution*. New York: Columbia University Press.

Winograd, K. (2003) The functions of teacher emotions: the good, the bad, and the ugly. *Teachers College Record*, 105(9), 1641–1673.

Zembylas, M. (2002) "Structures of feeling" in curriculum and teaching theorizing the emotional rules. *Educational Theory*, 52(2), 187–208.

Zembylas, M. (2003) Emotions and teacher identity: a poststructural perspective. *Teachers and Teaching: Theory and Practice*, 9(3), 214–238.

41 Learning among colleagues

Teacher community and the shared enterprise of education[1]

Joel Westheimer
University of Ottawa

In both Norwegian and Hebrew, the verbs "to teach" and "to learn" are etymologically inseparable.[2] Teaching and learning in these two highly distinct tongues are two sides of the same pedagogical coin. One who teaches is also one who learns. Yet teachers are rarely—on a daily basis—afforded formal or informal opportunities for learning. And teacher education programs do not always prepare future teachers to also be future learners. Most importantly—for the purposes of this chapter—too few teachers are adequately prepared to learn *from one another*, and too few schools create the conditions where learning from colleagues might be possible. As Seymour Sarason famously noted in his classic 1971 text, *The Culture of School and the Problem of Change*, teachers cannot possibly create and sustain productive learning environments for students when no such conditions exist for teachers. What do cultures of shared learning, dialogue, deliberation, debate, and community look like? How do such contexts affect teachers and students? How can we prepare future teachers to develop and benefit from professional interactions with colleagues?

This chapter reviews past and present conceptions of teacher professional communities as they relate to teacher learning. It conceptualizes teacher colleagues as a specific context for and resource to teacher learning. I emphasize empirical work that grounds these conceptions in actual teacher practice—in particular, the ways studying teacher practices exposes embedded values and competing ideologies. In what follows, I provide a brief history of these conceptions and review the multiple goals and enduring tensions inherent in studying and implementing teacher learning communities in practice.

A note about words

Many authors observe that terms such as "teacher community," "teacher professional community," and "professional learning community" are often used interchangeably in the literature that addresses teachers' work in schools (Furman & Mertz 1997; Little & Horn 2006). Talking about teachers' collaborative and collective work in schools, therefore, is slippery work. To make matters more complicated, these same terms are sometimes used to describe teachers' work *outside* of schools, in professional networks and summer workshops. For example, the professional community of English teachers and the Portfolio Assessment teacher community can both boast a constituency concerned with teaching and learning. Furthermore, "professional" is used in varied ways. For example, some use the term specifically to distinguish technical "training" that treats teachers like mindless rule-followers from respectful and thoughtful teacher education and practice (as in *the professionalization of teaching*). A number of authors also delineate friendly conversation from deeper dialogues aimed at mutual learning. Brian Lord (1994), for example, draws the distinction between *conviviality* and *critical colleagueship.* Getting along with one's colleagues, he argues, is not the same as seeing colleagues as a resource in the ongoing study and improvement of teaching and learning. Similarly, Lima (1997), and Jarzabkowski (2002) wrestle with the differences and similarities between teachers' *friendships* and their professional relationships.

In this chapter, I am concerned primarily with those interactions among teachers that are related to teacher learning. I use the term "teacher professional community" to designate a group of teachers engaged in professional endeavors together (those endeavors oriented specifically around teacher work). I will use "professional learning community" and "teacher learning community" to designate a subset of the former group—those specifically focused on learning with and from colleagues, generally within a school site.

TEACHING AND LEARNING TOGETHER

In the past three decades, assumptions about teaching and learning have changed substantially. Shifts in cognitive science and new theories of teaching and learning altered the way researchers and practitioners see the process of education unfolding. At the classroom level, researchers began to consider the ways students construct knowledge in relation to their surrounding contexts (e.g. Bruner, 1996; Gardner, 1985; Lave & Wenger, 1991; Vygotsky, 1978). And teacher educators began to emphasize the social and interdependent nature of teacher learning. Communities of learners became a popular way to think about not only students learning together but teachers collaborating as well (Barth, 1990; Sizer, 1992). Hoping to overcome the professional isolation so common in what Dan Lortie described as "egg-crate" schools (Lortie 1975)—where teachers are largely isolated from one another in their own classrooms—reformers began to advocate for new school structures and teacher practices that recognize the importance of learning within communities. By focusing on the environment in which teachers do their work, these reformers hoped to foster collegiality and increase professional dialogue.

The traditional view of schools as formal organizations began to give way, at least in some reform circles, to the notion of community. Research began to provide some evidence that examining schools as communities highlights "strategically different aspects of the school environment and fundamentally different levers for policy" (McLaughlin, 1993, p. 80; also Sergiovanni, 1994a). "The community metaphor," writes McLaughlin, "draws [policy] attention to norms and beliefs of practice, collegial relations, shared goals, occasions for collaboration, problems of mutual support and mutual obligation" (1993, p. 81). By attending to teacher professional communities, researchers argued, we gain an understanding of the ways in which teachers' relationships structure their work and their lives in schools. By the mid-1990s, creating professional conditions more conducive to a sense of collective mission and responsibility had become an essential component of many local, state, and national school reform efforts (Hargreaves, 1994; Lieberman, 1995; Meier, 1995; Sizer, 1992).

But while the goal of teacher learning within a community of colleagues is shared by many educators, the specifics of what these communities look like and of how to create and sustain them remain varied. The visions of teacher professional community implicit in school reform literature are numerous and diverse. Some variations are a matter of emphasis, creating complementary sets of lenses through which analysts can better study teacher communities in practice. Other visions, however, constitute competing ideologies about both the aims and means of professional learning communities in schools. The inability to pin down specific definitions of teacher collaboration and exchange within a professional community comes in part from the elusive nature of the term "community" itself.

The ambiguity of community

The anthropologist Herve Varenne (1986), while studying American conceptions of society and social diversity, concluded that there is tremendous theoretical confusion over notions of community. He found it difficult to reconcile ideals of individualism and community that coexist in the social psyche. Indeed, understanding the complexities inherent in these terms has been an ongoing project for more than two centuries. Contemporary examples of the tensions between individualism and community and between the borders of various communities abound. The readers of this book are undoubtedly part of multiple overlapping communities each of which has stronger or weaker bonds across numerous varied dimensions such as common beliefs, norms of interaction, participation, and space for dissent. Readers might be part of a "community of scholars," a "community of teacher educators," "the University of Pennsylvania community," a "tenants community," and their local neighborhood community, to name just a few.

For educators, the problems of conceptualizing community are multiplied. Necessarily occupying the space between theory and practice, researchers and reformers who study teacher professional communities often find conceptions of community rooted in practice to be oversimplified and those rooted in theory to be less than entirely convincing (Strike, 1999). Do three, four, or five characteristics constitute a way to identify communities, to verify that a particular alliance of individuals is or is not a community? Such a characterization would construe community as a static entity, and few social analysts would be comfortable with such a simplification. Many of the ethnographic accounts of teacher professional communities in practice go a considerable distance in providing a window into understanding the nature of experiences and interactions (Achinstein, 2002; Grossman *et al.*, 2001; Little, 2003). But while the features commonly identified by social theorists provide a common language for recognizing communities and their constitutive elements, they do not *define* the community with generalizable rigor. More importantly, identifying these features rarely convinces others—especially those resistant to these reforms—of the benefits of community. Reading about community is a bit like reading about love—it falls short of the experience. Used in conjunction with vignettes and ethnographic analysis, however, the features identified in different visions contribute a great deal to the construction of a coherent framework for enabling and understanding teacher professional communities in practice.

THE MULTIPLE AND OVERLAPPING GOALS OF PROFESSIONAL LEARNING COMMUNITIES

Achinstein adapts a definition of teacher professional community from organizational theorists Van Maanen and Barley that succinctly reflects many of the proposed levers for change pursued by those seeking to foster professional communities in schools:

> A teacher professional community can be defined as a group of people across a school who are engaged in common work; share to a certain degree a set of values, norms, and orientations towards teaching, students, and schooling; and operate

collaboratively with structures that foster interdependence (adapted from Van Maanen and Barley, 1984).

(Achinstein, 2002: 421–422)

The specific goals and processes suggested by particular visions of teacher professional community described in the research literature vary, but a number of them emphasize teacher learning and often refer to the teacher professional community as a professional *learning* community. As Mitchell and Sackney (2000) define it, teachers within professional learning communities "take an active, reflective, collaborative, learning-oriented, and growth-promoting approach toward the mysteries, problems and perplexities of teaching and learning" (Mitchell and Sackney, 2000). Below, I describe six umbrella categories that reflect common goals researchers and reformers have set for professional learning communities of teachers. Each of these perspectives draws on research findings that indicate the benefits and challenges for teaching and learning when teachers act in concert to "collectively question ineffective teaching routines, examine new conceptions of teaching and learning, find generative means to acknowledge and respond to difference and conflict, and engage actively in supporting one another's professional growth" (Little, 2003, p. 914).

Although this section of the handbook of teacher education research emphasizes teacher learning, it is worth noting that there are other ways to frame the importance of teacher community. And there are other ways to conceptualize teacher learning beyond the narrow goal of student achievement as measured by standardized tests. Indeed, there is a small but significant body of work that critiques instrumental conceptions of teacher learning on the grounds that a narrow focus on instrumental goals (usually the idea that teacher learning will lead to improved student learning) crowds out other compelling reasons for a focus on strong communal relationships in schools (see, for example, Fielding, 1999; Hargreaves, 1994; Jarzabkowski, 2002; Nias, 1999). At the same time, a number of scholars and practitioners observe that not all professional communities are productive or even desirable. A group of teachers who meet every day and share meals on weekends but use their shared time primarily to complain about or deride students might arguably experience strong communal bonds, but not of the kind most reformers seek (Little & Horn, 2006; McLaughlin & Talbert, 2001).

Although there is substantial overlap in the groupings that follow (these perspectives are not intended to constitute discreet categories), they prove helpful in examining the scope of work that engages notions of teachers learning within a professional community. The sections that follow describe six interconnected goals that researchers and reformers have frequently cited in the quest for building, sustaining, and examining professional learning communities in schools. Educators interested in developing professional learning communities hope to: (1) improve teacher practice so students will learn; (2) make ideas matter to both teachers and students by creating a culture of intellectual inquiry; (3) develop teacher learning about leadership and school management; (4) promote teacher learning among novice teachers; (5) reduce alienation as a precondition for teacher learning; and (6) pursue social justice and democracy.

Improve teacher practice so students will learn

The most central, and commonly referenced goal for teacher learning communities is, not surprisingly, to improve teaching (Lieberman & Miller, 2004; McLaughlin & Talbert, 2001). The vision of teacher learning community that seeks most directly to improve teacher practice is perhaps most simply reflected in Little's entreaty: "Imagine that you would become a better teacher, just by virtue of being on the staff of a particular school—just from that one fact alone" (1987: 493). In a profession marked by endemic norms of privacy and independence (Little, 1990; Lortie, 1975; Pomson, 2005), the opportunities for teachers to learn from their colleagues are rarer than many would like (Smylie & Hart, 2000). The "egg-crate" structure of schools, the schedule of the school day, and the multiple conflicting demands on teachers make collaborative practice and reflection difficult. Schools that seek to break these norms hope that teachers will share the problems and successes they have with other teachers and take collective responsibility for students' learning.

Kruse *et al.* (1995), for example, posit a framework for examining professional communities in schools in which "pedagogical growth and development of all teachers are considered a community-wide responsibility, and organizational structures such as peer coaching and time for conversation about practice are viewed as central" (1995: 27). The characteristics of successful professional learning communities, according to their framework, include a clear focus on student learning, reflective practice, deprivatized practice, collaboration, and shared values. Accordingly, the structural conditions necessary for teacher learning to occur include time to meet and talk, physical proximity to one another, interdependent teaching roles, structures for communication, and sufficient teacher autonomy (25). Professional learning communities like these nurture norms of collaboration and exchange that increase teachers' opportunities to improve classroom practice (Louis & Marks, 1998; Little, 1999).

The literature is replete with variations on this theme and most of these characterizations of teacher learning communities are similar and complementary. Indeed, a number of excellent studies support the notion that given the proper organizational conditions for professional communities to remain strong, instructional innovation can be dramatically strengthened. For example, the University of Chicago's Center for School Improvement studied elementary schools over a three year period and concluded that professional learning communities spur sustained reform in teaching practices in restructuring schools (Bryk *et al.*, 1999). Lee *et al.* (1995) report on studies conducted by the Center on Organization and Restructuring of Schools of 11,000 students enrolled in 820 U.S. secondary schools. They found that in those schools that demonstrated characteristics consistent with strong professional learning communities, teachers' classroom pedagogy was more likely to change in accordance with ongoing reform efforts. Similarly, McLaughlin and Talbert (1993) conducted longitudinal studies of high schools in California and Michigan and found that teacher professional learning communities are linked to instructional improvements and reform (see also McLaughlin & Talbert, 2001). Reyes *et al.* (1999) report on their work with Hispanic schools and also find that learning communities enabled teachers to improve their own practice. Over the past decade, other studies—both quantitative and qualitative—have supported these claims (Kruse & Louis, 1995; McLaughlin, 1993; Newmann & Wehlage, 1995; Sergiovanni, 1994b; Smylie & Hart, 2000; Thiessen & Anderson, 1999).

Student learning is also a central concern for those emphasizing teacher learning with and among colleagues. Accordingly, links to student achievement have been studied as well (Little, 1999; Louis & Marks, 1998; McLaughlin, 1993). In *Successful School Restructuring*, Newmann and Wehlage (1995) report on four large-scale studies that, together, include surveys of 1,500 elementary, middle, and high schools across the United States. The studies are notable for their extensive and careful data including surveys, three- and four-year longitudinal case studies, and compilation of student test results. Field research took place in 44 schools in sixteen states. In summarizing these studies (the National Educational Longitudinal Study of 1988, the School Restructuring Study, the

Study of Chicago School Reform, and the Longitudinal Study of School Restructuring), the authors link successful professional learning communities to reduced dropout rates among students, lower absenteeism rates, academic achievement gains (as measured by standardized tests) in math, science, history, and reading, and reduced gaps in achievement gains between students of varying socio-economic backgrounds. Together, these studies provide significant evidence that student learning depends, at least in part, on "the extent to which schools support the ongoing development and productive exercise of teachers' knowledge and skills" (Smylie & Hart, 2000: 421).

Another promising practice for school-based teacher learning communities involves teachers examining student work collectively rather than individually (Little *et al.*, 2003). A number of projects with that explicit focus have emerged in the past few years. One such project, for example, aims to "build the capacity of school faculties to improve the quality of instruction . . . through a continuous, comprehensive, and critical review of student work" (Academy for Education Development, 2006). Little and colleagues found useful aspects of professional learning communities built around examining student work to include: a process of localizing more generic tools for looking at student work, a healthy balance between comfort and challenge among the teachers, opportunities to use subject matter expertise, and strong and structured group facilitation to build relationships (2003: 189–190). Others have described similar teacher interactions around examinations of student work as fundamental to teacher (and student) learning within learning communities (see Ball & Cohen, 1999; Ball & Rundquist, 1992; Little, 1999; Sykes, 1999).

Studies have also made claims about the relationship between the specific nature and content of discussion among teachers (often called "teacher talk") and the benefits of such exchanges for teacher and student learning. These studies seek to distinguish teacher talk that is generative of teacher and student learning from simple conversation (e.g. Achinstein, 2002; Little & Horn, 2006). Brian Lord's model for "critical colleagueship," for example, specifies three concepts that should be reflected in teacher talk and exchange if the professional learning community is to reflect growth in teacher and student learning. First, teachers need to be open to discussing conflict and different views about teaching. He deems this conflict, if it is useful conflict, "productive disequilibrium" (Lord, 1994: 192). Second, he stresses that teachers need to become increasingly familiar (and comfortable) with ambiguity. And third, given the open conflict and ambiguity that he hopes will strengthen and not weaken the community, teachers must seek what Lord calls "collective generativity" (193) or a collective commitment to continuing their work together amidst ambiguity and conflict. Similarly, Ball and Cohen (1999) draw from case studies of teachers engaged in site-based professional development to provide thoughtful analysis of teachers' exchanges around both joint and individual work. They argue that teacher learning is greatly enriched by grounding professional development in the daily particulars of teacher practice. Meaningful teacher discussions around their practice, Ball and Cohen suggest, especially when situated within assumptions of critical collegiality, strengthen teacher learning opportunities and reinforce the practical basis for teacher growth (see also Gray & Rubenstein, 2004; Hord, 2003; King, 2002; Little & Horn 2006).

Make ideas matter—a culture of intellectual inquiry

Although improving teacher practice is often a primary goal of efforts to foster teacher learning communities in schools, conceptions of teacher learning communities do not all put this goal front and center. A number of other visions of collective teacher learning and practice hold strong sway in the literature. By focusing on teachers' lived experiences in schools, many school reforms and teacher community research efforts seek to highlight other levers for change. Some reformers, for example, imagine a successful school-based professional learning community in the way Peter Senge describes it: "a meeting ground for learning—dedicated to the idea that all those involved with it, individually and together, will be continually enhancing and expanding their awareness and capabilities" (2000, p. 6). Although the literature I refer to here is certainly concerned with improving teaching, the immediate goal is to foster a professional culture of intellectual inquiry in the workplace by engaging teachers in collective reflection and exchange in matters of pedagogy and practice.

For example, some advocate subject matter inquiry for teachers, focusing on the teachers as students of their own discipline. Professional development that aims at deepening teachers' disciplinary knowledge highlights a contrast "between the promise of direct applicability and the more distant goal of intellectual renewal" (Grossman et al., 2001: 952). The challenge, as Grossman and colleagues go on to explain, is "to maintain a focus on students while creating structures for teachers to engage as learners with the subject matters they teach . . . Teacher community must be equally concerned with student learning and with teacher learning" (952). Summer institutes for teachers have long provided intellectual stimulation for teachers in their subject areas, but this work necessarily occurs away from the professional community of the school. Having teachers engage in the difficult and rewarding work of intellectual renewal at the school site is an increasingly popular strategy for nurturing professional learning communities (Lieberman & Miller, 2004; Little et al., 2003; Smylie & Hart, 2000). Excellent examples of such practices abound, including a project bringing together humanities teachers to develop interdisciplinary curriculum through study of their own disciplines (Grossman et al., 2001), or subject-based reforms such as Project 2061 for changes in the science curriculum (American Association for the Advancement of Sciences, 1994).

These projects also meet with significant obstacles that I discuss in the section on enduring tensions. It is worth noting here, however, that those who study professional learning communities have become increasingly mindful about exploring and reporting on these tensions. One of the more detailed examples of this kind of reflective analysis can be found in Grossman and colleagues' (2001) description of the complexities they encountered when working with a mixed group of English and history teachers in an urban Seattle high school. Bringing together these teachers for an "intellectual experience" building an interdisciplinary humanities curriculum, they found, was both rewarding and also fraught with difficulty. For example, they found that teachers—often not used to learning among colleagues—initially formed a "pseudo-community" in which everyone tended to behave *as if* they all agreed while skirting the substance of important disagreements and suppressing conflict. They also found that as they moved from pseudo-community to more substantive discourse, old tensions within the professional community that had been handily suppressed quickly rose to the surface. Studies by Achinstein (2002), Gunn and King (2003), and Uline et al. (2003) discuss similar challenges. Those reform projects that do not shy away from the challenges described in studies like these seem far more likely to succeed in fostering authentic cultures of intellectual inquiry and learning among teachers (Gray & Rubinstein 2004; Little & Horn 2006).

Another example of intellectual culture-building comes from the tradition of teacher research and university-school research partnerships. The ground-breaking work of Cochran-Smith and Lytle (1992b), for example, articulates the ways teacher inquiry not only improves the individual practice of teachers but also improves the collective practices and culture of the entire professional community. More often than not, teacher research is concerned with the investigation of pedagogical practice rather than specific subject matter concerns. Teacher-scholars work together (often with the support and/or collaboration of university-based researchers) to examine their own practices, collectively study research done elsewhere, and challenge their own assumptions about teaching strategies, students, and broader educational policy issues (Hatch *et al.*, 2005; Noffke & Stevenson, 1995). As Lieberman and Miller explain, because the research is local, it "resonates with the dilemmas of practice that other teachers experience" (2004, 29). Some projects blend commitments to examining pedagogical and subject-matter concerns (see, for example, the Carnegie Foundation's K-12 Academy for the Scholarship of Teaching and Learning [CASTL], www.carnegiefoundation.org/programs/index.asp? key=32). Indeed, Center for Research on the Contexts of Teaching researchers McLaughlin and Talbert and others have repeatedly found that strong professional learning communities are characterized by in-depth and ongoing discussions about curriculum and pedagogy in which teachers collectively examine ineffective teaching, and critique and challenge common practices (McLaughlin & Talbert, 2001; Little, 2003). Teaching, in these schools, is regarded less as individualized, rote, and technocratic work, and more as "highly intellectual work, grounded in professional communities where teachers assume responsibility for the learning of their students and of one another . . . a profession that views itself as an intellectual and collective enterprise" (Lieberman & Miller, 2005: 153).

These rationales for recognizing teaching as intellectual work and for building teacher learning communities that encourage intellectual exchange and that "make ideas matter" are deeply rooted in a sense of ethics about teachers as human beings in addition to the alleged efficacy for better practice that may result (for example, Ball & Wilson 1996). In summarizing Katz and Feiman-Nemser's work on new teacher induction, for example, Goodlad and McMannon (2004) note that teachers are frequently told that they are in schools for students' well-being. They argue that although this point seems self-evident and ordinary, creating an intellectually and morally sustaining environment requires "caring attention to one another and opportunities for continued [adult] learning" (96) and that this is not only a good idea because it helps to retain new teachers but also because,

> it is simply the right thing to do. Sustaining a supportive environment should require no neon-lit slogans or ritualistic contingencies to remind us of the behavior our society should display. John Dewey taught us that traits such as civility, compassion, respect, and the like should be routine, reflective of cultural teaching and of learning what it means to be human.
>
> (96)

Promoting a supportive environment by developing teacher learning communities is a theme also found in the literature about new teacher induction and early teaching experiences which I address later on.

Teachers learning to be leaders

I have noted the ways teachers within school-based learning communities engage intellectually with disciplinary content and pedagogical strategies for improving practice. Collectively examining and making decisions about school policies, leadership strategies, and school reform more broadly is another means reformers have touted for building intellectual engagement and on-the-job teacher learning. Many teachers describe the larger political issues around schooling and discuss and write about their desire for change, but, as Cochran-Smith (2001) observes, opportunities for teachers to reflect on daily decisions, engage in thoughtful inquiry, or collaborate are few (285). For reformers advocating teacher leadership, inquiry goes beyond teachers learning their own disciplines or pedagogical approaches as described above. It has teachers learning to work together as leaders of the school site.

Educational policymakers have recognized the importance of organizational design and effective leadership in establishing and maintaining vibrant learning communities for both teachers and students (Lieberman & Miller, 2004). Shared decision-making, collective action regarding school policies, and reflection on broader school reform issues are seen as promising ways to engage teachers, foster collegiality, and improve practice. Many school reformers now hope that teachers will become instructional leaders who work and learn together across corridors, departments, and disciplines to foster educational reform (Barth, 2003; Lieberman, 1995; Leithwood, 2002; Maeroff, 1993). A professional learning community can be a pre-condition for effective teacher leadership and also be sustained by the collegial practices of teacher-led schools (Westheimer, 1998).

One of the enduring tensions in efforts to involve teachers in leadership positions is what Little and Bartlett (2002) referred to as the "Huberman Paradox." Michael Huberman studied teachers' career development and found that those teachers who became involved in school and district leadership roles tended to suffer greater "burnout" than those who remained content to work only in their own classrooms with their students (Huberman, 1993). As Lieberman and Miller (2004) summarize the paradox: "on the one hand, teachers were stimulated by their involvement in reform work and leadership in their school; on the other hand, that very work led to burnout, disaffection, professional conflict, and disappointment" (p. 19). Other studies come to similar conclusions (e.g. McLaughlin & Talbert, 2001; Johnson *et al.*, 2004).

To a large degree, researchers and reformers suspect that the difficulties experienced by teachers who take on leadership positions are due, in large part, to the absence of a professional culture that supports collaborative leadership in the schools and local districts. If, rather than individual teachers seeking to effect broad change, teachers worked together in leadership roles, the benefits of collective teacher engagement could be realized without the professional burnout that seemed to accompany individual efforts. Building a collaborative culture, therefore, became a goal of those seeking to engage teachers in leadership roles (Lieberman & Miller, 2004; McLaughlin & Talbert, 2001; Lambert, 2003). And a number of studies have examined the ways school and district administrators can create the conditions necessary for professional learning communities to flourish for example by adjusting the school schedule so that teachers could have time to meet together (Barth, 2003; Glickman, 2002). Working within professional learning communities, reformers argue, teacher leaders can reinvigorate the work of teaching for themselves and their colleagues, making it collaborative, purposeful, and dynamic (Fullan, 1994; Hargreaves & Fink, 2006; Lieberman & Miller, 2004). Furthermore, the kind of teacher learning that occurs in schools where teachers take on leadership roles can serve as an additional counterforce to teacher burnout. When teachers experience professional growth, they are more likely to stay in teaching (Nias, 1999; Strong & St. John, 2001; Thiessen & Anderson, 1999).

Teacher learning for novice teachers

Teaching has long been characterized by unusually high attrition rates, especially among new teachers (Lortie, 1975; Johnson *et al.*, 2004). A number of studies indicate that some

50 percent of new teachers leave within the first five years of teaching (Grissmer & Kirby, 1997; Murnane *et al.*, 1991). Moreover, teacher induction and retention programs have generally been far less structured and uniform than those of many other professional occupations. With some exceptions, a new teacher on her first day of school is often expected to perform the same or similar duties of a teacher who has been teaching for 25 years.

Further exacerbating the difficult first years of teaching, new teachers will spend a vast majority of their workday in isolation from colleagues in what many within the profession characterize as a "sink-or-swim" or "trial-by-fire" proposition (see Ingersoll & Kralik, 2004; Johnson *et al.*, 2004; Kardos *et al.*, 2001). This pervasive isolation leads to two kinds of recommendations pertinent to a discussion of teacher learning communities: first, new teachers require connections to veteran teachers in order to succeed in their first few years; and, second, most new and veteran teachers alike require a greater sense of connection and community to achieve the kind of personal and professional satisfaction that will keep them in the profession.

Susan Moore Johnson and colleagues in the Project on the Next Generation of Teachers at Harvard University conducted a longitudinal study of more than 50 teachers new to the teaching profession and found that the professional culture of the school greatly impacted novice teachers' decisions about whether to stay in teaching or move on to other careers (Johnson *et al.*, 2004). They identified three kinds of professional community (novice-oriented, veteran-oriented, and integrated) that offered varying levels of support to new teachers (Kardos *et al.*, 2001). The consequences of veteran-oriented professional cultures—in which the teachers tend to split into camps of novice and veteran teachers—are dramatic:

> In the first year of our study, twenty-one of the fifty new teachers taught within veteran-oriented professional cultures. Of those twenty-one, nine (43 percent) left their schools at the end of that year, and five (24 percent) left public school teaching altogether.
>
> (Johnson *et al.*, 2004: 150)

Similarly, in novice-oriented professional cultures—in which the community can be strong, but without a commitment to teacher learning—attrition can also be high. By contrast, in integrated professional cultures, novice and veteran teachers cohabit the professional community equally and orient their intertwined professional culture around sharing and improving practice. These schools emphasize "teachers as learners" (Johnson *et al.*, 2004: 158) and their ability to retain teachers appears considerably higher than in either of the other two orientations (14 of the 17 teachers in their study who began their career in integrated professional communities remain in teaching).

Important studies by Sharon Feiman-Nemser and others have similarly shown the importance of professional collaboration and exchange, especially for new teachers. Mentoring, in particular—when practiced within a strong professional community—strengthens teacher retention, teacher learning, and pedagogical innovation (Feiman-Nemser *et al.*, 1999; Gold, 1996; Katz & Feiman-Nemser, 2004; Strong & St. John, 2001; Smith & Ingersoll, 2004). It also helps novice teachers form and enact their own visions of good teaching and identify themselves with the teaching profession (Hammerness, 2006; Shulman & Shulman, 2004). This becomes especially important as routes into teaching proliferate and more new teachers enter the field without professional preparation.

Reduce alienation so teachers can learn from one another

Another issue affecting the ways both novice and veteran teachers learn on the job stems from broader cultural concerns over growing alienation (Bellah *et al.*, 1985; Selznick, 1992; Wehlage *et al.*, 1989). Scholars cite rampant individualism and isolation from one another as a growing impediment to our collective health (e.g. Putnam, 2000). Amitai Etzioni's communitarian movement, for example, seeks to remedy these ills (Etzioni, 1993). Through association and interaction, psychologists observe, human beings satisfy their need for attachment and social bonds (Bronfenbrenner, 1979; Erikson, 1963). Similarly, sociologists and political scientists emphasize the sense of identity and the commitments that result from participation in community. Human experience, notes Dewey (1938), is inherently social, and therefore depends on interpersonal contact and collaboration within community.

Schools, many argue, must provide this sense of connection and purpose since traditional sources for connectedness have diminished. And teachers, as much as students, require these attachments in order to live out satisfying professional lives in schools and create conditions of community for students. Reflecting the work of sociologists and anthropologists who have long been interested in the ties that bind people together, reformers aim to have teachers form learning communities that inspire their work and enrich the connections among themselves and their students (Lieberman, 1995). They hope teachers will work collaboratively on projects they find meaningful. Teachers might meet during lunch, after school, and during free periods of the day to discuss curriculum, pedagogy, and individual students. Rather than the isolation and professional alienation that is common in many schools, these teachers might experience a sense of membership and belonging, thereby strengthening the profession. Consequently, the role of trust (Bryk and Schneider, 2003) and friendship (Lima, 1997; Jarzabkowski, 2002; Hargreaves, 1994) among teachers in professional learning communities have also been explored. The central goal of these efforts is to nurture and sustain a professional culture that offers the sense of belonging, association, and fellowship that makes it possible for teachers to learn from one another and experience a sense of growing professional expertise (Bryk & Schneider, 2003; Pomson, 2005; Uline *et al.*, 2003).

However, it is not only to attract and retain teachers or to improve teacher practice and student test scores (all overly narrow and instrumental purposes some suggest) that scholars adopt the discourse of community. The community metaphor for educators, social theorists, and philosophers, is also intimately entwined with notions of democracy, social justice, and visions of the good society. I take up these views in the following section.

Pursuing social justice, democracy, and a communal way of life

A number of writers find the language of "professional" learning community potentially limiting in its focus on narrowly pragmatic or technocratic goals (e.g. Zeichner, 1991; Fielding, 1999; Hargreaves & Fink, 2006). Indeed, the word "professional" can demand attention to technical expertise rather than to broader social and socio-political commitments, especially when "professional" is tied to improving student test scores among students (as is increasingly the case among policy makers). Visions for teacher community, some authors suggest, should reflect the importance of democratic communities in pursuit of a better society. For example, Amy Gutmann, in her seminal work, *Democratic Education* (1987), argues that educators aiming at schooling that reinforces democratic notions of community must "create the conditions under which teachers can cultivate the capacity for critical reflection on democratic culture" (Gutmann, 1987: 79). Fielding (1999) ties his vision for teacher collegiality (which he calls "radical collegiality") to "an educational practice intentionally and demonstrably linked to the furtherance of democracy," "communal practice," and "educative engagement with each other and the world around us" (pp. 17–18). Fielding's suggestions are more thematic than tied to the actual practices of schooling (the power of peer learning, students as teachers and teachers as learners, reconstructing education as a democratic project, and so on), but he is aligned with other scholars and education writers who suggest similar ties between education, democracy, and teacher community in schools (Clark & Wasley, 1999; Furman & Mertz, 1997; Hargreaves, 1994; Meier, 1995; Pomson, 2005; Westheimer, 1998).

Democracy, in this sense, is more than a means for collective decision making. Rather it is consistent with what Strike (1999) describes as "thick democracy" signifying,

> a form of human community in which human flourishing is best realized and which is, therefore, essential to a good life. Thick democracy agrees that democratic practices promote fair decision making, but its value goes well beyond this. Thick democracy attaches significant value to such goods as participation, civic friendship, inclusiveness, and solidarity.
>
> (Strike, 1999: 60)

What, then, would it mean for schools to pursue as an educational goal, a vision of "thick democracy?" The intellectual origins of school community as a (thick) democratic endeavor stem at least as far back as John Dewey and fellow turn-of-the-century progressives. "Democracy," Dewey wrote, "is more than a form of government; it is primarily a mode of associated living, of conjoint communicated experience" (1916: 87). Schools thus require activities that have "social aims" and "utilize the materials of typical social situations. For under such conditions the school becomes itself a form of social life, a miniature community, and one in close interaction with other modes of associated experience beyond school walls" (Dewey, 1916: 360).

The path from Dewey's philosophy of education to discussion of the conditions under which teachers live, work, and learn in schools is becoming increasingly well-traveled. Teachers should participate in developing democratic communities in schools that derive from collective projects. "Things gain meaning," Dewey noted, "by being used in a shared experience or joint action" (1916: 16) and this line of argument can be found in a number of calls for greater attention to teacher professional communities in schools. As Hargreaves and Fink (2006) observe, it is either insincere or naïve to expect students to "learn the important skills of living together in a pluralist society from teachers who—within the school at least—all too often lack the kinds of interactions and relationships with colleagues that embody just such constructive discourse" (15).

Notions of democratic community also imply notions of social betterment and social justice. In *Democratic Education*, for example, Amy Gutmann (1987) includes nonrepression and nondiscrimination as essential principles to uphold in any democratic education. The principles of nonrepression and nondiscrimination allow families and other community members to shape, but not entirely constrain, children's future choices by obligating "professional educators to develop in children the deliberative capacity to evaluate competing conceptions of good lives and good societies" (46). Similarly, researchers and practitioners who view education as a means of transforming society often see teacher professional communities as a means of creating school cultures where both teachers and students learn how to promote just such transformation (Ayers, 2000; Fielding, 1999; Hargreaves, 1994).

Although some attention has been given to studying the possibilities for teacher community to advance a social-justice agenda, there has been little empirical work that seeks to assess the success or failure of such programs to effect change. Furthermore, much of the (non-empirical) discourse tends toward the saccharine—rhetorically sweet, but ideologically insipid. The values most often chosen as exemplars of teacher communities oriented towards social justice are those that produce maximum agreement, not necessarily those that are most reflective of philosophical or political notions of justice. "All children can learn" is far more likely to be a defining value of a teacher community aimed at "social justice" than values or goals that would likely engender controversy; and research to date has not, for the most part, sought to distinguish between teacher communities that pursue particular social justice agendas and those that do not. In other words, teacher communities (and studies that describe them) are more likely to boast a high degree of inclusiveness than strong adherence to a particular ideology that might foreground tensions around issues of social justice (see for example, Fielding, 1999).

ENDURING ISSUES AND CONCLUSIONS

Organizational management guru Peter Senge gained a great deal of attention for his 1990 book, *The Fifth Discipline*, which urged corporate America to consider developing "learning organizations." In learning organizations, Senge explained, people continually learn from each other, "new and expansive patterns of thinking are nurtured," and "collective aspiration is set free" (p. 3). The book made an impact on education researchers and practitioners who were engaged in their own efforts to effect change in schools. As Senge's notion of the learning organization became incorporated into the literature on school reform, "learning communities" became the more popular term among educators.[3]

But schools are not corporate boardrooms and they rarely run like them. School administrators, teachers, teacher educators, and education researchers seeking to foster professional communities in schools face obstacles that have outlasted periods of significant reforms. Some of these obstacles are widely recognized in the literature (isolation, lack of time, school architecture, and external pressures such as standardized testing). Others are given short-shrift or avoided altogether (persistent tensions between strong shared beliefs and inclusiveness, micro-politics and conflict, and macro-politics and power). In the remainder of this chapter, I explore these continuing challenges to teacher learning communities in practice. In seeking to better understand the connections between teacher professional communities and teacher learning, these are the areas I suggest are in need of further study.

Isolation and the culture of privacy

Isolation and a culture of privacy in teaching has been one of the most persistent threads of inquiry and commentary in the teacher community literature. Empirical studies have repeatedly shown the difficulties involved in breaking norms of autonomy and privacy at the same time that they have shown the potential benefits of doing so for teacher learning. For example, when Hargreaves and colleagues (2006) asked teachers about obstacles they encountered in seeking to effect school change, the most prominent response teachers gave was having to implement these changes alone without the benefit of collegial professional dialogue. Similarly, Elmore and Burney (1999) found that the greatest "enemy of instructional improvement" is the isolation that most teachers experience during the school day (p. 268). And the isolation is enforced not only by the structural conditions of teaching but also the cultural. What Little calls a "culture of isolation" is often internalized by teachers themselves who often feel too vulnerable or too busy to stop to learn from a colleague (Little, 1990, 1999). Pomson (2005: 787) sums up two explanations for teacher isolationism nicely—it is seen as either:

> (a) an adaptive strategy in environments where the resources required to meet instructional demands are in short supply or (b) an ecological condition, encouraged by workplace settings where physical isolation is pervasive.

Teachers cannot learn from each other if they rarely see or talk to one another. Yet these are the working conditions in which teachers in many if not most schools find themselves. Numerous studies reinforce these disconcertingly conjoined truths: there is much to be gained by teachers working and learning through collective practice and reflection, and the culture of teaching and the organizational constraints on schools mitigate against such practices (for example, Bryk *et al.*, 1999; Kruse & Louis, 1995). Indeed, as Cochran-Smith and Lytle found, the conditions of individual practice, on the whole, seem to be largely bolstered rather than challenged by organizational norms of the profession:

> As a profession, teaching is primarily defined by what teachers do when they are not with other teachers. When teachers are evaluated, it is individual classroom performance that is scrutinized. When contracts are negotiated, it is amount of instructional time that is often a key issue. In fact, when teachers are out of their classrooms or talking to other teachers, they are often perceived by administrators, parents, and sometimes even by teachers themselves as *not* working.
>
> (Cochran-Smith & Lytle, 1992a: 301)

Furthermore, the isolation is not limited to novice or veteran teachers, nor is it limited to schools of a particular demographic (Johnson *et al.*, 2004; Lytle & Fecho, 1991). Despite two decades of reform efforts aimed at bringing teachers together in schools, many educators still observe that teacher work remains primarily private (Barth, 2003; Bredeson, 2003; Grossman *et al.*, 2001).

Since the constraints on professional learning communities are not only organizational but also embedded in the professional culture, even when efforts to facilitate collaboration are implemented, resistance can be strong. In "Persistence of Privacy: Autonomy and Initiative in Teachers' Professional Relations," Little describes a phenomenon that is increasingly familiar to school reformers, staff developers, and teachers:

> The most common configurations of teacher-to-teacher interaction may do more to bolster isolation than to diminish it; the culture that Lortie described as individualistic, present-oriented, and conservative is thus not altered but is indeed perpetuated by the most prevalent examples of teacher collaboration or exchange.
>
> (1990, p. 511)

Feiman-Nemser and Floden (1986) reported similar disparity. The "cellular" nature of teaching in schools, they found, may be seen either as unfortunate lack of mutual support or as a welcome guarantee of professional autonomy (p. 517). Little and colleagues note that "Shared inquiry into student learning and teaching practice runs against the grain of typical professional talk and counter to the prevailing norms of non-interference, privacy, and harmony" (2003: 189–190). Management plans that grant teachers greater decision-making authority often free teachers from bureaucracy but do not connect them to one another.

Another common theme in explanations for the persistent isolation of teachers is teachers' own fears of exposure. In many schools, the expert teacher is considered to be the one who is confidently independent and self-sufficient (Cochran-Smith & Lytle, 1992b). Nervousness about evaluations or being embarrassed in front of peers or superiors result in many teachers preferring the isolation of their own classrooms to the perceived humiliation that might come from more collegial arrangements. Some teachers, even relatively novice ones, fear that if they ask too many questions, colleagues will perceive them to be less than competent (Richardson-Koehler, 1988; Pomson, 2005). These norms also help to explain the resistance to projects like video clubs, in which teachers videotape and discuss each other's teaching (see Grossman *et al.*, 2001).

How then do reformers address these obstacles? Researchers and school reformers have noted key strategies to overcoming the isolation so endemic to the profession of teaching. These include deliberately structured professional activities that require inte-grated work (Lieberman & Miller, 2004; Barth, 2003; Kahne & Westheimer, 2000), interdisciplinary teaching strategies that bring teachers together around content themes (Grossman *et al.*, 2001), action research projects around shared interests (Cochran-Smith & Lytle, 2001), and organizational structures around subject-matter such as high school departments that encourage the exchange of ideas and mutual learning (Little, 1999; McLaughlin, 1993). Each of these strategies assume both that bringing teachers together to learn from one another will help to overcome persistent professional isolation and also that reduced teacher isolation (by changing the organizational structures of schooling, for example) will allow teachers to learn from one another.

Notably, the most transient and least successful efforts at bringing teachers together in shared inquiry tend to be those whose focus is on community-building itself in the absence of more intellectually or pragmatically substantive goals. Team-building, sun-shine committees, shared lunchrooms, and after-school social gatherings are excellent supplements but poor substitutes for collective work on meaningful professional pro-jects. Planning a shared curriculum unit together has been found to be a better approach to fostering teacher learning and dialogue than a lone event of introduce-your-neighbor (Barth, 2003; Kahne & Westheimer, 2000). A detailed and rigorous study in elementary schools by Cousins *et al.* (1994) found, for example, that in-depth joint work on curric-ulum planning and implementation among teachers resulted in significant conceptual and affective gains while casual conversation or occasional advice did not.

Strategies that challenge the culture of isolation common in the teaching profession are similar in approach and kind to strategies for broader school reform advocated in the past several decades. Reform efforts that seek to address some of the most intractable obstacles to developing and maintaining professional learning communities in schools aim towards many of the same levers for change: the organizational and administrative conditions discussed above, and the temporal and architectural structures of schools which I discuss below.

Time and the pressures of standardization

Time is a precious commodity for most teachers (Lortie, 1975; Johnson, 1990) and relationship-building is not a speedy process. Furthermore, building a professional community, especially around opportunities for teacher learning, can take up many (often unpaid) hours (Cochran-Smith & Lytle, 1992b; King, 2002). A number of researchers suggest that school reforms to increase available professional time for teachers to spend together may well be a pre-condition for improved teacher learning (Bredson, 2003; Leithwood, 2002; Shollenberger-Swaim & Swaim, 1999). Teacher research, for example, is a prominent strategy to engage teachers in collective reflection on their own practice and widely understood as a potentially beneficial activity for teacher learning and community. But many teachers are hesitant to engage in teacher research for fear that it will take time away from their work with students (Cochran-Smith & Lytle, 1992b). Indeed, the most prominent examples of teacher learning take place outside of the school entirely. Teacher institutes and development seminars are most often stand-alone workshops in the summer or other non-instructional time. Teachers' developmental learning is rarely integrated into the daily rhythms of the school day (King, 2002; Little, 1999; Cochran-Smith and Lytle, 1992).

Recent emphasis on standards and testing benchmarks further magnify the scarcity of time for teachers to pursue collective work. Highly restrictive, state-level curriculum frameworks, standards-based evaluations, and high-stakes testing for teachers and students can severely curtail new teachers' capacities to teach as a community of colleagues who locate their teaching and curriculum development in the primacy of their own and their students' experiences. Standards, high-stakes testing, and competency testing for both students and teachers are currently the noisiest and most prevalent educational conversations, and calls for developing learning communities or innovative collective teaching can be lost in the din. In the U.S., forty-nine states have now adopted higher academic standards as one of the major strategies for educational improvement (Clark & Wasley, 1999). Test scores are frequently used for decisions with regard to tracking, promotion, and graduation (National Research Council, 1999). Especially in districts where low test scores and high-stakes policies threaten students, teachers, and principals, a test-centered pedagogy and curriculum will frequently dominate (Brabeck, 1999; Shepard, 1991; Wiggins, 1993). In many cases, opportunities for collective leadership and reflection are constrained or focused solely on raising students' test scores. In a study of 24 schools across 12 districts in six states, Berry and others found that "although high-stakes accountability systems help focus professional development efforts on the curricular needs of students, little evidence exists to support the claim that such systems help teachers change their practice to enhance student learning" (summarized in ASCD, 2004, p. 3). Furthermore, a "tendency exists—particularly in low-performing schools—to narrow the focus of professional development activities to tested subjects or provide general support that is disconnected from curricular needs" (3).

The inability of most teacher organizations to resist the onslaught of standards-based reforms and free up time to pursue broader visions of teacher and student learning hints at a related but infrequently mentioned issue regarding teacher professional community. Some authors express concern that the term "community" can be mis-used as a way to avoid the thornier issues of teacher professionalization, school funding, and low status of the profession (e.g. Meier, 2000; Zeichner, 1991). "Learning communities" cannot mitigate the fiscal crisis some schools now experience, these educators argue, and schools such as those described in Jonathan Kozol's *Savage Inequalities* need adequate funding before talk about "getting along" or having teachers volunteer their time after school hours. Time and money may not be sufficient to move teachers from talk that is friendly to discussions that are generative of teacher learning, but many argue that they are necessary preconditions (Ayers, 2000; Sizer, 1992; Westheimer, 2000).

Similarly, research conducted as part of the Project on the Next Generation of Teachers, at Harvard University, makes clear that teachers' lack of time impedes the formation of strong collaborative teacher professional cultures (Johnson *et al.*, 2004). They point out that it costs money to provide the time and space for both new and veteran teachers to meet and that matters of time and money are likely to be obstacles to community particularly in low-income and understaffed schools (see also Shollenberger-Swaim and Swaim, 1999 for the limitations of teachers' time). Narrowing of the curriculum in response to testing mandates and adding extra "drill" classes on top of already burdened teacher schedules further restricts teachers' opportunities for joint work and professional exchange (Kohn, 2000; Meier, 2000; Ohanian, 1999).

Architecture

Although public school reformers rarely have the opportunity to build a new school from scratch, many small-scale and private efforts have been able to make the architectural space of the school more conducive to both teacher–teacher and teacher–student interactions. And certainly, many educators have desired such changes (Meier, 1995; Barth, 1990; Sergiovanni 1994a). Probably owing to the lack of meaningful authority educators generally have over constructing the architectural plan of most schools, there have been few empirical studies of the effects of physical architecture on the learning environment and none of the effects on the capacities and predilections of teachers engaging in collegial learning activities. The small body of work that addresses the physical architecture of schools tends to narrowly emphasize healthy environments, air quality, heating, cooling, and so on (see, for example, Schneider, 2002).

There are some notable exceptions, such as *Architecture for Education: New School Designs from the Chicago Competition* (Sharp *et al.*, 2003) and *The Language of School Design* (2005) by Nair and Fielding. Both works aim to connect research on teaching and learning to school planning and design strategies. Effective learning environments, the authors of these works argue, are dependent as much on the spatial arrangements of the school as they are on the curriculum. Nair and Fielding, for example, draw from Christopher Alexander's classic work on "Pattern Language" to propose schools that reflect current concerns for learning communities, at least for students (see also Brubaker, 1997). Alexander's groundbreaking work in the world of architecture sought to identify "patterns" in the built environment that seem to nourish human relationships, interplay, and exchange. In *The Language of School Design*, the authors apply Alexander's theories to school design, hoping to address the "chasm between widely acknowledged best [educational] practice principles and the actual design of a majority of school facilities" (p. 2).

Other examples can be drawn from studies with foci on broader aspects of teacher professionalism and community. Scribner *et al.* (2002), for example, describe a school in which the principal decided to eliminate teacher classrooms and have teachers move around the school to their classes of students:

> One thing the principal did that I think is very good was to eliminate the teachers' desks in their rooms. Instead, we have a departmental concept. The teachers have all their desks in a room. The teachers didn't like that, but the new ones, they don't know any different. I don't even know if she anticipated the benefit, but just by putting the teachers with each other, the new teachers are going to push the old teachers in some new ideas that they've got, and the old teachers are going to show the new teachers some of the neat things that do work.
>
> (Veteran science teacher, quoted in Scribner *et al.*, 2002, p. 68)

Their example demonstrates the considerable influence even small and inexpensive "architectural" decisions can make on the professional culture of the school.

One final area of inquiry that considers the impact of school architecture and organization on professional learning community is the small schools literature (Ayers, 2000; Raywid, 1996; Stevens & Kahne, 2006). The increased personalization and diminished complexity of small schools enables less bureaucracy and more interdependence between and among teachers, administrators, and students. A number of studies reinforce the findings of Bryk *et al.* (1999): "Among all the factors considered, small school size stood out as being an important facilitator of professional community . . . Professional community was much more prevalent in elementary schools with less than 350 students than it was in larger schools" (Bryk *et al.* 1999: 767; see also Darling-Hammond *et al.*, 1995; Gladden, 1998; Raywid, 1996).

At the same time that certain forms of architecture may be correlated with teacher collaboration through the establishment of communal spaces, these spaces can also be seen as unwelcome efforts at containment or exclusion. School-within-school organizational structures, for example, can lead to tensions within the larger building and concerns over containment and isolation (Achinstein, 2002; Raywid, 1996). Moreover, in a study by Gunn and King (2003), one of the author's classrooms was relocated to another floor, under the assumption that "Gunn and the other team member on Gunn's floor were colluding together against the team leadership and that the close proximity of their classrooms was facilitating the formation of factions within the team" (Gunn & King, 2003: 182).

Overall, however, the literature on school architecture tends to be more metaphorical than literal. Bredeson (2003), for example, advocates new "architecture" for professional development in schools. Ideally, according to Bredeson, learning spaces for educators are not "isolated, self-contained spaces" but rather spaces that "support individual growth, foster collaborative learning, and build collective capacity" (p. 40). A number of others have observed the effects of spatial arrangements on teacher learning and collaboration as well (Glickman, 2002; Leithwood, 2002; Raywid, 1996; Rosenholtz, 1989). It is these often modest and/or metaphorical reforms to the physical space of the school coupled with the organizational and administrative reforms described earlier that have received substantial attention from educators and policy-makers interested in fostering learning communities for teachers.

Tension between community and liberal inclusiveness

Popular models for community generally demonstrate strong insights into the practical and theoretical tributaries that those interested in building community in schools must cross. Most, however, are less clear when discussing the social and political forces that often turn tributaries into quagmires. Nowhere is this more evident than in the considerable gloss that has consistently represented much of the literature on teacher professional community when it comes to issues of beliefs, ideology, and conflict. For example, conceptions of diversity have been central to most discussions about school and teacher community. The literature is replete with mentions of "tolerance," "multicultural perspective," and "diversity of ideas." But relatively few works address the tough dilemmas that emerge when practitioners pursue the ideals of democratic and egalitarian communities, hoping to become neither excessively insular nor aimlessly diffuse. Much of the research and practice relating teacher community to teacher learning advocates working together, overlooking differences, and creating friendlier, more open work settings for teachers. More work would be useful that studies power imbalances and the resulting sense of impotence that threaten to undo so many of these well-meaning reforms. In short, those of us who study teacher collaboration could benefit more from plodding through the muck, the ambiguity, and the mystery of how communities succeed and fail to manage conflict and how they ensure full participation of members with a diversity of backgrounds and interests. More specifically, studies are needed that address at least two persistent and overlapping tensions: the simultaneous pursuit of inclusiveness and community; and the reluctance to engage competing ideologies and conflict.

The tension between community and inclusiveness when it comes to professional learning communities is rooted in a gap in the broader schools-as-communities literature. This literature, as Strike (1999) points out, has not "adequately come to terms with the difficulties involved in sharing values in the public schools of a liberal democratic society" (p. 47). While most reformers advocate shared values as a basis for teacher community (Fielding, 1999; Little, 1999; Sergiovanni, 1994a), few engage what Strike notes is a tension between constitutive values and liberal inclusiveness. Constitutive values (values that are coherent enough to *constitute* communities among teachers and students), Strike explains, represent those beliefs and ideals people share about the good life and about ways schools might contribute to it. Catholic Schools are *prima facie* examples of schools with strong constitutive values because "those who are members of Catholic School communities can share a common educational project. They know what they are about because they have a shared vision of a good life and of how learning contributes to it" (p. 50). But, if we think towards extremes, no community can be wholly united by shared values and still be entirely inclusive. Indeed, anthropologists have long noted that communities are defined by their borders. Who is *excluded* is as important as who is included.

There have been a few responses to this dilemma, and I will describe just two here. Strike (1999) suggests a middle ground that calls for constitutive values that are "thick" enough to constitute community but vague enough to allow for competing ideas from all members of the community:

> the standard of liberal inclusiveness does not so much reject constitutive values as it wants to privatize them. Liberals often value community. They reject communities whose values are made obligatory . . . for those who do not share them.
>
> (Strike, 1999: 68)

Strike advocates building more opportunities for a middle ground that arises from greater freedom-of-association within public schools and public spaces. "Houses" within public schools, for example, could offer homes to students and teachers with varying but still constitutive conceptions of the good life. Given a number of different houses with varying degrees of constitutive ideals, no one, presumably, would be excluded from the school community entirely or branded second-class citizens.

A second response is illustrated by the work of Scribner *et al.* (2002). These authors argue that professional autonomy and individual needs, rather than being in conflict with community, might actually serve as necessary conditions that make professional community possible. They observe that much of the literature on professional community assumes a concordance between the health of the community and the degree to which collective identity supplants individual identity and needs (p. 49). They suggest that a more salient frame for examining the strength of professional community might be named a *shared identity* among heterogeneous individuals engaged in professional relationships rather than a *collective identity* that, as they see it, requires giving up individual autonomy and needs. Professional autonomy and attention to individual needs, the authors argue, are necessary conditions for strong professional communities where teachers can and do learn from one another. They describe one school in which the principal sought to impose a collective identity among teachers and was rebuffed. The teachers saw the imposition of collective action as a threat to their professional autonomy. In another (preferred) school, the principal encouraged a shared identity ("we-ness") that protected teachers' individual needs and their professional autonomy ("I-ness") and therefore resulted in a strong sense of professional community where shared teacher learning became the norm.

I make a related observation in *Among Schoolteachers: Community, Autonomy, and Individuality in Teachers' Work* (Westheimer, 1998). In describing two professional communities of teachers (Brandeis and Mills schools), I acknowledge a common tension and fear: that within a community with shared beliefs and interests, individuality will be suppressed and the individual submerged into a monolithic whole (p. 146). But the Mills community seemed to demonstrate something else at work entirely: individuality and community were unexpected bedfellows in the quest for a professional learning environment:

> Among the teachers, administrators, and staff at Mills are the usual gamut of individuals as well: the gregarious and the reserved, the associated and the isolated, those who stand out and those who prefer to blend in. [But these identities] call into question critics' customary polarization of the individual and the collective ... I learned an extraordinary amount about individuals' multiple roles in the community [and] their identities *in relation to* the community. Walter is known for speaking quietly. Paul builds wheelchairs. Mark is a workhorse. Sabrina is active in local community politics and can be counted on to bring important aspects of her work to bear in curriculum development for the school.

Collective projects at this school showcase teachers' talents and model the use of these talents for social purposes. Rather than submerging the individual within the group, collective work and frequent and engaged participation provide an opportunity and forum to develop an individual identity within and in relation to the group. This allowed teachers to learn from each other's different talents and capacities.

There are several other works that explore the tension between inclusiveness and community, and a small number do so empirically (Leithwood, 2002; Malen, 1995; Marshall & Scribner, 1995). This area, however, like the one that follows, is ripe for further investigation. In what ways can collective projects among teachers further teacher learning and development? How might communal identities be forged without sacrificing individual teachers' sense of autonomy? What role can school leaders play?

Reluctance to engage competing ideologies

The beliefs about teaching and learning that teachers, administrators, school board members, and parents share affect the curriculum, the organization, and the values conveyed to students about the purposes of education (Hargreaves & Fink, 2006; Strike, 1999). These beliefs and orientations are visible not only in the content of the curriculum but also in the organization and practices of the teacher professional community in each school (McLaughlin & Talbert, 2001) and or smaller units within the school such as high school departments (Siskin, 1994). Learning among teachers is accordingly affected by the embedded priorities and emphases of the broader professional community. One teacher professional community might emphasize teachers' individual autonomy, rights, and responsibilities to colleagues while another might be driven by a strong collective mission and collective values. One group of teachers might work together to develop interdisciplinary joint curriculum while another might convene in order to help individual teachers pursue individually-defined curricular goals. In contrast to so many school, both of these examples (and there are surely more) represent communities in which teachers do not feel isolated, share opportunities for learning from one another, and may be content in their jobs. But the differences are consequential: ideologically, different forms of learning communities embody differing beliefs about the purposes of professional communities, the philosophical, social, and political beliefs, values, and opinions that shape the way a group of teachers view the world, and the broad purposes of education in pursuing those beliefs.

Even the names various schools use to describe the ways their teachers work together can be revealing. A "team," for example denotes an instrumental group where individuals come together to accomplish a task. Other schools might divide teachers and students into "families," implying that individuals are part of a collective. In teams, individuals can accomplish goals together that may be unattainable alone. In families—ideally—individuals gain a sense of connection, belonging, and affinity.

When researchers study the effects of teacher communities on teacher learning, it would be useful to further distinguish empirically between teacher learning in these different kinds of learning communities. Many argue that teachers should share beliefs to form a robust professional community, but few articulate which beliefs might be worth sharing. "What beliefs should be shared?" is a thorny question almost always left to the imagination of practitioners and policy-makers. When it comes to specifying the kinds of beliefs that might lead to particular kinds of teacher learning and exchange, the literature on professional learning communities remains largely—to borrow Little's description of collegiality (1990)—"conceptually amorphous and ideologically sanguine" (p. 519).

Researchers and reformers often assert the role that *sharing beliefs* plays in community-building while ignoring the importance of the nature of the beliefs themselves and how these beliefs might bring about different kinds of learning. Developing not only clear conceptualizations of learning communities but also of the specific values, commitments, and ideologies that such conceptualizations embody could significantly strengthen practical efforts to build professional learning communities among teachers in schools (Cochran-Smith, 2001; Westheimer, 2000).

FUTURE RESEARCH

The literature on how teachers learn with and from colleagues has evolved significantly in the 20 years or so since discussions about professional learning communities became common. A variety of school reform efforts depend on teachers' ability to work with and learn from colleagues (Lieberman & Miller, 2004). Yet teacher education and development has only just begun to serve as a focus for developing learning communities. Schools led by communities of teachers who are responsible for making curricular, organizational, and sometimes financial decisions require that teachers learn from one another and become well versed about the benefits, commitments, tensions, and trouble spots that emerge when people learn and work together in demanding environments.

Research has demonstrated links between professional learning communities for teachers and improved teacher practice and student learning; a climate of intellectual inquiry; teachers' ability and willingness to serve as leaders; new teacher learning and retention; reduced alienation; and social justice and democracy. These studies provide significant rationale for continued work in the areas of professional learning communities.

Little and Horn (2006), for example, are currently studying teacher discourse to see what kinds of "teacher talk" are consequential and hold the greatest potential for teacher learning. More research of this nature would be beneficial to those seeking to understand the ways teachers learn from each other.

Moreover, enduring tensions persist and call for continued investigation. These include tensions around: isolation and privacy; time teachers have to engage in collaborative learning in a climate of standards and assessment; school architecture; inclusiveness; and varying ideologies. Research to date has indicated that amidst these tensions and without adequate preparation for teachers, expectations for teacher learning are easily thwarted (Lieberman & Miller, 2004).

Teacher learning among colleagues is a promising area for teacher development and reform. Further clarifying the substance and direction of teacher learning communities in practice is the task researchers and teacher educators now face.

NOTES

1 Research conducted for this chapter was supported by the University Research Chairs program at the University of Ottawa and through a grant from the Social Sciences and Humanities Research Council of Canada. Karen Emily Suurtamm provided outstanding research assistance, compiling and summarizing extensive swaths of literature. I would also like to thank Brad Cousins, Sharon Feiman-Nemser, Barbara Leckie, and Karen Emily Suurtamm for thoughtful comments on earlier drafts.
2 This observation is the subject of many biblical parables about teaching and is also described in Grossman *et al.* (2001).
3 Senge has a more recent book that addresses education directly: *Schools That Learn: A Fifth Discipline Fieldbook for Educators, Parents, and Everyone Who Cares About Education.* Doubleday, 2000.

REFERENCES

Academy for Educational Development (2006) Reviewing student work. Improving student achievement. Retrieved February 23, 2006 from http://scs.aed.org/rsw/.
Achinstein, B. (2002) *Community, diversity, and conflict among schoolteachers: the ties that bind.* Advances in contemporary educational thought series. New York: Teachers College Press.
Alexander, C. (1986) *A new theory of urban design.* New York: Oxford University Press.
American Association for the Advancement of Science (1994) *Benchmarks for science literacy.* New York: Oxford University Press.
ASCD, Association of Supervision and Curriculum Development (2004) Teacher professional development in high-stakes accountability systems. *ASCD Research Brief*, 2(13).
Ayers, W. (2000) *A simple justice: the challenge of small schools.* New York: Teachers College Press.
Ball, D. L. & S. Rundquist (1992) Collaboration as a context for joining teacher learning with learning about teaching. In D. K. Cohen, M. W. McLaughlin, & J. E. Talbert (eds.), *Teaching for understanding: challenges for practice, research, and policy* (pp. 13–42). San Francisco: Jossey-Bass.
Ball, D. L. & S. M. Wilson (1996) Integrity in teaching: recognizing the fusion of the moral and the intellectual. *American Educational Research Journal*, 33, 155–192.
Ball, D. L. & D. K. Cohen (1999) Developing practice, developing practitioners: toward a practice-based theory of professional education. In L. Darling-Hammond & G. Sykes (eds.), *Teaching as the learning profession: handbook of policy and practice.* San Francisco: Jossey-Bass.
Barth, R. S. (1990) *Improving schools from within.* San Francisco: Jossey-Bass.

Barth, R. S. (June 2003) *Lessons learned: shaping relationships and the culture of the workplace.* Thousand Oaks, CA: Sage.

Bellah, R., R. Masden, W. Sullivan, A. Swidler & S. Tipton (1985) *Habits of the heart: individualism and commitment in American life.* New York: Harper & Row.

Brabeck, M. (1999) Between Scylla and Charybdis: teacher education's odyssey. *Journal of Teacher Education,* 50(5), 346–351.

Bredeson, P. V. (2003) *Designs for learning: a new architecture for professional development in schools.* Thousand Oaks, CA: Corwin Press.

Bronfenbrenner, U. (1979) *The ecology of human development.* Cambridge, MA: Harvard University Press.

Brubaker, W. C. (1997) *Planning and designing schools.* New York: McGraw-Hill Professional.

Bruner, J. (1996) *The culture of education.* Cambridge, MA: Harvard University Press.

Bryk, A. & B. Schneider (2003). Trust in schools: a core resource for school reform. *Educational Leadership,* 60(6), 40–44.

Bryk, A., E. Camburn & K. S. Louis (1999) Professional community in Chicago elementary schools: facilitating factors and organizational consequences. *Educational Administration Quarterly,* 35, 751–781.

Clark, R. W. & P. A. Wasley (1999) Renewing schools and smarter kids: promises for democracy. *Phi Delta Kappan,* 80(8).

Cochran-Smith, M. (2001) Learning to teach against the (new) grain. *Journal of Teacher Education,* 52(1), 3–4.

Cochran-Smith, M. & S. L. Lytle (1992a) Communities for teacher research: fringe or forefront? *American Journal of Education,* 100(3), 298–324.

Cochran-Smith, M. & S. L. Lytle (1992b) *Inside/Outside: teacher research and knowledge.* New York: Teachers College Press.

Cochran-Smith, M. & S. L. Lytle (2001) Beyond certainty: taking an inquiry stance on practice. In Leiberman, A. & Miller, L. (eds.) *Teachers caught in the action: professional development that matters* (pp. 45–58). New York: Teachers College Press.

Cousins, J. B., J. A. Ross & F. J. Maynes (1994) The reported nature and consequences of teachers' joint work in three exemplary elementary schools. *The Elementary School Journal,* 94(4), 441–465.

Darling-Hammond, L. & M. McLaughlin (1999) Investing in teaching as a learning profession: policy problems and prospects. In Darling-Hammond, L. & G. Sykes (eds.) *Teaching as the learning profession: handbook of policy and practice* (pp. 376–412). San Francisco: Jossey-Bass.

Darling-Hammond, L., J. Ancess & B. Falk (1995) *Authentic assessment in action: studies of schools and students at work.* The series on school reform. New York: Teachers College Press.

Dewey, J. (1916) *Democracy and education: an introduction to the philosophy of education.* New York: Macmillan.

Dewey, J. (1938) *Experience and education.* New York: Macmillan.

Elmore, R. F. & D. Burney (1999) Investing in teacher learning: staff development and instructional improvement. In L. Darling-Hammond & G. Sykes (eds.), *Teaching as the learning profession: handbook of policy and practice* (pp. 263–291). San Francisco: Jossey-Bass.

Erikson, E. E. (1963) *Childhood and society.* New York: Norton.

Etzioni, A. (1993) *The spirit of community.* New York: Crown Publishers.

Feiman-Nemser, S. (2001) Helping novices learn to teach: lessons from an exemplary support teacher. *Journal of Teacher Education,* 52(1), 17–30.

Feiman-Nemser, S. & R. E. Floden (1986) The cultures of teaching. In M.C. Whittrock (ed.), *Handbook of Research on Teaching* (pp. 505–526). London: Collier-Macmillan.

Feiman-Nemser, S. & S. Schwille (1999) *A conceptual review of literature on new teacher induction.* Washington, DC: National Partnership for Excellence and Accountability in Teaching.

Fielding, M. (1999) Radical collegiality: affirming teaching as an inclusive professional practice. *Australian Educational Researcher,* 26(2), 1–34.

Fullan, M. G. (1994) Teacher leadership: a failure to conceptualize. In D. R. Walling (ed.) *Teachers as leaders: perspectives on the professional development of teachers* (pp. 241–253). Bloomington, IN: Phi Delta Kappa Educational Foundation.

Furman, G. & C. Mertz (1997) *Community and schools: promise and paradox.* New York: Teachers College Press.

Gardner, H. (1985) *The mind's new science: a history of the cognitive revolution.* New York: Basic Books.

Gladden, R. (1998) The small school movement: a review of the literature. In M. Fine & J. I. Somerville (eds.), *Small schools, big imaginations: a creative look at urban public schools* (pp. 113–137). Chicago: Cross City Campaign for Urban School Reform.

Glickman, C. D. (2002) *Leadership for learning: how to help teachers succeed.* Alexandria: Association for Supervision and Curriculum Development.

Gold, Y. (1996) Beginning teacher support: attrition, mentoring and induction. In C. B. Courtney (ed.) *Review of Research in Education,* 16, 548–594. Washington, DC: American Educational Research Association.

Goodlad, J. I. & T. J. McMannon (eds.) (2004) *The teaching career.* New York: Teachers College Press.

Gray, P. M. & L. Rubenstein (2004) Achieving and sustaining critical colleagueship. In B. August & M. Wolfe, *Looking both ways: studies in cross-institutional professional development, Vol. 2—facilitating collaboration* (pp. 45–58). New York: The City University of New York, Office of Academic Affairs.

Grissmer, D. & S. N. Kirby (1997) Teacher turnover and teacher quality. *Teachers College Record,* 99(1), 45–56.

Grossman, P., S. Wineburg, & S. Woolworth (2001). Toward a theory of teacher community. *Teachers College Record,* 103(6), 942–1012.

Gunn, J. H. & B. M. King (2003) Trouble in paradise: power, conflict, and community in an interdisciplinary teaching team. *Urban Education,* 38(2), 173–195.

Gutmann, Amy (1987) *Democratic education.* Princeton: Princeton University Press.

Hamerness, K. (2006) *Seeing through teachers' eyes: professional ideals and classroom practices.* New York: Teachers College Press.

Hargreaves, A. (1994) *Changing teachers, changing times: teachers' work and culture in the postmodern age.* New York: Teachers College Press.

Hargreaves, A. & D. Fink (2006) *Sustainable leadership.* San Francisco: Jossey-Bass.

Hatch, T., M. Eiler White & D. Faigenbaum (2005) Expertise, credibility, and influence: how teachers can influence policy, advance research, and improve performance. *Teachers College Record,* 107(5), 1004.

Hord, S. M. (2003) *Learning together, leading together: changing schools through professional learning communities.* New York: Teachers College Press.

Huberman, M. (1993) *The model of the independent artisan in teachers' professional relations.* In J. W. Little & M. W. McLauchlin (eds.) *Teachers' work: individuals, colleagues, and contexts.* New York: Teachers College Press.

Ingersoll, R. & J. M. Kralik (2004) *The impact of mentoring on teacher retention: what the research says.* Denver, CO: Education Commission of the States.

Jarzabkowski, L. M. (2002) The social dimensions of teacher collegiality. *Journal of Educational Enquiry,* 3(2), 1–20.

Johnson, S. M. (1990) *Teachers at Work.* New York: Basic Books.

Johnson, S. M. and the Project on the Next Generation of Teachers (2004) *Finders and keepers: helping new teachers survive and thrive in our schools.* San Francisco: Jossey-Bass.

Kahne, J. & J. Westheimer (2000) A pedagogy of collective action and reflection: preparing teachers for collective school leadership. *Journal of Teacher Education,* 51(5), 372–383.

Kardos, S. M., S. M. Johnson, H. G. Peske, D. Kauffman, & E. Liu (2001) Counting on colleagues: new teachers encounter the professional cultures of their schools. *Educational Administration Quarterly,* 37(2), 250–290.

Katz, D. & S. Feiman-Nemser (2004) New teacher induction in a culture of professional development. In J. I. Goodlad & T. J. McMannon (eds.) *The teaching career* (pp. 96–116). New York: Teachers College Press.

King, M. B. (2002) Professional development to promote schoolwide inquiry. *Teaching and Teacher Education*, 18(3), 243–257.

Kohn, A. (2000) *The case against standardized testing: raising the scores, ruining the schools.* Portsmouth, NH: Heinemann.

Kozol, J. (1992) *Savage inequalities: children in America's schools.* New York: HarperPerennial.

Kruse, S. & K. S. Louis (1995) *Developing professional community in new and restructuring schools.* In K. S. Louis, S. Kruse & Associates, *Professionalism and community: perspectives on reforming urban schools* (pp. 187–207). Thousand Oaks, CA: Corwin Press.

Kruse, S., K. S. Louis and A. Bryk (1995) An emerging framework for analyzing school-based professional community. In K. S. Louis & S. Kruse (eds.), *Professionalism and community: perspectives on reforming urban schools.* Thousand Oaks, CA: Sage.

Lambert, L. (2003) *Leadership capacity for lasting school improvement.* Alexandria, VA: ASCD.

Lave, J. & E. Wenger (1991) *Situated learning: legitimate peripheral participation.* Cambridge, UK: Cambridge University Press.

Lee, Valerie E., J. B. Smith & R. G. Croninger (1995) Another look at high school restructuring: more evidence that it improves student achievement, and more insight into why. *Issues in Restructuring Schools, Issue Report No. 9.* Madison, University of Wisconsin: Wisconsin Center for Education Research (pp. 1–10).

Leithwood, K. (2002) *Organizational learning and school improvement.* Greenwich, CT: JAI.

Lieberman, A. (ed.) (1995) *The work of restructuring schools: building from the ground up.* New York: Teachers College Press.

Lieberman, A. & L. Miller (2004) *Teacher leadership.* San Francisco: Jossey-Bass.

Lieberman, A. and L. Miller (2005) Teachers as leaders. *The educational forum.* v69, Winter.

Lima, Jorge Ávila de (1997) *Colleagues and friends. Professional and personal relationships among teachers in two portuguese secondary schools.* Ph.D. Dissertation, Ponta Delgada, Portugal: Serviços de Documentação da Universidade dos Açores.

Little, J. W. (1987) Teachers as colleagues. In V. Richardson-Koehler (ed.) *Educator's handbook* (pp. 491–518). White Plains: Longman.

Little, J. W. (1990) The persistence of privacy: autonomy and initiative in teachers' professional relations. *Teachers College Record*, 91, 509–536.

Little, J. W. (1999) Organizing schools for teacher learning. In L. Darling-Hammond & G. Sykes (eds.), *Teaching as the learning profession: handbook of policy and practice.* San Francisco: Jossey-Bass (pp. 233–262).

Little, J. W. (2003) Inside teacher community: representations of classroom practice. *Teachers College Record*, 105(6), 913–945.

Little, J. W. and Bartlett, L. (2002) Career and commitment in the context of comprehensive school reform. *Theory and Practice*, 8(3), 345–354.

Little, J. W. & I. S. Horn (2006) Resources for professional learning in talk about teaching: from "just talk" to consequential conversation. Paper presented at the annual meeting of the American Educational Research Association. San Francisco. April.

Little, J. W., M. Gearhart, M. Curry & J. Kafka (2003) Looking at student work for teacher learning, teacher community, and school reform. *Phi Delta Kappan*, 85(3), 184–192.

Lord, B. (1994) Teachers' professional development: critical colleagueship and the role of professional communities. In N. Cobb (ed.), *The future of education: Perspectives on national standards in America.* New York: College Entrance Examination Board.

Lortie, D. C. (1975) *Schoolteacher: a sociological study.* Chicago: University of Chicago Press.

Louis, K. S. & H. M. Marks (1998) Does professional community affect the classroom? Teachers' work and student experiences in restructuring schools. *American Journal of Education*, 106, 532–575.

Louis, K. S., S. D. Kruse & Associates (1995) *Professionalism and community: perspectives on reforming urban schools.* Thousand Oaks, CA: Corwin Press.

Louis, K. S., H. M. Marks & S. Kruse (1996) Teachers' professional community in restructuring schools. *American Educational Research Journal*, 33, 757–798.

Lytle, S. L. & R. Fecho (1991) Meeting strangers in familiar places: teacher collaboration by cross-visitation. *English Education*, 23(1), 5–28.

McLaughlin, M. W. (1993) What matters most in teachers' workplace context. In J. Little & M. McLaughlin (eds.), *Teachers' work: individuals, colleagues, and contexts* (pp. 79–203). New York: Teachers College Press.

McLaughlin, M. W. & J. E. Talbert (1993) *Contexts that matter for teaching and learning*. Stanford: Center for Research on the Context of Secondary School Teaching, Stanford University.

McLaughlin M. W. & J. E. Talbert (2001) *Professional communities and the work of high school teaching*. Chicago: University of Chicago Press.

Maeroff, G. (1993) Building teams to rebuild schools. *Phi Delta Kappan*, 74, 512–519.

Malen, B. (1995) The micropolitics of education: mapping the multiple dimensions of power relations in school policies. In J. D. Scribner & D. H. Layton (eds.) *The Study of Educational Politics*. Washington, DC: Falmer.

Marshall, C. & J. D. Scribner (1995) It's all political: inquiry into the micropolitics of education. *Education and Urban Society*, 23, 347–355.

Meier, D. (1995) *The power of their ideas: lessons for America from a small school in Harlem*. Boston: Beacon Press.

Meier, D. (2000) *Will standards save public education?* Boston: Beacon Press.

Mitchell, C. & L. Sackney (2000) *Profound improvement: building capacity for a learning community*. Lisse, The Netherlands: Swets & Zeitlinger.

Murnane, R. J., Singer, J. D., J. B. Willett, J. J. Kemple & R. J. Olsen (1991) *Who will teach? Policies that matter*. Cambridge, MA: Harvard University Press.

Nair, P. & R. Fielding (2005) *The language of school design: design patterns for 21st century schools*. New York: Designshare, Inc.

National Research Council (1999) *High stakes: testing for tracking, promotion, and graduation*. Washington, DC: National Academy Press.

Newmann, F. M. & G. G. Wehlage (1995) *Successful school restructuring: a report to the public and educators by the center on organization and restructuring of schools*. Washington, DC: American Federation of Teachers.

Nias, J. (1999) Teachers' moral purposes: stress, vulnerability, and strength. In R. Vanddenberghe & A. M. Huberman (eds.) *Understanding and preventing teacher burnout: a sourcebook of international research and practice* (pp. 223–237). Cambridge: Cambridge University Press.

Noffke, S.E. & R. B. Stevenson (eds.) (1995) *Educational action research: becoming practically critical*. New York: Teachers College Press.

Ohanian, S. (1999) *One size fits few: the folly of educational standards*. Portsmouth, NH: Heinemann.

Pomson, A. (2005) One classroom at a time? Teacher isolation and community viewed through the prism of the particular. *Teachers College Record*, 107(4), 783.

Putnam, R. D. (2000) *Bowling alone: the collapse and revival of American community*. New York: Simon & Schuster.

Raywid, M. A. (1996) *Taking stock: the movement to create mini-schools, schools-within-schools, and separate small schools*. Urban Diversity Series No 108. New York: ERIC Clearinghouse on Urban Education, Teachers College, Columbia University (ED 396 045).

Reyes, P., J. D. Scribner & A. Paredes Scribner (eds.) (1999) *Lessons from high-performing Hispanic schools: creating learning communities*. New York: Teachers College Press.

Richardson-Koehler, V. (1988) Barriers to effective student teaching: a field study. *Journal of Teacher Education*, 39(2), 28–34.

Rosenholtz, S. J. (1989) *Teacher's workplace: the social organization of schools*. White Plains, NY: Longman.

Sarason, S. (1971) *The culture of the school and the problem of change*. Boston: Allyn and Bacon.

Schneider, M. (2002) *Do school facilities affect academic outcomes?* Washington, DL: National Clearinghouse for Educational Facilities.

Scribner, J. P, D. R. Hager, & T. R. Warne (2002) The paradox of professional community: tales from two high schools. *Educational Administration Quarterly*, 38(1), 45–76.

Selznick, P. (1992) *The moral commonwealth: social theory and the promise of community*. Berkeley: University of California Press.

Senge, P. M. (1990) *The fifth discipline: the art and practice of the learning organization*. New York: Doubleday.

Senge, P. M. (2000) *Schools that learn: a fifth discipline fieldbook for educators, parents, and everyone who cares about education*. New York: Doubleday.

Sergiovanni, T. J. (1994a) *Building community in schools*. San Francisco: Jossey-Bass.

Sergiovanni, T. J. (1994b, May) Organizations or communities? Changing the metaphor changes the theory. *Educational Administration Quarterly*, 30(2), 214–226.

Sharp, R., C. Moelis, & M. Robbins (2003) *Architecture for education: new school designs from the Chicago competition*. Chicago: Business and Professional People for the Public Interest.

Shepard, L.A. (1991) The influence of standardized tests on the early childhood curriculum, teachers, and children. In B. Spodek & O.N. Saracho (eds.), *Issues in early childhood education. Yearbook in early childhood education* Vol. 2 (pp. 166–189). New York: Teachers College Press.

Siskin, L. (1994) *Realms of knowledge. Academic departments in secondary schools*. Philadelphia: Falmer Press.

Shollenberger Swaim, M. & S. C. Swaim (1999) *Teacher time: why teacher workload and school management matter to each student in our public schools*. Redbud Books.

Shulman, L. S. & J. H. Shulman (2004) How and what teachers learn: a shifting perspective. *Journal of Curriculum Studies*, 36(2), 257–271.

Sizer, T. R. (1992). *Horace's school*. Boston: Houghton Mifflin.

Smith, T. M. & R. M. Ingersoll (2004) What are the effects of induction and mentoring on beginning teacher turnover? *American Educational Research Journal*, 41(3).

Smylie, M. & A. W. Hart (2000) School leadership for teacher learning and change: a human and social capital development perspective. In J. Murphy & K. S. Louis (eds.), *Handbook of research on educational administration* (pp. 421–441). San Francisco: Jossey-Bass.

Stevens, W. D. & Kahne, J. (2006) *Professional communities and instructional improvement practices: a study of small high schools in Chicago*. A Report of the Chicago High School Redesign Initiative Research Project by the Consortium on Chicago School Research at the University of Chicago.

Strike, Kenneth A. (1999) Can schools be communities? The tension between shared values and inclusion. *Educational Administration Quarterly*, 35(1), 46–70.

Strong, M. and L. St. John (2001) *A study of teacher retention: the effects of mentoring for beginning teachers*. Santa Cruz, CA: University of California, Santa Cruz.

Sykes, G. (1999) Teacher and student Learning: strengthening their connection. In Darling-Hammond, L. & G. Sykes (eds.) (1999) *Teaching as the learning profession: handbook of policy and practice* (pp. 151–179). San Francisco: Jossey-Bass.

Thiessen, D. & S. E. Anderson (1999) *Transforming learning communities: getting into the habit of Change in Ohio schools—a cross-case study of 12 transforming learning communities*. Toronto: Ontario Insititute for Studies in Education of the University of Toronto.

Uline, C. L., M. Tshannen-Moran & L. Perez (2003) Constructive conflict: how controversy can contribute to school improvement. *Teachers College Record*, 105(5), 782–816.

Vaerenne, H. (1986) Part I: Telling America. In H. Varenne (ed.), *Symbolizing America* (pp. 13–45). Lincoln: University of Nebraska Press.

Van Maanen, J. & S. Barley (1984) Occupational communities: culture and control in organizations. *Research in Organizational Behaviour*, 6, 287–365.

Vygotsky, L. S. (1978) *Mind in society*. Cambridge, MA: Harvard University Press.

Wehlage, G. G., R. Rutter, G. A. Smith, N. Lesko & R. Fernandez (1989) *Reducing the risk: schools as communities of support*. Philadelphia: Farmer.

Westheimer, J. (1998) *Among school teachers: community, autonomy, and ideology in teachers' work*. New York: Teachers College Press.

Westheimer, J. (2000) Communities and consequences: an inquiry into ideology and practice in teachers' professional work. *Educational Administration Quarterly. Special Issue: School as Community*, 35(1), 71–105.

Wiggins, P. (1993) *Assessing student performance: exploring the purpose and limits of testing*. San Francisco: Jossey-Bass.

Zeichner, K. H. (1991) Contradictions and tensions in the professionalization of teaching and the democratization of Schools. *Teachers College Record*, 92(3), 363–377.

Part 6
Artifacts

6.1 The relation of theory to practice in education[1]

John Dewey

Source: In J. Boydston (ed.), *Essays on the New Empiricism 1903–1906*: Vol. 3. *The Middle Works of John Dewey 1899–1924*. Carbondale: Southern Illinois University Press, 1904, pp. 249–272

It is difficult, if not impossible, to define the proper relationship of theory and practice without a preliminary discussion, respectively, (1) of the nature and aim of theory; (2) of practice.

A. I shall assume without argument that adequate professional instruction of teachers is not exclusively theoretical, but involves a certain amount of practical work. The primary question as to the latter is the aim with which it shall be conducted. Two controlling purposes may be entertained so different from each other as radically to alter the amount, conditions, and method of practice work. On one hand, we may carry on the practical work with the object of giving teachers in training working command of the necessary tools of their profession; control of the technique of class instruction and management; skill and proficiency in the work of teaching. With this aim in view, practice work is, as far as it goes, of the nature of apprenticeship. On the other hand, we may propose to use practice work as an instrument in making real and vital theoretical instruction; the knowledge of subject-matter and of principles of education. This is the laboratory point of view.

The contrast between the two points of view is obvious; and the two aims together give the limiting terms within which all practice work falls. From one point of view, the aim is to form and equip the actual teacher; the aim is immediately as well as ultimately practical. From the other point of view, the *immediate* aim, the way of getting at the ultimate aim, is to supply the intellectual method and material of good workmanship, instead of making on the spot, as it were, an efficient workman. Practice work thus considered is administered primarily with reference to the intellectual reactions it incites, giving the student a better hold upon the educational significance of the subject-matter he is acquiring, and of the science, philosophy, and history of education. Of course, the *results* are not exclusive. It would be very strange if practice work in doing what the laboratory does for a student of physics or chemistry in way of securing a more vital understanding of its principles, should not at the same time insure some skill in the instruction and management of a class. It would also be peculiar if the process of acquiring such skill should not also incidentally serve to enlighten and enrich instruction in subject-matter and the theory of education. None the less, there is a fundamental difference in the conception and conduct of the practice work according as one idea or the other is dominant and the other subordinate. If the primary object of practice is acquiring skill in performing the duties of a teacher, then the amount of time given to practice work, the place at which it is introduced, the method of conducting it, of supervising, criticizing, and correlating it, will differ widely from the method where the laboratory ideal prevails; and *vice versa*.

In discussing this matter, I shall try to present what I have termed the laboratory, as distinct from the apprentice idea. While I speak primarily from the standpoint of the college, I should not be frank if I did not say that I believe what I am going to say holds, *mutatis mutandis*, for the normal school as well.

I. I first adduce the example of other professional schools. I doubt whether we, as educators, keep in mind with sufficient constancy the fact that the problem of training teachers is one species of a more generic affair—that of training for professions. Our problem is akin to that of training architects, engineers, doctors, lawyers, etc. Moreover, since (shameful and incredible as it seems) the vocation of teaching is practically the last to recognize the need of specific professional preparation, there is all the more reason for teachers to try to find what they may learn from the more extensive and matured experience of other callings. If now we turn to what has happened in the history of training for other professions, we find the following marked tendencies:

1. The demand for an increased amount of scholastic attainments as a prerequisite for entering upon professional work.

2. Development of certain lines of work in the applied sciences and arts, as centres of professional work; compare, for example, the place occupied by chemistry and physiology in medical training at present, with that occupied by chairs of "practice" and of *"materia medica"* a generation ago.

3. Arrangement of the practical and quasi-professional work upon the assumption that (limits of time, etc., being taken into account) the professional school does its best for its students when it gives them typical and intensive, rather than extensive and detailed, practice. It aims, in a word, at *control of the intellectual methods* required for personal and independent mastery of practical skill, rather than at turning out at once masters of the craft. This arrangement necessarily involves considerable postponement of skill in the routine and technique of the profession, until the student, after graduation, enters upon the pursuit of his calling.

These results are all the more important to us because other professional schools mostly started from the same position which training schools for teachers have occupied. Their history shows a period in which the idea was that students ought from the start to be made as proficient as possible in practical skill. In seeking for the motive forces which have caused professional schools to travel so steadily away from this position and toward the idea that practical work should be conducted for the sake of vitalizing and illuminating *intellectual* methods two reasons may be singled out:

a) First, the limited time at the disposal of the schools, and the consequent need of economy in its employ. It is not necessary to assume that apprenticeship is of itself a bad thing. On the contrary, it may be admitted to be a good thing; but the time which a student spends in the training school is short at the best. Since short, it is an urgent matter that it be put to its most effective use; and, relatively speaking, the wise employ of this short time is in laying scientific foundations. These cannot be adequately secured when one is doing the actual work of the profession, while professional life does afford time for acquiring and perfecting skill of the more technical sort.

b) In the second place, there is inability to furnish in the school adequate conditions for the best acquiring and using of skill. As compared with actual practice, the best that the school of law or medicine can do is to provide a somewhat remote and simulated copy of the real thing. For such schools to attempt to give the skill which comes to those adequately prepared, insensibly and unavoidably in actual work, is the same sort of thing as for grammar schools to spend months upon months in trying to convey (usually quite unsuccessfully) that skill in commercial arithmetic which comes, under penalty of practical failure, in a few weeks in the bank or counting-house.

It may be said that the analogy does not hold good for teachers' training schools, because such institutions have model or practice departments, supplying conditions which are identical with those which the teacher has to meet in the actual pursuit of his calling. But this is true at most only in such normal schools as are organized after the Oswego pattern—schools, that is to say, where the pupil-teacher is given for a considerable period of time the entire charge of instruction and discipline in the class-room, and does not come under a room critic-teacher. In all other cases, some of the most fundamentally significant features of the real school are reduced or eliminated. Most "practice schools" are a compromise. In theory they approximate ordinary conditions. As matter of fact, the "best interests of the children" are so safeguarded and supervised that the situation approaches learning to swim without going *too* near the water.

There are many ways that do not strike one at first glance, for removing the conditions of "practice work" from those of actual teaching. Deprivation of responsibility for the discipline of the room; the continued presence of an expert ready to suggest, to take matters into his own hands; close supervision; reduction of size of group taught; etc., etc., are some of these ways. The topic of "lesson plans" will be later referred to in connection with another topic. Here they may be alluded to as constituting one of the modes in which the conditions of the practice-teacher are made unreal. The student who prepares a number of more or less set lessons; who then has those lesson plans criticized; who then has his actual teaching criticized from the standpoint of success in carrying out the prearranged plans, is in a totally different attitude from the teacher who has to build up and modify his teaching plans as he goes along from experience gained in contact with pupils.

It would be difficult to find two things more remote from each other than the development of subject-matter under such control as is supplied from actual teaching, taking effect through the teacher's own initiative and reflective criticism, and its development with an eye fixed upon the judgment, presumed and actual, of a superior supervisory officer. Those phases of the problem of practice teaching which relate more distinctly to responsibility for the discipline of the room, or of the class, have received considerable attention in the past; but the more delicate and far-reaching matter of intellectual responsibility is too frequently ignored. Here centers the problem of securing conditions which will make practice work a genuine apprenticeship.

II. To place the emphasis upon the securing of proficiency in teaching and discipline *puts the attention of the student-teacher in the wrong place, and tends to fix it in the wrong direction*—not wrong absolutely, but relatively as regards perspective of needs and opportunities. The would-be teacher has some time or other to face and solve two problems, each extensive and serious enough by itself to demand absorbing and undivided attention. These two problems are:

1. Mastery of subject-matter from the standpoint of its educational value and use; or, what is the same thing, the mastery of educational principles in their application to that subject-matter which is at once the material of instruction and the basis of discipline and control;

2. The mastery of the technique of class management.

This does not mean that the two problems are in any way isolated or independent. On the contrary, they are strictly correlative. *But the mind of a student cannot give equal attention to both at the same time.*

The difficulties which face a beginning teacher, who is set down for the first time before a class of from thirty to sixty children, in the responsibilities not only of instruction, but of maintaining the required order in the room as a whole, are most trying. It is almost impossible for an old teacher who has acquired the requisite skill of doing two or three distinct things simultaneously—skill to see the room as a whole while hearing one individual in one class recite, of keeping the program of the day and, yes, of the week and of the month in the fringe of consciousness while the work of the hour is in its centre—it is almost impossible for such a teacher to realize all the difficulties that confront the average beginner.

There is a technique of teaching, just as there is a technique of piano-playing. The technique, if it is to be educationally effective, is dependent upon principles. But it is possible for a student to acquire outward form of method without capacity to put it to genuinely educative use. As every teacher knows, children have an inner and an outer attention. The inner attention is the giving of the mind without reserve or qualification to the subject in hand. It is the first-hand and personal play of mental powers. As such, it is a fundamental condition of mental growth. To be able to keep track of this mental play, to recognize the signs of its presence or absence, to know how it is initiated and maintained, how to test it by results attained, and to test *apparent* results by it, is the supreme mark and criterion of a teacher. It means insight into soul-action, ability to discriminate the genuine from the sham, and capacity to further one and discourage the other.

External attention, on the other hand, is that given to the book or teacher as an independent object. It is manifested in certain conventional postures and physical attitudes rather than in the movement of thought. Children acquire great dexterity in exhibiting in conventional and expected ways the *form* of attention to school work, while reserving the inner play of their own thoughts, images, and emotions for subjects that are more important to them, but quite irrelevant.

Now, the teacher who is plunged prematurely into the pressing and practical problem of keeping order in the schoolroom has almost of necessity to make supreme the matter of external attention. The teacher has not yet had the training which affords psychological insight—which enables him to judge promptly (and therefore almost automatically) the kind and mode of subject-matter which the pupil needs at a given moment to keep his attention moving forward effectively and healthfully. He does know, however, that he must maintain order; that he must keep the attention of the pupils fixed upon his own questions, suggestions, instructions, and remarks, and upon their "lessons." The inherent tendency of the situation therefore is for him to acquire his technique in relation to the outward rather than the inner mode of attention.

III. Along with this fixation of attention upon the secondary at the expense of the primary problem, *there goes the formation of habits of work which have an empirical, rather than a scientific, sanction.* The student adjusts his actual methods of teaching, not to the principles which he is acquiring, but to what he sees succeed and fail in an empirical way from moment to moment: to what he sees other teachers doing who are more experienced and successful in keeping order than he is; and to the injunctions and directions given him by others. In this way the controlling habits of the teacher finally get fixed with comparatively little reference to principles in the psychology, logic, and history of education. In theory, these latter are dominant; in practice, the moving forces are the devices and methods which are picked up through blind experimentation; through examples which are not rationalized; through precepts which are more or less arbitrary and mechanical; through advice based upon the experience of others. Here we have the explanation, in considerable part at least, of the dualism, the unconscious duplicity, which is one of the chief evils of the teaching profession. There is an enthusiastic devotion to certain principles of lofty theory in the abstract—principles of self-activity, self-control, intellectual and moral—and there is a school practice taking little heed of the official pedagogic creed. Theory and practice do not grow together out of and into the teacher's personal experience.

Ultimately there are two bases upon which the habits of a teacher as a teacher may be built up. They may be formed under the inspiration and constant criticism of intelligence, applying the best that is available. This is possible only where the would-be teacher has become fairly saturated with his subject-matter, and with his psychological and ethical philosophy of education. Only when such things have become incorporated in mental habit, have become part of the working tendencies of observation, insight, and reflection, will these principles work automatically, unconsciously, and hence promptly and effectively. And this means that practical work should be pursued primarily with reference to its reaction upon the professional pupil in making him a thoughtful and alert student of education, rather than to help him get immediate proficiency.

For immediate skill may be got at the cost of power to go on growing. The teacher who leaves the professional school with power in managing a class of children may appear to superior advantage the first day, the first week, the first month, or even the first year, as compared with some other teacher who has a much more vital command of the psychology, logic, and ethics of development. But later "progress" may with such consist only in perfecting and refining skill already possessed. Such persons seem to know how to teach, but they are not students of teaching. Even though they go on studying books of pedagogy, reading teachers' journals, attending teachers' institutes, etc., yet the root of the matter is not in them, unless they continue to be students of subject-matter, and students of mind-activity. Unless a teacher is such a student, he may continue to improve in the mechanics of school management, but he can not grow as a teacher, an inspirer and director of soul-life. How often do candid instructors in training schools for teachers acknowledge disappointment in the later career of even their more promising candidates? They seem to strike twelve at the start. There is an unexpected and seemingly unaccountable failure to maintain steady growth. Is this in some part due to the undue premature stress laid in early practice work upon securing immediate capability in teaching?

I might go on to mention other evils which seem to me to be more or less the effect of this same cause. Among them are the lack of intellectual independence among teachers, their tendency to intellectual subserviency. The "model lesson" of the teachers' institute and of the educational journal is a monument, on the one hand, of the eagerness of those in authority to secure immediate practical results at any cost; and, upon the other, of the willingness of our teaching corps to accept without inquiry or criticism any method or device which seems to promise good results. Teachers, actual and intending, flock to those persons who give them clear-cut and definite instructions as to just how to teach this or that.

The tendency of educational development to proceed by reaction from one thing to another, to adopt for one year, or for a term of seven years, this or that new study or method of teaching, and then as abruptly to swing over to some new educational gospel, is a result which would be impossible if teachers were adequately moved by their own independent intelligence. The willingness of teachers, especially of those occupying administrative positions, to become submerged in the routine detail of their callings, to expend the bulk of their energy upon forms and rules and regulations, and reports and percentages, is another evidence of the absence of intellectual vitality. If teachers were possessed by the spirit of an abiding student of education, this spirit would find some way of breaking through the mesh and coil of circumstance and would find expression for itself.

B. Let us turn from the practical side to the theoretical. What must be the aim and spirit of theory in order that practice work may really serve the purpose of an educational laboratory? We are met here with the belief that instruction in theory is merely theoretical, abstruse, remote, and therefore relatively useless to the teacher as a teacher, unless the student is at once set upon the work of teaching; that only "practice" can give a motive to a professional learning, and supply material for educational courses. It is not infrequently claimed (or at least unconsciously assumed) that students will not have a professional stimulus for their work in subject-matter and in educational psychology and history, will not have any outlook upon their relation to education, unless these things are immediately and simultaneously reinforced by setting the student upon the work of teaching. But is this the case? Or are there practical elements and bearings already contained in theoretical instruction of the proper sort?

I. Since it is impossible to cover in this paper all phases of the philosophy and science of education, I shall speak from the standpoint of psychology, believing that this may be taken as typical of the whole range of instruction in educational theory as such.

In the first place, beginning students have without any reference to immediate teaching a very large capital of an exceedingly practical sort in their own experience. The argument that theoretical instruction is merely abstract and in the air unless students are set at once to test and illustrate it by practice teaching of their own, *overlooks the continuity of the class-room mental activity with that of other normal experience.* It ignores the tremendous importance for educational purposes of this continuity. Those who employ this argument seem to isolate the psychology of learning that goes on in the schoolroom from the psychology of learning found elsewhere.

This isolation is both unnecessary and harmful. It is unnecessary, tending to futility, because it throws away or makes light of the greatest asset in the student's possession—the greatest, moreover, that ever will be in his possession—his own direct and personal experience. There is every presumption (since the student is not an imbecile) that he has been learning all the days of his life, and that he is still learning from day to day. He must accordingly have in his own experience plenty of practical material by which to illustrate and vitalize theoretical principles and laws of mental growth in the process of learning. Moreover, since none of us is brought up under ideal conditions, each beginning student has plenty of practical experience by which to illustrate cases of arrested development—instances of failure and maladaptation and retrogression, or even degeneration. The material at hand is pathological as well as healthy. It serves to embody and illustrate both achievement and failure, in the problem of learning.

But it is more than a serious mistake (violating the principle of proceeding from the known to the unknown) to fail to take account of this body of practical experience. Such ignoring tends also to perpetuate some of the greatest evils of current school methods. Just because the student's attention is not brought to the point of recognizing that *his own* past and present growth is proceeding in accordance with the very laws that control growth in the school, and that there is no psychology of the schoolroom different from that of the nursery, the playground, the street, and the parlor, he comes unconsciously to assume that education in the class-room is a sort of unique thing, having its own laws.[2] Unconsciously, but none the less surely, the student comes to believe in certain "methods" of learning, and hence of teaching which are somehow especially appropriate to the school—which somehow have their particular residence and application there. Hence he comes to believe in the potency for schoolroom purposes of materials, methods, and devices which it never occurs to him to trust to in his experience outside of school.

I know a teacher of teachers who is accustomed to say that when she fails to make clear to a class of teachers some point relative to children, she asks these teachers to stop thinking of their own pupils and to think of some nephew, niece, cousin, some child of whom they have acquaintance in the unformalities of home life. I do not suppose any great argument is needed to prove that breach of continuity between learning within and without the school is the great cause in education of wasted power and misdirected effort.

I wish rather to take advantage of this assumption (which I think will be generally accepted) to emphasize the danger of bringing the would-be teacher into an abrupt and dislocated contact with the psychology of the schoolroom—abrupt and dislocated because not prepared for by prior practice in selecting and organizing the relevant principles and data contained within the experience best known to him, his own.[3]

From this basis, a transition to educational psychology may be made in observation of the teaching of others—visiting classes. I should wish to note here, however, the same principle that I have mentioned as regards practice work, specifically so termed. The first observation of instruction given by model- or critic-teachers should not be too definitely practical in aim. The student should not be observing to find out how the good teacher does it, in order to accumulate a store of methods by which he also may teach successfully. He should rather observe with reference to seeing the interaction of mind, to see how teacher and pupils react upon each other—how mind answers to mind. Observation should at first be conducted from the psychological rather than from the "practical" standpoint. If the latter is emphasized before the student has an independent command of the former, the principle of imitation is almost sure to play an exaggerated part in the observer's future teaching, and hence at the expense of personal insight and initiative. What the student needs most at this stage of growth is ability to see what is going on in the minds of a group of persons who are in intellectual contact with one another. He needs to learn to observe psychologically—a very different thing from simply observing how a teacher gets "good results" in presenting any particular subject.

It should go without saying that the student who has acquired power in psychological observation and interpretation may finally go on to observe more technical aspects of instruction, namely, the various methods and instrumentalities used by a good teacher in giving instruction in any subject. If properly prepared for, this need not tend to produce copiers, followers of tradition and example. Such students will be able to translate the practical devices which are such an important part of the equipment of a good teacher over into their psychological equivalents; to know not merely as a matter of brute fact that they do work, but to know how and why they work. Thus he will be an independent judge and critic of their proper use and adaptation.

In the foregoing I have assumed that educational psychology is marked off from general psychology simply by the emphasis which it puts upon two factors. The first is the stress laid upon a certain end, namely, growth or development—with its counterparts, arrest and adaptation. The second is the importance attached to the social factor—to the mutual interaction of different minds with each other. It is, I think, strictly true that no educational procedure nor pedagogical maxim can be derived directly from pure psychological data. The psychological data taken without qualification (which is what I mean by their being pure) cover everything and anything that may take place in a mind. Mental arrest and decay occur according to psychological laws, just as surely as do development and progress.

We do not make practical maxims out of physics by telling persons to move according to laws of gravitation. If people move at all, they *must* move in accordance with the conditions stated by this law. Similarly, if mental operations take place at all, they *must* take place in accordance with the principles stated in correct psychological generalizations. It is superfluous and meaningless to attempt to turn these psychological principles directly into rules of teaching. But the person who knows the laws of mechanics knows the conditions of which he must take account when he wishes to reach a certain end. He knows that *if* he aims to build a bridge, he must build it in a certain way and of certain materials, or else he will not have a bridge, but a heap of rubbish. So in psychology. Given an end, say promotion of healthy growth, psychological observations and reflection put us in control of the conditions concerned in that growth. We know that if we are to get that *end*, we must do it in a certain way. It is the subordination of the psychological material to the problem of effecting growth and avoiding arrest and waste which constitutes a distinguishing mark of educational psychology.

I have spoken of the importance of the social factor as the other mark. I do not mean, of course, that general theoretical psychology ignores the existence and significance of the reaction of mind to mind—though it would be within bounds to say that till recently the social side was an unwritten chapter of psychology. I mean that considerations of the ways in which one mind responds to the stimuli which another mind is consciously or unconsciously furnishing possess a relative importance for the educator which they have not for the psychologist as such. From the teacher's standpoint, it is not too much to say that every habit which a pupil exhibits is to be regarded as a reaction to stimuli which some persons or group of persons have presented to the child. It is not too much to say that the most important thing for the teacher to consider, as regards his present relations to his pupils, is the attitudes and habits which his own modes of being, saying, and doing are fostering or discouraging in them.

Now, if these two assumptions regarding educational psychology be granted, I think it will follow as a matter of course, that only by beginning with the values and laws contained in the student's own experience of his own mental growth, and by proceeding gradually to facts connected with other persons of whom he can know little; and by proceeding still more gradually to the attempt actually to influence the mental operations of others, can educational theory be made most effective. Only in this way can the most essential trait of the mental habit of the teacher be secured—that habit which looks upon the internal, not upon the external; which sees that the important function of the teacher is direction of the mental movement of the student, and that the mental movement must be known before it can be directed.

II. I turn now to the side of subject-matter, or scholarship, with the hope of showing that here too the material, when properly presented, is not so *merely* theoretical, remote from the practical problems of teaching, as is sometimes supposed. I recall that once a graduate student in a university made inquiries among all the leading teachers in the institution with which he was connected as to whether they had received any professional training, whether they had taken courses in pedagogy. The inquirer threw the results, which were mostly negative, into the camp of the local pedagogical club. Some may say that this proves nothing, because college teaching is proverbially poor, considered simply as teaching. Yet no one can deny that there is *some* good teaching, and some teaching of the very first order, done in colleges, and done by persons who have never had any instruction in either the theory or the practice of teaching.

This fact cannot be ignored any more than can the fact that there were good teachers before there was any such thing as pedagogy. Now, I am not arguing for not having pedagogical training—that is the last thing I want. But I claim the facts mentioned prove that scholarship *per se* may itself be a most effective tool for training and turning out good teachers. If it has accomplished so much when working unconsciously and without set intention, have we not good reason to believe that, when acquired in a training school for teachers—with the end of making teachers held definitely in view and with conscious reference to its relation to mental activity—it may prove a much more valuable pedagogical asset than we commonly consider it?

Scholastic knowledge is sometimes regarded as if it were something quite irrelevant to method. When this attitude is even unconsciously assumed, method becomes an external attachment to knowledge of subject-matter. It has to be elaborated and acquired in relative independence from subject-matter, and *then* applied.

Now the body of knowledge which constitutes the subject-matter of the student-teacher must, by the nature of the case, be organized subject-matter. It is not a miscellaneous heap of separate scraps. Even if (as in the case of history and literature), it be not technically termed "science," it is none the less material which has been subjected to method—has been selected and arranged with reference to controlling intellectual principles. There is, therefore, method in subject-matter itself—method indeed of the highest order which the human mind has yet evolved, scientific method.

It cannot be too strongly emphasized that this scientific method is the method of mind itself.[4] The classifications, interpretations, explanations, and generalizations which make subject-matter a branch of study do not lie externally in facts apart from mind. They reflect the attitudes and workings of mind in its endeavor to bring raw material of experience to a point where it at once satisfies and stimulates the needs of active thought. Such being the case, there is something wrong in the "academic" side of professional training, if by means of it the student does not constantly get object-lessons of the finest type in the kind of mental activity which characterizes mental growth and, hence, the educative process. It is necessary to recognize the importance for the teacher's equipment of his own habituation to superior types of method of mental operation. The more a teacher in the future is likely to have to do with elementary teaching, the more, rather than the less, necessary is such exercise. Otherwise, the current traditions of elementary work with their tendency to talk and write down to the supposed intellectual level of children, will be likely to continue. Only a teacher thoroughly trained in the higher levels of intellectual method and who thus has constantly in his own mind a sense of what adequate and genuine intellectual activity means, will be likely, in deed, not in mere word, to respect the mental integrity and force of children.

Of course, this conception will be met by the argument that the scientific organization of subject-matter, which constitutes the academic studies of the student-teacher is upon such a radically different basis from that adapted to less mature students that too much preoccupation with scholarship of an advanced order is likely actually to get in the way of the teacher of children and youth. I do not suppose anybody would contend that teachers really can know more than is good for them, but it may reasonably be argued that continuous study of a specialized sort forms mental habits likely to throw the older student out of sympathy with the type of mental impulses and habits which are found in younger persons.

Right here, however, I think normal schools and teachers' colleges have one of their greatest opportunities—an opportunity not merely as to teachers in training, but also for reforming methods of education in colleges and higher schools having nothing to do with the training of teachers. It is the business of normal schools and collegiate schools of education to present subject-matter in science, in language, in literature and the arts, in such a way that the student both sees and feels that these studies *are* significant embodiments of mental operations. He should be led to realize that they are not products of technical methods, which have been developed for the sake of the specialized branches of knowledge in which they are used, but represent fundamental mental attitudes and operations—that, indeed, particular scientific methods and classifications simply express and illustrate in their most concrete form that of which simple and common modes of thought-activity are capable when they work under satisfactory conditions.

In a word, it is the business of the "academic" instruction of future teachers to carry back subject-matter to its common psychical roots.[5] In so far as this is accomplished, the gap between the higher and the lower treatment of subject-matter, upon which the argument of the supposed objector depends, ceases to have the force which that argument assigns to it. This does not mean, of course, that exactly the same subject-matter, in the same mode of presentation, is suitable to a student in the elementary or high schools that is appropriate to the normal student. But it does mean that a mind which is habituated to viewing subject-matter from the standpoint of the function of that subject-matter in connection with *mental* responses, attitudes, and methods will be sensitive to *signs of intellectual activity* when exhibited in the child of four, or the youth of sixteen, and will be trained to a spontaneous and unconscious appreciation of the subject-matter which is fit to call out and direct mental activity.

We have here, I think, the explanation of the success of some teachers who violate every law known to and laid down by pedagogical science. They are themselves so full of the spirit of inquiry, so sensitive to every sign of its presence and absence, that no matter what they do, nor how they do it, they succeed in awakening and inspiring like alert and intense mental activity in those with whom they come in contact.

This is not a plea for the prevalence of these irregular, inchoate methods. But I feel that I may recur to my former remark: if some teachers, by sheer plentitude of knowledge, keep by instinct in touch with the mental activity of their pupils, and accomplish so much without, and even in spite of, principles which are theoretically sound, then there must be in this same scholarship a tremendous resource when it is more consciously used—that is, employed in clear connection with psychological principles.

When I said above that schools for training teachers have here an opportunity to react favorably upon general education, I meant that no instruction in subject-matter (wherever it is given) is adequate if it leaves the student with just acquisition of certain information about external facts and laws, or even a certain facility in the intellectual manipulation of this material. It is the business of our higher schools in all lines, and not simply of our normal schools, to furnish the student with the realization that, after all, it is the human mind, trained to effective control of its natural attitudes, impulses, and responses, that is the significant thing in all science and history and art so far as these are formulated for purposes of study.

The present divorce between scholarship and method is as harmful upon one side as upon the other—as detrimental to the best interests of higher academic instruction as it is to the training of teachers. But the only way in which this divorce can be broken down is by so presenting all subject-matter, for whatever ultimate, practical, or professional purpose, that it shall be apprehended as an objective embodiment of methods of mind in its search for, and transactions with, the truth of things.

Upon the more practical side, this principle requires that, so far as students appropriate new subject-matter (thereby improving their own scholarship and realizing more consciously the nature of method), they should finally proceed to organize this same subject-matter with reference to its use in teaching others. The curriculum of the elementary and the high school constituting the "practice" or "model" school ought to stand in the closest and most organic relation to the instruction in subject-matter which is given by the teachers of the professional school. If in any given school this is not the case, it is either because in the *training class* subject-matter is presented in an isolated way, instead of as a concrete expression of methods of mind, or else because the *practice school* is dominated by certain conventions and traditions regarding material and the methods of teaching it, and hence is not engaged in work of an adequate educational type.

As a matter of fact, as everybody knows, both of these causes contribute to the present state of things. On the one hand, inherited conditions impel the elementary school to a certain triviality and poverty of subject-matter, calling for mechanical drill, rather than for thought-activity, and the high school to a certain technical mastery of certain conventional culture subjects, taught as independent branches of the same tree of knowledge! On the other hand traditions of the different branches of science (the academic side of subject-matter) tend to subordinate the teaching in the normal school to the attainment of certain facilities, and the acquirement of certain information, both in greater or less isolation from their value as exciting and directing mental power.

The great need is convergence, concentration. Every step taken in the elementary and the high school toward intelligent introduction of more worthy and significant subject-matter, one requiring consequently for its assimilation thinking rather than "drill," must be met by a like advance step in which the mere isolated specialization of collegiate subject-matter is surrendered, and in which there is brought to conscious and interested attention its significance in expression of fundamental modes of mental activity—so fundamental as to be common to both the play of the mind upon the ordinary material of everyday experience and to the systematized material of the sciences.

III. As already suggested, this point requires that training students be exercised in making the connections between the course of study of the practice or model school, and the wider horizons of learning coming within their ken. But it is consecutive and systematic exercise in the consideration of the subject-matter of the elementary and high schools that is needed. The habit of making isolated and independent lesson plans for a few days' or weeks' instruction in a separate grade here or there not only does not answer this purpose, but is likely to be distinctly detrimental. Everything should be discouraged which tends to put the student in the attitude of snatching at the subject-matter which he is acquiring in order to see if by some hook or crook it may be made immediately available for a lesson in this or that grade. What is needed is the habit of viewing the entire curriculum as a continuous growth, reflecting the growth of mind itself. This in turn demands, so far as I can see, consecutive and longitudinal consideration of the curriculum of the elementary and high school rather than a cross-sectional view of it. The student should be led to see that the same subject-matter in geography, nature-study, or art develops not merely day to day in a given grade, but from year to year throughout the entire movement of the school; and he should realize this before he gets much encouragement in trying to adapt subject-matter in lesson plans for this or that isolated grade.

C. If we attempt to gather together the points which have been brought out, we should have a view of practice work something like the following—though I am afraid even this formulates a scheme with more appearance of rigidity than is desirable:

At first, the practice school would be used mainly for purposes of observation. This observation, moreover, would not be for the sake of seeing how good teachers teach, or for getting "points" which may be employed in one's own teaching, but to get material for psychological observation and reflection, and some conception of the educational movement of the school as a whole.

Secondly, there would then be more intimate introduction to the lives of the children and the work of the school through the use as assistants of such students as had already got psychological insight and a good working acquaintance with educational problems. Students at this stage would not undertake much direct teaching, but would make themselves useful in helping the regular class instructor. There are multitudes of ways in which such help can be given and be of real help—that is, of use to the school, to the children, and not merely of putative value to the training student.[6] Special attention to backward children, to children who have been out of school, assisting in the care of material, in forms of hand-work, suggest some of the avenues of approach.

This kind of practical experience enables, in the third place, the future teacher to make the transition from his more psychological and theoretical insight to the observation of the more technical points of class teaching and management. The informality, gradualness, and familiarity of the earlier contact tend to store the mind with material which is unconsciously assimilated and organized, and thus supplies a background for work involving greater responsibility.

As a counterpart of this work in assisting, such students might well at the same time be employed in the selection and arrangement of subject-matter, as indicated in the previous discussion. Such organization would at the outset have reference to at least a group of grades, emphasizing continuous and consecutive growth. Later it might, without danger of undue narrowness, concern itself with finding supplementary materials and problems bearing upon the work in which the student is giving assistance; might elaborate material which could be used to carry the work still farther, if it were desirable; or, in case of the more advanced students, to build up a scheme of possible alternative subjects for lessons and studies.

Fourthly, as fast as students are prepared through their work of assisting for more responsible work, they could be given actual teaching to do. Upon the basis that the previous preparation has been adequate in subject-matter, in educational theory, and in the kind of observation and practice already discussed, such practice-teachers should be given the maximum amount of liberty possible. They should not be too closely supervised, nor too minutely and immediately criticised upon either the matter or the method of their teaching. Students should be given to understand that they not only are *permitted* to act upon their own intellectual initiative, but that they are *expected* to do so, and that their ability to take hold of situations for themselves would be a more important factor in judging them than their following any particular set method or scheme.

Of course, there should be critical discussion with persons more expert of the work done, and of the educational results obtained. But sufficient time should be permitted to allow the practice-teacher to recover from the shocks incident to the newness of the situation, and also to get enough experience to make him capable of seeing the *fundamental* bearings of criticism upon work done. Moreover, the work of the expert or supervisor should be directed to getting the student to judge his own work critically, to find out for himself in what respects he has succeeded and in what failed, and to find the probable reasons for both failure and success, rather than to criticising him too definitely and specifically upon special features of his work.

It ought to go without saying (unfortunately, it does not in all cases) that criticism should be directed to making the professional student thoughtful about his work in the light of principles, rather than to induce in him a recognition that certain special methods are good, and certain other special methods bad. At all events, no greater travesty of real intellectual criticism can be given than to set a student to teaching a brief number of lessons, have him under inspection in practically all the time of every lesson, and then criticise him almost, if not quite, at the very end of each lesson, upon the particular way in which that particular lesson has been taught, pointing out elements of failure and of success. Such methods of criticism may be adapted to giving a training-teacher command of some of the knacks and tools of the trade, but are not calculated to develop a thoughtful and independent teacher.

Moreover, while such teaching (as already indicated) should be extensive or continuous enough to give the student time to become at home and to get a body of funded experience, it ought to be intensive in purpose rather than spread out miscellaneously. It is much more important for the teacher to assume responsibility for the consecutive development of some one topic, to get a feeling for the movement of that subject, than it is to teach a certain number (necessarily smaller in range) of lessons in a larger number of subjects. What we want, in other words, is not so much technical skill, as a realizing sense in the teacher of what the educational development of a subject means, and, in some typical case, command of a method of control, which will then serve as a standard for self-judgment in other cases.

Fifthly, if the practical conditions permit—if, that is to say, the time of the training course is sufficiently long, if the practice schools are sufficiently large to furnish the required number of children, and to afford actual demand for the work to be done—students who have gone through the stages already referred to should be ready for work of the distinctly apprenticeship type.

Nothing that I have said heretofore is to be understood as ruling out practice teaching which is designed to give an individual mastery of the actual technique of teaching and management, provided school conditions permit it in reality and not merely in external form—provided, that is, the student has gone through a training in educational theory and history, in subject-matter, in observation, and in practice work of the laboratory type, before entering upon the latter. The teacher must acquire his technique some time or other; and if conditions are favorable, there are some advantages in having this acquisition take place in cadetting or in something of that kind. By means of this probation, persons who are unfit for teaching may be detected and eliminated more quickly than might otherwise be the case and before their cases have become institutionalized.

Even in this distinctly apprenticeship stage, however, it is still important that the student should be given as much responsibility and initiative as he is capable of taking, and hence that supervision should not be too unremitting and intimate, and criticism not at too short range or too detailed. The advantage of this intermediate probationary period does not reside in the fact that thereby supervisory officers may turn out teachers who will perpetuate their own notions and methods, but in the inspiration and enlightenment that come through prolonged contact with mature and sympathetic persons. If the conditions in the public schools were just what they ought to be, if all superintendents and principals had the knowledge and the wisdom which they should have, and if they had time and opportunity to utilize their knowledge and their wisdom in connection with the development of the younger teachers who come to them, the value of this apprenticeship period would be reduced, I think, very largely to its serving to catch in time and to exclude persons unfitted for teaching.

In conclusion, I may say that I do not believe that the principles presented in this paper call for anything utopian. The present movement in normal schools for improvement of range and quality of subject-matter is steady and irresistible. All the better classes of normal schools are already, in effect, what are termed "junior colleges." That is, they give two years' work which is almost, and in many cases quite, of regular college grade. More and more, their instructors are persons who have had the same kind of scholarly training that is expected of teachers in colleges. Many of these institutions are already of higher grade than this; and the next decade will certainly see a marked tendency on the part of many normal schools to claim the right to give regular collegiate bachelor degrees.

The type of scholarship contemplated in this paper is thus practically assured for the near future. If two other factors cooperate with this, there is no reason why the conception of relation of theory and practice here presented should not be carried out. The second necessary factor is that the elementary and high schools, which serve as schools of observation and practice, should represent an advanced type of education properly corresponding to the instruction in academic subject-matter and in educational theory given to the training classes. The third necessity is that work in psychology and educational theory make concrete and vital the connection between the normal instruction in subject-matter and the work of the elementary and high schools.

If it should prove impracticable to realize the conception herein set forth, it will not be, I think, because of any impossibility resident in the outward conditions, but because those in authority, both within and without the schools, believe that the true function of training schools is just to meet the needs of which people are already conscious. In this case, of course, training schools will be conducted simply with reference to perpetuating current types of educational practice, with simply incidental improvement in details. The underlying assumption of this paper is, accordingly, that training schools for teachers do not perform their full duty in accepting and conforming to present educational standards, but that educational leadership is an indispensable part of their office. The thing needful is improvement of education, not simply by turning out teachers who can do better the things that are now necessary to do, but rather by changing the conception of what constitutes education.

NOTES

* First published in Third Yearbook of the National Society for the Scientific Study of Education, 1904, Part I, pp. 9–30.

1 This paper is to be taken as representing the views of the writer, rather than those of any particular institution in an official way; for the writer thought it better to discuss certain principles that seem to him fundamental, rather than to define a system of procedure.

2 There is where the plea for "adult" psychology has force. The person who does not know himself is not likely to know others. The adult psychology ought, however, to be just as genetic as that of childhood.

3 It may avoid misapprehension if I repeat the word *experience*. It is not a *metaphysical* introspection that I have in mind, but the process of turning back upon one's own experiences, and turning them over to see how they were developed, what helped and hindered, the stimuli and the inhibitions both within and without the organism.

4 Professor Ella F. Young's *Scientific Method in Education* (University of Chicago Decennial Publications) is a noteworthy development of this conception, to which I am much indebted.

5 It is hardly necessary to refer to Dr. Harris's continued contention that normal training should give a higher view or synthesis of even the most elementary subjects.

6 This question of some real need in the practice school itself for the work done is very important in its moral influence and in assimilating the conditions of "practice work" to those of real teaching.

6.2 Growth of teachers in professional maturity

Lucy Sprague Mitchell

Source: Lucy Sprague Mitchell, *Our Children and Our Schools*.
New York: Simon and Schuster, 1950, pp. 323–338

An old professor once said that the proof of the pudding is not in the eating but comes several hours later. This holds true of more things than puddings! The results of an educational experiment such as the Bank Street Workshops do not show until several years later. It takes time to do what we were attempting—to explore what experiences, approaches, and techniques in an inservice situation are best adapted to further teachers' growth toward professional maturity. Both we and the teachers had to learn on the job. Growth is a slow process. One cannot expect quick results. In the second place, when one is immersed in the daily exigencies and details of a job, one cannot get far enough away from them to see things that are happening slowly. If one does not see a child for a number of years, one is actually startled at his growth—far more his parents, who have seen him daily. So is it with a long-term experiment. It is only later when one can study the day-by-day records with a detached attitude that one can get a total picture. That is the reason for keeping records—to have something more reliable than memory as a basis for an analysis. When records of several years are put together they form a kind of moving picture of what has happened.

In Part II we told the story of our Workshops largely as that of technicians. There we made a report based on the day-to-day records of what happened in six years. In such a report one can hardly see the forest for the trees. Now, in Part III, we shall turn from detailed reporting to analysis, from what the Workshops did to what we and the teachers learned through the doing.

We begin with an analysis of the growth of the teachers in understanding and enjoyment of their new job, which, as has been repeatedly said, was the central aim of out Workshop experiment. Throughout the experiment we measured the success or failure of our Workshop techniques in terms of their contribution to the teachers' professional growth. We shall go back to the initial attitudes of the teachers toward their job and what they wanted from the Workshop and analyze what kinds of situations hinder or aid the growth of teachers, and the stages of growth by which teachers progress toward professional maturity. This will take us rapidly over some of the same ground covered in Part II, since our analysis is necessarily based on the record of what happened in the Workshops.

INITIAL ATTITUDES TOWARD THEIR JOB AND WORKSHOP

Obviously, teachers cannot be lumped together as people with similar characteristics and personalities or attitudes toward life any more than can parents or miners or cooks or lawyers. What any of these groups have in common is not personality characteristics but a kind of work. When we come to analyze the growth of teachers we shall concentrate on professional thinking and attitudes and largely ignore the wide variations in personality, background, interests, and prejudices which they bring to the teaching job, though all these factors affect their professional growth. If we find a group of highly diversified personalities holding similar attitudes toward their work, we shall examine the conditions under which this work is carried on and ask how far these conditions explain the attitudes common to the group.

So we begin by recalling the initial attitudes of the Workshop teachers toward their job as shown by what they wanted from a Workshop. The situation in the New York schools when we began our Workshop was typical, we think, of the situations prevailing in many, perhaps most, of our schools throughout the country. The thinking and attitudes about children and curriculum to be planned for them were in a state of transition. The "new curriculum" embodying the new thinking and attitudes had been given to the teachers but in practice had not genuinely super-seded the old curriculum. In varying degrees the teachers clung to the familiar old curriculum (which to them meant largely subject matter) which had been set up over twenty years before under twenty or more separate courses of study. Within this old framework they were trying conscientiously to carry out the newer methods of teaching which, for a number of years, they had been instructed to use. A common complaint of the teachers was that, though they were willing to follow the new curriculum, they were handicapped by the conditions under which they worked—large classes, lack of space in the classrooms, old equipment, etc. They devoted "periods" to activity programs, units, trips, research, conferences, and "show and tell periods" in which children "expressed themselves," but for the most part these periods were thought of as extras, as episodes which interrupted the *real* work, "the desirable information" contained in the old syllabus.

Many teachers still depended largely upon the traditional source of "desirable information"—that is, textbooks which contained facts to be memorized. They were not tied to a single textbook as they were in the early traditional schools; but most of the added books were still heavily weighted with factual information—a variety of textbooks, encyclopedias, etc. For the most part, "research" meant reading one of these books. There was little use of genuine source material for research—pictures, maps, written materials which children were called upon to interpret, which challenged them to think out relationships for themselves. Few teachers thought of the function-ing world outside of the classrooms, the world in which their children lived, as a laboratory where children could have firsthand experiences, carry on investigations on a young level under teacher guidance, which would start new interests and give meaning to factual information contained in books.

The teachers had also been given instructions in regard to their attitude toward children and methods of "handling" them. Here, the teachers conscientiously tried to follow out these instruc-tions. In order to let the children freely express themselves in conferences, many teachers simply handed over the situation to the children and stepped out of any participation in or responsibility for these "free" periods. The children were both young and inexperienced in handling such responsibility. Without teacher guidance, they got nowhere and the listening children were simply bored. In subtler ways the new instructions concerning the "atmosphere" of classrooms brought difficulties to many teachers, In an attempt to let children be "free," they relaxed the old repressive kind of discipline before building up self-discipline within group or an individual child. They confused freedom with license, with disastrous results for both themselves and the children.

In this situation the teachers were practically unanimous in what they wanted from a Workshop. They wanted to be shown *how* to conduct the new teaching techniques they had been instructed to use, not *why*. Their primary interest was not to understand educational and psychological basis of the new curriculum better. They stated emphatically that they wanted "no theory" from us- that they had had enough theoretical talk. They wanted "practical help" in carrying out instruc-tions. These teachers obviously felt insecure as technicians in their "new job." This was only natural in this transition stage from old to new curriculum and was typical of teachers wherever school systems were trying to introduce new thinking and attitudes. For, broadly speaking, the experienced teachers nearly everywhere have been trained with major emphasis on subject methodology and have taught under a system which has upheld this traditional approach. These experienced teachers—who had self-confidence when officially supported by courses of study which gave detailed content to be covered in each term, by textbooks with recitation, by disciplinary punishment, gold star rewards—lost their self-confidence when their instructions became less rigid and less detailed. They attempted conscientiously to carry out whatever new instructions were given to them in the way of new techniques-units, trips, conferences, research, children committees, etc. But as a whole, these teachers felt little responsibility for studying their children and for planning experiences for them on the basis of such study. In some schools the teachers were told to be experimental, but few of them were or wanted to be.

In brief, the teachers' initial attitude toward their job was to follow instructions, to put new teaching techniques into practice without much responsibility for understanding the psychological and educational thinking that lay behind these techniques. What had brought about this attitude toward their job? It is important to try to answer this question. For such an attitude toward their job must profoundly affect the growth toward professional maturity of teachers everywhere who have a similar attitude. It is important to know whether psychological conditions under which the teachers carried on their job might explain the common attitude toward their job of a group of highly diversified personalities.

PSYCHOLOGICAL EFFECT OF ADMINISTRATIVE SYSTEM UPON TEACHERS' ATTITUDES

In telling the story of the development of our public school Workshops in Part II, we described the stage set of that six-year experiment with one important omission-the psychological effect upon teachers of the vast administrative system under which they worked and in which most of them had had all their teaching experience. A large proportion of the teachers of our country's children work under somewhat similar systems. So it seems well to attempt some analysis of the nature of administrative systems and how such systems psychologically condition the attitude of teachers toward their job and consequently their growth toward understanding and enjoyment in their new job.

A big school system is organized as an administrative hierarchy with responsibilities for decisions (which means instructions given or permission granted) belonging to a graded series of officials. At the top is the Superintendent of Schools; at the bottom are the teachers, whose job is directly with children, for whom the whole system has come into being. Each successive step up the graded responsibilities is one more step removed from children. A good principal knows the children in his school, but not in the intimate way the teachers do. He deals more with teachers than with children. A good district superintendent knows the children and the teachers in his district only as he sees them in occasional visits to the classrooms. He deals more with principals than with teachers and more with teachers than with children. Step by step up the administrative ladder, officials acquire wider and wider responsibilities and power and become more separated from children and their teachers. And promotion up the rungs of the ladder means increase in salary, which inevitably enhances the higher positions and stimulates the desire for promotion. Such is the nature of this hierarchical type of organization, whether in a school system, a government, an army, or anywhere else.

What psychological effect has this type of administrative organization upon the members who compose it? Since wider power and higher salary depend upon promotion to the next rung of the ladder, it tends to turn the eyes of the members at each level upwards to the occupants on the upper levels, to make them look to their immediate "superior" for instructions, to seek the superior's approval—all of which tends to mean following out *his* instructions, *his* thinking and planning, rather than concentrating their thinking and planning upon the responsibilities at their own level and acting according to their own judgments based upon their own experiences. At its worst, an administrative hierarchy can draw the attention and energies of an ambitious member at any level away from developing his immediate job, and make him an authoritarian in respect to those on the level below him, perhaps to offset the power exercised over him by his immediate superior. An ambitious teacher who is at the lowest level of administrative authority may have his eyes drawn from children to promotion; he, too, may become an authoritarian in his classroom to offset emotionally the power the principal has over him. How to conduct the complicated machinery of a vast school system without the evils of minimizing the importance of the job at each level and without breeding the authoritarian attitude is one of the major problems of public education.

At its best, any administrative ladder has to some extent a psychological effect upon all teachers-not merely upon the comparatively few who are more interested in their own promotion than anything else. The very nature of graded responsibilities (leaving out the salary aspect) is to make teachers who are on the lowest level look to their immediate superior, the principal, for instructions and to conceive of their job as following out his instructions and the instructions issued by those faraway supreme powers, the Board of Education and the Board of Super-intendents. Their whole experience within the administrative setup of a big school system has been away from their taking the responsibility for planning individually for their particular children, away from experimentation and initiative in their classrooms, away from trusting their own judg-ments based on their own experiences, away from taking part or even following educational efforts which do not affect them personally—in short, away from *taking their teaching job as a profession*. It is an anomaly inherent in this form of administration that the teachers, who are on the lowest level both in responsibility for educational decisions and in salary, are the ones who really control the school lives of the children for whom, presumably, the whole towering system has been erected. It was striking that, as the teachers relaxed in the informal atmosphere of the Workshop, they again and again expressed their sense of this anomaly. They posed this question as one of their greatest problems—How could they take responsibilities for educational thinking within their classrooms though they still remained on the lowest level as far as general decisions for educational thinking in the system ate concerned?

It may be that all of this is but a reflection of the total society in which our public school system evolved—a time when the hierarchical ladder prevailed in business, in family, in social organiza-tions. To succeed meant in all walks of life rising step by step, away from the actual work of the job nearer and nearer to management—to giving instead of taking orders. All institutions shifting from the old hierarchical form of structure to one more consistent with democratic ideals find difficulty in the transition. And this on every rung of the ladder, those on top trying to develop a more liberal approach as well as those below trying to use a new freedom. Historic lags are characteristic of all institutions in transition. It is all a part of the evolution of democracy.

STAGES OF TEACHERS' PROFESSIONAL GROWTH

As we came to know the teachers, we became sure that their early concentration of their interest on learning—teaching new techniques grew out of their attitude toward their job—an attitude which had been built up within an administrative ladder system in which they had been expected to follow instruction from "superior" officials rather than to think through educational and psycho-logical problems for themselves. Their new job asked many new things of them besides using new teaching techniques. It asked them to study their children's needs and interests. It asked them to be flexible, to adapt their programs to their children. It asked them to take responsibility for planning, to be experimental. But psychologically they had been conditioned by what had been asked of them under a hierarchical ladder system in which they stood on the lowest rung.

Their role had been to follow instructions handed down from above. No wonder that they did not trust themselves to take on new kinds of responsibilities and initiative, to be experimental. No wonder their anxieties centered upon learning *how* with only secondary interest in learning *why*.

First stage: self-confidence in thinking, planning, and experimenting

This, then, was where the Workshop began. The teachers, for all their differences in personality, in background content, were impatient of talk about what children are like and how fit a curriculum to children's needs; they said such basic concepts were "mere theory" and of "no practical use' " to them; they were unanimous in wanting from us practical help—to be told or shown *how* to handle "the activity program" or *how* to organize and conduct a "unit." Since we believed teachers, like everyone else, learn better by experience than by words, we began what they called "demonstration teaching" of children in the classrooms, followed in our Workshop meetings by discussions of the children's responses. We planned and took trips with a teacher and her children; we helped to get dramatic play started, or to organize and original play, or to make a map or a mural; we conducted a science experiment, and led follow-up discussions with the children.

After such demonstration teaching, the teachers tended *to repeat what we done* rather than to work out new experiences for the children adapted to a new situation. A few illustrations: After a staff member had planned and taken a trip a teacher and her children, a teacher repeated the same trip with her next group of children though a different trip would have contributed more to the current study. Teachers continued to use the source material we had brought rather than hunt for new materials themselves. After a staff member had helped a class of sixth-grade children to organize an original play by starting them off on writing jingles for each step in the process of making a woolen coat, from the sheep to buying the coat in a store, the teacher repeated this same pattern in the plays she later helped the children to write. That is, the teachers followed rather than taking initiative and experimenting along new lines. We were convinced that this pattern of following was not due to lack of originality or ability. Nor did we think the teachers were particularly resistant to a new way of teaching. Rather, they lacked self-confidence in what was genuinely a new job. We felt their pattern of following was a holdover of attitudes built up by their old job, in which they had been expected to follow in detail the instructions handed out to them. So long as they held to this old pattern, they could not throw themselves wholeheartedly into what was genuinely a new job. But to break this pattern they needed a degree of self-confidence, and that required time. The assurance that we were not supervisors trying to rate them was accepted only slowly. When it was finally accepted, they became less afraid of failure. The first stage in their growth was when they acquired enough self-confidence to experiment, to try out something new and not be unduly upset if their first trial was not altogether successful. Only then did tension begin to give way to satisfaction in this new way of teaching.

Naturally, it took some teachers longer than others to reach this first stage of self-confidence. We continued to give concrete suggestions and to encourage any attempt at independent planning until a teacher felt secure enough to use us as advisers rather than as guides to be followed.

Second stage: desire to acquire background content

At first we supplied the background content and source material necessary for any particular project or unit. Each of us arrived at school staggering under some load. We brought relevant books for both the children and the teachers. We brought pictures from our Bank Street files— even enormous graphic relief maps difficult to manipulate in the subway. We also brought some educational materials and tools such as simple science equipment and our Bank Street tubs of plasticine when the teachers modeled maps. In all our informal discussions with the children or at Workshop meetings, we naturally drew upon the background content which we had accumulated through years of teaching children and teachers. Much of it was new to the teachers. Most of them used our source materials and background content eagerly when saw how interested their children were and how children began to observe new things and ask questions which showed genuine intellectual curiosity.

By the end of our first Workshop year, a common remark was, "We don't know enough to teach this way—we haven't the background content." The group, as a whole, asked to devote considerable time the following year to talks on straight background content. Many asked for a list of readings for the summer. As a group they decided to work on gathering such material for a school source material library. Here was a big step forward in the teachers' growth—a step which meant an appreciation of how the use of all sorts of sources could enrich the children's curriculum experiences. It meant more than that, too. Eventually it meant an acceptance of more afterschool work as a part of their job. It meant a sharing of their experiences and problems and a sharing among themselves of precious "private" stores of pictures and other source materials. It meant an extension of their interest and their sense of responsibility from their own classroom to the school as a whole.

Third stage: growth of the concept of curriculum building

The teachers' understanding and interest in their new job broadened gradually along two lines—subject matter and child development—until they finally merged into the concept of curriculum building.

Their growth in thinking about child development had gone through several stages. At first their interest was largely limited to disturbed children. Nearly every teacher had some children whose behavior showed maladjustment, and some teachers had classes composed entirely of such children. The teachers' initial approach to child psychology was in terms of the troublesome problems they had to handle in their own classrooms. Many of the teachers began by rejecting children with behavior problems. "You can't do anything with such children." "You can't change their homes, so why try to do anything?" "They oughtn't to be in school anyway." This attitude of rejection gradually grew into an eagerness to understand why these children were so disturbed and disturbing, a challenging of a quick judgment that nothing could be done for them in school. Of course, a number of children *were* too unstable to be in school. But more and more, the teachers wished to give understanding help before saying, "They oughtn't to be in school."

From this limited interest in disturbed children the interest of most of the teachers eventually broadened until it included the total growth of all children. They came to recognize that all children have emotional needs which teachers must meet; also, that a child's ability to learn is closely tied up with a satisfying life. They began to question some of the old techniques of human relationships such as praise cards and gold stars. What did such rewards do to those unsuccessful in this competition? To those who succeeded? Did such rewards split the group into rival camps? Did they turn attention to achievements rather than to interest? Most of the teachers came to feel such rewards were harmful, that children were as genuinely interested in co-operation, group undertakings, as they were in competition. They told the principal how they felt and he accepted their point of view.

This growth in understanding children was brought about in a large measure by the Workshop discussions of actual children in this school—children these teachers were teaching—rather than of "the child" in general. The Bank Street psychologist observed the children in their classrooms and then discussed them in the Workshop. The principal had asked each teacher to make a case study of one child. Since most of these case studies were of disturbed children, the psychologist asked each teacher to make at least one study of a child the teacher felt was growing satisfactorily. Discussion of these case studies of their own children helped the teachers to understand the emotional needs of all children and the special needs at different stages of maturity as a basis of teacher-child relationships as well as the other human relationships in the home and with other children. Understanding children's emotional needs made a marked difference in the atmosphere of the classrooms of many teachers.

Another closely related aspect of child development was how children learn at various stages in their process of growing up. Such words as "children's interest drives," "direct experiences," "maturity levels," passed from the realm of theory into the realm of practical curriculum planning. Understanding how children learn had direct bearing upon teaching techniques. The teachers' interest in *how* to acquire skill in the new techniques broadened to *why* these techniques helped children to healthy all-around growth.

The teachers began by thinking of curriculum content as a series of separate courses of study and separate units. From this, bit by bit, they grew to think of a total program for their own children, a year's program built up of progressive experiences and activities centered around basic relationships in various kinds of information that the children were gathering. When the teachers began to reach this point we suggested that the Workshop plan curriculum materials in social studies for the whole school. The working out of this curriculum revealed a startling growth in the teachers whose interests only a year and a half before had been largely limited to the acquisition of new teaching techniques. Not only did they now think clearly and constructively about progressive steps in the total curriculum subject matter in social studies which children from kindergarten through sixth grade were ready to take: they extended their thinking to the children in the whole school system. That is, they did not want to do something for just their one school, though the Workshop had received permission to work out a fairly independent experimental curriculum. They distinctly wished to work within the prescribed framework of the official curriculum. But within this official framework they wished to experiment, to find out how to interpret the prescribed curriculum content in ways that were best for children's growth.

At this point, they were actually combining child development with curriculum content. Children's needs—physical, intellectual, and emotional—became a basis not only for teaching techniques but for selection of subject matter as well. When the two basic concepts—child development and fitting the curriculum to the child—became thus closely interrelated, the teachers were ready to *build* a curriculum. The social studies curriculum which the Workshop wrote (teachers, administration, and Bank Street staff) was based on the two fundamental concepts—what children are like and what subject matter, experiences, and activities best further their growth. These were exactly the basic concepts which at the beginning of our Workshop the teachers had said were "mere theory" and "of no practical use" to them. That the teachers were able so quickly to understand and apply these concepts shows, we think, that as a group they were learners. And what better can be said of a grownup than that he is still a learner?

Fourth stage: relating their job to the world outside the school

As their own jobs became more creative, we thought we noticed that the teachers were keeping more closely in touch with educational thinking and happenings elsewhere. Current books and magazine articles were constantly recommended by teachers at our meetings, as were interesting exhibits and lectures. We thought this indicated that the teachers felt more closely identified with the broad aspects of education everywhere.

As the teachers became more responsible for building their social studies curriculum, we heard more and more talk about national and world issues. We are in no position to judge whether their social thinking had been stimulated, for we had not known them in their lives outside the school. But this we think we can say: the social problems of the world had become more related to their job as teachers and they shared their thinking both as adults and as professional teachers. The suggestion that we ask someone to talk at a Workshop meeting about intercultural relations came from the teachers. One such meeting considered intercultural relations from the point of view of teaching techniques at various maturity levels. Another was frankly a thrashing out of points of view about the One-World concept on an adult level. We thought it significant that the teachers felt a Workshop for teachers in school was a suitable place for such discussions. We are reasonably sure that they would not have felt so at the beginning of our Workshop experiment.

TEACHERS DEVELOP A PROFESSIONAL ATTITUDE

All these growths, which we have somewhat arbitrarily enumerated as stages though many took place simultaneously, worked toward a professional attitude. Their attitude, their conception of their job, certainly expanded. And not merely in the kinds of work which, as we have indicated, they undertook in order to be better teachers. The most refreshing aspect of the growth of teachers as we watched it was subtle yet evident. There was an atmosphere of stimulation. Their new job was a challenge—not a frightening chore. Every Workshop teacher we met was bubbling over with some tale of "what her children had done." These teachers, as we have said, had a deep interest in their children. When they saw their children taking on new interests, new zest for observing and finding out, new habits of tackling a problem by thinking out relationships, new ways of expressing their thinking and feelings, the teachers themselves became excited. It worked, this new curriculum! They became inventive, experimental—and industrious, too. For this new way of teaching means hard work. The lazy, the indifferent will never teach this way except in superficial forms, but they are a small proportion of the teachers. Most of them got deep satisfaction in having a creative job. For that is exactly what their new job is. Creative jobs are always hard work, yes. But they are fun too.

We believe that only a negligible percentage of the teachers who have experienced creative teaching would wish to give it up. As they grow in creative power in their classrooms, they are more aware of and impatient at the practical handicaps under which their work is done and which are not inherent in this way of teaching—poor equipment, little space, large groups. Any school system that really wishes its teachers to do a creative job must implement its new curriculum. Any community that wishes its children to be taught by enthusiastic, creative teachers must insist that unnecessary handicaps be done away with. It may be that teachers themselves will become a force in bringing about clearer community thinking which will demand better working conditions for children and their teachers in our school. It may be that the teachers, once they are released from the psychological handicaps of authoritarian supervision to creative teaching, will become our educational leaders. They are closest to our children in their school lives. Is it too much to ask that we should look to them for educational guidance?

6.3 The nature of expertise in teaching

David C. Berliner

Source: In F. K. Oser, A. Dick and J-L. Patry (eds.),
Effective and Responsible Teaching: The New Synthesis.
San Francisco: Jossey-Bass, 1992, pp. 227–248

There are many reasons for studying expertise. For one, it is an interesting topic, and that alone is sufficient to promote a line of research. Expert mnemonists, chess players, taxi drivers, or mathematicians fascinate us, as idiot savants and geniuses do. Such individuals are rare, and their abilities seem mysterious to those of us who do not attain their levels of competence. In addition, the study of the perception and problem solving of experts sometimes provides insight into the cognitive processes and kinds of knowledge that they use, and these often differ substantially from the processes and knowledge base that are used by novices. Such information helps psychologists to understand more about the organization of memory, the way reasoning in a particular domain occurs, and the way judgments are made. This kind of knowledge can have practical benefits: it can be used to provide the scaffolding for the instruction of novices, to help them attain a greater degree of competence, though perhaps not expertise. Expertise, it should be remembered, is a characteristic that is ordinarily developed only after lengthy experience. It is descriptive of a level of performance ordinarily attained by only a small percentage of those who are competent at a task.

There are also other reasons for studying expertise in the area of teaching. With increased public criticism of teachers and schools, it has been a source of pride for teachers to learn that within the profession are individuals who resemble experts in other fields—bridge players, chess players, physicists, radiologists, and so forth (see Glaser, 1987; Chi *et al.*, 1988). In addition, information about pedagogical expertise can help policy makers concerned about teacher testing, merit pay, career ladders, and alternative certification programs, all of which require an understanding of the kinds of performance that characterize experts and novices (Berliner, 1989).

An additional reason for pursuing the study of expertise among teachers is to make clear that there are forms of pedagogical knowledge that are quite sophisticated and complex and take years to learn. Pedagogical knowledge—knowledge of organization and management of classrooms, of motivation, teaching methods, discipline, and individual differences among students—is not generally valued by the public. Virtually anyone who has ever raised a child or trained a dog thinks that teaching is easy. Such people have not had to work in public school classrooms, where high levels of managerial, organizational, and interpersonal social skills are required merely to be a competent provider of instruction for twenty-five or thirty distinctly different individuals. What studies of expertise in the pedagogical domain seek is a greater understanding of the sophisticated forms of pedagogical knowledge used by expert teachers to accomplish instructional goals in the complex social environment called the public school classroom.

Because studying expertise is interesting, because it enables us to learn more about cognition, because it builds morale, and because there is a lack of understanding of the complexity of pedagogical knowledge, a number of studies have been undertaken to examine expert knowledge in the pedagogical domain. Of primary interest have been studies about the differences between expert and novice teachers that affect instruction and achievement. Most of these studies have been concerned with teacher effectiveness, with focus on how these teachers might differ with regard to responsible teaching. This chapter attempts to change that by offering a selective review of some characteristics of expert pedagogues that highlight aspects of the literature that reflect on responsible teaching as well as effective teaching. This review is organized around seven propositions about expert and novice teachers for which empirical data exist.

PROPOSITIONS

Proposition one: experts excel mainly in their own domains and in particular contexts

The obvious reasons, Chi *et al.* (1988) state, that experts excel primarily in single domains, is that experts have a great deal more experience, probably reflected-on experience, in some domains than in others. Expert radiologists surveyed in studies by Lesgold and others (1988) were estimated to be looking at their one-hundred-thousandth x-ray. The chess experts studied in deGroot's (1965) seminal work and in other research (Newell and Simon, 1972; Chase and Simon, 1973) have been estimated to have spent ten to twenty thousand hours staring at chess positions. A perspective on this is offered by Posner (1988, p. xxxi): "a student who spends 40 hours a week for 33 weeks spends 1,320 hours studying. Imagine spending more than ten years in college studying one subject, chess, and you get some appreciation of the time commitment of master level players . . . It is reasonable to assume a chess master can recognize 50,000 different configurations of chess, not too far different from the number of different words an English reader may be able to recognize."

With lengthy time commitments necessary to become expert in complex areas of human functioning, it is no wonder that individuals generally excel in only a single area. In the study of teachers, we also note that time and experience play an important role in the development of expertise. On the basis of fragmentary evidence and anecdotal reports, some scholars propose that teachers do not hit their peak until they have at least five years of on-the-job experience. The expert teacher with ten years of experience has spent a minimum of ten thousand hours in classrooms as a teacher, preceded by at least fifteen thousand hours as a student. While not all such experienced teachers are experts, there are not likely to be many expert pedagogues who achieve their status without extensive classroom experience.

It is also likely that the domain-specific knowledge that is acquired through this experience is quite contextualized. For example, in one of our research studies, experts, advanced beginners, and novices were asked to teach a thirty-minute lesson on probability to a group of high school students (Berliner and others, 1988). While they taught the lesson, they were videotaped, and after the lesson, during stimulated recall, they were asked to tell us about their thinking and to justify their actions during teaching. The interesting thing about this study was the incredible level of anger that we triggered among all the expert teachers. We had assumed that they would breeze through the teaching task and that we would use their performance to assess the lesser skills to be shown by advanced beginners and novices. While the experts did, in fact, show more skills in a number of ways (Clarridge, 1988), all of them were angry about having to participate in the task. One of them walked out on the study, while another broke down and cried in the middle of it.

The reason for the teachers' anger was that we had moved them from their classrooms to a laboratory situation, and they did not feel that they could perform well under such conditions. We had allocated thirty minutes for planning, enough for the advanced beginners and the novices to feel comfortable, but the experts claimed that they needed more time—from three hours to as much as three weeks. From our interviews, we came to understand that experts rarely enter their classrooms without having taken all the time they need to thoroughly understand the content that they will teach and planning one or more activities to teach it. In addition, they did not know the students in this study.

Our interviews revealed that expert teachers' expertise depends in part on knowing their students in three ways: (1) They know the cognitive abilities of the students they teach, and this helps them to determine the level at which to teach. (2) They know their students personally, and this allows for personal rather than bureaucratic and informal mechanisms of control to be used in teaching. (3) They have a reputation with their students. In the teachers' own schools, their students knew that they were experts and had certain expectations about what their teaching would be like. These teachers had always had students who expected to be well taught and to learn a great deal, even if they were pushed to their intellectual limits. When they faced a group of strangers, none of these three aspects of "knowing the students" was present, and the teachers felt that they suffered from that. In addition, all the experts commented on the problems created by their inability to use routines, a basic part of any expert's performance (Bloom, 1985; Leinhardt and Greeno, 1986; Berliner, 1987). By taking them out of their classrooms, we had taken away the context in which these expert pedagogues excel.

There are aspects of this study revealing concern for responsible teaching that were not made evident in the primary analyses of the data. The first of these is the experts' demand for planning time sufficient for the instructional task. This concern need not just be thought of as a way for the experts to ensure more effective instruction. Another interpretation also fits these data. Compared to novices and advanced beginners, expert teachers appear to have such high self-respect and respect for their students that they consider it markedly unprofessional to show up in class without having mastered their material completely. They seem to feel that they owe that to their students and are embarrassed when they cannot fulfill that part of their social contract with them. Participation in this study may have been perceived as requiring the breaking of a moral obligation, and that may account for some of the unexpectedly high level of anger that was expressed. A second ethical concern among the experts was seen in their need to have one or more activities planned before initiating instruction. We think that this is because most of them strive for an instructional setting that is not lecture-oriented and teacher-dominated, which does not require a lot of planning time, but prefer instead, a more indirect method of teaching. This was less true of the novices and advanced beginners, who seemed much more direct in their instruction.

A third noteworthy aspect of the experts' behavior was their concern with knowing more about their students. The interviews revealed that this was required in order to accommodate instruction to their students' needs, a form of consideration not especially noted among the novice and advanced beginning teachers in this sample. Perhaps the most interesting aspect of the experts' behavior was their perception that their lack of personal knowledge about the students that they had to teach required them to use bureaucratic rather than informal mechanisms to control student behavior. All but one of the experts seemed upset by that. The task seemed to call for them to adopt more authoritarian roles than they had become accustomed to using, roles that they had generally discarded as they acquired expertise. This too may have contributed to their anger.

Another of our studies illustrates the nature of domain-specific, classroom-bound pedagogical knowledge, which is built up over time and may not be applicable to other domains in which individuals interact (Carter and others, 1987). It also reveals a humanistic side to experts that is yet to be demonstrated as clearly among novices and advanced beginners. Experts, advanced beginners, and raw novice teachers participated in a simulation in which information about a class was given to them. They received the tests that students had taken, homework assignments that students had turned in, and a set of student information cards containing typical academic information and some personal notes about the students, their families, and their social behavior. The simulation required the subjects to imagine taking over such a class in the fifth week of school, after the regular teacher had to leave because of an emergency. The novices in this study worked very hard trying to sort student information cards into piles. Here are some quotations from the protocols obtained in the study.

> I sorted the bad kids from the good kids from some of the ones that were just good natured, if they liked to work, that type of thing. And I would do that if I started writing my own comments. If I had the class for a while, I would tend to still categorize them.

> I went through her student cards and also went through the test scores and tried to divide the students into three groups, one group which I thought might be disruptive, one group which I thought would not be disruptive and that wouldn't need intense watching. The third group I really didn't know because the back of the card was blank. So it was classified later. I realized not all the disruptive students were getting bad grades. I decided to sort of rank cards from what I thought would be the best student from the top to the obviously poorer students going down the stack just to get some sort of an idea of ranking.

This behavior was in marked contrast to that of the experts. Experts were considerably less interested in remembering specific information about students than were the novices. Moreover, experts did not trust information left to them by a previous teacher. They believed that the information was useless because they knew that children make their own deals in every classroom. Information that the child was unmotivated or highly intelligent or disruptive was not thought to be as generalizable as, say, information on a medical record reporting the child to be hypertensive or hypoglycemic. The teachers had learned that every child takes on a different character in every classroom and that educational records, unlike medical records, cannot be trusted. Because of this and because of their generic view of students—seeing them all basically as alike and teachable (Calderhead, 1983)—the experts in our study had no reason to spend time on the particulars reported in the student information cards. The experts spent their time looking at the tests and the homework assignments that students had turned in, trying to understand, at some deep level, something about what students knew. When questioned about why they did not use the student information cards, the experts responded as follows:

> I just don't think names are important as far as this point in time. I haven't met the kids; there is no reason for me to make any value judgments about them at this time. And so she [the previous teacher] had a whole little packet of confidential material that I looked at, and it had trivial little things about where the parents worked and this kid was cute or something like that, and that to me is not relevant.

> Especially when I start fresh, I start from a clean slate. I usually always try to . . . I like getting a little background on the students in that there are going to be severe problems or someone may need special attention on certain things, you know, learning areas, but, in general, it's a conglomeration of the students. I like to learn from them and develop my own opinions.

> It was a typical classroom, some problem kids that need to be dealt with. And you have to take that into consideration when you're developing some kind of plan for them. There are the bright kids that were highly self-motivated. There were your shy kids. It was a typical class.

> I didn't read the cards. I never do unless there's a comment about a physical impairment such as hearing or sight or something I get from the nurse. I never want to place a judgment on the student before they start. I find I have a higher success rate if I don't.

Among the reasons given by the experts for their distrust of the information left for them about each student was their belief that students act differently in different environments—a belief in accord with that of most personality theorists. Their unwillingness to examine the records seems to be a conscious act by these teachers to prevent expectations from forming too early and to ensure that the beliefs they form about students are derived from their own personal experience. This is behavior that is quite considerate of students; it is responsible professional behavior. The experts may ignore student information also because they possess a sense of self-efficacy and have positive expectations. With some uniformity, the experts seem to believe that every child can learn and that they personally can teach every child assigned to them. They seem to attribute the level of student performance not to ability but to effort or family—external and alterable loci. For their own behavior, the locus of control appears to be internal. They take personal responsibility for their success and failure, an example of which was seen in the anger expressed by the expert teachers but not the novice or advanced beginners in the teaching situation described above.

That expert pedagogues use less information than novices or advanced beginners was also found when experienced and novice physicians reviewed applicants for internships and residencies and when experienced and novice financial advisers reviewed financial statements of companies (Johnson, 1988). Experience in a particular domain teaches one what is worth attending to and what is not.

It is hard to speculate on what someone would do in a new situation, but this kind of specialized knowledge probably does not transfer well across domains. It is very likely that when expert teachers join a social club, attend a professional conference, or register to take courses at graduate school, they act like novices. That is, they try to categorize people, grouping them into piles, as novice teachers do with their first class of students. We have increasing understanding that knowledge is, for the most part, contextually bound. As Brown, Collins, and Duguid (1989) put it, cognitions are situated; they are not adrift in the brain, unconnected to actions and situations. The road to transfer across situations appears to be a rocky one. Transfer does not usually appear spontaneously. It usually does not occur without cognitive work, some form of mental effort (Perkins and Salomon, 1989). Thus, we can anticipate that expert pedagogues, like other experts, will excel mainly in their own domain and in particular contexts within that domain. Their expert knowledge will not transfer automatically across domains.

Proposition two: experts often develop automaticity for the repetitive operations that are needed to accomplish their goals

Glaser (1987) notes the efficient decoding skill of the expert comprehender in reading as an example of the way automaticity frees working memory to allow other, more complex characteristics of the situation to be dealt with. Examples of the automaticity or routinization of some teaching functions among expert teachers are abundant. For example, Leinhardt and Greeno (1986), studying elementary school mathematics lessons, compared an expert's opening homework review with that of a novice. The expert teacher was quite brief, taking about one-third less time than the novice. This expert was able to pick up information about attendance and about who did or did not do the homework and was also able to identify who was going to need help later in the lesson. She elicited mostly correct answers throughout the activity and also managed to get all the homework corrected. Moreover, she did so at a brisk pace and never lost any control of the lesson. She had routines for recording attendance, for handling choral responding during the homework checks, and for hand raising to get attention. This expert also used clear signals to start and finish the lesson segments.

In contrast, when the novice was enacting an opening homework review as part of a mathematics lesson, she was not able to get a fix on who did and did not do the homework, she had problems with taking attendance, and she asked ambiguous questions that led her to misunderstand the difficulty of the homework. At one time, she lost control of the pace. She never learned which students were going to have more difficulty later on in the lesson. Of importance is that the novice showed lack of familiarity with well-practiced routines. She seemed not to have habitual ways to act. Students, therefore, were unsure of their roles in the class.

In a small study by Krabbe and Tullgren (1989), the routines of novice and well-regarded experienced teachers, whom I will call expert teachers, were assessed. English and language arts lessons at the junior high school level were analyzed. The experts took an average of fourteen minutes to introduce a literature lesson, while the novices took two minutes to do so. The experts needed that much time to follow a routine for the set inducement or introductory phase of the daily lesson. First, they briefly stated the immediate objective of the activity (for example, "We will discuss several ways that we can learn about the qualities of people"). Then they gave clear and explicit directions about what they wanted students to do (for example, "Put everything away; here are three situations for you to think about answering"). Then they created a positive environment for the phase of the lesson that would follow. The experts found ways to increase student involvement, often arousing curiosity through use of analogies that had something to do with the central concept and theme of the lesson. The goal of the lesson was apparent throughout their introduction. This three-step routine was also accompanied by a mood shift among the expert teachers from humorous and playful at the beginning of the introduction to serious and businesslike as the presentation, discussion, or oral reading phase of the lesson drew closer (Krabbe et al., 1988). This regularly occurring pattern of teaching, this routine, was not evident when the videotapes of the novice teachers were analyzed. Krabbe and Tullgren (1989) also identified a routine in the way that the presentation phase of the lesson was run by the experts. The expert teachers introduced material gradually and in hierarchical order, illustrated their points by using student background and daily experiences, and provided practice opportunities as they went along. Novice teachers during this phase of the lesson tended to ask text-specific factual questions until the lesson was over. No sense of a routine was noted in the way the novices taught a literature or language arts lesson.

The well-practiced routines of expert surgeons, ice skaters, tennis players, and concert pianists (Bloom, 1986), no less than expert teachers, are what give the appearance of fluidity and effortlessness to their performance. What looks to be so easy for the expert and so clumsy for the novice is the result of thousands of hours of reflected-on experience. But once again we may speculate that the expert teachers have more than just efficiency, effectiveness, and student achievement in mind as they develop their routines. Such routinization frees the mind so that people may attend to many aspects of the situation in which they find themselves. The mind is a very limited information processor. A concert pianist with no routines would be mechanical, paying little attention to the audience, the conductor, the acoustics, the subtle and unique elements that are present in each performance. Thus routines are so well honed that the pianist's mind is free to process much more than the position of her fingers on the keyboard. Similarly, if all the attention of a teacher were directed at simply keeping the instructional elements of a classroom moving along the proper course, the highest levels of thinking would rarely be in evidence, and the affective and moral dimensions of classrooms would be unnoticed.

Support for this thesis may be found in the classrooms of novice teachers such as the one studied by Leinhardt and Greeno (1986). With no routinization of the opening homework review, the novice could not find out which of the students had had a troubled night at home the evening before, though the expert teacher could. Routines among the experts studied by Krabbe and Tullgren (1989) may have allowed them to allocate attention to matching the content to be learned to the students' personal knowledge and common experience. That is, the quality of a teacher's pedagogical content knowledge (the teacher's explanations, metaphors, analogies, and other transformations of what is to be taught into something more easily learned) may depend in part on supportive routines. This is because pedagogical content knowledge is often developed on the run, during interactive instruction, when attention to simultaneous events is required. Thus, routinization may promote interpersonal and personal relations in classrooms as well as it promotes instructional goals.

Proposition three: experts are more sensitive than novices to task demands and the social situation when solving problems

Glaser (1987) notes that the mental models that experts develop to guide their behavior are constrained by the requirements of the situation in which they must work. Housner and Griffey (1985), in a study of experienced and novice physical education teachers, provide evidence of the sensitivity of experienced teachers to those issues. They found that the number of requests for information made by experienced and novice teachers during the time they were planning instruction was about the same. Each group made reasonable requests for information about the number of students they would be teaching, their gender, their age, and so forth. But in two areas, the experienced teachers made many more requests than did the novice teachers. They needed to know about the ability, experience and background of the students they were to teach, and they needed to know about the facility in which they would be teaching. In fact, five of the eight experienced teachers in this study of planning and instruction demanded to see the facility in which they would teach before they could develop their plan. Novices made no such requests. The experienced teachers were sensitive to the social and physical environment under which instruction was to take place.

When actually performing in the teaching role, the experienced teachers implemented changes in their instruction more often than did novices, using social cues to guide their inter-active instructional decision making. The experienced teachers used their judgment about student performance as a cue to change instruction 24 percent more often than did novices, their judgments about student involvement 41 percent more often, student enjoyment of the activities 79 percent more often, and their interpretation of mood and student feelings 82 percent more often. The novices used student verbal statements about the activity as their primary cue for instituting a change in their instructional activity, responding to these cues 131 percent more often than did the experienced teachers. Clearly, the novice teachers changed what they were doing primarily when asked to; they seemed unable to decode the social cues emitted by students about the ways in which instruction was proceeding. The experienced teachers, however, were far more sensitive to the social cues emitted in the situation and used these social cues for adjusting their instruction. Once again, we have evidence that experts behave in ways that we would judge more considerate of their students than the ways in which novices behave. Their experience has taught them how to read the more subtle cues emitted by their students, and this makes them more sensitive to the students' needs. Their reputations for effectiveness are likely to be due in part to their heightened social sensitivity.

Proposition four: experts are opportunistic in their problem solving

Glaser (1987) reports that experts are opportunistic in their planning and their actions. They take advantage of new information, quickly bringing new interpretations and representations of the problem to light. Novices are less flexible. Borko and Livingston (1988) discuss these same behaviors among novice and expert teachers. The term that these researchers use to character-ize the expert teacher whose lessons have an opportunistic quality is the improvisational per-former. They see the expert teacher as having a well-thought-out general script to follow but being very flexible in following it in order to be responsive to what students do. One expert, discussing his planning, made clear the improvisational aspect of teaching: "A lot of times I just put the objective in my book, and I play off the kids." This expert also described his interactive teaching as similar to a tennis match: "I sort of do a little and then they do a little. And then I do a little and they do a little. But my reaction is just that, it's a reaction. And it depends upon their action what my reaction's going to be."

Borko and Livingston (1988, p. 20) report that "the success of the expert teachers' improvisation seemed to depend upon their ability to quickly generate or provide examples and to draw connections between students' comments or questions and the lesson's objectives." This was not the case when the novices were teaching. All three of the novices in this study ran into problems when students made comments or asked questions requiring explanations that had not been planned for in advance. Novice teachers were sometimes unable to maintain the direction of the lesson when they had to respond to student comments or questions. This was true even when the issues brought up by the students were relevant to the topic of the lesson. Experiences such as this led two of the novices to prevent students from asking questions and making comments while they presented their lesson. Although he valued student responsiveness, Jim, one of the novices, reasoned this way (p. 26): "I think . . . because I'm not that proficient yet in handling questions, it's better to cut off the questions, just go through the material, because it'll be much clearer to them if they just let me go through it . . . I don't want to discourage questions, but there are times I'd rather get through my presentation and then get to the questions."

Opportunistic teaching is apparently much more difficult for the novice than for the expert. For novices, the pedagogical schemata necessary for improvisation or opportunism seem to be less elaborate, less interconnected, and clearly less accessible than are those of the experts. It is the flexibility arising out of self-confidence that allows the expert teacher to capitalize on the instructional opportunities that present themselves. They can personalize instruction, developing pedagogical content knowledge on the run, and this allows them to fit the lesson to the students' behavior in ways that the novice cannot. This ability must make an expert appear more sensitive and responsive to student needs than would a novice. The experience and confidence of the experts allow them to appear more considerate of students—more caring, flexible, interested in what their students know, and so forth. The display of such humanistic and effective interpersonal qualities is still beyond the reach of the typical novice.

Proposition five: experts' representations of problems and situations are qualitatively different from the representations of novices

Chi *et al.* (1988) note that experts seem to understand problems at a deeper level than do novices. Experts apply concepts and principles that are more relevant to the problem to be solved. Novices' understanding seems to be at a more superficial level; they show less evidence of principled reasoning. We find some support for this general statement in studies of expertise in the pedagogical domain. In one small study of ours, Hanninen (1983) created realistic scenarios about educational problems associated with gifted children. One scenario, for example, described Mark, an eight-year-old Asian boy with severe hearing deficits who likes mathematics and science and has a strong interest in computers. Scenarios describing educational problems of this type were presented to fifteen subjects. Five of the subjects were expert, experienced teachers of gifted children; another five were equally experienced teachers but without any background in gifted education; and five more were novice teachers of the gifted, still working on their certification.

The opening sentences of some of the protocols revealed much about the thinking of experts and novices. The opening sentence from one novice reads, "Mark seems like a very talented individual with many diverse interests." Another novice comments, "Mark should be encouraged by his teacher to continue his science experiments and work on the computer." From an experienced teacher who was a novice in the area of gifted education, we have "He should be able to pursue his interests in greater depth." In contrast to these banal, unsophisticated beginnings to essays that attempted to address Mark's needs, in which superficial characteristics of the problem were noted, one expert began right off with "Mark's needs can be broken into three broad areas: academic enrichment, emotional adjustment, and training to cope with his handicap." This essay was a more organized and sophisticated representation of the problem than was obtained from the novices. The experts also concentrated more on the affective characteristics of Mark's life than did the other teachers. This is a common pattern among experts and will be discussed in more detail below.

If one views pedagogical knowledge as a complex multidimensional domain of knowledge requiring sophisticated thinking, then it could be argued that the classification of a problem as solvable by using Newton's second law—that is, considering it a conservation-of-energy problem—is no different from classifying Mark's educational needs as falling into three categories and describing action relevant to each of those categories. This was an appropriate representation for a problem in the pedagogical domain.

The scenario methodology that we used to learn about teachers' thinking was used in a better-designed study by Nelson (1988), in which expert and novice physical education teachers were the subjects. She concluded that experts "displayed a greater variety of application of sound principles of teaching" (p. 25) than did novices. The experts were also more creative and thorough in describing ways to address teaching problems and provided more solutions to each problem that they addressed. In a different study, Peterson and Comeaux (1987) used videotapes to elicit comments from experienced and novice teachers. They found that the comments of experienced teachers "reflected an underlying knowledge structure in which they relied heavily on procedural knowledge of classroom events as well as on higher-order principles of effective classroom teaching" (p. 327).

Similarities in the two studies are quite apparent. An expert in Nelson's (1988) study says of a problem with an exercise program designed for an overweight child, "I'd find something positive about his workout . . . If I don't give him some positive reinforcement, I may lose his dedication to the task" (p. 25). And an experienced teacher in Peterson and Comeaux's (1987) study says about a teacher returning an essay test, "I guess before he handed them back, it might have been a good idea if there was an excellent paper there to have read it with no name, or excerpts from it, or at least on the board outline what a good answer would have been—that type of thing. He might have made some comments of errors that were made, again with no names, that were misconceptions, and clear those up with students right away. You can use the test as a learning experience rather than just hand it back, to put away, or throw away probably" (p.328).

In the comments of both the expert and experienced teachers, we see evidence of principled thought, the former enunciating a principle about reinforcement and motivation, the latter enunciating a pedagogical principle about the usefulness of tests as learning experiences separate from their function in evaluation. Such reasoning was not typical of the responses of novices. Moreover, the comments about motivation and the use of tests for learning experiences (not just for feedback, reward, or punishment) show interest in considerate teaching. The word *genuine* characterizes a good deal of the teaching that experienced teachers do. It is teaching primarily for growth and improvement rather than for sorting children out along an ability continuum.

In another study of ours (Stein *et al.*, forthcoming), we looked at the ways that expert teachers predict how students will respond to mathematics and science items used in the National Assessment of Educational Progress. From the protocols obtained while the subjects thought aloud, we learned that experts named or labeled items in a much more detailed and specific way than did novices or advanced beginners. The experts also engaged in a task analysis of the problem in a way that was quite sophisticated. They analyzed the demands of the task represented in the item to determine what sorts of problems students might experience with them. Task analysis was coded in their think-alouds when the subjects verbalized something about the reasons for an item's difficulty or when they traced out the various steps or competencies that a student would need to answer an item correctly. Eighty percent of the experts analyzed the task demands of the items; they did this for between one and four of the five items for which they had to think aloud. Among the novices and the advanced beginners, only 50 percent of each group engaged in task analysis of the items, and when they did so, it was for only one of the five items that they analyzed. The task analyses of the experts were also more elaborate or more clearly formed than those of others.

The experts also differed in their inferences about the student cognitions used in answering an item. Experts seemed to have a fund of knowledge about the way students thought and how that thinking interacted with the content of the specific mathematics or science items. In addition, the experts seemed able to think through the *mis*algorithms that students might apply. The experts had more experience dealing with student errors and therefore knew what types of errors students might make. Novices rarely discussed the issue of misalgorithms that students might apply to solve a problem. We concluded from this study that experts in mathematics and science teaching were more likely than novices and advanced beginners to represent the test items the students would address in a more sophisticated way because of their better labeling of problem types and that they gained insight into the nature of a particular problem type by more frequently doing a task analysis of it from the students' perspective. From the labeling and task analysis, the experts could more often predict the kinds of errors that students would make when attempting to answer test items. Since their predictions were more accurate, they appeared to be better explainers than novices or advanced beginners and more understanding of their students' ways of thinking.

Proposition six: experts have fast and accurate pattern-recognition capabilities; novices cannot always make sense of what they experience

Accurate interpretation of cues and recognition of patterns reduce a person's cognitive processing load and allow the person to instantaneously make sense of a field. For example, quick pattern recognition allows an expert chess player to spot areas of the board where difficulties might occur. Novices are not as good at recognizing such patterns, and when they do note them, they are less likely to make proper inferences about the situation.

In one of our studies, we showed subjects slides of classroom scenes and asked them to interpret what they saw. Each slide was viewed briefly three different times. After the second viewing of a slide, one expert in science said, "It's not necessarily a lab class. There just seemed to be more writing activity. There were people filling out forms. It could have been the end of a lab class after they started putting the equipment away." After the third viewing of the slide, the expert said, "Yeah—there was . . . very little equipment out and it almost appeared to be towards the end of the hour. The books appeared to be closed. Almost looked like it was a cleanup type of situation." Novices did not usually perceive the same cues in the classroom and therefore could not make the inferences that guided the expert's understanding of the classroom. The expert, by the way, was absolutely correct. It was a cleanup kind of activity.

In another study, novice, advanced beginner, and expert teachers simultaneously viewed three television screens, each depicting a different group working in the same class. We saw the same phenomena at work here as in the task using slides (Sabers *et al.*, 1991). During a think-aloud viewing of the videotape, one expert commented, "Left monitor again . . . I haven't heard a bell, but the students are already at their desks and seem to be doing purposeful activity, and this is about the time that I decided they must be an accelerated group because they came into the room and started something rather than just sitting down or socializing." In fact, the students in the scene shown on the left monitor did begin working as soon as they entered the classroom and continued working throughout the entire instructional period. To us, as well as to the experts, this group of students seemed to exhibit a lot of internal motivation. Further, just as this expert noted, this was an accelerated group: it was a science classroom for students identified as gifted and talented.

We regard the reading of a classroom, like the reading of a chess board, to be, in part, a matter of pattern recognition based on hundreds of thousands of hours of experience. The ability of novices or other relatively inexperienced teachers to reliably interpret classroom information is limited precisely because of their lack of experience. The information related to pedagogical events may be so rich and complex that novices and advanced beginners simply cannot agree on what is seen. In the study where they monitored three television screens simultaneously, novices and advanced beginners seemed to experience difficulty in making sense of their classroom observations and in providing plausible explanations of what was occurring within the classroom. For example, we obtained these two comments from advanced beginners who were asked to describe the learning environment in the class-room that they were observing:

> It looked . . . I wouldn't call it terribly motivating. It was, well, not bored, but not enthusiastic.

> Very positive as well as relaxed. Very positive . . . it's good to be able to focus [student] energy into a group situation, yet at the same time, accomplishing the work that they need to do for the class and also lending to the relaxed feeling of the classroom.

Such contradictions were common. Even more discrepancy was noted when these subjects were asked to describe the students' attitudes toward this class. For example,

> It didn't look like it was a favorite class for most of them. One boy looked kind of like, "Oh no, it's not this class again." They didn't look overwhelmingly enthusiastic to be there.

> They seemed pretty excited about the class, excited to learn and a lot of times it's hard to get students excited about science, but this teacher seems to have them so that they are excited about it. They're willing to work and they want to learn.

As a group, these advanced beginners, in their first year of teaching, seemed unable to make sense of what they saw. They experienced difficulty monitoring all three video screens at once. Thus, they often reported contradictory observations and appeared confused about what they were observing and the meaning of their observations. Because novices are much less familiar with classroom events than advanced beginners, they often appeared even more overwhelmed. Many of them expressed difficulty in monitoring all three video screens at once; generally, they appeared able to focus on and make sense of only one screen. Since this limited their observations, they also made errors and contradictions when they were asked about specific events. They were unable to see the overall patterns in the information presented to them.

Another of our studies also showed this difference in interpretive competency between experts and novices (Carter and others, 1988). In that study, subjects viewed a series of slides depicting science or mathematics instruction over a class period in a high school. The subjects held a remote control and were told to go through the fifty or so slides at their own pace, stopping to comment on any slides that they found interesting. Novices and advanced beginners seemed to show no particular pattern in what they stopped to comment on and showed the same kinds of contradictions in their interpretations that we found in the study using videotapes. That is, one novice might say "Everything looks fine, they're all paying attention," and another novice might say, "It looks like they're starting to go off task, they're starting to drift." A pattern was noted among the experts that was quite different. The experts, more often than the subjects in the other groups, found the *same* slides worth commenting about and had the *same* kinds of comments to make. For example, three experts made these comments on slide 5:

> It's a good shot of both people being involved and something happening.
>
> Everybody seems to be interested in what they're doing at their lab stations.
>
> Everybody working. A positive environment.

And two experts offered these comments on slide 51:

> More students with their books closed, their purses on their desks, hands folded, ready to go.
>
> Must be the end of class and everybody is getting ready for the bell to ring.
>
> This reduction in variance by the experts is particularly noteworthy. It means that they have learned to pay attention to some of the same things and to interpret visual stimuli in the same way. This similarity in what is attended to and how it is interpreted is what we hope for when we visit an expert ophthalmologist or automobile mechanic. Novices, advanced beginners—anyone in the early stages of skill acquisition—simply will not have acquired enough experience for that.

The ability to quickly make sense out of what is seen was demonstrated in a unique way by one of the experts in the study using slides. In the classroom that had been photographed, a girl had entered in a gray jacket, gone to her desk, put her purse down on the floor, and looked straight ahead throughout the lesson, neither opening a book nor engaging in any aspect of instruction or student conversation. She appeared clothed in a heavy mantle of grief. Near the end of the lesson, she silently started to cry. Tears streamed slowly down her cheeks, unnoticed by her teacher or her peers. As the bell rang, she bolted and ran from the class. From static slides, shot with a wide-angle lens, the girl's behavior could hardly be noticed. Yet one expert, as he got to a slide near the end of the tray, said, "There's something wrong with the girl in gray." And then, as he looked at the next slide, he said, "Yep, there's something really making her unhappy and it has nothing to do with this class." We think this is a remarkable example of accurate processing of subtle patterns in the visual field. We commented about this skill in social sensitivity when we discussed proposition three, above. And we will comment on a related phenomenon as we discuss proposition seven, next.

Proposition seven: experts perceive meaningful patterns in the domain in which they are experienced

Chi *et al.*, (1988) point out that the superior perceptual skills of experts are due not to any innate superior perceptual abilities but to the way that experience affects perception. After one hundred thousand x-rays or ten thousand hours observing students, what is attended to and how that information is interpreted are very likely to have changed. In another experiment with slides of classroom scenes (Carter and others, 1988), we flashed slides on the screen for only a very brief time and asked experts, novices, and advanced beginners to tell us what they saw. The responses of the novices and advanced beginners to the slides were clearly descriptive and usually quite accurate.

> *Novice:* A blond haired-boy at the table, looking at papers. Girl to his left reaching in front of him for something.

Advanced beginner: [It's] a classroom. Student with back to camera working at a table.

Advanced beginner: A room full of students sitting at tables.

In contrast to these literal descriptions, typical of novices and advanced beginners, some of our expert teachers often responded with inferences about what they saw:

> It's a hands-on activity of some type. Group work with a male and female of maybe late junior high school age.

> It's a group of students maybe doing small-group discussion on a project as the seats are not in rows.

For experts, the information that was often deemed important was information that had instructional significance, such as the age of the students or the teaching-learning activity in which they were engaged. They perceived more meaningful patterns than did novices. Nelson (1988) replicated these findings of ours, using expert and novice physical education teachers. When viewing a slide intended to show a common management problem, a student not dressing for the gym period, a novice teacher somehow misinterpreted the scene: "What I'm assuming is that this is an on-looker. Somebody [who's] just walked in. Maybe someone that's late to class or someone who's hesitant about doing gymnastics, a little scared so they're off in another area just watching" (p. 15). An expert viewing the same slide perceived more than the girl's lack of gym clothing. She saw the whole instructional situation in a more global way and made more meaning of it:

> Here is one girl I noticed earlier who is not dressed out [sic]. She could have a doctor's excuse or something, but she's far away from the remainder of the class and she should be involved, maybe with spotting, or at least in a closer proximity to the rest of the students. She needs to learn just like everyone else in the class. The teacher [then wouldn't] need to be worried about what she is doing, either. If something is missing from the teacher's desk or any of the students' belongings, [that girl] may have to take the responsibility. [Also], the doors are so close by, if she wants to leave there's always a possibility, and the teacher is responsible for her. She's just not involved in the class in any way.

(pp. 15–16)

In any field, the information that experts extract from the phenomena with which they are confronted stems, in part, from the concepts and principles that they use to impose meaning on phenomena in their domain of expertise. That is, experts in all domains appear to be top-down processors. They impose meaning on the stimuli in their domain of expertise. In education, one such concept used to interpret phenomena is attention, or involvement. The physical education expert quoted above is interpreting the slide with this concept in mind. In our study of the interpretation of slides, a focus of the experts was on the notion of work: "students *working* at the blackboard," "students *working* independently," "teacher looking over a person *working* in lab," and so on.

This work orientation, of course, is part of what promotes high rates of achievement among the students of experts. But some characteristics of the experts that are less clearly tied to effectiveness (though contributing to it) have also been found. These have more to do with the responsibility side of teaching. For example, we have found evidence from two studies of ours (Clarridge, 1988; Rottenberg and Berliner, forthcoming) that expert teachers take student responsibility in a lesson into account, expecting students to be in some way involved in the creation of their own knowledge, perhaps through discussion, perhaps through cooperative learning, perhaps through questions or projects. Somehow, the experts seem to communicate this sense of responsibility and are sensitive to it when discussing their views of classes. Evidence for this was found in Clarridge's (1988) study in which videotapes were rated by a specialist in non-verbal communication. The specialist found the expert teachers to be high in incorporative behavior, behavior that invites the students to work jointly with them. The specialist also found that novice and advanced beginners set up barriers to keep authority in their own hands. (The tapes, of course, were rated without knowledge of the experience level of the teachers that were viewed.) Furthermore, expert teachers seem to be unusually sensitive to the affective concerns of the students they teach (Nelson, 1988; Rottenberg and Berliner, forthcoming). The expert who recognized the unhappiness of the student from a minimum of cues in the study discussed above was displaying this kind of social sensitivity. This was also true of the physical education teachers described earlier.

A physicist may bring to bear Newtonian laws to make meaning of a problem in physics. A biologist may bring to bear concepts of homeostasis or ecological niche to make meaning of a problem in biology. A chemist, auto mechanic, and an engineer will also bring to bear on the problems that they face the most salient and useful concepts that they possess. Among the salient and useful pedagogical concepts with which teachers make meaning from the phenomena that they encounter in their work are attention, work, responsibility, and affect. While the first two of these concepts deal with effectiveness more than responsibility in teaching, the latter two concepts deal explicitly with issues of responsibility more than effectiveness. Perhaps of greater interest is that among experts, it appears that effectiveness and responsibility are fused concepts.

Conclusion

The results of the studies described in this selective review appear to be clear. First, expert teachers share characteristics with experts in other domains. Second, the domain-specific knowledge of experts is of a rather sophisticated nature. The collection of evidence supporting these two points is important for the profession. Finally, the evidence about experts suggests that their unique reputation is not based merely on their effectiveness as instructors. Certainly, the evidence supports the claim that they think and act differently from novices in ways that are likely to promote their effectiveness as instructors. But a review of the same data suggests that the experts also think and act differently in ways that promote responsible instruction. And these differences in thinking and acting do not appear to be attributable to differences in age and life experience, though such differences certainly exist; rather, they appear to result from reflected-upon classroom experience, which leads the experts, for the most part, to teach in ways consistent with the complementary synthesis model described in Chapter One of this book. The experts seem to understand better than other teachers that the two approaches are mutually interdependent. They appear to believe that effectiveness can be achieved through responsible teaching and that being responsible entails being effective. That is, a responsible teacher owes students the opportunity to obtain the knowledge and skill needed to succeed in life, and an effective teacher owes students civility and consideration. With rare exceptions, the experts that have been studied demonstrated this sense of obligation toward their students. They also had a positive motivational system at work in their classrooms, a recognition of individual differences among their students, a belief in their own efficacy and their students' ability to learn, and a concern with both the affective and the effective elements of the classroom environment in which they worked.

The research on expertise has proved to be useful in policy analysis. Understanding the contextualization of expertise helps us to understand the limits of what we can expect from teachers and the irrationality of the expectations that we sometimes have. Learning that it takes considerable time to acquire competence in the pedagogical domain, let alone expertise, changes the way we think about support systems for the beginning teacher and the limits of teacher education programs. Learning what experts attend to, what they find worth remembering, how they implement routines, and how they maintain a classroom that is considerate of their students can help in designing programs of teacher education that are more focused on the acquisition of the pedagogical knowledge needed to teach both responsibly and effectively. The research has also provided us with ways to think about the growth or development of different kinds of knowledge in the pedagogical domain. Theories about the development of pedagogical expertise have been proposed that fit the existing data quite well. An example is my own description of a five-stage theory of the development of expertise, which posits the stages of novice, advanced beginner, competent performer, proficient performer, and expert (Berliner, 1989; based on work by Dreyfus and Dreyfus, 1986). Developmental theories of knowledge growth have implications for the kinds of assessments, the content of assessments, and the timing of assessments that will be used in the evaluation of teachers.

Expertise in pedagogy is now seen as a synthesis of what we call responsible and effective instruction. It appears to be a complex and highly sophisticated kind of domain-specific knowledge and skill, developed slowly over many years by highly motivated individuals. It is not a level of development that is obtained by everyone. The small number of teachers who achieve this status should be honored. They are the people whom we should ask the public to watch when the public is criticizing education. Few among the critics could ever match the experts' pedagogical skills day after exhausting day, year after exhausting year.

REFERENCES

Berliner, D. C. "In Pursuit of the Expert Pedagogue." *Educational Researcher*, 1987, 15 (7), 5–13.

Berliner, D. C. "Implications of Studies of Expertise in Pedagogy for Teacher Education and Evaluation." In *New Directions for Teacher Assessment.* Princeton, NJ: Educational Testing Service, 1989.

Berliner, D. C. and others. "Implications of Research on Pedagogical Expertise and Experience for Mathematics Teaching." In D. A. Grouws and T. J. Cooney (eds.), *Perspectives on Research on Effective Mathematics Teaching.* Reston, VA: National Council of Teachers of Mathematics, 1988.

Bloom, B. S. (ed.). *Developing Talent in Young People.* New York: Ballentine, 1985.

Bloom, B. S. "Automaticity." *Educational Leadership*, Feb. 1986, 70–77.

Borko, H. and Livingston, C. "Expert and Novice Teachers' Mathematics Instruction: Planning, Teaching Arid Post-Lesson Reflections." Paper presented at the meeting of the American Educational Research Association, New Orleans, LA, Apr. 1988.

Brown, J. S., Collins, A., and Duguid, P. "Situated Cognition and the Culture of Learning." *Educational Researcher*, 1989, 18 (1), 32–42.

Calderhead, J. "Research into Teachers' and Student Teachers' Cognitions: Exploring the Nature of Classroom Practice." Paper presented at the meeting of the American Educational Research Association, Montreal, Canada, Apr. 1983.

Carter, K., and others. "Processing and Using Information About Students: A Study of Expert, Novice and Postulant Teachers." *Teaching and Teacher Education*, 1987, 3, 147–157.

Carter, K., and others. "Expert-Novice Differences in Perceiving and Processing Visual Information." *Journal of Teacher Education*, 1988, 39 (3), 25–31.

Chase, W. G. and Simon, H. A. "Perception in Chess." *Cognitive Psychology*, 1973, 4, 55–81.

Chi, M.T.H., Glaser, R., and Farr, M. (eds.). *The Nature of Expertise.* Hillsdale, NJ: Erlbaum, 1988.

Clarridge, P. B. "Alternative Perspectives for Analyzing Expert, Novice, and Postulant Teaching." Unpublished dissertation, University of Arizona, Tucson, 1988.

deGroot, A. D. *Thought and Choice in Chess.* The Hague, The Netherlands: Mouton, 1965.

Dreyfus, H. L. and Dreyfus, S. E. *Mind over Machine.* New York: Free Press, 1986.

Glaser, R. "Thoughts on Expertise." In C. Schooler and W. Schaie (eds.), *Cognitive Functioning and Social Structure over the Life Course.* Norwood, NJ: Ablex, 1987.

Hanninen, G. "Do Experts Exist in Gifted Education?" Unpublished manuscript, College of Education, University of Arizona, Tucson, 1983.

Housner, L. D., and Griffey, D. C. "Teacher Cognition: Differences in Planning and Interactive Decision Making Between Experienced and Inexperienced Teachers." *Research Quarterly for Exercise and Sport*, 1985, 56, 44–53.

Johnson, E. J. "Expertise and Decision Under Uncertainty: Performance and Process." In M. T. H. Chi, R. Glaser, and M. Farr (eds.), *The Nature of Expertise*. Hillsdale, NJ: Erlbaum, 1988.

Krabbe, M. A. and Tullgren, R. "A Comparison of Experienced and Novice Teachers' Routines and Procedures During Set and Discussion Instructional Activity Segments." Paper presented at the meeting of the American Educational Research Association, San Francisco, Mar. 1989.

Krabbe, M. A., McAdams, A. G., and Tullgren, R. "Comparisons of Experienced and Novice Verbal and Nonverbal Expressions During Preview and Directing Instructional Activity Segments." Paper presented at the meeting of the American Educational Research Association, New Orleans, LA, Apr. 1988.

Leinhardt, G. and Greeno, J. "The Cognitive Skill of Teaching." *Journal of Educational Psychology*, 1986, 78, 75–95.

Lesgold, A. and others. "Expertise in a Complex Skill: Diagnosing X-Ray Pictures." In M. T. H. Chi, R. Glaser, and M. Farr (eds.), *The Nature of Expertise*. Hillsdale, NJ: Erlbaum, 1988.

Nelson, K. R. "Thinking Processes, Management Routines and Student Perceptions of Expert and Novice Physical Education Teachers." Unpublished dissertation, Louisiana State University, Baton Rouge, 1988.

Newell, A. and Simon, H. A. *Human Problem Solving*. Englewood Cliffs, NJ: Prentice-Hall, 1972.

Perkins, D. N. and Salomon, G. "Are Cognitive Skills Contextually-Bound?" *Educational Researcher*, 1989, 18, 16–25.

Peterson, P. L. and Comeaux, M. A. "Teachers' Schemata for Classroom Events: The Mental Scaffolding of Teachers' Thinking During Classroom Instruction." *Teaching and Teacher Education*, 1987, 3, 319–331.

Posner, M. I. "Introduction: What Is It to Be an Expert?" In M. T. H. Chi, R. Glaser, and M. Farr (eds.), *The Nature of Expertise*. Hillsdale, NJ: Erlbaum, 1988.

Rottenberg, C. V. and Berliner, D. C. "Expert and Novice Conceptions of Everyday Classroom Activities," forthcoming.

Sabers, D., Cushing, K., and Berliner, D. C. "Differences Among Teachers in a Task Characterized by Simultaneity, Multidimensionality and Immediacy." *American Educational Research Journal*, 1991, 28, 63–88.

Stein, P., Clarridge, P. B., and Berliner, D. C. "Teacher Estimation of Student Knowledge: Accuracy, Content and Process," forthcoming.

Part 6
Commentaries

42 Rethinking the study of learning to teach

Renée T. Clift
University of Illinois at Urbana-Champaign

As the chapters and artifacts in this section illustrate, teacher learning is the core of the teacher education agenda both for prospective teachers and experienced teachers. In the 1980s and 1990s, teacher learning was also the explicit focus of the reform agenda. Federal funds through the Goals 2000: Educate America Act, passed in 1994, provided funds for teachers and administrators to learn how to improve student achievement. Title II of the Amendments to the Higher Education Act in 1988 provided three separate categories of grants to improve teaching quality, targeting prospective teachers' learning as well as that of experienced teachers. Foundations have also supported reform. For example, in 2002 the Carnegie Corporation of New York's Teachers for a New Era project (in partnership with the Ford Foundation and the Annenberg Foundation) began funding universities to work with local school districts to reform preservice teacher education and the support for continued teacher learning following graduation. There are now eleven universities involved, all striving to improve teacher learning and, therefore, student learning (www.teachersforanewera.org).

The issues surrounding teacher learning are the subjects of many arguments as critics of preservice teacher education continuously challenge the curriculum in schools, colleges, and departments of education. For example, in a recent column in *Newsweek,* George Will (2006) attacked teacher education curricula that deal with topics such as social justice and awareness of how identities are performed in school as "enemies of rigor." In the *Journal of Teacher Education,* Sandra Stotsky (2006) called for accountability of preservice teacher education to be moved to the departments housing the disciplines, which would offer a Master of Arts in Teaching (MAT) degree.

> If entry into teaching Grades 5 to 12 required the completion of an M.A.T. program consisting of, say, four authentic graduate courses in the discipline and no more than one methods course followed by an apprenticeship in the schools that included seminars on what was taking place in the classroom, neither teacher tests nor departmental exit exams at the undergraduate level would be necessary.
>
> (p. 263)

Although the academic home for teacher education, the nature of the curriculum, and the balance of subject matter and pedagogy have long been topics for debate, the research base—empirical evidence to support the location and nature of instruction, the curriculum, the qualifications of instructors, etc.—is very thin (Cochran-Smith & Zeichner, 2005). Indeed, even with the publication of the two previous handbooks on research on teacher education and with the proliferation of international journals devoted to teacher education in the past ten years (e.g. *Studying Teacher Education; Asia-Pacific Journal of Teacher Education and Development*) there is little data to provide links between an individual's knowledge, their learning within a teacher education program, their actual teaching in schools, and their students' learning. Using the chapters and artifacts in this section as a springboard, I will discuss five areas that we, as researchers, must consider in order to impact our ability to conduct rigorous research on teacher learning that can inform policy and practice.

DESIGNING AND CONDUCTING LONGITUDINAL STUDIES OF LEARNING TO TEACH

There is considerable agreement that the field of teacher education in general and the study of teacher learning in particular would benefit greatly from more longitudinal studies of teacher learning over time and how that learning plays out in practice (Wilson *et al.*, 2001; Clift & Brady, 2005). Since publication of the Clift & Brady review, a few more studies have been published. These studies relay mainly on qualitative designs and are based on interviews with several novice teachers or employ case study designs that include classroom observations. Several studies attempt to represent multiple perspectives on the learning and teaching of novice teachers, as the co-author is often the former student (now teacher) working with the researcher to make sense of the way in which learning opportunities within the preservice program were continued in practice. The texts include the voice of both the researcher and the novice teacher, thus providing two views of the transition from student to full time teacher. These case studies identified building level factors (e.g. Smagorinsky *et al.*, 2004; Bickmore *et al.*, 2005), district level factors (e.g. Grossman & Thompson, 2004), and personal factors (e.g. Smulyan, 2004) that influence teachers' learning and their teaching practice, including the decision by some novice teachers to move to contexts that are more congruent with their beliefs, practices and intentions regarding teaching and continued learning.

In one longitudinal, intensive study in the Boston area, Susan Moore Johnson and colleagues (2004) carefully documented school contexts that were able to recruit and retain talented novice teachers over five years. They studied the building level factors that encouraged fifty teachers to continue learning about how to best teach and reach their students most effectively, particularly in schools with well designed induction and mentoring programs.

> Notably each of these schools places a high value on adult learning and professional growth. There was an underlying assumption that students would benefit as teachers became more knowledgeable and skilled. Teachers' development was a purposeful, community endeavor, not the lone effort of a motivated, entrepreneurial individual.
>
> (p. 237)

As we think about the importance of longitudinal work, it is important to note that all of the lead researchers cited above are tenured professors at their respective institutions. They can invest several years in data collection and analysis because they are not under pressure of tenure review. It is also important to note that much of this research, including mine, has been externally funded, mostly through the federal grants.

To increase the number of longitudinal studies, funding is required, but additional factors impact longitudinal designs, particularly those involving more in-depth case studies. My own research team (Clift *et al.*, 2006) documented the challenges that we faced as we followed thirteen students through their teacher education program and into their first years of teaching (or not teaching). Ownership of the study, shifting roles and responsibilities, and the intersection of personal and professional goals affected the composition of the research team over time. As team members left the project because their professional goals did not include participating on one project over five or more years, knowledge was lost. Not only their knowledge of the project and all of the participants, but the knowledge they brought to the team because their areas of interest informed our discussions and interpretations of the data. As new members came on to the project, time was lost as they struggled to learn about methodology, the participants, and the team culture.

As we think about designing longitudinal studies, seeking funding, and forming a research team, we need to think carefully about ways to sustain participation over time by research team members, as well as by the participants who are allowing us to learn about their learning. There are few methods texts to guide us in this work, which means that the field of research on teacher learning must be as attentive to careful documentation and critique of methods as it is to asking the right questions.

LANGUAGE, POWER, AND VULNERABILITY

All of the chapters in this section, in agreement with the essay by Dewey, embrace the view that teachers are continuous students of teaching. Two of the chapters explicitly identify language as an important aspect of that study. Rodgers and Scott focus on the need for preservice teachers and teacher educators to examine how self and identity are formed and reformed as one develops as a teacher. They note that the terms others use to describe the self and the terms one uses to describe oneself work together to define identity in particular contexts and in particular relationships. Rosaen and Florio-Ruane unpack metaphors that overtly and covertly construct the nature of teacher education, teacher learning, and student learning. Their discussion details the ways in which social and cultural factors shape our interpretation of individuals, groups, and events. Both chapters make clear, in different ways, why teachers need to be mindful of the language that shapes their beliefs and practice and be engaged in continuous reflection on the helpful and harmful dimensions of language.

The international community that comprises teacher educators and teachers who are engaged in the self-study of teacher education has often raised questions about the social, emotional, and political facets of language in relation to studying one's own teaching and learning, as well as when studying others' learning. In writing about self-study by teacher educators, Bullough & Pinnegar (2004) caution

> The expressed form of self-study is always constructed in relation to the audience being addressed and it is tempered by the recognition of the deep moral obligation teachers have to students. It is here where vulnerability presents a genuine danger, but it is recognized as part of learning, which also involves unlearning. When unlearning, the vulnerability felt by the teacher educator must be managed so that in its expression in teaching and in the reporting of the research no harm is done.
>
> (p. 340)

An investigation of self as learner is an individual, personal, reflective, and political enterprise, particularly concerning those areas that one might like to unlearn. It is one thing when it is private, voluntary and under one's control. Required sharing of one's study of self with a teacher, a researcher, or even a peer is something else altogether. As we study learning to teach and teacher learning, and as we engage our students and colleagues in reflections on the role played by language in the construction of society and self, we do so in institutional and political contexts that may be hostile to what we are learning. Furthermore, as the Will essay quoted at the opening of this commentary illustrates, we must be mindful of the ideologies that oppose and scorn what we are attempting to enable. This makes the study of language, how it constructs and constrains world-views and how it is interpreted differently by different people, even more important. But we must also be mindful of the individual vulnerabilities that are created when a student explores his or her own practice or beliefs in the context of a classroom or research project and the individual and collective vulnerabilities that are created as we use language to challenge language use. As one of my research team members noted, "And I think I have become increasingly comfortable telling you how I feel, but I don't know if . . . there is definitely a very strong edit button," (Clift *et al.*, 2006, p. 93). In other words, research on learning to teach and teacher learning does not occur in a linguistic, political, ideological, or power vacuum; attending to this reality deliberately, rather than being surprised by it later, is an important aspect of research design.

INTRUSION AND THE PROTECTION OF HUMANS

Westheimer's chapter raises specific questions about the tenuous balance between respect, competing interpretations, and argument as teachers work in learning communities within their own schools.

> Much of the research and practice relating teacher community to teacher learning advocates working together, overlooking differences, and creating friendlier, more open work settings for teachers. More work would be useful that studies power imbalances and the resulting sense of impotence that threaten to undo so many of these well-meaning reforms.
>
> (p. 773)

The presence of a researcher, a documenter of agreements and disagreements, can exacerbate these threats. Even with pseudonyms, the audience who works in the school or community is very likely to read beyond the code names and to be able to identify individuals, places and events. The threat to self and professional identity may not come from being known to a national audience, but to the local audience. Thus, instances of an individual's learning that are negative or of contexts that are ineffective in terms of promoting learning may result in personal embarrassment or even hostility form one's colleagues.

For most institutional review boards, the question of any potential harm to human research participants is a key component of approval. Indeed, some boards have been known to disallow any research that involves a teacher studying his or her students (Hemming, 2006). In our review of studies of methods courses and field experiences (Clift & Brady, 2005), we found that many researchers who were studying their own students did not attend to the possibility that these students were engaging in behaviors that were advocated by professors, and that their findings were not tempered with cautions that learning or acting in a certain way occurred as a result of course expectations. Investigating one's own learning and one's students' learning necessitates collecting evidence of learning from multiple sources whenever possible. But even when the investigator is not part of the classroom setting, the study of teacher learning is still affected by the presence of the researcher or the knowledge that one is participating in a study.

Likewise, the researcher is changed by his or her participation. This is particularly evident when an investigator is accepted into a school community and invited to study professional learning with that community. Craig (2003), for example, documented the discomfort she felt when administrators approved of and encouraged her to study teachers' participation in a school reform effort, her attempts to become accepted, and her subsequent reflections on the situation. Accustomed to working in schools and with teachers, she was surprised to learn that while she was welcomed by the administration, she was not welcomed by many of the teachers. Many of them viewed her presence with suspicion and let her know they were hesitant to talk to her about their perceptions of the reforms. Her notions of working in schools and with teachers were fundamentally changed.

> Even as I was drawn in from the margins into YMS's reform vortex, as my work and my identity as a researcher became questioned in the episode by the school-based educators, and during and after the episode by the school-based educators and after the episode by me. Like the practitioners, I also sought ways to manoeuvre [sic] carefully on the landscape and to avoid landmines such as arriving at a gathering to which I was invited, but not fully welcome. The overall effect, as the reform effort shows, is not one of passing discomfort; it comprises full strength upheaval for all those whose professional lives take shape in reform active contexts with deeply etched social, narrative histories.
>
> (pp. 644–645)

Studies of teacher learning, whether smaller self-studies, studies of reform, or large scale longitudinal studies in which teacher educators work with others who are in different fields have the potential to challenge even as they inform. As we design and work with our students to design studies of teacher learning, we may need to think beyond the requirements of review boards to consider how our work may impact events, our findings, and our sense of who we are as teachers/researchers/learners.

CHANGES, CHANGES, AND MORE CHANGES

When I was an assistant professor, I was invited to participate in a reform of a teacher education program. Since my field of study was curriculum design and teacher education, it seemed like a natural invitation to accept. The processes and outcomes of our work were recorded in a book chapter (Clift *et al.*, 1992), along with the work of others across the country who were also engaged in teacher education curriculum reform. At the end of our chapter, we recount the dismantling of the program because of state mandates to restrict the curriculum hours devoted to professional education. I was disappointed about the lost opportunity. I had naively thought that once we had negotiated with faculty members and had passed through university and state approval processes, we would then be able to study the program, to investigate student outcomes, and to modify the program based on what we were learning about our students' learning. I have become more pragmatic over time as I talk with others who have sought to study a given program, only to learn that the program is being modified in the midst of their research. There are political, social, and individual factors that impact program stability over time and, therefore, the opportunity to evaluate program impact.

I now work in a nineteen-year-old department that has experienced eight department heads; five deans; six provosts; and one major reform of the early childhood, elementary, and secondary teacher education programs. Despite the changes in administration, my colleagues and I are committed to helping teachers learn to understand better and teach more effectively the students with whom they work. Many of us have engaged in the systematic study of our students' learning. I also work in a state that is divided into slightly less than 900 school districts and ranks in the bottom in terms of equality of education funding across districts. Seven out of every ten schools are operating with a deficit (Illinois Poverty Summit, 2005). Teachers leave high poverty schools and urban schools at higher rates than their counterparts (Klosterman *et al.*, 2003). As I write this, there are major state-wide debates concerning funding for education. Embedded within those debates is funding to support some level of mentoring and induction for new teachers and higher accountability for teachers' and schools' productivity. Internal change within institutions and external change brought about by policy are constants.

As we think about designing systematic studies of teacher learning and the contexts (university courses, community experiences, school-based experiences, etc.) designed to support that learning, we cannot ignore the continuous pressures for change that come from national, state, and local origins. We can either lament the presence of constant change or recognize that conditions for teaching and for teacher education are seldom stable. How teachers and teacher educators learn to resist effectively when change is harmful to students and communities and how they learn to adapt to change in ways that are helpful to students and communities are two areas of study that are not well documented in the literature on learning to teach. What is well documented is that the field of research on teacher learning, right now, is dominated by qualitative studies, most of which are small scale and many of which are some versions of self-study.

TRAINING FOR THE STUDY OF LEARNING TO TEACH

A growing number of scholars in teacher education are calling for a rethinking of how we prepare our graduate students to become the next generation of researchers. For example, in the final, synthesis chapter of the report of the AERA Panel on Research and Teacher Education, Zeichner (2005) called for a serious reconsideration of how educational researchers are prepared, including more funding for doctoral training programs for research in teacher education and post-doctoral opportunities to work with more experienced educators. Shulman *et al.* (2006) suggested that doctoral students in education who are preparing to be scholar practitioners should be prepared in fundamentally different ways from those who intend to devote most of their academic careers to research. Most of our doctoral students are exposed to a limited number of models of teacher education research, particularly in the areas of teacher and teacher educator learning.

In the introduction to this section, Sharon Feiman-Nemser concluded with a call for linking teacher learning to student learning and for better integration across programs of research. This is unlikely to happen unless researchers—whether in teacher education, student learning, organizational behavior, etc.—design programs of research that may incorporate, but go far beyond studies of their own classroom and students. Designs that involve researchers from different backgrounds who represent diverse theoretical orientations and teachers (at colleges and universities and in P-12 contexts) should work together to seek out funding to learn with one another and from one another's expertise—bringing graduate students into the work in meaningful ways. Indeed, many of these graduate students will be former teachers and, if their expertise and experience is tapped, research designs can become richer, more productive, and more respectful of all who are involved. Finally, given the issues of turnover I mentioned earlier, we may want to give more consideration to ways in which designs might anticipate some attrition, projects in which graduate students might engage in collaborative dissertations, cultures in which collaboration is expected and rewarded, and more publications (both in print and over the Internet) in which multiple perspectives, areas of consensus and dissent, and alternative interpretations are the norm.

The artifact from Dewey ends with the following plea, "The thing needful is improvement of education, not simply by turning out teachers who can do better the things that are now necessary to do, but rather by changing the conception of what constitutes education." With respect, I would like to end with a paraphrase of this quote. The thing needful is improvement of educational research and the education of educational researchers, not simply by turning out graduates who can do better the things that are now necessary to do, but rather by changing the conception of what constitutes meaningful research on teaching and learning to teach. At present, many researchers are comfortable working in their disciplines and replicating their own experiences as they work with their doctoral students. This is reinforced in many institutions that demand individual accountability for publications because they know how to evaluate this form of productivity. It is further reinforced by the absence of funds or professional structures that encourage multi-disciplinary, collaborative, cross-institutional, and long-term research. Re-learning and changing what we know and do in relation to the study of learning to teach is an important agenda for those of us who are committed to the continuous improvement of teaching and learning.

REFERENCES

Bickmore, S. T., Smagorinsky, P., & O'Donnell-Allen, C. (2005) Tensions between traditions: the role of contexts in learning to teach. *English Education*, 38(1), 23–52.

Bullough, Jr., R. V. & Pinnegar, S. E. (2004) Thinking about the thinking about self-study: an analysis of eight chapters. In J. J Loughran, M. L. Hamilton, V. K. LaBoskey, & T. Russell (eds.), *International handbook of self-study of teaching and teacher education practices*. Dordrecht, The Netherlands: Kluwer Academic Publishers (pp. 313–342).

Carnegie Foundation of New York (n.d.) *Teachers for a New Era*. Retrieved January 7, 2007 from http://www.teachersforanewera.org.

Clift, R. T. & Brady, P. (2005) Research on methods courses and field experiences. In M. Cochran-Smith & K. Zeichner (eds.), *Studying teacher education: the report of the AERA Panel on Research and Teacher Education*. Mahwah, NJ: Lawrence Erlbaum (pp. 309–424).

Clift, R. T., Houston, W. R., & McCarthy, J. (1992) Getting it RITE: A case of negotiated curriculum in teacher education. In L. Valli (ed.) *Reflective teacher education: case studies and critiques*. New York: SUNY (pp. 116–135).

Clift, R. T., Brady, P., Mora, R. A., Stegemoller, J., & Choi, S. J. (2006) From self-study to collaborative self-study to collaborative self-study of a collaboration: the evolution of a research team. In C. Kosnick, C. Beck, A. R. Freeze, & A. P. Samaras (eds.), *Making a difference in teacher education through self-study: studies of personal, professional, and program renewal*. Dordrecht, The Netherlands: Springer (pp. 85–100).

Cochran-Smith, M. & Zeichner, K. (eds.) *Studying teacher education: the report of the AERA Panel on Research and Teacher Education*. Mahwah, NJ: Lawrence Erlbaum.

Craig, C. J. (2003) Characterizing the human experience of reform in an urban middle-school context. *Journal of Curriculum Studies*, 35(5), 627–648.

Grossman, P. & Thompson, C. (2004) District policy and beginning teachers: a lens on teacher learning. *Educational Evaluation and Policy Analysis*, 26(4), 281–301.

Hemming, A. (2006) Great ethical divides: bridging the gap between institutional review boards and researchers. *Educational Researcher*, 35(4), 12–18.

Illinois Poverty Summit (2005) *2005 Report on Illinois Poverty*. Chicago, IL: Author Retrieved on January 22, 2007 from www.heartlandalliance.org/creatingchange/documents/2005RptonILPoverty.pdf.

Johnson, S.M. & the Project on the Next Generation of Teachers (2004) *Finders and keepers: helping new teachers survive and thrive in our schools*. San Francisco: Jossey-Bass.

Klosterman, B. K., Presley, J. B., Peddle, M. T., Trott, C. E., & Bergeron, L. (2003) *Teacher induction in Illinois: evidence from the Illinois Teacher Study*. Edwardsville, IL: Illinois Education Research Council. Retrieved on January 22, 2007 from http://ierc.siue.edu/documents/IERC_03_2.pdf.

Shulman, L., Golde, C. M., Bueschl, A. C., & Garabedian, K. J. (2006) Reclaiming education's doctorates: a critique and a proposal. *Educational Researcher*, 35(3) 25–32.

Smagorinsky, P., Cook, L. S., & Johnson, T. S. (2004) The twisting path of concept development in learning to teach. *Teachers College Record*, 105(8), 1399–1436.

Smulyan, L. (2004) Choosing to teach. *Teachers College Record*, 106 (3), 2004, 513–554. Retrieved on November, 29, 2005 from http://www.tcrecord.org.

Stotsky, S. (2006) Who should be accountable for what beginning teachers need to know? *Journal of Teacher Education*, 57(3), 256–268.

Will, G. (2006, January 16). Ed Schools vs. Education. Newsweek. Retrieved on January 28, 2007 from http://www.msnbc.msn.com/id/10753446/site/newsweek/.

Wilson, S., Floden, R., & Ferrini Mundy, J. (2001) *Teacher preparation research: current knowledge, gaps, and recommendations*. Washington, DC: University of Washington Center for the Study of Teaching and Policy.

Zeichner, K. M. (2005) A research agenda for teacher education. In M. Cochran-Smith & K. Zeichner (eds.), *Studying teacher education: the report of the AERA Panel on Research and Teacher Education*. Mahwah, NJ: Lawrence Erlbaum (pp. 761–759).

43 Perspectives on teacher learning
Normative, logical, empirical

Daniel Fallon
Carnegie Corporation

INTRODUCTION

My academic life began at Antioch College in the late 1950s and early 1960s with a rigorous liberal education interspersed with co-op jobs in the real world. I proceeded to the University of Virginia as a graduate student in experimental psychology. Learning and motivation was my principal field of study, primarily in tightly controlled experiments with laboratory animals. Using college students as subjects and procedures that would today be called cognitive science, I also conducted studies on human learning, memory, and retention.

As a new professor, I advocated strongly in the faculty senate for the admission of more students of color, and as these arguments met with success, I was drawn into academic administration. Prevented by the demands of my work schedule from conducting my own laboratory experiments, I shifted to writing about the experimental literature, relying on review and analysis done in libraries and at home.

As a dean of liberal arts and sciences at three universities, and later as a provost at a fourth, I changed my research focus from psychology to education. I wrote about curricular innovations within U.S. higher education, and on comparative higher education, focusing on the German research university. In 1989, as president of the Council of Colleges of Arts and Sciences, a national association, I undertook a partnership with the American Association of Colleges for Teacher Education to explore innovations in teacher education through Project 30, a Carnegie-funded national initiative.

I offer these brief paragraphs of background to illuminate the values that inform my commentary on this section of the *Handbook*. Reading the framing chapters and artifacts, I was stimulated to think about three perspectives on research and analysis on teacher learning: normative, logical, and empirical. As I began writing, I recalled with sympathy William James' observation in his classic 1890 text, *Principles of Psychology*, "I am often confronted by the necessity of standing by one of my empirical selves and relinquishing the rest. . . . All other selves thereupon become unreal, but the fortunes of this self are real. Its failures are real failures, its triumphs real triumphs . . ." (James, 1890, pp. 309–310).

Modes of reasoning

There are many ways to approach an analysis of teaching and the role of school teachers in bringing about pupils' learning. I organize this body of work by its contribution to three modes of reasoning: normative, logical, and empirical.

For persons trained in laboratory-based science and quantitative methods, the term "normative" usually means a central tendency in a population of measures around which variation occurs. Norm-referenced testing is an example of this use. In most educational discourse, however, the term normative has a technical meaning derived from the work of the sociologist Talcott Parsons (1937). This framework was most clearly brought into philosophical thought in the eighteenth century by David Hume, who contrasted descriptive statements (what *is*) with normative statements (what *ought to be*). Thus, normative refers to a mode of reasoning with values at its core. An example of a normative statement is that teachers should be competent, caring, and professional.

Logical reasoning is entirely dependent upon clearly stated and easily understood rules. With logic, knowledge is gained through the rational process called thinking and does not depend upon verification by observation. For example, if we know that a child cannot learn subject matter in the absence of that subject matter, we can deduce that if the teacher does not know the subject matter, the child cannot learn the subject matter from the teacher.

Empiricism refers to knowledge gained directly from observation based upon experience. Although essential to the procedures and reasoning associated with the scientific method, empirical knowledge by itself is not sufficient for science, which also requires systematic observation, usually in the form of designed experiments. Empirical reasoning can derive from qualitative methods, as in the examination and subsequent rating of portfolios of student work, or from quantitative methods, as in counting the number of arithmetic problems correctly solved by one student compared with other students.

Applying the modes to educational literature

Normative and logical conclusions could be subjected to empirical verification, but for many important purposes do not need to be. For example, we might choose to define successful teaching empirically as public evidence of student learning attributable to the teacher. Because this empirical definition has face validity in that most observers agree with it, I use it as a first screen when asking whether we have empirical evidence to support an assertion in the teacher education and teacher learning literature.

Now consider a normative proposition with which virtually everyone would agree: teachers should not abuse students. Conceptually we could imagine an empirical verification of whether abusive teachers are successful by measuring the learning of students assigned to abusive teachers in comparison with the learning of students assigned to non-abusive teachers; however, such a study is ethically unsupportable and in most places illegal. Many normative propositions are of this type, i.e. they define a threshold ethical context that overrules any empirical considerations.

The same arguments apply to most logical arguments, as illustrated in the proposition that teachers charged with teaching a subject matter domain should know the subject matter domain. Although many normative and logical propositions do not require empirical validation, empirical investigation often reveals matters of immense importance to the field of teacher learning, even when logical or normative arguments are seemingly very sound.

Consider the case of teacher subject-matter knowledge, for which we have established a logical foundation. In the domain of mathematics, there is compelling empirical evidence that student learning increases with the mathematical knowledge possessed by the teacher, but only up to a certain point, after which puzzling complications ensue. In an empirical study on a national longitudinal database (Monk, 1994), the number of college-level courses taken by the teacher served as the measure of mathematical knowledge, and scores on the National Assessment of Educational Progress provided a measure of student learning. Student learning of mathematics indeed increased with the number of courses taken by the teacher, but only up to an asymptote of about five courses. A second empirical study by Rowan *et al.* (2002) indicated that students taught by teachers with advanced degrees in mathematics learned less than those taught by teachers who had taken fewer courses in mathematics.

These findings are important in understanding the nature of teacher learning as it relates to student learning, but they could not have been persuasively revealed by logical argument alone. Empirical study was essential. Furthermore, these empirical findings call into question a normative assertion that teachers improve their teaching of subject matter by completing advanced academic work in the field of study they will be teaching. The findings do not necessarily contradict this assertion, but they suggest that important qualifications, based on empirical investigation, may be needed before we can determine how to qualify the assertion.

Empirical investigation can also reveal startling findings that may revolutionize a field. A vivid example is the progress made by medical science in the nineteenth century in developing the germ theory of disease (Ewald, 1994), which many regard as the most important contribution by science to the welfare of people. The critical breakthrough, pioneered by the work of Louis Pasteur, came in the early twentieth century and led to universal adoption of "scrubbing up," the practice of vigorous washing of hands before a clinical intervention. This simple practice immediately caused human mortality to plummet and life expectancies to increase. We now understand that germs cause disease, and that scrubbing up eliminates unseen microbiological vectors. The huge leap forward in saving lives was made possible by careful empirical investigation. Are such prospects possible for teaching? A persuasive answer depends on the kind of empirical inquiry that is now in its infancy in the field of teacher education and teacher learning.

Sensing a historic shift

Sharon Feiman-Nemser's lucid introduction to this section on teacher learning implicitly highlights my reading that the field of teacher education and teacher learning is deep and rich in normative and logical reasoning, but shallow in empirical knowledge. As Borko *et al.* (2007) point out, teacher education is a relatively new field of study and it is very expensive and complex to design and carry out the kind of empirical studies that would benefit the field. Although this is an accurate assessment, the current historical moment is driven by political, social and technical factors that now favor sound empirical research.

Advanced societies are passing through a revolutionary turning point. In 1910 the U.S. census found that 50 percent of adults reported that they had completed more than eight years of schooling. By 1968 more than 50 percent of U.S. adults reported that they had completed more than twelve years of schooling. The effects of this aggregation of intellectual capital in the late twentieth century is being felt dramatically in all sectors of the economy.

New knowledge-based industries such as information, technology, and services are producing wealth at a rapid pace. The mainstays of the U.S. economy formed more than a century ago such as agriculture, manufacturing and heavy industry now increasingly characterize the economies of developing countries. High-wage low-skill jobs are emigrating out of the U.S., and are being replaced within the U.S. by new jobs requiring relatively high levels of skill and education. Since these deep shifts in our underlying political economy are occurring in all advanced societies, the U.S. now competes with others for educated workers. These forces are the principle drivers behind today's pervasive standards-based pressure on schools and teachers. They are more likely to increase than to recede in the near future.

We have also seen a dramatic increase in physical technology primarily through computers, and in intellectual technology through advanced statistical analytic methods. We now have the capacity to store and sort very large quantities of numerical data in very little physical space and to retrieve information from these data warehouses with relative ease. The introduction of widespread mandatory statewide tests in the late 1980s, coupled with the capacity to store information, made possible the accumulation and management of longitudinal databases that linked test scores of individual students with the specific teachers who taught them during the preceding year. Researchers skilled in statistics began to refine hierarchical linear models to look at the relative contribution to student learning, as measured by standardized tests, of various factors in schooling. Thus, empirical methods led to now widely discussed value-added assessment measures and to the increasingly accepted conclusion that teachers are the most important school-related factor in producing student learning.

We are at a very early stage of accommodating these advances. Statistical techniques, more powerful than any before them, nonetheless remain at a primitive stage of development; measures are often taken from tests with unknown or unsatisfactory psychometric properties. We have not yet widely applied broader and more authentic assessments. Given the inexorable pressure from the society at large for improvement of academic performance by the nation's school children, as reflected in public policy, the time is ripe for significant government investment in educational research. The research community in the field of teacher education and teacher learning may be on the verge of an extraordinary opportunity to find the financing and conditions for research that will greatly expand our empirical knowledge.

The framing chapters

The chapters by Rodgers and Scott and by Rosaen and Florio-Ruane each reflect normative traditions within the profession. Each chapter also acknowledges the lack of empirical validation.

Proceeding from an insight-based tradition within clinical psychology, Rodgers and Scott state at the outset, "We hope that the introduction of a psychological frame will move the field of teacher education towards more empirical work in the development of self and identity in learning to teach" (p. 733). They conclude with the observation, "Clearly, what is still missing from the literature and the field is empirical work that seeks to better understand the role of psychology in teacher education" (p. 752). The chapter ends by asking the question, left unanswered, that is my primary filter for determining whether successful teaching has occurred, "What is the impact on [the teacher's] students' learning?"

Rosaen and Florio-Ruane state in their introduction, "We . . . call for empirical study of the alternative metaphors for designing and redesigning teacher education offered in the chapter . . ." (p. 708). In the concluding section they write, ". . . research on metaphors that reflect teachers' conceptions of teaching and sense of self provides a foundation for . . . empirical work" (p. 726). The authors then pose a series of questions about teacher learning that could be answered by empirical investigation, such as, "If teacher candidates have opportunities to investigate metaphorical language as part of study groups comprised of experienced teachers and teacher educators, what do these activities help novices notice and pay attention to?" The ultimate empirical question of what impact such education might have on the learning of these teachers students is not raised here.

Conspicuous in these chapters is the lack of empirical grounding for the ideas expressed. I have identified student learning as the critical dependent variable in studies of teacher learning and teacher education. What normative studies, such as those cited by Rodgers and Scott or Rosaen and Florio-Ruane, contribute is a strong theoretical framework for developing a set of independent variables. Until these independent variables have been connected to credible measurable dependent variables, they remain untested hypotheses joining others in a long queue of prospects for scientific examination.

Westheimer's chapter on learning communities surveys a wide research literature that focuses on empirical outcomes. For example, Westheimer cites a survey of four studies that show the effects of professional learning communities on a wide variety of dependent variables: "reduced dropout rates among students, lower absenteeism rates, academic achievement gains (as measured by standardized tests) in math, science, history, and reading, and reduced gaps in achievement gains between students of varying socio-economic backgrounds" (p. 761).

Westheimer's chapter also illustrates the tension between deductive approaches to collecting data and inductive approaches. Deductive reasoning involves working from a set of theoretical suppositions, and then designing data collection and analysis procedures to test them. In such a deductive mode, Westheimer asserts, "Highly restrictive, state-level curriculum frameworks, standards-based evaluations, and high-stakes testing for teachers and students can severely curtail new teachers' capacities to teach as a community of colleagues . . ." (p. 771). No citations of empirical evidence are provided in support of this statement. Later, he cites a non-empirical speculation ". . . that matters of time and money are likely to be obstacles to community, particularly in low-income and understaffed schools" (p. 772). The theoretical framework informing these statements could be subjected to empirical test.

Inductive reasoning asks questions in the reverse order. For example, in a set of well-conceived studies, Springboard Schools first identified sets of schools matched on several variables, including low socio-economic status, where one set had shown a rapid trajectory of strong improvement and the other set had not (Oberman, 2005). The question for the investigators was: what conditions differentiated these schools? The overriding common difference was the development in the high-performing schools of professional learning communities. Every one of these high-performing schools was characterized by low degrees of time and money and all were in precisely the kinds of public-policy environments that Westheimer speculates would curtail capacity to teach as a community. Thus an inductive approach built from the ground up on empirical observation creates what appears to be an insurmountable challenge to the hypothetico-deductive reasoning stemming from a popular but untested theory.

The artifacts

The artifacts are rich in normative reasoning and they also reflect a deep understanding of the value of empirical evidence.

Lucy Sprague Mitchell's inspiring, hortatory essay introduces empiricism in the very first paragraph, "So it is with a long-term experiment. It is only later when one can study the day-by-day records with a detached attitude that one can get a total picture. That is the reason for keeping records—to have something more reliable than memory as a basis for analysis" (p. 800). With respect to the dependent variable of student learning, Mitchell writes that her curriculum ". . . was based on two fundamental concepts—what children are like and what subject matter, experiences, and activities best further their growth" (p. 806). She concludes her essay by again stressing student learning, "Every Workshop teacher we met was bubbling over with some tale of 'what her children had done' " (p. 807). We see in this enthusiastic pioneer the reliance on empirical observation of student learning that was, in fact, what made her successful.

Dewey's dense, tightly interdependent rhetoric builds a convincing case for thinking of teaching as clinical practice, and for the development of clinical practice through guided and reflective experience. Writing about student teaching, he recommends that ". . . the wise employ of this short time is in laying scientific foundations" (p. 788). He stresses that the artificiality of practice teaching makes the situation unreal for teacher candidates in contrast with the teacher candidate who ". . . has to build up and modify his teaching plans as he goes along from experience gained in contact with pupils" (p. 789). With respect to the dependent variable, Dewey insists upon ". . . the stress laid upon a certain end, namely growth or development . . ." (p. 793). In a prescient observation, he says that a science of teacher learning demands ". . . consecutive and longitudinal consideration of the curriculum of the elementary and high school rather than a cross-sectional view of it" (p. 796). With Dewey, the necessity of an empirical orientation arising from direct experience is never in doubt.

Berliner's now classic account of his research into the difference between novice and expert teachers continues to be valuable in many ways. It is, of course, empirical in that it compares and contrasts the clinical practice of beginning teachers with those of more experienced ones. His work demonstrates convincingly how qualitative rather than quantitative dependent measures can be empirical, systematic, and productive of reliable new knowledge. Lending great persuasiveness to his arguments is his ability to frame his findings against a large experimental literature of novices and experts in domains far removed from teaching. With respect to the critical dependent variable, Berliner's findings are consistent with Mitchell and Dewey in pointing to student learning as the key measure of teacher quality. Berliner writes of experts, for example, that their teaching is ". . . primarily for growth and improvement rather than for sorting children out along an ability continuum" (p. 816). His studies are, like those of Springboard Schools, inductive rather than deductive. Berliner did not begin by attempting to prove a hypothesis derived from theory, but rather proceeded by careful observation of teachers differing along a continuum of low to high experience/expertise and let the empirical outcome dictate his theoretical considerations. Although this line of research outlines for us what the goal of teacher learning might look like, it does not tell us how to help novice teachers learn to be expert. It would be immensely valuable to replicate this line of work today, when we can use the technologies associated with value-added analysis to identify empirically highly effective teachers and contrast their clinical practice with that of novice teachers and experienced but low effective teachers.

Summary and conclusion

I have described three perspectives for approaching the research literature on teacher education and teacher learning. Normative reasoning is built upon values and describes what the enterprise of teaching should be. Logical reasoning ensures that a system of propositions about teaching is internally consistent. Empirical reasoning is dependent upon reliable observation of publicly observable events, and is usually advanced by careful measurement and quantitative analysis. Normative propositions can be valuable in their own right and need not always be validated empirically. Empirical validation is rarely necessary for logical propositions, since each proposition can be rationally determined from other propositions. Yet science cannot advance without empirical study. We cannot confidently determine a responsible program to ensure teacher learning without a solid empirical foundation.

The literature of teacher education and teacher learning is richly endowed with normative and logical argumentation, but empirical evidence to support a program of teacher learning is scarce. The richness of the normative literature ensures a plenitude of independent variables that might be employed in empirical study. The essential and necessary dependent variable to employ as a measure of teacher quality, and thus of teacher learning, is student learning attributable to the clinical practice of the teacher.

We are entering a historic period in which it may be possible to gain financial and academic support for rigorous high-quality empirical studies that advance the field of teacher learning. We have physical and intellectual technology that is far superior to any available even in the recent past. Thus there is good reason to resonate with the optimism expressed by William James that our empirical triumphs will be real triumphs.

REFERENCES

Borko, H., Liston, D., & Whitcomb, J. A. (2007) Editorial: genres of empirical research in teacher education. *Journal of Teacher Education*, 58, 3–11.

Ewald, P. W. (1994) *The evolution of infectious disease*. New York: Oxford University Press. Chapter 10.

James, W. (1890) *Principles of psychology. Volume I*. New York: Henry Holt and Co.

Monk, D. H. (1994) Subject area preparation of secondary mathematics and science teachers and student achievement. *Economics of Education Review*, 13, 125–145.

Oberman, I. (2005) *Challenged schools, remarkable results: three lessons from California's highest achieving high schools*. San Francisco: Springboard Schools.

Parsons, T. (1937) *The structure of social action*. New York: McGraw-Hill.

Rowan, B., Correnti, R., & Miller, R. J. (2002) What large-scale survey research tells us about teacher effects on student achievement: Insights from the Prospects study of elementary schools. *Teachers College Record*, 104, 1525–1777.

44 Teacher learning

A commentary by reform-minded teaching colleagues

Vivian Troen
Brandeis University

Katherine C. Boles
Harvard Graduate School of Education

When we were invited to comment on this section of the *Handbook of Research in Teacher Education*, we were pleased with the opportunity to respond to the powerful words of this diverse group of educators. It gave us a chance to reflect with a historical lens and an eye to the future on a topic that has engaged us for over 25 years—the topic of teacher learning.

What we value most about this collection is that each chapter emphasizes the intellectual nature of teaching, the prime importance of subject matter, the importance of understanding the student's mind and psychology, and giving teachers the opportunity to develop expertise in the company of other teachers. These works honor the layers and levels in teaching and learning to teach—weaving the recognition of complexity and valuing expertise—and realizing that all ideas about education must be nested in the culture of teaching and schools. Each chapter celebrates John Dewey's idea that we must prepare teachers to be "students of teaching" and, as the chapters make clear, it is at our peril if we do not create a teaching force of thinking, critical, highly intellectual and competent teachers with strong teacher identities. While the artifacts are mostly historical, and the three chapters present their ideas from a more "modern" perspective, they all demonstrate that, in the field of education, the difficulties and challenges faced by teachers and learners have not significantly changed in the past 100 years.

If one message connects all six pieces, it is that very little of what we call "deep learning" can occur without intellectual community. Joel Westheimer, reviewing the research of historians and sociologists who have examined teaching over the last century, says straightforwardly that the culture of teaching, both in the past and currently, has worked against creating this intellectual community. Too few teachers, he argues (echoing our own experience), are adequately prepared to learn from one another, and too few schools create the conditions where learning from colleagues might be possible.

Reading these chapters brought to mind the process of discovery we engaged in when, in 1985, the two of us formed a teaching partnership which led to the formation of the Learning/Teaching Collaborative—a collaboration among Boston and Brookline, Massachusetts public schools and Wheelock and Simmons Colleges—one of the nation's first professional development schools. We were fourth grade elementary school teachers, examining our professional lives and practice, and by extension, the culture of schools and schooling.

Being acutely aware of the debilitating norm of professional privacy and lack of collaboration that surrounded us as classroom teachers, even in the "congenial" school culture in which we taught, we sought structures that would help us address what we saw as fundamental weaknesses. The life of the classroom teacher with its inherent isolation supported neither collegiality nor intellectual stimulation. We were concerned with the one-step nature of the teaching career, a major factor in the deteriorating quality of student teachers now that there were so many options for educated women in the workforce. We were troubled as we watched children with learning problems—those who could least handle a fragmented day—taken out of the classroom for longer and more frequent periods of time. Working collaboratively as co-teachers who taught in the same classroom, we began to compile a list of things that needed change. We soon realized that we were looking at a blueprint for educational reform.

With a group of teacher colleagues we studied the "greats," starting with John Dewey. His ideas helped prepare the philosophical foundation for our school/college collaborative where we wanted to create a new culture of learning—one in which we were all "students of teaching." According to Dewey, ". . . unless they [teachers] continue to be students of subject-matter, and students of mind activity . . ." and unless ". . . a teacher is such a student, he may continue to improve in the mechanics of school management, but he can not grow as a teacher, an inspirer and director of soul-life." (Dewey, 1976) We agreed with Dewey, and through our collaboration and our efforts to improve our intellectual lives as teachers, we proved to ourselves and others that teaching could and indeed must be a profession in which growth and learning on the part of the teacher must parallel the growth and learning of children.

We wrote and published papers, and attempted to deliver our message in many venues. *Education Leadership* rejected one of our first articles because they "already had an article in that issue by a teacher." A respondent at an AERA session commented on our presentation by characterizing us as "the girls from Brookline with laudable goals." Many thought our ideas were too radical. Others questioned our credentials. We were only teachers. Who were we to suggest these reforms?

But thanks to a convergence of forces, notably the perseverance and the power of working collaboratively, the support of our principal Jerry Kaplan, and the invaluable assistance of Karen Worth, a professor at Wheelock College, The Learning/Teaching Collaborative eventually took shape and grew (Troen and Boles, 1994). The overarching goal of this collaborative was to create new professional roles for teachers while providing them with the opportunity to continue teaching in their own classrooms. There are four components to LTC: (1) a collaborative school-based model for pre-service teacher preparation; (2) team teaching; (3) integrated delivery of special education services; (4) alternative roles for teachers as part of the school day, utilizing what we called Alternative Professional Teaching time (APT). This team-teaching model altered the organization of instruction, mainstreamed special needs children, and created new professional roles for classroom teachers in research, curriculum development, and teacher preparation.

At the heart of the Learning/Teaching Collaborative is the continuum of learning to teach. Novices are inducted into the culture of the team and veterans and novices alike make their teaching practice public. This context of teacher learning, woven through and across levels of expertise and knowledge, provides rich intellectual excitement. All are involved in the study of teaching—veteran learning from novice, novice learning from veteran (Troen and Boles, 1997).

Joel Westheimer emphasizes that the culture of teaching currently and in the past has worked against creating this intellectual community. Our objective was to change the culture of schools and schooling, and we therefore set out to create a community of learning. Three over-arching themes in the chapters and artifacts that make up this section echo the beliefs that became the foci of the Learning/Teaching collaborative:

1   the creation of a collaborative context for successful teacher learning;
2   acknowledgment that learning to teach is an ongoing process;
3   recognition that teaching is complex, intellectual work.

The historic chapters agree on these points: Teaching is complex intellectual work that cannot be learned during a short internship, and teaching learned in collaboration with colleagues is richer than isolated learning. There are increasing levels of complexity to teaching and teachers go through stages toward mastery; but they are always students of teaching.

Lucy Sprague Mitchell addresses all three themes in Chapter 15 of her book, *Our Children and Our Schools* (1951) in which she describes how she used her Bank Street Workshops with New York City public school teachers to move away from rote learning and into deep curriculum understanding. The stages from examination and experimentation to creation of new curricula and intellectual teacher engagement is ably documented in her chapter—and was a significant aspect of LTC's work with both novice and veteran teachers.

Mitchell speaks eloquently of teachers' "growth toward professional maturity." As she describes it, a "new curriculum," replacing one that teachers had used for twenty years, was delivered to New York City public school teachers. It demanded newer methods without giving teachers adequate preparation, and thus the teachers maintained their earlier methods and used the newer methods as activities or add-ons while they continued to use the old syllabus for the real work of teaching. Mitchell notes ". . . these teachers felt little responsibility for studying their children and for planning experiences for them on the basis of such study. In some schools the teachers were told to be experimental, but few of them were or wanted to be."

Once the teachers engaged in workshops, they began asking questions about the situation within which they functioned. Mitchell wondered, though, "How could they take responsibilities for educational thinking within their classrooms though they still remained on the lowest level as far as general decisions for educational thinking in the system were concerned?" Mitchell describes the slow awakening of the teachers to the thoughtful use of the new materials provided for them in the workshops—the progress from imitation of activities and the use of source materials to learn more deeply. As the group developed it became more interested in background content and teachers began building their own curriculum that met the needs of their own children. The teachers' interest in *how* to acquire skill in the new techniques broadened to *why* these techniques helped children to healthy all-around growth.

In his chapter in *Effective and Responsible Teaching* (1992), David Berliner describes teaching and learning to teach as an ongoing process. He studied the elements of expertise, noting that expert teachers, just like experts in other fields, master the routine and develop automaticity "for the repetitive operations that are needed to accomplish their goals," thus freeing them to focus on the intellectual facets of teaching. Expert teachers can interpret cues, recognize patterns and "instantaneously make sense of a field." The ability of novices to perceive the same cues was limited. As Berliner concluded, "Learning that it takes considerable time to acquire competence in the pedagogical domain, let alone expertise, changes the way we think about support systems for the beginning teacher and the limits of teacher education programs." We used the Learning/Teaching Collaborative model to help our pre-service teachers learn, as Berliner suggests, ". . . what experts attend to, what they find worth remembering, how they implement routines, and how they maintain a classroom that is considerate of their students . . ." at the same time developing a pre-service model that ". . . focused on the acquisition of the pedagogical knowledge needed to teach both responsively and effectively."

The snapshots of teaching as intellectual work that we see in Dewey (1976), Mitchell (1951) and Berliner (1992) are repeated in the three new chapters. Westheimer's review of the development of communities of practice reverberates with Mitchell's workshop method—teachers thinking together—moving away from easy answers that respond to dicta from above. Westheimer does not ignore the tension that plagues efforts to forge communal identities without sacrificing individual teachers' sense of autonomy. A major challenge for us in our work with the Learning/Teaching Collaborative was striving for a balance between collaboration and teachers' individual needs. Westheimer's question, "In what ways can collective projects among teachers further learning and development?" reminded us of our motivation to create Alternative Professional Teaching time, the most innovative of the Learning/Teaching Collaborative's four components.

We designed Alternative Professional Teaching (APT) time to meet the teachers' expressed need to supplement their classroom work with wider intellectual and professional responsibilities. It also provided the opportunity for teachers to learn new skills and gain expertise in an area that interested them. Some very sophisticated professional development was (and still is being) undertaken and accomplished within the APT structure, in part because APT allows teachers to engage in complex work of the sort that demands sustained, concentrated effort over time. For teachers who have APT, professional development is no longer conceptualized as "afternoon workshops on mandated topics," which most teachers perceive as "deficit training" arranged by distant authorities. Rather, APT professional development work emerges from the interests and perceived needs of individual teachers and their students.

During their APT, some teachers conduct research to improve their own teaching or to test the assumptions of educational theory and practice. Others take on responsibility for teaching graduate student interns at the college and designing curricula that connect the theories and research studied at the college with actual classroom practice. A few develop, pilot, implement, and evaluate new curricula as part of town-wide curriculum initiatives, or develop curriculum with local educational consulting firms. As fully empowered partners in the team teaching process, they become improved classroom teachers and stronger advocates of education as well (Troen and Boles, 1996).

When we began to think about reforming the teaching career more than two decades ago, we based our ideas on some knowledge of theory and a great supply of empirical evidence. As we learned and worked for change, collaborated with the university and saw the value of theory, we recognized the importance of integrating theory and practice (Troen and Boles, 2003).

Lessons derived from the works of Dewey and Mitchell ring as true today as they did when they were written. Mitchell's workshop program in New York introduced the intellectual side of teaching new curricula and replicated Dewey's earlier drive to intellectualize teaching. Dewey and Mitchell highlight the importance of observation—teachers thoughtfully observing each other and learning from their work together. Berliner's propositions reinforce the earlier norms set by Dewey and Mitchell.

In the contemporary chapters, the same themes emerge—Rodgers and Scott's developmental look at the self resonates with the development of teaching skill emphasized in Berliner and Mitchell. How does this collection of essays inform our work in the twenty-first century? A beginning place is the focus on preparation of new teachers and the contexts in which they begin their teaching lives. What happens to new teachers when they enter teaching? What is the responsibility of teachers and teacher educators to create the communities so eloquently described by the authors of these six papers?

We recognize that none of these authors' ideas will come to fruition without a supportive context, without colleagues and a professional learning community where novice and veteran teachers receive appropriate, ongoing support. We have learned—and research continues to confirm—that teachers cannot learn to teach well on their own. We know that new teachers need supportive, collaborative learning communities (Troen and Boles, 2003).

But we observe the new teaching generation with dismay. As veteran teacher educators, we see too many novice teachers who, after three years of teaching, feel they have mastered teaching and can move "up" into administration (Boles and Troen, 2004). In response, it is the responsibility of teacher educators to renew the intellectual underpinnings so eloquently framed by Dewey, Mitchell and Berliner, and so well described in the modern context by Westheimer, Florio-Ruane & Rosaen, and Rogers & Scott. However, in a world bent on easily measurable accountability, on high standards that are difficult to attain (like the early twentieth-century curriculum that was poorly implemented in New York City, or the New Math that was ill-taught in the 1960s), there is the danger that we will ignore the lessons of these writers and thinkers and sacrifice the intellectual life of the teacher for the short-term gain of high test scores.

When policymakers ask what proof we have that any of these tools, methods, or theories made a difference in children's learning, will we have ready quantifiable answers? This is the point at which it is tempting to say that in order to answer those questions, "more research is required." But while research is always helpful, we don't need more research to tell us what we already know. Nor do we need more research to tell us what we have been doing wrong, and will continue to do wrong, if we perpetuate a school culture that serves to defeat our attempts to create communities of learning. We know what to do right, and models for success have been created. We need only follow their lead.

REFERENCES

Berliner, David C. (1992) The nature of expertise in teaching. In Fritz K. Oser, Andreas Dick, & Jean-Luc Patry (eds.) *Effective and responsible teaching: the new synthesis*. San Francisco: Jossey Bass.

Boles, K. & Troen, V. (2004) Don't let your babies grow up to be teachers. In *Recruiting, retaining and supporting qualified teachers*, Edited by Caroline Chauncey. Cambridge, MA: Harvard Education Press.

Dewey, John (1976) The relation of theory to practice. In Jo Ann Boydston (ed.) *The middle works, 1999–1924*. Carbondale, IL. Southern Illinois University Press.

Johnson, S.M. & The Project on the Next Generation of Teachers. *Finders and keepers: helping new teachers survive and thrive in our schools*. San Francisco: Jossey-Bass, 2004.

Mitchell, Lucy S. (1951) Growth of teachers in professional maturity. In *Our children and schools*. New York: Simon and Schuster.

Troen, V. & Boles, K. (1994) Two teachers examine the power of teacher leadership. In *Teachers as leaders: perspectives on the professional development of teachers*, ed. Donovan Walling. Bloomington, IN: Phi Delta Kappa Educational Foundation.

Troen, V. & Boles, K. (1996) Teachers as leaders and the problems of power: achieving school reform from the classroom. In *New directions for school leadership: every teacher a leader*, ed. Marilyn Katzenmeyer and Gayle Moller. San Francisco, CA: Jossey-Bass, Inc. Publishers.

Troen, V. & Boles, K. (1997) An examination of teacher leadership in a professional development school. In *Professional development schools*, (ed.) Marsha Levine and Roberta Trachtman. New York: Teachers College Press.

Troen, V. & Boles, K. (2003) *Who's teaching your children? Why the teacher crisis is worse than you think and what can be done about it*. New Haven, CT: Yale University Press.

Part 7

Who's in charge?

Authority in teacher education and licensure policy

Editor: Suzanne M. Wilson

Part 7
Framing chapters

45 The emperor's new clothes

Do we really need professional education and certification for teachers?

Suzanne M. Wilson
Michigan State University

We live in an age of heated disputes concerning the quality and control of teacher education. Teacher educators, believing that teaching is work that requires substantial preparation, call for professional training, including both university coursework and supervised field experiences. Skeptics wonder whether there is any "there" there, whether the emperor—as it were—has any clothes. They raise questions about the content, control, and quality of teacher preparation, worried—as many people are in this age—about the monopolization of the enterprise. This debate gets labeled in many ways—alternative vs. traditional teacher preparation, professionalism vs. deregulation, for example—often in ways that obscure or oversimplify important differences. These questions—about quality and control—are perennial ones in the history of teacher education and certification, and it would be fitting for us all to be well versed in those debates.

The purpose of this section is to explore the history, content, and character of these oft-passionate debates about teacher certification. The reasons for these are many, as authors of the chapters and responses in this section clearly demonstrate. For one, schooling is very much a local enterprise in the United States, and choosing our teachers has also been a local enterprise. Everyone wants a say—parents, administrators, the public—and yet they have vastly different ideas about what matters. I have heard a state senator proclaim that her niece, a fine young woman who "loves children," ought to be allowed to matriculate in a teacher education program, no matter her GPA. I have heard a father argue eloquently that all a teacher needs to know is the subject matter she is to teach, and at that keeping one chapter ahead of the children is okay.

The history of teacher education is also shaped by the field's on-going attempts to claim professional status, and the second force at play in these essays is the rocky road toward professionalization, with its associated questions concerning the knowledge base of teaching and the technology of assessing that knowledge base. These twin desires for public ownership and professional discretion, not surprisingly, have resulted in a long history of bracing discussions about how, when, and under what conditions teachers should be prepared, certified, and licensed.

In addition, the authors here highlight the significance of an additional force that might best be understood as American skepticism, albeit of two different forms. The first is the argument for deregulation, which in education is most often experienced as calls for choice, charter, and vouchers. The sentiment here is that deregulation will lead to higher productivity and efficiency. Another form of skepticism might best be understood as the "critical turn," which insists that we always ask, "Whose best interests are served by the current structures?" This form of skepticism asks questions about both the motivations of deregulation *and* the motivations for an autonomous profession for teachers and teacher educators.

These issues—public ownership, professional autonomy, and skepticism—are deeply rooted in political, intellectual, historical, cultural, and economic currents that run throughout U.S. history and culture, and the authors of the essays that follow illuminate how they have played out in the history of teacher certification. Michael Sedlak lays out the history of teacher certification and licensure up through the late 1970s. Sedlak's account highlights the multiple actors who have participated in teacher certification over time: local ministers, school administrators, the emerging education establishment, and generations of (often) sharp-tongued critics. Sedlak also documents the history of the "technology" of teacher assessment, most notably the content and evolution of various attempts to examine teachers. Like most good historians, Sedlak reminds us that much of our current world is not really new, the questions and concerns that plague teacher educators *and* their critics today have erupted throughout the history of teaching and teacher education in the U.S.

David Imig and Scott Imig pick up the story line, and provide an insiders' account of the last 25 years of D.C. politics around teacher education and certification. Theirs is a story of the contemporary struggles between teacher educators and their allies who are fighting the good fight for teacher professionalism, and the neoconservatives and Bush administration challenging the educational establishment's right to that jurisdictional control. Their argument, that we have moved from "traditional certification" to "competitive certification," provides us with a sense of the interconnected policy landscape in which teacher certification arguments play out, particularly with regards to the No Child Left Behind Act.

Wilson and Tamir propose a conceptualization of the battles over control that uses Bourdieu's theory of social field, habitus, and capital. From this perspective, the social field of education is constantly being renegotiated by actors and groups intent on seizing or maintaining control. Bourdieu, building on the work of Aristotle and the medieval Scholastics, argued that each person or group has a habitus—a set of values, beliefs, dispositions, cultural norms, and the like—that to a large extent defines actions, or as Bourdieu would have it, "position taking." Wilson and Tamir argue that a careful analysis of the criticisms leveled at teacher education might help the educational establishment, including teacher educators, interrogate our own habitus. By doing so, we might then be prepared to engage with those criticisms in productive ways.

Ed Crowe and Frank Murray offer thoughtful commentaries on the essays. Murray, a long time teacher educator leader, probes the question: Why is it so hard to find and retain over 3 million competent teachers for the purpose of assisting the nation's schools in their mission? Crowe asks the fundamental underlying question: Is it a reasonable goal to position teaching or teacher education as profession? It is not a question we teachers and teacher educators often want to ask.

The section ends with a handful of artifacts that illustrate the dynamics of the debates that Sedlak, the Imigs, and Wilson and Tamir address. Included are excerpts from several important historical and current critiques of the system. For instance, Bagley's (1919) account of teacher training describes a system with staggering low standards. Bagley, who understood teaching as an art, was deeply concerned that the poor investments in teacher preparation would lead to teaching becoming a mechanical practice, as more unqualified teachers entered the system with inadequate preparation. Bestor (1953a, b) offered another critical perspective. In *On the Education and Certification of Teachers*, he argues that we must make teacher preparation a university responsibility (not a college of education one). He argues also for limited preparation in pedagogy, deep exposure to the liberal arts and sciences, rigorous tests of disciplinary knowledge as a requirement for state certification, and an organized approach to field experiences.

Also included are past statements by teacher education "insiders" about the need to enhance the professionalism of teaching, including artifacts from meetings of the National Commission on Teacher Education and Professional Standards (NCTEPS). Peik (1948) spoke at the Bowling Green Conference, and provides an illuminating example of the interrelationships between the field of education, the professional preparation of teachers, and the assumed roles of teachers in preparing U.S. citizens to participate in the struggle for world leadership. Ralph McDonald (1956), then-President of Bowling Green State University and a leading figure in the professionalism movement, elaborates on the history and growth of teacher professionalism, from its inception as a vague idea to the organized meetings of the NCTEPS starting in 1946. We also provide two contemporary views of teacher professionalization, one by an insider, Allington (2005), and one by an outsider, Hess (2002). Allington argues that teacher education would be vastly improved if we ignored state and federal certification and accreditation policies: they often get in the way of high quality professional preparation. Hess also raises questions about the costs and benefits of teacher certification. His is a market-based argument, and he calls for competitive certification and "creative destruction" of policies and practices that compromise our search for high quality teachers.

Because alternative routes emerged as a policy solution to the problems recounted over and again in the history of teacher certification, we also offer several artifacts concerning alternative certification. Watts (1986) presents the educational establishment's arguments against the perils of alternate routes and questions the two main arguments made by proponents of these reforms: (1) that there is a teacher shortage and (2) that traditional teacher preparation programs are preventing talented individuals from becoming teachers. Cooperman and Klagholz's (1985) account of New Jersey's alternate route illustrates how general discussions and debates over teacher certification evolved within the political boundaries of a single state. This piece in particular helps us understand how big ideas about teacher quality and teacher knowledge are transformed to the language of educational policy.

Finally, because teacher testing has been a central issue in discussions of teacher certification, we offer two artifacts from teacher assessments. Tests of teachers have evolved and changed, in part due to shifting notions of our collective sense of what a good teacher is, what teachers need to know, and what kinds of tests might be the best predictors of future teacher effectiveness. Here we offer examples from two different eras: Stone's (1864) *Complete Examiner* and Fox's (1982) *National Teacher Examination*.

Together, the artifacts and essays that comprise this section tell a story of struggle for professional status, for control, for quality. There are resonances across time, with similar promises and complaints pronounced by insiders and outsiders. Yet there is also progress, painfully slow at times. We may not have a certification and accreditation system that guarantees us high quality new teachers for all of our U.S. children, but the landscape of teacher education is different in 2007 than it was in 1849 and 1919. Continued—perhaps even more satisfying—progress can only be made if teacher educators and critics alike learn from the present and the past. Hans Christian Andersen's *The Emperor's New Clothes*, as a morality play, reminds us all that the smallest question can hold profound meaning. Sometimes teacher educators think that only scoundrels, like those pestering the emperor, ask the questions raised here—about professional autonomy and status, about the role of the free market in teacher certification, about the challenges associated with deciding what to test teachers on and how. Hard as it might be to acknowledge, it behooves us, for now, to constantly ask ourselves about why we want to don the clothes of a profession, and whether we have that right.

REFERENCES

Bagley, W. C. (1919) The training of teachers. *Proceedings of the National Education Association*, 499–504.

Bestor, A. E. (1953a) *Educational wastelands: the retreat from learning in our public schools.* Urbana, IL: University of Illinois Press.

Bestor, A. E. Jr. (1953b) On the education and certification of teachers. *Education and Society*, 78 (2016), 81–87.

Cooperman, S. & Klagholz, L. (1985) New Jersey's alternative route to certification. *Phi Delta Kappan*, 66(10), 691–695.

Fox D. J. (1982). *National Teacher Examinations*. Arco Publishing, Inc. New York.

McDonald, R. W. (1956) The professional standards movement in teaching: evolution of an idea. The professional standards movement in teaching: progress and projection. *Proceedings of the National Commission on Teacher Education and Professional Standards, National Education Association of the United States, 8–21.* (Report of the Parkland Conference held at Pacific Lutheran College, Parkland, Washington, June 26–30).

Peik, W. E. (1948) Building a still better teaching profession for our times (abstract of conference keynote address). The education of teachers as viewed by the profession. *Proceedings of the National Commission on Teacher Education and Professional Standards, National Education Association of the United States, 9–17.* (Official group reports of the Bowling Green Conference held at Bowling Green State University, Bowling Green, Ohio, June 30–July 3).

Quillen, L. J. (1959) The education of teachers: quest for quality. The education of teachers: curriculum programs. *Proceedings of the National Commission on Teacher Education and Professional Standards, National Education Association of the United States, 31–40.* (Official report of the Kansas conference, University of Kansas, Lawrence, Kansas, June 23–26).

Stone, I. A. M. (1864) *The elementary and complete examiner; on candidate's assistant: prepared to aid teachers in securing certification from the board of examiners.* A. S. Barnes and Company: New York and London.

Watts, D. (1986) Alternate routes to teacher certification: a dangerous trend. *Action in Teacher Education*, 2, 25–29.

46 Competing visions of purpose, practice, and policy

The history of teacher certification in the United States

Michael W. Sedlak
Michigan State University

The history of the certification and licensure of teachers in the United States has always been contested: from the most intimate level, between employers and prospective teachers, to the broadest levels of national policy, between levels of government, between public and private organizations pursuing competing ambitions. Deciding who will be allowed to teach my child, your children, other people's kids, is a struggle rooted in competing visions of America itself and is driven by questions grounded in national identity and personal aspirations: What role should education play in constructing a democracy? Why would we want our children to attend school? Where should authority over our children's lives and futures reside? Who should we trust to care for our children? What, and how, should students learn in school anyway? The answers to such questions—inherently raised by the process of recruiting, selecting, and hiring a teacher—are even more important when the children attend compulsory, universal, tax-supported institutions.

Selecting teachers for one's child, or finding teachers for other people's children, has gone on since western Europeans began to migrate to this continent in the sixteenth and seventeenth centuries; indeed, the process was going on somewhere even before the First Peoples arrived. For centuries, finding teachers was primarily a matter of private and personal negotiation.

Entrusting one's children to the care and instruction of others reflected concern with the sort of larger questions presented above; and had always led to thoughtful and skeptical decision-making. A well-known exchange between colonial leaders from the middle colonies and the Indians of the Six Nations reflected this concern. As part of a treaty signed in 1744, leaders from the Six Nations were invited to send young men from their tribes to William and Mary College. The Indians declined the offer, and replied as follows:

> We know that you highly esteem the kind of learning taught in those Colleges, and that the Maintenance of our young Men, while with you, would be very expensive to you. We are convinced, that you mean to do us Good by your Proposal; and we thank you heartily. But you, who are wise must know that different Nations have different Conceptions of things and you will therefore not take it amiss, if our Ideas of this kind of Education happen not to be the same as yours. We have had some Experience of it. Several of our young People were formerly brought up at the Colleges of the Northern Provinces: they were instructed in all your Sciences; but, when they came back to us, they were bad Runners, ignorant of every means of living in the woods . . . neither fit for Hunters, Warriors, nor Counselors, they were totally good for nothing.

> We are, however, not the less oblig'd by your kind Offer, tho' we decline accepting it; and to show our grateful Sense of it, if the Gentlemen of Virginia will send us a Dozen of their Sons, we will take Care of their Education, instruct them in all we know, and make Men of them.

This touching, yet sassy, deflection suggests the depth of the meaning of decisions about *who* will teach *what, and* to *what* purpose, in our schools.[1]

White, European immigrants were also concerned about the purposes of education, and whenever possible they supported mechanisms to find and hire teachers who were properly fitted to instruct their children. Throughout the colonial period, until the early nineteenth century, schools served a fairly narrow but significant range of functions. From England, settlers brought with them an understandable preoccupation with their spiritual salvation, and very quickly enacted the sort of requirements that governed expectations of religious orthodoxy in their homeland. In the New World, they never actually replicated the dizzying policy shift that occurred in England between 1553 and 1581, when all of the Protestant teachers were replaced with Catholics, who were then replaced by Protestants following a regime change; and both were quickly replaced with an Anglican teaching corps several years later. But, in Massachusetts Bay, just a generation after the colony was established, the highest court—concerned as it was that youth be educated "not only in good literature but in sound doctrine"—recommended in 1654 that the selectmen who oversaw local schools rid their communities of teachers who were "lacking in faith and are scandalous in their lives and have not given satisfaction according to the rules of Christ" (Kinney, 1964, p. 39).

Like Massachusetts, most colonies authorized a variety of local actors—religious elders, prominent citizens, lay boards—to be responsible for finding and hiring teachers. Typically, these employers used informal approaches when making decisions about potential instructors. They relied on ministerial recommendations. They queried candidates about their beliefs and values. They assessed their physical strength and courage. They hired their relatives, with whom they were intimately familiar. And they occasionally tried to determine their potential teachers' academic expertise, largely by examining handwriting samples and listening to prospects read homilies or passages from the Bible. Conducting penetrating examinations of academic competence were often less important than gauging the other qualities, however, particularly because the prevailing approach to teaching—memorization and recitation—demanded literacy but not much more than a shallow understanding of what we would call school subjects.

This pattern of individual negotiation in a private market proved to be an enduring model, if not always a fully satisfactory way of recruiting and employing the most desirable teachers. It lasted two centuries, through the first few decades of the nineteenth century. Gradually, this tradition was undermined by abuses of nepotism and the fallout from lazy or uneducated examiners, yes, but more importantly it was challenged by the emergence of a new sense of purpose for education, whose advocates could no longer trust the consequences of private arrangements.

An array of social, economic, and demographic changes converged over the first third of the nineteenth century to galvanize reformers around a new vision for education. Economic change—highlighted by blossoming industrial capitalism, the first wave of the deskilling of labor, and the emergence of an American working class—convinced prominent citizens, business leaders, and some politicians that it was essential to begin building a labor force with a new form of work discipline, respect for property, commitment to new definitions of time and punctuality. Urbanization—represented not simply by increasing population density but by residential segmentation and stratification and the separation of home from work—led reformers to replace disintegrating forms of personal and neighborly social control with institutional supervision. And demographic change—symbolized by the arrival of the genuinely foreign Irish Catholic peasants—spurred civic authorities to establish mechanisms for intentional nation building and for developing common political and social values. Together, these dynamic changes demonstrated that there was considerable work to be done, and community and state leaders turned aggressively to the schools to undertake that work.[2]

These new social and economic ambitions for education demanded schools dedicated to expansive purposes beyond basic literacy and religious indoctrination. These new purposes would demand new forms of organization, curricula, and instruction. They would demand teachers with *professional* knowledge and commitment who were willing to invest in their own preparation, and able to contribute to what the reformers envisioned as an actual *system* of education.

The mid-nineteenth-century reformers moved to address the qualifications of the teaching force on several fronts. The most aggressive public policy actions focused on fashioning an embryonic certification system. Unwilling to tolerate the notorious abuses associated with local control and the "excesses of democracy," and not content simply to recommend better tests, they moved over the second third of the nineteenth century to launch the process of centralizing the licensure process. Governmental authorities, occasionally at the state level, but particularly at the county level, began to seize control of the examination system.[3]

They found many weaknesses in the prevailing examinations. The idiosyncrasies of many local laymen, the educational reformers were convinced, posed the greatest problems with the tradition of teacher testing. The folklore of assessments included too many examples like that recalled by John Swett in his memoir of teaching in California. The president of San Francisco's board of education himself—"a man of inordinate conceit"—prepared and administered a comprehensive examination. Swett reconstructed the geography section:

1 Name all the rivers of the globe.
2 Name all the bays, gulfs, seas, lakes and other bodies of water on the globe.
3 Name all the cities of the world.
4 Name all the countries of the world.
5 Bound each of the states in the United States.

He added that after the one hour allowed to answer these questions, some of the examinees were "still at work on the first question, some on the second question, a few on the third, and one on the fifth." Years later, after digging the results out of the board of education's archives, Swett learned that the board president issued a report indicating that "we all stood exactly alike, sixty percent" (Swett, 1911, p. 114). Sometimes examiners could not even answer their own questions. "What is the product of 25 cents by 25 cents," a candidate in Indiana was asked. After he responded that he did not know, the examiner, who appeared "a bit perplexed," said that he thought the answer "was six and one-fourth cents but he wasn't sure" (quoted in Elsbree, 1939, p. 183; Vold, 1985).

Local examiners were also under extraordinary pressure to falsify examination results in order to guarantee teaching positions to well-connected community members. One test administrator from Ohio, who would no doubt find appealing the campaign to centralize control of the testing apparatus, testified to the personal vulnerability of local examiners. "Not infrequently," he observed, candidates who have made an exhibition of their ignorance and utter incapacity will importune in the most urgent and pathetic way for certificates. Local directors, sometimes, plead that a candidate be spared rejection with an importunity like that of Abraham when praying for Sodom. A brawny brother has, more than once, intimated that a sad retribution would . . . overtake the examiners if his sister should be without a commission; though the girl could not repeat the multiplication table, if it were to save her from the doom of Gomorrah.

(*Fifth annual report* [Ohio], 1858, p. 99)

Because examinations were historically private events, attended only by the candidate and the examiners, both standards and individual performances remained discreet and flexible, which appealed to supporters of the patronage system of appointments. Since private examinations were so easily abused, however, some community leaders called for opening the events to the public. In addition to calming fears of favoritism, public examinations could offer other benefits. In an era of unprecedented community boosterism, when one educational institution competed against another to improve neighborhood status and attract settlers, examining teachers and students in public could be an attractive mechanism. One advocate of public examination in New Jersey in 1850 asked, "why should there not be a county competition, to exhibit the best teachers, the best schools, and the best-educated scholars, with far more propriety than which county can produce the fattest hog or the largest turnip?" (quoted in Elsbree, 1939, p. 184).

Agents of centralization, who were committed to deepening and extending the functions of education, confronted the notorious tradition of local examinations initially by requiring county and even state officials to take primary responsibility for testing prospective and returning teachers. Ohio, for example, moved—somewhat prematurely it turned out—to have the courts appoint three "examiners of common schools" in every county to "examine and certificate teachers" (Kinney, 1964, p. 46). Other Common School advocates pressed for more rigorous and standardized examinations, and encouraged the production and distribution of more systematic tests of academic and even professional knowledge. There emerged a small industry in publishing collections of widely used questions for the new examining boards (and for prospective teachers to study and review for their upcoming tests). These guides typically included questions covering introductory to advanced content in the entire array of school subjects.

John Swett's collection, which he released in 1872 to assist principals struggling to design productive questions for prospective employees, or even for inexperienced teachers needing to assess their own students' knowledge, was typical. The section on arithmetic began with questions like "divide $7.00 by half a cent. Multiply $5.00 by $5.00." It ended with more demanding questions like "find the greatest common divisor and the least common multiple of 18, 48, 72, 66." His English grammar questions asked examinees to "write sentences to show the correct use of the verbs lie, lay, sit and set in the future perfect (second future) tense, indicative mode," and "what do you mean by an idiom? Give an example." A simple geography question asked for the "four leading exports of California," while an advanced question asked "why is it warmer on the Pacific than on the Atlantic coast of the United States, in the same latitude?" His composition assignments were elaborate: the examinee was asked to write a two-page manuscript on subjects like the following:

Society: What is it? When did it begin to exist? Under what forms at first? Benefits? Effects on arts and sciences? Difference between a state of barbarism and of civilization. Evils of society. Vices. Illustrations from history.

Or

> *War*: When did war begin, and how originate? What kinds of wars? Is war justifiable? Evils of war; benefits of war. Illustrate both from history. Difference between barbarous and civilized warfare. Effect of inventions upon war. Will wars ever cease?
>
>   (all quotes from Swett, 1911, pp. 5, 18, 19, 38, 40, 50, 100, and 101)

The testing manuals also included sections on professional knowledge, which the county and state officials increasingly incorporated into the required examinations. Soon after the superintendents in Iowa's schools gathered to release a statement indicting the state's teachers for being "deficient in a knowledge of mind—its operation and how to control it," the legislature amended the examination law to include the "theory and practice of teaching" (Aurner, 1918, p. 298). Maine's examination in 1848, for example, asked candidates how they would deal with children who were "(1) obstinately disobedient? (2) physically and mentally indolent? (3) addicted to falsehood? (4) impulsive" (*Maine School Report* 1848, 57; quoted in Elsbree, 1939, 180)? One of the most famous collections of common questions, Isaac Stone's *The Elementary and Complete Examiner* (1864), begins its chapter on professional knowledge by stating that "The *principles* implied in the *foregoing questions* [about academic subjects] will be of but little avail to *Candidates*, unless they have a good *theory of imparting instruction*; a theory which they can practice" (Stone, 1864, p. 200). His taxonomy of professional knowledge ranged from routine questions like "What can you say of the ventilation of the school-room?" to complex, demanding questions about motivating students, pedagogy, and discipline:

> Is it *wise* or *otherwise* for a teacher to ask a mischievous or vicious pupil to do a favor for him?"
> Should a teacher be held responsible for the intellectual growth of his pupil?
> Which is preferable, the "*pouring in*," or "drawing out process?"
> What can you say of the relation of the teacher to the parents of his pupils?
> State briefly your idea of the *Science of Education*.
>
>   (Stone, 1864, pp. 200–201)

Among many other topics, Swett's anthology asked the following questions about the "theory and practice" of teaching:

> What position do you prefer to have your pupils take when reciting?
> For what particular offenses would you inflict corporal punishment?
> What do you conceive to be the relative advantages of public and private schools?
> What do you consider the aim of all educators to be?
>
>   (Swett, 1872, pp. 66–70)

In addition to standardizing the examination system, public authorities holding the new social vision for schooling also claimed that educators needed to become more professional and to have their knowledge, skills, and commitments developed through formal professional training. Historically, through the first half of the nineteenth century at least, the vast majority of teachers, few of whom taught more than a session or two, had little evident commitment to instruction, their pupils, or their employing communities. Teaching was largely a transient occupation, and probably no more than a handful possessed subject matter knowledge significantly greater than their students. There were few incentives for most teachers to invest in an extended academic or even introductory professional education. The minority of schoolmasters who were dedicated, successful instructors, would have acquired their professional knowledge about organizing schools, motivating and disciplining students, and evaluating recitations, from the important manuals published for teachers, whose experienced authors often traveled to conduct seminars and workshops.[4]

In order to address what they perceived as deficiencies in ambition, commitment, and skill, educational leaders at the county and state levels—from New England through the Midwest—called during the 1840s and 1850s for investing public resources in normal schools, which became the first distinct teacher education institutions. Historians have thoroughly reconstructed the origins and evolution of the normal schools and other local teacher institutes.[5] I want to make several simple points about this important stage in the development of preparation and certification policy. The most influential state leaders who fought to create and sustain programs of professional education shared an expansive, liberal vision of the function of public authority, particularly the potential for schools to improve social, economic, and individual conditions. And they were convinced that much prevailing instructional practice could do little to enable students to attain the levels of civic awareness and industrial capacity that the future would need. Schoolmasters who simply listened to memorized recitations, or who disciplined students into submission and compliance (practices leaders believed were common, even at the most respected academies) were not prepared or even willing to consider far more ambitious pedagogical techniques. Horace Mann's famous confrontation with Boston's senior schoolmasters revealed his preference for more engaging instruction, as did his many reports on new techniques surfacing in Europe (Church & Sedlak, 1976; Rury, 2002).

Furthermore, in a struggle that would be echoed in the mid-twentieth century, normal schools competed with liberal arts colleges and in some regions even with secondary academies for market share. In an era when the educational ladder was overlapping and an array of institutions served young men and women between 14 and 21, advocates of embryonic liberal arts colleges objected to the creation and expansion of the normal schools and their desire not only to usurp the teach training functions of these other institutions, but also to provide greater opportunities for adolescents outside the large urban centers to pursue academic study. Herbst's close analysis indicated, for example, that in western Massachusetts, Westfield Normal successfully competed with Mount Holyoke for young female students, and capitalized on its advantage as a public institution to attract students with lower tuition (Herbst, 1989, pp. 80–81).

The new professional education institutions were especially undesirable to those who held the traditional, narrow view of the limited function of education. Just after the moment of their creation in Massachusetts, for example, a political campaign erupted to eliminate the fledgling normal schools and to disband the state board of education. As Carl Kaestle and Maris Vinovskis noted in their study of this event, the challengers argued in their report that the "existing academies and high schools were 'fully adequate . . . to furnish a competent supply of teachers.' " The opposition committee's conclusion was rooted in a traditional view of educational purpose and operation:

> Considering that our District Schools are kept, on an average, for only three or four months in the year, it is obviously impossible, and perhaps, it is not desirable, that the business of keeping these schools should become a distinct and separate profession, which the establishment of Normal Schools seems to anticipate.
>
> (quoted in Kaestle & Vinovskis, 1980, p. 218; see also, Kaestle, 1983)

This is exactly the attitude and perspective that Mann and his generation of policy leaders fought over the ensuing decades.

After mid-century, then, ambitious public educational reformers had begun to shift arrangements for recruiting and hiring teachers. They not only voiced their objections to the traditions of diminished expectations for schooling and local control of, and dissatisfaction with, "unqualified teachers," but they were fashioning new policies—backed with unprecedented investments—designed to build a more standardized system capable of educating students for a new society and economy. They pressed for teacher quality policies that recognized and encouraged, if not always enforced, formal professional education. They launched an effort not only to elevate the certification process to the county and state levels, but also to expect and reward the possession of educational credentials. Over the latter half of the nineteenth century, this new pattern unfolded across the country. The balance between examinations and credentials fluctuated, as local authorities challenged higher-level officials by trying to exploit every opening in their state's certification laws. But state after state followed the lead of California, which in 1863 was the first state to accept professional educational credentials in lieu of examinations. By 1900, 41 states recognized *both* normal school diplomas and credentials from four-year colleges as acceptable alternatives to tests. In New England, and the deep South, where the colonial traditions of local control through examination were the strongest, the process was bumpier, but the shift reflected a clear national consensus by the early twentieth century (see Sedlak, 1989).

Teachers themselves began to join these constituencies concerned about the professional stature of education, and especially those who were troubled by the inadequacies of existing recruitment and hiring practices. As the campaign to spread this new vision of educational purpose gathered momentum in the 1850s and later, individuals attempting to fashion teaching jobs into actual careers resented the assumptions of transiency and amateurism embedded in the prevailing hiring arrangements. They grew frustrated by annual examinations, unpredictable standards, and temporary certificates. As teachers became more committed to effective education, they also pressed for the de-politicization of hiring, since patronage systems appeared to undermine the meritocratic ethos that was building within the educational enterprise. Reformers and many teachers alike believed that, as schools would perform increasingly indispensable social functions (including resolving social problems and expanding economic opportunity), they should more visibly and explicitly reject all traditions and trappings of ascription and embrace more defensible, standardized, uniform, professional practices.

The next phase in the history of certifying and hiring teachers witnessed the accelerating dominance of the professional educational credential model, and the steady increase in the minimal duration of prerequisite study. Appointing individuals to teaching positions remained at the local level, of course, but states gradually restricted the pool of legal prospects. And states increasingly granted certificates on the basis of educational attainment rather than examination performance. By 1873, according to a leading analyst of this issue, policy makers were beginning to recognize credentials from normal schools as "professional licenses," and several states were relying on them exclusively as the basis for certification. By 1897, 28 states accepted normal school diplomas, and by 1921 all but one state "recognized graduation from normal schools and universities as evidence of qualification for certification" (Cook, 1927, p. 3). By World War I, therefore, certification policies that bestowed licenses on the basis of credentials had become the rule nationwide.[6]

Despite the shift toward credentials in most regions, the examination tradition persisted in the South, where virtually every state continued to base certification on the basis of test performance as well as professional study. In other regions, developments were mixed. In Indiana and Wisconsin, for example, centralization proceeded more slowly because of a reluctance to deploy the states' plenary power in education. Many states also continued to require examinations for high school teaching certificates. But, as a reflection of the increasing impact of normal school and university programs of study, these tests increasingly included questions drawn from studying professional education, including pedagogy, management, and educational history and philosophy.

The expansion of the credential model grew dramatically as graduates of professional programs assumed leadership roles in state departments of education. Small-state departments were among the most highly professionalized sectors of the educational enterprise, and their staff members often owed their positions to their educational attainment, or were willing to respond to the lobbying of the professional education institutions. Many of those who owed their positions to their credentials distrusted examinations and wanted to reduce their impact on licensing. As one commentator observed: "The evil attendant upon the examination system that had been perfected to determine detailed knowledge of academic subject matter led to bitter opposition on the part of those trained in the newer professional school" (Morrison, 1928, p. 49).

Professionally trained educators objected to the view that it took only subject-matter knowledge in order to teach effectively. They were familiar with the tradition of abuse that continued to plague examinations, and were distressed about the gamesmanship and shallowness that contemporary testing practices tended to encourage and reward. Furthermore, during the late nineteenth and early twentieth centuries, other, more prestigious, occupations were abandoning informal idiosyncratic licensing practices for standardized educational credentials. Many believed that professionalization *itself* demanded advanced, formal professional education, sometimes as a substitute for examinations, sometimes in combination. Regardless of the reasons (some of which were sincere, while others were flagrantly self-protective), the movement of professionally educated teachers and administrators into positions of system-wide leadership and influence further undermined the tradition of simply testing aspiring professionals.

Raising standards—by requiring professional education or by making the examinations more challenging and professionally relevant—undoubtedly resulted in much individual pain. Heightened standards were assumed to limit access to teaching opportunities, particularly by closing off the mobility of youth from rural backgrounds. Shortly after World War I, for example, the Illinois superintendent for public instruction received a letter from an exasperated woman who was attempting to return to teaching at 46 after her husband died. She had been granted a temporary "Emergency Certificate" because of a spot shortage, but was unable to get "a certificate without 'Emergency' written on it," as she complained to—and pleaded with—the superintendent. The superintendent responded publicly to the letter in order to disclose the "strong appeals [that] can be made to the hearts of the certificating authorities and boards of education to relax or set aside the plain requirements of the law and to forget or subordinate the primal interests of the children who are to be taught." He raised the question of certification standards, arguing that, in teaching, traditions of licensing had too often been rooted in earlier days when it was common to select men who had some disability or handicap, "on the assumption that school teaching was an indoor occupation and required the minimum of physical health and completeness." The situation had changed, he commented, particularly since young middle-class women with strong academic qualifications began seeking and securing teaching positions:

Most young women, looking forward to teaching school, try to prepare themselves in a very conscientious way for the work. There still remains, however, the old idea that in selecting a teacher certain charitable ends should be kept in view. Every attempt to lift the scholastic and professional requirements for teachers in Illinois has met with the statement that higher standards will keep the poor man's daughter from teaching, overlooking entirely the fact that there is much greater charity, much more of the milk of human kindness, much more of sound common sense in trying to secure for poor men's children the very best teacher that can be had rather than in trying to get for a poor man's daughter a job for which she is not qualified.

(Ed., 1924, p. 761)

In sum, the enterprise of licensing teachers had changed in a variety of ways during the half-century prior to World War I. The practice of bestowing certificates to candidates on the basis of professional education rather than examinations exclusively was dramatically expanded. Whether through examination or educational attainment, certification was becoming centralized at the state level. The county superintendencies that had moved certification forward during the mid-nineteenth century were declining in power as states sought to tighten controls over the licensing of teachers, and because of a general movement toward centralization and standardization. This trend is evident in the table presented below, which indicates a progressively rapid process of centralizing certification to the state level (Cook, 1921; Cook, 1927; Cubberley, 1906; Jackson, 1903). Local certificates were also a victim of the effort to improve "reciprocity" that built during the late 19th century, especially in the North where groups of states made elaborate compacts to recognize one another's certificates (Barrett, 1902).

And, the number of categories of certificates increased dramatically. Differentiation of professional roles in schools contributed fundamentally to this process. The growing public and professional fascination with precision, order, and "scientific" classification schemes of all kinds undoubtedly contributed to this explosion as well. The annual, temporary certificates common during the mid-nineteenth century were replaced in some places in the twentieth century by permanent or life certificates (typically based on educational credentials).

Significantly, virtually all varieties of educational "progressives" in the late nineteenth and early twentieth centuries agreed with these changes in certification policy and practice, and many of the larger organizational reforms that were grounded in a new sense of purpose for education. The more liberal "pedagogical" progressives, who supported comparatively radical changes in methods of teaching and curricular design, were joined by more conservative "administrative" progressives, who shared enthusiasm for modernizing the curriculum, but also were committed to expanding state and county authority over local schools and deepening the hold of scientific rationalism over the schools.[7]

Although for possibly different reasons, both groups largely endorsed professional education for teachers and administrators. Pedagogical progressives wanted to reform teaching practice so that student learning would be deeper and more powerful than they perceived it was under the tradition of superficial factual memorization, which remained common into the twentieth century. They wanted students to be more engaged and personally connected to "relevant" curricula, and were distressed with the continued dominance of classical studies, especially at the high school level. They believed that the militantly classical curricula and teaching style of the nineteenth century was "undemocratic," and ill-suited to the diversifying profile of students that was enrolling in schools, particularly the waves of immigrant students, children of color, and working-class adolescents who were converting the high school into a mass institution. They pressed for preparing and hiring teachers who were dedicated to modern, diversified curricula, and with the depth of understanding of child development and psychology, repertoire of methods, and social vision to bring the schools into the twentieth century.

Administrative progressives aggressively challenged many manifestations and idio-syncratic practices of local democracy—the ward system of electing school board members insistent on representing neighborhood interests, unqualified personnel who found their way into teaching assignments through dubious routes—by "taking the schools out of politics," expanding the appointment of "experts" in administration and govern-ance, and centralizing control under the mantle of science wherever possible. They also embraced curricular modernization and differentiation—through the creation and rapid expansion of the practical arts and vocational classes—to increase efficiency and eco-nomic productivity. Concerned about the emerging disconnect between traditional school-ing and the modern industrial and corporate economy, these progressives held a larger sense of social purpose for education. Their vision—particularly those associated with the campaigns to create the junior high school and to transform secondary education—focused more on economic efficiency and vocational adaptation than the liberal progres-sives, who sought more individual opportunity. But both groups envisioned an ambitious, socially indispensable role for schools, a vision that depended on teachers with both academic and professional knowledge and commitments, whose abilities would be guar-anteed through expansive state certification policies.

Conservative educational scholars and administrative reformers were troubled by the residual—if declining—use of examinations to identify and hire prospective teachers and pressed to base eligibility to teach on higher educational attainment. The trans-formed high school obviously demanded significantly stronger academic credentials, they observed, and even the emergent efforts to individualize and personalize learning in the elementary school were revealing the weakness of typical teacher tests (Dutton and Snedden, 1908). In his systematic study of certification and licensure, E. L. Cubberley of Stanford University, the most influential educational reformer of the early twentieth century, argued forcefully that secondary teachers needed "advanced training beyond that given in the high schools or normal schools."

> The high school is the place for bringing the student into contact with new methods of instruction and news ways of thinking as well as new subject matter . . . Unless the teacher has come in contact with men who are masters of such subjects [espe-cially the new elective courses], and has learned something of the master's method of dealing with the great truths that lie in his field, he is not likely to carry much of a message to the young people who come under his direction in the secondary school.
> (Cubberley, 1906, pp. 59–60)

Cubberly argued that this advanced education could never be "enforced by means of a written examination." The only "safe way" of securing this level of talent, he continued, was to "impose a definite educational requirement, such as graduation from a college of recognized rank," as a prerequisite to certification. "Either certain work or courses in education," he added, "should be required to be taken as part of the college course" in order to guarantee the "strictly pedagogical part of the preparation" (pp. 60–61). Cubberley endorsed this expectation for all certificate levels. Even the work of the "kind-ergarten is special and requires special training," he stated, and endorsed "graduation from a reputable kindergarten training-school, or from the kindergarten department of a state normal school" (pp. 62–63). He held up California's recent elaborated state certi-fication code as a model, but admitted that few other states matched this vision in 1906.

Cubberley's disappointment about the state and pace of centralization and elevated academic standards for teacher certification resonated widely. Reformers across virtually all regions launched intense campaigns to convert their state policies in the direction of the California model. The following two tables reveal the consequences of their actions. First, the number of states requiring a bachelor's degree for teaching accelerated rapidly after 1910.

Level	Number of States Requiring the B.A. Degree						
	1900	1910	1920	1930	1940	1950	1960
Elementary	0	0	0	2	11	21	40
Secondary	2	3	10	32	40	42	51

As is evident, the spread of graduation requirements for certification spread most rapidly during the 1920s, a period of rapid standards-raising that occurred during a time of teacher shortage. The following table indicates the parallel expansion of professional studies at the four-year degree level (developed from Kinney, 1964, p. 83).

	Number of States	
	1921	1927
Four Years of College Required Total	12	32
Four Years of College, Professional Studies Required	4	25

California consistently set the pace for "progressive" licensure. In that state, the certification law of 1893 established a minimum of graduation from an accredited university with at least 12 semester hours in pedagogical courses for a high-school teaching certificate. This ambitious requirement was increased even further in 1906, when the state board of education restricted secondary certificates to those with one year of graduate credits (with a few subject-field restrictions, all of which were removed in 1928) (Frazier, 1938, p. 304).

The timing of events in many states in the North, East, and West lagged behind California, but paralleled those in Michigan. Responding to pressure from the Michigan State Teachers Association, the state moved to adopt a normal school graduation standard for elementary teachers during the early 1920s. At the secondary level, the North Central Association pressed the state to move beyond a simple baccalaureate requirement and endorse its proposal to redefine a "qualified" teacher as one who was certified to teach—and who taught—only in the subject(s) of his or her collegiate major or minor. The state gradually expanded the professional school requirements and standardized them, so that by 1925 they had begun to assume the dimensions that would serve throughout the twentieth century (Goodrich, 1928, p. 548; Davis, 1924b; Stinnett, 1969).

Southern states moved somewhat more slowly to raise standards of entry by centralizing the certification process and by abandoning the examination tradition for educational credentials. The region began to endorse normal school preparation after the turn of the century, but apparently imposed a relatively non-aggressive policy of "advising" attendance. Some states, like North Carolina, which held on to its examination system until the 1920s, attempted to strengthen the professional education of teachers by requiring them to attend two-week county institutes, and promoted summer-school classes for teachers (Stinnett, 1969, p. 398; ed. 1922, p. 304). Teacher training institutions were allowed to develop their own approaches to professional education with virtually no interference from the states. Over the course of the 1920s, standards in professional education throughout the South shifted, generally from summer-school and extension classes, brief institutes, and reading circles to formal pre-service educational programs (Stinnett, 1969, p. 398). Pressure for conformity in that region came from the professional education establishment rather than from state governments.

In addition to strengthening the expectation of formal professional education, the standards-raising movement of the 1920s began to articulate and enforce regulations concerning the *content* of teacher-education programs. The package of courses in social and psychological foundations, generic and subject matter pedagogy, and practice teaching began to assume the proportions that would constitute the preparation model until the wave of professionalization reform of the 1980s.

Raising standards had an immediate impact on the professional qualifications of the teaching force. A survey conducted early in 1925 revealed the extent to which states were approaching "the ideal of a trained teacher in every classroom." Between 1920 and 1925, for example, a number of states made substantial progress in raising the proportion of teachers with at least two years of normal schooling: North Carolina's "trained" teachers increased from 18 to 40 percent of the total force; Pennsylvania's grew from 50 to 78 percent; Oregon's jumped from 54 to 70 percent; and Wyoming's rose from 24 to 40 percent. The study's author attributed the improvement to "the influence of vigorous state policies" designed to raise certification and entry standards in teaching (Bagley, 1925, pp. 113–114; Morrison, 1928, p. 49; Rosier, 1925; Dynes, 1931; see also important surveys: Hood, 1916; Learned & Bagley, 1920; Cook, 1920; Deffenbaugh & Ziegel, 1932; Evenden *et al.*, 1933; Siedle, 1934; Slaughter, 1960; LaBue, 1960).

Once the professional education model was established and diffused nationally as the dominant route into teaching, the place and nature of examinations shifted considerably. They did not disappear entirely, but over the first third of the twentieth century they came to perform very specific functions for the educational enterprise. No one seriously advocated using them as a general mechanism for controlling entry into teaching. And no one believed that they could be used for bestowing general certificates, even under most emergency conditions. Virtually every analysis of the teaching force—its labor market and its demographics—elaborated the litany of familiar complaints about the examination tradition. Tests encouraged substandard preparation; examinations were "undependable in predicting teaching success;" and, tactfully, "undesirable local pressure for unmerited certification is often exerted when abuses in examinations are possible" (Anderson *et al.*, 1937 and 1934; Parkinson, 1932, pp. 422–448; Carnegie Foundation for the Advancement of Teaching, 1932, pp. 56ff.). They continued to be used in some rural districts, nevertheless, and occasionally for granting temporary access to teaching specific subjects, like music or drawing.

The most interesting and visible movement on the testing front before the 1980s surrounded the creation of the National Teacher Examination in 1940. Examinations could play a useful role in hiring and promoting teachers, argued critics who condemned bestowing initial licensure on the basis of a single test. Especially during the 1930s, a time when there was a surplus of teachers, pressure mounted to create an examination that would help popular districts to differentiate among many well-qualified applicants.

The National Teacher Examination was rooted in a series of three testing projects completed in the late 1920s and 1930s. The first developed an instrument to assess the professional and content knowledge of elementary teachers and was sold to personnel departments in many large school districts. The second was sold to more than a hundred teacher education institutions to evaluate college students who aspired to teach. The third, and most influential, project was sponsored by the Carnegie Foundation to assess the quality of secondary and higher education in Pennsylvania. Led by William Learned and Ben Wood, this effort contributed to a series of college and graduate testing initiatives, including the Graduate Record Examination.[8]

Learned and Wood's publicized their findings nationally and laid a foundation for dialogue about the intellectual and academic abilities of prospective teachers, even those who were graduating from Pennsylvania's strongest institutions of higher education. The average score of the teachers, they asserted, was below that of everyone else who took the examinations except those seeking careers in business, art, agriculture, and the secretarial sciences (Learned & Wood, 1938; Sedlak & Schlossman, 1986; Warren, 1985). Even worse, the prospective teachers in professional courses of study did poorly when compared with the *high-school* students who were tested. Learned and Wood's comparisons led them to stinging conclusions about the "limited mental ability of the individuals who are specially prepared for teaching positions," whom they identified as "narrower people" with "uninformed and incompetent minds" and skills, appropriate for elementary teaching perhaps, but unsuited for more-responsible positions in high schools (Learned & Wood, 1938, pp. 351–353). Commentators generally avoided calling attention to the painful comparisons, although Lewis Terman, a veteran of twentieth-century testing campaigns, classified some prospective teachers as "congenital ninth graders" (Terman, 1939, p. 112).

Ben Wood, one of the senior researchers in the Carnegie project, was appointed as director of the Cooperative Testing Service of the American Council on Education in 1930. With extended support from the Rockefeller-sponsored General Education Board, the service was charged with preparing, publishing, and distributing subject-matter examinations (McConn, 1931). In addition to cooperating with university testing bureaus across the nation, the service donated examinations to a variety of organizations, including the Carnegie project. Increasingly engaged in test construction and administration, school leaders in Providence, Rhode Island, requested a special edition of the service's examinations in 1932 "for use as one phase of their teacher selection procedure" (A. Wilson, 1985, p. 11). Other districts learned of the service's generosity, and within a few years, districts in Philadelphia, Pittsburgh, and Cleveland were being supplied with tests. Because the General Education Board funding was to expire in 1940, the service announced that it could no longer continue to supply districts with the tests. Disturbed by this threat, superintendents from several large districts met with the American Council on Education in 1939 and formed a National Committee on Teacher Examinations to ensure a continuous supply of tests to enable their personnel departments to identify and hire the best teachers.

Soon thereafter, the entrepreneurial Wood announced that his "teacher examination service" would help employers grapple with inconsistent certification standards. Trying to convince teacher educators that his service was not encouraging superintendents to circumvent the professional credentialing enterprise, Wood stressed that the examination was just "one phase" of the selection, hiring, and promotion process. But his tendency to condemn the "horde of semi-literates who flaunt their diplomas before the credulous eyes of employer superintendents," or his observation that "education classes are as much if not more amply populated with morons than other departments," did little to ease the skepticism teacher educators maintained about the service (Wood, 1936, p. 381; Wood & Beers, 1936, p. 498). Upon hearing about the new testing venture, for example, the president of Shippensburg (Pennsylvania) State Teachers College challenged Wood in the pages of the *Harvard Educational Review*. He feared that the prestige and power of the American Council of Education could make the proposed examinations popular and influential enough to cause a great deal of inadvertent damage: "A note of warning should be sounded against a procedure which, under the guise of providing an improved teaching service to our schools, may actually destroy the gains of several decades of intelligent planning for a better teaching personnel" (Rowland, 1940, pp. 277–288). Others feared that teacher education programs would be reduced to "tutoring schools for the passing of these tests." Pressured by his funding agency, Wood was forced to temper his enthusiasm for the tests and to do whatever he could to mend ties with the professional educators he had embarrassed and offended for several years. To an audience at the conference of the American Association of Teachers Colleges, he admitted that "objective examinations do not and cannot measure the total subtle complex which we call teaching ability" (quoted in A. Wilson, 1985, p. 15).

It took more than a year of focused effort to complete the battery of instruments that would comprise the first National Teacher Examination. The final incarnation consisted of a group of multiple-choice tests that totaled twelve hours in length. The set included an eight-hour common examination on reasoning, comprehension, expression, contemporary affairs, social problems, subject-matter fields, and a series of segments on professional issues like education and social policy, child development, and methods (Ryans, 1940, pp. 275ff.; A. Wilson, 1985, pp. 18–23; Wood & Beers, 1936). Most of the examination assessed prospective teachers' knowledge of basic college-course content and familiarity with current affairs, many questions being on military matters and New Deal politics. The "professional studies" component of the examination, totaling two hours out of twelve, was intentionally kept relatively small, Wood claimed, to avoid giving the impression that the testing service intended to exert "any undesirable influence on the teacher training curriculum." Professional knowledge items, consequently, were designed to assess familiarity with indisputable fundamentals: the awareness that John Dewey was the "chief contemporary exponent of the experimental method in philosophy," for example; or the recognition of various titles of "progressive" publications; or the knowledge that the best way to control adolescents was to exploit their obsession with "social approval." The superficial, definitive nature of such questions probably did little to calm the fears of the community of teacher educators. Once the examinations began to be administered during the 1940s, members of the teaching profession joined teacher educators in condemning the use of the National Teacher Examination as a measure of "good teaching" (A. Wilson, 1985, 1986a, p. 6).

From the moment of its inception, the "professional knowledge" component of the NTE faced criticism. Some complained that the professional segment was weighted far more heavily than its actual share of the exam warranted (A. Wilson, 1985). Others maintained that the questions were essential political, serving primarily as a form of loyalty oath to the tenets of progressivism. One reporter, who took the NTE and then interviewed other examinees during that first year of administration, observed that in the professional test, "one seemed to sense rather immediately that certain answers were expected."

Many questions in this area seemed to have reference to attitudes rather than to information," [he continued]. From the wording of the questions one would probably conclude that the answer desired that which would be given by one who stood somewhat to the left educationally, by one who would be classified as a liberal or a progressive.

He also found, as other reviewers of mass examinations had since World War I, that there was an "urban tonality" about many questions. Readers of New York City newspapers, he concluded, had a definite advantage. An "observant Easterner has a better chance to make a good score than an observant Midwesterner or Southerner." This "metropolitan cultural" bias was ultimately undemocratic he wrote. And he found the multiple-choice—forced single choice—format to be particularly ill suited for questions he considered "dogmatic." The new technology of the pencil lead reading scoring machines reinforced his frustration: answers that he wanted to explain or develop—out of a defiant attitude about their content—were simply marked right or wrong (Winetrout, 1941, pp. 480–481).

Just as the surplus of the 1930s spawned the National Teacher Examination, the abrupt conversion of the labor market to one of dramatic shortage—occasioned by World War II—derailed the movement to expand the NTE. Its initial role as an supplementary sorting instrument to help screen certified teachers for districts encumbered by too many applicants was undermined as the War drew off so many prospective teachers that even the largest districts had little use for such a device. In fact, backers of the NTE quickly reduced expenses by cutting the scope and scale of the examination sharply, from twelve hours to three and stopped preparing new questions for a number of years.

Ever the opportunist, Ben Wood took advantage of the South's determination to sustain racially based dual salary schedules that the U.S. Supreme Court invalidated in 1940 to keep the National Teacher Examination afloat. Immediately after the Court ruled, southern states began to consider new proposals for hiring and paying teachers. South Carolina, for example, established a new test-based certification system for both prospective and continuing teachers: it would bestow "graded" credentials (with different salaries attached) on the basis of performance on the "objective" NTE. Wood rethought the marketing strategy for his test, and, although he was privately concerned about "getting mixed up in the racial problem," he quickly saw the advantages of casting the NTE as a mechanism that would assist southern states in maintaining separate educational systems and opportunities while also meeting the objectivity challenges that the Court imposed (Baker, 1995, pp. 55ff.). He organized a series of conferences across the South to promote a scheme that would not award the same certificates to "persons of very unequal ability." He reassured his white audiences that African American teachers tended to score in the bottom quintile, and was pleased that superintendents from across the region believed that the NTE could be of "great assistance in working out a constructive solution to the problems brought to focus by the [Court's opposition to dual salary schedules in the] Norfolk decision" (Baker, 1995, p. 55).[9]

Wood's case was persuasive: within the next year, district after district, state after state, "began using test scores to legitimize so-called merit systems that reproduced salary differentials," according to John Baker's close analysis of the situation (Baker, 1995, p. 56). In Florida, for example, the use of the test led to patterns like the following: in Tampa, 84 percent of the white teachers, but only 6 percent of the African American teachers ranked on the highest rung of the pay scale; 80 percent of the blacks and only one percent of the whites occupied the lowest. In Palm Beach, 60 percent of the African American teachers were in the lowest salary group; no whites were in that group, and no blacks were at the highest salary rung (Baker, 1995, pp. 57–58). The courts endorsed this system because of its presumed "objectivity and validity." The NAACP and Thurgood Marshall were able to make no headway in blocking the new certification and merit-based schedules. Wood was most successful in South Carolina, where he "prepared the way" for the state to rely on the NTE in constructing its salary schedule (quoted in Baker, 1995, p. 59). A special committee that was convened to assess Wood's role in shaping state policy concluded that he helped to convince officials that since the tests could be scored "objectively and impartially," they would "not be subject to the accusation that they were used for the purpose of discrimination" (quoted in Baker, 1995, p. 60). Despite numerous claims that the NTE lacked validity—one investigator in South Carolina observed that that there was little assurance "that there is any close relationship between what a person can do on this examination and his excellence in teaching"—appeals to the scientific objectivity of the exam coupled with projected racial disparities in performance led the legislature to approve the NTE based salary policy in 1945 (quoted in Baker, 1995, p. 61).

Although Ben Wood became "rather frightened about further publicizing our [NTE's] relationship in this matter" of test-based differentiated salary schedules, his successors pressed to expand the exam's role in hiring and reward policies across the nation, particularly in the South. Ironically, after the NAACP's victories during the 1950s, the *Brown* decision in particular led to "greater use of the exams in the South" (quoted in Baker, 1995, pp. 63–64). Within just a few years, teacher and administrator testing was mandatory throughout the southern states, and was required in every major city. In addition to expanding differential salary schedules, the NTE was increasingly used, in the sobering analysis of Scott Baker, "to demote and dismiss thousands of African American teachers in desegregated school systems" (Baker, 1995, p. 64).

Nationally during this time, the continuing teacher shortage—instigated by the war and aggravated sharply by the arrival of the first wave of the Baby Boom generation into the elementary schools after 1952—influenced strategies for recruiting, licensing, and hiring teachers. Following a brief flirtation with "emergency" certificates, bestowed during the war on individuals otherwise unable to secure teaching positions through established licensure routes, states and districts tried to attract teachers with higher salaries, publicly supported financial aid and loan forgiveness programs, and deferments from the military draft. Paralleling the shortage of the 1920s, certification standards were actually raised during the period after World War II. By this time, almost all state policies were based on professional educational credentials, so attention focused on the scale, scope, and substance of the academic and professional preparation available to, and required of, prospective teachers. Between 1940 and 1967 the minimal professional component expanded very slightly, to roughly 28 semester hours at the elementary level and 18 at the secondary level. Most institutions offered programs that required more than these minimums, however: a survey of accredited institutions in 1958 revealed that elementary programs more typically required 36 hours, and secondary programs 24 (Stinnett, 1969, pp. 418–420; Armstrong, 1951; Woellner, 1946, 1949, 1952). Extended clinical experiences (as student teachers) became customary.

As these standards were raised, an intense struggle ensued during the 1950s and 1960s over teacher certification and preparation. In most respects, the struggle was ideological and rhetorical; the actual framework for licensure remained quite stable for the four decades following World War II. The hegemony of the loosely-coupled professional education enterprise—state education and certification authorities, teacher preparation institutions, K-12 teacher organizations, was increasingly challenged by another loose collection of intellectual, political, and professional interests, led for the most part by discipline-based academic faculty in colleges and universities.

Like the progressive factions that shaped policy during the early twentieth century, these two groups were driven by similar motivations: to impose their vision of educational purpose and teaching methodology on the nation's schools, and to advance their respective career interests. Unlike their progressive predecessors, however, the two groups in the 1950s and 1960s differed radically in their proposals for preparing, licensing, and recruiting K-12 teachers. The "educational trust," or "educationists," as the first group became known, continued their century long campaign for expanding and refining professional credentials based on increased levels of preparation, and for deepening the influence of practitioners in the training and hiring processes. The academic disciplinarians criticized the value of professional education, and opposed all of the burdensome state policies that based certification on extended professional preparation; they believed that a strong liberal arts education at a demanding four-year institution of higher learning was sufficient preparation to teach K-12 school subjects.[10]

This was the most vicious manifestation of what was becoming a perennial dispute between those who were committed to a broad, socially ambitious agenda for the schools, and those who advocated a narrower purpose, focused principally on ensuring the acquisition of school knowledge in the core academic subjects. Certainly since the 1920s, under the vision expressed most popularly in the *Cardinal Principles of Secondary Education* (1918) and subsequently through the policy and implementation statements associated with the "life adjustment movement" of the late 1930s and 1940s, the first group had grown more dominant. At least the American curriculum had adapted to this vision of serving the masses of children and adolescents that were attending the public schools. Other historians have thoroughly reconstructed this pronounced shift in the stated goals of schooling, away from concern with intellectual development and mastery of subject matter to concern for social and emotional development and to the adoption of "functional" objectives related to areas such as vocation, health, and family life (Ravitch, 1983, p. 55). So this chapter will address the movement away from elite, classical learning towards universal, inclusive (if highly differentiated) "socially relevant" learning only briefly, as assumptions about the education of children are intimately related to assumptions about the preparation of their teachers.[11]

The curriculum expanded aggressively to serve the presumed interests and needs of millions of working class and immigrant children who had traditionally abandoned systematic schooling during the elementary years. Claiming that it was undemocratic to force such children to endure the aggressive classical curriculum that had appeared to serve the needs of the handful of adolescents who would attend college or enter privileged economic and social positions, the reformers added an array of vocational, practical, and personal development experiences to the curriculum. And they fragmented the traditional disciplines, both to accommodate the students they thought were incapable of rigorous academic work, but also to infuse those subjects with new relevance and purpose. When they could afford it, many districts added social and health services. As they became less exclusive, many schools became far more internally stratified and differentiated. These innovations were essential, in the words of an influential report to the American Youth Commission of the American Council on Education, to meet the needs "of children of mediocre or inferior ability who lack interest in abstract and academic materials." Stimulating the final phase of the life adjustment movement, this study, released in 1937, posed the challenge of modern curriculum design by arguing that the course of study need not include subjects, or aspects of them, merely because they have made significant contributions to civilization. It is impractical to confuse, as is so commonly done, such values with the utility of subject matter for the education of the masses of young people today, however essential it may be that a small number of experts be well trained in these matters (quoted in Ravitch, 1983, pp. 60–61). The pressure towards life adjustment accelerated over the next few years. The prestigious Educational Policies Commission released its powerful argument to have schools meet "the imperative needs of youth" in 1944, called *Education for All American Youth*. Challenging the historical classical defense of traditional disciplines, the Commission claimed that in the future there should be "no aristocracy of 'subjects'," and that "mathematics and mechanics, art and agriculture, history and homemaking are all peers." Diane Ravitch has reconstructed this intensifying campaign through the late 1940s, and its impact on American schools, at least on their curricula (Ravitch, 1983, especially pp. 62–63).

It is not surprising that this expression of ambitious social expansionism through schooling provoked a variety of critics. Building on the narrower academic disciplinary objectives of William C. Bagley and the "Essentialists" of the 1930s, the critics coalesced during the early 1950s, and engaged the professional educational establishment in "the great debate," as it became known. Despite their radically varied motives and inspirations, the "anti-progressives" rallied around their common enemy—the life adjustment movement—which was a "bloated target," in Ravitch's memorable image (Ravitch, 1983, p. 70).

The more thoughtful critics shared Mortimer Smith's outrage regarding the progressive assumption of equality of knowledge. This former school board member rebelled at the notion that "no subject is intrinsically of any more value than any other subject . . . training in mechanical skills is put on a par with the development of mind and imagination . . . hairdressing and embalming are just as important, if not a little more so, than history and philosophy" (Smith, 1949, pp. 21–24, 42, 59–60, 92–93).

Critics rather quickly began to shift the blame towards the teacher education community, which they held accountable for the disturbing anti-intellectual hostility to the classical curricula and traditional teacher-directed methods. A liberal arts faculty member at the University of Illinois viciously attacked professors of education, who he argued converted teachers into "wet nurses, instructors in sex education, medical advisors, consultants to the lovelorn, umpires in the battle of the vertical versus the horizontal stroke in tooth-brushing, and professors of motor-vehicle operation." He thoroughly condemned faculty in education schools, from their enthusiasm for "socially relevant" curricula, to their "flatulent prose" masquerading as scholarship (H. Fuller, 1951, p. 34). One of his colleagues at Illinois at the time, history professor Arthur E. Bestor, Jr., moved quickly to address the essential problem: the usurpation of authority by the pedagogical faculty for teacher education in the university setting. In an address to the University of Wisconsin in early 1953, which would be later expanded in his comprehensive assault on prevailing educational practice and philosophy, *Educational Wastelands*, Bestor blasted professors of education who "represent themselves" to the public as the only legitimate segment of the university to speak about the broader aims and purposes of schooling. And this faculty group "contrived to put across the completely unfounded notion that the proper way to prepare for a career in teaching" was to take courses in "education, so-called, that is to say, in pedagogy" (Bestor, 1953, p. 82). He was not opposed to pedagogy as a research field, and claimed that as a history teacher he drew successfully on important scholarship of learning, textbook effectiveness, and adapting instruction to students of differing intellectual capacity. But, he continued, "the effective teacher of history requires many qualities of mind and personality, many varieties of knowledge, and many intellectual skills, among which pedagogy is only one." His main point was that "obviously every teacher must have some knowledge and skill in pedagogy just as a doctor must have some adeptness as what we call 'bedside manner.' " But such study is not what should be central in medical education, or in teacher education. "What counts in a doctor is his knowledge of medicine, and what counts in a teacher is his knowledge of the subject he is teaching. To expect to produce a good teacher by training him mainly in pedagogy is as foolish as to expect to produce a good doctor by loading him down with courses in bedside manner." If we operated medical schools as we did colleges of education, he stated, "we would all be done to death by cheery and plausible doctors who would know all about *how* to practice medicine but who would not be quite sure whether human beings have gizzards or not." Preparing teachers was one of the university's most critical functions, and it would never be done well until it was done by "the university as a whole." Delegating it to the department or college of education was a "principal cause of the alarming anti-intellectualism of so much public education today" (Bestor, 1953, p. 82).

Bestor blamed liberal arts and sciences faculty for allowing this troubling condition to develop. They had failed to be vigilant about public education, about the needs of teachers. Because they failed, the arrogant educationists had "rushed in to fill the vacuum." The academic disciplinarians must recapture authority over the structure and substance of the undergraduate curriculum, he said. Minimum study in teaching methods could be completed in an elective course or two. But, he warned, "under no circumstance should the department of pedagogy be permitted to exercise any sort of control over the undergraduate programs of prospective teachers" (Bestor, 1953, p. 83). Even at the graduate level, virtually all coursework needed to be in the academic disciplines, not in pedagogical fields. And research on pedagogy, learning, and administration should be shared among the social sciences. He then turned to the legal framework—state-imposed certification requirements—those stood as a barrier to his "rational program of teacher training." Sensitive to the institutional and personal economics of university-based teacher education, he argued that "these requirements are, in reality, special interest legislation—a kind of protective tariff—enacted for the most part at the behest of professional education-ists." He wanted to replace these codes with law that would "protect the schools against incompetent teachers rather than the professors of pedagogy against losses in enrollment" (Bestor, 1953, p. 85). Statutes that required minimum credits in professional education needed to be stripped. "Dethroning these requirements from their peculiarly privileged position" would help to open the teaching market to a "large and brilliant group of liberal arts graduates who are at present excluded from public-school employment by unjustifi-ably arbitrary pedagogical requirements." Finally, this realignment of certification and preparation would "bring to an end the aimless accumulation by experienced teachers of credits in pedagogical courses," and would do more than anything to "restore the repute" of public schools more than any other single reform. This change would appeal to those with genuine intellectual interest and capacity, who would not be "repelled at the outset by being asked to lay aside their intellectual interests and fritter away their time in the courses of pedagogues" (Bestor, 1953, p. 87). Such a teaching force would also be ready and able to resist the anti-intellectualism of the new wave of vacuous progressivism that was about to greet the baby boomers as they entered their first classrooms.

This argument of Bestor and his allies in the liberal arts departments reflected both a countervailing view of educational purpose, and a keen sense of their own political economics and career interests, a perspective that echoed the opposition of the liberal arts colleges and classical academies to the expansion of normal schools after the Civil War. Over the twentieth century, the expansion of professional studies for prospective teachers rose steadily, tripling from about 10 or 11 credits in the early 1900s, to well over 30 by 1950. The total size of the course of study leading to the bachelor's degree did not increase that much, so in many ways, in the zero-sum game of the undergraduate curric-ulum, the expansion of professional coursework displaced classes in the liberal arts and sciences disciplines (in general education, academic majors, and electives). As teacher education became an increasingly large segment of university work, the rise in influence of the faculties of education, and their influence over public discourse and policy, reduced the role of academic disciplinarians. Their aggressiveness in the 1950s represented in part a renewed quest for public legitimacy and institutional authority, just as had the quest of the professional educational community during the prior generation. There is no doubt that serious differences in philosophical and political visions divided the groups, and shaped the substance of their claims and campaigns. But private ambition and collective interests intensified the hostilities.

The rivalry deepened in the later 1950s and early 1960s, accelerated in part by the national response to the launch of Sputnik in 1957 and the concentrated campaign to restore disciplinary hegemony over the schools' academic curricula, particularly the effort to energize math and science teaching and learning. University faculty in the arts and sciences largely commandeered the public and foundation investments in the curricular and instructional reform movement—and the underlying research—of those years. This was another expression of the competition for resources and authority between the teacher education community and its university-based critics (Church & Sedlak, 1976).

The assault's intensity peaked in 1963, with the near simultaneous publication of two indictments of the state of K-12 schooling in general and of teacher education in particular, one sympathetic, the other scathing. James B. Conant, former Harvard president and author of the relatively liberal and supportive endorsement of the American high school, wrote *The Education of American Teachers*. For the times, this book was also surprisingly generous toward the teacher education and certification enterprises. He appreciated the difficult market conditions that shaped the constraints on schools of education, and he challenged the academic disciplinarians to care about improving the way that their subjects could be more effectively taught. Conant did anger teacher educators, however, by expecting them to share responsibility for preparing teachers with both their colleagues in the academic disciplines and practicing classroom instructors; his enthusiasm for the student-teaching apprenticeship experience also implicitly denigrated their higher education-based professional courses (Conant, 1963; Judge *et al.*, 1994; Stinnett, 1967).

Despite his claim to have studied teacher education "dispassionately" and "undogmatically," James D. Koerner, the author of the second book released in 1963, infuriated virtually everyone associated with preparing teachers, administrators, and other specialists for the educational system. His blunt and humiliating study, called *The Miseducation of American Teachers*, condemned teacher and administrator educators, students planning careers in education, and state licensing staff alike. Here are his most notorious complaints (Koerner, 1963; Labaree, 2004).

> 3 Education as an academic discipline has poor credentials ... [I]t has not yet developed a corpus of knowledge and technique of sufficient scope and power to warrant the field's being given full academic status. That it has been given this status in most of our colleges—or, more accurately, that it has achieved this status through the abdication of responsibility by the academic departments—does not make Education a genuine discipline; it only makes possible the building of more academic empires on sandy foundations.
>
> 5 It is an indecorous thing to say and obviously offensive to most educationists, but it is the truth and it should be said: the inferior intellectual quality of the education faculty is the fundamental limitation of the field, and will remain so ... [T]here is still a strong strain of anti-intellectualism that runs through the typical Education staff, despite their increasingly frequent apostrophes to academic quality.
>
> 6 Likewise, the academic caliber of students in Education remains a problem, as it always has. Fortunately, there is some progress here, more so, ironically enough, than with faculty. Many schools in the last few years have succeeded in raising the level of admission requirements to the teacher-training programs, which has been possible chiefly because the requirements were so low to begin with.
>
> 7 Course work in Education deserves its ill-repute. It is most often puerile, repetitious, dull, and ambiguous—incontestably. Two factors make it this way: the limitations of the instructor, and the limitations of subject-matter that has been

remorselessly fragmented, sub-divided, and inflated, and that in many cases was not adequate in its uninflated state . . . [T]he intellectual impoverishment of the course work remains a major characteristic of the field.

8 The quantity of Education courses in the typical teacher-training program also deserves the harsh things that have always been said about it. According to my survey of transcripts credit, secondary teachers of academic subjects take an average of 27 semester hours in Education. This is close to a year's work in most colleges and is clearly excessive. Elementary teachers take an average of 49 semester hours in Education. This is about 40 percent of their undergraduate careers, and is, I submit, wholly indefensible. These averages go even higher among teachers colleges and many university schools of Education; they are brought down nationally by the liberal arts colleges. The figures speak for themselves: a severe curtailment in the quantity of these courses is needed.

11 The academic component of a teacher's education, which remains, after all, the primary one, is also in need of attention. Course work in academic areas is sometimes not much stronger than in Education, a fact that academicians ought to face with candor . . . Although academic teachers have certain advantages over their Education colleagues in training and in the natural viability of their material, and although they are certainly more effective in their students' eyes than are Education professors, all indications are that course work in the liberal arts areas could immeasurably better than it is . . . If high school teachers are often incompetent, a large share of the responsibility must be accepted by the academic departments.

(Koerner, 1963, pp. 17–19)

Like many other critics of the educationist community, Koerner held a comparatively narrow and academic view of the purpose of education. "We have no choice but to assume Western civilization is good," he began. "Our civilization is the product of a long and painful process of taming, training, and refining the human animal, a process made possible by two characteristics that distinguish man from all other creatures: intelligence and compassion." Education could do its job of continuing to raise humankind out of savagery by "training the intellect of each new generation vigorously and systematically in those subjects that are the most fruitful for man's continuing development" (Koerner, 1963, pp. 6–7). Like others, he railed against the anti-intellectualism that he believed pervaded the most recent expression of progressive ideology. But, interestingly, Koerner differentiated sharply between educational purpose and the pedagogies that were most likely to achieve those ends. Although he opposed vocational, life adjustment, and other practical or utilitarian functions for education, he agreed with pedagogical romantics like Rousseau and even John Dewey. "How this kind of basic education can best be carried out in a classroom is another question," he said. "Let us by all means adopt those methods of progressivism that involve the student as actively as possible in the learning process. And let us by all means champion those views . . . that seek to reduce the cruelties or the senseless coercions of the classroom that, it is said, used to constitute education." And, unlike many of his contemporaries, he believed that the "great majority of people" could respond to the opportunities of a "liberal education when it is conducted well" (Koerner, 1963, pp. 9–10).

Although the academic disciplinarians played a compelling leadership role in the campaign, there were other constituencies, whose interests and aspirations were rooted in recent social and demographic changes, who tried to challenge the educational trust. In particular, the ambitious professional and middle classes, residentially concentrated in the flourishing suburbs, had grown uneasy about the erosion of academic focus in the schools. Many of them owed their career achievements, status, and modest wealth to their educational attainments and credentials. Many had graduated college, and had even earned professional and master's degrees, some with the aid of the G.I. Bill. They were committed to the installation of the emerging American meritocratic state, which recognized and rewarded educational accomplishments. They wanted to protect their children's futures by investing in advanced educational credentials, which would open access to privileged occupations. Thus, they resonated with the anti-life adjustment commentary and resisted the political movement to convert the high schools into terminal educational institutions dedicated to serving the social and vocational needs of the non-college bound masses. They were attracted to the arguments of Bestor and other academic faculty who endorsed the narrower, more elite college preparatory purpose for the K-12 system (Church & Sedlak, 1976, p. 422).

While this line of criticism was building, various constituencies of the unraveling educational trust were pressing ahead with distinct agendas of their own. The largest group, the classroom teachers, began mobilizing during the 1940s, just as World War II ended. David Angus has reconstructed the aggressive efforts of teachers, whose voices had eroded under the domination of their professional education partners—the teacher educators and state educational authorities. At the end of the war, the teaching corps was "grossly overworked, underpaid, and demoralized," Angus observed, and felt that after a half-century of educational investment and expansion of power in the educational enterprise, "the benefits had not trickled down to them" (2001, p. 19; see other "trickle down" imagery in E. Fuller, 1952, pp. 26–7). They turned quickly to the National Education Association, which had been gradually turning away from collegiate leadership, to create the National Commission on Teacher Education and Professional Standards (NCTEPS, TEPS for short) in 1946. Rooted in the NEA's department of classroom teachers, TEPS was the first initiative intended to fashion an "independent voice" for teachers that would begin to challenge the dominance of university-based professional school faculty "over teacher education and certification" (Angus, 2001, p. 20). Seeking to play a larger role in controlling entry to teaching, a critical ambition of all occupations undergoing professionalization, TEPS launched what has become known as the "professional standards movement" in education. The New Horizons Task Force, for example, was dedicated to achieving "a self-directing profession of teaching, which is capable of assuming responsibility for the competence of its members" (Kinney, 1964, p. 92; Topp, 1957; Benham, 1979).

For the next few years, TEPS organized conferences on a variety of certification and preparation issues. Under the banner of "democratizing" the discussion of professional licensing, the TEPS strategy was to expand the role of practitioners over state policy-making and to influence the content of teacher education. They largely succeeded in their effort to centralize all certification authority in the state departments, which were to be advised by advisory councils, whose membership was to include TEPS officers and classroom teachers, a maneuver to circumscribe the power traditionally held by education deans (Angus, 2001, p. 20). This led to a critical drive to overturn traditional state practices of allowing teacher education programs essentially to design themselves, which resulted in idiosyncratic approaches that made certification reciprocity very difficult and costly to teachers who wanted to pursue market opportunities across state lines (see E. Fuller, 1952, p. 27). Classroom teachers joined critics of education schools in condemning the low standards of admission and weaknesses in preparation. One of the TEPS leaders observed in 1950 that the teacher education system of the United States, with the exception of a very few states, is a hodgepodge of programs which are in the main a travesty upon professional education ... We even provide a better-planned and better-financed system of professional education for those who raise pigs than we do for those who teach children.

(quoted in Angus, 2001, p. 21)

Neither Arthur Bestor nor James Koerner could have phrased it more imaginatively.

Several organizations cooperated to promote an alternative to the state-by-state "approved program" approach. TEPS, the National Association of State Directors of Teacher Education and Certification (NASDTEC), and the recently formed American Association of Colleges for Teacher Education (AACTE) collaborated to establish in 1952 a national external accreditation body to develop and enforce national standards on the 1,200 institutions then preparing teachers. The resulting organization, the National Council for the Accreditation of Teacher Education (NCATE), was charged with raising preparation standards across the nation and to build "general public opinion in support of professional status for education" (National Council for Accreditation of Teacher Education, 1951; E. Fuller, 1952, p. 28; Russell, 1952; Tuttle, 1953; Lieberman, 1960, pp. 191–201). Modeled on councils operating in two dozen occupations at the time, NCATE was to operate initially under a shared leadership of classroom teachers, professional education faculty, and state certification officials. During the period of the "great debate," NCATE leadership respectfully addressed some of the concerns raised by Bestor and other academic disciplinarians. Aware of the critique that was rooted in the competition for space in the zero-sum higher education curriculum, for example, NCATE's director, W. Earl Armstrong laid out a model for a balanced "teacher education curriculum" (Armstrong, 1957). Speaking from a draft "thought piece" from the Council, in 1957 he argued that the ideal preparation would include a broad immersion in general-liberal studies, a subject matter major, a limited, coherent, and practice-based set of professional coursework. He noted emphatically how difficult this was to achieve in the typical four-year undergraduate program, and stated that *the period is rapidly approaching when a minimum of five years of college preparation will be regarded as essential for all fully qualified elementary and secondary school teachers*" (Armstrong, 1957, p. 241, emphasis in original). As society became more complex and knowledge expanded exponentially, as the social demands on education multiplied, and as the general public became more educated—and their confidence in the teachers in their communities depended upon equivalent credentials, he elaborated, "the need for more than four years to accomplish the total program becomes more apparent" (p. 241). Armstrong wanted to expand broad liberal arts learning by shifting some disciplinary specialization and professional education to the fifth year, which he also argued should be completed as an induction experience once the teacher was employed. He did not specify the relative scale of these essential components of the program, but said that the entire university community—liberal arts and professional education faculty alike—should come together to discuss the goals and size of the proportions (Armstrong, 1957, p. 241; see also Selden, 1960).

Armstrong's tentative proposal stimulated discussion, but little action. One of the most thorough responses was offered by educational philosopher Harry Broudy of the University of Illinois, who claimed that the NCATE proposal basically conceived of school teaching as "a genteel, white-collar craft" because it appeared to debase genuine, theory-driven professional knowledge, and substituted highly specialized but limited skill development in field settings. What sorts of "intellectual, economic, and social status" can mastery of such limited craft training command, he asked? If brevity and a low risk of failure is all there is to this corrupt "professional" education, he could "forsee the logical end of this trend:"

> The claim that a liberal arts degree plus some student teaching is enough; the liberal arts degree with apprenticeship in some school system at somewhat reduced salary will be suggested; then it may occur to someone that perhaps a high school diploma and apprenticeship might do . . . If teaching is merely a craft, then sooner or later the apprenticeship pattern of training will displace all others, because we learn a craft by doing it; the craft of teaching is best learned by teaching.
>
> (Broudy, 1959, p. 109)

Broudy concluded by noting that if the Council's proposal could lead to productive dialogue and the improvement and national upgrading of teacher education, "it will have contributed to the salvation of professional education." But if the proposal was taken as the solution, it would be "one step toward suicide—a lingering, gradual suicide but ultimately fatal, nevertheless" (Broudy, 1959, p. 112; see rejoinder by Bowers, 1959, pp. 112–116).

Possibly because of perspectives like those suggested in the Council's 1957 proposal, NCATE underwent restructuring several times over the next three decades, each time causing the classroom teachers to lose influence, and teacher educators to achieve a voting majority (Angus, 2001, p. 21; Kinney, 1964, pp. 92ff.; Armstrong, 1960, p. 9). And, as Angus observed, teacher militancy and unionism, both hallmarks of anti-professionalism during the 1960s, left practitioners in the NEA and AFT with even less voice over certification and teacher education.

NCATE accredited comparatively few of the nation's teacher education programs during the 1960s and 1970s, although it did engage many of the largest institutions. NCATE came to be seen as an expensive process that had not been able to fulfill its promise of substituting for state approval and ensuring national licensure reciprocity. Further complaints from many communities about the ability of the most notoriously weak programs either to avoid accreditation altogether or to slip through vulnerable enforcement procedures led the NEA and AACTE—both troubled by NCATE's deteriorating stature and influence—to institute new leadership and to fund a major three-year study of the organization in 1977. Led by Christopher Wheeler of Michigan State University's Institute for Research on Teaching, the analysis thoroughly probed all of the activities that occurred during the accreditation process (Wheeler, 2005; Wheeler, 1980; Watkins, 1980). Wheeler found that NCATE accreditation was actually improving some of the worst programs it examined; at least when the process was professional and taken seriously these institutions benefited from the review. But, more often, a variety of pressures led the NCATE visitation teams to conduct relatively superficial investigations. The composition and analytical depth of the teams was too easily manipulated and compromised, he found, because the institutions could veto team members, and often did so when a potential visitor had a reputation as too rigorous or had found too many problems with other programs (Wheeler, 1980, p. 57). The host institution's attitude about external accreditation also frustrated NCATE leaders and team members. "We saw NCATE as a problem to get over with in the least costly way," one program leader told Wheeler. He spoke candidly about the review:

> The faculty in our College of Education was hostile to NCATE, so we decided to keep the process as quiet as possible. Only the department chairperson and I knew it was coming up. I wrote the entire Institutional Report to cover over our problems.

Then we tried to get faculty members who might cause trouble out of town during the visit and we primed the others. We deliberately pushed for a small NCATE team on the assumption they would not be able to penetrate deeply because they would run out of time.

(Wheeler, 1980, p. 57)

This gamesmanship strategy worked: NCATE accredited all of his programs. Combined with vague and weak standards, the visiting teams were too often forced to conduct a shallow review, and were left with few alternatives to the prevailing practice of determining whether there was a "presence or absence" of a standard, or a problem: they could rarely comment on whether the teacher education program was doing well. Wheeler found this minimum standards approach to be a significant impediment to influencing moderately successful programs in positive directions (Wheeler, 2005; Tom, 1980a; Gubser, 1980; Wisniewski, 1981; Tom, 1981; Tom, 1980b). Provoked by this stinging critique about its processes, and by other substantial questions about its standards, NCATE devoted a number of years to revising its practices. Internally, NCATE leadership was challenged, and both the NEA and AACTE called for new leadership and directions. Art Wise, of the Rand Corporation, was brought in to shepherd the reforms, particularly to move the accreditation process towards revitalized standards and outcomes-based performance assessments.

Despite several decades of controversy and activity, the ways that teachers became licensed and hired had changed only modestly by the early 1960s. Over the prior 30 years, states increasingly relied on professional education credentials to certify new teachers. Even as the "Great Debate" was winding down, teacher educators remained solidly in control of most of the details of professional preparation. State officials did indeed define the basic requirements, but higher education institutions retained considerable autonomy in enacting the public guidelines. National accreditation spurred some efforts towards consistency across states and regions, and helped to elevate some of the weakest preparation programs. Resurrected through the National Teacher Exam, testing had begun to stagger out of the embarrassing awkwardness of southern racial politics, but was not yet meaningfully influential in models of initial certification. Certainly more constituencies had begun exercising their voices, but they were not yet affecting the policy landscape in significant fashion.

The immense shift in the political landscape that occurred during the 1960s, as the educational enterprise was drafted into the War on Poverty, delayed the convergence of ideologies and self-interests that would eventually reshape certification policy during the 1980s. President Lyndon Johnson's ambitious domestic agenda in 1964 and 1965 revitalized the languishing vision for expanding the social function of education, which had contracted during the 1950s. The aggressive focus on disadvantaged and non-college bound students derailed temporarily the so-called "elitist" initiatives that had received the bulk of publicity and investment for ten years. Members of the core educational communities who were committed to studying the sources and consequences of school failure, differential access to valuable knowledge, the relationship between educational achievement and adult mobility and success, and who were engaged in constructing compensatory programs, or curricula that were sensitive to class, race, and gender, were once again provided the opportunity to shape discussion and policy debates, and to have their ideas and projects privileged in competition for public and private funding. Pedagogical romanticism flourished during the late 1960s and 1970s, as schools experimented with new organizational forms like the "open classroom," or more child-centered instructional methods, such as the use of manipulatives in mathematics classes. These were never modal practices, and were rarely permanent, but they were popular, widely discussed in mass media, and were not as ridiculed as many expressions of the life adjustment movement had been.

After this extended period of policy consistency, coupled with growing rhetorical antagonism, the terrain of certification began to be reconfigured during the 1980s. Over the last two decades of the twentieth century, ambitious political and professional interests did not just sustain the rhetorical struggle that surfaced after World War II, but moved strategically to attempt to transform the mechanisms of preparation and licensure. This piece of the story is complicated, and this chapter concludes by just reconstructing its outline, leaving to other authors the unenviable responsibility of unraveling the subtleties and details.

The resurgence of the conservative criticism of the expanding educational vision during the 1960s, legitimized and funded aggressively for the first time by the federal government, found its initial voice in *A Nation at Risk*, released in 1983. It launched the first wave of accountability and standards reform by re-focusing attention on "excellence" and competitiveness, grounded—as was the anti-educationist perspective of the 1950s—in a comparatively narrow definition of educational purpose and achievement, associated, not surprisingly, with a rather conventional vision of pedagogy. Since the early 1980s this tension between visions of purpose and pedagogy has been integral to the policy struggles over certification. A "new Progressivism" has faced off against a "new Essentialism" in both the K-12 enterprise and in higher education. On the one side, advocates of broadening the function of education condemned the standards and excellence movement as elitist, likely to reinforce or exacerbate existing inequalities—if not intentionally, at least inadvertently as a consequence of misguided and narrow accountability initiatives. They argued that excessive and punitive testing of students often perverted teaching and learning, squandering opportunities for children to grow meaningfully through their experience in school, and contributing at best to improved scores that represented little beyond shallow test-taking gamesmanship. They advocated instead for various expressions like ambitious or "adventuresome teaching," "conceptual learning," or "teaching and learning for understanding." And they supported teacher certification standards that increasingly reflected such an instructional approach. On the other side, conservatives were troubled with the expansion of purpose and content, with the broadening of the curriculum to embrace multi-cultural and practical or peripheral coursework at the expense of traditional core academic disciplinary knowledge. They were increasingly enthusiastic about direct didactical, teacher-centered instruction, believing that the spread of group work and active or project-based instruction had left classrooms far too student-centered. And they wanted to restrict teacher certification requirements essentially to collegiate subject matter preparation, denigrating virtually all university-based professional education as irrelevant, costly, frivolous, and of unproven value. In contrast to earlier conflicts, leaders from traditionally under-served communities (African American religious and neighborhood organizations, for example), who saw merit in more traditional instruction and achievement in core academic subjects as a reasonable route to improved economic opportunity, aligned themselves politically with this conservative perspective.

Ironically, much of the largely conservative animosity of the 1980s and 1990s drew heavily from the radical left's anti-professionalism and consumerism sentiment of the late 1960s and 1970s. Scholars from a variety of disciplines (particularly sociology, political science, anthropology, and history) were joined by consumers' rights advocates in an assault on providers of health care, education, social welfare services, insisting that professionalization in such occupations insulated practitioners from the consequences of their work. Moreover, the early critique ran, these fields pressed for the right to control entry into the occupations, thereby enhancing professional arrogance and reducing client access and choice. More recently, conservatives and many otherwise liberal communities—again, African American civil rights leaders—resurrected this analysis and fashioned an array of market and choice solutions to weaken and derail professional ambition. In education, the anti- or competitive certification or deregulation, movement embraced the earlier perspective in calling for an end to the professional cartel or monopoly over entry into teaching.

In sum, the creation and evolution of certification standards in education has been shaped by deep and enduring differences of perspective about the purpose and place of schools in our society, about what we want children to become through their experiences as students, how we think schools can best have this effect, and what sorts of people we believe we can trust with our children's care and destinies. Certainly individual and organizational interests and ambitions have affected this evolution. *Everyone* in this story has had interests to advance, careers to create, enhance, and protect. Understanding and appreciating the power of those personal interests is important, but not as important as the task of beginning to disentangle these differing visions of purpose from conventional politics.

NOTES

1 This version of the treaty was recalled and captured by Benjamin Franklin, first in a letter to Peter Collison in 1753 (reprinted in Labaree, L. and Bell, 1961, p. 483); Franklin, 1784, translated the sentiment again in a pamphlet called "Remarks Concerning the Savages of North America," in 1784 (reprinted in Smyth, 1907, pp. 98–99). This is the version quoted here. The actual treaty was translated more briefly and formally, but the sentiment was the same (Van Doren and Boyd, 1938, pp. 72–73, 76).

　　Several authors have begun calling attention to the ways that differing definitions of purpose have influenced the politics of teacher licensure, but no one has effectively brought this to the place of prominence it deserves; see Angus, 2001; Imig and Imig, 2006. My colleague, Patrick Halladay, and I spent a good summer discussing this matter; I appreciate his suggestions.

2 This compressed and abbreviated description of social and economic developments of the early nineteenth century is based most conveniently on Rury, 2004; Church and Sedlak, 1976; Kaestle, 1983; Reese, 2005.

3 See Sedlak, 1989; Angus, 2001; S. Wilson and Youngs, 2005; Herbst, 1989 for informative introductions to this formative period of policy creation.

4 See Church and Sedlak, 1976; Sedlak, 1989; Elsbree, 1939.

5 The most thorough and convenient examples of the origins and early history of teacher education programs are Herbst, 1989; Labaree, D., 2004 although they appeared late to influence this chapter, see comprehensive studies by Ogren, C., 2005 and Fraser, J., 2007.

6 The following few paragraphs draw heavily from Sedlak, 1989, 266–267.

7 These are widely-known distinctions among "educational progressives;" see Tyack, 1974; Church and Sedlak, 1976; Rury, 2002.

8 The most accessible and valuable historical treatments of the National Teacher Examination include A. Wilson, 1985, 1986a, 1986b; Baker, 1995; Haney, Madaus, and Kreitzer, 1987; and Sedlak, 1989.

9 The case of South Carolina has received particular attention; see A. Wilson, 1986b; Baker, 1995; Sandifer, 1984.

10 Various historians have explored this phase of the controversy; see Ravitch, 1983; Church and Sedlak, 1976; Reese, 2005; Angus and Mirel, 1999.

11 In addition to the sources listed in Note 10, see Cohen and Neufeld, 1981; Ravitch, 2000.

REFERENCES

Anderson, E.W., Butsch, R.L.C., Ellsbree, W.S., & Torgerson, T.L. (eds.) (1934) Teacher personnel. *Review of Educational Research*, 4, 253–352.

Anderson, E.W., Butsch, R.L.C., Cooke, D.H., Ellsbree, W.S., Torgerson, T.L., & Umstatt, J.G. (eds.) (1937) Teacher personnel. *Review of Educational Research*, 7, 237–354.

Angus, D.L. (2001) *Professionalism and the public good: a brief history of teacher certification*. Washington, DC: Thomas B. Fordham Foundation.

Angus, D.L. & Mirel, J.E. (1999) *The failed promise of the American high school, 1890–1995*. New York: Teachers College Press.

Armstrong, W.E. (1951) *Tabular summary of teacher certification requirements in the United States*. U.S. Office of Education, Circular No. 233. Washington, DC: Government Printing Office.

Armstrong, W.E. (1957) The teacher education curriculum. *Journal of Teacher Education*, 8, 230–43.

Armstrong, W.E. (1960) The NCATE in 1960. *Journal of Teacher Education*, 9, 9–14.

Aurner, C.R. (1918) *History of education in Iowa*. Vol. II. Iowa City: State Historical Society.

Bagley, W. (1925) State progress in reducing the proportion of untrained teachers. *School and Society*, 22, 113–114.

Baker, S. (1995) Testing equality: the National Teacher Examination and the NAACP's legal campaign to equalize teachers' salaries in the South, 1936–63. *History of Education Quarterly*, 35, 49–64.

Barrett, R.C. (1902) Reciprocity in licensing teachers. *Proceedings and Addresses*, 299–305. Washington, DC: National Education Association.

Benham, B.J. (1979) *Teacher training: the futile 135-year search for a foolproof formula*. Paper presented at the annual meeting of the American Educational Research Association in San Francisco.

Bestor, A.E. (1953) On the education and certification of teachers. *School and Society*, 78, 81–87.

Bowers, H.J. (1959) The NCATE: suicide or salvation? *Journal of Teacher Education*, 10, 112–16.

Broudy, H.S. (1959) The NCATE statement on the teacher education curriculum. *Journal of Teacher Education*, 10, 107–112.

Carnegie Foundation for the Advancement of Education (1932) *State and higher education in California*. Sacramento: California State Printing Office.

Church, R.L. & Sedlak, M.W. (1976) *Education in the United States: an interpretive history*. New York: Free Press.

Cohen, D.K. & Neufeld, B. (1981) The failure of high schools and the progress of education. *Daedalus*, 110, 69–89.

Commission on the Reorganization of Secondary Education (1918) *Cardinal principles of secondary education: a report of the Commission on the Reorganization of Secondary Education*. Appointed by the National Education Association. Washington, DC: National Education Association.

Conant, J.B. (1963) *The education of American teachers*. New York: McGraw-Hill.

Cook, K.M. (1920) Certification by examination—the open door to the teaching profession. *American School Board Journal*, 61, 29–30.

Cook, K.M. (1921) *State laws and regulations governing teachers' certificates*. Washington, DC: U.S. Bureau of Education.

Cook, K.M. (1927) *State laws and regulations governing teachers' certificates*. Washington, DC: U.S. Bureau of Education.

Cubberley, E.P. (1906) *The certification of teachers: a consideration of present conditions with suggestions as to lines of future improvement*. Fifth Yearbook of the National Society for the Scientific Study of Education, Part III. Chicago: University of Chicago Press.

Davis, C.O. (1924a) The training and experience of teachers in the high schools accredited by the North Central Association. *School Review*, 30, 335–354.

Davis, C.O. (1924b) The training of teachers in North Central Association accredited high schools. *School and Society* 19, 390.

Deffenbaugh, W.S. & Zeigel, W.H. (1932) *Selection and appointment of teachers*. U.S. Department of the Interior, Bulletin No. 17, National Survey of Secondary Education. Washington, DC: Government Printing Office.

Dutton, S. & Snedden, D (1908) *The administration of public education in the United States*. New York: Macmillan.

Dynes, J.J. (1931) How certification is practiced in the various states. *Nation's Schools*, 7, 67–71.

Dynes, J.J. (ed.) (1922) Education of teachers in different states. *School and Society*, 15, 304.

Dynes, J.J. (ed.) (1924) Sympathy and the certification of teachers. *School and Society*, 19, 760–761.

Elsbree, W.S. (1939) *The American teacher: evolution of a profession in a democracy*. New York: American Book Co.

Evenden, E.S., Gamble, G.C., & Blue, H.G. (1933) *National survey of the education of teachers*. U.S. Office of Education, Bulletin No. 10. Washington, DC: Government Printing Office.

Franklin, B. (1784) *Remarks concerning the savages of North America*. In A.H. Smyth (1907), *The writings of Benjamin Franklin*, Vol. 10, pp. 97–105. New York: Macmillan.

Frazer, J. (2007) *Preparing America's teachers: a history*. New York: Teacher's College.

Frazier, B.W. (1938) *Development of state programs for the certification of teachers*. Washington, DC: Government Printing Office.

Fuller, E. (1952) Toward a qualified teaching profession. *Journal of Teacher Education*, 3, 26–28.

Fuller, H.J. (1951) The emperor's new clothes, or Prius Dementat. *Scientific Monthly*, 72, 32–41.

Goodrich, C.L. (1928) The annual convention of the North Central Association. *Michigan Educational Journal*, 5, 548.

Gubser, L. (1980) NCATE's director comments on Tom's critique. *Phi Delta Kappan*, 62, 117–119.

Haney, W., Madaus, G., & Kreitzer, A. (1987) Charms talismanic: testing teachers for the improvement of American education. *Review of Research in Education*, 14, 169–238.

Herbst, J. (1989) *And sadly teach: teacher education and professionalization in American culture*. Madison: University of Wisconsin Press.

Hood, W.R. (1916) *Digest of state laws relating to public education*, Part E: the examination and certification of teachers. U.S. Bureau of Education, Bulletin No. 47. Washington, DC: Government Printing Office.

Imig, D.G. & Imig, S.R. (2006) The teacher effectiveness movement: how 80 years of essentialist control have shaped the teacher education profession. *Journal of Teacher Education*, 57, 167–180.

Jackson, W.R. (1903) The present status of the certification of teachers in the United States. In, *Biennial Report on Education in the United States*. Washington, DC: Government Printing Office.

Judge, H., Lemosse, M., Paine, L., & Sedlak, M. (1994) *The university and the teachers: France, the United States, England*. Oxford: Triangle.

Kaestle, C.F. (1983) *Pillars of the republic: common schools and American society, 1780–1860*. New York: Hill and Wang.

Kaestle, C.F. & Vinovskis, M.A. (1980) *Education and social change in nineteenth-century Massachusetts*. New York: Cambridge University Press.

Kinney, L.B. (1964) *Certification in education*. Englewood Cliffs, NJ, Prentice-Hall, Inc.

Koerner, J.D. (1963) *The miseducation of American teachers*. Boston: Houghton Mifflin.

Labaree, D.F. (2004) *The trouble with ed schools*. New Haven: Yale University Press.

Labaree, L.W. & Bell, W.J. (1961) *The papers of Benjamin Franklin*, vol. 4. New Haven: Yale University Press.

LaBue, A.C. (1960) Teacher certification in the United States: a brief history. *Journal of Teacher Education*, 11, 147–172.

Learned, W.S. & Bagley, W.C. (1920) *The professional preparation of teachers for American public schools: a study based upon an examination of tax-supported normal schools in the state of Missouri*. New York: Carnegie Foundation for the Advancement of Teaching.

Learned, W.S. & Wood, B. (1938) *The student and his knowledge: a report to the Carnegie Foundation on the results of high school and college entrance examinations of 1928, 1930, and 1932*. Bulletin No. 29. New York: Carnegie Foundation for the Advancement of Teaching.

Lieberman, M. (1960) Considerations favoring national certification of teachers. *Journal of Teacher Education*, 11, 191–201.

McConn, M. (1931) The Co-Operative Test Service. *Journal of Higher Education*, 2, 225–232.

(Maine State Board of Education) (1848) *Maine school report*. Augusta: State Printing Office.

Morrison, J.C. (1928) Certification for improving professional leadership. *American School Board Journal*, 76, 49, 50, 169–70.

National Council for Accreditation of Teacher Education (1951) Proposal for the establishment of a National Council for Accreditation of Teacher Education. Reprinted in (1952). NEA to act on proposed council. *Journal of Teacher Education*, 3, 84.

Ogren, C.A. (2005) *The American state normal school: "an instrument of great good."* New York: Palgrave Macmillan

(Ohio State Board of Education) (1858) *Fifth annual report*. Columbus: State Printing Office.

Parkinson, B.L. (1932) Certification of teachers. In T.A. Schuttle (ed.), *Orientation in education*, 422–448. New York: Macmillan.

Ravitch, D. (1983) *The troubled crusade: American education, 1945–1980*. New York: Basic Books.

Ravitch, D. (2000) *Left back: a century of failed school reforms*. New York: Simon and Schuster.

Reese, W.J. (2005) *America's public schools: from the common school to "no child left behind."* Baltimore: The Johns Hopkins University Press.

Rosier, J. (1925) Report of the committee on standards, requirements, and credits of teachers in service. *Proceedings and Addresses*, 237–241. Washington, DC: National Education Association.

Rotherham, A.J & Mead, S. (2004) Back to the future: the history and politics of state teacher licensure and certification. In Hess, F.M., Rotherham, A.J., and Walsh, K. (eds.), *A qualified teacher in every classroom? Appraising old answers and new ideas*, 11–47. Cambridge: Harvard Education Press.

Rowland, A.L. (1940) The proposed Teacher Examination Service. *Harvard Educational Review*, 10, 277–288.

Rury, J.L. (2004) *Education and social change: themes in the history of American schooling*, 2nd ed. Mahwah, NJ: Lawrence Erlbaum Associates.

Russell, J.D. (1952) An analysis of the proposed National Council for Accreditation of Teacher Education. *Journal of Teacher Education*, 3, 87–93.

Ryans, D. (1940) The professional examination of teaching candidates: a report of the first annual National Teacher Examinations. *School and Society*, 52, 273–284.

Sandifer, P.D. (1984) *Teacher certification examinations in South Carolina, 1940 to 1984*. Paper presented at the annual meeting of the American Educational Research Association in New Orleans.

Sedlak, M.W. (1989) "Let us go and buy a schoolmaster:" historical perspectives on the hiring of teachers in the United States, 1750–1980. In D. Warren (ed.), *American teachers: histories of a profession at work*, 257–291. New York: Macmillan.

Sedlak, M.W. & Schlossman, S.L. (1986) *Who will teach? Historical perspectives on the changing appeal of teaching as a profession*. Santa Monica, CA: Rand Corporation.

Selden, W.K. (1960) Why accredit teacher education? *Journal of Teacher Education*, 11, 185–190.

Siedle, T.A. (1934) Trends in teacher preparation and certification. *Educational Administration and Supervision*, 20, 193–208.

Slaughter, E.E. (1960) The use of examinations for state certification of teachers. *Journal of Teacher Education*, 11, 231–238.

Smith, M. (1949) *And madly teach: a layman looks at public school education*. Chicago: Henry Regnery.

Smyth, A.H. (1907) *The writings of Benjamin Franklin*, Vol. 10, pp. 97–107. New York: Macmillan.

Stinnett, T.M. (1967) Teacher certification. *Review of Educational Research*, 37, 248–259.

Stinnett, T.M. (1969) Teacher education, certification, and accreditation. In J.B. Pearson & E. Fuller (eds.), *Education in the states: nationwide development since 1900*. Washington, DC: National Education Association.

Stone, I. (1864) *The elementary and complete examiner; or candidate's assistant: prepared to aid teachers in securing certificates from boards of examiners.* New York: A.S. Barnes & Co.

Swett, J. (1872) *Questions for written examinations: an aid to candidates for teachers' certificates and a handbook for examiners of teachers.* New York: American Book Co.

Swett, J. (1911) *Public education in California: its origins and development, with personal reminiscences of half a century.* New York: American Book Co.

Terman, L. (1939) An important contribution. *Journal of Higher Education*, 10, 112.

Tom, A.R. (1980a) NCATE standards and program quality: you can't get there from here. *Phi Delta Kappan*, 62, 113–116.

Tom, A.R. (1980b) Chopping NCATE standards down to size. *Journal of Teacher Education*, 31, 25–30.

Tom, A.R. (1981) An alternative set of NCATE standards. *Journal of Teacher Education* 32, 48–52.

Topp, L. (1957) The role of the National Education Association in the professional standards movement. *Progressive Education*, 34, 102–105.

Tuttle, E.M. (1953) The National Council for Accreditation of Teacher Education. *American School Board Journal*, 126, 55, 8, 10, 96.

Tyack, D.B. (1974) *The one best system: a history of American urban education.* Cambridge, MA: Harvard University Press.

Van Doren, C. & Boyd, J.P. (eds.) (1938) *Indian treaties printed by Benjamin Franklin.* Philadelphia: The Historical Society of Pennsylvania.

Vold, D.J. (1985) The roots of teacher testing in America. *Educational Measurement*, 4, 5–7.

Warren, D. (1985) Learning from experience: history and teacher education. *Educational Researcher*, 14, 5–12.

Watkins, B.T. (1980) Report criticizes teacher-education accreditation. *Chronicle of Higher Education*, 21, 4.

Wheeler, C.W. (1980) *NCATE: Does it matter?* East Lansing, MI: Institute for Research on Teaching, Research Series No. 92.

Wheeler, C.W. (2005) *Personal interview.*

Wilson, A.J. (1985) *Knowledge for teachers: the origin of the National Teacher Examinations program.* Paper presented at the annual meeting of the American Educational Research Association in Chicago.

Wilson, A.J. (1986a) *Historical issues of validity and validation: the National Teacher Examinations.* Paper presented at the annual meeting of the American Educational Research Association in San Francisco.

Wilson, A.J. (1986b) Historical issues of equity and excellence: South Carolina's adoption of the National Teacher Examinations. *Urban Educator*, 8, 77–82.

Wilson, S.M. & Youngs, P. (2005) Research on accountability processes in teacher education. In M. Cochran-Smith & K. Zeichner (eds.), *Studying teacher education: the report of the AERA Panel on Research and Teacher Education*, 591–643. Mahwah, NJ: Lawrence Erlbaum Associates.

Winetrout, K. (1941) The National Teacher Examinations, 1941. *Journal of Higher Education*, 12, 479–484.

Wisniewski, R. (1981) Quality in teacher education: a reply to Alan Tom. *Journal of Teacher Education*, 32, 53–55.

Woellner, R.C. (1946). Teacher certification. *Review of Educational Research*, 16, 279–282.

Woellner, R.C. (1949) Teacher certification. *Review of Educational Research*, 19, 250–253.

Woellner, R.C. (1952) Teacher certification. *Review of Educational Research*, 22, 182–185.

Wood, B. (1936) Teacher selection: tested intelligence and achievement of teachers-in-training. *Educational Record*, 17, 381.

Wood, B. & Beers, F.S. (1936) Knowledge versus thinking. *Teachers College Record*, 37, 487–499.

47 From traditional certification to competitive certification

A twenty-five year retrospective

David G. Imig
University of Maryland, College Park

Scott R. Imig
University of North Carolina, Wilmington

INTRODUCTION

Teacher certification has become the policy tool of choice for both liberals and conservatives as they seek to reshape teaching and teacher education. Webster's defines certification as "an official document awarded to somebody who has completed a course of study or training or passed a test or examination or conformed to a required standard." From the question of who should issue the certificate to the form and function of preparation leading to the certificate, from the setting of program standards to the means of assessing teacher candidate proficiency, every aspect of teacher certification has been contested over the past 25 years.

During this period, we have moved from consideration of the minimal requirements for initial certification (usually consisting of academic degrees and professional education courses) to a much more complicated array of certificates gained in multiple ways (NASDTEC, 1999). Perhaps surprisingly, however, this highly complex system demonstrates little variability across states—certification requirements in New York are remarkably similar to those in Washington. Issues of interstate reciprocity, the emergence of an assessment system for beginning teachers (the original National Teacher Examination), and common accreditation standards for teacher education programs have helped to foster a national system of quality assurance in teacher policymaking.

States have moved from analyzing the transcripts of teacher candidates to embracing completers from state approved programs. States have shifted from prescribing a course of study and requiring all collegiate preparation programs to comply with those prescriptions to focusing on competency testing, ceding authority for program approval to national accreditation agencies. Today, states have added state assessments of basic skills and subject matter knowledge as prerequisites to the awarding of teacher certificates. While state policies and state governance drive the current system of licensure and certification, federal policies now influence every aspect of the certification process.

There have been remarkable developments on the national level as well. The National Board for Professional Teaching Standards was created, as were three significant reform groups in teacher education: the National Network for Educational Renewal, the Holmes Group, and Project 30. The Council of Chief State School Officers created the Interstate New Teacher Assessment and Support Consortium (INTASC) and systemic or standards-based school reform came to dominate the educational discourse. The prominence of the teacher as the most significant in-school variable for the learning of all PK-12 students became widely accepted (Haycock, 1998; Sanders & Rivers, 1996).

Political parties and business coalitions alike embraced this theme, making good teachers a national priority. Underlying these movements and efforts was the assumption that if one changed certification laws, one could change teacher quality. In this chapter, we trace the contours of the shifts in policies concerning teacher quality from 1980 to 2005. We begin with a brief overview of trends in teacher licensure and certification.

TEACHER LICENSURE AND CERTIFICATION

The granting of a license to a prospective teacher probably came into being in the late 1660s as towns and villages in New England required tests of those who sought employment as teachers. It continues today as a means to ensure that candidates "will do no harm," that is, that they meet minimal requirements and are safe to place with young people. Certification came into existence in the mid-1800s and was influenced by the efforts of state normal schools to define a curriculum and for the state to grant a diploma or certificate for those who completed a set of state-approved conditions or requirements. County superintendents controlled access to teaching for a century (by designing and administering teacher tests) but state superintendents later exercised their leadership in defining standards and setting licensure requirements for prospective teachers (Stinnet, 1958; see also Sedlak, this volume).

While there have been efforts to maintain a distinction or differentiation between teacher licensure as a minimum condition for entry to the profession and certification as a standard for practice, the reality is that most people have continued to use the terms interchangeably (Cronin, 1983; Goodlad, 1990). However it is used, the term teacher certification has inspired a generation of activists to debate every aspect of the process of state certification and to question its effectiveness in defining high quality teaching (e.g. Asera & Chin, 2005; Ballou & Podgursky, 2000; Goldhaber & Brewer, 2002; Hanushek, 1997; Leigh & Mead, 2005; Rice, 2003; Rotherham & Mead, 2003; Walsh, 2001).

In these debates, some would increase the requirements and expectations for those seeking a teaching certificate; others would reduce the complexity of the current system, thus permitting greater access. On the one side are those who talk about certification as the means to increase teacher quality and contend that states, regional consortia of states, professional bodies, standards boards, or the federal government should exercise much greater control over who enters and advances in teaching. On the other side are those who contend that, if the current restrictions to teaching were reduced or even eliminated, schools and students would benefit by having a more diverse and talented teaching force.

Feeding the contention surrounding certification is the fact that state agencies must guarantee an adequate supply of teachers, while also ensuring that those teachers are well prepared. Some have argued that the responsibility for setting teaching standards must be separated and distanced from the state's responsibilities for guaranteeing an adequate supply (Goodlad, 1990). The recasting of the state's role in certification and the effort to assign standard-setting to professional entities is one of the important stories of the past 25 years, and the focus of the next section of this chapter.

One interesting aspect of the debate concerns the question of who should certify beginning teachers. Over time, teacher certification has moved from a local matter (often accompanied by locally-administered tests of teacher knowledge), to a matter for district or regional school superintendents to deal with, to state agencies. In the early 1900s, it was generally acknowledged that teacher certification was a matter of state policy and an integral part of the state's responsibilities to offer a free and public education to all (Learned & Bagley, 1920). Eventually, professionalists insisted that, as a profession, teaching and teachers needed to be overseen by professional practices or standards boards. In 1946, with the creation of the National Commission on Teacher Education and Professional Standards (TEPS) by the National Education Association (NEA), the matter of teacher certification was raised to a level of national discourse, which led to the establishment of the National Council for the Accreditation of Teacher Education (NCATE) to accredit teacher preparation institutions. Yet, it would take another two generations before teacher certification would be attracting the attention of federal legislators and governmental agencies.

Today, the matter of teacher certification is highly contested. Distinctions between liberals and conservatives blur as proponents for using certification as a national tool to reshape the teacher workforce or to redefine the knowledge and skills of beginning teachers emerge from across the political spectrum. Those who insist that states increase the rigor of the certification process are drawn from the left and right, as are those who would minimize its importance and delegate to building principals the authority to hire teachers (regardless of their qualifications). These differences have taken on particular importance with the emergence of the National Board for Professional Teaching Standards (NBPTS) and, later, the American Board for the Certification of Teacher Excellence (ABCTE), as well as the introduction of the concept of "alternative certification."

The founding of the NBPTS, through the efforts of a broad-based coalition of Republican and Democratic governors and other state legislators, the leadership of the two dominant teacher organizations, and an array of business and philanthropic leaders, created what the British call a quasi-non-governmental organization (quango) that had governmental involvement and support (in the ensuing dozen years, NBPTS would command nearly $100 million in federal appropriation) (Futrell, 2005). The NBPTS's articulation of five core propositions and the development of standards and assessments for numerous fields and courses of study attracted the interest and support of politicians and the public.

At the same time, the rise of alternative certification in New Jersey gave rise to a totally different approach to standards setting—a movement that would eventually be embraced by most states and lead to a reconsideration of the concept of certification (Michelli, 2005). Almost from its inception, alternative certification was promoted by the U.S. Education Department, the Republican Study Council, and numerous state policy groups and national "think tanks" as a better way to attract people to teaching (Gursky, 1989). While it was fashionable to contend that one effort was directed at advancing an agenda of greater rigor and quality in teaching while the other was intended to promote ready access, the reality was that there was enormous disagreement—within both groups—regarding what beginning teachers should know and how that knowledge was best acquired.

Teacher certification is a means to an end, a device used to guarantee a set of minimum conditions for teaching. It is one of several policy tools available to policymakers to regulate or control the "flow" of persons into teaching. While discussion of certification prompts consideration of an idealized vision of a beginning teacher, policymakers inevitably retreat to a set of minimal standards or the essentials of what a beginning teacher should know and be able to do (Sykes, 1990). Program approval and professional accreditation are also tools used to maintain quality. During the last 25 years, there were considerable shifts on all of these policy fronts. Before describing those, however, let us briefly turn to the role of demographics in teacher certification and licensure.

Demographics and teacher certification

Aside from the political and ideological battles over teaching and teacher education, the factor that most influenced the debate on teacher certification was a demographic one, that is, the prospect of a "looming" teacher shortage. As will be noted below, the report of the National Commission on Teaching and America's Future (NCTAF, 1996) galvanized the policy community to act on matters of teacher policy. International comparisons and stagnating K-12 student test scores promoted enormous concern about teacher quality. One premise of the NCTAF report that received the most attention was the projected need for local schools and districts to hire 2.2 to 2.4 million public school teachers during the decade following the release of that report (NCES, 1999). In the face of this shortage, the authors highlighted the quality-quantity conundrum facing policymakers (Berry *et al.*, 1998; Bradley, 1999; Darling-Hammond, 1996). In fact, President William Jefferson Clinton used his 1997 State of the Union address to highlight the need to both attract more people to teaching and to improve the quality of teachers in every classroom (The White House, 1997). Later, attention would focus on the need to find ways to stem the high attrition rates of beginning teachers, but policymakers rushed to address the shortage issue with incentive programs and loan forgiveness efforts designed to attract more people to teaching (Olson, 2003; Wayne, 2000).

CERTIFICATION BECOMES A STATE RESPONSIBILITY

Confounding observers of the certification scene has been the fact that state politicians and policymakers often call for higher standards for all candidates for teaching while reducing the requirements and lowering the barriers for some. Higher admission requirements (often in the form of GPAs, or SAT/ACT scores) are mandated for some while fewer prerequisites are expected of others in the name of alternative certification. State school boards (with most of the members elected in state elections or appointed by governors and/or state school superintendents) that control the certification process have found it difficult to maintain a uniform standard for all candidates. Particular teacher candidates are "advantaged" through abbreviated periods of training and reduced course requirements and shortened student teaching. In some states, where demand for beginning teachers has been the greatest, candidates are allowed to enter teaching with a few weeks of training—but then expected to accumulate professional development credits during the first years of teaching. It is the differentiation in requirements that strikes most teacher educators in "traditional" preparation programs as blatantly unfair.

Throughout this period, it appeared that many policymakers lacked understanding of the concept of teacher certification, in particular, the state's role. For some on the political right, state certification was little more than "a cartel operated by the teacher unions and colleges of education to enforce monopolies in what amounts to restraint of trade . . . It has most surely impaired the quality of teaching in the classroom" (Heritage Foundation, 1989). Rather than state systems and bureaucracies being blamed for this condition, the focal point for attention was "traditional" teacher preparation programs. In fact, George H. Bush would run for President in 1988 on a platform that advocated alternative certification as the means "to remove unnecessary barriers to qualified individuals who want to teach." Criticism of certification practices and teacher preparation was not limited to the political right. That same year, the National Governors Association (NGA, 1989) promoted alternative certification as a way to increase the number of teachers in mathematics and science.

The shift in authority for teacher education from the campus to the state occurred as campus-based education programs grew to meet the demand for PK-12 elementary and secondary school teachers. It was an explosion in numbers of beginning teachers that exceeded the capacity of state agencies to license individual teachers that resulted in the franchising of the responsibility to campuses in the form of program approval. Programs could not operate without state approval and campuses subjected themselves to a state-approved curriculum for teacher education and were given the right to operate. Three decades later, the federal government recognized that prevailing policies and practices were failing to produce quality teachers. However, while there was widespread agreement that the federal government should assume a new role in teacher preparation or certification, two very different ways of accomplishing this goal emerged. One was the professionalization agenda that viewed teaching as a learned occupation requiring extensive preparation and long-term commitment. The other agenda—which we will call the deprofessionalization agenda—treated teaching as a short-term job requiring little preparation and much emphasis on subject matter knowledge.

Professionalism vs. deprofessionalism

Many who promote advanced standards for teaching and teachers claim the mantle of teacher professionalism. If teachers are to be accorded the respect and remuneration enjoyed by other professionals, they argue, standards have to be raised. Deprofessionalists posit that, while minimal conditions for teaching are necessary, these should not be so restrictive as to prevent the "best and brightest" from entering teaching (even if only for a short time). Their contention is that current policies restrict entry, often citing the success of *Teach for America* in attracting such college graduates. Both professionalists and deprofessionalists look to the states to modify the certification processes to either increase or decrease the requirements to teach, as each sees certification as the policy tool of choice to recast the American teacher.

Perhaps the thing that most promoted the debate about good teaching was the movement to create a standards-based school system with aligned elements and policy levers (Fuhrman, 1994; O'Day & Smith, 1986). In the drive to accomplish systemic reform, teacher certification was a tool to ensure that teachers prepared to teach in a state-approved teacher preparation programs would teach the state PK-12 student standards. Teacher education was viewed as an integral part of a statewide reform effort and subject to the conditions and expectations imposed by the state. This was an important theme of NASDTEC (1992), as they articulated new certification standards based on program outcomes and demonstrable professional practice. Teachers who completed state approved programs were expected to be able to teach the state's approved course of study. Certification was a means to assess whether beginning teachers knew the material and were capable of presenting it to diverse youngsters in PK-12 schools.

But the policy proposal for teaching and teacher education most embraced by teacher educators—the professionalism agenda—has also been seen as an agenda in conflict with systemic reform. Professionalists have one set of expectations for beginning teachers, while those promoting a narrow conception of teaching as enabling all students to meet a prescribed set of outcome or performance standards often have another, and are more comfortably aligned at times with the deprofessionalists. Not only was the professionalization agenda out-of-step with the systemic reform efforts; it was also out-of-step with changes underway in higher education where college presidents were voicing their opposition to the organized teaching profession—most often represented by the teacher unions (Appleberry, 1994). Instead of embracing PK-12 teachers as peers, college presidents led a movement that blocked their involvement in specialized or professional accreditation, creating an alternative based on institutional mission rather than professional standards (Splete *et al.*, 1996). Not surprisingly, these same forces gave little credence to the efforts to extend teacher preparation to five-year programs or to promote professional schools of education. Unlike other professional preparation programs—housed primarily in post-baccalaureate, research-oriented, status-seeking, and self-sustaining professional schools—teacher education remained a low-status, campus-wide, baccalaureate-level, teaching-intensive program that commanded few resources and even less respect (Labaree, 2004).

Debates about teacher education

Thus, entwined in discussions of licensure and certification is an on-going debate about the role and purpose of education schools. One conception casts schools of education as extensions of the state system of PK-12 schooling, and therefore such professional schools need to prepare teachers to "deliver" the state's PK-12 curriculum. This conception is reflected in both how teacher education programs gain state approval and in the fact that 49 out of 50 states "house" teacher education in their PK-12 agency rather than the agency responsible for higher education. In this view, teacher educators are state employees with responsibilities to the state for ensuring that certified teachers teach to the PK-12 state standards.

An alternative view—one favored by higher education faculty—argues that schools of education are academic/disciplinary communities that reach beyond the state. This perspective positions teacher educators as university faculty who are charged with questioning the status quo—including the state's education agenda—and with conducting research on curriculum, teaching, learning, and policy. If the state prescribes a course of study or a particular instructional approach, in this vision of the professoriate, the academy is expected to question its appropriateness or to pose alternative directions.

As this chapter was being completed, numerous studies and opinion pieces again raised serious questions about the role of education schools in preparing and supporting beginning teachers. Styled as "an obituary for education schools" (Finn, 2005), *The New York Times* headlined an expansive story, "Who Needs Education Schools?", Finn observed that the author, Anemona Hartacollis (2005), concluded that the answer was "pretty much nobody." He then observed that "education schools have lost their way: 'social justice' and high-minded theory now trump academic mastery and skills in classroom management, and alternate routes to the teaching profession have arisen to challenge the monopolistic hold of the ed school cartel."

Finn and other neo-conservatives argue that teacher education and certification should be uncoupled, and that program approval should be abandoned. Competition between traditional and alternative providers, they posited, would lead to higher quality teachers. These debates about teacher education reform (and who should control access to teaching) are, at their heart, about professionalism and de-professionalism, regulation and deregulation (Allen, 2000; Cochran-Smith & Fries, 2001; Darling-Hammond, 2000). On the one hand, professionalists see certification, licensure, accreditation, and program approval—and the presumed higher status and renumeration that accompanies those things—as critical to providing both high quality and sufficient numbers of beginning teachers. Deprofessionalists decry these links, denouncing university-based teacher education, state systems of licensure, and national standards for advanced certification and teacher preparation. In particular, the critics raise questions about: (a) the epistemological and pedagogical underpinnings of contemporary teacher education, with outright attacks on constructivism, learner-centeredness, and critical theory; (b) the qualitative or narrative research paradigms used by education school faculty; and (c) higher education's long dominance of the "market" for teacher education (Herring, 2001; Izumi & Coburn, 2001; Kozloff, 2001).

INCREASING CENTRALIZATION

With the 1992 reauthorization of the Higher Education Act of 1965, we began to witness a consistent effort to use federal policy to direct changes in certification and teaching policy more generally. That reauthorization strengthened the role of state agencies in setting certification standards, while recognizing NBPTS as a non-governmental organization that would assess advanced candidates. It also increased investment in state agency efforts to strengthen teacher licensure, while encouraging states to add alternatives to their strategies for teacher certification. Simultaneously, the newly-formed *Teach for America*, another quango (designed to attract the "best and the brightest" into teaching), was also garnering considerable financial and political support.

The blurring of roles and distinctions between federal and national entities and state and campus authorities for teacher education was driven by policy proposals that often came from professional organizations and national entities. When NCATE articulated a vision of a national system of accreditation in 1992 (one that called for merging state program approval and national specialized accreditation into an integrated system), college and university presidents protested. Shortly thereafter, a resolution of opposition from the American Association of Colleges for Teacher Education was lodged, as well as the creation of an alternative accreditation approach. The Teacher Education Accreditation Council (TEAC) was created by a group of liberal arts college presidents (through the leadership of the Council of Independent Colleges). With its long tradition of independence and many small liberal arts colleges, Iowa became a focus for debates about the appropriate role of national bodies in setting standards for teaching and teacher education. Central to those discussions was the issue of localism vs. centralism, the latter of which was rejected by the opposition. It was not a coincidence that this was also a time when all of specialized accreditation was under attack, with college and university presidents claiming that specialized accreditors served only the interests of a particular preparation program or professional school. NCATE's standards and processes were the subject of particular concern, and leaders of various D.C.-based organizations offered support for TEAC or, at the very least, agreed not to take sides in what was cast as a contest between NCATE and TEAC.

Meanwhile, the NBPTS was expanding their assessments and vision. The development of new licensure tests by the Education Testing Service—the PRAXIS Series—reinforced efforts to conceptualize teaching as continuum of provisional to regular to advanced certification. The efforts to build an integrated national system of quality control, involving government and non-governmental agencies, as well as the private sector, offered much promise that a tightly coupled and aligned system of teaching and teacher education was possible through policy.

With the 1992 amendments to the Higher Education Act, the new Clinton administration embraced this agenda as well. Those who drafted the federal legislative proposals called for state plans that would lead to

> an integrated and coherent approach to attracting, recruiting, preparing and licensing teachers, administrators, and other educators so that there is a highly talented workforce of professional educators capable of preparing all students to reach challenging standards.
>
> (Cohen & Smith, 1993)

Teacher certification continued to be the policy tool of choice while debates about centralism vs. localism (Strike, 1997) continued to swirl.

The NCTAF report and its influence on certification

Streams of work began to coalesce. The Carnegie Corporation agenda of the 1980s had been translated into a national agenda of reform and innovation. Goodlad's (1990) *Teachers for Our Nation's Schools* and the ongoing efforts of the Holmes Group (1986) kept teacher education at the forefront of efforts to transform teaching. But it would be the work of yet another quango that would serve as the dominant policy vehicle for change in the 1990s. The National Commission on Teaching and America's Future (NCTAF) was formed in 1994. Linda Darling-Hammond led the efforts of the 26-person commission, funded by the Carnegie Corporation and the Rockefeller Foundation; the group took testimony, commissioned research products, and compiled research evidence. Its report, *What Matters Most: Teaching for America's Future*, called for a "competent, caring and knowledgeable teacher in every classroom in America by 2006" and was clearly based on the professionalization agenda. Its call—for high quality preservice preparation, continuous professional development for all school personnel, autonomous professional standards boards, advanced teacher certification, strengthened professional accreditation, empowered teachers, professional development schools, and new forms of assessment of both students and teachers—was appealing to teachers and teacher educators alike and attracted considerable media attention.

The report was widely embraced by many policymakers at the state and federal level and resulted in federal investments of more than $30 million for its implementation. Those investments were paralleled by unprecedented grant activity by philanthropic foundations and enormous support for the report's tenets. The NCTAF policy ideas were used in the half dozen legislative proposals introduced in Congress in 1998, relative to the reauthorization of teacher education programs in the Higher Education Act. The professionalization strategy—here based on the "three-legged stool" of accreditation, assessment, and certification—was popular with policymakers and was used at both the federal and state level to justify alignment across systems. Investments in the Interstate New Teacher Assessment and Support Consortium (INTASC) standards was championed, as was increased attention to the use of such work in a new system of per-formance-based teacher education accreditation introduced by NCATE. There was also widespread support for the use of the advanced certification standards of the NBPTS by state policymakers across the political spectrum (from Governors Tommy Thompson (R-WI) and John Engler (R-MI) to James Hunt (D-NC) and Gray Davis (D-CA)). It appeared to be a period of consensus and hope.

With the energy created by NCTAF, many anticipated that the key provisions in the NCTAF report would be incorporated into federal policy and replicated in every state, thereby serving to guarantee all children a competent and caring teacher. The localism-centralism tensions were resolved by the image of an overarching national system of quality assurance—shifting authority from local campuses to national entities—that was a "centralized-localized" system of professional controls and responsibilities. INTASC, NBPTS, and NCATE were increasingly aligned and there was much expectation that a national system of certification would emerge. NCTAF was a powerful instrument, and it should have resulted in substantial change.

The backlash

While the professionalization agenda was being embraced by the teacher organizations, other education associations, and by state and federal lawmakers, it was also generating enormous opposition. A well-organized opposition emerged, led by the Thomas B.

Fordham Foundation and a number of other right-of-center "think tanks." The Fordham Foundation issued a "manifesto" that was based on a set of studies challenging the empirical legitimacy of each plank in the professionalization platform (Ballou & Podgursky, 1998; Ballou & Soler, 1998; Finn, 1997; Petrilli, 1998). Similarly, the Capital Research Center (1998) issued a policy brief that criticized NCTAF's efforts:

> in the name of "professionalizing" the teaching field, a well-organized cadre of national teacher education groups, working in close cooperation with the two major teacher unions, seeks to transfer the authority over teacher training and certification away from states and communities to private managerial agencies that are run by the cadre's own members, who stand to gain much from a centralized teacher education system under their control and unaccountable to the public.

Better Teachers, Better Schools—a report issued by the Fordham Foundation—was even more appealing to both centrists and conservatives (Kanstoroom & Finn, 1999). Claiming that NCTAF was infatuated with "the romance of regulation," these neo-conservatives argued for deregulation and much greater local discretion in teacher certification, preparation, and hiring. Asserting that "the regulatory strategy being pursued today to boost teacher quality is seriously flawed," they argued for a minimalist approach. They contended, "The regulatory approach is also bound . . . to undermine the standards-and-accountability strategy for improving schools and raising student achievement." "Simplify the entry and hiring process," "Get rid of most hoops and hurdles," "Open more paths into the classroom" (Palmaffy, 1999) were among their slogans.

The Fordham proposal to "widen the entryway, deregulate the processes, and hold people accountable for their results—results judged primarily in terms of classroom effectiveness" attracted considerable interest. With prominent educators from the first Bush administration lobbying Congress, much of the steam went out of the professionalization agenda. Various policy briefs and position papers led to a recasting of various Congressional proposals—from efforts to expand federal support for preservice teacher education to an emphasis on attracting "better candidates to teaching . . . who possess much more robust content knowledge." Instead of an emphasis on capacity building for education schools, Congressional efforts emphasized alternative certification and non-traditional routes into teaching. Professionalization gave way to accountability as the dominant policy frame for teaching and teacher education.

A NEW AGE OF CENTRALIZED POLICYMAKING

It is important to understand that this combination of federal and state level policy proposals, when coupled with the profession's own efforts to use quangos to assert dominance over teacher education policymaking, shifted the agenda away from institutional practices and academic controls to external or centralized policies. Those policies applied to both public and private education schools and carried with them enormous implications for education school deans and their faculties. Authority for teacher education shifted away from the campus and state agencies and toward national entities that formulated policies and practices.

While some would argue that centralization came with the Bush administration, centralized goal setting comes through most insistently in the various announcements of the Clinton U.S. Education Department. Repeatedly, Education Secretary Richard Riley urged that extraordinary attention be devoted to issues of teacher quality. In one speech, he argued for the development of a common framework for teacher licensing, asserted that "we must make sweeping changes in how we prepare America's teachers," and claimed that too often colleges and departments of education are "sleepy little places" on the fringe of the campus "like forgotten stepchildren in our system of higher education" (Riley, 1999). He proposed a series of initiatives on teacher quality for college and university presidents including the appointment of a National Commission on Mathematics and Science Teaching for the 21st Century, chaired by former Senator John Glenn (D-OH), a national job bank for teacher recruitment, and a study of teacher tests by the National Academy of Sciences. With Clinton, teacher education became a national matter. Furthermore, as the dominant policy frame shifted from professionalism to accountability, colleges and universities came under increasingly intense scrutiny and were challenged in unprecedented ways to transform their teacher education programs. The regulatory focus of Sections 206 and 207 of the Higher Education Amendments of 1998 represented a sea-change in the role of the federal government as an overseer of teaching and teacher education.

The reauthorization of the Higher Education Act

The reauthorization of the Higher Education Act in a Republican-controlled Congress created a whole set of new accountability demands on teacher education. When Congress took up the matter of teacher education in February and March of 1998, it considered ten different legislative proposals. From these various proposals, a new Title II emerged to replace many existing programs with monies for states to revise teacher licensure requirements to increase expectations for teachers' subject matter competence and to develop alternative routes. In the name of accountability, Congress imposed a set of stipulations for public reporting and disclosure. Senator Jeff Bingaman (D-NM) noted that education schools had access to more than $2 billion in federal student aid money and claimed that there "is overwhelming evidence that we are not getting the return on that investment . . . [and that] institutions with . . . egregious pass rates [on state teacher tests] are committing a form of fraud on entering students who aspire to be teachers" (Bingaman, 1998). While Bingaman was a supporter of the professionalization agenda, his efforts led to the addition of a host of accountability measures.

Parallel to the efforts in the Senate, Representative George Miller (D-CA) introduced legislation in the House of Representatives that called for:

- strengthening teacher licensing requirements to improve the academic knowledge of beginning teachers;
- holding colleges and universities accountable for preparing teachers competent in the academic content areas in which they plan to teach;
- calling upon states to strengthen their alternative route programs; and
- creating opportunities for on-going professional development of teachers and other school personnel to increase their knowledge of academic content.

The measure that passed the House (on a bipartisan vote of 414 to 4 on May 6, 1998) had been written by the House majority staff and included provisions that required programs to demonstrate 70 percent pass rates on subject matter test for their graduates, as well as calling upon governors to "provid[e] prospective teachers alternatives to schools of education through programs at colleges of arts and sciences or at nonprofit organizations."

The Senate would add language to mandate the establishment of a national annual report card on the condition of teacher education. The U.S. Secretary of Education was to annually report on the qualifications of beginning teachers and show the national mean and median scores of these teachers on the standardized tests used for teacher licensure and certification. Also mandated were state and institutional report cards on the quality of teacher education. The college or university report card would include the following:

- passing rates of graduates on the teacher certification and licensure assessments of the state in which it is located;
- passing rates in comparison to the state's average pass rate;
- the number of students in each program, the average number of hours of supervised practice teaching, and the faculty-student ratio used in clinical experiences;
- an indication of whether the program is state-approved and nationally-accredited; and
- whether the program has been designated as low performing by the state, that is, failing to meet a baseline pass rate for its graduates on state licensing tests (Paige, 2002).

College presidents and their organizations rallied in opposition to the Bingaman-Miller provisions, particularly those connecting student aid eligibility to teacher candidate success rates on state tests, as well as those making NCATE accreditation mandatory. One leader described the political climate as "poisonous" and the mandates as "regulatory intrusion" (Magrath, 1998). While provisions concerning institutional eligibility for student financial aid and the mandating of NCATE accreditation were withdrawn (in exchange for the promise that the higher education community would address the matter of the quality of teacher education), the other accountability provisions were passed.

Following the enactment of the Higher Education Amendments of 1998, much of the focus of the Washington higher education policy community shifted to rule-making relative to the implementation of the amendments. This process was remarkably free of controversy. Regulations were drafted and shared with the higher education community. Teacher education was the focus of the greatest controversy as regulations were written to implement Section 207 of Title II of the Higher Education Act that sought to describe a methodology for gathering the required accountability data and generating common definitions for terms used in the mandatory annual state and institutional reports (e.g. credential, pass-rate, teaching candidate, etc.). Given the statutory requirement to seek input from states and colleges and universities, the National Center for Education Statistics (NCES) formed a consultative committee of academics, state officials, and interest group leaders that contributed to a report that appeared in the *Federal Register*.

Control of teaching and teacher education had clearly shifted to Washington. The newly-established national rules conceptualized teacher education as an all-campus responsibility and held universities or presidents responsible for program quality. The reliance on a series of report cards and teacher tests to drive Congressionally-determined reforms was consistent with forms of accountability previously used in states and applied to PK-12 schools. While these accountability provisions were mandatory, they were also unfunded, resulting in increased costs for teacher education. They also were threatening, as they imposed fines and sanctions for those who failed to report the relevant data.

Higher education's rejection of the professionalization agenda was most evident in a statement of principles issued by the American Association of State Colleges and Universities (AASCU) and the appeal for an alternative accreditation agency for teacher education. To many, AASCU's policy statement—calling for states to reassert their responsibilities for licensure and program approval—represented a bald rejection of the teacher professionalism movement (Appleberry, 1994). It is also important to note that these shifts took place in a broader context in which teacher unions were attempting to organize college faculties and university officials feared that the quangos—NBPTS, INTASC, NCTAF, NCATE—were largely controlled by the National Education Association and the American Federation of Teachers and, therefore, the "enemy."

College and university leaders, education school deans and their faculties began to recognize that a profound shift in responsibility for teacher preparation and teaching policies was underway. Whereas teacher education had become a state enterprise in the 1970s and early 1980s, teacher and teacher education policy was—in the late 1990s—increasingly national and "controlled" by the profession. Whereas teacher education had been a decentralized and often dispersed series of programs across a college campus, the 1998 amendments made teacher education a primary responsibility of the university president. With the encouragement of government authorities, responsibility for teacher education moved from university and college presidents and provosts having *de facto* responsibility for the conduct of teacher education to university leaders having a *de jure* responsibility for its success. There was also a shift from state to federal controls which heightened accountability expectations. The traditional responsibilities held by state agencies for teacher education, through program approval and beginning teacher licensure, was gradually shifting to national and professional authorities. Some have described this move as the "federalization" of teacher education policy. While embraced by an array of stakeholders across the political spectrum, it would take the policies of the Bush administration to solidify it.

The education agenda of the Bush administration

In his campaign for the presidency in 2000, G. W. Bush repeatedly pointed to the "near miraculous progress of Texas schools in reducing dropouts and increasing achievement," offering it as the model for American education (Haney, 2000). Bush insisted that the miracle was a result of changes in teacher certification, the expansion of alternative certification, tenure reforms for teachers, and the creation of differentiated staffing and bonus pay programs for teachers in high need schools. In addition, there was a heavy emphasis on using strategies "grounded in scientific research" (Fenoglio & Cannon, 2001).

During the first month of his presidency, Bush made education his first and most visible initiative. He introduced an education plan that he suggested would "overhaul federal education policy" (Milbank, 2001). The president's plan closely resembled what he had promised on the campaign trail and called for increasing student accountability, focusing on "what works," reducing bureaucracy, increasing flexibility, and empowering parents. The president's plan called for states to "select and design assessments of their choosing" for all students in grades three through eight, and required schools to publicly report results disaggregated by race, gender, English language proficiency, disability and socioeconomic status. States were to be more accountable for student performance.

In a climate of intense partisanship and attention to electoral politics, the one piece of domestic legislation that was enacted by the Congress during the first two years of the Bush administration was the *No Child Left Behind Act* (P.L. 107-N110, NCLB). In a rare display of bipartisanship, both chambers and both parties completed work on the education legislation, sending it to Bush for his signature by the end of December 2001. Though opposed by most of the organized education community and considered too intrusive or too flawed, in the aftermath of the September 11th crisis NCLB was signed into law on January 8, 2002. It was an act that only a Republican president could get passed because of its challenges to localism and local control (Alvarez, 2001; Beadle, 2001; Cardman, 2001).

The final version of NCLB was opposed by the teacher organizations, school board representatives, the National Conference of State Legislators, and the American Association of School Administrators. Opposition focused on "the unfunded mandates" and the lack of flexibility in the bill for schools and school districts. Virtually everyone agreed that the new law was both the most ambitious and most intrusive piece of educational legislation since the original enactment of the Elementary and Secondary Education Act of 1965 (ESEA), with both liberals and conservatives praising the intent but voicing their disapproval about the federal intrusion into local education policymaking. Conservatives argued that NCLB gives too much control to Washington, while liberals contended that it does little to close the discrepancy between rich and poor schools or address the achievement gap. While there were significant differences between the House and Senate with regard to teacher education and professional development (e.g. over definitions of "high quality" teachers and whether these should apply to both beginning and experienced teachers), these differences were resolved very early and the final bill had much of consequence for education schools and teacher education. Just one aspect of this would be that professional development provided with ESEA monies should be based on "scientifically-based" research. Also, traditional sources of grant support from Washington would now be combined with current and new school-based professional development monies and education schools would have to redirect their energies to acquiring monies from local education authorities.

NCLB and teacher policy

The other reality of this legislation was the ascendancy of teacher quality as a guiding principle for public policy formulation. Teacher quality dominated the policy debates regarding education and was at the core of NCLB. There were cross-sector conferences on teacher quality. Business leaders issued reports on ways to achieve it, foundations built program agendas and sponsored collaboratives, state policymakers enacted legislation, "think tanks" offered alternative strategies. Indeed, much of the Bush education agenda during the first term was built on the assumption that high quality teachers were essential to realizing education reform.

The belief that highly qualified teachers were the essential element of any strategy to help PK-12 students learn became widespread. According to the Bush administration, highly qualified teachers possessed subject matter competence in core academic subjects and are able to significantly raise PK-12 students' achievement. This definition was premised on evidence derived from the "value-added" assessment model of William Sanders (e.g. Sanders & Horn, 1998; Sanders & Rivers, 1996). Value-added methodology was embraced by numerous groups and many in the philanthropic community as a means for reforming teacher education professional development, licensure, certification, and accreditation. For instance, The Teaching Commission—an independent entity convened by former IBM Executive Lou Gerstner—described the value-added methodology as "the most promising technique available," calling for "some version of the 'value-added' method [being] used to measure student achievement in every school" (The Teaching Commission, 2004).

The Bush administration used teacher certification as a policy tool to change teaching and encouraged states to align state licensure provisions with NCLB and to gather information on highly qualified teachers, with a particular focus on teacher's verbal ability and content major as the indicators of high quality. NCLB defines a highly qualified teacher (HQT) as:

> [A college graduate who] has obtained full State certification as a teacher (including certification obtained through alternative routes to certification) or passed the State teacher licensing examination, and holds a license to teach in such State [and who has] not had certification or licensure requirements waived on an emergency, temporary, or provisional basis.

Many have attempted to interpret the law to put a premium on subject matter knowledge at the expense of almost everything else. These efforts have brought criticism from various groups, including the Education Trust, a centrist advocacy group which has often been described as the primary source for most of the ideas in NCLB. For example, Education Trust (2003) issued *Telling the Whole Truth (or Not) About Highly Qualified Teachers*, which condemned federal and state efforts to gather data and information on the condition of teaching. The group's president, Kati Haycock (2003), suggested that the teacher quality provisions have at various times been "ignored, misinterpreted, and misunderstood," contending that the Education Department prompted a lowering of standards at the state level by ignoring the challenge of placing high quality teachers in schools in need of improvement. The Education Trust document paralleled an earlier General Accounting Office study on teacher quality entitled, *No Child Left Behind Act: More Information Would Help States Determine Which Teachers Are Highly Qualified*, which reported that states needed much more information about ways to evaluate the subject matter knowledge of current teachers (Bright & Harmeyer, 2002). That study also found that there was little consensus on what constitutes effective or high-quality teaching, and that various studies indicated that teacher effectiveness is dependent upon variables such as years of experience, advanced degrees, teaching assignments (in-field or out-of-field), state certification, preparation and professional development, teacher scores on standardized tests, and verbal ability. Despite the fact that studies sponsored by the U.S. Education Department consistently have failed to narrow the range of indicators of teacher effectiveness, policymakers continued to insist on the need for highly qualified teachers.

The U.S. Education Department vigorously responded to Haycock's criticism, citing a number of initiatives including the new Teacher Assistance Corps, a *Toolkit for Teachers*, projects such as American Board for the Certification of Teacher Excellence, the creation of the *What Works Clearinghouse*, and technical assistance from the Council of Chief State School Officers and the National Association of State Directors of Teacher Education Certification to provide guidance in meeting the law's requirements.

Given the absence of better indicators of highly qualified teachers, recent policy has focused on two measures: scores on standardized tests of subject matter knowledge and degree attainment in a particular core or academic subject. With the support of dozens of advocacy groups across the political spectrum, the Bush administration is likely to continue to press the case for highly qualified teachers using this narrow conception.

The Bush administration sought to realize its vision of education by using a blend of rules and regulations, admonishments and funding strategies. In particular, they have promoted greater access to teaching as the way to improve teacher quality, embracing both "competitive" and "alternative" certification as policy tools. They also championed greater regulation of "traditional" teacher education (with institutional reporting of candidate scores on state administered tests and mandates to assess the achievement of program graduates' K-12 students) while promoting efforts to bypass teacher education (through sponsorship of on-line teacher preparation programs, for example, Western Governors University, for traditional aged college students, *Troops to Teachers* programs for military personnel, and *Teach for America* for college graduates from prestigious colleges). The results are that Congress and the U.S. Education Department currently hold traditional programs to higher levels of accountability while supporting initiatives that reduce—if not eliminate—those standards for alternative route programs.

The Bush agenda for teacher education

The Bush administration used a surprising array of policy tools to push for the reform of teacher education as well. Reports of the Education Secretary cast aspersions on traditional teacher education and promoted alternative routes. Seventy-seven million dollars was invested in conservative efforts to by-pass "traditional" teacher education and promoted a host of new efforts for professional development and teacher education (Bradley, 2003). Nearly 3 billion dollars was awarded to states and local school districts to fashion new models of teacher education. These efforts were reinforced by other actions that were included in both the reauthorization of Individuals with Disabilities Education Act (IDEA) and in the various proposals to reauthorize the Higher Education Act. If fully enacted, these policy proposals would redirect existing federal support for teacher education to other providers, including local school districts, and seriously impair the capacity of education schools to prepare and support sufficient numbers of high quality beginning teachers.

The most comprehensive statement of those policy proposals was contained in a seriously flawed report to the Congress by the U.S. Department of Education entitled *The Secretary's Annual Report on Teacher Quality: Meeting the Highly Qualified Teachers Challenge* (Paige, 2002). The report offered four far-reaching policy proposals:

- support the development of new models of "teacher training" that are "local," "based on the best alternative route programs of today," and "produce teachers with those skills that are in high demand";
- support state initiatives to end the "exclusive franchise" of schools of education and to curtail the "shocking number" of mandated education courses or assist state efforts to uncouple education school courses from state licensure, making "attendance at schools of education . . . optional";
- help states to "streamline" licensure requirements to place a premium on verbal ability and content knowledge, develop new and "challenging assessments" for teacher candidates, and require "content area majors"; and
- promote state efforts to shift authority for determining the qualifications of beginning teachers "from state certification officials . . . to local school principals."

While these policy proposals were largely drawn from an earlier report issued by the Progressive Policy Institute (Hess, 2001), the proposed policies represented the direction the Bush administration intended to take. The institute's report also served as the frame for the March 2002 White House conference on teacher preparation. Fundamental where a set of claims about research on and practice in teaching and teacher preparation, including:

- rigorous research indicates that verbal ability and content knowledge are the most important attributes of highly qualified teachers;

- there is little evidence that education school course work leads to improved student achievement;
- today's certification system discourages some of the most talented candidates from entering the profession while allowing too many poorly qualified individuals to teach; and
- alternative routes to certification demonstrate that streamlined systems can boost the quantity of teachers while maintaining—or even improving—their quality.

The flaws in Paige (2002) were legion. For an administration that had repeatedly pressed for research evidence to be "scientifically-based," little such evidence was used to substantiate the report. The studies that were cited had a decidedly ideological bent, were primarily funded by a single source, and failed the requirement for being peer reviewed or relying on randomized experiments. Further, the report—which was ostensibly about the performance of education schools in meeting HEA Title II, Sec.207 requirements—gave little attention to the matter of candidate performance or the pass rates of candidates enrolled in education schools. It essentially dismissed the mandate to do so, citing the low quality of the tests used. Paige (2003) later asserted that low cut scores and "10th-grade level" tests characterizes the current system, arguing that "standards for teachers, in far too many states" are "extremely low."

Meanwhile, the Bush administration also signaled its intent to influence state boards of education and other state agencies that control teacher licensure and certification to adopt policies more conducive to the provisions of NCLB. Uncoupling courses in teacher education from state licensure requirements was one goal. Described as an alternative to regular or traditional teacher certification, competitive certification was offered as effective means for ensuring a highly qualified teacher workforce. In effect, competitive certification promotes many different certifications (by states, professional standards bodies, local education agencies, NBPTS and ABCTE, teacher organizations and others), ceding to local school officials the authority to hire those they feel are best qualified to meet the staffing needs of their local schools. Competitive certification would come to be widely debated but to date has few adherents and even fewer adopters.

The Bush administration also set out to create a genuine alternative certification program that would be national in scope and serve as a substitute for state licensure, the American Board for Certification of Teaching Excellence (ABCTE). Patterned after the National Board for Professional Teaching Standards, this new quango was formed to develop a new licensure and advanced certification test for both beginning and practicing teachers. This was to be a non-state, independent agency to which states would have to cede authority to test and then certify beginning teachers using standards and assessments based not on state but rather national standards.

ABCTE was one of the most ambitious Bush administration proposals, as well as one of its most controversial. In contrast to teacher tests developed by the Education Testing Service, the National Evaluation Systems, and other testing houses, this new assessment would not be aligned to specific teacher standards of a particular state but would instead be based on a set of generic standards (derived from teacher standards in Virginia, California, and New York) and a set of guiding principles derived from a carefully constructed knowledge base on teacher education. An initial grant of $5 million was made to the Education Leaders Council to undertake this work, which was followed by a $35 million non-competitive discretionary grant to the National Council for Teacher Quality to advance this alternative (Cardman, 2003).

The initial focus of ABCTE was on beginning teachers, offering college graduates—with at least a bachelor's degree—the opportunity to earn a Passport Certificate if they possessed written language skills, a fundamental knowledge of teaching, and could pass a criminal background check and a series of examinations demonstrating subject-matter proficiency, as well as document a high quality classroom-based field experience. ABCTE would also attempt to compete with NBPTS by offering a Master Teaching Certificate for experienced teachers who passed "a rigorous test and [had] a track record of teaching excellence as demonstrated by student achievement."

ABCTE promoted the use of its assessments by seeking the endorsement of state legislatures, boards of education, and professional standards boards. ABCTE would gain adherents among Education Leadership Council members in a half dozen states in its first years of operation and—after changing testing contractors—launched a vigorous campaign for acceptance and adoption (Bradley, 2003). Its importance, for our purposes here, was less its structure and aggressive campaign for acceptance and more the fact that ABCTE represents a genuine effort by the Bush administration to create an alternative to state licensure and, like NBPTS, suggested a profound shift in the practice of certification.

The underlying logic was that, since the state had to guarantee an adequate supply of beginning teachers, its certification policies were dictated not by matters of high quality but rather by the exigencies of supply and demand. If demand was high and supply was low, then states recast their teacher certification policies to promote greater access to teaching. The Bush administration challenged state authority and promoted reliance on non-state entities to certify beginning teachers.

ABCTE carried with it enormous consequences for education schools; it was one of the most thoughtful and imaginative ways presented by neo-conservatives to remake teaching and the teacher workforce. Just as they were promoting the idea of competitive certification, so also were they endorsing the concept of competition between specialized accreditation bodies. While officials in earlier U.S. Education Departments had supported the idea of multiple accreditors for a particular sector or professional preparation area, this had not occurred in teacher education because of the absence of such an entity. The Bush administration encouraged the development of the alternative teacher education accreditor by granting federal funding and recognition to the Teacher Education Accrediting Council in October 2003.

The technician teacher argument

Finally, members of the Bush administration pressed for a different type of teacher to staff the schools. Grover R. Whitehurst, the Director of the Institute for Education Sciences, advanced the idea that there were two types of teachers: long-term teaching professionals who were prepared in education schools to assume numerous roles in promoting the learning of students and technicians who implement prescribed learning modules and training. Whitehurst suggested that the success of NCLB was dependent upon having enough "good enough teachers" who were skilled at teaching a lesson, maintaining discipline, and ensuring that PK-12 students do well on whatever performance measure used. Whitehurst contended that professional teachers present a costly burden to high-needs schools; technician teachers were more cost effective.

CONCLUSION: COMPETITIVE CERTIFICATION AND POLICY FOR TEACHING

The argument here is that the proliferation of quality assurance and control policies and bodies for teachers and teacher education is a legacy of policies broadly embraced by the teaching profession (and teacher educators) in the 1980s and 1990s. NBPTS and NCATE, NCTAF and national standards-setting bodies were hailed as extra-state, professional agencies to control access to and promote high quality in teaching. The idea that a competing set of such agencies would emerge (often with competing agendas and philosophies) was never anticipated. The reality that teaching and teacher education face in 2006 is far different that what was anticipated 25 years ago. Neo-conservative policies that champion competition, free-markets, and deregulation exploit those efforts and seek to refashion teaching policy by relying on competitive certification. With policy for education schools increasingly being set in Washington, education deans and faculty have to be particularly concerned with the attitudes of Congress and White House. In a study commissioned by AACTE and the American Council on Education, it was found that members of Congress are "increasingly angry toward schools of education" and are insisting that they demonstrate a commitment to both high quality and "improved interaction with K-12 schools and follow-up with their [graduates] who have become teachers" (Gunderson, 2003).

Changing attitudes and shaping policy is imperative. It is particularly important in 2005 as Congress continues the process of reauthorizing the Higher Education Act of 1965 (PL 105-244)—with the explicit goal of connecting HEA to NCLB and renewing the *Individuals with Disabilities Education Act* (PL 105–17). What all of these pieces of federal legislation have in common is the opportunity for federal policymakers to recast teacher certification and reinforce policies and practices that appear to undermine education schools.

These developments lead to the unmistakable conclusion that the Bush administration is determined to greatly reduce the influence of education schools in teacher preparation and certification. Some see this as an intentional effort to put the teaching profession at risk, to undermine the professional status of teaching, and to dismantle the conditions for professional work. These efforts include the well-orchestrated effort to sponsor alternative routes to the classroom, to redefine "highly qualified teachers" as teachers with subject matter knowledge alone, and to denigrate the research and training undertaken by education researchers. It is both an overt challenge, with few education schools exempted from attack, and an implicit threat to everything that education school faculty believe and understand about good teaching and learning.

For 25 years, many have worked to create a profession of teaching. The codification of a knowledge base of teaching; the expansion of the life-space for the preparation of professional practitioners, role differentiation, and opportunities for advancement and increased responsibility; the appeal for autonomy over practice are important elements of this professional agenda. The NBPTS, INTASC, and NCATE were the policy vehicles to be used to realize this agenda. In the 1990s, NCTAF reinforced earlier efforts of the TEPS Commission and the Bicentennial Commission of the AACTE. By the late-1990s, there was a surprising degree of consensus and uniformity represented by these various agencies and efforts, and the government was poised to embrace this agenda.

The fact that neo-conservatives were able to derail these efforts and promote an alternative agenda—one of public accountability, deregulation, competition, and reliance on market forces to control teaching and teacher education—is remarkable. They shifted the dialogue from one that focused on professional standards and progressive ideas—with attention to the role of school in providing "access to knowledge" and "enculturating the young into a political democracy"—to an agenda that centered attention on "good enough" teachers (Finn *et al.*, 1999; Goodlad, 1990; Whitehurst, 2003). At the same time, the Bush administration focused on recasting teacher certification from a "safe to practice" criterion to a matter of "high quality." It sought to move certification from a narrowly construed state responsibility to an array of national entities. Ultimately, its efforts were to give school principals greater choice in the selection of beginning teachers, although the connection between this practice and teacher quality was tenuous at best. While professional consensus was the basis for both the INTASC and NBPTS standards for teachers and NCATE's teacher education standards, the efforts of the neo-conservatives have undermined that agenda and put the profession of teaching at even greater risk.

The solution? Education professionals have to embrace an agenda of teacher effectiveness and promote a common set of performance standards or their voice will be lost in the debate. Teacher effectiveness is measured by the success of PK-12 students in scoring well on tests of student achievement. Gaining consensus on measures that promote such teaching is a necessary starting point in any long term discussion of the role of teaching and teaching policy for America's schools. Absent serious effort at rebuilding a profession of teaching, teaching will be cast as a skilled occupation or semi-profession and will lack, therefore, public status and accord. Using teacher certification as a policy tool to promote PK-12 student learning as the ultimate teacher role is the place to begin.

REFERENCES

Allen, M. (2000) *Two paths to quality teaching: implications for policymakers.* Denver, CO: Education Commission of the States.

Alvarez, L. (2001, June 15) Senate passes bill for annual tests in public schools. *The New York Times*, A1.

Appleberry, J. (1994) *Statement on responsibilities for teacher education.* Washington, DC: American Association of State Colleges and Universities.

Asera, R. & Chin, E. (2005) *Teacher certification: multiple treatment interactions on the body politic.* Draft Paper for the International Policy Handbook. Palo Alto, CA: Carnegie Foundation for the Advancement of Teaching.

Ballou, D. & Podgursky, M. (1998) *The case against teacher certification.* National Affairs Inc. The Public Interest.

Ballou, D. & Podgursky, M. (2000) Reforming teacher preparation and licensing: continuing the debate. *Teachers College Record*, 102(1), 5–27.

Ballou, D. & Soler, S. (1998) *Addressing the looming teacher crunch: the issue is quality.* Washington, DC: The Progressive Policy Institute.

Beadle, A. (2001) Education conferees prepare for final exam. *CQ Daily Monitor*, 37(94), 1–3.

Berry, B., Darling-Hammond, L., & Hasselkorn, D. (1998) *Teacher recruitment, selection and induction: strategies for transforming the teaching profession.* New York, NY: National Commission on Teaching and America's Future.

Bingaman, J. (1998) The role the Federal government can play in improving teacher quality. *Educational Horizons*, 78, 3 (spring), 115–116.

Bradley, A. (1999, September 2). States' uneven teacher supply complicates staffing of schools. *Education Week*, 17, 1, 7.

Bradley, A. (2003, October 8). Federal funding for teacher test. *Education Week*, 23, 6, 1–17.

Bright, K. & Harmeyer, S. (2002) *Higher education: activities underway to improve teacher training, but reporting on these activities could be enhanced.* Washington, DC: United States General Accounting Office.

Capital Research Center (1998) *Professional teaching standards: a policy brief.* NCPA: Washington, DC.

Cardman, M. (2001) K-12 bill ready for its closeup with the House. *Education Daily*, 34(15), 1.

Cardman, M. (2003, September 29) Alternative certification groups gets $35M ED grant. *Education Daily*, 36(181), 1.

Cochran-Smith, M. & Fries, M. K. (2001) Sticks, stones, and ideology: the discourse of reform in teacher education. *Educational Researcher*, 30(8), 3–15.

Cohen, M. & Smith, M. (1993) *Goals 2000: Educate America Act*. (Draft of March 18.) Washington, DC: U.S. Education Department.

Cronin, J. M. (1983) State regulation of teacher preparation. In L. S. Shulman & G. Sykes (eds.), *Handbook of teaching and policy* (pp. 171–192). New York, NY: Longman.

Darling-Hammond, L. (1996) What matters most: a competent teacher for every child. *Phi Delta Kappan*, 77(7), 193–200.

Darling-Hammond, L. (2000) Teaching for America's future: national commissions and vested interests in an almost profession. *Educational Policy*, 14(1), 162–183.

Education Trust (2003) *Telling the whole truth (or not) about high school graduation, and telling the whole truth (or not) about highly qualified teachers*. Washington, DC: Author.

Finn, C. E. (2005, August 25) An obit for ed schools, *Gadfly*. http://www.edexcellence.net/foundation/gadfly/issue.cfm?id=267

Finn, C. E. & Madigan, K. (2001) Removing the barriers for teacher candidates. *Educational Leadership*, 58, 8, 29–31.

Fuhrman, S. H. (1994) Politics and systemic education reform, *CPRE Policy Briefs*. New Brunswick, NJ: Consortium for Policy Research in Education.

Futrell, M. H. (2005) The National Board for Professional Teaching Standards. In S. Cimburek (ed.), *Leading a profession: defining moments in the AACTE agenda, 1980–2005*. Washington, DC: American Association of Colleges for Teacher Education.

Goldhaber, D. D. & Brewer, D. J. (2002) Does teacher certification matter? High school teacher certification status and student achievement. *Educational Evaluation and Policy Analysis*. 22, 129–146.

Goodlad, J. I. (1990) *Teachers for our nation's schools*. San Francisco, CA: Jossey Bass.

Gunderson, S. (2003) *Teacher preparation and the reauthorization of the Higher Education Act*. Arlington, VA: The Greystone Group, Inc.

Gursky, D. (1989) Looking for a short-cut. *Teacher Magazine* (December), 59–64.

Haney, W. (2000) The myth of the Texas miracle in education. *Education Policy Analysis Archives*, 8(41). Retrieved from http://epaa.asu.edu/epaa/v8n41/.

Hanushek, E. A. (1986) The economics of schooling: production and efficiency in public schools. *Journal of Economic Literature*, 24, 1147–1177.

Hanushek, E. A. (1997) Assessing the effects of school resources on student performance: an update. *Education Evaluation and Policy Analysis*, 19(2), 141–164.

Hartocollis, A. (2005, July 31) Who needs education schools? *The New York Times*.

Haycock, K. (1998) Good teaching matters . . . A lot. *Thinking K-12*, 3(2), 1–8. Washington, DC: The Education Trust.

Herring, M. Y. (2001) *At the core of the problem-reforming teacher preparation in Oklahoma*. Princeton, NJ: National Association of Scholars.

Hess, F. M. (2001) *Tear down this wall: the case for a radical overhaul of teacher certification*. Washington, DC: Progressive Policy Institute.

Higher Education Amendments of 1998, Conference Report to Accompany H.R. 6, 106th Congress, 2nd Session. (September 25, 1998).

Holmes Group (1986) *Tomorrow's teachers*. East Lansing, MI: Author.

Izumi, L. & Coburn, K. G. (2001) *Facing the classroom challenge: teacher quality and teacher training in California's schools of education*. San Francisco, CA: Pacific Research Institute for Public Policy.

Kanstoroom, M. & Finn, C. F., Jr. (eds.) (1999) *Better teachers, better schools*. Washington, DC: Thomas B. Fordham Foundation.

Kozloff, M. A. (2001, July 31) A direct and focused approach: necessary conditions for fundamental reform of schools of education. *EducationNews.org*.

Labaree, D. F. (2004) *The trouble with ed schools*. New Haven, CT: Yale University Press.

Learned, W. S., Bagley, W. C., McMurry, C. A., Strayer, G. D., Dearborn, W. F., Kandel, I. L., & Josselyn, H. W. (1920) *The professional preparation of teachers for American public schools: a study based upon an examination of tax-supported normal schools in the State of Missouri.* New York, NY: Carnegie Foundation for the Advancement of Teaching.

Leigh, A. & Mead, S. (2005) *Lifting teacher performance policy report.* Washington, DC: Progressive Policy Institute.

Magrath, P. (1998) *Community letter.* Washington, DC: National Association of State Universities and Land Grant Colleges.

Mathematical Policy Research (2004) *The effects of Teach for America on students: findings of a national evaluation.* Princeton, NJ: Author.

Michelli, N. (2005) Alternative routes to certification. In S. Cimburek (ed.), *Leading a profession: defining moments in the AACTE Agenda, 1980–2005.* Washington, DC: American Association of Colleges for Teacher Education.

Milbank, D. (2001, January 24) Bush makes education 1st initiative. *Washington Post,* 1.

National Association of State Directors of Teacher Education and Certification (1992) *Promoting systemic change in teacher education and certification.* Seattle, WA: Author.

National Association of State Directors of Teacher Education and Certification (1999) *Manual on the preparation and certification of educational personnel, 1998–1999.* Dubuque, IA: Kendal/Hunt Publishing Company.

National Center for Education Statistics (1999) *Data system for accountability provisions of the Higher Education Amendments of 1998, Title II.* Washington, DC: Author.

National Commission on Teaching and America's Future (1996) *What matters most: teaching for America's future.* New York, NY: Author.

National Council for the Accreditation of Teacher Education (2000) *NCATE 2000 unit standards.* Washington, DC. Author.

No Child Left Behind Act of 2001, Pub. L. No. 107–110, 115 Stat. 1425.

Olson, L. (2003, January 9) The great divide: ensuring a highly qualified teacher for every classroom. *Education Week's Quality Counts,* 22(17), 9–18.

Paige, R. (2002) *Meeting the highly qualified teacher challenge: the Secretary's annual report on teacher quality.* Washington, DC: U.S. Department of Education.

Paige, R. (2003) *Meeting the highly qualified teachers challenge: the Secretary's second annual report on teacher quality.* Washington, DC: U.S. Department of Education.

Petrilli, M. (1998) *Reinventing teacher education.* Indianapolis, IN: The Hudson Institute.

Rice, J. K. (2003) *Teacher quality: understanding the effectiveness of teacher attributes.* Washington, DC: Economic Policy Institute.

Riley, R. (1999, February 16) *Putting standards of excellence into action* (Sixth Annual State of American Education Address). California State University, Long Beach, CA.

Rotherham, A. J. & Mead, S. (2003) *Back to the future: The history and politics of state teacher licensure and certification.* Washington, DC: Progressive Policy Institute.

Sanders, W. & Horn S. (1998) Research findings from the Tennessee Value-Added Assessment System Database: implications for educational evaluation and research. *Journal of Personnel Evaluation in Education,* 12, 247–256.

Sanders, W. L. & Rivers, J. C. (1996) *Cumulative and residual effects of teachers on future student academic achievement.* Knoxville: University of Tennessee Value-Added Research and Assessment Center.

Scannell, M. M. & Scannell, D. P. (1994) Teacher certification and standards. In T. Husen & T. N. Postlethwaite (eds.), *International Encyclopedia of Education* (2nd ed.). London: Pergamon, 1994.

Splete, A. (1996) *Revised draft for the Teacher Education Accreditation Council* (TEAC). Washington, DC: Council for Independent Colleges.

Stinnett T. (1958) *The education of teachers: new perspectives.* Washington: National Education Association.

Strike, K. (1997) Centralized goal formation and systemic reform: reflections on liberty, localism and pluralism. *Education Policy Analysis Archives,* 5(11), 1–35.

Sykes, G. (1990) Licensure and certification of teachers: an appraisal. In J. Millman & L. Darling-Hammond (eds.), *The new handbook of teacher evaluation: assessing elementary and secondary teachers* (pp. 62–75). Newbury Park, CA: Corwin Press.

The Teaching Commission (2004) *Teaching at risk: a call to action.* Report of the Teaching Commission. New York: The Teaching Commission.

Walsh, K. (2001) *Teacher certification reconsidered: stumbling for quality.* Baltimore, MD: Abell Foundation.

Wayne, A. J. (2000) Teacher supply and demand: surprises from primary research. *Education Policy Analysis Archives*, 8, 47.

The White House. (1997, January 19) *Background on President Clinton's agenda for the nation: State of the Union Address.* Washington, DC: Author.

Whitehurst, G. (2003) Scientifically-based research on teacher quality: research on teacher preparation and professional development. In *Meeting the highly qualified teachers challenge: the Secretary's second annual report on teacher quality* (pp. 39–54). Washington, DC: U.S. Department of Education.

48 The evolving field of teacher education

How understanding challenge(r)s might improve the preparation of teachers

Suzanne M. Wilson
Michigan State University

Eran Tamir
Brandeis University

> The surest, quickest way to add quality to primary and secondary education would be addition by subtraction: Close all the schools of education.
>
> (Will, 2006)

INTRODUCTION

We live in an age of lively discussions concerning the value of "traditional" teacher education, which includes teacher preparation programs, teacher certification and licensing practices, and accreditation processes for programs. Teacher education programs are "intellectually barren," teacher educators are "arrogant" and "inept" (Hess, 2005). "There is a built-in institutional vapidity in ed schools" (Rochester, 2002). Refrains echo past criticisms leveled at the teacher education enterprise. Concerns like these were raised at least as far back as the 1930s, gaining a great deal of public exposure in the 1950s and 1960s with books like Bestor's (1953) *Educational Wastelands*, Lynd's (1953) *Quackery in the Public Schools*, Smith's (1949) *And Madly Teach*, Conant's (1964) *The Education of American Teachers*, and Koerner's (1963) *The Miseducation of American Teachers*. Koerner (1963) concluded that education school courses were "vague, insipid, time wasting adumbrations of the obvious" (p. 56). And Bestor (1953) proclaimed that there was a "preposterous overemphasis upon pedagogy that produces teachers who can talk glibly about how to teach, but who know too little about any given subject to teach it satisfactorily."

The teacher establishment does not always take such criticism well. Defenders of teacher education characterize the critics as "an alliance of thugs" or "marketeers" who seek to turn children into "sources of profit" and who are "at war with the public schools" (Hess, 2005); accusations are made about misrepresentations and misinterpretations of research and practice. Teacher educators and critics seem equally ready and likely to hurl accusations.[1] In so doing, important differences are obscured: critics are cast as political conservatives who do not care about social justice, for example, as assumptions about one's political values are considered coterminous with one's concerns about education and teacher quality.[2] Teacher educators are lumped together as a unified bloc of subject matter-deficient worshippers at the altar of progressive ideals who care only about process and never about content.

And everyone seems to want a piece of the action. The Secretary of Education has weighed in with reports on teacher quality (U.S.D.E., 2002, 2003); the National Board for Professional Teaching Standards jockeys for power in defining and certifying teacher excellence. States attempt to take over control of the content of teacher preparation (Prestine, 1991); the federal government attempts to close colleges of education and open up alternative routes into teaching, such as the certification available through the American Board for the Certification of Teaching Excellence (ABCTE) which received considerable financial support from the federal government under the Bush administration. Reports are issued and studies funded by the Thomas B. Fordham Foundation, American Federation of Teachers, Department of Education, American Educational Research Association, National Council on Teacher Quality, and National Academy of Education. Conferences are sponsored by think tanks, including the American Enterprise Institute, Hoover Institute, Brookings Institution, Progressive Policy Institute, and Manhattan Institute. Columnists from the *New York Times* (Kristof, 2006) and *Newsweek* (Will, 2006) have thrown in their two cents as well. The most recent of these reports, Levine's (2006) *Educating School Teachers*, while largely reiterating previous critiques and analyses of the problems of teacher preparation, drew enough attention to remind us all that teacher education remains promising fodder for critique in the profession, public, and press.

Our aim is to understand and map the critics and their concerns. Thus, in this chapter, we explore two questions: Who are the critics? What are their concerns? By examining the contemporary jurisdictional challenges to teacher preparation and certification—that is, the different individuals, groups, and institutions that struggle for power—we hope to gain insight into the social arrangements and transactions of power that shape, build, and redefine who controls the preparation and licensing of teachers.

Our approach, albeit more modest, is inspired by Bourdieu's (1988) canonical work on the French higher education system, *Homo Academicus*. In laying out this argument, we aim to develop a useful conceptual framework that would allow a better understanding of the teacher education field, both for challengers and defenders. In this sense, we face a problem similar to the one Bourdieu faced as he tried to understand—as an insider—the ways in which different groups and individuals struggled for power and control in a field that he himself belonged to. Bourdieu's attempt to portray his academic community led to harsh criticism from many of his colleagues. It is our hope that conceptualizing the debates over teacher education as a power struggle within what Bourdieu (1985, 1988; Bourdieu & Wacquant, 1992) has called a "social field" will allow for a more "objective"—or, at the very least, a somewhat distanced—evaluation of contemporary activity around teacher licensing and certification. In the midst of a heated and divisive struggle, where both challengers and defenders fight fiercely, at times presenting intentionally-biased research and evaluations, there is a clear need for an analysis that takes one step back in an attempt to provide—perhaps—a more "balanced" approach.[3] Here we take a first step by mapping out the challengers and their critiques. While it is equally important to consider the establishment's responses to those critiques, we leave that analysis for later (Tamir, 2006; Wilson, in progress).

TEACHER EDUCATION AS A SOCIAL FIELD

Let us start by introducing the notion of the social field, its general structure, logic of action, and components. According to Bourdieu and Wacquant (1992), the social space is comprised of "configuration of objective relations":

These positions are objectively defined, in their existence and in the determinations they impose upon their occupants, agents or institutions, by their present and potential situation (situs) in the structure of the distribution of species of power (or capital) whose possession commands access to the specific profits that are at stake in the field.

(p. 97)

In other words, a field is a space where social agents—individuals, groups, and institutions—interact, work, and struggle over power. These social agents possess a shared set of understandings, beliefs, values, and norms that constitute the logic and rules of the game for that field (Bourdieu, 1985).

These shared understandings of the field by social agents differ from one field to another. However, one thing that is always shared among social agents of a given field is the importance they ascribe to their field and to the importance of continuing to manufacture the products of their field. Artists, for example, share a general belief that their work matters. There is also the self-serving aspect, that is, all members of a field are invested in and thus dependent on the field thriving. This, however, does not mean that they do not struggle fiercely among themselves. The same is true for social agents who operate in the field of teacher education. They all believe that education is important and that teacher education is essential. They differ, however, in their beliefs about the nature of effective teacher preparation. We return to the question of how much "shared" belief, values, and knowledge the field of teacher education needs later in our discussion.

The orthodoxy

So who might be in this network of relations in the social field of teacher education? We will begin with the "teacher education establishment."[4] There is the American Association of Colleges of Teacher Education (AACTE), created in 1948 from the merger of six teacher educator associations, as well as the Association of Teacher Educators (ATE), which was founded in 1920, and includes members from over 700 colleges and universities, 500 school systems, and most state departments of education. The evolution, as well as past and current history of those collectivities, is explicated by Angus (2001), Imig and Imig (this volume), and Sedlak (this volume).

But not all teacher educators align themselves with those communities, and so we need to add also the Holmes Group, a consortium of research universities concerned with the state of teacher education in the wake of the publication of *A Nation at Risk* (National Commission on Excellence and Education, 1983), which later became the Holmes Partnership in 1996, and the American Educational Research Association (AERA), especially Division K, Teaching and Teacher Education, which attracts faculty from across teacher education programs who are often interested in the practice of and research about teacher education. We might then add the National Council for Accreditation of Teacher Education (NCATE) and the Teacher Education Accreditation Council (TEAC), the two accrediting institutions within teacher education, as well as state departments of education, which make decisions about individual teacher certification and licensure, as well as program accreditation. Most state departments of education are staffed with personnel who have been trained as educators and thus are naturally aligned with the education establishment. Critics often understand the establishment as those individuals who embrace progressive education ideas (Hirsch, 1996; Null, 2006; Ravitch, 2000). However, there is considerable variability in how aligned state department personnel are with university teacher educators or with K-12 teachers and administrators. Sometimes these groups collaborate extensively and share common ideas and ideals; at other times, they are at odds, struggling amongst themselves for power. This may be increasingly the case with the growing interest of states and the federal government in regulating and controlling public education and teacher quality in particular (Prestine, 1991; Ramirez, 2004; Tamir, 2006). The fact that state departments, as well as other groups, shift position helps remind us that Bourdieu's notions of a social field, with its orthodoxies and heterodoxies, are fluid, ever-changing.

Let us pause and consider this partial mapping of relations and groups. These institutions include many individuals who are considered members of the traditional teacher education establishment: university-based teacher educators; state department staff who license and certify teachers; accreditation organizations; leaders of the professional associations and movements, like David Imig and Sharon Robinson from AACTE, Art Wise from NCATE, Judith Lanier, Frank Murray, and Robert Yinger from the Holmes Group and later Holmes Partnership, as well as Murray's leadership of TEAC.[5] There are also networks like the Urban Network to Improve Teacher Education (UNITE), as well as alternative preparation programs created by the orthodoxy, including the DeWitt Wallace-Reader's Digest Fund's Pathways to Teaching Careers Program.

The network fills in quickly as one also considers foundations and other groups that fund work by these organizations, other scholars and advocates who organize efforts to improve teaching and teacher education, and the like. So, for example, Linda Darling-Hammond, who has long collaborated with Art Wise, is closely associated with the professionalization movement in teaching through her work in organizations like the National Commission on Teaching and America's Future (NCTAF, 1996, 2003). There is also Lee Shulman, current president of the Carnegie Foundation for the Advancement of Teaching (CFAT), whose ideas of teachers' professional knowledge greatly influenced the development of the National Board for Professional Teaching Standards, as well as the standards and assessments developed by the Chief State School Officers (CCSSO) through their Interstate New Teacher Assessment and Support Consortium (INTASC). Other teacher education leaders, like Marilyn Cochran Smith, Robert Floden, Pamela Grossman, and Gloria Ladson-Billings, exercise influence through holding offices in and winning awards from professional organizations like the American Education Research Association and AACTE. There is also the complication that the ideas and arguments of these actors shift over time. While portraits such as that offered here momentarily "freeze" an ever-evolving landscape, this ought not be construed as a portrait of a static field.

And then there are the professional journals acting as the organs for ideas about teacher education, including *Action in Teacher Education* (sponsored by ATE, the sponsor of this handbook), the *Journal of Teacher Education* (sponsored by AACTE), and the *International Journal of Teaching* and *Teacher Education* (TATE), as well as other journals like *Educational Researcher* and the *American Education Research Journal* (AERJ) in which many AERA members publish. And, as previously mentioned, there are the state level organizations, which also have their own journals.

While these are certainly not the only participants and organizations within this community (we apologize to any group or individual who is not named; our intent here is to evoke—not inventory—the character of the field), these networks of people, institutions, and professional organizations represent what Bourdieu (1984, 2005) would call the "orthodoxy" of the social field, the aggregation of individuals, groups, and institutions that hold and preserve a coherent line of ideas, interests, practices, and visions that dominate a given field.

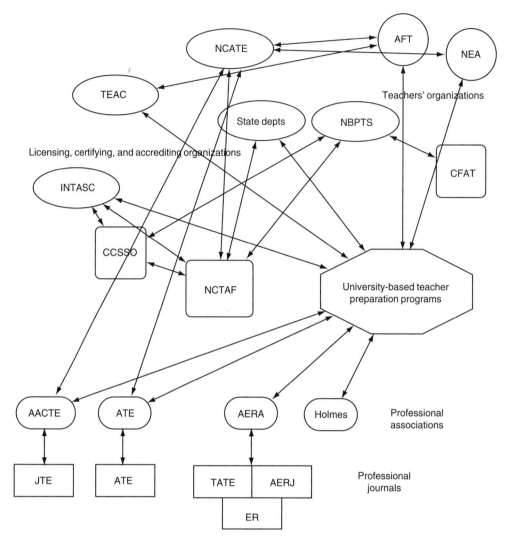

Figure 48.1 The orthodoxy of teacher education.

The heterodoxy

While these agents might account for the bulk of the teacher education establishment, there are other actors—what Bourdieu (2005) calls the "heterodoxy"—who also have strong opinions about teacher quality, preparation, and certification. According to Bourdieu, these agents too have a stake in the field, but they do not necessarily possess the shared norms and assumptions—Bourdieu's (1986) "cultural capital"—that are used to legitimate authority in the field. The heterodoxy, then, attempts to challenge the status quo.

Who are these "others?" First, there are the alternative routes that have been established by school districts and states. There is also the National Center for Education Information (NCEI) and the newly established National Center for Alternative Certification (NCAC), headed by Emily Feistritzer, which keeps track of the data on alternate routes and hosts annual conferences to disseminate knowledge, practices, and policies concerning alternative routes through www.teach-now.org. There are also programs designed to attract specific populations to teaching, including Wendy Kopp's Teach for America (TFA), Troops to Teachers (TTT), and the New York City Teaching Fellows Program (NYTCF). Although these "alternative" programs are sometimes characterized as being in opposition to "traditional" teacher education, they do not comprise some monolithic community, for there is a great deal of variability among them (just as there is within "traditional" teacher education) (Cochran-Smith & Zeichner, 2006; Humphrey & Wechsler, 2005; Johnson *et al.*, 2005; Schulte & Zeichner, 2001; Wilson *et al.*, 2001; Zeichner, 2005). In fact, under the auspices of many such programs, recruits eventually complete a relatively traditional path into teaching to gain certification. Thus, even though housed in alternative *settings*, so called "alternatives" can be staffed by members of the orthodoxy.

Then there is also the newly created American Board for Certification of Teaching Excellence (ABCTE)—funded by the U.S. Department of Education (which has also funded Teach for America and Troops to Teachers)—which offers its recruits an alternative "passport" into teaching. There are also smaller reforms like the Knowledge is Power Program (KIPP) schools that are frustrated with the traditional preparation of teachers and have expressed some interest in branching out into teacher preparation.

Then there are individuals and organizations that have released reports, held conferences, and raised questions about the quality of teacher preparation and the necessity of certification or accreditation. The Abell Foundation, the Pacific Research Institute, and the Progressive Policy Institute have issued reports (e.g. Izumi & Coburn, 2001). The Thomas B. Fordham Foundation (1999) issued a "manifesto" entitled *The Teachers We Need and How To Get More of Them*, which was signed by various critics of the teacher education establishment. The Hoover Institute has sponsored conferences; Frederick Hess (2001, 2002) from the American Enterprise Institute (an organization considered one of the leading architects of the current Bush administration's public policies) has written reports, books, and op eds arguing that we need to "tear down the walls" of traditional teacher certification. Other critics like E. D. Hirsch (1996, 2006) and Diane Ravitch (2000) have raised questions about quality of the content of teacher preparation programs. Economists Dale Ballou and Michael Podgursky (Ballou & Podgursky, 1998, 2000a, 2000b; Podgursky, 2004) have challenged the monopolistic rationale of teacher certification and the irrelevance and intellectual shallowness of teachers' tests. Kate Walsh of the National Council on Teacher Quality (whose advisory members include Hess, Hirsch, Kopp, among others), has written critiques of the teacher education establishment, including the recent *What Education Schools Aren't Teaching about Reading and What Elementary Teachers Aren't Learning* (Walsh *et al.*, 2006). Recently, mathematicians and scientists concerned about teachers' content knowledge have joined in as well. Their diagnosis, like that of the critics in the 1950s and 1960s, is that prospective teachers spend too much time in teacher education courses, thus compromising prospective teachers' chances to learn content in university disciplinary departments. A mapping of these agents can be seen in Figure 48.2.

Boundary crossers

Some challengers take a stance in strong opposition to the orthodoxy; others, while critical, seem less radically so. The American Federation for Teachers, for example, embraces the idea of teachers as professionals, which the critics do not always do. But the AFT (1998) nonetheless has concerns about the quality of "traditional" teacher preparation, as laid out in their report, *Building a Profession: strengthening Teacher Preparation and*

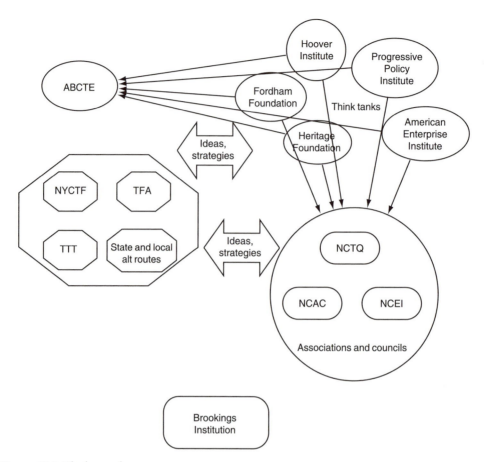

Figure 48.2 The heterodoxy.

Induction. Similarly, the Education Commission of the States (Allen, 2003), and the National Research Council (NRC), with its new teacher preparation study (as well as its study of the National Board for Professional Teaching Standards), appear to be concerned interest groups, but not clearly part of the orthodoxy or heterodoxy. Indeed, using the terms of "orthodoxy" and "heterodoxy" might communicate a static quality that is not intended. (And, of course, there is also the fact that the same person or organization can be seen as liberal, centrist, conservative, and radical by different agents in the social field at the same time.) The boundaries between the orthodoxy and heterodoxy are permeable, and groups and their alliances shift over time, as do the ideas, assumptions, and values that guide their work. Furthermore, some individuals and groups being pigeonholed: Lee Shulman (2005), for instance, champion of the professionalization agenda has also recently declared that teacher education "does not exist." We return to this point later in our discussion.

The Education Trust, led by Katy Haycock, serves as another example of groups that blur the lines between the establishment and its challengers, as does the National Governors Association (NGA). These organizations embrace ideas that resonate with the establishment—like certification, teacher preparation, the NBPTS—while simultaneously being open to alternatives offered by challengers. The NGA, for example, embraces a range of strategies associated with the orthodoxy and the heterodoxy: "high-quality and relevant professional development activities for teachers; teacher testing and certification against high standards . . . and merit or performance pay, teacher academies, alternative routes to certification" (NGA, 2006).

This stance—embracing ideas of both traditional teacher educators and their critics— is also taken by foundations and other organizations that invest heavily in education reforms, supporting initiatives by groups and institutions from both sides of the aisle. The Carnegie Corporation of New York has provided generous support for TFA, while at the same time supporting an ambitious effort to reform teacher preparation, Teachers for a New Era (TNE), which is largely a collection of institutions within the establishment. The National Science Foundation (NSF) also supports the work of challengers *and* the establishment, sometimes asking oppositional groups to collaborate. The Brookings Institution, a nonpartisan think tank (although it is thought of by some as "liberal" or centrist, and by others as conservative) also takes positions that cross boundaries between the orthodoxy and heterodoxy. Arthur Levine, in his recent critique of teacher education programs intentionally took this stance, although he declared himself an insider wanting to offer a critical perspective. It may be that this category of boundary crosser also includes boundary blurrers. Together, these agents suggest a third configuration of inter- ests groups that blurs the already-permeable boundaries between the teacher education establishment and its challengers (see Figure 48.3):

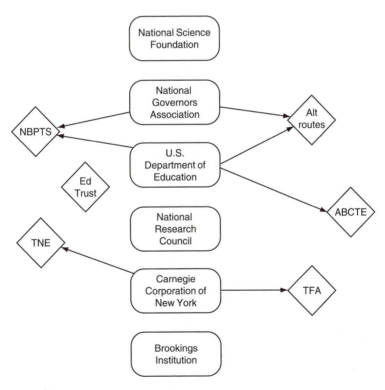

Figure 48.3 Boundary crossers.

In sum, the social field of teacher education is a large, shifting, crowded space with multiple communities, organizations, individuals, interest groups, and institutions. We do not offer these maps as static representations of positions, for the locations of various groups and institutions shifts over time. Nor do we want to fall into the habit—all too

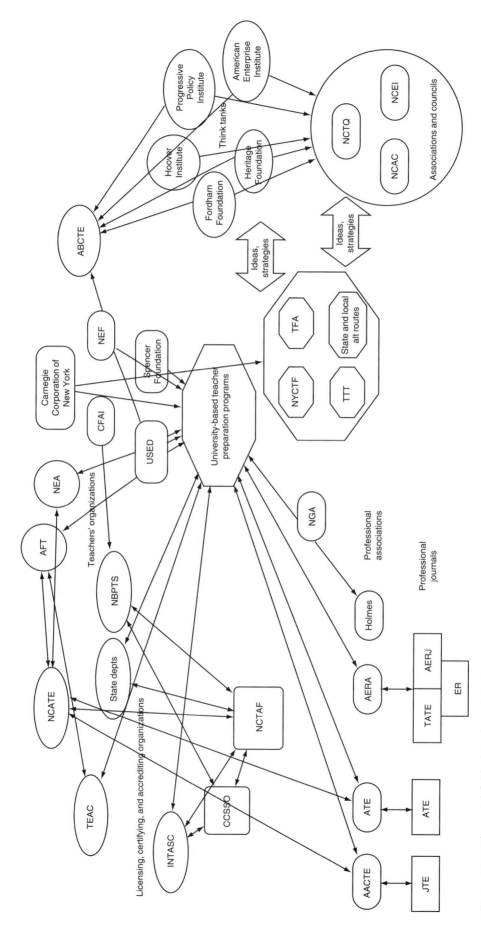

Figure 48.4 The social field of teacher education.

often present in the contemporary discourse—of implying that all individuals and organizations within a group are of like mind. There is considerable disagreement within these groups; all teacher educators do not agree with one another. Nor do the challengers.

Understanding, then, that we offer this mapping as a heuristic, not as a static entity, we now turn to the content of the challengers' critiques. We organize our comments around four major themes that run throughout challenges to the teacher education system.[6]

THE CHALLENGES

Bourdieu (1988, 2005) argues that challengers question and redefine the value of the "products" currently "manufactured" in a field. In our case, the challengers' critique is relatively straightforward: the current teacher education system does not "produce" high quality teachers. However, in diagnosing the root cause of the problem, four overlapping themes can be identified. Aspects of these themes have been discussed by other analysts of these debates as well, including Cochran-Smith (2006), Cochran-Smith & Fries (2001), Grossman (2004), Labaree (2004), and Zeichner (2003). Our analysis complements those.

"The cleansing winds of competition": The problems of regulation and bureaucracy

One criticism of the teacher education establishment draws on the larger discourse of "choice." Here critics note that, like everything else in the educational establishment, teacher education is conservative, mired in tradition, inflexible and, worse, not working. For example, Finn (2003) argues that the public education system needs to "open more gates, welcome people from many different directions to enter them, minimize the hoops and hurdles and regulatory hassles, look for talent rather than paper credentials" (p. 5). To his dismay, this is not what educators do: "The education field has developed a conventional wisdom . . . [which] boils down to: more of the same. We're told to improve the [schools] by adding more formal training and certification requirements to those already in place" (p. 5).

Zeichner (2003) and Cochran-Smith and Fries (2001) call this general line of criticism the "deregulation" reform (the advocates call it a "common sense" reform (Hess, 2004)). Several subthemes run throughout this "market" or anti-/de-regulatory argument. First, there is the matter of unnecessary costs. The traditional system of teacher education is expensive. Prospective teachers "pay tuition, sacrifice the opportunity to work in order to attend courses, practice teach for eight to twelve weeks without compensation, and endure the red tape of obtaining additional certification if one wants to work in a state other than the one in which they trained" (Hess, 2001, p. 15). Requiring prospective teachers "to jump through . . . time-consuming but little regarded hoops," he argues, discourages the "entrepreneurial and energetic" (p. 15).

Second is the presumed inherent positive potential of alternatives. Those who argue for an open market of teacher preparation and certification believe wholeheartedly that traditional teacher education keeps people out, especially "smart" people, career changers, and people of color. Finn (2001) claims that "this training and certification cycle is so burdensome and full of 'Mickey Mouse' courses and requirements that it discourages able would-be teachers from making their way into the public schools" (p. 129). If we tear down the walls, making the boundaries to the profession more permeable, we will attract better—and different—people to teaching:

> [S]ince good teachers can be found in many places, prepared in many ways, and channeled into schools via many pathways, states should scrap nearly all the hoops and hurdles that discourage good candidates from entering the classroom. Deregulating teaching in this way will not only expand the pool but also raise its quality. [p. 144] ... The popularity of such programs as Teach for America, which places liberal arts graduates without formal education coursework in public school classrooms in poor rural communities and inner cities, indicates that the prospect of teaching without first being obliged to spend years in pedagogical study appeals to some of our brightest college graduates.
>
> (p. 145)

The argument here is that alternatives are inherently good, and the very existence of alternatives will attract a population "turned off" by "traditional" approaches to teacher education.

A third reason offered by the challengers for the market argument concerns a perceived lack of internal or external accountability within the social field. Critics have long noted that teacher education has been resistant to any criticism:

> One of the most shocking facts about the field of education is the almost complete absence of rigorous criticism from within. Among scientists and scholars, criticism of one another's findings is regarded as a normal and necessary part of the process of advancing knowledge. But full and frank criticism of new educational proposals rarely comes from other professional educationists.
>
> (Bestor, 1953)

Ten years later, Conant (1964) made a similar observation, noting that "the [education] establishment is overly defensive; it views any proposal for change as a threat ... In short, there is too much resentment of outside criticism and too little effort for vigorous internal criticism" (p. 40).

And today's challengers are equally concerned. As Hess (2005) notes in his meditations of the unnecessarily hostile (from every direction) discussions of teacher education, "In responding to such malicious onslaughts, the teacher preparation community does itself no favors by presuming that sharp critiques are necessarily malicious or illegitimate" (p. 197). Even when critiques are not malicious, some members of the teacher education establishment are quick to accuse challengers of less-than-noble intentions. Opening up the field to market forces would, presumably, change these tendencies. Criticism would be encouraged (not discouraged), and teacher educators would be pushed to "improve their product."

The stridency of this deregulation and open market argument varies. Some proponents like Hess (2001, 2005) have been careful to note—unlike George Will—that opening up the market is not synonymous with closing *all* schools of education. Indeed, several challengers claim that there exist high quality teacher education programs. These "good" programs will, no doubt, withstand the challenges presented by a market competition. Institutions that do not offer high quality preparation will, on the other hand, fold.

In sum, the market/anti-bureaucracy argument lines up powerful ideas like deregulation, efficiency and effectiveness, free choice, accountability, and high quality (ideas that became the coin of the political and educational realm in the 1980s), and associates these ideas in a convincing, logical—for some, almost unquestionable—way to argue for the necessity of a free market approach to improve teacher education. We note also that this criticism of teacher education is tightly aligned with a similar line of argument offered by critics of the educational system more generally (e.g. Ballou & Podgursky, 1998, 2000a, b; Finn, 2001; Hess, 2002; Hess *et al.*, 2004). These challenges (to the larger education establishment) argue that the solution to the inherent failures of public education is privatization (through the introduction of market-based mechanisms). When an open market exists, critics argue, the rigid, constraining, suffocating divisions of bureaucracy dissolve, social structures and self-serving groups with excessive power tend to diminish, and—as a direct result—the system's productivity and efficiency flourish since the system's "fat" gets trimmed and money is spent in more sensible ways. Of course, these critiques are not reserved for discussions of education alone, since the market argument is part of the long, historical U.S. struggle over the distribution of wealth and power in a society that also proclaims a commitment to equity and equality.

Our goal here is to understand the heterodoxy's complaints, and so we will not explore in detail the orthodoxy's response, nor do we describe these challenges so as to then critique them here. That we save for future analyses; one can also see Cochran Smith (2006), Cochran-Smith and Fries (2001), and Zeichner (2003). We do briefly note, however, that in response to the market critique, the teacher education establishment often points out that public education is committed to equality; the market is not, as can be seen in the growing chasm between rich and poor in the U.S. While markets might stimulate competition, and competition might stimulate healthy innovation and change, the teacher education establishment argues that competition also stimulates sorting and selection, and might—in so doing—thwart access to knowledge and, therefore, equal opportunity, the hallmark aspiration of the U.S. public education system.

The research-base argument

A second challenge leveled at the teacher education establishment concerns the "evidence" that there is a value-added of "traditional" teacher education preparation. Cochran-Smith and Fries (2001) describe these as arguments over the "evidentiary warrant":

> Each side endeavors to construct its own warrant but also to undermine the warrant of the other by pointing out in explicit detail where methodological errors have been made, where the data reported are incorrect and incomplete, and/or where faulty logic or reasoning have led to inaccuracies and errors about the nature or size of effects.
>
> (p. 6)

The evidence that is used to make arguments about the quality of traditional teacher preparation varies, including test scores of students intending to enroll in teacher education programs and/or licensure examination scores for graduating potential teachers. For example, in the 1980s, policymakers in New Jersey compared the licensure examination scores of alternate routes individuals and those of their traditionally prepared counterparts, showing how the latter lagged behind the former. These data were then used as an evidence to support the alternate route program (Tamir, 2006). As this debate intensified, both the orthodoxy and heterodoxy pushed for the development of better databases in order to find the best, perhaps ultimate, proof of their perspective. Science, in this case, gradually ceased to be seen as a tool to improve an objective understanding of the social reality—like some would like to believe it should—and was exploited instead as the final arbiter for decisions concerning social policy.

More recent national debates about research evidence concern the value-added of teacher education and certification (e.g. Ballou & Podgursky, 2000b; Darling-Hammond,

2000a; Goldhaber & Brewer, 2000, 2001; Darling-Hammond *et al.*, 2001; and Abell Foundation (2001a, b) and Darling-Hammond (2002), as well as Darling-Hammond & Youngs (2002)). Other organizations jumped into the discussion: the U.S. Department of Education commissioned a synthesis of five questions concerning research on teacher preparation (Wilson *et al.*, 2001). The Education Commission of the States followed up with their own report (Allen, 2003). More reports have followed, including the most recent AERA report (Cochran-Smith & Zeichner, 2005), and the National Academy of Education report edited by Darling-Hammond and Bransford (2005). A recent report from the National Council on Teacher Quality (Walsh *et al.*, 2006)—which examines whether teacher education programs have integrated the findings of the National Reading Panel (2000) into their reading courses—offers yet another example.

Challengers' questions about the research base for teacher preparation include: What does the research say about the qualities of an effective/accomplished teacher? Do such teachers need to have subject matter knowledge? Do they need pedagogical knowledge or other forms of professional knowledge? Do teacher education programs teach new teachers what "scientifically-based" research tells us about the teaching of reading or mathematics? Is there evidence that teachers who are certified through traditional paths are better or worse than teachers who are certified through alternative paths into teaching? Are there any observable effects of teacher education programs—holistically or in terms of program components like field experience and student teaching?[7]

Researchers interested in these questions often employ statistical databases that attempt to align teachers according to the type of certification they hold with their students' achievements on standardized tests, while trying to control for personal/group characteristics like socioeconomic status (SES) and race, as well as teacher characteristics like grade point averages, subject matter knowledge or major, type of university, teaching experience, and having a graduate degree in education (e.g. Darling-Hammond, 2000b; Felter, 1999; Goldhaber & Brewer, 2000; Monk, 1994). Overall, the aim of these studies has usually been to compare the teaching effectiveness (as measured by students' test scores) of teachers who enter teaching through alternative pathways and teachers prepared in traditional programs.

Darling-Hammond and Bransford (2005) take a slightly different approach. They include research results of the sort described above, but they also ask the question: What knowledge of significant domains exists—research on learning or research on teaching, for instance? One can make a logical argument that teacher education programs ought to include such knowledge because of the nature of the work, not because a researcher found that teacher education programs that introduced such ideas produced more effective teachers (see Cochran-Smith (2006) for an elaboration of this perspective).

Even with these more generous attempts to stipulate the knowledge base of teacher education, it is fair to ask: What research-based conclusions can be drawn about the value of teacher preparation? Evidence is uneven, spotty, stronger in some domains than others. One can make a case for deep knowledge of how people learn (e.g. Bransford *et al.*, 1999). One can make a weaker case for an established knowledge base concerning how to teach reading (NRP, 2000) or mathematics (NRC, 2001). But in general, research offers few definitive conclusions about the effects of teacher preparation or certification, field experience, subject matter and pedagogy classes, program accreditation and the like (see Allen, 2003; Cochran-Smith & Zeichner, 2005; Wilson & Floden, 2002; Wilson *et al.*, 2001). Challengers use the lack of definitive research on the value-added of teacher education, and the uneven quality of teacher education research to support the market argument: open the gates of teacher education and certification until we have sufficient research to justify market closure. Optimistic about the effects of the open market, they also argue that competition will speed progress in the development of better evidence.

Complicating the critiques are questions about the quality of teacher education research as well. Challengers argue that teacher educators do not, in general, conduct high quality research, use appropriate research designs, or critically appraise the research they use to support their claims. "Research that seems to support teacher certification is selectively cited, while research that does not is overlooked," the Abell Foundation (2001a) writes:

> Analyses are padded with imprecise measures in order to conceal the lack of evidence in support of certification . . . Researchers focus on variables that are poor measures of the qualities they are interested in, sometimes ignoring variables that are better measures . . . Research that has not been subjected to peer review is treated without skepticism.

These criticisms too are part of a broader conversation about the value-added of education research. Both inside and outside of the education establishment, questions have been raised about what constitutes high quality education research more generally (e.g. Erickson, & Gutiérrez, 2002; NRC, 2002; Raudenbush, 2005; Whitehurst, 2002).

As we noted earlier, one challenge to portraying the social field of teacher education is that it is a moving target. With regard to research on teacher education, this is especially true. For example, while the research base on teacher education is considered weak by many, there are currently several important projects underway that promise to shed light on the value-added of various approaches to teacher preparation. These include the Pathways into Teaching Project (Boyd *et al.*, 2006) and the Ohio Teacher Quality Partnership (Lasley *et al.*, 2006), both of which are designed to compare the outcomes of different teacher preparation programs.

These discussions of warrants and "scientific" evidence very much resonate with other, larger national conversations. The uneasy commingling of science and politics can be seen in many aspects of American life. We are reminded of recent debates concerning the place of creationism in the public school science curriculum as well as arguments about the pros and cons of stem cell research. This is an old debate, for science has always been shaped by politics, religion, and power; and so it is not surprising that in the political battle for control over the teacher education field, themes of whose science, what science, and how science should be used are very much part of the discussion.

Again, we will not explore the orthodoxy's response in any depth. We note, however, that teacher educators respond by critiquing the heterodoxy's (sometimes) narrow view of science, most notably the claim that experimental design is a "gold standard." They also argue that teaching is moral and ethical work, and inherently complex, and cannot therefore be adjudicated by empirical evidence alone. For some in the teacher education establishment, the "laser-like" focus on "what does the research say" can be seen as an effort to impose a totalitarian technocracy on education.

The professionalism argument

A third challenge concerns the "professionalism" agenda.[8] Challenges aimed at professionalism are multiple. First, there are critics who claim that teaching is not a profession, but more like labor or civil service, especially given its unions (e.g. Mitchell & Kerchner, 1983). Other challengers suggest that teaching *could* be a profession, save for its failure to meet certain standards for professionalism. For example, Chubb (2001) argued that the education profession, like any other profession should have been built on the principles of autonomy and accountability. Alas, none exist:

> A professional system has two hallmarks, autonomy and accountability. Professionals are given tasks when the requirements of doing them well dictate the exercise of ample discretion. The freedom to exercise discretion—autonomy—is then checked by the system with provisions for accountability. These provisions generally focus on the results of the tasks, not on how the tasks themselves are carried out. A professional model of education would recognize that teachers and schools need to decide how best to educate each student. The system would not monitor or particularly care how each school provided education; the system would care about and monitor what students learn.
>
> (p. 37)

So the challenge here is not that teaching ought not be considered a profession, but that it remains more a pseudo- or quasi-profession. A similar challenge concerns the lack of agreement concerning professional knowledge. Again, critics point out that a hallmark of professions is a shared, specialized knowledge base. Challengers note that teaching does not have the agreed-upon body of professional knowledge and skill that the professions of medicine and law have:

> The problem is that no comparable body of knowledge and skills exists in teaching. Debate rages over the merits of various pedagogical strategies, and even teacher educators and certification proponents have a hard time defining a clear set of concrete skills that makes for a good teacher.
>
> (Hess, 2002)

While not critics, both Cusick (1992) and Labaree (2004) make similar points about the "soft" technical core of teaching. Within this critique, challengers are impatient with the teacher education establishment's inability or unwillingness to describe teacher knowledge and skill in concrete terms. Vague language is used to describe good teaching: Good teachers "reflect" and "listen," they take "global perspectives," they "model." This "educationese" frustrates critics who want to know what these terms mean, and how they can be measured. They want a better articulation of the "technology" of good teaching, as perhaps best illustrated by the report of the National Reading Panel (National Institute of Child Health and Human Development, 2000). Furthermore, challengers ask for evidence that the knowledge and behavior valued by the establishment is positively correlated with student learning (Hess, 2001). If the orthodoxy cannot or will not explicitly and clearly lay out measurable standards for what teachers need to know, the challengers suggest, "we ought not keep people out. . . . This is not to say that we think incompetence is acceptable in such a profession—only that we recognize licensing as ineffective and potentially pernicious way to control quality" (p. 11).

Much of the discussion about teacher knowledge focuses on issues of teacher content knowledge, largely because everyone—members of both the orthodoxy and heterodoxy—agrees that teachers need to know something about the subject matters they will teach. But discussions about teachers' content knowledge (its content and character, adequacy, balance with other forms of professional knowledge) are equally fraught. This may be because some challengers implicitly or explicitly claim or are misunderstood to be claiming that content knowledge (and verbal ability) are really *all* that matters in teaching, either because there is no professional knowledge base or because teaching is a practical art, one best learned through and in practice, not in professional schools (e.g. Whitehurst, 2002). The fact that many teachers—especially elementary teachers (e.g. Ball *et al.*, 1990; Ball *et al.*, 2001; Ma, 1999) and misassigned secondary teachers (e.g. Ingersoll, 1996)—do not have adequate content knowledge leads some challengers to accuse teacher educators of spending too much time on education courses and not enough time enhancing the liberal and disciplinary education of future teachers. Teacher licensure tests only serve to reinforce this sense of low standards for teacher content knowledge. In one study, for example, Mitchell and Barth (1999) found that most of the tests were multiple choice, aimed at high school level knowledge. "We found no evidence of content [knowledge] at the baccalaureate level" (p. 8).

In sum, there exists a deep suspicion among critics that there is no articulated, measurable knowledge base for teaching, and that the teacher education establishment wants the entitlements due professionals, but not the obligations.

The stridency of these challenges vary, with some critics admitting that teaching might be a profession, but that it still has important work to do to meet the minimum requirements of a profession (e.g. an agreed upon professional knowledge base, internal accountability), and others claiming that teachers need verbal ability and some content knowledge, nothing more, nothing less. Even critics who argue that teaching is a profession and that teachers do need professional knowledge nonetheless challenge the orthodoxy for the mediocre content preparation of teachers, as well as the lack of rigorous licensing examinations (see Crowe (this volume) for further elucidation on these issues).

Social justice: the "ideology" argument

> Many education schools discourage, even disqualify, prospective teachers who lack the correct "disposition," meaning those who do not embrace today's "progressive" political catechism. Karen Siegfried had a 3.75 grade-point average at the University of Alaska Fairbanks, but after voicing conservative views, she was told by her education professors that she lacked the "professional dispositions" teachers need. She is now studying to be an aviation technician.
>
> (Will, 2006)

The final challenge involves the accusation that the educational establishment is held hostage by a suffocating ideology that—despite its protestations to be liberal—does not welcome alternative perspectives. Hirsch (1996) writes of an "orthodoxy masquerading as reform" and "totalitarian intellectual dominion"; Finn and Ravitch (1996) have accused the education establishment of a "pedagogical correctness" (p. 41). Let us begin by considering what challengers perceive as this ideology.

The teacher education establishment long ago embraced a progressive stance toward K-12 education (Dewey, 1902; Hirsch, 1996; Ravitch, 2000), and one subtheme of the "ideology challenge" concerns the perceived effects of progressivism on the quality of the curriculum and what students learn. Ravitch (2000) argues that the teacher education establishment's progressivism led to "unrelenting attacks on the academic mission of the schools," which—she argues—account for why so many children are "left back": "Such [progressive] policies, packaged in rhetoric about democracy and 'meeting the needs of the individual child,' encouraged racial and social stratification in American schools" (p. 15).

Hirsch (1996) makes a similar argument, but avoids the language of "ideology" because he sees the educational establishment as taken over by a *set* of ideas (rather than a single "ideology"). Instead, he asserts that the education establishment exists within a "thoughtworld," composed of three "intellectual impulses"—Romanticism, American exceptionalism, and professionalism—all of which are problematic when applied to educating children:

> The psychological and ethical assumptions of Romanticism have not worked out the way their originators had hoped and predicted. Romanticism may have created some of the greatest poetry in our language, but its theories of education have been wrong theories. American exceptionalism does have some basis in reality in that our democratic political traditions and our habits of intellectual independence are special in world history; but exceptionalism can become mere complacency that evades the challenges of learning from the experiences of other peoples. Professionalism in the noblest sense denotes both heightened pride in one's work and a heightened sense of responsibility; but extreme professionalism becomes narrow and separatist.
>
> (p. 126)

It is important to note that both Ravitch's and Hirsch's condemnation of the progressive ideology is rooted in their firm belief that these ideas have worked against the "social justice" agenda that many members of the teacher education establishment hold dear. Their critique, in other words, is not of the orthodoxy's commitment to equal, high quality education for all. Rather, it is a critique of the strategies that the educational establishment has used to achieve that equality. For critics of the establishment, progressivism is not synonymous with equitable education.

In addition to its failure to make good on its commitment to high quality education for all children, some challengers feel as if the orthodoxy is attempting to impose a Romantic, Progressive, constructivist values on everyone. Hess (2005) explains:

> [M]any critics are concerned that leading voices in teacher preparation ... have unapologetically argued that teacher education is inescapably about championing certain values.... Ladson-Billings, current AERA president, has said that her personal vision of good teaching is promoting an "anti-racist, anti-sexist, anti-homophobic ... Anti-oppressive social justice pedagogy," despite her acknowledgement that such teaching will inevitably entail "unpopular and politically dangerous" curriculum and pedagogical decisions.

Why is this dangerous? Because many teachers, Hess (2001) argues, are young and impressionable, and because the teacher education establishment's values do not reflect those of the larger society:

> By entrusting schools of education with control over entry into teaching, certification lends the instructors a privileged position in sensitive social and moral discussions. This would be of little concern if education faculty mirrored the divisions with the larger society, but this is not the case. Professors of education tend to espouse a "constructivist" conception of pedagogy, curriculum, and schooling. It is received wisdom in teacher education that aggressive multiculturalism is a good thing, that aspiring white teachers ought to be forced to confront society's ingrained racism.

Recently, challengers have focused their critiques on the increasing emphasis on "dispositions" in teacher education and program accreditation. Anecdotes abound about prospective teachers who are removed from teacher education programs because they reject the progressive ideas of constructivism, oppression, and social justice. Damon

(2005) observes that NCATE's standards "imply that a successful candidate must demonstrate the right kind of beliefs and attitudes" (p. 2) in terms of "dispositions" like caring and social justice. What is more, the NCATE standards suggest that teacher candidates must not only have such beliefs, but their actions must be guided by them. What concerns Damon is that NCATE's use of the language of "disposition" does not reflect knowledge of the work of social scientists on dispositional traits, which emphasize behavioral tendencies, not moral values or socio/political ideologies. This is problematic:

> Those who have been given the authority to assess teaching candidates have been given unbounded power over what candidates may think and do, what they may believe and value, and those who are subject to this authority (the candidates) must guard their every expression of moral belief and commitment.
>
> (Damon, 2005)

So, do the challengers want U.S. schoolteachers to ignore racism or to be sexists? Do challengers think that teachers should treat children or their parents differently depending on their gender, race, class, or sexual orientation? Perhaps some do. But it is overly simplistic to presume that challengers are racists who want to maintain the status quo. Essentializing this critique obscures the complexity within. Our country *is* deeply divided over issues of gay marriage, welfare, religion. Teachers are, in many ways, caught in the middle, for as public employees they must respect and work across those differences. However, the discourse proclaims that teachers have to have one set of values (anti-sexist, anti-racist, etc.); the very act of marginalizing those who have different values is, paradoxically, illiberal. Or, as Finn and Ravitch (1996) once noted, "the pedagogical tent, as it turns out, is not very big at all" (p. 41). While we cannot explore this complexity in all of its depth here, we offer a few observations.

Arguments about teacher education are predicated on assumptions about what teachers should do in schools and who they are. Assumptions about teachers are predicated on assumptions about the purposes of schools. Americans do not agree on this fundamental issue. There are those who see schools as the place where we hand down to children the heritage of our glorious past and present; for others, who are (often) more skeptical of U.S. claims to greatness, schools are places where teachers work as change agents, preparing students to reinvent the world, to radically overhaul society's inequities, and to reimagine our country. Further, we do not only disagree on our assumptions about schooling, we differ on a range of other values as well; one sees the on-going battle for whose social values will triumph in debates about social security and health care, in stem cell research and intelligent design.

When some challengers critique the "social justice" agenda of the teacher education orthodoxy, they are reacting to what they see as a homogeneity among teacher educators and their radical social vision. Challengers experience this homogeneity as a form of "Orwellian mind control" which first captures and brainwashes the young minds of prospective teachers, and later—through them—threatens to control the minds of children. Those prospective teachers who dare to resist—according to the challengers—are aggressively condemned, stigmatized, and denied the opportunity to become teachers.

This challenge raises two philosophical issues; the first concerns cultural relativism, the second touches on the controversy between the rights of professionals to promote a normative value system through their practice that might stand in contrast to the common normative perspective of the layman. There are no easy answers to the dilemmas raised by these issues, and those who raise them cannot be dismissed as simply conservative, racist, and xenophobic (even though there are among the challengers a range of such views). This critique, if taken seriously, suggests that some groups feel like their core value system is violated and disregarded by the orthodoxy's agenda. Ironically, as critics will point out, this oppression of difference in viewpoint goes directly against the commitment to multiculturalism and diversity that the teacher education establishment seeks to nurture when it comes to other groups like minorities, immigrants, and other oft-times marginalized populations.

The Progressive ideas seem even more dangerous and oppressive to the critics, since they enter the discourse through the agenda of professionals who use their professional power to make their ideas and knowledge look authoritative, objective, and "true." In the case of education—where knowledge and truth are so seriously contested—challengers see this as an irresponsible and undemocratic misuse of power by a liberal minority who tries to impose their ideas on the entire society.

Again, the challengers vary in their stridency. Damon (2005) explicitly notes that it is not clear whether the decision to write the NCATE standards in this way was simply sloppy scholarship or an "intentional dictatorial effort at mind and behavior control" (p. 5). Other challengers—like the positions articulated by Will (2006) and Hess (2006)—are quicker to draw conclusions that the teacher education establishment is intentionally enacting an "Orwellian mind control" (Damon, 2005).

These discussions have undertones of our larger national discussions about "moral values." While at times, challengers say that they are mainly concerned with the "imbalance" of views and values that are reflected in the teacher preparation curriculum, at other times, the critiques sound more like accusations that the progressives (like the larger liberal Democratic Party) lost their moral compass, and that schools—and teacher education establishment more specifically—need to return to "moral"—it is unclear whether this means "Christian"—values. It is not surprising, then, that one theme in challenges to the orthodoxy concerns the predominant values of that community, including Progressivism, constructivism, Romanticism, social justice, equal opportunity, equality, and equity.

RE-VISIONING THE TEACHER EDUCATION ESTABLISHMENT

Our goal in the chapter was modest: to examine the usefulness of Bourdieu's ideas about social fields to help us understand the current jurisdictional challenges to teacher preparation and certification, focusing on the criticisms to the establishment, not the orthodoxy's responses to those challenges. While some might dismiss the ideas of orthodoxy and heterodoxy out of hand, for us, the Bourdieuian frame is helpful. We are persuaded that there is an orthodoxy, albeit loosely coupled and constantly shifting, and that the social field of teacher education is characterized by a dominant set of norms, values, ideas, ideologies, and assumptions that shape the ways that social agents operate. Bourdieu would call this socialized behavior of agents their "habitus." Put simply, habitus is the set of dispositions, behaviors, beliefs, and norms that one acquires through life. These are affected by one's sources of capital—economic, cultural, and social—and the position one occupies in the social field. The habitus conditions the way social agents understand the field, or as Bourdieu put it, the habitus is the agent's "feel for the game." According to Bourdieu, then, our rationality is bound and defined by the sources of capital we possess, our habitus, and the position we occupy in the social field(s).

Based on this theory, we argue that although the teacher education establishment is relatively remote from some of the heterodoxy's agents and thus often resistant and dismissive to their ideas, the teacher education establishment would benefit from understanding with more acuity the structure of our field, the types of agents that operate in it, and the positions that these agents currently occupy. The problem with one's habitus is that one is often not aware of it; norms and values are implicit and tacitly accepted. Thus critics play an invaluable role by helping us "see" our norms and assumptions through their challenges. Indeed, we have found stepping back and examining the critiques very helpful in examining our own assumptions and world views. (We rely here on the old anthropological premise that understanding the other helps us better understand ourselves.) We conclude by first summarizing how the challengers perceive the orthodoxy and then reflecting on the major criticisms to the teacher education field.[9]

So what do the challengers "see" when they experience the teacher education establishment? (And remember, the teacher education establishment includes the 1,300+ teacher education programs that currently exist.) They see a set of omnipresent ideas—ideas that are, at times, experienced as oppressive and stifling, despite their liberatory intent. Those ideas include Progressivism—with its hallmark belief that the purpose of government is the good of the people as exemplified in the work of Jane Addams and Hull-House (Bentham, 1879; Himmelfarb, 1991). More specifically, they also see progressive education ideology, with its attention to the child and experience; its "naturalistic" and Romantic ideas about learning; its hands-on, project-oriented pedagogy; and its skepticism about authority (teachers are, after all, not lecturers but guides, facilitators, and collaborators). Critics also see, at best, ignorance of, and at worst, an active resistance to ideas antithetical to or different from their own progressive notions, including empirical evidence about the "science" of learning and teaching. Challengers also see a commitment to a particular version of social justice, one that argues that all teachers should have certain values, beliefs, and dispositions, including a commitment to becoming change agents, to remedying inequalities in society, and to giving each and every child access to future economic, intellectual, professional, and personal success. They also see a rhetoric of teachers-as-professionals without the attendant obligations that accompany that status. And they see a bureaucracy—swollen, slow, conservative.

Equally important is considering what some of the challengers fail to see. Many among them do not see a field where teachers leaving preparation programs are highly qualified. Many do not see teachers with impressive—or even sufficient—content knowledge. Many do not see teacher educators critiquing or closing down preparation programs that are mediocre. Many do not see innovation or responsiveness. Many do not see the critique of progressivism or skepticism about particular progressive pedagogies. Many do not see some hallmarks of professions: internal accountability, an agreed upon knowledge base, specialized and rigorous training, challenging licensure examinations. Many do not see agreement about what the content of teacher education programs should be, nor do many see evidence that the field keeps up with current research-based knowledge about effective teaching.

So what? For one, Bourdieu helps us understand that, whether we would like it or not, the borders between the orthodoxy and heterodoxy are permeable, ever shifting. According to Bourdieu (2005), the struggle for domination in the field is constant, and continues as long as the field can provide space for challengers to operate and manifest their ideas. In this process, agents who were disenfranchised in the past are the potential challengers looking for opportunity to take control over the field in the future. Indeed, the social field of teacher education looks very different than it did 20 years ago. A case in point: The 500+ alternative routes into teaching, which currently exist in 48 states and the District of Columbia. Alternative routes are now part of the establishment, as is Teach For America, Troops to Teachers, and the like. Accountability and standards that were seen by many in the establishment as inappropriate ideas that impose a business mindset on the field are now part of the education landscape. So are more than ever before ideas of merit pay, which can be seen on the agendas of the NBPTS and the ABCTE.

As Bourdieu (2005) claimed, outsiders can change, (sometimes) dramatically, the way fields operate. Domination of certain groups depends on the value of the different sources of capital they possess—economic, social, cultural, bureaucratic. When the value of a capital (its "rate of exchange") deteriorates, the authority that was based on it is questioned too. This means that other agents who bring with them new ideas—based on other sorts or combinations of capital—are able to gain more authority. So, for instance, alternative routes became a legitimate part of the structure of power in the field of teacher education when they were able to successfully question the structure of capital that supported and justified the "old" teacher preparation system run by the orthodoxy. Instead of the cultural capital of teacher educators that praised the importance of progressive pedagogy, the serious alternate routes suggest an alternative which argues for the importance of broad liberal art education and disciplinary specific content background for teachers. And with very little research to rely on—either research that explicates the professional knowledge base of teaching/teacher education or research that demonstrates the value-added of teacher education—the orthodoxy's capital further erodes.

So how do we—as members of the "old" orthodoxy—respond, especially as the value of our capital shifts? Not, we contend, by dismissing all criticism out of hand as wrong-headed, anti-democratic, conservative, or oppressive. Nor is it helpful to politely accept all criticism on face value. Certainly, all critics and criticisms are not equally worthy of serious engagement, but many are. And their criticism might help us see what forms of capital we need to develop. While Bourdieu argues that economic capital will trump all other forms of capital, he also noted the power of cultural capital.

If the traditional cultural capital of the teacher education establishment has eroded, what new forms of capital might we acquire? Perhaps it is time to agree upon a knowledge base that all teachers should acquire in teacher preparation programs. A common knowledge base has not thwarted the commitments of medical or law or architecture schools to tailor their professional programs to particular foci; it should be possible for us to have a national collective commitment while also leaving room for programs to have particular strengths. The development of such a knowledge base would also require a commitment to sound educational research that produces both publicly credible and professional responsible results. If we had a collective answer to the question, "What do teachers need to know and be able to do?" and we had some evidence of the effects of that teacher knowledge on students' learning and development, then it would not be as easy for our challengers to take over aspects of our work (teacher preparation or licensure). Such cultural capital would lead to other forms of capital, including more control over the bureaucracy.

But building up more cultural capital is not sufficient. We might also need to become much more open to internal and external critique, for democracies and vital institutions depend on dialectical tension. To the extent that there is even a kernel of truth in the image of the teacher education establishment reflected back to us by our challengers, we have some serious work to do.

But the dialogue we suggest is by no means an invitation for challengers to take over the positions of power in the field, nor is such a dialogue our idea alone (the voices of insiders and outsiders in this volume is testimony to that). Conserving the relative autonomy of the field of teacher education from the grasp of other fields (like the state bureaucracy, business corporations, and religions) is essential for the future of public education, for teacher preparation needs to be protected from control by a singular ideology (including from within). Thus, while autonomy does not necessarily mean conserving the old order, it definitely does not mean caving to the narrow interests and ideology of the economic elite whose interests are powerful and invasive. We cannot disregard the fact that some of the challengers' arguments were cultivated in conservative think tanks funded by these interests; there might be those among the challengers whose interest is solely in the demolition of the politically powerful teachers' unions (and they see teacher education as the softest spot in the system). Indeed, Bourdieu noted the tendency of economic elites to use their economic capital to establish their interests in a seemingly legitimate acceptable order that can supposedly be profitable to everybody. But we know that the open market does not lead to a more equitable society; the gap between the rich and the poor of this country only continues to yawn.

We also know that the challenges and the challengers are not a monolithic bloc. The jurisdictional challenges to teacher education of the last 20 years is not a simple story of a battle between the narrow ideas of an economic, conservative, sometime religious elite and the democratic, progressive, liberal teacher education establishment. We believe that the reality is much more complex. Some challenges do not represent the interests of economic elites, but rather the interests of other groups that have been systematically excluded from the discourse by the orthodoxy, because their ideas are simply different. Examples for these kinds of groups are the ABCTE in the area of certification; TEAC in the area of accreditation; and Teach for America in teacher preparation. Each of these organizations has been battered by some representatives of the teacher education orthodoxy who out-of-hand have dismissed the value of such alternatives. But if we care about democracy, these organizations (and others) should be allowed to participate in the conversation about how best to prepare high quality teachers. Disregarding and alienating these groups is far more dangerous, as other challengers who *do* represent narrow undemocratic interests can argue that the current system is authoritarian and undemocratic and thus should be replaced altogether. Indeed, all professions carry the burden of being self-serving, monopolistic, and exclusionary. They talk about their mission to serve society, while focusing on fortifying their privileges.

Neo-Weberians argue that professionals tend to monopolize their work environment and its associated benefits, thus increasing social inequality. This criticism is based on a conflict perspective that views the social reality as a place where individuals and groups struggle to gain control over various kinds of resources (Weber, 1952). Among and within professions, then, there is a constant tension between "insiders" (the professionals who wants to act as gatekeepers and restrict access to prevent oversupply) and "outsiders" (those who cannot overcome the obstacles put by professionals and therefore are denied of the benefits associated with membership). Collins (1990) argues that "instead of merely responding to market dynamics . . . occupations attempt to control market conditions. Those which are especially successful are the ones which we have come to call the professions" (p. 25). Professions look to secure and preserve their privileges from the instability of the labor market and possible competition of other professions by surrounding their work with social rituals and turning their everyday practice into one that generates sacred symbols (Abbott, 1988; Collins, 1990). Education and credentials are among the social rituals that establish public legitimacy, which—in turn—enables professionals to follow practices of market closure and exclusion of non-members (Collins, 1990; also see Tamir & Wilson, 2005).

These two contradicting approaches emphasize the ambivalent/ambiguous nature of professions, which might serve public interests, but at the same time might attempt to better its members. Pels (1995) conceptualizes it as a "Janus face": the concept of professional autonomy "came to display an intrinsic duplicity or duality in which good and evil, functional necessity and dysfunctional domination, appeared to conspire closely" (p. 81).

While there is reason to believe that, on some occasions, the public is better served by a professional entity rather of being solely exposed to the political and economic interests of state administration and business community, professionals—at the same time—must protect that public from the dangers of the profession's power and monopoly.

Can research help us here? Research and science will never be objective or disinterested. They are, by definition, part of the field that they seek to study. And the politics of the field have deep effects on the subject of study, the research questions, the method and design, and presentation of the outcomes. All the while, it would be unfair to stigmatize all research as an advocacy work. There is work that is productive and illuminating in the sense that researchers aim to promote and advance the field as a whole irrespectively of its current political structure. We do believe that work like the scholarship represented in this handbook, which is designed to help the members of our field think and act responsively and critically, in ways that might help foster a more open climate to diverse ideas (while keeping and developing a professional autonomous core that aims to serve the public good in a comprehensive and democratic way) is potentially contributive to the public. We believe that other scholarship—of different genres and about different questions—can also help, if done with methodological acuity and moral grace.

In the end, in our continuing efforts to build a teacher education system that prepares and nurtures well-prepared teachers, we must engage other groups in our discussion. This does not mean that we should strive for a false unity or a consensus, for these are unrealistic, paralyzing, and sometimes undemocratic practices. Every field needs some diversity of ideas and an active heterodoxy in order to stay vibrant, productive, and in the case of a "professional" field, a real servant of the public good. Moreover, as Bourdieu and Wacquant (1992) have argued, the whole notion of a social field rests on the premise of a struggle between social agents (when there is no heterodoxy, the field simply ceases to exist as a field). Nevertheless, the price to pay for more openness on the part of the current orthodoxy is not insignificant. Diversity and openness to other ideas and approaches means navigating more persistent and impassioned political dynamics and less likelihood of the old elite preserving and perpetuating its positions of power and ideas. On the other hand, the field as a whole can benefit from a more democratic struggle that would surely act first, as a fodder and catalyst of needed change, and second as a mechanism to garner more public legitimacy for the field. This kind of evolution might better position members of the ever-evolving teacher education orthodoxy in the social space, as a professional field that might become a better servant of the public good, enjoy more legitimacy, while significantly reducing its self-serving practices, the immanent ills of any and all professions. In the end, the social field of teacher education will only thrive to the extent that we embrace these challenges, sort through them carefully, and respond to those that will help us prepare better teachers for America's children.

NOTES

1 For one analysis of these arguments, see Cochran-Smith (2005) and Cochran-Smith and Fries (2001), as well as the entire issue of the *Journal of Teacher Education* devoted to the politics of teacher education (volume 56, number 3). Cochran-Smith and Fries (2001) assert that the critics are more inappropriate in their criticism; we are not as sanguine about this.

2 This phenomenon is common in the "culture wars," especially those concerning curriculum. For instance, political liberals who align with educationally conservative ideas (e.g. teach the "canon") are often misrepresented as political conservatives (Wilson, 2003). This can be frustrating for critics, and lead to further alienation from the teacher education establishment.

3 We are aware of the problematic nature of the use of terms like "objective" or "balanced," but

we believe that it is both possible and helpful to attend to multiple perspectives simultaneously all the while acknowledging that no perspective is purely objective.

4 We do not use the language of "establishment" in a derogatory way as sometimes is presumed given its connotation. But we do use it to capture the perspectives of critics who experience and interpret the sometimes loosely coupled system that supports traditional teacher preparation as a unified bloc, as articulated by Conant (1964). Conant and others also used the language of "educationists."

5 In drawing these maps, we draw both on the work of Bourdieu and that of Spring (1997). We do not aim here for a comprehensive map of all agents and associations. Indeed, such a map would be very difficult to read. However, we hope here to evoke some sense of the complexities of the social field of teacher education. A further complication is that the teacher education establishment is embedded in the larger education establishment, full of even more agents and relations. Similarly, while this picture focuses on the national landscape, there are state level and local associations and actors as well (where Murray (this volume) argues that most of the action actually takes place), and the considerable variation across states and localities is also not captured here.

6 Throughout the essay, we use teacher education "establishment," "system," or "orthodoxy" as shorthand for the loosely coupled set of individuals and organizations portrayed in Figure 48.1.

7 The questions that the challengers do not ask are equally important to the establishment. For instance, critics have not asked: To what extent do teacher education programs prepare teachers to teach diverse student populations and students with disabilities? This kind of question is very important to members of the teacher education establishment, and reviews of relevant research can be found in Cochran-Smith and Zeichner (2005) and Darling-Hammond and Bransford (2005).

8 Zeichner (2003) argues that there are three approaches to recruiting teachers: professionalism, deregulation, and social justice. These approaches roughly parallel three themes of the critiques we describe here. However, Zeichner folds the argument that teachers need nothing more than content knowledge into the deregulation critique. We prefer a different conceptualization since not all de-regulators argue that there is no professional knowledge save for content knowledge.

9 We note also as Merleau-Ponty's (1945/1962) explains in *Phenomenology of Perception*, meaning is derived from understanding our own and others' *perceptions*. Perceptions can be true or false; that is of no matter, for understanding from a phenomenological point of view is dependent on understanding people's objective experiences and interpretations of the world. Here we are not arguing that the challengers' perceptions are "true," only that they are important perceptions for us to seriously consider, for our social field changes, due in no small part to these forces.

REFERENCES

Abbott, D. A. (1988) *The system of professions: essay on the division of expert labor*. Chicago: University of Chicago Press.

Abell Foundation (2001a, October) *Teacher certification reconsidered: stumbling for quality*. Retrieved 26 December 2001 from http://www.abell.org

Abell Foundation (2001b, November) *Teacher certification reconsidered: stumbling for quality: a rejoinder*. Retrieved 26 December 2001 from http://www.abell.org

Allen, M. (2003) *Eight questions on teacher preparation: what does the research say?* Denver, CO: Education Commission of the States.

American Federation of Teachers (1998) *Building a profession: strengthening teacher preparation and induction: a report of the K-16 Teacher Education Task Force*. Washington, DC: Author.

Angus, D. L. (2001) *Professionalism and the public good: a brief history of teacher certification* (J. Mirel, ed.). Washington, DC: Thomas B. Fordham Foundation.

Ball, D. L. (1990) The mathematical understandings that prospective teachers bring to teacher education. *Elementary School Journal*, 90, 449–466.

Ball, D. L., Lubienski, S., & Mewborn, D. (2001) Research on teaching mathematics: the unsolved problem of teachers' mathematical knowledge. In V. Richardson (ed.), *Handbook of research on teaching* (4th ed., pp. 433–456). New York: Macmillan.

Ballou, D. & Podgursky, M. (1998) *The case against teacher certification*. National Affairs Inc. The Public Interest.

Ballou, D. & Podgursky, M. (2000a) Gaining control of professional licensing and advancement. In T. Loveless (ed.), *Conflicting missions? Teachers unions and educational reforms* (pp. 69–109). Washington, DC: The Brookings Institution.

Ballou, D. & Podgursky, M. (2000b) Reforming teacher preparation and licensing: what is the evidence? *Teachers College Record*, 102(1), 5–27.

Bentham, J. (1879) *An introduction to the principles of morals and legislation*. Oxford: Clarendon Press.

Bestor, A. E. (1953) *Educational wastelands: the retreat from learning in our public schools*. Urbana, IL: University of Illinois Press.

Bourdieu, P. (1984) *Distinction: a social critique of the judgment of taste*, trans. Richard Nice. Cambridge, MA: Harvard University Press.

Bourdieu, P. (1985) The social space and the genesis of groups. *Theory and Society*, 14(6), 723–744.

Bourdieu, P. (1986) The forms of capital. In J. Richardson (ed.), *Handbook of theory and research for the sociology of education* (pp. 241–260). Westport: Greenwood Press.

Bourdieu, P. (1988) *Homo academicus*. Stanford: Stanford University Press.

Bourdieu, P. (2005) *Questions in sociology*, trans. A. Lahav. Tel Aviv: Resling.

Bourdieu, P. & Wacquant, L. J. D. (1992) *An introduction to reflexive sociology*. Chicago: University of Chicago Press.

Boyd, D. J., Grossman, P., Lankford, H., Loeb, S., Michelli, N. M., & Wyckoff, J. (2006) Complex by design: investigating pathways into teaching in New York City schools. *Journal of Teacher Education*, 57, 155–166.

Bransford, J. D., Brown, A. L., & Cocking, R. R. (1999) *How people learn: brain, mind, experience, and school*. Washington, DC: Commmittee on Developments in the Science of Learning, Commission on Behavioral and Social Sciences and Education, National Research Council.

Chubb, J. E. (2001) The system. In T. M. Moe (ed.), *A primer on America's schools* (pp. 15–42). Stanford, CA: Hoover.

Cochran-Smith, M. (2005) Introduction to the issue: the politics of teacher education. *Journal of Teacher Education*, 56(4), 332–342.

Cochran-Smith, M. (2006) *Policy, practice and politics in teacher education: editorials for the Journal of Teacher Education*. Thousand Oaks, CA: Corwin Press, Sage Publications, and American Association of Colleges for Teacher Education.

Cochran-Smith, M. & Fries, M. K. (2001) Sticks, stones, and ideology: the discourse of reform in teacher education. *Educational Researcher*, 30(8), 3–15.

Cochran-Smith, M. & Zeichner, K. (eds.) (2005) *Studying teacher education: the report of the American Educational Research Association panel on research and teacher education*. Mahwah, NJ: Lawrence Erlbaum Associates.

Collins, R. (1990) Market closure and the conflict theory of the professions. In M. Burrage & R. Torstendahl (eds.), *Professions in theory and history: rethinking the study of the professions* (pp. 24–42). London, Newbury Park, and New Delhi: Sage Publications.

Conant, J. B. (1964) *The education of American teachers*. New York: McGraw Hill.

Cusick, P. A. (1992) *The educational system: its nature and logic*. New York: Addison-Wesley.

Damon, W. (2005) Personality tests: the dispositional dispute in teacher preparation today and what to do about it. *Fwd:*, 2(3). Retrieved 10 March, 2006 from http://www.edexcellence.net/institute/publication/publication.cfm?id=343

Darling-Hammond, L. (2000a) Reforming teacher preparation and licensing: debating the evidence. *Teachers College Record*, 102(1), 28–56.

Darling-Hammond, L. (2000b) Teacher quality and student achievement: a review of state policy evidence. *Education Policy Analysis Archives*, 8, http://epaa.asu.edu/epaa/v8n1/

Darling-Hammond, L. (2002) Research and rhetoric on teacher certification: a response to "Teacher Certification Reconsidered." *Education Policy Analysis Archives*, 10(36), 1–54.

Darling-Hammond, L. & Youngs, P. (2002) Defining "highly qualified teachers": what does the "scientifically-based research" actually tell us? *Educational Researcher*, 31, 13–25.

Darling-Hammond, L., Berry, B., & Thoreson, A. (2001) Does teacher certification matter? Evaluating the evidence. *Educational Evaluation and Policy Analysis*, 23(1), 57–77.

Darling-Hammond, L. & Bransford, J. with LePage, P., Hammerness, K., & Duffy, H. (eds.) (2005) *Preparing teachers for a changing world: what teachers should learn and be able to do*. San Francisco: Jossey-Bass.

Dewey, J. (1902) *The child and the curriculum*. Chicago: The University of Chicago Press.

Erickson, F. & Gutierrez, K. (2002) Culture, rigor, and science in educational research. *Educational Researcher*, 31(8), 21–24.

Felter, M. (1999) High school staff characteristics and mathematics test results. *Education Policy Analysis Archives*, 7, http://epaa.asu.edu/epaa/v7n9.html

Finn, C. E. (2001) Getting better teachers. In T. Moe (ed.), *A primer on America's schools*. Stanford: Hoover Institution Press.

Finn, C. E. (2003) Foreword. In Broad Foundation and the Thomas B. Fordham Foundation, *Better leaders for America's schools* (pp. 5–8). Washington, DC: Thomas B. Fordham Foundation.

Finn, C. E. & Ravitch, D. (1996) *Education reform, 1995–1996: a report from the Educational Excellence Network to its Education Policy Committee and the American people*. Indianapolis: Hudson Institute.

Goldhaber, D. D. & Brewer, D. J. (2000) Does teacher certification matter? High school teacher certification status and student achievement. *Educational Evaluation and Policy Analysis*, 22, 129–145.

Goldhaber, D. D. & Brewer, D. J. (2001) Evaluating the evidence on teacher certification: a rejoinder. *Educational Evaluation and Policy Analysis*, 23(1), 79–86.

Grossman, P. L. (2004, April) *The research we want, the research we need: a teacher educator's perspective*. Paper present at the annual meeting of the American Educational Research Association. San Diego, CA.

Hess, F. H. (2001) *Tear down this wall: the case for a radical overhaul of teacher certification*. Washington, DC: Progressive Policy Institute.

Hess, F. H. (2002) Break the link. *Education Next*. Retrieved 15 October, 2005 from http://www.educationnext.org/20021/22.html

Hess, F. H. (2004) *Common sense school reform*. Hampshire, UK: Palgrave Macmillan.

Hess, F. H. (2006, February 5) Schools of reeducation? *Washington Post*. B07.

Hess, F. H. (2005) The predictable, but unpredictably personal, politics of teacher licensure. *Journal of Teacher Education*, 56(3), 192–198.

Hess, F. H., Rotherham, A. J., & Walsh, K. (eds.), (2004) *A qualified teacher in every classroom? Appraising old answers and new ideas*. Cambridge, MA: Harvard Education Publishing Group.

Himmelfarb, G. (1991) *Poverty and compassion: the moral imagination of the late Victorians*. New York: Knopf.

Hirsch, E. D. (1996) *The schools we need and why we don't have them*. New York: Doubleday.

Hirsch, E. D. (2006) *The knowledge deficit: closing the shocking education gap for American children*. New York: Houghton Mifflin.

Humphrey, D. C. & Wechsler, M. E. (2005, September 2) Insights into alternative certification: initial findings from a national study. *Teachers College Record*.

Ingersoll, R. (1996) *Out-of-field teaching and educational equality*. Washington, DC: National Center for Education Statistics.

Izumi, L. T. with Coburn, K. G. (2001) *Facing the classroom challenge: teacher quality and teacher training in California's schools of education*. San Francisco: Pacific Research Institute for Public Policy.

Johnson, S. M., Birkeland, S. E., & Peske, H. G. with Munger, M. S. (2005) *A difficult balance: incentives and quality control in alternative certification programs*. Cambridge, MA: Harvard Graduate School of Education.

Koerner, J. S. (1963) *The miseducation of American teachers*. Boston: Houghton Mifflin.

Kristof, N. D. (2006, April 30) Opening classroom doors. *The New York Times.*

Labaree, D. F. (2004) *The trouble with ed schools.* New Haven, CT: Yale University Press.

Lasley III, T. J., Siedentop, D., & Yinger, R. (2006) A systemic approach to enhancing teacher quality. *Journal of Teacher Education,* 57(1), 13–21.

Levine, A. (2006) *Educating school teachers.* Washington, DC: The Education Schools Project.

Lynd, A. (1953) *Quackery in the public schools.* Boston: Little, Brown.

Ma, L. (1999) *Knowing and teaching elementary mathematics: teachers' understanding of fundamental mathematics in China and the United States.* Mahwah, NJ: Lawrence Erlbaum.

Merleau-Ponty, M. (1945/1962) *Phenomenology of perception,* trans. C. Smith. London: Routledge & Kegan Paul.

Mitchell, D. E. & Kerchner, C. T. (1983) Labor relations and teacher policy. In L. S. Shulman & G. Sykes (eds.), *Handbook of teaching and policy* (pp. 214–238). New York: Longman.

Mitchell, R. & Barth, P. (1999) How teacher licensing tests fall short. *Thinking K-16,* 3(1), 3–23.

Monk, D. H. (1994) Subject area preparation of secondary mathematics and science teachers and student achievement. *Economics of Education Review,* 13, 125–145.

National Commission on Excellence and Education (1983) *A nation at risk: the imperative for educational reform.* Washington, DC: U.S. Government Printing Office.

National Commission on Teaching and America's Future (1996) *What matters most: teaching for America's future.* Washington, DC: Author.

National Commission on Teaching and America's Future (2003) *No dream denied: a pledge to America's future.* Washington, DC: Author.

National Governor's Association (2006) *Education reform policy.* Retrieved 20 April, 2006 from http://www.nga.org/portal/site/nga. Washington, DC: Author.

National Reading Panel (2000) *Report of the National Reading Panel: teaching children to read: an evidence-based assessment of the scientific research literature on reading and its implications for reading instruction* (NIH Publication No. 00–4769). Washington, DC: National Institute of Child Health and Development. *Report of the National Reading Panel.*

National Research Council (2001) *Adding it up: helping children learn mathematics,* J. Kilpatrick, J. Swafford & B. Findell (eds.). Washington, DC: Mathematics Learning Study Committee, Center for Education, Division of Behavioral and Social Sciences and Education. National Academy Press.

National Research Council (2002) *Scientific research in education,* Shavelson, R. J. & Towne, L. (eds.). Washington, DC: National Academy Press.

Null, J. W. (2006) We must start over: a new vision for the profession of teaching. In J. W. Null & D. Ravitch (eds.), *Forgotten heroes of American education: the great tradition of teaching teachers* (pp. xix–xxix). Greenwich, CT: Information Age Publishing.

Pels, D. (1995) Knowledge politics and anti-politics: toward a critical appraisal of Bourdieu's concept of intellectual autonomy. *Theory and Society,* 24(1), 79–104.

Podgursky, M. (2004) Improving academic performance in U.S. public schools: why teacher licensing is (almost) irrelevant. In F. M. Hess, A. J. Rotherham, & K. Walsh (eds.), *A qualified teacher in every classroom? Appraising old answers and new ideas* (pp. 255–277). Cambridge, MA: Harvard Education Publishing Group.

Prestine, N. A. (1991) Political system theory as an explanatory paradigm for teacher education reform. *American Educational Research Journal,* 28, 237–274.

Ramirez, H. A. (2004) The shift from hands-off: the federal role in supporting and defining teacher quality. In F. M. Hess, A. J. Rotherham, & K. Walsh (eds.), *A qualified teacher in every classroom? Appraising old answers and new ideas* (pp. 49–79). Cambridge, MA: Harvard Education Publishing Group.

Raudenbush, S. W. (2005) Learning from attempts to improve schooling: the contribution of methodical diversity. *Educational Researcher,* 34, 25–31.

Ravitch, D. (2000) *Left back: a century of battles over school reform.* New York: Simon & Schuster.

Rochester, J. M. (2002) *Class warfare: besieged schools, bewildered parents, betrayed kids and the attack on excellence*. San Francisco: Encounter Books.

Schulte, A. K. & Zeichner, K. M. (2001) What we know and don't know from peer-reviewed research about alternative teacher certification programs. *Journal of Teacher Education*, 52, 266–282.

Shulman, L. S. (2005) Teacher education does not exist. *Stanford Educator*, 7. Retrieved 12 March, 2006 from http://www.ed.stanford.edu/suse/news-bureau/educator-newsletter.html

Smith, M. (1949) *And madly teach: a layman looks at public education*. Chicago: Henry Regnery.

Spring, J. (1997) *Political agendas for education: from the Christian Coalition to the Green Party*. Mahwah, NJ: Lawrence Erlbaum Associates.

Stoddart, T. & Floden, R. E. (1995) *Traditional and alternative routes to teacher certification: issues, assumptions, and misconceptions*. National Center for Research on Teacher Learning, Michigan State University.

Tamir, E. (2006) *The politics of education reform: state power and the field of educational policy in New Jersey*. Unpublished doctoral dissertation, Michigan State University, East Lansing, MI.

Tamir, E. & Wilson, S. M. (2005) Who should guard the gates? Evidentiary and professional warrants for claiming jurisdiction. *Journal of Teacher Education*, 56(4), 332–342.

Thomas B. Fordham Foundation (1999) *The teachers we need and how to get more of them: a manifesto*. Washington, DC: Author.

U.S. Department of Education (2002) *Meeting the highly qualified teachers challenge: the secretary's annual report on teacher quality*. Washington, DC: Author.

U.S. Department of Education (2003) *Meeting the highly qualified teachers challenge: the secretary's second annual report on teacher quality*. Washington, DC: Author.

Walsh, K., Glaser, D., & Wilcox, D. D. (2006) *What education schools aren't teaching about reading and what elementary teachers aren't learning*. Washington, DC: National Council on Teacher Quality.

Weber, M. (1952) *Economy and society: an outline of interpretive sociology (Vol. 1–3)*. New York: Bedminster Press.

Whitehurst, G. R. (2002) *Scientifically based research on teacher quality: research on teacher preparation and professional development*. Paper presented at the White House Conference on Preparing Tomorrow's Teachers. Washington, DC.

Will, G. (2006, January 16) Ed schools versus education. *Newsweek*.

Wilson, S. M. (2003) *California dreaming: reforming mathematics education*. New Haven: Yale University Press.

Wilson, S. M. (in progress) *Jurisdictional challenges to teacher education*.

Wilson, S. M. & Floden, R. F. (2002, May) Addendum to *Teacher preparation research: current knowledge, recommendations, and priorities for the future*. Report commissioned by the Education Commission of the States. Also available *as Creating effective teachers: concise answers for hard questions*. Washington, DC: ERIC Clearinghouse on Teaching and Teacher Education.

Wilson, S. M., Floden, R. F., & Ferrini-Mundy, J. (2001, March) *Teacher preparation research: current knowledge, recommendations, and priorities for the future*. Center for the Study of Teaching Policy, University of Washington, Seattle, WA. (Available online at http://www.depts.washington.edu/ctpmail/.Reports.html# TeacherPrep)

Zeichner, K. M. (2003) The adequacies and inadequacies of three current strategies to recruit, prepare, and retain the best teachers for all students. *Teachers College Record*, 105(3), 490–519.

Zeichner, K. M. (2005) Research on alternate routes into teaching. In M. Cochran-Smith & K. M. Zeichner (eds.), *Studying teacher education: the report of the American Educational Research Association panel on research and teacher education* (pp. 656–689). Mahwah, NJ: Lawrence Erlbaum.

Zumwalt, K. (2005) Teachers' characteristics: research on indicators of quality. In M. Cochran-Smith & K. Zeichner (eds.) (2005) *Studying teacher education: the report of the American Educational Research Association panel on research and teacher education* (pp. 157–260). Mahwah, NJ: Lawrence Erlbaum Associates.

Part 7
Artifacts

7.1 The elementary and the complete examiner[1]

Isaac Stone, A.M.,
Principal Kenosha High School

Source: Isaac Stone, *The Elementary and the Complete Examiner; or Candidate's Assistant: Prepared to Aid Teachers in Securing Certificates from Boards of Examiners*. New York and Chicago: A. S. Barnes and Company, 1864

DIVISION OF FRACTIONS

1 How do you proceed when either of the fractions is a mixed number or a compound fraction?
2 Divide $3/4$ by $2/5$ and give *clearly* the rule and reason.
3 What is the sum and difference of $\frac{49\,5/8}{97}$ and $\frac{34\,3/5}{146\,3/11}$?
4 A man being asked how many sheep he had, said he had them in three fields; in the first he had 63, which was $7/8$ of what he had in the second, and that $5/3$ of what he had in the second was just 4 times what he had in the third. How many sheep had he in all?

DUODECIMALS

1 If one inch be divided into 12 equal parts, what is each part called?
2 Give rule and reason for multiplication and division of duo-decimals.

DECIMAL FRACTIONS

1 How does the value change from the left toward the right?

THEORY AND PRACTICE

1 How would you organize a school?
2 What spirit should one possess who has access to the *sanctuary* of the mind?
3 What motive should govern the teacher, moral or pecuniary?
4 What especial preparation does he need who is to play upon the "harp whose tones, *whose living tones,* are left forever in the strings?"
5 What can you say of the responsibility of the *teacher*?
6 What can you say of the ventilation of the school-room?
7 What should be the appearance of the school-room?
8 What can you say of the teacher's responsibility for the health of a child?
9 Would a knowledge of *Mental Philosophy* be a valuable acquisition for a teacher? Why?
10 Should a teacher be held responsible for the intellectual growth of his pupil?
11 Describe the ORDER OF STUDIES to be pursued by the pupil.
12 Should the teacher be responsible for the moral and religious training of his pupil?

NOTE

1 For space limitation we only present a sample of questions from the original text.

7.2 Training of teachers

W. C. Bagley
Teachers College, Columbia University, New York

Source: W. C. Bagley, Training of teachers. *Proceedings of the National Education Association, USA*, 1919, pp. 499–504

American policies regarding the professional preparation of teachers have pretty faithfully reflected the attitude of the public toward teaching as a career. It is unnecessary in this audience to rehearse the facts regarding our backwardness in this, the most important function of a democracy. We all know that our normal schools, generally speaking, are more penuriously supported than any other institutions of similar grade or approximate significance and responsibility. We know that they do not hold a place in the public esteem that is comparable to that of the colleges of liberal arts, engineering, agriculture, medicine, or law. We know that they suffer in consequence, both in the advantages that they are able to offer and in their attractiveness to ambitious youth.

All this is clear enough to us, but for some reason it is not clear to the public. There are certain fundamental facts that deserve to be reiterated until their deep significance has sunk home. There are four upon which I should lay particular emphasis.

In the first place the high-school graduates now entering the normal schools to prepare for public-school service represent a significantly lower level of mental ability than do the high-school graduates who are looking toward other professions. This fact is definitely suggested by investigations that have been undertaken in one large and typical state; that the same condition obtains in many if not most of the other states is voucht for by the testimony of those long familiar with the situation. Not only are the great masses of public-school teachers relatively short-lived in the service—half of all teachers remaining in the schools but four years or less, and fully one-fourth of all leaving at or before the close of the second year—not only are the majority of these teachers without professional training, but even the relatively few who are now preparing with any degree of seriousness for the work do not represent, as a group, the best available material. There is no doubt that this condition has developed chiefly within the past ten or fifteen years, and that the normal schools before that time were selective of a relatively better grade of student; but with the ever increasing opportunities for women to enter other callings, the situation in the public-school service is certain to become more and more serious unless immediate steps are taken to make classroom teaching a permanent, attractive, honored, and well-rewarded profession.

Another fact of which the public should become thoroughly aware is the low rank that we hold among the civilized nations with respect to the preparation of our public-school teachers. Just before the war began, for example, two-thirds of the elementary teachers in England were professionally prepared for their responsible work. I mean by this that these teachers had had a preparation that would be equivalent in this country to graduation from a four-year high school plus two years of normal-school training. In the United States not more than one-fifth of the elementary teachers have had so extended a preparation.

Nor is our standing low only in comparison with countries like England and France. One of our South America sister-republics, Chile, supports sixteen normal schools for a population of 4,000,000—five more than Massachusetts operates for a population about equal to that of Chile. While these Chilean normal schools do not require our equivalent of high-school graduation for admission, they keep their students in residence for six years and provide for them not only tuition but board, lodging, and clothing during this long period of professional study and training. Today 40 percent of the teachers in the elementary schools of Chile are graduates of these extended professional curricula, and the remaining 60 percent have had some professional preparation.

It is clear that if our people wish to continue their leadership in a democratic world they must be awakened to the significance of this most important democratic function of providing competent teachers for the children of the nation. Practically every other civilized country has adopted for the education of its public-school teachers the same liberal policy that we have adopted for the training of our officers for the army and the navy; that is, the selection of candidates upon a rigorous basis of merit and the careful education of these candidates at public expense. In the United States as in other countries the overwhelming majority of the public-school teachers are recruited from families that are unable at their own expense to send their children to normal schools for extended periods of professional preparation. There are two ways out of the difficulty. One is to require adequate professional preparation and limit certification to those individuals who can afford to secure this preparation. The other is to require professional preparation and then keep the profession open to all qualified candidates by providing the training at public expense. Our people have adopted neither method. They have kept the standards of certification so low that candidates readily secure licenses without any preparation worthy of the name, and they have established normal schools with the expectation that students will enroll voluntarily in large numbers for the privilege of securing training at their own expense and then competing with those who have been permitted to enter the profession by the back door. The result is one that could easily be predicted. Not only do the normal schools, as we have seen, fail to attract the best available talent, but they graduate less than one-sixth of the number of recruits needed each year to fill the vacancies in the elementary schools alone. Most of the graduates go into those city systems that are progressive enough to demand some measure of professional preparation, leaving to immature and untrained recruits the rural and village schools, in which more than one-half of the nation's children receive all of their schooling.

A third fact that should be brought before our people is that the kind of education that they expect the public schools to provide for their children can never be provided unless the standards for the preparation of teachers are raised far beyond what they are today even in our most progressive city school systems. Of course not all of the miracles that some people expect from the public schools can ever be brought about, any more than anyone can ever square the circle, or construct a cube that will be double the contents of a given cube, or devise a machine for perpetual motion. The sooner we recognize some of these impossibilities the better it will be for our cause, for good school men and even professors of education sometimes lose their heads over beautiful dreams that could be realized only if we were able to go back to the beginnings of things and reconstruct the human race on a different pattern. But even modest and eminently sane hopes of educational betterment must await a general level of teaching skill and teaching insight now to be found only in the rarest cases. Many parents who have a vague but sincere conviction that their children are not getting what they should from the schools are not expecting miracles, but they are expecting goods that cannot be delivered by a teacher whose equipment comprises at most a four-year high-school education, with a little professional training which has attempted in one or two years to prepare her to teach every subject and supervise every activity in an eight-year educational program.

A fourth fact deserves especially serious consideration. Our neglect of adequate preparation for teachers has led to the creation of a system which was designed to compensate for this neglect, but which in itself bears the seeds of very great evils. I mean frankly the effort to compensate for poor preparation thru elaborate systems of supervision. This is rapidly bringing into being a group of superteachers, if I may use the term, better trained and much better paid than the classroom teachers and bearing to the latter a relation akin to that of the foreman of a factory to the "hands" of the factory. More and more the plans and specifications for teaching are being prepared by these superteachers. While they have been selected in the past very largely upon the basis of their success in doing actual first-hand teaching, this condition is rapidly passing, and in any case their work means a detachment from the real first-hand problems of teaching and managing boys and girls. The classroom teacher, instead of looking upon his work as a fine art, is forced to look upon it as a mechanical trade; instead of being the artist that he should be, the present tendency is forcing him more and more insistently into the position of the artisan.

Now if a painter achieves success he does not forthwith surrender his pigments and his palette to a group of amateurs and expect them to paint great pictures under his direction. Nor does the successful actor retire permanently to the wings, with the expectation that the stage hands and the scene shifters can, even under his direction, read his lines to crowded houses. Nor does the successful novelist hire a group of hacks to put together his next great book. But if the great artist still agonizes over his first-hand materials, if the successful actor, not in spite of, but because of, the transcendent fame that he has won, still acts before the footlights, if the novelist still constructs his own plots and delineates his own characters, it is because they know that each added increment of success brings its corresponding reward and recognition. Until in the work of education we can insure that the teacher can profitably capitalize his success and still remain in first-hand contact with the materials of his art, teaching will remain the sorriest of the trades.

It may be too late to correct in industry the evils that the factory system has brought about. It is not too late in education. The problem is immediately to place teaching in the only position in which it can hope to render its all-important service—to give the actual work of first-hand teaching its true status as a fine art. This means above all a vast extension of our agencies for the initial preparation of teachers. This will solve the problem, and nothing else will.

I am convinced that it is the most shortsighted of policies to attempt to prepare a teacher in two years to fit successfully into any grade that happens to have a vacancy when she seeks appointment. What the child of eight or nine or ten years needs in the way of teaching is not what the beginner needs or what the eighth-grade pupil needs. The teaching difficulties that are involved in only a circumscribed range of school work are enormous when one comes to catalog them. The demands upon even a fourth-grade teacher who would do well the work of that grade are as severe and as exacting as any individual should be expected to bear. Until we dispel the fatuous delusion that the equipment of the teacher must vary directly as the age of the pupil, we shall never have in the elementary school the level of expert service that we must have if these basic schools are to do their basic work. If the people will give our normal schools four years to prepare each type of teacher—rural-school, primary, intermediate, upper-grade, or junior high-school and high-school; if they will provide scholarships for qualified students seeking entrance to these normal schools; if they will limit teachers' licenses to graduates of these normal schools; if they will insist that the normal school is to train teachers, and that this job is big enough and important enough to absorb all of its energies; if they will insist that every normal school is operated for the benefit of the whole people and not for the pecuniary advantage of the local community in which it has been placed; if they will determine, in consequence, that all the schools of every community having a normal school shall be available as laboratories of teaching, and will be firm in their determination to the point of moving the school to another place if the profiteers are obstinate; if they will pay to normal-school instructors salaries just a trifle higher than instructors in any other group of higher or professional institutions receive (for this, in view of their tremendous responsibilities, is no more than the due of those who prepare teachers for the public schools); if the people will take these simple steps the problem will be solved, and with it will be solved a host of other irritating and perplexing problems that beset public education.

I have purposely characterized these as "simple" steps, for they are simple. In the aggregate they bear no comparison in difficulty to any one of a half-dozen collective achievements of our people during the past two years: the establishment of the selective draft, the floating of Liberty Loans, the inauguration of the shipbuilding program, the feeding of the Allies, the sending of two million soldiers to France. Nor would the cost be prohibitive, even in this day of high taxes. The nation has spent for intoxicating liquors in the past years no less than $1,500,000,000 annually. It seems that this is to be saved in the future. It will be augmented by the increase production due to the disuse of intoxicants. Let us assume, conservatively, that the available wealth of the nation will be increased by an annual increment of two billion dollars because of prohibition. Where should this increase go? Is it improper to suggest that a fair portion—say one-half—should go to public education? Certainly the public schools have done their share to bring about this consummation. We are told, of course, that the prime cause of prohibition in this country has been the great development of industry; but other countries have undergone industrial development—are much more thoroughly industrialized even than we are. Yet there seems to be no visible movement toward prohibition. In this country one factor, however, has operated in a measure unapproached elsewhere. For two generations the schools have explicitly and systematically indoctrinated the children of the nation against alcohol. The mills of education grind slowly, but eventually they grind exceeding small.

Is it unreasonable to claim for education one-half of the impending saving? A billion dollars added to our annual educational budget would solve our problem in a trice. We could raise the level of public-school services to a point unapproacht and unapproachable by any other nation. We could put into every classroom in the country within a decade—into the rural and village schools as well as the urban schools—a teacher adequately prepared to do in a masterly way the work that that school involves. We could pay to that teacher a salary that would make him not only content but anxious to make the work a real and permanent career. We could pay to the rural-school teacher the differential that is needed to get into these schools and keep in them the men and women who, in these strategic positions, can do more for the future of our country than any other group. We could make our normal schools into great educational West Points, where the best talent that the country produces could be instructed and trained and inspired to do the most important work that can be done in a great democracy.

7.3 Building a still better teaching profession for our times[1]

W. E. Peik
Dean, College of Education, University of
Minnesota

Source: W. E. Peik, The education of teachers as viewed by the
profession. *Proceedings of the National Commission on Teacher
Education and Professional Standards, National Education
Association of the United States*, 1948, pp. 9–17. (Official group
reports of the Bowling Green Conference held at Bowling Green State
University, Bowling Green, Ohio, June 30–July 3.)

The assignment to us here is extraordinarily crucial and timely. At Chautauqua, two years ago, we emphasized the emergency in the supply of teachers. At Oxford, we stressed the improvement of teaching service for advancement of democratic standards of living through education.

Here at Bowling Green, we are now to come to closer grips with teachers' full, pre-service preparation for professional service.

We shall need a working philosophy of education as a frame of reference for teacher education. What is the over-all objective of teacher education today? I tried to state it for my own satisfaction recently and this is what I put down:

We must build to still higher levels of competence a profession of teachers. They must be better selected; broadly, functionally, and well educated; especially competent, responsible, and scholarly in teaching fields. They must be zealous and professionally both more informed and more skilled than they have been before. These competencies they must have that they may educate the children of America to their full growth and development that as future citizens and free men they may carry forward the democratic way of life in our homes, in our communities, and in our country; may earn security for themselves and become, also, more able than we seem to be, to meet their full responsibility to world citizenship; then, if there still be time and opportunity, may prevent any world war from ever happening again.

In ability, we can be matched many times from a great profession of 1,200,000 elementary, secondary and higher, public and private teachers, which includes the greatest minds of our times. However, in official leadership (which the contingent here holds at this time), in legal and organizational positions, you leaders can barely be matched once over again. It is that leadership, your representativeness of state and national positions, that makes this conference significant for American education. It is our new world role as a leading nation that makes this conference important now. It is the world in which we are leaders, and which is in part a rubble heap, for the most part miserable and three-fifths illiterate, while it is sitting on an atomic bomb, that makes this meeting of American teachers important now. It is the fact that, in this world leadership, democracy itself is on trial, that it often appears to be bungling along, and that it may not always have the chance to bungle along in the future, which makes this conference of teachers important. Never in the history of teacher education in our nation have so many leaders sat together to review the basic, undergraduate, professional education of American teachers in terms of the job that lies ahead. That is why Bowling Green must not fail the American teaching profession and through them, perhaps, America's destiny in world relations.

EVALUATE TEACHER PREPARATION, INSTITUTIONAL ACCREDITATION, AND CERTIFICATION STANDARDS

As practitioners who are in daily contact with our work, we must develop the standards and content of our preparation. Let us examine a few of these about which we ought to be united throughout the nation:

Require selection and limitation of supply to demand

Society has not screened out sufficiently those who are not endowed for so high a service and so difficult a vocation as that of the teacher. Too many teachers still come from the lower half of high school senior scholastic ability. Too many still do not have those human qualities which do endear good teachers to pupils. A few care too little about ethical or cultural standards. With the oversupply of secondary teachers, but not of well-selected, completely prepared secondary teachers which is developing now, state departments and colleges must have the wisdom and courage to do something more than they have in the past about selection and oversupply.

Bowling Green must show the way. Have we the courage to speak plainly to our institutions? Seventeen hundred junior colleges, arts colleges, teachers colleges, and universities can destroy the quality, status, and support of our profession. No single institution of our land has the right to prepare just anybody for teaching, in any convenient way, in any amount, unless it meets actual needs of supply, high standards of selection and preparation, which the teaching profession itself should now promote with specificity and with unanimity.

Evaluate and promote the teacher's education and training for his duties as a teacher

The teacher's education consists of four closely related areas: (1) the common general education of all; (2) additional professionalized general education for respective jobs; (3) specialization in teaching fields; and (4) the professional theory and practice of teaching.

INSTITUTIONAL RESPONSIBILITY AND COOPERATION IN TEACHER EDUCATION

Teachers colleges are becoming state colleges. Teacher education should not and need not suffer in the process. In fact a state college, larger and broader than a small teachers college, can do a better job of selection, of guidance, of general education, of professionalizing subject matter and of professional orientation and training, because there are larger enrollments for better specialization, for easier adjustment to special group needs, and for more economic unit costs. But the education of teachers must never become a neglected side line in a state college; of this there is danger and evidence of occurrence. The teaching profession is larger than all other learned professions combined. It is a main function of any institution that undertakes it.

Liberal arts colleges, which desire to prepare teachers, must win this right by appropriate provision for it in curriculum reorganization, guidance, selection, supervised student teaching, clinics for special child study, strengthened departments of education, and participation by their staffs in state associations, public school conferences. Teacher education is professional education in addition to liberal education. If a faculty does not wish to do vocational preparation, and does not mingle with the profession, it should not want to prepare teachers for certification.

In general, there should be fewer but stronger, more carefully accredited teacher preparing institutions of all types in our country. A college or department of education must cooperate with the whole institution for teacher education in a fine spirit of leadership and coordination. The whole institution must cooperate with the department or college of education in the same spirit. The time for making faces at each other is long past.

Upon the consciences of well-meaning but sometimes erring staffs must be placed the responsibility for retarding development of the professionalization of teaching. The presence of a staff antagonistic to professional preparation, especially if it is in a position to cripple it, should be considered *prima facie* evidence of a failure to meet standards. Fortunately this situation is clearing up rapidly.

A LONGER PERIOD OF PROFESSIONAL PREPARATION

The pre-service education of teachers within the pattern of adequate general education, professionalized subjects, competency in broad fields, adequate preparation in the theory and practice of education, together with sufficient electives to permit individualized adjustments to interest, special talents, and deficiencies, cannot be done in four years. It requires a minimum of five years. The five-year curriculum for teaching can best be met by an expansion of all elements of the undergraduate pattern described before. I believe it should be met with the award of an advanced professional degree by the professional school itself and not by the graduate school.

I have referred to the size of the assignments in terms of number of teachers, pupils, and laymen to be reached; in terms of the special problems of action-planning, publicity, public relations, unification of our profession through nationwide organization; the trimming of supply to demand; better selection, functional general education, broad specialization for the teacher's work, more complete professional orientation and training; the extension of the period of preparation for all teachers; better graduate training for research specialists; and to other problems that are related to these. I believe that the signs are favorable and that an outstanding contribution will be made by us. We must plan to build a still stronger profession of teachers for our times.

NOTE

1 Excerpts from abstract of conference keynote address.

7.4 On the education and certification of teachers[1]

Arthur E. Bestor, Jr.
University of Illinois

Source: Arthur E. Bestor, Jr., On the education and certification of teachers. *School and Society* 78(2016), 1953, pp. 81–87

The division between elementary and secondary education on the one hand and higher education on the other is an administrative fact, natural and probably inescapable. In recent years in the United States, however, it has been converted into a momentous intellectual schism, threatening the soundness of our public educational system and even the intellectual welfare of the nation. The schism has spread to the universities, where the education of teachers has come almost completely under the control of departments or colleges of education, so-called, which are affected little, if at all, by the educational thinking of the rest of the university faculties.

This process has been facilitated by a misuse and misapplication of the word *education*. The Department of Education actually concerns itself with "the art, practice or profession of teaching; especially, systematized learning or instruction concerning principles and methods of teaching." The quoted words are the dictionary definition, not of *education*, but of *pedagogy*. What calls itself a Department or College of Education is, properly speaking, only a Department of Pedagogy.

This is not a mere matter of words. The faulty terminology at present used has warped, in subtle but dangerous ways, the thinking of almost everyone in America concerning public educational policy. The fact—obvious, undeniably, and yet forgotten—is that the university *as a whole* is concerned with education. Every department in it is a department of education in the legitimate sense of that word. My own department is actually a Department of Education in Historical Thinking. The term Department of History is merely a convenient abbreviation of this concept. The division that calls itself a Department of Education is in reality a Department of Education in Pedagogical Methods. It has no right whatever to abbreviate its name to Department of Education and thereby to imply that it has a greater concern with education than some other department.

The abuses to which this faulty terminology has led are numerous and obvious. Taking advantage of the unfortunate laxness of academic terminology, professors of education represent themselves to the general public as the only members of university faculties who need to be consulted with respect to the ultimate aims and purposes of education. And they have contrived to put across the completely unfounded notion that the proper way to prepare for a career in teaching is to take course work in education, so-called, that is to say, in pedagogy.

Let me not be misunderstood. Pedagogy itself—that is to say, the careful investigation of the processes of teaching and learning—is a legitimate field of research. Important work has been done, and it must continue to be done, in investigating the psychology of learning, in developing effective textbooks and teaching aids, in experimenting with classroom procedures, in adapting instruction to students of differing intellectual capacity. As a teacher of history, I am directly interested in every improvement that increases the effectiveness with which history is being taught. But the effective teacher of history requires many qualities of mind and personality, many varieties of knowledge, and many intellectual skills, among which pedagogy is only one.

Obviously every teacher must have some knowledge and skill in pedagogy just as a doctor must have some adeptness at what we call "bedside manner." It is far from certain that the best way to acquire these skills is by listening to lectures about them. But granting that it is, such courses are not the central thing in the preparation for either profession. What counts in a doctor is his knowledge of medicine, and what counts in a teacher is his knowledge of the subject he is teaching. To expect to produce a good teacher by training him mainly in pedagogy is as foolish as to expect to produce a good doctor by loading him down with courses in bedside manner. And yet at one midwestern university there is a course entitled "Science in the Elementary School," the catalogue description of which says frankly, "no science background is assumed and no attempt is made to cover content." If medical schools were run as colleges of education are, we would all be done to death by cheery and plausible doctors who would know all about *how* to practice medicine but who would not be quite sure whether human beings have gizzards or not.

The preparation of teachers for the public schools is one of the most important functions of the American university. It is a function of the university as a whole. It will never be satisfactorily performed until it is performed by the university as a whole. The fact that it has largely been delegated to the department or school or college of education is a principal cause of the alarming anti-intellectualism of so much public education today.

Faculties of liberal arts and sciences must retrieve their past mistakes. At the undergraduate level the education of the future teacher should be an education in the liberal arts and sciences. This ought to be self-evident. The ideal of liberal education is to produce men and women with disciplined minds, cultivated interests, and a wide range of fundamental knowledge. Who in our society needs these qualities more than the teacher? We increasingly recognize that the doctor, the lawyer, and the engineer, if they are to achieve true professional eminence, must receive balanced training in many intellectual disciplines which are not directly related to their professions. How much more does a teacher need such an education? For him the fundamental intellectual disciplines are not supplements to, but the very essence of, his professional stock in trade. The teacher never knows when he may be called upon to give instruction in any or all of them. The students whose work he directs have a right to expect of him a genuine and sympathetic understanding of their various intellectual interests and ambitions. The last profession in which narrow vocational considerations should be allowed to interfere with thorough and well-balanced undergraduate preparation in the liberal arts and sciences is the teaching profession. Opportunity to satisfy minimum pedagogical requirements should be provided through electives that are a normal complement of a college program of liberal education, but under no circumstances should the department of pedagogy be permitted to exercise any sort of control over the undergraduate programs of prospective teachers.

Continued training in the fundamental intellectual disciplines is the recognized and proper purpose of graduate work. American universities, it seems to me, have failed, and failed most miserably, to apply even rudimentary common sense to the problem of devising a sound and useful graduate program for public-school teachers. We force the teacher to choose between a research program that is thorough and scholarly but too highly specialized for his needs, and a pedagogical program that is superficial and blatantly anti-intellectual and that solemnly and tediously reinstructs him in vocational skills he already possesses. The university ought not to compel the teacher to choose between such unacceptable alternatives. It should offer him a program that satisfies the highest academic standards and at the same time faces realistically the actual facts of secondary and elementary school teaching.

We must begin by considering the actual situation of the public-school teacher. He is usually called upon to teach two or more distinct disciplines. Even in a single course he ought to be bringing to bear upon the subject in hand appropriate information from other fields. A wide range of accurate knowledge is his most useful asset, rather than an intensive knowledge of a limited though rapidly advancing segment of learning within which he may hope to make original contributions of his own. In simplest terms, the graduate work of a school teacher ought to be a prolongation and deepening of the liberal education which he received (or should have received) as an undergraduate. The university ought to provide him an opportunity to continue that liberal education for as long as he is willing to pursue it, and it ought to reward him with a suitable degree for conscientious and thoughtful work when rationally directed to that end.

Let me illustrate by a specific example. A student, let us assume, has received a four-year liberal education, in the course of which he has met the pedagogical requirements for teaching. He has majored, perhaps, in history, and has done a considerable amount of work in English. He has taken introductory courses in the sciences, economics, and political science, and acquired a reading knowledge of one foreign language. His first teaching assignment is to a course in the social studies, to a course in English, and to one in algebra. He is to return for several summers to the university for advanced work. What should the university encourage him to do?

The university should permit him, first of all, to take courses that will really round out his knowledge of the various fields of history. For this purpose many undergraduate courses may be more appropriate than the graduate courses offered to research students, and he should be permitted to elect these. When he has completed a sound program in history, he should be permitted to go back to the point at which he dropped mathematics in college, and work that field up systematically in the way in which undergraduate majors in mathematics would do. So it should be with each of the fields in which he has done previous work, or in which he is required to teach, or in which, perhaps, he develops an interest for the first time.

The results of such study would be an exceptionally well-prepared teacher. More than that, the results would be a liberally educated man or woman, with a far deeper and wider range of knowledge than a four-year undergraduate program could give him. Study directed in such a way and to such ends is advanced study, no matter what parts of it may have been pursued in nominally undergraduate courses. It is the kind of education which a university should be proud to offer, and which it has a legitimate right to reward with an advanced degree. A student who pursues such a well-thought-out program for a full academic year beyond college graduation and who brings his command of two subjects up to certain pre-established standards should receive a Master's degree. A student who pursues it with distinction for three years beyond college graduation and who brings his command of five subjects up to the standards set should be entitled to a doctorate.

Much careful thought must go into the establishment of these standards in each subject. In order to receive a degree, a student should be required to demonstrate, in each proffered subject, a comprehension at least equal to that which an able undergraduate might be expected to obtain through a strong major program in the discipline. Course credits might aggregate about 30 semester hours, including undergraduate work. But the number of courses should not be the principal criterion. A comprehensive written examination in each of the subjects offered for the degree would be indispensable. In addition, an oral examination for the doctorate should cover all the five fields presented. A careful reading of certain basic works—the classics of the discipline— should be specifically required and tested. No thesis would be submitted for either degree, but a student should have been required to write at least one substantial original essay in each of his fields during the course of his studies, and these should be part of the record upon which his degree is awarded.

The traditional research program of the university, and the teaching program that I have just described, should be considered parallel but distinct. Both should be under the administration of the graduate school of the university, but the degrees ought to be different. Corresponding to the traditional degrees of M.A. and Ph.D. which would continue to be awarded in the research pro-gram, the university might make use of the degrees of Master and Doctor of Education (M.Ed. and Ed.D.) for the teaching program. These degrees, of course, already exist. The present pro-posal, however, would put them under the jurisdiction of the university as a whole, not the department of education or pedagogy, and would permit a student to earn them by work in any regular department of liberal arts or science in the university.

This new all-university faculty would also assume direct authority over the curriculum in the demonstration and laboratory schools which the university maintains. To the general public a university school signifies an institution of elementary or secondary education devoted to the ideals of science and scholarship for which the university stands. It must be made precisely that. Its program should be determined by scholars, scientists, and educationists together, and it should concentrate its experimental work upon the problem of effectively teaching the basic intellectual disciplines, organized as they are in the real world of science and learning.

Advanced research in educational problems will be conducted, as it ought to be, by the university as a whole and on an interdisciplinary basis. In other words, psychologists, sociologists, and statisticians will be asked to collaborate in investigating various problems of teaching and learning. Historians, political scientists, and economists will co-operate in studying various aspects of educational administration. The university will serve public education, not by delegating its responsibilities to a department of pedagogy, but by itself providing the opportunity, the facilities, and the funds to bring specialists from various disciplines together for co-operative research without detaching them permanently from the departments to which they belong.

One great barrier stands in the way of a rational program of teacher training—the certification requirements which are imposed by the state. These requirements are, in reality, special-interest legislation—a kind of protective tariff—enacted for the most part at the behest of professional educationists. As the very first step toward educational reform, citizens, scientists, scholars, professional men, and classroom teachers must unite in demanding that the legislatures of the 48 states review, carefully and realistically, the statutes governing the certification of teachers. The present laws must be replaced by ones which will protect the schools against incompetent teachers rather than the professors of pedagogy against losses in enrollment.

Looked at from the point of view of logic or common sense, the present arrangements for certifying teachers are completely topsy-turvy. Local school authorities, who can interview teachers individually as well as examine their credentials, are in a far better position to judge a candidate's probable skill and competence as a teacher than can a bureaucrat who works solely from records of courses taken. Conversely, an agency of the state is far better equipped than a local school board to determine a student's competence in his chosen subject, for it can compare his academic record with hundreds of others, it can administer standardized examinations, and it can call upon specialists in all the fields of knowledge for advice and assistance. Under the existing system, however, the responsibilities are completely reversed. The matters that local authorities are competent to determine for themselves are precisely the ones that the state educational bureaucracy insists on controlling from above; and the kinds of minimum requirements which the state is in the best position to enforce are precisely the ones that are left largely to local discretion, or to quasi-official accrediting agencies.

The first step to reform is to clear the statute books of those provisions which specify a fixed number of hours in education (that is, in pedagogy) as a requirement for certification. This means simply dethroning these requirements from their peculiarly privileged position. Then a new system must be worked out which will give assurance that a certified teacher is both proficient in teaching and well-prepared in the subjects he or she is to teach.

Different certificates should deal with these different matters. One certificate should testify to the teacher's proficiency in teaching. There ought to be several ways of earning this certificate. An experienced teacher ought to be granted it simply upon presentation of satisfactory evidence of a successful teaching career of a specified length of time. For a candidate without previous experience, successful completion of a period of practice teaching should be the principal requirement. The institution that supervises practice teaching usually specifies certain pedagogical courses as prerequisites, hence the state has no need to lay down pedagogical course requirements of its own in granting certificates of teaching proficiency. Provision should be made for students without either experience or practice teaching to obtain a temporary certificate enabling them to offer instruction in specially designated schools, which would guarantee to give on-the-job training and special guidance and supervision to those without experience. Such programs might well be financed by the state to aid in the recruitment of teachers, or they might be conducted by the extension departments of universities. After completing a specified period of teaching under such conditions, an instructor should be entitled to a permanent certificate of teaching proficiency. An arrangement of this kind would enable the schools to draw upon a large and brilliant group of liberal arts graduates who are at present excluded from public-school employment by unjustifiably arbitrary pedagogical requirements. After the basic certificate in teaching proficiency has been earned, further course work in pedagogy should be entirely optional with the individual teacher.

Another certificate should be provided for each of the fundamental disciplines of public-school instruction. Ideally these certificates should be granted on the basis of state-administered comprehensive examinations in the subject, periodically offered to all persons who believe themselves qualified. There should be at least two levels of such examinations, one leading to limited, the second to advanced certification in the subject or discipline. Pending the development of such examinations, limited certification might be granted on the basis of 15 or 20 semester hours of college work in the subject, advanced certification for 30 or 40 hours. The certification should be in specific subjects rather than general areas. In other words, there should be certificates in history, in political science, and in economics; a teacher of social studies would be expected to possess at least limited certification in two or three of these subjects.

A prospective teacher would be encouraged to meet certification requirements in as many subjects as possible during his undergraduate years. The teacher already in service who returned to the university for advanced work during summer sessions and regular terms would have a definite purpose in view: to bring his certification in the subjects he had been teaching from the limited to the advanced classification, or to secure certification in additional subjects. The recognition or accrediting standards applied to schools themselves could easily be geared to this system of certification. The ideal school would be one in which every course was being conducted by a teacher possessing advanced certification in the subject or subjects covered by the course. Every deviation from this would lessen the standing of the school.

Salary increments could likewise be effectively tied to this scheme. The term "professional growth" frequently appears among the criteria for the promotion and the advancement in salary of teachers. At present this is a vague phrase. It could easily be endowed with a definite meaning. Under the proposed system, a teacher would be giving tangible evidence of professional growth every time he raised his certification from limited to advanced in a given subject and every time he acquired a limited certificate in a new field. Each such step might well entitle him to an increment in salary.

Besides the certificate of teaching proficiency and the certificates in the various subjects, provision would have to be made for various types of special certificates. Elementary school teaching, for example, presents special problems. A certificate in Educational Psychology for Elementary School Teachers, in addition to the general certificate in teaching proficiency, might well be established. Care should be taken to make its requirements clear and specific. This certificate should not be granted for a mere potpourri of pedagogical courses, but only for a carefully designed program comprising extensive work in the regular academic department of psychology. Another certificate in Educational Administration should also be offered, to be obtained by specified work primarily in the departments of political science (or public administration), economics, and law, with only such work in the department of pedagogy as seemed clearly justifiable. Other special certificates—and several will doubtless be needed—should be set up on analogous principles.

A reorganization of teacher training and certification requirements along the lines here outlined would correct some of the gravest abuses in the present situation. It would bring to an end the aimless accumulation by experienced teachers of credits in pedagogical courses. It would restore to teacher training a realism and a clear sense of purpose that it has lost. It would, in fact, make teacher training "functional" once more.

A new curriculum for the education of teachers, based firmly upon the liberal arts and sciences rather than upon the mere vocational skills of pedagogy, will do more to restore the repute of the public schools than any other step that can be taken. Not only will teachers be adequately trained in the disciplines they undertake to teach, but they will also be imbued with respect for those disciplines and will be prepared to resist the anti-intellectualism that currently threatens the schools. And when the tide begins to turn, young men and women of genuine intellectual interest and capacity will be attracted in increasing numbers into the profession of public-school teaching. They will not be repelled at the outset by being asked to lay aside their intellectual interests and fritter away their time in the courses of the pedagogues. Under a well-ordered plan, the gateway to teaching will be the gateway of learning itself.

NOTE

1 Excerpts from an address at the University of Wyoming, July 29, 1953, to be expanded in the author's "Educational Wastelands," scheduled for publication October 26 by the University of Illinois Press.

7.5 The professional standards movement in teaching

Evolution of an idea[1]

Ralph W. McDonald
President, Bowling Green State University

Source: Ralph W. McDonald, The Professional Standards Movement in Teaching: Progress and Projection. *Proceedings of the National Commission on Teacher Education and Professional Standards, National Education Association of the United States*, 1956, pp. 8–21. (Report of the Parkland Conference held at Pacific Lutheran College, Parkland, Washington, June 26–30.)

The inquiring mind of man has produced several hypotheses as to the forces that determine the course of human events. There are those who have argued that military conquest has largely determined the ebb and flow of world history. There are those who have held that the mighty forces of nature—the sea, the mountains, the minerals, the elements—have really made our civilization or lack of it. A closer and more penetrating analysis of the evolution of human society brings us closer to the truth, in my judgment. The most powerful force in the shaping of human destiny is an idea.

On the canvas of history the picture of human progress is painted in the strokes of ideas—great ideas, lesser ideas, and ideas so fine in their tracing that they seem to disappear in the halo or the shadow. The entire canvas, however, is done in ideas.

The professional standards movement in teaching is an idea on the march. It is the idea that teaching is truly a professional endeavor, and that in the public interest the rank and file of qualified practitioners engaged in teaching must be organized as a profession to determine and apply appropriate standards to govern the selection, preparation, licensing, ethical conduct, and service of those who enter upon this profession.

CONTRIBUTION OF OTHER PROFESSIONS

The concept of practitioner responsibility for professional standards did not originate in the field of teaching. The same basic idea had long before been accepted and implemented in the fields of medicine, dentistry, law, and other major professions. Practice in these fields has become truly professional as the same basic idea had moved to fruition in the respective areas of service. Although teaching is in fact the mother of all the professions, it is years behind the others in becoming a profession. Since 1946, the organized body of American teachers has been engaged in the same kind of evolution or metamorphosis as has been taking place in other major professions in the United States. As individuals, many educational leaders long before 1946 had been striving to improve teacher selection, preparation, certification, and growth in service. Their individual efforts, however, were insufficient to produce widespread and lasting progress.

GROWTH OF THE IDEA

It was only natural that I should carry my driving convictions into the broader relationships with the organized teaching groups of the country.

A necessary first step had already been taken in 1945: an effort to bring the respected and scholarly leadership of American higher education into the working organization of the NEA. One of the major steps in the emergence of all of the other professions has been the establishment of a partnership between the organizations of practitioners and the administrations and faculties of the universities of the country. Medicine, law, engineering, forestry, journalism, and the other major professions had emerged to real professional strength and status as the programs of preparation for those professions had gradually shifted from separate technical schools and institutes to professional colleges on the university campuses, where they gained new strength and stature through the breadth of university life and firm integration with time-honored programs of liberal arts education.

I knew that teaching could achieve major professional status only if the same kind of transition and alliance could be encouraged in the field of teacher education. The NEA Department of Higher Education, the name of which was later changed to the Association for Higher Education, presented the opportunity to develop a broad liaison between the organized teachers at the elementary and secondary levels and the faculty leadership of the great colleges and universities of the country.

FORERUNNER OF NCTEPS—THE CHAUTAUQUA CONFERENCE

The professional standards movement began in earnest when the NEA Executive Committee approved the request of the Committee on Preparation and Certification for an emergency national conference to be held immediately preceding the 1946 Delegate Assembly of the NEA. The Chautauqua Conference came at a crucial time. Conditions in the public schools, particularly as regards teaching staffs, had reached a stage so serious that the word "crisis" was too mild a term to describe it. There had been almost a mass exodus of teachers from the classroom. Figures reported by the U.S. Office of Education revealed that 633,200 persons had quit classrooms in which they had been employed as teachers during the six years preceding 1946. Even more serious was the heavy decline in the percent of college students choosing to prepare for teaching. There had been a widespread effort to get more teachers into the classrooms by lowering the standards of preparation and certification, to the point that in many states any breathing human could legally be employed as a "teacher." With each downward step in standards more good teachers had left the classrooms and fewer capable students had chosen teaching as a career. In their desperation to keep the schools open, the American people did not seem to realize that they were making matters worse by these actions; and the organized teachers were standing idly by.

The Chautauqua Conference was deliberately structured to produce professional consciousness and professional conscience. For the first time in our history, highly trained primary teachers and high school teachers sat down around the table to consider common problems with scholars from the faculties of leading colleges and universities. At the conference table every person was held in equal respect and his opinions given equal consideration by all others around the table. They were earnest, intelligent leaders from all branches and levels of education in the United States. Every detail in the planning of the conference was geared to produce action. The questions were direct and to the point. Around every table the time was "now." The questions started with "How . . ." and "In what manner . . .," instead of "Should . . ." and "Would it be a good idea . . ." Even the revolutionary proposal that the organized teaching profession accredit colleges for teacher education was approached in the same manner by a carefully selected group under the chairmanship of Ernest Melby.

NCTEPS IS CREATED

It is difficult for us to realize ten years later just how revolutionary the Chautauqua Conference approach was. I shall always look back upon that conference and the ensuing events at the Buffalo Delegate Assembly as the American teachers' finest hour. In one bold and unprecedented series of events, the teachers of this nation overcame more than a century of inertia and staked out the ground upon which the structure of a real profession could be erected, beam by beam and stone upon stone.

The spark that had been kindled in the classroom teachers' regional meetings became a flaming torch at Chautauqua, and became at Buffalo a continuing lighthouse for the guidance of teaching into the harbor of true professionalism. The heart of Chautauqua was an idea. The idea was the important thing. It is the important thing now. It must ever be the essence of this movement.

NCTEPS BEGINS ITS WORK

The work of organizing and developing a program to implement the idea began in earnest after the Buffalo meeting. The newly appointed members of the Commission realized the toil and sweat had just begun. The tasks were many and arduous: Alert the American people to what was happening to their schools and particularly to the teaching profession. Secure complete acceptance of the idea at the very grass roots in all branches of the teaching profession at all levels and in all parts of the United States. Develop goals and policies applying the idea to every major factor related to the practice of teaching, from the recruitment of candidates to the standards covering salaries and working conditions. Conduct research to get the facts on all aspects of the problem and to provide criteria for evaluating progress. Establish cooperative machinery for engaging in direct action at national, state, and local levels. Initiate specific action programs directed to the selection, preparation, licensing, admission to practice, growth in service, and professional service of teachers.

Through national, regional, state, and district conferences and countless meetings at the local level the idea became, in a few short years, a commitment and an article of faith of the organized teaching profession.

PROGRESS IN THE PROFESSIONAL STANDARDS MOVEMENT

It was as if the leadership of the organized teachers across the country had been waiting merely for the signals to be called. The leadership, the resourcefulness, and the statesmanship of the officers and executive secretaries of the state education associations began immediately to be felt as a mighty force in carrying the idea forward. Likewise, most of the leaders of the national organizations in education and of the powerful lay allies of the teaching profession were soon joined in the movement. Within two or three years a vast organization for cooperative effort in the achievement of professional standards had come into existence. There were parallel state commissions in nearly all the states. Practically every national association affiliated with the NEA had a special program for the advancement of professional standards. One of the most important groups in American education, the National Association of State Directors of Teacher Education and Certification, had been nurtured by the Commission to a new stature of national leadership and service.

Literature

Imbued with the idea and organized for action, the profession began to achieve results. Within one year from Chautauqua the tide began to turn. The organized teachers began to bring emergency certification under control and to reduce its extent. The downward trend of certification standards, battered and weakened in the years before Chautauqua, was first halted and then reversed in state after state by the determined efforts of an aroused profession. Research studies, such as the annual national teacher supply and demand study by Ray C. Maul, began to reveal hitherto unknown facts about teaching and to focus attention upon the points where action was most imperative. Under the leadership of the Commission, a literature of professional standards began to emerge in the form of policy statements, *The Journal of Teacher Education*, the reports of the national and regional conferences, and numerous other publications. Steadily and surely the upward drive proceeded from Chautauqua to Oxford to Bowling Green to New Hampshire to Indiana to Palo Alto to Kalamazoo to Miami Beach to Albany to DeKalb, and now to Parkland.

Certification

From 15 states requiring the completion of a four-year degree preparation for minimum certification in 1946, the number had risen to 31 in 1955. The progress in elevating certification standards has been much wider and deeper, however, than even this impressive statistic would indicate. There is not a state in the Union that has failed to strengthen its teacher certification standards during this ten-year period. Even more important, I doubt that there is a state in the Union which does not have, at the present time, a going and vigorous program of action to elevate still further its teacher certification standards.

Teacher preparation

The chief gain in preservice teacher education since 1946 has been the strengthening of the liberal education foundation of the teacher. While a four-year prepared teacher usually has much better training in professional subject matter, the principal gain in his preparation for teaching is in the fact that he is a much better educated person in the broad sense. The most important earmark of the qualified teacher is a broad, liberal education. Even in medicine, law, business, engineering, theology, and other occupations that have risen to professional stature, the fundamental requirement of a broad, liberal education is practically universal, with the specialized professional preparation built upon or interwoven with this foundation. In preparation for teaching, sound liberal or general education is even more essential and should be even broader, deeper, and more thorough.

The elevation of preparation and certification standards has produced substantial improvement also in professional welfare, financial compensation, and conditions of service of teachers. Higher standards for teaching have produced a higher level of respect and prestige for those engaged in teaching. Parents and citizens generally have been willing, yes insistent, that more adequate salaries and better working conditions be provided for those engaged in teaching.

The march of an idea has become the forward salient of the great body of American teachers rising ever nearer to the level of a true profession.

DEVELOPMENT OF NCATE

From the beginning, even before Chautauqua, the core of the movement has been to establish and secure adherence to high standards in college programs for the preparation of teachers. As in other occupations that have achieved professional status in our democratic society, the voluntary professional accrediting process is the only effective means of achieving this goal. The steps in this direction have, in every profession, been the most difficult to achieve. Relationships in this area of progress are the most delicate, and the cooperation of all sincere interested groups is imperative. Progress in this area is the most profoundly significant contribution of the professional standards movement in teaching.

After long, patient, and cooperative efforts on the part of the Commission and AACTE, the latter agreed to yield the professional accrediting function to a broadly representative council rooted in the organized teaching profession of the United States. In April, 1951, I invited key representatives of the AACTE, NCTEPS, the National Council of Chief State School Officers, the National Association of State Directors of Teacher Education and Certification, and the National School Boards Association to meet at NEA headquarters. At this meeting and a meeting later that year, the National Council for Accreditation of Teacher Education was forged out and came into existence upon the official confirmation of the groups whose representatives had assembled. The Council was to begin its work on July 1, 1954. Through a stroke of great good fortune, W. Earl Armstrong became associated with the Council as its executive director a few months prior to the date when the Council was scheduled to take over the national professional accrediting function. Under the leadership of Mr. Armstrong the Council is on the way to achieving the structure and status necessary to perform its valuable function.

ROLE OF PROFESSIONAL ORGANIZATIONS

I should like to add a fifth major problem area to our agenda, not just for this conference, but for all conferences and all organized efforts to achieve professional status and professional standards in teaching. This problem area is perhaps the most crucial of all. It relates to the development of a strong and truly professional organization of the teachers in this country.

The National Education Association is one of the world's great organizations. Its progress is a source of pride to all of us. It is but a mere beginning, however, toward the kind of professional organization we need and must have if teaching is to rise to a professional level in our democratic society.

Our professional membership dues, when national, state, and local associations are considered as one, are pitifully small when measured against the needs and the demands of a truly professional organization. A doubling of the present level of our professional dues would still leave us far short of the financial support essential to a professional organization program. For one, I believe the teachers of the United States are ready and willing to go forward in this matter. Certainly we can blame no one but ourselves if we claim to be a profession and fail to provide even the minimum financial resources for a professional program.

Another fundamental weakness in our professional organization is that it is not professional by its own standards of admission to membership. You may recall, as I do, the great furor a few years ago when President Roosevelt's dog, Falla, was reported to have been duly admitted to membership in the NEA. How can we claim to be a profession when anybody, anywhere, with any qualifications or no qualifications, is admitted to membership in our so-called professional organization by merely turning over a five-dollar bill for membership dues? For so long as we continue such an admission policy, we shall *ipso facto* convict ourselves of being hypocrites and traitors to our own professed belief that teaching is a profession. Have you tried to join a medical society lately? Can you go to your local bar association and become a member merely by paying a fixed sum of money as annual dues? Can you join the American Institute of Architects or any of its local branches and call yourself an architect by the mere gesture of paying a sum of money and giving your name to the secretary? Of course you can do none of these things, because those organizations are professional bodies.

I challenge this conference and the entire leadership and membership of our profession in the United States to place as the number one item on your agenda this question: *When are we going to start making an honest effort to achieve a truly professional organization of teachers in the United States?*

As I pointed out in the beginning of this presentation, the professional standards movement in teaching is the march of an idea: the idea that teaching is truly a professional endeavor, and that in the public interest the rank and file of qualified practitioners engaged in teaching must be organized as a profession to determine and apply appropriate standards to govern the selection, preparation, licensing, ethical conduct, and service of those who enter upon this profession.

Dedicated to this idea, let us say with Jamie Sexton Holme:

> Do not come and look for me, I shall be gone;
> My bed will be empty, my door standing open—
> I have a pilgrimage to make before the dawn!
>
> There is a hill against the far horizon,
> Where the heavens dip down, and at last disappear.
> If I climb to the top, when the stars are just setting,
> I know I can reach them, they will be so near!

NOTE

1 For space limitations, the original text was excerpted.

7.6 National Teacher Examinations (NTE)

David J. Fox
City College, City University of New York

Source: David J. Fox, *National Teacher Examinations*. New York: Arco Publishing, Inc., 1982

PROFESSIONAL EDUCATION EXAMINATION
(Sample of 6 questions)

1   The high school of today may be considered the *common school*, just as in earlier days the elementary school was the common school in the United States. This statement is true because

   (A)   more students entering high school still need instruction in basic reading and arithmetic skills
   (B)   the great majority of American youth attend high school
   (C)   high school curricula have become stabilized after a period in which many new courses were added
   (D)   more students now continue their study into college
   (E)   students of higher social class attend college preparatory academies

2   A very young child learns that the small, furry, purring objects in his house is a "kitty." While visiting another house, this child points to a small dog there and says, "Kitty." This illustrates

   (A)   immediate reinforcement
   (B)   simultaneous discrimination
   (C)   an unconditioned response
   (D)   primary stimulus generalization
   (E)   secondary stimulus generalization

3   It has been found that intellectually gifted children tend to surpass average children in

   (A)   personal and social adjustment
   (B)   physical size and health
   (C)   social maturity and poise
   (D)   all of the above
   (E)   none of the above

4   The recommendation that a poem be read over in its entirety before memorizing individual lines illustrates an awareness of the principles of

   (A)   proactive inhibition
   (B)   gestalt organization
   (C)   massed practice
   (D)   secondary reinforcement
   (E)   retroactive inhibition

5   Within learning theorist's frame of reference, probably the best way of approaching the organization of subject matter is to move from the

(A)   familiar to the unfamiliar
(B)   general to the particular
(C)   logical to the psychological
(D)   societal to the individual
(E)   complex to the simple

6   Which instrument would be most desirable for testing the general mental ability of a second-grade pupil, aged seven years three months?

(A)   Lorge-Thorndike Intelligence Test
(B)   Goodenough Intelligence Test
(C)   Vineland Social Maturity Test
(D)   Wechsler Intelligence Scale for Children (Revised)
(E)   Wechsler-Bellevue Scale

ANSWER KEY

1 B   2 D   3 D   4 B   5 A   6 D

Mathematics education
(Sample of 7 questions)

1   The *chief* way in which programs for arithmetic teaching in most public school systems differ today from those of fifty years ago is in

(A)   rejection of drill and memorization
(B)   use of computers
(C)   integration of arithmetic with other curriculum areas
(D)   stress upon social utility
(E)   emphasis upon mathematical meanings

2   Select from the following number statements the one statement in which the mathematical sign < would be appropriately placed within the circle.

(A) $4 + 9$ O $8 + 5$
(B) $51 + 40$ O $10 + 80$
(C) $64 - 16$ O $41 + 13$
(D) $20 + 40$ O $30 + 10$
(E) $5 + 16$ O $17 + 4$

3   The "3" in the upper right-hand corner of a newspaper page denotes the

(A)   ordinal meaning of the number
(B)   cardinal meaning of the number
(C)   total collection at a particular point
(D)   place-value
(E)   fractional part of the total paper

4   The associative law in the process of multiplication states that

(A) $a \times a = a^2$

(B) $(a \times b) \times c = a \times (b \times c)$

(C) $a \times b = b \times a$

(D) $a \times (b \times c) = (a \times b) + (a \times c)$

(E) $a + b \times a = a + a \times b$

5   A student subtracts 3y from 5y and obtains the answer 2. Her error probably stems from the failure to recognize the meaning of the

(A)   additive inverse postulate

(B)   associative postulate

(C)   commutative postulate

(D)   distributive postulate

(E)   generalization postulate

6   On a number line, the sum of a number and its inverse is always

(A)   greater than either number

(B)   a positive number

(C)   zero

(D)   the greater of two numbers

(E)   one

7   The pupils in your class are having difficulty understanding what you are teaching. Of the following, it would be *least* desirable to stress

(A)   the meaning of mathematical concepts

(B)   rigorous proof of mathematical principles

(C)   motivation for mathematical principles

(D)   applications of mathematical principles

(E)   the need to practice the mathematical processes involved

ANSWER KEY

Mathematics

1 E   2 C   3 A   4 B   5 D   6 C   7 B

7.7 New Jersey's alternate route to certification[1]

Saul Cooperman and Leo Klagholz

Source: Saul Cooperman and Leo Klagholz, New Jersey's alternate route to certification. *Phi Delta Kappan*, 66(10), 1985, pp. 691–695

By next fall, New Jersey school districts will be able to offer the first district-administered training programs in the U.S. leading to teacher certification. The architects of this controversial program discuss its genesis and implementation.

> The blunt fact is that many of our teachers arc not properly qualified to handle the responsibility we have placed on them ... This is, in my view, the major weakness of American education.[2]
>
> Sterling M. McMurrin, Former U.S. Commissioner of Education, 1963

> Nothing in American education is in greater need of reform than the way we educate and certify classroom teachers.[3]
>
> Emily Feistritzer, 1984

In September 1985, local school districts in New Jersey will be able to offer the first district-administered training programs in the U.S. leading to teacher certification. The districts offering such programs will be able to hire on provisional contracts college graduates who have not been certified through traditional education programs and who have passed competency tests in the subject areas they are going to teach. Moreover, these districts will be able to recommend for state certification those individuals who successfully complete the district-administered programs.

This alternate route to certification is the outcome of more than two years of and discussion of teacher preparation and certification in New Jersey. But, in another way, this alternate route reflects 20 years of thinking about the need to reform teacher evaluation in the U.S.

Over the last quarter-century, critics of teacher education have played only minor variations on the same themes. These critics have complained that students majoring in education do not rank among the most academically talented, that both the quality and the quantity of education courses required of majors make for an inferior college education, and that districts are able to grant "emergency" certification to people not adequately prepared to teach—a situation that undermines attempts at school reform.[4]

As long ago as 1963 the critics also began to suggest alternatives to the teacher preparation programs offered by colleges and universities. In *The Miseducation of American Teachers*, published that year, James Koerner suggested "giving local boards complete freedom in staffing their school" through "some system of qualifying examinations whereby teachers, in order to be licensed, would demonstrate their mastery of the subject they propose to teach." Such a system "could operate in a number of different ways," Koerner wrote, "but the principle of *demonstrated mastery* would be paramount whatever the other details."[5]

Koerner felt that this kind of system—combining a qualifying examination and a demonstration of teaching ability—could provide an antidote for both "the low level of teaching that many communities now get with fully certified and licensed teachers" and "the tenuous connection between the training that teachers are exposed to and the performance they turn in on the job."[6]

> Whatever system of licensing prevails, the great majority of new teachers will undoubtedly continue for the indefinite future to come through organized programs in colleges and universities. An examination system would merely shift the emphasis for admission to teaching from stipulated preparatory programs to demonstrated ability, would afford a possible means of making teaching an open instead of a closed field, and would exert substantial pressure on the formal programs in the direction of high academic standards.[7]

If anything has changed since 1963, it is the possibility of implementing such a plan. At the time Koerner wrote about an alternate system of certification, he rejected his own proposal as politically impossible. A "free market for local boards in hiring teachers might on balance be a great gain for public education," he said. "Of course, no such thing is going to happen."[8]

More recently, the Education Commission of the States recommended that "state certification rules be sufficiently flexible to encourage service in the public schools by qualified persons from business, industry, the scientific and technical communities, and institutions of higher learning."[9] Similarly, Donna Kerr suggested that we test an alternative to the current certification system that would allow students who score in the top 10 percent on the National Teacher Examinations to enter teaching without taking courses in education.[10]

Clearly, educators are more open to change today than they were in Koerner's time. An alternative to traditional teacher preparation programs is more than possible today. It is happening in New Jersey.

New Jersey embarked on the process of creating this alternate route to certification in July 1982, when the state board of education expressed concern about the procedures by which "emergency" certification was being granted. The Department of Education responded to the board's concern by initiating a comprehensive examination of procedures for teacher preparation and certification in New Jersey. In the main, the Department of Education arrived at the same conclusions that similar studies by other researchers have yielded.

QUALITY OF EDUCATION MAJORS

One area on which the New Jersey study focused was the quality of students entering teacher education programs in the state. In 1982 the Scholastic Aptitude Test (SAT) scores of New Jersey high school graduates who planned to major in education were lower than those of graduates who planned to major in 22 of 24 fields of study at the college level. Moreover, among the high school seniors who intended to major in education and who had been admitted to community and state colleges in New Jersey (which provide 70 percent of all new teachers hired in New Jersey from in-state institutions of higher education), 19 percent scored 299 or lower on the verbal portion of the SAT, 60 percent scored 399 or lower, and only 12 percent scored 500 or better on this 800-point subtest.[11] In 1982 the average score on the verbal portion of the SAT for all New Jersey high school students was 416.

Nationally, students who major in education don't do much better.[12] For example, SAT scores in 1982 for students preparing to teach were 80 points below the national average.[13]

Not surprisingly, the New Jersey Department of Education found itself concurring with Ernest Boyer's conclusion that U.S. schools "cannot adequately prepare the coming generation if the least able students enter the profession."[14] As Jere Brophy has suggested, effective teachers "are probably brighter and more dedicated than average." He added that effective teachers need to be brighter because they must engage in complex tasks, such as planning, analyzing, organizing classroom time, and suspending judgment.[15] If the least-able college students decide to become teachers, will they be likely to address such complex tasks in ways that will excite children and motivate them to learn?

U.S. schools must educate young people to participate effectively in a high-tech society. Thus the first question posed by the New Jersey Department of Education was, How can we attract more academically talented people to teach in our public schools and identify those among them who have the personal characteristics that suit them to this task?

INCONSISTENT PREPARATION

The Department's study of teacher preparation and certification in New Jersey brought to light another concern as well: the widespread inconsistencies among teacher preparation programs with regard to the coursework required of students. For example, a survey of the six colleges that prepare a majority of the teachers employed in New Jersey schools showed that these colleges listed 120 education courses and that some colleges were *requiring* education majors to take courses not even *offered* by the other colleges. Such inconsistencies suggest a lack of consensus on what knowledge is essential for beginning teachers and on which qualities characterize effective teachers.

This finding in New Jersey is in step with other research on consistency among teacher education programs. Feistritzer has noted that the courses included in "too many teacher education programs . . . are ill-defined and impractical."[16] Boyer has suggested that education majors be required to take a four-year program of general academic study, followed by a fifth year of coursework in a carefully defined education core curriculum.[17]

Nor is concern over consistency across teacher education programs a particularly recent phenomenon. As early as 1963, James Bryant Conant noted that students who completed the sequence of education courses in one college may not have considered "the same, or even a similar, set of facts or principles as their contemporaries in another institution even in the same state."[18]

From its own survey and the observations of other researchers, the New Jersey Department of Education saw a clear need to identify a body of knowledge essential to all beginning teachers. This would be the point at which the Department would begin to build its alternate route to teacher certification.

"EMERGENCY" CERTIFICATION

Since 1942, a system of "emergency" certification has allowed New Jersey school districts to hire unqualified individuals to teach, if certified individuals are not available. Nearly 20 percent of all newly employed New Jersey teachers in 1982 had entered the education system in this fashion—many of them lacking adequate subject preparation as well as professional training. In some cases, individuals hired on emergency certificates did not even have college degrees. Emergency certification was a sink-or-swim situation; despite their lack of professional preparation, emergency teachers were guaranteed neither in-school support nor necessary professional training. Further, school districts could turn to this weak alternative system only when there was a quantitative shortage. There was nothing they could do when the *quality* of certified candidates was poor, except employ them as teachers.

As early as 1963, Conant condemned substandard certification. "To anyone who takes state requirements seriously, this is surely a national scandal," he wrote.[19] One of the most important functions of alternate certification in New Jersey will be to replace emergency certification in all but a few specific fields: special education, vocational education, bilingual education, and English as a second language.

Ironically, while in case of shortage New Jersey school districts could assign unprepared teachers to subjects they were unqualified to teach, without support or training, the New Jersey Department of Education was receiving a steady stream of inquiries from people who were interested in teaching in the public schools and who had talent and knowledge in those very subjects. These people included accountants and mathematicians, as well as teachers in colleges or in private schools. But unless there was a teacher shortage, and regardless of the quality of certified applicants, these people could not be considered for teaching positions—this at a time when the real "emergency" is one of quality as well as quantity.

THE INITIAL PROPOSAL

After carefully studying the problems inherent in the New Jersey teacher certification process, staff members of the Department of Education developed a proposal for an alternate route to certification.[20] This proposal was intended to begin a process of public development of a program to open classroom doors to talented and enthusiastic but noncertified individuals. However, unlike the unstructured nature of emergency certification, this alternate route would provide a rigorous, district-administered training program. The proposal was first announced to the public in September 1983. Among its suggested reforms were:

- a clear definition of the coursework essential for *all* beginning teachers;
- a more careful definition of effective teaching, which would be used both to improve the quality of teacher education programs in colleges and universities and to shape the district-administered training program;
- the replacement of emergency certification (except in a few specified teaching specialties) with a carefully developed, rigorous alternative to college teacher training programs, intended to attract talented college graduates who had not been certified through such traditional programs; and
- the establishment of new standards that would require *all* prospective teachers in New Jersey to have bachelor's degrees and to demonstrate "content competency" on tests covering the subjects they intend to teach.

THE OPEN PROCESS

By attending to the wide range of opinions, concerns, and experiences represented by these interests, the Department staff was able to strengthen the proposal. The open process for defining the alternate route also convinced almost all the interests that the final proposal addressed their particular concerns. Indeed, some of the groups most vociferously opposed to alternate certification when the proposal was first announced have since become supporters of the plan.

The Boyer Report

To identify the basic knowledge and skills essential for all beginning teachers, New Jersey Gov. Thomas Kean appointed a panel of 10 distinguished leaders in teacher education, headed by

Ernest Boyer.[21] The mission of this group was to determine (1) what things beginning teachers must know and (2) how effective teachers teach.

The panel defined an effective teacher as one who has clear goals and who delivers instruction in small increments but at an appropriate pace, interspersing questions to check on comprehension and providing many detailed examples and clear directions. An effective teacher provides sufficient successful practice for all students, sees to it that all students are involved in learning, provides opportunities for independent work, and evaluates the progress of each student, according to the panel. An effective teacher must also be able to stimulate creative thought, help students evaluate what they have learned, and prepare students to use their knowledge wisely.[22] The panel concluded that, while most teacher educators would agree with these findings, the knowledge and skills it had identified are often neither "conveyed effectively to new teachers nor applied in practice."[23]

To make teacher education more effective, the panel recommended a more practical curriculum—one that moves "from real-life problems to theory, rather than the other way around."[24]

The State Commission

As the next step in developing alternate certification, the state commissioner of education appointed an advisory commission.

After lengthy deliberation, the commission almost unanimously recommended "state-approved district training programs." Its report suggests that local school districts develop three-phase training programs and submit written program plans to the New Jersey Department of Education for approval.[25] The three phases are intended to provide progressive training in the knowledge and skills identified by the Boyer panel and in actual classroom teaching. By simultaneously conducting 200 hours of instruction—80 of them before the provisional teacher takes charge of a classroom—and a year of supervised teaching, the district training programs are expected to enable new teachers to integrate theory with practice more readily.

The commission also recommended that each candidate for "provisional" employment as a teacher should have:

- earned a bachelor's degree;
- passed a competency test on the subject matter that he or she has been hired to teach;
- earned 30 credit hours or have equivalent work experience in the subject that he or she has been hired to teach (at the secondary level) or 30 credit hours in any single field (in the case of elementary teachers); and
- been approved by district personnel after a screening interview that would focus on background, academic experience, and certain ethical and personal characteristics as identified as essential by the Boyer panel.

In September 1984, following extensive public hearings, the state board of education approved this alternative route to certification, as one of several revisions of the administrative code on teacher preparation and certification.

ANTICIPATED BENEFITS

The alternate route to teacher certification seems likely to benefit education in New Jersey in several ways. First, it will expand the pool of qualified candidates from which local school districts can choose their teachers. Second, it will bring into teaching a new cadre of knowledgeable, enthusiastic individuals, who are likely to bring with them new ways of looking at the classroom experience. Third, it will emphasize the importance of having teachers know well the subjects they teach.

The alternate route to certification will also give traditional teacher education programs competition that could invigorate the entire profession.

Perhaps most important, the alternate route to certification will do away with the 40-year tradition of emergency certification in New Jersey. A common theme in the current dialogue on U.S. education is the need to professionalize teaching. As Linda Darling-Hammond put it in her Rand Corporation study of the crisis in teaching, "Until teaching becomes a more attractive career alternative, the problems of attracting and retaining talented teachers will undermine the success of other reforms intended to upgrade educational programs and curricula."[26] And the key to making teaching more attractive, she concluded, is to make teaching more professional. Emily Feistritzer concurred. "If teaching is to become a true profession, it needs to act like one," she wrote.[27] Yet teaching can never act like a profession without developing more rigorous entry and training requirements.

That is the goal in New Jersey. The revisions to the teacher certification code require that all traditional teacher education students in New Jersey also complete an academic major and that all teacher education programs cover the essential knowledge identified by the Boyer panel. The revised code requires that all candidates for certification—whether from the traditional or the alternate route—pass a test of subject-matter competency. The alternate route to certification will complement these changes in the code by attracting a new group of individuals to New Jersey classrooms and by eliminating the abuses of emergency certification.

NOTES

1 For space limitations, the original text was excerpted.

2 Quoted in James Koerner, *The miseducation of American teachers* (Boston: Houghton-Mifflin, 1963). p. 4.

3 C. Emily Feistritzer, *The making of a teacher: a report on teacher education and certification* (Washington, D.C.: National Center for Education Information, 1984), p. 54.

4 James Bryant Conant, *The education of American teachers* (New York: McGraw-Hill, 1963). pp. 51, 81. See also W. Timothy Weaver, "In search of quality: the need for talent in teaching," *Phi Delta Kappan*, September 1979, pp. 29–32, 46. Evidence suggests that the lower academic talent of schoolteachers as a group is a long-standing phenomenon, going back as much as 50 years. See, for example, Ernest L. Boyer, *High school: a report on secondary education in America* (New York: Harper & Row, 1983), p. 171.

5 Koerner, p. 252.

6 Ibid.

7 Ibid., p. 262.

8 Ibid., p. 252.

9 Task Force on Education for Economic Growth, *Action for excellence: a comprehensive plan to improve our nation's schools* (Denver: Education Commission of the States, 1983), p. 39.

10 Donna H. Kerr, "Teaching Competence and Teacher Education in the United States," *Teachers College Record*, Spring 1983, p. 546.

11 "Executive Summary," *An alternative route to teacher selection and professional quality assurance* (Trenton: New Jersey State Department of Education, September 1983), p. 1.

12 See, for example, Weaver, "In search of quality . . ."; and Victor S. Vance and Phillip C. Schlechty, "The distribution of academic ability in the teaching force: policy implications." *Phi Delta Kappan*, September 1982, pp. 22–27.

13 Task Force on Education for Economic Growth, p. 27.

14 Boyer, p. 172.

15 Jere Brophy, "Successful teaching strategies for the inner-city child," *Phi Delta Kappan*, April 1982, p. 529.

16 Feistritzer, pp. 59–60.

17 Boyer, pp. 175–76.

18 Conant, p. 141.

19 Conant, p. 51.

20 *An alternative route . . ., passim.*

21 In addition to Ernest Boyer, who is president of the Carnegie Foundation for the Advancement of Teaching, with headquarters in Princeton. N. J., the panel included: David Berliner, professor of educational psychology at the University of Arizona, Tucson; Frank Brown, dean of education at the University of North Carolina, Chapel Hill; Edgar Epps, professor of urban education at the University of Chicago; Emily Feistritzer, director of the National Center for Education Information, Washington, D.C.; Jay Gottlieb, professor of educational psychology at New York University, New York City; Lawrence Lezotte, director of the Center for School Improvement, Michigan State University, East Lansing; Archie Lapointe, executive director of the Center for the Assessment of Educational Progress, Educational Testing Service, Princeton, N.J.; Kathryn Maddox, director of the Multi-Institutional Teacher Education Center, Kanawha County Schools. Charleston, W. Va.; and Barak Rosenshine, professor of education, University of Illinois, Urbana.

22 *Report of a panel on the preparation of beginning teachers*, Ernest L. Boyer, chairman (Princeton: New Jersey State Department of Education, March 1984).

23 Ibid.

24 Ibid., p. 2.

25 *Report of the State Commission on Alternative Teacher Certification*, Harry Jaroslaw, chairman (Trenton: New Jersey State Department of Education, May 1984).

26 Linda Darling-Hammond, *Beyond the commission report: the coming crisis in teaching* (Santa Monica, Calif: Rand Corporation, July 1984), p. v.

27 Feistritzer, p. 52.

7.8 Alternate routes to teacher certification
A dangerous trend

Doyle Watts

Source: Doyle Watts, Alternate routes to teacher certification: a dangerous trend. *Action in Teacher Education*, 2, 1986, pp. 25–29

INTRODUCTION

The teaching profession has been plagued by the existence of a variety of substandard certificates including emergency, temporary and provisional. As undesirable as they are, these credentials are at least recognized as being inferior to standard teaching certificates. Persons issued substandard credentials are usually limited in the length of time they can teach and, if they wish to remain in the classroom, they have to meet standard certification requirements. The recent development of alternate routes to standard teacher certification poses a much greater threat to the quality of the teaching profession and our educational system. Unfortunately, it appears that the practice of issuing substandard credentials is being replaced with substandard preparation programs which lead to standard teaching certificates.

Persons who complete an alternate plan are issued the same professional certificate as teachers who are prepared through a standard program. This would not be of concern if alternate routes to teacher certification were of equal or superior quality. Regrettably, existing alternate certification programs are inferior. Indeed, alternate routes only appear to be short cuts for unqualified individuals to obtain teaching credentials and, thus, ill-prepared teachers are placed in charge of children's education.

The commissioner of education in New Jersey described his state's alternate route to certification in this fashion, "the reforms . . . were intended to replace the emergency system with a rigorous and legitimate alternate system . . ." (Cooperman, 1985, p. 24). Wonderful, if you believe that replacing a temporary substandard certificate with a substandard route to standard certification is an improvement. As Haberman (1985) pointed out, the New Jersey plan that Mr. Cooperman was praising requires less preservice practice for teacher candidates than that state mandates for cosmetologists, manicurists, barbers, private detectives or funeral directors. It does not appear, therefore, that New Jersey is leading the charge to achieve excellence in education through its alternate program for teacher preparation.

The requirements for alternate routes to teacher certification are inferior to those for standard preparation programs in at least one of four areas. First, applicants may be permitted to teach in subject fields where they have less academic preparation than is required for standard programs. In addition, alternate routes may require less college preparation in academic foundations. Also, teacher candidates in alternate programs may be required to have little or no pedagogical preparation. Finally, regulations for alternate preparation programs may not require participants to pass competency examinations and achieve performance standards which are mandatory for teacher trainees in standard preparation programs. An excellent illustration of how quality standards are lower for alternate routes to teacher certification is Texas House Bill 72. This legislation specifically exempts those who progress through an alternate program for teacher certification from being required to take the competency examination in pedagogical knowledge which is required of all teacher candidates prepared through standard certification programs. It seems the Texas legislature has taken the peculiar position that a teacher prepared through an alternative program does not need to know how to teach.

WHY ALTERNATE PROGRAMS EXIST

The authority to establish standards and regulations for teacher preparation programs rests with state legislatures and state departments of education. Consequently, they must bear full responsibility for creating substandard credentialing processes which place the educational welfare of children in the hands of teachers who have not been properly prepared. The reasons given for opening these poorly defended back doors to teacher certification are not tenable.

One of the justifications frequently cited is the alleged shortage of teachers. But does a teacher shortage mean that there are fewer qualified teachers than there are available teaching positions; or does it indicate there is only a shortage of qualified teachers who are willing to accept available teaching positions in certain school systems? Although accurate data are difficult to obtain, it seems that colleges of education are continuing to prepare far more teachers than there are available teaching positions. For example, during the 1980–81 school year 3,257 teacher candidates graduated from Oklahoma colleges and universities but of that number only 1883 were employed in Oklahoma schools (Oklahoma State Department of Education, 1982). On the national level, there were 159,485 graduates completing teacher preparation in 1980 for the 71,425 open positions (NEA, 1981). During the 1980–81 school year, 140,639 graduates completed teacher preparation programs with only 76,550 available positions (NEA, 1983). Although these data are not current, they do indicate a continuing trend to prepare more teachers than there are available teaching positions. Consequently, it appears that, overall, vacant teaching positions are not due to a lack of qualified teachers but, instead, to a district's inability to attract those teachers.

Why then, do teacher shortages exist in some areas? For what reasons are we unable to staff certain schools with properly prepared teachers? The reasons are unclear. However, Goodlad (1983) found that teachers leaving the profession cited excessive administrative requirements, lack of professional autonomy, poor parental support and the absence of a practitioner-client relationship between teacher and students as their principal reasons for deciding to resign. And, of course, poor salaries have been cited extensively as being a factor in creating teacher shortages.

It seems that large inner city districts are the ones experiencing the most difficulty in attracting qualified teachers. As a result, these systems are having to depend more and more upon teachers with limited preparation to staff their schools. In striving to solve the problem of teacher shortages, these systems and state departments of education would be well advised to direct their efforts toward the solution of conditions which keep qualified teachers out of these classrooms instead of attempting to unearth means by which standards can be circumvented and poorly prepared teachers placed in schools. Inner city school systems might be more successful in attracting and retaining qualified teachers if funds presently earmarked to import teachers from abroad and to provide superficial teacher training to unprepared adults were used to improve conditions which make the inner city schools an unattractive place for teachers to practice.

A second justification is the claim that pedagogical preparation is unnecessary and that any educated person can teach effectively. This is an odd notion. Other professions are not subjected to this kind of attack. Few would profess that knowledge and skills developed in medical school are unnecessary for the successful practice of medicine or that dental schools contribute nothing worthwhile to the practice of dentistry. Yet, in the teaching profession, weak preparation programs are justified with the absurd assumption that teachers have no need of formal preparation in pedagogical knowledge and skills.

The belief that standard teacher preparation programs are somehow preventing outstanding individuals from entering the profession also exists. One hears the complaint that Socrates could not pass teachers competency examinations or meet present teacher certification requirements and, consequently, would not be permitted to teach in a modern American school. It is therefore concluded that present teacher certification standards are keeping potentially excellent teachers out of the classroom. But it is also true that Hippocrates would likely have trouble passing a modern medical examination and Plato would probably be unable to answer a majority of the questions on a current bar exam. However, in the case of medicine and law, this condition is not used as a justification to eliminate standards for entrance into those professions.

Also, those who favor substandard routes to teacher certification maintain that having a poorly qualified adult in the classroom is better than having no one there. But is a poor teacher better than no teacher? We must consider that extensive damage may be done to students through ignorance on the part of poorly trained teachers. In addition, the use of ill-prepared teachers encourages delays in seeking effective solutions to the causes of these shortages. Of all the professions, teaching seems to be the only one where a shortage of practitioners is solved by reducing the quality and duration of professional preparation. Understandably, the American Association of Colleges for Teacher Education's Task Force on Certification has called for "a halt to the practice of admitting unqualified persons into the profession through emergency certification procedures or 'alternatives' " (AACTE Task Force on Teacher Certification, 1984, p. 23).

HOW ALTERNATE PROGRAMS ARE ESTABLISHED

Unlike other professions, substandard credentials and short-cut routes to certification have not only been tolerated by the teaching profession but accepted by state departments of education and employing school districts as being legitimate. I know of no state that provides substandard credentials or allows substandard routes to standard credentials for the practice of medicine, law or pharmacy. Yet a great majority of the states provide ways a person may acquire a teaching credential through some short-cut strategy (Watts, 1982).

No distinctions are made in terms of salary, benefits, status, or professional authority and responsibility based on the type of preparation program the person completes. Those who progress through weak alternate certification procedures are granted the same professional rights and privileges as teachers who complete standard programs. Consequently, many less capable persons may be attracted to alternate preparation routes that are shorter and less demanding than standard programs. The big losers, of course, are students who receive inferior pedagogical services.

Unlike other practicing professionals who publicly display their professional licenses, teachers' certificates are almost never publicly displayed but are, instead, filed away in personnel folders in central administrative offices. Neither parents nor students are informed concerning the type of certificate held by the practicing teacher or how it was acquired.

THE RESULTS OF ALTERNATE PROGRAMS

Although there is little empirical research information concerning the effects that teachers prepared through alternate programs are having on the teaching profession and the quality of our educational system, the impact is not likely to be favorable. Such investigations are needed now.

Long term, harmful effects on students are possible. Incompetent practice can have a damaging influence on the educational and psychological welfare of students. We take steps to ensure that the dentist who fills our child's tooth has the proper training to accomplish that task. Anyone who practices as a dentist without such training would be subject to criminal charges. Yet we permit persons without proper training to practice as teachers of our children. The effects incompetent teachers have on our youth and society may be much more serious and destructive than permitting an ill-prepared person to fill a tooth.

Because of inadequate professional preparation, teachers may use inappropriate or ineffective pedagogical strategies and techniques resulting in students' inferior academic achievement. The effects could be devastating. Consequently, many students will fail to achieve their potential because of their lack of essential knowledge and skills. Not so obvious but equally important is the negative impact that poor academic achievement can have on students' attitudes, self-confidence and self-concept. Thus, we must take special care to ensure that those charged with the responsibility of delivering educational services to our youth have the necessary professional preparation to deliver those services in a competent fashion which incorporates much more than a simplistic notion that teaching is the delivery of facts and information.

The use of substandard routes to credentialing teachers also keeps teaching from progressing as a profession. When persons who have little or no professional training are issued credentials to teach, it is difficult to convince anyone that teaching is an important or difficult task. This incorrect perception inhibits the development of preparation programs comparable in scope and quality with those of other professions. Thus, the notion is perpetuated that most of a teacher's pedagogical training can be picked up on the job and that pedagogical knowledge and skills are not necessary anyway. Consequently, the progress of the profession is constantly stymied. In the long run, such stagnation will only hurt the children.

At a time when many schools of education are expanding their teacher preparation programs to five and six years, poorly designed alternate certification schemes are also springing up. If the trend continues and if alternate preparation programs continue to be inferior, in the near future, school systems in small cities and suburbs may be staffed with teachers who have completed extended teacher preparation programs while inner city districts are only able to attract as teachers persons who have much less professional training. As a result, the gap in the quality of education in urban and suburban districts will widen. Those students who need the most capable, best trained teachers will be served by weak, poorly prepared counterfeits.

CONCLUSION

If alternate routes to teacher certification actually meant a higher quality preparation system, then these programs would merit support. Unfortunately, they only appear to be a quick-fix scheme designed to place any adult, regardless of his/her professional preparation, in vacant classrooms. Consequently, they are another obstacle to efforts to advance the teaching profession and to achieve excellence in our educational system.

REFERENCES

1 AACTE Task Force on Teacher Certification. (1984) Emergency teacher certification: Summary and recommendations. *Journal of Teacher Education*, 35 (2), 21–25.
2 Cooperman, S. (June 5, 1985) In defense of New Jersey's alternate certification plan. *Education Week*, p. 24.
3 Goodlad, J. (1983) Access to knowledge. *Teachers College Record*, 84 (4), 787–800.

4   Haberman, M. (October, 1985) Skewed standards (Letter to the editor). *Phi Delta Kappan*, 67 (2), 167.

5   NEA Research Memo (1981) *Teacher supply and demand in public schools, 1980–81.* Washington, D.C.: National Education Association.

6   NEA Research Memo (1983) Teacher supply and demand in public schools, 1981–82.

7   Oklahoma State Department of Education (1982) *Teacher supply and demand in Oklahoma public schools.* Oklahoma City, Oklahoma.

8   Watts, D. (1982) Can campus-based preservice teacher education survive? *Journal of Teacher Education*, 33 (4) 35–39.

7.9 Break the link

Frederick M. Hess

Source: Frederick M. Hess, Break the link. *Education Next*, 2002.
Downloaded January 2006 from http://www.educationnext.org/
20021/22.html

The fact that schools of education could no longer rely on a captive body of aspiring teachers would expose them to the cleansing winds of competition

Picture Gerard, a 28-year-old business consultant who majored in economics at Williams College and graduated with a 3.7 GPA. Gerard has been working for a consulting firm in Stamford, Connecticut, but is looking for a new, more fulfilling position. He has demonstrated strong interpersonal skills and work habits. In addition, though he didn't major in math, he aced several calculus courses in college. Yet if Gerard were to apply through normal channels to teach math at a junior high school in the Hartford public school system, his application wouldn't even be considered. Why? Because he isn't a certified teacher.

Why shouldn't a principal or a faculty hiring committee in the Hartford schools even be allowed to look at Gerard's application, to judge his qualifications against those of other candidates? The assumption undergirding the contemporary approach to teacher certification is that public school hiring personnel are either unable or unwilling to gauge the quality of applicants. Our response has been to embrace a bureaucratic solution that handcuffs the capable and incapable alike and supposedly keeps weak teachers out of the classroom. As a result, having discouraged or turned away Gerard and hundreds like him, many large school systems resort to last-minute fill-ins who teach on emergency certificates.

This is not to suggest, even for a moment, that candidates with "real world" experience or high GPAs are necessarily qualified or equipped to become teachers or that professional preparation for teachers is unimportant. It is only to say that some potential applicants *might* be more effective teachers than the alternatives that are currently available to public schools.

The central premise underlying teacher certification is that—no matter what their qualifications are—anyone who has not completed the specified training is unsuited to enter a classroom and must be prohibited from applying for a job. Presumably, the danger is that, in a moment of weakness, a school official otherwise will mistakenly hire such an applicant rather than an appropriately trained teacher. It is essential to remember what we often seem to forget, which is that allowing someone to apply for a job is not the same as guaranteeing him employment. Making applicants eligible for a position simply permits an employer to hire them *in the event that they are deemed superior to the existing alternatives*. The argument against certification is not that unconventional applicants *will* be good teachers; it is only that they *might* be. If one believes this, case-by-case judgments are clearly more appropriate than an inflexible bureaucratic rule.

Imagine if colleges and universities refused to hire anyone who lacked a Ph.D. They would lose the talents and insights of "lay practitioners" like poet Maya Angelou, journalist William Raspberry, or former public officials such as Alan Simpson, Julian Bond, and Al Gore. The artists and writers "in residence" at dozens of public universities would fail to meet the criteria implicit in the public school certification model. Do we really believe that these universities are ill-serving their students by hiring people whom the public schools would consider unqualified?

COMPETITIVE CERTIFICATION

The theory behind certifying or licensing public school teachers is that this process elevates the profession by ensuring that aspiring teachers master a well-documented and broadly accepted body of knowledge and skills important to teaching. Supporters of teacher certification often make analogies to professions like law and medicine, where being an effective professional requires the acquisition of vast knowledge and skills. Licensure in these professions ensures at least minimal competency and boosts the public's confidence in members of the profession.

The problem is that no comparable body of knowledge and skills exists in teaching. Debate rages over the merits of various pedagogical strategies, and even teacher educators and certification proponents have a hard time defining a clear set of concrete skills that makes for a good teacher. Yet most aspiring teachers are still forced to run a gauntlet of courses, requirements, and procedures created by accredited training programs that vary dramatically in quality.

This is not to deny that teacher education can provide valuable training. After all, one may think that journalism schools produce better journalists without requiring all journalists to complete a mandatory set of courses before seeking work in the profession. Instead, it is assumed that a candidate's training is factored into the hiring process, along with considerations like aptitude, diligence, and energy.

Clearly some sort of screening process for aspiring teachers is essential; parents and the public rightly expect safeguards for those working with youngsters. What is needed is a competitive certification process that establishes key criteria for entry into the teaching profession; gives public schools greater freedom to hire and fire teachers; and treats teachers like professionals and their schools like professional institutions by allowing them to tailor professional development to meet the needs of teachers. Under such a model, aspiring teachers ought to be able to *apply* for a teaching job if they:

- Possess a B.A. or B.S. degree from a recognized college or university.
- Pass a test that demonstrates competency in knowledge or skills essential to what they seek to teach. The definition of "essential" knowledge or skills is obviously a loose one that can be interpreted in myriad ways and rightly should be different for those wishing to teach younger children or older students. The key point is to demand that teachers at least have an appropriate academic knowledge of the material they will be teaching.
- Pass a rigorous criminal background check. States conduct such checks now, but they tend to be compromised by the state's need to engage simultaneously in related certification paperwork.

Beyond these minimal qualifications, the competitive approach presumes that preparation and training are not only desirable but also essential, as is true in other professions where subtle skills and interpersonal dynamics are essential to effective performance. The questions are where to obtain this training and who should pay for it. Contemporary teacher preparation imposes nearly all of the costs on candidates by forcing them into a system of training that removes key incentives for quality and relevance in teacher preparation. The competitive model instead treats teachers as autonomous professionals able to make informed decisions about developing their skills and expertise. In short, the competitive model would substitute meaningful professional development for what is essentially a guild system funded by levying a significant tuition-based tax on aspiring teachers before permitting them to enter the profession.

THE ASSUMPTIONS OF CERTIFICATION

Over the years, an array of studies has sought to determine whether certified teachers serve students more effectively than uncertified teachers. There are two problems with this line of work. First, the methodological wrangling has often obscured the larger questions and the central assumptions of the certification model. Second, the case for certification is thin *whether or not* certified teachers boost student achievement more than their uncertified peers. The issue is *not* whether teacher education improves the performance of graduates, but whether we ought to—as best we are able—bar from teaching those who have not completed an approved preparatory program. Certification systems deny school administrators the ability to take their context or the promise of a particular applicant into account when hiring. Even if certified teachers are generally more effective than uncertified teachers, such a policy only makes sense if we believe that uncertified applicants are uniformly incompetent to teach or that school administrators cannot be trusted to assess their competence.

The allure of certification rests on three implicit assumptions. They are the beliefs that: (1) the training one receives while getting certified is so useful that the uncertified will be relatively ill-prepared; (2) certification weeds out unsuitable candidates; and (3) certification makes teaching more "professional" and therefore a more attractive career. However, each of these presumptions is problematic in the case of teacher certification.

As a general principle, certification is most effective when the licensing body ensures that aspiring professionals have mastered essential skills or knowledge and denies a license to inadequate performers. Licensure is most essential when a professional's tasks are critical and when clients may have trouble assessing a provider's qualifications. For instance, licensure is considered particularly appropriate for engineers, doctors, and attorneys because those who design bridges, tend us when we are ill, or defend our rights all perform tasks essential to our well-being and are frequently charged with aiding us at our most vulnerable. Moreover, it can be difficult for members of the public to know whether a bridge is properly designed, whether a doctor is performing appropriately, or whether an attorney is knowledgeable in the law. Licensing is not an assurance that these professionals are talented practitioners, but it does ensure that they have demonstrated an established degree of professional knowledge.

Educators are also charged with a crucial task. However, the oversight challenge is very different in education, where we have not established a specific, measurable body of skills or knowledge that teachers must master. Educational "experts" themselves argue that teaching is so complex that it can be difficult to judge a good teacher outside of a specific classroom context. This makes it difficult, if not impossible, to determine abstractly which aspirants possess satisfactory "teaching skills." Meanwhile, there is widespread agreement that colleagues, supervisors, and families have at least a proximate ability to gauge whether a teacher is effective. Given these circumstances, it is unclear how standardized licensing helps to safeguard teacher quality.

Such a conclusion does not require refuting the claims of teacher educators or the supporters of certification. It actually follows if one simply accepts their claims. Professional educators themselves have thus far been unable to explain in any concrete sense what makes a teacher competent or what teachers need to know and be able to do.

Consider the widely praised standards that the National Board for Professional Teaching Standards (NBPTS) has painstakingly constructed in 27 distinct fields, standards that certification's proponents have hailed as a breakthrough in quality control. The area where the NBPTS ought to have the easiest time creating straightforward standards is high school math and science teaching, where there is widespread consensus as to what teachers are supposed to do. Even in these areas, however, the NBPTS's "exemplary" standards are so broad and vague as to make concrete judgments of competence nearly impossible. For instance, to receive National Board certification to teach high-school math, teachers are to demonstrate mastery of

11 standards, including: commitment to students and their learning, the art of teaching, reflection and growth, and reasoning and thinking mathematically. The board tries to clarify these standards by explaining, for instance, that "commitment" is interpreted as meaning that "accomplished mathematics teachers value and acknowledge the individuality and worth of each student, believe that all students can learn," and so on. Mastering the "art of teaching" is taken to mean that teachers "stimulate and facilitate student learning by using a wide range of formats and procedures." While these are certainly admirable sentiments, nowhere in the National Board's rarified standards is it clear how we are to gauge just what constitutes "competence" in these tasks. The result, unsurprisingly, is that the board has been assailed for the capricious way in which the standards are being interpreted and applied. Despite the best of intentions in the drafting of the INTASC standards, which Mary Diez discusses, a cursory read makes clear that they are plagued by the same ambiguities evident in the NBPTS standards.

For another prominent example, consider education professors Gerald Grant and Christine E. Murray's award-winning 1999 Harvard University Press book, *Teaching in America*. They identify five "essential [teaching] acts" that can be analyzed and taught: listening with care; motivating the student; modeling caring by hearing and responding to the pain of others, and by creating a sense of security in their classrooms; evaluating by clarifying, coaching, advising, and deciding on an appropriate challenge for this boy or that girl; and reflecting and renewing. How one is to teach these five "essential acts," much less determine whether a teacher has satisfactorily mastered them, are questions that Grant and Murray never address.

If clear standards of professional competence do not exist, we typically (and appropriately) hesitate to prohibit some individuals from practicing a profession. This is not to say that we think incompetence is acceptable in such a profession—only that we recognize licensing as an ineffective and potentially pernicious way to control quality. While licensure could protect community members (including children) from exposure to "bad" entrepreneurs or journalists, we do not prohibit some people from seeking to start businesses or work for a newspaper. Instead, we trust that potential investors or employers are the best judges of who ought to be supported or hired. If an aspiring writer or entrepreneur is unsuccessful, we trust that they will eventually be persuaded to find a line of work for which they are better suited. This free-flowing process fosters diversity and ensures that unconventional workers are given a chance to succeed.

Even in professions with clear knowledge- or performance-based benchmarks for certification, as in law or medicine, licensure is useful primarily as a way of establishing minimal competence. A medical or a law license is not imagined to ensure competence in ambiguous, subtle skills like comforting a patient or swaying a jury—skills analogous to the interpersonal relations thought crucial to teaching. Basing certification on such traits is difficult, because we may disagree about what they entail or how they can be assessed devoid of context. The skills that teacher educators deem most important—listening, caring, motivating—are not susceptible to standardized quality control. Emphasis on these qualities is the norm in professions like marketing, journalism, consulting, or policymaking, where a subtle blend of people skills, knowledge, and relevant expertise is required. In professions like these, where there are a number of ways for practitioners to excel but where it is difficult to know in advance how any particular practitioner will perform, the most sensible way to find talent is to allow aspirants to seek work and to permit employers to screen on a variety of criteria—such as education, experience, and references.

A DUBIOUS SCREEN

While certification can serve to screen out aspirants who fail to meet a minimal performance standard, our current system is not designed to do so. Generally speaking, schools of education are not selective, flunk out few if any students for inadequate performance, and see that many of their teacher education graduates receive teacher licenses. The licensing exams are simple, and standards for passage are generally so low that the Education Trust concluded they exclude only the "weakest of the weak" from classrooms.

More than 1,300 institutions provide the training required for licensure. While defenders of the current approach to certification often focus on the certification programs at elite institutions, the top 25 education schools train less than 5 percent of the roughly 200,000 new graduates that teacher programs produce each year. It is the regional colleges, such as Illinois State University, Cal State–Hayward, and Southwest Texas State University—not the Stanfords and the Ohio States—that train and license the vast majority of teachers. The value of certification turns not on the quality of elite programs but on that of regional colleges.

Teacher-preparation programs neither screen out nor weed out weak candidates. Even at elite schools, such as UCLA or the University of North Carolina, where admissions rates are about 5 percent for medical school and 25 percent for law school, the M.Ed. programs (which include those seeking postgraduate training for teacher certification) accept more than half of their applicants. Moreover, education-school officials often make it clear that they do not see their mission as weeding out students during their course of study. Notes one such official, "We're here to develop teachers, not to screen people out. For the most part, everyone who enters the program is going to complete it, unless they decide that teaching's not for them."

THE COSTS OF CERTIFICATION

Especially for anyone who didn't complete a teacher-training program as an undergraduate, the costs of certification can be significant. It is not unusual for postgraduate teacher training programs to require a full-time commitment of 16 or even 24 months or a part-time commitment that can stretch to three years or more. The cost of training and the loss of salary due to time spent out of the workforce can easily reduce a teacher's real compensation during her first five years by 25 percent or more.

These barriers make other professions relatively more attractive, so that potentially talented teachers who are unsure about their interest are less likely to try teaching. Whereas candidates can readily try journalism or consulting or marketing for a year, they must make an extensive commitment before they can try public school teaching. The result is that many who might make fine teachers never enter the profession. There is disturbing evidence that certification may especially dissuade accomplished minority candidates—who have a number of attractive career options and who are often less well situated to absorb the costs of teacher preparation—from entering teaching.

This would pose no real problem if we were blessed with a surplus of good teachers. In such a case, we might scoff "good riddance" to those dissuaded from teaching. However, we have a desperate need for competent teachers. Moreover, rather than a lack of commitment to teaching, a reluctance to pursue certification may indicate that individuals have attractive alternatives. It is the most talented and hardest working individuals who have the most career options and who sacrifice the most by entering a profession where compensation is unlinked to performance and where opportunities for advancement are few. They may wish to teach but be unwilling to forgo work for a year, sit through poorly regarded courses, or jump through procedural hurdles. It is candidates with fewer attractive options who will find the tedious but intellectually undemanding requirements of certification less problematic. In fact, by suppressing the supply of teachers, certification provides teachers with enhanced job security. Coupled with a compensation scale that rewards seniority rather than performance, certification may well make the profession more attractive to graduates seeking a less demanding line of work. In this way, certification can actually harm the public's perception of teaching as a profession—the very opposite of what certification proponents wish to do.

CREATIVE DESTRUCTION

In a world without certification as we know it, districts and schools would have more flexibility to ensure that their new teachers are prepared, inducted, and supervised in a manner appropriate to the challenges at hand. Because aspiring teachers would no longer have to attend formal teacher-preparation programs in order to teach, they would be free to make professional decisions about training in the same manner as business school or journalism school students. Weaker teacher-preparation programs would likely fall by the wayside. The fact that schools of education could no longer rely on a captive body of aspiring teachers would expose them to the cleansing winds of competition. Schools would have to contribute value—by providing teacher training, services, or research that created demand and attracted support—or face significant cutbacks. Teacher-preparation programs would find it in their own self-interest to ensure that their graduates were knowledgeable and skilled, as this would help graduates to win desirable jobs amid increased competition, making preparatory institutions more attractive.

Under a competitive certification system, little is likely to change in many of our high-performing suburban districts, where officials are inundated with applicants and are unlikely to tamper with a formula that is "working." In such districts, except in rare cases, we would expect that administrators would continue to cherry-pick from the nation's top teacher-education graduates. It is in the less desirable and more troubled systems, the nation's urban and rural school districts, that administrators currently have tremendous difficulty finding sufficient numbers of certified teachers. This is doubly true in the areas of math and science education. It is in these districts and subjects, where critics have fretted about the numbers of long-term substitutes and "burned out" veterans, where the wave of new teachers will most likely be recruited and welcomed. While many of the resultant applicants will no doubt be deemed unprepared or unsuited for the jobs they pursue, there are few urban or rural principals who would not welcome the chance to pick and choose from their ranks.

Critics may fear that the elimination of licensure requirements will mean the end of teacher preparation and professional development. Such concern is unfounded. First, allowing uncertified individuals to become teachers does not mean that they must be viewed as "completed" professionals. Such a mindset is one of the vestiges of our current system, which is erected on a premise that all teachers are certified and therefore competent. Here, a better model might be medicine or law, where entering professionals begin their career with a trial period (serving as a hospital resident or as a junior partner in a law firm, for instance) during which their full panoply of skills is developed and monitored. Beginning teachers might serve on a probationary basis, receiving substantial monitoring and counseling. However, legal and contractual language ought to make it much simpler to terminate ineffective teachers or to mandate that they engage in support activities designed to improve their performance.

Second, moving to competitive certification does not mean doing away with professional teacher-education programs. Many applicants attend journalism school or business school, even though such training is not officially required, because it may make graduates more effective and can help them find better employment more readily. Likewise, aspiring teachers would presumably continue to attend those teacher-training programs thought to enhance their employability. This change would introduce some much-needed market pressure in this area, as schools would be forced to compete for students based on the usefulness of their course offerings.

Giving districts more leeway to hire promising candidates does not mean they will always make good decisions. Some ineffective teachers will inevitably continue to be hired. However, if entry to the profession is eased, it is appropriate that exit be eased as well. If administrators are to have more leeway to make hiring decisions, they also must be given more leeway to fire—and they must be held accountable for both sets of decisions.

At the end of the day, the individuals best equipped to assess the qualifications of prospective teachers are the principals who will be responsible for them. These same principals ought to have the strongest incentive to see that teachers are effective. If we believe that the administrators charged with managing and supervising schools either are unequipped to evaluate prospective teachers or are unwilling to do so, teacher certification will not suffice to protect our children from such profound systemic dysfunction. If we trust administrators, then certification is unnecessary and entails significant costs. If we don't trust administrators, let us address that issue directly and not rely on the hollow promise of flimsy parchment barriers. Regardless, it is past time to fully acknowledge the nuanced, multifaceted, and professional nature of teaching and to move beyond a system that restricts professional entry with procedural barriers characterized by ambiguity that are the result of an inability to clearly define the skills, knowledge, or training essential to good teaching.

7.10 Ignoring the policy makers to improve teacher preparation

Richard L. Allington
University of Tennessee

Source: Richard L. Allington, Ignoring the policy makers to improve teacher preparation. *Journal of Teacher Education*, 56(3), 2005, pp. 199–204

I think it is time for those of us in teacher education to consider ignoring the educational policy makers that are undermining our efforts to develop thoughtful, autonomous, and effective teachers. Current federal teaching and learning policy is more likely to undermine teacher quality than improve it (Cochran-Smith, 2002; Darling-Hammond & Youngs, 2002). Federal and state mandates on standards and testing are narrowing the curriculum and are focused on the lowest levels of learning (Elmore & Rothman, 1999; Hillocks, 2002; Paris & Urdan, 2000). Federal efforts to establish so-called "proven" programs as the mandated curriculum (Allington & Nowak, 2004) work against filling classrooms with powerful teaching provided by engaged, expert teachers. In addition, each of these policies flies in the face of what the research says about effective teaching and learning.

I suggest that it is a rare policy maker that shares my understandings of how we might best foster expertise and personal professional accountability in teachers. It is even rarer to find a policy maker who cares one whit about what the research says (unless it supports personal views or the findings are reflected in polling data). Federal and state policy makers routinely ignore the research evidence on improving teaching and learning and offer, instead, grand schemes that simply cannot be expected to achieve the meritorious goals suggested in the bipartisan advocacy for the federalization of teaching and teacher education (Allington, 1999, 2001, 2002).

I have watched as federal and state policies concerning improved reading instruction have been enacted across the nation—policies that often have little base in research and little credibility among those who work in the complex organizations we call schools. I have watched as educational research has been savaged and redefined as a narrow set of quantitative schemes. I have watched as the two states where I have recently worked (Florida and New York) have crafted tighter and tighter regulations for teacher education, often with the support of the National Council for Accreditation of Teacher Education (NCATE), while at the same time deregulating entry into the profession for those who have never set foot in a college of education.

It was during my first NCATE/Florida Department of Education accreditation review, as I watched faculty expend enormous time and effort sitting in meetings to learn the process developing matrices, targeted assessments, standardized course outlines, and such, the college expended substantial funds for consultants and lots of administrator and support staff time, that I began to wonder if the irony of the process of earning accreditation had occurred to others.

As far as I can tell, the whole point to accreditation, as now conceived by NCATE and state education agencies, is to homogenize teacher preparation, usually in the direction of the lowest common denominator. We are pressed to accept statewide course syllabi, assignments, and assessments, even statewide college textbook adoptions. Our students are pressed to develop standardized electronic portfolios (seems oxymoronic to me), to prepare to take standardized group achievement tests of professional and content knowledge, and to elect as their under-graduate majors one of five or six core disciplines (but child development, linguistics, and sociology are not among those majors suggested).

Art Wise (1979), now NCATE executive director, wrote some years ago about "goal reduction" as one outcome of bureaucratic rationalization and centralization. Goal reduction evolves as an unintended effect of rationalizing education. Setting goals results in minimal expectations and the exclusion of some goals (those on which not everyone would agree or those not amenable to group standardized testing). Preeminence is given to goals that seem to address pressing social problems versus individual goals (national economy vs. individual fulfillment). He concluded that

> in the drive to make educational institutions accountable, goals have become narrow, selective, and minimal. That which is measurable is preferred to that which is immeasurable.
>
> (p. 59)

I would suggest that he described what is happening in teacher education today.

My response, the only one that seems viable to me, in fact, is that we begin a campaign to ignore state and federal bureaucrats and policy makers who would dumb down our work. I think teacher educators need to seriously consider what benefits to them (or their students), if any, are actually accrued by earning accreditation for their programs. In other words, I am arguing that we disassociate our programs, our institutions, and ourselves from the whole accreditation process. We would do well to also consider disassociating ourselves from the teacher credentialing process. I am convinced that we must document that the courses and experiences offered in our teacher education programs do matter. Unfortunately, the teacher educator's role in credentialing has become more a matter of assuring the right course distribution than documenting graduates' expertise and effectiveness. All those completed matrices may look official but they are, fundamentally, bureaucratic ruses rather than convincing evidence of competence.

BENEFITS OF IGNORING STATE AND FEDERAL ACCREDITATION AND CREDENTIALING MANDATES

I see potential benefits from electing to ignore state and federal policies regarding accreditation and credentialing.

A renewed focus on what is important in teacher development

Is there anyone who has been through an NCATE/Department of Education review who cannot document the trivialization of teacher education (Johnson *et al.*, in press)? How many thousands of hours are taken from other activities to create mindless matrices of standards from state education agencies, the NCATE, and one or more specialized professional associations (e.g. National Council of Teachers of English, Association for Childhood Education International, International Reading Association, National Science Teachers Association)? Or to attempt "to document," that is, assess, whether students have acquired the appropriate "dispositions" required to be credentialed? And what research suggests that only certain dispositions are found in effective teachers? Or that anyone can reliably assess a disposition?

What evidence demonstrates that accredited teacher education programs more often prepare effective teachers than nonaccredited programs (about half of the teacher education programs in the United States are not accredited by the NCATE or the Teacher Education Accreditation Council)? We do know that graduates of traditional (but not necessarily NCATE-accredited) teacher education programs differ on several qualities important to both their employers and their students (Darling-Hammond & Youngs, 2002; Ferguson, 1991; Hoffman & Roller, 2001). But there is no convincing evidence that national program accreditation reliably predicts the development of more effective teachers.

Perhaps this lack of research is irrelevant. My primary concern is that by participating in state and national accreditation processes, we are eliminating our best opportunity to develop programs that produce effective teachers even more reliably. Given the federal fervor surrounding "scientific evidence" as the basis for educational decision making, I have taken the stance that without substantially better evidence that a national, corporate model of accreditation is an effective option, we have an obligation to continue to explore just what sorts of courses and experiences develop the teachers this nation needs.

Deciding to pass on the accreditation of our teacher education programs produces that opportunity to experiment with "homegrown" teacher education plans. It is, in my view, experimentation that is the engine that drives improvement. It is exploration, not mindless adherence to mandates, that offers us the best option for improving teacher education. Personal professional accountability should be the standard for both teachers and teacher educators. But such accountability rarely arises when we simply do what we are told to do. If I am given the syllabus, the textbook requirement, and a set of assessments that I must complete for each of my teacher education students, why would I feel accountable if few of them actually become effective teachers?

Perhaps we would be satisfied to let the marketplace determine our success under this model. That is, do our candidates get hired and are school districts satisfied with their performance? The lack of research support for the accreditation model suggests that gaining professional employment under a marketplace model would differ little from what already exists. Schools would continue to hire graduates of institutions known to reliably produce effective teachers, accredited or not.

We should work to capture accreditation process money and time for use in far more frequently and rigorously evaluating just what sort of teachers we are preparing. The time, energy, and money that are now spent preparing for and passing through an accreditation process could be used, instead, to fund and staff ongoing studies of the effects of our work. The costs of pursuing NCATE accreditation have been estimated to fall in the US$100,000 to US$800,000 range, without accounting for faculty time spent preparing all those standard syllabi and matrices of accomplishments (Johnson et al., in press). That is a lot of money and faculty time buyout to do research to assist us in deciding what sorts of things really matter in the preparation of effective teachers. And because we would be using internal funding (which means we should not have to turn over that 50 percent of a grant now assigned to indirect costs and overhead), we could employ a wide range of research methods, not just those now deemed "fundable" by federal research agencies.

Imagine the sort of studies that might be done with the resources allocated to an accreditation review. In my experience, that would mean a couple of full-time consultants for a period of 3 years or more, a secretary position, several graduate research assistants, a project director (using the administrative line usually assigned to head the accreditation process), and substantial release time and "borrowed" time from faculty members, including many from outside the college of education (e.g. art, music, agriculture, history, and health and human development departments). An interdisciplinary research team with financial and faculty resources focused on improving our current efforts. I can imagine any number of creative and powerful studies that might be accomplished with such support. It is not that such resources are not available but rather, that those resources are currently allocated to the accreditation process. Capturing those resources to support a continuous program of research on teacher education is, in my view, more likely to improve our teacher preparation than if we elect to simply continue complying with dumbed-down bureaucratic demands.

What I am suggesting is that there is a professional imperative to provide good, local evidence of effects of teacher preparation. We cannot simply continue to comply with norms and processes formulated by state and federal bureaucrats and policy makers and consider ourselves professional. In fact, compliance suggests that we are attempting to abdicate responsibility to study what we do and the effect our work has on our students. What I am arguing for is greater personal professional accountability among teacher educators and better evidence of the impact of our efforts on those who would be teachers.

AND THEN, OF COURSE, THERE ARE THOSE CONCERNS

But our graduates won't be certified!

Perhaps so. However, I do not see the problem with that. Most states offer a variety of avenues to become credentialed and these avenues are not nearly as rigorous as the traditional teacher education program process. Consider the modest demands placed on those in the Teach for America, Troops to Teachers, and other "fast-track" credentialing options. Consider the recent New York State option that allows anyone with a baccalaureate degree to work for 40 days as a teacher and, with college supervision, earn licensure. Or the similar recent legislation in Texas that literally bars requiring a teacher credential in hiring a teacher. I fully expect that such options will be expanded as the need for teachers grows in the coming decade. My advice: Counsel students to use the alternative routes and leave credentialing as a matter to be negotiated between the state education agency and the student.

We can use the federal policy makers' fascination with the "marketplace" (Podgursky, 2004) model—hire anyone and fire those that do not work out—to our advantage, all the while producing research that demonstrates the value of our work. Teachers are already hired more by where they came from (which institution of higher education) than by whether they graduated from an accredited program. Producing substantive evidence of our graduates' proficiencies and expertise will but enhance the attractiveness of our graduates in the marketplace. Of course there is an associated risk—that we will not be able to produce credible positive evidence of our program effects. But that is a risk I am willing to take.

Won't this deprofessionalize teaching?

Others worry that my stance suggests that teaching is not a profession and that disassociating ourselves from the accreditation process will undermine efforts to bolster the professionalism of teachers and of teacher education. Lots of folks use medicine and medical education as a model to pursue. But the idealized version of medical professional education seems more than a bit overblown. The research on medical practice suggests that evidence, as in experimental studies, might be a primary factor in only about 20 percent of all medical decisions doctors make (Hitt, 2001). Furthermore, as Frohlich (2003) noted in his editorial in the *New England Journal of Medicine*, a basic problem with experimental medical intervention studies is that they are at best a proxy for the care provided to individual patients by their own physicians (a point largely unconsidered in experimental education research). Frohlich observed that although researchers

> focus on responses at the population level in order to develop therapeutic guidelines, health care providers must deal with the specific relationship between the physician and the patient. This relationship is where the therapeutic tire meets the road, and there is no place for absolute or categorical answers. Population-based studies of therapies help point the way but are not analogous to the care of individual patients.

(p. 640)

Beyond the hyperbole about the merits of medical education and its role in professional licensure as a model for the education profession, there is the problem of scale. With only 85 medical schools in the United States, the process of monitoring medical education is far less complex than the problem of monitoring nearly 1,300 teacher education programs and their graduates (Johnson *et al.*, in press). And then there is the problem of the length of time it takes to become a physician compared to the time it takes to become a teacher.

We participate in the teacher credentialing process largely as dupes. Someone else sets the criteria, creates the budgets, monitors the outcomes, and tells us what else must be done or what must be done differently. We endure the criticisms that our graduates are underprepared, even though they have met all the state and federal requirements and were educated within the system those policy makers developed and mandated. It is my contention that the additional degrees of autonomy my proposal provides would stimulate better teacher preparation programs. Taking on these responsibilities would enhance the professionalism of teacher educators and teachers, especially if we involve teachers as something other than experimental subjects in the research we do on our programs.

The college of education would go out of business if we don't offer a credential

Perhaps, but only if we (a) fail to produce effective teachers and (b) fail to develop convincing evidence of our graduates' expertise and effectiveness. In either scenario, getting out of the teacher education business might not be a bad idea.

But following the arguments above, I suggest that the sheer demand for teachers will likely ensure the life of colleges of education. Continued employment of our graduates is all but ensured given the professional and general population demographics. In addition, most school-based educators are products of colleges of education and seem largely skeptical of the "y'all come into teaching" craze that accompanies a marketplace mindset. However, the proof will have to be the effectiveness of graduates.

I am willing to leave credentialing wholly up to someone else. Perhaps the teacher unions would be the most appropriate credentialing agency, because it is their members who have the most to gain or lose when ineffective teachers are credentialed. Perhaps local school districts should have the power to credential candidates (they already have the power of granting tenure in most states). Again, local education agencies have more at stake than state or federal agencies (or colleges of education under the existing schemes) in ensuring that only the effective candidates are credentialed. I am convinced that teacher educators should focus more on developing and evaluating the effects of teacher education programs and less on attempting to ensure that program participants will be credentialed by some other agency or organization.

In any event, given that the less cumbersome, alternative routes to obtaining a credential are fast expanding, colleges of education may soon lose students and faculty to alternate route providers. Whether we like it or not, there will be an intensifying pressure on colleges of education to prove their worth. But how do we prove our worth? We can continue to be hindered by participating in the accreditation and credentialing sham or begin the harder work of providing clear evidence of the effects of our efforts. Unfortunately, I see no way to do both.

REFERENCES

Allington, R. L. (1999) Crafting state educational policy: the slippery role of educational research and researchers. *Journal of Literacy Research*, 31, 457–482.

Allington, R. L. (2001) Does state and federal reading policymaking matter? In T. Loveless (ed.), *The great curriculum debate* (pp. 268–298). Washington, DC: Brookings Institution.

Allington, R. L. (2002) *Big brother and the national reading curriculum: how ideology trumped evidence.* Portsmouth, NH: Heinemann.

Allington, R. L. & Nowak, R. (2004) "Proven programs" and other unscientific ideas. In C. C. Block, D. Lapp, E. J. Cooper, J. Flood, N. Roser, & J. V. Tinajero (eds.), *Teaching all the children: strategies for developing literacy in an urban setting* (pp. 93–102). New York: Guilford.

Cochran-Smith, M. (2002) Reporting on teacher quality: the politics of politics. *Journal of Teacher Education*, 53, 379–382.

Darling-Hammond, L. & Youngs, P. (2002) Defining "highly qualified teachers": what does the "scientifically-based research" actually tell us? *Educational Researcher*, 31, 13–25.

Elmore, R. F. & Rothman, R. (eds.). (1999) *Testing, teaching, and learning: a guide for states and school districts*. Washington, DC: National Academy Press.

Ferguson, R. F. (1991) Paying for public education: new evidence on how and why money matters. *Harvard Journal on Legislation*, 28, 465–497.

Frohlich, E. D. (2003) Treating hypertension—what are we to believe? *New England Journal of Medicine*, 348(7), 639–642.

Hillocks, G. (2002) *The testing trap: how state writing assessments control learning*. New York: Teachers College Press.

Hitt, J. (2001, December 9) Evidence-based medicine. *The New York Times Magazine*, p. 22.

Hoffman, J. V. & Roller, C. M. (2001) The IRA Excellence in Reading Teacher Preparation Commission report: current practices in teacher education at the undergraduate level. In C. M. Roller (ed.), *Learning to teach reading: setting the research agenda* (pp. 32–79). Newark, DE: International Reading Association.

Johnson, D. D., Johnson, B., Farenga, S. J., & Ness, D. (2005) *Trivializing teacher education: the accreditation squeeze*. Lanham, MD: Rowman & Littlefield.

Paris, S. G. & Urdan, T. (2000) Policies and practices of high-stakes testing that influence teachers and schools. *Issues in Education: Contributions From Psychology*, 6, 5–26.

Podgursky, M. (2004) Model 4: Improving academic performance in U.S. public schools: why teacher licensing is (almost) irrelevant. In F. M. Hess, A. J. Rotherham, & K. Walsh (eds.) *A qualified teacher in every classroom? Appraising old answers and new ideas* (pp. 231–252). Cambridge, MA: Harvard Education Publishing Group.

Wise, A. E. (1979) *Legislated learning: the bureaucratization of the American classroom*. Berkeley: University of California Press.

Part 7
Commentaries

49 Teaching as a profession
A bridge too far?

Edward Crowe
The Bench Group LLC

For George Bernard Shaw, "all professions are conspiracies against the laity." The history of teaching in the U.S. is the story of a struggle for professional status. For teacher preparation, it is a quest for respect as a form of professional education. This essay will argue that teaching is not yet a profession. It will suggest that teaching and by extension, teacher preparation have not taken the key steps by which occupations attain professional status.

To say that teaching is not yet a profession—and to argue that teacher preparation is not a form of professional education—is *emphatically not* to make the case that our children and schools do not need or deserve the benefits of professional status for teachers and teacher educators. The struggle to improve teaching and learning in the United States would be helped immeasurably if teaching were to become a true profession.

BECOMING A PROFESSION

Professions have certain characteristics. Professions develop and maintain consensus around a set of values that shape core activities including who enters, how they are trained, how they practice, how they are regulated, and how they defend themselves. Entry standards are established and enforced by the profession through regulatory bodies such as licensing boards. For this to happen, governments must accept the norms of the profession itself with regard to which individuals "deserve" entry. Those who seek entrance must perceive sufficient returns to justify the costs. These returns to professionalization include status, authority, and earnings (Kleiner, 2000).

Acquiring professional status is a struggle. Those who seek to transform their field into a profession must act together to create and enforce consensus about training and working practices. They must find ways to link education, accreditation, and licensure so that all three processes are driven by similar values and desired outcomes. This is a steep hill to climb. This chapter considers professionalization from several perspectives. Economists focus on the costs and benefits. Sociologists study the process of acquiring professional status, and its implications. Both perspectives shed light on the increasingly difficult battle facing teaching and teacher preparation.

LEGITIMACY AS THE BASIS FOR PROFESSIONAL STATUS

Successful professions function as communities (Begun & Lippincott, 1993, p. 30). Members are "bonded to each other by virtue of the similar education and training they receive and the type of work they do" (p. 31). This makes professions different from occupations. Occupations acquire professional status through a complex process that entails a struggle for unity. Out of this contest, a professional community arises with shared norms, training, working practices, and regulatory mechanisms. In the wider world, there is a struggle with potential competitors, with purchasers of goods and services, and with agencies of government (legislatures, board and commissions, the courts). When this community is strong enough, the same values can be found in training programs, accreditation and approval processes, licensure policies, and professional practice. This results in coherence, unifies the profession, sets it apart from others, and provides a means of defense against "incursions" into one or more realms of the professional community. These strengths are economic and social assets (Begun & Lippincott, 1993; Starr, 1982).

Wilson and Tamir (this volume) describe the struggle for legitimacy in teaching and teacher education as "lively discussions" that often pit the "teacher establishment" against its critics. The jurisdictional challenges they portray are incursions into the "turf" of would-be professions. They adopt Bourdieu's concept of a "social field" to examine the present-day role of teaching as a profession. While Bourdieu argues that the social field is a space where individuals and groups both work and struggle for power, economists have a different take. For them, professionalization is fundamentally about economic power and returns—who pays the costs and who reaps the benefits (Stigler, 1971). Thus economists would say that professions are *economic* constructs, with measurable benefits and costs both inside and outside the field.

The regulation of occupations by the state is a quintessential case of professionalization as an economic process (Kleiner, 2000). For sociologists, professions are *political* communities and *scientific* constructs, especially in the health professions where the political and social power of the profession rest on claims of scientific knowledge (Begun & Lippincott, 1993; Starr, 1982). The social field concept overlaps with economics and the sociology of occupations in that the social field is *one part* of the economic and sociological apparatus of professions. Economists and other scholars of the professions would claim that the internal social field—whatever its value to "residents"—only matters if it confers economic benefits on members and is accepted as a legitimate space by the wider world of regulators, consumers, and potential competitors.

The long course of teaching's quest for status in the U.S. is about the twists and turns of efforts to define a field, create and maintain boundaries, and use education, accreditation, and licensure as components of professionalization. Sedlak (this volume) makes clear how these efforts have failed: "Everyone in this story has had interests to advance, careers to create, enhance, and protect." Those in the field, and many outside it, continue to have "deep and enduring differences of perspective" (Sedlak, this volume).

Professional legitimacy implies acceptance by others. It gives the profession influence with "outsiders" such as the public and government. In health care, legitimacy is built from a scientific knowledge base, and supported by successful diagnosis and treatment of disease. Complexity of the knowledge base is a source of legitimacy (Begun & Lippincott, 1993). But if "complexity is not accompanied by results," legitimacy is undercut by skepticism about the profession's claims (Begun & Lippincott, p. 65). Here, then, is an important point of departure between teaching and the recognized professions. The knowledge base for teaching may be complex, but there is little credible evidence that links claims of expertise to teaching or learning results (Cochran-Smith & Zeichner, 2005). The jurisdictional challenges described by all three chapters concern legitimacy. The robustness of these battles and the inability to resolve them means that teaching and teacher education have failed to establish and protect their jurisdictions. For the economist and the sociologist, this is the absence of legitimacy.

CREDENTIALING

Education, accreditation, and licensure are the components of credentialing. Credentialing is an indispensable source of professional legitimacy. The rigor and consistency of training provided to members of the professional community, particularly when that training claims a basis in scientific knowledge, helps to confer professional status on those who complete training. It is particularly persuasive when all members of the profession experience the same preparation regimen. Credentialing as a source of professional legitimacy also includes the receipt of degrees or certificates by individual members of the profession, licensure by the state, and accreditation of education programs by some external organization. Thus, credentialing involves three sets of "organized stakeholders—educational sites, accreditation agencies, and government institutions" (Begun & Lippincott, p. 59).

The intersection of these interests—and their unity of purpose—is clearest in the health professions (Starr, 1982). Medical education is the classic example. Following the Flexner Report and other social forces (Brown, 1979; Cox & Irby, 2006; Flexner, 1910, 1940; Starr, 1982), U.S. medical schools standardized their training programs. Teacher education programs have not. Large-scale studies of "pathways" into teaching through various preparation routes have found more variation within pathways than between them (Boyd *et al.*, 2006). Teacher training programs can be so different from each other that a leading scholar recently claimed, "there is no such thing as teacher education" (Shulman, 2006).

Sedlak (this volume) makes the point that, from the beginning of teaching as an occupation, significant pressures to strengthen credentialing and tie its key elements together (especially education and licensure) generally came from *outside* the field—except in the South where the preservation of racial separation was an important function of the education system. Later, the "teacher education establishment" (to use Wilson's and Tamir's phrase) was attacked from within the academy mostly by discipline-based academics. These events took place well into the 1960s—and, one can argue, the challenges continue today. Sedlak's "loosely-coupled professional education enterprise" is Wilson and Tamir's "orthodoxy." From the perspective of real professions, however, being "loosely-coupled" is to fail at professionalization.

Imig and Imig (this volume) see teacher preparation at the receiving end of policy makers' attempts to impose standards. However, for professions, the relationship goes in the other direction: credentialing is a means whereby a profession sets and enforces standards through influence over policy makers. It is my contention that many of the external policy pressures on teacher education over the years have resulted from the refusal of teacher educators to set standards or to enforce the few standards that did exist (Wilson and Tamir, this volume). There is no common set of values, collectively shared, and this is reflected in the existence of multiple credentialing entities for teaching and teacher preparation programs. As Begun and Lippincott note, successful credentialing involves three sets of "organized stakeholders" (p. 59) with *unity* of purpose (Starr, p. 115).

The third leg of credentialing is the system of training and education that produces members who are socialized into a set of common attitudes and values. Here, Wilson and Tamir document thoroughly the almost systematic absence of shared values, ideas, training methods, and outcomes. For Wilson and Tamir, arguments over the quality of teacher preparation are tied to the "commingling of science and politics" (p. 25). They describe a "political battle for control over the teacher education field" (p. 26), which includes preparation, regulation, and research about teaching and learning. Even a casual reader of the professional press—*Education Week, Education Next,* or the *Journal of Teacher Education*—witnesses the sound and fury of these arguments. From the perspective of scholarship on the professions, however, there is no teacher education "field." The absence of internal cohesion, the weak knowledge base, and the multiple "pathways" sanctioned by regulators (and increasingly by universities), suggest that the field as a concept in teacher education is so abstract as to lack meaning.

THE ROLE OF SCIENTIFIC KNOWLEDGE

Scientific knowledge is an essential foundation for professional status in the health professions. The claim to have and use scientific knowledge enables one group (e.g. traditional medicine) to control incursions by others (like alternative medicine), especially when the use of this knowledge can be shown to have beneficial results (Begun & Lippincott, 1993; Starr, 1982).

Wilson and Tamir describe the critics' belief that there is a complete absence of scientific knowledge from teaching and teacher preparation. Yet we now have increasingly sophisticated scientific knowledge about teaching and learning (e.g. National Research Council, 1999, 2005; National Reading Panel, 2000; Halpern, 2003; Halpern & Hakel, 2003). What we do not have yet is the systematic application of science to teaching, or to the process of learning how to teach.

This may be because important segments of the teaching and teacher preparation communities challenge the legitimacy of science as the basis for knowledge (Fallon, 2006). Critical theorists, for example, have long been concerned about the "objectivity" of "science." As Wilson and Tamir note, critics of the teacher education establishment decry the preoccupation of some teacher educators with "social justice" as a set of attitudes and beliefs that should be inculcated in future teachers if they are to teach all children well. Yet this ideology is not supported by research. One study of California schools that closed the black-white achievement gap found no relationship between successful learning outcomes and "teacher attitudes and beliefs" (Walsh Symonds, 2004). Teachers who failed at educating children were as likely to believe that "the achievement gaps can be closed and that all children can learn regardless of race or ethnicity," as were teachers whose teaching actually increased achievement levels for minority children (p. 16).

As a substitute for empirically-based and scientifically-acceptable knowledge, the set of values loosely coupled into "social justice" may be best understood as the latest manifestation of "pedagogical romanticism" (Sedlak, this volume) to beset the field. And the connection between these values and student learning is unclear. The "social justice mission" of the American Educational Research Association, for instance, does not refer to student achievement. NCATE's "dispositions" give great emphasis to teacher attitudes and self-efficacy concepts that have no empirically demonstrable bearing on whether students in the classroom are learning anything that can be measured objectively.

The endless argument about the "moral basis of education" undercuts claims of legitimacy and professional status. As Fallon (2006) noted recently, the definition of high quality teaching "requires that pupil learning growth be present as an indicator" (p. 147). Evidence about the impact of teacher content knowledge and teaching skills on pupil achievement puts science at the forefront of claims on professional status (Bransford *et al.*, 2005; Grossman *et al.*, 2005; Ma, 1999), a foundation more stable than the quicksand of ideological debate.

The academy may revel in discussions about knowledge and truth and morality, but schools and policy leaders have real world problems to solve. Because parents and policy makers are not experts, they—like patients in the medical world—must rely on arguments rooted in science and linked to results (Begun & Lippincott, 1993; Starr, 1982).

ENTRY INTO TEACHING: THE OPEN DOOR

One consequence of professional legitimacy is success in using the government's regulatory power to establish and enforce entry standards. A second consequence is the ability to set and enforce practice standards within the profession. The usual vehicle is licensing boards dominated by members of the regulated profession. Starr (1982) explains the implications of professional status in his study of medicine: "A profession differs from other occupations in part by its ability to set its own rules and standards" (p. 80). The capacity to exert control is Shaw's "conspiracy against the laity." Licensure enables practitioners to capture "monopoly profits," but it may also function to protect consumers (e.g. patients, pupils, customers, clients) (Starr, 1982; Stigler, 1971; Kugler & Sauer, 2002). This suggests that teacher licensure has benefits as well as costs.

Establishing and maintaining authority through the professional community cannot happen, "unless its members agree, first, on criteria for belonging to the profession and, second, on what its rules and standards ought to be" (Starr, p. 80). The absence of these agreements is a defining characteristic of teaching in the U.S. where both the "orthodoxy" and its challengers oppose entry standards. As Wilson and Tamir comment, "if the orthodoxy cannot or will not explicitly and clearly lay out measurable standards . . . the challengers say 'we ought not to keep people out' " (p. 922).

PROFESSIONAL TRAINING

The initial education of professionals generally takes place in academic institutions. Because colleges and universities have credibility in the broader society, this locus of training confers status on those who complete the process. The academic setting thus "validates education based on science" (Begun & Lippincott, p. 61). Over its tortured history, teacher education moved from the schoolhouse to the normal school, and then came to reside in the university (Sedlak, this volume). Today, the locus of training is moving away from the university through "alternate routes" managed by a variety of providers. Without a respected base of scientific knowledge, university-based programs have little but perceived self-interest as a weapon to defend their monopoly on teacher training.

Fights over curriculum are part of the professionalization process in most fields. For teacher education, Sedlak's discussion of these struggles portrays the combatants and the issues within the academy: "There is no doubt that serious differences in philosophical and political visions divided the groups, and shaped the substance of their claims and campaigns. But private ambitions and collective interests intensified the hostilities" (Sedlak, this volume). As a result of these arguments, teaching never gained the hold over regulators achieved by medicine, engineering, law, and other professions (Begun *et al.*, 1981). This has resulted in approval by the state of alternative sites and agents for the preparation of teachers.

For teacher preparation to be a form of professional education, *all* education of

prospective teachers must reside within the orthodoxy. Training is an essential component of the credentialing process by which a profession establishes and sustains itself
(Begun & Lippincott, 1993; Starr, 1982). But teacher training within the orthodox
"social field" takes place at 1323 institutions of higher education in the U.S. (Spellings,
2005). Aside from the huge variety of programs, pathways, course sequences, and degree
requirements, never-ending battles over program content successfully undercut claims
that training has a scientific knowledge base.

Currently, however, teacher training also exists *outside* the teacher education establishment. Bourdieu's "heterodoxy" includes a growing number of teacher training
programs operated by non-profit organizations such as Teach for America, individual
school districts (the New York City Teaching Fellows is just one example), and for-profit
institutions (the American College of Education in Chicago). Although there is no reliable national estimate for the number of these programs and their graduates, it does seem
clear that both programs and new graduates are growing rapidly. The very existence of
these disparate training sites is empirical evidence for the absence of professional status
for teaching and teacher education.

What stands out even to the advocates of university-based teacher preparation is the
powerful role of curricular "fads," and their influence on accreditation. The history of
teaching and teacher education often seems to be the story of various "progressive" ideas
and their influence (Ravitch, 2000). Among the examples where teacher training seemed
more about fads than science, Sedlak describes the "life adjustment" movement in the
1930s, the drift away from subject matter to "methods," preparing clinical practitioners
in programs almost devoid of clinical training, various forms of "pedagogical
romanticism" in the 1960s and 1970s, and continual tinkering with ways to teach
content areas like mathematics. Many of the most important demands for rigor and
coherence in teacher training have come from outside (Sedlak, this volume; Imig and
Imig, this volume).

QUALITY CONTROL: ACCREDITATION AND LICENSURE

Program accreditation is part of the process by which a profession sets and applies its
own standards and rules. To be effective and respected inside and outside the field,
program accreditation must also be rooted in rational and scientific ideas. The same ideas
must be embedded in education, licensure, and other form of professional oversight
(Starr, 1982; Begun & Lippincott, 1993). Any disjuncture is a barrier to professionalization. Accreditation standards, therefore, must also be seen by those outside the field as
effective mechanisms of quality control.

For teacher preparation, these preconditions do not exist. The disarray, conflicts,
and shifting rules make accreditation and licensure liabilities in teaching's quest for
professional status (Sedlak, this volume). In contrast to professions, the claims to professional authority of teacher preparation accreditation and licensure do not rest on agreement within the field on rules and standards. Nor do they have the required links with
scientific knowledge or with results that benefit the public (Begun & Lippincott). There
now are two accrediting bodies, but hundreds of programs neither have nor seek
approval through accreditation. Only about half of the university-based programs are
accredited by the NCATE or by TEAC. No serious argument can be sustained that these
programs are all high quality. Many states do not require that new teachers complete
accredited programs, breaking the link (if it ever existed) between training and licensing
that professions have established.

The weak knowledge base behind teaching and teacher preparation also means there is no demonstrable relationship between accreditation and program quality. This undermines the case for accreditation. Nor is there much evidence of empirical relationships between the programs themselves and teaching or learning outcomes. Without scientific knowledge—and in the absence of consensus about values or training practices—the argument that all teachers should be trained in a certain way cannot be sustained by teacher educators. Perhaps as a result, teacher education, program accreditation, and government regulation are loosely coupled at best.

Licensure is the standard vehicle for determining entry into a profession (Stigler, 1971; Kleiner, 2000). Stigler argues, "every industry or occupation that has enough political power to utilize the state will seek to control entry" (p. 5). Many of the largest and longest-running controversies in teacher preparation relate to entry standards that may or may not be the object of licensing rules. The Imigs (this volume) note that "there is little agreement on the way to ensure a highly qualified teacher for every student." This is at least as true *within the field* as in the wider world of policy makers and the public. The inability of the field of teacher education to adopt and enforce a set of standards that are understood by professionals and the public to be connected to results left the door open to others who were equally worried about schools and students.

The bewildering array of licensing categories, teacher tests, and exceptions to the rules makes it clear that licensing does not contribute to professionalization in teaching. Unlike recognized professions, every state has its own set of laws and rules—and its own way of circumventing them to admit people to practice that are otherwise not qualified. The National Research Council has documented over 600 different teacher tests, with varying content, cut scores for passing, and psychometric properties (NRC, 2001). If the regulatory gate to the classroom is not wide open, it stands ajar in most states.

When the "intense interest" of policy makers and others in teacher education culminated in efforts to develop meaningful national accountability standards during reauthorization of the Higher Education Amendments (HEA) in the late 1990s, many in the field regarded this as meddling (Imig & Imig, this volume). This response drove even a liberal friend of education to comment that "institutions with . . . egregious pass rates [on state teacher tests] are committing a form of fraud on entering students who aspire to be teachers" (Imig & Imig, this volume, p. 895, quoting Senator Jeff Bingaman, D-NM). As Imig and Imig note, the higher education establishment fought diligently against any form of federal accountability for teacher preparation program quality. The battle against disclosure and sanctions for weak programs was led by the nation's teacher education organizations. Having failed to develop professional standards themselves, they sought to defeat policy makers who acted from outside.

While they could not prevent Title II of the 1998 HEA from including a "report card" on teacher preparation programs, teacher educators had a useful fallback position. The state licensing agencies—which in medicine, the law, engineering and elsewhere use their regulatory authority to set standards based on a recognized body of knowledge tied to results—used their powers to make sure that Title II had no impact on teacher preparation programs under their purview. Of the 1323 university-based teacher preparation programs in the U.S. in 2004, states classified four of them as low performing and 15 "at risk of becoming" low performing (Spellings, 2005). These 19 programs represent just over 1.4 percent of all programs. One has not heard of the teacher education field protesting this abrogation of state responsibility.

Both economists and sociologists make the point that entry standards enshrined in law or regulation protect practitioners from competition. In contrast to the occupations that attained professional status, teaching has been unable to protect itself from other entrants into the field. This suggests that teaching has failed to establish itself as a professional community, that its knowledge base lacks scientific authority or public credibility, that teacher education is too divided to develop the standard content and pedagogy that characterize professions, and that its strategies for establishing legitimacy are weak. Critics "do not see some of the hallmarks of professions: internal accountability, an agreed upon knowledge base, specialized and rigorous training, challenging licensure examinations" (Wilson & Tamir, this volume, p. 927). These facets of professionalism do not exist in teaching or teacher preparation. Accreditors, teacher educators, and regulators have, in fact, worked diligently to ensure they are not developed or sustained.

CHICKEN OR EGG

Teacher education likes to portray itself as a victim of outside forces. The full story is more complex. As the review of professionalization literature shows, professional status for an occupation is not a gift from the wider world, bestowed by a grateful public in recognition of invaluable contributions to society. Rather, professional status is sought avidly by those in the field, fought for in practice settings and the political arena, and fiercely protected once attained.

Social forces and political developments have inhibited teaching in achieving these same goals. The fact that teaching is a female-dominated occupation is surely one factor (Begun & Lippincott). Frequent changes in state rules do not help. Panic over "teacher shortages" undercut efforts to develop and enforce entry standards (NCTAF, 2003). States and school districts manipulate policy levers to widen the pool of those allowed to teach (Carey, 2006). Licensure regulations are routinely altered to confer legal status on practitioners, no matter their training (NCTAF, 2003). In 2006, the concept "highly qualified teacher" is stretched to cover every teacher in some states, reducing its meaning to the lowest common denominator (Carey, 2006).

While many factors contribute to the problem of professional status for teaching, teaching and teacher preparation themselves have contributed as well. Just as some nineteenth-century physicians and medical educators believed that medicine was more art than science (Flexner, 1910; Flexner, 1940; Starr, 1982), highly individualistic and idiosyncratic notions of teaching contribute to its weaknesses as a professional community. Its professional associations function as trade unions, enforcing the rigid salary structures and contract-based work rules of the factory. High rates of teacher turnover add to the challenge of building a cohesive community with shared, and high, standards. The sometime rejection of science as the basis for teaching and learning and the lack of a widely accepted body of professional knowledge also undercut cohesion.

CROSSING THE BRIDGE TO PROFESSIONAL STATUS

The evidence mounts that teachers are the single most important influence on student achievement (Hanushek & Rivkin, 2001; Cochran-Smith & Zeichner, 2005; Rivkin et al., 2005; Fallon, 2006). Policymakers are moving toward defining teacher effectiveness in terms of pupil learning gains instead of relying on the efficacy of "process outcomes" such as degrees and certificates, preparation pathways, program accreditation, and state licensing standards. This is an implicit recognition that credentialing (training, licensure, accreditation) has failed as a professionalization strategy for teaching and teacher preparation.

Control of the external political environment and consensus on specific sets of values within teaching and teacher preparation are beyond us at this moment in time. The most productive strategy for moving toward professional status is to build a base of scientific knowledge about teaching and learning—and apply it to teacher training.

What does this mean for teaching and teacher preparation early in the twenty-first century? It means building on and utilizing findings flowing from efforts to understand the impact of teaching on pupil learning through high quality research designs and sophisticated methodologies. Examples abound: the New York Pathways Project (www.teacherpolicyresearch.org), the Texas Schools Project (www.tsp.org), the North Carolina Education Research Data Center, and the Ohio Teacher Quality Partnership (www.tqpohio.org). Quantitative analyses demonstrate the impact of teachers on pupils, as well as variations within and across preparation "pathways." Mixed methods research strategies "go behind" large-scale quantitative studies and tease out why certain schools are closing the achievement gap (Walsh Symonds, 2004), and *how* teaching performance produces pupil learning (Pianta *et al.*, 2006). Raudenbush (2004) explains the value of these contributions to the knowledge base.

Skeptics argue that data from pupil achievement tests are not good enough yet, that methods used in large-scale studies are not relevant to every classroom or every student's needs, that politics will twist findings and use them against schools and against preparation programs. This may all be true to some extent, but it is beside the point. We can resolve the dilemma of professional status by recognizing the limitations of where we have been, using the new tools and technologies to build an evidence base for sound decisions about the design and delivery of teacher education.

Commitment to scientific inquiry and to the use of evidence has the power to move us in the direction of professional legitimacy. This does not mean that teaching is a mechanistic function where creativity and innovation have no place. In "*Science as a Vocation*," Max Weber told his students that science was crucial for artists and musicians of the Renaissance like Leonardo da Vinci. "Science meant the path to true art, and that meant for them the path to true *nature*. Art was to be raised to the rank of a science, and this meant at the same time and above all to raise the artist to the rank of doctor" (Weber, 1922, 17).

Weber also wrote: "The primary task of a useful teacher is to teach his students to recognize 'inconvenient' facts" (Weber, 24). Since there is no widespread commitment by teacher education to anchor education, accreditation, licensure, and practice in scientifically-based knowledge and the use of evidence, each teacher education program must come to grips with the dilemma of professional status.

What to do? Demand of the state that program requirements and teacher performance expectations be raised in the name of quality. Create a teacher education program that subjects itself publicly to higher standards, whether or not the state agrees to strengthen its policies. These steps amount to the same strategy of professionalization that other fields have pursued over the years—putting scientific knowledge, credentialing, training programs, quality control, and policy under the umbrella of a single set of coherent values, enforcing standards that derive from these values, and keeping the focus on outcomes for which the public has respect. Acting on these challenges is the hallmark of a real profession.

REFERENCES

Begun, J.W. & Lippincott, R. C. (1993) *Strategic adaptation in the health professions: meeting the challenges of change*. San Francisco: Jossey-Bass.

Begun, J., Crowe, E., & Feldman, R. (1981) Occupational regulation in the states: a causal model. *Journal of Health Politics, Policy and Law*, 6(2), 229–254.

Boyd, D., Grossman, P., Lankford, H., Loeb, S., & Wyckoff, J. (2006) *How changes in entry requirements alter the teacher workforce and affect student achievement*. American Finance Association.

Bransford, J., Darling-Hammond, L., & LePage, P. (2005) *Introduction*. In L. Darling-Hammond & J. Bransford (eds.), *Preparing teachers for a changing world*, pp. 1–39. San Francisco: John Wiley & Sons.

Brown, E. R. (1979) *Rockefeller medicine men: medicine and capitalism in America*. Berkeley: University of California Press.

Carey, K. (2006) *Hot air: how states inflate their educational progress under NCLB*. Education Sector, May 2006.

Cochran-Smith, M. & Zeichner, K. (eds.) (2005). *Studying teacher education: the report of the AERA Panel on Research and Teacher Education*. Berkeley: Lawrence Erlbaum Associates.

Cox, M. & Irby, D. (2006) American medical education 100 years after the Flexner Report. *New England Journal of Medicine*, 355, 1339–1344.

Fallon, D. (2006) The buffalo upon the chimneypiece: the value of evidence. *Journal of Teacher Education*, 57(2), 139–54.

Flexner, A. (1910) *Medical education in the United States and Canada* (Bulletin No. 4). New York: Carnegie Foundation for the Advancement of Teaching.

Flexner, A. (1940) *I remember: the autobiography of Abraham Flexner*. New York: Simon and Schuster.

Grossman, P. & Schoenfeld, A. with Lee, C. (2005) Teaching subject matter. In L. Darling-Hammond & J. Bransford (eds.) *Preparing teachers for a changing world* (pp. 205–231). San Francisco: John Wiley & Sons.

Halpern, D. (2003) *Teaching for the future: fostering the twin abilities of knowing how to learn and think critically*. Paper prepared for National Summit on High Quality Teacher Preparation, National Commission on Teaching and America's Future.

Halpern, D. & Hakel, M. (2003) Applying the science of learning to the university and beyond. *Change*, 35(4), 36–41.

Hanushek, E. & Rivkin, S. (2001) Teacher quality and school reform in New York. *Proceedings from the symposium on the teaching workforce*. Education Finance Research Consortium.

Hess. F. (2005) The predictable, but unpredictably personal, politics of teacher licensure. *Journal of Teacher Education*, 56(3), 192–198.

Kleiner, M. (2000) Occupational licensing. *Journal of Economic Perspectives*, 14, 189–202.

Kugler, A. & Sauer, R. (2002) *Doctors without borders: the returns to an economic license for Soviet immigrant physicians in Israel*. Bonn, Germany: Institute for the Study of Labor, Discussion Paper No. 634.

Ma, L. (1999) *Knowing and teaching elementary mathematics: teachers' understanding of fundamental mathematics in China and the United States*. Berkeley: Lawrence Erlbaum Associates.

National Commission on Teaching and America's Future (2003) *No dream denied: a pledge to America's children*. Washington, DC: Author.

National Reading Panel (2000) *Teaching children to read: an evidence-based assessment of the scientific research literature on reading and its implications for reading instruction*. Washington, DC: National Institute of Child Health and Human Development.

National Research Council (1999) *How people learn: brain, mind, experience, and school*. Washington, DC: National Academies Press.

National Research Council (2001) *Testing teacher candidates: the role of licensure tests in improving teacher quality*. Washington, DC: Board of Testing and Assessment, National Academies Press.

National Research Council (2005) *How students learn: history, mathematics, and science in the classroom*. Washington, DC: National Academies Press.

National Research Council (2006) *Rising above the gathering storm: energizing and employing America for a brighter economic future*. Washington, DC: National Academies Press.

Pianta, R., Belsky, J., Houts, R., & Morrison, F. (2006) *Observed classroom experiences in elementary school: a day in fifth grade and stability from grades 1 and 3*. Unpublished manuscript. University of Virginia, Charlottesville, VA.

Raudenbush, S. W. (2004) *Learning from attempts to improve schooling: the contribution of methodological diversity*. Paper prepared for presentation to the forum on "Applying Multiple Social Science Research Methods to Educational Problems," convened by the Center for Education of the National Research Council.

Ravitch, D. (2000) *Left back: a century of failed school reforms*. New York: Simon and Schuster.

Rivkin, S., Hanushek, E., & Kain, J. (2005) Teachers, schools, and academic achievement. *Econometrica*, 73(2), 417–458.

Shaw, G. B. (1911) *The doctor's dilemma*. London: Constable and Company, Ltd.

Shulman, L. (2005) *The signature pedagogies of the professions of law, medicine, engineering, and the clergy: potential lessons for the education of teachers*. Palo Alto, CA: Carnegie Foundation for the Advancement of Teaching.

Shulman, L. (2006) Teacher education does not exist. *Stanford University School of Education Alumni Newsletter*. Retrieved from http://ed.stanford.edu.

Spellings, M. (2006) *A highly qualified teacher in every classroom: the Secretary's fifth annual report on teacher quality, 2006*. Washington, DC: U.S. Department of Education.

Starr, P. (1982) *The social transformation of American medicine*. New York: Basic Books.

Stigler, G. (1971) The theory of economic regulation. *Bell Journal of Economics*, 2, 137–146.

Walsh Symonds, K. (2004) *After the test: closing the achievement gaps with data*. Naperville, IL: Learning Points Associates.

Weber, Max. (1922) *Science as a vocation*. Retrieved from www.molsci.org/files/Max_Weber,_Science_a15767A.pdf

50 Jurisdictional issues in teacher education

Frank B. Murray
University of Delaware

Inspired by Bourdieu's analysis of the forces that shaped the French higher education system, Wilson and Tamir set out a heuristic for understanding the national forces and counter-forces at play in what would seem to be a simple, straightforward challenge: how to insure that each K-12 student has a competent teacher. Sedlak provides a sweeping historical account of how these forces interacted and evolved from the 1700s onward. The Imigs pick up the story line and provide a microanalysis of these same forces as they shaped teacher policies in the last 25 years.

The analytic framework Wilson and Tamir propose is that teacher education is a *social field*—in the sense of a force field in physics or a field in sports. The field is populated with forces, agents, or players, who share the field's logic and rules; who ascribe importance to the "game"; who share some beliefs; who have vested interests in the game's success and in winning it (in this case, determining who gets to teach). Using Bourdieu, Wilson and Tamir propose that there are two loosely assembled teams: the *orthodoxy* and their challengers, the *heterodoxy*. Without each, there is no field, no game, no evolution, and no sustainable solution to the problem.

What *is* the problem? How to find and retain over 3 million competent teachers. Why is it such a hard one to solve? First, the school's very mission is contested. Do schools perpetuate the heritage and norms of the past? Prepare productive citizens for the economy and military? Forge a patriotic national identity out of the diversity of those living in the U.S.? Subvert the norms of the past and build a new nation free of injustices and shortcomings? Maximize each individual's intellectual and social development and potential? Liberate the mind from false doctrine? Second, the logistics of any solution are numerically staggering since there simply are not enough people who are well above the norms on any available measure of teaching talent to fill the needed positions. Third, not enough of those with the requisite talent are willing to do the work, nor are adequate resources available to draw them into teaching. Fourth, we may not have a knowledge base sufficient to the task of making teachers out of non-teachers, regardless of the school's particular mission or the level of the prospective teacher's talent.

Wilson and Tamir vividly describe the key national players and their positions: the shifting strategies, arguments, and maneuvers each attempt to put into play; the constant recruitment of players from one side to the other; the defections and realignment of players and strategies. The snapshot of the social field is illuminating and should help those in the field—whether they are the orthodox establishment educationists or the heterodox challengers—to better understand the national field and, more importantly, to better understand and sharpen their own view of teacher quality.

However, the story Wilson and Tamir tell is a national one. But the action—indeed, the social field itself—may better be understood in the local setting of one or another of the nation's 15,000 school districts and 1,300 teacher education programs. The edicts and theories debated at the national level invariably have a different character at the local level. On the ground, constructivism becomes synonymous with hands on activity; cooperative learning is a furniture arrangement; standards-based instruction is the addition of a standardized test to traditional instruction; the slogan "less is more" yields only less; "all kids can learn" means no tracking, but differentiated instruction reintroduces it with a new name; and process writing becomes a prescribed number of drafts. More often than not, the new idea is clearer in what it is *not* than what it is. As a result, activities undertaken in the name of reform tend to only reinforce past practices, for no local actor is really sure what the new idea is; only what it is not. David Cohen (1990) describes Mrs. Oublier, a teacher nominated as the embodiment of California mathematics reforms, who—under scrutiny—was shown to have implemented nearly the opposite of each reform she espoused. In the busy, cacophonous world of the local, one would expect nothing else.

There is a risk to seeing power struggles within the social field as embodiments of universal forces when they are more likely to be rooted in messy localities where ordinary and basic matters drive behavior. The ending of the Cold War revealed, for example, that there really was no monolithic communist threat, but rather a loosely assembled group of individual national aspirations—often in conflict with each other—striving for individual gains. Teacher education and teacher selection goes on with barely an awareness of the agents so clearly delineated in the Wilson and Tamir analysis or in the Imig and Imig catalog of the dynamics of recent events in Washington, D.C. Decisions are driven by the press to fill a particular position, budgetary concerns about sufficient enrollments, and other local values and obligations.

Sedlak's exposition of the evolution of teaching from a private arrangement between families and tutors to something approaching a teaching profession shows how the seemingly current argument between the orthodoxy and heterodoxy about who should teach is a re-working of earlier tensions. His account also illuminates a host of local factors that shaped whether teachers were best selected from those who could pass a test showing their mastery of the school's curriculum or those—more or less after 1863—who completed a course of study in pedagogy. Often these factors, like the local factors mentioned above, had little to do with the policy tool itself—teacher testing vs. teacher credentialing—and more to do with local advantage, greed, racism, privilege, and corruption. While Sedlak makes clear that the license to teach by credentials (completion of a teacher education program) became orthodox, the heterodox alternative of the license by testing remains a viable challenge. And not just because the underlying issues remained unresolved. The technology that enabled the earlier widespread teacher testing regime, as Sedlak notes, rested on the invention of the pencil (specifically the No. 2) and the possibility of massive machine scoring. Similarly, contemporary computer simulation technologies promise to make more authentic, embedded, and credible teacher testing possible.

Of course, the current teacher testing policy alternative to the credential still has the limitations Sedlak cites: weak preparation is sufficient to pass the tests, tests with low or no predictive validity, and corruption or incompetence in test administration and execution. The credential, it should be noted, is not without its own examinations and predictive validity. In fact, it has within it some 100 hours of course-based tests in any teacher's undergraduate preparation, conducted by some 40 independent professors over a four to five year span, and on many samples of behavior and skill. The current standardized teacher tests have two to three hours of one sample and one point in time, hardly the psychometric equivalent of the assessments in the credential. Emerging interactive computer assessment programs might strengthen both heterodox challenge (ABCTE, for instance) or the orthodox practices (assessments embedded in teacher preparation programs) so that, as Sedlak makes clear, the historical past is not a sure guide to how these issues play out in the future.

The Imigs offer an insider and orthodox interpretation of the forces and counter-forces at work in the social field of teacher education and policy. In their view, the hard-won prior policy tool of certification, which Sedlak documented, became the policy tool of choice by the both the orthodoxy and heterodoxy (along with the other policy devices including, accreditation, board certification, professional tests, academic degrees and diplomas, and so forth). For the orthodoxy, these devices are the linchpins of a genuine profession, the means—regrettably more than a knowledge base itself—to bring status and respect, remuneration and recognition to teaching. In the Imigs' compellingly information-rich account, the heterodoxy has taken on each policy device and cleverly supplanted it with a look-alike counterfeit device that allows the heterodoxy to select the most able as teachers (the heterodoxy's own view) or to select teachers who are merely "good enough" technocrats (the orthodoxy's view of the heterodoxy's plan). Perhaps more remarkable than the orthodoxy's and heterodoxy's acceptance of certification as the policy tool of choice, according to the Imigs, was the enthusiastic acceptance of the federal government as the preferred instrument of teacher education policy.

The "federalization of teacher education policy" (Imig & Imig, this volume), however, is symptomatic of perhaps a deeper common ground of agreement between the orthodoxy and heterodoxy—an acknowledgment of the severity and magnitude of the problem of low quality teachers and teaching. Throughout our history, federal responses have rarely been sought willingly, but when they are, they concern disasters: stock market crashes, economic depressions, war-like aggression, epidemics, natural catastrophe. What is it that both the orthodoxy and the heterodoxy see about teachers and those who educate them as a national threat that warrants federal policy? Why would section 211 of Title II of the Higher Education Act require, for example, that *only* programs of teacher education (not programs in accounting, law, medicine, engineering, physical therapy, or nursing) report the pass rate of their graduates on state licensing examinations?[1]

Perhaps, it is because teaching is different from the other professions. By comparison, it is massive (over 3,000,000 practitioners compared with law's 400,000) and less well compensated. Perhaps it is because there are over 1,300 schools of education, nearly half unaccredited, in contrast to 180 law schools and 125 medical schools, all of which are accredited. In teaching, unlike most professions, the client does most of the work (students must learn; a lawyer's clients can do very little to produce justice). Moreover, teachers do not set or control the profession's standards. The skills of teaching, in contrast to those of other professions, seem quite accessible to lay persons. Indeed, teaching is seen as a natural act. Finally, professional training in teaching is apparently not very difficult, because unlike the other professions, persons of modest abilities are admitted to teacher education programs and almost all earn top marks.

While teaching, as both the orthodoxy and heterodoxy have noted, has all the modern quality assurance mechanisms of the other professions—licenses, certificates, academic degrees, accreditation, standardized examinations, standards boards, prize-awarding professional associations, and so forth—no mechanism has the result we see in other professions. In teaching, at least in the heterodoxy's mind, there are more false positives. Further, the heterodoxy believes, while many teachers with degrees from accredited schools of education and teaching certificates are not competent, those without those credentials could easily be successful teachers. Departing from the practice of other professional national boards, the formerly heterodox, now orthodox, National Board for

Professional Teaching Standards (NBPTS) apparently agrees since NBPTS certification requires neither a degree in teacher education nor a state teaching license.

As mentioned previously, what is puzzling is why teaching is held to standards that exceed those of the other professions. Other professions have no better evidence of the effectiveness of their training and licensing regimes. Grades in medical and law school, or scores on medical and law license tests, for example, have no greater relationship to the numbers of patients cured or court cases won than the teacher's grades and license scores have on the number of students who pass state achievement tests. While there are hard-to-teach children and high academic failure rates in impoverished schools, there are also high rates for some diseases (even intractable and incurable diseases) and persistent legal conundrums that require the highest court's adjudication and readjudication.

The Imigs lament that the "surprising degree of consensus and uniformity" in the late 1990s for the professionalism agenda (based on the National Commission on Teaching for America's Future (NCTAF) reports) collapsed under the heterodoxy's orchestrated calls for accountability and autonomy, competition and choice. They overlook the illuminating and emblematic role of the National Partnership for Excellence and Accountability in Teaching (NPEAT) in the collapse. This partnership, lavishly funded at $23 million by the Office of Educational Research and Improvement in 1997, promised that it would ensure the implementation of the NCTAF reform agenda by grounding it in research and marshalling the orthodoxy's considerable capacity to implement aligned change. The NPEAT was abandoned—unnoticed and without comment—less than two years after its formation. There were many reasons for the collapse, but central was the coexistence of two competing NPEAT goals: (1) the study of the NCTAF agenda *and* (2) its implementation. NPEAT was to do research about the NCTAF agenda, but apparently only to confirm it so that it might be implemented. The hypothesis, announced as NCTAF propositions, was that the NBPTS, INTASC, and NCATE standards were what mattered most for improving the nation's schools and they should be required and aligned with all relevant policies and practices. It remained an open question whether NPEAT's role was to test this hypothesis, or simply assume it was true and move toward the research necessary for implementation. Alternate and competing policy initiatives—alternate routes to certification, vouchers, Teach for America, charter schools, alternative accreditation, or unregulated private school achievement—were never considered or subjected to comparative inquiry. Thus, no effort was made to interrogate, disconfirm, or falsify the NCTAF values and beliefs, and an essential ingredient in scientific and intellectual advancement was lost.

Apart from confusion about whether NPEAT's point was confirmation or inquiry, the principal issue that remained unresolved was whether NPEAT was fundamentally about (1) building and designing an enduring national partnership, (2) being that partnership, or (3) conducting rigorous research testing the implicit hypotheses in NCTAF's propositions. Education policy in the U.S. is generally grounded on the orthodoxy's consensus and the wishes of its powerful constituent groups. NPEAT, in one view, was about grounding education policy in research findings rather than on well-intentioned political consensus. Thus, NPEAT could have changed the norms and values of the social field, providing the means to investigate contentious political issues, like social promotion or class size. This was the value-added of the NPEAT agenda. The policy community would finally have authoritative evidence for its policies, particularly teaching policies.

What is so striking about the NPEAT debacle is not that the orthodoxy's funder disbanded it, but that the orthodoxy did not continue the partnership on it own as the promised outcomes were essential to its collective agenda. The Imigs describe "a backlash" set out in a heterodoxy's manifesto, "based on a set of studies and findings that found all the planks of the so-called professionalization [NCTAF] proposal to be without merit" (p. 12). What the Imigs do not discuss is the empirical merit of those concerns (although they found Secretary Paige's 2002 *Annual Report* was hopelessly flawed and without merit). Was the research base of the manifesto sound or not?

The Holmes Group, charter schools, alternative routes into teaching, the National Board for Professional Teaching Standards, Praxis, TEAC have all been summarily rejected by many in the orthodoxy on the grounds that they were allegedly divisive, elitist, insensitive to diversity, unprofessional, and allied with the many enemies of the teaching profession. So too are the orthodoxy's ideas dismissed by the heterodoxy. The fact that proposals from the orthodoxy and heterodoxy are so single-mindedly and passionately opposed by each other—often without the benefit of investigation—does not help the matter.

Because all known measures and sources of evidence in education are subject to documented distortions and flaws, it is critical that the social field have independent lines of evidence that are beyond reproach on the various aspects of teachers' competence—whether they have studied and mastered what matters, whether they are entitled to a license, whether they should be hired and tenured, whether they deserve merit payments, promotions, and awards. A rise of public confidence in teaching and its professional license depends on the verification that the field's jurisdictional systems of the quality control are sound and capable of producing trustworthy evidence. When evidence instead of dogma is central to the rules of engagement—and when independent lines of evidence converge—confidence that the right people are teaching our children might increase and the tensions in the social field might become more mannerly and honorable.

NOTE

1 The Congressional goal was subverted by teacher education programs submitting misleading pass rates of 100 percent because they used the tests as entrance requirements.

REFERENCE

Cohen, D. (1990) A revolution in one classroom: the case of Mrs. Oublier. *Educational Evaluation and Policy Analysis*, 12(3), 311–329.

Part 8

How do we know what we know?

Research and teacher education

Editors: Marilyn Cochran-Smith and Kelly E. Demers

Part 8
Framing chapters

51 How do we know what we know?

Research and teacher education

Marilyn Cochran-Smith
and Kelly E. Demers
Boston College

There have been debates about how, where, by whom, and for what purposes teachers should be educated ever since teacher education emerged in mid-nineteenth-century America. For just as long, there have also been debates about what kind of an activity teaching is and what knowledge and skills teachers need to have in order to teach well. And almost from the beginning, research has played a prominent role in discussions and debates, particularly in disputes about which disciplines are appropriate to the study of education, what counts as educational scholarship, and how evidence should be used to make the case for or against particular approaches to the professional preparation of teachers.

The history and development of research on, in, about, and for teacher education is nested inside of, but also braided with, larger developments in the history of education research generally and in the development of education as a field of study within the university. As Lagemann (2000) points out, the history of educational research throughout the twentieth century was a troubling one, with the "science" of education, based on empirical rather than logical or ideological grounds, a complex and elusive objective. This section of the handbook, "How We Know What We Know: Research and Teacher Education," makes it clear that the history of research on teacher education has been at least as complex and troubling and the development of a "science" of teacher education at least as elusive.

This section explores the role of research in and on teacher education with a particular focus on changing emphases and major developments over the last fifty years. Woven through the chapters, artifacts and commentaries are explorations of the most enduring questions related to research and teacher education: What can we know about teaching and teacher education from empirical research? What does it mean to talk about a "science" of education/teacher education? How have changing views of science influenced teaching and teacher education over time? What is the history of research in teacher education? What kinds of research are being done and what kinds of research are missing from the field? What is the place of practitioner research, conceptual/analytic work, and critical studies relative to traditional forms of empirical research? How are issues of research methodology related to knowledge access? Whose voices and perspectives have been dominant in the research on teacher education, whose have been ignored or omitted? What are the most important questions to ask empirically? Which concepts and arrangements of school and society should be made problematic, which should be taken as given's in the research? What are the research designs most appropriate to answer these questions? What purposes and goals should be served by research?

There have been many changes over the last 50 years that have influenced the nature and development of education policy, practice and research generally. Three of these have had a particularly strong impact on teacher education research: shifts in the major research paradigms and methods used to study educational issues; changes in our understandings of teacher learning and teacher development; and changing notions of educational accountability.

SHIFTS IN PARADIGMS OF EDUCATIONAL RESEARCH

Not surprisingly, the major paradigm shift from positivism to postmodernism in education research generally (and in many other areas of the humanities, arts, and social sciences) had a major impact on teacher education research. Lagemann (2000) suggests that the key influences were: the development of cognitive science, the application to education of research perspectives from anthropology and other interpretive traditions, new relationships between educational research and practice (such as teacher research and design experiments), and the shift from a linear to a systemic view of how research influenced policy. Research on teacher education was shaped by these and by the expanded array of questions, multiple research designs, and broadened problematics of research on teaching, learning and schooling that characterized education research during this time.

Beginning in the late 1970s, there was a great deal of interest in what Erickson (1986) called "a whole family of approaches to participant observational research" (p. 119), which researchers used to study the ecology of classrooms—the social organization of classroom life, how teachers and students together constructed local meanings, and how teaching and learning were embedded within layers of context and culture. Teaching came to be understood as much more than transmitting information. It also included representing complex knowledge in accessible ways, asking good questions, forming relationships with students and parents, collaborating with other professionals, interpreting multiple data sources, meeting the needs of students with widely varying abilities and backgrounds, and both posing and solving problems of practice. Likewise, learning was understood as not just receiving information. Rather the science of learning showed that learning was a process of developing usable knowledge (not just isolated facts) by building on previous knowledge and experience, understanding and organizing information in a conceptual framework, and monitoring progress toward learning goals. Research on teaching began to focus on pedagogy as a social exchange among participants rather than simply the transmission of information from teacher to pupils.

This same general shift was evident in the research on teacher education. Research on teacher education shifted from teacher behavior to teachers' knowledge, learning, thinking and ideas. Researchers explored how teachers' attitudes, beliefs and values changed (or not) over time. Although programs and paradigms of research that were considered seminal—even revolutionary—during one period often seemed narrow and wrong-headed later, it was not the case that developments in educational research followed a linear path with new and "better" ways of conceptualizing and studying the issues replacing those that had come before. Rather, the major paradigms of educational research had a dynamic and fluid relationship, with certain approaches to research evolving and continuing in slightly altered forms rather than simply appearing and disappearing.

CHANGES IN UNDERSTANDINGS OF TEACHER LEARNING

In keeping with the larger paradigm shifts noted above, there were major changes in the ways the educational community came to understand teacher learning, teacher development, and the roles teachers could and did play in educational reform. During the decades from the 1970s onward, what some people referred to as a "new image" of teacher learning, a "new model" of teacher education, and even a "new paradigm" of professional development emerged. For prospective teachers, teacher learning was no longer seen as a one-time process of "teacher training" wherein undergraduates were equipped with methods in the subject areas and sent out to "practice" teaching. Similarly, for experienced teachers, teacher learning was no longer seen as a process of periodic "staff development" wherein experienced teachers were congregated to receive the latest information about the most effective teaching processes and techniques. New images of professional development were informed by research about how teachers thought about their work, and emphasis shifted from what teachers did to what they knew, what their sources of knowledge were, and how those sources influenced their work in classrooms.

The general orientation of the "new" approach to teacher learning and professional education was more constructivist than transmission-oriented—the recognition that both prospective and experienced teachers (like all learners) brought prior knowledge and experience to all new learning situations, which are social and contextually specific. In addition, it came to be generally understood that teacher learning took place over time rather than in isolated moments in time, and that active learning required opportunities to link previous knowledge with new understandings. It also was widely acknowledged that professional development needed to be linked to educational reform and needed to focus as much on the cultures of schools and the cultures of teaching as it did on skills training. It was also generally agreed that professional development that was linked to student learning and curricular reform had to be embedded in the daily life of schools in order to be effective and needed to feature opportunities for teachers to inquire systematically about how teaching practices constructed learning opportunities for students and thus supported or constrained access to knowledge.

Very broadly speaking, this new vision of teacher learning was shared by many of those responsible for designing, implementing, and researching programs, projects, and other initiatives that intended to promote teacher learning (Hawley & Valli, 1999). However, "the new professional education" was less monolithic and consensual than was claimed. Beneath the surface, as this section of the handbook reflects, new visions of professional education were different from one another, depending upon differing underlying assumptions about knowledge and practice and differing ideas about the purposes and goals of education (Cochran-Smith & Lytle, 1999).

SHIFTS IN NOTIONS OF EDUCATIONAL ACCOUNTABILITY

The third larger development that influenced research on teacher education was a major change in the way that educators, policy makers and the public understood educational accountability. Along these lines, Cuban (2004) points out that, contrary to the current popular belief that accountability is a relatively new development in education, public schools have, in actuality, never been "*un*-accountable." Rather, as Cuban argues, definitions of accountability and quality schooling changed. Prior to and immediately following World War II, what was most important to school boards, administrators and the public was the efficient use of resources to accommodate all those going to school. School leaders were accountable for providing equipment, supplies and facilities. Schools that did so were considered good schools. After the war, however, social, economic and political changes produced what Cuban calls a "more dramatic" notion of accountability that hinged on results.

The turning point was passage of the Elementary and Secondary Act (ESEA) of 1965 and the many events, acts and court cases leading up to or concurrent with it, including Brown v. Board of Education, the launching of Sputnik, and the Coleman Report (Cuban, 2004). The idea with ESEA was not only to provide funds for improving education but also to attach those funds to new accountability requirements. The reform reports of the 1980s that linked mediocre pupil performance on national and international tests to mediocre economic performance globally spurred new standards and accountability measures in nearly every state, including revised curricula, increased graduation requirements, and new performance standards. There were somewhat parallel developments in higher education.

The standards and accountability movement influenced the shift in teacher education policy and research from inputs to outcomes that occurred during the late 1990s and into present day. As several of the pieces in this section of the handbook make clear, although the current emphasis in teacher education research is on the outcomes and results of teacher education, this was not the case prior to the mid-1990s, when the emphasis was on process—how prospective teachers learned to teach, how their beliefs and attitudes changed over time, what contexts supported their learning, and what kinds of knowledge they needed. During this time, teacher education assessment focused on what is now retrospectively referred to as "inputs" rather than outcomes—institutional commitment, qualifications of faculty, content and structure of courses and fieldwork experiences, and the alignment of all of these with professional knowledge and standards. The shift in teacher education research and policy from inputs to outcomes was part of a shift in notions of educational accountability writ large.

ORGANIZATION OF THIS SECTION

Like preceding sections in this handbook, this section is comprised of three key framing chapters and three artifacts that reflect the enduring nature of questions and issues related to the roles, methods, and uses of research on teacher education. These are followed by three commentaries from authors who bring different perspectives to the topic.

The three framing chapters focus, respectively, on the genres of research most common to the study of teacher education, the history of research on the problem of teacher education, and the epistemological bases of race-based and other alternative critical and qualitative approaches to teacher education research. These three chapters, which represent different takes on the general topic of research and teacher education, were chosen very intentionally. Each offers an overview and a valuable update on issues in the field. Individually, each is worthwhile. But taken together, these three chapters provide a set of complementary lenses for understanding many of the most complex and perplexing questions that have permeated the discourse about research and teacher education for many years. The first two chapters explore traditional territory in research on teacher education with a number of overlapping and complementary points. However the first chapter—on genres—concentrates on research methods, pointing to the persistent use of particular research designs for particular purposes, and linking research on teacher education to larger methodological developments in educational research. This chapter makes it clear that method and purpose are inextricably linked and explores possibilities for linking across genres. The second chapter—on the history of teacher education research—works from a different angle, concentrating on changes in the prevailing constructions of teacher education as a research and policy problem over time and linking these to contemporary political and policy contexts. The second chapter complexifies judgments about the quality or relevance of the research conducted during one historical period from the hindsight perspective of another. The third chapter—on alternative critical and qualitative research perspectives in teacher education—challenges many of our traditional notions about both the questions and the genres of research on teacher education. It also explores research on teacher education from the perspective of the Black intellectual tradition, concentrating on genres of critical and qualitative research that have implications for social and racial justice.

In the first of the three framing chapters, Borko *et al.* analyze the genres of research that are most common in teacher education research, analyzing the strengths and disadvantages of each, and connecting these to larger methodological developments in educational and psychological research. The authors offer a thoughtful analysis of how their discussion of genres fits in with previous discussions, suggesting that part of what previous reviews had in common was a sense of participation in and documentation of a new field of study. Borko *et al.*'s chapter examines four genres of research on teacher education, which they refer to as the effects of teacher education, interpretive, practitioner, and design. Part of what is unique about this chapter is that it offers both a much-needed update of the first two genres, which are reasonably well-established in research on teaching and teacher education, and an examination of practitioner research and design research as emerging and important genres in the field. Their discussion helps to legitimize the importance of these genres and acknowledges the array of approaches researchers have taken to the study of teacher education. For each genre, the authors identify central features and offer detailed analysis of a contemporary example from teacher education. This is followed by an even-handed discussion of the contributions and limitations of each genre. The authors' thoughtful discussion of the potential of emerging mixed methods and multiple methods studies concludes the chapter.

In the second chapter, Cochran-Smith and Fries shift the focus from research genres to the history of research on teacher education during the early decades of the twentieth century and into the turn of the twenty-first. The Cochran-Smith and Fries chapter focuses on the dominant approach to conceptualizing and studying teacher education during each of four historical periods and links these to the policy, political, and accountability contexts of the times. Although the Cochran-Smith and Fries chapter acknowledges that there were alternative research paradigms as well as trenchant critiques of the dominant approaches during each of these historical periods, it focuses on the dominant ways the problem of teacher education was constructed and studied during each. The chapter argues that we can understand the history of research on teacher education by conceptualizing it as a "problem"—both a research problem to be investigated and the problem or challenge of providing the quantity and quality of teachers needed by the nation—that changed with changing times: teacher education as a curriculum problem, a training problem, a learning problem, and a policy problem. Using the major research syntheses of each time period as historical artifacts, the chapter shows that each conceptualization of the problem of teacher education was constructed in part as a response to the perceived limitations of the previous conceptualization and in part as a response to national concerns about the schools, teaching and teachers. The chapter provides two historical examples for each period as well as a chart that provides valuable detailed information about the key research syntheses from each.

The final framing piece is Joyce King's chapter on alternative critical and qualitative approaches to research on teacher education. In previous reviews of teacher education research, critical approaches of the sort King discusses here, have either been omitted or included as the last genre or the final paradigm of research reviewed, often with fewer concrete examples or less full discussions than the others. We have chosen to make this work a separate chapter in this section of the handbook in order to draw full attention to this perspective and thus to counter some of the ways it has previously been marginalized in the field. King argues that the traditional formats and paradigms of teacher education research—which includes most of the research discussed in the first two chapters of this section—have consistently failed to address the mis-education of teachers and students in the nation's schools where racism and social injustice are perpetuated. Drawing on the interdisciplinary tools of Black studies, King offers an analysis of how critical and quali-tative research related to teacher education supports democratic social change and chal-lenges the ideology of white supremacy racism. King describes four interrelated genres of critical and qualitative research on teacher education to show how conceptions of race, identity and culture are implicated in teacher education research—critical race theorizing in teacher education, whiteness studies and teacher learning, critical ethnography, and practitioner inquiry, including action research. King's provocative chapter suggests that collectively this work can build a "blues epistemology" for teacher education, intended to promote the cultural well-being of diverse populations and counter the dominant ideology. This chapter also includes a very useful chart comparing critical social theory, critical feminist theory pedagogy and methodology; and, critical race theory pedagogy and methodology.

Following the framing chapters, we have included three artifacts that explore some of the central enduring questions concerning how we know what we know about teacher education. The first artifact, "Applying What We Know: The Field of Teacher Education," is a chapter from *The Scientific Basis of the Art of Teaching* (1978), Nate Gage's seminal discussion of the logic and methods of process-product research on teach-ing. In this chapter, Gage argued that the traditional low status of teacher education was due not so much to its mode of governance or its relative emphasis on liberal arts or pedagogy, but its failure to develop a scientific basis for teaching. In discussing the application of research on teaching to teacher education, Gage explicitly stated that the independent variables of research on teaching (specific teaching behaviors, including teacher-pupil interactions) needed to be regarded as the dependent variables of research on teacher education. We include this artifact in this section of the handbook because it concentrates on one of the most enduring issues related to research and teacher education—the possibility of creating a "science" of teaching and teacher education wherein strategies and methods are based on empirical rather than logical, ideological or traditional grounds. Although now 30 years old, this piece also foresaw many of the issues being debated as part of the current preoccupation with "scientifically-based research" and "evidence-based practice" in education, calling for more connection between research on teacher education strategies and teaching strategies empirically linked to pupil achievement.

The second artifact is Susan Florio-Ruane's article, "More Light: An Argument for Complexity in Studies of Teaching and Teacher Education." Florio-Ruane's article was juxtaposed with Suzanne Wilson, Robert Floden and Joan Ferrini-Mundy's review of knowledge and gaps in research on teacher preparation (2002) in *The Journal of Teacher Education*'s special issue on "evidence and inquiry." This issue of the journal explored from many perspectives the then-emerging press in teacher education to utilize empirical research and evidence as ways to identify and solve policy problems. In her article, Florio-Ruane wrote against this trend, cautioning the community not to narrow the scope of research on teacher education in the quest to provide answers to very specific—and urgent—questions about "what works" in teacher education across contexts and institutions. Florio-Ruane argued instead for recognizing the broad and complex aspects of teaching, learning, and learning to teach and for engaging in inquiry on many aspects of teaching. Drawing on provocative examples from anthropology, medical research, and literacy, Florio-Ruane pointed out that in other fields, bearing down on particular practical problems with all of the resources of a discipline did not necessarily yield the insights and solutions imagined. On the other hand, she also suggested that close studies of complex processes in particular contexts sometimes yielded new conceptual understandings that were important and relevant far beyond the immediate context. We include this article here because of the enduring issues in research on teacher education it raises—What questions should researchers ask? What disciplinary and methodological perspectives are most likely to yield results that will have far-reaching implications? Who decides which questions get the resources needed for research?

The third artifact is Magdalene Lampert's article, "Knowing Teaching: The Intersection of Research on Teaching and Qualitative Research," which appeared in *Harvard Educational Review* in the year 2000. In the article, Lampert reflected on her own history as an educator and researcher and also on the history of research on teaching as a field to argue that teachers could be active participants in research on teaching, drawing on insider knowledge and experience. She suggested that the inclusion of practitioners in the community of researchers raised particularly knotty questions for qualitative research—the persons or groups responsible for the generation of professional knowledge, the possibilities but also pitfalls of involving the self in social science research, and the ways practitioner research is presented and how its claims are made and supported. Lampert concluded that the inclusion of practitioners in the community of those conducting research on teaching would change both the kinds of data collected and the kinds of analyses and interpretations generated. We chose Lampert's article for this section of the handbook because, like the other artifacts we have included here, it touches on enduring and complex issues related to research on teacher education. These include questions about voice, presentation and representation in the discourse of research; epistemological issues about what and how we can know about teaching and teacher education and what kinds of evidence it takes to support knowledge claims; and, ongoing debates about who is a legitimate knower and how to account for the tangled relationships of the knower and the known.

This section of the handbook concludes with commentaries from three scholars with different perspectives on the topic of research and teacher education. Robert Floden considers the intertwining of research methods and questions, suggesting that these have a bi-directional relationship. Floden charges that we need to build trust in all kinds of research on teacher education through greater clarity about data collection and analysis methods, more explication of the chains of reasoning leading to conclusions, and explicit distinctions between researchers' roles as experts and advocates. John Loughran takes on the perennial issues of research and teacher education from the perspective of pedagogy, which, in the European tradition, is not simply synonymous with teaching, but involves relationships, personal engagement, and attention to the conditions and contexts that make educative relationships between teachers and students possible. Loughran suggests that self study is an approach to research on teacher education that draws on insider questions, insights and analyses in ways not possible in research conducted by those outside of teacher education. David Monk offers a practical discussion about what we need to know about teacher effectiveness and preparation that will improve and transform the lives of students. In order to do this Monk suggests that, rather than privileging one type of research method over another, educational researchers should consider what questions are the most important and then choose the most appropriate research strategy.

REFERENCES

Cochran-Smith, M. & Lytle, S. (1999) Relationship of knowledge and practice: teacher learning in communities. In A. Iran-Nejad & C. Pearson (eds.), *Review of Research in Education* (Vol. 24, pp. 249–306). Washington, DC: American Educational Research Association.

Cuban, L. (2004) Looking through the rearview mirror at school accountability. In K. Sirotnik (ed.), *Holding Accountability Accountable* (pp. 18–34). New York: Teachers College Press.

Erickson, F. (1986) Qualitative methods on research on teaching. In M. Wittrock (ed.), *Handbook of Research on Teaching* (3rd ed., pp. 119–161). New York: Macmillan.

Hawley, W. & Valli, L. (1999) The essentials of effective professional development: a new consensus. In L. Darling-Hammond & G. Sykes (eds.), *Teaching as the learning profession: Handbook of policy and practice* (pp. 127–150). San Francisco, CA: Jossey-Bass.

Lagemann, E. (2000) *An elusive science: the troubling history of education research*. Chicago, IL: University of Chicago Press.

52 Genres of research in teacher education[1]

Hilda Borko, Jennifer A. Whitcomb,
and Kathryn Byrnes

University of Colorado at Boulder

INTRODUCTION

In this chapter we provide teacher educators, educational researchers, and policymakers with an overview to common methods of research in teacher education, emphasizing the affordances, contributions, and limitations of different methods. The development of this relatively new field coincides with a sustained period of vigorous epistemological and methodological debate within the educational research community; in essence, this conversation has involved both calls for and challenges to methodological pluralism. In this larger context, the field of teacher education research has emerged and established itself. While not yet a mature field, and indeed the quality of the research base in teacher education is contested, the rapidly growing body of research reflects the broad range of methods debated in the larger community. Given the challenging questions and problems the field of teacher education seeks to understand, we find this breadth of approaches essential to the field's vitality and continued development and argue in this chapter for an ongoing commitment to a plurality of approaches.

In preparing this chapter, we first reviewed how other scholars charged with taking a broad look at the field defined its contours. We refer readers to Cochran-Smith and Fries' chapters in this volume and in *Studying Teacher Education* (2005), for they provide a useful historical overview to teacher education research. We turn now to highlight other reviews that explicitly address issues and concerns regarding the purposes and methods of teacher education research, and we locate our review in relationship to them.

Reflecting the close connection the field of research on teacher education has had with research on teaching, both the second and third editions of the *Handbook of Research on Teaching* include chapters addressing research on teacher education (Lanier & Little, 1986; Peck & Tucker, 1973). Peck and Tucker focused their review on experimental studies in teacher education, an approach that reflects the dominance of this method in educational research conducted in the late 1960s and early 1970s; in hindsight, this narrow focus indicates the relative immaturity of the field. Coming thirteen years later at roughly the same time that Division K was established by the American Educational Research Association (AERA), Lanier and Little's comprehensive review reveals a much more dynamic, multidisciplinary, and contested field. They elaborated enduring problems of teacher education and offered explanations for their persistence. Their review continues to be a landmark for both the elegance of its framework and the impressive number of studies included; as such, it seems to confirm the arrival of research on teacher education as a field. Yet because their purpose was to summarize what research had to say to practitioners, researchers, and policymakers about chronic dilemmas in teacher education, their review is less explicit in its commentary on the nature and quality of the research itself.

In the 1990s three handbooks of research on teacher education were published, marking a new level of maturity of the field (Houston *et al.*, 1990; Murray, 1996; Sikula *et al.*, 1996). Within them, four chapters are devoted specifically to the nature of research (Doyle, 1990; Kennedy, 1996; Lee & Yarger, 1996; Yarger & Smith, 1990). The variation in approaches taken by these authors signals the "intellectual turbulence" (Doyle, 1990, p. 18) of this decade. Yarger and Smith (1990) used their review to call for an organizing framework based on an "antecedent-process-outcome paradigm"; they argued that in order for the field of teacher education research to advance, researchers should pursue an agenda in which studies, from a variety of methodological approaches, examine these three domains and the linkages among them. In contrast, Doyle (1990) seemed encouraged by the growing scholarly interest in teachers' knowledge and the loosening of the dominance of "quality control" and "effectiveness" as core themes. He also noted an important methodological shift in teacher education research, as researchers acknowledge the limitations of process-product research designs in helping people understand ". . . how meanings are constructed in classroom settings. To do this kind of analysis, one must have a powerful language to describe both *events* and the *interpretations* made of these events" (p. 20, emphasis in original). Six years later, in the second edition of the *Handbook of Research on Teacher Education*, Lee and Yarger (1996) framed their review by summarizing the recent and swift growth in methodologies employed in teacher education research. They described seven dominant modes of research in teacher education: *experimental and quasi-experimental, correlational, survey, case study, ethnographic, historical*, and *philosophical* research. In their conclusion they evaluated the relative impact of findings from studies conducted within these different modes and discussed general issues of quality. They questioned the contribution of the rapid rise in qualitative and narrative modes of inquiry in the field and closed with a call for more interdisciplinary research. Kennedy's (1996) review takes an intellectually playful look at the credibility of five different empirical approaches to examine the effectiveness of teacher education: She labeled these genres *contributions to student learning, comparing the haves and the have nots, ask the teacher, experiments in teacher education*, and *watch the teacher candidate*. What stands out in these reviews is the methodological pluralism of the field and a willingness to critique the methodological rigor of existing studies.

Four more reviews published as the twentieth century gave way to the twenty-first convey even greater urgency regarding the nature and quality of research in this field. Attention to quality reflects the recent policy context in which increasingly vigorous challenges to the effectiveness of teacher education threaten to narrow the questions and methods employed by researchers in this field. Zeichner (1999) used his AERA Vice-Presidential Address to Division K to take stock of the old and new scholarship in teacher education. He closed with his optimistic appraisal of the emergence of self-study as a category of research and with an admonishment to the field to be more globally aware in its search for quality research in teacher education. Sleeter (2001) organized her chapter in *Review of Research in Education* around four epistemological frameworks found in teacher education research—positivism, phenomenology, narrative research, and emancipatory research. She evaluated each framework for its potential to illuminate the problems associated with preparing dominant-culture teacher candidates to work with the increasingly heterogeneous K-12 learners. Her chapter closes with recommendations to improve research in this critical area, including developing multicultural research teams with expertise in several methodologies and epistemologies, and pursuing more longitudinal studies. Finally, in 2002 the *Journal of Teacher Education, Volume 53 (No. 3)* explored the theme "evidence and inquiry in teacher education." Anchoring the issue are essays by Wilson *et al.* (2002) and Florio-Ruane (2002). Wilson and colleagues called on the field to examine the rigor of its work: "We, as a field, must make changes that will, in the coming years, give us a better grounding for the practices we believe in or perhaps give us reasons to rethink some practices" (Wilson *et al.*, 2002, p. 201). Some suggestions they offered to ensure high-quality research include: aiming for peer-reviewed journals, making research design and methods more explicit and public, evaluating the quality of studies before citing them, developing more sound impact measures, and designing more large-scale quantitative research. Florio-Ruane's (2002) essay takes as its point of departure the acknowledged complexity of teaching and learning to teach, and she warned that research must also be complex and varied in its methodological approach.

> Unless we keep teaching and teacher education complex, we will fall prey to some or all of the following: pitting approaches of research against one another in the name of rigor; privileging natural science-based approaches solely because of their compatibility with the language and assumptions of policy; failing to recognize that all approaches to research have limited purview; and disregarding insights from critical, alternative approaches.
>
> (p. 214)

Overall, though the purposes, goals, and approaches in these reviews of research on teacher education vary, all convey a certain excitement associated with working on the frontier of establishing a field. Themes that emerge across the reviews include the importance of methodological pluralism, the ongoing concern for rigor and credibility of research, and the desire for the research to have a genuinely constructive impact on teacher education practice and policy. We trust that these themes will be evident in this chapter as well, as we address our charge to explore the various genres that have been central in research on teacher education, considering the central features, contributions, and limitations of each.

In this review of research methods, we feature four genres—*effects of teacher education, interpretive, practitioner*, and *design*. The first two—effects and interpretive—are established genres that have contributed substantially and over many years to the knowledge base on teacher education, while the latter two—practitioner and design—have been more recent additions and therefore were not addressed explicitly in previous handbooks (Doyle, 1990; Lee & Yarger, 1996). In choosing these four, we recognize that we leave out research that Sleeter (2001) placed within the "emancipatory" epistemology; others have called this research "critical, feminist, and post-structural" (Zeichner, 1999). We do so because King's chapter in this handbook addresses this genre. Also, while a number of our predecessors have treated survey research as a mode of inquiry (e.g. Lee & Yarger, 1996; Wilson *et al.*, 2001; Zeichner, 1999), we have not included it as a distinctive genre because we see surveys as a research tool. Studies in any of the genres we feature might, in principle, incorporate surveys in their design.

For each research genre we discuss its purpose and intellectual roots and its central features. We follow this general description with an analysis of a specific study or research program that exemplifies the genre's key features. We used the following criteria to identify an illustrative study within each genre: (1) *quality*, that is, the study demonstrates established criteria for rigor within the genre; (2) *recency*, by which we mean a study published in a refereed publication in the last five years; and (3) *topical focus*, where the study addresses a current or major issue in teacher education. Within each genre there were several, and sometimes many, studies that met these criteria; where alternatives were available, we chose to feature research programs rather than individual studies. Given that we could not highlight all studies that met our criteria, our intention is that each example serves as a useful guide to the genre it represents. We close each section with an analysis of the genre's contributions and limitations. In the chapter's conclusion, we compare and contrast possibilities of the genres and suggest worthwhile avenues for future research in the field.

"EFFECTS OF TEACHER EDUCATION" RESEARCH

Introduction: purpose and intellectual roots of "effects of teacher education"

Research

"Effects of teacher education" research refers to a body of scholarship concerned with understanding the relationships between teacher education experiences and student learning. With roots in the scientific method of the natural sciences (Guba & Lincoln, 1994; Wardekker, 2000), this research genre seeks to identify generalized patterns of relationships between characteristics of teacher candidates, features of teacher education practices and programs, and learning of teacher candidates and K-12 students through experimental, quasi-experimental, and correlational research methods. Its establishment as a major genre of research was assured by E. L. Thorndike's argument early in the twentieth century that experimental psychological research and statistical analyses should guide educational research. As founding editor of the *Journal of Educational Psychology*, in his introduction to the *Journal's* first issue Thorndike (1910) wrote,

> A complete science of psychology would tell every fact about every one's intellect and character and behavior, would tell the cause of every change in human nature, would tell the result which every educational force—every act of every person that changed any other or the agent himself—would have.
>
> (p. 6)

The legacy of this cause-and-effect orientation is evident in the process-product studies that dominated inquiry in teaching and teacher education in the late 1960s and the 1970s.

Early research on effects of teaching was based on a model of looking for relationships between *processes* (e.g. variables describing classroom practices including teacher and student behaviors) and *products* (typically measures of student performance on achievement tests). Grounded in the logic of the descriptive-correlational-experimental loop (Rosenshine & Furst, 1973), process-product programs of research sought to describe phenomena of teaching practice, isolate variables that were correlated with student achievement scores, create interventions to train teachers to engage in identified teaching behaviors, and conduct experiments to study the effect of these training interventions (Good & Grouws, 1979). For example, several classic process-product studies identified effective teaching behaviors—such as developing explicit objectives, wait time, and guided practice—that were associated with student achievement (e.g. Dunkin & Biddle, 1974; Emmer *et al.*, 1980; Flanders, 1970; Good & Grouws, 1979; Rowe, 1974; for reviews of major programs of research on effects of teaching see Brophy & Good, 1986; Floden, 2001; Rosenshine & Stevens, 1986). As an extension of this line of thinking, these behaviors became outcome measures in teacher education studies of microteaching (Lanier & Little, 1986; Grossman, 2005).

Microteaching, as an early example of this genre within research on teacher education, reflects the genre's aim to simplify the complex processes of teaching and learning by identifying and isolating specific variables that influence a targeted outcome. Researchers, who wanted teacher candidates to incorporate proven instructional behaviors into their repertoire, utilized microteaching as an intervention. In a laboratory setting, candidates were introduced to target teaching behaviors, often through expert modeling; they were then videotaped as they practiced the targeted behavior and received explicit feedback during review of the videotape. Measures of teacher candidates' learning in these studies focused on pedagogical skills and knowledge. While teacher candidates were often able to enact these behaviors in the laboratory settings, they were seldom able to demonstrate transfer to actual classrooms (see Grossman, 2005, for a recent review of microteaching studies). Research on the effects of teacher education broadened over time to include studies examining the impact of components of teacher education such as subject matter preparation, foundations and methods courses, and field experiences (for reviews that include studies in this genre, see Wilson *et al.*, 2001; Clift & Brady, 2005; Floden & Meniketti, 2005).

Although studies within this genre have contributed to the field since its inception, recently, calls to identify "what works" in teacher education have spawned renewed interest in the genre. In the larger conversation about educational research, Slavin (2004) argued, "For questions that compare the outcomes of alternative programs or policies, there is no substitute for a well-designed experiment" (p. 27). This stance on educational research has also been adopted as part of the No Child Left Behind (NCLB, 2002) federal legislation. In their analysis of states' progress toward implementing NCLB, the Education Commission of the States noted that the act requires programs and practices to be based on "scientifically based research, a phrase that appears in the 2002 legislation 111 times" (Neumann, 2002). The quasi-experimental and experimental designs frequently employed in effects of teacher education research appeal because they align with the U.S. federal government's recent "*de facto* definition of good research as consisting of experimental studies that yield prescriptions for action" (Hostetler, 2005, p.16). While experimental studies are clearly encouraged, some of the most recent effects studies have used correlational or structural equation modeling methods because these allow for complex analyses of naturally varying phenomena.

Central features of effects of teacher education research

The fundamental purpose underlying effects of teacher education research is to examine relationships between teacher education experiences and student learning. In effects of *teaching* studies, the students are K-12 learners; in effects of *teacher education* studies, the students may be either teacher candidates or K-12 learners. Recent policy questions emphasize linkages between teacher education and K-12 students' learning. Researchers using the effects of teacher education genre draw upon designs and methods found in the natural sciences. Seeking to maintain objectivity, they specify variables and examine the relationships among them. The researcher looks at the event or phenomenon as an outsider, objectively recording and analyzing data (Florio-Ruane, 2002). Information sources may include pre- and post-tests; observation protocols; and surveys that gather demographic data on teacher candidates, programmatic data (e.g. how many courses in mathematics are required for elementary teacher candidates), and candidates' perceptions of their preservice experiences. Data analyses typically rely on various statistical methods to determine relationships among variables. These methods of data collection and analysis afford opportunities to include large numbers of participants in a research program. Data collected are instrumental for generalizing across settings and time to understand "what works."

Among the different approaches to effects of teacher education research, experimental studies seek to identify causal relationships between conditions and events through the systematic study of planned modifications to the natural world. Researchers manipulate independent variables and then measure the consequences of those manipulations on a set of dependent variables. Ideally, random assignment of participants to experimental groups allows the researcher to attribute changes to a causal relationship between the independent and dependent variables. For example, researchers may randomly assign candidates to two or more clearly defined pedagogical methods in a teacher preparation program, and then assess their knowledge and skills after completion of the program. Correlational research does not attempt to manipulate or control variations in groups; rather, it assesses relationships among naturally occurring variables. Both experimental and correlational research seek to understand relationships among the following: characteristics of teacher candidates, features of teacher education practices and programs, and learning of teacher candidates and K-12 students. The following example is a correlational study utilizing survey data to examine outcomes associated with different routes of teacher certification.

Does teacher certification matter? An example

Goldhaber and Brewer (2000, 2001) conducted a study to examine the relationship between teacher licensure and student outcomes. As they noted, "Although teacher certification is pervasive, there is little rigorous evidence that it is systematically related to student achievement" (p. 141). Furthermore, many states have recently developed alternative routes for teacher certification and for allowing individuals to enter into classroom teaching without having completed a formal teacher education program. These opportunities "make the issue of the relative effectiveness of different types of teacher certification and state certification policies an important one" (p. 141).

In their study, Goldhaber and Brewer compared achievement test performance by students of teachers with standard certification, probationary certification, emergency (temporary) certification, private school certification, and no certification in their subject areas. They also examined whether differences in state licensure requirements are related to student achievement in mathematics and science. The *National Educational Longitudinal Study of 1988* (NELS:88), a nationally representative survey of approximately 24,000 eighth-grade students conducted in the spring of 1988, was their primary data source. Additional sources included the NELS parental survey conducted in 1988, surveys of a subset of the students conducted in the spring of 1990 (when the students were tenth graders) and 1992 (when they were twelfth graders), and the NELS:88 twelfth-grade teacher survey. A major advantage of NELS:88 is that it provides teacher and class information that is tied to individual students by subject, thereby enabling researchers to link teacher preparation to teachers to students, and then to estimate value-added models of student outcomes.

In one set of analyses, Goldhaber and Brewer (2000, 2001) used a multiple regression approach to model students' twelfth-grade standardized test scores in mathematics and science as a function of individual and family background characteristics; and of school, teacher, and classroom characteristics. Consistent with previous research, they found that individual and family background variables explained the majority of variance in students' test scores. Type of teacher certification is also an important determinant of student outcomes. In their analyses, students of teachers who either were not certified in their subject or held private school certification did less well than students whose teachers held standard, probationary, or emergency certification in mathematics. However, students of teachers with standard certification in mathematics did no better than students of teachers with emergency certification. The pattern in science was similar, although the results were not as strong in magnitude or statistical significance.

In another set of analyses they investigated whether the effects of teacher licensing on students' standardized test scores varied by state. Goldhaber and Brewer tested for possible relationships between states' licensing requirements (e.g. whether they required any type of teacher exam, whether they required field experiences prior to student teaching) and student achievement. These analyses did not detect any relationships between state licensure policies and student achievement—perhaps, in part, because of limitations in the data set.

Goldhaber and Brewer's research was constrained by several limitations in the NELS:88 data set. The certification categories used in NELS:88 do not correspond perfectly to definitions of "traditional" and "alternative" licensure used by policymakers and academics. The data set does not contain information on the year or state in which teachers obtained their original certification, thus making it impossible to link state policies to particular teachers. These limitations, coupled with the small sample size of teachers in any particular state, suggest the need for caution in interpreting findings regarding the relationship between state certification requirements and student outcomes. Conclusions regarding emergency certification are also problematic because the subsample of teachers who held temporary and emergency credentials was small, the educational backgrounds of these teachers (e.g. subject matter and pedagogical preparation, previous teaching experience) varied, and requirements for emergency certification differ from state to state (Darling-Hammond et al., 2001). Thus, as Goldhaber and Brewer (2001) acknowledged, "there is not yet enough information to draw strong conclusions about the impacts of certification on the teacher applicant pool" (p. 79) or on student outcomes. Their study informs our understanding of the predictive validity of certification requirements in a context where the presence or absence of certification is fixed (Floden, 2006).

Despite these limitations, the study is noteworthy because it addresses a significant policy question—does teacher certification matter? Goldhaber and Brewer located their study in the ongoing debate regarding the value added by teacher licensure; at the time of the study, the National Commission on Teaching America's Future had recently issued a major report, *What Matters Most: Teaching for America's Future* (1996), which argued for the importance of professional preparation in accredited schools of education. The study's design illustrates an approach to using a large, publicly available data base to examine relationships between teacher certification and student learning outcomes. The authors provided clear explanations for their regression models and for limitations of these models and the database itself. Careful not to overstate the significance of the associations they identified, they couched their findings with speculative commentary. While not settling the matter of whether teacher certification matters, Goldhaber and Brewer's study points to the potential value of this type of research for guiding the development of educational policy, and to the importance of additional research that outlines linkages between teachers' experiences in teacher education and K-12 student learning.

Contributions and limitations of "effects of teacher education" research

Potential contributions of effects of teacher education research derive from the fact that research designs within this genre allow for precise, quantitative predictions; assessment of cause-and-effect or correlational relationships; and results that are relatively independent of the researcher. The high status afforded to research within the natural sciences extends to effects research within the social sciences in general, and within teacher education in particular. Perhaps the most lasting contributions of effects of teacher education research have occurred within the realm of policy. Educational decision makers find research in this genre useful and attractive because of the relevance and validity of its findings as a basis for designing and evaluating teacher education programs (Florio-Ruane, 2002). The compatibility of the language and assumptions of policy with the language and assumptions of effects of teacher education research also helps explain the intimate relationship between the two. As Cochran-Smith (2004a) explained, when teacher education is constructed as a policy problem the evidence desired to address this problem comes from "experimental or correlational studies with sophisticated statistical analyses, which indicate that certain aspects of teacher preparation do or do not have a systematic and positive impact on pupils' learning or on other outcomes" (p. 112). As a cautionary note, however, Florio-Ruane (2002) reminded us that the quest for generalizability within the effects of teacher education tradition is often thwarted by the contextual, local, and situated nature of teaching and learning.

Further, many educational scholars have questioned the ability of effects research to impact the practice of teacher education. Burkhardt and Schoenfeld (2003) observed, "Such research provides insights, identifies problems, and suggests possibilities. However, it does not itself generate practical solutions, even on a small scale" (p. 5). The knowledge generated through this research may be too abstract and general for direct application to specific local situations, programs, and individuals (Johnson & Onwuegbuzie, 2004).

In sum, the effects genre is a powerful approach for deriving law-like principles governing the teaching and learning process within the field of teacher education. Darling-Hammond *et al.* (2001) eloquently captured the potential value of effects of teacher education research:

> The field would be well served by thoughtful, well designed and adequately nuanced studies of how different kinds of knowledge matter for teaching, how these can be acquired in various types of teacher preparation programs, and how their acquisition can be represented by state certification policies that provide both useful leverage on training and good information for schools.
>
> (p. 72)

At the same time, there are limitations to the insights this genre can provide; for example, studies cannot always account for why something works or fails to work in particular contexts.

INTERPRETIVE RESEARCH

Introduction: purpose and intellectual roots of interpretive research

Of the four genres addressed in this chapter, interpretive research is perhaps the most expansive category; for example, ethnography, symbolic interactionism, narrative, educational connoisseurship, phenomenology, and discourse analysis all fall within the genre of interpretive research. Because this section cannot do justice to the variety of approaches within the interpretive tradition, we sketch a broad overview of basic assumptions interpretive researchers make and the basic logic of this genre's methods.

Interpretive research is, at its core, a search for local meanings (Bogdan & Biklen, 1992; Erickson, 1986; Hatch, 2002; Lincoln & Guba, 1985; Schwandt, 1994). In contrast to effects of teacher education research, which aims to identify stable propositions that apply to multiple situations, interpretive research seeks to perceive, describe, analyze, and interpret features of a specific situation or context, preserving its complexity and communicating the perspectives of the actual participants. Interpretive research searches for "understanding thoughtful action in context" (Florio-Ruane, 2002, p. 209). It seeks to capture local variation through fine-grained descriptions of settings and actions, and through interpretation of how actors make sense of their sociocultural contexts and activities. Given the emphasis on the local, the implications of an interpretive study may address any or all of the following: (1) improving practice, including program design; (2) informing policy by outlining salient contextual features that shape policy formulation or by illustrating successes and flaws in policy enactment; (3) guiding or complementing the design of studies in other research genres, particularly effects of teacher education studies; and (4) shaping theory development. Responsibility falls to readers to determine what explanatory power a study has within their local context(s).

The intellectual roots of interpretive research lie in nineteenth-century European thought, particularly German intellectuals' interests in understanding the lived world of society's disenfranchised and in using this understanding to guide social reform (Erickson, 1986; Hatch, 2002; Schwandt, 1994). German social theorists, notably Max Weber, adopted hermeneutical methods within the social sciences. Meanwhile, in the United States, the social sciences, including educational psychology and sociology of education, followed a different path, developing positivist methods and standards of research more closely aligned with the physical sciences (Lagemann, 2000). European thought most influenced anthropologists (e.g. Malinowski *et al.*) and urban sociologists at the University of Chicago (e.g. Park and Burgess), whose work, in turn, shaped the research of ethnographers interested in education (e.g. Spindler and Kimball). This legacy of nineteenth-century European social thought, though not influential in the field of education during the first two thirds of the twentieth century, garnered the interest of educational scholars in the last third, particularly those who challenged the dominance of experimental and correlational methods in educational research (Guba, 1990; Guba & Lincoln, 1994). Interpretive research has branched out considerably from the work done in the earlier part of the twentieth century and is now an established genre within the field of education (Delamont *et al.*, 2000; Denzin & Lincoln, 1994).[2]

Interpretive studies of teaching and teacher education came to the fore as the shortcomings of process-product research became increasingly apparent (Shulman, 1986). Several classic interpretive studies in research on teaching introduced this genre to research on teacher education (e.g. Cazden, 1988; Heath, 1983; Jackson, 1968; Mehan, 1979; Shultz *et al.*, 1982; Tharp & Gallimore, 1988). Collectively, in the 1980s, interpretive studies gave the field an image of teaching as a complex intellectual endeavor that unfolds in an equally complex sociocultural context. Moreover, as the diversity of the student population increased, attention turned to how teachers made sense of both the sociocultural organization of the classroom and the learning and development of students whose lived worlds and experiences were different from their own. One logical extension of this deepened understanding of teaching practice was inquiry into how beginning teachers learn to teach *all* youth and how different contexts and teacher educators' practices shape teacher candidates' learning. This redefined purpose for inquiry in teacher education—what Cochran-Smith and Fries (2005) have called the "learning problem"—was well suited for an interpretive approach.

Central features of interpretive research

Since the early 1980s, teacher education has seen a dramatic increase in the number of studies conducted within the interpretive tradition. Reflecting both the intellectual vitality of anthropology, linguistics, psychology, and sociology, and the blurring between social science and humanities research, more sophisticated conceptualizations of subject matter, language, learning, identity, and culture have been the focus of theory development. Researchers within the interpretive tradition have drawn upon this theoretical work to forge conceptual frameworks that guide inquiry into the processes of learning to teach and the nature of different approaches to teacher education. No single theoretical framework has dominated the genre, although most recent interpretive studies reflect a sociocultural or situative perspective on learning to teach.

Consistent and distinguishing features of interpretive research include the privileging of "insiders' " perspectives (Cochran-Smith & Lytle, 1993; Florio-Ruane, 2002) and a focus on understanding sociocultural processes in natural settings where individuals learn to teach. Participants' voice and discourse are critical to capture, so researchers record interactions in naturalistic settings, conduct interviews, and review written artifacts such as reflective journals and, more recently, web-based communication. They ask individuals directly involved in teacher preparation—candidates, school-based professionals working with candidates, and university-based teacher educators—to explicate their backgrounds and to share how they make sense of their practice. Interactions and activities are documented through field notes, artifacts, audiotapes, and videotapes, thus affording researchers opportunities to identify elements of the educational settings that foster, shape, and/or constrain teacher learning. Typically, the researcher defines his or her role as either an observer or a participant observer; that is, he or she comes to know the phenomena under study by spending extended time in the setting and interacting with participants. Interpretive researchers recognize the importance of context by attending to features of a setting, such as physical details; resources and materials; organizational structures of programs, schools, and classrooms; local policies, decisions, and values; and the expected norms of interaction and breaches in those norms. Data analysis is a recursive process that begins during data collection; themes and patterns are developed both inductively from the data and deductively from the conceptual framework.

Unlike effects of teacher education research, interpretive research aims for particularizability, not generalizability.

> The task of the analyst is to uncover the different layers of universality and particularity that are confronted in the specific case at hand—what is broadly universal, what generalizes to other situations, what is unique to the given instance. This can only be done, interpretive researchers maintain, by attending to the details of the concrete case at hand. Thus the primary concern of interpretive research is particularizability, rather than generalizability.
>
> (Erickson, 1986, p. 130)

What comprises the grain size or boundaries of the concrete case depends on the researcher's theoretical and practical focus. For example, a common way of framing a case is around individual candidates or dyads (e.g. mentor/teacher candidate); however, interpretive researchers have also examined specific instantiations of program components (e.g. effective field experiences), pedagogical approaches in teacher education (e.g. case methods or autobiographical writing), or programs or pathways (e.g. cohort-based program or alternative licensure program). Readers of interpretive studies judge their quality using criteria such as credibility, applicability, transferability, dependability, and confirmability (Eisenhart & Howe, 1992; Lincoln & Guba, 1985; Toma, 2006).

Appropriating tools for teaching literacy: an example

We feature a cross-institutional, longitudinal research program collaboratively led by Pam Grossman, Peter Smagorinsky, and Sheila Valencia.[3] The common problem studied by these researchers was the "disjuncture between values and practices in the different settings that comprise teacher education" (Grossman et al., 1999, p. 3). Following elementary and secondary candidates from student teaching into their initial years of teaching, the researchers examined "how beginning teachers adopt concepts and practices in the various settings of professional education and then modify and use them in their first few years of teaching" (Grossman et al., 2000, p. 632).

The research design is an elegant example of interpretive research for the following reasons. First, the studies that composed the program were grounded in a shared theoretical framework, activity theory.

> Activity theory is predicated on the assumption that a person's frameworks for thinking are developed through problem-solving action carried out in specific settings whose social structures have been developed through historical, culturally grounded actions. Activity theory is useful for understanding the process of learning to teach, particularly in illuminating how teachers choose pedagogical tools to inform and conduct their teaching. This framework focuses attention on the predominant value systems and social practices that characterize the settings in which learning to teach occurs.
>
> (Grossman et al., 1999, pp. 4–5)

The decision to examine teacher learning through the lens of activity theory guided the researchers toward the study of *activity settings*, including how individuals constructed them as well as their sociocultural history; *identity* formation; and *tools*, both conceptual and practical, that teachers *appropriate*. A second distinctive feature of the research program was the substantial data set. Across the sites, a relatively small number of teacher candidates were followed intensively through student teaching and, when possible, into the initial years of teaching. Data collection involved multiple interviews of the candidates/novice teachers, observation cycles in their classrooms, interviews with supporting players (e.g. university supervisors, cooperating teachers, school and district administrators), artifacts from concept map activities, and artifacts from classroom practice (e.g. lesson plans, written teaching materials). Third, the data were rigorously analyzed using a collaboratively developed coding scheme. Finally, publications from this research program presented findings through cases of individual teacher candidates, an accessible format well-suited to trace the particulars of each individual's development as it unfolded in different settings. Moreover, the multiple case studies enhanced the power of the research program by affording opportunities for cross-case analyses. In comparing cases, researchers identified patterns and trends along with individual variation; more important, they were able to explore contextual factors that helped explain both patterns and variation.

Conclusions from this research program have greater impact than smaller-scale efforts by individual researchers, in part because the studies were collaborative and coordinated, and in part because they were longitudinal. The studies make several contributions to a theoretical understanding of teacher learning; for example, the researchers presented a developmental continuum, "five degrees of appropriation," that explains how novice teachers appropriate conceptual and pedagogical tools such as constructivism or writing workshop (Grossman *et al.*, 1999). They also elaborated upon the tensions that inhere in teachers' identity formation during student teaching and beyond (Smagorinsky *et al.*, 2004; Smagorinsky *et al.*, 2007). Teacher educators who read the collection of studies from this program may draw insights into teacher education practice. For instance, Grossman and colleagues (2000) illustrated ways in which novice teachers might make sense of curriculum materials that are provided, or prescribed, by their districts; they suggested that teacher educators introduce commercially prepared curricula and invite teacher candidates to analyze these materials during their preservice experience. Finally, the studies inform both teacher education program design and district-level policies because they point out critical disjunctures in teacher candidates' experiences as they move through the different settings of university courses, student teaching, and induction. For example, Grossman and Thompson's (2004) comparative analysis of two district policy environments revealed that in participants' first year of teaching, district policies with regard to curriculum materials, professional development, and mentoring shaped their concerns about instructional and curricular decisions. Such findings have implications for how teacher educators and local school district personnel might work together to facilitate these transitions.

A limitation of this research program is that the transferability of findings depends on whether readers judge the teacher candidate population and contexts studied to be comparable to their own situations. For example, teachers' appropriation of literacy practices may differ from their appropriation of mathematics practices, or readers may find that the district contexts and policies described in the study are far removed from those they seek to examine and understand.

Contributions and limitations of interpretive research

The interpretive research genre has provided important windows into the thinking of teacher candidates. Teacher educators have drawn upon interpretive research to answer questions about how teacher candidates make sense of learning to teach, and manage the complexities of teaching and learning. Studies have illustrated the importance of candidates' beliefs and knowledge (e.g. beliefs about teaching and learning, subject matter knowledge), demonstrating how beliefs and knowledge shape and mediate their teacher education experiences.[4] A significant challenge for teacher education has been how to respond to the "demographic divide" (Banks *et al.*, 2005) and prepare teachers for diverse populations. Interpretive studies have provided important insights into the role that candidates' beliefs about culture, race, and language play in understanding and responding to diverse students, and they have illustrated promising practices in teacher education that help teacher candidates learn to teach in culturally responsive ways.[5] Interpretive studies have also contributed to a substantial body of work examining what occurs within methods courses and field experiences (Clift & Brady, 2005) and the practices of teacher educators (Grossman, 2005). Finally, interpretive studies have helped researchers identify features of high-quality teacher preparation programs (e.g. Darling-Hammond, 2000; Zeichner, 2005b). Taken together, studies within the interpretive genre have given teacher educators a more nuanced understanding of teacher candidates as learners, and have presented a complex portrait of the impact of teacher education programs and teacher educators' practices on candidates' learning to teach.

A central limitation of research in the interpretive genre is the lack of shared conceptual frameworks and designs, which makes it a challenging task to aggregate findings and to draw comparisons across studies, even when those studies are of similar phenomena. Also, though this is not a limitation of the genre per se, many studies make it to print with inadequate discussions of any or all of the following aspects of sound interpretive study design—context and participants, the researcher's subjective presence, triangulation or member checks, and disconfirming or negative cases. As a result, readers encounter difficulty determining whether and how the findings of a particular study may apply to the situations they work within. A final limitation of the body of interpretive research that has accrued is that it has focused primarily on the perspectives of teacher candidates, teacher educators, and school-based personnel involved in teacher preparation. Broadening an empirical eye to include other stakeholders in teacher preparation—such as university administrators, legislators and school board members, district administrators, those in state departments of education, excellent veteran teachers, parents, and K-12 learners—may yield important findings that speak to the current policy demands to link teacher preparation with student learning.

PRACTITIONER RESEARCH

Introduction: purpose and intellectual roots of practitioner research

In Zeichner's (1999) assessment of scholarship in teacher education, he hailed self-study research in teacher education—"research about teacher education [that] is being conducted by those who actually do the work of teacher education"—as "probably the single most significant development ever in the field of teacher education research" (p. 8). He characterized teacher educators' disciplined and systematic inquiry into their own practices as a new genre of research and predicted its growth in importance in the years to come. This genre, which we label "practitioner research," includes action research, participatory research, self-study, and teacher research.[6] Like interpretive research, it aims to understand human activity in situ and from the perspective of participants; however, it differs in two critical ways, namely the role of the researcher and the overarching purpose for the research. With the researcher as a central actor in the experiences studied, practitioner research examines practice from the inside; that is, instead of research *on* teacher education *by* an outside party, it is research *by* teacher educators *about* their practice. Implicit in this genre is the belief that practitioners are legitimate knowers who have gained important and valuable perspectives about the situations in which they practice.

Cochran-Smith and Lytle (1990) attributed this genre's underlying conception of teacher as reflective practitioner to Dewey's (1904, 1938) ideas about the relationship between theory and practice in teaching and teacher preparation. As early as 1904, Dewey emphasized the importance of teachers being students of teaching, and he advocated that they develop theoretical understandings of teaching and learning through reflection on their practice. More typically, scholars trace the intellectual roots of practitioner research conducted by teachers and teacher educators to the social science action research of the 1950s and 1960s (Cochran-Smith & Lytle, 1990). Lewin (1948), who coined the phrase "action research," described it as a spiral of cycles of planning, execution, fact-finding, and reflection leading to social action and social change. Stenhouse (1975), one of the most influential spokespersons for action research in education, encouraged teachers to engage in action research as a way of strengthening their judgment and improving their classroom practice.

The term practitioner research highlights both the personal value of studying one's own practice and the professional and collective implications of teacher educators formally researching their practice as teachers of teachers. As teacher educators, we have the potential to work at "purposefully unpacking [our] practice in response to the perplexities and uncertainties of teaching about teaching" (Loughran, 2005, p. 8). We do this to deepen our understanding of our own practice, improve our practice, and share our experiences with one another. The knowledge generated through practitioner inquiry is intended primarily to understand and improve practice within a local context. This knowledge may also prove useful beyond local contexts, for example by communicating the complexity of teacher education to the larger community of educators and scholars (Lytle & Cochran-Smith, 1992; Zeichner, 1999). Additionally, practitioner research conducted by teacher educators models for prospective teachers the premise that learning to teach is inherently connected to learning to inquire (Dinkelman, 2003).

Central features of practitioner research

The defining feature of this genre is the teacher educator's dual role as practitioner and researcher. In all variants of practitioner research, the researcher's professional context is the site for inquiry, and problems and issues within professional practice are the focus of investigation. Often these issues arise from discrepancies between what the practitioner intends and what actually occurs. Because the practitioner is a researcher and the professional context is the site for inquiry, the boundaries between research and practice often blur. Cochran-Smith and Lytle (2004) used the phrase "working the dialectic" to characterize the multifaceted relationship between research and practice inherent in practitioner research. Working the dialectic involves

> . . . reciprocal, recursive, and symbiotic relationships of research and practice, analysis and action, inquiry and experience, theorizing and doing, and being researchers and practitioners as well as the dialectic of generating local knowledge of practice while making that knowledge accessible and usable in other contexts and thus helping to transform it into public knowledge.
>
> (p. 635)

This unique relationship elevates "the local and immediate context to a position of prominence in investigations of teacher education" (Dinkelman, 2003, pp. 14–15), thus creating new opportunities for reflection on and improvement of the practice of teacher education.

All versions of practitioner research also share the features of intentionality and systematicity (Cochran-Smith & Lytle, 1993; Cochran-Smith & Donnell, 2006). Intentionality refers to the planned and deliberate nature of practitioner research, which can be contrasted to other versions of reflective practice that are typically more spontaneous in nature. Systematicity refers to organized ways of gathering information, keeping records of experiences and events, and analyzing the information that has been collected and recorded. Data collection in practitioner research incorporates methods of documentation such as observations, interviews, and artifact collection that are characteristic of many forms of qualitative research. Many practitioner researchers keep organized records of their planning and preparation, copies of instructional materials and assignments, samples of candidates' performances on formative and summative assessments, and written reflections about their teaching and their candidates' learning. Some studies also draw upon e-mail, recorded conversations, narratives, and other data sources that document participants' perspectives at particular moments in time (Cochran-Smith & Donnell, 2006).

Like many researchers in interpretive genres, practitioner researchers frequently employ both inductive and deductive approaches to data analysis. Occasionally, they use forms of analysis and interpretation that may be less familiar; for example, in "oral inquiry" data analysis is primarily oral, and meaning is collectively constructed in the social interactions of communities of practitioners (Cochran-Smith & Lytle, 1993, 2004). The interweaving of systematic analyses of candidates' learning (or other educational outcomes) with the teacher educator's intentions, decisions, interpretations, and reflections enables practitioner researchers to construct detailed accounts of teaching and learning that allow them to derive insights and conclusions not available to outside researchers. The power and authenticity of practitioner research requires multiple approaches to inquiry—multiple sources of data and approaches to data analysis—as well as assurances that the researcher articulates and examines his or her biases and how they may affect data collection and analysis.

One way researchers in this genre ensure quality and rigor is by considering their work to be community property and therefore available to others for review and critique (Shulman, 2000). For this to occur, reports of the research must follow basic conventions of reporting—for example, clearly stating research questions, providing sufficient detail regarding the conditions and contexts in which the study was conducted, and spelling out data collection and analysis procedures. LaBoskey (2004) argued, "We advance the field through the construction, testing, sharing, and re-testing of exemplars of teaching practice" (p. 821). She viewed practitioner research as a vital method for making the practices of teacher education available for deliberation, further testing, and judgment. As Shulman (2000) asserted, by engaging in a scholarship of teaching—by striving to make our documentation, assessment, and analysis of teaching more public and accessible—we not only support the improvement of our own teaching, but also increase the likelihood that the work will be useful to our professional peers.

In many versions of practitioner research, collaboration among teacher educators is also a key feature (Cochran-Smith & Donnell, 2006). Collaboration may involve a range of activities such as writing groups, critical friends, or joint data collection and/or analysis. Practitioner research conducted in isolation from other teacher educators limits the possibility that insights will be shared among colleagues or with wider audiences. Thus, collaboration enhances the likelihood that practitioner research will impact institutional as well as individual change, and will bring theoretical contributions into the public arena. The research program we feature offers an example of collaborative practitioner research.

Linda Valli and Jeremy Price: an example of practitioner research

Teacher educators engage in practitioner research at two levels. The first, which is the emphasis of this chapter, is research on one's own practice as a teacher educator; the second involves facilitating prospective teachers' experiences as researchers of their own practice. The example that we feature in this section illustrates how both levels can be, and sometimes are, intertwined by researchers who have a commitment to the value of practitioner research in both their own professional lives and in the preparation of their students. Linda Valli (2000) and Jeremy Price (2001) conducted parallel studies of their action research courses for preservice teachers at the University of Maryland. In addition, they collaborated in a study of their respective action research projects, examining how and what the prospective teachers in their courses were learning about teaching, inquiry, and change (Price & Valli, 2005). These two scholars referred to their research as action research, thereby highlighting their change orientation, which embraces both individual and social-political change.

Valli (2000) located her project in a capstone action research course taken by master's-level preservice teachers who were also employed as full-time instructional assistants in a local school system. As the instructor, she posed the following research question, "How can this course become more directly linked to school improvement while retaining a focus on the personal development of beginning teachers?" (p. 716). Drawing on data collected through participant observation, interviews with key informants, document review of course assignments, audiotaped class sessions, a reflective journal, and student questionnaires, she found that some students focused their action research on the school level while others focused on the classroom level. Despite her emphasis on both personal growth and school improvement, they were unable to fuse these two foci into one project. Valli concluded that the schools, the course design, and the textbook contributed to this either/or dichotomy, and that strategies for integrating conceptions of teacher and school development "are still in their infancy" (p. 729).

Price's (2001) action research course in an intensive one-year master's certification program aimed to provide opportunities for preservice teachers to examine their practice from a social justice perspective and to produce their own knowledge of teaching. His action research explored how experiences in four domains of teacher knowledge central to the course—reflection and inquiry, students, pedagogical content knowledge, and social justice and democracy—helped to shape the candidates' dispositions and practices as beginning teachers. Using data sources similar to Valli's, Price found that the action research course provided an opportunity for teacher candidates to develop and expand their ideas, skills, and commitments, and to translate them into teaching practices. He concluded that what teacher candidates learn in an action research course can impact "who they become as teachers and how they see the work of teaching" (p. 71).

Price and Valli (2005) collaborated to explore the pedagogical implications of teaching about and for change in preservice action research courses by looking for patterns and themes across their parallel action research projects. In addition to the multiple sources of data for their individual projects, data for this collaborative research included policy documents and notes from their research meetings. They individually analyzed their own prospective teachers' experiences with action research and developed descriptive case studies of four students, two from each class. Through a cross-case analysis Price and Valli identified five tensions or dilemmas inherent in the process and pedagogy of action research: individual and institutional change, action and understanding, support and challenge, passion and reason, and regulation and emancipation. They suggested that by working with these tensions, teacher educators can help prospective teachers to examine and reframe assumptions about themselves as teachers and change agents.

This multilayered project exemplifies the dual role as practitioner and researcher that is a defining feature of practitioner research. Further, the focus on individual and social change situates it within the tradition of action research. Price and Valli noted, ". . . like novice teachers, we had much to learn about teaching and that teaching is a complex, moral activity that warrants continuous inquiry and improvement" (p. 60). Their collaborative project demonstrates the value of teacher educators' action research for simultaneously revealing the complexity of teacher learning, providing a model of inquiry for prospective teachers, and contributing to a theory of the teaching and learning of action research in preservice teacher education.

Contributions and limitations of practitioner research

Practitioner research provides immediate benefits to the teacher educator who is studying his or her practice. These benefits include an increased understanding of content and pedagogy, commitment to a variety of teaching methods, confidence in one's own ability, and willingness to listen to and learn from students and others (Bullough & Gitlin, 1995; Hensen, 1996). These understandings and commitments derive from teacher educators' courage to confront and reflect upon "the shortcomings in their work and the gaps between their rhetoric and the reality of their practice" (Zeichner, 1999, p. 12). Hamilton and Pinnegar (2000) argued, "From self study we can evaluate individual practices, understand teaching better, change our practice to respond to the needs of our students, and, most importantly, create practice that stands as an embodied testament to our belief" (p. 238).

The benefits of practitioner research can also extend beyond the teacher educator. As the work by Valli and Price illustrates, "This disciplined and systematic inquiry into one's own teaching practice provides a model for prospective teachers and for teachers of the kind of inquiry that more and more teacher educators are hoping their students employ" (Zeichner, 1999, p. 11). Practitioner research has the potential to foster educational change and innovations and to open doors for collaboration between K-12 school practitioners and schools of education. Benefits can and should impact the preservice teacher, the teacher education program, the institution of higher education, and the wider community of educators, scholars, and policymakers.

Professionals who engage in research on their own practice face a number of substantial challenges. For teacher educators, challenges such as time and negotiating research agendas within a university culture may constrain systematic inquiry into one's practice (Bullough & Gitlin, 1995; Cochran-Smith & O'Donnell, 2006). In addition, teacher educators engaged in practitioner research are often called upon to address significant critiques of this research genre. Cochran-Smith and her colleagues (Cochran-Smith & Lytle, 2004; Cochran-Smith & Donnell, 2006) organized the critiques into five categories: the knowledge critique, the methods critique, the science critique, the political critique, and the personal/professional development critique. While a discussion of these critiques is beyond the scope of this chapter, it is important to note that they are fundamentally tied to questions about what counts as knowledge, evidence, effectiveness, and even research. Despite these questions and critiques, Zeichner's (1999) prediction has clearly come to pass. The genre has continued to grow in scope and impact, as evidenced by numerous publications including the two-volume *International Handbook of Self-Study of Teaching and Teacher Education Practices* (Loughran *et al.*, 2004) and the new journal *Studying Teacher Education*, edited by Loughran and Russell.

DESIGN RESEARCH

Introduction: purpose and intellectual roots

Design research is perhaps the most recent genre of research to be used in the study of teacher education and learning to teach. In the educational arena, design research began as a reaction to traditional psychological experimentation, conducted under carefully controlled laboratory conditions, which dominated early research on human learning. Committed to addressing questions about what works in practice, design researchers carried their work into real-life settings, giving up the notions of controlling variables and fixed procedures characteristic of psychological experimentation (Collins, 1999).

Instead, design experiments draw upon models from engineering and "design sciences" such as aeronautics and artificial intelligence to explore learning in context through the systematic design and study of instructional strategies and tools (Design-Based Research Collective [DBRC], 2003). Thus, this genre is characterized by an intimate relationship between the improvement of practice and the development of theory (Brown, 1992; Simon, 1996). The research team works to simultaneously improve practice and contribute to theory by creating models of successful innovations and developing explanatory frameworks about both the processes of learning and the tools that are designed to foster learning (Cobb *et al.*, 2003).

Within education, the most extensive design research projects have been conducted in K-12 mathematics classrooms. Influenced by classroom teaching experiments (Gravemeijer, 1994) and constructivist teaching experiments (Cobb & Steffe, 1983) as well as by design research methodology in other disciplines, classroom-based design experiments typically entail creating an educational innovation and systematically studying learning during its enactment. In teacher education the focus of design research shifts to preservice teachers and their experiences within a teacher education innovation. As Simon (2000) explained, the teacher development experiment methodology "provides a framework for researchers to work at the edge of their evolving knowledge" (p. 336) as they design and enact educational opportunities for preservice teachers, and study participants' learning and development in the context of those opportunities.

Central features of design research

A hallmark of design research is its commitment to iterative cycles of design, enactment, analysis, and redesign. These cycles are theory-driven; researchers begin with an initial set of conjectures about ways to foster a particular form of learning. These conjectures are refined as they are supported or refuted by systematic collection and analysis of data. New conjectures are similarly subjected to testing and refinement, resulting in iterative cycles of intervention and revision. Design research is process focused; researchers trace changes in an individual or group by examining successive patterns in their reasoning and learning, and assessing the impact of features of the instructional intervention on that reasoning and learning.

The success of design research in educational settings depends on the knowledge and efforts of practitioners as well as researchers. Thus, researchers typically collaborate closely with teachers or teacher educators to develop, enact, and revise an educational intervention. The researchers' ongoing, direct involvement in the setting is essential. They must have a clear view of the anticipated learning trajectories, a firm grasp of potential means of support, and a deep understanding of the educational setting. These understandings enable them both to facilitate logistics of the innovation and to conduct regular debriefing sessions in which past events are analyzed and interpreted and future ones are planned. Often, the educational practitioner participates fully as a member of the research team, sharing in the collective effort to develop the initial design, conduct the experiment, carry out the analyses, and redesign the innovation. (See, for example, Bowers *et al.*, 1999; McClain, 2003.)

Design research is often multileveled. In teacher education, innovations typically involve multiple elements such as the tasks or problems preservice teachers are asked to solve, pedagogical materials that support learning, norms of participation and discourse that are established, and instructional practices that teacher educators use to orchestrate relations among tasks, materials, and participation norms. In addition to these classroom-level elements, innovations may incorporate activities or structures in the teacher education program. In sum, design research is iterative, theory driven, process-focused, collaborative, interventionist, and often multileveled (Shavelson *et al.*, 2003).

Although growing out of different scholarly traditions, programs of design research and practitioner research often have several key features in common. A commitment to both improving local practice and contributing to the broader knowledge base, always present in design research, is characteristic of many practitioner research projects as well. When the teacher educator is a member of the design research team and outside researchers participate in practitioner research, the collaborative nature of the working relationships is similar. In addition, there are obvious similarities in both design and intent between action research's spiraling cycles of planning, execution, fact-finding, and evaluation (Lewin, 1948), and the iterative cycles of design, enactment, analysis, and redesign that are central to design research. Design research also bears more than a passing resemblance to lesson study, in which a professional learning community spends months, or even years, teaching and revising a series of classroom lessons (Cobb, 2000).

Data collected during a design experiment typically include a comprehensive record of the design process—for example, audio or video recordings of design meetings and logs to document evolving conjectures. Of equal importance are data on the learning processes and outcomes and the means by which learning is organized and supported. In a preservice teacher education course, documentation of the intervention typically entails the collection and coordination of multiple forms of data such as audio and video records of class sessions, instructional artifacts, assessment tools and student work, and other products of student learning.

Design research features two distinct levels of data analysis, ongoing and retrospective. During the course of a design experiment, ongoing analyses aim to enhance participants' learning; these analyses lead to modified conjectures and refined interventions. In a teacher development experiment, these analyses consider prospective teachers' knowledge and reasoning, and the activity system in which they are situated. Retrospective analyses occur after the intervention is completed and aim to place the design experiment in a broader theoretical context. Through a systematic reexamination of the data, these analyses continue the development of explanatory models of learning and the means by which it can be supported (Simon, 2000; Cobb *et al.*, 2003).

The construction of elementary mathematics project: an example

Almost all examples of educational design research that we found were conducted within K-12 classrooms and focused on student learning. We located a small but growing number of design experiments that addressed teacher learning within professional development (e.g. Clark *et al.*, in press; Lehrer & Schauble, 2000; Stein *et al.*, 1998) and preservice teacher education (e.g. Simon, 2000; McClain, 2003). We feature one of the research programs conducted within preservice teacher education, the Construction of Elementary Mathematics (CEM) Project.

The CEM Project was a three-year teacher development experiment that both generated a set of learning activities to support prospective elementary teachers' mathematical and pedagogical development and also extended theoretical models of quantitative reasoning and mathematical justification (Simon, 2000). Simon, Blume, and colleagues at Pennsylvania State University studied teacher candidates' development in the context of an experimental teacher preparation program that coordinated a mathematics course, a course on mathematics learning and teaching, and two related practicum experiences. Primary goals of the program were to increase the preservice teachers' mathematical knowledge and to foster their development of conceptions of mathematics, teaching, and learning consistent with reform documents such as the *Curriculum and Evaluation Standards for School Mathematics* (National Council of Teachers of Mathematics [NCTM], 1989) and *Professional Standards for Teaching Mathematics* (NCTM, 1991). Simon designed and taught the two courses; thus, this project is an example of design research in which the practitioner is an integral member of the research team (Cobb, 2000).

The design experiment that Simon and colleagues conducted in the mathematics course focused on prospective teachers' quantitative reasoning and understanding of multiplicative relationships. The research team began by generating a model of preservice teachers' mathematical and pedagogical development. Following each class session, they met to discuss their perspectives on the candidates' mathematical development and to decide on the instructional tasks for the next class. Over the course of the semester, they documented substantial changes in the nature of arguments that the prospective teachers used to justify and validate their mathematical ideas. For example, many of their early attempts to justify a mathematical idea involved invoking authorities such as past teachers and texts. Later attempts involved deductive proofs and taking on the role of arbitrators of validity (Simon & Blume, 1996). On the basis of these ongoing analyses, the research team refined their model of teacher development and revised the learning activities they created to foster preservice teachers' understanding of multiplicative relationships and conceptions of justification.

Issues that emerged in the ongoing analyses became the foci of retrospective analyses. One set of analyses addressed the development of classroom norms related to justification and validation. These analyses generated an explanation of how mathematical and social norms regarding justification and validation were negotiated in the classroom community, and a description of the factors that affected students' engagement in mathematical justification and the development of classroom norms (McNeal & Simon, 2000; Simon & Blume, 1996).

In keeping with the goals of design research, these ongoing and retrospective analyses yielded contributions to both practice and theory. Practical products include instructional tasks and pedagogical practices for supporting the development of preservice teachers' quantitative reasoning and conceptions of justification, and classroom mathematical, and social norms (McNeal & Simon, 2000; Simon, 2000; Simon & Blume, 1994a, 1994b, 1996). Theoretical contributions include an elaboration of a model of quantitative reasoning and an extension of existing taxonomies of mathematical justification. The project exemplifies the iterative, collaborative, and interventionist nature of design research. In addition, it illustrates the blurred boundaries between design research and practitioner research. In fact, in the *Handbook of Research Design in Mathematics and Science Education* (Kelly & Lesh, 2000), the CEM Project is discussed as an example of studying teaching "from the inside" by Ball (2000) and "teacher development experiments" by Simon.

Contributions and limitations of design research

As the Construction of Elementary Mathematics Project illustrates, the contributions of design research are both theoretical and practical. Teacher development experiments (like classroom-based design experiments) are conducted around specific interventions in specific contexts. However, the explanatory frameworks developed through ongoing and retrospective analyses enable researchers to compare different enactments of the innovation with respect to key features of the context, teaching and learning practices, and outcomes. These analyses produce detailed accounts of the innovation and its effects across multiple teacher education settings. Such accounts contribute to context-ualized theories of teacher learning—theories that address the elements of context that matter for learning and have implications for teacher education policies and practices (Cobb, 2000; DBRC, 2003).

From a practical perspective, an important goal of design research is that the edu-cational innovations developed in one setting lead to productive patterns of learning when enacted in other settings. The intention is not to develop instructional programs to be replicated in the same way in different contexts; rather, design research is grounded in a conception of teacher educators as professionals who continually adjust their plans on the basis of ongoing assessments of individual and collective activity in the classroom. The explanatory frameworks for analyzing an innovation make it possible to enact the innovation in different settings in ways that preserve its essential elements while adap-ting to specific features of those settings—that is, ways that do not constitute "fatal mutations" (Brown, 1992).

A key strength of design research is that it enables researchers to test theories and investigate educational innovations as they are enacted in real-world settings. This genre is not well suited to examine the broader sociopolitical context of reform, or to under-stand an individual's cognition independent of situation and purpose. Design research is labor intensive and costly. An appropriate time frame for studying teacher development is probably several years—comprising both a long intervention and a long period for retrospective data analysis (Cobb, 2000; Shavelson *et al.*, 2003).

CHALLENGES AND OPPORTUNITIES FOR ESTABLISHED, EMERGING, AND BLURRED GENRES

In this final section we consider the contexts of current policy and practice in teacher education and teacher education research and imagine how the complex questions the field faces will draw upon established and emerging genres and might well inspire the blurring of research genres. We close with suggestions for future directions for genres of teacher education research.

Responding to "dangerous times"

In a 2004 editorial for the *Journal of Teacher Education*, Cochran-Smith suggested that "these are dangerous times for teacher education" (Cochran-Smith, 2004b, p. 3). Our field faces difficult challenges such as recruiting and retaining a diverse teacher cohort and improving our ability to prepare teachers who ensure *all* children realize their full potential, especially those who have historically been poorly served in public schools (Darling-Hammond & Bransford, 2005; Florio-Ruane, 2002). At the same time, both critics and stakeholders insist that teacher education demonstrate its contribution to student learning. This current emphasis on accountability, often framed in rather limited terms, has given rise to an environment where learning is defined in terms of what is measurable on tests, where teacher quality is conceptualized as courses taken in a content area and as individual teachers' effectiveness in raising student test scores, where legisla-tion seeks both to deregulate entry points into teaching and to tighten regulation of university-based teacher education programs, and where legislation calls for science to solve problems in education through "scientifically based research" and "evidence-based education." The convergence of these developments pushes us toward a narrow concep-tion of teaching and teacher education—"a technical view of teaching, a training model of teacher education, ... [and] equating of learning with testing" (Cochran-Smith, 2004b, p. 3).

How can research help us to address these challenges in the current milieu? What kinds of research are most needed to inform the decision making of practitioners and policymakers? In this section we offer recommendations for directions in teacher education research—directions designed to produce knowledge that will be useful for policy and practice. The notion of complexity features prominently in our recommendations. While research over the last fifty years has given us an understanding of and appreciation for the complexity of teaching and learning to teach, researchers in the next decade must do more to tease out that complexity and relate it to broad notions of student learning. Cochran-Smith (2005) characterized the goal of such a research agenda as building a chain of evidence:

> To get from teacher education to impact on pupils' learning requires a chain of evidence with several critical links: empirical evidence demonstrating the link between teacher preparation programs and teacher candidates' learning, empirical evidence demonstrating the link between teacher candidates' learning and their practices in actual classrooms, and empirical evidence demonstrating the link between graduates' practices and what and how much their pupils learn. Individually, each of these links is complex and challenging to estimate. When they are combined, the challenges are multiplied.
>
> (p. 303)

Complex questions call for varied methods

To address these challenges—to build this chain of evidence—our research must be multidisciplinary and pluralistic in its methods and must take advantage of new tools for data collection and analysis. The questions implicit in building this chain of evidence are complex. The field will need to draw upon established genres such as effects of teacher education and interpretive research, continue to develop and experiment with practitioner and design research genres, and blur genres in studies using mixed methods. As Zeichner (2005a) wrote in the concluding chapter of the report of the AERA Panel on Research on Teacher Education, "Given the complexity of teacher education and its connections to various aspects of teacher quality and student learning, no single methodological or theoretical approach will be able to provide all that is needed to understand how and why teacher education influences educational outcomes" (p. 743).

As a field, we must also take advantage of methodological advances to design more complex studies and to engage in multifaceted analyses. New technologies for gathering, recording, and storing information make larger data sets available. New statistical techniques and tools enable multilevel analyses of complex data sets. The digital revolution in media gives researchers the ability to gather and store high-quality audio and video records of teaching and learning activities, and computer software provides new tools to code and analyze textual and video data.

The studies highlighted in this chapter illustrate ways in which both established and emerging genres are incorporating these methodological advances into innovative research designs and analysis plans. We find this work very encouraging. At the same time, we see that there is additional potential in conducting research that blurs the boundaries between genres. In previous decades, larger conversations within the educational research community informed developments in genres of teacher education research. We expect current discussions of multiple methods will similarly contribute to the field of teacher education research.

Research that incorporates multiple methods in a single project goes by many names—for example, multiple methods, mixed methods, multiple or mixed approaches, multiple or mixed models, or integrated methods (Smith, 2006). Sometimes characterized as the "third methodological movement" in social and behavioral research (Tashakkori & Teddue, 2003), such research is typically driven by practical concerns. Taking a pragmatic approach, researchers choose multiple methods and combine them in unique ways that offer the best opportunity to address thorny problems. In this sense, building on the central metaphor of this chapter, they are blurring genres to create a richer analysis and interpretation of complex events.

There is much debate about the appropriateness of research that incorporates a combination of methods. This debate examines a variety of issues such as the fit between theoretical perspectives and methods, the conceptual coherence of knowledge claims that are derived from different methods, and the practicalities of conducting studies that combine multiple designs and procedures. A discussion of these issues, most of which remain unresolved, is beyond the scope of this chapter.[7] Here, we illustrate the potential value of such research by briefly describing two studies currently under way—the *Teacher Pathways* and *Teacher Quality Partnership* projects. Although in early 2006 these projects were just beginning to publish findings in peer-reviewed venues, given the nature of the questions they address and the strength of their mixed-methods research designs, it is already clear they have the potential to make important contributions to building the chain of evidence that will link teacher education to student learning.

The *Teacher Pathways Project* is a multiyear investigation of different pathways into teaching in New York City schools; it examines how features of those pathways impact a variety of outcomes such as whether people teach, whether they stay in teaching, and what impact they have on student achievement (Boyd *et al.*, 2006). As such, it is impressive in its purpose and scope. The research team, composed of scholars from several disciplines, includes labor-market economists, teacher educators, and policy analysts. The project incorporates a variety of methods and multiple data sources including individual-level administrative data on characteristics of aspiring and practicing teachers, on teachers' career histories, and on test scores of elementary math and reading students; survey data on teacher candidates' characteristics and experiences, on first- and second-year teachers' experiences and descriptions of school learning environments, and on principals' descriptions of school learning environments; and interview and artifact data on features of teacher preparation programs and K-12 schools.

> All of these data sources are linked at the individual teacher level; survey data on program participants and new teachers are linked to administrative data on their teaching careers and to descriptive information on preparation programs; student test scores are linked to the teachers who taught them; and so on.
>
> (Boyd *et al.*, 2006)

Initial results suggest that teacher attrition varies by pathway. For example, Teach for America teachers experience the highest attrition after two or more years of teaching. The relative rate of attrition for Teaching Fellows and temporary-license teachers is roughly equal after three years of teaching, and is greater than the rate for either college-recommended or individual evaluation teachers. With respect to student achievement gains, in many cases a teacher's pathway makes little difference, though there are some differences when grade level and years of experience are considered. For example, in their first year of teaching, alternate-route teachers often provide smaller gains in student achievement than college-recommended teachers, but they typically catch up by their second or third year of teaching. In addition to these patterns identified across pathways, ongoing data collection and analysis are examining the substantial variation within pathways of teachers' ability to increase student achievement (Boyd *et al.*, 2005).

The *Teacher Quality Partnership* (2006) is a comprehensive, longitudinal study of how the preparation and development of new teachers in Ohio affects students' academic performance. The research team, which includes scholars with expertise in measurement, literacy, and teacher education, is conducting a series of studies to explore the relationships among variations in teacher preparation, characteristics and instructional practices of (novice and experienced) teachers, and student learning. Four interlocking research initiatives are under way, with formal data collection taking place from 2005 into 2008. The first initiative, or component, involves surveying student teachers, first-year teachers, and teachers with alternative licensure, asking them to evaluate the coherence and quality of their teacher preparation experiences, particularly as they relate to essential teaching responsibilities. Adapting a theoretical framework from Dunkin and Biddle's (1974) presage-process-outcome model and using data sources that include surveys, observation cycles, interviews, and artifacts, the second component seeks to "unpack the 'black box' of experienced teachers' classrooms" (Teacher Quality Partnership, 2006). The third traces 50 novice teachers over a three-year period. Using the same protocols as the experienced teacher study, it examines mentoring and induction activities and how those activities support novices' continued learning, especially their learning to engage K-12 students in tasks that result in their achievement. The fourth component uses structural-equation modeling to analyze the interrelationships among all the qualitative and quantitative data.

New York's *Pathways* project and Ohio's *Partnership* project aim to understand the wide variation in and impact of the teacher education routes in their respective states. The research designs in both projects address the complexity of the problem and will result in extensive, longitudinal data gathered from a representative sample. While the possibility of oversimplifying or misusing findings from large-scale studies cannot be dismissed, such studies have great potential to contribute to our understanding of several links in the "chain of evidence" Cochran-Smith (2005a) called for. Furthermore, we believe the findings will help teacher educators to critique and reflect on their practice and their programs. These studies utilize both effects of teacher education and interpretive research genres; we hope that the studies' findings will, in turn, inspire teacher educators to engage in practitioner research and design inquiries.

Future contributions for genres of teacher education research

To conclude this chapter, we offer the following recommendations to guide decisions about genres of research in the study of teacher education:

- *Select research genres and methods of inquiry appropriate for the research questions.* The analyses in this chapter illustrate that there are multiple sound research genres available to the teacher education research community, and that each genre is well suited for some questions more than others. The researcher's first and most essential role is to pose questions of practical and theoretical significance. Researchers then should evaluate which genre or combination of genres best fits the question(s) and the resources available to conduct a well-designed study.

- *Continue support for multiple genres of research in teacher education.* The analysis of research genres in this chapter shows that no single genre can address the varied and complex questions we pose about learning to teach. Many teacher educators have specialized in research methods most attuned for interpretive and practitioner studies; thus, as a field, teacher education has insufficient ability to conduct studies that both speak to policymakers' concerns and reflect teacher educators' deep knowledge about learning to teach. To ensure the vitality of the field, the teacher education community must prepare more researchers with expertise in sophisticated quantitative methodologies. Furthermore, we encourage researchers, no matter what genre they claim as their area of expertise, to recognize the affordances and limitations of each genre and to champion the legitimate contributions each makes to illuminate persistent dilemmas in teacher education.
- *Build capacity to conduct collaborative research.* To conduct the multifaceted, large-scale studies of teacher education that are being called for by many policymakers will require collaboration among researchers with different areas of expertise. In addition to the challenges associated with any collaboration, teams conducting mixed-methods research will need to respond to methodological dilemmas noted earlier in our discussion. While we encourage more attention to mixed-methods design, we recognize that this complex approach to research is still relatively new terrain for researchers in teacher education—terrain whose navigation will require listening and negotiating across disciplinary boundaries (Eisenhart & Borko, 1991).
- *Demonstrate a strong commitment to rigor in both the conduct and the reporting of research.* The value of research hinges on the quality of the design and conduct of each study. As scholars, we must demand that methods of data collection and analysis are carried out with attention to the genre's major assumptions and quality criteria. Furthermore, research methods and findings must be reported in sufficient detail that quality is evident to consumers. The recently released *Standards for Reporting on Empirical Social Science Research in AERA Publications* (AERA, 2006) provides useful guidance. An emphasis on the quality of research is especially relevant to the emerging genres—practitioner and design research—as the field is still developing criteria for rigor that honors the innovative features of this research.

As we have argued throughout this chapter, the challenges facing teacher education are numerous and complex. It is all too common for teacher educators and policymakers to attempt to address these challenges—to design and implement programs and policies— without turning to research for guidance (Zeichner, 2005a). In order for research to influence the crafting of wise policy, the improvement of practice, and the development of theory, we must ensure that the research base in teacher education draws from multiple disciplines, is pluralistic in its methods, and is rigorously conducted and reported. Similar recommendations recently have been offered by many other scholars (cf. Borko, 2004; Cochran-Smith & Fries, 2005; Shavelson & Towne, 2002; Sleeter, 2001; Wilson *et al.*, 2002; Zeichner, 2005a). Nonetheless, they bear repeating, as they are essential to ensure that research will play a prominent role in addressing the challenges of policy and practice currently facing teacher education.

NOTES

1 The authors wish to thank Marilyn Cochran-Smith, Bob Floden, and Karen Hammerness for their thoughtful commentaries on earlier versions of this chapter: their astute observations

sharpened arguments and strengthened the piece. The authors, however, take full responsibility for any inadequacies or errors that remain.

2 As evidence of this growth, we note the following: (1) Since 1992 four major handbooks on qualitative research in education have been published (LeCompte *et al.*, 1992; Denzin & Lincoln, 1994, 2000, 2005). (2) Numerous textbooks and guides to conducting this research are available (e.g. Hatch, 2002; Miles & Huberman, 1994), and qualitative methods are an established and expected part of doctoral training in education. (3) New journals have been established to discuss qualitative methods and to publish qualitative work (e.g. *Journal of Qualitative Studies*). (4) Dynamic epistemological and methodological debates have taken place within established journals (e.g. *Educational Researcher*).

3 The work of this research program, carried out at two institutions, has been published in several journals. The 1999 article by Grossman *et al.*, "Appropriating Tools for Teaching English: A Theoretical Framework on Learning to Teach," laid out the program's collaboratively developed theoretical framework. Findings from the different studies that compose the research program include Cook *et al.* (2002), Grossman *et al.* (2000), Grossman and Thompson (2004), and Smagorinsky *et al.* (2002, 2004, 2006).

4 For example, see the following specific studies: Ball (1990), Borko *et al.* (1992), Eisenhart *et al.* (1993), Grossman (1990), Hollingsworth (1989), Holt-Reynolds (1999), Peressini *et al.* (2004), Stoddart *et al.* (1993), Wilson and Wineburg (1998). And see the following reviews of literature: Borko and Putnam (1996); Munby *et al.* (2001); Putnam and Borko (1997); Richardson and Placier (2001); Wideen *et al.* (1998).

5 For example, see the following specific studies: Burrant (1999); Escamilla and Nathenson-Mejia (2003); Fry and McKinney (1997); Gomez *et al.* (2000); Goodwin (1994); Weiner (1993). Also, see the following reviews of this literature: Hollins and Guzman (2005), Sleeter (2001), Weiner (2000), and Zeichner and Hoeft (1996).

6 Because a thorough discussion of similarities and differences among the forms of practitioner research is beyond the scope of this chapter, we direct readers to Cochran-Smith and Donnell (2006) and Zeichner and Noffke (2001).

7 We refer interested readers to Johnson and Ouwuegbuzie (2004). Smith (2006), and the *Handbook of Mixed Methods in Social and Behavioral Research* edited by Tashakkori and Teddue (2003).

REFERENCES

AERA (2006) Standards for reporting on empirical social science research in AERA publications. *Educational Researcher*, 35(6), 33–40.

Ball, D. L. (1990) The mathematical understandings that prospective teachers bring to teacher education. *Elementary School Journal*, 90, 449–466.

Ball, D. L. (2000) Working in the inside: using one's own practice as a site for studying teaching and learning. In A. Kelly & R. Lesh (eds.), *Handbook of research design in mathematics and science education* (pp. 365–402). Dordrecht, The Netherlands: Kluwer.

Banks, J., Cochran-Smith, M., Moll, L., Richert, A., Zeichner, K., LePage, P., Darling-Hammond, L., & Dully, H. (2005) Teaching diverse learners. In L. Darling-Hammond & J. Bransford (eds.), *Preparing teachers for a changing world: what teachers should learn and be able to do* (pp. 232–274). San Francisco: Jossey-Bass.

Bogdan, R. C. & Biklen, S. K. (1992) *Qualitative research for education: an introduction to theory and methods*. Boston: Allyn & Bacon.

Borko, H. (2004) Professional development and teacher learning: mapping the terrain. *Educational Researcher*, 33(8), 3–15.

Borko, H. & Putnam, R. (1996) Research in learning to teach. In D. Berliner & R. Calfee (eds.), *Handbook of research on educational psychology* (pp. 673–699). New York: Macmillan.

Borko, H., Eisenhart, M., Brown, C. A., Underhill, R. G., Jones, D., & Agard, P. C. (1992) Learning to teach hard mathematics: do novice teachers and their instructors give up too easily? *Journal for Research in Mathematics Education*, 21, 132–144.

Bowers, J., Cobb, P., & McClain, K. (1999) The evolution of mathematical practices: a case study. *Cognition and Instruction*, 17(1), 25–64.

Boyd, D., Grossman, P., Lankford, H., Loeb, S., & Wyckoff, J. (November 2005) *How changes in entry requirements alter the teacher workforce and affect student achievement.* Research Paper, Teacher Policy Research. http://www.teacherpolicyresearch.org

Boyd, D., Grossman, P., Lankford, H., Loeb, S., Wyckoff, J., & McDonald, M. (2006). *Examining teacher preparation: does the pathway make a difference?* Retrieved February 4, 2006 from http://www.teacherpolicyresearch.org/portals/1/pdfs/Examining_Teacher_Preparation_Full-Description.pdf

Boyd, D., Grossman, P., Lankford, H., Loeb, S., Michelli, N., & Wyckoff, J. (2006) Complex by design: investigating pathways into teaching in New York City schools. *Journal of Teacher Education,* 57, 155–166.

Brophy, J. E. & Good, T. L. (1986) Teacher behavior and student achievement. In M. C. Wittrock (ed.), *Handbook of research on teaching* (3rd ed., pp. 328–375). New York: Macmillan.

Brown, A. (1992) Design experiments: theoretical and methodological challenges in creating complex interventions in classroom settings. *Journal of the Learning Sciences,* 2(2), 141–178.

Bullough, R. V., Jr., & Gitlin, A. (1995) *Becoming a student of teaching: methodologies for exploring self and school context.* New York: Garland.

Burkhardt, H. & Schoenfeld, A. H. (2003) Improving educational research: toward a more useful, more influential, and better-funded enterprise. *Educational Researcher,* 32(9), 3–14.

Burrant, T. J. (1999) Finding, using, and losing voice: a preservice teacher's experiences in an urban educative practicum. *Journal of Teacher Education,* 50, 209–220.

Cazden, C. (1988) *Classroom discourse.* Portsmouth, NH: Heinemann.

Clark, K. K., Borko, H., Frykholm, J., Jacobs, J., Schneider, C., & Eiteljorg, E. (in press). The problem-solving cycle: a model to support the development of teachers' professional knowledge. *Mathematical Thinking and Learning.*

Clift, R. & Brady, P. (2005) Research on methods courses and field experiences. In M. Cochran-Smith & K. Zeichner (eds.), *Studying teacher education: the report of the AERA Panel on Research and Teacher Education* (pp. 309–424). Mahwah, NJ: Erlbaum.

Cobb, P. (2000) Conducting teaching experiments in collaboration with teachers. In A. E. Kelly & R. A. Lesh (eds.), *Handbook of research design in mathematics and science education* (pp. 307–333). Mahwah, NJ: Erlbaum.

Cobb, P. & Steffe, L. P. (1983) The constructivist researcher as teacher and model builder. *Journal for Research in Mathematics Education,* 14, 83–94.

Cobb, P., Confrey, J., diSessa, A., Lehrer, R., & Schauble, L. (2003) Design experiments in educational research. *Educational Researcher,* 32(1), 9–13.

Cochran-Smith, M. (2004a) Ask a different question, get a different answer: the research base for teacher education. *Journal of Teacher Education,* 55(2), 111–115.

Cochran-Smith, M. (2004b) Taking stock in 2004: teacher education in dangerous times. *Journal of Teacher Education,* 55(1), 3–7.

Cochran-Smith, M. (2005a) Studying teacher education: what we know and need to know. *Journal of Teacher Education,* 56(4), 301–306.

Cochran-Smith, M. & Lytle, S. L. (1990) Research on teaching and teacher research: the issues that divide. *Educational Researcher,* 19(2), 2–11.

Cochran-Smith, M. & Lytle, S. L. (1993) *Inside/outside: teacher research and knowledge.* New York: Teachers College Press.

Cochran-Smith, M. & Lytle, S. L. (2004) Practitioner inquiry, knowledge, and university culture. In J. Loughran, M. L. Hamilton, V. K. LaBoskey, & T. Russell (eds.) *International handbook of self-study of teaching and teacher education practices* (pp 601–649). Dordrecht, The Netherlands: Kluwer.

Cochran-Smith, M. & Fries, K. (2005) Researching teacher education in changing times: politics and paradigms. In M. Cochran-Smith & K. Zeichner (eds.). *Studying teacher education: the report of the AERA Panel on Research and Teacher Education* (pp. 69–109). Washington, DC: American Educational Research Association.

Cochran-Smith, M. & Donnell, K. (2006) Practitioner inquiry: blurring the boundaries of research and practice. In J. Green, Camilli, G., & P. B. Elmore (eds.) *Handbook of complementary methods in education research* (pp. 503–518) Mahwah, NJ: Erlbaum.

Collins, A. (1999) The changing infrastructure of education research. In E. C. Lagemann & L. S. Shulman (eds.) *Issues in education research: problems and possibilities* (pp. 289–298). San Francisco: Jossey-Bass.

Cook, L. S., Smagorinsky, P., Konopak, B., & Moore, C. (2002) Problems in developing a constructivist approach to teaching: one teacher's transition from teacher preparation to teaching. *Elementary School Journal*, 102(5), 389–413.

Darling-Hammond, L. (2000) *Studies of excellence in teacher education*. New York: National Commission on Teaching and America's Future.

Darling-Hammond, L. & Bransford, J. (eds.) (2005) *Preparing teachers for a changing world*. San Francisco: Jossey-Bass.

Darling-Hammond, L., Berry, B., & Thorensen, A. (2001) Does teacher certification matter? Evaluating the evidence. *Educational Evaluation and Policy Analysis*, 23(1), 5–77.

Delamont, S., Coffey, A., & Atkinson, P. (2000) The twilight years? Educational ethnography and the five moments model. *Qualitative Studies in Education*, 13(3), 223–238.

Denzin, N. & Lincoln, Y. (1994) *Handbook of qualitative research*. Thousand Oaks, CA: Sage.

Denzin, N. & Lincoln, Y. (2000) *Handbook of qualitative research* (2nd ed.). Thousand Oaks, CA: Sage.

Denzin, N. & Lincoln, Y. (2005) *The Sage handbook of qualitative research* (3rd ed.). Thousand Oaks, CA: Sage.

Design-Based Research Collective (2003) Design-based research: an emerging paradigm for educational inquiry. *Educational Researcher*, 32(1), 5–8.

Dewey, J. (1904) The relation of theory to practice in education. In J. Dewey, S. C. Brooks, F. M. McMurry, & C. A. McMurry (eds.), *The relation of theory to practice in the education of teachers: Third yearbook of the National Society for the Study of Education, Part 1*. Bloomington, IL: Public School Publishing.

Dewey, J. (1938) *Experience and education*. New York: Collier Books.

Dinkelman, T. (2003) Self-study in teacher education: a means and ends tool for promoting reflective teaching. *Journal of Teacher Education*, 54(1), 6–18.

Doyle, W. (1990) Themes in teacher education research. In W. R. Houston (ed.), *Handbook of research on teacher education* (pp. 3–24). New York: Macmillan.

Dunkin, M. & Biddle, B. (1974) *The study of teaching*. New York: Holt, Rinehart & Winston.

Eisenhart, M. & Borko, H. (1991) In search of an interdisciplinary collaborative design for studying teacher education. *Teaching and Teacher Education*, 7, 137–157.

Eisenhart, M. & Howe, K. (1992) Validity in educational research. In M. D. LeCompte, W. L. Millroy, & J. Priessle (1992) *The handbook of qualitative research in education* (pp. 643–680). San Diego, CA: Academic Press.

Eisenhart, M., Borko, H., Underhill, R., Brown, C., Jones, D., & Agard, P. (1993) Conceptual knowledge falls through the cracks: complexities of learning to teach mathematics for understanding. *Journal for Research in Mathematics Education*, 24(1), 8–40.

Emmer, E., Evertson, C., & Anderson, L. (1980) Effective classroom management at the beginning of the school year. *Elementary School Journal*, 80, 219–231.

Erikson, F. (1986) Qualitative methods in research on teaching. In M. C. Wittrock (ed.), *Handbook of research on teaching* (3rd ed., pp. 119–161). New York: Macmillan.

Escamilla, K. & Nathenson-Mejia, S. (2003) Preparing culturally responsive teachers: using Latino children's literature in teacher education. *Equity and Excellence in Education*, 36(3), 238–248.

Flanders, N. (1970) *Analyzing teacher behavior*. Reading, MA: Addison-Wesley.

Floden, R. E. (2001) Research on effects of teaching: a continuing model for research on teaching. In V. Richardson (ed.), *Handbook of research on teaching* (4th ed., pp. 3–16). Washington, DC: American Educational Research Association.

Floden, R. E. (2006) Personal communication.

Floden, R. E. & Meniketti, M. (2005) Research on the effects of coursework in the arts and sciences and in the foundations of education. In M. Cochran-Smith & K. M. Zeichner (eds.),

Studying teacher education: the report of the AERA Panel on Research and Teacher Education (pp. 261–308). Washington, DC: American Educational Research Association.

Florio-Ruane, S. (2002) More light: an argument for complexity in studies of teaching and teacher education. *Journal of Teacher Education*, 53(3), 205–215.

Fry, P. G. & McKinney, L. J. (1997) A qualitative study of preservice teachers' early field experiences in an urban, culturally different school. *Urban Education*, 32(2), 184–201.

Goldhaber, D. & Brewer, D. (2000) Does teacher certification matter? High school teacher certification status and student achievement. *Educational Evaluation and Policy Analysis*, 22(2), 129–145.

Goldhaber, D. & Brewer, D. (2001) Evaluating the evidence on teacher certification: a rejoinder. *Educational Evaluation and Policy Analysis*, 23(1), 79–86.

Gomez, M. L., Walker, A. B., & Page, M. L. (2000) Personal experience as a guide to teaching. *Teaching and Teacher Education*, 16(7), 731–747.

Good, T. L. & Grouws, D. A. (1979) The Missouri Mathematics Effectiveness Project: an experimental study in elementary classrooms. *Journal of Educational Psychology*, 71, 355–362.

Goodwin, L. (1994) Making the transition from self to other: what do preservice teachers really think about multicultural education? *Journal of Teacher Education*, 45, 119–130.

Gravemeijer, K. (1994) Educational development and developmental research in mathematics education. *Journal for Research in Mathematics Education*, 25, 443–471.

Grossman, P. (1990) *The making of a teacher: teacher knowledge and teacher education*. New York: Teachers College Press.

Grossman, P. (2005) Research on pedagogical approaches in teacher education. In M. Cochran-Smith & K. M. Zeichner (eds.), *Studying teacher education: the report of the AERA Panel on Research and Teacher Education* (pp. 425–476). Mahwah, NJ: Erlbaum.

Grossman, P. & Thompson, C. (2004) District policy and beginning teachers: a lens on teacher learning. *Educational Evaluation and Policy Analysis*, 26, 281–301.

Grossman, P., Smagorinsky, P., & Valencia, S. (1999) Appropriating tools for teaching English: a theoretical example for research on learning to teach. *American Journal of Education*, 108, 1–29.

Grossman, P., Valencia, S., Evans, K., Thompson, C., Martin, S., & Place, N. (2000) Transitions into teaching: learning to teach writing in teacher education and beyond. *Journal of Literacy Research*, 32, 631–662.

Guba, E. G. (ed.). (1990) *The paradigm dialog*. Thousand Oaks, CA: Sage.

Guba, E. G. & Lincoln, Y. S. (1994) Competing paradigms in qualitative research. In N. K. Denzin & Y. S. Lincoln (eds.), *Handbook of qualitative research* (pp. 105–117). Thousand Oaks, CA: Sage.

Hamilton, M. L. & Pinnegar, S. (2000) On the threshold of a new century: trustworthiness, integrity, and self-study in teacher education. *Journal of Teacher Education*, 51(3), 234–240.

Hatch, J. A. (2002) *Doing qualitative research in education settings*. Albany: State University of New York Press.

Heath, S. B. (1983) *Ways with words: language, life, and work in communities and classrooms*. Cambridge, UK: Cambridge University Press.

Henson, K. T. (1996) Teachers as researchers. In Sikula, J. (ed.), *Handbook of research on teacher education* (pp. 53–64). New York: Simon & Schuster Macmillan.

Hollingsworth, S. (1989) Prior beliefs and cognitive change in learning to teach. *American Educational Research Journal*, 26(2), 160–189.

Hollins, E. R. & Guzman, M. T. (2005) Research on preparing teachers for diverse populations. In M. Cochran-Smith & K. M. Zeichner (eds.), *Studying teacher education: the report of the AERA Panel on Research and Teacher Education* (pp. 477–548). Mahwah, NJ: Erlbaum.

Holt-Reynolds, D. (1999) Good readers, good teachers? Subject matter expertise as a challenge in learning to teach. *Harvard Educational Review*, 69, 29–50.

Hostetler, K. (2005) What is "good" education research? *Educational Researcher*, 34(6), 16–21.

Houston, W. R., Haberman, M., & Sikula, J. (eds.) (1990) *Handbook of research on teacher education*. New York: Macmillan.

Jackson, P. W. (1990, originally published 1968) *Life in classrooms.* New York: Teachers College Press.

Johnson, R. B. & Onwuegbuzie, A. J. (2004) Mixed methods research: a research paradigm whose time has come. *Educational Researcher*, 33(7), 14–26.

Kelly, A. & Lesh, R. (eds.) (2000) *Handbook of research design in mathematics and science education.* Dordrecht, The Netherlands: Kluwer.

Kennedy, M. (1996) Research genres in teacher education. In F. Murray (ed.), *The teacher educator's handbook: building a knowledge base for the preparation of teachers* (pp. 120–152). San Francisco: Jossey-Bass.

LaBoskey, V. (2004) The methodology of self-study and its theoretical underpinnings. In J. Loughran, M. L. Hamilton, V. K. LaBoskey, & T. Russell (eds.), *International handbook of self-study of teaching and teacher education practices* (pp. 817–870). Dordrecht, The Netherlands: Kluwer.

Lagemann, E. (2000) *An elusive science: the troubling history of education research.* Chicago: University of Chicago Press.

Lanier, J. E. & Little, J. W. (1986) Research on teacher education. In M. C. Wittrock (ed.), *Handbook of research on teaching* (3rd ed., pp. 527–569). New York: Macmillan.

LeCompte, M. D., Millroy, W. L., & Preissle, J. (eds.) (1992) *The handbook of qualitative research in education.* New York: Academic Press.

Lee, O. & Yarger, S. J. (1996) Modes of inquiry in research on teacher education. In J. P. Sikula, T. J. Buttery, & E. Guyton (eds.), *Handbook of research on teacher education: a project of the Association of Teacher Educators* (2nd ed., pp. 14–37). New York: Macmillan.

Lehrer, R. & Schauble, L. (2000) Modeling in mathematics and science. In R. Glaser (ed.), *Advances in instructional psychology: educational design and cognitive science* (pp. 101–159), Mahwah, NJ: Erlbaum.

Lewin, K. (1948) *Researching social conflicts.* New York: Harper & Row.

Lincoln, Y. S. & Guba, E. G. (1985) *Naturalistic inquiry.* Beverly Hills, CA: Sage.

Loughran, J. (2005) Researching teaching about teaching: self-study of teacher education practices. *Studying Teacher Education*, 1(1), 5–16.

Loughran, J. J., Hamilton, M. L., LaBoskey, V. K., & Russell, T. L. (eds.) (2004) *The international handbook of self-study of teaching and teacher education practices* (Vols. 1 & 2). Dordrecht, The Netherlands: Kluwer.

Lytle, S. & Cochran-Smith, M. (1992) Teacher research as a way of knowing. *Harvard Educational Review*, 62(4), 447–474.

McClain, K. (2003) Supporting pre-service teacher change: understanding place value and multi-digit addition and subtraction. *Journal of Mathematical Thinking and Learning*, 5, 281–306.

McNeal, B. & Simon, M. (2000) Mathematics culture class: negotiating new classroom norms with preservice teachers. *Journal of Mathematical Behavior*, 18(4), 475–509.

Mehan, H. (1979) *Learning lessons.* Cambridge, MA: Harvard University Press.

Miles, M. B. & Huberman, A. M. (1994) *Qualitative data analysis: a sourcebook of new methods.* Newbury Park, CA: Sage.

Munby, H., Russell, T., & Martin, A. K. (2001) Teachers' knowledge and how it develops. In V. Richardson (ed.), *Handbook of research on teaching* (pp. 877–904). Washington, DC: American Educational Research Association.

Murray, F. (ed.) (1996) *The teacher educator's handbook.* San Francisco: Jossey-Bass.

National Commission on Teaching and America's Future (1996) *What matters most: teaching for America's future.* New York: Author.

National Council of Teachers of Mathematics (1989) *Curriculum and evaluation standards for school mathematics.* Reston, VA: Author.

National Council of Teachers of Mathematics (1991) *Professional standards for teaching mathematics.* Reston, VA: Author.

NCLB (No Child Left Behind) (2002) U.S. Department of Education. Retrieved from http://www.ed.gov/nclb/landing.jhtml

Neumann, S. (2002) Elementary and secondary education scientifically based research seminar. February 6, 2002. Washington, DC: Retrieved November 6, 2005 from http://www.ed.gov/nclb/methods/whatworks/research/index.html

Peck, R. F. & Tucker, J. A. (1973) Research on teacher education. In R. M. W. Travers (ed.), *Second handbook of research on teaching* (pp. 940–978). Chicago: Rand McNally.

Peressini, D., Borko, H., Romagnano, L., Knuth, E., & Willis, C. (2004) A conceptual framework for learning to teach secondary mathematics: a situative perspective. *Educational Studies in Mathematics*, 56(1), 67–96.

Price, J. N. (2001) Action research, pedagogy and change: the transformative potential of action research in pre-service teacher education. *Journal of Curriculum Studies*, 33(1), 43–74.

Price, J. N. & Valli, L. (2005) Preservice teachers becoming agents of change: pedagogical implications for action research. *Journal of Teacher Education*, 56(1), 57–72.

Putnam, R. & Borko, H. (1997) Teacher learning: implications of new views of cognition. In B. J. Biddle (ed.), *International handbook of teachers and teaching* (pp. 1223–1296). Dordrecht, The Netherlands: Kluwer.

Richardson, V. & Placier, P. (2001) Teacher change. In V. Richardson (ed.), *Handbook of research on teaching* (4th ed., pp. 905–947). Washington, DC: American Educational Research Association.

Rosenshine, B. V. & Furst, N. (1973) The use of direct observation to study teaching. In R. Travers (ed.), *Second handbook of research on teaching* (pp. 122–183). Chicago: Rand McNally.

Rosenshine, B. & Stevens, R. (1986) Teaching functions. In M. C. Witrock (ed.), *Handbook of research on teaching* (3rd ed., pp. 376–391). New York: Macmillan.

Rowe, M. B. (1974) Wait-time and rewards as instructional variables: their influence on language, logic and fate control. Part 1: Wait-time. *Journal of Research in Science Teaching*, 11, 81–94.

Schwandt, T. A. (1994) Constructivist, interpretivist approaches to human inquiry. In N. K. Denzin & Y. S. Lincoln (eds.), *Handbook of qualitative research* (pp. 118–137). Thousand Oaks, CA: Sage.

Shavelson, R. J. & Towne, L. (eds.) (2002) *Scientific research in education*. Committee on Scientific Principles for Education Research. Washington, DC: National Academy Press.

Shavelson, R. J., Phillips, D. C., Towne, L., & Fuerer, M. J. (2003) On the science of education design studies. *Educational Researcher*, 32(1), 25–28.

Shulman, L. (1986) Paradigms and research programs in the study of teaching: a contemporary perspective. In M. C. Wittrock (ed.), *Handbook of research on teacher education* (3rd ed., pp. 3–36). New York: Macmillan.

Shulman, L. (2000) From Minsk to Pinsk: why a scholarship of teaching and learning? *Journal of the Scholarship of Teaching and Learning*, 1(1), 43–53.

Shultz, J. J., Erickson, F., & Florio, S. (1982) "Where's the floor?": aspects of social relationships in communication at home and at school. In O. K. Garnica & M. L. King (eds.), *Language, children, and society*. New York: Pergamon.

Sikula, J. P., Buttery, T. J., & Guyton, E. (eds.) (1996) *Handbook of research on teacher education: a project of the Association of Teacher Educators* (2nd ed.). New York: Macmillan.

Simon, H. A. (1996) *The sciences of the artificial*. Cambridge, MA: MIT Press.

Simon, M. A. (2000) Research on the development of mathematics teachers: the teacher development experiment. In A. Kelly & R. Lesh (eds.), *Handbook of research design in mathematics and science education* (pp. 335–359). Dordrecht, The Netherlands: Kluwer.

Simon, M. A. & Blume, G. W. (1994a) Building and understanding multiplicative relationships: a study of prospective elementary teachers. *Journal of Research in Mathematics Education*, 25, 472–494.

Simon, M. A. & Blume, G. W. (1994b) Mathematical modeling as a component of understanding ratio-as-measure: a study of prospective elementary teachers. *Journal of Mathematical Behavior*, 13, 183–187.

Simon, M. & Blume, G. (1996) Justification in the mathematics classroom: a study of prospective elementary teachers. *Journal of Mathematical Behavior*, 15, 3–31.

Slavin, R. E. (2004) Education research can and must address "what works" questions. *Educational Researcher*, 33(1), 27–28.

Sleeter, C. (2001) Epistemological diversity in research on preservice teacher preparation for historically underserved children. In W. G. Secada (ed.), *Review of research in education* (Vol. 25, pp. 209–250). Washington, DC: American Educational Research Association.

Smagorinsky, P., Lakly, A., & Johnson, T. S. (2002) Acquiescence, accommodation, and resistance to learning to teach within a prescribed curriculum. *English Education*, 34, 187–213.

Smagorinsky, P., Cook, L. S., Jackson, A. Y., & Fry, P. G. (2004) Tensions in learning to teach: accommodation and development of a teaching identity. *Journal of Teacher Education*, 55(1), 8–24.

Smagorinsky, P., Wright, L., Augustine, S. M., O'Donnell-Allen, C., & Konopak, B. (2007) Student engagement in the teaching and learning of grammar: a case study of an early-career secondary school English teacher. *Journal of Teacher Education*, 58(1), pp. 76–90.

Smith, M. L. (2006) Multiple methodology in education research. In J. Green, G. Camilli, & P. B. Elmore (eds.), *Handbook of complementary methods in education research* (pp. 457–475). Mahwah, NJ: Erlbaum.

Stein, M. K., Silver, E. A., & Smith, M. S. (1998) Mathematics reform and teacher development: a community of practice perspective. In J. G. Greeno & S. V. Goldman (eds.), *Thinking practices in mathematics and science learning* (pp. 17–52). Mahwah, NJ: Erlbaum.

Stenhouse, L. (1975) *Introduction to curriculum research and development*. London: Heinemann Education.

Stoddart, T., Connell, M., Stofflett, R., & Peck, D. (1993) Reconstructing elementary teacher candidates' understanding of mathematics and science content. *Teaching and Teacher Education*, 9, 229–241.

Tashakkori, A. & Teddue, C. (2003) *Handbook of mixed methods in social and behavioral research*. Thousand Oaks, CA: Sage.

Teacher Quality Partnership (2006) http://www.teacherqualitypartnership.org/

Tharp, R. G. & Gallimore, R. (1988) *Rousing minds to life: teaching, learning, and schooling in social context*. Cambridge: Cambridge University Press.

Thorndike, E. L. (1910) The contribution of psychology to education. *Journal of Educational Psychology*, 1, 5–12.

Toma, J. D. (2006) Approaching rigor in applied qualitative research. In C. Conrad & R. C. Serlin (eds.), *The Sage handbook for research in education: engaging ideas and enriching inquiry* (pp. 405–423). Thousand Oaks, CA: Sage.

Valli, L. (2000) Connecting teacher development and school improvement: ironic consequences of a pre-service action research course. *Teaching and Teacher Education*, 16, 715–730.

Wardekker, W. L. (2000) Criteria for the quality of inquiry. *Mind, Culture, and Activity*, 7(4), 259–272.

Weiner, L. (1993) *Preparing teachers for urban schools*. New York: Teachers College Press.

Weiner, L. (2000) Research in the 90s: implications for urban teacher preparation. *Review of Educational Research*, 70(3), 369–406.

Wideen, M., Mayer-Smith, J., & Moon, B. (1998) A critical analysis of the literature on learning to teach: making the case for an ecological perspective on inquiry. *Review of Educational Research*, 68(2), 130–178.

Wilson, S. & Wineburg, S. (1998) Peering at American history through different lenses: the role of disciplinary knowledge in teaching. *Teachers College Record*, 89, 529–539.

Wilson, S., Floden, R., & Ferrini-Mundy, J. (2001) *Teacher preparation research: current knowledge and recommendations*. Seattle, WA: Center for the Study of Teaching and Policy.

Wilson, S., Floden, R., & Ferrini-Mundy, J. (2002) Teacher preparation research: an insider's view from the outside. *Journal of Teacher Education*, 53, 190–204.

Yarger, S. J. & Smith, P. L. (1990) Issues in research on teacher education. In W. R. Houston (ed.), *Handbook of research on teacher education* (pp. 25–41). New York: Macmillan.

Zeichner, K. (1999) The new scholarship in teacher education. *Educational Researcher*, 28(9), 4–15.

Zeichner, K. (2005a) A research agenda for teacher education. In M. Cochran-Smith & K. M. Zeichner (eds.), *Studying teacher education: the report of the AERA Panel on Research and Teacher Education* (pp. 737–759). Mahwah, NJ: Erlbaum.

Zeichner, K. (2005b) Studying teacher education programs. In C. Conrad & R. C. Serlin (eds.), *The*

Sage handbook for research in education: engaging ideas and enriching inquiry (pp. 79–94). Thousand Oaks, CA: Sage.

Zeichner, K. (2006) Reflections of a university-based teacher educator on the future of college- and university-based teacher education. *Journal of Teacher Education*, 57(3), 326–340.

Zeichner, K. & Hoeft, K. (1996) Teacher socialization for cultural diversity. In J. Sikula, T. J. Buttery, & E. Guyton (eds.), *Handbook of research on teacher education* (2nd ed., pp. 525–547). New York: Macmillan.

Zeichner, K. & Noffke, S. (2001) Practitioner research. In V. Richardson (ed.), *Handbook of research on teaching* (4th ed., pp. 298–330). New York: Macmillan.

53 Research on teacher education

Changing times, changing paradigms

Marilyn Cochran-Smith
Boston College

Kim Fries
University of New Hampshire

For almost a century and a half, teacher education in the United States has been an identifiable activity with various programs, courses of study, and orientations for prospective teachers and offered by normal schools, colleges, universities, community colleges, and through alternative routes and for-profit providers. And for almost as long, there have been efforts to describe, analyze and improve teacher education by studying it empirically. Over time, the objects of empirical study have varied, including, among other things: the teacher education curriculum, effective methods of teacher training, the knowledge base for teaching, how teachers learn to teach, preparing teachers for diverse populations, the impacts of local and state-level teacher education policies and practices, and the recruitment, selection and retention of teachers. It would be an understatement to say that there has been disagreement over the years about how the nation's teachers ought to be prepared and how teacher education ought to be studied. Indeed, since its beginnings, teacher education has been a contested enterprise, and research has often played a prominent role in disputes by documenting the current status of the profession, suggesting directions for change, and providing ammunition for major debates.

In this chapter, we outline the recursive but nuanced history of empirical research on teacher education in the United States over most of the last century, from roughly 1920 through 2005.[1] Our major argument is that during these dramatically changing times, the dominant paradigms for conceptualizing and studying teacher education also changed dramatically. We suggest that there were four distinct approaches or shifts during this time period in how "the problem" of teacher education was framed and studied. How a problem or question is framed determines to a great extent how it is answered, which influences how human, fiscal and other resources are expended, what kinds of regulations are established, and what we think we know about a profession. Table 53.1 provides an overview of the four time periods, laying out the rough contours of how the problem of teacher education was constructed and the empirical research that was conducted in keeping with changing constructions.

STUDYING TEACHER EDUCATION

Although it was during the 1950s that research on teacher education (as well as research on teaching) began to proliferate in scope and quantity, we take the 1920s as the beginning point for our analysis. This decade marked the burgeoning of a national effort to upgrade the teaching profession with numerous advisory councils and organizations,

Table 53.1 Research on teacher education, 1920s–2000s

	Time period (approximate)	Policy/accountability contexts	How "the problem" of teacher education was conceptualized	How "the problem" of teacher education was studied	Selected examples and key syntheses
Teacher education as a curriculum problem	1920s–1950s	• Concern about lack of consistency and rigor in K-12 curriculum • Post WWI expansion of TE programs • Debates about appropriate location of TE—normal schools or colleges/universities? • Efforts to upgrade teaching profession and unify teacher education	• Improving teacher education was conceptualized as a matter of systematizing and standardizing the TE curriculum across programs and states, consistent with research on the traits of effective teachers	• Large-scale surveys were the primary research design • Survey and other data were intended to identify key teacher characteristics and determine whether these were being taught in the TE curriculum • Calls for statistical summaries of survey data and correlational studies applied to curriculum • First syntheses of empirical research on TE published	Selected chapter examples: Charters & Waples (1929) Evendon (1933) Key syntheses: Butsch (1931, 1934) Peik & Hurd (1937b) Peik (1940, 1943, 1946)
Teacher education as a training problem	1960s–1980s	• 1957 Sputnik launch exacerbated public concern about schools • "Educationists" responsible for TE were harshly criticized • Calls for more liberal arts, less pedagogy in TE • New federal support for teacher training, recruitment, and R&D centers for TE	• Improving teacher education was conceptualized as a matter of identifying transportable training strategies that produced desired teaching behaviors in teacher candidates, consistent with research on teaching	• Process-product research on TE was the primary research design • 1+ treatment groups of teacher candidates with different kinds of training compared to control groups • Intention was to establish the "science" of teaching and teacher education based on experimental and correlational research • Research was linked to the competency-based TE movement	Selected chapter examples: Allen (1967) Baker (1969) Key syntheses: Cyphert & Spaights (1964) Denemark & Macdonald (1967) Peck & Tucker (1973)

(Continued overleaf)

Table 53.1 Continued

	Time period (approximate)	Policy/accountability contexts	How "the problem" of teacher education was conceptualized	How "the problem" of teacher education was studied	Selected examples and key syntheses
Teacher education as a learning problem	1980s–2000s	• 1983 Nation at Risk and other reports linked failure of schools to concerns about the economy • Calls for professionalized teaching force and a new national board on professional teaching standards • Holmes Group and National Network for Educational Renewal established to reform teacher education	• Improving teacher education was conceptualized as a matter of codifying the professional knowledge base for teaching and understanding how teachers learned to teach over the professional lifespan	• Focus on TE research shifted from training procedures to learning processes • Multiple research paradigms and perspectives on TE emerged, including qualitative and critical approaches for studying teachers' attitudes, beliefs, experiences, knowledge acquisition and use • Programs of research on teacher knowledge, thinking, learning developed at major research centers • Attention to multicultural TE and how teachers learned to teach for diversity	Selected examples: Grossman (1990) Laframboise & Griffith (1997) Key syntheses: Lanier & Little (1986) Houston (1990) Sikula et al. (1996) Borko & Putnam (1996) Wideen et al. (1998)
Teacher education as a policy problem	1990s–present	• Shifting global economy and persistent achievement gap prompted concerns about schools, teachers, TE • Increasing role of conservative foundations and think tanks in TE research and policy • Competing reform agendas for TE— professionalization vs. deregulation • Standards movement shifted to accountability movement shifted to testing movement	• Improving teacher education was conceptualized as a matter of identifying and implementing cost-effective, outcomes-focused policies at the institutional, state, and federal levels	• Focus of TE research shifted from inputs and teacher learning processes to pupil outcomes • Major research designs included econometric, cost-benefit, and other analyses of TE policies and practices with goal of identifying policy levers likely to correlate with higher pupil test scores • Emergence of innovative mixed methods research designs, linking value-added and similar designs with case studies, surveys and interview data	Selected chapter examples: Decker et al. (2004) Boyd et al. (2005) Key syntheses: Darling-Hammond (2000a) Darling-Hammond & Youngs (2002) Abell Foundation (2001a) Ballou & Podgursky (2000) Allen (2003) Wilson et al. (2001) Cochran-Smith & Zeichner (2005)

national conferences, annual yearbooks, and multiple institutional self-studies. This was also the decade during which several major empirical reports on the status of teacher education programs and curriculum were issued. Our analysis extends through the turn of the twenty-first century and concludes with research on teacher education published in the early years of the 2000s, with 2005 the publication date of our most recent reports.

We identify four dominant approaches to conceptualizing and studying "the problem" of teacher education during four overlapping time periods: studying teacher education as a curriculum problem during the 1920s through the 1950s; studying teacher education as a training problem from the late 1950s through the early 1980s; studying teacher education as a learning problem from the early 1980s and into the early 2000s; and studying teacher education as a policy problem from the mid-1990s and continuing to the present day. We do not use the phrase, "the problem of teacher education," in a pejorative sense here, but rather to draw attention to teacher education as the problem or challenge every nation faces in providing teachers for its children and also to refer to how teacher education has been formulated over time as a research problem. Although these four constructions of the problem of teacher education capture the dominant approach of each period, we also note that the history of research on teacher education, like the history of education research generally, is not a steady march over time in which one perspective supplants another (Lagemann, 2000), but is instead more like a "conversation" (Shulman, 1986a, 1986b) among alternative viewpoints and approaches that is dynamic and interactive.

In this chapter, we make a distinction between research on teaching, which refers primarily to investigations of aspects of teaching in K-12 schools where the teachers in question are K-12 teachers and the learners are K-12 pupils, and, on the other hand, research on teacher education, which refers to studies of the preparation of K-12 teachers where the teachers in question are university- or program-based teacher educators and the learners are teacher candidates (and/or sometimes their K-12 pupils). Based on this distinction, we regard research on teacher education as a sub-set of research on teaching.

Since the 1920s, hundreds of empirical studies of teacher education have been conducted. To make this chapter manageable, we drew on this massive literature in two ways. First, we used major syntheses of empirical research on teacher education as historical artifacts, assuming that they reflected the ways of defining and studying teacher education that prevailed in particular periods. We located 38 such syntheses of research on teacher education published between 1920 and 2004. Table 53.2 provides an overview of these syntheses, divided by the time periods during which the problem of teacher education was constructed differently, indicating the kind and quantity of empirical studies reviewed and the general conclusions reached. Second, we used the syntheses from each period to identify two illustrative examples of empirical studies from the period. These provide a way to take a more detailed look at how research questions were posed and how research studies were designed and interpreted.

When we refer to the historical contexts of each period, we mean the larger political, professional and policy contexts that influenced the development of teacher education research. These include public concern about the economy, the welfare of the nation in a changing society and the capacity of the schools to meet the needs of future citizens and leaders. Our discussion of the larger context also includes major commissioned reports about the education of elementary and secondary teachers as well as critiques of existing teacher education programs and educational research. We also consider the governmental and non-governmental regulations and resources that constrain and support teacher education practice and research.

Table 53.2 Syntheses of research on teacher education, 1920s–2005

Synthesis/year	Literature reviewed	Purpose	Conclusions
	TEACHER EDUCATION AS A CURRICULUM PROBLEM		
Butsch (1931)	44 studies published between 1920 and 1930. A description of studies included or excluded from this review was not provided.	To summarize the studies of the general and specialized preparation of teachers in institutions, the state and local requirements for preparation, and the devices for in-service training.	• While there is some evidence that the general level of training that teachers receive is improving, it varies greatly between different states, school systems of different sizes, and different classes of teachers. • There is little agreement on the courses best suited for the preparation of teachers. • The standards set by the state certification laws are becoming higher, although still low.
Butsch (1934)	78 studies on the preparation of teachers, published between 1931 and 1933, including the *National Survey of the Education of Teachers* (Evendon, 1933). Criteria used to select studies for this synthesis were not discussed.	To synthesize empirical work on TE.	• No overall conclusions were drawn; rather annotations of studies were provided.
Peik & Hurd (1937a)	500 curriculum reports on higher education at the teacher training, college, and university levels. Studies included were those of "status with historical background, analytic opinion, consensus, experimentation, and measurement" (p. 178). Examination studies were not included unless definitely pertaining to the curriculum.	To review published reports on curricula implemented in liberal arts colleges, junior colleges, general academic subject fields, TE, and curriculum in professional schools.	Yielded 66 concepts found consistently across the reports. Generalizations included: • Changing life and knowledge necessitate continuous curriculum change. • Curriculum depends fundamentally upon their purposes, objectives, and functions. • Individual growth and development are controlling curriculum objectives. • More and better curriculum research, experimentation, and evaluation are needed.

			• Broad, distributed, comprehensive curriculum are basic to distinctly specialized curriculums.
			• Correlation between theory and practice is a vital consideration.
			• Organization and departmental division are important features of curriculum operation and function.
			• Basic principles should guide the solution of specific curriculum problems.
Peik & Hurd (1937b)	200 studies on the preparation of teachers published between 1934 and 1936. Studies included were those with "factual data" or had been published elsewhere. Of the 200 studies reviewed, 50 referred to general TE curriculum or course considerations. The remaining studies examined the scope of teacher training, practices and policies, innovations, extracurriculum, graduate work, student teaching, faculty personnel, summer session, college teachers, guidance and personnel, and special fields.	To review studies relative to the preparation of teachers.	• Much of the discussion on teacher preparation during this time period focused on the findings of the *National Survey of the Education of Teachers* (Evendon, 1933). • There is a need for more research relative to curriculum-pattern analysis, evaluation of innovations, and established practices • More curriculum building based upon actual studies of student needs, social needs, and higher levels of desired outcomes is needed.
Peik (1940)	155 studies on the preparation of teachers published between 1937 and 1939. Included studies that employed "research procedures;" omitted all unpublished graduate theses.	To review studies on the preparation of teachers.	• More research that focused on graduate work; the personal, social-civic, and professional needs of teachers is needed. • The development and evaluation of orientation or survey courses as constituents of teacher-repairing programs, educational guidance, and personality development is also needed.

(Continued overleaf)

Table 53.2 Continued

Synthesis/year	Literature reviewed	Purpose	Conclusions
			• All evidence pointed to the need for better scholarship in the profession and for a lengthened period of preparation for every type of position. The trend was definitely away from department majors and minors to broad field majors. • There was a growing interest in the internship.
Peik (1943)	138 studies published on the preservice preparation of teachers between 1940 and 1942. Included in this review were a number of extensive descriptions of experimental programs. Not included were unpublished graduate theses.	To review studies on the preparation of preservice teachers.	• An upgrade in the selection of teachers relative to "scholarship and personality" is needed. • An improved broad, functional, and somewhat professionalized general education is needed specialized by broad fields rather than by subjects. • An increase in the amount of well-supervised practice teaching or a year of supervised internship is needed.
Peik (1946)	73 studies on the preservice preparation of teachers published between 1943 and 1946. Studies included in this review came from historical sources, expert opinion, and analyses of legal documents, student records, curriculum, or courses-of-study. Also included were studies that used data from questionnaires, interviews, rating scales, and tests or examinations.	To review studies on the preservice preparation of teachers.	• An improved and broader teacher-training curriculum in both the professional and subject matter areas is needed. • Longer periods of practice teaching with more adequate supervision and more direct and practical work with children is needed. • A wider consideration of the problems faced by teachers and improvement of instruction in teacher-training institutions is needed, allowing for more student participation.

- The most important factors for better outcomes of teacher preparation programs are: more careful selection of persons with native competence and good personal qualifications, a functional general education related to our times and conditions, emphasis upon laboratory school experience with children, and more training in professional aspects of teaching that may develop into art and skill.

TEACHER EDUCATION AS A TRAINING PROBLEM

Cyphert & Spaights (1964)	182 studies published on TE between 1953 and 1963 Included studies came from the following sources: journals, *Dissertation Abstracts*, U.S. Office of Education studies, yearbooks of professional organizations, known researchers in the field of teacher education, data retrieval services, and professional organizations associated with teacher education Studies concerning teacher behavior and teacher effectiveness (rather than TE per se) were excluded.	To survey, summarize, and annotate examples of research efforts in TE in an un-biased and non-critical manner.	• The extant research in TE is neither extensive nor profound. • TE research traditionally has been classified in the following ways: historical development, scope, functions of teacher education; organization/administration of teacher education, college faculty/staff; curriculum; instruction/field; student personnel in teacher education; teachers and profession of teaching.
Denemark & Macdonald (1967)	Reviewed studies on the preservice and in-service education of teachers published between 1962 and 1966. Criteria used to select studies for this synthesis were not discussed	To review the research literature on the education of preservice and inservice teachers.	• Large grants for TE have been given for program development and not for theory development or research activity. • TE still appears to be fragmented and detached from teaching and from programs of liberal or general education.

(Continued overleaf)

Table 53.2 Continued

Synthesis/year	Literature reviewed	Purpose	Conclusions
			• Promising areas of research development include: preservice-inservice relationships, teacher role differentiation, programs for teachers of culturally disadvantaged youth, and programs built around the integrated use of newer media.
Peck & Tucker (1973)	Reviewed studies published on TE between 1955 and 1971. Studies included only those utilizing experimental research designs on the process of teacher education (i.e. designs that accurately identify, measure, and account for all of the factors put forth, as well as these factors' complex and interacting effects). Studies came from journals, books, dissertation abstracts, and final reports of contracted research.	To synthesize studies on TE.	• A quantum leap occurred, somewhere between 1963 and 1965, in the quality of both the design and the reporting of research in this field. • An accelerating trend toward linking TE to the cognitive, affective, or behavior learning of the teachers' pupils. • Researchers are "in sight" of the theoretical principles, the operational measures, and even the developmental technology for moving onto a performance-based method of appraising teaching.

TEACHER EDUCATION AS A LEARNING PROBLEM

Koehler (1967, 1985)	220 studies on preservice TE from the ERIC database published between 1980 and 1984. These included surveys of existing practices, evaluations of existing or experimental practices, surveys of practitioners or students concerning their competencies/attitudes acquired from preservice teacher education, measurement studies, ethnographies, and research reviews.	To summarize and analyze the existing research on preservice teacher education.	• More work is needed on conceptualizing the relationship between teacher preparation and teaching practice in order to provide goals and objectives which are possible to attain and have the potential to improve teaching.

Lanier & Little (1986)	Research published between the mid-1960s and the mid-1980s. Studies of teacher educators, of prospective and experienced teachers, of the TE curriculum, and of the milieu in which TE takes place were included. Studies on instructional models, modeling, corrective feedback, concept acquisition, and micro-teaching as training strategies in TE were systematically excluded.	To explore how and in what ways might the research on TE not only inform researchers, but also policymakers, professors, administrators, and teachers.	• The body of research leading to a better understanding of those who teach teachers is modest at this time. • The overall number of preservice teachers has become substantially smaller and composed of fewer academically-talented students than before. • The relationships between the study of teaching and the curriculum for teachers have received major attention from scholars. • Institutional policies, structures, and resources that might be expected to foster the quality of teaching and TE appear to do the opposite.
Houston (1990)	A synthesis of the knowledge base of TE organized in 48 chapters around the following themes: TE as a field of inquiry; governance of TE; contexts and models of TE; participants in TE; curriculum of TE; processes of TE; evaluation and dissemination; TE in the curricular areas; and broadened perspectives of TE.	The purpose of this "first-ever" handbook on TE was to provide those responsible for preservice and inservice TE with critical syntheses and a careful interpretation of research.	• The conceptual and research base for decisions about TE has never been as strong as it its today. • There has been notable recent progress, but the research basis is still extremely thin. • Research and practice needs to be based on what we currently know about TE in order to implement an agenda for consistent, continued development of the field.
Borko & Putnam (1996)	Studies selected were representative of research approaches relative to the following conceptual framework: • The role of knowledge in thinking, acting, and learning. • Learning as an active, constructive process. • Knowledge and learning as situated in contexts and cultures.	To examine how knowledge and beliefs change over time as novice teachers learn to teach and experienced teachers attempt to make changes in their teaching practices.	• Learning to teach is influenced by a complex array of factors. • Prospective teachers' knowledge and beliefs about teaching, learning, and learners are shaped by years of their own school experience and can be highly resistant to change.

(Continued overleaf)

Table 53.2 Continued

Synthesis/year	Literature reviewed	Purpose	Conclusions
	Studies on teacher socialization or career development were not examined. Although the number of empirical studies reviewed was not made explicit, the authors' bibliography cites more than 190 references from a variety of sources (i.e. conceptual, empirical, syntheses).		• Experienced teachers' attempts to learn to teach in new ways also are highly influenced by what they already know and believe about teaching, learning, and learners. • Research shows that with focused and sustained instruction, both preservice and inservice teachers can develop richer and more powerful understandings of subject matter content and transform their beliefs about the nature of the subjects that they teach. • Novices have limited knowledge of subject-specific instructional strategies and thinking of their students about particular subject matter content. • Experienced teachers typically have more knowledge of instructional strategies and of their students, but they often do not have appropriate knowledge and beliefs in the areas to support successful teaching for understanding. • Teachers can learn to teach in new ways, but they require considerable and sustained support to do so.
Sikula *et al.* (1996)	Building on the first handbook (Houston, 1990), the second handbook addressed new developments, changing contexts, and emerging new authorities via 48 research syntheses organized around the	To aggregate the most recent analyses of teaching and TE.	• Schooling and teacher preparation in America are not high-priority items. • Educational reform efforts in America are disjointed, uncoordinated, and often contradictory.

break following themes: TE as a field of study; recruitment, selection, and initial preparation; contextual influences on TE; TE curriculum; continuing professional growth, development, and assessment; diversity and equity issues; and emerging directions in TE

- The prospects for educational improvement in America in the near future are bleak.
- In recent history, Americans have been unwilling to invest adequate dollars for high-quality public education.

Also presented are two declaratives:

- Improvement in schooling and TE in the United States will be successful to the extent that educators establish via research and make known to the public and to budget controlling authorities the clear relationships that exist between investment in education and productive citizenship.
- Until educators become more proactive, demanding, political, and willing to serve as *American Reconstructioneers of Culture* (ARCs), educational institutions will continue to drift with the tide of mediocrity as resources flow to other more visible and vocal areas.

Wideen, Mayer-Smith, & Moon (1998)	93 empirical studies, primarily published after 1990 on learning to teach. The source of these studies included journal articles, electronic databases (i.e. RITE, ERIC), mainstream teacher education journals, and papers presented at conferences including the Annual Meeting of the American Educational Research Association (AERA).	To establish what is currently known about how people learn to teach and to critique the quality of reporting of that research.	- Beginning teachers enter preservice TE with firmly held views about teaching. - Beginning teachers are little influenced by the interventions that occur in preservice teacher education. - The homogeneous population of beginning teachers is under-prepared to teach the increasingly heterogeneous population of students.

(Continued overleaf)

Table 53.2 Continued

Synthesis/year	Literature reviewed	Purpose	Conclusions
	Excluded were position papers, conceptual studies, and papers judged to be overly vague in terms of data collection, presentation, or interpretation.		

TEACHER EDUCATION AS A POLICY PROBLEM

Synthesis/year	Literature reviewed	Purpose	Conclusions
Ballou & Podgursky (2000)	Examined 4 major studies cited in the National Commission on Teaching and America's Future's (NCTAF) (1996) document.	To re-examine the studies put forth by NCTAF which were used as evidence to propose a policy agenda to professionalize teaching, shifting the power to regulate teacher training and licensing from public officials to private organizations.	• The article refuted the research put forth by NCTAF, arguing that in many cases the research cited was misrepresented. • The evidence on expertise and qualifications offers little support for NCTAF's specific proposals. • The evidence that teacher effectiveness is enhanced by advanced degrees earned in schools of education is weak.
Darling-Hammond (2000a)	Re-examined the 4 studies cited by Ballou and Podgursky (2000). Also addressed the other 88 studies cited in NCTAF's two studies (1996, 1997).	To re-examine and respond to Ballou and Podgursky's (2000) claims that the NCTAF has misrepresented research data and findings.	• This article claimed that Ballou and Podgursky (2000) misrepresented most of the existing evidence base in order to argue that TE makes no difference to teacher performance or student learning and that students would be better off without state efforts to regulate entry into teaching or to provide supports for teachers' learning.
Abell (2001a)	150 published studies, papers, and unpublished dissertations cited by prominent national advocates of teacher certification over the past 50 years were examined in relationship to student achievement.	To explore the relationship between teacher preparation and student achievement. To examine whether or not existing research proves that certified teachers produce greater student achievement than uncertified teachers.	• The academic research attempting to link teacher certification with student achievement is astonishingly deficient. • Certification is incapable of providing any insight into an individual's ability, intellectual curiosity, affinity for children,

and/or instructional skills.
- Calls for the elimination of coursework requirements for teacher certification.
- Recommends that the average verbal ability score be reported on teachers (by school district) and teacher candidates (by school's of education).
- Calls for the responsibility of teacher selection and qualification to be moved from the state level to the district level (placing hiring decisions in the hands of principals).
- Suggests that school districts and principals rely on more productive methods for helping teachers gain the instructional skills and knowledge needed to be effective.

Wilson, Floden, & Ferrini-Mundy (2001)	57 empirical studies, published between 1985 and 2000, were examined after initially scrutinizing 313 studies. Studies were discarded from the original set of 313 for four reasons: they were not directly related to the questions; they lacked sufficient rigor; they consisted of arguments based on opinion or principles without empirical evidence; or they were based on a single course in a particular TE program.	To summarize what rigorous, peer-reviewed research tells us about key issues in teacher preparation. 5 key questions were posed related to subject-matter preparation, pedagogical preparation, clinical training, teacher quality, and alternative certification programs.	• Showed a positive connection between teacher preparation in their subject matter and their performance and impact in the classroom. • The pedagogical aspects of teacher preparation matter. • Clinical experiences are a powerful element of teacher preparation. • Too few studies exist that can draw significant conclusions about the effect of policies on the quality of preservice teacher education. • Recent data suggests that most states now have an alternative route into teaching.
Darling-Hammond & Youngs (2002)	Examined the research base surrounding 4 assertions put forth	To assess whether the 4 assertions and policy recommendations put	• None of the assertions presented has strong empirical support.

(Continued overleaf)

Table 53.2 Continued

Synthesis/year	Literature reviewed	Purpose	Conclusions
	by the U.S. Secretary of Education in the *Annual Report on Teacher Quality* (U.S. Department of Education, 2002).	forth by the U.S. Secretary of Education's *Annual Report on Teacher Quality* (2002) were supported by scientifically-based research.	• The report did not cite the scientific literature that addresses them.
Allen (2003)	92 studies were reviewed out of a total of more than 500 that were originally considered. The 92 chosen studies were all examples of research that met the following criteria: directly relevant to the questions under consideration; published in a scientific journal; published within the past two decades; studied TE in the United States; empirical and rigorous Unpublished reports were not included as well as "a good deal of the local research that teachers or teacher educators conduct in relative obscurity" (p. viii).	To determine the most effective strategies for educating and training the nation's teachers. Eight questions were posed around the topics of subject-matter knowledge, pedagogical coursework, field-based experiences, alternative routes, teacher effectiveness in hard-to-staff and low-performing schools, entrance requirements for TE programs, accreditation, and institutional warranties.	• Making education research more responsive to the needs of policymakers and practitioners and more accessible to all stakeholders. • Strengthening research capacity by increasing overall investment and defining strategies and a coordinated research agenda. • Ensuring that the research on teacher preparation defines more precisely the questions that need to be addressed and the data that need to be gathered. • Making the connection to student achievement as explicit as possible. • Creating a culture in which all education stakeholders use solid research, and use it fairly, in making policy decisions.
Cochran-Smith & Zeichner (2005)	3 overarching chapters and 9 research syntheses. These nine syntheses provided a review of the empirical research, primarily looking at the impact of TE on teacher learning, performance, and pupil learning relative to the following topics: • Demographics and teacher quality (90 studies published between 1985 and 2002).	To examine what the research says (and does not say) about preservice TE in the United States To provide an even-handed analysis of the empirical research on the impact of TE with regard to questions of high interest to policy makers and practitioners. To recommend a research agenda to the TE community.	Findings relative to each of the 9 topics are highlighted below: • *Demographics*: teachers are predominantly female, White, and monolingual; most are prepared in baccalaureate programs at public institutions; teacher turnover is the largest single determinant of demand for new teachers.

- The effects of coursework in the arts and sciences and in the foundations of education (40 studies published between 1990 and 2002).
- Methods courses and field experiences (107 studies published between 1995 and 2001).
- Pedagogical approaches in TE (38 studies published between 1985 and 2001).
- Preparing teachers for diverse populations (99 studies published between 1980 and 2000).
- Preparing teachers to work with students with disabilities (17 studies published between 1990 and 2002).
- Accountability processes (24 studies published between 1990 and 2002).
- TE Programs (38 studies published between 1986 and 2002).

More than 450 empirical studies were included in these 9 syntheses following criteria laid out by Shavelson and Towne (2002) as well as Wilson, Floden, and Ferrini-Mundy (2001).

- *Teacher Quality*: by graduation, TE program completers have higher average SAT/ACT scores than general pool of college students. Those in the top SAT/ACT quartile are less likely to take jobs as teachers, and once teaching, are less likely to stay.
- *Arts and sciences*: There is very little research on teachers' subject-specific study except in math. Studies of teachers' study of math show positive correlation with high school pupils' mathematics learning.
- *Methods and field experiences*: Most research is on how new teachers' are socialized into the profession, or how beliefs and actions do /do not change after methods courses and field experiences.
- *Pedagogy*: Five pedagogies have been studied: laboratory experiences, case studies, video/ hypermedia, and portfolios. Studies show shifts in perceptions, knowledge and beliefs, changes in ability to reflect or identify issues, changes in attitudes toward pedagogy or feelings of self-efficacy.
- *Preparing teachers to work with diverse populations*: Most studies are qualitative, conducted in a single course or field experience, drawing on narrative data. Quantitative studies employ surveys or

(Continued overleaf)

Table 53.2 Continued

Synthesis/year	Literature reviewed	Purpose	Conclusions
			questionnaires focused on candidates' beliefs or attitudes. Studies show short-term changes in beliefs and attitudes toward diversity. • *Preparing teachers to work with students with disabilities*: Studies indicate preservice teachers have positive attitudes about acquiring knowledge and skills to be successful with students with disabilities. • *Accountability*: Research on certification is limited, but the weight of the evidence generally favors certification over noncertification or undercertification, as measured by student achievement. 42 states require teacher testing, but there is little evidence these have predictive validity. Studies on the impact of accreditation are almost nonexistent. • *TE Programs*: Regardless of the type of TE program, subject matter specialization influences teacher retention. Studies comparing the effectiveness of traditional and alternative, 4-year versus 5-year programs have inconsistent or conflicting findings. This report lays out a research agenda including: • (a) research situated in relevant theoretical frameworks; (b) clear and consistent definition of terms;

(c) a fuller description of data collection and analysis methods and research contexts; (d) the development of more programs of research; (e) attention to the impact of TE on teachers' learning and professional practice; (f) research that links TE to pupil's learning; (g) multidisciplinary and mixed-methods studies; (h) reliable measures of teachers' knowledge and skills; (i) experimental research comparing programmatic alternative in terms of outcomes

- Research on these topics: (a) preparing teachers to close the achievement gap; (b) contexts and participants in teacher education; (c) TE curriculum, instruction, and organization; (d) organizational and structural alternatives for teacher preparation; (e) predictive validity of TE program admissions criteria; (f) national databases on teacher candidates, teachers, and reserve pools; (g) research on teacher preparation in various subject areas; (h) systematic analyses of alternative preparation programs and routes; (i) in-depth case studies of programs; (j) research that links preparation with practice and pupils' learning.

We want to make it clear that our discussion of the history of teacher education research represents only the dominant approaches to conceptualizing the study of teacher education and in no way is intended to suggest that these were the only approaches. In fact, during every period, there were also alternative approaches, thoughtful critics of the dominant views, and differing constructions of the problem of teacher education. We, ourselves, for example have critiqued the policy approach to teacher education research (Cochran-Smith & Fries, 2001, 2005a, 2005b). Historically these critiques and alternative approaches were less visible in the published literature and, with little or no funding, were often marginalized in the discourse. Thus, although the four constructions we describe here capture the predominant approach of each period, it is important to note that, like the history of educational research generally, the history of research on teacher education was not a steady march over time in which one perspective supplanted another. Rather, as noted earlier, the development of research on teacher education involved a dynamic relationship among alternative viewpoints and approaches, with some in the foreground and others more in the background or on the margins.

TEACHER EDUCATION AS A CURRICULUM PROBLEM: EARLY 1920s TO LATE 1950s

By 1921, in order to supply enough teachers, all but one state in the U.S. recognized normal school graduation as evidence of qualification to teach; by the World War I era, this was the practice nationwide (Labaree, 2004). As teacher preparation expanded, studies of the teacher preparation curriculum also began to emerge. One way to make sense of the research produced from the early 1920s to the late 1950s is to acknowledge that teacher education was constructed primarily as a curriculum problem during this time.

Political, professional and policy contexts

The industrialization, urbanization, and immigration of the late nineteenth and early twentieth centuries prompted a shift in the elementary and secondary curriculum—from one that emphasized the classics and was geared for the elite few who were college bound to one that included more subjects and was intended to meet the needs of the mass population (Commission on the Reorganization of Secondary Education, 1918). As a result, however, critics suggested that the curriculum was too broad and inconsistent, with no uniformity in subjects, time allotments, or placement of topics across schools (Thayer & Levit, 1966). Between 1893 and 1895, the National Education Association (NEA) organized committees to examine curricular issues, including: (1) the Committee of Fifteen on Elementary Education; (2) the Committee of Ten on Secondary School Studies; and (3) the Commission on College Entrance Requirements. These committees were dominated by subject-matter specialists. The Committee of Fifteen stressed the three Rs and subject matter compartmentalization at the elementary level (Dewey, 1916), rejecting both kindergarten and child-centered curriculum (Schwartz, 1996). The Committee of Ten recommended nine core subjects for the high school curriculum with "tracking" of students and no art, music, physical education, or vocational education. The Committee on College Entrance Requirements influenced the high school curriculum by recommending a specific number of credits in each subject and requiring the classics for college admission.

Constructing teacher education as a curriculum problem

Not surprisingly, debates about elementary and secondary curriculum had major impli-cations for teacher preparation, especially with regard to the appropriate curriculum for high school teachers (Monroe, 1952). Most agreed that high school teachers needed a thorough education in the disciplines, but disagreed about whether normal schools or colleges and universities should provide this training (Bullough, 2001). Those who sup-ported the normal school model argued that college and university graduates had aca-demic but not pedagogical training and did not know how to manage classrooms or work with children effectively (Brooks, 1907). Those who supported teacher education at the college and university level argued that normal schools trivialized education by emphasizing method, gearing the curriculum to the lowest level students, and not provid-ing the deep scholarship and liberal education that universities did (Bolton, 1907).

During the 1910s and 1920s (and continuing for much of the century), Teachers College laid out a "union of progressivism and professionalism" (p. 159) as a blueprint for the curriculum of teacher preparation (Labaree, 2004), which included: "general culture" (general knowledge), "special scholarship" (learning across several disciplines), "professional knowledge" (a systematic inquiry into the theory and practice of educa-tion), and "technical skills" (practical pedagogical skills) (Cremin, 1978; Lucas, 1999). Interestingly but not surprisingly, none of these recommendations was based on empir-ical evidence that time spent in preparation programs or time studying curricular theories actually led to the outcomes that were desired (Herbst, 1989; Lucas, 1999). Between 1920 and 1940, there was a push to upgrade the teaching profession by studying the core traits of effective teachers and adjusting the teacher education curriculum accordingly so there would be a more unified and consistent approach across institutions.

Studying teacher education as a curriculum problem

The push to upgrade the profession prompted several massive investigations into the teacher education curriculum. Using surveys, interviews, and observations of teacher preparation schools, the point was to identify the key characteristics and skills of effect-ive teachers and find out whether these were being taught in the curriculum across institutions. Inspired by the Flexner report on medical education, the Learned-Bagley (1920) report recommended that teachers' work be evaluated on the basis of pupil growth and that all teacher preparation courses be professionalized and offered at single-purpose college level institutions (Imig & Imig, 2006). The two most important studies of the period were the Commonwealth Teacher-Training Study (Charters & Waples, 1929) and the National Survey of the Education of Teachers (Evendon, 1933), which are detailed below.

Between 1930 and 1945, there were efforts to codify and unify teacher preparation, a movement stimulated by changing curricular and certification requirements (Haskew, 1960). The push to collect more than simple descriptions of programs and curricula was followed by a call for statistical summaries, surveys by experts, and correlational studies applied to curricula (Travers, 1983). The first syntheses of research on teacher education were published in the *Review of Educational Research* during the late 1930s.

Butsch (1931), for example, summarized "studies of general and special preparation of teachers in institutions, the state and local requirements for preparation, and the devices for in-service training" (p. 76). He found little agreement on the courses and/or curric-ulum best suited for the preparation of teachers. Several years later, Butsch provided a second synthesis drawing primarily on the data from the National Survey of the Education of Teachers, Peik's summary of the National Survey, and several more regionalized studies (Butsch, 1934). He examined the demographic studies on teachers, their levels of training, where they obtained training, and the professional coursework required for state licensure (e.g. educational psychology, general survey courses, student teaching, history of education, special methods, and tests and measurement).

Later in the decade, Peik and Hurd (1937b) reviewed more than 500 reports relative to higher education curricula. Studies of teacher education focused on curriculum building, subject matter divisions, professional courses, and the integration of theory and practice. The authors called for more and better curriculum research, experimentation, and evaluation as well as the establishment of centers for cooperative curriculum research. In later reviews, Peik and Hurd (1937a) and then Peik (1940, 1943, 1946) called for a broader curriculum in both professional and subject matter areas with longer periods of practice, better supervision, more experience with students, more attention to teaching problems, and improved teacher training instruction. These reviews also recommended studies of students' and social needs, clearer and more rigorous outcomes, and carefully planned experimentation along with valid and reliable evaluations.

Studying teacher education curriculum: two examples

We offer two examples of research on teacher education, conceptualized and studied as a curriculum problem. The Commonwealth Teacher-Training Study (Charters & Waples, 1929) was intended to use scientific means to identify key teacher traits in order to improve teacher preparation across the nation. The National Survey of the Education of Teachers (Evendon, 1933) was conducted under the auspices of the U.S. Commissioner of Education based on a mandate from Congress that a nationwide survey of the education of teachers be carried out.

The point of the Commonwealth Study was to find out scientifically what the most important traits of teachers were, isolate and represent these traits on charts, lists, and formulae including minute behavioral components, and then use these to guide teacher preparation. Charters and Waples (1929), researchers from the University of Chicago and the principal investigators of the study, led a large team of researchers who took as a premise that curriculum development should be guided by scientific principles (Zeichner, 2005b). As Zeichner suggests, this investigation was based on the assumption that the teacher education curriculum ought to be "radically reorganized" because it did not operate from "a clear definition of objectives and logical plans of procedure" (p. 7).

Charters and Waples and a large team of researchers used the research method of "consensus" wherein they interviewed teachers, administrators, parents, professors of education, and students in order to find out what these stakeholders believed to be the key characteristics of teachers in different contexts (Zeichner, 2005b). Their nominations were then reviewed by a large panel of judges, and 83 traits of effective teachers were defined, rank-ordered by importance, and matched with multiple indicators. Interestingly, as Imig and Imig (2006) point out, the idea of drawing on research and experience to develop professional consensus about the knowledge and skills teachers need to be effective is a strategy that has been used many times throughout the history of teacher education research, including the development by Goodlad (2002) and other professionals and policymakers of "postulates" to guide the teacher education curriculum and, most recently, the development by Darling-Hammond and Bransford (2005) and a large committee of experts of the major knowledge domains that the curriculum for all beginning teachers should include.

Charters and Waples' list of teaching traits included adaptability, alertness, inspiration, leadership, tact, wittiness, calmness, and magnetism, each of which had multiple indicators—some as many as 12 (Zeichner, 2005b). The process for developing this list was extensive and what many people would term "excessively" quantitative, involving multiple tabulations, categorizations, and sub-categorizations of traits, characteristics, and indicators. Zeichner (2005b) described the research process this way:

> Following the identification of the traits of good teachers, Charters and Waples employed job analysis techniques and collected a comprehensive list of the activities of teachers by mailing surveys to teachers in 42 states. The final list of 1,001 activities was subdivided into seven major divisions such as instruction and classroom management. Over 200,000 statements were analyzed to get to the final list. Some of these activities get right to the heart of teaching and can be found in contemporary teacher standards such as the INTASC standards.
>
> (p. 8)

Although Charters and Waples concluded that teacher-training institutions should use their lists of traits to guide the curriculum and to help determine course revisions and program offerings (Kliebard, 1973; Lagemann, 2000; Travers, 1983), their report had little impact on the curriculum of teacher education programs. Interestingly, however, and for better or worse, the Charters and Waples' (1929) report was the beginning of the development of performance-based standards development in teacher education, an approach that is alive and well today.

The second example of research on teacher education as a curriculum problem is the National Survey of the Education of Teachers (Evendon, 1933), which relied primarily on surveys as a research method. In 1929, following the Commonwealth Study, Congress mandated that the U.S. Commissioner of Education undertake a nationwide survey of the education of teachers. This mandate was supported by a number of organizations that were involved in larger efforts to professionalize teaching and teacher education—the American Association of Teachers Colleges (established in 1923), the National Council of State Superintendents and Commissions of Education, the Association of Deans of School of Education and the North Central Association of Colleges and Secondary Schools.

This six-volume report, put together by a team of researchers led by Evendon, was the outcome of the first-ever national survey on teacher education in the United States. The study utilized the prevailing education research design of the time—the survey method—to study the curriculum of teacher education by collecting and organizing data in a scientific manner (Lagemann, 2000). This report provided extensive information about the standards and status of training institutions, the demographics of teachers, and the policies and patterns of recruitment, selection, and licensure. However, its main emphasis was on the teacher education curriculum, particularly what was actually being provided to and required of teacher candidates in the variety of programs throughout the United States.

The National Survey of the Education of Teachers (Evendon, 1933) called for: (a) an increase in the amount of teacher preparation, academic studies, professional studies, and classroom practice; (b) more research on teacher education; and (c) preparation programs that reflected the proven characteristics of effective teaching. As a result, teacher preparation programs increased curricular requirements in general education, separated secondary from elementary methods, and deemphasized general methods in favor of subject-specific methods. In addition, coursework in the history of education lost out to courses in philosophy, psychology, and measurement (Cottrell *et al.*, 1956; Cremin, 1953).

The value of studying teacher education as a curriculum problem

The period of time when teacher education was defined as a curriculum problem marked the first attempts to study teacher education empirically and to use "scientific" methods to improve preparation. Those who carried out the curriculum studies during the 1920s, 1930s and 1940s were involved in early efforts to establish professional consensus—based on empirical data and professional experience—about what teachers should know and be able to do, a quest that has endured throughout the history of research on teacher education. As illustrated, the curriculum studies revealed that specific groups of stakeholders and professionals in the field could indeed come to a fair amount of consensus about what good teachers should know and do and that their ideas could be reported in the form of recommendations with identifiable indicators. It is important to note that there were also, of course, dissenters during this time. Different groups did not always agree with one another, so the notion of "consensus" was always contested.

As our examples reveal, however, what was recommended as a result of the early curriculum studies was too general to be of direct use to educators and so complex (and some would say, trivial) that it was impossible to implement and track. As the next section of this chapter reveals, in the years following the curriculum studies (and today in the early years of the 2000s), there were caustic attacks on teaching and teacher education, charging anti-intellectualism and myopic viewpoints held by the teachers in public schools. Educators were criticized for sharing a collective allegiance to the monolithic doctrine of progressivism (e.g. Bestor, 1953; Lynd, 1953; Smith, 1954), and there were calls for a new curriculum for teacher education, rooted in the liberal arts and sciences rather than the "mere vocational skills of pedagogy" (1953, p. 142). That there was tension—even contradiction—between the criticism of teacher education as too progressive and, simultaneously, the criticism that teacher education was too vocationalist reflects enduring disagreements within the field as well as disagreements between insiders and outside critics of the profession. This also reflects the fact that how the "problem" of teacher education was constructed and studied was continuously contested during the long history of research on teacher education.

TEACHER EDUCATION AS A TRAINING PROBLEM: LATE 1950s TO EARLY 1980s

The history of research on teacher education since World War II has been characterized by a recurring pattern: A confluence of events and/or blue-ribbon reports charges that the schools are in trouble and teachers are failing. Teacher preparation is condemned by both internal and external critics for its lack of intellectual rigor, standards, arrangements, research base, and/or failure to achieve positive results in schools. There are many calls for reform (that may be, but often are not, research-based), including calls for stronger and better-funded research. New initiatives are implemented that may or may not have lasting value, and new research programs develop with and without funding. This pattern was clear throughout the period of the 1950s to the early 1980s, when teacher education was defined primarily as a training problem.

Political, professional and policy contexts

The 1957 launch of Sputnik by the Soviets exacerbated already existing public concerns about the quality of the schools following World War II. Public education was intensely criticized for having become "soft" and "mediocre" (Lagemann, 2000, p. 159) and for emphasizing students' interests and life adjustment over rigor and excellence.

Not surprisingly, public perceptions of school failure were linked to similar conclusions about the failure of the "educationists" who were preparing the nation's teachers. Arthur Bestor (1953), for example, declared that educationists were making the schools into an "educational wasteland." James Conant's (1963) two-year study of teacher preparation concluded that the "science of education" had not yet come of age and that educational requirements for teachers were generally low. He recommended more liberal arts and humanities and less pedagogy and methods. Considerably more damning, Koerner's (1963) study of the "mis-education" of American teachers concluded that education faculty were intellectually inferior and that the evidence regarding the value of teacher preparation was weak, if not non-existent.

Notwithstanding these critiques, new federal support programs for teacher training and recruitment were developed in the 1960s and 1970s. The Teacher Corps was enacted in 1965 as part of Title V of the Higher Education Act to address teacher shortages, particularly in high poverty areas. The Education Professions Development Act of 1967 was intended to improve educator recruitment and training. Concern about the failure of the nation's teachers coupled with new federally-supported programs (Earley & Schneider, 1996) shaped the dominant research agenda on teacher training that emerged during this time period.

Constructing teacher education as a training problem

During this period, process-product research on teaching became prominent; this program of research had the goal of developing "the scientific basis for the art of teaching" (Gage, 1978) by specifying teacher behaviors correlated with student achievement and applying them as treatments to classroom situations. Research on teacher education also emerged as an identifiable program of empirical study. The federal research and development centers, the regional education laboratories, and large research programs played major roles in developing new lines of research on teacher education. The agenda of the University of Texas (Austin) R&D Center for Teacher Education, for example, focused on developing technologies for the training of teachers and analyzing the conditions under which these technologies were effective (Freiberg & Waxman, 1990), a line of research which was linked to the Competency Based Teacher Education movement of the 1970s (Urban, 1990).

Generally speaking, the intention of the research during this time was "answer[ing] the question of how the behavior of an individual in preparation for teaching can be made to conform to acceptable patterns" (Smith, 1971, p. 2), or, similarly, "optimiz[ing] that portion of teacher work success attributable to teacher preparation" (Turner, 1975, p. 87). The assumptions underlying "teacher education as training" mirrored the assumptions of the process-product research on teaching generally: teacher training was regarded as a technical transmission activity, teacher training and teacher behavior were assumed to be related to one another in a linear way, and training was taken to be the starting point with teacher behavior the endpoint of teacher education. With the training model, researchers concentrated on teacher rather than pupil outcomes, usually in the form of classroom behaviors. The target behaviors for prospective teachers were assumed to be correlated with pupils' achievement, based on the process-produce and other research on effective teaching, and thus teacher behaviors were assumed to be a correlate or a reasonable proxy for pupil outcomes.

Studying teacher education as a training problem

The objective of research on teacher education as a training problem was the identification of transportable training procedures that had an impact on teacher behaviors. The independent variables of process-product research on teaching (i.e. teacher behaviors that had been shown to be effective, such as clearly stated objectives for learning or certain question-asking techniques) became the dependent variables in research on teacher preparation. Teacher training procedures themselves (i.e. various procedures for training teachers to exhibit these behaviors, such as microteaching, lecture, demonstration with and without feedback) were the independent variables. The preferred method was experimental design, featuring a control and one or more treatment groups of prospective teachers who received different training, based on the presence, absence or combination of specific training techniques.

A number of research reviews were published during this time (Cyphert & Spaights, 1964; Denemark & Macdonald, 1967; Haberman & Stinnett, 1973; Hodenfield & Stinnett, 1961; Turner, 1975; Wilk *et al.*, 1967), but the definitive synthesis of the period was the chapter on teacher education research by University of Texas, Austin, researchers, Peck and Tucker (1973) in the second *Handbook of Research on Teaching* (Travers, 1973). Peck and Tucker concluded that a "quantum leap" (p. 941) had occurred in the quality and reporting of research on teacher education between 1963 and 1965 due in part to increased federal funding for research. Based on a synthesis of "experimental research on the process of teacher education" (p. 942), they concluded that prospective teachers could learn to master specific teaching behaviors during the pre-service program using a "systems approach" or "instructional design" training procedures (p. 943).

Although the training research was dominant during this time, it was not without critics. Major critiques suggested that: the empirical base for specific teaching behaviors was itself quite thin (Haberman & Stinnett, 1973); the empirical-analytic paradigm was inadequate, uncritical, and unhelpful in improving teacher education (Popkewitz *et al.*, 1979); and, there were major obstacles to establishing causal relationships between teacher preparation and performance given the many intervening variables and the long time lag between teacher training and later school outcomes (Turner, 1971).

Despite the critiques, training was the dominant approach to research on teacher education until it ebbed in influence by the mid-1980s when researchers became more interested in studying teacher education as a "learning problem." This is described and analyzed below.

Studying teacher training: two examples

Below we describe in some detail two examples of research on teacher education, conceptualized and studied as a training problem. The first was part of a much larger program of research on teacher training using the strategy of "microteaching," which was developed at Stanford University during the 1960s and 1970s, and was highly visible in the teacher education research and practice community. The second is an individual study of the impact on pupils' learning of training prospective teachers to perform certain teaching competencies derived from the research on effective teaching. These examples, each of which illustrates some of the major characteristics of studies of teacher education during this period, provide an avenue for fleshing out this approach to research.

Along with its versions and variants, the teacher education technique of microteaching may well have the distinction of being the most "studied" teacher training strategy of all time. Intended for use in training prospective teachers to perform discrete teaching skills, microteaching was first developed and applied as a combined training and diagnostic tool during Stanford's teacher intern program in the early 1960s (Allen, 1967; Gage, 1978; Perlberg, 1987). According to Allen (1967), who was the chief architect of the technique and of the research on it, "microteaching [was] a scaled-down teaching encounter that serve[d] three purposes: (1) as a preliminary experience and practice in teaching, (2) as a research vehicle to explore training effects under controlled conditions, and (3) as an inservice training instrument for experienced teachers" (p. 2). Allen elaborated on microteaching as a training technique as follows:

> the technique allows teachers to apply clearly defined teaching skills to carefully prepared lessons in a planned series of five to ten minute encounters with a small group of real students, often with an opportunity to observe the results on videotape. Its distinction lies in the opportunity it provides teachers for immediate and individual diagnostic evaluation of teacher performance by colleagues, supervisors, and participating students and for measuring progress in specific teaching techniques.
>
> (unpaginated preface)

Allen's (1967) report on the technique was published following the fourth microteaching clinic at Stanford and listed the discrete teaching skills the clinic aimed to teach to prospective teachers: reinforcement, varying the stimulus, illustrating and using examples, using student-initiated questions, and presentation skills such as set induction, lecturing, the use of audiovisuals, and closure.

The report also detailed the teach-reteach cycle, which had been presented to 145 teacher interns at the clinic: (1) teach for 5 minutes; (2) critique for 10 minutes; (3) break for 15 minutes so the intern could plan for changes in the re-taught lesson; (4) reteach a different group of students for 5 minutes; and (5) critique for 10 minutes. Using the Stanford Teacher Competence Appraisal Guide (a thirteen item, seven interval, forced-choice scale), both the students taught by the intern and the supervisors who were overseeing the intern rated the intern's performance at the conclusion of each phase. One-way multivariate analysis of variance was performed, which revealed statistically significant improvements between the first and final "diagnostics" (p. 20) for the interns.

Although Allen's report praised microteaching, it also indicated that the data revealed that students' ratings were a more accurate measure of interns' behavioral change than were the supervisors' ratings. The report also called for further development and more intense training in the use of the Appraisal Guide with more focus on the exact technical skills that were being taught in the micro-teaching clinic. These were subsequently developed.

In a review of research on the pedagogy of teacher education, Grossman (2005) points out that the research on microteaching is similar in many ways to research on the effectiveness of other laboratory experiences in teacher training (e.g. Copeland, 1982; McIntyre *et al.*, 1996; Metcalf *et al.*, 1996; Vare, 1994; Wilkinson, 1996; Winitzky & Arends, 1991). However, although researchers have investigated microteaching from a number of different angles to tease out the effects of subject matter, grade level, forms of feedback, and various models, Grossman concluded, as did MacLeod (1987) almost two decades earlier, that, given the lack of reliability and validity analyses of the instruments and existing discrepancies between students' and supervisors' appraisals and other technical issues, few definitive conclusions could be drawn regarding the effects and effectiveness of microteaching. From a historical perspective, it is also worth noting that although the technique of microteaching became a subject of national attention in teacher training discussions during the late 1960s and the 1970s (Copeland, 1975; Kallenbach & Gall, 1969), it had virtually disappeared by the early 1980s (Lucas, 1999) when teacher education began to be defined as a learning problem, and there was much less interest in training strategies.

Our second example of research on teacher education, conceptualized and studied as a training problem, is Eva Baker's (1969) study of the impact on students' performance of teachers' use of particular instructional principles. Conducted during the late 1960s, this study occurred in the context of Competency-Based Teacher Education (CBTE), a movement to conceptualize teachers' roles and functions in terms of particular skills or "competencies." Underlying CBTE was the assumption that ensuring that teacher candidates obtained "mastery" of specific pre-determined teaching competencies was more important than specifying the coursework they should complete.

Despite the push for CBTE, Baker found that there was little empirical research that had actually investigated the relationship between teachers' classroom behaviors in keeping with the CBTE competencies and behavioral changes in their students. She hypothesized that teachers' use of certain principles extrapolated from educational psychology courses and also required in a teacher education program would be positively related to the performance gains of students. Forty Peace Corps volunteers, who were in training to be teachers, participated in the study. The independent variables were prospective teachers' use of five teaching principles or practices (i.e. appropriate practice, individual differentiation, perceived purposes, graduated sequence, and knowledge of results) that were assumed to be effective teaching strategies. Each prospective teacher was given a chance to practice and then present lesson plans that demonstrated these principles to a group of students and observers. Four trained observers recorded instances of the instructional use of these principles. The dependent variable was pupil gain in achievement, measured by a 15-minute multiple-choice test administered as a pre- and post-test of students' knowledge. Analysis revealed that the prospective teachers' use of three of the five principles was statistically significant in terms of pupils' achievement gains: (1) appropriate practice, (2) individual differentiation, and (3) knowledge of results.

As these two examples reveal, research on teacher education as a training problem assumed that much of the complexity of teaching could be broken down into simpler, more easily trainable skills and techniques. The idea was that researchers who were studying teaching could empirically identify and label those teaching behaviors and skills that produced desirable pupil behaviors or increased pupil achievement. Then researchers who were studying teacher education could develop and test with experimental trials, specific training protocols and techniques that were most effective in teacher preparation programs. Use of these protocols and techniques could then be used across programs and at the preservice and inservice levels to help teachers achieve mastery of effective teaching behaviors.

The value of studying teacher education as a training problem

To their credit, those who carried out the training research in the 1960s and 1970s were attempting to develop and disseminate what, in the parlance of contemporary policy, might be called evidence-based practice. That is, they were developing a body of empirical research about how to produce effective teachers so that decisions could be empirically rather than normatively based. This is precisely what is called for in the early 2000s by critics of collegiate teacher preparation who argue that there is little compelling evidence about the most effective approaches to teacher preparation. The training research revealed that prospective teachers could indeed be trained to exhibit targeted behaviors and that some training techniques were more effective than others. Assuming that teaching is in part a technical activity, it may well be that research on training can be used to establish evidence-based teacher preparation practices for some of the routine and technical tasks of teaching, such as certain aspects of classroom management and organization.

As the next two sections of this chapter reveal, however, the training research did not connect the technical aspects of teaching to its many intellectual and decision-making aspects nor did it account for how teachers' knowledge, beliefs and prior experiences mediated their behavior in classrooms. Furthermore, the training research did not acknowledge the complex cultures of classrooms and schools or the influence of the policy and accountability contexts in which teachers' work is embedded. Last but definitely not least in light of today's policy context, for the most part, the training studies did not connect teacher candidate training directly to pupil learning outcomes.

TEACHER EDUCATION AS LEARNING PROBLEM: EARLY 1980s TO EARLY 2000s

During the 20 years following the training period, the pattern of critique and reform that had shaped teacher education research during the previous decades continued. Concerns about the public schools surfaced again in the 1980s, followed by critique of teacher preparation, reform of programs, and development of new lines of research.

Political, professional and policy contexts

As the 1980s began, the dire predictions of *A Nation At Risk* (National Commission on Excellence in Education, 1983) triggered many reforms. The Task Force on Teaching as a Profession of the Carnegie Forum on Education and the Economy (1986) called for a professionalized teaching force prepared to help redesign the schools, which would require role differentiation among teachers—with certification for some from the newly-envisioned National Board for Professional Teaching Standards (1988).

The Holmes Group report (Holmes Group, 1986) called for undergraduate liberal arts and graduate level professional preparation, teaching career ladders, high entry standards, and professional development schools linking schools of education with K-12 schools. The National Network for Educational Renewal (NNER), founded in 1986 to extend the work of the Center for Educational Renewal (Goodlad, 1990; Goodlad *et al.*, 1990), worked from the premise that school improvement and teacher education renewal should proceed in partnership (Patterson *et al.*, 1999).

Committed to the idea of a professional teaching force, many researchers and organizations worked to codify the professional knowledge base (e.g. Gardner, 1989; Murray, 1996; Richardson-Koehler, 1987; Shulman, 1986a). NCATE's new standards focused on how the curriculum incorporated the professional knowledge base (Christensen, 1996), and a series of RAND studies suggested that well-prepared teachers were more effective than those without professional preparation (Darling-Hammond, 1984, 1988; Darling-Hammond & Berry, 1987; Wise, 1988). Meanwhile, Goodlad's (1990) study of teacher education institutions called for more coherent programs and teachers prepared to meet the challenges of a changing society.

Goodlad, the Holmes Group, the Carnegie Task Force and other reformers both inside and outside the profession, advocated teacher education reform linked to the needs of the nation and to school reform and renewal. All of these assumed that a well-educated professional teacher, who was engaged in ongoing learning, was the linchpin.

Constructing teacher education as a learning problem

During the 1980s and into the 2000s, research on teacher education was influenced by the professionalization agenda, an expanded array of research perspectives (Erickson, 1986; Lagemann, 2000), and emerging research programs on teaching and teacher knowledge, such as the program at Michigan State University spearheaded by Judith Lanier and Lee Shulman in the late 1970s. During this time, the concepts and language of "learning to teach" (Feiman-Nemser, 1983) more or less replaced the language of "teacher training." Researchers studied the knowledge, attitudes and beliefs of prospective teachers as they began formal preparation; how these changed over time; the kinds and sources of knowledge teachers needed to teach well; how teachers learned that knowledge; and, how teachers interpreted their experiences in courses, fieldwork and other contexts.

To a great extent, constructing teacher education as a learning problem meant explicitly rejecting the technical view of teaching and the training view of teacher education that had been prevalent (Lanier, 1982; Tom, 1980). Not everybody agreed of course. How to conceptualize and conduct research on teaching and teacher education was hotly debated during this period, referred to by some as "the paradigm wars" (Gage, 1989). Notwithstanding the debates, the general shift from training to learning was quite evident. Some of the research on teacher learning derived from cognitive psychology, with emphasis on teachers' subject matter and pedagogical knowledge. Other work drew on perspectives from anthropology and sociology, with a focus on culture and its role in learning and schooling. All of these approaches presumed that teaching was a cognitive and intellectual practice that was situated, complex, and uncertain. This meant that it was important for teachers to learn how to make decisions, apply strategies differently in different situations, and reflect on their work. It is important to note, however, that differing theoretical perspectives were affiliated with quite different ideas about the impact of teacher preparation and the types of research that were most needed.

Studying teacher education as a learning problem

Not surprisingly and in keeping with the different disciplinary roots noted above, methods for studying teacher education as a learning problem involved multiple research questions and methods rather than adherence to a single paradigm. Although there were still studies of training, many researchers examined teachers' attitudes, beliefs, knowledge structures, predispositions, perceptions and understandings as well as their intellectual, social and organizational contexts. A major program of research also developed about how teachers learned to teach for diversity (e.g. Bennett, 1995; Ladson-Billings, 1995; Zeichner, 1993). In addition to new research perspectives from the social sciences and humanities, there were also new investigators of teacher education, including teacher educators who studied their own practices (e.g. Hamilton, 1998; Loughran, 1998) and studies from critical and feminist perspectives (e.g. Britzman, 1991; Gore, 1993; Ladson-Billings, 1999; Luke, 1992).

During the 1980s and 1990s, there were several major syntheses and short reviews of research on teacher education (e.g. Koehler, 1985; Richardson & Placier, 2001). Reflecting the evolving shift from training to learning, Lanier and Little's (1986) chapter in the third *Handbook of Research on Teaching* excluded experimental research and instead synthesized interdisciplinary research. They concluded that teacher preparation was pervaded by conservatism and a student body expecting a technical model. Houston's (1990) *Handbook of Research on Teacher Education* synthesized research in all the areas in Lanier and Little's review in addition to teacher education governance, models, evaluation, and curriculum. Both Houston's handbook and its second edition (Sikula *et al.*, 1996) suggested that the thin research base on teacher education was the result of the low priority the nation placed on schooling and teacher education. Borko and Putnam's synthesis (1996) focused on the psychological aspects of learning to teach, concluding it was a complex process requiring multiple knowledge bases, skills and understandings. Wideen *et al.*'s (1998) synthesis concluded not only that initial beliefs were difficult to change, a finding that continues to be supported in contemporary research, but also that there was a fundamental tension between teacher educators' desire to change their students' beliefs and prospective teachers' desire to learn how to "do" teaching.

Studying teacher learning: two examples

Below we discuss two examples of research on teacher education, conceptualized and studied as a learning problem. The first, Pam Grossman's (1990) study, was part of a larger program of research on the knowledge needed for teaching and how teachers learn to teach, particularly how they develop and use various kinds of knowledge including pedagogical content knowledge. This program of research grew out of work by Lee Shulman and colleagues that began at Michigan State University in the late 1970s and was further developed by Shulman and his students and colleagues at Stanford University in the 1980s (e.g. Grossman, 1990; Grossman *et al.*, 1989; Wilson *et al.*, 1987). Grossman's research used a case study method to investigate both the nature of pedagogical content knowledge among beginning English teachers and the role of subject-specific teacher education coursework in contributing to graduates' knowledge and beliefs about teaching English. She studied six first-year English teachers from the San Francisco Bay area including three who had graduated from the same teacher education program and three who entered teaching without formal training. Data collection included semi-structured interviews and multiple classroom observations. Analysis involved coding of all data within each case as well as cross-case analyses.

Grossman's research suggested that those with a teacher education background were flexible, open to innovative methods, and better able to comprehend students' perspectives. Those without such experience tended to rely on teaching techniques borrowed from undergraduate and graduate courses or on memories from their own K-12 schooling. This analysis suggested that a coherent and consistent vision of teaching and learning was important. Grossman suggested that four general features of a teacher education program seemed to contribute to the beginning teachers' learning included:

> a coherent vision of teaching and learning, organized around the specific subject matter to be taught; a collaborative relationship among professor, supervisors, and students, in which prospective teachers helped construct their evolving knowledge concerning the teaching of English for which they could feel a sense of ownership; the existence of necessary support, or "scaffolding" for prospective teachers as they acquired skills and pedagogical perspective for teaching and developed a reflective stance toward practice; and a developmental perspective on learning to teach, in which the curriculum provided the knowledge and skills appropriate for both the current and future needs and concerns of prospective teachers.
>
> (p. 139)

Our second example (Laframboise & Griffith, 1997) of studying teacher education as a learning problem, was conducted by a pair of researchers who were part of a group of teacher educators at the University of South Florida who worked with teacher candidates at a professional development school. Their study focused on how and what teacher candidates learned about culture and cultural conflict by reading literature cases. More specifically they used teaching cases or problem-based stories of teaching practice written by either a teacher or an observer who collaborated with the classroom teacher about teaching events in his or her classroom. The intention of these cases was to help preservice teachers reflect and problem solve with the goal of integrating information from course readings, observations in other classrooms, and course discussions that highlighted multiple perspectives, enabling students in a teacher education course "to view themselves as part of a culturally diverse society, to confront their own subjectivity, and to examine critical issues related to children and schooling" (p. 369). Additionally, the researchers were interested in how undergraduate students made meaning from instances of cultural conflict that were portrayed in juvenile novels and how they used that information to develop appropriate practice for case-based instruction in teacher education courses.

Twenty-two preservice teachers (four White males and 18 White females, ranging in age from 20 to 40) in their first semester of a five-semester undergraduate teacher education program were studied while they participated in an early field experience and site-based course at a PDS. The PDS was a K-5 school in a rural section of a large school district serving a population that was 24 percent White, 10 percent African American, and 66 percent either Mexican or Mexican-American.

Data sources included audio-taped discussions centered around problem-centered stories (teaching cases) and juvenile novels as well as the interns' written work, including literature logs, postwriting, and write-ups from classroom observations. Data were coded using Olneck's (2001) categories of cultural discontinuity—gender, student-to-student, student-to-teacher, student-to-family and cultural community, and student-to-community outside the cultural group—and six categories of interns' meaning making that emerged—paraphrasing, connecting to own knowledge, comparing, inferring, critiquing, and connecting to course content. Researchers concluded that students were able to correctly identify many sources of cultural discontinuity for characters in a book, to make connections to their own experiences, and to think critically about issues of cultural conflict. In most cases, stating and paraphrasing the information from the text was the initial step in discussions and writing, but researchers found this was often not sufficient to make sense of discontinuities. Discussion groups appeared to need someone to act as a challenger, to force the thinking of the group past literal levels, and to help students examine their own subjectivities. The researchers also concluded that preservice teachers needed to confront issues of diversity in ways that encouraged reflection and allowed students to have vicarious experiences of people and situations beyond the context of their immediate lives. The literature case discussions created an environment where students could examine their own values and attitudes, express divergent views, and learn reflective practices.

The value of studying teacher education as a learning problem

In his 1986 review of paradigms and research programs on teaching, Shulman (1986a) suggested that what was missing from the research on teaching was research on how teachers understood and used subject matter knowledge. Since that time, however, research on teachers' cognition, knowledge use, beliefs, and experiences has been so plentiful that some scholars (e.g. Wilson *et al.*, 2001) have suggested that what is now missing is research that connects teachers' knowledge and beliefs to pupils' learning and other outcomes. Even Shulman (2002) has acknowledged this limitation, concluding recently that research on teachers' knowledge and use "reflects the theoretical import-ance of the three Cs of content, cognition and context [but] continued to ignore a fourth C, consequences for students" (p. 251). This assessment of the research on teaching also applies to research on teacher education. When teacher education is primarily con-structed and studied as a learning problem, understanding teachers' knowledge and beliefs is considered an important research purpose in its own right and there is often little or no attention to pupil achievement or to the link between teachers' knowledge and beliefs and pupils' learning and other desirable educational outcomes.

As we argue in the next section, during the late 1990s and into the 2000s, research on teacher education shifted from teacher knowledge and learning issues to educational policy issues with a focus on the outcomes and consequences of teacher education pol-icies and practices. It is important to note that in many policy-related critiques, much of the research on knowledge and beliefs is not regarded as particularly useful because it does not examine causal questions or make the link to pupil achievement and thus, it is claimed, has limited implications for policy.

TEACHER EDUCATION AS A POLICY PROBLEM: MID-1990s TO PRESENT

From the mid-1990s and into the 2000s, the focus on high standards and accountability was intense. The emphasis in research on teacher education shifted from learning to policy, and the problem of teacher education was constructed and studied as a matter of specifying the policies and practices warranted by empirical evidence and cost-benefit analyses linked to pupils' achievement.

Political, professional, and policy contexts

By the mid-1990s, the shifting global economy coupled with the continuing achievement gap had created an urgency about improving education. As in previous eras, these concerns were linked to public demands for reforms in teaching and teacher education. In 1994 the Rockefeller Foundation and the Carnegie Corporation supported the new National Commission on Teaching and America's Future (NCTAF), which asserted that teaching and teacher education mattered more than anything else in improving school achievement (National Commission on Teaching & America's Future, 1996). Along with other professional organizations, NCTAF aimed to improve teacher prepar-ation through systematic professionalization and high standards across the professional lifespan. In addition, the American Council on Education's President's Task Force on Teacher Education (1999) promoted increased higher education responsibility for teacher preparation.

Meanwhile conservative foundations advocated deregulation of teacher education and redirection of public authority for teacher quality by significantly reducing college- and university-based teacher education and state-level certification bureaucracies. The Fordham Foundation (Kanstoroom & Finn, 1999) and others called for market-based reforms including alternate routes that focused only on results.

In nearly every state, new curricular frameworks were implemented coupled with new standards for K-12 student achievement and new standardized tests. The goal was to hold schools accountable to internationally competitive standards and assessments (National Education Goals Panel, 1997). Between 1987 and 1998, the number of states requiring tests for entry into teaching greatly increased and became more standardized (SRI International, 2000), and based on legislation enacted in 1998, institutions and states were required to report annually to the government on the credentials of all teachers they certified.

CONSTRUCTING TEACHER EDUCATION AS A POLICY PROBLEM

During this period, advocates of competing agendas for the reform of teacher education claimed to have an empirical research base. One result of highly publicized and politicized debates was to draw sharp attention to research on teacher education. With more and higher level policy makers working on policies related to teaching and teacher education, education came to be constructed primarily as a policy problem rather than as a curriculum, training, or learning problem as the previous decades had done.

The assumption behind constructing teacher education as a policy problem is that one important way policy makers can meet the challenges of providing a high-quality teaching force is by manipulating those broad aspects of teacher preparation (e.g. teacher tests, subject matter requirements, entry routes) most likely to affect pupil achievement. Although the intention here is to use empirical research to identify those aspects most likely to boost achievement, as is argued below, the research to support any particular policy is not necessarily straightforward. Several of the most debated research syntheses during this time examined the impact of teacher education as part of analyses of state-level policies regarding certification, licensure, teacher tests and other accountability mechanisms (Ballou & Podgursky, 2000; Darling-Hammond, 2000b). Some used econometric models and techniques, including cost-benefit and other analyses, to draw conclusions about the impact of school resources, including teacher qualifications (e.g. Hanushek, 1997). Others examined the research base for state or institutional policies regarding teacher requirements such as subject matter preparation, coursework and field experiences (Allen, 2003; Rice, 2003). Underlying the construction and study of teacher education as a policy problem is the assumption that empirical evidence linking teacher preparation and desirable student outcomes can and should shape policies and practices regarding teacher preparation.

STUDYING TEACHER EDUCATION AS A POLICY PROBLEM

As noted above, many research syntheses since 2000 have constructed teacher education as a policy problem, but reached different conclusions about what the evidence says. Darling-Hammond's (2000a, 2000b, 2002) analyses of evidence related to teacher quality and achievement, for example, concluded that teacher preparation and certification, regarded as important aspects of a cluster of variables that comprise teachers' qualifications, contributed at least as much as, if not more than, other variables to educational outcomes including teacher effectiveness and students' achievement. In contrast, a second group of syntheses and responses (e.g. Abell Foundation, 2001a, 2001b; Ballou & Podgursky, 2000; Whitehurst, 2002) concluded that while there was evidence that teachers' verbal ability and subject matter knowledge had an impact on pupil achievement, there was little evidence to support collegiate teacher preparation, the study of pedagogy, teacher certification, or program approval and accreditation.

A third group of syntheses (e.g. Allen, 2003; Cochran-Smith & Zeichner, 2005; Lauer, 2001; Rice, 2003; Wilson *et al.*, 2001) concluded that although there was some evidence that teacher preparation and certification had a positive impact on educational outcomes in some content areas and at certain school levels, the research base related to teacher preparation as policy was generally neither deep nor robust. Results were mixed in many areas, inconclusive in others, and there was virtually no reliable research in still other areas. These syntheses called for greater investments in research on teacher preparation and in developing qualified teachers. Although their language and emphases differ, the syntheses in this third group were generally consistent in their conclusion that although the teacher education research base about outcomes was thin, but there was also no evidence supporting full-scale elimination of credentialing requirements and no conclusive evidence about the best structures or pathways for preparing teachers.

Studying teacher education policy: two examples

Below we describe in some detail two examples of research on teacher education, conceptualized and studied as a policy problem. The first, a study sponsored in part by the Carnegie Corporation of America and conducted by the Mathematica Policy Research, Inc., compared the effectiveness of teachers prepared in the "Teach for America" (TFA) teacher recruitment program with that of non-TFA teachers (Decker *et al.*, 2004). The second example is somewhat similar—using mixed research methods, included a value-added model, this study examined six pathways into teaching in the New York Public Schools including prospective teachers entering via the Teach for America (TFA) program and the Teaching Fellows Program (Boyd *et al.*, 2005).

TFA has been a hot-button issue among teacher educators and policy makers since its inception in 1989. Indeed in many contentious debates, TFA has been constructed as both the poster child for alternative routes into teaching (even though it is technically not an alternative route, but a teacher recruitment and initial training program) and a major battleground for larger discussions about who should teach, what they should know, how and where they should be prepared, and who should decide. TFA is a publicly- and privately-funded organization that has established a national "corps" of recent college graduates with a variety of academic majors, recruited at Ivy League and other highly academically-rated colleges and universities across the nation. TFA volunteers make a commitment to teach in hard-to-staff urban and rural public schools for a minimum of two years. The organization's mission is to contribute to the elimination of educational inequity by recruiting into teaching in low-income schools some of the nation's most promising future leaders. The idea is that TFA alumni work for change from within education and from other sectors to ensure that all children have opportunities to learn (Smith, 2005).

A team of researchers from Mathematica Policy Research (Decker *et al.*, 2004) compared the reading and mathematics test scores of pupils taught by TFA teachers with those taught by non-TFA teachers to address the question, "Do TFA teachers improve (or at least not harm) student outcomes relative to what would have happened in their absence?" (p. ix). The test scores of pupils randomly assigned to TFA teachers and non-TFA teachers (with non-TFA teachers defined as all those who were never part of TFA, including traditionally certified, alternately certified, and uncertified teachers) were compared, as were test scores of pupils with novice TFA and novice non-TFA teachers (with novices defined as teachers in the first three years of teaching).

Following a pilot study in Baltimore, the investigation focused on 1800 pupils in grades 1–5 in 17 schools—all of which served economically disadvantaged students and faced substantial teacher shortages—in Chicago, Los Angeles, Houston, New Orleans, and the Mississippi Delta. The schools were chosen to be broadly representative of the schools where TFA teachers were placed at the time of the study, and the pupils were randomly assigned to classrooms with TFA teachers and control group teachers. Measures of student achievement were the Iowa Tests of Basic Skills in reading and mathematics. A baseline achievement test was administered in the fall, and a follow-up test was administered in the spring to each of the classes with over 90 percent of students completing both tests. Researchers found significant differences in mathematics, with the average scores of students taught by non-TFA teachers falling into the 15th percentile in the fall and remaining in the 15th percentile in the spring, while average scores of students with TFA teachers falling into the 14th percentile in the fall and increasing to the 17th percentile in the spring. Differences were also significant for students in different grades and those with differing ethnic backgrounds as well as for novice teachers in the two groups. In reading, students taught by TFA and non-TFA teachers experienced the same average growth rate—one percentile point during the school year.

Our second example of teacher education as a policy problem is a study by Boyd *et al.* (2005) examining the impact of pathways into teaching on the teacher workforce in the New York City Schools where many different entry routes are in place, including the Teaching Fellows Program and Teach For America (TFA). The Fellows Program (2006), described as "the largest alternative certification program in the country," aims to attract mid-career professionals, recent college graduates, and retirees to teach in under-performing schools. TFA (2006) is a national corps of top recent college graduates, as described in the Decker example above.

Boyd and colleagues (2005) identified six pathway into teaching in NYC: (1) college-recommended; (2) individual evaluation; (3) Teaching Fellows Program; (4) Teach For America; (5) temporary license; and (6) other. The study addressed two questions: (1) how the achievement gains of students differ by the teacher pathway; and more specifically, (2) whether students of teachers who enter the classroom through alternative routes with reduced coursework and field experiences achieve gains that are higher or lower than they would have if taught by traditionally certified or temporary licensed teachers? The student database (students in grades 3–8 between 1998 and 2004) included demographic and exam information. The teacher database included demographics, test performance, and pathway. Using a value-added model for analysis, the researchers examined trends in teachers by pathway, characteristics of classes, student achievement, effects of pathways relative to achievement, and teacher attrition.

Findings were reported relative to supply, teachers' general knowledge, teaching at the elementary and middle school levels, and rates of attrition: The composition and overall supply of teachers in NYC changed as a result of certification requirements that included alternative pathways, largely eliminating uncertified teachers. Many teachers in alternative pathways had strong academic training and performed well on tests of general knowledge. There was some evidence that elementary teachers in alternate routes did not teach mathematics or English Language Arts as well as teachers from the college-recommended path during their first year. However, their mathematics teaching improved differentially between their first and second years and was approximately equivalent to that of the college- recommended teachers during the second year. Alternative route middle school teachers did better than alternate route elementary teachers. TFA members did a better job of teaching mathematics to middle school students than either temporary license or college-recommended teachers during their first year, while Fellows performed as well as these teachers. By their third year of experience Fellows out-performed college-recommended and temporary licensed mathematics teachers. But results for English Language Arts in middle school were not as strong; the students of both Fellows and TFA teachers in their first year had lower achievement gains than college-recommended or temporary licensed teachers. Fellows showed differentially strong improvement in teaching between their second and third years.

In terms of attrition, the results from this study indicated that the differences in attrition rates across pathways were significant and meaningful. The attrition rate (when controlled for fixed school effects) of Fellows was roughly comparable to college-recommended teachers after two years but exceeded them after three or four years. Those entering through TFA also were relatively more likely to return in their second year. The retention of TFA teachers beyond the second year fell off dramatically, both relative to the traditional routes and the Fellows pathway. This study predicted that after four years fewer than 20 percent of TFA teachers would remain teaching in these schools.

In conclusion, Boyd and colleagues suggested that teachers' varying experiences prior to beginning as the teacher of record and differing coursework might have influenced outcomes. They also highlighted policy questions not addressed such as the attributes of preparation that are most important in increasing student achievement and how the size and composition of the college-recommended pool of teachers would change if financial incentives or reduced tuition towards a masters degree were available.

The value of studying teacher education as a policy problem

The essence of studying teacher education as a policy problem is to identify which broad parameters of teacher education policy that can be controlled by policy makers are most likely to lead to desirable student outcomes. In the midst of the current accountability context, it now seems "obvious" that state and institutional policy decisions should be driven, at least in part, by empirical evidence. But there are also many questions about the bases of comparisons in policy studies (e.g. Wilson & Youngs, 2005; Zeichner, 2005a). Although we need to invest in the capacity to conduct rigorous research on teacher education as a policy problem, we also need to acknowledge its limitations. The aspects of teacher education studied from this perspective are often "crude quantifiable indicators" (Kennedy, 1999, p. 85) that cannot be used to make meaningful distinctions across institutions, pathways, and programs. In addition, policy studies do not account for the contexts and cultures of K-12 schools or for how these support or constrain teachers' abilities to apply knowledge and skills.

Finally, it is worth noting that when teacher education is constructed as a policy problem, the focus is almost always on pupil achievement, defined as test scores, as the most important educational outcome. While this is important, it is not the only goal of preparation programs. Such outcomes as pupils' social and emotional growth and their preparedness to live in a democratic society and engage in civic discourse are also important as are goals such as teacher placement and retention in hard-to-staff schools and as advocates for educational equity.

RESEARCHING TEACHER EDUCATION IN CHANGING TIMES: DIRECTIONS FORWARD

We have suggested that the history of research on teacher education over the last century can be explained at least in part by identifying how "the problem" of teacher education is constructed and how that problem is studied, analyzed and interpreted. Different ways of constructing and studying teacher education—as a curriculum problem, a training problem, a learning problem, or a policy problem–are influenced by the changing political, professional and policy contexts of the times. Particularly important are public concerns and policies about teachers and schooling linked to larger economic and social issues, internal and external critiques of teacher education coupled with demands for reform, and new directions in educational research. It is also important to acknowledge that the quality of some published research on teacher education is poor. This judgment holds across research paradigms and methods. As in any field, poor quality research contributes to the impression that the research base is weak.

It is also important, however, to note that some of those who have concluded that the research base for teacher education is weak have done so because they were interested in a particular construction of the "problem" of teacher education about which there has been little research, even though large amounts of worthwhile research have been conducted on different constructions of the problem. Some reviewers have reached different conclusions about the research base because they worked from different constructions of the problem. This means that simply asking a different question about the quality and depth of the research base on teacher education can produce a different answer (Cochran-Smith, 2004). At other times, however, reviewers have asked similar questions but worked from differing assumptions about what counted as research, what levels of data aggregation were appropriate, or what educational outcomes mattered.

For example, although Peck and Tucker's (1973) review (discussed in the section on "training") focused exclusively on experimental research on the instructional methods used in teacher education, Whitehurst's brief review in 2002 (noted in the section on teacher education as a policy problem) complained that experimental research methods had not yet been discovered in research on teacher education. Peck and Tucker were working from the perspective that teacher education was a training problem and thus reviewed experimentally-verifiable techniques for training teachers to perform certain behaviors assumed to be effective. On the other hand, Whitehurst, who worked from a construction of teacher education as a policy problem, was looking for causal or correlational evidence about the impact of teacher preparation policies on pupils' achievement that could guide policymakers' decisions. The contrasts in the conclusions of these and other syntheses about the strength and depth of the research base for teacher education reflect both historical and contemporary issues.

Some researchers assume that teachers' learning (e.g. enhanced subject matter knowledge, changes in beliefs and attitudes about diverse populations, increased skill) is a justifiable outcome of teacher preparation because of its impact on instructional decisions, relationships with pupils and families, and quality of classroom learning opportunities. This approach is based on the premise that teachers' knowledge frames and beliefs are filters through which teachers' practices and decisions are made and through which they decide how to apply the various skills they have learned. The assumption is that knowledge and beliefs always mediate practice and the application of skills and thus knowledge and beliefs always influence pupils' learning opportunities, achievement, and other educational outcomes. From this perspective, teacher learning itself is an important outcome of teacher preparation. When teacher learning is the focus of teacher education research, it is not the case, as some have claimed, that pupils' learning is considered unimportant. Rather the link between teachers' learning and pupils' learning is not the focus of that particular line of research. Instead the link between teacher preparation components and organizational structures, on the one hand, and teachers' development of knowledge, skills, and/or rethinking of beliefs and attitudes, on the other, is the focus. One needed line of research currently is research that examines and untangles the relationships between and among teachers' knowledge and beliefs, their professional skill and performance in classrooms, and their pupils' learning.

In this chapter we have tried to make the case that historically there have been different constructions of the problem of teacher education coupled with different assumptions about how to study that problem. These reflect larger political, professional and policy contexts but also help to explain some of the differences in the conclusions of contemporary syntheses. These divergent conclusions may suggest the need for new initiatives in teacher education research that combine various constructions of the problem of teacher education as curriculum, training, learning and policy and examine the relationships among these.

It is also important to point out, as our analysis suggests, that some of what are considered serious failings in the research on teacher education are more rightly understood as reflections of the field's relative youth. Empirical research on teacher education really developed as an identifiable line of research only during the last half century. Even if we count, as we have in this chapter, the early institutional self-studies and surveys of normal schools and colleges and universities conducted in the 1920s and 1930s, the field is no more than 70 to 80 years old. Some of the strengths and limitations of the research reflect this newness. Other strengths and weaknesses reflect the priorities and viewpoints of the time. For example, in the early and middle of the twentieth century, there was harsh critique of the "educationists" and the "scientism" they were pursuing, particularly the notion that science rather than philosophy or moral education should suggest solutions to the problems of teacher education. In the early years of the twenty-first century, however, science has skyrocketed in importance. It is now written into federal law that scientific evidence ought to be the grounding for educational practice, policy and resource allocation. Changing times have an influence on changing paradigms for research on teacher education.

Finally, our discussion of the shift in research on teacher education from curriculum to training to learning to policy coupled with our analysis of the value and limits of each approach suggest that studies that link these aspects of teacher preparation could prove worthwhile. A few initiatives in their early stages are attempting to study the impact of teacher education policies that have built into them differing degrees and kinds of support for teachers' learning, thus tying together the constructions of teacher education as learning and teacher education as policy in sophisticated and intriguing new ways. As research on teacher education continues to evolve, we will need much more sophisticated scholarship that builds theory as well as generalizable knowledge about effectiveness. That means we will continue to need rich and detailed case studies as well as large-scale surveys. The emphasis needs to be on asking the important questions—and constructing the problem of teacher education in thoughtful, appropriate ways—and then on selecting the appropriate methods of data collection and analysis.

NOTE

1 This chapter draws on our analysis of teacher education research from the 1950s through the 2000s (Cochran-Smith & Fries, 2005a).

REFERENCES

Abell Foundation (2001a) Teacher certification reconsidered: stumbling for quality. Retrieved May 8, 2002 from http://www.abell.org

Abell Foundation (2001b) Teacher certification reconsidered: Stumbling for quality. A rejoinder. Retrieved May 8, 2002 from http://www.abell.org

Allen, D. (1967) *Micro-teaching: a description* (No. ED019224—ERIC Document). Palo Alto, CA: Stanford University.

Allen, M. (2003) *Eight questions on teacher preparation: what does the research say?* (An ECS Teaching Quality Report). Denver, CO: Education Commission of the States.

American Council on Education. (1999) *To touch the future: transforming the way teachers are taught: an action agenda for college and university presidents.* Washington, DC: American Council on Education.

Baker, E. (1969) Relationship between learner achievement and instructional principles stressed during teacher preparation. *Journal of Educational Research*, 63(3), 99–102.

Ballou, D. & Podgursky, M. (2000) Reforming teacher preparation and licensing: What is the evidence? *Teachers College Record*, 102(1), 5–27.

Bennett, C. (1995) *Comprehensive multicultural education: theory and practice* (3rd ed.). Boston, MA: Allyn and Bacon.

Bestor, A. (1953) *Educational wastelands: the retreat from learning in our public schools.* Urbana, IL: University of Illinois Press.

Bolton, F. (1907) The preparation of high-school teachers. *National Education Association Journal of Proceedings and Addresses*, 600–615.

Borko, H. & Putnam, R. (1996) Learning to teach. In D. Berliner & R. Calfee (eds.), *Handbook of Educational Psychology* (pp. 673–708). New York, NY: Macmillan.

Boyd, D., Lankford, H., Grossman, P., Loeb, S., & Wyckoff, J. (2006) How changes in entry requirements alter the teacher workforce and affect student achievement. *Education Finance and Policy*, Vol. 1, No. 2, Spring 2006.

Britzman, D. (1991) *Practice makes practice: a critical study of learning to teach.* Albany, NY: State University of New York Press.

Brooks, S. (1907) Preparation of high school teachers. *National Education Association Journal of Proceedings and Addresses*, (pp. 547–551).

Bullough, R. (2001) Pedagogical content knowledge circa 1907 and 1987: a study in the history of an idea. *Teaching and Teacher Education*, 17(6), 655–666.

Butsch, R. (1931) The preparation of teachers. *Review of Educational Research*, 1(2), 76–82.

Butsch, R. (1934) The preparation of teachers. *Review of Educational Research*, 4(3), 273–280.

Carnegie Forum on Education and the Economy (1986) *A nation prepared: teachers for the 21st century.* New York, NY: Carnegie Corporation.

Charters, W. & Waples, D. (1929) *The Commonwealth Teacher-Training Study.* Chicago, IL: University of Chicago Press.

Christensen, D. (1996) The professional knowledge-research base for teacher education. In J. Sikula, T. Buttery & E. Guyton (eds.), *Handbook of research on teacher education* (2nd ed., pp. 38–52). New York, NY: Macmillan.

Cochran-Smith, M. (2004) Editorial: ask a different question, get a different answer: The research base for teacher education. *Journal of Teacher Education*, 55(2), 111–115.

Cochran-Smith, M. & Fries, K. (2001) *The politics of teacher education: sticks, stones, and ideology.* Paper presented at the Annual Meeting of the American Educational Research Association, Seattle, WA.

Cochran-Smith, M. & Fries, K. (2005a) Researching teacher education in changing times: politics and paradigms. In M. Cochran-Smith & K. Zeichner (eds.), *Studying teacher education: the report of the AERA panel on research and teaching* (pp. 69–110). Mahwah, NJ: Lawrence Erlbaum Associates Inc.

Cochran-Smith, M. & Fries, K. (2005b) The AERA panel on research and teacher education: context and goals. In M. Cochran-Smith & K. Zeichner (eds.), *Studying teacher education: the report of the AERA panel on research and teacher education* (pp. 37–68). Mahwah, NJ: Lawrence Erlbaum Associates Inc.

Cochran-Smith, M. & Zeichner, K. (eds.) (2005) *Studying teacher education: the report of the AERA panel on research and teacher education.* Mahwah, NJ: Lawrence Erlbaum Associates Inc.

Commission on the Reorganization of Secondary Education: (1918) *Cardinal principles of secondary education.* Washington, DC: U.S. Government Printing Office.

Conant, J. (1963) *The education of American teachers.* New York, NY: McGraw-Hill.

Copeland, W. (1975) The relationship between microteaching and student teacher classroom performance. *Journal of Educational Research, 68,* 289–293.

Copeland, W. (1982) Laboratory experiences in teacher education. In *Encyclopedia of Educational Research* (5th ed., Vol. 2, pp. 1008–1019). New York, NY: Free Press.

Cottrell, D., Cooper, R., Hunt, C., Maaske, R., Sharpe, D., Shaw, J., *et al.* (eds.) (1956) *Teacher education for a free people.* Oneonta, NY: AACTE.

Cremin, L. (1953) The heritage of American teacher education. *Journal of Teacher Education, 4,* 163–164.

Cremin, L. (1978) *The education of the educating profession.* Washington, DC: AACTE.

Cubberly, E. (1920) *The history of education.* Boston, MA: Houghton Mifflin.

Cyphert, F. & Spaights, E. (1964) *An analysis and projection of research in teacher education.* Columbus, OH: Ohio State University.

Darling-Hammond, L. (1984) *Beyond the commission reports: the coming crisis in teaching.* Santa Monica, CA: Rand Corporation.

Darling-Hammond, L. (1988) Teacher quality and educational equality. *College Board Review, 148,* 16–23, 39–41.

Darling-Hammond, L. (2000a) Reforming teacher preparation and licensing: debating the evidence. *Teachers College Record, 102*(1), 28–56.

Darling-Hammond, L. (2000b) Teacher quality and student achievement: a review of state policy evidence. *Educational Policy Analysis Archives, 8*(1).

Darling-Hammond, L. (2002) Research and rhetoric on teacher certification: a response to "Teacher certification reconsidered." *Educational Policy Analysis Archives, 10*(36).

Darling-Hammond, L., & Berry, B. (1987) *The evolution of teacher policy* (No. RJRE-01). Santa Monica, CA: RAND Corporation.

Darling-Hammond, L. & Youngs, P. (2002) Defining "highly qualified teachers": what does "scientifically-based research" actually tell us? *Educational Researcher, 31*(9), 13–25.

Darling-Hammond, L. & Bransford, J. (eds.) (2005) *Preparing teachers for a changing world: what teachers should learn and be able to do.* San Francisco, CA: Jossey-Bass.

Decker, P., Mayer, D., & Glazerman, S. (2004) *The effects of Teach For America on students: findings from a national evaluation.* Princeton, NJ: Mathematica Policy Research, Inc.

Denemark, G. & Macdonald, J. (1967) Preservice and inservice education of teachers. *Review of Educational Research, 37*(3), 233–247.

Dewey, J. (1916) *Democracy and education: an introduction to the philosophy of education.* New York, NY: The Free Press.

Earley, P. & Schneider, J. (1996) Federal policy and teacher education. In J. Sikula (ed.), *Handbook of research on teacher education* (2nd ed., pp. 306–322). New York, NY: Macmillan.

Erickson, F. (1986) Qualitative methods in research on teaching. In M. Wittrock (ed.), *Handbook of research on teaching* (3rd ed., pp. 119–161). New York, NY: Macmillan.

Evendon, E. (ed.) (1933) *National survey of the education of teachers (6 volumes)* (Vol.). Washington, DC: U.S. Department of the Interior.

Feiman-Nemser, S. (1983) Learning to teach. In L. S. Shulman & G. Sykes (eds.), *Handbook of teaching and policy* (pp. 150–170). New York, NY: Longman.

Freiberg, H. & Waxman, H. (1990) Changing teacher education. In R. Houston (ed.), *Handbook of research on teacher education* (pp. 617–635). New York, NY: Macmillan

Gage, N. (1978) *The scientific basis of the art of teaching.* New York, NY: Teachers College Press.

Gage, N. (1989) The paradigm wars and their aftermath: a "historical" sketch of research on teaching since 1989. *Teachers College Record*, 91(2), 135–150.

Gardner, W. (1989) Preface. In M. Reynolds (ed.), *Knowledge base for the beginning teacher*. New York, NY: Pergamon Press.

Goodlad, J. (1990) Studying the education of educators: from conception to findings. *Phi Delta Kappan*, 71(9), 698–701.

Goodlad, J. (2002) Teacher education research: the outside and the inside. *Journal of Teacher Education*, 53(3), 216–221.

Goodlad, J., Soder, R., & Sirotnik, K. (eds.) (1990) *Places where teachers are taught*. San Francisco, CA: Jossey-Bass.

Gore, J. (1993) *The struggle for pedagogies: critical and feminist discourses as regimes of truth*. New York, NY: Routledge.

Grossman, P. (ed.) (1990) *The making of a teacher: teacher knowledge and teacher education*. New York, NY: Teachers College Press.

Grossman, P. (2005) Research on pedagogical approaches in teacher education. In M. Cochran-Smith & K. Zeichner (eds.), *Studying teacher education: the report of the AERA panel on research and teacher education* (pp. 425–476). Mahwah, NJ: Lawrence Erlbaum Associates Inc.

Grossman, P., Wilson, S., & Shulman, L. (1989) Teachers of substance: subject matter knowledge for teaching. In M. Reynolds (ed.), *Knowledge base for the beginning teacher* (pp. 23–36). Elmsford, NY: Pergamon Press.

Haberman, M. & Stinnett, T. (1973) *Teacher education and the new profession of teaching*. Berkeley, CA: McCutchen Publishing Company.

Hamilton, M. (ed.) (1998) *Reconceptualizing teaching practice: self-study in teacher education*. Bristol, PA: Falmer Press.

Hanushek, E. (1997) Assessing the effects of school resources on student performance: an update. *Educational Evaluation and Policy Analysis*, 19(2), 141–164.

Haskew, L. (1960) Teacher education—organization and administration In C. Harris (ed.), *Encyclopedia of education research* (3rd ed., pp. 1454–1461). New York, NY: Macmillan.

Herbst, J. (1989) *And sadly teach: teacher education and professionalization in American culture*. Madison, WI: University of Wisconsin Press.

Hodenfield, G. & Stinnett, T. (1961) *The education of teachers: conflict and consensus*. Englewood Cliffs, NJ: Prentice-Hall, Inc.

Holmes Group (1986) *Tomorrow's teachers*. East Lansing, MI: Author.

Houston, R. (ed.) (1990) *Handbook of research on teacher education* (1st ed.). New York, NY: Macmillan.

Imig, D. & Imig, S. (2006) The teacher effectiveness movement: how 80 years of essentialist control has shaped teacher education. *Journal of Teacher Education*, 57(2), 167–180.

Kallenbach, W. & Gall, M. (1969) Microteaching versus conventional methods in training elementary intern teachers. *Journal of Educational Research*, 63, 136–141.

Kanstoroom, M. & Finn, C. (1999) *Better teachers, better schools*. Washington, DC: Thomas B. Fordham Foundation.

Kennedy, M. (1999) The role of preservice teacher education. In L. Darling-Hammond & G. Sykes (eds.), *Teaching as the learning profession: handbook of policy and practice* (pp. 54–85). San Francisco, CA: Jossey-Bass.

Kliebard, H. (1973) The question in teacher education. In D. McCarty (ed.), *New perspectives on teacher education* (pp. 8–24). San Francisco, CA: Jossey-Bass.

Koehler, V. (1985) Research on preservice teacher education. *Journal of Teacher Education*, 36(1), 23–30.

Koerner, J. (1963) *The miseducation of American teachers*. Boston, MA: Houghton Mifflin.

Labaree, D. (2004) *The trouble with ed schools*. New Haven, CT: Yale University Press.

Ladson-Billings, G. (1995) Toward a theory of culturally relevant pedagogy. *American Educational Research Journal*, 32(3), 465–491.

Ladson-Billings, G. (1999) Preparing teachers for diverse student populations: a critical race theory perspective. In A. Iran-Nejad & D. Pearson (eds.), *Review of research in education* (Vol. 24, pp. 211–248). Washington, DC: American Educational Research Association.

Laframboise, K. & Griffith, P. (1997) Using literature cases to examine diversity issues with preservice teachers. *Teaching and Teacher Education*, 13(4), 369–382.

Lagemann, E. (2000) *An elusive science: the troubling history of education research.* Chicago, IL: University of Chicago Press.

Lanier, J. (1982, May) *Teacher education: needed research and practice for the preparation of teaching professionals.* Paper presented at the Future of Teacher education: Needed Research and Practice Conference, College Station, TX.

Lanier, J. & Little, J. (1986) Research on teacher education. In M. Wittrock (ed.), *Handbook of research on teaching* (3rd ed., pp. 527–569). Washington, DC: American Educational Research Association.

Lauer, P. (2001) *A secondary analysis of a review of teacher preparation research.* Denver, CO: Education Commission of the States.

Learned, W. & Bagley, W. (1920) *The professional preparation of teachers for American public schools* (Vol. 14). New York, NY: Carnegie Foundation for the Advancement of Teaching.

Loughran, J. (1998) Processes and practices of self-study: introduction. In M. Hamilton (ed.), *Reconceptualizing teaching practice: self-study in teacher education* (pp. 195–197). Bristol, PA: Falmer Press.

Lucas, C. (1999) *Teacher education in America: reform agendas for the twenty-first century.* New York, NY: St. Martin's Press.

Luke, C. (1992) Feminist politics in radical pedagogy. In C. Luke & J. Gore (eds.), *Feminisms and critical pedagogy* (pp. 25–53). New York, NY: Routledge.

Lynd, A. (1953) *Quackery in the public schools.* New York, NY: Greenwood.

MacLeod, G. (1987) Microteaching: end of a research era? *International Journal of Educational Research* 11(5), 531–541.

McIntyre, J., Byrd, D., & Fox, S. (1996) Field and laboratory experiences. In J. Sikula, T. Buttery, & E. Guyton (eds.), *Handbook of research on teacher education* (2nd ed., pp. 171–193). New York, NY: Macmillan.

Metcalf, K., Hammer, M., & Kahlich, P. (1996) Alternatives to field-based experiences: the comparative effects of on-campus laboratories. *Teaching and Teacher Education* 12(3), 271–283.

Monroe, W. (1952) *Teacher-learning theory and teacher education 1890–1950.* Urbana, IL: University of Illinois Press.

Murray, F. (ed.) (1996) *The teacher educator's handbook: building a knowledge base for the preparation of teachers.* Washington, DC: AACTE.

National Board for Professional Teaching Standards (1988) *Hearing before the US Congress, Senate Committee on labor and human resources, Subcommittee on Education, Art, and the Humanities.* Washington, DC: US Congress.

National Commission on Excellence in Education (1983) *A nation at risk: the imperative for educational reform.* Washington, DC: U.S. Government Printing Office.

National Commission on Teaching and America's Future (1996) *What matters most: teaching for America's future.* New York, NY: Author.

National Commission on Teaching and America's Future (1997) Doing what matters most: investing in quality teaching (Electronic Version). Retrieved December 1, 2000 from http://www.nctaf.org

National Education Goals Panel (1997) *National education goals report.* Washington, DC: Author.

New York City Teaching Fellows Program (2006) New York City Teaching Fellows Program. Retrieved July 10, 2006 from http://www.nycteachingfellows.org/

Olneck, M. (2001). Immigration and education. In J. Banks & C. Banks (eds.), *Handbook of research on multicultural education.* San Francisco, CA: Jossey-Bass.

Patterson, R., Michelli, N., & Pacheco, A. (1999) *Centers of pedagogy: New structures for educational renewal*. San Francisco, CA: Jossey-Bass.

Peck, R. & Tucker, J. (1973) Research on teacher education. In R. Travers (ed.), *Handbook of Research on Teaching* (2nd ed., pp. 940–978). Chicago, IL: Rand McNally.

Peik, W. (1940) The preparation of teachers. *Review of Educational Research*, 10(3), 191–198.

Peik, W. (1943) The preservice preparation of teachers. *Review of Educational Research*, 13(3), 228–240.

Peik, W. (1946) The preservice preparation of teachers. *Review of Educational Research*, 16(3), 217–227.

Peik, W. & Hurd, A. (1937a) Curriculum investigations at the teacher-training, college, and university levels. *Review of Educational Research*, 7(2), 178–184.

Peik, W. & Hurd, A. (1937b) The preparation of teachers. *Review of Educational Research*, 7(3), 253–262.

Perlberg, A. (1987) Microteaching: conceptual and theoretical bases. In M. Dunkin (ed.), *The international encyclopedia of teaching and teacher education* (pp. 715–720). Oxford: Pergamon Press.

Popkewitz, T., Tabachnick, B., & Zeichner, K. (1979) Dulling the senses: research in teacher education. *Journal of Teacher Education*, 30(5), 52–60.

Rice, J. (2003) *Teacher quality: understanding the effectiveness of teacher attributes*. Washington, DC: Economic Policy Institute.

Richardson, V. & Placier, P. (2001) Teacher change. In V. Richardson (ed.), *Handbook of research on teaching* (4th ed., pp. 905–950). Washington, DC: American Educational Research Association.

Richardson-Koehler, V. (1987) *Educator's handbook: a research perspective*. New York, NY: Longman.

Schwartz, H. (1996) The changing nature of teacher education. In J. Sikula, T. Buttery, & E. Guyton (eds.), *Handbook of research on teacher education* (2nd ed., pp. 3–13). New York, NY: Macmillan.

Shavelson, R. & Towne, L. (eds.) (2002) *Scientific research in education*. Washington, DC: National Academy Press.

Shulman, L. (1986a) Paradigms and research programs in the study of teaching: a contemporary perspective. In M. C. Wittrock (ed.), *Handbook of research on teaching*. (3rd ed., pp. 3–36). New York: Macmillan.

Shulman, L. (1986b) Those who understand: knowledge growth in teaching. *Educational Researcher*, 15(2), 4–14.

Shulman, L. (2002) Truth and consequences? Inquiry and policy in research on teacher education. *Journal of Teacher Education*, 53(3), 248–253.

Sikula, J., Buttery, T., & Guyton, E. (eds.) (1996) *Handbook of research on teacher education* (2nd ed.). New York, NY: Macmillan.

Smith, A. (2005, November) Equity within reach: insights from the front lines of America's achievement gap. Retrieved January 1, 2006 from http://www.teachforamerica.org

Smith, B. (ed.) (1971) *Research in teacher education: a symposium*. Englewood Cliffs, NJ: Prentice-Hall, Inc.

Smith, M. (1954) The stranglehold of the educationists. In M. Smith (ed.), *The diminished mind: a study of planned mediocrity in our public schools* (pp. 76–99). Chicago, IL: Henry Regnery Company.

SRI International (2000) *Preparing and supporting new teachers: a literature review*. Menlo Park, CA: SRI International.

Teach For America (2006). Teach For America Retrieved July 10, 2006 from http://www.teachforamerica.org

Thayer, V. & Levit, M. (1966) *The role of school in American society* (2nd ed.). New York, NY Dodd, Mead.

Tom, A. (1980) The reform of teacher education through research: a futile quest. *Teachers College Record*, 82(1), 15–29.

Travers, R. (1973) *Handbook of research on teaching* (2nd ed.). Chicago, IL: Rand McNally.

Travers, R. (1983) *How research has changed American schools: history from 1840 to the present.* Kalamazoo, MI: Mythos Press.

Turner, R. (1971) Conceptual foundations of research in teacher education. In B. Smith (ed.), *Research in teacher education: a symposium* (pp. 10–36). Englewood Cliffs, NJ: Prentice-Hall, Inc.

Turner, R. (1975) An overview of research in teacher education. In K. Ryan (ed.), *Teacher education, 74th Yearbook of the National Society for the Study of Education* (pp. 87–110). Chicago, IL: University of Chicago Press.

U.S. Department of Education (2002) *Meeting the highly qualified teachers challenge: the Secretary's annual report on teacher quality.* Washington, DC: Author.

Urban, W. (1990) Historical studies of teacher education. In W. Houston (ed.), *Handbook of research on teacher education* (pp. 59–71). New York, NY: Macmillan.

Vare, J. (1994) Partnership contrasts: microteaching activity as two apprenticeships in thinking. *Journal of Teacher Education,* 45(3), 209–217.

Whitehurst, G. (2002, April 4) *Research on teacher preparation and professional development.* Paper presented at the White House Conference on Preparing Tomorrow's Teachers, Washington, DC.

Wideen, M., Mayer-Smith, J., & Moon, B. (1998) A critical analysis of the research on learning to teach: making the case for an ecological perspective on inquiry. *Review of Educational Research,* 68(2), 130–178.

Wilk, R., Edson, W., & Wu, J. (1967). Student personnel research in teacher education. *Review of Educational Research,* 37, 219–232.

Wilkinson, G. (1996) Enhancing microteaching through additional feedback from preservice administrators. *Teaching and Teacher Education,* 12(2), 211–221.

Wilson, S. & Youngs, P. (2005) Research on accountability processes in teacher education. In M. Cochran-Smith & K. Zeichner (eds.), *The AERA Panel on Research and Teacher Education* (pp. 591–644). Mahwah, NJ: Lawrence Erlbaum Associates Inc.

Wilson, S., Shulman, L., & Richert, A. (1987) "150 different ways" of knowing: Representations of knowledge in teaching. In J. Calderhead (ed.), *Exploring teachers' thinking* (pp. 104–124). London: Cassell.

Wilson, S., Floden, R., & Ferrini-Mundy, J. (2001) *Teacher preparation research: current knowledge, gaps, and recommendations.* Washington, DC: Center for the Study of Teaching and Policy.

Winitzky, N. & Arends, R. (1991). Translating research into practice: the effects of various forms of training and clinical experience on preservice students' knowledge, skill, and reflectiveness. *Journal of Teacher Education,* 42(1), 52–65.

Wise, A. (1988) *Impacts of teacher testing: state educational governance through standard-setting* (No. NIE-G-83-0023). Santa Monica, CA: Rand Corporation.

Zeichner, K. (1993) *Educating teachers for cultural diversity* (National Center for Research on Teacher Learning Special Report No. ED 359 167). East Lansing, MI: Michigan State University.

Zeichner, K. (2005a) A research agenda for teacher education. In M. Cochran-Smith & K. Zeichner (eds.), *Studying teacher education: the report of the AERA panel on research and teacher education* (pp. 737–760). Mahwah, NJ: Lawrence Erlbaum Associates Inc.

Zeichner, K. (2005b) Learning from experience with performance-based teacher education. In F. Peterman (ed.), *Designing performance assessment systems for urban teacher preparation* (pp. 3–19). Mahwah, NJ: Lawrence Erlbaum Associates, Publishers.

54 Critical and qualitative research in teacher education

A blues epistemology for cultural well-being and a reason for knowing

Joyce E. King
Georgia State University

Defenders of white blues are often proponents of "color-blindness" as the ultimate weapon of anti-racism, but many of these color-blind whites are really resisting the importance of consciousness of race and race matters, with all the nagging reminders of racism contained therein. They believe that by refusing to use race as a criterion for anything, they are being the ultimate non-racists, but they are actually blinding themselves to the complexity of racial issues.

Paul Garon, 1995

I think we're at a moment now in which a blues nation has to learn from a blues people.
Cornell West, Interview with Toni Morrison, 2005

People who have no choice but to live their life in their black skins know racism when they see it. Racism is never subtle to the victim. Only White people say race doesn't matter.
Carrie Morris, Pathways School Faculty Member, 1996[1]

Nobody's coming to get us . . . Nobody's coming to get us.
Aaron Broussard, President, Jefferson Parish, Louisiana, 2005[2]

But can you expect teachers to revolutionize the social order for the good of the community? Indeed, we must expect this very thing. The educational system of a country is worthless unless it accomplishes this very task.
Carter G. Woodson, 1933/1977[3]

INTRODUCTION

A growing body of teacher education research documents the fact that many experienced and future teachers resist a critically transformative understanding of race and racial inequity. This resistance, which can be understood as a result of mis-education, is an ongoing challenge for the profession and for teacher education research. Emergent inquiry-based pedagogical approaches that use the knowledge traditions and lived experiences of marginalized and oppressed groups in teacher learning (and un-learning racism) with community members suggest possible ways out of this knowledge crisis. However, research on teacher education has yet to address the belief structure of race in ideologically biased school/academic knowledge and research that contributes to the mis-education of teachers, although a tradition of Black scholarship has long recognized this epistemological problem (McDaniels, 2006).

Writing nearly a century ago in 1917, for example, Black sociologist, lawyer, and historian, George Washington Ellis, pinpointed the hegemonic role of ideological knowledge in maintaining the mythology of race and perpetuating racial injustice. For Ellis "scholarly activity had to be moved from the ideological position of racism to the ideological position of democracy" for the benefit of the entire society (Childs, 1989, p. 87). A few years later, the research of another Black historian, educator, and activist scholar, Carter G. Woodson, who founded "Black History Week/Month" in 1927, showed how ideological school knowledge obstructs democratic community in the U.S. His analysis of mis-education, that is, how ideologically biased school knowledge systematically teaches whites to feel superior and Black people to feel inferior, led Woodson (1933) to call for teachers to "revolutionize the social order".

The integrity of Black culture, including its African roots, was fundamental in these scholarly challenges that Ellis, Woodson, and others have launched to combat the hegemony of ideologically biased knowledge (Gleason, 2006; King, 1992, 1995). Scholarly defense of Black culture and heritage has been necessary, not solely to set the historical record straight on behalf of African Americans, but also as an investment in human freedom from dehumanizing supremacist ideologies. The "convergence of critical thought and action" (King, 2004, p. 351) and the inextricable connection between the general welfare of humanity and Black people's cultural well-being are defining qualities of this Black intellectual tradition that have been carried forward in the modern discipline of Black Studies (B. Gordon, 1990, 1995). A Black Studies theoretical analysis is employed in this chapter to consider how (and how well) critical and qualitative research (and practice) in teacher education produces knowledge, understanding, and social action for racial-social justice. This hyphenated term is used in order not to lose sight of Black people's group survival needs, that is, the "requirements for black existence," in transformative visions of equity and democratic inclusion (Cone, 1972, p. 27).

Focus of the chapter

This chapter focuses on four inter-related genres of critical and qualitative research in teacher education with racial-social justice aims: (1) critical race theorizing, (2) whiteness studies, (3) critical ethnography, and (4) practitioner inquiry, including action research "in, on, and for" teacher education (Cochran-Smith & Lytle, 2004). The Black Studies theoretical analysis that informs the discussion of these modes of inquiry focuses analytical attention on the belief structure of race in ideologically biased knowledge in schools and academe and epistemologies and indigenous knowledge traditions from the ideological position of democracy. One example, the epistemology of the Black experience embodied in the African American blues tradition, will be used as a heuristic framework to suggest cultural well-being as a measure of what/how these modes of research can contribute to equity and democratic inclusion in education and society. It will be argued that a crisis of knowledge in teacher education research (and practice) exists because of the absence of marginalized and oppressed people's epistemologies as a foundation of knowledge for teacher learning and for teaching. Thus, the discussion of these genres of research goes beyond a focus only on the mis-education of teachers. Rather, the emphasis also is on producing knowledge for the benefit of marginalized communities and the general society's welfare. Several overlapping questions will illuminate this missing cultural well-being framework: (1) What/whose social vision does research honor and project? (2) Is the cultural well-being of marginalized groups a consideration? (3) What is missing in the theory and methods of these genres of inquiry, given their group survival needs, that is, the "requirements of black existence," for example? (4) Can research informed by the blues epistemology of the Black experience advance understanding of the interconnections among Black people's cultural well-being, positive inter-group relations, and humanity's general welfare?

Organization of the chapter

The chapter is divided into four parts. The first part, "Epistemologies and Knowledge Traditions for Cultural Well-Being," introduces the Black Studies analysis of the ideology of race and the blues epistemology of the Black experience. "Decolonizing" methodology and theory articulated and used by indigenous peoples that complement the blues epistemology are also presented. The second part of the chapter, "From Critical Social Theories/Theorizing to Critical Research Methods," briefly reviews the genealogy of critical theory and methods in the social sciences and teacher education. The research examples discussed illustrate various critical methods, including critical race theory, critical ethnography, as well as investigations of the discourse of "whiteness," and selected feminist research approaches. The third section of the chapter, "A Continuum of Practitioner Inquiry: Learning to Teach for Social Change," examines the use of various qualitative research methods in teacher education research—from individual narratives to ethnography to action research in community settings. The final section, "Beyond the Crisis of Knowledge in Teacher Education Research and Practice," presents teacher education methods that incorporate community knowledge and new roles for community members that support mutually beneficial teacher learning and development.

EPISTEMOLOGIES AND KNOWLEDGE TRADITIONS FOR CULTURAL WELL-BEING

In spite of a burgeoning body of multicultural education literature (Banks & Banks, 2004; Goodwin & Swartz, 2004; McAllister & Irvine, 2000), teacher education research has produced no accepted consensus about what teachers should "know, be able to do and be like" to promote and safeguard the cultural well-being, sense of belonging, and agency of African American learners (King, 1994; Lee, 2001) or other marginalized students. Murrell (2001) offers this cogent description of "capable" urban teachers who:

> ... must be aware that there is a deep and profound violence embedded in the fabric of American popular and institutional culture that is a significant and toxic part of children's school experience. Where there is not an anti-racist awareness and explicit pedagogy for working with African American children and families, there persists an insidious violence that even the most well-meaning teacher will be a participant in despite beliefs and values to the contrary.
>
> (p. 75)

In this vein S. King and Castenell (2001) assert: "the task of fighting racism has to be the bottom line" if educational institutions are going to prepare "teachers with the will and the strategies to teach all children" (p. 10). Assaults on "blackness as a cultural reality," as in the following example, is one form that racism takes (Murrell, 1997, p. 33). A student teacher related in one of my courses how a white teacher at an award-winning elementary school described the Black children in her classroom. The teacher said that there were two groups of Black children in her assigned classroom: the "black-Blacks" and the "white-Blacks." The teacher informed her that attempting to teach the "black-Blacks" would be a waste of time because they have "black values." Teaching the "white-Blacks," on the other hand, who have "white values," would be worthwhile.[4] The student was shocked and chagrined because she was among those credential candidates who had resisted the focus on racial inequity in the required cross-cultural communications course.

Knowledge for cultural well-being: a task for research

To combat such beliefs Murrell (2001) calls for a pedagogy "grounded in the history, traditions, and cultural heritage of African Americans" (p. 33). However, this will require re-writing academic and school knowledge (Loewen, 1995; Stevens *et al.*, 2005; Wynter, 2006). Following are three examples of ideologically biased academic/school knowledge, including misrepresentations of slavery in textbooks and classroom discourse that contribute to the mis-education of teachers and assaults on cultural blackness. First, an ethnographic investigation in predominately white suburban middle school classrooms reveals the limits of the white teachers' knowledge and pedagogical skills regarding teaching about the enslavement of African people and the heritage of Native Americans. Classroom discourse renders African Americans "present in the curriculum" but only as slaves, and, thus, "absent in history" (Wills *et al.*, 2004, p. 107).

Second, in my work with teachers I ask if anyone can name the three universities that existed in West Africa before Columbus arrived in the Americas (Gao, D'jenné, and Sankoré at Timbuktu in present-day Mali). Nearly always the response is: "No." Kincheloe (2004) reports a similar experience when he asks whether teachers have studied "the story of the European colonization of Africa and the effects of the slave trade" (p. 1). In fact, the structure of knowledge in the discipline that separates African history from American history circumscribes what teachers (and their students) can learn about Africa, slavery, and the development of U.S. society. Teachers learn little if anything concerning the vital role not just of African labor but also the sophisticated knowledge and skills African people possessed that made the nation's development and wealth possible (Carney, 2001; King, 2006). Fragmentation of historical knowledge thus obstructs the critical understanding teachers need to explain African descent people's continuing impoverishment given the nature and function of global capitalism—then and now (Maiga, 2005). The devastation of urban communities that has undermined traditional African American culture, community viability, and beneficial socialization practices— conditions that are portrayed as a "culture of poverty" and as culturally deficient "black-values" (Heath, 1989; King & Wilson, 1994).

A third example is the way "dysconsciousness," the term I introduced to describe such "limited and distorted understandings" of racial inequity, is used in multicultural teacher education and critical race scholarship (King, 1991a). Though it is often cited in discussions of racism, none of these publications reference the key finding of the original study of dysconsciousness: pre-service teachers typically explained racial inequality "as a historically inevitable consequence of slavery or as a result of prejudice and discrimination" (King, 1991a, p. 138), which they also linked to slavery. None of their explanations showed any recognition of the systemic nature of racism (Duncan, 2004) or the "structural underpinnings of inequity" (Cochran-Smith *et al.*, 2004, p. 956).

Generating forms of knowledge and effective pedagogy that teachers need to address such ideological constructions of race is a task for teacher education research. As Hilliard (2001) cautions, however, researchers have unfortunately been "following the detour of race rather than the ideology that propels it" (p. 2). In a Black Studies analysis of the ideological belief structure of race Wynter (2003, 2006) argues that racism is a logical outcome, an effect of "law-like" societal cultural rules and ideas that govern our behaviors and shape our perceptions of reality (King, 2005b). This system of knowledge and representation defines "conceptual blackness" as the "alter ego" of "conceptual whiteness" (Wynter, 2003). Although "whiteness" studies have begun to proliferate, this understanding of what "race" does and which grasps the epistemic roots of assaults on cultural blackness, is under-theorized in education (Bush, 2004; Ignatiev, 1995; Jensen, 2005; Kent, 1972; Prager, 1982; Roediger, 1998).

The blues epistemology of the Black experience

The task of fighting racism, then, entails the production of knowledge to combat this system of representation. It seems reasonable to expect that such research would benefit from the inclusion of epistemologies of marginalized peoples. Researchers of color recognize the intimate connection between epistemology and methodology when justice is the objective (Bernal, 1998; Pizarro, 1998). The African American blues tradition, discussed next, offers such an epistemological vantage point from which to document, interrogate, and transmit knowledge of the existential Black experience. This discussion is intended to illuminate four key characteristics of the blues epistemology that: (a) embraces the contradictions in the Black struggle for being; (b) functions as a unifying impetus for community building; and (c) provides clarifying social explanation, political knowledge, and spiritual understanding that is not solely for race consciousness but also (d) to connect Black suffering with the universal ideal of the human spirit of freedom. The following historical overview presents the rich, underutilized potential of this epistemology for teacher learning and research about and also through African American cultural perspectives.

Critical social explanation/theorizing

McLaren and Farahmandpur (2001) define theory as a "living aperture through which specific histories are made visible and intelligible" (p. 301, cf. Grande, 2004, p. 28). The blues tradition constitutes a form of critical Black working class theorizing or social explanation. Woods (1998) argues that the blues constitutes an epistemology of African American thought that embodies "African American daily life, social explanation, [and] social action," that is, "how to act," solve problems, and behave (p. 101). Blues lyrics, which typically address themes of love and mistreatment, have often been misinterpreted as a "music of resignation." On the contrary, as Titon (1990) posits, the core of the blues is about "freedom from mistreatment, not submission to it" (p. 2). Whereas Black people have been subjected to unspeakable dehumanization, the blues response is love.

The record of African American cultural resilience and critical social thought conveyed in the blues contrasts with the culture of poverty deficit "theories" of Black life and culture that emerged in the social sciences in the U.S. around the same time that the blues moved along with Black people from rural areas of the Mississippi Delta to the urban north. Woods provides this illuminating account of the emergence of the blues tradition of "cultural transmission and social explanation":

> Emerging out of the rich tradition of African song-centered orature, and under conditions of intense censorship, secular and sacred songs became fountainheads of cultural transmission and social explanation. Furthermore, as a result of the extremely hierarchical class structure of Southern plantations, African-American working class thought would come to find its fullest expression in the blues: a "collective

expression of the ideology and character of Black people situated at the bottom of the social order in America."

(Woods, 1998, p. 56, *cf.* Barlow, 1989, p. xii)

Black Studies scholarship recognizes in the "historic commitment to social and personal investigation, description and criticism present in the blues" a resource for critical knowledge and a source of theory (Woods, 1998, p. 30). In one program teacher educators and future teachers have studied blues culture, history, lyrics, and the lives of blues performers as aesthetics education (Asher *et al.*, 2006; Love, 2006). Considering the subjugated knowledge traditions of Black people (or any other marginalized cultural group) as an epistemological resource for pedagogy, theory, or methodology in research, however, requires a revolutionary break with the dominant societal episteme or system of knowledge.

A people's marginalized history

The blues emerged in the 1890s during the violent repression following the brief period of "freedom" between the end of the Civil War and the end of Reconstruction. Political "compromise" and betrayal resulted in the removal of Black troops and militia ("the Black and Blues") and the reinstatement of planter power and racial terror throughout the south (Cone, 1972; Ortiz, 2005; Woods, 1998). It was during this period that the "hollers" that became the central elements of the blues emerged, as the formerly enslaved were savagely forced back to labor in unfreedom (again) on the levées, in the "fields, prisons, docks and streets" (Woods, 1998, p. 82). Levine (1977), in *Black Culture, Black Consciousness*, situates this blues tradition within the heritage of Black community building:

> Black secular song, along with other forms of oral tradition allowed [Black people] to express themselves communally and individually, to derive great aesthetic pleasure, to perpetuate traditions, to keep values from eroding, and to begin to create new expressive modes. Black secular song revealed a culture which kept large elements of its own autonomous standards alive, which includes a rich internal life, which interacted with a larger society that deeply affected it.
>
> (p. 297, see Woods, pp. 56–57)

As the following passage explains, the blues represents a collective response to this repression in the form of the "conscious codification of African American folk wisdom" and knowledge out of which other musical forms also evolved:

> The derivative of these forms such as jazz, gospel, rock and roll, rhythm and blues, funk, and rap all refer back to these anchors and their insights. These new musical genres are documentary in nature. That is, they must still explicitly, or implicitly, address African American consciousness of this period and the intellectual/ performance traditions that emerged during it.
>
> (p. 83)

As an indigenous "American" art form (native to this country), which remains deeply rooted in an African ethos (values, functionality, and worldview) that survived among African Americans, the blues constitutes a unique social vision and critique of injustice that has been marginalized in, if not totally erased from, history. A wholly authentic but often maligned and misinterpreted musical form through which Black people have expressed a refusal to accept mistreatment, the blues can be understood philosophically as a "black point of view in song" (Davis, 1995, p. 69). The educational relevance of the blues is suggested in one artist's understanding of the meaning of the blues:

> To me, the blues is a literary and musical form and also a basic philosophy. When I get ready to study the mystical aspect of black people, I go to the blues, then I feel like I'm in touch with the root of black people.
>
> (Palmer, 1982, pp. 276–277)

According to Woods (1998), this blues epistemology represents "the beginnings of a *method of investigation*" (p. 21) that can recover "heroic movements" of Black cultural resistance that have been purged from "both historical texts and popular memory" (p. 4, emphasis added). This critical knowledge tradition is a cultural constant in Black music, including the blues as well as some forms of rap music and "conscious" hip-hop (Fisher, 2003, 2006). In the aftermath of Hurricane Katrina, for example, hip-hop artist Kanye West's criticism that President George Bush "doesn't care about Black people" has been "sampled," widely disseminated, and immortalized in a rap video/song via the Internet. In *Blues People* Jones (1963) explains that "the most expressive [Negro] music of any given period will be an exact reflection" of Black existence (p. 137). Following this line of reasoning, this chapter explores theoretical and methodological implications of this epistemology for group-affirming research in teacher education.

More than a musical genre

If language refers to a shared system of communication used by a nation, a people, or other distinct community, the blues "speaks" a communal language of the lived culture, material reality, and existential philosophy of Black existence. The blues gives voice to Black cultural ideals in a spoken record of Black suffering and transcendence that remains relevant and instructive. When visiting the Maori people in New Zealand, Bernice Johnson Reagon, African American historian, cultural activist, and founder of the incomparable female a cappella ensemble "Sweet Honey and the Rock," offered this insightful observation about Black music that also applies to the blues. Taking part in a discussion of "the significance of land to Maori identity," Reagon described the African American community "as one held together by song rather than by territory" (L. Smith, 1999, p. 126). Reagon's research and performances have revealed the deeper meaning embodied in the language of the African American sacred song tradition. When Christianity was being used explicitly to justify Black people's enslavement, for example, sacred songs—"Negro spirituals"—made use of Christian religious language and concepts with great critical insight and intelligence to repudiate this dominant ideology. A profoundly meaningful verse, "Everybody talkin' bout heaven ain't going there," in one of these "sorrow songs," *All God's Chillun Got Wings*, illustrates the subversive "reading" of the "Word" and the world encoded in these songs.[5] The injustice that Black people have suffered has also given blues singers and song writers opportunities to explore universal human themes made "specific through the African American experience" (Titon, 1990, p. 11).

The blues vision

The vision of social, cultural, interpersonal, economic, and racial justice in the blues implies certain conditions of freedom from mistreatment. As expressed, for example, in the blues song, "Further on up the road . . . someone is gonna hurt you like you hurt me," the blues conveys a universal philosophy of how people should be treated. The spirit of love in the blues honors humanity's triumphal capacity to transcend dehumanization without diminishing or relinquishing the "space of being" in which Black people exist (Grande, 2004). Whether expressed in the determination to overcome heartbreak or hopelessness ("Been down so low, down don't bother me ..."), the refusal to accept mistreatment (by a lover, a sheriff, or a bossman) affirms the singer's "somebodiness," that is to say, Black people's humanity (Cone, 1972). This vision of inclusion (in the human family) is neither "raceless" nor distorted by the mythology of race. Like the proverbial "crossroads" of the "deep blues," where the most accomplished performance of the art that any artist aspires to achieve is possible, the blues vision of humanity suggests a powerfully transformative reason for knowing: to honor individuality, group heritage, and human freedom—all at the same time—in spite of the depredations heaped upon one for being Black and poor. This is the essence of the unique democratic contribution of the blues.

The white blues

A long-standing controversy in the music world about the "white blues" concerns whether, given the traditional themes and content of the lyrics, the blues as played by white performers is "authentic." Some white performers argue that race should not matter in appreciating a virtuoso performance. Music critics and musicians remain at odds (Garon, 1995). This debate recalls persistent ruminations regarding "color-blindness" in teacher education literature. Within a guilt/innocence either/or mindset white pre-service teachers may profess to being and may prefer to remain "color-blind." These teachers resist the goals of racial-social justice teaching by proclaiming racial innocence and a commitment to a notion of raceless equity, but with no vision of an end to racial oppression. For another example, in research and teaching contexts, critical theorizing that privileges social class and capitalist relations of production posit a class versus race theoretical explanation that, in effect, privileges "hybrid" conceptions of being and identity as opposed to Black identity and cultural integrity. Researchers or practitioners who embrace "color-blindness" call to mind the standpoint of "white blues" aficionados who "refuse to see race as a criterion for anything." The "decolonizing" research methods of indigenous peoples, as discussed below, affirm transformative research possibilities that aim to ensure their cultural well-being, free from racial mistreatment, "annihilation and absorption into the democratic mainstream" (Grande, 2004, p. 172).

Decolonizing methodology/indigenous epistemologies

The importance of identity, cultural rights, community building, and belonging in the Black intellectual tradition is mirrored in methodological and epistemological alternatives to denigrating culture that indigenous education offers (Loveland, 2003). For example, "decolonizing" research methods and scholarship in Maori, Native Hawaiian, and Indian education and research practice prioritize community and student well-being in the context of a communal future, a sense of peoplehood, and indigenous people's culturally sovereign "space of being" (Grande, 2004; Kana'iaupuni, 2005; Kaomea, 2005; L. Smith, 1999; G. Smith, 2004). In these approaches educational purpose goes beyond the traditional value system promulgated in U.S. public schools that emphasizes competitive individualism and individual academic success, high stakes test scores, materialism, etc. These outcomes imply values that are deemed "alien" to the culture of achievement of indigenous peoples as well as African Americans (Murrell, 1997).

Proponents of the cultural rights of dispossessed and indigenous peoples in education use methods that are intended to illuminate "curricular silences" regarding the cultural and historical circumstances of indigenous communities and recover their collective heritages. Kaomea (2005) notes that such knowledge has been "buried, written over, or erased" and sometimes distorted beyond remembrance or recognition. One consequence has been the alienation of indigenous peoples from their own identity and heritage (Rollo, 2006). Native Americans and other indigenous educators, including the Maori of New Zealand, are using their heritages, languages, and other forms of "local knowledge" as pedagogical and methodological resources to: counter alienation, provide direction to research, preserve their culture, foster student achievement, and to ensure their collective survival as distinct peoples.

L. Smith describes Kaupapa Maori, or research by Maori people of New Zealand, for example, as more than a "paradigm." That is to say, it is also a social project "related to being Maori" that is "connected to Maori philosophy and principles" and "takes for granted the validity and legitimacy of Maori." The reason for knowing in Kaupapa Maori research also concerns Maori people's struggle for autonomy and "cultural well being" (Smith, 1999, p. 185). Kauppa Maori does not exclude non-Maori researchers but provides opportunities for their participation via equitable, authentic relationships with Maori partners. Along these same lines, as Angayuqaq Oscar Kawagley, Yupiak Elder and professor of education at the University of Alaska, Fairbanks, observes: "The tide has turned and the future of indigenous education is clearly shifting toward an emphasis on providing education *in and through the culture, rather than about the culture*. Critical to such indigenous approaches to education and research is language, which is "the living artifact of a culture" (Loveland, 2003).

Grande (2004), another indigenous scholar, clarifies the difference between indigenous people's cultural well-being and the vision of social change/equity/democracy in progressive/ revolutionary/ critical theory and pedagogy. From the epistemological vantage point of "Red pedagogy," according to Grande, regardless of the choices of particular individuals:

> . . . what distinguishes the indigenous struggle for (group) self-determination from others is . . . their collective effort to protect the rights of their peoples to live in accordance with traditional . . . ancestral ways.
>
> (p. 172)

Moreover, "this allegiance to traditional knowledge," including the preservation and use of indigenous language that conveys the peoples' "thought-world," has protected American Indians from total "annihilation and absorption" into the homogenizing, "democratic" European-centered "mainstream."[6]

Given that white teachers are the majority in the teaching force and given the various ways many white teachers (and parents) resist equity in education, it is not surprising that so much social justice-oriented teacher education research is directed toward understanding the "ideologies of privilege" of white teachers (Oakes *et al.*, 2006, p. 95). These efforts typically focus on the needs of experienced and prospective white teachers (e.g. their resistance or cultural encapsulation). One alternative is to create authentic research partnerships and methods of inquiry as "communities of practice" in which the epistemologies of community people are made relevant in the assessment of these efforts (Murrell, 2001). The problematic belief structures of white teachers can also be addressed via theory, research methods, and pedagogy that illuminate the "ideologies of otherness" that are at the epistemic root of race-based inequities in schools and society. Before examining this epistemic problematic using the conceptual tools of Black Studies, the trajectory of critical social theorizing from social science to educational approaches is discussed next.

FROM CRITICAL SOCIAL THEORIES/THEORIZING TO CRITICAL RESEARCH METHODS

In constrast to positivism, critical research approaches share a connection with the emancipatory aims of critical social theories (e.g. neo-Marxist, feminist, postcolonial). Qualitative educational research has common roots in the interpretive traditions in sociology and anthropology that bear the influence of various post-positive theory and methods, including phenomenology, structuralism, semiotics, hermeneutics, symbolic interactionism, and ethnomethodology (DeMarrais & LeCompte, 1999).

Critical roots in common

Carr and Kemmis (1989) made a relevant distinction between critical social theory and critical social science. Critical theory is the result of a process of critical analysis. Critical social science is a form of practice in which consciousness (the enlightened human agency of individual social actors) "comes to bear directly in their transformed social action" (p. 144). Critical educational theory has been criticized for a "tendency toward social critique" without theorizing action that practitioners can use to "develop a 'counter-hegemonic' practice" to challenge domination (Anderson, 1989, p. 257). Other scholars view critical educational research as a mode of inquiry to collect data about "schooling practices and their relationship to the social order" of power in order to "ultimately undermine and transform that order" (Morrell, 2005, p. 42).

Critical social science rejects the epistemology, ontology, and determinism of logical positivism. The goal of positive social science is to explain social life, while the alternative offered by interpretive social science is to facilitate understanding of domination and alienation. Following Marx, critical social science is informed by a moral obligation to understand social reality in order to change it. Thus, the dual aim of critical social science is simultaneously to explain and to combat dominating relations of power in favor of democracy and human freedom. The notion of "critical" applied to theory and methods of inquiry and in education (and teacher education) can also be traced to Marx's understanding of the necessity of "ideology critique" for social change. Critical pedagogy (Giroux, 1988; Sleeter & Bernal, 2004), which is the analytical tool of critical theory applied to pedagogy, is indebted also to the Brazilian educator, Paulo Freire (1970/1993). Critical consciousness is a goal of Freire's revolutionary pedagogy of liberation. In addition to these European, Euro-American, and Latin American roots of critical and qualitative research methods and theory, this chapter draws on the work or a number of scholars of color whose scholarship is influenced by the principles of critical social science. Table 54.1 (below) compares the common central features and distinct assumptions and concerns of critical social theory with feminist, critical multicultural, and race-central methods, theory, and pedagogy in social and education research.

Feminists, scholars of color and race-centered theorists criticize the lack of explicit attention to gender and women's oppression, race, ethnicity, and cultural sovereignty of indigenous peoples in critical theory and critical pedagogy (Ellsworth, 1998; hooks, 1997; Ladson-Billings, 1997; Leonardo, 2004; Lynn, 1999). However, critical theorists strenuously reject the allegation that in giving primacy to social class, critical theorizing

Table 54.1 Comparison of critical social theory and critical approaches in education

	Critical social theory	Critical feminist theory, pedagogy, and methodology	Critical race theory, pedagogy, and methodology
1 General aims	1 CST opposes positivism . . . (a moral obligation).	1 Feminist (liberal/socialist) theorizing identifies/describes women's oppression, its foundations and effects to conceive ways to generate strategies for women's liberation" (Brady, 2000, p. 369). "This entails identifying and articulating both objective oppression in practices and relationships and the male blindness to women's experience" (Weiler, 1988, p. 59).	1 CRT opposes "color-blind" critical social theory and affirms the centrality of race and racism and their intersectionality with other forms of subordination. CRT examines the roles of race and racism in as a central feature in the social and economic organization of the United States and, therefore, in education.
2 A social role for the knowledge research and theory produce	2 CST distinguishes between past and present, largely characterized by domination, exploitation, and oppression, and a possible future rid of these phenomena . . . The future society can be realized through concerted political action. The role of CST is to raise consciousness about . . . oppression and demonstrate the possibility of a qualitatively different future society.	2 Feminist pedagogy should present students with a language of critique and possibility . . . that challenges racist assumptions and calls into question taken for granted definitions of gender and other forms of domination (Brady, p. 372).	2 "Story telling is a significant part of the law and disenfranchised people have different stories and ways of telling them than enfranchised people(s). Counter stories can raise consciousness to challenge dominant ideology, initiate the necessary cognitive conflict to "jar dysconscious" racism and stimulate action (Ladson-Billings, 2000, p. 366).

	CST	Feminist	CRT
3 Explanatory constructs	3 CST argues that domination is structural. That is, people's everyday lives are affected by larger social institutions such as politics, economics, culture, discourse, gender, and race. CST illuminates these structures in helping people understand the national and global roots of their oppression.	3 A critical feminist pedagogy intersects a postmodern feminism with critical praxis understood within the context of economic, politic, and cultural constructs (Brady). A critical feminist methodology can illuminate the dual process of social and cultural reproduction and resistance—as in critical educational theory (Weiler, 1988, p. 59).	3 Race is a social construct, not biological.
4 Conceptions of consciousness	4 CST argues that structures of domination are reproduced through people's false consciousness, promoted by ideology (Marx), reification (Lukacs), hegemony (Gramsci), one-dimensional thinking (Marcuse), and the metaphysic of presence (Derrida) . . . CST pierces false consciousness by insisting on the power of agency, both personal and collective, to transform society.	4 Women should reject male supremacist thinking; to be female is to be a victim—and embrace their shared commonalities, the ability for self-determination, and communal agency (Brady) . . . Students should be offered the knowledge and the skills that allow them to reclaim their voice and their history . . . to enable them to name new identities . . . to assume ownership, and become active agents in their own lives (Brady, 2000).	4 Elites act against racist behavior in society only when it serves them, thus a critique of Liberalism's belief in steady but incremental processes of social change is an important component of CRT.
5 Key assumptions	5 CST argues social change begins . . . in people's every day lives—sexuality, family roles, workplace . . .	5 Feminist anti-racist teachers and administrators hold certain beliefs about justice and equality that they try to put into effect in their work to redefine the curriculum and social relationships (e.g. feminist counter-hegemony) (Weiler, 1988, p. 101).	5 Racist behavior is not an aberration, but is normal practice.

(Continued overleaf)

Table 54.1 Continued

	Critical social theory	Critical feminist theory, pedagogy, and methodology	Critical race theory, pedagogy, and methodology
6 Conceptions of justice	6 Following Marx . . . CST conceptualizes the bridge between structure (structural determinants) and agency (individual consciousness) as dialectical. That is, although structure conditions everyday experience, knowledge of structure can help people change social conditions. CST builds this bridge by rejecting economic determinism.	6 Feminist research emphasizes lived experience and the significance of everyday life (Brady). The contradictions of everyday life and consciousness can become the focus of a radical pedagogy (Weiler, 1988, p. 23).	6 Characteristics ascribed to a particular race will change, for example, African American people have been called "happy go lucky and childlike" historically in order to rationalize slavery, but are now most commonly called "threatening and criminal" in order to rationalize increased control through police, etc.
7 Implications for social struggle	7 . . . By focusing on the dialectical connection between everyday life and structure, CST holds people responsible for their own liberation and admonishes them not to oppress others in the name of distant future liberation . . . Adapted from: Agger (1998)	7 Postmodern feminism represents a politics in which people actively participate in the shaping of theories and practices of liberation by acknowledging both diversity and unity, focusing on people who work and live in a multiracial and multicultural society (Brady) . . . . Adapted from: J. F. Brady (2000, pp. 369–74) and K. Weiler (1988).	7 People have intersecting identities, i.e. there is more than one way that they are affected by disenfranchisement or inequality. We all have multiple lenses through which we experience the world (and are experienced by others). Adapted from: http://en wikipedia.org/wiki/ Critical_race_theory

fails to address forms of oppression other than that of social class (McLaren, 2000; Scatamburlo-D'Annibale & McLaren, 2004). These critical theorists assert that such "misguided" criticism incorrectly assumes the working class is white. Also, within a class-based (e.g. class-first) radical political economy framework the meanings of socially constructed categories of difference or subjectivities (e.g. gender, race and ethnicity) are produced by the class-based relations of production that define the capitalist system. Thus, these categories of lived experience and identity are interrogated and interpreted through the lens of the material (objective) relations of social class, power, and privilege linked to the relations of production (pp. 188–189).

Ongoing class versus race (or gender) debates illustrate the complexity of competing theories of social change. A radical Black Marxist tradition also exists that posits a class-first analysis. Multicultural and feminist approaches offer various interpretive frameworks to transcend this debate. Given that race is a social construction, scholars also posit that "hybridity" is a more useful conceptualization of being and identity than race (McCarthy, 1998). African-centered theorists and indigenous scholars, on the other hand, give primacy to peoplehood (Bernal, 1998; Grande, 2004; L. Smith, 1999). Identifying with one's group heritage is considered neither an epiphenomenon of social class (or gender), a reactionary form of in-group solidarity, false consciousness born of societal exclusion (Hilliard, 2001; King, 2005b), self-deceptive "fictive" kinship, nor misguided, romanticized identification with "dead civilizations" on foreign continents (King, 2005b). In fact, recent research documents the power of "race-ethnic self-schema" to buffer students from the racial vulnerabilities of alienating schooling (Oyserman et al., 2003).

CRITICAL RACE THEORY AND METHODS

According to Lynn (1999), in asserting that critical pedagogy had "failed to adequately address the question of race," Tate (1994) and Ladson-Billings (1997) helped put "race back into critical pedagogy" (p. 153) by applying the principles of critical race theory (CRT) in education. First articulated by legal scholars, then applied to education, critical race theory is an analytical lens developed by scholars of color to place race at the center of social analysis (Ladson-Billings & Tate, 1995; Parker & Stovall, 2004; Solórzano, 1997). Four precepts, delineated by Ladson-Billings (2005), define CRT in education. Critical race theory (CRT): (1) presumes that racism is normal not an aberration; (2) employs story telling as a mode analysis; (3) necessarily includes a critique of liberalism; and (4) points out that whites have been the primary beneficiaries of liberal/reform efforts (Ladson-Billings, 2006, pp. 300–302). In their introduction to a theme issue of *Qualitative Inquiry*, for example, Lynn et al. (2002) describe CRT as an "ontological and epistemological framework with which to analyze race" (p. 5). Sleeter and Bernal (2004) emphasize that CRT, in addition to addressing the "intersectionality of racism, classism, sexism, and other forms of oppression," challenges Eurocentric epistemologies and dominant ideologies (e.g. meritocracy, objectivity, and neutrality) using "counterstorytelling as a methodological and pedagogical tool" (p. 245). Also, Pizzaro (1998) uses a CRT framework to develop research methods that are consistent with a Chicano/a epistemology.

A theme issue of *Race and Ethnicity* considers the impact of CRT in the ten years since the publication of Ladson-Billings and Tate's seminal article on critical race theory in education and teacher education (Dixson & Rousseau, 2005). While CRT theorists criticize the idealized standpoint of "color-blindness" in the dominant discourse (Dixson & Rousseau, 2005; Ladson-Billings, 1997), other scholars who have studied race and ethnicity in the social sciences argue for some degree of caution with respect to use of the construct race. The concern is not to argue for a class-first analysis but to emphasize that focusing on race as an analytical category can displace a needed critique of supremacist ideology and thereby reify a *false*, ideological construct (Hilliard, 2001; Stanfield & Dennis, 1993). However, critical race theorists argue back that CRT illuminates the "everyday-ness" of racism and values and represents the voices, strengths, and complexity of the experiences of people of color (Chapman, 2005, p. 28; Lynn, 1999). Proponents of CRT use methods such as narrative inquiry, counterstories, historical ethnographies, autobiography, autoethnography, critical ethnography, and portraiture in teacher education research. In the passage below Duncan (2005) describes links between the use of these methods used by critical race theorists and Freire's liberation pedagogy:

> The centrality of narrative and storytelling in critical race approaches to educational research is consonant with Paulo Freire's (1995) view that changing language "is part of the process of changing the world" (pp. 67–68). Along these lines proponents of CRT in general emphasize aesthetic and emotional dimensions in their stories to stimulate the imagination and to inspire empathy to allow others to imagine the mind of the oppressed and to see, and perhaps vicariously experience, the world through their eyes.
>
> (p. 102)

Thus, these scholars argue that critical race theory has the capacity to convey to others "insider" knowledge of race as difference.

A CRT framework for qualitative inquiry

Critical race theory also provides a framework for qualitative inquiry in teacher education (Duncan, 2002; Ortiz & Rhoads, 2000; Parker *et al.*, 1999; Sleeter & Bernal, 2004; Smith-Maddox & Solórzano, 2002; Solórzano, 1997). Emergent CRT "offshoots" include "critical race pedagogy" (Lynn, 1999) and "critical race ethnography" (Duncan, 2005). CRT has also generated a number of other complementary "connecting parts": LatCrit (Latina/o critical race theory), Tribal Crits, FemCrits (critical race feminists), Asian American poststructural critical legal positions, and critical race feminism (Brayboy, 2005; Parker & Stovall, 2004; Sleeter & Bernal, 2004). Following are examples of how Black, Latina/o, as well as white teacher educator-researchers employ the CRT framework to study their professional practice. These researchers use "counterstories" and narratives to analyze their experiences teaching mostly white future teachers. For instance, Duncan (2002) describes pedagogical strategies he employed in an urban ethnography course that "rendered race visible." That is, CRT has the power to bring "subtle forms of racial oppression . . . into bold relief" (p. 102). Other frameworks that are combined with CRT include Freire's problem-posing method (Smith-Maddox & Solórzano, 2002), portraiture (Chapman, 2005), and Black feminism, which is discussed in the next section.

Black feminism and CRT in teacher education

In an article titled "The Burden of Teaching Teachers" Williams and Evans-Winters (2005), two African American women teacher educators, use the "lenses" of both Black feminism and CRT in reflective narratives of teaching white students. Reflecting on this experience they ask:

(1) [H]ow can those of us, who are on the side of social justice, bring race talk back into the public forum of the teacher education classroom and (2) how can we get the message to be digested, interpreted, and critically examined by teacher education students who benefit from systematic inequality?

(p. 202)

The authors describe Black feminism/womanism as an ideology and political movement "that examines issues affecting African American women in the United States as part of the global struggle for women's emancipation" (p. 204). Black feminism and CRT are presented as "the hope for teacher education." Black feminism (BF), as an extension of critical social theory, is concerned with "fighting against economic, political, and social injustice for Black women and other oppressed groups" (pp. 203–204; also, Collins, 2000, p. 9). The authors use these frameworks in a complementary fashion to examine their professional practice.

Williams and Evans-Winters take a morally engaged, activist stance toward "the powers that be" (department chairs, academic deans, provosts) and concerns that arose when their mostly white female student teachers and their supervisors questioned, "interrogated and dismissed" their teaching practices. Their recommendations to improve the climate for Black women professors engaged in social justice-oriented teacher education include suggestions for: (1) an alternative method of evaluation that takes students' retaliatory resistance into account; (2) mentoring to support the retention of faculty of color; and (3) holding open discussions about "learning from and with faculty of color" to address "who [which professors] students resist and why" (pp. 216–217). Challenging and changing institutional practice fulfills an important principle of critical race theory and is a central tenet of critical social science. As Dixson and Rousseau (2005) note:

It is not enough to simply tell the stories of people of colour. Rather the educational experiences revealed through these stories must be the subject of deeper analysis using the CRT lens. Furthermore, CRT mandates that social activism be a part of any CRT project. To that end the stories must move us to action and the qualitative and material improvement of the educational experiences of people of colour.

(p. 13)

The research examples discussed next illustrate critical ethnographic research methods in K-12 venues.

Critical ethnographies: engaging Xicana[7] teachers and urban youth

According to Anderson (1989), the "overriding goal of critical ethnography," unlike other interpretivist research in sociology and anthropology "is to free individuals from sources of domination and repression" (p. 249). Two examples of critical ethnographic research, which provide opportunities for empowering learning in high school contexts, illustrate very different conceptualizations of race in critical research for educational and social change. Xicana high school teachers and Black and Latino/a "urban" students who are trained as "apprentices" study their own experiences using a combination of critical ethnography and participatory research (Carspecken, 1996).

Xicana teachers as agents of change

Berta-Avila (2004) combines the methods of critical ethnography and participatory research to provide an environment for self-identified "Xicana" teachers to participate in an emancipatory "dialogic process." This research experience illuminates connections between these teachers' identity and their mode of critical (raza/race) pedagogy. Berta-Avila uses dialogues, journal entries, and observations to understand how these teachers perceive their role in the classroom when teaching Raza students. Language and (collective) self-identity emerged as important considerations in exploring these practitioners' self-conceptualization of being "critical Xicana" teachers. They view how and why they teach as a "political act for social transformation and the emancipation of Raza students." For instance, one teacher participant links her role as a teacher to her "Xicana" identity in a way that embraces her ethnicity, including her "indigenous roots":

> Xicana is how I identify myself culturally, historically, politically, and socially. I would expect a person who identifies him/herself as Xicana/Xicano to know her/his history and take pride in their indigenous roots. I would expect them to have a sense of responsibility to their community and be an advocate for those who have no voice and are silenced. I would expect them to understand what being political means . . .
>
> (p. 70)

Berta-Avila concludes that "grounding themselves in pedagogy for social change" and engaging the issues of race, class, and gender enables these teachers to expand their role in the classroom. Beyond being a "role model," who uncritically emulates a Euro-dominant consciousness and individual upwardly mobile success, these teachers see themselves as "change agents," who "critically challenge and address power relations" that affect their students and their communities (p. 68). As another teacher explains:

> If a Xicana/Xicano enters the classroom and has no social and/or political understanding of the institutions they are entrenched in, they then lack the skills needed to understand how educational systems and the dominant society are intertwined. He or she falls into the danger of perpetuating messages that Raza life experiences are not valid and they should forsake their identity in order to succeed in the United States.

Thus, Xicana/Xicano identity influences the relations between these teachers, their students, and the students' parents, from whom they learn and for whom they choose to serve as advocates and cultural models. For these teachers, then, "it is not enough to be just a teacher of color."

The descriptions of the "critical Xicana" practitioners in this study are consistent with other researchers' reports of the political clarity of teachers of color (Beauboeuf-Lafontant, 1999; Irvine, 2003; King, 1991b; Ladson-Billings, 2000b; Lynn, 1999; Murrell, 1997, 2001). On the other hand, the research literature also describes Black and Latina/o educators (and researchers) who favor assimilation and who are highly critical of their own culture and language (Wills et al., 2004). Parents, too, who favor assimilationist goals, may adopt the dominant unfavorable view of their home language and culture.

Berta-Avila does not represent this study of Xicana teachers as an explicit investigation of or for teacher learning and development. However, the participatory research methodology employed afforded opportunities for these practitioners to reflect on their practice together and to examine the data and share their observations with each other. These opportunities for reflection engaged the teachers and the researcher in intentional and unanticipated mutual learning. This study also indicates another important ability that scholars emphasize as essential for social justice outcomes for African American students and other marginalized students: developing students' race-ethnic identities and identification with their communities and heritage are important resources for academic engagement (Oyserman *et al.*, 2003). In the next example, however, high school students experience "becoming critical" without such a strong emphasis on race consciousness.

Urban youth becoming critical researchers

Morrell (2004), Morell and Collatos (2002), and Oakes *et al.* (2006) describe participatory social inquiry and organizing activities as learning opportunities that build communities of practice for pre-service and in-service teacher education, urban school reform, and community change using critical research methods. These collaborative research activities engage practitioners and community members as well as students in significant roles as co-researchers/change agents. For example, Morrell and Collatos (2002) trained a multi-racial team of urban high school "student sociologists" who participated in this program of:

> . . . critical teacher education that forefronts authentic dialogue between pre-service teachers and urban teens . . . who have been trained in the sociology of education [and who] provide mentoring to pre-service teachers enrolled in a teacher credential program.
>
> (p. 61)

In this four-year project Black and Latino/a urban high school students studied social theory and completed "critical research projects related to equity and access to education" (p. 63). This critical ethnography of students' literacy learning is situated within a postmodern cultural studies analysis of popular culture (e.g. neo-Marxian and Freire-influenced theories). Because racial "essentialism" is a concern, Black and Latino/a youth are described as "members of multiple cultures and communities" (Morrell, 2005, p. 5). Although Morrell affirms the existence of racial inequities and the utility of culturally relevant and multicultural pedagogy, this researcher argues against "conceptions of culture as mono-racial identity" (p. 39). In fact, a somewhat color-blind category, "popular culture"[8] is one object of analysis. The question/dilemma Morrell poses for "critical educators who seek to educate for empowerment and access" is: "How do we effectively educate marginalized students in a way that addresses the impact of race yet transcends the social construction of race . . . and unifies rather than divides?" (p. 15).

To summarize, research employing the framework of critical race theory and critical ethnography is contributing to a growing knowledge base on teacher education with critical social justice aims. We know less, however, about the design and effectiveness of teacher preparation experiences that contribute to the coherence of pedagogy, identity, and political understanding, particularly for teachers of color. This includes knowledge about how such learning experiences can intervene against internalized racism to "empower students of color to see the specific ways that whiteness causes them to think less of their individual and collective selves" (Allen, 2004, p. 128). A related problem is the support needed by faculty and "accomplished practitioners" who supervise and mentor these future teachers (Quiocho & Rios, 2000). Research is also needed that addresses how teachers and teacher educators can thrive in increasingly constraining and hostile educational contexts in schools and teacher preparation programs where technicist rationality and assimilationist priorities predominate (Kincheloe, 2004; King, 2005b; Okpodoku, 2003; Scott, 2003; West-Olatunji, 2005; Wilson, 2005).

The change agent role the Xicana teachers in Berta-Avila's study embrace suggests particular implications for teacher preparation. It would have been interesting to know something about how these Xicana teachers experienced their professional preparation. Did study of critical pedagogy, for example, inform their practice and shape their identity as Xicana teachers? Did Chicano Studies play any role in their professional development and identity? Morrell's student co-researchers studied sociology of education texts. Would learning about racism through the lens of a Black Studies analysis of the blues epistemology, or studying Mexican *corridos* (ballads) that express Chicano values and history enhance the students' abilities as mentors of pre-service teachers (Garcia, 2000; Pizzaro, 1998)? Can studying such forms of cultural expression illuminate important points of intersections in the social histories of people of color?[9] In the research that concludes this section the focus is on how teachers can learn about racism. White women teacher educators use critical race theory in studies by white women professors who situate the pre-service and experienced teachers' learning within the academic discourse of "Whiteness studies."

Interrogating the discourse of whiteness

An emerging genre of critical qualitative research for teacher learning interrogates "whiteness" and ways that critical pedagogy and practitioner inquiry can contest unearned white privilege. This genre of "whiteness studies" includes critical and qualitative inquiry methods—journal writing, reflective dialogue—focused on "enlightening" participants regarding the educational implications of "white racial identity" and "white privilege." The focus of these studies is the limited ways in which many white teachers understand issues of race and systemic racism, including their own racial identity and "privileged positionality" (Marx, 2004; McIntosh, 1993; McIntyre, 1997, 2002; Ortiz & Rhoads, 2000). This genre of research, which is an outgrowth of critical "Whiteness" studies in education, labor, and cultural studies, as well as critical race theory (CRT), interrogates the discourse of "whiteness" using practitioner and narrative inquiry. These studies can be situated along a continuum of focusing on teachers' "cultural competency" (Irvine, 2003), critical multicultural education (Sleeter, 2001), critical feminist pedagogy (Brady & Kanpol, 2000; Weiler, 1988), and anti-racist pedagogy (Berlak & Moyenda, 2001; Kailin, 1994; Urrieta & Reidel, 2006; Zeichner, 1996). Typically the data in these studies is collected using qualitative methods (e.g. interviews, focus groups, student reflections/narratives) collected in single courses to document pedagogical impacts on future teachers' self-identification and their understanding of societal or systemic (as contrasted with acts of interpersonal) racism. Data has also been gathered from multiple student cohorts, field placement experiences, and students' collages, for instance. Two examples of this genre that describe three research contexts will be discussed in this section.

Becoming critical of whiteness

McIntyre (2002) has analyzed 95 collaborative collages created by 450 students in 19 (four undergraduate and 15 graduate) education courses. McIntyre's students have constructed these collages and presented them in class to represent and explain their understanding of what whiteness means. In addition, two graduate courses also afforded the opportunity to engage students in critical readings and participatory community action research. One finding McIntyre reports is that many students came to "see whiteness as an integral aspect of discourse" and they became aware of its impact on education. In another study Marx and Pennington (2003) employed a CRT framework to explore the racialized, culture-deficit thinking and identity issues that limited the ability of white teachers "to meet the needs of students of color." These authors analyze their separate but complimentary exploratory efforts as self-described white teacher educators, who have "taken to heart the call of critical race theorists and critical Whiteness scholars to open up a White discourse on White racism" (p. 92).

Based on their understanding of the existing literature and their previous experiences teaching white student teachers, Marx and Pennington created "pedagogies of CRT that would draw the attention of white pre-service teachers to their own positionality and help them to become critical of it" (p. 92). These teacher educator-researchers indicate that they were cognizant of white (student teacher) resistance and resentments against "cultures of color." They interpreted this resistance and resentment as markers of an (un)productive stage of white racial identity development that is "mired in White guilt, fear or anger." (Such resistance, as discussed earlier in this chapter, continues to be a focus of the research of teacher educators of color, as well.) These experienced teacher educators engaged 12 white student teachers in two different settings in "supportive, trusting dialogical conversations" about the "taboo subjects" of race, "Whiteness," and "White racism."

Marx and Pennington describe the "sincere changes in attitudes" of student teacher/ participants in these studies, their adoption of "new language," their ability to see, name, and reject racism within themselves, and deficit thinking (about the children) "in everything from their teacher education classes, to the media, to their own home lives" (p. 105). Three student teachers participated in Pennington's study. These future teachers apparently were stymied in their development by the realization that they "lacked the cultural knowledge to be effective in the classroom and to be effective in interacting with parents" (pp. 104–105). By contrast, Marx's group of nine student teachers reportedly had empowering experiences by confronting racism in their teaching placements.

It deserves mention that the researchers in these three studies justify their pedagogical interventions on moral grounds rather than on the basis of demonstrated long- or short-term individual or institutional changes. The researchers do not report impacts on the actual practice of these future teachers nor are learning outcomes for the students they taught (and tutored) described. Despite student resistance, unsupportive university colleagues, and the warnings McIntyre received from a "disgruntled" administrator, she affirms her responsibility "as a white educator ... to continue to provide prospective teachers" with opportunities to "see whiteness as a 'center stage problem' ..." Marx and Pennington also articulate an explicit moral commitment to this "controversial work" on behalf of children of color:

> Much of the work on Whiteness implies that the construct is too controversial, too risky, too complex to be used with undergraduates ... We also see the effect on the children ... Only when we are brave enough to undertake this kind of controversial work with our students and to fortify ourselves with the knowledge and skills we need to lead, will we be able to foster the necessary changes. Without this courage, our children of color will continue to be the ones left to absorb the truly destructive effects of White racism.
>
> (p. 107)

The committed stance of these teacher education practitioner-researchers mirrors the politically engaged practice of other scholars that will also be discussed in this chapter.

Unexamined/unintended implications: intersectionalities of race/gender/identity

One implication of researchers' attempts to address white teachers' "color-blind" thought through pedagogical interventions and practitioner inquiry is that the focus on "whiteness" may obscure other relevant identity considerations like gender (Gore, 1993). Much of the research on "whiteness" in teacher education is reported by white women teacher educators/researchers who are teaching mostly white female students. Cochran-Smith (2000) recounts her experience of becoming critically aware of her own "blind vision" regarding the continuing significance of race and racism in her teaching and research. Upon reflection, however she was able to gain the insight that white women teacher educators need to address the intersections of race *and* gender identity issues that are inherent in social justice teacher education. What Cochran-Smith recalls with regard to her own practice is worth noting:

> "We," I came to realize, often referred not to "we who are committed to teaching elementary school differently and improving the life chances of all children," but to "we White people (*especially we White women*) who are trying to learn how to teach people who are different from us."
>
> (Cochran-Smith, 2000, p. 98, emphasis added)

In analyses of her teaching Cochran-Smith acknowledges that when the perspectives and experiences of the oppressed are not "sufficiently present" to inform the work, "blind-vision" can impair the efforts of white teacher educators to address issues of race, diversity, and social justice. She recalled, for example, discussions that had clearly focused attention on race in her work with future teachers. However, hindsight provided some understanding of what had escaped her vision and was missing in her approach:

> It is clear to me now, though, that these discussions [in the teacher education program] were framed primarily for the benefit of White students who were invited to learn more about racism through stories of other people's oppression.
>
> (p. 92)

Two other research contexts are relevant in illuminating perspective blindness with respect to race/gender intersectionalities. First, in revisiting the data presented in their book, *The Feminist Classroom*, Maher and Tetrault (1997) acknowledge that they lacked the interpretive framework needed to "see" the ways that a (feminist) "pedagogy of positionality" must also excavate whiteness (p. 322). Using whiteness/race as a lens, their re-analysis reveals what had previously escaped their vision. Second, Berlak and Moyenda's (2001) collaborative analysis of a classroom encounter with "whiteness" precipitated a reflective dialogue between the two women—a white Jewish radical teacher educator and a "militant" Black teacher. Their dialogue represents a unique examination of the intersectionality of race, identity, and gender in a teacher education context. Black and Latino/a teachers and teacher educators too often bear the "burden" of seeing what whites often do not see regarding the "taboo" work of dealing with race, often without adequate support from their white colleagues and administrators (Jervis, 1996; Williams & Evans-Winters, 2005).

This discussion of the intersectionality of race, gender, and identity suggests needed directions for research. For instance, do white women teachers and teacher educators experience racialized anxieties, "resentments" or "blind vision" in gendered ways that differ from the experiences of white males? Do these dispositions affect their ability to work with families and communities of color? With boys and girls in their classrooms? Do Black women and Black men working with white women in teaching and research contexts experience particular antagonisms or vulnerabilities with regard to "whiteness" (or "blackness") that are exacerbated by their differing historical experiences of race and gender? Finally, critical social theory defines ideology as "an organized belief system that represents social change as impossible, even if it suggests modes of individual betterment within the frame of reference of the existing social system" (Agger, 1998, p. 8). Sleeter and Bernal (2004) refer to ideology as "consciousness formation" of individuals, "particularly their consciousness about how the society works" (p. 242). Do educators—no matter what their background—who are using a critical theoretical framework envision a collective future for children of color? Examples of practitioner inquiry in which the focus is on teachers learning to teach for social change in urban and culturally diverse communities are presented the next section of the chapter.

A CONTINUUM OF PRACTITIONER INQUIRY: LEARNING TO TEACH FOR SOCIAL CHANGE

The genre of practitioner inquiry usually refers to practice-based research conducted by practicing teachers. Also included is the study of practice *for* teacher education by teacher educators. The forms of practitioner inquiry discussed below include collaborative action research partnerships and guided community-mediated inquiry experiences to support pre-service and in-service teacher learning. These research approaches can be located along a continuum of practice-centered knowledge about teaching and teacher learning (in schools and teacher preparation programs) from individual self-study to collective action research to guided community-based inquiry in which learning from and with community members takes precedence.

Several major analyses of the various types of practitioner inquiry are available (Anderson *et al.*, 1994; Cochran-Smith & Lytle, 2004; Zeichner & Noffke, 2001). Practitioner inquiry, that is, "systematic, intentional inquiry by teachers" (Lytle & Cochran-Smith, 1999, p. 84), is the term Cochran-Smith and Lytle (2004) use as a "conceptual and linguistic umbrella" to cover a number of research genres and modes of inquiry in which teachers engage in practice-centered investigation. Their extensive review of the literature demonstrates multiple and varying descriptions of forms of practitioner inquiry. Included are genres of research focused on teacher knowledge about teaching, pre-service teachers' experiences while learning to teach (Britzman, 1991), collaborative investigations with practitioners and teacher educators, as well as the practice of teacher educators as the focus of inquiry. Rosiek and Atkinson (2005) identify three practitioner inquiry approaches related to understanding teacher knowledge and the process of learning to teach: (1) narrative inquiry/analysis, (2) action research, and (3) teacher research. These categories of practitioner inquiry are discussed below.

Narrative inquiry

Narrative inquiry, also referred to as self-narrative inquiry (Garcia, 1997), is multifaceted and includes various methods of practitioner inquiry, such as teacher reflective writing (in journals and diaries, for instance) and autobiographical writing. Autoethnography can also be included in this genre (Olsen, 2000). Forms of narrative inquiry such as teachers' stories and life narratives reveal aspects of teacher knowledge and the experience of learning to teach in different contexts (Clandinin & Connelley, 1990, 2000). For example, these methods have been used to explore the experiences of teacher support groups for novice teachers (Stanislaus *et al.*, 2002) and the learning trajectories of pre-service teachers in "inner-city" teaching situations (Kea & Bacon, 1999; Rushton, 2001). Narrative inquiry reveals rich details of practical teacher knowledge and beliefs about teaching and learning. Like other forms of practitioner inquiry, studies of teacher learning using narrative forms seek their validation in the ways that "inquiry transforms practice" (Rosiek & Atkinson, 2005, p. 425; see also Feldman, 2003).

As the following journal reflection demonstrates, however, practitioner inquiry studies may show no evidence of teacher learning to transform their practice from the point of view of the lived experiences and epistemologies of diverse "others." Consider the lack of insight, empathy, and critical understanding in this journal entry, for example:

> What do you do with children who will not do their work, and every time somebody even brushed them they "explode in anger" but yet you know that their daddy is a drug dealer and they probably only get two hours of sleep a night?
>
> (Rushton, 2004, p. 74)

This study reports this student teacher's "unfavorable" classroom journey in an inner-city school resulted in a decision not to pursue a teaching career. Several studies by Cochran-Smith (1995; 1991), which have been collected in the volume *Walking the Road: Race Diversity and Social Justice in Teacher Education*, represent powerful examples of learning to teach for social change (Cochran-Smith, 2004) in ways that address such deficit thinking. In this body of work Cochran-Smith draws on teacher narratives to document the experiences of teachers learning to "teach against the grain." The narrative accounts of these future teachers demonstrate how they come to see themselves as "both educators and activists." Cochran-Smith provides a coherent theoretical rationale for this pedagogical approach.

Practitioner (narrative) inquiry research that documents the "voice" of pre-service teachers working in inner city schools, in particular, which has frequently involved single case-studies, is limited with respect to developing broader theoretical understandings (or generalizations) across contexts and situations (Rushton, 2004). Although forms of practitioner research have gained considerable ascendancy, this genre of research remains engaged for the most part with a "narrow range" of theory (Noffke, 1999). Indeed, largely missing from pre-service practitioner inquiry studies are forms of teacher knowledge and practice-centered theory generated from within the cultural realities and epistemologies of students of color, their families, and communities. Cochran-Smith's (2004) research documents teacher learning in this direction. She suggests that teacher educators-researchers may also need to rethink what and how they teach in this regard and notes that "theories of practice developed by and about persons of color, as well as rich and detailed analyses of successful teachers of children of color, particularly poor children of color . . ." were missing from her work (p. 97, originally published in 2000). Alternatively, Ball's study of the knowledge teachers need to effectively teach writing to African American vernacular English speakers recognizes the need not only for high expectations in the dominant society's terms "but also standards of the students' subcultures" (Ball, 1999, p. 243). Finding ways to draw upon and incorporate the perspectives and lived experience of community members in teacher learning and practitioner research in community contexts is an important dimension of the example of action research that is discussed next.

Action research as community-mediated inquiry

Action research, which can take many forms, has provided opportunities for both experienced teachers and future teachers to gain access to and to learn from community knowledge and perspectives (Gore & Zeichner, 1991). Noffke, one of the leading practitioners of action research in the field of teacher education, describes action research as "political, theorized practice" (Noffke, 1995, p. 3). This method of practitioner inquiry consists of a cyclical process of planning, acting, observing, and reflecting. Noffke and Somehk (2005) identify three types of action research: (1) the professional action research (focused on "improving services in a professional setting"), (2) the personal (focused on attaining "greater self-knowledge" and "a deeper understanding of one's own practice"), and (3) the political (focused on "social action to combat oppression").

The example of action research that will be discussed here is Hyland and Noffke's (2005) long-term collaborative teacher education action research program. These teacher educator-researchers have studied their own practice with white pre-service teachers by combining teaching with two levels of practitioner inquiry focused on: (a) their own practice and (b) the learning-to-teach for change experiences of their pre-service students. Hyland and Noffke state that their aim was to deepen their understanding of "how community-based pre-service work may be used to develop a critical multicultural approach to the teaching of social studies" (p. 370). In collaborative inquiries in their social studies methods courses, taught in their respective teacher education programs at two different institutions, Hyland and Noffke use examples of the students' learning as well as focus group discussions, journal writing responses to assigned critical readings, and community inquiry experiences as data. These teacher educator-researchers use these multiple data sources to ask about the impact of "critical study of injustice in history, politics, economics, and geography" (p. 371). They ask, for example, "In what ways do community inquiry assignments influence pre-service teachers' understanding of marginality?" And "how do students see themselves in relation to the communities they investigate?"

According to Hyland and Noffke, teachers "need to understand and interrogate oppression in order to act against it in their classrooms." Their action research program also demonstrates their belief that "teachers need to become allied with marginalized communities in the fight for social justice" (p. 379). For instance, they asked students at one of their institutions to develop a relationship with a community member and to collaborate on a lesson that used the perspective, life history, knowledge, talents or interests of the community member in that lesson. By using learning-to-teach experiences that involve community-mediated practitioner inquiry, Hyland and Noffke consciously model for their students some of the ways that curriculum and teaching can address social justice goals. These researchers report new understandings of ways to incorporate inquiry methods into their own teaching.[10]

Developing pre-service teachers' self-understanding (and self-efficacy) in relation to teaching students from "historically marginalized" groups is one goal of the community-mediated inquiry activities Hyland and Noffke studied through collaborative action research. They note the fundamental importance of gaining "historical perspective" about the group being investigated for "making sense" of these inquiry experiences. The assigned critical readings provide "authentic perspectives of the group being studied" and are "essential to the inquiry experience" (p. 378).[11] Some level of prejudice reduction among the student teachers is one result of these inquiry experiences that is documented in students' oral and written narratives, collaborative reflections, and seminar discussions. However, these researchers also call attention to an important drawback in their approach. In their efforts as critical educators who are conscious of gender issues from a feminist perspective, Hyland and Noffke attempt to resolve the contradiction of power and authority in their classrooms by giving their pre-service students the freedom to choose (comfortable) "cultural boundaries" to "cross." They acknowledge that students sometimes choose the least "challenging" cross-cultural community inquiry experiences.

In addition, Hyland and Noffke report that community learning experiences can re-inscribe various forms of privileged positionality related to the student teachers' race, gender, and class identity. In fact, pre-service students' fear of going into urban neighborhoods is a recurring theme in the literature (Buck & Sylvester, 2005; Duncan, 2002; Swartz, 2003). Moreover, practitioner inquiry focused on teachers learning to center students of color in their own cultural identities and heritages, as well as the needs of their communities, is still largely missing from this genre of research (Goodwin & Swartz, 2004). Practitioner inquiry also tends to neglect teachers' cultural and historical knowledge, that is, the mis-education of teachers that contributes to the problems of "whiteness" and dysconsciousness (King, 1991a). A number of teacher educator-researchers with considerable experience using anti-racism approaches in their courses speculate that college-level teacher preparation may actually be too late to change the deficit thinking and dysconsciousness of some future teachers (Berlak & Moyenda, 2001; McIntyre, 2002; Swartz, 2003). As will be discussed below, in contrast to course-based learning, teacher inquiry in the context of ethnographic study groups, learning communities, and communities of practice seem to provide support for more critical learning.

Ethnographic methods, practitioner inquiry and communities of color

Ethnographic research that engages experienced practitioners as co-researchers (Allen & Labbo, 2001; Bernal, 2002; Moll & Gonzáles, 2004) has generated forms of practical knowledge for teaching that build upon the "funds of knowledge" in the households of marginalized students (Gonzáles *et al.*, 2005). This research recognizes that successful teachers of low-income students and students of color respect, have knowledge of, and establish relationships with students' home communities (Irvine, 2003; Ladson-Billings, 1994; Moll *et al.*, 1995; Zeichner & Melnick, 1996). As Moll (2005) has noted:

> Teacher education is . . . a matter of developing not only technical competence and solid knowledge of subject matter but also sociocultural competence in working with the diversity of student that characterize contemporary schooling.

(p. 244)

Torres-Guzmán, Mercado, Quintero, and Viera (with Moll, 1994) are among a new breed of researchers of color who have designed new roles for students, parents, and teachers to participate in collaborative ethnographic research. Their research project in New York City and Puerto Rico, and supported both teacher and student learning in and about Puerto Rican communities in new ways. Moll and Gonzáles have led this program of collaborative ethnographic practitioner research for more than two decades in Arizona and other locales. Practitioner inquiry experiences are combined with ethnographic home visits in order to identify social and cultural practices that can inform classroom instruction. Researchers and their practitioner co-researchers report that these forms of collaborative inquiry deepen teachers' understanding of structural inequities by positioning them to "view urban communities as reservoirs of strength, possibility, and talent"

(Buck & Sylvester, 2005, cited in Moll & Hopffer, 2005, p. 246). This is an important dimension of the way the cultural "funds of knowledge" research program makes the intellectual, social, and cultural assets in families "pedagogically viable."

In summary, the growing acceptance of teacher education research produced in collaboration with practitioners represents a "hard-won paradigm shift" in the field (Cochran-Smith & Lytle, 2004). Significant strides have been made in giving "voice" to teachers as researchers of their own practice, including accomplished teachers and teacher educators of color. In addition, with varying results practitioner inquiry mediated by community knowledge takes many forms using various methods. For example, Allan and Labbo (2001) as well as Hyland and Noffke (2005) report that action research in urban communities has positively impacted prospective teachers' learning when they use what they learned from self-reflective, community inquiries to develop lessons. Relatively brief excursions and more extensive immersion experiences include both observation and inquiry activities designed to "shake up" students' deficit views in order to foster more critical awareness and understanding (Bernal, 2002; Duncan, 2002; Garcia, 1997; Wiest, 1998). Hyland and Noffke (2005) stress an important dimension of the need for such approaches in teacher education: "Unless our White, heterosexual students learn to understand diversity in new ways, the children from these [underserved] groups in their classrooms will continue to have to live within the dominant culture everyday of their schooling" (p. 378). Assets or strengths-based approaches are gaining coherence in a growing body of research and scholarship that demonstrates the value of community-mediated inquiry experiences for teacher learning (Boyle-Baise & Sleeter, 2000; Oakes, Rogers & Lipton, 2006). Less systematically developed, however, are modes of inquiry in which full-fledged reciprocal research partnerships incorporate community knowledge and perspectives in the purposes and conduct of collaborative inquiry. A vision of critical and qualitative research in teacher education for the cultural survival of marginalized students and their communities, as well as for teacher learning, is taken up next in the last part of the chapter.

BEYOND THE CRISIS OF KNOWLEDGE IN TEACHER EDUCATION RESEARCH AND PRACTICE

Teacher education research is only beginning to address the complexities that developing theory and practice in authentic democratic partnerships among researchers, teachers, and urban/indigenous community members entails. Noffke's (1999) observation nearly a decade ago is worth repeating: "Theory generated within the work and lives of people of colour has only marginally been addressed" in teacher education research (p. 27). Murrell (2001) has made a similar observation that remains pertinent: the failure of educators "to draw on the local knowledge, perspectives, and cultural frameworks of people of color in diverse urban communities" is nothing less than a crisis of knowledge in urban education (p. 20). As Zeichner and Noffke (2001) point out, teacher education research is inherently connected to conceptualizations of teachers' work and also to "debates about the overall goals of education in society" (p. 298). Preparing teachers who have the knowledge, competence, and the will to meet the needs of underserved students of color in K-12 classrooms and who can center their students' learning in the epistemological perspectives of their families and communities remains beyond the purview of the high-stakes standardized testing regime's "conservative agenda to produce 'highly qualified teachers' " (Banks, 2004, p. ix; Malveaux, 2005).

Valuing/using community knowledge: a task for liberatory research

The "community nomination" method that Ladson-Billings (1994), following Foster (1993), employed to identify successful teachers of African American students illustrates how researchers can honor community knowledge, goals, and perspectives on education. Ladson-Billings relied upon the knowledge of community members to identify the criteria she used to select the teachers in her study of culturally relevant pedagogy. These criteria imply educational goals and pedagogy that transcend "conventional notions of the students getting good grades, scoring well on standardized tests, graduating from high school, going on to college, and securing good jobs . . ." (Ladson-Billings, 1994, p. 147). The parents Ladson-Billings interviewed "expressed an interest in an education that would help their children maintain a positive identification with their own culture." As one parent stated: "I just want [my child] to hold his own in the classroom without forgetting his own in the community" (p. 147).

This parent's goal, which expresses the communal ideal and social vision of the epistemology of African American achievement, can be understood as a "requirement for black existence." Whether in the classroom or a blues performance, the traditional African American cultural ideal values individual accomplishment in the context of community well-being. This ideal contradicts prevailing conceptions of educational purpose and quality (Heath, 1982; Murrell, 1997). Boggs's (1974) classic description of Black "education to govern" for the benefit of a transformed, more just, democratic society is consistent with Tedla's (1997) articulation of "community mindfulness" as a goal of Black education and socialization. Following are examples of teacher education practice that value and use community knowledge in various ways and which suggest research questions and modes of inquiry for cultural well-being that are missing in "mainstream" teacher education research and practice.

First, in the "Community Teacher" model for effective urban teaching that Murrell (2002) has developed teachers, parents, school leaders, and community members participate as full-fledged partners in ongoing, collaborative practice-based community-mediated inquiry that supports teachers' and African American students' learning. Second, Hyland and Meacham (2004) propose a Community Knowledge Centered model of transformative teacher education that is centered on the "important and vital knowledge" that community members possess and that educators can learn with and from them (p. 123). "Community Scholars," a project of New Ways to Learn, is a third model for teacher learning with and from community members. In this project (summarized in Figure 54.1) "low-income" public housing residents: (1) teach the teachers and teacher candidates how to respect low-income family members in schools and (2) decide to become schoolteachers themselves. Ishibashi describes this program:

> Between 2002-present several classes of established teachers, teacher candidates, and aspiring teachers in classes at San Francisco State University and the City College of San Francisco have experienced learning with and from Community Scholars. In collaboration with tenant associations in publicly subsidized housing, educational organizations, public schools, service learning and mentoring programs, partnerships have created collaborative spaces where "low-income" community members teach the teachers how to respect them, their children, and extended family/community members, and they decide to become formal (credentialed) teachers themselves.
>
> (Jean Ishibashi, 2006, Personal communication)[12]

Community Scholars was born out of the cross-cultural growth pains among low-income residents of publicly subsidized housing in the San Francisco Bay Area of Northern California, USA, Turtle Island, North America. At a training meeting conducted by Featherston & Associates, Jean Ishibashi, one of the participants, asked: "Do you want to teach the teachers in the schools of your family members how to cross-culturally respect you and your families?" The overwhelming answer was, "YES." Dean Perea of San Francisco State University asked Acting Chair of the Department of Administration and Interdisciplinary Studies, Vanessa Sheared (currently the Dean of the School of Education at California State University, Sacramento), if there were any classes that could include such a project in its curriculum. A multicultural/cross-cultural and bilingual education class was identified.

The methodology for the Community Scholars project is oral her/his/our story where low-income residents—parents, significant adults, guardians, extended family members—share and document stories of what worked and did not work for them in their formal schooling experience/s and what they are experiencing in relationship to the schools now with their children and grandchildren. It is significant that most of the Community Scholars are and have been mothers who face the challenges of the schools and the toll of mainstream oppression on their and their children's lives. The toll of racism and its intersection with class, gender, sexual orientation, religion/spirituality, family structure, language, dis/abilities and more are documented in stories that include ways that the m/others have been able to survive the attacks on their dignity and humanity. These attacks have included intergenerational poverty, drugs, and guns, and institutional policies that have targeted their families and communities and rarely benefited anyone from their communities.

In addition, the oral his/her/ourstories methodology in this project is participatory action research where the dialogues, conversations, and storytelling challenge, name, and transform perspectives of teachers and teacher candidates so that cross-cultural respect can be present in the classroom. The oral his/her/our story methodology includes emotional knowledge and cross-cultural knowledge that is often made invisible in printed form. Therefore, its potential to transform by speaking to the whole person is great. Body gestures/postures, tones, rhythms/cadences, silences, and facial expressions are significant indicators of how or whether or not cross-cultural respect is present. These indicators are often ignored much to the detriment of the student, the learning environment, and the greater community. Most schools of education do not include cross-cultural or critical multicultural curriculum where these critical indicators are taught, addressed, and presented by low-income community members. Power imbalances, often the root of disrespect, are not addressed. The cultural naming of policies such as "No Child Left Behind" is made invisible so that the master (universal) narrative becomes the one and only game in town. Freedom of choice and intellectual rigor are left outside the classroom door.

Figure 54.1 The community scholars program: a project of new ways to learn.

What distinguishes these three teacher education program approaches just discussed from the research in previous sections of this chapter? With the possible exception of the "funds of knowledge" ethnographic research collaboratives, each incorporates "authentic cultural knowledge of students' home communities" (Hyland & Meacham, 2004, p. 114) through sustained, reciprocal engagement with community participants' knowledge and ways of being. To the extent that community knowledge is salient as both content and process, these model approaches demonstrate important tenets of teacher education *practice* for cultural well-being. As such, these teacher education approaches represent *emergent* venues for cultural well-being *research* informed by the blues epistemology of the Black experience. Research within a cultural well-being framework from this epistemological perspective: benefits both teachers and the community; connects teaching and teacher education with the "Black struggle for being"; creates social inquiry spaces for (teachers and communities to be engaged in) the mutual investigation of the epistemic roots of the ideology of race (e.g. assaults on cultural blackness); and community building and social action in alliance with other groups are thus grounded in group-affirming heritage knowledge. Finally, these social inquiry spaces will provide opportunities for critical social and political investigation of community needs, for spiritual ways of knowing and healing for Black consciousness and to identify with humanity's struggle for freedom.

The crux of the matter is whose social vision prevails in racial-social justice-oriented research and how can this research be a liberating resource for social change? That is, what is the role of culture, heritage, and identity in research to combat the system of knowledge that propels racism and other forms of oppression? This question must be asked of various collaborative research-for-change efforts that engage students, teachers, and families as "critical" co-researchers (Cahill, 2004; Hammond, 2001; Morrell, 2004). My own research, which has not been identified in earlier publications using the terms "cultural well-being," has created "research-as-pedagogy" contexts that have engaged educators, parents, and researchers in reciprocal inquiry activities that have helped to illuminate the "requirements of black existence" understood as a condition of the general welfare (King, 1991b, 1992, 2005a, 2006; King & Mitchell, 1995). An important consideration in this body of work, as noted below, is to devise research methods that afford opportunities for critical investigation of community needs and cultural practice as well as teachers' knowledge and pedagogy:

> This methodology recognizes that particular knowledge of the world contained in people's daily cultural practice and social experience is not merely distorted by the dominant ideology. Rather, knowledge generated from and grounded in people's culture and experience can be liberating as well.
>
> (King & Mitchell, 1995, p. 67)

Black Studies and Ethnic Studies programs, an under-utilized resource for teacher learning and research, can provide opportunities for future teachers to gain access to community knowledge traditions and to interrogate the limitations of dominant knowledge. For example, Kiang (2004) describes a range of programmatic strategies using Asian American studies in a K-12/university partnership program that engaged Asian American prospective teachers in the recovery and affirmation of their cultural heritage. This program also provided African American and other teachers of color with valuable lessons about cultural diversity. Kiang concludes that ethnic studies programs can lead to and sustain powerful interventions in these areas precisely because of their foundational commitments to educational equity and social justice and their holistic relationships to diverse students, families, and communities.

Oakes *et al.* (2006) developed and describe various university-supported social "design experiments" that involve collaborative public inquiry and organizing for school and community change. This "learning power" program includes numerous examples of teachers, teacher educators, researchers, parents, and students engaged in sustained, "empowering" inquiry-based learning and "teaching for change" using critical and qualitative methods of research. (Morrell's (2004) critical ethnography is a previously discussed example.) These scholars cite the democratic grassroots organizing of civil rights movement leader/teacher Ella Baker as a model for this "learning power" approach. However, Baker's democratic social change methodology included coalition building from a "strong autonomous" African American community base (Ransby, 2003, p. 100). In Baker's practice this meant developing people's knowledge of and appreciation of their own history, culture, and identity—in the worker education curricula and in the Freedom Schools that she inspired, for example. As Woodson understood, such knowledge, from the ideological position of democracy, can facilitate multi-racial alliances but is also required to support the "space of being" marginalized groups need in a democratic society.

Teacher education research documents white teachers' resistance to investigating their "emotional investment in particular beliefs, assumptions, and worldviews" (Urrieta & Reidel, 2006, p. 282) and their resistance adversely affects teacher educators of color and others who are committed to equitable education (Scott, 2003). However, framing teacher education research within the limited terms of a demographic imperative impelled by the predominate number of white teachers is an epistemologically inadequate "logic of inquiry" (Stanfield & Dennis, 1993). Such a rationale risks remaining circumscribed within the limits of white teachers' mis-education and dysconsciousness (King, 2005b). Teachers need knowledge and skills that will enable them to teach in ways that foster students' intellectual and social development without diminishing the cultural identities, languages, and heritages of people of color. Educational and research purposes need to be broadened to include community perspectives. However, community participants involved in teacher learning also need opportunities to develop a critical understanding of their lived realities, cultural practice, and social histories. Researchers need methods of inquiry that can capture the beneficial effects of such knowledge and that provide support for community members' roles in contributing to and assessing the social utility of teachers' knowledge and pedagogical skills in the context of community change and survival needs (Patillo-McCoy, 1999). Knowledge of the societal episteme is required for all. The opportunity to use this liberating knowledge in inquiry-based partnerships for professional teacher preparation is akin to the mutuality between the audience and the blues performer. Such new forms of knowledge and accountability in collaborative teacher education research and practice within a cultural well-being framework have implications for "the very notion of knowledge and how our definitions of what counts as knowledge produce hierarchies of power that have both real and symbolic effects on people's lives" (Hyland & Meacham, 2004, p. 177).

CONCLUSION

Through the lens of a Black Studies analysis of the ideology of race, this chapter examines selected examples of critical and qualitative research in teacher education with racial-social justice aims. A focus on the value of community knowledge and marginalized epistemologies informs the discussion of four interrelated genres of critical and qualitative research "in, on, and for" teacher education. The chapter considers how and how well critical and qualitative methods of teacher education research value and use the social vision and epistemological perspectives of people of color. Also considered are models for collaborative research and practice that engage teachers and parents and community members in mutual learning.

The relevance of the blues epistemology for teacher education research is the authentic knowledge for cultural well-being this worldview perspective offers. The blues has been described as "a dispossessed people's alternative to suffering and silence" (Davis, 1995, p. 84). What is missing in critical and qualitative teacher education research and practice? Effective ways to use the "subjugated knowledge" of the dispossessed as a liberating educational tool for cultural well-being and human freedom are lacking (Hyland & Meacham, 2004, p. 123). Also needed are spaces for social inquiry in which teachers, researchers, and community members can seek understanding in order to challenge the epistemic foundations of ideological racism in knowledge, research, and pedagogy. Historical understanding is crucial to address this crisis of knowledge in teacher education. At a time when "many people have lost hope in the possibility of liberal reform" in the U.S. (Bush, 2004, p. 11), West observes that it is time for a "blues nation to learn from a blues people"—Black Americans. Yet, Black people's cultural survival has never been in greater jeopardy. Duncan (2002) remarks that it is "fashionable nowadays to downplay and even dismiss race as a fact shaping the quality of life in the United States ... in favor [of] class-based and gender-based approaches to understanding social oppression" (p. 93). It is even more fashionable to eschew anything that has to do with humanity's debt to Africa and the African heritage of African American people (Robinson, 2000).

Critical educators, as well as liberals and conservatives share a concern about whether racial/ethnic cultural identification "unifies" rather than "divides." Allen (2004) suggests a role for the subjugated knowledge of the oppressed in bringing about unity but within a transformed society:

> ... people of color must provide the major source of knowledge, inspiration, and sacrifice in humanity's collective liberation from white racism ... As people of color around the world engage in the struggle against global white supremacy, they should work to humanize both themselves and whites, *when strategic*. They should avoid the pull to follow the white model of humanity and instead replace repression with radical love ...
>
> (p. 134, emphasis added)

This is the universal message the blues epistemology conveys regarding another possible way of "being in the world" (Reagon, 2001)—a way of being that is an urgently needed alternative to the "western bourgeois model" of the human (Wynter, 2006). This model falsely defines being human in terms of the anachronistic construct of race.

The spectacle of a white man, a prominent community leader, weeping openly on national television because rescuers had failed to arrive in New Orleans after hurricane Katrina to save not only Black lives but white people as well, suggests a vital lesson the blues has affirmed for quite a long time:

> If we are ever going to be a civilized [nation], we are going to have to begin to work as hard for the weakest and most maligned among us as we do for the strongest and most sympathetic. If we don't, any of us could one day face the consequences.
>
> (Sothern, 2005, p. 22)

Methods for transformative engagement with the Black experience, including study of the overcoming human spirit and conditions that continue to give rise to the hopeful determination of the blues, expressed in the most maligned of American languages (African American Home Language), offer a possible way out of the "utter terribleness of our new millennium" (Baker, 2001, p. 10). A "blues epistemology" for critical and qualitative teacher education research acknowledges Black people's humanity, articulates cultural well-being as a reason for knowing, and allays a white discourse of guilt/innocence. We are all implicated.

Coda

It's all my fault / I musta / Did somebody wrong ...
Everything that's happened / You know I am to blame.
I'm gonna find me a doctor / Maybe my luck will change.
My mother told me these days / Would surely come.

I wouldn't listen to her / Said I gotta have some fun.
I musta / Did somebody wrong . . .

Elmore James, Blues Artist Extraordinaire

NOTES

1 Kathe Jervis, "How Come There Are No Brothers on that List?" (1996, p. 2.).
2 Aaron Broussard, President, Jefferson Parish, Louisiana, Interview with Tim Russert, "Meet the Press," MSNBC, September 4, 2005.
3 Cited by Susan E. Noffke, (1999, p. 29).
4 This student-teacher shared this information in class, with an apology, after she and other students had vehemently complained that this "cross-cultural communication" course was a "waste of time". See King & Ladson-Billings, 1990.
5 This song is also titled, "Going to Shout All Over God's Heaven." See http://www.negrospirituals.com, retrieved November 1, 2006.
6 I use American Indian and Native American to refer to the indigenous peoples of the Americas, including the United States.
7 The "X" in the Xicana/Xicano movement, which replaces the "Ch" in Chicana/o, symbolizes the "all encompassing" political and spiritual struggle connecting different indigenous peoples throughout North, Central and South America, some of whom identify ancestral connections with the ancient Aztecs. A Xicana/Xicano movement "without borders" has evolved out of the Mexican American (Chicano/a) movement in the U.S. Southwest. "Raza" means race in Spanish. See Berta-Avila (2004), Note 1.
8 On the other hand, Elam and Jackson (2005) in *Black Cultural Traffic* examine "mass popular culture" using the category of "black popular culture" without denying aspects of its dynamic "hybridity."
9 See Horne's (2005) illuminating research on intersecting Black American, Mexican, and Mexican American histories in the U.S. and Mexico. Also, activist Yuri Kochiyama's memoir illustrates Black and Asian relations in the struggle for human rights (Fujino, 2005; Kochiyama, 2004). See also http://www.aasc.ucla.edu/archives/passingitonpress.htm. Retrieved on November 1, 2006.
10 Buck and Sylvester (2005) report a similar approach using "community liaisons" to mediate pre-service students' "entry" into urban communities. These community members facilitate pre-service students' community ethnographies focused on identifying "funds of knowledge" or community assets.
11 "Blues in the Schools," a program that is available in many schools, would also facilitate such learning. See http://www.blues.org/bits/index.php4. Retrieved November 1, 2006.
12 The Board of Directors are: Jacqueline Elaine Featherston (formerly Elena Featherston), Alexandra Featherston Gomez, Virginia R. Harris, Jean Ishibashi, Margo Okazawa-Rey, Gwen Orro, Sylvia Ramirez, Noemi Sohn, and Diana Vielmann. This group of women of color, including low-income women, named the organization: New Ways To Learn. The project name, "Community Scholars," was suggested by the late Dr. Beverly Robinson, of UCLA, an oral historian from the San Francisco Bay Area. (J. Ishibashi, personal communication).

REFERENCES

Agger, B. (1998) *Critical social theories: an introduction*. Boulder, CO: Westview Press.

Allen, R. L. (2004) Whiteness and critical pedagogy. *Educational Philosophy and Theory*, 36(2), 122–136.

Allen, J. & Labbo, L. (2001) Giving it a second thought: making culturally engaged teaching culturally engaging. *Language Arts*, 79(1), 40–52.

Anderson, G. L. (1989) Critical ethnography in education: origins, current status and new directions. *Review of Educational Research*, 59(3), 249–270.

Anderson, G., Herr, K., & Hihlen, A. (1994) *Studying your own school: an educator's guide to qualitative practitioner research*. Thousand Oaks, CA: Corwin Press.

Asher, R., Fairbank, H., & Love, A. (2006) *Creating community: aesthetic education at Queens College*. Queens, New York: Queens College Publication Series.

Ball, A. (1999) Evaluating the writing of culturally and linguistically diverse students: the case of the African American vernacular English speaker. In C.R. Cooper & L. Odell (eds.) *Evaluating writing: the role of teachers' knowledge about text, learning and culture* (pp. 225–248). Urbana, IL: National Council of Teachers of English.

Baker, H. A. (2001) *Turning South again: re-thinking modernism/re-reading Booker T.* Durham, NC: Duke University Press.

Banks, J. (1991) Teaching multicultural literacy to teachers. *Teacher Education*, 4(1), 135–144.

Banks, J. (2004) Series Foreword. In M. Cochran-Smith, *Walking the road: race, diversity and social justice in teacher education* (pp. vii–x). New York: Teachers College.

Banks, J. & Banks, C. M. (2004) (eds.) *Handbook of research on multicultural education* (2nd edition). San Francisco: Jossey-Bass.

Barlow, W. (1989) *Looking up, looking down: the emergence of blues culture*. Philadelphia: Temple University Press.

Beauboeuf-Lafontant, T. (1999) Movement against and beyond boundaries: "politically relevant teaching" among African American teachers. *Teachers College Record*, 100(4), 702–723.

Berlak, A. & Moyenda, S. (2001) *Taking it personally: racism in the classroom from kindergarten to college*. Philadelphia: Temple University Press.

Bernal, D. D. (1998) Using a Chicana epistemology in educational research. *Harvard Educational Review*, 68(4), 555–582.

Bernal, D. D. (2002) Critical race theory, Latino critical theory and critical raced-gendered epistemologies: recognizing students of color as holders and creators of knowledge. *Qualitative Inquiry*, 8(1), 105–126.

Berta-Avila, M. I. (2004) Critical Xicana/Xicano educators: is it enough to be a person of color? *High School Journal*, 87(4), 66–79.

Boggs, G. L. (ed.) (1974) Education: the great obsession: institute for the Black world. Education and Black struggle: notes from the colonized world, *Harvard Educational Review* (pp. 61–68), Monograph No. 2.

Boyle-Biase, M. & Sleeter, C. (2000) Community based service learning for multicultural education: an exploratory study. *Educational Foundations*, 14(2), 33–50.

Brayboy, B. (2005) Towards a tribal critical race theory in education. *The Urban Review*, 37(5), 425–446.

Brady, J. F. (2000) Critical feminist pedagogy. In D. Gabbard (ed.) *Knowledge and power in the global economy: politics and rhetoric of school reform* (pp. 369–74). Mahwah, NJ: Erlbaum.

Brady, J. F. & Hammett, R. F. (1999) Reconceptualizing leadership from a feminist postmodern perspective. *The Review of Education, Pedagogy, Cultural Studies*, 21(1), 41–61.

Brady, J. F. & Kanpol, B. (2000) The role of critical multicultural education and feminist thought in teacher preparation: putting theory into practice. *Educational Foundations*, 14(3), 39–50.

Britzman, D. (1991) *Practice makes practice: a critical study of learning to teach*. Albany: SUNY Press.

Buck, P. & Sylvester, P. S. (2005) Pre-service teachers enter urban communities: coupling funds of knowledge research and critical pedagogy in teacher education. In N. Gonzales, L. C. Moll, & C. Amanti (eds.), *Funds of knowledge: theorizing practices in households, communities, and classrooms* (pp. 213–232). Mahwah, NJ: Lawrence Erlbaum Associates, Inc.

Bush, M. (2004) *Breaking the code of good intentions: everyday forms of whiteness*. Lanham, MD: Rowman & Littlefield.

Cahill, C. (2004) Defying gravity? Raising consciousness through collective research. *Children's Geographies*, 2(2), 273–286.

Carspecken, P. F. (1996) *Critical ethnography in educational research: a theoretical and practical guide*. New York: Routledge.

Carney, J. A. (2001) *Black rice: the African origins of rice cultivation in the Americas*. Cambridge, MA: Harvard University Press.

Carr, W. & Kemmis, S. (1986) *Becoming critical: education, knowledge and action research.* London: The Falmer Press.

Chapman, T. K. (2005) Expressions of "voice" in portraiture. *Qualitative Inquiry*, 11(1), 27–51.

Childs, J. B. (1989) *Leadership, conflict and cooperation in African-American social thought.* Philadelphia: Temple University Press.

Clandinin, D. J. & Connelley, M. F. (1990) Stories of experiences and narrative inquiry. *Educational Researcher*, 19(5), 2–14.

Clandinin, D. J. & Connelley, M. F. (2000) *Narrative inquiry: experiences and story in qualitative research.* San Francisco: Jossey-Bass.

Cochran-Smith, M. (1991) Learning to teach against the grain, *Harvard Educational Review* 51(3) 279–310.

Cochran-Smith (1995) Color blindness and basket making are not the answer: confront the dilemmas of race, culture, and language diversity in teacher education. *American Educational Research Journal*, 32(3), 493–522.

Cochran-Smith, M. (2000) Blind vision: unlearning racism in teacher education. *Harvard Educational Review*, 70(2), 157–190.

Cochran-Smith, M. (2004) *Walking the road: race, diversity and social justice in teacher education.* New York: Teacher's College Press.

Cochran-Smith, M. (2005) Studying teacher education: what we know and what we need to know. *Journal of Teacher Education*, 56(4), 301–306.

Cochran-Smith, M. & Lytle, S. (1990) Research on teaching and teacher research: the issues that divide. *Educational Researcher*, 19(2), 2–11.

Cochran-Smith, M. & Lytle, S. (2004) Practitioner inquiry, knowledge, and university culture. In J. Loughran, M. L. Hamilton, V. LaBoskey, & T. Russell (eds.), *International handbook of research of self-study of teaching and teacher education practices* (pp. 2–74). Norwell, MA: Kluwer Publishers.

Cochran-Smith, M., Davis, D., & Fries, K. (2004) Multicultural teacher education: research, practice and policy. In J. A. Banks, & C. M. Banks (eds.) *Handbook of research on multicultural education* (2nd edition, pp. 931–975). San Francisco: Jossey-Bass.

Collins, P. H. (2000) *Black feminist thought: knowledge, consciousnesss, and the politics of empowerment.* New York: Routledge.

Cone, J. (1972) *The spirituals and the blues: an interpretation.* Maryknoll, NY: The Seabury Press.

Connelley, M. F. & Clandinin, D. J. (1999) *Shaping a professional identity: stories of educational practice.* San Francisco: Jossey-Bass.

Davis, F. (1995) *The history of the blues: the roots, the music, the people.* Cambridge, MA: Da Capo Press.

DeMarrais, K. B. & LeCompte, M. (1999) *The way schools work: a sociological analysis of education.* New York: Longman.

Dixson, A. & Rousseau, C. K. (2005) And we are still not saved: critical race theory in education ten years later. *Race & Ethnicity*, 8(1), 7–27.

Duncan, G. A. (2002) Critical race theory and method: rendering race in urban ethnographic research. *Qualitative Inquiry*, 8(1), 85–104.

Duncan, G. A. (2004) Systemic analysis. In S. Goodwin & S. Swartz (eds.), *Teaching children of color: seven constructs of effective teaching in urban schools* (pp. 66–75). Rochester, NY: Rochester Teacher Association Press.

Duncan, G. A. (2005) Critical race ethnography in education: narrative, inequality and the problem of epistemology. *Race, Ethnicity and Education*, 8(1), 93–114.

Elam, H. J. & Jackson, K. (2005) *Black cultural traffic: crossroads in global performance and popular culture.* Ann Arbor: The University of Michigan Press.

Ellsworth, E. (1998) Why doesn't this feeling empowering? Working through the repressive myths of critical pedagogy. *Harvard Educational Review*, 59, 297–327.

Feldman, A. (2003) Validity and quality in self-study. *Educational Researcher*, 32(3), 26–28.

Fisher, M. T. (2003) Open mics and open minds: spoken word poetry in African Diaspora participatory literacy communities. *Harvard Educational Review*, 73(3), 362–389.

Fisher, M. T. (2006) Building a literocracy: diaspora literacy and heritage knowledge in participatory literacy communities. In A. Ball (ed.), *With more deliberate speed: achieving equity and excellence in education—realizing the full potential of Brown v. Board of Education*. 105th Yearbook of the National Society for the Study of Education (pp. 361–381). Chicago: NSSE.

Foster, M. (1993) Educating for competence in community and culture. *Urban Education*, 27(4), 300–412.

Freire, P. (1970/1993) *Pedagogy of the oppressed*. New York: Continuum Press.

Fujino, D. (2005) *Heartbeat of the struggle: the revolutionary life of Yuri Kochiyama*. Minneapolis: University of Minnesota Press.

Garcia, S. (1997) Self-narrative inquiry in teacher development: living and working in just institutions. In J. E. King, E. R. Hollins, & W. C. Hayman (eds.), *Preparing teachers for cultural diversity* (pp. 146–155). New York: Teachers College Press.

Garcia, S. (2000) Education and ambigous borders in Mexican corridos thriving in the United States. In H. von Sigrid Rieuwerts & H. Stein (eds.), *Bridging the cultural divide: our common ballad heritage* (pp. 124–134). New York: Georg Olms Hildesheim.

Garon, P. (1995) White Blue. *Race Traitor*, 4 (Winter). Retrieved November 1, 2007 from http://racetraitor.org/blues.html

Giroux, H. (1988) *Schooling and the struggle for public life: critical pedagogy in the modern age*. Minneapolis: University of Minneapolis Press.

Gleason, T. (2006) Beyond bondage: situating "Africa" in the mind of Carter G. Woodson. In R. Burkett, P. McDaniels III, & T. Gleason. *The mind of Carter G. Woodson as reflected in the books he owned, read and published*. Exhibition Catalogue (pp. 43–52). Atlanta, GA: Emory University.

Goodwin, S. & Swartz, E. (2004) *Teaching children of color: seven constructs of effective teaching in urban schools*. Rochester: Rochester Teachers Association Press.

Gonzáles, N., Moll, L. C., & Amanti, C. (eds.) (2005) *Funds of knowledge: theorizing practices in households, communities, and classrooms*. Mahwah, NJ: Lawrence Erlbaum Associates, Inc.

Gonzáles, N., Moll, L., Tenery, M. F., Rivera, A., Rendón, P., Gonzales, R., & Amanti, C. (2005) Funds of knowledge for teaching in Latino households. In Gonzáles, N., Moll, L. C., & Amanti, C. (eds.), *Funds of knowledge: theorizing practices in households, communities, and classrooms* (pp. 89–111). Mahwah, NJ: Lawrence Erlbaum Associates, Inc.

Gordon, B. M. (1990) The necessity of African American epistemology for educational theory and practice. *Journal of Education*, 172(3), 88–106.

Gordon, B. M. (1995) Knowledge construction, competing critical theories, and education. In J. A. Banks & C. M. Banks (eds.), *The handbook on research in multicultural education* (pp. 184–199). New York: Macmillan.

Gore, J. (1993) *The struggle for pedagogies: critical and feminist discourses as regimes of truth*. New York: Routledge.

Gore, J. & Zeichner, K. M. (1991) Action research and reflective teaching in preservice teacher education: a case study from the United States. *Teaching and Teacher Education*, 7, 119–136.

Grande, S. (2004) *Red pedagogy: Native American social and political thought*. Lanham, MA: Rowman and Littlefield Publishers.

Hammond, L. (2001) Notes from California: an anthropological approach to urban science education for language minority student families. *Journal of Research in Science Teaching*, 38(9), 983–999.

Heath, S. B. (1982) What no bedtime story means: narrative skills at home and school. *Language in Society*, 11(1), 49–76.

Heath, S. B. (1989) Oral and literate traditions among Black Americans living in poverty. *American Psychologist*, 44(2), 367–373.

Hensley, M. (2005) Empowering parents of multicultural backgrounds. In Gonzáles, N., Moll, L. C., & Amanti, C. (eds.). *Funds of knowledge: theorizing practices in households, communities, and classrooms* (pp. 143–151). Mahwah, NJ: Lawrence Erlbaum Associates, Inc.

Hilliard, A. G. (2001) "Race," identity, hegemony and education: what do we need to know now?

In H. Watkins, J. H. Lewis, & V. Chou (eds.), *Race and education: the roles of history and society in educating African American students* (pp. 7–33). Needham, MA: Allyn & Bacon.

hooks, b. (1997) *Teaching to transgress: education as the practice of freedom.* New York: Routledge.

Horne, G. (2005) *Black and Brown: African Americans and the Mexican Revolution, 1910–1920.* New York: NYU Press.

Hyland, N. E. & Meacham, S. (2004) Community-centered teacher education: a paradigm for socially just education transformation. In J. L. Kincheloe, A. Bursztyn, & S. Steinberg (eds.), *Teaching teachers: building a quality school of urban education* (pp. 113–134). New York: Peter Lang.

Hyland, N. E. & Noffke, S. E. (2005) Understanding diversity through social and community inquiry: an action research study. *Journal of Teacher Education*, 56(4), 367–381.

Ignatiev, N. (1995) *How the Irish became white.* New York: Routledge.

Irvine, J. J. (2003) *Educating teachers for diversity: seeing with a cultural eye.* New York: Teachers College Press.

Jenks, C., Lee, J.-O., & Kanpol, B. (2001) Approaches to multicultural education in preservice teacher education: philosophical frameworks and models for teaching. *The Urban Review*, 33(2), 87–105.

Jensen, R. (2005) *The heart of whiteness.* San Francisco: New Light Books.

Jervis, K. (1996) How come there are no brothers on that list? Hearing the hard questions all children ask. *Harvard Educational Review*, 66(3), 546–575.

Jones, L. (1963) *Blues people.* New York: William & Morris.

Kailin, J. (1994) Anti-racist staff development for teachers: considerations of race, class and gender. *Teaching and Teacher Education*, 10(2), 169–184.

Kailin, J. (1999) How white teachers perceive the problem of racism in their schools: a case study in "liberal" Lakeview. *Teachers College Record*, 100, 724–750.

Kaomea, J. (2003) "Reading erasure and making the familiar strange: defamiliarizing methods for research in formerly colonized and historically oppressed communities." *Educational Researcher*, 32(2), 14–25.

Kana'iaupuni, S. M. (2005) Ka'akālai kū kanaka: a call for strengths-based approaches from a Native Hawaiian perspective. *Educational Researcher*, 34(5), 32–38.

Kea, C. D. & Bacon, E. H. (1999) Journal reflections of preservice education students on multicultural experiences. *Action in Teacher Education*, 21(2), 34–50.

Kent, G. (1972) *Blackness and the adventure of western culture.* Chicago: Third World Press, 1972.

Kiang, P. N. (2004) Linking strategies and interventions in Asian American Studies to K-12 classrooms and teacher preparation. *International Journal of Qualitative Studies in Education*, 17(2), 199–225.

Kincheloe, J. L. (2004) The bizarre, complex, and misunderstood world of teacher education. In J. L. Kincheloe, A. Bursztyn, & S. Steinberg (eds.), *Teaching teachers: building a quality school of urban education* (pp. 1–50). New York: Peter Lang.

King, J. E. (1991a) Dysconscious racism: ideology, identity, and the miseducation of teachers. *Journal of Negro Education*, 60(2), 133–146.

King, J. E. (1991b) Unfinished business: Black student alienation and Black teachers' emancipatory pedagogy. In M. Foster (ed.), *Readings on equal education. Volume II: qualitative investigations into schools and schooling* (pp. 245–271). New York: AMS Press.

King, J. E. (1992) Diaspora literacy and consciousness in the struggle against mis-education in the Black community. *Journal of Negro Education*, 61(3), 317–340.

King, J. E. (1994) The purpose of schooling for African American children: including cultural knowledge. In E. R. Hollins, J. E. King, & W. C. Hayman (eds.), *Teaching diverse populations: formulating a knowledge base* (pp. 25–56). Albany: SUNY Press.

King, J. E. (1995) Culture-centered knowledge: Black studies, curriculum transformation and social action. In J. A. Banks & C. M. Banks (eds.), *The handbook of research on multicultural education* (pp. 265–290). New York: Macmillan.

King, J. E. (1997) "Thank you for opening our minds": on praxis, transmutation and Black studies in teacher development. In J. E. King, R. Hollins, & W. C. Hayman (eds.), *Preparing teachers for cultural diversity* (pp. 156–169). New York: Teachers College Press.

King, J. E. (1999a) In search of a method for liberating education and research: the half (that) has not been told. In C. A. Grant (ed.), *Multicultural research: a reflective engagement with race, class, gender and sexual orientation* (pp. 101–119). Philadelphia: Falmer Press.

King, J. E. (1999b) Race. In D. A. Gabbard (ed.), *Knowledge and power in the global economy? Politics and the rhetoric of school reform* (pp. 141–148). New York: Lawrence Erlbaum.

King, J. E. (2004) Culture-centered knowledge: Black studies, curriculum transformation and social action. In J. A. Banks & C. M. Banks (eds.), *The handbook of research on multicultural education* (2nd ed., pp. 349–378), 2nd edition. San Francisco: Jossey-Bass.

King, J. E. (ed.) (2005a) *Black education: a transformative research and action agenda for the new century.* Mahwah, NJ: Erlbaum.

King, J. E. (2005b) Rethinking the Black/White duality of our times. In A. Bogues (ed.), *Caribbean reasonings: after man, toward the human—critical essays on Sylvia Wynter* (pp. 25–56). Kingston, Jamaica: Ian Randle Publishers.

King, J. E. (2006) "If our objective is justice": diaspora literacy, heritage knowledge, and the praxis of critical studyin' for human freedom. In A. Ball (ed.), *With more deliberate speed: achieving equity and excellence in education—realizing the full potential of Brown v. Board of Education.* 105th Yearbook of the National Society for the Study of Education (pp. 337–357). Chicago: NSSE.

King, J. E. & Ladson-Billings, G. (1990) The teacher education challenge in elite university settings: developing critical perspectives for teaching in a democratic and multicultural society. *European Journal of Intercultural Studies*, 1(2), 15–30.

King, J. E. & Mitchell, C. A. (1995) *Black mothers to sons: juxtaposing African American literature with social practice.* New York: Peter Lang.

King, J. E. & Wilson, T. L. (1990) Being the soul-freeing substance: a legacy of hope in Afro humanity, *Journal of Education*, 172(2), 9–27.

King, S. & Castenell, L. (2001) Tenets to guide antiracist teacher education practice. In S. King & L. Castenell (eds.), *Racism and racial identity: implications for teacher education.* Washington, DC: American Association of Colleges for Teacher Education.

Kochiyama, Y. (2004) *Passing it on: a memoir.* Los Angeles: UCLA Center for Asian American Studies.

Ladson-Billings, G. (1994) *The dreamkeepers: successful teachers of African American children.* San Francisco: Jossey-Bass.

Ladson-Billings, G. (1995) Toward a theory of culturally relevant pedagogy. *American Educational Research Journal*, 32(3), 464–491.

Ladson-Billings, G. (1996) Silence as weapons: challenges of a Black professor teaching white students. *Theory Into Practice*, 35(2), 79–85.

Ladson-Billings, G. (1997) I know why this doesn't feel empowering: a critical race analysis of critical pedagogy. In Freire, P., Fraser, J. W., Macedo, D., & McKinnon, T. (eds.), *Mentoring the mentor: a critical dialogue with Paulo Friere* (pp. 127–141). New York: Peter Lang.

Ladson-Billings, G. (1999) Preparing teachers for diverse student populations: a critical race theory perspective. *Review of Research in Education*, 24, 211–247.

Ladson-Billings, G. (2000a) Critical race theory. In D. Gabbard (ed.), *Knowledge and power in the global economy: politics and rhetoric of school reform* (pp. 363–367). Mahwah, NJ: Lawrence Erlbaum Associates.

Ladson-Billings, G. (2000b) Fighting for our lives: preparing teachers to teach African American students. *Journal of Teacher Education*, 51(3), 206–214.

Ladson-Billings, G. (2000c) Racialized discourses and ethnic epistemologies. In N. Denzin & Y. Lincoln (eds.), *Handbook of qualitative research* (2nd edition, pp. 257–278). Thousand Oaks: Sage.

Ladson-Billings (2003) It's your world. I'm just trying to explain it: understanding our epistemological and methodological challenges. *Qualitative Inquiry*, 9(1), 5–12.

Ladson-Billings, G. (2005) *Beyond the big house: African American educators on teacher education.* New York: Teachers College Press.

Ladson-Billings, G. (2006) The meaning of Brown ... for now. In A. Ball (ed.), *With more deliberate speed: achieving equity and excellence in education—realizing the full potential of Brown v. Board of Education.* 105th Yearbook of the National Society for the Study of Education (298–315). Chicago: NSSE.

Ladson-Billings, G. & Tate, W. F. (1995) Toward a critical race theory of education. *Teachers College Record,* 97, 47–63.

Ladson-Billings, G. & Grant, C. A. (eds.) (1997) *Dictionary of multicultural education.* Phoenix, AZ: Oryx Books.

Lee, C. D. (2001) Comment. Unpacking culture, teaching, and learning: a response to the "power of pedagogy." In. W. H. Watkins, J. H. Lewis, & V. Chou (eds.), *Race and* education: *the roles of history and society in educating African American students* (pp. 87–99). Needham, MA: Allyn & Bacon.

Leonardo, Z. (2004) The color of supremacy: beyond the discourse of "White privilege." *Educational Philosophy and Theory,* 36(2), 137–152.

Levine, L. (1977) *Black culture and black consciousness: Afro-American folk thought from slavery to freedom.* Oxford: Oxford University Press.

Loewen, J. W. (1995) *Lies my teacher told me: everything your American history textbook got wrong.* New York: New Press.

Love, A. (2006) Teaching is learning: teacher candidates reflect on aesthetic education. *Teaching Artist Journal,* 4(2), 112–121.

Loveland, E. (2003, February) Achieving academic goals through place-based learning: students in five states show how to do it. *Roots,* 4(1). Retrieved February 15, 2005 from www.ruraledu.org/roots/roots03.htm#rr4.1

Lynn, M. (1999) Toward a critical race pedagogy. *Urban Education,* 33(5), 606–626.

Lynn, M., Yosso, T. J., Solórzano, D. G., & Parker, L. (2002) Guest editors' introduction: critical race theory and education: qualitative research in the new millennium. *Qualitative Inquiry* 8(1), 3–4.

Lytle, S. & Conchran-Smith, M. (1990) Learning from teacher research: a working typology. *Teachers College Record,* 92, 82–102.

Maher, F. A. & Thompson Tetreault, M. K. (1997) Learning in the dark: how assumptions of whiteness shape classroom knowledge. *Harvard Educational Review,* 67(2), 321–349.

McIntosh, P. (1993) Examining unearned privilege, *Liberal Education,* 79(1), 62ff.

McAllister, G. & Irvine, J. J. (2000) Cultural competency and multicultural teacher education. *Review of Educational Research,* 70(1), 3–24.

McCarthy, C. (1998) *The uses of culture: education and the limits of ethnic affiliation.* New York: Routledge.

McDaniels III, P. (2006) To move the masses and liberate the folk: the prophetic vision of Carter Godwin Woodson. In R. Burkett, P. McDaniels III, & T. Gleason, *The mind of Carter G. Woodson as reflected in the books he owned, read & published.* Exhibition Catalogue (pp. 25–43). Atlanta, GA: Emory University.

McLaren, P. (1995) White terror and oppositional agency: towards a critical multiculturalism. In C. Sleeter & P. McLaren (eds.), *Multicultural education, critical pedagogy and the politics of difference* (pp. 33–70). New York: SUNY Press.

McLaren, P. (2000) Critical pedagogy. In D. Gabbard (ed.), *Knowledge and power in the global economy: politics and the rhetoric of school reform* (pp. 345–353). Mahwah, NJ: Lawrence Erlbaum.

McLaren, P. & Farahmandpur, R. (2001) The globalization of capitalism and the new imperialism: notes toward a revolutionary pedagogy. *Review of Education, Pedagogy, Cultural Studies,* 23, 271–315.

McIntyre, A. (1997) *Making meaning of whiteness: exploring the racial identity of white teachers.* Albany: SUNY Press.

McIntyre, A. (2002) Exploring whiteness and multicultural education with prospective teachers. *Curriculum Inquiry,* 32(1), 32–48.

Maiga, H. (2005) What happens when the language of education is not the language of culture? In J. E. King (ed.), *Black education: a transformative research and action agenda for the new century*. Mahwah, NJ: Erlbaum.

Malveaux, J. (2005) Is the Department of Justice at war with diversity? *Diverse Issues in Higher Education*, 22(22), December 15, p. 39.

Marx, S. (2004) Regarding whiteness: exploring and intervening in the effects of white racism in teacher education. *Equity & Excellence in Education*, 37(1), 31–43.

Marx, S. & Pennington, J. (2003) Pedagogies of critical race theory: experimentations with white preservice teachers. *Qualitative Studies in Education*, 16(1), 91–110.

Mehan, H., Lintz, A., Okamoto, D. & Wills, J. (1995) Ethnographic studies of multicultural education in classrooms and schools. In J. A. Banks & C. M. Banks (eds.), *Handbook of research on multicultural education* (pp. 129–144). New York: Macmillan.

Moll, L. C. & Gonzáles, N. (2004) Engaging life: a funds of knowledge approach to multicultural education. In J. A. Banks & C. M. Banks (eds.), *Handbook of research on multicultural education* (pp. 699–715). San Francisco: Jossey-Bass.

Moll, L. C. & Arnot-Hopffer, E. (2005) Sociocultural competence in teacher education. *Journal of Teacher Education*, 56(3), 242–247.

Montecitos, C. (1994) Teachers of color and multiculturalism. *Equity & Excellence in Education*, 27(3), 34–42.

Morrell, E. (2004) *Becoming critical researchers: literacy and empowerment for urban youth*. New York: Peter Lang.

Morrell, E. & Collatos, A. M. (2002) Toward a critical teacher education: high school student sociologists as teacher educators. *Social Justice*, 29(4), 60–70.

Murrell, P. C., Jr. (1997) Digging again the family wells: a Freirian literacy framework as emancipatory pedagogy for African American children. In P. Freire, J. Fraser, D. Macedo, & T. McKinnon, (eds.), *Mentoring the mentor: a critical dialogue with Paulo Freire* (pp. 19–58). New York: Peter Lang.

Murrell, P. C., Jr. (2001) *The community teacher: a new framework for effective urban teaching*. New York: Teachers College Press.

Murrell, P. C., Jr. (2002) *African-centered pedagogy*. Albany: State University of New York Press.

Narode, R. & Rennie-Hill, L. (1994) Urban community study by preservice teachers. *Urban Education*, 29(1), 5–22.

Noffke, S. E. (1995) Action research and democratic schooling. In S. E. Noffke & R. B. Stevenson (eds.), *Educational action research: becoming practically critical* (pp. 1–10). New York: Teachers College.

Noffke, S. E. (1999) What's a nice theory like yours doing in a practice like this? And other impertinent questions about practitioner research. *Change: Transformations in Education*, 2(1), 25–35.

Noffke, S. E. & Brennan, M. (1997) Reconstructing the politics of action in action research. In S. Hollingsworth (ed.), *International action research: a casebook for educational reform* (pp. 63–68). New York: Falmer Press.

Noffke, S. E. & Somehk, B. (2005) Action research. In B. Somehk & C. Lewin (eds.), *Research methods in the social sciences* (pp. 89–96). London: Sage.

Noffke, S. E., Clark, B. G., Palmeri-Sautiago, J., Sadler, J., & Suujaa, M. (1996) Conflict, learning and change in a school/university partnership. *Theory Into Practice*, 35(3), 165–173.

Oakes, J., Rogers, J., & Lipton, M. (2006) *Learning power: organizing for education and justice*. New York: Teachers College Press.

Okpokodu, O. N. (2003) Teaching multicultural education from a critical perspective: challenges and dilemmas. *Multicultural Perspectives*, 5(4), 17–23.

Ortiz, P. (2005) *Emancipation betrayed: the hidden history of Black organizing and white violence in Florida from Reconstruction to the bloody election of 1920*. Berkeley: University of California Press.

Ortiz, A. M. & Rhoads, R. A. (2000) Deconstructing whiteness as part of a multicultural educational framework: from theory to practice. *Journal of College Student Development*, 41(1), 81–93.

Oyserman, D., Kemmelmeier, M., Fryberg, S., Brosh, H., & Hart-Johnson, T. (2003) Racial-ethnic self-schemas. *Social Psychology Quarterly*, 66(4), 333–347.

Palmer, R. (1982) *Deep blues: a musical and cultural history, from the Mississippi Delta to Chicago's South Side to the world*. New York: Penguin Books.

Parker, L. (2001) Comment: the social "deconstruction" of race to build African American education. In H. Watkins, J. H. Lewis, & V. Chou (eds.), *Race and education: the roles of history and society in educating African American students* (pp. 34–39). Needham, MA: Allyn & Bacon.

Parker, L. & Stovall, D. O. (2004) Actions following words: critical race theory connects to critical pedagogy. *Educational Philosophy and Theory*, 36(2), 167–183.

Parker, L., Deyhle, S., & Villenas, S. (eds.) (1999) *Race is . . . race isn't: critical race theory and qualitative studies in education*. Boulder, CO: Westview Press.

Pattillo-McCoy, M. (1999) *Black picket fences: privilege and peril among the Black middle class*. Chicago: University of Chicago Press.

Pizzaro, M. (1998) "Chicano/a Power!" epistemology and methodology for social justice and empowerment in Chicana/o communities. *Qualitative Studies in Education*, 11(1), 57–80.

Prager, J. (1982) American racial ideology as collective representation. *Ethnic and Racial Studies*, 5(1), 99–119.

Quiocho, A. & Rios, F. (2000) The power of their presence: minority group teachers and schooling. *Review of Educational Research*, 70(4), 485–528.

Ransby, B. (2003) *Ella Baker and the Black freedom movement: a radical democratic vision*. Chapel Hill: University of North Carolina Press.

Reagon, B. (2001) *If you don't go, don't hinder me: the African American sacred song tradition*. Lincoln: The University of Nebraska Press.

Robinson, R. (2000) *The debt: what America owes Black people*. New York: Dutton Books.

Roediger, D. (1998) *Black on white: Black writers on what it means to be white*. New York: Schocken Books.

Rogan, A. & de Kock, D. M. (2005) Chronicles from the classroom: making sense of the methodology and methods of narrative analysis. *Qualitative Inquiry*, 11(4), 628–649.

Rollo, A. (2006, November 2) The learning path of Patty Loew. *Diverse*, 23(19), 22–24.

Rosiek, J. & Atkinson, B. (2005) Bridging the divide: the need for a pragmatic semiotics of teacher knowledge research. *Educational Theory*, 55(4), 421–442.

Rushton, S. (2004) Using narrative inquiry to understand a student teacher's practical knowledge while teaching in an inner-city school. *The Urban Review*, 36(1), 61–79.

Scatamburlo-D'Annibale, V. & McLaren, P. (2004) Class dismissed? Historical materialism and the politics of "difference." *Educational Philosophy and Theory*, 36(2), 183–199.

Scott, K. A. (2003) My students think I'm Indian: the presentation of an African-American self to pre-service teachers. *Race, Ethnicity and Education*, 6(3), 211–226.

Sleeter, C. (1992, Spring) Resisting racial awareness: how teachers understand the social order from their racial, gender, and social class locations. *Educational Foundations*, 2, 7–32.

Sleeter, C. (2001) Epistemological diversity in research on preservice teacher preparation for historically underserved children. In W. Secada (ed.), *Review of Research in Education*, 25, 209–250.

Sleeter, C. & Grant, C. (1987) An analysis of multicultural education in the United States. *Harvard Educational Review*, 57(4), 421–444.

Sleeter, C. & Bernal, D. G. (2004) Critical pedagogy, critical race theory and anti-racist education. In J. A. Banks & C. A. McGee Banks (eds.). *Handbook of research on multicultural education* (pp. 240–258). San Francisco: Jossey-Bass.

Smith, G. H. (2004) Mai i te maramatanga ki to putanga mai o te tahuritana: from conscientization to transformation, 37(1), 46–52. Special Edition edited by M. Maaka. *Educational Perspectives: Journal of the College of Education/University of Hawaii at Manoa*.

Smith, L. T. (1999) *Decolonizing methodologies: Research and indigenous peoples*. London: Zed Books.

Smith-Maddox, R. & Solórzano, D. (2002) Using critical race theory, Paulo Freire's problem-posing method, and case study research to confront race and racism in education. *Qualitative Inquiry*, 8(1), 66–84.

Solórzano, D. (1997) Images and words that wound: critical race theory, racial stereotyping and teacher education. *Teacher Education Quarterly*, 24, 5–19.

Solórzano, D. & Yosso, T. (2002) Critical race methodology: counter-storytelling as an analytical framework for education research. *Qualitative Inquiry*, 8(1), 23–44.

Sothern, B. (2005, January) Left to die: how New Orleans abandoned its citizens in a flooded jail and a flawed system. *The Nation*, 282(1), 18–22.

Stanfield, J. & Dennis, R. M. (1993) *Race and ethnicity in research methods*. Newbury Park, CA: Sage Publications.

Stanislaus, R. N., Fallona, C., & Pearson, C. A. (2002) "Am I doing what I am supposed to be doing?" Mentoring novice teachers through the uncertainties and challenges of the first year of teaching. *Mentoring & Tutoring*, 10(1), 71–81.

Stevens, R., Wineburg, S., Herrenkohl, L. R., & Bell, P. (2005) "Comparative understanding of school subjects: past, present and future." *Review of Educational Research*, 75(2), 125–158.

Swartz, E. (2003) Teaching white preservice teachers: pedagogy for change. *Urban Education*, 38(3), 255–278.

Tate, W. F. (1996) Critical race theory. *Review of Research in Education*, 22, 201–247.

Tedla, E. (1977) Sankofan education for development of personhood. *Raising Standards: Journal of the Rochester Teachers Association*, 5 (1), 19–25.

Titon, J. T. (1990) *Down home Blues lyrics: an anthology from the post-World War II era*. Urbana: University of Illinois Press.

Torres-Guzman, M., Mercado, C. I., Quintero, A. H., Viera, D. R., & Moll, L. (1994) Teaching and learning in Puerto Rican Latino collaboratives: implications for teacher education. In E. R. Hollins, J. E. King, & W. C. Hayman (eds.), *Teaching diverse populations: formulating a knowledge base*. Albany: SUNY Press.

Urrieta, Jr. & Reidel, M. (2006) Avoidance, anger, and convenient amnesia: White supremacy and self-reflection in social studies teacher education. In E. W. Ross (ed.), *Race, ethnicity, and education: racism and anti-racism in education* (pp. 279–299). Westport, CT: Greenwood Publishers.

Weiler, K. (1988) *Women teaching for change: gender, class and power*. South Hadley, MA: Bergin & Garvey.

Weiler, K. (1991) Freire and a feminist pedagogy of difference. *Harvard Educational Review*, 61, 449–474.

West-Olatunji, C. (2005) Incidents in the lives of Harriet Jacobs's children—a reader's theatre: disseminating the outcomes of research on the Black experience in the academy. In J. E. King (ed.), *Black Education: a transformative research and action agenda for the new century* (pp. 329–340). Mahwah, NJ: Lawrence Erlbaum.

Wiest, L. R. (1998) Using immersion experiences to shake up pre-service teachers' views about cultural differences. *Journal of Teacher Education*, 49(5), 358–365.

Wills, J., Lintz, A., & Mehan, H. (2004) Ethnographic studies of multicultural education in U.S. classrooms and schools. In J. A. Banks & C. M. Banks (eds.), *Handbook of research on multicultural education* (pp. 163–183). San Francisco: Jossey-Bass.

Williams, D. G. & Evans-Winters, V. (2005) The burden of teaching teachers: Memoirs of race discourse in teacher education. *The Urban Review*, 37(3), 201–219.

Wilson, R. (2005, December 16). We don't need that kind of attitude: education schools want to make sure prospective teachers have the right "disposition." *Chronicle of Higher Education*, LII (17), pp. A8–A11.

Woods, C. (1998) *Development arrested: the blues and plantation power in the Mississippi Delta*. London: Verso.

Woodson, C. G. (1933) *The Mis-education of the Negro*, Washington, DC: Associated Publishers.

Wynter, S. (2003) Unsettling the coloniality of Being/Power/Truth/Freedom: towards the Human, after Man, its overrepresentation—an argument. *CR: The New Centennial Review*, 3 (3).

Wynter, S. (2006) On how we mistook the map for the territory and re-imprisoned ourselves in our unbearable wrongness of being, of désêtre. In L. Gordon & J. A. Gordon (eds.), *Not only the master's tools: African-American studies in theory and practice* (pp. 107–169). Boulder, CO: Paradigm Publishers.

Zeichner, K. M. (1996) Educating teachers for cultural diversity. In K. M. Zeichner, S. Melnick, & M. L. Gomez (eds.), *Currents of reform in pre-service teacher education* (pp. 133–175). New York: Teachers College Press.

Zeichner, K. M. (2003) Teacher research as professional development for P-12 educators in the U.S.A. *Educational Action Research*, 11(2), 301–326.

Zeichner, K. M. & Melnick, S. (1996) The role of community field experiences in preparing teachers for cultural diversity. In K. M. Zeichner, S. Melnick, & M. Gomez (eds.), *Currents of reform in preservice teacher education* (pp. 176–198). New York: Teachers College Press.

Zeichner, K. M. & Noffke, S. E. (2001) Practitioner research. In V. Richardson (ed.), *Handbook of research on teaching* (4th ed., pp. 298–330). New York: American Educational Research Association/Macmillan.

Part 8
Artifacts

8.1 Applying what we know

The field of teacher education[1]

Nathaniel L. Gage

Source: N. Gage, *The Scientific Basis of the Art of Teaching*. New York, NY: Teachers College Press, 1978, pp. 42–62

In considering how a scientific basis for the art of teaching can be applied, we obviously become concerned with teacher education. It is in that field that the application takes place—in preservice teacher education, where prospective teachers are prepared, and in inservice teacher education, where teachers already on the job improve their ability to do the job.

The importance of teacher education is commensurate with the importance of teaching itself. We do not want our children to be influenced by persons to whom we have failed to give the best possible preparation for their task. Nor do we want our enormous investment in teaching to yield anything but the best possible returns for our society.

THE STATE OF TEACHER EDUCATION

As everyone knows, teacher education has a long history of low status. It is possible to find statements concerning its poor condition in the nineteenth century and all through the twentieth. In our own time, that undesirable state of affairs has been set forth in volumes by James Bryant Conant (1963) and James Koerner (1963), and in *Teacher Education*, a yearbook of the National Society for the Study of Education edited by Kevin Ryan (1975).

Many of the criticisms of teacher education deal with its governance and only incidentally with its content. The debates on content are concerned with relative emphasis on liberal education and subject matter competence as against more strictly "education" courses, such as those in curriculum and teaching methods. The problem of content is seen in turn to be involved with governance—the distribution of power over teacher education. Liberal arts faculties, education faculties, organizations of teachers and administrators, and state education departments engage in struggles for this power. Such struggles were expressed in the 1950s in the writings of Arthur Bestor and Harold Hand.

Yet in a recent series of articles (Messerli, 1977; Wallace, 1977; LoPresti, 1977; Spencer & Boyd, 1977; King, Hayes, & Newman, 1977) it was repeatedly recognized that the power struggle is not more important than the research struggle for knowledge about teaching. Who determines what teachers should learn does not matter so much as what kinds of knowledge and what skills in teaching have been identified as worth learning. In short, although no armistice between the warring camps should be expected, the competition for control of teacher education should take second place to our concern with establishing a scientific basis for the art of teaching.

Thus, the poor state of teacher education is attributable, in part at least, to an insufficiency of the kind of scientific basis I have tried to sketch. This kind of explanation can be seen in the history of medical education. That field was diagnosed by Abraham Flexner (1910), in his epochal *Medical Education in the United States*, as extremely sick. He was able to bring about a cure, however, because even in his time medicine was "part and parcel of modern science." The scientific basis for the art of medical practice was imperfect in 1910—even more so, of course, than it is today. In Flexner's words, medical science dealt "not only with certainties but also with probabilities, surmises, theories." Yet, because medicine had a scientific basis, the weakness of medical education in 1910 could be contrasted with the strength of the scientific knowledge that medical research had built. We all know that the Flexner Report was able to raise medical education to a wholly new level because of the strength of that profession's scientific basis.

Clifford (1973) has documented in detail the forlorn "history of the impact of research on teaching." That history is a record of premature hopes dashed upon the realities of inadequate scientific bases. Educational innovations can indeed spread and become widely adopted—often to an extent and with a rapidity unjustified by the scientific basis for the innovation. The Roman-candle history of teaching machines (Markle, 1976) provides just one example. But more solidly established bases for change in teacher education in the application of scientific knowledge about teaching—can lead to a happier history. Teacher education should rise to a wholly new level as the scientific basis of the art of teaching becomes stronger.

KNOWLEDGE THAT vs. KNOWLEDGE HOW

It is important at the outset to make clear the need for knowledge of a new kind of relationship if teacher education is to apply what we have by way of a scientific basis for the art of teaching. This new relationship is one between teacher education policies, procedures, and techniques, on the one hand, and teaching methods and styles, on the other. Until now we have been concerned with teacher behavior—in all its ramifications, including teacher–pupil interaction and the creation of classroom environments—as the independent variable. But when we come to teacher education, we must look upon teacher behavior as the dependent variable.

Further, we are not so much concerned here with the teacher's' "knowing that" as with his or her "knowing how." This distinction, made by the analytic philosopher Gilbert Ryle (1949), refers to the difference between being able to state factual propositions and being able to perform skills or operations. The one kind of knowledge does not necessarily follow from the other. For example, we may know *that* reinforcers strengthen responses but not know *how* to reinforce a pupil so as to strengthen the child's tendency to participate in class discussions. Similarly, we may know *that* criticism in very small amounts may be good for the achievement of more academically oriented pupils but not know *how* to limit our criticism to those small amounts for that kind of pupil.

Much of the teacher education program is given over to providing teachers with a great deal of knowledge *that* certain things are true: in the subjects to be taught; in the historical, philosophical, social, and psychological foundations of education; in the curriculum and instruction of various subject matter fields; and so on. This kind of knowledge is acquired by prospective teachers in the courses taught by teacher education faculties, with all the paraphernalia and methods used in college teaching in general. For the most part, this aspect of teacher education has proceeded along much the same lines as those that have been followed in courses in the sciences and humanities—in English, history, philosophy, chemistry, or mathematics—at the college level.

In recent years, however, an additional approach toward helping teachers know and understand concepts has been used. This is the "protocol materials" approach. It consists of developing films or videotapes to be viewed by the teacher. The materials show instances, occurring in real or almost real settings, of particular categories of teacher behavior (e.g. approving or probing). After viewing the materials, the teacher should be able to recognize instances of a particular category and to categorize occurrences in real classrooms appropriately.

In one program for developing protocol materials, Gliessman and Pugh (1976) produced films showing instances of the concepts of *approving, disapproving, probing, informing. reproductive (lower-order) questioning*, and *productive (higher-order) questioning*. Shown to students in educational psychology courses, the films raised scores on tests of ability to categorize these behaviors and received favorable ratings from the instructors and their students. It seems clear that protocol materials can go a long way toward reducing the hitherto almost total reliance on words as the medium by which teachers are helped to understand the concepts and phenomena entailed in their work.

When it comes to providing prospective or already employed teachers with knowledge *how*, we know that practice is required—as another analytic philosopher, Jane Roland (1961), has pointed out. "Jones could not know how to swim or speak French unless he had at some time practiced swimming or tried to speak French" (p. 61). It is this realization of the need for practice that has led from the very beginning to the inclusion in teacher education programs of opportunities for practice teaching.

Yet common sense and research results agree in finding that practice alone is not enough. If it were, teachers would automatically improve in performance as they gained more years on the job. But the fact is that at least nine studies have shown only a very low correlation, if any, between years of teaching experience and the average achievement of the teacher's students (Rosenshine, 1971, pp. 201–205).

Those studies were made with teachers already in service. What about the practice of budding teachers? Here the practice is accompanied by the observation, guidance, and advice of the regular classroom teacher, who provides a model as well—one from which the student teacher can presumably learn.

Student teaching has been the subject of much thinking, writing, and even some research over the decades. In general, it has been considered to be the single best, though far from faultless, component of teacher education programs. It has often been indicted as too unsystematic or unplanned, as unmanageable in its complexity, and as too much at the mercy of the idio-syncrasies of the cooperating and supervising teachers. Some appraisals have shown that student teachers hardly change their ways of teaching at all, from the beginning to the end of the student teaching period—and even that their attitudes and behavior tend to deteriorate, at least in the view of those who value nonauthoritarianism and nonpunitiveness in teaching.

It has been demonstrated that skill in simple and complex motor tasks continues to improve over hundreds and even thousands of trials (Hudgins, 1974). Apparently, knowledge of results continues to operate to improve motor skills even over protracted practice. In student teaching, however, such feedback or knowledge of results seldom comes through clearly or quickly enough to improve performance. The feedback may be delayed for days or weeks, or never appear at all.

Hudgins (1974) has derived from research on the learning of complex skills certain principles that should apply to the acquisition and use of teaching skills, such as the teaching of concepts (Clark, 1971). In teaching concepts, the teachers should first assess the pupil's preinstructional knowledge. Second, the teacher should define the concept and offer clear, positive instances along with indications of their critical characteristics. Third, the teacher should gradually mix negative instances into the examples, asking the student to indicate whether each does or does not meet the criteria of the concept, and give the student feedback after each response. Finally, the teacher should evaluate the student's learning of the concept.

To prepare teachers to carry out such steps, teacher education should provide for the teacher's (a) learning the general model of the teaching skill; (b) practicing the skill in a self-contained setting, one that is easily arranged and does not require students and supervisors but does provide the teacher with feedback; and (c) practicing the skill in the actual classroom. Using this conception of teacher preparation led Hudgins to a restatement of the already well-established concept of self-contained materials for teacher education—a concept we shall consider in vari-ous forms. Here we note only that this concept represents a major effort to overcome the limita-tions of the student teaching arrangement that was for too long the sole vehicle of practice for prospective teachers.

TECHNIQUES FOR CHANGING TEACHER BEHAVIOR

Thus we see that the limitations of student teaching made teacher education receptive when alternatives began to be offered. The time for more varied and manageable approaches had come.

Microteaching

In the 1960s, teacher educators fell hungrily upon the innovation called microteaching. Micro-teaching caught on rapidly. Within a few years it was being used, in one form or another, in 176 programs for educating secondary school teachers in the United States (B. E. Ward, 1970). I am also aware of its being used in several other countries, including Australia, Canada, England, West Germany, Israel, Nigeria, and Sweden.

As is well known, microteaching is scaled-down teaching—teaching conducted for only five or ten minutes at a time, with only five or ten students, and focused on only one or a few aspects of the teacher's role. The teacher tries, say, reinforcing participation or making an assignment, rather than undertaking the whole of what a teacher does, in all its multifaceted complexity, with a class of 30 for a whole period of instruction.

The advantages of microteaching become evident as soon as one encounters this intriguing idea. Such an arrangement is at the least more manageable and controllable. It does not take up whole hours and classes in order to give the neophyte an introduction to teaching. It does not induce the anxiety that accompanies facing a whole class for a whole period. It allows concentra-tion on one part of teaching at a time—just as the violinist can play the same few bars again and again.

Not only was microteaching widely adopted; it was closely studied. The technique lends itself to easy variation and manipulation, and many of the possibilities were quickly tried. For example, the value of providing the microteaching teacher with a model was investigated, and different kinds of models—live, videotaped, or merely printed—were compared to determine their effectiveness in promoting the teacher's acquisition of a given skill. Also, the feasibility of teach-ing peers rather than actual pupils was investigated. The number of pupils taught was varied. The kinds of supervision and feedback provided the teacher were studied, particularly as to the value of videotaped feedback. And the interval between the first and second microteaching sessions was permitted to range from a few minutes to a week.

The results of many of these investigations have been reviewed by Turney, Clift, Dunkin, and Traill (1973), writing in Australia. I mention this work only to indicate the enthusiasm and industry that greeted this first major departure from the traditional sole reliance on student teaching as the vehicle by which the prospective teacher could get some practice. For our purposes, let it suffice to say that microteaching has generally been found to be effective in the sense that teachers do exhibit the kinds of behavior at which the microteaching is aimed—not only in the hours or days immediately following the microteaching but in the subsequent months and at the end of the first year of actual teaching as well (Trinchero, 1975). Compared with traditional observation and teaching experience, microteaching produced teachers judged to have higher degrees of competence and more favorable attitudes toward their teacher education programs.

Nonetheless, microteaching research has not yielded many firm conclusions concerning the value of the many variations possible within this approach to teacher practice. It may be that such research has erred in regarding the technique too much as a vehicle for increasing *knowledge how* and too little as a means for influencing *knowledge that*. Such a conclusion seems to follow from the studies conducted and reviewed by MacLeod and McIntyre (1977). Their work led them to a new rationale for microteaching as a teacher education technique—a rationale that emphasizes teachers' cognitions. Microteaching can thus be regarded as primarily a way of influencing cognitive structures that are important in teaching. Such structures, they held, should give teachers conceptually simple guides by which to govern their behavior in the hundreds of interpersonal interactions occurring in a day's classroom work.

Minicourses

Microteaching was developed primarily for use in preservice teacher education. It was relatively unwieldy in inservice teacher education, where supervisors and videotape recording machine operators were usually hard to come by. What was needed was a relatively self-administrable version of the microteaching idea. This was soon forthcoming in the form of Minicourses (Borg, Kelley, Langer, & Gall, 1970). Minicourses are packages of materials, including manuals, self-administered tests, and films, intended for use with videotape or audiotape recorders in rooms and with pupils furnished by the school.

With one typical Minicourse the teacher can acquire training in "Organizing Independent Learning: Primary Level." First, the teacher reads about a set of skills in the teacher's handbook; second, she views a film explaining and illustrating those skills; third, she plans and teaches a lesson in which she practices the skills; and fourth, she evaluates her lesson. The practice is performed both in a microteaching format, with only three or four pupils outside the regular classroom, and in the regular classroom with the entire class. This Minicourse takes about an hour a day for 16 days over about a four-week period. In general, the course is aimed at helping teachers to establish with pupils the concept of working independently, to give pupils facility in solving problems that arise during independent work periods, to develop appropriate expectations about the promptness or delay of teacher response to pupil work, and finally to combine independent work, problem solving, and delayed response into a learning environment that facilitates independent activity and small-group instruction.

All in all, about a dozen Minicourses have been developed, tested, and marketed. The testing consists of an experiment in which teachers are first observed to determine the preexisting level of the teaching skills at which the Minicourse is aimed. Then the Minicourse is individually self-administered by the teachers. The teachers are observed again by trained observers who determine the quality of the behaviors in the teacher's actual classroom some time after the end of the Minicourse.

Borg (1972) carried out what may be the most convincing demonstration of Minicourse effectiveness thus far. Among the behaviors influenced were "Redirecting the same question to several pupils," "Framing questions that call for longer pupil responses," "Seeking further clarification and pupil insight," and "Not repeating pupil answers." He made videotape recordings of each of 24 teachers before, immediately after, 4 months after, and 39 months after training. Analyses of the recordings showed that the Minicourse significantly changed most of the 10 question-asking behaviors that the Minicourse was intended to influence. Borg concluded that "after 39 months, the performance of the subjects was still significantly superior to their pre-course performance on 8 of the 10 behaviors that were scored" (p. 572). It might be objected that the teachers knew their behaviors were being recorded and hence behaved as they had been influenced to behave only to please the investigator. But this possibility seems remote simply because the behaviors cannot be turned on and off that easily. It seems improbable that teachers could exhibit these 10 behaviors unless the behaviors had become fairly well established in the teacher's normal practice.

Other methods of changing teacher behavior

With microteaching and Minicourses, teacher educators acquired tools that seemed to have demonstrable effectiveness in improving the teacher's "knowledge how." These approaches received the widest attention and were subjected to the most research. But they were not the only procedures that appeared on the teacher education scene during the sixties and seventies. For example, Flanders (1970) had accumulated much evidence about teachers who learned and used his interaction analysis categories to observe and analyze their own behavior or who received information about their behavior in terms of these categories. Such teachers usually made some successful attempt to change their behavior to make it accord more closely with their own previously unarticulated conceptions of desirable teaching.

Similarly, Wagner (1973) compared the effectiveness of microteaching and cognitive discrimination training in bringing about student-centered teaching on the part of undergraduates (prospective teachers). The discrimination training consisted of presenting the undergraduates, four at a time, with 33 recorded teacher replies to student comments. The prospective teachers had been supplied with a brief description of six subcategories of teacher replies (namely, "asking for clarification," "restating," and "using students' ideas"—all considered to be parts of *student*-centered teaching—and "asking a directive question," "arguing," and "ignoring"—all considered to be aspects of *teacher*-centered teaching). The undergraduates coded the taped teacher responses one at a time and then, after each coding, were told the correct answer and given a short explanation. The training lasted about 30 minutes. Another group of undergraduates engaged in microteaching for about 30 minutes. Subsequently, both groups of undergraduates prepared and taught a new lesson. It turned out that the discrimination training was significantly more effective than the microteaching in bringing about student-centered teaching. Thus, learning to discriminate was sufficient to bring about behavioral change. In this instance, and perhaps in many others, the more elaborate microteaching procedure could be replaced by this less expensive kind of training.

Another demonstration of the possibility that simple techniques can change teacher behavior was provided by Good and Brophy (1974). They used a single interview to provide a teacher with feedback based on observations of the teacher—feedback intended to help change teacher behavior toward selected students. Each teacher was at once informed and advised about his or her own behavior toward various pupils. Thus in making suggestions for improvement the authors were in effect saying, "You are doing a fine job with Mary; now try to do the same kinds of things with Jane." This is much less threatening and more acceptable than "your way is wrong, do it my way" (p. 291).

Using this approach, Good and Brophy identified pupils who participated much less than the average and also pupils who seldom were encouraged by the teacher to make a second or an extended response to a question. The teachers were given the names of these pupils as well as the names of pupils whom the teachers *were* treating appropriately. As a result of the interview, the teachers agreed to seek responses more persistently from the appropriate pupils and also, although less readily, to call more frequently on pupils who were infrequent participants and to initiate more private interactions with them. Subsequent observations in each classroom showed that the teacher had changed substantially in the directions intended.

There is another way to change teacher behavior that is even less expensive than the discrimination training provided by Wagner or the interviews conducted by Good and Brophy. The technique has been used, especially at the college level, and found to be moderately effective. It consists of using students' descriptions of their teachers on rating scales as feedback to the teachers. Such feedback has been used with sixth-grade teachers given their pupils' ratings (Gage, Runkel, & Chatterjee, 1963), with elementary school principals given their teachers' ratings (Daw & Gage, 1967; Bums, 1977), and with social studies department chairmen given the department members' ratings (Hovenier, 1966).

Discrepancy influences the technique's effectiveness. Thus, Centra (1973) showed that the feedback to teachers of college students' ratings produced change in the teachers' behavior only when there were marked discrepancies between the teacher's self-rating, or self-perception, and the students' ratings. Similarly, the greater the discrepancy between teacher's ratings of their ideal and their actual department chairman, the greater the change in the department chairman's behavior as a consequence of the feedback, as compared with the change in a group that did not receive the feedback (Hovenier, 1966).

Such ratings are altogether inexpensive. The technique requires no interviews or observations by professional staff whose salaries must be paid. Thus the feedback of students' ratings can be regarded as a feasible approach to teacher change—but only under certain conditions. For one thing, the pupils must be mature enough to make usable and reliable ratings; the fifth or sixth grade is probably the lower limit in this sense. Second, the teachers must be motivated to change by virtue of their respect for student opinion. Third, as McKeachie (1976) has pointed out, teachers are more likely to change if they receive initial ratings that are moderate rather than extremely high or extremely low. McKeachie considers this finding to be consistent with achievement motivation theory—theory that predicts greater success or change when expectations are neither too high to be realistic nor too low to instigate action. Finally, the feedback may be expected to have an effect only when the teacher has the indicated changes in behavior within his or her repertoire of behaviors—in other words, when the teachers *can* change in the desired direction if they want to. Here, the microteaching and Minicourse techniques could be useful in equipping teachers with desired ways of behaving that they do not already possess.

One last approach seems worth mentioning if only because it rests on the ever-attractive conception of teaching as a performing art. What Stanislavski did to help his actors realize their roles may help teachers comprehend and enact theirs. Travers and Dillon (1975) have worked on this appealing idea. They summarized Stanislavski's method and then presented scenarios for careful study by future teachers. They intend the study to consist of more than reading—the student should analyze the role characteristics, reread the scenario, put himself into the teacher's shoes, act out and speak the parts, and try to experience the appropriate feelings and ideas. Rather than focusing on the teacher's observable performance, this approach emphasizes "inner behavior." It assumes the correct inner behavior will be reflected in appropriate "outer behavior."

In another part of their treatment, Travers and Dillon seem to contradict themselves by telling teachers that, if they will relax their muscles (outer behavior), they will reduce their feelings of tension and anxiety (inner behavior). Here the outer behavior is assumed to control the inner. Also, the authors offer no research evidence that their techniques work. Nonetheless, if it can be put into forms that can be experimentally tested, the idea of training teachers as if they had much in common with actors seems to be worth trying.

THE FIELD OF TEACHER EDUCATION PRODUCTS

Let us turn now to a more general view of the effort to apply a scientific basis for the art of teaching to teacher education. This view takes in the field of teacher education products. These are materials packaged in a form that makes them transportable and relatively self-administrable for use in changing and, it is hoped, improving teaching in some way. Such products have been developed by the hundreds during the last decade, largely as a result of the emphasis on developmental work by the Federal government's Office of Education and National Institute of Education. That emphasis influenced university research and development centers, regional educational laboratories, and many other organizations and workers to produce curriculum packages and materials to help teachers and administrators. The whole enterprise was an attempt to make readily available and highly usable the ideas and techniques that educational research and development workers had formulated. In the past, these ideas had usually gone unused and neglected by the practitioners to whom they could conceivably be helpful.

The Stanford catalog

The teacher-training products became so numerous that several catalogs of these materials appeared. Finally, the Program on Teaching Effectiveness (1974) at Stanford, in order to meet its own research and development needs, compiled a master catalog stored on computer tape. That catalog identified and described more than 800 products. A teacher-training product was defined as material intended to equip teachers with skills, or knowledge of how to do certain things, rather than merely knowledge that certain things are true. As we put it in a monograph describing the field,

> teacher training products must require the trainee to be active, in the sense of performing, practicing, or trying out the skills to be acquired. Such a requirement rules out training materials that merely ask the trainee to receive information through reading, listening, or viewing.
>
> (Program on Teaching Effectiveness, 1974, pp. 3–4)

The Stanford catalog described the hundreds of products in terms of nine dimensions:

1   The product's subject matter specificity. (Did it apply to the teaching of English, mathematics, science, social studies, or school subjects in general?)
2   The target audience. (Was the product intended for preservice trainees, inservice teachers, or both?)
3   The grade-level specificity. (Was the teaching skill pertinent to early childhood education, to the high school level, to something in between, or to all levels?)
4   The so-called target outcome. (Which aspects of teaching—such as planning, presentation, interaction with pupils, attitude toward teaching, or the teacher's self-concept—was the product concerned with?)
5   The target outcomes for students. (Which of various kinds of cognitive and social-emotional outcomes?)
6   The training situation. (What materials were provided with the product and what materials and equipment had to be provided by the user?)
7   The time and number of persons required to administer training with the product. (How many trainees could use the product at one time?)
8   The kind of practice provided. (Was it paper-and-pencil exercises, or classifying incidents in a film, or playing a simulated teaching game, or teaching actual students?)
9   The phase of teaching in which the acquired skills would be used. (Did the training apply to the teacher's work before, during, or after interaction with students?)

The NEA/Far West Laboratory Project

The main purpose of the Stanford catalog was to determine in detail what was already available in order to plan the work of the Stanford Center's Program on Teaching Effectiveness. For this reason the catalog was not readily usable by teachers and teacher educators who were interested in considering the products.

The need for putting the information into a more usable form eventually led to a new project conducted by Robert McClure and Robert Luke of the National Education Association with the support of the National Institute of Education and the collaboration of Beatrice Ward of the Far West Laboratory for Educational Research and Development. In this "Pilot Project on Practitioner Selection, Use und Critique of Inservice Education Projects" (McClure, 1976), many products were examined by teachers, teacher educators, and other potential users. McClure characterized the products as ranging from simple to complex; as providing either individual or large-group instruction; as ranging from cheap to expensive; as using either a single medium or several media; as ranging from homemade to "slickly professional"; as being subject-centered or process-oriented or both; as being oriented toward all levels from early childhood education to college and adult education; as ranging from those that offered undocumented, simply derived claims for effectiveness to those that had been subjected to rigorous field tests; and as varying between empirically based and theoretically based.

From working with practitioners, McClure and his coworkers gained the impression that most teachers were unaware of the existence of the products. Further, it seemed that the most successful products clearly matched teachers' stated needs in such activities as individualizing instruction, managing classrooms, or teaching reading. These products could be used without an outside resource person, could be used and completed over a period of several weeks, employed methods other than merely presenting reading matter, and were attractively but not expensively packaged. Some persons who knew about the products rejected them on the grounds that they imposed others' views of teaching or were unrelated to a local problem. But others viewed the products as "one resource that can help to solve some persistent problems with inservice education" (McClure, 1976, p. 15). This was the view adopted by the NEA/Far West Laboratory Project.

What do these products consist of? The NEA/Far West project described them in terms readily understandable by teachers. Let us consider products intended to help teachers in motivating students, since that problem received the highest average rating for level of interest in an NEA Assessment of Teacher Inservice Education Needs conducted in 1975. Student motivation is one of four categories into which the NEA/Far West project has grouped the more than 50 products it has described in detail. (The other three categories were individualizing instruction, language arts, and classroom management.)

One product, entitled "Motivation Theory for Teachers," was developed in 1967 by Madeline Hunter. It consists of a film and an optional programmed book aimed at interpreting motivation theory so that it can be useful in the daily decisions of teachers. The film deals with six factors that can influence motivation: anxiety in the form of concern for the task; the interest of the task; the feeling tone of the task; the level of difficulty of the task; knowledge of results; and intrinsic rewards. The describer's critique of the film states that it "is appropriate to the objectives stated at the beginning of the film. The technical quality is good . . . The content of the film appears to be accurate and socially fair."

A second product in this category is entitled "Individually Guided Motivation." It was developed at the Wisconsin Research and Development Center for Cognitive Learning, under the direction of Herbert Klausmeier. It deals with four motivational procedures to be used with elementary school children: adult-child conferences to encourage independent reading; teacher -child conferences for goal setting; older children tutoring younger children; and small-group conferences to encourage self-directed desirable social behavior. The product consists of a textbook to be studied and five films to be viewed and discussed by the teachers. It requires five two-hour sessions or a two-day workshop. Large-group sessions are used to communicate information, show films, and administer self-assessment exercises. Large- or small-group sessions are used to criticize and apply information, discuss practice exercises, and engage in role playing.

This pair of descriptions must suffice to illustrate what is meant by teacher-training products. In general, they have the advantages and disadvantages of textbooks or any other standardized set of instructional materials. The advantage is that they can incorporate more careful thought, planning, and scholarship than most teachers or teacher educators can muster when left to their own resources. Their disadvantage is that they cannot be custom tailored to the needs and capabilities of each teacher who may use them. Thus they run the risk of missing the mark for a particular teacher.

Nevertheless, teacher-training products deserve to be better known and more extensively tried. Toward that end the NEA group, under the direction of Robert Luke, has organized a "Project on Utilization of Inservice Education R & D Outcomes." The project serves teachers and other local users in approximately 80 local education associations and school districts in 16 states across the country. It is intended to assist teachers in identifying problems in teaching the basic skills, to build an information system on training products aimed at improving teaching in the basic skills, to assist in setting criteria for selecting products, and to provide help in adapting the products to local conditions. Descriptions of products are kept in central files at the NEA. An information specialist is available via a toll-free telephone line to help users track down the products that seem most promising. All in all, the system is administratively elaborated and coordinated in such a way that the obstacles of ignorance and information lack should be substantially overcome. Then teacher-training products can be given the fair try they deserve.

TEACHER CENTERS

It should be obvious by now that more is involved in teacher education, both preservice and inservice, than a scientific basis for the art of teaching. We need more than the knowledge and tools that will make teacher education procedures influence teacher behavior and, in turn, make teacher behavior contribute more to student achievement and desirable attitudes. Teacher education products of the kind just described are in themselves only part of what is needed. Beyond them organizational and administrative arrangements are needed to bring together productive combinations of leadership, personnel, time, and money.

One idea for organizing such combinations is the teacher center. As is well known, the idea was born in England (see Thornbury, 1974). It was brought to this country by Americans who saw it there and liked what they saw (Rogers, 1976). In brief, teacher centers are places where teachers can come together with other teachers, and perhaps with other useful persons, such as professors, to do things that will help them teach better.

It would not be appropriate to my topic to attempt a full-scale analysis of the alternative kinds of teacher centers that have been proposed and of the political pulling and hauling that have accompanied their development in this country. These matters have been discussed by Eugenia Kemble (1973) from the point of view of the American Federation of Teachers. She has quoted both the AFT's David Selden and the NEA's David Darland as being opposed to the kind of forced and mandated inservice teacher education that teacher centers would presumably replace. To my mind also, teacher centers should be initiated and controlled by teachers. Other kinds of participants, such as administrators, parents, and professors, should come to them only by invitation. Just as practitioners of medicine, law, and engineering take responsibility for their own continuing education, so teachers should have the right to do the job for themselves. This proposition seems to me to follow from any decent respect for the professionalism of teachers.

Teacher-governed teacher centers should learn about teacher education products and procedures as these may commend themselves. Thus these approaches should get a fair chance to prove themselves; and that is all that their developers should ask. In short, these ways of applying knowledge about teaching ought, it seems to me, to stand or fall on their ability to impress teachers favorably and to improve teaching, with only such consultation with research workers and other scholars as teachers may see fit to invite.

Teacher centers that focus on teacher education products have been termed "behaviorally oriented" by Feiman (1977), who also identified two other kinds: the humanistic and the developmental. Both of these involve teachers in less structured activities. The humanistic centers try to help teachers share their own expertise with one another in a secure, supportive, and informal atmosphere; teachers adapt materials on display and talk about how things were made. The developmental centers use advisors and curriculum workshops to get teachers to think about the ways in which they organize their experience and their classrooms and to reexamine their beliefs and teaching behavior.

Each of Feiman's three kinds of centers seems to have advantages. It will be regrettable if the "ideological" differences between the types prevent centers from gaining the advantages of all three types: the structure and focus of behavioral centers using teacher education products; the teacher-centeredness and informality of humanistic centers using unprogrammed encounters; and the conceptual orientation of developmental centers providing advisory services. If I have emphasized teacher education products, it is only because they have most obviously represented ways of applying a scientific basis for the art of teaching. But teacher centers can make those applications in other ways, such as discussion and encounter groups, workshops, advisory services, and the simple process of helping teachers talk to one another.

THE CONNECTIONS BETWEEN TEACHER EDUCATION AND EDUCATIONAL OUTCOMES

Two kinds of causal connections are part of the logic of teacher education. The first kind was considered in Chapter I, where it was argued that something is indeed known about relationships between teaching behaviors and methods, on the one hand, and pupil achievement and attitudes, on the other. The second kind of connection is that between teacher education procedures and teacher behaviors.

Now there ought to be a good connection between the two kinds of connections. That is, (a) teacher education should be aimed at producing (b) the kinds of teacher behaviors that have been shown to be related—preferably causally related—to (c) valued kinds of student knowledge, understanding, sensibility, and attitude. Then the a → b connections would contribute to achieving the b → c connections.

The hiatus between the two connections

Strangely enough, the work on each of the two kinds of connections has proceeded almost completely independently of the other. Developers of teacher education procedures have gone ahead with their a → b work without waiting for empirical evidence on b → c connections—evidence that the kinds of teacher behaviors they were trying to bring about were indeed conducive to the achievement of educational goals. There has been too little unification of effort of the kind that would bring research and development on teacher effects, or the effects of different kinds of teacher behavior, into close contact with research and development on ways to bring about those kinds of behavior. In short, the right hand of research on teaching effectiveness has too seldom informed the left hand of research on teacher education of what it has been up to. In other words, we have not had enough a → b → c research.

An example of this kind of divorcement can be seen in the work on teachers' questions. Research has thrown serious doubt on the desirability of so-called higher-order questions—questions that call for thinking and problem-solving rather than mere recall. A fair number of correlational studies and experiments (see especially Rosenshine, 1976, pp. 355–356; Gall, Ward, Berliner, Cahen, Crown, Elashoff, Stanton, & Winne, 1976; Program on Teaching Effectiveness, SCRDT, 1976) have failed to show what many educational thinkers had expected, namely, that teachers who ask more "thought" questions produce pupils with better understanding of the subject matter. Indeed they have more often shown the reverse. Higher proportions of *lower*-order, or recall, questions have usually been accompanied by higher pupil scores on tests of both knowledge and understanding of the subject matter. The research is not yet conclusive on this matter, and more sensitive forms of both the questioning and the achievement variables may eventually yield the results that many writers have led us to expect. Nonetheless, we do not at present have any firm empirical basis for advocating that teachers ask more higher-order questions than they presently ask (a rather low proportion).

The explanation may well be that the give-and-take of the classroom recitation is no place for higher-order questions. Such questions, by definition, require deliberation, which takes time. And pupils feel too harried by social pressures in this setting to benefit from the opportunity to think. This explanation implies that higher-order questions *should* improve understanding when encountered in the course of reading prose, in a setting congenial to quiet deliberation. And this implication is supported by evidence that "higher-order inserted questions are of greater benefit than factual ones" (Faw & Waller, 1976, p. 712).

Notwithstanding this state of affairs with respect to higher-order questions in classroom discussions, teacher education research and development have proceeded to develop techniques, such as Minicourses, for instructing teachers to frame more "questions that require the pupil to use higher cognitive processes" (Borg, 1972). Many other objectives of teacher education have also been adopted and acted upon prior to any demonstration that the particular kinds of behavior were desirable in the sense of fostering achievement and desirable attitudes.

An illustration of unified effort

What is needed is work that unites the effort to show that a certain kind of teacher behavior is desirable with the effort to show that such behavior can be brought about through teacher education. Let me illustrate what is needed by describing an experiment in 33 third-grade classes conducted by the Program on Teaching Effectiveness at Stanford University. Put very briefly, the aim of the experiment was to determine whether teachers instructed to behave in certain ways produce pupils with higher levels of achievement and more desirable attitudes than do teachers who have not received such instruction. The noteworthy feature of the experiment in relation to the point concerning unification of effort is that the teacher education objectives were derived in detail from the results of previous correlational studies. The results of those studies were examined, variable by variable, in terms of (a) the exact operational definitions of the teacher behaviors observed, (b) the correlations of those behaviors with adjusted measures of pupil achievement in reading, (c) the average and the variability across teachers of the frequencies of the given kind of teacher behavior, and (d) the implications of the empirical findings for what might be considered desirable in teacher education, given the criterion of pupil achievement in reading (see Table 2, in Chapter 1).

This kind of detailed sifting of the evidence concerning hundreds of teacher behavior variables in four recent, relatively large-scale correlational studies provided the basis for the formulation of the "teacher-should" statements presented in Chapter 1. That formulation, in turn, was expressed in five sets of reading matter, presented at the rate of one per week to the teachers in the instructed group. The instructed teachers were themselves divided at random into two subgroups. One subgroup received the instruction in a "minimal" form consisting merely of the reading matter and self-scored quizzes on the reading matter. The other subgroup received the instruction in a more traditional, and much more expensive, workshop format. These teachers not only read the material and took the quizzes but they participated in weekly group meetings with an instructional staff. At these meetings, the teachers engaged in role playing, viewed videotape records, and discussed the content and problems considered in the teacher education materials.

This experiment illustrates the kind of linkage between teacher education and teacher effectiveness research that seems to be obviously logical and desirable. Yet only a few examples of it are known. Still fewer of these have developed the linkage with detailed attention to the correlational findings on teaching effectiveness.

It should also be noted that each of the teachers in both the instructed and the uninstructed groups was observed in detail for 18 full school days during the school year—that is, one day every one to three weeks before, during, and after the teacher education program. And, of course, the pupils and their teachers took batteries of tests of cognitive and noncognitive variables at the beginning and end of the school year.

The broad purposes of the experiment should by now be obvious: It is intended, first, to determine whether teacher behaviors that correlate with pupil achievement have causal efficacy in improving pupil achievement. It will also determine how a cheap and easy way of instructing teachers compares in effectiveness with one that requires a professional and hence expensive teacher education staff.

In summary, to restate the main proposition of this chapter, there are many ways to give teachers knowledge of how to teach. These ways, in all their variety, have been found to work in the sense of getting teachers to behave in ways congruent with the aims of the teacher education effort. Accordingly, the tools needed to apply what we know of a scientific basis for the art of teaching are relatively well in hand. They are being further developed and tested in field programs, such as that of the NEA, and they should receive fair consideration in the teacher centers of the kind being advocated by the AFT. The main need in this field is a closer connection between the work of the teacher education researchers and that of the teacher effectiveness researchers. That closer connection can be seen in efforts to use the findings of correlational studies in experiments whose effects on both teacher behavior and student achievement and attitude are determined.

NOTE

1 The citations in this chapter are located in the general reference listing at the end of *The Scientific Basis of the Art of Teaching* (N. Gage, 1978).

8.2 More light

An argument for complexity in studies of teaching and teacher education

Susan Florio-Ruane
Michigan State University

Source: Susan Florio-Ruane, More light: an argument for complexity in studies of teaching and teacher education. *Journal of Teacher Education*, 53(3), 2002, pp. 205–215

ABSTRACT

This article borrows an analogy from Michael Cole's *Cultural Psychology: A Once and Future Discipline*. A man loses his car keys and searches unsuccessfully for them only in the area illuminated by the streetlight. Cole urged psychology to study thought by illuminating human activity in cultural and historical context. Lanier and Shulman similarly urged the study of teaching as multidisciplinary research. An applied field, our research is responsive to problems of practice. However, when these problems are framed rhetorically as crises, we are apt to respond to their urgency by seeking simplicity, authority, and order in our research. Paradoxically, this move reduces the sources of light diverse research traditions and genres can offer. We should resist (a) pitting approaches to research against one another, (b) privileging approaches merely because they are compatible with the language of policy, (c) accepting uncritically any approach to research, and (d) disregarding research emphasizing local knowledge.

> It takes a lot of variables to describe a man, or for that matter a virus; and you cannot often usefully study these variables two at a time. Animate nature also exhibits very confusing instabilities, as students of history, the stock market, or genetics are well aware.
>
> (Weaver, cited in Mead, 1976, p. 904)

The title of this article borrows a metaphor used by Michael Cole (1996) in his book *Cultural Psychology: A Once and Future Discipline*. Describing the historic "marginality of cross-cultural research to mainstream psychology" (p. 62), Cole commented,

> Such a position is uncomfortably reminiscent of the man who searches for his lost car keys only within the arc of light provided by the street lamp, except that psychologists who fail to encounter culture in their carefully designed experiments declare, in effect, that the keys have ceased to exist because they are not under the lamppost.
>
> (p. 68)

Cole urged "approaches that enlarge the 'circle of light' in which to look for the keys to relationships between culture and cognition" (p. 68) and illustrated with examples of psychological research taking into account the role of culture in human thought and activity. American educational research in the 20th century is a child of the field of psychology. As such, it shares many of the challenges Cole described. Broadly speaking, research on teaching and teacher education is concerned with the study of mind, culture, and activity. Its focus is the nexus of these in what Erickson (1982) called "taught cognitive learning."

A hallmark of our species, explicit teaching is a skilled craft as well as a cultural tool. By means of teaching, knowledge is encoded, passed on, and transformed over time. This process of teaching operates in the life history of the individual as well as the history of a society. It acts reflexively to conserve a society's norms and standards while enabling individuals' agency and the possibility of social transformation (Eisenhart, 1995). In making teaching and teacher education topics of research during the 20th century, scholars responded to optimism that social science could be mobilized to serve human needs and problems. Their efforts can usefully be thought of in terms of Cole's (1996) metaphor.

Social scientific efforts to understand the complexities of teaching and teacher education—for purposes of improving pupil as well as teacher learning—add more light to a complex subject. However, applied research does not occur in a vacuum. As a social, discursive practice in its own right, research is sensitive to the ebb and flow of resources and problems in society's history and its politics. Thus, what counts as research for informing policy and practice in teaching or teacher education shifts with perception of the problems it might inform, the availability of resources to support it, and the particular interests and values of powerful practitioners and policy makers who use it in their decision making. The remainder of this article is about the light shed by research on the complexities of teaching and teacher education in our time. It is also about circumstances that change the light by which researchers view teaching and teacher education. The article closes with some cautionary thoughts about the tendency to narrow the scope of research to focus only on the spaces immediately relevant to a pressing problem framed by powerful consumers and benefactors of research.

CONSIDERING COMPLEXITY

While on sabbatical in the mid-1980s, I audited an inquiry course at Harvard University taught by Eleanor Duckworth. In it, fledgling researchers were treated to many intriguing and challenging activities. We tracked the behavior of the moon as it made its way through a month of skies. We responded to poems and paintings. We played with mirrors to figure out how they work. We investigated permutation, combination, and probability by sorting poker chips and jellybeans. I enjoyed this new and different way of thinking about learning. But I admit to having shared a bit of anxiety with the bright, earnest doctoral students in the class. What, we wondered, does all this have to do with educational research?

With characteristic ability to turn academic assumptions on end, Duckworth (1991) addressed this question in an essay titled "Twenty-Four, Forty-Two, and I Love You: Keeping It Complex." In it, she retold the following vignette:

> My favorite radio show is "A Hitchhiker's Guide to the Galaxy." In one episode, a computer is built expressly for the purpose of answering the question, "What is the meaning of life, the universe, and everything?" When it is ready, they ask if it can answer that question. It says, yes, it can, but that it will take, as I recall, seven million years. They say, "Well, OK, go to it." Seven million years later, whoever is around goes to learn the answer. The computer says that it does have the answer, but that it might be a little disappointing. "No, no," they say, "go ahead, what is it?" "Forty-two," the computer says.
>
> (p. 7)

Duckworth speculated, "Who knows? Maybe forty-two is the answer. But such an answer is of no more help to us than no answer at all. It does not speak to our level of interaction with the mysteries of our existence" (p. 7).

In the same essay, Duckworth (1991) offered another anecdote, this one from research conducted by Lisa Schneier, an urban high school teacher, in her ninth grade English class. Schneier described her students reading aloud the balcony scene from Romeo and Juliet. Taking Shakespeare's difficult language in stride, they enjoyed acting out the parts. Schneier was aware from their intonation and gestures that they understood some but not all of what they were reading. The activity went so well that Schneier did not interrupt it for discussion. She reported, however, that

> our last Romeo of the day finally did interrupt it. We had started the scene again to give more readers a turn, and he had begun to wade through his first speech. In the midst of it, he broke off, shook his head impatiently, and turned to me. "He loves her. That's what he's saying. So why all that other stuff? Why not just say it? 'I love you!' [to the current Juliet]. There!" And then in a memorable tone, a mixture of humor, frustration, and honest confusion: "Why can't he just say what he means?"
>
> (pp. 7–8)

Duckworth remarked,

> Of course that's what [Shakespeare] is saying: "what he means," is complex. The words he chooses are the best he can choose to say what he wants to say, . . . There is a parallel here between a poet and a teacher: the universe is complex; science is complex; the poet's thoughts and feelings are complex. "Forty-two" doesn't do the trick . . . Nor, in this case, does "I love you."
>
> (p. 8)

Sometimes the most helpful thing research can offer is thoughtful exploration of complexity. This may take a bit of both the computer and the poet. Margaret Mead (1976) alluded to this in her presidential address to the American Association for the Advancement of Science. Discussing the nature of what she called "a human science," Mead described the dual forces at work in the scientific study of human understanding as "our capacity to explore human responses to events in which we and others participate through introspection and empathy, as well as . . . our capacity to make objective observations on physical and animate nature" (p. 905).

When we look back on more than a half century of research on teaching and a generation of research on teacher education, we notice scholars using both capacities. As they have done so, a variety of questions have been addressed, methods plied, and theories framed. Learning and practicing the craft of teaching has been researched, for example, as action that causes learning, a process of clinical decision making, negotiated sociolinguistic interaction, a force for cultural praxis, and much more. What does the accumulation of these studies tell us about teaching and learning? What does it tell us about our views of knowledge, our history and values as a society, our biases and blind spots, our work as researchers? Although these may not be questions our various audiences and benefactors ask us, they are questions we ask ourselves. Such epistemological stocktaking is different from other important scholarly responsibilities, such as the setting of standards for studies within any particular research tradition applied to understanding teaching or teacher education. Lave (1996) commented that self-examination concerning the origins, topics, and purposes of our studies is an important part of our scholarship precisely because our inquiry is not disinterested. Of this she wrote,

> In education, in the social sciences, we have moved in the last quarter century from implicit

to explicit theory, increasing our ability to reflect critically on our own research practice. It seems crucial . . . to base the field of education on explicit accounts of its different theoretical perspectives.

(pp. 149–150)

Critical reflection on our own practice as researchers helps us assume responsibility for the questions we ask, the investigative methods we use, and the answers we devise. This self-monitoring activity is important for responsible research in an applied field such as ours. It helps us to be modest and circumspect in our claims to truth and reminds us to balance rigorous search for knowledge with responsiveness to problems of practice.

LOOKING FOR TEACHING

In the public schools of the late 19th and early 20th centuries, bureaucrats collected a lot of information about education. However, little of it explicitly and self-consciously addressed teaching, either its practice or the process of learning that practice. The history of teaching in the public schools of the United States offers a picture of a craft more or less taken for granted in the educational equation. Many teachers had only their own schooling to rely on as they faced their own pupils. In some cases, this schooling was limited to grammar school. In others, it also included "normal" training in teaching at the high school level. In a history of urban education, Tyack (1974) noted that "given the widespread assumption among school superintendents that teachers should be subordinate—should toe the line as their students did—this limited training was an advantage" (p. 59). Implicit in this belief was not only faith in emerging modern management techniques to regulate the behaviors of teachers and pupils but also a theory of mind in which neither teaching nor learning required more than prior experience and direct instruction in a limited range of contexts and contents. This led to both constancy in practice and a sense that teaching was determined and limited by social tradition (Cuban, 1984, p. 8).

Without deviation from this tradition, especially by innovation, there seemed to be little need to make teaching explicit in the recorded history of education in the early part of the 20th century. Thus, when Cuban (1984) studied the historical record of teaching in the early 20th century, he found little systematic documentation of its practice. However, he did find traces of teaching in anecdotal records of practice, especially in the ephemera of schooling such as classroom photographs, student reminiscences, school newspapers and yearbooks, reports of administrator visits to the classroom, and so forth. Apparently, teaching and teacher education were practices about which people held commonsense or folk theories and from which little in the way of complexity was expected. Still, Cuban acknowledged that like pottery shards to an archaeologist, the traces of teaching he accumulated and studied suggest a practice more complex than its record. And even with a richer data set from which to infer what teaching must have felt and looked like, Cuban asked, "How . . . can I capture only one slice of this whirl after it has disappeared?" (p. 8).

Figuring out how to study the "whirl" of classroom life and the teacher's role was the focus of research on teaching as it came of age in mid-20th century. The rise of applied social science and the advent of electronic technologies for recording and reviewing classroom activity helped make the study of teaching a focus of research. It also afforded the means to experiment with different approaches to teaching. Early studies of teachers' instructional behavior and its effects on pupil learning are reviewed in Dunkin and Biddle's (1974) book, *The Study of Teaching*. The review emphasized the need for standards for research, stressing methods, guiding concepts, and data collection and analysis. Reflecting on the historic absence of a scientific study of teaching, they sought research-based knowledge on which to build effective teaching practice.

Moving teaching front and center, researchers hoped to make its study systematic and accountable not only to the social scientific community but, as an applied field, to decision makers responsible for designing teacher education programs and evaluating teachers' competency. In doing this, educational researchers joined others in what Cohen and Garet (1975) called the "applied social sciences." Research on teaching and teacher education framed in the manner of natural science provides knowledge useful to administrators in that it offers information gathered objectively, reviewed by peers, and conducted rigorously and in sufficiently large populations to warrant general conclusions. What this ray of light illuminated was, in Dunkin and Biddle's (1974) terms, "teaching as researchers have conceptualized it ... the classroom behavior of teachers, the response of pupils, and the determinants and effects of these events" (p. 1). This orientation to research considered scientifically rigorous only those studies conducted in the "nomological tradition" (Wardekker, 2000). As such, the research they reviewed is premised on the idea that

> acting means creating the conditions that enable a natural law to work in a way that will produce desired results. Thus, a teacher creates conditions under which learning processes, in a way, must happen. If students do not learn, that means that the right conditions for those processes were not created in that situation.
>
> (Wardekker, 2000, p. 262)

This way of studying teaching is an outside-in process wherein the researcher, a classroom outsider, objectively records and analyzes behavior as data. Teacher thinking, what Clark and Yinger (1979) termed the "hidden world of teaching," is not a focal problem in this research. Because it is not explicitly concerned with moment-to-moment judgments of the teachers whose actions are observed, teachers are not considered informants in the development of observational categories. Also framed out of view in this genre of research on teaching is close investigation of the nested, negotiated contexts—from interpersonal to social and historical—constraining teaching. Thus, absent in this view of teaching is investigation of teachers' learning to act within and often despite vicissitudes of their working lives, cultural norms, and social institutions (Erickson, 1986). It is important to mention these limitations not because we should hold a study accountable for all of teaching's complexities but to illustrate the need to look within and also outside the area illuminated by any single approach to research. Moreover, recalling Cole's (1996) metaphor, the areas framed out of view, or left outside of the realm of inquiry, should not be assumed to be irrelevant to the inquiry.

The idea of applying the nomological paradigm to the study of social problems was ascendant at mid-century and remains extremely salient in contemporary research on teaching. Its research is especially useful and attractive to educational decision makers when they are designing and evaluating programs—a phenomenon of modern educational life. For example, Cohen and Garet (1975) characterized its authority in the eyes of policy makers in terms of its offering relevance, validity, and a "believable and consistent basis for social action" (p. 25). We can study human thought and activity in the light of this paradigm, seeking law-like generalizations about how teachers think and also what kinds of knowledge they need to make good pedagogical decisions. However, it is of limited use for purposes of understanding thoughtful action in context, a kind of research useful to teachers and administrators more locally.

To understand local knowledge in teaching and teacher education, we needed in-depth studies of individual teachers at work and of the variety of ways that teachers think about and do that work (e.g. Lampert, 1985, 2001). For example, we can use ethnographic research to study meaning in teachers' thought and action, specifically, "what meanings people construct, how they construct them, and how these constructions guide their actions." This kind of research, in what is called the "interpretive paradigm," yields "a relatively loosely ordered collection of interpretive schemes" often of interest and use to practitioners (Wardekker, 2000, p. 266). As we will see below, like the nomological paradigm, the interpretive paradigm has particular strengths and limitations. It illuminates different aspects of teaching and teacher education, and it does so in different ways and for different audiences and purposes.

In the 1970s, researchers tackled the problem of studying the local knowledge informing practice. Early on, the computer was viewed as both a metaphor and a conceptual model for studying local knowledge because it was able to make thinking both contingent and visualizeable. Psychologists became interested in studying human thinking in context as "information processing" (Bruner, 1996). Yet when researchers used this metaphor to understand pedagogy, information processing needed to be further complicated to capture the reflexivity and indeterminacy of teaching practice (Spiro, Feltovich, Jacobson, & Coulson, 1993/1995). Of this Shulman (2001) recalled,

> I was struck by this incredible anomaly that while physicians were being studied as complex, autonomous, thoughtful, reflective, strategic problem-solvers, teaching was studied as if it were a series of mindless behaviors emitted by teachers in response to students as stimuli. It grew out of a totally different conception of the behavioral sciences. And so I began to raise the question: What would research on teaching actually look like if we thought about teachers with the same kind of respect and complexity that we hold for physicians and other professionals?
>
> (p. 11)

Because a teacher works with many students within emergent, normative, and negotiated settings, his or her knowledge is not simply instantiated in patterns of observed behavior, nor is it simply invisibly scripted and in the head. Instead, its norms are taught and learned, and they are shared sufficiently for us to recognize and even assess teaching. But these norms are not determinative. Teachers retain sufficient agency to act in new, creative ways. As such, teaching is both ordered and responsive to norms and standards and also improvisational and responsive to other participants (Gee, 1991; Shulman, 1986).

This way of understanding teaching and the approach to studying teaching that it implies are illuminated by sociolinguistic theory and its descriptions of communication as a cultural process in which language is grammatical, whereas its use (or speech)—constrained by grammar—is creative, context-sensitive, and thus both situationally appropriate and comprehensible (Cazden, 1986). Teaching, when viewed in this light, is a complicated craft to teach and learn. It requires skill, experience, mentoring, apprenticeship, and knowledge. The teacher as professional cannot be assumed to be prepared to teach simply because he or she has attended school as a pupil. Thus, the study of teaching and teacher education needs additional light from fields concerned with the social and cultural organization of thought and learning. Moreover, it needs a focus on the explicit preparation of teachers. In an introductory review of research in teacher education, Lanier (1986) noted that some of this research on teaching as a learned profession would necessarily be interdisciplinary and that it would need examination of the language, thought, and activity of the often overlooked "teachers of teachers" (p. 528).

Proposing multidisciplinary research on teachers' clinical thinking, Lanier and Shulman (1975) sought to understand teaching complexity in ways that would inform the education of both pupils and teachers at the levels of both practice and policy. For them, absent a coherent, contextualized theory of teacher thinking in action, it would be difficult to envision a curriculum or means of assessment for teacher education that cultivated the habits of mind of a professional educator. Thus, seeking to complicate the prevailing nomological view of teaching, Lanier and Shulman wrote,

> It is not merely doing which defines teaching. It is knowing what to do and when to do it that

constitutes the clinical aspect of teaching and defines the features of teaching that serve as the subject matter for research on teaching as clinical work.

(p. B-I-6)

Some of the research genres applied to studying teacher thinking as clinical work have been in the nomological tradition (e.g. experimental, quasi-experimental, and correlational studies). Others have been interpretive (e.g. ethnographies, clinical interviews, and discourse analyses). Eclectic in style, research on teacher thought and action includes studies framed and conducted by university-based researchers and teacher educators (e.g. Brophy, 1989), practitioners (e.g. Ballenger, 1999; Lytle & Cochran-Smith, 1992), and teachers and university-based researchers working in collaboration (e.g. Raphael *et al.*, 2001). These diverse inquiries share the idea that teaching is, in Bruner's (1996) words, "inevitably based on notions about the nature of the learner's mind." Bruner elaborated on this perspective as follows:

> In theorizing about the practice of education in the classroom (or any other setting for that matter), you had better take into account the folk theories that those engaged in teaching and learning already have. For any innovations that you, as "proper pedagogical theorist," may wish to introduce will have to compete with, replace, or otherwise modify the folk theories that already guide both teachers and pupils.

(p. 46)

Notwithstanding its concern for teachers' folk theories and its inclusion of teachers as participants in the inquiry process, research on teacher thought and action in context is limited in the view of teaching that it affords. For example, its bias toward typicality in descriptions of local knowledge tends to freeze actors in the "ethnographic present." This makes envisioning difference, variation, or change difficult. Its reports tend to generalize within groups, leading to texts that can stereotype individuals and groups. Its descriptive language can reify limiting images of the teacher (as Caucasian, monolingual, and suburban, for example), the teacher's work (as isolated or bounded in the classroom), or the teacher's time and place (contemporary, suburban). Thus, although their research aims at descriptions of local knowledge in use, biases, methodological choices, and limitations in styles of research reporting can leave very little room for examination of difference or, ultimately, for consideration of praxis (Florio-Ruane, 2001; Ladson-Billings, 2000; Oakes & Lipton, 1999).

To redress some of these problems of theory, ideology, method, and representation, researchers have again widened the arc of light in research on teaching and teacher learning to include explication of local knowledge(s) in contact, conflict, and transformation. This is intertextual work, drawing on literature, literary criticism, political theory, history, and social analysis to examine difference, conflict, power, and change. In this light, research involves critical dialogue among various participants and stakeholders in the teaching and learning process, from parent to politician, novice teacher to policy maker, child to administrator. Attempting discursive research of this sort within an urban preservice teacher education setting, Morrell and Collatos (2001) applied critical theory to educational research, asserting that "true teacher learning and classroom transformations will not occur until teacher-students and student-teachers engage in critical and liberating dialogue where each group informs the other as both grow in consciousness and sensitivity" (p. 6). The view of teaching and research on teaching as dialogue stands to add yet more light to a field of research that has been centered on the teacher. It may decenter teaching, finding other ways to explore the complexity of the educational process. In addition, it identifies other centers for our gaze if we aim to understand the teacher's work. For example, we need to know a good deal more about the experience of teaching from learners' perspectives (Shultz & Cook-Sather, 2001) and also from the perspectives of the families and communities from which learners come (Moll & Greenberg, 1990) if we are to discover and understand new and perhaps more effective ways to serve students of and for the future. Doing this entails shifts in researchers' points of view, admits of more voices and methods of inquiry, and teaches us anew about teaching and the education of teachers.

In this critical light, teaching is open to reconceptualization. Many tacitly held ideas about the role of the teacher, the nature of knowledge, and the purpose of education are called into question when teacher and learner come together in dialogue and where knowledge is not something to be produced in the student by means of teacher thought and action but is a joint construction, continuously negotiated and developed as a part of life in a learning community (see, e.g. Lave & Wenger, 1991).

WHAT WORKS? THE USE OF COMPLEXITY

Entertaining complexity is difficult under any circumstances and especially in situations of urgency. Although our problems in education are urgent, we must be cautious about the ways that urgency can limit inquiry and understanding. What works? is the question most often asked by practitioners and policy makers of our applied research on teaching and teacher education. Sometimes we can answer this question helpfully and wisely. Sometimes we do not answer it, choosing to reframe it. Sometimes information useful to practitioners and policy makers comes from research on questions they had not thought to ask or from modest, easily overlooked studies of ancillary or exploratory nature. Sometimes we bear down on a practical problem with all of our resources only to have it elude us within the limits of our theory and research design. At other times, serendipity leads the prepared mind to unanticipated findings that are of both theoretical importance and practical value.

Teacher education faces difficult problems as we begin the new century—recruiting a diverse teacher cohort, preparing teachers better to serve our pupil population, enriching our canon with accounts of teaching in diverse contexts, and improving our effectiveness to educate all children, especially those in poverty who are poorly served by public education. Yet if a climate of crisis prevails in the face of such problems, the public may look to research for authority, efficiency, and simplicity. Although the temptation to succumb to this seductive position may be strong, researchers need to remember that it is a misrepresentation of what we can provide, a distortion of our efforts to provide information that is useful and carefully expressed. To illustrate, I will make brief reference to two examples that may seem far afield from teaching and teacher education: research on cancer and research on literacy in Liberia, West Africa.

First, cancer. Recently I read an article in *The New Yorker* magazine. Although it critiqued the U.S. "war on cancer" of the late 20th century, it also spoke to a national tendency to choose the metaphor of war (with all the discipline and urgency it implies) to solve difficult social problems (e.g. the war on drugs, the war on poverty) (Groopman, 2000). This critique haunted me because of its applicability to our field. Using the 20-year war on cancer as his case example, Groopman (2000) reported that the coming together of serious problems, philanthropy, and political power led to the development of a federally funded program of research that aimed to hasten the finding of cures to cancer by means of particular lines of inquiry thought to be most relevant. Thus, research proposals funded in the war on cancer targeted with laser-like precision areas of inquiry thought to hold the answers to cancers of many kinds.

More than 20 years later, although there have been modest successes, we can hardly say that the war on cancer has been won. Perhaps the war was itself a casualty of its own narrowness of mind. By targeting cancer narrowly and perhaps selecting its targets with insufficient information, it became difficult to get funding for research that widened the arc of light on the complex of diseases we call cancer. And more troubling, some of the funded studies had prematurely closed in on experimental treatments, sometimes with dire results to patients. Paradoxically, some of what researchers learned in the war on cancer did not help us cure cancer but helped us understand other difficult diseases outside the manifest scope of work (e.g. HIV). And finally, in a number of cases, research undertaken at the fringes of or entirely outside the cancer centers in the United States had unanticipated findings of use to cancer researchers (Groopman, 2000).

Now to Vai literacy. The late Sylvia Scribner (1984) was a pioneer not only in her commitment to scholarship addressing policy makers but also in her awareness of the need for critical, reflective action as an applied researcher. Her essay "Literacy in Three Metaphors" was addressed to policy makers in international development. Based on her research on the local meaning and use of literacy among the Vai in Liberia, Scribner combined methods drawn from anthropology and psychology to locate literacy in culture. Scribner's vignettes of Vai literacy illustrate different ways people use written language. Taken this way, Scribner's accounts offer only one limited and reproductive account to policy makers. Readers do not learn about their own thinking, or the frames of reference within which they are enmeshed. Implicitly, they think of teaching literacy as helping others not to become literate but to "become like me."

Instead, however, Scribner (1984) used her research-based vignettes of Vai literacies as metaphors (literacy as a state of grace, as a functional tool, as power). Not every reader of the Vai accounts cares specifically about programs for literacy education in Liberia. But to the extent that readers care about what it means to presume to design, administer, or assess educational programs of any sort, they learn from the metaphors Scribner offered: that literacy is not a unitary practice and that it is intimately tied to context of use and also to history, politics, and culture. She used figurative language to link the reader not only to the expected declarative description of the "other" (what Margaret Mead would likely consider fulfilling the necessary objectivity of observation), but poetically to images of people using script in many ways and for many purposes (what Mead would identify as the empathy also required of good human science). This blend of mind and heart invites the reader to reflect on his or her own folk wisdom and local knowledge by asking, What does literacy mean in my life, time, and society? How do my tacitly held norms and values for its practice limit my thinking about other literacies? What responsibilities do I have, as a person empowered to make decisions affecting the literate lives of others, to be thoughtful about not only the limits of their knowledge but also the limits of my own? To the pragmatic question, What works? we can think of Scribner answering by means of her research, it depends on what you mean by literacy. And, by the way, defining literacy is not a simple, once-and-for-all act.

We can miss the point in applied research by focusing too tightly and prematurely on a problem or by misconstruing the nature of the problem. Describing research as the lens through which we view complex problems of our practice, Purcell-Gates (2000) offered us four rigorous lenses, each useful in different ways in educational research: experimental, correlational, descriptive, and ethnographic. Noting the strengths and limitations of these approaches, she made a strong case for multiple views of complexity that deserve to be used in concert rather than in competition to enhance our understanding of literacy teaching and learning. She pointed out that

> many educational issues and problems clearly require research that draws on multiple perspectives, approaches, and procedures . . . To restrict educational research to one or two paradigms . . . would unacceptably restrict our ability to address the complex challenges of educating all learners in this complex, multicultural society of ours to their full potential.
>
> (p. 4)

In many ways, that is the legacy of research on teaching and teacher education in the 20th century.

It is a paradoxical feature of social interaction that in times of stress or urgency, we are apt to limit the light on the subject rather than to open up possible avenues of exploration. In contemporary times, we are not only metaphorically at war with complex social and educational problems but functionally at war (though at this writing not formally declared), not with a bounded nation-state but with a complex, indeterminate collective of terrorists. In response to the urgency of our situation, we have made many moves toward focus and hierarchical order. Yet curiously, out in the desert, where the enemy is not marching in flanks but hiding in caves, we have had to rely on small, stealthy, and nonhierarchical groups to locate intelligence by which we can direct our forces. Perhaps this is one reason the war on terrorism seems strangely new to our senses and sensibilities.

In a classic essay on the concept of role, Goffman (1961) described the idea of "role distance" or the different ways a formal role is enacted in different situations. He noted that whereas there are many ways to behave in enacting a formal role, these tend to move closer to the role's putative definition when crisis or urgency is perceived. Thus, the surgeon may joke and banter with scrub nurses and interns prior to the incision but utter only clipped, highly compact imperatives ("Clamp." "Scalpel.") as the patient's entrails are exposed. Bernstein (1975) similarly argued that the work of people can be more flexibly and horizontally organized in situations of low stress. However, when resources are limited or there is external pressure, organizations tend to work in more specialized, hierarchical ways. To the extent that formality, what Frake (n.d.) called "the black tie of scholarship," is highly valued, these moves serve to confer a sense of efficiency, quality, even virtue, to particular genres of research, ironically at the very moment when it would seem that a wide and varied exploration is needed most. The moves toward discipline, formality, and hierarchy are, by definition, moves that stratify. They are moves that mute or eliminate some voices and exaggerate the power of others. In this way, paradoxically, the calling of a crisis can lead to the exclusion of the perspectives and voices of people closest to the problem under study—or at least those most directly implicated in the solutions proffered by research.

IN CONCLUSION: KEEPING IT COMPLEX

Each new venture in research is neither a sign of progress toward some Aristotelian truth nor a stop on the way to a wished-for grand synthesis. However, studies of the messiness of practice are not de facto messy studies. As applied researchers in the human sciences, we work to illuminate teaching and teacher education in an ongoing way and by means of sustained, expansive, responsive, critical, and multivoiced scholarship. Yet this process seems paradoxical in the present moment, when our field is under great pressure from our various publics and a political rhetoric of crisis permeates discussion of teaching, teacher education, and teacher quality. Researchers, at times, seem to be proceeding at too leisurely a pace. We sometimes fail to synthesize our work and apply what we have learned to problems of practice. Yet our deliberative pace and care with respect to truth claims are not efforts to dodge the responsibility of an applied field. They are part and parcel of our discipline, forcing us to slow down sufficiently to be sure that we balance what Margaret Mead (1976) took to be the dual commitments of practitioners of a human science—empathy and objectivity.

In addition to studies supported or contracted for by powerful agencies and benefactors, we need, as a field, inquiry into the very nature of the crises to which we are asked to respond as well as consideration of those interests and problems left outside such a scope of work. In short, we need thoughtful dialogue about the ways that teaching and teacher education problems are identified, understood, queried, and helpfully addressed by our research. By means of this dialogue, we may continue to grow our field and its potential not only to solve practical problems but also to create new knowledge and to entertain problems as yet undiscovered. Unless we take the time and the responsibility to keep our work—and our field—complex, we will be unable to resist crisis-driven, regressive behaviors that harden the lines of power and authority and limit educational inquiry. Unless we keep teaching and teacher education complex, we will fall prey to some or all of the following: pitting approaches to research against one another in the name of rigor; privileging natural science-based approaches solely because of their compatibility with the language and assumptions of policy; failing to recognize that all approaches to research have limited purview; and disregarding insights from critical, alternative approaches that seek to increase the light in our studies of teaching and teacher education.

ACKNOWLEDGMENT

I thank P. David Pearson, with whom I have been privileged to teach a seminar on language, literacy, and learning, for helping me to think about the topic of this article.

REFERENCES

Ballenger, C. (1999) *Teaching other people's children: literacy and learning in a bilingual classroom.* New York: Teachers College Press.

Bernstein, B. (1975) *Class, codes, and control* (Vol. 3). London: Routledge.

Brophy, J. (ed.) (1989) *Advances in research on teaching* (Vol. 1). Greenwich, CT: JAI.

Bruner, J. (1996) *The culture of education.* Cambridge, MA: Harvard University Press.

Cazden, C. B. (1986) *Classroom discourse.* New York: Teachers College Press.

Clark, C. M. & Yinger, R. (1979) *Three studies of teacher planning* (IRT Research Series No. 55). East Lansing: Michigan State University.

Cohen, D. K. & Garet, M. S. (1975) Reforming educational policy with applied research. *Harvard Educational Review*, 43(1), 17–43.

Cole, M. (1996) *Cultural psychology: a once and future discipline.* Cambridge, MA: Harvard University Press.

Cuban, L. (1984) *How teachers taught.* New York: Longman.

Duckworth, E. (1991) Twenty-four, forty-two, and I love you: keeping it complex. *Harvard Educational Review*, 61(1), 1–26.

Dunkin, M. J. & Biddle, B. J. (1974) *The study of teaching.* New York: Holt.

Eisenhart, M. (1995) The fax, the jazz player, and the self-story teller. How do people organize culture? *Anthropology and Education Quarterly*, 26(1), 3–26.

Erickson, E. (1982) Taught cognitive learning in its immediate environments: a neglected topic in the anthropology of education. *Anthropology and Education Quarterly*, 13(2), 149–180.

Erickson, F. D. (1986) Qualitative methods in research on teaching. In M. C. Wittrock (ed.), *Handbook of research on teaching* (3rd ed., pp. 119–161). New York: Macmillan.

Florio-Ruane, S. (with deTar, J.) (2001) *Teacher education and the cultural imagination: autobiography, conversation and narrative.* Mahwah, NJ: Erlbaum.

Frake, C. (n.d.) A cultural analysis of "formal." Unpublished manuscript, Stanford University, CA.

Gee, J. (1991) *The social mind: language, ideology, and social practice.* New York: Bergen and Garvey.

Goffman, E. (1961) *Encounters: two studies in the sociology of interaction.* New York: Bobbs-Merrill.

Groopman, J. (2000, June 4) The 30 years war. *The New Yorker*, 77(14), 52–63.

Ladson-Billings, G. (2000) Fighting for our lives: preparing teachers to teach African American students. *Journal of Teacher Education*, 51(3), 206–214.

Lampert, M. (1985) How do teachers manage to teach? *Harvard Educational Review*, 55(2), 178–194.

Lampert, M. (2001) *Teaching problems and the problems of teaching.* New Haven, CT: Yale University Press.

Lanier, J. E. (with Little, J. W.) (1986) Research on teacher education. In M. Wittrock (ed.), *Handbook of research on teaching* (3rd ed., pp. 527–569). New York: Macmillan.

Lanier, J. E. & Shulman, L. S. (1975) *Technical proposal.* East Lansing: Michigan State University, Institute for Research on Teaching.

Lave, J. (1996) Teaching, as learning, in practice. *Mind, Culture, and Activity*, 3(3), 149–164.

Lave, J. & Wenger, E. (1991) *Situated learning: legitimate peripheral participation.* Cambridge, UK: Cambridge University Press.

Lytle, S. L. & Cochran-Smith, M. (1992) Teacher research as a way of knowing. *Harvard Educational Review,* 62(4), 447–474.

Mead, M. (1976) Towards a human science. *Science,* 191(4230), 903–909.

Moll, L. & Greenberg, J. B. (1990) Creating zones of possibilities: combining social contexts for instruction. In L. C. Moll (ed.), *Vygotsky and education: instructional and applications of sociohistorical psychology* (pp. 319–348). Cambridge, UK: Cambridge University Press.

Morrell, E. & Collatos, A. (2001, April) *Toward a critical pedagogy: utilizing student sociologists as teacher educators.* Paper presented at the annual meeting of the American Educational Research Association, Seattle, WA.

Oakes, J. & Lipton, M. (1999) *Teaching to change the world.* Boston: McGraw-Hill.

Purcell-Gates, V. (2000) The role of qualitative and ethnographic research in educational policy. *Reading Online,* 4(1). Retrieved from http//readingonline.org/articles/purcell-gates/

Raphael, T. E., Florio-Ruane, S., Kehus, M., George, M., Hasty, N. L., & Highfield, K. (2001) Thinking for ourselves: literacy learning in a diverse teacher inquiry network. *Reading Teacher,* 54(6), 596–607.

Scribner, S. (1984) Literacy in three metaphors. *American Journal of Education,* 93(1), 7–22.

Shulman, L. S. (1986) Paradigms and research programs in the study of teaching: a contemporary perspective. In M. C. Wittrock (ed.), *Handbook of research on teaching* (3rd ed., pp. 3–36). New York: Macmillan.

Shulman, L. S. (2001) Those who understand, teach: Lee Shulman champions the cause of understanding teachers and their learning. *New Educator,* 7(1), 10–13.

Shultz, J. and Cook-Sather, A. (eds.). (2001) *In our own words: student perspectives on school.* Lanham, MD: Rowan & Littlefield.

Spiro, R., Feltovich, P. J., Jacobson, M. D., & Coulson, R. L. (1993/1995) *Cognitive flexibility, constructivism, and hypertext: random access instruction for advanced knowledge in ill-structured domains.* Available from Webmaster@ilt.columbia.edu

Tyack, D. (1974) *The one best system: a history of American urban education.* Cambridge, MA: Harvard University Press.

Wardekker, W. L. (2000) Criteria for the quality of inquiry. *Mind, Culture, and Activity,* 7(4), 259–272.

8.3 Knowing teaching

The intersection of research on teaching and qualitative research

Magdalene Lampert
University of Michigan, Ann Arbor

Source: Magdalene Lampert, Knowing teaching: the intersection of research on teaching and qualitative research. *Harvard Educational Review*, 70(1), 2000, pp. 86–99

In this article, Magdalene Lampert argues that teachers can be both initiators and active partici-pants in a research agenda, adding valuable insider knowledge. She considers three points: "the potential for teacher research to change ideas about who is responsible for producing profes-sional knowledge, the benefits and dangers of inserting the self into social science, and the challenges of presenting the problems of a practice from inside that practice."

Educational researchers struggle incessantly with the relationship between knowledge and action. What does it mean to do scholarship in an applied field? What methodologies are appropriate to capture the problems of the field? Are these practitioners' problems? Are they problems worthy of scholarly inquiry? What is the relevance of the findings of scholarly research for improving practice? In wrestling with these questions, educational research and qualitative research have intertwined and influenced one another, raising issues that mix content questions with methodological problems. In the halls of academe, questions about voice, about the rela-tionship between the researcher and the researched, and about the relevance of scholarship to the solution of social problems have always been high on the agendas of both qualitative research and educational research. In the corners where educational research attends to teach-ing, these questions have been particularly prominent.

WHAT IS RESEARCH ON TEACHING?

I started teaching in the 1960s, inspired by contemporary commentaries about what was wrong with schools. Among the most influential of these commentaries were stories about teaching written in the first person by reformers who taught school to find out what was going on there and what could be done about it.[1] My experience as a teacher in an urban high school confirmed what I had been reading. But, when I turned from classroom teaching to the academic study of teach-ing in 1978, I discovered that books like these were not found on the assigned reading lists in my graduate school courses. Only in a history seminar did I encounter some writing about practice by teachers from the 1920s and 1930s, teachers who started schools, designed curricula, and studied children.[2] In the contemporary writing about teaching that I was assigned, the teacher's voice was not to be heard.

I am not the only one who has been puzzling about the teacher's role in research on teaching. In *Educational Researcher*, the monthly journal of the American Educational Research Associ-ation (AERA), the question of who in my research community speaks appropriately of teaching and how they should go about studying practice has been raised repeatedly over the last decade.[3] Most recently, Gary Anderson and Kathryn Herr examined the problem of making room for "rigorous practitioner knowledge" in schools and universities.[4] They pointed to the classic relationship between professional knowledge and "systematic knowledge produced by schools of higher learning" as one of the sticking points in defining appropriate methods of research on teaching, as well as in determining who is qualified to do it. As scholars argue about both the purposes and the validity of research on teaching, the question of who should do research on teaching spills over into questions about method and mixes with assertions about appropriate genres for reporting research. Is research on teaching a scholarly effort to understand a complex practice? Is it only of interest if applying it produces student learning? Is it an instrumental project, identifying problems, proposing solutions, and testing them in practice? Is it meant to produce knowledge for teachers? Or for those who prepare teachers? Or for those who control teachers' working conditions?

In the midst of all these questions, not only paradigms but also products and venues for communicating findings have proliferated. The AERA established a new division (Division K) for research on "Teaching and Teacher Education" in June 1984. It quickly became the largest division in the association, with seven different sections. From a practitioner's perspective, the boundaries among the sections are somewhat puzzling: one deals with research on teaching "subject matter," one with research on "collaborative or partnership settings" for teaching, one with research on teaching in multicultural settings, and one with research on "teaching and learning in the contexts of teachers' work," which is further divided into a subsection for pedagogical aspects and a subsection for organizational aspects. A separate section is devoted to "self-study and practitioner inquiry and scholarship on teachers and teaching."[5] In all of the sections of Division K, research is "construed broadly to include but not be limited to, philosophical, historical, ecological, ethnographic, descriptive, correlational, or experimental studies." Research on teaching and qualitative research have grown and developed together, and the hodgepodge that has resulted from their interaction has become an institution.

TEACHER RESEARCH

One element in this jumble of practice-focused inquiry stands out as especially worthy of commentary. The formal addition of practitioners to the community of researchers on teaching, indicated by their inclusion in the AERA as well as other scholarly institutions, seems to raise the most interesting questions for qualitative research. The shift from thinking of research as something that is done *on* teachers to a kind of work that is done *by* teachers could not have happened without the concurrent growth in appreciation of the contributions of qualitative research to the field of educational scholarship in recent years. In the 1970s, qualitative research helped to open educational research to questions of meaning, perspective, ownership, and purpose, and into this opening came teacher research.

Teachers have become participants in academic communities of research in several different ways. Some who make their living by teaching full time K-12 schools conduct inquiry in their own and in one another's classrooms.[6] Others collaborate with university researchers while retaining their teaching positions, contributing the perspective of daily practice to the questions under study.[7] In a few cases, teachers regard inquiry to be part of their day-to-day work in classrooms. In other cases, it is one among many opportunities for "professional development," offered alongside summer institutes on subject matter, workshops on classroom management techniques, and conference sessions on new curricula. And then there are faculty members of colleges and universities who choose to teach in K-12 schools as a means to create a site for pursuing investigations of practice.[8] Some teach part of every day, others teach full time for a year or more.

A multitude of books and articles are produced by this conglomeration of practitioners, some published in academic presses and journals, some in popular media. A few hybrid presses and journals have emerged that would be hard to identify as one or the other, and which count a majority of teachers among their authors. Conferences are devoted to teacher research, and funding agencies are making money available to support it.[9] The genres used to convey the findings of teacher research are as varied as the ways in which this work is structured.

ISSUES RAISED FOR QUALITATIVE RESEARCH BY TEACHER RESEARCH

Teacher research raises numerous issues for scholars who do qualitative research. Here I will consider only three: the potential for teacher research to change ideas about who is responsible for producing professional knowledge, the benefits and dangers of inserting the self into social science, and the challenges of presenting the problems of a practice from inside that practice.

Professional responsibility

If teachers are doing research on their own practice, might they assume a central role in professional knowledge production? If teaching problems were considered to be the responsibility of the profession, rather than private trials for individuals to endure or mechanical defects for outsiders to repair, a great deal of expertise could be mustered in the service of improving practice. Such a move would redefine power relationships between practitioners and researchers, and raise questions about what nonpractitioners have to add to the "knowledge base." Practitioners doing research on practice could change the kinds of questions that are asked and the new understanding that is produced. If teachers write about their work from the inside, including both personal and professional perspectives on the problems of practice, their work could substantially alter what we now think of as appropriate conventions in the discourse of applied research.[10] As they communicated about their inquiry, teachers would develop a new syntax and a new semantics to add to those of the academic disciplines in the study of educational phenomena. Just as sociologists, anthropologists, and psychologists now both use and modify a variety of qualitative methods, practitioners would test and contribute to the development of these approaches to producing new knowledge.

Although appealing, looked at through an outsider's lens, this scenario is not without its problems. One of them has to do with where we draw the line between research and thoughtful practice. As Ken Zeichner has asked, "Is it proper to call it research when teachers examine their practice in a systematic and intentional manner?"[11] I will not take on that issue here, as Zeichner has already done so, and he is more qualified to give it adequate treatment than I. Another problem has to do with the social arrangements around teaching that tend to stifle inquiry. Creating a professional discourse in teaching has been a persistent challenge in the United States. In 1975, Dan Lortie wrote:

> The preparation of teachers does not seem to result in the analytic turn of mind one finds in other occupations whose members are trained in colleges and universities . . . One hears little mention of the disciplines of observation, comparison, rules of inference, sampling, testing hypotheses through treatment and so forth. Scientific modes of reasoning and pedagogical practice seem compartmentalized; I observed this even among science teachers. This intellectual segregation puzzles me; those in other kinds of "people work" (e.g. clinical psychology, psychiatry, social work) seem more inclined to connect clinical issues with scientific modes of thought. This separation is relevant because it militates against the

development of an effective technical culture and because its absence means that conserva-tive doctrines receive less factual challenge; each teacher is encouraged to have a personal version of teaching truth.[12]

In the past twenty-five years, many questions have been raised about the value and character of "the scientific method." But the problem that Lortie calls "intellectual segregation" persists among teachers, as does the rarity of observation, comparison, rules of inference, sampling, and testing hypotheses through treatment.[13] What Lortie calls "a personal version of teaching truth" con-tinues to exist for most teachers alongside of and often untouched by the "teaching truths" that are produced by university researchers.[14] No professional language for describing and analyzing practice has developed in the United States, even as teachers reject the descriptions and analy-ses of scholars.[15] This deficit is particularly alarming when it is considered in light of recent psychological and linguistic work on the relationships between shared language, the develop-ment of understanding, and problem-solving activity.[16] It is notable that teacher educators are not drawn from the ranks of accomplished teachers and that "practice teaching" is rarely conducted as the kind of apprenticeship that doctors and lawyers experience as they work on practical problems together with more experienced members of their intended profession. What this means is that the language of practice remains flat or nonexistent.

That teachers do not learn simply by engaging in collaborative professional inquiry has as much to do with the structure of their work as it does with a disposition toward privacy and intuition. Currently, few teachers in the United States have the time and space in their work lives to think about the dynamics of teaching, let alone the resources to document their work and study the problems of their practice. Collaborations among practitioners to work on the problems of practice are considered "luxuries," rather than essential components of the work, as they would be in other professions such as medical or legal practice.[17] In Japan, by contrast, the structure of professional development in teaching is built on the assumption that teaching is a collaborative process rather than a private enterprise, and that it is improved through teachers' collaborative inquiry, including peer planning of curriculum and instruction.[18] In K-12 classrooms, Japanese teachers regularly teach "research lessons" to their students that are designed, recorded, and discussed by groups of practitioners working together on a particular problem of curriculum and instruction. Such work—which occurs at the school and district level as well as in national profes-sional organizations—is thought not only to improve classroom practice, but also to connect classroom practice to broader educational goals and to explore conflicting ideas. Similarly, in China, a decades-long tradition and a well-articulated structure has new and experienced teachers collaborating in inquiry and practical problemsolving.[19] In the United Kingdom, a strong tradition of "action research" by teachers began in the 1960s and continues today.[20] The teachers who produce and communicate knowledge of teaching in these cultures are not a special brand of "teacher researchers," they do what they do as part of their everyday practice, accepting the study of teaching and the solving of its problems as a professional responsibility.

Although the structural supports for it are still weak, teacher research on practice seems to be gaining ground. As teachers talk at conferences and write for their peers, they are beginning to create a genre of professional inquiry. As scholars who teach make their teaching experiments available for common investigation, they develop a shared text for analysis by others and a language of conceptual frames based in practice. This work is part of a modest but growing set of complementary institutional efforts, including teachers' collaborative assessment of student work, district-level teacher research groups, professional development schools, and the presen-tation of practice for assessment by fellow teachers in teacher portfolios, all of which might qualify as forms of "qualitative research." As these new professional venues become opportunities for teachers to conduct inquiry and communicate their findings, how will their work be regarded in relation to the larger picture of "knowledge production"? Should practitioners' research meet the same standards of method as scholarly research? If they invent their own methods, will these methods make their way into academic discourse? Should they?

Bringing the self into scholarly activity

Writing academic texts in the first person is a current trend in many of the social sciences. Teacher research is but one small example of this phenomenon, but it gives qualitative researchers in education a context in which to examine the potential and the problems of this kind of writing. There are at least three issues of interest to qualitative researchers that arise from getting the self into a central position in research on teaching: the potential and pitfalls of auto-biographical narrative as a scholarly genre; the capacity to uncover invisible, relational aspects of the work that have not been recognized by outsiders; and the mixture of responsibility and analysis that such work entails. In 1985, as a justification for writing about my teaching in the first person as a form of scholarship, I argued:

> Who the teacher is has a great deal to do with both the way she defines problems and what can and will be done about them. The academician solves problems that are recognized in some universal way as being important, whereas a teacher's problems arise because the state of affairs in the classroom is not what she wants it to be. Thus, practical problems, in contrast to theoretical ones, involve someone's wish for a change and the will to make it. Even though the teacher may be influenced by many powerful sources outside herself, the responsibility to act lies within. Like the researcher and the theoretician, she identifies problems and imagines solutions to them, but her job involves the additional personal burden of doing something about these problems in the classroom and living with the consequences of her actions over time. Thus, by way of acknowledging this deeply personal dimension of teaching practice, I have chosen not only to present the particular details of [other] teachers' problems, but to draw one of these problems from my own experience.[21]

In the 1980s, research on teacher thinking expanded to include the teacher's voice alongside the researcher's, as scholars sought to understand why practitioners act the way they do. In naming the teacher thinking that this approach revealed as "practical knowledge," researchers like Freema Elbaz, Jean Clandinin, and Michael Connelly raised new epistemological questions, as well as new questions about what sorts of research methods were appropriate for the study of teaching.

Another way to bring teachers' voices into the research literature has occurred through the publication of autobiographical narratives, but several scholars have advised proceeding cautiously with this approach. In a keynote address to the International Study Association on Teacher Thinking in 1995, Ivor Goodson observed that it was dangerous to believe "that merely by allowing people to 'narrate' that we in any serious way give them voice and agency."[22] Goodson quotes Cynthia Chamber's review of Connelly and Clandinin's book, *Teachers as Curriculum Planners: Narratives of Experience:*

> These authors offer us the naive hope that if teachers learn "to tell and understand their own story" they will be returned to their rightful place at the center of curriculum planning and reform. And yet, their method leaves each teacher a "blackbird singing in the dead of night"; isolated, and sadly ignorant of how his/her song is part of a much larger singing of the world.[23]

He notes as well that Kathy Carter celebrated the insertion of teachers' voices into educational research in 1993, but she also observed:

For those of us telling stories in our work, we will not serve the community well if we sanctify story-telling work and build an epistemology on it to the point that we simply substitute one paradigmatic domination for another without challenging the domination itself. We must, then, become much more self-conscious than we have been in the past about the issues involved in narrative and story, such as interpretation, authenticity, normative value, and what our purposes are for telling stories in the first place.[24]

Working in the fields of psychology and sociology, Louise Kidder and Michelle Fine have made similar critical comments about the celebration of the insider's narrative. They assert that is it is the responsibility of researchers who stand outside the context of practice to "assert interpretive authority," placing the actor's story in relation to other actors and the world of ideas. Citing Joyce Ladner's commentaries on race research, they observe, "For Ladner, the very point of conduct-ing social research is to interrupt the 'common sense' frames, ideologically driven by social arrangements or what she calls 'the system,' and to provide alternative lenses for viewing social behavior."[25] Kidder and Fine suggest that multiple lenses of this sort are possible and desirable in researchers' interpretations of practitioners' stories: they call this work "kaleidoscopic."

How we regard the personal in teacher research is both a practical and a deeply epistemo-logical question, forcing us back to the enduring puzzles educational researchers deal with about how to relate what is learned from a single "case" in all its complexity to other situations in which similar problems arise. What does it mean for problems that arise for particular people in particu-lar contexts to be similar across settings? What additional skill or knowledge does a practitioner, or for that matter a scholar, need to have to take knowledge from one case into another?

Problem of representation

Once you know teaching from the inside, how do you communicate what you know so that there can be an accumulation of knowledge in the field? Writing about first-person teacher research in mathematics education, Deborah Ball goes beyond the importance of inserting the teacher's voice into the discourse of teaching and raises questions about the nature of autobiographical argument: on what basis are claims made by first-person writers, and on what evidence do readers accept them? Ball observes that teachers writing about teaching force us to ask what we mean by "truth" and to examine the writer's purposes as we define it. She draws on Ruth Behar's work, which describes the changing discourse of anthropology to emphasize that autobiograph-ical scholarly writing is more difficult than more familiar academic argument. Behar issues a caution to which all who are involved in such projects would be wise to attend:

> As is the case with any intellectual trend, some experiments work out better than others. It is far from easy to locate oneself in one's own text. Writing vulnerably takes as much skill, nuance, and willingness to follow through on the ramifications of a complicated idea as writing invulnerably and distantly. I would say it takes greater skill.[26]

Why would the teacher researcher be "writing vulnerably"? What is it about this kind of writing that requires so much skill, given that it is the telling of one's own story? As a teacher writing about my own teaching, I certainly have access to special knowledge, but at the same time, I am constrained by the limitations of any medium to express the multiple aspects of what I know. Although it is my aim to retain the richness and complexity of what is going on in what I write about my teaching, being in the middle of it makes me painfully aware of the impossibility of telling the whole story. Language, even supplemented by other media, is simply inadequate to capture my experience and knowledge of teaching practice. It is inadequate even to capture all of the aspects of an event, to say nothing of representing the constellations of feelings and intentions imbedded in that event. That I can have more of a sense of the whole of what is going on than any observer is both a blessing and a curse when I try to write about it.

Practice is doing. As I have argued, the study of practice thus begins in the setting in which a particular practitioner acts. To study practice means that I cannot succeed by limiting the focus of my inquiry, since a limited focus hinders practical problem-solving. Yet, in the course of attempting to tell about any practice, even if the telling is in the first person, one necessarily formalizes what has been learned, leaving out some aspects of the experience highlighting others. It is not only the outsider who can bring what Kidder and Fine call "kaleidoscopic interpretations." For any inquiry into one's own practice, there are many possible stories to tell. For every story that is told, there are many possible meanings to interpret. Stories about practice are mirrors of experience: like all texts, they are constructed by the author with certain intentions in mind.[27] When one is writing about oneself, no description seems adequate to the experience, and yet without description, what is learned remains private and unexamined.

This judgment about the inadequacy of language to represent my multi-faceted experience of practice is more than scrupulous self-criticism. My audience can hold me to a higher standard of verisimilitude than they would other authors of case studies of teaching because I am the teacher I am portraying. Other kinds of writers about teaching are excused for leaving out considerations of gender or political context or parental relations or subject matter because these are outside of their area of expertise. As a teacher I cannot ignore any of these domains, and I am also expected not to ignore them as a self-referential writer. In 1987, I turned to video as a possible solution to the problem of representing the complex nature of my teaching to others. I reasoned that, with video, the viewer would have greater access to the complex interactions occurring in the classroom even if they were limited by my editorial selection of a few minutes of the lesson from a longer stream of activity or by the angle of the videographer's lens. Such representations of the practices of teaching and studying seem authentic because what is going on for the participants seems to be available to the viewer all at once, rather than filtered through the interests of a describer.[28] In contrast to writing, video makes it possible to have a running image of the teacher–student–subject interaction without isolating these into single elements that need to be put back together in some way to convey the whole.

When I show a videotape of my classroom, the question of how much "background" I need to provide and what to tell people before showing the tape always worries me. I am never satisfied that I have figured it out. Invariably, I run up against the frustration of wanting to show and say more than I have time for, and wish I could say, "You had to have been there to understand what that was about." Once viewers start to comment on what they see me doing on the tape, the video seems to represent so little of what I know about what is going on. And what I know from "being there" has a lot to do with reasoning about the actions we are seeing on the tape. Speculating about why I did what I did and evidence of the reasonableness of those actions would need to be grounded in much more information than what was available. The possibility of real-time representations of teaching on video seems to exacerbate the problem of communicating about my practice rather than solving it.

My experiences with video pushed me to want to invent a better representation of teaching practice to serve as a basis for collaborative analysis and problem-solving. Working as elementary teachers, teacher educators, and researchers on teaching, Deborah Ball and I began to experiment in 1989 with multimedia. We assembled multiple records of our practice in an electronically accessible database that could be used by a teacher and her audience as the text to be interpreted in analytic discussions about practice. Although the promise of the technology has been greater than the reality, this representation of teaching continues to be both practically and conceptually appealling.[29] Multimedia technology has the potential to enable us to represent the kind of knowing that Ball and I find essential to our own teaching but lacking in research on teaching—what Lee Shulman has called "strategic" modes of knowing in practice.[30] Shulman's characterization of strategic knowing is strikingly similar to the rhetoric used by developers of multimedia technologies.[31] He observes that propositional knowledge is what is most conventionally delivered in academic settings to be "applied" in practice. He claims that case knowledge, with its vivid detail, makes the propositions it illustrates more memorable, but is still clearly distinguishable from strategic knowledge—knowledge as it is used in actual situations of practice:

> Both propositions and cases share the burden of unilaterality, the deficiency of turning the reader or user toward a single, particular rule or practical way of seeing. Strategic knowledge comes into play as the teacher confronts particular situations or problems, whether theoretical, practical, or moral, where principles collide and no simple solution is possible. Strategic knowledge is developed when the lessons of single principles contradict one another, or the precedents of particular cases are incompatible.[32]

It is precisely this sort of representation of practices of teaching that multimedia is supposed to make possible. It appealed to us because it could capture the complexity of practice that we saw from the inside, the strategic piece that required both thinking and doing but did not have a simple face. And perhaps it is this desire to understand the strategies teachers use in practice that drives the development of teacher research more broadly.

WHERE NEXT?

In 1990, the research team that I was working with conjured up the idea of a computer supported database called the "Investigator's Working Environment" (IWE), which would further the study of teaching by enabling the activities of browsing, organizing, annotating, and displaying records of classroom teaching and learning in multiple media, along with individual and group commentaries on these records. The IWE was to be designed so that classroom practitioners and educational researchers, as well as students, parents, school administrators, and policymakers, could have access to the same set of records and add their interpretations to those records for access by others in both synchronous and asynchronous conversations about the problems of teaching. In 1999, we are closer to the IWE becoming a reality than we were ten years ago, and perhaps it represents an idea of where qualitative research on teaching might be going. New technologies for recording and archiving video and audio data and increasingly sophisticated communications and database technologies have great promise for integrating broad sweeps with deep analyses. Decreased financial and cognitive costs of access means that communication between scholars and practitioners can be more readily established on a common base of information. Electronic communications enable participation in conversations about a common text among participants that are not limited by time and place. And new database technologies make possible links between primary sources and interpretations of those sources, opening up new ground on the old questions of how "results" of research are to be reported and their validity judged.

What research on teaching has become, particularly in the hands of teacher researchers, opens up new prospects and new puzzles for qualitative research. The new tools that practitioners and researchers have at their disposal will change both what kind of data can be collected and how analyses of that data can be carried out and communicated. As qualitative research on teaching evolves, practitioners and researchers will need to take account of the contributions of teachers who take on the responsibility of using these tools as a basis for generating context-specific professional knowledge. Practitioners and researchers will need to consider what counts as a "good" interpretation of events as the stories of practitioners about those events are placed alongside interpretive scholarship of various sorts. And practitioners and researchers will need to face the representational challenges of communicating about practice when it has been "known" from the inside. As we allow more voices into the conversation and enable the juxtaposition of their analyses, we will struggle with understanding the nature of practice, the nature of knowledge, and what knowledge is good for.

NOTES

1 For example, George Dennison, *The Lives of Children* (New York: Random House, 1969); James Herndon, *The Way It Spozed to Be* (New York: Simon & Schuster, 1968); John Holt, *How Children Fail* (New York: Pitman, 1964) and *How Children Learn* (New York: Pitman, 1967); Herb Kolh, *36 Children* (New York: New American Library, 1967); Jonathan Kozol, *Death at An Early Age* (New York: Houghton Mifflin, 1967).

2 *The Dewey School*, written by teachers at Chicago Lab School (Katherine Camp Mahew and Anna Camp Edwards [New York: Appleton-Century, 1936]), is a particularly interesting example of this genre.

3 See, for example, Marilyn Cochran-Smith and Susan Lytle, "Research on Teaching and Teacher Research: The Issues that Divide," *Educational Researcher*, 19, No.2 (1990), 2–11; Kathy Carter, "The Place of Story in the Study of Teaching and Teacher Education," *Educational Researcher*, 22, No.1 (1993), 5–12, 18; Virginia Richardson, "Conducting Research on Practice," *Educational Researcher*, 23, No.5 (1994), 5–10; D. Jean Clandinin and F. Michael Connelly, "Teachers' Professional Knowledge Landscapes: Teacher Stories—Stories of Teachers—School Stories—Stories of Schools," *Educational Researcher*, 25, No.3 (1996), 24–30.

4 Gary R. Anderson and Kathryn Herr, "The New Paradigm Wars: Is There Room for Rigorous Practitioner Knowledge in Schools and Universities?" *Educational Researcher*, 28, No.5 (1999), 12–21, 40.

5 See "2000 Annual Meeting Call for Proposals," *Educational Researcher*, 28, No.4 (1999), 39.

6 See, for example, Joan Krater, Jane Zeni, and Nancy Devlin Cason, *Mirror Images: Teaching Writing in Black and White* (Portsmouth, NH: Heinemann, 1994); Karen Hale Hankins, "Cacophony to Symphony: Memoirs in Teacher Research," *Harvard Educational Review*, 68 (1998), 80–95; and Karen Gallas, *Talking Their Way into Science: Hearing Children's Questions and Theories and Responding with Curricula* (New York: Teachers College Press, 1995).

7 See, for example, Sarah Warshauer Freedman, E. R. Simons, J. S. Kalnin, A. Casareno, and the M-CLASS Teams, *Inside City Schools: Investigating Literacy in Multicultural Classrooms* (New York: Teachers College Press, 1999).

8 See, for example, Timothy J. Lensmire, *When Children Write: Critical Re-visions of the Writing Workshop* (New York: Teachers College Press, 1994); Deborah Lowenberg Ball and Suzanne M. Wilson, "Integrity in Teaching: Recognizing the Fusion of the Moral and Intellectual," *American Educational Research Journal*, 33, No.1 (1996), 155–192; Magdalene Lampert, "When the Problem Is Not the Question and the Solution Is Not the Answer," *American Educational Research Journal*, 27, No.1 (1990), 29–64.

9 For example, "Voices from the Classroom," sponsored by The Center for Research on Evaluation, Standards and Student Testing (CRESS), Davis, CA; the teacher research section of the Ethnography Forum, University of Pennsylvania; The International Conference on Teacher Research, held annually by the National Writing Project; The Spencer Foundation; National Council for Teacher Education (NCTE).

10 See Susan Florio-Ruane, "Conversation and Narrative in Collaborative Research: An Ethnography of the Written Literacy Forum," in *Stories Lives Tell: Narrative and Dialogue in Education*, ed. Carol Witherell and Nel Noddings (New York: Teachers College Press, 1991), p. 247.

11 Kenneth Zeichner and Susan Noffke, "Practitioner Research," in *Fourth Handbook of Research on Teaching*, ed. Virginia Richardson (Washington, DC: American Educational Research Association, in press).

12 Dan Lortie, *Schoolteacher* (Chicago: University of Chicago Press, 1975), p. 230.

13 Michael Huberman, "The Model of the Independent Artisan in Teachers' Professional Relations," in *Teacher's Work*, ed. Judith Warren-Little and Milbrey McLaughlin (New York: Teachers College Press, 1993), pp. 11–50; Judith Warren Little, "The Persistence of Privacy: Autonomy and Initiative in Teachers' Professional Relations," *Teachers College Record*, 91 (1990), 509–536.

14 Zeichner and Noffke, "Practitioner Research"; Michael Huberman, "Moving Mainstream: Taking a Closer Look at Teacher Research," *Language Arts*, 73 (1996), 124–140.

15 The potential of National Board for Professional Teaching Standards (NBPTS), Interstate New Teachers Assessment and Support Consortium (INTASC), and National Council for the Accreditation of Teacher Education (NCATE) to support this development are described in *What Matters Most: Teaching for America's Future* (New York: National Commission on Teaching and America's Future, 1996). For a discussion of the difference and relationship between local and professional language, see Donald Freeman, "Renaming Experience/Reconstructing Practice: Developing New Understandings of Teaching," *Teaching and Teacher Education*, 9 (1993), 485–497.

16 For an application of this idea to teacher development, see Mary K. Stein, Edward A. Silver, and Margaret Schwan Smith, "Mathematics Reform and Teacher Development: A Community of Practice, Perspective," in *Thinking Practices in Mathematics and Science Learning*, ed. James Greeno and Shelly Goldman (Mahwah, NJ: Lawrence Erlbaum, 1998), pp. 17–52.

17 See Deborah Lowenberg Ball and Sylvia Rundquist, "Collaboration as a Context for Joining Teacher Learning with Learning about Teaching," in *Teaching for Understanding: Challenges for Policy and Practice*, ed. David K. Cohen, Milbrey W. McLaughlin, and Joan E. Talbert (San Francisco: Jossey-Bass, 1993), pp. 13–42; Suzanne Wilson, Carol Miller, and Carol Yerkes, "Deeply Rooted Change: A Tale of Learning to Teach Adventurously" in *Teaching for Understanding: Challenges for Policy and Practice*, ed. David K. Cohen, Milbrey W. McLaughlin, and Joan E. Talbert (San Francisco: Jossey-Bass, 1993), pp. 84–129.

18 Catherine Lewis and Ineko Tsuchida, "A Lesson Is Like a Swiftly Flowing River," *American Educator*, 22, No.4 (1998), 12–17, 50–51; N. Ken Shimahara, "The Japanese Model of Professional Development: Teaching as Craft," *Teaching and Teacher Education*, 14 (1998), 451–462.

19 Lynne Paine and Liping Ma, "Teachers Working Together: A Dialogue on Organizational and Cultural Perspectives of Chinese Teachers," *International Journal of Educational Research*, 19 (1993), 675–698.

20 See John Elliot, "School-Based Curriculum Development and Action Research in the United Kingdom," in *International Action Research: A Casebook for Educational Reform*, ed. Sandra Hollingsworth (London: Falmer Press, 1997), pp. 17–28.

21 I refer to "How Do Teachers Manage to Teach?" *Harvard Educational Review*, 55 (1985), 180; see also footnotes to this article and its brief review of supporting literature.

22 This address was published as Ivor Goodson, "Representing Teachers: Bringing Teachers Back In," in *Changing Research and Practice: Teachers' Professionalism, Identity, and Knowledge*, ed. Michael Kompf, W. Richard Bond, Don Dworet, and R. Terrance Boak (London: Falmer Press, 1966), pp. 211–221. The quote is on pp. 215–216.

23 Cynthia Chambers, "Review of Teachers as Curriculum Planners: Narratives of Experience," *Journal of Educational Policy*, 6 (1991) 353–354 (p. 354 quoted in Goodson, "Representing Teachers," p. 216).

24 Kathy Carter, "The Place of Story in the Study of Teaching and Teacher Education," *Educational Researcher*, 22, No.1 (1993), 11 (quoted in Goodson, "Representing Teachers," p. 220).

25 Louise Kidder and Michelle Fine, "Qualitative Inquiry in Psychology: A Radical Tradition," in *Critical Psychology: An Introduction*, ed. Dennis R. Fox and Isaac Prilltensky (Thousand Oaks, CA: Sage, 1997), pp. 34–50.

26 Deborah Lowenberg Ball, "Working in the Inside: Using One's Own Practice as a Site for Studying Teaching and Learning," in *In Research Design in Mathematics and Science Education*, ed. Anthony Kelly and Richard Lesh (Amsterdam: Kluwer, 1999), p. 400.

27 For examples of multiple stories being told about the same teaching events, see Harriet Bjerrum Nielsen, "Seductive Texts with Serious Intentions," *Educational Researcher*, 24, No.1 (1995), 4–12.

28 Katherine Merseth and Catherine Lacey, "Weaving Stronger Fabric: The Pedagogical Promise of Hypermedia and Case Methods in Teacher Education," *Teaching and Teacher Education*, 9 (1993), 283–299; Gary Sykes and Tom Bird, "Teacher Education and the Case Idea," in *Review of Research in Education*, ed. Gerald Grant (Washington, DC: American Educational Research Association, 1992), pp. 457–521; Deidre LeFevre, "'Why Video?" Unpublished manuscript, University of Michigan, 1999.

29 For a full description of this project and references to similar projects, see Magdalene Lampert and Deborah Ball, *Teaching, Multimedia and Mathematics: Investigations of Real Practice* (New York: Teachers College Press, 1998).

30 Lee Shulman, "Those Who Understand: Knowledge Growth in Teaching," *Educational Researcher*, 15, No.2 (1986), 4–14.

31 See, for example, the essays in Sueann Ambron and Kristina Hooper, *Interactive Multimedia: Visions of Multimedia for Developers, Educators, and Information Providers* (Redmond, WA: Microsoft Press, 1988).

32 Shulman, "Those Who Understand," p. 12.

Part 8
Commentaries

55 Toward a better understanding of teaching and learning about teaching

John Loughran
Monash University

Because a teacher works with many students within emergent, normative, and negotiated settings, his or her knowledge is not simply instantiated in patterns of observed behaviour, nor is it simply invisibly scripted and in the head. . . . Teachers retain sufficient agency to act in new, creative ways. As such, teaching is both ordered and responsive to norms and standards and also improvisational and responsive to other participants.

(Florio-Ruane, 2002, pp. 209–210)

As Florio-Ruane (above) makes abundantly clear, teaching is multifaceted. Yet paradoxically, although a recognition of the skills, competencies and knowledge that are enmeshed in practice may be helpful for looking into that which teaching comprises, simply reducing it to individual elements only serves to detract from an appreciation of its underlying complexity. A teacher's ability to improvise, adapt and respond in different ways to different pedagogical situations offers insight into the creativity, necessary professional autonomy and expertise inherent in quality practice, while simultaneously highlighting its somewhat ethereal nature. Clearly, as teaching is so complex it stands to reason that it must be difficult to capture, analyse and portray.

Teacher education then, in its attempt to mediate both teaching *and* learning about teaching must explicitly grapple with the complexity of practice while at the same time being sensitive to the fact that teaching is largely tacit by nature (Polanyi, 1962). In light of this, it is little wonder that teaching about teaching is often so poorly understood and misrepresented (both within and outside of the profession). Therefore, as a consequence of this situation, it is important that teacher educators are responsive to critique (rather than ignoring or naively accommodating it) in order to ensure that the work of teacher education is better understood.

Criticism of teacher education has been a recurrent theme for many years. Sadly, part of the implicit criticism of teacher education is linked to the taken for granted nature of teaching (and by extension, teacher education) which reinforces the notion of teaching as an undervalued profession. But as the introduction to this chapter suggests, this situation may itself be exacerbated by a lack of understanding of all that teaching and teacher education really involves. For example, Gage (1978) stated that "the importance of teacher education is commensurate with the importance of teaching" (p. 42) and he drew on Ryle's (1949) distinction between "knowing that" and "knowing how" as one way of interrogating teacher education practices in order to illustrate that "knowing about" teaching and "doing teaching" are not necessarily one and the same.

In many ways, Gage's argument reflects long held concerns for teaching and teacher education dating back to the work of Dewey in the Chicago Laboratory School: ". . . Dewey (1938) drew attention to the need for experience to be seen as a shaping force in the development of thoughtful and alert students of education as opposed to an entrée to a rudimentary proficiency in teaching" (Loughran, 2006, p. 22). Unfortunately, the distinction between technical proficiency and professional practice has largely served to establish arguments about teacher education based on a dichotomy rather than exploring the problematic nature of teaching; something that is compounded when considering teaching about teaching.

If teaching is viewed as problematic, then things that are viewed as absolute through the dichotomous approach noted above such as: developing the *best* way of responding to a given teaching and learning situation; creating the *right* curriculum for teacher education; choosing the *ideal* candidates for teaching; or, constructing *the* model of teacher education, are able to be translated into possibilities for enhancing understandings *for* practice (as opposed to measures *of* practice), thus leading to more meaningful and responsive approaches to teaching and learning about teaching. Perhaps one reason why conceptualizing teacher education at the (constantly) varying points along a continuum is so difficult is related to the intricacies of genuinely responding to the reality of learning; and all that that entails for teaching.

Myers (2002) has argued that teacher education has long been dominated by a "telling, showing, and guided approach" to practice. This phrase captures how teacher education practices are played out when the dilemmas and tensions borne of the complexity of teaching about teaching are glossed over by inappropriately conceptualizing quality teaching as "better telling." Indeed, the use of telling, showing and guided practice is based on an assumption that learning is simple and uncomplicated and that the knowledge and experiences of teacher educators can be transplanted into students of teaching. It is through such superficial views of the relationship between teaching and learning that much of the critique (both founded and unfounded) of the work of teacher education is based. Thus there is a pressing need for teacher education to respond more fully to the implications inherent in better understanding the interplay between teaching and learning. A considered response is crucial which means a serious focus on pedagogy is essential.

UNDERSTANDING PEDAGOGY

The use of the term pedagogy in countries such as the United Kingdom, United States, Australia and New Zealand is often as a synonym for teaching. However, drawing on the long tradition of pedagogy in Europe, it more readily "describes the relational values, the personal engagement, [and] the pedagogical climate . . . [It involves] problematizing the conditions appropriate [to] educational practices and aims to provide a knowledge base for professionals in their work with children [students]" (van Manen, 1999, p. 14). Teacher education obviously goes to the heart of the study of pedagogy. Teacher education therefore must be, by definition, at the cutting edge of understandings of pedagogy as it attempts to make clear for students of teaching the value of the how, what and why of teaching for understanding. Inevitably then, teacher education must purposefully embed learning about the complexity of teaching within experiences of its problematic nature so that pedagogy itself is the central focus for both teachers and students of teaching; and this should be reflected in the manner in which learning about teaching is constructed.

Lampert (2000) illustrates this very point through her explanation of what it means to her to be a teacher researcher. By paying attention to the opportunities for enhancing professional responsibility, introducing the self into scholarly activities and addressing problems associated with representing the complexity of practice she focuses attention on the importance of studying practice from the inside. In so doing, she highlights how a teacher's perspective on practice creates the "capacity to uncover invisible, relational aspects of the work that have not been recognized by outsiders; and the mixture of responsibility and analysis that such work entails" (p. 91). As a teacher researcher and concurrently being a teacher educator, Lampert works within the crucible of teaching and learning thus privileging her access to, and understanding of, pedagogy in ways that observers of teaching cannot. As she teaches her students and researches the influence of learning on teaching and teaching on learning, she develops new ways of seeing into the world of pedagogy. She is able to frame and reframe (Schön, 1983) situations, to create new and different vantage points and, in so doing, develop much deeper understandings of the complex relationship between teaching and learning.

Lampert's work appears to be driven by concerns for practice similar to those involved in self-study of teaching and teacher education practices (Hamilton, 1998). Self-study is a field that opens up the complex world of teaching and learning about teaching in ways that can only be done by those who are participants in the work of teacher education. Hence, self-study offers a fresh way of responding to the dichotomous views of teacher education practices that have persisted for so long by presenting "an approach to researching practice that has facilitated the development of more informed understanding of teacher educators' practice" (Berry, 2004a, p. 149).

In her extensive inquiry through self-study into her developing understanding of the demands associated with being a teacher educator, Berry (2004b) uncovered and described a number of tensions salient to learning about practice for teacher educators when they:

> ... attempt to match their goals for their students' learning with the needs and concerns that student teachers express for their own learning. These at times conflicting purposes are part of the ever-present ambiguity of teachers' (and teacher educators') work and are, as Lampert (1985, p. 194) observes, "more manageable than solveable."
>
> (Berry, 2004b, p. 1313)

Berry goes on to list in detail six tensions that she describes as crucial to shaping her teacher education practices that, together, illustrate some of the wisdom and expertise inherent in creating teaching situations through which to explore with students of teaching both "knowing that" and "knowing how." Her tensions are those of: Telling and Growth; Confidence and Uncertainty; Working with and Against; Discomfort and Challenge; Acknowledging and Building upon Experience; and, Planning and Being Responsive. Through these tensions, Berry captures the essence of that which teacher educators experience when confronted by the juxtaposition of simplistic and complex conceptualizations of teaching and learning about teaching.

In recognizing and responding to these tensions, contradictions and uncertainties of practice, pedagogical expertise becomes immediately apparent. However, managing this situation is not something that can be easily taught. It is difficult work and involves creating situations that must be experienced from both a teacher's and a student's perspective if it is to be fully apprehended and genuinely valued. Herein lies the challenge in teaching about teaching. There is a constant need for pedagogy to be a site for inquiry and growth. Clearly, both teaching and learning influence one another and, just as a teacher needs to be a learner so too a learner needs to be a teacher. Investigating and seeking to better understand the reciprocity necessary in this complex relationship is what makes it so difficult to accept that teacher education practices can (or should) be simply codified. But that does not mean that teacher education practices should not be well articulated. In fact, articulating teacher education practices matters and is central to that that which has been described as a pedagogy of teacher education (Korthagen *et al.*, 2001).

PEDAGOGY OF TEACHER EDUCATION

> In teaching and learning about teaching, the content, or subject matter, comprises at least the "theoretical" aspects of the "knowledge" of teaching (some might describe it as the *discipline of teaching*). Typically, much of this subject matter is distilled and offered through some form of curriculum ... and is what Russell (1997) has described as the *content turn* in teacher education. However, an issue that is often easily overlooked in teaching and learning about teaching is the concurrent need to also pay careful attention to the practices employed in presenting the subject matter—the *pedagogical turn* (Russell, 1997). Hence, for both the teacher and the student of teaching, ongoing and conflicting roles continually complicate the competing agendas of *teaching and learning* about teaching. Not only must both teachers and students of teaching pay careful attention to the subject matter being taught, they must also simultaneously pay attention to the manner in which that knowledge is being taught; and both must overtly be embraced in a *pedagogy of teacher education*.
> (Loughran, 2006, pp. 3–4, emphasis in original)

The importance of the notion of a pedagogy of teacher education is rooted in an expectation that teacher educators need to articulate their knowledge of practice in ways that will offer insights into what they do, how they do it and why as they teach teaching. Developing a pedagogy of teacher education is not a veiled call for a "complete book of rules" about how to teach teaching, rather, it is a way of focusing serious attention on the need for teacher educators' knowledge of practice to be more formally shared and critiqued in line with other scholarly traditions.

A pedagogy of teacher education involves a knowledge of teaching about teaching and a knowledge of learning about teaching and how the two influence one another in the pedagogic episodes that teacher educators create to offer students of teaching experiences that might inform their developing views of practice. Articulating that which comprises a pedagogy of teacher education therefore requires teacher educators to look into their teaching in ways that might capture and offer insights about the subtleties and nuances of their practice so that others might learn from, and build on, these research outcomes. Just as King (this volume) illustrates, that which might be "critical" to the research of learning about teacher education needs to be open to debate. If teacher educators share their approach to, and conceptualizations of, practice, they create opportunities for others to adopt, adapt and creatively respond to those insights in their own practice.

In developing a pedagogy of teacher education, the community of teacher educators needs to be able to illustrate how it is that students of teaching are educated (as opposed to trained). Through education, students of teaching might see that developing confidence in their own professional judgments as a consequence of explicating their pedagogical reasoning matters.

A pedagogy of teacher education offers the promise that teacher educators can demonstrate in their practice with their students of teaching that the core of expert practice is embedded in the need to make subtle judgements in unique situations (Hagger & McIntyre's, 2000). In so doing, teacher education can create a worthwhile goal for students of teaching to strive to achieve through their career long professional learning. To that end, looking into teacher education takes on new meaning so that the concept of teacher preparation might be better understood as just that; a beginning not an end unto itself.

LOOKING IN TO TEACHER EDUCATION

Cochran-Smith and Fries (this volume) "identify four dominant approaches to conceptualizing and studying "the problem" of teacher education during four overlapping time periods." They highlight studying teacher education as a: curriculum problem; training problem; learning problem; and, policy problem. Through these different lenses for looking into teacher education divergent responses emerge and clearly represent very different expectations of the field over time. Importantly, they conclude that there is a growing need for "constructing the problem of teacher education in thoughtful, appropriate ways" and this is obviously most desirable. However, as has been alluded in both their work and this commentary chapter, "who it is" that constructs the problem impacts dramatically what is looked for and why.

A rich knowledge of teaching enmeshed in the subtle nuances of practice emerges from deeper understandings of pedagogy when the problems *of* teacher education are illustrated and worked with, mediated and managed, in the practices of teacher education itself. What a teacher educator frames as a given problem of practice at a given time may still revolve around any or all of the problems noted by Cochran-Smith and Fries; yet responding to each individually does not necessarily resolve *the* problem.

It is time for teacher educators to explicitly frame teacher education as being problematic in such a way as to illustrate that what they know, how they know it, why it matters and what it looks in practice is central to that which might be described as quality in teaching about teaching. Teacher educators are daily confronted by issues associated with (at least): the tacit nature of teaching (Polanyi, 1962); the theory-practice gap (Korthagen *et al.*, 2001); the complexity of practice (Florio-Ruane, 2002); the tensions between developing students' authority of experience and the allure of their authority of position (Munby & Russell, 1994); and, many more issues that impact what teaching about teaching looks like, and how learning about teaching is experienced. Each of these dilemmas, tensions, issues and concerns can of course easily be ignored so that *the* problem with teacher education can be framed by others. However, in a profession that understands what it does, how and why, the ability to speak for itself, to shape its own destiny and to seriously grapple with the expectations, needs and demands placed upon it is of paramount importance. Clearly, it is time for the work of teacher educators to boldly shape that which is the problem *of* teacher education and to respond in positive, well informed and meaningful ways. Seriously pushing ahead with an agenda for the development of a pedagogy of teacher education, I would suggest, is one such way.

REFERENCES

Berry, A. (2004a) Confidence and uncertainty in teaching about teaching. *Australian Journal of Education*, 48(2), 149–165.

Berry, A. (2004b) Self-study in teaching about teaching. In J. Loughran, M. L. Hamilton, V. LaBoskey, & T. Russell (eds.), *International handbook of self-study of teaching and teacher education practices* (Vol. 2, pp. 1295–1332). Dordrecht: Kluwer.

Florio-Ruane, S. (2002) More light: an argument for complexity in studies of teaching and teacher education. *Journal of Teacher Education*, 53(3), 205–215.

Gage, N. (1978) Applying what we know: the field of teacher education. In *The scientific basis of the art of teaching*, (pp. 42–62). New York: Teachers College Press.

Hagger, H. & McIntyre, D. (2000) What can research tell us about teacher education? *Oxford Review of Education*, 26(3 & 4), 483–494.

Hamilton, M. L. (ed.) (1998) *Reconceptualizing teaching practice: Self-study in teacher education*. London: Falmer Press.

Korthagen, F. A. J., with Kessels, J., Koster, B., Langerwarf, B., & Wubbels, T. (2001) *Linking practice and theory: the pedagogy of realistic teacher education*. Mahwah, New Jersey: Lawrence Erlbaum Associates, Publishers.

Lampert, M. (2000) Knowing teaching: the intersection of research on teaching and qualitative research. *Harvard Educational Review*, 70(1), 86–99.

Loughran, J. J. (2006) *Developing a pedagogy of teacher education: understanding teaching and learning about teaching*. London: Routledge.

Munby, H. & Russell, T. (1994) The authority of experience in learning to teach: messages from a physics method class. *Journal of Teacher Education*, 4(2), 86–95.

Myers, C. B. (2002) Can self-study challenge the belief that telling, showing and guided practice constitute adequate teacher education? In J. Loughran & T. Russell (eds.), *Improving teacher education practices through self-study* (pp. 130–142). London: RoutledgeFalmer.

Polanyi, M. (1962) *Personal knowledge: towards a post-critical philosophy*. London: Routledge and Kegan Paul.

Russell, T. (1997) Teaching teachers: how I teach IS the message. In J. Loughran & T. Russell (eds.), *Teaching about teaching: purpose, passion and pedagogy in teacher education* (pp. 32–47). London: Falmer Press.

Ryle, G. (1949) *The Concept of Mind*. Chicago: The University of Chicago Press.

Schön, D. A. (1983) *The reflective practitioner: how professionals think in action*. New York: Basic Books.

van Manen, M. (1999) The language of pedagogy and the primacy of student experience. In John Loughran (ed.), *Researching teaching: methodologies and practices for understanding pedagogy* (pp. 13–27). London: Falmer Press.

56 Improving methods for research on teacher education

Robert E. Floden
Michigan State University

INTRODUCTION

The framing chapters for this section distinguish among the variety of methods used to do research on teacher education. Distinguishing among categories of research helps scholars understand changes in the field over time. More important, the categories can help researchers think about how they might engage in studies of teacher education. The categories are rough, but serviceable, groupings of research methods, purposes, and questions.

Much has been written about the strengths and weaknesses of varying research approaches, sometimes with the aim of promoting or defending an approach; sometimes with the aim of clarifying differences in fundamental assumptions. Discussions occur with an underlying sense that the quality of education research needs to be improved. Reports by the National Research Council (2002, 2005) have argued that the route toward improving "scientific" education research—a phrase chosen to acknowledge the legitimacy of non-scientific forms of education scholarship such as philosophy of education—is to adhere to general principles important to all scientific inquiry:

> pos[ing] significant questions that can be investigated empirically . . .
> linking research to relevant theory . . .
> using methods that permit direct investigation of the questions posed . . .
> provid[ing] a coherent and explicit chain of reasoning . . .
> replicat[ing] and generaliz[ing] across studies . . .
> disclos[ing] research to encourage professional scrutiny and critique.
> (National Research Council, 2002, pp. 3–4)

The categories of research sketched in the preceding chapters aid in seeing differences among the groupings of questions, theories, and methods. That is, they show how some types of questions are linked to associated theories (implicit or explicit) and methods. Understanding these associations makes it easier to identify what questions fit with what methods and theories, helping researchers plan their work and helping readers decide whether a study has taken an appropriate approach.

Comparing categories of research on teacher education highlights issues connected to all of these principles. Rather than going through each principle, the discussion below considers three issues, each cutting across several principles: first, the issue of criteria for determining which research questions are significant; second the ways in which methodological constraints affect the choice of questions; third, the need for building trust in teacher education research.

HOW SHOULD RESEARCH QUESTIONS BE SELECTED?

A perennial issue in research on teacher education is how to determine what questions should be addressed. Ideally, questions should be both educationally and theoretically significant. That is, they should address issues of substantive value to the educational enterprise and add to the general understanding of education in ways that extend beyond the particular subjects and objects of study. The methods selected should then be ones that will yield the most trustworthy answers to the questions, given the resources available.

The framing papers and exhibits vary in the suggestions they make about how questions and methods should be selected. Gage (this volume) argues that research on teacher education should address the causal questions about what ways of teaching lead to pupil learning and what approaches to teacher education will, in turn, lead teachers to teach in those effective ways. The substantive value of the question stems from its focus on pupil learning, assumed to be a widely shared goal for education. The theoretical value of the question comes from the assumption that the causal connections identified will be found across a wide range of contexts. Gage's article presumes that questions in research on teacher education should be selected by researchers, who gauge what issues are of educational importance and which theories should structure investigations.

King (this volume) takes issue with the idea that leading researchers should pick research questions, arguing that research on teacher education should address questions identified by those who have been ill-served by current education practices—especially questions identified by people of color. She also differs from Gage in the substantive touchstone for judging the significance of a question. For her, questions are not significant unless they are linked to critical understandings that will lead toward democracy and human freedom. Questions should be connected to critical social theory, highlighting the differences in power and privilege. Rather than having researchers with standing in the traditional social structure determine what questions should be addressed, King contends that those outside the dominant social structure should play the leading role.

Lampert (this volume), like King, believes that judgments about significance should be made by a group other than mainstream researchers. She says that education practitioners, rather than university academics, have "inside" knowledge of teaching that should guide the formulation of research questions. Those questions will often be context-specific, of immediate educational importance to the teacher. Theoretical contributions come through accumulating understandings about the nature of practice, rather than through learning about widely applicable causal linkages. Florio-Ruane (this volume) likewise views problems of practice as an important source of research questions.

Where Gage, King, Lampert, and Florio-Ruane promote attention to particular domains of research questions, the framing papers by Cochran-Smith and Fries (this volume) and by Borko, Whitcomb, and Byrnes (this volume) take a more neutral approach, distinguishing among several approaches, listing advantages and disadvantages of each. They optimistically recommend pulling approaches together, making links and drawing on the best from each option. Cochran-Smith and Fries cast differences as variations on the teacher education problem being addressed. Borko, Whitcomb, and Byrnes cast the differences as varying "genres" of research. Their effects and practitioner genres correspond roughly to the stances of Gage and Lampert, respectively. Their design genre is blend of these, with successive practitioner-oriented studies leading toward broader generalization.

Decisions about how questions should be selected, with related decisions about method, are obviously complex. They depend on value judgments, as well as reasoned analyses about what is already known, how answering additional questions would contribute to theory and practice, and what chance a projected study has of yielding informative and credible answers. The value judgments themselves are complex. If the goal is social justice, does that imply selecting questions provided by students, teachers, or scholars from groups out of power? Or, as Sandra Harding (1992) claims, are marginalized groups also likely to be deceived about what will benefit them most? Will including diverse voices in setting research questions lead to greater equity or to a more accurate representation of teacher education's operations and effects? Should these voices be included on democratic grounds? Or is science, and ultimately society, better served by allowing those recognized as experts within the research community to guide selection of questions? Such questions are vitally important, but contested. The quality of research depends on posing significant questions, but doing so, even deciding who should do so, requires careful thought.

WHICH COMES FIRST, THE METHOD OR THE QUESTION?

The theme of this section of the handbook is research methodology. The chapters and artifacts that make up the section demonstrate how closely intertwined are research methods and research questions. As discussions of how to improve education research (e.g. National Research Council, 2002) consistently emphasize, research methods should match the questions to be addressed. Questions about cause may be best addressed by experiments; questions about constructed meaning suggest ethnographic methods. And so on.

Standard advice in education research is to choose a research method to match the research question. Faculty cringe when a doctoral student begins a discussion of possible dissertation topics by saying what method they want to use, whether that be hierarchical linear modeling, auto-ethnography, or mixed methods. The professor will push back with, "What is the question you are trying to answer?" The presumption is that a student's dissertation will be improved by formulating the question first, then designing research to answer that question.

Such admonitions are based on kernels of truth, but they create the impression that research plans are best formulated by selecting questions that seem most important or compelling first, then devising methods to address them. But doctoral students who take the advice literally often find that the question they develop cannot serve as the focus of a dissertation because it cannot be answered with the time and tools available. A question such as whether pupil learning is improved by having teachers complete programs accredited by NCATE, for example, matches current policy interests, but cannot be answered with much credibility by a doctoral student with only a year or two to devote to a study.

As, or perhaps before, researchers begin to pose significant questions, they should reflect on what methods are available to them, given their research skills, their talents, and the time they can devote. Their advisors will still likely push for clarity about the particular focal questions, or may suggest some investment in gaining additional research skills, but in any case planning for research requires joint consideration of question and method.

This reconsideration of the ordering of questions and methods should be undertaken by experienced scholars, as well as by doctoral students. For research on teacher education at any career stage, investigators should plan their studies through joint consideration of what questions are important and what methods are feasible. As Cochran-Smith and Fries show, the history of the research domain can be characterized by changes in the central research questions, but historical development of the field has been simultaneously affected by changes in the research methods scholars prefer. The choice of method is affected by what questions seem important, but it will also be affected by the capacity for using methods and by the contemporary views about a method's potential for producing trustworthy answers.

The bi-directional influence of question and method is consistent with the admonition that question and method should match. Recognizing that methods sometimes come first helps explain some of the disjuncture between what research is carried out and what questions are most often asked. Policy questions about the relative effectiveness of different approaches to teacher preparation, for example, are the dominant contemporary questions. Yet most research publications address other questions. The difference between dominant questions and current studies is explained, at least in part, by the methods most scholars prefer to use, or are constrained to use by the resources and tools available. The research methods appropriate for answering questions about effects of teacher education policies include econometric analyses of nationally representative data sets or controlled experimental comparisons of competing pathways to teacher certification. These approaches require a combination of specialized skills and data that only a fraction of current education researchers possess. Hence most of those doing research on teacher education will choose to address other questions, whether or not they agree that these policy questions are important.

Most faculty engaged in teacher education have teaching loads that give them limited time to carry out research. Moreover, they have few institutional resources, such as graduate assistants, survey research units, or travel funds, to support large-scale investigations. When these faculty engage in research, they are therefore constrained in the research methods they can use. The emergence of inexpensive internet based survey tools reduces some of the costs of large-scale research, but limited time allocated to research makes it difficult to invest time in developing valid and reliable survey scales and to carry out the follow-up needed to get high response rates. It is, then, reasonable for many faculty to select research questions that might be answered using small scale, inexpensive research methods. The appeal of practitioner research is obvious.

If limited research resources mean that most studies of teacher education will be modest, practitioner studies, then it is no surprise that most published research on teacher education addresses the questions to which these studies are suited. These include questions about what the practice of teacher education means to those who engage in it, how prospective teachers interpret their opportunities to learn, and what they learn from the particular experiences in their programs. Such work is what Lampert and Florio-Ruane advocate and what the framing chapter, Borko *et al.*, classifies as interpretive. The examples Cochran-Smith and Fries offer to illustrate work on the problem of teacher learning likewise address such questions.

As the authors in this section note, interpretive and practitioner research poses particular challenges for communicating what is learned in ways that allow readers to go beyond the single case. As studies in disciplines from anthropology to political science demonstrate, close analysis of single cases can shed light extending beyond that case (Firestone, 1993; King *et al.*, 1994). To provide trustworthy bases for generalization, it is particularly important for researchers to attend to the principles regarding an explicit chain of reasoning, generalization and replication, and disclosing research to critical scrutiny.

BUILDING TRUST IN RESEARCH ON TEACHER EDUCATION

A persistent complaint about education research is that its quality is low (e.g. Kaestle, 1993). Recent syntheses found that research on teacher education is no exception; for research on central questions such as the effect of subject matter courses or the effects of teacher education policies, few studies were found to be of high quality.

Greater trust in education research is needed across all areas. To build trust, it will be important to provide explicit chains of reasoning, to give enough information to allow for replication and generalization, and to disclose research methods to professional scrutiny. Too often, interpretive and practitioner research studies do not describe enough about the research methods used or the analyses done to make the chain of reasoning leading to conclusions clear to the reader. This is a failing of the individual research articles, not of the research method itself. As Erickson (1986) has argued, rigorous procedures can be used to give readers of qualitative research reports a good basis for trusting the interpretations and conclusions drawn. Both Lampert and Florio-Ruane recognize this problem, noting that practitioner research too often results in storytelling without sufficient attention to the details needed to understand the basis of the story or the connections to theory and without enough discussion of the other research that would put the story into context and make its purpose clear.

The need for greater clarity about methods used in data collection and analysis is not unique to practitioner and interpretive research. Teacher education studies using large samples, surveys, and structured interviews and observations also need to be explicit about the bases for drawing conclusions from their studies. An endemic problem is that the surveys and other data collection instruments used are not accompanied by information about the degree to which they have been tested for reliability and validity.

For research on effects or on policy, reports often offer too little explanation of the chain of reasoning from data to conclusions. Gaps in the chain may come from unclarity about the connections between the names for features and outcomes under study and the tools used to measure them. Lack of connection to theory is often a problem here, too. Studies are guided by implicit theories that seem to have a basis in common sense, but lack conceptualization of the ways in which the components are believed to interconnect. For example, studies of teacher certification presume some connection between certification and teacher effectiveness, but the basis for that connection is ambiguous at best. One possible connection would be that completing the requirements for certification makes it likely that a teacher can produce at least some minimum amount of pupil learning. That presumes that requirements and minimum scores on teacher tests are set with the *intent* to ensure that all teachers have attained a minimum level of knowledge and skill. But the *intent* of those setting minimum test scores is seldom known.

One final way in which trust in research is undercut comes when researchers also become advocates. Because education is an applied field, researchers are often asked about what should be done. Some researchers initiate entry into debates about best policy and practice. Because of their expertise, researchers should have a role in policy debates. Their credibility, however, can be undercut when they are identified as advocates, rather than experts. Researchers must, as much as possible, make clear when they are speaking as experts and when they are speaking as advocates.

CONCLUSION

Research on teacher education can be usefully divided into several categories. The categories have distinctive clusters of questions, purposes and methods. Understanding the differences among these categories gives researchers a better sense of the choices they can make. Those choices should attend to what is already known and to the issues that are current in the field. Choices should also be driven by the educational values an investigator wishes to promote.

The questions that researchers will address are also dependent on their own skills and the resources on which they can draw. Some questions can only be productively addressed by costly, large-scale studies. Such studies require the support of major institutions, whether these be universities or funding agencies. Only a small fraction of those interested in studying teacher education will have the opportunity to lead such studies, though many others may be involved in some way. For many people who wish to do teacher education research, the resources they have available will lead them to do small scale studies focused on practices in particular courses or experiences.

The authors in this section argue that such studies can make valuable contributions to our understandings of practice, but they also warn of the difficulties in doing interpretive work that allows for understandings that go beyond a single particular case. Such intensive work can add to collective understanding, but only if reports include the detail needed for readers to evaluate the reasoning about the case and to think about the light it sheds on other cases.

Those working on studies in other genres also face challenges to making their work credible to a variety of audiences. For all research genres, it is critical to give the reader enough information to understand the chain of reasoning. Chains of reasoning in survey studies, for example, include assumptions about how respondents interpreted the questions, what motivated their responses (e.g. trying to please the researcher, trying to give the socially acceptable answer), how individual survey items were combined to make up broader scales, and so on. Readers need to see that chain of reasoning to have a basis for trusting a report's conclusions.

Many approaches to research on teacher education can make productive contributions. With appropriate levels of support, trustworthy answers may be offered for the central questions in today's debates. Critical interpretive studies can contribute to our understandings of the complexities of teacher education and may change the terms of debate.

REFERENCES

Erickson, F. (1986) Qualitative methods in research on teaching. In M. C. Wittrock (ed.), *Handbook of Research on Teaching* (3rd ed., pp. 119–161). New York: Macmillan.

Firestone, W. A. (1993) Alternative arguments for generalizing from data as applied to qualitative research. *Educational Researcher*, 22(4), 16–23.

Harding, S. (1992) After the neutrality ideal: science, politics, and "strong objectivity." *Social Research*, 59(3), 567–589.

Kaestle, C. F. (1993) The awful reputation of education research. *Educational Researcher*, 22(1), 26–31.

King, G., Keohane, R. O., & Verba, S. (1994) *Designing social inquiry: scientific inference in qualitative research*. Princeton, NJ: Princeton University Press.

National Research Council (2002) *Scientific research in education*, R. J. Shavelson & L. Towne (eds.). Washington, DC: National Academy Press.

National Research Council (2005) *Advancing scientific research in education*, L. Towne, L. L. Wise, & T. M. Winters (eds.). Washington, DC: National Academies Press.

57 Notes from a pragmatist

Learning what we need to know about teacher effectiveness and preparation

David H. Monk
Pennsylvania State University

I begin with a disclaimer and a confession of sorts. I come to teacher preparation as a researcher from a rather far-removed field. I have always been interested in education and teaching as a field partly because I grew up in the home of a high school English teacher. At the same time, the focus and practicality of economics as a way of thinking was attractive to me from an early age. I became an undergraduate economics major, but continued to be interested in teaching and learning, and pursued what by today's standards would count as an alternative route into teaching. As a third grade teacher, I was very struck by how many resource allocation decisions I was making and all this prompted me to try and combine my interests in the fields of education and economics in a graduate program.

I first encountered the process-product teacher effectiveness research literature as a novice graduate student, and recall being determined to master the literature and to become quite knowledgeable about what we know about links between processes in classrooms and learning outcomes for students. I struggled unsuccessfully to understand the process-product literature. I have memories of making endless charts about what seemed to make a difference under what circumstances. I have further memories of failing to make sense of these charts and ultimately feeling there was something wrong with me since others seemed so convinced that progress was being made. Scarred though I was, I soldiered on.

DISCERNING THE EDUCATION PRODUCTION FUNCTION

Given my economic disciplinary orientation, I tried to square the process-product research tradition in education with the production function research tradition within economics. Permit me to use the production function terminology as a shorthand for whatever there is about teaching and learning that is systematic and predictable. Notice that by formulating the concept in this fashion I am introducing the possibility that there really may be no such thing as an education production function.

It is abundantly clear that there is no such thing as a simple or straightforward education production function (Monk, 1989, 1992). If it did exist, simple and straight forward interventions like providing additional training of a particular type for teachers or hiring teachers with certain pre-specified characteristics would translate with considerable certainty into desired outcomes like increased pupil performance. The fact that the evidence is so inconsistent with the idea of a simple production function introduces complexity into the debate, a point Florio-Ruane (2002) articulates quite clearly.

Complexity makes life more difficult for the analyst and we must find ways to control for the sources of complexity. This sets the stage for more powerful research techniques—experimental studies and multivariate statistical designs being some examples. It also sets the stage for narrowing the focus of questions with the attendant risk of losing the ability to answer the more general questions that tend to be of interest to practitioners and policy makers. Several of the authors in this section of the Handbook comment on this dilemma. For example, Borko and her colleagues note the limitations of process product research because of its failure to deal with how people construct meaning in classroom settings (Borko *et al.*, this volume). Florio-Ruane (2002) observes that efforts to generalize the results of teacher effectiveness studies are often thwarted by the contextual, local, and situated nature of teaching and learning. I am reminded of the old quip about academics knowing more and more about less and less until they know everything about nothing.

Complexity also sets the stage for an infinite regress as when we go on and on, slicing things ever more finely in our efforts to discern regularities. Disappointing results prompt efforts to go deeper and there really are no well worked out rules for assessing whether or not actual progress is being made toward understanding the properties of the elusive production function. Economists (and others) have limited tolerance for delving ever more deeply into the black box. Some finesse the problem by focusing on outcomes and emphasizing the importance of creating clear goals and the proper incentives for the various players, including teachers, who have influence over the endeavor (see, for example, the volume edited by Hanushek and Jorgenson, 1996). From this perspective, it matters less how one gets to the goal than being able to show that the goal has been achieved—with rewards distributed accordingly.

Education researchers, in contrast, are a hearty lot and seem undaunted, even in the face of very discouraging results. Pam Grossman's conclusion about there being few definitive conclusions that can be drawn about the effectiveness of micro teaching, as reported by Cochran-Smith and Fries (this volume), is quite devastating in my mind since she calls attention to a host of serious problems including a lack of reliability and validity analyses of the instruments and discrepancies between appraisals. But notice there is nothing in Grossman's conclusion to preclude new efforts to understand micro teaching, presumably using instruments with better reliability and validity properties.

THE POLICY CONTEXT

Not all questions about the effectiveness of teaching and the preparation of teachers are equally important to answer, and for me the questions that matter the most are those whose answers make a difference in the life chances of learners. I do not worry as much as Florio-Ruane (2002) about privileging one research tradition over another. If one research tradition is better equipped to answer the pressing questions of the day, so be it and let us embrace the approach and take advantage of what we learn. However, it is also important to be on guard for pretenders and the ease of convenience. Just because something is relatively easy to measure should not entitle it to predominance in the debate.

Moreover, the mixing of research methodologies for its own sake has little appeal to me. Researchers come from different orientations and know about and embrace different research strategies. They work in different parts of the field and properly focus on honing their skills as researchers. They learn from one another and do so largely by reading and critiquing each others' work and participating in the overarching scholarly debates. Even if we grant the premise that all these multiple perspectives have value to add, it does not follow that the best strategy involves simply mixing them together. Effective collaborations and inter-disciplinary studies are more difficult to achieve than the rhetoric sometimes suggests. Where the question needing an answer lends itself to cross disciplinary efforts, it makes sense to pursue these, but we should resist falling in to the trap of thinking that just getting people from different perspectives together will somehow lead to useful results. For me the key is to settle upon what questions are the most important and to then choose the relevant research strategies.

My practical bent is also rooted in my current set of responsibilities since I am in an administrative role in a research oriented college of education with a quite large pre-service teacher preparation program. I find myself engaged in making design decisions with remarkably little research based evidence to provide guidance. For example, we recently decided to change the type of supervision we provide during our student teaching experience. Heretofore, we relied upon generic supervisors who worked with student teachers in many different content areas. A given supervisor might be supervising a student teacher in secondary mathematics one day and a student teacher in secondary English the next. As part of our effort to strengthen the content preparation of our aspiring teachers, we shifted to supervisors with content-specific expertise so that one supervisor with a background in secondary mathematics would supervise only student teachers preparing to become secondary mathematics teachers. While this seems like a desirable change on its face, I was very struck by how little guidance there was in the literature to support making such a change.

I hasten to point out that the change was not without its critics. A number of our students were unhappy with the change since it basically meant that we had to group student teachers geographically by subject area. Currently at Penn State, if you wish to become a secondary mathematics teacher, you need to student teach in the Pittsburgh area where we have located our secondary mathematics supervisors. Previously, there were more degrees of freedom regarding the location of student teaching sites and this was a benefit for students since it is not convenient for all of our mathematics education students to move to Pittsburgh. When quizzed by students about why we made the change, I found myself talking about how research has demonstrated the importance of subject-specific pedagogical knowledge. While I can certainly point to some studies that reach this sort of conclusion, I must also concede that I am not aware of any study that assessed the impact of changing student teacher supervision in precisely this fashion.

Other costs were associated with the change and perhaps the most obvious is the increase in the salary we needed to pay supervisors. It is easier to find generically trained supervisors and as a consequence we had to increase our stipends to attract reasonable pools of candidates. Can I demonstrate additional benefits to justify these increased costs of our program? Not really. Perhaps this will become possible as we become better at tracking the successes of our students, but it is hard to demonstrate currently. The bottom line is that we made a fairly significant and costly change in our teacher preparation program with only limited support from the research literature. And yet, I think it was the right move to make, largely because of the compelling nature of the face validity of the underlying logic.

SOME IMPORTANT TWISTS TO KEEP IN MIND

As I ponder questions about what we need to know about teacher effectiveness and preparation, I am reminded of a taunt a colleague was fond of making to teachers. He would take some delight in making the assertion that "teaching is a weak treatment." If we strip away the hyperbole and self-serving rhetoric that is so often on such bright display in our field and focus on the mind-numbing nonsense that sometimes goes on in the name of teaching, many will be tempted to think he is right, but grudgingly so. And here comes an important twist: even in at its drab, mind-numbing worst, teaching on occasion can prove itself to be truly transformational. Teachers and educational institutions in the real world and even in the face of all the pressures of the day can and do transform lives.

A second twist to keep in mind is that just because current practice has a drabness associated with it, nothing says that it has to be this way. Just because the education production function we are living with is complicated and ill-behaved and perhaps a bit drab, it does not follow that it has to stay this way. In other words, the production function itself is something we have created and it is not immutable. We can change it and make deliberate efforts to change how it is that teaching and learning take place. So, in addition to trying to study and deduce the properties of the education production function, the task at hand can be extended to include efforts to try and change its nature. This could have horrific implications as in trying to make learners compliant to ill-designed teacher proof curricula or quite empowering as in stimulating genuine inquiry on the part of teachers, students, and administrators.

SOME SUGGESTIONS TO CONSIDER

As we seek to learn more about the impact of teachers and teaching so that we can improve practice and more routinely achieve transformational results, I offer the following suggestions:

> Be clear about the question you are trying to answer, frame it narrowly and be clear about why it is important;
> Be explicit about methods and why you are choosing them;
> Be willing to make your data available to others;
> Anticipate critiques and do what you can a priori to address them;
> Be measured in drawing conclusions;
> Situate your study in the existing literature so that your study builds on previous efforts; and
> Be mindful of the political environment into which your findings will emerge and recognize that you have some obligation to assist consumers in understanding the results of your research.

The design studies described by Borko *et al.* (this volume) are consistent with these ideals and seem quite promising for the field. It is heartening to see instances like these of powerful studies that are so rich in potential for improving the practice of teaching.

REFERENCES

Florio-Ruane, S. (2002) More light: an argument for complexity in studies of teaching and teacher education. *Journal of Teacher Education*, 53(3), 205–215.

Hanushek, Eric & Dale W. Jorgenson (1996) *Improving america's schools: the role of incentives.* Washington, DC: National Academy Press.

Monk, David. H. (1992) The education production function: its evolving role in policy analysis. *Education Evaluation and Policy Analysis*, 11, 31–45.

Monk, David H. (1992) Education productivity research: an update and assessment of its role in education finance reform. *Education Evaluation and Policy Analysis*, 14, 307–332.

Part 9

What good is teacher education?

The place of teacher education in teachers' education

Editor: Mary M. Kennedy

Part 9
Framing chapters

58 The place of teacher education in teachers' education

Mary M. Kennedy
Michigan State University

One of the most enduring and most contentious questions involving the education of teachers has to do with defining an education that would genuinely enhance the quality of teaching practice. One problem is that, as a society, we hold different ideals for good teaching. In one ideal, the teacher plays a cultural role, representing an educated person. In another ideal the teacher is a nurturer who helps young people grow, learn and develop. In another the teacher is a political actor, striving to right social wrongs, and in yet another the teacher is a professional with specialized expertise. With so many different notions of what makes someone a good teacher, it should not be surprising that there are different notions about the kind of education that would produce a good teacher.

Colleges and universities respond to this dilemma by providing a bit of everything to the aspiring teacher. Teachers are not educated in isolated programs such as those attended by aspiring lawyers, doctors or architects, but instead are educated by the entire institution. The full institutional program is presumed to make teachers into educated adults, while one part, which is explicitly labeled "the teacher education program," is presumed to make them into professionals with specialized expertise. Labeling the professional portion of the program "teacher education" is somewhat misleading, since teachers presumably benefit from their entire college education, not just from that narrow segment that is labeled as such. But because we hold so many different ideals for good teaching, this segment of teachers' education, the piece that is called "teacher education," is the most contested part of teachers' education and is the focus of the papers presented here. Let's call this the Official Teacher Education Program, or OTEP. Questions of interest here are: Is the OTEP really necessary? Does it improve the quality of teaching? What does it accomplish, or what should it accomplish?

The papers in this section address these questions. They recognize that the OTEP is one part of teachers' education, and they recognize that there are enduring questions about this piece. In light of the rest of teachers' education, perhaps this part isn't really needed. How can we be sure that it provides something that really adds value to teachers' overall education? These are the questions taken up here.

There are at least two dimensions to arguments about the OTEP portion of teachers' education. One dimension has to do with the character of the knowledge needed for teaching, and whether that knowledge is essentially vocational or liberal. Vocational knowledge is usually presumed to have a direct application to specific situations, whereas liberal knowledge is presumed to provide ways of perceiving and understanding situations. Disagreements on this issue reflect not only different ideas about teaching, but also differences in assumptions about how knowledge influences human activity in general. The second dimension of the dispute has to do with the content of the knowledge needed for teaching. Here, advocates debate the relative importance of specific courses. A common argument, for instance, has to do with the relative importance of knowing the content to be taught versus knowing about teaching itself. Usually, content is offered by the institution as a whole, but the OTEP portion may focus only on teaching itself. Arguments about the value of specific content differ from arguments about the character of teachers' education in that advocates on both sides tend to focus on the vocational value of the content, so that the liberal value of being an educated person is obscured.

These two dimensions are rarely cleanly separated in arguments about teacher education, but each yields distinct criticisms of the OTEP portion of teachers' education. Advocates for a liberal education dislike the OTEP because it is generally perceived to be vocational rather than liberal. They also fear that these courses may actually deter bright, liberally-inclined young people from choosing teaching careers because such people are not interested in vocational courses. Advocates for the value of content knowledge as a vocational ingredient tend to dislike the OTEP because they don't believe it is really vocationally necessary. In addition, they worry that the time required for the OTEP may replace time that would have been better spent acquiring more subject matter content. In each case, the value of the OTEP is challenged, though the reasons for the challenge are quite different.

The phenomenon of the OTEP is like the famous duck/rabbit optical illusion shown in Figure 58.1, whose entire interpretation can shift from moment to moment even though the phenomenon itself remains unchanged. Different perceptions of the OTEP often follow from different assumptions about the nature of teaching, different assumptions about the nature of knowledge, and different assumptions about how knowledge influences human actions. It should not be surprising, then, that different people draw different conclusions about the role and value of the OTEP.

This section aims to both examine and illuminate these different perspectives regarding the role of the Official Teacher Education Program plays in the overall education of

Figure 58.1 The Official Teacher Education Program as a duck/rabbit problem.
Source: Jastrow (1899), cited at http://mathworld.wolfram.com/Rabbit-DuckIllusion.html

teachers. Both the historical artifacts and the new contributions reflect different points of view and different assumptions about how that particular piece of teachers' education adds to their entire educational experience and what it adds, if anything.

FRAMING CHAPTERS

We have three framing chapters, each with a different slant on the question of how to educate teachers.

The first paper, from Steve Weiland, examines the OTEP—not as a vocational training opportunity but as an opportunity for young adults to be liberated from the confines of their own narrow experiences. An advocate for liberal education, Weiland also acknowledges that the keepers of liberal education, the liberal arts faculty, are themselves in a quandary now, as they re-examine fundamental questions about canon, knowledge and the role of education. Weiland examines different interpretations of the term, "liberal education" and argues that liberal education is important for teachers because their authority as teachers derives from their education. In an interesting turn-around, Weiland also notes, though, that contemporary higher education has not done a good job of providing any of its students with a strong liberal education and argues that the OTEP could enhance teachers' overall education by stepping in and filling this gap. That is, Weiland's view of the role of the OTEP is not to provide a technical, research based education but to provide a liberal education, one that helps intending teachers learn to see multiple points of view, to critique arguments, to reason, and to see connections among ideas. His argument is that the OTEP would be stronger if it became more liberalizing, rather than more professionalizing.

The second paper, by Frank Murray, focuses on the need for OTEP by asking about the nature of teaching itself. He suggests that critics of the OTEP assume that teaching is a process that comes naturally to human beings and that requires no special training. But, he notes, the kind of teaching that comes naturally, a form of "show and tell," is not very well suited to the institutional context in which contemporary teaching occurs, nor to the kind of abstract content that comprises our curriculum. Murray suggests that, if teachers are to produce genuinely educated students, with deep understanding of school content, they do indeed need the OTEP. And, more specifically, Murray's view of the value of OTEP is that it should provide teachers with a technical education, filled with vocationally-relevant content largely deriving from research.

These papers, as a pair, reveal the tension between liberal and vocational education even within the OTEP. Both of these authors argue that teachers' overall education needs to include the OTEP, but they see its value in very different ways. Yet they both argue that this piece of teachers' education needs improving. So even though both believe there is a genuine need for the OTEP, they define the need in quite different ways and neither believes the OTEP, as currently configured, achieves the needs they identify for it.

The third paper, by Kennedy, Ahn and Choi, looks for evidence that educational course content actually benefits teachers' pupils. It asks, to what extent do the courses teachers take in college make a difference to their students' learning once they become practicing teachers? It takes up three hypotheses about teachers' education: that they need the pedagogical knowledge provided by the OTEP, that they need content knowledge provided outside the OTEP, and that they need, more than any specific courses, to be generally bright and well-educated people. The authors seek out and examine empirical studies for evidence that different types of educational backgrounds, and specific portions of the college curricula, demonstrate greater benefit than others educational backgrounds do, when we look at how much teachers' pupils learn from them.

ARTIFACTS

The earliest paper we present was originally published in 1920, and then reprinted in 1965 in a collection of readings edited by Merle Borrowman. The original authors, William Learned and William Bagley, were asked to assess the status of normal schools in Missouri but they used the occasion to consider the deeper question of role and purpose for teacher education. They note that normal schools were initially designed to provide a purely vocational education for teachers, not a general education, and moreover, this vocational preparation was almost entirely devoted to matters of technique, not content. Content was provided only in cases where the teacher clearly needed basic education. However, over time, normal schools started thinking of themselves as local colleges, or as stepping stones to other colleges. Students began attending normal schools not to prepare for teaching, but to prepare for a college education. Learned and Bagley are unhappy about this drift in purpose. They argue that normal schools should return to their original mission and should make all curriculum decisions from the perspective of a genuinely professional purpose. The programmatic details of teacher education have changed substantially since Learned and Bagley wrote this paper–indeed, the evolution is now complete as virtually all normal schools have evolved into regional state colleges or universities, offering general education programs to all students. But their paper provides a good example of an argument for a purely professional approach to teacher education, a good sense for the tension between liberal and vocational education, and an interesting picture of what teacher education looked like in the early 1900s.

The second historical artifact was originally published in 1963 as a chapter in a book examining the role of the OTEP within a teacher's college education (Conant, 1963). Like Learned and Bagley, Conant was also conducting a Carnegie-commissioned study of teacher education. His book summarizes his findings and includes a number of recommendations, mostly directed toward state education agencies. But his opening chapter, "A quarrel among educators," reprinted here, describes the animosity he sees between education faculty and disciplinary faculty. He finds that discipline faculty want to minimize education courses, but at the same time, they don't want to sully their hands with problems of public education. Conant's examination of teacher education helps us see how much teacher education had changed since Learned and Bagley's examination. By the time Conant conducted his investigation, normal schools had evolved into colleges and universities and were subject to numerous state rules about their curricula. But Conant's examination also shows us that the argument about what the OTEP should look like was even more bitter in the early 1960s than it had been 45 years earlier. Conant suggests that debates within the professorate, and the eventual entry of laymen into that debate, led to certification rules in most states, which did not resolve the question but merely added yet another layer to it.

The third artifact, by Gary Sykes, was originally published in 1984, and provides a view of teacher education after another pair of decades has passed. Sykes examines the difficulty teacher education has had in establishing itself as a legitimate occupant of the higher education community, and the difficulty it has had establishing its legitimacy in the broader education community. He examines a number of reform efforts that rose and fell since Conant's examination of teacher education and reviews the reasons for their failures.

RESPONSES

Three discussants respond to these papers and the discussants also represent different points of view. Diane Ravitch, a historian, puts both the papers and the issue into a historical perspective. Linda Darling-Hammond, a teacher educator, puts the issue into a professional perspective, considering the question of teacher education in light of the professionalism granted the graduates of teacher education programs. Frederic Hess, a policy analyst, examines the papers from a policy perspective, re-casting the issue in terms of options available to policy makers who must respond to these disagreements.

A reading of the entire set of papers helps us understand why this issue is never entirely resolved. The optimal education for teachers depends in part on social values, in part on the financing and management of schools, in part on the interaction between different departments within the university. Ultimately, though, it also depends on our ability to understand the mystery of teaching, the things that enable teachers to enter the minds of other human beings and cause learning to occur in those minds. If this ability results from a specific knowledge base, we are still at a loss as to what is in that knowledge base.

REFERENCES

Borrowman, M. L. (ed.) (1965) *Teacher education in America: a documentary history*. New York: Teachers College Press.

Conant, J. B. (1963) *The education of American teachers*. New York: McGraw Hill.

Jastrow, J. (1899) The Mind's Eye. *Popular Science Monthly* 54, 299–312.

Learned, W. S., W. C. Bagley *et al.* (1920/1965) Purposes of a Normal School. In M. L. Borrowman (ed.), *Teacher education in America: a documentary history*. New York: Teachers College Press.

59 Teacher education toward liberal education

Steven Weiland
Michigan State University

Are we meeting our educational obligations to prospective teachers? Consider how Bard College president Leon Botstein (1997), also a scholar of European history and leading figure in classical music, described the situation of students entering American higher education, including of course, those planning on teaching careers.

> Is there for the American adolescent the social supports for the love of learning, for curiosity, for the discipline that must accompany inquiry and then access to the pleasure of the life of the mind? . . . In fact, in our history as a nation, we have never had a comparable moment in which, at any level of schooling, the encouragement of learning and curiosity has received less support, spiritually and practically, from the adult world.

As Botstein knows, relations between liberal education and professional studies have confounded college and university faculty and administrators, students, and higher education policy makers for decades. Teacher educators of course align themselves with Botstein's attitude toward learning. But like their students, they are increasingly remote from liberal education and the intellectual opportunities if offers, if not indifferent to it. The goal of this chapter it so explore how liberal education might be made more important in teacher education, to teacher educators and prospective teachers alike.

For most American college students the undergraduate curriculum is simply a sequence of courses leading to a degree. Its rationale is as obscure as its origins in the liberal arts as they were formulated in antiquity. The part of the curriculum that came to be called "liberal education" in the U.S. more than a century ago signified the hope that a college degree would provide something durable for young adults, a course of study in the humanities and the social and natural sciences, that would "liberate" them from the limits of their experience and add historical, philosophical, and other perspectives to what was learned in preparation for a career. Liberal education stood primarily for knowledge of the past, great works of literature (the controversial "canon" in the "Culture Wars" of recent decades), principles of science, and other domains presumed to be valuable for individuals and for democratic society. In a paradox, liberal education conveyed tradition and represented ways of being critical of it. It has been, at its best, a resource for intellectual independence, personal development, and reflective citizenship.

When aspiring teachers think about the teacher education curriculum they are like other students; primary attention goes to completing the requirements for launching a career. They seek certification in courses on teaching methods and some form of supervised classroom teaching, but are generally asked to be only minimally prepared in academic subjects, much less in liberal education. Indeed, between the now well known "apprenticeship of observation" (Lortie, 1975) preceding college, when prospective teachers learn about elementary and secondary teaching as students, and "induction" into the profession as a teacher learning from practice (Hoy & Spero, 2005), the undergraduate years can appear to be merely an interlude in which the practical value of prior classroom experience is suspended while the academic and bureaucratic machinery of certification performs its state-sponsored functions, primarily focused on matters of teaching methods. We can expect most teacher education students to wonder, if they don't actually ask, "What should I know that will make me an effective teacher?"

In the view of the Carnegie Corporation teacher education shows little interest in liberal education, thus this recent statement of its meaning for prospective teachers is surprisingly direct, based as it is on the place of learning in any legitimate profession.

> [Teachers'] professional authority will rest in a significant extent upon their ability to demonstrate that they are themselves educated persons. Therefore, teacher candidates must be expected to know more in the way of subject matter than just what they are charged with teaching. Teacher candidates must command general education, liberal education, and the liberal arts.
>
> (Carnegie Corporation, 2001, p. 3)

But the Corporation's eagerness for better educated "Teachers for a New Era" (the name given to the major reform project it is sponsoring) reflects expectations for a part of the undergraduate curriculum that is by no means as secure as it once was. Teacher education is asked to make more concrete and visible the uses of liberal education *for its own purposes*. This chapter takes up conditions for such a change in the teacher education curriculum.

The timing does not appear right for such a commitment. Recent accounts of what teachers should learn as undergraduates ignore liberal education (Hiebert *et al.*, 2002; Brouwer & Korthhagen, 2004; Darling-Hammond & Bransford, 2005). And liberal education is now an uncertain enterprise without a consensus about its goals and practices, or how the prescribed curriculum of the past can be fitted to the proliferation of new fields and majors generally indifferent to intellectual tradition (Edmundson, 1997; Brint, 2002). American colleges and universities, with our elementary and secondary schools, now mainly serve "vocationalism" (Grubb & Lazerson, 2004). Thus, despite the optimism of some observers (Lemann, 2004) most students appear to see little value in courses beyond what contributes to their majors and, in their view, to their prospects for jobs and careers. If the Carnegie outlook is correct, then prospective teachers, and their teachers in teacher education programs, should be among those resisting such a trend. Thus, this chapter addresses the question "What role should liberal education play in teacher education?" It argues that the best opportunity for liberal education in teacher education will come from within the latter in conjunction with whatever else makes up a student's degree program. Thus, teacher education should adopt those goals of liberal education which can strengthen its programs and their impact, and its institutional and social position.

The chapter offers a review of the meanings associated with the phrase "liberal education" as it is offered at the different kinds of institutions with teacher education programs. The review identifies those features of liberal education that have made loyalty to it so durable and practice of it so contested. There has been, seemingly, a "crisis" in liberal education since Harvard adopted the elective system more than a hundred years ago and prompted a debate about what all American undergraduates should be asked to study. Attention then turns to teacher education and its stake in liberal education, focusing first on the question of professionalism and the teacher's "knowledge base," a necessary framework for considering any role for liberal learning. The longest section of the chapter explores how teacher education might move toward liberal education, by incorporating into its curriculum attention to practices proposed recently by leading scholars in the humanities who have also demonstrated interest in teaching at all levels, and by applying such ideals and practices to the education of teacher educators. A brief conclusion is based on the chapter's title and what will be required if there is to be any closing of the distance between teacher education and liberal education.

LIBERAL EDUCATION: THE GOLDEN AGE AND AFTER

The influential psychologist Jerome Bruner (1996) identifies many of the problems of the curriculum with these questions:

> Should education reproduce the culture, or should it enrich and cultivate human potential? Should it be based on cultivating differentially the inherent talents of those with the best native endowment, or should it give priority to equipping all with a cultural toolkit that can make them fully effective? Should we give priority to the values and ways of the culture as a whole, or give pride of place to the identities of the subcultures that comprise it?
>
> (p. 80)

In its reflection of these choices the college curriculum resembles the elementary and secondary ones, Bruner's primary concern. Thus, school subjects and then academic disciplines (old and new) are made to represent a variable configuration of complementary and competing interests. And the curriculum is a product too of history and social change, making the coordination of its intentions with what actually happens in the classroom often problematic and never perfect. Liberal education has been celebrated and reviled for its role in "cultural reproduction," though most of its partisans would abjure such a phrase. Bruner does not mean to suggest that choosing between the options he proposes is a simple matter. He knows that no curriculum represents a precise and unambiguous response to any or all of his questions.

Despite the fact that many teachers have presumably been educated to teach the primary subjects of the liberal arts (literature, history, etc.) there has never been a strong role for liberal education in teacher education, with many teacher educators seeing it as elitist or indifferent to the demands of "practice" or "pedagogy." In the late 1960s, the organizer of a national conference on the liberal arts and teacher education did ask "why the two are not essentially one and the same thing." But the book derived from the conference carried the less optimistic and more honest title, *The Liberal Arts and Teacher Education: A Confrontation* (Bigelow, 1971). They "confront" each other because of their seemingly contrary assumptions about the purposes of the undergraduate curriculum, the academic vocations, and the nature and uses of the university. Traditional liberal education, centered on the humanities and the social and natural sciences, favors the history of ideas and theories, the authority of the disciplines, and an image of the university as apart from society, or detached enough to support critical perspectives toward its social institutions. Teacher education favors practice, has on campus an intellectually subordinate relation to the disciplines of the liberal arts and sciences, and, because of its relations with schooling represents the university's obligations to society. In the 1990s the influential philosopher of education Nel Noddings' recommendation that liberal education (or what was left of it) be abandoned in favor of "care" as the primary subject of the curriculum was well received by teacher educators. "Relation," she argued, "precedes any engagement with subject matter" (p. 36).

Since the middle of the last century there have been periodic expressions among teacher educators for more integration of their efforts with liberal education (recent examples include Reagan, 1990; Coleman & DeBay, 2002; and Trubowitz, 2004) and occasional expressions of regard for the work of K-12 teaching among scholars in the disciplines of the arts and sciences (e.g. Graff, 2003). But the gap between the two academic domains appears to be unbreachable. The differences are not absolute of course; scholars cross boundaries, as examples later in this chapter demonstrate, and projects of reform sometimes include cooperation across the liberal and teacher education divide (e.g. Murray & Porter, 1996). Yet, as is often lamented, specialization reigns in academic work together with territorial prerogatives and suspicions, even when developments in the organization and production of knowledge, like the new information and communications technologies, pose compelling problems of teaching and learning across sectors.

What is liberal education?

Perhaps if there was a universal definition of liberal education it would be easier to enlist teacher educators in supporting its role in the curriculum. But defining liberal education is as challenging as defending it in a time of increasing focus on the college years as merely preparation for jobs and careers. In the Carnegie Corporation statement, for example, as is often the case, general education and the liberal arts appear to be conflated with liberal education. There are reasons to do so reflecting intention if not practice in American colleges and universities.

Yet, general education is better understood as something different from liberal education, reflecting a pattern of distribution requirements, as in Harvard's recent adoption of a format popular at many other institutions. Students choose from a menu of courses, rather than taking a prescribed group of courses in arts and sciences disciplines that represent a particular idea about learning goals.

The "Report" announcing Harvard's latest reform includes a useful statement of difference. Thus, general education represents "an overview of knowledge [that] insists on the value of learning in more than one discipline and specialization," while liberal education—though it can contribute to such an integrating function—has as its goal demonstrating "the value of 'disinterested' learning-knowledge for self-development-aside from any specific informational or use value the learning may also supply" (Committee, p. 4). Finally, the phrase "liberal arts" can suggest work in the humanities and the fine and performing arts if it is not amended to recognize also what is required in the study of science and mathematics. And the phrase "liberal learning" also deserves consideration, signifying as it does an activity taking place beyond the years of formal degree-seeking education, or "professional development" in the case of teachers.

Liberal education is still the best phrase to describe what is desired of students before or outside the college major, or ideally (and certainly for teachers) in conjunction with it. Definitions come in many forms. Some scholars prefer a genealogical approach, focusing on how liberal education in the U.S. today still reflects its origins in the debates over it in England in the nineteenth century. Thus, historian William Carnochan (1993) finds there the wish to heal "the deep, twin wounds of commercialism and professionalization, an argument that has survived and flourished in the commercial and professional setting of the modern university, where liberal education is looked upon as a way of staying human in a world of inhuman practices" (p. 29). Others recast such foundations in more recent intellectual vocabularies, as in the judgment of American liberal education as an expression of Pragmatism, the nation's distinctive form of academic philosophy (Kimball, 1995). In this version, seen from the perspective of increasing institutional and public uncertainty about the meanings and uses of liberal education when it is organized around classical forms of learning, there are key roles for multi-culturalism, community services, and assessment.

Whatever the origins of liberal education, the steady growth of the "practical arts" threatens their durability simply because a smaller and smaller percentage of American students have any sustained exposure to them (Brint 2002). In fact, at all but the leading research universities, the "practical arts" (including education) now make up the core of teaching and learning as the liberal arts did in the middle years of the twentieth century. These are the institutions where most American teachers are educated (at least formally), the locations of the "Education Gospel" giving increasing priority to "vocationalism" above all other educational values (Grubb & Lazerson, 2004). And many of their students are transfers who wind up cobbling together whatever liberal education they can gain (or are required to have) apart from any idea about its uses including its relation to teaching (Schneider, 2005).

Contemporary uncertainty about a definition of liberal education reflects a breach between approaches to undergraduate learning that specify what a student should know, or what he or she should be able to do. Thus, for some advocates, liberally educated students should have knowledge of the past, of durable works of literature, of essential scientific ideas and theories, and of the habits of mind characteristic of the disciplines in which these are studied. For historian Donald Kagan (1999), such a prescribed curriculum yields "serious talk on serious subjects based on shared knowledge." Inevitably, he favors knowledge of the past as the core of liberal learning, of "human experience through the ages, of what has been tried, of what has succeeded and what has failed, of what is the price of cherishing some values as opposed to others or of how values relate to one another" (pp. 222–223). There is here a strong normative tone, typical of many critics of higher education who find a lack of substance (or subject matter) in what is now mis-identified as "liberal education."

In arguments for liberal education, of course, scholars and teachers often speak with the authority of their own educational accomplishments. Charles Anderson (1993), a political theorist, believes that the meanings of liberal education are most visible in professional behavior.

> The true professional does not simply follow doctrine but *examines* doctrine, critically, aware of it as an imperfect, flawed structure that always begs for improvement. Such a professional must be liberally educated. This person must come to see the discipline as a human construct, a rough approximation of an ideal form. To be liberally educated is to pass through the relativizing experience taught by the skeptic, the debunker, the postmodern critical theorist, the pragmatic idealist. But the aim of this teaching is not estrangement from a discipline but an enticement to creativity within it.
>
> (p. 128; emphasis in original)

"Passing through" may not name clearly enough how the liberal education curriculum is taught but it suggests the kind of intellectual opportunity envisioned by the Carnegie Corporation.

Liberal education is also defined in the vocabularies of institutions, colleges and universities themselves, and organizations acting as advocates for their collective purposes.

The Association of American Colleges and Universities (AAC&U), which devotes considerable resources to making the case for liberal education among it members—many of them as former teachers' colleges now preparing the majority of American teachers— has named these essential "outcomes":

- Strong analytical, communication, quantitative, and information skills.
- Deep understanding of hands-on experience with the inquiry practices of disciplines that explore the natural, social, and cultural realms.
- Intercultural knowledge and collaborative problem-solving skills.
- A proactive sense of responsibility for individual, civic, and social choices.
- Habits of mind that foster integrative thinking and the ability to transfer skills and knowledge from one setting to another.

Source: American Association of Colleges and Universities,
Our Students' Best Work (2004)

No courses or other parts of the curriculum are named, no particular kind of knowledge is specified, and the Association ignores the specific intellectual practices named by Anderson, those that might prompt disagreements among members with its endorsement of "relativizing." As an important contribution to the recent history of liberal education reveals (Orrill, 1995), the conflicting premises, goals, and practices even among those— in and out of the mainstream disciplines of the arts and sciences—favoring increased attention and support for liberal education makes such curricular pieties inevitable.

The vocabulary of the AAC&U definition, in its attention to pluralism and social responsibility, reflects shared goals with teacher education (as it does with many other forms of university-based professional education), or the view that teachers are "change agents" and teaching is an activity aimed primarily at achieving social justice. But critics of teacher education, including those who find teachers "miseducated," often lament that the part of liberal education focused on "important issues" and the "intellectual world," are of less interest to teacher educators who cannot see very far beyond their own professional interests and the conventions of progressive pedagogy and curriculum development (Hirsch, 1996; Ravitch, 2000; Mason, 2000).

Specifying what a liberally educated teacher would know and be able to do is also difficult because of the different ways that teacher education units organize their work. These include all of the types of four year institutions, from the small liberal arts college to the large research university. The majority of teachers are educated at regional "comprehensive" universities (in the Carnegie classification) where vocationalism usually dominates liberal education. As their statements of mission and curriculum reveal, most pledge loyalty to the kind of liberal education defined by the AAC&U. The problem, of course, characteristic of large institutions with many purposes and kinds of students, is to identify how such ideals are made part of professional education and practice. Given the variety of forms of teacher education, reflecting institutional differences (Howey and Zimpher, 1989), liberal education can hardly be the prescriptive activity its traditional partisans desire. In fact, as Paul Dressel (1954) noted during another reform period, "One great difficulty is that the ideal of a liberal education untainted by vocationalism exists more in the imagination of conservatives than in the reality of the past" (p. 291).

Custom and ruin

Bruner's questions about the aims of the curriculum are late twentieth-century ones. What answers does the history of liberal education offer? According to Carnochan's account, one of the best, "The aggregation of practices sanctioned by custom, and incorporating the multiplicity of purposes embedded in the idea of liberal education, has made it next to impossible to think matters back to the beginning" (Carnochan, p. 119). Even so, he works his way back from a curricular episode in the Culture Wars of the 1990s to present a familiar sequence of events, now characterized as a "long term struggle of contested ideas," or more dramatically as a "battleground." The determining nineteenth-century U.S. engagement (a version of earlier ones in England) began when Harvard President Charles Eliot, thinking he was strengthening institutional and student responsibility, replaced the prescribed curriculum with the elective system. A key rationale was Eliot's belief that his initiative would yield the self-reliance necessary in a democracy with a changing and fast growing economy. But Eliot's move was challenged by other influential leaders (like President McGosh of Princeton) and the disagreement prefigured episodes of reform and, inevitably, more disagreement for decades.

Without degree requirements (or with minimal ones) the developing American university could respond to the rapid growth of knowledge in old and new disciplines and expand its sponsorship of science and scholarship. The new curriculum, if it could be called that, also prompted individual responsibility among students whose choices, ideally at least, reflected judgments about what was most important to know. According to Eliot: "That all branches of sound knowledge are of equal dignity and equal educational value for mature students is the only hopeful and tenable view in our day" (cited in Carnochan, p. 17). Eliot could be mistaken for a late twentieth-century spokesmen for the proliferation of majors whose utility is wholly defined by their relation to the marketplace. But setting the limits of the new system at "sound knowledge" represented in his view the high standards that remained in the revolutionary elective-based curriculum.

The famed innovations associated with (in the 1920s) Columbia's world civilization sequence and then (in the 1930s) Chicago's commitment to the "Great Books" signified resistance to Eliot's vision on behalf of faith in the long term value of required courses and what they added *generally* (to borrow for the moment the strategy of "general education") to any student's education. A degree made only of electives ultimately lost out to the intentions of liberal education represented by these programs, though the versions of them that appeared across the variety of American colleges and universities were often poor cousins of the originals. Even so, the status hierarchy of American education helped to keep the prescriptive system in place despite the lack of any empirical evidence that the required liberal education curriculum had the effects administrators and faculty thought that it did (Pascarella and Terenzini, 1991). Recently, elective freedom has returned as a popular choice, particularly at elite institutions.

By the end of the twentieth century literary critic and cultural historian Louis Menand (1997) was one of a chorus of voices breaking through key assumptions about liberal education. Speaking of the teaching of literature in such programs he said:

> Where the texts are not compelled to point toward a contemporary moral, the argument is commonly made that they are being read to teach the skill of reading. But reading a literary text is a *particular* skill, not a generalizable one. Not everyone can do it well; it takes a lot of practice and experience to get it right; and the skill is nontransferable. Knowing how to read a poem enables people to do one thing, which is to read more poems.

(p. 9)

The last of the AAC&U's "outcomes" for liberal education confidently assumes broad powers of "transfer." Menand's dismissal of such an effect stands for how little can be said for sure about the impact of liberal education, including how it has contributed to teacher education, largely via courses in the disciplines (Floden & Meneketti, 2005).

Menand (2001) himself has proclaimed traditional liberal education to be now an artifact of the "golden age" of American higher education prior to its remaking by vocationalism (or the "Education Gospel"), particularly at the large public institutions where many teachers are trained. Other influential scholars have found it threatened as a resource for intellectual vitality by catering to students' desires to be treated as "consumers" (Edmundson, 1997), the proliferation of electronic media (Gitlin, 1998), and management of higher education according to the practices of the corporation (Lears, 2003). And it has been declared to be "in ruins" today due to its neglect by the influential research universities, reflecting the faculty's professional preoccupation with disciplinary specialization and indifference to undergraduates (Katz, 2005). Whatever the causes, there is simply less liberal education now, as a percentage of undergraduate instruction, than ever before in our history (Brint *et al.*, 2005). Teacher education students, as do others in the "practical arts," experience the change in the form of the reduction of degree requirements outside the major, as the major itself—adopting in newer fields the preference for specialization in the older ones—claims more of the total hours required for graduation. In the special case of prospective teachers there is this paradox: public skepticism about their qualifications and performance has prompted more work in an academic (as opposed to a pedagogically focused) major, typically a discipline in the liberal arts and sciences, without producing teachers who can be said to be "well educated" according to the Carnegie Corporation's enlightened expectations. In effect, some observers find consolation in the long view. Thus, Carnochan says: "However numerous the trials of American higher education, and however unstable it may seem in the aftershocks of the nineteenth century rupture, [its] trials and instabilities . . . have given it . . . tensility and strength" (p. 5). Yet, with the triumph of the "practical arts" the strength of American higher education is being redefined. The place of liberal education throughout the undergraduate curriculum remains one of its most compelling problems. "Tensility" is presumably protection from breaking into parts. It cannot be said that teacher education and liberal education were ever fruitfully unified. Whatever can be done to move one toward the other will have to reflect historical burdens and be attentive to how much pressure the teacher education curriculum—now responding to new Federal initiatives, demographic change, impending teacher shortages, and the fiscal uncertainties of the public schools—can bear from one more necessary reform.

THE LEARNED PROFESSIONS AND TEACHERS' KNOWLEDGE

All American teachers have some experience of liberal education, but it has not counted for very much in their self-images or society's regard for them. For, every effort to improve teaching and the social standing of teachers reflects the problem of professionalism. Teachers and their advocates have struggled for more than a century to gain recognition as genuine professionals, having authority over their work and in the community commanded by doctors, lawyers, and others.

The practice of expert pedagogy has always been seen as the central element of the claim for teaching as a "major" profession, together with knowledge of school subjects and, ideally, of child and adolescent development. Thus, for most of the past century the question "What do teachers know?" was answered with a version of the straightforward response, "How to teach." Teachers themselves will claim that much of what they know about teaching derives from classroom experience. But that has never satisfied critics and skeptics in the post World War Two decades from focusing on the flaws of teacher education. Thus, for them, the "miseducation" of teachers, largely according to progressive principles, has long been an obstacle to reform (e.g. Kramer, 1991). Arthur Bestor (1953), whose well known case for liberal education derived from his frustration with the consequences of progressive ideas in the administration of schools, also found teachers wanting in intellectual capacity—a reflection of what was asked of them by anti-intellectual teacher educators.

In fact, as Lee Shulman (1998) reminds us, Dewey's vision of progressivism, still the dominant ideology in colleges of education, included the preparation of teachers in academic subjects in the form of liberal education. It reflected his commitment to the ethos of the emerging American research university, and new roles for research and theoretical inquiry. By late in the twentieth century, as higher education diversified and became more and more vocational (e.g. in the form of the "minor professions" [Glazer, 1974]), resistance to this ideal had become common. The appeal of practice obscured what could be learned from "theory," or any subject not perceived by students as practical, in this case prospective teachers expecting a curriculum focused on methods of teaching.

Thus, Shulman registers what he believes teacher education shares with other true professions, including those based on what are called the "practical arts"

> We who have tried to educate future professionals understand the challenge that is created when one's starting point for an education in a learned profession is immersion in vast bodies of academic knowledge. We prepare professionals in universities because we make the strong claim that these are *learned* professions and that academic knowledge is absolutely essential to their performance.
>
> (p. 517; emphasis in the original)

Shulman welcomes Dewey's insistence on the value of liberal education as a prerequisite for the study of teaching but can only ask, before going on to matters of practice: "What are the liberal arts and sciences per se whose grasp would identify an individual as 'educated' or 'learned' and therefore entitled to pursue a learned profession?" (p. 518).

By the end of his account of professionalism and the education of teachers, Shulman appears to find at least as much value in "situated practice" as a resource for becoming a teacher than anything deriving from liberal education, or the benefits of study outside the immediate interests of teacher education programs. But he does not give up on it. It was Dewey's own situation as he gained academic influence, Shulman proposes, that made him emphasize the kind of liberal education that could be provided by the new research oriented universities eager to control professional education. "While he was certainly justified in valuing a more rigorous, skeptical, and investigation-based foundation for the professions, he gave inadequate attention to the need to nurture such activities and perspectives *within the communities of the professions themselves*" (Shulman, 1998, p. 524; emphasis added).

Thus, in the late 1980s, with pressure for educational reform from the inflammatory national report *A Nation at Risk* (1983), and the problems of maintaining belief in the authority in the academic disciplines deriving from the advent of the Culture Wars, Shulman himself devised the theory of "Pedagogical Content Knowledge" as a way to consolidate subject matter learning—allied as it is with liberal education—with the practice and knowledge of teaching. "Pedagogical content knowledge," he declared, "is the category most likely to distinguish the understanding of the content specialist from that of the pedagogue" (Shulman, 1987, p. 8). But it was also to represent what teachers knew of the "sources" of the "content" of teaching. Thus, "The teacher must have not only depth of understanding with respect to the particular subjects taught but also a *broad liberal education that serves as a framework for old learning and as a facilitator for new understanding*" (p. 9; emphasis added).

Presumably, the "broad liberal education" would come from the teacher education student's experience in the institution's prescribed liberal or general education curriculum. In effect, Shulman was enlisting the entire faculty in teacher education, a familiar gesture for overcoming any "miseducation." Indeed, as he says later in his essay, "The emphasis on the integral relationships between teaching and the scholarly domains of the liberal arts makes clear that teacher education is the responsibility of the entire university, not the schools or departments of education alone" (p. 20). An important book (Clifford & Guthrie, 1988) had advised against regarding such a view as much more than a slogan but Shulman's confidence reflects that of his allies in the Holmes Group (1988) and other reform activities of the time aimed at strengthening campus relations between education and the liberal arts (e.g. "Project 30," a Carnegie Corporation project of the 1990s).

There were (and are) of course, some leaders of colleges of education who were eager to guard what they perceived as their "unique" mission. Recognizing the appeal of arguments for better curricular integration and fresh academic alliances prompted one to bemoan the fact that "the historical vulnerability of teacher education has once again induced sycophantic gesturing toward the liberal arts" (Gore, 1987, p. 2). But interest in fortifying liberal education across the increasingly popular professional curriculum was a key theme in Ernest Boyer's comprehensive and widely cited study of undergraduate education. He identified the predominant mood in this remark by a freshman: "This year I have all these 'general education' courses to complete. I wish I could concentrate on what I really need to get a job" (Boyer, 1987, p. 84). Even so, like Shulman, Boyer found a resource for optimism, admiring the "longing among undergraduates for a more coherent view of knowledge" (p. 85).

Shulman could not, it turns out, speak on behalf of his liberal education colleagues for what it was exactly that they would contribute to the "knowledge base" for teaching. "We may be able to offer a compelling argument for the broad outlines and categories of the knowledge base for teaching. It will, however, become abundantly clear that much, if not most, of the proposed knowledge base remains to be discovered, invented, and refined" (Shulman, 1987, p. 12). His "New Reform," supported at last by dedication to subject matter, provided just the right setting for specification of the contributions of liberal education to teacher education which would, ideally, be woven into what teachers come to know from their encounters with educational "theory."

But since the 1980s no such account of the distinctive professional knowledge of teaching has established itself definitively in teacher education, though Shulman's formulation of "pedagogical content knowledge" continues to prompt considerations of the problems and possibilities of achieving one (Segall, 2004). As Mary Kennedy (1999) has demonstrated, the question of the kind of knowledge necessary for teaching will not yield to a simple dichotomy of "expert" and "craft" knowledge (or what others often call "theory" and "experience"). In her view there is a third form of knowledge mediating the two—"expertise"—that is the actual domain of teacher education. In this way she invites a fresh contribution from liberal education which can be at once propositional as in "expert" knowledge and particular as in what is known from the practice of a "craft." It can contribute to "expertise," in Kennedy's terms, or to "creativity within a discipline" outside the liberal arts and sciences in the formulation (above) of Charles Anderson. New accounts of what teachers know and how they come to know it may follow from inquiries into mature cognition and the social conditions of epistemology. And scholars of teacher education, seeking to theorize the consequences of emerging conditions of schooling (e.g. more standardized testing and pressure on the qualifications of teachers), will likely seek to explain how teachers knowledge and beliefs are changing accordingly.

"GOOD ENOUGH" LIBERAL EDUCATION

What can we do now? What form of liberal education would be of most value to teacher education and, according to Shulman and others, give it more intellectual authority and durability? Presumably, it would be the one that has been shown to be the most effective—if we only knew enough to make such a judgment. Psychologist David Winters (with colleagues) acknowledged twenty five years ago that "It is sobering to realize that we have little firm evidence one way or the other about the actual effects of liberal arts education, this most enduring and expensive Western educational ideal" (Winter *et al.*, 1981, p. 9). And, Ernest Pascarella, who has helped us to learn a good deal about the general effects of undergraduate learning (Pascarella & Terenzini, 1991), asserted recently that "there is little evidence of [liberal education's] long term impact" (cited in Blaich *et al.*, 2004, p. 7).

Winters focused on the small and selective liberal arts college to demonstrate the value of liberal education. He looked also at a regional university (and former teachers college) where he found that despite having learning goals influenced by liberal educa-tion, its actual curriculum and impact on students turned out to embody the "practical, utilitarian tradition." There is little reason to assume that things are any different today at the institutions training most American teachers. Since the early 1980s, there is only scant evidence of the impact of liberal education on any form of professional education though there have been well organized efforts aimed at just such a goal (e.g. Stark & Lowther, 1989). However, the status of liberal education in the professions, including the "minor" ones other than teacher education, remains high, as is demonstrated by their wish to claim a share in the goals of liberal learning (e.g. Flanagan, 2000; Durden, 2003; Hermann, 2004).

Historian David Labaree (2004) has proposed these alternatives for teacher education. It can either rely on the academic disciplines to provide liberal education, or, in excessive dedication to its role in training for teaching "actually displace and discount the liberal learning" students bring to their more specialized pre-professional studies (p. 105). Labaree believes that "teacher educators have neither the time nor the academic expertise to give students a deep understanding of individual subjects, much less a broad under-standing of culture, language, history, and theory" (p. 105). There is, in other words, according to Labaree, little to draw on in teacher education itself to meet Carnegie's high standard for "educated" teachers. But surely there is enough for a selective effort based largely on the current curriculum and adjusted for a small group of themes central to liberal education, or a path other than (on Labaree's terms) deference or dismissal.

Taking my cue from Shulman's reformulation of Dewey, I propose below potential elements of an effort to strengthen liberal education *within* teacher education. Liberal education of this kind is, admittedly, some distance from "golden age" versions of it. It cannot be based on any "canon," prescribed courses, or a list of necessary dispositions, but it can represent intellectual opportunities that would "liberate" teacher education students from the limits of merely (or mainly) the professionalism of the "practical arts." In any case, as noted by Paul Dressel in the 1950s (above), nostalgia for liberal education can obscure the fact that it only approximated what its most passionate advocates believed about its influence on students.

It is worth potential misunderstanding—and misunderstanding compounded when the context is status conscious teacher education—to refer to the results of such an effort as "good enough" liberal education. Wendy Luttrell (2000), borrowing from the psychoanalyst Donald Winnicott, adapted that phrase to explain her approach to ethnography. He had argued that the "perfect mother" is only a fantasy of childhood and that efforts to attain "perfection" distracted from recognition of the inevitability and value of "good enough" mothering, which is what most children actually get. Thus, "good enough" liberal education refers to what is possible within a professional curriculum and what can, given the abilities, interests, and willingness of the faculty, express selectively how the teacher education curriculum can be deepened from within, or as part of the work that teacher educators already do. Here are four proposals presented as contributions from prominent scholars in liberal education who are also sympathetic to the goals of teacher education.

The clueless, the cultivated, and the uses of argument

The history of liberal education is a record of competing interests and ideas. But it is only rarely that students understand the disagreements behind any particular curriculum, or any clash of ideas or theories in a discipline, or any dispute over the interpretation of a text, idea, event, or work of art. Accordingly, Gerald Graff (1992), the literary critic and historian of English as a discipline, proposed that we "teach the conflicts" in order to move "beyond the culture wars" and toward a timely pedagogy for liberal education. While this approach has had an uneven history (see Symposium, 2003) it might still be usefully applied to the teacher education curriculum as it is taught, particularly by faculty members, as I suggest in a later section, willing to see value in the arguments of opponents of the progressive ideology of pedagogy.

Unlike many scholars who turn to problems of education, Graff has given priority to practical matters of teaching and learning, making the perspective of the typical undergraduate student—generally bewildered by the interests of the faculty—a position from which to suggest reform. He refined his views in *Clueless in Academe* (2004), suggesting that students' "cluelessness," if not quite a badge of academic honor, was still an innocent sign of the inability or unwillingness of the faculty to teach what is needed before anything else in liberal education. That is, students must learn the rudiments of "argument," how ideas are expressed in serious "conversation," or the discourses of the academic disciplines. Graff believes in the capacity of all students to mount prose arguments: "[They] can argue competently when there is a real conversation that requires [them] to be persuasive" (p. 155).

Clueless in Academe is part argument itself (about the border of academic and popular communications) and part primer on the tasks of student writers. Throughout there is a focus on writing as participation in a "conversation," or the role in any text of views and voices other than the author's. Graff urges student writers to recognize the opposition for the contributions it makes to any argument.

> [P]lanting a naysayer in your text, a move in which you deliberately make trouble for yourself, is likely to seem counterintuitive if you have been socialized to think of school as a place you get through by *staying out* of trouble. The five paragraph theme and other typical assignments reinforce this view by influencing students to think of writing (and academic study generally) as a business of stringing together true statements, statements that can't be challenged. Teachers need to help students see why this apparent common sense is not only misleading, but a sure-fire recipe for

dull writing and student boredom. Unless we produce some problem, trouble or instability, we have no excuse for writing at all.

(pp. 160–1)

Graff's general method (he does not of course claim it is original), the oldest of liberal education's conventions, used in "liberating" students from their habits of thinking, is formulated as a pedagogy available to anyone who assigns student papers, including of course teacher educators.

Philosopher Martha Nussbaum also encourages better undergraduate education in making arguments but it is part of an inclusive view of the "abilities" reflected in the thinking and action of an educated teacher or any other liberally educated person. In her learned but accessible "classical defense" of reform in liberal education, Nussbaum (1997) favors the Greek and Roman Stoics who believed, again, that education properly "liberates the mind from the bondage of habit and custom." For her, liberal education is "cultivation of the whole human being for the functions of citizenship and life generally." In her combined representation of the origins of the endeavor, and the recent efforts at institutions of different kinds to renew liberal education according to freshly conceived purposes, Nussbaum identifies three primary "abilities" as the core of liberal education needed in all fields of higher education, including the ability to critically examine oneself and one's own traditions, or the habit of questioning all beliefs and accepting only those that meet the demand for arguments and explanations.

For each of the abilities Nussbaum identifies a pattern of Stoic thought and action standing behind it and anticipating our interests and problems. The present, and the curriculum she proposes, can be seen as continuous with the past directly and practically, even in the maxims she favors from Marcus Aurelius, particularly one that might be a motto for liberal education: "Generally, one must learn many things before one can judge another's action with understanding" (*Meditations*, 11.18, cited in Nussbaum, 1997, p. 63). While proponents of liberal education still rely on its role in "liberating" students, Nussbaum sees beyond the slogan to the productive constraints that come from educated abilities. Thus, she says,

> Reason . . . constructs the personality in a very deep way, shaping its motivations as well as its logic. Argument doesn't just provide students with reasons for doing thus and so; it also helps to make them more likely to act in certain ways, on the basis of certain motives . . . [I]t produces people who are responsible for themselves, people whose reasoning and emotion are under their own control.

(pp. 29–30)

Nussbaum acknowledges the limits of her approach, it largely neglects the sciences, as does Graff's, even if argument is essential to scientific inquiry. The arguments that interest him most are the ones new and intellectually inexperienced students can learn to make as they prepare for work in the disciplines, or of professional programs like teacher education. Nussbaum's approach is conveniently complementary, focused as it is on how teaching and learning the "abilities" that "liberalize," as her examples from different kinds of institutions is meant to show, can be woven into virtually any instructional program.

Like their colleagues in other fields, teacher educators wish for students who can write with skill and pleasure. But the problem of "arguments" is compounded by a classroom ethos reflecting the relativizing habits of progressivism and the priority it gives to "experience." At the same time, as "writing across the curriculum" projects have demonstrated, any subject can be more fruitfully taught with attention to the nature and significance of composing arguments. Graff's "bottom line goal for education" is to bring more students into "the club" of intellectuals and mature discourse. Liberal education has always represented, for better or worse, associations with academic status. Graff and Nussbaum would democratize it as an accessible goal represented at the very least in the faculty's commitment to student writing.

Our talk, our texts, our terms

If the goals and organization of writing is recognized as an essential and realizable goal of liberal education in teacher education then inevitably attention to language itself can be made part of the curriculum. The goal would be, as Orwell (1950) put it in his famous essay "Politics and the English Language," to make visible to students the dangers of their "half conscious belief that language is a natural growth and not an instrument which we shape for our own purposes." Orwell was primarily interested in the "decadence" of contemporary language, its imprecision and careless reliance on overused metaphors, obscure terms, and slogans. He believed that language was concealing as much as it was expressing and that inattention to precise meanings and accessible syntax (if not outright deceit) could be cured with "conscious action." Orwell's essay has become a staple of liberal education, a sign of its expressive goals and the uses today of his insistence that "To think clearly is a necessary first step toward political regeneration."

Where would such a project begin in teacher education? Historian Peter Stearns (2004), who has been a leading figure in the organization of the history curriculum in the schools, has urged for some time that "cultural analysis" be placed at the center of liberal education since it contributes "a way of thinking about aspects of human and social behaviors that shows the culturally contingent underpinnings of many qualities often regarded as fixed and immutable" (p. 10). He recognizes too that "culture," is one of the most widely used, complex and demanding of terms in education and other fields. Thus, an influential trend in intellectual life, the "cultural turn," multiplied the problems as well as the prospects of "culture" as the key term in guiding research and teaching. However far they might come in "cultural analysis," the term "culture" itself is essential to education. Bruner, for example, says that "Education is a major embodiment of a culture's way of life, not just preparation for it," and in *The Culture of Education* (1996) he finds several meanings of "culture," just as culture quite variably guides us toward the meanings we find in education and in living.

It was the history of the term "culture" that prompted the British scholar (of several fields) Raymond Williams to codify his practice of a new form of historical semantics. The result was *Keywords: A Vocabulary of Culture and Society* (1976; Rev. ed. 1985; see also Bennet *et al.*, 2005) which represents a fundamental activity of liberal education, gaining understanding of the operations of particular terms in the making of knowledge and social relations. Williams recognized that what makes it so difficult to work straightforwardly with the key terms in our talk and writing was that "the problem of a term's meaning is inextricably bound up with the problems it is used to discuss" (p. 15). What issues and problems are "inside" our most widely used terms, Williams asked, and what does the difficulty in defining many of them tell us about our experience?

Student authors and their teachers more attentive to the making and uses of arguments will make language itself a subject of teacher education. The well known "linguistic turn" that came to the humanities and some sectors of the social sciences in the last decades of the past century urged the study of discourse for knowledge of how the world is produced, or how language represents the history of human experience as a competition of interests as well as a desire for solidarity. Professional vocabularies became the subject of scrutiny, particularly in the academic movement known as "Rhetoric of Inquiry" (Nelson, 1987). In his account of "Standards," for example, Williams notes how "an authoritative example of correctness" became associated with "a concept of graded progress within a hierarchy." Since then "standards" has been used commonly as both an ordinary plural term and as a plural singular. Thus, "it is often impossible . . . to disagree with some assertion of 'standards' without appearing to disagree with the very idea of quality." The case is further complicated by our derogatory use of "standardization" alongside our laudatory use of "standards." Pedagogical exploration of such a paradox, a model exercise in liberal education, can derive from the study of almost any keyword. In any language, Williams says, "and especially in periods of change, a necessary confidence and concern for clarity can quickly become brittle, if the questions involved are not faced" (p. 16).

The "interrogation" of our terms, to borrow a popular term of postmodern discourse, must be seen as steady and often slow work. No single exercise, or social history of any particular word, will transform the intellectual habits of prospective teachers. What matters in assimilating liberal education to teacher education in this instructional format is a stance or attitude toward language that makes students historians and critics of their own discourse. If, as Graff claims (and Nussbaum implies) education in any academic field means entering a particular "argument culture," then there is a complementary "vocabulary culture" as well, or agreement among the culture's "natives" to use words in certain ways. But habit can be the enemy of clarity or even honesty—and slogans abound in teacher education. Ethnography is familiar enough to teacher educators to offer an image of empathic but still critical inquiry in the undergraduate classroom. Education's "keywords" are a platform from liberal education precisely because so many are rarely scrutinized for what they reveal about the fate of ideas subordinated to contemporary styles progressive pedagogy.

Teachers as users and critics of technology

The student arguments that Graff and Nussbaum hope for reflect the print world in which they were educated. But as they were writing their books—no doubt on computers—the foundations of literacy were being altered by the new information and communications technologies. We have access today to more resources for learning—liberal and practical—than ever before. But as is often pointed out, information is not the same thing as knowledge, a lesson in liberal education to be learned with increasing urgency in the Age of the Internet. It is one that classicist and former technology administer James O'Donnell (1998) features in his historical account of those "avatars" of oral and written language that have transformed the ways we use and think about both.

Information and Communication Technology (ICT) is still a new enough phenomenon that its novelty can obscure how fundamentally it will change our habits of literacy and learning. But it will soon be taken for granted, as it should be, and teacher education students can then pay attention to the best ways to use it and to the consequences of doing so. For technologies are not neutral instruments for teaching and learning, as we are reminded by O'Donnell and philosophers of education in the vanguard of understanding and capitalizing on new opportunities: "The capacity for transformation is not intrinsic to the technology itself" (Burbules & Callister, 2000, p. 7). The key is a relational view of ICT, thus,

Tools may have certain intended uses and purposes, but they frequently acquire new, unexpected uses and have new, unexpected effects . . . [W]e never simply use tools, without the tools also "using" us. We never use technologies to change our surroundings without being changed ourselves, sometimes in recognized, sometimes in entirely unrecognized and unexpected ways. The relationship with technology is not just one way and instrumental, but two way

(p. 6)

Building the classroom "identities" of prospective teachers is a favored strategy of teacher education but no working psychology will now be complete without attention to the impact of ICT on how we think about professional roles. Teacher education students have a large stake—as students and then as teachers—in guiding their own students in the uses of ICT as well as contributing to their understanding of what its uses mean for learning and living. The strategy favored in teacher education has been to study the new classroom technologies for the ways they can be used in projects of learning. But what of the social and educational practices that derive from the adoption of ICT? These are new problems for liberal education as they are for teacher education. They direct us, for example, to the nature of texts and textuality. The terms "Hypertext" and "Hypermedia" are widely used but poorly understood as signs of what digitalization invites us to do as writers and readers. As users of the Internet we have an allied critical obligation. Thus, to be "literate" on the Web means to have powers of discrimination suitable for making durable educational uses of its abundant resources.

Liberal education has always struggled with what to make of the expansion of knowledge in the disciplines and the increasing difficulty in gaining an integrative perspective. The Internet, with its rapid access to every kind of knowledge, magnifies this dilemma and especially so for teachers hoping to make their students lifelong learners. We see frequent calls for "digital" or "silicon" literacy (Gilster, 1997; Snyder, 2002; Kelly, 2003), perhaps qualifying as another "ability" to be represented in any "new" liberal education. Certainly it is in the interests of technology's enthusiasts to identify the newest part of the curriculum with the oldest. Innovation is made safe by association. Thus,

Information literacy should in fact be conceived more broadly as a new liberal art that extends from knowing how to use computers and access information to critical reflection on the nature of information itself, its technical infrastructure, and its social, cultural, and even philosophical context and impact—as essential to the mental framework of the educated information-age citizen as the trivium of basic liberal arts was to the educated person in medieval society.

(Shapiro & Hughes, 1996)

The practical value of "information literacy" is plain, for example in understanding what it means to use a library in both old and new ways. But it would remain the task of teacher educators to make their students adept in the new ICT, just as they themselves adapt to what can be called the new "scholarly literacy" reflecting the influence of digitalization on academic work (e.g. Bell, 2005).

In the same way that liberal education has always included attention to the meanings of civic life, of living and working in groups, knowledgeable and thoughtful use of ICT requires understanding of how the phrase "virtual community" signifies new forms of electronic communication and of how people work and live together. It resembles other spaces for learning in their good and bad effects. Accordingly, a critical user of the new technology would be someone alert to how the host of new terms associated with

ICT (e.g. the "Information Society," "surfing the Web," etc.) represent a complex meta-phorical effort to characterize and control the new digital environment, sometimes for purposes inconsistent with liberal education and the mission of teacher education (Meyer, 2005). Teachers will use this language as much or more than any other professional group and they should be equipped to do so as critics who, in their interactions with students, illuminate the meanings of new technology as they use it. All teacher education courses using technology—and soon there will be few that don't—should contribute to students' growth as critics as well as users, or for mastery of "educational technology" in the spirit of liberal education.

A via media for foundations of education

It was only a few years ago that the phrase "cultural literacy" appeared as often as "information literacy" in accounts of what needed attention in education. The new information and communications technologies swept over American higher education just as the most important trend of the late twentieth century—the Culture Wars—appeared to be losing some of its force. But a generation of teachers has been educated during the Culture Wars and teaching will continue to show the effects of public disputes over what belongs in the curriculum (Hunter, 1991) and the results of widespread and politically partisan censorship of textbooks (Ravitch, 2003).

Prospective teachers often encounter the "foundations of education" in attention to the history and social relations of schooling, sometimes in encounters (typically via textbooks) with history's most influential philosophers of teaching and learning. As such, foundations can be understood to be an extension of liberal education, or perhaps in some cases a surrogate for it in the teacher education curriculum. In the late 1980s a group of scholars in foundations did in fact propose that teacher education was a form of liberal education. They argued that "the practice of teaching should be taken as a central object of liberal study and liberal study should be taken as the object of teaching" (Beyer *et al.*, 1989, p. 14). Their program, however, is cast in the vocabulary of postmodernism and the wish to overturn what is foundational (if you will) about the disciplines of the arts and sciences. Thus, they urge that teacher education join in the movement to "deflect rationality from its Enlightenment trajectory" (p. 103). This is a betrayal of liberal education rather than a case for it.

A recent guide to the field of "foundations" offers scholars speaking with virtually a single political voice. "It is now common," we are told, "for teacher education programs to focus on social justice across the curriculum. It is widely understood that schools will tend to reproduce the divisions of race, class, and gender unless teachers are explicitly taught to challenge oppressive assumptions and behaviors" (Martusewicz and Edmundson, 2005, p. 76). Another contribution puts the assumptions this way: "[A]s foundationists we are working to widen the reach of justice . . . Our schools are ideal locations to conduct such an enterprise . . . and the social foundations classroom sets the path for prospective teachers to embark on that journey" (Edmundson & Bushnell Greiner, 2005, p. 153).

There is of course always the need for more justice in education and all other social institutions. But how that might come about is a question that cannot be fully answered if "social reproduction" is named as the only, or even primary, activity of schooling and the task of prospective teachers who pass unenlightened through teacher education programs. "Foundations" is essential to any effort in teacher education in the direction of liberal education if reflection on habits of thinking is to include attention to tradition as well as transformation.

The situation of philosophers of education is symptomatic, caught as they are between contrary professional identifications and practices, and the uncertain status of liberal education in the teacher education curriculum. According to Christopher Higgins (2000), "We would seem to be unique insofar as we speak a philosophical language to an educational audience, or bring philosophical tools to educational problems. The problem is that we are able to reach our educational audience only in inverse proportion to how well we speak philosophy's strange tongue, and the problems that plague education do not strike most people as the type to admit philosophical solution" (p. 275). He acknowledges the "waning of the metaphor of philosophical foundations." Even so, and echoing Graff, he proposes that "What teachers need is [an] invitation to be intellectuals themselves."

Higgins would accomplish this by capitalizing on educational philosophy as a "paradigm of liberal teacher education." This would come about by recognizing in philosophy essential questions of the ends and means of human development central to teaching: "What is human nature? What constitutes human flourishing? What facilitates growth for beings like us toward that which is good for us" (p. 278). Philosophers of education bring to teacher education their "love" of such questions and invite prospective teachers into the "conversation" of liberal learning based on "the historically removed, humanistic texts which maintain, in their treatment of questions of human becoming, an untimely relation to the present's foreclosed and shrunken questions." In effect, a liberally educated teacher would redirect some part of political activism toward intellectual curiosity. "It encourages them to be more circumspect about the social fabric they have been enlisted to renew, and, at the same time, to convert from a practice that runs on the fast burning fuel of altruism to the sustainable commitment of an ongoing apprenticeship to questions worth loving" (p. 280).

I find this a most timely and salutary proposal, aimed as it is at the insistence in schools of education on a role for schooling, and thus for aspiring teachers, in transformational social reform. Henry Giroux (1992) and others working in "critical theory" want teachers to be "public intellectuals" but he can only advocate liberal education for what it contributes to "a curriculum committed to reclaiming higher education as an agency of social justice and critical democracy and to developing forms of pedagogy that affirm and engage the often-silenced voices of subordinate groups" (p. 124). "Foundations" has new work to do in modifying the activist ideology of teacher education enough to make the conflict between tradition and transformation more than a location for the display of the progressive virtues of teacher educators. Thus, the social and political relations of education might be represented by the "via media" proposed by political theorist Jean Bethke Elshtain (1997). Like her heroes Jane Addams and Camus, she has little patience with comfortable theorists of injustice and recommends the *via media* not as a "tepid compromise" but as a form of intellectual pluralism and realism. "We arrive at democracy and our understanding of education in our own way, framed within a horizon of limited, not limitless possibility dictated by our historic time and place" (p. 363). She urges criticism of "tradition" and recognition that education is always "political" because it "is never outside a world of which politics—how human beings govern and order a way of life in common—is a necessary feature" (p. 365). But the "middle way" is the "rare but now and then attainable fruit of the democratic imagination" (p. 371).

CONCLUSION: TEACHER EDUCATION AND THE
INTELLECTUAL LIVES OF TEACHERS

"Good enough" liberal education refers to opportunities for teacher education to enhance its curriculum from within by complementing professional preparation (or the "practical arts") with attention to themes representing the liberal arts in old and new ways. In the reforms Shulman proposes he assumes there to be the necessary curricular leadership and classroom talent among the teacher education faculty. But teacher educators, often associated with the anti-intellectual legacy of educational "progressivism," can be said to work in the university as "aliens," perceived as "marginal" to its primary purposes (Labaree, 2004). These are not promising positions from which to advance liberal education and the commitment to academic tradition it requires. Indeed, even a sympathetic portrait of teacher educators includes the disappointing news that hardly any of the professors interviewed could respond concretely to a question asking that they name books they would have their students read so as to "make them better teachers and better people." One confessed that "Provincialism is probably the central problem in teacher education" (Ducharme, 1980). Perhaps that is why Eliot Eisner (1995) underlined the fact that teacher education provides little more than an initiation into teaching, the only hope, presumably, for better educated teachers being in what they learn as classroom professionals.

The abundance of research in education, most of it the product of faculty in colleges of education, has not led to widespread confidence that it plays a key role in improving schools or learning. Nor does it provide images of teaching that reflect its intellectual responsibilities rather than its pedagogical and social ones. In effect, scholarly teacher educators can behave as yet another group of faculty members indifferent to the shared purposes of the university and of liberal education, with the advantage of having no apparent curricular responsibility for it either. That is what lies behind the Carnegie Corporation's intended intervention based on a lofty intellectual standard for a career in teaching.

It remains to ask if teacher educators can in fact move their curriculum toward liberal education. Current commitments and habits suggest not, or at least that it can only be done with extensive re-education and re-thinking of the position of teacher education in higher education. But anyone who believes in lifelong learning and the change that can accompany it, as all scholars must, should be able to master what is needed to contribute. And some teacher educators already make one or more of the approaches I have named part of their teaching, though likely without identifying it—to themselves or their students—as liberal education. It is not, in any case, a matter of specialists in math or science education, for example, taking responsibility for knowledge of literary history. In the approaches to liberal education I have named, it is not new fields of learning that matter but how teacher educators position what they already know—with resources (as in what is offered by Graff, Nussbaum and others) aimed at those scholars inclined to give themselves a role in major curricular [problems] of their time, and ones that also have considerable social significance. What does Marilyn Cochran-Smith (2005) mean when she refers to teacher educators as "public intellectuals" if they can not be asked to do so?

Those teacher educators who enlist in such an effort would benefit from institutional activities in colleges of education that make visible the significance of liberal education for prospective teachers—and for *their* students. In his first reform manifesto, Gerald Graff (1992) smartly noted that not every new idea or method needed to be organized as a course, presenting as that would problems for an already crowded curriculum. Instead, reforms can be built into existing courses and be represented in the curriculum by guest speakers, workshops, small-scale conferences (some combining courses for joint purposes), and other occasions for introducing new ideas to students and faculty alike.

I do not think that the attitudes Labaree (and others) identify—a measure of anti-intellectualism in colleges of education and resentment over the fact that teacher educators have any place at all in academic culture—will change soon. There are many critics of the schools, like Leon Botstein, who plead for greater regard for teachers and the abandonment of pedagogy as an undergraduate subject of study. And claims for introducing liberal education into the teacher education curriculum would no doubt be greeted with skepticism by departments believing it to be their peculiar role by virtue of their more cosmopolitan academic practices. But if it is done well, liberal education in teacher education would signify, in an unlikely corner of academic life, willingness to address a serious problem facing all institutions. Taking the high road is no guarantee of collegiate success and individual rewards. But it is consistent with the long time self-image of teacher education as vanguard project, in this case mobilizing its own curriculum for the purpose of deepening the intellectual lives of teachers.

There is frequent recognition of teaching as a peculiarly complex activity and of the demands placed on teacher education, named as an "impossible role" itself requiring new ways of understanding its possibilities and limits (Ben-Peretz, 2001). Thus, the durability of the problem of the teacher education curriculum, and fitting it to social and demographic change and to the purposes of both undergraduate education and professional practice. Even successful programs can produce what Arthur Powell calls "passive achievement," signifying the narrowing of school reform to "measured student achievement" (reflecting primary interest in economic and vocational goals) and the neglect of lasting habits of mind. "Few educators in the elementary-secondary sector have been seriously concerned about passive achievement and the resulting weak dispersion of enduring intellectual interests in the population" (Powell, p. 15).

A version of this view might be applied to higher education and the gap between teacher education and liberal education. Powell specifies institutionally the problem Botstein had named socially and culturally, suggesting that teaching, and I would add teacher education, is the place to inspire "enduring intellectual interests." However new definitions of liberal education adjust the role of the "canon" and study of the past, and promote instead skills or service, there is always the hope that students will have the advantage of such interests over the course of their careers—and rectify the pattern of relations between educational generations identified by Botstein and Powell. Working within teacher education to move it toward liberal education is a pragmatic strategy for adding to what is necessarily practical in the minds of students learning to teach.

REFERENCES

American Association of Colleges and Universities (2004) *Our students' best work*. Washington, DC: Association.

Anderson, C. (1993) *Prescribing the life of the mind: an essay on the purpose of the university, the aims of liberal education, the competence of citizens, and the cultivation of practical reason.* Madison, WI: University of Wisconsin Press.

Astin, A. W., S. A. Parrott, W. S. Korn, & L. Sax (1997) *The American freshman: thirty-year trends.* Los Angeles, CA: UCLA Higher Education Research Institute.

Bell, D. (2005) The bookless future: what the internet is doing to scholarship. *The New Republic*, May 2 and 9: 27–33.

Ben-Peretz, M. (2001) The impossible role of teacher educators in a changing world. *Journal of Teacher Education*, 52(1): 48–56.

Bennet, T., L. Grossberg, & M. Morris (eds.) (2005) *New keywords: a revised vocabulary of culture and society*. Malden, MA: Blackwell.

Bestor, A. (1953) *Educational wastelands: the retreat from learning in our public schools*. Champaign, IL: University of Illinois Press.

Beyer, L., W. Feinberg, J. Whitson, & J. Pagano (1989) *Preparing teachers as professionals: the role of educational studies and other liberal disciplines*. New York: Teachers College Press.

Bigelow, D. N. (1971) *The liberal arts and teacher education: a confrontation*. Lincoln, NE: University of Nebraska Press.

Blaich, C., Bost, A., Chan, E., & Lynch, R. (2004) Defining liberal arts education. Retrieved May, 2005 from http://liberal arts.wabash.edu/home.cfm?news_id=1400

Boyer, E. (1987) *College: the undergraduate experience in America*. New York: Harper and Row.

Botstein, L. (1997) *Jefferson's children: education and the promise of American culture*. New York: Doubleday.

Brint, S. (2002) The rise of the "practical arts." In Brint (ed.), *The future of the city of intellect: the changing American university*, pp. 231–259. Stanford, CA: Stanford University Press.

Brint, S., M. Riddle, L. Turk-Bicakci, & C. S. Levy (2005) From the liberal to the practical arts in American colleges and universities: organizational analysis and curricular change. *Journal of Higher Education*, 76(2): 151–180.

Brouwer, N. & F. Korthagen (2004) Can teacher education make a difference? *American Educational Research Journal*, 42(1): 153–224.

Bruner, J. (1996) *The culture of education*. Cambridge, MA: Harvard University Press.

Burbules, N. & T. Callister. (2000) *Watch IT: the risks and promises of information technologies for education*. Boulder, CO: Westview.

Carnegie Corporation of New York (2001) "Prospectus: 'Teachers for a New Era.' " Retrieved from www.teachersforanewera.org/index.cfm?fuseaction=home.prospectus

Carnochan, W. B. (1993) *The battleground of the curriculum: liberal education and American experience*. Stanford, CA: Stanford University Press.

Clifford, G. J. & J. W. Guthrie (1988) *Ed school: a brief for professional education*. Chicago, IL: University of Chicago Press.

Cochran-Smith, M. (2005) The new teacher education: for better or for worse? *Educational Researcher*, 34(7): 3–17.

Coleman, D. & M. DeBay (2000) Weaving teacher education into the fabric of a liberal arts education. *Kappa Delta Pi Record*, 36(3): 116–120.

Committee on General Education (2005) Harvard College curricular review: report of the Committee on General Education. Retrieved from www.fas.harvard.edu/curriculum-review

Darling-Hammond, L. & J. Bransford (2005) *Preparing teachers for a changing world: what teachers should learn and be able to do*. San Francisco, CA: Jossey-Bass.

Dressell, P. (1954) General and liberal education. *Review of Educational Research*, 24(4) 285–294.

Ducharme, Edward R. (1980) Liberal arts in teacher education. *Journal of Teacher Education*, 31(3): 7–12.

Ducharme, Edward R. (1993) *The lives of teacher educators*. New York: Teachers College Press.

Durden, W. (2003) The liberal arts as a bulwark of business education. *Chronicle of Higher Education*, July 18: B20.

Edmundson, J. & M. B. Greiner (2005) Social foundations within teacher education. In D. Butin (ed.), *Teaching social foundations of education: context, theories, and issues*. Mahwah, NJ: Erlbaum.

Edmundson, M. (1997) On the uses of liberal education. *Harper's Magazine*, September: 39–49.

Eisner, E. (1995) Preparing teachers for schools of the 21st century. *Peabody Journal of Education*, 70(3): 99–111.

Elshtain, J. B. (1997) *Real politics: at the center of everyday life*. Baltimore: Johns Hopkins University Press.

Flanagan, T. (2000) Liberal education and the criminal justice major. *Journal of Criminal Justice Education*, 11(1): 1–13.

Floden, R. E. & M. Meniketti (2005) Research on the effects of coursework in the arts and sciences and in the foundations of education. In Marilyn Cochran-Smith & Kenneth Zeichner (eds.), *Studying teacher education: the AERA panel on research and teacher education*. Washington, DC: American Educational Research Association.

Gilster, P. (1997) *Digital literacy*. New York: Wiley.

Giroux, H. (1992) *Border crossings: cultural workers and the politics of education*. New York: Routledge.

Gitlin, T. (1998) The liberal arts in the age of info-glut. *Chronicle of Higher Education*, May 1, B4–5.

Glazer, N. (1974) The schools of the minor professions. *Minerva*, 12(3): 346–364.

Gore, J. (1987) Liberal and professional education: keep them separate. *Journal of Teacher Education*, 38(1): 2–5.

Graff, G. (1992) *Beyond the culture wars: how teaching the conflicts can revitalize American education*. New York: Norton.

Graff, G. (2003) *Clueless in academe: how schooling obscures the life of the mind*. New Haven, CT: Yale University Press.

Grubb, W. N. and M. Lazerson (2004) *The education gospel: the economic power of schooling*. Cambridge, MA: Harvard University Press.

Hermann, M. L. (2004) Linking liberal and professional learning in nursing education. *Liberal Education*, 90(4): 42–47.

Hiebert, J., R. Gallimore, & J. W. Stigler (2002) A knowledge base for the teaching profession: what would it look like and how can we get one? *Educational Researcher*, 31(5): 3–15.

Higgins, C. (2000) Educational philosophy as liberal teacher education: charting a course beyond the dilemma of relevance. *Philosophy of Education 2000*, (pp. 271–282).

Hirsch, E. D., Jr. (1996) *The schools we need and why we don't have them*. New York: Doubleday.

Holmes Group (1988) The role of liberal arts in teacher education. East Lansing, MI: Holmes Group.

Howey, K. & N. Zimpher (1989) *Profiles of preservice teacher education: inquiry into the nature of programs*. Albany, NY: State University of New York Press.

Hoy, A. W. & R. B. Spero (2005) Changes in teacher efficacy during the early years of teaching: a comparison of four measures. *Teaching and Teacher Education*, 21(4): 343–356.

Hunter, J. D. (1991) *Culture wars: the struggle to define America*. New York: Basic Books.

Kagan, D. (1999) What is a liberal education? In E. Fox-Genovese and E. Lasch-Quinn (eds.), *Reconstructing history: the emergence of a new historical society*. New York: Routledge, 1999.

Katz, S. (2005) Liberal education on the ropes. *Chronicle of Higher Education*, April 1: B6–9.

Kelly, T. M. (2003) Remaking liberal education: the challenges of new media. *Academe*, 89(1): 28–31.

Kennedy, M. M. (1999) Ed schools and the problem of knowledge. In J. D. Raths & A. C. McAnich (eds.), *Advances in teacher education*, (Vol. 5, pp. 29–45). Stamford, CT: Ablex.

Kimball, B. (1995) *The condition of American liberal education: pragmatism and a changing tradition*. New York: College Entrance Examination Board.

Kliebard, H. M. (1992) The liberal arts curriculum and its enemies: the effort to redefine general education. In Kliebard, *Forging the American curriculum: essays in curriculum history and theory*, pp. 27–50. New York: Routledge.

Kramer, R. (1991) *Ed school follies: the miseducation of American teachers*. New York: Free Press.

Labaree, D. F. (2004) *The trouble with ed schools*. New Haven, CT: Yale University Press.

Lears, J. (2003) The radicalism of the liberal arts tradition. *Academe*, 89(1): 23–27.

Lehman, N. (2004) Liberal education and professionals. *Liberal Education*, 90(2): 12–17.

Lortie, D. (1975) Schoolteacher: a sociological study. Chicago, IL: University of Chicago.

Luttrell, W. (2000) "Good enough" methods for ethnographic research. *Harvard Educational Review*, 70(4): 499–523.

McGrath, C. (2006) What every school student should know: even Harvard, as it replaces its well-known core, isn't quite sure. *New York Times Education Life*. January 8: 33–35.

Martusewicz, R. & J. Edmundson (2005) Social foundations as pedagogies of responsibility and eco-ethical commitment. In D. Butin (ed.), *Teaching social foundations of education: context, theories, and issues*. Mahwah, NJ: Erlbaum.

Mason, S. F. (2000) Do colleges of liberal arts and science need schools of education? *Educational Policy*, 14(1): 121–128.

Menand, L. (1997) Re-imagining liberal education. In R. Orrill (ed.), *Education and democracy: re-imagining liberal leaning in America*. NY: The College Board.

Menand, L. (2001) College: the end of the golden age. *New York Review of Books*, October 18: 18–23.

Meyer, K. (2005) Common metaphors and their impact on distance education: what they tell and what they hide. *Teachers College Record*, 107(8): 1601–1625.

Murray, F. B. (1998) Reforming teacher education: issues and the joint effort of education and liberal arts faculty. *The History Teacher*, 31(4): 503–519.

Murray, F. B. & D. Fallon (1989) *The reform of teacher education for the 21st century: project 30 year one report*. Newark, DE: College of Education.

Murray, F. B. & A. Porter (1996) Pathway from the liberal arts curriculum to lessons in the schools. In F. B. Murray (ed.), *The teacher educator's handbook: building a knowledge base for the preparation of teachers*. San Francisco, CA: Jossey-Bass.

Nelson, J., A. Megill, & D. McCloskey (1987) The rhetoric of the human sciences: language and argument in scholarship and public affairs. Madison, WI: University of Wisconsin Press.

Noddings, N. (1992) *The challenge to care in schools: an alternative approach to education*. New York: Teachers College Press.

Nussbaum, M. (1997) *Cultivating humanity: a classical defense of liberal education*. Cambridge, MA: Harvard University Press.

O'Donnell, J. J. (1998) *Avatars of the word: from papyrus to cyberspace*. Cambridge, MA: Harvard University Press.

Orrill, R. (ed.) (1995) *The condition of liberal education: pragmatism and a changing tradition*. New York: College Entrance Examination Board.

Orwell, G. (1950) *Shooting an elephant and other essays*. New York: Harcourt Brace and World. The essay was first published in 1946.

Pascarella, E. & P. Terenzini (1991) *How college effects students: findings and insights from twenty years of research*. San Francisco, CA: Jossey-Bass.

Powell, A. (2003) *American high schools and the liberal arts tradition*. Washington, DC: Brookings Institution.

Ravitch, D. (2000) *Left back: a century of failed school reform*. New York: Simon and Schuster.

Ravitch, D. (2003) *The language police: how pressure groups restrict what children learn*. New York: Knopf.

Reagan, G. (1990) Liberal studies and the education of teachers. *Theory into Practice*, 29(1): 30–35.

Schneider, C. (2005) Liberal education: slip-sliding away? In R. Hersh & J. Merrow (eds.), *Declining by degrees: education at risk*. New York: Palgrave Macmillan.

Segall, A. (2004) Revisiting pedagogical content knowledge: the pedagogy of content/the content of pedagogy. *Teaching and Teacher Education*, 20: 489–504.

Shapiro, J. J. & S. Hughes (1996) Information literacy as a liberal art: enlightenment proposals for a new curriculum. *Educom Review*, 31(2).

Shulman, L. (1987) Knowledge and teaching: foundations of the new reform. *Harvard Educational Review*, 57(1): 1–22.

Shulman, L. (1998) Theory, practice, and the education of professionals. *Elementary School Journal*, 98(5): 511–526.

Snyder, I. (2002) *Silicon literacies: communication, innovation and education in the electronic age*. New York: Routledge.

Stark, J. S. & M. A. Lowther (1989) Exploring common ground in liberal and professional education. In R. A. Armour & B. Fuhrmann (eds.), Integrating liberal learning and professional education. *New Directions in Teaching and Learning*, 40 (1989): 7–20.

Stearns, P. N. (1993) *Meaning over memory: recasting the teaching of culture and history*. Chapel Hill, NC: University of North Carolina Press.

Stearns, P. N. (2004) Teaching culture. *Liberal Education*. Summer: 6–14.

Symposium: teaching the conflicts at twenty years (2003). *Pedagogy*, 3(2): 245–275.

Trubowitz, S. (2004) The marriage of liberal arts departments and schools of education. *Educational Horizons*, 82(2): 114–117.

Williams, R. (1983) *Keywords: a vocabulary of culture and society*. Rev. ed. New York: Oxford University Press.

Winter, D. G., D. C. McClelland, & A. Stewart (1981) *A new case for the liberal arts: assessing institutional goals and student development*. San Francisco, CA: Jossey-Bass.

60 The role of teacher education courses in teaching by second nature

Frank B. Murray
University of Delaware

The argument against professional teacher education courses is rooted in the undeniable fact that teaching is a naturally occurring human behavior, a wholly natural act that is an enduring and universal feature[1] of the repertoire of human behaviors. We are, in other words, a teaching species, a species whose young cannot, and do not, survive unless they are taught, invariably by persons with no formal schooling in teaching or in teacher education. Some have argued (e.g. Gilbert & Borish, 1997) that teaching is so basic to life that it can be found at the cellular level, but most researchers find that teaching is a constellation of distinctly human behaviors that entails an intention to teach, an awareness and ascription of a knowledge differential between the student and teacher, and the teacher's implicit theory of the student's mind (Strauss & Ziv, 2004; Premack & Premack, 1996). Even when teaching is taken to have occurred merely when an "activity is performed that imparts information to another that would not be obtained through the normal performance of the activity alone," there are few documented cases of teaching in non-humans (Visalberghi & Fragaszy, 1996, p. 286).

With regard to humans, Ashley and Tomasello (1998) found evidence of teaching in children as young as three years old, and Strauss *et al.* (2002) found that children's style of teaching a new board game or building something changed from demonstration and modeling at 3–4 years to predominately verbal explaining at five and six years. Seven year olds can adapt their teaching on occasion to their perception of their pupil's proficiency and knowledge. They also introduce the new teaching strategy of asking the learners if they understood, and they then adapt their *teaching* to the learners' mistakes. Children's pedagogy is also influenced by schooling itself. Maynard (2004) found that older Mayan children (6–11 years), who had been to school, were also able to adopt "school-like" teaching with their younger siblings (didactic teaching at a distance) in place of indigenous teaching practices used in families for cooking and weaving (close-up interactive demonstrations).

FEATURES OF NATURAL TEACHING

J. M. Stephens (1967) catalogued the features of naturally occurring teaching in his theory of spontaneous schooling. His argument was that schooling, a feature of all known anthropological groups,[2] was dependent on a set of natural human tendencies that some persons had in greater degrees than others. Those who had these tendencies in generous proportions would be seen, whether they intended to teach or not, as teachers by the members of their communities. Teaching and learning would take place naturally, spontaneously, non-deliberatively, and not necessarily with any particular motive or intention to benefit the pupil. They would occur merely because the tendencies, which fundamentally serve only the teacher's needs, led incidentally and inevitably to learning in those persons in the teacher's company. Teaching, in other words, was natural and spontaneous; it occurred whenever a person with these tendencies was with any other person for a protracted period, and it occurred to satisfy some need of the teacher, not some need of the student.

The particular tendencies, which sustain natural teaching and schooling, were thought by Stephens to occur in two categories—manipulative and communicative:

Spontaneous manipulative tendency

(1) A tendency in all people to collect and manipulate things, classify them, dwell on them, play with simple and basic ideas, and create systems for grouping things— all done with no immediate tangible payoff.

Spontaneous communicative tendencies

(2) A tendency of a person to talk about what he or she knows because an unshared experience is painful and a burden that must be eased through telling.
(3) A tendency to applaud, commend, and to correct and disapprove others' performance, but not with any a motive to making them better persons. An error, for example—whether in a book or spoken on television—is spontaneously corrected even when the correction cannot possibly affect or benefit the author, publisher, or actor.
(4) A tendency to supply an answer that someone else is groping for, not to help the person exactly, but to meet one's own need to provide the answer and to fill the void of silence. (This deeply rooted tendency is perhaps why *wait time* must be a learned and practiced skill in teacher education programs so that waiting for the answer *can be done by second nature*.)
(5) A tendency to "point the moral," to show others how things are related, to show that *x* leads to *y* as in "*I told you that would happen.*"

The theory of spontaneous schooling, incidentally, is meant to account for two pervasive, and otherwise unexplained, findings in the research literature on schooling— (1) the universality and constancy of schooling, and (2) the fact that educational research overwhelmingly finds insignificant and small differences between educational treatments. The theory accounts for universality by arguing that wherever there are people, there are these five spontaneous tendencies, and in whomever these reside, there will be a teacher— whether in a formal school or outside one. The features of schooling, in other words, can be parsimoniously derived from the spontaneous tendencies.

The pervasive no difference findings in educational research are explained as the natural outcome of the fact that the tendencies were operating in both the treatment and control groups (e.g. in large and small classes, in computer-assisted and conventional instruction, in mixed and segregated ability groups, in classrooms with textbooks *A* and *B*, and so forth). The tendencies, by themselves, caused powerful learning effects that swamped any differential effects that could be attributed to the researcher's treatment. These effects were explained adequately by the prevailing large scale learning theories because the spontaneous tendencies forged the defining stimulus-response learning link. They caused the stimulus to be presented, they permitted the opportunity to respond to it, and they rewarded and shaped the listener's response to the stimulus. At the time, these conditions were thought to be the sufficient for all school learning.

The theory, like other socio-biological theories, provides a convenient base for arguing that knowledge of subject matter, derived from the manipulative tendencies, and in the company of the communicative tendencies will outfit a person as a teacher, especially in situations where the teacher and the pupil are a lot like each other and share common goals—as they are in families and other anthropological groups. It is not important that Stephen's speculations on the specific character of the natural or spontaneous tendencies are correct in every detail, but only that there are natural teaching abilities and that these seem to be adequate for most contemporary teaching and schooling.

The question of the moment is whether university- and college-based teacher education courses, coming on the scene in the late 1800s, offer anything that can take novices much beyond the natural teaching skills possessed by all persons, including children.

Education Life (*New York Times*, July 31, 2005), to take only a recent example, makes a case that teachers need only be well-meaning and well-informed liberal arts graduates who are willing to work in today's schools. The natural teaching view is also reinforced by the fact that many effective private school teachers have not taken education courses, nor have professors, who were trained only to research, not teach, their subjects (Judge *et al.*, 1994). A close look at contemporary higher education, however, might show that the educational weaknesses driving the public school reforms in the post *Nation-at-risk* period, now culminating in *No Child Left Behind*, can be seen as well in contemporary higher education (Murray, 1985), but the point is that university professors meet their teaching responsibilities satisfactorily without the benefit of engaging the content of education courses.

Policy-makers raise the related question: Even if formal teacher education can refine and improve natural teaching somewhat, can the nation's needs for teachers still be met, less expensively and adequately, by the natural teaching techniques and styles we all seem to possess?

THE MANY INADEQUACIES OF NATURAL TEACHING

The theory of spontaneous schooling, and the view of teaching that is based on it, have a number of problematical consequences for contemporary schooling because schooling now takes place on larger scales than that found in families and other anthropological groups, and because schooling increasingly takes place in circumstances where the teacher and the pupils have less and less in common. As a result, reliance on the theory of natural teaching can be expected to lead to serious pedagogical mistakes for both weak and superior students. Quite apart from the matter of scale and the degree of similarity between the teacher and the pupil, the theory promotes a direct mode of instruction that is unduly limiting in terms of modern views of cognition and cognitive development. Finally, the theory provides insufficient guidance for the solution of difficult and novel problems in schooling that go beyond the natural teacher's exclusive reliance on "*showing and telling*," the core of the natural style of teaching found in children and adults.

Low expectations

When the teacher and the pupil are not alike and when the teacher has, as a result, lower expectations for the *different* pupil, the natural tendencies lead to very unfortunate consequences (Brophy & Good, 1986; Evertson *et al.*, 1985). When the teacher and the pupil have dissimilar backgrounds, we can expect the natural teaching mechanisms that support familial instruction will not operate to benefit the student.

American teachers are a relatively homogenous set of lower-middle class suburban white women, and the American pupil is increasingly variable with regard to every demographic feature (Howe, 1990; Choy, 1993). Thus, the teacher, even if he or she were to rely exclusively on the spontaneous tendencies, would still need to come to terms with the findings in a maturing literature on sexism, racism, bilingualism, cultural, ethnic, and class diversity.

Even if the teacher had acquired this information about the diverse groups in the classroom, information alone is often an insufficient basis for overcoming the natural teaching tendencies. Even experienced teachers fail to act on relevant information in an appropriate manner. Cohen (1990), for example, reports a case of an enthusiastic teacher, *Mrs. O*, who believed she understood and had adopted an innovative teaching approach only to have it shown that her *innovative* teaching was stubbornly hobbled with traditional and natural techniques.

Natural teaching leads to a predictable number of pedagogical mistakes that novices, and regrettably some licensed teachers, make unless they also have had the opportunity to learn and practice extensively some counterintuitive and *unnatural* teaching techniques. For example, it is certain that the natural teacher, well-meaning and well-read with good college grades, will still make the following pedagogical mistakes with their pupils for whom they have low expectations, regardless of how benignly they came to have these expectations. They will treat these pupils not as individuals but as a group, seat them further away and outside the classroom zone of frequent teacher-pupil interaction, look at them less, ask them low-level questions, call on them less often, give them less time to respond, give them fewer hints when they are called upon, and give them less praise and more blame than other pupils. And the natural teachers will do all this out of a mistaken sense of kindness that is seemingly oblivious to the pedagogical harm their undisciplined actions have caused their pupils (Hawley & Rosenholtz, 1984; Murray, 1996).

This untrained, natural, and kind person, believing the pupil does not know very much, will not want to embarrass the pupil by calling on the pupil often, will ask *appropriately* easy questions when the pupil is called upon, will give fewer hints and less time when the pupil fails to respond as it would be unkind to prolong the pupil's embarrassment and so on. The educated teacher, like all professionals, and in contrast with the *spontaneous* or *natural* teacher, must discipline many of his or her kinder instincts and implement an equitable and disciplined professional approach to bring about high levels of achievement from those pupils for whom the teacher would otherwise have low expectations (Oakes, 1985). These professional actions are frequently counterintuitive and as a result require extensive practice so that they can be performed by *second nature*.

Higher-order forms of learning

Kantor and Lowe (2004) argue persuasively that historically the schools, with a few exceptions that proved the rule, were inattentive to quality education and higher order subject matter understanding. Teaching was largely *showing and telling* coupled with rapid fire teacher questions and student recitation and memorization, all practices consonant with the natural teaching regime.

A further limitation of the natural teaching regime, apart from the harm caused to weaker pupils, is that it doesn't take the superior pupil much beyond the kind of information that can be told and demonstrated and conforms to the stimulus-response and imitative forms of learning. While such declarative knowledge is important, the forms of knowledge that are constructed by the pupil, not merely transmitted to the pupil, are increasingly seen as key to the student's performance at the advanced levels of the disciplines (Murray, 1992; Ogle *et al.*, 1991). A pupil can be told and shown, for example, that *A* is greater than *B*, and that *B* is also greater than *C*, but the knowledge that *A must be* greater than *C*, and that one could know that without ever looking directly at *A* and *C*, cannot be simply given to the pupil. Not only is *A* truly greater than *C*, but more than that, it *has to be* greater. The notion of necessity has its origins elsewhere. Showing and telling have not been found, except in very unusual circumstances, to be effective means of "teaching" necessity (Beilin, 1971; Murray, 1978, 1990; Smith, 1993). It is one thing to know that a statement is true, but quite another to know that it *must be* true. The origins of necessity, and other pivotal concepts, like irony or justice, seem to lie in *dialectical* instruction, which demands intellectual action on the part of the teacher and the student. While more demanding on the student, dialectic or maieutic teaching, is a less direct and more subtle form of instruction than that supported by the natural "*show and tell*" teaching tendencies.

The naive theory of mind

Along with the natural teaching techniques there often comes a naive and serviceable, but limited, theory of the human mind (Heider, 1958; Baldwin, 1980). The pupil's school achievement in the naive or common sense theory is tied to four common place factors—ability, effort, task difficulty, and luck. With these four factors, the natural teacher can explain completely the pupil's success or failure in school by attributing the level of the pupil's work to his/her ability or effort, or to the difficulty of the school task, or to plain luck. The problem with naive theory, apart from the circularity in the four factors, is that more sophisticated theories have been developed in which it can be shown that ability, to take only one example, is not fixed or stable, and that it varies from moment to moment interactively with many other mental factors, not just the few in the naive theory (Baldwin, 1980; Murray, 1991).

Naive theories also yield such maxims as "*practice makes perfect*," when it is clearer that "*practice only makes tired*" as it is reinforced practice that makes perfect. Moreover, these naive theories give contradictory maxims like "*he who hesitates is lost*" and its converse, "*fools rush in where angels fear to tread*." Naive theories, to take another example, see forgetting as the inevitable decay of stored knowledge, when the educated view is that forgetting is an active thinking process of interference and reorganization (Rose, 1993).

Naive pedagogy. Natural teaching is essentially *showing and telling* (see Olson and Bruner 1996 for an account of folk pedagogy). Naive pedagogy is based upon a *transmission of intact packets of information* model of teaching. Strauss and Shilony (1994) interviewed experienced and novice science and humanities teachers about how they would teach a topic of their choosing to children of various ages (7–17 years). Both novice and experienced teachers in each discipline conceptualized teaching only as the flow of information from their heads to their pupils' heads, acknowledging their own role was only to devise manageable and interesting ways of entry into the student's mind so the information could be stored and anchored appropriately. The student is passive, a receptacle waiting to be filled, and if the information fails to flow to its destination, the receptacle was taken to be too small and/or the student was inattentive. Because novices and experienced teachers were indistinguishable in their responses, Strauss and Shilony attributed the teachers' responses to their pre-training and pre-existing common sense naive views of pedagogy.

In other contexts, however, there is clear evidence that experienced teachers perform differently from novices (Berliner, 1988), but mostly in the reading of highly contextualized cues that contribute to the smooth functioning of the class and were seemingly learned *on the job*. The effects of teacher training seem negligible in this area.

Astington and Pelletier (1996) catalogued the following tenets of naive pedagogy: (1) children are born with abilities and capacities that unfold linearly in time, (2) instructional sequences should match developmental sequences, (3) learning occurs sequentially within a hierarchy of skills, and (4) student errors are attributable to incomplete learning or inattention. When the pupil needs to do something, the teacher need only demonstrate or model it, and when the pupil needs to learn something, the teacher need only tell the pupil what they need to know.

On the whole, these folk or naive pedagogical techniques and beliefs frustrate modern pedagogies based on dialectic, discovery, invention and collaboration. They are also at variance with some contemporary research findings: developmental pathways, for example, are rarely linear and often show fits and starts, oscillations, and even reversals, particularly when performance is at an optimal level or when a new skill is being developed (Fischer & Bidell, 1998).

These naive views of how the mind works coupled with equally naive views about the nature of the academic subject matters as received and objective truth further limit the benefits that can be expected from nonprofessional or natural teaching (see Amsler & Stotko, 1996, for examples of the possible and legitimate variations in what constitutes correct subject matter knowledge). The naive view of subject matter also shows itself principally in the area of assessment of the student's understanding of a subject matter.

Classroom assessment

The natural or naive teacher's evaluation of the pupil's correct and incorrect responses provides a telling and targeted arena for distinguishing naive and educated teachers. A pupil's reasoning may look illogical to a naive teacher, while the educated teacher will see that the pupil's reasoning is intact, but operating on different premises from those of the set problem. The naive teacher will be distressed when a pupil who had pluralized *mouse* correctly suddenly pluralizes it as *mouses*, while the educated teacher will see the new plural, not as an unfortunate regression, but as a positive sign of cognitive advancement in which the pupil is exhibiting a newly developed appreciation of a linguistic rule that is merely over-generalized in this instance.

Other decrements in performance may also indicate educational progress; for example, readers, as opposed to nonreaders, perform quite poorly when they are asked to identify the red color of the ink in the printed word, *blue*, while nonreaders have little difficulty with the task (the Stroup effect). Along similar lines, some six-year-old pupils not only maintain incorrectly that the longer row of two rows of five beans has more beans, but also maintain that the longer row must have more beans and would always have more beans. These errors occur even after the pupil has just counted the equal number of beans in each row. It happens that the error, "there *must* be more beans," which seems the more serious error, is indicative of more developed reasoning than the error, "there are more beans" (Murray & Zhang, 2005). Naturally, it is very difficult for the naive or natural teacher to accept any error or poor performance as a marker of progress, yet the failure to see some errors as markers of progress is another serious pedagogical mistake that stems from the naive theory of teaching and learning (see Bruner, 1961, on *creative errors*).

The student's superior performance may also be misinterpreted by the naïve teacher (see Strauss & Stavy, 1982, for examples where correct performance actually rests on immature and incorrect reasoning). Murray (1990) found that young children's success on a developmentally advanced task was, despite the appearances, not an indication of the same level of cognitive development as older children's success on the same task.

The teacher's scoring rubric, by which the student's accomplishments and progress are noted, reveals even more about the teacher's naive theory of subject matter knowledge. If a child arrives at the correct answer to a multiplication problem through serial addition, how would the naive teacher score the response—as superior or inferior to the response of a child who arrives at an incorrect answer through multiplication? Do college students, who correctly calculate the mean, median, and mode, operate at different standards of sophistication if their reasoning is based on a calculation algorithm, a mechanical model of balance, an algebraic deduction, or a special case in the calculus? Upon what theory, and by what means, would the naive teacher determine whether some solutions are more sophisticated, elegant, significant, and so forth, than other solutions. By what criteria would the teacher even see his/her teaching as successful and/or high quality (see Fenstermacher & Richardson, 2005, on these distinctions)?

The naive or natural approaches to teaching, pedagogy, and subject matter provide misleading and limited guidance to any of these questions. More thoughtful answers require deeper study than that afforded in naive theories and regrettably in many contemporary teacher education courses.

Problems with courses in teacher education

Problems in the academic major courses

The fact that many liberal arts graduates have engaged in deeper study of their subject matter and have succeeded in meeting the expectations of the faculty in their fields of study, should not be taken as evidence that they, having taken the traditional major in a subject matter, are ready to take up work as teachers, because many of these graduates, despite their high grades, have still not mastered many of the fundamental ideas of their disciplines (McDiarmid, 1992; Tyson, 1994). Surprisingly large numbers of undergraduate majors in science and engineering, for example, are simply unable to write an equation to represent the fact that there were six times as many cows in the field as farmers. Their errors are systematic. They write the equation as *6 cows = 1 farmer*, rather than correctly as *1 cow = 6 farmers*. Most undergraduates, including math majors, cannot think of a real world example of the division of one fraction by another (e.g. 1¾ ÷ ½). Many, in fact, get the mathematics wrong in this school problem and give examples of "1¾ ÷ 2," not "½" (Ball, D., 1991).

The naive or educated teacher's mistakes in subject matter knowledge and its assessment are a problem under any view of teacher employment. Additional study in the subject matter would seem the obvious remedy, and nearly every reform initiative in teacher education recommends additional and deeper subject matter preparation. The exact nature of the study, however, has been shown to be complex (Wilson *et al.*, 2001; Rice, 2003; Floden & Meniketti, 2005). Generally more preparation in the subject, particularly mathematics, is positively related to student learning, but there are inconsistencies in which additional subject matter preparation weakens student learning in some circumstances.

The problem of abbreviated study

The research on the efficacy of pedagogical courses is weaker than that for subject matter courses, but also shows some positive association with student teaching (Rice, 2003).

The strengthening of subject matter preparation, however, often comes at the expense of pedagogical and clinical training. It is doubtful, however, that a sufficient level of pedagogical training can be reached in a short period. For example, on a simple reading of Skinner, as might be found in a survey course in education, prospective teachers could believe that positive reinforcement (or reward) is an effective and preferred way to increase the likelihood of desirable pupil behavior. Without an awareness of the important exceptions and qualifications in which rewards actually weaken a response (the *over-justification phenomenon*), teachers will make mistakes by implementing procedures that run counter to their intentions (Cameron & Pierce, 1994).[3]

Similarly, upon a quick reading, the prospective teacher could come to believe that student grades should be normally distributed or that reliability is a property of a test rather than a property of those who took the test. These professional lessons cannot be easily abridged or rushed because many educational innovations are counterintuitive and subtly tied to hidden factors.

For example, it makes a difference whether addition problems, like *8 + 5 =_*, are presented horizontally or vertically. While a seven-year-old child, to take another example, may understand that the amount of clay in a ball would be unaffected if the ball were flattened into a pancake, she would more than likely believe incorrectly that the same pancake would weigh more and take up less space, despite the fact that the child had claimed the ball and pancake have the same amount of clay. Furthermore, it is now acknowledged that many research findings are inherently provisional and must be qualified by context and the cohort or generation of subjects who participated in the study, as different results are obtained from different cohorts and contexts on such basic questions as whether intellectual performance decreases after a certain age. Thus, having studied the research literature at one time is not a guarantee that the results can be applied at a later time with regard to such nagging and recurring issues as social promotion, skipping grades, ability grouping, optimal class size, delayed instruction, and so forth. Current and deeper study is required throughout the teaching career.

The problem of insufficient time

Sudden or effortless changes in behavior are taken by developmental psychologists as a sign that the change was not fundamental, but rather a temporary change, caused by a peripheral mechanism (e.g. fatigue, inattention, misperception, etc.), and not authentic. Protracted and extended practice and experience is needed to overcome the acquisitions of a prior stage of development or of the naive or natural teaching regime, which seems to be deeply rooted in behavior.

Smith (1989) has shown that highly motivated, knowledgeable, and experienced teachers were still unsure and shaky after ten months of practice in their efforts to implement a *conceptual change* science teaching technique, even though they practiced the new technique extensively under ideal teacher education conditions (extended coaching one on one). Such protracted experience is rarely afforded in the traditional teacher education course. Despite having practiced the technique in a variety of settings, having video and stimulated recall analysis of their teaching performance, and having personal feedback of their efforts, the teachers regressed to their earlier teaching style whenever the lesson took an unusual and unexpected turn (Smith & Neale, 1990). Their regression to *show and tell* sometimes undermined the entire point of the science lesson and science itself, because the teachers would deny or ignore an unexpected outcome in a science demonstration in favor of the outcome that was supposed to have happened. In a light and shadow lesson, when a single shadow was expected and predicted, but a double shadow appeared, the teacher would deny it or ignore it and continue with the demonstration as if the single predicted and expected shadow had appeared, all in opposition to the new teaching technique and the tenets of science.

The classic defense against this kind of *regression under stress* to the more primitive and older strategies is *over-learning* or practice well beyond what is needed to simply learn the new skill or approach. Regrettably, few teacher education programs make the necessary provisions for over-learning.

The problem of backward design

Teacher education programs are remarkably the same in their four part format across the country—(1) general/liberal arts courses, (2) subject matter courses, (3) pedagogical or methods courses and (4) clinical experience courses. It is the substance of the courses, not the format, which varies so widely that Shulman (2005) argues that there really isn't any teacher education curriculum in the United States. The problem is that the curricular content that is in place, varied as it is, is typically not clearly connected to the educational needs of children and adolescents. The content needs to be backwardly designed from the needs of children to the program's content. These needs, of course, should be the driving principle in the design of teacher education courses, but the influence of other factors is more clearly seen (Gardner, 1991).

The overriding question, whose answer legitimizes any course content, is—can the content be connected, on some line of reasoning, to the teacher's response to an educational need the child or adolescent truly has? The more distant the connection, the less convincing the course content is to the candidates and the public. The more distant the connection to the child's needs, the less university-based teacher education is actually warranted because naive or natural teaching would be adequate, because it primarily serves the needs of the teacher, not the pupil's.

Educational scholarship is also not currently organized around the needs of children and adolescents, but rather around the professor's needs as expressed in the academic disciplines, the separate clinical methods, clinical practice and the norms of higher education. Were educational scholarship organized around children's needs and the teacher's responses to them, prospective teachers would be guided by the view that the curriculum must be shaped so that it actually solves a problem the student has. The teacher's art is in organizing the activities of the classroom so that the student's academic work solves a genuine problem the student brings to the classroom. As it is now, students work on problems that others have brought to the classroom, problems imposed by the school and largely artificial, viz., the student has to avoid school failure by taking actions that meet the teacher's expectations no matter how unrelated they are to anything the student directly cares about. To connect the curriculum to problems students truly have is an exceptionally demanding task for the teacher, which is another reason why teachers need more than their natural teaching skills. Natural teaching, at least as Stephens set it out, is organized solely around the teacher's needs and flows from innate dispositions the teacher has.

Olson and Bruner (1996) conclude that the shift from the simplest pedagogies of natural teaching to the more sophisticated ones available in scholarship entails a focus on what the student, not the teacher can do, on what the student thinks, on the student's view of teaching itself, and on knowledge as an emergent event in the dialectic between the teacher and the student.

The problem of failed confidence in quality assurance

Ironically, the teaching education program is held back by the very fact that teaching has all the attributes of the other professions—accreditation, professional associations, standardized tests, licenses and credentials, advanced degrees, and so forth. Teachers, since the end of the Second World War, have been required to have college degrees (in some cases, graduate degrees), pass standardized examinations, meet state license standards, fulfill the school district's requirements for tenure, complete annual update courses and show other evidence of professional growth. While there is some fragile evidence for the efficacy of the license in the teaching field and advanced degrees (Rice, 2003), none of these requirements, all demanding in their appearance, has credibility within or outside the profession as each is routinely waived when there are shortages of otherwise qualified persons for the public schools. In the case of the private schools, many states typically set and require no standards at all, a practice that only reinforces the lack of standing the current standards have.

To take one example of the low regard in which these bureaucratic standards are held, the National Board for Professional Teaching Standards (NBPTS), departing from the practice of other professional national boards, elected *not* to require a degree in teacher education, a state teaching license, or study at an accredited institution for those permitted to sit for its certification examinations. National Board certification, itself, is not even required for advancement in the field or promotion to higher levels of professional responsibility.

None of the standards for teaching, collectively or separately, apparently provides the public any assurance that the teacher is competent. Few feel the nation is at risk over these lax professional standards because, sadly, the naive view of teaching is held by large numbers of policy-makers and the public. Yet, many feel the nation is still at risk, and it is largely over the fact that neither today's graduates nor their teachers seem to understand very much of what they have learned.

Going beyond natural teaching

While there are the many weaknesses in the naive approach to teaching, a strong case for professional education courses is also difficult to make owing to the failure of educational scholarship and teacher education to coalesce around any powerful and generative theory of schooling and teaching (Shulman, 2005). Although it is unfortunately a negative example, one test of the tentative and embryonic nature of educational scholarship in this regard is that there is still no consensus among educational scholars and practitioners about what would constitute educational malpractice (Collis, 1990).

Apart from teachers' acts that are expressly illegal, there is surprisingly no accepted view, except in a few extreme instances (like no longer forcing lefthanders to switch hands for penmanship), about what educational practices should never be employed in classrooms. Even competing practices, like *whole word* and *phonics* instruction in initial reading methods, have reasonable levels of current scholarly support and adherents. Without a sure sense of what constitutes educational malpractice, teaching and teacher education are behind other professions, which have fairly well-articulated codes of good practice, and which by extension define malpractice as the failure to follow good practice (see Cochran-Smith, 2005, for an argument that teacher education is still somewhat ahead of other professional fields in demonstrating its effectiveness).

Challenges for educational scholarship

On the whole, the accumulated record of educational scholarship has not yet yielded a coherent academic discipline of teacher education (Cochran-Smith & Zeichner, 2005). Until the last three decades, scholarship in education relied heavily upon findings from other disciplines, particularly the behavioral sciences. The transfer of those findings, collected in non-school settings, to issues of educational practice has been generally unsatisfying. Within the last thirty years, however, the powerful methodologies of other disciplines have been turned on classrooms themselves with the result that life in classrooms has been studied in such a way that some fairly convincing and counterintuitive conclusions about schooling rise to level of the standards of a university course.

Even though there are significant gaps in it, over the last thirty years, a body of scholarly literature has developed that supports the teacher's reasoning about some educational practices and allows the teacher to evaluate the merits of some educational innovations, techniques, and policies. This literature does provide sound advice about some matters, such as whether a teacher should adopt ita (the initial teaching alphabet) that regularizes spelling by having 44 letters, one for each of the phonemes of English. The argument is that ita facilitates early reading by reducing the discrepancies between English orthography and pronunciation. The teacher who had studied Osgood's transfer surface, unlike the thousands of teachers in the USA and Britain who adopted the innovation in the 1970s or in the 1860s (when the innovation was called *phonotaby*), would know what the likely benefits to reading and harm to spelling of the innovation.

Similarly there is a substantial literature on the controversial question of whether failing pupils should repeat a grade or be *socially* promoted to the next grade, or whether a gifted pupil should skip a grade, enter school early, be grouped separately from less gifted pupils. How could the *natural* teacher decide whether or not pupils should use calculators in their arithmetic lessons and homework? How can the naive teacher avoid making mistakes in answering questions like these unless they study the relevant scholarly literature on these matters, and in the cases where the literature is unhelpful or absent, unless they have also acquired ways of thinking and inquiring about their own teaching?

Despite these fragmentary examples of useful scholarship, the lack of an encompassing, systematic and authoritative body of scholarly knowledge about teaching, let alone about the education of teachers, presents a formidable obstacle to the study of teaching earning a place in the college curriculum and to teaching becoming the genuine profession it aspires to be (Cochran-Smith & Zeichner, 2005). Cochran-Smith (2006) poses a more expansive list of unanswered questions about teaching that would also take the prospective teacher well-beyond answers that could be derived from natural teaching, an apprenticeship in the school, or the study of current scholarship about teaching. Much fundamental work needs to be done, including an enlarged view of what constitutes scholarly evidence.

The challenge of education as a university subject

Owing to the natural teaching skills, it is possible to perform many routine teaching tasks without the benefit of experience and great theoretical sophistication, but errors of judgment multiply when events in the classroom are not routine and when past practice is an insufficient guide. The question is how to provide the aspiring teacher with a way of thinking and a set of skills that will take the new teacher beyond the ancient skills of natural teaching that are proving to be insufficient for the challenges of contemporary schooling.

Teacher education courses, however, are probably not warranted at the university level if the teacher is held only to the standard of presenting material truthfully and clearly, to giving students an opportunity to practice, and to testing the student's grasp of the material (*teach, test, hope for the best*). Teacher education is also probably not warranted at the university level if the needed ways of thinking and skills can be acquired in an apprenticeship during an internship in a school. It is discipline based scholarship that informs practice and leads to the practitioner's understanding of practice that uniquely commends teacher education as a college or university course of study.

The modern teacher's obligation is at a high level. It is not enough to have today's students simply learn the subject matter; they must *understand* it (Gardner, 1991). On this argument the teacher's own education must have the same attributes as their future students. Understanding, it would appear, cannot be produced by didactic telling, or by showing and coaching, although the pupil may learn and remember what the teacher said and may imitate what the teacher did. Understanding seems to be dependent upon the student's active investigation and experimentation, guided by *dialectic*—the teacher's skillful questioning and conversation aimed at the student's misconceptions and provoking the student to resolve discrepancy—forging, thereby, a coherent understanding of the events at hand. Unlike *solutions* that are learned, the dialectical outcomes are personal and extraordinarily resistant to forgetting.

Neither pupils, nor teacher education candidates, will understand their lessons if the teacher's or professor's role is merely to deliver information and imitate action. While dialectic requires the pupil to do something overtly—to speak, respond, and question—there are other features of teaching for understanding that require the teacher to abandon the naive and spontaneous techniques as the prime teaching style in which the teacher is more active than the students.

Modern views of intelligence and cognition, for example, are clear that knowing is negotiated, distributed, situated, constructed, developmental, and affective—all features of knowing that entail greater degrees of student action than is found in natural teaching. As Olson and Bruner (1996) put it

> truths are the product of evidence, argument, and construction rather than holding by dint of authority whether textual or pedagogic. The model of education is dialectical, more concerned with interpretation and understanding, than in the achievement of factual knowledge or skilled performance.
>
> (p. 19)

The challenge of the content for pedagogy courses

Of course, the first challenge for university courses in teacher education is to address the weaknesses and inadequacies in natural teaching. This is not an easy problem to solve because many of the documented weaknesses associated with natural teaching were found not only in novices but in experienced teachers, who, even though they had taken many traditional education courses, apparently regressed to the natural teaching techniques under the pressure of teaching.

All teachers know that the subject matter they teach is inevitably different from the subject matter they learned from their professors. The teacher must transform the subject matter into something else—a teachable subject that has its own structure and logic and is something that will make sense to the pupil. The question is: what body of scholarship guides the teacher in selecting an appropriate logic and structure? The knowledge that supports this conversion of the storehouse of knowledge into the school curriculum, into something that has meaning for the pupil, is sometimes called, *pedagogical content knowledge*, and ought to be the unique and signature content of the modern education course (see Murray, 1991, for an account of various structures available for the content of a teacher education program in elementary education).

The specification of pedagogical content knowledge entails the appropriate ways of organizing information and knowledge. It is the search for structures, ways of representing the subject matter, analogies and metaphors, that will take *each* pupil well beyond what can be held together temporally and spatially through rote memorization. Pedagogical content knowledge is fundamentally about those structures that confer some appropriate level of understanding, and it is ultimately about those structures that actually advance understanding.

Discussions of pedagogical content knowledge are at the heart of university and college pedagogy courses. *Hamlet* will at some point be taught (Grossman, 1990), but how should it be represented, and what should teachers claim it is about—the use of language to talk about language, the pathology of indecision, the unconscious mind of the adolescent, the re-creation of an historical event, or something else? How is the teacher candidate to think about these questions and who can best guide the candidate to compelling answers?

Some structures are merely scaffolds, and as scaffolds they are provisional and designed solely to advance the pupil to another place. Thus, it may be appropriate to introduce the *1812 Overture*, and by implication all classical music, as the re-creation of an event, as programme music, in which the two national anthems battle each other in the overture as the armies did on the battlefield. But, then again, this may not be an appropriate scaffold. This representation, or structure, which is hopelessly inadequate for any later understanding of musical composition, may engage and propel the student to further study, or it may provide a distorting foundation for later study. How is the naive teacher to know?

In teaching *Huckleberry Finn*, the teacher inevitably interprets the book as a story of gender and race relations, or generation gaps, or a historical period, or latent homosexuality on the frontier, or injustice, and so on (Graff & Phelan, 1995). Science teachers often attempt to clarify the nature of electric current by comparing it to the behavior of water currents in various sized pipes, or they compare the circulation of blood to the circulation of hot and cold home heating system, and so forth. Is this a good way to think about electricity or arterial circulation? How would the naive teacher or apprentice know? The answer to the question is not to be found in physics, biology, or in education, but in a qualitatively different kind of knowledge that comes from a new academic discipline of education built on inquiry by disciplinarians and pedagogues. This knowledge—the knowledge of what is a telling example, a good analogy, a provocative question, a compelling theme—is a proper object of study and could yield a deep and generative understanding of the disciplines. To have multiple ways of representing a subject matter, to have more than one example or metaphor, to have more than one mode of explanation requires a high order and demanding form of subject matter understanding.

In the teaching of descriptive statistics, for example, it may make sense to introduce the notions of central tendency and variation with physical models of equilibrium, or with computer graphics representations of data points, or as calculation formulae, or as the solution to certain questions in the behavioral sciences, or as derivations of algebraic equations, or as part of a system of expressions in calculus or some other branch of mathematics. These pedagogical options merit academic study by an approach that is as serious as the approach to any question in any academic discipline.

Few have seen that this kind of knowledge advances the academic discipline itself. At the cutting edge of a discipline, pedagogical content knowledge and theoretical breakthrough may be the same thing. What happens on the frontiers of a discipline? The researchers invent ways to communicate with each other about the phenomenon under study; they invent ways to make sense of the phenomenon. The "double helix," for example, was as much pedagogical content knowledge as a Nobel Prize winning description because it provided a means for researchers to teach each other, to converse about the genetic code.

When the teacher invents a structure that organizes and gives meaning to a field of study, he or she is doing *exactly* what the scholar or researcher does when the scholar provides a novel or generative structure for his or her peers about some problem in their field. Thus, the study of pedagogical content knowledge can be a study on the cutting edge of a field, insofar as new modes of representing the subject matter and new ways of making it interesting and meaningful are formulated.

The challenge in designing contemporary pedagogy courses also entails the incorporation of other information that also has not traditionally been part of them (see Murray, 1991). By way of somewhat lengthy example of this kind of information, consider what a teacher would need to know about physics and the student to teach the concept of *weight*.

The young child can be shown to operate with the following "system" for weight (Murray & Johnson, 1970, 1975): Weight for the pupil in the early grades can be shown to be a function of the following aspects of an object:

1   The object's mass, with additions of mass yielding greater weight, etc. and no change in mass yielding no change in weight.
2   Size, with larger objects weighing more, etc.
3   Shape, with some shapes weighing more and some less (e.g. flattening increases weight).
4   Texture, with the rougher weighing more and the smoother weighing less.
5   Temperature, with the colder weighing more and the warmer weighing less.
6   Hardness, with the harder weighing more and the softer weighing less.
7   Continuity, with whole weighing more than the sum of the components.
8   Label, with the object labeled, *bigger*, weighing more than the object labeled, *smaller*.

Some factors that are potential members of the system can be shown to have no influence on the child's physics of weight of an object; for example,

1   Object's horizontal position, with an object weighing the same at either end of the table.
2   Object's vertical position, with an object weighing the same in deep hole or at the top of the tallest mountain.

The young child's view of weight is based upon a consistent child-logic in which the factors above influence weight lawfully and dependably (Murray, 1982; Murray & Markessini, 1982). Adolescents and many adults operate with the following simpler and to some degree more sophisticated "system": Weight is a function of only the object's mass, the only influential factor to survive the child's system. In other words, the only way adults can think of to change an object's weight is to alter its mass, that is, add something or take something away from the object. The young child can imagine many other ways for altering weight, all unfortunately incorrect, however reasonable they seem to the child (and as it happens, to some adults on some occasions).The educated person operates within another system of the following factors organized as a mathematical expression of the product of the first two factors below divided by the square of the third:

1   Mass of the object (as above).
2   Mass of the planet (the largest nearest object), with larger planets yielding increased weight.
3   The distance between the centers of the above two factors, with weight decreasing with increases in the distance. In addition the educated person may be able to convert the expression into a genuine equation *via* a value, [g], for the gravitational constant which permits algebraic manipulation of the terms in the expression.

At this point other factors may be introduced into the expression to treat certain buoyant forces or variations in the earth's g, etc. After lengthy further education, gravitation is seen as an aspect of a space-time continuum in relativity physics and weight can only be determined once the time and space frame of the object is determined (as the weight of an object that is falling in space).

There is a similar developmental progression for the child's understanding of the beam balance in which the young child's understanding of "weighing" is controlled solely by the effects of adding or subtracting weight from a beam balance pan without regard to the influence of any other factor (Siegler, 1981). Later the distance of the balance pan from the fulcrum is gradually factored into the child's scheme for the operation of the balance, and after several more developmental steps we see the product moment law in place in the adolescent's thinking.

Similar scholarship exists for other concepts and relationships in the school curriculum. The information, unlike much of the current teacher education curriculum, has face validity because it contains precisely the kinds of information that prospective teachers readily accept as clearly relevant for their future work. It is also the kind of information that would not be found in an apprenticeship approach to teacher education. It is the kind of information at a university standard that also supports the teacher who holds a *developmentally appropriate* perspective on instruction.

Conclusion

The skepticism and cynicism that accompanies contemporary university-based teacher education courses is rooted in the fact that some forms of teaching are natural human behaviors that seem deeply rooted in our species. However, the forms of teaching we seem to have by nature are largely limited to *showing and telling* and are most effective only when the teacher and the student share common cultural assumptions and goals. These natural forms of teaching, however, are less effective, and on occasion even harmful, when the goals of education go beyond the kind of information and understanding that cannot be simply imitated and copied.

If the goals of schooling are restricted to what can be imitated and copied, then teacher education as a university subject is probably not warranted as the natural and spontaneous teaching regime can be relied on to accomplish the school's mission. If the goal of teacher education is to merely have persons who can teach by performing new techniques by second nature, teacher education as a university subject is probably not warranted either. If the goal, however, is to have teachers who can understand their practice and inquire into its purpose and efficacy, then the study of teaching practice, based upon scholarship and scholarly investigation, warrants space in the higher education curriculum.

Regrettably, many of today's education courses are weak because they are not organized around the pupil's educational needs or the newer scholarship about the development of the student understanding of the concepts in the curriculum. They also devote insufficient time to the candidate's unlearning some of the limiting aspects of natural teaching before supplanting them with the newer pedagogical techniques.

The remedy for advancing beyond natural teaching and the weaknesses in today's education courses, however, is not to abandon the courses in pedagogy, the hallmark of any genuine profession of teaching, but to strengthen these courses along the lines advocated by an array of reform groups, inside and outside the education schools. These reforms all reduce to a demand for a much higher standard for the teacher's work—namely having *all* their students *understand* the curriculum—and requiring a teacher education program that can deliver that outcome for their graduates.

NOTES

1 Draper (1976) and Konner (1976) show there are complex limits to universality of teaching in anthropological groups. In some cultures children are taught to eat but not to sit and to walk and vice versa in other cultures.
2 Prenack and Premack (1996, p. 315) point out that "pedagogy is not an official anthropological category: no catalogue lists the pedagogical practices of different groups . . . the anthropology of pedagogy is largely nonexistent; its proper study has yet to begin."
3 See further comment on the over-justification phenomenon in the Spring, 1996 issue of the *Review of Educational Research*, 66, No. 1, 1–51.

REFERENCES

Amsler, M & Stotko, E. M. (1996) Changing the subject: teacher education and language arts. In F. Murray (ed.), *The teacher educator's handbook*. San Francisco: Jossey-Bass (pp. 194–216).

Astington, J. W. & Pelletier, J. (1996) The language of mind. In D. R. Olson & N. Torrance (eds.), *The handbook of education and human development*. Oxford: Blackwell (pp. 591–619).

Ashley, J. & Tomasello, M. (1998) Cooperative problem solving and teaching in preschoolers. *Social Development*, 7, 143–163.

Baldwin, A. (1980) *Theories of child development* (2nd edition). New York: John Wiley.

Ball, D. (1991) Teaching mathematics for understanding: what do teachers need to know about subject matter? In M. Kennedy (ed.), *Teaching academic subjects to diverse learners*. New York: Teachers College Press (pp. 63–83).

Beilin, H. (1971) The training and acquisition of logical operations. In L. Rosskopf, L. P. Steffe & S. Taback (eds.), *Piagetian cognitive-development research and mathematical education*. Washington, DC: National Council of Teachers of Mathematics, Inc.

Berliner, D. (1988) Implications of studies of expertise in pedagogy for teacher education and evaluation. *New directions for teacher assessment: proceedings of the 1988 ETS invitational conference*, Princeton, NJ: Educational Testing Service (pp. 39–68).

Brophy, J. & Good, T. (1986) Teacher behavior and student achievement. In M. Wittrock (ed.), *Handbook of research on teaching*, 3rd edition. New York: Macmillan (pp. 328–375).

Brown, R. (1991) *Schools of thought: how the politics of literacy shape thinking in the classroom*. San Francisco: Jossey-Bass Publishers.

Bruner, J. (1961) *The process of education*. Cambridge, MA: Harvard University Press.

Cameron, J. & Pierce, D. (1994) Reinforcement, reward, and intrinsic motivation: a meta-analysis. *Review of Educational Research*, 64, No. 3, 363–423.

Cochran-Smith, M. (2005) Studying teacher education: what we know and need to know. *Journal of Teacher Education*, 56(1), 301–306.

Cochran-Smith, M. (2006) Evidence, efficacy, and effectiveness. *Journal of Teacher Education*, 57(1), 3–5.

Cochran-Smith, M. & Zeichner, K. (2005) (eds.) *Studying teacher education*. Mawah, NJ: Lawrence Erlbaum & Associates.

Cohen, D. (1990) A revolution in one classroom: the case of Mrs. Oublier. *Educational Evaluation and Policy Analysis*, 12, 311–330.

Collis, J. (1990) *Educational malpractice*. Charlottesville, Virginia: The Michie Co.

Evertson, C., Hawley, W., & Zlotnick, M. (1985) Making a difference in educational quality through teacher education. *Journal of Teacher Education*, 36(3): 2–12.

Cox, M. (1980) *Are young children egocentric?* New York: St. Martin's Press.

Draper, P. (1976) Docail and economic constraints on child life among the !Kung. In B. Lee & I. Devore (eds.), *Kahlahari hunter-gatherers*. Cambridge, MA: Harvard University Press (pp. 199–217).

Fensternacher, G. D. & Richardson, V. (2005) On making determinations of quality teaching. *Teachers College Record*, 107(1), 186–213.

Fischer, K. & Bidell, T. (1998) Dynamic development of psychological structures in action and thought. In W. Damon (ed.) and R. Lerner (Vol. ed.) *Handbook of child psychology* (Volume I). New York: John Wiley & Sons (pp. 467–561).

Floden, R. E. & Meniketti, M. (2005) Research on the effects of coursework in the arts and sciences in the foundations of education. In M. Cochran-Smith and K. Zeichner (eds.) *Studying teacher education*. Mahwah, NJ: Lawrence Erlbaum & Associates (pp. 251–308).

Fosnot, C. (1989) *Enquiring teachers, enquiring learners: a constructivist approach for teaching*. New York: Teachers College Press.

Gardner, H. (1991) *The unschooled mind: how children think and how schools should teach*. New York: Basic Books.

Gilbert, S. F. & Borish, S. (1997) How cells learn, How cells teach: Education in the body. In E. Amsel and A. K. Renniger (eds.), *Change and Development: issues in method, and application*. Mahwah, NJ: Lawrence Erlbaum Associates (pp. 61–76).

Graff, G. (1992) *Beyond the culture wars: how teaching the conflicts can revitalize American education*. New York: W.W. Norton.

Graff, G. & Phelan, J. (eds.) (1995) *Mark Twain, Adventures of Huckleberry Finn: a case study in critical controversy*. New York: Bedford Books of St. Martin's Press.

Grossman, P. (1990) *The making of a teacher: teacher knowledge and teacher education*. New York: Teachers College Press.

Hawley, W. & Rosenholtz, S. (1984) Good schools: what research says about improving student achievement. *Peabody Journal of Education*, 61 (4).

Heider, F. (1958) *The psychology of interpersonal relations*. New York: Wiley,

Henke, R., Choy, S., Xianglei, C., Geies, S., & Alt, M. (1991) *America's Teachers: Profile of a Profession 1993–4*. DC: National Center for Education Statistics.

Howe, H. (1990) Thinking about the forgotten half. *Teachers College Record*, 92, 293–305.

Judge, H., Lemosse, M., Paine, M., & Sedlak, M. (1994) The university and the teachers. *Oxford Studies in Comparative Education*, 4 (1&2).

Kantor, H. & Lowe, R. (2004) Reflections on history and quality education. *Educational Researcher*, 33(5), 6–10.

Konner, M. (1976) Maternal care, infant behavior and development among the !Kung. In B. Lee & I. Devore (eds.), *Kahlahari hunter-gatherers*. Cambridge, MA: Harvard University Press, 218–245.

McDiarmid, G. W. (1992) The arts and sciences as preparation for teaching. *Issue Paper 92–3*, E. Lansing: National Center for Research on Teacher Learning.

Maynard, A. (2004) Cultures of teaching in childhood: formal schooling and Maya sibling teaching at home. *Cognitive Development*, 19, 517–535.

Murray, F. (1978) Teaching strategies and conservation training. In A. M. Lesgold, J. W. Pellegrino,

S. Fokkema, & R. Glaser (eds.), *Cognitive psychology and instruction*. New York: Plenum (pp. 419–428).

Murray, F. (1982) The pedagogical adequacy of children's conservation explanations. *Journal of Educational Psychology*, 74(5), 656–659.

Murray, F. (1985) Paradoxes of a university at risk. In J. Blits (ed.), *The American university: problems, prospects and trends*. Buffalo, NY: Prometheus Books (pp. 101–120).

Murray, F. (1986) Teacher education. *Change Magazine*, September/October, 18–21.

Murray, F. (1990) The conversion of truth into necessity. In W. Overton (ed.), *Reasoning, necessity and logic: developmental perspectives*, 183–203. Hillsdale, NJ: Lawrence Erlbaum Associates.

Murray, F. (1991a) Questions a satisfying developmental would answer: the scope of a complete explanation of developmental phenomena. In H. Reese (ed.), *Advances in child development and behavior* (volume 23). New York: Academic Press, Inc. (pp. 39–47).

Murray, F. (1991b) Alternative conceptions of academic knowledge for prospective elementary teachers. In M. Pugach and H. Barnes (eds.), *Changing the practice of teacher education: the role of the knowledge base*. Washington, DC: AACTE (pp. 63–82).

Murray, F. (1992) Restructuring and constructivism: the development of American educational reform. In H. Beilin and P. Pufall (eds.), *Piaget's theory: prospects and possibilities*. Hillsdale, NJ: Lawrence Erlbaum Associates (pp. 287–308).

Murray, F. (1996) Beyond natural teaching: the case for professional education. In F. B. Murray (ed.), *The teacher educator's handbook*, San Francisco: Jossey-Bass, 3–13.

Murray, F. & Johnson, P. (1970) A note on using curriculum models in analyzing the child's concept of weight. *Journal of Research in Science Teaching*, 7, 377–381.

Murray, F. & Johnson, P. (1975) Relevant and some irrelevant factors in the child's concept of weight. *Journal of Educational Psychology*, 67, 705–711.

Murray, F. & Markessini, J. (1982) A semantic basis of nonconservation of weight. *The Psychological Record*, 32, 375–379.

Murray, F. & Zhang, Y. (2005) The role of necessity in cognitive development. *Cognitive Development*, (20), 235–241.

Oakes, J. (1985) *Keeping track: how schools structure inequality*. New Haven: Yale University Press.

Ogle, L., Alsalam, N., & Rogers, G. (1991) *The condition of education 1991*. Washington, DC: National Center for Educational Statistics.

Olson, D. & Bruner, J. (1996) Folk psychology and folk pedagogy. In D. R. Olson & N. Torrance (eds.). *The handbook of education and human development*. Oxford: Blackwell (pp. 9–27).

Premack, D. & Premack, A. J. (1996) Why animals lack pedagogy and some cultures have more of it than others. In D. R. Olson & N. Torrance (eds.), *The handbook of education and human development*. Oxford: Blackwell, 302–323.

Rose, S. (1993) *The making of memory*. New York: Anchor Books.

Rushcamp, S. & Roehler, L. (1992) Characteristics supporting change in a professional development school. *Journal of Teacher Education*, 43 (1), 19–27.

Rice, J. K. (2003) *Teacher quality: understanding the effectiveness of teacher attributes*. Washington, DC: Economic Policy Institute.

Scardamalia, M. & Bereiter, C. (1991) Higher levels of agency for children in knowledge building: a challenge for the design of new knowledge media. *Journal of the Learning Sciences*, (1), 37–68.

Sheingold, K. (September, 1991) Restructuring for learning with technology: the potential for synergy. *Phi Delta Kappan*, (73), 17–27.

Shulman, L. S. (2005) Teacher education does not exist. The Stanford Educator (Stanford University School of Education Alumni Newsletter), Fall, 2005, p. 7 (also at http://ed.stanford.edu/suse/news-bureau/educator-newsletter.html).

Siegler, R. (1981) Developmental sequences within and between concepts. *Monographs of the Society for Research in Child Development*, 46 (No. 189).

Smith, D. (1989) *The role of teacher knowledge in teaching conceptual change science lessons.* Unpublished doctoral dissertation, University of Delaware.

Smith, D. & Neal, D. (1990) The construction of subject matter in primary science teaching. In J. Brophy (ed.), *Advances in research on teaching subject matter knowledge.* Greenwich, CT: JAI Press.

Smith, L. (1993) *Necessary knowledge: Piagetian perspectives on constructivism.* Hillsdale, NJ: Erlbaum.

Stephens, J. (1967) *The process of schooling: a psychological examination.* New York: Holt, Rinehart & Winston.

Strauss, S. & Stavy, R. (1982) U-shaped behavioral growth: implications for developmental theories. In W. W. Hartap (ed.), *Review of developmental research.* Chicago, IL: University of Chicago Press (pp. 547–599).

Strauss, S. & Shilony, T. (1994) Teachers' models of children's mind and learning: implications for teacher education. In L. A. Hirschfeld and S. A. Gelman (eds.), *Mapping the mind: domain specificity in cognition and culture.* New York: Cambridge University Press (pp. 455–473).

Strauss, S. & Ziv, M. (2004) Teaching: ontogenesis, culture, and education. *Cognitive Development* (19), 451–456.

Strauss, S., Ziv, M. & Stein, A. (2002) Teaching as a natural cognition and its relation to preschoolers' developing theory of mind. *Child Development,* 17, 1473–1487.

Synder, T. (1993) *120 Years of American Education: A Statistical Portrait.* Washington, DC: National Center for Education Statistics.

Tyson, H. (1994) *Who will teach the children: progress and resistance in teacher education.* New York: Jossey-Bass.

Visalberghi, E. & Fragaszy, D. M. (1996) Pedagogy and imitation in monkeys: yes, no or maybe? In D. R. Olson and N. Torrance (eds.), *The handbook of education and human development.* Oxford: Blackwell (pp. 277–301).

Wilson, S. M., Floden, R. E., & Ferrini-Mundy, J. (2001) Teacher preparation research: current knowledge, gaps, and recommendations. University of Washington: Center for the Study of Teaching and Policy.

61 The value added by teacher education

Mary M. Kennedy,[1]
Soyeon Ahn and Jinyoung Choi
Michigan State University

Teaching is the sort of work that both inspires and mystifies, and many people have tried to articulate the qualities they believe make someone a good teacher. Some say a good teacher is bright, others that she is caring, others something else. These speculations take on a more practical quality when the conversation turns to how to prepare good teachers, for the preparation question can lead to detailed curriculum and program specifications. So literature on the question of how to produce good teachers includes philosophical inquiries, program designs, and empirical tests of hypotheses.

Arguments about how to prepare teachers have become especially shrill in recent years, as observers become increasingly concerned about the quality of the education system as a whole. Debates have also been stimulated by a new body of work called "value-added" analyses, which examine variations among teachers' classroom effectiveness. From these analyses, we know that teachers vary considerably in the amount their students learn, so much so that if a student had two or three consecutive weak teachers, his overall academic achievement would be seriously compromised (Aaronson *et al.*, 2003; Rokoff, 2003; Sanders & Horn, 1998). These studies demonstrate that teachers differ substantially in their effectiveness, and raise to prominence the question of how to better prepare teachers.

The aim of this paper is to examine empirical evidence regarding the merits of the most prominent hypotheses about educational backgrounds that will improve teacher effectiveness.[2] One hypothesis, the one that dominates most state regulations, is that teachers need specialized knowledge about issues directly pertinent to teaching—things like classroom management, techniques for teaching, the role of school in society and other educational issues. We call this hypothesis the *Pedagogical Knowledge* hypothesis. Virtually every state subscribes to this hypothesis by requiring prospective teachers to take courses from departments of teacher education whose mission is to prepare people specifically for teaching careers. But even though this hypothesis is widely represented in state regulations, it is not without its detractors. In particular, two other hypotheses are offered, either as alternatives or as supplements. One argues that teachers need *Content Knowledge* more than pedagogical knowledge. Proponents of this hypothesis frequently note that teachers cannot teach content if they do not know it. While it is possible in principle for teachers to obtain pedagogical knowledge as well as content knowledge, advocates for content knowledge frequently pit the two against one another under the assumption that courses providing pedagogical knowledge take up too much space in the college curriculum and hence remove space for courses providing content knowledge that would ultimately be more beneficial to prospective teachers. There is, among those outside the teacher education community, a general skepticism about the merit and value of courses taken in teacher education programs per se (Conant, 1963; Damerell, 1985; Hess, 2001; Kramer, 1991; Labaree, 2004; Lagemann, 1999).

In the past two decades, a third hypothesis has been put forward that suggests that teachers need a blend of pedagogical and content knowledge, something called *Pedagogical Content Knowledge*. This knowledge consists of such things as how students understand, or misunderstand, particular substantive ideas, how to present particular substantive ideas in a way that makes them more accessible to different types of students, or how to use particular resources in lessons about particular content. This third hypothesis, then, suggests that there is a relationship between pedagogy and content that teachers need to understand.

All of these hypotheses focus on the college curriculum, suggesting that there are particular domains of knowledge that can make a difference, and that teachers should take courses in these domains. There is another hypothesis that challenges the validity of all of these. This fourth hypothesis argues that the best teachers are Bright, well-educated people who are smart enough and thoughtful enough to figure out the nuances of teaching in the process of doing it. For people subscribing to this hypothesis, the route to improving the quality of teaching lies in recruitment, not in specific courses that will prepare people for this work.

Advocates of the first hypothesis tend to acknowledge all of the rest as well. That is, they rarely argue *against* content knowledge, *against* pedagogical content knowledge, or *against* the value of having bright, well-educated people teaching in the nation's classrooms (see, e.g. National Commission on Teaching and America's Future, 1996). However, advocates for content knowledge and for bright, well-educated people often do argue against the pedagogical knowledge and against pedagogical content knowledge hypotheses. So the debate really focuses mainly on the merits of allocating college curriculum space to courses specifically about teaching and learning.

We take the view that all of these hypotheses need to be examined. Therefore, we seek evidence about all of them, rather than confining ourselves to the most controversial one. For the first three hypotheses, we examine studies of teachers' college course-taking histories. We assume that courses in education represent pedagogical knowledge, courses in mathematics represent content knowledge, and courses in mathematics education represent pedagogical content knowledge. Because our fourth hypothesis deals more with recruitment than with college curriculum per se, we test this not by looking at studies of college courses, but instead at studies that examine the selectivity of the teachers' alma maters.

In this investigation, we confine our inquiry to the content area of mathematics, and take student achievement in mathematics as our indicator of teachers' effectiveness. This limitation is necessary in part to ensure that all curricular options are tested against a common outcome. We test hypotheses only about teachers' educational background, not about their tested knowledge.

The studies reviewed here come from a larger collection of literature addressing the role of a wide range of teacher qualifications to the quality of teaching. Below we describe our search procedures for gathering this literature and discuss some of the methodological problems in this literature. We then review findings for college curricula and for recruitment.

LITERATURE SEARCH PROCEDURES

Literature for this paper was drawn from a larger literature data base gathered as part of the *Teacher Qualifications and the Quality of Teaching* (TQQT) study. The TQQT data base includes studies that examine the relationship between at least one teacher qualification and at least one indicator of the quality of teaching. Our original search criteria defined *qualifications* to include such aspects of teachers' backgrounds as their college curricula, test scores, credentials, grade point averages and degrees. Indicators of teaching *quality* included such things as direct observation of classroom practice, student achievement, and principal ratings, as long as these indicators were obtained after the teacher had a full time teaching position.[3]

Excluded from this compilation were studies of student teachers, preschool teachers, and teachers of college students and adults. Also excluded were studies published prior to 1960 and studies conducted outside the United States, on the grounds that these contexts may be too different from contemporary United States to be applicable. For our tests of the four hypotheses about educational backgrounds, we also eliminate studies published before 1980, on the grounds that curricula change over time and earlier studies may no longer be applicable.

Literature was obtained by searching the Education Resource Information Center (ERIC), PsycInfo, Dissertation Abstracts International, and EconLit. Search terms included those commonly used to define either qualifications of teaching quality, such as assessment, certification, teacher education, teacher effectiveness and so forth. In addition, we searched the bibliographies of these articles as well as those of literature reviews and policy analyses in this area and searched recent issues of entire journals whose domain encompassed this area. Studies were screened to ensure that they included at least one qualification and at least one indicator of quality, and that their analysis explicitly linked the two. Links could be established with group comparisons (e.g. a group of traditionally certified teachers versus a group of alternatively certified teachers); correlations, various multivariate strategies, or through qualitative approaches. As of this writing (Summer 2006) the data base included about 480 studies. More details about the study and the data base can be found at http://www.msu.edu/~mkennedy/TQQT.

To test our four hypotheses about teachers' educational backgrounds, we searched this literature for two types of studies. First, to test hypotheses about the college courses, we sought studies that tried to assess the relationship between the courses teachers took in college and the teachers' current effectiveness. We sought tallies of courses taken in education, mathematics, or mathematics education. We also sought tallies of whether teachers had majored or minored in either of these subjects or held advanced degrees in them. The bright, well-educated person hypothesis cannot readily be tested by examining college curricula, but we did find two types of studies that are relevant to that hypothesis: those that measure of the status, or selectivity, of the institution which teachers had attended for their college education, and those that looked at the effectiveness of teachers who were recruited by Teach for America. Because the TFA recruits from prestigious colleges and universities (Raymond & Fletcher, 2002b), we consider these studies to be tests of the bright, well-educated person hypothesis.

Methodological issues

Research on the relative value of different kinds of teacher preparation has been impeded by some very difficult methodological problems. One problem is that many of the credentials of interest don't really vary much. For example, the value of a bachelor's degree would be difficult to assess in the United States because some 99 percent of teachers already have a bachelor's degree (National Center for Education Statistics, 2003). A test of the value of this degree would require an extensive search to find teachers who *lacked* the degree, to serve as a comparison group for those who have it. In many important respects, the teaching population in the United States is quite homogenous, a phenomenon that is hard to reconcile with the large differences in effectiveness that we see. For example, we know that about 75 percent of them are women and 84 percent are white (National Center for Education Statistics, 2003). We also know that 99 percent of teachers have a bachelor's degree and that 90 percent of teachers are certified.

On the other hand, bachelor's degrees and teaching certificates can have quite different meanings across educational institutions and across states. The United States has hundreds of institutions offering college degrees and they vary in size, quality, religious affiliation, research orientation and so forth. In addition, states have a plethora of certifications on their books, often exceeding a hundred. And they differ in the curricula they require for any given certificate (Ballou & Podgursky, 1999; Council of Chief State School Officers, 1988; Rotherman & Mead, 2003). We avoid ambiguous measures such as certification and degree level and focus instead on the number of course teachers take in particular subjects and on the selectivity of their alma mater. Of course these also can have different meanings in different places but we think their meaning is more clear than certification is. This strategy helps increase the variability in measured educational background, and at the same time improves the clarity of their meaning.

Another problem affecting all studies of qualifications is that teachers decide for themselves which qualifications they will obtain. Researchers do not randomly assign teachers to colleges or universities, nor to their college majors. Thus measurements such as the number of courses taken on topic X or Y reflect not only the knowledge teachers gained from these courses but also their initial interest in those topics. We can never separate teachers' initial interest in a subject from the knowledge they have acquired about it. Thus, if we find that courses in a certain topic seem to lead to better-quality teaching, we cannot infer that if states *require* teachers to take those courses, that the same results will obtain. Only after the courses are required can we see their effect on teachers who have no interest in them. This problem plagues the present examination as much as every other examination of teachers' qualifications. Prospective teachers take some college courses because they are required to, but they take others because they want to, and it is likely that these two reasons bear on the degree of benefit that teachers derive from their courses.

A similar self-selection phenomenon occurs when teachers seek employment, for their assignment to schools is also not at all random. In fact, there is now considerable evidence regarding the way teachers and schools become matched. We know, for instance, that most young people who choose teaching as a career are white women who come from rural and suburban communities. We also know that, upon graduation, they seek positions in schools that are similar to those they attended when they were students themselves (Boyd *et al.*, 2003). They engage in a process of *differential migration*, such that college graduates who grew up in the suburbs seek teaching positions in the suburbs, and those who grew up in small towns seek teaching positions in small towns. We also know that school systems give preferences to their own graduates (Strauss, 1999), so that both schools and teachers are seeking to match each others' cultural and demographic fundamentals. Finally, we know that urban schools, and other schools serving lower income and non-white populations, have greater difficulty filling their vacancies, have higher turnover in their teaching staffs, and are more likely to employ teachers with fewer qualifications (Boyd *et al.*, 2002; Lankford *et al.*, 2002; Wykoff, 2001). As a result they tend to have more novices than other schools and to have less-qualified teachers as well. These processes, taken together, suggest that the positions teachers eventually take are likely to be *affinity assignments*, such that their social backgrounds and their qualifications match the social backgrounds and qualifications of their students.

Now imagine how these processes influence research. We want to see if teachers with different types of qualifications have different influences on their students. But teachers with different qualifications have already been matched to students with different qualifications, through these natural processes of differential migration and affinity assignments. One result of these processes is that the schools whose students need the most educational help—that is, those who are the least qualified as students—are allocated the least qualified teachers, while those who are the most advantaged are allocated teachers with more qualifications. If we examine a simple correlation between, say, the prestige of the teachers' alma mater and their students' achievement test scores, we would likely see a relationship *even if the teachers have had no impact at all on their students*, simply because they have been matched to their students through these processes of differential migration and affinity assignments. The migration and assignment processes make it difficult for researchers to tell whether teachers created their students' achievement levels or whether, instead, students with different achievement levels have attracted different kinds of teachers.

We address this problem of non-random assignment by limiting our review to studies that use relatively sophisticated statistical methods. We seek studies in which researchers try to separate out these various influences statistically, by measuring all the things they expect to influence teachers' effectiveness, and include them in a statistical model. These more sophisticated models include not only teachers' qualifications, but also measures of students' socio-economic status, race or ethnicity, perhaps measures of school size, finances, or demographic makeup, and perhaps other characteristics of the teachers themselves, such as their beliefs or values. In these studies, the goal is to find a relationship between teachers' qualifications and the quality of their teaching practice *after measuring and accounting for other relevant influences*. They cannot guarantee that they are documenting causal influences, of course, but they are more able to measure and take into account competing explanations for their data. We also strengthen our inference by examining multiple studies, each with its own statistical model.

Finally all studies of teachers' qualifications are complicated by numerous influences that intervene between teachers' prior college experiences and their current teaching practices. Any given sample of teachers will include some relatively new teachers, some with a few years of experience and some with many years of experience. Many things may have influenced their teaching since they obtained their original college degrees and certifications. They may have worked in different schools, taken different kinds of professional development courses, confronted parents with different expectations for their children. Any of these experiences may have influenced their practices and their effectiveness. Yet our research is ignorant of these influences and seeks evidence of only one influence, their college education, and that may have occurred years ago. Indeed, time itself is an intervening influence, for teachers who obtained their certificates 20 years ago may have experienced very different educational programs than teachers who obtained their certificates five years ago. And studies that were published 20 years ago may have included teachers whose preparation was quite different from that of teachers prepared today (Metzger *et al.*, 2004).

We address these problems in part by limiting ourselves to stronger research studies, studies that are more likely to have addressed these issues. We include only those studies that meet these important criteria.

1 *The studies must use relatively sophisticated models*, models that allow the researcher to take account of numerous other possible influences. These studies typically rely on either multiple regression or hierarchical linear models, both of which allow more opportunity than do simple correlations or group comparisons to measure additional influences and take them into account.

2 *The studies must include a pretest as one of their factors.* Measures of student

achievement are like snapshots taken at a specific time. They measure student knowledge at a particular time, but that knowledge reflects the sum of everything students have learned throughout their entire lives, from parents, other teachers, other adults and from each other. Moreover, they can present a relationship that reflects the effect of affinity assignments more than the effects of teachers' influence on student learning. We therefore prefer studies that incorporate a pretest score as one of the factors in their model, or as part of a gain score. The inclusion of some measure of prior achievement enables the researcher to separate the knowledge students gained prior to studying under the teacher who is the focus of the study.

3 *The studies must focus on individual students or teachers rather than institutional collections of teachers.* Some researchers rely on school averages or district averages of teachers and students, rather than using data from individual teachers. Aggregated data are often used when researchers borrow data bases that belong to school districts or states. Such data bases may not include individual-level information, or may restrict access to it to protect teachers' privacy. These aggregated data conceal all of the variations among teachers within each school or district and focus on variations among schools that may be due to many things other than instructional influences, things researchers have no knowledge of (for more on this issue, see Murnane, 1981; Hanushek *et al.*, 1996). As a result, they may lead to erroneous estimates of the relationship between teachers' qualifications and the quality of teaching practices. We therefore limit our attention to studies that focus on individual teachers and students.

One final note is needed about the findings we present here. A synthesis of this sort requires us not only to define our criteria for including studies, but also to define criteria for selecting specific findings from each study. Researchers frequently present multiple statistical models, each with unique features. They sometimes provide findings for multiple subgroups (e.g. high-achieving and low-achieving students) or for multiple achievement sub-tests. To avoid over-representation of any one study, we selected a single model from each grade or sample examined. Our decision rules were to first seek models that met our criteria of including a pretest and focusing in individual teachers rather than aggregations. If an author presented one model using a gain score and another using the pretest as a covariate, we chose the covariate model. We selected fixed effects over random effects. We selected total samples rather than subgroups and total test scores rather than sub-test scores. We avoided models that included interaction terms. If different models from the same sample are presented in different publications, we selected the most recent version. Otherwise we selected the model that included the largest number of curriculum measures or, absent differences in this, the one that was most complete with respect to other variables. We preferred one-year gains to two-year or partial-year gains.

Final sample

The studies we examine here represent what we consider to be the best evidence of the relationship between teachers' qualifications and their students' mathematics achievement. By limiting our review to these studies we gain more confidence in our findings. Our criteria have been recognized by numerous other researchers as indicators of better research designs (see, e.g. Goldhaber & Anthony, 2003; Hanushek, 1971, 1996; Murnane, 1981). In this respect, we follow Slavin's (1984, 1986) suggestion that reviewers should focus on best evidence, and we agree with him that what constitutes best evidence depends on the research questions and contexts. Table 61.1 lists the studies that meet our criteria for best evidence.

Table 61.1 Studies included in this synthesis

| Citation | Hypo-thesis | Educational background of interest | | Sample | | No. of statistical controls | No. of estimates of influence |
		Indicator	Content area	Grade level	No. of students		
Aaronson, Barrow, & Sander (2003)	CK* PK	Major in:	Math Education	9	52991	27 27	1 1
	BWE	Level of:	Institutional Status	9	52991	22	6
*Betts, Zao, & Rice (2003)	CK	BA in:	Math	Elem Middle High	36927 30226 26697	83 83 83	1 1 1
		Minor in:	Math	Elem Middle High	36927 30226 26697	83 83 83	1 1 1
Brewer & Goldhaber (1996); Goldhaber & Brewer (1996a, 1997a, 1997, 1999, 2000)	CK PK CK PK	Major in: MA in:	Math Education Math Education	10, 12 12 10, 12 12	5149, 3786 3786 5149, 3786 3786	41, 37 37 41, 37 36	1, 1 1 1, 1 2
*Chiang (1996); Rowan, Chiang, & Miller (1997)	CK	Double degree in: Any degree in:	Math Math	12 10	4751 5341	15 23	1 1
Clotfetler, Ladd, & Vigdor (2004a, 2004b, 2006)	BWE	Levels of:	Institutional Status	5	60656	46	3
Darling-Hammond, Holtzman, Gatlin, & Hellig (2005a, 2005b)	BWE	Program entry:	TFA	4–5	Range from 11437 to 105511	15	4
Decker, Mayer, & Glazerman (2004)	BWE	Program entry:	TFA	1–5	1715	60	1
Eberts & Stone (1984)	PCK	N of courses in:	Math Ed	4	Over 14,000	34	1
Fagnano (1988)	CK PCK PK	N of courses in:	Math Math Ed Education	8	211	~100 ~100 ~100	1 1 1
Guarino, Hamilton, Lockwood, & Rathbun (2006)	PCK	N of courses in:	Math Ed	K	16308	29	6
Harris & Sass (2006)	PCK	N of courses in:	Math Ed	4–5 6–8 9–10	74103 116673 83516	12 12 11	1 1 1
	CK		Math	4–5 6–8 9–10	74103 116673 83516	12 12 11	1 1 1
	CK		Subject Content	4–5 6–8 9–10	74103 116673 83516	12 12 11	1 1 1
	PK		General Ed Theory	4–5 6–8 9–10	74103 116673 83516	12 12 11	1 1 1

(Continued overleaf)

Table 61.1 Continued.

Citation	Hypo-thesis	Educational background of interest		Sample		No. of statistical controls	No. of estimates of influence
		Indicator	Content area	Grade level	No. of students		
	PCK		Pedagogical Content	4–5	74103	12	1
				6–8	116673	12	1
				9–10	83516	11	1
	PK	Major in:	Education	4–5	74103	1	1
				6–8	116673	3	1
				9–10	83516	3	1
	PCK		Math Ed	6–8	116673	3	1
				9–10	83516	3	1
	CK		Math	6–8	116673	3	1
				9–10	83516	3	1
Hill, Rowan, & Ball (2005)	CK+ PCK	N of courses in:	Math and/or Math Ed	1, 3	1190, 1773	17, 17	1, 1
Monk (1994); Monk & King (1994)	CK PCK	N of courses in:	Math Math Ed	10, 11	1492, 983	10, 10 13, 14	4, 5 1, 1
	CK	More than 5 courses in:	Math	11	983	11	1
	CK PCK	N of graduate courses in:	Math; Math Ed	10, 11	1492, 983	13, 14 13, 14	1, 1 1, 1
	CK	Major in:	Math	10, 11	1492, 983	13, 14	2, 2
Raymond & Fletcher (2002a, 2002b); Raymond *et al.* (2001)	BWE	Program entry:	TFA vs. All	4–5	81814	12	1
				6–8	96276	12	1
			TFA vs. New	4–5	11321	11	1
				6–8	19521	11	1
Rowan, Correnti, & Miller (2002)	CK	BA/MA in:	Math	1–6	NA	NA	2
Rowley (2004)	PK	N of courses in:	Elementary Ed	K	12873	31	1
	PK		Early Ed			31	1
	PK		Child Dev			31	1
	PCK		Math Teaching			31	1
Taddese (1997)	CK	Major in:	Math	12	20840	22	1

* Betts *et al.* estimates for minors are not included in this analysis.
Chiang *et al.* double degree is not included in Figure 4 because it confounds Bachelors degree and Masters degree.
Rowan *et al.* not included in Figure 4 because we could not convert the data into a gain score metric.
CK = Content Knowldge; PCK = Pedagogical Content Knowledge; PK = Pedagogical Knowledge; BWE = Bright Well-Educated.

DATA ANALYSIS

We have devised a novel yardstick for defining influences on student test scores. We want to see whether teachers who took more courses have students with higher achievement gains than other students. But the apparent influence of a college course will look different when student achievement is measured on a 50-point scale than when it is measured with a 10-point scale. The conventional solution to this problem is to divide all effects by the group's standard deviation, thus creating a scale that puts all effects on a common metric. But this approach can only work when all researchers derive their standard deviations in the same way (see Hedges, 1986 for more on this). If one researcher provides a pooled within-school estimate of variation while another provides an estimate that includes between-school variation, then the standard deviations will not convert effect sizes to a comparable metric. Moreover, even if the standard deviations were comparable, we face another problem when studies rely on national data bases and their associated tests, for these tests are not aligned with local curricula. They will likely measure some content that was not taught and fail to measure some content that was taught. Because they miss some areas the teacher has influenced, and measure some areas teachers have not tried to influence, we expect these tests to underestimate teachers' actual instructional influence on students. This is not due to inadequacies in the teacher but to a lack of alignment between the teachers' curriculum and the test content. Hence effects based on national tests may not be comparable to effects that are based on state or local tests which are designed to reflect the local curriculum. In fact, this underestimation is apparent in the average annual gains shown in national data bases, which are often just one or two points for the entire school year.

Our solution to this "yardstick" problems is to define all outcomes relative to the average amount that students gain during a given school year. That is, instead of standardizing effects by dividing them with the standard deviation, we standardize by dividing them with the average annual gain for the population.[4] For instance, if majoring in mathematics adds 1 point to students' achievement scores, and if students typically gain 3 points during the year, then we would say that the effect of the major was equivalent to 1/3, or 33 percent, of students' annual gain. Our estimates of effects, then, are based on the following equation:

$$\frac{b_i}{\bar{Y}_{post} - \bar{Y}_{pre}}$$

where b_i is the unstandardized regression slope for a particular qualification taken from a particular sample; and $\bar{Y}_{post} - \bar{Y}_{pre}$ is the gain in mathematics achievement for the population from which the sample was taken.

This strategy offers certain advantages over other standardizing strategies. We do not have to eliminate studies because they calculate their standard deviations in different ways, for instance. And we do not have to worry about how closely student tests are aligned to local curricula because these are equalized by the use of average gains as our yardstick.

FINDINGS

Findings are presented in two sections. In the first, we summarize research that examines the influence of teachers' curricula on their students' mathematics achievement. These studies allow us to evaluate hypotheses about the relative importance of pedagogical knowledge, content knowledge, and pedagogical content knowledge. In the second section, we examine two sets of literature that are relevant to the bright, well-educated person hypothesis. These include multiple regressions that measure the status or selectivity of the institutions that teachers attended, and a handful of studies that contrast TFA teachers with other teachers.

Evidence for the influence of college courses

When people suggest that teachers need more knowledge of, say classroom management, they really mean more knowledge of this *relative to other areas of knowledge*. And when people argue that teachers do not need knowledge in an area, they rarely mean that this knowledge is absolutely lacking in value, but rather that it is not as valuable as some other knowledge would be. Defined in this way, the empirical question then becomes one of identifying the value added by different parts of the teachers' total college education, where one part might be courses in education, another might be courses in subject matter (in our case, mathematics), and a third might be courses in math education, or how to teach mathematics.

Because estimates of effects can depend statistical models—that is, on the combination of other variables the researcher measure and control in their model—it is not possible to directly compare one study's estimate of effects with another's. We solve this problem in two ways. First, we examine studies that test more than one hypothesis within a single statistical model. These studies allow a direct comparison of different course content under the same methodological conditions. Our second strategy arrays findings from studies conducted under more varying statistical conditions. We have already made these studies somewhat more comparable by requiring that they all fall within our best-evidence boundaries. We also increase comparability by examining all effects relative to student achievement gains on that particular test.

Within-study comparisons

Here we examine two studies that meet our best-evidence standards and also test multiple hypotheses within a single study. The first (Monk, 1994) examines secondary mathematics teachers and the second (Harris and Sass, 2006) examines all grade levels of teachers.

Monk used multiple regression, a statistical technique that allows researchers to estimate the contributions of several different potential influences within a single equation. Monk's equations included student background variables as well as several measures of teachers' educational backgrounds. He estimated the influence of individual courses teachers took as well as the influence of majoring in mathematics. Since Monk studied both sophomores and juniors, we review two equations, one for each group. Figure 61.1 displays his findings.

Each hatch-mark in Figure 61.1 represents the amount that students' test scores increased (or decreased) with each additional course their teachers took in math or math education, assuming that everything else that was measures is held constant. Recall that the "amount" is measured relative to the average gain for all students in the population, so it reads as a percentage of that gain. So, for example, assuming no change in students' backgrounds and assuming no other measured differences among teachers, the top line indicates that, among teachers of sophomores, each additional course taken in math education—that is, in methods of teaching mathematics—is associated with an increase in student achievement equivalent to about 16 percent of sophomores' average achievement gains.

The general pattern, for both sophomores and juniors, is to see the largest benefits in mathematics education courses, somewhat smaller benefits in mathematics courses, and a negative effect for majoring in mathematics. In this sample of mathematics teachers, the average teacher took about eight courses in mathematics but only two in mathematics education.

Monk suspected that there might be a pattern of diminishing returns as teachers took

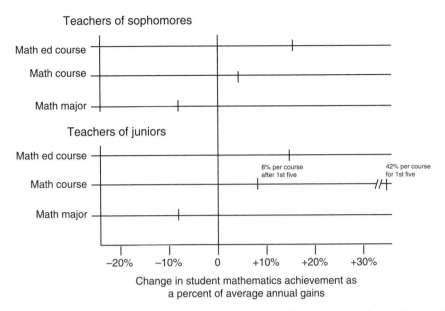

Figure 61.1 Estimates of the relationship between teachers' college coursework and their students' achievement gains in mathematics (from Monk, 1994).

more and more courses in mathematics, and tested this idea by distinguishing early course-taking from more advanced course-taking. He found that the benefits of courses in mathematics tapered off after about five courses. In Figure 61.1, the large positive effect of teachers' college math courses for juniors represents added benefit for each of the first five courses teachers took, while the smaller number (8 percent) represents the additional benefit for each course taken beyond the first five.

The most surprising finding here is that, at both grade levels, when teachers majored in mathematics, their students actually gained *less* than students whose teachers did not major in mathematics—about 8 percent less for each group of students. This apparent negative result is a surprise since most of the debate about teachers' curriculum focuses on the value of courses in education, not on courses in content knowledge. Even Monk's diminishing returns hypothesis cannot explain this outcome.

Here we face one of the difficulties of squaring research findings with our common sense. It is hard to imagine that additional study in any topic could actually make someone a less effective teacher. The implication would be that these courses are providing harmful knowledge. We seek an alternative explanation for this pattern. Many explanations are possible, including possible flaws in the statistical model, but the one that seems most probable to us is that teachers who chose to take more courses in mathematics were already different from other college students even before they took the courses, and the difference is one that leads to less effective teaching. Perhaps college students who choose to major in mathematics have different personalities, values or beliefs that render them less effective as teachers, and it is these initial differences that explain for the apparent negative effects of additional courses, not the courses themselves. This pattern of findings reminds us of the two important interpretive difficulties in this type of research: the effects we see in these studies must be interpreted in the context of the entire statistical model, and that these measures of course-taking reflect *both* the knowledge gained from the courses *and* the teachers' original interests and dispositions that motivated her to take these courses in the first place.

Now let's look at the Harris and Sass (2006) study. This study is distinctive in part because it offers an unusually large collection of estimates of effects and because it is an unusually high-quality study. These authors use hierarchical linear modeling, an analytic strategy that better accommodates the nested organization of teachers and students in schools, and they also used fixed effects, a strategy that better accommodates hidden differences (such as subtle personality differences or school climate differences) among teachers and schools that might interfere with interpretations of findings. The sample for this study is limited to a single state (Florida), however, it provides great detail regarding teachers' college coursework and the data are available for elementary, middle and secondary teachers.

Figure 61.2 shows the array of effects that Harris and Sass reported. It can be read in the same way as Figure 61.1, except that these authors examined course credits rather than courses per se. Each hatch mark represents the effect of an additional credit of study in a particular knowledge domain, measured as a percentage of students' one-year achievement gains, again assuming all other variables in the model are held constant. The figure shows a large number of estimates because these authors were able to include multiple grade levels and to distinguish specific course content—for instance, they could separate out courses in one aspect of education versus another. Like Figure 61.1, this one suggests a great variety in size and direction of effects. As we argued when reviewing the Monk study, we are not inclined to hypothesize that knowledge itself can be harmful, and therefore suspect that the apparent negative effects shown in this chart reflect either a statistical anomaly or a pre-existing difference among teachers who chose to take different patterns of courses.

Looking first at elementary teachers, Figure 61.2 suggests that credits in education and in math education are somewhat more beneficial than credits in mathematics per se (Again we assume that negative effects do not really mean that the additional knowledge has harmful effects). However, when we examine the patterns for middle and secondary teachers, the effects are far more various and difficult to interpret. All three domains of

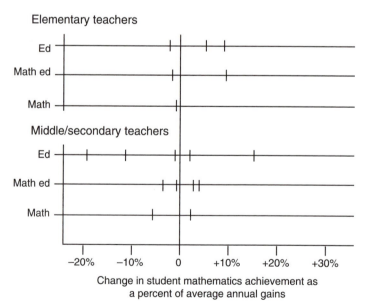

Figure 61.2 Estimates of the relationship between course credits teachers earned in college and their students' achievement gains in mathematics (from Harris and Sass, 2006).

knowledge show both positive and negative effects. While the math education courses tend to balance between positive and negative effects, education courses strongly lean toward negative and mathematics courses also lean slightly toward negative.

Harris and Sass did not test for the possibility of diminishing returns for courses taken in different content areas. However we may still imagine that people with different prior inclinations tended to take different patterns of courses and these prior differences could account for the patterns we see here. For instance, since the estimates within education refer to specific content (class management vs. instructional strategies, etc.) it is possible that teachers who chose these courses had prior personalities or beliefs that render them relatively more or less successful as teachers, independent of the effect of the credits per se.

All best-evidence studies

Our second approach to reviewing studies of teachers' educational backgrounds gathers together all the research findings that examine courses into a single graph. Figure 61.3 summarizes all the best evidence regarding the number of courses teachers took (it does not include the Harris and Sass data since that examined course credits rather than courses per se), and Figure 61.4 summarizes all the best evidence regarding intensive study in a particular area. In these figures, each hatch mark represents one estimate from one study. Together, they represent many different populations and statistical models.

The most important reason for examining all of the studies in a single graph is to search for broad patterns of effects that may rise above the variations in statistical models and other study details. Such a pattern might give us an idea of the true relationship between teachers' educational backgrounds and their students' achievement, one that is not an artifact of the individual studies.

Figure 61.3 still reveals quite a variety of outcomes, though they do lean toward positive at all grade levels and subjects. However, with the exception of Monk's findings,

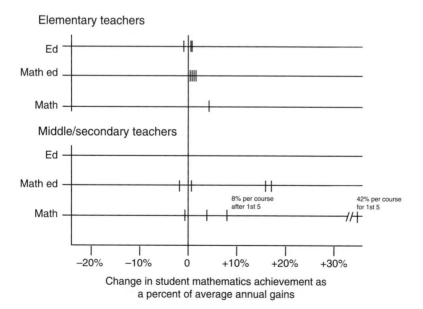

Figure 61.3 Estimates of the relationship between courses teachers took in college and their students' achievement gains in mathematics, all studies, 1980–2006.

most effects are relatively small. Since these hatch marks represent the effect of individual courses, we might expect small effects which could accumulate as teachers took more courses. As we saw in the Harris and Sass study, there does seem to be more dispersion in effects of courses for secondary teachers than for elementary.

Figure 61.4 summarizes all estimates of the effect of obtaining a full major in either subject, or of obtaining an advanced degree in either subject. Since these hatch-marks represent the effects of extensive study in one of these domains, we might expect them to be substantially larger than those of individual courses summarized in Figure 61.3. Indeed, most of these effects are larger than those in Figure 61.3, but not by much. Moreover, many are negative as well as large.

No researcher other than Monk has tested for the possibility of diminishing returns for additional courses in a given subject but such a relationship might help us understand this pattern of outcomes. For example, among elementary teachers, majoring in either education or mathematics is apparently detrimental to student achievement, a finding that contradicts the more generally positive pattern shown in Figure 61.3 of effects of individual courses. Moreover, we found another negative effect of majoring in mathematics (from Rowan *et al.*, 2002) which we were unable to convert to our metric and so are not displaying here. But the contradiction between the apparent benefits of individual courses and the apparent detriment of extensive study is at least partially reconciled if we assume that there are diminishing returns as teachers accumulate more and more courses in any one domain. Suppose, for instance, that additional courses benefit teachers up to a specific point, but add little or no benefit after that point. Since researchers rarely devise models to accommodate curvilinear relationships, we might expect to see the effects of a college

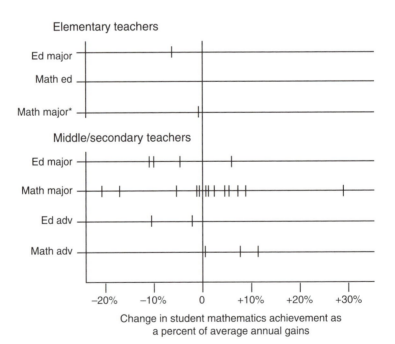

Figure 61.4 Estimates of the relationship between teachers' college majors and fields of advanced study and their students' achievement gains in mathematics, all studies, 1980–2006.

* One additional study (Rowan *et al.*, 2002) reported an achievement loss for elementary students whose teachers were majoring in mathematics. It is not shown here because we were unable to convert the data to this metric.

major flipping from positive to negative as different researchers use different statistical models. Or we might assume that the people who choose to major in either subject are somehow different from those who take a few courses in each area but major in neither.

Only at the level of advanced degrees do we begin to see a clear difference across domains of knowledge. Though there are fewer estimates of the effect of advanced degrees, the pattern in education clearly differs from that in mathematics. Both estimates of the effect of an advanced degree in education are negative and all three estimates of the effect of an advanced degree in mathematics are positive. We need to add one caveat to this observation: all of these estimates of the effect of advanced degrees come from a single data base, the National Educational Longitudinal Study of 1988. It is possible that these results are an anomaly unique to this data base. Ludwig and Bassie (1999) are convinced that the pretest used in this data base is not adequately controlling for non-random assignment of students to their teachers. However, if the finding is real and generalizable, it raises an important question about the value of obtaining a masters degree in education. We offer two speculations here. First, since most school districts provide salary benefits to teachers who earn advanced degrees, practicing teachers have an incentive to seek them out, and education programs may try to oblige them by offering degrees that are not very rigorous or beneficial to their teaching practice. Hence the degrees themselves may be relatively weak. Second, it is possible that the type of person who chooses to obtain an advanced degree in education differs from other teachers in being less effective to begin with and that the degree does nothing to improve their effectiveness.

Summary

In this section, we have examined evidence regarding three hypotheses about the kind of knowledge teachers need. We are interested in the relative merits of pedagogical knowledge, pedagogical content knowledge, and content knowledge. We used coursework in education to test the hypothesis that pedagogical knowledge makes a difference, coursework in mathematics education to test the hypothesis that pedagogical content knowledge makes a difference, and coursework in mathematics to test the hypothesis that content knowledge makes a difference.

Despite variability among study findings, we see some broad patterns. First, courses in all three domains of knowledge appear capable of improving elementary teachers' effectiveness. For elementary teachers, the modal benefit of additional courses in education and in mathematics education appears to be around 0–3 percent of students' annual achievement gains, with courses in mathematics and in mathematics education adding somewhat more than that. Second, estimates are far more variable among middle and secondary teachers than among elementary teachers, whether we are looking at individual courses or intensive study in a domain. This may be because there are more anomalies in secondary-level data bases, perhaps more confounding variables in secondary studies due to local practices of assigning students and teachers. Still we can make out some trends. In particular, the differences between Figures 61.3 and 61.4, suggest that courses in all three domains have diminishing returns, such that the effects of majors, in either education or mathematics, are highly variable but on average very close to zero. Finally, we see a clear difference between mathematics and education in the benefits of advanced degrees, and suspect this difference may be due to both the differences among teachers who choose to seek out these degrees as well as differences in the benefits of the degrees themselves.

Throughout this text we have considered a variety of hypotheses to account for the patterns we see. The hypothesis of interest, of course, is that knowledge in these domains benefits teaching. But the presence of negative effects raises the question of whether knowledge can be detrimental to teaching. We are inclined to believe that these apparent negative effects are not due to the courses themselves, but rather to either pre-existing differences among people who chose these different curricular paths, or to statistical anomalies, perhaps resulting from the presence of curvilinear relationships or multicollinearity on the statistical models employed.

Evidence for the bright, well-educated person hypothesis

We rely on two very different types of studies to test the bright well-educated person (BWE) hypothesis. One group of studies examines the influence of the status, or selectivity, of teachers' alma maters on their current students' achievement. The other examines the effectiveness of teachers who were recruited into the profession via the Teach for America (TFA) program, a program that explicitly recruits people presumed to be bright and well educated, but who have not necessarily studied teaching.

Institutional status

Two studies examined indicators of institutional status, or selectivity, in their attempts to account for teacher effectiveness. They differ in how they define and measure institutional status, however, so each must be examined separately. Figure 61.5 and 61.6 show the pattern of changes in students' mathematics achievement that are associated with the status of their teachers' alma maters.

The first study (Clotfelter *et al.*, 2004a, 2004b) is the only study in our data base to explicitly recognize that teachers and students may already be matched by their social class and qualifications even before any data are collected. These authors checked individual schools to see how students were assigned to teachers. They found that many schools had assignment policies that placed less advantaged students with different teachers than more advantaged students. In Figure 61.5, we see the difference in the apparent benefit of the status of teachers' alma maters, as classified by Barrons' College

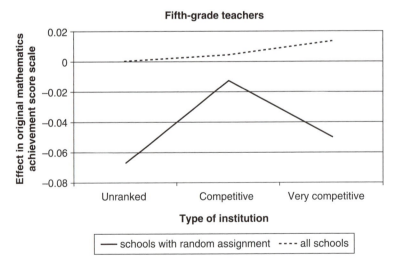

Figure 61.5 Relationship between the prestige of teachers' alma maters and their students' gains in mathematics achievement (from Clotfelter *et al.*, 2004a, 2004b, 2006). All estimates are compared to teachers from "less competitive universities."

Ranks, when examined with the full sample and again when examined only in those schools that relied on random assignment practices. The figure suggests that higher alma mater status is indeed associated with higher student achievement in the full sample, where students and teachers are matched, but that the opposite pattern appears when the study is restricted to schools that randomly assign students to teachers. In schools where students are not matched to their teachers, teachers from the most prestigious alma maters appear to be less able to foster learning in their fifth grade students.[5]

Figure 61.6 summarizes findings from the second study (Aaronson *et al.*, 2003), which focuses on ninth grade mathematics teachers and defines institutional status with a scale based on US News and World Reports classifications. We might expect affinity assignments to be even more prevalent in secondary schools than in elementary schools, since secondary schools tend to engage in more tracking, but Aaronson and colleagues tested for this possibility by comparing their observed classroom assignments with a variety of simulated assignment possibilities. Based on these analyses, the authors argue that their data did not suggest systematic classroom sorting. With respect to outcomes, the pattern suggests that students' mathematics achievement tests scores were usually higher when their teachers had attended higher-status institutions. But the pattern is also uneven and suggests that only the level 5 institutions stand clearly apart from the others. This may be due to unusually anamolous samples in some of the status categories. Since the first study was conducted in elementary schools and this one in secondary schools, it is possible that institutional status has a greater impact in secondary school than in elementary school.

Teach for America recruits

The second type of study that is relevant to the BWE hypothesis examines teachers who were recruited into the profession by Teach for America (TFA). On its website, TFA defines its recruitment strategy as follows:

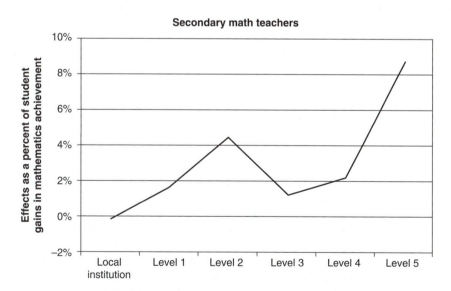

Figure 61.6 Relationship between the prestige of teachers' alma maters and their students' gains in mathematics achievement (from Aaronson *et al.*, 2003). All estimates are compared to teachers graduating from universities ranked by *US News and World Reports* as "other."

> Each year, Teach For America launches an aggressive effort to recruit the most out-standing graduating college seniors and recent college graduates—people who will be the future leaders in fields such as business, medicine, politics, law, journalism, education, and social policy. We seek a diverse group—socio-economically, racially, ethnically, politically, and in every other respect. We seek leaders who can describe significant past achievements and who operate with an exceptional level of personal responsibility for outcomes. Because our corps members face such tremendous challenges, we seek applicants who have demonstrated determination and persist-ence when confronted with obstacles in the past. Lastly, we seek people with the specific skills—from critical thinking to organizational ability—that we have seen characterize our most successful teachers.
> (retrieved June 27, 2005 from http://www.teachforamerica.org/looking.html)

TFA does not assume its recruits will take up teaching for their entire careers, but does ask for a two-year commitment and most recruits apparently honor that commitment.

Once admitted into the program, TFA enrolls candidates in a 5-week summer institute that requires them to teach summer school students while concurrently taking courses in such topics as classroom management, learning theory, student diversity and so forth. To test the benefits of this program, researchers usually contrast TFA recruits with other teachers.

There is considerable muddle about what one is learning from such a comparison. Some researchers think that this comparison informs them about the value of *peda-gogical knowledge*, assuming that the comparison group of traditionally-certified teachers has taken courses in pedagogy that TFA recruits have not taken. But TFA teachers are not completely lacking in pedagogical knowledge because TFA does provide some of this content to its teachers. In addition, TFA candidates must also meet state requirements for certification and many states require that teachers who enter the field without a traditional certificate must work toward obtaining one during their first few years of practice. In these cases, differences in pedagogical knowledge between TFA recruits may be small at the outset and may disappear completely as TFA recruits take the courses required for traditional certificate.

There is another reason why these comparisons don't inform us about pedagogical knowledge: in the studies we review here, most teachers in the "other" category *also lack a full certificate*. The non-TFA teachers in these studies represent an eclectic mix of emergency-certified, alternatively-certified and traditionally-certified teachers. For all these reasons, then, contrasts of TFA teachers with other teachers are not very informa-tive about the value of pedagogical knowledge, traditional certification, or any other aspect of teachers' college course work. We cannot be sure how much pedagogical knowl-edge either group actually has.

But the contrast does inform us about the value of different *recruitment strategies*, since TFA focuses its recruitment on more selective institutions. So an examination of TFA graduates offers us a good opportunity to test the bright, well-educated person hypothesis in situations where pedagogical knowledge may not be substantially different.

We found three studies that meet our evidence standards and that examine the influ-ence of TFA recruits on student math achievement scores.[6] In each of these studies, the number of TFA teachers available for study was relatively small. The first two studies were both conducted in Houston, Texas, using data that belonged to the school district. These two studies both used multiple cohorts of teachers and students, and were not able to control students' classroom assignments. They both used multiple regression to try to statistically adjust for other differences among students.

The first Houston study was conducted by Raymond and Fletcher (Raymond & Fletcher, 2002a, 2002b; Raymond *et al.*, 2001). These authors used 1996–2000 data from upper elementary and middle school grade levels. During this period, Houston hired between 350 and 420 new teachers each year, but only about 20–25 per year, or less than 10 percent, were TFA teachers. The researchers note that TFA teachers were placed in schools with higher percentages of Latinos and with higher percentages of students receiving free or reduced-price lunches. Test scores were also lower in the schools where TFA teachers taught.

The second Houston study (Darling-Hammond *et al.*, 2005a) was explicitly designed to replicate and extend the first by paying more attention to the specific credentials of the comparison group. These authors found over 100 different certification categories in Houston's data base and, after studying the state's code, reduced these to seven categories: standard, alternative, emergency/temporary, certified out of field, certified no test, uncertified, and unknown. Because we are interested in the TFA as a means of testing a *recruitment* strategy, we do not report findings from this study that address the *certification* value of the TFA program.[7]

The third study of TFA recruits was an experiment in which students within each grade level and school were randomly assigned to either a TFA teacher or another teacher (Decker *et al.*, 2004). Because experiments entail random assignments of students to programs (in this case, to teachers with different kinds of credentials) they remove the confounding caused by affinity assignments that tends to occur in natural settings and they increase the chances of seeing an unbiased estimate of the effect of the program of interest.

Because the Decker *et al.* study is an experiment, it is stronger than the other two, but there are certain problems it shares with the other studies. In all three studies, the number of TFA teachers is rather small, so that researchers had to combine grade levels to obtain reasonable group sizes. And in all three studies, the non-TFA teachers represented an eclectic mix of credentials. For example, in their comparison group of novice teachers, Decker *et al.* found that 31 percent had a full traditional certificate, 28 percent had a temporary certificate, and another 25 percent had emergency certificates. Hence the comparison is not a good test of alternative credentials. However, the contrast remains a reasonable test of the bright, well-educated person hypothesis, since the main distinction between these two groups lies in TFAs recruitment strategies. Less than 4 percent of the novices in the Decker *et al.*'s "all other" group graduated from a competitive college or university, whereas 70 percent of TFA teachers graduated from such schools.

Figure 61.7 shows the effects of TFA recruits relative to other teachers in each of these three studies. Each hatch mark represents a particular estimate of the influence of TFA

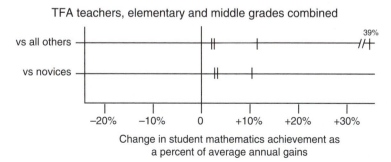

Figure 61.7 Effects on students' achievement gains in mathematics when teachers are recruited via Teach for America Program, all studies.

recruits on their pupils' mathematics achievement. They are all positive, ranging from 3 percent of annual growth to 21 percent. These findings are encouraging for the bright, well-educated person hypothesis, in part because we are more confident that the normal processes of differential migration and affinity matching have been disrupted in one case by an experiment and in the other two by the TFA recruitment and placement strategy. So these findings are more persuasive than those about institutional status that were displayed in Figures 61.5 and 61.6. However, the most persuasive findings, those from Decker *et al.*, also yielded the smallest effect.

Summary

Evidence regarding the bright, well-educated person hypothesis comes both from studies of the institutional status of teachers' alma maters and from studies of TFA, which can be considered as more of a recruitment strategy than a different approach to certification. Studies in the first group are more susceptible to biases associated with affinity assignments, but those in the second group correct for these biases by systematically drawing teachers from elite institutions and placing them in schools with less-qualified students. The second group, however, is limited to very small samples of bright, well-educated teachers which are then compared with large, amorphous samples of teachers with highly variable backgrounds. If we can assume that more selective institutions tend to produce brighter, more well-educated people, then both sets of studies provide some support for the hypothesis that bright, well-educated people do help students learn more.

For those who argue for the BWE hypothesis as an alternative to pedagogical knowledge, this evidence is reassuring but not entirely satisfying. The strongest study in our set, the experiment, suggests that bright well-educated people add about 3 or 4 percent to students' average annual achievement gains, an amount roughly equal to the benefit of a single course in education or in mathematics education. The comparability of findings across hypotheses suggest that casting the question as one of either/or will not lead to an optimal approach to teacher education.

DISCUSSION

Since teachers are in the business of educating students, we want to believe that their own education is relevant to their effectiveness. Many researchers have tried to test the effects of teachers' educational backgrounds on their students' achievement and they have had to solve a wide range of methodological problems to do so. In this synthesis we have focused only on relatively high-quality studies and we have rendered their findings comparable by using average population gains in achievement as a common yardstick. Based on these studies, we suggest that individual courses do indeed add to elementary teachers' effectiveness, and that this is true for all three domains of knowledge—mathematics, education, and mathematics education. Secondary students also benefit when their teachers have taken additional courses in mathematics and in mathematics education. However, there is reason to believe that additional courses eventually have diminishing returns, so that the early courses teachers take would have a relatively larger impact, but more advanced courses would add little or no further benefit. This may explain the wide variability in apparent benefits of majoring in either mathematics or education. Majoring in either subject appears to have negative effects on elementary teachers' effectiveness and also on secondary teachers' effectiveness, though the secondary estimates are far more variable.

There is also evidence that teachers with different personal qualities may have differential effectiveness. For example, students learn more from teachers who graduate from more selective institutions. We base this conclusion mainly on TFA studies, since the two regression studies of institutional status yielded inconsistent findings. The effects of TFA's selective recruitment are somewhat larger than those of individual courses teachers take across all colleges, but they do appear to be consistently positive.

Finally, there appears to be a negative effect associated with obtaining an advanced degree in education, and a positive effect associated with obtaining an advanced degree in mathematics. We suspect that this pattern may also reflect differences in the personal qualities of teachers who seek out these degrees, which are not required for an initial teaching certificate, but for which there are often financial incentives to pursue.

Particularly surprising here is the difference between the observed patterns of effects and the conventional wisdom about teacher knowledge. Among the four hypotheses that motivated this analysis, the most contentious is pedagogical knowledge. Teacher educators believe they have meritorious and important content that teachers need to know, but skeptics fear that these courses are rarely beneficial and that teachers would be better educated if the space currently reserved for education courses were released. The least contentious hypothesis is that content knowledge is essential: virtually all advocates support the importance of content knowledge. Yet the differences we see in these data do not suggest such a differential conclusion. Data in Figure 61.1 suggests that mathematics education is more beneficial than mathematics per se, and data in Figure 61.2 suggests virtual comparability across the content domains, with mixed results in all three domains and at both elementary and secondary level. Data in Figure 61.3 shows a modest benefits to courses in all content domains, while data in Figure 61.4 shows marked variability in estimates of the benefits of majoring in either education or in mathematics. It is not until we get to the level of advanced degree that we see a clear difference between education and mathematics, and these differences are based on a single data base.

Taken as a whole, our evidence does not suggest that education courses are harmful except at the graduate level. Indeed our evidence suggests that, in moderation, education courses are beneficial. At the same time, our evidence also does not suggest that mathematics courses are entirely beneficial. Instead, it suggests that that there may also be a limit to the number of courses in mathematics that will benefit teachers. Perhaps a good next step for researchers would be to consider non-linear models when testing these hypotheses, and to examine their models more closely for aberrations that might be influencing outcomes.

We suggested at the outset that, although most advocates for coursework in education are also in favor of courses in other domains, and are in favor of bright, well-educated teachers, whereas advocates for these other hypotheses tend to be quite skeptical of education coursework. In an adversarial setting, it will be tempting to dismiss equivocal findings about one domain while embracing equivocal findings about another. A better response to the data would be to begin a program of research that more closely examines the content actually taught in various courses and to generate more nuanced hypotheses about what it takes to learn to teach. Both mathematics and teacher education departments could benefit from a closer examination of the content they offer to prospective teachers, with an eye toward its relevance. Mathematics departments might want to examine the relevance of advanced mathematics coursework for teaching. Teacher education departments certainly need to examine the content they provide in their advanced degree courses.

NOTES

1 Work for this paper was supported by a grant from the U.S. Department of Education, Institute for Educational Sciences, and by the National Science Foundation, Program on Research, Evaluation and Communication. Responsibility for the content and quality of the paper reside solely with the authors.

2 Though we use the term "value added" in our title, we use it in a more general sense than it is sometimes used. In the literature, this phrase sometimes refers to a very specific analytic approach (Kupermintz, 2002; Sanders & Horn, 1994) and sometimes to the general approach of using pretests to control for prior achievement in a statistical model (Cunningham & Stone, 2005). We use it here in the more general sense.

3 We eventually expanded our list of qualifications to include some things that typically are acquired *after* teachers obtain full-time teaching positions because these things may be relevant in district hiring or salary decisions. These include, for instance, teachers' years of experience, whether or not they possess an advanced degree, whether they had been certified by the National Board of Professional Teaching Standards, and how they responded to a commercial hiring interview such as the Teacher Perceiver Interview. These later additions have no bearing on the present study.

4 There were a few cases in which authors did not provide this information. When they did not, we sometimes found relevant information in another research report that used the same data base and sometimes from a web site that presented population statistics. The general goal was to find a population average pre- and post-test score that could be used as a benchmark for examining the size of teachers' effects on students.

5 Since these authors did not provide information on average students' change during the year, we present their findings using raw scores. We are unable to say whether or not these differences are substantial relative to average gains.

6 Another recent study, by Laczko-Kerr (2002a, 2002b; Laczko and Berliner, 2001; Laczko-Kerr and Berliner, 2002) was rejected because it did not employ a pretest.

7 The Darling-Hammond *et al.* study actually includes effects as measured by several different tests, and the authors argue that, in the Houston situation, the other tests may be better indicators of student learning. However, we prefer the TAAS test because it is the assessment that is aligned with the state curriculum and that teachers are accountable for. Since, in all cases, we take only one model per study sample, to avoid data dependency among effects, this is the only estimate we take from that study.

REFERENCES

*Aaronson, D., Barrow, L., & Sander, W. (2003) *Teachers and student achievement in the Chicago public high schools.* Chicago: Federal Reserve Bank of Chicago.

Ballou, D. & Podgursky, M. (1999) Teacher training and licensure: a layman's guide. In M. Kanstoroom & C. Finn (eds.), *Better teachers, better schools* (pp. 31–82). Washington, DC: Thomas B. Fordham Institute.

*Betts, J. R., Zau, A. C., & Rice, L. A. (2003) *Determinants of student achievement: new evidence from San Diego.* San Francisco CA: Public Policy Institute of California.

Boyd, D., Lankford, H., Loeb, S., & Wyckoff, J. (2003) *The draw of home: how teachers' preferences for proximity disadvantage urban schools.* Cambridge, MA: National Bureau of Economic Research.

Boyd, D., Lankford, H., Loeb, S., & Wykoff, J. (2002) *Analyzing the determinants of the matching of public school teachers to jobs.* Albany, NY: State University of New York at Albany.

*Brewer, D. J. & D. D. Goldhaber (1996) Educational achievement and teacher qualifications: new evidence from microlevel data. In B. S. Cooper and S. T. Speakman (eds.), *Optimizing educational resources* (pp. 243–264). Greenwich, CT: JAI.

*Cavalluzo, L. (2004) *Is National Board certification an effective signal of teacher quality?* Washington, DC: The CNA Corporation.

*Chiang, F.-S. (1996) Ability, motivation, and performance: a quantitative study of teacher effects on student mathematics achievement using NELS:88 data. Unpublished Dissertation, University of Michigan.

*Clotfelter, C., Ladd, H., & Vigdor, J. (2004a) *Teacher quality and minority achievement gaps.* Durham NC: Duke University Sanford Institute of Public Policy.

*Clotfelter, C., Ladd, H., & Vigdor, J. L. (2004b) *Teacher sorting, teacher shopping, and the assessment of teacher effectiveness.* Retrieved June, 2005 from http://trinity.aaaas.duke.edu/~vigdor/TSAOR5.pdf

*Clotfelter, C., Ladd, H. F., & Vigdor, J. L. (2006) *Teacher-student matching and the assessment of teacher effectiveness.* Retrieved February 14, 2006 from http://www.nber.org/papers/w11936

Council of Chief State School Officers (1988) State Education Indicators, 1988. Washington, DC: Author.

Conant, J. B. (1963) *The Education of American Teachers.* New York: McGraw Hill.

Cunningham, G. K. & Stone, J. E. (2005) *Value-added assessment of teacher quality as an alternative to the national board for professional teaching standards: what recent studies say.* Arlington, VA: Education Consumers Clearinghouse.

Damerell, R. G. (1985) *Education's smoking gun: how teachers colleges have destroyed education in America.* New York: Freundlich Publishers.

*Darling-Hammond, L., Holtzman, D. J., Gatlin, S. J., & Hellig, J. V. (2005a) *Does teacher certification matter? Evidence about teacher certification, teach for America, and teacher effectiveness.* Stanford University. Retrieved April 16, 2005 from http://www.schoolredesign.net/sm/server.php?idx=934

*Darling-Hammond, L., Holtzman, D. J., Gatlin, S. J., & Heilig, J. V. (2005b) Does teacher preparation matter? Evidence about teacher certification, teach for America, and teacher effectiveness. *Education Policy Analysis Archives,* 13 (42).

*Decker, P. T., Mayer, D. P., & Glazerman, S. (2004) *The effects of Teach For America on students: findings from a national evaluation.* Princeton, NJ: Mathematical Policy Research.

*Eberts, R. W. & Stone, J. A. (1984) *Unions and public schools.* Lexington, MA: Lexington Books.

*Fagnano, C. L. (1988) *An investigation into the effects of specific types of teacher training on eighth grade mathematics students' mathematics achievement.* Unpublished Dissertation, University of California at Los Angeles.

*Goldhaber, D. D. & Brewer, D. J. (1996) *Evaluating the effect of teacher degree level on educational performance.* Washington, DC: National Center for Education Statistics, U.S. Department of Education.

* Goldhaber, D. D. & Brewer, D. J. (1997a) Evaluating the effect of teacher degree level on educational performance. In W. Fowler (ed.), *Developments in school finance,* 1996 (pp. 197–210). Washington, DC: U.S. Department of Education National Center for Education Statistics.

*Goldhaber, D. D. & Brewer, D. J. (1997b) Why don't schools and teachers seem to matter? Assessing the impact of unobservables on educational productivity. *Journal of Human Resources,* 32(3), 505–523.

*Goldhaber, D. D. & Brewer, D. J. (1999) Teacher licensing and student achievement. In M. Kanstoroom and C. F. J. Finn (eds.), *Better teachers, better schools* (pp. 83–102). Washington, DC: Thomas B. Fordham Foundation.

*Goldhaber, D. D. & Brewer, D. J. (2000) Does teacher certification matter? High school teacher certification status and student achievement. *Educational Evaluation and Policy Analysis* 22 (2): 129–45.

Goldhaber, D. D. & Anthony, E. (2003) *Teacher quality and student achievement.* New York: ERIC clearinghouse on urban education.

*Guarino, C. M., Hamilton, L. S., Lockwood, J. R., & Rathbun, A. H. (2006) *Teacher qualifications, instructional practices, and reading and mathematics gains of kindergartners.* Washington, DC: National Center for Education Statistics.

Hanushek, E. (1971) Teacher characteristics and gains in student achievement: estimation using micro data. *American Economic Review,* 61(2), 280–288.

Hanushek, E., Rivkin, S. G., & Taylor, L. L. (1996) Aggregation and the estimated effects of school resources. *The Review of Economics and Statistics* 78(4), 611–627.

*Harris, D. & Sass, T. R. (2006) *The effects of teacher training on teacher value-added*. Paper presented at the American Education Finance Association.

Hedges, L. V. (1986) Issues in meta-analysis, *Review of Research in Education* (Vol. 13, pp. 353–398). Washington, DC: American Educational Research Association.

Hess, F. (2001) *Tear down this wall: the case for a radical overhaul of teacher certification*. Washington, DC: Progressive Policy Institute.

*Hill, H., Rowan, B., & Ball, D. L. (2005) Effects of teachers' mathematical knowledge for teaching on student achievement. *American Educational Research Journal*, 42(2), 371–406.

Kramer, R. (1991) *Ed school follies: the miseducation of America's teachers*. New York: The Free Press.

Kupermintz, H. (2002) Value-added assessment of teachers: the empirical evidence. In A. Molnar (ed.), *School reform proposals: the research evidence*. Greenwich, CT: Information Age Publishing.

Labaree, D. F. (2004) *The trouble with ed Schools*. New Haven, CT: Yale University Press.

Laczko-Kerr, I. I. (2002a) The effects of teacher certification on student achievement: an analysis of Stanford Nine achievement for students with emergency and standard certified teachers. Paper presented at the American Educational Research Association, New Orleans, LA.

Laczko-Kerr, I. I. (2002b) *Teacher certification does matter: The effects of certification status on student achievement*. Unpublished Dissertation, Arizona State University.

Laczko-Kerr, I. I. & Berliner, D. C. (2001) The effects of teacher certification on student achievement: an analysis of the Stanford Nine. Paper presented at the American Educational Research Association, Seattle, WA.

Laczko-Kerr, I. I. & Berliner, D. C. (2002) The effectiveness of "Teach for America" and other under-certified teachers on student academic achievement: a case of harmful public policy. *Education Policy Analysis Archives*, 10(37).

Lagemann, E. C. (1999) Whither schools of education? Whither educational research. *Journal of Teacher Education*, 50(5), 373–376.

Lankford, H., Loeb, S., & Wykoff, J. (2002) Teacher sorting and the plight of urban schools: a descriptive analysis. *Education Evaluation and Policy Analysis*, 24(1), 37–62.

Ludwig, J. & Bassie, L. J. (1999) The puzzling case of school resources and student achievement. *Educational Evaluation and Policy Analysis*, 21(4), 385–403.

Metzger, S. A., Qu, Y., & Becker, B. J. (2004) An examination of literature on teacher qualifications: influence of ill-defined constructs on synthesis outcomes. Paper presented at the American Educational Research Association, San Diego.

*Monk, D. H. (1994) Subject area preparation of secondary mathematics and science teachers and student achievement. *Economics of Education Review*, 13(2), 125–145.

*Monk, D. H. & King, J. A. (1994) Multilevel teacher resource effects on pupil performance in secondary mathematics and science: the case for teacher subject-matter preparation. In R. G. Ehrenberg (ed.), *Choices and consequences: contemporary policy issues in education* (pp. 29–58). Ithaca, NY: ILR Press.

Murnane, R. J. (1981) Interpreting the evidence on school effectiveness. *Teachers College Record*, 83(1), 19–35.

National Commission on Teaching and America's Future (1996) *What matters most: teaching for America's future*. New York: National Commission on Teaching & America's Future.

National Center for Education Statistics (2003) Digest of educational statistics: Author. Retrieved June 20, 2005 from http://nces.ed.gov/programs/digest/d03/tables/dt067.asp

Raudenbush, S. W. & Bryk, A. S. (1988) Methodological advances in analyzing the effects of schools and classrooms on student learning. In E. K. Rothkopf (ed.), *Review of Research in Education* (Vol. 15, pp. 423–475). Washington, DC: American Educational Research Association.

*Raymond, M. & Fletcher, S. (2002a) Education Next summary of CREDO's evaluation of teach

for America. Education Next. Retrieved April 2006 from www.teachforamerica.org/pdfs/
TFA_final.pdf

*Raymond, M. & Fletcher, S. (2002b) The Teach for America evaluation. *Education Next*
(Spring), 62–68.

*Raymond, M., Fletcher, S. H., & Luque, J. (2001) *Teach for America: an evaluation of teacher
differences and student outcomes in Houston, Texas.* Houston TX: CREDO.

Rokoff, J. E. (2003) The impact of individual teachers on student achievement: evidence from
panel data. Retrieved April, 2006 from econwpa.wustl.edu/eps/pe/papers/0304/0304002.pdf

Rotherman, A. & Mead, S. (2003, October 23–24) Back to the future: the history and politics
of state teacher licensure and certification. Paper presented at A Qualified Teacher in Every
Classroom: Appraising Old Answers and New Ideas, Washington, DC.

*Rowan, B., Chiang, F.-S., & Miller, R. J. (1997) Using research on employees' performance to
study the effects of teachers on students' achievement. *Sociology of Education*, 70(4), 256–284.

*Rowan, B., Correnti, R., & Miller, R. J. (2002) What large-scale survey research tells us about
teacher effects on student achievement: insights from the Prospects Study of elementary schools.
Teachers College Record, 104(8), 1525–1567.

*Rowley, K. J. (2004, April) Teacher experience, certification, & education: characteristics that
matter most in kindergarten math achievement. Paper presented at the American Educational
Research Association, San Diego, CA.

Sanders, W. L. & Horn, S. P. (1998) Research findings from the Tennessee Value-Added Assessment
System (TVAAS) data base: Implications for Educational Evaluation and Research. *Journal of
Personnel Evaluation in Education*, 12(3), 247–256.

Sanders, W. L. & Horn, S. P. (1994) The Tennessee Value-Added Assessment System: mixed model
methodology in educational assessment. *Journal of Personnel Evaluation in Education*, 8(1),
299–311.

Slavin, R. E. (1984) Meta-Analysis in education: how has it been used. *Educational Researcher*,
13(8), 6–15.

Slavin, R. E. (1986) Best-evidence synthesis: an alternative to meta-analytic and traditional
reviews. *Educational Researcher*, 15(9), 5–11.

Strauss, R. P. (1999) Who gets hired? The case of Pennsylvania. In M. Kanstoroom & C. E. Finn, Jr.
(eds.), *Better Teachers, Better Schools* (pp. 103–130). Washington, DC: The Thomas B Fordham
Foundation.

*Taddese, N. (1997) *The impact of teacher, family and student attributes on mathematics achieve-
ment.* Unpublished Dissertation, University of Cincinnati.

Wykoff, J. (2001) *The geography of teacher labor markets: implications for policy.* Albany: SUNY.

* Included in Table 61.1.

Part 9
Artifacts

9.1 Purposes of a normal school

William S. Learned,
William C. Bagley and others

Source: W. S. Learned, W. C. Bagley and others. Purposes of a normal
school. In M. L. Borrowman (ed.), *Teacher Education in America: A
Documentary History*. New York: Teachers College Press, 1965

In 1914, Governor Elliott W. Major of Missouri obtained the support of the Carnegie Foundation
for a study of the teacher education problems of his state. In organizing the study, William S.
Learned, of the Foundation's staff, enlisted the services of people who were, or were destined to
become, shapers of "professional" thought about American education. Among them were: William
C. Bagley of Teachers College, Columbia University, whose students established the field of
teacher education as an area of specialized scholarship; Charles A. McMurry of Illinois Normal
University, George Peabody College for Teachers, and Teachers College, an expert on "methods
of instruction" who had led the early Herbartian movement in America; Ned Dearborn of Harvard
University, one of the early advocates of scientific measurement in education; and George D.
Strayer of Teachers College, who perhaps as much as any one man made the school survey a
permanent feature of American life.

Missouri was their laboratory, the nation their audience. Their survey was the first of several
massive studies of American teacher education. Paradoxically, though their techniques represented the wave of the future, their basic values and assumptions were quickly to wane. In no
subsequent major study will be found so complete a consensus in favor of the single-purpose
teachers college.

1 THE EXISTING CONCEPTION

"What should a normal school be?" This is a question which, according to Joseph Baldwin, the
first president at Kirksville, "only the angels can answer." Whatever the accuracy of this verdict, it
is possible at least to discover what the function of the institution has been as worked out in
practice in Missouri.

Early conception of the function of a normal school

The question may be reduced to the following alternatives: the normal school shall either provide
a general education, making its professional features more or less incidental, or it shall undertake
to give an intensive professional training, exclusively for teachers. Of these alternatives, Missouri
at any time in her early normal school history would have emphatically asserted the latter. From
the beginning, the movement was in the hands of men who had unlimited faith in the professional
idea. Its appeal was founded on the prevailing low state of training among common school
teachers, and it was promoted by teachers, superintendents, and associations of these, who had
definitely in mind the elevation of the class as a whole. So in 1871 the State Teachers Association
at Chillicothe resolved "that the normal schools should be at the head of our educational system;

that the course should be purely professional; and that all preparatory work should be done in the public schools and universities."[1] The early curricula exhibit this predominant idea very clearly: it was never a question of giving or of not giving the professional subjects, but always of how much academic material would suffice to supplement the defective preparation with which most students came equipped. All subjects were presented or reviewed from the standpoint of their most effective presentation to a class, and the practical usages of instruction received heavy emphasis. "No effort has been spared to make the institution exclusively a school for teachers."[2] "In arranging the course of instruction strict regard has been paid to the requirements of the public schools of Missouri, and in carrying out that course our constant aim has been to give such training as will best qualify the graduate both intellectually and morally for effective work as a teacher."[3] These statements from Warrensburg in 1878 and 1886 reveal the attitude of the other schools as well. President Baldwin, at Kirksville, declared in 1872 that "every energy is directed to preparing for the public schools of Missouri the largest number of good teachers in the shortest time,"[4] and in 1880: the aim of the school is "to give culture and learning, not for the benefit of the student, but that it may be used in the education of the masses."[5] Especially instructive are the observations of State Superintendent Monteith, who was in office when the schools were started:

> It is a pretty well-defined result of experience, too, that normal schools should be quite elementary in respect to the subject matter and curriculum of study. In a school system which embraces high schools and universities, there is not the slightest reason why the normal school should duplicate the instruction of these more advanced institutions. I am thoroughly convinced, in observing the mistakes of other states, that the normal school is disappointing the object of its design when it drifts away from the common schools of the country. With this object steadily in view, our Board of Regents are endeavoring to adjust the two schools already established to the special conditions and wants of the state. The higher mathematics and dead languages, except within a certain eminently practical limit, are to give way to a more generous attention to natural science, drawing, and the perfecting of teachers in the best methods of conducting the common branches of the common school.[6]

Missouri normal schools, therefore, were founded to train teachers. To say "exclusively" would be technically wrong, as certain readjustments were occasionally made here and there; for example, special classes in Greek were sometimes offered to accommodate a few who wished to go to the university, and certain individuals were occasionally present who did not declare their intention to teach. But the clear and consistent aim apparent under all circumstances was to provide teachers, actual or prospective, with special skill for their duties, and in their reports to the legislature all the schools were solicitous to show that the largest possible proportion of their students were actually teaching in the state.

Subsequent variations

This fixed purpose of the first thirty years has wavered in some schools during the subsequent period. The three original institutions furnish an interesting contrast in this respect. In 1909, under the caption "People's College," Kirksville announced itself as follows:

> The State Normal School, Kirksville, Mo., is attempting to do a great work for the people of the state by giving studies reaching from the kindergarten through the most advanced college courses. This wide range of work—meeting the demands of all the people—is found in very few first class schools. While advanced common school courses are given in this institution for the benefit of those who are preparing to teach in the rural and ungraded schools, academic degrees are conferred upon those who have completed the work offered

by our best colleges. This brings the school in close touch with the people by giving an elaborate education to those who want to enter the professions, and a vocational education for those who want to take practical business courses. It cannot be denied that the Normal School comes nearer the people than other schools and may therefore be justly called the People's College.[7]

This statement is followed by an extensive program of courses that are clearly not intended for teachers—one year curricula chiefly in farming and commerce. Nowhere in this bulletin, furthermore, is there a clear statement that the school is of a limited professional character, or that a declaration of intention to teach is required. It holds out rather an alluring vision of a sort of educational lunch counter where everything "the people" wish, may be had in portions suited to their convenience.

The "People's College" idea does not appear to have thrived; at any rate, nothing more is heard of it, and the catalogue of the following year goes back plainly to the original aim: "The Normal School is not a college for general culture. It is a vocational institution of college rank. Under the law its students declare their intention to teach in the public schools." The subsequent catalogues have shown a single, strong professional purpose.

At Cape Girardeau an enlargement of scope was announced in the same year as at Kirksville. The catalogue of 1909 declares: "The Normal School has a larger mission in Southeast Missouri than that of a state college for teachers . . . The institution must be to this section of the state their one great college. It is fully equipped to meet the demands that are naturally made upon it. In its college courses; in its agricultural courses; in its Manual Training School; in its domestic science and domestic art courses; in its School of Music; in its business courses; and in its teachers' college the people of Southeast Missouri will find the opportunity to educate themselves for their life work."

Tho placing its teachers college last in the above list, the school elsewhere in the catalogue clearly defines its legal teacher-training function as a portion of its activity. In the catalogue of 1910 its "Field of Service" is formally described as comprising "A School for Teachers," a "Subcollegiate" department, and "A State College," the latter offering (since 1907) courses leading to the degree of A.B. and requiring in them no work in education whatever. Here we have, therefore, an institution deliberately revising its organization throughout and introducing, not one-year vocational courses as at Kirksville, but an elaborate curriculum with a new and alien purpose. It is difficult to see how either school could reconcile these departures with the law's demand for an exaction from each student of a declaration of intention to teach in the schools of Missouri. Cape Girardeau, and possibly Kirksville, has been saved from embarrassment thru the fact that but for a single case no graduate has taken the courses except prospective teachers who could also avow their intention to teach; that, however, scarcely justifies the appeal for students distinctly excluded by law. This divided purpose at Cape Girardeau has never been abandoned. On the contrary, it has been officially reaffirmed in the school's magazine publications of 1913 and 1914,[8] where the pledge to teach is declared to be out of date, and it is frankly proposed to adapt the institution to the needs of men and women who will teach but a short time, if at all, and whose professional interest is therefore incidental at best.

Warrensburg, on the other hand, has consistently adhered to the original plan, to the extent, at least, of an unequivocal announcement of her special aim in every catalogue down to the present year. An expression in the school's biennial report of 1885 is a fair sample of the early attitude: "On all proper occasions we have taken pains to spread abroad the impression that this school is designed for the training of teachers and for no other purpose whatever." In the catalogue of 1904 the "Object of the School" is defined in the following paragraphs:

In the law creating Normal Schools in this State the following passages occur:
"The course of instruction shall be confined to such branches of science only as are

usually taught in Normal Schools and which may be necessary to qualify the students as competent teachers in the public schools of this State.

"Every applicant for admission shall undergo an examination in such manner as may be prescribed by the Board [of Regents], and they shall require the applicant to sign and file with the Secretary of the Board a declaration of intention to follow the business of teaching in the public schools of this State."

The following is the pledge required of every student upon entrance and registration:

"I hereby declare that it is my intention to follow the business of teaching in the public schools of this State, and that I voluntarily enroll myself as a student in the State Normal School at Warrensburg for the purpose of preparing for that work."

The limits prescribed for the course of study and the form of the pledge show that but one purpose was contemplated by the State in establishing these schools, viz.: The training of teachers for the public schools of the State.[9]

Similarly in 1905 and after, the school's "sole function is the preparation of teachers for the schools of Missouri." "The school does not exist for the benefit of its students, but for the benefit of the whole people."[10] And in 1912: The school's "sole purpose is to confer on its students that education, discipline, professional training, and practical skill which will best fit them for teaching in the public schools of the State."[11]

The schools at Springfield and Maryville, founded in 1906, have in general followed the exclusively professional ideal also, as their catalogues attest. Southwest Missouri has been an unusually fruitful field for such single-minded service, and the school at Springfield has prospered remarkably. Maryville, in 1914, devotes two pages of its catalogue to the exposition of this distinctly professional aim. It is with some surprise, therefore, that one sees it weakened in 1916. The school now calls itself simply "an educational institution," and, besides enumerating the various teacher-groups that are provided for, invites also those who are "seeking to secure the preliminary college academic requirement" for the university, or students from other colleges who seek "to extend their credits in college," and finally observes "that many persons not immediately concerned with teaching find pleasure and profit in becoming enrolled in our classes." There is no reference to the declaration of intention to teach required by law.

Special considerations affecting a normal school's conception of its function

Before discussing the merits of the question involved in these divergent proposals, there are certain additional facts to be considered. In spite of the professional ideal that, with the above exceptions, has dominated the schools, the notion of a general education has almost unconsciously, and for historical reasons, influenced their purpose. From the beginning the students in these normal schools have been exceedingly heterogeneous, with a preponderance of mature minds of good ability but with very defective preparation due to lack of opportunity. The all-important preliminary process was therefore necessarily one of fundamental education, and it is impressive to note how consistently the Missouri normal schools have urged this principle, even tho at times they appear to have failed to practise it. Throughout their history they seem to have been ardent advocates of having something to teach as compared with certain schools in other states that sacrificed their character on the altar of "method."

Pressure for academic credit

Furthermore, it should be noted that as purveyors to that occupation of teaching whereby chiefly needy and ambitious boys and girls obtained the means for further education, these institutions stood in tempting relation to the fuller education that their students sought. It was a matter of course that the kind of student who came to the normal school had taught or would teach; teaching was his most obvious resource for temporary support. Hence in very many cases the student accepted professional work as a necessary incident, while his real attention was upon the academic work that would be accepted for credit in another and higher institution. It was but a step, and a very natural step, for the normal school to develop its requirements with such an end in view. A genuine desire to prove serviceable to hard-working students who were using the teaching profession merely as a ladder, and a less worthy feeling that such students brought to the school not only numbers but prestige, combined to enhance the "college" idea as a legitimate goal. Aside from Cape Girardeau's wholly non-professional curriculum already mentioned, the sixty-hour curriculum for high school graduates at Maryville, in 1914, illustrates such a purpose: in the effort to offer only subjects that might be used for credit elsewhere, no special study of the history, geography, and arithmetic that these students were presumably later to teach was required, except as it appeared fragmentarily in ten semester hours of practice teaching.[12]

That pressure of this sort has been and still continues to be severe seems evident from the replies made by students to enquiries at the various schools. Sixty per cent of the students in attendance at the time of inspection declared that they did not intend to teach permanently. With the women the factor of prospective marriage probably weighs heavily; this cannot, however, be true of the men, seventy-eight per cent of whom make the negative reply. Such students naturally have little interest in an intensive professional training; those studies please them best which give them the most credit for future use. Even the men who are intending to continue in the field of education find but little inducement in the work properly expected from most of the women. The latter expect to teach, while the men hope to go directly into administrative positions. As a group the men in the normal schools seem to be a disintegrating element, yet the efforts made to attract and retain them indicate that their presence is nevertheless much preferred to a homogeneous professional group more largely made up of women.

Effect of local control

A third motive for stress on general education has arisen from the complete local attachment and control of the schools. The town or county has paid a heavy bonus for the location, and naturally exercises proprietorship. The schools are severally in the hands of local boards, who really own them in behalf of their respective districts. They are maintained largely, to be sure, out of state funds, but the amount of such appropriations depend upon the energy and influence of their board members and friends who lobby vigorously, and is never in any sense the considered proposal of a state authority directing the institution solely for the good of the whole state. They become, therefore, the local public educational institutions; and the fundamental theory of a school to train public servants for the benefit of the state is largely obscured by the more attractive idea of a place where local youth may prepare for college, or even pursue collegiate studies and acquire degrees. Town or sectional pride urges this interpretation on the institution, which in turn is anxious to recruit its numbers because of its feeling of responsibility to the local community.[13] Regents with pet notions find an easy field of influence, and often have slight perception of the larger purpose of the school. One of these urged that, as his school had an old telescope in its possession, it should undertake collegiate courses in astronomy. Administrators naturally yield most quickly to the forces that feed and affect the school, and when dependent solely upon such local influences can scarcely be blamed if truer ideals seem distant and impracticable. It is easy, under these circumstances, to include the professional idea, because, as already pointed out, it fits the economic situation of most of the student patrons; but to make it really the sole and sufficient reason for the school's existence is less easy, and probably cannot be fully accomplished under the present system of control.

"Democracy": the justification

The situation described in the foregoing paragraph has, of course, developed a theory, or the interpretation of a theory, for its justification. Great emphasis is placed on the perfectly valid creed that the people know what they want, and that democracy in education consists in gratifying their desires. But from this creed there is then drawn the inference that because the people desire good teachers, the people are therefore competent to direct the institution that provides them, and that the institution is most "democratic" that yields itself most completely to the popular local fancy. Such, unfortunately, are the terms on which it is often possible, thru spectacular features, to develop a large school; but such is not the way to give the people what they, at heart, desire. An intelligent society has learned not to interfere with competent professional service when it would be healed or seek justice at court; that service commands the maximum confidence which, for a selected end, most completely refines and dominates its choice of means. This temper is superlatively characteristic of a good school; it must mould and dominate public opinion in its field; it must guard its aims and processes from public interference precisely in order that the public may get the service that it wants. No other interpretation of public service is worthy of a democracy, but the present system of local control makes such detached and efficient service difficult if not impossible.

Professional training: long uncertain as to its method

Finally, the development of professional training itself has involved the conception of general education in an ambiguous and confusing manner. When the Missouri normal schools were established, two theories existed as to their operation. According to the first, the purpose of the schools should be solely to teach subject-matter properly; it was said that students would teach precisely as they had been taught, and could shift for themselves if filled with ideas to be communicated. According to the second theory, only the indispensable subject-matter should be given; the main purpose should be to develop the philosophy of method and to test the skill of the candidate in using methods. The latter theory was the one adopted and chiefly followed,[14] although, as has been said, the schools appear to have insisted usually that the foundation of subject-matter should be substantial. Little by little, however, both in Missouri and elsewhere, the whole normal school practice seems to have hardened into a formalized method from which the schools were aroused thru criticism by the universities. The latter had been persistent adherents of the first of the two doctrines noted; consequently the cult of "method" received little but ridicule, and in so far as it had developed a pose to hide its insufficient learning, its pretensions were quickly punctured. Under the fire of this attack many unworthy accretions of "professional" lore disappeared—sentimentalism, mystic reverence for formulae, a not infrequent quackery; while such conceptions as survived the refining process were eventually accepted for use in normal school and university alike.

Apart from this salutary process, however, and somewhat preceding it, came an increased mechanical emphasis on what the university primarily stood for, namely, content. In Missouri this is illustrated by the change that came over all the institutions about 1900, when within two years the headship in each was transferred to a new man. The university high school inspector and former state superintendent of public schools went to Kirksville with a commission from the president of the university to "go and put scholarship into that school." The president of Central College at Fayette, Missouri, went to Warrensburg, and a successful school superintendent, a graduate of the state university, went to Cape Girardeau. The effect of this infusion of fresh academic blood became immediately apparent in the announcements of the schools: the cultural idea; the proposal, in order to make teachers, to make "first educated men and women;" the notion of "a broad academic foundation" are all insistently emphasized. Accordingly, the studies

THE PURPOSES OF A NORMAL SCHOOL **1281**

considered "academic" were set off sharply from those termed "professional," and commanded a certain special respect if only because they were terms shared in common with the higher academic world; and this distinction has in general been pronounced even to the present day.

The influence of this development has been marked both on the students and on the institutions. In effect the school has unconsciously said to the student: "This academic foundation is your education; it is of prime importance, it has nothing to do with teaching, it is what you want for life, it will serve you if you proceed to college or professional school; as a teacher-preparing agency we are obliged to hang in your belt certain tools that will get you a license and may be useful if you teach, but they are not big enough to be in the way if you do not, and an educated person ought to have them anyhow." Thus its very endeavors to meet more satisfactorily its professional purpose by strengthening the academic foundation have created in the normal school a divided aim which it has not known how to unify, and of which the various other centrifugal tendencies already enumerated have taken full advantage.

In its effect upon the institution itself this situation has been positively disastrous. With the emphatic division of subjects into academic and professional groups came naturally a corresponding division of the staff. Teachers of educational subjects, including the practice-school director and supervisors, should be the core of the institution; distinct from them are the academic instructors, who generally will have nothing to do with the practice school or its works. In members of the academic staff, pride of subject, and often of better training, has bred not a little scorn (carried over, perhaps, from the universities from whence they came) for the department of "pedagogy" and the ill-paid supervisors of the training school. At any rate, these academic instructors have rarely been selected for their knowledge of how to teach young children; their interests and sympathies are elsewhere, and the organization of the school has usually failed to exact of them responsibility for this phase of their duty.

In some normal schools, not in Missouri, the faculty is split from top to bottom on this line, and even in Missouri, with the sole exception of Springfield, the cleavage is apparent. The inevitable tendency of such division of sympathy and purpose is to reproduce itself in the mind of the student. His strictly educational courses lack conviction because they lack relation, and fail of the illustrative and cumulative force latent in the so-called "content" subjects; the latter, in turn, conceived as ends in themselves for "general education," terminate often in a series of blind alleys whence the student neither gets further nor sees how his achievement affects his main purpose.

2 NORMAL SCHOOLS SHOULD TRAIN TEACHERS

It is the judgment of the authors of this report that institutions established by the state to prepare teachers as public servants for its schools should make that business their sole purpose and concern. The character of such preparation is a question of administrative knowledge and policy. It will depend upon the amount of financial support available, and will be modified by the varying need for teachers in the state and by the rewards offered in the communities to be served. But with their method and specific goal thus defined, no consideration whatever should divert such schools from their task.

The grounds for this conclusion are simple and obvious. The question is one of institutional economy. Each school has a certain amount of energy expressed in terms of its annual appropriation plus its organization and permanent plant. With this energy it confronts a definite and difficult task contemplated in the statute,[15] namely, with the help of four similar schools and of the university, to place a competent teacher in every teaching position in the state. This is a task with which these six schools have scarcely begun to cope. It is a task so great that large and important portions of it have temporarily to be farmed out, as in the inevitable allotment for the present of the teachers of the large cities to the city training schools, and of rural teachers to the high school training classes. Hitherto the schools have trained a few teachers thoroughly, and have given a meager smattering to a vast number. Even the few have received a generalized training which will not be tolerable longer if the reasonable demands of educated communities are to be met in Missouri as they are already met in some other states. There is an overwhelming need for more prolonged and more intensive training, extended to include as many as can be reached. In the face of this heavy obligation which the state lays upon the normal schools, it is difficult to justify the proposal of any school, say of Cape Girardeau, to use its share of the all too scanty training funds to develop a local university. This means, as indicated in the prospectus already quoted, to relegate its training of teachers to an inconspicuous department; to promote the other phases of collegiate work for their own sake and not alone as they produce better teachers; to fill classes, as college classes are now filled, with some who will teach, some who will farm, some who will be politicians, and many who have no specific purpose; in other words, to sacrifice the enormous advantage of momentum and morale that inheres in a single fine idea well worked out, for a round of inevitable mediocrity. For the school has at best wholly insufficient funds for its present logical purpose—the preparation of a competent teacher for every position in its district. To take over other projects, as these are conceived in modern education, is not only to fail in its proper task but to fail altogether.

The case of Cape Girardeau is especially interesting, inasmuch as for many years both regents and administration have made every effort to realize this "larger" nation. Elaborate advanced "college" curricula, special scholarships "for graduates from other colleges," and an enthusiastic literature have all pushed the idea. But only a single graduate has as yet (1917) gone out from such courses; the school is still as solely a normal school as is any of the other four. And with good reason: Cape Girardeau has taken pride in being a good school, and both teachers and students have dimly perceived that it was impossible to be a good normal school and a "great college" on the same appropriation. There is doubtless truth in the claim that, as college attendance is in great part local, more southeast Missourians would go to college if they had one nearby. But it is just as true that a good normal school is a professional school throughout and cannot be an arts college; if it wishes to conduct a college that is self-respecting, it must have double funds, separate classes, another faculty selected for that purpose, and so on. The combination is not a happy one in any place where it is now on trial, and the logic both of theory and experience is against it. The college agitation at Cape Girardeau has probably done good rather than harm; some public interest has been aroused, and a college foundation may some time seize the imagination of the wealthy men of that region or be developed from the local high school by way of a junior college as elsewhere in Missouri; but the obvious way to help in bringing about this result is for the present institution to discharge its own peculiar task well, and to fix its ambitions on becoming the best purely professional training school for teachers in the Middle West.

Cape Girardeau is an excellent illustration of a school-appropriated body and soul by the local community in the hope of making it the engine of local ambitions. The town and county bought the school in the first place, and can scarcely be blamed for owning it now. Fortunately state control of the funds, by forcing it into comparison with the other schools, still determines ill general line of action, but it can probably never reach its maximum power until it acquires a controlling board disentangled from local concerns and sympathetic with its proper purpose. Reimbursement of this and the other counties for their original outlay would be a small price to pay as compared with the benefit of independent management.

Obstacles to professional training are disappearing

Other obstacles to an exclusive and intensive professional development in normal schools are happily vanishing. Secondary work, to which the normal schools have hitherto of necessity been tied, seems destined early to disappear from them. The phenomenal increase in high school facilities has brought secondary education within the possible reach of nearly every student,[16] and the higher institution owes it to the lower to turn back every pupil of high school age who can attend a local or neighboring school before coming to the normal school. Many of these country high schools have large contingents who come in for the week from the surrounding territory. Especially where training classes are installed, every consideration appears to favor the development of local training centres for secondary work. Mature persons, for whom the high school makes unsatisfactory provision, should be given opportunities elsewhere.[17]

The question of relation with other higher institutions is likewise being disposed of successfully. As this problem has existed, however, an important distinction should be made clear. It is one thing for those who have taken a strictly professional course and who expect to give themselves seriously to teaching to urge that they be allowed to continue their preparation in other institutions without loss of credit; it is quite another thing for persons who have no such intention to demand that the normal school give them a general education that will see them into college and professional school. For the first group adjustment has already been accomplished. Two-year graduates of the normal school may enter the School of Education at the university without serious loss of credit, and the recent conference arrangement between normal schools and university provides that students doing four years of standard work at a normal school may be admitted to graduate work in education at the university. The second group should be dealt with drastically, as the institution values its professional integrity. If elementary and high school instruction in this country is ever to be cleared of its traditionally random and trivial reputation, training agencies must insist on a curriculum so specific in character as to make its choice a fateful step in an individual's career. There will doubtless always be quondam teachers who fail and practise law, just as there are quondam physicians who fail and sell insurance, but it is intolerable for an honest training school so to relax its administration and enfeeble its courses as to put the transient at ease. Every normal school student should feel behind him a full tide of pressure from every quarter urging him to teach and to do nothing else, and he should contribute the impetus of his own clear decision to the general impulse.

Unity of aim increasing

Finally, in the professional training itself there are discernible strong tendencies making for unity. The present schism in staff and curriculum was the result, at first, of the difficulty of securing competent teachers of academic subjects who possessed likewise a thorough training in education and successful experience in teaching children and youth. This is still an unusual combination, but, thanks to rapid growth of schools of education and to improved product in the normal schools, it is becoming less rare. In the case of the curriculum, the result seems to have been due partly to unsympathetic instructors, but more largely to a desire on all sides to swing as far as possible toward the collegiate idea and away from the earlier attitude. It is now evident that this emphasis has been greatly overdone. The normal school that is true to itself finds it impossible to be a college. A genuine professional purpose makes itself felt much further than the purely technical subjects; it governs the selection of material for every curriculum, it grips every course that is offered, and that in no perfunctory fashion as formerly, but with a clear, scientific conception of the ultimate aim in view. "With a mission like this, why waste time trying to be a college?" is the convincing retort of the modern training school. Again, if this clearer definition of aim affects the attendance of men at the schools, let the situation be faced frankly. There is nothing to be gained for the profession of teaching by catering to a set of individuals who definitely intend to make their normal school course and a year's teaching a step to other work. Such a procedure cheapens the course for its proper candidates, and advertises most effectually that teaching is a makeshift occupation and preparation therefore a farce. It is certainly most desirable to make the teaching profession attractive to men; but, given higher financial rewards, the surest way to convince them that there is something to it is to make it genuinely selective in respect to length and character of preparation. If they cannot be held on these terms, there is no help for it; any other condition is illusory and dishonest.

A normal school's obligation to the state

The efficient teacher-training school of any grade is not to be measured by college, university, law, medical, or other liberal or professional institutions. These operate indirectly for the general good, but their direct aim is rather the intellectual or vocational benefit of the individual. The school for teachers, on the other hand, is the immediate instrument of the state for providing a given number and quality of public servants to discharge the main collective obligation of society to the next generation. Salaried staffs of physicians or lawyers supported by state or city for the whole people would imply a similar function in medical and law schools. Even so, the large number of teachers required, in proportion to the number of doctors and lawyers, would tend to elaborate and standardize the teacher-training agencies above other schools, Private and out-side sources would not play so large a part, nor would such wide individual variation be acceptable in preparing five thousand as in furnishing three hundred.

In view of this peculiar relation to the state it is evident that, to be effective, the training institution should have two characteristics in a preeminent degree. First, it should have a vivid purpose. Its sole aim being to train teachers, every item of its organization should contribute either to the final excellence of its product, or to the creation and maintenance of conditions in its region that will make its product most successful. Irrelevant work that can be done elsewhere should be discontinued as soon as possible; bogus or uncertain candidates should be rejected; diversions of aim, however attractive, should be avoided. The school should do one thing and do it mightily. In the second place, it should be wholly responsive. First and last it serves the state and not individuals; as an efficient instrument it must be sensitive to control. New types or altered numbers of teachers, fresh courses to be added, higher standards to be set,—all of these should find the training school prepared for continual and automatic readjustment. The informed and authorized directors of the state's educational policy—and the state should obviously have such directors—should not find themselves helpless because of institutional conservatism, opposition of alumni, or local entanglements. To ensure this, the school clearly should not be entrusted to an irresponsible head for personal exploitation; the measure of excellence in administration should be a quiet and rapid accommodation to the changing demands of the state's educational author-ity. The loyalty of alumni should be won, not for persons or places, but for the skill with which the school does its work and for its flexible adaptation to its duties; the head of an institution who, by personal appeal to numerous or powerful graduates, seeks to swing his own policy at all costs is abusing his trust. Finally, to be responsive, the school must be free from local pressure and interference. The state as a whole invariably wants for itself better things, and defines those wants more wisely than can be the case in any but highly developed urban districts. To tie a school down to the limited vision of a small area is to deprive the community of that margin of superiority which the whole state has achieved and formulated.

NOTES

1 *Report of the Superintendent of Public Schools*, 1871, page 19.
2 Ibid., 1878, page 224.
3 Ibid., 1886, page 108.
4 Ibid., 1872, page 166.

5 Ibid., 1880, page 159.

6 Ibid., 1872, page 37.

7 *Bulletin* (Supplement), Kirksville, June, 1909, page 1.

8 *The Educational Outlook*, October, 1913, page 136.

9 *Catalogue, Warrensburg*, 1904, page 15.

10 Ibid., 1905, page 20.

11 Ibid., 1912, page 16.

12 Good normal schools elsewhere were at the same time requiring 12–15 semester hours in these subjects aside from a full semester of practice work.

13 An everywhere vigorous and vocal expression of this town pride rises from the vested interests dependent on the schools—boardinghouses, stores, churches, and so on. Thus, a writer in the local newspaper of one of the normal school towns struck a responsive chord when he declared that the present study would undoubtedly discourage the attendance of men at the school, and send both men and women to "enrich the boarding houses of some other place." *Kirksville Express*, December 10, 1914.

14 These two points of view are well stated in one of Superintendent Monteith's discussions. See *State Report*, 1872, page 37.

15 The Revised Statutes of 1909 declare that "the course of instruction in each normal school shall be confined to such subjects in the sciences and arts as are usually taught in normal schools and necessary to qualify the students to become competent teachers In the public schools." See Chap. 106, Art. 14, Sect. 11071. An Act of 1919 extends this to include "such subjects in the arts and sciences as are usually taught in teachers' colleges, normal schools or school of education," Sect. 11075.

16 See William S. Learned, William C. Bagley, *et al.*, *The Professional Preparation of Teachers for American Public Schools*, page 297.

17 See ibid., page 300.

9.2 A quarrel among educators

James Bryant Conant

Source: James Bryant Conant, *The Education of American Teachers*.
New York: McGraw Hill, 1963

Universities have existed for nearly a thousand years. Their periods of vitality have been marked by passionate debates among professors. A clash of opinion has often been the prelude to a fruitful development of new ideas. Bitter theological disputes in the Middle Ages, as well as the violent controversy over Darwin's theory a century ago, might be cited as examples of quarrels among educators. But the quarrel I have in mind in writing this volume is of an entirely different kind. Neither factual evidence nor theoretical speculations provide the battleground. Rather, this quarrel might be described as a power struggle among professors, which has come to involve parents, alumni, legislators, and trustees. Let me illustrate the nature of the battle by recording my own involvement during the course of nearly fifty years.

Early in my career as a professor of chemistry, I became aware of the hostility of the members of my profession to schools or faculties of education. I shared the views of the majority of my colleagues on the faculty of arts and sciences that there was no excuse for the existence of people who sought to teach others how to teach. I felt confident that I was an excellent teacher and I had developed my skill by experience, without benefit of professors of education. I saw no reason why others could not do likewise, including those who graduated from college with honors in chemistry and who wished to teach in high school. As joint author, with my former chemistry teacher, of a high school chemistry textbook, I was quite certain I knew all about the way the subject should be presented; I doubted that my understanding was shared by any professors of education. When any issues involving benefits to the graduate school of education came before the faculty of arts and sciences, I automatically voted with those who looked with contempt on the school of education.

Suddenly, after being a member of one faculty for fifteen years, I found myself in a new position. I became the presiding officer of all the faculties of Harvard University. I was responsible to the governing boards for the budgets and the welfare of all our undertakings, including that of training teachers. It soon became evident that the antithesis between the views of the professors who taught the usual college subjects and those who were instructing future teachers was not as simple as I had thought. In the circumstances, it seemed reasonable to attempt to increase mutual understanding between the two hostile groups by establishing some arrangement through which they might exchange views and, if possible, learn to cooperate in their endeavors. The idea was obvious enough, though in the mid-1930s it was so unorthodox that a leading scholar in another university wrote the dean of the Harvard School of Education that "a shotgun would be needed to carry the wedding off."

As a matter of fact it did not prove too difficult for a new president to persuade the two faculties to agree to the establishment of a joint board to administer a new joint degree, the master of arts in teaching. One faculty, that of arts and science, was to certify through its usual departments that the candidate was well prepared in the subject to be taught in school—English, for example. The other faculty, that of education, was to certify that the candidate had successfully completed the courses in education that the administrative board had agreed were necessary. Since the School of Education, like the other professional schools at Harvard, was a graduate school, the question of offering courses in education to undergraduates did not arise. The candidates for the joint degree, it was assumed, would already have received a bachelor's degree.

The scheme was accepted by the two faculties, but I can hardly say it was accepted with enthusiasm. Before more than a few years had passed, some of the members of the joint administrative board asked for a new committee to review the whole arrangement. The committee, composed of a few professors of education and a few from the faculty of arts and sciences, raised a fundamental issue. Had it not been a mistake to force a Harvard undergraduate to postpone his work with professors of education until after he had received the A.B. degree? Obviously he had started his preparation as a future teacher early in his college course by studying the subject matter to be taught. Why not arrange for a continuous five-year program with professors from both faculties involved in the undergraduate as well as the graduate work? Such a modification of the joint venture did not appeal to me as president of the University. I knew far too well the degree of hostility felt toward professors of education by the majority of the faculty of arts and sciences. It would be fatal to the whole idea to present a scheme based on the premise that a candidate for the bachelor's degree could include in his program courses in education. Furthermore, the University had decided years before that professional preparation should be wholly at the graduate level. The School of Business Administration, for example, established a generation earlier, had rigidly adhered to this decision, and functioned only as a graduate school.

The entry of the United States into World War II so disorganized American colleges and universities that all concerned at Harvard lost interest in a second reformation of the education of teachers. After the war was over, the original concept of the degree of master of arts in teaching was accepted without question. And under the leadership of Dean Keppel the new system began to prosper. As the years went by, the hostility between the two Harvard faculties gradually diminished. I feel sure that a similar change was taking place in other institutions, yet from what my collaborators and I observed in the 77 institutions we visited in 1961–63, I am equally sure that the quarrel between educators is not yet over. As one dean of education remarked to me, "The boys have at least agreed to check their hatchets with their hats at the Faculty Club coatroom when they lunch together."

While I am not prepared to say that there was, or is, actual hostility between educational and academic professors on every campus, there has always been a considerable gap between the two groups in a majority of institutions. Such a gap often exists in spite of fine word spoken by administrators about "an all-university approach" to the education of teachers, and the existence of a committee that symbolized the approach.

As long ago as 1944, I took the occasion of an invitation to speak on the 50th Anniversary of Columbia's Teachers College to call for a "Truce Among Educators." By that time, I had been thoroughly exposed to the views of the two camps, including their views about each other. After pointing out that, as is always the case in academic matters, errors had been committed by both sides, I suggested the terms for a cease-fire order. In brief, they were that the professors of education admit their failure to be sufficiently concerned with the type of youth who should go to college, and that the professors of the college subjects such as English or chemistry admit their ignorance of the nature of the high school problems of the 1940s, which were quite different from those of the 1900s. Indeed, the warfare had started primarily because of the revolution in secondary education. I reminded the audience that the expansion of the high schools of the country since the 1880s has been nothing short of astronomical. Instead of being concerned with the education of a very small proportion of the boys and girls from fourteen to eighteen years of age, the high schools now must accommodate nearly three-fourths of the entire age group. The mere physical expansion, the mere change in scale, would in itself have presented a major problem to the institutions of higher education concerned with the training of teachers, but another and still more important factor entered in.

At the turn of the century, the high schools and their equivalents—the private academies and preparatory schools—were essentially concerned with a group of young people who were studying languages and mathematics, science and history. The enrollment in these schools in the nineties usually represented either impecunious youths with high scholastic aptitude and a keen desire for book learning, or children of well-to-do families who for social reasons were bent on having their offspring acquire a college education. The combination of social motivation on the one hand and high scholastic aptitude on the other presented the teachers of that day with a relatively simple problem. What we now call an old-fashioned curriculum enabled the graduates of those schools of the last century to enter college well prepared for further work in languages, in mathematics, and in the sciences. Those who could take it found the formal instruction excellent; those who couldn't or wouldn't dropped by the wayside as a matter of course. From the point of view of those on the receiving end-the professors in the colleges-this was a highly satisfactory situation. What sort of education the rest of the fourteen-to-eighteen-year-olds received was none of their affair!

In reviewing this bit of history in 1944, I was, of course, only reminding my audience of what most of them already knew. Professors of education had been pointing out for several decades that the faculties of arts and sciences had shown little interest in school problems. In the nineteenth century they had been quite ready to leave to the normal schools the task of preparing teachers for the elementary grades. When social changes in this century transformed the nature of the high school, the typical college professor himself was viewing with disgust and dismay what was happening in the schools. (I am reporting on personal observation of fifty years.) With few exceptions, college professors turned their backs on the problem of mass secondary education and eyed with envy Great Britain and the Continent, where such problems did not exist.

My plea for a truce, made while World War II was still in progress, had little if any effect. In fact the quarrel intensified in the 1950s because laymen entered the fray in increasing numbers and with increasing vehemence. Schools have always been subject to criticism by parents, but after the close of World War II, the criticism became more general and more bitter. The Russian success with Sputnik triggered a veritable barrage of denunciation of those in charge of public education. These attacks served to embitter the professors of education, who considered that the work of their former students—classroom teachers, principals, and superintendents—was being unfairly appraised. Since practically all public school administrators have studied at one time or another in teacher-training institutions or a school or department of education, they are bound by history and sympathy to the faculties of education. The same is true of a substantial proportion of classroom teachers. Mutual loyalty between professors and former students has led to the formation of something approaching a guild of professors of education and their erstwhile students. An attack on public education is therefore automatically an attack on schools and faculties of education. As a matter of fact, the connection is not always so indirect. Many a violent critic of our public schools has specifically attacked the professors of education.

One can understand the reaction of the members of the faculties of education, yet the criticism to which they were being exposed was not without its justification. The deficiencies in our public schools, particularly in our high schools, to which a number of writers (among whom I must include myself) have called attention, were in no small part a consequence of their activities. Despite the fact (often overlooked) that public school teachers and administrators have spent many more hours in the classrooms of professors of arts and sciences than in classes taught by professors of education, their attitude toward education has been largely shaped by the latter. The writings of education professors have also influenced the outlook of many parents. The emphasis on education for citizenship, on the socially unifying effects of the comprehensive high school, and on the public schools as instruments of democracy, the recognition of individual differences, and of the need for including practical courses in high school elective programs—all these characteristics, which I applaud, were the fruits of the labors of professors of education. These men, most of them now no longer active, are entitled to a large measure of credit for making American schools what they are. But by the same token, the historian must charge against them some of those features of our schools that their younger successors and the general public have recently criticized so heavily. In particular, the failure to challenge the academically talented youth, to provide adequate courses in modern foreign languages, and to emphasize English composition—now widely recognized as faults of the 1930s and 1940s—are in process of being corrected.

What happened after Sputnik might be characterized as the entry of the layman in force into a battle of professors. What is now involved is more than a quarrel among educators. The academic professors[1] have consciously or unconsciously enlisted the support of their alumni. We are therefore today dealing with two hostile camps. One camp is composed of professors of education allied with classroom teachers and public school administrators (though, like all alliances, it has its strains); the other is composed of professors of the sciences and the humanities and of influential collegiate alumni. Since the latter group includes radio and television commentators, editors, and publishers, the public school people and their mentors in some communities have faced a powerful set of forces. Along with the indignation of the professors of education frequently goes a sense of anxiety. "We who have shaped and improved our public schools are now being unfairly attacked, and there is danger that the public will be led astray!" Such thoughts are in the mind of more than one aging and honored individual who proudly carries the title of emeritus professor of education.

Why are the academic professors angry? What are they angry about? Many academic professors believe that the courses given by professors of education are worthless, and that the degrees granted students who have devoted much of their time to these courses are of little value. It is generally the case that the academic professors who advance these arguments know far too little about education courses. And unfortunately, what some professors of education have written about education can be labeled anti-intellectual. But what particularly irritates the academic professors is what professors of education say about teaching. After all, those who are engaged in college teaching usually pride themselves on their skill as teachers. And here are those who call themselves "professional educators" claiming that they and only they know what is good teaching! They imply, and sometimes openly state, that if all professors had taken their courses they would be better teachers! To make matters worse, in more than one state no one is permitted to teach in a junior college unless he has taken courses in education. If this is justified, the opponents ironically demand, why not require all teachers of freshmen and sophomores in four-year colleges to study under professors of education? To this question, professors of education often answer, "Such a requirement ought to be on the books."

And here we come to the issue about which emotions are most easily aroused—the issue of state requirements. Time was, not long ago, when in some states a school board could hire a teacher, and give him a permanent position, even if he had never even seen a professor of education. But those days are past. As a consequence, a graduate who has majored in an academic field must by hook or by crook meet the state requirements in education. (I shall be considering in a later chapter the various hooks and crooks now in use.) The fact that schools of education are beneficiaries of a high protective tariff wall is the single aspect of the present-day education of teachers that is most maddening to the academic professors.

In most states private schools can legally hire those they want. There is in these schools a free choice between teachers trained without benefit of courses in education and those trained as the state requires. Why shouldn't there be the same free choice in our public schools? The question is implicit in many of the attacks on schools of education. It is at the base of much of the hostility of lay critics, many of whom can cite examples of high-standing college graduates who are forced by state requirements to devote a certain number of hours to courses given by professors of education. It is hard to overestimate the bitterness of those who attack schools of education with such cases in their minds.

An inquiry into the history of certification reveals that this issue has long been a breeding ground of controversy. The struggle to control entrance to the teaching office is an old one, destined perhaps to continue indefinitely. The motives for certification were clearly recognized when modern state systems of education first emerged from the medieval systems of church schools, town or guild schools, and universities. With respect to all these schools, first clerical and later secular authorities assumed responsibility to protect the young from teachers whose influence might be morally—in those days considered inseparable from religiously—destructive. As far as the lower schools were concerned, their function was viewed primarily as one of religious indoctrination. The public interest was deemed insured when competent authority attested to the religious orthodoxy and moral reliability of potential teachers. As far as the universities were concerned, a second factor—mastery of the material to be taught—was considered necessary. This mastery was attested to by the university faculty through examinations leading to a university degree.

But the university faculty was in origin a medieval guild—indeed *universitas* was a rather general term for an organized guild—and hence the granting of a degree took on the added meaning of controlling membership in a group granted exclusive vocational rights to conduct a particular social service. Thus the combination of licensure and degree-granting power served three purposes: first, it protected the students from immoral influence; second, it insured mastery of the material to be taught; and third, it defined a group to which exclusive vocational rights to the teaching office were given.

On the university level the guild was able, in some periods, to playoff secular and religious authorities against each other in such a way that the guild established exclusive control of certification for persons in higher education. On the lower levels the result varied from nation to nation and school to school. In some cases religious authority held, in others secular, and in still others a blending of the two.

In the United States local secular authorities early established control, with respect to publicly supported schools, of the total process of certification, though, of course, religious leaders sometimes acted as agents of the secular community. These authorities utilized two screening devices: character witnesses, and oral or written examinations. But since local boards were often hard pressed to find any teacher, they were sorely tempted to tailor the examinations to whatever candidate became available. Indeed in some rural areas the examiners themselves were too unschooled to develop and evaluate rigorous examinations even if they were inclined to do so. Finally, local ethnic or religious prejudices, personal favoritism on the part of some board members, and, it must be said, simple graft often entered the process.

As state systems of education developed in the middle decades of the nineteenth century, the emerging state Departments of Education began to take over the examination function. The rate of change varied from state to state, and in some cases the system of local examination persisted well into the present century. Though the legal sovereignty of the state in educational matters is clearly recognized, the state has never assumed total control of the actual certification processes from such major communities as New York City, Chicago, Philadelphia, and St. Louis.

In many states, public normal schools (later teachers colleges), controlled by the state Departments of Education, emerged simultaneously with the state system of public schools. Before 1850, state Departments of Education had begun to accept as a basis for certification completion of a course of instruction in one of the normal schools or colleges they controlled. This alternative to examinations simplified their tasks. Thus, by 1850 several states had two certification devices: first, completion of an approved course of studies in a state-regulated institution; and second, examinations.

When, at the turn of the century, American education expanded in terms of the number of students and schools, a further complicating factor entered the picture: the amount of knowledge available increased explosively; and the amount required for effective citizenship and employment rose rapidly as the social and economic system grew more complex and technologically oriented. The question raised in England by Thomas Arnold and Herbert Spencer about "what knowledge is of greatest worth" became acute in American education generally, and in teacher education explicitly.

Among the bodies of knowledge, or literature, that grew most rapidly, was that having to do with the process of education itself. The normal-school people developed an extensive literature concerning the "science and art of teaching," and as university departments of education developed, research and speculation flourished both in them and in the related social science fields. Instructional materials ostensibly tailored to the growing interests and aptitudes of school-age youngsters came to abound. By 1900 the field of "education" had so developed that doctoral degrees were being awarded, and shortly thereafter one could specialize on the doctoral level in such fields as educational psychology, school administration, curriculum and instruction, and the history or philosophy of education.

In the normal schools, material concerning curriculum and instructional problems secured a major place. In universities in which a minority of the students and professors were directly concerned with teacher education, and in which the atmosphere was traditionally hostile to vocational education of any kind, the process moved more slowly. Since the state came more and more to depend for its supply of teachers on graduates of the universities and of colleges with traditional academic orientation, those who believed in the desirability of pedagogical courses found it necessary to utilize forces outside the colleges and universities. Their solution was a series of laws establishing requirements for courses in education to be taken by all candidates for certification. These early laws tended to assume that the collegiate and university faculties would make certain that the candidate was liberally educated and had adequately studied the subjects he proposed to teach. But college and university faculties were unwilling to tailor their academic requirements to the teaching assignments their graduates were to undertake, and as a result it often happened that teachers were not properly prepared in their subjects. When this became evident, the state certification officers began to require teaching "majors" of one sort or another. By this time, a new certification device had emerged: certification based on the successful completion of a specified set of courses taken in a collegiate institution which might or might not have been subject to state inspection and regulation.

It is important to note that such certification regulations were in a sense imposed on the universities and colleges as the result of pressure from a coalition of state Department officials and public school people. Just as the professors of the academic subjects had not, in general, been willing to assume active responsibility toward the public elementary and secondary schools, they did not welcome the responsibility for the professional preparation of teachers. Moreover, the academic faculties often felt that the professors of education employed to offer this instruction would not have been hired if it had not been for the state regulations, and resented what seemed to them external coercion. The professors of education, for their part, found that their own convictions coincided with those of state Department and public school personnel, and realized, too, that their source of greatest support was outside the university faculty; as a result, they were more careful to cultivate the outside group.

In modem form the traditional patterns of certification are all at present in contention. What is essentially new is the determination of academic professors, and their allies in the larger community, to minimize the influence that professors of education, State Department personnel, and other public school forces have traditionally held over the certification process.

I have perhaps stated the issue too simply. In some instances, quarrels ostensibly about teacher education serve to mask more fundamental conflicts over economic, political, racial, or ideological issues. Furthermore, there are professors of the arts and sciences who warmly support education courses, and there are professors of education and public school people among the leaders in the movement to strengthen the teachers' academic preparation. Moreover, in some institutions and states, the university faculties-academic and professional in concert-struggle to extend the institution's autonomy against attempts by the public school people, the state Departments, and other interest groups to control its programs.

Yet it remains true that certification requirements rank high among the sources of hostility between professors of education and their colleagues in academic faculties. This should not be surprising, for the importance of these requirements on campuses throughout the country is enormous.

One would like to look at the education of future teachers in terms of a free market of ideas, and this I endeavored to do in my visits to teacher-training institutions during this study. But I came to the conclusion that such an inquiry lacks reality. The idea of state certification is so thoroughly accepted that I have found it hard to get a serious discussion of the question "What would you recommend if there were no state requirements?"

As for the attitude of the students taking state-required courses, I must report that I have heard time and time again complaints about their quality. To be sure, by no means all students I interviewed were critical; so many were, however, that I could not ignore their repeated comments that most of the educational offerings were "Mickey Mouse" courses. There can be no doubt that at least in some institutions the courses given by professors of education have a bad name among undergraduates, particularly those intending to be high school teachers. To some extent, perhaps, this is simply because the courses are required. I am well aware, from my years of experience as a teacher of a subject required for admission to a medical school, that any required course has two strikes against it in the student's mind. I am also aware that in some institutions the critical attitude of the students toward the education faculty is fed by the devastating comments they hear from certain academic professors.

The subject of teacher education is not only highly controversial, but also exceedingly complicated. The complexities are hardly ever acknowledged by those who are prone to talk in such slogans as "those terrible teachers colleges" or "those reactionary liberal-arts professors." These slogans invariably represent a point of view so oversimplified as to be fundamentally invalid. This is not to say that either academic or education professors cannot be criticized. It is to say that neither side can be criticized to the exclusion of the other. *In the course of my investigations, I have found much to criticize strongly on both sides of the fence that separates faculties of education from those of arts and sciences.*

Earlier in this chapter I referred to the fact that the quarrel among educators had come to involve laymen. I had in mind, first of all, that teachers for our public schools are employed by local boards of education on the recommendation of the superintendent. Local boards are composed of laymen; therefore, these citizens are intimately concerned with the training of the teachers whom the boards employ. I had in mind also the fact that the freedom of the school board is limited by state requirements, which directly or indirectly are determined by laymen-the members of the legislature in each state. Indeed, the role of the state has been so important in shaping the development of teacher education that I am going to consider, in the next two chapters, first of all the way certification requirements are brought about in some of the more populous states, and then some of the policies that are actually employed today.

Unless one considers the relation of the state authorities to the school boards on the one hand, and the teacher-training institutions on the other, one is apt to miss what I consider a fundamental element in any plan for improving teacher education. The essential questions are: What role should the state play in the supervision of teacher education? And to what extent should universities and colleges be left free to experiment with new and different programs for educating teachers? My own answers to these questions will follow my report in Chapters 2 and 3 on current practices. Thereafter, I shall devote the remainder of the book to suggestion for a fresh approach to a four-year college program for teachers, and for improvements in current programs for teacher education beyond college.

I am aware that many educators resent the idea that laymen should have anything to do with education except to provide the funds. I do not agree with this point of view. What goes on in schools and colleges is far too important to be left entirely to the educators. The layman as a responsible member of a school board, a board of trustees, a legislature, or any public body, has a vital part to play. The layman as a citizen who votes and pays taxes has every reason to make his voice heard; as a parent and as an alumnus he should have concern with teacher education. What he says, however, should be based on an informed opinion. It is with the hope of developing such opinions that I have undertaken to write this book.

NOTE

1 The word "academic" has varying connotations; I shall use it to refer to those subjects traditionally taught in faculties of arts and sciences.

9.3 Teacher education and the predicament of reform

Gary Sykes

Source: Gary Sykes, Teacher education and the predicament of reform. In C. E. J. Finn, D. Ravitch and R. T. Fancher (eds.), *Against Mediocrity: The Humanities in America's High Schools*. New York: Holmes and Meier, 1984, pp. 172–194

A paradox lies at the heart of teacher education in America. For nearly half a century critics of all persuasions have scolded, even reviled, teacher education as a benighted and ill-starred enterprise, the very heel of our schooling system. Yet over this period teacher education has remained largely unchanged in important respects despite a variety of efforts at reform. True, the institution of teacher education has shifted from the normal school to the teachers college to the multipurpose university and the general educational level of teachers has risen. In 1961, nearly 15 percent of the teacher work force still held less than a bachelor's degree, while less than a quarter had earned a master's degree. By 1981, nearly one-half of all teachers held a master's degree (or more) while the other half were at least college graduates.[1] This may be counted true progress (although it paralleled a general rise in U.S. educational attainment over these two decades), but the debate over teacher education has never slackened, nor has the sense of malaise, of something badly amiss, lifted appreciably.

WHAT TROUBLES TEACHER EDUCATION

Teacher education involves a smorgasbord of enduring, unresolved difficulties along which critics in each era pass, making selections to fit the mood and spirit of the times. The central conflict has always involved the proper balance and relationship among what nearly everyone regards as the four necessary (and sufficient) components of a program: a strong liberal arts education, solid grounding in at least one subject area (particularly for secondary teachers), an introduction to education as a subject of inquiry and to an emerging science of pedagogy, and the opportunity to practice and experience teaching in a real yet controlled setting. So much appears self-evident as hardly to require elaborate justification for either individual parts or their constituency into a coordinated program of study and experience. Yet no practical synthesis has resolved the dialectics of this professional quadrivium, while the politics of teacher education have remained a zero-sum game featuring imperialist forays from the contending faculties of arts and sciences and of education.

An ambiguity of competence[2] lies at the core of this territorial dispute. Teaching, like many undertakings, involves the employment of both special and ordinary knowledge, but stands apart in its reliance on the extraordinary use of ordinary knowledge. Teaching style appears to depend largely on personality and on tacit, idiosyncratic approaches to human relations. To many, teaching, like parenting, is a "natural," "spontaneous," "organic" human activity. Knowing subject matter and caring about children are the primary ingredients for success, around which some technical embellishments can marginally matter. Given this basic view, the notion of a "scientific basis of the art of teaching,"[3] or of "sources of a science of education"[4] seems dubious, a mystification of an essentially simple, universal activity.

By another view, however, teaching is an enormously complicated act whose full import has eluded the increasingly sophisticated methodological and conceptual tools of the social sciences. In the last decade, however, progress has been made and the rudiments of a paradigm have emerged, giving promise for the steady advance that characterizes the coming of age of a scientific field. The great hope—a scientifically validated knowledge base, an emergent science of pedagogy—seems less forlorn now, and the modest successes with applications suggest that stronger links between knowledge and practice are in the offing. But these steps are neither widely known nor credited, and the grounding of competence in science is a project still open to doubt and to counterclaims about the kinds of knowledge most useful to the aspiring teacher.

There is, too, in teacher education an unhappy legacy to live down. Visitors to college campuses have too often come away with a low opinion of the actual quality of faculty, students, courses, and standards in schools and departments of education. The paint has long since dried this portrait of mediocrity, of insipid if not anti-intellectual fare, of pseudo scientific "methods courses" and a "professional" jargon which apes social science. (Koerner labeled it "educanto.") While the fraternity of teacher educators and researchers doggedly issues analyses proclaiming an imminent millennium if only the resources will be made available and the purposes properly fixed, the fleet of disconcerting reports sailing from the nation's campuses has belied such optimism. Conservatives, perennialists, and devotees of the liberal arts have gleefully contributed to or seized on this literature to support their position, but a close look at reports on education usually uncovers an indictment of higher education in general, with the faculties of arts and sciences coming in for their share of blame and criticism. Yet teacher education's position at the bottom of the academic pecking order is undisputed—a terrible handicap for those whose project is to raise up this enterprise via the fruits of science.

Complicating the indignities of internecine strife is the tenuous relation of teacher education programs to the schools. One dilemma here is common to professional education in all fields: to accept the conditions of practice, warts and all, preparing novices to fit a sadly imperfect status quo, or to take a critical stance toward current practice, imbuing the next generation with the need for change, with the imperative to make, not take, the role assigned. In teaching, though, there is evidence that suggests that socialization plays a far stronger role than formal training in shaping a teaching style. Research on the subject parcels formative influences into four sets of factors:[5] the "apprenticeship of observation" that teachers undergo during their fifteen thousand hours of experience as students;[6] the bureaucratic aspects of schools and the ecology of the classroom;[7] supervisors' and colleagues' impress on teachers;[8] and the impact of students as unintended agents of socialization.[9] So, while the stance to be taken toward the schools is a genuine vexation to teacher educators, alternately provoking calls for closer collaboration or ringing manifestos to raise consciousness and stimulate reform, teacher education appears such a "weak treatment" as to make moot the argument.

As a practical matter, however, schools of education must nurture relations with the schools, which after all serve as the training ground for beginners, provide a shadowy extension of the faculty in the form of "cooperating teachers," and supply the chief clientele for postbacalaureate course work and the consulting that supplements faculty incomes. This relationship remains uneasy at best, with little coincidence of interests. School men complain about how out of touch university faculty are, students typically find only their practice teaching helpful, and the professors who know how it should be done express dismay at the gap between their ideals and the realities of life in the classroom. Each point of view is valid; but the means for reconciliation or accommodation have not emerged. Hence, these laments persist generation after generation.

The shifting tasks and protean agenda of the schools make the relationship between the universities and the schools as unstable as it is uneasy. The remarkable growth of the school system has created serious strains, as educators have come to be expected to serve the full spectrum of the social structure. Likewise the transformation of the secondary school into a multipurpose social service agency has complicated the teacher's role and expanded the domain of responsibilities to this larger, more diverse clientele. Underlying these changes, however, has been a deeper conflict over the priority of excellence, equity, or efficiency in the school's mission. As the emphasis among these central cultural values has shifted from one era to the next, so too have the terms of criticism of the schools.

Teacher education is vulnerable in its own right to fluid social imperatives. While the training institutions must now prepare teachers for "the real world" of inner-city schools, for multicultural education, for educating the handicapped, for distinguishing the subtle bases for sex and race iniquities in their own and others' behavior, for the computer revolution, and so on, they must also act affirmatively in hiring and admissions while maintaining high standards and producing a teaching elite capable of training the advanced manpower for mastery in world technology markets. Neither schools nor universities can serve up such a volatile brew. After a while, both institutions may be permitted a modest dispensation for hunkering down and resisting change.

The status, wages, and other valuables associated with teaching constitute a final difficulty for teacher education. Teaching has always suffered an equivocal status compounded of respect and disdain, reverence and mockery, as amply depicted in the writings of Hofstadter, Elsbree, Waller, Lortie, and others. Moreover, some evidence suggests that teaching's occupational status actually declined between 1963 and 1980; according to one survey, teaching lost more ground than any other occupation ranked.[10] One telling indication of this trend comes from a Gallup Poll item. When asked "Would you like to have a child of yours take up teaching in the public schools as a career?" 75 percent of those surveyed responded yes in 1969, 67 percent in 1972, and only 48 percent in 1980.[11] To enhance the status and prospects of teacher education independently of the teaching occupation seems unlikely. Similarly, proposals to extend professional education for teachers run up against objections that few students would be willing to undergo a genuine training ordeal such as medicine requires or bear the costs of further schooling for the meager annual salaries and lifetime earnings teaching supplies.

That teaching is the closest thing to a mass profession may alone preclude a more elite status. Until the last decade, teaching regularly consumed 20 percent of the college labor market (35 percent of the market for college-educated women),[12] and training institutions were hard-pressed simply to supply the requisite numbers, regardless of quality. Indeed, easy access to teaching has historically served as both a potent recruitment incentive for individuals and a guarantee that supply would not lag too far behind demand in a tight labor market. The route to sovereignty in the true professions of law and medicine—restricted access under the protective mantle of a meritocratic ideology—was never available to an occupation whose single, overriding imperative was growth.

TWENTY YEARS' WORTH OF TEACHER EDUCATION

The oft called-for transformation of teacher education has failed through no lack of effort. Nearly everyone, it seems, has tried to reform teacher education; and our history is filled with task force and commission reports, with studies and recommendations, with association resolutions, government programs, foundation initiatives, legislation, and the rest. Teacher education has been the target for improvement both as an end in itself and as a means to effect other sorts of change in the schools and in the society at large. No assessment about what ails teacher education has yielded a consensus on what should be done, though, and the profession has proven vulnerable to a variety of enthusiasms, most of which has left little trace in their passing. A brief look at four reforms—The Master of Arts in Teaching, the Teacher Corps, Competency Based Teacher

Education, and recent state regulatory efforts—will serve to illustrate the trends over the past two decades.

Recruiting an elite: the master of arts in teaching

Beginning in the early 1950s and extending well into the 1960s, the Ford Foundation sponsored a bold new approach to teacher education. Over a fifteen-year period Ford committed some seventy million dollars in awards to over seventy universities to underwrite the establishment of a new teacher training program, the Master of Arts in Teaching (MAT). More specifically, Ford supported three types of programs: undergraduate training in a handful of liberal arts colleges, a five-year or fifth-year program, and the MAT. Most awards went to MAT programs to train secondary school teachers. These were alternatives, not sequels, to regular teacher education programs. They aimed at graduates of liberal arts programs and typically involved a summer school orientation on campus, then either a full- or half-time internship in a local school, supplemented by seminars and additional course work and perhaps a summer of course work after the internship. These postbaccalaureate programs resulted in a master's degree and a teaching certificate; the five-year programs yielded only the certificate but were integrated with the undergraduate course of study.

The significance of these programs lay not so much in their innovative approach to the education of teachers (although the programs accommodated a variety of experiments) as in their impact on recruitment. Ford's strategy was to enlist the elites among American universities to train a new cadre of teachers. Ford hoped that academically rigorous, selective programs at the nation's best universities would set a new standard for teacher education and would lure the best and brightest among college graduates. At the institutional level the elite universities would influence their less prestigious brethren via higher education's "snakelike progression" (David Riesman's phrase), the status hierarchy impelling lesser institutions to follow the leaders. At the individual level, programs offered both an inducement and the removal of a disincentive: to study with the finest faculty and peers at the finest universities, and to avoid the dreariness of education courses. The grant strategy, then, called for bypassing the existing system in favor of an elite alternative, and implicitly viewed the status quo as part of the problem.

Additionally, these programs aimed to strengthen the ties of teacher training to the schools and to the liberal arts. The internship provided an extended yet controlled opportunity to work in classrooms under apprenticeship conditions—a genuine improvement over the usual, meager practice teaching experience. And, most proposals promised a renewed commitment to a liberal education through involvement of Arts and Sciences faculty in planning and implementing the program. Beneath the diversity in individual programs lurked the fundamental assumption James Bryant Conant made in his study of teacher education: that a strong liberal arts education, an extended, well-supervised practicum, and a modest dose of course work in education constitute the ideal.

Essentially a recruitment strategy, the MAT suffered some obvious limits as a paradigm of reform. First, the allure of the program consisted not in some technical breakthrough that the elites could model for others, but in the cachet associated with the places themselves. The glamor of Harvard's simply being Harvard was not available in Pomona, Pierre, or Des Moines. Furthermore, the strategy relied on counteridentification with the status quo. Ford was consciously elitist in culling universities east of the Mississippi and north of the Mason-Dixon line that represented a liberal arts tradition very different from that of the mainline teacher training institutions. The aim, in part, was to enrich the pool of liberal arts graduates willing to teach by skirting the standard course of teacher education. The immediate appeal of such a strategy to education school deans and professors was not readily apparent.

The MAT failed to spread much beyond those few institutions that received Ford funds. Evidence on numbers completing MAT programs is fragmentary, but one study reported that in the three-year period 1961–1962 through 1963–1964, 4,114, students graduated, as compared with an annual production figure in those years of some 200,000 new teachers. MAT programs, then, accounted for less than 1 percent of the nation's new teachers.[13]

That only a handful of MAT programs are left testifies to their tenuous hold in the elite universities. Declining student enrollments and the teacher surplus of the 1970s hastened their demise. But even though the MAT programs were lively and exciting while they lasted, and anecdotal evidence suggests they were successful in attracting bright liberal arts graduates to teaching,[14] the handwriting was on the wall from the beginning. Teacher training had little enduring appeal for either liberal arts professors or faculty in graduate schools of education who wished to get on with training administrators and researchers. The mission of training teachers never gained much legitimacy, never secured core support, never engaged the faculty in the crucial roles of supervising interns, spending time in the schools, or conducting the companion seminars and courses. Teaching's low status ultimately confounded the attempt to enlist higher education's elite, who returned gratefully to traditional pursuits after this brief flirtation with teacher training.

Welcoming the great society: the teacher corps

Prior to the 1960s, the federal government was little involved with teacher education, but in the late 1950s it began what amounted to a sizable investment in the 1960s and 1970s. National defense provided the rationale.[15]

Initial government ventures aimed chiefly at improving teachers' subject matter competence via in-service activities. The programs operated through the existing institutional structure and eschewed fundamental reform. But as the conservative tenor of the 1950s gave way to the social activism of the 1960s, the federal government sponsored a range of more far-reaching programs, often in conjunction with the decade's major equity mandates. The government initiated or intensified training expenditures in vocational, compensatory, and higher education, in special education, and in bilingual education. Much of the funding went to teachers' in-service; but a number of programs were aimed at preservice training as well. In 1967, Congress passed the first piece of comprehensive legislation aimed at the development of educators, the Education Professions Development Act (EPDA). The act consolidated several existing program (e.g. Teacher Corps) and spawned twenty-five programs of its own. In its nine-year life (1967 to 1976), these programs accounted for expenditures of $781 million on a wide range of innovative projects.[16]

Over these decades Washington controlled the agenda for reform and set a brisk pace. Directly or indirectly the federal government provided the funds and mandates, the strategies, the leadership, and the influence networks through which flowed a powerful current of reform and innovation. By 1981 forty-three federal programs expended nearly $6 billion on personnel development with nine formula grant programs accounting for 90 percent of this total.[17] (The Reagan administration, however, has eliminated or consolidated and reduced the budget of many of these programs.) No other development in this period so profoundly influenced teacher education as this centralization of reform. The Teacher Corps represents a small but significant piece of this history, and is worth examining both in its own right and for its lessons about federal programmatic reform.

Created in 1964, the Teacher Corps was touted initially as a domestic Peace Corps. In its early years the project supported a two-year internship for liberal arts graduates who wished to serve in low-income schools. The original purposes included strengthening the education of disadvantaged children, attracting and preparing persons to teach such children through coordinated work-study experiences, and encouraging colleges and universities, schools, and state departments of education to work together in improving teacher education. The program's rationale stressed that there are critical differences between the skills, attitudes, and experiences required to teach successfully in low-income schools and in middle-class schools. The corps sought to recruit idealistic young people and to provide them with mediated entry to teaching in schools where they were most needed. The typical program involved from thirty to forty liberal arts graduates (interns) and five experienced teachers who acted as team leaders. Following a summer preservice training program at a college or university, each team was assigned to a school serving a poverty area. Interns spent some 60 percent of their weekly time in schools, 20 percent in academic work at the university, and 20 percent in community activities. This two-year course resulted in certification and a master's degree.

Due to its entrepreneurial leadership, the Teacher Corps enjoyed a chameleonlike existence over its sixteen-year history. Program guidelines emphasized a series of vanguard themes, including, "performance based teacher education, training complexes, portal schools, research adaptation, education of the handicapped, multicultural education, youth advocacy, basic skills, organization theory, and models of teaching."[18] When the teacher shortage of the 1960s turned into a teacher surplus in the 1970s, the program secured congressional authority in its 1974 reauthorization to work with in-service teachers, and in 1978 extended the time span of local projects from two to five years. Initiated as a service program, the focus shifted after 1975 to a demonstration strategy for training and retraining experienced teachers and teacher aides.[19]

The Teacher Corps had undergone seven major evaluations over the years, and its effectiveness as a reform strategy is unusually well documented.[20] During its ten years as a service program, the Teacher Corps, like the MAT programs, proved an effective recruitment strategy. Evidence from several projects in the early program cycles suggests that the corps successfully attracted bright, change-oriented college graduates. With backgrounds in the liberal arts, the early interns displayed academic aptitudes above those of graduate students in education (but still below the median of all graduate students).[21] Initially, the Corps attracted white, upper middle-class youth, but determined efforts to recruit minorities increased their representation in later cycles. Imbued with the spirit of the times, the new recruits were more change-oriented, politically liberal, independent, and aggressive than their veteran counterparts. However, those drawn to teaching exclusively by the Teacher Corps program were also most likely to drop out. While a majority of interns went into teaching upon graduation, most did not anticipate a career in the classroom but intended to take on other roles in education.[22] So it appears the Corps attracted a new breed of teachers but could not hold them long in the classroom.

Teacher Corps was less successful in altering institutional patterns within the schools, colleges, or universities. The program's early rhetoric urged the intern teams to serve as change agents within the schools, but the sources of resentment and resistance proved too strong. Veteran teachers regarded interns merely as apprentices useful in assisting with normal duties. Filled with the program's reform rhetoric the interns sought greater influence and often threatened the regular teachers with their radical ideas. The intern status could not easily accommodate the dual roles of change agent and apprentice. Interns possessed neither the technical knowledge nor the formal position to support their posture, so the schools shrugged them off. Some interns became radical and alienated in the process, while others were co-opted.

Colleges and universities, too, made few concessions to the program and resisted a more enduring involvement with the schools. Teacher Corps projects stimulated the addition of some new courses and raised consciousness about the special problems of teaching in low-income schools but failed to promote closer ties with higher education. The interns were more critical of the universities than any other aspect of the program. They found their courses irrelevant and judged that their professors knew little about teaching the disadvantaged and were less academically qualified than their undergraduate professors. The faculty acutely felt their inadequacies in educating the interns but themselves had no contact with the schools, no relevant, special knowledge to impart, and no solid commitment to the projects.

Teacher Corps projects also had difficulty overcoming the social isolation between schools and universities and could not supply the incentives for true collaboration. Vested interests within the higher education community resisted new missions, new priorities, or any reallocation of resources. When changes occurred, they tended to be superficial add-ons. Boundary-spanning personnel—the project director, team leaders, or unusually dedicated university faculty—sometimes created effective partnerships, but, "the hoped-for 'hybrid' professional, trained in the social sciences but concerned with the application of knowledge to educational practice, seldom appeared."[23] In short,

> The institutions operated under different incompatible incentive systems and had independent publics and resources. The schoolteachers were precariously trying to maintain daily teaching schedules with inadequate resources, often in the face of challenges from both students and the community. They were not primarily responsible for training and resisted being used as laboratories unless they had been provided with assistance or other benefits. University professors were oriented to an academic status system and were insulated from the operational pressures of school teaching and from the unruly or dull classrooms. Therefore, they could not provide the practical guidance and necessary leadership that interns needed. The interns were trapped between the university, which controlled their professional certification and the schools, which controlled their professional experiences.[24]

Ambitious in scope, complex in conception and execution, the Teacher Corps took on a number of long-standing problems plaguing both teaching and teacher education: the difficulty of recruiting talented college graduates to teach in low-income schools, the lack of attention to pedagogy suited to disadvantaged and minority students, the remoteness of colleges and universities purporting to train teachers from the schools, the strong resistance to change in the public schools themselves. Like other helping professions in the 1960s, teaching proved vulnerable to government intervention on behalf of society's neglected and oppressed. The profession could not resist these external pressures; but in a decentralized system and without a consensus, federal authority was not strong enough to affect institutional patterns and reward systems. Working within the existing system, subject to the constraints of special interest politics and of organizational inertia within the schools, the program had but modest long-term impact.

Quest for certainty: competency based teacher education

In the late 1960s a number of themes in our political culture converged in a reform known as Competency Based Teacher Education (CBTE). The movement toward this reform drew support from the U.S. Office of Education, from several state departments of education, from the American Association of Colleges for Teacher Education (AACTE), from a handful of vanguard universities eager to innovate, and from a group of educational researchers. These groups stimulated intense interest in CBTE for a time, but the reform failed to attract widespread support and faded away in the face of retrenchment pressures in the 1970s. CBTE, however, represents a persistent strain in American education: a powerful yearning for method, for system, for certainty. Moreover, the fact of this reform illustrates education's difficulty with establishing a knowledge base. It is, then, worthy of attention beyond its impact.

Competency Based Teacher Education was an attempt to gain technical control over the preparation of teachers, to ground a professional curriculum in science, and to establish its measure for purposes of public accountability. The method, behaviorist in spirit, had the straightforward appeal of an engineering feat. Steps in the process called for, first, the decomposition of teaching into a set of discrete competencies, empirically validated through their connection to learning outcomes; then development of a training program within which students would learn the appropriate behaviors, via practice and coaching; close evaluation of students to determine their mastery of the competencies, with additional training prescribed for those who required it; and finally, certification based on mastery of the mandated competencies.

Proponents of this approach did not claim that teaching is simply a finite bundle of skills, nor did they deny that teaching is an artistic activity involving improvisation. Rather they argued that effective teachers exhibit skills that can be precisely identified and transmitted. The business of an initial training program is to provide such skills to novices as the foundation for development of a mature teaching style. This rationale at once supplied an implicit critique of current practice, a powerful appeal based on culturally authoritative symbols, and an orderly agenda for progress.

Status-quo training programs suffered, according to competency advocates, from two major shortcomings: a failure to base the professional curriculum on empirically validated knowledge, and a lack of precision and specificity in setting forth the skills of teaching to be mastered. Teacher education was at once too abstract, too impractical, and too trivial. Coursework failed to connect theory to practice, while methods courses deserved their ill repute as whimsical collections of gimmicks. A competency-based approach would remedy these defects through introduction of scientific rigor. Teaching would be systematically analyzed, and its core elements extracted, then validated through research. The result would be a training program organized around a set of competencies enjoying science's imprimatur.

CBTE as a rallying point had a number of obvious appeals, the primary one being that it promised to establish the intellectual legitimacy of teacher education through a grounding in science. In an era marked by increasing accountability demands on public service providers, CBTE offered the means and a commitment from educators for such an accounting. A fully developed program would utilize social science's most powerful and sophisticated technology— testing—to monitor progress, to diagnose difficulties, and to certify graduates. Professional educators would have the tools to gauge student progress, to prescribe extra and remedial work, and to identify those who lacked all aptitude and should therefore be counseled out of teaching. Rigor, precision, and control: these were the virtues around which to reconstitute a course of training.

CBTE possessed a further virtue as well. The design of teacher education around a set of competencies was a development largely internal to schools and departments of education, strengthening their claim to professional standing within the university. CBTE was a technical reform involving an orderly agenda of research and development. If the movement's leadership could establish the paradigm's power and gain a consensus within the educational community on its general outline, then widespread, concerted efforts could go forward and "normal science" (in Thomas Kuhn's sense)[25] could take shape. Furthermore, a technical breakthrough would strengthen the hand of educators seeking to secure greater resources for pedagogical education. CBTE's proponents recognized that at the time there was no set of empirically validated, generic teaching competencies, but hoped that a sustained, united commitment to the approach from the profession would gradually yield such knowledge.

Creating competency programs required a substantial initial investment of faculty time and cooperation, but in the late 1960s several universities undertook such efforts, stimulated by modest funds from foundations and the U.S. Office of Education (which expended some $12 million, mostly for conferences, dissemination, model building, and the like). Some schools, including Weber State College, the University of Houston, Toledo University, and Florida International, recast their entire programs; others, notably Brigham Young University, the University of Texas-El Paso, and Western Washington State University, established alternative programs. There was never a careful account of how many institutions participated, but a 1972 AACTE survey of 783 institutions turned up 125 that claimed to have such programs, with 366 others in the developmental stage.[26] (What "developmental stage" meant, though, was not clear.) Another AACTE publication provides details on seventeen programs located in thirteen institutions, with the range of effort from modest experiments to total conversion.[27] The slender record suggests that the reform stirred up enormous interest, spawned a large volume of talk and publication, but had near negligible impact in the universities themselves.

Competency education's difficulties are instructive both for the technical problems that proved insurmountable and for the opposition that the reform provoked. The yearning for a knowledge base could not compensate for its absence. In the face of multiple conceptions of teaching, multiple interpretations of classroom realities, and multiple educational aims, the hoped-for consensus on a unifying paradigm never emerged. Without the discipline of relatively unambiguous, fixed ends, the technical project of securing the means-ends relationship could not advance. And the attempt to validate teaching competencies through their association with student outcomes soon provoked challenges on grounds:[28] the evidence was impeachable and the research community divided on its worth.

Furthermore, the notion of a teaching competency itself proved more troublesome than helpful. There was no agreement on whether a competency was big or small, referred to "knowing how" as well as "knowing that," or was subject-specific or generic. The effort to provide behavioral specificity yielded nearly a thousand competencies by one reckoning.[29] To avoid the traditionally loose, abstract, and behaviorally unanchored accounts of teaching, competency logic drove to a ludicrously atomized conception which in the same manner failed to provide guidance to teacher training. Just as overwhelming was the task of assessment. Reform rhetoric promised both accountability and individualization via a measurement and tracking system to chart each student's progress toward mastery of hundreds of competencies. But the measures were fallible to nonexistent, and the management burdens enormous. In short, the behaviorist approach, so appealing in its promise of rigor, system, and method, could not carry the intended freight.

As the CBTE vanguard grappled with these problems, opposition also took form. Humanists quickly became suspicious of competency education on a number of counts. Harry Broudy, for example, worried that the approach reduced teaching to the imparting of information and thus sacrificed its other modes and dimensions.[30] He argued that teaching involves more than skillful behavior, that teachers must develop understanding of their actions as educators and must be able to consider ends as well as employ skills. If teachers were to be more than craftsmen following set routines, asserted Broudy, then their education must include theory and must aim at creating a capacity for reflection and flexible action. Yet he saw little appreciation for this in the competency approach. In his view, CBTE actually threatened to deprofessionalize teaching by turning out proficient technicians, not full professionals.

Yet another critic feared a bias against intellect, against what was "merely academic." He first asked, "Does competence based education reduce the teacher to a coach merely drilling people to pass exams? Does the competence approach kill all true education or deeper thinking?"[31] Not necessarily, he thought. A more moderate rhetorical question expresses his view: "Does competence based education lead students and teachers to be predominantly pragmatic? Not simple-minded or trivial or blindly mechanical, mind you, but does it lead to a slight narrowing in the range of human styles, away from creativity, intuition, play, humor, and purely disinterested curiosity? Is the spirit of competence, in short, the spirit of instrumentalism?"[32] Thus did humanists come to characterize competency education as at worst illiberal, anti-intellectual, and technicist, and at best merely an admonition to teacher educators to think harder about what they were doing.

CBTE was a bootstrap operation by déclassé teacher training institutions to gain credibility and prestige in an era of accountability, a technical reform internal to the school of education, whose rhetoric drew upon powerful cultural themes. Its proponents hoped this sort of inexpensive, nonthreatening innovation would support their argument for a truly professional school and for more "life space" in the university. However, the requisite technical knowledge never appeared at the party thrown in its honor, and program conversion along competency lines proved more expensive than anticipated. One calculation, likely an underestimate, placed the cost at $5–6 million per institution, with a total system cost over twenty years of $100 million.[33] During CBTE's brief period of fashionability, most institutions found it cheaper to adopt little but the rhetoric.

Faced with philosophical and political opposition and fraught with technical difficulties, this reform's liabilities outweighed its benefits in the eyes of most teacher educators. Championed by lesser institutions, CBTE failed to enlist opinion leaders in higher education's pantheon. It was, in short, a very shallow ripple on a large pond, one that illustrated the difficulties in establishing a knowledge base for teaching and the danger in premature sponsorship of an ill-conceived technical reform.

Crisis of confidence: state regulation of teaching

As foundations, universities, and the federal government have all attempted to recast teacher education in various images, so too have state policymakers intermittently taken an interest. Their tools, however, have been regulations rather than programs, funds, or new knowledge, and the history of state regulation reflects teacher education's uneasy regard among the public. State certification and licensing laws have the dual potential to protect the public interest via standard setting and to enhance professional status by restricting entry and requiring special courses of study. The legitimacy of such laws rests on the public's perception of an equivalence between these functions, but the relationship is weak. Without scientific breakthroughs or potent technologies, teacher education must rely to a considerable degree on trust that its mission is valuable and useful. Perceptions that the schools, hence the teachers, are failing threaten this trust and impel state regulation as protection *from*, not protection *of*, professional autonomy.

Over the decades, the states have tirelessly tinkered with the certification law. Early on, many states and localities used literacy tests to screen candidates. In the 1830s, for example, Illinois state legislator Abraham Lincoln voted in favor of a teacher exam,[34] which became common by the century's turn. But as schooling levels rose and normal schools sprang up, states began to require years of schooling, then courses in education for certification. By 1940 the course requirements approach had largely superseded examinations, with additive reform—more years of schooling, more required courses in education—the progression thereafter.[35] Twenty years later, however, Conant reflected much public opinion in labeling such policy bankrupt. The low repute of education courses made their mandate through state policy an embarrassment. States, it appeared, were conspiring with the "education establishment" to require a fraudulent set of courses that had failed to demonstrate their worth.

This mounting criticism posed a crisis of legitimacy for teacher educators. Their clients (the students) expressed great dissatisfaction, Arts and Sciences faculties decried the wasteland of teacher education, and policymakers were becoming uneasy. However, two events forestalled action. First, the teacher shortages of the 1950s and 1960s turned to a surplus. Enrollments declined in teacher education, and few new teachers entered the schools. Concern consequently shifted from preservice education to renewal of an aging work force already in place. And, second, the 1960s' preoccupation with equity and civil rights intervened to shift the ground of criticism and the agenda for public policy. Relevance and rights, not rigor, became the watchwords, and the critiques of Conant, Koerner, and Silberman[36] for the moment lost their salience. The locus of reform shifted, as well, from the state to the federal level and over the next decade state policy took shape largely in response to the cascade federal initiatives.

Enrollment declines and the social ferment of the 1960s and 1970s merely deferred the fundamental dissatisfaction with the quality of teacher education expressed earlier. By the mid-1970s, public worry over the test score drop, over reports of lax discipline in the schools, and over a general decline in standards was paramount. The academic adequacy of teachers became an issue as the press reported cases of teachers who wrote and spoke ungrammatically and who could not spell. The suspicion also took hold that some training institutions, faced with enrollment declines, had lowered entry standards to maintain their share of students. The demand for quality control led to the reintroduction of testing in state after state, so that at present thirty-six states have mandated some form of test for entry to a teacher education program and/or for certification.[37]

Some jurisdictions have extended their concern for teacher quality further still. Georgia sends observers into beginning teachers' classrooms to rate their performance on fourteen teaching competencies. South Carolina has required increased practice teaching, more observation and evaluation of teachers, and additional credits for recertification. Oklahoma's new Bill 1706 similarly mandates more clinical fieldwork and an entry-year internship during which a committee composed of a principal, a consulting teacher, and a teacher educator regularly monitors the first-year teacher and recommends either certification or further supervision at year's end.

The states have emerged as standard bearer for teacher education. While the older "approved-program approach" to certification—i.e. graduates of approved programs were certified simply because they were graduates of approved programs—implicitly reposed confidence in the training institutions, this new body of law regulates teaching in the name of public protection. Through tests, the states have extended their influence indirectly to the curriculum of teacher education, as training institutions must now ensure that their graduates can pass the tests. States are no longer willing to trust the profession to set standards. They have intervened firmly and in the name of accountability. To some extent, teacher education's interests have benefited from the new legislation which they have helped shape, but in many respects state regulatory action reflects the lack of public confidence in teaching and the loss of esteem for teachers. By emphasizing basic skills and general rather than professional knowledge, the tests themselves are demeaning and seem to imply that any reasonably bright college graduate can teach.

For years teacher organizations have pressed a professional governance model on state policymakers, and a half dozen states currently support professional practice boards with teacher membership. But vesting regulation of the teaching occupation in its practitioners enjoys no widespread support, and the unions' use of professional rhetoric and strategy is not credible anywhere. Unions exist to protect the rights of their members; but the rationale for professional control, especially among public employees, rests not on an assertion of rights but on claims of technical expertise and of the public interest.

The states, though, can do little else through a regulatory approach than set minimums and thereby symbolize a concern for standards. Though the most academically deficient will be denied access to teaching, at the program level little is likely to change. These recent state responses fail to address one of the fundamental dilemmas facing teacher education: that without additional resources, it cannot demonstrate its worth; yet without such a demonstration, it cannot secure additional resources. This dilemma ultimately frames teacher education's relation to the state and makes vivid the crisis of confidence.

Prospects for an enlightened future

These various efforts over the years to reform teacher education achieved some limited and temporary success, but could not effect a thoroughgoing transformation. The enterprise as a whole seems fixed by a range of institutional, demographic, and economic forces at an unacceptably low level of quality, incapable of setting and enforcing—or even of articulating and projecting—high standards. Invidious distinctions of status among the institutions of higher education, among departments and schools within the university, and between the universities and the schools frustrate the search for a common cause. Despite decades of earnest labor and some progress, no research paradigm has emerged to order the pursuit of knowledge and no cognitive base organizes, unifies, and legitimates the professional curriculum. Inevitably the mission is shortchanged. Teacher education is underfunded and lacks institutional "life space." It is a small, old outboard propelling a very large cabin cruiser through the water at an unsurprisingly slow rate.

Several recent developments have complicated these woes. Unionism has replaced professionalism as a strategy for advancement among teachers. An overlay on existing status tensions, unionism has further estranged teachers from teacher educators in terms of their organizational interests and public posture, rendering even more suspect the rhetoric of professionalism. And, as enrollments in teacher education dropped 50 percent between 1972 and 1980, thereby threatening the survival of many programs, coping with decline superseded programmatic reform. Retrenchment proved inhospitable to the quest for excellence. Simultaneously the states intensified their regulation of teacher education, exposing its vulnerability to external control. This policy development revealed teacher education's inherent weakness in relation to the state: the public confidence required for control over teaching to be vested in teacher education institutions has been based more on inattention than approval.

Most friendly critics appreciate that reforms of teacher education stand little chance unless linked to changes in the schools, in the teaching occupation, and in the policy framework shaping the whole enterprise. They emphasize that teacher salaries must be higher, that working conditions must better support teachers,[38] that teaching must attract and hold more academically able recruits, and that state policy—particularly allocation formulas to the universities—must supply more resources.[39]

If the past is prologue in teacher education, then widespread, comprehensive reform is unlikely. The prospect of converting teacher education to a postbaccalaureate program (whether integrated with the undergraduate curriculum or not) appears slim. To require an extended program of training for all new teachers without a corresponding increase in the rewards of teaching is not feasible: market pressure will continue to dominate standards. Likewise, no major reallocation or infusion of resources to teacher education is likely. The training venture has not gained sufficient warrant for this, in part because its rationale is derivative: teacher education exists to improve teaching. With ever-present arguments that both teaching and teacher education are underfunded, and without an impressive demonstration of the latter's potency, policymakers will most often direct funds to teaching itself. Finally, social science knowledge is unlikely to rationalize a technical transformation of the professional curriculum. No paradigm orders inquiry in education, no "sciences of the artificial" nor eclectic arts conjoin basic knowledge and design;[40] rather, the technical base grows fitfully and in small increments.

Short of ambitious reforms, though, teacher education has several modest prospects. Both the MAT strategy and the Teacher Corps demonstrated that special programs can enhance status, supply an esprit otherwise lacking, and recruit able college graduates despite teaching's low pay. For a limited number of prospective teachers a selective postbaccalaureate program highly regarded by the university and by the community will be attractive. The MAT approach never received much trial in the mainline institutions, yet might well serve as an alternative on more campuses.

Efforts to extend training into the first year of teaching point to another promising trend. State-mandated induction or intern programs such as Oklahoma's join the university and the schools in providing more support, supervision, and evaluation for first-year teachers, a step intermediate to and less costly than a full extended program. Intern programs have several virtues: they are job-related, do not defer income for young teachers, can involve experienced teachers in passing along their lore, and provide a performance base for certification. The Teacher Corps experience underscored the importance of boundary spanners between universities and schools, and the new state mandates may help provide a framework within which such positions will develop. They appear crucial to effective collaboration.

Finally, the gradual accumulation of usable pedagogical knowledge provides a more spacious avenue for technical improvements in the professional curriculum. For some time advocates have faulted the training programs for failing to stay abreast and failing to use the best available knowledge, arguing that the translation and use of knowledge, not its quality or quantity, are the fundamental problems. Progress in the coming decades, then, will take the form of better knowledge use in the training program, and stronger connections between research and training.

The neglected dimension

Interpreted in broad outline, teacher education appears trapped in a force-field admitting only small movements in any direction. Yet other histories and interpretations are available. This broad interpretation of teacher education's status omits consideration of the individual institutions where stories of success and failure, triumph and tragedy, progress and stasis have played out over the decades. A bit of determinism often accompanies history as global sweep, denying the choices and maneuvering room actually open to individuals. But let us step down from the slow movements of history and the grand strategies of reformers to the prospects for renewal and excellence in particular institutions and glimpse other possibilities.

Worry over what is lacking in teacher education often centers on such things as funds, status, standards, life space, and knowledge, with corresponding attention to these resources in reform proposals. Yet this emphasis on the instrumental neglects an important dimension in the lives of individuals and institutions. What is most fundamentally missing in teacher education is both a conception and conviction of its value. The enterprise of preparing teachers in our society is not esteemed, and the consequences of this lack of esteem are devastating. Without sufficient caring we have no appreciative framework for teacher education, no shared conception of quality, no capacity to recognize or vocabulary to describe excellence, nor occasions to celebrate it. The process of educating teachers is essentially invisible, a sure sign of its undervaluation in our culture.

The outward manifestations of this problem should now be clear, but there is a toll on the inner life as well. Every professional practice requires a discourse continuously enriched through reference to transcendent ideals. Central to human services is a sense of mission powerful enough to inspire and sustain, to give meaning and significance to the work. Without occasions for pride and a sense of connection to important values, the vicissitudes of human service work can be great. As any teacher will acknowledge, working with others has both a light and dark side, an inevitable feature in the pursuit of ideals that at once compel but admit no easy realization. Teaching can provide joy and fulfillment, but can be frustrating and enervating, too. Visions of excellence nourish the light side, enabling buoyancy and resilience. Their absence leads to low morale, failure of nerve, loss of expectations.

Missing from the rhetoric of reform in teacher education is much attention to this expressive side, to the inner life of the enterprise. Consider, by contrast, the emphasis in some recent writing on management that hails the creation of corporate cultures as a hallmark of excellence.[41] In these accounts of successful businesses and business leaders, it is not technological breakthroughs or rational management schemes that matter, but attention to the human side of enterprise. The corporate exemplars stand for and communicate a set of values through rites and rituals, organizational sagas, and proud traditions filled with heroes and champions. The new language used to describe corporate life is remarkably primitive, smacking more of Margaret Mead on Samoa than of Harold Geneen at ITT. It is an anthropological language redolent of mythology and symbolism, a language appropriate to the centrality of values.

"Companies succeed," claims one observer, "because their employees can identify, embrace, and act on the values of the organization."[42] So, too, do programs of teacher education, yet preoccupations there are unrelievedly literal, instrumental, and parochial. The rhetoric is too often plaintive, too seldom inspirational. Needed is not another six-point program of reform complete with arguments pro and con and steps toward implementation, but eloquently rendered visions of excellence. To repeat: what the leadership has most sadly neglected in teacher educa-tion is not resource calculations or the mechanics of reform but reasons and ways to care.

This concern for value, for meaning, is no mere froth on the bracing brew of hard-headed practice. Rather it is something more serious, more fundamental to the life of an institution. Although I have argued that the larger predicament of teacher education is in a sense tragic—the show must go on but with no promise of greatness on a grand scale—there is room for affirmation and progress at any institution that prepares teachers. But the starting point for those who are interested—the university president, the dean, the professors—must be with the value of the enterprise itself, even in the face of public indifference, narrow institutional confines, and resource poverty. Teacher education needs its heroes, its sagas, its proud traditions that embody and convey what is valuable in the undertaking. This, I judge, is the place to start.

NOTES

1 National Education Association, *Status of the American Public School Teacher, 1980–81* (Washington, DC: National Education Association, 1982), p. 21.

2 For this phrase and the related ideas, I am indebted to David Cohen. See his unpublished manuscript, "Commitment and Uncertainty," May 1982 (available from D. Cohen, Harvard Graduate School of Educa-tion, Harvard University, Cambridge, MA 02139).

3 N. L. Gage, *The Scientific Basis of the Art of Teaching* (New York: Teachers College Press, 1978).

4 John Dewey, *The Sources of a Science of Education* (New York: Liveright, 1929).

5 For a good brief summary of evidence on teacher socialization, see K. M. Zeichner and B. R. Tabachnick, "Are the Effects of University Teacher Education 'Washed Out' by School Experiences?" *Journal of Teacher Education* 32, no. 3 (May–June 1981), 7–11; and K. M. Zeichner, "Myths and Realities: Field-Based Experiences in Preservice Teacher Education," *Journal of Teacher Education* 31, no. 6 (November–December 1980), 45–55.

6 See chapter 3 in Dan Lortie, *Schoolteacher* (Chicago: University of Chicago Press, 1975).

7 Research by Wayne Hoy and colleagues emphasizes how the bureaucratic aspects of school shape teachers' pupil control ideology. See W. Hoy, "The Influence of Experience on the Beginning Teacher," *School Review* 76 (1968), 312–323; W. Hoy, "Pupil Control Ideology and Organizational Socialization: A Further Examination of the Influence of Experience on the Beginning Teacher," *School Review* 77 (1969), 257–265; and W. Hoy and R. Rees, "The Bureaucratic Socialization of Student Teachers," *Journal of Teacher Education* 28, no. 1 (January–February 1977), 23–26. A variety of studies explore the struc-tural characteristics of classrooms that affect teachers. See, for example, P. Jackson, *Life in Classrooms* (New York: Holt, Rinehart, and Winston, 1968); R. Dreeben, "The School as Workplace," in R. Travers, ed., *The Second Handbook of Research on Teaching* (Chicago: Rand McNally, 1973); R. Sharp and A. Green, *Education and Social Control* (London: Routledge & Kegan Paul, 1975); and W. Doyle, "Learn-ing the Classroom Environment: An Ecological Analysis," *Journal of Teacher Education* 28, no. 6 (November 1977), 51–55.

8 See D. Edgar and R. Warren, "Power and Autonomy in Teacher Socialization," *Sociology of Education* 42 (1969), 386–399; for a study of superteachers see G. McPherson, *Small Town Teacher* (Cambridge: Harvard University Press, 1972). See also R. Parelius, "Faculty Cultures and Instructional Practices," unpublished manuscript, Rutgers University, September 1980.

9 See, for example, W. D. Copeland, "Student Teachers and Cooperating Teachers: An Ecological Relation-ship," *Theory into Practice* 18 (June 1979), 194–199; and S. S. Klein, "Student Influence on Teacher Behavior," *American Educational Research Journal* 8 (1971), 403–421.

10 G. R. Reinhart, "The Persistence of Occupational Prestige," paper presented at the Southern Sociological Society, Louisville, KY, 1981.

11 "The 12th Annual Gallup Poll of the Public's Attitudes Toward Public Schools," *Phi Delta Kappan* 62 no. 1 (September 1980), 38.

12 National Center for Education Statistics, *Projections of Education Statistics to 1988–89* (Washington, DC: NCES, 1980), pp. 63–64.

13 James Stone, *Breakthrough in Teacher Education* (San Francisco, CA: Jossey-Bass, 1968), pp. 156–157.

14 For example, Stone, ibid., p. 158, reports that in 1961–1962 and 1962–1963, 2,187 teachers successfully completed experimental programs, of whom 78 percent were teaching in the subsequent year. During the same period 16,117 completed the conventional program in these same institutions, of whom only 49 percent were teaching in the following year. He further reports that a six-year follow-up of University of California-Berkeley MAT graduates, 1956 to 1962, reveals a sizable number still teaching, with a similar report from Harvard in the first decade following World War II (under President Conant, Harvard had established its MAT program before the Ford Foundation became involved).

15 Wayne Welch, "Twenty Years of Science Curriculum Development: A Look Back," in *Review of Research in Education*, ed. D. Berlinger, vol. 7 (Washington, D.C.: American Educational Research Association, 1979), pp. 282–306.

16 Roy Edelfelt and Margo Johnson, "A History of the Professional Development of Teachers," in *The 1981 Report on Educational Personnel Development* ed. E. Feistritzer (Washington, DC: Feistritzer Publications, 1980), pp. 44–56. See also Don Davies, "Reflections on EPDA," *Theory into Practice*, 13 (June 1974), 210–217.

17 Feistritzer, pp. 134–135.

18 Edelfelt and Johnson, p. 54.

19 Gary Sykes, "An Overview of the Teacher Corps Program, 1965–1982" (Washington, DC: U.S. Department of Education, unpublished report, undated), pp. 22, 25.

20 For a succinct review of six of these seven studies, see G. Thomas Fox, "Limitations of a Standard Perspective on Program Evaluation: The Example of Ten Years of Teacher Corps Evaluations" in James Steffenson, *et al.*, *Teacher Corps Evaluation* (Omaha: University of Nebraska, 1978), pp. 11–86.

21 Ronald Corwin, *Reform and Organizational Survival: The Teacher Corps as an Instrument of Educational Change* (New York: John Wiley, 1973), pp. 81ff.

22 See Corwin, p. 93, and Fox, p. 54.

23 Corwin, p. 378.

24 Ibid., pp. 370–371.

25 The distinction between "normal" and paradigm-shattering science is made in Thomas Kuhn, *The Structure of Scientific Revolutions* (Chicago: University of Chicago Press, 1970).

26 W. Robert Houston, "Competency Based Education," in *Exploring Competency Based Education*, ed. W. B. Houston (Berkeley, CA: McCutchan Publishing Corporation, 1974), p. 4.

27 Iris Elfenbein, "Performance-Based Teacher Education Programs: A Comparative Description," PBTE Series, no. 8 (Washington, DC: AACTE), October 1972.

28 See, for example, R. W. Heath and M. A. Neilson, " 'The Research Basis for Performance-Based Education," *Review of Educational Research* 44 no. 4 (Fall 1974), 463–484.

29 See Normal Dodl, *et al.*, *The Florida Catalog of Teacher Competencies* (Tallahassee, FL: Florida State Department of Education, 1973).

30 Harry Broudy, "A Critique of Performance-Based Teacher Education," PBTE Series, no. 4 (Washington, DC: AACTE, May 1972).

31 Peter Elbow, "Trying to Teach While Thinking About the End," in *On Competence: A Critical Analysis of Competence-Based Refoms in Higher Education*, ed. Gerald Grant *et al.* (San Francisco, CA: Jossey-Bass, 1979), p. 125.

32 Ibid.

33 Bruce Joyce, *Estimating Costs of Competency Orientation* (New York: Teachers College, Columbia University, 1973).

34 This historical fact is cited in Joseph Cronin, "State Regulation of Teacher Preparation," in *Handbook of Teaching and Policy*, ed. L. Shulman and G. Sykes (New York: Longman, 1983), p. 178.

35 See Willard Elsbree, *The American Teacher* (New York: American Book Co., 1939), chapter 24.

36 These three authors overlapped substantially in their critique of the status quo in teacher education. See James B. Conant, *The Education of American Teachers* (New York: McGraw-Hill, 1963); James D. Koerner, *The Miseducation of American Teachers* (Boston: Houghton Mifflin Company, 1963); and Charles E. Silberman, *Crisis in the Classroom* (New York: Random House, 1971).

37 J. T. Sandefur has been tracking the development of teacher competency tests. He reports that the turn to teacher tests began in 1977, and that of the 36 states involved, 21 test or plan to test applicants for

admission to teacher education programs, while 28 states test or plan to test prior to certification. Ten states now also require some on-the-job assessment, usually a one-year internship or induction program for beginning teachers. See J. T. Sandefur, "Teacher Competency Assessment Plans 'Little Short of Phenomenal' " (Washington, D.C.: AACTE Briefs, November 1982).

38 See Donna H. Kerr, "Teaching Competence and Teacher Education in the United States," in Shulman and Sykes, pp. 143–144, and Hendrick D. Gideonse, "The Necessary Revolution in Teacher Education," *Phi Delta Kappan* 64 no. 1 (September 1982), 15–18.

39 B. O. Smith, "Pedagogical Education: How About Reform?" *Phi Delta Kappan* 62, no. 2 (October 1980), 87–90.

40 See Herbert Simon, *The Sciences of the Artificial.* (Cambridge, MA: The MIT Press, 1969); and Joseph J. Schwab, "The Practical: A Language for Curriculum," *School Review* 58 (November 1969), 1–20, and "The Practical: Arts and 'The Eclectic," *School Review* 59 (November 1970), 493–542.

41 See, for example, T. E. Deal and A. A. Kennedy, *Corporate Cultures* (Reading, MA: Addison-Wesley Publishing Co., 1982): and T. J. Peters and R. H. H. Waterman, Jr., *In Search of Excellence: Lessons from America's Best-Run Corporations* (New York: Harper and Row, 1982).

42 Deal and Kennedy, p. 21.

Part 9
Commentaries

62 A reflection on the professional preparation of teachers

Diane Ravitch
New York University

This is an interesting group of papers, which tackle some of the thorniest issues that bedevil teacher education. The long history of teacher education has been beset with debates about how it should be organized, whether it should stress content or pedagogy, whether it should be professional or vocational, and even whether it is necessary at all. In the nineteenth century, when the first teacher training institutions and normal schools were established, teaching was a humble occupation indeed. Itinerant teachers were commonplace, as were schools managed by anyone with a bit of book learning. At the beginning of the twentieth century, there was a concerted effort by the various professions to set standards for entry, to establish professional schools to prepare those who would qualify for the profession, and to administer entry tests to the profession. So, while it was possible in the nineteenth century to read for the bar or to become a doctor by apprenticeship, those informal routes into the legal and medical professions were eventually closed, and admission was restricted to those who had taken a specified educational program and passed their qualifying examinations. In medicine, of course, the requirements for admission to the profession included a clinical training period as well.

Education stood outside that paradigm. As William S. Learned, William C. Bagley, *et al.*, show in what came to be known as "the Learned report," schools of education were usually seen as multi-purpose; their students might be preparing to teach, or they might not. In any case, schools were usually so eager for teachers that they were likely to hire someone with no training in a normal school. The entirety of the Learned report, commissioned by the Carnegie Foundation, was supposed to do for teacher education what Abraham Flexner's report had done for medical education. Learned and his colleagues argued that normal schools should evolve into single-purpose institutions to educate future teachers; they thought that the normal schools should be the education profession's equivalent of law school and medical school, with the same fixity of purpose and the same high prestige. In their view, the curriculum for future teachers should combine content and pedagogy; every course would demonstrate how to teach subject matter to students, regardless of their grade. At the end of a four-year prescribed course of studies, marked by a case-based approach and practice teaching in training schools, future teachers would be examined for their readiness to teach. Learned's goal was not to "vocationalize" teacher training, as the entry to this section says, but to professionalize it. Interestingly, David Imig and Scott Imig wrote about the farsightedness of the Learned report in *Change* magazine, calling it "a vision delayed."[1] The Imigs suggest that teacher education might have been transformed—and the current debate obviated—if education leaders had taken seriously Learned's ideas and created truly professional preparation programs for teachers. As it happened, however, the normal schools evolved into comprehensive colleges, leaving open the question of how best to train teachers and whether to train them at all.

Steven Weiland's paper wrestles with the age-old problem of making sure that future teachers are liberally educated. He writes at a time when leaders of higher education seem less sure than ever about what a liberal education is and how to teach it. In addition to the uncertainty introduced by postmodernism, relativism, and various other -isms, there is the upsurge of vocationalism among college-age youth. Anyone who reviews statistics on college majors cannot but be struck, and possibly depressed, by the decline of majors in traditional liberal arts subjects and the increase in majors in business and other fields that promise immediate economic payoff. There was a time, though it now seems like ancient history, when academicians had a shared understanding of the meaning and purpose of the liberal arts. That was before the Culture Wars and the Canon Wars. Now, as Weiland shows, we must all engage in a sort of academic archeology, trying to figure out or remember what it is, what it was, what it should be, why it matters. Weiland suggests that teacher education might profitably "move . . . toward liberal education" and that students will thereby develop "enduring intellectual interests," but it is not clear how this will happen in the current situation of teacher education, what might be added, what subtracted from the curriculum.

Frank B. Murray maintains that "teaching by second nature" is a skill that many people have, without any specific training or preparation. They just know how to do it. He also persuasively argues that this kind of teaching is usually inadequate; he draws a useful distinction between a "naive" teacher and an "educated" teacher, with the latter having a deeper understanding of how students learn and what their mistakes mean. As I read his essay, I thought of certain young people I know who had a superb education, decided to teach, and found that they were unable to get across what they wanted their students to learn. They had a secure knowledge of their subject, but were unable to figure out how to teach it in ways that adolescents understood.

The most surprising paper in this section, from my point of view, is the one written by Mary M. Kennedy, Soyeon Ahn, and Jinyoung Choi. The authors set out to compare the value-added by different educational backgrounds, as reflected in students' learning gains. They looked at variations in what teachers had studied before they became teachers and sought to compare the value added by the following kinds of knowledge: pedagogical knowledge, pedagogical content knowledge, and content knowledge.

One would have expected that a paper written by researchers at a major school of education might conclude in a defense of pedagogical studies. But this was not the case. Indeed, the authors arrived at some interesting and unexpected findings. One is that individual courses, whether in mathematics, mathematics education, or pedagogy, have positive effects, but pedagogical courses have a smaller effect than the other two domains. Also, advanced degrees in education are negatively correlated with student achievement, but advanced subject-matter degrees in mathematics have a positive effect (except in elementary school). The authors caution that these findings derive from a single data base.

When they looked at evidence for what they call "the Bright, Well-educated Person hypothesis" or BWE, they found that BWE teachers from highly selective colleges were associated with higher student achievement; but when they looked at schools where students were randomly assigned to teachers, the BWE teachers did not achieve good results with their fifth-grade students. The authors then looked at Teach for America teachers as examples of BWE teachers. They did indeed find gains in student learning for the BWE who were TFA (there is a certain resonance to those acronyms!). However, their conclusions were confounded by the fact that BWE teachers often did have pedagogical knowledge that they gained in their training program or in graduate courses, and the comparison group of teachers had a wide range of educational backgrounds. In short, they found it nearly impossible to conclude that they had truly compared the raw educated talent of a pure BWE—untouched by pedagogy—with teachers who had been thoroughly immersed in pedagogical training. Ultimately, the authors conclude that all three domains of knowledge—mathematics (course content), pedagogy, and pedagogical knowledge (mathematics education)—have positive effects.

At the end of reading these articles, I was left with a picture of what the future teacher should know and be able to do. Yes, future teachers should have a liberal education, but it was not clear where they would get it or what it might consist of. Yes, future teachers need a certain foundation of pedagogical content knowledge so that they can know how to teach what they know to the children in their care. And yes, it would be best if all future teachers were bright and well-educated. I was not persuaded—at least not by the evidence in the Kennedy research study—that future teachers need an advanced degree in education.

These provocative articles seem to me to be complementary, but they leave questions hanging. What is the liberal education that our future teachers need? Where should they get it? Do future mathematics teachers need to study literature and history as well as mathematics? How can the profession attract greater numbers of bright, well-educated people to its ranks, not just for a two-year experience, but for a professional commitment? Do current state requirements for pedagogical courses enhance teachers' capacity or are they excessive? Are these requirements actually a deterrent to recruiting bright, well-educated college graduates to teaching? Should these state requirements be reviewed to make sure that they are infused with content knowledge as well as pedagogy?

We are left at the end of the discussion, as I see it, back at the place where William Learned and William Bagley left off. They thought that teacher education would become truly professional, that it might eventually become a post-baccalaureate professional study, akin to the study of law and medicine. That it did not may be seen either as a cause or an effect of the lesser status of teaching as a profession.

One can only dream of what a Learned School of Education might be in the twenty-first century. An institution where future teachers become masters of their craft; where they learn the best ways to teach their subjects; where every course is infused with the ideals of liberal education; where there is no distinction made between what to teach and how to teach it; where the entire institution is organized to attract, prepare, and educate the best teachers in the land.

In my imagination, school districts would vie for the graduates of such an institution, indeed would offer bonuses to attract them. If this seems utopian, it is because pedagogy never became what Learned and Bagley believed it must. It was marginalized for reasons partly of its own making. It did not develop a research-based, scientific approach to its work. The pedagogical individualism that reigned in pedagogical circles during the 1920s was one cause of its self-imposed isolation. The periodic need for vast numbers of new teachers, regardless of qualifications, was another. There were others as well. Whatever the reason, education never achieved the professional status that it needed and deserved.

As more and more states adopt alternative routes into teaching, this is a propitious time for teacher educators to think about these issues and to begin to reconsider the professional preparation of future teachers.

NOTE

1 David Imig and Scott Imig, "The learned report on teacher education: a vision delayed," *Change*, September/October 2005.

63 Knowledge for teaching
What do we know?

Linda Darling-Hammond
Stanford University

In her thoughtful introduction to this section, Mary Kennedy identifies two dimensions of the long-standing debates over teacher education: One has to do with whether teachers benefit from specific preparation for teaching or need only a strong liberal education; the other has to do with the extent to which teachers benefit from specific courses in, for example, subject matter or teaching methods. She points out that views about what teachers need are generally framed in either/or terms: more of one kind of preparation means less of another, and notes the worry that "bright, liberally-inclined young people" might not choose teaching careers "because such people are not interested in vocational courses" or that such courses might take time away from acquiring more content.

WHAT ARE THE ISSUES THAT DRIVE THE DEBATE?

The relative merits of different kinds of coursework for teachers are certainly contended within the academy as well as in policy circles. Yet, the recurring arguments over teacher education and certification have their roots in much larger societal issues having to do with the role of education and teaching in society, the governance of educational decision making, and the costs and purposes of public education. Among these deep-seated disagreements are whether teaching should be treated as a profession, with the higher salaries and greater decision making authority for teachers this implies; whether education should be regarded as a public good available to all on equal terms, with the reallocations of resources that would accompany such a view; and—perhaps most contentious—who should decide what is taught and how. Resolving empirical questions about the utility of specific courses or programs of study is unlikely to settle these larger questions.

Frank Murray provides vivid examples of some of the things that teachers need to know beyond the liberal arts and subject matter content if they are to teach effectively. His illustrations are buttressed by exhaustive reviews of contemporary research on teaching and learning recently compiled by the National Research Council (Bransford *et al.*, 1999) and the National Academy of Education (Darling-Hammond & Bransford, 2005). However, if teaching were to be regarded as a profession, with expectations that teachers master the kinds of knowledge these reports highlight, the question would shift from whether prospective teachers should study content or pedagogy within a short period of undergraduate education to how they should be enabled to study both and the intersections between them, with implications for the incentives needed to enable this more extensive preparation.

Indeed, "bright, liberally-inclined young people" seem plenty willing to engage in extensive vocational coursework for professions like law, medicine, engineering, and architecture. And in a number of other countries, like Australia, Finland, France, Germany,

New Zealand, Norway, and Taiwan, top candidates are eager to undertake the two to three years of graduate level teacher education that follow the one or two disciplinary majors they have already completed at the undergraduate level. The issue is not whether these teacher education courses are vocational but whether they open the door to a well-respected, well-compensated occupation that demands such study. It may not hurt that these extensive programs of teacher education are often completely subsidized by the state on the theory that society benefits when all teachers are well-prepared with strong subject matter and pedagogical training.

Teaching has failed to achieve professional status in the United States as much because low standards enable smaller investments in education, as because empirical evidence is unclear about the relative value of different kinds of coursework. The option of lowering standards for entry into teaching when salaries and working conditions are inadequate to bolster supply—especially in districts where poor and minority students attend school—reduces pressures for education spending and supports the current unequal allocation of resources (Darling-Hammond, 2004). Those interested in maintaining low cost teacher education and the unfettered hiring of untrained teachers have also argued against school funding reforms that would enable equal access to fully-prepared teachers and create larger investments in public education, particularly in poor urban and rural areas (e.g. Hanushek, 1996, 2000; Podgursky, 2000).

While opponents of teacher education often argue for recruiting bright people into teaching (and who could disagree with that?), their proposals do not offer incentives for attracting talented individuals into the occupation other than the removal of preparation requirements. While they present the removal of teacher education "barriers" as an attraction to teaching, evidence suggests that lack of preparation actually contributes to high attrition rates (Darling-Hammond & Sykes, 2003) and thereby becomes a disincentive to long-term teaching commitments and to the creation of a stable, high ability teaching force.

These same critics of teacher education often object to what is seen as its progressive ideology—for example, approaches that consider multiple intelligences or multicultural education, and pedagogies that emphasize critical thinking, comprehension, and problem solving, such as "whole language" instruction in reading (caricatured as a method "in which the teacher stands by while the student tries to guess what the word is") or inquiry-oriented approaches in mathematics (described as "wasting time" when students must try to discover mathematical ideas that are already known) (Ballou & Podgursky, 1999, p. 41). At root here are issues about what will be taught in public schools and who will decide. To the extent that teachers are untainted by education schools, it is thought, they will be less likely to support these kinds of wrong-headed ideas. And to the extent that teaching is a high-turnover occupation whose members have little shared knowledge of learning and teaching, it is less likely that a legitimate claim to professionalism giving teachers greater voice in curriculum decisions will emerge.

These concerns about a too-powerful profession of teaching would be exacerbated if teachers routinely experienced Murray's vision of professional education or the kind of liberal education for critical intellectual inquiry that Steven Weiland describes. For such teachers would be prepared to wrestle deeply with curricular questions and assume leadership based on serious examination of the social and pedagogical implications of different decisions.

These much larger philosophical, financial, and political issues are the ones that ultimately drive the debate on teacher education. It is no coincidence that the issues of whether teacher education matters and whether teacher certification should be required are at the heart of school funding litigation in many states where unqualified teachers are hired in the under-resourced, lower-paying districts that serve the most disadvantaged students. Similarly, teacher education is regularly implicated in the great curriculum wars that are waged across the country. Readings of the research on teacher education are thus informed by the strongly held views of proponents and opponents of teacher professionalism, a well-financed and equitable public education system, and distinctive views of educational purposes.

WHAT DOES RESEARCH SAY ABOUT HOW TEACHER EDUCATION MATTERS?

Recent reviews of research have concluded that the weight of the evidence suggests that teachers who have more complete preparation are better rated and more effective than those who do not have this preparation, finding the evidence for the value of additional pedagogical training is at least as strong as for subject matter (Darling-Hammond, 2000; Wilson *et al.*, 2001).

Kennedy, Ahn, and Choi seek to quantify one aspect of this question by examining the coefficients associated with different amounts of subject matter or pedagogical coursework in studies that have sought to predict individual student achievement gains in mathematics. Their chapter offers some interesting findings about the relative magnitude and direction of the influences of specific coursework and majors, which appear largely mixed. The strategy, if further refined, could be a potentially useful one. However, as implemented, it does not help us clarify the value-added effects of different kinds of teacher education, because the analysis does not report or interpret the set of teacher qualifications variables in each study, taking account of what is controlled in each model.

Evaluating effects: the need to disentangle preparation measures

Although the chapter provides a very useful treatment of the importance of examining statistical controls in studies, its later discussion of studies does not discuss their models or report on the other qualifications variables controlled in the estimates. The authors do not discuss the fact that the coefficient on a given variable is importantly related to the other qualifications already considered in that model. So, for example, if individual courses in mathematics are considered after mathematics majors have been controlled, the coursework coefficient will be likely to be much smaller than it would be in a model that did not include the major as a variable as well. The variance claimed by one qualifications measure will be offset by other related measures, and can cause a given variable to have a smaller coefficient if the underlying construct of interest has already been well represented in the model. In addition, since certification status includes many of the subcomponents of traditional teacher education (including subject matter and pedagogical requirements as well as tests of verbal and basic skills), its presence or absence in a given model will influence the size of other measures. Without this information it is difficult to meaningfully interpret and compare the findings of the studies on single measures of teacher preparation.

A more helpful kind of analysis is one that weighs and balances a set of qualifications variables in light of one another, as Goldhaber and Brewer (2000) did in their analysis of the effects of teacher qualifications on student achievement gains in math and science. The authors noted, for example, that

> having a teacher with a standard certification in mathematics rather than a private

school certification or a certification out of subject results in at least a 1.3 point increase in the mathematics test. This is equivalent to about 10 percent of the standard deviation on the 12th grade test, a little more than the impact of having a teacher with a BA and MA in mathematics.

(p. 139)

In this case, the study included both majors and certification status, so the effect of each is estimated independent of the effect of the other. The fact that the study found a significant effect of certification status in mathematics even after controlling for whether teachers had a degree in their field (and certified teachers were more likely to have a major in the field) suggests that the knowledge represented by the certification variable has an influence above and beyond the influence of content knowledge.

Evaluating teacher effectiveness: "compared to what?"

Similarly, it is important to know whether preparation variables are controlled when comparing teachers with different background characteristics, such as the Teach for America candidates Kennedy, Ahn, and Choi examine as evidence for the "bright person" hypothesis. Early in their paper, Kennedy and colleagues write that "comparisons of TFA teachers and regularly certified teachers . . . offer us another way to test the bright, well-educated person hypothesis." However, when they summarize studies that have examined TFA they ignore the findings that compare TFA teachers to certified teachers. In two of the studies they mention, which found evidence that TFA recruits' students achieved comparable (in reading) or better (in math) gains in student learning when compared to other teachers (Raymond *et al.*, 2001; Decker *et al.*, 2004), the comparison group teachers were *less* likely to be prepared and certified than the TFA teachers. Most of the TFA teachers had had to enter a teacher education program when hired and became certified in the first two or three years of teaching if they stayed. Neither of these studies explicitly compared TFA teachers to teachers with standard training and certification, controlling for other student, teacher, and school variables.

The third study did look at certification (Darling-Hammond *et al.*, 2005), but Kennedy and colleagues do not report its central findings. Looking at student achievement gains on six different reading and mathematics tests over a six-year period, this study found that certified teachers consistently produced stronger student achievement gains than did uncertified teachers of similar experience levels working in similar schools, including uncertified TFA recruits. On five of the six tests, the negative effect of having an uncertified TFA teacher was greater than the negative effect of having another uncertified teacher, depressing student achievement by up to three months annually compared to a fully certified teacher. The negative effects of TFA recruits were generally larger in reading than in mathematics. Similarly, a recent study in New York City found that beginning TFA teachers, along with other alternative pathway teachers, had a strong negative effect on student achievement in reading in the elementary grades relative to beginners from traditional teacher education programs; in mathematics, the effects were mixed (Boyd *et al.*, 2005).

Like the other studies, Darling-Hammond and colleagues found that in three of the six years TFA teachers were more qualified than comparison teachers in Houston. In these years only, TFA teachers appeared to be as effective as other teachers when certification was not controlled. However, as the proportion of fully certified teachers in Houston grew over the years in our study, and as the proportion of TFA teachers who were certified declined, the observed effects of TFA teachers relative to other teachers became increasingly negative. Thus, we found that interpreting the relative influence of TFA teachers on student achievement depended on knowing about the characteristics of the comparison group of teachers. The relative effectiveness of any group of teachers must be evaluated in a specific context at a particular point in time, with close understanding of the qualifications and characteristics of the comparison groups of teachers employed in that same setting at that point in time.

Thus, the "bright person" hypothesis appears to hold up only in the instances where untrained "bright person" recruits are compared to other untrained entrants, without taking preparation into account. It appears that general academic ability does not offset the need for professional training or render it irrelevant. While uncertified TFA recruits were less effective than certified beginning teachers in teaching both reading and math, they appeared to benefit from preparation, and were as effective as others on most measures when they became certified. On one of the six test measures—the TAAS in mathematics—*certified* TFA recruits appeared more effective than other certified teachers. This finding—and a similar finding from the recent study of teacher education pathways in New York (that experienced TFA recruits had a positive effect on student mathematics gains by their third year of practice, relative to traditionally trained teachers, though they continued to have a negative effect on reading scores)—might be attributed to the strong liberal arts background of TFA teachers. It is plausible that candidates who have attended selective colleges may have a stronger basic mathematics background in high school and college than the average elementary teaching candidate, and that this strength in prior knowledge might translate into greater effectiveness when teaching skills have been mastered.

WHAT CAN (AND SHOULD) TEACHER EDUCATION DO?

Even if one were to accept that teacher education courses have some value, including for "bright persons" entering teaching, there is no dispute that there is a wide range of quality among teacher education programs. As the chapters in this section point out, the movement of teacher education from normal schools to the university has created serious dilemmas for both the identity of teacher education and the development of those teaching skills that require intensive, long-term engagement with practice. Murray notes that "the curricular content that is in place . . . is typically not clearly connected to the educational needs of children and adolescents." His suggestion for a kind of backward mapping from the needs of children to the content of preparation for teachers is exactly the process undertaken by the National Academy of Education's Committee on Teacher Education in its four-year process of developing recommendations for a teacher education curriculum based on what we have come to know about how children learn, as well as what we have learned about how teachers teach (Darling-Hammond and Bransford, 2005).

The Committee's work identified key concepts within several domains of knowledge that are critical for teachers:

- knowledge of *learners* and how they learn and develop within social contexts, including knowledge of language development;
- understanding of *curriculum content and goals*, including the subject matter and skills to be taught in light of disciplinary demands, student needs, and the social purposes of education; and
- understanding of and skills for *teaching*, including content pedagogical knowledge and knowledge for teaching diverse learners, as these are informed by an understanding of assessment and of how to manage a productive classroom.

The Academy's proposals go beyond the questions raised here about teacher education coursework to argue that the clinical experiences embedded in and linked to coursework are equally important. Indeed, learning to teach requires that new teachers not only learn to "think like a teacher" but also to "*act* as a teacher"—posing what Mary Kennedy (1999) has termed "the problem of enactment." Teachers need not only to understand but also to *do* a wide variety of things, many of them simultaneously. One of the perennial dilemmas of teacher education is how to integrate theoretically-based knowledge that has traditionally been taught in university classrooms with the experience-based knowledge that has traditionally been located in the practice of teachers and the realities of classrooms and schools. The challenge may be less one of adding on more courses or sharpening their content in the abstract and more one of connecting them appropriately to the problems of practice. This is where the absorption of normal schools into universities—and the predominant focus on coursework with little attention to strong clinical opportunities—weakened many teacher education programs. Traditional teacher education has often had students taking batches of front-loaded coursework in isolation from practice and then adding a short dollop of student teaching to the end of the program—often in classrooms that did not model the strategies that had previously been described in abstraction.

In order to help teachers enact good practices, close connections between theory and practice, coursework and clinical work are necessary, along with access to high-quality modeling, practical strategies, useful tools, and repeated opportunities for practice. Many teacher educators have argued that novices who have experience in classrooms are more prepared to make sense of the ideas addressed in their academic work and that student teachers understand both theory and practice differently if they take coursework concurrently with fieldwork. A growing body of research confirms this belief, finding that teachers-in-training who participate in fieldwork with coursework are better able to apply concepts they are learning in their coursework and to support student learning (Darling-Hammond & Bransford, 2005, p. 398).

Similarly, a study examining seven exemplary teacher education programs that produce graduates who are extraordinarily well-prepared from their first days in the classroom found that all of these programs had built a more powerful clinical curriculum than is typically found in teacher education (Darling-Hammond *et al.*, 2006). Candidates spend extensive time in the field throughout the entire program—and complete many kinds of performance assessments and analyses of teaching and learning—examining and applying the concepts and strategies they are simultaneously learning about in their courses alongside teachers who can show them how to teach in ways that are responsive to learners. These programs typically require at least a full year of student teaching under the direct supervision of one or more teachers who model expert practice with students who have a wide range of learning needs, with the candidate gradually assuming more independent responsibility for teaching. This allows prospective teachers to grow "roots" on their practice, which is especially important if they are going to learn to teach in ways that are attentive to learning and require diagnosis, adaptations to learners' needs, intensive assessment and planning, and a complex repertoire of practices, judiciously applied.

It has often been the lack of this kind of serious clinical work in schools of education that has led some to view them as irrelevant, and it may be that the lack of connections between coursework and clinical work in many programs render the coursework much less powerful and productive than might otherwise be the case.

Finally, as we consider the nature of knowledge for teaching, we should contemplate the ways in which knowledge for practice is to be used. Murray notes that "competing practices, like whole word and phonics instruction in initial reading methods, have reasonable levels of current scholarly support and adherents," suggesting that, without disposition of these kinds of questions and clarity about "codes of good practice," teaching is "behind" other professions. However, other professions also have many potentially competing techniques supported by research—and often try to reconcile these viewpoints by exploring whether there are circumstances in which one is to be preferred to the other or how they may be used in combination for particular purposes, rather than seeking to land solely on a single answer. Consider the recent debates and competing studies in medicine about issues ranging from hormone replacement therapy to very distinctive schools of treatment for a range of cancers. Doctors are expected to evaluate the evidence and make judgments based on their view of the reach and constraints of the research and the needs of individual clients with different situations at different points in time. Indeed, the goal of professional education in these other fields is not the acquisition of a body of settled knowledge but the understanding of underlying principles, the ability to read and interpret continually emerging research, and the diagnostic skill to assess when various strategies are likely to be most useful.

Similarly, rather than learning the pre-determined right answers to questions about strategy (or learning to implement one or another prescribed orthodoxy), teachers need highly refined knowledge and skills for assessing pupil learning, and they need a wide repertoire of practices—along with the knowledge to know when to use different strategies for different purposes. Rather than being subject to the pendulum swings of polarized teaching policies that rest on simplistic ideas of best practice—"whole language" vs. "phonics," for example, or inquiry learning vs. direct instruction—research suggests that teachers need to know how and *when* to use a range of practices—often in different combinations—to accomplish their goals with different students in different contexts.

Teaching will not wait to become a profession until a larger basket of right answers has been assembled and incorporated into their training. Teachers will be armed with useful professional knowledge when they are given the kind of preparation, as Weiland notes, that enables them to respond to Higgins invitation to be intellectuals themselves—weighing and balancing the appropriateness of practical actions in light of what is suggested in theory and what is consistent with the needs of individual children. That blend of analytic thinking, borne of liberal education at the intersection of content and pedagogy, and of clinical insight, borne of thoughtful work in classrooms connected to a practical, professional knowledge base, will arm teachers with the knowledge they need to become increasingly successful.

REFERENCES

Ballou, D. & Podgursky, M. (1999) Teacher training and licensure: a layman's guide. In M. Kanstoroom and C. E. Finn (eds.), *Better teachers, better schools*. Washington, DC: The Fordham Foundation.

Boyd, D., Grossman, P., Lankford, H., Loeb, S., & Wyckoff, J. (2005, November) *How changes in entry requirements alter the teacher workforce and affect student achievement*. New York: City University of New York.

Bransford, J.D., Brown, A.L. & Cocking, R.R. (1999) *How people learn: brain, mind, experience, and school*. Washington, DC: National Academy Press. http://www.nap.edu/html/howpeople1/

Darling-Hammond, L. (2000) Teacher quality and student achievement: a review of state policy evidence. *Education Policy Analysis Archives*, 8 (1). Retrieved from http://epaa.asu.edu/epaa/v8n1

Darling-Hammond, L. (2004) The color line in American education: race, resources, and student achievement. *W.E.B. Du Bois Review: Social Science Research on Race*, 1 (2): 213–246.

Darling-Hammond, L. & Sykes, G. (2003) Wanted: a national teacher supply policy for education: the right way to meet the "highly qualified teacher" challenge. *Educational Policy Analysis Archives*, 11 (33). http://epaa.asu.edu/epaa/v11n33/

Darling-Hammond, L. & Bransford, J. (2005). *Preparing teachers for a changing world: what teachers should learn and be able to do.* San Francisco: Jossey-Bass.

Darling-Hammond, L. (2006) *Powerful teacher education: lessons from exemplary programs.* San Francisco: Jossey-Bass.

Darling-Hammond, L., Holtzman, D., Gatlin, S. J., & Helig, J. V. (2005) Does teacher preparation matter? Evidence about teacher certification, Teach for America and teacher effectiveness. *Education Policy Analysis Archives*, 13(42). http://epaa.asu.edu/epa//v13n42/

Decker, P. T., Mayer, D. P., & Glazerman, S. (2004) *The effects of teach for America on students: findings from a national evaluation.* Princeton, NJ: Mathematical Policy Research, Inc.

Goldhaber, D. D. & Brewer, D. J. (2000) Does teacher certification matter? High school certification status and student achievement. *Educational Evaluation and Policy Analysis*, 22: 129–195.

Hanushek, E. (1996) *School resources and achievement in Maryland.* Baltimore, MD: Maryland State Department of Education.

Hanushek, E. (2000, May 17) *The structure of analysis and argument in plaintiffs' expert reports.* Report for the defense in *Williams v. California.* http://www.decentschools.org/expert_reports/hanushek_report.pdf

Kennedy, M. (1999) The role of preservice teacher education. In L. Darling-Hammond & G. Sykes (eds.), *Teaching as the learning profession: handbook of policy and practice* (pp. 54–85). San Francisco, CA: Jossey-Bass Publishers.

Podgursky, M. J. (2000, May 17) *Access to teacher quality in California public schools.* Report for the defense in *Williams v. California.* http://www.decentschools.org/expert_reports/podgursky_report.pdf

Raymond, M., Fletcher, S., & Luque, J. (2001) *Teach for America: an evaluation of teacher differences and student outcomes in Houston, Texas.* CREDO, The Hoover Institution, Stanford University: www.rochester.edu/credo

Wilson, S. M., Floden, R. E., & Ferrini-Mundy, J. (2001) *Teacher preparation research: current knowledge, gaps, and recommendations: a research report prepared for the U.S. Department of Education.* Seattle: Center for the Study of Teaching and Policy.

64 Teacher education and the education of teachers

Frederick M. Hess
American Enterprise Institute

For the sake of clarity—but recognizing that it requires foregoing potentially instructive nuance—I want to suggest that two competing perspectives dominate thought on the relationship of teacher education and the education of teachers.

One perspective holds that there is a definable body of knowledge, thought, and practice that teachers need to possess. Regarding teaching as a "profession" in which practitioners are obliged to have mastered essential skills prior to entry, proponents deem teacher education to be essential and invaluable for aspiring teachers. These "essentialists" argue that all teachers need to have completed an appropriate program of "teacher education" in the course of their training. There are some in this camp who would go even further, suggesting that preparation should also help teachers cultivate the "dispositions" and worldviews deemed necessary for effective practice.

The second perspective is skeptical of claims that there is an understood body of knowledge that responsible professionals must master. This camp tends to be even more wary of the notion that there are identified dispositions or values necessary for effective teaching and learning. Consequently, members of the "elective" camp—while acknowledging that teacher instruction can be very useful for some teachers, at some times, when provided by certain instructors or institutions—doubt that formal teacher education is essential to the education of teachers.

There is a third, peripheral school of thought, composed of a handful of vocal education school critics who believe that teacher education is an intellectually corrupt enterprise dominated by progressive ideologues, and that formal teacher education should be dismantled. However, because they are engaged more in a cultural critique than in a debate over the nature and role of teacher education, I will set them aside for the purpose of this essay.

What may seem a modest disagreement between the "essentialists" and the "electivists" grows impassioned because the stakes are larger than they may at first appear. In addition to questions of funding, jobs, and political influence, the status of teaching as a conventional "profession" hinges on the answer. For those who work in schooling or teacher education, this makes the stakes very high indeed. There is a natural inclination to insist that one's work requires careful preparation and cloak it in the garb of "professionalism," if possible. For these reasons, the "essentialist" camp tends to find much sympathy among educators and education professors, all of whom have good reason to embrace arguments that elevate their profession's import. Unsurprisingly, those of the "electivist" persuasion find a much cooler reception in those quarters. For these reasons, the dispute frequently pits those inside the world of teaching and teacher preparation against those outside this world.

However, the two camps do not break down neatly along ideological or partisan lines. For instance, some groups frequently perceived as hostile to conventional teacher education—such as Teach For America and "conservative" proponents of "scientifically-based research"—are amenable to the claim that there are things teachers must believe or need to know before entering the classroom. In other words, they *are* members of the "essentialist" camp; their disagreement with many in that camp is more about what those things are, how to identify them, and what kind of formal programs should teach them.

To varying degrees, members of the "essentialist" and "electivist" camps disagree about the skills and knowledge that aspiring teachers need, how to cultivate good teaching, what effect various licensing requirements have on the quality of applicants, and what the evidence says about these questions. Ultimately, the merits of the two perspectives turn on a variety of claims. Because supporters tend to put these forward on both normative and empirical grounds, sorting out the arguments requires distinguishing the mingled claims.

Moreover, the empirical basis for making strong claims regarding "what we know" about the value of teacher education is extremely tenuous. In their review of the research, Kennedy, Ahn and Choi are careful to acknowledge the data limitations, self-selection issues, and related caveats that warrant caution in judging the utility of preparation based on the handful of studies that meet even minimal requirements for rigor and validity. For that reason, it was somewhat surprising to see them seemingly brush away this sensible caution in concluding that the evidence shows even modest value in taking education and math education courses in the area of math instruction. While it's not unlikely that additional professional training may yield some benefits—one would be astounded if teacher education was never beneficial—it seems rash to draw such a conclusion based on the existing evidence.

In short, while various scholars and practitioners can frequently judge an existing body of research differently, I suggest that it is very difficult to justify the "essentialist" position on empirical grounds. Consequently, it's worth carefully considering the assertions underlying the "essentialist" position. In reading the essays I was asked to respond to, I was struck by four key "essentialist" claims deserving of scrutiny. And because the "electivist" position merely suggests that the significance of such preparation is contingent, the burden of proof in this discourse lies with those who claim that teacher education is essential. If teacher preparation is only helpful in some cases, for some people, when teaching some subjects, or in some schools, then it is difficult to prove that it is essential.

The first "essentialist" claim, voiced by Frank Murray, is that absent professional training, teachers will have low expectations for students. In making this point, Murray quotes two studies, both more than two decades old, and he goes on to suggest that "natural" teachers (those who have not benefited from teacher education) will systematically treat disadvantaged pupils in ways that inhibit academic growth. But he never explains just why or how it is that teacher education serves to raise expectations. In a familiar refrain, Murray also suggests that today's teacher education programs may not have the desired effect, but this is a fixable glitch rather than a real challenge to the "essentialist" position.

There is, however, cause to believe that teachers who complete teacher education are among those whose expectations for students, including poor and minority students, are disappointingly low. For instance, a 2005 survey of Teach For America (TFA) teachers—almost none of whom had completed a recognizable course of teacher education—found that they had demanding standards for their students, themselves, and their schools. Similarly, some schools that have relied on large numbers of teachers without formal preparation—such as the KIPP Academies and many parochial schools—have seen disadvantaged students make achievement gains that dramatically exceed those posted by students with formally trained teachers. Now, the significance of such anecdotal claims is primarily illustrative, so I do not intend to overstate their particular import. Rather, I mean to suggest that the argument in general—that teacher education infuses future teachers with a burning sense of mission or a passion for demanding standards—seems to run in the face of much experience.

A second "essentialist" claim is that we have a reasonably coherent idea of what teachers need to know or be able to do, and that any aspiring professional ought to be educated accordingly. But in reality, a close look at the state of research-based knowledge on instruction, pedagogy, and learning suggests that, as a general rule, we know very little about what teachers need to know or what skills will make them more effective. While today's teacher educators claim to have assembled a body of knowledge equal to the task, these same claims have been made for decades. Consider, just to take one example, the award-winning 1999 Harvard University Press book, *Teaching in America*, penned by education scholars Gerald Grant and Christine E. Murray. In the volume, Grant and Murray identify five "essential acts" that should be analyzed and taught: listening with care; motivating the student; modeling caring by hearing and responding to the pain of others and creating a sense of security in the classroom; evaluating by clarifying, coaching, advising, and deciding on appropriate challenges for individual students; and reflecting and renewing. The authors never even addressed how these five "essential acts" are to be taught, much less how to determine whether a teacher has mastered them. Under scrutiny, claims about research-based knowledge and established instructional or pedagogical methods typically prove to be a stew of theory, intuition, anecdote, and inconclusive findings.

Third, "essentialists" frequently argue that effective teachers need to be educated on the subjects and effects of "sexism," "racism," "classism," "bilingualism," "heterosexism," "white privilege," the "language of oppression," and other, related, biases. The National Council for the Accreditation of Teacher Education has made the cultivation of appropriate dispositions and the promotion of "diversity" central to its standards for teacher education. But there is no unanimity on the importance or effectiveness of such instruction. Skeptics question the pedagogical or instructional utility of such concepts, noting the lack of evidence supporting claims that teachers educated in these modes of thought are more effective by any discernible metric.

Leading voices in teacher preparation, including Nel Noddings, the president of the National Academy of Education, have unapologetically argued that teacher education is about championing certain values—without suggesting that there is evidence that these values enhance teaching and learning. As Marilyn Cochran-Smith (2004), former president of the American Educational Research Association (AERA) has argued, "Education (and teacher education) are social institutions that pose moral, ethical, social, philosophical, and ideological questions. It is wrong-headed—and dangerous—to treat these questions as if they were value neutral and ideology free" (p. 6). Gloria Ladson-Billings, another former AERA president, has said that she believes good teaching entails promoting an "anti-racist, anti-sexist, anti-homophobic . . . anti-oppressive social justice pedagogy" (in Kumashiro, 2004, p. xiv). The reality is that instruction in this area frequently amounts to advocacy of particular perspectives. Given the lack of evidence on the value of promoting certain perspectives, and the possibility that students with a variety of backgrounds and views may benefit from encountering teachers with heterogeneous beliefs, skeptics are dubious of the utility of this instruction.

A fourth claim, again eloquently advanced by Murray, is that untrained teachers are pedagogically unsophisticated and unable to construct the kinds of lessons or provide the kind of instruction that trained teachers can provide. For instance, Murray asserts that untrained teachers are overly prone to "showing and telling" and devote too little attention to engaging students, cultivating student thinking, or addressing the full range of social and intellectual development. Of course, one problem with this argument is the scant evidence that teacher preparation has a profound or lasting impact on how teachers actually teach. Murray, for instance, is unable to present any evidence that those who have completed teacher education are more likely to utilize "dialectical" methods or are more likely to use them effectively.

The more fundamental question, however, may be whether emphasizing concrete mastery and factual knowledge is necessarily bad for students. There is certainly a school of thought that schools ought to deemphasize teacher-centered instruction and employ pedagogies based on discovery, invention, and collaboration; but it is a mistake to suggest that this is rooted in a body of established, uncontested knowledge rather than personal judgment. Moreover, exactly when "showing and telling" is excessive or inappropriate, as opposed to a useful component of disciplined instruction, is a subject of legitimate dispute. In short, it is not a settled matter that the pedagogical and instructional practices that Murray associates with teacher education graduates are more effective than those of teachers who have not received such an education.

Finally, a critical problem for the "essentialist" position is that even its leading proponents are generally critical of much contemporary teacher education—though they are quick to explain that its disappointments ought not tarnish the "essentialist" school of thought. Even staunch defenders of the "essentialist" position, including thoughtful scholars like Linda Darling-Hammond and Gary Sykes, concede that there are many teacher education programs that fail to embody the standards they have in mind. It may indeed be possible to imagine teacher education that could be integral to the education of teachers. However, decades of efforts have failed to realize that vision in more than a small number of the nation's 1,300 preparation programs. As Lee Shulman (2005), president of the Carnegie Foundation for the Advancement of Teaching, argued in late 2005, we have not yet created a coherent system of teacher education in the United States. Shulman acidly observed,

> Teacher education does not exist in the United States. There is so much variation among all programs in visions of good teaching, standards for admission, rigor of subject matter preparation, what is taught and what is learned, character of supervised clinical experience, and quality of evaluation that compared to any other academic profession, the sense of chaos is inescapable.
>
> (p. 7)

There comes a point where persistent and widespread institutional failure ceases to be a question of implementation and gives cause for a fundamental rethinking of the institution. It's at least worth asking, if this is all we have to show after 150 years of efforts and five decades of sustained institution building, whether there might not be something about teacher education that will almost inevitably frustrate "essentialist" efforts to formalize and institutionalize its delivery.

It is certainly possible to imagine circumstances under which both camps might regard teacher education as more critical for the proper education of teachers. If educational researchers were to make meaningful strides in identifying practices that consistently deliver educational benefits for children, aspiring educators should clearly be expected to know and be able to apply the relevant findings. As research proceeds, it increasingly yields important insights into cognition, learning, and brain development. If teacher education begins to teach this new knowledge in a disciplined and relevant manner, then it may indeed come to be essential for educating teachers.

Of course, teacher education under those conditions may look very differently than it looks today. Importantly, there's no guarantee that those academics that have fought so hard to preserve teacher education in its contemporary shape will be pleased with the form it takes under such circumstances, or even that they will be equipped to provide the requisite instruction. In the meantime, teacher education remains a nonessential but potentially useful exercise that can contribute to the education of some teachers, at some times, and for some purposes.

REFERENCES

Cochran-Smith, M. (2004). Taking stock in 2004: teacher education in dangerous times. *Journal of Teacher Education*, 55(1), 3–7.

Grant, G. & Murray, C. E. (1999) *Teaching in America: the slow revolution*. Cambridge, MA: Harvard University Press.

Kumashiro, K. K. (2004) *Against common sense: teaching and learning toward social justice*. New York: RoutledgeFalmer.

Smith, A. (2005) *Equity within reach: insights from the front lines of Americas achievement gap*. New York: Teacher for America.

Shulman, L. (2005) Teacher education does not exist. *The Stanford Educator*, Fall, available online at http://ed.stanford.edu/suse/educator/fall2005/EducatorFall05.pdf

Name index

Subject index